NEW ENGLISH DICTIONARY AND THESAURUS

GEDDES & GROSSET

Published by Geddes & Grosset, an imprint of
Children's Leisure Products Limited

© 1994 Children's Leisure Products Limited,
David Dale House, New Lanark ML11 9DJ, Scotland

First published 1994
Reprinted 1995, 1998, 1999, 2000

ISBN 1 85534 324 X

Printed and bound in Finland

Contents

List of Abbreviations

abbr	abbreviation	*myth*	mythology
adj	adjective	*n*	noun
adv	adverb	*naut*	nautical
anat	anatomy	*neut*	neuter
approx	approximately	*news*	news media
arch	archaic	*nf*	noun feminine
archit	architecture	*npl*	noun plural
astrol	astrology	*n sing*	noun singular
astron	astronomy	*obs*	obsolete
Austral	Australia, Australasia	*orig*	original, originally, origin
aux	auxiliary	*p*	participle
biol	biology	*pers*	person, personal
bot	botany	*philos*	philosophy
Brit	Britain, British	*photog*	photography
c	circa, about	*pl*	plural
cap	capital	*poet*	poetical
cent	century	*poss*	possessive
chem	chemical, chemistry	*pp*	past participle
compar	comparative	*prep*	preposition
comput	computing	*pres t*	present tense
conj	conjunction	*print*	printing
demons	demonstrative	*pron*	pronoun
derog	derogatory, derogatorily	*pr p*	present participle
dimin	diminutive	*psychol*	psychology
econ	economics	*pt*	past tense
eg	exempli gratis, for example	*RC*	Roman Catholic
elect	electricity	*reflex*	reflexive
esp	especially	*Scot*	Scotland
fog	figuratively	*sing*	singular
geog	geography	*sl*	slang
geol	geology	*superl*	superlative
geom	geometry	*theat*	theatre
gram	grammar	*TV*	television
her	heraldry	*UK*	United Kingdom
hist	history	*US*	United States
ie	id est, that is	*USA*	United States of America
imper	imperative	*usu*	usually
incl	including	*vb*	verb
inf	informal	*vb aux*	auxiliary verb
interj	interjection	*vi*	intransitive verb
math	mathematics	*vt*	transitive verb
mech	mechanics	*vti*	transitive or intransitive verb
med	medicine	*vulg*	vulgar, vulgarly
mil	military	*zool*	zoology
mus	music		

Dictionary

A

A *abbr* = ampere(s).

Å *abbr* = ångström(s).

a *adj* the indefinite article; one; any; per.

A1 *adj* (*inf*) in perfect condition; physically fit; excellent.

AA *abbr* = Alcoholics Anonymous; anti-aircraft; Automobile Association.

AAA *abbr* = Automobile Association of America; Amateur Athletics Association.

aardvark *n* a nocturnal African mammal with a long snout that feeds on termites.

aardwolf *n* (*pl* aardwolves) the earth wolf, a South African carnivore like a hyena.

ab *prep* from, as in *ab initio*.

ab- *prefix* away, from, apart.

abaca *n* Manila hemp.

aback *adv* taken aback startled.

abacus *n* (*pl* abaci, abacuses) a frame with sliding beads for doing arithmetic.

Abaddon *n* a destroying angel, the devil; hell.

abaft *adv, prep* (*naut*) behind.

abalone *n* an edible mollusc having an ear-shaped shell lined with mother-of-pearl.

abandon *vt* to leave behind; to desert; to yield completely to an emotion or urge. * *n* freedom from inhibitions.—abandonment *n*.

abandoned *adj* (*behaviour*) showing abandon, unrestrained.—abandonedly *adv*.

abase *vt* to degrade, humiliate.—abasement *n*.

abash *vt* to cause a feeling of shame, embarrassment or confusion.—abashment *n*.

abashed *adj* ashamed, embarrassed.

abate *vti* to make or become less; (*law*) to end.—abatement *n*.

abatis *n* (*pl* abatis, abatises) a defence work of fallen trees with the branches towards the enemy.

abattoir *n* a slaughterhouse.

abbacy *n* (*pl* abbacies) the office or rights of an abbot.

abbatial *adj* of an abbey or abbot.

abbé *n* a French ecclesiastic.

abbess *n* the woman who heads a convent of nuns.

abbey *n* a building occupied by monks or nuns; a church built as part of such a building; the community of monks or nuns.

abbot *n* the head of an abbey of monks.

abbreviate *vt* to make shorter, esp to shorten (a word) by omitting letters.

abbreviation *n* the process of abbreviating; a shortened form of a word.

ABC[1] *n* the alphabet; the basic facts of a subject.

ABC[2] *abbr* = American Broadcasting Corporation; Australian Broadcasting Corporation.

abdicate *vti* to renounce an official position or responsibility, etc.—abdication *n*.

abdomen *n* the region of the body below the chest containing the digestive organs; the belly; (*insects, etc*) the section of the body behind the thorax.—abdominal *adj*.—abdominally *adv*.

abducent *adj* (*anat*) (*limb, etc*) drawn from its natural position.

abduct *vt* to carry off (a person) by force; (*anat*) to draw (a limb, etc) from its natural position.—abduction *n*.—abductor *n*.

abeam *adv* (*naut*) at right angles to a ship's length, abreast.

abecedarian *adj* of the ABC, elementary; arranged alphabetically. * *n* one learning the ABC, a beginner, a learner.

abed *adv* in bed.

abelmosk *n* an Asian herb of the mallow family yielding musk.

aberrant *adj* deviating from that regarded as normal or right.—aberrance, aberrancy *n*.

aberration *n* a deviation from the normal; a mental or moral lapse.

abet *vt* (abetting, abetted) to encourage or assist, esp to do wrong.—abetment *n*.—abetter, (*esp law*) abettor *n*.

abeyance *n* (*usu preceded by* in) (*law, etc*) suspended temporarily.

abhor *vt* (abhorring, abhorred) to detest, despise.

abhorrence *n* detestation.

abhorrent *adj* detestable.

abide *vt* (abiding, abode *or* abided) to endure; to put up with.

abiding *adj* permanent.—abidingly *adv*.

abigail *n* a lady's maid.

ability *n* (*pl* abilities) the state of being able being able; power to do; talent; skill.

ab initio (*Latin*) from the beginning.

abiogenesis *n* spontaneous generation.—abiogenetic *adj*.

abject *adj* wretched; dejected.—abjection *n*.—abjectly *adv*.

abjure *vt* to renounce.—abjuration *n*.—abjurer *n*.

ablactation *n* the act of weaning a child from the breast.

ablate *vti* (ablating, ablated) to remove surgically; (*astrophysics*) to melt or vaporize when entering the earth's atmosphere; (*geol*) to erode, to waste or wear away.—ablation *n*.

ablative *adj* (*gram*) expressing source, instrumentality, etc; (*astrophysics*) ablating. * *n* one of the cases of Latin nouns, expressing chiefly separation and instrumentality and sometimes place.

ablative absolute *n* a particular construction in Latin of a noun and a participle in the ablative case, agreeing in gender and number, and forming a clause by themselves, but unconnected gramatically with the rest of the sentence.

ablaut *n* (*linguistics*) a vowel permutation, the change of a root vowel in the derivation of a word, as *do, did* or *sing, sang, sung, song.*

ablaze *adj* burning, on fire.

-able *adj suffix* capable of, as in *suitable.*

able *adj* having the competence or means (to do); talented; skilled.—**ably** *adv.*

able-bodied *adj* fit, strong.

able-bodied seaman *n* a trained seaman in the (merchant) navy.—*also* **able seaman.**

abloom *adv* in bloom, blooming.

ablution *n* (*usu pl*) a washing or cleansing of the body by water; the ritual cleansing of vessels or hands.—**ablutionary** *adj.*

ably *adv* in an able manner.

ABM *abbr* = antiballistic missile.

abnegate *vt* to deny oneself (a right, etc); to renounce.—**abnegation** *n.*

abnormal *adj* unusual, not average or typical; irregular.—**abnormality** *n.*—**abnormally** *adv.*

abnormality *n* (*pl* **abnormalities**) deformity; irregularity; difference or departure from a regular type or rule.

aboard *adv* on or in an aircraft, ship, train, etc.—*also prep.*

abode[1] *n* a home, residence.

abode[2] *see* **abide.**

abolish *vt* to bring to an end, do away with.—**abolisher** *n.*—**abolishment** *n.*

abolition *n* the act of abolishing; (*with cap*) in UK, the ending of the slave trade (1807) or slavery (1833), in US, the emancipation of the slaves (1863).

abolitionist *n* one who is in favour of the repeal or abolition of some existing law or custom; (*often with cap*) one in favour of Abolition.

abomasum *n* (*pl* **abomasa**) the fourth stomach of a ruminant animal.—**abomasal** *adj.*

A-bomb *n* atomic bomb.

abominable *adj* despicable, detestable; (*inf*) very unpleasant.—**abominably** *adv.*

abominable snowman *n* a huge creature of legend resembling a man or an animal, said to be found in the Himalayas.—*also* **yeti.**

abominate *vt* to abhor; to regard with feelings of disgust or hatred.—**abominator** *n.*

abomination *n* detestation; a loathsome person or thing.

aboriginal *adj* existing in a place from the earliest times; of aborigines. * *n* the species of animals or plants presumed to have originated within a given area.

aborigine *n* any of the first known inhabitants of a region; (*with cap*) one of the original inhabitants of Australia before the arrival of European settlers.

abort *vti* to undergo or cause an abortion; to terminate or cause to terminate prematurely. * *n* the premature termination of a rocket flight, etc.

abortion *n* the premature expulsion of a foetus, esp if induced on purpose.

abortionist *n* a person who performs abortions, esp illegally.

abortive *adj* failing in intended purpose; fruitless; causing abortion.—**abortively** *adv.*

aboulia *see* **abulia.**

abound *vi* to be in abundance; to have in great quantities.

about *prep* on all sides of; near to; with; on the point of; concerning. * *adv* all around; near; to face the opposite direction.

about-turn, about-face *n* a complete reversal in direction or opinion, etc. * *vi* to make an about-turn.

above *prep* over, on top of; better or more than; beyond the reach of; too complex to understand. * *adv* in or to a higher place; in addition; (*text*) mentioned earlier.

aboveboard *adj, adv* without trickery; in open sight.

abracadabra *n* a cabbalistic word used as a charm, a spell; gibberish.

abradant *adj* having the property of rubbing away. * *n* a substance employed for abrading or scouring.

abrade *vt* to wear or rub away; to remove as by friction or abrasion; to corrode, as by acids.—**abrader** *n.*

abranchiate, abranchial *adj* (*zool*) devoid of gills. * *n* an animal without gills.

abrasion *n* the act or process of rubbing away by friction, etc; a scraped area, esp on the body.

abrasive *adj* causing abrasion; harsh, irritating. * *n* a substance or tool used for grinding or polishing, etc.—**abrasively** *adv.*

abreact *vt* (*psychoanal*) to remove (a complex) by acting it out or talking it out.—**abreaction** *n.*—**abreactive** *adj.*

abreast *adv* side by side and facing the same way; informed (of); aware.

abridge *vt* to shorten by using fewer words but keeping the substance.

abridgment, abridgement *n* the state of being contracted or curtailed; a shortened version of a text; an epitome.

abroach *adj, adv* letting out; broached, pierced so as to let the liquor run.

abroad *adv* in or to a foreign country; over a wide area; out in the open; in circulation, current.

abrogate *vt* to repeal, cancel.—**abrogator** *n.*

abrogation *n* the act of abrogating; the repeal or annulling of a law.

abrupt *adj* sudden; unexpected; curt.—**abruptly** *adv.*—**abruptness** *n.*

abruption *n* a separation with violence; a sudden or abrupt termination.

abscess *n* an inflamed area of the body containing pus.

abscissa *n* (*pl* **abscissas, abscissae**) (*geom*) one of the two coordinates fixing the position of a point.

abscission *n* the act of severance; (*bot*) the shedding of parts; the breaking off in a sentence, leaving the rest to be implied.

abscond *vi* to hide, run away, esp to avoid punishment for a wrongdoing.

abseil *vi* to descend a rock face by means of a double rope attached to a higher point.—**abseiling** *n.*

absence *n* the state of not being present; the time of this; a lack; inattention.

absent[1] *adj* not present; not existing; inattentive.—**absently** *adv.*

absent[2] *vt* to keep (oneself) away.

absentee *n* a person who is absent, as from work or school.

absenteeism *n* persistent absence from work, school, etc.

absently *adv* in an abstracted manner.

absent-minded *adj* inattentive; forgetful.

absinthe, absinth *n* a potent, green, brandy-based liqueur flavoured with wormwood.

absit omen (*Latin*) may the foreboding caused by some unlucky word or event not come to pass.

absolute *adj* unrestricted, unconditional; complete; positive; perfect, pure; not relative; (*monarch, ruler, etc*) authoritarian, despotic; (*inf*) utter, out-and-out.

absolutely *adv* completely; unconditionally; (*inf*) I completely agree, certainly.

absolution *n* forgiveness; remission of sin or its penalty.

absolutism *n* the state of being absolute; the principle or system of absolute government.—**absolutist** *n, adj*.

absolve *vt* to clear from guilt or blame; to give religious absolution to; to free from a duty, obligation, etc.

absolver *n* one who absolves, or pronounces absolution.

absorb *vt* to take in; to soak up; to incorporate; to pay for (costs, etc); to take in (a shock) without recoil; to occupy one's attention or interest completely.—**absorber** *n*.—**absorptive** *adj*.

absorbable *adj* capable of being absorbed.—**absorbability** *n*.

absorbefacient *adj* inducing or causing absorption. * *n* something that causes absorption.

absorbent *adj* capable of absorbing moisture, etc.—**absorbency** *n*.

absorbent cotton *n* raw cotton that has been bleached and sterilized for use as a dressing, etc.—*also* **cotton wool**.

absorbing *adj* engrossing.—**absorbingly** *adv*.

absorption *n* the process or act of absorbing; the state of being absorbed; entire preoccupation of the mind.—**absorptive** *adj*.

absorption lines *npl* dark lines in the spectrum produced by the absorption of cool vapours through which the light has passed.

absorptivity *n* the power of absorption; (*physics*) the rate of absorption of radiation by a material.

abstain *vi* to keep oneself from some indulgence, esp from drinking alcohol; to refrain from using one's vote.

abstainer *n* one who abstains, especially from intoxicants.

abstemious *adj* sparing in consuming food or alcohol.—**abstemiously** *adv*.—**abstemiousness** *n*.

abstention *n* the act of holding off or abstaining; the withholding of a vote.—**abstentious** *adj*.—**abstentionist** *n*.

abstergent *adj* possessing cleansing or purging properties. * *n* that which cleanses or purges; a detergent.

abstinence *n* an abstaining or refraining, esp from food or alcohol.

abstinent *adj* refraining from over-indulgence, esp with regard to food and drink. * *n* an abstainer.—**abstinently** *adv*.

abstract *adj* having no material existence; theoretical; (*art*) non-representational. * *n* (*writing, speech*) a summary or condensed version. * *vt* to remove or extract; to separate; to summarize.

abstracted *adj* not paying attention.—**abstractedly** *adv*.—**abstractedness** *n*.

abstraction *n* preoccupation, inattention; an abstract concept.—**abstractive** *adj*.

abstractionism *n* the theory and art of the abstract, esp non-representational painting.—**abstractionist** *adj, n*.

abstract noun *n* the name of a state or quality considered apart from the object to which it belongs.

abstruse *adj* obscure; hidden; difficult to comprehend; profound.—**abstrusely** *adv*.—**abstruseness** *n*.

absurd *adj* against reason or common sense; ridiculous.—**absurdly** *adv*.

absurdity *n* (*pl* **absurdities**) the state of being absurd; that which is absurd.

abulia *n* (*psychol*) loss of willpower.—*also* **aboulia**.—

abulic *adj*.

abundance *n* a plentiful supply; a considerable amount.

abundant *adj* plentiful; rich (in).—**abundantly** *adv*.

abuse *vt* to make wrong use of; to mistreat; to insult, attack verbally. * *n* misuse; mistreatment; insulting language; immoderate or illegal use of drugs or other stimulants.—**abuser** *n*.

abusive *adj* insulting.—**abusively** *adv*.—**abusiveness** *n*.

abut *vi* (**abutting, abutted**) to adjoin, border or lean (on, against).

abutment, abuttal *n* that which borders upon something else; the solid structure that supports the extremity of a bridge or arch.

abutter *n* (*law*) the owner of an adjoining property.

abuzz *adv* filled with buzzing sounds; active, alive.

abysm *n* (*arch*) an abyss, a gulf.

abysmal *adj* extremely bad, deplorable.—**abysmally** *adv*.

abyss *n* a bottomless depth; anything too deep to measure; hell.

abyssal *adj* pertaining to oceanic depths.

AC, ac *abbr* = alternating current.

Ac (*chem symbol*) actinium.

a/c *abbr* = account; account current.

ac- *prefix* the form of *ad-* before *c, k, g*.

acacia *n* a genus of shrubby or arboreous leguminous plants of warmer regions with white or yellow flowers, several species of which yield gum.

academic *adj* pertaining to a school, college or university; scholarly; purely theoretical in nature. * *n* a member of a college or university; a scholarly person.

academically *adv* theoretically, unpractically.

academician *n* a member of an Academy.

academy *n* (*pl* **academies**) a school for specialized training; (*Scot*) a secondary school; (*with cap*) a society of scholars, writers, scientists, etc.

Acadian *adj* of Acadia, a region of Canada, Nova-Scotian.

acanthine *adj* pertaining to or resembling the plant acanthus. * *n* ornamentation in the shape of the acanthus leaf.

acanthus *n* (*pl* **acanthuses, acanthi**) a genus of herbaceous plants with sharp-toothed leaves; (*archit*) ornamentation adopted in the capitals of the Corinthian and Composite orders, and resembling the foliage of the acanthus.

a cappella *adv* (*mus*) after the style of church or chapel music, without accompaniment.

acarid *n* a tick or mite of the *Acarina* order of insects, etc, in which the divisions of head, thorax and abdomen are not apparent.—*also adj*.

acarpellous, acarpelous *adj* (*bot*) without carpels.

acarpous *adj* (*bot*) not producing fruit; sterile or barren.

acatalectic *adj* (*verse*) with a complete number of syllables, not catalectic.—*also* n.

acaudal, acaudate *adj* (*zool*) without a tail.

acaulescent *adj* (*bot*) stemless or with a very short stem.—**acaulescence** *n*.

acc. *abbr* = according; account; accusative.

Accadian *see* **Akkadian**.

accede *vi* to take office; to agree or assent to (a suggestion).

accelerando *adv, adj* (*mus*) with gradual increase of speed. * *n* (*pl* **accelerandos**) a piece of music played in this way.

accelerate *vti* to move faster; to happen or cause to happen more quickly; to increase the velocity of (a vehicle, etc).—**accelerative, acceleratory** *adj.*

acceleration *n* the act of accelerating or condition of being accelerated; the rate of increase in speed or change in velocity; the power of accelerating.

accelerator *n* a device for increasing speed; a throttle; (*physics*) an apparatus that imparts high velocities to elementary particles.

accent *n* emphasis on a syllable or word; a mark used to indicate this; any way of speaking characteristic of a region, class, or an individual; the emphasis placed on something; rhythmic stress in music or verse. * *vt* to express the accent, or denote the vocal division of a word by stress or modulation of the voice; to pronounce; to mark or accent a word in writing by use of a sign; to dwell upon or emphasize, as a passage of music.

accentuate *vt* to emphasize.

accentuation *n* the act of accentuating by stress or accent; speaking or writing with emphasis or distinction.

accept *vt* to receive, esp willingly; to approve; to agree to; to believe in; to agree to pay.

acceptable *adj* satisfactory; welcome; tolerable.—**acceptability** *n.*—**acceptably** *adv.*

acceptance *n* the act of accepting; the act of being accepted or received with approbation; agreement; the subscription to a bill of exchange; the bill accepted or the sum contained in it.

acceptation *n* the act of accepting or state of being accepted or acceptable; the meaning or sense of a word or statement in which it is to be understood.

accepter, acceptor *n* one who accepts; the person who accepts a bill of exchange.

access *n* approach, or means of approach; the right to enter, use, etc. * *vt* (*comput*) to retrieve (information) from a storage device; to gain access to.

accessible *adj* able to be reached; open (to).—**accessibility** *n.*—**accessibly** *adv.*

accession *n* the act of reaching or assuming a rank or position.—**accessional** *adj.*

accessory *adj* additional; extra. * *n* (*pl* **accessories**) a supplementary part or item, esp of clothing; a person who aids another in a crime.—**accessorial** *adj.*

acciaccatura *n* (*pl* **acciaccaturas, acciaccature**) a half-note or grace note below the principal note, struck at the same time as the principal note and immediately released while the latter is held.

accidence *n* (*linguistics*) the part of grammar that deals with the inflections of words, which are accidents, not essentials; a book containing the rudiments of grammar; the rudiments themselves.

accident *n* an unexpected event; a mishap or misfortune, esp one resulting in death or injury; chance.

accidental *adj* occurring or done by accident; non-essential; (*mus*) a sign prefixed to a note indicating a departure from the key signature.—**accidentally** *adv.*

accidie *n* sloth, torpor, apathy.

accipiter *n* a generic name for birds of prey, as the common hawk.

accipitrine *adj* hawk-like, rapacious.

acclaim *vt* to praise publicly (the merits of a person or thing); to welcome enthusiastically. * *vi* to shout approval. * *n* a shout of welcome or approval.

acclamation *n* a shout of applause or other demonstration of hearty approval, loud united assent; an outburst of joy or praise; the adoption of a resolution *viva voce*; a mode of papal election.—**acclamatory** *adj.*

acclimatize *vt* to adapt to a new climate or environment * *vi* to become acclimatized.—**acclimatization** *n.*

acclivity *n* (*pl* **acclivities**) an ascent or upward slope of the earth; the talus of a rampart.—**acclivitous** *adj.*

accolade *n* praise; approval; an award; a ceremonial touch on the shoulder with a sword to confer knighthood.

accommodate *vt* to provide lodging for; to oblige, supply; to adapt, harmonize.

accommodating *adj* obliging, willing to help.—**accommodatingly** *adv.*

accommodation *n* lodgings; the process of adapting; willingness to help.

accommodation bill *n* a bill or note endorsed by one or more parties to enable the drawer to raise money upon it.

accommodation ladder *n* a ladder or stairway suspended at the gangway of a ship.

accommodative *adj* disposed or tending to accommodate.

accompaniment *n* an instrumental part supporting a solo instrument, a voice, or a choir; something that accompanies.

accompanist, accompanyist *n* one who plays a musical accompaniment.

accompany *vt* (**accompanying, accompanied**) (*person*) to go with; (*something*) to supplement.

accomplice *n* a partner, esp in committing a crime.

accomplish *vt* to succeed in carrying out; to fulfil.

accomplished *adj* done; completed; skilled, expert; polished.

accomplishment *n* a skill or talent; the act of accomplishing; something accomplished.

accord *vi* to agree; to harmonize (with). * *vt* to grant. * *n* consent; harmony.

accordance *n* agreement; conformity.

accordant *adj* corresponding; of the same mind.

according *prep* as stated by or in; (*with* **to**) in conformity with; (*with* **as**) depending on whether. * *adj* agreeing, harmonious.

accordingly *adv* consequently; therefore; suitably.

accordion *n* a portable keyboard instrument with manually operated folding bellows that force air through metal reeds.—**accordionist** *n.*

accost *vt* to approach and speak to, often to accuse of crime or to solicit sexually.

account *n* a description; an explanatory statement; a business record or statement; a credit arrangement with a bank, department store, etc; importance, consequence. * *vt* to think of as; consider. * *vi* to give a financial reckoning (to); (*with* **for**) to give reasons (for); (*with* **for**) to kill, dispose of.

accountable *adj* liable; responsible; explainable.—**accountability** *n.*—**accountably** *adv.*

accountancy *n* the profession or practice of an accountant.

accountant *n* one whose profession is auditing business accounts.

account book *n* a book for the entering of accounts, or in which particulars of sales, purchases, etc, are kept.

accounting *n* the maintaining or auditing of detailed business accounts; accountancy.

accoutre, accouter *vt* to dress; to equip; to array in military dress; to furnish with accoutrements.—**accoutrement, accouterment** *n.*

accoutrements, accouterments *npl* equipage; dress; military equipment.

accredit vt to give credit or authority to; to have confidence in; to authorize; to stamp with authority; to believe and accept as true.—**accreditation** n.

accredited adj authorized officially; accepted as valid; certified as being of a prescribed quality.

accrescent adj increasing; growing.

accrete vi to adhere, to grow together; to be added. * vt to cause to grow or unite. * adj (bot) grown into one.

accretion n an increase by natural growth; the addition of external parts; the growing together of parts or members naturally separate.—**accretive, accretionary** adj.

accrue vi (accruing, accrued) to come as a natural increase or addition; (money, etc) to accumulate or be added periodically.—**accrual, accrument** n.

accumbent adj (bot) reclining or recumbent, (hist) of the Roman style of reclining on a couch at meals.—**accumbency** n.

accumulate vti to collect together in increasing quantities, to amass.

accumulation n the act of accumulating or amassing; the addition of interest to principal; the mass accumulated.

accumulative adj cumulative; acquisitive.

accumulator n a rechargable battery; (horseracing) a bet that accumulates in value over successive races; (comput) a storage register.

accuracy n (pl accuracies) the quality of being accurate; exactness or correctness.

accurate adj conforming with the truth or an accepted standard; done with care, exact.—**accurately** adv.

accursed, accurst adj under or subject to a curse; ill-fated, doomed to destruction; detestable; execrable.

accusation n the act of accusing or being accused; an allegation; the charge of guilt brought against a person.

accusative n (gram) the case expressing the direct object of a word.

accusatorial, accusatory adj accusing, or containing an accusation; (of legal procedure) in which prosecutor and judge are not the same (opposite to inquisitorial).

accuse vt to charge with a crime, fault, etc; to blame.—**accuser** n.—**accusingly** adv.

accused n (law) (with the) the defendant in court facing a criminal charge.

accuser n one who accuses; one who formally charges an offence against another.

accustom vt to make used (to) by habit, use, or custom.

accustomed adj usual, customary; used to.

ace n the one spot in dice, playing cards, dominoes, etc; a point won by a single stroke, as in tennis; an expert. * adj (inf) excellent.

-acea n suffix forming the plural names for orders of animals, eg Crustacea, Crustaceae.

-aceae n suffix forming plural names for families of plants, eg Rosaceae.

acedia n an abnormal condition of the mind, characterized by lassitude, listlessness, and general indifference.

acentric adj away from the centre; having no centre.

acephalous adj headless; without a leader; an ovary of a plant that has its style springing from the base instead of the apex.

acerbic adj bitter and harsh to the taste; astringent.

acerbity n (pl acerbities) sharpness of speech or manner; (of taste) bitterness.

acerose adj (bot) like a needle, very narrow, rigid, and tapering to a point.

acervate adj growing in closely compacted clusters.

acet-, aceto- prefix vinegar.

acetabulum n (pl acetabula, acetabulums) the cavity of the hip bone into which the femur fits; one of the cuplike suckers on the arms of the cuttlefish; the posterior sucker of the leech; the saucer-shaped fructification of certain lichens; the receptacle of various fungi; a cup to hold vinegar.

acetanilide, acetanilid n a pungent white powder, formed by the action of acetyl choride on aniline, used in medicine as an antipyretic.

acetate n a salt or ester of acetic acid; a fabric made from cellulose acetate.

acetic adj of acetic acid or vinegar.

acetic acid n a clear liquid with a strong acid taste and sharp smell, present in a dilute form in vinegar

acetify vt (acetifying, acetifed) to turn into vinegar.—**acetification** n.—**acetifier** n.

acetometer n an instrument for gauging the strength or purity of vinegar or acetic acid.

acetone n a clear flammable liquid used as a solvent.

acetous, acetose adj of the nature of vinegar; sour; causing acetification.

acetylene n a gas that burns with a hot flame, used for welding, etc.

Achates n a faithful friend, from Aeneas's friend in Virgil's Aeneid.

ache n a dull, continuous pain. * vi to suffer a dull, continuous mental or physical pain; (inf) to yearn.—**achy** adj.

achieve vt to perform successfully, accomplish; to gain, win. —**achievable** adj.—**achiever** n.

achievement n a thing achieved, esp by great effort, courage, determination, etc; accomplishment; (her) an escutcheon in memory of a distinguished feat.

Achilles' heel n a person's vulnerable or weak point.

Achilles' tendon n a tendon attaching the heel to the calf muscles.

achlamydeous adj having neither calyx nor corolla.

achromatic adj colourless; transmitting light without decomposing it.—**achromatically** adv.—**achromaticity, achromatism** n.

achromatize vt to deprive of the power of transmitting colour; to render achromatic.—**achromatization** n.

acicula n (pl aciculae) a spine or prickle.

acicular adj needle-shaped.

aciculate, aciculated adj in the shape of a needle; acicular.

acid adj sharp, tart, sour; bitter. * n a sour substance; (chem) a corrosive substance that turns litmus red; (sl) LSD.—**acidly** adv.

acid house n a party where people take drugs and dance to House music; the style of popular music played.

acidic adj containing a large proportion of the acid element; opposed to basic.

acidifier n a substance having the property of imparting an acid quality.

acidify vti (acidifying, acidified) to make or become acid.—**acidification** n.

acidimeter n an instrument for measuring the strength of acids.—**acidimetric** adj.—**acidimetrically** adv.—**acidimetry** n.

acidity n (pl acidities) the quality or condition of being acid.

acidosis n an acid condition of the blood.—**acidotic** adj.

acid rain n rain made acidic by air pollution from

power stations, etc.

acid test *n* a crucial or conclusive test.

acidulate *vt* to render slightly acid. * *adj* acidulous.— acidulation *n*.

acidulous, acidulent *adj* somewhat acid; tart; peevish.

acierate *vt* (**acierating, acierated**) to change into steel.— acieration *n*.

acinaciform *adj* (*bot*) resembling a scimitar in shape, as an acinaciform leaf or pod.

aciniform *adj* grape-like; clustered like grapes.

-acious *adj suffix* forming adjectives meaning full of, inclined to, as mendacious.

-acity *n suffix* forming corresponding nouns of quality, as mendacity.

acknowledge *vt* to admit that something is true and valid; to show that one has noticed or recognized.

acknowledgment, acknowledgement *n* the act of acknowledging; the admission or recognition of a truth; confession; the expression of appreciation of a favour or benefit conferred; a printed recognition by an author of others' works used or referred to; a receipt.

aclinic line *n* the imaginary point near the equator where the magnetic needle has no dip, the magnetic equator.

acme *n* the peak or highest point; the height of perfection.

acne *n* inflammation of the skin glands producing pimples.

acolyte *n* an assistant or follower, esp of a priest.

aconite, aconitum *n* the plant wolf's-bane or monk's-hood; the drug prepared from the plant.—aconitic *adj*.

acorn *n* the nut of the oak tree.

acotyledon *n* (*bot*) a plant with seeds (spores) that have no cotyledons (seed lobes).—**acotyledonous** *adj*.

acoustic, acoustical *adj* of the sense of hearing or sound; of acoustics; (*mus*) not amplified, eg a guitar.—acoustically *adv*.

acoustician *n* one skilled in acoustics.

acoustics *npl* (*room, concert hall, etc*) properties governing how clearly sounds can be heard in it; (*in sing*) the physics of sound.—**acoustician** *n*.

acquaint *vt* to make (oneself) familiar (with); to inform; (*with* **with**) to introduce (to).

acquaintance *n* a person whom one knows only slightly.

acquainted *adj* having personal knowledge; (*with* **of, with**) familiar, known.

acquiesce *vi* (*with* **in**) to comply with readily, or put up no opposition to.

acquiescence *n* compliance; assent.—**acquiescent** *adj*.

acquire *vt* to gain by one's own efforts; to obtain.—acquirable *adj*.

acquirement *n* the act of acquiring; that which is acquired; mental attainment.

acquisition *n* the act of gaining, acquiring; someone or something that is acquired, often of special worth or talent.

acquisitive *adj* eager or greedy for possessions.—acquisitively *adv*.—acquisitiveness *n*.

acquit *vt* (**acquitting, acquitted**) to free from an obligation; to behave or conduct (oneself); to declare innocent.

acquittal *n* the act of releasing or acquitting, the state of being acquitted; a judicial discharge from accusation; the performance (of duty).

acquittance *n* a discharge or release from debt or other

liability; a receipt barring a further demand.

acre *n* land measuring 4840 square yards.

acreage *n* area measured in acres.

acrid *adj* sharp and bitter of taste or smell; caustic, critical in attitude or speech.—**acridity** *n*.—**acridly** *adv*.

acrimony *n* (*pl* **acrimonies**) bitterness of manner or language.—**acrimonious** *adj*.—**acrimoniously** *adv*.

acro- *prefix* topmost, extreme.

acrobat *n* a skilful performer of spectacular gymnastic feats.—**acrobatic** *adj*.—**acrobatically** *adv*.

acrobatics *npl* acrobatic feats.

acrocarpous *adj* (*bot*) having (like the mosses) the fruit at the end of the primary axis.

acrogen *n* (*bot*) a nonflowering plant increasing by growth from the top, as ferns and mosses.— **acrogenic, acrogenous** *adj*.

acrolith *n* a sculptured figure, with head and extremities of stone and the rest of wood.

acromegaly *n* a hormonal disease resulting in overdeveopment of the extremities.—**acromegalic** *adj*.

acronycal, acronical *adj* (*astron*) (*stars*) rising at sunset and setting at sunrise.

acronym *n* a word formed from the initial letters of other words (as *laser*).

acrophobia *n* dread of heights.—**acrophobe** *n*.—**acrophobic** *adj, n*.

acropolis *n* the highest part or citadel of a Grecian city; the citadel itself.

acrospire *n* (*bot*) the sprout of a seed.

across *prep* from one side to the other of; on or at an angle; on the other side of. * *adv* crosswise; from one side to the other.

across-the-board *adj* (*wage increase, cut, etc*) applying equally to all; (*horseracing*) winning a bet if the horse comes first, second or third.

acrostic *n* a poem or word puzzle in which certain letters of each line spell a complete word, etc.— **acrostically** *adv*.

acrylic *adj* of or derived from acrylic acid. * *n* an acrylic fibre or resin.

act *vi* to perform or behave in a certain manner; to perform a specific function; to have an effect; to perform on the stage; (*with* **up**) (*inf*) to misbehave; to malfunction. * *vt* to portray by actions, esp on the stage; to pretend, simulate; to take the part of, as a character in a play. * *n* something done, a deed; an exploit; a law; a main division of a play or opera; the short repertoire of a comic, etc; something done merely for effect or show.

acting *n* the art of an actor. * *adj* holding an office or position temporarily.

actinia *n* (*pl* **actiniae, actinias**) any of a genus of sea anemones that resemble flowers when the tentacles of the mouth are spread out.

actiniform, actinoid *adj* having the form of rays; star-shaped.

actinism *n* the property of light by which chemical changes are caused, as in photography.—**actinic** *adj*.—**actinically** *adv*.

actinium *n* a radioactive element occurring as a decay product of uranium.

actinozoan *see* **anthozoan**.

action *n* the process of doing something; an operation; a movement of the body, gesture; a land or sea battle; a lawsuit; the unfolding of events in a play, novel, etc; (*inf*) (*with* **the**) the centre of (social) activity.

actionable *adj* providing grounds for legal action.—**actionably** *adv*.

action painting *n* expressionist art produced by daubing, dribbling, splashing, throwing, etc, paint on to the canvas.

activate *vt* to make active; to set in motion; to make radioactive.—**activation** *n*.—**activator** *n*.

active *adj* lively, physically mobile; engaged in practical activities; energetic, busy; (*volcano*) liable to erupt; capable of producing an effect; radioactive; (*armed forces*) in full-time service. * *n* (*gram*) the verb form having as its subject the doer of the action.—**actively** *adv*.—**activeness** *n*.

active service, active duty *n* full-time service in a military force, esp during a war.

activist *n* an advocate of direct or militant action, esp in politics.—**activism** *n*.

activity *n* (*pl* **activities**) the state of being active; energetic, lively action; specific occupations (*indoor activities*).

act of God *n* a direct and unforeseeable act of nature that could not reasonably have been guarded against.

actor *n* a person who acts in a play, film, etc.—**actress** *nf*.

actual *adj* real; existing in fact or reality.

actuality *n* (*pl* **actualities**) the state of being real or actual; that which is in full existence; reality

actualize *vt* to realize in action; to describe realistically; to make actual.—**actualization** *n*.

actually *adv* as an existing fact, really; strange though it seems.

actuary *n* (*pl* **actuaries**) a person who calculates insurance risks, premiums, etc.—**actuarial** *adj*.

actuate *vt* to move or incite to action; to put in motion; to impel, influence.—**actuation** *n*.—**actuator** *n*.

acuity *n* sharpness of thought or vision.

aculeate *adj* pointed; (*zool*) equipped with a sting; (*bot*) having aculei or sharp prickles.

aculeus *n* (*pl* **aculei**) a prickle.

acumen *n* sharpness of mind, perception.

acuminate *adj* ending in a sharp point. * *vt* (**acuminating, acuminated**) to sharpen.—**acumination** *n*.

acupuncture *n* the insertion of the tips of fine needles into the skin at certain points to treat various common ailments.—**acupuncturist** *n*.

acute *adj* perceptive; sharp-witted; (*hearing*) sensitive; (*pain*) severe; very serious; (*angles*) less than 90 degrees; (*disease*) severe but not long lasting.—**acutely** *adv*.—**acuteness** *n*.

acute accent *n* a mark (´) over a vowel in certain languages to indicate emphasis or special quality.

-acy *n suffix* forming nouns of state or quality, eg piracy.

ad[1] *abbr* = advertisement.

ad[2] *prep* to, as in *ad absurdum*.

ad- *prefix* to, as in *adhere*.

AD *abbr* = *anno domini* (in the year of Our Lord) in dates of the Christian era, indicating the number of years since the birth of Christ.

ad absurdum (*Latin*) to absurdity.

adactylous *adj* without toes or fingers.

adage *n* a proverb, old saying.

adagio *adv* (*mus*) slowly, gracefully. * *n* (*pl* **adagios**) a slow movement.

adamant *adj* inflexible, unyielding. * *n* adamantine, an extremely hard substance.

adamantine *adj* made of adamantine; impenetrable, very hard. * *n* an extremely hard substance; the diamond (—*also* **adamant**).

Adamite *n* a child of Adam; a member of a sect who went naked; a nudist.—**Adamitic** *adj*.

Adam's apple *n* the hard projection of cartilage in the front of the neck.

Adam's needle *n* a popular name of the yucca.

adapt *vti* to make or become fit; to adjust to a new purpose or circumstances.—**adaptability** *n*.—**adaptable** *adj*.—**adapter** *n*.

adaptation *n* the process or condition of being adapted; something produced by modification; a version of a literary composition rewritten for a different medium.

adaptor *n* a device that allows an item of equipment to be put to new use; a device for connecting parts of differing size and shape; an electrical plug using one socket for different appliances.

adaxial *adj* towards the axis.

ADC *abbr* = aide-de-camp.

add *vt* to combine (two or more things together); to combine numbers or amounts in a total; to remark or write further. * *vi* to perform or come together by addition.

addax *n* (*pl* **addaxes, addax**) a large North African antelope with twisted horns.

addendum *n* (*pl* **addenda**) a thing to be added; supplementary text appended to a book, etc.

adder *n* the venomous viper.

adder's-tongue *n* a kind of fern whose spike resembles the tongue of a snake.

addict *n* a person who is dependent upon a drug. * *vt* to devote or give oneself up to; to practise sedulously (usu pejorative).—**addiction** *n*.—**addictive** *adj*.

addition *n* the act or result of adding; something to be added; an extra part.

additional *adj* added, extra; supplementary.—**additionally** *adv*.

additive *adj* produced by addition. * *n* a substance added (to food, etc) to improve texture, flavour, etc.

addle *vb* (**addling, addled**) *vt* to make corrupt, putrid or confused. * *vi* to become addled. * *adj* rotten.

addle-headed, addle-pated *adj* stupid, weak-brained; muddled.

address *vt* to write directions for delivery on (a letter, etc); to speak or write directly to; to direct one's skills or attention (to); (*golf*) to adjust one's stance and aim before hitting the ball; * *n* a place where a person or business resides, the details of this on a letter for delivery; a speech, esp a formal one; (*comput*) a specific memory location where information is stored.—**addressable** *adj*.

addressee *n* a person or company to whom a letter is addressed.

Addressograph *n* (*trademark*) an addressing machine.

adduce *vt* to offer as an example or evidence.

adducent *adj* bringing forward or together.

adducible, adduceable *adj* capable of being adduced.

adduct *vt* to pull towards; (*of muscles*) to draw to a common centre.—**adduction** *n*.—**adductive** *adj*.

adductor muscle *n* a muscle that draws certain parts to a common centre.

ademption *n* (*law*) the revocation of a grant; the lapse of a legacy.

aden-, adeno- *prefix* gland.

adenitis *n* inflammation of a gland.

adenoids *npl* enlarged masses of tissue in the throat behind the nose.—**adenoidal** *adj*.

adenoma *n* (*pl* **adenomas, adenomata**) a gland-like benign tumour.

adept *adj* highly proficient. * *n* a highly skilled person.—**adeptly** *adv.*—**adeptness** *n.*

adequacy *n* adequateness; sufficiency for a particular purpose.

adequate *adj* sufficient for requirements; barely acceptable.—**adequately** *adv.*—**adequateness** *n.*

à deux (*French*) for two; intimate.

adhere *vi* to stick, as by gluing or suction; to give allegiance or support (to); to follow.

adherence *n* the act or state of adhering; unwavering attachment.

adherent *adj* sticking, attached. * *n* a supporter of a political party, idea, etc.

adhesion *n* the action or condition of adhering; the attachment of normally separate tissues in the body.

adhesive *adj* sticky; causing adherence. * *n* a substance used to stick, such as glue, paste, etc.—**adhesiveness** *n.*

ad hoc *adj* for a particular purpose.

ad hominem (*Latin*) to the man, personal.

adiabatic *adj* (*physics*) not gaining or losing heat.—**adiabatically** *adv.*

adiaphorous *adj* (*theol*) tolerant in nonessential points of religion; morally indifferent; (*med*) neither helping nor harming.

adieu *n* (*pl* **adieux, adieus**) farewell, goodbye; good wishes at parting.

ad infinitum *adv* without end, forever.

ad interim (*Latin*) for the meantime.

adipocere *n* a fatty substance resulting from decomposition of animal bodies in moist places.—**adipocerous** *adj.*

adipose *adj* of, like or containing animal fat; fatty.—**adiposity** *n.*

adit *n* an entrance or passage; an entrance to a mine more or less horizontal.

adjacent *adj* nearby; adjoining, contiguous.—**adjacency** *n.*

adjective *n* a word used to add a characteristic to a noun or pronoun.—**adjectival** *adj.*—**adjectivally** *adv.*

adjoin *vt* to unite or join. * *vi* to lie next to.

adjoining *adj* beside, in contact with.

adjourn *vt* to suspend (a meeting) temporarily. * *vi* (*inf*) to retire (to another room, etc).—**adjournment** *n.*

adjournment *n* the act of adjourning; the postponement of a meeting.

adjudge *vt* (**adjudging, adjudged**) to decide or award judicially; to sentence; to determine in a controversy, to adjudicate.—**adjudgment, adjudgement** *n.*

adjudicate *vt* (*law*) to hear and decide (a case). * *vi* to serve as a judge (in or on).—**adjudicator** *n.*

adjudication *n* the act of determining judicially; a judicial sentence; a court's decision.

adjunct *n* something joined or added but inessential.—**adjunctive** *adj.*

adjuration *n* the solemn charging on oath; the oath used.

adjure *vt* to command on oath under pain of a penalty; to charge solemnly, request earnestly.

adjust *vt* to arrange in a more proper or satisfactory manner; to regulate or modify by minor changes; to decide the amount to be paid in settling (an insurance claim). * *vi* to adapt oneself.—**adjustable** *adj.*—**adjuster** *n.*

adjustment *n* the act of adjusting; arrangement.

adjutancy *n* (*pl* **adjutancies**) the office of an adjutant.

adjutant *n* a military staff officer who assists the commanding officer.

adjutant general *n* (*pl* **adjutants general**) the chief staff officer of an army, through whom all orders, etc, are received and issued by the general commanding.

adjuvant *adj* assisting, helpful. * *n* a helper, an auxiliary.

ad-lib *vti* (**ad-libbing, ad-libbed**) (*speech, etc*) to improvise. * *n* an ad-libbed remark. * *adv* spontaneously, freely.—**ad-libber** *n.*

adman *n* (*pl* **admen**) (*inf*) a person who works in the advertising business.

admass *n* the public targeted by or influenced by advertising.

admeasure *vt* (**admeasuring, admeasured**) to measure dimensions; to apportion.

admeasurement *n* a measurement by a rule; adjustment of proportions; dimensions.

admin *n* (*inf*) administration.

administer *vt* to manage, direct; to give out as a punishment; to dispense (medicine, punishment, etc); to tender (an oath, etc).

administrate *vti* to manage or control the affairs of a business, institution, etc.

administration *n* management; the people who administer an organization; the government; (*with cap*) the executive officials of a government, their policies, and term of office.

administrative *adj* of management; executive.—**administratively** *adv.*

administrator *n* a person who manages or supervises; (*law*) one appointed to settle an estate.

admirable *adj* deserving of admiration or approval.—**admirably** *adv.*

admiral *n* the commanding officer of a fleet; a naval officer of the highest rank.

admiralty *n* (*pl* **admiralties**) the department of a government having authority over naval affairs; the building in which naval affairs are transacted; the office of an admiral.

admiration *n* a feeling of pleasurable and often surprised respect or approval; an admired person or thing.

admire *vt* to regard with honour, approval and pleasure; to express admiration for.—**admirer** *n.*—**admiring** *adj.*—**admiringly** *adv.*

admissible *adj* that may be admitted or allowed.—**admissibility, admissibleness** *n.*

admission *n* an entrance fee; a conceding, confessing, etc; a thing conceded, confessed, etc.—**admissive** *adj.*

admit *vb* (**admitting, admitted**) *vt* to allow to enter or join; to concede or acknowledge as true. * *vi* to give access; (*with* **of**) to allow or permit.

admittance *n* the act of admitting; the right to enter.

admittedly *adv* acknowledged as fact, willingly conceded.

admix *vt* to mix with something else; to add as an extra ingredient.

admixture *n* a mixture, a compound of substances mixed together.

admonish *vt* to remind or advise earnestly; to reprove gently.

admonition *n* a friendly reproof or warning.—**admonitory** *adj.*

adnate *adj* (*bot*) with organic cohesion of unlike parts.

ad nauseam *adv* to a sickening degree.

ado *n* fuss, excitement, esp over trivial matters.

adolescence *n* the period of life between puberty and maturity; youth.

adobe n a brick made of sun-dried clay; clay for making adobe bricks; a building using such bricks.

adolescent adj pertaining to the stage between childhood and maturity; (inf) immature. * n an adolescent person.

adopt vt to take legally into one's family and raise as one's child; to select and pursue, eg a course of action; to take as one's own.—**adoption** n.

adoptive adj made or related by adoption.

adorable adj worthy of being adored; extremely charming.—**adorably** adv.

adoration n worship, homage; profound regard.

adore vt to worship; to love deeply.—**adoringly** adv.

adorn vt to decorate; to make more pleasant or attractive.—**adornment** n.

ad rem adj, adv to the point or purpose.

adrenal adj of or near the kidney. * n an adrenal gland.

adrenal gland n one of two glands situated above the kidneys that secretes adrenaline.

adrenaline n a hormone that stimulates the heart rate, blood pressure, etc in response to stress and that is secreted by the adrenal glands or manufactured synthetically.

adrift adj, adv afloat without mooring, drifting; loose; purposeless.

adroit adj skilful and clever, sharp-witted.—**adroitly** adv.—**adroitness** n.

adscititious adj taken in addition; added from without; additional, supplementary.

adsorb vti to accumulate on a surface, to collect by adsorption.—**adsorbable** adj.

adsorbent n an adsorbing substance.

adsorption n the action of a solid in condensing and holding a gas upon it.

adulate vt to flatter excessively or basely.—**adulator** n.—**adulatory** adj.

adulation n excessive flattery.—**adulatory** adj.

adult adj fully grown; mature; suitable only for adults, as in pornography, etc. * n a mature person, etc.—**adulthood** n.

adulterant adj adulterating. * n the person or thing that adulterates.

adulterate vt to make impure or inferior, etc by adding an improper substance.—**adulteration** n.—**adulterator** n.

adulterer n a person who commits adultery.—**adulteress** nf.

adulterine adj resulting from adulterous intercourse; fake, spurious; illegal.

adulterous adj guilty of adultery.

adultery n (pl **adulteries**) sexual intercourse between a married person and someone other than their legal partner.

adumbral adj overshadowing; shady.

adumbrate vt to foreshadow; to overshadow; to give a faint semblance of.—**adumbration** n.—**adumbrative** adj.

ad valorem adj, adv according to value; (customs, duties) levied on the value of goods as sworn to by the owner.

advance vt to bring or move forward; to promote; to raise the rate of; (money) to lend. * vi to go forward; to make progress; to rise in rank, price, etc. * n progress; improvement; a rise in value; payment beforehand; (pl) friendly approaches, esp to please. * adj in front; beforehand.

advanced adj in front; old; superior in development or progress.

advancement n promotion to a higher rank; progress in development.

advantage n superiority of position or condition; a gain or benefit; (tennis) the first point won after deuce. * vt to produce a benefit or favour to.

advantageous adj producing advantage, beneficial.—**advantageously** adv.

advent n an arrival or coming; (with cap) (Christianity) the coming of Christ; the four-week period before Christmas.

Adventist n a person who believes in Christ's second coming to set up a kingdom on earth.—**Adventism** n.

adventitious adj happening by chance; casual; fortuitous; accidental; produced out of normal and regular order; growing in an abnormal position.—**adventitiously** adv.—**adventitiousness** n.

Advent Sunday n the Sunday nearest (before or after) to St Andrew's Day (30 November).

adventure n a strange or exciting undertaking; an unusual, stirring, often romantic, experience.

adventure playground n a children's playground equipped with materials and objects for building, climbing, hiding in, etc.

adventurer n a person who seeks adventure; someone who seeks money or power by unscrupulous means.—**adventuress** nf.

adventurous adj inclined to incur risk; full of risk; rash; enterprising; daring.—**adventurously** adv.

adverb n a word that modifies a verb, adjective, another adverb, phrase, clause or sentence and indicates how, why, where, etc.—**adverbial** adj.—**adverbially** adv.

adversary n (pl **adversaries**) an enemy or opponent.

adversative adj (words) denoting opposition or contrariety; expressing opposition.

adverse adj hostile; contrary or opposite; unfavourable.—**adversely** adv.

adversity n (pl **adversities**) trouble, misery, misfortune.

advert[1] vt to refer (to); to turn attention (to).

advert[2] n (inf) an advertisement.

advertence, advertency n attention; heedfulness.—**advertent** adj.

advertently adv in an intentional manner.

advertise, advertize vt to call public attention to, esp in order to sell something, by buying space or time in the media, etc. * vi to call public attention to things for sale; to ask (for) by public notice.—**advertiser, advertizer** n.

advertisement, advertizement n advertising; a public notice, usu paid for by the provider of a good or service.

advertising, advertizing n the promotion of goods or services by public notices; advertisements; the business of producing adverts.

advice n recommendation with regard to a course of action; formal notice or communication.

advisable adj prudent, expedient.—**advisability** n.

advise vt to give advice to; to caution; to recommend; to inform. * vi to give advice.—**adviser, advisor** n.

advised adj acting with caution; deliberate; judicious.—**advisedly** adv.

advisory adj having or exercising the power to advise; containing or giving advice.

advocaat n a sweet egg-based liqueur.

advocacy n (pl **advocacies**) the function of an advocate; a pleading in support (of).

advocate n a person who argues or defends the cause of

another, esp in a court of law; a supporter. * *vt* to plead in favour of, to recommend.

adynamia *n* want of vital power, prostration, weakness.—**adynamic** *adj*.

adze, adz *n* a type of axe with a blade at right angles to the handle for cutting and shaping wood.

aedile, *n* a Roman magistrate who exercised supervision over the temples, public and private buildings, the markets, public games, sanitation, etc, hence a municipal officer.—*also* **edile**.

aegis *n* protection, sponsorship.—*also* **egis**.

Aeolian *adj* pertaining to Aeolis in Asia Minor or to the Aeolic race; of Aeolus, the Greek god of winds.

aeolian harp *n* a stringed instrument, the wires of which are set in motion and sounded by the wind.

Aeolic *adj* of Aeolis. * *n* the Aeolic dialect of ancient Greece.

aeon *n* a period of immense duration; an age.—*also* **eon**.

aeonian *adj* everlasting.—*also* **eonian**.

aerate *vt* to supply (blood) with oxygen by respiration; to supply or impregnate with air; to combine or charge a liquid with gas.—**aeration** *n*.

aerator *n* an apparatus for making aerated waters.

aerial *adj* belonging to or existing in the air; of aircraft or flying. * *n* a radio or TV antenna.

aerialist *n* a trapeze or high-wire artist.

aerie *see* **eyrie**.

aeriform *adj* having the form of air; gaseous; like air; unsubstantial.

aerify *vt* (**aerifying, aerified**) to combine with air.—**aerification** *n*.

aero- *prefix* aviation; air vessel

aerobatics *npl* stunts performed while flying an aircraft.

aerobe, aerobium *n* (*pl* **aerobes, aerobia**) a microbe that cannot live without air.

aerobic *adj* (*exercise*) that conditions the heart and lungs by increasing the efficient intake of oxygen by the body.

aerobics *npl* aerobic exercises.

aerodrome *n* an airfield.

aerodynamics *n* the study of the forces exerted by air or other gases in motion, esp around solid bodies such as aircraft.—**aerodynamic** *adj*.—**aerodynamically** *adv*.

aerofoil *n* a wing, the lifting surface of an aeroplane.

aerogram, aerogramme *n* a radio telegraphic message.

aerolite *n* a stone falling from the air, a meteorite.

aerology *n* the science that deals with the air and the atmosphere.—**aerologic, aerological** *adj*.—**aerologist** *n*.

aerometer *n* an instrument for weighing the air.—**aerometric** *adj*.

aerometry *n* the branch of physics concerned with air, pneumatics.

aeronaut *n* an aviator; the pilot or navigator of an aircraft.

aeronautical, aeronautic *adj* of or pertaining to aeronatics or an aernonaut.—**aeronautically** *adv*.

aeronautics *n* the science dealing with the operation of aircraft; the art or science of flight.

aeroplane *n* a power-driven aircraft.—*also* **airplane**.

aerosol *n* a suspension of fine solid or liquid particles in gas, esp as held in a container under pressure, with a device for releasing it in a fine spray.

aerospace *n* the earth's atmosphere and the space beyond. * *adj* technology for flight in aerospace.

aerostat *n* a balloon; a balloonist.

aerostatics *n* (*used as sing*) the science that studies the equilibrium of bodies sustained in air; the science of air navigation.—**aerostatic, aerostatical** *adj*.

aerostation *n* ballooning.

aeruginous *adj* of or like verdigris or copper rust.

aery *see* **eyrie**.

Aesculapian *adj* of or pertaining to Aesculapius, the Roman god of medicine, or to medicine.

aesthete *n* a person who is or pretends to be highly sensitive to art and beauty.—*also* **esthete**.

aesthetic, aesthetical *adj* of or pertaining to aesthetics; concerned with beauty rather than practicality.—*also* **esthetic, esthetical**.—**aesthetically, esthetically** *adv*.

aestheticism *n* the cult of the beautiful, esp a fantastic art movement at the end of the 19th century.—*also* **estheticism**.

aesthetics *n* the philosophy of art and beauty.—*also* **esthetics**.

aestival *adj* of or occurring in summer.—*also* **estival**.

aestivation *n* (*bot*) the arrangement of petals in a flower bud; (*zool*) the spending of the dry season in a dormant state.—*also* **estivation**.

aet., aetat. *abbr = aetatis*, of, at, the age of.

aetiology, aetiological, aetiologist *see* **etiology**.

af- *prefix* the form of *ad-* before *f*.

afar *adv* at, to, or from a great distance.

affable *adj* friendly; approachable.—**affability** *n*.—**affably** *adv*.

affair *n* a thing done or to be done; (*pl*) public or private business; (*inf*) an event; a temporary romantic or sexual relationship.

affaire (de coeur) *n* a love affair.

affect[1] *vt* to have an effect on; to produce a change in; to act in a way that alters or affects the feelings of.

affect[2] *vt* to pretend or feign (an emotion); to incline to or show a preference for.

affect[3] *n* an emotion, feeling or desire associated with a certain stimulus.

affectation *n* a striving after or an attempt to assume what is not natural or real; pretence.

affected *adj* (*manner, etc*) assumed artificially.—**affectedly** *adv*.—**affectedness** *n*.

affecting *adj* having power to excite the emotions; moving; pathetic.—**affectingly** *adv*.

affection *n* tender feeling; liking.—**affectional** *adj*.

affectionate *adj* showing affection, loving.—**affectionately** *adv*.

affective *adj* arousing the emotions, emotional.—**affectivity, affectiveness** *n*.

afferent *adj* conveying inwards or to a part.

affettuoso *adv* (*mus*) with feeling, tender, pathetic.

affiance *vt* to promise in marriage, betroth. * *n* faith, trust; a marriage contract.

affiche *n* a paper affixed to a wall, a poster.

affidavit *n* a statement written on oath.

affiliate *vt* to connect as a subordinate member or branch; to associate (oneself with). * *vi* to join. * *n* an affiliated person, club, etc.—**affiliation** *n*.

affinity *n* (*pl* **affinities**) attraction, liking; a close relationship, esp by marriage; similarity, likeness; (*chem*) a tendency in certain substances to combine.

affirm *vt* to assert confidently or positively; to confirm or ratify; (*law*) to make an affirmation.

affirmation *n* affirming; an assertion; a solemn declaration made by those declining to swear an oath, eg on religious grounds.

affirmative *adj* confirming; indicating agreement. * *n* a positive word or statement, eg *yes*.—**affirmatively** *adv*.

affix *vt* to fasten; to add, esp in writing; to attach.

afflatus *n* a breath or blast of wind; poetic or divine inspiration; creative power.

afflict *vt* to cause persistent pain or suffering to; to trouble greatly.—**afflictive** *adj*.

affliction *n* persistent pain, suffering; a cause of this.

affluence *n* an abundant supply, as of thoughts, words, riches; wealth.

affluent *adj* rich, well provided for.—**affluently** *adv*.

affluenza *n* a psychological disease resulting from an excess of affluence.

afflux *n* a flowing towards; an increase; an influx.

afford *vt* to be in a position to do or bear without much inconvenience; to have enough time, money, or resources for; to supply, produce.

afforest *vt* to plant trees to cover with forest.—**afforestation** *n*.

affranchise *vt* to free from an obligation or slavery; to enfranchise.—**affranchisement** *n*.

affray *n* a noisy fight.

affreightment *n* the hire of a ship for the transportation of goods or freight.

affright *vt* (*arch*) to frighten, to terrify; to alarm; to confuse.

affront *vi* to insult or offend openly or deliberately. * *n* such an insult or offence.

affusion *n* the act of pouring upon, esp in baptism.

Afghan *adj* pertaining to Afghanistan. * *n* a native of Afghanistan (—*also* **Afghani**).

aficionado *n* (*pl* **aficionados**) a devotee of a particular sport, activity, etc.

afield *adv* far away from home; to or at a distance; astray.

afire *adj*, *adv* on fire.

aflame *adj*, *adv* flaming, ablaze, in a glow.

afloat *adj* floating; at sea, on board a ship; debt-free; flooded.—*also adv*.

afoot *adj*, *adv* on foot; astir; on the move; in operation.

afore *adv*, *prep* in front, before; previously.

aforementioned *adj* mentioned previously.

aforesaid *adj* referred to previously.

aforethought *adj* premeditated.

a fortiori (*Latin*) with stronger reason, more conclusively.

afraid *adj* full of fear or apprehension; regretful.

afreet *n* (*Arabian myth*) an evil demon.

afresh *adv* anew, starting again.

African *adj* pertaining to Africa. * *n* a native of Africa.

African violet *n* any of various African plants popular as houseplants, with purple, pink or white flowers and velvet-textured leaves.

Afrikaans *n* a language derived from Dutch used in South Africa.

Afrikander, Africander *n* (any of) a breed of southern African beef cattle.

Afrikaner *n* a South African native white, esp of Dutch descent.

Afro *n* (*pl* **Afros**) a bushy hairstyle.

Afro- *prefix* Africa or African.

Afro-American *n* a Black American. * *adj* of or relating to Black Americans, or their culture, history, etc.

afrormosia *n* a hard wood similar to teak, used in furniture.

aft *adv* at, near, or towards the stern of a ship or rear of an aircraft.

after *prep* behind in place or order; following in time, later than; in pursuit of; in imitation of; in view of, in spite of; according to; about, concerning; subsequently. * *adv* later; behind. * *conj* at a time later than. * *adj* later, subsequent; nearer the stern of a ship or aircraft.

afterbirth *n* the placenta expelled from the womb after giving birth.

afterbrain *n* that portion of the brain behind the hindbrain, the medulla oblongata.

afterburner *n* a device in a jet engine used to provide extra thrust by igniting additional fuel.

aftercare *n* care following hospital treatment, etc.

afterdamp *n* the carbonic acid found in coal mines after an explosion of fire damp; choke damp.

aftereffect *n* an effect that occurs some time after its cause.

afterglow *n* the glow in the sky after sunset.

afterimage *n* the image that remains momentarily after the eye has been withdrawn from a bright object.

afterlife *n* life after death.

aftermath *n* the result, esp an unpleasant one.

aftermost *adj* hindmost; farthest aft, nearest to the stern.

afternoon *n* the time between noon and sunset or evening.—*also adj*.

afternote *n* the second or unaccented note, which takes its time from the first or accented note.

afterpains *npl* pains after childbirth.

aftershave *n* lotion for use after shaving.

aftertaste *n* the taste that remains after eating or drinking.

afterthought *n* a thought or reflection occurring later.

afterwards, afterward *adv* at a later time.

afterwit *n* wisdom that comes too late.

Ag (*chem symbol*) silver.

ag- *prefix* the form of *ad-* before *g*.

aga *n* in Turkey, a commander or chief officer; a title of respect.—*also* **agha**.

again *adv* once more; besides; on the other hand.

against *prep* in opposition to; unfavourable to; in contrast to; in preparation for; in contact with; as a charge on.

agalloch *n* a fragrant resinous heartwood.—*also* **eaglewood**.

agama *n* a short-tongued lizard found in India and Africa.

agami *n* a South American bird allied to the cranes; a trumpeter bird.

agamic *adj* (*biol*) produced without sexual action, asexual.—**agamically** *adj*.

agamogenesis *n* (*biol*) asexual reproduction.—**agamogenetic** *adj*.—**agamogenetically** *adv*.

agapanthus *n* an ornamental plant with bright blue flowers.

Agape *n* the love feast of the early Christians at communion time.

agape *adj* open-mouthed.

agar *n* a preparation of seaweed used for jelly, glue and bacteria culture.

agaric *n* a mushroom or other fungus of the genus *Agaricus*.

agate *n* stone with striped or clouded colouring used as a gemstone.

agave *n* a genus of plants of which the chief species is the century plant.

age *n* the period of time during which someone or something has lived or existed; a stage of life; later years of life; a historical period; a division of geological time; (*inf: often pl*) a long time. * *vti* (**ageing** *or* **aging, aged**) to grow or make old, ripe, mature, etc.

aged *adj* very old; of a specified age. * *n* (*with* **the**) the elderly.

ageism *n* discrimination on grounds of age.—*also* **agism**.—**ageist, agist** *adj*.

ageless *adj* timeless; appearing never to grow old.

age-long *see* **age-old**.

agency *n* (*pl* **agencies**) action; power; means; a firm, etc empowered to act for another; an administrative government division.

agenda, agendum *n* (*pl* **agendas, agendums**) a list of items or matters of business that need to be attended to.

agenesis *n* imperfect development of the body.—**agenetic** *adj*.

agent *n* a person or thing that acts or has an influence; a substance or organism that is active; one empowered to act for another; a government representative; a spy.

agent provocateur *n* (*pl* **agents provocateurs**) a person hired to tempt or provoke suspected persons into illegal acts so to incriminate themselves.

age-old *adj* ancient.—*also* **age-long**.

agglomerate *vti* to gather into a heap; to accumulate; to collect into a mass. * *n* a heap or mass; a rock consisting of volcanic fragments.—**agglomeration** *n*.—**agglomerative** *adj*.

agglutinate *vti* to stick or fuse together; to form words into compounds. * *adj* glued together.—**agglutination** *n*.—**agglutinative** *adj*.

agglutination *n* the act or condition of being united or joined together; the formation of words by combination, not inflexion.

aggrandize *vt* to increase the power, rank, wealth, or reputation of.—**aggrandizement** *n*.

aggravate *vt* to make worse; (*inf*) to annoy, irritate.—**aggravation** *n*.

aggravated *adj* (*law*) denoting a grave form of a specified offence.

aggravating *adj* making worse or more heinous; (*inf*) annoying, irritating.

aggregate *adj* formed of parts combined into a mass or whole; taking all units as a whole. * *n* a collection or sum of individual parts; sand, stones, etc mixed with cement to form concrete. * *vt* to collect or form into a mass or whole; to amount to (a total).—**aggregation** *n*.

aggression *n* an unprovoked attack; a hostile action or behaviour.

aggressive *adj* boldly hostile; quarrelsome; self-assertive, enterprising.—**aggressively** *adv*.—**aggressiveness** *n*.

aggressor *n* a person or country that attacks first.

aggrieve *vt* to pain; to injure; to have a grievance; to bear heavily upon; to oppress.—**aggrieved** *adj*.—**aggrievedly** *adv*.

aggro *n* (*sl*) aggression.

agha *see* **aga**.

aghast *adj* utterly horrified.

agile *adj* quick and nimble in movement; mentally acute.—**agility** *n*.

agio *n* (*pl* **agios**) the premium on changing paper money into cash or for exchanging one currency for another.—**agiotage** *n*.

agism *see* **ageism**.

agitate *vt* to shake, move; to disturb or excite the emotions of. * *vi* to stir up public interest for a cause, etc.—**agitation** *n*.—**agitator** *n*.

agitato *adj, adv* (*mus*) in a hurried or agitated manner.

agitator *n* one who starts or keeps up a political or other agitation; an implement for stirring.

aglet *n* a tag (of a shoelace, etc); a spangle, a metallic ornament; a catkin.—*also* **aiglet**.

aglow *adj* radiant with warmth or excitement.

agnail *n* a sore under or near the nail, a hangnail.

agnate *adj* related by the father's side or with the same male ancestor. * *n* a relative by the father's side.—**agnatic** *adj*.

agnomen *n* (*pl* **agnomina**) the fourth name of a person in ancient Rome; an additional name or epithet, as *Milton, the poet*.—**agnominal** *adj*.

agnostic *n* one who believes that knowledge of God is impossible. * *adj* pertaining to the agnostics or their teachings; expressing ignorance.—**agnostically** *adv*.—**agnosticism** *n*.

Agnus Dei *n* a figure of a lamb bearing a banner or cross, symbolic of Christ and associated emblematically with St John the Baptist; the lamb and flag; a medal of wax or precious metal stamped with the figure of the Agnus Dei and blessed by the pope for distribution on Low Sunday.

ago *adv* in the past. * *adj* gone by; past.

agog *adj, adv* in agitation or expectation; eager, on the lookout.

agonic *adj* making no angle.

agonistic *adj* of athletic contests; athletic; polemic; melodramatic; strained; unnatural.

agonize *vti* to suffer or cause to suffer agony; to strive.—**agonizingly** *adv*.

agony *n* (*pl* **agonies**) extreme mental or physical suffering.

agony aunt *n* a person who replies to readers' problem letters in an agony column.

agony column *n* the column of a newspaper devoted to advertisements relating to lost friends, etc; a column in a magazine containing readers' letters with helpful replies to problems.

agoraphobia *n* abnormal fear of crossing open places.—**agoraphobic** *adj, n*.

agouti *n* (*pl* **agoutis, agouties**) a rodent similar to the guinea pig found in the West Indies and South America.

AGR *abbr* = advanced gas-cooled reactor.

agraphia *n* the inability to write due to mental illness.

agrarian *adj* of or relating to fields, or their cultivation; of or relating to farmers or agricultural life. * *n* an advocate of redistribution of property in land.

agrarianism *n* the principle of a uniform division of land; agitation with respect to land tenure.

agree *vb* (**agreeing, agreed**) *vi* to be of similar opinion; to consent or assent (to); to come to an understanding about; to be consistent; to suit a person's digestion; (*gram*) to be consistent in gender, number, case, or person. * *vt* to concede, grant; to bring into harmony; to reach terms on.

agreeable *adj* likeable, pleasing; willing to agree.—**agreeableness** *n*.—**agreeably** *adv*.

agreement *n* harmony in thought or opinion, correspondence; an agreed settlement between two people, etc.

agrestic *adj* rustic; uncouth.

agriculture *n* the science or practice of producing crops and raising livestock; farming.—**agricultural** *adj.*—**agriculturally** *adv.*—**agriculturist, agriculturalist** *n.*

agrimony *n* (*pl* **agrimonies**) a yellow-flowered plant.

agronomics *n* (*used as sing*) the part of economics concerned with the management and distribution of farming lands.—**agronomic, agronomical** *adj.*

agronomy *n* the science of land cultivation and management, husbandry.—**agronomist** *n.*

agrostology *n* the branch of botany that treats of the grasses.

aground *adj, adv* on or onto the shore.

aguardiente *n* an inferior Spanish brandy.

ague *n* malaria, an intermittent fever; the cold fit of the intermittent fever.—**aguish** *adj.*

ah *interj* an exclamation of sudden emotion.

AH *abbr* = *anno Hegira* (in the year of the Hegira) used in dates of the Muslim era.

aha *interj* an exclamation of satisfaction, triumph or mockery.

ahead *adj* in or to the front; forward; onward; in advance; winning or profiting.—*also adv.*

ahem *interj* an exclamation to call attention.

ahoy *interj* a term used in hailing a vessel.

A.I. *abbr* = artificial insemination; artificial intelligence.

ai *n* (*pl* **ais**) a South American three-toed sloth.

AID *abbr* = Agency for International Development; artificial insemination (by) donor.

aid *vti* to help, give assistance to. * *n* anything that helps; a specific means of assistance, eg money, equipment; a helper.

aide *n* an aide-de-camp; assistant.

aide-de-camp *n* (*pl* **aides-de-camp**) a military officer serving as an assistant to a senior officer.

aide-mémoire *n* (*pl* **aides-mémoire**) a summarized document; a memorandum, etc, as an aid to the memory.

AIDS, Aids *n* (*acronym for* acquired immune deficiency syndrome) a condition caused by a virus, in which the body loses its immunity to infection.

AIDS-related complex *n* a condition in which mild symptoms of AIDS (e.g. fever, weight loss) precede development of the full-blown disease.

aiglet *see* **aglet**.

aigrette, aigret *n* a small white heron; a plume arranged in imitation of the feathers of the heron, worn on helmets and as a hat decoration.

aiguille *n* a sharp peak of rock.

aiguillette *n* an ornamental tag or lace worn on uniforms and liveries.

AIH *abbr* = artificial insemination (by) husband.

ail *vt* to give or cause pain. * *vi* to feel pain; to be afflicted with pain.

aileron *n* a hinged section on the wing of an aircraft used for lateral control.

ailing *adj* unwell.

ailment *n* a slight illness.

ailurophobia *n* cat fear; a morbid dread of cats and a consciousness of their presence even when they are not in sight.—**ailurophobe** *n.*

aim *vti* to point or direct towards a target so as to hit; to direct (one's efforts); to intend. * *n* the act of aiming; purpose, intention.

aimless *adj* without purpose or object.—**aimlessly** *adv.*—**aimlessness** *n.*

ain't = am not, is not, are not, has not, have not.

air *n* the mixture of invisible gases surrounding the earth; the earth's atmosphere; empty, open space; a

light breeze; aircraft, aviation; outward appearance, demeanour; a pervading influence; (*mus*) a melody; (*pl*) an affected manner. * *vt* to expose to the air for drying, etc; to expose to public notice; (*clothes*) to place in a warm place to finish drying.

airbag *n* a safety device in a motor vehicle that automatically inflates to protect the occupants in the event of an accident.

air base *n* a base for military aircraft.

air bath *n* a lengthened exposure of the body to the action of the air and sun; an arrangement for drying articles by exposing them to air of any regulated temperature.

air bed *n* an inflatable mattress usu of plastic or rubber.

airborne *adj* carried by or through the air; aloft or flying.

air box *n* a tube for conveying fresh air to a mine; a flue supplying air to a furnace; a chamber behind the fire box of a furnace to assist combustion by supply of air.

air brake *n* a brake operated by compressed air.

air brick *n* a brick with holes in the sides through which air for ventilation can pass.

airbrush *n* a device for spraying paint by compressed air.

airbus *n* a jet aircraft designed for short-distance intercity flights.

air conditioning *n* regulation of air humidity and temperature in buildings, etc.

air-cooled *adj* cooled by having air passed over, into, or through.

air course *n* a ventilating passage in a mine.

air cover *n* protection for ground forces given by fighter aircraft; the aircraft giving this protection.

aircraft *n* (*pl* **aircraft**) any machine for travelling through air.

aircraft carrier *n* a warship with a large flat deck, for the carrying, taking off and land of aircraft.

aircrew *n* the crew of an aircraft.

air cushion *n* an inflatable cushion usu of plastic or rubber.

air drop *n* a dropping by parachute of troops and supplies.

Airedale *n* a large rough-coated terrier.

airfield *n* a field where aircraft can take off and land.

air force *n* the aviation branch of a country's armed forces.

air gas *n* an illuminating gas made from air charged with the vapour of petroleum, naphtha, etc.

airgun *n* a gun that fires pellets by compressed air.

airhead *n* (*sl*) a stupid person.

air hostess *n* a stewardess on a passenger aircraft.

airing *n* exposure to the open air for drying or freshening; exercise in the open air; exposure to public view.

airless *adj* stuffy; sultry.—**airlessness** *n.*

air letter *n* a sheet of light writing paper that is folded and sealed for sending by airmail.

airlift *n* the transport of cargo, troops, passengers, etc by air, esp in an emergency.—*also vt.*

airline *n* a system or company for transportation by aircraft; a beeline.

airliner *n* a large passenger aeroplane.

airlock *n* a blockage in a pipe caused by an air bubble; an airtight compartment giving access to a pressurized chamber.

airmail *n* mail transported by aircraft.

airman *n* (*pl* **airmen**) a male civilian or military pilot, etc.—**airwoman** *nf* (*pl* **airwomen**).

airmiss *n* the near collision of aircraft in flight.

airplane *see* **aeroplane**.

air plant *n* a plant that derives its nourishment from the air, an epiphyte.

airplay *n* the playing of a recording over radio or TV.

air pocket *n* a patch of rarefied air causing aircraft to drop abruptly.

airport *n* a place where aircraft can land and take off, with facilities for repair, etc.

air pump *n* a machine for exhausting the air from a receiver; the pump used to exhaust the water and gases from the condenser of a steam engine.

air raid *n* an attack by military aircraft on a surface target.

airs *npl* affected behaviour for the purpose of impressing others.

airship *n* a self-propelled steerable aircraft that is lighter than air.

airsick *adj* nauseated due to the motion of an aircraft.

airspace *n* the space above a nation over which it maintains jurisdiction.

airspeed *n* the speed of an aircraft relative to the outside air.

airstrip *n* an area of land cleared for aircraft to land on; a runway.

airtight *adj* too tight for air or gas to enter or escape; (*alibi, etc*) invulnerable.

airtime *n* (*radio, TV*) the time alotted to a programme, item, commercial, etc; the time at which the broadcast begins.

air-to-air *adj* (*weaponry, communications, etc*) activated between aircraft in flight.

air valve *n* a valve regulating the supply of air to a boiler or pipe.

air vesicle *n* a dilatation of the trachea of certain insects enabling them to ascend or descend by its inflation or expiration; a vesicle filled with air in certain fishes, connected with the swim bladder.

airway *n* an aircraft route; a ventilation passage, as in a mine; a passage for air into the lungs; (*med*) a device to maintain the airway of an unconscious person.

airworthy *adj* safe to fly.—**airworthiness** *n*.

airy *adj* (**airier, airiest**) open to the air; breezy; light as air; graceful; lighthearted; flippant.—**airily** *adv*.—**airiness** *n*.

aisle *n* a passageway, as between rows of seats; a side part of a church.

ait *n* a small island in a river or lake.—*also* **eyot**.

aitch *n* the letter H.

aitchbone *n* the rump bone; the cut of meat lying over it.

ajar *adv* partly open, as a door.

AK *abbr* = Alaska.

aka, a.k.a *or* **AKA** *abbr* = also known as.

akimbo *adv* having the hands on the hips and the elbows bent outwards.

akin *adj* related; essentially similar, compatible.

Akkadian *n* an ancient Babylonian language preserved in cuneiform inscriptions. * *adj* of Akkad or Accad, the Babylonian city.—*also* **Accadian**.

al- *prefix* the form of *ad-* before *l*.

-al *adj suffix* of, of the nature of, as in *mortal, colossal*. * *n suffix* esp of verbal action, as in *approval*.

AL *abbr* = Alabama.

Al (*chem symbol*) = aluminium.

Ala. *abbr* = Alabama.

à la *prep* in the style of.

alabaster *n* a type of soft, chalky stone used in orna-

ments.—**alabastrine** *adj*.

à la carte *adj* (*menu*) with dishes listed and priced as separate items.

alack *interj* an exclamation of blame, sorrow, or surprise.

alacrity *n* promptness, eager readiness.—**alacritous** *adj*.

alameda *n* a public promenade planted with trees.

à la mode *adv* in the fashion. * *adj* fashionable.

alamode *n* a thin, light, glossy black silk.

alar *adj* of wings; winged; winglike; wing-shaped.—*also* **alary**.

alarm *n* a signal warning of danger; an automatic device to arouse from sleep or to attract attention; the fear arising from the apprehension of danger. * *vt* to give warning of danger; to fill with apprehension or fear.

alarm clock *n* a clock with an apparatus that can be set to ring loudly at a particular time.

alarming *adj* frightening, disconcerting.—**alarmingly** *adv*.

alarmist *n* one who keeps prophesying danger, a panicmonger.—**alarmism** *n*.

alarum *n* (*arch*) an alarm.

alary *see* **alar**.

alas *interj* expressive of misery, unhappiness, grief, etc.

alate *adj* having wings or winglike side appendages.

alb *n* a white priestly vestment reaching to the feet, worn at the celebration of the Eucharist in the RC Church and in some Anglican churches.

albacore *n* a large species of mackerel or tunny found in the Atlantic and Pacific Oceans.

albata *n* an alloy imitating silver; German silver.

albatross *n* any of various large web-footed seabirds; a heavy burden, as of debt, guilt, etc; (*golf*) a score of three under par.

albeit *conj* although, even though, notwithstanding.

albescent *adj* shading into white; whitish; becoming white.—**albescence** *n*.

albino *n* (*pl* **albinos**) a person lacking normal coloration, so that they have white skin and pink eyes; an animal or plant with abnormal pigmentation.

Albion *n* (*arch*) Britain.

album *n* a book with blank pages for the insertion of photographs, autographs, etc; a long-playing record, cassette, or CD.

albumen *n* the white of an egg.

albumenize *vt* to coat (paper) with an albuminous solution.

albuminoid *adj* like albumen. * *n* a class of organic compounds that form the chief part of the organs and tissues of animals and plants; proteids.

albuminous *adj* like, or containing, albumin.

albuminuria *n* the presence of albumin in the kidneys and the urine.

alburnum *n* the white and softer part of wood between the bark and the heartwood; sapwood.

alchest *see* **alkahest**.

Alcaic *n* a kind of lyric verse form consisting of four lines of four feet devised by the 7th-century BC Greek poet Alcaeus.—*also adj*.

alcaide *n* the commander of a castle in Spain; the warder of a Spanish jail.

alcalde, alcade *n* a magistrate or justice in Spain or Portugal.

alcazar *n* a Spanish or Moorish palace or castle.

alchemist *n* one who studies or practises alchemy.

alchemize *vt* to transmute.

alchemy *n* (*pl* **alchemies**) chemistry as practised during medieval times, with the aim of transmuting base metals into gold.—**alchemic, alchemical** *adj*.—**alchemist** *n*.

alcohol *n* a liquid, generated by distillation and fermentation, that forms the intoxicating agent in wine, beer and spirits; a liquid containing alcohol; a chemical compound of this nature.

alcoholic *adj* of or containing alcohol; caused by alcohol. * *n* a person suffering from alcoholism.

alcoholism *n* a disease caused by excessive consumption of alcohol.

alcoholize *vt* to subject to the influence of alcohol; to rectify (spirits of wine).—**alcoholization** *n*.

alcoholometer *n* an instrument for determining the strength of spirits.

Alcoran *n* the Koran, the Muslim bible.

alcove *n* a recess off a larger room.

aldehyde *n* a volatile fluid with a suffocating smell, obtained from alcohol.

al dente *adj* cooked but still firm to the teeth.

alder *n* a genus of plants growing in moist land and related to the birch.

alderman *n* (*pl* **aldermen**) in US, a member of certain municipal councils; (*formerly*) in England and Wales, a senior councillor.—**aldermanic** *adj*.

ale *n* beer.

aleatory *adj* depending on dice or chance.

alee *adj, adv* (*naut*) on the lee, to leeward.

alegar *n* vinegar made from ale.

alehouse *n* a place where ale is sold.

alembic *n* an apparatus formerly used in distilling.

Alençon *n* a fine lace made at Alençon in France.

alert *adj* watchful; active, brisk. * *n* a danger signal. * *vt* to warn of impending danger, put in a state of readiness.—**alertly** *adv*.—**alertness** *n*.

alexandrine *n* a heroic verse of six iambic feet, or twelve syllables.—*also adj*.

alexia *n* the inability to read, due to mental illness.

alexin *n* a disease-resisting protein in blood serum.

alfalfa *n* a deep-rooted leguminous plant grown widely for hay and forage.—*also* **lucerne**.

alfresco *adj* taking place outside in the open.—*also adv*.

alga *n* (*pl* **algae**) any of a group of chiefly aquatic lower plants classified according to colour.—**algal** *adj*.

algarroba, algaroba *n* the carob tree and bean; St John's bread.

algebra *n* the branch of mathematics dealing with the properties and relations of numbers; the generalization and extension of arithmetic.—**algebraic, algebraical** *adj*.—**algebraist** *n*.

Algerian *adj* pertaining to Algeria or Algiers. * *n* a native of Algeria or Algiers.

Algerine *adj* Algerian.

-algia *n suffix* pain.—**algic** *adj*.

algid *adj* cold, chilly.

ALGOL *n* (*comput*) a high-level programming language used for solving general problems in science and mathematics.

algology *n* the study of algae.—**algologist** *n*.

algor *n* the rigor or chill on the onset of fever.

algorism *n* the arabic (decimal) numeration; arithmetic.—**algorismic** *adj*.

algorithm *n* (*math*) any method or procedure for computation.—**algorithmic** *adj*.—**algorithmically** *adv*.

alias *adv* otherwise called. * *n* (*pl* **aliases**) an assumed name.

alibi *n* (*pl* **alibis**) (*law*) the plea that a person charged with a crime was elsewhere when it was committed; (*inf*) any excuse.

alien *adj* foreign; strange; distasteful to, counter to. * *n* a person from another country, place, etc; a person of foreign birth who has not been naturalized; a being from outer space.

alienable *adj* (*law*) (*property*) that may be transferred.—**alienability** *n*.

alienage *n* the state or legal status of an alien.

alienate *vt* to render hostile or unfriendly; to make less affectionate or interested.

alienation *n* estrangement; transference; diversion to another purpose; mental derangement.

alienee *n* (*law*) one to whom property is transferred.

alienism *n* the study and treatment of mental alienation.—**alienist** *n*.

alienor *n* (*law*) one who transfers property to another.

aliform *adj* wing-shaped.

alight[1] *vi* (**alighting, alighted** *or* **alit**) to come down, as from a bus; to land after a flight.

alight[2] *adj* on fire; lively.

align *vt* to place in a straight line, to bring into agreement, etc. * *vi* to line up.—**alignment** *n*.

alignment *n* the act of laying out or adjusting by a line; the ground plan of a railway or road.

alike *adj* like one another. * *adv* equally; similarly.

aliment *n* food; the necessaries of life generally; an allowance for support by decree of court. * *vt* to make provision for the maintenance of; to make provision for the support of parents or children respectively.—**alimental** *adj* .

alimentary *adj* pertaining to nourishment, food.

alimentary canal *n* the tube extending within the body from the mouth to the anus through which food passes and is absorbed.

alimentation *n* the act of giving nourishment; the function of the alimentary canal.—**alimentative** *adj*.

alimony *n* (*pl* **alimonies**) an allowance for support made by one spouse to the other, esp a man to his wife or former wife, pending or after a legal separation or divorce.—*also* **maintenance**.

aliped *adj* having wing-like limbs, as the bat.

aliphatic *adj* (*chem*) of fat.

aliquant *adj* (*math*) being a part of a number that does not divide it without a remainder, as 8 is the aliquant part of 25.—*also n*.

aliquot *adj* (*math*) being a part of a number of quantity that will divide it without a remainder, as 8 is the aliquot part of 24.—*also n*.

alive *adj* having life; active, alert; in existence, operation, etc.

alizarin *n* a red colouring matter found in madder but now produced from anthracene.

alkahest *n* the supposed universal solvent of the alchemists.—*also* **alcahest**.

alkali *n* (*pl* **alkalis, alkalies**) (*chem*) any salt or mixture that neutralizes acids.—**alkaline** *adj*.

alkalify *vb* (**alkalifying, alkalified**) *vt* to form or convert into alkali. * *vi* to become an alkali.

alkalimeter *n* an instrument used to determine the relative strength of alkalis.

alkalimetry *n* the process of determining the strength of an alkaline mixture or liquid.—**alkalimetric** *adj*.

alkaline *adj* pertaining to, or having the properties of, an alkali.—**alkalinity** *n*.

alkalize *vt* to convert into an alkali or render alkaline.—**alkalizable** *adj*.

alkaloid n a body or substance containing alkaline properties; (pl) nitrogenous compounds met with in plants in combination with organic acids. * adj resembling an alkali in its properties.

alkanet n a rich red dye; the plant the root of which yields it.

all adj the whole amount or number of; every one of. * adv wholly; supremely, completely; entirely. * n the whole number, quantity; everyone; everything.

alla breve adv (mus) in quick time, with one breve to a measure.

Allah n the Muslim name of God.

all along adv throughout.

allantoid adj of or pertaining to the allantois; (bot) sausage-shaped. * n the allantois.—**allantoidal** adj.

allantois n (pl **allantoides**) a membranous appendage of most vertebrate embryos.

allay vt to lighten, alleviate; to pacify or make calm.

all but adv almost.

all clear n a signal indicating that a danger has passed or that it is safe to proceed.

allegation n the act of alleging; assertion; declaration; that which is asserted or alleged; that which is offered as a plea, an excuse, or justification; the statement as yet unproved of a party to a suit.

allege vt to assert or declare, esp without proof; to offer as an excuse.

allegedly adv asserted without proof.

allegiance n the obligation of being loyal to one's country, etc; devotion, as to a cause.

allegorical, allegoric adj pertaining to, consisting of, or in the nature of allegory; figurative.—**allegorically** adv.

allegorize vt to put in the form of an allegory.—**allegorization** n.

allegory n (pl **allegories**) a fable, story, poem, etc in which the events depicted are used to convey a deeper, usu moral or spiritual, meaning.—**allegorist** n.

allegretto adv (mus) moderately fast. * n (pl **allegrettos**) a piece of music played in this way.

allegro adv (mus) fast. * n (pl **allegros**) a piece of music played in this way.

allele n (genetics) either of a pair of contrasting characteristics one or the other of which is found unmixed in descendants of a cross between parental forms respectively possessing them.—also **allelomorph**.—**allelic** adj.—**allelism** n.

alleluia see **hallelujah**.

allemande n a German national dance in three-quarter time.

allergen n a substance inducing an allergic reaction.

allergenic adj causing an allergic reaction.

allergy n (pl **allergies**) an abnormal reaction of the body to substances (certain foods, pollen, etc) normally harmless; antipathy.—**allergic** adj.

allerion n (her) an eagle displayed without feet or beak.

alleviate vt to lessen or relieve (pain, worry, etc).—**alleviation** n.—**alleviator** n.

alleviative adj tending to alleviate. * n that which alleviates.

alley n a narrow street between or behind buildings; a bowling lane.

all fours adv on hands and knees.

All-hallowe'en n Hallowe'en.

All-hallows npl All Saints' Day, celebrated on 1 November, in honour of all the saints.

alliaceous adj of the nature or property of garlic or the onion.

alliance n a union by marriage or treaty for a common purpose; an agreement for this; the countries, groups, etc in such an association.

allied see **ally**.

alligator n a large reptile similar to the crocodile but having a short, blunt snout.

alligator pear n the avocado.

all in adj (price, etc) all-inclusive.

all-in adj (inf) exhausted.

all-inclusive adj including everything.

alliteration n the repetition of the same sound at the beginning of two or more words in a phrase, etc.—**alliterative** adj.

allocate vt to distribute or apportion in shares; to set apart for a specific purpose.

allocation n the act of alloting, allocating, or assigning; an allotment or assignment; an allowance made on an account.

allocution n a formal address, esp as one delivered by the Pope to his clergy or to the Church generally.

allodial adj freehold; not feudal. * n land thus held.

allodium, allod n (pl **allodia, allods**) freehold estate; land that is the absolute property of the owner.

allogamy n (biol) cross-fertilization.—**allogamous** adj.

allograph n a signature by one person on behalf of another, opposite of autograph.—**allographic** adj.

allomorphism n (chem) the property in certain substances of assuming a different form while remaining the same in constitution.

all one adj, n in effect the same.

allopath, allopathist n one who favours or practises allopathy.

allopathy n the orthodox medical practice of treating disease by inducing an action opposite to the disease it is sought to cure, opposite of homoeopathy.—**allopathic** adj.—**allopathically** adv.

allot vt (**allotting, allotted**) to distribute, allocate.

allotment n allotting; a share allotted; a small area of land rented for cultivation.

allotropy, allotropism n the capability shown by certain chemical elements to assume different forms, each characterized by peculiar qualities, as the occurrence of carbon in the form of the diamond, charcoal and plumbago respectively.—**allotropic** adj.—**allotropically** adv.

allottee n one to whom an allotment or share is granted or assigned; a plot-holder.

all out adv with maximum capacity.

all-out adj using maximum effort.

all-over adj covering the whole surface.

allow vt to permit; to acknowledge, admit as true; (money) to give, grant as an allowance at regular intervals; to estimate as an addition or deduction. * vi to admit the possibility (of).

allowable adj permissible.—**allowably** adv.

allowance n an amount or sum allowed or given at regular times; a discount; a portion of income not subject to income tax; permission; admission, concession.

alloy n a solid substance comprising a mixture of two or more metals; something that degrades the substance to which it is added. * vt to make into an alloy; to degrade or spoil by mixing with an inferior substance.

all-purpose adj suitable for many uses.

all right adv good enough, acceptable; without doubt. *

adj satisfactory; safe, well; agreeable. * *interj* (*used to express consent*).—*also* **alright**.

all-round *adj* efficient in all respects, esp sport.

All Saints' Day *n* (*Christian Church*) 1 November, a festival in honour of all the saints.

All Souls' Day *n* (*RC Church*) the day, celebrated 2 November, in honour of the departed.

allspice *n* an aromatic spice made from the berry of a West Indian tree.

all-star *adj* made up entirely of outstanding performers.

all there *adj* (*sl*) not mentally wanting.

all-time *adj* unsurpassed until now.

all told *adv* with all counted; all in all.

allude *vi* to refer indirectly to.

allure *vt* to entice, charm. * *n* fascination; charm.— **allurement** *n*.

alluring *adj* attractive.

allusion *n* alluding; an implied or indirect reference.— **allusive** *adj*.

allusive *adj* having reference to something not definitely expressed.—**allusively** *adv*.—**allusiveness** *n*.

alluvion *n* the wash of the sea or river against a shore; land added to a shore or riverbank by the action of the water; an overflow.

alluvium *n* (*pl* **alluviums, alluvia**) earth, sand, gravel, etc deposited by moving water.—**alluvial** *adj*.

ally *vti* (**allying, allied**) to join or unite for a specific purpose; to relate by similarity of structure, etc. * *n* (*pl* **allies**) a country or person joined with another for a common purpose.

Almagest *n* the great astronomical treatise of Ptolemy of the 2nd century AD; (*without cap*) other similar treatises.

alma mater *n* one's school, college, or university.

almanac *n* a calendar with astronomical data, weather forecasts, etc.

almanack *n* (*arch*) an almanac.

almandine *n* a violet-red variety of garnet, tinged sometimes with blue or yellow.

almighty *adj* all-powerful. * *n* (*with cap*) God, the all-powerful.—**almightly** *adv*.—**almightiness** *n*.

almond *n* the edible kernel of the fruit of a tree of the rose family; the tree bearing this fruit. * *adj* (*eyes, etc*) oval and pointed at one or both ends.

almoner *n* (*formerly*) one who dispenses or distributes alms or charity; an alms purse; a pouch or purse which in early times was suspended from the girdle.

almost *adv* all but, very nearly but not quite all.

alms *npl* money, food, etc given to the poor.

almshouse *n* a house endowed by private or public charity and appropriated to the use of the poor.

aloe *n* (*pl* **aloes**) a succulent plant with tall spikes of flowers.

aloes *n* (*used as sing*) the bitter juice of the aloe plant used in medicine.

aloft *adv* in the air, flying; high up.

alone *adj* isolated; without anyone or anything else; unassisted; unique. * *adv* exclusively.

along *adv* onward, forward; over the length of; in company and together with; in addition. * *prep* in the direction of the length of; in accordance with.

alongside *prep* close beside. * *adv* at the side.

aloof *adv* at a distance; apart. * *adj* cool and reserved.— **aloofness** *n*.

alopecia *n* baldness; loss of hair through skin disease.

aloud *adv* with a normal voice; loudly; spoken.

alow *adv* (*naut*) to or in a lower part; below.

alp *n* a mountain peak.

alpaca *n* a Peruvian llama with long fine wool; a fabric made of this wool.

alpenglow *n* a peculiar purple glow on the snow on the Alps seen just before sunrise and after sunset.

alpenhorn *n* a long and nearly straight horn used by the mountaineers of the Alps.

alpenstock *n* a stout staff with an iron spike, used by mountain climbers.

alpha *n* the first letter of the Greek alphabet.

alphabet *n* the characters used in a language arranged in conventional order.

alphabetical, alphabetic *adj* pertaining to an alphabet; in the order of the alphabet.—**alphabetically** *adv*.

alphabetize *vt* to arrange in alphabetical order.—**alphabetization** *n*.

alphanumeric, alphameric *adj* containing letters of the alphabet and numerals.—**alphanumerically, alphamerically** *adv*.

alpha particle *n* a particle of helium given off by radium.

alpha ray *n* radiation of alpha particles.

alpine *adj* (*with cap*) of the Alps; of high mountains. * *n* a mountain plant, esp a small herb.

alpinist *n* a mountaineer who climbs in the Alps or in areas of similar mountains.—**alpinism** *n*.

Alps *npl* a high mountain range in south central Europe.

already *adv* by or before the time specified; before the time expected.

alright *adv* a frequent spelling of all right.

Alsatian *n* a German shepherd; a native of Alsace.

also *adv* in addition, besides.

also-ran *n* a defeated contestant in a race, an election, etc.

alt *n* (*mus*) the high notes above the treble staff.

Alta. (*abbr*) = Alberta.

Altaic *adj* pertaining to the Altaic mountain regions, partly bounding Russia and China. * *n* the language of the region.

altar *n* a table, etc for sacred purposes in a place of worship.

altarage *n* the offerings placed upon the altar to be devoted to the church, or appropriated by the priest as stipend.

altar cloth *n* a general term for the coverings of the altar.

altar ledge *n* a step or ledge behind the altar of a church, slightly raised above it for holding lights, flowers, and other symbolical ornaments; a retable.

altarpiece *n* a painting, decorative screen, or other work of art, placed over or behind an altar.

altarscreen *n* a screen or partition separating the altar from the choir; a reredos.

altar slab *n* the top of an altar; the consecrated part of an altar (the mensa).

altarwise *adv* placed in the usual position of an altar, with the ends towards the north and south, and the front to the west.

altazimuth *n* an instrument for determining the altitudes and azimuths of the stars and planets.

alter *vti* to make or become different in a small way; to change.—**alterable** *adj*.—**alterability** *n*.

alteration *n* the act of altering or changing; the change or modification effected.

alterative *adj* producing change; having the power to alter. * *n* a medicine that restores the healthy functions of the body.

altercate *vi* to contend in words; to wrangle; to dispute with anger or heat.

altercation *n* an angry or heated quarrel.

alter ego *n* one's other self; a constant companion.

alternant *adj* alternating; composed of alternate layers.

alternate[1] *vt* to do or use by turns. * *vi* to act, happen, etc by turns; to take turns regularly.—**alternation** *n*.

alternate[2] *adj* occurring or following in turns.—**alternately** *adv*.

alternate angles *npl* the internal angles made by two lines with a third on opposite sides of it.

alternating current *n* an electric current that reverses its direction at regular intervals.

alternation *n* the act of alternating, or state of being alternate; reciprocal succession; antiphonal singing or reading.

alternative *adj* presenting a choice between two things. * *n* either of two possibilities.—**alternatively** *adv*.

alternative comedy *n* a form of comedy that avoids conventional humour (e.g. racist and sexist jokes), characterized by aggressively delivered and blackly humourous stand-up routines that usu challenge political and social orthodoxy.

alternative medicine *n* any technique of medical treatment without use of drugs, eg osteopathy, acupuncture, dieting.

alternator *n* an electric generator that produces alternating current.

althaea, althea *n* a genus of plants including the marshmallow and the hollyhock.

althorn *n* a musical instrument of the saxhorn class, frequently used in military bands.

although *conj* though; in spite of that.

altimeter *n* an instrument for measuring altitude.

altimetry *n* the art of measuring altitudes by the use of the altimeter.—**altimetrical** *adj*.

altissimo *adj* (*mus*) of the part or notes situated above F in alt.

altitude *n* height, esp above sea level.—**altitudinal** *adj*.

alto *n* (*pl* **altos**) the range of the highest male voice; a singer with this range; a contralto. * *adj* high.

alto clef *n* the C clef placed on the third line of the staff.

altogether *adv* in all; on the whole; completely.

alto-relievo, alto-rilievo *n* (*pl* **alto-relievos, alto-rilievos**) high relief; figures or other objects that stand out boldly from the background, and having more than half their thickness projecting.

altruism *n* unselfish concern for or dedication to the interests or welfare of others.—**altruist** *n*.—**altruistic** *adj*.—**altruistically** *adv*.

aludel *n* one of the pear-shaped glass or earthenware pots, open at both ends, used in sublimation.

alum *n* a double sulphate formed of aluminium and some other element, usually an alkali metal.

alumina *n* the single oxide of aluminium, the most abundant of the earths; a notable constituent of common clay, alumina is largely used in dyeing and calico printing as a mordant.

aluminiferous *adj* containing or yielding alum, alumina, or aluminium.

aluminous *adj* of, containing or resembling alum or alumina.

aluminium, aluminum *n* a silvery-white malleable metallic element notable for its lightness.

alumna *n* (*pl* **alumnae**) a female graduate or pupil of a university or college.

alumnus *n* (*pl* **alumni**) a former pupil or student.—

alumna *nf* (*pl* **alumnae**).

alum root *n* a popular name given to certain astringent roots of saxifrages.

alum schist *n* a thin-bedded fissile rock from which alum is procured.

alunite *n* subsulphate of alumina and potash.

alveolar *adj* of tooth sockets.

alveolate *adj* with deep pits or cells resembling the honeycomb.—**alveolation** *n*.

alveolus *n* (*pl* **alveoli**) a small pit, cell, cavity, or socket; the socket in which a tooth is fixed; the cell of a honeycomb.

alvine *adj* pertaining or belonging to the intestines or belly.

always *adv* at all times; in all cases; repeatedly; forever.

Alzheimer's disease *n* a degenerative disorder of the brain resulting in progressive senility.

am *see* **be**.

a.m. *abbr* = *ante meridiem*, before noon.

amadou *n* a styptic and a tinder prepared by steeping the solid portions of a fungus affecting trees in a solution of saltpetre; German tinder.

amah *n* an East Indian nurse or female servant.

amalgam *n* an alloy of mercury and another metal; a mixture.

amalgamate *vt* to combine, unite.

amalgamation *n* the act or process of compounding mercury with another metal; the separation of precious metals from the mother rock by means of quicksilver; the blending or mixing of different elements or things; the union or consolidation of two or more companies or businesses into one concern, a merger.

amanuensis *n* (*pl* **amanuenses**) one who is employed to write at the dictation or direction of another; a secretary.

amaranth *n* an imaginary flower said by poets to be unfading; a plant of the genus *Amarantus*; a colour mixture in which magenta is the chief ingredient; red colouring added to some foods.

amaranthine *adj* pertaining to the amaranth; never-fading, like amaranth; purplish.

amaryllis *n* a genus of bulbous flowering plants to which the belladonna lily and narcissus belong.

amass *vt* to bring together in a large quantity; to accumulate.—**amasser** *n*.—**amassment** *n*.

amateur *n* one who engages in a particular activity as a hobby, and not as a profession. * *adj* of or done by amateurs.—**amateurism** *n*.

amateurish *adj* lacking expertise.—**amateurishly** *adv*.—**amateurishness** *n*.

amatol *n* a high explosive.

amatory, amatorial *adj* relating to or expressive of love.

amaurosis *n* loss or decay of sight due to partial, periodic, or complete paralysis of the optic nerve.—**amaurotic** *adj*.

amaze *vt* to fill with wonder, astonish.—**amazing** *adj*.—**amazingly** *adv*.

amazement *n* the state of being amazed; astonishment; perplexity arising from sudden surprise.

Amazon *n* (*Greek myth*) a race of women warriors; a tall strong athletic woman.—**Amazonian** *adj*.

amazon ant *n* a species of ant found in Europe and America, which seizies the neuters of other species in the pupa stage and brings them up with their own larvae.

amazonite *n* the amazon stone gemstone.

amazon stone *n* a beautiful green feldspar found near

the Amazon.

ambary, ambari *n* (*pl* **ambaries, ambaris**) a plant of Asia that produces a jute-like fibre; the fibre.

ambassador *n* the highest-ranking diplomatic representative from one country to another; an authorized messenger.—**ambassadorial** *adj*.—**ambassadress** *nf*.

ambassador extraordinary *n* an ambassador sent on a special mission.

ambassador plenipotentiary *n* an ambassador sent with full powers to make a treaty.

amber *n* a hard yellowish fossil resin, used for jewellery and ornaments, etc; the colour of amber; a yellow traffic light used to signal "caution".

ambergris *n* a waxy substance found in tropical seas, which is secreted by sperm whales and is used in perfumery as a fixative.

amberoid, ambroid *n* pressed amber; synthetic amber.

amber tree *n* the common name for various species of African evergreen shrubs with fragrant leaves.

ambidextrous *adj* able to use the left and the right hand equally well.—**ambidexterity** *n*.

ambience, ambiance *n* surrounding influence, atmosphere.

ambient *adj* surrounding.

ambiguity *n* (*pl* **ambiguities**) double or dubious significance; vagueness.

ambiguous *adj* capable of two or more interpretations; indistinct, vague.—**ambiguously** *adv*.—**ambiguousness** *n*.

ambit *n* a circuit or compass; the line or sum of the lines by which a figure is bounded; the perimeter; sphere of action.

ambition *n* desire for power, wealth and success; an object of ambition.

ambitious *adj* having or governed by ambition; resulting from or showing ambition; requiring considerable effort or ability.—**ambitiously** *adv*.

ambivalent *adj* having mixed feelings toward the same object.—**ambivalence** *n*.

amble *vi* to walk in a leisurely way. * *n* an easy pace.—**ambler** *n*.

amblyopia *n* dimness of vision; amaurosis.—**amblyopic** *adj*.

ambo *n* (*pl* **ambos, ambones**) a pulpit; a reading desk.

amboyna, amboina *n* a beautifully mottled and curled variegated wood used in cabinet work.

ambrosia *n* (*Classical myth*) the food of the gods; anything exquisitely pleasing to taste or smell; a genus of weeds allied to wormwood.—**ambrosial, ambrosian** *adj*.

ambrotype *n* (*photog*) a process by which the light parts of a photograph are produced in silver, the dark parts showing as a background through the clear glass.

ambry *n* (*pl* **ambries**) a recess in a church wall for sacred vessels; a repository for arms; a cupboard for money tools, etc.

ambsace *n* two ones, the lowest throw at dice; bad luck.

ambulacrum *n* (*pl* **ambulacra**) a perforation in the shell of echinoderms through which the tube feet are protruded.—**ambulacral** *adj*.

ambulance *n* a special vehicle for transporting the sick or injured.

ambulance chaser *n* one who attempts to profit from disaster.

ambulant *adj* (*patient*) able to walk, not bed-ridden; moving from place to place.

ambulate *vi* to walk about; to move about; to wander.—

ambulation *n*.

ambulatory *adj* of or pertaining to walking; movable; temporary; capable of walking. * *n* (*pl* **ambulatories**) a place for walking in; a covered way.

ambuscade *n* a strategic disposition of troops in ambush.

ambush *n* the concealment of soldiers, etc to make a surprise attack; the bushes or other cover in which they are hidden. * *vti* to lie in wait; to attack from an ambush.

ambush marketing *n* the practice of taking advantage of another's official event to advertise one's own products.—*also* **ambushing**.

ameba *see* **amoeba**.

ameer *see* **amir**.

ameliorate *vti* to make or become better.—**ameliorative** *adj*.—**ameliorator** *n*.

amelioration *n* the making or growing better; improvement.

amen *interj* may it be so!

amenable *adj* easily influenced or led, tractable; answerable to legal authority.—**amenability** *n*.—**amenably** *adv*.

amend *vt* to remove errors, esp in a text; to modify, improve; to alter in minor details.—**amendable** *adj*.—**amender** *n*.

amendatory *adj* tending to amend; corrective.

amende honorable *n* (*pl* **amendes honorables**) a public apology and reparation; a punishment formerly inflicted in France on traitors and the sacrilegious.

amendment *n* the act of amending, correction; an alteration to a document, etc.

amends *npl* (*used as sing*) compensation or recompense for some loss, harm, etc.

amenity *n* (*pl* **amenities**) pleasantness, as regards situation, convenience, or service.

amenorrhoea, amenorrhea *n* abnormal absence of menstruation.

ament, amentum *n* (*pl* **aments, amenta**) a catkin, as of the willow.

amentia *n* want of reason; mental deficiency.

amerce *vt* to punish by an arbitrary fine.—**amerceable** *adj*.—**amercement** *n*.

Amerenglish *n* the English language as spoken in the United States.

American *adj* belonging to or characteristic of America. * *n* an inhabitant of the US.

Americanism *n* a form of expression peculiar to the US; a custom peculiar to the US; attachment to the US.

Americanize *vt* to render American; to assimilate to the political and social institutions of the US.—**Americanization** *n*.

americium *n* a white radioactive metallic element derived from plutonium.

Amerindian, Amerind *n* an American Indian.—**Amerindic** *adj*.

ametabolic *adj* (*certain insects*) not undergoing metamorphosis.

amethyst *n* a gemstone consisting of bluish-violet quartz; the colour of an amethyst.—**amethystine** *adj*.

amiable *adj* friendly in manner, congenial.—**amiability** *n*.—**amiably** *adv*.

amianthus *n* earth or mountain flax, a fibrous variety of asbestos.—**amianthine, amianthoid, amianthoidal** *adj*.

amicable *adj* friendly; peaceable.—**amicability, amicableness** *n*.—**amicably** *adv*.

amice n a square of white linen formerly worn on the head but now worn about the neck and shoulders by celebrant priests while saying Mass; a pilgrim's cloak.

amicus curiae n (pl **amici curiae**) (law) a friend of the court; a disinterested adviser.

amid, amidst prep in or to the middle of; during.

amide n any of several compounds produced by the replacement of a hydrogen atom of ammonia by an acid radical or metal atom.

amidships adv in the middle of a ship.

amine n any of several organic compounds formed by replacing hydrogen atoms of ammonia by one or more univalent hydrocarbon radicals.

amino acid n any of a group of organic acids that occur in proteins.

amir n (formerly) the Muslim ruler of Afghanistan.—also **ameer**.

amiss adj wrong, improper. * adv in an incorrect manner.

amity n (pl **amities**) friendship.

ammeter n an instrument for measuring electric current in amperes.

ammo n (sl) ammunition.

ammonal n a highly explosive compound.

ammonia n a pungent colourless gas composed of nitrogen and hydrogen.

ammoniac[1] n a gum resin.—also **gum ammoniac**.

ammoniacal, ammoniac[2] adj of, pertaining to, like or containing ammonia.

ammonite n a fossil shell, twisted like a ram's horn; snakestone.—**ammonitic** adj.

ammonium n the hypothetical base of ammonia.

ammunition n bullets, shells, rockets, etc; any means of attack or defence; facts and reasoning used to prove a point in an argument.

amnesia n a partial or total loss of memory.—**amnesiac, amnesic** n, adj.

amnesty n (pl **amnesties**) a general pardon, esp of political prisoners; a pardon granted for a limited time. * vt (**amnestying, amnestied**) to pardon (an offence).

amniocentesis n the extraction by hollow needle of a sample of amniotic fluid from the womb to test for foetal abnormalities.

amnion n (pl **amnions, amnia**) the thin innermost membrane surrounding the foetus in the womb of mammals, birds, and reptiles.—**amniotic** adj.

amoeba n (pl **amoebae, amoebas**) a unicellular microorganism found in water, damp soil and the digestive tracts of animals.—also **ameba**.—**amoebic, amebic** adj.

amoebaean, amoebean adj (verse form) alternately answering.

amok adj, adv **run amok** to run about armed, in a state of frenzy, attacking all that come in the way; indiscriminate slaughter; headstrong violence.—also **amuck**.

among, amongst prep in the number of, surrounded by; in the group or class of; within a group, between; by the joint efforts of.

amontillado n (pl **amontillados**) a dry kind of light-coloured sherry.

amoral adj neither moral nor immoral; without moral sense.—**amorality** n.—**amorally** adv.

amoretto, amorino n (pl **amoretti, amorini**) (art) a figure of cupid and representations of children.—also **putto**.

amorist n an amateur in love, a philanderer.

amoroso adj (mus) in a tender, amatory style.

amorous adj displaying or feeling love or desire.—**amorously** adv.—**amorousness** n.

amor patriae n love of one's country.

amorphous adj lacking a specific shape, shapeless; unrecognizable, indefinable.—**amorphism** n.

amortization n the extinction of a debt by means of a sinking fund; the act of alienating lands to a corporation in mortmain.—**amortizement** n.

amortize vt to put money aside at intervals for gradual payment of (a debt, etc).—**amortization** n.

amount vi to be equivalent (to) in total, quantity or significance. * n the total sum; the whole value or effect; a quantity.

amour n a love affair; an intrigue.

amour propre n self-love, vanity; self-respect.

amp n an ampere; (inf) an amplifier.

ampelopsis n kinds of vine creeper, incl the Virginia creeper.

amperage n the strength of an electric current measured in amperes.

ampere n the standard SI unit by which an electric current is measured.

ampersand n the sign (&) meaning "and".

amphetamine n a drug used esp as a stimulant and to suppress appetite.

amphi- prefix of both kinds; on both sides; around.

amphibian n an animal living on land but breeding in water; an aircraft that can take off and land on water or land; a vehicle that can travel on land and through water.

amphibious adj living on both land and in water; (mil) involving both sea and land forces.

amphibology, amphiboly n (pl **amphibologies, amphibolies**) an ambiguous phrase, as a sentence that may be construed in two distinct ways, as "The duke yet lives that Henry shall depose"; a quibble.

amphibrach n (verse) a foot of three syllables, the middle long, the first and last short.—**amphibrachic** adj.

amphimacer n (verse) a foot of three syllables, the middle short, the first and last long.

amphimixis n (pl **amphimixes**) a mingling of male and female gametes in sexual reproduction.

amphioxus n (pl **amphioxi, amphioxuses**) the name of the lancelet, a fish with a body tapering at both ends, the lowest in organization of the vertebrates.

amphipod n any of the *Amphipoda* order of crustaceans having feet for both walking and swimming, including the sandhoppers and sand fleas.

amphiprostyle adj (archit) with a portico at both ends. * n a building of this kind, esp a temple.—**amphiprostylar** adj.

amphisbaena n (pl **amphisbaenae, amphisbaenas**) a fabled serpent with a head at each end; a kind of lizard or worm.—**amphisbaenic** adj.

amphitheatre, amphitheater n an oval or circular building with rising rows of seats around an open arena.

amphora n (pl **amphorae, amphoras**) a two-handled vessel of oblong shape, used by the ancients for holding wine, etc; a Greek and Roman liquid measure, the former 9 gallons, the latter 6 gallons.

ample adj large in size, scope, etc; plentiful.—**amply** adv.

amplification n the act of amplifying or expanding; enlargement.

amplifier *n* a device that increases electric voltage, current, or power, or the loudness of sound.

amplify *vt* (**amplifying, amplified**) to expand more fully, add details to; (*electrical signals, etc*) to strengthen.

amplitude *n* largeness of extent, scope; abundance; the maximum deviation of an oscillation from the mean or zero.

amplitude modulation *n* (the transmitting of information by) the modulation of the amplitude of a radio carrier wave in accordance with the amplitude of the signal carried.

ampoule, ampul, ampule *n* a small sealed glass vessel containing liquid, esp for injection.

ampulla *n* (*pl* **ampullae**) an ancient vessel which contained unguents for the bath; a drinking vessel; a vessel for consecrated oil or chrism used in church rites and at the coronation of sovereigns.—**ampullar, ampullary** *adj*.

amputate *vt* to cut off, esp by surgery.—**amputation** *n*.

amuck *see* **amok**.

amulet *n* something worn as a charm against evil.

amuse *vt* to entertain or divert in a pleasant manner; to cause to laugh or smile.—**amusing** *adj*.

amusement *n* that which amuses; the state of being amused; an entertainment; a pastime.

amusement arcade *n* an indoor or roofed area with mechanical games for entertainment.

amusement park *n* an outdoor area with fairground entertainments.

amygdalate *adj* of or belonging to the almond.

amygdalin *n* a white crystalline substance obtained from the kernels of almonds.

amygdaloid *adj* almond shaped. * *n* an igneous rock containing almond-shaped nodules of some mineral.

amyl *n* (*formerly*) the alcohol radical of many chemical compounds.

amylase *n* an enzyme that breaks down starch and glycogen.

amyl nitrite *n* a drug inhaled to relieve spasms.

amylaceous *adj* of starch, starchy.

amylene *n* a hydrocarbon obtained by the removal of water from amyl alcohol.

amyloid *n* a starchy food.

amylopsin *n* a pancreatic ferment converting starch into sugar.

an- *prefix* the form of *ad-* before *n*.

an *adj* the indefinite article ("a"), used before words beginning with the sound of a vowel except "u".

-an, -ain, -ane *adj suffix* of, of the nature of, as in *suburban, certain, humane*.

-ana, -iana *n suffix* sayings of, publications about, as *Shakespeariana*, etc.

ana- *prefix* up, anew, again.

Anabaptist *n* one who believes in the rebaptizing of adults on their profession of faith; one who holds the invalidity of infant baptism; (*pl*) the sect of Baptists.—**Anabaptism** *n*.

anabas *n* a genus of Indian fishes allied to the perch, remarkable for their power of living a long time out of water and of travelling on land.

anabasis *n* (*pl* **anabases**) the name given to Xenophon's account of the expedition of Cyrus the Younger (401BC); an inland military expedition.

anabatic *adj* (*of wind*) caused by upward current of air.

anabiosis *n* a coming to life again, resuscitation.

anableps *n* (*pl* **anableps**) a genus of the perch family found in Guiana, remarkable for the structure of its eye.

anabolic steroid *n* any of various synthetic steroid hormones that promote rapid muscle growth.

anabolism *n* constructive metabolism, in which simple molecules synthesize into more complex ones.—**anabolic**.

anabranch *n* a stream that leaves a river and rejoins it lower down.

anachronism *n* a person, custom, or idea regarded as out of date or out of its period.—**anachronistic** *adj*.—**anachronistically** *adv*.

anacoluthia *n* want of grammatical sequence, esp in a sentence.—**anacoluthic** *adj*.

anacoluthon *n* (*pl* **anacolutha**) a sentence in which one part belongs to a different construction from the other.

anaconda *n* a large South American semiaquatic snake that kills its prey by constriction.

Anacreontic *adj* after the manner of Anacreon, the Greek poet (6th century BC); amatory, erotic. * *n* a poem in praise of love and wine.

anacrusis *n* (*pl* **anacruses**) (*linguistics*) an unstressed syllable at the beginning of a verse.—**anacrustic** *adj*.

anadiplosis *n* (*rhetoric*) the repetition of the last word of a line or clause at the beginning of the next.

anadromous *adj* (*fish*) ascending from the sea to freshwater rivers to deposit spawn, as the salmon, etc.

anaemia *n* a condition in which the blood is low in red cells or in haemoglobin, resulting in paleness, weakness, etc.—*also* **anemia**.

anaemic *adj* suffering from anaemia; weak; pale; listless.—*also* **anemic**.

anaerobe, anaerobium *n* (*pl* **anaerobes, anaerobia**) a microbe that can live without air.

anaerobiosis *n* life devoid of oxygen.—**anaerobic** *adj*.—**anaerobically** *adv*.

anaesthesia *n* a partial or total loss of the sense of pain, touch, etc.—*also* **anesthesia**.

anaesthetic *n* a drug, gas, etc used to produce anaesthesia, as before surgery. * *adj* of or producing anaesthesia.—*also* **anesthetic**.

anaesthetist *n* a person trained to give anaesthetics.—*also* **anesthetist**.

anaesthetize *vt* to administer an anaesthetic.—*also* **anesthetize**.—**anaesthetization, anesthetization** *n*.

anaglyph *n* an ornament or work of art carved in low relief, as distinguished from intaglio.—**anaglyphic, anaglyphical, anaglyptic, anaglyptical** *adj*.

anagnorisis *n* (*pl* **anagnorises**) the denouement in a drama.

anagoge, anagogy *n* an allegorical or mystical interpretation, a hidden sense.—**anagogic, anagogical** *adj*.—**anagogically** *adv*.

anagram *n* a word or sentence formed by rearranging another word or sentence.—**anagrammatic, anagrammatical** *adj*.—**anagrammatically** *adv*.

anagrammatize *vt* to make into an anagram. * *vi* to construct anagrams.—**anagrammatism** *n*.—**anagrammatist** *n*.

anal *adj* of or situated near the anus.

analects, anelecta *npl* literary passages or extracts selected from published works by different authors.—**analectic** *adj*.

analeptic *adj* restorative. * *n* a restorative drug.

analgesia *n* insensibility to pain without loss of consciousness.

analgesic *adj* relieving pain. * *n* a pain-relieving drug.

analogism *n* a reasoning from the cause to the effect; study and examination of matters and things by reference to their analogies.—**analogist** *n*.

analogize *vt* to reason or expound by reference to analogy, to draw comparisons. * *vi* to treat or investigate by use of analogy.

analogous *adj* corresponding in certain respects (to).—**analogously** *adv*.

analogue, analog *n* a word or thing analogous to something else.

analogy *n* (*pl* **analogies**) a similarity or correspondence in certain respects between two things.—**analogical, analogic** *adj*.

analysand *n* anyone undergoing psychoanalysis.

analysis *n* (*pl* **analyses**) the process of analysing; a statement of the results of this; psychoanalysis.

analyst *n* a person who analyses; a psychoanalyst.

analytic, analytical *adj* pertaining to analysis.—**analytically** *adv*.

analysable, analyzable *adj* capable of being resolved by, or that may be subjected to, analysis.

analyse, analyze *vt* to separate (something) into its constituent parts to investigate its structure and function, etc; to examine in detail; to psychoanalyse.

anamnesis *n* (*pl* **anamneses**) recollection; a patient's case history.—**anamnestic** *adj*.—**anamnestically** *adv*.

anamorphosis *n* (*pl* **anamorphoses**) the irregular and distorted representation of an object as viewed directly, but which is corrected and reduced to its proper proportion when regarded from a different point of view, or reflected by a curved mirror; the abnormal or monstrous development of a portion of a plant or flower; a gradual progression from one type to another.

ananas *n* a genus of tropical plants to which the pineapple belongs.

anandrous *adj* without stamens.

ananthous *adj* without flowers.

anapaest, anapest *n* a foot comprising two short syllables and one long syllable.—**anapaestic, anapestic** *adj*.

anaphora *n* (*rhetoric*) the repetition at the beginning of the succeeding clauses of sentences of the word or words used in beginning the first; that part of the Eucharistic service which starts with the Sursum Corda; the oblique ascension of a star.—**anaphoric** *adj*.—**anaphorically** *adv*.

anaphrodisia *n* impotence of the sexual organs; absence of venereal desire.

anaphrodisiac *adj* tending to diminish sexual desire. * *n* a remedy that produces such an effect.

anaphylaxis *n* excessive sensitivity to a substance or germ due to prior inoculation with it, an allergy.—**anaphylactic** *adj*.—**anaphylactically** *adv*.

anaplasty *n* the repairing of wounds by the transplantation of adjacent healthy tissue, plastic surgery.—**anaplastic** *adj*.

anarchism *n* lawlessness; confusion; anarchy; the doctrines of the anarchists.

anarchist *n* a person who believes that all government is unnecessary and should be abolished.—**anarchistic** *adj*.

anarchy *n* the absence of government; political confusion; disorder, lawlessness.—**anarchic, anarchical** *adj*.

anarthrous *adj* without the article; destitute of joints; without articulated limbs.

anasarca *n* (*med*) dropsy.—**anasarcous** *adj*.

anastigmat *n* a lens corrected of astigmatism.—**anastigmatic** *adj*.

anastomosis *n* (*pl* **anastomoses**) a cross-connection of arteries, rivers, etc.—**anastomotic** *adj*.

anastrophe *n* (*rhetoric*) an inversion of the sequence of words in a sentence, as "echoed the hills", for "the hills echoed".

anathema *n* (*pl* **anathemas**) anything greatly detested; an ecclesiastical curse or denunciation accompanied by excommunication.

anathematize *vt* to pronounce a decree of excommunication against. * *vi* to curse.—**anathematization** *n*.

anatomist *n* one possessing a knowledge of anatomy by dissection.

anatomize *vt* to dissect; to study the structure of; to analyse.—**anatomization** *n*.

anatomy *n* (*pl* **anatomies**) the science of the physical structure of plants and animals; the structure of an organism.—**anatomical** *adj*.—**anatomically** *adv*.

anbury *n* (*pl* **anburies**) a soft wart or tumour on horses and cattle; a disease in turnips.

ANC *abbr* = African National Congress.

-ance *n suffix* denoting quality or action, as in *arrogance, penance*.

ancestor *n* one from whom a person is descended, a forefather; an early animal or plant from which existing types are descended; something regarded as a forerunner.—**ancestress** *nf*.

ancestral *adj* belonging to, or connected with, one's ancestors; derived from one's progenitors; lineal.

ancestry *n* (*pl* **ancestries**) ancestors collectively; lineage.

anchor *n* a heavy metal implement that lodges at the bottom of the sea or a river to hold a ship in position; something that gives support or stability. * *vt* to fix by an anchor; to secure firmly.

anchorage *n* a safe anchoring place for ships; the charge for anchoring.

anchorite *n* one who voluntarily secludes him or herself from society and lives a solitary life devoted to religious or philosophic meditation; a recluse; a hermit.—**anchoress** *nf*.

anchorman *n* (*pl* **anchormen**) (*sport*) the last man in a team to compete and whose contribution is vital; the compere of a television broadcast.

anchor stock *n* the crossbar at the top of the shank, at right angles to the arms.

anchor watch *n* the watch on board ship when at anchor; the seamen on this watch.

anchovy *n* (*pl* **anchovies, anchovy**) a small Mediterranean fish resembling a herring with a very salty taste.

anchovy pear *n* a West Indian fruit like the mango, used as a pickle.

anchylose *see* **ankylose**.

anchylosis *see* **ankylosis**.

ancien régime *n* (*pl* **anciens régimes**) the old order, esp that ruling France before the Revolution.

ancient *adj* very old; dating from the distant past; of the period and civilizations predating the fall of the Roman Empire; old-fashioned. * *n* a person who lived in the ancient period; (*pl*) the members of the classical civilizations of antiquity, esp of Greece and Rome.

Ancient of Days *n* (*Bible*) God, as described in the Book of Daniel.

ancillary *adj* subordinate (to); auxiliary; supplementary. * *n* (*pl* **ancillaries**) a subordinate or auxiliary person or thing.

ancipital, ancipitous *adj* (*biol*) two-edged and sharp.

ancon, ancone *n* (*pl* **ancones**) (*archit*) a bracket or projection for the support of a cornice; the elbow.—**anconal, anconeal** *adj*.

and *conj* in addition to; together with; plus; increasingly; as a consequence, afterwards; expressing contrast.

andalusite *n* a silicate of alumina.

andante *adj* (*mus*) moderately slow; naturally and easily. * *n* a movement written and to be played in andante time.

andantino *adj* rather slower than andante. * *n* (*pl* **andantinos**) a movement slower than an andante.

andesite *n* a silicate of alumina, soda, and lime.

andiron *npl* metal standards used for open fires to support the logs; fire dogs.

androgen *n* a male sex hormone.—**androgenic** *adj*.

androgenous *adj* (*biol*) having only male offspring.

androgynous *adj* combining both sexes or bearing both male and female organs; hermaphroditical.—**androgyne** *n*.—**androgyny** *n*.

android *n* (*science fiction*) a robot in human form.—*also adj*.

androsphinx *n* (*pl* **androsphinxes, androsphinges**) a sphinx with the body of a lion and the head of a man.

anecdotal *adj* relating to anecdotes; (*evidence, etc*) obtained from experience, not scientific.

anecdote *n* a short entertaining account about an amusing or interesting event or person.

anemia *see* **anaemia**.

anemic *see* **anaemic**.

anemograph *n* an instrument for registering the force or direction of the wind.

anemography *n* the scientific description of winds, and the measurement and registration of their force and direction.—**anemographic** *adj*.—**anemographically** *adv*.

anemology *n* the science and literature of the winds.

anemometer *n* an instrument for measuring the force or speed of the wind.

anemone *n* a plant of the buttercup family.

anemophilus *adj* (flowers, etc) fertilized by pollen carried by the wind, wind-pollinated.—**anemophily** *n*.

anemoscope *n* an apparatus for exhibiting the direction of the wind.

anent *prep, adv* (*Scot*) with regard or respect to; concerning.

aneroid *adj* having no liquid, as quicksilver. * *n* a barometer shaped like a watch, the action depending on the varying pressure of the atmosphere on the top of an elastic metal box.

aneroid barometer *n* a barometer that measures air pressure by its effect on the flexible lid of a box containing a partial vacuum.

anesthesia *see* **anaesthesia**.

anesthetic *see* **anaesthetic**.

anesthetist *see* **anaesthetist**.

anesthetize *see* **anaesthetize**.

aneurysm, aneurism *n* the permanent abnormal swelling of an artery.

anew *adv* afresh; again, once more; in a new way or form.

anfractuous *adj* winding, intricate.—**anfractuosity** *n* (*pl* **anfractuosities**).

angary *n* a belligerent's right to seize and use neutral property, for which it pays indemnity.

angel *n* a messenger of God; an image of a human figure with wings and a halo; a very beautiful or kind person; (*inf*) one who gives financial backing to an enterprise.

angel cake *n* a small round cake with a round fruit on the top.

Angeleno *n* (*pl* **Angelenos**) (*inf*) an inhabitant of the city of Los Angeles.

angelfish *n* (*pl* **angelfish, angelfishes**) a species of shark with large pectoral fins, which give to it a winged appearance.

angelic, angelical *adj* belonging to or resembling an angel in nature or function.—**angelically** *adv*.

angelica *n* the candied stalks of a fragrant plant used esp in cake decoration.

Angelus *n* (*RC Church*) a devotional exercise commemorating the Incarnation, during which the Ave Maria is twice repeated, said morning, noon, and night; the bell that is rung to announce the time of such devotions.

anger *n* strong displeasure, often because of opposition, a hurt, etc. * *vti* to make or become angry.

angina *n* sharp stabbing pains in the chest, usu caused by angina pectoris.

angina pectoris *n* a heart disease causing a spasmodic gripping pain in the chest.

angiology *n* the branch of anatomy that deals with the blood vessels and lymphatics.

angioma *n* (*pl* **angiomas, angiomata**) a tumour caused by the enlargement of a blood vessel.—**angiomatous** *adj*.

angiosperm *n* (*bot*) a plant having its seeds protected by a covering.—**angiospermous** *adj*.

angle[1] *n* a corner; the point from which two lines or planes extend or diverge; a specific viewpoint; an individual method or approach (eg to a problem). * *vt* to bend at an angle; to move or place at an angle; to present information, news, etc from a particular point of view.

angle[2] *vi* to fish with a hook and line; to use hints or artifice to get something.—**angler** *n*.

angler *n* one who fishes with rod and line; the name of a fish with filamentary appendage that attracts smaller fish on which it feeds.

Anglican *adj* belonging to or of the Church of England and other churches in communion with it. * *n* a member of the Anglican Church; a ritualist.

Anglicanism *n* the principles and ritual of the Anglican Church.

Anglicism *n* a form of speech, an English idiom; a principle or mannerism peculiar to England.

anglicize *vt* to make or to render into English; to accord with English manners and customs.—**anglicization** *n*.

angling *n* the art or act of fishing with rod and line.

Anglo- *prefix* English, British.

Anglo-American *adj* pertaining to England and the United States conjointly, as to commerce or population. * *n* an American citizen of English descent.

Anglo-Catholic *adj* Catholic according to the teachings and ritual of the English Church; in the strictest Catholic sense; high church. * *n* a member of the English Church, popularly a ritualist or high churchman, who repudiates the term "Protestant".

Anglo-Catholicism *n* the principles and ritual of the Anglican Church interpreted in their strictest Catholic sense.

Anglo-French *adj* English and French. * *n* the old French language introduced into England by the Normans.

Anglo-Indian *adj* pertaining to England and India conjointly. * *n* one of English descent born or residing in India.

Anglo-Irish *adj* pertaining to England and Ireland, or to the English settled in Ireland and their descendants; having the father or mother of English or Irish race. * *npl* English born or resident in Ireland.

Anglomania *n* a predilection carried to excess for everything that is English, in the sense of being peculiar to England.

Anglo-Norman *adj* common to England and Normandy. * *n* one of the Norman settlers in England after the Conquest (AD 1066).

Anglophile *n* a person who loves England or anything English.—*also* **Anglophil**.

Anglophobe *n* one who hates or fears England and the English.

Anglophobia *n* an intense aversion or fear of everything English.—**Anglophobe** *n*.

Anglo-Saxon *adj* pertaining to the Saxon settlers in England prior to the Conquest, or to their language. * *n* one of the Saxon settlers in England as distinguished from those on the Continent; Old English, the language of the settlers; (*pl*) the English race.

angora *n* a long-haired variety of cat, rabbit or goat; fabric made from the hair of angora goats or rabbits.

angostura bark *n* a bitter aromatic bark used for medicinal purposes.

angostura bitters *npl* a bitter flavouring made from the bark of a South American tree.

angry *adj* (**angrier, angriest**) full of anger; inflamed.—**angrily** *adv*.

angst *n* a feeling of anxiety, fear or remorse.

angstrom, ångström *n* one hundred millionth of a centimetre, a unit used in measuring the length of light waves.

anguilliform *adj* shaped like an eel or a serpent.

anguine *adj* snakelike.

anguish *n* agonizing physical or mental distress.

angular *adj* having one or more angles; forming an angle; measured by an angle; stiff and clumsy in manner, thin and bony.

angularity *n* (*pl* **angularities**) the quality of being angular in any sense.

angulate *adj* constructed of angles; having the form of an angle.

angulation *n* the exact measurement of angles; an angular shape.

anhydride *n* an oxygen compound formed by substituting an acid radicle for the whole of the hydrogen in one or two molecules of water.

anhydrite *n* anhydrous sulphate of lime.

anhydrous *adj* without water, applied to minerals in which the water of crystallization is not present.

ani *n* (*pl* **anis**) a tropical American bird of the cuckoo family.

aniconic *adj* (*idols*) not of human or animal form.

anil *n* the indigo plant; a dye yielded by it.

anile *adj* resembling an old woman; aged.—**anility** *n*.

aniline *n* a base used in the formation of many rich dyes obtained from coal tar but more extensively from benzole. * *adj* of or pertaining to aniline.

animadversion *n* the act of observing; capacity for perception; censure; criticism; stricture.

animadvert *vi* to give the mind to; to pass comment or stricture upon, to criticize.

animal *n* any living organism except a plant or bacterium, typically able to move about; a lower animal as distinguished from man, esp mammals; a brutish or bestial person. * *adj* of or like an animal; bestial; sensual.

animalcule, animalculum *n* (*pl* **animalcules, animalcula**) one of a class of minute or microscopic organisms abounding in water and infusions.—**animalcular** *adj*.

animalism *n* the state of being animal, or actuated by animal instincts or appetites; the theory that regards humankind as merely animal; sensuality.—**animalist** *n*.—**animalistic** *adj*.

animality *n* the state or quality of being an animal, or possessing animal characteristics, animal nature.

animalize *vt* to make animal; to impart animal life, form, and attributes; to sensualize or bestialize; to convert into animal substance by assimilation.—**animalization** *n*.

animal kingdom *n* beings endowed with animal life and regarded collectively, one of the three great divisions of nature.

animal liberation *n* freeing animals from captivity and exploitation (eg in laboratories) by humans, action esp associated with organizations such as the Animal Liberation Front.

animal magnetism *n* another name for mesmerism; attractiveness, esp to the opposite sex.

animal rights *n* a movement that seeks to extend certain rights, such as freedom from captivity and exploitation by humans, to animals.

animal spirits *npl* vivacity; liveliness of disposition.

animal worship *n* the worship of animals as symbols of deities, as among the ancient Egyptians, Hindus, etc.

animate *vt* to give life to; to liven up; to inspire, encourage. * *adj* alive; lively.

animated *adj* lively, full of spirit.

animated cartoon *n* a film made by photographing a series of drawings, giving the illusion of movement.

animation *n* liveliness; movement; the skill of making animated films.

animato *adv, adj* (*mus*) with vigour.

animator, animater *n* an artist who draws and produces animated cartoons.

animé *n* an amber-coloured resin, resembling copal, obtained from a tropical American tree and used in varnish.

animism *n* in primitive religion, the belief that natural effects are due to spirits and that inanimate objects have spirits; the belief in a human apparitional soul, having the form and appearance of the body, existing after death as semi-human.—**animist** *n*.—**animistic** *adj*.

animosity *n* (*pl* **animosities**) strong dislike; hostility.

animus *n* an actuating spirit; a bitter or hostile feeling (against); hostility.

anion *n* the element in a body decomposed by voltaic action, which is evolved at the positive pole or anode.—**anionic** *adj*.

anise *n* the common name for a plant (indigenous in Egypt) yielding the seeds used in aniseed.

aniseed *n* the seed of the anise plant, used as a flavouring.

anisette *n* a liqueur prepared from aniseed.

ankh *n* an Egyptian cross with a loop or handle at the

top, the symbol of life.—*also* **crux ansata**.

ankle *n* the joint between the foot and leg, the part of the leg between the foot and calf.

anklet *n* an ornamental chain worn round the ankle.

ankylose *vt* to consolidate or join by bony growth; to stiffen as a joint. * *vi* to grow together; to become stiff.—*also* **anchylose**.

ankylosis *n* (*zool*) the joining or consolidation of parts formerly or normally separate or movable by means of bony growth; (*med*) the stiffening of a joint by fibrous bands or union of bones.—*also* **anchylosis**.— **ankylotic, anchylotic**.

anna *n* an Indian coin, one sixteenth of a rupee.

annals *npl* a written account of events year by year; historical records; periodical reports or records of a society.—**annalist** *n*.—**annalistic** *adj*.

annates *npl* (*RC Church*) the sum paid to the pope by an abbot or bishop on his appointment to a benefice or see and consisting of the first year's revenue of the living, now chiefly supplied by Peter's Pence.

anneal *vt* to fix by heat; to temper and render malleable; to bake or fuse.—**annealer** *n*.

annelid *n* any of a class of invertebrates which includes the worms, whose bodies are composed of numerous segments or ring-like divisions.—**annelidan** *adj*.

annex *vt* to attach, esp to something larger; to incorporate into a state the territory of (another state).

annexation *n* the act of annexing; that which is annexed.—**annexational** *adj*.—**annexationism** *n*.— **annexationist** *n*.

annexe *n* an extension to a main building; something added, a supplement.

annihilate *vt* to destroy completely; (*inf*) to defeat convincingly, as in an argument.—**annihilable** *adj*.—**annihilative** *adj*.—**annihilator** *n*.

annihilation *n* the act of annihilating; nonexistence.

anniversary *n* (*pl* **anniversaries**) the yearly return of the date of some event; a celebration of this.—*also adj*.

anno Domini *adv* (*abbr* AD) in the year of our Lord, dating from the birth of Christ. * *n* (*inf*) advancing age.

annotate *vti* to provide with explanatory notes.—**annotative** *adj*.—**annotator** *n*.

annotation *n* the act of noting or commenting upon; a note, remark, or criticism made in a book.

announce *vt* to bring to public attention; to give news of the arrival of; to be an announcer for. * *vi* to serve as an announcer.

announcement *n* the act of announcing; that which is announced; a proclamation.

announcer *n* a person who reads the news, etc on the radio or TV.

annoy *vt* to vex, tease, irritate, as by a repeated action.—**annoyingly** *adv*.

annoyance *n* the act of annoying or causing vexation; the state of being annoyed; the thing or act that annoys.

annual *adj* of or measured by a year; yearly; coming every year; living only one year or season. * *n* a plant that lives only one year; a periodical published once a year.—**annually** *adv*.

annuitant *n* one who is in receipt of, or is entitled to receive, an annuity.

annuity *n* (*pl* **annuities**) an investment yielding fixed payments, esp yearly; such a payment.

annul *vt* (**annulling, annulled**) to do away with; to deprive of legal force, nullify.

annular *adj* ring-like; in the form of a ring or annulus.

* *n* the ring of light surrounding the moon's body in an annular eclipse of the sun

annulate *adj* ringed; having ring-like bands or circles.

annulation *n* a ring-like formation.

annulet *n* a small ring; (*archit*) a small fillet encircling a column.

annulment *n* the act of reducing to nothing; abolition; invalidation.

annulose *adj* composed of a succession of rings; segmented.

annunciate *vt* to make known officially or publicly; to announce, proclaim.—**annunciation** *n*.— **annunciative, annunciatory** *adj*.

Annunciation *n* (*Bible*) the intimation of the Incarnation made by the angel Gabriel to the Virgin Mary (Luke 1:28-33); the Church festival (Lady Day, 25 Mar) commemorating this.

annunciator *n* a signalling apparatus; an indicator connected with bells and telephones, to show where attendance is required.

anode *n* the positive electrode by which electrons enter an electric circuit.

anodyne *n* a drug that relieves pain; anything that relieves pain or soothes.

anoestrus *n* the period of sexual inactivity in mammals between periods of estrus.—*also* **anestrus**.— **anoestrous, anestrous** *adj*.

anoint *vt* to rub with oil; to apply oil in a sacred ritual as a sign of consecration.—**anointment** *n*.

anomalistic year *n* the time occupied by the earth in passing through its orbit (365 days, 6 hours, 13 minutes, 48 seconds), from perihelion to perihelion.

anomalous *adj* deviating from the common order, abnormal.

anomaly *n* (*pl* **anomalies**) abnormality; anything inconsistent or odd.—**annomalistic** *adj*.—**anomalistically** *adv*.

anon *adv* soon; at another time; (*arch*) anonymous.

anonym *n* an unnamed person; an assumed name.

anonymous *adj* having or providing no name; written or provided by an unnamed person; lacking individuality.—**anonymity** *n*.—**anonymously** *adv*.

anopheles *n* (*pl* **anopheles**) any of a genus of mosquitos, which transmits the microbe of malaria.

anorak *n* a waterproof jacket with a hood.

anorexia *n* loss of appetite.—**anorexic** *adj*.

anorexia nervosa *n* the psychological condition causing fear of becoming overweight and reluctance to eat even to the point of starvation and death.

anosmia *n* the inability to smell.—**anosmatic, anosmic** *adj*.

another *adj* a different or distinct (thing or person); an additional one of the same kind; some other.—*also pron*.

ansate *adj* with a handle, as a vase.

Anschluss *n* the union of Nazi Germany with Austria in 1938; the annexation of one territory by another for the benefit of the more powerful.

anserine, anserous *adj* of, relating to or resembling a goose; stupid as a goose.

answer *n* a spoken or written reply or response; the solution to a problem; a reaction, response. * *vt* to speak or write in reply; to satisfy or correspond to (eg a specific need); to justify, offer a refutation of. * *vi* to reply; to act in response (to); to be responsible (for); to conform (to).

answerable *adj* capable of being refuted; (*with* **for** *or* **to**) responsible, accountable.—**answerability** *n.*—**answerableness** *n.*

answering machine *n* an apparatus that records incoming telephone calls.

-ant *adj suffix* as in *repentant.* * *n suffix* denoting agent, as in *celebrant.*

ant *n* any of a family of small, generally wingless insects of many species, all of which form and live in highly organized groups.

anta *n* (*pl* **antae**) (*archit*) a square pilaster at either corner of a building, or at either side of a door.

antacid *n* a substance that counters excessive acidity.

antagonism *n* antipathy, hostility; an opposing force, principle, etc.

antagonist *n* an adversary; an opponent.

antagonistic *adj* acting in opposition; opposed.—**antagonistically** *adv.*

antagonize *vt* to arouse opposition in.—**antagonization** *n.*

antalkali *n* (*pl* **antalkalis**, **antalkalies**) a substance that counteracts the presence of alkali in the system; an acid.—**antalkaline** *adj, n.*

Antarctic *adj* of the South Pole or its surroundings. * *n* the Antarctic regions; the Antarctic Ocean.

ant bear *n* the aardvark.

ant bird *n* one of an extensive group of South American birds.

ant cow *n* an aphid or similar insect collected by ants for the sweet secretion in its body.

ante *n* a player's stake in poker; (*inf*) money contributed as a share in a joint project.

ante- *prefix* in front of; earlier than.

anteater *n* an ant-eating animal, as the pangolin.

antecede *n* to precede or go before in time or space.

antecedence *n* precedence; going before; priority.

antecedent *adj* prior in time, previous. * *n* a preceding event or happening; (*pl*) ancestry; (*pl*) the previous events of a person's life.

antechamber *n* an anteroom.

antedate *vt* to carry back to an earlier period; to anticipate. * *n* a date esp on a document earlier than the actual date.

antediluvian *adj* of or pertaining to the world before the Flood; belonging to very ancient times; antiquated, primitive. * *n* one who lived before the Flood; an old-fashioned person.

antelope *n* (*pl* **antelopes**, **antelope**) any of the family of fast-running and graceful deer-like animals of Africa and Asia.

ante meridiem *n* (*abbr* a.m.) the period between midnight and noon.—**antemeridian** *adj.*

antenatal *adj* occurring or present before birth.

antenna *n* (*pl* **antennae**) either of a pair of feelers on the head of an insect, crab, etc; (*pl* **antennas**) a metal device for transmitting and receiving radio waves.

antennule *n* a little antenna.

antependium *n* (*pl* **antependia**) a covering for the front of an altar.

antepenult *n* the last but two, usu of syllables.

antepenultimate *adj* pertaining to the last but two. * *n* that which is last but two, antepenult.

anterior *adj* at or towards the front; earlier; previous.

anteroom *n* an outer room leading into a larger or main room.

anthelion *n* (*pl* **anthelia**) (*meteorol*) a luminous halo, opposite the sun, formed around the shadow of the head of the observer, as projected on a cloud or fog bank.

anthem *n* a religious choral song; a song of praise or devotion, as to a nation.

anther *n* the part of a flower's stamen containing pollen.—**antheral** *adj.*

anthill *n* a mound thrown up by ants or termites in digging their nests.

anthologize *vt* to compile or include in an anthology.

anthology *n* (*pl* **anthologies**) a collection of poetry or prose.—**anthological** *adj.*—**anthologist** *n.*

anthozoan *n* any of a class of radiated soft marine zoophytes, which includes the sea anemones, corals, etc.—*also* **actinozoan**.

anthracene *n* a complex hydrocarbon obtained from coal tar, the source of a red dye.

anthracite *n* a hard coal that gives off a lot of heat and little smoke.—**anthracitic** *adj.*

anthrax *n* (*pl* **anthraces**) a contagious bacterial disease of cattle and sheep, etc that can be transmitted to people.

anthropo- *prefix* man.

anthropocentric *adj* centring in man.—**anthropocentrism** *n.*

anthropoid *adj* resembling man. * *n* one of the higher apes resembling man.—**anthropoidal** *adj.*

anthropology *n* the scientific study of human beings, their origins, distribution, physical attributes and culture.—**anthropological** *adj.*—**anthropologist** *n.*

anthropometry *n* the measurement of the human body; the branch of anthropology relating to such measurement of persons at various ages and in different tribes, races, occupations, etc.—**anthropometric**, **anthropometrical** *adj.*—**anthropometrist** *n.*

anthropomorphism *n* the ascription of human behaviour to other animals or to things.—**anthropomorphic** *adj.*—**anthropomorphist** *n.*

anthropomorphize *vt* to invest with human qualities.

anthropomorphous *adj* in the form of a human being.

anthropophagi *npl* (*sing* **anthropophagus**) cannibals, men-eaters.

anti- *prefix* opposed to; against.

anti-aircraft *adj* for use against aircraft.

antiar *n* the upas tree of Java; a poison obtained from one species of it.

antibiotic *n* any of various chemical, fungal or synthetic substances used against bacterial or fungal infections.

antibody *n* (*pl* **antibodies**) a protein produced by an organism in response to the action of a foreign body, such as the toxin of a parasite, that neutralizes its effects.

antic *n* a ludicrous action intended to amuse.

Antichrist *n* (*Bible*) an opponent of Christ, esp the great personal opponent expected to appear before the end of the world (1 John 2:22).

Antichristian *n* one who is an opponent of the Christian religion. * *adj* pertaining to Antichrist; opposed to the Christian religion.

anticipant *adj* operating beforehand. * *n* one who looks forward.

anticipate *vt* to give prior thought and attention to; to use, spend, act on in advance; to foresee and take action to thwart another; to expect. * *vi* to speak, act, before the appropriate time.

anticipation *n* the act of taking beforehand; expectation; hope; preconception.

anticlerical *adj* opposed to the power of the clergy or church, esp in secular affairs. * *n* a person opposed to the power of the church.—**anticlericalism** n.

anticlimax n a sudden drop from the important to the trivial; an ending to a story or series of events that disappoints one's expectations.—**anticlimactic** adj.—**anticlimactically** adv.

anticlinal adj (strata) inclining or folding with the convex side upwards; inclined in opposite directions.

anticlockwise see **counterclockwise**.

anticoagulant n a substance that inhibits blood clotting.

anticyclone n a body of air rotating about an area of high atmospheric pressure.—**anticyclonic** adj.

antidepressant n any of various drugs used to alleviate mental depression.—also adj.

antidote n a remedy that counteracts a poison; something that counteracts harmful effects.

antifebrile adj capable of allaying fever. * n a medicine for allaying fever.

antifreeze n a substance used, as in a car radiator, to prevent freezing up.

antigen n a substance introduced into the blood to stimulate production of antibodies.—**antigenic** adj.—**antigenically** adv.

antihero n (pl **antiheroes**) a leading character in a book, film, etc who lacks the conventional heroic attributes.

antihistamine n any of a group of drugs that inhibit the action of histamines, used in treating allergic conditions.

antilog n an antilogarithm.

antilogarithm n a number which a logarithm represents.—**antilogarithmic** adj.

antilogy n (pl **antilogies**) a contradiction.

antimacassar n an ornamental covering for chairbacks, etc, to prevent their being soiled (formerly by macassar oil, once used as a pomade).

antimatter n matter composed of antiparticles.

antimasque n a droll or grotesque interlude between parts of a more serious nature in a masque.

antimere n (biol) one of two or more corresponding parts or organs on opposite sides of animals.—**antimeric** adj.—**antimerism** n.

antimonic, antimonous adj relating to, composed of, or obtained from antimony.

antimony n (pl **antimonies**) a brittle metallic element used in making alloys.—**antimonial** adj, n.

antinomy n (pl **antinomies**) contradiction in law or authorities or conclusions; the opposition of one law or part of a law to another.—**antinomic** adj.—**antinomically** adv.

antiparallel adj running parallel, but in an opposite direction. * n one of two or more lines making equal angles with two other lines, but in contrary order.

antiparticle n an elementary particle with the same mass as its corresponding particle but having an equal and opposite electric charge, resulting in mutual destruction when brought into contact.

antipathetic, antipathetical adj possessing or causing a natural antipathy or aversion (to).—**antipathetically** adv.

antipathy n (pl **antipathies**) a fixed dislike; aversion; an object of this.

antiperiodic adj preventive of a return in periodic or intermittent disease. * n a medicine for periodic diseases.

antipersonnel adj (weapon) used to destroy people rather than objects.

antiperspirant n a substance used to stem excessive perspiration.

antiphlogistic adj efficacious in counteracting fever or inflammation. * n any remedy that checks inflammatory symptoms.

antiphon n a verse or sentence sung by one choir in response to another, as in church services; an anthem.

antiphonal adj characterized by responsive singing; sung alternately. * n a collection of antiphons.—**antiphonally** adv.

antiphonary n (pl **antiphonaries**) a book of responses used in church services; an antiphonal. * adj antiphonal or responsive.

antiphony n (pl **antiphonies**) the alternate or responsive rendering of psalms or chants by a dual choir; a musical setting of sacred verses arranged for alternate singing.

antiphrasis n (rhetoric) the use of words in a sense opposite to the true one.

antipodes npl the regions on the earth's surface opposite each other; (with cap preceded by **the**) Australia and New Zealand.—**antipodean** adj.

antipope n one who usurps or is elected to the papal office in opposition to a pope canonically elected; a rival pope.

antipyretic adj preventive of, or remedial to fever. * n a fever-allaying drug.—**antipyresis** n.

antipyrine n a drug obtained from coal tar and used to relieve neuralgia, etc, and to reduce heat in fevers.

antiquarian adj connected with the study of antiquities. * n an antiquary.

antiquary n (pl **antiquaries**) a person who studies or collects antiquities.

antiquated adj old-fashioned; obsolete.

antique adj from the distant past; old-fashioned. * n a relic of the distant past; a piece of furniture, pottery, etc dating from an earlier historical period and sought after by collectors.

antiquity n (pl **antiquities**) the far distant past, esp before the Middle Ages; (pl) relics dating from the far distant past.

antirrhinum n snapdragon.

antisabbatarian adj opposed to the observance of the Sabbath.—also n.

antiscorbutic n a remedy against scurvy.—also adj.

anti-Semite n one who is hostile toward or discriminates against Jews as a religious or racial group.—**anti-Semitic** adj.—**anti-Semitism** n.

antiseptic n a substance that destroys or prevents the growth of disease-producing microorganisms. * adj destroying harmful organisms; very clean; (inf) unexciting.—**antiseptically** adv.

antiserum n (pl **antiserums, antisera**) blood serum containing antibodies.

antisocial adj avoiding the company of other people, unsocial; contrary to the interests of society in general.

antispasmodic adj counteractive to or curative of spasms. * n a medicine having such an effect.

antistatic adj (material, agent) counteracting the effects of static electricity.

antistrophe n a stanza or movement of a Greek chorus alternating with the strophe, sung in moving to the right.—**antistrophic** adj.

antithesis n (pl **antitheses**) a contrast or opposition, as of ideas; the exact opposite.—**antithetical, antithetic** adj.

antitoxin n a substance that acts against a specific toxin in the body; a serum containing an antitoxin, injected into a person to prevent disease.—**antitoxic** *adj*.

antitrade *n* a tropical wind blowing steadily in an opposite direction to the trade wind.

antitrust *adj* (*laws, regulations*) restricting or opposing the activities of cartels and monopolies.

antitype *n* that which a type or symbol stands for; that which preceded the type and of which the type is the representation.

antivenin *n* an antidote to snake poison.

antivivisectionist *n* a person who opposes scientific experimentation on live animals.

antler *n* the branched horn of a deer or related animal.—**antlered** *adj*.

antlion *n* a neuropterous insect whose larva constructs a pitfall for ants and other insects.

antonomasia *n* (*rhetoric*) the use of an attribute or epithet, or style of dignity or office, in place of the proper noun, eg "the Stagirite" for Aristotle, or the reverse, of a proper noun for a common noun, eg "some mute inglorious Milton".—**antonomastic** *adj*.—**antonomastically** *adv*.

antonym *n* a word that has the opposite meaning to another.

antrum *n* (*pl* **antra**) (*anat*) a cavity, esp in the upper jawbone.

anurous *adj* (*zool*) tailless.

anus *n* the excretory orifice of the alimentary canal.

anvil *n* the heavy iron block on which metal objects are shaped with a hammer.

anxiety *n* (*pl* **anxieties**) the condition of being anxious; eagerness, concern; a cause of worry.

anxious *adj* worried; uneasy; eagerly wishing; causing anxiety.—**anxiously** *adv*.—**anxiousness** *n*.

any *adj* one out of many, some; every.

anybody *pron* any person; an important person.

anyhow *adv* in any way whatever; in any case.

any more, anymore *adv* now; nowadays.

anyone *pron* any person; anybody.

anything *pron* any object, event, fact, etc. * *n* a thing, no matter what kind.

anyway *adv* in any manner; at any rate; haphazardly.

anywhere *adv* in, at, or to any place.

Anzac *abbr* = Australian and New Zealand Army Corps. * *n* a member of this corps.—*also adj*.

aorist *n* (*gram*) an indeterminate past tense of the verb expressing completed action. * *adj* indefinite; pertaining to the aorist tense.—**aoristic** *adj*.—**aoristically** *adv*.

aorta *n* (*pl* **aortas, aortae**) the main artery that carries blood from the heart to be distributed through the body.—**aortic, aortal** *adj*.

aoudad *n* a wild sheep-like animal of North Africa, somewhat resembling the chamois.

ap- *prefix* the form of *ad-* before *p*.

apace *adv* at a swift pace.

Apache *n* (*pl* **Apaches, Apache**) a tribe of North American Indians.

apache *n* a Parisian street ruffian, a hooligan;

apagoge *n* (*logic*) the establishing of a proposition by demonstrating the untenability of its opposite.—**apagogic, apagogical** *adj*.—**apagogically** *adv*.

apanage *see* **appanage**.

apart *adv* at a distance, separately, aside; into two or more pieces.

apartheid *n* a policy of racial segregation implemented in South Africa.

apartment *n* a room or rooms in a building; a flat.

apathetic *adj* devoid of or insensible to feeling or emotion.—**apathetically** *adv*.

apathy *n* lack of feeling; lack of concern, indifference.—**apathetic** *adj*.—**apathetically** *adv*.

apatite *n* a crystalline phosphate of lime.

ape *n* a chimpanzee, gorilla, orangutan, or gibbon; any monkey; a mimic. * *vt* to imitate.

apeak *adv* (*naut*) nearly vertical in position.

apeman *n* (*pl* **apemen**) an extinct creature supposedly intermediate in development between apes and man.

aperçu *n* a first view; a rapid survey; a brief outline.

aperient *adj* gently laxative; opening the bowels. * *n* a mild laxative medicine.

aperiodic *adj* without periodicity.—**aperiodically** *adv*.—**aperiodicity** *n*.

aperitif, apéritif *n* an alcoholic drink taken before a meal as an appetizer.

aperture *n* an opening; a hole; a slit; in optical instruments, the (diameter of the) opening allowing or controlling the amount of light or radiation to enter.

apery *n* (*pl* **aperies**) mimicry.

apetalous *adj* without petals or corolla.—**apetaly** *n*.

apex *n* (*pl* **apexes, apices**) the highest point, the tip; the culminating point; the vertex of a triangle.

aphaeresis *n* (*pl* **aphaereses**) (*linguistics*) the removal of a letter or syllable from the beginning of a word.—*also* **apheresis**.

aphagia *n* the inability to swallow.

aphasia *n* loss of the power of speech or the appropriate use of words due to disease or injury of the brain.—**aphasic** *adj*.

aphelion *n* (*pl* **aphelia**) that point in the orbit of a planet or a comet which is farthest from the sun.

apheliotropic *adj* (*bot*) turning away from the sun.

apheresis *see* **aphaeresis**.

aphesis *n* (*linguistics*) the gradual loss of an unaccented vowel at the beginning of a word, as in "squire" for "esquire".—**aphetic** *adj*.—**aphetically** *adv*.

aphid *n* any of various small insects, such as the greenfly, that suck the juice of plants.

aphis *n* (*pl* **aphides**) an aphid.

aphonia, aphony *n* dumbness, loss of voice.—**aphonic** *adj*.

aphorism *n* a brief, wise saying; an adage.—**aphoristic** *adj*.

aphrodisiac *adj* arousing sexually. * *n* a food, drug, etc that excites sexual desire.

aphtha *n* (*pl* **aphthae**) the small round white ulcers infesting the interior of the mouth; thrush.

aphyllous *adj* (*bot*) without leaves.—**aphylly** *n*.

apian *adj* of, pertaining to, or like bees.

apiarian *adj* of or relating to beekeeping.

apiarist *n* a beekeeper.

apiary *n* (*pl* **apiaries**) a place with hives where bees are kept.

apical *adj* of, pertaining to, belonging to, or at the apex.—**apically** *adv*.

apices *see* **apex**.

apiculate *adj* terminated abruptly by a point, as leaves.

apiculture *n* beekeeping.—**apicultural** *adj*.—**apiculturist** *n*.

apiece *adv* to, by, or for each one.

apish *adj* like an ape in manners; foolish; imitative.—**apishness** *n*.

apivorous *adj* feeding on bees.

aplacental *adj* without a placenta.

aplanatic *adj* (*physics*) free from, or correcting, spherical or chromatic aberration.—**aplanatically** *adv*.

aplastic *adj* without plasticity; not easily moulded.

aplomb *n* poise; self-possession.

apnea, apnoea *n* partial suspension of breathing; suffocation.—**apnoeic** *adj*.

apo- *prefix* off, from, away; un-; quite.

apocalypse *n* a cataclysmic event, the end of the world; revelation, esp that of St John; (*with cap*) the last book of the New Testament.—**apocalyptic** *adj*.—**apocalyptically** *adv*.

apocarpous *adj* (*bot*) having the carpels of the ovary separate or distinct.

apochromat *n* a highly achromatic lens.—**apochromatic** *adj*.

apocopate *vt* to cut off or drop the last letter or syllable of a word.—**apocopation** *n*.

apocope *n* (*linguistics*) the cutting off or deletion of the last letter or syllable of a word.

Apocrypha *npl* (*used as sing*) books of the Old Testament, eg Ecclesiasticus, accepted as an authentic part of the Holy Scriptures by the RC Church but not by Protestants.

apocryphal *adj* doubtful; untrue; invented; (*with cap*) of the Apocrypha.—**apocryphally** *adv*.

apodal *adj* without feet.

apodeictic, apodictic *adj* clearly established, unquestionable true.—**apodeictically, apodictically** *adv*.

apodosis *n* (*pl* **apodoses**) (*gram*) the latter portion, or consequent clause, of a conditional sentence.

apogamy *n* the absence of sexual reproduction; asexual reproduction.—**apogamic** *adj*.—**apogamous** *adj*.

apogee *n* the point in the orbit of the moon or any planet where it is most distant from the earth; the highest point.

apolitical *adj* uninterested or uninvolved in politics.

Apollo *n* (Greek, Roman myth) a sun god and god of music; (*pl* **Apollos**) a young handsome man.

apologetic *adj* expressing an apology; contrite; presented in defence.—**apologetically** *adv*.

apologetics *n* (*used as sing*) the defence and vindication of the principles and laws of Christian belief.

apologia *n* a written defence of one's principles or conduct.

apologist *n* a person who makes an apology; a defender of a cause.

apologize *vi* to make an apology.

apologue *n* a moral fable; a fiction or allegory embodying a moral application, as *Aesop's Fables*.

apology *n* (*pl* **apologies**) an expression of regret for wrongdoing; a defence or justification of one's beliefs, etc; (*with* **for**) a poor substitute.

apophthegm *n* a pithy saying embodying a wholesome truth or precept, a maxim.—*also* **apothegm**.

apophyge *n* (archit) the small hollow curve of a column where it springs from the base or top of the shaft.

apoplectic *adj* of, causing, or exhibiting symptoms of apoplexy; (*inf*) furious.

apoplexy *n* a sudden loss of consciousness and subsequent partial paralysis, usu caused by a broken or blocked artery in the brain.

aport *adv* (*naut*) on or towards the port or left side of a ship.

aposiopesis *n* (*pl* **aposiopeses**) (*rhetoric*) a sudden breaking off in speech for effect, eg "Bertrand is— what I dare not name".—**aposiopetic** *adj*.

apostasy *n* (*pl* **apostasies**) abandonment of one's religion, principles or political party.

apostate *n* a person who commits apostasy.

apostatize *vi* to abandon one's faith, church or party; to change one's religion for another.

a posteriori *adj* (*logic*) inductively, from effect to cause, founded on observation of facts, effects or consequences.

apostil *n* a marginal note.

apostle *n* the first or principal supporter of a new belief or cause; (*with cap*) one of the twelve disciples of Christ.

Apostles' Creed *n* the shortest of the three creeds, so named as containing a summary of apostolic doctrine.

apostle spoon *n* a spoon having a figure of one of the Apostles at the top of the handle.

apostolate *n* the dignity or office of an apostle, now restricted to that of the pope.

apostolic *adj* of or relating to the Apostles or their teachings; of or relating to the pope as successor to the Apostle St Peter.

Apostolic Church, Apostolic See *n* the Christian church as founded and governed by the Apostles on their doctrine and order. The name originally applied to the Churches of Rome, Antioch, Ephesus, Alexandria and Jerusalem.

Apostolic succession *n* the regular and uninterrupted transmission of ministerial authority by bishops from the Apostles.

apostrophe[1] *n* a mark (') showing the omission of letters or figures, also a sign of the possessive case or the plural of letters and figures; a breaking off in speech to appeal to someone dead or absent.—**apostrophic** *adj*.

apostrophe[2] *n* (*rhetoric*) a digression made in a speech or address, esp one directed at a person.

apostrophize *vt* to address by apostrophe; to omit a letter or letters; to mark an omission by the sign ('). * *vi* to make an apostrophe or short digressive address in speaking.

apothecaries' weight *n* a system of weights used for dispensing drugs, comprising the pound (12 oz), the ounce (8 drachms), the drachm (3 scruples), the scruple (20 grains), and the grain.

apothecary *n* (*pl* **apothecaries**) (*arch*) one who prepares and dispenses medicines and drugs, a pharmacist.

apothecium *n* (*pl* **apothecia**) the shield-like receptacle of lichens.—**apothecial** *adj*.

apothegm *see* **apophthegm**.

apotheosis *n* (*pl* **apotheoses**) deification; glorification of a person or thing; the supreme or ideal example.

apotheosize *vt* to exalt to the rank of a god; to deify.

appal, appall *vt* (**appals** *or* **appalls, appalling, appalled**) to fill with terror or dismay.

appalling *adj* shocking, horrifying.—**appallingly** *adv*.

appanage *n* provision for the younger sons of kings, etc; a perquisite; a dependency; an attribute.—*also* **apanage**.

apparatus *n* (*pl* **apparatus, apparatuses**) the equipment used for a specific task; any complex machine, device, or system.

apparel *n* clothing, dress. * *vt* (**apparelling, apparelled** *or* **appareling, appareled**) to dress; to clothe.

apparent *adj* easily seen, evident; seeming, but not real.—**apparently** *adv*.

apparition *n* an appearance or manifestation, esp something unexpected or unusual; a ghost.

appassionato *adj, adv* (*mus*) with passion.

appeal *vi* to take a case to a higher court; to make an earnest request; to refer to a witness or superior authority for vindication, confirmation, etc; to arouse pleasure or sympathy. * *n* the referral of a lawsuit to a higher court for rehearing; an earnest call for help; attraction, the power of arousing sympathy; a request for public donations to a charitable cause.—**appealable** *adj.*—**appealer** *n.*—**appealing** *adj.*

appear *vi* to become or be visible; to arrive, come in person; to be published; to present oneself formally (before a court, etc); to seem, give an impression of being.

appearance *n* the act or occasion of appearing; that which appears; external aspect of a thing or person; outward show, semblance.

appease *vt* to pacify; to allay; to conciliate by making concessions.—**appeasement** *n.*

appellant *n* a person who makes an appeal to a higher court.

appellate *adj* pertaining to appeals; dealing with appeals. * *n* the person appealed against or called upon to appear.

appellation *n* the name, title or designation by which a person or thing is called or known; the act of appealing.

appellative *n* (*gram*) a common, as distinguished from a proper, name; the designation of a class. * *adj* serving to distinguish, as a name or denomination of a group or class; common, as a noun.

appellee *n* the person appealed against; the defendant in an appeal.

append *vt* to attach; to add, esp to the end as a supplement, etc.

appendage *n* something appended; an external organ or part, as a tail.

appendant *adj* attached or annexed; attached in a subordinate capacity to another. * *n* that which is appended or added.

appendicectomy, appendectomy *n* (*pl* **appendicectomies, appendectomies**) surgical removal of the appendix that grows from the intestine.

appendicitis *n* inflammation of the appendix that grows from the intestine.

appendicle *n* a small appendage.

appendix *n* (*pl* **appendixes, appendices**) a section of supplementary information at the back of a book, etc; a small tube of tissue that forms an outgrowth of the intestine (—*also* **vermiform appendix**).

apperception *n* (*psychol*) perception with consciousness of self.—**apperceptive** *adj.*

appertain *vi* to belong or pertain to, as by relation or custom.

appetence, appetency *n* (*pl* **appetences, appetencies**) desire, craving; affinity.

appetite *n* sensation of bodily desire, esp for food; (*with* **for**) a strong desire or liking, a craving.

appetizer *n* a food or drink that stimulates the appetite; something that whets one's interest.

appetizing *adj* stimulating the appetite.—**appetizingly** *adv.*

applaud *vt* to show approval, esp by clapping the hands; to praise.

applause *n* approval expressed by clapping; acclamation.

apple *n* a round, firm, fleshy, edible fruit.

apple brandy *n* a liqueur distilled from cider.

applecart *n* **upset the applecart** to spoil one's plans.

applejack *n* apple brandy.

apple-pie bed *n* a bed made with the sheets folded so that one's legs cannot get down.

apple-pie order *n* perfect order.

apple sauce *n* a sauce of stewed apples usu served with pork; (*sl*) nonsense, flattery.

applicative *adj* capable of being applied.

applicatory *adj* fit to be applied.

appliance *n* a device or machine, esp for household use.

applicable *adj* that may be applied; appropriate, relevant (to).—**applicability** *n.*

applicant *n* a person who applies, esp for a job.

application *n* the act of applying; the use to which something is put; a petition, request; concentration, diligent effort; relevance or practical value.

applicator *n* a device for applying something.

applied *adj* practical.

appliqué *n* ornamental fabricwork applied to another fabric. * *vt* (**appliquéing, appliquéed**) to decorate with appliqué.

apply *vb* (**applying, applied**) *vt* to bring to bear; to put to practical use; to spread, lay on; to devote (oneself) with close attention. * *vi* to make a formal, esp written, request; to be relevant.

appoggiatura *n* (*pl* **appoggiaturas, appoggiature**) (*mus*) a grace note immediately preceding a principal note with which it is connected, and taking its time from the latter.

appoint *vt* to fix or decide officially; to select for a job; to prescribe.

appointed *adj* equipped; furnished.

appointee *n* a person appointed.

appointment *n* an appointing; a job or position for which someone has been selected; an arrangement to meet.

apportion *vt* to divide into shares; allot.—**apportionable** *adj.*—**apportioner** *n.*—**apportionment** *n.*

appose *vt* to apply; to place opposite or in juxtaposition.

apposite *adj* (*remarks*) especially pertinent, appropriate.—**appositely** *adv.*

apposition *n* the act of adding; addition by application, or placing together; (*gram*) the placing of a second noun in the same case in juxtaposition to the first, which it characterizes or explains, as St Mark, the Evangelist.—**appositional** *adj.*

appraisal, appraisement *n* the act of appraising or valuing, esp the putting of a price upon with a view to sale; a valuation.

appraise *vt* to estimate the value or quality of.—**appraiser** *n.*

appreciable *adj* capable of being perceived or measured; fairly large.—**appreciably** *adv.*

appreciate *vt* to value highly; to recognize gratefully; to understand, be aware of; to increase the value of. * *vi* to rise in value.

appreciation *n* gratitude, approval; sensitivity to aesthetic values; an assessment or critical evaluation of a person or thing; a favourable review; an increase in value.—**appreciative** *adj.*

apprehend *vt* to arrest, capture; to understand, to perceive.

apprehension *n* anxiety; the act of arresting; understanding; an idea.

apprehensive *adj* uneasy; anxious.—**apprehensively** *adv.*

apprentice *n* one being taught a trade or craft; a novice.

apprise * *vt* to take on as an apprentice.—**apprenticeship** *n.*

apprise, apprize *vt* to give notice to; to inform.

approach *vi* to draw nearer. * *vt* to make a proposal to; to set about dealing with; to come near to. * *n* the act of approaching; a means of entering or leaving; a move to establish relations; the final descent of an aircraft.

approachable *adj* within approaching distance; easy to approach; inviting friendship.—**approachability** *n.*—**approachably** *adv.*

approbation *n* formal approval; sanction.

appropriate *adj* fitting, suitable. * *vt* to take for one's own use, esp illegally; *(money, etc)* to set aside for a specific purpose.—**appropriately** *adv.*—**appropriateness** *n.*

appropriation *n* the act of setting apart or reserving for one's own use; a sum of money set aside for a particular purpose.

approval *n* the act of approving; favourable opinion; official permission.

approve *vt* to express a good opinion of; to authorize. * *vi (with* **of**) to consider to be favourable or satisfactory.

approx. *abbr* = approximate(ly).

approximate *adj* almost exact or correct. * *vt* to come near to; to be almost the same as. * *vi* to come close.—**approximately** *adv.*

approximation *n* a close estimate; a near likeness.

appulse *n* a coming towards; (astron) the near approach of a planet to a conjunction with the sun or any fixed star.—**appulsive** *adj.*

appurtenance *n* that which belongs or relates to something else; an adjunct or appendage; that which belongs it, is accessory to; an estate or property.—**appurtenant** *adj, n.*

APR *abbr* = annual percentage rate.

Apr. *abbr* = April.

après-ski *n* social activity after skiing.—*also adj.*

apricot *n* a small, oval, orange-pink fruit resembling the plum and peach.

April *n* the fourth month of the year, having 30 days.

April Fool *n* the victim of a trick played on 1 April, **April Fool's Day.**

a priori *(Latin)* deductively, from cause to effect.

apron *n* a garment worn to protect clothing; anything resembling the shape of an apron used for protection; the paved surface on an airfield where aircraft are parked, etc.

apropos *adv* at the right time; opportunely; appropriately. * *adj* appropriate. * *prep (with* **of**) regarding, in reference to.

apse *n* a domed or vaulted recess, esp in a church.

apsis *n (pl* **apsides**) *(astron)* one of two points in the orbit of a planet situated at the furthest or the least distance from the central body or sun; the imaginary line connecting these points.—**apsidal** *adj.*

apt *adj* ready or likely (to); suitable, relevant; able to learn easily.—**aptness** *n.*

apteral *adj (archit)* without side columns.

apterous *adj* without wings.

apterygial *adj* lacking wings or fins.

apteryx *n* the kiwi, a New Zealand bird with rudimentary wings and no tail.

aptitude *n* suitability; natural talent, esp for learning.

apyretic *adj* without fever, or with intermission of fever.

aq *abbr* = aqua.

aqua *n (pl* **aquae, aquas**) water as used in pharmacy.

aquaculture *n* the cultivation and breeding of fish and other marine organisms.—*also* **aquiculture.**—**aquacultural** *adj.*—**aquaculturist** *n.*

aqua fortis *n* impure nitric acid.

aqualung *n* portable diving gear comprising air cylinders connected to a face mask.

aquamarine *n* a variety of bluish-green beryl used as a gemstone; its colour.

aquaplane *n* a plank towed at high speed. * *vi* to ride on one.

aqua regia *n* a mixture of nitric and hydrochloric acids, capable of dissolving gold.

aquarelle *n* a style of painting in Chinese ink and thin watercolours; a painting so executed.—**aquarellist** *n.*

aquarium *n (pl* **aquariums, aquaria**) a tank, pond, etc for keeping aquatic animals or plants, a building where collections of aquatic animals are exhibited.

Aquarius *n (astrol)* the eleventh sign of the zodiac, the water-carrier, operative 20 January–18 February.—**Aquarian** *adj, n.*

aquatic *adj* of or taking place in water; living or growing in water.

aquatics *npl* water sports.

aquatint *n* a style of etching resembling a watercolour drawing in Indian ink or in sepia; an engraving produced by this process. * *vt* to etch or engrave in aquatint.

aqua vitae *n* unrectified alcohol; brandy and other ardent spirits.

aqueduct *n* a large pipe or conduit for carrying water; an elevated structure supporting this.

aqueous *adj* of, like, or formed by water.

aqueous humour *n* a limpid fluid of the eye, filling the space between the crystalline lens and the cornea.

aquiculture *n* hydroponics; another name for aquaculture.—**aquicultural** *adj.*—**aquiculturist** *n.*

aquilegia *n* columbine.

aquiline *adj* of or like an eagle; *(nose)* hooked, like an eagle's beak.

ar- *prefix* the form of *ad-* before *r.*

-ar *adj suffix* of, belonging to, as in *angular, popular.*

AR *abbr* = Arkansas.

Ar *(chem symbol)* argon.

Arab *n* a native of Arabia; one of the Arabic races spread over the African and Syrian deserts. * *adj* pertaining to Arabia or the Arabs.

arabesque *n* a decorative design incorporating organic motifs, such as leaves and flowers, in an intricate pattern; *(ballet)* a posture in which the dancer balances on one leg with one arm extending forwards and the other arm and leg extending backwards.

Arabian *adj* of Arabia, Arab. * *n* an Arab.

Arabian camel *n* a camel with a single hump.

Arabic *n* the Arabian language. * *adj* of or pertaining to the Arabic language and the countries in which it is spoken.

Arabic numeral *n* one of the numbers 0, 1, 2, 3, 4, 5, etc.

arable *adj (land)* suitable for ploughing or planting crops.—*also n.*

arachnid *n* any of a class of animals including spiders, scorpions, mites and ticks.—**arachnidan** *adj, n.*

arachnoid *adj* pertaining to spiders; resembling the web of a spider. * *n* the enveloping membrane of the brain and spinal cord, between the dura mater and the pia mater.

aragonite *n* a variety of carbonate of lime.

arak *see* **arrack.**

Aramaic *n* the language of Palestine at the time of Christ.

araneid *n* a member of the Arachnida order, the spider family.

araucaria *n* one of a genus of coniferous trees, found principally in South America and Australia, which includes the monkey puzzle.

arbalest *n* a crossbow with a drawing mechanism.

arbiter *n* a person having absolute power of decision or absolute control.

arbitrage *n* the rapid purchase and resale of stocks to maximize price discrepancy, often using confidential knowledge.—*also* **index arbitrage**.

arbitrament *n* an arbiter's judgment; an authoritative decision.

arbitrary *adj* not bound by rules; despotic, absolute; capricious, unreasonable.—**arbitrarily** *adv.*—**arbitrariness** *n*.

arbitrate *vi* to act as an arbitrator. * *vt* to submit to an arbiter; to act as an arbiter upon.

arbitration *n* the settlement of disputes by arbitrating.

arbitrator *n* a person chosen to settle a dispute between contending parties.

arbor¹ *see* **arbour**.

arbor² *n* the main support of a machine; an axis, a spindle.

Arbor Day *n* a day legally set apart in certain states of the US for planting trees.

arboraceous *adj* pertaining to, or of the nature of, a tree or trees; living on or among trees.

arboreal *adj* of or living in trees.

arboreous *adj* wooded.

arborescent *adj* growing or formed like a tree.—**arborescence** *n*.

arboretum *n* (*pl* **arboreta, arboretums**) a botanical tree garden where rare trees are cultivated and exhibited.

arboriculture *n* the cultivation of trees and shrubs, forestry.

arborization, arborisation *n* a tree-like appearance.

arbor vitae *n* an evergreen tree extensively cultivated in gardens, etc.

arbour *n* a place shaded by trees, foliage, etc; a bower.—*also* **arbor**.

arbutus *n* (*pl* **arbutuses**) one of a genus of tree-like evergreen shrubs to which the strawberry tree belongs.

ARC *abbr* = AIDS-related complex.

ARC *acronym for* AIDS-related condition.

arc *n* a portion of the circumference of a circle or other curve; a luminous discharge of electricity across a gap between two electrodes or terminals. * *vi* to form an electric arc.

arcade *n* a series of arches supported on columns; an arched passageway; a covered walk or area lined with shops.

Arcadia, Arcady *n* (*poet*) ideal countryside.

Arcadian *adj* of or pertaining to Arcadia, a department of Greece, or its inhabitants; rurally simple. * *n* an inhabitant of Arcadia.

arcane *adj* secret or esoteric.

arcanum *n* (*pl* **arcana**) a secret, a mystery; a valuable elixir.

arch¹ *n* a curved structure spanning an opening; the curved underside of the foot. * *vti* to span or cover with an arch; to curve, bend into an arch.

arch² *adj* (*criminal, etc*) principal, expert; clever, sly; mischievous.—**archly** *adv.*—**archness** *n*.

Archaean *adj* of the earliest geological period or strata.—*also* **Archean**.

archaeology *n* the study of past human societies through their extant remains.—*also* **archeology.**—**archaeological, archeological** *adj.*—**archaeologist, archeologist** *n*.

archaeopteryx *n* oldest fossil bird.

archaic *adj* belonging to ancient times; (*language*) no longer in common use.

archaism *n* an archaic word or phrase.—**archaistic** *adj*.

archaize *vti* to affect the archaic; to make archaic.—**archaizer** *n*.

archangel *n* a principal angel.—**archangelic** *adj*.

archbishop *n* a bishop of the highest rank.

archbishopric *n* the jurisdiction, office or see of an archbishop.

archdeacon *n* a clergyman ranking next under a bishop.

archdeaconry *n* (*pl* **archdeaconries**) the office, rank, jurisdiction, or residence of an archdeaon.

archdiocese *n* the diocese of an archbishop.—**archdiocesan** *adj*.

archducal *adj* of or pertaining to an archduchess, an archduchy or an archduke.

archduchess *n* a daughter of the emperor of Austria; the wife or widow of an archduke.

archduchy *n* (*pl* **archduchies**) the territory or rank of an archduke or an archduchess.

archduke *n* a prince of the imperial house of Austria.

Archean *see* **Archaean**.

archegonium *n* (*pl* **archegonia**) (*bot*) the pistillidium or female organ of the higher cryptogams (ferns, etc).

archenemy *n* (*pl* **archenemies**) a principal enemy; Satan.

archeology *see* **archaeology**.

archer *n* a person who shoots with a bow and arrow.

archerfish *n* (*pl* **archerfish, archerfishes**) a scaly-finned fish of the Java seas, which catches insects by darting drops of water upon them.

archery *n* the art or sport of shooting arrows from a bow.

archetype *n* the original pattern or model; a prototype.—**archetypal, archetypical** *adj*.

archfiend *n* a chief fiend; Satan.

archidiaconal *adj* of or pertaining to an archdeacon or to his office.

archidiaconate *n* the office of an archdeacon.

archiepiscopate, archiepiscopacy *n* the rule or dignity of an archbishop.

archiepiscopal *adj* of or pertaining to an archbishop or to his office.

archimagus, archimage *n* the high priest of the Persian magi or fire-worshippers; a chief magician.

archil *see* **orchil**.

archimandrite *n* (*Greek Orthodox Church*) the abbot of a monastery, or an abbot-general having the charge and superintendence of several monasteries.

Archimedean screw *n* an instrument for raising water, consisting of a flexible tube wound spirally around or within a cylinder in the form of a screw. When placed in an inclined position, with the lower end immersed in water, by the revolution of the screw the water is raised to the upper end.

archipelago *n* (*pl* **archipelagoes, archipelagos**) a sea filled with small islands; a group of small islands.—**archipelagic, archipelagian** *adj*.

architect *n* a person who designs buildings and supervises their erection; someone who plans something.

architectonic *adj* pertaining to design or construction;

skilled in architecture; expert in constructing; of the systematizing of knowledge.—**architectonically** *adv*.

architectonics *n* (*used as sing*) the science of architecture; structure.

architecture *n* the art, profession, or science of designing and constructing buildings; the style of a building or buildings; the design and organization of a computer's parts.—**architectural** *adj*.—**architecturally** *adv*.

architrave *n* an epistyle, the lowest division of an entablature, the part resting immediately on a column; the parts round a door or window.

archives *npl* the location in which public records are kept; the public records themselves.—**archival** *adj*.

archivist *n* a keeper of public records.

archivolt *n* the undercurve of an arch or the moulding on it.

archpriest *n* a chief priest; a rural dean.

archway *n* an arched or vaulted passage, esp that leading into a castle.

arc light *n* light produced by a current of electricity passing between two carbon points placed a short distance from each other.

arctic *adj* (*often with cap*) of, near, or relating to the North Pole or its surroundings; (*inf*) very cold, icy.

Arctic Circle *n* an imaginary circle around the arctic regions parallel to the equator.

arctic fox *n* a small species of fox, whose fine fur is used for muffs, trimmings, etc.

Arctic Ocean *n* the ocean that washes the northern coasts of Europe, Asia and North America.

arcuate *adj* bent or curved in the form of a bow.

arcuation *n* the act of bending; the state of being bent or curved; a method of propagating trees by bending branches to the ground and covering portions of them with earth.

arc welding *n* welding using an electric arc.

ardent *adj* passionate; zealous.—**ardency** *n*.—**ardently** *adv*.

ardent spirits *npl* alocholic beverages, as brandy, whisky, etc.

ardour, ardor *n* warmth of feeling; extreme intensity.

arduous *adj* difficult, laborious; steep, difficult to climb. —**arduously** *adv*.—**arduousness** *n*.

are[1] *see* be.

are[2] *n* a metric unit of measure equal to 100 square metres.

area *n* an expanse of land; a total outside surface, measured in square units; a specific part of a house, district, etc; scope or extent.

areca *n* a genus of lofty palms, including the tree from which the betelnut and the astringent juice Catechu are obtained.

arena *n* an area within a sports stadium, etc where events take place; a place or sphere of contest or activity.

arenaceous *adj* sandy; abounding in, or having the properties of, sand.

aren't = are not.

areola *n* (*pl* **areolae, areolas**) a very small area; an interstice in tissue; the coloured circle or halo surrounding the nipple of the breast.—**areolar, areolate** *adj*.—**areolation** *n*.

arête *n* the sharp ridge or spur of a mountain.

argali *n* (*pl* **argalis, argali**) a large wild Asiatic sheep, remarkable for its huge curved horns.

argent *n* (*her*) silver, represented in a drawing or engraving of a coat of arms by a plain white surface, symbolic of purity, beauty, etc. * *adj* made of or resembling silver; silvery white; bright like silver.

argentiferous *adj* producing or containing silver.

argentine *adj* pertaining to or resembling silver; silvery. * *n* a silvery-white slaty variety of calcite; white metal coated with silver, imitation silver.

argil *n* clay, esp potter's clay or earth.

argillaceous *adj* of or containing clay, clayey.

argilliferous *adj* producing or containing clay.

argillite *n* clay-slate.—**argillitic** *adj*.

argol *n* a deposit of crude tartar on the sides of wine vessels; crude tartar from which cream of tartar is prepared.

argon *n* an inert gaseous element.

argosy *n* (*pl* **argosies**) a large, richly laden merchant ship.

argot *n* the special vocabulary of any set of persons, as of lawyers, criminals, etc.—**argotic** *adj*.

arguable *adj* debatable; able to be asserted; plausible.— **arguably** *adv*.

argue *vb* (**arguing, argued**) *vt* to try to prove by reasoning; to debate, dispute; to persuade (into, out of). * *vi* to offer reasons for or against something; to disagree, exchange angry words.—**arguer** *n*.

argufy *vi* (**argufying, argufied**) (*sl*) to argue tediously, to wrangle.

argument *n* a disagreement; a debate, discussion; a reason offered in debate; an abstract, summary.

argumentation *n* systematic reasoning; argument, discussion.

argumentative *adj* prone to arguing.—**argumentatively** *adv*.—**argumentativeness** *n*.

argy-bargy *n* (*pl* **argy-bargies**) a tedious discussion. * *vi* to argue at length.

aria *n* a song for one voice accompanied by instruments, eg in opera.

Arian *adj* pertaining to the doctrines of the Arian sect, which held that Christ is not divine.—**Arianism** *n*.

arid *adj* very dry, parched; uninteresting; dull.—**aridity** *n*.—**aridly** *adv*.

Aries *n* (*astrol*) the first sign of the zodiac, the Ram, operative 21 March–21 April.—**Arian** *adj, n*.

arietta *n* a short aria, song or air.

aright *adv* correctly.

aril *n* (*bot*) an accessory covering or appendage of certain seeds.

arioso *adj, adv* (*mus*) like an air; in a smooth melodious style.

arise *vi* (**arising, arose**, *pp* **arisen**) to get up, as from bed; to rise, ascend; to come into being, to result (from).

arista *n* (*pl* **aristae**) the awn or beard of grasses; a bristle.

aristate *adj* bearded; having a beard or bristle, as certain grasses.

aristocracy *n* (*pl* **aristocracies**) (a country with) a government dominated by a privileged minority class; the privileged class in a society, the nobility; those people considered the best in their particular sphere.

aristocrat *n* a member of the aristocracy; a supporter of aristocratic government; a person with the manners or taste of a privileged class.

aristocratic *adj* relating to or characteristic of the aristocracy; elegant, stylish in dress and manners.— **aristocratically** *adv*.

Aristotelian *adj* pertaining to, or characteristic of, Aristotle (384—322 BC) or his philosophy.

arithmetic *n* (*math*) computation (addition, subtraction, etc) using real numbers; calculation.—**arithmetic, arithmetical** *adj.*—**arithmetically** *adv.*

arithmetician *n* one skilled in the science of numbers.

Ariz. *abbr* = Arizona.

ark *n* (*Bible*) the boat in which Noah and his family and two of every kind of creature survived the Flood; a place of safety; an enclosure in a synagogue for the scrolls of the Torah.

Ark. *abbr* = Arkansas.

ark of the covenant *n* (*Bible*) the chest containing the two stone tablets inscribed with the Ten Commandments.

arm[1] *n* the upper limb from the shoulder to the wrist; something shaped like an arm, as a support on a chair; a sleeve; power, authority; an administrative division of a large organization.

arm[2] *n* (*usu pl*) a weapon; a branch of the military service; (*pl*) heraldic bearings. * *vt* to provide with weapons, etc; to provide with something that protects or strengthens, etc; to set a fuse ready to explode. * *vi* to prepare for war or any struggle.

armada *n* a fleet of warships or aircraft.

armadillo *n* (*pl* **armadillos**) a small animal from South America with a body covering of small bony plates.

Armageddon *n* (*Bible*) the site of the last decisive battle between good and evil; any great decisive battle.

armament *n* (*often pl*) all the military forces and equipment of a nation; all the military equipment of a warship, etc; the process of arming or being armed for war.

armature *n* a piece of iron connecting the poles of a magnet or electromagnet to preserve and increase the magnetic force; the revolving part of a dynamo; arms, armour, that which serves as a means of defence; iron bars or framework used to strengthen a building; a framework supporting clay, etc, in sculpture or modelling.

armchair *n* a chair with side rests for the arms. * *adj* lacking practical experience.

armed forces *npl* the military forces of a nation.—*also* **armed services.**

armful *n* as much as the arms can hold.

armhole *n* an opening for the arm in an item of clothing.

armiger *n* one entitled to use heraldic bearings, an esquire.—**armigerous** *adj.*

armillary *adj* of or resembling a bracelet; consisting of circles or rings.

armillary sphere *n* a skeleton celestial globe showing the relative positions of the stars, etc.

Arminianism *n* a Christian Protestant doctrine that denies Calvin's doctrine of predestination.—**Arminian** *adj, n.*

armistice *n* a truce, preliminary to a peace treaty.

armlet *n* an ornamental or protective band worn around the arm; a badge worn on the arm; a small arm of the sea.

armorial *adj* pertaining to armour or the arms or escutcheon of a family. * *n* a book or dictionary of heraldic devices and the names of persons entitled to use them.

armour, armor *n* any defensive or protective covering.

armoured, armored *adj* covered or protected with armour; equipped with tanks and armour vehicles.

armourer, armorer *n* the custodian of the arms of a bat-

tleship, etc; (formerly) a maker of arms or armour; one who had charge of the armour of another.

armour plate, armor plate *n* a plate of iron or steel affixed to a ship or tank as part of a casing for protection against shellfire.

armoury, armory *n* (*pl* **armouries, armories**) an arsenal; a place where armour or ammunition is stored.

armpit *n* the hollow underneath the arm at the shoulder.

arms *see* **arm**[2].

army *n* (*pl* **armies**) a large organized body of soldiers for waging war, esp on land; any large number of persons, animals, etc.

army worm *n* the larva of a moth that devastates grain and other crops, esp destructive in North America; the larva of a European small two-winged fly.

arnica *n* a genus of perennial herbs, esp mountain tobacco, whose roots and flowers are used to make a tincture for treating bruises.

aroma *n* a pleasant smell; a fragrance.

aromatherapy *n* the massage of fragrant oils into the skin to relieve tension and promote wellbeing.

aromatic *adj* giving out an aroma; fragrant, spicy; odoriferous. * *n* a plant, herb or drug yielding a fragrant smell.—**aromatically** *adv.*

aromatize *vt* to render fragrant, to perfume, to scent.—**aromatization** *n.*

arose *see* **arise**.

around *prep* on all sides of; on the border of; in various places in or on; approximately, about. * *adv* in a circle; in every direction; in circumference; to the opposite direction.

arousal *n* the act of awakening or stimulating; the state of being awakened or stimulated.

arouse *vt* to wake from sleep; to stir, as to action; to evoke.

arpeggio *n* (*pl* **arpeggios**) (*mus*) the playing of notes of a chord in rapid succession, instead of simultaneously; a passage or chord so played.

arquebus *n* an old-fashioned handgun fired from a forked rest.—*also* **harquebus**.

arrack *n* an alcoholic spirit distilled in some Asian countries from rice, molasses, the juice of the date palm, etc.—*also* **arak**.

arraign *vt* to put on trial; to indict, accuse; to censure publicly; to impeach.—**arraigner** *n.*—**arraignment** *n.*

arrange *vt* to put in a sequence or row; to settle, make preparations for; (*mus*) to prepare a composition for different instruments other than those intended.* *vi* to come to an agreement; to make plans.—**arranger** *n.*

arrangement *n* the act of putting in proper form or order; that which is ordered or disposed; the method or style of disposition; a preparatory measure; preparation; settlement; classification; adjustment; adaptation; (*pl*) plans.

arrant *adj* notorious; unmitigated; downright, thorough; shameless.

arras *n* a tapestry; hangings made of a rich figured fabric.

array *n* an orderly grouping, esp of troops; an impressive display; fine clothes; (*comput*) an ordered data structure that allows information to be easily indexed. * *vt* to set in order, to arrange; to dress, decorate.—**arrayal** *n.*

arrears *npl* overdue debts; work, etc still to be completed.

arrest *vt* to stop; to capture, apprehend esp by legal authority; to check the development of a disease; to catch and hold the attention of. * *n* a stoppage; seizure by legal authority.

arrestee *n* one who has been arrested.

arrester *n* one who or that which stops or seizes, or causes to be detained.

arresting *adj* striking or attracting to the mind or eye; impressive.—**arrestingly** *adv*.

arrière-pensée *n* (*pl* **arrière-pensées**) a mental reservation.

arris *n* (*pl* **arris, arrises**) (*archit*) the line or sharp edge in which two curved or straight surfaces, forming an exterior angle, meet each other.

arrival *n* arriving; a person or thing that has arrived.

arrive *vi* to reach any destination; to come; (*with* **at**) to reach agreement, a decision; to achieve success, celebrity.

arriviste *n* an ambitious person, a self-seeker.

arrogance *n* an exaggerated assumption of importance.

arrogant *adj* overbearing; aggressively self-important.—**arrogantly** *adv*.

arrogate *vt* to assume or lay claim to unduly or presumptuously.—**arrogation** *n*.—**arrogative** *adj*.—**arrogator** *n*.

arrondissement *n* a subdivision of a French department; a municipal subdivision of Paris, etc.

arrow *n* a straight, pointed weapon, made to be shot from a bow; a sign used to indicate direction or location.

arrowhead *n* the head or barb of an arrow; an aquatic plant so named from the shape of its leaves.

arrowroot *n* a starch obtained from the rootstocks of several species of West Indian plants.

arrowwood *n* a wood once used for arrows by American Indians.

arroyo *n* a watercourse or rivulet; the dry bed of a small stream.

arse *n* (*vulg*) the buttocks.

arsenal *n* a workshop or store for weapons and ammunition.

arsenate *n* a salt formed by combination of arsenic acid with any base.

arsenic *n* a soft grey metallic element, highly poisonous.

arsenical *adj* pertaining to or containing arsenic.

arsenious, arsenous *adj* pertaining to or containing arsenic.

arsenite *n* a salt of arsenious acid.

arsis *n* (*poet*) the part of a metrical foot where the accent is placed.

arson *n* the crime of using fire to destroy property deliberately.—**arsonist** *n*.

art[1] *n* human creativity; skill acquired by study and experience; any craft and its principles; the making of things that have form and beauty; any branch of this, as painting, sculpture, etc; drawings, paintings, statues, etc; (*pl*) the creative and nonscientific branches of knowledge, esp as studied academically.

art[2] (*arch*) the second person singular indicative mood and present tense of the verb to be.

art deco *n* a style of design and architecture popular in the 1920s and 1930s and characterized by bold geometrical lines.

artefact *see* **artifact**.

artel *n* a workers' guild in the former USSR.

artemisia *n* a large genus of plants to which the common wormwood belongs, yielding a volatile oil (the chief ingredient of absinthe).

arterial *adj* pertaining to an artery or the arteries; contained in an artery; (*blood*) oxygenated, of a lighter red colour than venous blood; (*road*) major, with many branches.

arterialize *vt* to convert as venous blood into arterial blood by exposure to oxygen in the lungs.—**arterialization** *n*.

arteriosclerosis *n* (*med*) hardening of the walls of the arteries due to the action of fatty deposits, which impairs blood circulation.—**arteriosclerotic** *adj*.

artery *n* (*pl* **arteries**) a tubular vessel that conveys blood from the heart; any main channel of transport or communication.

artesian well *n* a well in which water rises to the surface by internal pressure.

artful *adj* skilful at attaining one's ends; clever, crafty.—**artfully** *adv*.—**artfulness** *n*.

arthritis *n* painful inflammation of a joint.—**arthritic** *adj*.

arthropod *n* a member of the largest group of invertebrate animals with jointed legs, such as the butterfly, spider, crab, centipede.

artichoke *n* a thistle-like plant with a scaly flower head, parts of which are eaten as a vegetable.

article *n* a separate item or clause in a written document; an individual item on a particular subject in a newspaper, magazine, etc; a particular or separate item; (*gram*) a word placed before a noun to identify it as definite or indefinite.

articled *adj* apprenticed to, as an articled clerk to a solicitor.

articular *adj* of a joint or structural components in a joint.

articulate *adj* capable of distinct, intelligible speech, or expressing one's thoughts clearly; jointed. * *vti* to speak or express clearly; to unite or become united (as) by a joint.—**articulatedly** *adv*.—**articulateness** *n*.

articulated lorry, articulated truck *n* a large vehicle composed of a tractor and one or more trailers connected by flexible joints for greater manoeuvrability.—*also* **trailer truck**.

articulation *n* the act of jointing; the act of speaking distinctly; a distinct utterance; the state of being articulated; a joint or juncture between bones; the point of separation of organs or parts of a plant; a node or joint of the stem, or the space between two nodes.—**articulatory** *adj*.

articulator *n* one who pronounces distinctly; any organ of the mouth, etc, that moves to produce speech sounds.

artifact *n* a product of human craftsmanship, esp a simple tool or ornament.—*also* **artefact**.

artifice *n* a clever contrivance or stratagem; a trick, trickery.

artificer *n* a skilled or artistic worker; a maker or constructor; an inventor.

artificial *adj* lacking natural qualities; man-made.—**artificiality** *n*.—**artificially** *adv*.

artificial insemination *n* injection of semen into the womb by artificial means so that conception takes place without sexual intercourse.

artificial intelligence *n* (*comput*) the ability to imitate intelligent human behaviour.

artificial respiration *n* the forcing of air into and out of the lungs of somebody whose breathing has stopped.

artillery *n* (*pl* **artilleries**) large, heavy guns; the branch of the army that uses these.

artisan *n* a skilled workman.

artist *n* one who practises fine art, esp painting; one who does anything very well.—**artistic** *adj*.

artiste *n* a professional, usu musical or theatrical, entertainer.

artistic *adj* pertaining to art or to artists; characterized by aesthetic feeling or conformity to the principles of a school of art or design.—**artistically** *adv*.

artistry *n* artistic quality, ability, work, etc.

artless *adj* simple, natural; without art or skill.—**artlessly** *adv*.—**artlessness** *n*.

art nouveau *n* a style of art and decoration that developed in the late 19th century, characterized by flowing curves and designs in imitation of nature.

arty *adj* (**artier, artiest**) (*inf*) having a pretentious or affected interest in art.

arty-crafty, artsy-craftsy *adj* (*inf*) relating to arts and crafts, esp when affecting a simple, traditional style.

arum *n* a genus of plants with small flowers within a hood-shaped leaf.

arundinaceous *adj* pertaining to or resembling a reed or cane.

-ary *adj suffix*, *n suffix* connected with, as *dictionary*.

Aryan *n* a member of the Indo-European race; according to Nazi belief, a Caucasian, esp of the Nordic type, with no Jewish blood. * *adj* pertaining to the Aryans, or to their language.

As (*chem symbol*) arsenic.

as[1] *adv* equally; for instance; when related in a certain way. * *conj* in the same way that; while; when; because. * *prep* in the role or function of.

as[2] *n* (*pl* **asses**) a Roman weight equivalent to the libra or pound; a Roman copper coin.

asafoetida, asafetida *n* a foul-smelling gum resin obtained from the roots of several large umbelliferous plants and used in medicine.

ASAP, a.s.a.p. *abbr* = as soon as possible.

asbestos, asbestus *n* a fine fibrous mineral used for making incombustible and chemical-resistant materials.

asbestosis *n* (*med*) a disease of the lungs caused by the inhalation of asbestos fibres.

ascend *vti* to go up; to succeed to (a throne).

ascendancy, ascendency *n* governing or dominating influence; power; sway.

ascendant, ascendent *adj* rising upwards; dominant.

ascender *n* one who ascends; the top part of letters such as b, d, h.

ascension *n* the act of ascending or rising.—**ascensional** *adj*.

Ascension *n* the ascent of Christ into heaven after the Resurrection.

Ascension Day *n* a movable feast commemorating the Ascension, celebrated on the Thursday next but one before Whit Sunday.—*also* **Holy Thursday**.

ascent *n* an ascending; an upward slope; the means of, the way of ascending.

ascertain *vt* to acquire definite knowledge of, to discover positively.—**ascertainable** *adj*.

ascetic *adj* self-denying, austere. * *n* a person who practises rigorous self-denial as a religious discipline; any severely abstemious person.—**ascetically** *adv*.—**asceticism** *n*.

ascidian *n* a type of mollusc with a leathery tunic resembling a double-necked bottle, a sea squirt.—*also adj*.

ascidium *n* (*pl* **ascidia**) (*bot*) a pitcher-shaped or flask-shaped organ peculiar to certain plants, as the pitcher plants.

ASCII *acronym* (*comput*) = American Standard Code for Information Interchange, a standard code of 128 alphanumeric characters for storing and exchanging information.

ascomycete *n* one of a family of the fungi, including most of the lichens, which form free spores within elongated spore cases.—**ascomyetous** *adj*.

ascorbic acid *n* vitamin C, found esp in citrus fruit and fresh green vegetables.

ascribe *vt* to attribute, impute or refer; to assign.—**ascribable** *adj*.—**ascription, adscription** *n*.

ascus *n* (*pl* **asci**) the spore case of lichens and fungi.

asdic *n* an apparatus for locating submarines; an echo sounder; sonar.

asepsis *n* an absence of disease or putrefaction; a surgical method aiming at this.—**aseptic** *adj*.

asexual *adj* lacking sex or sexual organs; (*reproduction*) produced without the union of male and female germ cells.—**asexuality** *n*.—**asexually** *adv*.

ash[1] *n* a tree with silver-grey bark; the wood of this tree.

ash[2] *n* powdery residue of anything burnt; fine, volcanic lava.

ashamed *adj* feeling shame or guilt.—**ashamedly** *adv*.

ash can *n* a container for household refuse, a garbage can.

ashen *adj* like ashes, esp in colour; pale.

Ashkenazi *n* (*pl* **Ashkenazim**) a Jew from Germany or eastern Europe.

ashlar, ashler *n* a squared stone used in building; masonry of this; thin slabs of building stone squared for facing walls.

ashlaring *n* a wall faced with ashlar; a low wall of a garret, built close to where the rafters reach the floor.

ashore *adv* to or on the shore; to or on land.—*also adj*.

ashram *n* a Hindu religious retreat.

ashtray *n* a small receptacle for tobacco ash and cigarette stubs.

Ash Wednesday *n* the first day of Lent; a special day set apart for fasting.

ashy *adj* (**ashier, ashiest**) of ashes; ash-coloured, pale.

Asian *adj* of or relating to the continent of Asia, its inhabitants or languages.—*also n*.

Asiatic cholera *n* a virulent form of cholera.

aside *adv* on or to the side; in reserve; away from; notwithstanding. * *n* words uttered and intended as inaudible, esp as spoken by an actor to the audience and supposedly unheard by the other actors on the stage.

asinine *adj* silly, stupid.—**asininity** *n*.

ask *vt* to put a question to, inquire of; to make a request of or for; to invite; to demand, expect. * *vi* to inquire about.—**asker** *n*.

askance, askant *adv* with a sideways glance; with distrust.

askew *adv* to one side; awry.—*also adj*.

aslant *adv* not at right angles; obliquely. * *prep* slantingly across, athwart.

asleep *adj* sleeping; inactive; numb. * *adv* into a sleeping condition.

asocial *adj* not capable of or avoiding social contact; antisocial.

asp *n* a small poisonous snake.

asparagus *n* a plant cultivated for its edible young shoots.

aspartame *n* an artificial sweetener derived from an amino acid.

aspect *n* the look of a person or thing to the eye; a particular feature of a problem, situation, etc; the direction something faces; view; (*astrol*) the position of the planets with respect to one another, regarded as having an influence on human affairs.

aspen *n* a species of poplar with leaves that have tremble in the slightest breeze. * *adj* (*arch*) quivering.

aspergillus *n* (*pl* **aspergilli**) a genus of microscopic fungi, to which several of the moulds belong.

asperity *n* (*pl* **asperities**) hardship, severity; sharpness of temper.

asperse *vt* to slander; (*rare*) to besprinkle, to bespatter.—**asperser** *n.*—**aspersive** *adj.*

aspersions *npl* slander; an attack on a person's reputation.

aspersorium *n* (*pl* **aspersoria, aspersoriums**) a vessel containing holy water for sprinkling; a brush or metallic instrument used for sprinkling the water.

asphalt *n* a hard, black bituminous substance, used for paving roads, etc. * *vt* to surface with asphalt.—**asphaltic** *adj.*

asphodel *n* one of several plants of the lily family; (*poet*) the daffodil; (*poet*) an immortal, unfading flower that bloomed in the meadows of Elysium (possibly the narcissus).

asphyxia *n* unconsciousness due to lack of oxygen or excess of carbon dioxide in the blood.

asphyxiate *vt* to suffocate.—**asphyxiation** *n.*—**asphyxiator** *n.*

aspic *n* a savoury jelly used to coat fish, game, etc.

aspidistra *n* an Asian plant with broad leaves, grown as a house plant.

aspirant *n* someone who aspires to something.

aspirate[1] *n* the sound of *h*.

aspirate[2] *vt* to pronounce with an *h*; to suck out using an aspirator.

aspiration *n* strong desire; ambition; the act of aspirating; the act of breathing; the withdrawal of air or fluid from a body cavity.—**aspiratory** *adj.*

aspirator *n* a device used to suck (air, fluid, etc) from a (body) cavity.

aspire *vi* to desire eagerly; to aim at high things.—**aspirer** *n.*—**aspiring** *adj.*

aspirin *n* (*pl* **aspirin, aspirins**) acetylsalicylic acid, a pain-relieving drug.

asquint *adv, adj* with a squint, to or out of the corner of the eye; obliquely.

ass *n* a donkey; a silly, stupid person; (*sl*) the arse, the buttocks.

assagai *see* **assegai**.

assai *adv* (*mus*) very, more, extremely.

assail *vt* to attack violently either physically or verbally.—**assailable** *adj.*—**assailer** *n.*—**assailment** *n.*

assailant *n* an attacker.

assassin *n* a murderer, esp one hired to kill a leading political figure, etc.

assassinate *vt* to kill a political figure, etc; to harm (a person's reputation, etc).—**assassination** *n.*

assault *n* a violent attack; (*law*) an unlawful threat or attempt to harm another physically. * *vti* to make an assault (on); to rape.—**assaulter** *n.*

assault course *n* an obstacle course used for military training .

assay *n* the analysis of the quantity of metal in an ore or alloy, esp the standard purity of gold or silver; a test.

* *vt* (**assaying, assayed**) to subject to analysis; to determine the quantity or proportion of one or more of the constituents of a metal.—**assayable** *adj.*—**assayer** *n.*

assegai, assagai *n* (*pl* **assegais, assagais**) (*S Africa*) a light hardwood javelin or spear for casting or stabbing.

assemblage *n* a gathering of persons or things; (*art*) a form of collage.

assemble *vti* to bring together; to collect; to fit together the parts of; (*comput*) to translate using an assembler.

assembler *n* (*comput*) a program that converts low-level mnemonic symbols into machine code.

assembly *n* (*pl* **assemblies**) assembling or being assembled; a gathering of persons, esp for a particular purpose; the fitting together of parts to make a whole machine, etc.

assembly line *n* a series of machines, equipment and workers through which a product passes in successive stages to be assembled.

assemblyman *n* (*pl* **assemblymen**) a member of a legislative assembly.—**assemblywoman** *nf* (*pl* **assemblywomen**)

assent *vi* to express agreement to something. * *n* consent or agreement.—**assentor, assenter** *n.*

assentation *n* compliance with the opinion of another, in flattery or obsequiousness.

assert *vt* to declare, affirm as true; to maintain or enforce (eg rights).—**assertible** *adj.*

assertion *n* an asserting; a statement that something is a fact, usu without evidence.

assertive *adj* self-assured, positive, confident; dogmatic.—**assertively** *adv.*—**assertiveness** *n.*

assess *vt* to establish the amount of, as a tax; to impose a tax or fine; to value, for the purpose of taxation; to estimate the worth, importance, etc of.—**assessable** *adj.*

assessment *n* the act of assessing or determining an amount to be paid; an official valuation of property, or income, for the purpose of taxation; the specific sum levied as tax, or assessed for damages.

assessor *n* a person appointed to assess property or persons for taxation; an expert appointed to assist a judge or magistrate as an adviser on special points of law.—**assessorial** *adj.*

asset *n* anything owned that has value; a desirable thing; (*pl*) all the property, accounts receivable, etc of a person or business; (*pl*) (*law*) property usable to pay debts.

asset-stripping *n* the practice of buying a company in order to sell off its assets at a profit.—**asset-stripper** *n.*

asseverate *vt* to declare solemnly; to affirm or aver positively.—**asseveration** *n.*

asshole *n* (*sl*) a stupid person; (*vulg*) the anus.

assibilate *vt* (*phonetics*) to pronounce with a hissing sound; to alter to a sibilant.—**assibilation** *n.*

assiduity *n* (*pl* **assiduities**) close application, steady attention; diligence; (*usu pl*) constant attentions.

assiduous *adj* persistent or persevering; diligent.—**assiduously** *adv.*—**assiduousness** *n.*

assign *vt* to allot; to appoint to a post or duty; to ascribe; (*law*) to transfer (a right, property, etc).—**assignable** *adj.*—**assigner** *n.*

assignat *n* a money or currency bond secured on state lands, issued by the French Revolutionary Government (1789–96).

assignation *n* the act of assigning; a meeting, esp one made secretly by lovers.

assignee *n* (*law*) one to whom an assignment of anything is made, either in trust or for his or her own use and enjoyment.

assignment *n* the act of assigning; something assigned to a person, such as a share, task, etc.

assignor *n* (*law*) one who assigns or transfers an interest.

assimilate *vt* to absorb; to digest; to take in and understand fully; to be ascribed; to be like.—**assimilable** *adj.*—**assimilation** *n*.

assimilative, assimilatory *adj* having the power of assimilating, or causing assimilation, tending to produce assimilation.

assist *vti* to support or aid.—**assister** *n*.

assistance *n* help; furtherance; aid; succour; support.

assistant *n* one who or that which assists; a helper; an auxiliary; a subordinate. * *adj* helping; lending aid; auxiliary.

assize *n* (*pl* **assizes**) a court or session of justice for the trial by jury of civil or criminal cases; (*usu pl*) (*formerly*) the sessions held periodically in each county of England by judges of the Supreme Court; (*usu pl*) the time or place of holding the assize.

associable *adj* capable of being joined or associated; liable to be affected by sympathy with kindred parts or organs.

associate *vt* to join as a friend, business partner or supporter; to bring together; to unite; to connect in the mind. * *vi* to combine or unite with others; to come together as friends, business partners or supporters. * *adj* allied or connected; having secondary status or privileges. * *n* a companion, business partner, supporter, etc; something closely connected with another; a person admitted to an association as a subordinate member.

association *n* an organization of people joined together for a common aim; the act of associating or being associated; a connection in the mind, memory, etc.

association football *n* football played with a round ball that is not handled, soccer.

associationism *n* (*psychol*) the mental connection existing between an object and the ideas related to it.

associative *adj* tending to or characterized by association; (*math*) having elements whose result is the same despite the grouping.

assonance *n* a correspondence in sound between words or syllables.—**assonant** *adj, n.*—**assonantal** *adj*.

assort *vt* to arrange in groups according to kind. * *vi* to agree in kind.—**assortative, assortive** *adj.*—**assorter** *n*.

assorted *adj* distributed according to sorts; miscellaneous.

assortment *n* a collection of people or things of different sorts.

asst *abbr* = assistant.

assuage *vt* to soften the intensity of; to soothe.—**assuager** *n.*—**assuagement** *n.*—**assuasive** *adj*.

assume *vt* to take on, to undertake; to usurp; to take as certain or true; to pretend to possess.—**assumable** *adj.*—**assumer** *n*.

assuming *adj* presumptuous.

assumption *n* something taken for granted; the taking on of a position, esp of power; (*with cap*) the ascent of the Virgin Mary into heaven; (*RC Church*) the Christian feast in remembrance of this, celebrated 15 August.—**assumptive** *adj*.

assurance *n* a promise, guarantee; a form of life insurance; a feeling of certainty, self-confidence.

assure *vt* to make safe or certain; to give confidence to; to state positively; to guarantee, ensure.—**assurable** *adj.*—**assurer** *n*.

assured *adj* certain; convinced; self-confident.—**assuredness** *n*.

assuredly *adv* certainly.

assurgent *adj* ascending, rising; (*bot*) rising in a curve.

Assyrian *adj* pertaining to Assyria, an ancient kingdom of Mesopotamia, or to its inhabitants or language. * *n* the language spoken in Assyria; an inhabitant of Assyria.

Assyriology *n* the science or study of the extinct language and the antiquities of Assyria.—**Assyriologist** *n*.

astatic *adj* having a tendency not to stand still; unstable.—**astatically** *adv.*—**astaticism** *n*.

astatine *n* a radioactive element.

aster *n* a kind of plant with round composite flowers; a Michaelmas daisy.

-aster *n suffix* petty imitation, as in *poetaster*.

asteriated *adj* (*crystal, etc*) radiated; having the form of a star.

asterisk *n* a sign (*) used in writing or printing to mark omission of words, a footnote or other reference, etc. * *vt* to mark with an asterisk.

asterism *n* a group or cluster of stars; three asterisks placed in the form of a triangle (∴) or (⁂) to direct attention to a particular passage; the star-like appearance in certain crystals.

astern *adv* behind a ship or aircraft; at or towards the rear of a ship, etc; backward.

asternal *adj* (*anat*) (*ribs*) not joined to the sternum or breastbone.

asteroid *n* any of the small planets between Mars and Jupiter. * *adj* star-like; star-shaped (—*also* **asteroidal**).

asthenia *n* debility, weakness.—**asthenic** *adj*.

asthma *n* a chronic respiratory condition causing difficulty with breathing.—**asthmatic** *adj.*—**asthmatically** *adv*.

asthmatic *adj* of or suffering from or good for asthma, * *n* an asthmatic person.—**asthmatically** *adv*.

astigmatism *n* a defective condition of the eye or lens causing poor focusing.—**astigmatic** *adj.*—**astigmatically** *adv*.

astir *adv* moving or bustling about; out of bed.

astomatous *adj* (*biol*) lacking a mouth; without breathing pores.

astonish *vt* to fill with sudden or great surprise.—**astonishing** *adj.*—**astonishment** *n*.

astound *vt* to astonish greatly.—**astounding** *adj.*—**astoundingly** *adv*.

astraddle *adv* astride, straddling.

astragal *n* (*archit*) a small moulding or bead of semicircular form; a ring of moulding round the top or bottom of a column.

astragalus *n* (*pl* **astragali**) the ball of the ankle joint; the lower bone into which the tibia articulates.

astrakhan *n* the dark curly fleece of lambs from Astrakhan in Russia; a cloth with a curled pile made from or imitating this.

astral *adj* of or from the stars.

astray *adv* off the right path; into error.

astride *adv* with a leg on either side. * *prep* extending across.

astringent *adj* that contracts body tissues; stopping

blood flow, styptic; harsh; biting. * *n* an astringent substance—**astringency** *n*.

astro- *prefix* (*astrophysics*) of a star or stars.

astrodome *n* a large sports stadium covered with a domed translucent roof.

astrolabe *n* an instrument formerly used for taking altitudes of the sun and stars.

astrology *n* the study of planetary positions and motions to determine their supposed influence on human affairs.—**astrologer, astrologist** *n*.—**astrological** *adj*.—**astrologically** *adv*.

astrometry *n* the art by which the apparent relative magnitude of the stars is determined.—**astrometric, astrometrical** *adj*.

astronaut *n* one trained to make flights in outer space.

astronautics *npl* (*used as sing*) the scientific study of space flight and technology.

astronomical, astronomic *adj* enormously large; of or relating to astronomy.—**astronomically** *adv*.

astronomical clock *n* a clock that keeps sidereal time.

astronomical year *n* a year the length of which is determined by astronomical observations.

astronomy *n* the scientific investigation of the stars and other planets.—**astronomer** *n*.

astrophotography *n* photography of the heavenly bodies.—**astrophotographic** *adj*.

astrophysics *n* (*used as sing*) the branch of astronomy that deals with the physical and chemical constitution of the stars.—**astrophysical** *adj*.—**astrophysicist** *n*.

astute *adj* clever, perceptive; crafty, shrewd.—**astutely** *adv*.—**astuteness** *n*.

asunder *adv* apart in direction or position; into pieces.

asylum *n* a place of safety, a refuge; (*formerly*) an institution for the blind, the mentally ill, etc.

asymmetric, asymmetrical *adj* lacking symmetry.—**asymmetrically** *adv*.

asymmetry *n* a lack of symmetry or proportion between the parts of a thing.

asymptote *n* (*geom*) the line that continually approaches nearer to a given curve without ever meeting it.—**asymptotic, asymptotical** *adj*.

asyndeton *n* (*pl* **asyndetons, asyndeta**) (*gram*) a figure of speech in which conjunctions are omitted, as "I came, I saw, I conquered"; such a figure.

at- *prefix* the form of *ad-* before *t*.

At (*chem symbol*) astatine.

at *prep* on; in; near; by; used to indicate location or position.

ataraxia, ataraxy *n* impassivity; peace of mind.

atavism *n* the appearance in plants or animals of characteristics typical in more remote ancestors; reversion to a more primitive type.—**atavistic** *adj*.—**atavistically** *adv*.

ataxia *n* irregularities in the functions of the body, esp muscular coordination, or in the course of a disease.—**ataxic, atactic** *adj*.

-ate *adj suffix* having or furnished with, as *foliate*. * *n suffix* forming the equivalent of *pp*, as in *associate*.

ate *see* **eat**.

atelier *n* a workshop; the studio of a painter or sculptor.

a tempo, a tempo primo *n* (*mus*) a direction to a musician to restore the original time after acceleration or retardation.

a tempo giusto *n* (*mus*) a direction to a performer to sing or play in strict time.

Athanasian Creed *n* one of the three creeds thus named

as containing an exposition of the doctrines of the Trinty and incarnation of Christ, which Athanasius, bishop of Alexandria (*c*.296–373), defended.

atheism *n* belief in the nonexistence of God.—**atheist** *n*.—**atheistic, atheistical** *adj*.

atheling *n* an Anglo-Saxon title of honour conferred on royal children and young nobles.

athenaeum, atheneum *n* a public institution, club or building devoted to the purposes or study of literature, science and art; a literary club; (*with cap*) the temple of Athena in ancient Athens, where scholars met.

Athenian *adj* pertaining to Athens, the capital of Greece. * *n* a native or citizen of Athens.

athermanous *adj* resisting the passage of heat; nonconducting.—**athermany** *n*.

atherosclerosis *n* (*pl* **atheroscleroses**) a degenerative disease of the arteries characterized by deposition of fatty material on the inner arterial walls.—**atherosclerotic** *adj*.

athirst *adj* thirsty; eager (for).

athlete *n* a person trained in games or exercises requiring skill, speed, strength, stamina, etc.

athlete's foot *n* a fungal infection of the feet.

athletic *adj* of athletes or athletics; active, vigorous.—**athletically** *adv*.—**athleticism** *n*.

athletics *n* (*used as sing or pl*) running, jumping, throwing sports, games, etc.

athwart *prep* across, from side to side. * *adv* crosswise; obliquely; across the course or direction of a ship; adversely (to).

atilt *adv* in the position or with the action of a person making a thrust; tilted.

atlantes *see* **atlas**[2].

Atlantic *adj* of, near or relating to the Atlantic Ocean.

atlas[1] *n* a book containing maps, charts and tables.

atlas[2] *n* (*pl* **atlantes**) (*archit*) a figure or half-figure of a man, used in place of a column or pilaster to support an entablature.—*also* **telamon**.

-ation *n suffix* denoting action or its result, as in *flirtation, vacation*.

ATM *abbr* = automated teller machine.

atmo- *prefix* vapour, air, atmosphere.

atmometer *n* an instrument for measuring the rate and amount of evaporation from a moist surface.—**atmometry** *n*.

atmosphere *n* the gaseous mixture that surrounds the earth or the other stars and planets; a unit of pressure equal to the pressure of the atmosphere at sea level; any dominant or surrounding influence; special mood or aura.—**atmospheric, atmospherical** *adj*.

atmospherics *npl* interference in radio reception, etc caused by atmospheric disturbances.

at. no. *abbr* = atomic number.

atoll *n* a coral reef enclosing a central lagoon.

atom *n* the smallest particle of a chemical element; a tiny particle, bit.

atomic *adj* pertaining to or consisting of atoms; extremely minute.—**atomically** *adv*.

atomic bomb *n* a bomb whose explosive power derives from the atomic energy released during nuclear fission or fusion.—*also* **A-bomb**.

atomic energy *n* the energy derived from nuclear fission.

atomicity *n* the number of atoms in a molecule of an element; equivalence; the combining capacity of an element, valency.

atomic theory *n* the theory that elemental bodies consist of ultimate atoms of definite weight, and that atoms of different elements unite chemically with each other in fixed proportions.

atomic weight *n* the weight of the atom of any element as compared with another taken as a standard, usu hydrogen, taken as 1.

atomism *n* the doctrine of atoms, atomic theory.—**atomist** *n*.—**atomistic, atomistical** *adj*.

atomize *vt* to reduce to a fine spray or minute particles.—**atomization** *n*.

atomizer *n* a device for atomizing liquids, usu perfumes or cleaning agents.

atonal *adj* (*mus*) avoiding traditional tonality; not written in any established key.—**atonality** *n*.—**atonally** *adv*.

atone *vi* to give satisfaction or make amends (for).—**atonable, atoneable** *adj*.—**atoner** *n*.

atonement *n* satisfaction, reparation; (*Christianity: with cap*) the reconciliation of humankind with God through Christ's self-sacrifice.

atonic *adj* (*word, etc*) unaccented; lacking tone, or vital energy. * *n* an unaccented word or syllable; a medicine to allay excitement.—**atonicity** *n*.

atony *n* lack of tone; debility; weakness of any organ.

atop *adv* on or at the top.

atrip *adv* (*naut*) (*anchor*) just clear of the ground.

atrium *n* (*pl* **atria, atriums**) an auricle of the heart; the unroofed courtyard of a Roman house; an entrance hall that rises up several storeys, often with a glass roof.

atrocious *adj* extremely brutal or wicked; (*inf*) very bad, of poor quality.—**atrociously** *adv*.

atrocity *n* (*pl* **atrocities**) a cruel act; something ruthless, wicked, repellent.

atrophy *n* (*pl* **atrophies**) a wasting away or failure to grow of a bodily organ. * *vti* (**atrophying, atrophied**) to cause or undergo atrophy.

atropine, atropin *n* a crystalline alkaloid of a very poisonous nature extracted from the deadly nightshade (belladonna), having the singular property of producing dilatation of the pupil of the eye.

attacca *n* (*mus*) a direction to a performer at the end of a movement to follow on with the next without pause.

attach *vt* to fix or fasten to something; to appoint to a specific group; to ascribe, attribute. * *vi* to become attached; to adhere.—**attachable** *adj*.—**attacher** *n*.

attaché *n* a technical expert on a diplomatic staff.

attaché case *n* a flat case for carrying documents, etc.

attached *adj* fixed; feeling affection for.

attachment *n* a fastening; affection, devotion; something attached; a device or part fixed to a machine, implement, etc; the act of attaching or being attached.

attack *vt* to set upon violently; to assault in speech or writing; to invade, as of a disease. * *n* an assault; a fit of illness; severe criticism; an enthusiastic beginning of a performance, task, undertaking, etc.—**attacker** *n*.

attain *vt* to succeed in getting or arriving at; to achieve. * *vi* to come to or arrive at by growth or effort.—**attainable** *adj*.—**attainability** *n*.

attainder *n* loss of estate and civil rights following conviction for high treason.

attainment *n* something attained; an accomplishment.

attaint *vt* to subject to attainder; to infect; to stain, to disgrace.

attar *n* a fragrant essential oil extracted from rose petals and used in making perfume.

attempt *vt* to try to accomplish, get, etc. * *n* an endeavour or effort to accomplish; an attack, assault.—**attemptable** *adj*.—**attempter** *n*.

attend *vt* to take care of; to go with, accompany; to be present at. * *vi* to apply oneself (to); to deal with, give attention to.—**attender** *n*.

attendance *n* attending; the number of people present; the number of times a person attends.

attendant *n* a person who serves or accompanies another; someone employed to assist or guide. * *adj* accompanying, following as a result; being in attendance.

attention *n* the application of the mind to a particular purpose, aim, etc; awareness, notice; care, consideration; (*usu. pl*) an act of civility or courtesy; (*usu. pl*) indications of admiration or love; (*mil*) a soldier's formal erect posture.

attentive *adj* observant, diligent; courteous.—**attentively** *adv*.—**attentiveness** *n*.

attenuate *vt* to make thin; to weaken; to reduce the force or severity of. * *vi* to become thin; to weaken.—**attenuation** *n*.

attest *vt* to state as true; to certify, as by oath; to give proof of. * *vi* to testify, bear witness (to).—**attestable** *adj*.—**attestation** *n*.—**attester, attestor** *n*.

attestation *n* the act of attesting; testimony or evidence given on oath or by official declaration; swearing in.

attic *n* the room or space just under the roof; a garret.

Attic *adj* pertaining to Attica in Greece; classical; elegant. * *n* a dialect of ancient Athens.

atticism *n* an elegant expression; (*with cap*) a peculiarity of style or idiom characterizing the Attic rendering of the Greek language.

Attic order *n* a square column of any of the five Greek orders of architecture.

Attic salt, Attic wit *n* delicate wit.

attire *vt* to clothe; to dress up. * *n* dress, clothing.

attitude *n* posture, position of the body; a manner of thought or feeling; behaviour; the position of an aircraft or spacecraft in relation to certain reference points.—**attitudinal** *adj*.

attitudinize *vi* to assume affected postures, to pose for effect.—**attitudinizer** *n*.

attorn *vti* to transfer; to make legal acknowledgment of a new landlord.—**attornment** *n*.

attorney *n* (*pl* **attorneys**) one legally authorized to act for another; a lawyer.

attorney general *n* (*pl* **attorneys general, attorneys generals**) the chief law officer of of a state or nation acting as its legal representative and advising the chief executive on legal matters.

attract *vt* to pull towards oneself; to get the admiration, attention, etc of. * *vi* to be attractive.—**attractable** *adj*.—**attractor** *n*.

attraction *n* the act of attraction; the power of attracting, esp charm; (*physics*) the mutual action by which bodies tend to be drawn together.

attractive *adj* pleasing in appearance, etc; arousing interest; able to draw or pull.—**attractively** *adv*.—**attractiveness** *n*.

attribute *vt* to regard as belonging to; to ascribe, impute (to). * *n* a quality, a characteristic of.—**attributable** *adj*.

attribution *n* the act of attributing, esp a work of art, etc to a particular creator; a designation; a function.—**attributional** *adj*.

attributive *adj* expressing an attribute; (*gram*) qualifying. * *n* a word joined to and describing a noun; an adjective or adjective phrase.—**attributively** *adv*.

attributive *adj* pertaining to, of the nature of, or expressing, an attribute; (*gram*) qualifying. * *n* a word denoting an attribute; a word joined to and describing a noun; an adjective or adjectival phrase.

attrition *n* a grinding down by or as by friction; a relentless wearing down and weakening; natural wastage or reduction of a workforce by not employing replacements for those who resign or leave.—**attritional** *adj*.—**attritive** *adj*.

attune *vt* to bring (a person or thing) into harmony with; to adapt.

at. wt. *abbr* = atomic weight.

atypical *adj* not according to type; without definite typical character.—**atypically** *adv*.

Au (*chem symbol*) gold.

aubade *n* a musical announcement of dawn; a sunrise song.

auberge *n* an inn.

aubergine *n* a plant producing a smooth, dark-purple fruit; this fruit used as a vegetable.—*also* **eggplant**.

aubrietia, aubretia *n* a small purple-flowered perennial plant.

auburn *adj* reddish brown.

au contraire *adv* on the contrary.

au courant *adj* well-informed, esp in current affairs.

auction *n* a public sale of items to the highest bidder. * *vt* to sell by or at an auction.

auction bridge *n* a form of bridge in which the players contract to take a certain number of tricks, with extra tricks counting towards game.

auctioneer *n* one who conducts an auction.

audacious *adj* daring, adventurous; bold; rash; insolent.—**audaciously** *adv*.—**audaciousness** *n*.

audacity *n* (*pl* **audacities**) boldness; daring; spirit; presumptuousness; impudence; effrontery.

audible *adj* heard or able to be heard.—**audibility** *n*.—**audibly** *adv*.

audience *n* a gathering of listeners or spectators; the people addressed by a book, play, film, etc; a formal interview or meeting, esp one in which one's views are heard.

audile *adj* received through hearing.

audio *n* sound; the reproduction, transmission or reception of sound.

audio frequency *n* a frequency audible to the human ear.

audiometer *n* an instrument for gauging the power of hearing.—**audiometric** *adj*.—**audiometrically** *adv*.—**audiometry** *n*.

audiotypist *n* a typist who works from a recording.

audiovisual *adj* using both sound and vision, as in teaching aids.

audit *n* the inspection and verification of business accounts by a qualified accountant. * *vt* to make such an inspection.

audition *n* a trial to test a performer. * *vti* to test or be tested by audition.

auditor *n* a person qualified to audit business accounts.—**auditorial** *adj*.

auditorium *n* (*pl* **auditoriums, auditoria**) the part of a building allotted to the audience; a building or hall for speeches, concerts, etc.

auditory *adj* of or relating to the sense of hearing.

au fait *adj* fully informed about; competent.

au fond (*French*) fundamentally.

auf Wiedersehen *interj, n* till we meet again.

Aug. *abbr* = August.

auger *n* a tool for boring holes, a large gimlet.

aught *n* anything; any part. * *adv* (*arch*) in any degree, in any way; at all.—*also* **ought**.

augite *n* a variety of pyroxene of a black or dark green colour.—**augitic** *adj*.

augment *vti* to increase.—**augmentable** *adj*.—**augmenter, augmentor** *n*.

augmentation *n* enlargement, addition, increase; (*mus*) the increase in time value of the notes of a theme; (*her*) an additional charge to a coat of arms bestowed as a mark of honour.

augmentative *adj* having the quality or power of augmenting; (*gram*) increasing in force the idea of a word. * *n* a word or affix that expresses with greater force the idea conveyed by the term from which it is derived, opposite of diminutive.

au gratin *adj* topped with breadcrumbs or breadcrumbs and cheese, and cooked until crisp.

augur *vti* to prophesy; to be an omen (of).—**augural** *adj*.

augury *n* (*pl* **auguries**) the art or practice of foretelling events by reference to natural signs or omens; an omen; prediction; presage.

August *n* the eighth month of the year, having 31 days.

august *adj* imposing; majestic.

Augustan *adj* of or pertaining to Augustus Caesar, emperor of Rome, or his reign, during which Roman literature gained its highest point; of or pertaining to the period of the highest stage of literary excellence in other countries.

auk *n* a northern sea bird with short wings used as paddles.

au lait *adj* with milk.

auld lang syne *n* days of old; long ago.

au naturel *adj, adv* in the natural state; cooked plainly; raw; nude.

aunt *n* a father's or mother's sister; an uncle's wife.

auntie, aunty *n* (*pl* **aunties**) (*inf*) aunt.

au pair *n* a person, esp a girl, from abroad who performs domestic chores, child-minding, etc in return for board and lodging.

aura *n* (*pl* **auras, aurae**) a particular quality or atmosphere surrounding a person or thing.

aural[1] *adj* of the ear or the sense of hearing.—**aurally** *adv*.

aural[2] *adj* of the air or an aura.

aureate *adj* golden; gilded; golden yellow.

aureole, aureola *n* (*art*) a halo, radiance, or luminous cloud encircling the figures of Christ, the virgin and the saints in sacred pictures; anything resembling an aureole.

au revoir *n* goodbye for the present.

auric *adj* of or pertaining to gold.

auricle *n* the external part of the ear; either of the two upper chambers of the heart.

auricula *n* (*pl* **auriculas, auriculae**) a species of primrose with leaves the shape of a bear's ear.

auricular *adj* of or received by the ear; shaped like an ear; spoken privately; relating to the auricles of the heart.

auriculate *adj* ear-shaped; having ears or ear-like appendages.

auriferous *adj* gold-bearing; yielding or containing gold.

aurochs *n* (*pl* **aurochs**) an extinct wild ox of North Africa, Europe and Asia.

aurora *n* (*pl* **auroras, aurorae**) either of the luminous bands seen in the night sky in the polar regions.—*also* **northern lights**.

aurora australis *n* the aurora seen at the South Pole.

aurora borealis *n* the aurora seen at the North Pole.

aurous *adj* of or bearing gold.

auscultate *vt* to examine by auscultation.—**auscultator** *n*.—**auscultatory** *adj*.

auscultation *n* a listening to the sounds of the heart, lungs, etc in the chest for medical diagnosis.

auspex *n* (*pl* **auspices**) one who divined by observation of birds in ancient Rome.

auspice *n* (*pl* **auspices**) an omen; (*pl*) sponsorship; patronage.

auspicious *adj* showing promise, favourable.—**auspiciously** *adv*.

Aussie *n* (*sl*) an Australian.

austere *adj* stern, forbidding in attitude or appearance; abstemious; severely simple, plain.—**austerely** *adv*.—**austereness** *n*.

austerity *n* (*pl* **austerities**) being austere; economic privation.

austral *adj* southern; (*with cap*) Australian.

Australasian *adj* of or pertaining to Australasia (Australia, New Zealand and adjacent islands). * *n* a native or inhabitant of Australasia.

Australian *adj* of or pertaining to Australia. * *n* a native or inhabitant of Australia.

Australoid *adj* of the variety of human population that includes the Australian aborigines. * *n* an Australoid person.

autarchy *n* (*pl* **autarchies**) absolute or autocratic rule or sovereignty; a country governed in such a way; autarky.—**autarchic, autarchical** *adj*.

autarky *n* (*pl* **autarkies**) self-sufficiency, esp in the economic sphere; the policy of encouraging economic self-sufficiency.—**autarkic, autarkical** *adj*.

authentic *adj* genuine, conforming to truth or reality; trustworthy, reliable.—**authentically** *adv*.—**authenticity** *n*.

authenticate *vt* to demonstrate the authenticity of; to make valid; to verify.—**authentication** *n*.—**authenticator** *n*.

author *n* a person who brings something into existence; the writer of a book, article, etc. * *vt* to be the author of.—**authoress** *nf*.—**authorial** *adj*.

authoritarian *adj* favouring strict obedience; dictatorial. * *n* a person advocating authoritarian principles.—**authoritarianism** *n*.

authoritative *adj* commanding or possessing authority; accepted as true; official.—**authoritatively** *adv*.

authority *n* (*pl* **authorities**) the power or right to command; (*pl*) officials with this power; influence resulting from knowledge, prestige, etc; a person, writing, etc cited to support an opinion; an expert.

authorize *vt* to give authority to, to empower; to give official approval to, sanction.—**authorization** *n*.

Authorized Version *n* the version of the Bible published by the sanction of James I of England in 1611 and appointed to be read in churches.—*also* **King James Bible, King James Version**.

authorship *n* the writing profession; origin (of book).

autism *n* (*psychiatry*) a mental state, usu of children, marked by disregard of external reality—**autistic** *adj*.

auto *n* (*pl* **autos**) (*inf*) an automobile.

auto- *prefix* self; by oneself or itself.

autobahn *n* a German, Austrian or Swiss motorway.

autobiography *n* (*pl* **autobiographies**) the biography of a person written by himself or herself.—**autobiographer** *n*.—**autobiographical** *adj*.

autocephalous *adj* having its own head; independent.

autochondriac *n* a person who is preoccupied with his or her car.

autochthon *n* (*pl* **autochthons, autochthones**) an earliest known inhabitant, an aboriginal.

autochthonous, autochthonal *adj* pertaining to primitive inhabitants; indigenous, native to the soil.—**autochthonism, autochthony** *n*.

autoclave *n* a strong container used for chemical reactions at high temperatures and pressures; a device for sterilizing implements using steam at high pressure.

autocracy *n* (*pl* **autocracies**) government by one person with absolute power.

autocrat *n* an absolute ruler; any domineering person.—**autocratic** *adj*.—**autocratically** *adv*.

autocross *n* cross-country motor racing.

Autocue *n* (*trademark*) a prompting device used in TV, etc, which provides speakers with a script that remains invisible to the audience.—*also* **Teleprompter**.

auto-da-fé *n* (*pl* **autos-da-fé**) a public judgment by the Spanish Inquisition upon prisoners tried for heresy and other offences against the religious or civil law; the subsequent execution of such sentences by burning.

autoeroticism, autoerotism *n* self-produced sexual emotion.—**autoerotic** *adj*.

autogamy *n* self-fertilization.—**autogamous** *adj*.

autogenesis, autogeny *n* spontaneous generation.—**autogenetic** *adj*.

autogenous *adj* self-generated; produced independently.

autogyro, autogiro *n* (*pl* **autogyros, autogiros**) an aircraft like a helicopter but with unpowered rotor blades.

autograph *n* a person's signature. * *vt* to write one's signature in or on.—**autographic** *adj*.—**autographically** *adv*.

autography *n* one's own handwriting; a lithographic process by which copies of writings or drawings are reproduced in facsimile.

autolysis *n* the destruction of cells of a body by the action of its own serum.—**autolytic** *adj*.

automaker *n* a manufacturer of automobiles.

automat *n* in US, a restaurant equipped with slot machines for dispensing food and drink; a vending machine.

automate *vt* to control by automation; to convert to automatic operation.

automated telling machine *n* a device that provides cash and other banking services automatically when activated by a plastic card issued to customers; a cash dispenser.—*also* **autoteller**.

automatic *adj* involuntary or reflexive; self-regulating; acting by itself. * *n* an automatic pistol or rifle.—**automatically** *adv*.

automatic pilot *n* a device that can maintain an aircraft or ship on a previously set course.—*also* **autopilot**.

automatic transmission *n* a system in a motor vehicle for changing gears automatically.

automation *n* the use of automatic methods, machinery, etc in industry.

automatism *n* automatic action; involuntary action; mechanical routine; the doctrine that assigns all animal functions to the active operation of physical laws.—**automatist** n.

automaton n (pl **automatons, automata**) any automatic device, esp a robot; a human being who acts like a robot.

automatous adj spontaneous; of the nature of an automaton.

automobile n a usu four-wheeled vehicle powered by an internal combustion engine.—also **motor car**.

automotive adj relating to motor vehicles.

autonomy n (pl **autonomies**) freedom of self-determination; independence, self-government.—**autonomous** adj.

autopilot n automatic pilot.

autoplasty n the process of repairing lesions by application of tissue removed from another part of the same body.—**autoplastic** adj.

autopsy n (pl **autopsies**) a post-mortem examination to determine the cause of death.

autoroute n a French motorway.

autostrada n an Italian motorway.

autosuggestion n (psychoanal) self-applied suggestion.—**autosuggestive** adj.

autoteller see **automated telling machine**.

autotoxin n a poisonous substance produced by changes within an organism.—**autotoxic** adj.

autumn n the season between summer and winter.—also **fall**.

autumnal adj belonging or peculiar to autumn or fall; produced or gathered in autumn; pertaining to the period of life when middle age is past. * n a plant that flowers in autumn.

aux. abbr = auxiliary.

auxiliary adj providing help, subsidiary; supplementary. * n (pl **auxiliaries**) a helper; (gram) a verb that helps form tenses, moods, voices, etc of other verbs, as have, be, may, shall, etc.

AV abbr = ad valorem; audiovisual; Authorized Version.

avadavat n a small Asian finch-like bird, kept as a caged bird for its song.

avail vti to be of use or advantage to. * n benefit, use or help.

available adj ready for use; obtainable, accessible.—**availability** n.—**availably** adv.

avalanche n a mass of snow, ice, and rock tumbling down a mountainside; a sudden overwhelming accumulation or influx.

avant-garde n (arts) those ideas and practices regarded as in advance of those generally accepted. * adj pertaining to such ideas and practices and their creators.—**avant-gardism** n.

avarice n greed for wealth.—**avaricious** adj.—**avariciously** adv.

avast interj (naut) stop! cease! hold!

avatar n (Hinduism) the descent to earth of a deity in an incarnate form; manifestation or embodiment; transference of personality.

avdp. abbr = avoirdupois.

ave interj hail; farewell. * n an Ave Maria; a salutation.

Ave, ave abbr = avenue.

Ave Maria n (RC Church) Hail Mary.

avenge vt to get revenge for.—**avenger** n.

avens n (pl **avens**) the popular name of plants to which the herb bennet belongs.

aventurine n a brown, gold-spangled kind of Venetian glass; a variety of micaceous quartz or feldspar.

avenue n a street, drive, etc, esp when broad; means of access; the way to an objective.

aver vt (**averring, averred**) to state as true; to assert.—**averment** n.

average n the result of dividing the sum of two or more quantities by the number of quantities; the usual kind, amount, quality, etc. * vt to calculate the average of; to achieve an average number of.

averse adj unwilling; opposed (to).

aversion n antipathy; hatred; something arousing hatred or repugnance.

avert vt to turn away or aside from; to prevent, avoid.—**avertible, avertable** adj.

avian adj of or pertaining to birds.

aviary n (pl **aviaries**) a building or large cage for keeping birds.

aviate vi to pilot or travel in an aircraft.

aviation n the art or science of flying aircraft.

aviator n a pilot, esp in the early history of flying.

aviculture n the breeding and rearing of birds.—**aviculturist** n.

avid adj eager, greedy.—**avidly** adv.

avidity n greediness; eagerness; strong appetite.

avifauna n (pl **avifaunae**) the birds of a region regarded collectively.—**avifaunal** adj.

avionics n (used as sing) the application of electronics in aviation.—**avionic** adj.

avocado n (pl **avocados**) a thick-skinned, pear-shaped fruit with yellow buttery flesh.

avocet n one of several species of wading birds, characterized by very long legs and an extremely slender curved bill.

avoid vt to keep clear of, shun; to refrain from.—**avoider** n.

avoidable adj able to be avoided.

avoidance n the act of annulling or making void; the act of shunning; the state of being vacant.

avoirdupois n the system of weights based on the pound of 16 ounces; (inf) excess weight.

avow vt to declare confidently; to acknowledge.—**avowed** adj.—**avowedly** adv.—**avower** n.

avowal n an open declaration; a frank acknowledgment; a confession.

avulsion n a separation by violence; the sudden removal of land, without change of ownership, caused by a flood, etc.

avuncular adj like an uncle.

await vti to wait for; to be in store for.

awake vb (**awaking, awoke** or **awaked, pp awoken** or **awaked**) vi to wake; to become aware. * vt to rouse from sleep; to rouse from inaction. * adj roused from sleep, not asleep; active; aware.

awaken vti to awake.

awakening n the act of rousing from sleep; a revival of religion, or activity of a particular religious sect. * adj rousing; exciting; alarming.

award vt to give, as by a legal decision; to give (a prize, etc); to grant. * n a decision, as by a judge; a prize.

aware adj realizing, having knowledge; conscious; fully conversant with and sympathetic towards (ecologically aware).—**awareness** n.

awash adj filled or overflowing with water.

away adv from a place; in another place or direction; off, aside; far. * adj absent; at a distance.

awe n a mixed feeling of fear, wonder and dread. * vt to fill with awe.

aweather adv (naut) on the weather side, or towards the wind. * n opposed to the alee.

aweigh *adj, adv* (*naut*) (*anchor*) atrip, just drawn out of the ground and hanging perpendicularly.

awesome *adj* inspiring awe; (*inf*) marvellous, terrific.

awestricken, awestruck *adj* struck with awe.

awful *adj* very bad; unpleasant. * *adv* (*inf*) very.—**awfulness** *n*.

awfulize *vt* to envisage a situation as being worse than it is.—*also* **catastrophize**.

awfully *adv* in an awful manner; excessively; (*inf*) very.

awhile *adv* for a short time.

awkward *adj* lacking dexterity, clumsy; graceless; embarrassing; embarrassed; inconvenient; deliberately obstructive or difficult to deal with.—**awkwardly** *adv*.—**awkwardness** *n*.

awl *n* a small pointed tool for boring or piercing, used by shoemakers, etc.

awn *n* the beard or bristle-like appendage of the outer glume of wheat, barley, and numerous grasses.

awning *n* a structure, as of canvas, extended above or in front of a window, door, etc to provide shelter against the sun or rain.

awoke *see* **awake**.

AWOL *abbr* = absent without leave.

awry *adv* twisted to one side. * *adj* contrary to expectations, wrong.

axe, ax *n* (*pl* **axes**) a tool with a long handle and bladed head for chopping wood, etc. * *vt* to trim, split, etc with an axe.

axial *adj* of, forming or round an axis.—**axially** *adv*.

axil *n* (*bot*) the angle formed by the upper side of an organ or branch with the stem or trunk to which it is attached.

axile *adj* (*bot*) of, lying or situated in, or attached to, an axis.

axilla *n* (*pl* **axillae, axillas**) the armpit, or cavity in the junction of the arm and shoulder; the axil of a leaf.

axillary *adj* of or pertaining to the armpit; (*bot*) pertaining to, springing from, or situated in, the axil. * *n* (*pl* **axillaries**) a feather from the axilla of a bird.

axiom *n* a widely held or accepted truth or principle.

axiomatic *adj* pertaining to, or of the nature of, an axiom.—**axiomatically** *adv*.

axis[1] *n* (*pl* **axes**) a real or imaginary straight line about which a body rotates; the centre line of a symmetrical figure; a reference line of a coordinate system; (*with cap*) a partnership, alliance, esp of Germany and Italy, 1936 to the end of World War II.—**axial** *adj*.

axis[2] *n* (*pl* **axises**) a small deer of India and Asia with slender antlers.

axle *n* a rod on or with which a wheel turns; a bar connecting two opposite wheels, as of a car.

axletree *n* a bar connecting the opposite wheels of a carriage, on the rounded ends of which the wheels revolve.

axolotl *n* a Mexican amphibian like the salamander, having gills.

ay[1], **aye**[1] *adv* (*arch*) for ever, always; continually.

ayah *n* a native Indian nurse or lady's maid.

ayatollah *n* a Shiite Muslim leader; a title of respect.

aye[2], **ay**[2] *adv, interj* yes; even so; indeed. * *n* (*pl* **ayes**) an affirmative answer or vote in a parliamentary division; the members so voting..

aye-aye *n* a small nocturnal quadruped, native to Madagascar and allied to the lemurs.

AZ *abbr* = Arizona.

azalea *n* a flowering shrub-like plant.

azan *n* the call to public prayers in Islamic countries.

azedarach *n* an Asian tree, the bark or root of which was formerly used as a drug.

Azilian *adj* of a Mesolithic geological stage characterized by bone harpoon heads and painted stone pebbles.

azimuth *n* (*astron*) a vertical arc from the zenith to the horizon; the angular distance of this from the meridian.—**azimuthal** *adj*.

azoic *adj* without life; (*geol*) without fossils, older than the lowermost series of rocks containing traces of organic life.

azote *n* an old name for nitrogen.

AZT *abbr* = azidothymidine, a drug that has been effective in alleviating symptoms in some AIDS sufferers.

Aztec *adj* pertaining to the Aztec race that ruled Mexico before the Spanish conquest. * *n* a member of the Aztec race.

azure *adj* sky-blue.

azurite *n* blue carbonate of copper; blue malachite or chessylite; lazulite.

azygous *adj* (*anat*) single, as a muscle or vein; not one of a pair.

B

B *abbr* = boron.

b *abbr* = born; billion.

BA *abbr* = Bachelor of Arts; British Airways; British Academy.

Ba *abbr* = barium.

baa *n* the bleat of a sheep. * *vi* to bleat as a sheep.

baba *n* a small sponge cake soaked in (usu rum) flavoured syrup.

Babbitt metal *n* an anti-friction alloy of copper, tin and zinc, used in crank and axle bearings, etc.

Babbittry *n* (*derog*) businessman's or middle-class person's standards or blinkered outlook.—**Babbitt** *n*.

babble *vi* to make sounds like a baby; to talk incoherently, endlessly or senselessly; to give away secrets; to murmur, as a brook. * *n* incoherent talk; chatter; a murmuring sound.—**babbler** *n*.

babe *n* a baby; a naive person; (*sl*) a girl or young woman.

Babel *n* (*Bible*) the tower in Shinar (Genesis 11); a lofty structure; a confused and meaningless sound of voices; a scene of confusion and noise.

babirusa, babiruossa, babirussa *n* the wild hog of Eastern Asia.

baboon *n* a large, short-tailed monkey.

babul *n* the rind of the East Indian acacia.

baby *n* (*pl* **babies**) a newborn child or infant; a very young animal; (*sl*) a girl or young woman; a personal project. * *vt* (**babying, babied**) to pamper.—*also adj.*—**babyish** *adj*.

baby boom *n* a sharp rise in the birth rate.

baby-boomer *n* a person born in the period immediately after World War II when the birthrate increased sharply (*baby boom*).

baby break *n* a period, often five years, when a parent raises children before returning to work.

baby burst *n* a sudden fall in birth rate.

baby carriage *n* a perambulator.

baby grand *n* a small grand piano.

Babylonian *adj* of or pertaining to the ancient kingdom of Babylonia; magnificent; luxurious. * *n* an inhabitant of Babylonia; its language.

baby-sit *vti* (**baby-sitting, baby-sat**) to look after a baby or child while the parents are out.—**baby-sitter** *n*.

baby snatcher *n* (*inf*) one who marries or has a liaison with a much younger person; a person who steals a baby.

baby wipe *n* a disposable paper towel, ready moistened.

baccalaureate *n* the university degree awarded to a Bachelor of Arts etc; a commencement address.

baccarat *n* a card game where players bet against the banker.

baccate *adj* having many berries; berry-shaped.

bacchanal *n* a priest of Bacchus, the god of wine; a drunken reveler; a drunken feast.—**bacchanalian** *adj*.

bacchanalia *npl* drunken revels.

bacchant *n* (*pl* **bacchants, bacchantes**) a priest or votary of Bacchus; a drunkard.—**bacchante** *nf* (*pl* **bacchantes**).

Bacchic *adj* pertaining to Bacchus or the feasts in his honour; riotous, or mad with drink.

bacciferous *adj* bearing or producing berries.

bacciform *adj* berry-shaped.

baccivorous *adj* eating or subsisting on berries.

bachelor *n* an unmarried man; a person who holds a degree from a college or university.—**bachelorhood** *n*.

bachelor's buttons *npl* the popular name for a double-flowered buttercup with blossoms resembling buttons.

bacillary, bacillar *adj* of, like, caused by, or consisting of bacilli; rod-shaped.

bacilliform *adj* rod-shaped, like a bacillus.

bacillus *n* (*pl* **bacilli**) any of a genus of rod-shaped bacteria; (*loosely*) bacteria in general.

back[1] *n* the rear surface of the human body from neck to hip; the corresponding part in animals; a part that supports or fits or makes firm the back of anything; the part farthest from the front; (*sport*) a player or position behind the front line. * *adj* at the rear; (*streets, etc*) remote or inferior; (*pay, etc*) of or for the past; backward. * *adv* at or towards the rear; to or towards a former condition, time, etc; in return or requital; in reserve or concealment. * *vti* to move or go backwards; to support; to bet on; to provide or be a back for; to supply a musical backing for a singer; (*with* **down**) to withdraw from a position or claim; (*with* **off**) to move back (or away, etc); (*with* **out**) to withdraw from an enterprise; to evade keeping a promise, etc; (*with* **up**) to support; to move backwards; to accumulate because of restricted movement; (*comput*) to make a copy (of a data file, etc) for safekeeping.

back[2] *n* a large shallow cistern or vat used by brewers, etc, for liquids.

backache *n* an ache or pain in the back.

backbencher *n* in UK, Australia, etc, a member of parliament who does not hold office.

backbite *vt* (**backbiting, backbit**, *pp* **backbitten** *or* **backbit**) to talk spitefully or ill of behind a person's back.—**backbiter** *n*.—**backbiting** *n*.

backboard *n* a board at the back of a cart; a board worn at the back to support the back; a thin wooden backing used for picture frames, mirrors, etc.

backbone *n* the spinal column; main support; strength, courage.

backbreaking *adj* arduous; physically exhausting.

backchat *n* (*inf*) cheeky repartee.

backcomb *vt* (*hair*) to comb towards the roots to give body.

backdate *vt* to declare valid from some previous date.

backdoor *adj* indirect, concealed, devious.

backdown *n* the act of backing down; the withdrawal of a claim, etc.

backdrop *n* a curtain, often scenic, at the back of a stage; background.

back end *n* (*dial*) autumn.

backer *n* a patron; one who bets on a contestant.

backfire *vi* (*cars*) to ignite prematurely causing a loud bang from the exhaust; to have the opposite effect from that intended, usu with unfortunate consequences.—*also n*.

backgammon *n* a board game played by two people with pieces moved according to throws of the dice.

background *n* the distant part of a scene or picture; an inconspicuous position; social class, education, experience; circumstances leading up to an event.

backhand *n* (*tennis, etc*) a stroke played with the hand turned outwards.

backhanded *adj* backhand; (*compliment*) indirect, ambiguous.—*also adv*.—**backhandedly** *adv*.

backhander *n* a backhanded stroke; (*inf*) a backhanded remark; (*sl*) a bribe.

backing *n* support; supporters; a lining to support or strengthen the back of something; musical accompaniment to a (esp pop) singer.

backlash *n* a violent and adverse reaction; a recoil in machinery.

backlist *n* books published in past years that are still in print.

backlog *n* an accumulation of work, etc still to be done.

back number *n* a former issue (of a magazine, etc); an out-of-date person.

backpack *n* a rucksack; an equipment pack carried on the back of an astronaut, etc. * *vi* to travel, hike, etc wearing a backpack.

back pay *n* an increase in wages or salary paid retrospectively.

back-pedal *vi* (**back-pedalling, back-pedalled** *or* **back-pedaling, back-pedaled**) to work the pedals of a bicycle backwards; to modify or withdraw one's original argument or action.

back-seat driver *n* a passenger in a car who irritates the driver with persistent unwanted advice.

backside *n* (*inf*) buttocks.

backslide *vi* (**backsliding, backslid,** *pp* **backslid** *or* **backslidden**) to return to one's (bad) old ways.—**backslider** *n*.

backspace *vi* to move a typewriter carriage or cursor of a word processor back one space.

backspin *n* (*sport*) a backward spin in a ball to slow it down.

backstage *adv* behind the stage of a theatre in areas hidden from the audience; (*inf*) away from public view.—*also adj*.

backstairs *npl* stairs in the back part of a house; stairs for private use. * *adj* indirect; underhand; secret; intriguing.

backstay *n* (*naut*) a long rope extending from the masthead to the side of a ship, supporting the mast.

backstitch *n* an overlapping stitch. * *vt* to sew with this stitch.

backstroke *n* (*swimming*) a stroke using backward circular sweeps of the arms whilst lying face upwards.

backsword *n* a sword with one sharp edge, a broadsword; a stick with a basket handle used in the game of singlestick.

back-to-back *adj* facing in opposite directions, often with the backs touching.

backtrack *vi* to return along the same path; to reverse or recant one's opinion, action, etc.

backup *n* an alternate or auxiliary; support, reinforcement; (*comput*) a copy of a data file, etc.

backward *adj* turned toward the rear or opposite way; shy; slow or retarded. * *adv* backwards.—**backwardness** *n*.

backwards *adv* towards the back; with the back foremost; in a way opposite the usual; into a less good or favourable state or condition; into the past.

backwash *n* water receding from the action of an oar, propeller, etc; the consequences of an event.

backwater *n* a pool of still water fed by a river; a remote, backward place.

backwoods *npl* uncleared forest land; an isolated, thinly populated area.—**backwoodsman** *n* (*pl* **backwoodsmen**).

backyard *n* a yard at the back of a house.

baclava *see* **baklava**.

bacon *n* salted and smoked meat from the back or sides of a pig; **to bring home the bacon** to succeed; to help materially; **to save one's bacon** to have a narrow escape.

bacteria *npl* (*sing* **bacterium**) microscopic unicellular organisms usu causing disease.—**bacterial** *adj*.

bactericide *n* a substance that destroys bacteria.—**bactericidal** *adj*.

bacteriology *n* the scientific study of bacteria.—**bacteriological** *adj*.—**bacteriologist** *n*.

bacteriolysis *n* destruction of bacteria by a serum.—**bacteriolytic** *adj*.

bacterium *see* **bacteria**.

Bactrian camel *n* a camel with two humps.

bad[1] *adj* (**worse, worst**) not good; not as it should be; inadequate or unfit; rotten or spoiled; incorrect or faulty; wicked; immoral; mischievous; harmful; ill; sorry, distressed.—**badness** *n*.

bad[2] *see* **bid**.

bad blood *n* enmity, hostility.

bad debt *n* a debt that is not recoverable.

baddie, baddy *n* (*pl* **baddies**) (*inf*) a villain.

badderlocks *n* a large dark-green edible seaweed.

bade *see* **bid**.

badge *n* an emblem, symbol or distinguishing mark.

badger *n* a hibernating, burrowing black and white mammal related to the weasel. * *vt* to pester or annoy persistently.

badinage *n* light or playful raillery or banter.

badly *adv* (**worse, worst**) poorly; inadequately; unsuccessfully; severely; (*inf*) very much.

badminton *n* a court game for two or four players played with light rackets and a shuttlecock volleyed over a net.

badmouth *vt* (*sl*) to speak ill of; to slander.

baffle *vt* to bewilder or perplex; to frustrate; to make ineffectual. * *n* a plate or device used to restrict the flow of sound, light or fluid.—**bafflement** *n*.—**baffling** *adj*.

bag *n* a usu flexible container of paper, plastic, etc that can be closed at the top; a satchel, suitcase, etc; a handbag; a purse; game taken in hunting; a bag-like shape or part; (*derog*) an old, unpleasant or ugly woman; (*inf: in pl*) plenty (of). * *vti* (**bagging, bagged**) to place in a bag; to kill in hunting; (*inf*) to get; to make a claim on; to hang loosely.

bagasse *n* sugar-cane refuse after crushing, used as a fuel.

bagatelle *n* something of little value; a piece of light music usu for piano; a board game in which balls struck with a cue or by a spring are aimed at holes or pinned spaces.

bagel *n* a ring-shaped bread roll, hard and glazed on the outside, soft in the centre.

bagful *n* (*pl* **bagfuls**) as much as will fill one bag.

baggage *n* suitcases; luggage; **bag and baggage** with one's entire possessions; entirely.

bagging *n* the act of putting into bags; a coarse cloth or other material used for bags; filtration through canvas bags.

baggy *adj* (**baggier, baggiest**) hanging loosely in folds.—**baggily** *adv.*—**bagginess** *n.*

bag lady *n* (*pl* **bag ladies**) a homeless woman who wanders the streets carrying her possessions in shopping bags or carrier bags.

bagman *n* (*pl* **bagmen**) (*formerly*) a travelling salesman who carried his wares in saddlebags; a person who collects or distributes illegally obtained money for another.

bagnio *n* (*pl* **bagnios**) a brothel; a bath house; an oriental prison.

bagpipe *n* (*often pl*) a musical instrument consisting of an air-filled bag fitted with pipes.

bail¹ *n* money lodged as security that a prisoner, if released, will return to court to stand trial; such a release; the person pledging such money. * *vt* to free a person by providing bail; (*with* **out**) to help out of financial or other difficulty; (*government, bank, etc*) to assist a floundering business.—**bailable** *adj.*

bail² *vti* (*usu with* **out**) to scoop out (water) from (a boat).

bail³ *n* (*cricket*) either of two wooden crosspieces that rest on the three stumps; a bar separating horses in an open stable; a metal bar that holds the paper against the roller of a typewriter.

bailee *n* (*law*) the person to whom goods are delivered in trust.

bailey *n* the outer wall of a castle; a castle yard.

Bailey bridge *n* a prefabricated bridge of steel easily and quickly assembled for temporary use.

bailie *n* (*Scot*) a municipal officer corresponding to an alderman.

bailiff *n* in UK, the agent of a landlord or landowner; a sheriff's officer who serves writs and summonses; a minor official in some US courts, usu a messenger or usher.

bailiwick *n* the district within which a bailiff has jurisdiction; a person's special sphere of knowledge or activity or jurisdiction.

bailment *n* (*law*) a delivery of goods in trust to another; the action of becoming surety for one in custody.

bailor *n* (*law*) one who delivers goods in trust.

bail-out *n* assistance by a bank, government, etc, to help (a company) in financial trouble.

bailsman *n* (*pl* **bailsmen**) one who gives bail for another.

bain-marie *n* (*pl* **bains-marie**) a vessel that holds hot water for cooking or warming food.

bairn *n* (*Scot*) a child.

bait *n* food attached to a hook to entice fish or make them bite; any lure or enticement. * *vt* to put food on a hook to lure; to set dogs upon (a badger, etc); to persecute, worry or tease, esp by verbal attacks; to lure, to tempt; to entice.

baize *n* a coarse, green woollen fabric used to cover

snooker tables.

bake *vt* (*pottery*) to dry and harden by heating in the sun or by fire; (*food*) to cook by dry heat in an oven. * *vi* to do a baker's work; to dry and harden in heat; (*inf*) to be very hot. * *n* all the food baked at one time or baking; a party or picnic featuring one baked item, eg a *clambake.*

baked beans *npl* cooked haricot beans canned in tomato sauce.

bakehouse *n* a bakery.

Bakelite *n* (*trademark*) a hard synthetic resin used for dishes, etc.

baker *n* a person who bakes and sells bread, cakes, etc.

baker's dozen *n* thirteen.

bakery *n* (*pl* **bakeries**) a room or building for baking; a shop that sells bread, cakes, etc; baked goods.

baking powder *n* a leavening agent containing sodium bicarbonate and an acid-forming substance.

baking soda *n* sodium bicarbonate.

baklava *n* a cake made with thin, flaky pastry, honey and nuts.—*also* **baclava.**

baksheesh *n* a present of money as a bribe or tip to expedite service.

balaclava (helmet) *n* a woollen hood that covers the ears and neck.

balalaika *n* a Russian, three-stringed guitar with a triangular body.

balance *n* a device for weighing, consisting of two dishes or pans hanging from a pivoted horizontal beam; equilibrium; mental stability; the power to influence or control; a remainder.—**in the balance** a state of uncertainty.—**on balance** having considered all aspects or factors. * *vt* to weigh; to compare; to equalize the debit and credit sides of an account. * *vi* to be equal in power or weight, etc; to have the debits and credits equal.—**balanceable** *adj.*—**balancer** *n.*

balance of payments *n* the difference between a country's total receipts from abroad and total payments abroad over a given period.

balancer *n* one who or that which keeps anything in equilibrium; an acrobat; (*pl*) halter.

balance sheet *n* a statement of assets and liabilities.

balance wheel *n* a wheel that regulates the speed of a clock or watch.

balas *n* a variety of spinel ruby of a pale rose-red colour.

balata *n* dried gum from a South American tree, used as a substitute for guttapercha.

balcony *n* (*pl* **balconies**) a projecting platform from an upper storey enclosed by a railing; an upper floor of seats in a theatre, etc, often projecting over the main floor.—**balconied** *adj.*

bald *adj* lacking a natural or usual covering, as of hair, vegetation, or nap; (*tyre*) having little or no tread; (*truth*) plain or blunt; bare, unadorned.—**baldly** *adv.*—**baldness** *n.*

baldachin *n* a canopy, esp over a throne or altar; a rich brocade fabric used for this.

balderdash *n* nonsense.

balding *adj* becoming bald.

baldric *n* a broad belt, often richly ornamented, worn round the waist, or over one shoulder and across the breast.

bale¹ *n* a large bundle of goods, as raw cotton, compressed and bound. * *vt* (*hay etc*) to make into bales. * *vi* (*with* **out**) to parachute from an aircraft, usu in an emergency.

bale² *n* a great evil; woe.

baleen *n* whalebone.

baleful *adj* evil; harmful; deadly; ominous.—**balefully** *adv*.—**balefulness** *n*.

balk *see* **baulk**.

ball[1] *n* a spherical or nearly spherical body or mass; a round object for use in tennis, football, etc; a throw or pitch of a ball; a missile for a cannon, rifle, etc; any rounded part or protuberance of the body; (*pl*: *sl*) testicles; nonsense. * *interj* (*pl*) (*sl*) nonsense! * *vti* to form into a ball; (*vulg sl*) to have sexual intercourse with.

ball[2] *n* a formal social dance; (*inf*) a good time.—**ballroom** *n*.—**ballroom dancing** *n*.

ballad *n* a narrative song or poem; a slow, sentimental, esp pop, song.—**balladeer** *n*.—**balladry** *n*.

ballade *n* a poem of (usu) three eight-line stanzas and an envoy, all with the same rhymes and refrain.

balladmonger *n* a dealer in ballads; an inferior poet, a poetaster.

ballast *n* heavy material carried in a ship or vehicle to stabilize it when it is not carrying cargo; crushed rock or gravel, etc used in railway tracks.

ball bearing *n* a device for lessening friction by having a rotating part resting on small steel balls; one of these balls.

ball boy *n* (*tennis*) a boy who retrieves balls that go out of play.—**ball girl** *nf*.

ballcock *n* a device that uses a floating ball to regulate the flow of water in a cistern, tank, etc.

ballerina *n* a female ballet dancer.

ballet *n* a theatrical representation of a story, set to music and performed by dancers; the troupe of dancers.

balletomane *n* an enthusiastic lover of ballet.—**balletomania** *n*.

ballistic *adj* relating to the flight of projectiles.

ballistic missile *n* a missile whose trajectory is initially guided then ballistic.

ballistics *n* (*used as sing*) the scientific study of projectiles and firearms.

ballonet *n* a small balloon; a subdivision of a balloon's or an airship's gasbag for controlling descent.

balloon *n* a large airtight envelope that rises up when filled with hot air or light gases, often fitted with a basket or gondola for carrying passengers; a small inflatable rubber pouch used as a toy or for decoration; a balloon-shaped line enclosing speech or thoughts in a strip cartoon. * *vti* to inflate; to swell, expand; to travel in a balloon.—**balloonist** *n*.

balloon jib, balloon sail *n* (*naut*) a light triangular sail used by yachts in a slight breeze.

ballooning *n* the art or practice of managing balloons or making balloon ascents.

ballot *n* a paper used in voting; the process of voting; the number of votes cast; the candidates offering themselves for election. * *vi* (**balloting, balloted**) to vote.—**balloter** *n*.

ballot box *n* a secure container for ballot papers.

ballpoint pen *n* a pen with a tiny ball, which rotates against an inking cartridge, as its writing tip.

ball valve *n* a valve that is opened or shut by the rising or falling of a ball.

ballyhoo *n* vulgar, noisy publicity or advertisement.

ballyrag *vb* (**ballyragging, ballyragged**) *vt* to hustle, to jeer at. * *vi* to indulge in horseplay.—*also* **bullyrag**.

balm *n* a fragrant ointment used in healing and soothing; anything comforting and soothing.

balm of Gilead *n* any of various fragrant resins, as that of the evergreen terebinth tree of Arabia or the bal-

sam fir; a North American poplar with broad heart-shaped leaves.

balmoral *n* a laced boot; a Scottish bonnet of wool; a petticoat.

balmy *adj* (**balmier, balmiest**) having a pleasant fragrance; soothing; (*weather*) mild, warm.

balneology *n* the science of therapeutic baths and their effect.—**balneological** *adj*.—**balneologist** *n*.

baloney *n* (*inf*) foolish talk; nonsense.—*also* **boloney**.

balsa *n* lightweight wood from a tropical American tree.

balsam *n* a fragrant, resinous substance; the tree yielding it.—**balsamic** *adj*.

balsam fir *n* a North American evergreen pine with flat needles and yielding balsam.

balsamiferous *adj* producing or yielding balsam.

Baltimore oriole *n* an American bird nearly related to the starlings with bright orange and black plumage.

baluster *n* any of the small posts of a railing, as on a staircase.—**balustered** *adj*.

balustrade *n* an ornamental row of balusters joined by a rail.

bambino *n* (*pl* **bambinos, bambini**) a child or baby; (*RC Church*) a figure of the infant Christ wrapped in swaddling clothes, exhibited in churches from Christmas to Epiphany.

bamboo *n* (*pl* **bamboos**) any of various, often tropical, woody grasses, used for furniture.

bamboo shoots *npl* the edible shoots of certain bamboos.

bamboozle *vt* (*inf*) to deceive; to mystify.—**bamboozlement** *n*.—**bamboozler** *n*.

ban[1] *n* a condemnation, an official prohibition. * *vt* (**banning, banned**) to prohibit, esp officially; to forbid.

ban[2] *n* (*feudal*) a public proclamation or summons to arms.

banal *adj* trite, commonplace.—**banally** *adj*.

banality *n* (*pl* **banalities**) anything trite or trivial; a commonplace remark, etc.

banana *n* a herbaceous plant bearing its fruit in compact, hanging bunches.

banana republic *n* (*derog*) a small country, esp in Central America, that is dominated by foreign interests.

banana skin *n* (*inf*) an unforeseen occurrence that causes embarrassment.

banana split *n* ice cream served on a lengthwise sliced banana and topped with syrup, nuts, cream, etc.

banausic *adj* merely mechanical; mean, illiberal.

band[1] *n* a strip of material used for binding; a stripe; (*radio*) a range of wavelengths.

band[2] *n* a group of people with a common purpose; a group of musicians playing together, an orchestra. * *vti* to associate together for a particular purpose.

bandage *n* a strip of cloth for binding wounds and fractures. * *vt* to bind a wound.

bandanna, bandana *n* a large coloured handkerchief.

bandbox *n* a light box of pasteboard, etc, for holding collars or hats.

bandeau *n* (*pl* **bandeaux**) a band for the hair; a fitting band inside a hat.

banderilla *n* a barbed dart, used by a banderillero in bullfights to exasperate the bull.

banderillero *n* (*pl* **banderilleros**) a bullfighter's assistant.

banderole, banderol *n* a long narrow flag with a cleft end; a streamer; a small flag carried at the head of a lance or mast; a scroll or band with an inscription.—*also* **bannerol**.

bandicoot *n* a large rat, native to India and Sri Lanka, very destructive to rice fields and gardens; the name given to rat-like marsupials of several species found in Australia and Tasmania.

bandit *n* (*pl* **bandits, banditti**) a robber.—**banditry** *n*.

bandmaster *n* the conductor of a musical, esp brass, band

bandoleer, bandolier *n* a belt worn over the chest with pockets for holding ammunition.

bandore, bandora *n* an ancient stringed instrument resembling a zither.—*also* **pandora, pandore**.

band saw *n* a motorized, toothed steel belt used for sawing.

bandsman *n* (*pl* **bandsmen**) a player in a musical, esp brass, band.

bandstand *n* a platform for a musical band.

bandwagon *n* a wagon for carrying a band in a parade; a movement, idea, etc that is (thought to be) heading for success.

bandwidth *n* the range of frequencies within a given waveband for radio or other types of transmission.

bandy[1] *vt* (**bandying, bandied**) to pass to and fro; (*often with* **about**) (*rumours, etc*) to spread freely; to exchange words, esp angrily.

bandy[2] *adj* (**bandier, bandiest**) having legs curved outwards at the knee.

bandy-legged *adj* bandy.

bane *n* a person causing distress or misery; something bringing destruction or death; a poison.—**baneful** *adj*.

baneberry *n* (*pl* **baneberries**) a plant of the buttercup family bearing white or red poisonous berries; its berry.—*also* **herb Christopher, cohosh**.

bang[1] *n* a hard blow; a sudden loud sound. * *vt* to hit or knock with a loud noise; (*door*) to slam. * *vi* to make a loud noise; to hit noisily or sharply. * *adv* with a bang, abruptly; successfully; (*inf*) precisely.

bang[2] *n* (*pl*) hair cut straight across the forehead to form a fringe; false hair so worn. * *vt* to cut the hair across the forehead to form a fringe.

bang[3] *see* **bhang**.

banger *n* an exploding firework; (*sl*) a sausage; (*sl*) an old car.

bangle *n* a bracelet worn on the arm or ankle.

banian *see* **banyan**.

banish *vt* to exile from a place; to drive away; to get rid of.—**banishment** *n*.

banister *n* the railing or supporting balusters in a staircase.—*also* **bannister**.

banjo *n* (*pl* **banjos, banjoes**) a stringed musical instrument with a drum-like body and a long fretted neck.—**banjoist** *n*.

bank[1] *n* a mound or pile; the sloping side of a river; elevated ground in a lake or the sea; a row or series of objects, as of dials, switches. * *vti* to form into a mound; to cover (a fire) with fuel so that it burns more slowly; (*aircraft*) to curve or tilt sideways.

bank[2] *n* an institution that offers various financial services, such as the safekeeping, lending and exchanging of money; the money held by the banker or dealer in a card game; any supply or store for the future, such as a *blood bank*. * *vti* (*cheques, cash, etc*) to deposit in a bank; to work as a banker.

bank account *n* money deposited in a bank and credited to the depositor.

bank bill *n* a note or a bill of exchange of a bank payable on demand or at a future specified time.

bankbook *n* a book in which a record is kept of deposits and withdrawals of money into a personal account.

bank discount *n* a deduction made according to the current rate of interest.

banker *n* a person who runs a bank; the keeper of the bank at a gaming table.

banker's card *see* **cheque card**.

bank holiday *n* in UK, a weekday when banks are officially closed; a day observed as a public holiday.

banking *n* the activity or occupation of running a bank. * *adj* of or concerning a bank.

banknote *n* a promissory note issued by a bank, which serves as money.

bank rate *n* the rate at which a central bank will discount bills.

bankrupt *n* a person, etc legally declared unable to pay his debts; one who becomes insolvent. * *adj* judged to be insolvent; financially ruined; devoid of resources, ideas, etc. * *vt* to make bankrupt.—**bankruptcy** *n*.

banksia *n* any of an Australian genus of flowering shrubs with evergreen leaves.

banner *n* a flag or ensign; a headline running across a newspaper page; a strip of cloth bearing a slogan or emblem carried between poles in a parade.

banneret *n* (*hist*) an order of knighthood conferred on the field of battle for distinguished service or a deed of valour; the person on whom the degree was conferred and who ranked between a baron and a knight.

bannerette *n* a little banner or flag.

bannerol *see* **banderole**.

bannister *see* **banister**.

bannock *n* a thick flat cake made of oatmeal or barley and baked on a griddle.

banns *npl* public declaration of intention, esp in church, to marry.

banquet *n* a feast; an elaborate and sometimes formal dinner in honour of a person or occasion. * *vt* (**banqueting, banqueted**) to hold a banquet.—**banqueter** *n*.

banquette *n* a cushioned bench; a step along the inside of a parapet on which soldiers stood to fire upon the enemy; the footway of a bridge when raised above the carriageway.

banshee *n* (*folklore*) a female fairy whose wail portends a death in the family.

bantam *n* a dwarf breed of domestic fowl; a small, aggressive person; (*boxing*) a bantamweight.

bantamweight *n* a boxing weight (112–118 lbs; 51–53.5 kg) between featherweight and flyweight.

banter *vt* to tease good-humouredly.—**banterer** *n*.

Bantu *n* (*pl* **Bantu, Bantus**) one of a group of Southern African peoples or their language.

banyan *n* an Indian fig tree with vast, rooting branches.—*also* **banian**.

banzai *interj* a Japanese greeting or salute.

baobab *n* an African tree with an enormously thick trunk.

bap *n* a large soft bread roll.

baptism *n* the sprinkling of water on the forehead, or complete immersion in water, as a rite of admitting a person to a Christian church; any initiating experience.—**baptismal** *adj*.—**baptismally** *adv*.

Baptist *n* a member of a Protestant Christian denomination holding that the true church is of believers only, who are all equal, that the only authority is the Bible, and that adult baptism by immersion is necessary.

baptistry, baptistery *n* (*pl* **baptistries, baptisteries**) the part of a church where baptism takes place.

baptize *vt* to christen, to name.—**baptizer** *n*.

bar[1] *n* a straight length of wood or metal; a counter where alcoholic drinks or other refreshments are served; a place with such a counter; an oblong piece, as of soap; anything that obstructs or hinders; a band or strip; a strip or bank of sand or mud near and in line with the shore or across a river or harbour; (*mil*) a badge signifying a second award; (*with cap*) barristers or lawyers collectively; the legal profession; (*mus*) a vertical line dividing a staff into measures; (*mus*) a measure. * *vt* (**barring, barred**) to secure or fasten as with a bar; to exclude or prevent; to oppose. * *prep* except for.

bar[2] *n* a unit of atmospheric pressure.

barathea *n* a type of fine woollen material.

barb *n* the sharp backward point of a fish-hook, etc; one of the sharp parts combined to form barbed wire; a pointed or critical remark; a beard-like growth. * *vt* to provide with a barb.—**barbed** *adj*.

barbarian *n* an uncivilized, primitive person; a cruel vicious person.—*also adj*.

barbaric *adj* of or suitable for barbarians.—**barbarically** *adv*.

barbarism *n* a barbarous act; the state of being a barbarian; an expression or word that is tasteless or not standard; an object or act that offends.

barbarity *n* (*pl* **barbarities**) savage cruelty; a vicious act.

barbarize *vti* to make or become barbarous.

barbarous *adj* uncivilized, cruel, coarse.—**barbarously** *adv*.

Barbary ape *n* a tailless macaque monkey of North Africa and Gibraltar.

barbate *adj* tufted, bearded.

barbecue *n* a metal frame for grilling food over an open fire; an open-air party where barbecued food is served. * *vt* (**barbecuing, barbecued**) to cook on a barbecue.

barbed wire *n* wire with barbs at close intervals.—*also* **barbwire**.

barbel *n* a freshwater fish with beard-like filaments at its mouth; such a filament.—**barbelled** *adj*.

barbell *n* a metal rod with weights at each end, used in weightlifting.

barber *n* a person who cuts hair and shaves beards.

barberry *n* (*pl* **barberries**) a thorny shrub with yellow flowers; its red berry.

barbershop *n* the business premises of a barber.

barbet *n* a tropical bird with tufts of feathers at the base of the bill.

barbette *n* a raised platform for guns to fire over a parapet; a type of armoured turret in a warship.

barbican *n* a defensive tower over the gate or drawbridge of a castle or fortification.

barbitone, barbital *n* a habit-forming, toxic, hypnotic and sedative drug.

barbiturate *n* a sedative drug.

barbule *n* a minute barb; a filament fringing the barb of a feather.

barbwire *see* **barbed wire**.

barcarole, barcarolle *n* a Venetian gondolier's song; an instrumental piece resembling this.

bar code *n* a striped pattern on a package, book cover, etc, containing information about the price that can be read by a computer for stock control, etc.

bard *n* a poet.—**bardic** *adj*.

bare *adj* without covering; unclothed, naked; simple, unadorned; mere; without furnishings. * *vt* to uncover; to reveal.—**bareness** *n*.

bareback *adj* on a horse with no saddle.—*also adv*.

barefaced *adj* with the face shaven or uncovered; shameless.—**barefacedly** *adv*.

barefoot, barefooted *adj* with the feet bare.—*also adv*.

barège, barege *n* a thin gauze-like fabric, usu of silk and worsted.

barehanded *adj* without using weapons.

barely *adv* openly; merely, scarcely.

bargain *n* an agreement laying down the conditions of a transaction; something sold at a price favourable to the buyer; **into the bargain** as well; in addition. * *vt* to make a bargain, to haggle; (*with* **for**) to expect or hope for.

barge *n* a flat-bottomed vessel, used to transport freight along rivers and canals; a large boat for excursions or pleasure trips. * *vi* to lurch clumsily; (*with* **in**) to interrupt (a conversation) rudely; (*with* **into**) to enter abruptly.

bargeboard *n* a board placed at a gable to conceal the roof timbers.

barge couple *n* one of two beams bounding a gable, mortised and tenoned together and used for strengthening a building.

barge course *n* the tiling that projects beyond the principal rafters in a building; a wall coping constructed of bricks set on edge.

bargee *n* the owner of or one employed on a barge; a bargeman.

barilla *n* an alkali made from kinds of marine plant or seaweed.

barite *see* **barytes**.

baritone *n* the adult male voice ranging between bass and tenor; a singer with such a voice.—*also adj*.

barium *n* (*chem*) a white metallic element.

barium sulphate *n* a white insoluble fine heavy powder which is opaque to X-rays, swallowed by a patient before X-ray of the alimentary canal.

bark[1] *n* the harsh or abrupt cry of a dog, wolf, etc; a similar sound, such as one made by a person. * *vi* to make a loud cry like a dog; to speak or shout sharply or angrily.

bark[2] *n* the outside covering of a tree trunk. * *vt* to remove the bark from; to scrape; to skin (the knees, etc).

bark[3] *see* **barque**.

barkentine *see* **barquentine**.

barker *n* one who or that which barks; a person who shouts his wares, etc, usu at a fairground.

barking *n* the process of stripping bark from trees; the process of tanning leather or dyeing with bark.

barley *n* a grain used in making beer and whisky, and for food.

barleycorn *n* a grain of barley; (*formerly*) a measure of length, one-third of an inch (0.85 cm).

barley sugar *n* a transparent amber-coloured sweet.

barm *n* the froth on fermenting liquor used as leaven in breadmaking, yeast.

barmaid *n* a female serving alcohol in a bar.

barman *n* (*pl* **barmen**) a man serving alcohol in a bar.

Barmecide, Barmedcidal *adj* like the Barmecide's feast in *The Arabian Nights*; imaginarily satisfying; unreal, illusory.

bar mitzvah *n* (*Judaism*) the ceremony marking the thirteenth birthday of a boy, who then assumes full religious obligations; the boy himself.

barn *n* a farm building used for storing grain, hay, etc, and sheltering animals.

barnacle *n* a marine crustacean that attaches itself to rocks and ship bottoms.

barnacle goose *n* a wild European grey-winged goose that breeds in the Arctic.

barn dance *n* a social dance featuring several dance forms (as square dancing).

barn owl *n* any of a genus of owl with brownish plumage above and white plumage below.

barnstorm *vi* to tour (rural areas) as an actor, or making speeches in a political campaign, or demonstrating flying stunts.—**barnstormer** *n*.

barograph *n* a self-recording aneroid barometer.—**barographic** *adj*.

barogram *n* the record traced by a barograph.

barometer *n* an instrument for measuring atmospheric pressure and imminent changes in the weather; anything that marks change.—**barometric** *adj*.—**barometrically** *adv*.

baron *n* a member of a rank of nobility, the lowest in the British peerage; a powerful businessman.—**baroness** *nf*.

baronage *n* the whole body of barons; the dignity or rank of a baron.

baronet *n* the lowest hereditary title of honour in Britain.

baronetage *n* the collective body of baronets; the dignity or rank of a baronet.

baronetcy *n* (*pl* **baronetcies**) the dignity or rank of a baronet.

baronial *adj* pertaining to or suitable for a baron.

barony *n* (*pl* **baronies**) the rank or lands of a baron; (*Scot*) a large manor; (*Ir*) a division of a county.

baroque *adj* extravagantly ornamented, esp in architecture and decorative art.

baroscope *n* an instrument for indicating variations in the pressure of the atmosphere without actual measurement of its weight.—**baroscopic** *adj*.

barouche *n* a 19th-century roomy four-wheeled carriage for four with a folding top.

barque *n* (*poet*) a ship; a three-masted vessel with the foremast and main mast square-rigged and the mizzen fore-and-aft.—*also* **bark**.

barquentine, barquantine *n* a three-masted vessel with the foremast square-rigged and the main mast and mizzenmast fore-and-aft or schooner-rigged.—*also* **barkentine**.

barrack *vti* to shout or protest at.—**barracker** *n*.

barracks *n* (*used as sing*) a building for housing soldiers.

barracuda *n* (*pl* **barracuda, barracudas**) a fierce fish with edible flesh.

barrage *n* a man-made dam across a river; heavy artillery fire; (*of protests, questions, etc*) continuous and heavy delivery.

barrage balloon *n* a large balloon anchored to the ground and trailing cables or nets, used as a defence against low-flying enemy aircraft.

barranca, barranco *n* (*pl* **barrancas, barrancos**) a deep mountain gully or ravine.

barratry *n* the defrauding or injury of a ship's owner, freighter or insurer by the master or crew; the practice of inciting and encouraging lawsuits or litigation.—**barrator** *n*.—**barratrous** *adj*.

barre *n* a horizontal rail used for ballet practice.

barred *see* **bar**[1].

barrel *n* a cylindrical container, usu wooden, with bulging sides held together with hoops; the amount held by a barrel; a tubular structure, as in a gun. * *vt* (**barrelling, barrelled** *or* **barreling, barreled**) to put into barrels.

barrel organ *n* a mechanical piano or organ played by a revolving cylinder with pins that operate the keys or valves to produce sound.

barren *adj* infertile; incapable of producing offspring; unable to bear crops; unprofitable; (*with* **of**) lacking in.

barricade *n* a barrier or blockade used in defence to block a street; an obstruction. * *vt* to block with a barricade.

barrier *n* anything that bars passage, prevents access, controls crowds, etc, such as a fence; obstruction; hindrance.

barrier reef *n* an exposed coral reef separated from the shore by a navigable channel.

barring *prep* excepting; leaving out of account.

barrister *n* a qualified lawyer who has been called to the bar in England.

barrow[1] *n* a wheelbarrow or hand-cart used for carrying loads.

barrow[2] *n* a prehistoric burial mound.

Barsac *n* a French white wine.

bar sinister *n* (*her*) in error for **bend sinister**, the badge of illegitimacy.

Bart *abbr* = baronet.

barter *vt* to trade commodities or services without exchanging money. * *vi* to haggle or bargain. * *n* trade by the exchanging of commodities.—**barterer** *n*.

bartizan *n* an overhanging turret at the top of a tower or wall.

barytes *n* a white crystalline mineral of great weight, consisting mainly of barium sulphate.—*also* **barite, heavy spar**.

baryon *n* an elementary particle (nucleon or hyperon) with a mass greater than or equal to that of the proton.

basal *adj* pertaining to, at or forming the base; fundamental. * *n* a basal part.—**basally** *adv*.

basalt *n* hard, compact, dark-coloured igneous rock.—**basaltic** *adj*.

bascule *n* a mechanical arrangement on the seesaw principle by which the lowering of one end raises the other; a kind of drawbridge so operated.

base[1] *n* the bottom part of anything; the support or foundation; the fundamental principle; the centre of operations (eg military); (*baseball*) one of the four corners of the diamond. * *vt* to use as a basis; to found (on); (*with* **at, in**) to place, to station.—**basal** *adj*.

base[2] *adj* low in morality or honour; worthless; menial.—**basely** *adv*.—**baseness** *n*.

baseball *n* the US national game, involving two teams that score runs by hitting a ball and running round four bases arranged in a diamond shape on the playing area.

baseborn *adj* (*arch*) of low or mean birth; illegitimate; mean.

baseless *adj* without a base; unfounded.

baseline *n* the line at each end of a games court marking the limit of play; (*baseball*) the line between any two consecutive bases; a measured line in a survey area from which triangulations are calculated.

baseman *n* (*pl* **basemen**) (*baseball*) a fielder placed at the first, second, and third bases respectively.

basement *n* the part of a building that is partly or wholly below ground level.

base metal *n* any metal other than the precious metals.

bash *vt* (*inf*) to hit hard; to dent by striking. * *n* (*inf*) a heavy blow; (*inf*) a try or attempt; (*sl*) a party.

bashful *adj* easily embarrassed, shy.—**bashfully** *adv.*—**bashfulness** *n.*

bashibazouk *n* a volunteer or irregular in the Turkish army.

BASIC *n* (*comput*) a simple programming language: Beginners' All-purpose Symbolic Instruction Code.

basic *adj* fundamental; simple. * *n* (*often pl*) a basic principle, factor, etc; the rudiments.—**basically** *adv.*

basicity *n* the state of being a base; (*chem*) the power of an acid to unite with one or more atoms of a base.

basic slag *n* the phosphates of lime and oxidized impurities left as a brittle powder in steelmaking and used as a fertilizer.

basidium *n* (*pl* **basidia**) the cell to which the spores of certain fungi are attached.—**basidial** *adj.*

basify *vt* (**basifying, basified**) to convert into a base, make basic.

basil *n* a plant with aromatic leaves used for seasoning food.

basilar, basilary *adj* (*anat*) pertaining to or situated at the base, esp of the skull.

basilica *n* a church with a broad nave, side aisles, and an apse; (*RC Church*) a church with special ceremonial rites.—**basilican** *adj.*

basilisk *n* a fabulous creature dealing death by its gaze, sometimes identified with the cockatrice; a lizard with an inflatable crest. * *adj* pertaining to the basilisk; penetrating or malignant.

basin *n* a wide shallow container for liquid; its contents; any large hollow, often with water in it; a tract of land drained by a river.

basinet *n* a light steel helmet of medieval times, often with a visor.

basis *n* (*pl* **bases**) a base or foundation; a principal constituent; a fundamental principle or theory.

bask *vi* to lie in sunshine or warmth; to enjoy someone's approval.

basket *n* a container made of interwoven cane, wood strips, etc; the hoop through which basketball players throw the ball to score.

basketball *n* a game in which two teams compete to score by throwing the ball through an elevated net basket or hoop; this ball.

basket hilt *n* the hilt of a sword shaped like a basket.

basking shark *n* a large shark of northern seas, which is harmless and has the habit of basking at the surface in the sun.

basque *n* a woman's jacket with a short skirt.

Basque *n* one of a people inhabiting the western Pyrenees; their language.

bas-relief *n* a low relief; a form of relief in which the figures stand out very slightly from the ground.—*also* **basso-rilievo.**

bass[1] *n* (*mus*) the range of the lowest male voice; a singer or instrument with this range. * *adj* of, for or in the range of a bass.

bass[2] *n* (*pl* **bass**) any of numerous freshwater food and game fishes.

bass clef *n* (*mus*) the character C placed at the beginning of the bass staff.

basset[1], **basset hound** *n* a smooth-haired hound with short legs.

basset[2] *vi* (**basseting, basseted**) (*geol*) to crop out at the surface. * *n* an outcrop.

basset horn *n* a tenor clarinet.

bassinet *n* a wickerwork or wooden cradle with a hood; a pram.

bassist *n* a player of the double bass.

basso *n* (*pl* **bassos, bassi**) one who sings bass.

bassoon *n* an orchestral, deep-toned woodwind instrument.—**bassoonist** *n.*

basso profundo *n* (*pl* **basso profundos**) the lowest bass voice; a singer with such a voice.

basso-rilievo *n* (*pl* **basso-rilievos**) a bas-relief.

bass viol *n* a large stringed instrument of the violin class for playing bass, the violoncello.

bast *n* the tough inner fibrous bark of various trees, especially of the lime; rope or matting made from this bark.

basta *interj* enough!

bastard *n* a person born of unmarried parents; (*offensive*) an unpleasant person; (*inf*) a person (*lucky bastard*); (*inf*) a difficult task, situation, etc. * *adj* illegitimate (by birth); false; not genuine.—**bastardy** *n.*

bastardize *vt* to declare illegitimate; to falsify or corrupt.—**bastardization** *n.*

baste[1] *vt* to drip fat over (roasting meat, etc).

baste[2] *vt* to sew with long loose stitches as a temporary seam.

bastinado *n* (*pl* **bastinadoes**) a caning of the soles of the feet as a form of torture. * *vt.* (**bastinadoing, bastinadoed**) to torture in this way.

bastion *n* a tower at the corner of a fortification; any strong defence; one who strongly upholds or supports a principle, etc.—**bastioned** *adj.*

basuco *n* the dregs of cocaine after refining, which are packaged and sold in Colombia.

bat[1] *n* a wooden club used in cricket, baseball, etc; a batsman; a paddle used in table tennis. * *vb* (**batting, batted**) *vt* to hit as with a bat. * *vi* to take one's turn at bat.

bat[2] *n* a nocturnal, mouse-like flying mammal with forelimbs modified to form wings.

bat[3] *vt* (**batting, batted**) (*one's eyelids*) to wink or flutter.

batch *n* the quantity of bread, etc produced at one time; one set, group, etc; an amount of work for processing by a computer in a single run.

bate *vt* to lessen or reduce; to deduct.

bateau *n* (*pl* **bateaux**) a light boat used esp on Canadian rivers.

bath *n* water for washing the body; a bathing; a bathtub; (*pl*) a building with baths for public use; a municipal swimming pool. * *vti* to give a bath to; to bathe.

bath chair *n* a wheeled chair for invalids.

bathe *vt* to dampen with any liquid. * *vi* to have a bath; to go swimming; to become immersed.—**bather** *n.*

bathometer *n* an apparatus for measuring depths.

bathos *n* anticlimax; descent from the elevated to the ordinary in speech or writing.

bathrobe *n* a loose-fitting garment of absorbent fabric for use after bathing or as a dressing gown.

bathroom *n* a room with a bath or shower and usually a lavatory and washbasin.—*also* **lavatory.**

bathtub *n* a usu fixed tub for bathing.

bathymetry *n* the art or science of sounding or of measuring sea depths.—**bathymetric** *adj.*—**bathymetrically** *adv.*

bathyscaphe *n* a submersible vessel for deep-sea observation and exploration.

bathysphere *n* a hollow steel sphere for descending to great depths in the sea.

batik *n* a method of printing coloured designs on fabric; fabric produced by this method.

batiste *n* a kind of cambric; a fabric like cambric.

batman *n* (*pl* **batmen**) (*mil*) in UK, an officer's servant.

baton *n* a staff serving as a symbol of office; a thin stick used by the conductor of an orchestra to beat time; a hollow cylinder carried by each member of a relay team in succession; a policeman's truncheon.

batrachian *n* one of the amphibians, which includes frogs and toads. * *adj* of or pertaining to frogs or toads.

batsman *n* (*pl* **batsmen**) (*cricket, baseball*) the player whose turn it is to bat.

battalion *n* an army unit consisting of three or more companies; a large group.

batten[1] *n* a strip of wood or metal; a strip of wood put over a seam between boards. * *vt* to fasten or supply with battens.

batten[2] *vt* to make fat by rich living; to fertilize or enrich. * *vi* to grow or become fat; to thrive at the expense of others.

batter *vt* to beat with repeated blows; to wear out with heavy use; to criticize strongly and at length. * *vi* to strike heavily and repeatedly. * *n* a mixture of flour, egg, and milk or water used in cooking.—**batterer** *n*.

battering ram *n* (*hist*) a military machine for breaching the walls of besieged places, consisting of a large beam with an iron head resembling the head of a ram.

battery *n* (*pl* **batteries**) a set of heavy guns; a small unit of artillery; an electric cell that supplies current; an unlawful beating; an arrangement of hens' cages designed to increase egg laying.

battle *n* a combat or fight between two opposing individuals or armies; a contest; any struggle towards a goal. * *vti* to fight; to struggle.—**battler** *n*.

battle-axe, battle-ax *n* (*pl* **battle-axes**) an old-fashioned two-headed axe; (*inf*) a domineering woman.

battle cruiser *n* a heavy-gunned ship with higher speed and lighter armour than a battleship.

battle cry *n* a war cry; a slogan used to rally supporters of a political campaign, etc.

battledore *n* a wooden bat used in washing, baking, etc; a bat used in **battledore and shuttlecock**, a forerunner of badminton.

battlefield *n* the land on which a battle is fought.

battlement *n* a parapet or wall with indentations, from which to shoot.

battle royal *n* (*pl* **battles royal**) a fight with many combatants; a general engagement; a melee.

battleship *n* a large, heavily armoured warship.

battue *n* (*hunting*) the driving up of game by beaters towards the guns; wholesale slaughter.

batty *adj* (**battier, battiest**) (*inf*) crazy; eccentric.—**battiness** *n*.

bauble *n* a showy toy; a shining ball hung on a Christmas tree as a decoration; a worthless trifle or ornament.

baud *n* (*comput*) a unit used in measuring the speed of electronic data transmissions.

baulk *vt* to obstruct or foil. * *vi* to stop and refuse to move and act.—*also* **balk**.

bauxite *n* aluminium ore.

bawd *n* a woman who runs a brothel; a prostitute.

bawdy *adj* (**bawdier, bawdiest**) humorously indecent; obscene, lewd.—**bawdily** *adv*.—**bawdiness** *n*.

bawl *vti* to shout; to weep loudly. * *n* a loud shout; a noisy weeping.—**bawler** *n*.—**bawling** *n*.

bay[1] *n* a type of laurel tree:

bay[2] *n* a wide inlet of a sea or lake; an inward bend of a shore.

bay[3] *n* an alcove or recess in a wall; a compartment used for a special purpose.

bay[4] *vti* to bark (at). * *n* the cry of a hound or a pursuing pack.—**at bay** the position of one forced to turn and fight.

bay[5] *adj* reddish brown. * *n* a horse of this colour.

bayberry *n* (*pl* **bayberries**) any of various shrubs, esp the wax myrtle of North America; the grey waxy berry of the wax myrtle; a West Indian tree with fragrant leaves used in bay rum.

bay leaf *n* the leaf of the laurel dried and used as a flavouring for food.

bayonet *n* a blade for stabbing attached to the muzzle of a rifle. * *vt* (**bayoneting, bayoneted** *or* **bayonetting, bayonetted**) to kill or stab with a bayonet.

bayou *n* in the southern US, the marshy inlet or outlet of a lake or river.

bay rum *n* a perfumed cosmetic obtained from the leaves of the bayberry.

bay window *n* a window projecting from the outside wall of a house.

bazaar *n* a marketplace; a street full of small shops; a benefit sale for a church, etc.

bazooka *n* a portable anti-tank weapon that fires rockets from a long tube.

B and B *abbr* = bed and breakfast.

BBC *abbr* = British Broadcasting Corporation.

BC *abbr* = Before Christ; British Columbia.

BD *abbr* = Bachelor of Divinity.

bdellium *n* a fragrant gum used medicinally and as a perfume; the African and Asian tree yielding it.

be- *prefix* all over, thoroughly, as in *bespatter*; to make, as in *bedim*; to call, as in *bedevil*; to form a transitive verb from an intrasitive, as *bewail*.

Be (*chem symbol*) beryllium.

be *vi* (*pr t* **am, are, is**, *pt* **was, were**, *pp* **been**) to exist; to live; to take place.

beach *n* a flat, sandy shore of the sea. * *vi* to bring (a boat) up on the beach from the sea.

beachcomber *n* a person who hangs about the shore on the lookout for wreckage or plunder; a long curling wave rolling in from the ocean.—**beachcombing** *n*.

beachhead *n* an area of seashore captured from the enemy by an advance force in preparation for a full-scale landing of troops and equipment.

beach music *n* a style of pop music originating on the coast of South Carolina, based on soul music and rhythm and blues.

beacon *n* a light, esp on a high place, tower, etc, for warning or guiding. * *vi* to guide, to act as a beacon.

bead *n* a small ball pierced for stringing; (*pl*) a string of beads; (*pl*) a rosary; a bubble or droplet of liquid; the sight of a rifle.—**beaded** *adj*.

beading *n* moulding or edging in the form of a series of beads; a wooden strip, rounded on one side, used for trimming.—*also* **beadwork**.

beadle *n* an officer of a parish or church; a mace-bearer; (*formerly*) an officer in a law court.

beady *adj* (**beadier, beadiest**) (*eyes*) small, round and bright, sometimes calculating or unfriendly.—**beadily** *adv*.—**beadiness** *n*.

beagle *n* a small hound with short legs and drooping ears.

beak *n* a bird's bill; any projecting part; the nose.—**beaked** *adj*.

beaker *n* a large drinking cup, or the amount it holds; a cylindrical vessel with a pouring lip used by chemists and pharmacists.

beam *n* a long straight piece of timber or metal; the crossbar of a balance; a ship's breadth at its widest point; a slender shaft of light, etc; a radiant look, smile, etc; a steady radio or radar signal for guiding aircraft or ships. * *vt* (*light, etc*) to send out; to smile with great pleasure.

beamy *adj* (**beamier, beamiest**) emitting rays of light; resembling a beam in size and weight; (*ship*) broad; (*inf*) having broad hips.

bean *n* a plant bearing kidney-shaped seeds; a seed or pod of such a plant; any bean-like seed.

bean bag *n* a small cloth bag filled with dried beans and used in games; a larger cloth bag filled with plastic granules and used for sitting on.

bean curd *n* soft cheese made from soya milk.—*also* **tofu**.

beanfeast *n* (*inf*) an annual dinner given by an employer for his employees; (*inf*) any festive meal.

bean sprout *n* the shoot of the mung bean used in Chinese cooking.

bear[1] *vb* (**bearing, bore**, *pp* **borne**) *vt* to carry; to endure; to support, to sustain; to conduct (oneself); to produce or bring forth; (*with* **out**) to show to be true, confirm. * *vi* to be productive; (*with* **down**) to press or weigh down; to overwhelm; (*with* **on** *or* **upon**) to have reference to, be relevant to; (*with* **out**) to confirm the truth of; (*with* **up**) to endure with courage; (*with* **with**) to listen to patiently.

bear[2] *n* (*pl* **bears, bear**) a large mammal with coarse black, brown or white fur, short legs, strong claws and feeding mainly on fruit and insects; a gruff or ill-mannered person; a teddy bear; a speculator who sells stock in anticipation of a fall in price so that he may buy them back at a lower price.

bearable *adj* endurable.—**bearably** *adv*.

bear baiting *n* the former sport of setting dogs to attack captive bears.

beard *n* hair covering a man's chin; similar bristles on an animal or plant. * *vt* to defy, oppose openly.—**bearded** *adj*.

beardless *adj* without a beard; youthful.

bearer *n* a person who bears or presents; a person who carries something (a coffin, etc).

bear garden *n* (*formerly*) a place where bears were kept for sport; any scene or place of tumult or disorder.

bear hug *n* (*wrestling*) a hold in which the opponent's arms and chest are pinned in a tight embrace; any tight embrace.

bearing *n* demeanour; conduct; a compass direction; (*with* **on, upon**) relevance; a machine part on which another part slides, revolves, etc; (*usu pl*) one's position, orientation.

bearing rein *n* a short fixed rein for holding up the head of a horse.—*also* **checkrein**.

bearish *adj* resembling a bear in qualities; rude, surly.—**bearishly** *adv*.—**bearishness** *n*.

bear's breech *n* one of two tall plants of the acanthus genus with purple-tinged white flowers.

bear's ear *see* **auricula**.

bearskin *n* the skin of a bear used as a garment, rug, etc; a tall furry cap worn by a guardsman in the British army.

beast *n* a large, wild, four-footed animal; a brutal, vicious person; (*inf*) something difficult, an annoyance.

beastings *see* **beestings**.

beastly *adj* (**beastlier, beastliest**) (*inf*) disagreeable. * *adv* (*inf*) very (*beastly cold*).

beat *vb* (**beating, beaten**, *pp* **beat**) *vt* to strike, dash or pound repeatedly; to flog; to overcome or counteract; to win against, to arrive first; to find too difficult for; (*mus*) to mark (time) with a baton, etc; (*eggs, etc*) to mix by stirring vigorously; (*esp wings*) to move up and down; (*a path, way, etc*) to form by repeated trampling; (*sl*) to baffle; (*with* **up**) (*inf*) to cause grievous bodily harm to by severe and repeated blows and kicks. * *vi* to hit, pound, etc repeatedly; to throb; (*naut*) to sail against the wind. * *n* a recurrent stroke, pulsation, as in a heartbeat or clock ticking; rhythm in music or poetry; the area patrolled by a police officer.—**beatable** *adj*.

beaten *adj* defeated; (*metal*) shaped or formed by pounding; (*a path*) formed by constant trampling.

beater *n* an implement for beating, such as an attachment for an electric food mixer; one who rouses game birds from cover.

beatific *adj* showing great happiness; making blessed.—**beatifically** *adv*.

beatify *vt* (**beatifying, beatified**) (*RC Church*) to declare that one who has died is among the blessed in heaven; to make blissfully happy.—**beatification** *n*.

beating *n* the act of striking or thrashing; throbbing or pulsation; a defeat.

beatitude *n* blessedness; heavenly happiness; (*with cap*) (*Bible*) one of Christ's eight sayings in the Sermon on the Mount (Matthew 5).

beau *n* (*pl* **beaus, beaux**) a woman's suitor or sweetheart.

Beaufort scale *n* an international system of indicating wind strength, from 0 (calm) to 12 (hurricane).

beau geste *n* (*pl* **beaux gestes**) a fine gesture; a gesture that appears noble but is meaningless.

beau ideal *n* (*pl* **beaux ideals**) ideal excellence, a standard of perfection.

beaujolais *n* (*often with cap*) a popular fruity red or white wine from Burgundy in France.

beau monde *n* the fashionable world.

beaut *adj* (*sl*) good. * *n* (*sl*) beauty.

beauteous *adj* (*poet*) beautiful.

beautician *n* one who works in a beauty salon offering cosmetic treatments.

beautiful *adj* having beauty; very enjoyable.—**beautifully** *adv*.

beautify *vti* (**beautifying, beautified**) to make or become beautiful.—**beautification** *n*.

beauty *n* (*pl* **beauties**) the combination of qualities in a person or object that cause delight or pleasure; a very attractive woman or girl; good looks; a very fine specimen.

beauty salon, beauty parlour, beauty shop *n* an establishment that offers cosmetic beauty treatments.

beauty sleep *n* sleep taken before midnight, supposed to be more restorative than that taken later.

beauty spot *n* a scenic location; a small birthmark or artificial patch on the cheek, regarded as a mark of beauty.

beaver¹ *n* a large semi-aquatic dam-building rodent; its fur; a hat made from beaver fur. * *vi* (*often with* **away**) to work hard (at).

beaver² *n* the lower or moveable part of a helmet's face guard.

bebop *see* bop.

becalm *vt* to make calm; to make (a ship) motionless from lack of wind.—**becalmed** *adj*.

became *see* become.

because *conj* since; for the reason that.

because of *prep* by reason of.

beccafico *n* (*pl* beccaficos) a small bird of the warbler family, eaten as a delicacy in Italy.

béchamel sauce *n* a thick, rich white sauce.

bêche-de-mer *n* (*pl* bêches-de-mer) the trepang, a sea slug dried and eaten as a food in China; a form of pidgin English used in the islands of the Pacific (— *also* beach-la-mar).

beck¹ *n* a wave or nod with the finger or head.

beck² *n* a brook, a mountain stream.

becket *n* (*naut*) a rope loop, a hook, or a bracket for securing sails, tackle, etc.

beckon *vti* to summon by a gesture.—**beckoner** *n*.— **beckoning** *adj*.

becloud *vt* to obscure by clouds, to dim.

become *vb* (**becoming, became,** *pp* **become**) *vi* to come or grow to be. * *vt* to be suitable for.

becoming *adj* appropriate; seemly; suitable to the wearer.—**becomingly** *adv*.

becquerel *n* the SI unit of radiation activity.

bed *n* a piece of furniture for sleeping on; the mattress and covers for this; a plot of soil where plants are raised; the bottom of a river, lake, etc; any flat surface used as a foundation; a stratum. * *vt* (**bedding, bedded**) to put to bed; to embed; to plant in a bed of earth; to arrange in layers.

BEd *abbr* = Bachelor of Education.

bed and breakfast *n* overnight accommodation and breakfast the following morning, as offered in hotels and guesthouses, etc.—**bed-and-breakfast** *adj*.

bedaub *vt* to smear all over.

bedbug *n* a bloodsucking wingless insect that infests dirty bedding.

bedchamber *n* a bedroom.

bedclothes *npl* sheets, blankets, etc for a bed.

bedding *n* bedclothes; litter (straw, etc) for animals; a bottom layer, foundation.

bedding plant *n* a young plant suitable for a garden bed.

bedeck *vt* to cover with finery, to adorn.

bedevil *vt* (**bedevilling, bedevilled** *or* **bedeviling, bedeviled**) to plague or bewilder.—**bedevilment** *n*.

bedew *vt* to moisten, to sprinkle.

bedfellow *n* a sharer of a bed; an associate, ally, etc, esp a temporary one.

bedim *vt* (**bedimming, bedimmed**) to make dim.

bedizen *vt* to adorn or dress gaudily.—**bedizenment** *n*.

bedlam *n* (*arch*) a madhouse; uproar.

Bedouin *n* (*pl* **Bedouins, Bedouin**) an Arab desert nomad; a gypsy.

bedpan *n* a vessel used as a lavatory by a bedridden person; a warming pan.

bedplate *n* the base plate or frame or platform on which a machine is fixed.

bedraggle *vt* to make untidy or dirty by dragging in the wet or dirt.—**bedraggled** *adj*.

bedridden *adj* confined to bed through illness.

bedrock *n* solid rock underlying soil, etc; the base or bottom; fundamentals.

bedroom *n* a room for sleeping in. * *adj* suggestive of sexual relations; (*area, suburb, etc*) inhabited by commuters.

bedside *n* the space beside a bed. * *adj* situated or conducted at the bedside; suitable for someone bedridden.

bedsitter, bedsit, bedsitting room *n* a single room with sleeping and cooking facilities.

bedsore *n* an ulcerous sore caused by pressure, common in bedridden persons.

bedspread *n* a covering for a bed, usu decorative.

bedstead *n* a frame for the spring and mattress of a bed.

bedstraw *n* a plant of the madder family used formerly as straw for stuffing beds.

bee¹ *n* a social, stinging four-winged insect that is often kept in hives to make honey; any of numerous insects that also feed on pollen and nectar and are related to wasps.

bee² *n* a social meeting for work on behalf of a neighbour or a charitable object.

bee³ *n* (*naut*) strips of wood bolted each side of a bowsprit, through which the fore topmast stays are reeved.

beebread *n* a brown bitter substance consisting of the pollen of flowers collected and stored by bees as food for larvae.

beech *n* a tree with smooth silvery-grey bark; its wood.

beechmast *n* beechnuts collectively.

beechnut *n* the triangular nut of the beech, which yields an oil.

bee-eater *n* any of the numerous species of bee-eating birds.

beef *n* (*pl* **beefs**) the meat of a full-grown cow, steer, etc; (*inf*) muscular strength; (*inf*) a complaint, grudge; (*pl* **beeves**) cows, ox, steers, etc bred for their meat. * *vt* (*with* **up**) to add weight, strength or power to.

beefburger *n* a flat grilled or fried cake of minced beef.

beefcake *n* (*sl*) muscular men displayed provocatively, esp in photographs.

beefeater *n* an eater of beef; (*inf*) in UK, a yeoman of the royal guard, attending the sovereign on state occasions.

beef tea *n* stewed beef juice.

beefy *adj* (**beefier, beefiest**) brawny, muscular.

beehive *n* a container for keeping honeybees; a scene of crowded activity.

beekeeper *n* one who keeps bees for producing honey.—**beekeeping** *n*.

beeline *n* the straight course pursued by a bee returning laden to the hive; a direct line or course.

Beelzebub *n* the devil, Satan; a fallen angel, next in power to Satan.

bee moth *n* a moth that lays its eggs in beehives, and whose larvae feed upon the wax.

been *see* be.

beep *n* the brief, high-pitched sound of a horn or electronic signal. * *vti* to make or cause to make this sound.

beer *n* an alcoholic drink made from malt, sugar, hops and water fermented with yeast.

beery *adj* (**beerier, beeriest**) smelling or tasting of beer.

beestings *npl* the first milk given by a cow after calving.—*also* **biestings, beastings**.

beeswax *n* wax secreted by bees, refined and used for polishing.

beeswing *n* a gauze-like crust that occurs in port and some other wines, indicative of age.

beet *n* a red, edible root used as a vegetable, in salads, etc; a source of sugar.

beetle[1] *n* any of an order of insects having hard wing covers.

beetle[2] *n* a heavy wooden mallet for driving wedges, etc; a club for beating linen, etc, in washing. * *vt* to use a beetle on; to beat with a heavy wooden mallet.

beetle[3] *vi* to be prominent; to jut out, overhang, as a cliff.—**beetling** *adj*.

beetroot *n* (*pl* **beetroot**) the fleshy root of beet used as a vegetable, in salads, etc.—*also* **red beet**.

beeves *see* **beef**.

beezer *n* (*sl*) a fellow; (*sl*) a nose.

befall *vti* (**befalling**, **befell**, *pp* **befallen**) to happen or occur to.

befit *vt* (**befitting**, **befitted**) to be suitable or appropriate for; to be right for.—**befittingly** *adv*.

befog *vt* (**befogging**, **befogged**) to involve in a fog, to confuse.

befool *vt* to make a fool of.

before *prep* ahead of; in front of; in the presence of; preceding in space or time; in preference to; rather than. * *adv* beforehand; previously; until now. * *conj* earlier than the time that; rather than.

beforehand *adv* ahead of time; in anticipation.

befoul *vt* to make foul, to soil.—**befouler** *n*.—**befoulment** *n*.

befriend *vt* to be a friend to, to favour.

befuddle *vt* to confuse, stupefy, often with drink.

beg *vti* (**begging**, **begged**) to ask for money or food; to ask earnestly; to implore.

began *see* **begin**.

beget *vt* (**begetting**, **begot** *or* **begat**, *pp* **begotten** *or* **begot**) to become the father of; to cause.—**begetter** *n*.

beggar *n* a person who begs or who lives by begging; a pauper; (*inf*) a person. * *vt* to reduce to poverty; (*description*) to render inadequate.

beggarly *adj* like, or in the condition of, a beggar; poor; mean, contemptible.—**beggarliness** *n*.

beggary *n* the state of a beggar; extreme poverty; beggars collectively.

begin *vti* (**beginning**, **began**, *pp* **begun**) to start doing, acting, etc; to originate.

beginner *n* one who has just started to learn or do something; a novice.

beginning *n* source or origin; commencement.

begird *vt* (**begirding**, **begirded** *or* **begirt**) to gird round, to encompass, surround.

begone *interj* go away! be off!

begonia *n* a tropical plant cultivated for its showy petalless flowers and ornamental lopsided leaves.

begorra *interj* by God.

begot, **begotten** *see* **beget**.

begrime *vt* to make grimy, to soil deeply.

begrudge *vt* to grudge; to envy.—**begrudgingly** *adv*.

beguile *vt* (**beguiling**, **beguiled**) to cheat or deceive; to charm; to fascinate.—**beguilement** *n*. —**beguiler** *n*.—**beguilingly** *adv*.

beguine *n* a West Indian dance in bolero rhythm; the music for this.

begum *n* a Muslim queen or lady of high rank.

begun *see* **begin**.

behalf *n* **in** *or* **on behalf of** in the interest of; for.

behave *vti* to act in a specified way; to conduct (oneself) properly.

behaviour, **behavior** *n* way of behaving; conduct or action.—**behavioural**, **behavioral** *adj*.

behaviourism, **behaviorism** *n* the doctrine that human action is governed by external stimuli.—**behaviourist**, **behaviorist** *adj*, *n*.—**behaviouristic**, **behavioristic** *adj*.

behead *vt* to cut the head off.

beheld *see* **behold**.

behemoth *n* (*Bible*) an enormous animal described in Job, possibly the hippopotamus.

behest *n* a command; a precept.

behind *prep* at the rear of; concealed by; later than; supporting. * *adv* in the rear; slow; late.

behindhand *adj*, *adv* late, in arrears.

behold *vb* (**beholding**, **beheld**) *vt* to look at; to observe. * *vi* to see.—**beholder** *n*.

beholden *adj* indebted to; bound under an obligation.

behoof *n* advantage; interest; profit; use; behalf.

behove, **behoove** *vt* to be necessary or fit for, to be incumbent.

beige *n* a very light brown.

being *n* life; existence; a person or thing that exists; nature or substance.

bejewel *vt* (**bejewelling**, **bejewelled** *or* **bejeweling**, **bejeweled**) to ornament or furnish with jewels.

bel *n* a unit equal to 10 decibels.

belabour, **belabor** *vt* to beat soundly, to thump; to criticize severely.

belated *adj* coming late.—**belatedly** *adv*.

belay *vti* (**belaying**, **belayed**) to secure (a rope) by winding it round a spike, piton; to secure by a rope.

belch *vti* to expel gas from the stomach by the mouth; to eject violently from inside.—*also* *n*.

beleaguer *vt* to besiege, to blockade; to harass.

belemnite *n* a pointed fossil internal bone or shell of an extinct family of cuttlefish.

bel esprit *n* (*pl* **beaux esprits**) a person of wit or genius.

belfry *n* (*pl* **belfries**) the upper part of a tower, in which bells are hung.

Belgian *adj* of or pertaining to Belgium or its inhabitants. * *n* a native or inhabitant of Belgium.

Belial *n* a demon or devil; a fallen angel.

belie *vt* (**belying**, **belied**) to show to be a lie; to misrepresent; to fail to live up to (a hope, promise).—**belier** *n*.

belief *n* a principle or idea considered to be true; religious faith.

believe *vt* to accept as true; to think; to be convinced of. * *vi* to have religious faith.—**believable** *adj*.—**believer** *n*.

believing *adj* trustful.

belittle *vt* (*a person*) to make feel small; to disparage.—**belittlement** *n*.—**belittler** *n*.—**belittlingly** *adv*.

bell[1] *n* a hollow metal object which rings when struck; anything bell-shaped; the sound made by a bell.

bell[2] *n* the cry of a stag in rut. * *vi* to make this cry.

belladonna *n* the deadly nightshade plant, whose flowers, leaves and stalk are poisonous.

bellbird *n* an American bird whose note resembles a bell; an Australian bird with a similar call.

bell buoy *n* a buoy with a warning bell activated by wave movement.

belle *n* a pretty woman or girl.

belles-lettres *n* (*used as sing*) artistic literature, including poetry, essays, etc.—**belletrist** *n*.—**belletristic** *adj*.

bellfounder *n* a person who casts bells.—**bellfoundry** *n*.

bellhop, bellboy *n* one who carries luggage, runs errands, etc in a hotel or club.

bellicose *adj* war-like; ready to fight.—**bellicosity** *n*.

belligerent *adj* at war; of war; war-like; ready to fight or quarrel.—**belligerence** *n*.—**belligerently** *adv*.

bell jar *n* a protective glass cover in the shape of a bell.

bellman *n* (*pl* **bellmen**) one who uses a bell for public announcement, a town crier.

bell metal *n* an alloy of copper and tin, used for the manufacture of bells.

bellow *vi* to roar; to make an outcry. * *vt* to utter loudly. * *n* the roar of a bull; any deep roar.

bellows *n* (*used as pl or sing*) a device for creating and directing a stream of air by compression of its collapsible sides.

bellpull *n* a rope or handle for a bell.

bell punch *n* a punch with a signal bell used for punching tickets and checking the number of fares issued.

bellpush *n* a button that operates a bell.

bellwether *n* the leading sheep of a flock with a bell round its neck.

belly *n* (*pl* **bellies**) the lower part of the body between the chest and the thighs; the abdomen; the stomach; the underside of an animal's body; the deep interior, as of a ship. * *vti* (**bellying, bellied**) to swell out; to bulge.

bellyache *n* (*inf*) a pain in the stomach. * *vi* (*sl*) to complain constantly.

bellyband *n* a band that encircles the belly of a horse, a saddle girth.

bellybutton *n* (*inf*) the navel.

belly dance *n* a solo dance performed by a woman with sinuous, provocative movements of the belly and hips.—**belly dancer** *n*.

belly-flop *vt* (**belly-flopping, belly-flopped**) to dive in such a way that the body lands almost flat against the water.—**belly flop** *n*.

bellyful *n* (*sl*) as much as one can tolerate of something.

belong *vi* to have a proper place; to be related (to); (*with* **to**) to be a member; to be owned; (*inf*) to fit in socially.

belongings *npl* personal effects, possessions.

beloved *adj* dearly loved. * *n* one who is dearly loved.

below *prep* lower than; unworthy of. * *adv* in or to a lower place; south of; beneath; later (in a book, etc).

belt *n* a band of leather, etc worn around the waist; any similar encircling thing; a belt as an award for skill, eg in boxing, judo; a continuous moving strap passing over pulleys and so driving machinery; a distinctive region or strip; (*sl*) a hard blow. * *vt* to surround, attach with a belt; to thrash with a belt; (*sl*) to deliver a hard blow; (*sl*) to hurry; (*with* **out**) (*sl*) to sing or play loudly; (*with* **up**) to fasten with a belt. * *vi* (*with* **up**) (*inf*) to wear a seat belt; (*sl:often imper*) to be quiet.

Beltane *n* a Celtic festival formerly observed in Scotland on old May Day and in Ireland on June 21 by the kindling of huge bonfires.

beluga *n* a large sturgeon; its caviar; a white whale.

belvedere *n* a raised turret or summerhouse for viewing scenery.

bema *n* the inner part of the chancel in a Greek church; a speaker's platform; a platform in a synagogue from which services are led.

bemire *vt* to soil with mire; to be stuck in mud.

bemoan *vti* to lament.

bemuse *vt* to muddle; to preoccupy.—**bemused** *adj*.—**bemusement** *n*.

ben *n* (*Scot*) a mountain.

bench *n* a long hard seat for two or more persons; a long table for working at; the place where judges sit in a court of law; the status of a judge; judges collectively; (*sport*) the place where reserves, etc, sit during play.

bench mark *n* a surveyor's mark for making measurements; something that serves as a standard.

bencher *n* one who sits on a bench; in UK, a senior member of an Inn of Court, one of a group that has the government of the society.

bench warrant *n* a warrant issued by a court or judge for someone's arrest.

bend *vb* (**bending, bent**) *vt* to form a curve; to make crooked; to turn, esp from a straight line; to adapt to one's purpose, distort. * *vi* to turn, esp from a straight line; to yield from pressure to form a curve; (*with* **over** *or* **down**) to curve the body; to give in. * *n* a curve, turn; a bent part; (*pl: used as sing or pl*) decompression sickness in divers.—**bendable** *adj*.

bend sinister *n* (*her*) a bar or band drawn from the upper corner of the shield at the left (sinister) to the opposite base at the right (dexter), a sign of illegitimacy.

bender *n* one who or that which bends; (*sl*) a bout of drinking.

beneath *prep* underneath; below; unworthy. * *adv* in a lower place; underneath.—*also adj*.

benedict *n* a newly married man, esp if previously a confirmed bachelor.

benedicite *n* a blessing, a grace; (*with cap*) a Christian hymn or canticle sung at morning prayer when the Te Deum is not used.

Benedictine *adj* of or relating to the order of St Benedict. * *n* a monk of the Benedictine order; a kind of liqueur made from herbs and spices.

benediction *n* a blessing; an invocation of a blessing, esp at the end of a church service.—**benedictory** *adj*.

Benedictus *n* the Song of Zacharias (Luke 1) used as a canticle after the second lesson at morning prayer when the Jubilate is not sung.

benefaction *n* the act of doing good; the money or help given.

benefactor *n* a patron.—**benefactress** *nf*.

benefice *n* a church office yielding an income to a clergyman.

beneficence *n* active kindness, the act of doing good; benefaction.

beneficent *adj* generous; conferring blessings.—**beneficence** *n*.—**beneficently** *adv*.

beneficial *adj* advantageous.—**beneficially** *adv*.

beneficiary *n* (*pl* **beneficiaries**) a person who receives or will receive benefit, as from a will, etc.

benefit *n* advantage; anything contributing to improvement; (*often pl*) allowances paid by a government, insurance company, etc; a public performance, bazaar, etc, the proceeds of which are to help some person or cause. * *vb* (**benefiting, benefited**) *vt* to help. * *vi* to receive advantage.

benefit of clergy *n* a sanctioning by the church; (*hist*) exemption from trial by a secular court.

benefit society, benefit association *n* an association for mutual insurance against sickness, etc.

benevolence *n* inclination to do good; kindness; generosity; (*formerly*) a royal tax levied under the guise of a gratuity to the sovereign.—**benevolent** *adj*.—**benevolently** *adv*.

Bengali *n* a native or inhabitant of the Bengal province of India; the language spoken in Bengal. * *adj* of or pertaining to Bengal, its inhabitants or language.

Bengal light n a firework used also for signals, giving a steady bright blue light.

benighted adj overtaken by night; in moral darkness or ignorance.

benign adj favourable; kindly; gentle or mild; (med) not malignant.—**benignly** adv.

benignant adj kind; benign.—**benignancy** n.

benignity n (pl **benignities**) kindliness.

benison n (arch) a benediction or blessing.

benne n the sesame, an Asian annual cultivated for its seeds, which yield a valuable oil.

bent[1] see **bend**.

bent[2] n aptitude; inclination of the mind. * adj curved or crooked; (with on) strongly determined; (sl) dishonest; sexually deviant.

bent[3] n a kind of coarse stiff grass; a withered grass stalk; a heath.

benthos n the flora and fauna at the bottom of the sea; the sea bottom itself.—**benthic, benthonic** adj.

bentwood adj (furniture) made of wood that is bent and shaped by heat.

benumb vt to make numb.—**benumbed** adj.

benzene n a mixture of hydrocarbons from petroleum used as a solvent, in the manufacture of plastics, and as motor fuel.

benzine, benzol n a volatile mixture of lighter hydrocarbons from petroleum, used as a solvent and as motor fuel.

benzoin n a resin of the benjamin tree of Sumtra, used chiefly in cosmetics, perfumes and incense.—**benzoic** adj.

bequeath vt (property, etc) to leave by will; to pass on to posterity.—**bequeathal** n.—**bequeather** n.

bequest n act of bequeathing; something that is bequeathed, a legacy.

berate vt to scold severely.

berberine n an alkaloid used in dyeing and medicine, and obtained as a bitter yellow substance from the barberry and other plants.

berceuse n (pl **berceuses**) a cradle song; a tender or soothing musical composition.

bereave vt to deprive (of) a loved one through death.—**bereaved** adj.—**bereavement** n.

bereft adj deprived; bereaved.

beret n a flat, round, brimless, soft cap.

berg n an iceberg.

bergamot n a variety of lemon, the rind of which yields a valuable oil used in perfumery; the oil of the bergamot; a variety of pear; a variety of mint; a coarse kind of tapestry.

bergschrund n a crevasse between a glacier and the side of its valley.

beriberi n a disease of the nervous system, due to lack of vitamin B.

berkelium n a radioactive metallic element derived from americium.

berlin n a fine dyed knitting wool; an 18th-century four-wheeled carriage with a hood behind.

berm, berme n a ledge between a ditch and rampart; a narrow shelf along a slope; a shoulder of a road.

Bermuda grass n a valuable variety of pasture grass.

Bermuda-rigged adj (naut) rigged with a high tapering mainsail.

Bermuda shorts npl close-fitting knee-length shorts.

berry n (pl **berries**) any small, juicy, stoneless fruit (eg blackberry, holly berry). * vti (**berrying, berried**) to bear, produce or gather berries.

berserk adj frenzied; destructively violent.—also adv.

berth n a place in a dock for a ship at mooring; a built-in bed, as in a ship or train; (inf) a job. * vt to put into or furnish with a berth; to moor a ship. * vi to occupy a berth.

bertha n a wide lace collar.

Bertillon system n a method of identifying criminals by body measurements.

beryl n a (usu green) precious stone.

beryllium n a hard lightweight silvery-white metallic element used in making alloys.

beseech vt (**beseeching, beseeched** or **besought**) to implore, to entreat; to beg earnestly for.

beset vt (**besetting, beset**) to surround or hem in; to attack from all sides; to harass.

besetting adj constantly harassing.

beside prep at, by the side of, next to; in comparison with; in addition to; aside from; **beside oneself** extremely agitated.

besides prep other than; in addition; over and above. * adv in addition; also; except for that mentioned; moreover.

besiege vt to hem in with armed forces; to close in on; to overwhelm, harass, etc.

besmear vt to smear with sticky stuff; to soil.

besmirch vt to sully; to make dirty, to soil.

besom n a broom made of twigs; (Scot) a naughty or silly woman.

besotted adj muddled with drunkenness or infatuation; dull, stupid.—**besottedly** adv.

besought see **beseech**.

bespangle vt to adorn with spangles; to dot or sprinkle with something that glitters.

bespatter vt to soil by spattering; to spot with mud; to asperse with calumny.

bespeak vt (**bespeaking, bespoke**, pp **bespoken** or **bespoke**) to speak for beforehand; to order or arrange in advance; to be evidence of; to indicate, as by signs or marks.

bespoke adj (clothes) custom-made; (tailor) making such clothes.

besprent adj (poet) sprinkled; scattered.

besprinkle vt to sprinkle over (with).

best adj (superl of **good**) most excellent; most suitable, desirable, etc; largest; above all others. * n one's utmost effort; the highest state of excellence. * adv (superl of **well**) in or to the highest degree. * vt to defeat, outdo.

bestial adj brutal; savage.—**bestially** adv.

bestiality n (pl **bestialities**) brutal or brutish behaviour; a brutal or savage action or practice; sexual intercourse by a person with an animal.

bestialize vt to make like a beast; to degrade to the level of a brute.

bestiary n (pl **bestiaries**) a medieval treatise on beasts.

bestir vt (**bestirring, bestirred**) to put into brisk or vigorous action; to rouse, exert (oneself).

best man n the principal attendant of the bridegroom at a wedding.

bestow vt to present as a gift or honour.--**bestowal** n.—**bestower** n.

bestrew vt (**bestrewing, bestrewed**, pp **bestrewed** or **bestrewn**) to strew or scatter over; to lie scattered over.

bestride vt (**bestriding, bestrode**, pp **bestridden**) to stand, sit on or mount with the legs astride.

best seller n a book or other commodity that sells in vast numbers; the author of such a book.—**best-selling** adj.

bet n a wager or stake; the thing or sum staked; a person or thing likely to bring about a desired result; (inf) belief, opinion. * vti (**betting, bet** or **betted**) to declare as in a bet; to stake (money, etc) in a bet (with someone).

beta n the second letter of the Greek alphabet; (astron) the second star in a constellation; (chem) the second of two or more isomerous modifications of the same compound; (biol) the second subspecies or permanent variety of a species.

beta blocker n a drug that subdues cardiac activity, used in the treatment of high blood pressure.

betake vt (**betaking, betook,** pp **betaken**) to have recourse (to), to resort; to take oneself (to), to go.

beta particle n an electron or positron ejected from the nucleus of an atom during radioactive disintegration.

beta ray n a stream of penetrating rays emitted by radioactive substances.

beta wave n an electrical rhythm of the brain associated with normal waking consciousness.

betel n an Asian pepper, the leaves of which are mixed with betel nuts and chewed as a stimulant or narcotic.

betel nut n the seed of the betel palm.

betel palm n a palm tree of tropical Asia with feathery leaves and scarlet or orange fruit.

bête noir n (pl **bêtes noires**) pet hate.

bethel n a hallowed spot; a seamen's church; in UK, a nonconformist chapel.

betide vt to happen to, to befall. * vi to come to pass.

betimes adv (arch) in good time; before it is too late; early; soon.

bêtise n folly; an ill-chosen remark.

betoken vt to signify, to indicate by signs; to augur, to foreshadow.

betony n (pl **betonies**) a purple-flowered woodland plant formerly used in medicine and as a dye.

betook see betake.

betray vt to aid an enemy; to expose treacherously; to be a traitor to; to reveal unknowingly.—**betrayal** n.—**betrayer** n.

betroth vt to promise in marriage.

betrothal n the state of being engaged to marry; a mutual promise for future marriage made between a man and a woman.

betrothed adj affianced, engaged to be married. * n a fiancé or fiancée.

better[1] adj (compar of **good**) more excellent; more suitable; improved in health; larger. * adv (compar of **well**) in a more excellent manner; in a higher degree; more. * n a person superior in position, etc; a more excellent thing, condition, etc. * vt to outdo; to surpass.

better[2] n someone who bets.

betterment n an improvement.

between prep the space, time, etc separating (two things); (bond, etc) connecting from one or the other.

betweentimes, betweenwhiles adv at or during intervals.

betwixt prep between; in the space that separates.

bevel n an angle other than a right angle; the inclination that one surface makes with another when not at right angles; a tool for setting of angles. * vb (**bevelling, bevelled** or **beveling, beveled**) vt to cut on the slant. * vi to slant or incline.

bevel gear n a gear in which the axis or shaft of the driving wheel forms an angle with the shaft of the wheel driven.

beverage n a drink, esp one other than water.

bevy n (pl **bevies**) a flock of quails; a large group (esp of girls).

bewail vt to mourn or weep aloud for, to lament. * vi to express grief.—**bewailer** n.—**bewailing** n.

beware vti to be wary or careful (of).

bewilder vt to perplex; to confuse hopelessly.—**bewilderingly** adv.—**bewilderment** n.

bewitch vt to cast a spell over; to fascinate or enchant.

bewitching adj fascinating, enchanting, captivating, alluring.—**bewitchingly** adv.

bey n a Turkish title of respect; a title similar to Mr; (formerly) a governor of a province or district in the Turkish dominions.

beyond prep further on than; past; later than; outside the reach of (beyond help). * adv further away. * n (with the) life after death.

bezant n a gold coin of Byzantium or Constantinople, issued in the Middle Ages and current in Europe until the fall of the Eastern Empire, 1472; (her) a small circle of gold representing the coin.

bezel n the sloping edge of a chisel; the rim that holds a gem in its setting; the groove in which the glass of a watch is fitted.

bezique n a game of cards for two, three, and four persons using two decks of cards with sixes and cards below omitted.

bezoar n a calcareous concretion found in the intestines of certain animals.

bhang n the dried leaves of Indian hemp, chewed or smoked as an intoxicant or narcotic, hashish.—also **bang**.

bhp abbr = brake horsepower.

bi- prefix having two; doubly; happening twice during; every two; using two or both; joining or involving two; having twice the amount of acid or base.

Bi (chem symbol) bismuth.

biannual adj occurring twice a year.—**biannually** adv.

bias n a slanting or diagonal line, cut or sewn across the grain in cloth; a weight inside a bowl in a game of bowls slanting its course when rolled; partiality; prejudice. * vt (**biasing, biased** or **biassing, biassed**) to prejudice.

biathlon n (sport) an athletic event combining cross-country skiing and rifle shooting.

biauriculate, biauricular adj having two auricles, as the heart of the higher vertebrates; (bot) having two earlike projections at the base, as a leaf.

biaxial adj having two (optic) axes.—**biaxially** adv.

bib[1] n a cloth or plastic cover tied around a baby or child to prevent food spillage on clothes; the upper part of dungarees or an apron.

bib[2] vi (**bibbing, bibbed**) (arch) to drink, to tipple.

bib[3] n a kind of fish, whiting pout.

bibelot n a trinket, a knickknack.

Bible n the sacred book of the Christian Church; the Old and New Testaments; (without cap) an authoritative book on a particular subject.

biblical adj of or referring to the Bible.—**biblically** adv.

Biblicist n a biblical scholar; a fundamentalist.—**Biblicism** n.

biblio- prefix book or books.

bibliography n (pl **bibliographies**) a list of writings on a given subject or by a given author; the study of the history of books and book production. —**bibliogra-pher** *n*.—**bibliographic** *adj*.—**bibliographical** *adj*.

bibliolatry *n* book worship; excessive reverence for the letter of the Bible.—**bibliolater** *n*.—**bibliolatrous** *adj*.

bibliomania *n* a mania for acquiring rare and curious books.—**bibliomaniac** *adj, n*.

bibliophile, bibliophil *n* a book lover.—**bibliophilistic** *adj*.—**bibliophism** *n*.

bibliopole, bibliopolist *n* a bookseller, esp one who deals in rare works.—**bibliopolic** *adj*.—**bibliopoly** *n*.

bibliotheca *n* (*pl* **bibliothecas, bibliothecae**) a library; a list of books.

bibulous *adj* readily absorbing or imbibing fluids; spongy; addicted to drink.—**bibulously** *adv*.—**bibu-lousness** *n*.

bicameral *adj* (*legislature*) having two chambers.

bicarbonate *n* sodium bicarbonate.

bicentenary *adj* occurring every two hundred years. * *n* (*pl* **bicentenaries**) a two hundredth anniversary or its celebration.

bicentennial *adj* lasting or occurring every two hun-dred years. * *n* a bicentenary, the two hundredth an-niversary of an event, or its celebration.

bicephalous, bicephalic *adj* (*biol*) two-headed.

biceps *n* (*pl* **biceps, bicepses**) the muscle with two points of origin, esp the large muscle in the upper arm.

bichloride *n* (*chem*) a compound of two or more atoms of chlorine combined with a base; dichloride.

bicipital *adj* (*anat*) having two heads, as a biceps mus-cle; dividing into two parts at either extremity.

bicker *vi* to squabble, quarrel.—*also n*.—**bickerer** *n*.

bicoastal *adj* pertaining to both the west and east coasts of the United States.

biconcave *adj* hollow on both sides.—**biconcavity** *n*.

biconvex *adj* rounded on both sides.

bicorn, bicornuate *adj* having two horns.

bicuspid *adj* having two points or prominences (—*also* **bicuspidate**). * *n* one of the two double-pointed teeth forming the first pair of molars on either side of the jaw, above and below.

bicycle *n* a vehicle consisting of a metal frame on two wheels, driven by pedals and having handlebars and a seat. * *vti* to ride or travel on a bicycle.—**bicyclist, bicycler** *n*.

bid[1] *n* an offer of an amount one will pay or accept; (*cards*) a statement of the number of tricks that a player intends to win. * *vi* (**bidding, bid**) to make a bid.—**bidder** *n*.

bid[2] *vt* (**bidding, bade** *or* **bid**, *pp* **bidden** *or* **bid**) to com-mand or ask; to summon; (*farewell, etc*) to express.

biddable *adj* docile, obedient; worth bidding on.—**biddability** *n*.—**biddably** *adv*.

bidding *n* an order; command; an invitation; the act of offering a price at auction.

biddy[1] *n* (*pl* **biddies**) (*inf*) a woman, esp an old or med-dlesome one.

biddy[2] *n* (*pl* **biddies**) (*dial*) a fowl or chicken.

bide *vb* (**biding, bided** *or* **bode**) *vi* to wait; to dwell. * *vt* to endure, suffer; to wait for.

bidentate *adj* having two teeth, or two tooth-like proc-esses.

bidet *n* a low, bowl-shaped bathroom fixture with run-ning water for bathing the crotch and anus.

biennial *adj* lasting two years; occurring every two years. * *n* a plant that lasts for two years.—**biennially** *adv*.

bier *n* a portable framework on which a coffin is put.

biestings *see* **beestings**.

bifacial *adj* having two faces or fronts; (*leaves*) having upper and lower surfaces that are dissimilar; having opposite surfaces alike.

bifarious *adj* (*bot*) two-fold; two-rowed; pointing in two ways.

biff *n* (*sl*) a blow. * *vt* to hit, strike.

bifid *adj* divided by a deep cleft, partially divided into two.—**bifidity** *n*.—**bifidly** *adv*.

bifilar *adj* two-threaded; fitted with two threads.—**bifilarly** *adv*.

bifocal *adj* (*spectacles*) having two different focuses.

bifocals *npl* spectacles with bifocal lenses for near and distant vision.

bifoliate *adj* (*bot*) having two leaves.

bifurcate *vti* to divide into two branches.—**bifurcation** *n*.

big *adj* (**bigger, biggest**) large; of great size; important; influential; grown-up; pregnant; generous; boast-ful.—**bigness** *n*.

bigamist *n* a person guilty of bigamy.

bigamy *n* (*pl* **bigamies**) the act of marrying a second time when one is already legally married.—**biga-mous** *adj*.—**bigamously** *adv*.

big bang theory *n* (*astron*) the theory that the universe originated in a cataclysmic explosion and is still ex-panding.

big brother *n* an older brother; a person who fills that protective role; (*with caps*) a ruthless and sinister dic-tator, corporation, etc that wields absolute power.

big business *n* large corporations and enterprises col-lectively, esp when regarded as exploitative.

big cat *see* **cat**.

big deal *n* an important achievement. * *interj* (*sl*) an ex-pression of scorn or contempt.

big dipper *n* a roller coaster; (*with caps*) the seven main stars in the constellation Ursa Major.

big dry *n* a period of drought longer than normal.

big game *n* large animals or fish hunted for sport; an important, usu risky objective.

biggin[1] *n* a close-fitting child's hood or cap.

biggin[2] *n* a small building; a cottage.

bighead *n* (*inf*) a boastful or conceited person.—**big-headed** *adj*.

bighorn *n* (*pl* **bighorns, bighorn**) the wild sheep of the Rocky Mountains.

bight *n* a loop or bend of a rope, in distinction from the ends; a bend in a coastline forming an open bay; a small bay between two headlands.

bigmouth *n* (*inf*) a loud-mouthed, bragging or indis-creet person.

big name *n* a famous person, esp in entertainment.

bigot *n* an intolerant person who blindly supports a particular political view or religion.—**bigoted** *adj*.

bigotry *n* (*pl* **bigotries**) the state or condition of a nar-row-minded, intolerant person; blind and obstinate attachment to a particular creed, party or opinion; in-tolerance; fanaticism.

big screen *n* (*inf*) the cinema (industry).

big shot *n* (*inf*) an important person.

big stick *n* the threat of force.

big time *n* the top level in any profession.

big top *n* a large circus tent.

bigwig *n* (*inf*) an important person.

bijou *n* (*pl* **bijoux**) a jewel; any small and elegantly fin-ished article. * *adj* (*often derog*) small and elegant.

bijouterie n bijoux collectively, jewellery.

bijugate, bijugous adj (bot) having two pairs of leaflets; having two heads in profile, one of which overlaps the other.

bike n (inf) a bicycle; a motorcycle.

bikini n (pl **bikinis**) a scanty two-piece swimsuit for women.

bilabiate adj (bot) having two lips, as a flower.

bilateral adj having two sides; affecting two parties reciprocally.—**bilaterally** adv.

bilberry n (pl **bilberries**) an edible dark-blue berry.

bilbo n (pl **bilboes**) a rapier or sword; (pl) a long bar of iron with sliding shackles for the feet and a lock at the end, formerly used as fetters.

bile n a gall, a thick bitter fluid secreted by the liver; bad temper.

bilge n the lowest part of a ship's hull; filth that collects there.

bilge keel n a piece of timber secured edgeways under the bottom of a vessel to prevent heavy rolling.

bilge water n foul water in a ship's bilge.

bilharzia n a tropical disease caused by a parasitic worm.

biliary adj of or pertaining to the bile; conveying bile.

bilingual adj written in two languages; able to speak two languages.—**bilingualism** n.—**bilingually** adv.

bilious adj suffering from or caused by disorder of the bile; peevish.—**biliously** adv.—**biliousness** n.

bilirubin n an orange or yellow pigment in the bile.

biliverdin n a green pigment in the bile, the oxidized form of bilirubin.

bilk vt to deceive or defraud, as by evading a payment; to leave in the lurch; (cribbage) to spoil the score of an opponent. * n a swindler; the act of spoiling the score of an opponent at cribbage.—**bilker** n.

bill[1] n a bird's beak.

bill[2] n a statement for goods supplied or services rendered, the money due for this; a list, as a menu or theatre programme; a poster or handbill; a draft of a proposed law, to be discussed by a legislature; a bill of exchange; a piece of paper money; (law) a written declaration of charges and complaints filed. * vt to make out a bill of (items); to present a statement of charges to; to advertise by bills; (a performer) to book.

billabong n an Australian word for a pond or a stagnant pool connected to a river.

billboard n a large panel designed to carry outdoor advertising; a hoarding.

billet[1] n a written order to provide lodging for military personnel; the lodging; a position or job. * vt (**billeting, billeted**) to assign to lodging by billet.

billet[2] n a small stick or log of wood, as for fuel; (archit) a moulding ornament, resembling a billet of wood.

billet-doux n (pl **billets-doux**) a love letter.

bill fold n a notecase or wallet.

billhook n a small curved cutting tool with a hooked point.

billiards n a game in which hard balls are driven by a cue on a felt-covered table with raised, cushioned edges.

billing n the order in which actors' names are listed.

billingsgate n coarse or profane language; virulent abuse.

billion n (pl **billions, billion**) a thousand millions, the numeral 1 followed by 9 zeros; in UK, a million million, a trillion.—**billionaire** n.—**billionth** adj, n.

bill of exchange n a written order to pay a certain sum

of money to the person named.

bill of fare n a menu.

bill of health n a ship's certificate of health; a report on a situation or condition, usu favourable.

bill of lading n a receipt issued to a shipper by a carrier, listing the goods received for shipment.

bill of rights n a charter or summary of basic human rights.

bill of sale n a written statement transferring ownership by sale.

billon n an alloy of gold and silver, with a large proportion of copper or other base metal, used in coinage of low value.

billow n a large wave; any large swelling mass or surge, as of smoke. * vi to surge or swell in a billow.—**billowy** adj.

billposter n a person who pastes up bills.

billsticker n a billposter.

billy, billycan n (pl **billies, billycans**) (Austral) a can used as a kettle by campers.

billy-goat n a male goat.

bilobate, bilobed adj divided into two lobes or segments, with two lobes.

bilocular, biloculate adj divided into, or containing, two cells.

biltong n (S Africa) strips of meat, salted and dried in the sun.

bimanous adj (zool) having two hands.

bimbo n (pl **bimbos, bimboes**) (sl) an attractive, but brainless, young woman, often one who has an affair with a prominent person.

bimetallic adj of or containing two metals; of or based on bimetallism.

bimetallism n a monetary system using both gold and silver as a standard currency at a fixed relative value.—**bimetallist** n.

bimonthly adj every two months; loosely twice a month.

bin n a box or enclosed space for storing grain, coal, etc; a dustbin. * vt (**binning, binned**) to put or store in a bin; (inf) to discard, throw away.

binary adj made up of two parts; double; denoting or of a number system in which the base is two, each number being expressed by using only two digits, specifically 0 and 1.

binary star n a double star or sun whose members revolve round their common centre of gravity.

binate adj (bot) occurring or growing in pairs.—**binately** adv.

binaural adj of or used with both ears; (sound) transmitted from two sources.—**binaurally** adv.

bind vb (**binding, bound**) vt to tie together, as with rope; to hold or restrain; to encircle with a belt, etc; to fasten together the pages of (a book) and protect with a cover; to obligate by duty, love, etc; (with over) to compel, as by oath or legal restraint; (often with up) to bandage. * vi to become tight or stiff; to stick together; to be obligatory; (sl) to complain. * n anything that binds; (inf) a difficult situation.

binder n a folder for keeping loose papers together; a bookbinder; something used to bind; a sheaf-binding machine.

bindery n (pl **binderies**) a bookbinder's workshop.

binding n the covering of a book holding the pages together.

bindweed n a common name for twining plants belonging to the genus Convolvulus.

bine n the slender stem of a twining plant, esp hop; one of these plants.

binge n (inf) a heavy drinking session; immoderate indulgence in anything.

bingo n a game of chance in which players cover numbers on their cards according to the number called aloud. * interj, n a cry of delight, surprise or success.

binnacle n a turret-shaped box containing a ship's compass.

binocular adj for or using both eyes.

binoculars npl a viewing device for use with both eyes, consisting of two small telescope lenses joined together.

binomial n (math) an expression or quantity consisting of two terms connected by the sign plus (+) or minus (-). * adj consisting of two terms; pertaining to binomials; (biol) using two names, esp of classification by genus and species.—**binomially** adv.

binomial theorem n the general algebraic formula, discovered by Newton, by which any power of a binomial quantity may be found with performing the progressive multiplication.

binturong n a prehensile-tailed civet of India.

binucleate, binucleated, binuclear adj having two nuclei.

bio- prefix life.

biochemistry n the chemistry of living organisms.—**biochemical** adj.—**biochemist** n.

biodegradable adj readily decomposed by bacterial action.

bioengineering n the application of engineering principles in the biological and medical sciences.—**bioengineer** n.

biofeedback n the practice of monitoring and recording involuntary mental and physiological processes (eg brainwaves) in order to attempt to bring them under conscious control.

biogenesis n the theory that only living matter can produce living matter; the science of life development.—**biogenetic** adj.—**biogenetically** adv.

biography n (pl biographies) an account of a person's life written by another; biographical writings in general.—**biographer** n.—**biographical** adj.

biology n the study of living organisms.—**biological** adj.—**biologically** adv.—**biologist** n.

biometry, biometrics n (used as sing) the statistics of biology or probable duration of life.—**biometric, biometrical** adj.—**biometrically** adv.—**biometrician** n.

bionics n the study of electronically operated mechanical systems that function like living organisms.—**bionic** adj.

bionomics n (used as sing) ecology.—**bionomic, bionomical** adj.—**bionomist** n.

biophysics n the application of physics to biology.—**biophysical** adj.—**biophysicist** n.

bioplasm n living germinal matter, living protoplasm.—**bioplasmic** adj.

biopsy n (n biopsies) the removal of parts of living tissue for medical diagnosis.

biorhythm n a cyclical pattern in physiological activity said to determine a person's intellectual, emotional and physical moods and behaviour.—**biorhythmic** adj.

biosphere n the regions of the earth's surface and atmosphere inhabited by living things.

biosynthesis n (pl biosyntheses) the formation of chemical compounds by living organisms.—**biosynthetic** adj.—**biosynthetically** adv.

biotechnology n the commercial and industrial application of biological processes, such as the use of microorganisms to dye cloth.

biotic adj of life or specific life conditions.

biotin n a factor of the vitamin B group found in liver and egg yolk.

biparous adj producing two at once in time or place; (zool) producing two at a birth; (bot) having two branches.

bipartisan adj of, representing or supported by two political parties.—**bipartisanship** n.

bipartite adj having two parts; involving two.—**bipartition** n.

biped n an animal having two feet.—also adj.—**bipedal** adj.

bipinnate adj (bot) having lobes that are lobed themselves.—**bipinnately** adv.

biplane n an aeroplane with two sets of wings.

bipod n a stand with two legs for supporting a weapon, etc.

bipolar adj having two poles or opposite extremities; of or affecting both the earth's poles; having or expressing two directly opposite ideas or qualities.—**bipolarity** n.

biquadratic adj (math) pertaining to the fourth power. * n the fourth power, arising from the multiplication of a square number or quantity by itself.

birch n a tree with a smooth white bark and hard wood; a bundle of birch twigs used for thrashing. * vt to flog.—**birchen** adj.

bird n any class of warm-blooded, egg-laying vertebrates with a feathered body, scaly legs, and forelimbs modified to form wings; (sl) a woman; (sl) time in prison; **for the birds** useless, worthless, unimportant; **get** or **give the bird** (inf) to boo an entertainer off the stage.

birdbrain n (inf) a stupid or frivolous person.—**birdbrained** adj.

birdie n (inf) a small bird; (golf) a score of one stroke under par for a hole.

birdlime n a viscous substance used for snaring small birds; a thing that snares. * vt to smear or trap with birdlime.

bird of passage n a migratory bird; a transient person.

bird of prey n a meat-eating bird (as a hawk, owl, falcon, etc) that hunts other animals for food.

birdseed n a mixture of seeds for feeding wild or caged birds.

bird's-eye adj seen from above; dappled to resemble the eye of a bird. * n any of several plants with flowers resembling a bird's eye.

bird watcher n one who makes a study of birds in the wild.—**bird watching** n.

bireme n an ancient galley with two tiers of oars.

biretta n a square cap with three corners worn by Roman Catholic clergy.

Biro n (trademark) (pl Biros) a ball-point pen.

birr vi to make a whirring sound, like that of a spinning wheel. * n a whirring sound.

birth n the act of being born; childbirth; the origin of something; lineage, ancestry.

birth control n the use of contraceptive drugs or devices to limit reproduction.

birthday n the day of birth; the anniversary of the day of birth.

birthmark *n* a patch or blemish on the body dating from birth.

birth rate *n* the number of births per thousand of population per year.

birthright *n* privileges or property that a person is believed entitled to by birth.

birthstone *n* a gem symbolizing the month of one's birth.

bis *adv* twice; (*mus*) for a second time; encore.

biscuit *n* a small, flat, dry, sweet or plain cake baked from dough.—*also* **cookie**. * *adj* pale brown in colour.

bise *n* a piercing dry northeast wind prevalent in Switzerland.

bisect *vt* to split into two equal parts; (*geom*) to divide into two equal parts.—**bisection** *n*.

bisector *n* a line bisecting.

bisexual *adj* sexually attracted to both sexes; having the characteristics of both sexes. * *n* a person sexually attracted to both sexes.—**bisexualism, bisexuality** *n*.

bishop *n* a high-ranking clergyman governing a diocese or church district; a chessman that can move in a diagonal direction.

bishopric *n* the office, dignity or jurisdiction of a bishop; a diocese.

bismuth *n* one of the elements, a light reddish-coloured metal of brittle texture.—**bismuthal, bismuthic** *adj*.

bison *n* (*pl* **bison**) a wild ox of Europe and America.—*also* **buffalo**.

bisque[1] *n* a thick cream soup made from shellfish.

bisque[2] *n* an unglazed white porcelain, used for statuettes, etc, biscuit porcelain.

bisque[3] *n* (*croquet, tennis, golf*) a stroke allowed to an inferior player or side.

bissextile *n* a leap year. * *adj* pertaining to a leap year.

bister *see* **bistre**.

bistort *n* a herb with twisted roots, snakeweed.

bistoury *n* (*pl* **bistouries**) a surgeon's knife, a scalpel.

bistre *n* a warm brown pigment made from wood soot. * *adj* of this colour.—*also* **bister**.

bistro *n* (*pl* **bistros**) a small restaurant.

bisulcate *adj* having two furrows or grooves; cloven-footed.

bisulphate, bisulfate *n* a salt of sulphuric acid in which half of its hydrogen is replaced by a positive element.

bisulphite, bisulfite *n* a salt of sulphurous acid, half the hydrogen of which is replaced by the base.

bit[1] *n* a small amount or piece; in US, a small coin worth one eighth of a dollar; a small part in a play, film, etc, a bit part.—**a bit** slightly, rather.

bit[2] *n* a metal mouthpiece in a bridle used for controlling a horse; a cutting or boring attachment for use in a brace, drill, etc. * *vt* (**bitting, bitted**) to put a bridle upon; to put the bit in the mouth of.

bit[3] *n* (*comput*) a unit of information in binary notation equivalent to either of two digits, 0 or 1.

bit[4] *see* **bite**.

bitch *n* a female dog or wolf; (*sl*) a spiteful woman; (*inf*) an unpleasant or difficult situation. * *vi* (*inf*) to grumble; to act spitefully; (*with* **up**) to make a mess of, to ruin.

bite *vb* (**biting, bit, pp bitten**) *vt* to grip or tear with the teeth; to sting or puncture, as an insect; to cause to smart; to take the bait. * *vi* to press or snap the teeth (into, at, etc); (*with* **back**) to stop oneself from saying something offensive, embarrassing, etc. * *n* the act of biting with the teeth; a sting or puncture by an insect.

biting *adj* severe; critical, sarcastic.—**bitingly** *adv*.—**bitingness** *n*.

bit part *n* a small acting role in a play, film, etc.

bitt *n* (*usu pl*) (*naut*) a post of wood or iron to which cables are made fast. * *vt* to put round the bitts.

bitter *adj* having an acrid or sharp taste; sorrowful; harsh; resentful; cynical; (*weather*) extremely cold.—**bitterly** *adj*.—**bitterness** *n*.

bitter end *n* final extremity.

bittern[1] *n* a wading bird of the heron family, with a booming cry.

bittern[2] *n* the liquid that remains after cystallization of common salt from sea water or the brine of salt springs.

bitters *npl* liquor in which herbs or roots are steeped.

bittersweet *n* the woody nightshade, the roots and leaves of which when chewed produce first a bitter then a sweet taste; a variety of apple. * *adj* simultaneously sweet and bitter; pleasantly sad.

bituminize *vt* to make into or mix with bitumen.—**bituminization** *n*.

bitty *adj* (**bittier, bittiest**) small, tiny; made up of scraps of something.

bitumen *n* any of several substances obtained as residue in the distillation of coal tar, petroleum, etc, or occurring naturally as asphalt.—**bituminous** *adj*.

bivalent *adj* (*chem*) having a valency of two; (*genetics*) having two homologous chromosomes; (*logic*) having two truth values. * *n* an element, one of the atoms of which can replace two atoms of hydrogen; (*genetics*) a pair of homologous chromsomes.—**bivalency** *n*.

bivalve *n* any mollusc having two valves or shells hinged together, as a clam.—**bivalvular** *adj*.

bivouac *n* a temporary camp, esp one without tents or other cover. * *vi* (**bivouacking, bivouacked**) to spend the night in a bivouac.

biweekly *adj* every two weeks; twice a week. * *n* (*pl* **biweeklies**) a periodical published every two weeks.

bizarre *adj* odd, unusual.

Bk (*chem symbol*) berkelium.

blab *vti* (**blabbing, blabbed**) to reveal (a secret); to gossip. * *n* a gossip.—**blabber** *n*.

black *adj* of the darkest colour, like coal or soot; having dark-coloured skin and hair; without light; dirty; evil, wicked; sad, dismal; sullen; angry; (*coffee, etc*) without milk. * *n* black colour; (*often with cap*) a Negro, Australian Aborigine; black clothes, esp when worn in mourning; (*chess, draughts*) black pieces.—**in the black** without debts, in credit. * *vt* to make black; to blacken; (*shoes*) to polish with blacking; to boycott; (*with* **out**) (*lights*) to extinguish, obliterate; (*broadcast*) to prevent transmission. * *vi* (*with* **out**) to lose consciousness or vision.—**blackly** *adv*.—**blackness** *n*.

black-and-blue *adj* livid with bruises.

black and white *n* writing, print; a line drawing; a photograph not in colour. * *adj* black-and-white.

black-and-white *adj* (*film, photography*) in black and white, not colour; (*ideas, etc*) highly simplistic.

black art *n* black magic, witchcraft.

blackball *vt* to ostracize.

black belt *n* a black belt awarded to an expert of the highest skill in judo or karate; a person who holds a black belt.

blackberry *n* (*pl* **blackberries**) a woody bush with thorny stems and berry-like fruit; its black or purple edible fruit (—*also* **bramble**). * *vt* to gather blackberries.

blackbird *n* any of various birds, the male of which is almost all black.

blackboard n a black or dark green board written on with chalk.

black book n a record of offenders; **in someone's black books** in disfavour; **little black book** (sl) an address book with names and telephone numbers of women.

black box n a flight recorder on an aircraft.

black bread n rye bread.

black bryony n a European climbing plant with small green flowers and poisonous red berries.

blackcap n the popular name of several black-crested birds.

blackcock n the male of the European black grouse or black game.

black comedy n a comedy with a tragic theme.

Black Death n the name given to the bubonic plague that ravaged Europe and Asia in the 14th century.

black economy n undeclared economic activity.

blacken vt to make black; to defame.

black eye n (inf) discoloration around the eye caused by a blow; (sl) shame.

blackfish n (pl **blackfish**, **blackfishes**) a female salmon immediately after spawning; a common name for several species of British and American fish.

black flag n the flag of a pirate with a skull and crossbones emblazoned upon it.

blackfly n (pl **blackflies**) any of various dark insects, esp a North American fly that sucks the blood of mammals.

black frost n a severe frost without a rime that damages vegetation.

blackguard n a villain, scoundrel.—**blackguardism** n.—**blackguardly** adj.

blackhead n a small spot or pimple clogging a pore in the skin.

black hole n a hypothetical, invisible region in space.

black ice n a thin transparent coating of ice on roads or other surfaces.

blacking n black shoe polish.

blackish adj rather black.—**blackishly** adv.—**blackishness** n.

blackjack[1] n a gambling game with cards in which players try to obtain points better than the banker's but not more than 21.—also **pontoon**, **twenty-one**, **vingt-et-un**.

blackjack[2] n a large leather vessel or drinking cup; a short leather club with a flexible handle. * vt to hit with a blackjack.

blackjack (oak) n a dark shrubby oak of North America.

black lead n plumbago, graphite.

blackleg n a person who takes a striker's place, a scab; a person who endeavours to obtain money by cheating at races or cards, a rook; a disease affecting sheep and cattle. * vti (**blacklegging**, **blacklegged**) to act or injure, as a blackleg.

black letter n the old English or Gothic type used in early manuscripts and the first printed books. * adj written or printed in black letter.

blacklist n a list of those censored, refused employment, regarded as suspicious politically or generally not to be trusted. * vt to put on such a list.

black magic n sorcery, witchcraft.

blackmail vt to extort money by threatening to disclose discreditable facts. * n the crime of blackmailing.—**blackmailer** n.

Black Maria n a prison van, a patrol wagon.

black market n the illegal buying and selling of goods, esp banned goods, eg drugs, or when rationing is in force.—**black marketeer**, **black marketer** n.

black mass n a travesty of the Mass used by Satanists.

blackout n the darkness when all lights are switched off; temporary loss of consciousness or electricity; a breakdown of communications between a spacecraft and ground control; a closing down of radio or TV broadcasting due to strike action or government ban.

black power n a movement of black people whose goal is political, social and economic equality with whites.

black pudding n a dark sausage with a large proportion of blood.

Black Rod n in UK, the usher belonging to the order of the Garter and the House of Lords, so called from the black rod of the office.

black sheep n a person regarded as disreputable or a disgrace by their family.

Blackshirt n a fascist, esp a member of Mussolini's Italian Fascist party.

blacksmith n a metal worker, esp one who shoes horses.

black spot n an area where traffic accidents frequently happen; a difficult or dangerous place; a disease affecting leaves, esp of roses.

blackthorn n the sloe; a walking stick cut from the stem of the sloe.

black widow n a poisonous spider found in America, the female of which devours its mate.

bladder n a sac that fills with fluid, esp one that holds urine flowing from the kidneys; any inflatable bag.

bladderwort n any of a genus of water plants, some of which trap insects.

bladderwrack n a type of seaweed with trailing fronds containing small air bladders.

blade n the cutting edge of a tool or knife; the broad, flat surface of a leaf; a straight, narrow leaf of grass; the flat part of an oar or paddle; the runner of an ice skate.—**bladed** adj.

blah[1] n (sl) nonsense, exaggeration; a blunder.

blah[2] adj (sl) boring; mediocre.

blain n an inflamed sore, a blister.

blame vt to hold responsible for; to accuse. * n responsibility for an error; reproof.—**blamable**, **blameable** adj.

blameful adj meriting blame; guilty.—**blamefully** adv.—**blamefulness** n.

blameless adj innocent; free from blame.—**blamelessly** adv.—**blamelessness** n.

blameworthy adj deserving blame.—**blameworthiness** n.

blanch vt to whiten or bleach; to make pale; (vegetables, almonds, etc) to scald. * vi to turn pale.

blancmange n a dessert made from gelatinous or starchy ingredients (as cornflour) and milk.

bland adj mild; gentle; insipid.—**blandly** adv.—**blandness** n.

blandish vti to flatter in order to coax; to cajole.

blandishment n (usu pl) a winning expression or action, an artful caress, cajolery.

blank adj (paper) bearing no writing or marks; vacant; (mind) empty of thought; (look) without expression; (denial, refusal) utter, complete; (cheque) signed but with no amount written in. * n an empty space, esp one to be filled out on a printed form; an empty place or time.—**blankly** adv.—**blankness** n.

blank (cartridge) n a powder-filled cartridge without a bullet.

blank cheque, blank check *n* a signed cheque with the amount left blank to be filled by the payee; complete freedom of action.

blanket *n* a large, soft piece of cloth used for warmth, esp as a bed cover; (*of snow, smoke*) a cover or layer. * *adj* applying to a wide variety of cases or situations. * *vt* to cover.

blank verse *n* unrhymed verse.

blare *vti* to sound harshly or loudly. * *n* a loud, harsh sound.

blarney *n* wheedling talk, flattery. * *vt* (**blarneying, blarneyed**) to influence or talk over by soft wheedling speeches; to humbug with flattery.

Blarney Stone *n* a stone in the wall of Blarney Castle, Cork, on kissing which a person is said to become an adept in flattery.

blasé *adj* bored, indifferent; sated with pleasure.

blaspheme *vt* to speak irreverently of (God, a divine being or sacred things). * *vi* to utter blasphemy.—**blasphemer** *n*.

blasphemous *adj* impious, grossly insulting (to God, etc).

blasphemy *n* (*pl* **blasphemies**) impious speaking; speaking irreverently of God, a divine being or sacred things.

blast *n* a sharp gust of air; the sound of a horn; an explosion; an outburst of criticism. * *vt* to wither; to blow up, explode; to criticize sharply. * *vi* to make a loud, harsh sound; to set off explosives, etc; (*with* **off**) to be launched.

blasted *adj* withered; (*inf*) damned.

blastema *n* (*pl* **blastemas, blastemata**) (*biol*) the point of growth of an organ as yet unformed, from which it is developed.—**blastemal, blastemic, blastematic** *adj*.

blast furnace *n* a smelting furnace using compressed air.

blasto- *prefix* bud; germination.

blastoderm *n* a layer of embryonic cells in an egg from which an organism is formed.—**blastodermic** *adj*.

blastoff *n* the launch of a space vehicle or rocket; the time when this takes place.

blastogenesis *n* reproduction by budding.—**blastogenic, blastogenetic** *adj*.

blatant *adj* noisy; glaringly conspicuous.—**blatancy** *n*.—**blatantly** *adv*.

blather *see* **blether**.

blatherskite *n* a blethering or blustering person.

blaze[1] *n* an intensive fire; a bright light; splendour; an outburst (of emotion). * *vi* to burn brightly; to shine with a brilliant light; to be excited, as with anger.

blaze[2] *n* a white mark on the face of a horse or other quadruped; a white mark cut on a tree to serve as a guide. * *vt* to mark, as trees, by removing a portion of the bark; to indicate, as a path or boundary, by blazing trees; **blaze a trail** to act as a pioneer.

blaze[3] *vt* to proclaim, to publish widely.

blazer *n* a lightweight jacket, often in a bright colour representing membership of a sports club, school, etc.

blazon *vt* to proclaim publicly; to adorn; to describe (heraldic or armorial bearings) in technical terms. * *n* the terminology of coats of arms.—**blazoner** *n*.—**blazonment** *n*.

blazonry *n* (*pl* **blazonries**) a heraldic device; the art of describing and explaining coats of arms; decoration, as with heraldic devices; a bright display.

bldg. *abbr* = building.

bleach *vti* to make or become white or colourless. * *n* a substance for bleaching.—**bleachable** *adj*.—**bleacher** *n*.

bleachers *npl* the unroofed seats at a baseball field or sports ground.

bleaching powder *n* a white powder, chloride of lime, used for bleaching.

bleak[1] *adj* cold; exposed; bare; harsh; gloomy; not hopeful.—**bleakly** *adv*.—**bleakness** *n*.

bleak[2] *n* (*pl* **bleak, bleaks**) a small European river fish with brilliant silvery scales.

blear *adj* (*eyes*) sore or dim with inflammation. * *vt* to make (eyes) sore or watery; to dim or blur.

bleary *adj* (**blearier, bleariest**) (*eyesight*) dim with water or tears; obscure, indistinct.—**blearily** *adv*.—**bleariness** *n*.

bleary-eyed *adj* with eyes dulled by tears or tiredness; dull.

bleat *vi* to cry as a sheep, goat or calf; to complain. * *n* a bleating cry or sound.—**bleater** *n*.—**bleatingly** *adv*.

bleb *n* a small blister; a bubble in water or glass.

bleed *vb* (**bleeding, bled**) *vi* to lose blood; to ooze sap, colour or dye; to die for a country or an ideal; to sympathize (often ironically). * *vt* to remove blood or sap from; (*inf*) to extort money or goods from.

bleeder *n* one who bleeds, esp blood from another; (*inf*) a person with haemophilia; (*sl*) an annoying person.

bleep *vi* to emit a high-pitched sound or signal (eg a car alarm). * *n* a small portable electronic radio receiver that emits a bleep to convey a message.—*also* **bleeper**.

blemish *n* a flaw or defect, as a spot. * *vt* to mar; to spoil.

blench *vi* to flinch; to blanch.

blend *vt* (*varieties of tea, etc*) to mix or mingle; to mix so that the components cannot be distinguished. * *vi* to mix, merge; to shade gradually into each other, as colours; to harmonize. * *n* a mixture.

blende *n* any of various minerals composed mainly of metallic sulphides; a yellow to brownish-black zinc ore, sphalerite.

blender *n* something or someone that blends; an electrical device for preparing food.—*also* **liquidizer**.

blenny *n* (*pl* **blennies, blenny**) a small elongated spiny-finned sea fish.

blepharitis *n* inflammation of the eyelids.—**blepharitic** *adj*.

blesbok *n* (*pl* **blesboks, blesbok**) a South African white-faced antelope.

bless *vt* (**blessing, blessed** *or* **blest**) to consecrate; to praise; to call upon God's protection; to grant happiness; to make the sign of the cross over.

blessed *adj* holy, sacred; fortunate; blissful; beatified.—**blessedly** *adv*.—**blessedness** *n*.

blessing *n* a prayer or wish for success or happiness; a cause of happiness; good wishes or approval; a grace said before or after eating.

blest *see* **bless**.

blet *n* a decayed spot in fruit.

blether *vi* (*inf*) to talk foolishly. * *n* (*inf*) foolish talk; one who talks it.—*also* **blather**.

blew *see* **blow**[2].

blight *n* any insect, disease, etc that destroys plants; anything that prevents growth or destroys; somone or something that spoils. * *vt* to destroy; to frustrate.

blimp *n* a small, nonrigid airship; any airship; a soundproof cover for a camera.

blind *adj* sightless; unable to discern or understand; not directed by reason; (*exit*) hidden, concealed; closed at one end. * *n* something that deceives; a shade for a window; (*sl*) a drinking bout. * *vti* to make sightless, to deprive of insight; to dazzle (with facts, a bright light, etc); to deceive.—**blindly** *adv*.—**blindness** *n*.

blind alley *n* a street closed at one end; an occupation or inquiry that leads to nothing.

blind date *n* a date between two individuals who have never met before; either individual on a blind date.

blinder n a horse's blinkers.

blindfish *n* (*pl* **blindfish, blindfishes**) a diminutive fish of a pale colour and with rudimentary eyes, which inhabits underground waters.

blindfold *n* a cloth or bandage used to cover the eyes. * *adj* having the eyes covered, so as not to see; reckless. * *vt* to cover the eyes with a strip of cloth, etc; to hamper sight or understanding; to mislead.

blind man's buff *n* a game in which a blindfold person tries to catch and identify others.

blind spot *n* a point on the retina of the eye that is insensitive to light; a place where vision is obscured; a subject on which someone is ignorant.

blindstorey, blindstory *n* (*pl* **blindstoreys, blindstories**) (*archit*) the storey below the clerestory, admitting no light.

blindworm *n* the slowworm, a small, slender limbless lizard with very small eyes.

blini, blinis *npl* (*sing* **blin**) buckwheat pancakes.

blink *vi* to open and close the eyes rapidly; (*light*) to flash on and off; (*with* at) to ignore. * *vt* (*with* at) to be amazed or surprised. * *n* a glance, a glimpse; a momentary flash.

blinker *n* one who blinks; that which obscures the sight or mental perception; (*pl*) a screen for a horse's eye, to prevent it from seeing sideways; (*sl*) the eyes.

blip *n* a trace on a radar screen; a recurring sound; a temporary setback. * *vi* (**blipping, blipped**) to make a blip.

bliss *n* supreme happiness; spiritual joy.—**blissful** *adj*.—**blissfully** *adv*.

blister *n* a raised patch on the skin, containing water, as caused by burning or rubbing; a raised bubble on any other surface. * *vti* to cause or form blisters; to lash with words.

blistering *adj* (*criticism*) scornful, cruel.

BLit, BLitt *abbr* = Bachelor of Literature.

blithe *adj* happy, cheerful, gay.—**blithely** *adv*.—**blitheness** *n*.

blithering *adj* (*inf*) stupid, idiotic.

blithesome *adj* blithe, merry.—**blithesomely** *adv*.—**blithesomeness** *n*.

blitz *n* heavy aerial bombing; any sudden destructive attack; a determined effort. * *vt* to subject to a blitz.

blitzkrieg *n* warfare in which blitz is employed; any swift combined action.

blizzard *n* a severe storm of wind and snow.

bloat *vti* to swell as with water or air; to puff up, as with pride; to cure or dry (fish) in smoke.—**bloated** *adj*.

bloater *n* a herring or mackerel smoked and partially dried, but not split open.

blob *n* a drop of liquid; a round spot (of colour, etc).

bloc *n* a group of parties, nations, etc united to achieve a common purpose.

block *n* a solid piece of stone or wood, etc; a piece of wood used as a base (for chopping, etc); a group or row of buildings; a number of things as a unit; the main body of a petrol engine; a building divided into offices; an obstruction; a child's building brick; (*sl*) the head. * *vt* to impede or obstruct; to shape; (*often with* out) to sketch roughly. * *vi* to obstruct an opponent in sports.—**blocker** *n*.

blockade *n* (*mil*) the obstruction of an enemy seaport by warships; any strategic barrier. * *vt* to obstruct in this way.—**blockader** *n*.

blockage *n* an obstruction.

blockbuster *n* (*sl*) a very heavy bomb of great penetrative power; a conspicuously powerful or effective person or thing; one who engages in blockbusting.

blockbusting *n* the practice of persuading house owners to sell their houses quickly by convincing them that property values will drop.

blockhead *n* a dolt, a stupid person.

blockhouse *n* a small fort, usu of timber; a log house; a concrete fortification with loopholes for observation or firing from.

block letter *n* a handwritten capital letter similar to a printed letter.

block vote *n* at a conference, a total vote represented by one delegate.

bloke *n* (*inf*) a man.

blond, blonde *adj* having light-coloured hair and skin; light-coloured. * *n* a blond person.—**blondness, blondeness** *n*.

blonde lace *n* a silk lace.

blood *n* the red fluid that circulates in the arteries and veins of animals; the sap of a plant; the essence of life; kinship; descent; hatred; anger; bloodshed; guilt of murder.

blood-and-thunder *adj* melodramatic. * *n* a sensational story or play.

blood bank *n* a place where blood is taken from blood donors and stored.

blood bath *n* a massacre.

blood brother *n* one of two men or boys pledged to treat the other as a brother, as confirmed by the ceremonial mingling of blood.

blood cell *n* a red or white cell present in the blood.

blood count *n* the determination of the numbers of red and white corpuscles in a sample of blood.

bloodcurdling *adj* exciting terror, horrifying, chilling.

blood donor *n* a person who donates his or her blood for transfusion.

blooded *adj* having a specific kind of blood (*hot-blooded*); of fine breed; initiated.

blood group *n* any of the classes of human blood.—*also* **blood type**.

blood heat *n* the normal heat of the human blood in health (37° C, 98.4° F).

bloodhound *n* a large breed of hound used for tracking; a detective.

bloodletting *n* phlebotomy; bloodshed, eg a massacre.

bloodless *adj* without blood or slaughter; unfeeling.—**bloodlessly** *adv*.—**bloodlessness** *n*.

blood money *n* money obtained at the cost of another's life; the reward paid for the discovery or capture of a murderer; compensation paid to the next of kin of a person slain by another.

blood poisoning *n* septicaemia.

blood pressure *n* the pressure of the blood in the arterial system.

blood pudding *n* blood sausage.

blood-red *adj* red as blood.

blood relation, blood relative *n* a person related by descent, not marriage.

blood sausage *n* a dark sausage with a large proportion of blood.

bloodshed *n* killing.

bloodshot *adj* (*eye*) suffused with blood, red and inflamed.

blood sport *n* any sport in which an animal is hunted and killed.

bloodstain *n* a stain made by blood.

bloodstained *adj* stained with blood; responsible for killing.

bloodstock *n* thoroughbred horses collectively.

bloodstone *n* a dark green quartz flecked with red jasper; heliotrope.

bloodstream *n* the flow of blood through the blood vessels in the human body.

bloodsucker *n* an animal that sucks blood, a leech; a person who sponges or preys on another, an extortionist.—**bloodsucking** *adj, n*.

blood test *n* an examination of a blood specimen to ascertain blood group, alcohol intake, etc.

bloodthirsty *adj* (**bloodthirstier, bloodthirstiest**) eager for blood, cruel, warlike.—**bloodthirstiness** *n*.

blood type *see* **blood group.**

blood vessel *n* in the body, a vein, artery, or capillary.

bloody *adj* (**bloodier, bloodiest**) stained with or covered in blood; bloodthirsty; cruel, murderous; (*sl*) as an intensifier (*a bloody good hiding*). * *vt* (**bloodying, bloodied**) to cover with blood.—**bloodily** *adv*.—**bloodiness** *n*.

Bloody Mary *n* (*pl* **Bloody Marys**) a drink made with vodka and tomato juice.

bloody-minded *adj* (*inf*) deliberately obstructive.—**bloody-mindedness** *n*.

bloom[1] *n* a flower or blossom; the period of being in flower; a period of most health, vigour, etc; a youthful, healthy glow; the powdery coating on some fruit and leaves. * *vi* to blossom; to be in one's prime; to glow with health etc.

bloom[2] *n* a rough mass of incandescent iron for hammering or rolling into bars. * *vt* to make (iron) into bloom.

bloomer, blooper *n* (*inf*) a stupid mistake.

bloomers *npl* (*inf*) baggy knickers.

blooming *adj* blossoming, flowering; flourishing; (*sl*) confounded, bloody.—**bloomingly** *adv*.

blossom *n* a flower, esp one that produces edible fruit; a state or time of flowering. * *vi* to flower; to begin to develop.—**blossomy** *adj*.

blot *n* a spot or stain, esp of ink; something that diminishes or spoils the beauty of; a blemish in reputation. * *vt* (**blotting, blotted**) to spot or stain; to obscure; to disgrace; to absorb with blotting paper.

blotch *n* a spot or discoloration on the skin; any large blot or stain. * *vt* to cover with blotches.—**blotched** *adj*.—**blotchily** *adv*.—**blotchy** *adj*.

blotter *n* a piece of blotting paper.

blotting paper *n* absorbent paper used to dry freshly written ink.

blotto *adj* (*sl*) very drunk.

blouse *n* a shirt-like garment worn by women.

blow[1] *n* a hard hit, as with the fist; a sudden attack; a sudden misfortune; a setback.

blow[2] *vb* (**blowing, blew,** *pp* **blown**) *vi* to cause a current of air; to be moved or carried (by air, the wind, etc); (*mus*) to make a sound by forcing in air with the mouth; (*often with* **out**) to burst suddenly; to breathe hard; (*with* **out**) to become extinguished by a gust of air; (*gas or oil well*) to erupt out of control; (*with* **over**) to pass without consequence. * *vt* to move along with a current of air; to make a sound by blowing; to inflate with air; (*a fuse, etc*) to melt; (*inf*) to spend (money) freely; (*sl*) to leave; (*sl*) to divulge a secret; (*sl*) to bungle; (*often with* **up**) to burst by an explosion; (*with* **out**) to extinguish by a gust; (*storm*) to dissipate (itself) by blowing; (*with* **over**) to pass over or pass by; (*with* **up**) to enlarge a photograph; (*with* **up**) (*inf*) to lose one's temper.

blow[3] *vi* (**blowing, blew,** *pp* **blown**) to blossom, to flower. * *n* a mass of blossom; the state or condition of flowering.

blow-by-blow *adj* told or shown in great detail.

blow-dry *vt* (**blow-drying, blow-dried**) to style recently washed hair with a hand-held drier.

blower *n* one who blows; a braggart; a device for producing a stream of gas or air.

blowfly *n* (*pl* **blowflies**) a fly that lays its eggs in rotting meat.

blowhole *n* a nostril of a whale; a vent for the escape of gas, air, etc; a hole in ice used for breathing by whales, seals, etc; a hole of gas in metal capturing during the solidifying process.

blow job *n* (*sl*) fellatio.

blowlamp, blowtorch *n* a gas-powered torch that produces a hot flame for welding, etc.

blown *adj* swollen or bloated.

blowout *n* (*inf*) a festive social event; a bursting of a container (as a tyre) by pressure on a weak spot; an uncontrolled eruption of a gas or oil well.

blowpipe *n* a tube through which a current of air or gas is driven upon a flame to concentrate its heat on a substance, eg glass, to fuse it; a long tube of cane or reed used to discharge arrows by the force of the breath.

blowup *n* an explosion; an enlarged photograph; (*sl*) an angry outburst.

blowy *adj* (**blowier, blowiest**) breezy, windy.

blowzy, blowsy *adj* (**blowzier, blowziest** *or* **blowsier, blowsiest**) (*esp a woman*) fat and ruddy, slatternly.—**blowzily, blowsily** *adv*.—**blowziness, blowziness** *n*.

blubber[1] *vi* to weep loudly.

blubber[2] *n* whale fat; excessive fat on the body.

bludgeon *n* a short, heavy stick used for striking. * *vti* to strike with a bludgeon; to bully or coerce.

blue *adj* (**bluer, bluest**) of the colour of the clear sky; depressed; (*film*) indecent, obscene. * *n* the colour of the spectrum lying between green and violet; (*with* **the**) the sky, the sea; (*pl: with* **the**) (*inf*) a depressed feeling; (*pl: with* **the**) a style of vocal and instrumental jazz; a representative in a sport of a university, esp Oxford or Cambridge; the badge worn or honour bestowed; in UK, a member or adherent of the Tory party. * *vt* (**blueing** *or* **bluing, blued**) to make or dye blue; to dip in blue liquid; (*sl*) to squander.

blue baby *n* one born with a heart condition causing a blueness of the skin.

bluebell *n* any of several plants with a one-sided cluster of blue bell-shaped flowers.

bluebird *n* any of various small songbirds prevalent in North America.

blue blood *n* royal or aristocratic descent.

bluebonnet *n* a Scottish cap of blue cloth; a name given to the Scottish troops before the Union, 1707; a Scotsman.

blue book *n* a governmental official report, etc, bound in blue paper covers; a directory of socially prominent persons; a booklet in which students answer examination questions.

bluebottle *n* a large fly; (*inf*) a policeman.

blue cheese *n* cheese with veins of blue mould.

blue chip *adj* (*stocks, shares*) providing a reliable return.

blue-collar *adj* of or pertaining to manual workers.

blue devils *npl* low spirits; mental depression; delirium tremens.

bluegrass *n* any of several rich pasture grasses with bluish green blades, esp in Kentucky; improvisatory country music played on unamplified instruments.

blue gum *n* a lofty eucalyptus tree of Australia, valuable for its timber and essential oil.

blueing *n* the process of imparting a blue tint; the indigo, etc, used by washerwomen.—*also* **bluing**.

bluejacket *n* a seaman in the British or US navy.

blue mould *n* a minute fungus that attacks bread and other foodstuffs.

bluenose *n* a puritanical person; a Nova Scotian.

blue peter *n* a small blue flag with a white square in the centre, hoisted when a ship is about to sail.

blueprint *n* a blue photographic print of plans; a detailed scheme, template of work to be done; basis or prototype for future development.

blue ribbon *n* in UK, the broad ribbon of a dark blue colour worn by members of the order of the Garter; a prized distinction; a mark of success; a thin blue strip worn as a badge of teetotalism.

blue rinse *n* a rinse giving a blue tint to grey hair.

blue-rinse *adj* (*inf*) describing mature, assured, social women and their background.

blues *npl* (*used as sing or pl*) depression, melancholy; a type of melancholy folk music originating among Black Americans.

bluestocking *n* a woman of literary tastes or occupation.

bluestone *n* a grey sandstone used for building, etc; copper sulphate in crystalline form.

blue whale *n* a rorqual, the largest mammal known.

bluey *n* (*Austral*) a bushman's bundle.

bluff[1] *adj* rough in manner; abrupt, outspoken; ascending steeply with a flat front. * *n* a broad, steep bank or cliff.—**bluffness** *n*.

bluff[2] *vti* to mislead or frighten by a false, bold front.* *n* deliberate deception.—**bluffer** *n*.

bluing *see* **blueing**.

blunder *vi* to make a foolish mistake; to move about clumsily. * *n* a foolish mistake.—**blunderer** *n*.—**blundering** *adj*.—**blunderingly** *adv*.

blunderbuss *n* (*hist*) a short gun or firearm with a wide bore, firing many balls; a clumsy person.

blunge *vt* (*pottery*) to mix clay with water.

blunt *adj* not having a sharp edge or point; rude, outspoken, unsubtle. * *vti* to make or become dull.—**bluntly** *adv*.—**bluntness** *n*.

blur *n* a stain, smear; an ill-defined impression. * *vti* (**blurring, blurred**) to smear; to make or become indistinct in shape, etc; to dim.—**blurred** *adj*.—**blurredly** *adv*.—**blurry** *adj*.

blurb *n* a promotional description, as on a book cover; an exaggerated advertisement.

blurt *vt* (*with* **out**) to utter impulsively.

blush *n* a red flush of the face caused by embarrassment or guilt; any rosy colour. * *vi* (*with* **for, at**) to show embarrassment, modesty, joy, etc involuntarily, by blushing; to become rosy.

blusher *n* a cosmetic that gives colour to the cheeks.

blush wine *n* rosé wine, a blend of red and white wines.

bluster *vi* to make a noise like the wind; to bully. * *n* a blast, as of the wind; bullying or boastful talk, often to hide shame or embarrassment.—**blusterer** *n*.—**blustery** *adj*.—**blusteringly, blusterously** *adv*.

Blvd *abbr* = Boulevard.

B-movie *n* (*cinema*) a film made as a supporting feature, esp in the 1940s and 1950s.

BMus *abbr* = Bachelor of Music.

bn *abbr* = battalion; billion.

BO *abbr* = (*inf*) body odour.

boa *n* any of various large South American snakes that crush their prey; a long fluffy scarf of feathers.

boa constrictor *n* the largest boa, remarkable for its length and power of destroying its prey by constriction.

boar *n* a male pig, a wild hog.

board *n* meals, esp when provided regularly for pay; a long, flat piece of sawed wood, etc; a flat piece of wood, etc for some special purpose; pasteboard; a council; a group of people who supervise a company; the side of a ship (*overboard*). * *vt* to provide with meals and lodging at fixed terms; to come onto the deck of (a ship); to get on (a train, bus, etc). * *vi* to provide with meals, or room and meals, regularly for pay; (*with* up) to cover with boards; **to take on board** to appoint to a position; to adopt new ideas.

boarder *n* one who is provided with board.

board game *n* a game as chess, chequers, etc, played by moving pieces on a marked board.

boarding *n* light timber collectively; a covering of planks; the act of supplying, or state of being supplied with, food and lodging for a stipulated sum; the act of entering a ship or aircraft.

boarding house *n* a house for boarders.

boarding school *n* a school where the students are boarded.

boardroom *n* a room where meetings of a company's board are held.

board rule *n* a figured scale for finding the number of square feet in a board without calculation.

boardwalk *n* a footway of boards, esp by the sea.

boarish *adj* coarse; brutal; cruel.

boart *see* **bort**.

boast[1] *vi* to brag. * *vt* to speak proudly of; to possess with pride. * *n* boastful talk.—**boaster** *n*.—**boastingly** *adv*.

boast[2] *vt* to dress stone with a broad chisel and mallet; to dress a block in outline for a statue, etc, prior to more detailed or delicate work.

boastful *adj* given to boasting.—**boastfully** *adv*.—**boastfulness** *n*.

boat *n* a small, open, waterborne craft; (*inf*) a ship. * *vi* to travel in a boat, esp for pleasure.

boatbill(ed heron) *n* a South American wading bird with a boat-shaped bill.

boater *n* a stiff flat straw hat.

boathook *n* a hooked pole for drawing a boat to land, fending off, etc.

boathouse *n* a shed for boats.

boating *n* rowing, sailing, etc, for pleasure.

boatman *n* (*pl* **boatmen**) a person who works on, deals in, or operates boats.

boat people *npl* refugees fleeing by boat.

boatswain *n* a ship's officer in charge of hull maintenance and related work.—*also* **bosun**.

boat train *n* a train for steamer or ferry passengers.

bob *vb* (**bobbing, bobbed**) *vi* to move abruptly up and down, often in water; to nod the head; to curtsey. * *vt* (*hair*) to cut short. * *n* a jerking motion up and down; the weight on a pendulum, plumb line, etc; a woman's or girl's short haircut.

bobbery *n* (*pl* **bobberies**) a rumpus, a row, a noisy disturbance; a pack of hunting dogs.

bobbin *n* a reel or spool on which yarn or thread is wound.

bobbinet *n* a machine-made cotton netting or lace in imitation of pillow lace.

bobble *n* a small woolly ball used for ornament or trimming; a bobbing movement; (*inf*) a mistake; a fumble. *vti* to bob up and down; to make a mistake; to fumble with (a ball).

bobby *n* (*pl* **bobbies**) (*sl*) a policeman.

bobby pin *n* a clip for holding hair in position; a hairgrip.

bobcat *n* (*pl* **bobcats, bobcat**) a medium-sized feline of eastern North America with a black-spotted reddish-brown coat and a short tail.

bobolink *n* an American migratory songbird.—*also* **reedbird, ricebird.**

bobsled, bobsleigh *n* a long racing sled. * *vi* (**bobsledding, bobsledded**) to ride or race on a bobsled.

bobstay *n* (*naut*) a rope holding the bowsprit down to the stem.

bobtail *n* a short tail or a tail cut short; an animal with a docked tail; the rabble (*rag-tag and bobtail*). * *adj* with a docked tail.—**bobtailed** *adj*.

Boche *n* (*pl* **Boche**) (*sl*) a German, esp a soldier.

bock *n* a variety of lager beer of double strength; a glass of beer.

bode *vt* to be an omen of.

bodega *n* a wine vault, cellar or shop where wine is sold from the cask; a store specializing in Hispanic groceries.

bodice *n* the upper part of a woman's dress.

bodiless *adj* without a body, incorporeal.—**bodilessness** *n*.

bodily *adj* physical; relating to the body. * *adv* in the flesh; as a whole; altogether.

bodkin *n* a large blunt needle, a tool for piercing holes; a pin for fastening hair; a small dagger.

body *n* (*pl* **bodies**) the whole physical substance of a person, animal, or plant; the trunk of a person or animal; a corpse; the principal part of anything; a distinct mass; substance or consistency, as of liquid; a richness of flavour; a person; a distinct group of people. * *vt* (**bodying, bodied**) to give shape to.

body bag *n* a large plastic sack, usu zipped, to carry a corpse from the scene of a disaster.

bodybuilding *n* strengthening and enlarging the muscles through exercise and diet for competitive display.— **bodybuilder** *n*.

bodyguard *n* a person or persons assigned to guard someone.

body language *n* gestures, unconscious bodily movements, etc, that function as a means of communication.

body politic *n* the collective body of people living under an organized political government.

body-snatcher *n* (*formerly*) one who stole corpses from graves for dissection by anatomists.

body stocking *n* a woman's tight-fitting garment that covers the torso and sometimes the legs.

body warmer *n* a sleeveless, quilted outer garment.

bodywork *n* the outer shell of a motor vehicle.

Boeotian *adj* pertaining to Boeotia in central Greece, noted for its moist and heavy atmosphere; dull, stupid. * *n* an inhabitant of Boeotia; a dull, stupid person.

Boer *n* a Dutch-descended South African.—*also adj*.

boffin *n* (*inf*) a military research scientist.

boffo *adj* (*sl*) wonderful, amazing.

bog *n* wet, spongy ground; quagmire. * *vb* (**bogging, bogged**) *vt* to sink or submerge in a bog or quagmire. * *vi* to sink or stick in a bog.—**boggy** *adj*.

bogey[1] *n* (*pl* **bogeys**) (*golf*) one stroke more than par on a hole.

bogey[2] *n* (*pl* **bogeys**) a goblin; a cause of worry.—*also* **bogy** (*pl* **bogies**).

bogeyman *n* (*pl* **bogeymen**) an imaginary monster commonly used to frighten children.

boggle *vi* to be surprised; to hesitate (at). * *vt* to confuse (the imagination, mind, etc).

bogie *n* an assembly of four or six wheels on a rail carriage.

bogle *n* a goblin, a spectre; a scarecrow.

bogus *adj* counterfeit, spurious.

bogy *see* **bogey**[2].

bohea *n* a black China tea of the lowest quality.

Bohemian *adj* of or pertaining to Bohemia in Czechoslovakia; unconventional. * *n* an inhabitant of Bohemia; a person who disregards social conventions or evinces a wild or roving disposition; a gipsy.

Bohemianism *n* the life or habits of a person, usu artistic or literary, who by natural inclination leads a free and easy unconventional existence.

boil[1] *vi* to change rapidly from a liquid to a vapour by heating; to bubble when boiling; to cook in boiling liquid; to be aroused with anger; (*with* **down**) to reduce by boiling; to condense; (*with* **over**) to overflow when boiling; to burst out in anger. * *vt* to heat to boiling point; to cook in boiling water.—**boilable** *adj*.

boil[2] *n* an inflamed, pus-filled, painful swelling on the skin.

boiler *n* a container in which to boil things; a storage tank in which water is heated and steam generated; a device for providing central heating and hot water.

boilersuit *n* coveralls.

boiling point *n* the temperature at which a liquid boils; the point at which a person loses his temper; the point of crisis.

boisterous *adj* wild, noisy; stormy; loud and exuberant.—**boisterously** *adv*.

bola, bolas *n* a South American hunting implement consisting of two or more balls of iron or stone attached to the ends of a leather cord, used to entangle the legs of an animal.

bold *adj* daring or courageous; fearless; impudent; striking to the eye. * *n* boldface type.—**boldly** *adv*.—**boldness** *n*.

boldface type *n* type characters with thickened, heavy strokes.

bole[1] *n* the trunk or stem of a tree.

bole[2] *n* friable clay or clayey shale, usu coloured by oxide of iron.

bolection *n* (*archit*) a raised moulding on a panel.

bolero *n* (*pl* **boleros**) a lively Spanish dance; the music accompanying such a dance; a short jacket-shaped bodice.

boletus *n* (*pl* **boletuses, boleti**) any of a large genus of thick-stemmed fungi containing edible or poisonous species.

bolide *n* a large meteor that explodes on coming into contact with air, a fire ball.

boll *n* the pod of a plant, esp of cotton or flax.

bollard *n* a strong post on a wharf around which mooring lines are secured; one of a line of posts closing off a street to traffic; an illuminated marker on a traffic island.

bollocks *npl* (*sl*) testicles. * *interj* used to express utter disbelief, ridicule, etc.

boll weevil *n* an American weevil that infests cotton bolls.

bolometer *n* an instrument for measuring radiation.—**bolometric** *adj*.—**bolometrically** *adv*.

boloney *see* **baloney**.

Bolshevik *n* (*pl* **Bolsheviks, Bolsheviki**) a Russian communist; a revolutionary; an opponent of an existing social order.

Bolshevism *n* the doctrines and practices of the Bolsheviks; the communist form of government adopted in Russia in March 1917.—**Bolshevist** *adj, n*.

bolshie, bolshy *adj* (*sl*) left-wing; rebellious. * *n* (*pl* **bolshies**) (*often with cap*) a Bolshevik; a revolutionary.

bolster *n* a long narrow pillow; any bolster-like object or support. * *vt* (*often with* **up**) to support or strengthen.—**bolsterer** *n*.—**bolsteringly** *adv*.

bolt[1] *n* a bar used to lock a door, etc; an arrow for a crossbow; a flash of lightning; a threaded metal rod used with a nut to hold parts together; a roll (of cloth, paper, etc); a sudden dash. * *vt* to lock with a bolt; to eat hastily; to say suddenly; to blurt (out); to abandon (a party, group, etc). * *vi* (*horse*) to rush away suddenly * *adv* erectly upright.—**bolter** *n*.

bolt[2] *vt* to sift or separate coarser from finer particles; to examine with care, to investigate; to separate.—*also* **boult.**—**bolter** *n*.

bolthole *n* an escape route; a safe and secret hiding place; a person's private refuge.

boltrope *n* (*naut*) a rope to which the edges of sails are sewn.

bolus *n* (*pl* **boluses**) a medicine in the form of a soft rounded mass, larger than an ordinary pill, to be swallowed at once; anything disagreeable, which must be accepted.

bomb *n* a projectile containing explosives, incendiary material, or chemicals used for destruction; (*with* **the**) the hydrogen or atomic bomb; (*sl*) a lot of money. * *vt* to attack with bombs. * *vi* to fail, to flop.

bombard *vt* to attack with bombs or artillery; to attack verbally.—**bombardment** *n*.

bombardier *n* the crew member who releases the bombs in a bomber; in Britain and Canada, a noncommissioned artillery officer.

bombardier beetle *n* any of various coleopterous insects that, when irritated, expel a fluid from the abdomen with a slight report.

bombast *n* pretentious or boastful language.—**bombastic** *adj*.—**bombastically** *adv*.

bombazine *n* a twilled fabric of which the warp is silk and the weft worsted.

bombe *n* a frozen dessert moulded into a round shape.

bomber *n* a person who bombs; an aeroplane that carries bombs.

bomber jacket *n* a waist-length bloused jacket with a zip.

bombshell *n* a shocking surprise.

bombsight *n* a manual or electronic device for aiming bombs.

bomb site *n* an area devastated by bombing; a vacant area cleared after a bombing raid.

bombycid *n* any of a family of moths, including the silkworm moth.

bona fide *adj* in good faith; genuine or real.

bona fides *n* good faith; honourable dealing.

bonanza *n* a rich vein of ore; any source of wealth; unexpected good fortune or luck.

bonbon *n* a small piece of candy, a sweet.

bond *n* anything that binds, fastens, or unites; (*pl*) shackles; an obligation imposed by a contract, promise, etc; the status of goods in a warehouse until taxes are paid; an interest-bearing certificate issued by the government or business, redeemable on a specified date; surety against theft, absconding, etc. * *vt* to join, bind, or otherwise unite; to provide a bond for; to place or hold (goods) in bond; to put together bricks or stones so that they overlap to give strength. * *vi* to hold together by means of a bond.—**bondable** *adj*.—**bonder** *n*.

bondage *n* slavery, captivity.

bondstone *n* a long stone runing through a wall and so binding it.

bone *n* the hard material making up the skeleton; any constituent part of the skeleton; (*pl*) the skeleton; the essentials or basics of anything. * *vti* to remove the bones from, as meat; (*with* **up**) (*inf*) to study hard.—**boneless** *adj*.

bone black *n* a black pigment made partly from charcoal obtained by roasting animal bones.

bone china *n* china made from clay mixed with bone ash.

bone-dry *adj* completely dry.

bonehead *n* (*sl*) a fool.

bone meal *n* fertilizer or feed made of crushed or ground bone.

bone of contention *n* a source of strife.

bonesetter *n* one who treats fractures or dislocated limbs without medical qualification to do so.

bonfire *n* an outdoor fire.

bongo[1] *n* (*pl* **bongos**) either of a pair of small drums of different pitch struck with the fingers.

bongo[2] *n* (*pl* **bongo, bongos**) a large striped African antelope.

bonhomie *n* good-heartedness; a frank good-natured manner.—**bonhomous** *adj*.

bonito *n* (*pl* **bonitos, bonito**) one of several species of warm-sea game fishes allied to the tuna.

bonk *vt* (*inf*) to hit; (*inf*) to have sexual intercourse with.—**bonking** *n*.

bon mot *n* (*pl* **bons mots**) a witty saying, a fitting remark.

bonne *n* a French nursemaid.

bonnet *n* a hat with a chin ribbon, worn by women and children; a case or covering, usu of sheet metal, placed over a motor (—*also* **hood**).

bonny, bonnie *adj* (**bonnier, bonniest**) healthy, attractive looking.

bonsai *n* (*pl* **bonsai**) a miniature tree or shrub that has been dwarfed by selective pruning; the art of cultivating bonsai.

bonspiel *n* (*Scot*) a curling match between players of different clubs.

bontebok *n* (*pl* **bonteboks, bontebok**) a pied antelope of South Africa.

bon ton *n* the style of persons in high life; good breeding; fashionable society; height of fashion.

bonus *n* (*pl* **bonuses**) an amount paid over the sum due as interest, dividend, or wages.

bon vivant *n* (*pl* **bons vivants**) a gourmet.

bon voyage *n, interj* an expression used to wish travellers a pleasant trip.

bony *adj* (**bonier, boniest**) of or resembling bones; having large or prominent bones; full of bones.

bonze *n* a Buddhist monk.

boo *interj* an expression of disapproval. * *n* (*pl* **boos**) hooting. * *vb* (**booing, booed**) *vi* to low like an ox; to groan. * *vt* to hoot at.

boob *n* a stupid awkward person; a blunder; (*sl*) a female breast.

booby *n* (*pl* **boobies**) a foolish person; the loser in a game.

booby prize *n* a prize of little value for the lowest score.

booby trap *n* a trap for playing a practical joke on someone; a camouflaged explosive device triggered by an unsuspecting victim.

boodle *n* money paid for votes or undue political influence; graft; lot, caboodle.

boogie *vi* (**boogieing, boogied**) to dance to pop music or jazz. * *n* fast, rhythmic music for dancing.

boogie-woogie *n* a style of jazz piano.

boohoo *vi* (**boohooing, boohooed**) to weep noisily or to pretend to do so. * *n* (*pl* **boohoos**) the sound of noisy weeping.

book *n* a bound set of printed or blank pages; a literary composition of fact or fiction; the script or libretto of a play or musical; (*pl*) written records of transactions or accounts; a book or record of bets. * *vt* to make a reservation in advance; to note a person's name and address for an alleged offence. * *vi* to make a reservation.

bookcase *n* a piece of furniture with shelves for books.

book club *n* an organization that sells books to its members at cheaper prices, usu by mail order.

book end *npl* a prop at the end of a row of books to keep them upright.

bookie *n* (*inf*) a bookmaker.

bookish *adj* fond of reading.—**bookishness** *n*.

bookkeeping *n* the systematic recording of business accounts.—**bookkeeper** *n*.

book learning *n* theoretical, not practical, knowledge.—**book-learned** *adj*.

booklet *n* a small book, usu with a paper cover; a pamphlet.

bookmaker *n* a person who takes bets on horse races, etc and pays out winnings; a manufacturer or publisher of books.

bookman *n* (*pl* **bookmen**) a literary man, a scholar; one who works in publishing.

bookmark(er) *n* a thing to mark a place in a book.

bookplate *n* a label in a book with the owner's name on it.

bookseller *n* a person who sells books.

bookstall *n* a stall for the sale of books, magazines, etc.

bookworm *n* an insect that feeds on books; a person who reads a lot.

Boolean algebra *n* (*math*) a system of symbolic logic used in the manipulation of sets and other mathematical entities, and in computing science.

boom¹ *n* a spar on which a sail is stretched; a barrier across a harbour; a long pole carrying a microphone.

boom² *vi* to make a deep, hollow sound. * *n* a resonant sound, as of the sea.

boom³ *vi* to flourish or prosper suddenly. * *n* a period of vigorous growth (eg in business, sales, prices).

boomer *n* the male of the great kangaroo; one who starts or promotes a boom; (*sl*) a migratory worker.

boomerang *n* a curved stick that, when thrown, returns to the thrower; an action that unexpectedly rebounds and harms the agent.—*also vi*.

boom town *n* a town that suddenly grows and increases in economic prosperity.

boon¹ *n* something useful or helpful; a blessing; a favour.

boon² *adj* bountiful; convivial, jolly; specially friendly (*boon companion*).

boondocks *npl* (*sl*) a wild, inhospitable area; a dull, provincial region.—**boondock** *adj*.

boor *n* an ill-mannered or coarse person.—**boorish** *adj*.—**boorishly** *adv*.—**boorishness** *n*.

boost *vt* (*sales, etc*) to increase; to encourage, to improve; to push; to help by advertising or promoting. * *n* a push.

booster *n* a thing or person that increases the effectiveness of another mechanism; the first stage of a rocket, which usually breaks away after launching; a substance that increases the effectiveness of medication.

boosterism *n* the practice of boosting an image or product commercially.

booster shot, booster injection *n* a supplementary dose of medicine, esp a vaccine.

boot¹ *n* a strong covering for the foot and lower part of the leg; (*sl: with* **the**) dismissal from employment; the rear compartment of a car used for holding luggage, etc (—*also* **trunk**). * *vt* to kick; to get rid of by force; (*comput*) to bring a program from a disc into the memory.

boot² *n* (*arch*) advantage, use; **to boot** as well. * *vi* (*arch*) to avail.

bootblack *n* one who shines shoes.

booted *adj* wearing boots.

bootee *n* a knitted or soft shoe for a baby.

booth *n* a stall for selling goods; a small enclosure for voting; a public telephone enclosure.

bootjack *n* an appliance for drawing off boots.

bootleg *vt* (**bootlegging, bootlegged**) to smuggle illicit alcohol; to deal in illegally made records and tapes of live music, etc.—**bootlegger** *n*.

bootless *adj* useless, unavailing.—**bootlessly** *adv*.—**bootlessness** *n*.

bootlicker *n* a person who ingratiates himself or herself to gain favour, a toady.

boots *n* (*pl* **boots**) in UK, the servant in an hotel who cleans the boots of the guests.

boots and saddles *n* a cavalry signal to mount.

booty *n* (*pl* **booties**) spoils obtained as plunder.

booze *vi* (*inf*) to drink alcohol excessively. * *n* alcohol.—**boozer** *n*.

boozy *adj* (**boozier, booziest** (*sl*) addicted to drink; drunk.—**boozily** *adv*.

bop *n* a style of 1940s jazz music.—*also* **bebop**.

bora *n* a fierce dry northeast wind that blows on the coasts of the Adriatic Sea.

boracic *see* **boric**.

boracic acid *see* **boric acid**.

borage *n* a blue-flowered herb used in salads, etc.

borax *n* a mineral composed of the sodium salt compounded of boracic acid chiefly from the dried beds of certain lakes, used in the manufacture of glass, enamel, antiseptics, soaps, etc; (*sl*) shoddy merchandise.

Bordeaux *n* any of several red, white or rosé wines from around Bordeaux in France.

bordello *n* (*pl* **bordellos**) a brothel.

border *n* the edge, rim, or margin; a dividing line between two countries; a narrow strip along an edge. * *vi* (*with* **on, upon**) to be adjacent; to approach, to verge on. * *vt* to form a border.

bordereau *n* (*pl* **bordereaux**) a memorandum of contents, a docket.

borderer *n* a dweller on a frontier.

borderland *n* land forming a border or frontier; an uncertain or debatable district; an intermediate state.

borderline *n* a boundary. * *adj* on a boundary; doubtful, indefinite.

bordure *n* (*her*) a border round a shield.

bore[1] to drill so as to form a hole; to weary, by being dull or uninteresting. * *n* a hole made by drilling; the diameter of a gun barrel; a dull or uninteresting person.

bore[2] *see* **bear**[1].

bore[3] *n* a tidal wave that breaks in the estuaries of some rivers and, impeded by a narrowing channel, rises in a ridge and courses along with great force and noise.

boreal *adj* of or pertaining to the north, or to the north wind; situated on the northern side; of a northern character.

Boreas *n* the north wind personified.

boredom *n* tedium.

boric *adj* of or yielding boron.—*also* **boracic**.

boric acid *n* a white solid acid used in manufacturing and as a mild antiseptic.

boring *adj* dull, tedious; making holes.

born *pp* of **bear**[1]. * *adj* by birth, natural.

born-again *adj* having undergone a revival of personal faith or conviction.

borne *see* **bear**[1].

bornite *n* a valuable ore of copper.

boron *n* a nonmetallic element found in borax.

borough *n* a self-governing, incorporated town; an administrative area of a city, as in London or New York.

borough English *n* (*formerly*) a custom existing in some parts of England by which an estate descended to the youngest son instead of the eldest, or, if there were no son, to the youngest brother.

borrow *vt* to obtain (an item) with the intention of returning it; (*an idea*) to adopt as one's own; (*loan, money*) to obtain from a financial institution at definite rates of interest.—**borrower** *n*.

borscht, borsch *n* a type of soup (orig from Russia) made with beetroot.

borstal system *n* (*often cap*) (*formerly*) a reformatory system by which the sentence depended on the prisoner's conduct; now called a youth custody centre.

bort, bortz *n* an imperfect or inferior diamond used for polishing other stones; a fragment of diamond made in the cutting.—*also* **boart**.

borzoi *n* (*pl* **borzois**) a tall hound with a long, silky coat and a long head, a Russian wolfhound.

boscage, boskage *n* ground covered with trees and shrubs; woods; thickets; a wooded landscape.

bosh *n* (*inf*) nonsense.—*also interj*.

bosk *n* a small wood, a thicket.

bosky *adj* (**boskier, boskiest**) wooded, bushy.—**boskiness** *n*.

bosom *n* the breast of a human being, esp a woman; the part of a dress that covers it; the seat of the emotions. * *adj* (*friend*) very dear, intimate.

bosun *see* **boatswain**.

boss[1] *n* (*inf*) the manager or foreman; a powerful local politician. * *vt* to domineer; to be in control.

boss[2] *n* a protuberant part; a stud or knob, an ornamental projection of a ceiling. * *vt* to ornament with studs or knobs.

bossa nova *n* a dance from Brazil similar to the samba; the music for this.

bossy *adj* (**bossier, bossiest**) (*inf*) domineering, fond of giving orders.—**bossily** *adv*.—**bossiness** *n*.

bot *n* the larva of the botfly, which infests horses, cattle, sheep, etc; (*pl*) the disease that it causes.—*also* **bott**.

botanical, botanic *adj* pertaining to plants and botany.—**botanically** *adv*.

botanize *vi* to study plants, esp on a field trip.—**botanizer** *n*.

botany *n* (*pl* **botanies**) the study of plants.—**botanist** *n*.

botch *n* a poorly done piece of work. * *vt* to mend or patch clumsily; to put together without sufficient care.—**botcher** *n*.

botchy *adj* (**botchier, botchiest**) clumsily made or done; marked with botches.—**botchily** *adv*.—**botchiness** *n*.

botfly *n* (*pl* **botflies**) any of many winged insects with larvae parasitic on humans and livestock.

both *adj, pron* the two together; the one and the other. * *conj* together equally.—*also adv*.

bother *vt* to perplex or annoy; to take the time or trouble. * *n* worry; trouble; someone who causes problems, etc.

botheration *n* bother.—*also interj*.

bothersome *adj* causing bother.

bothy *n* (*pl* **bothies**) (*Scot*) a small cottage or hut, esp a hut or barrack serving as farm servants' quarters; a shelter for climbers on mountains.

bo tree *n* the peepul, the sacred tree of the Buddhists.

botryoidal *adj* resembling a bunch of grapes.—**botryoidally** *adv*.

bott *see* **bot**.

bottle[1] *n* a glass or plastic container for holding liquids; its contents; (*sl*) courage, nerve. * *vt* to put in bottles; to confine as if in a bottle.

bottle[2] *n* (*dial*) a quantity of hay or grass bundled up.

bottle green *adj* dark green.

bottleneck *n* a narrow stretch of a road where traffic is held up; a congestion in any stage of a process.

bottlenose *n* a dolphin with a sharp protruding beak; a moderately large toothed whale with a prominent beak.

bottom *n* the lowest or deepest part of anything; the base or foundation; the lowest position (eg in a class); the buttocks; (*naut*) the part of a ship's hull below water; the seabed. * *vt* to be based or founded on; to bring to the bottom, to get to the bottom of. * *vi* to become based; to reach the bottom; (*with* **out**) to flatten off after dropping sharply.

bottomlands *npl* rich flat low-lying land along watercourses in the western states of the US.

bottomless *adj* very deep; without limit.

bottom line *n* the crux; the line at the bottom of a financial report that shows the net profit or loss; the final result.—**bottom-line** *adj*.

bottomry *n* (*pl* **bottomries**) the borrowing of money by the owner on the security of his or her ship. * *vt* to pledge (a ship) thus.

botulism *n* a type of severe food poisoning.

bouclé, boucle *n* a type of looped yarn or fabric.

boudoir *n* a woman's bedroom.

bouffant *adj* puffed out; (*of hair*) backcombed.

bougainvillea, bougainvillaea *n* a tropical plant with large rosy or purple bracts.

bough *n* a branch of a tree.

bought *see* **buy**.

bougie *n* a wax candle; (*med*) a slender flexible tube for inserting into the gullet, etc; a catheter.

bouillabaisse *n* a French fish stew.

bouillon *n* a clear seasoned stock or broth.

boulder *n* a large stone or mass of rock rounded by the action of erosion.

boule¹ *n* an imitation gemstone.

boule² *n* in ancient Athens, a higher popular assembly, (*with cap*) the lower house of the modern Greek legislative assembly.

boule³ *see* **boulle**.

boules *n* (*used as sing*) a French game similar to bowls played with small, hard balls.

boulevard *n* a broad, often tree-lined road.

boulevardier *n* a frequenter of a boulevard, esp a Parisian; a man about town.

bouleversement *n* an overturning, overthrow.

boulle *n* decorative inlaying for cabinetwork, consisting of brass or other metal, tortoiseshell, etc, worked into scrolls or other patterns; the articles so ornamented.—*also* **boule, buhl**.

boult *see* **bolt**².

bounce *vi* to rebound; to jump up suddenly; (*sl: cheque*) to be returned because of lack of funds; (*with* **back**) to recover easily, eg from misfortune or ill health. * *vt* to cause a ball to bounce; (*sl*) to put (a person) out by force; (*sl*) to fire from a job. * *n* a leap or springiness; capacity for bouncing; sprightliness; boastfulness, arrogance.

bouncer *n* (*sl*) a man hired to remove disorderly people from nightclubs, etc.

bouncing *adj* big, healthy, etc.

bouncy *adj* able to spring or bound; elastic; vigorous, lively.—**bouncily** *adv*.—**bounciness** *n*.

bound¹ *see* **bind**.

bound² *n* (*usu pl*) the limit or boundary. * *vt* to limit, confine or surround; to name the boundaries of.

bound³ *n* a jump or leap. * *vi* to jump or leap.

bound⁴ *adj* (*with* **for**) intending to go to, on the way to.

boundary *n* (*pl* **boundaries**) the border of an area; the limit; (*cricket*) the limit line of a field; a stroke that goes beyond the boundary line.

bounden *adj* (*duty*) obligatory.

bounden duty *n* a moral obligation.

bounder *n* one who or that which bounds; (*inf*) an insolent, ill-bred man, who makes himself disagreeable to those whom he meets.

boundless *adj* unlimited, vast.—**boundlessly** *adv*.—**boundlessness** *n*.

bounteous *adj* giving freely, bountiful, generous; plentiful.—**bounteously** *adv*.—**bounteousness** *n*.

bountiful *adj* generous in giving.—**bountifully** *adv*.—**bountifulness** *n*.

bounty *n* (*pl* **bounties**) generosity in giving; the gifts given; a reward or premium.

bouquet *n* a bunch of flowers; the perfume given off by wine.

bouquet garni *n* (*pl* **bouquets garnis**) herbs tied in a small bundle used for flavouring stews, soups, sauces, etc.

bourbon *n* a whiskey distilled in the US from corn mash.

bourdon *n* the bass drone of the bagpipe; a bass stop of an organ.

bourgeois *n* (*pl* **bourgeois**) a member of the bourgeoisie or middle class; a conventional and unimaginative individual. * *adj* smug, respectable, conventional; mediocre.

bourgeoisie *n* the class between the lower and upper classes, mostly composed of professional and business people.—*also* **middle class**.

bourn, bourne¹ *n* a small stream, a rivulet.

bourn, bourne² *n* (*arch*) a boundary; a destination, goal; a realm.

bourrée *n* (*mus*) a composition of a lively character, similar to the gavotte; the music for this.

bourse *n* a stock exchange for the transaction of business; (*with cap*) the stock exchange of Paris.

bouse *vi* (*naut*) to pull or haul hard.—*also* **bowse**.

boustrophedon *n* an ancient mode of writing lines alternately from left to right and from right to left.—**boustrophedonic** *adj*.

bout *n* a spell, a turn, a period spent in some activity; a contest or struggle, esp boxing or wrestling; a time of illness.

boutique *n* a small shop, usually selling fashionable clothing and accessories.

boutonniere, boutonnière *n* a buttonhole; a spray of flowers worn in it.

bouzouki *n* (*pl* **bouzoukis**) a Greek stringed instrument similar to the mandolin.

bovine *adj* relating to cattle; dull; sluggish. * *n* an ox, cow etc.

bow¹ *vi* to bend the knee or to lean the head (and chest) forward as a form of greeting or respect or shame; (*with* **before**) to accept, to submit; (*with* **out**) to withdraw or retire gracefully. * *vt* to bend downwards; to weigh down; to usher in or out with a bow. * *n* a lowering of the head (and chest) in greeting.

bow² *n* a weapon for shooting arrows; an implement for playing the strings of a violin; a decorative knot of ribbon, etc. * *vti* to bend, curve.

bow³ *n* the forward part of a ship.

bow compass *n* (*geom*) a compass with jointed legs.

bowdlerize *vt* to expurgate, to remove indelicate words from.—**bowdlerism** *n*.—**bowdlerization** *n*.

bowel *n* the intestine; (*pl*) entrails; (*pl*) the deep and remote part of anything.

bower¹ *n* an arbour, a shady recess; (*poet*) dwelling.

bower² *n* (*naut*) an anchor carried at the bow of a ship.

bower³ *n* (*cards*) one of the two highest cards in some card games, or the second and third highest (when the joker is used).

bowerbird *n* one of various Australian birds belonging to the starling family.

bowhead *n* an Arctic whale with a large mouth; Greenland whale.

bowie knife *n* a long hunting knife, a sheath knife.

bowing *n* a playing upon an instrument of the violin class with a bow; the particular style of execution.

bowl¹ *n* a wooden ball having a bias used in bowling; (*pl*) a game played on a smooth lawn with bowls. * *vti* to play the game of bowls; (*cricket*) to send a ball to a batsman; to dismiss (a batsman) by hitting the wicket with a bowled ball; (*with* **over**) to knock over; (*inf*) to astonish.

bowl² *n* a deep, rounded dish; the rounded end of a pipe; a sports stadium.

bow-legged *adj* having legs that curve outwards between the thigh and the ankle; bandy.

bowler¹ *n* a person who plays bowls; (*cricket*) the player who delivers the ball.

bowler² *n* a stiff felt hat.—*also* **derby**.

bowline *n* (*naut*) a knot used in making a fixed end loop; (*naut*) a rope from the weather side of a square sail to the bow to keep the ship near the wind.

bowling *n* a game in which a heavy wooden ball is bowled along a bowling alley at ten wooden skittles; the game of bowls.

bowling alley *n* a long narrow wooden lane, usu one of several in a building designed for them.

bowling green *n* a smooth lawn for bowls.

bowman¹ *n* (*pl* **bowmen**) an archer.

bowman² *n* (*pl* **bowmen**) (*naut*) the oarsman nearest the bow.

bowsaw *n* a saw with a blade under tension for cutting curves.

bowse *see* **bouse**.

bowsprit *n* a large boom or spar running out from the stem of a (sailing) ship to carry its sails forward.

bowstring *n* the string of a bow.

bow tie *n* a necktie tied in the shape of a bow.

bow window *n* a curved bay window.

bow-wow *n* a dog's bark; a child's name for a dog. * *vi* to bark like a dog.

bowyer *n* a maker or seller of archery bows.

box¹ *n* a container or receptacle for holding anything; (*theatre*) a compartment with seats; (*inf*) a television set. * *vt* to put into a box; to enclose; (*with* in) to restrict.

box² *vt* to hit using the hands or fists. * *vi* to fight with the fists.* *n* a blow on the head or ear with the fist.

box³ *n* an evergreen shrub or small tree yielding a hard close-grained wood; the wood. * *adj* of box or boxwood.

boxcar *n* an enclosed freight car.

boxer *n* a person who engages in boxing; a breed of dog with smooth hair and a stumpy tail.

boxer shorts *npl* loose underpants that resemble the pants worn by boxers.

box girder *n* a girder constructed from rectangular metal plates.

boxing *n* the skill or sport of fighting with the fists.

Boxing Day the weekday following December 25, Christmas, when traditionally presents are given to tradesmen, employees, etc.

box office *n* a theatre ticket office; the popularity of a play, film, actor.—**box-office** *adj*.

box pleat *n* a double pleat in cloth made by two facing folds.

boxwood *n* the hard wood of the box tree; the tree itself.

boy *n* a male child; a son; a lad; a youth. * *interj* an exclamation of surprise or joy.

boyar *n* (*formerly*) a Russian landed proprietor of an old aristocratic order abolished by Peter I.

boycott *vt* to refuse to deal with or trade with in order to punish or coerce.—*also n*.

boyfriend *n* a male friend with whom a person is romantically or sexually involved.

boyhood *n* the time, or state, of being a boy.

boyish *adj* like a boy; puerile; with the appeal of a boy.—**boyishly** *adv*.—**boyishness** *n*.

Boy Scout *n* a scout; (*without cap*) (*inf*) a man with a strong sense of duty.

boysenberry *n* (*pl* **boysenberries**) (the fruit of) a hybrid shrub developed by crossing the loganberry and various blackberries and raspberries.

BP, B/P *abbr* = blood pressure.

Bq (*symbol*) bequerel.

Br *abbr* = British; (*chem symbol*) bromine; brother.

bra *n* a brassiere.

brace *n* a prop; a support to stiffen a framework; a hand tool for drilling; (*pl* **brace**) a pair, esp of game; (*pl*) straps for holding up trousers; a dental appliance for straightening the teeth. * *vt* to steady.

brace and bit *n* a revolving tool for boring.

bracelet *n* an ornamental chain or band for the wrist; (*pl*: *sl*) handcuffs.

bracer¹ *n* something that braces; a pick-me-up.

bracer² *n* a wrist guard in archery.

brachial *adj* of, pertaining to, or like the arm.

brachiate *adj* having arms; (*bot*) having branches in pairs, nearly horizontal and each pair at right angles to the next.—**brachiation**.

brachiopod *n* an animal like a mollusc with two spirally coiled armlike appendages, one on each side of the mouth.

brachy- *prefix* short.

brachycephalic, brachycephalous *adj* (*anat*) having the skull short in proportion to its breadth, short-headed.—**brachycephaly** *n*.

brachylogy *n* (*pl* **brachylogies**) conciseness; a condensed expression.—**brachylogous** *adj*.

brachypterous *adj* (*insects*) short-winged.

brachyuran *adj* of or belonging to a group of ten-footed crustaceans, including the crabs, marked by an undeveloped abdomen (—*also* **brachyurous**) * *n* a member of this group.

bracing *adj* refreshing, invigorating.—**bracingly** *adv*.

bracken *n* a large, coarse fern; a wide area of these growing on hills or moorland.

bracket *n* a projecting metal support for a shelf; a group or category of people classified according to income; (*pl*) a pair of characters (), [], {}, used in printing or writing as parentheses. * *vt* to support with brackets; to enclose by brackets; (*people*) to group together.

brackish *adj* somewhat salty; nauseating.—**brackishness** *n*.

bract *n* a modified leaf growing from a flower stem or enveloping a head of flowers.—**bracteal** *adj*.

bracteate *adj* (*plant*) furnished with bracts. * *n* a plate or dish made of a thin beaten precious metal and decorated.

brad *n* a slender flat nail with a projection on one side.

bradawl *n* a small boring tool for making holes for brads.

brady- *prefix* slow.

brae *n* (*Scot*) a hillside; sloping ground.

brag *vti* (**bragging, bragged**) to boast. * *n* a boast or boastful talk.—**bragger** *n*.

braggadocio *n* (*pl* **braggadocios**) bragging talk, empty boasting; a boaster, braggart.

braggart *n* a loud arrogant boaster.

Brahma¹ *n* (*Hinduism*) a supreme god; divine essence.

Brahma² *n* a useful variety of large domestic fowl with feathered legs.

Brahman¹ *n* (*pl* **Brahmans**) (*Hinduism*) a member of the highest caste, formerly consisting only of priests; Brahma.—**Brahmanic, Brahmanical** *adj*.

Brahman² *n* (*pl* **Brahmans, Brahman**) a breed of Indian cattle with a large hump used in crossbreeding beef cattle.

Brahmani *n* (*pl* **Brahmanis**) a female Brahman.

Brahmanism *n* the religion or doctrines of the Brahmans.—**Brahmanist** *n*.

Brahmin *n* a Brahman; a member of an upper-class New England family.

braid *vt* to interweave three or more strands (of hair, straw, etc); to make by such interweaving. * *n* a narrow band made by such interweaving for decorating clothing; a plait.—**braider** *n*.

brail *n* (*naut*) one of certain ropes used to gather up the foot and leeches of a sail prior to furling. * *vt* (*usu with* **up**) to haul in by the brails.

Braille *n* printing for the blind, using a system of raised dots that can be understood by touch.—*also adj*.

brain *n* nervous tissue contained in the skull of vertebrates that controls the nervous system; intellectual ability; (*inf*) a person of great intelligence; (often *pl*) the chief planner of an organization or enterprise. * *vt* to shatter the skull of; (*sl*) to hit on the head.

brainchild *n* (*pl* **brainchildren**) the result of creative thought; a clever and original idea or plan.

brain death *n* the irreversible cessation of brain activity, but not of the heartbeat, widely accepted as a criterion of death.

brain drain *n* the loss of highly skilled scientists, technicians, academics, etc through emigration.

brainless *adj* (*inf*) stupid.—**brainlessness** *n*.

brainpan *n* the cranium.

brainstorm *n* a violent mental disturbance; a brain wave.

brainteaser *n* a mathematical puzzle; a difficult problem.

brainwash *vt* to change a person's ideas or beliefs by physical or mental conditioning, usu over a long period.—**brainwasher** *n*.—**brainwashing** *n*.

brain wave *n* an electrical impulse in the brain; (*inf*) a bright idea.

brainy *adj* (**brainier**, **brainiest**) (*inf*) having a good mind; intelligent.—**braininess** *n*.

braise *vt* (*meat, vegetables, etc*) to sauté lightly and cook slowly in liquid with the lid on.

brake[1] *n* a device for slowing or stopping the motion of a wheel by friction. * *vt* to retard or stop by a brake. * *vi* to apply the brake on a vehicle; to become checked by a brake.

brake[2] *n* bracken.

brake[3] *n* a place overgrown with brushwood, etc; a thicket.

brake horsepower *n* the rate of work of an engine measured in terms of its resistance to a brake.

brakeman *n* (*pl* **brakemen**) a person in charge of a brake; a guard on a train; the person at the back of a bobsled team.

brake shoe *n* that part of a brake which presses against the wheel.

bramble *n* a prickly shrub or vine, esp of blackberries and raspberries.—**brambly** *adj*.

brambling *n* a migratory European finch with bright plumage.

bran *n* the husks of grain separated by sieving from the flour; a food containing these.

branch *n* an offshoot extending from the trunk or bough of a tree or from the parent stem of a shrub; a separately located subsidiary or office of an enterprise or business; a part of something larger, eg a road or railway. * *vi* to possess branches; to divide into branches; to come out (from a main part) as a branch; (*with* **out**) to extend or enlarge one's interests, activities, etc.

branchia *n* (*pl* **branchiae**) a respiratory organ of fishes and some amphibians, a gill.—**branchial** *adj*.

branchiate *adj* having permanent gills.

branchio- *prefix* gills.

branchiopod *n* one of a group of crustaceans, including the water flea, the gills of which are situated on the feet.

brand *n* an identifying mark on cattle, imprinted with hot iron; a burning piece of wood; a mark of disgrace; a trademark; a particular make (of goods). * *vt* to burn a mark with a hot iron; to fix in the memory; to denounce.

brandish *vt* (*a weapon, etc*) to wave or flourish in a threatening manner.—**brandisher** *n*.

brandling *n* a small brownish-red earthworm used as bait by freshwater anglers.

brand name *n* the name by which a certain commodity is known.—**brand-name** *adj*.

brand-new *adj* entirely new and unused.

brandy *n* (*pl* **brandies**) an alcoholic liquor made from distilled wine or fermented fruit juice.

brant *n* the brent goose, the smallest species of the wild goose.

brash[1] *adj* bold; loud-mouthed; reckless.—**brashly** *adv*.—**brashness** *n*.

brash[2] *n* broken, loose and angular fragments of rock underlying alluvial deposits; small broken pieces of ice; hedge clippings.

brash[3] *n* acid eructation, a fit of sickness; a rash; a burst of rain.

brasilin *see* **brazilin**.

brass *n* an alloy of copper and zinc; (*inf*) impudence; nerve; cheek; money; (*often pl*) the brass instruments of an orchestra or band; (*sl*) officers or officials of high rank.

brassard, brassart *n* armour for the upper arm; an armlet for the upper arm.

brass band *n* a band that uses brass and percussion instruments.

brasserie *n* a bar and restaurant.

brassica *n* any of a group of plants that includes cabbages, turnips and mustards.—**brassicaceous** *adj*.

brassie *n* (*golf*) a wooden club orig with a brass sole, now No.2 wood.

brassiere *n* a woman's undergarment for protecting and supporting the breasts, a bra.

brass tacks *npl* (*inf*) basic facts.

brassy *adj* (**brassier**, **brassiest**) like brass; brazen, cheeky.—**brassily** *adv*.—**brassiness** *n*.

brat *n* an ill-mannered, annoying child.

bratpack *n* a group of precociously young actors, writers, etc.

brattice *n* (*mining*) a wooden partition or separating wall in a level or shaft to form an air passage. * *vt* to divide by a brattice.

bratwurst *n* a type of seasoned German sausage made from pork.

bravado *n* (*pl* **bravadoes**, **bravados**) pretended confidence; swaggering.

brave *adj* showing courage; not timid or cowardly; fearless; handsome; of excellent appearance. * *vt* to confront boldly; to defy. * *n* a North American Indian warrior.—**bravely** *adv*.

bravery n (pl **braveries**) the quality of being brave; courage, fearlessness; finery, magnificence.

bravo interj well done! * n (pl **bravoes, bravos**) a cry or shout of "bravo!"

bravura n bold daring; dash; (mus) a passage requiring spirit and technical brilliance.

brawl n a loud quarrel; a noisy fight. * vi to quarrel loudly.—**brawler** n.

brawn n strong, well-developed muscles; physical strength; pickled pork.

brawny adj (**brawnier, brawniest**) muscular, tough.—**brawnily** adv.—**brawniness** n.

bray[1] n the sound of a donkey; any harsh sound. * vi (**braying, brayed**) to make similar sounds.—**brayer** n.

bray[2] vt (**braying, brayed**) to pound or beat fine or small.

brayer n (print) a hand roller used to rub down and temper ink.

braze[1] vt to solder with an alloy of brass and zinc.—**brazer** n.

braze[2] vt to cover or ornament with brass; to colour like brass.

brazen adj made of brass; shameless. * vt (usu with out) to face a situation boldly and shamelessly.—**brazenness** n.

brazier[1] n a metal container for hot coals.

brazier[2] n a worker in brass.

brazil n brazilwood; a dye of various tints of esp red and orange obtained from brazilin.

brazilin n the colouring substance extracted from brazilwood.—also **brasilin.**

brazil nut n a large three-cornered nut, the seed of a tall tree of Brazil.

brazilwood n a very heavy wood of a red colour from various species of Central and South American trees.

breach n a break or rupture; violation of a contract, promise, etc; a break in friendship. * vt to make an opening in.

breach of promise n the breaking of a promise to marry.

breach of the peace n a public disturbance.

bread n a dough, made from flour, yeast and milk, that is baked; nourishment; (sl) money; **bread and butter** (inf) one's livelihood. * vt to coat meat, fish, etc with breadcrumbs before cooking.

bread-and-butter adj (job) providing a basic income; (issues, etc) fundamental, basic; (letter) thanking for hospitality.

breadbasket n a basket for holding bread; (sl) the stomach; a source of food.

breadboard n a wooden board for cutting bread on; board used for constructing experimental electric circuits.

breaded adj coated with breadcrumbs.

breadfruit n (pl **breadfruits, breadfruit**) the fruit of a tree growing in the Pacific islands, which, when roasted, is eaten as bread.

breadline n a queue for bread ration; **on the breadline** poverty-stricken, only just able to subsist.

breadth n measurement from side to side, width; extent; liberality (eg of interests).

breadthways, breadthwise adv from side to side.

breadwinner n the principal wage-earner of a family.

break vb (**breaking, broke**, pp **broken**) vt to smash or shatter; to tame; (rules) to violate; to discontinue; to cause to give up a habit; (fall) to lessen the severity of; to ruin financially; (news) to impart; to decipher or solve; (with **down**) to crush or destroy; to analyse; (with **in**) to intervene; to train. * vi to fall apart; (voice) to assume a lower tone at puberty; to cut off relations with; to suffer a collapse, as of spirit; (news) to become public in a sudden and sensational way; (with **down**) to fail completely; to succumb emotionally; (with **even**) to suffer neither profit nor loss (after taking certain action); (with **in**) to force a way in; (with **out**) to appear, begin; to erupt; to throw off restraint, escape; (with **up**) to disperse; to separate; to collapse. * n a breaking; an interruption; a gap; a sudden change, as in weather; a rest or a short holiday; an escape; (snooker, billiards) a continuous run of points; (sl) a fortunate opportunity.

breakable adj able to be broken. * n a fragile object.

breakage n the action of breaking; something broken.

breakaway n secession, disassociation.

break dancing n dancing that involves acrobatic movements.

breakdown n a mechanical failure; failure of health; nervous collapse; an analysis.

breakdown truck n a vehicle for towing away smashed or damaged cars, etc.

breaker[1] n a large wave that crashes onto the shore, reef, etc.

breaker[2] n (naut) a small cask for holding water.

breakeven n the point at which costs are covered but no profit is made.

breakfast n the first meal of the morning; the food consumed. * vi to have breakfast.

break-in n the unlawful entering of premises, esp by thieves.

breakneck adj dangerously steep or fast.

break of day n dawn.

break-out n an escape, esp from prison.

breakthrough n the action of breaking through an obstruction; an important advance or discovery.

break-up n separation; collapse; dispersal.

breakwater n a barrier that protects a harbour or area of coast against the force of the waves.

bream[1] n (pl **bream**) a freshwater fish.

bream[2] vt (naut) to clear (a ship's bottom) of shells, seaweed, etc, by heating and scraping.

breast n the chest; one of the two mammary glands; the seat of the emotions. * vt to oppose, confront; to arrive at the top of; to confess (make a clean breast of).

breastbone n (anat) the flat narrow bone in the centre of the chest that connects the ribs, the sternum.

breast-feed vt (**breast-feeding, breast-fed**) to allow a baby to suck milk from the breast.

breastplate n armour covering the front of the body; a part of the vestment of a Jewish high priest.

breaststroke n a swimming stroke in which both arms are brought out sideways from the chest.

breastwork n a hastily constructed work thrown up breast-high for defence; the parapet of a building.

breath n the inhalation and exhalation of air in breathing; the air taken into the lungs; life; a slight breeze; (scandal) a hint.

Breathalyzer, Breathalyser n (trademark) a device for measuring the amount of alcohol in a person's breath.

breathe vi to inhale and exhale, to respire air; to take a rest or pause; to exist or live; to speak or sing softly; to whisper. * vt to emit or exhale; to whisper or speak softly.

breather n a pause during exercise to recover one's breath.

breathing n respiration; air in gentle motion; a gentle influence; a pause; (*phonetics*) an accent (') whether an initial vowel is aspirated or not.

breathing space n a pause in which to recover, get organized or get going.

breathless *adj* out of breath; panting; gasping; unable to breathe easily because of emotion.—**breathlessly** *adv.*—**breathlessness** n.

breathtaking *adj* very exciting.

breathy *adj* (**breathier, breathiest**) (*voice*) not clear sounding.—**breathily** *adv.*—**breathiness** n.

breccia n a rock of angular fragments cemented by lime, etc.—**brecciated** *adj.*

bred *see* **breed.**

bree n (*Scot*) broth; juice or liquor in which something has been steeped or boiled.

breech n the back part of a gun barrel.

breech delivery, breech birth n the birth of a baby buttocks or feet first.

breeches *npl* trousers extending just below the knee.

breeches buoy n a lifebuoy on a hawser to take people off a wreck.

breeching n the harness that passes round a horse's hindquarters; a strong rope to check the recoil of a gun.

breechloader n a gun loaded at the breach.—**breechloading** *adj.*

breed *vb* (**breeding, bred**) *vt* to engender; to bring forth; (*dogs*) to raise; to give rise to. * *vi* to produce young; to be generated. * n offspring; lineage or race; species (of animal).—**breeder** n.

breeder reactor n a nuclear reactor that produces more fissile material than it consumes.

breeding n the bearing of offspring; one's education and training; refined behaviour.

breeze[1] n a light gentle wind; something easy to do. * *vi* (*inf*) to move quickly or casually.

breeze[2] n sifted ashes and cinders used in burning bricks; house sweepings, refuse.

breeze block n a lightweight building brick composed mainly of the ashes of coal and coke.

breezy *adj* (**breezier, breeziest**) windy; nonchalant; light-hearted, cheerful.—**breezily** *adv.*—**breeziness** n.

brent (goose) n the smallest species of the wild goose.—*also* **brant.**

br'er n (*dial*) brother.

brethren *see* **brother.**

Breton *adj* of or relating to Brittany, its people or language. * n an inhabitant of Brittany; the Celtic language of Brittany.

breve n a mark (^) used to indicate a short vowel; (*mus*) the longest note now used, equal to two whole notes (two semibreves or four minims).

brevet n (*mil*) a commission to an officer in the army conferring a higher rank but without increase of pay; a warrant; a licence. * *adj* conferred by brevet; nominal, honorary. * *vt* (**brevetting, brevetted** *or* **breveting, breveted**) to confer brevet rank on.—**brevetcy** n.

brevi- *prefix* short.

breviary n (*pl* **breviaries**) (*RC Church*) a book containing the daily offices and prayers.

brevirostrate *adj* (*birds*) short-billed.

brevity n (*pl* **brevities**) briefness; conciseness.

brew *vt* to make (beer, ale, etc) from malt and hops by boiling and fermenting; to infuse (tea, etc); to plot, scheme. * *vi* to be in the process of being brewed; to

be about to happen. * n a brewed drink.

brewage n something made by brewing; the brewing process.

brewer n a person who brews, usu beer.

brewery n (*pl* **breweries**) a place where beer, etc is brewed.

briar *see* **brier.**

bribe n money or gifts offered illegally to gain favour or influence; the gift to achieve this. * *vt* to offer or give a bribe to.—**bribable** *adj.*—**briber** n.

bribery n (*pl* **briberies**) the giving or taking of bribes.

bric-a-brac n curios, ornamental or rare odds and ends.

brick n a baked clay block for building; a similar shaped block of other material. * *vt* to lay or wall up with brick.

brickbat n a piece of brick, esp one used as a weapon; an unfavourable remark.

bricklayer n a person who lays bricks.

brick red n a greyish red colour.—**brick-red** *adj.*

brickwork n a structure formed of bricks.

bridal *adj* relating to a bride or a wedding.

bride n a woman about to be married or recently married.

bridegroom n a man about to be married or recently married.

bridesmaid n a young girl or woman attending the bride during a wedding.

bridge[1] n a structure built to convey people or traffic over a river, road, railway line, etc; the platform on a ship where the captain gives directions; the hard ridge of bone in the nose; an arch to raise the strings of a guitar, etc; a mounting for false teeth.* *vt* to be or act as a bridge; to be a connecting link between.—**bridgeable** *adj.*

bridge[2] n a card game for two teams of two players based on whist.

bridgeboard n a notched board into which the ends of the steps of wooden stairs are fastened.

bridgehead n a defensive work covering the end of a bridge nearest the enemy; a foothold in enemy territory.

bridgework n a false tooth or teeth secured to the natural teeth.

bridging n a piece of wood between two beams to keep them apart.

bridging loan n a loan, usu short-term, advanced to cover the gap between the settlement of two transactions, esp between buying a new house and selling the old one.

bridle n the headgear of a horse, controlling its movements; a restraint or check; (*naut*) a mooring cable. * *vt* to put a bridle on (a horse); to restrain or check. * *vi* to draw one's head back as an expression of anger, scorn, etc.—**bridler** n.

bridle path n a trail suitable for horse riding.

bridoon n the light snaffle and rein of a military bridle.

Brie n creamy white soft cheese.

brief n a summary of a client's case for the instruction of a barrister in a trial at law; an outline of an argument, esp that setting out the main contentions; (*pl*) men's or women's close-fitting underpants or knickers. * *vt* to provide with a precise summary of the facts. * *adj* short, concise.—**briefly** *adv.*—**briefness** n.

briefcase n a flat case for carrying documents, etc.

brier n a plant with a thorny or prickly woody stem; a mass of these; a tobacco pipe made from the root of the brier.—*also* **briar.**—**briery, briary** *adj.*

brig *n* a two-masted square-rigged vessel; a naval prison, esp on a ship.

brigade *n* an army unit, smaller than a division, commanded by a brigadier; a group of people organized to perform a particular function.

brigadier *n* an officer commanding a brigade and ranking next below a major general.

brigand *n* a bandit, usu one of a roving gang.

brigantine *n* a small two-masted vessel, square-rigged on the foremast only and with raking masts.

bright *adj* clear, shining; brilliant in colour or sound; favourable or hopeful; intelligent, illustrious. * *adv* brightly.—**brightly** *adv.*—**brightness** *n*.

brighten *vti* to make or become brighter.—**brightener** *n*.

Bright's disease *n* a kidney disease characterized by the presence of albumin in the urine.

brill *n* (*pl* **brill, brills**) a European flatfish resembling the turbot.

brilliance *n* intense radiance, lustre, splendour.

brilliancy *n* the quality of being brilliant; shining quality, lustrousness, shining brightness.

brilliant *adj* sparkling, bright; splendid; very intelligent.—**brilliantly** *adv*.

brilliantine *n* a cosmetic oil giving a gloss to the hair; a shiny fabric of cotton and mohair.

brim *n* the rim of a hollow vessel; the outer edge of a hat. * *vti* (**brimming, brimmed**) to fill or be filled to the brim; (*with* **over**) to overflow.

brimful *adj* completely full; overflowing.

brimstone *n* sulphur; a yellow butterfly.

brindled *adj* streaked brown or grey, or with flecks of a darker colour.

brine *n* salt water; the sea.

bring *vt* (**bringing, brought**) to fetch, carry or convey "here" or to the place where the speaker will be; to cause to happen (eg rain, relief), to result in; to lead to an action or belief; to sell for; (*with* **about**) to induce, to effect; (*with* **down**) to cause to fall by or as if by shooting; (*with* **forth**) to give birth to; (*with* **forward**) to present something for consideration; to transfer a total figure from the bottom of a page to the top of the next page; (*with* **in**) to yield a profit or return; to return a verdict in court; to introduce (a legislative bill); to earn (an income); (*with* **off**) to achieve a success, often against odds; accomplish; (*with* **out**) to cause to appear; to produce (a play) or publish (a book); to demonstrate clearly, expose to view; to help someone with encouragement; (*with* **over**) to convince a person to change their loyalties; (*with* **round**) to convince a person to change their opinion; to get someone to agree or give support; to restore a person to consciousness, revive; (*with* **up**) to educate, rear a child; to raise (a matter) for discussion; to vomit.—**bringer** *n*.

brink *n* the verge of a steep place; the edge of the sea; the point of onset; the threshold of danger.

brinkmanship, brinksmanship *n* the pursuing of a policy, esp in international relations, that brings serious risk of danger in order to gain advantage.

briny *adj* (**brinier, briniest**) salty. * *n* the sea.—**brininess** *n*.

brio *n* vivacity.

brioche *n* a small, slightly sweet, bread roll.

briony *see* **bryony**.

briquette, briquet *n* a compacted brick usu of fine compressed material, esp charcoal.

brisk *adj* alert; quick; vigorous; sharp in tone.—**briskly** *adv.*—**briskness** *n*.

brisket *n* meat from the breast of an animal.

brisling *n* a small fish like a sardine.

bristle *n* a short, coarse hair. * *vi* to stand up, as bristles; to have the bristles standing up; to show anger or indignation; to be thickly covered (with).

bristly *adj* (**bristlier, bristliest**) covered with bristles; rough.—**bristliness** *n*.

Bristol board *n* a thick smooth white pasteboard.

brit *n* the young of the herring and sprat; small animals upon which whales feed.

Brit *n* (*inf*) a British person.

Brit. *abbr* = Britain; British.

Britannia *n* Britain or its former empire personified.

Britannia metal *n* a white metal alloy of tin, copper, antimony and bismuth, resembling pewter.

Britannic *adj* of Britain; British.

Briticism *n* a word, phrase, etc, peculiar to or characteristic of British English.

British *adj* of or pertaining to Great Britain or its inhabitants; pertaining to the ancient Britons. * *n* the people of Britain; the language of the ancient Britons.

Britisher *n* a British subject.

Britishism *n* a Briticism.

Briton *n* a native of Great Britain, esp before the Anglo-Saxon conquest.

brittle *adj* easily cracked or broken; fragile; sharp-tempered.—**brittleness** *n*.

britzka, britzska *n* an open carriage with a hooded top and space for reclining.

bro *n* (*inf*) mate, buddy.

broach *vt* (*a topic*) to introduce for discussion; to pierce (a container) and draw out liquid.

broad *adj* of large extent from side to side; wide; spacious; giving an overall view or idea; (*humour*) coarse; strongly marked in dialect or pronunciation. * *n* (*sl*) a woman.—**broadly** *adv.*—**broadness** *n*.

broad arrow *n* an arrow with a broad barbed head; a UK government mark to distinguish its property.

broad bean *n* a plant widely grown for its large flat edible seed.

broadcast *n* a programme on radio or television. * *vti* (**broadcasting, broadcast**) to transmit on radio or television; to make known widely; to scatter seed.—**broadcaster** *n*.

Broad Church *n* a section or party intermediate between the High and the Low Church of England; any group that opposes rigid dogma.—**Broad-Church** *adj*.

broadcloth *n* a fine woollen cloth with a smooth finished surface.

broaden *vti* to grow or make broad; to widen.

broadloom *adj* (*carpets*) woven on a wide loom.

broad-minded *adj* tolerant; liberal in outlook.—**broadmindedly** *adv.*—**broad-mindedness** *n*.

broad seal *n* the official seal of a nation.

broadsheet *n* a large sheet of paper printed on one side only; a large format newspaper, approx 15 by 24 inches (38 by 61cms).

broadside *n* the entire side of a ship above the waterline; a simultaneous volley from one side of a warship; a sheet printed on one side containing information of a popular nature or an attack on some public person; any verbal or written attack.

broad-spectrum *adj* efficacious against a wide range (of diseases, microorganisms).

broadsword n a cutting sword with a broad straight blade.

Brobdingnagian adj resembling one of the giant inhabitants of the land of Brobdingnag in Swift's *Gulliver's Travels*; gigantic.

brocade n a heavy fabric woven with raised patterns, orig in gold and silver. * vt to work with a raised pattern.

brocatelle, brocatel n a figured brocade of silky texture; a variegated marble from Italy and Spain.

broccoli n (pl **broccoli**) a kind of cauliflower with loose heads of tiny green buds.

broch n (Scot) a dry-built circular tower of the Iron Age.

brochette n (food cooked on) a skewer or small spit.

brochure n an advertising booklet.

brock n (dial) a badger.

brogan n a sturdy ankle-high work shoe.

brogue n a sturdy shoe; a dialectical accent, esp Irish.

broil[1] vti to cook by exposure to direct heat; to grill.

broil[2] n a noisy quarrel, a tumult. * vi to be heated with passion.

broiler n a pan, grill, etc for broiling; a bird fit for broiling.

broke pt of **break**. * adj (inf) hard up, having no money.

broken pp of **break**. * adj splintered, fractured; violated; ruined; tamed; disconnected, interrupted; overwhelmed by sorrow or ill fortune; (speech) imperfect.—**brokenly** adv.—**brokenness** n.

broken-down adj extremely infirm; worn out.

brokenhearted adj grief-stricken; very sad.

broken-winded adj (horse) having the heaves.

broker n an agent who negotiates contracts of purchase and sale (as of commodities or securities); a power broker; a stockbroker.

brokerage n a broker's business; the commission charged by a broker.

bromate n a salt of bromic acid.

brome (grass) n any of a genus of oat-like grasses with drooping clusters of spikelets.

bromic acid n a compound of bromine and oxygen.

bromide n a compound of bromine; a sedative; (sl) a bore; a trite remark.

bromine n an evil-smelling nonmetallic element related to chlorine and iodine.—**bromic** adj.

bronchi see **bronchus**.

bronchia npl (sing **bronchium**) the bronchial tubes.

bronchial adj of or pertaining to the bronchial tubes.

bronchial tube n either of the two main branches of the windpipe.

bronchitis n inflammation of the lining of the bronchial tubes.—**bronchitic** adj.

bronchopneumonia n diffuse inflammation of the lungs and bronchi.

bronchus n (pl **bronchi**) one of the two principal branches of the windpipe or trachea.

bronco n (pl **broncos**) a wild or half-tamed horse of North America.

broncobuster n a cowboy who breaks in broncos.—**broncobusting** n.

brontosaur, brontosaurus n (pl **brontosauruses**) a large plant-eating dinosaur.—**brontosaurian** adj.

Bronx cheer n (inf) a rude sound made with the lips; a raspberry.

bronze n a copper and tin alloy, sometimes other elements; any object cast in bronze; a reddish-brown colour. * adj made of, or like, or of the colour of bronze; (skin) tanned.—**bronzy** adj.

Bronze Age n the age succeeding the Stone Age, the ornaments and weapons of that period being made of bronze.

brooch n an ornament held by a pin or a clasp.

brood vi to incubate or hatch (eggs); to ponder over or worry about. * n a group having a common nature or origin, esp the children in a family; the number produced in one hatch.

broody adj (**broodier, broodiest**) contemplative, moody; (inf) wanting to have a baby.—**broodily** adv.—**broodiness** n.

brook[1] n a freshwater stream.

brook[2] vt to tolerate.—**brookable** adj.

brooklet n a small brook.

broom[1] n a bundle of fibres or twigs attached to a long handle for sweeping.

broom[2] n a shrub bearing large yellow flowers.

broomstick n the handle of a broom.

Bros abbr = Brothers.

brose n (Scot) a kind of porridge made by pouring boiling water or milk or meat liquor on oatmeal.

broth n a thin or thick soup made by boiling meat, etc in water.

brothel n a house where prostitutes work.

brother n a male sibling; a friend who is like a brother; a fellow member of a group, profession or association; a lay member of a men's religious order; (pl **brethren**) used chiefly in formal address or in referring to the members of a society or sect.

brother-in-law n (pl **brothers-in-law**) the brother of a husband or wife; the husband of a sister.

Brother Jonathan n (hist) a humorous personification of the US.

brotherhood n the state or quality of being a brother, brotherliness; a fraternity, an association.

brotherly adj like a brother; kind; affectionate.—**brotherliness** n.

brougham n a light closed four-wheeled carriage for one or two horses.

brought see **bring**.

brouhaha n a fuss; uproar.

brow n the forehead; the eyebrows; the top of a cliff; the jutting top of a hill.

browbeat vt (**browbeating, browbeat**, pp **browbeaten**) to intimidate with threats, to bully.

brown adj having the colour of chocolate, a mixture of red, black and yellow; tanned. * n a brown colour. * vti to make or become brown, esp by cooking.—**brownish** adj.—**brownness** n.

brown bear n a large wild bear of a brownish colour that lives in forests in temperate areas of Asia, North America and Europe.

brown bread n bread made from wholemeal flour.

brown coal n lignite.

browned-off adj (sl) fed up, depressed.

Brownian movement n a rapid whirling movement frequently seen in microscopic particles suspended in water or other liquids.

brownie n a square of flat, rich chocolate cake; a friendly helpful elf; (with cap) a member of the junior branch of the Girl Scout or Guide movement.

Brownie point n a credit gained by having scored some success.

Browning n an automatic or semi-automatic gas-operated rifle; an automatic machine gun.

brown rice n unpolished rice.

brownshirt n (often cap) a member of the Nazi Party; a

storm trooper.

brownstone *n* a kind of sandstone; a house built of this.

brown study *n* a reverie.

brown sugar *n* sugar that is unrefined or partially refined.

browse *vti* to nibble, to graze; to examine (a book) at one's leisure or casually.—**browser** *n*.

brucellosis *n* an infectious disease of livestock, esp cattle, which can be passed to human beings.

bruin *n* the brown bear personified.

bruise *vt* to injure and discolour (body tissue, surface of fruit) without breaking the skin; to break down (as leaves and berries) by pounding; to inflict psychological pain on. * *vi* to inflict a bruise; to undergo bruising. * *n* contusion of the skin; a similar injury to plant tissue; an injury, esp to the feelings.

bruiser *n* a tough, pugnacious man; a boxer.

bruit *n* a report; a rumour; fame. * *vt* to report; to noise abroad.

brumal *adj* of or like winter, wintry.

brume *n* fog, mist; a thick vapour.—**brumous** *adj*.

brunch *n* breakfast and lunch combined.

brunette, brunet *adj* having dark-brown or black hair, often with dark eyes. * *n* a brunette person.

brunt *n* the main force or shock of a blow; the hardest part.

brush[1] *n* a device made of bristles set in a handle, used for grooming the hair, painting or sweeping; a short unfriendly meeting or exchange of words; a fox's bushy tail; a light stroke or graze, made in passing. * *vt* to groom or sweep with a brush; to remove with a brush; (*with* **aside**) to ignore, to regard as little account; (*with* **up**) to refresh one's memory of or skill in a subject; to wash and tidy oneself. * *vi* to touch lightly or graze; (*with* **up**) to smarten one's appearance.—**brusher** *n*.

brush[2] *n* brushwood.

brush-off *n* a curt dismissal.

brush-up *n* a smartening of one's appearance; refreshment of memory or skill.

brushwood *n* rough, close bushes; a thicket, a coppice; small wood or twigs suitable for the fire.

brushwork *n* a particular or characteristic style of painting.

brusque *adj* blunt and curt in manner.—**brusquely** *adv*.—**brusqueness** *n*.

Brussels carpet *n* a strong kind of woollen carpet.

Brussels lace *n* a fine, expensive lace with a floral pattern made orig in Brussels.

Brussels sprout *n* a plant of the cabbage family with a small edible green head.

brut *adj* (*wines*) dry, unsweetened.

brutal *adj* inhuman; savage, violent; severe.—**brutally** *adv*.

brutality *n* (*pl* **brutalities**) the quality of being brutal; pitiless cruelty; a brutal act.

brutalize *vt* to treat brutally; to degrade.—**brutalization** *n*.

brute *n* any animal except man; a brutal person; (*inf*) an unpleasant or difficult person or thing. * *adj* (*force*) sheer, physical.

brutish *adj* brutal; stupid; savage, violent; coarse.—**brutishly** *adv*.—**brutishness** *n*.

bryology *n* the scientific study of mosses.—**bryological** *adj*.—**bryologist** *n*.

bryony *n* (*pl* **bryonies**) any of several climbing plants of Europe and North Africa; black bryony; white

bryony.—*also* **briony**.

bryozoan *n* any small animal belonging to the class Polyzoa, forming moss-like colonies by budding.

BSc *abbr* = Bachelor of Science.

Bt. *abbr* = Baronet.

bub *n* (*inf*) a boy; brother.

bubble *n* a film of liquid forming a ball around air or gas; a tiny ball of gas or air in a liquid or solid; a transparent dome; a scheme that collapses. * *vi* to boil; to rise in bubbles; to make a gurgling sound.

bubble and squeak *n* meat and vegetables fried together.

bubble bath *n* perfumed crystals or liquid added to a bath to soften the water and produce foam; a bath to which this has been added.

bubble gum *n* chewing gum that can be blown into large bubbles.

bubbly *adj* (**bubblier, bubbliest**) having bubbles, effervescent; cheerful, high-spirited. * *n* (*inf*) champagne.

bubo *n* (*pl* **buboes**) an inflamed swelling in the groin or armpit.—**bubonic** *adj*.

bubonic plague *n* a highly infectious often fatal disease contracted from fleas from infected rats.

bubonocele *n* a rupture or hernia in the groin.

buccal *adj* pertaining to the cheek or the mouth.

buccaneer *n* a sea robber, a pirate. * *vi* to be a pirate.

buccinator *n* a flat muscle of the cheek, also called the trumpeter's muscle from its use in blowing wind instruments.

Buchmanism *see* **Oxford Group**.

buck *n* the male of animals such as the deer, hare, rabbit, antelope; (*inf*) a dashing young man; (*sl*) a dollar. * *vti* (*horse*) to rear upwards quickly; (*inf*) to resist; (*with* **up**) (*inf*) to make or become cheerful; to hurry up.

buckaroo *n* (*pl* **buckaroos**) a cowboy.

buckbean *n* a water plant with pinkish flowers.

buckboard *n* a light four-wheeled carriage with a flexible board bearing the seats.

bucket *n* a container with a handle for carrying liquid or substances in small pieces; (*comput*) a direct-access storage area from which data can be retrieved; (*inf*) a wastepaper bin. * *vt* to drive fast or recklessly; to pour with rain.

bucket seat *n* a single, contoured seat with an adjustable back as in a car, etc.

bucket shop *n* (*sl*) a dishonest brokerage firm; a business that sells cheap airline tickets.

buckeye *n* a North American tree with white or reddish flowers growing in clusters, the American horse chestnut; its nut; a native of Ohio.

buckjumper *n* a vicious untrained horse that endeavours to throw its rider by arching its back and drawing its feet together.

buckle *n* a fastening or clasp for a strap or band; a bend or bulge. * *vti* to fasten with a buckle; to bend under pressure, etc; (*with* **down**) (*inf*) to apply oneself diligently.

buckler *n* a small shield; protection. * *vt* to defend.

bucko *n* (*pl* **buckoes**) (*naut: sl*) a swaggering bully; (*Irish*) a young man.

buckpasser *n* (*inf*) one who regularly shifts the blame or responsibility to someone else.

buckram *n* a coarse linen or cotton cloth stiffened with dressing. * *adj* made of, or resembling, buckram; stiff, precise. * *vt* (**buckraming, buckramed**) to stiffen with or bind in buckram.

buckshee n (sl) an extra allowance, a windfall. * adj, adv free, for nothing.

buckshot n shot of a large size for shooting game.

buckskin n a soft leather of deerskin, etc; (pl) breeches or shoes made of this; (hist) a native American. * adj made of buckskin.

buckthorn n any of several shrubs or trees with small greenish flowers, black berries and thorny branches.

bucktooth n (pl buckteeth) a projecting front tooth.

buckwheat n a plant cultivated for its triangular seeds, which are ground into meal and used as a cereal.

bucolic adj pastoral; rustic. * n a pastoral poem; a rustic.—**bucolically** adv.

bud[1] n an embryo shoot, flower, or flower cluster of a plant; an early stage of development. * vi (**budding, budded**) to produce buds, to begin to develop.

bud[2] n (inf) buddy.

Buddha n one who has arrived at the state of perfect enlightenment; an image of Siddharta Gautama, founder of Buddhism.

Buddhism n a system of ethics and philosophy based on teachings of Buddha.

Buddhist n a follower of Buddhism.

budding adj being in an early stage of development; promising or showing promise.

buddle n an inclined trough in which ore is separated from earth by the action of running water. * vt to wash ore in a buddle.

buddleia n a shrub with lilac or yellow flowers.

buddy n (pl buddies) (inf) a friend; a term of informal address; one who helps and supports another, esp an AIDS sufferer. * vi (**buddying, buddied**) to help as a buddy.

budge[1] vti to shift or move.

budge[2] n lambskin dressed with the wool outwards.

budgerigar n a small Australian parrot bred as a cage bird in many varieties of different colours.

budget n an estimate of income and expenditure within specified limits of a country, a business, etc; the total amount of money for a given purpose; a stock or supply; **on a budget** restricting one's expenditure. * vb (**budgeting, budgeted**) vi to make a budget. * vt to put on a budget; to plan; (with for) to allow for or save money for a purpose or aim.—**budgetary** adj.

budgie n (inf) a budgerigar.

buff n a heavy, soft, brownish-yellow leather; a dull brownish yellow; (inf) a devotee, fan; (inf) a person's bare skin. * adj made of buff; of a buff colour. * vt to clean or shine, orig with leather or a leather-covered wheel.

buffalo n (pl buffalo, buffaloes or buffalos) a wild ox; a bison.

buffer[1] n anything that lessens shock, as of collision; something that serves as a protective barrier; a temporary storage area in a computer.

buffer[2] n (sl) a good-tempered somewhat foolish person; an elderly man.

buffer zone, buffer state n an area intended to separate; a neutral area.

buffet[1] n a blow with the hand or fist. * vb (**buffeting, buffeted**) vt to hit with the hand or fist; to batter (as of the wind). * vi to make one's way esp under difficult conditions.—**buffeter** n.

buffet[2] n a counter where refreshments are served; a meal at which guests serve themselves food.

buffet car n a railway coach where light refreshments are served.

buffeting n repeated battering.

buffo n (pl buffi, buffos) a comic actor, esp in an opera. * adj comic; burlesque.

buffoon n a clown, a jester; a silly person.

buffoonery n ridiculous behaviour.

bug[1] n a continuing source of irritation.

bug[2] n an insect with sucking mouth parts; any insect; (inf) a germ or virus; (sl) a defect, as in a machine; (sl) a hidden microphone; an obsession, an enthusiasm. * vt (**bugging, bugged**) (sl) to plant a hidden microphone; (sl) to annoy, anger, etc.

bugbear n an object that causes great fear and anxiety.

bugger n a sodomite; (sl) a contemptible or annoying person or thing. * vt to practise buggery with; (sl) to ruin; to exhaust; (with off) to leave. * interj an exclamation of annoyance.

buggery n anal sexual intercourse.

buggy n (pl buggies) a light four-wheeled, one-horse carriage with one seat; a small pushchair for a baby; a small vehicle.

bughouse n (sl) a mental home. * adj crazy.

bugle[1] n a valveless brass instrument like a small trumpet, used esp for military calls. * vti to signal by blowing a bugle.—**bugler** n.

bugle[2] n an elongated glass bead, usu black.

bugle[3] n bugleweed.

bugleweed n a plant of Europe and Asia with spikes or clusters of small blue or white flowers.

bugloss n any of various plants with hairy leaves and stems.

buhl see boulle.

build vb (**building, built**) vt to make or construct, to establish, base; (with up) to create or develop gradually. * vi to put up buildings; (with up) to grow or intensify; (health, reputation) to develop. * n the way a thing is built or shaped; the shape of a person; the physical appearance or weight or size of a person.—**builder** n.

building adj the skill or occupation of constructing houses, boats, etc. * n something built with walls and a roof.

building society n a company that pays interest on deposits and issues loans to enable people to buy their own houses.—also **savings and loan association**.

built-in adj incorporated as an integral part of a main structure; inherent.

built-up adj made higher, stronger, etc with added parts; having many buildings on it, eg built-up area.

bulb n the underground bud of plants such as the onion and daffodil; a glass bulb in an electric light; a rounded shape.—**bulbous** adj.

bulbiferous adj (plants) producing bulbs.

bulbil n (bot) a small bulb formed at the side of an old one; a small solid or scaly bud, which detaches itself from the stem, becoming an independent plant.

bulbul n an Eastern songbird; (poet) the Persian nightingale.

bulge n a swelling; a rounded projected part; a significant rise in numbers (of population). * vti to swell or bend outward.—**bulgy** adj.

bulimia n insatiable hunger, voracity.

bulimia nervosa n an illness characterized by bouts of compulsive eating followed by self-induced vomiting.

bulk n magnitude; great mass; volume; the main part; **in bulk** in large quantities. * adj total, aggregate; (goods) not packaged.

bulk buying n the large-scale buying of one commodity

usu at a cost reduction; the purchase by one country of the total output of a product of another country.

bulk carrier *n* a ship carrying as cargo one unpackaged commodity.

bulkhead *n* a wall-like partition in the interior of a ship, aircraft or vehicle.

bulky *adj* (**bulkier, bulkiest**) large and unwieldy.—**bulkily** *adv*.—**bulkiness** *adj*.

bull¹ *n* an adult male bovine animal; a male whale or elephant; a speculator who buys in anticipation of reselling at a profit; the bull's-eye; (*sl*) nonsense; bullshit. * *adj* male; rising in price.

bull² *n* an official edict issued by the pope, with the papal seal on it.

bull³ *n* a ludicrous inconsistency in language.—*also* **Irish bull**.

bulla *n* (*pl* **bullae**) a lead seal on a papal document; a blister.—**bullous** *adj*.

bullace *n* a wild European species of plum cultivated as the damson.

bullate *adj* blistered; puffy.

bulldog *n* a variety of dog of strong muscular build, remarkable for its courage and ferocity, formerly used for baiting bulls; a short-barrelled pistol with a large calibre. * *adj* characterized by the courage of a bulldog; tenacious.

bulldog clip *n* a spring clip with a powerful grip.

bulldoze *vt* to demolish with a bulldozer; (*inf*) to force.

bulldozer *n* an excavator with caterpillar tracks for moving earth.

bullet *n* a small metal missile fired from a gun or rifle.

bulletin *n* an announcement; a short statement of news or of a patient's progress.

bulletin board *n* a board on which notices are posted.

bulletproof *adj* providing protection against bullets.

bullfight *n* a combat between armed men and a bull or bulls.

bullfighting *n* the sport of goading and then killing bulls, popular in Spain, etc.—**bullfighter** *n*.

bullfinch *n* a common brightly coloured European songbird.

bullfrog *n* a large North American frog found in marshy places, remarkable for its loud bellowing croak.

bullheaded *adj* stubborn; stupid.—**bullheadedly** *adv*.—**bullheadedness** *n*.

bullion *n* gold or silver in mass before coinage.

bull-necked *adj* having a short thick neck.

bullock *n* a gelded bull; steer.

bullring *n* an arena for bullfighting.

bull's-eye *n* (*darts, archery*) the centre of a target; something resembling this; a direct hit; a large round peppermint boiled sweet.

bullshit *n* (*vulg sl*) nonsense; exaggeration, pretentious talk. * *vti* (**bullshitting, bullshitted**) (*vulg sl*) to claim knowledge that is lacking; to talk boastfully.—**bullshitter** *n*.

bull terrier *n* a dog bred by a cross between the bulldog and the terrier.

bullwhip *n* a whip with a long lash for driving cattle. * *vt* (**bullwhipping, bullwhipped**) to whip with this.

bully *n* (*pl* **bullies**) a person, adult or child, who hurts or intimidates others weaker than himself or herself. * *vb* (**bullying, bullied**) *vt* to intimidate, oppress or hurt. * *vi* (*with* **off**) (*hockey*) to cross sticks in a bully-off to start a match. * *adj* (*inf*) very good, as in *bully for you*.

bully (**beef**) *n* canned corned beef.

bully boy *n* a hoodlum, a ruffian, usu one hired to beat up someone.

bullyrag *see* **ballyrag**.

bulrush *n* a tall marsh plant.

bulwark *n* a defensive wall or rampart; (*naut*) a fence-like structure projecting above the deck of a ship; an object or person acting as a means of defence.

bum *n* (*inf*) a tramp; an idle person; (*inf*) a devotee, as of skiing or tennis; (*sl*) buttocks or anus. * *adj* broken; useless. * *vti* (**bumming, bummed**) to beg, to sponge; to live as a vagabond; (*with* **around**) to be idle, to loaf about.

bumble *vi* to do or say something clumsily or in a confused way; to stumble.—**bumbler** *n*.

bumblebee *n* a large, furry bee.

bumboat *n* a boat used for conveying provisions, fruit, etc, for sale to vessels lying off shore.

bummer *n* a worthless person who sponges on others; a low politician; an unpleasant experience, esp due to drug taking.

bump *vi* to knock with a jolt. * *vt* to hurt by striking or knocking; (*inf*) to refuse a booked passenger a seat on a flight because of overbooking by the airline; (*with* **into**) to collide with; (*inf*) to meet by chance; (*with* **off**) (*sl*) to kill, murder; (*with* **up**) (*inf*) to increase prices, size or bulk. * *n* a jolt; a knock; the noise made by a bump or a collision; a swelling or lump; one of the bulges on the head supposedly indicating a special faculty.

bumper *n* a shock-absorbing bar fixed to the front and rear of a motor vehicle; a brimming glass for a toast. * *adj* exceptionally large.

bumpkin *n* an awkward or simple country person.

bumptious *adj* offensively conceited or self-assertive.—**bumptiously** *adv*.—**bumptiousness** *n*.

bumpy *adj* (**bumpier, bumpiest**) having many bumps; rough; jolting, jerky.—**bumpily** *adv*.—**bumpiness** *n*.

bum steer *n* (*sl*) false or deceptive information or advice.

bun *n* a roll made of bread dough and currants, spices and sugar; a bun-shaped coil of hair at the nape of the neck.

bunch *n* a cluster; a number of things growing or fastened together; (*inf*) a group of people. * *vi* to group together; * *vt* to make into a bunch.—**bunchy** *adj*.—**bunchiness** *n*.

buncombe *see* **bunkum**.

bund¹, **Bund** *n* (*pl* **bunds, Bünde**) a league, a confederacy.

bund² *n* an embankment to protect land against inundation.

bundle *n* a number of things fastened together; a fastened package; (*sl*) a large sum of money. * *vt* to put together in bundles; to push hurriedly into.—**bundler** *n*.

bung *n* a cork or rubber stopper. * *vt* to close up with or as with a bung; (*sl*) to throw, toss.

bungalow *n* a one-storey house.

bungle *n* a mistake or blunder; something carried out clumsily. * *vt* to spoil something through incompetence or clumsiness.—**bungler** *n*.—**bungling** *adj, n*.

bunion *n* a lump on the side of the first joint of the big toe.

bunk¹ *n* a narrow, shelf-like bed; a bunk bed.

bunk² *n* (*sl*) a hurried departure.

bunk³ *n* (*sl*) buncombe.

bunk bed *n* one of two or three single beds arranged one above the other in a compact unit.

bunker *n* a large storage container, esp for coal; a sand pit forming an obstacle on a golf course; an underground shelter.

bunkum *n* idle or showy speech; nonsense.—*also* **buncombe**.

bunny *n* (*pl* **bunnies**) a pet name for a rabbit; a nightclub waitress dressed to resemble a rabbit.

Bunsen burner *n* a burner that mixes gas and air to produce a smokeless flame of great heat.

bunt[1] *vti* (*animal*) to butt; (*baseball*) to tap (the ball) within the infield. * *n* this stroke.

bunt[2] *n* a species of fungus that produces the smut disease in wheat.

bunt[3] *n* the bulge of a sail, net, etc.

bunting[1] *n* a cotton fabric used for making flags; a line of pennants and decorative flags.

bunting[2] *n* a bird allied to the finches and sparrows.

buntline *n* (*naut*) one of the ropes attached to the foot rope of a square sail to draw the sail up to the yard.

buoy *n* a bright, anchored, marine float used for mooring and for making obstacles. * *vt* to keep afloat; (*usu with* **up**) to hearten or raise the spirits of; to mark with buoys.

buoyancy *n* ability to float or rise; cheerfulness; resilience.

buoyant *adj* able to float; light, elastic; not easily depressed, cheerful.—**buoyantly** *adv*.

bur *n* a prickly seed-case of a plant; a person hard to shake off; a rough edge left after drilling or cutting; a burr. * *vt* (**burring, burred**) to pick burs off.

burble *vi* to make a gurgling sound; to speak incoherently, esp from excitement.—**burbler** *n*.

burbot *n* (*pl* **burbot, burbots**) a freshwater fish like the eel.

burden[1] *n* a load; something worrisome that is difficult to bear; responsibility. * *vt* to weigh down, to oppress.

burden[2] *n* the chorus or refrain of a song; a topic dwelt on in speech or writing.

burdensome *adj* onerous; oppresive; heavy.—**burdensomely** *adv*.

burdock *n* a large wayside weed with prickly flowers and rough broad leaves.

bureau *n* (*pl* **bureaus, bureaux**) a writing desk; a chest of drawers; a branch of a newspaper, magazine or wire service in an important news centre; a government department.

bureaucracy *n* (*pl* **bureaucracies**) a system of government where the administration is organized in a hierarchy; the government collectively; excessive paperwork and red tape.

bureaucrat *n* an official in a bureaucracy, esp one who adheres inflexibly to this system.—**bureaucratic** *adj*.—**bureaucratically** *adv*.

burette, buret *n* a graduated glass tube, usu with a tap, for measuring the volume of liquids.

burg *n* a town; (*formerly*) a fortified town.

burgee *n* a swallow-tailed flag or pennant flown on the mast of a yacht to show membership of a club or of a merchant vessel to show ownership.

burgeon *vt* to start to increase rapidly; (*plant*) to bloom copiously.

burger *n* (*inf*) hamburger.

burgess *n* in UK, a citizen or freeman of a borough; (*formerly*) a member of parliament for a borough or university; in US, a representative sent by a town to the colonial legislative body of Virginia or Maryland.

burgh *n* (*Scot*) a borough.—**burghal** *adj*.

burgher *n* a citizen or freeman of a burgh or borough; a prosperous person of the middle classes.

burglar *n* a person who trespasses in a building with the intention of committing a crime, such as theft.

burglary *n* (*pl* **burglaries**) the act or crime of breaking into a house or any building with intent to commit a felony, esp theft.

burgle, burglarize *vti* to commit burglary (in or on).

burgomaster *n* the chief magistrate of a municipal town in Holland, Belgium or Germany.

burgonet *n* a kind of steel cap or helmet of the 16th century.

Burgundy *n* (*pl* **Burgundies**) a dryish wine, red or white, made in the Burgundy region of eastern France; a similar wine produced elsewhere; a dark purplish red colour.

burial *n* the act of burying; interment of a dead body.

burial ground *n* a graveyard.

burin *n* a chisel used for engraving metal, wood or marble; (*archaeol*) a primitive tool with a chisel-shaped head.

burke *vt* to murder by suffocation; to dispose of quietly; to hush up.

burl *n* a small knot or lump in thread or cloth; a knot in wood; a wood veneer with knots in it. * *vt* to pick knots, etc, from, as in finishing cloth.

burlap *n* a coarse fabric made of jute, hemp, etc, used for bagging or in upholstery.

burlesque *n* a caricature; a literary or dramatic satire. * *vti* (**burlesquing, burlesqued**) to make fun of, to caricature. * *adj* of or like burlesque; mockingly imitative.

burly *adj* (**burlier, burliest**) heavily built; sturdy.—**burliness** *n*.

burn[1] *vb* (**burning, burned** *or* **burnt**) *vt* to destroy by fire; to injure by heat. * *vi* to be on fire; to feel hot; to feel passion; (*inf*) to suffer from sunburn; (*with* **off**) to clear ground by burning all vegetation; to get rid of (surplus gas, energy) by burning or using up; (*with* **out**) (*fire*) to go out; (*person*) to lose efficiency through exhaustion, excess or overwork. * *n* a scorch mark or injury caused by burning.

burn[2] *n* (*Scot*) a small stream, a brook.

burner *n* the part of a lamp or stove that produces a flame.

burnet *n* a brown-flowered plant of the rose family.

burning *adj* intense, passionate; urgent.—**burningly** *adj*.

burning glass *n* a double convex lens used to focus the sun's rays on combustible substances to ignite them.

burnish *vt* to make shiny by rubbing; to polish. * *n* lustre; polish.—**burnishable** *adj*.—**burnisher** *n*.

burnous, burnoose *n* a long, hooded cloak worn by Arabs.

burnt *see* **burn**.

burnt offering *n* something offered and burnt upon an altar as a sacrifice or an atonement for sin.

burnt sienna *n* an orange-reddish pigment used in painting.

burro *n* (*pl* **burros**) a donkey.

burp *vi* to belch. * *vt* to pat a baby on the back to cause it to belch. * *n* a belch.

burr[1] *see* **bur**.

burr[2] *n* a whirring sound; a gruff pronunciation of the letter *r*. * *vti* to pronounce with a burr.

burrito *n* a tortilla baked with a savoury filling.

burrow *n* an underground hide or tunnel dug by a rabbit, badger or fox, etc for shelter. * *vi* to dig a burrow; to live in a burrow; to hide (oneself); to grope into the depths of one's pockets.—**burrower** *n*.

burry *adj* (**burrier**, **burriest**) full of burs; rough; prickly.

bursa *n* (*pl* **bursae**, **bursas**) (*anat*) a sac or sac-like cavity, esp between joints, full of a fluid that lessens friction.—**bursal** *adj*.

bursar *n* a treasurer; a person in charge of the finances of a college or university; a student holding a bursary.—**bursarial** *adj*.

bursary *n* (*pl* **bursaries**) a scholarship awarded to a student.—**bursarial** *adj*.

burst *vb* (**bursting**, **burst**) *vt* to break open; to cause to explode. * *vi* to emerge suddenly; to explode; to break into pieces; to give vent to. * *n* an explosion; a burst; a volley of shots; a sudden increase of activity; a spurt.—**burster** *n*.

burton *n* (*naut*) a tackle formed of two or more blocks or pulleys; **go for a burton** to die; to be no longer useful.

bury *vt* (**burying**, **buried**) (*bone*, *corpse*) to place in the ground; to inter; to conceal, to cover; to blot out of the mind; **bury the hatchet** to make peace; to be reconciled.

bus *n* (*pl* **buses**, **busses**) a motor coach for public transport. * *vti* (**busing**, **bused** *or* **bussing**, **bussed**) to transport or travel by bus; to take by bus children from one area to another, esp to balance racial numbers.

busby *n* (*pl* **busbies**) a tall, fur hat, esp one worn by a guardsman.

bush¹ *n* a low shrub with many branches; a cluster of shrubs forming a hedge; woodland; (*with* **the**) uncultivated land, esp in Africa, Australia, New Zealand, Canada; a thick growth, eg of hair; a fox's tail or brush.

bush² *n* a metal lining of a hole in which an axle turns to reduce wear by friction (—*also* **bushing**). * *vt* to furnish with a bush.

bushbaby *n* (*pl* **bushbabies**) a small tree-dwelling nocturnal lemur from Africa.

bushed *adj* (*inf*) tired, exhausted; (*Austral*) lost in the bush.

bushel¹ *n* a dry measure containing eight gallons (UK) or 64 pints (US); a vessel of such a capacity; a large quantity.

bushel² *vt* (**bushelling**, **bushelled** *or* **busheling**, **busheled**) to patch or repair, esp clothes.—**busheller**, **busheler** *n*.

bushfire *n* a fire, often widespread, in bush or scrubland.

bushing *see* **bush²**.

bushman *n* (*pl* **bushmen**) a woodsman; (*Austral*) a settler in the bush or newly opened country; (*with cap*) one of a tribe of South African aboriginals near the Cape of Good Hope.

bushmaster *n* a large deadly South American snake with brown and grey markings.

bushranger *n* a frontiersman; (*Austral: formerly*) a criminal who escaped and lived a lawless life in the bush.

bush telegraph *n* a means of communicating news by drumbeat across a large area; (*inf*) a means of spreading gossip.

bushwhack *vi* to work one's way through the bush; to ambush.

bushwhacker *n* a backwoodsman; a guerrilla fighter;

an implement for cutting brushwood.

bushy *adj* (**bushier**, **bushiest**) covered with bushes; (*hair*) thick.—**bushiness** *n*.

business *n* trade or commerce; occupation or profession; a firm; a factory; one's concern or responsibility; a matter; the agenda of a business meeting.

businesslike *adj* efficient, methodical, practical.

businessman *n* (**businessmen**) a person who works for an industrial or commercial company, esp as an executive.—**businesswoman** *nf* (*pl* **businesswomen**).

busing *see* **bussing**.

busker *n* a street entertainer.—**busking** *n*.

buskin *n* a half boot or high shoe; a high boot once worn by tragic actors to increase their height; a tragic drama.

busman's holiday *n* a holiday spent doing what one usually does at work.

buss *n* a smacking kiss. * *vt* to kiss.

bussing *n* the transport of children to a school in another district to achieve racially balanced classes.— *also* **busing**.

bust¹ *n* the chest or breast of a human being, esp a woman; a sculpture of the head and chest.

bust² *vti* (**busting**, **busted** *or* **bust**) (*inf*) to burst or break; to make or become bankrupt or demoted; to hit; to arrest. * *n* (*inf*) a failure; financial collapse; a punch; a spree; an arrest.

bustard *n* any of a genus of large swift-running birds of Europe and Africa.

buster *n* a person or thing that busts; something very large; a frolic; a violent wind; (*with cap*) (*inf*) boy, man, a form of address.

bustle¹ *vi* to move or act noisily, energetically or fussily. * *n* noisy activity, stir, commotion.—**bustler** *n*.—**bustling** *adj*.

bustle² *n* a pad placed beneath the skirt of a dress to cause it to puff up at the back.

bust-up *n* (*inf*) a fight or quarrel; a noisy brawl; the permanent ending of a relationship.

busy *adj* (**busier**, **busiest**) occupied; active; crowded; full; industrious; (*painting*) having too much detail; (*room*, *telephone*) engaged, in use. * *vt* (**busying**, **busied**) to occupy; to make or keep busy (esp oneself).— **busily** *adv*.—**busyness** *n*.

busybody *n* (*pl* **busybodies**) a meddlesome person.

but *prep* save; except. * *conj* in contrast; on the contrary, other than. * *adv* only; merely; just. * *n* an objection.

butane *n* an inflammable gas used as a fuel.

butch *adj* (*sl*) tough; aggressively male; (*often of a woman*) male-looking.

butcher *n* a person who slaughters meat; a retailer of meat; a ruthless murderer. * *vt* to slaughter; to murder ruthlessly; to make a mess of or spoil.

butcherbird *n* any of a genus of shrikes that suspend their slaughtered prey from thorns.

butcher's-broom *n* a low-growing evergreen shrub with rigid branched stems and spiny leaves.

butchery *n* (*pl* **butcheries**) the preparation of meat for sale; slaughter.

butler *n* a manservant, usu the head servant of a household, etc.

butt¹ *vti* to strike or toss with the head or horns, as a bull, etc; (*with* **in**) to interfere, to enter into unasked. * *n* a push with the head or horns.—**butter** *n*.

butt² *n* a large cask for wine or beer.

butt³ *n* a mound of earth behind targets; a person who is the target of ridicule or jokes; (*pl*) the target range.

butt⁴ *n* the thick or blunt end; the stump; (*sl*) a cigarette; fag end; (*sl*) the buttocks. * *vti* to join end to end.

butte *n* an abrupt isolated hill or ridge.

butter *n* a solidified fat made from cream by churning. * *vt* to spread butter on; (*with* **up**) (*inf*) to flatter.

butter bean *n* a variety of lima bean cultivated for its large flat pale edible seeds.

buttercup *n* any of various plants with yellow, glossy, cup-shaped flowers.

butterfingers *n* (*used as sing*) a person who lets (a ball, etc) slip through his or her fingers.—**butterfingered** *adj*.

butterfly *n* (*pl* **butterflies**) an insect with a slender body and four usu brightly coloured wings; a swimming stroke.

buttermilk *n* the sour liquid that remains after separation from the cream in buttermaking.

butternut *n* a North American tree of the walnut family; its large oily nut; its hard wood; the colour of the butternut, a brownish grey, the colour of the Confederate uniform in the American Civil War; one who wore the uniform of the Confederate army.

butterscotch *n* a sauce made of melted butter and brown sugar; a kind of hard toffee made from this; its flavour; a brownish-yellow colour.

butterwort *n* a violet-flowered bog plant with leaves that secrete a viscid fluid to entrap small insects.

buttery¹ *adj* like or tasting of butter; insincere.

buttery² *n* (*pl* **butteries**) a storeroom for wine or food.

buttock *n* either half of the human rump.

button *n* a disc or knob of metal, plastic, etc used as a fastening; a badge; a small button-like sweet; an electric bell push; a knob at the point of a fencing foil. * *vti* to fasten with a button or buttons.

buttonhole *n* the slit through which a button is passed; a single flower in the buttonhole. * *vt* to make buttonholes; to sew with a special buttonhole stitch; (*person*) to keep in conversation.

buttonhook *n* a tool for fastening buttons on shoes or gloves.

buttress *n* a projecting structure for strengthening a wall. * *vt* to support or prop.

butyraceous *adj* like butter in consistency, appearance or properties..

butyrate *n* a salt of butyric acid.

butyric acid *n* a colourless liquid obtained from butter, also present in cod-liver oil and sweat glands.

buxom *adj* plump and healthy; (*woman*) big-bosomed.—**buxomness** *n*.

buy *vt* (**buying, bought**) to purchase (for money); to bribe or corrupt; to acquire in exchange for something; (*inf*) to believe; (*with* **off**) to pay (someone) to ensure that some undesired action is not taken; (*with* **out**) to purchase a controlling interest in or share of; to secure the release of (e.g. a person from the army) by payment; (*with* **up**) to purchase the total supply of something; to acquire a controlling interest in. * *n* a purchase.

buyer *n* a person who buys; a customer; an employee who buys on behalf of his or her employer, esp a company or store.

buyer's market *n* a market in which, because the supply exceeds the demand, the buyers control the price.

buzz *vi* to hum like an insect; to gossip; to hover (about). * *vt* spread gossip secretly; (*inf*) to telephone. * *vi* (*with* **off**) to go away. * *n* the humming of bees or flies; a rumour; (*sl*) a telephone call; (*sl*) a thrill, a kick.

buzzard *n* a large bird of prey of the hawk family.

buzzer *n* a device producing a buzzing sound.

buzz saw *n* a circular saw.

buzzword *n* (*inf*) a vogue or jargon word; a word or phrase that was once a technical or specialist term and which has suddenly become popular, often used mainly for effect.—*also* **fuzzword**.

bwana *n* (*E Africa*) an employer, a boss; (*with cap*) a form of address.

by-, bye- *prefix* subordinate, side, secret.

by *prep* beside; next to; via; through the means of; not later than. * *adv* near to; past; in reserve, aside.

by and by *adv* presently, before long; later; eventually; in the future.—**by-and-by** *n*.

by and large *adv* on the whole.

by-blow *n* a side blow; a bastard.

bye *n* something subordinate or incidental; an odd man in a knockout competition; (*cricket*) a run scored without the ball being hit by the batsman; (*golf*) holes left after a match is decided; (*lacrosse*) a goal.

bye-bye¹ *interj* (*inf*) goodbye.

bye-bye² *n* sleep; bed.

by-election, bye-election *n* an election held other than at a general election.

bygone *adj* past. * *n* (*pl*) past offences or quarrels.

bylaw, bye-law *n* a rule or law made by a local authority or a company.

by-line *n* a line under a newspaper article naming its author.

bypass *n* a main road built to avoid a town; a channel redirecting the flow of something around a blockage; (*med*) an operation to redirect the flow of blood into the heart. * *vt* (**bypassing, bypassed**) to go around; to avoid, to act by ignoring the usual channels.

bypath *n* a secluded path.

byplay *n* action or dumb show aside from the main action.

byproduct, by-product *n* something useful produced in the process of making something else.

byre *n* a shed for cows.

byroad *n* an unfrequented or side road.

byssus *n* (*pl* **byssuses, byssi**) a tuft of long soft silky filaments by which certain molluscs attach themselves to rocks; a fine linen used by the ancient Egyptians for wrapping mummies.

bystander *n* a chance onlooker.

byte *n* (*comput*) a set of eight bits treated as a unit.

by the by, by the bye *adv* incidentally.

by the way *adv* incidentally.

byway *n* a side road; a specialist or abstruse interest or area of study.

byword *n* a well-known saying; a perfect example; an object of derision.

Byzantine *adj* of or pertaining to Byzantium, the ancient capital of the Eastern Roman Empire; (*archit*) in the style of the Eastern Empire. * *n* an inhabitant of Byzantium.

C

C *abbr* = Celsius, centigrade; (*math*) third known quantity; (*roman numerals*) 100; (*chem symbol*) = carbon.

c. *abbr* = carat; cent(s); century.

c. *abbr* = *circa*, about.

© (*symbol*) = copyright.

CA *abbr* = California; Chartered Accountant.

Ca (*chem symbol*) = calcium.

cab *n* a taxicab; the place where the driver sits in a truck, crane, etc.

cabal *n* a conspiracy, a secret plot; a small group of people united in perpetrating this; a clique. * *vi* (**caballing, caballed**) to form a cabal, to plot.

cabala, cabbala *n* a mystic interpretation of Scripture by Jewish rabbis; occult lore.—*also* **kabala, kabbala.**—**cabalism, cabbalism** *n.*—**cabalist, cabbalist** *n.*—**cabalistic, cabbalistic** *adj.*

caballero *n* (*pl* **caballeros**) a Spanish knight or gentleman; a horseman; a Spanish dance.

cabaret *n* entertainment given in a restaurant or nightclub.

cabbage *n* a garden plant with thick leaves formed usu into a compact head, used as a vegetable.

cabbage rose *n* a large full rose.

cabby, cabbie *n* (*pl* **cabbies**) (*inf*) a person who drives a cab for hire.

caber *n* a rough pole, usu cut from a tree, tossed as a trial of strength at Highland games.

cabin *n* a small house, a hut; a room in a ship; the area where passengers sit in an aircraft.

cabin cruiser *n* a powerful motorboat with living accommodation.

cabinet *n* a case or cupboard with drawers or shelves; a case containing a TV, radio, etc; (*often with cap*) a body of official advisers to a government; the senior ministers of a government.

cabinetmaker *n* a person who makes fine furniture.

cable *n* a strong thick rope often of wire strands; an anchor chain; an insulated cord that carries electric current; a cablegram; a bundle of insulated wires for carrying cablegrams, TV signals, etc; (*naut*) a cable length. * *vti* to send a message by cablegram.

cable car *n* a car drawn by a moving cable, as up a steep incline.

cablegram *n* a message transmitted by telephone line, submarine cable, satellite, a cable.

cable-laid *adj* (*rope*) composed of three triple strands.

cable length *n* (*naut*) (*UK*) a unit of length, about 100 fathoms, 608 feet or one tenth of a nautical mile, (*US*) 120 fathoms, 720 feet

cable stitch *n* a pattern of knitting stitches resembling a cable.

cable television *n* TV transmission to subscribers by cable.

cabman *n* (*pl* **cabmen**) the driver of a cab.

cabochon *n* a precious stone polished but not faceted.

caboodle *n* (*sl*) a lot, a set (*the whole caboodle*).

caboose *n* the guard's car at the rear of a freight train; a kitchen on a ship's deck.

cabriolet *n* a covered carriage with two or four wheels drawn by one horse; a car body with a folding hood and fixed sides.

cacao *n* a tropical tree; its seed, from which cocoa and chocolate are obtained.

cachalot *n* the sperm whale.

cache *n* a secret hiding place; a store of weapons or treasure; a store of food left for use by travellers, etc. * *vt* to place in a cache.

cache (memory) *n* a small high-speed memory for easy access and frequent reference to computer data.

cachepot *n* an ornamental pot to hold a flowerpot.

cachet *n* a mark of authenticity; any distinguishing mark; prestige.

cachexia, cachexy *n* (*med*) a bad state of general health, weakness.—**cachectic** *adj.*

cachinnate *vi* to laugh loudly and unrestrainedly.—**cachinnation** *n.*

cachou[1] *see* **catechu.**

cachou[2] *n* a lozenge for sweetening the breath.

cachucha *n* a quick Spanish dance; the music for it.

cacique *n* a West Indian or American Indian chief; a political boss.

cackle *n* the clucking sound of a hen; shrill or silly talk or laughter. * *vi* to utter with a cackle.

caco- *prefix* bad.

cacodemon, cacodaemon *n* an evil spirit.

cacodyl *n* an evil-smelling compound of arsenic and methyl.

cacoethes *n* a bad habit or propensity of the body or mind; an uncontrollable urge.—**cacoethic** *adj.*

cacography *n* bad handwriting or spelling, the opposite of calligraphy and orthography.—**cacographic** *adj.*

cacophonous *adj* harsh, ill-sounding, discordant.

cacophony *n* (*pl* **cacophonies**) an ugly sound, a discord.

cactus *n* (*pl* **cactuses, cacti**) a plant with a thick fleshy stem that stores water and is often studded with prickles.

cad *n* (*inf*) a man who behaves in an ungentlemanly or dishonourable way.—**caddish** *adj.*—**caddishly** *adv.*—**caddishness** *n.*

cadastre, cadaster *n* a register of the real estate of a district or county as a basis for taxation.—**cadastral** *adj.*

cadaver *n* a dead body.—**cadaveric** *adj.*

cadaverous *adj* gaunt, haggard; pallid, livid.—**cadaverousness** *n.*

caddis *n* the larva of the mayfly used as bait.

caddie, caddy *n* (*pl* **caddies**) a person who carries a golfer's clubs.—*vi* (**caddying, caddied**) to perform as a caddie.

caddy *n* (*pl* **caddies**) a small box or tin for storing tea.

cade *n* a lamb, etc, bred by hand.

cadence *n* a falling of the voice; the intonation of the voice; rhythm; measured movements as in marching.

cadent *adj* rhythmic; falling.

cadenza *n* (*mus*) an ornamental flourish at the close of a movement.

cadet *n* a student at an armed forces academy, police college, etc; a school pupil in a school army training corps.

cadge *vti* to beg or obtain by begging.—**cadger** *n*.

cadi *n* a minor Mohammedan judge.

cadmium *n* a whitish metallic element.

cadre *n* a permanent nucleus or framework of a political or military unit.

caduceus *n* (*pl* **caducei**) the winged wand of Hermes (Mercury) entwined with two serpents, the emblem of the medical profession, an ancient herald's wand.

caducity *n* the quality or condition of being caducous; senility.

caducous *adj* (*biol*) (*parts of a plant*) falling off quickly or before maturity; fleeting; perishable.

caecum *n* (*pl* **caeca**) the pouch at the beginning of the large intestine containing the vermiform appendix.—*also* **cecum.**—**caecal** *adj*.

Caesar *n* the title of Roman emperors, esp Julius Caesar (*c*. 100–44 BC); (*without cap*) any ruler.

Caesarean section, Cesarean section *n* the removal of a child from the womb by a surgical operation involving the cutting of the abdominal wall.

caesium *n* a rare silvery alkaline metal.—*also* **cesium.**

caesura *n* (*pl* **caesuras, caesurae**) a natural pause in the rhythm of a verse line.—**caesural** *adj*.

cafe, café *n* a small restaurant, a coffee bar, a nightclub, etc.

café au lait *n* coffee with milk; a light brown colour.

café noir *n* coffee without milk.

cafeteria *n* a self-service restaurant.

cafetière *n* a usu glass coffee pot with a plunger to press down coffee grounds.

caffeine *n* a stimulant present in coffee and tea.—**caffeinic** *adj*.

caftan *n* a long-sleeved, full-length, voluminous garment originating in the Middle East.—*also* **kaftan.**

cage *n* a box or enclosure with bars for confining an animal, bird, prisoner, etc; a car for raising or lowering miners. * *vt* to shut in a cage, to confine.

cagey, cagy *adj* (**cagier, cagiest**) (*inf*) wary, secretive, not frank.—**cagily** *adv*.—**caginess** *n*.

cahier *n* sheets of paper put loosely together, a notebook.

cahoots *npl* partnership; **in cahoots** in league or partnership.

CAI *abbr* = computer-aided instruction.

caiman *n* (*pl* **caimans**) an alligator of South and Central America.—*also* **cayman.**

caique, caïque *n* a skiff or light rowing boat used on the Bosphorus in Turkey.

cairn *n* a stone mound placed as a monument or marker.

cairngorm *n* (a gemstone of) a yellow or brown variety of quartz or rock crystal.

caisson *n* a watertight chamber used for carrying out underwater repairs or construction work; an apparatus for floating or lifting a vessel.

caitiff *n* (*arch*) a coward; a rascal. * *adj* (*arch*) base, despicable, cowardly.

cajole *vti* to persuade or soothe by flattery or deceit.—**cajoler** *n*.—**cajolingly** *adv*.

cajolery, cajolement *n* (*pl* **cajoleries, cajolements**) the action or practice of cajoling; persuasion by false arts.

Cajun, Cajan *n* an inhabitant of Louisiana descended from 18th-century French-Canadian immigrants; the dialect spoken by Cajuns.

cake *n* a mixture of flour, eggs, sugar, etc baked in small, flat shapes or a loaf; a small block of compacted or congealed matter. * *vti* to encrust; to form into a cake or hard mass.

cakewalk *n* an elaborate step dance; a task accomplished without difficulty.

Cal *abbr* = California; Calorie.

cal *abbr* = calendar; calibre; calorie.

Calabar bean *n* a West African plant; its poisonous bean.

calabash *n* the fruit of the calabash tree of tropical America, used when dried as a vessel for liquids, etc.

calaboose *n* (*inf*) a jail.

calamanco *n* (*pl* **calamancoes, calamancos**) a glossy woollen fabric, brocaded or checkered.

calamander *n* a fine variety of Indian ebony of a very hard texture.

calamari *n* squid eaten as a food.

calamary *n* (*pl* **calamaries**) squid.

calamine *n* a zinc oxide powder used in skin lotions, etc for its soothing effect.

calamint *n* an aromatic herb of the mint family.

calamite *n* a fossil plant resembling a horsetail.

calamitous *adj* producing or resulting from calamity; disastrous.—**calamitously** *adv*.—**calamitousness** *n*.

calamity *n* (*pl* **calamities**) a disastrous event, a great misfortune; adversity.

calamus *n* (*pl* **calami**) any of a genus of palms producing the rattan canes; the sweet flag.

calando *adv* (*mus*) gradually; slower and softer.

calash *n* a light carriage with low wheels and a folding removable top; (*Canada*) a two-wheeled single-seater carriage; a hood formerly worn by women.—*also* **caleche.**

calcar *n* (*pl* **calcaria**) a tube or spur at the base of a petal or sepal; a furnace used in glass-making.

calcareous *adj* of the nature of, or containing, lime.—**calcareousness** *n*.

calceiform, calceolate *adj* (*bot*) slipper-shaped.

calceolaria *n* any of a genus of South American ornamental plants with slipper-shaped flowers.

calcic *adj* of or containing calcium.

calciferous *adj* containing or yielding carbonate of lime.

calcify *vb* (**calcifying, calcified**) *vt* to convert into lime. * *vi* to harden by conversion into lime.

calcimine *n* a white or tinted wash for walls or ceilings.—*also* **kalsomine.**

calcination *n* the act or process of reducing to powder by heat.

calcine *vt* to reduce a substance to chalky powder by the action of heat; to burn to ashes. * *vi* to undergo calcination.

calcite *n* crystallized carbonate of lime.—**calcitic** *adj*.

calcium *n* the chemical element prevalent in bones and teeth.

calcium carbide *n* a fusion of coal or coke with lime in an electrical furnace, which, with water, produces acetylene gas.

calcium carbonate *n* a compound occurring naturally in limestone, chalk, and in bones and shells.

calcsinter *n* a crystalline deposit from lime springs.

calcspar *n* calcite, a crystalline carbonate of lime.

calculate *vti* to reckon or compute by mathematics; to suppose or believe; to plan.—**calculable** *adj*.

calculated *adj* adapted or suited (to); deliberate, cold-blooded, premeditated.—**calculatedly** *adv*.

calculating *adj* shrewd, scheming.—**calculatingly** *adv*.

calculation *n* the act of calculating; the result obtained from this; an estimate.—**calculational** *adj*.

calculator *n* a device, esp a small, electronic, hand-held one, for doing mathematical calculations rapidly; one who calculates.

calculous *adj* stony; gritty.

calculus *n* (*pl* **calculi, calculuses**) an abnormal, stony mass in the body; (*math*) a mode of calculation using symbols.

caldera *n* a deep caldron-like cavity on the summits of extinct volcanoes.

caldron *see* **cauldron**.

caleche *see* **calash**.

Caledonian *adj* pertaining to Caledonia, the ancient name of Scotland; Scottish. * *n* a native of Scotland.

calefacient *adj* producing or exciting heat. * *n* a heat-producing substance.—**calefaction** *n*.

calendar *n* a system of determining the length and divisions of a year; a chart or table of months, days and seasons; a list of particular, scheduled events.

calendar month *n* a solar month reckoned according to the calendar, as distinguished from the lunar month.

calender[1] *n* a press with rollers for finishing the surface of cloth, paper, etc. * *vt* to press in a calender.—**calenderer** *n*.

calender[2] *n* a mendicant dervish.

calends *npl* in the Roman calendar, the first day of each month.—*also* **kalends**.

calendula *n* any of a genus of plants, including the marigold, from which a medical tincture is obtained.

calenture *n* a tropical fever with delirium.

calf[1] *n* (*pl* **calves**) the young of a cow, seal, elephant, whale, etc; the leather skin of a calf.

calf[2] *n* (*pl* **calves**) the fleshy back part of the leg below the knee.

calf love *n* puppy love; an immature infatuation.

calfskin *n* the skin of a calf made into leather.

calibrate *vt* to measure the calibre of a gun; to adjust or mark units of measurement on a measuring scale or gauge.—**calibration** *n*.—**calibrator** *n*.

calibre, caliber *n* the internal diameter of a gun barrel or tube; capacity, standing, moral weight.

calico *n* (*pl* **calicoes, calicos**) a kind of cotton cloth. * *adj* made of this.

calif *see* **caliph**.

Calif. *abbr* = California.

califate *see* **caliphate**.

californium *n* an artificial radioactive metallic element.

calipash *n* the part of a turtle belonging to the upper shell, enclosing a dull greenish gelatinous edible substance.

calipee *n* the part of a turtle belonging to the lower shell, enclosing a light yellow gelatinous edible substance.

caliper *see* **calliper**.

caliph *n* the former title assumed by the successors of Mohammed as rulers; title of a Turkish sultan.—*also* **calif**.

caliphate *n* the office, dignity or government of a caliph.—*also* **califate**.

calisthenics *npl* light gymnastic exercises.—*also* **callisthenics**.—**calisthenic, callisthenic** *adj*.

calix *n* (*pl* **calices**) a chalice; a cup-like cavity or organ.

calk[1] *see* **caulk**.

calk[2] *n* the part of a horseshoe that projects downwards to prevent slipping; a semicircular piece of iron nailed to the heel of a boot.

call *vi* to shout or cry out; to pay a short visit; to telephone; (*with* **in**) to pay a brief or informal visit; (*with* **on**) to pay a visit; to ask, to appeal to. * *vt* to summon; to name; to describe as specified; to awaken; to give orders for; (*with* **down**) to invoke; (*with* **in**) to summon for advice or help; to bring out of circulation; to demand payment of (a loan); (*with* **off**) to cancel; (*an animal*) to call away in order to stop, divert; (*with* **out**) to cry aloud; to order (workers) to come out on strike; to challenge to a duel; to summon (troops) to action; (*with* **up**) to telephone; to summon to military action, as in time of war; to recall. * *n* a summons; the note of a bird; a vocation, esp religious; occasion; a need; a demand; a short visit; the use of a telephone; a cry, a shout.

calla (lily) *n* an ornamental plant of the arum family with a large white spathe that enfolds a yellow spadix.

callant, callan *n* (*Scot*) a lad, a youth.

call box *n* a telephone booth; a roadside box containing a telephone for making emergency calls.

callboy *n* a prompter's attendant who tells actors when to go on.

caller[1] *n* one who calls, esp by telephone; one who pays a brief visit.

caller[2] *adj* (*Scot*) (*food*) cool, fresh; in season; (*fish*) recently caught.

call girl *n* (*inf*) a prostitute who makes appointments by telephone.

calligraphy *n* handwriting; beautiful writing.—**calligrapher, calligraphist** *n*.—**calligraphic** *adj*.—**calligraphically** *adv*.

calling *n* the act of summoning; a summons or invitation; a vocation, trade or profession; the state of being divinely called.

calliope *n* a steam organ; (*with cap*) the muse of epic poetry.

calliper *n* a metal framework for supporting a crippled or weak leg; paper thickness measured in microns; (*pl*) a two-legged measuring instrument. * *vt* to measure with or use callipers.—*also* **caliper**.

callisthenics *see* **calisthenics**.

call loan *n* a loan subject to recall without notice.

callosity *n* (*pl* **callosities**) the state or quality of being hardened; a callus.

callous *adj* (*skin*) hardened; (*person*) unfeeling.—**calloused** *adj* —**callously** *adv*.—**callousness** *n*.

callow *adj* inexperienced, undeveloped.—**callowness** *n*.

call sign *n* a signal identifying a particular radio transmitter.

call-up *n* a summons to military service.

callus *n* (*pl* **calluses**) a hardened, thickened place on the skin.

calm *adj* windless; still, unruffled; quiet, peaceful. * *n* the state of being calm; stillness; tranquillity. * *vti* to become or make calm.—**calmly** *adv*.—**calmness** *n*.

calmative *adj* (*med*) sedating. * *n* a sedative.

calomel *n* a preparation of mercury used as a purgative.

caloric *adj* of or pertaining to heat or calories.—**calorically** *adv*.

Calorie *n* a unit of heat equalling 1,000 calories.

calorie *n* a unit of heat; a measure of food energy.—*also* **calory**.

calorific *adj* heat-producing; (*inf*) causing fat.—**calorifically** *adv*.

calorimeter *n* an instrument for measuring quantities of heat.—**calorimetric, calorimetrical** *adj*.—**calorimetry** *n*.

calory *see* **calorie**.

calotte *n* a small plain skullcap of satin, etc, worn by priests.

calotype *n* a photographic process in which the image is received on paper prepared with iodide of silver.

caloyer *n* a Greek monk of the order of St Basil.

calpac, calpack *n* a tall brimless sheepskin cap worn by Turks and Armenians.—*also* **kalpak**.

caltrop, caltrap, calthrop *n* any of various plants with prickly fruit; an iron instrument with four spikes, placed in ditches, etc, to hinder the advance of troops.

calumet *n* the tobacco pipe of the North American Indians, smoked as a symbol of peace or to ratify treaties.

calumniate *vt* to accuse falsely and maliciously. * *vi* to utter calumnies.—**calumniation** *n*.—**calumniator** *n*.

calumny *n* (*pl* **calumnies**) a slander; a lie, a false accusation.—**calumnious** *adj*.—**calumniously** *adv*.

calvados *n* apple brandy distilled in Normandy in France.

calvary *n* (*pl* **calvaries**) a place or representation of the crucifixion of Christ; an experience of intense mental suffering; (*with cap*) the place where Christ was crucified.

calve *vti* to give birth to a calf; (*glacier, iceberg*) to break up and release ice.

calves *see* **calf**.

Calvinism *n* the doctrines of John Calvin (1509–64) the French theologian and reformer, esp those relating to predestination and election.—**Calvinist** *n*.—**Calvinistic** *adj*.

calvities *n* (*med*) baldness.

calx *n* (*pl* **calxes, calces**) the powder left when a metal or mineral has been subjected to great heat.

calycine, calycinal *adj* having a calyx; of or on the calyx.

calycle, calyculus *n* (*pl* **calycles, calyculi**) a whorl of small bracts forming a secondary calyx below the true one.

calypso *n* (*pl* **calypsos**) a West Indian folk song that comments on current events or personalities.

calyptra *n* (*bot*) the hood-like covering of the spore case of mosses.—**calyptrate** *adj*.

calyx *n* (*pl* **calyxes, calyces**) the outer series of leaves that form the cup from which the petals of a flower spring.

cam *n* a device to change rotary to reciprocating motion.

camaraderie *n* friendship, comradeship.

camarilla *n* a political clique, a cabal.

camber *n* a slight upward curve in the surface of a road, etc. * *vti* to curve upwards slightly.—**cambered** *adj*.

cambist *n* an expert in exchanges; a dealer in bills of exchange.

cambium *n* (*pl* **cambiums, cambia**) the formative layer of cellular tissue that lies between the young wood and the bark of exogenous trees.—**cambial** *adj*.

Cambrian *adj* of Wales; (*geol*) of the earliest Palaeozoic period, before the Silurian. * *n* the strata underlying the Silurian rocks, now classed with them.

cambric *n* a fine white linen or cotton cloth.

camcorder *n* a portable video recorder with built-in sound recording facilities.

came *see* **come**.

camel *n* a large four-footed, long-necked animal with a humped back; a fawny-beige colour.—*also adj*.

cameleer *n* a camel driver.

camellia *n* an oriental evergreen shrub with showy blooms.—*also* **japonica**.

camelopard *n* the giraffe.

camel's hair, camelhair *n* the hair of a camel; cloth from this; its fawn-tan colour; the hair from a squirrel's tail used as a paintbrush.—**camel's-hair, camelhair** *adj*.

Camembert *n* a soft white cheese originating in Normandy.

cameo *n* (*pl* **cameos**) an onyx or other gem carved in relief, often showing a head in profile; an outstanding bit role, esp in a motion picture; a short piece of fine writing.

camera *n* the apparatus used for taking still photographs or television or motion pictures; a judge's private chamber; **in camera** in private, esp of a legal hearing exluding the public; **off camera** outside the area being filmed; **on camera** being filmed, before the camera.

cameraman *n* (*pl* **cameramen**) a film or television camera operator.

camera obscura *n* a darkened chamber or box in which, by means of lenses, external objects are exhibited on paper, glass, etc.

camera-ready *adj* (*printing*) ready for photographic platemaking.

camera-shy *adj* unwilling to, or against, being filmed or photographed.

camion *n* a heavy truck, a wagon.

camise *n* a light loose robe, a chemise.

camisole *n* a woman or girl's loose sleeveless underbodice.

camlet *n* a kind of light cloth.

camomile *see* **chamomile**.

Camorra *n* a secret terrorist organization in southern Italy; a lawless clique.

camouflage *n* a method (esp using colouring) of disguise or concealment used to deceive an enemy; a means of putting people off the scent. * *vt* to conceal by camouflage.

camp[1] *n* the ground on which tents or temporary accommodation is erected; the occupants of this, such as holiday-makers or troops; the supporters of a particular cause. * *vi* to lodge in a camp; to pitch tents.—**camping** *n*.

camp[2] *adj* (*sl*) theatrical, exaggerated; effeminate; homosexual. * *vi* (*with* **up**) to make or give an exaggerated display of camp characteristics.

campaign *n* a series of military operations; a series of operations with a particular objective, such as election of a candidate or promotion of a product; organized course of action. * *vi* to take part in or conduct a campaign.—**campaigner** *n*.

campanile *n* a bell tower detached from the body of a church.

campanology *n* the art of bell ringing.—**campanologist** *n*.

campanula *n* a plant with bell-shaped flowers.

campanulate *adj* (*flower*) bell-shaped.

camper *n* one who lives in a tent; a person on a camping holiday; a vehicle equipped with all domestic facilities.

campfire *n* an outdoor fire at a camp; a social gathering around such a fire.

camp follower *n* a civilian, esp a prostitute, who provides unofficial services to military personnel; a person who is sympathetic to the aims of a particular group but is not a member.

camphene *n* rectified oil of turpentine.

camphor *n* a solid white transparent essential oil with a pungent taste and smell used to repel insects, as a stimulant in medicine, etc.—**camphoric** *adj*.

camphor tree *n* a species of laurel that yields camphor.

camphorate *vt* to saturate or treat with camphor.

campion *n* any of various wild plants of the pink family, the commonest having red or white flowers.

camp meeting *n* an oudoor religious meeting.

campsite *n* a camping ground, often with facilities for holiday-makers.

campstool *n* a folding stool or seat.

campus *n* (*pl* **campuses**) the grounds, and sometimes buildings, of a college or university.

camshaft *n* the rotating shaft to which cams are fitted to lift valves in engines.

Can *abbr* = Canada; Canadian.

can¹ *vt* (*pt* **could**) to be able to; to have the right to; to be allowed to.

can² *n* a container, usu metal, with a separate cover in which petrol, film, etc is stored; a tin in which meat, fruit, drinks, etc are hermetically sealed; the contents of a can; (*sl*) jail; (*sl*) a lavatory; **in the can** (*film*) shot and edited and ready for showing; (*inf*) accomplished, agreed, tied up. * *vti* (**canning, canned**) to preserve (foods) in a can.—**canner** *n*.

Canada balsam *n* a resin obtained from a species of fir.

Canada Day *n* a national Canadian holiday, July 1, commemorating its dominion status (established 1867).

Canada goose *n* a large grey goose with a black head and neck and a white throat patch.

Canadian *adj* of or pertaining to Canada. * *n* a native of Canada.

canaille *n* a rabble, the lowest orders.

canal *n* an artificial waterway cut across land; a duct in the body. * *vt* (**canalling, canalled** *or* **canaling, canaled**) to provide with canals.

canalize, canalise *vt* to provide with a canal or channel. * *vi* to flow in or into a channel; to establish new channels or outlets.—**canalization, canalisation** *n*.

canapé *n* a small piece of pastry, bread or toast with a savoury spread or topping.

canard *n* a false report, an absurd story, a baseless rumour.

canary *n* (*pl* **canaries**) a small finch, usu greenish to yellow in colour, kept as a songbird.

canasta *n* a card game played with two packs of cards, for two to six players.

cancan *n* an energetic dance performed by women, involving high kicks and the lifting of frothy petticoats.

cancel *vt* (**cancelling, cancelled** *or* **canceling, canceled**) to cross out; to obliterate; to annul, suppress; (*reservation, etc*) to call off; to countermand; (*with* **out**) to make up for.—**canceller, canceler** *n*.

cancellation, cancelation *n* the act of cancelling; annulment; something that has been cancelled; the mark made by cancelling.

cancellous, cancellate, cancellated *adj* (*med*) marked with cross lines or ridges.

Cancer *n* (*astron*) the Crab, a northern constellation; (*astrol*) the 4th sign of the zodiac, operative 21 June–21 July.—**Cancerian** *adj*.

cancer *n* the abnormal and uncontrollable growth of the cells of living organisms, esp a malignant tumour; an undesirable or dangerous expansion of something.—**cancerous** *adj*.

cancroid *adj* resembling a cancer; like a crab.

candela *n* a unit of luminous intensity.

candelabrum *n* (*pl* **candelabra**) a branched and ornamented candlestick or lampstand.

candescent *adj* glowing; white-hot.—**candescence** *n*.

candid *adj* frank, outspoken; unprejudiced; (*photograph*) informal.—**candidly** *adv*.—**candidness** *n*.

candidate *n* a person who has nomination for an office or qualification for membership or award; a student taking an examination.—**candidacy** *n*.—**candidature** *n*.

candid camera *n* a small camera for photographing people unexpectedly or unknowingly.

candied *adj* preserved in or encrusted with sugar.

candle *n* a stick of wax with a wick that burns to give light. * *vt* to check the freshness of eggs by examining in front of a light.

candlelight *n* the light produced by a candle or candles.

Candlemas (Day) *n* the Feast of the Purification of the Virgin Mary (2 February).

candlepower *n* a unit of measurement of the intensity of a light source, measured in candelas.

candlestick *n* a holder for one or more candles.

candlewick *n* a cotton fabric with raised pattern of tufted yarn.—*also adj*.

candour, candor *n* sincerity, openness, frankness.

candy *n* (*pl* **candies**) a solid confection of sugar or syrup with flavouring, fruit, nuts, etc, a sweet. * *vb* (**candying, candied**) *vt* to preserve by coating with candy; to encrust with crystals. * *vi* to become candied.

candyfloss *n* a confection of spun sugar.—*also* **cotton candy**.

candy-striped *adj* (*cloth*) with narrow stripes of colour on a white background.

candytuft *n* a plant with pink, white or purple tufted flowers.

cane *n* the slender, jointed stem of certain plants, as bamboo; a plant with such a stem, as sugar cane; (*usu with* **the**) a stick of this used for corporal punishment; strips of this used in furniture making etc or for supporting plants; a walking stick. * *vt* to thrash with a cane; to weave cane into; (*inf*) to beat, eg in a game.

canebrake *n* a thicket of canes.

canella *n* an aromatic and tonic bark of a West Indian tree.

canescent *adj* (*biol*) growing white, hoary.

cane sugar *n* sugar made from sugar cane.

cangue *n* (*formerly*) a square wooden collar worn as a punishment by criminals in China.

canine *adj* of or like a dog; of the family of animals that includes wolves, dogs and foxes; pertaining to a canine tooth. * *n* a dog or other member of the same family of animals; in humans, a pointed tooth next to the incisors.

canister *n* a small box or container usu of metal for storing tea, flour, etc; a tube containing tear gas which explodes and releases its contents on impact.

canker *n* an erosive or spreading sore; a foot disease in horses; an ear disease in cats and dogs; a fungal disease of trees; a corrupting influence.—**cankerous** *adj*.

cankerworm *n* a caterpillar destructive to trees or plants.

canna *n* a showy American tropical plant.

cannabin *n* a narcotic resin extracted from hemp.

cannabis *n* a narcotic drug obtained from the hemp plant; the hemp plant.—*also* **hashish, marijuana.**—**cannabic** *adj*.

canned *adj* stored in sealed tins; recorded for reproduction; (*sl*) drunk.

canned hunt *n* (*sl*) an organized big-game hunt carried out within an area from which the quarry cannot escape.

cannel (coal) *n* a hard bituminous coal burning with a clear bright flame.

cannelloni *npl* stuffed pasta tubes.

cannelure *n* a groove or fluting.

cannery *n* (*pl* **canneries**) a building, etc, where foods are canned.

cannibal *n* a person who eats human flesh; an animal that feeds on its own species. * *adj* relating to or indulging in this practice.—**cannibalism** *n*.—**cannibalistic** *adj*.

cannibalize *vti* to strip (old equipment) of parts for use in other units.—**cannibalization** *n*.

cannikin *n* a small can.

cannon *n* (*pl* **cannon**) a large mounted piece of artillery; an automatic gun on an aircraft; (*pl* **cannons**) (*billiards*) a carom. * *vi* to collide with great force (with into); to rebound; (*billiards*) to make a carom.

cannonade *n* a heavy, continuous artillery attack. * *vti* to attack with cannon.

cannonball *n* the heavy, round shot fired from a cannon; (*tennis*) a low, fast service stroke. * *vi* to move along at great speed.

cannoneer *n* an artilleryman.

cannon fodder *n* soldiers regarded as expendable in war.

cannonry *n* (*pl* **cannonries**) artillery.

cannot = can not.

cannula *n* (*pl* **cannulas, cannulae**) (*med*) a small tube for inspecting or withdrawing fluids.

canny *adj* (**cannier, canniest**) knowing, shrewd; cautious, careful; thrifty.—**cannily** *adv*.—**canniness** *n*.

canoe *n* a narrow, light boat propelled by paddles.—*also* *vi* (**canoeing, canoed**).—**canoeist** *n*.

canon *n* a decree of the Church; a general rule or standard, criterion; a list of the books of the Bible accepted as genuine; the works of any author recognized as genuine; a list of canonized saints; a member of a cathedral chapter; a part of the mass containing words of consecration; (*mus*) a round.

canoness *n* (*RC Church*) one of a number of women living under canon law but not compelled to take religious vows.

canonical *adj* pertaining to a rule or canon; according to or established by ecclesiastical laws; belonging to the canon of scripture. * *n* (*pl*) the official dress of the clergy.—**canonically** *adv*.

canonical hour *n* (*RC Church*) one of the hours appointed by ecclesiastical law for daily prayer: matins with lauds, prime, sext, nones, vespers, and compline.

canonist *n* an expert in canon law.—**canonistic** *adj*.

canonize *vt* (*RC Church*) to officially declare (a person) a saint.—**canonization** *n*.

canon law *n* rules or laws relating to faith, morals and discipline that regulate church government, as laid down by popes and councils.

canonry *n* (*pl* **canonries**) the office of a cathedral canon.

canoodle *vti* (*sl*) to cuddle, to fondle.

canopy *n* (*pl* **canopies**) a tent-like covering over a bed, throne, etc; any roof-like structure or projection; the transparent cover of an aeroplane's cockpit; the tops of trees in a forest; the sky regarded as a covering. * *vt* (**canopying, canopied**) to cover with or as with a canopy.

cans *npl* (*sl*) headphones.

cant[1] *n* insincere or hypocritical speech; language specific to a group (eg thieves, lawyers); cliched talk, meaningless jargon. * *vi* to talk in or use cant.

cant[2] *n* an inclination or tilt; a slanting surface, bevel. * *vti* to slant, to tilt; to overturn by a sudden movement.

can't = can not.

cantabile *adv* (*mus*) in a lyrical flowing style.

Cantabrigian *n* a student or graduate of Cambridge University; an inhabitant of Cambridge.—*also adj*.

cantaloupe, cantaloup *n* a variety of melon with orange flesh.

cantankerous *adj* ill-natured, bad-tempered, quarrelsome.—**cantankerously** *adv*.—**cantankerousness** *n*.

cantata *n* (*mus*) a composition for voices of a story or religious text.

cantatrice *n* a female singer, esp one who sings in operas.

canteen *n* a restaurant attached to factory, school, etc, catering for large numbers of people; a flask for carrying water; (a box containing) a set of cutlery.

canter *n* a horse's three-beat gait resembling a slow, smooth gallop.—*also vti*.

Canterbury bell *n* a large variety of campanula with handsome bell-shaped blossoms.

cantharides *npl* (*sing* **cantharis**) (*med*) a diuretic preparation made from dried Spanish flies, formerly considered an aphrodisiac.—*also* **Spanish fly**.

canthus *n* (*pl* **canthi**) the angle made by the meeting of the eyelids.

canticle *n* a song taken from the Bible (eg the Magnificat).

cantilever *n* a projecting beam that supports a balcony, etc.

cantilever bridge *n* a bridge supported by cantilevers springing from piers.

cantle *n* a corner; a piece; the rising rear part of a saddle.

canto *n* (*pl* **cantos**) a division of a long poem.

canton *n* a political and administrative division of Switzerland.—**cantonal** *adj*.

Cantonese *n* (*pl* **Cantonese**) a Chinese language deriving from Canton; an inhabitant or native of Canton.—*also adj*.

cantonment *n* a part of a town or village alloted to a body of troops; in India, a permanent military station.

cantor *n* a singer of liturgical solos in a synagogue; the leader of singing in a church choir.

cantorial *adj* of or pertaining to a precentor's or the north side of the choir of a church.

cantrip *n* a prank, a piece of mischief; a magic spell.

Canuck *n* (*inf*) a Canadian.—*also adj*.

canvas *n* a strong coarse cloth of hemp or flax, used for tents, sails, etc, and for painting on; a ship's sails collectively; a tent or tents; an oil painting on canvas.

canvasback *n* (*pl* **canvasbacks, canvasback**) a North American duck esteemed for the delicacy of its flesh.

canvass *vti* to go through (places) or among (people)

asking for votes, opinions, orders, etc.—also *n*.—**canvasser** *n*.

canyon *n* a long, narrow valley between high cliffs.

canzone, canzona *n* (*pl* **canzoni, canzone**) a song or air resembling the madrigal; an instrumental piece in the style of a madrigal.

canzonet, canzonette *n* a short light song.

caoutchouc *n* rubber.—*also adj*.

cap *n* any close-fitting headgear, visored or brimless; the special headgear of a profession, club, etc; the top of a mushroom or toadstool; a cap-like thing, as an artificial covering for a tooth; a top, a cover; a percussion cap in a toy gun; a type of contraceptive device; (*sport*) the head gear presented to a player chosen for a team. * *vt* (**capping, capped**) to put a cap on; to cover (the end of); to award a degree at a university; to seal (an oil or gas well); to equal, outdo or top; to limit the level of a tax increase, etc; (*sport*) to choose a player for a team.

capability *n* (*pl* **capabilities**) the quality of being capable; an undeveloped faculty.

capable *adj* able or skilled to do; competent, efficient; susceptible (of); adapted to.—**capably** *adv*.

capacious *adj* able to hold a great deal; roomy.—**capaciousness** *n*.

capacitance *n* (a measure of) the ability of a system to store an electric charge.

capacitate *vt* to make capable; to enable; to qualify.—**capacitation** *n*.

capacitor *n* a device for storing electric charge.

capacity *n* (*pl* **capacities**) the power of holding or grasping; cubic content; mental ability or power; character; the position held; legal competence; the greatest possible output or content.

cap-a-pie *adv* from head to foot.

caparison *n* an ornamental covering for a horse; rich clothing. * *vt* to cover (a horse) with rich clothing; to adorn with rich dress.

cape[1] *n* a headland or promontory running into the sea.

cape[2] *n* a sleeveless garment fastened at the neck and hanging over the shoulders and back.

capelin, caplin *n* a small sea fish of the smelt family, largely used as bait for cod.

caper[1] *vi* to skip about playfully, to frolic. * *n* a playful leap or skip; (*sl*) an escapade; (*sl*) a criminal activity.

caper[2] *n* a low, prickly Mediterranean shrub; its pickled flower buds, used in cooking (eg caper sauce).

capercaillie, capercailzie *n* the largest Old World grouse.

Capetian *adj* of or pertaining to the dynasty founded by Hugh Capet, who ascended the French throne in 987.

capias *n* (*law*) a writ for arrest.

capillarity *n* (*pl* **capillarities**) the power possessed by porous bodies of drawing up a fluid; surface tension.

capillary *adj* of or as fine as a hair; (*tube, pipe*) of a hair-like calibre; (*anat*) of the capillaries. * *n* (*pl* **capillaries**) one of the very fine blood vessels connecting arteries and veins.

capital[1] *adj* of or pertaining to the head; (*offence*) punishable by death; serious; chief, principal; leading, first-class; of, or being the seat of government; of capital or wealth; relating to a large letter, upper case; (*inf*) excellent. * *n* a city that is the seat of government of a country; a large letter; accumulated wealth used to produce more; stock or money for carrying on a business; a city, town, etc pre-eminent in some special activity.—**capitally** *adv*.

capital[2] *n* the head or top part of a column or pillar.

capital gain *n* the profit made on the sale of an asset.

capital goods *npl* goods (eg machinery) used to produce other goods.

capitalism *n* the system of individual ownership of wealth; the dominance of such a system.

capitalist *n* a person who has money invested in business for profit; a supporter of capitalism. * *adj* of or favouring capitalism.—**capitalistic** *adj*.

capitalize *vti* (*with* **on**) to use (something) to one's advantage; to convert into money or capital; to provide with capital; to write in or print in capital letters.—**capitalization** *n*.

capitally *adv* in a capital manner; excellently.

capital punishment *n* the death penalty for a crime.

capitate *adj* (*bot*) shaped like a head; head-like.

capitation *n* a direct, uniform tax imposed on each person, a tax per head.

Capitol *n* (*with* **the**) the building where the US Congress meets; the temple of Jupiter on the Capitoline in Rome.

capitular *adj* of or pertaining to a chapter. * *n* a member of a cathedral chapter.

capitulary *n* (*pl* **capitularies**) a statue passed in a chapter, as of knights or canons; (*pl*) the body of statues of a chapter or of an ecclesiastical council.

capitulate *vi* to surrender on terms; to give in.—**capitulation** *n*.—**capitulator** *n*.—**capitulatory** *adj*.

capo *n* (*pl* **capos**) a device attached across the fingerboard of a guitar to raise the pitch of the strings.

capon *n* a castrated cockerel fattened for eating.

caponize *vt* to make a cock a capon by castration.

caporal *n* a French tobacco.

capote *n* a long coarse cloak; a long mantle for women.

cappuccino *n* (*pl* **cappuccinos**) frothy, milky coffee usu served sprinkled with chocolate powder.

capreolate *adj* (*bot*) furnished with tendrils.

capriccio *n* (*pl* **capriccios, capricci**) a light musical composition in a fantastic, whimsical style.

capriccioso *adv* (*mus*) in a free, fantastic style.

caprice *n* a passing fancy; an impulsive change in behaviour, opinion, etc; a whim.

capricious *adj* unstable, inconstant; unreliable.—**capriciously** *adv*.—**capriciousness** *n*.

Capricorn *n* (*astron*) the Goat, a southern constellation; (*astrol*) the tenth sign of the zodiac, operative 21 December–19 January.—**Capricornean** *adj*.

caprification *n* a process of accelerating the ripening of the fig by puncturing it.

caprine *adj* of, pertaining to, or like a goat.

capriole *n* a leap of a horse made without advancing; a caper. * *vi* to execute a capriole, to kick up the heels.

capsaicin *n* an alkaloid extracted from several species of capsicum.

capsicum *n* a tropical plant with bell-shaped fruits containing hot or mild seeds; the fruit of this plant used as a vegetable.—*also* **red** *or* **green pepper**.

capsize *vti* to upset or overturn.

capstan *n* an upright drum around which cables are wound to haul them in; the spindle in a tape recorder that winds the tape past the head.

capsulate, capsulated *adj* furnished with or enclosed in a capsule.—**capsulation** *n*.

capsule *n* a small gelatin case enclosing a drug to be swallowed; a metal or plastic container; (*bot*) a seed case; the orbiting and recoverable part of a spacecraft.—**capsular** *adj*.

capsulize vt to present (information) in a concise or condensed form.—**capsulization** n.

captain n a chief, leader; the master of a ship; the pilot of an aircraft; a rank of army, naval and marine officer; the leader of a team, as in sports; a leading employer in industry; a policeman responsible for a precinct. * vt to be captain of.—**captaincy** n.

captaincy, captainship n (pl **captaincies, captainships**) the rank, post, or commission of a captain.

caption n a heading in a newspaper, to a chapter, etc; a legend or title describing an illustration; a subtitle. * vti to provide with a caption.

captious adj ready to find fault or take offence; carping, quibbling.—**captiously** adv.

captivate vt to fascinate; to charm.—**captivating** adj.—**captivation** n.—**captivator** n.

captive n one kept confined; a prisoner; a person obsessed by an emotion. * adj taken or kept prisoner; unable to avoid being addressed (a captive audience); unable to refuse (a product) through a lack of choice (a captive market); captivated.

captivity n (pl **captivities**) the state of being a captive; a period of imprisonment.

captor n a person or animal who takes a prisoner.

capture vt to take prisoner; (fortress, etc) to seize; to catch; to gain or obtain by skill, attraction, etc, to win. * n the act of taking a prisoner or seizing by force; anything or anyone so taken.

capuche n a monk's hood or cowl; the hood of a cloak.

capuchin n a monkey with hair resembling a cowl; a pigeon with cowl-like feathers; a woman's cloak and hood; (with cap) a Franciscan monk of the mendicant order.

capybara n a large South American rodent that lives mostly in water.

car n a self-propelled motor vehicle, an automobile, a motorcar; the passenger compartment of a train, airship, lift, cable railway, etc; a railway carriage.

carabineer, carabinier see **carbineer**.

carabiner n (climbing) a type of shackle with a snap link, used to secure a rope.

caracal n a kind of lynx; its fur.

caracole, caracol vi (horse) to make a half turn to the right or left. * n a half turn, right or left; a spiral staircase.

carafe n an open-topped bottle for serving water or wine at table.

caragheen see **carragheen**.

caramel n burnt sugar, used in cooking to colour or flavour; a type of sweet tasting of this.

caramelize vti to turn or be turned into caramel.

carapace n the upper shell of the tortoise, turtle, crab, etc.

carat n a measure of weight for precious stones; a measure of the purity of gold.—also **karat**.

caravan n a large enclosed vehicle that is equipped to be lived in and may be towed by a car (—also **trailer**); a band of merchants travelling together for safety. * vi (**caravanning, caravanned**) to travel with a caravan, esp on holiday.

caravanserai, caravansary n (pl **caravanserais, caravansaries**) in the East, a large inn surrounding a spacious courtyard, where caravans rest at night.

caravel, caravelle n an ancient small light fast Spanish ship with broad bows, a narrow high poop, four masts and lateen sails.—also **carvel**.

caraway n a biennial plant with pungent aromatic seeds used as a flavouring.

carbide n a compound of carbon with another element, esp calcium carbide.

carbine n a light, semiautomatic or automatic rifle.

carbineer n a mounted soldier armed with a carbine.—also **carabineer, carabinier**.

carbo-, carb- prefix carbon.

carbohydrate n a compound of carbon, hydrogen and oxygen, esp in sugars and starches as components of food. * npl starchy foods.

carbolic acid n phenol.

carbolize vt to sterilize with carbolic acid.

carbon n a nonmetallic element, a constituent of all organic matter; a duplicate made with carbon paper.

carbon-12 n an isotope of carbon, used as the standard for atomic weight.

carbon-14 n a radioisotope used in medicine as a tracer and in carbon dating.

carbonaceous adj pertaining to, composed of or resembling carbon.

carbonado n (pl **carbonadoes, carbonados**) a piece of meat cut crossways for grilling.

carbonate n a salt of carbonic acid. * vt to treat with carbon dioxide, as in making soft, fizzy drinks.—**carbonated** adj.

carbon copy n a copy of typed or written material made by using carbon paper; (inf) an exact copy of something or someone.

carbon dating n a scientific method of dating material by measuring the amount of carbon-14 it contains.

carbon dioxide n a gas formed by combustion and breathing and absorbed by plants.

carbonic adj of or obtained from carbon.

carbonic acid n a weakly acidic solution of carbon dioxide in water.

carboniferous adj coal-bearing, yielding carbon; (with cap) of or relating to strata of the Palaeozoic Age from which coal is derived.

carbonize vt to convert into carbon or a carbon residue.—**carbonization** n.

carbon monoxide n a colourless, odourless, highly poisonous gas.

carbon paper n a sheet of paper covered with a dark, waxy pigment inserted between sheets of paper for making copies of writing or typing.

Carborundum n (trademark) a compound of carbon and silicon used for polishing and grinding.

carboy n a, usu cushioned, container of glass, plastic or metal for the safe transportation of liquids.

carbuncle n a red, knob-shaped gemstone, esp a garnet; a large inflamed boil; a pimple.—**carbuncular** adj.

carburet vt (**carburetting, carburetted** or **carbureting, carbureted**) to combine with carbon.

carburetor, carburettor n a device in an internal-combustion engine for making an explosive mixture of air and fuel vapour.

carburize vt to combine with carbon.—**carburization** n.

carcanet n (arch) a collar of jewels.

carcass n the dead body of an animal; a framework, skeleton or shell; (derog) the body of a living person.

carcinogen n a substance that produces cancer.—**carcinogenic** adj.

carcinoma n (pl **carcinomas, carcinomata**) a tumour caused by a cancer.

card[1] n a small piece of cardboard; a piece of this with a figure or picture for playing games or fortune-telling; a piece of this filed in a card index; a membership card; a piece of card with a person or firm's name, address or with an invitation, greeting, message, etc; (*inf*) an entertaining or eccentric person; a small piece of plastic identifying a person for banking purposes, eg a cheque card, credit card; (*pl*) card games; (*pl*) card playing; (*pl*) employees insurance and tax documents held by the employer.

card² *n* a toothed instrument for combing cotton, wool or flax fibres off. * *vt* (*wool, etc*) to comb.

cardamom, cardamum, cardamon *n* a tropical Asian plant the seed pods of which are used as a spice.

cardboard *n* thick stiff paper, often with a clay coating, for boxes, cartons, etc. * *adj* made of this; lacking substance; makeshift.

card-carrying *adj* being an official member of a political party, organization, etc.

card catalogue *n* a catalogue, each item of which is entered on a separate card.

card file *n* a filing system in which each item is entered separately on a single card.

cardi- *prefix* heart.

cardiac *adj* relating to the heart. * *n* a person suffering a disorder of the heart; a drug to stimulate the heart.

cardiac arrest *n* heart failure.

cardialgia *n* heartburn.—**cardialgic** *adj*.

cardigan *n* a knitted sweater fastening up the front.

cardinal *adj* of chief importance, fundamental; of a bright red. * *n* an official appointed by the Pope to his councils; bright red.—**cardinally** *adv*.

cardinalate, cardinalship *n* the office, rank, or dignity of a cardinal; the body of cardinals.

cardinal numbers *npl* numbers that express how many (1, 2, 3, 4 etc).

cardinal points *npl* the four chief points of the compass: north, south, east, west.

cardinal virtues *npl* justice, prudence, temperance, and fortitude.

cardio- *prefix* heart.

cardiogram *n* an electrocardiogram.

cardiograph *n* a device for recording heart movements; an electrocardiograph.

cardiology *n* the branch of medicine concerned with the heart and its diseases.—**cardiological** *adj*.—**cardiologist** *n*.

cardiopulmonary *adj* of or concerned with or affect the heart and lungs.

cardiovascular *adj* of or pertaining to the heart and the blood vessels.

carditis *n* inflammation of the muscular tissue of the heart.

cardoon *n* a plant related to and resembling the artichoke and used as a vegetable in Spain and France.

cards *see* **card¹**.

cardsharp(er) *n* a person who cheats at cards.

care *n* anxiety; concern; serious attention, heed; consideration; charge, protection; the cause or object of concern or anxiety. * *vt* to feel concern; to agree, like, or be willing (to do something); **care of** at the address of, c/o; **in, into care** (*person*) taken charge of by a local authority by court order. * *vi* (*usu with* **for** *or* **about**) to feel affection or regard; to have a desire (for); to provide for, have in one's charge.

careen *vt* to bring (a ship) over on one side for calking, cleansing, or repairing. * *vi* to incline to one side, as a ship under press of sail.

career *n* progress through life; a profession, occupation, esp with prospects for promotion. * *vi* to rush rapidly or wildly.

careerist *n* a person who is ambitious to advance in a chosen profession.

career woman *n* a woman primarily interested in her job and in furthering her career.

carefree *adj* without cares, lively, light-hearted.

careful *adj* painstaking; cautious; thoughtful.—**carefully** *adv*.—**carefulness** *n*.

careless *adj* not careful; unconcerned, insensitive; carefree.—**carelessly** *adv*.—**carelessness** *n*.

carer *n* one who takes on (professionally) the care of a dependent person.

caress *n* any act or expression of affection; an embrace. * *vt* to touch or stroke lovingly.—**caresser** *n*.—**caressingly** *adv*.

caret *n* a mark (^) showing where something omitted in text is to be inserted.

caretaker *n* a person put in charge of a place or thing; (*government*) one temporarily in control.

careworn *adj* showing signs of stress, worry.

cargo *n* (*pl* **cargoes, cargos**) the load carried by a ship, truck, aircraft, etc; freight.

Carib *n* (*pl* **Caribs, Carib**) a member of an Indian people of the Lesser Antilles and neighbouring parts of the South American coast, or of their descendants; their language * *adj* of or pertaining to the Carib people or language.

Caribbean *adj* of or pertaining to the Caribbean Sea and its islands. * *n* the Caribbean Sea.

caribou *n* (*pl* **caribou, caribous**) a large North American reindeer.

caricature *n* a likeness made ludicrous by exaggeration or distortion of characteristic features. * *vt* to make a caricature of, to parody.—**caricaturist** *n*.

caries *n* (*pl* **caries**) decay of bones or teeth.

carillon *n* a chime of bells diatonically tuned and played by hand or machinery; a simple air adapted for playing on a set of bells.

carina *n* (*pl* **carinae, carinas**) a keel; the two lower petals of a papilionaceous flower (as the furze) partially joined; the keel of the breastbone of birds.

carinate, carinated *adj* shaped like a keel.

caring *adj* compassionate; of or dealing with people's welfare, usu professionally.

carious *adj* affected with caries; decayed.

carling *n* a ship's timber running fore and aft from one transverse deck beam to another, serving as a foundation for the planks of the deck.

Carlovingian *see* **Carolingian**.

carmagnole *n* a popular song and dance of the time of the French Revolution; a costume adapted by the revolutionists; a bombastic report from the French armies during the Revolution.

Carmelite *n* a member of a mendicant order founded on Mount Carmel in the 12th century, a white friar; a variety of pear; a kind of fine woollen cloth. * *adj* of or belonging to the order of Carmelites.

carminative *n* a medicine that expels wind and relieves colic and flatulence. * *adj* expelling wind.

carmine *n* a rich crimson pigment; the essential colouring principle of cochineal.

carnage *n* great slaughter.

carnal *adj* of the flesh; sexual; sensual; worldly.—**carnality** *n*.—**carnally** *adv*.

carnal knowledge *n* sexual intercourse.

carnation *n* a garden flower, the clove pink.

carnelian *see* **cornelian**.

carnet *n* a customs permit or licence, esp for a vehicle; a book of tickets, etc.

carnival *n* public festivities and revelry; a travelling fair with sideshows, etc.

carnivore *n* a flesh-eating mammal.

carnivorous *adj* (*animals*) feeding on flesh; (*plants*) able to trap and digest insects.

carob *n* an edible, sugary pod of a Mediterranean tree.

carol *n* a joyful song or hymn; a Christmas hymn. * *vi* (**carolling, carolled** *or* **caroling, caroled**) to sing carols; to sing with happiness.

Caroline, Carolean *adj* belonging to the period of Charles I or Charles II.

Carolingian *adj* of or pertaining to the medieval Frankish dynasty that once ruled France. * *n* a member of this dynasty.—*also* **Carlovingian**.

Carolinian *adj* of or pertaining to either North or South Carolina.

carom *n* (*billiards*) a shot in which the cue ball hits two others successively. * *vi* to make a carom.—*also* **cannon**.

carotid (artery) *n* one of the two principal arteries, one on either side of the neck, which convey blood from the aorta to the head.—**carotidal** *adj*.

carousal *n* a feast or festival; a noisy drinking bout or revel.

carouse *vi* to drink and have fun.—**carousal** *n*.—**carouser** *n*.

carousel *n* a merry-go-round; a revolving circular platform, as in an airport luggage conveyor.

carp[1] *vi* to find fault, esp continually.

carp[2] *n* (*pl* **carp, carps**) a brown and yellow freshwater fish.

carpal *adj* pertaining to the carpus or wrist.

car park *n* a parking lot.

carpe diem (*Latin*) seize the day; take advantage of a present opportunity.

carpel *n* a simple pistil, or one of the parts of a compound pistil or ovary of a flower.—**carpellary** *adj*.

carpellate *adj* having a carpel.

carpenter *n* a person skilled in woodwork, esp in house building.—**carpentry** *n*.

carpenter bee *n* a bee that makes nests in wood.

carpentry *n* the art of cutting, framing, and joining timber; work done by a carpenter.

carpet *n* a woven fabric for covering floors; any thick covering * *vt* to cover with carpet; (*inf*) to issue a reprimand, to have on the carpet to rebuke.

carpetbag *n* a carrying bag formerly made of carpeting.

carpetbagger *n* an outsider, esp a nonresident who meddles in politics.

carpeting *n* cloth for carpets; carpets in general.

carpet sweeper *n* a mechanical device for removing dirt, etc, from a carpet.

carphone *n* a cellular telephone fitted in and operated from a car.

carpology *n* the branch of botany that treats of the structure of fruits in general.—**carpological** *adj*.—**carpologist** *n*.

carpophore *n* (*bot*) a slender prolongation of the axis that bears the carpels.

carport *n* an open-sided shelter for a car extending from the side of a house.

carpus *n* (*pl* **carpi**) the bones between the forearm and the hand, forming the wrist in man and the corresponding bones in other animals.

carrack *n* a large round-built vessel formerly used by the Portuguese and Spaniards in the East Indian and American trade.

carrageen, carragheen *n* a seaweed very common on the rocks of the Irish coast that, when dried and bleached, is known as Irish moss and is used for blancmanges, soup, etc.—*also* **carageen**.

carrel *n* a small study room or cubicle, esp in a library.

carriage *n* the act of carrying, transport; the cost of this; deportment, bearing; behaviour; a rail coach or compartment; a wheeled coach drawn by horses; a frame with wheels to carry a gun; the moving part of a typewriter.

carriage dog *n* the spotted Dalmatian.

carrick bend *n* (*naut*) a particular kind of knot for splicing two hawsers together.

carrick bitt *n* (*naut*) one of the bitts supporting the windlass.

carrier *n* one who carries or transports goods, esp for hire; a device for carrying; a person or animal transmitting an infectious disease without being affected by it; an aircraft carrier; a plastic or paper bag with handles for holding things; a portable seat for a baby, a carrycot.

carrier pigeon *n* a homing pigeon used to carry messages.

carrier wave *n* an electromagnetic wave that can be modulated in frequency, amplitude, etc, to transmit (radio, TV, etc) signals.

carrion *n* the dead putrefying flesh of an animal.

carrion crow *n* the common crow of Europe.

carronade *n* a short cannon of large bore for close range, formerly used in the navy.

carron oil *n* a mixture of linseed oil and lime water used as a liniment for burns.

carrot *n* a plant grown for its edible, fleshy orange root; an inducement, often illusory.

carroty *adj* orange-red in colour.

carry *vb* (**carrying, carried**) *vt* to convey or transport; to support or bear; to involve, have as a result; to hold (oneself); to extend or prolong; to gain by force; to win over; to stock; to be pregnant; (*with* **away**) to delight; to arouse to extreme enthusiasm; to remove violently; (*with* **forward**) (*book-keeping*) to transfer (a total) to the next column, page, etc; (*with* **off**) to cause to die; to remove by force, capture; (*situation*) to handle successfully; (*with* **out**) to perform (a task, etc); to accomplish; (*with* **over**) to carry forward; (*with* **through**) to complete. * *vi* (*with* **away**) to be filled with joy or emotion; (*with* **on**) to persevere; to conduct a business, etc; (*inf*) to have an affair; (*inf*) to cause a fuss; (*with* **through**) to enable to survive; to persist.

carryall *n* an overnight or holdall bag.

carrycot *n* a baby carrier, a portable cot.

carry-out *n* food or drink sold by a restaurant but consumed elsewhere.—*also adj*.

carsick *adj* ill or queasy from the motion of a moving vehicle.—**carsickness** *n*.

cart *n* a two-wheeled vehicle drawn by horses; any small vehicle for carrying loads. * *vt* to carry in a cart; (*inf*) to transport with effort.

cartage *n* conveyance in a cart; the charge made for this.

carte blanche *n* (*pl* **cartes blanches**) full authority to act as one thinks best.

cartel *n* an association of business firms to coordinate production, prices, etc to avoid competition and maximize profits; a union of political parties to achieve common aims.

Cartesian *adj* pertaining to the French philosopher

René Descartes (1596–1650) or his philosophy. * *n* a follower of Descartes or his philosophy.

Carthaginian *adj* pertaining to ancient Carthage, a city of North Africa.

Carthusian *n* one of an order of monks founded (1086) by St Bruno in the Grande Chartreuse, France.

cartilage *n* tough, elastic tissue attached to the bones of animals; gristle.—**cartilaginous** *adj*.

cartload *n* the amount a cart will hold.

cartogram *n* a map showing statistical information in diagrammatic form.

cartography *n* the drawing and publishing of maps.—**cartographer** *n*.—**cartographic, cartographical** *adj*.

carton *n* a cardboard box or container.

cartoon *n* a humorous picture dealing with current events; a comic strip; an animated cartoon; a full-size preparatory sketch for reproduction on a fresco, etc.—**cartoonist** *n*.

cartouche, cartouch *n* a cartridge; a canvas cartridge case; an ornament in the form of an unrolled scroll; on Egyptian monuments, etc, an oval figure containing the name or title of a sovereign or deity.

cartridge *n* the case that contains the explosive charge and bullet in a gun or rifle; a sealed case of film for a camera; the device containing the stylus on the end of the pick-up arm of a record player.

cartridge belt *n* a belt with loops for holding spare cartridges.

cartridge clip *n* a detachable container for cartridges in an automatic firearm.

cartulary *n* (*pl* **cartularies**) a collection or register of charters.—*also* **chartulary**.

cartwheel *n* an acrobatic handspring in which the body revolves with the weight on each hand in turn and the legs spread like the spokes of a wheel.

caruncle *n* a small fleshy excrescence on a bird's head, as the comb or wattle of a fowl; an appendage surrounding the hilum of a seed.—**caruncular, carunculate** *adj*.

carve *vt* to shape by cutting; to adorn with designs; to cut up (meat, etc); (*with* **up**) to cut into pieces or shares; (*sl*) to share out illegal proceeds; to slash someone with a knife or razor.

carvel *see* **caravel**.

carvel-built *adj* (*vessel*) with the outer boards or plates meeting flush, not overlapping.

carving *n* a figure or design carved from wood, stone, etc; the act of carving.

caryatid *n* (*pl* **caryatids, caryatides**) a figure of a woman in long robes supporting an entablature.—**caryatic, caryatidic, caryatidal, caryatidean** *adj*.

caryophyllaceous *adj* (*flowers*) belonging to the pink family.

caryopsis *n* (*pl* **caryopses, caryopsides**) a small dry fruit with the thin pericarp adherent to the seed, as in wheat, etc.

casaba *n* a variety of winter melon with a yellow rind and sweet flesh.—*also* **cassaba**.

Casanova *n* a man of amorous reputation.

cascade *n* a small, steep waterfall; a shower, as of sparks, etc. * *vti* to fall in a cascade.

cascara *n* Californian bark used as an aperient; a bark canoe.

cascarilla *n* the bark of a West Indian shrub, possessing aromatic and bitter properties; the shrub itself, from which is obtained a white bitter crystalline substance, cascarillin.

case[1] *n* a covering; a suitcase; its contents; the binding covering a book.

case[2] *n* an instance; a state of affairs; a condition, circumstance; a lawsuit; an argument for one side; (*sl*) a character; a person of a specific type; (*med*) a patient under treatment; (*gram*) the relationship between nouns, pronouns and adjectives in a sentence; **in case** in order to prevent, lest.

case-harden *vt* to make the surface (of iron or steel) harder than the interior.

case-hardened *adj* with a hard surface; made callous.

case history *n* a record of a person's medical background, etc.

casein *n* a protein in the curd matter of milk.

case knife *n* a sheath knife.

case law *n* law as settled by precedent.

casemate *n* a bomb-proof vault or battery in a fortification; an armoured enclosure for a gun in a warship; a hollow moulding.

casement *n* a window or its frame with a side hinge for opening.

caseous *adj* like cheese, cheesy.

casern, caserne *n* a lodging or barrack for soldiers in a garrison town.

case study *n* an analysis arrived at from studying more than one case history.

casework *n* social work based on the close monitoring of individuals or families.—**caseworker** *n*.

cash[1] *n* money in coins or notes; immediate payment, as opposed to that by cheque or on credit. * *vt* to give or get cash for; (*with* **in**) to exchange something for money; (*inf*) to gain an advantage or seize an opportunity to profit from; (*sl*) to die. * *vi* (*with* **in**) to exploit for profit; to take advantage of.—**cashable** *adj*.

cash[2] *n* (*pl* **cash**) the name of various Eastern coins of low value.

cash and carry *n, adj* (a policy of) selling for cash without delivery of goods.

cash-book *n* a book in which a register is kept of money received or paid out.

cash crop *n* a crop grown for market not for consumption.

cashew *n* the small, edible nut of a tropical tree.

cash flow *n* money which is paid into and out of a business during its operations.

cashier[1] *n* a person in charge of the paying and receiving of money in a bank, shop, etc.

cashier[2] *vt* to dismiss (an officer) from military service; to discharge.

cashmere *n* a fine wool from Kashmir goats; a material made from this.

cash on delivery *n* delivery to be paid for to a postman or carrier.

cash register *n* an automatic or electronic machine that shows and records the amount placed in it.

casimere *see* **cassimere**.

casing *n* any protective or outer covering; the material for this.

casino *n* (*pl* **casinos**) a room or building where gambling takes place.

cask *n* a barrel of any size, esp one for liquids; its contents.

casket *n* a small box or chest for jewels, etc; a coffin.

casque *n* (*poet*) a helmet.

cassaba *see* **casaba**.

cassava *n* a plant of tropical America and Africa cultivated for its tuberous roots, which yield a nutritious starch from which cassava bread and tapioca are made.

casserole *n* a covered dish for cooking and serving; the food so cooked and served. * *vt* to cook in a casserole.

cassette *n* a case containing magnetic tape or film for loading into a tape recorder or camera.

cassia *n* one of several tropical leguminous plants, the leaves of several species of which constitute the drug senna.

cassimere *n* a thin twilled woollen cloth used for men's garments.—*also* **casimere**.

cassiterite *n* a native tin dioxide; the principal ore of tin.

cassock *n* a long close-fitting black garment worn by certain clergy and by choristers.

cassowary *n* (*pl* **cassowaries**) a large running bird resembling the ostrich, inhabiting Australia and New Guinea.

cast *vb* (**casting, cast**) *vt* to throw or fling; to throw off or shed; to record; to direct; to shape in a mould; to calculate; to select actors, etc for a play; to throw a fishing line into the water. * *vi* to throw, hurl; (*with* **off**) to untie a ship from its moorings; (*knitting*) to loop off stitches from a needle without letting them unravel; (*with* **on**) to loop the first row of stitches onto a needle. * *n* act of casting; a throw; a plaster form for immobilizing an injured limb; a mould for casting; type or quantity; a tinge of colour; the actors assigned roles in a play; the set of actors; a slight squint in the eye.

castanets *npl* hollow shell-shaped pieces of wood held between the fingers and rattled together, esp to accompany Spanish dancing.

castaway *adj* shipwrecked; discarded. * *n* a shipwrecked person.

cast down *adj* depressed.

caste *n* any of the Hindu hereditary social classes; an exclusive social group.

castellan *n* the governor of a castle.

castellated *adj* having turrets and battlements, as a castle.

caster *see* **castor**.

castigate *vt* to chastise; to punish; to correct.—**castigation** *n*.

casting vote *n* the deciding vote used by the chairman of a meeting when the votes on each side are equal.

cast iron *n* an iron-carbon alloy melted and run into moulds.

cast-iron *adj* made of cast iron; untiring; rigid, unadaptable.

castle *n* a fortified building; a chess piece (—*also* **rook**).

castoff *n* a rejected item; a rough estimate of the number of pages of a finished book, etc.

cast-off *adj* laid aside or rejected.—**castoff** *n*.

castor *n* a small container with a perforated top for sprinkling salt, sugar, etc; a small swivelled wheel on a table leg, etc.—*also* **caster**.

castor oil *n* a vegetable oil used as a cathartic and lubricant.

castrate *vt* to remove the testicles of, to geld.—**castration** *n*.—**castrator** *n*.

castrato *n* (*pl* **castrati, castratos**) a male castrated in childhood to prevent a change of voice at the age of puberty; an artificial male soprano.

casual *adj* accidental, chance; unplanned; occasional; careless, offhand; unmethodical; informal. * *n* someone who works occasionally; (*pl*) informal or leisure clothing, shoes.—**casually** *adv*.—**casualness** *n*.

casualty *n* (*pl* **casualties**) a person injured or killed in a war or in an accident; something damaged or destroyed.

casuarina *n* a tree of Australia and southeast Asia having jointed branches.

casuist *n* one who studies or resolves cases of conscience; one skilled in casuistry.—**casuistic, casuistical** *adj*.—**casuistically** *adv*.

casuistry *n* (*pl* **casuistries**) the study or application of rules of right and wrong; sophistical or equivocal reasoning, esp on moral matters.

casus belli *n* (*pl* **casus belli**) an act or occurrence justifying war.

CAT (*acronym*) computerized axial tomography (—*also* **computer-aided** *or* **computer-assisted tomography**); the production of detailed three-dimensional images from scans of cross-sections of internal organs (**CAT scans**) using a computer-controlled X-ray machine (**CAT scanner**).

cat *n* a small, domesticated feline mammal kept as a pet; a wild animal related to this; lions, tigers, etc (—*also* **big cat**); (*inf*) a spiteful woman; (*sl*) a man.

cata- *prefix* down; wrongly; thoroughly.

catabolism *n* a downward series of changes by which complex bodies are broken down into simpler forms.—**catabolic** *adj*.—**catabolically** *adv*.

catabolize *vti* to subject to or undergo catabolism.

catachresis *n* (*pl* **catachreses**) misapplication of words; formation of words on a false analogy.—**catachrestic** *adj*.—**catachrestically** *adv*.

cataclysm *n* a violent disturbance or disaster.—**cataclysmic** *adj*.

catacomb *n* (*usu pl*) an underground burial place.

catadromous *adj* going down to the sea to spawn.

catafalque *n* a temporary structure erected, usu in a church, to support the coffin on the occasion of a lying in state.

Catalan *adj* of or pertaining to Catalonia, a province of Spain, or to its inhabitants or language. * *n* an inhabitant of Catalonia; the language of Catalonia.

catalectic *adj* (*poetry*) lacking a syllable in the last foot.

catalepsy *n* (*pl* **catalepsies**) a state of temporary rigidity and unconsciousness.—**cataleptic** *adj*.

catalogue, catalog *n* a list of books, names, etc in systematic order. * *vti* to list, to make a catalogue of.—**cataloger, cataloguer** *n*.

catalogue raisonné *n* a catalogue of books, paintings, etc, classed according to their subjects.

catalpa *n* an American tree with trumpet-shaped flowers.

catalysis *n* (*pl* **catalyses**) the acceleration or retardation of a chemical reaction by the action of a catalyst. — **catalytic** *adj*.

catalyst *n* a substance which accelerates or retards a chemical reaction without itself undergoing any permanent chemical change; a person or thing which produces change.

catalytic converter *n* a filter device in vehicles to reduce pollution from exhaust produced by combustion, eg carbon monoxide, nitrogen oxide, etc.

catalyze *vt* to accelerate or retard (a chemical reaction) by catalysis.—**catalyzer** *n*.

catamaran *n* a (sailing) boat with twin hulls; a raft of logs.

catamenia *n* menstruation.—**catamenial** *adj*.

catamite *n* a boy kept by a sodomite.

catamount, catamountain *n* the wild cat; the puma, cougar, or mountain lion.

cataplasm *n* a poultice.

cataplexy *n* (*pl* **cataplexies**) a sudden shock to the nerves causing paralysis.

catapult *n* a slingshot; a device for launching aircraft from the deck of an aircraft carrier. * *vt* to shoot forwards as from a catapult.

cataract *n* a waterfall, esp a large sheet one; a disease of the eye causing dimming of the lens and loss of vision.

catarrh *n* inflammation of a mucous membrane, esp in the nose and throat, causing a flow of mucus.—**catarrhal** *adj*.

catarrhine *adj* of or pertaining to a group of monkeys and apes of the Old World, which have the nostrils close together and pointing downwards.

catastrophe *n* a great disaster.—**catastrophic** *adj*.—**catastrophically** *adv*.

catastrophize *vt* to envisage a situation as being worse than it is.—*also* **awfulize**.

catatonia *n* a form of schizophrenia in which a trance-like state is punctuated by periods of hyperactivity.—**catatonic** *adj*.

Catawba *n* (*pl* **Catawba, Catawbas**) a member of a North American Indian people formerly of North and South Carolina; a light red variety of American grape; a light wine made from this grape.

catbird *n* a kind of American thrush.

catboat *n* a small boat with one sail on a single mast near the bows.

cat burglar *n* a burglar who enters by climbing.

catcall *n* a shrill whistle or cry used to express disapproval. * *vt* to express disapproval by a catcall.

catch *vb* (**catching, caught**) *vt* to take hold of, to grasp; to capture; to ensnare or trap; to be on time for; to detect; to apprehend; to become infected with (a disease); to attract (the eye); (*inf*) to see, hear, etc; to grasp (a meaning); (*with* **out**) (*inf*) to detect (a person) in a mistake; (*cricket*) to catch a ball hit by a batsman before it touches the ground, making him "out". * *vi* to become entangled; to begin to burn; (*with* **on**) (*inf*) to become popular; to understand; (*with* **up**) to reach or come level with (eg a person ahead); to make up for lost time, deal with a backlog. * *n* the act of catching; the amount or number caught; a device for fastening; someone worth catching; a hidden difficulty.

catch-all *adj, n* (something) intended to cover all eventualities.

catcher *n* (*baseball*) the player who stands behind the batter to catch the ball.

catching *adj* infectious; attractive.

catchment *n* the collecting or the drainage of water.

catchment area *n* the area from which a body of water is fed, eg a river or reservoir; a geographic area served by a particular institution.

catchpenny *n* (*pl* **catchpennies**) an article of little value got up attractively to effect a quick sale.

catch phrase *n* a well-known phrase or slogan, esp one associated with a particular group or person.

catchpole *n* a sheriff's officer; a constable in medieval England.

catch-22 *n* a predicament from which a victim is powerless to escape due to conditions beyond his or her control.

catchup *see* **ketchup**.

catchweight *n* a weight left to the choice of an owner of a horse. * *adv* without being handicapped.

catchword *n* a guide word; a word or expression, briefly popular, representative of a person or point of view; a cue in the theatre.

catchy *adj* (**catchier, catchiest**) easily remembered, as a tune.—**catchiness** *n*.

catechetical, catechetic *adj* instructing orally; proceeding by question and answer; of catechism.—**catechetically** *adv*.

catechin *n* a tannic acid extracted from catechu.

catechism *n* a simple summary of the principles of religion in question and answer form, used for instruction; continuous questioning.—**catechismal** *adj*.

catechize *vt* to instruct by question and answer.—**catechization** *n*.—**catechist, catechizer** *n*.

catechu *n* a brown astringent substance obtained from tropical plants and used in the arts and as a medicine.—*also* **cachou, cutch**.

catechumen *n* one who is under religious instruction prior to receiving baptism; a beginner in the first principles of knowledge.

categorical *adj* unconditional, absolute; positive, explicit.—**categorically** *adv*.

categorical imperative *n* (*philos*) the absolute and unconditional command of moral law.

categorize *vt* to place in a category.—**categorization** *n*.

category *n* (*pl* **categories**) a class or division of things.

catena *n* (*pl* **catenae, catenas**) a series of notions; things connected with each other like the links of a chain; a systematic arrangement of selections from authors to illustrate a doctrine.

catenary *n* (*pl* **catenaries**) a curve formed by a hanging chain. * *adj* of or resembling a chain (—*also* **catenarian**).

catenate *vt* (*biol*) to link together.—**catenation** *n*.

catenulate *adj* (*bot*) consisting of little links.

cater *vi* (*with* **for** *or* **to**) to provide with what is needed or desired, esp food and service, as for parties.—**caterer** *n*.

cateran *n* a kern; a Highland or Irish irregular soldier; a Highland freebooter.

caterpillar *n* the worm-like larvae of a butterfly or moth; the ribbed band in place of wheels on a heavy vehicle; a vehicle (eg tank, tractor) equipped with such tracks.

caterwaul *vi* to make a howling noise like a cat. * *n* such a cry.

catfish *n* (*pl* **catfish, catfishes**) a large, usu freshwater, fish with whisker-like feelers around the mouth.

catgut *n* a strong cord made from animal intestines, used for the strings of musical instruments, sports rackets, and surgical ligatures.

catharsis *n* (*pl* **catharses**) emotional relief given by art, esp tragedy; (*med*) purgation; (*psychoanal*) relief obtained by the uncovering of buried repressions, etc.

cathartic *adj* bringing about catharsis; purgative. * *n* a purgative medicine.—**cathartically** *adv*.

cathead *n* a beam projecting from a ship's bows to which the anchor is secured.

cathedra *n* (*pl* **cathedrae**) a bishop's throne in the cathedral of his diocese; an official or professional chair.

cathedral *n* the chief church of a diocese. * *adj* having or belonging to a cathedral.

Catherine wheel *n* a rotating firework.—*also* **pinwheel**.

catheter *n* a flexible tube inserted into the bladder for drawing off urine.

catheterize *vt* to insert a catheter into.—**catheterization** *n*.

cathode *n* (*elect*) the negative terminal; the electrode by which current leaves.—**cathodal** *adj.*—**cathodic, cathodical** *adj.*

cathode rays *n* (one of the electrons in) a stream of electrons emitted by a cathode in a vacuum tube.

cathode-ray tube *n* a vacuum tube in which electron beams are directed onto a fluorescent screen to produce luminous images, as used in television sets.

Catholic *n* a member of the Roman Catholic Church. * *adj* relating to the Roman Catholic Church; embracing the whole body of Christians.—**Catholicism** *n.*

catholic *adj* universal, all-embracing; broad-minded, liberal; general, not exclusive.

Catholic Epistles *npl* the Epistles of the Apostles addressed to believers generally, ie James 1 and 2, Peter 1, 2 and 3, John, and Jude.

Catholicism *n* the belief of, or adherence to, the Catholic Church or faith, esp to that of the Roman Catholic Church.

catholicity *n* the quality of being catholic; universality, comprehensiveness; accordance with Catholic, esp Roman Catholic, church doctrine.

catholicize *vt* to convert to the Roman Catholic Church.—**catholicization** *n.*

catholicon *n* a universal remedy, a panacea.

cathouse *n* a brothel.

cation *n* a positively charged ion.—**cationic** *adj.*

catkin *n* a hanging spike of small flowers, eg on birch, willow and hazel trees.

cat-like *adj* like a cat; stealthy, noiseless.

catmint, catnip *n* a strongly-scented plant attractive to cats.

catnap *n* a short, light or intermittent sleep, a snooze, a doze.—*also vi* (**catnapping, catnapped**).

cat-o'-nine-tails *n* (*pl* **cat-o'-nine-tails**) a whip with nine lashes of knotted cord, formerly used as a punishment in the army and navy.

catoptric, catoptrical *adj* of or pertaining to mirrors or reflected light.

Cat scan, Cat scanner *see* **CAT.**

cat's cradle *n* a game of making designs with string looped over the fingers.

cat's-eye *n* a hard semi-transparent variety of quartz.

cat's-paw *n* a person used as a tool by another, a dupe; (*naut*) a light breeze that slightly ripples the surface of the water.

catsup *see* **ketchup.**

cattery *n* (*pl* **catteries**) a place for boarding or breeding cats.

cattle *npl* domesticated bovine mammals such as bulls and cows.

cattle-grid *n* a metal grid over a ditch allowing the passage of people and vehicles, but not cattle, sheep, etc.

cattleman *n* (*pl* **cattlemen**) one who tends or drives cattle; a breeder of cattle.

cattle prod *n* an electrified prod for driving cattle.

catty[1] *adj* (**cattier, cattiest**) (*inf*) spiteful, mean.—**cattily** *adv.*—**cattiness** *n.*

catty[2] *n* (*pl* **catties**) an East Indian weight equal to one and a third pounds; a name applied to a Chinese kin or pound; a Siamese coin.

catwalk *n* a narrow, raised pathway on a stage, bridge, etc; fashion modelling (*with* **the**).

Caucasian *adj* of the light-skinned racial group of humankind; of or relating to the Caucasus Mountains. * *n* a Caucasian person.—**Caucasoid** *adj.*

Caucasus *n* a mountain range in the southwest USSR (*with* **the**).—*also* **Caucasus Mountains.**

caucus *n* (*pl* **caucuses**) a private meeting of leaders of a political party or faction, usu to plan strategy.

caudal *adj* of or pertaining to a tail.—**caudally** *adv.*

caudate, caudated *adj* having a tail; having a tail-like appendage.

caudex *n* (*pl* **caudices, caudexes**) the main trunk or axis of a plant.

caudle *n* a warm drink made of wine or ale, spiced or sugared, and mixed with bread, eggs, etc.

caught *see* **catch.**

caul *n* the membrane covering a foetus; part of this covering the head of some infants at birth.

cauldron *n* a large kettle or boiling pot; a state of violent agitation.—*also* **caldron.**

caulescent *adj* having a true stem or stalk.

caulicle *n* a small or rudimentary stem.

cauliflower *n* a kind of cabbage with an edible white flower-head used as a vegetable.

cauliflower ear *n* a thickening condition of the ear, common to boxers, caused by repeated blows.

cauline *adj* of, on or belonging to a stem.

caulk *vt* to make (a boat) watertight by stopping up the seams with pitch.—*also* **calk.**—**caulker, calker** *n.*

causal *adj* forming or being a cause; involving, expressing or implying a cause.—**causally** *adv.*

causality *n* (*pl* **causalities**) the relationship between cause and effect.

causation *n* causality; the act of causing something to happen.—**causational** *adj.*

causative *adj* that causes; effective as a cause; expressing causation.

cause *n* that which produces an effect; reason, motive, purpose, justification; a principle for which people strive; a lawsuit. * *vt* to bring about, to effect; to make (to do something).—**causer** *n.*

cause célèbre *n* (*pl* **causes célèbres**) a famous lawsuit, trial or celebrated issue.

causeless *adj* without cause; groundless.

causerie *n* a discursive conversational article; an informal chat.

causeway *n* a raised road across wet ground or water.

caustic *adj* burning tissue, etc by chemical action; corrosive; sarcastic, cutting. * *n* a caustic substance.—**caustically** *adv.*—**causticness, causticity** *n.*

caustic potash *n* potassium hydroxide, a white substance acting as a powerful bleach, much used in medicine and manufacturing.

caustic soda *n* sodium hydroxide, a white solid substance, largely used in soapmaking.

cauterize *vt* to burn with a caustic substance or a hot iron so as to destroy dead tissue, stop bleeding, etc; to deaden.—**cauterization** *n.*

cautery *n* (*pl* **cauteries**) a burning or searing; an instrument or drug used for such a purpose.

caution *n* care for safety, prudence; a warning, esp a formal one, to a suspect or accused person. * *vt* to warn (against); to admonish.

cautionary *adj* of a warning nature.

cautious *adj* careful, circumspect.—**cautiously** *adv.*—**cautiousness** *n.*

cavalcade *n* a procession of riders on horseback; a dramatic sequence or procession.

cavalier *adj* free and easy, careless; offhand, brusque. * *n* a horseman; a lady's escort; (*with cap*) a royalist in the English Civil War.—**cavalierly** *adv.*

cavalry *n* (*pl* **cavalries**) combat troops originally mounted on horseback.

cavatina *n* (*pl* **cavatine**) a short simple melody.

cave *n* a hollow place inside the earth open to the surface. * *vti* (*with* **in**) to collapse or make collapse; (*inf*) to yield, submit.—**cave-in** *n*.

caveat *n* (*law*) a process to suspend proceedings; a warning.

caveat emptor (*Latin*) let the buyer beware.

cavefish *n* (*pl* **cavefish, cavefishes**) a fish belonging to the family Amblyopsidae, species of which inhabit cave streams of the US.

caveman *n* (*pl* **cavemen**) a prehistoric cave dweller; (*inf*) a person who acts in a primitive or crude manner.

cavern *n* a large cave.—**cavernous** *adj*.

cavetto *n* (*pl* **cavetti**) (*archit*) a round concave moulding.

caviar, caviare *n* salted roe of the sturgeon or other large fish.

cavil *vi* (**cavilling, cavilled** *or* **caviling, caviled**) to make trifling objections, to find fault. * *n* a trifling objection.—**caviller** *n*.

caving *n* the sport of exploring caves.—**caver** *n*.

cavity *n* (*pl* **cavities**) a hole; a hollow place, esp in a tooth.

cavort *vi* to frolic, prance.

cavy *n* (*pl* **cavies**) one of several kinds of small rodent including the guinea pig.

caw *n* the cry of the crow, rook, or raven. * *vi* to utter this cry.

cay *n* a small low island.

cayenne, cayenne pepper *n* a hot red pepper made from capsicum.

cayman *see* **caiman**.

Cayuse *n* (*pl* **Cayuse, Cayuses**) a member of an American Indian tribe of Oregon and Washington; their language.

CB *abbr* = citizens' band.

CBC *abbr* = Canadian Broadcasting Corporation.

CD *abbr* = compact disc; corps diplomatique.

Cd (*chem symbol*) = cadmium.

cd *abbr* = candela.

CD-ROM *abbr* = compact disc read only memory: a CD used for distributing text and images in electronic publishing, for computer software, and for permanent storage of computer data.

Ce (*chem symbol*) = cerium.

cease *vti* to stop, to come to an end; to discontinue.

ceasefire *n* a period of truce in a war, uprising, etc.

ceaseless *adj* without ceasing; incessant.—**ceaselessly** *adv*.

cecum *see* **caecum**.

cedar *n* a large coniferous evergreen tree; its wood.—**cedarwood** *n*.

cede *vt* to yield to another, give up, esp by treaty; to assign or transfer the title of.—**ceder** *n*.

cedilla *n* a character written under a c in certain languages (ç) to indicate that it is pronounced as an (s) not (k).

ceil *vt* to overlay or cover the inner surface of a roof; to furnish with a ceiling.

ceiling *n* the inner roof of a room; the lining of this; any upper limit; the highest altitude a particular aircraft can fly.

celadon *n* a soft pale sea-green colour; porcelain or fine earthenware of such a colour. * *adj* having the colour of celadon.

celandine *n* one of several kinds of wild plant with star-shaped yellow flowers.

celebrant *n* one who celebrates, esp the principal offici-ating priest in offering mass or celebrating the Eucharist.

celebrate *vt* to make famous; to praise, extol; to perform with proper rites; to mark with ceremony; to keep (festival).—**celebrant** *n*.

celebrated *adj* famous.

celebration *n* the act of celebrating; an observance or ceremony to celebrate anything.

celebrity *n* (*pl* **celebrities**) fame; a famous or well-known person.

celeriac *n* a variety of celery with a turnip-like root.

celerity *n* quickness, dispatch.

celery *n* (*pl* **celeries**) a vegetable with long juicy edible stalks.

celesta, celeste *n* a kind of glockenspiel with a keyboard.

celestial *adj* in or of the sky; heavenly; divine.—**celestially** *adv*.

celestite *n* native strontium sulphate.

celiac *see* **coeliac**.

celibacy *n* (*pl* **celibacies**) the unmarried state; complete sexual abstinence.

celibate *n* a person who remains unmarried, esp one who has taken religious vows; a person who abstains from sexual intercourse.—*also adj*.

cell *n* a small room for one in a prison or monastery; a small cavity as in a honeycomb; a device that converts chemical energy into electricity; a microscopic unit of living matter; a small group of people bound by common aims within an organization or political party.—**cellular** *adj*.

cellar *n* a basement; a stock of wines.

cellarage *n* cellars collectively; the space occupied by cellars; a charge for storage in cellars.

cellarer *n* an official in a monastery who superintends the cellar and distribution of provisions; an official of the chapter who has charge of the temporals.

cellarete, cellaret *n* a case for holding bottles of wine or liquor.

cellnet *n* a portable radio telephone used in cellular radio.

cello *n* (*pl* **cellos**) the violoncello, a large four-stringed bass instrument of the violin family, held between the knees.—**cellist** *n*.

cellophane *n* a thin transparent paper made from cellulose, used for wrapping.

Cellphone *n* (*trademark*) a cellular telephone, a portable mobile telephone operated by cellular radio.

cellular *adj* of, resembling or containing cells; (*textiles*) of an open texture.

cellular radio *n* a computer-controlled radio communications system for Cellphones, etc, using a network of transmitters serving small zones called cells, as users move between cells the transmitters/receivers are transferred automatically.

cellule *n* a small cell or cavity.

cellulite *n* a form of fat on the hips, thighs and buttocks that causes puckering of the skin surface.

celluloid *n* a type of plastic made from cellulose nitrate and camphor; a plastic coating on film; cinema film.

cellulose *n* a starch-like carbohydrate forming the cell walls of plants, used in making paper, textiles, film, etc.

cellulose acetate *n* a compound used in the manufacture of artificial textiles, film, and varnishes.

Celsius *adj* pertaining to a thermometer scale with a freezing point of 0 degrees and a boiling point of 100 degrees.

Celt n a member of an ancient people who inhabited pre-Roman Britain, Gaul and Spain.

celt n a prehistoric edged instrument or weapon of stone or bronze, resembling a chisel or blade of an axe, found in ancient tumuli.

Celtic adj of or relating to the Celts; the language of the Celts, including Scots or Irish Gaelic, Manx, Welsh, Cornish and Breton.

Celticist, Celtist n a student of Celtic antiquities, languages, etc.

cement n a powdered substance of lime and clay, mixed with water, etc to make mortar or concrete, which hardens upon drying; any hard-drying substance. * vt to bind or glue together with or as if with cement; to cover with cement.—**cementer** n.

cementation n the act of cementing; a process for converting iron into steel, glass into porcelain, etc.

cemetery n (pl **cemeteries**) a place for the burial of the dead.

cenobite see **coenobite**.

cenotaph n a monument to a person who is buried elsewhere.—**cenotaphic** adj.

Cenozoic adj of the third geological period, Tertiary.

cense vt to perfume with incense.

censer n a covered cup-shaped vessel pierced with holes in which incense is burned.

censor n an official with the power to examine literature, films, mail, etc and remove or prohibit anything considered obscene, objectionable, etc. * vt to act as a censor.—**censorable** adj.—**censorial** adj.—**censorship** n.

censorious adj expressing censure; fault-finding.—**censoriously** adv.—**censoriousness** n.

censure n an expression of disapproval or blame. * vt to condemn as wrong; to reprimand.—**censurable** adj.

census n (pl **censuses**) an official count of the population, including details of age, sex, occupation, etc; any official count.

cent n a hundredth of a dollar; (inf) a negligible amount of money.

centaur n a fabulous monster, half man, half horse; an expert horseman; (astron) a southern constellation.

centaury n (pl **centauries**) a medicinal herb.

centavo n (pl **centavos**) the hundredth part of a dollar or peso in use in the South American republics.

centenarian n one who is one hundred years old or more.—also adj.

centenary n (pl **centenaries**) a hundredth anniversary or its celebration. * adj of a hundred years.

centennial adj happening every hundred years. * n a centenary.

center see **centre**.

centerboard see **centreboard**.

centerfold see **centrefold**.

centerpiece see **centrepiece**.

centesimal adj counting or counted by hundredths. * n a hundredth part.

centi- prefix one hundredth.

centiare, centare n a square metre, equal to the hundredth part of an are.

centigrade adj Celsius.

centigram, centigramme n one hundredth of a gram.

centilitre, centiliter n one hundredth of a litre.

centime n a small french coin, the hundredth part of a franc.

centimeter, centimetre n one hundredth of a metre.

centimetre-gram-second n a unit system in which the centimetre, the gram and the mean solar second are taken respectively as the units of length, mass, and time (usu abbreviated **cgs units**).

centipede n a crawling creature with a long body divided into numerous segments each with a pair of legs.

centner n a weight divisible first into a hundred parts and then into smaller parts; in many European countries the commercial name for a hundredweight.

cento n (pl **centos**) a literary or musical composition formed by selections from various authors or composers and arranged in a new order.

central adj in, at, from or forming the centre; main, principal; important.—**centrally** adv.—**centrality** n.

central bank n a national bank that handles government transactions as opposed to private business.

central heating n a system of heating by pipes from a central boiler or other heat source.

centralism n the policy or process of bringing under central control.—**centralist** adj, n.

centralize vt to draw to the centre; to place under the control of a central authority, esp government.—**centralization** n.

central nervous system n in vertebrates, the brain and spinal cord which coordinates an animal's activity.

central processing unit n (comput) the part of a computer that performs logical and arithmetical operations on data in accordance with program instructions.

centre n the approximate middle point or part of anything, a pivot; interior; point of concentration; a place where a particular activity goes on (shopping centre); source; political moderation; (sport) a player at the centre of the field, etc, a centre-forward. * adj of or at the centre. * vt (**centring, centred**) to place in the centre; to concentrate; to be fixed; (football, hockey) to kick or hit the ball into the centre of the pitch.—also **center**.

centre bit n a carpenter's tool turning upon a centre, for boring holes.

centreboard n a keel so constructed that it may be raised within the hull of a vessel or lowered, extensively used by racing craft; a yacht with this.—also **centerboard**.

centrefold n a colour illustration spread across the two facing pages in the middle of a newspaper or magazine.—also **centerfold**.

centre of gravity n that point of a body through which the resultant of all the forces acting upon it in consequence of the earth's attraction will pass.

centrepiece n a central ornament or decoration.—also **centerpiece**.

centric, centrical adj placed in the centre; central.—**centricity** n.

centrifugal adj moving away from the centre of rotation.—**centrifugally** adv.

centrifugal force n an imaginary force which acts outwards on a rotating body or one moving along a curved path.

centrifuge n a device used to separate milk, blood, etc, by rotating at very high speed.—**centrifugation** n.

centripetal adj tending to move towards the centre.—**centripetally** adv.

centrist n a person of moderate political opinions, etc.—**centrism** n.

centrobaric adj relating to the centre of gravity or to the method of its determination.

centroid n the centre of mass or gravity of a body.

centurion *n* an officer commanding a hundred Roman soldiers.

century *n* (*pl* **centuries**) a period of a hundred years; a set of a hundred; (*cricket*) 100 runs made by a batsman in a single innings; a company of a Roman legion.

century plant *n* a name of the American aloe, from the supposition that it flowered once only in a hundred years.

cep *n* an edible woodland fungus with a shiny brown cap and a white underside.

cephalagia *n* a headache.

cephalic *adj* of the head.

cephalic index *n* the relation of the length of the head to its breadth.

cephalization *n* the tendency in animal development to localize important parts or organs in or near the head.

cephalopod *n* a marine mollusc, such as an octopus, characterized by a well-developed head and eyes and a ring of sucker-bearing tentacles.—**cephalopodan** *n*, *adj*.

cephalothorax *n* (*pl* **cephalothoraxes, cephalothoraces**) the anterior part of the body in the higher crustaceans, spiders, etc.

ceraceous *adj* resembling wax.

ceramic *adj* of earthenware, porcelain, or brick. * *n* something made of ceramic; (*pl*) the art of pottery.

ceramics *n* (*sing*) work executed wholly or partly in clay and baked; the art of pottery.—**ceramist, ceramicist** *n*.

cerastes *n* (*pl* **cerastes**) the horned viper.

cerate *n* a thick ointment of wax, etc.

ceratodus *n* (*pl* **ceratoduses**) a genus of Australian fishes containing the barramunda, or native salmon.

cere[1] *n* a wax-like membrane at the base of the bill of many birds, as the parrot.

cere[2] *vt* to cover or close with cerecloth.

cereal *n* a grass grown for its edible grain, eg wheat, rice; the grain of such grasses; a breakfast food made from such grains. * *adj* of corn or edible grain.

cerebellum *n* (*pl* **cerebellums, cerebella**) a part of the brain below and behind the cerebrum which coordinates voluntary movements.—**cerebellar** *adj*.

cerebral *adj* of or relating to the cerebrum; intellectual.—**cerebrally** *adv*.

cerebral hemisphere *n* one of the two lateral halves of the cerebrum.

cerebral palsy *n* a disability caused by brain damage before, during or immediately after birth resulting in poor muscle coordination.

cerebrate *vi* to use the brain; to think.

cerebration *n* the conscious or unconscious action of the brain; thought or thinking.

cerebrospinal *adj* of the brain and spinal cord.

cerebrum *n* (*pl* **cerebrums, cerebra**) the front part of the brain of vertebrates; the dominant part of the brain in man, associated with intellectual function; the brain as a whole.

cerecloth *n* a cloth saturated with wax or some gummy substance, used for wrapping embalmed bodies in.

cerement *n* a grave cloth or shroud; (*pl*) grave clothes.

ceremonial *adj* of or with ceremony; formal. * *n* a set of rules for ceremonies.—**ceremonially** *adv*.

ceremonialism *n* adherence to, or fondness for, ceremonial observance; ritualism.—**ceremonialist** *n*.

ceremonious *adj* observant of ceremony; marked by formality; overpolite.—**ceremoniously** *adv*.

ceremony *n* (*pl* **ceremonies**) a sacred rite; formal observance or procedure; behaviour that follows rigid etiquette.

cerise *n* a light and clear red.—*also adj*.

cerium *n* a grey metallic element used in various metallurgical and nuclear applications.

cero- *prefix* wax.

cert *abbr* = certified; certificate; (*sl*) certainty.

certain *adj* sure, positive; unerring, reliable; sure to happen, inevitable; definite, fixed; some; one; unnamed, unspecified.

certainly *adv* without doubt; yes.

certainty *n* (*pl* **certainties**) something undoubted, inevitable; the condition of being certain.

certificate *n* a document formally attesting a fact; a testimonial of qualifications or character.—**certificated** *adj*.

certified public accountant *n* an accountant who has qualified by passing official examinations; a chartered accountant.

certify *vt* (**certifying, certified**) to declare in writing or attest formally; to endorse with authority.—**certification** *n*.

certiorari *n* a writ issuing from a superior court calling for the records of an inferior court, or to remove a case from a court below.

certitude *n* freedom from doubt.

cerulean *adj* deep blue.

cerumen *n* wax of the ear.—**ceruminous** *adj*.

ceruse *n* white lead used as a pigment and from which a cosmetic is prepared.

cervical *adj* of the neck of the womb.

cervical smear *n* (*med*) a sample of cells taken from the cervix for detection of cancer; the taking of the sample.

cervine *adj* of or pertaining to the deer family; of a tawny or fawn colour.

cervix *n* (*pl* **cervixes, cervices**) the neck of the womb.

cesium *see* **caesium**.

cespitose *adj* (*bot*) growing in tufts.

cess[1] *vt* to impose a tax; to assess. * *n* a rate or tax, esp the land tax.

cess[2] *n* (*Irish*) luck or fortune.

cessation *n* a stoppage; a pause.

cession *n* a giving up, a surrender; something ceded.

cessionary *n* (*pl* **cessionaries**) (*law*) a giving or yielding up.

cesspool, cesspit *n* a covered cistern for collecting liquid waste or sewage; (*fig*) a place of sin and depravity.

cestoid *adj* of or pertaining to the Cestoda, an order of parasitic flat worms to which the tapeworms belong. * n a flat intestinal worm.

cetacean *n* a member of an order of aquatic, usu marine, mammals that includes whales, dolphins and porpoises. * *adj* belonging to this order (—*also* **cetaceous**).

ceteris paribus (*Latin*) other things being equal.

Cf (*chem symbol*) californium.

cf. *abbr* = compare (Latin *confer*).

CFC *abbr* = chlorofluorocarbon.

cgs *abbr* = centimetre-gram-second.

ch. *abbr* = chapter; church; (*chess*) check.

cha-cha(-cha) *n* a ballroom dance orig from Latin America; the music for this.

chablis *n* (*often with cap*) a dry white wine from Chablis, France.

chacma *n* a South African baboon.

chaconne *n* an old Spanish dance; the music for such a dance.

chad *n* (*comput*) the little scraps of paper or cardboard left by the punching of holes in computer cards or paper tape.

chafe *vti* to restore warmth by rubbing; to make or become sore by rubbing; to irritate; to feel irritation, to fret.

chafer *n* any of various large beetles.

chaff[1] *n* husks of grain separated from the seed by threshing or winnowing; cut hay or straw; worthless stuff.

chaff[2] *vt* to banter; to make a game of. * *vi* to use bantering language. * *n* good-natured teasing, banter.

chaffer *vi* to bargain, haggle. * *n* the act of bargaining.

chaffinch *n* a European songbird.

chaffy *adj* resembling, or full of, chaff; anything light or worthless.

chafing dish *n* a vessel for heating or cooking food on a table; a small portable grate for coals.

chagrin *n* annoyance; vexation; disappointment.

chain *n* a series of connected links or rings; a continuous series; a series of related events; a bond; a group of shops, hotels, etc owned by the same company; a unit of length equal to 66 feet; a range of mountains; a group of islands; (*pl*) anything that restricts or binds; fetters. * *vt* to fasten with a chain or chains.

chain gang *n* a group of prisoners chained together.

chain mail *n* flexible armour formed of metal links interwoven.

chain reaction *n* a process in which a chemical, atomic or other reaction stimulates further reactions, eg combustion or nuclear fission; a series of events, each of which stimulates the next.

chain saw *n* a power-driven saw with teeth linked as in a chain.

chain-smoke *vti* to smoke (cigarettes) one after the other.—**chain-smoker** *n*.

chain stitch *n* an embroidery stitch that resembles the links of a chain.

chain store *n* one of a series of retail stores owned by one company.

chair *n* a separate seat for one, with a back and legs; a seat of authority; a chairman; a professorship; the electric chair. * *vt* to preside as chairman of.

chair lift *n* a series of seats suspended from a cable for carrying sightseers or skiers uphill.

chairman *n* (*pl* **chairmen**) a person who presides at a meeting; the president of a board or committee.—**chairwoman** *nf* (*pl* **chairwomen**).—*also* **chairperson**.

chaise *n* a light two-wheeled carriage; any carriage.

chaise longue *n* (*pl* **chaise longues, chaises longues**) a couch-like chair with a long seat.

chalcedony *n* (*pl* **chalcedonies**) a form of quartz used as a gemstone.

chalco- *prefix* copper.

chalcopyrite *n* a copper ore.

Chaldean, Chaldaean *adj* pertaining to Chaldea, or ancient Babylon, or its language. * *n* the language of ancient Babylon.

chalet *n* a Swiss hut; any similar building used in a holiday camp, as a ski lodge, etc.

chalice *n* a large cup with a base; a communion cup.

chalk *n* calcium carbonate, a soft white limestone; such a stone or a substitute used for drawing or writing. * *vt* to write, mark or draw with chalk; (*with* **up**) (*inf*)

to score, get, achieve; to charge or credit.

chalky *adj* (**chalkier, chalkiest**) containing or resembling chalk.—**chalkiness** *n*.

challenge *vt* to summon to a fight or contest; to call in question; to object to; to hail and interrogate; to demand proof of identity. * *n* the act of challenging; a summons to a contest; a calling in question; a problem that stimulates effort.—**challenger** *n*.—**challenging** *adj*.

challis *n* a light all-wool fabric.

chalybeate *adj* (*water*) impregnated with iron.

chamber *n* a room, esp a bedroom; a deliberative body or a division of a legislature; a room where such a body meets; a compartment; a cavity in the body of an organism; part of a gun cylinder holding the cartridge; (*pl*) a judge's office.

chamberlain *n* an official in charge of the household of a monarch or nobleman; a steward, treasurer or factor of a municipal corporation.

chambermaid *n* a woman employed to clean bedrooms in a hotel, etc.

chamber music *n* music for performance by a small group, as a string quartet.

chamber of commerce *n* (*often cap*) an organization of representatives from local businesses formed to promote and protect their interests.

chamber pot *n* a vessel for urine.

chameleon *n* a lizard capable of changing colour to match its surroundings; a person of variable moods or behaviour; an adaptable person.—**chameleonic** *adj*.

chamfer *n* a flat surface made in wood or metal by paring off an angle, a bevel. * *vt* to groove, channel or flute.—**chamferer** *n*.

chamois *n* (*pl* **chamois**) a small antelope found in Europe and Asia; a piece of chamois leather.

chamois leather, chammy (leather) *n* a soft, pliable leather formerly made from chamois skin, and now obtained from sheep, goats and deer; a piece of this for polishing.—*also* **shammy (leather)**.

chamomile *n* an aromatic plant with daisy-like flowers used medicinally for its soothing property and as a hair lightener, and in making camomile tea.—*also* **camomile**.

champ[1] *vti* to munch noisily, chomp; **champ at the bit** to be impatient.

champ[2] *n* (*inf*) a champion.

champagne *n* a sparkling white wine; a pale straw colour.

champaign *n* flat open country, a level expanse. * *adj* level, open.

champerty *n* (*pl* **champerties**) (*law*) the maintenance of a party in a suit on condition that, if successful, the property is shared; the offence of aiding another's lawsuit in order to share in gains from it.—**champertous** *adj*.

champignon *n* an edible mushroom that grows in circular clusters.

champion *n* a person who fights for another; one who upholds a cause; a competitor successful against all others. * *adj* first-class; (*inf*) excellent. * *vt* to defend; to uphold the cause of.

championship *n* the act of championing; the process of determining a champion; a contest held to find a champion.

champlevé *n* enamel bearing indentations filled with colour.—*also adj*.

chance *n* a course of events; fortune; an accident, an unexpected event; opportunity; possibility; probability; risk. * *vti* to risk; to happen; to come upon unexpectedly. * *adj* accidental, not planned.

chancel *n* the part of a church around the altar, for the clergy and the choir.

chancellery, chancellory *n* (*pl* **chancelleries, chancellories**) a chancellor's department or office; an office attached to an embassy.

chancellor *n* a high government official, as, in certain countries, a prime minister; in some universities, the president or other executive officer.—**chancellorship** *n*.

chance-medley *n* (*law*) justifiable homicide in self-defence; inadvertency.

chancery *n* (*pl* **chanceries**) originally in England, next to Parliament the highest court of justice, since 1873 a division of the High Court of Justice; the office for public records; in US a court of equity.

chancre *n* a syphilitic ulcer.—**chancrous** *adj*.

chancy *adj* (**chancier, chanciest**) (*inf*) risky, uncertain.—**chancily** *adv*.

chandelier *n* an ornamental hanging frame with branches for holding lights.

chandler *n* a dealer or merchant, esp in candles, oil, soap, etc.

chandlery *n* (*pl* **chandleries**) a chandler's shop or stock.

change *vt* to make different, to alter; to transform; to exchange; to put fresh clothes on. * *vi* to become different, to undergo alteration; to put on fresh clothes; to continue one's journey by leaving one station, etc, or mode of transport and going to and using another. * *n* alteration, modification; substitution; variety; a fresh set, esp clothes; money in small units; the balance of money returned when given in a larger denomination as payment.—**changer** *n*.

changeable *adj* able to be changed; altering rapidly between different conditions; inconstant.—**changeability** n.—**changeably** *adv*.

changeful *adj* often changing.

changeless *adj* constant, immutable.—**changelessly** *adv*.—**changelessness** *n*.

changeling *n* a child secretly left in place of another.

change of life *n* the menopause.

changeover *n* a complete change of system, method, state, attitude, etc.

channel[1] *n* the bed or the deeper part of a river, harbour, etc; a body of water joining two larger ones; a navigable passage; a means of passing or conveying or communicating; a band of radio frequencies reserved for a particular purpose, eg television station; a path for an electrical signal; a groove or line along which liquids, etc may flow. * *vt* (**channelling, channelled** *or* **channeling, channeled**) to form a channel in; to groove; to direct.

channel[2] *n* a projection from a ship's side to spread the shrouds and keep them clear of the bulwarks.

chanson *n* (*pl* **chansons**) a song.

chant *vti* to sing; to recite in a singing manner; to sing or shout (a slogan) rhythmically. * *n* sacred music to which prose is sung; sing-song intonation; a monotonous song; a rhythmic slogan, esp as sung or shouted by sports fans, etc.

chanter *n* a person who chants; the tenor or treble pipe of a bagpipe on which the melody is played.

chanterelle *n* an edible yellow mushroom.

chantey, chanty *n* (*pl* **chanteys, chanties**) a shanty.

chanticleer *n* a rooster.

chantry *n* (*pl* **chantries**) a chapel endowed for the saying or singing mass daily for the soul of the founder; such an endowment.

chaology *n* the study of chaos theory.—**chaologist** *n*.

chaos *n* utter confusion, muddle.

chaos theory *n* (*physics*) the theory that the behaviour of dynamic systems is haphazard rather than mathematical.

chaotic *adj* completely without order or arrangement.—**chaotically** *adv*.

chap[1] *vti* (**chapping, chapped**) (*skin*) to make or become split or rough in cold weather. * *n* a chapped place in the skin.

chap[2] *n* (*inf*) a man.

chap[3] *n* (*usu pl*) one of the jaws or its fleshy covering; the mouth of a channel.

chaparejos *npl* a cowboy's leather leg coverings.—*also* **chaps**.

chaparral *n* a dense thicket.

chapatti, chapati *n* (*pl* **chapattis, chapatis**) in Indian cookery, flat unleavened bread.

chapbook *n* a small book of ballads, romances, etc, formerly hawked by a chapman.

chape *n* the metal tip of a scabbard; the part attaching a scabbard to a belt.

chapeau *n* (*pl* **chapeaux, chapeaus**) a hat or head covering.

chapel *n* a building for Christian worship, not as large as a church; an association or trade union of printers in a printing office.

chaperon, chaperone *n* a woman who accompanies a girl at social occasions for propriety. * *vt* to attend as a chaperon.—**chaperonage** *n*.

chapfallen *adj* with the jaw hanging down, dejected, dispirited.—*also* **chopfallen**.

chapiter *n* (*archit*) the upper part or capital of a column.

chaplain *n* a clergyman serving in a religious capacity with the armed forces, or in a prison, hospital, etc.—**chaplaincy** *n*.

chaplet *n* a wreath or garland encircling the head; a rosary; a round moulding carved into beads, olives, etc.—**chapleted** *adj*.

chapman *n* (*pl* **chapmen**) formerly a merchant or trader; a hawker.

chaps *npl* chaparejos.

chapter *n* a main division of a book; the body or meeting of canons of a cathedral or members of a monastic order; a sequence of events; an organized branch of a society or association.

chapterhouse *n* a room for the meetings of a cathedral chapter.

char[1] *n* a charwoman. * *vti* (**charring, charred**) to work as a charwoman.

char[2] *vb* (**charring, charred**) *vt* to burn to charcoal or carbon. * *vti* to scorch.

char[3] *n* (*pl* **char, chars**) a red-bellied fish allied to the salmon.—*also* **charr**.

character *n* the combination of qualities that distinguishes an individual person, group or thing; moral strength; reputation; disposition; a person of marked individuality; an eccentric; (*inf*) a person; a person in a play or novel; a guise, role; a letter or mark in writing, printing, etc.

characterful *adj* full of character, unusual.

characteristic *adj* marking or constituting the particular nature (of a person or thing). * *n* a characteristic or distinguishing feature.—**characteristically** *adv*.

characterize *vt* to describe in terms of particular qualities; to designate; to be characteristic of, mark.—**characterization** *n*.

characterless *adj* ordinary, undistinguished.

charade *n* a travesty; an absurd pretence; (*usu pl*) a game of guessing a word from the acted representation of its syllables and the whole.

charcoal *n* the black carbon matter obtained by partially burning wood and used as fuel, as a filter or for drawing.

chard *n* a type of beet with edible leaves and stalks.

charge *vt* to ask as the price; to record as a debt; to load, to fill, saturate; to lay a task or trust on; to burden; to accuse; to attack at a run; to build up an electric charge (in). * *n* a price charged for goods or service; a build-up of electricity; the amount which a receptacle can hold at one time; the explosive required to fire a weapon; trust, custody; a thing or person entrusted; a task, duty; accusation; an attack.

chargeable *adj* liable to be charged.—**chargeability** *n*.

charge account *n* an account with a store, etc, to which the cost of goods are charged for later payment.

charge card *n* a type of credit card issued by a chain store or other organization.

chargé d'affaires *n* (*pl* **chargés d'affaires**) an ambassador's deputy; a minor diplomat.

charger *n* a cavalry horse; a device for charging a battery.

charily *adv* reluctantly; cautiously.

chariness *n* a being chary.

chariot *n* a two-wheeled vehicle driven by two or more horses in ancient warfare, races, etc.—**charioteer** *n*.

charisma, charism *n* (*pl* **charismata, charisms**) personal quality enabling a person to influence or inspire others; a God-given power or gift.—**charismatic** *adj*.

charitable *adj* of or for charity; generous to the needy, benevolent; lenient in judging others, kindly.—**charitableness** *n*.—**charitably** *adv*.

charity *n* (*pl* **charities**) leniency or tolerance towards others; generosity in giving to the needy; a benevolent fund or institution.

charivari *n* a mock serenade of discordant music; hurly-burly.—*also* **shivaree**.

charlatan *n* a person who pretends to be what he or she is not; one who professes knowledge dishonestly, esp of medicine.—**charlatanism, charlatanry** *n*.

Charleston *n* a lively dance with sidekicks from the knee.

charlock *n* wild mustard.

charlotte *n* a pudding of stewed fruit covered with breadcrumbs.

charlotte russe *n* whipped cream custard enclosed in a sponge cake.

charm *n* an alluring quality, fascination; a magic verse or formula; something thought to possess occult power; an object bringing luck; a trinket on a bracelet. * *vt* to delight, captivate; to influence as by magic.—**charmer** *n*.

charming *adj* delightful, attractive.—**charmingly** *adv*.

charnel house *n* a vault containing corpses or bones.

charpoy *n* a light portable Indian bedstead.

charqui *n* beef cut into strips and sun-dried.

charr *see* **char**[3].

chart *n* a map, esp for use in navigation; an information sheet with tables, graphs, etc; a weather map; a table, graph, etc; (*pl with* **the**) a list of the most popular mu-sic recordings. * *vt* to make a chart of; to plan (a course of action).

charter *n* a document granting rights, privileges, ownership of land, etc; the hire of transportation. * *vt* to grant by charter; to hire.

chartered accountant *n* an accountant who has qualified by passing the official examinations; a certified public accountant.

Chartism *n* a democratic reforming movement in England for the extension of political power to the working class, embodied in the People's Charter of 1838.—**Chartist** *adj, n*.

Chartreuse *n* (*trademark*) a yellowish green liqueur; (*without cap*) its colour.

chartulary *see* **cartulary**.

charwoman *n* (*pl* **charwomen**) a woman employed to clean a house.

chary *adj* (**charier, chariest**) cautious; sparing; (*with* **of**) unwilling to risk.

chase[1] *vt* to pursue; to run after; to drive (away); to hunt; (*inf: usu with* **up**) to pursue in a determined manner. * *n* pursuit; a hunt; a quarry hunted; a steeplechase.

chase[2] *n* a frame for securing a page of type; a groove; that part of a cannon in front of the trunnions.

chase[3] *vt* to work or emboss precious metals; to cut a screw.

chaser *n* a horse used in steeplechasing; a person that chases; (*inf*) a drink taken after another, as in beer after a whisky.

chasm *n* a deep cleft, an abyss, a gaping hole; a wide difference in opinions, etc.—**chasmal, chasmic** *adj*.

chassé *n* a rapid gliding step in dancing. * *vi* to perform a chassé.

chasseur *n* a French light-armed foot or cavalry soldier; a domestic dressed in military or hunting costume.

chassis *n* (*pl* **chassis**) the frame, wheels, engine of a car, aeroplane or other vehicle.

chaste *adj* pure, abstaining from unlawful sexual intercourse; virgin; modest; restrained, unadorned.—**chastely** *adv*.—**chasteness** *n*.

chasten *vt* to correct by suffering, discipline; to restrain.—**chastener** *n*.

chastise *vt* to punish; to beat; to scold.—**chastisement** *n*.

chastity *n* sexual abstinence; virginity; purity.

chasuble *n* a rich sleeveless vestment worn over the alb by a priest celebrating mass.

chat *vti* (**chatting, chatted**) to talk in an easy or familiar way; (*with* **up**) (*inf*) to talk in a flirtatious way with another person. * *n* informal conversation.

chateau, château *n* (*pl* **chateaus, châteaux**) a castle or large country estate in France.

chatelaine *n* the lady of a country house; a bunch of chains to which are attached keys, etc, worn at the waist by ladies.

chatoyant *adj* changing in colour or lustre.—**chatoyancy** *n*.

chat show *n* a television or radio programme with informal interviews and conversation.

chattel *n* (*usu pl*) goods, possessions; (*law*) personal property except freehold.

chatter *vi* to talk aimlessly and rapidly; (*animal, etc*) to utter rapid cries; (*teeth*) to rattle together due to cold or fear. * *n* idle rapid talk; the sound of chattering.—**chatterer** *n*.

chatterbox *n* an incessant talker.

chatty *adj* (**chattier, chattiest**) talkative, full of gossip.—**chattily** *adv.*—**chattiness** *n*.

chauffeur *n* a person who drives a car for someone else. * *vt* to drive as a chauffeur.—**chauffeuse** *nf*.

chauvinism *n* aggressive patriotism; excessive devotion to a belief, cause, etc, esp a man's belief in the superiority of men over women.—**chauvinist** *n*.—**chauvinistic** *adj*.

chaw *vt* (*dial*) to chew, to munch, esp tobacco. * *n* a plug of tobacco.

cheap *adj* low-priced, inexpensive; good value; of little worth, inferior; vulgar.—**cheaply** *adv.*—**cheapness** *n*.

cheapen *vti* to make or become cheap; to lower the value, worth or reputation of.

cheap-jack *n* (*inf*) a person who sells cheap or worthless goods. * *adj* worthless, inferior.

cheapskate *n* (*inf*) a mean or dishonourable person.

cheat *vti* to defraud, to swindle; to deceive; to play unfairly. * *n* a fraud, deception; a person who cheats.—**cheater** *n*.

check *vti* to bring or come to a stand; to restrain or impede; to admonish, reprove; to test the accuracy of, verify; (*with* in) to sign or register arrival at a hotel, work, an airport, etc; (*with* out) to settle the bill and leave a hotel; to investigate. * *n* repulse; stoppage; a pattern of squares; a control to test accuracy; a tick against listed items; a bill in a restaurant; a cheque; (*chess*) a threatening of the king; a money order to a bank (—*also* **check**).

checkbook *see* **chequebook**.

check digit *n* (*comput*) a digit added to data digits to test accuracy and check for corruption.

checker[1] *see* **chequer**.

checker[2] *n* a cashier in a supermarket.

checkerboard *n* a draughtboard.

checkered *see* **chequered**.

check list *n* a list of items, used for reference or verification.

checkmate *n* (*chess*) the winning position when the king is threatened and unable to move; utter defeat. * *vt* (*chess*) to place in checkmate; to defeat, foil.

checking account *n* a bank account, usu with no interest, from which money is withdrawn by cheques or cash cards; a current account.

checkout *n* a place where traffic may be halted for inspection; the place in a store where goods are paid for.

checkpoint *n* a place where visitors' passports or other official documents may be examined.

checkrein *see* **bearing rein**.

checkroom *n* a temporary repository for luggage, coats, etc.

checkup *n* a thorough examination; a medical examination, usu repeated at intervals.

Cheddar *n* a type of hard, white or yellow cheese originally made in Cheddar, England.

cheek *n* the side of the face below the eye; (*sl*) buttock; impudence.

cheeky *adj* (**cheekier, cheekiest**) disrespectful, impudent.—**cheekily** *adv.*—**cheekiness** *n*.

cheep *n* the frail squeak of a young bird. * *vi* to make such a sound.

cheer *n* a shout of applause or welcome; a frame of mind, spirits; happiness. * *vt* to gladden; to encourage; to applaud.

cheerful *adj* in good spirits; happy.—**cheerfully** *adv.*—**cheerfulness** *n*.

cheerleader *n* a person who leads organized cheering, esp at a sports event.

cheerless *adj* dismal, depressing.

cheers *interj* (*inf*) an expression used in offering a toast, as a form of farewell or thanks.

cheery *adj* (**cheerier, cheeriest**) lively, genial, merry.—**cheerily** *adv.*—**cheeriness** *n*.

cheese *n* the curds of milk pressed into a firm or hard mass; a boss or important person (*big cheese*).

cheeseburger *n* a hamburger with melted cheese on top.

cheesecake *n* a cake made with cottage or cream cheese; (*sl*) attractive women or men displayed as sex objects in photographs, etc.

cheesecloth *n* a thin cotton fabric.

cheeseparing *adj* niggardly, mean.

cheesy *adj* (**cheesier, cheesiest**) like cheese.—**cheesiness** *n*.

cheetah *n* a large spotted cat, similar to a leopard.

chef *n* a professional cook.

chef-d'oeuvre *n* (*pl* **chefs-d'oeuvre**) a masterpiece.

cheiro-, chiro- *prefix* hand.

chela *n* (**chelae**) a claw-like pincer of the crab, etc.—**cheliferous** *adj*.

chelonian *n* any of the order of reptiles, including turtles and tortoises.—*also adj*.

chemical *n* a substance used in, or arising from, a chemical process. * *adj* of, used in, or produced by chemistry.—**chemically** *adv*.

chemical engineering *n* the branch of engineering dealing with the design, construction, and manufacture of plant used in industrial chemical processes.

chemical warfare *n* warfare in which poison gases and other chemicals are used.

chemin de fer *n* a gambling game, a kind of baccarat.

chemise *n* a woman's undergarment; a loose-fitting dress.

chemisette *n* a short bodice worn over the breast; lace, etc, filling the neck opening of a dress.

chemist *n* a pharmacy; a manufacturer of medicinal drugs; a person skilled in chemistry.

chemistry *n* (*pl* **chemistries**) the science of the properties of substances and their combinations and reactions; chemical structure.

chemotherapy *n* the treatment of disease, esp cancer, by drugs and other chemical agents.

chenille *n* silk or worsted cord.

cheque *see* **check**.

chequebook *n* a book containing blank cheques to be drawn on a bank.—*also* **checkbook**.

chequer *n* a pattern of squares (—*also* **checker**); a flat counter used in the game of checkers (—*also* **draughtsman**); (*pl*) a game for two players who each move twelve round flat pieces over a checkerboard (—*also* **draughts**).

chequered *adj* marked with a variegated pattern; having a career marked by fluctuating fortunes.—*also* **checkered**.

cherish *vt* to tend lovingly, foster; to keep in mind as a hope, ambition, etc.—**cherisher** *n*.

cheroot *n* a cigar cut square at each end.

cherry *n* (*pl* **cherries**) a small red, pitted fruit; the tree bearing it; a bright red colour.

cherry picker *n* a crane, usu on a truck, with a long elbow-jointed arm carrying a platform that can be raised and lowered.

chersonese *n* (*poet*) a peninsula.

chert *n* an impure flint-like quartz or hornstone.— **cherty** *adj*.

cherub *n* (*pl* **cherubim**) an angel of the second order; a winged child or child's head; (*pl* **cherubs**) an angelic, sweet child.—**cherubic** *adj*.

chervil *n* an aromatic herb used for flavouring.

Cheshire cheese *n* a mild flavoured cheese, originally made in Cheshire, England.

chess[1] *n* a game played by two people with 32 pieces on a chessboard.

chess[2] *n* one of the flooring planks of a pontoon bridge.

chessboard *n* a board chequered with 64 squares in two alternate colours, used for playing chess or draughts.

chessman *n* (*pl* **chessmen**) any of the 16 pieces used by each player in chess.

chest *n* a large strong box; the part of the body enclosed by the ribs, the thorax.

chesterfield *n* a large, stuffed couch with straight ends; a man's overcoat.

chestnut *n* a tree or shrub of the beech family; the edible nut of a chestnut; the wood of the chestnut; a horse with chestnut colouring; (*inf*) an old joke. * *adj* of the colour of a chestnut, a deep reddish brown.

chest of drawers *n* a piece of furniture containing several drawers.

chesty *adj* (**chestier, chestiest**) (*inf*) prone to chest infections; having a large chest or bosom.—**chestily** *adv*.—**chestiness** *n*.

cheval-de-frise *n* (*pl* **chevaux-de-frise**) a fence constructed of a bar armed with long spikes.

cheval glass *n* a full-length mirror which can swivel in its frame.

chevalier *n* a knight; a horseman; a member or knight of an honourable order; the lowest title or rank of the old French nobility; a gallant.

chevet *n* an apse; a group of apses.

cheviot *n* a rough cloth made from the wool of sheep bred on the Cheviot Hills along the border between England and Scotland.

chevron *n* the V-shaped bar on the sleeve of a uniform, showing rank.

chevrotain *n* a small musk deer.

chew *vt* to grind between the teeth, to masticate; (*with* **over**) to ponder, think over; (*with* **up**) to spoil by chewing. * *n* the act of chewing; something to chew, as a sweet or tobacco.—**chewable** *adj*.—**chewer** *n*.

chewing gum *n* a flavoured gum made from chicle, for chewing.

chewed-up *adj* (*sl*) made nervous or worried.

chewy *adj* (**chewier, chewiest**) needing to be chewed.

chez *prep* at the home of.

chi *n* the 22nd letter of the Greek alphabet.

Chianti *n* a dry red or white wine from Italy.

chiaroscuro *n* (*pl* **chiaroscuros**) the effects of light and shade; the treatment of this in painting, drawing, or engraving; the use of contrast and relief in literature. * *adj* pertaining to such treatment.—**chiaroscurism** *n*.—**chiaroscurist** *n*.

chiasma, chiasm *n* (*pl* **chiasmas, chiasmata, chiasms**) the central body of nervous matter formed by the junction and the crossing of the fibres of the optic nerves.—**chiasmal** *adj*.—**chiasmic** *adj*.

chiasmus *n* (*pl* **chiasmi**) a figure of speech by which the order of words in the first of two parallel clauses is reversed in the second, eg "to stop too fearful and too faint to go".—**chiastic** *adj*.

chibouk, chibouque *n* a long Turkish tobacco pipe.

chic *n* elegance, style. * *adj* stylish.

chicane *n* a hand at bridge without trumps; a barrier or obstacle on a motor-racing course; chicanery.

chicanery *n* (*pl* **chicaneries**) underhand dealing, trickery; verbal subterfuge.

Chicano *n* (*pl* **Chicanos**) a Mexican-American.—*also adj*.

chick *n* a young bird; (*sl*) a young attractive woman or girl.

chickadee *n* the American blackcap titmouse.

chickaree *n* the American red squirrel.

chicken *n* a young, domestic fowl; its flesh. * *adj* cowardly, timorous. * *vi* (*with* **out**) (*inf*) to suffer a failure of nerve or courage.

chicken feed *n* poultry food; (*inf*) a trifling amount of money.

chicken-hearted, chicken-livered *adj* cowardly.

chickenpox *n* a contagious viral disease that causes a rash of red spots on the skin.

chicken wire *n* light wire netting with a hexagonal mesh.

chickpea *n* (the seed eaten as a vegetable of) an Asian leguminous plant.

chickweed *n* a small white-flowered plant of the pink family.

chicle *n* the milky gum of a tropical American tree used to make chewing gum.

chicory *n* (*pl* **chicories**) a salad plant; its dried, ground, roasted root used to flavour coffee or as a coffee substitute.

chide *vt* (**chiding, chided** *or* **chid**; *pp* **chided, chid** *or* **chidden**) to rebuke, scold.—**chider** *n*.—**chidingly** *adv*.

chief *adj* principal, most important. * *n* a leader; the head of a tribe or clan.

chiefly *adv* especially; mainly; for the most part.

chieftain *n* the head of a Scottish clan; a chief.

chiffchaff *n* a European warbler.

chiffon *n* a thin gauzy material. * *adj* made of chiffon; (*pie filling, etc*) having a light fluffy texture.

chiffonier, chiffonnier *n* a high chest of drawers; a wide, low cupboard.

chignon *n* a mass of hair worn in a roll at the back of the head, a bun.

chigoe *n* a species of West Indian and South American flea that burrows beneath the skin of the feet, causing irritation and ulcers.—*also* **jigger**.

Chihuahua *n* a tiny dog with erect ears, originally from Mexico.

chilblain *n* an inflamed swelling on the hands, toes, etc, due to cold.

child *n* (*pl* **children**) a young human being; a son or daughter; offspring; an innocent or immature person.

child abuse *n* physical, mental or sexual maltreatment of a child by parents or any other adult.

childbearing *n* pregnancy and childbirth.—*also adj*.

childbirth *n* the process of giving birth to children.

child care *n* care by an authority of homeless children or those from a disturbed home background.

childe *n* a term formerly applied to the scions of knightly houses before their admission into knighthood; a youth of noble birth.

childhood *n* the period between birth and puberty in humans.

childish *adj* of, like or suited to a child; foolish.—**childishly**.—**childishness** *n*.

child labour n illegal employment of children below a certain age.

childless adj having no children.

child-like adj like a child; innocent, simple, candid.

children see **child**.

child's play n an easy task.

chili n (pl **chilies**) the hot-tasting pod of some of the capsicums, dried and used as flavouring.

chiliad n a thousand; a thousand years.—**chiliadal, chiliadic** adj.

chiliasm n the doctrine of the milennium.—**chiliast** n.—**chiliastic** adj.

chili con carne n a spicy stew of minced beef, beans, onions and tomatoes flavoured with chilli powder or chillies.

chill n a sensation of coldness; an illness caused by exposure to cold and marked by shivering; anything that dampens or depresses. * adj shivering with cold; feeling cold; unemotional, formal. * vti to make or become cold; to harden by cooling; to depress.

chillum n the bowl of a hookah; a hookah; smoking.

chilly adj (**chillier, chilliest**) cold; unfriendly.—**chilliness** n.

chilopod n any of an order of the class Myriopoda, containing the centipedes.

chime[1] n the harmonious sound of a bell; accord; harmony; (pl) a set of bells or metal tubes, etc tuned in a scale; their ringing. * vi to ring (a bell); (with **in**) (inf) to join in in agreement; to interrupt a conversation; (with **with**) to agree. * vt to indicate the hour by chiming, as a clock.

chime[2], **chimb** n the rim formed by the ends of the staves of a cask.

chimera, chimaera n (Greek myth) a fire-breathing monster with body parts from various different animals; a fantastic hybrid; an impossible fancy.

chimere n a loose silk robe worn by an Anglican bishop, either sleeveless or with lawn sleeves.

chimerical, chimeric adj merely imaginary; fantastic, visionary; unreal.—**chimerically** adv.

chimney n (pl **chimneys**) a passage for smoke, hot air or fumes, a funnel; a chimney stack; the vent of a volcano; a vertical crevice in rock large enough to enter and climb.

chimneypiece n a mantelpiece.

chimneypot n a pipe extending a chimney at the top.

chimney stack n the chimney above roof level.

chimney sweep n a person who removes soot from chimneys.

chimp n (inf) chimpanzee.

chimpanzee n an African anthropoid ape.

chin n the part of the face below the mouth.

china n fine porcelain; articles made from this.

china clay n kaolin.

Chinatown n the Chinese quarter of any city.

chinch n a tropical American insect destructive to corn crops; a bedbug.

chinchilla n a small South American rodent with soft grey fur; a breed of domestic cat; a breed of rabbit.

chine n the backbone or spine of an animal; a piece of the backbone of an animal with adjacent parts cut for cooking; a ridge; a rocky ravine or large fissure in a cliff.

Chinese adj of or pertaining to China. * n (pl **Chinese**) an inhabitant of China.

Chinese chequers n a board game played with marbles.

Chinese gooseberry see **kiwi fruit**.

Chinese lantern n a collapsible paper lantern.

Chinese puzzle n an intricate puzzle based on fitting boxes within boxes; any very difficult puzzle or complex problem.

Chinese restaurant syndrome n an ailment characterized by chest pain, dizziness, flushing, allegedly caused by consuming in quantity monosodium glutamate found in Chinese food.

Chinese white n a white pigment; white zinc oxide.

chink[1] n a narrow opening; a crack or slit.

chink[2] n the sound of coins clinking together.

chino n (pl **chinos**) a strong, hardwearing twilled cotton; (pl) trousers made of this fabric.

chinoiserie n (an object or objects in) a style of decoration copying Chinese motifs.

Chinook n a jargon of native and foreign words used on the northwest Pacific coast by Indians and whites.

chinook n a warm dry southwesterly wind of the eastern slopes of the Rocky Mountains; a warm moist wind blowing onto the northwest coast of America.

chinquapin n the dwarf chestnut of the US; its nut.

chintz n a glazed cotton cloth printed with coloured designs.

chintzy adj (**chintzier, chintziest**) of or describing furniture, decor, etc covered in chintz; cheap; tasteless in a flowery way.

chinwag vi (**chinwagging, chinwagged**) (sl) to talk, to gossip. * n (sl) a chatty conversation, a gossip.

chip vt (**chipping, chipped**) to knock small pieces off; to shape or make by chipping. * n a small piece cut or broken off; a mark left by chipping; a thin strip of fried potato, french fry; a potato chip; a counter used in games; a tiny piece of semiconducting material, such as silicon, printed with a microcircuit and used as part of an integrated circuit.

chipboard n a thin stiff material made from compressed wood shavings and other waste pieces combined with resin.

chipmunk n a small, striped, squirrel-like animal of North America.

Chippendale adj of the light style of furniture introduced in the middle of the 18th century by the furniture maker and designer, Thomas Chippendale (1718–79).

chipper adj active; lively, cheerful.

chip shot n a short, lofted approach shot in golf.

chiro-, cheiro- prefix hand.

chirography n the art of writing, calligraphy; judgment of character by the handwriting.—**chirographer** n.—**chirographic, chirographical** adj.

chiromancy n palmistry.—**chiromancer** n.

chiropody n the care and treatment of the feet.—**chiropodist** n.

chiropractic n the manipulation of joints, esp of the spine, to alleviate nerve pressure as a method of curing disease.—**chiropractor** n.

chirp n the sharp, shrill note of some birds or a grasshopper. * vi to make this sound.—**chirper** n.

chirpy adj (**chirpier, chirpiest**) lively, cheerful.—**chirpily** adv.—**chirpiness** n.

chirr n the shrill rasping sound of a grasshopper. * vi to make this sound.—also **churr**.

chirrup vi (birds) to twitter; to make a clicking sound to a horse. * n chirruping sound.—**chirruper** n.—**chirrupy** adj.

chisel n a tool with a square cutting end. * vt (**chiselling, chiselled** or **chiseling, chiseled**) to cut or carve with a chisel; (*sl*) to defraud.—**chiseller** *n*.

chit[1] *n* a voucher or a sum owed for drink, food, etc; a note; a requisition.

chit[2] *n* a child; (*derog*) an impudent girl.

chitchat *n* gossip, trivial talk.

chitin *n* the white horny substance that forms the outer covering of many invertebrate animals.—**chitinoid** *adj*.—**chitinous** *adj*.

chiton *n* in ancient Greece, a knee-length tunic; a full-length woman's dress; a genus of molluscs.

chitterlings, chitlins, chitlings *npl* the small edible entrails of pigs.

chivalrous *adj* relating to chivalry; war-like; high-spirited; brave, gallant; generous to the weak.—**chivalrously** *adv*.

chivalry *n* (*pl* **chivalries**) the medieval system of knighthood; knightly qualities, bravery, courtesy, respect for women.—**chivalric** *adj*.—**chivalrous** *adj*.—**chivalrously** *adv*.

chive, chives *n* a plant whose onion-flavoured leaves are used in cooking and salads.

chivvy, chivy *vt* (**chivvying, chivvied** *or* **chivying, chivied**) to annoy, harass, nag.

chloral (hydrate) *n* a bitter white crystalline compound used as a sedative or anaesthetic.

chlorate *n* a salt of chloric acid.

chlor-, chloro- *prefix* green.

chloric *adj* pertaining to or containing chlorine.

chloric acid *n* an acid containing hydrogen, oxygen, and chlorine.

chloride *n* any compound containing chlorine.—**chloridic** *adj*.

chloride of lime *n* a compound of chlorine with lime used in bleaching.

chlorinate *vt* to treat or combine with chlorine; to disinfect with chlorine.—**chlorination** *n*.

chlorine *n* a nonmetallic element, a yellowish-green poisonous gas used in bleaches, disinfectants, and in industry.

chloro-, chlor- *prefix* green.

chlorofluorocarbon *n* any of various compounds containing carbon, chlorine, fluorine and hydrogen, used in refrigerants, aerosol propellants, etc, and thought to be harmful to the earth's atmosphere.

chloroform *n* a colourless volatile liquid formerly used as an anaesthetic.

chlorophyll, chlorophyl *n* the green photosynthetic colouring matter in plants.

chlorosis *n* a disease affecting young women, characterized by anaemia.—**chlorotic** *adj*.

chock *n* a block of wood or other material used as a wedge. * *vt* to secure with a chock.

chock-a-block *adj* completely full.—*also* **chock-full**.

chocolate *n* a powder or edible solid made of the roasted, pounded cacao bean; a drink made by dissolving this powder in boiling water or milk; a sweet with a centre and chocolate coating. * *adj* flavoured or coated with chocolate; dark reddish brown.—**chocolaty** *adj*.

chocolate-box *adj* sweetly pretty; oversentimental.

choice *n* act of choosing; the power to choose; selection; alternative; a thing chosen; preference; the best part. * *adj* of picked quality, specially good.—**choicely** *adv*.—**choiceness** *n*.

choir *n* an organized group of singers, esp of a church; the part of a church before the altar used by them.

choirboy *n* one of the young trebles in a choir.

choirmaster *n* one who trains and conducts the singers in a choir.

choke *vti* to stop the breath of, stifle; to throttle; to suffocate; to block (up); to check, esp emotion, to choke back or up. * *n* a fit of choking; a choking sound; a valve that controls the flow of air in a carburettor.

chokebore *n* a shotgun with a bore narrowing towards the muzzle.

chokedamp *n* carbonic acid gas generated in mines.

choker *n* a necklace worn tight round the neck; a high collar.

choler *n* bile; irascibility, anger.

cholera *n* a severe, infectious intestinal disease.

choleric *adj* irascible; tending to anger; angry.

cholesterol, cholesterin *n* a substance found in animal tissues, blood and animal fats, thought to be a cause of hardening of the arteries.

chomp *vt* to chew noisily and with relish, champ.

chondr-, chondri-, chondro- *prefix* cartilage.

chondrify *vti* (**chondrifying, chondrified**) to change into cartilage.—**chondrification** *n*.

choose *vb* (**choosing, chose,** *pp* **chosen**) *vt* to select (one thing) rather than another. * *vi* to decide, to think fit.—**chooser** *n*.

choosy *adj* (**choosier, choosiest**) (*inf*) cautious; fussy; particular.—**choosily** *adv*.—**choosiness** *n*.

chop[1] *vt* (**chopping, chopped**) to cut by striking; to cut into pieces. * *n* a cut of meat and bone from the rib, loin, or shoulder; a downward blow or motion; **get the chop** (*sl*) to be dismissed from one's employment; to be killed.

chop[2] *n* a mark or brand denoting quality.

chopfallen *see* **chapfallen**.

chopper *n* a tool for chopping; a cleaver; a small hand axe; (*sl*) a helicopter.

choppy *adj* (**choppier, choppiest**) (*sea*) running in rough, irregular waves; jerky.—**choppily** *adv*.—**choppiness** *n*.

chops *npl* the jaws or cheeks.

chopsticks *n* a pair of wooden or plastic sticks used in Asian countries to eat with.

chop suey *n* a Chinese-American dish consisting of stir-fried vegetables and meat or seafood served with rice.

choral[1] *adj* relating to, sung by, or written for, a choir or chorus.—**chorally** *adv*.

chorale, choral[2] *n* a slow hymn or psalm sung to a traditional or composed melody, esp by a choir.

chord[1] *n* (*mus*) three or more notes played simultaneously.—**chordal** *adj*.

chord[2] *n* a straight line joining the ends of an arc; a feeling of sympathy, recognition or remembering (*strike a chord*).

chore *n* a piece of housework; a regular or tedious task.

chorea *n* a neurological disorder characterized by jerky involuntary movements, esp of the arms, legs and face.—**choreal, choreic** *adj*.

choreograph *vt* to devise the steps for a ballet, dance, etc.

choreography *n* the art of devising ballets or dances.—**choreographer** *n*.—**choreographic** *adj*.—**choreographically** *adv*.

choric *adj* of or for a Greek chorus.

chorion *n* the exterior membrane of a seed or foetus.—**chorionic, chorial** *adj*.

chorister *n* a member of a choir.

chorizo *n* (*pl* **chorizos**) a spicy pork sausage.

chorography *n* the geographical description of a region.—**chorographer** *n.*—**chorographic, chorographical** *adj.*

choroid *n* the vascular membrane of the retina.

chorology *n* the study of the geographical distribution of plants and animals.

chortle *vi* to chuckle exultantly.—*also n.*

chorus *n* (*pl* **choruses**) a group of singers and dancers in the background to a play, musical, etc; a group of singers, a choir; music sung by a chorus; a refrain; an utterance by many at once. * *vt* (**chorusing, chorused**) to sing, speak or shout in chorus.

chorus girl *n* one who sings and dances in the chorus of a musical.—**chorus boy** *nm.*

chose, chosen *see* **choose.**

chough *n* a red-legged crow.

chow *n* a breed of thick-coated dog, originally from China (—*also* **chow chow**); (*sl*) food.

chowder *n* a thick clam and potato soup.

chow mein *n* a Chinese-American dish of fried, crispy noodles with meat and vegetables.

chrestomathy *n* (*pl* **chrestomathies**) a collection of extracts for learning a foreign language; a phrasebook; an anthology.

chrism *n* consecrated oil.—**chrismal** *adj.*

chrisom *n* an infant's baptismal robe.

Christ *n* Jesus of Nazareth, regarded by Christians as the Messiah.

christen *vt* to enter the Christian Church by baptism; to give a name to; (*inf*) to use for the first time.—**christener** *n.*—**christening** *n.*

Christendom *n* all Christians, or Christian countries regarded as a whole.

Christian *n* a person who believes in Christianity. * *adj* relating to, believing in, or based on the doctrines of Christianity; kind, gentle, humane.

Christian Era *n* the present era reckoned from the birth of Christ.

Christianity *n* the religion based on the teachings of Christ.

Christianize *vt* to convert to Christianity.—**Christianization** *n.*—**Christianizer** *n.*

Christianly *adj* like or befitting a Christian.

Christian name *n* a name given when one is christened; (*loosely*) any forename.

Christian Science *n* a system of religion founded by Mary Baker Eddy, 1866, in which sin and disease are regarded as mental errors to be overcome by faith.—**Christian Scientist** *n.*

Christlike *adj* resembling Christ.

Christmas *n* (*pl* **Christmases**) an annual festival (25 December) in memory of the birth of Christ.

Christmas card *n* a greeting card, usu decorative, sent at Christmas.

Christmas Eve *n* the day and esp the night before Christmas Day.

Christmas rose *n* the black hellebore.

Christmastide *n* Christmas Eve (24 December) to Epiphany (6 January).

Christmas tree *n* an evergreen tree decorated at Christmas; an imitation tree.

Christology *n* the branch of theology that studies Christ's nature.—**Christological** *adj.*—**Christologist** *n.*

chrom-, chromo- *prefix* colour.

chromate *n* a salt or ester of chromic acid.

chromatic *adj* of or in colour; (*mus*) using tones outside the key in which the passage is written.—**chromatically** *adv.*—**chromaticism** *n.*

chromatics *n* (*sing*) the science of colour.

chromatic scale *n* a twelve-note musical scale that proceeds by semitones.

chromatin *n* a protoplasmic substance in a cell nucleus forming chromosomes.—**chromatinic** *adj.*

chromatography *n* the separation of the components of a substance by passing it over or through a substance that absorbs selectively.—**chromatograph** *n.*—**chromatographer** *n.*—**chromatographic** *adj.*—**chromatographically** *adv.*

chrome *n* chromium; a chromium pigment; something plated with an alloy of chromium.

-chrome *adj suffix* coloured. * *n suffix* colour, pigment.

chrome green *n* a green pigment made from a compound of chromium.

chrome red *n* a red pigment made from a compound of chromium.

chrome yellow *n* a yellow pigment made from a compound of chromium.

chromic *adj* of chromium.

chromium *n* a hard metallic element used in making steel alloys and electroplating to give a tough surface.

chromo-, chrom- *prefix* colour.

chromogen *n* the colouring matter of plants.—**chromogenic** *adj.*

chromolithography *n* the art of printing in colours from stone.—**chromolithograph** *n.*—**chromolithographer** *n.*—**chromolithographic** *adj.*

chromosome *n* any of the microscopic rod-shaped bodies bearing genes.

chromosphere *n* the rose-coloured outer gaseous envelope of the sun above the photosphere.—**chromospheric** *adj.*

chron-, chrono- *prefix* time.

chronic *adj* (*disease*) long-lasting; regular; habitual;.—**chronically** *adv.*—**chronicity** *n.*

chronicle *n* a record of events in chronological order; an account; a history. * *vt* to record in a chronicle.—**chronicler** *n.*

chronogram *n* an inscription which includes in it the date of some event.—**chronogrammatic, chronogrammatical** *adj.*

chronograph *n* an instrument for recording minute intervals of time; a stopwatch.—**chronographer** *n.*—**chronographic** *adj.*

chronological, chronologic *adj* arranged in order of occurrence.—**chronologically** *adv.*

chronology *n* (*pl* **chronologies**) the determination of the order of events, eg in history; the arrangement of events in order of occurrence; a table of events listed in order of occurrence.—**chronologist** *n.*

chronometer *n* a very accurate instrument for measuring time exactly.

chronometry *n* the scientific measurement of time.—**chronometric, chronometrical** *adj.*—**chronometrically** *adv.*

chronoscope *n* an instrument for measuring by electricity the velocity of a projectile.—**chronoscopic** *adj.*

chrys-, chryso- *prefix* gold.

chrysalis *n* (*pl* **chrysalises, chrysalides**) the pupa of a moth or butterfly, enclosed in a cocoon.

chrysanthemum *n* a plant with a brightly coloured flower head.

chryselephantine *adj* composed (or overlaid) partly with gold and partly with ivory.

chrysoberyl *n* a yellowish-green gem.

chrysolite *n* a green-coloured and sometimes transparent gem.—**chrysolitic** *adj*.

chrysoprase *n* a variety of chalcedony of an apple-green colour.

chthonian, chthonic *adj* (*Greek gods*) of the underworld, as opposed to Olympian.

chub *n* (*pl* **chub, chubs**) a small freshwater fish of the carp family.

chubby *adj* (**chubbier, chubbiest**) plump.—**chubbiness** *n*.

chuck¹ *vt* to throw, to toss; (*inf*) to stop, to give up. * *n* (*usu with* **the**) a giving up; dismissal.

chuck² *n* a device on a lathe, etc, that holds the work or drill; a cut of beef from the neck to the ribs.

chuck³ *vt* to make a noise like a hen calling to her chickens. * *n* a hen's call.

chuck⁴ *n* (*dial*) darling.

chuckle *vt* to laugh softly; to gloat. * *n* a quiet laugh.—**chuckler** *n*.

chuck wagon *n* a provision cart.

chuff¹ *n* a surly fellow, a boor.

chuff² *vi* to make a puffing sound, as a steam engine. * *n* such a sound.

chug *n* the explosive sound of a car exhaust, etc. * *vi* (**chugging, chugged**) to make such a sound.

chukker, chukka *n* each period of play in a game of polo.

chum *n* (*inf*) a close friend, esp of the same sex. * *vi* (**chumming, chummed**) to be friendly (with); to room together.

chummy *adj* (**chummier, chummiest**) friendly, close to.—**chummily** *adv*.—**chumminess** *n*.

chump *n* (*inf*) a stupid person; a fool.

chunk *n* a short, thick piece or lump, as wood, bread, etc.—**chunky** *adj*.

chunky *adj* (**chunkier, chunkiest**) short and thick; (*clothing*) of heavy material.—**chunkily** *adv*.—**chunkiness** *n*.

Chunnel *n* (*inf*) the Channel Tunnel linking England and France.

church *n* a building for public worship, esp Christian worship; the clerical profession; a religious service; (*with cap*) all Christians; (*with* **the**) a particular Christian denomination.

churchgoer *n* one who goes to church regularly.—**churchgoing** *adj, n*.

churchman *n* (*pl* **churchmen**) a member of the Church; a clergyman.—**churchwoman** *n* (*pl* **churchwomen**).

churchwarden *n* in the Anglican church, an elected lay representative who administers the secular matters of a parish church.

churchyard *n* the yard around a church often used as a burial ground.

churl *n* formerly one of the lowest orders of freemen; a peasant; a surly ill-bred person.

churlish *adj* surly, ill-mannered.—**churlishly** *adv*.—**churlishness** *n*.

churn *n* a large metal container for milk; a device that can be vigorously turned to make milk or cream into butter. * *vt* to agitate in a churn; to make (butter) this way; to stir violently; (*with* **out**) (*inf*) to produce quickly or one after the other or without much effort.

churr *see* **chirr**.

chute *n* an inclined trough or a passage for sending down water, logs, rubbish, etc; a fall of water, a rapid; an inclined slide for children; a slide into a swimming pool.

chutney *n* a relish of fruits, spices, and herbs.

chutzpah, chutzpa *n* shameless audacity, presumption, or gall.

chyle *n* a milk-like fluid separated from digested matter in the stomach, absorbed by the lacteal vessels and assimilated into the blood.—**chylaceous, chylous** *adj*.

chyme *n* the pulpy mass of digested food prior to the separation of the chyle.

Ci (*symbol*) curie.

CIA *abbr* = Central Intelligence Agency.

ciao *interj* (*Italian*) used to express greeting or farewell.

ciborium *n* (*pl* **ciboria**) a covered chalice for holding the sacrament; a canopy over an altar.

cicada, cicala *n* (*pl* **cicadas, cicadae** *or* **cicalas, cicale**) a large fly-like insect with transparent wings, the male producing a loud chirp or drone.

cicatrix *n* (*pl* **cicatrices**) the scar remaining after a wound has healed; a scarlike mark.—**cicatricial** *adj*.—**cicatricose** *adj*.

cicatrize *vt* to heal a wound by inducing the skin to form a cicatrix; to mark with scars.—**cicatrization** *n*.—**cicatrizer** *n*.

cicely *n* (*pl* **cicelies**) a species of umbelliferous plants allied to chervil.

cicerone *n* (*pl* **cicerones, ciceroni**) a guide who explains the antiquities and chief features of a place.

CID *abbr* = Criminal Investigation Department.

-cide *n suffix* killing, or killer of, as in *regicide*.

cider *n* fermented apple juice as a drink.

cigar *n* a compact roll of tobacco leaf for smoking.

cigarette *n* shredded tobacco rolled in fine paper for smoking.

cilia *npl* (*sing* **cilium**) the hair of the eyelids; long minute hair-like appendages on the margins of vegetable bodies; the minute vibrating filaments lining or covering certain organs.—**ciliated** *adj*.

cilice *n* haircloth.

Cimmerian *adj* intensely dark; gloomy; pertaining to the Cimmerii, a legendary people mentioned by Homer as living in perpetual darkness.

C in C *abbr* = Commander in Chief.

cinch *n* (*sl*) a firm hold, an easy job; a saddle band or girth.

cinchona *n* a South American tree that yields quinine and other drugs.

cinchonism *n* a medical condition characterized by buzzing in the ears, deafness, etc, caused by the excessive use of quinine.

cincture *n* a belt or girdle worn round the waist; a raised or carved ring at the bottom and top of a pillar.

cinder *n* a tiny piece of partly burned wood, etc; (*pl*) ashes from wood or coal.—**cindery** *adj*.

cine- *prefix* motion picture or cinema, as in *cinecamera*, *cinefilm*.

cineast, cineaste *n* a film enthusiast.

cinema *n* a place where motion pictures are shown; film as an industry or art form.—**cinematic** *adj*.—**cinematically** *adv*.

cinematography *n* the art or science of motion-picture photography.—**cinematographic** *adj*.—**cinematographer** *n*.

cinéma vérité *n* cinema photography of real-life scenes and situations, etc, to create realism.

cineraria *n* a genus of garden plants of the aster family with bright flowers.

cinerarium n (pl **cineraria**) a place for keeping a person's ashes after cremation.

cinerary adj of, pertaining to, or containing, ashes.

cinereous adj ash-grey.

cingulum n (pl **cingula**) belt.

cinnabar n red sulphide of mercury. * adj vermilion.

cinnamon n a tree of the laurel family; its aromatic edible bark; a spice made from this; a yellowish-brown colour. * adj yellowish brown.—**cinnamonic, cinamic** adj.

cinnamon stone n a variety of the garnet.

cinque n a five at dice or cards.

cinquecento n the 16th century and Italian fine art of that period. * adj designed or executed in such Italian style.

cinquefoil n a plant with leaves divided into five lobes; (archit) ornamentation resembling five leaves.

cipher n the numeral 0, zero; any single Arabic numeral; a thing or person of no importance, a nonentity; a method of secret writing. * vt to convert (a message) into cipher.—also **cypher**.

circa prep about.

circadian adj of or pertaining to biological processes that occur in 24-hour cycles.

circinate adj (leaf) rolled up with the tip inwards.

circle n a perfectly round plane figure; the line enclosing it; anything (built) in the form of a circle; the curved seating area above the stalls in a theatre; a group, set or class (of people); extent, scope, as of influence. * vti to encompass; to move in a circle; to revolve (round); to draw a circle round.—**circler** n.

circlet n a small circle; a circular band or hoop.

circuit n a distance round; a route or course; an area so enclosed; the path of an electric current; a visit to a particular area by a judge to hold courts; the area itself; a chain or association, eg of cinemas controlled by one management; sporting events attended regularly by the same competitors and at the same venues; a motor-racing track.—**circuital** adj.

circuit breaker n a switch that interrupts an electric circuit under certain abnormal conditions.

circuitous adj roundabout, indirect.—**circuitously** adv.

circuitry n (pl **circuitries**) the plan of an electric circuit; the components of a circuit.

circular adj shaped like a circle, round; (argument) using as evidence the conclusion which it is seeking to prove; moving round a circle. * n an advertisement, etc addressed to a number of people.—**circularity, circularness** n.

circularize vt to make circular; to send circulars to; to canvass.—**circularization** n.—**circularizer** n.

circular saw n a power-driven saw with a circular blade.

circulate vti to pass from hand to hand or place to place; to spread or be spread about; to move round, finishing at the starting point.—**circulative** adj.—**circulator** n.—**circulatory** adj.

circulating decimal n the recurring decimal.

circulating library n a lending library.

circulation n the act of circulating; a movement to and fro; the regular cycle of blood flow in the body; the number of copies sold of a newspaper, etc; currency.

circum- prefix round, about.

circumambient adj enclosing, or being surrounded, on all sides.—**cicumambience, cicumabiency** n.

circumcise vt to cut off the foreskin of (a male) or the clitoris of (a female), esp as a religious rite.

circumcision n the act of circumcising; spiritual purification.

circumference n the line bounding a circle, a ball, etc; the length of this line.—**circumferential** adj.

circumflex n an accent (^) placed over a vowel to indicate contraction, length, etc.—**circumflexion** n.

circumfuse vt to pour or spread around; to bathe (with).—**circumfusion** n.

circumlocution n the use of more words than are necessary; a roundabout or evasive expression.—**circumlocutory** adj.

circumnavigate vt to sail or fly completely round (the world).—**circumnavigable** adj.—**circumnavigation** n.—**circumnavigator** n.

circumnutate vi (bot) to turn successively to all points of the compass.—**circumnutation** n.

circumpolar adj near the north or south pole; (astron) always above the horizon.

circumscribe vt to draw a line around; to enclose; to limit or restrict.—**circumscription** n.

circumspect adj prudent, cautious; careful; discreet.—**circumspection** n.—**circumspective** adj.

circumstance n an occurrence, an incident; a detail; ceremony; (pl) a state of affairs; condition in life.

circumstantial adj detailed; incidental; (law) strongly inferred from direct evidence.—**circumstantially** adv.

circumstantiality n (pl **circumstantialities**) the state of being circumstantial; fullness of detail.

circumstantiate vt to describe or verify in detail.—**circumstantiation** n.

circumvallate vt to surround with a rampart.—**circumvallation** n.

circumvent vt to evade, bypass; to outwit.—**circumventer, circumventor** n.—**circumvention** n.

circumvolution n the act of rolling round; the state of being rolled round; a coil.—**circumvolutory** adj.

circus n (pl **circuses**) a large arena for the exhibition of games, feats of horsemanship, etc; a travelling show of acrobats, clowns, etc; a company of people travelling round giving displays; houses built in a circle; an open space in a town where streets meet; (inf) noise, disturbance; loud, extravagant behaviour.

cirque n a natural amphitheatre or ring.

cirrhosis n a hardened condition of the tissues of an organ, esp the liver.—**cirrhosed** adj.—**cirrhotic** adj.

cirriped, cirripede adj having feet resembling cirri; pertaining to the Cirripedia, a subclass of parasitic crustaceans, as the barnacles and acorn shells.

cirrocumulus n (pl **cirrocumuli**) a cloud broken up into small fleecy masses.

cirrostratus n (pl **cirrostrati**) a horizontal or slightly inclined light fleecy cloud.

cirrouse, cirrous adj terminating in a curl, tuft, or tendril.

cirrus n (pl **cirri**) thin, wispy clouds.

CIS abbr = Commonwealth of Independent States: a federation of former Soviet republics, such as Russia, Ukraine, who wish to retain voluntary links with one another.

cis- prefix on this side of.

cisalpine adj this side of the Alps with regard to Rome, south of the Alps.

cisco n (pl **ciscoes, ciscos**) the Canadian lake herring.

cismontane adj on this (northern) side of the Alps.

cist n a prehistoric stone tomb consisting of two rows of stone and covered with a flat stone slab; a box or chest.

Cistercian n one of a Benedictine order of monks, founded 1098 at Citeaux, France. * adj pertaining to the Cistercians.

cistern n a tank or reservoir for storing water, esp in a toilet.

citadel n a fortress in or near a city.

citation n a quotation; a source or authority cited; a commendation, esp for bravery; (law) a summons to appear.

cite vt to summon officially to appear in court; to quote; to give as an example or authority.—**citable, citeable** adj.

cithara n an ancient lyre.—also **kithara**.

citify vt (**citifying, citifed**) to assume city ways, habits, dress.

citizen n a member of a city, state or nation.—**citizenship** n.

citizenry n (pl **citizenries**) citizens collectively.

citizen's band n a shortwave band reserved for private radio communication.

citrate n a salt or ester of citric acid.

citric adj of or obtained from citrus fruits or citric acid.

citric acid n a sour acid found in fruits and used as a flavouring.

citrine adj lemon-coloured.

citron n a large fruit-like a lemon; the tree bearing it; a yellow-green colour.

citronella n a fragrant Asian grass which yields an aromatic oil used in soap, perfumes, and in insect repellents.

citrus n (pl **citruses**) a genus of trees including the lemon, orange, etc; the fruit of these trees. * adj of or relating to citrus trees or shrubs or their fruit.

cittern n a medieval stringed instrument.

city n (pl **cities**) an important or cathedral town; a town created a city by charter; the people of a city; business circles, esp financial services.—also adj.

city editor n the editor in charge of local news.

city fathers npl the people who take part in running a city.

city hall n the townhall; the government of a city or its officers; (inf) bureaucracy.

city slicker n (inf) one who adopts city ways; a suave, unreliable person.

city-state n (hist) a sovereign state comprising a city and its surrounding territory.

civet n a cat-like animal of central Africa and South Asia; the pungent substance secreted by this animal used in perfumery.

civic adj of a city, citizen or citizenship. * npl the principles of good citizenship; the study of citizenship.—**civically** adv.

civil adj of citizens or the state; not military or ecclesiastical; polite, obliging; (law) relating to crimes other than criminal ones or to private rights.—**civilly** adv.

civil defence n the organization of civilians against enemy attack.

civil disobedience n refusal to pay taxes, etc, as part of a political campaign; nonviolent protest to achieve an end.

civil engineer n an engineer who designs and constructs roads, bridges, etc.

civilian n a person who is not a member of the armed forces.

civility n (pl **civilities**) good manners, politeness.

civil rights npl the personal rights of a citizen.

civil service n those employed in the service of a state apart from the military.—**civil servant** n.

civil war n a war between citizens of the same state or country.

civilization n the state of being civilized; the process of civilizing; an advanced stage of social culture; moral and cultural refinement.

civilize vt to bring out from barbarism; to educate in arts and refinements.—**civilizer** n.

civilized adj no longer in a savage or uncultured state.

civvy adj (sl) civilian. * n (pl **civvies**) (sl) civilian clothes.

Cl (chem symbol) = chlorine.

cl abbr = centilitre(s).

clack vt to make a sudden, sharp sound; to chatter rapidly and continuously. * n a sudden, sharp sound as of wood striking wood.

clad¹ see **clothe**.

clad² vt (**cladding, clad**) to bond one material to another for protection (iron cladding).—**cladding** n.

claim vt to demand as a right; to call for; to require; to profess (to have); to assert; to declare to be true. * n the act of claiming; a title, right to something; a thing claimed, esp a piece of land for mining.—**claimable** adj.—**claimer** n.

claimant n a person who makes a claim.

clairvoyance n the power of seeing things not present to the senses, second sight.

clairvoyant n a person with the gift of clairvoyance. * adj possessing clairvoyance; having remarkable insight.

clam n an edible marine bivalve mollusc. * vb (**clamming, clammed**) vt to gather clams. * vi (with **up**) (inf) to remain silent, refuse to talk.

clamant adj insistent, crying; clamorous.

clambake n clams baked with seaweed; a picnic at which baked clams form the chief dish.

clamber vi to climb with difficulty, using the hands as well as the feet. * n a climb performed in this way.—**clamberer** n.

clammy adj (**clammier, clammiest**) damp and sticky.—**clammily** adv.—**clamminess** n.

clamour, clamor n a loud confused noise; an uproar; an insistent demand. * vi to demand loudly; to make an uproar.—**clamorous** adj.

clamp n a device for gripping objects tightly together. * vt to grip with a clamp; to attach firmly. * vi (with **down**) to put a stop to forcefully. * vt to attach a wheelclamp to a wheel to immobilize an illegally parked car.

clan n a group of people with a common ancestor, under a single chief; people with the same surname; a party or clique.

clandestine adj done secretly; surreptitious; sly.—**clandestinely** adv.

clang n a loud metallic sound. * vti to make or cause to make a clang.

clangour, clangor n a sharp clang; repeated clanging.—**clangourous, clangorous** adj.—**clangourously, clangorously** adv.

clank n a short, harsh metallic sound. * vt to make or cause to make a clank.

clannish adj closely united and excluding others.—**clannishly** adv.

clansman n (pl **clansmen**) a member of a clan.—**clanswoman** nf (pl **clanswomen**).

clap¹ vti (**clapping, clapped**) to strike (the hands) together sharply; to applaud in this way; to slap; to flap (wings) loudly; to put or place suddenly or vigorously. * *n* the sound of hands clapping; a sudden sharp noise; a sudden sharp slap.

clap² *n* (*vulg*) venereal disease, gonorrhoea.

clapboard *n* a narrow, thin board used for building by overlapping each piece.

clapper *n* the tongue of a bell.

claptrap *n* flashy display, empty words.

claque *n* an organized body of people paid to applaud or express disapproval at theatres; interested admirers.

clarence *n* a closed four-wheeled carriage with a curved front.

claret *n* a dry red wine of Bordeaux in France; its purple-red colour.

claret cup *n* a summer drink composed of iced claret, lemon, brandy, etc.

clarify *vti* (**clarifying, clarified**) to make or become clear or intelligible; to free or become free from impurities.—**clarification** *n*.—**clarifier** *n*.

clarinet *n* an orchestral woodwind instrument.—**clarinettist** *n*.

clarion *n* a shrill trumpet formerly used in war; a rousing sound. * *adj* ringing.

clarity *n* clearness.

clarkia *n* a bright-flowered garden plant.

clary *n* (*pl* **claries**) meadow and wild sage.

clash *n* a loud noise of striking weapons, cymbals, etc; a contradiction, disagreement; a collision. * *vti* to make or cause to make a clash by striking together; to conflict; to collide; to be at variance (with); (*colours*) to be unsuitable or not pleasing when put together.—**clasher** *n*.

clasp *n* a hold, an embrace; a catch or buckle. * *vt* to grasp firmly, to embrace; to fasten with a clasp.—**clasper** *n*.

clasp knife *n* a knife with a blade or blades that shut into the handle.

class *n* a division, a group; a kind; a set of students who are taught together; a grade of merit or quality; standing in society, rank; (*inf*) high quality, excellence; style. * *vt* to put into a class.

class-conscious *adj* aware of and taking part in the conflict between labouring and other classes.—**class-consciousness** *n*.

classic *adj* of the highest class or rank, esp in literature; of the best Greek and Roman writers; of music conforming to certain standards of form, complexity, etc; traditional; authoritative. * *n* a work of literature, art, cinema, etc of the highest excellence; a definitive work of art.

classical *adj* influenced by, of or relating to ancient Roman and Greek art, literature and culture; traditional; serious; refined.—**classicality** *n*.—**classically** *adv*.

classicism, classicalism *n* the use of ancient Roman and Greek style.

classicist, classicalist *n* a scholar of the classics.—**classicistic** *adj*.

classics *n* (*with* **the**) the study of ancient Greek and Roman literature; any literature considered to be a model of its type.

classification *n* the organization of knowledge into categories; a category or a division of a category into which knowledge or information has been put.—**classificational** *adj*.—**classificatory** *adj*.

classified *adj* arranged by a system of classification; (*information*) secret and restricted to a select few; (*advertisements*) grouped according to type.

classify *vt* (**classifying, classified**) to arrange in classes, to categorize; to restrict for security reasons.—**classifiable** *adj*.—**classifier** *n*.

classless *adj* not divided into classes; not belonging to a particular class.—**classlessness** *n*.

classmate *n* a member of the same class in a school, college, etc.

classroom *n* a room where pupils or students are taught.

classy *adj* (**classier, classiest**) (*sl*) stylish; elegant.—**classily** *adv*.—**classiness** *n*.

clastic *adj* (*geol*) composed of fragments.

clatter *n* a rattling noise; noisy talk. * *vti* to make or cause a clatter.—**clattery** *adj*.

clause *n* a single article or stipulation in a treaty, law, contract, etc; (*gram*) a short sentence; a division of a sentence.—**clausal** *adj*.

claustral *adj* of or pertaining to a cloister, cloistral.

claustrophobia *n* a morbid fear of confined spaces.—**claustrophobe** *n*.—**claustrophobic** *adj*.—**claustrophobically** *adv*.

clavate, claviform *adj* club-shaped.

clavichord *n* a medieval keyboard instrument, the predecessor of the piano.—**clavichordist** *n*.

clavicle *n* one of the two bones that connect the shoulder blades with the breast bone, the collarbone.—**clavicular** *adj*.

clavier *n* a musical instrument with a keyboard; the keyboard.

claw *n* the sharp hooked nail of an animal or bird; the pointed end or pincer of a crab, etc; a claw-like thing. * *vti* to seize or tear with claws or nails; to clutch or scratch (at); (*with* **back**) to recover (something) with difficulty; to get back money by taxing; to take back part of what was handed out, esp by taxation.—**clawer** *n*.

claw hammer *n* a hammer with a claw for drawing out nails.

clay *n* a sticky ductile earthy material.—**clayey** *adj*.

claymore *n* a large two-edged sword formerly used in Scotland.

clay pigeon *n* a brittle clay disc or other object propelled into the air as a shooting target; someone in a vulnerable position.

clean *adj* free from dirt or impurities; unsoiled; morally or ceremonially pure; complete, decisive; free of errors; free of suggestive language; not carrying firearms or drugs. * *adv* entirely; outright; neatly. * *vti* to remove dirt from; (*with* **out**) to remove dirt out of; (*sl*) to take away everything from someone, esp money; (*with* **up**) to leave clean; (*sl*) to get rid of corrupt people, a system, etc; to gain a large profit.—**cleanable** *adj*.—**cleanness** *n*.

clean-cut *adj* sharply defined, clear-cut; well-shaped.

cleaner *n* a substance or device used for cleaning; a person employed to clean; (*pl*) a dry cleaner.

clean-limbed *adj* having well-proportioned or shapely limbs.

cleanly *adj* (**cleanlier, cleanliest**) clean in habits or person; pure; neat. * *adv* in a clean manner.—**cleanliness** *n*.

cleanse *vt* to make clean or pure.—**cleansable** *adj*.

cleanser *n* something that cleanses, esp a detergent, face cream, etc.

clear *adj* bright, not dim; transparent; without blemish; easily seen or heard; unimpeded, open; free from clouds; quit (of); plain, distinct, obvious; keen, discerning; positive, sure; without debt. * *adv* plainly; completely; apart from. * *vti* to make or become clear; to rid (of), remove; to free from suspicion, vindicate; to disentangle; to pass by or over without touching; to make as a profit; (*with* **off**) (*inf*) to depart; (*with* **up**) to explain; to tidy up; (*weather*) to become fair.—**clearness** *n*.

clearance *n* the act of clearing; permission, authority to proceed; the space between two objects in motion.

clear-cut *adj* having a sharp, clearly defined outline, as if chiselled; straightforward and open.

clear-headed *adj* showing sense, alertness, judgment.—**clear-headedly** *adv*.—**clear-headedness** *n*.

clearing *n* a tract of land cleared of trees, etc for cultivation.

clearing bank *n* a bank that uses a clearing house to exchange cheques and credits with other banks.

clearing house *n* an office where cheques are sorted and exchanged by the clearing banks; a central agency for the collection, classification and distribution of information.

clearly *adv* in a clear manner; evidently.

clear-sighted *adj* discerning, objective.

clearstory *see* **clerestory**.

cleat *n* a wedge; a strip of wood nailed crossways to a footing, etc; a projection for making ropes fast to.

cleavage *n* the way a thing splits; divergence; the hollow between the breasts.

cleave[1] *vti* (**cleaving, cleft, cleaved** *or* **clove**, *pp* **cleft, cleaved** *or* **cloven**) to divide by a blow; split; to sever.—**cleavable** *adj*.

cleave[2] *vi* (**cleaved, clave**) to be faithful to; to stick.

cleaver *n* a butcher's heavy chopper.

cleavers *n* goose-grass.

cleek *n* an iron-headed golf club with a narrow straight face; (*Scot*) a large hook or crook.

clef *n* a sign on a music stave that indicates the pitch of the notes.

cleft *n* a fissure or crack.

cleft palate *n* a congenital fissure of the hard palate in the roof of the mouth.

cleistogamy *n* (bot) self-fertilization without opening of the flower.—**cleistogamous, cleistogamic** *adj*.

clematis *n* a climbing plant with large colourful flowers.

clemency *n* (*pl* **clemencies**) mercy, leniency; mildness, esp of weather.

clement *adj* merciful, gentle; (*weather*) mild.

clench *vt* (*teeth, fist*) to close tightly; to grasp. * *n* a firm grip.

clerestory *n* (*pl* **clerestories**) the upper story, with windows, of the nave of a church.—*also* **clearstory**.—**clerestoried, clearstoried** *adj*.

clergy *n* (*pl* **clergies**) ministers of the Christian church collectively.

clergyman *n* (*pl* **clergymen**) a member of the clergy.

cleric *n* a member of the clergy.

clerical *adj* of or relating to the clergy or a clergyman; of or relating to a clerk or a clerk's work.—**clerically** *adv*.

clerical collar *n* a narrow stiff white collar buttoned at the back and worn by the clergy.—*also* **dog collar**.

clericalism *n* clerical influence, esp of an undue kind.

clerihew *n* a short nonsensical or satirical poem, usu in four lines of varying length, eg Sir Christopher Wren / Said, "I'm going to dine with some men. / If anyone calls, / Say I'm designing St Paul's."

clerk *n* an office worker who types, keeps files, etc; a layman with minor duties in a church; a public official who keeps the records of a court, town, etc.—**clerkdom** *n*.—**clerkship** *n*.

clerkly *adj* (**clerklier, clerkliest**) pertaining to a clerk, or to penmanship. * *adv* in a scholarly manner.

clever *adj* able; intelligent; ingenious; skilful, adroit.—**cleverly** *adv*.—**cleverness** *n*.

clew *n* a ball of thread; the corner of a sail to which a sheet is attached. * *vt* to truss up (sails) to the yard of a ship.

cliché *n* a hackneyed phrase; something that has become commonplace.—**cliché'd, clichéd** *adj*.

click *n* a slight, sharp sound. * *vi* to make such a sound; (*inf*) to establish immediate friendly relations with; to succeed; (*inf*) to become plain or evident; to fall into place.—**clicker** *n*.

client *n* a person who employs another professionally; a customer.—**cliental** *adj*.

clientele *n* clients, customers.

cliff *n* a high steep rock face.

cliffhanger *n* the perilous situation at the climax of each episode of a serialized film or book; any dramatic or suspenseful situation.—**cliffhanging** *adj*.

climacteric *n* a critical period, a turning point, esp in the life of an individual; the male menopause. * *adj* forming a crisis (—*also* **climacterical**).

climate *n* the weather characteristics of an area; the prevailing attitude, feeling, atmosphere.—**climatic, climatical, climatal** *adj*.

climatology *n* the science of climates.—**climatologic, climatological** *adj*.—**climatologist** *n*.

climax *n* the highest point; a culmination; sexual orgasm; the highlight or most interesting part of a story, drama or music. * *vti* to reach, or bring to a climax.—**climactic, climactical** *adj*.

climb *vti* to mount with an effort; to ascend; to rise; (*plants*) to grow upwards by clinging onto walls, fences or other plants; (*with* **down**) to descend from a higher level; to retreat from a position previously held, eg in a debate or argument; to yield. * *n* an ascent.

climber *n* a mountaineer or rock climber; a climbing plant; a socially ambitious person.

clime *n* (*poet*) a country, region, or tract.

clinch *vt* (*argument, etc*) to confirm or drive home. * *vi* (*boxing*) to grip the opponent with the arms to hinder his punching. * *n* the act of clinching; (*inf*) an embrace.

clincher *n* a decisive point in an argument.

cling *vi* (**clinging, clung**) to adhere, to be attached (to); to keep hold by embracing or entwining.—**clinger** *n*.

clingstone *n* a fruit, eg the peach, with pulp adhering to the stone.—*also adj*.

clinic *n* a place where outpatients are given medical care or advice; a place where medical specialists practise as a group; a private or specialized hospital; the teaching of medicine by treating patients in the presence of students.

clinical *adj* of or relating to a clinic; based on medical observation; plain, simple; detached, cool, objective.—**clinically** *adv*.

clink[1] *n* a slight metallic ringing sound. * *vti* to make or cause to make such a sound.

clink[2] *n* (*sl*) prison.

clinker *n* very hard-burnt brick; a mass of partly vitrified brick; slag; a fine specimen.

clinker-built adj built so that the planks of a boat overlap each other like weather-boarding.

clinkstone n an igneous rock that emits a clinking sound when struck.

clinometer n an instrument for measuring the angles of slopes or the dip of rock strata; a kind of plumb level.—**clinometric, clinometrical** adj.—**clinometry** n.

clinquant adj glittering. * n tinsel.

clip[1] vt (**clipping, clipped**) to cut or trim with scissors or shears; to punch a small hole in, esp a ticket; (words) to shorten or slur; (inf) to hit sharply. * n the piece clipped off; a yield of wool from sheep; an extract from a film; (inf) a smart blow; speed.

clip[2] vt (**clipping, clipped**) to hold firmly; to secure with a clip. * n any device that grips, clasps or hooks; a magazine for a gun; a piece of jewellery held in place by a clip.

clipboard n a writing board with a spring clip for holding paper.

clip joint n (sl) a place, such as nightclub or restaurant, that overcharges or defrauds its customers.

clipper n a fast sailing ship.

clippers n a hand tool, sometimes electric, for cutting hair; nail clippers.

clipping n an item cut from a publication, film, etc, a cutting.

clique n a small exclusive group, a set.—**cliquey, cliquish** adj.

clitoridectomy n (pl **clitoridectomies**) the excision of the clitoris.

clitoris n a small sensitive erectile organ of the vulva.—**clitoral** adj.

cloaca n (pl **cloacae**) a sewer; the cavity receiving the alimentary canal and urinary duct in birds, reptiles, many fishes, and the lower mammals.—**cloacal** adj.

cloak n a loose sleeveless outer garment; a covering; something that conceals, a pretext. * vt to cover as with a cloak; to conceal.

cloak-and-dagger adj involving intrigue or espionage; undercover.

cloakroom n a room where overcoats, luggage, etc, may be left.

clobber vt (sl) to hit hard and repeatedly; to defeat; to criticize severely.

cloche n a bell-shaped glass or plastic cover for food or outdoor plants; a woman's bell-shaped hat.

clock[1] n a device for measuring time; any timing device with a dial and displayed figures; a dandelion head after flowering. * vt to time (a race, etc) using a stopwatch or other device; (inf) to register a certain speed; (sl) to hit; (with **off, out**) to stop work, esp by registering the time of one's departure on a card; (with **on, in**) to start work, esp by registering the time of one's arrival on a card.

clock[2] n a woven or embroidered ornament on a sock or stocking.

clockwise adv moving in the direction of a clock's hands.—also adj.

clockwork n the mechanism of a clock or any similar mechanism with springs and gears. * adj mechanically regular.

clod n a lump of earth or clay; a stupid person.

cloddish adj stupid; phlegmatic.

clodhopper n (inf) a clumsy person; (usu pl) a large heavy shoe.

clog n a wooden-soled shoe. * vt (**clogging, clogged**) to cause a blockage in; to impede, obstruct.

cloggy adj (**cloggier, cloggiest**) lumpy, clogging; adhesive, sticky.—**clogginess** n.

cloisonné n enamel decoration with the colours of the pattern set in spaces partitioned off by wires. * adj inlaid with partitions; decorated in outline with bands of metal.

cloister n a roofed pillared walk, usu with one side open, in a convent, college, etc; a religious retreat. * vt to confine or keep apart as if in a convent.

cloistered adj solitary, secluded.

cloistral adj pertaining to or confined in a cloister; secluded; claustral.

clone n a group of organisms or cells derived asexually from a single ancestor; an individual grown from a single cell of its parent and genetically identical to it; (inf) a person or thing that resembles another. * vt to propagate a clone from; to make a copy of.—**clonal** adj.

clonus n (pl **clonuses**) (med) a series of convulsive spasms.—**clonic** adj.—**clonicity** n.

close[1] adj near; reticent, secret; nearly alike; nearly even or equal; dense, compact; cut short; sultry, airless; narrow; careful; restricted. * adv closely; near by. * n a courtyard; the entrance to a courtyard; the precincts of a cathedral.—**closely** adv.—**closeness** n.

close[2] vt to make closed; to stop up (an opening); to draw together; to conclude; to shut; (with **down**) to wind up, eg a business. * vi to come together; to complete; to finish. * n a completion, end.

close call n a close shave, a narrow escape.

close(d) corporation n a corporation in which vacancies are filled up by its members.

closed adj shut up; with no opening; restricted; not open to question or debate; not open to the public, exclusive.

closed book n something too difficult to understand; something put aside for ever.

closed circuit n the transmission of TV signals by cable to receivers connected in a particular circuit.

closed shop n a firm employing only members of a trade union.

close-fisted adj mean with money.

close-hauled adj with sails trimmed to keep as near to the wind as possible.

close(d) season n certain months in the year in which it is illegal to kill certain game, protected wild birds, fish, etc.

close shave, close thing n a close call, a narrow escape.

closet n a small room or a cupboard for clothes, supplies, etc; a small private room. * vt to enclose in a private room for a confidential talk.

close-up n a film or television shot taken from very close range; a close examination.

closure n closing; the condition of being closed; something that closes; (parliament, etc) a decision to end further debate and move to an immediate vote.

clot n a thickened mass, esp of blood; (sl) an idiot.* vti (**clotting, clotted**) to form into clots, to curdle, coagulate.

cloth n (pl **cloths**) woven, knitted or pressed fabric from which garments, etc are made; a piece of this; a tablecloth; clerical dress; (with **the**) the clergy.

cloth binding n a book binding of linen over cardboard.

clothe vt (**clothing, clothed** or **clad**) to cover with garments; to dress; to surround, endow (with).

clothes npl garments, apparel.

clotheshorse *n* a wooden or metal frame for drying linen, etc; a dressy person.

clothesline *n* a rope on which washing is hung to dry.

clothespin *n* a plastic, wooden or metal clip for attaching washing to a line.

clothier *n* one who manufactures or sells cloth and clothes.

clothing *n* clothes.

cloud *n* a visible mass of water vapour floating in the sky; a mass of smoke, etc; a threatening thing, a gloomy look; a multitude; **on cloud nine** (*inf*) blissfully happy; **under a cloud** suspected of wrongdoing, disgraced. * *vt* to darken or obscure; to confuse; to depress.—**cloudless** *adj*.

cloudberry *n* (*pl* **cloudberries**) a species of wild dwarf raspberry.

cloudburst *n* a sudden rainstorm.

cloud chamber *n* (*physics*) a chamber filled with vapour used for detecting the tracks of high-energy particles.

cloud-cuckoo-land *n* a realm of fantasy, imagination and impossible dreams.

cloudlet *n* a small cloud.

cloudy *adj* (**cloudier, cloudiest**) of or full of clouds; not clear; gloomy.—**cloudily** *adv*.—**cloudiness** *n*.

clout *n* a blow; (*sl*) power, influence.

clove[1] *see* **cleave**.

clove[2] *n* a segment of a bulb, as garlic.

clove[3] *n* the dried flower bud of a tropical tree, used as a spice.

clove hitch *n* a knot used to secure a rope around a spar or pole.

cloven *adj* divided; split.—*see also* **cleave**.

cloven hoof *n* the split hoof of oxen, sheep, etc; the mark of the Devil; an evil influence.

clove pink *n* the carnation.

clover *n* a low-growing plant with three leaves used as fodder; a trefoil; **in clover** (*inf*) luxury.

cloverleaf *n* connecting roads built in the shape of a clover leaf.

clown *n* a person who entertains with jokes, antics, etc, esp in a circus; a clumsy or boorish person. * *vi* to act the clown, behave comically or clumsily.—**clownish** *adj*.

cloy *vt* to sicken with too much sweetness or pleasure.—**cloyingly** *adv*.

club *n* a heavy stick used as a weapon; a stick with a head for playing golf, etc; an association of people for athletic, social, or common purposes; its premises; a suit of playing cards with black clover-like markings. * *vb* (**clubbing, clubbed**) *vt* to beat with or use as a club. * *vi* to form into a club for a common purpose.

clubbable, clubable *adj* suitable for a club, sociable.

clubfoot *n* a congenital malformation of the foot.

clubhaul *vt* (*naut*) to tack by dropping the lee anchor as soon as the wind is out of the sails, bringing the ship's head to the wind.

clubhouse *n* premises used by a club.

club moss *n* the lycopodium.

club sandwich *n* a three-layered sandwich.

cluck *n* the call of a hen. * *vi* to make such a noise.

clue *n* a guide to the solution of a mystery or problem. * *vt* (**cluing, clued**) (*with* **in, up**) to provide with helpful information.

clueless *adj* (*inf*) stupid, incompetent.

clumber *n* a breed of spaniel, a field spaniel.

clump *n* a cluster of trees; a cluster of bacteria; a lump; (*of hair*) a handful; the sound of heavy footsteps.

clumsy *adj* (**clumsier, clumsiest**) unwieldy; awkward; lacking tact, skill or grace.—**clumsily** *adv*.—**clumsiness** *n*.

clung *see* **cling**.

clunk *n* a dull metallic sound. * *vi* to make this sound.

clupeid *n* one of the genus of fishes to which the herring belongs.—*also adj*.

cluster *n* a bunch, esp of things growing or tied together; a swarm; a group. * *vti* to form or arrange in a cluster.—**clustery** *adj*.

clutch[1] *vt* to seize, to grasp tightly; to snatch at. * *n* a tight grip; a device for throwing parts of a machine into or out of action; the pedal operating this device; (*pl*) power.

clutch[2] *n* a nest of eggs; a brood of chicks.

clutter *n* a disordered mess; confusion. * *vti* to litter; to put into disorder.

Clydesdale *n* a heavy breed of carthorse.

clypeal, clypeate *adj* shield-shaped.

clypeus *n* (*pl* **clypei**) a shield-like part of an insect's head.

clyster *n* a liquid injected into the lower intestines by a syringe, an enema.

Cm (*chem symbol*) curium.

cm *abbr* = centimetre.

CNN *abbr* = Cable News Network.

CO *abbr* = Colorado; Commanding Officer.

Co (*chem symbol*) = cobalt.

Co. *abbr* = Company; County.

co- *prefix* together with, jointly.

c/o *abbr* = care of.

coach *n* a long-distance bus; a railway carriage; a large, covered four-wheeled horse-drawn carriage; a sports instructor; a tutor in a specialized subject. * *vti* to teach or train.

coach dog *n* a Dalmatian dog.

coachman *n* (*pl* **coachmen**) the driver of a horse carriage.

coaction *n* compulsion; an acting together.—**coactive** *adj*.—**coactivity** *n*.

coadjutor *n* a helper; an assistant to a bishop.—**coadjutrix** *nf*.

coadunate *adj* (*bot*) united, growing together.—**coadunation** *n*.—**coadunative** *adj*.

coagulant *n* a substance that causes coagulation.

coagulate *vti* to change from a liquid to partially solid state, to clot, curdle.—**coagulation** *n*.—**coagulative** *adj*.—**coagulator** *n*.

coagulum *n* (*pl* **coagula**) a clot (of blood); a curdled mass.

coal *n* a black mineral used for fuel; a piece of this; an ember.

coalesce *vi* to come together and form one, to merge.—**coalescence** *n*.—**coalescent** *adj*.

coalfield *n* a region yielding coal.

coalfish *n* (*pl* **coalfish, coalfishes**) the pollock.

coal gas *n* gas obtained from coal and formerly used for lighting and heating.

coalition *n* a temporary union of parties or states.—**coalitional** *adj*.—**coalitionist, coalitioner** *n*.

Coal Measure *n* that part of the Carboniferous series in which coal is found.

coal oil *n* petroleum; kerosene.

coal tar *n* a thick opaque liquid distilled from bituminous coal and from which many rich dye colours are obtained.

coaming *n* the raised wood or iron border round the outside of a ship's hatch.

coaptation n the adjustment or adaptation of parts to one another.

coarse adj rough; large in texture; rude, crude; inferior.—**coarsely** adv.—**coarseness** n.

coarse-grained adj having a coarse grain; ill-tempered; gross.

coarsen vti to make or become coarse.

coast n an area of land bordering the sea; the seashore. * vi to sail along a coast; to travel down a slope without power; to proceed with ease.—**coastal** adj.

coaster n a ship engaged in coastal trade; a tray for a decanter; a small mat for drinks; a roller coaster.

coastguard n an organization which monitors the coastline and provides help for ships in difficulties, prevents smuggling, etc.

coastline n the outline of the shore.

coat n a sleeved outer garment; the natural covering of an animal; a layer. * vt to cover with a layer or coating.

coat hanger n a piece of wood, wire or plastic curved to fit the shoulders for hanging a garment from a hook.

coati, coatimundi n a raccoon-like South American animal.

coating n a surface coat or layer; material for coats.

coat of arms n the heraldic bearings of a family, city, institution, etc.

coat of mail n chain mail.

coax vt to persuade gently; to obtain by coaxing; to make something work by patient effort.—**coaxer** n.—**coaxingly** adv.

coaxial adj having a common axis.

coaxial cable n a transmission cable having a double conductor separated by insulating material, as for a television.

cob[1] n a sturdy riding horse; a corn cob; a round lump of coal; a male swan.

cob[2] n a composition of clay and straw used for building.

cobalt n a metallic element; a deep blue pigment made from it.

cobalt-60 n a radioisotope used in radiotherapy.

cobalt-blue n a greenish-blue pigment derived from cobalt.

cobalt bomb n a radioisotope (cobalt-60) used in radiotherapy; a nuclear weapon made from a hydrogen bomb encased in cobalt.

cobber n (Austral) (sl) a chum, a pal.

cobble[1] n a cobblestone, a rounded stone used for paving. * vt to pave with cobblestones.

cobble[2] vt to repair, to make (shoes); to put together roughly or hastily.

cobbler n a person who mends shoes; a clumsy workman.

cobbler[2] n an iced drink of wine or spirits, fruit and sugar; fruit covered with a rich crust as a pudding.

cobelligerent n a power cooperating with another in carrying on a war.

cobnut n a large hazelnut.

Cobol n (comput) a high-level programming language for general business use (Common Business Orientated Language).

cobra n a venomous hooded snake of Africa and India.

cobweb n a spider's web; a flimsy thing; an entanglement.—**cobwebbed** adj.—**cobwebby** adj.

coca n either of two South American shrubs; their leaves, chewed as a stimulant.

Coca-Cola n (trademark) a brown-coloured carbonated soft drink flavoured with coca leaves, etc.

cocaine, cocain n an intoxicating addictive drug obtained from coca leaves, used in anaesthesia.

cocainism n a morbid state resulting from excess of cocaine.

cocainize vt to subject to, or render insensible by, cocaine; to treat with cocaine.—**cocainization** n.

cocci see **coccus**.

coccus n (pl **cocci**) a spherical bacterium; one of the separable carpels of a dry fruit.—**coccal, coccoid** adj.

coccyx n (pl **coccyges**) a small triangular bone at the base of the spine.—**coccygeal** adj.

cochineal n a scarlet dye obtained from dried insects.

cochlea n (pl **cochleae**) the spiral-shaped cavity of the inner ear.

cochleate, cochleated adj shell-shaped, screw-like.

cock[1] n the adult male of the domestic fowl; the male of other birds; a tap or valve; the hammer of a gun; a cocked position; (vulg) the penis. * vt to set erect, to stick up; to set at an angle; to bring the hammer (of a gun) to firing position; (with **up**) to make a complete mess of.—**cockup** n.

cock[2] n a small pile of hay.

cockade n a rosette worn on the hat as a badge.

cock-a-hoop adj elated, exultant.

Cockaigne n an imaginary land of plenty.—also **Cockayne**.

cock-a-leekie n soup made of chicken boiled with leeks, etc.

cockalorum n a young cock; a perky or self-important person.

cock-and-bull story n an incredible story.

cockatoo n (pl **cockatoos**) a large crested parrot.

cockatrice n a fabulous serpent possessing the power of killing by a glance of its eye, a basilisk.

Cockayne see **Cockaigne**.

cockchafer n a large winged beetle.

cockcrow n the time of dawn, early morning.

cocked hat n a hat with turned-up brims pointed in front and behind; **to knock into a cocked hat** to beat easily.

cockerel n a young cock, rooster.

cocker spaniel n a small breed of spaniel.

cockeyed adj (inf) having a squint; slanting; daft, absurd.

cockfight n an organized fight between gamecocks.

cockhorse n a rocking horse.

cockle[1] n an edible shellfish with a rounded shell.

cockle[2] vti to curl up, to pucker. * n a wrinkle, a bulge.

cockle[3] n a purple-flowered weed, the plant corncockle or darnel.

cockleshell n the shell of a cockle; a frail boat.

cockloft n a small upper loft; a garret.

cockney n (pl **cockneys**) a person born in the East End of London; the dialect of this area.

cockpit n the compartment of a small aircraft for the pilot and crew, the flight deck; an arena for cock fighting; the driver's seat in a racing car.

cockroach n a nocturnal beetle-like insect.

cockscomb n a cock's crest; a jester's cap resembling a cock's comb; a decorative plant with red or yellow flowers; a vain young fop.—also **coxcomb**.

cockshy n (pl **cockshies**) a thing set up to be thrown at; a throw at a cockshy.

cocksure adj quite certain; over-confident.

cocktail n an alcoholic drink containing a mixture of spirits or other liqueurs; an appetizer, usu containing shellfish, served as the first course of a meal.

cocky *adj* (**cockier, cockiest**) cheeky; conceited; arrogant.—**cockily** *adv.*—**cockiness** *n.*

coco *n* (*pl* **cocos**) the coconut palm.

cocoa *n* a powder of ground cacao seeds; a drink made from this.

cocoa bean *n* the seed of the cacao plant.

cocoa butter *n* a waxy substance derived from cocoa beans and used in perfumery, confectionery, etc.

coconut matting *n* rough matting made from the fibrous outer husks of coconuts.

coconut *n* the fruit of the coconut palm.

coconut palm *n* a tall palm tree that is grown widely in the tropics for its fruit, the coconut.

coconut shy *n* a fairground stall where coconuts are set up as targets.

cocoon *n* a silky case spun by some insect larvae for protection in the chrysalis stage; a cosy covering. * *vt* to wrap in or as in a cocoon; to protect oneself by cutting oneself off from one's surroundings.

cocotte[1] *n* a small fireproof dish for cooking and individual serving of food.

cocotte[2] *n* a promiscuous woman.

COD *abbr* = cash on delivery; collect on delivery.

cod *n* (*pl* **cod, cods**) a large edible fish of the North Atlantic.

coda *n* (*mus*) a passage at the end of a composition or section to give a greater sense of finality; a supplementary section at the end of a novel.

coddle *vt* to treat as an invalid, to pamper; to cook (eggs) in lightly boiling water.—**coddler** *n.*

code *n* a system of letters, numbers or symbols used to transmit secret messages, or to simplify communication; a systematic body of laws; a set of rules or conventions; (*comput*) a set of program instructions. * *vt* to put into code.

codeine *n* an analgesic substance.

codeword, codename *n* a word used in planning and when referring to a secret operation.

codex *n* (*pl* **codices**) a volume of ancient manuscripts.

codger *n* (*sl*) a buffer, an old man.

codicil *n* an addition to a will modifying, adjusting, or supplementing its contents.—**codicillary** *adj.*

codify *vt* (**codifying, codified**) to collect or arrange (laws, rules, regulations, etc) into a system.—**codifier** *n.*—**codification** *n.*

codlin *n* a kind of stewing apple.

codling *n* a young cod.

cod-liver oil *n* oil derived from the livers of cod and related fish which is rich in vitamins A and D.

codpiece *n* a baggy appendage once worn in front of men's breeches.

codswallop *n* (*sl*) nonsense.

co-ed *adj* (*inf*) coeducational. * *n* (*inf*) a girl attending a coeducational school or college.

coeducation *n* the teaching of students of both sexes in the same institution.—**coeducational** *adj.*—**coeducationally** *adv.*

coefficient *n* (*math*) a numerical or constant factor in an algebraic term.

coelacanth *n* a type of primitive fish that is extinct except for one species.

coelenterate *n* any of a group of aquatic creatures with a bulbous or tube-shaped body and a mouth surrounded by tentacles, such as sea anemones, jellyfish and corals.—*also adj.*

coeliac *adj* of or pertaining to the abdomen. * *n* a person

with celiac disease.—*also* **celiac.**

coeliac disease *n* a chronic digestive disease of young children, causing malnutrition and diarrhoea.

coenobite *n* one of a religious order living in a convent or in community.—*also* **cenobite.**

coequal *adj* having complete equality.—**coequality** *n.*—**coequally** *adv.*

coerce *vt* to compel; to force by threats.—**coercible** *adj.*—**coercion** *n.*

coercion *n* the act of coercing; forcible compulsion; government by force.—**coercionary** *adj.*—**coercionist** *n.*

coercive *adj* having the power to force; compelling.—**coerciveness** *n.*

coessential *adj* of the same substance.—**coessentiality, coessentialness** *n.*

coeternal *adj* equally eternal.—**coeternally** *adv.*

coeval *adj* contemporaneous. * *n* a person of the same age, a contemporary.—**coevality** *n.*—**coevally** *adv.*

coexist *vi* to exist together at the same time; to live in peace together.—**coexistence** *n.*—**coexistent** *adj.*

coextensive *adj* extending over the same space or time; equally extensive.

C of E *abbr* = Church of England.

coffee *n* a drink made from the seeds of the coffee tree; the seeds, or the shrub; a light-brown colour.

coffee bean *n* the seed of the coffee plant.

coffee house, coffee bar, coffee shop *n* a refreshment house where coffee is served.

coffee mill *n* a machine for grinding coffee beans.

coffeepot *n* a pot for making coffee in.

coffee table *n* a low table for holding drinks, books, etc.

coffee table book *n* a large book for display, not reading.

coffer *n* a strong chest for holding money or valuables.

cofferdam *n* a watertight structure enclosing a submerged area which can be pumped dry to allow construction or essential repair work.

coffin *n* a box for a dead body to be buried or cremated in.

coffin bone *n* a bone inside a horse's hoof.

coffle *n* a gang of slaves, animals, etc chained together.

cog[1] *n* a tooth-like projection on the rim of a wheel.

cog[2] *vti* (**cogging, cogged**) to load dice in order to cheat. * *n* a trick.

cogent *adj* persuasive, convincing.—**cogently** *adv.*—**cogency** *n.*

cogitate *vi* to think deeply, to ponder.—**cogitation** *n.*—**cogitator** *n.*

cognac *n* a superior grape brandy distilled in France.

cognate *adj* having a common source or origin; kindred, related.—**cognation** *n.*

cognition *n* the mental act of perceiving; knowledge.—**cognitive** *adj.*

cognizable *adj* knowable; (*law*) within the cognizance of a court.

cognizance *n* judicial knowledge or notice; extent of knowledge; awareness, perception; (*her*) a distinctive crest or badge.

cognizant *adj* aware, informed (of).

cognize *vt* to have cognition of.

cognomen *n* (*pl* **cognomens, cognomina**) a surname; a nickname.

cognoscente *n* (*pl* **cognoscenti**) (*usu pl*) a connoisseur.

cogwheel *n* a wheel with a toothed rim for gearing.

cohabit *vi* to live together as husband or wife.—**cohabitant, cohabiter** *n.*—**cohabitation** *n.*

cohere *vi* to stick together; to remain united; to be consistent.

coherent *adj* cohering; capable of intelligible speech; consistent.—**coherently** *adv*.—**coherence** *n*.

cohesion *n* the act of cohering or sticking together; the force that causes this; interdependence.—**cohesive** *adj*.

cohort *n* a tenth part of a Roman legion; any group of persons banded together; a follower, a comrade.

coif *n* a close-fitting cap.

coiffeur *n* a hairdresser.—**coiffeuse** *nf*.

coiffure *n* a hairstyle.

coil[1] *vti* to wind in rings or folds; to twist into a circular or spiral shape. * *n* a coiled length of rope; a single ring of this; (*elect*) a spiral wire for the passage of current; an intrauterine contraceptive device.—**coiler** *n*.

coil[2] *n* (*arch*) tumult, disturbance.

coin *n* a piece of legally stamped metal used as money. * *vt* to invent (a word, phrase); to make into money, to mint; to make a lot of money quickly.

coinage *n* the act of coining; the issue of coins, currency; a coined word.

coincide *vi* to occupy the same portion of space; to happen at the same time; to agree exactly, to correspond.

coincidence *n* the act of coinciding; the occurrence of an event at the same time as another without apparent connection.

coincident *adj* coinciding.

coincidental *adj* happening by coincidence.—**coincidentally** *adv*.

coin-op *n* a self-service launderette, etc where the machines are operated by coins.

Cointreau (*trademark*) *n* a clear liqueur with orange flavouring.

coir *n* the prepared fibre of the husks of coconuts.

coitus, coition *n* sexual intercourse.—**coital** *adj*.

coitus interruptus *n* the interruption of coitus by withdrawal of the penis before ejaculation.

Coke *n* (*trademark*) short for Coca-Cola.

coke[1] *n* coal from which gas has been expelled. * *vt* to convert (coal) into coke.

coke[2] *n* (*sl*) cocaine.

col *n* a pass between mountain peaks; an atmospheric depression between two anticyclones.

col- *prefix* the form of *com-* before *l*.

Col. *abbr* = Colonel.

cola[1] *see* **colon**[1].

cola[2] *n* a carbonated drink flavoured with extracts from the kola nut and coca leaves.—*also* **kola**.

colander *n* a bowl with holes in the bottom for straining cooked vegetables, pasta, etc.

cola nut *see* **kola nut**.

colcannon *n* an Irish dish of boiled cabbage and potatoes mashed together and seasoned with salt, pepper, etc.

colchicum *n* meadow saffron; a narcotic made from its seeds.

colcothar *n* red peroxide of iron used as a pigment.

cold *adj* lacking heat or warmth; lacking emotion, passion or courage; unfriendly; dead; (*scent*) faint; (*sl*) unconscious. * *adv* (*inf*) without prior knowledge or preparation; completely. * *n* absence of heat; the sensation caused by this; cold weather; a virus infection of the respiratory tract.—**coldish** *adj*.—**coldly** *adv*.—**coldness** *n*.

cold-blooded *adj* having a body temperature that varies with the surrounding air or water, as reptiles and fish; without feeling; callous; ruthless; in cold blood.—**cold-bloodedness** *n*.

cold chisel *n* a tempered chisel for cutting cold iron.

cold cream *n* a creamy preparation for cleansing and softening the skin.

cold feet *n* (*inf*) fear.

cold frame *n* an unheated plant frame with a glass top for protecting seedlings, etc.

cold front *n* the forward edge of a cold air mass approaching a warmer mass.

cold-shoulder *vt* (*inf*) to treat with indifference or hostility.—**cold shoulder** *n*.

cold sore *n* one or more blisters appearing near the mouth, caused by the virus herpes simplex.

cold storage *n* storage in refrigerated areas; (*with* in) (*inf*) abeyance, being set aside for future use.

cold sweat *n* a cooling and moistening of the skin usually associated with fear or shock.

cold turkey *n* (*sl*) sudden withdrawal of narcotic drugs from an addict as a cure; the symptoms (eg nausea, vomiting, cramps) resulting from this withdrawal.

cold war *n* enmity between two nations characterized by military tension and political hostility.

cole *n* cabbage plants in general.

coleopteran *n* (*pl* **coleopterans, coleoptera**) any of the beetles, an order of insects having the outer pair of wings formed into hard sheaths for the inner pair.—**coleopterous** *adj*.

coleslaw *n* raw shredded cabbage, carrots, onions in a dressing, used as a salad.

coleus *n* (*pl* **coleuses**) a plant cultivated for its variegated foliage.

colic *n* acute spasmodic pain in the abdomen.—**colicky** *adj*.

coliseum *n* a large building, such as a stadium, used for sports events and other public entertainments; (*with* cap) the Colosseum.

colitis *n* inflammation of the colon.—**colitic** *adj*.

collaborate *vi* to work jointly or together, esp on a literary project; to side with the invaders of one's country.—**collaboration** *n*.—**collaborator** *n*.—**collaborative** *adj*.

collage *n* art made up from scraps of paper, material and other odds and ends pasted onto a hard surface.

collagen *n* a protein present in connective tissue and bones which yields gelatin when boiled.

collapse *vi* to fall down; to come to ruin, to fail; to break down physically or mentally. * *n* the act of collapsing; a breakdown, prostration.

collapsible, collapsable *adj* designed to fold compactly.—**collapsibility** *n*.

collar *n* the band of a garment round the neck; a decoration round the neck, a choker; a band of leather or chain put round an animal's neck. * *vt* to put a collar on; (*inf*) to seize; to arrest.

collarbone *n* one of the two bones that connect the shoulder blades with the breast bone, the clavicle.

collate *vt* to examine and compare (manuscripts, etc); to put (pages) together in sequence; (*bishop*) to appoint to a benefice.—**collation** *n*.—**collator** *n*.

collateral *n* security pledged for the repayment of a loan. * *adj* side by side; accompanying but secondary; descended from the same ancestor but not directly.—**collaterally** *adv*.

collation *n* the act of collating, a comparison; a light meal; the presentation to a benefice by a bishop, who is the patron.

colleague *n* an associate in the same profession or office; a fellow worker.

collect¹ *vti* to bring together, gather or assemble; to regain command of (oneself); to concentrate (thoughts, etc); to ask for or receive money or payment. * *adj* (*telephone call*) paid for by the person called.

collect² *n* a short comprehensive prayer for a particular occasion.

collectible, collectable *adj* (*antiques, etc*) of interest to a collector. * *n* an object worth collecting.

collectanea *npl* passages selected from various authors; a miscellany.

collected *adj* self-possessed, cool.—**collectedly** *adv.*

collection *n* act of collecting; an accumulation; money collected at a meeting, etc; a group of things collected for beauty, interest, rarity or value; the periodic showing of a designer's fashions; a regular gathering of post from a postbox.

collective *adj* viewed as a whole, taken as one; combined, common; (*gram*) used in the singular to express a multitude. * *n* a collective enterprise, as a farm.—**collectively** *adv.*

collective bargaining *n* negotiations on working conditions between representatives of employees and management.

collective farm *n* a farm or number of smallholdings run on a cooperative basis, usually under state supervision.

collective noun *n* a singular noun covering a number of person or things (eg *family, flock*).

collectivism *n* the political or economic theory of collective ownership of the means of production and distribution by the state or people.—**collectivist** *n.*—**collectivistic** *adj.*

collectivize *vt* to bring into public ownership in accordance with the principle of collectivism.—**collectivization** *n.*

collector *n* a person who collects things, eg stamps, butterflies, as a hobby or so as to inspect them, as tickets.

colleen *n* (*Irish*) a girl.

college *n* an institution of higher learning; a school offering specialized knowledge; the buildings housing a college; an organized body of professionals.

collegian *n* a student or recent graduate of a college.

collegiate, collegial *adj* of or belonging to a college; containing, connected with or having the status of a college.

collet *n* the part of a ring in which the stone is set.

collide *vi* to come into violent contact (with); to dash together; to conflict; to disagree.

collie *n* a breed of dog with a pointed muzzle and long hair, used as a sheepdog.

colligate *vt* to bind together; to bring (isolated facts) under a general principle.—**colligation** *n.*—**colligative** *adj.*

collimate *vt* to bring into the same line; to make parallel.—**collimation** *n.*

collinear *adj* in the same straight line.—**collinearity** *n.*

collision *n* state of colliding together; a violent impact of moving bodies, a crash; a clash of interests, etc.

collision course *n* one that, if continued on, will end in disaster.

collocate *vt* to place together; to arrange.

collocation *n* a placing in a particular order; an arrangement, relative situation.

collodion *n* a preparation of soluble pyroxylin with ether, used in photography.

colloid *adj* like glue or jelly; (*chem*) of a gummy noncrystalline kind. * *n* a viscid inorganic transpar-

ent substance.—**colloidal** *adj.*—**colloidality** *n.*

collop *n* a slice of meat.

colloquial *adj* used in familiar but not formal talk, not literary.—**colloquially** *adv.*

colloquialism *n* a colloquial word or phrase.

colloquium *n* (*pl* **colloquiums, colloquia**) a conference, seminar.

colloquy *n* (*pl* **colloquies**) a conversation; a written dialogue.

collotype *n* a gelatine photographic plate used for printing from in ink.—**collotypic** *adj.*

collude *vi* to act together; to conspire, esp to defraud.

collusion *n* the act of colluding; an agreement to commit fraud or deception.—**collusive** *adj.*

collyrium *n* (*pl* **collyria, collyriums**) an eye salve.

collywobbles *npl* (*sl*) abdominal pain or discomfort; nervousness.

colobus *n* any of a genus of long-tailed African monkeys with shortened or absent thumbs.

colocynth *n* a kind of cucumber; the pulp it yields dried and powdered and used as a purgative.

cologne *n* eau-de-Cologne, a scented liquid.

colon¹ *n* (*pl* **colons, cola**) the part of the large intestine from the caecum to the rectum.—**colonic** *adj.*

colon² *n* (*pl* **colons**) a punctuation mark (:) between the semicolon and the full stop, usu written before an explanation or a list.

colonel *n* a commissioned officer junior to a brigadier but senior to a lieutenant colonel.—**colonelcy, colonelship** *n.*

colonial *adj* of or pertaining to a colony or colonies; (*with cap*) pertaining to the thirteen British colonies that became the US. * *n* a person who takes part in founding a colony, a settler.—**colonially** *adv.*

colonialism *n* the policy of acquiring and governing colonies.—**colonialist** *adj, n.*

colonist *n* a person who settles in a colony.

colonize *vt* to establish a colony in; to settle in a colony.—**colonization** *n.*—**colonizer** *n.*

colonnade *n* a range of columns placed at regular intervals; a similar row, as of trees.

colony *n* (*pl* **colonies**) an area of land acquired and settled by a distant state and subject to its control; a community of settlers; a group of people of the same nationality or interests living in a particular area; a collection of organisms in close association.

colophon *n* a publisher's imprint or decorative device on a book; (*formerly*) an inscription at the end of a book giving the printer's or writer's name.

color *see* **colour.**

colorable *see* **colourable.**

colored *see* **coloured.**

colorfast *see* **colourfast.**

colorful *see* **colourful.**

coloring *see* **colouring.**

colorist *see* **colourist.**

colorize *see* **colourize.**

colorless *see* **colourless.**

Colorado beetle *n* a yellowish beetle with ten longitudinal black stripes on its back, destructive to potatoes.

colorant *n* a colouring matter.

coloration *n* colouring.

coloratura, colorature *adj* (*mus*) highly ornamented or florid. * *n* a vocal passage sung in this way.

colorific *adj* producing colour.

colorimeter *n* an instrument for measuring the intensity of colour, strength of dyes, etc.—**colorimetric, colorimetrical** adj.—**colorimetry** n.

Colosseum n a large amphitheatre in Rome built in the 1st century.

colossal adj gigantic, immense; (inf) amazing, wonderful.—**colossally** adv.

colossus n (pl **colossi, colossuses**) a gigantic statue; something immense.

colostomy n (pl **colostomies**) a surgical opening into the bowel forming an artificial anus.

colostrum n the first milk secreted after parturition; biestings.—**colostral** adj.

colotomy n (pl **colotomies**) an incision in the colon.

colour n the eye's perception of wavelengths of light with different colours corresponding to different wavelengths; the attribute of objects to appear different according to their differing ability to absorb, emit, or reflect light of different wavelengths; colour of the face or skin; pigment; dye; paint; (literature) use of imagery, vividness; (mus) depth of sound; (pl) a flag; a symbol of a club, team, etc. * vt to give colour to, paint; to misrepresent; to influence. * vi to emit colour; (face) to redden in anger or embarrassment; to blush; to change colour, to ripen.—also **color**.

colourable adj capable of being coloured; specious, plausible.—also **colorable**.

colour bar n discrimination based on race, esp by White races against other races.

colour-blind adj unable to distinguish colours, esp red and green.—**colour blindness** n.

colour code n a system of identifying by colours, eg of electrical wires.

coloured adj possessing colour; biased, not objective; of a darker skinned race. * n a person of a darker skinned race.—also **colored**.

colourfast adj of a material made with non-running or non-fading colours after washing.—also **colorfast**.

colour filter n (photog) a thin plate or layer for adjusting depth and brightness of required colours.

colourful adj full of colour; vivid.—also **colorful**.—**colourfully** adv.

colouring n appearance in term of colour; disposition or use of colour; a substance for giving colour.—also **coloring**.

colourist n an artist whose works are characterized by beauty of colour.—also **colorist**.—**colouristic** adj.

colourize vt to add colour to a black-and-white film using a Colorizer device.—also **colorize**.

colourless adj lacking colour; dull, uninteresting, characterless.—also **colorless**.—**colourlessly** adv.—**colourlessness** n.

colporteur n a person who hawks books, esp bibles.

colt n a young male horse; a young, inexperienced person; an inexperienced player of a sport.

colter see **coulter**.

coltish adj like a colt; frisky; inexperienced.

coltsfoot n (pl **coltsfoots**) a yellow-flowered weed.

colubrine adj of, like or pertaining to snakes.

columbarium n (pl **columbaria**) a dovecote; a place with niches for cinerary urns.

Columbian adj pertaining to the US.

Columbine n a female character or dancer in a pantomime, sweetheart of Harlequin.

columbine[1] adj pertaining to or like a dove or pigeon.

columbine[2] n a garden plant, aquilegia.

columbium n a metallic element now called niobium.

Columbus Day n a legal holiday in most US states, 12 October, commemorating Columbus' landing in the Americas, 1492.

columella n (pl **columellae**) (biol) a central axis or column.—**columellar** adj.

column n a round pillar for supporting or decorating a building; something shaped like this; a vertical division of a page; a narrow-fronted deep formation of troops; a long line of people; a feature article appearing regularly in a newspaper, etc.—**columnar** adj.—**columned, columnated** adj.

columnist n a journalist who contributes a regular newspaper or magazine column.

colza n rape seed.

colza oil n an oil made from rape seed.

coma[1] n (pl **comas**) deep prolonged unconsciousness.

coma[2] n (pl **comae**) (astron) the nebulous hair-like envelope around the nucleus of a comet; (bot) the silky hairs at the end of a seed; the branches forming the leafy head of a tree.—**comal** adj.

comate adj (bot) hairy.

comatose adj in a coma; lethargic, sleepy.

comb n a toothed instrument for separating hair, wool, etc; a part of a machine like this; the crest of a cock; a honeycomb. * vt to arrange (hair) or dress (wool) with a comb; to seek for thoroughly.

combat vti to strive against, oppose; to do battle. * n a contest; a fight; struggle.—**combatable** adj.—**combater** n.

combatant adj fighting. * n a person engaged in a fight or contest.

combative adj aggressive, keen to fight.

comber n a wool-combing machine; a long curling wave, a breaker.

combination n the act of combining; a union of separate parts; persons allied for a purpose; a sequence of numbers which opens a combination lock; a motorcycle and sidecar.

combination lock n a lock which can only be opened by moving a set of dials to show a specific sequence of numbers.

combinations npl an all-in-one undergarment also covering the arms and legs.

combine vti to join together; to unite intimately; to possess together; to cooperate; (chem) to form a compound with. * n an association formed for commercial or political purposes; a machine for harvesting and threshing grain.—**combinable** adj.—**combiner** n.

combo n (pl **combos**) a small jazz band; (inf) any small group.

combust vt to burn.

combustible adj capable of burning; easily set alight; excitable. * n a combustible thing.—**combustibility, combustibleness** n.

combustion n the process of burning; the process in which substances react with oxygen in air to produce heat.

combustion chamber n the space in the cylinder of an engine in which the gas compressed by the piston is exploded.

come vi (**coming, came,** pp **come**) to approach; to arrive; to reach; to happen (to); to originate; to turn out (to be); to occur in a certain order; to be derived or descended; to be caused; to result; to be available; (sl) to experience a sexual orgasm; (with **about**) to happen; (naut) to change to a new tack; (with **across**) to meet with unexpectedly; to communicate the intended information or impression; to provide what is expected; (*sl*) to pay up; (*with* **along**) to make progress; (*with* **at**) to find out; to attack; (*with* **away**) to get detached; to leave with; (*with* **between**) to cause the estrangement of (two people); (*with* **by**) to obtain, esp by chance; to pass; (*with* **down**) to descend; to fall; to suffer an illness; to leave university; (*with* **down on**) to reprimand; (*with* **forward**) to offer oneself for some duty, volunteer; (*with* **from**) (*inf*) to have an awareness of the circumstances causing one's attitudes or actions; to understand what someone means; (*with* **in**) to enter, arrive; (*race*) to finish in a certain position; to perform a certain function; to become popular or fashionable; (*money*) to be received as income; to turn out to be; (*with* **into**) to enter; to receive as an inheritance; (*with* **of**) to result from; (*with* **off**) to become detached; to fall from; to emerge from or finish something in a specified way; to succeed; to be reduced in price, etc; (*inf*) to happen; (*inf*) to have the intended effect; (*with* **on**) to advance, make progress; (*electricity, etc*) to begin functioning; to enter on to the stage or set; (*with* **out**) to become public or be published; to go on strike; to declare oneself in public; to present oneself openly as homosexual; to transpire; to make one's debut; (*with* **over**) to change sides; to communicate effectively; to make an impression; (*inf*) to become affected with a certain feeling; (*with* **round, around**) to recover one's normal state; to look in as a visitor; to regain consciousness; to change one's opinion, accede to something; (*with* **to**) to regain consciousness, revive; (*total*) to amount to; (*with* **through**) to overcome; to survive; (*with* **under**) to be subjected to; to be classed among; (*with* **up**) to approach; to grow; to come to a higher place or rank; (*sun*) to rise; to occur; to arise for discussion, etc; (*with* **upon**) to discover or meet unexpectedly; (*with* **up with**) to overtake; to put forward for discussion.

comeback *n* (*inf*) a return to a career or to popularity; (*inf*) a witty answer.

comedian *n* an actor of comic parts; an entertainer who tells jokes; a person who behaves in a humorous manner.

comedienne *nf* a female comedian.

comedown *n* a downfall; a disappointment.

comedy *n* (*pl* **comedies**) an amusing play or film; drama consisting of amusing plays; an amusing occurrence; humour.—**comedic** *adj*.

comehither *adj* (*sl*) flirtatious; charmingly seductive.

comely *adj* (**comelier, comeliest**) pleasing to the eye, good-looking.—**comeliness** *n*.

come-on *n* (*inf*) an enticement, lure.

comer *n* (*inf*) a person or thing showing promise of success.

comestible *n* (*usu pl*) anything to eat.

comet *n* a celestial body that travels round the sun, with a visible nucleus and a luminous tail.—**cometary, cometic** *adj*.

comeuppance *n* (*inf*) a deserved retribution.

comfit *n* a candy; a sugared almond.

comfort *vti* to bring consolation to; to soothe; to cheer. * *n* consolation; relief; bodily ease; (*pl*) things between necessities and luxuries.—**comforting** *adj*.

comfortable *adj* promoting comfort; at ease; adequate; (*inf*) financially well off.—**comfortably** *adv*.

comforter *n* one who comforts; a woollen scarf; a baby's dummy teat; a quilted bedcover.

comfort station *n* (*inf*) a public lavatory.

comfrey *n* a tall bell-flowered hairy plant.

comfy *adj* (**comfier, comfiest**) (*inf*) comfortable.

comic *adj* of comedy; causing amusement. * *n* a comedian; an entertaining person; a paper or book with strip cartoons.

comical *adj* funny, laughable; droll, ludicrous.—**comically** *adv*.

comic book *n* a book or magazine containing stories told in strip cartoons.

comic opera *n* a musical play with a comic theme.

comic relief *n* a humorous scene or character in a tragedy that alleviates tension.

comic strip *n* a series of drawings that depict a story in stages.

coming *adj* approaching next; of future importance or promise.

comitia *n* (*pl* **comitia**) one of the three Roman public assemblies for passing laws, declaring war, etc.

comity *n* (*pl* **comities**) civility, politness; acts of international courtesy.

comma *n* a punctuation mark (,) that indicates a slight pause or break in a sentence or separates items in a list.

command *vti* to order; to bid; to control; to have at disposal; to evoke, compel; to possess knowledge or understanding of; to look down over; to be in authority (over), to govern. * *n* an order; control; knowledge; disposal; position of authority; something or someone commanded; an instruction to a computer.

commandant *n* an officer in command of troops or a military establishment, esp a fortress.

commandeer *vt* to seize for military purposes; to appropriate for one's own use.

commander *n* a person who commands, a leader; a naval officer ranking next below a captain.—**commandership** *n*.

commander in chief *n* the commander of a state's entire forces.

commanding *adj* in command; dominating; impressive.

commandment *n* a command; a divine law, esp one of the Ten Commandments in the Bible.

command module *n* the operational part of a spacecraft.

commando *n* (*pl* **commandos, commandoes**) a member of an elite military force trained to raid enemy territory.

comme il faut (*French*) as it should be; correct; well bred.

commemorate *vt* to keep in the memory by ceremony or writing; to be a memorial of.—**commemoration** *n*.—**commemorative, commemoratory** *adj*.—**commemorator** *n*.

commence *vti* to begin.

commencement *n* a start; a ceremony of conferring degrees; the day of this.

commend *vt* to speak favourably of, to praise; to recommend; to entrust.—**commendable** *adj*.—**commendably** *adv*.—**commendatory** *adj*.

commendation *n* the act of commending, praise; an award.

commensal *adj* (*biol*) living together, but not at the expense of another; (*person, organization*) living and feeding with another. * *n* one of two commensal plants or animals; a dinner companion.—**commensalism, commensality** *n*.

commensurable *adj* measurable by the same standard; divisible without a remainder by the same quantity; proportionate (to).—**commensurability** *n*.

commensurate *adj* having the same extent or measure; proportionate.—**commensuration** *n*.

comment *n* a remark, observation, criticism; an explanatory note; talk, gossip. * *vi* to make a comment (upon); to annotate.—**commenter** *n*.

commentary *n* (*pl* **commentaries**) a series of explanatory notes or remarks; a verbal description on TV or radio of an event as it happens, esp sport (—*also* **running commentary**).—**commentarial** *adj*.

commentate *vt* to act as a commentator.

commentator *n* one who reports and analyses events, trends, etc, as on television.

commerce *n* trade in goods and services on a large scale between nations or individuals.

commercial *adj* of or engaged in commerce; sponsored by an advertiser; intended to make a profit. * *n* a broadcast advertisement.—**commerciality** *n*.—**commercially** *adv*.

commercial art *n* art designed for use in all aspects of advertising and packaging.—**commercial artist** *n*.

commercialism *n* commercial methods or principle.—**commercialist** *n*.—**commercialistic** *adj*.

commercialize *vt* to put on a business basis; to exploit for profit.—**commercialization** *n*.

commercial traveller *n* a sales representative or travelling salesman.

commie *n* (*pl* **commies**) (*derog*) a communist.

commination *n* a threatening of divine punishment and vengeance, denunciation, cursing.—**comminatory** *adj*.

commingle *vti* to mix together, to mingle.

comminute *vt* to reduce to minute particles or powder.—**comminution** *n*.

commiserate *vti* to sympathize (with); to feel pity for.—**commiseration** *n*.—**commiserator** *n*.

commissar *n* (*formerly*) a head of a government department in the USSR.

commissariat *n* a supply of provisions; the department in charge of this, as for an army.

commissary *n* (*pl* **commissaries**) a store, as in an army camp, where food and supplies are sold; a restaurant in a film studio, factory, etc.—**commissarial** *adj*.

commission *n* authority to act; a document bestowing this; appointment as a military officer of the rank of lieutenant or above; a body of people appointed (by government) for specified duties; a task or duty or business committed to someone; a special order for something, esp a picture or other art object; a percentage on sales paid to a salesman or agent; brokerage. * *vt* to empower or appoint by commission; to employ the service of; to authorize.—**commissional, commissionary** *adj*.

commissioner *n* a person empowered by a commission; various types of civil servant; a member of a commission.

commissure *n* (*anat*) a line of junction, a seam; the point of union between two bodies.—**commissural** *adj*.

commit *vti* (**committing, committed**) to entrust; to consign (to prison); to do, to perpetrate a crime, etc; to pledge, to involve.—**committer** *n*.

commitment *n* the act of committing; an engagement that restricts freedom; an obligation; an order for imprisonment or confinement in a mental institution (—*also* **committal**).

committed *adj* dedicated; pledged by a commitment.

committee *n* a body of people appointed from a larger body to consider or manage some matter.

commode *n* a chamber pot enclosed in a stool; a chest of drawers.

commodious *adj* roomy; (*arch*) useful.

commodity *n* (*pl* **commodities**) an article of trade; a useful thing; (*pl*) goods.

commodore *n* a naval officer ranking below a rear admiral and above a captain; the senior commander of a fleet; the president of a yacht club.

common *adj* belonging equally to more than one; public; usual, ordinary; widespread; familiar; frequent; easily obtained, not rare; low, vulgar; (*noun*) applying to any of a class. * *n* a tract of open public land; (*pl*) the common people; the House of Commons.—**commonality** *n*.—**commonly** *adv*.—**commonness** *n*.

commonage *n* the right of pasturing on common land.

commonalty, commonality *n* (*pl* **commonalties, commonalities**) the common people.

common chord *n* a note accompanied by its third and fifth.

common denominator *n* a common multiple of the denominators of two or more fractions; a characteristic in common.

commoner *n* an ordinary person, not a member of the nobility.

common law *n* the body of law developed in England based on custom and judicial precedents, as distinct from statute law. * *adj* denoting a marriage recognized in law not by an official ceremony, but after a man and woman have cohabited for a number of years.

common market *n* a grouping of nations formed to facilitate trade by removing tariff barriers; (*with caps*) the European Economic Community.

common measure *n* a number that will divide two or more numbers without a remainder.

commonplace *adj* ordinary, unremarkable. * *n* a platitude; an ordinary thing.

Commons *n* (*with* **the**) the House of Commons, the lower House of the British Parliament.

common sense *n* ordinary, practical good sense.—**common-sense** *adj*.

common time *n* (*mus*) two or four beats in a bar.

commonweal *n* the public good.

commonwealth *n* a political community; a sovereign state, republic; a federation of states; (*with cap*) an association of sovereign states and dependencies ruled or formerly ruled by Britain.

commotion *n* a violent disturbance; agitation; upheaval.—**commotional** *adj*.

communal *adj* of a commune or community; shared in common.—**communality** *n*.—**communally** *adv*.

communalism *n* a political system based on local self-government.—**communalist** *n*.—**communalistic** *adj*.

communalize *vt* to make over to a community.—**communalization** *n*.

communard *n* one who advocates government by communes.

commune[1] *n* a group of people living together and sharing possessions; the smallest administrative division in several European countries.

commune[2] *vi* to converse intimately; to communicate spiritually.

communicable *adj* able to be communicated; (*disease*) easily passed on.—**communicability, communicableness** *n*.

communicant *n* a person who receives Holy Communion.

communicate *vti* to impart, to share; to succeed in conveying information; to pass on; to transmit, esp a disease; to be connected.—**communicator** *n*.—**communicatory** *adj*.

communication *n* the act of communicating; information; a connecting passage or channel; (*pl*) connections of transport; (*pl*) means of imparting information, as in newspapers, radio, television.

communications satellite *n* an artificial satellite orbiting the earth used to relay telephone, radio and TV signals.

communicative *adj* inclined to talk and give information.

communion *n* common possession, sharing; fellowship; an emotional bond with; union in a religious body; (*with cap*) Holy Communion, the Christian sacrament of the Eucharist when bread and wine are consecrated and consumed.—**communional** *adj*.

communiqué *n* an official communication, esp to the press or public.

communism *n* a social system under which private property is abolished and the means of production are owned by the people; (*with cap*) a political movement seeking the overthrow of capitalism based on the writings of Karl Marx; the system as instituted in the former USSR and elsewhere.—**communistic** *adj*.

communist *n* a supporter of communism; (*with cap*) a member of a Communist party.

community *n* (*pl* **communities**) an organized political or social body; a body of people in the same locality; the general public, society; any group having work, interests, etc in common; joint ownership; common character; a group of plants and animals of a region, dependent on each other for life and survival.

community centre *n* a place providing social and recreational facilities for a local community.

commutative *n* relating to or involving substitution; (*math*) having a result that is independent of the order in which the elements are combined; (*addition, etc*) showing this property.

commutator *n* a device for reversing the direction of electric current.

commute *vti* to travel a distance daily from home to work; to exchange (for); to change (to); to reduce (a punishment) to one less severe.—**commutable** *adj*.—**commutation** *n*.

commuter *n* a person who commutes to and from work.

comose *adj* hairy; tufted.

compact[1] *n* an agreement; a contract, a treaty.

compact[2] *adj* closely packed; condensed; terse; firm; taking up space neatly. * *vt* to press or pack closely; to compose (of). * *n* a small cosmetic case, usu containing face powder and a mirror.—**compacter** *n*.—**compactly** *adv*.—**compactness** *n*.

compact disc *n* a small mirrored disc containing music (or audio-visual material) encoded digitally in metallic pits which are read optically by a laser beam.

compact video disc *n* a laser disc, similar to an audio compact disc, which plays sound and pictures.

companion[1] *n* an associate in an activity; a partner; a friend; one of a pair of matched things; a low-ranking member of an order of knighthood.—**companionship** *n*.

companion[2] *n* a wooden shelter over a companionway.

companionable *adj* friendly, sociable.—**companionability** *n*.—**companionably** *adv*.

companionway *n* a ladder or staircase on a ship.

company *n* (*pl* **companies**) any assembly of people; an association of people for carrying on a business, etc; a society; a military unit; the crew of a ship; companionship, fellowship; a guest, visitor(s).

comparable *adj* able or suitable to be compared (*with* with); similar.—**comparably** *adv*.—**comparability** *n*.

comparative *adj* estimated by comparison; relative, not absolute; (*gram*) expressing more.—**comparatively** *adv*.

compare *vt* to make one thing the measure of another; to observe similarity between, to liken; to bear comparison; (*gram*) to give comparative and superlative forms of (an adjective). * *vi* to make comparisons; to be equal or alike.—**comparer** *n*.

comparison *n* the act of comparing; an illustration; a likeness; (*gram*) the use of *more* or *er* with an adjective.

compartment *n* a space partitioned off; a division of a railway carriage; a separate section or category.—**compartmental** *adj*.—**compartmented** *adj*.

compartmentalize *vt* to divide into categories, esp excessively.—**compartmentalization** *n*.

compass *n* a circuit, circumference; an extent, area; the range of a voice; an instrument with a magnetic needle indicating north, south, east, west; (*often pl*) a two-legged instrument for drawing circles, etc.—**compassable** *adj*.

compassion *n* sorrow for another's sufferings; pity.

compassionate *adj* showing compassion; merciful.—**compassionately** *adv*.

compass points *n* north, south, east, west, etc.

compatible *adj* agreeing or fitting in (with); of like mind; consistent; (*body organ*) able to be transplanted successfully.—**compatibly** *adv*.—**compatibility** *n*.

compatriot *n* a fellow countryman.—*also adj*.—**compatriotic** *adj*.

compeer *n* an equal; a companion.

compel *vt* (**compelling, compelled**) to force, constrain; to oblige; to obtain by force.—**compeller** *n*.

compelling *adj* evoking powerful feelings, eg interest, admiration.

compendious *adj* containing much in a small space, succinct.

compendium *n* (*pl* **compendiums, compendia**) an abridgement; a summary; a collection; an assortment of things in one box.

compensate *vti* to counterbalance; to make up for; to recompense.—**compensator** *n*.—**compensatory, compensative** *adj*.

compensation *n* the act of compensating; a sum given to compensate, esp for loss or injury; an exaggerated display of ability in one area as a cover-up for a lack in another.

compete *vi* to strive; to contend; to take part in a competition, esp sporting.

competence *n* the quality of being capable; sufficiency; capacity; an adequate income to live on.

competency *n* (*pl* **competencies**) competence; (*law*) the capacity to testify in court.

competent *adj* fit, capable; adequate; with enough skill for; legally qualified.—**competently** *adv*.

competition *n* act of competing; rivalry; a contest in skill or knowledge; a match.

competitive *adj* of, or involving, competition; of sufficient value in terms of price or quality to ensure success against rivals.—**competitively** *adv*.—**competitiveness** *n*.

competitor *n* a person who competes; an opponent; a rival.

compile *vt* to collect or make up from various sources; to amass; to gather data, etc for a book; (*comput*) to translate high-level program instructions into machine code using a compiler.—**compilation** *n*.

compiler *n* a person who compiles a book, etc; (*comput*) a program that translates high-level program instructions into machine code.

complacency, complacence *n* (*pl* **complacencies, complacences**) self-satisfaction; gratification.

complacent *adj* self-satisfied.—**complacently** *adv*.—**complacency, complacence** *n*.

complain *vi* to find fault, to grumble; to be ill; (*poet*) to express grief, to make a mourning sound.—**complainer** *n*.

complainant *n* (*law*) a plaintiff.

complaint *n* a statement of some grievance; a cause of distress or dissatisfaction; an illness.

complaisant *adj* disposed to please, obliging; compliant.–**complaisance** *n*.

complement *n* something making up a whole; a full allowance (of equipment or number); the entire crew of a ship, including officers. * *vt* to make complete.

complementary *adj* completing; together forming a balanced whole.

complete *adj* entire; free from deficiency; finished; thorough. * *vt* to make complete; to finish.—**completeness** *n*.—**completer** *n*.—**completive** *adj*.

completely *adv* entirely, utterly.

completion *n* the act of completing; accomplishment; fulfilment.

complex *adj* having more than one part; intricate, not simple; difficult. * *n* a complex whole; a collection of interconnected parts, buildings or units; a group of mostly unconscious impulses, etc strongly influencing behaviour; (*inf*) an undue preoccupation; a phobia.—**complexity** *n* (*pl* **complexities**).

complex fraction *n* (*math*) a fraction with fractions for the numerator or denominator or both.

complexion *n* a colour, texture and look of the skin; aspect, character.

complexity *n* (*pl* **complexities**) the state of being complex, complexness.

complex number *n* (*math*) a number having both real and imaginary parts.

complex sentence *n* a sentence with one principal clause and one or more subordinate clauses.

compliance, compliancy *n* the act of complying with another's wishes; acquiescence.

compliant *adj* yielding, submissive.—**compliantly** *adv*.

complicate *vt* to make intricate or involved; to mix up.

complicated *adj* intricately involved; difficult to understand.

complication *n* a complex or intricate situation; a circumstance that makes (a situation) more complex; (*med*) a condition or disease following an original illness.

complicity *n* (*pl* **complicites**) partnership in wrongdoing.

compliment *n* a polite expression of praise, a flattering tribute; (*pl*) a formal greeting or expression of regard. * *vt* to pay a compliment to, to flatter; to congratulate (on).

complimentary *adj* conveying or expressing a compliment; given free of charge.

complin, compline *n* (*RC Church*) the last service of the day following vespers.

comply *vi* (**complying, complied**) to act in accordance (with); to yield, to agree.—**complier** *n*.

compo *n* (*pl* **compos**) a mixture of plaster, stucco, etc; (*sl*) compensation.

component *adj* going to the making of a whole, constituent. * *n* a component part.—**componential** *adj*.

comport *vti* to conduct (oneself); to be compatible, to accord (with).—**comportment** *n*.

compose *vt* to make up, to form; to construct in one's mind, to write; to arrange, to put in order; to settle, to adjust; to tranquillize; (*print*) to set up type * *vi* to create musical works, etc.

composed *adj* calm, self-controlled.—**composedly** *adv*.

composer *n* a person who composes, esp music.

composite *adj* made up of distinct parts or elements; (*archit*) blending Ionic and Corinthian orders; (*bot*) having many flowers in the guise of one, as the daisy. * *n* a composite thing or flower.

composition *n* the act or process of composing; a work of literature or music, a painting; a short written essay; the general make-up of something; a chemical compound.—**compositional** *adj*.

compositor *n* a person who puts together, or sets up, type for printing.

compos mentis *adj* of sound mind, sane.

compost *n* a mixture of decomposed organic matter for fertilizing soil.

composure *n* the state of being composed, calmness.

compote *n* fruit preserved in syrup.

compound[1] *n* a substance or thing made up of a number of parts or ingredients, a mixture; a compound word made up of two or more words. * *vt* to combine (parts, elements, ingredients) into a whole, to mix; to intensify by adding new elements; to settle (debt) by partial payment. * *vi* to become joined in a compound; to come to terms of agreement. * *adj* compounded or made up of several parts; not simple.—**compounder** *n*.

compound[2] *n* an enclosure in which a building stands.

compound eye *n* the eye in insects consisting of numerous separate visual units.

compound fracture *n* a fracture in which the shattered bone protrudes through the skin.

compound interest *n* interest paid on the principal sum of capital and the interest that it has accrued.

compound sentence *n* a sentence with more than one principal clause.

comprador *n* a native agent for a foreign company in China or Japan.

comprehend *vt* to grasp with the mind, to understand; to include, to embrace.—**comprehendible** *adj*.—**comprehension** *n*.

comprehensible *adj* capable of being understood.—**comprehensibly** *adv*.—**comprehensibility** *n*.

comprehensive *adj* wide in scope or content, including a great deal; (*car insurance policy*) covering most risks including third party, fire, theft. * *n* a comprehensive school.—**comprehensively** *adv*.—**comprehensiveness** *n*.

compress *vt* to press or squeeze together; to bring into a smaller bulk; to condense. * *n* a soft pad for compressing an artery, etc; a wet or dry bandage or pad for relieving inflammation or discomfort.—**compressed** *adj*.—**compressible** *adj*.—**compressive** *adj*.

compression *n* the act of compressing; the increase in pressure in an engine to compress the gases so that they explode.—**compressional** *adj*.

compressor n a machine for compressing air or other gases.

comprise vt to consist of, to include.—**comprisable** adj.—**comprisal** n.

compromise n a settlement of a dispute by mutual concession; a middle course or view between two opposed ones. * vti to adjust by compromise; to lay open to suspicion, disrepute, etc.—**compromiser** n.

compromised adj (reputation) open to disrepute, tarnished.

comptroller n the form of controller used in some titles.

compulsion n the act of compelling; something that compels; an irresistible urge.

compulsive adj compelling; acting as if compelled.—**compulsively** adv.

compulsory adj enforced, obligatory, required by law, etc; involving compulsion; essential.—**compulsorily** adv.

compunction n pricking of the conscience; remorse; scruple.—**compunctious** adj.

computation n the act or process of computing; a reckoning, an estimate.—**computational** adj.

compute vt to determine mathematically; to calculate by means of a computer. * vi to reckon; to use a computer.—**computability** n.—**computable** adj.—**computation** n.

computer n an electronic device that processes data in accordance with programmed instructions.

computer-aided tomography, computer-asisted tomography see **CAT**.

computer game n a game on cassette or disk to play on a home computer by means of operating the keys according to the images appearing on the screen.

computer graphics n the production and manipulation of pictorial images on a computer screen.

computerize vt to equip with computers; to control or perform (a process) using computers; to store or process data using a computer.—**computerization** n.

computerized axial tomography see **CAT**.

computer language n a code used to provide instructions and data to a computer.

computer literate adj capable of or proficient in using computers.

computer virus n a program introduced into a computer system with the intention of sabotaging or destroying data.

comrade n a companion; a fellow member of a Communist party.—**comradely** adv.—**comradeship** n.

comsat n communications satellite.

con[1] vt (**conning, conned**) (inf) to swindle, trick. * n (inf) a confidence trick.

con[2] n against, as in **pro and con**.

con[3] prep with.

con[4] vt (**conning, conned**) to direct the course of (a ship).

con[5] vt (**conning, conned**) to study; to learn by heart.

con[6] n (sl) a convict.

con- prefix com-.

con amore adj, adv (mus) with love.

conation n (psychol) the faculty of voluntary agency, including volition and desire.

conative adj (verb) expressing endeavour or effort; pertaining to the faculty of conation.

con brio adj, adv (mus) with spirit.

concatenate vt to link together. * adj linked.

concatenation n a string of connected ideas or events.

concave adj curving inwards, hollow. * n a concave line or surface.—**concavity** n (pl **concavities**).

concavo-concave adj hollow on both surfaces, as a lens.

concavo-convex adj concave on one side, convex on the other.

conceal vt to hide, to keep from sight; to keep secret.—**concealment** n.

concede vt to grant; to admit to be true, to allow; to agree to be certain in outcome.—**conceder** n.

conceit n an over-high opinion of oneself; vanity; a far-fetched comparison, a quaint fancy.

conceited adj full of conceit, vain.—**conceitedly** adv.

conceivable adj capable of being imagined or believed; possible.—**conceivably** adv.

conceive vti to become pregnant (with); to form in the mind; to think out, to imagine; to understand; to express.

concenter see **concentre**.

concentrate vt to bring or converge together to one point; to direct to a single object or purpose; to collect one's thoughts or efforts; (chem) to increase the strength of by diminishing bulk, to condense. * n a concentrated product, esp a food reduced in bulk by eliminating fluid; a foodstuff relatively high in nutrients.—**concentrator** n.

concentration n the act or process of concentrating; the direction of attention to a single object; a drawing together of forces; the simultaneous firing of many weapons.—**concentrative** adj.

concentration camp n a camp where persons (as prisoners of war, political prisoners, and refugees) are detained or confined.

concentre vti to bring or come to a common centre.—also **concenter**.

concentric, concentrical adj having a common centre.—**concentrically** adv.—**concentricity** n.

concept n a general idea, esp an abstract one.

conceptacle n (bot) that which holds anything; a follicle.

conception n the act of conceiving; the fertilizing of an ovum by a sperm; a thing conceived; an idea, a notion.—**conceptional** adj.

conceptual adj of mental conception or concepts.

conceptualism n (philos) the theory that universal truths exist in the mind apart from any concrete embodiment.—**conceptualist** n.—**conceptualistic** adj.

conceptualize vt to form a concept of in the mind based on evidence, experience, etc.—**conceptualization** n.

concern vt to relate or apply to; to fill with anxiety; to interest (oneself) in; to take part, to be mixed up (in). * n a thing that concerns one; anxiety, misgiving; interest in or regard for a person or thing; a business or firm.

concerned adj troubled, worried; interested.—**concernedly** adv.

concerning prep about; regarding.

concert n a musical entertainment; harmony; agreement or union; **in concert** working together; (musicians) playing together.

concerted adj planned or arranged by mutual agreement; combined; (mus) arranged in separate parts for musicians or singers.

concertina n a hexagonal musical instrument, similar to an accordion, which produces sound by squeezing bellows which pass air over metal reeds.

concertino n (pl **concertini**) a short concerto.

concerto n (pl **concertos, concerti**) a musical composition for a solo instrument and orchestra.

concert pitch n a pitch slightly above normal; a state of exceptional efficiency.

concession *n* the act of conceding; something conceded; a grant of rights, land, etc by a government, corporation, or individual; the sole right to sell a product within an area; a reduction in price (of admission, travel, etc) for certain people.—**concessionary** *adj.*—**concessible** *adj.*

concessionaire, concessioner *n* a person holding a concession.

concessive *adj* of or expressing concession.

conch *n* (*pl* **conchs, conches**) a tropical marine spiral shell, sometimes used as a trumpet.

concha *n* (*pl* **conchae**) the external ear or its cavity; (*archit*) the dome of a semicircular apse.—**conchal** *adj.*

conchiferous *adj* producing shells.

conchology *n* the branch of zoology that studies molluscs and their shells.—**conchological** *adj.*—**conchologist** *n.*

concierge *n* a resident doorkeeper or janitor, esp in France.

conciliar *adj* of or pertaining to ecclesiastical councils.

conciliate *vt* to win over from hostility; to make friendly; to appease; to reconcile.—**conciliation** *n.*—**conciliator** *n.*—**conciliatory** *adj.*

concinnity *n* (*pl* **concinnities**) neatness, elegance, esp in speech or writing.—**concinnous** *adj.*

concise *adj* brief, condensed, terse.—**concisely** *adv.*—**conciseness** *n.*

concision *n* conciseness; (*arch*) mutilation.

conclave *n* a private or secret meeting; a meeting of cardinals in seclusion to choose a pope; the meeting place.—**conclavist** *n.*

conclude *vti* to bring or come to an end, to finish; to effect, to settle; to infer; to resolve.

conclusion *n* concluding; the end or close; an inference; a final opinion; (*logic*) a proposition deduced from premises.

conclusive *adj* decisive; convincing, removing all doubt.—**conclusively** *adv.*

concoct *vt* to make by combining ingredients; to devise, to plan; to invent (a story).—**concocter, concoctor** *n.*—**concoctive** *adj.*

concoction *n* the act of concocting; something concocted; a mixture; a lie.

concomitance *n* the state of being concomitant; coexistence.

concomitant *n* an accompanying thing or circumstance.—*also adj.*

concord *n* agreement, harmony; a treaty; grammatical agreement.—**concordant** *adj.*

concordance *n* agreement; an alphabetical index of words in a book or in the works of an author with their contexts.

concordant *adj* agreeing, harmonious.

concordat *n* a compact or agreement, esp between church and state.

concourse *n* a crowd; a gathering of people or things, eg events; an open space or hall where crowds gather, eg a railway or airport terminal.

concrescence *n* (*biol*) a growing together, coalescence.—**concrescent** *adj.*

concrete *adj* having a material existence; (*gram*) denoting a thing, not a quality, not abstract; actual, specific (*a concrete example*); made of concrete. * *n* anything concrete; a mixture of sand, cement, etc with water, used in building. * *vti* to form into a mass, to solidify; to build or cover with concrete.

concretion *n* a solidified mass; a stone-like mass found in some parts of the body, calculus.—**concretionary** *adj.*

concubinage *n* the act of living with a woman without being legally married.

concubine *n* a secondary wife (in polygamous societies); (*formerly*) a mistress of a king or nobleman.—**concubinage** *n.*

concupiscence *n* sexual desire, lust.—**concupiscent** *adj.*

concur *vi* (**concurring, concurred**) to happen together, to coincide; to cooperate; to be of the same opinion, to agree.—**concurrence** *n.*

concurrence *n* the act of concurring; agreement; consent.

concurrent *adj* existing, acting or occurring at the same time; coinciding.—**concurrently** *adv.*

concuss *vt* to shake violently, to agitate; to cause concussion of the brain to.

concussion *n* the violent shock of an impact or explosion; loss of consciousness caused by a violent blow to the head.—**concussive** *adj.*

condemn *vt* to express strong disapproval of; to find guilty; to blame or censure; to declare unfit for use; to force into unwillingly.—**condemnable** *adj.*—**condemnation** *n.*—**condemnatory** *adj.*—**condemner** *n.*

condense *vt* to reduce to a smaller compass, to compress; to change from a gas into a liquid; to concentrate; to express in fewer words. * *vi* to become condensed.—**condensable, condensible** *adj.*—**condenser** *n.*—**condensation** *n.*

condensed milk *n* milk that has been sweetened and reduced by evaporation.

condenser *n* an apparatus for reducing gases or vapour to a liquid or solid form; a device for storing electricity; a lens for concentrating light.

condescend *vi* to waive one's superiority; to deign, to stoop; to act patronizingly.—**condescension** *n.*

condescending *adj* kindly in a lordly fashion to inferiors; patronizing.

condescension *n* a condescending act or manner.

condign *adj* deserved, merited; suitable.

condiment *n* a seasoning or relish.

condition *n* the state or nature of things; anything required for the performance, completion or existence of something else; physical state of health; an abnormality, illness; a prerequisite; (*pl*) attendant circumstances. * *vt* to be essential to the happening or existence of; to stipulate; to agree upon; to make fit; to make accustomed (to); to bring about a required effect by subjecting to certain stimuli.

conditional *adj* depending on conditions; not absolute; (*gram*) expressing condition. * *n* a conditional clause or conjunction.—**conditionality** *n.*—**conditionally** *adv.*

conditioner *n* a person or thing that conditions; a creamy substance for bringing the hair into a glossy condition.

conditioning *n* a bringing into a required state or state of fitness for an objective.

condo *n* (*pl* **condos, condoes**) (*inf*) a condominium.

condole *vt* (*with* **with**) to express sympathy for another.—**condolatory** *adj.*—**condoler** *n.*

condolence, condolement *n* sympathy.

con dolore *adv* (*mus*) mournfully.

condom *n* a sheath for the penis, used as a contraceptive and to prevent infection.

condominium *n* (*pl* **condominiums**) a block of apartments, each apartment being individually owned; joint rule; a country ruled by more than one other country.

condone *vt* to overlook, to treat as nonexistent; to pardon an offence.—**condonation** *n*.—**condoner** *n*.

condor *n* a large South American vulture.

condottiere *n* (*pl* **condottieri**) a military adventurer, a captain of mercenaries.

conduce *vi* to tend to bring about, to contribute (to).—**conducer** *n*.

conducive *adj* leading to or helping to cause or produce a result.

conduct *vti* to lead; to guide; to convey; to direct (an orchestra); to carry on or manage (a business); to transmit (electricity, heat); to behave (oneself). * *n* management, direction; behaviour.—**conductible** *adj*.—**conductibility** *n*.

conductance *n* the ability of a specified system to conduct electricity.

conduction *n* the conducting or transmission of heat or electricity through a medium; the transmission of nerve impulses.

conductive *adj* having the power to transmit heat or electricity.—**conductivity** *n* (*pl* **conductivities**).

conductor *n* a person who conducts an orchestra; one in charge of passengers on a train, or who collects fares on a bus; a substance that conducts heat or electricity.—**conductress** *nf*.

conduit *n* a channel or pipe that carries water, etc.

conduplicate *adj* (*bot*) folded lengthwise along the middle.—**conduplication** *n*.

condyle *n* the rounded head at the end of a bone fitting into another bone.—**condylar** *adj*.

condyloid *adj* shaped like, resembling or connected with a condyle.

cone *n* a solid pointed figure with a circular or elliptical base; any cone-shaped object (*an ice-cream cone*); a warning ballard on roads, etc; the scaly fruit of the pine, fir, etc.

coney *see* **cony**.

confab *n* (*inf*) an informal talk, chat.

confabulate *vi* to talk familiarly together.—**confabulation** *n*.—**confabulator** *n*.—**confabulatory** *adj*.

confection *n* candy, ice cream, preserves, etc; anything overfussy, fanciful or ornate.

confectionary *n* (*pl* **confectionaries**) a place where confectionery is made or sold. * *adj* of or pertaining to confectionery.

confectioner *n* a person who makes or sells confectionery.

confectionery *n* (*pl* **confectioneries**) candies.

confederacy *n* (*pl* **confederacies**) a union of states, an alliance; a combination of persons for illegal purposes; (*with cap*) the Confederate States of America.

confederate *adj* banded together by treaty, united in confederation. * *vti* to bring or come into alliance or confederacy. * *n* a member of a confederacy; a partner in design, an accomplice; an ally.

Confederate States *npl* in US history, the eleven Southern States that seceded from the Union in 1861, leading to the Civil War in which they were defeated in 1865.

confederation *n* the act or state of confederating; an alliance of individuals, organizations, states or cantons (as in Switzerland).—**confederationism** *n*.—**confederationist** *n*.

confer *vt* (**conferring, conferred**) to grant or bestow; to compare views or take counsel; to consult.—**confer-**

ment, conferral *n*.—**conferrable** *adj*.—**conferrer** *n*.

conferee, conferree *n* one on whom something is conferred; a member of a conference.

conference *n* a meeting for discussion or consultation.—**conferential** *adj*.

conferva *n* (*pl* **confervae, confervas**) a genus containing green freshwater algae.—**conferval** *adj*.—**confervoid** *adj*.

confess *vt* to acknowledge or admit; to disclose (sins) to a confessor; (*priest*) to hear confession of. * *vi* to make or hear a confession.

confessedly *adv* avowedly.

confession *n* admission or acknowledgement of a fault or sin, esp to a confessor; a thing confessed; a statement of one's religious beliefs, creed.—**confessionary** *adj*.

confessional *n* an enclosure in a church where a priest hears confessions.

confessor *n* a priest who hears confessions and grants absolution; one who confesses.

confetti *npl* small bits of coloured paper thrown at weddings.

confidant *n* a person trusted with one's secrets.—**confidante** *nf*.

confide *vti* to put confidence (in); to entrust; to impart a confidence or secret.—**confider** *n*.

confidence *n* firm trust, faith; belief in one's own abilities; boldness; something revealed confidentially.

confidence trick *n* the persuading of a victim to hand over valuables as proof of confidence.

confident *adj* full of confidence; positive, assured.—**confidently** *adv*.

confidential *adj* spoken or written in confidence, secret; entrusted with secrets.—**confidentiality, confidentialness** *n*.—**confidentially** *adv*.

confiding *adj* unsuspicious.—**confidingly** *adv*.

configuration *n* arrangement of parts; external shape, general outline; aspect; (*astrol*) the relative position of the planets; the make-up of a computer system.—**configurational, configurative** *adj*.

confine *vt* to restrict, to keep within limits; to keep shut up, as in prison, a sickbed, etc; to imprison. * *n* (*pl*) borderland, edge, limit.—**confinable, confineable** *adj*.

confined *adj* narrow, enclosed, of limited space.

confinement *n* a being confined; the period of childbirth.

confirm *vt* to make stronger; to establish firmly; to make valid, to ratify; to corroborate; to administer rite of confirmation to.

confirmation *n* the act of confirming; convincing proof; the rite by which people are admitted to full communion in Christian churches.

confirmatory, confirmative *adj* giving extra proof; corroborative.

confirmed *adj* habitual; settled in belief, mode of life, etc; having undergone the rite of confirmation.

confiscate *vt* to appropriate to the state as a penalty; to seize by authority.—**confiscable** *adj*.—**confiscation** *n*.—**confiscator** *n*.—**confiscatory** *adj*.

conflagration *n* a massively destructive fire.—**conflagrative** *adj*.

conflation *n* a fusing together; a combining of two variant readings of a text into one.—**conflate** *vt*.

conflict *n* a fight; a contest; strife, quarrel; emotional disturbance. * *vi* to be at variance; to clash (with); to struggle.—**confliction** *n*.—**conflictive, conflictory** *adj*.

conflicting *adj* contradictory.

confluence, conflux *n* the point where two rivers meet; a coming together.

confluent *adj* flowing or running together. * *n* a tributary river or stream.

confocal *adj* having a common focus.

conform *vi* to comply, to be obedient (to); to act in accordance with. * *vt* to adapt; to make like.—**conformer** *n*.

conformable *adj* compliant; corresponding, adapted (to); in parallel order.—**conformability, conformableness** *n*.—**conformably** *adv*.

conformation *n* arrangement of parts, structure; adaptation.

conformist *n* one who conforms to established rules, standards, etc; compliance with the rites and doctrines of an established church.—**conformism** *n*.

conformity, conformance *n* (*pl* **conformities, conformances**) correspondence; agreement; conventional behaviour; compliance.

confound *vt* to mix up, to obscure; to perplex, to astound; to overthrow; to mistake one thing for another.—**confounder** *n*.

confounded *adj* astonished; confused; annoying; (*inf*) damned.—**confoundedly** *adv*.

confraternity *n* (*pl* **confraternities**) a brotherhood or society of men associated for a common purpose.—**confraternal** *adj*.

confrère *n* an associate, a colleague.

confront *vt* to stand in front of, to face; to bring face to face (with); to encounter; to oppose.—**confronter** *n*.

confrontation *n* the coming face to face with; hostility without actual warfare, esp between nations.

Confucian *adj* pertaining to Confucius, the Chinese philosopher. * *n* a follower of the teachings of Confucius.

confuse *vt* to throw into disorder; to mix up; to mistake one thing for another; to perplex, to disconcert; to embarrass; to make unclear.—**confusable** *adj*.—**confusing** *adj*.—**confusingly** *adv*.

confused *adj* perplexed; disordered; mentally unbalanced.—**confusedly** *adv*.

confusion *n* the act or state of being confused; disorder; embarrassment, discomfiture; lack of clarity.

confute *vt* (*argument, etc*) to prove wrong; to convict of error; to overcome in argument.—**confutation** *n*.—**confutative** *adj*.—**confuter** *n*.

conga *n* a Cuban dance in which the dancers move along in a long line; music for this. * *vi* (**congaing, congaed**) to do this dance.

congé *n* dismissal; (*arch*) a formal bow, esp at parting.

congeal *vti* to change from a liquid to a solid by cooling, to jell.—**congealment** *n*.

congelation *n* the act of congealing; a congealed state or substance.

congener *n* a person or thing of the same kind as another.

congeneric *adj* of the same genus or origin.

congenial *adj* of a similar disposition or with similar tastes, kindred; suited, agreeable (to).—**congenially** *adv*.—**congeniality, congenialness** *n*.

congenital *adj* existing or dating since birth, as in certain defects.—**congenitally** *adv*.

conger eel *n* a large marine eel.

congeries *n* (*used as sing or pl*) a gathered mass, a heap; a conglomeration.

congest *vt* to overcrowd. * *vi* (*med*) to affect with congestion.—**congested** *adj*.—**congestible** *adj*.

congestion *n* an overcrowding; (*med*) an excessive accumulation of blood in any organ; an accumulation of traffic causing obstruction.—**congestive** *adj*.

conglobate *vti* to form into a mass.—**conglobation** *n*.

conglomerate *adj* stuck together in a mass. * *vt* to gather into a ball. * *n* a coarse-grained rock of embedded pebbles; a large corporation consisting of companies with varied and often unrelated interests.—**conglomeratic, conglomeritic** *adj*.

conglomeration *n* the act of conglomerating; a mass stuck together; a miscellaneous collection.

conglutinate *vt* to glue together. * *adj* glued together; united by an adhesive substance.—**conglutination** *n*.—**conglutinative** *adj*.

congou *n* a kind of black Chinese tea.

congratulate *vt* to express sympathetic pleasure at success or good fortune of, to compliment; to feel satisfied or pleased with oneself.—**congratulation** *n*.—**congratulator** *n*.—**congratulatory** *adj*.

congratulations *npl* an expression of joy or pleasure.

congregate *vti* to flock together, to assemble; to gather into a crowd or mass.—**congregator** *n*.

congregation *n* a gathering, an assembly; a body of people assembled for worship.

congregational *adj* of a congregation; (*with cap*) of or pertaining to Congregationalism.

Congregationalism *n* a form of church government in which each congregation has management of its own affairs.—**Congregationalist** *adj, n*.

congress *n* an association or society; an assembly or conference, esp for discussion and action on some question; (*with cap*) the legislature of the US, comprising the Senate and the House of Representatives.

congressional *adj* of, or relating to, a congress.—**congressionalist** *n*.

Congressman *n* (*pl* **Congressmen**) a member of Congress.—**Congresswoman** *nf* (*pl* **Congresswomen**).

congruent *adj* in agreement; harmonious; (*geom*) having identical shape and size so that all parts correspond.—**congruence, congruency** *n*.

congruous *adj* accordant; fit.—**congruity** *n*.

conic, conical *adj* of a cone; cone-shaped.

conics *n* (*used as sing*) the branch of geometry that deals with conic sections.

conic section *n* a curve formed from a cone—an ellipse, a parabola, or a hyperbola.

conidium (*pl* **conidia**) a reproductive cell formed of certain fungi.—**conidial** adj.

conifer *n* any evergreen trees and shrubs with true cones (as pines) and others (as yews).—**coniferous** *adj*.

coniferous *adj* bearing fruit cones.

conine, conin *n* a very poisonous alkaloid existing in the hemlock.

conium *n* a genus of biennial poisonous plants including the hemlock.

conjectural *adj* depending on conjecture, doubtful.—**conjecturally** *adv*.

conjecture *n* a guess, guesswork. * *vt* to make a conjecture, to guess, surmise.—**conjecturer** *n*.—**conjecturable** *adj*.—**conjectural** *adj*.

conjoin *vt* to join together; to connect or associate. * *vi* to be joined.—**conjoinedly** *adv*.—**conjoiner** *n*.

conjoint *adj* united, combined; cooperating.—**conjointly** *adv*.

conjugal *adj* of or relating to marriage.—**conjugality** *n*.—**conjugally** *adv*.

conjugate *vt* to give the parts of (a verb); to unite.—**conjugable** *adj.*—**conjugation** *n.*—**conjugator** *n.*—**conjugative** *adj.*

conjugation *n* the act of conjugating; a group of verbs with the same inflections; the union of cells in reproduction.—**conjugational** *adj.*

conjunct *adj* joined together; associated.

conjunction *n* (*gram*) a word connecting words, clauses or sentences; a union; a simultaneous occurrence of events; the apparent proximity of two or more planets.—**conjunctional** *adj.*

conjunctiva *n* (*pl* **conjunctivas, conjunctivae**) the mucous membrane that lines the inner surface of the eyelids and the exposed area of the eyeball.—**conjunctival** *adj.*

conjunctive *adj* serving to unite; closely connected, (*gram*) of or pertaining to conjunctions. * *n* a conjunction.—**conjunctively** *adv.*

conjunctivitis *n* inflammation of the conjunctiva.

conjuncture *n* a combination of many circumstances or causes; a critical time.—**conjunctural** *adj.*

conjuration *n* the act of conjuring or invoking; an incantation; an enchantment; a solemn entreaty.

conjure *vti* to practise magical tricks; to call up (spirits) by invocation.

conjurer, conjuror *n* one who conjures or is skilled in sleight of hand.

conk *n* (*sl*) the nose or head. * *n* a blow to the nose or head. * *vt* to hit, esp on the head. * *vi* (*with* out) (*sl*) (*machine*) to break down entirely; to collapse suddenly from exhaustion.

conker *n* (*inf*) the horse chestnut; (*pl*) a children's game using conkers on a string.

con man *n* (*inf*) a swindler, one who defrauds by means of a confidence trick.

con moto *adj* (*mus*) spirited.

connate *adj* inborn, congenital; (*leaves*) united at the base.

connatural *adj* congenital; having the same nature.

connect *vti* to fasten together, to join; to relate together, to link up; (*trains, buses, etc*) to be timed to arrive as another leaves so that passengers can continue their journey; to establish a link by telephone; (*sl*) to punch or kick; to uncover (a source of drugs).—**connectible, connectable** *adj.*—**connector, connecter** *n.*

connection *n* the act of connecting; the state of being connected; a thing that connects; a relationship, bond; a train, bus, etc timed to connect with another; an opportunity to transfer between trains, buses, etc; context; a link between components in an electric circuit; a relative; (*sl*) a supply or the supplier of illicit drugs; (*pl*) clients, customers.—**connectional** *adj.*

connective *adj* serving to connect.—**connectively** *adv.*

connectivity *n* the ability of computers of different kinds to communicate.

conning tower *n* the armoured pilot house of a submarine.

conniption *n* (*sl*) a fit of hysteria or rage.

connivance *n* the act of conniving; pretence of ignorance; passive cooperation in a crime or fault; collusion.

connive *vi* to permit tacitly; to wink (at); to plot.—**conniver** *n.*

connivent *adj* converging.

connoisseur *n* a trained discriminating judge, esp of the fine arts.

connotation *n* a consequential meaning, an implication—**connotative, connotive** *adj.*

connote *vt* to imply; to indicate; to mean.

connubial *adv* of or relating to marriage.—**connubiality** *n.*—**connubially** *adv.*

conoid *n* (*geom*) a solid formed by revolution of a conic section about its axis. * *adj* somewhat conical (—*also* **conoidal**).

conquer *vt* to gain victory (over), to defeat; to acquire by conquest; to overcome, to master. * *vi* to be victor.—**conqueror** *n.*

conquest *n* conquering; the winning of a person's affection; a person or thing conquered.

conquistador *n* (*pl* **conquistadors, conquistadores**) a member of the Spanish forces that conquered Mexico and Peru in the 16th century.

consanguineous, consanguine *adj* related by blood or birth.—**consanguinity** *n.*

conscience *n* the knowledge of right and wrong that affects action and behaviour; the sense of guilt or virtue induced by actions, behaviour, etc; an inmost thought; conscientiousness.

conscience clause *n* a clause in an act giving relief to persons having religious scruples to some requirement in it.

conscience investment *n* the investment in companies whose activities do not offend the investor's moral principles.—*also* **ethical investment**.

conscience money *n* money paid, usu anonymously, to atone for some dishonest act or illegal monetary gain.

conscience-stricken *adj* feeling extreme guilt or remorse.

conscience-stricken *adj* feeling pangs of guilt.

conscientious *adj* following the dictates of the conscience; scrupulous; careful, thorough.—**conscientiously** *adv.*—**conscientiousness** *n.*

conscientious objector *n* a person who refuses to serve in the military forces on moral or religious grounds.

conscionable *adj* governed by conscience, just.—**conscionably** *adv.*

conscious *adj* aware (of); awake to one's surroundings; (*action*) realized by the person who does it, deliberate.—**consciously** *adv.*

consciousness *n* the state of being conscious; perception; the whole body of a person's thoughts and feelings.

conscript *adj* enrolled into service by compulsion; drafted. * *n* a conscripted person (as a military recruit). * *vt* to enlist compulsorily.

conscription *n* compulsory military or naval service; the persons enrolled.—**conscriptional** *adj.*

consecrate *vt* to set apart as sacred, to sanctify; to devote (to).—**consecration** *n.*—**consecrator** *n.*—**consecratory, consecrative** *adj.*

consecration *n* the act of consecrating; a setting apart or devoting to a sacred use or office; (*with cap*) (*RC Church*) the part of Mass when the bread and wine are blessed.

consecution *n* a following on; a logical sequence.

consecutive *adj* following in regular order without a break; successive; (*gram*) expressing consequence.—**consecutively** *adv.*

consensual *adj* caused by sympathetic action.

consensus *n* an opinion held by all or most; general agreement, esp in opinion.

consent *vi* to agree (to); to comply; to acquiesce * *n* agreement, permission; concurrence.—**consenter** *n.*

consequence *n* a result, an outcome; importance; (*pl*) an unpleasant result of an action; a game in which each player writes part of a story without knowing what has gone before.

consequent *adj* occurring as a result.

consequential *adj* pompous, self–important; resultant.—**consequentiality, consequentialness** *n*.—**consequentially** *adv*.

consequently *adv* as a result, therefore.

conservancy *n* (*pl* **conservancies**) in UK, an authority controlling a river or port; conservation.

conservation *n* the act of conserving; preservation of the environment and natural resources.—**conservational** *adj*.—**conservationist** *n*.

conservation of energy *n* the fact that the amount of energy in a closed system remains the same although its form changes.

conservatism *n* opposition to change; a political ideology favouring preservation and defence of tradition.

conservative *adj* traditional, conventional; cautious; moderate. * *n* a conservative person; (*with cap*) a member of the Conservative Party in Britain and other countries.—**conservatively** *adv*.

conservatoire *n* an institution for instruction in music.

conservator *n* a custodian, a keeper; a preserver; a member of a conservancy.

conservatory *n* (*pl* **conservatories**) a greenhouse attached to a house; a conservatoire.

conserve *vt* to keep from loss or injury; to preserve (a foodstuff) with sugar. * *n* a type of jam using whole fruit.—**conservable** *adj*.—**conserver** *n*.

consider *vti* to reflect (upon), to contemplate; to examine, to weigh the merits of; to take into account; to regard as; to be of the opinion; to act with respect; to allow for.—**considerer** *n*.

considerable *adj* a fairly large amount; worthy of respect.—**considerably** *adv*.

considerate *adj* careful of the feelings of others.—**considerately** *adv*.

consideration *n* the act of considering; deliberation; a point of importance; an inducement; thoughtfulness; deference; a payent.

considered *adj* well thought out.

considering *prep* in view of. * *adv* all in all. * *conj* seeing that.

consign *vt* to hand over, to commit; to send goods addressed (to).—**consignable** *adj*.—**consignation** *n*.

consignee *n* the person to whom goods are consigned.

consignment *n* consigning; goods, etc consigned.

consignor *n* the person by whom goods are consigned.

consist *vi* to be made up (of); to be comprised (of).

consistency *n* (*pl* **consistencies**) degree of density, esp of thick liquids; the state of being consistent.

consistent *adj* compatible, not contradictory; uniform in thought or action.—**consistently** *adv*.

consistory *n* a solemn assembly or the place where it meets; the ecclesiastical court of the pope and cardinals, of an Anglican bishop, or of Presbyterian presbyters.—**consistorial, consistorian** *adj*.

consolation *n* someone or something that offers comfort in distress.—**consolatory** *adj*.

consolation prize *n* a prize for the runner up or loser in a competition.

console[1] *vt* to bring consolation to, to cheer in distress.—**consolable** *adj*.—**consoler** *n*.

console[2] *n* a desk containing the controls of an electronic system; the part of an organ containing the pedals, stops, etc; an ornamental bracket supporting a shelf or table.

consolidate *vti* to solidify; to establish firmly, to strengthen; to combine into a single whole.—**consolidator** *n*.

consolidation *n* the act of consolidating; solidification.

consols *npl* British government securities consolidated into a single stock.

consommé *n* a clear soup made from meat stock.

consonance, consonancy *n* (*pl* **consonance, consonancies**) agreement of sounds; harmony; concord.

consonant *n* a letter of the alphabet that is not a vowel; the sound representing such a letter. * *adj* consistent, in keeping (with).—**consonantal** *adj*.

consort *n* a husband or wife, esp of a reigning queen or king; a ship sailing with another. * *vti* to associate, to keep company with (often dubious companions).—**consorter** *n*.

consortium *n* (*pl* **consortia**) an international banking or financial combination.—**consortial** *adj*.

conspectus *n* a general sketch or digest of some subject, a synopsis.

conspicuous *adj* easily seen, prominent; outstanding, eminent.—**conspicuousness** *n*.—**conspicuously** *adv*.

conspiracy *n* (*pl* **conspiracies**) a secret plan for an illegal act; the act of conspiring.

conspirator *n* one who conspires.—**conspiratorial, conspiratory** *adj*.—**conspiratorially** *adv*.

conspire *vti* to combine secretly for an evil purpose; to plot, to devise.

con spirito *adj, adv* (*mus*) with spirit.

constable *n* in UK, a policeman or policewoman of the lowest rank; a governor of a royal castle.

constabulary *n* (*pl* **constabularies**) in UK, a police force.—*also adj*.

constancy *n* being constant; steadfastness; fidelity.

constant *adj* fixed; unchangeable; unchanging; faithful; firm and steadfast; continual. * *n* (*math, physics*) a quantity that does not vary.

constantly *adv* continually, continuously, often.

constellate *vti* to form into a constellation.

constellation *n* a group of fixed stars; an assembly of the famous.—**constellatory** *adj*.

consternate *vt* to dismay.

consternation *n* surprise and alarm; shock; dismay.

constipate *vt* to cause constipation in.—**constipated** *adj*.

constipation *n* infrequent and difficult movement of the bowels.

constituency *n* (*pl* **constituencies**) a body of electors; the voters in a particular district or area.

constituent *adj* forming part of a whole, component; having the power to revise the constitution. * *n* a component part; a member of an elective body; a voter in a district.

constitute *vt* to set up by authority, to establish; to frame, to form; to appoint; to compose, to make up.—**constituter, constitutor** *n*.

constitution *n* fundamental physical condition; disposition; temperament; structure, composition; the system of basic laws and principles of a government, society, etc; a document stating these specifically.

constitutional *adj* of or pertaining to a constitution; authorized or limited by a constitution, legal; inherent, natural. * a walk for the sake of one's health.—**constitutionally** *adv*.—**constitutionality** *n*.

constitutionalism *n* constitutional government; adherence to constitutional principles.—**constitutionalist** *n*.

constitutive *adj* having the power to enact, constituent; elemental; essential; productive.

constrain *vt* to compel, to force; to hinder by force; to confine, to imprison.—**constrainer** *n*.

constrained *adj* enforced; embarrassed, inhibited; showing constraint.

constraint *n* compulsion; forcible confinement; repression of feeling; embarrassment; a condition that restricts freedom.

constrict *vt* to draw together, to squeeze, to compress.

constricted *adj* narrowed, cramped.

constriction *n* compression; tightness.—**constrictive** *adj*.

constrictor *n* a constrictive muscle; a snake that crushes its prey.

construct *vt* to make, to build, to fit together; to compose. * *n* a structure; an interpretation; an arrangement, esp of words in a sentence.—**constructible** *adj*.—**constructor, constructer** *n*.

construction *n* a constructing; anything constructed; a structure, building; interpretation, meaning; (*gram*) two or more words grouped together to form a phrase, clause or sentence.—**constructional** *adj*.

constructive *adj* helping to improve, promoting development.—**constructively** *adv*.

constructivism *n* nonrepresentational art, esp sculpture based on movement and using machine-made materials.

construe *vti* (**construing, construed**) to translate word for word; to analyse grammatically; to take in a particular sense, to interpret.—**construer** *n*.

consubstantiation *n* the doctrine that the body and blood of Christ are in a mysterious manner substantially present in the Eucharistic elements after Consecration.

consuetude *n* an established custom.—**consuetudinary** *adj*.

consul *n* a government official appointed to live in a foreign city to attend to the interests of his country's citizens and business there.—**consular** *adj*.

consulate *n* the official residence of a consul; the office of a Roman consul.

consult *vti* to seek advice from, esp a doctor or lawyer; to seek information from, eg a work of reference; to deliberate, to confer.—**consulter, consultor** *n*.

consultant *n* a specialist who gives professional or technical advice; a senior physician or surgeon in a hospital; a person who consults another.—**consultancy** *n* (*pl* **consultancies**).

consultation *n* the act of consulting; a conference, esp with a professional adviser.—**consultative, consultatory, consultive** *adj*.

consultative, consultatory *adj* advisory; deliberative.

consumable *adj* able to be consumed. * *n* (*usu pl*) something bought to be used.

consume *vti* to destroy; to use up; to eat or drink up; to waste away; to utilize economic goods.

consumer *n* a person who uses goods and services, the end user.

consumer goods *npl* commodities for domestic consumption which are not used for the production of other goods and services.

consumerism *n* protection of the interests of consumers; encouragement to buy consumer goods.

consumer price index *n* an index of the prices of the food, clothing and housing necessary for life.

consummate[1] *vt* to bring to perfection, to be the crown of; (*marriage*) to complete by sexual intercourse.—**consummation** *n*.—**consummative, consummatory** *adj*.—**consummator** *n*.

consummate[2] *adj* complete, perfect, highly skilled.

consumption *n* the act of consuming; the state of being consumed or used up; (*econ*) expenditure on goods and services by consumers; tuberculosis.

consumptive *adj* tending to consume; affected with consumption. * *n* a person with tuberculosis.

contact *n* touch, touching; connection; an acquaintance, esp one willing to provide help or introductions in business, etc; a connection allowing the passage of electricity; (*med*) a person who has been in contact with a contagious disease.* *vti* to establish contact with.—**contactual** *adj*.

contact lens *n* a thin correctional lens placed over the cornea of the eye.

contagion *n* the communicating of a disease by contact; a disease spread in this way; a corrupting influence.

contagious *adj* (*disease*) spread by contact; capable of spreading disease by contact; (*influence*) catching, infectious.—**contagiousness** *n*.

contain *vt* to hold, to enclose; to comprise, to include; to hold back or restrain within fixed limits.

container *n* a receptacle, etc designed to contain goods or substances; a standardized receptacle used to transport commodities.

containerize *vt* to put or convey (cargo) in large standardized containers.

containment *n* the prevention of the expansion of a hostile power; the prevention of the release of dangerous quantities of radioactive material from a nuclear reactor.

containment building *n* a building enclosing a nuclear reactor to limit the spread of radiation, esp in the event of an accident.

contaminate *vt* to render impure by touch or mixing, to pollute, esp by radioactive contact.—**contaminant** *n*.—**contaminator** *n*.

contamination *n* the act of contaminating; the state of being contaminated; a thing that contaminates.

conte *n* a short story.

contemn *vt* to despise; to disregard scornfully.—**contemner, contemnor** *n*.—**contemnible** *adj*.

contemplate *vti* to look at steadily; to reflect upon, to meditate; to have in view, to intend.—**contemplator** *n*.

contemplation *n* the act of contemplating; pious meditation; intention.

contemplative *adj* thoughtful, meditative, of or given to contemplation; dedicated to religious contemplation.—**contemplatively** *adv*.—**contemplativeness** *n*.

contemporaneous *adj* existing or occurring at the same time; of the same period.—**contemporaneously** *adv*.—**contemporaneity** *n*.

contemporary *adj* living or happening at the same time; of about the same age; present day; of or following present-day trends in style, art, fashion, etc. * *n* (*pl* **contemporaries**) a person living at the same time; a person of the same age.—**contemporarily** *adv*.

contempt *n* the feeling one has towards someone or something considered low, worthless etc; the condition of being despised; disregard.

contemptible *adj* deserving contempt.—**contemptibly** *adv*.—**contemptibility** *n*.

contemptuous *adj* showing or feeling contempt; disdainful.—**contemptuously** *adv.*—**contemptuousness** *n.*

contend *vti* to take part in a contest, to strive (for); to quarrel; to maintain (that), to assert or argue strongly for.—**contender** *n.*

content[1] *n* (*usu pl*) what is in a container; (*usu pl*) what is in a book; substance or meaning.

content[2] *adj* satisfied (with), not desiring more; willing (to); happy; pleased. * *n* quiet satisfaction. * *vt* to make content; to satisfy.—**contentment** *n.*

contented *adj* content; gratified, satisfied.—**contentedly** *adv.*

contention *n* contending, struggling, arguing; a point in dispute; an assertion in an argument.—**contentional** *adj.*

contentious *adj* tending to argue; likely to cause dispute, controversial.—**contentiously** *adv.*

conterminous *adj* having a common boundary (with), contiguous.—*also* **coterminous**.

contest *vti* to call in question, to dispute; to fight to gain, to compete for; to strive. * *n* a struggle, an encounter; a competition; a debate; a dispute.—**contestable** *adj.*—**contestation** *n.*—**contester** *n.*

contestant *n* a competitor in a contest; a person who contests.

context *n* the parts of a written work or speech that precede and follow a word or passage, contributing to its full meaning; associated surroundings, setting.—**contextual** *adj.*—**contextually** *adv.*

contextualize *vt* to place in or treat as part of a context.

contexture *n* a structure; a fabric; a style of composition.—**contextural** *adj.*

contiguous *adj* touching, adjoining; near; adjacent.—**contiguity** *n.*

continent[1] *n* one of the six or seven main divisions of the earth's land; (*with cap*) the mainland of Europe, excluding the British Isles; a large extent of land.

continent[2] *adj* able to control urination and defecation; practising self-restraint; chaste.—**continence, continency** *n.*

continental *adj* of a continent; (*with cap*) of or relating to Europe, excluding the British Isles; of or relating to the former thirteen British colonies later forming the USA. * *n* an inhabitant of the Continent.—**continentalism** *n.*—**continentalist** *n.*—**continentally** *adv.*

continental breakfast *n* a light morning meal of coffee and rolls.

continental drift *n* (*geol*) the (theoretical) gradual process of separation of the continents from their original solid land mass.

continental shelf *n* the sea bed, under relatively shallow seas, bordering a continent.

contingency *n* (*pl* **contingencies**) a possibility of a future event or condition; something dependent on a future event.

contingent *adj* possible, that may happen; chance; dependent (on); incidental (to). * *n* a possibility; a quota of troops.—**contingently** *adv.*

continual *adj* frequently repeated, going on all the time.—**continuality** *n.*—**continually** *adv.*

continuance *n* uninterrupted succession; duration.

continuant *n* a consonant whose sound can be prolonged, as *f, v.*

continuation *n* a continuing; prolongation; resumption; a thing that continues something else, a sequel, a further instalment.

continue *vt* to go on (with); to prolong; to extend; to resume, to carry further. * *vi* to remain, to stay; to last; to preserve.—**continuable** *adj.*—**continuer** *n.*—**continuingly** *adv.*

continuity *n* (*pl* **continuities**) continuousness; uninterrupted succession; the complete script or scenario in a film or broadcast.

continuous *adj* continuing; occurring without interruption.—**continuously** *adv.*—**continuousness** *n.*

continuum *n* (*pl* **continua, continuums**) a continuous and homogeneous whole.

contort *vti* to twist out of a normal shape, to pull awry.—**contorted** *adj.*—**contortion** *n.*—**contortional** *adj.*

contortionist *n* a person who can twist his or her body into unusual postures, esp as entertainment.—**contortionistic** *adj.*

contour *n* the outline of a figure, land, etc; the line representing this outline; a contour line. * *adj* made according to a shape or form (*contour chair*).

contour line *n* a line on a map that passes through all points at the same altitude.

contra *n* a thing that may be argued against.

contra- *prefix* against.

contraband *n* smuggled goods; smuggling. * *adj* illegal to import or export.—**contrabandist** *n.*

contraband of war *n* certain commodities used in warfare; the traffic in them with belligerent states; goods supplied to one belligerent and seizable by another.

contrabass *n* an instrument sounding an octave lower than another instrument of the same class; the largest instrument of the violin class, the double bass.—**contrabassist** *n.*

contrabassoon *n* the largest instrument of the oboe class.—**contrabassoonist** *n.*

contraception *n* the deliberate prevention of conception, birth control.

contraceptive *n* a contraceptive drug or device.—*also* *adj.*

contract *vt* to draw closer together; to confine; to undertake by contract; (*debt*) to incur; (*disease*) to become infected by; (*word*) to shorten by omitting letters. * *vi* to shrink; to become smaller or narrower; to make a contract; (*with* out) to decide not to take part in or join, eg a pension scheme. * *n* a bargain; an agreement to supply goods or perform work at a stated price; a written agreement enforceable by law.—**contractibility** *n.*—**contractible** *adj.*

contract bridge *n* a form of bridge in which the players contract to take a certain number of tricks.

contractile *adj* able or causing to grow smaller.—**contractility** *n.*

contraction *n* the act of contracting; the state of being contracted; a contracted word; a labour pain in childbirth.—**contractional** *adj.*—**contractive** *adj.*

contractor *n* a person who makes a business contract, esp a builder; something that draws together, eg a muscle.

contractual *adj* of a contract.—**contractually** *adv.*

contradance *see* **contredanse**.

contradict *vti* to assert the contrary or opposite of; to deny; to be at variance (with); to lack consistency.—**contradictable** *adj.*—**contradicter, contradictor** *n.*

contradiction *n* the act of contradicting; a denial.—**contradictory** *adj.*

contradistinction *n* a distinction by opposite qualities.—**contradistinctive** *adj.*

contradistinguish *vt* to mark the difference between two things by contrasting their opposite qualities.

contralto *n* (*pl* **contraltos**) a singing voice having a range between tenor and mezzo-soprano; a person having this voice.

contraposition *n* opposition, antithesis.

contraption *n* (*inf*) a device, a gadget.

contrapuntal *adj* of or according to counterpoint.—**contrapuntally** *adv*.

contrapuntist *n* one skilled in the rules of counterpoint.

contrariety *n* (*pl* **contrarieties**) opposition; inconsistency, discrepancy.

contrariwise *adv* on the other hand; conversely.

contrary *adj* opposed; opposite in nature; wayward, perverse. * *n* (*pl* **contraries**) the opposite. * *adv* in opposition to; in conflict with.—**contrarily** *adv*.—**contrariness** *n*.

contrast *vi* to show marked differences. * *vt* to compare so as to point out the differences. * *n* the exhibition of differences; difference of qualities shown by comparison; the degree of difference between colours or tones when put together.

contravene *vt* to infringe (a law), to transgress; to conflict with, to contradict.—**contravener** *n*.—**contravention** *n*.

contredanse *n* a dance in which the partners are arranged in opposite lines; the music for this.—*also* **contradance**.

contretemps *n* (*pl* **contretemps**) a confusing, embarrassing or awkward occurrence.

contribute *vti* to give to a common stock or fund; to write (an article) for a magazine or newspaper; to furnish ideas, etc.—**contributive** *adj*.

contribution *n* the act of contributing; something contributed; a literary article; a payment into a collection.

contributor *n* a person who contributes, esp the writer of an article for a newspaper, etc; a factor, a contributory cause.—**contributorial** *adj*.

contributory *adj* giving, donating; partly responsible, sharing in.

con trick *n* (*inf*) confidence trick.

contrite *adj* deeply repentant, feeling guilt.—**contritely** *adv*.—**contrition** *n*.

contrivance *n* something contrived, esp a mechanical device, invention; inventive ability; an artificial construct; a stratagem.

contrive *vt* to plan ingeniously; to devise, to design, to manage; to achieve, esp by some ploy or trick; to scheme.—**contriver** *n*.

contrived *adj* skilful but overdone; (*writing*) not spontaneous or natural or flowing.

control *n* restraint; command, authority; a check; a means of controlling; a standard of comparison for checking an experiment; (*pl*) mechanical parts by which a car, aeroplane, etc is operated. * *vt* (**controlling, controlled**) to check; to restrain; to regulate; to govern; (*experiment*) to verify by comparison.

controllable *adj* able to be controlled.—**controllably** *adv*.

controller *n* a person who controls, esp one in charge of expenditure or finances.

control tower *n* a tower at an airport from which flight directions are given.

controversial *adj* causing controversy, open to argument.—**controversialism** *n*.—**controversialist** *n*.—**controversially** *adv*.

controversy *n* (*pl* **controversies**) a discussion of contrary opinions; dispute, argument.

controvert *vt* to contend against; to refute; to disprove.—**controverter** *n*.—**controvertible** *adj*.

contumacious *adj* resisting authority, insubordinate; obstinate.

contumacy *n* (*pl* **contumacies**) stubborn resistance to authority, esp contempt of court.—**contumacious** *adj*.

contumelious *adj* haughtily contemptuous or offensive; supercilious.

contumely *n* (*pl* **contumelies**) haughty and contemptuous rudeness; scornful and insolent abuse; reproach, disgrace.

contuse *vt* to wound or bruise without breaking the skin.—**contusive** *adj*.

contusion *n* a wound that does not break the skin, a bruise.—**contusioned** *adj*.

conundrum *n* a riddle involving a pun; a puzzling question.

conurbation *n* a vast urban area around and including a large city.

convalesce *vi* to recover health and strength after an illness; to get better.—**convalescence** *n*.

convalescent *adj* recovering health; aiding the recovery of full health. * *n* a patient recovering after an illness.

convection *n* the transmission of heat through a liquid by currents; the process whereby warmer air rises while cooler air drops.—**convectional** *adj*.—**convective** *adj*.

convector *n* a heater that circulates warm air.

convene *vti* to call together for a meeting.—**convenable** *adj*.—**convener** *n*.

convenience *n* what suits one; a useful appliance.

convenience food *n* food that is easily and quickly prepared.

convenient *adj* handy; suitable; causing little or no trouble.—**conveniently** *adv*.

convent *n* a house of a religious order, esp an establishment of nuns.

conventicle *n* a meeting house; a secret meeting; an assembly for worship, usu by a schism; (*formerly*) a prohibited meeting of Nonconformists or Covenanters.

convention *n* a political or ecclesiastical assembly or meeting; an agreement between nations, a treaty; established usage, social custom.

conventional *adj* of or based on convention or social custom; not spontaneous; lacking imagination or originality; following accepted rules; (*weapons*) non-nuclear.—**conventionality** *n* (*pl* **conventionalities**).—**conventionally** *adj*.

conventionalism *n* that which is received as established by usage, etc; adherence to established usage.—**conventionalist** *n*.

conventionalize *vt* to make conventional.—**conventionalization** *n*.

conventual *adj* belonging to a convent. * *n* a member or inmate of a convent.

converge *vti* to come or bring together.—**convergence, convergency** *n*.—**convergent** *adj*.

conversable *adj* disposed to converse, sociable.

conversant *adj* well acquainted; proficient; familiar (with).—**conversance, conversancy** *n*.

conversation *n* informal talk or exchange of ideas, opinions, etc between people.—**conversational** *adj*.—**conversationally** *adv*.

conversationalist, conversationist *n* a person who is good at conversation.

conversation piece *n* originally an 18th-century picture showing a group in an outdoor or indoor setting; something unusual or novel that provokes conversation; a play that focuses interest on dialogue as much as on action.

conversazione *n* (*pl* **conversazioni, conversaziones**) a meeting for conversation, esp on literary or scientific topics.

converse[1] *vi* to engage in conversation (with). * *n* familiar talk, conversation.—**converser** *n*.

converse[2] *adj* opposite, contrary. * *n* something that is opposite or contrary.—**conversely** *adv*.

conversion *n* change from one state, or from one religion, to another; something converted from one use to another; an alteration to a building undergoing a change in function; (*rugby*) a score after a try by kicking the ball over the crossbar.—**conversional, conversionary** *adj*.

convert *vt* to change from one thing, condition or religion to another; to alter; to apply to a different use; (*rugby*) to make a conversion after a try. * *n* a converted person, esp one who has changed religion.

converter, convertor *n* one who converts; an iron retort used for converting pig iron into steel in the Bessemer process; a kind of electrical induction coil.

converter reactor *n* a nuclear reactor that changes fertile material to fissile material.

convertible *adj* able to be converted. * *n* an automobile with a folding or detachable roof.—**convertibility** *n*.

convex *adj* curving outward like the surface of a sphere.—**convexly** *adv*.—**convexity** *n*.

convexo-concave *adj* convex on one side, concave on the other.

convexo-convex *adj* curving outwards on both sides, as a lens.

convey *vt* to transport; to conduct, to transmit; to make known, to communicate; (*law*) to make over (property).—**conveyable** *adj*.—**conveyor, conveyer** *n*.

conveyance *n* the act of conveying; a means of transporting, a vehicle; (*law*) the act of transferring property.—**conveyancer** *n*.

conveyancing *n* the business of drawing up deeds, leases, etc, and investigating titles to property.

conveyor belt *n* a continuous moving belt or linked plates for moving objects in a factory.

convict *vt* to prove or pronounce guilty. * *n* a convicted person serving a prison sentence.

conviction *n* act of convicting; a settled opinion; a firm belief.

convince *vt* to persuade by argument or evidence; to satisfy by proof.—**convincer** *n*.—**convincible** *adj*.

convincing *adj* compelling belief.—**convincingly** *adv*.

convivial *adj* sociable, jovial.—**conviviality** *n*.—**convivially** *adv*.

convocation *n* the act of convoking an assembly, esp of bishops, clergy or heads of a university; an assembly of clergy.—**convocational** *adj*.—**convocator** *n*.

convoke to call or summon together; to convene.—**convoker** *n*.

convolute *vt* to form into a rolled or coiled shape. * *adj* (*bot*) rolled upon itself; coiled.

convoluted *adj* twisted; coiled; complicated, difficult to understand.

convolution *n* a rolling together, a coiling; a fold, a twist; a complicated or confused matter.

convolve *vt* to roll together.

convolvulus *n* (*pl* **convolvuluses, convolvuli**) a twin-ing plant with bell-shaped flowers.

convoy *n* a group of ships or vehicles travelling together for protection. * *vt* to travel thus.

convulse *vt* to agitate violently; to shake with irregular spasms. * *vi* (*inf*) to cause to shake with uncontrollable laughter.—**convulsive** *adj*.—**convulsively** *adv*.

convulsion *n* a violent involuntary contraction of a muscle or muscles; an agitation, tumult; (*pl*) a violent fit of laughter.

cony, coney *n* (*pl* **conies, coneys**) rabbit, or the skin or fur of a rabbit used in making clothes.

coo *n* the note of the pigeon; a soft murmuring sound. * *vt* (**cooing, cooed**) to utter the cry of a dove or pigeon; to speak softly; to act or murmur in a loving manner.

cook *vt* to prepare (food) by heat; (*inf*) to fake (accounts, etc); to subject to great heat. * *vi* to be a cook; to undergo cooking; (*with* **up**) to plot; to make up a story. * *n* a person who cooks; one whose job is to cook.—**cookable** *adj*.

cookbook, cookery book *n* a book of recipes and other information for preparing food.

cook-chill *n* (*catering*) a method in which meals are precooked, chilled rapidly and then reheated as required.

cooker *n* an electric or gas appliance for cooking.

cookery *n* the art or practice of cooking.

cookhouse *n* a kitchen, esp outdoors.

cookie, cooky *n* (*pl* **cookies**) a small flat sweet cake; (*sl*) a person.

cookout *n* a meal cooked and eaten outdoors, a barbecue.

cool *adj* moderately cold; calm; indifferent; unenthusiastic; cheeky. * *vti* to make or become cool. * *n* coolness; composure.—**coolly** *adv*.—**coolness** *n*.

coolant *n* a fluid or other substance for cooling machinery.

cooler *n* that which cools; a vessel for cooling liquids, etc; a drink of spirits; (*sl*) prison.

cool-headed *adj* not easily excited.

coolie, cooly *n* (*pl* **coolies**) an Indian or Chinese hired labourer.

cooling tower *n* a tall hollow construction used in some industries, in which water is cooled and reused.

coon *n* a raccoon; (*derog*) a black person.

cooncan *n* a card game for two.

coop *n* a small pen for poultry. * *vt* to confine as in a coop.

co-op *n* a cooperative.

cooper *n* one who makes and repairs barrels, etc.

cooperage *n* the business or workshop of a cooper; the price for a cooper's work.

cooperate *vi* to work together, to act jointly.—**cooperation** *n*.—**cooperator** *n*.

cooperative *adj* willing to cooperate; helpful. * *n* an organization or enterprise owned by, and operated for the benefit of, those using its services.—**cooperatively** *adv*.

co-opt *vt* to elect or choose as a member by the agreement of the existing members.—**co-optation, co-option** *n*.—**co-optative, co-optive** *adj*.

coordinate *vt* to integrate (different elements, etc) into an efficient relationship; to adjust to; to function harmoniously. * *n* an equal person or thing; any of a series of numbers that, in a given frame of reference, locate a point in space; (*pl*) separate items of clothing intended to be worn together. * *adj* equal in degree or status.—**coordinately** adv.—**coordinator** n.

coordination n the act of coordinating; the state of being coordinated; balanced and harmonious movement of the body.

coot n a European water-bird with dark plumage and a white spot on the forehead; a silly person.

cootie n (sl) a louse.

cop[1] vb (**copping, copped**) vt (sl) to arrest, catch. * vi (with out) (sl) to fail to perform, to renege. * n (sl) capture; a policeman.

cop[2] n a conical ball of thread on a spindle.

copaiba n an aromatic resinous balsam from various South American and West Indian trees.

copal n a gum resin used in varnishes.

coparcenary n joint heirship.

coparcener n a coheir.

copartner n a joint partner.—**copartnership** n.

cope[1] vi to deal successfully with; to contend on even terms (with).

cope[2] n a large semicircular ecclesiastical vestment worn by bishops and priests over the surplice; a canopy, esp of heaven.

Copernican adj of or relating to Copernicus and his teaching that the earth and planets revolve around the sun.

copestone n the top stone of a structure; a crowning touch.

copier n a copying machine, a photocopier.

copilot n a second pilot in an aircraft.

coping n the top masonry of a wall.

coping saw n a saw with a U-shaped frame and narrow blade used for cutting outlines in wood.

copious adj plentiful, abundant.—**copiously** adv.—**copiousness** n.

cop-out n (sl) an evasion; a means of avoiding responsibility.

copper[1] n a reddish ductile metallic element; a bronze coin. * adj made of, or of the colour of, copper. * vt to cover with copper.—**coppery** adj.

copper[2] n (sl) a police officer.

copper-bottomed adj to be trusted; financially sound.

copperhead n a South American snake.

copperplate n a polished plate of copper for engraving or printing; a print from this; copybook writing.

coppersmith n a worker in copper.

copra n the dried kernel of the coconut after the oil has been removed.

copro- prefix dung.

coprolite n fossil dung.—**coprolitic** adj.

coprophagous adj feeding on dung, as certain beetles.—**coprophagy** n.

coprophilia n an abnormal interest in faeces; love of obscenity.

coprophilous adj growing in dung.

copse n a thicket of small trees and shrubs.

Copt n a native Egyptian Christian.

copter n a helicopter.

Coptic adj pertaining to the Copts, their church or their language. * n the language spoken by Copts.

copula n (pl **copulas, copulae**) a link, a connecting part; (gram) a word that joins the subject and predicate in a sentence or proposition.—**copular** adj.

copulate vi to have sexual intercourse.—**copulation** n.—**copulatory** adj.

copulative adj joining, uniting; (gram) serving as a copula; uniting ideas as well as words. * n a copulative conjunction.

copy n (pl **copies**) a reproduction; a transcript; a single specimen of a book; a model to be copied; a manuscript for printing; newspaper text; text for an advertisement; subject matter for a writer. * vt (**copying, copied**) to make a copy of, to reproduce; to take as a model, to imitate.

copybook n a book of handwriting exercises.

copy-edit vt to correct and prepare text for printing.

copyhold n (English law) a tenure of estate by copy of the court roll or custom of the manor.

copyholder n a tenant by copyhold; (print) a reader's assistant.

copyist n one who copies.

copyright n the exclusive legal right to the publication and sale of a literary, dramatic, musical, or artistic work in any form. * adj protected by copyright.

copywriter n a writer of advertising or publicity copy.—**copywriting** n.

coq au vin n a dish of chicken cooked in wine.

coquet vi (**coquetting, coquetted**) to flirt with; to seek to attract attention or admiration; to trifle.

coquetry n (pl **coquetries**) the act of coquetting; flirtatious behaviour.

coquette n a woman who trifles with men's affections.—**coquettish** adj.

coquito n (pl **coquitos**) a tall Chilean palm producing edible nuts and palm honey.

coracle n a boat with a wicker frame covered with leather.

coracoid n a hook-like process of the scapula or bladebone.

coral n the hard skeleton secreted by certain marine polyps. * adj made of coral, esp jewellery; of the colour of coral, deepish pink.

coralline, coralloid adj consisting of, or like, coral; of a colour like coral. * n a coral-like seaweed or animal.

coral reef n a formation or bank of coral.

coral tree n an American tree with blood-red flowers.

corban n an offering to God in fulfilment of a vow.

corbeil n (archit) a sculptured basket of flowers, fruit, etc.

corbel n a stone or timber projection from a wall to support something. * vt (**corbelling, corbelled** or **corbeling, corbeled**) to furnish with or support by corbel.

corbicula n (pl **corbiculae**) the receptacle for pollen in the honey bee.

cord n a thick string or thin rope; something that binds; a slender electric cable; a ribbed fabric, esp corduroy; (pl) corduroy trousers; any part of the body resembling string or rope (spinal cord).

cordage n a quantity of cores or ropes; ropes and rigging collectively.

cordate adj heart-shaped.

cordial adj hearty, warm; friendly; affectionate. * n a fruit-flavoured drink.—**cordially** adv.—**cordialness** n.

cordiality n (pl **cordialities**) sincere sympathetic geniality; sincerity; heartiness.

cordiform adj heart-shaped.

cordillera n a continuous ridge or chain of mountains, esp of the Andes mountains.

cordite n an explosive used in bullets and shells.

cordless adj (electrical device) operated by a battery.

cordon n a chain of police or soldiers preventing access to an area; a piece of ornamental cord or ribbon given as an award. * vt (with off) (area) to prevent access to.

cordon bleu *n* the highest distinction in any profession; a first-class cook.—*also adj.*

cordon sanitaire *n* a barrier around an infected area; a buffer zone.

cordovan *n* a Spanish leather made of goatskin or split horsehide, tanned and dressed.—*also* **cordwain**.

cords *npl* (*inf*) corduroy trousers.

corduroy *n* a strong cotton fabric with a velvety ribbed surface; (*pl*) trousers of this.

corduroy road *n* a roadway formed of logs laid crosswise across swampy ground, etc.

cordwain *see* **cordovan**.

cordwainer *n* (*arch*) a worker in leather; a shoemaker.

core *n* the innermost part, the heart; the inner part of an apple, etc containing seeds; the region of a nuclear reactor containing the fissile material; (*comput*) a form of magnetic memory used to store one bit of information. * *vt* to remove the core from.—**corer** *n*.

coreopsis *n* a kind of plant with rayed flowers and seeds with two small horns at the end.

corespondent *n* (*law*) a person named as having committed adultery with the husband or wife from whom a divorce is sought.—**corespondency** *n*.

corgi *n* (*pl* **corgis**) a Welsh breed of dog with short legs and a sturdy body.

coriaceous *adj* of leather; leathery.

coriander *n* a plant with aromatic seeds used for flavouring food.

Corinthian *adj* of or pertaining to Corinth, a Greek city noted for its luxury and licentiousness; luxurious; conducted by amateurs; (*archit*) denoting the Corinthian order. * *n* a man about town; a gentleman yachtsman or sportsman.

Corinthian order *n* the lightest and most ornate of the classic orders of architecture, with a bell-shaped capital and ornamented with acanthus leaves.

corium *n* (*pl* **coria**) the innermost layer of skin of the cuticle.

cork *n* the outer bark of the cork oak used esp for stoppers and insulation; a stopper for a bottle, esp made of cork. * *adj* made of cork. * *vt* to stop up with a cork; to give a taste of cork to (wine).

corkage *n* a charge made by a restaurant for serving wine, esp when brought in by the customer from outside.

corked *adj* (*wine*) contaminated by a decayed cork.

corker *n* (*sl*) something conclusive or superlatively good; a flagrant lie.

corkscrew *n* a tool for drawing corks from wine bottles. * *adj* spiral-shaped, resembling a corkscrew.

corky *adj* made of, or like, cork.

corm *n* the bulb-like underground stem of the crocus, etc; a solid bulb.—**cormous** *adj.*

cormel *n* a new corm developing from a mature one.

cormorant *n* a large voracious sea bird with dark plumage and webbed feet.

corn[1] *n* a grain or seed of a cereal plant; plants that yield grain; maize; (*sl*) something corny.

corn[2] *n* a small hard painful growth on the foot.

corn[3] *vt* to preserve or cure, as with salt.

corn(ed) beef *n* cooked salted beef.

corn circle *see* **crop circle**.

corncob *n* the central part of an ear of maize to which the corn kernels are attached; a corncob pipe.

corncockle *n* a plant with purplish flowers that grows among corn.

corncrake *n* a bird with a harsh cry, the landrail.

corncrib *n* a storehouse for corn.

cornea *n* (*pl* **corneas, corneae**) the transparent membrane in front of the eyeball.—**corneal** *adj.*

cornel *n* the cornelian cherry or dogwood, yielding an acrid edible red berry.

cornelian *n* a dull-red semi-transparent form of chalcedony.—*also* **carnelian**.

corneous *adj* horny.

corner *n* the point where sides or streets meet; an angle; a secret or confined place; a difficult or dangerous situation; (*football, hockey*) a free kick from the corner of the pitch; a monopoly over the supply of a good or service giving control over the market price; one of the opposite angles in a boxing ring. * *vt* to force into a corner; to monopolize supplies of (a commodity). * *vi* to turn round a corner; to meet at a corner or angle.

cornerstone *n* the principal stone, esp one at the corner of a foundation; an indispensable part; the most important thing or person.

cornet *n* a tapering valved brass musical instrument; a cone-shaped wafer for ice cream.

cornetist, cornettist *n* a performer on the cornet.

cornfield *n* a field planted with corn or other cereal plants.

cornflakes *npl* a breakfast cereal made from split and toasted maize.

cornflour *n* a type of corn or maize flour used for thickening sauces.—*also* **cornstarch**.

cornflower *n* a blue-flowered wild plant growing in cornfields.

cornice *n* a plaster moulding round a ceiling or on the outside of a building.

corniche *n* a coastal road, esp one along a cliff offering spectacular views.

corniculate *adj* horned; spurred.

Corn Laws *npl* British laws (1436–1834) for regulating the import and export of corn, repealed 1846–9.

corn pone *n* a type of Indian cornbread made with milk and eggs.

cornstalk *n* a stem of corn; (*sl*) a youth or girl of Australian birth.

cornstarch *see* **cornflour**.

cornucopia *n* a horn-shaped container overflowing with fruits, flowers, etc; great abundance, an inexhaustible store.

cornute, cornuted *adj* (*biol*) horned; horn-like.

corny *adj* (**cornier, corniest**) (*inf*) hackneyed; banal; trite; overly sentimental.—**cornily** *adv.*—**corniness** *n.*

corolla *n* the inner envelope of a flower composed of two or more petals.

corollary *n* (*pl* **corollaries**) an additional inference from a proposition already proved; a result.

corona *n* (*pl* **coronas, coronae**) a top; a crown; a luminous halo or envelope round the sun or moon; the flat projecting part of a cornice.

coronal *adj* pertaining to the corona. * *n* a crown or garland.

coronary *adj* pertaining to the arteries supplying blood to the heart. * *n* (*pl* **coronaries**) a coronary artery; coronary thrombosis.

coronary thrombosis *n* blockage of one of the coronary arteries by a blood clot.

coronation *n* the act or ceremony of crowning a sovereign.

coroner *n* a public official who inquires into the causes of sudden or accidental deaths.—**coronership** *n.*

coronet *n* a small crown; an ornamental headdress.

corpora *see* corpus.

corporal[1] *n* a noncommissioned officer below the rank of sergeant.—**corporalship** *n*.

corporal[2] *adj* of or relating to the body; physical, not spiritual.—**corporality** *n*.—**corporally** *adv*.

corporal[3] *n* a communion cloth.

corporate *adj* legally united into a body; of or having a corporation; united.—**corporately** *adv*.

corporation *n* a group of people authorized by law to act as one individual; a city or town council.—**corporative** *n*.

corporator *n* a member of a corporation.

corporeal *adj* having a body or substance, material.—**corporeality, corporealness** *n*.—**corporeally** *adv*.

corposant *n* a flame-like electric discharge from a ship's mast and rigging in thundery weather, St Elmo's fire.

corps *n* (*pl* corps) an organized subdivision of the military establishment; a group or organization with a special function (*medical corps*).

corps de ballet *n* all the dancers in a ballet company.

corps diplomatique *n* all the ambassadors at a particular capital, the diplomatic corps.

corpse *n* a dead body. * *vi* (*theat sl*) to laugh or create laughter mischievously on stage.

corpulent *adj* fleshy, fat.—**corpulence, corpulency** *n*.

corpus *n* (*pl* corpora) a body or collection, esp of written works; the chief part of an organ.

Corpus Christi *n* (*RC Church*) a festival in honour of the Eucharist, held on the Thursday after Trinity Sunday.

corpuscle *n* a red or white blood cell.—**corpuscular** *adj*.

corpus delicti *n* (*law*) the essence of a crime charged.

corral *n* a pen for livestock; an enclosure with wagons; a strong stockade. * *vt* (**corralling, corralled**) to form a corral; to put or keep in a corral.

correct *vt* to set right, to remove errors from; to reprove, to punish; to counteract, to neutralize; to adjust. * *adj* free from error; right, true, accurate; conforming to a fixed standard; proper.—**correctable, correctible** *adj*.—**correctly** *adv*.—**correctness** *n*.—**corrector** *n*.

correction *n* the act of correcting; punishment.—**correctional** *adj*.

correctitude *n* correctness, esp of conduct.

corrective *adj* serving to correct or counteract. * *n* that which corrects.—**correctively** *adv*.

correlate *vti* to have or to bring into mutual relation; to correspond to one another. * *n* either of two things so related that one implies the other.—**correlation** *n*.—**correlative** *adj*.

correlation *n* reciprocal relation; similarity or parallelism of relation or law; the interdependence of functions, organs, natural forces, or phenomena.—**correlational** *adj*.

correlative *adj* having or expressing reciprocal or mutual relation. * *n* the antecedent to a pronoun.—**correlativeness, correlativity** *n*.

correspond *vi* to answer, to agree; to be similar (to); to tally; to communicate by letter.

correspondence *n* communication by writing letters; the letters themselves; agreement.

correspondence school *n* an institution offering tuition (**correspondence courses**) by post.

correspondent *n* a person who writes letters; a journalist who gathers news for newspapers, radio or television from a foreign country. * *adj* similar, analogous.

corridor *n* a long passage into which compartments in a train or rooms in a building open; a strip of land giving a country without a coastline access to the sea.

corrie *n* (*Scot*) a round hollow on a hillside.

corrigendum *n* (*pl* corrigenda) an error in a book, etc, for which a correction slip is printed.

corrigible *adj* capable of being amended, correct, or reformed.—**corrigibility** *n*.

corroborant *adj* corroborating. * *n* a corroborating fact.

corroborate *vt* to confirm; to make more certain; to verify.—**corroboration** *n*.—**corroborative** *adj*.—**corroborator** *n*.

corroboree *n* an Australian festivity and dance.

corrode *vti* to eat into or wear away gradually, to rust; to disintegrate.—**corrodant, corrodent** *n*.—**corroder** *n*.—**corrodible** *adj*.—**corrosion** *n*.

corrosion *n* the act of corroding; a corroded condition.

corrosive *adj* causing corrosion. * *n* a corrosive substance, as acid.—**corrosively** *adv*.—**corrosiveness** *n*.

corrosive sublimate *n* a poisonous compound of mercury.

corrugate *vt* to form into parallel ridges and grooves.—**corrugated** *adj*.—**corrugation** *n*.

corrugated iron *n* sheet iron pressed in alternate parallel ridges and grooves and galvanized.

corrugated paper *n* paper used for packaging with one surface in parallel ridges.

corrupt *adj* dishonest; taking bribes; depraved; rotten, putrid. * *vti* to make or become corrupt; to infect; to taint.—**corrupter, corruptor** *n*.—**corruptive** *adj*.—**corruptly** *adv*.—**corruptness** *n*.

corruptible *adj* open to corruption.—**corruptibility** *n*.

corruption *n* the act of corrupting; the state of being corrupted; physical dissolution.—**corruptionist** *n*.

corsage *n* a small bunch of flowers for pinning to a dress; the part of a woman's dress covering the bust.

corsair *n* a pirate; a pirate ship.

corse *n* (*poet*) a corpse.

corselet, corslet *n* light body armour, esp for the breast.

corset *n* a close-fitting undergarment, worn to support the torso.

corsetière *n* a woman who makes and fits corsets.—**corsetier** *nm*.

cortege, cortège *n* a train of attendants; a retinue; a funeral procession.

Cortes *n* the national and legislative assembly of Spain and (formerly) Portugal.

cortex *n* (*pl* cortices) an outer layer of tissue of any organ, eg the outer grey matter of the brain; the outer tissue of a plant stem; bark of a tree.—**cortical** *adj*.

corticate, corticated *adj* covered with bark or a bark-like substance.—**cortication** *n*.

cortisone *n* a hormone produced by the adrenal glands, the synthetic version of which is used to treat arthritis, allergies and skin disorders, etc.

corundum *n* a hard mineral of many colours used as an abrasive and as gemstones.

coruscate *vi* to sparkle, to flash.—**coruscation** *n*.

corvée *n* the exacting of unpaid labour in the feudal system.

corves *see* corf.

corvette *n* a fast escort warship.

corvine *adj* of or pertaining to a crow or raven.

corymb *n* an inflorescence with the flowers all nearly at the same level and the lower stalks are the longest.—**corymbose, corybous** *adj*.

coryphaeus *n* (*pl* coryphaei) the leader of the chorus in ancient Greek drama.

coryphée *n* a ballet dancer.

coryza *n* a severe cold in the head with inflammation of the mucous membrane of the nose.

cos *abbr* = cosine.

cosec *abbr* = cosecant.

cosecant *n* (*geom*) the secant of the complement of the given angle or arc of 90°.

coseismal, coseismic *adj* showing simultaneous shocks of an earthquake.

cosh *vt* (*sl*) to bludgeon.

cosher *vt* to pamper, to coddle.

cosignatory *n* a person signing along with another.

cosine *n* a trigonometrical function of an angle that in a right-angled triangle is equal to the ratio of the length of the adjacent side to the hypotenuse.

cosmetic *n* a preparation for improving the beauty, esp of the face. * *adj* beautifying or correcting faults in the appearance.—**cosmetically** *adv*.

cosmetic surgery *n* surgery carried out to improve the appearance.

cosmic, cosmical *adj* of or pertaining to the universe and the laws that govern it; vast in extent, intensity, or comprehensiveness.—**cosmically** *adv*.

cosmo- *prefix* universe.

cosmogony *n* (*pl* **cosmogonies**) the origin of the universe; a theory or treatise on this.—**cosmogonal** *adj*.—**cosmogonic, cosmogonical** *adj*.—**cosmogonist** *n*.

cosmography *n* the description and mapping of the universe or the earth as a whole.—**cosmographer, cosmographist** *n*.—**cosmographic, cosmographical** *adj*.

cosmology *n* the science of the nature, origins, and development of the universe.—**cosmological, cosmologic** *adj*.—**cosmologist** *n*.

cosmonaut *n* a Russian astronaut.

cosmopolitan *adj* of all parts of the world; free from national prejudice; at home in any part of the world. * *n* a well-travelled person; a person without national prejudices.—**cosmopolitanism** *n*.

cosmopolite *n* a citizen of the world, a person without patriotism; an animal or plant found worldwide.—**cosmopolitism** *n*.

cosmos *n* the universe as an ordered whole; any orderly system.

Cossack *n* a member of a Russian people skilled as horsemen. * *adj* pertaining to Cossacks.

cosset *vt* to make a pet of; to pamper.

cost *vt* (**costing, cost**) to involve the payment, loss, or sacrifice of; to have as a price; to estimate and fix the price of. * *n* a price; an expense; expenditure of time, labour, etc; a loss, a penalty; (*pl*) the expenses of a lawsuit.

costa *n* (*pl* **costae**) a rib.—**costal** *adj*.

costard *n* a large kind of English apple; (*arch*) a head.

costate *adj* ribbed.

cost-effective *adj* giving a satisfactory return for the amount spent on outlay.

costive *adj* constipated.

costly *adj* (**costlier, costliest**) expensive; involving great sacrifice.—**costliness** *n*.

costmary *n* (*pl* **costmaries**) a perennial plant with fragrant leaves, formerly used for flavouring ale.

cost-of-living index *n* consumer price index.

costume *n* a style of dress, esp belonging to a particular period, fashion, etc; clothes of an unusual or historical nature, as worn by actors in a play, etc; fancy dress.

costume jewellery *n* imitation gems or cheap jewellery worn for decorative effect.

costumer, costumier *n* a dealer in fancy dress for the theatre, etc.

cosy *adj* (**cosier, cosiest**) warm and comfortable; snug; friendly for an ulterior motive. * *n* a cover to keep a thing warm.—*also* **cozy**.—**cosily** *adv*.—**cosiness** *n*.

cot[1] *n* a child's box-like bed; a narrow collapsible bed.

cot[2] *abbr* = cotangent.

cotangent *n* a trigonometrical function of an angle that in a right-angled triangle is equal to the ratio of the length of the adjacent side to the opposite side.

cot death *n* the sudden death of a baby during sleep from an unexplained cause.—*also* **crib death**.

cote *n* a shed or shelter for animals or birds, esp doves.

cotenant *n* a joint tenant.—**cotenancy** *n*.

coterie *n* a small circle of people with common interests; a social clique.

coterminous *see* **conterminous**.

cotidal *adj* (*chart lines*) joining those places where high tide occurs at the same time.

cotillion *n* a brisk, lively dance for eight or more people; music for such a dance; a formal ball.

cotoneaster *n* an ornamental shrub of the rose family with red or orange berries.

cotta *n* (*pl* **cottae, cottas**) a short surplice.

cottage *n* a small house, esp in the country.

cottage cheese *n* a soft cheese made from loose milk curds.

cottage industry *n* manufacture carried out in the home, eg weaving, basketry.

cottager *n* a person who lives or holidays in a cottage.

cotter[1], **cottar** *n* a farm labourer who has the use of a cottage for which he works in lieu of rent.

cotter[2] *n* a bolt, wedge, etc used to secure parts of machinery to prevent movement.

cotter pin *n* a split pin that secures (a cotter, etc) by spreading the ends after insertion.

cotton *n* soft white fibre of the cotton plant; fabric or thread made of this; thread. * *adj* made of cotton. * *vi* (*with* **on**) (*inf*) to realize the meaning of, to understand; to take a liking to.—**cottony** *adj*.

cotton candy *see* **candyfloss**.

cotton grass *n* a plant with long silky hairs.

cottontail *n* an American rabbit.

cotton wool *n* raw cotton that has been bleached and sterilized for use as a dressing, etc; absorbent cotton; a state of being protected.

cotyledon *n* a seed lobe or rudimentary leaf or leaves of an embryo; kinds of plant, chiefly evergreens.—**cotyledonal** *adj*.—**cotyledonary** *adj*.—**cotyledonous, cotyledonoid** *adj*.

cotyloid, cotyloidal *adj* cup-shaped.

couch *n* a piece of furniture, with a back and armrests, for seating several persons; a bed, esp as used by psychiatrists for patients. * *vt* to express in words in a particular way; to lie down; to deposit in a bed or layer; (*arch*) to crouch ready for springing; to depress or remove (a cataract in the eye).—**coucher** *n*.

couchant *adj* (*her*) lying down with the head up.

couch grass *n* a kind of coarse grass that spreads rapidly.

couching *n* the operation of removing a cataract from the eye by depressing or removing the crystalline lens; a style of embroidery.

couch potato *n* (*sl*) a person who would rather watch television in leisure time than participate in sports, etc.

cougar *n* a puma.

cough *vi* to expel air from the lungs with a sudden effort and noise; (*with* **up**) (*inf*) to hand over or tell unwillingly. * *n* the act of coughing; a disease causing a cough.

cough drop *n* a lozenge that when sucked relieves a cough.

cough syrup *n* a medicinal liquid to relieve coughing.

could *see* **can**[1].

couldn't = could not.

coulee *n* a dry ravine with sloping sides; a flow of lava.

coulisse *n* a piece of grooved timber in which anything slides; one of the side scenes of a stage; (*pl*) the space between the side scenes.

couloir *n* a steeply ascending gorge in a mountainside.

coulomb *n* an SI unit of electric charge; the quantity of electricity conveyed by a current of one ampere in one second.

coulter *n* a vertical blade at the front of a ploughshare.—*also* **colter**.

coumarin *n* an aromatic crystalline substance obtained from the tonka bean and used in perfumes and medicines.—**coumaric** *adj*.

council *n* an elected or appointed legislative or advisory body; a central body uniting a group of organizations; an executive body whose members are equal in power and authority.—**councillor, councilor** *n*.—**councillorship, councilorship** *n*.

councillor, councilor *n* a member of a council.—**councillorship, councilorship** *n*.

councilman *n* (*pl* **councilmen**) a member of a council, a councillor.

counsel *n* advice; consultation, deliberate purpose or design; a person who gives counsel, a lawyer or a group of lawyers; a consultant. * *vb* (**counselling** *or* **counseling, counselled** *or* **counseled**) *vt* to advise; to recommend. * *vi* to give or take advice.

counselling, counseling *n* professional guidance for an individual or a couple from a qualified person.

counsellor, counselor *n* an adviser; a lawyer.

counsellor, counselor *n* one who gives advice, esp legal advice, an adviser.

count[1] *n* a European noble.

count[2] *vt* to number, to add up; to reckon; to consider to be; to call aloud (beats or time units); to include or exclude by counting; (*with* **against**) to have an adverse effect. * *vi* to name numbers or add up items in order; to mark time; to be of importance or value; to rely (upon); (*with* **on**) to rely on: (*with* **out**) (*inf*) to exclude, leave out; to pronounce after a count a floored boxer to be the loser. * *n* an act of numbering or reckoning; the total counted; a separate and distinct charge in an indictment; rhythm.

countdown *n* the descending count backwards to zero, eg to the moment a rocket lifts off.

countenance *n* the whole form of the face; appearance; support. * *vt* to favour, give approval to.

counter[1] *n* one who or that which counts; a disc used for scoring, a token; a table in a bank or shop across which money or goods are passed.

counter[2] *adv* contrary; adverse; in an opposite direction; in the wrong way. * *adj* opposed; opposite. * *n* a return blow or parry; an answering move. * *vti* to oppose; to retort; to give a return blow; to retaliate.

counter- *prefix* rival; opposed; reversed; matched.

counteract *vt* to act in opposition to so as to defeat or hinder; to neutralize.—**counteraction** *n*.—**counteractive** *adj*.

counterattack *n* an attack in response to an attack. * *vt* to make a counterattack.

counterattraction *n* a rival attraction; attraction in an opposite direction.

counterbalance *n* a weight balancing another. * *vt* to act as a counterbalance; to act against with equal power.

counterchange *vti* to interchange; to chequer.

countercharge *n* an opposing charge, esp by an accused person against his or her accuser. * *vt* to charge in opposition to another.

countercheck *n* a check on a check; an opposing check; (*arch*) a retort.

counterclaim *n* an opposing claim, esp by a defendant in a lawsuit.—**counterclaimant** *n*.

counterclockwise *adj* moving in a direction contrary to the hands of a clock as viewed from the front.—*also adv*.—*also* **anticlockwise**.

counterespionage *n* spying on or exposing enemy spies.

counterfeit *vt* to imitate; to forge; to feign, simulate. * *adj* made in imitation, forged; feigned, sham. * *n* an imitation, a forgery.—**counterfeiter** *n*.

counterfoil *n* a detachable section of a cheque or ticket, kept as a receipt or record; a stub.

counterintelligence *n* activities intended to frustrate enemy espionage and intelligence-gathering operations.

counterirritant *n* an application or action irritating the body surface to relieve internal inflammation.—**counterirritation** *n*.

countermand *vt* to revoke or annul, as an order or command; to cancel the orders of another. * *n* a command cancelling another.

countermarch *vti* to march in the reverse direction. * *n* such a march.

countermeasure *n* an action taken to neutralize or retaliate against some threat or danger, etc.

countermine *n* a mine made to intercept that of an enemy. * *vi* to make a countermine; to counterplot.

counteroffensive *n* a counterattack, esp by defenders of a position.

counterpane *n* a bedspread.

counterpart *n* a thing exactly like another, a duplicate; a corresponding or complementary part or thing.

counterplot *n* a plot to defeat another plot. * *vi* (**counterplotting, counterplotted**) to plot in retaliation.

counterpoint *n* (*mus*) a melody added as an accompaniment to another. * *vt* to set in contrast.

counterpoise *n* a weight, force or influence that balances another; equilibrium. * *vt* to counterbalance.

counterproductive *adj* producing a contrary effect on productivity or usefulness; hindering the desired end.

Counter-Reformation *n* the reforming movement in the Roman Catholic Church following the Protestant Reformation.

counter-revolution *n* a revolution undoing the work of a previous one.—**counter-revolutionary** *adj*, *n*.

countersign *vt* to authenticate a document by an additional signature. * *n* an additional signature to a document to attest it; a word to be given in answer to a sentry's challenge; an additional mark.—**countersignature** *n*.

countersink *vt* (**countersinking, countersunk**) to enlarge the upper part of a hole so that the screw head will sit flush with, or below, the surface; to drive (a screw) into such a hole. * *n* a tool for countersinking.

countertenor *n* a high tenor voice with an alto range; a person who sings countertenor.

counterterrorism *n* terrorist act(s) perpetrated in revenge for former terrorist act(s).

countervail *vt* to counterbalance, compensate for.

counterweight *n* a counterbalancing weight or power.

countess *n* a woman with the rank of count or earl; the wife or widow of a count.

counting house *n* a book-keeping office or department.

countless *adj* innumerable.

countrified, countryfied *adj* in the manner of the country; rural.

country *n* (*pl* **countries**) a region or district; the territory of a nation; a state; the land of one's birth or residence; rural parts; country-and-western. * *adj* rural.

country-and-western *n* a style of white folk music of the southeastern US.—*also* **country music.**

country club *n* a social and sporting facility in a rural setting.

country dance *n* a dance with the couples face to face in two lines.

country house *n* a gentleman's country residence.

countryman *n* (*pl* **countrymen**) a person who lives in the country; a person from the same country as another.—**countrywoman** *nf* (*pl* **countrywomen**).

countryside *n* a rural district.

county *n* (*pl* **counties**) in US, an administrative subdivision of a state; in UK, an administrative subdivision for local government.—*also adj.*

county palatine *n* a county having royal powers in the administration of justice.

county town, county seat *n* the capital of a county.

coup *n* a sudden telling blow; a masterstroke; a coup d'état.

coup de grâce *n* (*pl* **coups de grâce**) a finishing or fatal blow.

coup d'état *n* (*pl* **coups d'état**) a sudden and unexpected bold stroke of policy; the sudden overthrow of a government.

coup de théâtre *n* (*pl* **coups de théâtre**) a sudden dramatic or sensational action.

coupé *n* a closed, four-seater, two-door automobile with a sloping back.

couple *n* two of the same kind connected together; a pair; a husband and wife; a pair of equal and parallel forces. * *vt* to link or join together. * *vi* to copulate.

couplet *n* two consecutive lines of verse that rhyme with each other.

coupling *n* a device for joining parts of a machine or two railway carriages.

coupon *n* a detachable certificate on a bond, presented for payment of interest; a certificate entitling one to a discount, gift, etc.

courage *n* bravery; fortitude; spirit.—**courageous** *adj.*—**courageously** *adv.*—**courageousness** *n.*

courgette *n* a zucchini.

courier *n* a messenger, esp diplomatic; a tourist guide; a carrier of illegal goods between countries.

course *n* a race; a path or track; a career; a direction or line of motion; a regular sequence; the portion of a meal served at one time; conduct; behaviour; the direction a ship is steered; a continuous level range of brick or masonry of the same height; the chase of a hare by greyhounds; a length of time; an area set aside for a sport or a race; a series of studies; any of the studies. * *vt* to hunt. * *vi* to move swiftly along an indicated path; to chase with greyhounds.

courser *n* one who courses; a dog trained for coursing; (*poet*) a swift and spirited horse.

coursing *n* the sport of pursuing game with hunting dogs.

court *n* an uncovered space surrounded by buildings or walls; a short street; a playing space, as for tennis, etc; a royal palace; the retinue of a sovereign; (*law*) a hall of justice; the judges, etc engaged there; address; civility; flattery. * *vt* to seek the friendship of; to woo; to flatter; to solicit; to risk. * *vi* to carry on a courtship.

courteous *adj* polite; obliging.—**courteously** *adv.*—**courteousness** *n.*

courtesan *n* (*formerly*) a prostitute, or mistress of a courtier.

courtesy *n* (*pl* **courtesies**) politeness and kindness; civility; a courteous manner or action.

courthouse *n* a public building that houses law courts.

courtier *n* one in attendance at a royal court.

courtly *adj* (**courtlier, courtliest**) well-mannered, polite; of a court.—**courtliness** *n.*

court martial *n* (*pl* **courts martial, court martials**) a court of justice composed of naval or military officers for the trial of disciplinary offences.

court-martial *vt* (**court-martialling, court-martialled** *or* **court-martialing, court-martialed**) to try by court martial.

court plaster *n* a superior kind of sticking plaster, originally used by ladies at court for ornamental patches on the face.

courtship *n* the act of wooing.

courtyard *n* an enclosed space adjoining or in a large building.

couscous *n* a North African dish of cracked wheat steamed and served with a meat and vegetable stew.

cousin *n* the son or daughter of an uncle or aunt.—**cousinly** *adj.*—**cousinship**

couture *n* the design and manufacture of expensive fashion clothes.

couturier *n* a designer of expensive fashion clothes.—**couturière** *nf.*

couvade *n* a primitive custom by which when a child is born the father takes to his bed, where he receives the attentions usu given to the mother.

cove *n* a small sheltered bay or inlet in a body of water; a curved moulding at the juncture of a wall and ceiling (—*also* **coving**).

coven *n* an assembly of witches.

covenant *n* a written agreement; a solemn agreement of fellowship and faith between members of a church; an agreement to pay annually a sum to a charity. * *vt* to promise by a covenant. * *vi* to enter into a formal agreement.—**covenantal** *adj.*—**covenanted** *adj.*

covenantee *n* one in whose favour a covenant is made.

covenantor *n* one who enters into a covenant.

cover *vt* to overspread the top of anything with something else; to hide; to save from punishment; to shelter; to clothe; to understudy; to insure against damage, loss, etc; to report for a newspaper; to include; to make a journey over; (*male animal*) to copulate. * *vi* to spread over, as a liquid does; to provide an excuse or alibi (for); to work, eg as a salesman, in a certain area; to have within firing range. * *n* that which is laid on something else; a bedcover; a shelter; a covert; an understudy; something used to hide one's real actions, etc; insurance against loss or damage; a place laid at a table for a meal.—**coverer** *n.*

coverage *n* the amount, extent, etc covered by something; the amount of reporting of an event for newspaper, television, etc.

coverall *n* (*usu pl*) a one-piece garment that completely covers and protects one's clothing.

cover charge *n* a charge made by a restaurant over and above the cost of the food and service.

cover girl *n* an attractive girl whose picture is used on magazine covers.

covering *n* that which covers or protects; dress.

covering letter *n* a letter containing an explanation of an accompanying item.

coverlet *n* a bedspread.

coversine *n* the versed sine of the complement of an angle or arc.

covert *adj* covered; secret, concealed. * *n* a place that protects or shelters; a thicket; shelter for game.—covertly *adv*.

coverture *n* a cover; shelter; (*law*) the status of a married woman.

cover-up *n* something used to hide one's real activities, etc; a concerted effort to keep an act or situation from being made public.

covet *vt* to desire earnestly; to lust after; to long to possess (what belongs to another).—coveter *n*.—covetous *adj*.—covetousness *n*.

covetous *adj* avaricious, grasping, acquisitive.—covetousness *n*.

covey *n* a hatch or brood of birds, esp partridges.

coving *n* a curved moulding at the juncture of a wall and ceiling.—*also* cove.

cow[1] *n* the mature female of domestic cattle; the mature female of various other animals, as the whale, elephant, etc; (*sl*) a disagreeable woman.

cow[2] *vt* to take the spirit out of, to intimidate.

coward *n* a person lacking courage; one who is afraid.

cowardice *n* lack of courage.

cowardly *adj* of, or like, a coward.—cowardliness *n*.

cowbane *n* water hemlock.

cowbird *n* an American blackbird so called from its accompanying cattle.

cowboy *n* a person who tends cattle or horses (—*also* cowhand); (*inf*) one who is engaged in dubious business activities.

cowcatcher *n* a wedge-shaped iron frame on the front of a locomotive to push aside obstacles.

cower *vi* to crouch or sink down through fear, etc; to tremble.

cowfish *n* (*pl* cowfish, cowfishes) a name given to various fishes and other marine animals, as the dolphin.

cowgirl *n* a woman who works as a cowhand.

cowherd *n* a person employed to tend cattle.

cowhide *n* the tanned and dressed skins of cows; a stout flexible whip made of rawhide.

cowl *n* a hood; the hooded habit of a monk; the draped neckline of a woman's dress or sweater; a chimney corner.

cowlick *n* a tuft of hair turned up or brushed over the forehead.

cowling *n* the metal covering of an aeroplane engine.

coworker *n* a fellow worker.

cow pat *n* a piece of cow dung.

cow pony *n* a mustang used by cowboys.

cowpox *n* a disease of cows that produces vesicles from which the vaccine for inoculation against smallpox is obtained.

cowpuncher, cowpoke *n* a cowboy.

cowry, cowrie *n* (*pl* cowries) a marine mollusc with a glossy, brightly speckled shell.

cowslip *n* a common wild plant with small fragrant yellow flowers.

cox *n* a coxswain. * *vt* to act as a coxswain.

coxa *n* (*pl* coxae) the hip joint.—coxal *adj*.

coxalgia *n* a pain in, or disease of, the hip joint.—coxalgic *adj*.

coxcomb *n* a cockscomb; a vain conceited person, a fop.

coxcombry *n* (*pl* coxcombries) affected airs, foppishness.

coxswain *n* a person who steers a boat, esp a lifeboat or racing boat.—*also* cockswain.

coy *adj* playfully or provocatively demure; bashful.—coyly *adv*.—coyness *n*.

coyote *n* (*pl* coyotes, coyote) a small prairie wolf of North America.

coypu *n* (*pl* coypus, coypu) an aquatic beaver-like animal, originally from South America.

coz *n* (*arch*) cousin.

cozen *vt* to cheat, to beguile; to act deceitfully.—cozenage *n*.—cozener *n*.

cozy *see* cosy.

CP *abbr* = Communist Party.

cp. *abbr* = compare.

Cpl *abbr* = Corporal.

CPU *abbr* = central processing unit.

Cr (*chem symbol*) chromium.

cr. *abbr* = credit; creditor.

crab *n* any of numerous chiefly marine broadly built crustaceans. * *vi* (crabbing, crabbed) to fish for crabs; to complain.

crab-apple *n* a wild apple.

crabbed *adj* bad-tempered, morose; (*writing*) cramped; hard to decipher.

crabby *adj* bad-tempered.—crabbily *adv*.—crabbiness *n*.

crab louse *n* a species of body louse.

crabstick *n* a cudgel; a surly person.

crack *vt* to burst, break or sever; to utter a sharp, abrupt cry; to injure; to damage mentally; to open a bottle; (*sl*) to make (a joke); (*inf*) to break open (a safe); to decipher (a code). * *vi* to make a sharp explosive sound; (*inf*) to lose control under pressure; to shift erratically in vocal tone; (*with* up) (*inf*) to be unable to cope; (*sl*) to take the drug crack. * *n* a chink or fissure; a narrow fracture; a sharp sound; a sharp resonant blow; an altered tone of voice; a chat, gossip; a wisecrack; (*inf*) an attempt; an expert; (*sl*) the drug cocaine packaged in the form of pellets.

crackbrained *adj* crazy.

crackdown *n* repressive action to quell disorder, etc.

cracked *adj* split, broken; blemished; insane; legally imperfect.

cracker *n* a firework that explodes with a loud crack; a paper tube that when pulled explodes harmlessly and releases a paper hat and plastic toy; a thin, crisp biscuit; (*sl*) a person or thing of great ability or excellence.

crackerjack *n* (*sl*) a fine specimen.

crackers *adj* (*sl*) crazy.

crackhead *n* (*sl*) a person who is addicted to the drug crack.

crack house *n* (*sl*) a place where the drug crack is made available by dealers.

cracking *adj* (*inf*) fast-moving; excellent. * *n* the act of hacking into computer games; **to get cracking** to start to do something with vim and vigour.

crackle vi to make a slight, sharp explosive noise. * vt to cover with a delicate network of minute cracks. * n a noise of frequent and slight cracks and reports; a surface glaze on glass or porcelain.—**crackly** adj.

crackling n (usu pl) the browned crisp rind of roast pork.

cracknel n a thick puffy dry fancy biscuit.

crackpot n (inf) an eccentric, a crazy person. * adj (inf) crazy, unpractical.

cracksman n (pl **cracksmen**) a burglar.

-cracy n suffix government by, as in democracy.

cradle n a baby's crib or a small bed, often on rockers; infancy; birthplace or origin; a case for a broken limb; a framework of timbers, esp for supporting a boat; the rest for a telephone handset. * vt to rock or place in a cradle; to nurse or train in infancy.

cradlesong n a lullaby.

cradling n the open timbers or ribs of a vaulted ceiling.

craft n manual skill; a skilled trade; the members of a skilled trade; cunning; (pl **craft**) a boat, ship, or aircraft.

craftsman n (pl **craftsmen**) a person skilled in a particular craft.—**craftsmanship** n.—**craftswoman** nf (pl **craftswomen**).

crafty adj (**craftier, craftiest**) cunning, wily.—**craftily** adv.—**craftiness** n.

crag n a rough steep rock or cliff.

craggy, cragged adj (**craggier, craggiest**) full of crags; rugged.—**cragginess** n.

crake n the corncrake.

cram vb (**cramming crammed**) vt to pack tightly, to stuff; to fill to overflowing; (inf) to prepare quickly for an examination. * vi to eat greedily.

crambo n (pl **cramboes**) a game in which rhymes have to be found for a given word.

cramp n a spasmodic muscular contraction of the limbs; (pl) abdominal spasms and pain; a clamp. * vt to affect with muscular spasms; to confine narrowly; to hamper; to secure with a cramp. * vi to suffer from cramps.

cramped adj restricted, narrow; (handwriting) small and irregular.

crampon, crampoon n a metal frame with spikes attached to boots for walking or climbing on ice.

cranberry n (pl **cranberries**) a small red sour berry; the shrub it grows on.

crane n a large wading bird with very long legs and neck, and a long straight bill; a machine for raising, shifting, and lowering heavy weights. * vti to stretch out (the neck).

crane fly n the daddy-longlegs.

cranesbill n a kind of wild geranium.

craniology n the scientific study of skulls and their characteristics.—**craniological** adj.—**craniologist** n.

craniometer n an instrument for measuring the skull.

craniometry n the measurement and study of skulls.—**craniometric, craniometrical** adj.

craniotomy n (pl **craniotomies**) the operation of crushing the head of a dead fetus for facilitating delivery; the operation of opening the skull for neurosurgery.

cranium n (pl **craniums, crania**) the skull, esp the part enclosing the brain.—**cranial** adj.

crank n a right-angled arm attached to a shaft for turning it; (inf) an eccentric person, usu one with strange or unorthodox opinions; an irritable or rude person.

* vt to provide with a crank; to turn or wind; (with **up**) (engine) to start with a crank handle; (inf) to speed up; (sl) to inject a narcotic drug.

crankcase n the housing for a crankshaft in an internal combustion engine, etc.

crankpin n a cylindrical pin parallel with the shaft axis of a crank upon which the connecting rod acts to turn the crank.

crankshaft n a shaft with one or more cranks for transmitting motion.

cranky adj (**crankier, crankiest**) (inf) eccentric; shaky; cross.—**crankily** adv.—**crankiness** n.

cranny n (pl **crannies**) a fissure, crack, crevice.

crap n (sl) nonsense; (vulg) faeces. * vi (**crapping, crapped**) (vulg) to defecate.—**crappy** adj.

crape n crepe; a black gauze-like crimped silk material used for mourning.

craps n (sing or pl) a gambling game played with two dice.

crapshooter n a player of craps.

crapulence n sickness from drinking to excess.—**crapulent, crapulous** adj.

craquelure n a network of tiny cracks found on old paintings caused by cracking of the varnish.

crash n a loud, sudden confused noise; a violent fall or impact; a sudden failure, as of a business or a computer; a collapse, as of the financial market. * adj done with great speed, suddenness or effort. * vti to clash together with violence; to make a loud clattering noise; (aircraft) to land with a crash; to involve a car in a collision with one or more other vehicles or with a hard object; to collapse, to ruin; (inf) to intrude into (a party); (with **out**) vi (sl) to fall asleep; to pass out; to stay the night somewhere other than home.

crash dive n an emergency dive by a submarine.

crash helmet n a cushioned helmet worn by airmen, motorcyclists, etc for protection.

crash-land vti (aircraft) to make an emergency landing without lowering the undercarriage, or to be landed in this way.—**crash-landing** n.

crass adj gross; dense; very stupid.—**crassly** adv.—**crassness, crassitude** n.

-crat n suffix a supporter or member of a particular form of government or class.

cratch n a rack for fodder.

crate n an open box of wooden slats, for shipping; (sl) an old vehicle or aircraft. * vt to pack in a crate.

crater n the mouth of a volcano; a cavity caused by the landing of a meteorite, the explosion of a bomb, shell, etc; an ancient Greek goblet.—**craterous** adj.

cravat n a neckcloth.

crave vt to have a strong desire (for); to ask humbly, to beg.—**craving** n.

craven adj spiritless, cowardly. * n a coward.

craw n a bird's crop.

crawfish n (pl **crawfish**) a crayfish; the spiny lobster.

crawl vi to move along the ground on hands and knees; to move slowly and with difficulty; to creep; (inf) to seek favour by servile behaviour; to swarm (with). * n the act of crawling; a slow motion; a racing stroke in swimming.—**crawler** n.

crayfish n (pl **crayfish**) any of numerous freshwater crustaceans; the spiny lobster.

crayon n a stick or pencil of coloured chalk; a drawing done with crayons. * vt to draw with a crayon.—**crayonist** n.

craze n a passing infatuation; excessive enthusiasm; a

crack in pottery glaze. * vt to produce cracks; to render insane.—**crazed** adj.

crazy adj (**crazier**, **craziest**) (inf) mad, insane; foolish; ridiculous; unsound; madly in love with; (paving) composed of irregular pieces.—**crazily** adv.—**craziness** n.

creak vi to make a shrill grating sound. * n such a sound.

creaky adj (**creakier**, **creakiest**) apt to creak.—**creakiness** n.

cream n the rich, fatty part of milk; the choicest part of anything; a yellowish white colour; a type of face or skin preparation; any preparation of the consistency of cream (eg shoe cream). * vt to add or apply cream to; to beat into a soft, smooth consistency; to skim cream from; to remove the best part of. * vi to form cream or scum; to break into a creamy froth.

cream cheese n soft cheese made from soured milk or cream.

creamer n a machine or dish for separating cream from milk; a jug for cream or milk; a powder used as a substitute for cream in drinks.

creamery n (pl **creameries**) a place where dairy products are made or sold.

cream of tartar n purified tartar or argol, potassium bitartrate.

creamy adj (**creamier**, **creamiest**) like cream.—**creaminess** n.

crease n a line made by folding; a wrinkle; (cricket) a line made by a batsman or bowler marking the limits of their position. * vti to make or form creases; to become creased; (sl) to find something very funny.

create vt to cause to come into existence; to form out of nothing. * vi to make something new, to originate; (sl) to make a fuss.

creatine, creatin n a white crystalline substance in muscular tissue.

creation n the act of creating; the thing created; the whole world or universe; a production of the human mind; (with cap) the universe as created by God.—**creational** adj.

creationism n the belief in special creation, not evolution; the belief that God creates a soul for every human being at birth.—**creationist** adj, n.

creative adj of creation; having the power to create; imaginative, original, constructive.—**creatively** adv.—**creativeness** n.—**creativity** n.

creator n one who creates, esp God.

creature n a living being; a created thing; one dependent on the influence of another.—**creatural, creaturely** adj.

crèche n a day nursery for very young children.

credence n belief or trust, esp in the reports or testimony of another.

credentials npl documents proving the identity, honesty or authority of a person.

credibility gap n a gap between what is claimed in official statements and the true facts of a situation.

credible adj believable; trustworthy.—**credibility, credibleness** n.—**credibly** adv.

credit n belief; trust; honour; good reputation; approval; trust in a person's ability to pay; time allowed for payment; a sum at a person's disposal in a bank; the entry in an account of a sum received; the side of the account on which this is entered; (educ) a distinction awarded for good marks in an examination; (pl) a list of those responsible for a film, television pro-

gramme, etc. * vt to believe; to trust; to have confidence in; to attribute to; to enter on the credit side of an account.

creditable adj worthy of praise.—**creditableness, creditability** n.—**creditably** adv.

credit card n a card issued by a bank, department store, etc authorizing the purchase of goods and services on credit.

creditor n a person to whom money is owed.

credit rating n an appraisal of a person's or a business's creditworthiness.

credits npl a list of those involved in the production of a film or television show.

creditworthy adj worthy of being given credit as judged by the capacity to earn, repay debts promptly, etc.—**creditworthiness** n.

credo n (pl **credos**) a creed.

credulous adj over-ready to believe; easily imposed on.—**credulously** adv.—**credulity** n.

creed n a system of religious belief or faith; a summary of Christian doctrine; any set of principles or beliefs.—**creedal, credal** adj.

creek n a natural stream of water smaller than a river.

creel n a wicker fishing basket; a wickerwork cage.

creep vi (**creeping, crept**) to move slowly along the ground, as a worm or reptile; (plant) to grow along the ground or up a wall; to move stealthily or slowly; to fawn; to cringe; (flesh) to feel as if things were creeping over it. * n (inf) a dislikable or servile person; (pl: inf) shrinking horror.

creeper n a creeping or climbing plant.

creepy adj (**creepier, creepiest**) making one's flesh crawl; causing fear or disgust.—**creepily** adv.—**creepiness** n.

creepy-crawly n (pl **creepy-crawlies**) (inf) a small crawling insect.

cremate vt to burn (a corpse) to ashes.—**cremation** n.—**cremationism** n.—**cremationist** n.

crematorium n (pl **crematoriums, crematoria**) a place where bodies are cremated.

crematory adj pertaining to cremation. * n (pl **crematories**) a place for burning the dead, a crematorium.

crème, creme n cream.

crème de la crème n the cream of the cream, the very best.

crème de menthe n a green-coloured peppermint liqueur.

crenate, crenated adj (leaves) scalloped.—**crenation, crenature** n.

crenellated, crenelated adj having battlements.—**crenellation, crenelation** n.

crenulate, crenulated adj (leaves) finely notched, indented.—**crenulation** n.

Creole n a descendant of European settlers in the West Indies or South America; a white descendant of French settlers in the southern US; a person of mixed European and Negro ancestry; the language of any of these groups.

creole n a language combining two or more original languages, one of which is European.

creosol n an oily liquid resembling phenol, a constituent of creosote.

creosote n an oily substance derived from tar used as a wood preservative. * vt to treat with creosote.—**creosotic** adj.

crepe, crêpe n a thin, crinkled cloth of silk, rayon, wool, etc (—*also* **crape**) ; thin paper like crepe; a thin pancake.

crepe de Chine *n* a silk crepe.

crepe paper, crêpe paper *n* a thin soft coloured paper that resembles crepe.

crepe rubber *n* a type of ribbed rubber used for the soles of shoes.

crêpe suzette *n* (*pl* **crêpes suzettes**) a thin orange-flavoured pancake with a hot liqueur sauce.

crepitate *vi* to make a slight, sharp crackling noise.—**crepitation** *n*.

crept *see* **creep**.

crepuscular *adj* pertaining to or resembling twilight; active at twilight, as certain animals.

crescendo *adv* (*mus*) gradually increasing in loudness or intensity; moving to a climax. * *n* (*pl* **crescendos, crescendi**) a crescendo passage or effect.

crescent *n* the figure of the moon in its first or last quarter; a narrow, tapering curve; a curving street. * *adj* crescent-shaped; (*arch*) increasing.—**crescentic** *adj*.

cresol *n* a phenol obtained from coal and wood tar.

cress *n* any of various plants with pungent leaves, used in salads.

cresset *n* a light set on a beacon; an open frame of iron containing fire, used as a torch.

crest *n* a plume of feathers on the head of a bird; the ridge of a wave; the summit of a hill; a distinctive device above the shield on a coat of arms. * *vti* to mount to the top of; to take the form of a crest; to provide or adorn with a crest, to crown.—**crested** *adj*.

crestfallen *adj* dejected.

cresting *n* an ornamental finish, esp along a rooftop; ornamentation on top of furniture, a mirror, etc.

Cretaceous *n* a geological group between the Jurassic and Tertiary formations. * *adj* of the last Mesozoic era.

cretaceous *adj* composed of or like chalk; chalky.

Cretan *adj* of or pertaining to Crete or its inhabitants.

cretin *n* a person suffering from mental and physical retardation due to a thyroid disorder; (*inf*) an idiot.—**cretinism** *n*.—**cretinoid, cretinous** *adj*.

cretonne *n* an unglazed cotton fabric printed with coloured patterns on one side.

crevasse *n* a deep cleft in a glacier; a deep crack.

crevice *n* a crack, a fissure.

crew *n* the people operating a ship or aircraft; a group of people working together. * *vi* to act as a member of the crew of a ship, etc.

crewcut *n* a very short hairstyle for men.

crewel *n* a fine twisted or worsted yarn used in embroidery.—**crewelist** *n*.

crew neck *n* a plain closely-fitting neckline in sweaters.

crib *n* a rack for fodder, a manger; a child's cot with high sides; a model of the manger scene representing the birth of Jesus; (*inf*) something copied from someone else; (*inf*) a literal translation of foreign texts used (usu illicitly) by students in examinations, etc. * *vti* (**cribbing, cribbed**) (*inf*) to copy illegally, plagiarize.

cribbage *n* a card game for two to four players.

crib death *see* **cot death**.

cribellum *n* (*pl* **cribella**) a spinning organ in front of the spinnerets of certain spiders.

cribriform adj with small holes like a sieve.

crick *n* a painful stiffness of the muscles of the neck. * *vt* to produce a crick in.

cricket[1] *n* a leaping grasshopper-like insect.

cricket[2] *n* a game played with wickets, bats, and a ball,

by eleven players on each side.—**cricketer** *n*.

cried *see* **cry**.

crier *n* one who cries; an officer who makes public proclamations.

crime *n* a violation of the law; an offence against morality or the public welfare; wrong-doing; (*inf*) a shame, disappointment.

criminal *adj* of the nature of, or guilty of, a crime. * *n* a person who has committed a crime.—**criminality** *adv*.—**criminally** *adv*.

criminal conversation *n* (*formerly*) a legal action for damages for illegal sexual intercourse; adultery.

criminology *n* the scientific study of crime.—**criminological, criminologic** *adj*.—**criminologist** *n*.

crimp[1] *vt* to press into small folds; to frill; to corrugate; (*hair*) to curl.—**crimper** *n*.

crimp[2] *n* a person luring or pressganging sailors aboard a vessel. * *vt* to decoy thus.

crimson *n* a deep-red colour inclining to purple. * *adj* crimson-coloured. * *vti* to dye with crimson; to blush.

cringe *vi* to shrink in fear or embarrassment; to cower; to behave with servility; to fawn.

cringle *n* a loop of rope containing a metal ring for another rope to pass through.

crinite *adj* hairy.

crinkle *vt* to wrinkle; to corrugate; to crimp; to rustle. * *vi* to curl; to be corrugated or crimped. * *n* a wrinkle.—**crinkly** *adj*.

crinoid *adj* lily-shaped. * *n* a stone lily, a kind of sea urchin.

crinoline *n* a hooped skirt made to project all round; a stiff fabric for stiffening a garment.

crinum *n* any of several handsome tropical plants.

cripple *vt* to deprive of the use of a limb; to disable. * *n* a lame or otherwise disabled person. * *adj* lame.

crippling *adj* harmful; unbearable.

crisis *n* (*pl* **crises**) a turning point; a critical point in a disease; an emergency; a time of serious difficulties or danger.

crisp *adj* dry and brittle; bracing; brisk; sharp and incisive; decided; very clean and tidy. * *n* a potato snack; in US, a potato chip. * *vt* to make crisp.—**crisply** *adv*.—**crispness** *n*.

crispate, crispated *adj* curled; (*bot*) with a wavy margin.—**crispation** *n*.

crispy *adj* (**crispier, crispiest**) crisp.—**crispily** *adv*.—**crispiness** *n*.

crisscross *vti* to intersect; to mark with cross lines. * *n* an intersecting; a mark of a cross; a game of noughts and crosses. * *adj* crossing; in cross lines. * *adv* crosswise.

cristate, cristated *adj* crested; tufted.

criterion *n* (*pl* **criteria**) a standard, law or rule by which a correct judgment can be made.

critic *n* a person skilled in judging the merits of literary or artistic works; one who passes judgment; a faultfinder.

critical *adj* skilled in criticism; censorious; relating to the turning point of a disease; crucial.—**critically** *adv*.

criticism *n* being critical; an adverse comment; a review or analysis of a book, play, work of art, etc by a critic.

criticize *vt* to pass judgment on; to find fault with; to examine critically.—**criticizer** *n*.

critique *n* a critical article or review.

critter *n* (*dial*) a creature.

croak *n* a deep hoarse discordant cry. * *vti* to utter a croak; (*inf*) to die, to kill.—**croakily** *adv*.—**croakiness** *n*.—**croaky** *adj*.

Croatian, Croat *adj* of or pertaining to Croatia, its people or language. * *n* an inhabitant of Croatia; the language of Croatia, a dialect of Serbo-Croatian.

crochet *n* a kind of knitting done with a hooked needle. * *vti* (**crocheting, crocheted**) to do this; to make crochet articles.—**crocheter** *n*.

crocidolite *n* blue asbestos.

crock¹ *n* an earthenware pot.

crock² *n* a broken-down horse; (*sl*) a worn-out or unfit person. * *vti* to become or make unfit.

crock³ *n* soot on a kettle, etc. * *vt* to blacken with soot.

crockery *n* china dishes, earthenware vessels, etc.

crocket *n* a small curved ornament on the angles of spires, canopies, etc.

crocodile *n* a large amphibious reptile, similar to an alligator; its skin, used to make handbags, shoes, etc; a line of schoolchildren walking in pairs.

crocodile tears *npl* insincere grief.

crocodilian *adj* pertaining to crocodiles. * *n* any of the order of reptiles that includes alligators and crocodiles.

crocus *n* (*pl* **crocuses**) a bulbous plant with yellow, purple, or white flowers.

croft *n* a small plot of land with a rented farmhouse, esp in Scotland.—**crofter** *n*.

croissant *n* a rich bread roll.

Cro-Magnon man *n* a race of man living in late Palaeolithic times.

cromlech *n* a prehistoric monument of rough stones in a circle and usu surrounding a lofty pillar of stone.

crone *n* a withered old woman.

crony *n* (*pl* **cronies**) an intimate friend.

crook *n* a shepherd's hooked staff; a bend, a curve; a swindler, a dishonest person. * *adj* (*sl*) unwell. * *vti* to bend or to be bent into the shape of a hook.

crooked *adj* bent, twisted; dishonest.—**crookedly** *adv*.—**crookedness** *n*.

croon *vi* to hum in a low gentle voice. * *vt* to sing songs in a soft gentle manner.—**crooner** *n*.

crop *n* a year's or a season's produce of any cultivated plant; harvest; any collection of things appearing at the same time; a pouch in a bird's gullet; a hunting whip; hair cut close or short. * *vti* (**cropping, cropped**) to clip short; to bite off or eat down (grass); (*land*) to yield; to sow, to plant; (*geol*) to come to the surface; to sprout; (*with* **up**) (*inf*) to occur or appear by chance or unexpectedly.

crop circle *n* a circular patch of corn in a cornfield that has been flattened by an as yet unexplained whirling movement.

crop-eared *adj* with clipped ears; short-haired.

cropper *n* a thing that crops; a cloth-facing machine; a pouter pigeon; (*sl*) a heavy fall.

croquet *n* a game played with mallets, balls and hoops. * *vt* (**croqueting, croqueted**) to drive away an opponent's ball by striking one's own placed in contact with it.

croquette *n* a ball of minced meat, fish or potato seasoned and fried brown.

crosier *n* the pastoral staff of a bishop.—*also* **crozier**.

cross *n* a figure formed by two intersecting lines; a wooden structure, consisting of two beams placed across each other, used in ancient times for crucifixion; the emblem of the Christian faith; a symbol or mark (X); a focal point in a town; a burden, or affliction; a device resembling a cross; a cross-shaped medal; a hybrid. * *vti* to pass across; to intersect; to meet and pass; to place crosswise; to mark with a cross; to make the sign of the cross over; to thwart, to oppose; to modify (a breed) by intermixture (with). * *adj* transverse; reaching from side to side; intersecting; out of temper, peevish.—**crosser** *n*.—**crossly** *adv*.—**crossness** *n*.

crossbar *n* a horizontal bar, as that across goal posts or a bicycle frame.

crossbill *n* a bird whose mandibles cross when the bill is closed.

crossbow *n* a bow set crosswise on the stock from which bolts are shot along a groove.

crossbreed *vt* (**crossbreeding, crossbred**) to breed animals by mating different varieties. * *n* an animal produced in this way.

crosscheck *vt* to verify by checking different opinions or sources.

cross-country *adj* across fields; denoting cross-country racing or skiing.—*also* *n*.

crosscurrent *n* a current that flows across another in water or air; ideas running counter to those generally held.

crosse *n* a long-handled racket in which the ball is caught and carried in lacrosse.

cross-examine *vt* to question closely; (*law*) to question (a witness) who has already been questioned by counsel on the other side.—**cross-examiner** *n*.—**cross-examination** *n*.

cross-eyed *adj* squinting.—**cross-eye** *n*.

cross-fertilization *n* fertilization of the ovules of a flower by the pollen of another.

cross-fertilize *vt* to fertilize (a plant) with pollen from another.

crossfire *n* converging gunfire from two or more positions; animated debate or argument.

cross-grained *adj* contrary or awkward; with an irregular grain or fibre.

crosshatch *vt* to shade with crossed lines.

crossing *n* an intersection of roads or railway lines; a place for crossing a street; the crossbreeding of animals and plants.

cross-legged *adj* seated with one leg crossed over the other.

crosspatch *n* (*inf*) a bad-tempered person.

crosspiece *n* a transverse piece.

cross-purpose *n* a contrary purpose; **be at cross-purposes** to talk without either party realizing that the other is talking about a different thing.

cross-question *vt* to question to elicit details or test the accuracy of an account already given.—**cross-questioning** *n*.

cross-refer *vt* to mark (text, a book, etc) in such a way as to direct the reader to another page, etc with more information.

cross-reference *n* a note directing the reader to a different section of a book or document.

crossroad *n* a road crossing another; (*pl*) where two roads cross; (*fig*) the time when a decisive action has to be made.

cross section *n* a cutting at right angles to length; the surface then shown; a random selection of the public.—**cross-sectional** *adj*.

cross-stitch *n* a stitch formed of two stitches of the same length, one crossing the other.

crosstalk *n* interference in lines of communication, esp telephone lines; a quick-witted flow of conversation; repartee.

crosstie *n* a railway sleeper.

crosstree *n* (*naut*) one of several pieces of timber across the head of a lower mast to support the mast above.

crosswalk *n* a street crossing for pedestrians.

crosswind *n* a side or unfavourable wind.

crosswise, crossways *adv* in the manner of a cross.

crossword (puzzle) *n* a puzzle in which interlocking words to be inserted vertically and horizontally in a squared diagram are indicated by clues.

crotch *n* the region of the body where the legs fork, the genital area; any forked region.

crotchet *n* (*mus*) a note equal to the duration of a half-minim.—*also* **quarter note**.

crotchety *adj* peevish, ill-tempered.—**crotchetiness** *n*.

crouch *vi* to squat or lie close to the ground; to cringe, to fawn.

croup[1] *n* inflammation of the windpipe causing coughing and breathing problems, esp in children.—**croupous, croupy** *adj*.

croup[2], **croupe** *n* the rump or buttocks of certain animals; the place behind the saddle of a horse.

croupier *n* a person who presides at a gaming table and collects or pays out the money won or lost.

crouton *n* a small piece of fried or toasted bread sprinkled onto soups.

crow *n* any of various usu large, glossy, black birds; a cawing cry, the shrill sound of a cock. * *vi* (**crowing, crowed** *or* **crew**) to make a sound like a cock; to boast in triumph; to utter a cry of pleasure.—**crower** *n*.

crowbar *n* an iron bar for use as a lever.

crowd *n* a number of people or things collected closely together; a dense multitude, a throng; (*inf*) a set; a clique. * *vti* to press closely together; to fill to excess; to push, to thrust; to importune.—**crowded** *adj*.

crowfoot *n* (*pl* **crowfoots**) any of several kinds of buttercup with yellow or white flowers and leaves like a crow's foot.

crown *n* a wreath worn on the head; the head covering of a monarch; regal power; the sovereign; the top of the head; the top of a tree; a summit; a reward; the part of a tooth above the gum. * *vt* to invest with a crown; to adorn or dignify; to complete; to reward; to put an artificial crown on a tooth; (*sl*) to strike on the head.

crown colony *n* a British colony subject to the control of the home government.

crown glass *n* a fine, thick kind of glass.

crown land *n* in the UK, land or real property belonging to the sovereign.

crown prince *n* the heir apparent to a throne.

crown princess *n* the heiress apparent to a throne; the wife of a crown prince.

crown saw *n* a kind of circular saw.

crownwork *n* the covering or replacement of the crown of a tooth; the making of crowns; a fortified outwork.

crow's-foot *n* (*pl* **crow's-feet**) a wrinkle at the corner of the eye; an arrangement of cords to suspend an awning; a decorative embroidery stitch.

crow's-nest *n* a lookout or watchtower on the main top-mast of a sailing vessel.

crozier *see* **crosier**.

CRT *abbr* = cathode-ray tube.

cruces *see* **crux**.

crucial *adj* decisive; severe; critical.—**crucially** *adv*.

cruciate *adj* (*bot*) cross-shaped.

crucible *n* a heat-resistant container for melting ores, etc.

crucifer *n* any of many plants with four petals arranged like a cross, as the mustard, etc; the bearer of a large cross in a religious procession.

crucifier *n* one who crucifies.

crucifix *n* a cross with the sculptured figure of Christ.

crucifixion *n* a form of execution by being nailed or bound to a cross by the hands and feet; (*with cap*) the death of Christ in this manner.

cruciform *adj* cross-shaped.

crucify *vt* (**crucifying, crucified**) to put to death on a cross; to cause extreme pain to; to defeat utterly in an argument; to ridicule mercilessly.

crud *n* (*sl*) a deposit of encrusted filth; nuclear waste; a contemptible person.

crude *adj* in a natural state; unripe; raw; immature; harsh in colour; unfinished, rough; lacking polish; blunt; vulgar. * *n* crude oil.—**crudely** *adv*.—**crudeness** *n*.

crude oil *n* unrefined petroleum.

crudités *npl* coarsely chopped raw vegetables eaten with a dip.

crudity *n* (*pl* **crudities**) crudeness; a crude act or expression.

cruel *adj* (**crueller, cruellest**) disposed to give pain to others; merciless; hard-hearted; fierce; painful; unrelenting.—**cruelly** *adv*.—**cruelty** *n*.

cruelty *n* (*pl* **cruelties**) inhumanity; savageness; a cruel act.

cruet *n* a small glass bottle for vinegar and oil, used at the table; a set of containers holding salt, pepper, vinegar.

cruise *vi* to sail to and fro; to wander about; to move at the most efficient speed for sustained travel. * *vt* to cruise over or about. * *n* a voyage from place to place for military purposes or in a liner for pleasure.

cruise missile *n* a subsonic low-flying guided missile.

cruiser *n* fast warship smaller than a battleship; a pleasure yacht or motorboat.

crumb *n* a fragment of bread; the soft part of bread; a little piece of anything; (*sl*) a despicable person. * *vi* to cover food with breadcrumbs before cooking.

crumble *vt* to break into crumbs; to cause to fall into pieces. * *vi* to disappear gradually, to disintegrate.—**crumbly** *adj*.

crumby *adj* (**crumbier, crumbiest**) in crumbs; soft.—**crumbiness** *n*.

crummy *adj* (**crummier, crummiest**) (*sl*) dirty, squalid, worthless; slightly ill.—**crumminess** *n*.

crump *n* a bursting shell; the crunching or exploding sound of this. * *vi* to explode. * *vt* to shell; to hit (a ball) hard.

crumpet *n* a soft cake with holes on one side, often eaten toasted; (*sl*) a sexually attractive woman.

crumple *vti* to twist or crush into wrinkles; to crease; to collapse. * *n* a wrinkle or crease made by crumpling.—**crumply** *adj*.

crunch *vti* to crush with the teeth; to tread underfoot with force and noise; to make a sound like this; to chew audibly. * *n* the sound or act of crunching; (*with the*) (*inf*) the crucial moment, the time of vital decision.

crunchy *adj* (**crunchier, crunchiest**) crisp; able to be crunched.—**crunchily** *adv*.—**crunchiness** *n*.

crupper *n* a looped leather band attached to the back of a saddle and passing under the horse's tail; the hindquarters of a horse.

crural *adj* of the leg or thigh; leg-shaped.

crus *n* (*pl* **crura**) the leg proper; a part resembling a leg.

crusade *n* a medieval Christian military expedition to recover the Holy Land; a vigorous concerted action for the defence of a cause or the advancement of an idea. * *vi* to engage in a crusade.—**crusader** *n*.

cruse *n* a small earthenware pot or dish for holding liquids.

crush *vt* to press between two opposite bodies; to squeeze; to break by pressure; to bruise; to ruin; to quell, to defeat; to mortify. * *vi* to be pressed out of shape or into a smaller compass. * *n* a violent compression or collision; a dense crowd; (*inf*) a large party; a drink made from crushed fruit; (*sl*) an infatuation.—**crushable** *adj*.—**crusher** *n*.

crust *n* any hard external coating or rind; the exterior solid part of the earth's surface; a shell or hard covering; (*sl*) a means of livelihood. * *vti* to cover or become covered with a crust.—**crusty** *adj* (**crustier, crustiest**).—**crustily** *adv*.—**crustiness** *n*.

crustacean *n* any aquatic animal with a hard shell, including crabs, lobsters, shrimps, and barnacles .—*also adj*.—**crustaceous** *adj*.

crutch *n* a staff with a crosswise head to support the weight of a lame person; something that supports; a prop; the crotch.

crux *n* (*pl* **cruxes, cruces**) a difficult problem; the essential or deciding point.

cry *vb* (**crying, cried**) *vi* to call aloud; to proclaim; to exclaim vehemently; to implore; to shed tears; (*with* **off**) (*inf*) to cancel (an agreement, arrangement, etc), to renege; (*with* **out**) to shout due to fear or pain. * *vt* to utter loudly and publicly; (*with* **out for**) to be in dire need of. * *n* (*pl* **cries**) an inarticulate sound; an exclamation of wonder or triumph; an outcry; clamour; an urgent appeal; a spell of weeping; a battle cry; a catchword; the particular sound made by an animal or bird.

crybaby *n* (*pl* **crybabies**) a child who weeps easily; a person who cries or complains often.

cryo- *prefix* frost; freezing.

cryoextraction *n* the extraction of juice from grapes that have been frozen before pressing to obtain a higher level of sugar and fruitier taste.

cryogen *n* a substance for producing freezing temperatures.

cryogenics *n* (*sing*) the science of very low temperatures and their effects.

cryolite *n* a mineral from which aluminium is produced.

cryometer *n* an instrument for measuring very low temperatures.—**cryometry** *n*.

cryonic suspension *n* the process of freezing a corpse in the hope that it may be restored to life in the future.

cryonics *n* (*sing*) the use of extreme cold to preserve living tissue (eg organs) for future use.

cryosurgery *n* surgery involving freezing to destroy or remove diseased tissue.

crypt *n* an underground chamber or vault, esp under a church, used as a chapel or for burial.

crypt-, crypto- *prefix* hidden.

cryptaesthesia, cryptesthesia *n* clairvoyance; extrasensory perception.

cryptic, cryptical *adj* hidden, secret; mysterious.

cryptogam *n* a plant without stamens or pistil, a nonflowering plant, as mosses, ferns, etc.—**cryptogamic, cryptogamous** *adj*.

cryptogram *n* a coded message, cipher.

cryptograph *n* a piece of writing in cipher.

cryptography *n* the art of code writing and breaking.—**cryptographer** *n*.—**cryptographic** *adj*.

cryptozoology *n* the study of creatures whose existence has yet to be proved, eg the yeti, the Loch Ness monster.

crystal *n* a solid piece, eg of quartz, geometrically shaped owing to regular arrangement of its atoms; very clear, brilliant glass; articles of such glass, as goblets; (*sl*) the drug methamphetamine packaged and sold as a stimulant in powdered form (—*also* **crystal meth**). * *adj* made of crystal.—**crystalline** *adj*.

crystal gazing *n* fortune telling by peering into a ball of crystal.

crystalline *adj* pertaining to or having the form of a crystal; clear; transparent.—**crystallinity** *n*.

crystalline lens *n* a transparent biconvex solid body enclosed in a capsule between the vitreous and acqueous humours of the eye.

crystallize *vti* to form crystals; to give definite form; to express clearly the theme and content of an argument, proposition, etc.—**crystallization** n.

crystallography *n* the science of the forms and structure of crystals.—**crystallographer** *n*.—**crystallographic** *adj*.

crystalloid *adj* resembling a crystal; of a crystalline structure, opposite to colloid. * *n* a crystalloid substance; one of certain bodies that in solution diffuse readily through animal membranes.

Cs (*chem symbol*) = caesium.

c/s *abbr* = cycles per second.

CS gas *n* an irritant gas used in quelling riots and disturbances.

CST *abbr* = Central Standard Time.

CT *abbr* = Connecticut.

ct *abbr* = carat; cent; court.

ctenidium *n* *pl* **ctenidia**) one of the respiratory organs of molluscs.

ctenoid *adj* having a comb-like margin.

Cu (*chem symbol*) = copper.

cu. *abbr* = cubic.

cub *n* a young carnivorous mammal; a young, inexperienced person; (*with cap*) a Cub Scout. * *vi* (**cubbing, cubbed**) to bring forth cubs.

cubage, cubature *n* the act of determining the contents of a solid; the contents so measured.

cubbyhole *n* a small or snug place; a pigeonhole.

cube *n* a solid body with six equal square sides or faces; a cube-shaped block; the product of a number multiplied by itself twice. * *vt* to raise (number) to the third power, or cube; to cut into cube-shaped pieces.

cubeb *n* a species of pepper of Asia; its small spicy berry dried and used as a stimulant.

cube root *n* the number that gives the stated number when cubed.

cubic *adj* having the form or properties of a cube; three-dimensional.

cubical *adj* of or pertaining to volume; cube-shaped.

cubicle *n* a small separate sleeping compartment in a dormitory, etc.

cubiculum *n* (*pl* **cubicula**) a burial chamber in a catacomb.

cubism *n* a style of painting in which objects are depicted as fragmented and reorganized geometrical forms.—**cubist** *n*.—**cubistic** *adj*.—**cubistically** *adv*.

cubit *n* an ancient measure of about 18 inches; the forearm from the elbow to the wrist.

cubital *adj* of the forearm.

cuboid *adj* like a cube. * *n* a regular solid contained by parallelograms.

Cub Scout *n* a junior branch of the Scout Association.

cuckold *n* a man whose wife has committed adultery.—**cuckoldry** *n*.

cuckoo *n* a bird with a dark plumage, a curved bill and a characteristic call that lays its eggs in the nests of other birds. * *adj* (*inf*) crazy, silly.

cuckoo clock *n* a clock that strikes the hours with a cuckoo call.

cuckoopint *n* a European plant with large leaves, purple flowers and bearing red berries.

cuckoo spit *n* a white froth exuded by froghopper larvae on the leaves of plants.

cucullate, cucullated *adj* hooded; hood-shaped.

cucumber *n* a long juicy fruit used in salads and as a pickle; the creeping plant that bears it.

cucurbit *n* any of an order of succulent, climbing, tendril-bearing plants with a fleshy fruit, including cucumbers, pumpkins, melons, etc.

cud *n* the food that a ruminating animal brings back into the mouth to chew again; **chew the cud** to consider and mull over.

cudbear *n* a purple dye made from lichens.

cuddle *vt* to embrace or hug closely. * *vt* to nestle together. * *n* a close embrace.

cuddlesome *adj* tempting to cuddle.

cuddly *adj* (**cuddlier, cuddliest**) given to cuddling; tempting to cuddle.

cuddy *n* (**cuddies**) (*naut*) the cabin of a half-decked boat; a small cabin, a galley.

cudgel *n* a short thick stick for beating. * *vt* (**cudgelling, cudgelled** *or* **cudgeling, cudgeled**) to beat with a cudgel.—**cudgeller, cudgeler** *n*.

cudweed *n* a plant with a fine down, belonging to the aster family.

cue[1] *n* the last word of a speech in a play, serving as a signal for the next actor to enter or begin to speak; any signal to do something; a hint. * *vt* (**cueing** *or* **cuing, cued**) to give a cue to.

cue[2] *n* a tapering rod used in snooker, billiards, and pool to strike the cue ball.

cue ball *n* (*snooker, etc*) the ball that a player strikes in order to hit other balls.

cuff[1] *n* a blow with the fist or the open hand. * *vt* to strike such a blow.

cuff[2] *n* the end of a sleeve; a covering round the wrist; the turn-up on a trouser leg.

cufflink *n* a decorative clip for fastening the edges of a shirt cuff.

cuirass *n* defensive armour for the breast and back, a breastplate.

cuirassier *n* a cavalry soldier armed with a cuirass.

cuisine *n* a style of cooking or preparing food; the food prepared.

cuisse *n* defensive armour for the thighs.

culch *n* materials forming a spawning bed for oysters; oyster spawn.

cul-de-sac *n* (*pl* **culs-de-sac, cul-de-sacs**) a street blocked off at one end; a blind alley; a position, job leading nowhere.

-cule *n suffix* forming diminutives, as *animalcule*.

culinary *adj* of or relating to cooking.

cull *vt* to select; to pick out, gather. * *n* the selection of certain animals with the intention of killing them.—**culler** *n*.

cullet *n* broken or refuse glass for recycling.

culm[1] *n* the stem of grasses.

culm[2] *n* inferior anthracite coal.

culminate *vti* to reach the highest point of altitude, rank, power, etc; (*astron*) to reach the meridian; to bring to a head or the highest point.—**culminant** *adj*.—**culmination** *n*.

culottes *npl* a women's flared trousers that resemble a skirt.

culpable *adj* deserving censure; criminal; blameworthy.—**culpably** *adv*.—**culpability** *n*.

culprit *n* a person accused, or found guilty, of an offence.

cult *n* a system of worship; devoted attachment to a person, principle, etc; a religion regarded as unorthodox or spurious; its body of adherents; a current fashion.—**cultic** *adj*.—**cultism** *n*.—**cultist** *n*.

cultivate *vt* to till and plant; to improve by care, labour, or study; to seek the society of; to civilize or refine.—**cultivated** *adj*.

cultivation *n* the act of cultivating; the state of being cultivated; tillage; culture.

cultivator *n* a machine for breaking up soil for cultivation; someone who cultivates.

cultrate, cultrated *adj* (*bot*) shaped like a pruning knife; pointed and sharp-edged.

cultural *adj* pertaining to culture.—**culturally** *adv*.

culture *n* appreciation and understanding of the arts; the skills, arts, etc of a given people in a given period; the entire range of customs, beliefs, social forms, and material traits of a religious, social, or racial group; the scientific cultivation of plants to improve them and find new species; improvement of the mind, manner, etc; a growth of bacteria, etc in a prepared substance.* *vt* to cultivate bacteria for study or use.

cultured *adj* educated to appreciate the arts; having good taste; artificially grown, as cultured pearls.

cultured pearl *n* a pearl induced to grow artificially by the injection of a foreign body into the closed shell.

culture shock *n* loss of bearings and distress caused by an uprooting from a familiar environment or culture.

culverin *n* a 16th-century long cannon with serpent-shaped handles.

culvert *n* a drain or conduit under a road.

cum *prep* with.

cumarin *see* **coumarin**.

cumber *vt* to hamper, to burden. * *n* a hindrance.

cumbersome *adj* inconveniently heavy or large, unwieldy.

cumin, cummin *n* a plant cultivated for its seeds which are used as a spice.

cummerbund *n* a sash worn as a waistband, esp with a man's tuxedo.

cumshaw *n* in China, a present or bonus.

cumulate *vt* to accumulate; to combine into one; to build up by adding new material.—**cumulation** *n*.

cumulative *adj* augmenting or giving force; growing by successive additions; gathering strength as it grows.—**cumulatively** *adv*.

cumulative voting *n* a system of voting in which each voter has as many votes as there are candidates, and may give all to one candidate.

cumulus *n* (*pl* **cumuli**) a cloud form having a flat base and rounded outlines.

cuneate *adj* wedge-shaped.

cuneiform *adj* wedge-shaped (—*also* **cuneal**). * *n* the wedge-shaped characters of ancient Assyrian and Persian writing.

cunnilingus *n* sexual stimulation of the female genitals by the tongue.

cunning *adj* ingenious; sly; designing; subtle. * *n* slyness, craftiness.

cunt *n* (*vulg*) the female genitals, the vagina; (*derog*) a woman; (*offensive*) an obnoxious person.

cup *n* a small, bowl-shaped container for liquids, usu with a handle; the amount held in a cup; a drink made from a mixture of drinks with one main ingredient (eg *claret cup*); one of two shaped supporting parts of a brassiere; an ornamental cup used as a trophy. * *vt* (**cupping, cupped**) to take or put as in a cup; to curve (the hands) into the shape of a cup.

cupbearer *n* one who serves wine at a banquet, esp an officer of a royal household.

cupboard *n* a closet or cabinet with shelves for cups, plates, utensils, food etc.

cupel *n* a small flat vessel used to assay precious metals. * *vt* (**cupelling, cupelled** *or* **cupeling, cupeled**) to refine precious metals from lead in a cupel.

cupful *n* (*pl* **cupfuls**) as much as a cup will contain.

Cupid *n* the god of love in Roman mythology.

cupidity *n* greed of gain; covetousness.

cupola *n* a dome, esp a pointed or bulbous shape; a furnace for melting metals.—**cupolated** *adj*.

cupreous *adj* of or like copper; coppery.

cupric, cuprous *adj* containing copper.

cupriferous *adj* yielding copper.

cuprite *n* red oxide of copper.

cupule *n* (*biol*) a cup-shaped part, as of the acorn.

cur *n* a mongrel dog; a despicable person.

curable *adj* able to be cured, remediable.—**curability** *n*.—**curably** *adv*.

curaçao *n* an orange-flavoured liqueur.

curacy *n* (*pl* **curacies**) the office or district of a curate.

curare, curari *n* a substance extracted from vines and used by South American Indians to poison arrows.

curarine *n* an alkaloid extract of curare used as a muscle relaxant.

curarize *vt* to poison with curare.—**curarization** *n*.

curassow *n* a large turkey-like bird of South America.

curate *n* an assistant of a vicar or rector.

curative *adj* tending to cure. * *n* a curative agent or drug.

curator *n* a superintendent of a museum, art gallery, etc.—**curatorial** *adj*.

curb *vt* to restrain; to check; to keep in subjection. * *n* that which checks, restrains, or subdues; a line of raised stone forming the edge of a pavement (—*also* **kerb**).

curbing *n* curbstones collectively; material for curbstones.—*also* **kerbing**.

curb roof *n* a roof with a double slope, the lower being steeper.

curbstone *n* the stone edge of a path.—*also* **kerbstone**.

curcuma *n* one of several kinds of plant including turmeric.

curd *n* the coagulated part of soured milk, used to make cheese.—**curdy** *adj*.—**curdiness** *n*.

curdle *vti* to turn into curds; to coagulate; (*with* **the blood**) to cause terror.—**curdler** *n*.

cure *n* the act or art of healing; a remedy; restoration to health. * *vt* to heal; to rid of; to preserve meat or fish by drying, salting, etc.

curé *n* a French parish priest.

curettage *n* surgical scraping to remove growths or dead tissue, etc.

curette, curet *n* a surgical instrument for scraping a body cavity. * *vt* (**curetting, curetted**) to scrape with this.

curfew *n* a signal, as a bell, at a fixed evening hour as a sign that everyone must be indoors; the signal or hour.

curia *n* (*pl* **curiae**) the papal court; a senate house of ancient Rome; one of the divisions of the Roman people; a medieval court of justice.

curie *n* a unit of radioactivity.

curio *n* (*pl* **curios**) an item valued as rare or unusual.

curiosity *n* (*pl* **curiosities**) the quality of being curious; inquisitiveness; a strange, rare or interesting object.

curious *adj* anxious to know, prying, inquisitive, strange, remarkable, odd.—**curiously** *adv*.—**curiousness** *n*.

curium *n* an artificially made radioactive metallic element derived from plutonium.

curl *vti* to form into a curved shape, to coil; to twist into ringlets; to proceed in a curve, to bend; to play at curling; (*with* up) to rest with the body in a curved shape and the legs drawn up; to relax in a comfortable place; (*inf*) to give up; to be embarrassed and sickened by. * *n* a ringlet of hair; a spiral form, a twist; a bend or undulation.

curler *n* a small pin or roller used for curling the hair; a person who plays curling.

curlew *n* a bird with a long curved bill and long legs.

curlicue *n* an exaggerated ornamental curl.

curling *n* a Scottish game in which two teams slide large smooth stones on ice into a target circle.

curling stone *n* a heavy round flat stone with a handle used in curling.

curling tongs *n* a pair of tongs heated to curl hair.

curly *adj* (**curlier, curliest**) full of curls.—**curliness** *n*.

curmudgeon *n* an ill-natured churlish person; a miser.—**curmudgeonly** *adj*.

currant *n* a small variety of dried grape; a shrub that yields a red or black fruit.

currency *n* (*pl* **currencies**) the time during which a thing is current; the state of being in use; the money current in a country.

current *adj* generally accepted; happening now; presently in circulation. * *n* a body of water or air in motion, a flow; the transmission of electricity through a conductor; a general tendency.

current account *n* a bank account, usu with no interest, from which money is withdrawn by cheques or cash cards; a checking account.

currently *adv* at the present time.

curricle *n* a two-wheeled open carriage drawn by two horses abreast.

curriculum *n* (*pl* **curricula, curriculums**) a prescribed course of study.—**curricular** *adj*.

curriculum vitae *n* (*pl* **curricula vitae**) a brief survey of one's career.

currier *n* a leather dresser.—**curriery** *n*.

currish *adj* snappy; quarrelsome; rude.

curry[1] *n* (*pl* **curries**) a spicy dish with a hot sauce; curry seasoning. * *vt* (*pl* **currying, curried**) to flavour with curry.

curry[2] *vt* (**currying, curried**) to rub down and groom (a horse); to dress leather after tanning; to beat; (*with* **favour**) to use flattery to ingratiate.

currycomb *n* a metal comb for grooming horses.

curse n a calling down of destruction or evil; a profane oath; a swear word; a violent exclamation of anger; a scourge. * vti to invoke a curse on; to swear, to blaspheme; to afflict, to torment.

cursed adj damnable.

cursive adj running; flowing. * n a script with the letters joined, as in handwriting.

cursor n a flashing indicator on a computer screen indicating position; the transparent slide on a slide rule.

cursorial adj (bird) with limbs adapted for running or walking.

cursory adj hasty, passing; superficial, careless.—**cursorily** adv.

curt adj short; abrupt; concise; rudely brief.—**curtly** adv.—**curtness** n.

curtail vt to cut short; to reduce; to deprive of part (of).—**curtailment** n.

curtain n a cloth hung as a screen at a window, etc; the movable screen separating the stage from the auditorium; (pl: sl) the end, death. * vt to enclose in, or as with, curtains.

curtain call n (theat) a call from the audience for performers to appear at the end to receive applause.

curtain lecture n a private reprimand from a wife to her husband.

curtain-raiser n a short play preceding the main one; an introductory item.

curtilage n (law) a yard, garden or enclosure of a house, included in the same fence.

curtsy, curtsey n (pl **curtsies, curtseys**) a formal gesture of greeting or respect, involving bending the knees, made by women. * vi (**curtsying, curtsied** or **curtseying, curtseyed**) to make a curtsy.

curvaceous adj (inf) having an attractive body with shapely curves.

curvature n a bending; a curved form.

curve n a bending without angles; a bent form or thing; (geom) a line of which no part is straight. * vti to form into a curve, to bend.—**curvy** adj (**curvier, curviest**).

curvet n a particular leap of a horse; a frisk or bound. *vi (**curvetting, curvetted** or **curveting, curveted**) to leap as a horse; to frisk or bound.

curvilinear, curvilineal adj consisting of or bounded by curved lines.—**curvilinearity** n.

cusec n a unit of flow of one cubic foot of water per second.

cushion n a case stuffed with soft material for resting on; the elastic border around a snooker table; the air mass supporting a hovercraft. * vt to furnish with cushions; to protect by padding; to give protection against difficulties, etc; to soften the effect of.—**cushiony** adj.

cushy adj (**cushier, cushiest**) (inf) easy, comfortable.

cusp n an apex or point; the point at each end of a crescent moon; (astrol) the transitional point of a house; (archit) the pointed intersection between two arcs; a cone-shaped point on a tooth; a fold or flap of a heart valve.

cuspid n a canine tooth.

cuspidate, cuspidal adj of, like or having a cusp; (leaves, etc) ending in a point.

cuspidor n a spittoon.

cuss n (sl) an annoying person; a curse. * vt (sl) to curse.

cussed adj (sl) cursed; stubborn, perverse.

cussedness n (sl) contrariness.

custard n a sauce mixture of milk, eggs and sugar.

custard apple n a West Indian tree; its dark fruit with a soft edible pulp.

custodian n one who has the care of anything; a keeper; a caretaker.

custody n (pl **custodies**) guardianship; imprisonment; security.—**custodial** adj.

custom n a regular practice; usage; traditions of a people or a society; frequent repetition of the same act; business patronage; (pl) duties on imports.

customary adj habitual; conventional; common.—**customarily** adv.

custom-built adj made to a customer's specifications.

customer n a person who buys from a shop or business, esp regularly; (inf) a person.

custom house n an office or building where duties are paid on exported or imported goods and vessels are entered and cleared.

cut vb (**cutting, cut**) vt to cleave or separate with a sharp instrument; to make an incision in; to wound with a sharp instrument; to divide; to trim; to intersect; to abridge; to diminish; to pass deliberately without recognition; to wound the feelings deeply; to reduce or curtail; to grow a new tooth through the gum; to divide (a pack of cards) at random; to switch off (a light, an engine); (inf) to stay away from class, school, etc; (with **back**) to prune vegetation; to economize; (with **down**) to fell a tree; to reduce expenditure, consumption, etc; to make a smaller garment from an old one; to kill; (with **off**) to take away by cutting or slicing; to stop abruptly, esp a telephone conversation; to sever relations; to be so placed as to foil something, eg an escape; (with **out**) to delete; to cut into shapes; (inf) to force out a rival; to give up an indulgence or habit; (with **up**) to cut into pieces; to wound with a knife; (inf) to affect deeply. * vi to make an incision; to perform the work of an edged instrument; to grow through the gums; (cinema) to change to another scene, to stop photographing; (with **in**) to butt in; to interpose oneself; to interrupt with comments; to drive between two vehicles, leaving insufficient space; (with **out**) (engine) to stop working. * n an incision or wound made by a sharp instrument; a gash; a sharp stroke; a sarcastic remark; a passage or channel cut out; a slice; a block on which an engraving is cut; the fashion or shape of a garment; the deliberate ignoring of an acquaintance; the division of a pack of cards; a diminution in price below another merchant; (sl) a share, as of profits. * adj divided or separated; gashed; having the surface ornamented or fashioned; not wrought or hand-made; reduced in price.

cutaneous adj pertaining to the skin.

cutaway n a drawing (of a machine) with part of the exterior covering cut away to show the internal mechanism; (film) a scene shot separately from but relevant to the main action.

cutback n a reduction, esp in expenditure; a flashback.

cutch see **catechu**.

cute adj (inf) acute, shrewd; pretty or attractive, esp in a dainty way.—**cutely** adv.—**cuteness** n.

cut glass n flint glass cut into facets or figures.

cuticle n the skin at the base of the fingernail or toe nail; epidermis.—**cuticular** adj.

cutie n (sl) a bright smart girl.

cutis n (pl **cutes, cutises**) the vascular layer of the skin, below the epidermis.

cutlass n a sailor's short heavy sword.

cutler n a maker of or dealer in knives.

cutlery n knives, forks, etc for eating and serving food.

cutlet *n* a neck chop of lamb, etc; a small slice cut off from the ribs or leg; minced meat in the form of a cutlet.

cutoff *n* a short or straight road; a new shorter channel cut by a river across a bend; a device for stopping steam from entering a cylinder.

cutout *n* a switch to cut off an electric light from a circuit.

cutpurse *n* a pickpocket.

cutter *n* someone or something that cuts; a small, swift sailing vessel; a light boat carried by larger ships.

cutthroat *n* a murderer. * *adj* merciless; (*razor*) having a long blade in a handle.

cutting *n* a piece cut off or from; an incision; a newspaper clipping; a slip from a plant for propagation; a passage or channel cut out; the process of editing a film or recording; a recording. * *adj* (*wind*) sharp, biting; (*remarks*) hurtful.

cuttlebone *n* the internal bone of the cuttlefish, used for polishing, etc.

cuttlefish *n* (*pl* **cuttlefish, cuttlefishes**) a marine creature with a flattened body that squirts ink when threatened.

cutwater *n* the fore part of a ship's prow.

cutwork *n* appliqué work.

CV *abbr* = curriculum vitae.

cwt. *abbr* = hundredweight.

cyan *n* a blue colour, one of the primary colours.

cyanamide, cyanamid *n* a chemical compound of calcium carbide and nitrogen, used as a fertilizer.

cyanate *n* a compound of cyanic acid with a base.

cyanic acid *n* a strong acid composed of cyanogen and oxygen.

cyanide *n* a poison.

cyanogen *n* a colourless poisonous gas burning with a purple flame and with the odour of peach blossom.

cyanosis *n* a condition of the body in which its surface becomes blue due to insufficient aeration of the blood.—**cyanotic** *adj*.

cyanotype *n* a photographic process in which the picture is taken in Prussian blue; a blueprint.

cybernetics *n* (*sing*) the study of communication and control functions in living organisms, and in mechanical and electronic systems.—**cybernetic** *adj*.

cyberphobia *n* a morbid fear or intense dislike of computers.—**cyberphobic** *adj*.

cyclamen *n* a plant of the primrose family, with pink, purple or white flowers.

cycle *n* a recurring series of events or phenomena; the period of this; a body of epics or romances with a common theme; a group of songs; a bicycle, motorcycle, or tricycle. * *vi* to go in cycles; to ride a bicycle or tricycle.

cyclic, cyclical *adj* moving or recurring in cycles.—**cyclically** *adv*.

cyclist *n* a person who rides a bicycle.

cycloid *n* a curve traced by a point on a circle as it rolls along a straight line.—**cycloidal** *adj*.

cyclometer *n* an instrument for registering the revolutions of a wheel.—**cyclometry** *n*.

cyclone *n* a violent circular storm; an atmospheric movement in which the wind blows spirally round towards a centre of low barometric pressure.—**cyclonic** *adj*.

Cyclopean *adj* pertaining to the Cyclops, the legendary one-eyed giant; one-eyed; huge and rough; vast, massive; (*archit*) built of huge stones without mortar.

cyclopedia, cyclopaedia *n* an encyclopedia.—**cyclopedic, cyclopaedic** *adj*.

cyclorama *n* a series of moving pictures extended circularly so as to appear in natural perspective to the viewer standing in the centre.—**cycloramic** *adj*.

cyclotron *n* an apparatus for accelerating charged particles in a magnetic field.

cygnet *n* a young swan.

cylinder *n* a hollow figure or object with parallel sides and circular ends; an object shaped like a cylinder; any machine part of this shape; the piston chamber in an engine.—**cylindrical** *adj*.—**cylindrically** *adv*.

cylindroid *adj* like a cylinder. * *n* a solid body resembling a cylinder but with the ends elliptical.

cyma *n* (*pl* **cymae, cymas**) (*archit*) ogee moulding of a cornice.

cymbal *n* (*mus*) one of a pair of two brass plates struck together to produce a ringing or clashing sound.—**cymbalist** *n*.

cyme *n* a flower cluster in which the main stem ends in a flower, while from each side of the main stem secondary stems branch off to end a flower, and tertiary stems from those, etc.—**cymose** *adj*.

Cymric *adj* pertaining to the Cymry, or the Welsh. * *n* the Welsh language.

cynic *n* a morose, surly, or sarcastic person; a sceptic about people, motives and actions; one of a sect of ancient Greek philosophers.—**cynicism** *n*.

cynical *adj* sceptical of or sneering at goodness; shameless in admitting unworthy motives.—**cynically** *adv*.

cynosure *n* a centre of attraction or admiration.

cypher *see* **cipher**.

cypress *n* an evergreen tree with hard wood.

Cyprian *adj* of Cyprus; of Aphrodite, the Greek goddess of love; wanton, lascivious. * *n* a native of Cyprus; a prostitute.

cyprinid *n* any of a family of freshwater fishes, including the carp.

cyprinoid *adj* of or resembling a cyprinid; carp-like.

Cypriot *adj* pertaining to Cyprus, or to its inhabitants. * *n* a native of Cyprus.

Cyrillic *adj* of or pertaining to St Cyril, or to the Slavonic alphabet. * *n* the alphabet of the Slavonic languages.

cyst *n* a closed sac developing abnormally in the structure of plants or animals.—**cystic** *adj*.

cystic fibrosis *n* a congenital disorder in young children characterized by chronic respiratory and digestive problems.

cystitis *n* inflammation of the urinary bladder.

cystocele *n* a hernia caused by protrusion of the bladder.

cystoid *adj* cyst-like. * *n* a growth resembling a cyst.

cystolith *n* a stone in the bladder.

cystoscope *n* an instrument for examining the urinary bladder.—**cystoscopic** *adj*.—**cystoscopy** *n*.

cystotomy *n* (*pl* **cystotomies**) the opening of the human bladder for the removal of a stone, etc.

cyt-, cyto- *prefix* cell.

cytogenesis, cytogeny *n* cell formation in plants and animals.

cytology *n* the scientific study of cells; cell structure.—**cytological** *adj*.—**cytologist** *n*.

cytoplasm *n* the substance of a cell as opposed to its nucleus.—**cytoplasmic** *adj*.

cytoscreening *n* the examination of smear tests for indications of cervical cancer.

czar *see* **tsar**.

czardas *n* a Hungarian national dance with varying tempos; the music for it.

czarevitch *see* **tsarevitch**.

czarina, czaritsa *see* **tsarina, tsaritsa**.

Czech *n* a native, or the language, of the Czech Republic.

D

D (*symbol*) (*mus*) the second note of the C major scale; (*chem*) deuterium; five hundred.

d *abbr* = penny or pennies (UK currency before 1971)

DA *abbr* = District Attorney.

dab[1] *vt* (**dabbing, dabbed**) to touch lightly with something moist or soft. * *n* a quick light tap; a small lump of anything moist or soft.—**dabber** *n*.

dab[2] *n* a species of European flounder.

dab[3] *n* (*inf*) a dab hand.

dabble *vi* to move hands, feet, etc gently in water or another liquid; (*usu with* **at, in, with**) to do anything in a superficial or dilettante way. * *vt* to splash.—**dabbler** *n*.

dabchick *n* a water bird, the little grebe.

dab hand *n* (*inf*) an adept person, an expert.

da capo *adj, adv* (*mus*) from the beginning.

dace *n* (*pl* **dace**) a small freshwater fish of the carp family.

dacha *n* in Russia, a house in the country used as a holiday and summer residence.

dachshund *n* a breed of short-legged, long-bodied hound.

dacoit *n* one of a group of robbers in India and Burma, who plunder in bands.—*also* **dakoit**.

dactyl *n* a poetic foot of three syllables, one long and two short.—**dactylic** *adj, n*.

dactylogram *n* a fingerprint.

dactylography *n* the science of fingerprints.—**dactylographer** *n*.—**dactylographic** *adj*.

dactylology *n* the art of communicating ideas with the fingers; sign language.

dad *n* (*inf*) father.

Dada *n* a school of art and literature that aims at suppressing all relations between thought and expression.—**Dadaism** *n*.— **Dadaist** *n*—**Dadaistic** *adj*.

daddy *n* (*pl* **daddies**) (*inf*) father.

daddy longlegs *n* (*inf*) any of various spiders or insects with long, slender legs, esp a crane fly.

dado *n* (*pl* **dadoes**) the lower part of a room wall when separately panelled or decorated.

daff *vi* (*Scot*) to sport, to play.

daffodil *n* a yellow spring flower, a narcissus; its pale yellow colour.

daft *adj* (*inf*) silly, weak-minded; giddy; mad.—**daftly** *adv*.—**daftness** *n*.

dagger *n* a short weapon for stabbing; a reference mark used in printing (†) (—*also* **obelisk**).

dago *n* (*pl* **dagos, dagoes**) (*offensive*) a foreigner, esp from Spain or Portugal.

daguerreotype *n* an early photographic process using a copper plate; a picture taken by this process.—**daguerreotypy** *n*.

dahlia *n* a half-hardy tuberous perennial of the aster family grown for its colourful blooms.

daily *adj, adv* (happening) every day; constantly, progressively. * *n* (*pl* **dailies**) a newspaper published every weekday; (*inf*) a charwoman.

dainty *adj* (**daintier, daintiest**) delicate; choice; nice, fastidious. * *n* (*pl* **dainties**) a titbit, a delicacy.—**daintily** *adv*.—**daintiness** *n*.

daiquiri *n* (*pl* **daiquiris**) a cocktail of rum, sugar and lime juice.

dairy *n* (*pl* **dairies**) a building or room where milk is stored and dairy products made; a shop selling these; a company supplying them.

dairy cattle *npl* cows reared for milk production.

dairying *n* the business or occupation of a dairy farmer.

dairyman *n* (*pl* **dairymen**) a person who works in a dairy or deals in dairy products.

dairy products *npl* milk and products made from it, eg butter, cheese, yogurt.

dais *n* a low platform at one end of a hall or room.

daisy *n* (*pl* **daisies**) any of various plants with a yellow centre and white petals.

daisywheel *n* (*comput*) a flat, wheel-shaped, printing device with characters at the ends of spokes.

dal *n* a split-grain pulse commonly used in Indian cooking.—*also* **dhal**.

Dalai Lama *n* the chief lama of Tibet.

dale *n* a valley.

dalliance *n* idle or frivolous time-wasting; trifling; flirtation.

dally *vi* (**dallying, dallied**) to lose time by idleness or trifling; to play or trifle (with); to flirt.—**dallier** *n*.

dallymoney *n* (*sl*) alimony paid by one partner in a former sexual relationship to the other.

Dalmatian *n* a large short-haired dog with black spot-like markings on a white body.

dalmatic *n* a loose vestment with open sides worn esp by a bishop.

dam[1] *n* an artificial embankment to retain water; water so contained. * *vt* (**damming, dammed**) to retain (water) with such a barrier; to stem, obstruct, restrict.

dam[2] *n* the mother of a four-footed animal.

damage *n* injury, harm; loss; (*inf*) price, cost; (*pl*) (*law*) payment in compensation for loss or injury. * *vt* to do harm to, to injure.—**damageable** *adj*.—**damager** *n*.—**damaging** *adj*.

damask *n* a reversible, figured, woven fabric, esp linen or silk. * *adj* made of this; having a pinkish colour like a damask rose.

damask rose *n* a rose with greyish-pink blooms and a sweet fragrance used in perfume making.

dame *n* the comic, female role in a pantomime usu played by a man; (*sl*) a woman; (*with cap*) the title of a woman who has been awarded an order of chivalry equivalent to the title of a Knight; the wife of a knight or baronet.

dammar, damar *n* a resin used for varnish.

damn *vt* to condemn, censure; to ruin; to curse; to consign to eternal punishment. * *vti* to prove guilty. * *interj* (*sl*) expressing irritation or annoyance. * *n* (*sl*) something having no value. * *adj, adv* damned.

damnable *adj* deserving damnation; despicable; hateful; offensive; wicked; (*inf*) annoying.—**damnably** *adv*.

damnation *n* the state of being condemned to hell; the act of damning. * *interj* expressing annoyance, irritation, etc.

damnatory *adj* assigning to, or containing a threat of, damnation.

damned *adj* (*inf*) damnable; extremely.—*also adv*.

damnify *vt* (**damnifying, damnified**) (*law*) to cause loss or damage to.

damp *n* humidity, moisture; in mines, poisonous or foul gas. * *adj* slightly wet, moist. * *vt* to moisten; (*with* **down**) to stifle, reduce.—**damply** *adv*.—**dampness** *n*.

dampen *vti* to make or become damp. * *vt* to stifle.—**dampener** *n*.

damper *n* a depressive influence; a metal plate in a flue for controlling combustion; (*mus*) a device for stopping vibration in stringed instruments; (*Austral*) unleavened bread.

damsel *n* (*formerly*) a girl.

damselfly *n* (*pl* **damselflies**) an insect resembling the dragonfly but having wings that fold when at rest.

damson *n* a small, dark-purple variety of plum; the colour of this; the tree on which this fruit grows.

dance *vti* to move rhythmically, esp to music; to skip or leap lightly; to execute (steps); to cause to dance or to move up and down. * *n* a piece of dancing; a dance performance of an artistic nature; a party with music for dancing; music for accompanying dancing.—**dancer** *n*.—**dancing** *adj, n*.

D and C *n* (*med*) dilation (of the cervix) and curettage (of the womb).

dandelion *n* a common wild plant with ragged leaves, a yellow flower and a fluffy seed head.

dander[1] *n* scurf from various animals, eg cats, dogs, that may be allergenic; temper; fighting spirit.

dander[2] *vi* (*Scot*) to saunter. * *n* a sauntering stroll.

Dandie Dinmont *n* a breed of terrier.

dandify *vt* to give the character or style of a dandy to; to make trim or smart like a dandy.—**dandification** *n*.

dandle *vt* to play with (a baby) on the knee, to fondle.—**dandler** *n*.

dandruff *n* scales of skin on the scalp, under the hair, scurf.—**dandruffy** *adj*.

dandy *n* (*pl* **dandies**) a man who likes to dress too fashionably. * *adj* (**dandier, dandiest**) (*inf*) excellent, fine.—**dandyish** *adj*.—**dandyism** *n*.

dandy-brush *n* a stiff brush for grooming horses.

Dane *n* a native or citizen of Denmark.

Danegeld *n* an annual tax imposed in England in the reign of Ethelred II to maintain forces against the Danes.

Danelaw, Danelagh *n* the code of laws established by the Danes on their settlement in England; that part of the country where these laws were in force.

dang *adj, adv, interj, n* a euphemistic form of **damn**.

danger *n* exposure to injury or risk; a source of harm or risk.

dangerous *adj* involving danger; unsafe; perilous.—**dangerously** *adv*.—**dangerousness** *n*.

dangle *vi* to hang and swing loosely. * *vt* to carry something so that it hangs loosely; to display temptingly.—**dangler** *n*.

Danish *adj* of the people or language of Denmark. * *n* the language of Denmark.

Danish pastry *n* a sweet pastry topped with fruity icing and nuts.

dank *adj* disagreeably damp.—**dankly** *adv*.—**dankness** *n*.

danseur *n* a professional dancer, a ballet dancer.—**danseuse** *nf*.

dap *vb* (**dapping, dapped**) *vi* to drop bait gently into water * *vt* to dip lightly; to bounce (a ball) * *n* a bounce.

daphne *n* a genus of small evergreen shrubs with fragrant flowers, allied to the laurel.

dapper *adj* nimble; neat in appearance, spruce.

dapple *vti* to mark with or show patches of a different colour; to variegate. * *adj* marked in such a way. * *n* something so marked.

dapple-grey *adj* mottled with darker grey. * *n* a horse of this colour.

Dardanian, Dardan *adj* pertaining to Dardania, an ancient city of Troy, in Asia Minor, or its people. * *n* a Trojan.

dare *vti* (**daring, dared** *or* **durst**) to be bold enough; to venture, to risk; to defy, to challenge. * *n* a challenge.—**darer** *n*.

daredevil *n* a rash, reckless person. * *adj* daring, bold; courageous.—**daredevilry, daredeviltry** *n*.

daring *adj* fearless; courageous; unconventional. * *n* adventurous courage.—**daringly** *adv*.

dark *adj* having little or no light; of a shade of colour closer to black than white; (*person*) having brown or black skin or hair; gloomy; (*inf*) secret, unknown; mysterious. * *n* a dark state or colour; ignorance; secrecy.—**darkly** *adv*.—**darkness** *n*.

darken *vti* to make or become dark or darker.—**darkener** *n*.

dark horse *n* a competitor about whom little is known; a person of reserved character; a surprise political candidate.

darkish *adj* quite dark.

darkroom *n* a room for processing photographs in darkness or safe light.

darksome *adj* gloomy.

darling *n* a dearly loved person; a favourite. * *adj* lovable; much admired.

darn[1] *vt* to mend a hole in fabric or a garment with stitches. * *n* an area that has been darned.—**darner** *n*.

darn[2] *interj* a form of **damn** as a mild oath.—*also adj*.

darnel *n* a kind of rye grass.

darning *n* a patch made by darning; material, garments, etc to be darned.

dart *n* a small pointed missile; a sudden movement; a fold sewn into a garment for shaping it; (*pl*) an indoor game in which darts are thrown at a target. * *vti* to move rapidly; to send out rapidly.

dartboard *n* a circular cork or wooden target used in the game of darts.

darter *n* one of several kinds of bird or fish.

Darwinian *adj* pertaining to Charles Darwin, the naturalist (1809–82) or Darwinism. * *n* an evolutionist.

Darwinism *n* the theory of natural selection advocated by Darwin.—**Darwinist** *n*.

dash *vti* to fling violently; to rush quickly; (*hopes*) to shatter; (*one's spirits, etc*) to depress, confound; to write quickly. * *n* a short race; a rush; a small amount of something added to food; a tinge; a punctuation mark (—); a dashboard; vigour, verve; display.

dashboard *n* an instrument panel in a car.

dasher *n* one who or that which dashes; a dashing person; the part of a churn that agitates cream.

dashing *adj* debonair; spirited, stylish, dapper.—**dashingly** *adv*.

dastard *n* a malicious coward.

dastardly *adj* mean, cowardly; base.—**dastardliness** *n*.

dasyure *n* a small carnivorous Australian marsupial.

DAT *abbr* = digital audio tape.

data *npl* (*sing* **datum**) (*often used as sing*) facts, statistics, or information either historical or derived by calculation or experimentation.

data bank, database *n* a large store of information for analysis, esp one held in a computer.

data capture *n* the process of translating information into computer-readable form.

data processing *n* the analysis of information stored in a computer for various uses, eg stock control, statistical research, mathematical modelling, etc.

date[1] *n* a day or time of occurrence; a statement of this in a letter, etc; a period to which something belongs; a duration; an appointment, esp with a member of the opposite sex. * *vt* to affix a date to; to note the date of; to reckon the time of; (*inf*) to make a date with; (*inf*) to see frequently a member of the opposite sex. * *vi* to reckon from a point in time; to show signs of belonging to a particular period.—**datable, dateable** *adj*.—**dater** *n*.

date[2] *n* the sweet fruit of the date palm, a palm tree of tropical regions.

dated *adj* old-fashioned; out of style; bearing a date.—**datedness** *n*.

dateless *adj* without a date; timeless; classic.

dateline *n* a line on a newspaper story giving the date and place of writing. * *vt* to provide with a dateline.

date line *n* the line running north to south along the 180-degree meridian, east of which is one day earlier than west of it.—*also* **International Date Line**.

dative *adj* (*gram*) denoting an indirect object. * *n* the dative case.—**datival** *adj*.—**datively** *adv*.

datum *n* (*pl* **data**) a single unit of information; a thing given or taken for granted; something known or assumed as fact and made the basis of reasoning or calculation; an assumption or premise from which inferences are drawn; (*pl* **datums**) (*geol*) a level, line or point used as a reference in surveying.

datura *n* any of several kinds of strongly scented narcotic plant.

daub *vt* to smear or overlay (with clay, etc); to paint incompetently. * *n* a smear; a poor painting.—**dauber** *n*.

daughter *n* a female child or descendant; a female member of a family, race, etc; a woman in relation to her native country or place; (*physics*) a nucleus, particle, etc, produced from another by radioactive decay; (*biol*) a cell produced by the division of another.

daughter-in-law *n* (*pl* **daughters-in-law**) the wife of one's son.

daughterly *adj* of or befitting a daughter.—**daughterliness** *n*.

daunt *vt* to intimidate; to discourage.—**daunter** *n*.—**dauntingly** *adv*.

dauntless *adj* incapable of being discouraged; intrepid, fearless.—**dauntlessly** *adv*.—**dauntlessness** *n*.

dauphin *n* the title of the eldest son of the king of France, 1349–1830.

dauphine, dauphiness *n* the wife of the dauphin.

davenport *n* a large sofa, often able to be converted into a bed; a small ornamental writing desk.

davit *n* a small crane with tackle for raising or lowering a lifeboat, etc over a ship's side.

Davy Jones *n* the spirit of the sea.

Davy Jones's locker *n* the seabed, the deep, esp as the grave of those who die at sea.

daw *n* a bird of the crow family; a jackdaw.

dawdle *vi* to move slowly and waste time, to loiter.—**dawdler** *n*.

dawn *vi* (*day*) to begin to grow light; to begin to appear. * *n* daybreak; a first sign.

day *n* the time when the sun is above the horizon; the twenty-four hours from midnight to midnight; daylight; a particular period of success or influence; (*usu pl*) a period, an epoch.

daybook *n* a diary; an account book for recording the day's transactions.

daybreak *n* the first appearance of daylight, dawn.

daydream *n* a reverie. * *vi* to have one's mind on other things; to fantasize.—**daydreamer** *n*.

daylight *n* the light of the sun; dawn; publicity; a visible gap; the dawning of sudden realization or understanding.

days *adv* during the day regularly.

daytime *n* the time of daylight.

day-to-day *adj* daily; routine.

daze *vt* to stun, to bewilder. * *n* confusion, bewilderment.—**dazedly** *adv*.—**dazedness** *n*.

dazzle *vt* to confuse the sight of or be partially blinded by strong light; to overwhelm with brilliance. * *n* the act of dazzling; a thing that dazzles; an overpoweringly strong light; bewilderment.—**dazzlement** *n*.—**dazzler** *n*.—**dazzlingly** *adv*.

dB, db *abbr* = decibels.

DBS *abbr* = direct broadcasting by satellite.

DC District of Columbia.

dc, DC *abbr* = direct current.

DD *abbr* = Doctor of Divinity.

D-day *n* the date (June 6, 1944) of the Allied cross-channel invasion of France during World War II; any date set aside for an important event.

DDT *abbr* = dichlorodiphenyltrichloroethane, a chemical used as an insecticide.

de *prep* from, concerning; of.

de- *prefix* down; off; completely; un-.

de-accessioning *n* the disposal, usu by selling, of an artefact or painting in a public collection.

deacon *n* (*Anglican, RC churches*) an ordained member of the clergy ranking below a priest; (*Presbyterian churches*) a lay church officer who assists the minister.—**deaconship** *n*.

deaconess *n* a churchwoman appointed to do work in a parish; a member of an institution or order trained to carry on systematic charitable work; in a convent, the nun who attends to the altar.

deactivate *vt* (*bomb*) to make inactive or harmless.—**deactivation** *n*.—**deactivator** *n*.

dead *adj* without life; inanimate, inert; no longer used; lacking vegetation; emotionally or spiritually insensitive; without motion; (*fire, etc*) extinguished; (*limb, etc*) numb; (*colour, sound etc*) dull; (*a ball*) out of play; complete, exact; unerring. * *adv* in a dead manner; completely; utterly. * *n* a dead person; the quietest time.—**deadness** *n*.

deadbeat *n* (*inf*) a lazy or socially inept person; a vagrant.

dead duck *n* (*sl*) a person or thing destined to fail.

deaden vt to render numb or insensible; to deprive of vitality; to muffle.—**deadener** n.—**deadeningly** adv.

dead end n a cul-de-sac; a hopeless situation.

dead-end adj (job) holding no chance of advancement; having no hope of success in the future (dead-end kids).

deadening n material for soundproofing a room.

deadeye n an expert marksman; (naut) a round, laterally flattened wooden block pierced with three holes through which the lanyards are passed, used for extending the shrouds.

deadfall n a trap with a falling weight, which can kill or disable; a tangled mass of fallen trees.

deadhead n a person who has a free pass on trains or to places of amusement, etc; a transport vehicle travelling empty. * vt to remove dead flower heads from (a plant); to provide free admission to. * vi to travel or gain admission without payment; to drive an empty transport vehicle.

dead heat n a race in which two or more finish equal, a tie.

dead letter n a law or rule that is no longer enforced; a letter that cannot be delivered and is returned to the sender.

deadlight n (naut) a storm shutter for a cabin window; a skylight not made to open.

deadline n the time by which something must be done.

deadlock n a clash of interests making progress impossible; a standstill.—also vt.

deadly adj (**deadlier, deadliest**) fatal; implacable; (inf) tedious. * adv death-like; intensely.—**deadliness** n.

deadly nightshade n a poisonous plant with purple flowers and black berries.—also **belladonna**.

deadpan adj (inf) deliberately expressionless or emotionless.—also adv.

dead reckoning n the taking of a ship's position by log and compass, not astronomical observations.

dead set adv with determination.

dead weight n a very heavy load; an oppressive burden.

dead wood n (inf) a useless person or thing.

deaf adj unable to hear; hearing badly; not wishing to hear.—**deafly** adv.—**deafness** n.

deafen vt to deprive of hearing.—**deafeningly** adv.

deaf-mute n a deaf and dumb person.

deal[1] vb (**dealing, dealt**) vt (a blow) to deliver, inflict; (cards, etc) to distribute; (with **with**) to do business with; (problem, task) to solve. * vi to do business (with); to trade (in). * n a portion, quantity; (inf) a large amount; a dealing of cards; a business transaction.

deal[2] n fir or pine wood.—also adj.

dealer n a trader; a person who deals cards; (sl) a seller of illegal drugs.

dealings npl personal or business transactions.

dealt see **deal**.

dean n the head of a cathedral chapter; a college fellow in charge of discipline; the head of a university or college faculty.—**deanship** n.

deanery n (pl **deaneries**) the office or residence of a dean.

dear adj loved, precious; charming; expensive; a form of address in letters. * n a person who is loved. * adv at a high price.—**dearness** n.

dearie, deary n (pl **dearies**) (inf) a darling, a dear.

dearly adv with great affection; at a high price or rate.

dearth n scarcity, lack.

death n the end of life, dying; the state of being dead; the destruction of something.

deathbed n the bed in which a person dies or is about to die.

deathblow n a blow causing death.

death duty n a tax paid on an inheritance after a death.—also **death tax**.

deathless adj immortal.—**deathlessly** adv.—**deathlessness** n.

deathly adj like death, pale, still; deadly. * adv in a manner causing or tending to death; to a degree resembling death; (inf) extremely (deathly quiet).—**deathliness** n.

death mask n a plaster cast of a face taken immediately after death.

death rate n the yearly proportion of deaths to population.—also **mortality rate**.

death rattle n a deep gurgling noise sometimes made by a dying person.

death row n the section of a prison housing inmates sentenced to death.

death's head n a skull or representation of a skull, emblematic of death.

death's-head moth n a large moth with skull-like markings.

death tax see **death duty**.

deathtrap n an unsafe place, thing or structure.

death warrant n official authorization for the execution of a person condemned to death; anything that guarantees the destruction of hope or expectation.

deathwatch beetle n a small beetle that makes a ticking sound, superstitiously supposed to forebode death.

deathwatch n a vigil beside a dying person; a guard over a criminal prior to execution.

death wish n a usu unconscious wish for one's own death or that of another.

deb n (inf) a debutante.

debacle n a sudden disastrous break-up or collapse; a break-up of river ice.

debar vt (**debarring, debarred**) to exclude, to bar.—**debarment** n.

debark vti to land from a ship, to disembark.—**debarkation** n.

debase vt to lower in character or value; (coinage) to degrade.—**debasement** n.—**debaser** n.

debatable adj open to question, disputed.—**debatably** adv.

debate n a formal argument; a discussion, esp in parliament. * vt to consider, contest. * vi to discuss thoroughly; to join in debate.—**debater** n.

debauch vti to corrupt, dissipate; to lead astray, to seduce.—**debaucher** n.

debauchee n a dissolute person, a libertine.

debauchery n (pl **debaucheries**) depraved over-indulgence; corruption; profligacy.

debenture n a bond with guaranteed interest and forming a first charge on assets; a certificate acknowledging a debt; a certificate entitling a refund of customs duty.

debilitate vt to weaken, to enervate.—**debilitation** n.—**debilitative** adj.

debility n (pl **debilities**) weakness, infirmity.

debit n the entry of a sum owed, opposite to the credit; the left side of a ledger used for this. * vt to charge to the debit side of a ledger.

debonair, debonnaire adj having a carefree manner; courteous, gracious, charming.—**debonairly** adv.

debouch *vi* to march or to flow out from a narrow space to open ground.—**debouchment** *n*.

debrief *vt* (*diplomat, etc*) to make a report following a mission; to obtain such information.—**debriefing** *n*.

debris *n* (*pl* **debris**) broken and scattered remains, wreckage.

debt *n* a sum owed; a state of owing; an obligation.

debtor *n* a person, company, etc who owes money to another.

debug *vt* (**debugging, debugged**) (*inf*) (*room, etc*) to clear of hidden microphones; (*machine, program, plan, etc*) to locate and remove errors from; to remove insects from.

debunk *vt* (*inf*) (*claim, theory*) to expose as false.—**debunker** *n*.

debut *n* a first appearance as a public performer or in society. * *vi* to make one's debut.

debutant *n* one making a debut, esp a sportsman.

debutante *n* a young woman making her first appearance in upper-class society; a young woman regarded as wealthy, aristocratic and indolent.

Dec. *abbr* = December.

decade *n* a period of ten years; a group of ten.—**decadal** *adj*.

decadence, decadency *n* a state of deterioration in standards, esp of morality.

decadent *adj* deteriorating; self-indulgent.—**decadently** *adv*.

decaffeinated *adj* (*coffee, tea, carbonated drinks, etc*) with caffeine reduced or removed.

decagon *n* a ten-sided plane figure.—**decagonal** *adj*.

decahedron *n* a solid with ten faces.—**decahedral** *adj*.

decalcify *vt* (**decalcifying, decalcified**) to deprive (bone etc) of its lime.

decalitre, decaliter *n* a unit of ten litres.

Decalogue *n* the Ten Commandments.

decametre, decameter *n* a unit of ten metres.

decamp *vi* to leave suddenly or secretly.—**decampment** *n*.

decanal *adj* of a dean or his office; of the south side of the choir of a church, etc.

decant *vt* (*wine, etc*) to pour from one vessel to another, leaving sediment behind.—**decantation** *n*.

decanter *n* an ornamental bottle (usu glass) for holding wines, etc.

decapitate *vt* to behead.—**decapitation** *n*.—**decapitator** *n*.

decapod *adj* having ten feet or ten arms. * *n* a ten-footed crustacean, or ten-armed cephalopod.—**decapodal, decapodan, decapodous** *adj*.

decarbonate *vt* to deprive of carbon dioxide.—**decarbonation** *n*.

decarbonize *vt* take carbon or carbon deposit from.—**decarbonization** *n*.

decare *n* a measure of 1,000 square metres.

decasyllable *n* a ten-syllabled line or word.—**decasyllabic** *adj, n*.

decathlon *n* a track-and-field contest consisting of ten events.—**decathlete** *n*.

decay *vti* to rot, to decompose; to deteriorate, to wither. * *n* the act or state of decaying; a decline, collapse.

decease *n* death. * *vi* to die.

deceased *adj* dead. * *n* the dead person.

deceit *n* the act of deceiving; cunning; treachery; fraud.

deceitful *adj* treacherous; insincere; misleading.—**deceitfully** *adv*.—**deceitfulness** *n*.

deceive *vt* to cheat; to mislead; to delude; to impose upon.—**deceivable** *adj*.—**deceiver** *n*.—**deceivingly** *adv*.

decelerate *vt, vi* to reduce speed.—**deceleration** *n*.—**decelerator** *n*.

December *n* the twelfth and last month of the year with 31 days.

Decembrist *n* one of the conspirators who took part in the insurrection against Tsar Nicholas I of Russia, on his accession, December 1825.

decency *n* (*pl* **decencies**) being decent; conforming to accepted standards of proper behaviour.

decennial *adj* lasting for, or occurring, every ten years.—**decennially** *adv*.

decennium *n* (*pl* **decenniums, decennia**) a ten-year period, a decade.

decent *adj* respectable, proper; moderate; not obscene; (*inf*) quite good; (*inf*) kind, generous.—**decently** *adv*.

decentralize *vt* (*government, organization*) to divide among local centres.—**decentralist** *adj, n*.—**decentralization** *n*.

deception *n* the act of deceiving or the state of being deceived; illusion; fraud.

deceptive *adj* apt to mislead; ambiguous; unreliable.—**deceptively** *adv*.—**deceptiveness** *n*.

deci- *prefix* one tenth.

decibel *n* a unit for measuring sound level.

decide *vti* to determine, to settle; to give a judgment on; to resolve.—**decidable** *adj*.

decided *adj* unhesitating; clearly marked.

decidedly *adv* definitely, certainly.

decider *n* a deciding round, a final heat.

deciduous *adj* (*trees, shrubs*) shedding all leaves annually, at the end of the growing season.—**deciduousness** *n*.

decilitre, deciliter *n* a unit equal to one-tenth of a litre.

decillion *n* in UK, the tenth power of a million, a unit followed by 60 zeros; in US, the eleventh power of a thousand, a unit followed by 33 zeros.—**decillionth** *adj*.

decimal *adj* of tenths, of numbers written to the base 10. * *n* a tenth part; a decimal fraction.—**decimally** *adv*.

decimal classification *see* **Dewey Decimal System**.

decimal currency *n* currency in which units are divisible by ten.

decimal fraction *n* a fraction whose denominator is ten or a power of ten, indicated by figures after a decimal point.

decimalize *vt* to express as a decimal or to convert to a decimal system.—**decimalization** *n*.

decimal point *n* a dot written before the numerator in a decimal fraction (eg $0.5 = 1/2$).

decimal system *n* a system of weights and measures in which units are related in multiples or submultiples of ten.

decimate *vt* to kill every tenth person; to reduce by one tenth; to kill a great number.—**decimation** *n*.—**decimator** *n*.

decimetre, decimeter *n* a measure of length, one tenth of a metre.

decipher *vt* to decode; to make out (indistinct writing, meaning, etc).—**decipherable** *adj*.—**decipherer** *n*.—**decipherment** *n*.

decision *n* a settlement; a ruling; a judgment; determination, firmness; (*boxing*) a win on points.—**decisional** *adj*.

decisive *adj* determining the issue, positive; conclusive, final.—**decisively** *adv*.—**decisiveness** *n*.

deck *n* the floor on a ship, aircraft, bus or bridge; a pack of playing cards; the turntable of a record-player; the playing mechanism of a tape recorder; (*sl*) the ground, the floor. * *vt* to cover; to adorn.

deck chair *n* a folding chair made of canvas suspended in a frame.

deck hand *n* a seaman who performs manual tasks.

deckle edge *n* the ragged edge, as on handmade paper.—**deckle-edged** *adj*.

deckle *n* a gauge on a papermaking machine for determining the width.

declaim *vti* to state dramatically; to recite.—**declaimer** *n*.

declamation *n* the art of declaiming according to rhetorical rules; impassioned oratory; distinct and correct enunciation of words in vocal music.

declamatory *adj* pertaining to, or characterized by, declamation; noisy in style; appealing to the passions.—**declamatorily** *adv*.

declaration *n* the act of declaring or proclaiming; that which is declared; an assertion; publication; a statement reduced to writing.

declarative *adj* making a declaration.—**declaratively** *adv*.

declaratory *adj* declarative; explanatory, affirmative.—**declaratorily** *adv*.

declare *vt* to affirm, to proclaim; to admit possession of (dutiable goods). * *vi* (*law*) to make a statement; (*with* **against, for**) to announce one's support.—**declarable** *n*.

déclassé *adj* fallen in the social scale.

declassify *vt* (**declassifying, declassified**) to remove a document, etc from the list of official secrets.—**declassification** *n*.

declension *n* (*gram*) variation in the form of a noun and its modifiers to show case and number; a complete set of such variations of a noun, etc.—**declensional** *adj*.

declination *n* a downward bend; (*astron*) the angular distance of a star and the celestial equator; (*compass*) the angle between true north and the magnetic north..—**declinational** *adj*.

decline *vi* to refuse; to move down; to deteriorate, fall away; to fail; to diminish; to draw to an end; to deviate. * *vt* to reject, to refuse; (*gram*) to give the cases of a declension. * *n* a diminution; a downward slope; a gradual loss of physical and mental faculties.—**declinable** *adj*.—**decliner** *n*.

declivity *n* (*pl* **declivities**) a downward slope.—**declivitous** *adj*.

decoct *vt* to boil anything to extract its essence.

decoction *n* an extract obtained by boiling or digesting in hot water; the act of decocting.

decode *vt* to translate a code into plain language.

decoder *n* one who decodes; (*comput*) a device for converting data from one form to another, eg binary to decimal.

decollate *vt* to separate (collated papers); (*arch*) to behead.—**decollator** *n*.

decollation *n* the act of decollating; (*art*) a representation of a beheading, esp of St John the Baptist.

décolletage *n* a low-cut dress or neckline.

décolleté *adj* having a low neckline.

decolonize *vt* to allow a colony to become independent.

decolorize *vt* to remove colour from, to bleach.—**decoloration** *n*.—**decolorization** *n*.

decompose *vti* to separate or break up into constituent parts, esp as part of a chemical process; to resolve into its elements. * *vi* to decay.—**decomposable** *adj*.—**decomposition** *n*.

decompress *vt* to decrease the pressure on, esp gradually; to return (a diver, etc) to a condition of normal atmospheric pressure.—**decompression** *n*.—**decompressive** *adj*.—**decompressor** *n*.

decompression sickness *n* a condition affecting divers, astronauts, etc, resulting from too rapid a return from high pressure to atmosphere and characterized by cramps and paralysis.

decongestant *n* a medical preparation that relieves congestion, eg catarrh.

deconsecrate *vt* to transfer (a church) from ecclesiastical use.—**deconsecration** *n*.

decontaminate *vt* to free from (radioactive, etc) contamination.—**decontamination** *n*.—**decontaminator** *n*.

decontrol *vt* (**decontrolling, decontrolled**) to release from control, esp government control.

décor, decor *n* general decorative effect, eg of a room; scenery and stage design.

decorate *vt* to ornament; to paint or wallpaper; to honour with a badge or medal.

decoration *n* decorating; an ornament; a badge or an honour.

decorative *adj* ornamental, pretty to look at.—**decoratively** *adv*.—**decorativeness** *n*.

decorator *n* a person who decorates, esp houses.

decorous *adj* proper, decent; showing propriety and dignity.—**decorously** *adv*.—**decorousness** *n*.

decorticate *vt* to remove the bark, rind, or husk from; to remove the cortex of an organ by surgery. * *vi* to peel or come off, as bark, skin.—**decortication** *n*.—**decorticator** *n*.

decorum *n* what is correct in outward appearance, propriety of conduct, decency.

decoy *vt* to lure into a trap. * *n* anything intended to lure into a snare.—**decoyer** *n*.

decrease *vti* to make or become less. * *n* a decreasing; the amount of diminution.—**decreasingly** *adv*.

decree *n* an order, edict or law; a judicial decision. * *vt* (**decreeing, decreed**) to decide by sentence in law; to appoint.—**decreeable** *adj*.—**decreer** *n*.

decrement *n* a decrease; the amount of this; (*math*) a negative increment of a variable.—**decremental** *adj*.

decrepit *adj* worn out by the infirmities of old age; in the last stage of decay.—**decrepitly** *adv*.

decrepitate *vti* to heat (a salt, mineral) until it crackles; to crackle under extreme heat.—**decrepitation** *n*.

decrepitude *n* the state or condition of being decrepit; feebleness and decay, esp that due to old age.

decrescendo *n* (*pl* **decrescendos**) (*mus*) a sign (>) that the volume of sound is to be gradually reduced; a gradual decrease in force of tone or a passage where this occurs. * *adj* gradually diminishing in loudness.—*also* **diminuendo**.

decrescent *adj* growing less; (*moon*) waning.—**decrescence** *n*.

decretal *n* (*RC Church*) a papal decree; a book of edicts. * *adj* of a decree or decretal.

decry *vt* (**decrying, decried**) to disparage, to censure as worthless.—**decrial** *n*.—**decrier** *n*.

dectet *n* a group of eight musicians or voices.

decumbent *adj* lying down, prostrate, reclining; (*bot*) resting on the ground, trailing.—**decumbence, decumbency** *n*.

decuple *adj* tenfold * *n* a number repeated ten times * *vt* to increase tenfold.

decurion *n* a Roman officer commanding ten men.

decurrent *adj* (*plant*) running or extending downward.

decussate *vti* to intersect in the form of an X * *adj* X-shaped; (*leaves*) in pairs, at right angles to those above and below.—**decussation** *n*.

dedicate *vt* to consecrate (to some sacred purpose); to devote wholly or chiefly; to inscribe (to someone).—**dedicatee** *n*.—**dedicator** *n*.—**dedicatory, dedicative** *adj*.

dedicated *adj* devoted to a particular cause, profession, etc; single-minded; assigned to a particular function.

dedication *n* the act of dedicating; a dedicatory inscription in a book, etc; devotion to a cause, ideal, etc.

deduce *vt* to derive (knowledge, a conclusion) from reasoning; infer.—**deducible** *adj*.

deduct *vt* to take (from); to subtract.

deductible *adj* capable of being deducted; allowable as a deduction against income tax.—**deductibility** *n*.

deduction *n* deducting; the amount deducted; deducing; a conclusion that something is true because it necessarily follows from a set of general premises known to be valid.—**deductive** *adj*.—**deductively** *adv*.

deed *n* an act; an exploit; a legal document recording a transaction.

deem *vti* to judge; to think, to believe.

deep *adj* extending or placed far down or far from the outside; fully involved; engrossed; profound, intense; heartfelt; penetrating; difficult to understand; secret; cunning; sunk low; low in pitch; (*colour*) of high saturation and low brilliance. * *adv* in a deep manner; far in, into. * *n* that which is deep; the sea.—**deeply** *adv*.—**deepness** *n*.

deepen *vt* to make deeper in any sense; to increase. * *vi* to become deeper.—**deepener** *n*.

deepfreeze *n* a refrigerator in which food is frozen and stored.

deep-freeze *vt* (**deep-freezing, deep-froze** *or* **deep-freezed,** *pp* **deep-frozen, deep-freezed**) to freeze (food) so that it keeps for a long period of time; to store in a freezer. * *n* a freezer.

deep-fry *vt* (**deep-frying, deep-fried**) to fry food in deep fat in order to cook or brown it without turning.—**deep-fryer** *n*.

deep-laid *adj* (*plans, etc*) secret and elaborate.

deep-rooted *adj* (*feelings, opinions, etc*) firmly established; ingrained; deep-seated.

deep-seated *adj* having its seat far beneath the surface; deep-rooted.

Deep South *n* the southeastern states of the USA.

deep space *n* the region of outer space beyond our solar system.

deer *n* (*pl* **deer, deers**) a four-footed animal with antlers, esp on the males, including stag, reindeer, etc.

deerhound *n* a large rough-haired greyhound.—*also* **Scottish deerhound**.

deerstalker *n* a person who hunts deer; a soft hat peaked at the front and back.

de-escalate *vti* to reduce the intensity of.—**de-escalation** *n*.

deface *vt* to disfigure; to obliterate.—**defaceable** *adj*.—**defacement** *n*.—**defacer** *n*.

de facto *adv* in fact; in reality.—*also adj*.

defalcate *vi* to embezzle money held in trust.—**defalcation** *n*.—**defalcator** *n*.

defamation *n* the act of injuring someone's good name or reputation without justification, either orally or in writing; the condition of being defamed.

defamatory *adj* containing that which is injurious to the character or reputation of someone.—**defamatorily** *adv*.

defame *vt* to destroy the good reputation of; to speak evil of.—**defamer** *n*.

default *n* neglect to do what duty or law requires; failure to fulfil a financial obligation; (*comput*) a basic setting or instruction to which a program reverts. * *vi* to fail in one's duty (as honouring a financial obligation, appearing in court).

defaulter *n* one who defaults; one who fails to appear in court when required, or to make a proper account of money or property entrusted to his charge; on the Stock Exchange, one who fails to meet his engagements.

defeasance *n* (*law*) annulment; a condition annexed to a deed, which being performed renders the deed void.

defeasible *adj* able to be annulled.—**defeasibility** *n*.

defeat *vt* to frustrate; to win a victory over; to baffle. * *n* a frustration of plans; overthrow, as of an army in battle; loss of a game, race, etc.—**defeater** *n*.

defeatism *n* disposition to accept defeat.—**defeatist** *n, adj*.

defecate *vi* to empty the bowels. * *vt* (*chem*) to free from impurities, to refine.—**defecation** *n*.—**defecator** *n*.

defect *n* a deficiency; a blemish, fault. * *vi* to desert one's country or a cause, transferring one's allegiance (to another).—**defector** *n*.

defection *n* desertion of duty or allegiance.

defective *adj* having a defect; faulty; incomplete. * *n* a person defective in physical or mental powers.—**defectively** *adv*.—**defectiveness** *n*.

defence, defense *n* resistance or protection against attack; a means of resisting an attack; protection; vindication; (*law*) a defendant's plea; the defending party in legal proceedings; (*sport*) defending (the goal, etc) against the attacks of the opposing side; the defending players in a team.—**defenceless, defenseless** *adj*.—**defencelessness, defenselessness** *n*.

defend *vt* to guard or protect; to maintain against attack; (*law*) to resist, as a claim; to contest (a suit).—**defendable** *adj*.—**defender** *n*.

defendant *n* a person accused or sued in a lawsuit.

defensible *adj* able to be defended or justified.—**defensibly** *adv*.—**defensibility** *n*.

defensive *adj* serving to defend; in a state or posture of defence.—**defensively** *adv*.—**defensiveness** *n*.

defer[1] *vt* (**deferring, deferred**) to put off to another time; to delay.—**deferrable, deferable** *adj*.—**deferrer** *n*.

defer[2] *vi* (**deferring, deferred**) to yield to another person's wishes, judgment or authority.

deference *n* a deferring or yielding in judgment or opinion; polite respect.

deferent *adj* deferential (*anat*) conveying (a fluid, etc) away.

deferential *adj* expressing deference or respect.—**deferentially** *adv*.

deferment *n* a delay; postponement.

deferral *n* a deferment.

deferred *adj* postponed; (*stock, shares*) having its dividend payable after other shares.

defiance *n* the act of defying; wilful disobedience; a challenge.

defiant *adj* characterized by defiance; challenging.—**defiantly** *adv*.

deficiency *n* (*pl* **deficiencies**) being deficient; lack, shortage; deficit.

deficient *adj* insufficient, lacking.—**deficiently** *adv*.

deficit *n* the amount by which an amount falls short of what is required; excess of expenditure over income, or liabilities over assets.

defilade *vt* to raise (a rampart) to protect defensive lines from guns placed in a high position. * *n* protection provided in this way.

defile[1] *vt* to pollute or corrupt.—**defilement** *n*.—**defiler** *n*.

defile[2] *n* a long, narrow pass or way, through which troops can pass only in single file. * *vt* to march in single file.

define *vt* to fix the bounds or limits of; to mark the limits or outline of clearly; to describe accurately; to fix the meaning of.—**definable** *adj*.—**definer** *n*.

definite *adj* defined; having distinct limits; fixed; exact; clear.—**definiteness** *n*.

definitely *adv* certainly; distinctly. * *interj* used to agree emphatically.

definition *n* a description of a thing by its properties; an explanation of the exact meaning of a word, term, or phrase; sharpness of outline.—**definitional** *adj*.

definitive *adj* defining or limiting; decisive, final.—**definitively** *adv*.—**definitiveness** *n*.

definitude *n* the quality of being definite; definiteness, precision.

deflagrate *vt* to set fire to * *vi* to cause to burn with sudden and sparkling combustion.—**deflagration** *n*.

deflate *vt* to release gas or air from; to reduce in size or importance; to reduce the money supply, restrict credit, etc to reduce inflation in the economy.—**deflator** *n*.

deflation *n* deflating; a reduction in the supply of money, causing a fall in prices.—**deflationary** *adj*.—**deflationist** *adj*, *n*.

deflect *vti* to turn or cause to turn aside from a line or proper course.—**deflective** *adj*.—**deflector** *n*.

deflection *n* the action of deflecting or the state of being deflected from a straight line or regular path; deviation; the turning of a magnetic needle away from its zero; the amount of this.

defloration *n* a deflowering.

deflower *vt* to deprive of virginity; to corrupt the beauty, innocence of.—**deflowerer** *n*.

defoliant *n* a chemical that kills foliage.

defoliate *vt* to strip (a plant or tree) of its leaves.—**defoliation** *n*.—**defoliator** *n*.

deforce *vt* (*law*) to keep (property) out of the legal owner's possession by force; (*Scots law*) to resist (an officer of law in execution of his duty).—**deforcement** *n*.

deforest *vt* to clear of trees.—**deforestation** *n*.—**deforester** *n*.

deform *vt* to spoil the natural form of; to put out of shape.—**deformer** *n*.

deformation *n* the act of deforming; a change for the worse; a perverted form of word.

deformed *adj* misshapen; warped.

deformity *n* (*pl* **deformities**) the condition of being deformed; a deformed part of the body; a defect.

defraud *vt* to remove (money, rights, etc) from a person by cheating or deceiving.—**defraudation** *n*.—**defrauder** *n*.

defray *vt* to provide money (to pay expenses, etc).—**defrayable** *adj*.—**defrayal** *n*.—**defrayer** *n*.

defrock *vt* to expel from the priesthood, to unfrock.

defrost *vt* to unfreeze; to free from frost or ice.* *vi* to become unfrozen.

deft *adj* skilful, adept; nimble.—**deftly** *adv*.—**deftness** *n*.

defunct *adj* no longer being in existence or function or in use.—**defunctive** *adj*.

defuse *vt* to disarm an explosive (bomb or mine) by removing its fuse; to decrease tension in a (crisis) situation.

defy *vt* (**defying**, **defied**) to resist openly and without fear; to challenge (a person) to attempt something considered dangerous or impossible; to resist attempts at, to elude.—**defier** *n*.

dégagé *adj* unconstrained, at ease.

degauss *vt* to neutralize or remove a magnetic field.—**degausser** *n*.

degeneracy *n* (*pl* **degeneracies**) the condition or quality of being degenerate; an instance of degeneracy; something that is degenerate.

degenerate *adj* having declined in physical or moral qualities; sexually deviant. * *vi* to become or grow worse. * *n* a degenerate person.—**degenerately** *adv*.

degeneration *n* the act, state, or process of growing worse; degeneracy; decline; the morbid impairment of any structural tissue or organ.

degenerative *adj* of the nature of, or tending to, degenerate.—**degeneratively** *adv*.

deglutinate *vt* to extract gluten from; to unglue.—**deglutination** *n*.

deglutition *n* the power to swallow, a swallowing.

degradable *adj* capable of being broken down by biological or chemical action.

degradation *n* a degrading or being degraded in quality, rank or status; a degraded state; (*geol*) a lowering of land by erosion; (*RC Church*) the unfrocking of a priest.

degrade *vt* to reduce in rank or status; to disgrace; to decompose; to be lowered by erosion.—**degrader** *n*.

degrading *adj* humiliating; (*geol*) eroding.—**degradingly** *adv*.

degree *n* a step in an ascending or descending series; a stage in intensity; the relative quantity in intensity; a unit of measurement in a scale; an academic title awarded as of right or as an honour.

degression *n* a going down; a decrease, esp in taxation rate.—**degressive** *adj*.

dehisce *vi* (*fruits, seed pods, etc*) to burst open.

dehiscent *adj* (*fruits*) opening to release seeds.—**dehiscence** *n*.

dehorn *vt* to cut back, or deprive of, horns.—**dehorner** *n*.

dehumanize *vt* to remove human qualities from; to deprive of personality or emotion, to render mechanical.—**dehumanization** *n*.

dehydrate *vt* to remove water from. * *vi* to lose water, esp from the bodily tissues.—**dehydration** *n*.—**dehydrator** *n*.

dehypnotize *vt* to rouse from a hypnotic state.

de-ice *vt* to prevent the formation of or to remove ice from a surface.—**de-icer** *n*.

deicide *n* the killing of a god; the killer of a god.—**deicidal** *adj*.

deictic *adj* (*gram*) demonstrative; (*logic*) proving directly.—**deictically** *adv*.

deific *adj* making, or tending to make, divine.

deify vt (**deifying, deified**) to make into a god; to worship as a god, glorify.—**deification** n.—**deifier** n.

deign vi to condescend; to think it worthy to do (something).

deil n (Scot) the devil.

deism n belief in the existence of God, but not religious revelation.—**deist** n.—**deistic, deistical** adj.

deity n (pl **deities**) a god or goddess; the rank or essence of a god; (with cap and **the**) God.

déjà vu n the illusion that you have already experienced the present situation.

deject vt to have a depressing effect on.

dejecta npl excrement, droppings.

dejected adj morose, depressed.—**dejectedly** adv.—**dejectedness** n.

dejection n depression; lowness of spirits.

de jure adv according to the law, by right.

delaine n a light fabric of wool and cotton.

delate vt (formerly) to inform against (a person); to report (an offence).—**delation** n.—**delator** n.

delay vt to postpone; to detain, obstruct. * vi to linger. * n a delaying or being delayed; the time period during which something is delayed.—**delayer** n.

dele vt (**deleing, deled**) (print) to take out a letter, etc, in proofreading. * n a mark that a letter, etc, is to be deleted.

delectable adj delightful, delicious.—**delectability** n.—**delectably** adv.

delectation n delight, enjoyment.

delegate vt to appoint as a representative; to give powers or responsibilities to (an agent or assembly). * n a deputy or an elected representative.—**delegable** adj.

delegation n the act of delegating; a group of people empowered to represent others.

delete vt to strike out (something written or printed); to erase.

deleterious adj harmful or destructive.

deletion n the act of deleting; a word, passage, etc, deleted from a text; the absence of a normal part of a chromosome.

delft, delftware n a type of blue-glazed earthenware, originally from Delft in Holland.

deli n (pl **delis**) (inf) a delicatessen.

deliberate vt to consider carefully. * vi to discuss or debate thoroughly; to consider. * adj well thought out; intentional; cautious.—**deliberately** adv.—**deliberateness** n.—**deliberator** n.

deliberation n careful consideration; thorough discussion; caution.

deliberative adj of or appointed for deliberation; as a result of deliberation.—**deliberatively** adv.

delicacy n (pl **delicacies**) delicateness; sensibility; a luxurious food.

delicate adj fine in texture; fragile, not robust; requiring tactful handling; of exquisite workmanship; requiring skill in techniques.—**delicately** adv.—**delicateness** n.

delicatessen n a store selling prepared foods, esp imported delicacies.

delicious adj having a pleasurable effect on the senses, esp taste; delightful.—**deliciously** adv.—**deliciousness** n.

delict n a legal offence.

delight vt to please greatly. * vi to have or take great pleasure (in). * n great pleasure; something that causes this.—**delighter** n.

delighted adj very pleased; filled with delight.—**delightedly** adv.—**delightedness** n.

delightful adj giving great pleasure.—**delightfully** adv.—**delightfulness** n.

delimit, delimitate vt to fix or mark the boundaries of.—**delimitation** n.—**delimitative** adj.

delineate vt to describe in great detail; to represent by drawing.—**delineation** n.—**delineative** adj.

delineator n one who delineates; an adjustable tailor's pattern.

delinquency n (pl **delinquencies**) neglect of or failure in duty; a misdeed; a fault; antisocial or illegal behaviour, esp by young people (—also **juvenile delinquency**).

delinquent adj negligent; guilty of an offence. * n a person guilty of a misdeed, esp a young person who breaks the law.

deliquesce vi to melt and become liquid by absorbing moisture from the atmosphere.—**deliquescence** n.—**deliquescent** adj.

delirious adj mentally confused, light-headed; wildly excited.—**deliriously** adv.—**deliriousness** n.

delirium n (pl **deliriums, deliria**) a state of mental disorder, esp caused by a feverish illness; wild enthusiasm.

delirium tremens n a disorder of the brain, causing delusions and violent trembling, as the result of excessive drinking.

deliver vt (goods, letters, etc) to transport to a destination; to distribute regularly; to liberate, to rescue; to give birth; to assist at a birth; (blow) to launch; (baseball) to pitch; (speech) to utter.—**deliverable** adj.—**deliverer** n.

deliverance n the act of rescuing or liberating.

delivery n (pl **deliveries**) the act of delivering; anything delivered or communicated; the manner of delivering (a speech, etc); the manner of bowling in cricket, etc; the act of giving birth.

dell n a small hollow, usu with trees.

delocalize vt to deprive of local character; to remove from a locality.—**delocalization** n.

delouse vt to rid the lice from.

Delphic, Delphian adj relating to the ancient Greek city or its famous oracle which imparted enigmatic prophecies; obscure or ambiguous in meaning.

delphinium n a garden plant with spikes of, usu blue, flowers.

delta n the fourth letter of the Greek alphabet; an alluvial deposit at the mouth of a river.—**deltaic** adj.

delta wing n a triangular-shaped aircraft wing.

deltoid adj of the shape of the letter delta; triangular * n (anat) a muscle that lifts the upper arm.

delude vt to mislead, to deceive.—**deluder** n.

deluge n a flood; anything happening in a heavy rush. * vt to inundate.

delusion n a false belief; a persistent false belief that is a symptom of mental illness.—**delusional** adj.

delusive adj deluding or tending to delude; deceptive; false.—**delusively** adv.

delusory adj delusive.

deluxe adj luxurious, of superior quality.

delve vti to search deeply; to dig.—**delver** n.

demagnetize vt to remove the magnetic properties of.—**demagnetization** n.—**demagnetizer** n.

demagogic, demagogical adj of, pertaining to, or characteristic of a demagogue.—**demagogically** adv.

demagogue, demagog n a political orator who derives power from appealing to popular prejudices.

demagoguery *n* demagogy; the rhetoric of a demagogue.

demagogy *n* the principles or practice of a demagogue; rule by a demagogue.

demand *vt* to ask for in an authoritative manner. * *n* a request or claim made with authority for what is due; an urgent claim; desire for goods and services shown by consumers.—**demandable** *adj.*—**demander** *n.*

demandant *n* a plaintiff.

demanding *adj* constantly making demands; requiring great skill, concentration or effort.—**demandingly** *adv.*

demantoid *n* an emerald green garnet used as a gem.

demarcate *vt* to delimit; to define or mark the bounds of.—**demarcator** *n.*

demarcation, demarkation *n* the act of marking off a boundary or setting a limit to; a limit; the strict separation of the type of work done by members of different trade unions.

démarche *n* a diplomatic announcement of policy or plan.

demark *vt* to demarcate.

dematerialize *vti* to deprive of or give up material form.—**dematerialization** *n.*

deme *n* a territorial subdivision or township of ancient Greece; (*biol*) a group within a species with similar cell structure, etc.

demean *vt* to lower in dignity.—**demeaning** *adj.*

demeanour, demeanor *n* behaviour; bearing.

dement *vt* to make insane, to drive mad.

demented *adj* crazy, insane.—**dementedly** *adv.*

dementia *n* the failure or loss of mental powers.

demerge *vt* to separate a previously merged business corporation into several companies.—**demerger** *n.*

demerit *n* a fault, a defect; a mark recording poor work by a student, etc.

demersal *adj* (*zool*) found in deep water or on the sea bottom.

demesne *n* (*law*) one's own land; (*hist*) a landed estate attached to a manor; a domain.

demi- *prefix* half.

demigod *n* a being that is part mortal part god; a godlike individual.—**demigoddess** *nf.*

demijohn *n* a large bottle, often in a wicker case.

demilitarize *vt* to remove armed forces, weapons systems, etc from.—**demilitarization** *n.*

demimondaine *n* a member of the demimonde, a courtesan.

demimonde *n* a class of women not recognized by society, esp in 19th-century France, because of promiscuity; any socially disreputable group.

demise *n* (*formal*) death; termination, end. * *vt* to give or grant by will. * *vi* to pass by bequest or inheritance.—**demisable** *adj.*

demisemiquaver *n* (*mus*) a note with a time value of half a semiquaver.—*also* **thirty-second note.**

demitasse *n* a small cup (of black coffee).

demiurge *n* in Platonic philosophy, the creator of the world; in Gnostic philosophy, an agent of the Supreme Being in the creation of man and the material universe; in ancient Greece, the chief magistrate of some states.—**demiurgic** *adj.*

demo *n* (*pl* **demos**) (*inf*) a demonstration.

demob *vt* (**demobbing, demobbed**) (*inf*) to demobilize. * *n* (*inf*) demobilization.

demobilize *vt* to discharge from the armed forces.—**demobilization** *n.*

democracy *n* (*pl* **democracies**) a form of government by the people through elected representatives; a country governed by its people; political, social or legal equality.

democrat *n* a person who believes in or promotes democracy; (*with cap*) a member of the Democratic Party in the US.

democratic *adj* of, relating to, or supporting the principles of democracy; favouring or upholding equal rights; (*with cap*) of or pertaining to the Democratic Party in the US.—**democratically** *adv.*

democratize *vt* to make democratic. * *vi* to become democratic.—**democratization** *n.*

démodé *adj* out of fashion.

demodulate *vt* to extract a modulating (radio, video, etc) wave or signal from a modulated carrier wave.—**demodulator** *n.*—**demodulation** *n.*

demography *n* the study of population statistics concerning birth, marriage, death and disease.—**demographer, demographist** *n.*—**demographic** *adj.*—**demographically** *adv.*

demoiselle *n* a damsel; a small crane of North Africa, southeast Europe and central Asia.

demolish *vt* (*a building*) to pull down or knock down; (*an argument*) to defeat; (*inf*) to eat up.—**demolisher** *n.*—**demolishment** *n.*

demolition *n* a demolishing or being demolished, esp by explosives.—**demolitionist** *adj, n.*

demon *n* an evil spirit; a cruel person; someone who is very skilled, energetic, hard-working, etc.—**demonic** *adj.*—**demonically** *adv.*

demonetize *vt* to withdraw (coin) from circulation; to abandon (gold etc) as a currency.—**demonetization** *n.*

demoniac, demoniacal *adj* of or like a demon; possessed by evil; frenzied, energetic. * *n* a person possessed by a demon.—**demoniacally** *adv.*

demonism *n* belief in demons; the nature of a demon.—**demonist** *n.*

demonize *vt* to make into or represent as a demon.

demonolater *n* a demon worshipper.—**demonolatry** *n.*

demonology *n* the study of demons and superstitions about them.—**demonologist** *n.*

demonstrable *adj* able to be demonstrated or proved.—**demonstrability** *n.*—**demonstrably** *adv.*

demonstrate *vt* to indicate or represent clearly; to provide certain evidence of, prove; to show how something (a machine, etc) works. * *vi* to show one's support for a cause, etc by public parades and protests; to act as a demonstrator of machinery, etc.—**demonstrational** *adj.*

demonstration *n* proof by evidence; a display or exhibition; a display of feeling; a public manifestation of opinion, as by a mass meeting, march, etc; a display of armed force.

demonstrative *adj* displaying one's feelings openly and unreservedly; indicative; conclusive; (*gram*) describing an adjective or pronoun indicating the person or thing referred to.—**demonstratively** *adv.*—**demonstrativeness** *n.*

demonstrator *n* a person who shows consumer goods to the public; one who or that which shows how a machine, etc works; a person who takes part in a public protest.

demoralize *vt* to lower the morale of, discourage.—**demoralization** *n.*—**demoralizer** *n.*

demos *n* in ancient Greece, the common people of a

state; the population personified.

demote vt to reduce in rank or position.—**demotion** n.

demotic adj pertaining to the people; in the simplified style of ancient Egyptian writing.

demulcent adj softening; soothing. * n a medicine that allays irritation.

demur vi (**demurring, demurred**) to raise objections.—**demurral** n.

demure adj modest, reserved; affectedly quiet and proper; coy.—**demurely** adv.—**demureness** n.

demurrage n a charge for keeping a ship, truck, etc beyond the time agreed for unloading.

demurrer n (law) a plea that an opponent's facts are irrelevant; exception taken.

demy n (pl **demies**) a size of paper for printing ($22^1/_2$ x $17^1/_2$ ins) or writing (20 x $15^1/_2$ ins).

demystify vt (**demystifying, demystified**) to remove the mystery from; clarify.—**demystification** n.

den n a cave or lair of a wild beast; a place where people gather for illegal activities; a room in a house for relaxation or study.

denarius n (pl **denarii**) in ancient Rome, a silver coin; a gold coin worth 25 silver denarii.

denary adj of ten; decimal.

denationalize vt to transfer (industry, etc) from state control to private ownership.—**denationalization** n.

denaturalize vt to make unnatural; to deprive of acquired citizenship.—**denaturalization** n.

denature vt to modify the nature of; to change the properties of (a protein) by the action of an acid or heat; to render (alcohol) unfit for consumption.—**denaturant** n.—**denaturation** n.

dendriform adj branching, like a tree.

dendrite n a stone or mineral with tree-like markings; a fine branch of one of the nerve cells that conduct impulses.—**dendritic** adj.

dendrochronology n the dating of past events by studying the annual growth rings in trees.—**dendrochronological** adj.

dendroid adj resembling a tree in appearance.

dendrology n the scientific study of trees.—**dendrologic, dendrological** adj.—**dendrologist** n.

dene n a low sandy tract near sea, a dune.

denegation n a denial.

dengue n a tropical disease transmitted by the mosquito, causing fever and pain in the joints.

deniable adj able to be denied; questionable.—**deniably** adv.

denial n the act of denying; a refusal of a request, etc; a refusal or reluctance to admit the truth of something.

denier[1] n a unit of weight used to measure the fineness of silk, nylon or rayon fibre, esp as used in women's tights, etc.

denier[2] one who denies.

denigrate vt to disparage the character of; to belittle.—**denigration** n.—**denigrator** n.

denim n a hard-wearing cotton cloth, esp used for jeans; (pl) denim trousers or jeans.

denizen n an inhabitant, resident; an animal or plant established in a region where it is not native.

denominate vt to give a name to; to designate.

denomination n a name or title; a religious group comprising many local churches, larger than a sect; one of a series of related units, esp monetary.

denominational adj of, belonging to or controlled by a religious denomination.—**denominationally** adv.

denominationalism n denominational spirit, policy or

principles; adherence to these.—**denominationalist**.

denominative adj giving a name; (gram) formed from a substantive or adjectival stem; connotative. * n a verb formed from a substantive or adjectival stem.

denominator n the part of a fractional expression written below the fraction line.

denotation n the action of denoting; expression by marks, signs or symbols; a sign, indication; a mark by which a thing is made known; designation, meaning.

denotative adj having the power to denote or point out; significant.—**denotatively** adv.

denote vt to indicate, be the sign of; to mean.—**denotement** n.

denouement, dénouement n the resolution of a plot or story; the solution, the outcome.

denounce vt to condemn or censure publicly; to inform against; to declare formally the ending of (treaties, etc).—**denouncement** n.—**denouncer** n.

dense adj difficult to see through; massed closely together; dull-witted, stupid.—**densely** adv.—**denseness** n.

density n (pl **densities**) the degree of denseness or concentration; stupidity; the ratio of mass to volume.

dent n a depression made by pressure or a blow. * vti to make a dent or become dented.

dental adj of or for the teeth.—**dentally** adv.

dental floss n waxed thread for cleaning between the teeth.

dental hygienist n a professionally trained and qualified person who checks and cleans teeth.—also **hygienist**.

dentate adj toothed, notched.

denticle n a small tooth or tooth-like projection.

denticulate adj (leaf) having small teeth.

dentiform adj tooth-shaped.

dentifrice n toothpowder or toothpaste.

dentil n (arch) a small, square, projecting block on a moulding.

dentin, dentine n the hard, bone-like substance forming the main part of teeth.

dentist n a person qualified to treat tooth decay, gum disease, etc.

dentistry n the area of medicine dealing with the care of teeth and the treatment of diseases of the teeth and gums; the practice of this as a profession.

dentition n the process or period of cutting the teeth; the arrangement of the teeth.

dentoid adj tooth-shaped.

denture n (usu pl) a set of artificial teeth.

denude vt to make naked; to deprive, strip.—**denudation** n.—**denuder** n.

denunciate vt (rare) to denounce.—**denunciator** n.

denunciation n the act of denouncing; a threat.—**denunciator** n.—**denunciatory** adj.

deny vt (**denying, denied**) to declare to be untrue; to repudiate; to refuse to acknowledge; to refuse to assent to a request, etc.

deodand n (law) (hist) a chattel that, having caused death, was forfeited to the crown.

deodar n a tall Himalayan cedar tree yielding a valuable timber.

deodorant n a substance that removes or masks unpleasant odours.

deodorize vt to remove the odour or smell from.—**deodorization** n.—**deodorizer** n.

deoxidize vt to deprive of oxygen.

depart vi to go away, leave; to deviate (from).

departed adj (time, etc) long past; (person) recently dead.

department n a unit of specialized functions into which an organization or business is divided; a province; a realm of activity.

departmental adj of, having, or organized into departments.—**departmentally** adv.

departmentalism n departmental structure, esp a bureaucratic one.

departmentalize vt to split into departments; to subdivide.—**departmentalization** n.

department store n a large store divided into various departments selling different types of goods.

departure n a departing; a deviating from normal practice; a new venture, course of action, etc.

depend vi to be determined by or connected with anything; to rely (on), put trust (in); to be reliant on for support, esp financially.

dependable adj able to be relied on.—**dependably** adv.—**dependability** n.

dependant, dependent n a person who is dependent on another, esp financially.

dependence, dependance n the state of being dependent; reliance, trust; a physical or mental reliance on a drug, person, etc.

dependency n (pl **dependencies**) dependence; a territory controlled by another country.

dependent, dependant adj relying on another person, thing, etc for support, money, etc; contingent; subordinate.

depersonalize vt to eliminate the individual character from a person, organization, etc; to make impersonal.—**depersonalization** n.

depict vt to represent pictorially; to describe.—**depicter, depictor** n.—**depiction** n.

depilate vt to remove hair from.—**depilation** n.—**depilator** n.

depilatory n (pl **depilatories**) a substance for removing superfluous hair. * adj removing hair.

deplane vti to alight or unload from an aircraft.

deplete vt to use up a large quantity of.—**depletion** n.—**depletive** adj.

deplorable adj shocking; extremely bad.—**deplorably** adv.

deplore vt to regret deeply; to complain of; to deprecate.—**deplorer** n.—**deploringly** adv.

deploy vt (military forces) to distribute and position strategically. * vi to adopt strategic positions within an area.—**deployment** n.

deplume vt to strip of feathers, to pluck; to strip of position, honour, etc.—**deplumation** n.

depolarize vt to deprive of or counteract the polarity of.—**depolarization** n.

depone vti (Scot) to testify upon oath, to depose.

deponent adj (gram) (verb) passive in form but active in meaning. * n (gram) a deponent verb; (law) one who makes a deposition.

depopulate vt to reduce the population of.—**depopulation** n.—**depopulator** n.

deport vt to expel (an undesirable person) from a country; to behave (in a certain manner).—**deportable** adj.

deportation n forcible removal from a country, esp of an undesirable person.

deportee n a deported person.

deportment n manners; bearing; behaviour.

depose vt to remove from power; to testify, esp in court.—**deposable** adj.—**deposer** n.

deposit vt to place or lay down; to pay money into a bank or other institution for safekeeping, to earn interest, etc; to pay as a first instalment; to let fall, leave. * n something deposited for safekeeping; money put in a bank; money given in part payment or security; material left in a layer, eg sediment.

depositary n (pl **depositaries**) the person to whom something is entrusted; a depository.

deposition n the act of depositing or deposing; a being removed from office or power; a sworn testimony, esp in writing.

depositor n a person who deposits money in a bank, etc.

depository n (pl **depositories**) a place where anything is deposited; a depositary.

depot n a warehouse, storehouse; a place for storing military supplies; a military training centre; a bus or railway station.

deprave vt to pervert; to corrupt morally.—**depravation** n.—**depraver** n.

depraved adj morally debased; corrupt; made bad or worse.—**depravedly** adv.

depravity n (pl **depravities**) moral corruption; extreme wickedness.

deprecate vt to criticize, esp mildly or politely; to belittle.—**deprecation** n.—**deprecative** adj.—**deprecator** n.

deprecative adj deprecatory.

deprecatory adj apologetic; disapproving, belittling.

depreciate vti to make or become lower in value.—**depreciator** n.—**depreciatory, depreciative** adj.

depreciation n a fall in value, esp of an asset through wear and tear; an allowance for this deducted from gross profit; disparagement.

depredate vt to pillage; to rob; to lay waste; to prey upon.—**depredator** n.

depredation n plundering; pillage.

depress vt to push down; to sadden, dispirit; to lessen the activity of.—**depressing** adj.—**depressingly** adv.

depressant adj causing depression. * n a substance that reduces the activity of the nervous system; a drug that acts as a depressant.

depressed adj cast down in spirits; lowered in position; flattened from above, or vertically.

depression n excessive gloom and despondency; an abnormal state of physiological inactivity; a phase of the business cycle characterized by stagnation, widespread unemployment, etc; a falling in or sinking; a lowering of atmospheric pressure, often signalling rain.

depressive adj depressing; tending to suffer from mental depression.—**depressively** adv.

depressor n one who or that which depresses; a muscle that draws down an organ or part.

deprive vt to take a thing away from; to prevent from using or enjoying.—**deprivation** n.

deprived adj lacking the essentials of life, such as adequate food, shelter, education, etc.

dept. abbr = department.

depth n deepness; the distance downwards or inwards; the intensity of emotion or feeling; the profundity of thought; intensity of colour; the mid point of the night or winter; the lowness of sound or pitch; the quality of being deep.

depth charge n a bomb designed to explode under water, used against submarines.

depurate vti to free or become free from impurities.—**depuration** n.—**depurative** adj.—**depurator** n.

deputation *n* a person or group appointed to represent others.

depute *vt* to appoint as one's representative; to delegate.

deputize *vi* to act as deputy.—**deputization** *n*.

deputy *n* (*pl* **deputies**) a delegate, representative, or substitute.

deracinate *vt* to tear up by the roots.—**deracination** *n*.

derail *vti* (*train*) to cause to leave the rails.—**derailment** *n*.

derailleur *n* a system of gearing on a bicycle.

derange *vt* to throw into confusion; to disturb; to make insane.—**deranged** *adj*.—**derangement** *n*.

derby *n* (*pl* **derbies**) a bowler hat.

deregulate *vt* to remove (eg government) regulations or controls from (an industry, etc).—**deregulation** *n*.

derelict *adj* abandoned, deserted and left to decay; negligent. * *n* a person abandoned by society; a wrecked ship or vehicle.

dereliction *n* neglect (of duty); abandonment.

deride *vt* to scorn, mock.

de rigueur *adj* required by fashion or etiquette.

derisible *adj* open to derision.

derision *n* ridicule.

derisive *adj* full of derision; mocking, scornful.—**derisively** *adv*.—**derisiveness** *n*.

derisory *adj* showing or deserving of derision.

derivation *n* the tracing of a word to its root; origin; descent.—**derivational** *adj*.

derivative *adj* derived from something else; not original. * *n* something that is derived; a word formed by derivation; (*math*) the rate of change of one quantity with respect to another.—**derivatively** *adv*.

derive *vt* to take or receive from a source; to infer, deduce (from). * *vi* to issue as a derivative (from).—**derivable** *adj*.—**deriver** *n*.

dermal *adj* of the skin; consisting of skin.

dermatitis *n* inflammation of the skin.

dermatology *n* the science of the skin and its diseases.—**dermatologic, dermatological** *adj*.—**dermatologist** *n*.

dermic *adj* dermal.

dermis *n* the fine skin below the epidermis containing blood vessels.

derogate *vti* to detract (from); to lose face; to degenerate; to take a part (from).—**derogation** *n*.

derogatory *adj* disparaging; deliberately offensive.—**derogatorily** *adv*.

derrick *n* any crane-like apparatus; a tower over an oil well, etc, holding the drilling machinery.

derring-do *n* bravery, reckless valour.

derringer *n* a pocket pistol with a short barrel of very large calibre.

dervish *n* a member of a Muslim religious order vowing chastity and poverty, noted for frenzied, whirling dancing.

desalinate *vt* to remove the salt from (seawater, etc).—**desalination** *n*.—**desalinator** *n*.

descant *n* a musical accompaniment sung or played in counterpoint to the main melody.—*also vi*.

descend *vi* to come or climb down; to pass from a higher to a lower place or condition; (*with* **on, upon**) to make a sudden attack upon, or visit unexpectedly; to sink in morals or dignity; to be derived. * *vt* to go, pass, or extend down.

descendant *n* a person who is descended from an ancestor; something derived from an earlier form.

descendent *adj* descending; sinking.

descendible *adj* (*law*) that may be inherited; transmissible.

descent *n* a descending; a downward motion or step; a way down; a slope; a raid or invasion; lineage, ancestry.

describe *vt* to give a verbal account of; to trace out.—**describable** *adj*.—**describer** *n*.

description *n* a verbal or pictorial account; a sort, a kind.

descriptive *adj* tending to or serving to describe.—**descriptively** *adv*.—**descriptiveness** *n*.

descry *vt* (**descrying, descried**) to catch sight of.

desecrate *vt* to violate a sacred place by destructive or blasphemous behaviour.—**desecration** *n*.—**desecrator, desecrater** *n*.

desegregate *vt* to abolish (racial or sexual) segregation in.—**desegregation** *n*.

desert[1] *n* (*often pl*) a deserved reward or punishment.

desert[2] *vt* to leave, abandon, with no intention of returning; to abscond from the armed forces without permission.—**deserter** *n*.—**desertion** *n*.

desert[3] *n* a dry, barren region, able to support little or no life; a place lacking in some essential quality.

desertification *n* the transformation of fertile land into arid waste or desert through soil erosion, overcultivation, etc.

desertion *n* deserting; being forsaken.

deserve *vt* to merit or be suitable for (some reward, punishment, etc).

deserved *adj* justly earned, merited.—**deservedly** *adv*.—**deservedness** *n*.

deserving *adj* worthy of support, esp financially.

deshabille *see* **dishabille**.

desiccate *vti* to dry or become dried up; to preserve (food) by drying.—**desiccation** *n*.—**desiccative** *adj*.

desiccator *n* an apparatus for drying foods and other substances.

desiderate *vt* to feel the lack of, to desire earnestly.—**desideration** *n*.—**desiderative** *adj*.

desideratum *n* (*pl* **desiderata**) anything desired; a want or desire generally felt and recognized.

design *vt* to plan; to create; to devise; to make working drawings for; to intend. * *n* a working drawing; a mental plan or scheme; the particular form or disposition of something; a decorative pattern; purpose; (*pl*) dishonest intent.

designate *vt* to indicate, specify; to name; to appoint to or nominate for a position, office. * *adj* (*after noun*) appointed to office but not yet installed.—**designator** *n*.

designation *n* the act of designating; nomination; a distinguishing name or title.

designedly *adv* intentionally.

designer *n* a person who designs things; a person who is renowned for creating high-class fashion clothes. * *adj* (*inf*) trendy, of the latest, esp expensive, fashion.

designer drug *n* a synthetic narcotic or hallucinogenic substance which mimics the chemical structure and effects of banned drugs but is not yet covered by anti-drug laws.

designing *adj* crafty, scheming. * *n* the art or practice of making designs.

desirable *adj* arousing (sexual) desire; advisable or beneficial; worth doing.—**desirability** *n*.—**desirably** *adv*.

desire *vt* to long or wish for; to request, ask for. * *n* a longing for something regarded as pleasurable or satisfying; a request; something desired; sexual craving.

desirous *adj* desiring; craving.

desist *vi* to stop (doing something).—**desistance** *n*.

desk *n* a piece of furniture with a writing surface and usu drawers; a counter behind which a cashier, etc sits; the section of a newspaper responsible for a particular topic.

desktop publishing *n* the use of a microcomputer with sophisticated page-layout programs and a laser printer to produce professional-looking printed matter.

desman *n* (*pl* **desmans**) a small amphibious animal similar to a mole.

desmoid *adj* having the characteristics of, or resembling, a ligament; (*tumour*) fibrous.

desolate *adj* solitary, lonely; devoid of inhabitants; laid waste; forlorn, disconsolate; overwhelmed with grief. * *vt* to depopulate; to devastate, lay waste; to make barren or unfit for habitation; to leave alone, forsake, abandon; to overwhelm with grief.—**desolately** *adv*.—**desolateness** *n*.—**desolator, desolater** *n*.

desolated *adj* wretched, lonely, miserable.

desolation *n* destruction, ruin; a barren state; loneliness; wretchedness.

despair *vi* to have no hope. * *n* utter loss of hope; something that causes despair.

despatch *see* **dispatch**.

desperado *n* (*pl* **desperadoes, desperados**) a violent criminal.

desperate *adj* (almost) hopeless; reckless through lack of hope; urgently requiring (money, etc); (*remedy*) extreme, dangerous.—**desperately** *adv*.—**desperateness** *n*.

desperation *n* loss of hope; recklessness from despair.

despicable *adj* contemptible, worthless.—**despicableness** *n*.—**despicably** *adv*.

despise *vt* to regard with contempt or scorn; to consider as worthless, inferior.

despite *prep* in spite of.

despoil *vt* to plunder, rob.—**despoiler** *n*.—**despoilment** *n*.

despoliation *n* despoilment; pillage.

despond *vi* to lose hope, to be dejected. * *n* despondency.

despondency, despondence *n* a being despondent; depression or dejection of spirits through loss of resolution or hope.

despondent *adj* dejected, depressed.—**despondently** *adv*.

despot *n* a ruler possessing absolute power; a tyrant.

despotic, despotical *adj* of, pertaining to, or of the nature of a despot or of despotism; arbitrary, tyrannical.—**despotically** *adv*.

despotism *n* absolute power, tyranny; a state governed by a despot.

desquamate *vti* to peel or scale off.—**desquamation** *n*.

dessert *n* the sweet course at the end of a meal.

dessertspoon *n* a spoon in between a teaspoon and a tablespoon in size, used for eating desserts.

destination *n* the place to which a person or thing is going.

destine *vt* to set aside for some specific purpose; to predetermine; intend.

destiny *n* (*pl* **destinies**) the power supposedly determining the course of events; the future to which any person or thing is destined; a predetermined course of events.

destitute *adj* (with **of**) lacking some quality; lacking the basic necessities of life, very poor.

destitution *n* extreme poverty.

destroy *vt* to demolish, ruin, to put an end to; to kill.

destroyer *n* one who or that which destroys; a fast small warship.

destruct *vt* to destroy deliberately (a missile, etc). * *n* the act of destructing (a missile, etc).

destructible *adj* subject to destruction; able to be destroyed.—**destructibility** *n*.

destruction *n* the act or process of destroying or being destroyed; ruin.

destructionist *n* an anarchist.

destructive *adj* causing destruction; (with **of** or **to**) ruinous; (*criticism*) intended to discredit, negative.—**destructively** *adv*.—**destructivity** *n*.

destructor *n* a furnace for burning up rubbish, etc; an explosive device for blowing up a malfunctioning rocket, etc.

desuetude *n* disuse, discontinuance.

desultory *adj* going aimlessly from one activity or subject to another, not methodical.—**desultorily** *adv*.—**desultoriness** *n*.

detach *vt* to release; to separate from a larger group; (*mil*) to send off on special assignment.

detachable *adj* able to be detached.—**detachability** *n*.—**detachably** *adv*.

detached *adj* separate; free from bias or emotion; (*house*) not joined to another; aloof.

detachment *n* indifference; freedom from emotional involvement or bias; the act of detaching; a thing detached; a body of troops detached from the main body and sent on special service.

detail *vt* to describe fully; (*mil*) to set apart for a particular duty. * *n* an item; a particular or minute account; (*art*) treatment of smaller parts; a reproduction of a smaller part of a picture, statue, etc; a small detachment for special service.

detailed *adj* giving full details; thorough.

detain *vt* to place in custody or confinement; to delay.—**detainment** *n*.

detainee *n* a person who is held in custody.

detainer *n* the (wrongful) detaining of person or goods; a writ for holding on another charge a person already arrested.

detect *vt* to discover the existence or presence of; to notice.

detectable *adj* able to be detected.—**detectability** *n*.

detection *n* a discovery or a being discovered; the job or process of detecting.

detective *n* a person or a police officer employed to find evidence of crimes.

detector *n* a device for detecting the presence of something.

detent *n* a catch for locking machinery or regulating the striking of a clock.

détente, detente *n* relaxation of tension between countries.

detention *n* the act of detaining or withholding; a being detained; confinement; the act of being kept in (school after hours) as a punishment.

deter *vt* (**deterring, deterred**) to discourage or prevent (from acting).—**determent** *n*.

deterge *vt* to cleanse, as a wound.

detergent *n* a cleaning agent, esp one made from a chemical compound rather than fats, as soap. * *adj* having cleaning power.

deteriorate *vt* to make or become worse.—**deterioration** *n*.—**deteriorative** *adj*.

determinable *adj* capable of being definitely ascertained; defined with clearness; terminable.—**determinability** *n*.—**determinably** *adv*.

determinant *adj* determining. * *n* something that determines, a decisive factor; (*math*) an algebraic term expressing the sum of certain products arranged in a square or matrix.

determinate *adj* definitely bounded in time, space, position, etc; fixed; clearly defined; distinct; resolute, decisive; (*bot*) having the terminal flower bud opening first, followed by those on lateral branches.—**determinately** *adv*.—**determinateness** *n*.

determination *n* the act or process of making a decision; a decision resolving a dispute; firm intention; resoluteness.

determinative *adj* determining, limiting, or defining; tending to define the genus or species * *n* that which serves to determine the quality or character of something else; a demonstrative pronoun; an ideograph.—**determinatively** *adv*.

determine *vt* to fix or settle officially; to find out; to regulate; to impel. * *vi* to come to a decision.

determined *adj* full of determination, resolute.—**determinedly** *adv*.—**determinedness** *n*.

determiner *n* one who or that which determines; (*gram*) a word that limits the meaning of a noun, esp an article or possessive pronoun.

determinism *n* the theory that all events, including human actions, are determined by preceding causes, thereby precluding free will.—**determinist** *n*.—**deterministic** *adj*.—**deterministically** *adv*.

deterrent *n* something that deters; a nuclear weapon that deters attack through fear of retaliation. * *adj* deterring.—**deterrence** *n*.

detest *vt* to dislike intensely.—**detester** *n*.

detestable *adj* intensely disliked, abhorrent.—**detestably** *adv*.

detestation *n* extreme dislike; a detestable person or thing.

dethrone *vt* to remove from a throne, to depose.—**dethronement** *n*.—**dethroner** *n*.

detinue *n* (*law*) a writ for recovery of property wrongfully detained.

detonate *vti* to explode or cause to explode rapidly and violently.

detonation *n* a sudden explosion with a loud report.

detonator *n* a device that sets off an explosion.

detour *n* a deviation from an intended course, esp one serving as an alternative to a more direct route. * *vti* to make or send by a detour.

detoxification centre *n* an institution that treats alcoholism or drug addiction.

detoxify *vt* (**detoxifying, detoxified**) to extract poison or toxins from.—**detoxification** *n*.

detract *vt* to take away. * *vi* to take away (from).—**detractor** *n*.

detraction *n* defamation; slander; depreciation.—**detractive** *adj*.—**detractively** *adv*.

detrain *vt, vi* to set down or alight from a train.—**detrainment** *n*.

detriment *n* (a cause of) damage or injury.

detrimental *adj* harmful.—**detrimentally** *adv*.

detrition *n* a wearing down by rubbing or friction.

detritus *n* debris; loose matter, esp formed by rubbing away or erosion of a larger mass (eg a rock).—**detrital** *adj*.

de trop *adj* too much; out of place; (*person*) not wanted.

detumescence *n* the diminution of a swelling, esp of an erect penis.—**detumescent** *adj*.

deuce[1] *n* a playing card or dice with two spots; (*tennis*) the score of forty-all.

deuce[2] *interj* (*inf*) the devil!—an exclamation of surprise or annoyance.

deuced *adj* (*inf*) confounded.

deus ex machina *n* divine intervention; an artificial solution of difficulties, esp in a play.

deuter(o)- *prefix* second.

deuteragonist *n* (*Greek drama*) the second principal actor.

deuterium *n* heavy hydrogen, used as a moderator in nuclear reactors to slow the rate of fission.

deuterocanonical *adj* of or belonging to a second canon or to the Apocrypha.

deuterogamy *n* a second marriage.

deuteron *n* the nucleus of a heavy hydrogen atom.

deutoplasm *n* the albuminous part of the yolk that provides food for the embryo in an egg.—**deutoplasmic** *adj*.

Deutschmark, Deutsche Mark *n* the monetary unit of Germany.

deutzia *n* a small shrub of the saxifrage family with clusters of white flowers.

deva *n* (*Hinduism*) a god.

devaluate *vt* to devalue.

devalue *vt* (**devaluing, devalued**) to reduce the exchange value of (a currency).—**devaluation** *n*.

devastate *vt* to lay waste; to destroy; to overwhelm.—**devastatingly** *adv*.—**devastation** *n*.—**devastator** *n*.

develop *vt* to evolve; to bring to maturity; to show the symptoms of (eg a habit, a disease); to treat a photographic film or plate to reveal an image; to improve the value of. * *vi* to grow (into); to become apparent.

developer *n* a person who develops; a person or organization that develops property; a reagent for developing photographs.

developing country *n* a poor country that is attempting to improve its social conditions and encourage industrial growth.

development *n* the process of growing or developing; a new situation that emerges; a piece of land or property that has been developed.—**developmental** *adj*.

deviant *adj* that which deviates from an accepted norm. * *n* a person whose behaviour deviates from the accepted standards of society.—**deviance, deviancy** *n*.

deviate *vi* to diverge from a course, topic, principle, etc.—**deviator** *n*.

deviation *n* a deviating from normal behaviour, official ideology, etc; deflection of a compass needle by magnetic disturbance; (*statistics*) difference from a mean.

device *n* a machine, implement, etc for a particular purpose; an invention; a scheme, a plot.

devil *n* (*with cap*) in Christian and Jewish theology, the supreme spirit of evil, Satan; any evil spirit; an extremely wicked person; (*inf*) a reckless, high-spirited person; (*inf*) someone or something difficult to deal with; (*inf*) a person. * *vb* (**devilling, devilled** or **deviling, deviled**) *vt* to cook food with a hot seasoning. * *vi* to act as a drudge to someone; to do research for an author or barrister.

devilfish *n* (**devilfish, devilfishes**) the manta, a very large ray; a large species of octopus.

devilish *adj* fiendish; mischievous. * *adv* (*inf*) very.—**devilishly** *adv*.—**devilishness** *n*.

devil-may-care *adj* audacious, contemptuous of authority.

devilment *n* mischievous behaviour.

devilry *n* (*pl* **devilries**) wickedness; malicious mischief.

devil's advocate *n* a person who advocates an opposing cause, esp for the sake of argument.

devious *adj* indirect; not straightforward; underhand, deceitful.—**deviously** *adv*.—**deviousness** *n*.

devisable *adj* capable of being imagined; (*law*) (*real estate*) capable of being bequeathed.—**devisability** *n*.

devise *vt* to invent, contrive; to plan; (*law*) to leave (real estate) by will. * *n* (*law*) a bequest (of real estate); property so bequeathed.—**deviser** *n*.

devisee *n* (*law*) a person to whom (real estate) has been bequeathed.

devisor *n* (*law*) a person who bequeathes, esp real estate.

devitalize *vt* to deprive of vitality or vigour.—**devitalization** *n*.

devitrify *vt* (**devitrifying, devitrified**) to deprive of glassy quality, to make opaque.—**devitrification** *n*.

devoid *adj* (*with* **of**) lacking; free from.

devoirs *npl* civilities; one's best.

devolution *n* a transfer of authority, esp from a central government to regional governments; a passing on from one person to another.

devolve *vti* to hand on or be handed on to a successor or deputy.—**devolvement** *n*.

devote *vt* to give or use for a particular activity or purpose.

devoted *adj* zealous; loyal; loving.—**devotedly** *adv*.—**devotedness** *n*.

devotee *n* (*with* **of** *or* **to**) a person who is enthusiastically or fanatically devoted to something; a religious zealot.

devotion *n* given to religious worship; piety; strong affection or attachment (to); ardour; (*pl*) prayers.

devotional *adj* of devotions; devout. * *n* a brief religious service.

devour *vt* to eat up greedily; to consume; to absorb eagerly by the senses or mind.

devout *adj* very religious, pious; sincere, dedicated.—**devoutly** *adv*.—**devoutness** *n*.

dew *n* air moisture, deposited on a cool surface, esp at night.

dew point *n* the air temperature at which dew forms.

dewberry *n* (*pl* **dewberries**) a kind of trailing blackberry plant; its dark blue fruit.

dewclaw *n* a rudimentary toe above a dog's paw or above the hoof of a deer, etc.

Dewey Decimal System *n* a method of classifying library books into ten main subject areas.—*also* **decimal classification**.

dewlap *n* a flap of skin hanging under the throat of some animals, eg cows; loose skin on the throat of an elderly person.

dewy *adj* (**dewier, dewiest**) wet with dew.—**dewily** *adv*.—**dewiness** *n*.

dewy-eyed *adj* sentimental, naive.

dexter *adj* right; (*her*) to the viewer's left and the wearer's right.

dexterity *n* manual skill, adroitness.

dexterous *adj* possessing manual skill; quick, mentally or physically; adroit; clever.—**dexterously** *adv*.—**dexterousness** *n*.

dextral *adj* on the right-hand side; right-handed; (*shell*) with whorls going to the right.—**dextrality** *n*.—**dextrally** *adv*.

dextrin, dextrine *n* a white gummy substance found in plant sap, etc, and used as gum and a thickening agent.

dextrorotation *n* right-handed or clockwise rotation.—**dextrorotary, dextrorotatory** *adj*.

dextrorse *adj* (*bot*) twining spirally from left to right.—**dextrorsely** *adv*.

dextrose *n* a form of glucose found in fruit, honey and animal tissues.

dextrous *adj* dexterous.

DFC *abbr* = Distinguished Flying Cross.

dhak *n* an Indian tree with brilliant red flowers.

dhal *see* **dal**.

dharma *n* (*Hinduism, Buddhism*) the law requiring virtue and righteousness; its practice in daily life.

dhobi *n* (*pl* **dhobis**) in India, a laundryman.

dhole *n* (*pl* **dholes, dhole**) an Asian wild dog that hunts in packs.

dhoti *n* (*pl* **dhotis**) a loincloth worn by men in India.

dhow *n* an Arab coastal vessel with a triangular sail.

di- *prefix* two; twice; double.

diabase *n* dolerite, a dark coloured igneous rock.

diabetes *n* a medical disorder marked by the persistent and excessive discharge of urine.

diabetes mellitus *n* a breakdown in the body's ability to absorb carbohydrates caused by a deficiency of insulin, which results in abnormally high levels of sugar in the blood and urine.

diabetic *adj* of or suffering from diabetes. * *n* a person with diabetes.

diablerie *n* a devil's work, sorcery; devil-lore; mischief.

diabolic *adj* devilish; cruel, wicked.—**diabolically** *adv*.—**diabolicalness** *n*.

diabolical *adj* diabolic; (*inf*) extremely bad or annoying.

diabolism *n* devil worship; witchcraft.—**diabolist** *n*.

diabolize *vt* to make into or represent as a devil.

diaconal *adj* of or pertaining to a deacon.

diaconate *n* the office or dignity of a deacon; deacons collectively.

diacritic *adj* diacritical. * *n* a diacritical mark.

diacritical *adj* distinguishing, distinctive, esp of accents, etc attached to letters to indicate pronunciation.—**diacritically** *adv*.

diacritical mark *n* a mark, such as an accent, used above or below a letter to indicate differences in sound.

diactinic *adj* transparent to actinic rays.—**diactinism** *n*.

diadelphous *adj* (*flowers*) with stamens in two bundles.

diadem *n* a crown or jewelled headband worn by royalty.

diaeresis *see* **dieresis**.

diagnose *vt* to ascertain by diagnosis.—**diagnosable, diagnoseable** *adj*.

diagnosis *n* (*pl* **diagnoses**) the identification of a disease from its symptoms; the analysis of the nature or cause of a problem.—**diagnostician** *n*.

diagnostic *adj* of or aiding diagnosis; characteristic * *n* a symptom distinguishing a disease; a characteristic; (*pl*: used as sing) the art of diagnosing.—**diagnostically** *adv*.

diagonal *adj* slanting from one corner to an opposite corner of a polygon. * *n* a straight line connecting opposite corners.—**diagonally** *adv*.

diagram *n* a figure or plan drawn in outline to illustrate the form or workings of something. * *vt* (**diagramming, diagrammed** *or* **diagraming, diagramed**) to demonstrate in diagram form.

diagrammatic, diagrammatical *adj* having the form or

nature of a diagram; of or pertaining to diagrams.—**diagrammatically** *adv*.

diagraph *n* an instrument for enlarging maps, etc mechanically.

dial *n* the face of a watch or clock; a graduated disk with a pointer used in various instruments; the control on a radio or television set indicating wavelength or station; the numbered disk on a telephone used to enter digits to connect calls; an instrument for telling the time by the sun's shadow. * *vt* (**dialling, dialled** *or* **dialing, dialed**) to measure or indicate by a dial; to make a telephone connection by using a dial or numbered keypad.

dialect *n* the form of language spoken in a particular region or social class.—**dialectal** *adj*.—**dialectally** *adv*.

dialectic *n* the pursuit of truths in philosophy through logical debate.—**dialectical** *adj*.—**dialectically** *adv*.

dialectology *n* the study of dialects.—**dialectological** *adj*.—**dialectologist** *n*.

dialogue, dialog *n* a conversation, esp in a play or novel; an exchange of opinions, negotiation.

dial tone *n* a sound heard over the telephone indicating that the line is clear.

dialyse, dialyze *vt* to separate crystalline from colloid parts of a mixture by filtration.—**dialysation, dialyzation** *n*.

dialyser, dialyzer *n* a machine for dialysing, esp one that act as a kidney.

dialysis *n* (*pl* **dialyses**) the removal of impurities from the blood by filtering it through a membrane.—**dialytic** *adj*.—**dialytically** *adv*.

diamagnetic *adj* cross-magnetic, tending to point east and west.—**diamagnetically** *adv*.

diamagnetism *n* the property of certain bodies when under the influence of magnetism and freely suspended of taking a position at right angles to the magnetic meridian.

diamanté *adj* glittering with rhinestones, sequins or imitation jewels. * *n* a material ornamented in this way.

diameter *n* a straight line bisecting a circle; the length of this line.

diametric, diametrical *adj* of or along a diameter; completely opposed.—**diametrically** *adv*.

diamond *n* a valuable gem, a crystallized form of pure carbon; (*baseball*) the playing field, esp the infield; a suit of playing cards denoted by a red lozenge. * *adj* composed of, or set with diamonds; shaped like a diamond; denoting the 60th (or 75th) anniversary of an event.

diamondback *n* a large rattlesnack with diamond-shaped markings.

dianthus *n* (*pl* **dianthuses**) any of a large genus of ornamental plants, including carnations and pinks.

diapason *n* the entire compass of a voice or instrument; a recognized musical standard of pitch; the foundation stops of an organ.

diaper *n* a nappy.

diaphanous *adj* (*fabrics*) delicate, transparent.—**diaphanously** *adv*.—**diaphanousness** *n*.

diaphoretic *adj* causing profuse perspiration. * *n* a diaphoretic drug.

diaphragm *n* the midriff, a muscular structure separating the chest from the abdomen; any thin dividing membrane; a device for regulating the aperture of a camera lens; a contraceptive cap covering the cervix; a thin vibrating disk used in a telephone receiver, microphone, etc.—**diaphragmatic** *adj*.—**diaphragmatically** *adv*.

diarchy *n* (*pl* **diarchies**) government by two independent authorities.—*also* **dyarchy**.

diarist *n* one who keeps a diary; the author of a diary.

diarrhoea, diarrhea *n* excessive looseness of the bowels.—**diarrhoeal, diarrheal, diarrhoeic, diarrheic** *adj*.

diary *n* (*pl* **diaries**) a daily record of personal thoughts, events, or business appointments; a book for keeping a daily record.

Diaspora *n* the dispersion of the Jews after the Babylonian captivity; the Jewish communities outside Israel; (*without cap*) the dispersion of any peoples outside their native area.

diastase *n* any enzyme that converts starch into sugar.—**diastatic, diastasic** *adj*.

diastole *n* the dilation of the chambers of the heart during which they fill with blood.—**diastolic** *adj*.

diatessaron *n* the combination of the four Gospels into a single narrative.

diathermancy *n* the property of transmitting radiant heat.—**diathermanous** *adj*.

diathermic *adj* having diathermancy; allowing heat rays to pass freely.

diathermy *n* the use of electric current to warm or destroy body tissues as part of medical treatment.

diathesis *n* (*pl* **diatheses**) a constitutional tendency, esp to disease; a predisposing factor.

diatom *n* a microscopic alga found in fresh and seawater and in soil.—**diatomaceous** *adj*.

diatomite *n* soft earth formed from the shells of diatoms and used as a filter, etc.

diatonic *adj* (*mus*) using only the major and minor scales, as opposed to the chromatic scale.—**diatonically** *adv*.—**diatonicism** *n*.

diatribe *n* a lengthy and abusive verbal attack.

dib *vti* (**dibbing, dibbed**) to dibble; (*fishing*) to drop bait gently into water; to dip lightly.

dibasic *adj* containing two atoms of hydrogen replaceable by a basic radical.—**dibasicity** *n*.

dibber *n* a dibble.

dibble *n* a pointed tool used to make holes in the ground for seedlings. * *vt* to make a hole in the ground with a dibber.

dicast *n* in ancient Athens, a juryman.

dice *n* (*the pl of* **die**[2] *but used as sing*) a small cube with numbered sides used in games of chance. * *vt* to gamble using dice; to cut (food) into small cubes.

dicentra *n* a member of a genus of perennial plants with heart-shaped flowers.

dicephalous *adj* two-headed.

dicey *adj* (**dicier, diciest**) (*inf*) risky.

dichloride *see* **bichloride**.

dichogamous, dichogamic *adj* (*bot*) with stamens and pistils maturing at different times, preventing self-fertilization.—**dichogamy** *n*.

dichotomy *n* (*pl* **dichotomies**) a division into two parts.—**dichotomous, dichotomic** *adj*.

dichroic, dichroitic *adj* (*crystal*) showing two colours; dichromatic.

dichroism *n* the property by which a crystallized body exhibits different colours according to the direction of light transmitted through it.

dichromatic *adj* two-coloured (—*also* **dichroic**); being able to see only two of the three primary colours, colour-blind; (*biol*) having one of two varieties of seasonal coloration.—**dichromatism** *n*.

dichromic *adj* seeing only two of the three primary colours, dichromatic.

dick *n* (*sl*) a detective; (*sl*) a person; (*vulg*) a penis.

dickens *interj* (*inf*) the devil.

dicker *vi* to barter or trade on a small scale; to haggle.* *n* a barter; a deal; haggling.

dicky, dickey[1] *n* (*pl* **dickies, dickeys**) a false shirt-front; a seat at the back of a sports car.

dicky, dickey[2] *adj* (**dickier, dickiest**) (*sl*) shaky, unsound.

dicrotic *adj* having a double or secondary pulse beat.— **dicrotism** *n*.

dicta *see* **dictum**.

Dictaphone *n* (*trademark*) a machine that records dictation and later reproduces it for typing.

dictate *vt* to say or read for another person to write or for a machine to record; to pronounce, order with authority. * *vi* to give dictation; to give orders (to). * *n* an order, rule, or command; (*usu pl*) an impulse, ruling principle.

dictation *n* the act of dictating words to be written down by another; the thing dictated; an authoritative utterance.

dictator *n* a ruler with absolute authority, usu acquired by force.

dictatorial *adj* like a dictator; tyrannical; domineering.—**dictatorially** *adv*.

dictatorship *n* the office or government of a dictator; a country governed by a dictator; absolute power.

diction *n* a way of speaking, enunciation; a person's choice of words.

dictionary *n* (*pl* **dictionaries**) a reference book containing the words of a language or branch of knowledge alphabetically arranged, with their meanings, pronunciation, origin, etc.

Dictograph *n* (*trademark*) a sound recording instrument used for recording or monitoring telephone conversations.

dictum *n* (*pl* **dictums, dicta**) an authoritative pronouncement.

did *see* **do**.

Didache *n* the title of a 2nd-century AD treatise on Christian doctrine and order, discovered 1883.

didactic *adj* intended to teach; instructive; in a lecturing manner.—**didactically** *adv*.—**didacticism** *n*.

didactics *n* (*used as sing*) the art of teaching.

diddle *vi* (*sl*) to cheat.—**diddler** *n*.

didn't = did not.

didymium *n* a mixture of rare earths, formerly thought to be an element, used for colouring glass.

didymous *adj* (*biol*) growing in pairs; paired or double.

die[1] *vb* (**dying, died**) *vi* to cease existence; to become dead; to stop functioning; to feel a deep longing; (*with* **out**) to become extinct. * *vi* to experience a particular form of death.

die[2] *n* a dice.

die[3] *n* (*pl* **dies**) an engraved stamp for pressing coins; a casting mould; a tool used in cutting the threads of screws or bolts, etc.

diecious *see* **dioecious**.

diehard *n* a person who prolongs futile resistance, usu an extreme conservative.

dielectric *adj* nonconducting * *n* any medium, as glass, that transmits electric force by induction.

dieresis *n* (*pl* **diereses**) a sign (¨) placed over the second of two separate vowels to show that each has a separate sound in pronuniation, as Zoë; a division in a line of verse.—*also* **diaeresis**.—**dieretic, diaeretic** *adj*.

diesel *n* a vehicle driven by a diesel engine.

diesel engine *n* an internal combustion engine in which ignition is produced by the heat of highly compressed air alone.

diesel oil *n* a form of petroleum for diesel engines, ignited by the heat of compression.

diesis (*pl* **dieses**) *n* the double dagger used in printing (¥); (*mus*) the difference between a greater and lesser semitone.

diet[1] *n* food selected to adjust weight, to control illness, etc; the food and drink usually consumed by a person or animal. * *vt* to put on a diet. * *vi* to eat according to a special diet.—**dieter** *n*.

diet[2] *n* a legislative assembly in some countries.

dietary *adj* pertaining to a diet.

dietetic, dietetical *adj* regulating food or diet.— **dietetically** *adv*.

dietetics *n* (*used as sing*) the science of diet.

dietetics *n* (*used as sing*) the scientific study of diet and nutrition.

differ *vi* to be unlike, distinct (from); to disagree.

difference *n* the act or state of being unlike; disparity; a distinguishing feature; the amount or manner of being different; the result of the subtraction of one quantity from another; a disagreement or argument.

different *adj* distinct, separate; unlike, not the same; unusual.—**differently** *adv*.

differentia *n* (*pl* **differentiae**) (*logic*) what distinguishes a thing from others, esp one subclass from another of the same class.

differential *adj* of or showing a difference; (*math*) relating to increments in given functions. * *n* something that marks the difference between comparable things; the difference in wage rates for different types of labour, esp within an industry.—**differentially** *adv*.

differential calculus *n* the branch of calculus dealing with the rate of change of given functions with respect to their variables.

differential gear *n* a type of gear that allows powered wheels in a motor vehicle to turn at different speeds (eg when cornering).

differentiate *vt* to make different; to become specialized; to note differences; (*math*) to calculate the derivative of.

differentiation *n* the act of differentiating; (*biol*) specialization; (*math*) the calculation of a differential.

difficult *adj* hard to understand; hard to make, do, or carry out; not easy to please.

difficulty *n* (*pl* **difficulties**) the state of being difficult; a problem, etc that is hard to deal with; an obstacle; a troublesome situation; a disagreement.

diffidence *n* lack of confidence in one's own ability; shyness, modesty.

diffident *adj* shy, lacking self-confidence, not assertive.—**diffidently** *adv*.

diffract *vti* to cause, or cause to undergo, diffraction.— **diffractive** *adj*.

diffraction *n* the breaking up of a ray of light into coloured bands of the spectrum, or into a series of light and dark bands.

diffuse *vt* to spread widely in all directions. * *vti* (*gases, fluids, small particles*) to intermingle. * *adj* spread widely, not concentrated; wordy, not concise.—**diffusely** *adv*.

diffusion *n* the act of diffusing; a spreading abroad; the passing by osmosis through animal membranes.

diffusive *adj* extending; spreading widely.—**diffusively** *adv*.—**diffusiveness** *n*.

dig *vt* (**digging, dug**) to use a tool or hands, claws, etc in making a hole in the ground; to unearth by digging; to excavate; to investigate; to thrust (into); to nudge; (*sl*) to understand, approve. * *n* (*sl*) a thrust; an archaeological excavation; a cutting remark.

digamist *n* one who marries for a second time.—**digamous** *adj*.—**digamy** *n*.

digamma *n* a letter of the ancient Greek alphabet, in sound approaching that of V or W.

digastric *adj* (*muscle*) with two swollen ends. * *n* a neck muscle that helps lower the jaw.

digenesis *n* (*biol*) an alternating process of reproduction, sexual in one generation, asexual in the following.—**digenetic** *adj*.

digest[1] *vt* to convert (food) into assimilable form; to reduce (facts, laws, etc) to convenient form by classifying or summarizing; to form a clear view of (a situation) by reflection. * *vi* to become digested.

digest[2] *n* an abridgment of any written matter; a periodical synopsis of published or broadcast material.

digester *n* one who makes a digest; a thing that digests; an apparatus for extracting the essence of a substance by heat.

digestible *adj* capable of being digested.—**digestibility, digestibly** *adv*.

digestion *n* the act or process of digesting.—**digestional** *adj*.

digestive *adj* pertaining to, performing, or aiding, digestion. * *n* a thing that aids digestion; a sweet wholemeal biscuit.

digger *n* an implement or machine for digging; (*inf*) an Australian or New Zealander (used as a form of address).

digit *n* any of the basic counting units of a number system, including zero; a human finger or toe.

digital *adj* of, having or using digits; using numbers rather than a dial to display measurements; of or pertaining to a digital computer or digital recording.—**digitally** *adv*.

digital audio tape *n* a magnetic tape capable of being used in digital recording, giving high-quality audio reproduction.

digital clock *n* a clock that displays the time in figures.

digital computer *n* a computer that processes information in the form of characters and digits in electronic binary code.

digitalin *n* a poison extracted from foxglove leaves.

digitalis *n* a drug derived from foxglove leaves, used as a heart stimulant.

digital recording *n* the conversion of sound into discrete electronic pulses (representing binary digits) for recording.

digital watch *n* a watch that displays the time in figures.

digitate, digitated *adj* having separate fingers or toes.—**digitation** *n*.

digitigrade *adj* (cats, dogs, etc) walking on the toes. * *n* an animal that walks in this way.

digitize *vt* (*data, images*) to translate into digital form for input into a computer.—**digitization** *n*.

diglot *adj* bilingual. * *n* a book with the text in two languages.

dignified *adj* possessing dignity; noble; serious.—**dignifiedly** *adv*.

dignify *vt* (**dignifying, dignified**) to confer dignity; to exalt; to add the appearance of distinction (to something).

dignitary *n* (*pl* **dignitaries**) a person in a high position or rank.

dignity *n* (*pl* **dignities**) noble, serious, formal in manner and appearance; sense of self-respect, worthiness; a high rank, eg in the government.

digraph *n* a combination of two sounds or characters to represent one simple sound, as *ph* in *phone*.—**digraphic** *adj*.—**digraphically** *adv*.

digress *vi* to stray from the main subject in speaking or writing.—**digression** *n*.

digressive *adj* tending to digress; deviating from the subject.—**digressively** *adv*.—**digressiveness** *n*.

dihedral *adj* (*angle*) having two intersecting plane faces or sides. * *n* a dihedral angle; the angle between aircraft wings for improving stability.

dik-dik *n* a small East African antelope.

dike *see* **dyke**[2].

dike[1] *n* an embankment to prevent flooding or form a barrier to the sea; a ditch; a causeway.—*also* **dyke.**

dilapidate *vt* to bring into partial ruin by neglect or misuse. * *vi* to become dilapidated.

dilapidated *adj* in a state of disrepair; shabby.

dilapidation *n* a state of damage or disrepair.

dilatation *n* a dilating, esp as part of a medical procedure; an abnormal enlargement of an organ, etc.—**dilatational** *adj*.

dilatation and curettage *n* a surgical procedure for opening the cervix and scraping the uterus.

dilate *vti* to make wider or larger; to increase the width of; to expand, amplify, enlarge; to extend in time, protract, prolong, lengthen. * *vi* to become wider or larger; to spread out, widen, enlarge, expand; to discourse or write at large; to enlarge.—**dilatable** *adj*.—**dilatabilty** *n*.

dilation *n* the action or process of dilating; something dilated.

dilator *n* that which dilates; a surgical instrument for opening or expanding an orifice; a muscle that dilates the parts on which it acts.

dilatory *adj* tardy; causing or meant to cause delay.—**dilatorily** *adv*.—**dilatoriness** *n*.

dildo *n* (*pl* **dildos**) an artificial penis used for sexual stimulation.

dilemma *n* a situation where each of two alternative courses is undesirable; any difficult problem or choice.—**dilemmatic** *adj*.

dilettante *n* (*pl* **dilettantes, dilettanti**) a person who dabbles in a subject for amusement only.

diligence[1] *n* careful attention; assiduity; industry.

diligence[2] *n* (*formerly*) a French stagecoach.

diligent *adj* industrious; done with proper care and effort.—**diligently** *adv*.

dill *n* a yellow-flowered herb whose leaves and seeds are used for flavouring and in medicines.

dillydally *vi* (**dillydallying, dillydallied**) (*inf*) to dawdle, loiter.

dilute *vt* to thin down, esp by mixing with water; to weaken the strength of. * *adj* diluted.—**diluter, dilutor** *n*.—**diluteness** *n*.

dilution *n* the act of diluting; a weak liquid.

diluvial, diluvian *adj* pertaining to, produced by, or resulting from, a deluge or flood, esp the Flood of the Bible.

diluvium (*pl* **diluviums, diluvia**) *n* (*formerly*) geological deposits caused by water action, drift.

dim *adj* (**dimmer, dimmest**) faintly lit; not seen, heard, understood, etc clearly; gloomy; unfavourable; (*inf*) stupid. * *vti* (**dimming, dimmed**) to make or cause to become dark.—**dimly** *adv.*—**dimness** *n*.

dime *n* a US or Canadian coin worth ten cents.

dimension *n* any linear measurement of width, length, or thickness; extent; size.

dimensional *adj* of or pertaining to dimension or magnitude; (*geom*) of or pertaining to (a specified number of) dimensions.—**dimensionality** *n*.—**dimensionally** *adv*.

dimerous *adj* (*flowers*) having two members in each whorl; (*insects*) having a foot composed of two parts.

dimeter *n* (a line of) verse of two measures, a measure being one or two feet, according to the metre.

diminish *vti* to make or become smaller in size, amount, or importance.—**diminishable** *adj.*—**diminishment** *n*.

diminuendo *see* **decrescendo**.

diminution *n* act or process of being made smaller.

diminutive *adj* very small. * *n* a word formed by a suffix to mean small (eg *duckling*) or to convey affection (eg *Freddie*).

dimity (*pl* **dimities**) *n* a light, strong striped or figured cotton cloth used for curtains, etc.

dimmer *n* a switch for reducing the brightness of an electric light.

dimorphism *n* the quality of assuming, crystallizing or existing in two forms.—**dimorphic, dimorphous** *adj*.

dimple *n* a small hollow, usu on the cheek or chin. * *vti* to make or become dimpled; to reveal dimples.—**dimply** *adj*.

dimwit *n* (*inf*) an idiotic person, a fool.—**dimwitted** *adj.*—**dimwittedly** *adv.*—**dimwittedness** *n*.

din *n* a loud persistent noise. * *vt* (**dinning, dinned**) to make a din; (*with* **into**) to instil by continual repetition.

dinar *n* the monetary unit of Yugoslavia and various North African countries.

dine *vi* to eat dinner. * *vt* to entertain to dinner.

diner *n* a person who dines; a dining car on a train; a small, cheap eating place.

dinette *n* a small area in a house for eating in.

ding *vi* to sound, as a bell, with a continuous monotonous tone. * *vt* to impress by noisy repetition. * *n* the ringing sound of a bell.

ding-dong *n* the sound of a metallic body produced by blows, as a bell; (*inf*) a violent argument. * *adj* characterized by a rapid succession of blows; (*insults, etc*) vigorously maintained. * *vi* to ring as or like a bell. * *vt* to assail with constant repetition; to repeat with mechanical regularity.

dinghy *n* (*pl* **dinghies**) a small open boat propelled by oars or sails; a small inflatable boat.

dingle *n* a small wooded hollow.

dingo *n* (*pl* **dingoes**) an Australian wild dog.

dingy *adj* (**dingier, dingiest**) dirty-looking, shabby.—**dingily** *adv.*—**dinginess** *n*.

dining car *n* a restaurant car on a train.

dining room *n* a room used for eating meals.

dinkum *adj* genuine, honest.

dinky *adj* (**dinkier, dinkiest**) (*inf*) small; of no consequence, unimportant; (*Scot*) neat and attractive, smart.

dinner *n* the principal meal of the day; a formal meal in honour of a person or occasion.

dinner jacket *n* a tuxedo.

dinosaur *n* any of an order of extinct reptiles, typically enormous in size; (*inf*) a person or thing regarded as outdated.

dinothere *n* a huge, extinct animal like an elephant.

dint *n* (*arch*) a mark left by a blow, a dent; **by dint of** by force of. * *vt* make a dint in.

diocesan *adj* of or pertaining to a diocese; the bishop of a diocese.

diocese *n* the district over which a bishop has authority.

diode *n* a semiconductor device for converting alternating to direct current; a basic thermionic valve with two electrodes.

dioecious *adj* (*bot, zool*) having male and female organs respectively in separate individuals.—*also* **diecious**.

dioptase *n* a vitreous emerald green ore of copper.

dioptre, diopter *n* a unit for measuring the refractive power of a lens.

dioptric, dioptrical *adj* assisting vision by means of the refraction of light in viewing distant objects.

dioptrics *n* (*used as sing*) the area of optics dealing with the refraction of light.

diorama *n* a miniature three-dimensional scene, esp in a museum; any small-scale model with figures; a device for producing changing effects using special lighting on a translucent picture.—**dioramic** *adj*.

diorite *n* a granite-like rock consisting of felspar and hornblende.

dioxide *n* an oxide with two molecules of oxygen to one molecule of the other constituents.

dip *vt* (**dipping, dipped**) to put (something) under the surface (as of a liquid) and lift quickly out again; to immerse (as a sheep in an antiseptic solution). * *vi* to go into water and come out quickly; to suddenly drop down or sink out of sight; to read superficially; to slope downwards. * *n* a dipping of any kind; a sudden drop; a mixture in which to dip something.

dip., Dip. *abbr* = diploma.

diphtheria *n* an acute infectious disease causing inflammation of the throat and breathing difficulties.—**diphtherial** *adj*.

diphtheritic, diphtheric *adj* of or like diphtheria; affected by diphtheria.

diphthong *n* the union of two vowel sounds pronounced in one syllable; a ligature.—**diphthongal** *adj*.

diphyllous *adj* (*bot*) having two leaves.

diploblastic *adj* (*zool*) with two germ layers.

diplodocus *pl* **diplodocuses**) *n* an extinct reptile with a very long tail and neck and a small head.

diploe *n* the soft spongy tissue between the two layers of the skull.—**diploic** *adj*.

diploma *n* (*pl* **diplomas**) a certificate given by a college or university to its graduating students; the course of study leading to a diploma; (*pl often* **diplomata**) an official document, a charter.

diplomacy *n* (*pl* **diplomacies**) the management of relations between nations; skill in handling affairs without arousing hostility.

diplomat *n* a person employed or skilled in diplomacy.

diplomatic, diplomatical *adj* of diplomacy; employing tact and conciliation; tactful.—**diplomatically** *adv*.

diplomatic corps *n* all the ambassadors at a particular capital, the corps diplomatique.

diplomatic immunity *n* the exemption from local laws and taxes accorded to foreign diplomats in the country where they are stationed.

diplomatist *n* a diplomat.

dipole n two equal and opposite electric charges or magnetic poles a small distance apart; a molecule in which the centres of negative and positive charge do not coincide; a directional aerial consisting of two metal rods.—**dipolar** adj.

dipper n a ladle; any of various diving birds.

dippy n (**dippier, dippiest**) (sl) eccentric; crazy.

dipso n (pl **dipsos**) (inf) a dipsomaniac.

dipsomania n a compulsive craving for alcohol.

dipsomaniac n a person with an uncontrollable craving for alcohol. * adj of or having dipsomania.—**dipsomaniacal** adj.

dipstick n a rod with graduated markings to measure fluid level.

dipteral adj (archit) having a double row of columns, as a temple, etc.

dipteran n any of a large order of insects including flies, mosquitoes, midges, having one pair of true wings and piercing or sucking mouthparts.

dipterous adj (insects) two-winged; (seeds) with appendanges resembling wings.

diptych n a pair of paintings or carvings on two panels hinged together.

dire adj dreadful; ominous; desperately urgent.—**direly** adv.—**direness** n.

direct adj straight; in an unbroken line, with nothing in between; frank; truthful. * vt to manage, to control; to tell or show the way; to point to, to aim at; (a letter or parcel) to address; to carry out the organizing and supervision of; to train and lead performances; to command. * vi to determine a course; to act as a director.—**directness** n.

direct current n an electric current that flows in one direction only.

direction n management, control; order, command; a knowing or telling what to do, where to go, etc; any way in which one may face or point; (pl) instructions.

directional adj relating to direction in space; (aerial) transmitting in one direction only.—**directionality** n.—**directionally** adv.

direction finder n a device used to locate the direction of incoming radio signals, used in navigation.

directive adj directing; authoritatively guiding or ruling. * n an order, instruction.

directly adv in a direct manner; immediately; in a short while.

Directoire adj of or imitating the low-necked high-waisted dress or curving oriental furniture of the Directoire period in France (1795–99).

director n person who directs, esp the production of a show for stage or screen; one of the persons directing the affairs of a company or an institution.—**directorial** adj.—**directorship** n.

directorate n a board of directors; the position of a director (—also **directorship**).

directory n (pl **directories**) an alphabetical or classified list, as of telephone numbers, members of an organization, charities, etc.

direct tax n a tax paid by the actual person or organization on which it is levied.

direful adj dreadful, dire.—**direfully** adv.

dirge n a song or hymn played or sung at a funeral; a slow, mournful piece of music.

dirigible adj able to be steered. * n an airship.

dirk n a small dagger, esp as formerly worn by Scottish Highlanders.

dirndl n a woman's full skirt with a tight waistband.

dirt n filth; loose earth; obscenity; scandal. * adj made of dirt.

dirt-cheap adj (inf) very cheap.

dirty adj (**dirtier, dirtiest**) filthy; unclean; dishonest; mean; (weather) stormy; obscene. * vti (**dirtying, dirtied**) to make or become dirty.—**dirtily** adv.—**dirtiness** n.

dis- prefix not, the reverse of; away from, apart; deprive of.

disability n (pl **disabilities**) a lack of physical, mental or social fitness; something that disables, a handicap.

disable vt to make useless; to cripple; (law) to disqualify.—**disablement** n.

disabled adj having a physical handicap.

disabuse vt to free from a mistaken impression.

disaccord vi to disagree, to be at variance. * n disagreement, incongruity.

disadvantage n an unfavourable condition or situation; loss, damage. * vt to put at a disadvantage.

disadvantaged adj deprived or discriminated against in social and economic terms.

disadvantageous adj causing disadvantage; unfavourable.—**disadvantageously** adv.

disaffected adj discontented, no longer loyal.—**disaffectedly** adv.—**disaffection** n.

disaffirm vt (law) to set aside, to reverse.—**disaffirmation** n.

disafforest vt to change from the legal state of forest to that of ordinary land; to remove forest from.—**disafforestation** n.

disagree vi (**disagreeing, disagreed**) to differ in opinion; to quarrel; (with with) to have a bad effect on.—**disagreement** n.

disagreeable adj nasty, bad tempered.—**disagreeableness** n.—**disagreeably** adv.

disagreement n refusal to agree; a difference; a quarrel or dispute.

disallow vt to refuse to allow or to accept the truth or value of.—**disallowance** n.

disannul vt (**disannulling, disannulled**) to annul completely; to make void.

disappear vi to pass from sight completely; to fade into nothing.—**disappearance** n.

disappoint vt to fail to fulfil the hopes of (a person).—**disappointed** adj.—**disappointing** adj.—**disappointingly** adv.

disappointment n the frustration of one's hopes; annoyance due to failure; a person or thing that disappoints.

disapprobation n disapproval, condemnation.

disapproval n the action or fact of disapproving; condemnation of what is wrong.

disapprove vti to express or have an unfavourable opinion (of).—**disapprovingly** adv.

disarm vt to deprive of weapons or means of defence; to defuse (a bomb); to conciliate. * vi to abolish or reduce national armaments.

disarmament n the reduction or abolition of a country's armed forces and weaponry.

disarming adj allaying opposition, conciliating; ingratiating, endearing.—**disarmingly** adv.

disarrange vt to make untidy; to disorganize.—**disarrangement** n.

disarray n disorder, confusion; undress. * vt to put into disorder.

disarticulate vt to separate, to take to pieces.—**disarticulation** n.—**disarticulator** n.

disaster *n* a devastating and sudden misfortune; utter failure.—**disastrous** *adj*.—**disastrously** *adv*.

disavow *vt* to deny, disclaim; to repudiate.—**disavowal** *n*.—**disavower** *n*.

disband *vt* to disperse; to break up and separate.—**disbandment** *n*.

disbar *vt* (**disbarring, disbarred**) to deprive (a barrister) of the right to practice.—**disbarment** *n*.

disbelief *n* a disbelieving; mental rejection of a statement or assertion; positive unbelief.

disbelieve *vt* to believe to be a lie. *vi* to have no faith (in).—**disbeliever** *n*.

disburden *vt* to throw off a burden; to relieve of anything annoying or oppressive * *vi* to ease one's mind.—**disburdenment** *n*.

disburse *vt* to pay out.—**disburser** *n*.

disbursement *n* a paying out (of money); expenditure.

discalced *adj* (*friars, etc*) barefoot, wearing sandals.

discard *vti* to cast off, get rid of; (*cards*) to throw away a card from one's hand. * *n* something discarded; (*cards*) a discarded card.

disc brake, disk brake *n* a brake in which two flat discs press against a central plate on the wheel hub.

discern *vt* to perceive; to see clearly.—**discernible** *adj*.—**discernibly** *adv*.

discerning *adj* discriminating; perceptive.—**discerningly** *adv*.—**discernment** *n*.

discharge *vt* to unload; to send out, emit; to release, acquit; to dismiss from employment; to shoot a gun; to fulfil, as duties. * *vi* to unload; (*gun*) to be fired; (*fluid*) to pour out. * *n* the act or process of discharging; something that is discharged; an authorization for release, acquittal, dismissal, etc.

disciple *n* a person who believes in and helps to spread another's teachings, a follower; (*with cap*) one of the twelve apostles of Christ.—**discipleship** *n*.

disciplinarian *n* a person who insists on strict discipline.

disciplinary *adj* of or for discipline.

discipline *n* a field of learning; training and conditioning to produce obedience and self-control; punishment; the maintenance of order and obedience as a result of punishment; a system of rules of behaviour. * *vt* to punish to enforce discipline; to train by instruction; to bring under control.—**disciplinable** *adj*.—**disciplinal** *adj*.

disc jockey *n* (*inf*) a person who announces records on a programme of broadcast music, or in discotheques.

disclaim *vi* to deny connection with; to renounce all legal claim to.

disclaimer *n* a denial of legal responsibility; a written statement embodying this.

disclose *vt* to bring into the open, to reveal.—**disclosure** *n*.

disclosure *n* the act of revealing anything secret; discovery; an uncovering.

disco *n* (*pl* **discos**) (*inf*) a discotheque.

discography *n* (*pl* **discographies**) a classified list or survey of gramophone records or CDs.—**discographer** *n*.

discoid *adj* round and flat like a disc (—*also* **discoidal**). * *n* anything with the shape of a disc.

discolour, discolor *vti* to ruin the colour of; to fade, stain.—**discolouration** *n*.

discomfit *vt* to defeat; to rout; to frustrate; to thwart; to disconcert.

discomfiture *n* defeat; disappointment; confusion.

discomfort *n* uneasiness; something causing this. * *vt* to make uncomfortable; to make apprehensive or uneasy.

discommode *vt* to put to inconvenience.

discompose *vt* to disturb the calmness of; to ruffle.—**discomposure** *n*.

disconcert *vt* to confuse; to upset; to embarrass.—**disconcerting** *adj*.—**disconcertingly** *adv*.

disconnect *vt* to separate or break the connection of.—**disconnection** *n*.

disconnected *adj* not connected, detached; disjointed; incoherent.—**disconnectedly** *adv*.—**disconnectedness** *n*.

disconsolate *adj* miserable; dejected.—**disconsolately** *adv*.—**disconsolation** *n*.

discontent *n* lack of contentment, dissatisfaction (—*also* **discontentment**). * *adj* not content; dissatisfied; discontented. * *vt* to deprive of contentment; to dissatisfy.

discontented *adj* feeling discontent; unhappy, unsatisfied.—**discontentedly** *adv*.

discontinuance *n* a discontinuing or breaking off; interruption; (*law*) the termination of a suit by the plaintiff.

discontinuation *n* a discontinuing; discontinuance; a breach or interruption of continuity.

discontinue *vti* to stop or come to a stop; to give up, esp the production of something; (*law*) to terminate (a suit).

discontinuity *n* (*pl* **discontinuities**) a being discontinuous; lack or failure of continuity or sequence; a break or gap in a structure; (*geol*) a point at which the character of the earth alters abruptly; (*math*) a function that is discontinuous.

discontinuous *adj* not continuous, incoherent, intermittent; (*math*) of a function that varies discontinuously and whose differential coefficient may therefore become infinite.—**discontinuously** *adv*.

discord *n* lack of agreement, strife; (*mus*) a lack of harmony; harsh clashing sounds.

discordant *adj* at variance; inharmonious; jarring; incongruous.—**discordance, discordancy** *n*.—**discordantly** *adv*.

discotheque, discothèque *n* an occasion when people gather to dance to recorded pop music; a club or party, etc where this takes place; equipment for playing such music.

discount *n* a reduction in the amount or cost; the percentage charged for doing this. * *vt* to deduct from the amount, cost; to allow for exaggeration; to disregard; to make less effective by anticipation. * *vi* to make and give discounts.—**discountable** *adj*.—**discounter** *n*.

discountenance *vt* to refuse moral support to; to discourage, frown upon.

discourage *vt* to deprive of the will or courage (to do something); to try to prevent; to hinder.—**discouragingly** *adv*.

discouragement *n* the action or fact of discouraging; the state or feeling of being discouraged; something that discourages; a disheartening or deterring influence.

discourse *n* a formal speech or writing; conversation. * *vi* to talk or write about.

discourteous *adj* lacking in courtesy, rude.—**discourteously** *adv*.—**discourteousness** *n*.

discourtesy *n* (*pl* **discourtesies**) lack of courtesy or consideration; rudeness; an inconsiderate or rude act.

discover *vt* to see, find or learn of for the first time.—**discoverable** *adj.*—**discoverer** *n*.

discovert *adj* (*law*) (*single woman, divorcée, widow*) without a husband.—**discoverture** *n*.

discovery *n* (*pl* **discoveries**) the act of discovering or state of being discovered; something discovered; (*law*) a process obliging on the parties to an action to disclose relevant facts or documents.

discredit *n* damage to a reputation; doubt; disgrace; lack of credibility. * *vt* to damage the reputation of; to cast doubt on the authority or credibility of.

discreditable *adj* bringing discredit or disgrace.—**discreditably** *adv*.

discreet *adj* wisely cautious, prudent; unobtrusive.—**discreetly** *adv.*—**discreetness** *n*.

discrepancy *n* (*pl* **discrepancies**) difference; a disagreement, as between figures in a total.

discrepant *adj* inconsistent; not tallying.—**discrepantly** *adv*.

discrete *adj* individually distinct; discontinuous.—**discretely** *adv.*—**discreteness** *n*.

discretion *n* the freedom to judge or to choose; prudence; wise judgment; skill.

discretionary *adj* left to or done at one's own discretion.

discriminate *vi* to be discerning in matters of taste or judgment; to make a distinction; to treat differently, esp unfavourably due to prejudice.

discriminating *adj* judicious; discerning; discriminatory.—**discriminatingly** *adv*.

discrimination *n* prejudicial treatment of a person, minority group, etc, based on sex, religion, race, etc; penetration, discernment.

discriminative *adj* serving to discriminate or distinguish; discerning; discriminatory.—**discriminatively** *adv*.

discriminator *n* one who or that which discriminates; (*electronics*) a circuit that converts a property of a signal into an amplitude variation.

discriminatory *adj* discriminating; showing prejudice or favouritism; biased.—**discriminatorily** *adv*.

discursive *adj* wandering from one subject to another; digressive.—**discursively** *adv.*—**discursiveness** *n*.

discus *n* (*pl* **discuses, disci**) a heavy disk with a thickened middle, thrown by athletes.

discuss *vt* to talk over; to investigate by reasoning or argument.—**discussible, discussable** *adj*.

discussion *n* an argument; a debate; the airing of a question.

disdain *vt* to scorn, treat with contempt. * *n* scorn; a feeling of contemptuous superiority.—**disdainful** *adj.*—**disdainfully** *adv*.

disdainful *adj* showing or feeling disdain; contemptuous; haughty.—**disdainfully** *adv.*—**disdainfulness** *n*.

disease *n* an unhealthy condition in an organism caused by infection, poisoning, etc; sickness; a harmful condition or situation.—**diseased** *adj*.

disembark *vti* to land from a ship, debark.—**disembarkation** *n*.

disembarrass *vt* to free from embarrassment; to relieve (of); to disentangle.—**disembarrassment** *n*.

disembody *vi* (**disembodying, disembodied**) to free (a soul, spirit, etc) from the body.—**disembodiment** *n*.

disembogue *vti* (**disemboguing, disembogued**) (*river etc*) to discharge, pour forth (its water).

disembowel *vt* (**disembowelling, disembowelled** *or* **disemboweling, disemboweled**) to remove the en-

trails of; to remove the substance of.—**disembowelment** *n*.

disenchant *vt* to disillusion.—**disenchantment** *n*.

disencumber *vt* to free from burden or hindrance.

disendow *vt* to deprive (a church) of endowments.—**disendowment** *n*.

disenfranchise *see* **disfranchise**.

disengage *vt* to separate or free from engagement or obligation; to detach, to release.—**disengaged** *adj.*—**disengagement** *n*.

disentail *vt* to release from entail.—*also n*.

disentangle *vt* to untangle; to free from complications.—**disentanglement** *n*.

disenthrall, disenthral *vt* (**disenthralling, disenthralled**) to free from bondage, to emancipate.

disestablish *vt* to displace from a settled position; to sever (church) from connection with the state.—**disestablishment** *n*.

disesteem *vt* to regard with disfavour, to dislike. * *n* lack of favour or regard.

diseur *n* a reciter of monologues for entertainment.—**diseuse** *nf*.

disfavour, disfavor *n* dislike; disapproval. * *vt* to treat with disfavour.

disfeature *vt* to disfigure.

disfigure *vt* to spoil the beauty or appearance of.—**disfigurer** *n*.

disfigurement, disfiguration *n* the act of disfiguring; a disfigured state; a thing that disfigures; a blemish, a defect.

disfranchise *vt* to deprive of the right to vote.—*also* **disenfranchise**.—**disfranchisement, disenfranchisement** *n*.

disgorge *vt* to emit violently from the throat, to vomit; to empty; to surrender (eg stolen property).—**disgorgement** *n*.

disgrace *n* a loss of trust, favour, or honour; something that disgraces. * *vt* to bring disgrace or shame upon.—**disgracer** *n*.

disgraceful *adj* causing or deserving disgrace, shameful.—**disgracefully** *adv.*—**disgracefulness** *n*.

disgruntled *adj* dissatisfied, resentful.—**disgruntlement** *n*.

disguise *vt* to hide what one is by appearing as something else; to hide what (a thing) really is. * *n* the use of a changed appearance to conceal identity; a false appearance.—**disguisedly** *adv.*—**disguiser** *n*.

disgust *n* sickening dislike; repugnance; aversion. * *vt* to cause disgust in.—**disgustedly** *adv*.

dish *n* any of various shallow concave vessels to serve food in; the amount of food served in a dish; the food served; a shallow concave object, as a dish aerial; (*inf*) an attractive person. * *vt* (*with* **out**) (*inf*) to distribute freely; (*with* **up**) (*inf*) to serve food at mealtimes; (*inf*) to present (eg facts).

dishabille *n* a partly clad state, undress.—*also* **deshabille**.

dish aerial, dish antenna *n* a microwave antenna used in radar, telescopes, telecommunications, etc having a concave reflector.

disharmonize *vt* to put out of harmony; to set at variance.

disharmony *n* (*pl* **disharmonies**) a lack of harmony between sounds; discord; a discordant situation, etc.—**disharmonious** *adj*.

dishcloth *n* a cloth for washing dishes.

dishearten *vt* to discourage.—**dishearteningly** *adv.*—**disheartenment** *n*.

dishevelled, disheveled adj rumpled, untidy.—**dishevelment** n.

dishonest adj not honest.—**dishonestly** adv.—**dishonesty** n.

dishonour, dishonor n loss of honour; disgrace, shame. * vt to bring shame on, to disgrace; to refuse to pay, as a cheque.

dishonourable, dishonorable adj lacking honour, disgraceful.—**dishonourably, dishonorably** adv.

dishtowel n a towel for drying dishes.

dishwasher n an appliance for washing dishes; a person employed to wash dishes.

dishwater n water used for washing dishes; something that looks like or tastes like this.

dishy adj (**dishier, dishiest**) (inf) physically attractive, good-looking.

disillusion vt to free from (mistaken) ideals or illusions. * n the state of being disillusioned.—**disillusionment** n.

disincentive n a discouragement to action or effort.

disinclination n reluctance, unwillingness.

disinclined adj unwilling.

disinfect vt to destroy germs.—**disinfection** n.

disinfectant n any chemical agent that inhibits the growth of or destroys germs.

disinformation n false information given out by intelligence agencies to mislead foreign spies.

disingenuous adj insincere, not candid or straightforward.—**disingenuously** adv.—**disingenuousness** n.

disinherit vt to deprive of the right to an inheritance.—**disinheritance** n.

disintegrate vti to break or cause to break into separate pieces.—**disintegration** n.—**disintegrator** n.

disinter vt (**disinterring, disinterred**) to take out of a grave; to bring out from obscurity, to unearth.—**disinterment** n.

disinterest n lack of partiality or bias. * vt to cease to concern (oneself).

disinterested adj impartial; objective.—**disinterestedly** adv.—**disinterestedness** n.

disjoin vt to separate. * vi to become detached.

disjoint vt to dislocate; to take to pieces. * adj (math) having no elements in common; (obs) disjointed.

disjointed adj incoherent, muddled, esp of speech or writing.—**disjointedly** adv.—**disjointedness** n.

disjunction n severance, disconnection (—also **disjuncture**); (logic) a compound proposition presenting alternative terms only one of which is true.

disjunctive adj disjoining; alternative; (gram) marking an adverse or oppositional sense; syntactically independent; (logic) presenting alternative terms.—**disjunctively** adv.

disk[1] n a disc; a cylindrical pad of cartilage between the vertebrae; a gramophone record.

disk[2] n any flat, thin circular body; something resembling this, as the sun; (comput) a storage device in a computer, either floppy or hard.

disk brake see **disc brake**.

disk drive n (comput) a mechanism that allows a computer to read data from, and write data to, a disk.

dislike vt to consider unpleasant. * n aversion, distaste.—**dislikable, dislikeable** adj.

dislocate vt to put (a joint) out of place, to displace; to upset the working of.

dislocation n the act of dislocating; a joint put out of its socket; an imperfection in a crystalline structure; (geol) a displacement of stratified rocks, a fault.

dislodge vt to force or move out of a hiding place, established position, etc.—**dislodgment, dislodgement** n.

disloyal adj unfaithful; false to allegiance, disaffected.—**disloyally** adv.

disloyalty (pl **disloyalties**) n the state of being unfaithful; a disloyal act.

dismal adj gloomy, miserable, sad; (inf) feeble, worthless. —**dismally** adv.

dismantle vt to pull down; to take apart.—**dismantlement** n.

dismast vt to deprive (a ship) of a mast or masts.

dismay n apprehension, discouragement. * vt to fill with dismay.

dismember vt to cut or tear off the limbs from; to cut or divide into pieces.—**dismemberment** n.

dismiss vt to send away; to remove from an office or employment; to stop thinking about; (law) to reject a further hearing (in court); (cricket) to bowl a batsman or side out.—**dismissible** adj.

dismissal n the act of dismissing; a removal from office, etc.

dismissive adj rejecting; offhand.—**dismissively** adv.

dismount vti to alight from a horse or bicycle; to remove from a mount or setting.

disobedience n the withholding of obedience; a refusal to obey; violation of a command by omitting to conform to it, or of a prohibition by acting in defiance of it; an instance of this.

disobedient adj failing or refusing to obey.—**disobediently** adv.

disobey vt (**disobeying, disobeyed**) to refuse to follow orders.

disoblige vt to ignore the wishes of; to inconvenience.—**disobligingly** adv.

disorder n lack of order; untidiness; a riot; an illness or interruption of the normal functioning of the body or mind. * vt to throw into confusion; to upset.

disorderly adj untidy; unruly, riotous.—**disorderliness** n.

disorganize vt to confuse or disrupt an orderly arrangement.—**disorganization** n.

disorient, disorientate vt to cause the loss of sense of time, place or identity; to confuse.—**disorientation** n.

disown vt to refuse to acknowledge as one's own.

disparage vt to belittle.—**disparagingly** adv.—**disparagement** n.

disparate adj unequal, completely different.—**disparately** adv.—**disparateness** n.

disparity n (pl **disparities**) essential difference; inequality.

dispassionate adj unemotional; impartial.—**dispassionately** adv.—**dispassionateness** n.

dispatch vt to send off somewhere; to perform speedily; to kill. * n a sending off (of a letter, a messenger etc); promptness; haste; a written message, esp of news.—also **despatch**.—**dispatcher** n.

dispel vt (**dispelling, dispelled**) to drive away and scatter.

dispensable adj able to be done without; unimportant.—**dispensability** n.

dispensary n (pl **dispensaries**) a place in a hospital, a chemist shop, etc where medicines are made up and dispensed; a place where medical treatment is available.

dispensation n the act of distributing or dealing out; exemption from a rule, penalty, etc.

dispense vt to deal out, distribute; to prepare and distribute medicines; to administer.

dispenser n a person who dispenses medicines; a machine, etc, that dispenses measured quanitites or units of something.

dispermous adj (bot) two-seeded.

dispersal n the act of dispersing; dispersion.

disperse vt to scatter in different directions; to cause to evaporate; to spread (knowledge); to separate (light, etc) into different wavelengths. * vi to separate, become dispersed.—**dispersedly** adv.

dispersion n a dispersing, or state of being dispersed; (physics) the separation of light into colours by diffraction or refraction; (statistics) the scattering of data about a mean.

dispersive adj tending to disperse; producing dispersion.—**dispersively** adv.

dispirit vt to depress the spirits of; to dishearten; to render cheerless.

dispirited adj depressed, discouraged.—**dispiritedly** adv.

displace vt to take the place of, to oust; to remove from a position of authority.

displaced person n a person who has become a refugee from their own country, eg due to war or famine.

displacement n the act of displacing; substitution; apparent change of position; the weight of water displaced by a solid body immersed in it.

display vt to show, expose to view; to exhibit ostentatiously. * n a displaying; an eye-catching arrangement, exhibition; a computer monitor for presenting visual information.

displease vt to cause offence or annoyance to.

displeasure n a feeling of being displeased; dissatisfaction.

disport vt to amuse or divert (oneself) * vi to display gaily.

disposable adj designed to be discarded after use; available for use. * n something disposable, eg a baby's nappy.

disposal n a disposing of something; order, arrangement.

dispose vt to place in order, arrange; to influence. * vi to deal with or settle; to give, sell or transfer to another; to throw away.

disposed adj inclined (towards something).

disposition n a natural way of behaving towards others; tendency; arrangement.—**dispositional** adj.

dispossess vt to deprive, rid (of); to eject.—**dispossession** n.— **dispossessor** n.

dispraise vt to disparage; to censure. * n depreciation; a reproach.—**dispraisingly** adv.

disproof n a disproving or refuting; evidence that refutes.

disproportion n a lack of symmetry, a being out of proportion. * vt to render or make out of due proportion.—**disproportional** adj.—**disproportionally** adv.

disproportionate adj out of proportion.—**disproportionately** adv.

disprove vt to prove (a claim, etc) to be incorrect.—**disprovable** adj.

disputable adj likely to cause dispute, arguable.—**disputability** n.—**disputably** adv.

disputant n a person involved in a dispute.

disputation n an argument; an exercise in debate.

disputatious adj fond of argument, contentious.—**disputatiously** adv.—**disputatiousness** n.

dispute vt to make the subject of an argument or debate; to query the validity of. * vi to argue. * n an argument; a quarrel.

disqualify vt (**disqualifying, disqualified**) to make ineligible because of a violation of rules; to make unfit or unsuitable, to disable.—**disqualifier** n.—**disqualification** n.

disquiet vt to trouble, disturb; to make uneasy or restless. * n disturbance; uneasiness, anxiety, worry; restlessness. * adj restless; uneasy; disturbed.—**disquieting** adj.

disquietude n restlessness; disturbance; a feeling, occasion or cause of disquiet.

disquisition n a careful examination of a subject.

disregard vt to pay no attention to; to consider as of little or no importance. * n lack of attention, neglect.

disrelish vt to dislike.—also n.

disrepair n a worn-out condition through neglect of repair.

disreputable adj of bad reputation; not respectable; discreditable.—**disreputably** adv.

disrepute n disgrace, discredit.

disrespect n lack of respect, rudeness.—**disrespectful** adj.—**disrespectfully** adv.

disrobe vti to undress; to uncover.

disrupt vti to break up; to create disorder or confusion; to interrupt.—**disruption** n.

disruptive adj causing disruption.—**disruptively** adv.

dissatisfaction n disapproval; discontent; something that dissatisfies.

dissatisfactory adj unsatisfactory.

dissatisfy vt (**dissatisfying, dissatisfied**) to fail to please, to make discontented.

dissect vt to cut apart (a plant, an animal, etc) for scientific examination; to analyse and interpret in fine detail.—**dissection** n.—**dissector** n.

disseise, disseize vt to deprive of possession; to dispossess unlawfully.—**disseisor, disseizor** n.

disseisin, disseizin n the act of unlawfully dispossessing a person or an estate.

dissemble vti to pretend or to conceal (eg true feelings) by pretence.—**dissemblance** n.—**dissembler** n.

disseminate vt to spread or scatter (ideas, information, etc) widely.—**dissemination** n.—**disseminator** n.

dissension n disagreement, esp when resulting in conflict.

dissent vi to hold a different opinion; to withhold assent. * n a difference of opinion.—**dissenter** n.

dissentient adj disagreeing with the majority. * n a person who dissents.

dissepiment n (biol) a calcareous or membraneous partition, a septum.

dissertate vi to hold forth, to discourse.—**dissertator** n.

dissertation n a written thesis, esp as required for a university degree, etc.

disservice n an ill turn, a harmful action.

dissever vti to cut apart, to disunite.—**disseverance, disseverment** n.

dissident adj disagreeing. * n a person who disagrees strongly with government policies, esp one who suffers harassment or imprisonment as a result.—**dissidence** n.

dissimilar adj unlike, different.—**dissimilarly** adv.

dissimilarity n (pl **dissimilarities**) lack of similarity; a difference, distinction.

dissimulate vt to dissemble.—**dissimulation** n.—**dissimulator** n.

dissipate *vt* to scatter, dispel; to waste, squander (money, etc). * *vi* to separate and vanish.—**dissipater, dissipator** *n*.

dissipated *adj* dissolute, indulging in excessive pleasure; scattered, wasted.—**dissipatedly** *adv*.—**dissipatedness** *n*.

dissipation *n* dispersion; wastefulness; frivolous or dissolute living.

dissociate *vti* to separate or cause to separate the association of (people, things, etc) in consciousness; to repudiate a connection with.—**dissociation** *n*.

dissociation *n* a dissociating or being dissociated; (*chem*) decomposition of a molecule into single atoms, etc; (*psychol*) the separation of an attitude, belief, etc, from the rest of the personality.

dissoluble *adj* soluble.—**dissolubility** *n*.

dissolute *adj* lacking moral discipline, debauched.—**dissolutely** *adv*.—**dissoluteness** *n*.

dissolution *n* separation into component parts; the dissolving of a meeting or assembly (eg parliament); the termination of a business or personal relationship; death; the process of dissolving.

dissolve *vt* to cause to pass into solution; to disperse (a legislative assembly); to melt; (*partnership, marriage*) to break up legally, annul. * *vi* to become liquid; to fade away; to be overcome by emotion.—**dissolvable** *adj*.—**dissolver** *n*.

dissolvent *adj* able to dissolve. * *n* a substance that dissolves.

dissonance *n* a harsh or inharmonious sound; discord; lack of agreement; (*mus*) an incomplete or unfulfilled chord requiring resolution into harmony.

dissonant *adj* inharmonious; discordant; disagreeing; (*mus*) producing dissonance.—**dissonantly** *adv*.

dissuade *vt* to prevent or discourage by persuasion.—**dissuasion** *n*.—**dissuasive** *adj*.

dissyllable *n* a word of two syllables.—*also* **disyllable.**—**dissyllabic, disyllabic** *adj*.

dissymmetry (dissymmetries) *n* an absence or lack of symmetry; symmetry in opposite directions, like right and left hands.—**dissymmetrical, dissymmetric** *adj*.

distaff line *n* the female line of a family.

distaff *n* the stick on which wool for flax is wound for spinning; (*arch*) a woman, women.

distal *adj* (*anat*) relatively distant from the centre of the body or point of attachment.—**distally** *adv*.

distance *n* the amount of space between two points or things; a distant place or point; remoteness, coldness of manner. * *vt* to place at a distance, physically or emotionally; to outdistance in a race, etc.

distant *adj* separated by a specific distance; far-off in space, time, place, relation, etc; not friendly, aloof.—**distantly** *adv*.

distaste *n* aversion; dislike.

distasteful *adj* unpleasant, offensive.—**distastefully** *adv*.—**distastefulness** *n*.

distemper *n* an infectious and often fatal disease of dogs and other animals; a type of paint made by mixing colour with egg or glue instead of oil; a painting made with this.

distend *vti* to swell or cause to swell, esp from internal pressure.

distensible *adj* able to be distended.

distension, distention *n* a distending or being distended; a swelling.

distich *n* (*pl* **distichs**) (*poetry*) a couplet.

distichous *adj* (*bot*) arranged in two rows on opposite sides of an axis.—**distichously** *adv*.

distil, distill *vti* (**distils** *or* **distills, distilling, distilled**) to treat by, or cause to undergo, distillation; to purify; to extract the essence of; to let or cause to fall in drops.

distillate *n* a product of distillation.

distillation *n* the conversion of a liquid into vapour by heat and then cooling the vapour so it condenses again, separating the liquid's constituents or purifying it in the process; a distillate.—**distillatory** *adj*.

distiller *n* an individual or organization that distils, eg a brewery.

distillery *n* (*pl* **distilleries**) a place where distilling, esp of alcoholic spirits, is carried on.

distinct *adj* different, separate (from); easy to perceive by the mind or senses.—**distinctly** *adv*.—**distinctness** *n*.

distinction *n* discrimination, separation; a difference seen or made; a distinguishing mark or characteristic; excellence, superiority; a mark of honour.

distinctive *adj* clearly marking a person or thing as different from another; characteristic.—**distinctively** *adv*.—**distinctiveness** *n*.

distingué *adj* of superior manner, distinguished, striking.

distinguish *vt* to see or recognize as different; to mark as different, characterize; to see or hear clearly; to confer distinction on; to make eminent or known. * *vi* to perceive a difference.—**distinguishable** *adj*.

distinguished *adj* eminent, famous; dignified in appearance or manners.

Distinguished Flying Cross *n* a US military decoration for gallantry or heroism in flying operations.

distort *vt* to pull or twist out of shape; to alter the true meaning of, misrepresent.

distortion *n* a distorting or being distorted; a distorted feature; (*optics*) a faulty image; (*electronics*) an unwanted change in a signal, etc.—**distortional** *adj*.

distract *vt* to draw (eg the mind or attention) to something else; to confuse.—**distractingly** *adv*.

distracted *adj* bewildered, confused.—**distractedly** *adv*.

distraction *n* something that distracts the attention; an amusement; perplexity; extreme agitation.—**distractive** *adj*.—**distractively** *adv*.

distrain *vt* to seize and hold goods or chattels as security for payment of a debt.—**distrainer, distrainor** *n*.—**distrainment** *n*.

distrainee *n* a person who is distrained upon.

distraint *n* the act of distraining for debt; seizure.

distrait *adj* absent-minded, preoccupied.

distraught *adj* extremely distressed.

distress *n* physical or emotional suffering, as from pain, illness, lack of money, etc; a state of danger, desperation. * *vt* to cause distress to.—**distressingly** *adv*.

distressful *adj* suffering or causing distress.—**distressfully** *adv*.—**distressfulness** *n*.

distributary *n* (**distributaries**) a river branch that does not return to the main stream.

distribute *vt* to divide and share out; to spread, disperse throughout an area.—**distributable** *adj*.

distribution *n* a distributing or a being distributed; allotment; a thing distributed; diffusion; the geographical range or occurence of an organism; classification; (*law*) the apportioning of an estate among the heirs; (*commerce*) the marketing of goods to customers, their handling and transport; (*statistics*) the way numbers denoting characteristics in a statistical population are distributed.—**distributional** adj.

distributor n an agent who sells goods, esp wholesale; a device for distributing current to the spark plugs in an engine.

district n a territorial division defined for administrative purposes; a region or area with a distinguishing character.

district attorney n in US a lawyer who is the state's prosecutor in a judicial district.

District of Columbia n a federal area whose boundary is that of Washington, the capital.

distrust n suspicion, lack of trust. * vt to withhold trust or confidence from; to suspect.—**distrustful** adj.—**distrustfully** adv.—**distrustfulness** n.

disturb vt to interrupt; to cause to move from the normal position or arrangement; to destroy the quiet or composure of.

disturbance n a disturbing or being disturbed; an interruption; an outbreak of disorder and confusion.

disturbed adj showing symptoms of emotional illness.

disulphate, disulfate n a sulphate containing one atom of hydrogen, replaceable by a basic element.

disulphide, disulfide n a sulphide in which two atoms of sulphur are contained.

disunite vt to divide, disrupt. * vi to separate.

disuse n the state of being neglected or unused.—**disused** adj.

disyllable see **dissyllable**.

ditch n any long narrow trench dug in the ground. * vt to make a ditch in; (sl) to drive (a car) into a ditch; (sl) to make a forced landing of (an aircraft); (sl) to get rid of.

dither vi to hesitate, vacillate. * n a state of confusion; uncertainty.—**ditherer** n.

dithyramb n a hymn sung in honour of Dionysus, the Greek god of wine; an impassioned speech or writing.—**dithyrambic** adj, n.—**dithyrambically** adv.

dittany (pl **dittanies**) n an aromatic pink-flowered plant of the mint family formerly considered to have magical properties.

ditto n (pl **dittos**) the same again, as above—used in written lists and tables to avoid repetition. * vt (**dittoing, dittoed**) to repeat.

ditto marks npl two small marks (") placed under an item repeated.

ditty n (pl **ditties**) a simple song.

diuretic n a substance or drug that acts to increase the discharge of urine.—also adj.

diurnal adj occurring daily; of the daytime; having a daily cycle.—**diurnally** adv.

diva n (pl **divas, dive**) an accomplished female opera singer; a prima donna.

divalent adj (chem) having a valence of two.

divan n a long couch without back or sides; a bed of similar design.

dive vi (**diving, dived** or **dove, dived**) to plunge headfirst into water; (aircraft) to descend or fall steeply; (diver, submarine) to submerge; to plunge (eg the hand) suddenly into anything; to dash headlong, lunge. * n a headlong plunge; a submerging of a submarine, etc; a sharp descent, a steep decline; (sl) a disreputable public place.

dive bomber n an aircraft designed to release its bombs during a steep dive for superior accuracy.—**dive-bomb** vt.

diver n a person who dives; a person who works or ex-

plores underwater from a diving bell or in a diving suit; any of various aquatic birds.

diverge vi to branch off in different directions from a common point; to differ in character, form, etc; to deviate from a path or course.—**divergence** n.—**divergent** adj.

divers adj (arch) various; sundry.

diverse adj different; assorted, various.—**diversely** adv.—**diverseness** n.

diversify vb (**diversifying, diversified**) vt to vary; to invest in a broad range of securities to lessen risk of loss. * vi to engage in a variety of commercial operations to reduce risk.—**diversification** n.

diversion n turning aside from a course; a recreation, amusement; a drawing of attention away from the principal activity; a detour when a road is temporarily closed to traffic.—**diversionary** adj.

diversity n (pl **diversities**) the condition or quality of being diverse; unlikeness; a difference, distinction; variety.

divert vt to turn aside from one course onto another; to entertain, amuse.

diverticulitis n inflammation of a diverticulum.

diverticulum n (pl **diverticula**) a pocket or side branch off a passage or cavity in the body, esp the intestine.

divertimento n (pl **divertimenti, divertimentos**) a light, pleasant vocal or instrumental composition.

divertissement n an amusement; a recreation, a light entertainment, a ballet, etc, as an interlude between the acts of a play; an entr'acte; (mus) a divertimento.

divest vt to strip of clothing, equipment, etc; to deprive of rights, property, power, etc.—**divestiture, divestment** n.

divide vt to break up into parts; to distribute, share out; to sort into categories; to cause to separate from something else; to separate into opposing sides; (parliament) to vote or cause to vote by division; (math) to ascertain how many times one quantity contains another. * vi to become separated; to diverge; to vote by separating into two sides. * n a watershed; a split.—**dividable** adj.

divided highway see **dual carriageway**.

dividend n a number which is to be divided; the money earned by a company and divided among the shareholders; a bonus derived from some action.

divider n something that divides; a screen, furniture or plants, etc used to divide up a room; (pl) measuring-compasses.

divi-divi (pl **divi-divis**) n a South American tropical plant; its astringent husks used for dyeing and tanning.

divination n the art of foretelling the future or discovering hidden knowledge by supernatural means; intuitive perception.—**divinatory** adj.

divine adj of, from, or like God or a god; (inf) excellent. * n a clergyman; a theologian. * vt to foretell the future by supernatural means; to discover intuitively; to dowse. * vi to practise divination.—**divinely** adv.—**diviner** n.

diving bell n an open-bottomed chamber for working under water, supplied with compressed air.

diving board n a platform or springboard for diving from.

diving suit n a watertight suit with a helmet and air supply, used by divers.

divining rod n a forked twig used for dowsing.

divinity n (pl **divinities**) any god; theology; the quality of being God or a god.

divisible *adj* able to be divided.—**divisibility** *n*.

division *n* a dividing or being divided; a partition, a barrier; a portion or section; a military unit; separation; (*Parliament*) a separation into two opposing sides to vote; a disagreement; (*math*) the process of dividing one number by another.—**divisional** *adj*.

divisive *adj* creating disagreement or disunity.—**divisively** *adv*.—**divisiveness** *n*.

divisor *n* a number that is to be divided into another number (the dividend).

divorce *n* the legal dissolution of marriage; separation. * *vt* to terminate a marriage by divorce; to separate.

divorcé, divorcee *n* a divorced person.—**divorcée** *nf*.

divorcement *n* the act or process of divorcing.

divot *n* a lump of turf dug from the ground while making a golf swing, etc.

divulge *vt* to tell or reveal.—**divulgence** *n*.

divvy *n* (*pl* **divvies**) in the UK, a dividend; in the US, a portion. * *vt* (**divvying, divvied**) (*usu with* **up**) to share out.

Dixie *n* the southern States of the US.

Dixieland *n* Dixie; a New Orleans jazz style.

dizzy *adj* (**dizzier, dizziest**) confused; causing giddiness or confusion; (*sl*) silly; foolish. * *vt* to make dizzy; to confuse.—**dizzily** *adv*.—**dizziness** *n*.

DJ *abbr* = disc jockey; dinner jacket.

dl *abbr* = decilitre.

DM *abbr* = Deutschmark.

dm *abbr* = decimetre.

DMus *abbr* = Doctor of Music.

DMZ *abbr* = demilitarized zone.

DNA *abbr* = deoxyribonucleic acid, the main component of chromosomes that stores genetic information.

do *vt* (*pres t* **does, doing, did,** *pp* **done**) to perform; to work; to end, to complete; to make; to provide; to arrange, to tidy; to perform; to cover a distance; to visit; (*sl*) to serve time in prison; (*sl*) to cheat, to rob; (*sl*) to assault; (*with* **in**) (*inf*) to kill; to tire out. * *vi* to act or behave; to be satisfactory; to manage. * *n* (*pl* **dos, do's**) (*inf*) a party; (*inf*) a hoax. *Do* has special uses where it has no definite meaning, as in asking questions (*Do you like milk?*), emphasizing a verb (*I do want to go*), and standing for a verb already used (*My dog goes where I do*).

DOA *abbr* = dead on arrival.

Doberman (pinscher) *n* a breed of dog with a smooth glossy black-and-tan coat and docked tail.

doc *n* (*inf*) doctor.

docent *n* a person licensed to teach in a university, but of lower grade and authority than a professor.

docile *adj* easily led; submissive.—**docilely** *adv*.—**docility** *n*.

dock[1] *vt* (*an animal's tail*) to cut short; (*wages, etc*) to deduct a portion of.

dock[2] *n* a wharf; an artificial enclosed area of water for ships to be loaded, repaired, etc; (*pl*) a dockyard. * *vt* to come or bring into dock; to join (spacecraft) together in space.

dock[3] *n* an enclosed area in a court of law reserved for the accused.

dockage *n* the provision of accommodation for the docking of vessels; money paid for the use of a dock.

docker *n* a labourer who works at the docks.—*also* **longshoreman** *n*.

docket *n* a label or document recording the contents of a package, delivery instructions, payment advice, or details of payment of customs duties; in US, a list of lawsuits to be tried by a court. * *vt* (*goods*) to put a docket on; (*lawsuit*) to enter on a docket.

dockyard *n* an area with docks and facilities for repairing and refitting ships.

doctor *n* a person qualified to treat diseases or physical disorders; the highest academic degree; the holder of such a degree. * *vt* to treat medically; (*machinery, etc*) to patch up; to tamper with, falsify; (*inf*) to castrate or spay.—**doctoral** *adj*.

doctorate *n* the highest degree in any discipline given by a university, conferring the title of doctor.

doctrinaire *adj* obsessed by theory rather than by experience. * *n* a person so obsessed.—**doctrinairism** *n*.

doctrine *n* a principle of belief.—**doctrinal** *adj*.—**doctrinally** *adv*.

document *n* a paper containing information or proof of anything. * *vt* to provide or prove with documents.—**documental** *adj*.—**documentation** *n*.

documentary *adj* consisting of documents; presenting a factual account of an event or activity. * *n* (*pl* **documentaries**) a nonfiction film.

dodder *vt* to tremble or shake through old age or weakness; to walk slowly and shakily.—**dodderer** *n*.—**doddery** *adj*.

dodecagon *n* a geometric figure with twelve angles and sides.

dodecahedron *n* a solid figure with twelve faces.—**dodecahedral** *adj*.

dodge *vi* to move quickly in an irregular course. * *vt* to evade (a duty) by cunning; to avoid by a sudden movement or shift of position; to trick. * *n* a sudden movement; (*inf*) a clever trick.—**dodger** *n*.

dodgy *adj* (**dodgier, dodgiest**) (*inf*) cunning; risky.

dodo *n* (*pl* **dodos, dodoes**) a large, clumsy bird, now extinct.

doe *n* (*pl* **does, doe**) a female deer, rabbit, or hare.

doer *n* a person who acts, as opposed to thinking or talking; an active energetic person.

does *see* **do**.

doeskin *n* the skin of a doe; a fine woollen cloth with a smooth finish.

doesn't = does not.

doff *vt* to take off (esp one's hat) in greeting or as a sign of respect.

dog *n* a canine mammal of numerous breeds, commonly kept as a domestic pet; the male of the wolf or fox; a despicable person; a device for gripping things. * *vt* (**dogging, dogged**) to pursue relentlessly.—**doglike** *adj*.

dogcart *n* a light, two-wheeled carriage with cross seats back to back.

dog collar *n* a collar for a dog; (*inf*) a clerical collar.

dog days *npl* the warmest days of the year.

doge *n* (*formerly*) the chief magistrate in republican Venice and Genoa.

dog-eared *adj* worn, shabby; (*book*) having the corners of the pages turned down.—**dog-ear** *vt*.

dogfight *n* (*loosely*) a fiercely disputed contest; combat between two fighter planes, esp at close quarters.

dogfish *n* (*pl* **dogfish, dogfishes**) any of various small shark-like fish.

dogged *adj* tenacious.—**doggedly** *adv*.—**doggedness** *n*.

doggerel *n* trivial or worthless verse.

doggish *adj* like a dog, surly; (*sl*) showily stylish.—**doggishly** *adv*.—**doggishness** *n*.

doggo *adv* (*sl*) silent and still; **lie doggo** to lie low, stay hidden.

doggone *interj* (*sl*) darn, damn. * *adj* (*sl*) cursed, confounded. * *vt* (*sl*) to damn.

doggy *adj* (**doggier, doggiest**) of or like a dog; fond of dogs; (*sl*) showily stylish. * *n* (*pl* **doggies**) a pet name for a dog; a little dog (—*also* **doggie**).

doghouse *n* a dog kennel; **in the doghouse** (*inf*) in disgrace.

dogleg *n* something having a sharp angle or a sharp bend, as a road or fairway on a golf course. * *adj* crooked like a dog's hind leg (—*also* **doglegged**).

dogma *n* (*pl* **dogmas, dogmata**) a belief taught or held as true, esp by a church; a doctrine; a belief.

dogmatic, dogmatical *adj* pertaining to a dogma; forcibly asserted as if true; overbearing.—**dogmatically** *adv*.

dogmatics *n* (*used as sing*) the study of religious dogmas; doctrinal theology.

dogmatize *vt* to assert in a dogmatic manner.—**dogmatism** *n*.—**dogmatist** *n*.

do-gooder *n* a well-meaning person, esp if naive or ineffectual.—**do-gooding** *n*.

dog paddle *n* an elementary form of swimming in which the arms and legs paddle rapidly in the water.—**dog-paddle** *vi*.

dog rose *n* a prickly wild rose.

dogsbody *n* (*pl* **dogsbodies**) (*inf*) a drudge.

dogtooth (*pl* **dogteeth**) *n* a canine tooth; (*archit*) a small conical ornament resembling a petal in Early English architecture.

dogtrot *n* a gentle trot; a covered passageway.

dogwatch *n* (*naut*) one of two watches on board ship of two hours each, between 4 and 8 pm.

dogwood *n* any of several shrubs with clusters of small flowers.

doily *n* (*pl* **doilies**) a small ornamented mat, laid under food on dishes, eg cakes.—*also* **doyley**.

doing *n* an action or its result; (*pl*) things done; actions.

doit *n* a small old Dutch copper coin; a thing of little value.

do-it-yourself *n* domestic repairs, woodwork, etc undertaken as a hobby or to save money.—*also adj*.—**do-it-yourselfer** *n*.

dolabriform, dolabrirate *adj* (*bot*) hatchet-shaped.

Dolby *n* (*trademark*) an electronic noise-reduction system used in sound-recording and playback systems.

dolce *adj* soft. * *adv* (*mus*) gently.

doldrums *npl* inactivity; depression; boredom; the regions of the ocean about the equator where there is little wind.

dole *n* (*inf*) money received from the state while unemployed; a small portion. * *vt* to give (out) in small portions.

doleful *adj* sad, gloomy.—**dolefully** *adv*.—**dolefulness** *n*.

dolerite *n* a dark-coloured basic igneous rock composed of augite, felspar and iron; basaltic greenstone.

dolichocephalic *adj* with a skull long in proportion to its breadth, long-headed.—**dolichocephaly** *n*.

doll *n* a toy in the form of a human figure; a ventriloquist's dummy; (*sl*) a woman

dollar *n* the unit of money in the US, Canada, Australia and many other countries.

dollop *n* (*inf*) a soft mass or lump; a portion, serving.

dolly *n* (*pl* **dollies**) (*inf*) a child's word for a doll; a wheeled platform for a camera. * *vi* (**dollying, dollied**) to manouevre a camera dolly.

dolman *n* (*pl* **dolmans**) a loose robe; a short cloak.

dolman sleeve *n* a full, wide sleeve narrowing to a wristband.

dolmen *n* a prehistoric structure of two or more erect stones supporting a horizontal slab.

dolomite *n* a white mineral obtained from sedimentary rock; a sedimentary rock similar to limestone.—**dolomitic** *adj*.

doloroso *adv* (*mus*) sadly.

dolorous *adj* mournful, doleful.—**dolorously** *adv*.—**dolorousness** *n*.

dolour, dolor *n* grief, sorrow, distress.

dolphin *n* a marine mammal with a beak-like snout, larger than a porpoise but smaller than a whale.

dolphinarium *n* (*pl* **dolphinariums, dolphinaria**) a large pool or aquarium for keeping and displaying dolphins.

dolt *n* a dull or stupid person.—**doltish** *adj*.—**doltishly** *adv*.—**doltishness** *n*.

Dom *n* (*RC Church*) the title of certain dignitaries; a former Portuguese title of rank, as Don.

domain *n* an area under the control of a ruler or government; a field of thought, activity, etc.

dome *n* a large, rounded roof; something high and rounded.—*also vt*.

domed *adj* having, or shaped like, a dome.

domesday *n* the day of God's Last Judgment of mankind.—*also* **doomsday**.

Domesday Book *n* the record of William I's survey of England in 1086.

domestic *adj* belonging to the home or family; not foreign; (*animals*) tame. * *n* a servant in the home.—**domestically** *adv*.

domestic science *n* the study of household skills; home economics.

domesticate *vt* to tame; to make home-loving and fond of household duties.—**domestication** *n*.

domesticity *n* (*pl* **domesticities**) home life; being domestic.

domicile *n* a house; a person's place of residence. * *vt* to establish, to settle permanently.—**domiciliary** *adj*.

domiciliate *vt* to domicile.—**domiciliation** *n*.

dominant *adj* commanding, prevailing over others; overlooking from a superior height. * *n* (*mus*) the fifth note of a diatonic scale.—**dominance** *n*.—**dominantly** *n*.

dominate *vt* to control or rule by strength; to hold a commanding position over; to overlook from a superior height.—**domination** *n*.—**dominator** *n*.

domineer *vti* to act in an arrogant or tyrannical manner.—**domineeringly** *adv*.

dominical *adj* pertaining to Christ as Lord, or to Sunday.

dominie *n* (*Scot*) a schoolteacher; (*inf*) a clergyman.

dominion *n* a territory with one ruler or government; the power to rule; authority.

domino *n* (*pl* **dominoes, dominos**) a flat oblong tile marked with up to six dots; (*pl*) a popular game usu using a set of 28 dominoes; a loose cloak, usu worn with an eye mask, at masquerades.

Don *n* a Spanish title for a gentleman or nobleman.—**Doña** *nf*.

don[1] *vt* (**donning, donned**) to put on; to invest with; to assume.

don[2] *n* a head, fellow or tutor at Oxford or Cambridge universities; (*loosely*) any university teacher; a Mafia leader.

donate *vt* to give as a gift or donation, esp to a charity.—**donator** *n*.

donation *n* a donating; a contribution or gift, esp to a charity.

donative *n* a gift; largess, a donation. * *adj* given by donation.

done[1] *see* **do.**

done[2] *adj* completed; cooked sufficiently; socially acceptable; (*with* **for**) (*sl*) doomed; dead; exhausted; discarded.

donee *n* a person to whom a gift is made.

donjon *n* the central tower of a castle, a keep.

donkey *n* (*pl* **donkeys**) a small animal resembling a horse.

donkey engine *n* a portable auxiliary engine.

donkey jacket *n* a thick waterproof jacket, esp worn by labourers.

donkey's years *npl* (*inf*) a very long time.

donkey-work *n* the groundwork; drudgery.

Donna *n* a term of respect to a lady in Italy.

donnish *adj* (*inf*) resembling a university don.—**donnishly** *adv.*—**donnishness** *n.*

donor *n* a person who donates something, a donator; a person who gives their blood, organs, etc for medical use.

don't = do not.

donut *n* (*sl*) a doughnut.

doodad *n* (*inf*) a small item whose name is lost or forgotten.

doodle *vi* to scribble aimlessly. * *vt* to draw (something) absentmindedly. * *n* a meaningless drawing or scribble.—**doodler** *n.*

doom[1] *n* a grim destiny; ruin. * *vt* condemn to failure, destruction, etc.

doom[2] *see* **doum.**

doomsday *n* the day of God's Last Judgment of mankind.—*also* **domesday.**

door *n* a movable barrier to close an opening in a wall; a doorway; a means of entry or approach.

doorjamb *n* one of the two vertical sides of a door frame; a doorpost.

doorkeeper *n* a person guarding a door.

doorman *n* (*pl* **doormen**) a uniformed attendant stationed at the entrance to large hotels, offices, etc.

doormat *n* a mat placed at the entrance to a doorway for wiping one's feet; (*inf*) a submissive or easily bullied person.

doornail *n* (*formerly*) a large nail with which doors were studded; **dead as a doornail** most certainly dead.

doorplate *n* a plate with the name of the occupant of a building.

doorpost *n* the straight vertical side-post of a door, jamb.

doorstop *n* a device for preventing a door from moving or fixed to the bottom of a door to prevent it hitting a wall when opening, etc.

doorway *n* an opening in a wall, etc filled by a door.

dope *n* a thick pasty substance used for lubrication; (*inf*) any illegal drug, such as cannabis or narcotics; (*sl*) a stupid person; (*sl*) information. * *vt* to treat with dope. * *vi* to take addictive drugs.

dopey, dopy *adj* (**dopier, dopiest**) (*sl*) stupid; (*inf*) half asleep.—**dopiness** *n.*

doppelgänger, doppelganger *n* a ghostly double of a living person.

Dorian *adj* of or relating to an early Greek race that overthrew the Mycenaean civilization. * *n* a member of that race.

Doric *adj* of the Dorians or their dialect; of or belonging to the oldest and simplest style of Greek architecture. * *n* the dialect of the Dorians; any broad dialect.

dormant *adj* sleeping; quiet, as if asleep; inactive.—**dormancy** *n.*

dormer *n* an upright window that projects from a sloping roof.

dormitory *n* (*pl* **dormitories**) a large room with many beds, as in a boarding school.

dormouse *n* (*pl* **dormice**) a small mouse-like creature that hibernates in winter.

dorp *n* (*S Africa*) a small town.

dorsal *adj* of, on, or near the back.—**dorsally** *adv.*

dorsiventral *adj* (*leaves*) having a differentiated back and front.

dory[1] *n* (*pl* **dories**) a light flat-bottomed boat with a sharp bow and high sides.

dory[2] *n* (*pl* **dories**) an edible yellow seafish.—*also* **John Dory.**

dosage *n* the administration of a medicine in doses; the size of a dose; the operation of dosing.

dose *n* the amount of medicine, radiation, etc administered at one time; a part of an experience; (*sl*) a venereal disease. * *vt* to administer a dose (of medicine) to.

doss *vi* (*sl*) to sleep, esp in a dosshouse.

dossal, dossel *n* a hanging of silk or damask at the back and sides of an altar.

dosshouse *n* (*sl*) a cheap lodging house.

dossier *n* a collection of documents about a subject or person, a file.

dot *n* a small round speck, a point; the short signal in Morse code. * *vt* (**dotting, dotted**) to mark with a dot; to scatter (about).—**dotter** *n.*

dotage *n* weakness and infirmity caused by old age.

dotard *n* a person in their dotage.

dote *vi* (*with* **on** *or* **upon**) to show excessive affection.—**doter** *n.*

dot matrix printer *n* (*comput*) a printer in which each printed character is formed by pins selected from a rectangular array.

dotted *see* **dot.**

dotterel, dottrel *n* a small plover of Europe and Asia, now rare; a similar Australian bird.

dottle *n* a remnant of tobacco left in a smoked pipe.

dotty *adj* (**dottier, dottiest**) (*inf*) eccentric, slightly mad.—**dottily** *adv.*—**dottiness** *n.*

double *adj* twice as large, as strong, etc; designed or intended for two; made of two similar parts; having two meanings, characters, etc; (*flowers*) having more than one circle of petals. * *adv* twice; in twos. * *n* a number or amount that is twice as much; a person or thing identical to another; (*film*) a person closely resembling an actor and who takes their place to perform stunts, etc; (*pl*) a game between two pairs of players. * *vti* to make or become twice as much or as many; to fold, to bend; to bend sharply backwards; to sail around; to have an additional purpose.—**doubly** *adv.*

double agent *n* a spy secretly acting for two governments at the same time.

double-barrelled, double-barreled *adj* (*gun*) having two barrels; (*surname*) having two parts; (*question*) serving a double purpose.

double bass *n* the largest instrument of the violin family.—**double bassist** *n.*

double boiler *n* two saucepans fitting into each other so that the contents of the upper are cooked while boiling in the lower.

double-breasted *adj* (*suit*) having one half of the front overlap the other.

double cream *n* cream with a high fat content.

double-cross *vt* to betray an associate, to cheat. * **double cross** *n*.—**double-crosser** *n*.

double-dealing *n* treachery, deceit.—**double-dealer** *n*.

double-edged *adj* acting in two ways; (*remarks*) having two possible meanings (eg well-meaning or malicious).

double entendre *n* a word or phrase with two meanings, one of which is usu indecent.

double entry *n* (*bookkeeping*) a system where each transaction is entered as a debit in one account and a credit in another.—**double-entry** *adj*.

double-faced *adj* having two faces; hypocritical.

double-jointed *adj* having joints which allow the limbs, figures, etc an unusual degree of flexibility.

double-park *vt* to park alongside a car which is already parked beside the kerb.

double-quick *adj, adv* very quick. * *vti* to march quickly.

double standard *n* a principle that is applied more strictly to one person or group than to another.

doublet *n* (*formerly*) a man's close-fitting jacket; one of a pair of similar things.

doublethink *n* a belief in two conflicting ideas, principles, etc.

doubleton *n* two cards only of a suit (in a player's hand).

doubloon *n* an old Spanish gold coin.

doubt *vi* to be uncertain or undecided. * *vt* to hold in doubt; to distrust; to be suspicious of. * *n* uncertainty; (*often pl*) lack of confidence in something, distrust.—**doubter** *n*.

doubtful *adj* feeling doubt; uncertain; suspicious.—**doubtfully** *adv*.—**doubtfulness** *adv*.

doubtless *adv* no doubt; probably. * *adj* assured; certain.—**doubtlessly** *adv*.—**doubtlessness** *n*.

douce *adj* (*Scot*) sober; sedate; prudent; modest.

douceur *n* a gift for services rendered, or to secure favour; a bribe.

douche *n* a jet of water directed on or into a part of the body; a device for applying this. * *vt* to cleanse or treat with a douche.

dough *n* a mixture of flour and water, milk, etc used to make bread, pastry, or cake; (*inf*) money.

doughboy *n* a boiled dumpling; (*sl*) a soldier.

doughnut *n* a small, fried, usu ring-shaped, cake.—*also* **donut**.

doughty *adj* (**doughtier**, **doughtiest**) valiant; strong.—**doughtily** *adv*.—**doughtiness** *n*.

doughy (**doughier**, **doughiest**) *adj* soft, like dough.—**doughiness** *n*.

doum, doom *n* an Egyptian palm tree.

dour *adj* stern; sullen; grim.—**dourly** *adv*.—**dourness** *n*.

douse *vt* to plunge into or soak with water; to put out, extinguish.

dove[1] *see* dive.

dove[2] *n* a small bird of the pigeon family; (*politics, diplomacy*) an advocate of peace or a peaceful policy.

dovecote, dovecot *n* a shelter and breeding place for domesticated pigeons.

dovetail *n* a wedge-shaped joint used in woodwork. * *vt* to fit or combine together.

dowager *n* a widow possessing property or title from her husband; (*inf*) a dignified elderly woman.

dowdy *adj* (**dowdier**, **dowdiest**) poorly dressed, not stylish.—**dowdily** *adv*.—**dowdiness** *n*.

dowel *n* a headless wooden or metal pin used for fastening wood or stone. * *vt* (**doweling, doweled** *or* **dowelling, dowelled**) to fasten with dowels.

dower *n* a widow's share of her husband's estate.

down[1] *n* soft fluffy feathers or fine hairs.

down[2] *adv* towards or in a lower physical position; to a lying or sitting position; toward or to the ground, floor, or bottom; to a source or hiding place; to or in a lower status or in a worse condition; from an earlier time; in cash; to or in a state of less activity. * *adj* occupying a low position, esp lying on the ground; depressed, dejected. * *prep* in a descending direction in, on, along, or through. * *n* a low period (as in activity, emotional life, or fortunes); (*inf*) a dislike, prejudice. * *vti* to go or cause to go or come down; to defeat; to swallow.

down[3] *n* (*usu pl*) a tract of bare hilly land used for pasturing sheep; banks or rounded hillocks of sand.

downbeat *adj* (*mus*) the first beat in the bar, the downward gesture of a conductor's baton; (*inf*) dismal; relaxed.

downcast *adj* dejected; (*eyes*) directed downwards.

downer *n* (*sl*) a depressant drug, esp a barbiturate; a depressing experience or situation.

downfall *n* a sudden fall (from power, etc); a sudden or heavy fall of rain or snow.

downgrade *n* a descending slope. * *vt* to reduce or lower in rank or position; to disparage.

down payment *n* a deposit.

downpour *n* a heavy fall of rain.

downright *adj* frank; absolute. * *adv* thoroughly.

downscale, down-market *adj* (*goods, services*) of inferior quality.

downside *n* the less appealing or advantageous aspect of something.

downsize *vt* to produce a smaller version of (eg a car); to reduce the numbers in a workforce by means of redundancy.

Down's syndrome *n* a chromosomal abnormality resulting in a flat face, slanting eyes and mental retardation.

downstage *adv* to the front of the stage.

downstairs *adv* to or on a lower floor. * *adj* on the ground floor or a lower floor. * *n* (*used as sing or pl*) the lower part of a house, the ground floor.

down-to-earth *adj* practical, sensible.

downtown *n* the main business district of a town or city.—*also adj*.

downtrodden *adj* oppressed, trampled underfoot.

downturn *n* a decline in (economic) activity or prosperity.

down under *n* (*inf*) Australia or New Zealand.

downward *adj* moving from a higher to a lower level, position or condition. * *adv* towards a lower place, position, etc; from an earlier time to a later (—*also* **downwards**)

downwind *adv* in the direction the wind is blowing.—*also adj*.

downy *adj* (**downier**, **downiest**) like, covered with, or made of, down.

dowry *n* (*pl* **dowries**) the money or possessions that a woman brings to her husband at marriage.

dowse *vi* to search for water, treasure, etc with a divining rod.—**dowser** *n*.

doxology *n* (*pl* **doxologies**) a hymn of praise to God.

doxy *n* (*pl* **doxies**) (*arch*) a sweetheart, a prostitute.

doyen *n* a senior member of a group; an expert in a field; the oldest example of a category.—**doyenne** *nf*.

doyley *see* **doily**.

doze *vi* to sleep lightly. * *n* a light sleep, a nap.—**dozer** *n*.

dozen *n* a group of twelve.—**dozenth** *adj*.

dozy *adj* (**dozier, doziest**) drowsy; (*inf*) stupid.—**dozily** *adv*.—**doziness** *n*.

DPhil, D.Phil *abbr* = Doctor of Philosophy.

Dr *abbr* = Doctor; debtor.

drab *adj* (**drabber, drabbest**) dull, uninteresting; of a dull brown colour. * *n* a dull yellow brown colour; cloth of this colour.—**drably** *adv*.—**drabness** *n*.

drabble *vt* to make wet or dirty by dragging through mud or water.

dracaena *n* any of a genus of tropical liliaceous palm-like plants.

drachm *n* in UK, a unit of capacity ($1/8$th fluid ounce); in US, a dram; a drachma.

drachma *n* (*pl* **drachmas, drachmae**) the monetary unit of Greece.

draconian *adj* (*laws, etc*) very cruel, severe; (*with cap*) of the 7th-century Athenian statesman Draco or his extremely harsh laws.

draft *n* a rough plan, preliminary sketch; an order for the payment of money by a bank; a smaller group selected from a larger for a specific task; conscription. * *vt* to draw a rough sketch or outline of; to select for a special purpose; to conscript.—*also* **draught**.

draftboard, draftsboard *see* **draughtboard**.

draftee *n* a conscript.

draftsman *see* **draughtsman**.

drafty *see* **draughty**.

drag *vb* (**dragging, dragged**) *vt* to pull along by force; to draw slowly and heavily; to search (in water) with a dragnet or hook. * *vi* to trail on the ground; to move slowly and heavily; (*sl*) to draw on a cigarette. * *n* something used for dragging, a dragnet, a heavy harrow; something that retards progress; a braking device; (*sl*) something boring or tedious; (*sl*) women's clothes worn by a man; (*sl*) a draw at a cigarette.

dragée *n* a coated nut or ball of sugar; a silver coated ball used as a cake decoration; a pill coated with sugar.

draggle *vt* to wet or soil by dragging in the mud or along the ground * *vi* to become dirty or wet by dragging.

dragnet *n* a net for scouring a riverbed, pond, etc to search for anything; a coordinated hunt for an escaped criminal, etc.

dragon *n* a mythical winged reptile; an authoritarian or grim person, esp a woman.

dragonfly *n* (*pl* **dragonflies**) an insect with a long slender abdomen, large eyes and iridescent wings.

dragoon *n* a soldier on horseback, a cavalryman. * *vt* to force into submission by bullying commands.

drail *n* a weighted fishhook for dragging through water.

drain *vt* to draw off liquid gradually; to make dry by removing liquid gradually; to exhaust physically or mentally; to drink the entire contents of a glass * *vi* to flow away gradually; to become dry as liquid trickles away. * *n* a sewer, pipe, etc by which water is drained away; something that causes exhaustion or depletion.—**drainer** *n*.

drainage *n* a draining; a system of drains; something drained off.

draining board, drainboard *n* a sloping, usu grooved, surface beside a sink for draining washed dishes.

drainpipe *n* a pipe that carries waste liquid, sewage, etc out of a building.

drake *n* a male duck.

dram *n* a small drink of spirits; a small amount; a unit of capacity ($1/8$th fluid ounce); a unit of weight (avoirdupois 27.243 grains or 0.00265 ounce/apothecaries' weight 3 scruples or 60 grains).

drama *n* a play for the stage, radio or television; dramatic literature as a genre; a dramatic situation or a set of events.

dramatic *adj* of or resembling drama; exciting, vivid.—**dramatically** *adv*.

dramatics *n* (*used as sing or pl*) the producing or performing of plays; (*used as sing*) exaggerated behaviour, histrionics.

dramatis personae *n* the characters in a play.

dramatist *n* a person who writes plays.

dramatization *n* the action or process of dramatizing; an event or novel, etc, adapted to the form of a play.

dramatize *vt* to write or adapt in the form of a play; to express in an exaggerated or dramatic form.—**dramatizer** *n*.

dramaturge, dramaturg *n* a playwright; a literary adviser; an expert in dramaturgy.

dramaturgy *n* the art of dramatic composition; representation and stage effect.—**dramaturgic, dramaturgical** *adj*.

drank *see* **drink**.

drape *vt* to cover or hang with cloth; to arrange in loose folds; to place loosely or untidily. * *n* a hanging cloth or curtain; (*pl*) curtains.

draper *n* a seller of cloth.

drapery *n* (*pl* **draperies**) fabrics or curtains, esp as arranged in loose folds; the trade of a draper.

drastic *adj* acting with force and violence.—**drastically** *adv*.

drat *interj* (*sl*) a euphemism for damn.

dratted *adj* (*sl*) confounded; annoying.

draught *n* a current of air, esp in an enclosed space; the pulling of a load using an animal, etc; something drawn; a dose of medicine or liquid; an act of swallowing; the depth of water required to float a ship; beer, wine, etc stored in bulk in casks; a flat counter used in the game of draughts; (*pl*) (*used as sing*) a game for two players using 24 round pieces on a draughboard.

draughtboard *n* a square board identical to a chessboard used for playing draughts.—*also* **draftboard, draftsboard**.

draughtsman[1] *n* (*pl* **draughtsmen**) a person who makes detailed drawings or plans.—*also* **draftsman**.—**draughtsmanship, draftsmanship** *n*.

draughtsman[2] *n* (*pl* **draughtsmen**) *n* a flat counter used in the game of draughts.—*also* **checker, draftsman**.

draughty *adj* (**draughtier, draughtiest**) letting in or exposed to drafts of air.—*also* **drafty**.—**draughtiness, draftiness** *n*.

Dravidian *adj* pertaining to an ancient race and their languages, spoken in southern India and Sri Lanka. * *n* a member of this race; a family of languages spoken by the Dravidians.

draw *vti* (**drawing, drew**, *pp* **drawn**) to haul, to drag; to cause to go in a certain direction; to pull out; to attract; to delineate, to sketch; to receive (as a salary); to bend (a bow) by pulling back the string; to leave (a contest) undecided; to write up, to draft (a will); to produce or allow a current of air; to draw lots; to get information from; (*ship*) to require a certain depth to float; (*with* **on**) to approach; to use (a resource); to withdraw (money) from (an account, etc); to put on (clothes); (*with* **out**) to extract; to prolong, extend; to cause (someone) to speak freely; to take (money) from an account; (*with* **up**) to bring or come to a standstill; to draft (a document); to straighten oneself; to form soldiers into an array. * *n* the act of drawing; (*inf*) an event that attracts customers, people; the drawing of lots; a drawn game.

drawback *n* a hindrance, handicap.

drawbridge *n* a bridge (eg over a moat) designed to be drawn up.

drawee *n* one on whom an order, bill of exchange, or a draft is drawn.

drawer *n* a person who draws; a person who draws a cheque; a sliding box-like compartment (as in a table, chest, or desk); (*pl*) knickers, underpants.

drawing *n* a figure, plan, or sketch drawn by using lines.

drawing pin *n* a thumbtack.

drawing room *n* a room where visitors are entertained, a living room.

drawl *vt* to speak slowly and with elongated vowel sounds. * *n* drawling speech.—**drawler** *n.*—**drawlingly** *adv.*

drawn[1] *see* **draw**.

drawn[2] *adj* looking strained because of tiredness or worry.

drawstring *n* a string or tape threaded through fabric which when pulled gathers it up or closes an opening (eg in a purse).

dray *n* a low, stoutly built cart used for heavy loads.

dread *n* great fear or apprehension. * *vt* to fear greatly.

dreadful *adj* full of dread; causing dread; extreme (*dreadful tiredness*); (*sl*) bad, disagreeable.—**dreadfully** *adv* —**dreadfulness** *n*.

dreadlocks *npl* hair worn in long matted strands by male Rastafarians.

dreadnought, dreadnaught *n* a battleship with main armament entirely of big guns; a heavy cloth; an overcoat of this cloth.

dream *n* a stream of thoughts and images experienced during sleep; a day-dreaming state, a reverie; an ambition; an ideal. * *vb* (**dreaming, dreamt** *or* **dreamed**) *vi* to have a dream during sleep; to fantasize. * *vt* to dream of; to imagine as a reality; (*with* **up**) to devise, invent.—**dreamer** *n*.

dreamy *adj* (**dreamier, dreamiest**) given to dreaming, unpractical; (*inf*) attractive, wonderful.—**dreamily** *adv.*—**dreaminess** *n*.

dreary *adj* (**drearier, dreariest**) dull; cheerless.—**drearily** *adv.*—**dreariness** *n*.

dredge[1] *n* a device for scooping up material from the bottom of a river, harbour, etc. * *vt* to widen, deepen, or clean with a dredge; to scoop up with a dredge; (*with* **up**) (*inf*) to discover, reveal, esp through effort.

dredge[2] *vt* to coat (food) by sprinkling.

dredger[1] *n* a vessel fitted with dredging equipment.

dredger[2] *n* a container with a perforated lid for sprinkling.

dreggy (**dreggier, dreggiest**) *adj* full of dregs; like dregs.

dregs *npl* solid impurities that settle on the bottom of a liquid; residue; (*inf*) a worthless person or thing.

drench *vt* to soak, saturate.

dress *n* clothing; a one-piece garment worn by women and girls comprising a top and skirt; a style or manner of clothing. * *vt* to put on or provide with clothing; to decorate; (*wound*) to wash and bandage; (*animal*) to groom; to arrange the hair; to prepare food (eg poultry, fish) for eating by cleaning, gutting, etc; (*with* **up**) to attire in best clothes; to improve the appearance of. * *vi* to put on clothes; to put on formal wear for an occasion; (*with* **up**) to put on fancy dress, etc.

dressage *n* the training of a horse in deportment and obedience.

dress circle *n* the first tier of seats in a theatre above the stalls.

dresser *n* a person who assists an actor to dress; a type of kitchen sideboard.

dressing *n* a sauce or stuffing for food; manure spread over the soil; dress or clothes; the bandage, ointment, etc applied to a wound.

dressing-down *n* a severe scolding.

dressing gown *n* a loose garment worn when one is partially clothed.

dressmaker *n* a person who makes clothes.—**dressmaking** *n*.

dress rehearsal *n* rehearsal in full costume.

dressy *adj* (**dressier, dressiest**) stylish; elaborate; showy.—**dressily** *adv.*—**dressiness** *n*.

drew *see* **draw**.

dribble *vi* to flow in a thin stream or small drips; to let saliva trickle from the mouth. * *vt* (*soccer, basketball, hockey*) to move (the ball) along little by little with the foot, hand, stick, etc. * *n* the act of dribbling; a thin stream of liquid.—**dribbler** *n*.

driblet *n* a small amount; a drop, trickle.

dried *see* **dry**.

drier *see* **dry, dryer**.

drift *n* a heap of snow, sand, etc deposited by the wind; natural course, tendency; the general meaning or intention (of what is said); the extent of deviation (of an aircraft, etc) from a course; an aimless course; the action or motion of drifting. * *vt* to cause to drift. * *vi* to be driven or carried along by water or air currents; to move along aimlessly; to be piled into heaps by the wind.

driftage *n* matter that drifts ashore; deviation from a course caused by air or sea currents.

drifter *n* a person who wanders aimlessly.

driftwood *n* wood cast ashore by tides.

drill[1] *n* an implement with a pointed end that bores holes; the training of soldiers, etc; repetitious exercises or training as a teaching method; (*inf*) correct procedure or routine. * *vt* to make a hole with a drill; to instruct or be instructed by drilling.

drill[2] *n* a machine for planting seeds in rows; a furrow in which seeds are planted; a row of seeds planted in this way.—*also vt*.

drilling platform *n* the fixed or mobile structure supporting the equipment and accommodation facilities, etc for drilling an offshore oil well.

drilling rig *n* the machinery required to drill an oil well.

drily *see* **dry**.

drink *vb* (**drinking, drank,** *pp* **drunk**) *vt* to swallow (a liquid); to take in, absorb; to join in a toast. * *vi* to consume alcoholic liquor, esp to excess. * *n* liquid to be drunk; alcoholic liquor; (*sl*) the sea.—**drinker** *n*.

drip *vti* (**dripping, dripped**) to fall or let fall in drops. * *n* a liquid that falls in drops; the sound of falling drops; (*med*) a device for administering a fluid slowly and continuously into a vein; (*inf*) a weak or ineffectual person.—**dripper** *n*.

drip-dry *adj* (*clothing*) drying easily and needing relatively little ironing.—*also vti*.

dripping *n* fat that drips from meat during roasting.

drive *vb* (**driving, drove,** *pp* **driven**) *vt* to urge, push or force onward; to direct the movement or course of; to convey in a vehicle; to carry through strongly; to impress forcefully; to propel (a ball) with a hard blow. * *vi* to be forced along; to be conveyed in a vehicle; to work, to strive (at). * *n* a trip in a vehicle; a stroke to drive a ball (in golf, etc); a driveway; a military attack; an intensive campaign; dynamic ability; the transmission of power to machinery.

drive-in *n* a cinema, restaurant, etc, where customers are served in their cars.—*also adj*.

drivel *n* nonsense. * *vi* (**drivelling, drivelled** *or* **driveling, driveled**) to talk nonsense.—**driveller, driveler** *n*.

driven *see* **drive**.

driver *n* one who or that which drives; a chauffeur; (*golf*) a wooden club used from the tee.

driveway *n* a road for vehicles, often on private property.

drizzle *n* fine light rain.—*also vi*.—**drizzly** *adj*.

drogue *n* a sea anchor; a small parachute that slows down or stabilizes something (as a jet aircraft); a funnel-shaped device that enables an aeroplane to be refuelled from a tanker plane while in flight; a buoy at the end of a harpoon line; a windsock.

droit *n* equity; a right of ownership, esp in land; custom; duty.

droll *adj* oddly amusing; whimsical.—**drollness** *n*.—**drolly** *adv*.

drollery *n* (*pl* **drolleries**) the quality of being droll; buffoonery; a droll act.

dromedary *n* (*pl* **dromedaries**) a one-humped camel.

drone *n* a male honey-bee; a lazy person; a deep humming sound; a monotonous speaker or speech; an aircraft piloted by remote control. * *vi* to make a monotonous humming sound; to speak in a monotonous manner.

drool *vi* to slaver, dribble; to show excessive enthusiasm for.

droop *vi* to bend or hang down; to become weak or faint. * *n* the act or an instance of drooping.

droopy *adj* (**droopier, droopiest**) drooping; tending to droop; (*sl*) tired, depressed.—**droopily** *adv*.—**droopiness** *n*.

drop kick *n* a kick made by dropping the ball onto the ground and kicking as it bounces.—**drop-kick** *vt*.

drop *n* a small amount of liquid in a roundish shape; something shaped like this, as a sweet; a tiny quantity; a sudden fall; the distance down; (*pl*) liquid medicine, etc dispensed in small drops. * *vb* (**dropping, dropped**) *vi* to fall in drops; to fall suddenly; to go lower, to sink; to come (in); (*with* **in**) to visit (with) informally; (*with* **out**) to abandon or reject (a course, society, etc). * *vt* to let fall, to cause to fall; to lower or cause to descend; to set down from a vehicle; to mention casually; to cause (the voice) to be less loud; to give up (as an idea).—**dropper** *n*.

droplet *n* a tiny drop (as of liquid).

dropout *n* a student who abandons a course of study; a person who rejects normal society.

droppings *npl* animal dung.

dropsy *n* an unnatural accumulation of serious fluid in any cavity of the body or its tissues.—**dropsical** *adj*.

droshky, drosky *n* (*pl* **droshkies, droskies**) a light four-wheeled open Russian carriage.

dross *n* a surface scum on molten metal; rubbish, waste matter.

drought *n* a long period of dry weather.—**droughty** *adj*.

drove[1] *see* **drive**.

drove[2] *n* a group of animals driven in a herd or flock, etc; a large moving crowd of people.

drover *n* a person whose occupation is to drive cattle.

drown *vti* to die or kill by suffocation in water or other liquid. * *vt* to flood; to drench; to become deeply immersed in some activity; to blot out (a sound) with a louder noise; to remove (sorrow, etc) with drink.

drowse *vi* to be nearly asleep.

drowsy *adj* (**drowsier, drowsiest**) sleepy; soporific; lethargic; inactive.—**drowsily** *adv*.—**drowsiness** *n*.

drub *vt* (**drubbing, drubbed**) to thrash; to defeat convincingly.

drudge *vi* to do boring or very menial work. * *n* a person who drudges, esp a servant.—**drudger** *n*.—**drudgingly** *adv*.

drudgery *n* (*pl* **drudgeries**) dull, boring work.

drug *n* any substance used in medicine; a narcotic. * *vt* (**drugging, drugged**) to administer drugs to; to stupefy.

drugget *n* a coarse woollen or cotton fabric; a rug made of this.

druggist *n* a pharmacist.

drugstore *n* a retail store selling medicines and other miscellaneous articles such as cosmetics, film, etc.

druid *n* (*often with cap*) a priest of the ancient inhabitants (probably Celtic) of Britain, Gaul and Germany; a member of a modern society reviving druidism.—**druidic, druidical** *adj*.

druidism *n* the beliefs, manners, rites and customs of the druids.

drum *n* a round percussion instrument, played by striking a membrane stretched across a hollow cylindrical frame; the sound of a drum; anything shaped like a drum, as a container for liquids. * *vb* (**drumming, drummed**) *vi* to play a drum; to beat or tap rhythmically. * *vt* (*with* **in**) to instil (knowledge) into a person by constant repetition; (*with* **up**) to summon as by drum; to create (business, etc) by concerted effort; to originate.

drumhead *n* the membrane stretched across the end of a drum.

drummer *n* a person who plays a drum; (*inf*) a travelling salesman.

drumstick *n* a stick for beating a drum; the lower part of a cooked leg of poultry.

drunk[1] *see* **drink**.

drunk[2] *adj* intoxicated with alcohol. * *n* a drunk person.

drunkard *n* an habitual drunk.

drunken *adj* intoxicated; caused by excessive drinking.—**drunkenly** *adv*.—**drunkenness** *n*.

drupe *n* a fleshy fruit with a stone, as a plum.—**drupaceous** *adj*.

drupelet *n* a small drupe in a compound fruit, eg. raspberry.

druse *n* a crust of crystals; a rock cavity lined with this.

Druse, Druze *n* a member of a fanatical politico-religious sect in Syria and Lebanon.

dry *adj* (**drier, driest**) free from water or liquid; thirsty; marked by a matter-of-fact, ironic or terse manner of expression; uninteresting, wearisome; (*bread*) eaten without butter, etc; (*wine*) not sweet; not selling alcohol. * *vti* (**drying, dried**) to make or become dry; (*with out*) to be treated for alcoholism or drug addiction.—**drily, dryly** *adv.*—**dryness** *n.*

dryad *n* (*pl* **dryads, dryades**) (*Greek myth*) a wood nymph.

dry-clean *vt* to clean with solvents as opposed to water.—**dry-cleaner** *n.*—**dry-cleaning** *n.*

dry dock *n* a dock that can be drained of water to make ship repairs easier.

dryer *n* a device for drying, as a tumble-drier; a clothes horse.—*also* **drier.**

dry ice *n* solid carbon dioxide.

dry rot *n* decay of timber caused by a fungus; any form of moral decay or corruption.

dry run *n* (*inf*) a rehearsal.

dry-salt *vt* to cure (meat, etc) by salting and drying.

drysalter *n* (*formerly*) a dealer in dyes, oils, etc.—**drysaltery** *n.*

DSC *abbr* = Distinguished Service Cross.

DSM *abbr* = Distinguished Service Medal.

DSO *abbr* = Distinguished Service Order.

dt, DT *abbr* = delirium tremens.

DTP *abbr* = desktop publishing.

dual *adj* double; consisting of two.

dual carriageway *n* a road with traffic travelling in opposite directions separated by a central reservation.—*also* **divided highway.**

dualism *n* a twofold division; (*philos*) the doctrine that the universe is based on two principles, eg good and evil, mind and matter.—**dualist** *n.*—**dualistic** *adj.*—**dualistically** *adv.*

duality *n* (*pl* **dualities**) the condition or quality of being two or in two parts, dualism; dichotomy.

dub¹ *vt* (**dubbing, dubbed**) to confer knighthood on; to nickname.

dub² *vt* (**dubbing, dubbed**) to replace the soundtrack of (a film), eg with one in a different language; to add sound effects or music to (a film, broadcast, etc); to transfer (a recording) to a new tape.

dubbin, dubbing *n* a grease for softening and waterproofing leather.

dubiety *n* (*pl* **dubieties**) doubtfulness, uncertainty; a matter of doubt.

dubious *adj* doubtful (about, of); uncertain as to the result; untrustworthy.—**dubiously** *adv.*—**dubiousness** *n.*

ducal *adj* of or pertaining to a duke, a dukedom or a duchy.—**ducally** *adv.*

ducat *n* a gold or silver coin formerly in use in Europe; (*pl*) (*sl*) money.

duce *n* a chief, a leader; (*with cap*) the title used by the Italian Fascist dictator, Benito Mussolini (1922–43).

duchess *n* the wife or widow of a duke; a woman having the same rank as a duke in her own right.

duchy *n* (*pl* **duchies**) the territory of a duke, a dukedom.

duck¹ *vt* to dip briefly in water; to lower the head suddenly, esp to avoid some object; to avoid, dodge. * *vi* to dip or dive; to move the head or body suddenly; to evade a duty, etc. * *n* a ducking movement.

duck² *n* (*pl* **ducks, duck**) a water bird related to geese and swans; the female of this bird; its flesh used as food.

duck³ *n* a plain cotton cloth; (*pl*) trousers or light clothes made from this and worn in hot climates.

duckbill, duck-billed platypus *n* an Australian egg-laying furred mammal with webbed feet and a broad bill.—*also* **platypus.**

duckboard *n* a path of wooden slats laid over muddy or wet ground.

duckling *n* a young duck.

duckweed *n* a common floating freshwater plant.

ducky, duckie *adj* (**duckier, duckiest**) (*inf*) fine; satisfactory; cute. * *n* (*pl* **duckies**) (*inf*) a term of endearment, darling.

duct *n* a channel or pipe for fluids, electric cable, etc; a tube in the body for fluids to pass through.

ductile *adj* malleable; yielding.

dud *adj* (*sl*) worthless. * *n* (*sl*) anything worthless; an ineffectual person.

dude *n* a dandy; a city person on holiday in a ranch.

dudeen *n* a short clay tobacco pipe.

dudgeon *n* resentment, indignation; (*arch*) the hilt of a dagger.

due *adj* owed as a debt; immediately payable; fitting, appropriate; appointed or expected to do or arrive. * *adv* directly, exactly. * *n* something due or owed; (*pl*) fees.

duel *n* combat with weapons between two persons over a matter of honour, etc; conflict of any kind between two people, sides, ideas, etc. * *vi* (**duelling, duelled** or **dueling, dueled**) to fight in a duel.—**duellist, duelist** *n.*

duello *n* (*pl* **duellos**) the duelists' code.

duenna *n* an older woman acting as a chaperone of young women in Spanish or Portuguese families.

duet *n* a musical composition for two performers.—**duettist** *n.*

duffel, duffle *n* a coarse, heavy woollen cloth.

duffel bag, duffle bag *n* a large cylindrical drawstring bag for personal belongings.

duffel coat, duffle coat *n* a heavy, hooded overcoat, fastened with toggles.

duffer *n* an incompetent person, esp an elderly one.

dug *see* **dig.**

dugong *n* an aquatic herbivorous mammal resembling the seal and walrus; the sea cow.

dugout *n* a boat made from the hollowed out tree trunk; a rough underground shelter.

duiker *n* (*pl* **duikers, duiker**) a small South African antelope.

duke *n* the highest order of British nobility; the title of a ruler of a European duchy.

dukedom *n* a duchy; the rank, position or title of a duke.

dulcet *adj* sweet-sounding, melodious.—**dulcetly** *adv.*

dulcimer *n* a musical instrument with wire strings that are struck with a hammer; a folk-music instrument with usu three strings that are played by plucking (—*also* **dulcimore**).

dulia *n* the veneration paid to saints and angels as the servants of God.

dull *adj* not sharp or pointed; not bright or clear; stupid; boring; not active. * *vti* to make or become dull. —**dully** *adv.*—**dullness** *n.*

dullard *n* a slow-witted person.

dulse *n* a red edible seaweed found on rocks.

duly *adv* properly; suitably.

dumb *adj* not able to speak; silent; (*inf*) stupid.—**dumbly** *adv.*—**dumbness** *n.*

dumbbell *n* one of a pair of heavy weights used for muscular exercise; (*sl*) a fool.

dumbfound, dumfound *vti* to astonish, surprise.

dumbwaiter *n* a stand with revolving shelves for holding food; a revolving tray for holding food; a small elevator or lift for carrying food, etc, between floors.

dum-dum *n* (*sl*) a foolish person.

dumdum (bullet) *n* a soft-nosed, expanding bullet.

dumdum *n* (*sl*) a stupid person; a dummy.

dummy *n* (*pl* **dummies**) a figure of a person used to display clothes; (*sl*) a soother or pacifier for a baby; a stupid person; an imitation; (*bridge*) the exposed cards of the dealer's partner.

dump *vt* to drop or put down carelessly in a heap; to deposit as rubbish; to abandon or get rid of; to sell goods abroad at a price lower than the market price abroad; (*with* on) (*sl*) to censure strongly the words or actions of others. * *n* a place for refuse; a temporary store; (*inf*) a dirty, dilapidated place; (*pl*) (*inf*) despondency, low spirits.—**dumper** *n*.

dumpling *n* a rounded piece of dough cooked by boiling or steaming; a short, fat person.

dumpster *n* a large garbage can.

dumpy *adj* (**dumpier, dumpiest**) short and thick.—**dumpily** *adv*.—**dumpiness** *n*.

dun[1] *adj* (**dunner, dunnest**) greyish-brown.—**dunness** *n*.

dun[2] *vt* (**dunning, dunned**) to press persistently for payment of a debt.

dunce *n* a person who is stupid or slow to learn.

dunderhead *n* a stupid person, a dunce.—**dunderheaded** *adj*.

dune *n* a hill of sand piled up by the wind.

dung *n* excrement; manure; filth. * *vt* to spread with manure.—**dungy** *adj*.

dungaree *n* a coarse cotton cloth; (*pl*) overalls or trousers made from this.

dungeon *n* an underground cell for prisoners.

dunghill *n* a heap of dung.

dunk *vti* to dip (cake, etc) into liquid, eg coffee.

dunlin *n* a small red-backed sandpiper of northern regions.

dunnage *n* loose wood, etc, used to pack cargo or keep it out of bilge water in a ship's hold; baggage.

dunnite *n* a powerful explosive used esp in shells.

duo *n* (*pl* **duos, dui**) a pair of performers; (*inf*) two persons connected in some way.

duodecimal *adj* of twelve; proceeding by twelves. * *n* a twelfth; a system of computing by twelves.

duodecimo *n* (*pl* **duodecimos**) a book of sheets folded into twelve leaves; this book size.—*also* **twelvemo**.

duodenary *adj* duodecimal.

duodenum *n* (*pl* **duodena, duodenums**) the first part of the small intestine.—**duodenal** *adj*.

duologue *n* a play with two actors; a conversation between two people.

dup *vt* (**dupping, dupped**) (*arch*) to open.

dupe *n* a person who is cheated. * *vt* to deceive; to trick.—**dupable** *adj*.—**duper** *n*.—**dupery** *n*.

duple *adj* double; (*mus*) of two beats to the bar.

duplex *adj* having two parts, double. * *n* a flat or apartment on two floors.—**duplexity** *n*.

duplicate *adj* in pairs, double; identical; copied exactly from an original. * *n* one of a pair of identical things; a copy. * *vt* to make double; to make an exact copy of; to repeat.—**duplicable** *adj*.

duplication *n* the act of duplicating; a copy; multiplication by two.—**duplicative** *adj*.

duplicator *n* a machine for making copies, esp of a document.

duplicity *n* (*pl* **duplicities**) treachery; deception.—**duplicitous** *adj*.

durable *adj* enduring, resisting wear, etc.—**durability** *n*.—**durably** *adv*.

duralumin *n* a strong alloy of aluminium with copper, magnesium, manganese and silicon.

dura mater *n* the tough outer membrane that envelops the brain and spinal cord.

duramen *n* the inner heartwood of a tree.

durance *n* imprisonment.

duration *n* the time in which an event continues.

durbar *n* (*formerly*) a state levee or reception in India and Africa.

duress *n* compulsion by use of force or threat; unlawful constraint; imprisonment.

durian, durion *n* an oval fruit with a foul smell and a pleasant taste; the Asian tree that bears it.

during *prep* throughout the duration of; at a point in the course of.

durmast *n* a dark European oak yielding a tough wood.

durst *see* **dare**.

dusk *n* (the darker part of) twilight.

dusky *adj* (**duskier, duskiest**) having a dark colour.—**duskily** *adv*.—**duskiness** *n*.

dust *n* fine particles of solid matter. * *vt* to free from dust; to sprinkle with flour, sugar, etc.

dustbin *n* a container for household refuse.—*also* **garbage can, trash can**.

dust bowl *n* a drought area subject to dust storms.

dust cover *n* a dust jacket.

duster (coat), dustcoat *n* a coat for keeping off dust, worn esp by early motorists.

duster *n* a cloth for dusting; a device for dusting; a duster coat; a light housecoat.

dustman *n* (*pl* **dustmen**) a garbageman.

dust jacket *n* a paper cover for a book.

dust wrapper *n* a dust jacket.

dusty *adj* (**dustier, dustiest**) covered with dust.—**dustily** *adv*.—**dustiness** *n*.

Dutch *adj* pertaining to Holland, its people, or language. * *n* the Dutch language.

Dutch courage *n* courage obtained from alcohol; alcoholic drink.

Dutch elm disease *n* a fungal disease which withers the foliage of elm trees and eventually kills them.

Dutch oven *n* a metal box for cooking before an open fire.

Dutch treat *n* a meal, etc, where each pays for himself or herself.

Dutch uncle *n* a person with stern kindness.

duteous *adj* (*poet*) dutiful.—**duteously** *adv*.—**duteousness** *n*.

dutiable *adj* (*goods, etc*) subject to duty.—**dutiability** *n*.

dutiful *adj* performing one's duty; obedient.—**dutifully** *adv*.—**dutifulness** *n*.

duty *n* (*pl* **duties**) an obligation that must be performed for moral or legal reasons; respect for one's elders or superiors; actions and responsibilities arising from one's business, occupation, etc; a tax on goods or imports, etc.

duty-free *adj* free from tax or duty.

duumvir *n* (*pl* **duumvirs, duumviri**) in ancient Rome, either of two officers of high rank acting together in one capacity or public function; either member of a duumvirate.

duumvirate *n* a governing body of two; two such people.

duvet *n* a thick, soft quilt used instead of bedclothes.— *also* **continental quilt.**

dwarf *n* (*pl* **dwarfs, dwarves**) a person, animal or plant of abnormally small size. * *vt* to stunt; to cause to appear small.

dwarfish *adj* like a dwarf; very small.—**dwarfishness** *n.*

dwell *vi* (**dwelling, dwelt** *or* **dwelled**) to live (in a place); (*with* **on**) to focus the attention on; to think, talk, or write at length about.—**dweller** *n.*

dwelling *n* the house, etc where one lives, habitation.

dwindle *vi* to shrink, diminish; to become feeble.

Dy (*chem symbol*) dysprosium.

dyad *n* a pair; (*chem*) a bivalent atom, element, or radical.—**dyadic** *adj.*

dyarchy *see* **diarchy.**

dye *vt* (**dyeing, dyed**) to give a new colour to. * *n* a colouring substance, esp in solution; a colour or tint produced by dyeing.—**dyer** *n.*

dyeing *n* the process or work of giving colour to fabrics using dyes.

dyed-in-the-wool *adj* uncompromising in attitude or opinion.

dyestuff *n* material yielding a dye.

dying[1] *see* **die**[1].

dying[2] *adj* passing away from life; decaying physically; drawing to a close; expiring. * *n* death.

dyke[1] *see* **dike**[1].

dyke[2] *n* (*derog*) a lesbian.

dynamic *adj* relating to force that produces motion; (*person*) forceful, energetic.—**dynamically** *adv.*

dynamics *n* (*used as sing*) the branch of science that deals with forces and their effect on the motion of bodies.

dynamism *n* dynamic influence or power; (*philos*) the theory that the universe is constituted of forces.— **dynamist** *n.*—**dynamistic** *adj.*

dynamite *n* a powerful explosive; a potentially dangerous situation; (*inf*) an energetic person or thing. * *vt* to blow up with dynamite.—**dynamiter** *n.*

dynamo *n* (*pl* **dynamos**) a device that generates electric current.

dynamoelectric, dynamoelectrical *adj* of or denoting the production of electricity from mechanical energy or of mechanical energy from electricity.

dynamometer *n* an instrument for measuring energy expended.

dynast *n* a ruler, usu a hereditary one.

dynasty *n* (*pl* **dynasties**) a line of hereditary rulers or leaders of any powerful family or similar group.— **dynastic** *adj.*—**dynastically** *adv.*

dyne *n* a unit of force, causing in one gram an acceleration per second of one centimetre per second; the unit of force in the cgs system.

dys- *prefix* bad, unfavourable.

dysentery *n* painful inflammation of the large intestine with associated diarrhoea.—**dysenteric** *adj.*

dysergy *n* (*business*) the possibility that the merger of two companies will produce a combined operation of less productivity and efficiency, the opposite of synergy.

dysfunction *n* a failure in normal functioning.—**dysfunctional** *adj.*

dysgenic *adj* having a bad effect on the hereditary qualities of a race.

dysgenics *n* (*used as sing*) the study of the causes of reduction in quality of a race.

dyslexia *n* impaired ability in reading or spelling.— **dyslexic** *adj, n.*

dysmenorrhoea, dysmenorrhea *n* painful menstruation.—**dysmenorrhoeal, dysmenorrheal** *adj.*

dyspepsia *n* indigestion, esp chronic.

dyspeptic *adj* of or afflicted with indigestion. * *n* a dyspeptic sufferer.

dysphagia *n* difficulty in swallowing.—**dysphagic** *adj.*

dysphasia *n* a deficiency in the use or understanding of language.—**dysphasic** *adj.*

dysphoria *n* morbid restlessness, fidgets.—**dysphoric** *adj.*

dyspnoea, dyspnea *n* shortness of breath, difficulty in breathing.—**dyspnoeal, dyspneal, dyspneic, dyspnoeic** *adj.*

dysprosium *n* a soft metallic element used in lasers and magnetic alloys.

dystrophy *n* various hereditary disorders causing progressive weakening of the muscles (*muscular dystrophy*).—**dystrophic** *adj.*

dysuria *n* difficulty in passing urine.—**dysuric** *adj.*

E

E. *abbr* = east; eastern; Ecstacy.

E- *prefix* used to indicate a standard system (for packaging, weight, content, etc) within the European Community.

each *adj* every one of two or more.

eager *adj* enthusiastically desirous (of); keen (for); marked by impatient desire or interest.—**eagerly** *adv*.—**eagerness** *n*.

eager beaver *n* (*inf*) an exceptionally diligent person.

eagle *n* a bird of prey with keen eyes and powerful wings; (*golf*) a score of two strokes under par.

eagle-eyed *adj* having very sharp eyesight.

eagle owl *n* a type of large owl, also known as the great horned owl.

eaglet *n* a young eagle.

ear[1] *n* (the external part of) the organ of hearing; the sense or act of hearing; attention; something shaped like an ear.

ear[2] *n* the part of a cereal plant (eg corn, maize) that contains the seeds.

earache *n* a pain in the ear.

eardrum *n* the membrane within the ear that vibrates in response to sound waves.

eared *adj* having ears.

earing *n* (*naut*) a rope attaching the upper corner of a sail to a yard or stanchion.

earl *n* a member of the British nobility ranking between a marquis and a viscount.—**countess** *nf*.

earldom *n* the position or estate of an earl.

early *adj* (**earlier, earliest**) before the expected or normal time; of or occurring in the first part of a period or series; of or occurring in the distant past or near future.—*also adv*.—**earliness** *n*.

earmark *vt* to set aside for a specific use; to put an identification mark on. * *n* a distinguishing mark.

earn *vt* to gain (money, etc) by work or service; to acquire; to deserve; to earn interest (on money invested, etc).

earnest *adj* sincere in attitude or intention.—**earnestly** *adv*.—**earnestness** *n*.

earnings *npl* wages or profits; something earned.

earphone *n* a device held to or worn over the ear, through which sound is transmitted; a headphone.

earpiece *n* a telephone earphone.

earplug *n* a piece of wadding or wax inserted in the ear to prevent noise or water penetration.

earring *n* an ornament worn on the ear lobe.

earshot *n* hearing distance.

ear-splitting *adj* very loud.

earth *n* the world that we inhabit; solid ground, as opposed to sea; soil; the burrow of a badger, fox, etc; a connection between an electric device or circuit with the earth; (*inf*) a large amount of money. * *vt* to cover with or bury in the earth; to connect an electrical circuit or device to earth.

earthborn *adj* mortal.

earthbound *adj* confined to the earth; heading towards the earth.

earthen *adj* composed of earth; made of baked clay.

earthenware *n* pottery, etc made from baked clay.

earthly *adj* (**earthlier, earthliest**) of the earth; material, worldly.—**earthliness** *n*.

earthquake *n* a violent tremor of the earth's crust.

earth science *n* any of the sciences (eg geology) concerned with the nature and composition of the earth.

earthwards, earthward *adv* towards the earth.

earthwork *n* an excavation of earth; a fortification.

earthworm *n* any of various common worms that live in the soil.

earthy *adj* (**earthier, earthiest**) of or resembling earth; crude.—**earthiness** *n*.

earwax *n* cerumen, the brown wax found in the ear.

earwig *n* a small insect with a pincer-like appendage at the end of its body.

ease *n* freedom from pain, discomfort or disturbance; rest from effort or work; effortlessness; lack of inhibition or restraint, naturalness. * *vt* to relieve from pain, trouble, or anxiety; to relax, make less tight, release; to move carefully and gradually. * *vi* (*often with* **off**) to become less active, intense, or severe.

easeful *adj* restful.

easel *n* a supporting frame, esp one used by artists to support their canvases while painting.

easement *n* relief; something that gives ease or relief; (*law*) right of way over someone else's land.

easily *adv* with ease; by far; probably.

east *n* the direction of the sunrise; the compass point opposite west; (*with cap preceded by* **the**) the area of the world east of Europe. * *adj, adv* in, towards, or from the east.

Easter *n* the Christian festival observed on a Sunday in March or April in commemoration of the resurrection of Christ.

easterly *adj* situated towards or belonging to the east, coming from the east. * *n* (*pl* **easterlies**) a wind from the east.

eastern *adj* of or in the east.

easterner *n* someone from the east.

easternmost *adj* farthest to the east.

easting *n* the distance travelled by a vessel eastwards from a given meridian.

eastward *adj* towards the east.—**eastwards** *adv*.

easy *adj* (**easier, easiest**) free from pain, trouble, anxiety; not difficult or requiring much effort; (*manner*) relaxed; lenient; compliant; unhurried; (*inf*) open to all alternatives. * *adv* with ease.—**easiness** *n*.

easy chair *n* a comfortable chair.

easygoing *adj* placid, tolerant, relaxed.

eat *vt* (**eating, ate,** *pp* **eaten**) to take into the mouth, chew and swallow as food; to have a meal; to consume, to destroy bit by bit; (*also with* **into**) to corrode; (*inf*) to bother, cause anxiety to; (*with* **up**) to consume completely; (*inf*) to listen or absorb avidly; (*inf*) to preoccupy. * *vi* (*with* **out**) to eat away from home, esp in a restaurant. * *n* (*pl: inf*) food.—**eater** *n*.

eatable *adj* suitable for eating; fit to be eaten. * *n* (*pl*) food.

eau de Cologne *n* (*pl* **eaux de Cologne**) a perfume originally from Cologne.

eau de vie *n* brandy.

eaves *npl* the overhanging edge of a roof.

eavesdrop *vi* (**eavesdropping, eavesdropped**) to listen secretly to a private conversation.—**eavesdropper** *n*.

ebb *n* the flow of the tide out to sea; a decline. * *vi* (*tide water*) to flow back; to become lower, to decline.

ebon *n* (*poet*) ebony.

ebonite *n* a hard black rubber substance.

ebonize *vt* to make black by staining like ebony.

ebony *n* (*pl* **ebonies**) a hard heavy wood. * *adj* black as ebony.

ebracteate *adj* without bracts.

ebullient *adj* exuberant, enthusiastic; boiling.—**ebullience, ebulliency** *n*.—**ebulliently** *adv*.

ebullition *n* boiling; an outburst (of passion, feeling, etc).

EC *abbr* = European Community; East Central.

eccentric *adj* deviating from a usual or accepted pattern; unconventional in manner or appearance, odd; (*circles*) not concentric; off centre; not precisely circular. * *n* an eccentric person.—**eccentrically** *adv*.

eccentricity *n* (*pl* **eccentricities**) strangeness of behaviour; an eccentric or unusual habit.

ecclesiastic[1] *n* a member of the clergy.

ecclesiastic[2], **ecclesiastical** *adj* of or relating to the Christian Church or clergy.—**ecclesiastically** *adv*.

ecclesiasticism *n* excessive attachment to the forms, usages, organization and privileges of the Christian Church.

ecclesiology *n* the study of the Christian Church and its development; the study of church architecture and decoration.—**ecclesiological** *adj*.—**ecclesiologist** *n*.

ecdysis (*pl* **ecdyses**) *n* sloughing of skin, moulting.

ECG *abbr* = electrocardiogram.

echelon *n* a stepped formation of troops, ships, or aircraft; a level (of authority) in a hierarchy.

echidna *n* (*pl* **echidnas, echidnae**) an Australian nocturnal, toothless, spiny, egg-laying animal.

echinoderm *n* one of a class of animals which includes starfish and sea urchins.

echinus *n* (*pl* **echini**) a sea urchin.

echo *n* (*pl* **echoes**) a repetition of sound caused by the reflection of sound waves; imitation; the reflection of a radar signal by an object. * *vb* (**echoing, echoed**) *vi* to resound; to produce an echo. * *vt* to repeat; to imitate; to send back (a sound) by an echo.

echo chamber *n* a room with walls that reflect sound, used for making acoustic measurements and creating special sound effects.

echoic *adj* like an echo; imitative.

echolocation *n* finding unseen objects by means of reflected sound waves.

echo sounder *n* an instrument for determining the depth beneath a ship using sound waves.—**echo sounding** *n*.

éclair *n* a small oblong shell of choux pastry covered with chocolate and filled with cream.

eclampsia *n* (*med*) a serious condition occurring in the last three months of pregnancy, caused by toxins in the blood and causing convulsions.

éclat *n* success; applause; striking effect; social distinction.

eclectic *adj* selecting from or using various styles, ideas, methods, etc; composed of elements from a variety of sources. * *n* a person who adopts an eclectic method.—**eclectically** *adv*.—**eclecticism** *n*.

eclipse *n* the obscuring of the light of the sun or moon by the intervention of the other; a decline into obscurity, as from overshadowing by others. * *vt* to cause an eclipse of; to overshadow, darken; to surpass.—**eclipser** *n*.

ecliptic *n* the apparent path of the sun's motion relative to the stars.—**ecliptically** *adv*.

eclogue *n* a short, esp pastoral poem.

eco- *prefix* ecology; ecological.

ecology *n* (the study of) the relationships between living things and their environments.—**ecological** *adj*.—**ecologist** *n*.

econometrics *n* (*sing*) the application of mathematical and statistical methods in economics.

economic *adj* pertaining to economics or the economy; (*business, etc*) capable of producing a profit.

economical *adj* thrifty.—**economically** *adv*.

economics *n* (*sing*) the social science concerned with the production, consumption and distribution of goods and services; (*pl*) financial aspects.

economist *n* an expert in economics.

economize *vti* to spend money carefully; to save; to use prudently.—**economization** *n*.

economy *n* (*pl* **economies**) careful use of money and resources to minimize waste; an instance of this; the management of the finances and resources, etc of a business, industry or organization; the economic system of a country.

ecosphere *n* the parts of the universe where life can exist.

ecosystem *n* (*ecology*) a system comprising a community of living organisms and its surroundings.

ecru *n* beige.

ecstasy *n* (*pl* **ecstasies**) intense joy; (*sl: often with cap*) the synthetic amphetamine-based drug MDMA, which reduces social and sexual inhibitions.—**ecstatic** *adj*.—**ecstatically** *adv*.

ECT *abbr* = electroconvulsive therapy.

ecto-, ect- *prefix* outside.

ectoderm *n* the outer layer of an embryo or skin.

ectomorph *n* a person with a lightly built physique.—**ectomorphic** *adj*.—**ectomorphy** *n*.

-ectomy *n* *suffix* denoting surgical removal of a part.

ectopic *adj* (*anat*) in an abnormal position; (*fertilized egg*) developing abnormally outside the uterus.

ectoplasm *n* the outer layer of the cytoplasm of a cell; a substance supposedly exuded from the body of spiritualist mediums during trances.—**ectoplasmic** *adj*.

ectype *n* a reproduction or imitation of an original design.

ECU *abbr* = European currency unit.

ecumenical *adj* of the whole Christian Church; seeking Christian unity worldwide.—**ecumenicalism, ecumenicism** *n*.—**ecumenically** *adv*.

eczema *n* inflammation of the skin causing itching and the formation of scaly red patches.—**eczematous** *adj*.

edacious *adj* gluttonous, greedy.—**edacity** *n*.

Edam *n* a mild-flavoured round Dutch cheese, usu with a red waxy rind.

eddy *n* (*pl* **eddies**) a swiftly revolving current of air, water, fog, etc. * *vi* (**eddying, eddied**) to move round and round.

edelweiss *n* a small white-flowered alpine herb.

edema *see* **oedema**.

Eden *n* (*Bible*) the garden where Adam and Eve lived after the creation; a paradise.

edentate *adj* (*zool*) toothless.

edge *n* the border, brink, verge, margin; the sharp cutting side of a blade; sharpness, keenness; force, effectiveness. * *vt* to supply an edge or border to; to move gradually.—**edger** *n*.

edgeways, edgewise *adv* with the edge forwards; sideways.

edging *n* any border for decoration or strengthening.

edgy *adj* (**edgier, edgiest**) irritable.—**edgily** *adv*.—**edginess** *n*.

edible *adj* fit or safe to eat.—**edibility, edibleness** *n*.

edict *n* a decree; a proclamation.—**edictal** *adj*.

edifice *n* a substantial building; any large or complex organization or institution.—**edificial** *adj*.

edify *vt* (**edifying, edified**) to improve the moral character or mind of (a person).—**edification** *n*.—**edifier** *n*.—**edifyingly** *adv*.

edile *see* **aedile**.

edit *vt* to prepare (text) for publication by checking facts, grammar, style, etc; to be in charge of a publication; (*cinema*) to prepare a final version of a film by selection and arrangement of photographed sequences.

edition *n* a whole number of copies of a book, etc printed at a time; the form of a particular publication.

editio princeps (*pl* **editiones principes**) *n* the first printed edition of a book.

editor *n* a person in charge of a newspaper or other publication; a person who edits written material for publication; one who prepares the final version of a film; a person in overall charge of the form and content of a radio or television programme.—**editorship** *n*.

editorial *adj* of or produced by an editor.* *n* an article expressing the opinions of the editor or publishers of a newspaper or magazine.—**editorialist** *n*.—**editorially** *adv*.

EDP *abbr* = electronic data processing.

educable, educatable *adj* able to be educated.

educate *vt* to train the mind, to teach; to provide schooling for.—**educator** *n*.

education *n* the process of learning and training; instruction as imparted in schools, colleges and universities; a course or type of instruction; the theory and practice of teaching.—**educational** *adj*.—**educationally** *adv*.

educationalist, educationist *n* an expert in education.

educative *adj* educating.

educe *vt* to elicit (information, etc); to infer.—**educible** *adj*.

edulcorate *vt* to free from acids and other impurities by washing.—**edulcoration** *n*.

EEC *abbr* = European Economic Community (now European Community).

EEG *abbr* = electroencephalogram.

eel *n* a snake-like fish.

eelpout *n* a type of freshwater fish, found in Europe, North America and Asia; another name for the burbot.

e'en *n* (*poet*) evening.

e'er *adv* (*poet*) ever.

eerie *adj* (**eerier, eeriest**) causing fear; weird.—**eerily** *adv*.—**eeriness** *n*.

efface *vt* to rub out, obliterate; to make (oneself) humble or inconspicuous.—**effaceable** *adj*.—**effacement** *n*.—**effacer** *n*.

effect *n* the result of a cause or action by some agent; the power to produce some result; the fundamental meaning; an impression on the senses; an operative condition; (*pl*) personal belongings; (*pl: theatre, cinema*) sounds, lighting, etc to accompany a production. * *vt* to bring about, accomplish.—**effecter** *n*.—**effectible** *adj*.

effective *adj* producing a specified effect; forceful, striking in impression; actual, real; operative.—**effectively** *adv*.—**effectiveness** *n*.

effectual *adj* able to produce the desired effect.—**effectuality, effectualness** *n*.—**effectually** *adv*.

effectuate *vt* to make happen.—**effectuation** *n*.

effeminate *adj* (*man*) displaying what are regarded as feminine qualities.—**effeminacy, effeminateness** *n*.

effendi (*pl* **effendis**) *n* a Turkish title of respect, equivalent to sir or Mr.

efferent *adj* (*anat*) conveying or discharging outwards.

effervesce *vt* (*liquid*) to froth and hiss as bubbles of gas escape; to be exhilarated.—**effervescence** *n*.—**effervescent** *adj*.—**effervescible** *adj*.

effete *adj* decadent, weak.—**effeteness** *n*.

efficacious *adj* achieving the desired result.—**efficacy, efficaciousness** *n*.

efficient *adj* achieving results without waste of time or effort; competent.—**efficiently** *adv*.—**efficiency** *n* (*pl* **efficiencies**).

effigy *n* (*pl* **effigies**) a sculpture or portrait; a crude figure of a person, esp for exposure to public contempt and ridicule.

effloresce *vi* to blossom; (*chem*) to turn to powder when exposed to air, to crystallize; to become encrusted with crystals as a result of loss of water.—**efflorescence** *n*.—**efflorescent** *adj*.

effluence, efflux *n* something that flows out.

effluent *adj* flowing out. * *n* that which flows out, esp sewage.

effluvium *n* (*pl* **effluvia, effluviums**) an offensive vapour or smell.—**effluvial** *adj*.

effort *n* exertion; an attempt, try; a product of great exertion.—**effortful** *adj*.

effortless *adj* done with little effort, or seemingly so.—**effortlessly** *adv*.—**effortlessness** *n*.

effrontery *n* (*pl* **effronteries**) impudent boldness, insolence.

effulgent *adj* radiant, brilliant.—**effulgence** *n*.

effuse *vt* (*liquid, words*) to flow or pour out.

effusion *n* a pouring out; an unrestrained outpouring, as of emotion; something poured out.

effusive *adj* gushing, emotionally unrestrained; demonstrative.—**effusiveness** *n*.

eft *n* a newt.

e.g., eg, eg. *abbr* = for example (Latin *exempli gratia*).

egad *interj* (*arch*) an exclamation of surprise, pleasure or admiration.

egalitarian *adj* upholding the principle of equal rights for all.—*also n*.—**egalitarianism** *n*.

egest *vt* to excrete.—**egestion** *n*.

egesta *npl* excrement.

egg[1] *n* the oval hard-shelled reproductive cell laid by birds, reptiles and fish; the egg of the domestic poultry used as food; ovum.—**eggy** *adj*.

egg² *vt* (*with* **on**) to incite (someone to do something).

egger *n* a type of large moth.

egghead *n* (*inf*) an intellectual.

eggnog *n* a drink made from egg, beaten up with hot milk, sugar and brandy.

eggplant *see* **aubergine**.

eggshell *n* the hard outer covering of an egg. * *adj* fragile; (*paint*) having a slight sheen.

egis *see* **aegis**.

eglantine *n* the sweetbrier; the wild rose.

ego *n* (*pl* **egos**) the self; self-image, conceit.

egocentric *adj* self-centred.—**egocentricity** *n*.

egoism *n* self-concern; self-centredness.—**egoist** *n.*—**egoistic, egoistical** *adj.*—**egoistically** *adv*.

egotism *n* excessive reference to oneself; conceit.—**egotist** *n.*—**egotistic, egotistical** *adj.*—**egotistically** *adv*.

ego trip *n* (*inf*) an activity undertaken to boost one's own self-esteem or importance in the eyes of others.—**ego-trip** *vi*.

egregious *adj* outstandingly bad.—**egregiousness** *n*.

egress *n* the way out, exit.

egression *n* the act of going out or emerging; egress.

egret *n* a type of heron.

Egyptology *n* the study of Egyptian antiquities and hieroglyphics.—**Egyptologist** *n*.

eh *interj* an exclamation of inquiry or surprise.

eider *n* a large marine duck, the down of which has commercial value as a filling for quilts etc.

eiderdown *n* the down of the eider duck used for stuffing quilts, etc; a thick quilt with a soft filling.

eidolon *n* (*pl* **eidolons, eidola**) *n* an apparition or phantom.

eight *n, adj* one more than seven; the symbol for this (8, VIII, viii); (the crew of) an eight-oared rowing boat.

eighteen *n, adj* one more than seventeen; the symbol for this (18, XVIII, xviii).—**eighteenth** *adj*.

eighteenmo (*pl* **eighteenmos**) *n* a book whose sheets are folded into eighteen leaves.

eightfold *adj, adv* consisting of eight units; being eight times as great or many.

eighth *adj, n* one after seventh; one of eight equal parts.

eighty *n* (*pl* **eighties**) eight times ten; the symbol for this (80, LXXX, lxxx); (*pl*) the numbers from 80 to 89.—**eightieth** *adj, n*.

einsteinium *n* an artificial radioactive element.

eisteddfod *n* (*pl* **eisteddfods, eisteddfodau**) a Welsh competitive festival of the arts, esp singing.—**eisteddodic** *adj*.

either *adj, n* the one or the other of two; each of two. * *conj* correlative to *or*.

ejaculate *vti* to emit a fluid (as semen); to exclaim.—**ejaculation** *n.*—**ejaculator** *n.*—**ejaculatory** *adj*.

eject *vt* to turn out, to expel by force. * *vi* to escape from an aircraft or spacecraft using an ejector seat.—**ejection** *n.*—**ejector** *n*.

ejecta *npl* matter discharged by an erupting volcano.

ejector seat *n* an escape seat, esp in combat aircraft, that can be ejected with its occupant in an emergency by means of explosive bolts.

eke *vt* (*with* **out**) to supplement; to use (a supply) frugally; to make (a living) with difficulty.

elaborate *adj* highly detailed; planned with care and exactness. * *vt* to work out or explain in detail.—**elaborateness** *n.*—**elaboration** *n.*—**elaborative** *adj.*—**elaborator** *n*.

élan *n* verve, spirit.

eland *n* an African antelope with spirally twisted horns.

elapse *vi* (*time*) to pass by.

elasmobranch *n* (*pl* **elasmobranchs**) a member of a class of fish that includes sharks and skates.

elastic *adj* returning to the original size and shape if stretched or squeezed; springy; adaptable. * *n* fabric, tape, etc incorporating elastic thread.—**elastically** *adv.*—**elasticity** *n*.

elasticated *adj* made elastic by the use of elastic thread.

elate *vt* to fill with happiness or pride.—**elated** *adj.*—**elatedness** *n.*—**elation** *n*.

elbow *n* the joint between the forearm and upper arm; the part of a piece of clothing covering this; any sharp turn or bend, as in a pipe. * *vt* to shove away rudely with the elbow; to jostle.

elbow grease *n* (*inf*) effort, hard work.

elbowroom *n* space to move, scope.

elder¹ *n* a tree or shrub with flat clusters of white or pink flowers.

elder² *n* an older person; an office bearer in certain churches.—**eldership** *n*.

elderberry *n* (*pl* **elderberries**) (the fruit of) an elder.

elderly *adj* quite old.—**elderliness** *n*.

eldest *n* oldest, first born.

El Dorado, eldorado *n* an imaginary land of vast wealth.

eldritch, eldrich *adj* (*Scot*) weird; hideous.

elecampane *n* a plant of the aster family, from the roots of which a tonic medicine is made.

elect *vti* to choose by voting; to make a selection (of); to make a decision on. * *adj* chosen for an office but not installed.

election *n* the public choice of a person for office, esp a politician.

electioneer *vi* to work on behalf of a candidate for election.—**electioneering** *n*.

elective *adj* pertaining to, dependant on, or exerting the power of, choice.—**electivity, electiveness** *n*.

elector *n* a person who has a vote at an election.—**electorship** *n*.

electoral *adj* of elections or electors.

electorate *n* the whole body of qualified electors.

electric *adj* of, producing or worked by electricity; exciting, thrilling. * *npl* electric fittings.

electrical *adj* of or relating to electricity.—**electrically** *adv*.

electric chair *n* a chair used in executing condemned criminals by electrocution.

electric eel *n* an eel-like fish capable of giving an electric shock.

electric eye *n* a photoelectric cell.

electric guitar *n* a guitar that is electronically amplified.

electrician *n* a person who installs and repairs electrical devices.

electricity *n* a form of energy comprising certain charged particles, such as electrons and protons; an electric current.

electrify *vt* (**electrifying, electrified**) to charge with electricity; to modify or equip for the use of electric power; to astonish or excite.—**electrifiable** *adj.*—**electrification** *n.*—**electrifier** *n*.

electro-, electr- *prefix* of or by electricity.

electrocardiogram *n* the tracing made by an electrocardiograph.

electrocardiograph *n* a device for recording the electrical activity of the heart.—**electrocardiographic, electrocardiographical** *adj.*—**electrocardiography** *n*.

electrochemistry *n* the area of chemistry dealing with

chemical changes caused by electricity.—**electrochemical** adj.—**electrochemist** n.

electroconvulsive therapy n treatment of certain types of mental illness by passing an electric current through the brain.

electrocute vt to kill or execute by electricity.—**electrocution** n.

electrode n a conductor through which an electric current enters or leaves an electrolyte, gas discharge tube or thermionic valve.

electrodynamics n (sing) the area of physics dealing with electric currents.—**electrodynamic, electrodynamical** adj.

electroencephalogram n the tracing produced by an electroencephalograph.

electroencephalograph n a device for recording the electrical activity of the brain.—**electroencephalographic** adj.—**electroencephalographically** adv.—**electroencephalography** n.

electrokinetics n (sing) the area of physics dealing with electricity in motion.—**electrokinetic** adj.

electrolysis n the passage of an electric current through an electrolyte to effect chemical change; the destruction of living tissue, esp hair roots, by the use of an electric current

electrolyte n a solution that conducts electricity.

electrolyze vt to cause to undergo electrolysis.—**electrolyzation** n.—**electrolyzer** n.

electromagnet n a metal core rendered magnetic by the passage of an electric current through a surrounding coil.

electromagnetic adj pertaining to, or produced by, electromagnetism.—**electromagnetically** adv.

electromagnetism n magnetism produced by an electric current; the area of science dealing with the relations between electricity and magnetism.

electrometallurgy n metallurgy using a slow electric current to precipitate certain metals from their solutions, or to separate metals from their ores.—**electrometallurgical** adj.—**electrometallurgist** n.

electrometer n an instrument for measuring electricity.—**electrometric, electrometrical** adj.—**electrometry** n.

electromotive adj producing an electric current.

electromotive force n a source of energy producing an electric current; the amount of energy drawn from such a source per unit current of electricity passing through it, measured in volts.

electron n a negatively charged elementary particle that forms the part of the atom outside the nucleus.

electronegative adj with a negative electrical charge.

electronic adj of or worked by streams of electrons flowing through semiconductor devices, vacuum or gas; of or concerned with electrons or electronics.—**electronically** adv.

electronic mail n messages, etc, sent and received via computer terminals.

electronic publishing n the publication of information on CD-ROM, magnetic disks, on-line databases, etc, for access by computer.

electronics n (sing) the study, development and application of electronic devices; (pl) electronic circuits.

electron microscope n a powerful microscope that uses a stream of electrons instead of light to produce magnified images.

electronvolt n a unit of energy equivalent to the energy gained by an electron that has been accelerated through a potential difference of one volt.

electrophorus n (pl electrophori) an instrument for generating static electricity by induction.

electroplate vt to plate or cover with metal (eg silver) by electrolysis. * n electroplated objects.—**electroplater** n.

electropositive adj with a positive electrical charge.

electroscope n an instrument for showing the presence or quality of electricity.—**electroscopic** adj.

electrostatics n (sing) the branch of physics concerned with static electric charges.—**electrostatic** adj.—**electrostatically** adv.

electrotherapeutics n (sing) the area of medicine dealing with the use of electrotherapy.

electrotherapy n the treatment of disease using electricity.—**electrotherapist** n.

electrotype n (print) a facsimile made by covering a mould or plate of the original with a coating of copper or nickel. * vt to make a copy in this way.—**electrotyper** n.

electrum n an alloy of gold and silver.

electuary n (pl electuaries) a medicinal drug mixed with honey or syrup.

eleemosynary adj dependent on charity; (money) given as charity.

elegant adj graceful; refined; dignified and tasteful in manner and appearance.—**elegance, elegancy** n.—**elegantly** adv.

elegiac adj characteristic of elegy; mournful.

elegize vt to write an elegy about.—**elegist** n.

elegy n (pl elegies) a slow mournful song or poem.

element n a constituent part; any of the 105 known substances composed of atoms with the same number of protons in their nuclei; a favourable environment for a plant or animal; a wire that produces heat in an electric cooker, kettle, etc; any of the four substances (earth, air, fire, water) that in ancient and medieval thought were believed to constitute the universe; (pl) atmospheric conditions (wind, rain, etc); (pl) the basic principles, rudiments.

elemental adj of elements or primitive natural forces.—**elementally** adv.

elementary adj concerned with the basic principles of a subject.—**elementariness** n.

elementary particle n any of the subatomic particles, such as electrons, protons and neutrons, not made up of other particles.

elemi n (pl elemis) a resin used in medicines and varnishes.

elenchus n (pl elenchi) (logic) refutation of an argument.—**elenctic** adj.

elephant n (pl elephants, elephant) a large heavy mammal with a long trunk, thick skin, and ivory tusks.—**elephantoid** adj.

elephantiasis n (pl elephantiases) a disease in which the limbs or scrotum become enormously enlarged.—**elephantiasic** adj.

elephantine adj of or like elephants; very big or clumsy.

elevate vt to lift up; to raise in rank; to improve in intellectual or moral stature.

elevated adj raised; (fig) inflated; (inf) tipsy.

elevation n a raised place; the height above the earth's surface or above sea level; the angle to which a gun is aimed above the horizon; a drawing that shows the front, rear, or side view of something.

elevator n a cage or platform for moving something

from one level to another; a moveable surface on the tailplane of an aircraft to produce motion up and down; a lift; a building for storing grain.

eleven *adj, n* one more than ten; the symbol for this (11, XI, xi); (*soccer, etc*) a team of eleven players.—**eleventh** *adj, n.*

elf *n* (*pl* **elves**) a mischievous fairy.—**elfin** *adj.*—**elfish, elvish** *adj.*

elflock *n* an intricately twisted lock of hair.

elicit *vt* to draw out (information, etc).—**elicitable** *adj.*—**elicitation** *n.*—**elicitor** *n.*

elide *vt* (*linguistics*) to cut off a syllable or vowel.

eligible *adj* suitable to be chosen, legally qualified; desirable, esp as a marriage partner.—**eligibility** *n.*—**eligibly** *adv.*

eliminate *vt* to expel, get rid of; to eradicate completely; (*sl*) to kill; to exclude (eg a competitor) from a competition, usu by defeat.—**eliminable** *adj.*—**elimination** *n.*—**eliminative, eliminatory** *adj.*—**eliminator** *n.*

elision *n* (*linguistics*) the cutting off of a syllable or vowel.

elite, élite *n* a superior group; (*typewriting*) a letter size having twelve characters to the inch.

elitism *n* leadership or rule by an elite; advocacy of such a system.—**elitist** *n.*

elixir *n* (*alchemy*) a substance thought to have the power of transmuting base metals into gold, or of conferring everlasting life; any medicine claimed as a cure-all; a sweet syrup containing a medicine.

Elizabethan *adj* pertaining to Queen Elizabeth I of England and her reign (1558–1603), esp its architecture and literature; pertaining to Queen Elizabeth II of Great Britain and her reign (1952–). * *n* a person alive in the reign of Elizabeth I.

elk *n* (*pl* **elks, elk**) the largest existing deer of Europe and Asia.

ell *n* an old measure of length used for cloth, based on the length of a man's arm, approximately equal to 45 inches (1.15 metres).

ellipse *n* (*geom*) a closed plane figure formed by the plane section of a right-angled cone; a flattened circle.

ellipsis *n* (*pl* **ellipses**) the omission of words needed to complete the grammatical construction of a sentence; the mark (…) used to indicate such omission.

ellipsoid *n* (*geom*) an elliptical spheroid; an oval.—**ellipsoidal** *adj.*

elliptic, elliptical *adj* of or like an ellipse; having a part understood.—**elliptically** *adv.*

ellipticity *n* (*geom*) the extent of deviation of an oval from a circle or sphere.

elm *n* a tall deciduous shade tree with spreading branches and broad top; its hard heavy wood.

elocution *n* skill in public speaking.—**elocutionary** *adj.*—**elocutionist** *n.*

elongate *vti* to make or become longer.—**elongation** *n.*

elope *vi* to run away secretly with a lover, esp to get married.—**elopement** *n.*—**eloper** *n.*

eloquence *n* skill in the use of words; speaking with fluency, power or persuasiveness.

eloquent *adj* (*speaking, writing, etc*) fluent and powerful.

else *adv* besides; otherwise.

elsewhere *adv* in another place.

elucidate *vt* to make clear, to explain.—**elucidation** *n.*—**elucidative, elucidatory** *adj.*—**elucidator** *n.*

elude *vt* to avoid stealthily; to escape the understanding or memory of a person.—**eluder** *n.*—**elusion** *n.*

elusive *adj* escaping; baffling; solitary, difficult to contact.—**elusiveness** *n.*

elver *n* a young eel.

elves, elvish *see* **elf.**

Elysian *adj* of or resembling Elysium; paradisiacal, blissful.

Elysium *n* the ancient Greek paradise; a condition of perfect happiness.

elytron, elytrum *n* (*pl* **elytra**) one of the hard wing cases of a beetle.—**elytroid, elytrous** *adj.*

em *n* (*print*) a measure of width, equal to one sixth of an inch (approx 4 mm).

emaciate *vti* to make or become very thin and weak.—**emaciated** *adj.*—**emaciation** *n.*

emanate *vi* to issue from a source.—**emanative** *adj.*—**emanator** *n.*—**emanatory** *adj.*

emanation *n* something coming from or caused by something else.—**emanational** *adj.*

emancipate *vt* to liberate, esp from bondage or slavery.—**emancipative** *adj.*—**emancipator** *n.*—**emancipatory** *adj.*

emancipation *n* the act of freeing; freedom, liberation.—**emancipationist** *n.*

emarginate, emarginated *adj* (*leaf*) notched at the edges or tip.—**emargination** *n.*

emasculate *vt* to castrate; to deprive of vigour, strength, etc.—**emasculation** *n.*—**emasculative, emasculatory** *adj.*—**emasculator** *n.*

embalm *vt* to preserve (a dead body) with drugs, chemicals, etc.—**embalmer** *n.*—**embalmment** *n.*

embank *vt* to enclose or protect with an embankment.

embankment *n* an earth or stone mound made to hold back water or to carry a roadway.

embargo *n* (*pl* **embargoes**) an order of a government forbidding ships to enter or leave its ports; any ban or restriction on commerce by law; a prohibition, ban. * *vt* (**embargoing, embargoed**) to lay an embargo on; to requisition.

embark *vti* to put or go on board a ship or aircraft to begin a journey; to make a start in any activity or enterprise.—**embarkation** *n.*—**embarkment** *n.*

embarrass *vt* to make (a person) feel confused, uncomfortable or disconcerted.—**embarrassing** *adj.*—**embarrassment** *n.*

embassy *n* (*pl* **embassies**) a person or group sent to a foreign government as ambassadors; the official residence of an ambassador.

embattle *vt* to arrange troops for battle; to prepare for battle.—**embattled** *adj.*

embay *vt* to bring or drive a ship into a bay.

embed *vt* (**embedding, embedded**) to fix firmly in surrounding matter.—**embedment** *n.*

embellish *vt* to decorate, to adorn.—**embellisher** *n.*—**embellishment** *n.*

ember *n* a piece of glowing coal or wood in a fire; (*pl*) the smouldering remains of a fire.

embezzle *vt* to steal (money, securities, etc entrusted to one's care).—**embezzlement** *n.*—**embezzler** *n.*

embitter *vt* to cause to feel bitter.—**embitterment** *n.*

emblazon *vt* to make bright with colour; to ornament with heraldic devices.—**emblazonment** *n.*

emblazonry *n* heraldic decoration, blazonry.

emblem *n* a symbol; a figure adopted and used as an identifying mark.

emblematic, emblematical *adj* of emblems; symbolic.—**emblematically** *adv.*

emblements *npl* (*law*) the annual crops produced by the labour of the cultivator; the profit from these crops.

embody *vt* (**embodying, embodied**) to express in definite form; to incorporate or include in a single book, law, system, etc.—**embodiment** *n*.

embolden *vt* to inspire with courage; to make bold.

embolism *n* the obstruction of a blood vessel by a blood clot, air bubble, etc.—**embolismic** *adj*.

embolus *n* (*pl* **emboli**) material obstructing a blood vessel, eg a blood clot or air bubble.

embonpoint *n* plumpness.

emboss *vt* to ornament with a raised design.—**embosser** *n*.—**embossment** *n*.

embouchure *n* the mouth of a river; (*mus*) the mouthpiece of a wind instrument; the correct positioning of the mouth when playing a wind instrument.

embowel *vt* (**embowelling, embowelled** *or* **emboweling, emboweled**) (*arch*) to remove the intestines from, disembowel; to embed, to bury.

embower *vt* (*arch*) to cover with, or as with, a bower.

embrace *vt* to take and hold tightly in the arms as a sign of affection; to accept eagerly (eg an opportunity); to adopt (eg a religious faith); to include. * *n* the act of embracing, a hug.—**embraceable** *adj*.—**embracement** *n*.

embracer *n* one who embraces; (*law*) one who attempts to influence a jury corruptly.

embracery *n* (*law*) the act of attempting to corrupt or influence a jury.

embranchment *n* the act of branching out.

embrasure *n* an opening in a wall or parapet from which to fire guns; a window or door having its sides slanted on the inside.

embrocate *vt* to rub a diseased or injured part of the body with a lotion.

embrocation *n* a liniment for applying to, or rubbing, an injured part of the body.

embroider *vt* to ornament with decorative stitches; to embellish (eg a story).—**embroiderer** *n*.

embroidery *n* (*pl* **embroideries**) decorative needlework; elaboration or exaggeration (of a story, etc).

embroil *vt* to involve (a person) in a conflict, argument, or problem.—**embroiler** *n*.—**embroilment** *n*.

embryo *n* (*pl* **embryos**) an animal during the period of its growth from a fertilized egg up to the third month; a human product of conception up to about the second month of growth; a thing in a rudimentary state.—**embryoid** *adj*.

embryology *n* the scientific study of embryos.—**embryological, embryologic** *adj*.—**embryologist** *n*.

embryonic, embryonal *adj* immature, existing at an early stage.—**embryonically** *adv*.

emend *vt* to correct mistakes in written material.—**emendable** *adj*.—**emendation** *n*.

emerald *n* a rich green gemstone; its colour.

emerge *vi* to appear up out of, to come into view; to be revealed as the result of investigation.—**emergence** *n*.—**emergent** *adj*.

emergency *n* (*pl* **emergencies**) an unforeseen situation demanding immediate action; a serious medical condition requiring instant treatment.

emeritus *adj* retired but still holding one's title or rank.—*also n*.

emersed *adj* (*bot*) rising out of water.

emersion *n* the act of emerging.

emery *n* a hard granular mineral used for grinding and polishing; a hard abrasive powder.

emery board *n* a nailfile made from cardboard covered with powdered emery.

emery paper *n* a stiff paper covered with powdered emery.

emetic *n* a medicine that induces vomiting.—*also adj*.—**emetically** *adv*.

emf, EMF *abbr* = electromotive force.

emigrant *n* a person who emigrates.

emigrate *vi* to leave one's country for residence in another.—**emigration** *n*.

émigré *n* an emigrant, usually someone forced to emigrate.

eminence, eminency *n* (*pl* **eminences, eminencies**) high rank or position; a person of high rank or attainments; (*with cap*) the title for a cardinal of the RC Church; a raised piece of ground, a high place.

eminent *adj* famous; conspicuous; distinguished.—**eminently** *adv*.

emir *n* a ruler in parts of Africa and Asia.

emirate *n* the territory governed by an emir.

emissary *n* (*pl* **emissaries**) a person sent on a mission on behalf of another, esp a government.

emit *vt* (**emitting, emitted**) to send out (light, heat, etc); to put into circulation; to express, to utter.—**emission** *n*.—**emissive** *adj*.—**emitter** *n*.

Emmenthal(er), Emmental *n* a hard Swiss cheese with lots of holes.

emmet *n* (*dial*) an ant.

emollient *adj* softening and soothing, esp the skin. * *n* a preparation used for skin care.—**emollience** *n*.

emolument *n* a fee received, salary.

emote *vi* to display emotion theatrically.

emotion *n* a strong feeling of any kind.

emotional *adj* of emotion; inclined to express excessive emotion.—**emotionality** *n*.—**emotionally** *adv*.—**emotionalism** *n*.

emotive *adj* characterized by or arousing emotion.—**emotiveness, emotivity** *n*.

empale *see* impale.

empanel *vt* (**empanelling, empanelled** *or* **empaneling, empaneled**) (*law*) to enrol (for a jury); to enter on a jury list.—*also* **impanel**.

empathize *vi* to treat with or feel empathy.

empathy *n* the capacity for participating in and understanding the feelings or ideas of another.—**empathic, empathetic** *adj*.

emperor *n* the sovereign ruler over an empire.—**emperorship** *n*.

emperor penguin *n* an Antarctic penguin, the largest species known.

empery *n* (*pl* **emperies**) (*arch*) power, dominion.

emphasis *n* (*pl* **emphases**) particular stress or prominence given to something; force or vigour of expression; clarity of form or outline.

emphasize *vt* to place stress on.

emphatic *adj* spoken, done or marked with emphasis; forceful, decisive.—**emphatically** *adv*.—**emphaticalness** *n*.

emphysema *n* a medical condition marked by the distension of the air sacs in the lungs, causing breathlessness.—**emphysematous** *adj*.

empire *n* a large state or group of states under a single sovereign, usu an emperor; nations governed by a single sovereign state; a large and complex business organization.

empiric *adj* empirical. * *n* an empirical worker; a quack.

empirical *adj* based on observation, experiment or experience only, not theoretical.—**empirically** *adv*.—**empiricalness** *n*.

empiricism *n* (*philos*) the theory that experience is the only source of knowledge; the use of empirical methods.—**empiricist** *n*.

emplacement *n* a position prepared for a gun or artillery.

emplane *vti* to put on board a plane; to board a plane.

employ *vt* to give work and pay to; to make use of.—**employable** *adj*.

employee *n* a person who is hired by another person for wages.

employer *n* a person, business, etc that employs people.

employment *n* an employing; a being employed; occupation or profession.

empoison *vt* to taint, corrupt.

emporium *n* (*pl* **emporiums, emporia**) a large shop carrying many different items.

empower *vt* to give official authority to.—**empowerment** *n*.

empress *n* the female ruler of an empire; the wife or widow of an emperor.

empty *adj* (**emptier, emptiest**) containing nothing; not occupied; lacking reality, substance, or value; hungry. * *vb* (**emptying, emptied**) *vt* to make empty; to transfer or discharge (the contents of something) by emptying. * *vi* to become empty; to discharge contents. * *n* (*pl* **empties**) empty containers or bottles.—**emptily** *adv*.—**emptiness** *n*.

empty-handed *adj* with nothing in one's hands; without gain.

empty-headed *adj* scatterbrained.

empyema *n* (*pl* **empyemata**) a collection of pus, esp in the chest.—**empyemic** *adj*.

empyrean *n* (*arch*) the highest heaven. * *adj* pertaining to the highest heaven; celestial.

EMS *abbr* = European Monetary System.

EMU *abbr* = European Monetary Union.

emu *n* a fast-running Australian bird, related to the ostrich.

emulate *vt* to try to equal or do better than; to imitate; to rival or compete.—**emulation** *n*.—**emulative** *adj*.—**emulator** *n*.

emulous *adj* wanting to excel; competitive.

emulsify *vti* (**emulsifying, emulsified**) to make or become an emulsion.—**emulsification** *n*.—**emulsifier** *n*.

emulsion *n* a mixture of mutually insoluble liquids in which one is dispersed in droplets throughout the other; a light-sensitive substance on photographic paper or film.—**emulsive** *adj*.

emunctory *n* (*pl* **emunctories**) (*anat*) an excretory duct or canal. * *adj* excretory.

en *n* (*print*) a measure of width, equal to half an em.

enable *vt* to give the authority or means to do something; to make easy or possible.—**enabler** *n*.

enact *vt* to make into law; to act (a play, etc).—**enactive** *adj*.—**enactment** *n*.—**enactor** *n*.—**enactory** *adj*.

enamel *n* a glass-like substance used to coat the surface of metal or pottery; the hard outer layer of a tooth; a usu glossy paint that forms a hard coat. * *vt* (**enamelling, enamelled** *or* **enameling, enameled**) to cover or decorate with enamel.—**enameller, enameler, enamellist, enamelist** *n*.—**enamelwork** *n*.

enamour, enamor *vt* to inspire with love.—**enamoured, enamored** *adj*.

enarthrosis *n* (*pl* **enarthroses**) (*anat*) a ball-and-socket joint.

en bloc *adv* in a mass.

encage *vt* to shut up in, or as in, a cage.

encamp *vt* to place or stay in a camp.—**encampment** *n*.

encapsulate *vt* to enclose or be enclosed in, as a capsule; to summarize.—**encapsulation** *n*.

encase *vt* to enclose (as if) in a case.—**encasement** *n*.

encaustic *adj* (*ceramics*) with colours burned in. * *n* the art of painting in melted wax; a piece of work done by this method.

enceinte *adj* pregnant.

encephalic *adj* of the brain.

encephalitis *n* inflammation of the brain.—**encephalitic** *adj*.

encephalogram *n* an electroencephalogram.—**encephalograph** *n*.

enchain *vt* to hold fast with, or as with, a chain.—**enchainment** *n*.

enchant *vt* to bewitch, to delight.—**enchanter** *n*.—**enchantment** *n*.—**enchantress** *nf*.

enchase *vt* to engrave, to emboss.

encircle *vt* to surround; to move or pass completely round.—**encirclement** *n*.

enclasp *vt* to clasp.

enclave *n* an area of a country's territory entirely surrounded by foreign territory.

enclitic *adj* (*linguistics*) attached to the preceding word and treated as a suffix, *eg* "thee" in "prithee". * *n* an enclitic word.—**enclitically** *adv*.

enclose *vt* to shut up or in; to put in a wrapper or parcel, usu together with a letter.—**enclosable** *adj*.—**encloser** *n*.

enclosure *n* an enclosing; an enclosed area; something enclosed with a letter, in a parcel, etc.

encomiast *n* a composer of an encomium.—**encomiastic** *adj*.

encomium *n* (*pl* **encomiums, encomia**) a usu formal expression of high praise in speech or writing.

encompass *vt* to encircle or enclose; to include.—**encompassment** *n*.

encore *interj* once more! * *n* a call for the repetition of a performance.—*also vt*.

encounter *vt* to meet, esp unexpectedly; to fight, engage in battle with; to be faced with (problems, etc). * *n* a meeting; a conflict, battle.

encourage *vt* to inspire with confidence or hope; to urge, incite; to promote the development of.—**encouragement** *n*.—**encourager** *n*.—**encouragingly** *adv*.

encroach *vi* to infringe another's territory, rights, etc; to advance beyond an established limit.—**encroacher** *n*.—**encroachingly** *adv*.—**encroachment** *n*.

encrust *vt* to cover with a hard crust; to form a crust on the surface of; to decorate a surface with jewels.—**encrustation** *n*.

encumber *vt* to weigh down; to hinder the function or activity of.—**encumberingly** *adv*.

encumbrance *n* something that is a hindrance or burden.

encumbrancer *n* a person who has a legal claim on an estate.

encyclical *adj* circulated widely (—*also* **encyclic**). * *n* a letter addressed by the pope to all Roman Catholic bishops.

encyclopedia, encyclopaedia *n* a book or series of books containing information on all branches of knowledge, or treating comprehensively a particular branch of knowledge, usu in alphabetical order.

encyclopedic, encyclopaedic *adj* comprehensive.—**encyclopedically, encyclopaedically** *adv*.

encyclopedist, encyclopaedist *n* a compiler of an encyclopedia.

encyst *vti* (*biol*) to enclose, or become enclosed in, a cyst or vesicle.—**encystment** *n*.

end *n* the last part; the place where a thing stops; purpose; result, outcome. * *vt* to bring to an end; to destroy. * *vi* to come to an end; to result (in). * *adj* final; ultimate.

end-, endo- *prefix* within.

endanger *vt* to put in danger.—**endangerment** *n*.

endear *vt* to make loved or more loved.—**endearing** *adj*.—**endearingly** *adv*.

endearment *n* something that endears; a word or words of affection.

endeavour, endeavor *vi* to try or attempt (to). * *n* an attempt.

endemic *adj* (*disease*) locally prevalent; (*plant*) peculiar to a locality. * *n* an endemic disease; an endemic plant.—**endemicity** *n*.—**endemically** *adv*.

ending *n* reaching or coming to an end; the final part.

endive *n* an annual or biennial herb widely cultivated as a salad plant; a variety of chicory used in salads.

endless *adj* unending; uninterrupted; extremely numerous.—**endlessly** *adv*.—**endlessness** *n*.

endo-, end- *prefix* within.

endocarditis *n* inflammation of the endocardium.—**endocarditic** *adj*.

endocardium *n* (*pl* **endocardia**) the membrane lining the heart cavities.

endocarp *n* the inner coat or shell of a fruit.—**endocarpal, endocarpic** *adj*.

endocrine *adj* secreting internally, specifically producing secretions that are distributed in the body by the bloodstream (—*also* **endocrinal**). * *n* an endocrine gland.

endocrine gland *n* a gland that secretes hormones directly into the bloodstream, eg the pituitary and thyroid.

endocrinology *n* the scientific study of endocrine glands and hormones.—**endocrinologic, endocrinological** *adj*.—**endocrinologist** *n*.

endoderm *n* the inner layer of embryonic cells in an egg from which an organism is formed.—*also* **entoblast, entoderm**.—**endodermal, endodermic, entodermal, entodermic** *adj*.

endogamy *n* the practice of marrying only within the same tribe.—**endogamous** *adj*.

endogenous *adj* growing from or on the inside.—**endogeny** *n*.

endomorph *n* a mineral enclosed within another mineral; a person with a heavily built physique.—**endomorphic** *adj*.—**endomorphy** *n*.

endomorphism *n* (*geol*) metamorphosis of molten rock within older rock.

endoparasite *n* an internal parasite.—**endoparasitic** *adj*.

endoplasm *n* (*biol*) the inner layer of protoplasm.

endorse *vt* to write one's name, comment, etc on the back of to approve; to record an offence on a driving licence; to support.—**endorsable** *adj*.—**endorsee** *n*.—**endorsement** *n*.—**endorser** *n*.

endoscope *n* a medical instrument for examining the interior of the body.—**endoscopic** *adj*.—**endoscopist** *n*.—**endoscopy** *n*.

endosmosis *n* (*biol*) osmosis inwards through the porous membrane of a cell, etc, by a surrounding liquid.

endosperm *n* the albumen of a seed.—**endospermic** *adj*.

endothelium *n* (*pl* **endothelia**) (*anat*) a tissue which lines blood vessels.

endow *vt* to give money or property to provide an income for; to provide with a special power or attribute.—**endower** *n*.

endowment *n* an endowing; an income, etc settled on an individual or organization; a natural quality or gift.

endpaper *n* either of two folded sheets of paper pasted against the inside covers of a book and attached to the first and last pages.

end product *n* the final result of a manufacturing or other process.

endue *vt* (**enduing, endued**) to provide with a quality or power.—*also* **indue**.

endurance *n* the ability to withstand pain, hardship, strain, etc.

endure *vt* to undergo, tolerate (hardship, etc) esp with patience. * *vi* to continue in existence, to last out.—**endurable** *adj*.—**endurability** *n*.—**endurably** *adv*.

enduring *adj* lasting, permanent.—**enduringly** *adv*.

endways *adv* on end, with the end foremost.

enema *n* (*pl* **enemas, enemata**) the injection of a liquid into the rectum to void the bowels; the liquid injected.

enemy *n* (*pl* **enemies**) a person who hates or dislikes and wishes to harm another; a military opponent; something harmful or deadly.

energetic *adj* lively, active; done with energy.—**energetically** *adv*.

energetics *n* (*sing*) the science of energy.

energize *vt* to fill with energy; to invigorate; to apply an electric current to.—**energizer** *n*.

energy *n* (*pl* **energies**) capacity of acting or being active; vigour, power; (*physics*) capacity to do work.

enervate *vt* to lessen the strength or vigour of; to enfeeble in mind and body.—**enervation** *n*.—**enervative** *adj*.—**enervator** *n*.

enface *vt* to write or stamp on the face of a document.

enfant terrible *n* (*pl* **enfants terribles**) a person who makes awkward remarks.

enfeeble *vt* to make feeble.—**enfeeblement** *n*.—**enfeebler** *n*.

enfeoff *vt* (*law*) to give a freehold property to; to convey.—**enfeoffment** *n*.

enfilade *n* gunfire directed (at troops, etc) in a line from end to end.—*also vt*.

enfold *vt* to wrap up; to hug in the arms.—**enfolder** *n*.—**enfoldment** *n*.

enforce *vt* to compel obedience by threat; to execute with vigour.—**enforceable** *adj*.—**enforcement** *n*.—**enforcer** *n*.

enfranchise *vt* to admit to citizenship; to grant the vote to.—**enfranchisement** *n*.—**enfranchiser** *n*.

engage *vt* to pledge as security; to promise to marry; to keep busy; to hire; to attract and hold, esp attention or sympathy; to cause to participate; to bring or enter into conflict; to begin or take part in a venture; to connect or interlock, to mesh.—**engager** *n*.

engaged *adj* entered into a promise to marry; reserved, occupied or busy.

engagement *n* the act or state of being engaged; a pledge; an appointment agreed with another person; employment; a battle.

engaging *adj* pleasing, attractive.—**engagingly** *adv*.—**engagingness** *n*.

engender *vt* to bring into existence.—**engenderment** *n*.

engine *n* a machine by which physical power is applied to produce a physical effect; a locomotive; (*formerly*) a mechanical device, such as a large catapult, used in war.

engineer *n* a person trained in engineering; a person

who operates an engine, etc; a member of a military group devoted to engineering work; a designer or builder of engines. * *vt* to contrive, plan, esp deviously.

engineering *n* the art or practice of constructing and using machinery; the art and science by which natural forces and materials are utilized in structures or machines.

English *adj* of, relating to, or characteristic of England, the English people, or the English language. * *n* the language of the English people, the US and many areas formerly under British control; English language and literature as a subject of study.

engorge *vt* to congest with blood; to consume (food) greedily.—**engorgement** *n*.

engrained *see* **ingrained**.

engrave *vt* to produce by cutting or carving a surface; to cut to produce a representation that may be printed from; to lodge deeply (in the mind, etc).—**engraver** *n*.

engraving *n* a print made from an engraved surface.

engross *vt* to occupy (the attention) fully; to copy in large handwriting; to prepare the final text of.—**engrossing** *adj*.—**engrossment** *n*.

engulf *vt* to flow over and enclose; to overwhelm.—**engulfment** *n*.

enhance *vt* to increase in value, importance, attractiveness, etc; to heighten.—**enhancement** *n*.—**enhancer** *n*.

enigma *n* someone or something that is puzzling or mysterious.—**enigmatic, enigmatical** *adj*.—**enigmatically** *adv*.

enjoin *vt* to command, order someone with authority; to forbid, to prohibit.—**enjoiner** *n*.—**enjoinment** *n*.

enjoy *vt* to get pleasure from, take joy in; to use or have the advantage of; to experience.—**enjoyment** *n*.

enjoyable *adj* giving enjoyment.—**enjoyably** *adv*.

enkindle *vt* to set on fire; (*fig*) to inflame.

enlace *vt* to entwine; to enfold.—**enlacement** *n*.

enlarge *vti* to make or grow larger; to reproduce (a photograph) in a larger form; to speak or write at length (on).

enlargement *n* an act, instance, or state of enlarging; a photograph, etc that has been enlarged.

enlarger *n* a device for making photographic enlargements.

enlighten *vt* to instruct; to inform.—**enlightening** *adj*.—**enlightenment** *n*.

enlightened *adj* well-informed, tolerant, unprejudiced.

enlist *vt* to engage for service in the armed forces; to secure the aid or support of. * *vi* to register oneself for the armed services.—**enlistee** *n*.—**enlistment** *n*.

enliven *vt* to make more lively or cheerful.—**enlivening** *adj*.—**enlivenment** *n*.

en masse *adv* all together; in a large group.

enmesh *vt* to catch in a net; to entangle.—*also* **inmesh, immesh**.

enmity *n* (*pl* **enmities**) hostility, esp mutual hatred.

ennage *n* (*print*) the number of ens in a text.

ennea- *prefix* nine.

ennead *n* a set of nine.—**enneadic** *adj*.

enneagon *n* a plane figure with nine sides and nine angles.

ennoble *vt* to make noble, dignify; to raise (a person) to a rank of nobility.—**ennoblement** *n*.—**ennobler** *n*.

ennui *n* boredom, apathy.

enology *see* **oenology**.

enormity *n* (*pl* **enormities**) great wickedness; a serious crime; huge size, magnitude.

enormous *adj* extremely large.—**enormously** *adv*.

enough *adj* adequate, sufficient. * *adv* so as to be sufficient; very; quite. * *n* a sufficiency. * *interj* stop!

enounce *vt* to proclaim, to enunciate.

en passant *adv* in passing.

enquire, enquirer *see* **inquire**.

enquiry *see* **inquiry**.

enrage *vt* to fill with anger.—**enraged** *adj*.—**enragement** *n*.

enrapture *vt* to fill with pleasure or delight.

enrich *vt* to make rich or richer; to ornament; to improve in quality by adding to.—**enricher** *n*.—**enrichment** *n*.

enrol, enroll *vti* (**enrols** *or* **enrolls, enrolling, enrolled**) to enter or register on a roll or list; to become a member of a society, club, etc; to admit as a member.—**enrollee** *n*.—**enroller** *n*.—**enrolment, enrollment** *n*.

en route *adv* along or on the way.

ensanguine *vt* to smear or cover with blood.

ensconce *vt* to establish in a safe, secure or comfortable place.

ensemble *n* something regarded as a whole; the general effect; the performance of the full number of musicians, dancers, etc; a complete harmonious costume.

enshrine *vt* to enclose (as if) in a shrine; to cherish as sacred.—*also* **inshrine**.—**enshrinement** *n*.

enshroud *vt* to cover with, or as with, a shroud.

ensiform *adj* sword-shaped.

ensign *n* a flag; the lowest commissioned officer in the US Navy.

ensilage *n* storage in a pit or silo; silage.

ensile *vt* to store in a silo.—**ensilability** *n*.

enslave *vt* to make into a slave; to subjugate.—**enslavement** *n*.—**enslaver** *n*.

ensnare *vt* to trap in, or as in, a snare.—**ensnarement** *n*.

ensue *vi* (**ensuing, ensued**) to occur as a consequence or in time.—**ensuing** *adj*.

en suite *adv, adj* in a single unit.

ensure *vt* to make certain, sure, or safe.—**ensurer** *n*.

enswathe *vt* to wrap, swathe.

ENT *abbr* = ear, nose, and throat.

entablature *n* the part of a building resting on top of columns.

entablement *n* a platform for a statue, above the dado and base.

entail *vt* to involve, necessitate as a result; to restrict the inheritance of property to a designated line of heirs. * *n* the act of entailing or the estate entailed.—**entailer** *n*.—**entailment** *n*.

entangle *vt* to tangle, complicate; to involve in a tangle or complications.—**entanglement** *n*.—**entangler** *n*.

entelechy *n* (*pl* **entelechies**) (*philos*) actuality.

entente (cordiale) *n* a friendly understanding or relationship between two or more countries.

enter *vi* to go or come in or into; to come on stage; to begin, start; (*with* **for**) to register as an entrant. * *vt* to come or go into; to pierce, penetrate; (*an organization*) to join; to insert; (*proposal, etc*) to submit; to record (an item) in a diary, etc.—**enterable** *adj*.—**enterer** *n*.

enteric, enteral *adj* intestinal.—**enterally** *adv*.

enteritis *n* inflammation of the intestines, usu causing diarrhoea.

enteron (*pl* **entera**) the alimentary canal.

enterotomy *n* (*pl* **enterotomies**) dissection of, or an incision into, the bowels.

enterprise *n* a difficult or challenging undertaking; a business project; readiness to engage in new ventures.—**enterpriser** *n*.

enterprising *adj* adventurous, energetic and progressive.—**enterprisingly** *adv.*

entertain *vt* to show hospitality to; to amuse, please (a person or audience); to have in mind; to consider.

entertainer *n* a person who entertains in public, esp professionally.

entertaining *adj* amusing; diverting.—**entertainingly** *adv.*

entertainment *n* entertaining; amusement; an act or show intended to amuse and interest an audience, etc.

enthral, enthrall *vt* (**enthrals** *or* **enthralls, enthralling, enthralled**) to captivate.—**enthralment, enthrallment** *n.*

enthrone *vt* to install ceremonially, as a monarch or bishop.—**enthronement** *n.*

enthuse *vti* to fill with or express enthusiasm.

enthusiasm *n* intense interest or liking; something that arouses keen interest.

enthusiast *n* a person filled with enthusiasm for something.

enthusiastic *adj* filled with enthusiasm.—**enthusiastically** *adv.*

enthymeme *n* (*logic*) a syllogism in which one premise is suppressed.

entice *vt* to attract by offering some pleasure or reward.—**enticement** *n.*—**enticer** *n.*—**enticing** *adj.*

entire *adj* whole; complete.—**entireness** *n.*

entirely *adv* fully; completely.

entirety *n* (*pl* **entireties**) completeness; the total.

entitle *vt* to give a title to; to give a right (to).—**entitlement** *n.*

entity *n* (*pl* **entities**) existence, being; something that has a separate existence.

entoblast, entoderm *see* **endoderm**.

entomb *vt* to place in, or as in, a tomb.—**entombment** *n.*

entomic *adj* of insects.

entomo-, entom- *prefix* insect.

entomology *n* the branch of zoology that deals with insects.—**entomological, entomologic** *adj.*—**entomologist** *n.*

entomophagous *adj* insect-eating.

entomophilous *adj* fertilized by insects.

entopic *adj* (*anat*) in a normal position.

entourage *n* a retinue, group of attendants.

entozoic *adj* living within an animal.

entozoan *n* (*pl* **entozoa**) a parasite which lives inside an animal.

entr'acte *n* a light entertainment, a ballet, etc, as an interlude between the acts of a play or opera.

entrails *npl* the insides of the body, the intestines.

entrain *vti* to put or get onto a train.

entrance[1] *n* the act of entering; the power or authority to enter; a means of entering; an admission fee.

entrance[2] *vt* to put into a trance; to fill with great delight.—**entrancement** *n.*—**entrancing** *adj.*

entrant *n* a person who enters (eg a competition, profession).

entrap *vt* (**entrapping, entrapped**) to catch, as if in a trap; to lure into a compromising or incriminatory situation.—**entrapment** *n.*—**entrapper** *n.*

entreat *vt* to request earnestly; to implore, beg.—**entreaty** *n* (*pl* **entreaties**).

entrecôte *n* a boned cut of beef from between the ribs.

entrée, entree *n* a dish served before the main meal; in US, the principal dish of a meal; the right or power of admission.

entremets *n* (*pl* **entremets**) a dessert.

entrench *vt* to dig a trench as a defensive perimeter; to establish (oneself) in a strong defensive position.—**entrencher** *n.*—**entrenchment** *n.*

entrepôt *n* an intermediate centre of trade and transhipment.

entrepreneur *n* a person who takes the commercial risk of starting up and running a business enterprise.—**entrepreneurial** *adj.*—**entrepreneurship** *n.*

entresol *n* a floor between the ground and first floor, a mezzanine.

entropy *n* (*pl* **entropies**) a measure of the unavailable energy in a closed thermodynamic system; disorder, disorganization.

entrust *vt* (*usu with* **with**) to confer as a responsibility, duty, etc; (*usu with* **to**) to place something in another's care.—**entrustment** *n.*

entry *n* (*pl* **entries**) the act of entering; a place of entrance; an item recorded in a diary, journal, etc; a person or thing taking part in a contest.

entwine *vt* to twine together or around.—**entwinement** *n.*

enucleate *vt* to remove the nucleus from.

E number *n* a series of numbers with the prefix E used to identify food additives within the European Community.

enumerate *vt* to count; to list.—**enumeration** *n.*—**enumerator** *n.*

enunciate *vt* to state definitely; to pronounce clearly.—**enunciation** *n.*—**enunciator** *n.*—**enunciative** *adj.*

enure *see* **inure**.

enuresis *n* urinary incontinence; bedwetting.—**enuretic** *adj.*

envelop *vt* to enclose completely (as if) with a covering.—**envelopment** *n.*

envelope *n* something used to wrap or cover, esp a gummed paper container for a letter; the bag containing the gas in a balloon or airship.

envenom *vt* to put poison into; (*fig*) to embitter.

enviable *adj* causing envy; fortunate.—**enviably** *adv.*

envious *adj* filled with envy.—**enviously** *adv.*

environ *vt* to surround or enclose.

environment *n* external conditions and surroundings, esp those that affect the quality of life of plants, animals and human beings.—**environmental** *adj.*—**environmentally** *adv.*

environmentalist *n* a person who is concerned with improving the quality of the environment.—**environmentalism** *n.*

environs *npl* the surrounding area or outskirts of a district or town.

envisage *vt* to have a mental picture of.—**envisagement** *n.*

envoy *n* a diplomatic agent; a representative.

envy *n* (*pl* **envies**) resentment or discontent at another's achievements, possessions, etc; an object of envy. * *vt* (**envying, envied**) to feel envy of.—**envier** *n.*

enwrap *vt* to wrap up.

enzootic *adj* (*disease*) affecting animals in a particular district.

enzyme *n* a complex protein, produced by living cells, that induces or speeds chemical reactions in plants and animals.

eon *see* **aeon**.

eonian *see* **aeonian**.

eonism *n* (*psychiatry*) a tendency in a male to adopt female clothing and mannerisms, transvestitism.

eosin, eosine *n* a pink coal tar dye.—**eosinic** *adj*.

EP *abbr* = extended play (gramophone record).

epact *n* (*astron*) the difference between the solar and the lunar month, about eleven days in the year.

eparch *n* (*Greek Orthodox Church*) a metropolitan or other bishop; a governor of an eparchy.

eparchy, eparchate *n* (*pl* **eparchies, eparchates**) a Greek province; the diocese of an eparch.—**eparchial** *adj*.

epaulette, epaulet *n* a piece of ornamental fabric or metal worn on the shoulder, esp on a uniform.

épée *n* a sword used in fencing.—**épéeist** *n*.

epenthesis *n* (*pl* **epentheses**) *n* (*linguistics*) the insertion of a letter or syllable in the middle of a word.

epergne *n* a branched centrepiece or ornamental stand for a dinner table.

epexegesis *n* (*pl* **epexegeses**) (*linguistics*) the use of additional words to clarify a meaning.—**epexegetic, epexegetical** *adj*.

ephah *n* a Hebrew dry measure, equal to about one bushel (33 litres).

ephebe *n* a young citizen (aged 18 to 20) of ancient Greece.

ephedrine *n* an alkaloid used to treat asthma and hay fever.

ephemeral *adj* existing only for a very short time. * *n* an ephemeral thing or organism.—**ephemerality, empheralness** *n*.

ephemeris *n* (*pl* **ephemerides**) an astronomical almanac showing the daily positions of the sun, moon and planets.

ephod *n* a vestment worn by a Jewish priest.

ephor *n* (*pl* **ephors, ephori**) a magistrate in ancient Greece.

epi-, ep- *prefix* upon, at, in addition.

epiblast *n* the outer layer of the embryonic cells in an egg from which an organism is formed.—**epiblastic** *adj*.

epic *n* a long poem narrating the deeds of a hero; any literary work, film, etc in the same style. * *adj* relating to or resembling an epic.

epicarp *n* the outer skin of a fruit.

epicene *adj* having characteristics of both sexes; lacking characteristics of either sex, sexless.

epicentre, epicenter *n* the area of the earth's surface directly above the focus of an earthquake.—**epicentral** *adj*.

epicure *n* a person who has cultivated a refined taste in food, wine, literature, etc.—**epicurism, epicureanism** *n*.

epicurean *adj* given to sensuous enjoyment.

epicycle *n* (*geom*) a small circle, the centre of which is situated on the circumference of a larger circle.—**epicyclic** *adj*.

epicycloid *n* (*geom*) a curve described by a point in the circumference of one circle which rolls round the circumference of another circle.

epidemic *adj, n* (a disease) attacking many people at the same time in a community or region.—**epidemical** *adj*.

epidemiology *n* the area of medicine dealing with epidemic diseases.—**epidemiological** *adj*.—**epidemiologist** *n*.

epidermis *n* an outer layer, esp of skin.—**epidermal, epidermic, epidermoid** *adj*.

epidiascope *n* a projector for magnifying opaque as well as transparent pictures.

epidural *n* a spinal anaesthetic used for the relief of pain during childbirth.

epigastrium *n* (*pl* **epigastria**) the upper part of the abdomen.

epigenesis *n* the theory that an organism is created by the division or segmentation of a fertilized egg cell; a form of geological metamorphism of rock brought about by outside forces; the depositing of ore in already formed rock.—**epigenesist, epigenist** *n*.—**epigenetic** *adj*.—**epigentically** *adv*.

epiglottis *n* (**epiglottises, epiglottides**) a thin flap of cartilaginous tissue over the entrance to the larynx.—**epiglottal, epiglottic** *adj*.

epigram *n* a short witty poem or saying.—**epigrammatic** *adj*.—**epigrammatically** *adv*.

epigrammatize *vti* to compose an epigram (about).—**epigrammatist** *n*.

epigraph *n* a quotation at the beginning of a book or chapter; an inscription on a building or monument.—**epigraphic, epigraphical** *adj*.

epigraphy *n* the study of inscriptions.—**epigraphist, epigrapher** *n*.

epilepsy *n* a disorder of the nervous system marked typically by convulsive attacks and loss of consciousness.

epileptic *adj* of or affected with epilepsy. * *n* a person affected with epilepsy.—**epileptically** *adv*.

epilogue *n* the concluding section of a book or other literary work; a short speech addressed by an actor to the audience at the end of a play.—**epilogist** *n*.

epiphany *n* (*pl* **epiphanies**) a moment of sudden revelation or insight; (*with cap*) a festival of the Christian Church in commemoration of the coming of the Magi to Christ.

epiphenomenon *n* (*pl* **epiphenomena**) a by-product; (*med*) an attendant symptom.

epiphyte *n* (*bot*) a plant which grows on another plant but is not fed by it.—**epiphytic** *adj*.

episcopacy *n* (*pl* **episcopacies**) the system of church government by bishops.

episcopal *adj* of bishops; governed by bishops.—**episcopally** *adv*.

episcopalian *adj* pertaining to episcopacy * *n* a member or supporter of an episcopal church.—**episcopalianism** *n*.

episcopate *n* the office of a bishop.

episiotomy *n* (*pl* **episiotomies**) a cut made in the perineum during childbirth to prevent tearing.

episode *n* a piece of action in a dramatic or literary work; an incident in a sequence of events.

episodic, episodical *adj* happening at irregular intervals; digressive.—**episodically** *adv*.

epispastic *adj* producing a blister.

epistaxis *n* (*med*) nosebleed.

epistemology *n* the science of the processes and grounds of knowledge.

epistle *n* (*formal*) a letter; (*with cap*) a letter written by one of Christ's Apostles to various churches and individuals.

epistler *n* someone who reads the Epistle in the communion service; one who writes an epistle.

epistolary *adj* pertaining to, contained in, or conducted by letters.

epistrophe *n* (*rhetoric*) the practice of ending several successive clauses or sentences with the same word.

epistyle *n* an architrave.

epitaph *n* an inscription in memory of a dead person, usu on a tombstone.—**epitaphic** *adj*.—**epitaphist** *n*.

epithalamium *n* (*pl* **epithalamia**) a nuptial song or poem.—**epithalamic** *adj*.

epithelioma *n* (*pl* **epitheliomas, epitheliomata**) a cancer of the epithelium.—**epitheliomatous** *adj*.

epithelium *n* (*pl* **epithelia**) any of the cells that line the surface of the membranes of the body.—**epithelial** *adj*.

epithet *n* a descriptive word or phrase added to or substituted for a person's name (*Vlad the Impaler*).—**epithetic, epithetical** *adj*.

epitome *n* a typical example; a paradigm; personification; a condensed account of a written work.—**epitomic, epitomical** *adj*.—**epitomist** *n*.

epitomize *vt* to be or make an epitome of.—**epitomization** *n*.—**epitomizer** *n*.

epoch *n* a date in time used as a point of reference; an age in history associated with certain characteristics; a unit of geological time.—**epochal** *adj*.

epode *n* a kind of lyric poem; the last part of a lyric ode.—**epode** *adj*.

eponym *n* a person after whom something is named; a name so derived.—**eponymous, eponymic** *adj*.—**eponymy** *n*.

epopee *n* an epic poem; epic poetry.

EPOS *abbr* = electronic point of sale.

epos *n* early unwritten epic poetry; an epic poem; the subject of an epic poem.

epoxy *adj* (*chem*) of or containing an oxygen atom and two other groups, usually carbon, which are themselves linked with other groups.

epoxy resin *n* a strong synthetic resin containing epoxy groups, used in laminates and adhesives.

epsilon *n* the 5th letter of the Greek alphabet.

equable *adj* level, uniform; (*climate*) free from extremes of hot and cold; even-tempered.—**equability, equableness** *n*.—**equably** *adv*.

equal *adj* the same in amount, size, number, or value; impartial, regarding or affecting all objects in the same way; capable of meeting a task or situation. * *n* a person that is equal. * *vt* (**equalling, equalled** *or* **equaling, equaled**) to be equal to, esp to be identical in value; to make or do something equal to.—**equally** *adv*.

equality *n* (*pl* **equalities**) being equal.

equalize *vti* to make or become equal; (*games*) to even the score.—**equalization** *n*.—**equalizer** *n*.

equanimity *n* (*pl* **equanimities**) evenness of temper; composure.—**equanimous** *adj*.

equate *vt* to make, treat, or regard as comparable. * *vi* to correspond as equal.

equation *n* an act of equalling; the state of being equal; a usu formal statement of equivalence (as in logical and mathematical expressions) with the relations denoted by the sign =; an expression representing a chemical reaction by means of chemical symbols.—**equational** *adj*.

equator *n* an imaginary circle passing round the globe, equidistant from the North and South poles.—**equatorial** *n*.

equerry *n* (*pl* **equerries**) an officer in the British royal household.

equestrian *adj* pertaining to horses and riding; on horseback. * *n* a skilled rider.—**equestrienne** *nf*.—**equestrianism** *n*.

equi- *prefix* equal.

equiangular *adj* having equal angles.

equidistant *adj* at equal distances.—**equidistance** *n*.

equilateral *adj* having all sides equal.

equilibrate *vti* to balance.—**equilibration** *n*.—**equilibrator** *n*.

equilibrist *n* a tightrope walker; an acrobat.—**equilibristic** *adj*.

equilibrium *n* (*pl* **equilibriums, equilibria**) a state of balance of weight, power, force, etc.

equine *adj* of or resembling a horse.

equinox *n* the two times of the year when night and day are equal in length (around 21 March and 23 September).—**equinoctial** *adj*.

equip *vt* (**equipping, equipped**) to provide with all the necessary tools or supplies.—**equipper** *n*.

equipage *n* a carriage with horses and liveried attendants.

equipment *n* the tools, supplies and other items needed for a particular task, expedition, etc.

equipoise *n* balance, equilibrium.

equipollent *adj* equal in power.—**equipollence** *n*.

equiponderant *vti* to make or be equal in weight.—**equiponderant** *adj*.

equisetum *n* (*pl* **equisetums, equiseta**) a plant of the group that includes horsetails.

equitable *adj* just and fair; (*law*) pertaining to equity as opposed to common or statute law.—**equitableness** *n*.—**equitably** *adv*.

equitation *n* horsemanship.

equity *n* (*pl* **equities**) fairness; (*law*) a legal system based on natural justice developed into a body of rules supplementing the common law; (*pl*) ordinary shares in a company.

equivalence, equivalency *n* (*pl* **equivalences, equivalencies**) equality of value or power; (*chem*) the property of having equal valency.

equivalent *adj* equal in amount, force, meaning, etc; virtually identical, esp in effect or function. * *n* an equivalent thing.

equivocal *adj* ambiguous; uncertain; questionable; arousing suspicion.—**equivocality, equivocacy** *n*.—**equivocally** *adv*.

equivocate *vi* to use ambiguous language, esp in order to confuse or deceive.—**equivocation** *n*.—**equivocator** *n*.—**equivocatory** *adj*.

equivoque, equivoke *n* a pun; an ambiguous expression.

Er (*chem symbol*) erbium.

era *n* an historical period typified by some special feature; a chronological order or system of notation reckoned from a given date as a basis.

eradiate *vti* to emit rays, to radiate.—**eradiation** *n*.

eradicate *vt* to obliterate.—**eradicable** *adj*.—**eradication** *n*.—**eradicator** *n*.

erase *vt* to rub out, obliterate; to remove a recording from magnetic tape; to remove data from a computer memory or storage medium.—**erasable** *adj*.—**erasion** *n*.

eraser *n* a piece of rubber, etc for rubbing out marks or writing.

erasure *n* an erasing; something rubbed out.

erbium *n* a soft metallic element of the rare earth group.

ere *prep, conj* (*poet*) before.

erect *adj* upright; not leaning or lying down; (*sexual organs*) rigid and swollen with blood from sexual stimulation. * *vt* to construct, set up.—**erectable** *adj*.—**erecter, erector** *n*.—**erectness** *n*.

erectile *adj* (*penis, clitoris, etc*) able to become enlarged and rigid through sexual stimulation.—**erectility** *n*.

erection *n* construction; something erected, as a building; swelling, esp of the penis, due to sexual excitement.

erector *n* a person who, or a thing that, erects; a muscle that erects.

eremite *n* a hermit.—**eremitic, eremitical** *adj*.—**eremitism** *n*.

erethism *n* (*med*) an abnormal degree of excitement in an organ or tissue of the body.

erg *n* the unit for measuring work or energy.

ergo *adv* therefore.

ergometer *n* an instrument for measuring work performed or force produced.

ergonomics *n* (*sing*) the study of the interaction between people and their working environment with the aim of improving efficiency.—**ergonomic** *adj*.—**ergonomically** *adv*.—**ergonomist** *n*.

ergot *n* a disease of rye and other cereals caused by a fungus; this fungus; a medicine derived from an ergot fungus.

ergotism *n* a toxic condition in humans caused by ergot fungus or chronic excessive use of an ergot drug.

erica *n* a genus of flowering plants, including the heaths.

ericaceous *adj* of the heath family.

eristic, eristical *adj* (*logic*) seeking to win an argument rather than find the truth.

ermine *n* (*pl* **ermines, ermine**) the weasel in its winter coat; the white fur of the winter coat; a rank or office whose official robe is edged with ermine.

erne, ern *n* the sea eagle.

erode *vt* to eat or wear away gradually.

erogenous *adj* sexually arousing; sensitive to sexual stimulation.

erosion *n* the act of eroding; gradual destruction or eating away; an eroded part.—**erosive, erosional** *adj*.

erotic, erotical *adj* of sexual love; sexually stimulating.—**erotically** *adv*.

erotica *n* sexually explicit literature or art.

eroticism, erotism *n* erotic nature; sexually arousing themes in literature and art; sexual desire.

erotomania *n* excessive sexual desire.—**erotomaniac** *n*.

err *vi* to be or do wrong.

errand *n* a short journey to perform some task, usu on behalf of another; the purpose of this journey.

errant *adj* going astray, esp doing wrong; moving aimlessly.

errantry *n* (*pl* **errantries**) the state or conduct of a knight errant.

erratic *adj* capricious; irregular; eccentric, odd.—**erratically** *adv*.

erratum *n* (*pl* **errata**) a written or printed error; a page bearing a list of corrigenda (—*also* **corrigendum**).

erroneous *adj* incorrect; mistaken.—**erroneously** *adv*.

error *n* a mistake, an inaccuracy; a mistaken belief or action; (*statistics*) the difference between an approximation of a value and the actual value, usu expressed as a percentage.

ersatz *adj* made in imitation; synthetic.

Erse *n* Scottish Gaelic; Irish Gaelic.—*also adj*.

erstwhile *adv* formerly. * *adj* former.

eructation *n* the act of belching.

erudite *adj* scholarly, having great knowledge.—**eruditely** *adv*.—**erudition** *n*.

erupt *vi* to burst forth; to break out into a rash; (*volcano*) to explode, ejecting ash and lava into the air.—**eruptible** *adj*.

eruption *n* the ejection of lava from a volcano; an outbreak; a rash, pimples.—**eruptional** *adj*.—**eruptive** *adj*.

eryngo, eringo *n* (*pl* **eryngoes, eryngos, eringoes, eringos**) one of a genus of plants including the sea holly.

erysipelas *n* an acute bacterial disease, characterized by a fever and skin inflammation.—**erysipelatous** *adj*.

erythema *n* (*med*) a superficial patchy redness of the skin.—**erythematic, erythematous, erythemic** *adj*.

erythrocyte *n* a red blood corpuscle.—**erythrocytic** *adj*.

Es (*chem symbol*) einsteinium.

escalade *n* the act of scaling the walls of a fortified place by ladders.

escalate *vi* to increase rapidly in magnitude or intensity.—**escalation** *n*.

escalator *n* a motorized set of stairs arranged to ascend or descend continuously.

escallop *n* a scallop.

escalope *n* a thin cut of meat, esp veal.

escapade *n* a wild or mischievous adventure.

escape *vt* to free oneself from confinement, etc; to avoid, remain unnoticed; to be forgotten. * *vi* to achieve freedom; (*gas, liquid*) to leak. * *n* an act or instance of escaping; a means of escape; a leakage of liquid or gas; a temporary respite from reality.—**escapable** *adj*.—**escaper** *n*.

escapee *n* a person who has escaped, esp a prisoner.

escapement *n* a device in a watch or clock by which the motions of the pendulum or balance are regulated.

escape velocity *n* the minimum velocity required for a rocket, etc to escape the gravitational pull of the earth or other celestial body.

escapism *n* the tendency to avoid or retreat from reality into fantasy.—**escapist** *n, adj*.

escapologist *n* a performer who escapes from handcuffs, locked boxes, etc.—**escapology** *n*.

escargot *n* a snail prepared as food.

escarp *n* a steep bank in front of a rampart.

escarpment *n* a steep side of a ridge or plateau.

eschatology *n* (*pl* **eschatologies**) the study of death, judgment, heaven and hell, and how humanity relates to them.

escheat *n* (*law*) (*formerly*) the lapsing of property to the state in the absence of an heir or by forfeiture; property that passes to the state in this way. * *vt* to confiscate property by escheat. * *vi* to revert to the state by escheat.

eschew *vt* to avoid as habit, esp on moral grounds.—**eschewal** *n*.—**eschewer** *n*.

escort *n* a person, group, ship, aircraft, etc accompanying a person or thing to give protection, guidance, or as a matter of courtesy; a person who accompanies another on a social occasion. * *vt* to attend as escort.

escritoire *n* a writing desk.

escrow *n* (*law*) a contract kept by a third party until the fulfilment of a condition.

escudo *n* (*pl* **escudos**) the monetary unit of Portugal.

esculent *adj* edible.

escutcheon *n* a shield bearing a coat of arms.

esker, eskar *n* (*geol*) a ridge of gravel, glacially deposited.

Eskimo *n* (*pl* **Eskimos, Eskimo**) the Inuit people; a group of peoples of eastern Siberia; a member of these peoples; their language.—*also adj*.

Eskimo dog *n* a powerful type of dog with a thick coat bred to pull sledges.

esophagus *see* **oesophagus**.

esoteric *adj* intended for or understood by a select few; secret; private.—**esoterically** *adv*.—**esotericism** *n*.

ESP *abbr* = extrasensory perception.

esp. *abbr* = especially.

espadrille *n* a flat shoe usu having a fabric upper and rope soles.

espalier *n* a plant (as a fruit tree) trained to grow flat against a support; the trellis on which such plants are trained.

esparto *n* (*pl* **espartos**) either of two Spanish and Algerian grasses used esp in paper-making.

especial *adj* notably special, unusual; particular to one person or thing.—**especially** *adv*.

Esperanto *n* an artificial international language.

espionage *n* spying or the use of spies to obtain information.

esplanade *n* a level open space for walking or driving, esp along a shore.

espouse *vt* to adopt or support a cause.—**espousal** *n*.—**espouser** *n*.

espresso *n* (*pl* **espressos**) coffee brewed by forcing steam through finely ground darkly roasted coffee beans; an apparatus for making espresso.

esprit *n* wit; liveliness.

esprit de corps *n* a sense of loyalty and attachment to a group to which one belongs.

espy *vt* (**espying, espied**) to catch sight of.—**espial** *n*.—**espier** *n*.

Esq *abbr* = esquire.

esquire *n* a general courtesy title used instead of Mr in addressing letters.

essay *n* a short prose work usu dealing with a subject from a limited or personal point of view; an attempt. * *vt* (**essaying, essayed**) to try, to attempt.

essayist *n* an essay writer.

essence *n* that which makes a thing what it is; a substance distilled or extracted from another substance and having the special qualities of the original substance; a perfume.

essential *adj* of or containing the essence of something; indispensable, of the greatest importance. * *n* (*often pl*) indispensable elements or qualities.—**essentiality, essentialness** *n*.—**essentially** *adv*.

essential oil *n* any of various plant oils used in perfumery.

establish *vt* to set up (eg a business) permanently; to settle (a person) in a place or position; to get generally accepted; to place beyond dispute, prove as a fact.—**establisher** *n*.

established *adj* (*church, religion*) officially recognized as the national church or religion of a country.

establishment *n* the act of establishing; a commercial organization or other large institution; the staff and resources of an organization; a household; (*with cap*) those people in institutions such as the government, civil service and commerce who use their power to preserve the social, economic and political status quo.

establishmentarian *adj, n* of an established church; supporting the established church system. * *n* a person who advocates official recognition of a church or religion.—**establishmentarianism** *n*.

estaminet *n* a café.

estancia *n* a cattle ranch in Latin America.

estate *n* landed property; a large area of residential or industrial development; a person's total possessions, esp at their death; a social or political class.

estate agent *see* **realtor**.

estate car *n* a car with extra carrying space reached through a rear door.—*also* **station wagon**.

esteem *vt* to value or regard highly; to consider or think. * *n* high regard, a favourable opinion.

ester *n* (*chem*) a compound of acid and alcohol.

esthete, esthetics *see* **aesthete, aesthetics**.

estheticism *see* **aestheticism**.

estimable *adj* worthy of esteem; calculable.

estimate *vt* to judge the value, amount, significance of; to calculate approximately. * *n* an approximate calculation; a judgment or opinion; a preliminary calculation of the cost of a particular job.—**estimative** *adj*.

estimation *n* estimating; an opinion, judgment; esteem.

estimator *n* someone or something that estimates.

estival *see* **aestival**.

estivation *see* **aestivation**.

estivation *see* **aestivation**.

estop *vt* (**estopping, estopped**) (*law*) to prohibit by estoppel.

estoppel *n* (*law*) a legal impediment arising as a result of one's previous action.

estrange *vt* to alienate the affections or confidence of.—**estranged** *adj*.—**estrangement** *n*.

estrogen *see* **oestrogen**.

estrus *see* **oestrus**.

estuarine *adj* pertaining to, or formed in, an estuary.

estuary *n* (*pl* **estuaries**) an arm of the sea at the mouth of a river.

esurient *adj* voracious, greedy.—**esurience** *n*.

ETA *abbr* = estimated time of arrival.

eta *n* the 7th letter of the Greek alphabet.

étagère *n* an ornamental stand.

et al *abbr* =*et alii*, and others.

etc, etc. *abbr* = et cetera.

et cetera, etcetera *n* and so forth.

etceteras *npl* the usual extra things or persons.

etch *vti* to make lines on (metal, glass) usu by the action of acid; to produce (as a design) by etching; to delineate clearly.—**etcher** *n*.

etching *n* the art or process of producing designs on and printing from etched plates; an impression made from an etched plate.

ETD *abbr* = estimated time of departure.

eternal *adj* continuing forever without beginning or end, everlasting; unchangeable; (*inf*) seemingly endless.—**eternality, eternalness** *n*.—**eternally** *adv*.

eternalize *vt* to make eternal.—**eternalization** *n*.

eternity *n* (*pl* **eternities**) infinite time; the timelessness thought to constitute life after death; (*inf*) a very long time.

etesian *adj* (*winds*) blowing from the northwest in the Mediterranean for about forty days each summer.

ethane *n* a colourless gaseous hydrocarbon found in natural gas and used esp as fuel.

ethene *see* **ethylene**.

ether *n* (*chem*) a light flammable liquid used as an anaesthetic or solvent; the upper regions of space, the invisible elastic substance formerly believed to be distributed evenly through all space.—**etheric** *adj*.

ethereal *adj* delicate; spiritual; celestial.—**ethereality, etherealness** *n*.—**ethereally** *adv*.

etherealize *vt* to make ethereal; to regard as ethereal.—**etherealization** *n*.

etherize *vt* (*patient*) to anaesthetize, using ether.—**etherization** *n*.

ethic *n* a moral principle or set of principles. * *adj* ethical.

ethical *adj* of or pertaining to ethics; conforming to the principles of proper conduct, as established by society, a profession, etc; (*med*) legally available only on prescription.—**ethically** *adv*.—**ethicalness, ethicality** *n*.

ethical investment *n* the investment in companies whose activities do not offend the investor's moral principles.—*also* **conscience investment**.

ethics *n* (*sing*) the philosophical analysis of human morality and conduct; system of conduct or behaviour, moral principles.—**ethicist** *n*.

Ethiopian *adj* of or pertaining to Ethiopia, its languages or people.—*also n*.

ethmoid *adj* (*anat*) denoting a light, spongy bone that forms the roof of the nose (—*also* **ethmoidal**). * *n* the ethmoid bone.

ethnic, ethnical *adj* of races or large groups of people classed according to common traits and customs.—**ethnically** *adv*.

ethno- *prefix* indicating race; people; culture.

ethnography *n* the area of anthropology dealing with the scientific description of human races.—**ethnographer** *n*. **ethnographic, ethnographical** *adj*.

ethnology *n* the scientific study of the origins and culture, etc of different races and peoples.—**ethnologic, ethnological** *adj*.—**ethnologist** *n*.

ethology *n* the scientific study of animal behaviour.—**ethologic, ethological** *adj*.—**ethologist** *n*.

ethos *n* the distinguishing character, sentiment, moral nature, or guiding beliefs of a person, group, or institution.

ethyl *n* the radical from which common alcohol and ether are derived.

ethylene *n* a colourless sweet-smelling gaseous hydrocarbon obtained from petroleum and used to manufacture chemicals including polythene.—*also* **ethene**.

etiolate *vti* (*green plants*) to bleach by depriving of light; to make or become pale and sickly.—**etiolation** *n*.

etiology *n* (*pl* **etiologies**) the study of causation, esp causes of diseases.—*also* **aetiology**.—**etiological** *adj*.—**etiologist** *n*.

etiquette *n* the form of conduct or behaviour prescribed by custom or authority to be observed in social, official or professional life.

Etruscan *n* an inhabitant of ancient Etruria (now Tuscany); the language of ancient Etruscans.—*also adj*.

étude *n* (*mus*) a short study or exercise for a solo instrument.

étui *n* (*pl* **étuis**) a pocket case for sewing implements and other small articles.

etymology *n* (*pl* **etymologies**) the study of the source and meaning of words; an account of the source and history of a word.—**etymological, etymologic** *adj*.—**etymologist** *n*.

etymon *n* (*pl* **etymons, etyma**) the root of a word, or its original meaning.

Eu (*chem symbol*) europium.

eucalyptol *n* a liquid contained in eucalyptus oil.

eucalyptus, eucalypt *n* (*pl* **eucalyptuses, eucalypti** *or* **eucalypts**) any of a genus of mostly Australian evergreen trees cultivated for their resin, oil, and wood; a type of oil obtained from its leaves.

Eucharist *n* the Christian sacrament of communion in which bread and wine are consecrated; the consecrated elements in communion.—**Eucharistic, Eucharistical** *adj*.

euchre *n* a card game for two, three or four players.

Euclidean *adj* pertaining to or accordant with the geo-

metrical principles of Euclid, the Greek mathematician (*fl* 3rd century BC).

eudemonism, eudaemonism *n* the ethical doctrine that regards happiness as the chief end in moral conduct.

eudiometer *n* an instrument for measuring the amount of oxygen in the air.

eugenics *n* (*sing*) the science of improving the human race by selective breeding.—**eugenic** *adj*.—**eugenically** *adv*.—**eugenicist** *n*.

euhemerism *n* the theory that the classical deities are deified heroes and that the myths connected with them are based on real history.—**euhemerist** *n*.—**euhemeristic** *adj*.—**euhemeristically** *adv*.

eulogize *vt* to extol in speech or writing.—**eulogist, eulogizer** *n*.—**eulogistic, eulogistical** *adj*.—**eulogistically** *adv*.

eulogy *n* (*pl* **eulogies**) a speech or piece of writing in praise or celebration of someone or something.

eunuch *n* a castrated man.

euonymus *n* a genus of small trees, containing the spindle tree.

euphemism *n* a mild or inoffensive word substituted for a more unpleasant or offensive term; the use of such inoffensive words.—**euphemistic** *adj*.—**euphemistically** *adv*.

euphonic, euphonical *adj* sounding pleasant to the ear.—**euphonically** *adv*.

euphonium *n* a brass musical instrument with its oval bell pointed backwards.

euphony *n* (*pl* **euphonies**) a pleasing sound, esp words.—**euphonious** *adj*.

euphorbia *n* a member of the large genus of plants of the spurge family.

euphoria *n* a feeling of elation.—**euphoric** *adj*.—**euphorically** *adv*.

euphuism *n* an affected style of prose using elaborate antithesis, alliteration, and conceits; the pedantic or affected use of words or language.—**euphuist** *n*.—**euphuistic, euphuistical** *adj*.

Eurasian *adj* of Europe and Asia (Eurasia) taken as one continent; of mixed European and Asian descent.—*also n*.

eureka *interj* used to express triumph on a discovery.

eurhythmics *see* **eurythmics**.

Euro- *prefix* Europe; European.

Eurocrat *n* a member of the administration of the European Community.

Europe *n* a continent extending from Asia in the east to the Atlantic Ocean in the west.

European *adj* relating to or native to Europe. * *n* a native or inhabitant of Europe; a person of European descent.

European Economic Community *or* **European Community** *n* the official name of the European Common Market, whose members aim to eliminate all obstacles to the free movement of goods, services, capital and labour between the member countries and to set up common external commercial, agricultural, and transport policies.

europium *n* a soft metallic element of the rare earth group.

eurythmics *npl* the art of representing musical harmony by physical gestures.—*also* **eurhythmics**.

Eustachian tube *n* a tube that leads from the middle ear to the pharynx.

euthanasia *n* the act or practice of killing painlessly, esp to relieve incurable suffering.

eV *abbr* = electronvolt.

evacuate *vti* to move (people, etc) from an area of danger to one of safety; to leave or make empty; to discharge wastes from the body.—**evacuation** *n.*—**evacuative** *adj.*—**evacuator** *n.*

evacuee *n* an evacuated person.

evade *vt* to manage to avoid, esp by dexterity or slyness.—**evadable** *adj.*—**evader** *n.*

evaluate *vt* to determine the value of; to assess.—**evaluation** *n.*—**evaluator** *n.*

evanescent *adj* fading away, vanishing; ephemeral.—**evanescence** *n.*

evangel *n* the Christian gospel.

evangelical *adj* of or agreeing with Christian teachings, esp as presented in the four Gospels; pertaining to various Christian sects that believe in salvation through personal conversion and faith in Christ.—**evangelicalism** *n.*

evangelism *n* preaching the Christian gospel; missionary zeal.

evangelist *n* a person who preaches the gospel; one of the writers of the four Gospels.—**evangelistic** *adj.*—**evangelistically** *adv.*

evangelize *vt* to preach or spread the gospel; to seek converts to a particular cause.—**evangelization** *n.*—**evangelizer** *n.*

evaporate *vti* to change into a vapour; to remove water from; to give off moisture; to vanish; to disappear.—**evaporable** *adj.*—**evaporation** *n.*—**evaporative** *adj.*—**evaporator** *n.*

evaporated milk *n* tinned unsweetened milk thickened by evaporation.

evasion *n* the act of evading; a means of evading, esp an equivocal reply or excuse.—**evasive** *adj.*—**evasively** *adv.*—**evasiveness** *n.*

eve *n* the evening or the whole day, before a festival; the period immediately before an event; (*formerly*) evening.

evection *n* (*astron*) a periodical irregularity of the moon's motion.

even *adj* level, flat; smooth; regular, equal; balanced; exact; divisible by two. * *vti* to make or become even; (*with* **up**) to balance (debts, etc). * *adv* exactly; precisely; fully; quite; at the very time; used as an intensive to emphasize the identity of something (*he looked content, even happy*), to indicate something unexpected (*she refused even to look at him*), or to stress the comparative degree (*she did even better*).—**evenly** *adv.*—**evenness** *n.*

even-handed *adj* impartial, fair.—**even-handedness** *n.*

evening *n* the latter part of the day and early part of the night.

evening primrose *n* a plant with yellow flowers that open in the evening.

evens *npl* (*bet*) winning the same as the stake if successful; offered at such odds, as a horse.—*also* **even money**.

evensong *n* vespers; evening prayers.

event *n* something that happens; a social occasion; contingency; a contest in a sports programme.

even-tempered *adj* calm.

eventful *adj* full of incidents; momentous

eventide *n* (*formerly*) evening.

eventual *adj* happening at some future unspecified time; ultimate.—**eventually** *adv.*

eventuality *n* (*pl* **eventualities**) a possible occurrence.

eventuate *vi* to result.—**eventuation** *n.*

ever *adv* always, at all times; at any time; in any case.

evergreen *adj* (*plants, trees*) having foliage that remains green all year.—*also n.*

everlasting *adj* enduring forever; (*plants*) having flowers that may be dried without loss of form or colour.—**everlastingly** *adv.*

evermore *adv* forever.

evert *vt* to turn inside out.—**eversible** *adj.*—**eversion** *n.*

every *adj* being one of the total.

everybody, everyone *pron* every person.

everyday *adj* happening daily; commonplace; worn or used on ordinary days.

everything *pron* all things, all; something of the utmost importance.

everywhere *adv* in every place.

evict *vt* to expel from land or from a building by legal process; to expel.—**eviction** *n.*—**evictor** *n.*

evidence *n* an outward sign; proof, testimony, esp matter submitted in court to determine the truth of alleged facts. * *vt* to demonstrate clearly; to give proof or evidence for.

evident *adj* easy to see or understand.—**evidently** *adv.*

evidential *adj* relating to, providing, or based on evidence.—**evidentially** *adv.*

evil *adj* wicked; causing or threatening distress or harm. * *n* a sin; a source of harm or distress.—**evilly** *adv.*—**evilness** *n.*

evildoer *n* a wicked person.—**evildoing** *n.*

evil eye *n* a stare superstitiously believed to inflict harm; the power to cause harm in this manner.

evince *vt* to indicate that one has (eg a quality); to demonstrate.—**evincible** *adj.*—**evincive** *adj.*

eviscerate *vt* to take out the intestines of, disembowel.—**evisceration** *n.*—**eviscerator** *n.*

evocative *adj* serving to evoke.—**evocatively** *n.*

evoke *vt* to call forth or up.—**evocable** *adj.*—**evocation** *n.*—**evoker** *n.*

evolution *n* a process of change in a particular direction; the process by which something attains its distinctive characteristics; a theory that existing types of plants and animals have developed from earlier forms.—**evolutionary, evolutional** *adj.*

evolutionist *adj* pertaining to evolution. * *n* someone who believes in the theory of evolution.

evolve *vi* to develop by or as if by evolution.—**evolvable** *adj.*—**evolvement** *n.*

ewe *n* a female sheep.

ewer *n* a large pitcher or jug with a wide spout.

ex[1] *n* (*inf*) a former husband, wife, etc.

ex[2] *prep* out of, from.

ex- *prefix* out, forth; quite, entirely; formerly.

exacerbate *vt* to make more violent, bitter, or severe.—**exacerbatingly** *adv.*—**exacerbation** *n.*

exact *adj* without error, absolutely accurate; detailed. * *vt* to compel by force, to extort; to require.—**exactable** *adj.*—**exactness** *n.*—**exactor, exacter** *n.*

exacting *adj* greatly demanding; requiring close attention and precision.—**exactingness** *n.*

exaction *n* the extortion of money, etc; an outrageous demand; something exacted.

exactitude *n* (the state of) being exact.

exactly *adv* in an exact manner; precisely. * *interj* quite so!

exaggerate *vt* to enlarge (a statement, etc) beyond what is really so or believable.—**exaggeration** *n.*—**exaggerative** *adj.*—**exaggerator** *n.*

exalt *vt* to raise up, esp in rank, power, or dignity.—**exalted** *adj.*—**exalter** *n.*

exaltation *n* elevation; rapture; a flock of larks.

exam *n* (*inf*) an examination.

examination *n* an examining, close scrutiny; a set of written or oral questions designed as a test of knowledge; the formal questioning of a witness on oath.—**examinational** *adj*.

examine *vt* to look at closely and carefully, to investigate; to test, esp by questioning.—**examinable** *adj*.—**examiner** *n*.

examinee *n* a person who is being tested in an examination.

example *n* a representative sample; a model to be followed or avoided; a problem to be solved in order to show the application of some rule; a warning to others.

exanimate *adj* dead, defunct, lifeless.—**exanimation** *n*.

exarch *n* a bishop of the Eastern Orthodox Church; the governor of a province under the Byzantine Empire.

exarchate, exarchy *n* the area of jurisdiction of an exarch.

exasperate *vt* to annoy intensely.—**exasperatedly** *adv*.—**exasperating** *adj*.—**exasperation** *n*.

Excalibur *n* in legend, King Arthur's sword.

ex cathedra *adj* with authority.

excavate *vt* to form a hole or tunnel by digging; to unearth; to expose to view (historical remains, etc) by digging away a covering.—**excavation** *n*.—**excavator** *n*.

exceed *vt* to be greater than or superior to; to go beyond the limit of.—**exceedable** *adj*.—**exceeder** *n*.

exceedingly *adv* very, extremely.

excel *vb* (**excelling, excelled**) *vt* to outdo, to be superior to. * *vi* (*with* **in, at**) to do better than others.

excellence *n* that in which one excels; superior merit or quality; (*with cap*) a title of honour given to certain high officials (—*also* **Excellency**).

excellent *adj* very good, outstanding.—**excellently** *adv*.

excelsior *interj* higher. * *n* soft wood shavings for stuffing.

except *vt* to exclude, to take or leave out. * *prep* not including; other than.—**exceptable** *adj*.

excepting *prep* except, not including.

exception *n* the act of excepting; something excepted; an objection.

exceptionable *adj* open to objection.—**exceptionably** *adv*.

exceptional *adj* unusual, forming an exception; superior.—**exceptionally** *adv*.

excerpt *n* an extract from a book, film, etc. * *vt* to select or quote (a passage from a book).—**exerptible** *adj*.—**excerption** *n*.

excess *n* the exceeding of proper established limits; the amount by which one thing or quantity exceeds another; (*pl*) overindulgence in eating or drinking; unacceptable conduct.

excessive *adj* greater than what is acceptable, too much.—**excessively** *adv*.—**excessiveness** *n*.

exchange *vt* to give and take (one thing in return for another); to give to and receive from another person. * *n* the exchanging of one thing for another; the thing exchanged; the conversion of money in one currency into a sum of equivalent value in another currency; the system of settling commercial debts between foreign governments, eg by bills of exchange; a place where things and services are exchanged, esp a marketplace for securities; a centre or device in which telephone lines are interconnected.—**exchangeable** *adj*.—**exchangeability** *n*.—**exchanger** *n*.

exchange rate *n* the rate at which one foreign currency may be exchanged for another.

exchequer *n* (*with cap*) the British governmental department in charge of finances; (*inf*) personal finances.

excise[1] *n* a tax on the manufacture, sale, or use of certain articles within a country.—**excisable** *adj*.

excise[2] *vt* to remove by cutting out.—**excision** *n*.

exciseman *n* (*pl* **excisemen**) (*formerly*) an officer employed to collect and enforce excise.

excitable *adj* easily excited.—**excitability, excitableness** *n*.

excitant *n* a stimulant. * *adj* stimulating.

excitation *n* the act of exciting; the state of excitement.—**excitative, excitatory** *adj*.

excite *vt* to arouse the feelings of, esp to generate feelings of pleasurable anticipation; to cause to experience strong emotion; to stir up, agitate; to rouse to activity; to stimulate a physiological response, eg in a bodily organ.

excited *adj* experiencing or expressing excitement.—**excitedly** *adv*.—**excitedness** *n*.

excitement *n* a feeling of strong, esp pleasurable, emotion; something that excites.

exciting *adj* causing excitement; stimulating.—**excitingly** *adv*.

exclaim *vti* to shout out or utter suddenly and with strong emotion.—**exclaimer** *n*.

exclamation *n* a sudden crying out; a word or utterance exclaimed.—**exclamational** *adj*.

exclamation point, exclamation mark *n* the punctuation mark (!) placed after an exclamation.

exclamatory *adj* of or expressing exclamation.—**exclamatorily** *adv*.

exclave *n* a small part of a country lying within the territory of another country.

exclude *vt* to shut out, to keep out; to reject or omit; to eject.—**excluder** *n*.—**exclusion** *n*.

exclusive *adj* excluding all else; reserved for particular persons; snobbishly aloof; fashionable, high-class, expensive; unobtainable or unpublished elsewhere; sole, undivided.—**exclusively** *adv*.—**exclusiveness** *n*.—**exclusivity** *n*.

excogitate *vt* to devise, to invent; to discover by thinking.—**excogitation** *n*.—**excogitative** *adj*.

excommunicate *vt* to bar from association with a church; to exclude from fellowship.—**excommunication** *n*.—**excommunicative** *adj*.—**excommunicator** *n*.

excoriate *vt* to strip of the skin; to flay.—**excoriation** *n*.

excrement *n* waste matter discharged from the bowels.—**excremental, excrementitious** *adj*.

excrescence *n* an outgrowth, esp abnormal, from a plant or animal; a disfigurement.

excrescent *adj* pertaining to excrescence; superfluous.

excreta *npl* waste matter discharged from the body, faeces, urine.

excrete *vt* to eliminate or discharge wastes from the body.—**excreter** *n*.—**excretion** *n*.—**excretive, excretory** *adj*.

excruciate *vt* to inflict severe pain upon; to torture.—**excruciation** *n*.

excruciating *adj* intensely painful or distressful; (*inf*) very bad.—**excruciatingly** *adv*.

exculpate *vt* to free (a person) from alleged fault or guilt.—**exculpable** *adj*.—**exculpation** *n*.

exculpatory *adj* tending or serving to exculpate.

excurrent *adj* (*bot*) (*leaf*) having a midrib running beyond the edge; (*tree*) having a projecting stem; (*zool*) having a duct, etc, whose contents flow out.

excursion *n* a pleasure trip; a short journey.

excursionist *n* someone going on an excursion.

excursive *adj* digressing, rambling.—**excursively** *adv*.

excursus *n* (*pl* **excursuses, excursus**) a dissertation added as a supplement to a work, giving additional information on certain points; a digression from the main subject of a work.

excusable *adj* able to be excused.—**excusably** *adv*.

excuse *vt* to pardon; to forgive; to give a reason or apology for; to be a reason or explanation of; to let off. * *n* an apology, a plea in extenuation.

ex-directory *adj* (*telephone number*) not listed in the telephone directory by request.

execrable *adj* appalling.—**execrableness** *n*.

execrate *vt* to denounce as evil; to abhor.—**execration** *n*.—**execrative, execratory** *adj*.

executant *n* a person who executes or performs, esp an artist, musician, etc.

execute *vt* to carry out, put into effect; to perform; to produce (eg a work of art); to make legally valid; to put to death by law.—**executable** *adj*.—**executer** *n*.

execution *n* the act or process of executing; the carrying out or suffering of a death sentence; the style or technique of performing, eg music.

executioner *n* a person who executes a death sentence upon a condemned prisoner.

executive *n* a person or group concerned with administration or management of a business or organization; the branch of government with the power to put laws, etc into effect. * *adj* having the power to execute decisions, laws, decrees, etc.

executor *n* a person appointed by a testator to see the terms of a will implemented.—**executorial** *adj*.—**executorship** *n*.

executory *adj* (*law*) pertaining to the execution of laws; to be carried out at a future date.

executrix *n* (*pl* **executrices, executrixes**) a female executor.

exegesis *n* (*pl* **exegeses**) an explanation or interpretation of a text or passage, esp of the Bible.

exegetic, exegetical *adj* expository; interpretative.

exegetics *n* (*sing*) the study of exegesis.

exemplar *n* a model; a typical instance or example.

exemplary *adj* deserving imitation; serving as a warning.—**exemplarily** *adv*.—**exemplariness** *n*.

exemplify *vt* (**exemplifying, exemplified**) to illustrate by example; to be an instance or example of.—**exemplification** *n*.—**exemplifier** *n*.

exempt *adj* not liable, free from the obligations required of others. * *vt* to grant immunity (from).—**exemptible** *adj*.—**exemption** *n*.

exercise *n* the use or application of a power or right; regular physical or mental exertion for health, amusement or acquisition of some skill; something performed to develop or test a specific ability or skill; (*often pl*) manoeuvres carried out for military training and discipline. * *vt* to use, exert, employ; to engage in regular physical activity to strengthen the body, etc; to train (troops) by means of drills and manoeuvres; to engage the attention of; to perplex.—**exercisable** *adj*.

exergue *n* the space below the principal design on a coin or medal for the insertion of a date, etc.—**exergual** *adj*.

exert *vt* to bring (eg strength, influence) into use.

exertion *n* an exerting; a strenuous effort.—**exertive** *adj*.

exeunt (*Latin*) they go off, a stage direction.

exfoliate *vi* to flake off; (*tree*) to shed bark.—**exfoliation** *n*.

ex gratia *adj* given as a favour or where no legal obligation exists.

exhalant *adj* exhaling. * *n* a duct, organ, etc used for exhaling.

exhale *vt* to breathe out.—**exhalation** *n*.

exhaust *vt* to use up completely; to make empty; to use up, tire out; (*subject*) to deal with or develop completely. * *n* the escape of waste gas or steam from an engine; the device through which these escape.—**exhausted** *adj*.—**exhauster** *n*.—**exhaustible** *adj*.—**exhausting** *adj*.

exhaustion *n* the act of exhausting or being exhausted; extreme weariness.

exhaustive *adj* comprehensive, thorough.—**exhaustively** *adv*.

exhibit *vt* to display, esp in public; to present to a court in legal form. * *n* an act or instance of exhibiting, something exhibited; something produced and identified in court for use as evidence.—**exhibitor** *n*.—**exhibitory** *adj*.

exhibition *n* a showing, a display; a public show; an allowance made to a student.

exhibitioner *n* a student who holds an exhibition.

exhibitionism *n* an excessive tendency to show off one's abilities; a compulsion to expose oneself indecently in public.—**exhibitionist** *n*.—**exhibitionistic** *adj*.

exhilarant *adj* exhilarating. * *n* something that exhilarates.

exhilarate *vt* to make very happy; to invigorate.—**exhilarating** *adj*.—**exhilaration** *n*.—**exhilarator** *n*.

exhort *vt* to urge or advise strongly.—**exhortation** *n*.—**exhortative, exhortatory** *adj*.—**exhorter** *n*.

exhume *vt* to dig up (a dead person) for detailed examination.—**exhumation** *n*.—**exhumer** *n*.

exigency, exigence *n* (*pl* **exigencies, exigences**) a pressing need; emergency.

exigent *adj* urgent; exacting.—**exigently** *adv*.

exigible *adj* (*debt etc*) liable to be exacted.

exiguous *adj* very small in amount, meagre.—**exiguity, exiguousness** *n*.

exile *n* prolonged absence from one's own country, either through choice or as a punishment; an exiled person. * *vt* to banish, to expel from one's native land.—**exilic, exilian** *adj*.

exist *vi* to have being; to just manage a living; to occur in a specific place under specific conditions.

existence *n* the state or fact of existing; continuance of life; lifestyle; everything that exists.

existent *adj* real, actual; existing; current.

existential *adj* of or pertaining to existence; existentialist.

existentialism *n* (*philos*) a movement stressing personal freedom and responsibility in relation to existence.—**existentialist** *n*, *adj*.

exit *n* a way out of an enclosed space; death; a departure from a stage. * *vi* to leave, withdraw; to go off-stage.

ex libris *adj* from the library of. * *n* (*pl* **ex libris**) a book plate.

exocrine *adj* secreting though a duct; of or relating to exocrine glands or their secretions.

exocrine gland *n* a gland that releases secretions through a duct, eg a sweat gland.

exoderm *see* **ectoderm**.

exodus *n* the departure of many people; (*with cap*) the departure of the Israelites from Egypt led by Moses; (*Bible*) the second book of the Old Testament.

ex officio *adv, adj* by virtue of an official position.

exogamy *n* the practice of marrying only outside one's own tribe.—**exogamous** *adj*.

exogenous *adj* (*biol*) produced by external growth; a used or influenced by external factors.—**exogenously** *adv*.

exonerate *vt* to absolve from blame; to relieve from a responsibility, obligation.—**exoneration** *n*.—**exonerative** *adj*.—**exonerator** *n*.

exophthalmos, exophthalmus *n* protrusion of the eyeball.—**exophthalmic** *adj*.

exorbitant *adj* (*prices, demands, etc*) unreasonable, excessive.—**exorbitance** *n*.

exorcise, exorcize *vt* to expel an evil spirit (from a person or place) by ritual and prayer.—**exorciser, exorcizer** *n*.—**exorcism** *n*.—**exorcist** *n*.

exordium *n* (*pl* **exordiums, exordia**) the opening part of a speech or composition.—**exordial** *adj*.

exoteric *adj* accessible to ordinary people; external.—**exoterically** *adv*.—**exotericism** *n*.

exotic *adj* foreign; strange; excitingly different or unusual.—**exotically** *adv*.—**exoticism** *n*.—**exoticness** *n*.

exotica *npl* exotic items, esp as a collection.

expand *vt* to increase in size, bulk, extent, importance; to describe in fuller detail. * *vi* to become larger; to become more genial and responsive.—**expandable, expandible** *adj*.—**expander** *n*.

expanse *n* a wide area of land, etc; the extent of a spread-out area.

expansible *adj* capable of expansion, or of being expanded.—**expansibility** *n*.

expansile *adj* capable of expansion, or of causing expansion.

expansion *n* the act of expanding or being expanded; something expanded; the amount by which something expands; the fuller development of a theme, etc.—**expansionary** *adj*.

expansive *adj* able to or having the capacity to expand or cause expansion; comprehensive; (*person*) genial, communicative.—**expansively** *adv*.—**expansiveness** *n*.

ex parte *adj* (*law*) on behalf of one side only; partisan.

expatiate *vi* to speak or write at length; to enlarge.—**expatiation** *n*.—**expatiator** *n*.

expatriate *adj* living in another country; self-exiled or banished. * *n* an expatriate person. * *vti* to exile (oneself) or banish (another person). —**expatriation** *n*.

expect *vt* to anticipate; to regard as likely to arrive or happen; to consider necessary, reasonable or due; to think, suppose.

expectant *adj* expecting, hopeful; filled with anticipation; pregnant.—**expectantly** *adv*.—**expectancy, expectance** *n*.

expectation *n* the act or state of expecting; something that is expected to happen; (*pl*) prospects for the future, esp of inheritance.—**expectative** *adj*.

expectorant *n* a medicine that promotes expectoration.

expectorate *vti* to bring up (mucus) from the respiratory tract by coughing; to spit.—**expectoration** *n*.—**expectorator** *n*.

expediency, expedience *n* (*pl* **expediencies, expediences**) fitness, suitability; an inclination towards expedient methods.—**expediential** *adj*.

expedient *adj* suitable or desirable under the circumstances. * *n* a means to an end; a means devised or used for want of something better.—**expediently** *adv*.

expedite *vt* to carry out promptly; to facilitate.—**expediter, expeditor** *n*.

expedition *n* a journey to achieve some purpose, as exploration, etc; the party making this journey; speedy efficiency, promptness.

expeditionary *adj* of or constituting an expedition.

expeditious *adj* speedy; efficient.—**expeditiously** *adv*.

expel *vt* (**expelling, expelled**) to drive out, to eject; to banish.—**expellable** *adj*.—**expellee** *n*.—**expeller** *n*.

expend *vt* to spend (money, time, energy, etc); to use up, consume.—**expender** *n*.

expendable *adj* able to be consumed, not worth keeping; available for sacrifice to achieve some objective.—**expendability** *n*.

expenditure *n* the act or process of expending money, etc; the amount expended.

expense *n* a payment of money for something, expenditure; a cause of expenditure; (*pl*) money spent on some activity (eg travelling on business); reimbursement for this.

expense account *n* an account of expenses to be reimbursed to an employee.

expensive *adj* causing or involving great expense; costly.—**expensively** *adv*.—**expensiveness** *n*.

experience *n* observation or practice resulting in or tending towards knowledge; knowledge gained by seeing and doing; a state of being affected from without (as by events); an affecting event. * *vt* to have experience of.

experienced *adj* wise or skilled through experience.

experiential *adj* of or based on experience.

experiment *n* any test or trial to find out something; a controlled procedure carried out to discover, test, or demonstrate something. * *vi* to carry out experiments.—**experimentation** *n*.—**experimenter** *n*.

experimental *adj* of, derived from, or proceeding by experiment; empirical; provisional.—**experimentalism** *n*.—**experimentally** *adv*.

expert *adj* thoroughly skilled; knowledgeable through training and experience. * *n* a person with special skills or training in any art or science.—**expertly** *adv*.—**expertness** *n*.

expertise *n* expert knowledge or skill.

expiate *vt* to pay the penalty for; to make amends for.—**expiation** *n*.—**expiator** *n*.—**expiatory** *adj*.

expire *vti* to come to an end; to lapse or become void; to breathe out; to die.—**expiration** *n*.—**expirer** *n*.

expiry *n* (*pl* **expiries**) the ending of a period of validity, eg of a passport.

explain *vt* to make plain or clear; to give a reason for; account for.—**explainable** *adj*.—**explainer** *n*.

explanation *n* an act or process of explaining; something that explains, esp a statement.

explanatory, explanative *adj* serving as an explanation.—**explanatorily** *adv*.

expletive *n* a violent exclamation or swearword.

explicable *adj* able to be explained.

explicate *vt* to analyse the implications of; to explain in great detail.—**explication** *n*.—**explicative, explicatory** *adj*.—**explicator** *n*.

explicit *adj* clearly stated, not merely implied; outspoken, frank; graphically detailed.—**explicitly** *adv*.—**explicitness** *n*.

explode *vti* to burst or cause to blow up with a loud

noise, as in the detonation of a bomb; (*emotions*) to burst out; (*population*) to increase rapidly; to expose (a theory, etc) as false.—**exploder** *n*.

exploit *n* a bold achievement. * *vt* to utilize, develop (raw materials, etc); to take unfair advantage of, esp for financial gain.—**exploitable** *adj*.—**exploitation** *n*.—**exploitative** *adj*.

exploratory, explorative *adj* for the purpose of exploring or investigating.

explore *vti* to examine or inquire into; to travel through (a country) for the purpose of (geographical) discovery; to examine minutely.—**exploration** *n*.—**explorer** *n*.

explosion *n* an act or instance of exploding; a sudden loud noise caused by this; an outburst of emotion; a rapid increase or expansion.

explosive *adj* liable to or able to explode; liable or threatening to burst out with violence and noise. * *n* an explosive substance.—**explosively** *adv*.

exponent *n* a person who explains or interprets something; a person who champions, advocates, or exemplifies; (*math*) an index of the power to which an expression is raised.

exponential *adj* of, relating to or having an exponent; (*math*) having a variable in an exponent; able to be expressed by an exponential function. * *n* an exponential function.—**exponentially** *adv*.

exponential function *n* a mathematical function in which the constant quantity of the expression is raised to the power of a variable quantity, i.e. the exponent.

export *vt* to send out (goods) of one country for sale in another. * *n* the act of exporting; the article exported.—**exportable** *adj*.—**exportation** *n*.—**exporter** *n*.

exposé *n* a revelation of crime, dishonesty, etc.

expose *vt* to deprive of protection or shelter; to subject to an influence (as light, weather); to display, reveal; to uncover or disclose.—**exposable** *adj*.—**exposal** *n*.—**exposer** *n*.

exposed *adj* open to view; not shielded or protected.—**exposedness** *n*.

exposition *n* a public show or exhibition; a detailed explanation; a speech or writing explaining a process, thing, or idea.—**expositional** *adj*.

expositive, expository *adj* of, pertaining to or conveying exposition; explanatory.—**expositively, expositorily** *adv*.

ex post facto *adj* (*law*) enacted retrospectively. * *adv* after the fact.

expostulate *vi* to argue with, esp to dissuade.—**expostulation** *n*.—**expostulator** *n*.—**expostulatory, expostulative** *adj*.

exposure *n* an exposing or state of being exposed; time during which light reaches and acts on a photographic film, paper or plate; publicity.

expound *vt* to explain or set forth in detail.—**expounder** *n*.

express *vt* to represent in words; to make known one's thoughts, feelings, etc; to represent by signs, symbols, etc; to squeeze out. * *adj* firmly stated, explicit; (*train, bus, etc*) travelling at high speed with few or no stops. * *adv* at high speed, by express service. * *n* an express train, coach, etc; a system or company for sending freight, etc at rates higher than standard.—**expresser** *n*.—**expressible** *adj*.

expression *n* an act of expressing, esp by words; a word

or phrase; a look; intonation; a manner of showing feeling in communicating or performing (eg music); (*math*) a collection of symbols serving to express something.—**expressional** *adj*.—**expressionless** *adj*.

expressionism *n* a style of art, literature, music, etc that seeks to depict the subjective emotions aroused in the artist by objects and events, not objective reality.—**expressionist** *n*.—**expressionistic** *adj*.

expressive *adj* serving to express; full of expression.—**expressively** *adv*.—**expressiveness** *n*.

expressly *adv* explicitly; for a specific purpose.

expressway *n* a motorway.

expropriate *vt* to remove (property) from its owner, to dispossess.—**expropriable** *adj*.—**expropriation** *n*.—**expropriator** *n*.

expulsion *n* the act of expelling or being expelled.—**expulsive** *adj*.

expunge *vt* to obliterate, to erase.—**expunction** *n*.—**expunger** *n*.

expurgate *vt* to cut from a book, play, etc any parts supposed to be offensive or erroneous.—**expurgation** *n*.—**expurgator** *n*.—**expurgatory, expurgatorial** *adj*.

exquisite *adj* very beautiful, refined; sensitive, showing discrimination; acutely felt, as pain or pleasure.—**exquisitely** *adv*.

exsanguinate *vt* to drain of blood.—**exsanguination** *n*.

exsanguine *adj* bloodless.

exscind *vt* to cut off; to cut out, excise.

exsert *vt* to thrust outwards.—**exsertile** *adj*.—**exsertion** *n*.

exsiccate *vt* to dry up.—**exsiccation** *n*.

extant *adj* still existing.

extemporaneous, extemporary *adj* spoken, acted, etc without preparation.—**extemporaneously, extemporarily** *adv*.

extempore *adv, adj* without preparation, impromptu.

extemporize *vi* to do something extemporaneously.—**extemporization** *n*.

extend *vt* to stretch or spread out; to stretch fully; to prolong in time; to cause to reach in distance, etc; to enlarge, increase the scope of; to hold out (eg the hand); to accord, grant; to give, offer, (eg sympathy). * *vi* to prolong in distance or time; to reach in scope.

extended family *n* a family with three or more generations of blood relations living as a unit.

extendible, extendable *adj* able to be extended.—**extendibility, extendability** *n*.

extensible, extensile *adj* extendible.—**extensibility, extensibleness** *n*.

extension *n* the act of extending or state of being extended; extent, scope; an added part, eg to a building; an extra period; a programme of extramural teaching provided by a college, etc; an additional telephone connected to the principal line.

extensive *adj* large; having a wide scope or extent.—**extensively** *adv*. —**extensiveness** *n*.

extensometer *n* a type of micrometer for measuring the expansion of a body.

extensor *n* a muscle that extends or straightens a limb.

extent *n* the distance over which a thing is extended; the range or scope of something; the limit to which something extends.

extenuate *vt* to make (guilt, a fault, or offence) seem less.—**extenuating** *adj*.—**extenuator** *n*.—**extenuatory** *adj*.

extenuation *n* an extenuating or being extenuated, partial justification; something that extenuates, an excuse.

exterior *adj* of, on, or coming from the outside; external; (*paint, etc*) suitable for use on the outside. * *n* the external part or surface; outward manner or appearance.

exteriorize *vt* to externalize; (*med*) to move (an organ, etc) out of the body, usu to facilitate surgery.

exterminate *vt* to destroy completely.—**exterminable** *adj*.—**extermination** *n*.—**exterminatory** *adj*.

exterminator *n* one who or that which exterminates; a person who is employed to destroy pests, etc.

extern, externe *n* a non-resident doctor.

external *adj* outwardly perceivable; of, relating to, or located on the outside or outer part. * *n* an external feature.—**externally** *adv*.

externality *n* (*pl* **externalities**) a being external or externalized; something external; (*philos*) a being external to the perceiving mind.

externalize *vt* to make external; to attribute an external existence to; to express (feelings, etc) esp in words; (*psychol*) to project (opinions, feelings) onto others or one's surroundings.—**externalization** *n*.

exterritorial *adj* extraterritorial.—**exterritoriality** *n*.

extinct *adj* (*animals*) not alive, no longer existing; (*fire*) not burning, out; (*volcano*) no longer active.—**extinction** *n*.

extine *n* (*bot*) the outer coat of the pollen grain.

extinguish *vt* to put out (a fire, light, etc); to bring to an end.—**extinguishable** *adj*.—**extinguishment** *n*.

extinguisher *n* a device for putting out a fire.

extirpate *vt* to destroy totally, as by uprooting.—**extirpation** *n*.—**extirpative** *adj*.—**extirpator** *n*.

extol, extoll *vt* (**extols** *or* **extolls, extolling, extolled**) to praise highly.—**extoller** *n*.—**extollment, extolment** *n*.

extort *vt* to obtain (money, promises, etc) by force or improper pressure.—**extorter** *n*.—**extortive** *adj*.

extortion *n* the act or practice of extorting; the criminal instance of this; oppressive or unjust exaction.—**extortionary** *adj*.—**extortioner, extortionist** *n*.

extortionate *adj* exorbitant; excessively high in price.—**extortionately** *adv*.

extra *adj* additional. * *adv* unusually; in addition. * *n* something extra or additional, esp a charge; a special edition of a newspaper; a person who plays a non-speaking role in a film.

extra- *prefix* outside, beyond.

extract *vt* to take or pull out by force; to withdraw by chemical or physical means; to abstract, excerpt. * *n* the essence of a substance obtained by extraction; a passage taken from a book, play, film, etc.—**extractable, extractible** *adj*.—**extractability, extractibility** *n*.

extraction *n* the act of extracting; lineage; something extracted.

extractive *adj* tending or serving to extract.

extractor *n* one who extracts; a thing that extracts, esp a device for removing teeth or delivering a baby; a device for extracting stale air or fumes from a room (—*also* **extractor fan**).

extracurricular *adj* not part of the regular school timetable; beyond one's normal duties or activities.

extradite *vt* to surrender (an alleged criminal) to the country where the offence was committed.—**extraditable** *adj*.—**extradition** *n*.

extrados *n* (*pl* **extrados, extradoses**) (*archit*) the upper or outer curve of an arch.

extragalactic *adj* outside the Galaxy.

extrajudicial *adj* out of the ordinary course of legal proceedings.

extramarital *adj* occurring outside marriage, esp sexual relationships.

extramundane *adj* beyond the material world.

extramural *adj* (*course, studies*) outside the usual courses run by a university, etc; outside a city's walls or boundaries.—**extramurally** *adv*.

extraneous *adj* coming from outside; not essential.—**extraneously** *adv*.

extraordinary *adj* not usual or regular; remarkable, exceptional.—**extraordinarily** *adv*.—**extraordinariness** *n*.

extrapolate *vti* to infer (unknown data) from known data.—**extrapolation** *n*.—**extrapolator** *n*.

extrasensory perception *n* the claimed ability to obtain information by means other than the ordinary physical senses.

extraterritorial *adj* outside territorial boundaries; (*embassy etc*) outside the jurisdiction of the country in which it is.—*also* **exterritorial**.

extraterritoriality *n* exemption granted to foreign diplomats from the legal jurisdiction of the country to which they are posted; a country's jurisdiction over its nationals abroad.

extravagant *adj* lavish in spending; (*prices*) excessively high; wasteful; (*behaviour, praise, etc*) lacking in restraint, flamboyant, profuse.—**extravagantly** *adv*.—**extravagance** *n*.

extravaganza *n* an elaborate musical production; a spectacular show, play, film, etc.

extravagate *vi* (*arch*) to wander; to be extravagant.—**extravagation** *n*.

extravasate *vt* (*anat*) to force blood, etc out of its proper vessel; to exude. * *vi* to flow out.—**extravasation** *n*.

extraversion *see* **extroversion**.

extravert *see* **extrovert**.

extreme *adj* of the highest degree or intensity; excessive, immoderate, unwarranted; very severe, stringent; outermost. * *n* the highest or furthest limit or degree; (*often pl*) either of the two points marking the ends of a scale or range.—**extremely** *adv*.—**extremeness** *n*.

extremist *n* a person of extreme views, esp political.—**extremism** *n*.

extremity *n* (*pl* **extremities**) the utmost point or degree; the most remote part; the utmost violence, vigour, or necessity; the end; (*pl*) the hands or feet.

extricable *adj* able to be extricated.

extricate *vt* to release from difficulties; to disentangle.—**extrication** *n*.

extrinsic *adj* external; not inherent or essential.—**extrinsically** *adv*.

extrorse *adj* (*bot*) turned outwards.

extroversion *n* the state of having thoughts and activities directed towards things other than oneself.—*also* **extraversion**.

extrovert *n* a person more interested in the external world than his own thoughts and feelings.—*also* **extravert**.—**extroverted, extraverted** *adj*.

extrude *vt* to force or push out; to mould (metal or plastic) by forcing through a shaped die.—**extrusion** *n*.—**extrusive** *adj*.

exuberant *adj* lively, effusive, high-spirited; profuse.—**exuberance** *n*.—**exuberantly** *adv*.

exuberate *vi* to be exuberant; (*arch*) to abound.

exudate *n* exuded matter, eg sweat.

exudation *n* an exuding or being exuded; exuded matter, eg sweat.—**exudative** *adj*.

exude *vt* to cause or allow to ooze through pores or incisions, as sweat, pus; to display (confidence, emotion) freely.

exult *vi* to rejoice greatly.—**exultation** *n*.

exultant *adj* exulting, joyful; triumphant.—**exultantly** *adv*.

exuviae *npl* the cast-off skins, shells, etc, of animals.—**exuvial** *adj*.

exuviate *vt* (*skin*) to shed, slough.—**exuviation** *n*.

eyas *n* a young hawk.

eye *n* the organ of sight; the iris; the faculty of seeing; the external part of the eye; something resembling an eye, as the hole in a needle, the leaf-bud on a potato, etc. * *vt* (**eyeing** *or* **eying, eyed**) to look at; to observe closely.

eyeball *n* the ball of the eye. * *vt* (*sl*) to stare at.

eyebright *n* a plant with small white and purplish flowers, formerly used as a lotion to treat disorders of the eye.

eyebrow *n* the hairy ridge above the eye.

eye-catching *adj* attractive or striking in appearance.—**eye-catcher** *n*.

eyeful *adj* (*inf*) a close look, gaze; an attractive vision, esp a woman.

eyeglass *n* a lens for correcting defective vision, a monocle.

eyeglasses *npl* spectacles.

eyelash *n* the fringe of fine hairs along the edge of each eyelid.

eyeless *adj* without eyes; blind.

eyelet *n* a small hole for a rope or cord to pass through, as in sails, garments, etc.

eyelid *n* the lid of skin and muscle that moves to cover the eye.

eye-liner *n* a cosmetic used to apply a line round the eye.

eye-opener *n* something that comes as a shock or surprise.

eyepiece *n* the lens or lenses at the end nearest the eye of an optical instrument, eg a telescope.

eyeprint *n* the pattern of veins in the retina, which is unique to an individual and used as a means of identification.

eye-shadow *n* a coloured powder applied to accentuate or decorate the eyelids.

eyeshot *n* seeing distance.

eyesight *n* the faculty of seeing.

eyesore *n* anything offensive to the sight.

eyespot *n* a rudimentary visual organ; (*on butterflies, etc*) a marking resembling an eye.

eyetooth *n* (*pl* **eyeteeth**) a canine tooth in the upper jaw.

eyewash *n* (*inf*) nonsense, drivel.

eye-witness *n* a person who sees an event, such as an accident or a crime, and can describe what happened.

eyrie *n* the nest of an eagle or other bird of prey; any high inaccessible place or position.—*also* **aerie**.

F

F *abbr* = Fahrenheit; (*chem symbol*) fluorine.

f, F *n* the 6th letter of the English alphabet.

fa *n* (*music*) the fourth note in the sol-fa musical notation.—*also* **fah**.

fabaceous *adj* (*bot*) bean-like.

Fabian *adj* pertaining to the tactics of the Roman general, Fabius Maximus; cautiously persistent; watchful. * *n* a member of the Fabian Society.

Fabian Society *n* a society seeking socialism by moral persuasion.

fable *n* a story, often with animal characters, intended to convey a moral; a lie, fabrication; a story involving mythical, legendary or supernatural characters or events.

fabled *adj* related in fables; fictitious.

fabric *n* cloth made by knitting, weaving, etc; framework, structure.

fabricate *vt* to construct, manufacture; to concoct (eg a lie); to forge.—**fabrication** *n*.—**fabricator** *n*.

fabulist *n* a writer of fables; a liar.

fabulous *adj* told in fables; incredible, astonishing; (*inf*) very good.—**fabulously** *adv*.

façade, facade *n* the main front or face of a building; an outward appearance, esp concealing something hidden.

face *n* the front part of the head containing the eyes, nose, mouth, chin, etc; facial expression; the front or outer surface of anything; external show or appearance; dignity, self respect; impudence, effrontery; a coal face. * *vt* to be confronted by (a problem, etc); to deal with (an opponent, problem, etc) resolutely; to be opposite to; to turn (a playing card) face upwards; to cover with a new surface. * *vi* to turn the face in a certain direction; to be situated in or have a specific direction.

face card *n* the king, queen or jack in a pack of cards.

faceless *adj* lacking a face; anonymous.

face-lift *n* plastic surgery to smooth and firm the face; an improvement or renovation, esp to the outside of a building.

facer *n* someone who, or something which, faces; (*inf*) an unexpected setback.

face-saving *adj* allowing the preservation of dignity and prevention of humiliation.

facet *n* a small plane surface (as on a cut gem); an aspect of character, a problem, issue, etc.

facetiae *npl* witty sayings; books characterized by coarse wit.

face-time *n* (*sl*) a spell of duty, esp by US Secret Service agents guarding the President or others.

facetious *adj* joking, esp in an inappropriate manner.—**facetiously** *adv*.—**facetiousness** *n*.

face value *n* the value indicated on the face of (e.g. a coin or share certificate); apparent worth or significance.

facia *see* **fascia**.

facial *adj* of or pertaining to the face. * *n* a beauty treatment for the face.—**facially** *adv*.

facies *n* (*pl* **facies**) the general appearance of a person or a group of plants, animals or rocks; the face.

facile *adj* easy to do; superficial.

facilitate *vt* to make easier; to help forward.—**facilitator** *n*.—**facilitation** *n*.

facility *n* (**facilities**) the quality of being easily done; aptitude, dexterity; something, eg a service or equipment, that makes it easy to do something.

facing *n* a lining at the edge of a garment; a covering on a surface for decoration or protection.

facsimile *n* an exact copy of a book, document, etc; a method of transmitting printed matter (text and graphics) through the telephone system.—*also* **fax**.

fact *n* a thing known to have happened or to exist; reality; a piece of verifiable information; (*law*) an event, occurrence, etc as distinguished from its legal consequences.

faction[1] *n* a small group of people in an organization working together in a common cause against the main body; dissension within a group or organization.—**factional** *adj*.—**factionally** *adv*.—**factious** *adj*.

faction[2] *n* a book, film, etc based on facts but presented as a blend of fact and fiction.

factitious *adj* contrived, artificial.—**factitiously** *adv*.

factitive *adj* (*gram*) causative.

factor *n* any circumstance that contributes towards a result; (*math*) any of two or more numbers that, when multiplied together, form a product; a person who acts for another.

factor 8 *n* a blood-clotting agent used in the treatment of haemophilia.

factorage *n* a factor's commission.

factorial *n* (*math*) an integer multiplied by all lower integers, *eg* $4 \times 3 \times 2 \times 1$.

factorize *vt* to reduce to factors.—**factorization** *n*.

factory *n* (*pl* **factories**) a building or buildings where things are manufactured.

factory farm *n* a farm which rears livestock intensively using modern manufacturing processes.—**factory farming** *n*.

factory ship *n* a ship that processes the catch of a fishing fleet.

factotum *n* a person employed to do all kinds of work.

facts of life *npl* knowledge of human sexual reproduction.

factual *adj* based on, or containing, facts; actual.—**factually** *adv*.

facula *n* (*pl* **faculae**) a bright spot or streak on the surface of the sun.

facultative *adj* enabling; optional; contingent.

faculty *n* (*pl* **faculties**) any natural power of a living organism; special aptitude; a teaching department of a college or university, or the staff of such a department.

fad n a personal habit or idiosyncrasy; a craze.—**faddish, faddy** adj.—**faddism** n.—**faddist** n.

fade vi to lose vigour or brightness of colour gradually; to vanish gradually. * vt to cause (an image or a sound) to increase or decrease in brightness or intensity gradually.—also n.

fadeless adj unfading.

fading n decay; loss of colour; (radio) a deterioration in quality of reception.

faeces npl excrement.—also **feces**.—**faecal, fecal** adj.

faerie, faery n (pl **faeries**) (arch) the fairy world; enchantment.

Faeroese n (pl **Faeroese**) an inhabitant of the Faeroes in the North Atlantic; the language of the Faeroes.—also adj.—also **Faroese**.

fag vti (**fagging, fagged**) to become or cause to be tired by hard work. * n (formerly) a British public schoolboy who performs chores for senior pupils; (inf) drudgery; (sl) a homosexual; (sl) a cigarette.

fag-end n the useless remains of anything; (sl) a cigarette-end.

faggot[1], **fagot** n a bundle of sticks for fuel; (sl) a nasty old woman.

faggot[2] n (sl) in US, a male homosexual.

faggoting, fagoting n a method of decorating textile fabrics.

fah see **fa**.

Fahrenheit adj of, using, or being a temperature scale with the freezing point of water marked at 32° and the boiling point at 212°.

faïence, faience n a type of decorated earthenware.

fail vi to weaken, to fade or die away; to stop operating; to fall short; to be insufficient; to be negligent in duty, expectation, etc; (exam, etc) to be unsuccessful; to become bankrupt. * vt to disappoint the expectations or hopes of; to be unsuccessful in an exam, etc; to leave, to abandon; to grade (a candidate) as not passing a test, etc. * n failure in an examination.

failing n a fault, weakness. * prep in default or absence of.

faille n a soft silk, used for dresses and hat trimmings.

fail-safe adj designed to operate safely even if a fault develops; foolproof.

failure n failing, non-performance, lack of success; the ceasing of normal operation of something; a deficiency; bankruptcy; an unsuccessful person or thing.

fain adv (arch) willingly; gladly. * adj willing; glad.

fainéant, faineant adj indolent.

faint adj dim, indistinct; weak, feeble; timid; on the verge of losing consciousness. * vi to lose consciousness temporarily from a decrease in the supply of blood to the brain, as from shock. * n an act or condition of fainting.—**faintly** adv.—**faintness** n.

faint-hearted adj lacking courage and resolution.

fainting n a sudden and temporary loss of consciousness.

fair[1] adj pleasing to the eye; clean, unblemished; (hair) light-coloured; (weather) clear and sunny; (handwriting) easy to read; just and honest; according to the rules; moderately large; average. * adv in a fair manner; squarely.—**fairness** n.

fair[2] n a gathering for the sale of goods, esp for charity; a competitive exhibition of farm, household, or manufactured goods; a fun-fair.

fair game n a legitimate target for attack or ridicule.

fairground n an open area where fairs are held.

fairing n a structure attached to the exterior of an aircraft, ship, motor vehicle, etc to reduce drag.

fairly adv in a fair manner; justly; moderately.

fair play n justice, honesty; impartiality.

fairway n a navigable channel; the mowed part of a golf course between the tee and the green.

fair-weather adj (friend) unreliable in troubled times.

fairy n (pl **fairies**) an imaginary supernatural being, usu in human form; (sl) a male homosexual.

fairyland n the country of fairies; a beautiful, enchanting place.

fairy ring n a dark or bare ring in grass caused by fungi.

fairy story, fairy tale n a story about fairies; an incredible story; a fabrication.

fait accompli n (pl **faits accomplis**) something already done; an irreversible act.

faith n trust or confidence in a person or thing; a strong conviction, esp a belief in a religion; any system of religious belief; fidelity to one's promises, sincerity.

faithful adj loyal; true; true to the original, accurate.—**faithfully** adv.—**faithfulness** n.

faithless adj treacherous, disloyal; untrustworthy.—**faithlessly** adv.—**faithlessness** n.

fake vt to make (an object) appear more real or valuable in order to deceive; to pretend, simulate. * n a faked article, a forgery; an impostor. * adj counterfeit, not genuine.—**faker** n.

fakir n a Muslim or Hindu religious mendicant or ascetic.

Falangist n a supporter of the Spanish Falange, a fascist party founded in 1933.

falbala n a flounce on a dress.

falcate, falciform adj sickle-shaped.

falchion n a broad, curved sword.

falcon n a type of hawk trained for use in falconry.

falconer n a person who hunts with, or who breeds and trains hawks for hunting.—**falconry** n.

falconet n a small falcon.

falderal n a trifling ornament.

faldstool n an armless chair, used by a bishop.

fall vi (**falling, fell,** pp **fallen**) to descend by force of gravity; to come as if by falling; to collapse; to drop to the ground; to become lower, weaker, less; to lose power, status, etc; to lose office; to slope in a downward direction; to be wounded or killed in battle; to pass into a certain state; to become pregnant; to take place, happen; to be directed by chance; to come by inheritance; (with **about**) to laugh uncontrollably; (with **back**) to retreat; (with **behind**) to fail to keep up with; to become in arrears with; (with **for**) to fall in love with; to be fooled by (a lie, trick, etc); (with **out**) to quarrel; to leave one's place in a military formation; (with **through**) to fail to happen. * n act or instance of falling; something which falls; the amount by which something falls; a decline in status, position; overthrow; a downward slope; a decrease in size, quantity, value; (US) autumn; (wrestling) a scoring move by pinning both shoulders of an opponent to the floor at once.

fallacious adj misleading.—**fallaciously** adv.—**fallaciousness** n.

fallacy n (pl **fallacies**) a false idea; a mistake in reasoning.

fallal n a piece of finery, an ornament.

fallen adj sunk to a lower state or condition; overthrown.

fall guy n (*inf*) a person who is easily cheated; a scapegoat

fallible adj liable to make mistakes.—**fallibly** adv.—**fallibility** n.

Fallopian tube n either of the two tubes through which the egg cells pass from the ovary to the uterus.

fall-out n a deposit of radioactive dust from a nuclear explosion; a by-product.

fallow[1] adj (*land*) ploughed and left unplanted for a season or more.

fallow[2] adj yellowish-brown.

fallow deer n a small European deer with a brownish-yellow coat which becomes spotted with white in summer.

false adj wrong, incorrect; deceitful; artificial; disloyal, treacherous; misleading, fallacious.—**falsely** adv.—**falseness** n.

falsehood n a being untrue; the act of deceiving; a lie.

falsetto n (*pl* **falsettos**) an artificial tone higher in key than the natural compass of the voice.

falsify vt (**falsifying, falsified**) to misrepresent; to alter (a document, etc) fraudulently; to prove false.—**falsification** n.

falsity n (*pl* **falsities**) the quality of being false; an error, a lie.

falter vi to move or walk unsteadily, to stumble; to hesitate or stammer in speech; to be weak or unsure, to waver.—**falteringly** adv.

fame n the state of being well known; good reputation.—**famed** adj.

familiar adj well-acquainted; friendly; common; well-known; too informal, presumptuous. * n a spirit or demon supposed to aid a witch, etc; an intimate.—**familiarly** adv.—**familiarity** n.

familiarize vt to make well known or acquainted; to make (something) well known.—**familiarization** n.

family n (*pl* **families**) parents and their children; a person's children; a set of relatives; the descendants of a common ancestor; any group of persons or things related in some way; a group of related plants or animals; a unit of a crime syndicate (as the Mafia).

family circle n close relatives.

family name n a surname.

family planning n birth control.

family tree n a genealogical diagram.

famine n an acute scarcity of food in a particular area; an extreme scarcity of anything.

famish vti to make or be very hungry.

famous adj renowned; (*inf*) excellent.—**famously** adv.

famulus n (*pl* **famuli**) a magician's assistant.

fan[1] n a handheld or mechanical device used to set up a current of air. * vt (**fanning, fanned**) to cool, as with a fan; to ventilate; to stir up, to excite; to spread out like a fan.

fan[2] n an enthusiastic follower of some sport, hobby, person, etc.

fanatic n a person who is excessively enthusiastic about something.—**fanatical** adj.—**fanatically** adv.

fanaticism n excessive enthusiasm.

fanaticize vti to make or become fanatical.

fan belt n the belt that drives the cooling fan in a car engine.

fancied adj imaginary.

fancier n a person with a special interest in something, esp plant or animal breeding.

fanciful adj not factual, imaginary; indulging in fancy; elaborate or intricate in design.—**fancifully** adv.

fan club n an organized group of followers of a celebrity.

fancy n (*pl* **fancies**) imagination; a mental image; a whim; fondness. * adj (**fancier, fanciest**) not based on fact, imaginary; elegant or ornamental. * vt (**fancying, fancied**) to imagine; to have a fancy or liking for; (*inf*) to be sexually attracted to.

fancy dress n a costume worn at masquerades or parties, usu representing an animal, historical character, etc.

fancy-free adj uncommitted, carefree.

fancy man n (*sl*) a woman's lover; a pimp.

fancy woman n (*sl*) a mistress, prostitute.

fancywork n ornamental needlework.

fandango n (*pl* **fandangos**) a Spanish dance, music for this dance, tomfoolery.

fanfare n a flourish of trumpets.

fang n a long sharp tooth, as in a canine; the long hollow tooth through which venomous snakes inject poison.

fanlight n a semicircular window with radiating bars like the ribs of a fan.

fanny n (*pl* **fannies**) (*vulg*) the female genitals; (*US sl*) the buttocks.

fantail n a pigeon with a tail that opens out like a fan.

fantan n a Chinese gambling game in which players make guesses about hidden counters.

fantasia n an improvised musical or prose composition.

fantasize vt to imagine in an extravagant way. * vi to daydream.

fantast n a visionary or dreamer.

fantastic adj unrealistic, fanciful; unbelievable; imaginative; (*inf*) wonderful.—**fantastically** adv.

fantasy n (*pl* **fantasies**) imagination; a product of the imagination, esp an extravagant or bizarre notion or creation; an imaginative poem, play or novel.

fanzine n a magazine produced by and for the fans of a celebrity, football club, etc.

FAO abbr = Food and Agricultural Organization.

far adj (**farther, farthest** or **further, furthest**) remote in space or time; long; (*political views, etc*) extreme * adv very distant in space, time, or degree; to or from a distance in time or position, very much.—**farness** n.

farad n a unit of electrical capacitance.

faradic adj pertaining to the phenomenon of induced electricity, or to faradization.

faradize vt to treat by use of a faradic current.—**faradization** n.—**faradizer** n

farandole n a lively dance, originating in Provence.

faraway adj distant, remote; dreamy.

farce n a style of light comedy; a drama using such comedy; a ludicrous situation.—**farcical** adj.—**farcically** adv.

farceur, farceuse n a writer of or actor in a farce; a wit.

farcy n (*pl* **farcies**) a disease of horses, closely allied to glanders.

fardel n (*arch*) a bundle or burden.

fare n money paid for transportation; a passenger in public transport; food. * vi to be in a specified condition.

Far East n the countries of East and Southeast Asia including China, Japan, North and South Korea, Indochina, eastern Siberia and adjacent islands.

farewell interj goodbye.—*also* n.

far-fetched adj unlikely.

far-flung adj spread over a wide area; remote.

farina n flour or meal obtained by grinding the seeds of cereals and leguminous plants; starch.

farinaceous adj consisting of, or made from, farina; mealy.

farinose adj producing farina; resembling farina.

farm n an area of land (with buildings) on which crops and animals are raised. * vt to grow crops or breed livestock; to cultivate, as land; to breed fish commercially; (with out) to put out (work, etc) to be done by others, to subcontract.

farmer n a person who manages or operates a farm.

farm hand n a worker on a farm.

farmhouse n a house on a farm.

farming adj pertaining to, or engaged in, agriculture. * n the business or practice of agriculture.

farmstead n a farm with the buildings belonging to it.

farmyard n a yard close to or surrounded by farm buildings.

faro n a gambling card game.

farouche adj sullen; unsociable.

far-out adj (sl) weird, bizarre; fantastic, wonderful. * interj used to express delight.

farrago n (pl **farragoes**) a confused collection.—**farraginous** adj.

far-reaching adj having serious or widespread consequences.

farrier n a person who shoes horses.

farrow n a litter of pigs. * vti to give birth to (pigs).

far-seeing adj having foresight.

fart vi (vulg) to expel wind from the anus.—also n.

farther adj at or to a greater distance. * adv to a greater degree.

farthest adj at or to the greatest distance. * adv to the greatest degree.

farthing n a former British monetary unit.

farthingale n a hooped support worn beneath a skirt to expand it at the hip line.

fasces npl a bundle of rods with an axe used in ancient Rome as a symbol of authority.

fascia n (pl **fasciae**) the instrument panel of a motor vehicle, the dashboard; the flat surface above a shop front, with the owner's name, etc.—also **facia**.

fascicle n one part of a book published by instalments (—also **fascicule**); a small collection, group or bundle; (bot) a cluster of leaves, roots, etc.

fascicular, fasciculate adj (bot) arranged in fascicles.

fascicule n a fascicle.

fasciculus n (pl **fasciculi**) (anat) a bundle of nerve fibres; a fascicle.

fascinate vt to hold the attention of, to attract irresistibly.—**fascination** n.

fascinating adj having great interest or charm.

fascine n a long bundle of sticks bound together, used for fortifying ditches, building earthworks, etc.

Fascism n a system of government characterized by dictatorship, belligerent nationalism, racism, and militarism.—**Fascist** n, adj.

fash vti (Scot) to bother, worry. * n worry; trouble.

fashion n the current style of dress, conduct, speech, etc; the manner or form of appearance or action. * vt to make in a particular form; to suit or adapt.—**fashioner** n.

fashionable adj conforming to the current fashion; attracting or frequented by people of fashion.—**fashionably** adv.

fast[1] adj swift, quick; (clock) ahead of time; firmly attached, fixed; (colour, dye) non-fading; wild, promiscuous. * adv firmly, thoroughly, rapidly, quickly.

fast[2] vi to go without all or certain foods. * n a period of fasting.

fastback n a car with a roof that slopes to the back.

fast breeder reactor n a nuclear reactor that produces more fissile material than it uses.

fasten vti to secure firmly; to attach; to fix or direct (the eyes, attention) steadily.

fastener, fastening n a clip, catch, etc for fastening.

fast food n food, such as hamburgers, kebabs, pizzas, etc prepared and served quickly.

fast-forward vt to move (video or music tape, etc) on at high speed.

fastidious adj hard to please; daintily refined; over-sensitive.—**fastidiously** adv.—**fastidiousness** n.

fastigiate adj (biol) narrowing at the apex.

fastness n swiftness; colourfast quality; a stronghold.

fast track n a hectic and competitive lifestyle or career.—**fast-track** adj.

fat adj (**fatter, fattest**) plump; thick; fertile; profitable. * n an oily or greasy material found in animal tissue and plant seeds; the richest or best part of anything; a superfluous part.—**fatness** n.

fatal adj causing death; disastrous (to); fateful.—**fatally** adv.

fatalism n belief that all events are predetermined by fate and therefore inevitable; acceptance of this doctrine.—**fatalist** n.—**fatalistic** adj.

fatality n (pl **fatalities**) a death caused by a disaster or accident; a person killed in such a way; a fatal power or influence.

fat cat n (sl) a rich person.

fate n the ultimate power that predetermines events, destiny; the ultimate end, outcome; misfortune, doom, death.

fated adj doomed; destined by fate.

fateful adj having important, usu unpleasant, consequences.—**fatefully** adv.

Fates npl (Greek myth) the three goddesses of destiny, Atropos, Clotho and Lachesis.

fathead n (inf) an idiot.

father n a male parent; an ancestor; a founder or originator; (with cap) God; a title of respect applied to monks, priests, etc. * vt to be the father of; to found, originate.—**fatherhood** n.

father-in-law n (pl **fathers-in-law**) the father of one's husband or wife.

fatherland n one's native country.

fatherless adj without a living father.

fatherly adj pertaining to a father; kind, affectionate, as a father. * adv like a father.

fathom n a nautical measure of 6 feet (1.83 m). * vt to measure the depth of; to understand.

fatidic, fatidical adj having the gift of prophecy.

fatigue n tiredness from physical or mental effort; the tendency of a material to break under repeated stress; any of the menial or manual tasks performed by military personnel; (pl) the clothing worn on fatigue or in the field. * vti (**fatiguing, fatigued**) to make or become tired.

fatling n a young animal fattened for slaughter.

fatten vt to make fat or fleshy; to make abundant.—**fattening** adj.

fat transfer n a cosmetic surgery procedure to take fat from parts of the body, eg hips, and insert it in the face to reduce wrinkling.

fatty acid n any of various organic carboxylic acids (e.g. palmitic, stearic and oleic) present in fats and oils.

fatty adj (**fattier, fattiest**) resembling or containing fat. * n (pl **fatties**) (inf) a fat person.

fatuous *adj* foolish, idiotic.—**fatuously** *adv.*—**fatuousness** *n.*—**fatuity** *n.*

fatwa, fatwah *n* a decision by a mufti or Muslim judge.

faubourg *n* a suburb, esp of Paris in France.

faucal *adj* (*anat*) of the fauces; (*sound*) deeply guttural.

fauces *n* (*pl* **fauces**) (*anat*) the upper part of the throat.

faucet *n* a fixture for draining off liquid (as from a pipe or cask); a device controlling the flow of liquid through a pipe or from a container (—*also* **tap**).

faugh *interj* an expression of disgust or abhorrence.

fault *n* a failing, defect; a minor offence; (*tennis, etc*) an incorrect serve or other error; a fracture in the earth's crust causing displacement of strata. * *vt* to find fault with, blame. * *vi* to commit a fault.

fault-finding *adj* censorious, critical.—**fault-finder** *n.*

faultless *adj* without fault; perfect; blameless.—**faultlessly** *adv.*—**faultlessness** *n.*

faulty *adj* (**faultier, faultiest**) imperfect; defective; wrong.—**faultily** *adv.*—**faultiness** *n.*

faun *n* (*Roman myth*) a woodland deity, half man, half beast.

fauna *n* (*pl* **faunas, faunae**) the animals of a region, period, or specific environment.

faute de mieux in the absence of anything better.

fauteuil *n* an armchair; a stall in a theatre.

faux pas *n* (*pl* **faux pas**) an embarrassing social blunder.

faveolate *adj* honeycombed.

favonian *adj* of or pertaining to the west wind; (*poet*) favourable.

favour, favor *n* goodwill; approval; a kind or helpful act; partiality; a small gift given out at a party; (*usu pl*) a privilege granted or conceded, esp sexual. * *vt* to regard or treat with favour; to show support for; to oblige (with); to afford advantage to, facilitate.

favourable, favorable *adj* expressing approval; pleasing; propitious; conducive (to).—**favourably, favorably** *adv.*

favourite, favorite *n* a favoured person or thing; a competitor expected to win. * *adj* most preferred.

favouritism, favoritism *n* the showing of unfair favour.

fawn[1] *n* a young deer; a yellowish-brown colour. * *adj* fawn-coloured.

fawn[2] *vi* (*dogs, etc*) to crouch, etc in a show of affection; to flatter in an obsequious manner.—**fawner** *n.*—**fawning** *n.*

fax *n* a document sent by facsimile transmission; a device for sending faxes. * *vt* to send (a document) by facsimile transmission.

fay *n* a fairy.

faze *vt* (*inf*) to disturb; to discompose, to disconcert; to daunt.

FBI *abbr* = Federal Bureau of Investigation.

FC *abbr* (Brit) = Football Club.

Fe (*chem symbol*) iron.

fealty *n* (*pl* **fealties**) (*feudal society*) the loyalty due from a vassal to his feudal lord.

fear *n* an unpleasant emotion excited by danger, pain, etc; a cause of fear; anxiety; deep reverence. * *vt* to feel fear, be afraid of; to be apprehensive, anxious; to be sorry. * *vi* to be afraid or apprehensive.—**fearless** *adj.*—**fearlessly** *adv.*—**fearlessness** *n.*

fearful *adj* causing intense fear; timorous; apprehensive (of); (*inf*) very great, very bad.—**fearfully** *adv.*

fearless *adj* brave, intrepid.—**fearlessly** *adv.*—**fearlessness** *n.*

fearnought, fearnaught *n* a strong woollen cloth.

fearsome *adj* causing fear, frightful.

feasible *adj* able to be done or implemented, possible.—**feasibly** *adv.*—**feasibility** *n.*

feast *n* an elaborate meal prepared for some special occasion; something that gives abundant pleasure; a periodic religious celebration. * *vi* to have or take part in a feast. * *vt* to entertain with a feast.—**feaster** *n.*

feat *n* an action of remarkable strength, skill, or courage.

feather *n* any of the light outgrowths that form the covering of a bird, consisting of a hollow central shaft with a vane of fine barbs on each side; a plume; something resembling a feather; the water thrown up by the turn of the blade of an oar. * *vt* to ornament with feathers; to turn (an oar or propeller blade) so that the edge is foremost.—**feathering** *n.*—**feathery** *adj.*

feather bed *n* a mattress stuffed with feathers.

featherbrain, featherhead *n* (*inf*) a silly, forgetful person.

featherbrained *adj* frivolous, giddy.

featheredge *n* a thin piece of board with one wedge-shaped side.

featherstitch *n* a zigzag stitch with a featherlike appearance.

featherweight *n* a lightweight thing or person; an insignificant thing or person; a boxer weighing from 118–126 lbs (53.5–57 kg); a wrestler weighing from 127–137 lbs (58–62 kg).

feathery *adj* like or covered with feathers.—**featheriness** *n.*

feature *n* any of the parts of the face; a characteristic trait of something; a special attraction or distinctive quality of something; a prominent newspaper article, etc; the main film in a cinema programme. * *vti* to make or be a feature of (something).

featureless *adj* lacking prominent or distinctive features.

Feb. *abbr* = February.

febrifuge *n* a drug that reduces fever.—**febrifugal** *adj.*

febrile *adj* of fever; feverish.

February *n* (*pl* **Februaries**) the second month of the year, having 28 days (or 29 days in leap years).

feces *see* **faeces.**

feckless *adj* incompetent, untrustworthy.—**fecklessly** *adv.*—**fecklessness** *n.*

feculent *adj* muddy, turbid; full of dregs or sediment.—**feculence** *adj.*

fecund *adj* fertile, prolific.—**fecundity** *n.*

fecundate *vt* to impregnate.—**fecundation** *n.*

fed *see* **feed.**

fedayee *n* (*pl* **fedayeen**) an Arab commando or guerrilla.

federal *adj* designating, or of a union of states, etc, in which each member surrenders some of its power to a central authority; of a central government of this type.—**federalism** *n.*—**federalist** *n.*—**federally** *adv.*

federalize *vt* to unite (states, etc) in a federal union; to put under federal authority.—**federalization** *n.*

federate *vti* to unite in a federation. * *adj* united in a league; on a federal basis.—**federative.***adj.*

federation *n* a union of states, groups, etc, in which each subordinates its power to a central authority; a federated organization.

fedora *n* a soft felt hat with a curled brim and a crown creased lengthways.

fee *n* the price paid for the advice or service of a professional; a charge for some privilege, as membership of a club; (*law*) an inheritance in land.

feeble *adj* weak, ineffective.—**feebly** *adv.*—**feebleness** *n.*

feeble-minded *adj* mentally defective; of low intelligence.

feed *vb* (**feeding, fed**) *vt* to give food to; to give as food to; to supply with necessary material; to gratify. * *vi* to consume food. * *n* food for animals; material fed into a machine; the part of a machine supplying this material.

feedback *n* a return to the input of part of the output of a system; information about a product, service, etc returned to the supplier for purposes of evaluation.

feeder *n* a person or thing that feeds; a baby's feeding-bottle; a device for supplying material to a machine; a subsidiary road, railway, etc acting as a link with the central transport network.

feel *vb* (**feeling, felt**) *vt* to perceive or explore by the touch; to find one's way by cautious trial; to be conscious of, experience; to have a vague or instinctual impression of; to believe, consider. * *vi* to be able to experience the sensation of touch; to be affected by; to convey a certain sensation when touched. * *n* the sense of touch; feeling; a quality as revealed by touch.

feeler *n* a tactile organ (as a tentacle or antenna) of an animal; a tentative approach or suggestion to test another person's reactions.

feeling *n* the sense of touch; mental or physical awareness; a physical or mental impression; a state of mind; sympathy; emotional sensitivity; a belief or opinion arising from emotion; (*pl*) emotions, sensibilities.

feet *see* **foot.**

feign *vt* to invent; to pretend.

feint *n* a pretended attack, intended to take the opponent off his guard, as in boxing.—*also vi.*

feldspar *n* any member of the group of hard rock-forming minerals.—*also* **felspar.**—**feldspathic, felspathic** *adj.*

felicitate *vt* to congratulate.—**felicitation** *n.*

felicitous *adj* (*words, etc*) apt, well-chosen; agreeable in manner; happy.—**felicitously** *adv.*

felicity *n* (*pl* **felicities**) happiness; apt and pleasing style in writing, speech, etc.

feline *adj* of cats; cat-like.—**felinity** *n.*

fell[1] *see* **fall.**

fell[2] *vt* to cut, beat, or knock down; to kill, to sew (a seam) by folding one raw edge under the other.

fell[3] *n* a skin, hide, pelt.

fell[4] *adj* (*poet*) cruel, fierce, bloody, deadly.

fellah *n* (*pl* **fellahs, fellahin, fellaheen**) an Arab peasant.

fellatio *n* sexual stimulation of the penis with the mouth.

felloe, felly *n* (*pl* **felloes, fellies**) one of the curved pieces of wood which form the outer section of a wheel; the outer section of a wheel, the circumference.

fellow *n* an associate; a comrade; an equal in power, rank, or position; the other of a pair, a mate; a member of the governing body in some colleges and universities; a member of a learned society; (*inf*) a man or boy. * *adj* belonging to the same group or class.

fellowship *n* companionship; a mutual sharing; a group of people with the same interests; the position held by a college fellow.

felo de se *n* (*pl* **felones de se, felos de se**) the act of suicide; a person who commits suicide.

felon *n* a person guilty of a felony.

felonious *adj* done with the intention of committing a crime; criminal; malignant.—**feloniously** *adv.*—**feloniousness** *n.*

felony *n* (*pl* **felonies**) (*formerly*) a grave crime.

felspar *see* **feldspar.**

felt[1] *see* **feel.**

felt[2] *n* a fabric made from woollen fibres, often mixed with fur or hair, pressed together. * *vti* to make into or become like felt.

felting *n* the material from which felt is made; the process of manufacturing felt.

felucca *n* a small boat with oars and lateen sails, used in the Mediterranean.

female *adj* of the sex that produces young; of a woman or women; (*pipe, plug, etc*) designed with a hollow part for receiving an inserted piece. * *n* a female animal or plant.

feminine *adj* of, resembling, or appropriate to women; (*gram*) of that gender to which words denoting females belong.—**femininity** *n.*

feminism *n* the movement to win political, economic and social equality for women.—**feminist** *adj, n.*

feminize *vti* to make or become feminine.—**feminization** *n.*

femme de chambre *n* (*pl* **femmes de chambre**) a chambermaid.

femme fatale *n* (*pl* **femmes fatales**) a dangerously seductive woman.

femur *n* (*pl* **femurs, femora**) the thighbone.—**femoral** *adj.*

fen *n* an area of low-lying marshy or flooded land.

fence *n* a barrier put round land to mark a boundary, or prevent animals, etc from escaping; a receiver of stolen goods. * *vt* to surround with a fence; to keep (out) as by a fence. * *vi* to practise fencing; to make evasive answers; to act as a fence for stolen goods.—**fencer** *n.*

fencing *n* fences; material for making fences; the art of fighting with foils or other types of sword.

fend *vi* (*with* **for**) to provide a livelihood for.

fender *n* anything that protects or fends off something else, as old tyres along the side of a vessel, or the part of a car body over the wheel.

fenestrated, fenestrate *adj* having windows.

fenestration *n* the design and arrangement of windows in a building.

fennec *n* a type of small fox, found in Africa.

fennel *n* a European herb of the carrot family grown for its foliage and aromatic seeds; a herb grown for its edible bulbous stem tasting of aniseed.

fennelflower *n* one of a variety of Mediterranean plants, with white, blue or yellow flowers.—*also* **love-in-a-mist.**

fenny *adj* marshy.

fenugreek *n* a Mediterranean plant with white flowers and pungent seeds.

feoff *see* **fief.**

fer-de-lance *n* a yellowish, highly poisonous snake of tropical America.

feral, ferine *adj* wild, untamed; like a wild beast.

feretory *n* (*pl* **feretories**) a shrine for the relics of a saint; a chapel for keeping this.

ferial *adj* (*RC: Church*) (*a day*) ordinary, not a festival or a fast.

ferment *n* an agent causing fermentation, as yeast; excitement, agitation. * *vti* to (cause to) undergo fermentation; to (cause to) be excited or agitated.—**fermentable** *adj.*—**fermenter** *n.*

fermentation n the breakdown of complex molecules in organic components caused by the influence of yeast or other substances.

fermentative adj of or pertaining to fermentation; capable of or causing fermentation.

fermion n a type of subatomic particle.

fermium n an artificially-produced radioactive metallic element.

fern n any of a large class of nonflowering plants having roots, stems, and fronds, and reproducing by spores.—**ferny** adj.

fernery n (pl **ferneries**) a place for growing ferns.

ferny adj (**fernier, ferniest**) full of ferns; of or characteristic of ferns.

ferocious adj savage, fierce.—**ferociously** adv.—**ferocity, ferociousness** n.

ferrate n a salt of ferric acid.

ferret n a variety of the polecat, used in unearthing rabbits. * vt to drive out of a hiding-place; (with **out**) to reveal by persistent investigation. * vi to hunt with ferrets.—**ferreter** n.—**ferrety** adj.

ferriage n the act of conveying by ferry; the fare paid for this.

ferric adj of or containing iron.

ferriferous adj yielding iron.

Ferris wheel n a large upright revolving wheel with suspended seats, popular in amusement parks.

ferroconcrete n reinforced concrete.

ferrocyanic acid n an acid formed by the union of iron and cyanogen.

ferromagnetism n magnetism possessed by iron, and some other metals, which is retained even after the removal of the magnetizing field.—**ferromagnetic** adj.

ferromanganese n an alloy of iron and manganese.

ferrotype n a photograph taken on a sensitized iron plate.

ferrous adj containing iron.

ferruginous adj containing, or impregnated with, iron; rust-coloured, reddish brown.

ferrule n a metal ring or cap on a cane, umbrella, etc, to keep it from splitting.—also **ferule**.

ferry vt (**ferrying, ferried**) to convey (passengers, etc) over a stretch of water; to transport from one place to another, esp along a regular route. * n (pl **ferries**) a boat used for ferrying; a ferrying service; the location of a ferry.—**ferryman** n (pl **ferrymen**).

fertile adj able to bear offspring; (land) easily supporting plants and vegetation; (animals) capable of breeding; (eggs) able to grow and develop; prolific; (mind, brain) inventive.—**fertility, fertileness** n.

fertility n the state or quality of being fertile.

fertilize vt to make (soil) fertile by adding nutrients; to impregnate; to pollinate.—**fertilization** n.

fertilizer n natural organic or artificial substances used to enrich the soil.

ferula n (pl **ferulas, ferulae**) a genus of plants of the parsley family, from one of which asafoetida is produced.

ferule see **ferrule**.

fervency n earnestness; ardour.

fervent, fervid adj passionate; zealous.—**fervently, fervidly** adv.—**fervency** n.

fervour, fervor n intensity of feeling; zeal; warmth.

fescue n a kind of grass, often grown for pasture and fodder.

fesse n (her) a broad horizontal band across the middle of a shield.

festal adj of a feast or holiday; festive.—**festally** adv.

fester vti to become or cause to become infected; to suppurate; to rankle.

festival n a time of celebration; performances of music, plays, etc given periodically.

festive adj merry, joyous.—**festively** adv.—**festiveness** n.

festivity n (pl **festivities**) a festive celebration.

festoon n a decorative garland of flowers, etc hung between two points. * vt to adorn as with festoons.—**festoonery** n.

feta n a type of white goat's milk cheese, esp popular in Greece.

fetal adj pertaining to the fetus.—also **foetal**.

fetch[1] vt to go for and bring back; to cause to come; (goods) to sell for (a certain price); (inf) to deal (a blow, slap, etc); (with **up**) to come to stand, arrive at; **fetch and carry** to run errands for another.—**fetcher** n.

fetch[2] n an apparition of a living person, a wraith; a person's double.

fetching adj attractive.—**fetchingly** adv.

fête, fete n a festival; a usu outdoor sale, bazaar or entertainment in aid of charity. * vt to honour or entertain (as if) with a fête.

fetial n (pl **fetiales**) a priestly herald in ancient Rome who performed rites accompanying a declaration of war or peace.

feticide n the destruction of a fetus in the womb.—also **foeticide**.

fetid adj stinking.—also **foetid**.

fetish, fetich n an object believed by primitive peoples to have magical properties; any object or activity regarded with excessive devotion.

fetishism, fetichism n the transfer of sexual desire to an inanimate object, or to some part of the body other than the sexual organs; worship of, or belief in, fetishes—**fetishist, fetichist** n.

fetlock, fetterlock n the joint on a horse's leg behind and above the hoof.

fetter n (usu pl) a shackle for the feet; anything that restrains. * vt to put into fetters; to impede, restrain.—**fetterer** n.

fettle n good condition or repair.

fettucine, fettuccine, fettucini n a kind of pasta cut in strips.

fetus n (pl **fetuses**) the unborn young of an animal, esp in its later stages; in humans, the offspring in the womb from the fourth month until birth.—also **foetus** (pl **foetuses**).—**fetal, foetal** adj.

feud n a state of hostilities, esp between individuals, families, or clans; a dispute.—also vi.

feudal adj pertaining to feudalism; (inf) old-fashioned, redundant.

feudalism n the economic and social system in medieval Europe, in which land, worked by serfs, was held by vassals in exchange for military and other services to overlords.—**feudalist** n.—**feudalistic** adj.

feudality n (pl **feudalities**) the state of being feudal; a feudal estate.

feudalize vt to make feudal.—**feudalization** n.

feudatory adj pertaining to, or held by, feudal tenure.

feudist n someone taking part in a feud or argument.

feuilleton n in France, etc, the section of a newspaper containing reviews, fiction, etc; an article in this; serialization in a newspaper.—**feuilletonist** n — **feuilletonistic** adj

fever n an abnormally increased body temperature; any disease marked by a high fever; a state of restless excitement.—**fevered** adj.

feverfew n a perennial European herb, formerly used to reduce fevers.

feverish, feverous adj having a fever; indicating a fever; restlessly excited.—**feverishly** adv.—**feverishness** n.

few adj, n a small number, not many.—**fewness** n.

fey adj strange and unusual.—**feyness** n.

fez n (pl **fezzes**) a red brimless high cap, usu with black tassel, worn esp by men in eastern Mediterranean countries.

ff abbr = and the following pages; (mus) fortissimo—very loud.

fiacre n a type of horse-drawn carriage.

fiancé n a person engaged to be married.—**fiancée** nf.

fiasco n (pl **fiascos, fiascoes**) a complete and humiliating failure.

fiat n an order by authority; a decree.

fib n a lie about something unimportant. * vi (**fibbing, fibbed**) to tell a gib.—**fibber** n.

fibre, fiber n a natural or synthetic thread, eg from cotton or nylon, which is spun into yarn; a material composed of such yarn; texture; strength of character; a fibrous substance, roughage.—**fibred, fibered** adj.

fibreglass, fiberglass n glass in fibrous form, often bonded with plastic, used in making various products.

fibre optics, fiber optics n (sing) the transmission of information in the form of light signals along thin transparent fibres of glass.—**fibre-optic, fiber-optic** adj.

fibril, fibrilla n (pl **fibrils, fibrillae**) a small fibre.—**fibrilar, fibrillar, fibrillose** adj

fibrillation n the rapid and irregular twitching of muscle fibres, esp in the heart.

fibrin n a white protein in the blood, which causes coagulation.

fibrinous adj composed of, or resembling,fibrin.

fibroid adj (anat) containing or resembling fibre. * n a benign tumour in the uterus.

fibroin n a protein that is the main constituent of silk and cobwebs.

fibroma n (pl **fibromata, fibromas**) a benign fibrous tumour.

fibrosis n the abnormal growth of fibrous tissue in an organ or part of the body.

fibrositis n inflammation of fibrous tissues, esp muscles.

fibrous adj composed of fibres.—**fibrousness** n.

fibula n (pl **fibulae, fibulas**) the outer of the two bones of the lower leg.—**fibular** adj.

fiche n (pl **fiche**) a microfiche.

fichu n a woman's light three-cornered scarf worn over the neck and shoulders.

fickle adj inconstant; capricious.—**fickleness** n.

fictile adj moulded from clay; able to be moulded from clay.

fiction n an invented story; any literary work with imaginary characters and events, as a novel, play, etc; such works collectively.—**fictional** adj.—**fictionally** adv.

fictitious adj imaginary, not real; feigned.—**fictitiously** adv.

fictive adj pertaining to fiction; creating or created by the imagination.—**fictively** adv.

fid n (naut) an iron or wooden bar used to support a topmast; a pin used to open the strands of a rope.

fid. abbr = fidelity.

fiddle n (inf) a violin; (sl) a swindle. * vt (inf) to play on a violin; (sl) to swindle; to falsify. * vi to handle restlessly, to fidget.—**fiddler** n.

fiddle-de-dee interj an expression of incredulity or impatience.

fiddle-faddle n nonsense; trifles. * vi to fuss over unimportant matters.

fiddlehead n an ornament at the prow of a ship.

fiddler n one who fiddles; (inf) a violinist.

fiddlestick n a bow for playing the violin.

fiddlesticks interj nonsense!

fiddling adj trifling, petty.

fidelity n (pl **fidelities**) faithfulness, loyalty; truthfulness; accuracy in reproducing sound.

fidget vi to (cause to) move restlessly. * n nervous restlessness; a fussy person.—**fidgetingly** adv.—**fidgety** adj.

fiducial adj (physics) taken as a standard of reference; based on trust or faith.—**fiducially** adv.

fiduciary adj of, held or given in trust; (paper currency) depending on public confidence for value. * n a trustee.

fie interj for shame; an expression of disgust or dismay.

fief n (feudalism) heritable land held by a vassal; an area in which one has control or influence.—also **feoff**.

field n an area of land cleared of trees and buildings, used for pasture or crops; an area rich in a natural product (eg gold, coal); a battlefield; a sports ground; an area affected by electrical, magnetic or gravitational influence, etc; the area visible through an optical lens; a division of activity, knowledge, etc; all competitors in a contest; (comput) a section of a record in a database. * vt (cricket, baseball, etc) to catch or stop and return the ball as a fielder; to put (eg. a team) into the field to play; (inf) to handle (eg questions) successfully.

field[2] see **fjeld**.

field day n a day of sports and athletic competition; (inf) any day of unusual happenings or success.

fielder n (cricket, baseball, etc) a person who is not in the batting side, a person who fields.—also **fieldsman** (pl **fieldsmen**).

field event n (usu pl) an athletic competition involving jumping or throwing, as opposed to running.

fieldfare n a European thrush, which migrates to Britain for winter.

field glasses npl small, portable binoculars for use outdoors.

field hockey n an outdoor game played by two teams of 11 players with a ball and clubs curved at one end —also **hockey**.

fieldmouse n a small, noctural mouse that lives in woods and fields.

fieldwork n research done outside the laboratory or place of work by scientists, archaeologists, social workers, etc.—**fieldworker** n.

fiend n an evil spirit; an inhumanly wicked person; (inf) an avid fan.—**fiendish** adj.—**fiendishly** adv.

fierce adj ferociously hostile; angry, violent; intense; strong, extreme.—**fiercely** adv.—**fierceness** n.

fiery adj (**fierier, fieriest**) like or consisting of fire; the colour of fire; intensely hot; spicy; passionate, ardent; impetuous; irascible.—**fierily** adv.—**fieriness** n.

fiesta n a religious celebration, a festival, esp in Spain and Latin America.

fife *n* a type of small flute with a shrill sound used esp in military music to accompany drums.—**fifer** *n*.

fife rail *n* (*naut*) a rail round the mast holding belaying pins.

fifteen *adj, n* one more than fourteen; the symbol for this (15, XV, xv); the first point scored by a side in a game of tennis; a rugby football team.—**fifteenth** *adj, n*.

fifth *adj, n* last of five; (being) one of five equal parts; (*mus*) an interval of three tones and a semitone; a gear in a motor vehicle used when driving at speed.—**fifthly** *adv*.

fifth column *n* a subversive organization within a country, which is ready to give help to an enemy.—**fifth columnist** *n*.

fifty *adj, n* (*pl* **fifties**) five times ten; the symbol for this (50, L, l).—**fiftieth** *adj*.

fifty-fifty *adj, adv* (*inf*) evenly, equally; (*chance*) an equal possibility of winning.

fig *n* a tree yielding a soft, pear-shaped fruit; a thing of little or no importance.

fig. *abbr* = figure; figuratively.

fight *vb* (**fighting, fought**) *vi* to engage in battle in war or in single combat; to strive, struggle (for). * *vt* to engage in or carry on a conflict with; to achieve (one's way) by fighting; to strive to overcome; (*with* **off**) to repel; to ward off or repress through effort. * *n* fighting; a struggle or conflict of any kind; a boxing match.—**fighting** *n*.

fighter *n* a person who fights; a person who does not yield easily; an aircraft designed to destroy enemy aircraft.

fighting chance *n* a small chance of success given supreme effort.

figment *n* something imagined or invented.

figurant *n* a ballet dancer who performs as one of a group.—**figurante** *nf*.

figuration *n* the giving of form; representation; a figure, a shape; (*mus*) the use of florid counterpoint.

figurative *adj* metaphorical, not literal; using or full of figures of speech; emblematic; pictorial.—**figuratively** *adv*.

figure *n* a character representing a number; a number; value or price; bodily shape or form; a graphic representation of a thing, person or animal; a design; a geometrical form; a statue; appearance; a personage; (*dancing, skating*) a set of steps or movements; (*pl*) arithmetic. * *vt* to represent in a diagram or outline; to imagine; (*inf*) to consider; (*inf*) to believe; (*with* **out**) (*inf*) to solve. * *vi* to take a part (in), be conspicuous (in); to calculate.—**figurer** *n*.

figured *adj* depicted as a figure; adorned with figures.

figurehead *n* a carved figure on the bow of a ship; a nominal head or leader.

figure of speech *n* an expression not intended to be taken literally, as a metaphor or simile.

figure skating *n* ice skating in which prescribed figures are outlined.

figurine *n* a statuette.

filagree *see* **filigree**.

filament *n* a slender thread or strand; a fibre; the fine wire in an electric light bulb that is made incandescent by current; (*bot*) the anther-bearing stalk of a stamen.—**filamentary, filamentous** *adj*.

filar *adj* of or pertaining to thread; (*microscope, etc*) having fine threads in the eyepiece for measuring tiny distances.

filature *n* the reeling of silk from cocoons; a place where this is done.

filbert *n* the edible nut of the cultivated hazel.

filch *vt* to steal (something of little value), to pilfer.—**filcher** *n*.

file[1] a container for keeping papers, etc, in order; an orderly arrangement of papers; a line of persons or things; (*comput*) a collection of related data under a specific name. * *vt* to dispatch or register; to put on public record. * *vi* to move in a line; to apply.—**filer** *n*.

file[2] *n* a tool, usu steel, with a rough surface for smoothing or grinding. * *vt* to cut or smooth with, or as with, a file; to polish, improve.—**filer** *n*.

filefish *n* (*pl* **filefish, filefishes**) a tropical fish, of the family of triggerfish, with a narrow body and rough skin.

filester *see* **fillister**.

filet *n* a net with a square mesh.

filial *adj* of, or expected from, a son or daughter.—**filially** *adv*.—**filialness** *n*.

filiation *n* the relation of child to father; lineage, line of descent; the formation of branches of a society, etc; a branch so formed.

filibeg *n* a kilt.—*also* **philabeg**.

filibuster *n* a member of a legislature who obstructs a bill by making long speeches. * *vti* to obstruct (a bill) by such methods.—**filibusterer** *n*.

filiform *adj* threadlike.

filigree *n* a kind of lace-like ornamental work in precious metal. * *vt* (**filigreeing, filigreed**) to decorate with filigree.—*also* **filagree**.

filing *n* a particle rubbed off with a file.

Filipino *n* (*pl* **Filipinos**) a native or inhabitant of the Philippines.—*also adj*.

fill *vt* to put as much as possible into; to occupy wholly; to put a person into (a position or job, etc); (*US*) to supply the things called for (in an order, etc); to close or plug (holes, etc); (*with* **in**) to complete (a form, design, etc) by writing or drawing; (*inf*) to provide with the latest news or facts; (*with* **out**) to make fuller or heavier; to fill in (a form, etc). * *vi* to become full; (*with* **in**) to act as a substitute for; (*with* **out**) to become fuller or heavier. * *n* enough to make full or to satisfy; anything that fills.

filler *n* one who or that which fills; a substance used to plug a hole or increase the bulk of something.

fillet *n* a thin boneless strip of meat or fish; a ribbon, etc worn as a headband; (*archit*) a narrow band used between mouldings. * *vt* to bone and slice (fish or meat).

filling *n* a substance used to fill a tooth cavity; the contents of a sandwich, pie, etc. * *adj* (*meal, etc*) substantial.

filling station *n* a place where petrol is sold to motorists, a service station.

fillip *n* a blow with the nail of the finger; a stimulus.

fillister, filister *n* a plane used to cut grooves, rabbets, etc.—*also* **filester**.

filly *n* (*pl* **fillies**) a young female horse, usu less than four years.

film *n* a fine, thin skin, coating, etc; a flexible cellulose material covered with a light-sensitive substance used in photography; a haze or blur; a motion picture. * *vti* to cover or be covered as with a film; to photograph or make a film (of).—**filmic** *adj*.

film card *see* **microfiche**.

film star *n* a leading cinema actor or actress.

filmy *adj* (**filmier, filmiest**) gauzy, transparent; blurred, hazy.—**filmily** *adv*.—**filminess** *n*.

filose *adj* threadlike.

filter *n* a device or substance straining out solid particles, impurities, etc, from a liquid or gas; a device for removing or minimizing electrical oscillations, or sound or light waves, of certain frequencies; a traffic signal at certain road junctions that allows vehicles to turn left or right while the main lights are red. * *vti* to pass through or as through a filter; to remove with a filter.—**filterable, filtrable** *adj*.

filter tip *n* the porous tip of a cigarette designed to reduce the intake of tar during smoking.—**filter-tipped** *adj*.

filth *n* dirt; obscenity.

filthy *adj* (**filthier, filthiest**) dirty, disgusting; obscene; (*inf*) extremely unpleasant.—**filthily** *adv*.—**filthiness** *n*.

filtrate *vt* to filter. * *n* a liquid that has been filtered.—**filtration** *n*.

fimbriate, fimbriated *adj* (*bot*) fringed.

fin *n* an organ by which a fish, etc steers itself and swims; a rubber flipper used for underwater swimming; any fin-shaped object used as a stabilizer, as on an aircraft or rocket. * *vb* (**finning, finned**) *vi* (*fish, whale. etc*) to agitate the fins. * *vt* to furnish with fins.

finable, fineable *adj* liable to a fine.

finagle *vt* (*inf*) to obtain or achieve through cunning or deceit; to use trickery or deceit on someone.

final *adj* of or coming at the end; conclusive. * *n* (*often pl*) the last of a series of contests; a final examination.—**finally** *adv*.

finale *n* the concluding part of any public performance; the last section in a musical composition.

finalist *n* a contestant in a final.

finality *n* (*pl* **finalities**) the state or quality of being final; completeness, conclusiveness.

finalize *vt* to make complete, to bring to an end.—**finalization** *n*.

finally *adv* at last; lastly; completely.

finance *n* the management of money; (*pl*) money resources. * *vt* to supply or raise money for.

financial *adj* of finance.—**financially** *adv*.

financier *n* a person skilled in finance.

finback *n* a whale with a prominent dorsal fin; the rorqual.

finch *n* any of numerous songbirds of the *Fringillidae* family.

find *vb* (**finding, found**) *vt* to discover by chance; to come upon by searching; to perceive; to recover (something lost); to reach, attain; to decide and declare to be; (*with* **out**) to discover; to solve; to detect in an offence. * *vi* to reach a decision (as by a jury). * *n* a discovery, something found.—**findable** *adj*.

finder *n* one who or that which finds; a discoverer; a device for sighting the field of view of a camera, telescope, etc..

fin de siècle *adj* of or typical of the end of a century, esp the 19th century. * *n* the end of a century.

finding *n* a discovery; the conclusion reached by a judicial enquiry.

fine¹ *adj* very good; with no impurities, refined; (*weather*) clear and bright; not heavy or coarse; very thin or small; sharp; subtle; elegant. * *adv* in a fine manner; (*inf*) very well.—**finely** *adv*.—**fineness** *n*.

fine² *n* a sum of money imposed as a punishment. * *vt* to punish by a fine.—**finable, fineable** *adj*.

fine arts *npl* painting, sculpture, engraving, etc valued for their aesthetic qualities.

fine-draw *vt* (**fine-drawing, fine-drew**, *pp* **fine-drawn**) to sew up (a darn) so neatly that the join cannot be noticed; to draw out (wire) to an extreme fineness.—**fine-drawn** *adj*.

finely *adv* in a fine manner; discriminatingly; subtly; in tiny pieces.

fineness *n* the state or quality of being fine; the quantity of pure metal contained in an alloy.

finery *n* (*pl* **fineries**) elaborate clothes, jewellery, etc.

finespun *adj* delicate, fine; over-subtle.

finesse *n* delicacy or subtlety of performance; skilfulness, diplomacy in handling a situation; (*bridge*) an attempt to take a trick with a card lower than a higher card held by an opponent. * *vt* to achieve by finesse; to play (a card) as a finesse.

fine-tooth(ed) comb *n* a comb with closely set fine teeth for trapping nits, etc.

fine-tune *vt* to make fine adjustments to something in order to improve its effectiveness.

finger *n* one of the digits of the hand, usu excluding the thumb; anything shaped like a finger; (*inf*) the breadth of a finger. * *vt* to touch with fingers; (*mus*) to use the fingers in a certain way when playing; to mark this way on music; (*sl*) to inform against.—**fingerer** *n*.

fingerboard *n* the part of a violin, guitar, etc against which the strings are pressed by the fingers.

finger bowl *n* a small bowl containing water for rinsing the fingers at the table.

fingered *adj* marked by handling; having a finger or fingers; (*mus*) marked to show how the fingers are used.

fingering *n* the manner of using the fingers in playing a musical instrument; the indication of this in a musical score.

fingering² *n* a fine knitting yarn.

fingerling *n* a young fish, esp a trout.

fingernail *n* the nail on a finger.

fingerpost *n* a direction post in the shape of a pointing finger.

fingerprint *n* the impression of the ridges on a fingertip, esp as used for purposes of identification.—*also vt*.

fingerstall *n* a protective covering for a finger.

finial *n* (*archit*) a pointed ornament at the top of a spire, gable, etc.—**finialed** *adj*.

finical *adj* fastidious, over-particular, fussy; affectedly fine.—**finicality** *n*.—**finically** *adv*.

finicky, finicking *adj* too particular, fussy.

fining *n* the act or process of clarifying or refining; a liquid used to clarify wine, beer, etc.

finis *n* the end, used at the conclusion of books, films, etc.

finish *vt* to bring to an end, to come to the end of; to consume entirely; to perfect; to give a desired surface effect to. * *vi* to come to an end. * *n* the last part, the end; anything used to finish a surface; the finished effect; means or manner of completing or perfecting; polished manners, speech, etc.—**finisher** *n*.

finishing school *n* a private school for girls which teaches social etiquette.

finite *adj* having definable limits; (*verb form*) having a distinct grammatical person and number.—**finitely** *adv*—**finiteness** *n*.

Finn *n* a native of Finland.

finnan haddock, Finnan haddie *n* a kind of smoked haddock, named after *Findon*, a Scottish fishing village.

finned *adj* having a fin or fins.

Finnish *adj* of or relating to Finland or its language. * *n* the language of Finland.

finny *adj* (**finnier, finniest**) pertaining to, or abounding in, fish; having a fin or fins.

fino *n* (*pl* **finos**) a dry sherry.

fiord *see* **fjord**.

fir *n* a kind of evergreen, cone-bearing tree; its timber.

fire *n* the flame, heat and light of combustion; something burning; burning fuel in a grate to heat a room; an electric or gas fire; a destructive burning; a strong feeling; a discharge of firearms. * *vti* to ignite; to supply with fuel; to bake (bricks, etc) in a kiln; to excite or become excited; to shoot (a gun, etc); to hurl or direct with force; to dismiss from a position.—**fireable** *adj*.—**firer** *n*.

fire alarm *n* a device that uses a bell, hooter, etc to warn of a fire.

firearm *n* a handgun.

fireball *n* a ball of fire; a meteor; the hot gas cloud created by a nuclear explosion.

firebox *n* the furnace in a steam locomotive.

firebrand *n* a piece of burning wood; a person who starts trouble.

firebreak *n* a strip of land cleared of vegetation to halt the spread of a fire.

firebrick *n* a brick made of fireclay to withstand the action of fire.

fire brigade *n* an organized body specially trained and equipped for fighting fires.

firebug *n* (*inf*) an arsonist.

fireclay *n* a fire-resisting clay.

firecracker *n* a small explosive firework.

firedamp *n* a combustible mine gas, chiefly methane.

firedog *n* a metal standard used for open fires to support the logs; andirons.

fire-eater *n* a performer who pretends to eat fire; a quarrelsome person.—**fire-eating** *adj, n*.

fire engine *n* a vehicle equipped for fire-fighting.

fire escape *n* a means of exit from a building, esp a stairway, for use in case of fire.

fire extinguisher *n* a container with a spray nozzle, holding water or chemicals for putting out a fire

firefighter *n* a person who fights fires, esp a member of a fire department; fireman.

firefly *n* (*pl* **fireflies**) a winged nocturnal beetle whose abdomen glows with a soft intermittent light.

fireguard *n* a protective grating placed in frontof a fire.

fire insurance *n* insurance against loss by fire.

fire irons *npl* tools for tending a domestic fire, esp a poker, tongs, and shovel.

firelighter *n* a prepared block of ignitable material used for lighting a fire.

firelock *n* a flintlock.

fireman *n* (*pl* **firemen**) a member of a fire brigade; firefighter; a person employed to tend furnaces.

fireplace *n* a place for a fire, esp a recess in a wall; the area surrounding this.

fireplug *n* a connection in a water main for a hose; a hydrant.

fire power *n* the amount of fire that a military unit can deliver on a target.

fireproof *adj* not easily destroyed by fire. * *vt* to make fireproof.

fire raiser *n* an arsonist.—**fire raising** *n*.

firescreen *n* a movable ornamental screen for keeping the heat of a fire off the face; a screen for decorating an empty fireplace.

fireship *n* a ship filled with explosives to set an enemy's ships on fire.

fireside *n* the area in a room nearest the fireplace; home.

fire station *n* a building where firemen and fire-fighting equipment are based.—*also* **firehouse, station house**.

firetrap *n* a building easily set on fire or hard to get out of if on fire.

firewarden *n* an officer responsible for protecting forests.against fire.

firewater *n* (*inf*) strong alcoholic drink.

firewood *n* wood for fuel.

firework *n* a device packed with explosive and combustible material used to produce noisy and colourful displays; (*pl*) such a display; (*pl*) a fit of temper, an outburst of emotions.

firing *n* baking in intense heat, esp of clay; fuel; the act of discharging a firearm; the act of adding fuel to a fire.

firing line *n* the front line of a military position; the forefront of any activity.

firing squad *n* a detachment with the task of firing a salute at a military funeral or carrying out an execution.

firkin *n* a small wooden barrel containing butter, etc; (*Brit*) a measure of one quarter of a barrel (41 litres/9 gallons).

firm[1] *adj* securely fixed; solid, compact; steady; resolute; definite. * *vti* to make or become firm.—**firmly** *adv*.—**firmness** *n*.

firm[2] *n* a business partnership; a commercial company.

firmament *n* the sky, viewed poetically as a solid arch or vault.—**firmamental** *adj*.

first *adj* before all others in a series; 1st; earliest; foremost, as in rank, quality, etc. * *adv* before anyone or anything else; for the first time; sooner. * *n* any person or thing that is first; the beginning; the winning place, as in a race; low gear; the highest award in a university degree.

first aid *n* emergency treatment for an injury, etc, before regular medical aid is available.

first-born *adj* eldest. * *n* the eldest child in a family.

first-class *adj* of the highest quality, as in accommodation, travel. * *n* the best accommodation on a plane, train, etc; the highest class in an examination, etc.

first-degree burn *n* (*med*) a mild burn causing a painful reddening of the skin but no blistering or charring.

first fruits *npl* fruit which is the first to ripen; the earliest returns or results from an enterprise.

firsthand *adj* obtained directly from a source.

First Lady *n* the wife of the US president.

firstling *n* the first offspring.

firstly *adv* in the first place.

first night *n* the opening performance of a play.

first person *n* (*gram*) pronouns and verbs referring to the person speaking.

first-rate *adj, adv* of the best quality; (*inf*) excellent.

firth *n* an arm of the sea, esp a river mouth.—*also* **frith**.

fiscal *adj* of or relating to public revenue; financial. * *n* a prosecuting official in some countries.

fish *n* (*pl* **fish, fishes**) any of a large group of cold-blooded animals living in water, having backbones, gills for breathing and fins; the flesh of fish used as food. * *vi* to catch or try to catch fish; (*with* **for**) to try to obtain by roundabout methods. * *vt* (*often with* **out**) to grope for, find, and bring to view.—**fishable** *adj*.

fish² *n* a rigid strip of wood or metal used to strengthen a mast, joint, etc. * *vt* to strengthen or join with a fish.

fish-eye lens *n* a wide-angled lens with a curved protruding front.

fisher *n* a person who fishes; (*zool*) another name for the pekan, a marten found in North America.

fisherman *n* (*pl* **fishermen**) a person who fishes for sport or for a living; a ship used in fishing.

fishery *n* (*pl* **fisheries**) the fishing industry; an area where fish are caught.

fishfinger *n* a small oblong piece of fish covered in breadcrumbs.—*also* **fish stick**.

fishing *n* the art, sport or business of catching fish.

fishing rod *n* a wooden, metal or fibreglass rod used with a line to catch fish.

fish meal *n* granules of dried fish used as fertilizer and food for livestock.

fishmonger *n* a shop that sells fish.

fishnet *n* a coarse open-mesh fabric.—*also adj*.

fishplate *n* an iron plate, one of a pair used to join railway rails.

fishpond *n* a pond in which fish are kept.

fish stick *see* **fishfinger**.

fishwife *n* (*pl* **fishwives**) a woman who guts or sells fish; a coarse, scolding woman.

fishy *adj* (**fishier, fishiest**) like a fish in odour, taste, etc; (*inf*) creating doubt or suspicion.—**fishily** *adv*.—**fishiness** *n*.

fissile *adj* capable of undergoing nuclear fission; easily split.—**fissility** *n*.

fission *n* a split or cleavage; the reproductive division of biological cells; the splitting of the atomic nucleus resulting in the release of energy, nuclear fission.—**fissionable** *adj*.

fissiparous *adj* multiplying or propagating by fission.

fissiped, fissipedal *adj* (*zool*) having the toes separated, eg dogs, cats, etc.

fissirostral *adj* (*birds*) with a deeply cleft beak, eg swallows.

fissure *n* a narrow opening or cleft. * *vti* to split.

fist *n* the hand when tightly closed or clenched.

fistic *adj* (*joc*) of or pertaining to boxing.

fisticuffs *npl* a fight with the fists.

fistula *n* (*pl* **fistulas, fistulae**) an abnormal passage, as from an abscess to the skin.

fistulous *adj* resembling a fistula; hollow, like a pipe.

fit¹ *adj* (**fitter, fittest**) suited to some purpose, function, etc; proper, right; healthy; (*sl*) inclined, ready. * *n* the manner of fitting. * *vb* (**fitting, fitted**) *vt* to be suitable to; to be the proper size, shape, etc, for; to adjust so as to fit; (*with* **out**) to equip, to outfit. * *vi* to be suitable or proper; to have the proper size or shape.—**fittable** *adj*.—**fitly** *adv*.—**fitness** *n*.

fit² *n* any sudden, uncontrollable attack, as of coughing; an outburst, as of anger; a short period of impulsive activity; a seizure involving convulsions or loss of consciousness.

fitch *n* the polecat; the hair of a polecat; a brush made of this.

fitful *adj* marked by intermittent activity; spasmodic.—**fitfully** *adv*.—**fitfulness** *n*.

fitment *n* a piece of equipment, esp fixed furniture.

fitter *n* a person who specializes in fitting clothes; a person skilled in the assembly and operation of a particular piece of machinery.

fitting *adj* appropriate; suitable, right. * *n* an act of one that fits, esp a trying on of altered clothes; a small often standardized electrical part.—**fittingly** *adv*.—**fittingness** *n*.

five *adj, n* one more than four; the symbol for this (5, V, v).

fivefold *adj, adv* having five units or members; being five times as great or as many.

fiver *n* (*inf*) in UK, a £5 note; in US, a $5 bill.

fives *n* (*sing*) a ball game similar to squash, played in a walled court.

fix *vt* to fasten firmly; to set firmly in the mind; to direct (one's eyes) steadily at something; to make rigid; to make permanent; to establish (a date, etc) definitely; to set in order; to repair; to prepare (food or meals); (*inf*) to influence the result or action of (a race, jury, etc) by bribery; (*inf*) to punish. * *vi* to become fixed; (*inf*) to prepare or intend. * *n* the position of a ship, etc, determined from the bearings of two known positions; (*inf*) a predicament; (*inf*) a situation that has been fixed; (*inf*) something whose supply becomes continually necessary or greatly desired, as a drug, entertainment, activity, etc.—**fixable** *adj*.

fixated *adj* having a fixation.

fixation *n* a fixing; (*psychol*) an unhealthy obsession, esp one leading to arrested emotional development.

fixative *n* a substance used to fix things in position; a substance that prevents (colours, perfumes, etc) fading or evaporating.

fixed *adj* firm; not moving; lasting; intent.—**fixedly** *adv*.—**fixedness** *n*.

fixer *n* a chemical that fixes photographs, making the image permanent; (*sl*) a person who fixes something, esp by illegal means.

fixings *npl* trimmings.

fixity *n* (*pl* **fixities**) the state of being fixed; stability; permanence.

fixture *n* what is fixed to anything, as to land or to a house; a fixed article of furniture; a firmly established person or thing; a fixed or appointed time or event.

fizz *vi* to make a hissing or sputtering sound. * *n* this sound; any effervescent drink.—**fizzy** *adj*.—**fizziness** *n*.

fizzle *vi* to make a weak fizzing sound; (*with* **out**) (*inf*) to end feebly, die out, esp after a promising start.

fjeld *n* in Scandinavia, a high, barren plateau.—*also* **field**.

fjord *n* a long, narrow inlet of the sea between high cliffs, esp in Norway.—*also* **fiord**.

fl. *abbr* = fluid; floor; *floruit* (flourished).

flab *n* (*inf*) fat.

flabbergast *vt* (*inf*) to astonish, startle.

flabby *adj* (**flabbier, flabbiest**) fat and soft; weak and ineffective.—**flabbily** *adv*.—**flabbiness** *n*.

flabellate, flabelliform *adj* (*bot*) fan-shaped.

flabellum *n* (*pl* **flabella**) (*RC*) a large fan.

flaccid *adj* not firm or stiff; limp, weak.—**flaccidity** *n*.

flack *see* **flak**.

flacon *n* a small bottle or flask.

flag¹ *vi* (**flagging, flagged**) to grow limp; to become weak, listless.

flag² *n* a piece of cloth, usu with a design, used to show nationality, party, a particular branch of the armed forces, etc, or as a signal. * *vt* (**flagging, flagged**) to decorate with flags; to signal to (as if) with a flag; (*usu with* **down**) to signal to stop.

flag³ n a hard, flat stone used for paving, a flagstone. * vt (**flagging, flagged**) to pave with flagstones.

flag⁴ n a plant with a sword-shaped leaf, the iris; a long thin plant blade.

flag day n a day on which charitable donations are solicited in exchange for small flags; (with caps) in US, 14 June, the anniversary of the adoption of the stars and stripes, 1777.

flagellant n a person who scourges himself or herself or others as a sign of religious penance or for sexual gratification.—**flagellantism** n.

flagellate vt to scourge, to whip.—**flagellation** n.—**flagellator** n..

flagelliform adj long, tapering and flexible; shaped like the thong of a whip.

flagellum n (pl **flagella, flagellums**) (biol, zool) a whip-like appendage; (bot) a runner.

flageolet¹ n a small flute resembling the treble recorder.

flageolet² n a type of edible bean.

flagging n a pavement of flagstones.

flagitious adj atrocious, abominably wicked.—**flagitiously** adv.—**flagitiousness** n.

flag of convenience n a flag of a country flown by a ship registered there by the owners to benefit from less rigorous taxes or safety regulations.

flagon n a pottery or metal container for liquids with a handle and spout and often a lid.

flagrant adj conspicuous, notorious.—**flagrancy, flagrance** n.—**flagrantly** adv.

flagrante delicto adv in the very act, red-handed.

flagrante delicto see **in flagrante delicto**.

flagship n the ship that carries the admiral and his flag; the most important vessel of a shipping line; the chief or leading item of a group or collection.

flagstaff, flagpole n a pole on which a flag is displayed.

flagstone n hard, evenly stratified rock easily split into slabs for paving.

flag-waver n an excessively patriotic person, a jingoist.

flail n a tool for threshing by hand. * vt to beat with a flail. * vi (usu with **about**) to wave (the arms, etc) wildly.

flair n natural ability, aptitude; discernment; (inf) stylishness, sophistication.

flak n shells fired by anti-aircraft guns; criticism, opposition.—also **flack**.

flake n a small piece of snow; a small thin layer chipped from a larger mass of something. * vt to form into flakes. * vi (with **out**) (inf) to collapse or fall asleep from exhaustion.—**flaker** n.

flaky adj (**flakier, flakiest**) of or resembling flakes; liable to flake; (sl) nervous; (sl) odd, eccentric.—**flakily** adv.—**flakiness** n.

flam vt (**flamming, flammed**) (dial) to deceive.

flambé, flambée adj (food) covered with flaming brandy or other spirit.—also vt.

flambeau n (pl **flambeaux, flambeaus**) a lighted, flaming torch; a large ornamental candlestick.

flamboyant adj brilliantly coloured; ornate; strikingly elaborate; dashing, exuberant.—**flamboyance, flamboyancy** n.—**flamboyantly** adv.

flame n the burning gas of a fire, appearing as a tongue of light; the state of burning with a blaze; a thing like a flame; an intense emotion; (inf) a sweetheart. * vi to burst into flame; to become bright red with emotion.

flamen n (pl **flamens, flamines**) in ancient Rome, a priest devoted to the service of a special deity.

flamenco n (pl **flamencos**) a type of vigorous Spanish dance and music of gipsy origin.

flame-thrower n a weapon that shoots a jet of flaming liquid.

flaming adj emitting flames; very hot; gaudy; exaggerated; intense.—**flamingly** adv.

flamingo n (pl **flamingos, flamingoes**) any of several wading birds with rosy-pink plumage and long legs and neck.

flammable adj easily set on fire.—**flammability** n.

flamy adj (**flamier, flamiest**) resembling flame; flame-coloured.

flan n an open case of pastry or sponge cake with a sweet or savoury filling.

flânerie n idleness.

flâneur an idle person, a lounger.

flange n a raised edge, as on a wheel rim to keep it on a rail; a projecting rib. * vt to provide with a flange.—**flanged** adj.

flank n the fleshy part of the side from the ribs to the hip; the side of anything; the right or left side of a formation of troops. * vt to attack the flank of; to skirt the side of; to be situated at the side of.

flanker n (mil) a soldier or fortification used to protect a flank.

flannel n a soft light cotton or woollen cloth; a small cloth for washing the face and hands; (sl) nonsense, equivocation; (pl) trousers of such cloth. * vt (**flannelling, flannelled** or **flanneling, flanneled**) to wash with a flannel; (inf) to flatter.—**flannelly** adj.

flannelette n a soft cotton fabric.

flap vi (**flapping, flapped**) to move up and down, as wings; to sway loosely and noisily, as curtains in the wind, etc; to move or hang like a flap; (inf) to get into a panic or fluster. * n the motion or noise of a flap; anything broad and flexible, either hinged or hanging loose; a light blow with a flat object; (inf) agitation, panic.

flapdoodle n (inf) nonsense.

flapjack n a kind of pancake; a cake made with oats and syrup.

flapper n someone who, or something which, flaps; (inf) a fashionable young woman of the 1920s.

flare vi to burn with a sudden, bright, unsteady flame; to burst into emotion, esp anger; to widen out gradually. * n an unsteady flame; a sudden flash; a bright light used as a signal or illumination; a widened part or shape.

flare-up n a sudden burst of fire; (inf) a sudden burst of emotion.

flash n a sudden, brief light; a brief moment; a sudden brief display; (TV, radio) a sudden brief news item about an important event; (photog) a device for producing a brief intense light; a sudden onrush of water; **flash in the pan** a misfire; a showy start not followed up. * vi to send out a sudden, brief light; to sparkle; to come or pass suddenly; (sl) to expose the genitals indecently. * vt to cause to flash; to send (news, etc) swiftly; (inf) to show off. * adj (inf) flashy.—**flasher** n.

flashback n an interruption in the continuity of a story, etc, by telling or showing an earlier episode.

flashboard n a board placed on a dam to increase its height and hence the depth of the water contained.

flashbulb n a small bulb giving an intense light used in photography.

flash flood n a sudden brief flood caused by a heavy rainfall.

flash gun n (photog) a device for holding and operating a flashbulb.

flashing n a piece of lead or other metal, used to keep a roof watertight.

flashlight n an electric torch; a flash of electric light used to take photographs in dark conditions.

flashpoint n the lowest temperature at which vapour, as from oil, will ignite with a flash; the point where a situation will erupt into violence.

flashy adj (flashier, flashiest) pretentious; showy, gaudy.—**flashily** adv.—**flashiness** n.

flask n a slim-necked bottle; a vacuum flask.

flasket n a small flask; a long, shallow basket.

flat adj (flatter, flattest) having a smooth level surface; lying spread out; broad, even, and thin; not fluctuating; (tyre) deflated; dull, tedious; (drink) not fizzy; (battery) drained of electric current. * adv in a flat manner or position; exactly; (mus) below true pitch. * n anything flat, esp a surface, part, or expanse; a flat tyre; a set of rooms on one floor of a building (—also apartment).—**flatly** adv.—**flatness** n.

flatcar n an open, sideless rail truck.

flatfish n (pl flatfish, flatfishes) any of an order of marine fishes that as adults have both eyes on one side.

flatfoot n a condition in which the arch of the instep is flattened; (pl flatfeet, flatfoots) (sl) a policeman.

flat-footed adj having flatfoot; (inf) awkward; (inf) unprepared; (inf) determined, blunt.—**flat-footedly** adv.—**flat-footedness** n.

flatiron n an iron used for clothes, linen, etc, heated by being placed upon a hot stove, etc.

flat spin n a spin or manoeuvre in which an aircraft is more horizontal than vertical; (inf) a confused or agitated state.

flatten vti to make or become flat.—**flattener** n.

flatter vt to praise excessively or insincerely, esp out of self-interest or to win favour; to display to advantage; to represent as more attractive, etc than reality; to gratify the vanity of; to encourage falsely.—**flatterer** n.—**flattering** adj.—**flatteringly** adv.

flattery n (pl flatteries) compliments; insincere praise.

flattie n (inf) a woman's shoe with a flat heel.

flatting n (metallurgy) the process of rolling metal into flat sheets.

flatulence, flatulency n wind in the stomach; windiness, verbosity; pomposity.

flatulent adj causing or affected with intestinal gas; pretentious, vain.—**flatulently** adv.

flatways, flatwise adv flat side downwards.

flatworm n any of various parasitic worms having a flattened body.

flaunt vi to move or behave ostentatiously; (flag) to wave in the wind. * vt to display.—**flaunter** n.—**flauntingly** adv.

flaunty adj (flauntier, flauntiest) inclined to flaunting.

flautist n a flute player.—also **flutist**.

flavescent adj turning yellow; yellowish.

flavin, flavine n a yellow dye and antiseptic.

flavorous adj tasty.

flavour, flavor n the taste of something in the mouth; a characteristic quality. * vt to give flavour to.—**flavourer, flavorer** n.—**flavoursome, flavorsome**.adj.

flavouring, flavoring n any substance used to give flavour to food.

flaw n a defect; a crack. * vti to make or become flawed.

flaw[2] n a gust of wind, a squall.

flawless adj perfect.—**flawlessly** adv.—**flawlessness** n.

flax n a blue-flowered plant cultivated for its fibre and seed; the fibre of this plant.

flaxen, flaxy adj made of flax; pale yellow.

flaxseed n the seed of the flax plant, from which linseed oil is obtained.

flay vt to strip off the skin; to berate, criticize severely.—**flayer** n.

flea n a small wingless jumping bloodsucking insect.

fleabane n a plant of the aster family.

fleabite n the bite of a flea; a minor inconvenience.

fleabitten adj marked with fleabites; (inf) shabby, wretched; (horses) flecked with red spots on a light ground.

fleam n a lancet used for bleeding cattle.

flea market n an open-air street market, usu selling second-hand articles.

fleapit n (inf) a shabby cinema or theatre.

flèche n (archit) a slender spire, esp at the intersection of the nave and transept.

fleck n a spot or speckle of colour; a tiny particle. * vt to mark with flecks.

flection see **flexion**.

fled see **flee**.

fledge vt (birds) to rear until ready to fly; to cover or provide with feathers, esp an arrow.

fledgling, fledgeling n a young bird just fledged; an inexperienced person, a trainee.

flee vti (fleeing, fled) to run away from danger, etc; to pass away quickly, to disappear.—**fleer** n.

fleece n the woollen coat of sheep or similar animal. * vt to remove wool from; to defraud.

fleecy adj (fleecier, fleeciest) like a fleece, woolly.—**fleecily** adv.—**fleeciness** n.

fleer n a derisive look, sneer. * vti to sneer (at), to mock.

fleet[1] n a number of warships under one command; (often with cap) a country's navy; any group of cars, ships, buses, etc, under one control.

fleet[2] adj swift moving; nimble.—**fleetly** adv.—**fleetness** n.

fleeting adj brief, transient.—**fleetingly** adv.

Fleming n a native or inhabitant of Flanders.

Flemish adj of the people of Flanders, or their language.

flense, flench vt (whale, seal) to strip blubber from.

flesh n the soft substance of the body, esp the muscular tissue; the pulpy part of fruits and vegetables; meat; the body as distinct from the soul; all mankind; a yellowish-pink colour. * vt (usu with out) to give substance to.

fleshings npl flesh-coloured tights.

fleshly adj (fleshlier, fleshliest) having to do with the body and its desires, material, sensual.—**fleshliness** n.

flesh wound n a superficial wound.

fleshy adj (fleshier, fleshiest) of or resembling flesh; plump; succulent; sensual.—**fleshiness** n.

fleur-de-lis, fleur-de-lys n (pl fleurs-de-lis, fleurs-de-lys) a heraldic lily, the emblem of France.

fleury adj (her) decorated with a fleur-de-lis.—also **flory**.

flew see **fly**.

flews npl the pendulous lips of a bloodhound, etc.

flex vti to bend (a limb or joint, etc); to contract (a muscle). * n an insulated cable used to connect electric appliances to the mains (—also cord).

flexible adj easily bent, pliable; adaptable, versatile; docile.—**flexibility** n.—**flexibly** adv.

flexile adj supple; docile; flexible.—**flexility** n.

flexion n the act or process of bending; a curve; (gram) an inflection.—also **flection**.

flexitime, flextime *n* the staggering of working hours to enable each employee to work the full quota of time but at periods most convenient for the individual.

flexor *n* a muscle that acts to bend a joint or limb.

flexuous, flexose *adj* winding, sinuous; unsteady.—**flexuosity** *n*.

flexure *n* the act of bending; the state of being bent; (*math*) the curving of a line or surface.—**flexural** *adj*

flibbertigibbet *n* an impish, flighty or gossipy person.

flick *n* a light stroke or blow; (*inf*) a cinema film. * *vt* to strike or propel with a flick; a flicking movement.

flicker *vi* to burn unsteadily, as a flame; to move quickly to and fro. * *n* a flickering moment of light or flame; a flickering movement.—**flickeringly** *adv*.—**flickery** *adj*.

flick knife *n* a knife with a retractable blade released by pressing a button.

flier *see* **flyer**.

flies *see* **fly**.

flight[1] *n* the act, manner, or power of flying; distance flown; a group of creatures or things flying together; an aircraft scheduled to fly a certain trip; a trip by aircraft; a set of stairs, as between landings; a mental act of soaring beyond the ordinary; a set of feathers on a dart or arrow.

flight[2] *n* an act or instance of fleeing.

flight-deck *n* the cockpit of an aircraft.

flightless *adj* (*birds, insects*) incapable of flying.

flight recorder *n* a device that records information about the flight performance of an aircraft.

flighty *adj* (**flightier, flightiest**) irresponsible, capricious, frivolous.—**flightily** *adv*.—**flightiness** *n*.

flimflam *vt* (**flimflamming, flimflammed**) to deceive. * *n* nonsense; a trick.

flimsy *adj* (**flimsier, flimsiest**) weak, insubstantial; light and thin; (*excuse etc*) unconvincing. * *n* (*pl* **flimsies**) thin paper; copy written on this.—**flimsily** *adv*.—**flimsiness** *n*.

flinch *vi* to draw back, as from pain or fear; to wince.—**flincher** *n*.—**flinchingly** *adv*.

flinders *npl* fragments.

fling *vb* (**flinging, flung**) *vt* to cast, throw aside, esp with force; to put or send suddenly or without warning. * *vi* to kick out violently; to move or rush quickly or impetuously. * *n* the act of flinging; a lively dance; a period of pleasurable indulgence.—**flinger** *n*.

flint *n* a very hard rock that produces sparks when struck with steel; an alloy used for producing a spark in lighters.

flint glass *n* a lustrous kind of glass; lead glass.

flintlock *n* a type of old-fashioned gun fired by sparks from a flint.

flinty *adj* (**flintier, flintiest**) like flint, hard; cruel.—**flintily** *adv*.—**flintiness** *n*.

flip[1] *n* a drink made from any alcoholic beverage sweetened and mixed with beaten egg.

flip[2] *vb* (**flipping, flipped**) *vt* to toss with a quick jerk, to flick; to snap (a coin) in the air with the thumb; to turn or turn over. * *vi* to move jerkily; (*inf*) to burst into anger.

flip-flop *n* a backward handspring; an electronic circuit that can assume either of two states when activated; a rubber-soled sandal with a strap that fits between the toes (—*also* **thong**).

flippant *adj* impertinent; frivolous.—**flippancy** *n*.—**flippantly** *adv*.

flipper *n* a limb adapted for swimming; a flat rubber shoe expanded into a paddle, used in underwater swimming.

flip side *n* the reverse side of a gramophone record; the less attractive or well-known aspect of a person or thing.

flirt *vi* to make insincere amorous approaches; to trifle or toy (eg with an idea). * *n* a person who toys amorously with the opposite sex.—**flirtation** *n*.—**flirter** *n*.—**flirtingly** *adv*.

flirtatious *adj* fond of flirting, coquettish.—**flirtatiously** *adv*.

flit *vi* (**flitting, flitted**) to move lightly and rapidly; to vacate (a premises) stealthily. * the act of flitting, a removal.

flitch *n* a side of bacon, salted and cured; a plank cut from a tree.

flitter *vi* to flit about; to flicker, flutter.

flivver *n* (*sl*) an old or cheap car.

float *vi* to rest on the surface of or be suspended in a liquid; to move lightly; to wander aimlessly. * *vt* to cause to float; to put into circulation; to start up a business, esp by offering shares for sale. * *n* anything that floats; a cork or other device used on a fishing line to signal that the bait has been taken; a low flat vehicle decorated for exhibit in a parade; a small sum of money available for cash expenditures.—**floatable** *adj*.

floatage *see* **flotage**.

floatation *see* **flotation**.

floater *n* something that floats; a person lacking strong political convictions; (*inf*) a blunder.

floating *adj* swimming, or buoyed up, on the surface of a liquid; (*anat*) displaced; (*vote, etc*) not settled; (*capital*) in circulation, available for use.

floccose *adj* tufted.

floccule *n* a mass of fleecy material; a small tuft or flake.

flocculent *adj* woolly or flaky.—**flocculence, flocculency** *n*.

flocculus *n* (*pl* **flocculi**) a tufted mass; (*astron*) a mass of gas appearing as a mark on the sun (—*also* **plage**).

floccus *n* (*pl* **flocci**) down, such as that found on young birds; a tuft of hair.

flock[1] *n* a group of certain animals as birds, sheep, etc, living and feeding together; a group of people or things. * *vi* to assemble or travel in a flock or crowd.

flock[2] *n* a tuft of wool or cotton fibre; woollen or cotton waste used for stuffing furniture.—**flocky** *adj*.

floe *n* a sheet of floating ice.

flog *vt* (**flogging, flogged**) to beat harshly with a rod, stick or whip; (*sl*) to sell.—**flogger** *n*.—**flogging** *n*.

flong *n* (*printing*) paper used for stereotyping.

flood *n* an overflowing of water on an area normally dry; the rising of the tide; a great outpouring, as of words. * *vt* to cover or fill, as with a flood; to put too much water, fuel, etc on or in. * *vi* to gush out in a flood; to become flooded.—**floodable** *adj*.—**flooder** *n*.

floodgate *n* a gate for controlling the flow of water, a sluice.

floodlight *n* a strong beam of light used to illuminate a stage, sports field, stadium, building exterior, etc. * *vt* (**floodlighting, floodlit**) to illuminate with floodlights.

flood tide *n* the rising or inflowing tide.

floor *n* the inside bottom surface of a room, flooring; the bottom surface of anything, as the ocean; a storey in a building; the area in a legislative assembly where the members sit and debate; the lower limit, the base. * vt to provide with a floor; to knock down (a person) in a fight; (inf) to defeat; (inf) to shock, to confuse.

floorage n the area of a floor.

floorboard n one of the boards making up a floor.

flooring n material for making or covering a floor; a floor.

floor plan n a scale drawing of the layout of a floor of a building.

floor show n entertainment with singers and dancers, etc in a nightclub.

floozy, floozie, floosie n (pl **floozies, floosies**) (sl) a disreputable woman.

flop vi (**flopping, flopped**) to sway or bounce loosely; to move in a heavy, clumsy or relaxed manner; (inf) to fail. * n a flopping movement; a collapse; (inf) a complete failure.

floppy adj (**floppier, floppiest**) limp, hanging loosely. * n (pl **floppies**) a floppy disk.—**floppily** adv.—**floppiness** n.

floppy disk n (comput) a flexible magnetic disk in a protective casing used for data storage and retrieval.

flora n (pl **floras, florae**) the plants of a region or a period.

floral adj pertaining to flowers.—**florally** adv.

Florentine n a native or inhabitant of Florence.—also adj.

florescence n the process, state or time of flowering.

floret n one of the small flowers forming the head of a plant.

floriated, floreated adj ornamented with floral decorations; flowery.

floribunda n any of several varieties of hybrid roses with large clusters of flowers.

floriculture n the cultivation of flowers.—**floricultural** adj.—**floriculturist** n

florid adj flowery; elaborate; (complexion) ruddy.—**floridity** n.—**floridly** adv.

florist n a person who sells or grows flowers and ornamental plants.

flory see **fleury**.

floss n a mass of short silky fibres, as from the rough outside of the silkworm's cocoon; fine silk used in embroidery; dental floss.

flossy adj (**flossier, flossiest**) like floss, silky, downy; (sl) flashy.

flotage n flotation; a craft afloat; flotsam.—also **floatage**.

flotation n the act or process of floating; the launching of a business venture.—also **floatation**.

flotilla n a small fleet of ships.

flotsam n wreckage or debris found floating in the sea.

flounce[1] vi to move in an emphatic or impatient manner.* n the act of flouncing, a plunge.

flounce[2] n a frill of material sewn to the skirt of a dress. * vt to add flounces to.

flouncing n a material used for making flounces.

flounder[1] vi to move awkwardly and with difficulty; to be clumsy in thinking or speaking.

flounder[2] n (pl **flounder, flounders**) a small flatfish used as food.

flour n the finely ground powder of wheat or other grain. * vt to sprinkle with flour.—**floury** adj.

flourish vi (plants) to grow luxuriantly; to thrive, prosper; to live and work at a specified time. * vt to brandish dramatically. * n embellishment; a curve made by a bold stroke of the pen; a sweeping gesture; a musical fanfare.—**flourisher** n.

flout vt to treat with contempt, to disobey openly. * n an insult.—**flouter** n.—**floutingly** adv.

flow vi (liquids) to move (as if) in a stream; (tide) to rise; to glide smoothly; (conversation, etc) to continue effortlessly; to be characterized by smooth and easy movement; to hang free or loosely; to be plentiful. * n a flowing; the rate of flow; anything that flows; the rising of the tide.

flow chart n a diagram representing the sequence of and relationships between different steps or procedures in a complex process, eg manufacturing.

flower n the seed-producing structure of a flowering plant, blossom; a plant cultivated for its blossoms; the best or finest part. * vt to cause to bear flowers. * vi to produce blossoms; to reach the best stage.

floweret n a little flower.

flowerpot n a pot used to contain a growing plant.

flowery adj full of or decorated with flowers; (language) full of elaborate expressions.—**floweriness** n.

flown see **fly**.

fl. oz. abbr = fluid ounce.

flu n (inf) influenza.

fluctuate vi (prices, etc) to be continually varying in an irregular way.—**fluctuation** n.

flue[1] n a shaft for the passage of smoke, hot air, etc, as in a chimney.

flue[2] n soft downy matter; fluff.

flue[3] n a type of fishing net.

fluent adj able to write and speak a foreign language with ease; articulate, speaking and writing easily and smoothly; graceful.—**fluency** n.—**fluently** adv.

fluff n soft, light down; a loose, soft mass, as of hair; (inf) a mistake, bungle. * vt to pat or shake until fluffy; (inf) to forget, to bungle.

fluffy adj (**fluffier, fluffiest**) like fluff; soft and downy; feathery.—**fluffily** adv.—**fluffiness** n.

fluid n a substance able to flow freely, as a liquid or gas does. * adj able to flow freely; able to change rapidly or easily.—**fluidal** adj.—**fluidity** n.—**fluidly** adv.

fluid ounce n a US unit of capacity equal to one sixteenth of a US pint; a UK unit of capacity equal to one twentieth of an imperial pint

fluke[1] n a flatfish; a flattened parasitic worm.

fluke[2] n the part of an anchor that fastens in the sea bed, river bottom, etc; the barbed end of a harpoon; one of the lobes of a whale's tail.

fluke[3] n a stroke of luck. * vti to make or score by a fluke.

fluky, flukey adj (**flukier, flukiest**) obtained by luck; uncertain.—**flukiness** n.

flume n a channel for water; a ravine with a stream; a chute with a flow of water into a swimming pool. * vt to transport or divert by a flume.

flummery n (pl **flummeries**) (inf) an empty compliment; a pudding, a kind of custard or blancmange.

flummox vt (inf) to bewilder, perplex.

flung see **fling**.

flunk vti (sl) to fail, as in school work; to shirk.

flunky, flunkey n (pl **flunkies, flunkeys**) a servile person, toady; a person who does menial work; a liveried servant.

fluor see **fluorspar**.

fluoresce vi to display fluorescence.

fluorescence n the property of producing light when acted upon by radiant energy; light so produced.—**fluorescent** adj.

fluorescent lamp *n* a glass tube coated with a fluorescent substance that emits light when acted upon by ultraviolet radiation.

fluoridate *vt* to add fluoride to drinking water to reduce tooth decay.—**fluoridation** *n*.

fluoride *n* any of various compounds of fluorine.

fluorinate *vt* to treat or mix with fluorine.—**fluorination** *n*.

fluorine, fluorin *n* a chemical element, a pale greenish-yellow corrosive gas.

fluoroscope *n* an instrument with a fluorescent screen, used for studying X-ray images.—**fluoroscopy** *n*.

fluorspar *n* a transparent, or semi-transparent, material, composed of calcium fluoride.—*also* **fluor**.

flurry *n* (*pl* **flurries**) a sudden gust of wind, rain, or snow; a sudden commotion. * *vti* (**flurrying, flurried**) to (cause to) become flustered.

flush[1] *n* a rapid flow, as of water; sudden, vigorous growth; a sudden excitement; a blush; a sudden feeling of heat, as in a fever. * *vi* to flow rapidly; to blush or glow; to be washed out by a sudden flow of water. * *vt* to wash out with a sudden flow of water; to cause to blush; to excite. * *adj* level or in one plane with another surface; (*inf*) abundant, well-supplied, esp with money.—**flusher** *n*.

flush[2] *vt* to make game birds fly away suddenly.—**flusher** *n*.

flush[3] *n* (*poker, etc*) a hand of cards all of the same suit.

fluster *vti* to make or become confused. * *n* agitation or confusion.

flute *n* an orchestral woodwind instrument in the form of a straight pipe (with finger holes and keys) held horizontally and played through a hole located near one end; a decorative groove. * *vi* to play or make sounds like a flute; to cut grooves in.—**fluty** *adj*.

fluter *n* a person who makes flutes; a tool used in making flutes; a flute player.

fluting *n* decorative channels or grooves in pillars, etc; pleats like this in a skirt, etc.

flutist *n* a flute player, flautist.

flutter *vi* (*birds*) to flap the wings; to wave about rapidly; (*heart*) to beat irregularly or spasmodically. * *vt* to cause to flutter. * *n* rapid, irregular motion; nervous excitement; commotion, confusion; (*inf*) a small bet.—**flutterer** *n*.—**fluttery** *adj*.

fluty *adj* (**flutier, flutiest**) soft and clear like the sound of a flute.—**flutily** *adv*,—**flutiness** *n*.

fluvial, fluviatile *adj* of or found in streams and rivers.

flux *n* a continual flowing or changing; a substance used to help metals fuse together, as in soldering.

fluxion *n* a flowing; an excessive flow; (*math*) differential calculus.—**fluxional, fluxionary** *adj*.

fly[1] *n* (*pl* **flies**) a two-winged insect; a natural or imitation fly attached to a fish-hook as bait.

fly[2] *vb* (**flying, flew**, *pp* **flown**) *vi* to move through the air, esp on wings; to travel in an aircraft; to control an aircraft; to take flight, flee; to pass quickly; (*inf*) to depart quickly. * *vt* to cause to fly, as a kite; to escape, flee from; to transport by aircraft. * *n* a flap that conceals buttons, a zip, etc on trousers; material forming the outer roof of a tent; a device for regulating machinery, a flywheel.—**flyable** *adj*.

fly[3] *adj* (*inf*) sly, astute.

flyaway *adj* (*hair etc*) loose; (*person*) flighty.

flyblow *n* the egg or larva of a fly. * *vt* (**flyblowing, flyblew**, *pp* **flyblown**) to contaminate (meat, etc) by laying eggs (esp of a blowfly) in it.

flyby *n* (*pl* **flybys**) a flight past a target, esp by a spacecraft past a celestial body to collect scientific data.

fly-by-night *adj* (*inf*) unreliable, untrustworthy; transitory. * *n* an untrustworthy person, esp one who evades responsibilities or debts by flight.

flycatcher *n* a bird that catches insects on the wing.

flyer *n* something that flies or moves very fast; a pilot.—*also* **flier**.

fly fishing *n* fishing using artificial flies as lures.—**fly-fish** *vi*.

flying *adj* capable of flight; fleeing; fast-moving. * *n* the act of flying an aircraft, etc.

flying boat *n* a sea plane in which the boat forms the fuselage and float.

flying buttress *n* a buttress connected to a wall by an arch, serving to resist outward pressure.

flying colours *npl* great success; triumph.

flying doctor *n* a doctor who visits patients (e.g. in isolated communities) by aircraft.

flying fish *n* any of numerous fishes of warm seas with winglike fins used in gliding through the air.

flying fox *n* a large fruit bat of Africa and Asia.

flying saucer *n* an unidentified flying disc-shaped object, purportedly from outer space.

flying squad *n* a small detachment of police officers mobilized for swift action.

flying squirrel *n* a nocturnal squirrel with folds of skin joining its legs, enabling it to glide.

flying start *n* a start in a race when the competitor is already moving when passing the starting line; a promising start in anything.

flyleaf *n* (*pl* **flyleaves**) the blank leaf at the beginning or end of a book.

flyover *n* a bridge that carries a road or railway over another; a fly-past.

flypaper *n* paper with a sticky poisonous coating that is hung up to trap and kill flies.

fly-past *n* a processional flight of aircraft.

flyte *see* **flite**.

flytrap *n* any of various insect-eating plants; a device for catching flies.

flyweight *n* a boxer weighing not more than 112 pounds (51 kg).

flywheel *n* a heavy wheel which stores energy by inertia, used to regulate machinery.

FM *abbr* = Field Marshal; frequency modulation.

Fm (*chem symbol*) fermium.

f-number *n* (*photog*) a number used to calculate the ratio of light passing through a lens.

FO *abbr* = Foreign Office.

foal *n* the young of the horse or a related animal. * *vti* to give birth to a foal.

foam *n* froth or fine bubbles on the surface of liquid; something like foam, as frothy saliva; a rigid or springy cellular mass made from liquid rubber, plastic, etc. * *vi* to cause or emit foam.

foamy *adj* (**foamier, foamiest**) of, like, or covered with foam.—**foamily** *adv*.—**foaminess** *n*.

f.o.b. *abbr* = free on board.

fob[1] *n* the chain or ribbon for attaching a watch to a waistcoat; any object attached to a watch chain; a small pocket in a waistcoat for a watch.

fob[2] *vt* (**fobbing, fobbed**) (*with* **off**) to cheat; to put off; to palm off (upon).

focal *adj* of or pertaining to a focus.—**focally** *adv*.

focalize *vti* to (cause to) focus.—**focalization** *n*.

focal length *n* the distance between the focal point and optical centre of a lens or mirror.

fo'c's'le, fo'c'sle *see* **forecastle.**

focus *n* (*pl* **focuses, foci**) a point where rays of light, heat, etc meet after being bent by a lens, curved mirror, etc; correct adjustment of the eye or lens to form a clear image; a centre of activity or interest. * *vt* (**focusing, focused** *or* **focussing, focussed**) to adjust the focus of; to bring into focus; to concentrate.—**focusable** *adj.*—**focuser** *n.*

fodder *n* dried food for cattle, horses, etc.

FOE *abbr* = Friends of the Earth.

foe *n* an enemy, an adversary.

foehn *see* **föhn.**

foeman *n* (*arch*) an adversary in war.

foetal *see* **fetal.**

foeticide *see* **feticide.**

foetid *see* **fetid.**

foetus *see* **fetus.**

fog[1] *n* (a state of poor visibility caused by) a large mass of water vapour condensed to fine particles just above the earth's surface; a state of mental confusion; (*photog*) cloudiness on a developed photograph. * *vti* (**fogging, fogged**) to make or become foggy.

fog[2] *n* a second growth of grass in autumn; winter pasture; (*Scot*) moss.

fogbound *n* unable to function due to fog.

fogey, fogy *n* (*pl* **fogeys, fogies**) a person of old-fashioned or eccentric habits.—**fogeyish, fogyish** *adj.*

foggy *adj* (**foggier, foggiest**) thick with fog; mentally confused; indistinct, opaque.—**foggily** *adv.*—**fogginess** *n.*

foghorn *n* a horn (in a ship, etc) sounded in a fog as a warning.

fogy *see* **fogey.**

föhn *n* a warm, dry, Alpine wind.—*also* **foehn.**

foible *n* a slight weakness or failing; an idiosyncrasy; the weakest part of the blade of a sword.

foil[1] *vt* to defeat; to frustrate; to trample a trail to spoil scent. * *n* (*arch*) the trail of hunted game.—**foilable** *adj.*

foil[2] *n* a very thin sheet of metal; a backing for a mirror or gem; anything that sets off or enhances another by contrast; (*archit*)a small arc or space in the tracery of a window. * *vt* to cover, back or adorn with foil; to set off.

foil[3] *n* a long, thin blunted sword used for fencing.

foison *n* (*arch*) an abundance.

foist *vt* (*with* **in** *or* **into**) to introduce stealthily or without permission; (*with* **off** *or* **on**) to pass off as genuine.

folacin *see* **folic acid.**

fold[1] *vt* to cover by bending or doubling over so that one part covers another; to wrap up, envelop; to interlace (one's arms); to clasp (one's hands); to embrace; to incorporate (an ingredient) into a food mixture by gentle overturnings. * *vi* to become folded; to fail completely; to collapse, esp to go out of business. * *n* something folded, as a piece of cloth; a crease or hollow made by folding.—**foldable** *adj.*

fold[2] *n* a pen for sheep; a group of people or institutions having a common belief, activity, etc. * *vt* to pen in a fold.

-fold *suffix* times repeated, eg *tenfold.*

foldaway *adj* (*bed, etc*) collapsible.

folder *n* a folded cover or large envelope for holding loose papers.

folderol *see* **falderal.**

folding *n* the act or process of folding. * *adj* which folds or can be folded.

foliaceous *adj* resembling or having leaves; (*rock*) having thin layers.

foliage *n* leaves, as of a plant or tree.

foliar *adj* of or pertaining to leaves.

foliate *adj* resembling or having leaves. * *vti* to beat (metal) into foil; to divide into thin layers; to produce leaves; (*archit*) to decorate with foils; to number the leaves of (a book).

foliation *n* (*bot*) the act of producing leaves or the state of having leaves; the act or process of beating a metal into thin plates.

folic acid *n* a B-complex vitamin used in treating anaemia.—*also* **folacin.**

folio *n* (*pl* **folios**) a large sheet of paper folded once to make two leaves of a book; a book of sheets in this size, the largest commonly used; the number of a page in a book. * *vt* (**folioing, folioed**) to number the pages of.

foliose *adj* (*bot*) having many leaves; of or resembling leaves.

folk *n* (*pl* **folk, folks**) a people of a country or tribe; people in general, esp those of a particular area; relatives; folk music. * *adj* of or originating among the ordinary people.—**folkish** *adj.*

folk etymology *n* the perversion of a word in an attempt to explain it, as "sparrow grass" for "asparagus."

folklore *n* the traditional beliefs, customs, legends, etc of a people; the study of these.—**folkloric, folkloristic** *adj.*—**folklorist** *n.*

folk music *n* traditional music.

folk song *n* a traditional song.

folksy *adj* (**folksier, folksiest**) (*inf*) simple, plain; friendly.—**folksiness** *n.*

folktale *n* an anonymous, timeless, and placeless tale circulated orally among a people.

follicle *n* any small sac, cavity, or gland.—**follicular, folliculate, folliculated** *adj.*

follow *vt* to go or come after; to pursue; to go along (a path, road, etc); to copy; to obey; to adopt, as an opinion; to watch fixedly; to focus the mind on; to understand the meaning of; to monitor the progress of; to come or occur after in time; to result from; (*with* **through**) to pursue (an aim) to a conclusion; (*with* **up**) to pursue a question, inquiry, etc, that has been started. * *vi* to go or come after another; to result; (*with* **on**) (*cricket*) to take a second innings immediately after a first; (*with* **suit**) to play a card of the same suit; to do the same thing; (*with* **through**) (*sport*) to continue a stroke or motion of a bat, club, etc after the ball has been struck; (*with* **up**) to pursue steadily; to supplement.—**followable** *adj.*

follower *n* a disciple or adherent; a person who imitates another.

following *n* a body of adherents or believers. * *adj* next after; now to be stated.

follow-on *n* (*cricket*) an immediate return to bat by a side which has scored a certain number of runs fewer than its opponents in the first innings.

follow-through *n* (*golf, tennis, etc*) the continuation of a swing after hitting the ball.

follow-up *n* the continuing after a beginning; a steady pursuit.

folly *n* (*pl* **follies**) a lack of sense; a foolish act or idea; an extravagant and fanciful building which serves no practical purpose.

foment *vt* to stir up (trouble); to bathe with warm water or lotions.—**fomenter** *n.*

fomentation n the act of formenting; instigation; the application of a warm lotion to ease pain or swelling.

fond adj loving, affectionate; doting, indulgent; (arch) overcredulous, simple; (with of) having a liking for.—**fondly** adv.— **fondness** n.

fondant n a soft sugar mixture for sweets and icings; a sweet made from this.

fondle vt to caress.—**fondler** n.—**fondlingly** adv.

fondue n melted cheese used as a dip with small pieces of bread.

font[1] n a receptacle for baptismal water; a receptacle for holy water.—**fontal** adj.

font[2] see **fount**[1].

fontanameter n a device for measuring the pressure within the skull of a foetus in the womb.

fontanelle, fontanel n one of the open spaces in between the bones of an infant's skull.

food n any substance, esp a solid, taken in by a plant or animal to enable it to live and grow; anything that nourishes.

foodie n (pl **foodies**) (inf) a person who takes great delight in cooking and eating.

food poisoning n an acute illness caused by harmful bacteria or toxins in food.

food processor n an electric appliance used to perform various functions when preparing food, as chopping, mixing and grating.

foodstuff n a substance used as food.

fool n a person lacking wisdom or common sense; (Middle Ages) a jester; a dupe; a cold dessert made from whipped cream mixed with fruit purée. * vt to deceive, make a fool of. * vi to act jokingly; to spend time idly; to tease or meddle with.

foolery n (pl **fooleries**) foolish behaviour, buffoonery.

foolhardy adj (**foolhardier, foolhardiest**) foolishly bold; rash.—**foolhardiness** n.

foolish adj unwise; ridiculous; ill-judged.—**foolishly** adv.—**foolishness** n.

foolproof adj proof against failure; easy to understand; easy to use.

foolscap n a large size of writing paper.

fool's errand n a pointless undertaking.

fool's paradise n illusory happiness.

foot n (pl **feet**) the end part of the leg, on which one stands; anything a resembling foot, as the lower part of a chair, table, etc; the lower part or edge of something, bottom; a measure of length equal to 12 inches (30.48 cm); the part of a garment that covers the foot; an attachment on a sewing machine that grips the fabric; a group of syllables serving as a unit of metre in verse. * vi to dance. * vt to walk, dance over or on; to pay the entire cost of (a bill).

footage n measurement in feet, esp film exposed.

foot-and-mouth disease n a contagious disease of cattle.

football n a field game played with an inflated leather ball by two teams; the ball used.—**footballer** n.

footboard n a treadle on a machine; a step on a carriage.

footbridge n a narrow bridge for pedestrians.

footer n (sl) football.

footfall n the sound of a footstep.

foot-fault n (tennis) overstepping the base line when serving. * vi to commit a foot-fault.

footgear n shoes and socks, etc.

foothill n a hill at the foot of higher hills.

foothold n a ledge, etc for placing the foot when climbing, etc; a place from which further progress may be made.

footie see **footy**.

footing n the basis upon which something rests; status, relationship; a foothold; (archit) a projecting course at the base of a wall.

footle vi to potter.

footlights npl a row of lights in front of a stage floor.

footling adj trifling.

footloose adj free, untramelled.

footman n (pl **footmen**) a liveried servant or attendant.

footmark n a footprint.

footnote n a note or comment at the foot of a page.

footpad n (arch) a highwayman on foot.

footpath n a narrow path for pedestrians.

foot-pound n a unit of energy, equal to the work required to raise a one pound weight through one foot; equivalent to 0.042 joule.

footprint n the impression left by a foot.

foot-rot n an inflammation of the feet of sheep and cattle; a plant disease affecting stalks and trunks; (sl) athlete's foot.

foots npl the sediment of oil or sugar.

footsie n (inf) amorous touching together of feet; (inf) clandestine dealings.

footslog vt (**footslogging, footslogged**) (inf) to march.

footsore adj having painful feet from excessive walking.

footstalk n (bot) the supporting stem of a plant or flower; (zool) the attachment of a barnacle.

footstall n a woman's stirrup (used on a sidesaddle)

footstool n a stool for the feet of a seated person.

footwear n shoes and socks, etc.

footwork n skilful use of the feet in boxing, football, dancing, etc.

footy n (sl) football.—also **footie**.

foozle n (golf) a bungled shot. * vi to bungle (a shot).

fop n someone obsessed with fashion and appearance.

foppery n (pl **fopperies**) the appearance, manner or dress of a fop.

foppish adj affected in dress and manners.—**foppishly** adv.—**foppishness** n.

for prep because of, as a result of; as the price of, or recompense of; in order to be, to serve as; appropriate to, or adapted to; in quest of; in the direction of; on behalf of; in place of; in favour of; with respect to; notwithstanding, in spite of; to the extent of; throughout the space of; during. * conj because.

for- prefix expressing prohibition or neglect; bad effect; intensity.

forage n food for domestic animals, esp when taken by browsing or grazing; a search for provisions. * vi to search for food.—**forager** n.

foramen n (pl **foraminia, foramens**) a short passage or opening, esp in a bone.

foraminifer n a member of a group of protozoa having a shell with very minute apertures, through which parts of its body pass.

forasmuch as conj seeing that, since.

foray n a sudden raid. * vti to plunder.—**forayer** n.

forbad, forbade see **forbid**.

forbear vb (**forbearing, forbore**, pp **forborne**) vi to endure, to avoid. * vt to hold oneself back from.—**forbearer** n.—**forbearingly** adv.

forbearance n patience; self-control.

forbid vt (**forbidding, forbad** or **forbade**, pp **forbidden** or **forbid**) to command (a person) not to do something; to render impossible, prevent.—**forbiddance** n.—**forbidder** n.

forbidding *adj* unfriendly, solemn, strict.—**forbiddingly** *adv.*

forbore, forborne *see* **forbear.**

force *n* strength, power, effort; *(physics)* (the intensity of) an influence that causes movement of a body or other effects; a body of soldiers, police, etc prepared for action; effectiveness; violence, compulsion; legal or logical validity. * *vt* to compel or oblige by physical effort, superior strength, etc; to achieve by force; to press or drive against resistance; to produce with effort; to break open, penetrate; to impose, inflict; to cause (plants, animals) to grow at a greater rate than normal.—**forceable** *adj.*—**forcer** *n.*

forced *adj* compulsory; strained.—**forcedly** *adv.*—**forcedness** *n.*

force-feed *vt* (**force-feeding, force-fed**) to compel a person to swallow food.

forceful *adj* powerful, effective.—**forcefully** *adv.*—**forcefulness** *n.*

force majeure *n* compelling force, unavoidable circumstances.

forcemeat *n* finely chopped meat, seasoned and used as a stuffing.

force pump *n* a pump that forces water beyond the range of atmospheric pressure.

forceps *n* (*pl* **forceps, forcipes**) an instrument for grasping and holding firmly, or exerting traction upon objects, esp by jewellers and surgeons.

forcible *adj* powerful; done by force.—**forcibleness** *n.*—**forcibly** *adv.*

ford *n* a shallow crossing place in a river, stream, etc. * *vt* to wade across.—**fordable** *adj.*

fore *adj* in front. * *n* the front. * *adv* in, at or towards the front. * *interj* (*golf*) a warning cry to anybody who may be hit by the ball.

fore- *prefix* in front; beforehand.

fore-and-aft *adj* (*naut*) (situated) at both bow and stern.

forearm[1] *n* the arm between the elbow and the wrist.

forearm[2] *vt* to arm in advance.

forebear *n* (*usu pl*) an ancestor.

forebode *vt* to be a sign or warning (of trouble, etc) in advance; to have a premonition of (an event).—**foreboder** *n.*

foreboding *n* a feeling that evil is going to happen, a presentiment.

forecast *vt* (**forecasting, forecast** *or* **forecasted**) to predict (an event, the weather, etc) through rational analysis; to serve as a forecast of. * *n* a prediction, esp of weather; foresight.—**forecaster** *n.*

forecastle *n* the forward part of a ship containing the crew's quarters.—*also* **fo'c's'le, fo'c'sle**

foreclose *vt* to remove the right of redeeming (a mortgage); to bar, exclude; to hinder.—**foreclosable** *adj.*—**foreclosure** *n.*

forecourt *n* an enclosed space in front of a building, as in a filling station.

forefather *n* (*usu pl*) an ancestor.

forefinger *n* the finger next to the thumb.

forefoot *n* (*pl* **forefeet**) a front foot of an animal; (*naut*) the foremost piece of the keel.

forefront *n* the very front, vanguard.

foregather *see* **forgather.**

forego[1] *see* **forgo.**

forego[2] *vt* (**foregoing, forewent,** *pp* **foregone**) to precede.—**foregoer** *n.*

foregoing *adj* going before, preceding.

foregone conclusion *n* an inevitable result, easily predictable.

foreground *n* the part of a picture or view nearest the spectator's vision.

forehand *n* (*tennis, etc*) a stroke made with the hand facing forwards; the part of a horse in front of the rider. * *adj* (*tennis stroke*) made with the palm leading.

forehanded *adj* thrifty; well-off.—**forehandedness** *n.*

forehead *n* the part of the face above the eyes.

foreign *adj* of, in, or belonging to another country; involving other countries; alien in character; introduced from outside.

foreigner *n* a person from another country; a stranger.

foreignism *n.*a foreign mannerism, custom or saying, or an imitation of any of these.

foreign office *n* the government department which handles foreign affairs.—*also* **state department.**

forejudge *vti* to judge before hearing evidence.

foreknow *vt* (**foreknowing, foreknew,** *pl* **foreknown**) to know beforehand.—**foreknowledge** *n.*

foreland *n* a promontory, a headland.

foreleg *n* a front leg of an animal.

forelock *n* the lock of hair growing above the forehead.

foreman *n* (*pl* **foremen**) a person who supervises workers in a factory, etc; the spokesperson of a jury.—**forewoman** *nf* (*pl* **forewomen**).

foremast *n* the mast nearest the bow of a sailing vessel.

foremost *adj* first in importance; most advanced in rank or position. * *adv* in the first place.

forenoon *n* time before midday; morning.

forensic *adj* of, belonging to or used in courts of law.—**forensicality** *n.*—**forensically** *adv.*

forensic medicine *n* the application of medical expertise to legal and criminal investigations.

foreordain *vt* to arrange in advance; to predestine.—**foreordainment, foreordination** *n.*

forepeak *n* (*naut*) the end of a ship's hold in the angle of the bow.

foreplay *n* mutual sexual stimulation before intercourse.

forerun *vt* (**forerunning, foreran,** *pp* **forerun**) to precede, to foreshadow.

forerunner *n* a person or thing that comes in advance of another; a portent.

foresail *n* (*naut*) the largest sail on the foremast of a sailing vessel.

foresee *vt* (**foreseeing, foresaw,** *pp* **foreseen**) to be aware of beforehand.—**foreseeable** *adj.*—**foreseer** *n.*

foreshadow *vt* to represent or indicate beforehand.—**foreshadower** *n.*

foresheet *n* a rope for controlling a foresail; (*pl*) the inner part of a boat's bows.

foreshore *n* a strip of land next to the shore; the shore between the high and low water marks.

foreshorten *vt* in drawing, etc, to shorten some lines of (an object) to give the illusion of proper relative size.

foresight *n* foreseeing; the power to foresee; prudent provision for the future.—**foresighted** *adj.*—**foresightedness** *n.*

foreskin *n* the loose skin that covers the end of the penis.

forest *n* a thick growth of trees, etc covering a large tract of land; something resembling a forest. * *vt* to plant with trees; to make into forest.—**forestal, forestial** *adj.*

forestall *vt* to prevent by taking action beforehand; to anticipate.—**forestaller** *n.*—**forestalment, forestallment** *n.*

forestation *n* the planting of trees over a large area.

forestay n (*naut*) a strong rope reaching from the top of the foremast to the bow of a vessel.

forester n a person trained in forestry.

forestry n the science of planting and cultivating forests.

foretaste n partial experience in advance; anticipation. * vt to taste before possession; to have a foretaste of.

foretell vt (**foretelling, foretold**) to forecast, to predict.—**foreteller** n.

forethought n thought for the future; provident care.—**forethoughtful** adj.

foretime n the past, old times.

foretoken vt to portend, foreshadow. * n an omen.

foretop n (*naut*) a platform at the head of the foremast.

fore-topgallant mast n the mast above the fore-top-mast, carrying the fore-topgallant sail.

fore-topmast n (*naut*) the mast immediately above the foremast, carrying the fore-topsail.

for ever, forever adv for all future time; continually.

for evermore, forevermore adv for ever.

forewarn vt to warn beforehand.—**forewarner** n.—**forewarningly** adv.

forewent see **forego**².

forewind n (*naut*) a favourable wind.

forewoman n (*pl* **forewomen**) a person who supervises workers in a factory, etc; the spokesperson of a jury.

foreword n an introduction to a book to explain its purpose, often by someone other than the author.

forfeit n something confiscated or given up as a penalty for a fault; (*pl*) a game in which a player redeems a forfeit by performing a ludicrous task. * vt to lose or be penalized by forfeiture.—**forfeiter** n.—**forfeiture** n.

forfend vt to protect; (*arch*) to avert, ward off.

forficate adj (*zool*) scissor-shaped, forked.

forgather vi to assemble, meet.—*also* **foregather**.

forgave see **forgive**.

forge¹ n (a workshop with) a furnace in which metals are heated and shaped.* vt to shape (metal) by heating and hammering; to counterfeit (eg a signature). * vi to commit forgery.—**forgeable** adj.—**forger** n.

forge² vt to move steadily forward with effort.

forgery n (*pl* **forgeries**) fraudulently copying; a forged copy; a spurious thing.

forget vti (**forgetting, forgot,** *pp* **forgotten**) to be unable to remember; to overlook or neglect; **forget oneself** to lose self-control; to act unbecomingly.—**forgettable** adj.—**forgetter** n.

forgetful adj apt to forget, inattentive.—**forgetfully** adv.—**forgetfulness** n.

forget-me-not n a plant with bright-blue or white flowers.

forgive vt (**forgiving, forgave,** *pp* **forgiven**) to cease to feel resentment against (a person); to pardon. * vi to be merciful or forgiving.—**forgivable** adj.—**forgiveness** n.—**forgiver** n.

forgiving adj willing to forgive; merciful, kind.—**forgivingly** adv.

forgo vt (**forgoing, forwent,** *pp* **forgone**) to give up, abstain from.—*also* **forego**.—**forgoer** n.

forgot, forgotten see **forget**.

fork n a small, usu metal, instrument with two or more thin prongs set in a handle, used in eating and cooking; a pronged agricultural or gardening tool for digging, etc; anything that divides into prongs or branches; one of the branches into which a road or river divides; the point of separation. * vi to divide into branches; to follow a branch of a fork in a road, etc. * vt to form as a fork; to dig, lift, etc with a fork; (*with* out) (*sl*) to pay or hand over (money, goods, etc).

forked adj shaped like a fork; branching, opening into two or more parts; zigzag, eg lightning.

fork-lift truck n a vehicle with power-operated prongs for raising and lowering loads.

forlorn adj alone; wretched.—**forlornly** adv.

forlorn hope n a faint hope; a desperate enterprise.

form n general structure; the figure of a person or animal; a mould; a particular mode, kind, type, etc; arrangement; a way of doing something requiring skill; a conventional procedure; a printed document with blanks to be filled in; a class in school; condition of mind or body; a chart giving information about racehorses; changed appearance of a word to show inflection; (*sl*) a criminal record. * vt to shape; to train; to develop (habits); to constitute. * vi to be formed.—**formable** adj.

form²*see* **forme**.

formal adj in conformity with established rules or habits; regular; relating to the outward appearance only; ceremonial; punctilious; stiff.—**formally** adv.

formaldehyde n a colourless pungent gas used in solution as a disinfectant and preservative.

formalin n an aqueous solution of formaldehyde used as an antiseptic or preservative.—*also* **formol**.

formalism n strict observance of outward form or conventional usage.—**formalist** n.—**formalistic** adj.

formality n (*pl* **formalities**) strict observance of established rules or customs; an act or procedure required by law or convention.

formalize vt to make formal; to clothe with legal formality.—**formalization** n.

format n the size, form, shape in which books, etc are issued; the general style or presentation of something, eg a television programme; (*comput*) the arrangement of data on magnetic disk, etc for access and storage. * vt (**formatting, formatted**) to arrange in a particular form, esp for a computer.

formate n a salt of formic acid..

formation n form of making or producing; that which is formed; structure; regular array or prearranged order; (*geol*) a group of strata with common characteristics.—**formational** adj.

formative adj pertaining to formation and development; shaping; (*gram*) used in forming words.—**formatively** adv.—**formativeness** n.

forme n a frame with type assembled in it for printing.—*also* **form**.

former adj of or occurring in a previous time; the first mentioned (of two).—**formerly** adv.

formerly adv previously; heretofore.

formic adj of or pertaining to ants or formic acid.

Formica n (*trademark*) a heat-resistant laminated sheeting.

formic acid n a colourless pungent liquid found esp in ants and many plants.

formicary, formicarium n (*pl* **formicaries, formicaria**) an anthill.

formication n an irritation of the skin, resembling the sensation made by insects crawling over it.

formidable adj causing fear or awe; difficult to defeat or overcome; difficult to handle.—**formidability** n.—**formidably** adv.

formless adj without distinct form, shapeless.—**formlessness** n.

formol see **formalin**.

formula n (pl **formulas, formulae**) a set of symbols expressing the composition of a substance; a general expression in algebraic form for solving a problem; a prescribed form; a formal statement of doctrines; a list of ingredients, as for a prescription or recipe; a fixed method according to which something is to be done; a prescribed recipe for baby food.—**formulaic** adj.

formularize vt to formulate.—**formularization** n.—**formularizer** n.

formulary n (pl **formularies**) a book of prescribed forms, or of prayers, ritual, etc; (med) a book giving details of the formulas and preparation of pharmaceutical products. * adj of formulas or ritual.

formulate vt to express in a formula; to devise.—**formulation** n.—**formulator** n.

formulism n adherence to formulas.—**formulist** adj, n.

fornicate[1] vi to have sexual intercourse without being married.—**fornication** n.—**fornicator** n.

fornicate[2], **fornicated** adj (archit) vaulted, arched.

fornix n (pl **fornices**) (anat) an arch-shaped part.

forsake vt (**forsaking, forsook**, pp **forsaken**) to desert; to give up, renounce.—**forsaker** n.

forsooth adv (arch) in truth.

forswear vb (**forswearing, forswore**, pp **forsworn**) vt to reject, renounce; to deny; to perjure (oneself).

forsythia n a widely cultivated, yellow-flowered shrub.

fort n a fortified place for military defence.

forte[1] n something at which a person excels.

forte[2] adv (mus) loudly.

forte-piano adj, adv (music) loud, then soft.

forth adv forwards; onwards; out; into view; **and so forth** and the like.

forthcoming adj about to appear; readily available; responsive.—**forthcomingness** n.

forthright adv frank, direct, outspoken; decisive.—**forthrightly** adv.—**forthrightness** n.

forthwith adv immediately, without delay.

fortification n the act or process of fortifying; a wall, barricade, etc built to defend a position.

fortify vt (**fortifying, fortified**) to strengthen physically, emotionally, etc; to strengthen against attack, as with forts; to support; (wine, etc) to add alcohol to; (milk) to add vitamins to.—**fortifiable** adj.—**fortifier** n.

fortissimo adv (mus) very loud. * n (pl **fortissimos, fortissimi**) (mus) a passage played very loudly.

fortitude n courage in adversity; patient endurance, firmness.—**fortitudinous** adj.

fortnight n a period of two weeks or fourteen consecutive days.

fortnightly adj, adv once a fortnight.

Fortran n (comput) a high-level programming language used for scientific and mathematical problem-solving.

fortress n a strong fort or fortified town.

fortuitous adj happening by chance.—**fortuitously** adv.—**fortuitousness** n.

fortuity n (pl **fortuities**) fortuitousness; accident, chance.

fortunate adj having or occurring by good luck.—**fortunately** adv.

fortune n the supposed arbitrary power that determines events; luck; destiny; prosperity, success; vast wealth.

fortune hunter n someone who seeks to become rich, esp by marrying for money.

fortune-teller n a person who claims to foretell a person's future.—**fortune-telling** n.

forty n (pl **forties**) four times ten, the symbol for this (40, XL, xl).—also adj.—**fortieth** adj.

forty-five n a gramophone record played at 45 revolutions per minute; (with cap) the Jacobite rebellion of 1745.

forty-niner n a pioneer who went to California in 1849 to look for gold.

forty winks n (sing or pl) a nap.

forum n (pl **forums, fora**) an assembly or meeting to discuss topics of public concern; a medium for public debate, as a magazine; the marketplace and centre of public affairs in ancient Rome.

forward adj at, toward, or of the front; advanced; onward; prompt; bold; presumptuous; of or for the future. * vt to promote; to send on. * n (sport) an attacking player in various games. * adv toward the front; ahead.—**forwardness** n.

forwardly adv pertly; promptly; forwards.

forwards adv towards the front, in an onward direction

forwent see **forgo**.

forzando adv (music) with sudden emphasis.

fossa n (pl **fossae**) (anat) a groove, pit or cavity.

fosse, foss n a ditch or moat, esp in a fortification.

fossick vt to search for by picking over, to rummage.—**fossicker** n.

fossil n the petrified remains of an animal or vegetable preserved in rock; (inf) a thing or person regarded as outmoded or redundant. * adj of or like a fossil; dug from the earth.

fossiliferous adj containing fossils.

fossilize vti to change or become changed into a fossil.—**fossilization** n.

fossorial adj (zool) used for digging.

foster vt to encourage; to bring up (a child that is not one's own). * adj affording, giving, sharing or receiving parental care although not related.—**fosterer** n.

fosterage n the act of fostering.

fosterling n a foster child.

foudroyant adj sudden and overwhelming; dazzling, like lightning.

fought see **fight**.

foul adj stinking, loathsome; extremely dirty; indecent; wicked; (language) obscene; (weather) stormy; (sports) against the rules. * adv unfairly. * vt to make filthy; to dishonour; to obstruct; to entangle (a rope, etc); to make a foul against, as in a game; (with **up**) to contaminate; to ruin, bungle; to cause to become blocked or entangled. * vi to be or become fouled; (with **up**) to become blocked or entangled. * n (sports) a hit, blow, move, etc that is foul.—**foully** adv.—**foulness** n.

foulard n a light silk, or silk-cotton, fabric; a scarf made of this fabric.

foul-mouthed adj using abusive or obscene language.

foul play n fouls in sport; violent crime, murder.

found[1] see **find**.

found[2] vt to bring into being; to establish (as an institution) often with provision for future maintenance.

found[3] vt to melt and pour (metal) into a mould to produce castings.

foundation n an endowment for an institution; such an institution; the base of a house, wall, etc; a first layer of cosmetic applied to the skin; an underlying principle, etc; a supporting undergarment, as a corset.—**foundational** adj.—**foundationary** adj.

founder[1] n one who founds an institution, a benefactor.

founder[2] n a person who casts metal.

founder[3] vi (ship) to fill with water and sink; to collapse; to fail.

foundling n a deserted child whose parents are unknown.

foundry n (pl **foundries**) a workshop or factory where metal castings are produced.

fount[1] n a set of printing type or characters of one style and size.—also **font**.

fount[2] n a source.

fountain n a natural spring of water; a source; an artificial jet or flow of water; the basin where this flows; a reservoir, as for ink. * vti to (cause to) flow or spurt like a fountain.

fountainhead n a spring from which a stream flows; a first source.

fountain pen n a pen with an internal reservoir or cartridge of ink which supplies the nib.

four n one more than three; the symbol for this (4, IV, iv); the fourth in a series or set; something having four units as members (as a four-cylinder engine); a four-oared boat or its crew.—also adj.

fourchette n (anat) a fold of skin situated at the rear of the vulva.

four flush n a poker hand with four cards of one suit.

four-flusher n a bluffer.

fourfold adj having four units or members; being four times as great or as many.—also adv.

fourhanded adj for four players; (mus) for two players.

four-letter word n any of various words regarded as offensive or obscene typically containing four letters.

four-poster n a bed with four posts and a canopy.

fourscore n eighty.

foursome n a group or set of four; (golf) a game between two pairs in which each pair has one ball.

foursquare adj square; firm. * adv squarely; firmly.

four-stroke adj (internal-combustion engine) having a piston that operates a cycle of four strokes for every explosion.

fourteen n, adj four and ten; the symbol for this (14, XIV, xiv).—**fourteenth** adj.

fourth adj next after third. * n one of four equal parts of something.—**fourthly** adv.

fourth dimension n time as added to the three spatial dimensions (length, breadth, depth).

fourth estate n journalists or the press in general.

Fourth of July n Independence Day of U.S.A.

fowl n any of the domestic birds used as food, as the chicken, duck, etc; the flesh of these birds. * vi to hunt or snare wildfowl.—**fowler** n.—**fowling** n.

fox n (pl **foxes, fox**) any of various small, alert wild mammals of the dog family; the fur of the fox; a sly, crafty person. * vt to deceive by cunning. * vi (inf) to bemuse, puzzle.

foxglove n a tall plant with spikes of purple or white flowers.

foxhole n a pit dug in the ground as a protection against enemy fire.

foxhound n any of various large swift powerful hounds of great endurance used in hunting foxes.

foxtail n a type of grass found in Europe, Asia and South America.

fox-terrier n any of a breed of small lively terriers formerly used to dig out foxes.

foxtrot n a dance for couples in 4/4 time. * vi (**foxtrotting, foxtrotted**) to dance the foxtrot.

foxy adj (**foxier, foxiest**) reddish-brown; crafty; resembling a fox; physically attractive.—**foxily** adv.—**foxiness** n.

foyer n an anteroom; an entrance hallway, as in a hotel or theatre.

FP abbr = (US) fireplug; former pupil.

Fr (chem symbol) francium.

fr abbr = franc.

Fra n (title) a friar.

fracas n (pl **fracas, fracases**) uproar; a noisy quarrel.

fraction n a small part, amount, etc; (math) a quantity less than a whole, expressed as a decimal or with a numerator and denominator.—**fractionary** adj.—**fractionally** adv.

fractional adj of or pertaining to fractions; inconsiderable, very small.

fractional distillation n the process used for separating a mixture of liquids into component parts by distillation.

fractionate vt to separate (elements of a mixture) by distillation.—**fractionation** n.

fractionize vt to divide into fractions.—**fractionization** n.

fractious adj quarrelsome; peevish.—**fractiously** adv.—**fractiousness** n.

fracture n the breaking of any hard material, esp a bone. * vti to break; to cause or suffer a fracture.—**fracturable** adj.—**fractural** adj.

fragile adj easily broken; frail; delicate.—**fragilely** adv.—**fragility, fragileness** n.

fragment n a piece broken off or detached; an incomplete portion. * vti to break or cause to break into fragments.—**fragmentation** n.

fragmentary adj consisting of fragments; incomplete.—**fragmentarily** adv.—**fragmentariness** n.

fragrance, fragrancy n (pl **fragrances, fragrancies**) a pleasant scent, a perfume.

fragrant adj sweet-scented.—**fragrantly** adv.

frail[1] adj physically or morally weak; fragile.—**frailly** adv.—**frailness** n.

frail[2] n a rush basket; the quantity of fruit held in a frail.

frailty n (pl **frailties**) physical or moral weakness; infirmity; a failing.

fraise n a palisade of pointed sticks, used in a rampart; a type of neck ruff; a tool used to enlarge a drill hole.

framboesia, frambesia n an infectious tropical disease, causing red skin eruptions and joint pain.—also **yaws**.

frame vt to form according to a pattern; to construct; to put into words; to enclose (a picture) in a border; (sl) to falsify evidence against (an innocent person). * n something composed of parts fitted together and united; the physical make-up of an animal, esp a human body; the framework of a house; the structural case enclosing a window, door, etc; an ornamental border, as around a picture; (snooker) a triangular mould for setting up balls before play; (snooker) a single game.—**framable, frameable** adj.—**framer** n.

frame of reference n an arbitrary system of axes for describing the position or motion of something or from which physical laws are derived; a set or system (as of facts and ideas) serving to orient; a viewpoint, a theory.

frame-up n (sl) a conspiracy to have someone falsely accused of a crime.

framework n a structural frame; a basic structure (as of ideas); frame of reference.

franc *n* a unit of money in France, Belgium, and Switzerland.

franchise *n* the right to vote in public elections; authorization to sell the goods of a manufacturer in a particular area. * *vt* to grant a franchise.—**franchisement** *n.*

Franciscan *n* a member of the Order of Friars Minor founded by St Francis of Assisi in 1209.

francium *n* a radioactive metallic element.

Franco- *prefix* France; French.

francolin *n* a kind of partridge, found in Africa and Asia.

Francophile *n* a lover of France or its customs, etc.

frangible *adj* fragile, easily broken.—**frangibility** *n.*

frangipane *n* a paste or cake made with almonds and cream.

frangipani *n* (*pl* **frangipanis, frangipani**) a tropical American shrub, the flowers of which are used to make a perfume.

Frank *n* a member of a West Germanic people who conquered Gaul in the 4th century AD.—**Frankish** *adj.*

frank *adj* free and direct in expressing oneself; honest, open. * *vt* to mark letters, etc with a mark denoting free postage. * *n* a mark indicating free postage.—**frankly** *adv.*—**frankness** *n.*

Frankenstein *n* a work that ruins its originator.

frankfurter *n* a type of smoked sausage.

frankincense *n* a fragrant gum resin.

franklin *n* a middle-class landowner in 14th and 15th century England.

frantic *adj* violently agitated; furious, wild.—**frantically, franticly** *adv.*

frap *vt* (**frapping, frapped**) (*naut*) to bind tightly.

frappé *adj* iced; chilled.

frater[1] *n* a friar.

frater[2] *n* (*arch*) a refectory.

fraternal *adj* of or belonging to a brother or fraternity; friendly, brotherly.—**fraternalism** *n.*—**fraternally** *adv.*

fraternity *n* (*pl* **fraternities**) brotherly feeling; a society of people with common interests.

fraternize *vt* to associate in a friendly manner.—**fraternization** *n.*

fratricide *n* the murder of a brother; a person guilty of this.—**fratricidal** *adj.*

Frau *n* (*pl* **Frauen, Fraus**) (a title of) a married German woman.

fraud *n* deliberate deceit; an act of deception; (*inf*) a deceitful person; an impostor.

fraudulent *adj* deceiving or intending to deceive; obtained by deceit.—**fraudulence, fraudulency** *n.*—**fraudulently** *adv.*

fraught *adj* filled or loaded (with); (*inf*) anxious; difficult.

Fraülein *n* (*pl* **Fraülein, Fraüleins**) (a title of) an unmarried German woman.

fraxinella *n* a white-flowered Eurasian plant.

fray[1] *n* a fight, a brawl.

fray[2] *vti* (*fabric, etc*) to (cause to) wear away into threads, esp at the edge of; (*nerves, temper*) to make or become irritated or strained.

frazil *n* the ice that forms in a stream.

frazzle *vt* to exhaust; to fray, tatter. * *n* (*inf*) a state of exhaustion.

freak[1] *n* an unusual happening; any abnormal animal, person, or plant; (*inf*) a person who dresses or acts in a notably unconventional manner; an ardent enthusiast. * *vi* (*with* **out**) (*inf*) to hallucinate under the influence of drugs; to experience intense emotional excitement.—**freakish** *adj.*

freak[2] *vt* to variegate; to spot or streak.

freakish *adj* very unusual; changing suddenly.—**freakishly** *adv.*—**freakishness** *n.*

freckle *n* a small, brownish spot on the skin. * *vti* to make or become spotted with freckles.—**freckled, freckly** *adj.*

free *adj* (**freer, freest**) not under the control or power of another; having social and political liberty; independent; able to move in any direction; not burdened by obligations; not confined to the usual rules; not exact; generous; frank; with no cost or charge; exempt from taxes, duties, etc; clear of obstruction; not fastened. * *adv* without cost; in a free manner. * *vt* (**freeing, freed**) to set free; to clear of obstruction, etc.—**freely** *adv.*

freebie *n* (*sl*) something provided free of charge.

freeboard *n* the part of the side of a ship between the upper side of the deck and the water-line.

freebooter *n* a pirate; a plunderer.

freeborn *adj* born of free parents, as opposed to in slavery.

freedman *n* (*pl* **freedmen**) an emancipated slave.

freedom fighter *n* a person violently resisting an oppressive political regime.

freedom *n* being free; exemption from obligation; unrestricted use; a right or privilege.

free enterprise *n* the freedom of business from government intervention or control.

free fall *n* the descent of a body under the force of gravity alone, as a parachutist before the parachute opens.

free fight *n* an indiscriminate contest, a melée.

free-for-all *n* (*inf*) a disorganized fight or brawl involving as many participants as are willing.

free hand *n* freedom to act as desired.

freehand *adj* (*drawing, etc*) drawn by the hand without the aid of instruments.

freehanded *adj* generous; liberal.—**freehandedly** *adv.*—**freehandedness** *n.*

freehold *n* tenure without rent; absolute ownership; an estate so held.—**freeholder** *n.*

free house *n* in the UK, a public house which is allowed to sell drinks from more than one brewer.

free kick *n* (*soccer, rugby*) a place kick awarded because of a foul or infringement by an opponent.

freelance *n* a person who pursues a profession without long-term commitment to any employer (—*also* **freelancer**). * *vt* to work as a freelance.

free-living *n* (*organisms*) not parasitic.—**free-liver** *n.*

freeload *vi* to impose upon another's hospitality.—**freeloader** *n.*

free love *n* sexual intercourse without the restraints of marriage.

freeman *n* (*pl* **freemen**) someone who is not a slave; someone with civic rights.

freemartin *n* a sexually imperfect and sterile cow calf, born as the twin of a bull calf.

Freemason *n* a member of the secretive fraternity (Free and Accepted Masons) dedicated to mutual aid.

freemasonry *n* mutual help between persons of similar interests.

free port *n* a port where goods are received and shipped free of customs duty.

free-range *adj* (*hens*) allowed to roam freely, not confined in a battery; (*eggs*) produced by hens raised in this way.

freesheet *n* a newspaper distributed free of charge.

freesia *n* a sweet-scented African plant of the iris family.

freespoken *adj* outspoken, blunt.—**freespokenness** *n*.

freestanding *adj* (*furniture*) standing on its own; not attached.

freestone *n* a type of limestone or sandstone that is suitable for working.

freestyle *n* a swimming competition in which the competitor chooses the stroke.

freethinker *n* a person who rejects authority in religion, etc; a sceptic.

free trade *n* trade based on the unrestricted international exchange of goods with tariffs used only as a source of revenue.—**free-trader** *n*.

free verse *n* verse without a fixed metrical pattern.

freeway *n* in North America, a fast road, a motorway.

freewheel *n* a device for temporarily disconnecting and setting free the back wheel of a bicycle from the driving gear. * *vi* to ride a bicycle with the gear disconnected; to drive a car with the gear in neutral.—**freewheeler** *n*.

free will *n* voluntary choice or decision; freedom of human beings to make choices that are not determined by prior causes or by divine intervention.

freeze *vb* (**freezing, froze,** *pp* **frozen**) *vi* to be formed into, or become covered by ice; to become very cold; to be damaged or killed by cold; to become motionless; to be made speechless by strong emotion; to become formal and unfriendly. * *vt* to harden into ice; to convert from a liquid to a solid with cold; to make extremely cold; to act towards in a stiff and formal way; to act on usu destructively by frost; to anaesthetize by cold; to fix (prices, etc) at a given level by authority; to make (funds, etc) unavailable to the owners by authority.—**freezable** *adj*.

freeze-dry *vt* (**freeze-drying, freeze-dried**) to preserve (food) by rapid freezing and then drying in a vacuum.

freeze-frame *n* a frame of a motion picture or television film that is repeated to give the illusion of a static picture.

freezer *n* a compartment or container that freezes and preserves food for long periods.

freezing *adj* very cold.

freezing point *n* the temperature at which a liquid solidifies.

freight *n* the transport of goods by water, land, or air; the cost for this; the goods transported. * *vt* to load with freight; to send by freight.

freightage *n* the conveyance of cargo; the cargo conveyed; a charge made for transporting cargo.

freight car *n* a rail truck for carrying freight.

freighter *n* one who freights; a ship or aircraft carrying freight.

French *adj* of France, its people, culture, etc. * *n* the language of France.

French bread *n* bread in a long, slender loaf.

French chalk *n* a soapstone used as a dry lubricant and to mark cloth, etc.

French doors *see* **French windows.**

French dressing *n* a salad dressing made from vinegar, oil and seasonings.

French fries, french fries *npl* thin strips of potato fried in oil, etc, chips.

French horn *n* an orchestral brass instrument with a narrow conical tube wound twice in a circle, a funnel shaped mouthpiece, and a flaring bell.

Frenchify *vti* (**Frenchifies, Frenchifying, Frenchified**) (*inf*) to make or become French.

French leave *n* leave taken without permission; a hasty or secret departure.

French letter *n* a condom.

French polish *n* a shellac varnish for furniture.

French roof *n* a mansard roof.

French toast *n* toast with one side buttered and the other toasted; bread soaked in milk and batter and fried lightly.

French windows *npl* a pair of casement windows extending to the floor that are placed in an outside wall and open on to a patio, garden, etc.—*also* **French doors.**

frenetic *adj* frantic, frenzied.—**frenetically** *adv*.

frenzy *n* (*pl* **frenzies**) wild excitement; violent mental derangement. * *vt* (**frenzying, frenzied**) to infuriate, to madden.—**frenzied** *adj*.—**frenziedly** *adv*.

frequency *n* (*pl* **frequencies**) repeated occurrence; the number of occurrences, cycles, etc in a given period.

frequency modulation *n* the transmission of signals by radio waves whose frequency varies according to the amplitude of the signal.

frequent *adj* coming or happening often. * *vi* to visit often; to resort to.—**frequenter** *n*.—**frequently** *adv*.

frequentative *adj* (*gram*) expressing repetition and intensity (of a verb). * *n* a frequentative verb.

fresco *n* (*pl* **frescos, frescoes**) a picture painted on walls covered with damp freshly laid plaster. * *vt* (**frescoing, frescoed**) to paint in fresco.

fresh *adj* recently made, grown, etc; not salted, pickled, etc; not spoiled; lively, not tired; not worn, soiled, faded, etc; new, recent; inexperienced; cool and refreshing; (*wind*) brisk; (*water*) not salt; (*inf*) presumptuous, impertinent. * *adv* newly.—**freshly** *adv*.—**freshness** *n*.

freshen *vi* to make or become fresh.—**freshener** *n*.

fresher *n* (*pl* **freshers**) a freshman.

freshet *n* a flood caused by melting snow or heavy rain; a stream of fresh water.

freshman *n* (*pl* **freshmen**) a first year student at university, college or high school.

freshwater *adj* of a river; not sea-going.

fret[1] *vti* (**fretting, fretted**) to make or become worried or anxious; to wear away or roughen by rubbing.

fret[2] *n* a running design of interlacing small bars. * *vt* (**fretting, fretted**) to furnish with frets.

fret[3] *n* any of a series of metal ridges along the fingerboard of a guitar, banjo, etc used as a guide for depressing the strings.

fretful *adj* troubled; peevish; irritable; impatient.—**fretfully** *adv*.—**fretfulness** *n*.

fretsaw *n* a narrow saw held under tension in a frame used for cutting intricate designs in wood or metal.

fretwork *n* decorative carving consisting of frets.

Freudian *adj* of or pertaining to the psychoanalytic theories of Sigmund Freud. * *n* a psychoanalyst who follows the theories of Freud.—**Freudianism** *n*.

Freudian slip *n* a slip of the tongue said to betray an unconscious feeling.

Fri. *abbr* = Friday.

friable *adj* easily crumbled.—**friability** *n*.

friar *n* a member of certain Roman Catholic religious orders.

friarbird *n* an Australasian songbird with a tongue specially adapted to extract nectar.

friary n (pl **friaries**) a monastery of friars.

fribble vt to fritter away. * vi to trifle.—**fribbler** n.

fricandeau, fricando n (pl **fricandeaus, fricandeaux, fricandoes**) a dish made from spiced, stewed veal.

fricassee n a dish made of stewed poultry, rabbit, etc in a white sauce. * vt (**fricasseeing, fricasseed**) to cook in this way.

fricative n (phonetics) a sound, eg "f," produced by the friction of breath in a narrow opening. * adj pertaining to a fricative.

friction n a rubbing of one object against another; conflict between differing opinions, ideas, etc; the resistance to motion of things that touch.—**frictional** adj.

friction clutch n a clutch that transmits motion by friction.

Friday n the sixth day of the week.

fridge n (inf) a refrigerator.

fried see **fry**[1].

friend n a person whom one knows well and is fond of; an ally, supporter, or sympathizer. * vt (arch) to befriend.—**friendless** adj.—**friendship** n.

friendly adj (**friendlier, friendliest**) like a friend; kindly; favourable. * n a sporting game played for fun, not in competition.—**friendlily** adv.—**friendliness** n.

friendly society n an association for mutual insurance against sickness, etc.

friendship n the state of being friends; intimacy united with affection or esteem; mutual attachment; goodwill.

frier see **fry**[1].

frieze[1] n a decorative band along the top of the wall of a room; (archit) the part of an entablature between the architrave and cornice, often filled with sculpture.

frieze[2] n a coarse woollen cloth with a rough shaggy nap on one side.

frigate n a warship smaller than a destroyer used for escort, anti-submarine, and patrol duties.

frigate bird n a swift-flying tropical sea bird.

fright n sudden fear; a shock; (inf) something unsightly or ridiculous in appearance.

frighten vt to terrify, to scare; to force by frightening.—**frightener** n.—**frighteningly** adv.

frightful adj terrible, shocking; (inf) extreme, very bad.—**frightfully** adv.—**frightfulness** n.

frigid adj extremely cold; not warm or friendly; unresponsive sexually.—**frigidity** n.—**frigidly** adv.

Frigid Zone n either of the areas within the Arctic or Antarctic circles.

frigorific adj (arch) causing cold.

frijol n (pl **frijoles**) a type of bean, widely cultivated for eating in Mexico.

frill n a piece of pleated or gathered fabric used for edging; something superfluous, an affectation. * vt to decorate with a frill or frills.—**frilled** adj.—**frilly** adj.

fringe n a decorative border of hanging threads; hair hanging over the forehead; an outer edge; a marginal or minor part. * vt to be or make a fringe for. * adj at the outer edge; additional; minor; unconventional.

fringe benefit n a benefit given by an employer to supplement an employee's wages; any additional advantage.

frippery n (pl **fripperies**) cheap, gaudy clothes or ornaments; trivia.

Frisbee n (trademark) a plastic disc that is spun through the air for recreation or sport.

frisette n a curly fringe, esp of false hair.—also **frizette**.

frisk vi to leap playfully. * vt (inf) to search (a person) by feeling for concealed weapons, etc. * n a gambol, dance, or frolic.—**frisker** n.

frisky adj (**friskier, friskiest**) lively, playful.—**friskily** adv.—**friskiness** n.

frisson n an emotional thrill, a shiver of excitement.

frit, fritt n the mixture of sand and fluxes from which glass is made. * vt (**fritting, fritted**) to make into frit.

frith see **firth**.

frit fly n a small fly destructive to grain.

fritillary n (pl **fritillaries**) a flowering plant of the lily kind, the petals of which are variegated with purple, dice-shaped marks; a butterfly with brownish wings spotted with black or silver.

fritt see **frit**.

fritter[1] n a slice of fruit or meat fried in batter.

fritter[2] vt (with **away**) to waste; to break into tiny pieces.—**fritterer** n.

frivol vb (**frivolling, frivolled** or **frivoling, frivoled**) vi to behave in a frivolous way; to trifle. * vt to squander.

frivolity n (pl **frivolities**) a trifling act, thought, or action.

frivolous adj irresponsible; trifling; silly.—**frivolously** adv.—**frivolousness** n.

frizette n see **frisette**.

frizz vti (hair) to (cause to) form into small tight curls. * n hair that is frizzed.—**frizzer** n.

frizzle[1] vt to frizz. * n a small tight curl.—**frizzler** n.

frizzle[2] vti to sizzle, as in frying; to scorch by frying.

frizzy, frizzly adj (**frizzier, frizziest** or **frizzlier, frizzliest**) (hair) in tight wiry curls.—**frizziness, frizzliness** n.

fro adv away from; backward; **to and fro** back and forward.

frock n a dress; a smock; a loose wide-sleeved gown worn by a monk. * vt to put on a frock; to invest with the office of priest.

frock coat n a double-breasted skirted coat for men.

frog[1] n a small tailless web-footed jumping amphibian; (offensive) a French person.

frog[2] n a decorative loop used to fasten clothing; an attachment on a belt for carrying a sword.—**frogged** adj.

frog[3] n a section of rail where two lines cross.

frog[4] n a tender horny substance growing in the middle of the sole of a horse's foot.

frogfish n (pl **frogfish, frogfishes**) a variety of angler fish.

froggy adj (**froggier, froggiest**) resembling or containing a frog or frogs.

froghopper n a small jumping insect whose larvae secrete a spittle-like protective covering.

frogman n (pl **frogmen**) a person who wears rubber suit, flippers, oxygen supply, etc and is trained in working underwater.

frogmarch vt to carry an unwilling person by the legs and arms face down; to move (a person) by force.—also n.

frolic n a lively party or game; merriment, fun. * vi (**frolicking, frolicked**) to play happily.—**frolicker** n.

frolicsome, frolicky adj. fond of frolicking; playful.

from prep beginning at, starting with; out of; originating with; out of the possibility or use of.

fromage frais n a smooth white curd cheese eaten plain or with added fruit as a dessert.

fromenty see **frumenty**.

frond n a large leaf with many divisions, esp of a palm or fern.

frondescence n (bot) the act of producing leaves; foliage.—**frondescent** adj.

frons n (pl **frontes**) a plate found on the head of an insect.

front n outward behaviour; (inf) an appearance of social standing; etc; the part facing forward; the first part; a forward or leading position; the promenade of a seaside resort; the advanced battle area in warfare; a person or group used to hide another's activity; an advancing mass of cold or warm air. * adj at, to, in, on, or of the front. * vti to face; to stand or be situated opposite to or over against; to serve as a front (for); to have the front turned in a particular direction.

frontage n the front part of a building or plot of land; the width or extent of the front of a shop, building, piece of land, etc.

frontal adj of or belonging to the front; of or pertaining to the forehead. * n a decorative covering for the front of an altar; a small pediment over a window or door.—**frontally** adv.

front bench n in the British House of Commons, either of the two rows of benches occupied by the leading figures (**front benchers**) in the Government or Opposition.

front door n a main entrance to a building.

frontier n the border between two countries; the limit of existing knowledge of a subject.

frontispiece n an illustration opposite the title page of a book; (archit) the main face of a building.

frontlet n a band worn on the forehead; an animal's forehead.

frontrunner n the favourite to win a race, election, etc.

frontwards, frontward adj, adv towards the front.

frost n temperature at or below freezing point; a coating of powdery ice particles; coldness of manner. * vt to cover (as if) with frost or frosting; to give a frost-like opaque surface to (glass).

frostbite n injury to a part of the body by exposure to cold.—**frostbitten** adj.

frosting n icing for a cake.

frosty adj (**frostier, frostiest**) cold with frost; cold or reserved in manner, chilly, distant.—**frostily** adv.—**frostiness** n.

froth n foam; foaming saliva; frivolity. * vi to emit or gather foam.

frothy adj (**frothier, frothiest**) full of or composed of froth; frivolous; insubstantial.—**frothily** adv.—**frothiness** n.

froufrou n the rustling sound made by the material, esp silk, of a dress etc, when in motion.

froward adj (arch) obstinate; wayward.

frown vi to contract the brow as in anger or thought; (with **upon**) to regard with displeasure or disapproval. * n a wrinkled brow; a stern look.—**frowner** n.—**frowningly** adv.

frowst n (inf) a close, stuffy atmosphere.

frowsty adj stuffy; musty.

frowzy, frowsy adj (**frowzier, frowziest** or **frowsier, frowsiest**) dirty and untidy; unkempt.

froze see **freeze**.

frozen[1] see **freeze**.

frozen[2] adj formed into or covered by ice; damaged or killed by cold; (food, etc) preserved by freezing; motionless; made speechless by strong emotion; formal and unfriendly; extremely cold; (prices, wages, etc)

fixed at a given level; (funds, etc) unrealizable.

FRS abbr = Fellow of the Royal Society.

fructiferous adj (plant etc) bearing fruit.

fructify vb (**fructifies, fructifying, fructified**) vt to make fruitful, fertilize. * vi to bear fruit; to become fruitful.—**fructification** n.

fructose n a type of sugar found in ripe fruit and honey.

fructuous adj fruitful.

frugal adj economical, thrifty; inexpensive, meagre.—**frugality** n.—**frugally** adv.

frugivorous adj fruit-eating.

fruit n the seed-bearing part of any plant; the fleshy part of this used as food; the result or product of any action. * vti to bear or cause to bear fruit.

fruitage n the process of bearing fruit; a collective term for all fruits.

fruiter n a fruit grower; a fruit tree.

fruiterer n a dealer in fruit.

fruitful adj producing lots of fruit; productive.—**fruitfully** adv.—**fruitfulness** n.

fruition n a coming to fulfilment, realization.

fruitless adj unproductive; pointless; useless.—**fruitlessly** adv.—**fruitlessness** n.

fruit machine n a coin-operated gambling machine, using symbols of fruit to indicate a winning combination.

fruit salad n a dish of various fruits sliced and mixed.

fruity adj (**fruitier, fruitiest**) like, or tasting like, fruit; (inf) (voice) mellow; (inf) salacious.—**fruitiness** n.

frumenty n a sort of porridge, made from hulled wheat and boiled milk.—also **fromenty, furmenty**

frump n a drab and dowdy woman.—**frumpish, frumpy** adj.

frustrate vt to prevent from achieving a goal or gratifying a desire; to discourage, irritate, tire; to disappoint.—**frustrater** n.—**frustratingly** adv.—**frustration** n.

frustule n the shell of a diatom.

frustum n (pl **frustums, frusta**) (geom) the part of a cone, pyramid, etc, left after the top is cut off.

frutescent adj pertaining to, having the form of, or resembling a shrub.

fruticose adj resembling a shrub.

fry[1] vti (**frying, fried**) to cook over direct heat in hot fat. * n (pl **fries**) a dish of things fried.

fry[2] n (pl **fries**) recently hatched fishes; the young of a frog, etc.

fryer n a person who fries; a pan, etc, for frying in; a piece of meat for frying.—also **frier**.

f-stop n any of the standard settings of the aperture in a camera lens.

ft. abbr = foot or feet.

fuchsia n any of a genus of decorative shrubs with purplish-red flowers.

fuchsine, fuchsin n a crystalline substance, made into a dark red dye.

fuck vti (vulg) to have sexual intercourse with. * n (vulg) an act of sexual intercourse. * interj (vulg) expressing anger, frustration, etc.

fucus n (pl **fuci, fucuses**) a kind of large brown flat seaweed.—**fucoid, fucoidal** adj.

fuddle vt to make drunk; to make confused.

fuddy-duddy n (pl **fuddy-duddies**) a person with old-fashioned or staid views.

fudge[1] n a soft sweet made of butter, milk, sugar, flavouring, etc; (print) a piece of late matter inserted in the stop-press column of a newspaper; a made-up story. * vi to refuse to commit oneself; to cheat; to contrive by imperfect or improvised means. * vt to fake; to fail to come to grips with; to make or do anything in a bungling, careless manner.

fudge² n nonsense. * interj expressing annoyance or disbelief.

fuehrer see **führer**.

fuel n material burned to supply heat and power, or as a source of nuclear energy; anything that serves to intensify strong feelings. * vti (**fuelling, fuelled** or **fueling, fueled**) to supply with or obtain fuel.—**fueller, fueler** n.

fug n (inf) a hot, stale atmosphere.

fugacious adj fleeting; elusive; volatile; (bot) (petals, etc) falling off very early.—**fugaciously** adv.—**fugaciousness** n.

fugacity n fugaciousness; the property of a gas to escape or expand.

fugitive n a person who flees from danger, pursuit, or duty. * adj fleeing, as from danger or justice; fleeting, transient; not permanent.—**fugitively** adv.

fugleman n (pl **fuglemen**) (formerly) a soldier who stands in front of others to demonstrate drill; a ringleader.

fugue n a polyphonic musical composition with its theme taken up successively by different voices.—**fugal** adj.—**fugally** adv.

fuguist n a composer of fugues.

führer n (German) a leader, esp a dictator; (with cap) the title of Adolf Hitler (1889-1945), leader of the German Nazi party.

-ful adj suffix full of, eg doleful. * n suffix the amount needed to fill, eg cupful.

fulcrum n (pl **fulcrums, fulcra**) the fixed point on which a lever turns; a critical factor determining an outcome.

fulfil, fulfill vt (**fulfils** or **fulfills, fulfilling, fulfilled**) to carry out (a promise, etc); to achieve the completion of; to satisfy; to bring to an end, complete.—**fulfiller** n.—**fulfilment, fulfillment** n.

fulgent adj (poet) shining, radiant.—**fulgency** n.—**fulgently** adv.

fulgurate vi to flash (like lightning).—**fulgurant** adj.

fulgurite n rock or sand that has been vitrified by lightning.

fuliginous adj sooty, smoky.—**fuliginously** adv.

full adj having or holding all that can be contained; having eaten all one wants; having a great number (of); complete; having reached to greatest size, extent, etc. * n the greatest amount, extent etc. * adv completely, directly, exactly.

full² vt to clean and thicken (cloth) by beating.

fullback n (football, rugby, hockey, etc) one of the defensive players at the back; the position held by this player.

full-blooded adj vigorous, hearty.—**full-bloodedly** adv.

full-blown adj in full bloom; matured, fully developed.

full-bodied adj (flavour) characterized by richness and fullness.

full dress n dress worn for formal or ceremonial occasions.—**full-dress** adj.

fuller¹ n someone who fulls cloth.

fuller² n a tool used for grooving and shaping iron; a groove made by this.

fuller's earth n a type of clay used for fulling.

full face adj, adv seen from in front.

full-frontal adj (inf) (nude person or photograph) with the genitals clearly visible; unrestrained.—**full frontal** n.

full house n (poker) a hand with three cards of the same value and a pair (—also **full hand**); (theatre, etc) a performance for which all seats are sold; (bingo) a complete set of winning numbers.

full moon n the moon at its phase when the whole disc is illuminated; the period of this.

fullness n the state of being full; **fullness of time** the proper or destined time.—also **fulness**.

full-scale adj actual size.

full-stop n the punctuation mark (.) at the end of a sentence.—also **period**.

full time n the finish of a match.

full-time adj working or lasting the whole time.—**full-timer** n.

fully adv thoroughly, completely; at least.

fully-fledged adj (bird) mature; having full status.—also **full-fledged**.

fulmar n an Arctic sea bird.

fulminant adj fulminating; sudden; (pain) sharp, piercing.

fulminate vi to issue protests with violence or threats; to inveigh (against). * vt to utter or exclaim, as a denunciation. * n an explosive compound of fulminic acid.—**fulmination** n.—**fulminator** n.—**fulminatory** adj.

fulminic acid n an unstable acid composed of cyanogen and oxygen.

fulness see **fullness**.

fulsome adj excessively praising, obsequious.—**fulsomely** adv.—**fulsomeness** n.

fulvous adj tawny.

fumarole n a small hole in a volcano from which gases issue.

fumatorium n (pl **fumatoriums, fumatoria**) an airtight room where insects, plants, etc, are fumigated.

fumble vi to grope about. * vt to handle clumsily; to say or act awkwardly; to fail to catch (a ball) cleanly. * n an awkward attempt.—**fumbler** n.—**fumblingly** adv.

fume n (usu pl) smoke, gas or vapour, esp if offensive or suffocating. * vi to give off fumes; to express anger. * vt to subject to fumes.—**fumer** n.—**fumingly** adv.

fumigate vt to disinfect or exterminate (pests, etc) using fumes.—**fumigation** n.—**fumigator** n.

fumitory n (pl **fumitories**) a plant, found mainly in Europe, the leaves of which were formerly used as a treatment for skin diseases.

fun n (what provides) amusement and enjoyment. * vi (**funning, funned**) to joke.

funambulist n a tightrope walker.

function n the activity characteristic of a person or thing; the specific purpose of a certain person or thing; an official ceremony or social entertainment; (math) a quantity whose value depends on the varying value of another. * vi to perform a function; to act, operate.

functional adj of a function or functions; practical, not ornamental; (disease) affecting the functions only, not organic.—**functionally** adv.

functionalism n the theory and practice of design for practical application.—**functionalist** adj, n.

functionary n (pl **functionaries**) a person in an official capacity.

fund n a supply that can be drawn upon; a sum of money set aside for a purpose; (pl) ready money. * vt to provide funds for; to convert (a debt) into stock; to place in a fund.

fundament *n* foundation, basis; (*euphemism*) the buttocks; the anus.

fundamental *adj* basic; essential. * *n* that which serves as a groundwork; an essential.—**fundamentality, fundamentalness** *n*. —**fundamentally** *adv*.

fundamentalism *n* belief in the literal truth of the Bible, Koran etc.—**fundamentalist** *adj*, *n*.—**fundamentalistic** *adj*.

fundus *n* (*pl* **fundi**) (*anat*) the base or deepest part of an organ.

funeral *n* the ceremony associated with the burial or cremation of the dead; a procession accompanying a coffin to a burial.

funeral director *n* a person who manages funerals.

funereal *adj* suiting a funeral, dismal, mournful.—**funereally** *adv*.

fungal *adj* of or pertaining to a fungus; caused by a fungus.

fungible *adj* (*law*) replaceable by another, similar specimen. * *n* a fungible thing, eg a coin.

fungicide *n* a substance that destroys fungi.—**fungicidal** *adj*.

fungiform *adj* resembling a mushroom

fungoid *adj* resembling a fungus.

fungous *adj* of, pertaining to or like fungi; fungal; developing suddenly.

fungus *n* (*pl* **fungi, funguses**) any of a major group of lower plants, as mildews, mushrooms, yeasts, etc, that lack chlorophyll and reproduce by spores.—**fungic** *adj*.

funicular *adj* of rope or its tension. * *n* a cable railway ascending a mountain.

funiculus *n* (*pl* **funiculi**) (*anat*) a small cord, ligature or fibre.

funk *n* (*inf*) panic, fear; a coward; funky music. * *vti* (*inf*) to show fear; to shirk.—**funker** *n*.

funky[1] *adj* (**funkier, funkiest**) panicky; fearful.

funky[2] *adj* (**funkier, funkiest**) (*inf*) (*pop, jazz music, etc*) soulful, bluesy; fashionable.—**funkiness** *n*.

funnel *n* an implement, usually a cone with a wide top and tapering to a narrow tube, for pouring fluids, powders, into bottles, etc; a metal chimney for the escape of smoke, steam, etc. * *vti* (**funnelling, funnelled** *or* **funneling, funneled**) to pour or cause to pour through a funnel.

funny *adj* (**funnier, funniest**) causing laughter; puzzling, odd; (*inf*) unwell, queasy. * *n* (*pl* **funnies**) a joke; (*pl*) comic strips, esp in a newspaper.—**funnily** *adv*.—**funniness** *n*.

funny bone *n* the part of the elbow where a sensitive nerve rests close to the bone, producing a tingling sensation if struck.

fur *n* the short, soft, fine hair on the bodies of certain animals; their skins with the fur attached; a garment made of fur; a fabric made in imitation of fur; a furlike coating, as on the tongue. * *vti* (**furring, furred**) to cover or become covered with fur.

furbelow *n* a flounce or other trimming on clothing.

furbish *vt* to polish, to burnish; to renovate.—**furbisher** *n*.

furcate *vi* to fork, divide. * *adj* forked, branching.—**furcation** *n*.

furfur *n* (*pl* **furfures**) scurf, dandruff.

furfuraceous *adj*.resembling bran; resembling dandruff.

Furies *see* **fury**.

furioso *adv* (*mus*) wildly.

furious *adj* full of anger; intense; violent, impetuous.—**furiously** *adv*.—**furiousness** *n*.

furl *vt* to roll up (a sail, flag, etc) tightly and make secure; to fold up, close.—**furlable** *adj*.—**furler** *n*.

furlong *n* 220 yards, one-eighth of a mile (201 metres).

furlough *n* leave of absence from duty, esp for military personnel. * *vt* to grant a furlough to.

furmenty *see* **frumenty**.

furnace *n* an enclosed chamber in which heat is produced to burn refuse, smelt ore, etc.

furnish *vt* to provide (a room, etc) with furniture; to equip with what is necessary; to supply.—**furnisher** *n*.

furnishings *npl* furniture, carpets, etc.

furniture *n* the things in a room, etc that equip it for living, as chairs, beds, etc; equipment.

furore, furor *n* fury, indignation; widespread enthusiasm.

furrier *n* a dealer in furs.

furriery *n* (*pl* **furrieries**) the fur trade; a collective name for furs.

furrow *n* the groove in the earth made by a plough; a groove or track resembling this; a wrinkle. * *vti* to make furrows in; to wrinkle.—**furrower** *n*.—**furrowy** *adj*.

furry *adj* (**furrier, furriest**) like, made of, or covered with, fur.—**furrily** *adv*.—**furriness** *n*.

further *adv* at or to a greater distance or degree; in addition. * *adj* more distant, remote; additional. * *vt* to help forward, promote.—**furtherer** *n*.

furtherance *n* a helping forward.

furthermore *adv* moreover, besides.

furthermost *adj* most remote.

furthest *adj* at or to the greatest distance.

furtive *adj* stealthy; sly.—**furtively** *adv*.—**furtiveness** *n*.

furuncle *n* (*med*) a boil.—**furuncular** *adj*.

fury *n* (*pl* **furies**) intense rage; a frenzy; a violently angry person; (*with cap*) (*Greek, Roman myth*) one of the three winged goddesses of vengeance with serpents for hair, Alecto, Megaera, and Tisiphone.

furze *n* gorse.

fuscous *adj* dark-coloured, esp brownish-black.

fuse *vti* to join or become joined by melting; to (cause to) melt by the application of heat; to equip a plug, circuit, etc with a fuse; to (cause to) fail by blowing a fuse. * *n* a tube or wick filled with combustible material for setting off an explosive charge; a piece of thin wire that melts and breaks when an electric current exceeds a certain level.—*also* **fuze**.

fusee *n* a large-headed match; a conical spindle in a clock, around which the chain is wound.—*also* **fuzee**.

fuselage *n* the body of an aircraft.

fusel oil *n* a poisonous liquid mixture of various alcohols, formed as a byproduct of distillation.

fusible *adj* able to be fused; (*metal, alloy*) having a melting point below 148.9° C (300° F) and used in fuses, etc.—**fusibility** *n*.—**fusibly** *adv*.

fusiform *adj* spindle-shaped.

fusil *n* a light flintlock musket.

fusilier, fusileer *n* (*formerly*) a British soldier armed with a flintlock musket; a soldier in certain infantry regiments.

fusillade *n* a firing of shots in continuous or rapid succession; an outburst, as of criticism. * *vt* to attack or shoot down by fusillade.

fusion *n* the act of melting, blending or fusing; a product of fusion; union, partnership; nuclear fusion.

fuss *n* excited activity, bustle; a nervous state; (*inf*) a quarrel; (*inf*) a showy display of approval. * *vi* to worry over trifles; to whine, as a baby.—**fusser** *n*.

fussy *adj* (**fussier, fussiest**) worrying over details; hard to please; fastidious; over-elaborate.—**fussily** *adv*.—**fussiness** *n*.

fustian *n* a kind of coarse twilled cotton cloth, eg corduroy; ranting language, bombast. * *adj* made of fustian; turgid.

fustic *n* a large tropical American tree; its wood; the yellow obtained from it.

fusty *adj* (**fustier, fustiest**) smelling of mould or damp; outmoded in ideas or opinions.—**fustily** *adv*.—**fustiness** *n*.

futhark, futharc, futhork, futhorc *n* a phonetic alphabet made up of runes.

futile *adj* useless; ineffective.—**futilely** *adv*.—**futility** *n*.

futon *n* a light cotton mattress.

futtock *n* (*naut*) one of the upright curved ribs of a ship, springing from the keel.

future *adj* that is to be; of or referring to time yet to come. * *n* the time to come; future events; likelihood of eventual success; (*gram*) the future tense; (*pl*) commodities purchased at a prescribed price for delivery at some future date.

futurism *n* a movement in art, music, and literature begun in Italy about 1909 marked by an effort to give formal expression to the energy of mechanical processes; a point of view that finds meaning or fulfillment in the future.—**futurist** *adj, n*.

futuristic *adj* forward-looking in design, appearance, intention, etc.—**futuristically** *adv*.

futurity *n* (*pl* **futurities**) time or events yet to come.

futurology *n* the forecasting of future trends in human affairs.—**futurologist** *n*.

fuze *see* **fuse**.

fuzee *see* **fusee**.

fuzz *n* fine light particles of fibre (as of down or fluff); a blurred effect; fluff; (*sl*) police. * *vi* to fly off in minute particles; to become blurred.

fuzzword *see* **buzzword**.

fuzzy *adj* (**fuzzier, fuzziest**) like fuzz; fluffy; blurred.—**fuzzily** *adv*.—**fuzziness** *n*.

-fy *vb suffix* to make, eg *solidify*.

G

G (*symbol*) (*mus*) the 5th note of the scale of C; gravitational constant; (*physcs*) conductance; giga; (*sl*) grand ($1000 or £1000).

g *abbr* = gallons(s); gram(s); gravity; acceleration due to gravity.

Ga (*chem symbol*) gallium.

GA, Ga. (*US*) *abbr* = Georgia.

gab *vi* (gabbing, gabbed) (*inf*) to talk in a rapid or thoughtless manner, chatter. * *n* (*inf*) idle talk.—gabber *n*.

gabardine *n* a firm cloth of wool, rayon, or cotton; gaberdine.

gabble *vti* to talk or utter rapidly or incoherently; to utter inarticulate or animal sounds.—gabbler *n*.

gabbro *n* (*pl* gabbros) a dark igneous rock like granite.—gabbroic *adj*.

gabby *adj* (gabbier, gabbiest) (*inf*) talkative.

gabelle *n* (*formerly*) a tax on salt in France.

gaberdine *n* (*formerly*) a long, loose upper garment worn by pilgrims, Jews etc; a raincoat; gaberdine.

gabion *n* (*formerly*) a large cylindrical basket filled with earth or stones, used in military defence; a similar metal container used in engineering and underwater construction.

gable *n* the triangular upper part of a wall enclosed by the sloping ends of a pitched roof.—gabled *adj*.

gablet *n* a small ornamental gable used for the summit of niches etc.

gad *vi* (gadding, gadded) (*usu with* about) to wander restlessly or idly in search of pleasure.—gadder *n*.

gadabout *n* (*inf*) a person that wanders restlessly in search of pleasure or amusement.

gadfly *n* (*pl* gadflies) any of various flies that bite or annoy livestock; an irritating person.

gadget *n* a small, often ingenious, mechanical or electronic tool or device.—gadgety *adj*.

gadgetry *n* gadgets; the use of gadgets.

gadoid *adj, n* (a fish) of the cod family.

gadolinite *n* a silicate of yttrium.

gadolinium *n* a magnetic metallic element of the rare earth group.—gadolinic *adj*.

gadroon *n* an ornamental edge of inverted fluting; a decorative border, esp on silver.

gadwall *n* (*pl* gadwalls, gadwall) a large freshwater duck, prized as game.

Gael *n* a person who speaks Gaelic, esp a Scottish Highlander or Irishman.

Gaelic *n* the Celtic language of Ireland, the Scottish Highlands, and the Isle of Man.—*also adj*.

gaff *n* a pole with a sharp hook for landing large fish; (naut) a hgh boom or yard for hoisting a sail aft of a mast; (*sl*) one's home. * *vt* to land (a fish) with a gaff.

gaffe *n* a social blunder.

gaffer *n* an old man, often a countryman; an overseer or foreman; the senior electrician of a film crew.

gaff-topsail *n* (*naut*) a light sail set above a gaff.

gag *n* something put over or into the mouth to prevent talking; any restraint of free speech; a joke. * *vb* (gagging, gagged) *vt* to cause to retch; to keep from speaking, as by stopping the mouth of. * *vi* to retch; to tell jokes.

gaga *adj* (*inf*) senile; slightly crazy.

gage *see* gauge.

gaggle *n* a flock of geese when not in flight; (*inf*) a disorderly collection of people.

gahnite *n* a greenish and dark-brown mineral.

gaiety *n* (*pl* gaieties) happiness, liveliness; colourful appearance.

gaige *n* the Chinese word for "radical reform" or peristroika.

gaily *adv* in a cheerful manner; with bright colours.

gain *vt* to obtain, earn, esp by effort; to win in a contest; to attract; to get as an addition (esp profit or advantage); to make an increase in; to reach. * *vi* to make progress; to increase in weight. * *n* an increase esp in profit or advantage; an acquisition.

gainful *adj* profitable.—gainfully *adv*.—gainfulness *n*.

gainsay *vt* (gainsaying, gainsaid) (*formal*) to dispute; to deny.—gainsayer *n*.

gait *n* a manner of walking or running; the sequence of footsteps made by a moving horse.

gaiter *n* a cloth or leather covering for the lower leg.

gal[1] *n* (*sl*) a girl.

gal[2], gall. *abbr* = gallon.

gala *n* a celebration, festival.

galactic *adj* of a galaxy; huge.

galago *n* (*pl* galagos) an African genus of lemurs; a bushbaby.

galantine *n* a dish composed of chicken, veal or other white meat, boned, seasoned, tied up, boiled, shaped and served cold in its own jelly.

galatea *n* a cotton fabric, often with blue and white stripes.

Galatians *n sing* (*New Testament*) the epistles of St Paul addressed to the Galatians.

galavant *see* gallivant.

galaxy *n* (*pl* galaxies) any of the systems of stars in the universe; any splendid assemblage; (*with cap*) the galaxy containing the Earth's solar system; the Milky Way.

galbanum *n* an odorous and bitter gum resin used in medicine.

gale *n* a strong wind, specifically one between 32 to 63 mph; an outburst.

galea *n* (*pl* galeae) (*bot, zool*) a helmet-like structure.—galeate, galeated *adj*.

galena *n* a sulphide of lead.

Galenic *adj* of Galen (*c*.AD130*c*.200), the Greek physician and philosopher, or his works.

Galilean[1] *adj* of Galilee or its inhabitants * *n* a native of

Galilee; (*often pl*) a Christian; (*with* the) Jesus Christ.

Galilean[2] *adj* of or pertaining to Galileo (15641642), the Italian astronomer and mathematician.

galilee *n* a small chapel or porch at the western entrance to a church.

galingale, galangal *n* a kind of sedge; the aromatic root of an Asian plant.

galiot, galliot *n* a heavily built two-masted Dutch trading vessel; (*formerly*) a small light galley used in the Mediterranean.

galipot *n* a white resinous juice that exudes from pine trees.

galivant *see* **gallivant**.

gall[1] *n* bile; bitter feeling; (*inf*) impudence.

gall[2] *n* a diseased growth on plant tissue produced by fungi, insect parasites, or bacteria.

gall[3] *n* a skin sore caused by rubbing. * *vt* to chafe or hurt by rubbing; to irritate.

gallant *adj* dignified, stately; brave; noble; (*man*) polite and chivalrous to women.—**gallantly** *adv*.—**gallantness** *n*.—**gallantry** *n* (*pl* **gallantries**).

gallantry *n* (*pl* **gallantries**) (an act of) bravery, dashing courage; courtliness, a polite act.

gall bladder *n* a membranous sac attached to the liver in which bile is stored.

galleass *n* a large low-built three-masted vessel propelled by sails and oars, and carrying twenty or more guns.

galleon *n* a large sailing ship of the 15th–18th centuries.

gallery *n* (*pl* **galleries**) a covered passage for walking; a long narrow outside balcony; a balcony running along the inside wall of a building; (the occupants of) an upper area of seating in a theatre; a long narrow room used for a special purpose, eg shooting practice; a room or building designed for the exhibition of works of art; the spectators at a golf tournament, tennis match, etc.—**galleried** *adj*.

galley *n* a long, usu low, ship of ancient or medieval times, propelled by oars; the kitchen of a ship, aircraft; (*print*) a shallow tray for holding type; proofs printed from such type (—*also* **galley proof**).

galliard *n* a lively dance in triple time.

Gallic *adj* of or pertaining to France; of ancient Gaul or its people.

gallic *adj* of or made of gallnuts; (*chem*) of or containing gallium in the trivalent state.

Gallican *adj* of the Roman Catholic Church in France.

Gallicanism *n* the doctrine of the national party in the French Roman Catholic Church, tending to restrict papal control, opposed to Ultramontanism.

Gallice *adv* in French.

Gallicism *n* a French expression or idiom.

Gallicize, Gallicise *vt* to make French in manners, idiom etc.

galligaskins *n pl* trousers, leggings worn in the 16th and 17th centuries.

gallimaufry *n* (*pl* **gallimaufries**) a medley, a hotchpotch.

gallinaceous *adj* of or relating to a group of heavy-bodied largely land-loving birds including pheasants and domestic fowl.

galling *adj* irritating, exasperating.

gallipot *n* a small glazed pot, esp for medicine.

gallium *n* a metallic element that is liquid at room temperature and is used in thermometers, semiconductor devices, etc.

gallivant *vi* (*inf*) to go about in search of amusement.—*also* **galivant, galavant**.

galliwasp *n* a West Indian lizard.

gallnut *n* a round excrescence produced on the oak by the puncturing of the leaf buds by an insect, the gall beetle.

gallon *n* a unit of liquid measure comprising 4 quarts or 3.78 liters (in UK, 4.54 liters); (*pl*) (*inf*) a large amount.

galloon *n* a narrow braid or trimming of silk, gold lace, embroidery etc.

gallop *n* the fastest gait of a horse, etc; a succession of leaping strides; a fast pace. * *vti* to go or cause to go at a gallop; to move swiftly.—**galloper** *n*.

gallowglass *n* a heavily armed footsoldier; a chief's retainer in Ireland in the 13th-16th centuries.

gallows *n* (*pl* **gallowses, gallows**) a wooden frame used for hanging criminals.

gallstone *n* a small solid mass in the gall bladder.

Gallup poll *n* a sampling of public opinion, esp to help forecast an election.

galop *n* a dance.

galore *adv* in great quantity; in plentiful supply.

galosh *n* a waterproof overshoe.

galumph *vi* (*inf*) to prance triumphantly, or clumsily.

galvanic *adj* producing electricity by chemical action; stimulating (people) into action.—**galvanically** *adv*.

galvanism *n* (*arch*) electricity produced by the chemical action of certain bodies or an acid on a metal; the medical use of this.

galvanize *vt* to apply an electric current to; to startle; to excite; to plate (metal) with zinc.—**galvanization** *n*.—**galvanizer** *n*.

galvanometer *n* an instrument for detecting or measuring small electric currents.—**galvanometric, galvanometrical** *adj*.—**galvanometry** *n*.

galvanoscope *n* an instrument for measuring the direction and presence of electricity by movements of a magnetic needle.

gam[1] *n* a school of whales; a visit by one captain of a whaler to another; * *vb* (**gams, gammed, gamming**) *vt* to call upon the captain of a whaler. * *vi* (*whales*) to gather together in schools .

gam[2] *n* (*sl*) a well-shaped leg.

gambado (*pl* **gambados, gambadoes**) *n* a kind of leather legging used by horsemen; a flourish or curvet.

gambier, gambir *n* a vegetable extract used medicinally as an astringent, and also for tanning and dyeing.

gambit *n* (*chess*) an opening in which a piece is sacrificed to gain an advantage; any action to gain an advantage.

gamble *vi* to play games of chance for money; to take a risk for some advantage. * *vt* to risk in gambling, to bet. * *n* a risky venture; a bet.—**gambler** *n*.—**gambling** *n*.

gamboge *n* a yellow gum resin from SE Asia, used as a pigment and as a purgative (—*also* **cambogia**); a bright yellow colour.

gambol *vi* (**gambolling, gambolled** *or* **gamboling, gamboled**) to jump and skip about in play; to frisk. * *n* a caper, a playful leap.

gambrel *n* the hock of a horse; a bent stick of wood or metal resembling a horse's leg, used by butchers; a gambrel roof.

gambrel roof *n* a curved roof with a small gable at each end; a roof with a double slope on each side so that each side is shaped like a horse's leg.

game[1] *n* any form of play, amusement; activity or sport involving competition; a scheme, a plan; wild birds or animals hunted for sport or food, the flesh of such animals. * *vi* to play for a stake. * *adj* (*inf*) brave, resolute; (*inf*) willing.—**gamely** *adv*.—**gameness** *n*.

game² *adj* (*limbs*) injured, crippled, lame.

gamecock *n* (*formerly*) a cock bred and trained for fighting.

gamekeeper *n* a person who breeds and takes care of game birds and animals, as on an estate.—**gamekeeping** *n*.

game point *n* (*tennis*) the situation when the next point scored wins the game for one side or player.

gamesmanship *n* (*inf*) the art of winning games by questionable acts just short of cheating.

gamesome *adj* sportive.

gamester *n* a gambler.

gamete *n* a reproductive cell that unites with another to form the cell that develops into a new individual.—**gametal, gametic** *adj*.

gamic *adj* (*zool*) having a sexual character.

gamin *n* a mischievous urchin.

gamine *n* a boyish girl or woman with impish appeal.

gaming *n* the act of playing games for stakes; gambling. —*also adj*.

gamma *n* the third letter of the Greek alphabet.

gamma radiation, gamma rays *n* shortwave electromagnetic radiation from a radioactive substance.

gammer *n* (*rare*) (*usu humorous*) an old woman.

gammon *n* cured or smoked ham; meat from the hindquarters of a side of bacon.

gamogenesis *n* (*bot*) sexual reproduction.

gamopetalous *adj* with petals united at the base.

gamophyllous *adj* (*flowers*) with leaves cohering at the edges.

gamosepalous *adj* (*flowers*) with sepals united at the edges to form a calyx.

gamut *n* a complete range or series; (*mus*) the whole range of notes of a voice or instrument.

gamy, gamey *adj* (**gamier, gamiest**) having the strong smell or flavour of cooked game; (*inf*) spirited, lively.—**gaminess** *n*.

-gamy *n suffix* marriage; sexual union.

gander *n* an adult goose; (*inf*) a quick look.

gang *n* a group of persons, esp labourers, working together; a group of persons acting or associating together, esp for illegal purposes. * *vti* to form into or act as a gang.—**ganged** *adj*.

gangland *n* the criminal fraternity.

gangling, gangly *adj* tall, thin and awkward in appearance and movement.

ganglion *n* (*pl* **ganglia, ganglions**) a mass of nerve cells from which nerve impulses are transmitted.—**ganglionic** *adj*.

gangplank *n* a moveable ramp by which to board or leave a ship.

gangrene *n* death of body tissue when the blood supply is obstructed.—**gangrenous** *adj*.

gangster *n* a member of a criminal gang.

gangue, gang *n* the earth or matrix in which ore is found

gangway *n* a passageway, esp an opening in a ship's side for loading, etc; a gangplank.

ganister, gannister *n* a kind of silicious clay rock or hard sandstone; a refractory material used for lining furnaces.

ganja *n* marijuana.

gannet *n* any of various large voracious fish-eating sea birds.

ganoid *adj* (*fish*) having enamelled bony scales, like the sturgeon. * *n* a ganoid fish.

gantlet *see* **gauntlet.**

gantry *n* (*pl* **gantries**) a metal framework, often on wheels, for a travelling crane; a wheeled framework with a crane, platforms, etc for servicing a rocket to be launched.

gaol, gaolbird, gaoler *see* **jail, jailbird, jailer.**

gap *n* a break or opening in something, as a wall or fence; an interruption in continuity, an interval; a mountain pass; a divergence, disparity. * *vt* (**gapping, gapped**) to make a gap in.—**gappy** *adj*.

gape *vi* to open the mouth wide; to stare in astonishment, esp with the mouth open; to open widely. * *n* the act of gaping; a wide opening.—**gaping** *adj*.—**gapingly** *adv*.

gaper *n* a person who gapes; one of various types of shellfish that have a space between the valves.

gar *n* (*pl* **gar, gars**) a garfish.

garage *n* an enclosed shelter for motor vehicles; a place where motor vehicles are repaired and serviced, and fuel sold. * *vt* to put or keep in a garage.

garage sale *n* a sale of unwanted household goods, held in a garage or other part of the house.

garb *n* clothing, style of dress. * *vt* to clothe.

garbage *n* food waste; unwanted or useless material; rubbish; (*comput*) useless data.

garbageman *n* (*pl* **garbagemen**) a person employed to remove garbage.

garble *vt* to distort (a message, story, etc) so as to mislead.—**garbler** *n*.

garboard (strake) *n* (*naut*) the plank or plate on a ship's bottom next to the keel.

garbology *n* the study of the disposal of waste material.—**garbologist** *n*.

garçon *n* a waiter.

garden *n* an area of ground for growing herbs, fruits, flowers, or vegetables; a yard; a fertile, well-cultivated region; a public park or recreation area, usu laid-out with plants and trees. * *vi* to make, or work in, a garden.—**gardener** *n*.—**gardening** *n*.

gardenia *n* a tree or shrub with beautiful fragrant white or yellow flowers.

garfish *n* (*pl* **garfish, garfishes**) a long, slender freshwater fish with a spearlike snout and a thick-scaled body.

gargantuan *adj* colossal, prodigious.

garget *n* a disease in cattle.

gargle *vti* to rinse the throat by breathing air from the lungs through liquid held in the mouth. * *n* a liquid for this purpose; the sound made by gargling.—**gargler** *n*.

gargoyle *n* a grotesquely carved face or figure, usu acting as a spout to drain water from a gutter; a person with an ugly face.—**gargoyled** *adj*.

garibaldi *n* a type of loose blouse, orig red.

garish *adj* crudely bright, gaudy.—**garishly** *adv*.—**garishness** *n*.

garland *n* a wreath of flowers or leaves worn or hung as decoration. * *vt* to decorate with a garland.

garlic *n* a bulbous herb cultivated for its compound bulbs used in cookery; its bulb.—**garlicky** *adj*.

garment *n* an item of clothing.

garner *vt* to gather, store.

garnet *n* a semiprecious stone, red, yellow or green in colour.

garnish *vt* to decorate; to decorate (food) with something that adds colour or flavour. * *n* something used to garnish food.—**garnisher** *n*.—**garniture** *n*.

garnishee vt (**garnisheeing, garnisheed**) (*law*) to warn by garnishment. * n (*law*) the person into whose hands the property of another is attached pending the satisfaction of the claims of a third party.

garnishment n embellishment; (*law*) notice to holder of another's attached property not to give it to him but to account for it in court; a summons; (*arch*) notice to third party to appear in suit.

garniture n embellishment, trimmings (esp on a dish of food).

garpike n the garfish.

garret n an attic.

garrison n troops stationed at a fort; a fortified place with troops. * vt to station (troops) in (a fortified place) for its defence.

garrotte, garrote, garotte n a method of execution by strangling with an iron collar; the iron collar used. * vt to execute by garrotte; to half-throttle and rob.— **garrotter, garroter, garotter** n.

garrulous adj excessively talkative.—**garrulously** adv.— **garrulousness, garrulity** n.

garter n an elasticated band used to support a stocking or sock.

garth n a courtyard surrounded by a cloister; (*arch*) a yard, garden or paddock.

gas n (pl **gases, gasses**) an air-like substance with the capacity to expand indefinitely and not liquefy or solidify at ordinary temperatures; any mixture of flammable gases used for lighting or heating; any gas used as an anaesthetic; any poisonous substance dispersed in the air, as in war; (*inf*) empty talk; gasoline. * vt (**gases** or **gasses, gassing, gassed**) to poison or disable with gas; (*inf*) to talk idly and at length.

gasbag n (*inf*) an idle talker.

gas chamber n an airtight room where animals or people are killed by poisonous gas.

gasconade n (*rare*) boastful or blustering talk. * vi to bluster, to boast.

gaseous adj having the form of or being gas; of or being related to gases; lacking substance or solidity.—**gaseousness** n.

gash n a long, deep, open cut. * vt to cut deep.

gasholder n a circular hollow tank, open at the bottom and closed at the top, for storing gas prior to distribution

gasify vti (**gasifying, gasified**) to turn into gas.—**gasification** n.

gasket n a piece or ring of rubber, metal, etc sandwiched between metal surfaces to act as a seal.

gaslight n a type of lamp using a jet of gas to provide illumination.

gasman n (pl **gasmen**) an employee of a gas company who reads meters, etc.

gasolier, gaselier n a branched hanging support for gas lights.

gasoline, gasolene n (*US*) a liquid fuel or solvent distilled from petroleum.—*also* **petrol.**—**gasolinic** adj.

gasometer n an instrument for measuring gas; a gasholder.

gasometry n the science or process of measuring gas.

gasp vi to draw in the breath suddenly and audibly, as from shock; to struggle to catch the breath. * vt to utter breathlessly. * n the act of gasping.—**gaspingly** adv.

gassy adj (**gassier, gassiest**) impregnated with or like a gas; given to pretentious talk; inflated.

gastr-, gastro- prefix stomach.

gastric adj of, in, or near the stomach.

gastric juice n digestive fluid secreted by glands in the stomach lining.

gastric ulcer n an ulcer of the lining of the stomach.

gastritis n inflammation of the stomach.—**gastritic** adj.

gastroenteric adj of or pertaining to the stomach or intestinal tract.

gastroenteritis n inflammation of the mucous membrane of the stomach and intestines.—**gastroenteritic** adj.

gastrointestinal adj of or pertaining to the stomach or intestines.

gastrology, gastroenterology n the study of diseases of the stomach and intestinal tract.

gastronome, gastronomer, gastronomist n a connoisseur of food.

gastronomy n the art and science of good eating.—**gastronomic, gastronomical** adj.—**gastronomically** adj.

gastropod n any of a large class of molluscs (as snails) with a flattened foot for moving and usu with stalk-like sense organs.—**gastropodan** adj, n.— **gastropodous** adj.

gastrula n (pl **gastrulas, gastrulae**) the fertilized ovum at a certain period in its development.

gasworks n sing a place where gas is manufactured.

gate n a movable structure controlling passage through an opening in a fence or wall; a gateway; a movable barrier; a structure controlling the flow of water, as in a canal; a device (as in a computer) that outputs a signal when specified input conditions are met; the total amount or number of paid admissions to a football match, etc. * vt to supply with a gate; to keep within the gates (of a university) as a punishment.

gâteau, gateau n (pl **gâteaux, gateaux**) a large cream cake.

gate-crasher n a person who attends a party, etc without being invited.—**gatecrash** vi.

gatefold n an oversize page in a book or magazine that is folded in.

gatehouse n a house built over or beside a gate.

gatekeeper n a person who controls entrance to a gate.

gate-leg(ged) table n a table with drop leaves supported by movable legs.

gatepost n a post on which a gate is hung, or to which it is attached when closed.

gateway n an opening for a gate; a means of entrance or exit.

gather vt to bring together in one place or group; to get gradually; to collect (as taxes); to harvest; to draw (parts) together; to pucker fabric by pulling a thread or stitching; to understand, infer. * vi to come together in a body; to cluster around a focus of attention; (*sore*) to swell and fill with pus.—**gatherable** adj.—**gatherer** n.

gathering n the act of gathering or assembling together; an assembly; folds made in a garment by gathering.

Gatling gun n a machine gun with clustered barrels, which are discharged in succession by turning a handle.

GATT abbr = General Agreement on Tariffs and Trade.

gauche adj socially inept; graceless, tactless.—**gauchely** adv.—**gaucheness** n.

gaucherie n awkwardness, tactlessness; a tactless or awkward act.

gaucho n (pl **gauchos**) a cowboy of the pampas of South America.

gaud n a piece of finery, a trinket or ornament.

gaudery n (pl **gauderies**) cheap, showy finery.

gaudy adj (**gaudier, gaudiest**) excessively ornamented; tastelessly bright.—**gaudily** adv.—**gaudiness** n.

gauffer see **goffer**.

gauge n measurement according to some standard or system; any device for measuring; the distance between rails of a railway; the size of the bore of a shotgun; the thickness of sheet metal, wire, etc. * vt to measure the size, amount, etc of.—also **gage**.—**gaugeable, gagable** adj.—**gauger, gager** n.

Gaul n an ancient region of Western Europe corresponding roughly to modern France and Belgium; a native of Gaul.

Gaullism n the policies pertaining to General de Gaulle, first president of the Fifth Republic in France (1959–69); the political movement based on de Gaulle's policies and principles.—**Gaullist** n, adj.

gaunt adj excessively thin as from hunger or age; looking grim or forbidding.—**gauntness** n.

gauntlet[1] n a knight's armoured glove; a long glove, often with a flaring cuff.—also **gantlet** n.

gauntlet[2] n (formerly) a type of military punishment in which a victim was forced to run between two lines of men who struck him as he passed.

gaur n a large fierce, dark-coloured ox found in SE Asia and India.

gauss n (pl **gauss, gausses**) the unit of measurement for magnetic flux density.

gauze n any very thin, loosely woven fabric, as of cotton or silk; a firm woven material of metal or plastic filaments; a surgical dressing.

gauzy adj (**gauzier, gauziest**) like gauze, thin, transparent.—**gauzily** adv.—**gauziness** n.

gave see **give**.

gavel n a hammer used by a chairman, auctioneer, judge, etc to command proceedings.

gavial n an Indian crocodile with a long narrow snout.

gavotte n a lively dance of French peasant origin.

gawk vi to stare at stupidly.

gawky adj (**gawkier, gawkiest**) clumsy, awkward, ungainly.—**gawkily** adv.—**gawkiness** n.

gay adj joyous and lively; colourful; homosexual. * n a homosexual.—**gayness** n.

gaze vi to look steadily. * n a steady look.—**gazer** n.

gazebo n (pl **gazebos, gazeboes**) a summerhouse or belvedere, elevated to command a wide view.

gazelle n (pl **gazelles, gazelle**) any of numerous small swift Asian or African antelopes.

gazette n a newspaper, now mainly in newspaper titles; an official publication listing government appointments, legal notices, etc.

gazetteer n an index of geographical place names.

gazpacho n a Spanish soup of tomatoes and other vegetables, served cold.

GB abbr = Great Britain.

Gd (chem symbol) gadolinium.

GDP abbr = Gross Domestic Product.

Ge (chem symbol) germanium.

gear n clothing; equipment, esp for some task or activity; a toothed wheel designed to mesh with another; (often pl) a system of such gears meshed together to transmit motion; a specific adjustment of such a system; a part of a mechanism with a specific function. * vt to connect by or furnish with gears; to adapt (one thing) to conform with another.

gearbox n a metal case enclosing a system of gears.

gearing n a particular arrangement of gears.

gearshift n a lever used to engage or change gear, esp in a motor vehicle.

gearwheel n a cogwheel.

gecko n (pl **geckos, geckoes**) a small lizard of warm regions that feeds on insects.

gee vi (**geeing geed**) (often with **up**) to make a horse go faster. * interj a mild oath.

geese see **goose**.

geezer n (sl) an old man.

Geiger counter n an electronic device for detecting and measuring radioactive emissions.

geisha n (pl **geisha, geishas**) a Japanese girl trained as an entertainer to serve as a hired companion to men.

gel n a jelly-like substance, as that applied to style and sculpt hair before drying it. * vti (**gelling, gelled**) to become or cause to become a gel.—also **jell**.

gelatin, gelatine n a tasteless, odourless substance extracted by boiling bones, hoofs, etc and used in food, photographic film, medicines, etc.

gelatinize vt to make or become gelatinous; to coat with gelatin.—**gelatinization** n.—**gelatinizer** n.

gelatinous adj of or like gelatin; jelly-like in consistency.

gelation n solidification (of liquids) by cold.

geld vt (**gelding, gelded** or **gelt**) to castrate, esp a horse.

gelding n a castrated horse.

gelid adj intensely cold; icy.—**gelidity** n.

gelignite n an explosive consisting of nitroglycerin absorbed in a base of wood pulp mixed with sodium or potassium nitrate.

gem n a precious stone, esp when cut and polished for use as a jewel; a person or thing regarded as extremely valuable or beloved. * vt (**gemming, gemmed**) to decorate or set with gems.

geminate, geminated adj growing or occurring in pairs.

gemination n duplication; (rhetoric) the repetition of a word, etc, for effect.

Gemini n the third sign of the zodiac, represented by the twins Castor and Pollux, operative 21 May–20 June.—**Geminian** adj.

gemma n (pl **gemmae**) a growth on an animal or plant budding off as a separate individual.

gemmate vi to have buds; to propagate by gemmae.—**gemmation** n.—**gemmiparous** adj.

gemmule n a small bud or gemma; an ovule; a cell produced by certain moulds.

gemot, gemote n an assembly or local court in pre-Norman England.

gemsbok n (pl **gemsbok, gemsboks**) a large, straight-horned South African antelope with a broad black stripe along its length.

gemstone n a mineral or substance used as a gem.

gendarme n an armed policeman in France and Belgium.

gendarmerie, gendarmery n a force of gendarmes.

gender n the classification by which words are grouped as feminine, masculine, or neuter; (inf) the sex of a person.

gene n any of the complex chemical units in the chromosomes by which hereditary characteristics are transmitted.

genealogy n (pl **genealogies**) a recorded history of one's ancestry; the study of family descent; lineage.—**genealogical** adj.—**genealogist** n.

genera see **genus**.

generable adj capable of being generated.

general adj not local, special, or specialized; of or for a whole genus, relating to or covering all instances or individuals of a class or group; widespread, common to many; not specific or precise; holding superior rank, chief. * *n* something that involves or is applicable to the whole; a commissioned officer above a lieutenant general; a leader, commander; the title of the head of some religious orders.—**generalness** *n*.

general anaesthetic *n* an anaesthetic effecting the whole body and producing unconsciousness.

general delivery *n* the department of a post office that will hold mail until it is called for.—*also* **poste restante**.

general election *n* a national election to choose representatives in every constituency.

generalissimo *n* (*pl* **generalissimos**) a military commander of combined air, naval and ground forces.

generality *n* (*pl* **generalities**) the quality or state of being general; a vague or inadequate statement.

generalization *n* general inference; induction; a general notion formed by attributing the characteristic(s) of a particular part or member (of a class, community etc) to the whole.

generalize *vti* to form general conclusions from specific instances; to talk (about something) in general terms.—**generalization** *n*.—**generalizer** *n*.

generally *adv* widely; popularly; usually; not specifically.

general practitioner *n* a non-specialist doctor who treats all types of illnesses in the community.

general-purpose *adj* having all kinds of uses.

generalship *n* the office of general; military skill; management skill.

general staff *n* officers who advice and assist a military commander.

general strike *n* a strike of all workers in a city, region or country.

generate *vt* to bring into existence; to produce.

generation *n* the act or process of generating; a single succession in natural descent; people of the same period; production, as of electric current.

generation gap *n* the difference in attitudes and understanding between one generation and another.

generative *adj* pertaining to generation; having the power to generate.

generator *n* one who or that which generates; a machine that changes mechanical energy to electrical energy.

generic *adj* of a whole class, kind, or group.—**generically** *adv*.

generosity *n* (*pl* **generosities**) the quality of being generous; liberality; munificence; a generous act.

generous *adj* magnanimous; of a noble nature; willing to give or share; large, ample.—**generously** *adv*.—**generousness** *n*.

genesis *n* (*pl* **geneses**) the beginning, origin; (*with cap*) the first book of the Old Testament.

genet *n* an animal of southern Europe, western Asia and Africa, related to the civet and valued for its fur; any fur made in imitation of genet.

genetic, genetical *adj* of or relating to the origin, development or causes of something; of or relating to genes or genetics.—**genetically** *adv*.

genetic code *n* the order of genetic information in a cell, which determines hereditary characteristics.

genetic engineering *n* the modification of genetic information in the cell of a plant or animal to improve yield, performance, etc.

genetic fingerprinting *n* the analysis of bodily tissue or fluids to identify the unique genetic character of an individual, as used in criminal investigations, the determination of paternity, etc.

genetics *n sing* the branch of biology dealing with heredity and variation in plants and animals.—**geneticist** *n*.

genial[1] *adj* kindly, sympathetic and cheerful in manner; mild, pleasantly warm.—**geniality, genialness** *n*.—**genially** *adv*.

genial[2] *adj* of the chin.

geniculate, geniculated *adj* having knee-like joints; bent at a sharp angle.

genie *n* (*pl* **genies, genii**) (*fairy tales*) a spirit with supernatural powers which can fulfil your wishes.—*also* **jinni**.

genital *adj* of reproduction or the sexual organs.

genitals, genitalia *npl* the (external) sexual organs.—**genitalic** *adj*.

genitive *adj* (*gram*) of or belonging to the case of nouns, pronouns and adjectives expressing ownership or relation. * *n* the genitive case.—**genitival** *adj*.

genius *n* (*pl* **geniuses**) a person possessing extraordinary intellectual power; (*with* **for**) natural ability, strong inclination.

genocide *n* the systematic killing of a whole race of people.—**genocidal** *adj*.

genre *n* a distinctive type or category, esp of literary composition; a style of painting in which everyday objects are treated realistically.

gens *n* (*pl* **gentes**) in ancient Rome, a clan or house; one of a number of related families claiming a common ancestor or having a name or religious rites etc in common.

gent *n* (*inf*) a gentleman.

genteel *adj* polite or well-bred; affectedly refined.—**genteelly** *adv*.—**genteelness** *n*.

gentes *see* **gens**.

gentian *n* an alpine plant, usu with blue flowers.

gentian violet *n* a crystalline substance used as an antiseptic.

gentile *n* a person who is not a Jew.—*also adj*.

gentility *n* (*pl* **gentilities**) refinement, good manners.

gentle *adj* belonging to a family of high social station; refined, courteous; generous; kind; kindly; patient; not harsh or rough.—**gentleness** *n*.—**gently** *adv*.

gentleman *n* (*pl* **gentlemen**) a man of good family and social standing; a courteous, gracious and honourable man; a polite term of address.—**gentlemanly** *adj*.

gentleman-at-arms *n* (*pl* **gentlemen-at-arms**) one of the bodyguard of the UK sovereign on state occasions.

gentlewoman *n* (*pl* **gentlewomen**) a woman of noble or gentle birth; a lady.

gentrify *vt* (**gentrifying, gentrified**) to convert a working-class house or district to more expensive middle-class tastes.—**gentrification** *n*.

gentry *n* people of high social standing; (*formerly*) landed proprietors not belonging to the nobility.

genuflect *vi* to act in a servile way; to bend the knee in worship or respect.—**genuflection** *n*.—**genuflector** *n*.

genuine *adj* not fake or artificial, real; sincere.—**genuinely** *adv*.—**genuineness** *n*.

genus *n* (*pl* **genera**) (*biol*) a taxonomic division of plants and animals below a family and above a species; a class of objects divided into several subordinate species.

geo- *prefix* earth.

geocentric *adj* viewed as from the centre of the earth; having the earth as a centre.—**geocentrically** *adj*.

geod *abbr* = geodesic; geodesy; geodetic.

geode *n* a cavity lined with crystals, usu within a rock.

geodesic *adj* geodetic (—*also* **geodesical**). * *n* (*math*) the shortest distance between two points on a cruved surface, determined by triangulation.

geodesic dome *n* a lightweight domed structure made of interlocking polygons.

geodesy *n* the mathematical determination of the exact positions of geographical points and the shape and size of the earth.—**geodesic** *adj*.—**geodic** *adj*.

geodetic, geodetical *adj* of, pertaining to, determined by, or carried out by geodesy.

geography *n* (*pl* **geographies**) the science of the physical nature of the earth, such as land and sea masses, climate, vegetation, etc, and their interaction with the human population; the physical features of a region.—**geographer** *n*.—**geographical, geographic** *adj*.—**geographically** *adv*.

geologize *vti* to study geology or the geology of.

geology *n* the science relating to the history and structure of the earth's crust, its rocks and fossils.—**geological, geologic** *adj*.—**geologically** *adv*.—**geologist, geologer** *n*.

geomancy *n* divination by figures or lines.—**geomancer** *n*.—**geomantic** *adj*.

geometer, geometrician *n* one who studies or is skilled in geometry.

geometric, geometrical *adj* pertaining to, or done by, geometry; (*design, etc*) consisting of simple geometric shapes.—**geometrically** *adv*.

geometric progression *n* a sequence in which the terms differ by a constant ratio (e.g. 1, 2, 4, 8, 16…).

geometrize *vti* to work or make by geometrical methods; to study geometry.

geometry *n* the branch of mathematics dealing with the properties, measurement, and relationships of points, lines, planes, and solids.—**geometric, geometrical** *adj*.—**geometrically** *adv*.

geophagy, geophagia, geophagism *n* the practice of eating certain kinds of clay, earth or chalk.—**geophagist** *n*.—**geophagous** *adj*.

geophysics *n sing* the physics of the earth.— **geophysical.**—*adj*.—**geophysicist** *n*.

geopolitics *n sing* the study of the relationship between the geographical situation of a nation and its politics; the study of the effect of a nation's geography on its politics, esp in relation to that nation's relationship with other nations.

geoponic *adj* agricultural.

geoponics *n sing* the scientific study of agriculture.

georgette *n* a thin silk fabric.

Georgian *adj* of the times or reigns of the four Georges (1714–1830) or of George V (1910–36) who ruled Britain; pertaining to Georgia in the US; pertaining to Georgia in the Caucasus. * *n* a person from Georgia; a person who lived in Georgian times; one who lives as if he or she belonged to Georgian times.

georgic, georgical *adj* of or pertaining to husbandry; rural. * *n* a poem on agriculture; (*with cap: pl*) a poem on agriculture by Virgil.

geothermal, geothermic *adj* of, relating to, or using the heat of the earth's interior.

geotropism *n* (*bot*) a tendency in the roots of certain plants to turn in the direction of the earth.—**geotropic** *adj*.—**geotropically** *adv*.

geranium *n* a garden plant with red, pink or white flowers.

gerbil, gerbille *n* a type of burrowing desert rodent of Asia and Africa.—*also* **jerbil**.

gerent *n* (*rare*) a ruler, a manager.

gerfalcon *see* **gyrfalcon**.

geriatric *adj* relating to geriatrics or old people; (*inf*) old, decrepit. * an aged person.

geriatrics *n sing* a branch of medicine dealing with the diseases and care of old people.—**geriatrician, geriatrist** *n*.

germ *n* a simple form of living matter capable of growth and development into an organism; any microscopic, disease-causing organism; an origin or foundation capable of growing and developing.

German *adj* of or relating to Germany, its people or their language. * *n* a native of Germany.

german *adj* of the same stock or parentage; germane.

germander *n* a plant of the mint family.

germane *adj* relevant.—**germanely** *adv*.—**germaneness** *n*.

Germanic *adj* of Germans or Germany or of a German-speaking nation. * *n* the family of languages derived from Indo-European that comprises the English, Dutch, German, Scandinavian and Gothic languages.

Germanism *n* a German idiom, custom, or characteristic.

germanium *n* a rare metallic element used in transistors.

Germanize *vti* to make or become German in language, custom, manners etc.—**Germanization** *n*.

German measles *n* (*sing*) a mild contagious disease similar to measles.—*also* **rubella**.

Germanophile *n* a lover of Germany or its customs, etc.

Germanophobe *n* a person who has an irrational fear of Germany.—**Germanophobia** *n*.

German shepherd *n* any of a breed of large smooth-haired dogs often used by the police and for guarding property.—*also* **Alsatian**.

German silver *n* an alloy of nickel, copper and zinc.—*also* **nickel silver**.

germ cell *n* a reproductive cell.

germicide *n* a substance used to destroy germs.—**germicidal** *adj*.

germinal *adj* incipient; of or pertaining to a germ or germs or seed buds; in the French revolutionary calendar, the seventh month (March 22-April 20).

germinate *vti* to start developing; to sprout, as from a seed.—**germinable, germinative** *adj*.—**germination** *n*.—**germinator** *n*.

germ warfare *n* the use of disease-causing bacteria against enemy forces.

gerontocracy *n* (*pl* **gerontocracies**) government by old men.—**gerontocratic** *adj*.

gerontology *n* the study of aging and its effects and problems.—**gerontological** *adj*.—**gerontologist** *n*.

gerrymander *vt* to rearrange the boundaries of (voting districts) to favour a particular party or candidate.

gerund *n* the participle of a verb used as a noun.—**gerundial** *adj*.

gerundive *adj* of or like a gerund. * *n* a passive verbal adjective.

gesso *n* (*pl* **gessoes**) a prepared ground of plaster for painting on; plaster of Paris.

gestalt *n* (*pl* **gestalts, gestalten**) an integral pattern or system of phenomena forming a functional unit in which the whole is more than the sum of its parts.

Gestapo *n* the secret police of Nazi Germany.

gestate *vt* to carry (young) in the womb during pregnancy; to develop (a plan, etc) gradually in the mind.—**gestational, gestative** *adj.*—**gestatory** *adj.*

gestation *n* the act or period of carrying young in the womb; pregnancy.

gesticulate *vi* to make expressive gestures, esp when speaking.—**gesticulation** *n.*—**gesticulative** *adj.*—**gesticulator** *n.*

gesture *n* movement of part of the body to express or emphasize ideas, emotions, etc. * *vi* to make a gesture.—**gestural** *adj.*—**gesturer** *n.*

get *vb* (**getting, got,** *pp* **got, gotten**) *vt* to obtain, gain, win; to receive; to acquire; to go and bring; to catch; to persuade; to cause to be; to prepare; (*inf*) (*with vb aux* **have** *or* **has**) to be obliged to; to possess; (*inf*) to strike, kill, baffle; defeat, etc; (*inf*) to understand; (*with* **across**) to cause to be understood; (*with* **in**) to bring in; (*crops, etc*) to gather; to insert; (*with* **off**) to acquit, to secure favourable treatment of; (*letters*) to post; (*with* **out**) to cause to leave or escape; to cause to become known or published; (*with* **out of**) to avoid doing; (*with* **over**) to communicate effectively. * *vi* to come; to go; to arrive; to come to be; to manage or contrive; (*with* **about, around**) to be up and on one's feet, esp after being unwell; to be socially active; (*news, gossip*) to become circulated; (*with*) **across**) to be understood; (*with* **at**) to reach; (*inf*) to mean, imply; to irritate, pester relentlessly; (*inf*) to criticize; (*inf*) to corrupt, bribe, influence illegally; (*with* **away**) to escape; (*with* **by**) (*inf*) to manage, to survive; (*with* **in**) (*vehicle, etc*) to enter; to arrive; (*university, college, etc*) to be offered a place; (*with* **off**) to come off, down, or out of; to be acquitted; to escape the consequences of; to begin, depart; (*with* **on**) to go on or into; to put on; to proceed; to grow older; to become late; to manage; to succeed; (*with* **on with**) to establish a friendly relationship; (*with* **out**) to go out or away; to leave or escape; to take out; to become known or published; (*with* **over**) to overcome; to recover from; to forget; (*with* **round, around**) to evade, circumvent; to coax, cajole; (*with* **through**) to use up, spend, consume; to finish; to manage to survive; (*examination, test*) to succeed or pass; to contact by telephone; (*with* **up**) to rise to one's feet; to get out of bed; (*inf*) to organize; (*inf*) to dress in a certain style; (*inf*) to be involved in (mischief, etc).—**getable, gettable** *adj.*

get-at-able *adj* accessible.

getaway *n* the act of escaping; a start in a race, etc.

get-together *n* (*inf*) an informal social gathering or meeting.

get-up *n* (*inf*) dress, costume.

get-up-and-go *n* (*inf*) energy, enthusiasm.

getter *n* one who gets or acquires.

geum *n* a genus of the rose family, with yellow, orange, red or white flowers.

gewgaw *n* a showy ornament; a trinket.

geyser *n* a natural spring from which columns of boiling water and steam gush into the air at intervals; a water heater.

gharry, gharri *n* (*pl* **gharries**) a cart or carriage in India that is available for hire.

ghastly *adj* (**ghastlier, ghastliest**) terrifying, horrible; (*inf*) intensely disagreeable; pale, unwell looking.—**ghastliness** *n.*

ghat, ghaut *n* in India, a mountain pass or a chain of mountains; a landing-place with steps; a flight of steps to a river or a temple.

ghazi *n* (*pl* **ghazies**) a Muslim slayer of infidels; a Turkish title bestowed on distinguished commanders; a warrior champion.

ghee *n* clarified butter.

gherkin *n* a small cucumber used for pickling.

ghetto *n* (*pl* **ghettos, ghettoes**) a section of a city in which members of a minority group live, esp because of social, legal or economic pressure.

ghetto blaster *n* (*inf*) a large portable stereo cassette player and radio with built-in speakers.

ghillie *n* (*pl* **ghillies**) a gillie.

ghost *n* the supposed disembodied spirit of a dead person, appearing as a shadowy apparition; a faint trace or suggestion; a false image in a photographic negative. * *vt* to ghostwrite.

ghostly *adj* (**ghostlier, ghostliest**) of or like a ghost.—**ghostliness** *n.*

ghost town *n* a town abandoned by most or all of its inhabitants.

ghostwrite *vt* (**ghostwriting, ghostwrote,** *pp* **ghostwritten**) to writes books, speeches, articles, etc for another who professes to be the author.—**ghostwriter** *n.*

ghoul *n* (*Muslim folklore*) an evil spirit that robs graves and feeds on the dead; a person with macabre tastes or interests.—**ghoulish** *adj.*—**ghoulishly** *adv.*

GHQ *abbr* = General Headquarters.

GI *n* (*pl* **GI's, GIs**) (*inf*) a private soldier in the US Army.

giant *n* a huge legendary being of great strength; a person or thing of great size, strength, intellect, etc. * *adj* incredibly large.—**giantess** *nf.*

giant panda *n* a large black and white bear-like herbivore.—*also* **panda.**

giaour *n* (*derog*) a Muslim term for an unbeliever, esp a Christian.

gibber *vi* to utter meaningless or inarticulate sounds.

gibberish *n* unintelligible talk, nonsense.

gibbet *n* a gallows; a structure from which bodies of executed criminals were hung and exposed to public scorn.

gibbon *n* a small tailless ape of southeastern Asia and the East Indies.

gibbous *adj* protuberant; humped; irregularly rounded; (*moon*) between full and half.

gibe *n* a taunt, sneer. * *vti* to jeer, scoff (at).—*also* **jibe.**—**giber, jiber** *n.*—**gibingly, jibingly** *adv.*

giblets *npl* the edible internal organs of a bird.

gid *n* a disease in sheep, marked by staggering.

giddy *adj* (**giddier, giddiest**) frivolous, flighty; having a feeling of whirling around as if about to lose balance and fall; causing giddiness. * *vti* (**giddying, giddied**) to make giddy, to become giddy.—**giddily** *adv.*—**giddiness** *n.*

gie *vt* (*Scot*) to give.

GIFT (*acronym*) Gamete Intra-Fallopian Transfer: a technique that helps infertile couples to have children.

gift *n* something given; the act of giving; a natural ability. * *vt* to present with or as a gift.—**giftedness** *n.*

gifted *adj* having great natural ability.

gig[1] *n* a light two-wheeled horse-drawn carriage; a long, light boat.

gig[2] *n* (*inf*) a single booking for a jazz or pop band, etc; a single night's performance. * *vi* (**gigging, gigged**) to perform a gig.

giga- *prefix* one billion (10^9); (*comput*) 2^{30}.

gigantesque *adj* as if by or for a giant.

gigantic *adj* exceedingly large.—**gigantically** *adv.*—**giganticness** *n.*

giggle *vi* to laugh in a nervous or silly manner. * *n* a laugh in this manner; (*inf*) a prank, a joke.—**giggler** *n.*—**giggly** *adj.*

gigolo *n* (*pl* **gigolos**) a man paid to be a woman's escort.

gigot *n* a leg of mutton.

gigue *n* a lively tune; a dance similar to a jig.

gild[1] *see* **guild**.

gild[2] *vt* (**gilding, gilded** *or* **gilt**) to coat with gold leaf; to give a deceptively attractive appearance to.—**gilder** *n*

gilder *see* **guilder**.

gilding *n* the art or proceess of overlaying or covering with gold leaf; gold leaf applied to a surface; a superficial covering.

gill[1] *n* an organ, esp in fish, for breathing in water.

gill[2] *n* in US a liquid measure equal to 4 fluid ounces (0.25 pint) or 23.6 millimeters; in UK, 5 fluid ounces (0.25 pint) or 28.4 millimeters.

gillie, gilly *n* (*pl* **gillies**) (*Scot*) a Highland attendant, esp one who accompanies a shooting or fishing party.—*also* **ghillie**.

gills *npl* the wattle below the beak of a bird, as in certain domestic fowl; one of the radiating plates under the cap of a mushroom; a person's cheeks or jowls.

gillyflower *n* one of various scented plants of the mustard family, eg wallflower, stock, etc.

gilt[1] *see* **gild**.

gilt[2] *n* gilding; a substance used for this.

gilt-edged *adj* (*securities*) considered a secure investment.

gimbal *n* (*usu pl*) one of two rings moving within each other at right angles, used to suspend a ship's compass, etc.

gimcrack *adj* showy, cheap and useless.

gimlet *n* a small tool with a screw point for boring holes.

gimmick *n* a trick or device for attracting notice, advertising or promoting a person, product or service.—**gimmickry** *n.*—**gimmicky** *adj.*

gimp *n* an interlaced silk twist or trimming interwoven with wire or cord, used for furniture, dresses etc.—*also* **guimpe**.

gin[1] *n* an alcoholic spirit distilled from grain and flavoured with juniper berries.

gin[2] *n* a trap for catching small animals; a type of crane; a machine for separating the seeds from raw cotton. * *vt* (**ginning, ginned**) to trap with a gin; to separate seeds from cotton.

ginger *n* a tropical plant with fleshy roots used as a flavouring; the spice prepared by drying and grinding; (*inf*) vigour; a reddish-brown.—**gingery** *adj.*

ginger ale, ginger beer *n* a carbonated soft drink flavoured with ginger.

gingerbread *n* a cake flavoured with ginger.

gingerly *adv* with care or caution. * *adj* cautious.—**gingerliness** *n.*

ginger snap *n* a ginger-flavoured biscuit.

gingham *n* a cotton fabric with stripes or checks.

gingival *adj* of the gums.

gingivitis *n* inflammation of the gums.

ginglymus *n* (*pl* **ginglymi**) (*anat*) a joint like a hinge.

gink *n* (*sl*) a boy or man, esp an eccentric one.

ginkgo *n* (*pl* **ginkgoes**) a Japanese tree with handsome fan-shaped foliage; the maidenhair tree.

ginseng *n* a plant found in China and North America; its root, said to have an invigorating effect on the mind and body.

gip *see* **gyp**.

Gipsy *see* **Gypsy**.

giraffe *n* (*pl* **giraffes, giraffe**) a large cud-chewing mammal of Africa, with very long legs and neck.

girandole, girandola *n* a branched chandelier; a revolving firework or water jet; a pendant or earring with small stones around a larger one; one of several mines connected in a group.

girasol, girosol, girasole *n* a variety of opal; the fire opal.

gird *vt* (**girding, girded** *or* **girt**) to encircle or fasten with a belt; to surround; to prepare (oneself) for action.

girder *n* a large steel beam for supporting joists, the framework of a building, etc.

girdle *n* a belt for the waist.

girl *n* a female child; a young woman; (*inf*) a woman of any age.—**girlhood** *n.*—**girlish** *adj.*

girlfriend *n* a female friend, esp with whom one is romantically involved.

Girl Guide *n* a member of the Girl Guides, a scouting organization founded in Britain in 1910.

girlie *n* a little girl; a young woman; (*inf*) a woman.

girlie magazine *n* a magazine that contains photographs of nude or semi-nude females.

girlish *adj* of or like a girl.—**girlishly** *adv.*—**girlishness** *n.*

Girl Scout *n* a member of the Girl Scouts, a youth organization founded in the US in 1912.

giro (*pl* **giros**) a credit-transfer system between financial organizations; a payment so made.

Girondist *n* a member of the Gironde, the moderate Republican party during the Revolution in France (179193).

girt *see* **gird**.

girt[2] *adj* (*naut*) moored so taut by two cables as not to swing to the wind or tide.

girth *n* the thickness round something; a band put around the belly of a horse, etc to hold a saddle or pack.

gist *n* the principal point or essence of anything.

gîte *n* self-catering holiday accommodation in France.

give *vb* (**giving, gave,** *pp* **given**) *vt* to hand over as a present; to deliver; to hand over in or for payment; to pass (regards etc) along; to act as host or sponsor of; to supply; to yield; (*advice*) to offer; (*punishment, etc*) to inflict; to sacrifice; to perform; (*with* **away**) to make a gift of; to give (the bride) to the bridegroom; to sell cheaply; to reveal, betray; (*with* **in**) to deliver, hand in (a document, etc); (*with* **off**) to emit (fumes, etc); (*with* **out**) to discharge; to make public, to announce; to emit; to distribute; (*with* **over**) to devote time to a specific activity; to cease (an activity); to transfer to another; to set aside for a particular purpose; (*with* **up**) to hand over; to stop, renounce; to cease; to resign (a position); to stop trying; to despair of; to surrender; to devote oneself completely (to). * *vi* to bend, move, etc from force or pressure; (*inf*) to be happening; (*with* **in**) to concede, admit defeat; (*with* **out**) to become used up or exhausted; to fail; (*with* **over**) (*inf*) to stop (an activity). * *n* capacity or tendency to yield to force or strain; the quality or state of being springy; (*with* **in**) to submit; (*with* **out**) to become worn out; (*with* **up**) to accept defeat or failure to do something, to surrender.—**givable, giveable** *adj.*

give-and-take *n* mutual concessions; free-flowing exchange of ideas and conversation.

giveaway *n* (*inf*) an unintentional revelation; a free gift to encourage sales; a freesheet.

given[1] *see* **give**.

given[2] *adj* accustomed (to) by habit, etc; specified; assumed; granted.

giver *n* a person who gives.

gizzard *n* the second stomach of a bird, used for grinding food.

glabrous *adj* without hair, smooth-skinned.

glacé *adj* candied, covered in icing, as fruit. * *vt* (**glacéing, glacéed**) to cover with icing; to candy.

glacial *adj* extremely cold; of or relating to glaciers or a glacial epoch.—**glacially** *adv*.

glaciate *vti* to subject to glacial action; to cover or become covered with glaciers.—**glaciation** *n*.

glacier *n* a large mass of snow and ice moving slowly down a mountain.

glacis *n* (*pl* **glacis**) a sloping bank of earth in front of a fortification for its defence; a slope (on a tank) to throw off hostile shot.

glad *adj* (**gladder, gladdest**) happy; causing joy; very willing; bright.—**gladly** *adv*.—**gladness** *n*.

gladden *vti* to make or become glad.—**gladdener** *n*.

glade *n* an open space in a wood or forest.

gladiate *adj* sword-shaped.

gladiator *n* (*ancient Rome*) a person trained to fight with men or beasts in a public arena.—**gladiatorial** *adj*.

gladiolus *n* (*pl* **gladiolus, gladioli**) any of a genus of the iris family with sword-like leaves and tall spikes of funnel-shaped flowers.

gladsome *adj* joyous.

glair *n* white of egg; size made from this; a sticky substance; any sticky or glairy matter * *vt* to smear with glair.—**glaireous** *adj*.

glairy *adj* (**glairier, glairiest**) like or smeared with glair.—**glairiness** *n*.

glamorize, glamourize *vt* to make glamorous.—**glamorization, glamourization** *n*.—**glamorizer, glamourizer** *n*.

glamour, glamor *n* charm, allure; attractiveness, beauty.—**glamorous, glamourous** *adj*.—**glamorousness, glamourousness** *n*.

glance *vi* to strike obliquely and go off at an angle; to flash; to look quickly. * *n* a glancing off; a flash; a quick look.—**glancingly** *adv*.

gland *n* an organ that separates substances from the blood and synthesizes them for further use in, or for elimination from, the body.

glanders *n* (*sing or pl*) a contagious bacterial disease esp of horses, often fatal.—**glandered** *adj*.—**glanderous** *adj*.

glandular *adj* of, having or resembling glands; (*plants*) covered with hairs tipped with glands.

glare *n* a harsh uncomfortably bright light, esp painfully bright sunlight; an angry or fierce stare. * *vi* to shine with a steady, dazzling light; to stare fiercely.

glaring *adj* dazzling; obvious, conspicuous.—**glaringly** *adv*.—**glaringness** *n*.

glasnost *n* the Russian word for "openness," now applied to the policy, initiated by President Gorbachev of the former USSR, of greater frankness and openness in Soviet affairs.—**glasnostian** *adj*.

glass *n* a hard brittle substance, usu transparent; glassware; a glass article, as a drinking vessel; (*pl*) spectacles or binoculars; the amount held by a drinking glass. * *adj* of or made of glass. * *vt* to equip, enclose, or cover with glass.

glass-blowing *n* the art, skill or process of blowing air into molten glass and shaping it.—**glass-blower** *n*.

glassware *n* objects made of glass, esp drinking vessels.

glasswort *n* a fleshy plant of marshy areas, from which soda was formerly obtained for use in making glass.

glassy *adj* (**glassier, glassiest**) resembling glass; smooth; expressionless, lifeless.—**glassily** *adv*.—**glassiness** *n*.

glaucoma *n* a disease of the eye caused by pressure.—**glaucomatous** *adj*.

glaucous *adj* sea-green; covered with bloom of a blueish-white colour, green with a bluish-grey tinge.

glaze *vt* to provide (windows etc) with glass; to give a hard glossy finish to (pottery, etc); to cover (foods, etc) with a glossy surface. * *vi* to become glassy or glossy. * *n* a glassy finish or coating.—**glazer** *n*.

glazier *n* a person who fits glass in windows.—**glaziery** *n*.

glazing *n* a glaze; the operation of setting glass or applying a glaze; windowpanes; glass; semi-transparent colours passed thinly over other colours to tone down their effect.

gleam *n* a subdued or moderate beam of light; a brief show of some quality or emotion, esp hope. * *vi* to emit or reflect a beam of light.—**gleamingly** *adv*.

glean *vti* to collect (grain left by reapers); to gather (facts, etc) gradually.—**gleanable** *adj*.—**gleaner** *n*.

gleaning *n* the act of collecting after reapers; (*often pl*) that which is collected laboriously from various sources.

glee *n* joy and gaiety; delight; (*mus*) a song in parts for three or more male voices.—**gleeful** *adj*.—**gleefully** *adv*.—**gleefulness** *n*.

gleeful *adj* merry, joyous; triumphant.—**gleefully** *adv*.—**gleefulness** *n*.

gleet *n* a thin mucous discharge, esp from the urethra, resulting from gonorrhoeal disease.

glen *n* a narrow valley.

glengarry *n* (*pl* **glengarries**) (*often cap*) a boat-shaped cap originating in Scotland.

glib *adj* (**glibber, glibbest**) speaking or spoken smoothly, to the point of insincerity; lacking depth and substance.—**glibly** *adv*.—**glibness** *n*.

glide *vti* to move smoothly and effortlessly; to descend in an aircraft or glider with little or no engine power. * *n* a gliding movement.—**glidingly** *adv*.

glider *n* an engineless aircraft carried along by air currents.

gliding *n* the sport of flying gliders.

glim *n* (*sl*) a light, a candle.

glimmer *vi* to give a faint, flickering light; to appear faintly. * *n* a faint gleam; a glimpse, an inkling.

glimmering *n* a faint gleam; a glimpse, an inkling.

glimpse *n* a brief, momentary view. * *vt* to catch a glimpse of.—**glimpser** *n*.

glint *n* a brief flash of light; a brief indication. * *vti* to (cause to) gleam brightly.

glioma *n* (*pl* **gliomata, gliomas**) a tumour of rapid growth on the brain, spinal cord, or auditory nerve.

glissade *vi* to slide down a snow-covered slope without the aid of skis. * *n* a sliding ballet step.—**glissader** *n*.

glissando *n* (*pl* **glissandi, glissandos**) (*mus*) a run by sliding the fingers over the keys of a piano; a quick slur on a violin.

glisten *vi* to shine, as light reflected from a wet surface.—**glisteningly** *adv*.

glister *vi* (*poet*) to sparkle, to glitter.—*also n.*

glitch *n* a malfunction in a, usu electronic, system.

glitter *vi* to sparkle; (*usu with* **with**) to be brilliantly attractive. * *n* a sparkle; showiness, glamour; tiny pieces of sparkling material used for decoration.—**glittering** *adj.*—**glittery** *adj.*

glitz *n*(*sl*) gaudiness; ostentatious glamour.—**glitzy** *adj* (**glitzier, glitziest**)

gloaming *n* twilight.

gloat *vi* to gaze or contemplate with wicked or malicious satisfaction.—**gloater** *n.*—**gloatingly** *adv.*

global *adj* worldwide; comprehensive.—**globally** *adv.*

global warning *n* the process caused by a blanket of 'greenhouse gases' building up around the earth trapping heat from the sun. Carbon dioxide, released by burning fossil fuels is one of the main causes.—see **greenhouse effect.**

globate, globated *adj* globe-shaped.

globe *n* anything spherical or almost spherical; the earth, or a model of the earth.

globeflower *n* a plant with round yellow flowers.

globetrotter *n* a person who travels widely.—**globetrotting** *n, adj.*

globin *n* a constituent of red blood corpuscles.

globoid *adj* nearly globular. * *n* a globoid figure.

globose, globous *adj* globe-like, spherical.

globosity, globoseness *n*

globular *adj* spherical.

globule *n* a small spherical particle; a drop, pellet; a blood corpuscle.

globulin *n* an albuminous protein forming one of the constituents of blood, muscle, and the cellular tissue of plants.

glockenspiel *n* an orchestral percussion instrument with tuned metal bars, played with hammers.

glomerate *adj* gathered into a roundish head or mass; compactly clustered.

glomerule *n* a clustered flowerhead.

gloom *n* near darkness; deep sadness. * *vti* to look sullen or dejected; to make or become cloudy or murky.

gloomy *adj* (**gloomier, gloomiest**) almost dark, obscure; depressed, dejected.—**gloomily** *adv.*—**gloominess** *n.*

gloria *n* a halo or aureole; a light fabric of silk, etc; (*with cap*) a prayer of praise, esp the *Gloria in excelsis* and *Gloria patri*; a musical setting of these.

glorify *vt* (**glorifying, glorified**) to worship; to praise, to honour; to cause to appear more worthy, important, or splendid than in reality.—**glorifiable** *adj.*—**glorification** *n.*—**glorifier** *n.*

glorious *adj* having or deserving glory; conferring glory or renown; beautiful; delightful.—**gloriously** *adv.*—**gloriousness** *n.*

glory *n* (*pl* **glories**) great honour or fame, or its source; adoration; great splendour or beauty; heavenly bliss. * *vi* (**glorying, gloried**) (*with* **in**) to exult, rejoice proudly.

gloss¹ *n* the lustre of a polished surface; a superficially attractive appearance. * *vt* to give a shiny surface to; (*with* **over**) to hide (an error, etc) or make seem right or inconsequential.—**glosser** *n.*

gloss² *n* an explanation of an unusual word (in the margin or between the lines of a text); a misleading explanation; a glossary. * *vt* to provide with glosses; to give a misleading sense of.—**glosser** *n.*

glossa *n* (*pl* **glossae, glossas**) the tongue, esp of insects.—**glossal** *adj.*

glossary *n* (*pl* **glossaries**) a list of specialized or techni-cal words and their definitions.—**glossarial** *adj.*—**glossarist** *n.*

glossitis *n* inflammation of the tongue.

glossography *n* the making of glossaries or glosses.—**glossographer** *n.*

glossy *adj* (**glossier, glossiest**) having a shiny or highly polished surface; superficial; (*magazines*) lavishly produced. * *n* (*pl* **glossies**) a magazine with many colour pictures, printed on coated paper, esp a fashion magazine.—**glossily** *adv.*—**glossiness** *n.*

glottal *adj* of, pertaining to, or produced by the glottis.

glottis *n* (**glottises, glottides**) the opening between the vocal cords in the larynx.—**glottidean** *adj.*

glove *n* a covering for the hand; a baseball player's mitt; a boxing glove. * *vt* to cover (as if) with a glove.

glover *n* a maker or seller of gloves.

glow *vi* to shine (as if) with an intense heat; to emit a steady light without flames; to be full of life and enthusiasm; to flush or redden with emotion. * *n* a light emitted due to intense heat; a steady, even light without flames; a reddening of the complexion; warmth of emotion or feeling.

glower *vi* to scowl; to stare sullenly or angrily. * *n* a scowl, a glare.—**gloweringly** *adv.*

glow-worm *n* a beetle that emits light from the abdomen.

gloxinia *n* a tropical plant with showy bell-shaped flowers, cultivated as a houseplant.

glucose *n* a crystalline sugar occurring naturally in fruits, honey, etc.

glue *n* a sticky, viscous substance used as an adhesive. * *vt* (**gluing, glued**) to join with glue.—**gluer** *n.*

gluey *adj* (**gluier, glueist**) like glue, sticky.

glum *adj* (**glummer, glummest**) sullen; gloomy.—**glumly** *adv.*—**glumness** *n.*

glumaceous *adj* bearing or resembling glumes.

glume *n* the husk of corn or grasses.

glut *vt* (**glutting, glutted**) to over-supply (the market). * *n* a surfeit, an excess of supply.

gluteal *adj* pertaining to the buttocks.

gluten *n* a sticky elastic protein substance, esp of wheat flour, that gives cohesiveness to dough.—**glutenous** *adj.*

gluteus *n* (*pl* **glutei**) any of the three muscles that form the buttocks.

glutinous *adj* resembling glue, sticky.—**glutinousness, glutinosity** *n.*

glutton *n* a person who eats and drinks to excess; a person who has a tremendous capacity for something (eg for work); a wolverine.—**gluttonous** *adj.*

gluttony *n* the act or habit of eating and drinking to excess.

glyceride *n* an ester of glycerol.

glycerin, glycerine *n* the popular and commercial name for glycerol.

glycerol *n* a colourless, syrupy liquid made from fats and oils, used in making skin lotions, explosives, etc.—**glyceric** *adj.*

glycogen *n* a white insoluble starch-like substance obtained from the livers of animals and humans.

glycol *n* a viscid liquid intermediate between glycerine and alcohol; antifreeze.

glycosuria *n* a disease marked by excess sugar in the urine.—**glycosuric** *adj.*

glyph *n* (*arch*) a perpendicular fluting.—**glyphic** *adj.*

glyptic *adj* pertaining to engraving on gems; figured. * *n* the art of engraving designs on precious stones, ivory, etc.

glyptography *n* the art of cutting designs or engraving on a gem.

gm *abbr* = gram(s).

G-man *n* (*pl* **G-men**) (*inf*) an agent of the FBI.

GMT *abbr* = Greenwich Mean Time.

gnarl *n* a knot on the trunk or branch of a tree.

gnarled *adj* (*tree trunks*) full of knots; (*hands*) rough, knobbly; crabby in disposition.

gnash *vti* to grind (the teeth) in anger or pain. * *n* a grinding of the teeth.—**gnashingly** *adv*.

gnat *n* any of various small, two-winged insects that bite or sting.

gnathic, gnathial *adj* of or pertaining to jaws.

gnaw *vti* (**gnawing, gnawed**, *pp* **gnawed** *or* **gnawn**) to bite away bit by bit; to torment, as by constant pain.—**gnawable** *adj*.—**gnawer** *n*.

gneiss *n* a granite-like rock formed by layers of quartz, mica, etc.—**gneissic, gneissoid, gneissose** *adj*.

gnocchi *npl* small dumplings made from flour, semolina or potatoes.

gnome *n* (*folklore*) a dwarf who dwells in the earth and guards its treasure; a small statue of a gnome used as a garden decoration; a small and ugly person; (*sl*) an international banker or financier.—**gnomish** *adj*.

gnomic *adj* dealing in or containing pithy or sententious sayings; didactic.—**gnomically** *adv*.

gnomon *n* the indicator on a sundial that casts a shadow to indicate the time of day.—**gnomonic** *adj*.—**gnomonically** *adv*.

gnosis *n* (*pl* **gnoses**) higher knowledge, mysticism or insight.

gnostic *adj* of, pertaining to, or having knowledge; (*with cap*) pertaining to the Gnostics or Gnosticism (—also **gnostical**). * *n* (*with cap*) a member of an early Christian sect seeking salvation by knowledge, not faith.

Gnosticism *n* the doctrine of the Gnostics.

GNP *abbr* = Gross National Product.

gnu *n* (*pl* **gnus, gnu**) either of two large African antelopes with an ox-like head.—*also* **wildebeest**.

go[1] *vb* (**going, went**, *pp* **gone**) *vi* to move on a course; to proceed; to work properly; to act, sound, as specified; to result; to become; to be accepted or valid; to leave, to depart; to die; to be allotted or sold; to be able to pass (through); to fit (into); to be capable of being divided (into); to belong; (*with* **about**) to handle (a task, etc) efficiently; to undertake (duties, etc); (*sailing*) to change tack; (*with* **into**) to enter; to become a member of; to examine or investigate; to discuss; (*with* **off**) to explode; to depart; (*food, etc*) to become stale or rotten; to fall asleep; to proceed, occur in a certain manner; to take place as planned; to stop liking (something or someone); (*with* **on**) to continue; to happen; to talk effusively; to nag; to enter on stage; (*with* **out**) to depart; (*light, fire, etc*) to become extinguished; to cease to be fashionable; to socialize; (*radio or TV show*) to be broadcast; to spend time with, esp a person of the opposite sex; (*with* **over**) to change one's loyalties (to); to be received or regarded in a certain way; to examine and repair (something); (*with* **round**) to circulate; to be sufficient for everyone; (*with* **slow**) to work at a slow rate as part of an industrial dispute; (*with* **through**) to continue to the end (with); to be approved; to use up completely; to experience (an illness, etc); to search thoroughly; (*with* **together**) to match, to be mutually suited; (*inf*) to associate frequently, esp as lovers; (*with* **up**) in the UK, to enter or return to college or university; (*with* **with**) to

match; to accompany; to associate frequently, esp as lovers; (*with* **without**) to be deprived of or endure the lack of (something). * *vt* to travel along; (*inf*) to put up with. * *n* (*pl* **goes**) a success; (*inf*) a try; (*inf*) energy.

go[2] *n* a Japanese board game.

goa *n* an Asian gazelle, the male of which has horns that curve backwards.

goad *n* a sharp-pointed stick for driving cattle, etc; any stimulus to action. * *vt* to drive (as if) with a goad; to irritate, nag persistently.

go-ahead *n* (*inf*) permission to proceed. * *adj* (*inf*) enterprising, ambitious.

goal *n* the place at which a race, trip, etc is ended; an objective; the place over or into which the ball or puck must go to score in some games; the score made.

goalie *n* (*inf*) a goalkeeper.

goalkeeper *n* a player who defends the goal.—**goalkeeping** *n*.

goat *n* a mammal related to the sheep that has backward curving horns, a short tail, and usu straight hair; a lecherous man.

goatee *n* a small pointed beard.

goatherd *n* a person who looks after goats.

goatish *adj* pertaining to or like a goat; (*arch*) lustful; rank-smelling.—**goatishly** *adv*.—**goatishness** *n*.

goatsbeard, goat's-beard *n* a European grass-like plant with yellow flowers; an American plant with compound leaves and small white flowers.

goatskin *n* the skin of a goat; a bottle or garment made of this.

goatsucker *n* a nocturnal bird with dull mottled plumage.—*also* **nightjar**.

gob[1] *n* (*sl*) the mouth.

gob[2] *n* a lump or clot of something; (*inf*) spittle. * *vi* (**gobbing, gobbed**) (*inf*) to spit.

gobbet *n* a lump of something.

gobble *vt* to eat greedily; (*often with* **up**) to take, accept or read eagerly. * *vi* to make a throaty gurgling noise, as a male turkey.

gobbledygook, gobbledegook *n* (*sl*) nonsense, pretentious jargon.

gobbler *n* (*inf*) a turkey cock.

go-between *n* a messenger, an intermediary.

goblet *n* a large drinking vessel with a base and stem but without a handle.

goblin *n* an evil or mischievous elf.

goby *n* (*pl* **goby, gobies**) a sea fish with a large head and a long thin body.

go-cart *n* a small cart for children to play in or pull; a stroller; a handcart.

god *n* any of various beings conceived of as supernatural and immortal, esp a male deity; an idol; a person or thing deified; (*with cap*) in monotheistic religions, the creator and ruler of the universe.

godchild *n* (*pl* **godchildren**) the child a godparent sponsors.

goddaughter *n* a female godchild.

goddess *n* a female deity; a woman of superior charms or excellence.

godfather *n* a male godparent; the head of a Mafia crime family or other criminal organization.

god-fearing *adj* religious.

godforsaken *adj* desolate, wretched.

godhead *n* the divine nature, deity; God.

godhood *n* the quality or condition of being a god; divinity.

godless *adj* irreligious; wicked.—**godlessly** *adv*.—**godlessness** *n*.

godlike *adj* like a god, divine.

godly *adj* (**godlier, godliest**) religious; holy; devout; devoted to God.—**godliness** *n*.

godmother *n* a female godparent.

godown *n* in India and China, a warehouse or storeroom.

godparent *n* a person who sponsors a child, as at baptism or confirmation, taking responsibility for its faith.

godsend *n* anything that comes unexpectedly and when needed or desired.

godson *n* a male godchild.

Godspeed *n* success, good luck.

godwit *n* any of a genus of wading birds with a long bill, related to the snipes but resembling curlews.

goer *n* a regular attender; something, as a car, that goes fast; an enthusiastic person.

gofer *n* (*inf*) a person who runs errands, as in an office.

goffer *vt* to make wavy or frilly with a hot iron, to crimp.—*also* **gauffer**.

go-getter *n* (*inf*) an ambitious person.

goggle *vi* to stare with bulging eyes. * *npl* large spectacles, sometimes fitting snugly against the face, to protect the eyes.

goggle-eyed *adj* with wide staring eyes.

go-go dancer *n* a scantily-clad dancer employed in a disco or nightclub.

going *n* an act or instance of going, a departure; the state of the ground, eg for walking, horse-racing; rate of progress. * *adj* that goes; commonly accepted; thriving; existing.

going-over *n* (*pl* **goings-over**) (*inf*) a thorough inspection; (*sl*) a beating.

goings-on *npl* events or actions, esp when disapproved of.

goiter, goitre *n* an abnormal enlargement of the thyroid gland.—**goitrous** *adj*.

gold *n* a malleable yellow metallic element used esp for coins and jewellery; a precious metal; money, wealth; a yellow colour. * *adj* of, or like, gold.

goldbeater's skin *n* a membrane prepared from the large intestine of an ox used to separate layers of gold in goldbeating.

goldbeating *n* the process of beating gold until it is very thin.—**goldbeater** *n*.

gold card *n* a credit card that entitles the cardholder to extra benefits.

gold-digger *n* a person who mines gold; (*inf*) a woman who uses feminine charms to extract money or gifts from men.—**gold-digging** *adj*.

golden *adj* made of or relating to gold; bright yellow; priceless; flourishing.—**goldenly** *adv*.—**goldenness** *n*.

golden age *n* the fabled early age of innocence and perfect human happiness; the flowering of a nation's civilization or art.

golden calf *n* (*Bible*) a golden calf made by Aaron and worshipped by the Israelites; wealth worshipped as a god.

golden eagle *n* a large eagle of the Northern hemisphere.

golden fleece *n* (*Greek myth*) the ram's fleece in search of which Jason sailed with the Argonauts; an order of knighthood in Austria and Spain.

golden handcuffs *npl* financial incentives to induce an employee to remain in a particular job for an agreed period.

golden handshake *n* (*inf*) financial compensation awarded an employee for loss of employment.

golden mean *n* neither too much nor too little; moderation.

goldenrod *n* a tall plant of the aster family with yellow flowers.

golden rule *n* a guiding principle.

goldfield *n* a district containing gold deposits and diggings.

gold-filled *adj* coated with gold.

goldfinch *n* a common European finch with yellow and black wings.

goldfish *n* (*pl* **goldfish, goldfishes**) a small gold-coloured fish of the carp family, kept in ponds and aquariums.

goldilocks *n* any of various plants with yellow flowers, eg the buttercup; (*with cap*) a name for someone, usu female, with golden hair.

gold leaf *n* gold beaten into very thin sheets, used for gilding.

gold mine *n* a mine where gold is extracted; (*inf*) a source of wealth.

gold plate *n* vessels of gold; a thin covering of gold.—**gold-plated** *adj*.

gold rush *n* a rush to a new gold field, as to the Yukon in 1897.

goldsmith *n* a worker in gold; a dealer in gold plate.

gold standard *n* a monetary standard in which the basic currency unit equals a specified quantity of gold.

golf *n* an outdoor game in which the player attempts to hit a small ball with clubs around a turfed course into a succession of holes in the smallest number of strokes.—**golfer** *n*.

golf ball *n* a hard dimpled ball used in golf; the spherical printing head in some typewriters.

golf club *n* a club with a wooden or metal head used in golf; a golf association or its premises.

golf course, golf links *n* a tract of land laid out for playing golf.

golliard *n* a medieval wandering jester or scholar.

golliwog, golliwogg *n* a cloth doll with a black face.

golly[1] *n* (*inf*) a golliwog.

golly[2] *interj* expressing surprise.

gonad *n* a primary sex gland that produces reproductive cells, such as an ovary or testis.—**gonadal, gonadic** *adj*.

gondola *n* a long, narrow, black boat used on the canals of Venice; a cabin suspended under an airship or balloon; an enclosed car suspended from a cable used to transport passengers, esp skiers up a mountain; a display structure in a supermarket, etc.

gondolier *n* a person who propels a gondola with a pole.

gone[1] *see* **go**[1].

gone[2] *adj* departed; dead; lost; (*inf*) in an excited state; (*inf*) pregnant for a specified period.

goner *n* (*sl*) a person or thing that is ruined, dead, or about to die.

gonfalon *n* a banner, usu with streamers, hung from a crossbar, used in ecclesiastical processions; a military flag or standard with a pointed edge.

gong *n* a disk-shaped percussion instrument struck with a usu padded hammer; (*sl*) a medal. * *vi* to sound a gong.

Gongorism *n* (a passage of) a florid pedantic Spanish literary style resembling euphuism.

goniometer *n* an instrument for measuring solid angles; an instrument used to determine the location of a distant radio station.—**goniometry** *n*.

gonorrhoea, gonorrhea *n* a venereal disease causing a discharge of mucous and pus from the genitals.—**gonorrhoeal, gonorrheal, gonorrhoeic, gonorrheic** *adj*.

goo *n* (*sl*) sticky matter; sickly sentimentality.

good *adj* (**better, best**) having the right or proper qualities; beneficial; valid; healthy or sound; virtuous, honourable; enjoyable, pleasant, etc; skilled; considerable. * *n* something good; benefit; something that has economic utility; (*with* the) good persons; (*pl*) personal property; commodities; (*pl*) the desired or required articles. * *adv* (*inf*) well; fully.—**goodish** *adj*.

goodbye *interj* a concluding remark at parting; farewell.—*also n*.

good-for-nothing *adj* useless, worthless. * a worthless person.

Good Friday *n* the Friday before Easter, commemorating the Crucifixion of Christ.

good-humoured *adj* genial, cheerful.—**good-humouredly** *adv*.—**good-humouredness** *n*.

good-looking *adj* handsome.

goodly *adj* (**goodlier, goodliest**) considerable; ample.—**goodliness** *n*.

goodman *n* (*pl* **goodmen**) (*formerly*) the master of a house, a husband; a man not born into the aristocracy.

good-natured *adj* amiable, easy-going.—**good-naturedly** *adv*.—**good-naturedness** *n*.

goodness *n* the state of being good; the good element in something; kindness; virtue. * *interj* an exclamation of surprise.

Good Samaritan *n* a person who helps those in distress (after the compassionate figure mentioned in the Bible.—Luke 10:33).

good-tempered *adj* having a pleasant and kindly nature.

good turn *n* a favour; an act of kindness.

goodwill *n* benevolence; willingness; the established custom and reputation of a business.

goodwoman *n* (*pl* **goodwomen**) (*formerly*) the mistress of a house, a wife; a woman not born into the aristocracy.

goody *n* (*pl* **goodies**) something pleasant or sweet; a goddy-goody. * *interj* an expression (usu used by a child) signifying pleasure.

goody-goody *adj* insufferably virtuous. * *n* (*pl* **goody-goodies**) a goody-goody person.

gooey *adj* (**gooier, gooiest**) (*inf*) soft and sticky; sweet; sentimental.

goof *n* (*sl*) a stupid person; a blunder. * *vi* (*sl*) to bungle.

goofy *adj* (**goofier, goofiest**) (*sl*) silly, stupid.—**goofily** *adv*.—**goofiness** *n*.

goon *n* (*sl*) a thug; a stupid person.

goop *n* (*sl*) any sticky, semi-liquid substance; (*sl*) a rude person.

goosander *n* a web-footed migratory waterfowl.

goose[1] *n* (*pl* **geese**) a large, long-necked, web-footed bird related to swans and ducks; its flesh as food; a female goose as distinguished from a gander; (*inf*) a foolish person.

goose[2] *vt* (*sl*) to poke (a person) between the buttocks.

gooseberry *n* (*pl* **gooseberries**) the acid berry of a shrub related to the currant and used esp in jams and pies.

goose bumps, goose pimples, goose flesh *n* a roughening of the skin caused usu by cold or fear.

goosegrass *n* a species of creeping plant on which geese feed.

gooseneck *n* (*naut*) a bent iron fitted to the extremity of a boom or yard.

goose step *n* a stiff-legged marching step used by some armies when passing in review.

goose-step *vi* (**goose-stepping, goose-stepped**) to march in a stiff-legged manner using the goose step.

gopher *n* a North American burrowing, rat-like rodent; a ground squirrel; a burrowing tortoise.

gopherwood *n* the wood Noah's Ark is reputed to have been made from, possibly cypress; the yellowwood.

gore[1] *n* (clotted) blood from a wound.

gore[2] *n* a tapering section of material used to shape a garment, sail, etc.

gore[3] *vt* to pierce or wound as with a tusk or horns.

gorge *n* a ravine. * *vt* to swallow greedily; to glut. * *vi* to feed gluttonously.—**gorgeable** *adj*.—**gorger** *n*.

gorgeous *adj* strikingly attractive; brilliantly coloured; (*inf*) magnificent.—**gorgeously** *adv*.—**gorgeousness** *n*.

Gorgon *n* (*Greek myth*) one of three female monsters with live snakes for hair whose looks turned the beholder to stone; (*without cap*) any ugly or formidable woman.

gorgonian *n* any of a genus of flexible branching coral.

Gorgonzola *n* a semi-hard blue-veined cheese with a rich flavour, originating in Italy.

gorilla *n* an anthropoid ape of western equatorial Africa related to the chimpanzee but much larger.

gormand *see* **gourmand**.

gormandize *vti* to eat like a glutton.—**gormandizer** *n*.

gorse *n* a spiny yellow-flowered European shrub.

gory *adj* (**gorier, goriest**) bloodthirsty; causing bloodshed; covered in blood.—**gorily** *adv*.—**goriness** *n*.

gosh *interj* an exclamation of surprise.

goshawk *n* any of several long-tailed hawks with short rounded wings.

gosling *n* a young goose.

go-slow *n* a deliberate slowing of the work rate by employees as a form of industrial action.

gospel *n* the life and teachings of Christ contained in the first four books of the New Testament; (*with cap*) one of these four books; anything proclaimed or accepted as the absolute truth.

gospeller, gospeler *n* the reader of the gospel in a communion service; an evangelist.

gossamer *n* very fine cobwebs; any very light and flimsy material. * *adj* light as gossamer.

gossip *n* one who chatters idly about others; such talk. * *vi* to take part in or spread gossip.—**gossiper** *n*.—**gossipingly** *adv*.—**gossipy** *adj*.

gossipmonger *n* a gossip.

got *see* **get**.

Goth *n* any member of a Germanic people that conquered most of the Roman Empire in the 3rd–5th centuries AD.

Gothic *adj* of a style of architecture with pointed arches, steep roofs, elaborate stonework, etc. * *n* German black letter type; a bold type style without serifs.—**Gothically** *adv*.

gotten *see* **get**.

gouache *n* a method of painting with opaque watercolours.

Gouda *n* a type of large flat round Dutch cheese.

gouge *n* a chisel with a concave blade used for cutting grooves. * *vt* to scoop or force out (as if) with a gouge.

gouger n one who or that which gouges; a swindler.

goujons npl narrow fried strips of fish or chicken in breadcrumbs.

goulash n a rich stew made with beef or veal seasoned with paprika.

gourami n (pl **gourami, gouramis**) an oriental fish cultivated for food.

gourd n any trailing or climbing plant of a family that includes the squash, melon, pumpkin, etc; the fruit of one species or its dried, hollowed-out shell, used as a cup, bowl, etc or ornament.

gourmand n a person who likes good food and drink, often to excess.—also **gormand.**—**gourmandism** n.

gourmandise, gormandise n the (sometimes excessive) love of good food.

gourmet n a person who likes and is an excellent judge of fine food and drink.

gout n a disease causing painful inflammation of the joints; esp of the great toe.—**gouty** adj.—**goutiness** n.

Gov., gov abbr = government; governor.

govern vti to exercise authority over; to rule, to control; to influence the action of; to determine.—**governable** adj.—**governability, governableness** n.

governance n the action, function, or power of government.

governess n a woman employed in a private home to teach and train the children.

government n the exercise of authority over a state, organization, etc; a system of ruling, political administration, etc; those who direct the affairs of a state, etc.—**governmental** adj.

governor n a person appointed to govern a province, etc; the elected head of any state of the US; the director or head of a governing body of an organization or institution; (sl) an employer; a mechanical device for automatically controlling the speed of an engine.—**governorship** n.

Govt, govt abbr = government.

gowan n (Scot) the daisy.

gown n a loose outer garment, specifically a woman's formal dress, a nightgown, a long, flowing robe worn by clergymen, judges, university teachers, etc; a type of overall worn in the operating room. * vt to dress in a gown, to supply with a gown.

goy n (pl **goyim, goys**) (sl) Jewish for Gentile.

GP abbr = general practitioner.

GPO abbr = general post office.

Gr. abbr = Grecian; Greece; Greek.

grab vt (**grabbing, grabbed**) to take or grasp suddenly; to obtain unscrupulously; (inf) to catch the interest or attention of. * n a sudden clutch or attempt to grasp; a mechanical device for grasping and lifting objects.—**grabber** n.

grabble vi to feel about, to grope.—**grabbler** n.

grace n beauty or charm of form, movement, or expression; good will; favour; a delay granted for payment of an obligation; a short prayer of thanks for a meal. * vt to decorate; to dignify.

graceful adj having beauty of form, movement, or expression.—**gracefully** adv.—**gracefulness** n.

graceless adj unattractive; lacking sense of what is proper; clumsy.—**gracelessly** adv.—**gracelessness** n.

grace note n (mus) an ornamental note.

Graces npl (Greek myth) the three sister goddesses who are the givers of charm and beauty.

gracile adj slender.—**gracility** n.

gracious adj having or showing kindness, courtesy, etc; compassionate; polite to supposed inferiors; marked by luxury, ease, etc; interj an expression of surprise.—**graciously** adv.—**graciousness** n.

grackle n an Asian bird like a starling; an American bird with shiny black plumage; the crow blackbird.

grad n (sl) a graduate.

gradate vti to change or cause to change gradually from one stage, degree, colour, etc to another; to arrange by grade or degree.

gradation n a series of systematic steps in rank, degree, intensity, etc; arranging in such stages; a single stage in a gradual progression; progressive change.—**gradational** adj.

grade n a stage or step in a progression; a degree in a scale of quality, rank, etc; a group of people of the same rank, merit, etc; the degree of slope; a sloping part; a mark or rating in an examination, etc. * vt to arrange in grades; to give a grade to; to make level or evenly sloping.

grade crossing n a place where a road and rail line or two rail lines cross at the same level, a level crossing.

gradient n a sloping road or railway; the degree of slope in a road, railway, etc.

gradin, gradine n one of a tier of seats; a ledge at the back of an altar.

gradual adj taking place by degrees.—**gradually** adv.—**gradualness** n.

graduate n a person who has completed a course of study at a school, college, or university; a receptacle marked with figures for measuring contents. * adj holding an academic degree or diploma; of or relating to studies beyond the first or bachelor's degree.—**graduator** n.

graduation n graduating or being graduated; the ceremony at which degrees are conferred by a college or university; an arranging or marking in grades or stages.

Graeco- see **Greco-**.

graffiti npl (sing **graffito**) inscriptions or drawings, often indecent, on a wall or other public surface.

graft n a shoot or bud of one plant inserted into another, where it grows permanently; the transplanting of skin, bone, etc; the getting of money or advantage dishonestly.—**grafter** n.—**grafting** n.

grail n in medieval legend, the dish or chalice that was used by Christ at the Last Supper, and the object of many knights' quests.—also **Holy Grail.**

grain n the seed of any cereal plant, as wheat, corn, etc; cereal plants; a tiny, solid particle, as of salt or sand; a unit of weight, 0.0648 gram; the arrangement of fibres, layers, etc of wood, leather, etc; the markings or texture due to this; natural disposition. * vt to form into grains; to paint in imitation of the grain of wood, etc. * vi to become granular.—**grainer** n.

grainy adj (**grainier, grainiest**) resembling grains in form or texture.—**graininess** n.

gram¹ n the basic unit of weight in the metric system, equal to one thousandth of a kilogram (one twenty-eighth of an ounce).

gram² n any of various leguminous plants grown for their edible seeds.

gram. abbr = grammar; grammatical.

grama (grass) n a low pasture grass of western and southwestern USA and South America.

gramarye, gramary n (arch) magic, necromancy.

gramercy interj (arch) an expression of great thanks; expressing great surprise.

gramineous *adj* of or like grass; grassy.

graminivorous *adj* feeding on grasses.

grammar *n* the study of the forms of words and their arrangement in sentences; a system of rules for speaking and writing a language; a grammar textbook; the use of language in speech or writing judged with regard to correctness of spelling, syntax, etc.

grammarian *n* one who studies grammar; the author of a grammar.

grammatical *adj* conforming to the rules of grammar.—**grammatically** *adv*.

gramophone *n* a record player, esp an old mechanical model with an acoustic horn.—*also* **phonograph**.

grampus *n* (*pl* **grampuses**) a marine mammal, as the blackfish or killer whale.

granadilla *n* a passion-fruit.

granary *n* (*pl* **granaries**) a building for storing grain.

grand *adj* higher in rank than others; most important; imposing in size, beauty, extent, etc; distinguished; illustrious; comprehensive; (*inf*) very good; delightful. * *n* a grand piano; (*inf*) a thousand pounds or dollars.—**grandly** *adv*.—**grandness** *n*.

grand-aunt *n* a father's or mother's aunt.—*also* **great-aunt**.

grandchild *n* (*pl* **grandchildren**) the child of a person's son or daughter.

granddad *n* (*inf*) grandfather; an old man.

granddaughter *n* the daughter of a person's son or daughter.

grand duke *n* the ruler of a state or principality.

grandee *n* a high-ranking person.

grandeur *n* splendour; magnificence; nobility; dignity.

grandfather *n* the father of a person's father or mother.

grandfather clock *n* a large clock with a pendulum in a tall, upright case.

grandiloquent *adj* using pompous words.—**grandiloquence** *n*.

grandiose *adj* having grandeur; imposing; pompous and showy.—**grandiosely** *adv*.—**grandiosity** *n*.

grand jury *n* a jury in the US that examines evidence in a case to determine whether an indictment should be made.

grandma, grandmama *n* (*inf*) grandmother.

grand mal *n* severe epilepsy.

grandmaster *n* an expert player (as of chess) who has scored consistently well in international competition.

grandmother *n* the mother of a person's father or mother.

grandnephew *n* a nephew's or niece's son.—*also* **great-nephew**.

grandniece *n* a nephew's or niece's daughter.—*also* **great-niece**.

grand opera *n* opera in which the whole text is set to music.

grandpa, grandpapa *n* (*inf*) grandfather.

grandparent *n* a grandfather or grandmother.

grand piano *n* a large piano with a horizontal harp-shaped case.

Grand Prix *n* (*pl* **Grand Prix**) any of a series of formula motor races held in different countries throughout the season; an important contest in other sports, including horse racing, tennis, and athletics.

grand slam *n* (*tennis, golf*) a winning of all the major international championships in a season; (*bridge*) a bidding for and winning all the tricks in a deal; (*baseball*) a home run hit when there is a runner on each base.

grandson *n* the son of a person's son or daughter.

grandstand *n* the main structure for seating spectators at a sporting event.

grand tour *n* (*formerly*) a trip round Europe taken by the sons of wealthy Englishmen to complete their education; (*inf*) a sightseeing or educational tour.

grand-uncle *n* a father's or mother's uncle.—*also* **great-uncle**.

grange *n* a country house with outbuildings etc; a local lodge of a powerful agricultural association; (*with the*) this association; (*formerly*) an outlying farm building where a monastery or local lord stored crops or tithes; (*arch*) a granary.

grangerize *vt* interleave (a book) with illustrations taken from other books; to remove illustrations, etc, from books for this purpose.—**grangerism** *n*.—**grangerization** *n*.

granite *n* a hard, igneous rock consisting chiefly of feldspar and quartz; unyielding firmness of endurance.—**granitic, granitoid** *adj*.

granivorous *adj* grain-eating; living on seeds.—**granivore** *n*.

granny, grannie *n* (*pl* **grannies**) (*inf*) a grandmother; (*inf*) an old woman.

granny knot *n* a wrongly tied reef knot, which is insecure.

grant *vt* to consent to; to give or transfer by legal procedure; to admit as true. * *n* the act of granting; something granted, esp a gift for a particular purpose; a transfer of property by deed; the instrument by which such a transfer is made.

grantee *n* the person to whom property is transferred by deed, etc.

granter *n* one who grants.

grantor *n* one who transfers property by deed, etc.

granular *adj* consisting of granules; having a grainy texture.—**granularity** *n*.

granulate *vt* to form or crystallize into grains or granules. * *vi* to collect into grains or granules; to become roughened and grainy in surface texture.—**granulation** *n*.—**granulative** *adj*.—**granulator, granulater** *n*.

granule *n* a small grain or particle.

grape *n* a small round, juicy berry, growing in clusters on a vine; a dark purplish red.—**grapey, grapy** *adj*.

grape fern *n* a fern with cresent-shaped fronds, moonwort.

grapefruit *n* (*pl* **grapefruit, grapefruits**) a large, round, sour citrus fruit with a yellow rind.

grape hyacinth *n* any of various small plants of the lily family bearing tight clusters of blue grape-like flowers.

grapeshot *n* cannon shot packed in layers, scattering when fired.

grapevine *n* a type of woody vine on which grapes grow; an informal means of communicating news or gossip.

graph *n* a diagram representing the successive changes in the value of a variable quantity or quantities. * *vt* to illustrate by graphs.

-graph *n suffix* a writing or recording device; something written, drawn or recorded.

-grapher *n suffix* denoting a person with specified skills; denoting a person who writes or draws in a certain way.

graphic, graphical *adj* described in realistic detail; pertaining to a graph, lettering, drawing, painting, etc.—**graphically** *adv*.—**graphicalness, graphicness** *n*.

graphic arts *npl* the fine and applied arts involving design, illustration and printing.

graphics *n sing or pl* the use of drawings and lettering; the drawings, illustrations, etc used in a newspaper, magazine, television programme, etc; information displayed in the form of diagrams, illustrations and animation on a computer monitor.

graphite *n* a soft, black form of carbon used in pencils, for lubricants, etc.—**graphitic** *adj*.

graphology *n* the study of handwriting, esp as a clue to character.—**graphological** *adj*.—**graphologist** *n*.

graph paper *n* ruled paper for drawing graphs and diagrams.

-graphy *n suffix* denoting a form of writing, representation or description.

grapnel *n* a small anchor with multiple claws.

grapple *vt* to seize or grip firmly. * *vi* to struggle hand-to-hand with, to deal or contend with. * *n* a grapnel, an act of grappling, a wrestle; a grip.—**grappler** *n*.

grappling iron, grappling hook *n* an iron bar with claws at one end for anchoring a boat, securing a ship alongside or raising sunken objects.

grasp *vt* to grip, as with the hand; to seize; to understand. * *vi* to try to clutch, seize; (*with* at) to take eagerly. * *n* a firm grip; power of seizing and holding; comprehension.—**graspable** *adj*.—**grasper** *n*.

grasping *adj* greedy, avaricious.—**graspingly** *adv*.—**graspingness** *n*.

grass *n* any of a large family of plants with jointed stems and long narrow leaves including cereals, bamboo, etc; such plants grown as lawn; pasture; (*sl*) marijuana; (*sl*) an informer. * *vi* to cover with grass; (*sl*) to inform, betray.

grasshopper *n* any of a group of plant-eating, winged insects with powerful hind legs for jumping.

grassland *n* land reserved for pasture; land, such as prairie, where grass dominates.

grass roots *npl* (*inf*) the common people, the ordinary members of a political or other organization; the basic level, the essentials.

grass snake *n* a small nonpoisonous European snake with a greenish body and yellow markings.

grass widow, grass widower *n* (*inf*) a person whose spouse is frequently absent.

grassy *adj* (**grassier, grassiest**) abounding in, covered with, or like, grass.—**grassiness** *n*.

grate¹ *n* a frame of metal bars for holding fuel in a fireplace; a fireplace; a grating.

grate² *vt* to grind into particles by scraping; to rub against (an object) or grind (the teeth) together with a harsh sound; to irritate. * *vi* to rub or rasp noisily; to cause irritation.

grateful *adj* appreciative; welcome.—**gratefully** *adv*.—**gratefulness** *n*.

grater *n* a metal implement with a jagged surface for grating food.

gratification *n* the act of gratifying; satisfaction; pleasure; (*arch*) a reward or recompense.

gratify *vt* (**gratifying, gratified**) to please; to indulge.—**gratification** *n*.—**gratifier** *n*.—**gratifyingly** *adv*.

grating¹ *n* a open framework or lattice of bars placed across an opening.

grating² *adj* harsh; irritating.—**gratingly** *adv*.

gratis *adj, adv* free of charge.

gratitude *n* a being thankful for favours received.

gratuitous *adj* given free of charge; done without cause, unwarranted.—**gratuitously** *adv*.—**gratuitousness** *n*.

gratuity *n* (*pl* **gratuities**) money given for a service, a tip.

grav *n* a unit of acceleration equal to standard free fall (1 grav = 9.8 metres (32 feet) per second).

gravamen *n* (*pl* **gravamens, gravamina**) the principal part of a legal complaint or accusation.

grave¹ *n* a hole dug in the ground for burying the dead; any place of burial, a tomb.

grave² *adj* serious, important; harmful; solemn, sombre; (*sound*) low in pitch. * *n* an accent (´) over a vowel.—**gravely** *adv*.—**graveness** *n*.

gravel *n* coarse sand with small rounded stones. * *vt* (**gravelling, gravelled** *or* **graveling, graveled**) to cover or spread with gravel.—**gravelish** *adj*.

gravelly *adj* like gravel; (*voice*) deep and rough-sounding.

graven *adj* engraved; fixed indelibly.

graven image *n* an idol.

graver *n* an engraving tool.

gravestone *n* a stone marking a grave, usu inscribed with the name and details of the deceased.

graveyard *n* a burial-ground, cemetery.

gravid *adj* pregnant.—**gravidity, gravidness** *n*.—**gravidly** *adv*.

gravimeter *n* an instrument for measuring the specific gravity of liquid or solid bodies; an instrument for measuring gravity at particular geographical locations.—**gravimetry** *n*.

gravimetric, gravimetrical *adj* of or relating to measurement by weight; determined by weight.—**gravimetrically** *adv*.

gravitate *vi* to move or tend to move under the force of gravitation.—**gravitater** *n*.

gravitation *n* a natural force of attraction that tends to draw bodies together.—**gravitational** *adj*.—**gravitationally** *adv*.

gravitative *adj* pertaining to or determined by gravitation; likely to gravitate, causing something to gravitate.

gravity *n* (*pl* **gravities**) importance, esp seriousness; weight; the attraction of bodies toward the centre of the earth, the moon, or a planet.

gravy *n* (*pl* **gravies**) the juice given off by meat in cooking; the sauce made from this juice; (*sl*) money easily obtained.

gravy boat *n* a small boat-shaped dish for holding and serving gravy or sauces.

gravy train *n* (*sl*) a source of easy money.

gray *n* any of a series of neutral colours ranging between black and white; something (as an animal, garment, cloth, or spot) of a grey colour. * *adj* grey in colour; having grey-coloured hair; darkish; dreary; vague, indeterminate.—*also* **grey**.—**grayish** *adj*.—**grayness** *n*.

graybeard *n* an old man, esp one considered to be wise; an earthenware jug.—*also* **greybeard**.

graylag (goose) *n* the common wild goose of Europe and Asia.

grayling *n* (*pl* **grayling, graylings**) a freshwater fish.

gray matter *n* grey-coloured nerve tissue of the brain and spinal cord; (*inf*) brains, intelligence.

gray squirrel *n* a common squirrel with grey fur orig from North America.

graywacke *n* a hard conglomerate rock of pebbles and sand.—*also* **greywracke**.

graze¹ *vi* to feed on growing grass or pasture. * *vt* to put (animals) to feed on growing grass or pasture.—**grazer** *n*.

graze² *vt* to touch lightly in passing; to scrape, scratch.

* *n* an abrasion, esp on the skin, caused by scraping on a surface.—**grazingly** *adv*.

grazier *n* a person who grazes cattle and prepares them for the market.

grazing *n* pasture; the crops, plants, etc, growing on this for animals to feed from.

grease *n* melted animal fat; any thick, oily substance or lubricant. * *vt* to smear or lubricate with grease.

greasepaint *n* make-up used by actors.

greaser *n* (*sl*) a mechanic; a motorcyclist, often a member of a gang; a member of the engine room crew on a commercial ship; (*derog*) an unpleasant, fawning person, (*derog*) a person from Latin America or Mexico.

greasy *adj* (**greasier, greasiest**) covered with grease; full of grease; slippery; oily in manner.—**greasily** *adv*.—**greasiness** *n*.

great *adj* of much more than ordinary size, extent, etc; much above the average; intense; eminent; most important; more distant in a family relationship by one generation; (*often with* at) (*inf*) skilful; (*inf*) excellent; fine. * *n* (*inf*) a distinguished person.—**greatly** *adv*.—**greatness** *n*.

great-aunt *n* a parent's aunt.—*also* **grand-aunt**.

greatcoat *n* a large heavy coat.

Great Dane *n* a breed of very large smooth-haired dogs.

great divide *n* a watershed between major drainage systems; a significant point of division, esp death.

great-nephew *n* a nephew's or niece's son.—*also* **grand-nephew**.

great-niece *n* a nephew's or niece's daughter.—*also* **grandniece**.

great-uncle *n* a parent's uncle.—*also* **grand-uncle**.

great tit *n* a common yellow, black and white Eurasian tit.

Great War *n* the First World War 1914–18.

greave *n* armour for the lower leg.

greaves *npl* the sediment of melted tallow; (*often sing*) armour to protect the legs from the ankle to the knee.

grebe *n* any of a family of swimming and diving birds.

Grecian *adj* pertaining to Greece; in the Greek style; Greek. * *n* a native or inhabitant of Greece; a Greek scholar.

Grecism *n* a Greek idiom, phrase, spirit or style; a reverent imitation of these, eg in architecture or literature.

Grecize *vti* to give a Greek form to; to imitate Greek.

Greco- *prefix* Greek.

Greco-Roman *adj* of or relating to the ancient Greek and Romans.

greed *n* excessive desire, esp for food or wealth.

greedy *adj* (**greedier, greediest**) wanting more than one needs or deserves; having too strong a desire for food and drink.—**greedily** *adv*.—**greediness** *n*.

Greek *adj* of Greece, its people, or its language. * *n* a native of Greece; the language used by Greeks; (*inf*) something unintelligible.

Greek cross *n* a cross with four equal arms.

Greek fire *n* (*ancient history*) a weapon used in sea battles consisting of an unidentified substance that ignited on contact with water.

green *adj* of the colour green; covered with plants or foliage; having a sickly appearance; unripe; inexperienced, naive; not fully processed or treated; concerned with the conservation of natural resources; (*inf*) jealous. * *n* a colour between blue and yellow in the spectrum; the colour of growing grass; something of a green colour; (*pl*) green leafy vegetables, as spinach, etc; (*often with cap*) a person concerned with the future of the earth's environment; a grassy plot, esp the end of a golf fairway.—**greenish** *adj*.—**greenly** *adv*.—**greenness** *n*.—**greeny** *adj*.

greenback *n* a legal-tender note of US currency.

green bean *n* any of various beans with narrow edible pods.

green belt *n* a belt of parkland, farms, etc surrounding a community, designed to prevent urban sprawl.

greenery *n* (*pl* **greeneries**) green vegetation.

green-eyed *adj* jealous.

green-eyed monster *n* jealousy.

greenfinch *n* a European and Asian bird with yellow and green plumage.

green fingers *n* gardening expertise. Us and Canadian equivalent—**green thumb**.

greenfly *n* (*pl* **greenflies**) an insect pest that infests garden plants and crops.

greengage *n* a small greenish sweet variety of plum.

greenheart *n* a tropical American tree that yields a dark durable timber; the timber.

greenhorn *n* an inexperienced person; a person easily duped.

greenhouse *n* a heated building, mainly of glass, for growing plants.

greenhouse effect *n* action of radiant heat from the sun passing through the glass of greenhouses etc., warming the contents inside, where such heat is thus trapped; application of the same effect to a planet's atmosphere.—*see* **global warming**.

greening[1] *n* a type of cooking apple that is green when ripe.

greening[2] *n* growing awareness of the environment.

green light *n* permission to proceed with a plan, etc.

green pepper *n* the unripe fruit of the sweet pepper eaten raw or cooked.

greenroom *n* the actors' rest room in a theatre, the room where they can receive visitors.

greensand *n* a green sandstone

greenshank *n* a large European wading bird with greenish legs and feet.

greenstone *n* New Zealand jade; any green igneous rock that contains chlorite or epidote.

green thumb *see* **green fingers**.

greensward *n* (*arch*) (a stretch of) turf.

green tea *n* a drink made from dried unfermented tea leaves.

Greenwich Mean Time *n* the time of the meridian of Greenwich, England, used as the basis of worldwide standard time.

greenwood *n* leafy woodland.

greet *vt* to address with friendliness; to meet (a person, event, etc) in a specified way; to present itself to.—**greeter** *n*.

greeting *n* the act of welcoming with words or gestures; an expression of good wishes; (*pl*) a message of regards.

gregarious *adj* (*animals*) living in flocks and herds; (*people*) sociable, fond of company.—**gregariously** *adv*.—**gregariousness** *n*.

Gregorian *adj* pertaining to or established by Gregory, the name of various popes.

Gregorian calendar *n* the reformed calendar introduced in 1582 by Pope Gregory XIII and currently in use.

gremlin *n* an imaginary creature blamed for disruption of any procedure or of malfunction of equipment, esp in an aircraft.

grenade *n* a small bomb thrown manually or projected (as by a rifle or special launcher).

grenadier[1] *n* a soldier of the British Grenadier Guards, the first regiment of the household infantry; (*formerly*) a foot soldier who threw grenades; (*formerly*) a company made up of the tallest and strongest soldiers in the regiment.

grenadier[2] *n* a sea fish with a large head and a long, narrow tail.

grenadine[1] *n* a gauze-like dress fabric.

grenadine[2] *n* a syrup made from pomegranates; a red-orange colour.

gressorial *adj* adapted for walking; (*birds*) having three toes of the feet forward, two of them connected, and one behind.

grew *see* **grow**.

grey *see* **gray**.

greybeard *see* **graybeard**.

greyhound *n* any of a breed of tall and slender dogs noted for its great speed and keen sight.

greywracke *see* **graywracke**.

grid *n* a gridiron, a grating; an electrode for controlling the flow of electrons in an electron tube; a network of squares on a map used for easy reference; a national network of transmission lines, pipes, etc for electricity, water, gas, etc.

griddle *n* a flat metal surface for cooking.

griddlecake *n* a pancake.

gridiron *n* a framework of iron bars for cooking; anything resembling this, as a field used for American football.

gridlock *n* a traffic jam that halts all traffic at a street crossing; the breakdown of an organization or a system.

grief *n* extreme sorrow caused as by a loss; deep distress.

grief-stricken *adj* full of sorrow.

grievance *n* a circumstance thought to be unjust and cause for complaint.

grieve *vti* to feel or cause to feel grief.—**griever** *n*.—**grieving** *adj*, *n*.

grievous *adj* causing or characterized by grief; deplorable; severe.—**grievously** *adv*.—**grievousness** *n*.

griffin, griffon *n* a mythical animal with the body and tail of a lion and an eagle's beak and wings.—*also* **gryphon**.

griffon *n* a small dog with a wire-haired coat; a large hawk with a pale body and black wings, found in Africa, Asia and warm parts of Europe.

grig *n* an extravagantly vivacious person; the sandeel; a young eel; a hen with short legs; heather.

grill *vt* to broil by direct heat using a grill or gridiron; (*inf*) to question relentlessly. * *n* a device on a cooker that radiates heat downward for broiling or grilling; a gridiron; broiled or grilled food; a grille; a grill-room.—**griller** *n*.

grillage *n* an arrangement of planks and crossbeams forming a foundation in loose or marshy soil.

grille, grill *n* an open grating forming a screen.

grillroom *n* a restaurant that specializes in grilled food.

grilse *n* (*pl* **grilses, grilse**) a young salmon returning from the sea to spawn for the first time.

grim *adj* (**grimmer, grimmest**) hard and unyielding, stern; appearing harsh, forbidding; repellent, ghastly in character.—**grimly** *adv*.—**grimness** *n*.

grimace *n* a contortion of the face expressing pain, anguish, humour, etc. * *vi* to contort the face in pain,

etc.—**grimacer** *n*.—**grimacingly** *adv*.

grimalkin *n* an old she-cat; a spiteful, bad-tempered old woman.

grime *n* soot or dirt, rubbed into a surface, as the skin. * *vt* to dirty, soil with grime.

grimy *adj* (**grimier, grimiest**) dirty, soiled.—**griminess** *n*.

grin *vi* (**grinning, grinned**) to smile broadly as in amusement; to show the teeth in pain, scorn, etc. * *n* a broad smile.—**grinner** *n*.

grind *vb* (**grinding, ground**) *vt* to reduce to powder or fragments by crushing; to wear down, sharpen, or smooth by friction; to rub (the teeth) harshly together; to oppress, tyrannize; to move or operate by a crank. * *vi* to be crushed, smoothed, or sharpened by grinding; to jar or grate; to work monotonously; to rotate the hips in an erotic manner. * *n* the act or sound of grinding; hard monotonous work.

grinder *n* someone or something that grinds; a molar tooth.

grindstone *n* a circular revolving stone for grinding or sharpening tools.

gringo *n* (*pl* **gringos**) (*offensive*) among Hispanics, a foreigner, esp North Americans.

grip *n* a secure grasp; the manner of holding a bat, club, racket, etc; the power of grasping firmly; mental grasp; mastery; a handle; a small travelling bag. * *vt* (**gripping, gripped**) to take firmly and hold fast.

gripe *vt* to cause sharp pain in the bowels of; (*sl*) to annoy. * *vi* (*sl*) to complain.—**griper** *n*.—**gripingly** *adv*.

grippe *n* (*formerly*) influenza.

gripper *n* one who or that which grips; a mechanical device for seizing and holding.

grisaille *n* a method of painting in grey tints so as to represent a solid body in relief; a decorative painting in grey monochrome, esp on glass.

griseous *adj* bluish-grey.

grisette *n* a lively young French working girl, esp a flirtatious one; an edible toadstool.

griskin *n* the lean part of a loin of pork.

grisly *adj* (**grislier, grisliest**) terrifying; ghastly; arousing horror.—**grisliness** *n*.

grison *n* a carnivorous mammal of Central and South America, which resembles a weasel.

grist *n* grain that is to be or has been ground; matter forming the basis of a story or analysis.

gristle *n* cartilage, esp in meat.—**gristly** *adj*.—**gristliness** *n*.

grit *n* rough particles, as of sand; firmness of spirit; stubborn courage. * *vt* (**gritting, gritted**) to clench or grind together (eg the teeth); to spread grit on (eg an icy road).

grits *npl* oats, hulled and coarsely ground; coarsely ground maize, boiled in water or milk as a food (—*also* **hominy grits**).

gritty *adj* (**grittier, grittiest**) composed of, containing, or resembling, grit; courageous.—**grittily** *adv*.—**grittiness** *n*.

grivet *n* a green and white Ethiopian monkey with a long tail.

grizzle *vt* (*inf*) to fret; to complain. * *vti* to (cause to) become grey * *n* a grey colour; hair that is, or is becoming, grey; a wig of grey hair.—**grizzled** *adj*.

grizzled *adj* streaked with grey; grey-haired.

grizzly *adj* (**grizzlier, grizzliest**) greyish; grizzled. * *n* (*pl* **grizzlies**) the grizzly bear.

grizzly bear *n* a large powerful bear of North America.

groan *vi* to utter a deep moan; to make a harsh sound (as of creaking) under sudden or prolonged strain. * *n* a deep moan; a creaking sound.—**groaner** *n.*—**groaningly** *adv.*

groat *n* (*formerly*) a British silver coin worth fourpence; a trifling sum.

groats *npl* hulled grain broken into fragments, esp oats.

grocer *n* a dealer in food and household supplies.

grocery *n* (*pl* **groceries**) a grocer's shop; (*pl*) goods, esp from a grocer.

grog *n* rum diluted with water, often spiced and served hot.

groggy *adj* (**groggier**, **groggiest**) (*inf*) weak and unsteady, usu through illness, exhaustion or alcohol.—**groggily** *adv.*—**grogginess** *n.*

grogram *n* a coarse cloth of silk or silk and mohair or wool.

groin *n* the fold marking the junction of the lower abdomen and the thighs; the location of the genitals.

grommet *n* a plastic or rubber ring used to protect wire, a cable, etc passing through a hole; a ring formed of a strand of rope laid round, used in pipe joints or sails (—*also* **grummet**); (*formerly*) a cannon-wad made of rope, and rammed between the powder and the ball.

gromwell *n* a herb of the borage family.

groom *n* a person employed to care for horses; a bridegroom. * *vt* to clean and care for (animals); to make neat and tidy; to train (a person) for a particular purpose.—**groomer** *n.*—**grooming** *n.*

groomsman *n* (*pl* **groomsmen**) one who attends a bridegroom; a best man.

groove *n* a long, narrow channel; a spiral track in a gramophone record for the stylus; a settled routine. * *vt* to make a groove in.

groovy *adj* (**groovier**, **grooviest**) (*sl*) excellent.

grope *vi* to search about blindly as in the dark; to search uncertainly for a solution to a problem. * *vt* to find by feeling; (*sl*) to fondle sexually. * *n* the act of groping.—**groper** *n.*—**gropingly** *adv.*

grosbeak *n* any finch-like bird of Europe or America with a large stout conical bill.

groschen *n* (*pl* **groschen**) a 10-pfennig coin used in Germany; a silver coin formerly current in Germany; in Austria, a coin with a value of one hundredth of a schilling.

grosgrain *n* a stout double-corded silk; a fabric or ribbon of this.

gros point *n* a large needlepoint stitch covering two vertical and two horizontal threads; a piece of needlework done in this.

gross *adj* fat and coarse-looking; flagrant, dense, thick; lacking in refinement; earthy; obscene; total, with no deductions. * *n* (*pl* **grosses**) an overall total; (*pl* **gross**) twelve dozen. * *vt* to earn as total revenue.—**grossly** *adv.*—**grossness** *n.*

gross domestic product *n* the total value of goods and services produced by a country in one year.

gross national product *n* the gross domestic product plus income earned from abroad.

grot[1] *n* (*poet*) a grotto.

grot[2] *n* (*Brit sl*) unpleasant mess.—**grotty** *adj* (**grottier**, **grottiest**) nasty, unattractive; in bad condition; unsatisfactory.

grotesque *adj* distorted or fantastic in appearance, shape, etc; ridiculous; absurdly incongruous. * *n* a grotesque person or thing; a decorative device combining distorted plant, animal and human forms.—**grotesquely** *adv.*—**grotesqueness** *n.*

grotesquery, **grotesquerie** *n* (*pl* **grotesqueries**) *n* something that is fantastic or distorted in shape, etc.

grotto *n* (*pl* **grottoes**, **grottos**) a cave, esp one with attractive features.

grotty *see* **grot**.

grouch *vi* (*inf*) to grumble or complain. * *n* (*inf*) a grumble; a person who grumbles.—**groucher** *n.*

grouchy *adj* (**grouchier**, **grouchiest**) bad-tempered.—**grouchily** *adv.*—**grouchiness** *n.*

ground *n* the solid surface of the earth; soil; the background, as in design; the connection of an electrical conductor with the earth; (*pl*) a basis for belief, action, or argument; the area about and relating to a building; a tract of land; sediment. * *vti* to set on the ground; to run aground or cause to run aground; to base, found, or establish; to instruct in the first principles of; to prevent (aircraft) from flying.

ground control *n* the communications and tracking equipment and staff that monitor aircraft and spacecraft in flight and during takeoff and landing.

ground cover *n* low-growing shrubs, plants and other foliage on the ground.

ground floor *n* the floor of a building on a level with the ground.

ground hog *n* a woodchuck.

grounding *n* basic general knowledge of a subject.

ground ivy *n* a trailing Eurasian plant with bluish-purple flowers.

groundless *adj* without reason.—**groundlessly** *adv.*

groundnut *n* a climbing plant of North America with an underground nut; a peanut.

ground rule *n* a fundamental rule or principle.

groundsel *n* a weed of the aster family with yellow flowers.

groundsheet *n* a waterproof sheet placed on the ground in, or as part of, a tent.

groundsman *n* (*pl* **groundsmen**) a man who looks after a cricket pitch, football pitch, park, etc.

groundswell *n* a large rolling wave; a wave of popular feeling.

groundwork *n* foundation, basis.

group *n* a number of persons or things considered as a collective unit; a small musical band of players or singers; a number of companies under single ownership; two or more figures forming one artistic design. * *vti* to form into a group or groups.

grouper *n* (*pl* **grouper**, **groupers**) an edible sea fish.

groupie *n* a devoted fan.

group therapy *n* (*psychol*) the simultaneous treatment of patients with similar problems through mutual discussion and exchange of experiences.

grouse[1] *n* (*pl* **grouse**, **grouses**) a game bird; its flesh as food.

grouse[2] *vi* (*inf*) to complain.—**grouser** *n.*

grout *n* a thin mortar used as between tiles. * *vt* to fill with grout.—**grouter** *n.*

grove *n* a small wood, generally without undergrowth.

grovel *vi* (**grovelling**, **grovelled** *or* **groveling**, **groveled**) to lie and crawl in a prostrate position as a sign of respect, fear or humility.—**groveller**, **groveler** *n.*—**grovellingly**, **grovelingly** *adv.*

grow *vb* (**growing**, **grew**, *pp* **grown**) *vi* to come into being; to be produced naturally; to develop, as a living thing; to increase in size, quantity, etc; (*with* **on**) to become more accustomed or acceptable to; (*with* **up**) to mature; to arise, develop. * vt to cause or let grow; to raise, to cultivate.—**growable** adj.—**grower** n.

growing pains npl muscular discomfort sometimes experienced by growing children; difficulties experienced in the early stages of a project.

growl vi to make a rumbling, menacing sound such as an angry dog makes. * vt to express in a growling manner. * n a growling noise; a grumble.—**growler** n.

growler n one who growls; (arch) a four-wheeled cab; a small iceberg; a beer jug or beer can.

grown-up n a fully grown person, an adult. * adj mature, adult; fit for an adult.

growth n the act or process of growing; progressive increase, development; something that grows or has grown; an abnormal formation of tissue, as a tumour.

groyne n a timber structure to stop the shifting of sand on a beach.

grub vb (**grubbing, grubbed**) vi to dig in the ground; to work hard. * vt to clear (ground) of roots; to uproot. * n the worm-like larva of a beetle; (sl) food.

grubber n one who or that which grubs; a grub hoe.

grubby adj (**grubbier, grubbiest**) dirty.—**grubbily** adv.—**grubbiness** n.

grudge n a deep feeling of resentment or ill will. * vt to be reluctant to give or admit something.—**grudger** n.—**grudging** adj.—**grudgingly** adv.

gruel n a thin porridge cooked in water or milk.

grueling, gruelling adj severely testing, exhausting.

gruesome adj causing horror or loathing.

gruff adj rough or surly; hoarse.—**gruffly** adv.—**gruffness** n.

grugru n the larva of a South American weevil, cooked for food as a delicacy; the palm tree on which this lives.

grumble vti to mutter in discontent; to make a rumbling sound. * n a complaint; a grumbling sound.—**grumbler** n.—**grumblingly** adv.

grump n (inf) a bad-tempered person.

grumpy adj (**grumpier, grumpiest**) bad-tempered, peevish.—**grumpily** adv.—**grumpiness** n.

grunt vi to make a gruff guttural sound like a pig; to say or speak in such a manner. * n a low gruff sound; (sl) a US infantry man.

grunter n one who or that which grunts; an edible marine American fish; a pig; (Austral sl) a woman who is promiscuous.

Gruyère n a hard, pale yellow Swiss cheese usu with holes.

gryphon see **griffin**.

G-string n a string on an instrument tuned to the note G; a string or strip worn round the waist and between the legs.

G-suit n a (gravity) suit designed to counteract the physiological effects of acceleration on airmen and astronauts.

GT abbr = gran turismo, a sporty touring car.

guaco n (pl **guacos**) a tropical American plant, used as an antidote to snakebites.

guaiacum n any of various tropical and West Indian shrubs or trees; the wood from these; a gum obtained from them, used medicinally and in the manufacture of varnishes.

guan n an American bird similar to a turkey.

guanaco n (pl **guanacos, guanaco**) the wild llama of South America.

guanine n a nitrogenous base component of the nucleic acids, DNA and RNA, also found in guano.

guano n (pl **guanos**) dung of sea birds used as manure; a similar artificially produced fertilizer.

guarantee n a pledge or security for another's debt or obligation; a pledge to replace something if it is substandard, etc; an assurance that something will be done as specified; something offered as a pledge or security; a guarantor. * vt (**guaranteeing, guaranteed**) to give a guarantee for; to promise.

guarantor n a person who gives a guaranty or guarantee.

guaranty n (pl **guaranties**) (law) a guarantee.

guard vt to watch over and protect; to defend; to keep from escape or trouble; to restrain. * vi to keep watch (against); to act as a guard. * n defence; protection; a posture of readiness for defence; any device to protect against injury or loss; a person or group that guards; (boxing, fencing, cricket) a defensive attitude; a railway official in charge of a train; (with cap: pl) a regiment of British or European household troops.—**guardable** adj.—**guarder** n.

guarded adj discreet; cautious.—**guardedly** adv.—**guardedness** n.

guardhouse n a building used by a military guard when not walking a post; a military jail for temporary confinement.

guardian n a custodian; a person legally in charge of a minor or someone incapable of taking care of their own affairs.—**guardianship** n.

guardrail n a railing, eg at the side of a road, to prevent falling; a short metal rod placed inside the rails to keep a train's wheels on the track.

guardsman n (pl **guardsmen**) an officer or soldier of the British Guards; an officer or solider of the US National Guard.

guard's van n the railway carriage where the guard travels, usu at the back of a train.—also **caboose**.

guava n a tropical American shrubby tree widely cultivated for its sweet acid yellow fruit.

gubernatorial adj pertaining to a governor or to his office.

gudgeon n a small edible freshwater fish; a fish used as bait in fishing; a person who is easily imposed upon; an iron pin or shaft on which a wheel revolves; (naut) one of the sockets into which a rudder is fixed.

guelder-rose n a cultivated variety of cranberry bush with large heads of sterile flowers.

Guelph, Guelf n a member of a powerful Italian political party in the Middle Ages, which supported the pope and sought the independence of Italy; a member of a secret society in 19th-century Italy, supporting Italian independence.

guerdon n (poet) reward. * vt to reward, to recompense.

guernsey n a particular breed of dairy cattle originally from the island of Guernsey; a close-fitting knitted woollen jersey; (Austral) a woollen top worn by a football player.

guerrilla, guerilla n a member of a small force of irregular soldiers, making surprise raids.—also adj.

guess vt to form an opinion of or state with little or no factual knowledge; to judge correctly by doing this; to think or suppose. * n an estimate based on guessing.—**guessable** adj.—**guesser** n.

guesstimate n (inf) an estimate based mainly on guesswork.

guesswork n the process or result of guessing.

guest n a person entertained at the home, club, etc of another; any paying customer of a hotel, restaurant, etc; a performer appearing by special invitation.

guesthouse *n* a private home or boarding-house offering accommodation.

guestroom *n* a room kept for guests.

guffaw *n* a crude noisy laugh. * *vi* to laugh boisterously.

guidance *n* leadership; advice or counsel.

guide *vt* to point out the way for; to lead; to direct the course of; to control. * *n* a person who leads or directs others; a person who exhibits and explains points of interest; something that provides a person with guiding information; a device for controlling the motion of something; a book of basic instruction; a Girl Guide.—**guidable** *adj*.—**guider** *n*.—**guiding** *adj*, *n*.

guidebook *n* a book containing directions and information for tourists.

guided missile *n* a military missile whose course is controlled by radar or internal instruments, etc.

guideline *n* a principle or instruction which determines conduct or policy.

guidepost *n* a direction post; a guiding principle.

guidon *n* a forked or pointed military flag, used esp by troops of light cavalry.

guild *n* a club, society; an association of people with common interests formed for mutual aid and protection, as craftsmen in the Middle Ages.—*also* **gild**.

guilder *n* a coin of the Netherlands, or of Netherlands Antilles and Surinam; a gold or silver coin formerly in circulation in Germany, Austria and the Netherlands.—*also* **gilder, gulden**.

guildhall *n* the meeting place of a guild or corporation.

guile *n* craftiness, deceit.—**guileful** *adj*.—**guilefully** *adv*.—**guilefulness** *n*.

guileless *adj* without guile; ingenuous.—**guilelessly** *adv*.—**guilelessness** *n*.

guillemot *n* a small sea bird of the auk family.

guilloche *n* (*archit*) an ornament resembling braided ribbons.

guillotine *n* an instrument for beheading by a heavy blade descending between grooved posts; a device or machine for cutting paper; a rule for limiting time for discussion in a legislature. * *vt* to execute (someone) by guillotine.—**guillotiner** *n*.

guilt *n* the fact of having done a wrong or committed an offence; a feeling of self-reproach from believing one has done a wrong.

guiltless *adj* innocent.

guilty *adj* (**guiltier, guiltiest**) having guilt; feeling or showing guilt.—**guiltily** *adv*.—**guiltiness** *n*.

guimpe *n* a short blouse worn under a pinafore dress; a piece of cloth used to disguise a low-cut neckline; the starched cloth that covers the shoulders and front of a nun's habit; gimp.

guinea *n* a former English gold coin equal to 21 shillings (£1.05).

guinea fowl *n* a domestic African bird of the pheasant family.

guinea pig *n* a rodent-like animal commonly kept as a pet, and often used in scientific experiments; a person or thing subject to an experiment.

guipure (lace) *n* a coarse lace in which the pattern is supported by bars connecting the motifs rather than founded on a net base; a kind of gimp.

guise *n* an external appearance, aspect; an assumed appearance or pretence.

guitar *n* a stringed musical instrument with a long, fretted neck, and a flat body, which is plucked with a plectrum or the fingers.—**guitarist** *n*.

gular *adj* of, in or pertaining to the gullet or throat.

gulch *n* a deep, narrow ravine.

gulden *see* **guilder**.

gules *n* (*her*) the colour red, also indicated by vertical parallel lines.

gulf *n* a large area of ocean reaching into land; a wide, deep chasm; a vast separation.

Gulf Stream *n* a warm ocean current flowing from the Gulf of Mexico northward towards Europe.

gulfweed *n* brown seaweed with air bladders which floats in dense masses in warm Atlantic waters.—*also* **sargasso, sargasso weed**.

gull *n* any of numerous long-winged web-footed sea birds.

gullet *n* the esophagus; the throat.

gullible *adj* easily deceived.—**gullibility** *n*.—**gullibly** *adv*.

gully *n* (*pl* **gullies**) a narrow trench cut by running water after rain; (*cricket*) a fielding position between the slips and point. * *vt* (**gullying, gullied**) to make gullies in.

gulp *vt* to swallow hastily or greedily; to choke back as if swallowing. * *n* a gulping or swallowing; a mouthful.—**gulper** *n*.—**gulpingly** *adv*.

gum[1] *n* the firm tissue that surrounds the teeth.

gum[2] *n* a sticky substance found in certain trees and plants; an adhesive; chewing gum. * *vb* (**gumming, gummed**) *vt* to coat or unite with gum. * *vi* to become sticky or clogged; (*with* **up**) (*inf*) to mess up, prevent from working properly.

gum ammoniac *n* a gum resin.—*also* **ammoniac**.

gum arabic *n* the gum obtained from certain species of acacia trees and used in the manufacture of adhesives and in pharmacy.

gumbo *n* (*pl* **gumbos**) a rich soup thickened with okra.

gumboil *n* an abscess in the gum.

gumboot *n* a rubber, waterproof boot, a wellington.

gumma *n* (*pl* **gummas, gummata**) a syphilitic tumour.—**gummatous** *adj*.

gummy *adj* (**gummier, gummiest**) sticky; revealing the gums, toothless.—**gummily** *adv*.—**gumminess** *n*.

gumption *n* (*inf*) shrewd practical common sense; initiative.

gum resin *n* a mixture of gum and resin exuded from certain plants and trees.

gumtree *n* a eucalyptus, or one of various other trees that yield gum.

gun *n* a weapon with a metal tube from which a projectile is discharged by an explosive; the shooting of a gun as a signal or salute; anything like a gun. * *vb* (**gunning, gunned**) *vi* to shoot or hunt with a gun; (*with* **for**) to search out in order to hurt or kill. * *vt* (*inf*) to shoot (a person); (*sl*) to advance the throttle of an engine.

gunboat *n* a small armed ship.

gunboat diplomacy *n* the threat of force used to back diplomatic activity.

guncotton *n* a highly explosive substance formed by the action of nitric and sulphuric acid upon cotton, or some other vegetable fibre.

gun dog *n* a dog trained to flush out or retrieve game shot by hunters.

gunfire *n* repeated and consecutive gunshots; the use of guns, etc, rather than other military options.

gunk *n* (*inf*) dirty, greasy, matter; gunge.

gunman *n* (*pl* **gunmen**) an armed gangster; a hired killer.

gunmetal *n* bronze with a dark tarnish; its dark-grey colour.

gunnel *see* **gunwale**.

gunner *n* a soldier, etc who helps fire artillery; a naval warrant officer in charge of a ship's guns.

gunnery *n* the science of the design and operation of large guns.

gunny *n* (*pl* **gunnies**) a strong coarse fabric made from jute used for sacking.

gunpoint *n* the muzzle of a gun; the threat of being shot.

gunpowder *n* an explosive powder used in guns, for blasting, etc.

gunrunning *n* the smuggling of firearms into a country.—**gunrunner** *n*.

gunshot *n* the range of a gun; the instance of shooting a gun or the shot fired from it.

gun-shy *adj* afraid of a loud noise; markedly distrustful.

gunslinger *n* (*sl*) a gunman or gunfighter.

gunstock *n* the wooden or metal mounting of a gun barrel.

gunwale *n* the upper edge of a ship's or boat's side.—*also* **gunnel**.

guppy *n* (*pl* **guppies**) a small vividly-coloured fish of South America and the West Indies popular for aquariums.

gurgitation *n* a whirling motion, a surging.

gurgle *vi* (*liquid*) to make a low bubbling sound; to utter with this sound. * *n* a bubbling sound.—**gurglingly** *adv*.

gurnard *n* (*pl* **gurnard, gurnards**) a spiny sea fish with an armoured head.

guru *n* (*pl* **gurus**) a Hindu or Sikh spiritual teacher; an influential leader or teacher, esp of a religious cult.

gush *vi* to issue plentifully; to have a sudden flow; to talk or write effusively. * *vt* to cause to gush. * *n* a sudden outpouring.—**gushingly** *adv*.

gusher *n* an effusive person; an oil well from which oil spouts forth.

gushy *adj* (**gushier, gushiest**) expressing excessive admiration.—**gushily** *adv*.—**gushiness** *n*.

gusset *n* a small triangular piece of cloth inserted in a garment to strengthen or enlarge a part.

gust *n* a sudden brief rush of wind; a sudden outburst. * *vi* to blow in gusts.

gustation *n* the act of tasting; the ability to taste; taste.—**gustatory** *adj*.

gusto *n* great enjoyment, zest.

gusty *adj* (**gustier, gustiest**) windy; irritable.—**gustily** *adv*.—**gustiness** *n*.

gut *n* (*often pl*) the bowels or the stomach; the intestine; tough cord made from animal intestines; (*pl*) (*sl*) daring; courage. * *vt* (**gutting, gutted**) to remove the intestines from; to destroy the interior of.

gutless *adj* (*inf*) cowardly, lacking determination.—**gutlessness** *n*.

gutsy *adj* (**gutsier, gutsiest**) (*sl*) brave, courageous; passionate; greedy.

gutta *n* (*pl* **guttae**) (*archit*) a small loop-like ornament, esp in a Doric entablature; (*med*) (*formerly*) a drop.

gutta-percha *n* the flexible hardened juice of a tropical tree; one of several trees yielding this.

guttate, guttated *adj* (*plants*) spotted; drop-like.

gutter *n* a channel for carrying off water, esp at a roadside or under the eaves of a roof; a channel or groove to direct something (as of a bowling alley); the lowest condition of human life. * *adj* marked by extreme vulgarity or indecency. * *vt* to provide with a gutter. * *vi* to flow in rivulets; (*candle*) to melt unevenly; (*candle flame*) to flutter.—**guttering** *n*.

guttering *n* the system of gutters, pipes, etc, on exterior walls for carrying off rainwater; material for making gutters.

guttersnipe *n* a dirty child who plays in the streets, esp slum areas.

guttural *adj* formed or pronounced in the throat; harshsounding.—**gutturally** *adv*.—**gutturalness, gutturality, gutturalism** *n*.

gutturalize *vt* to form (a sound) in the throat; to speak in a harsh manner.—**gutturalization** *n*.

guy[1] *n* a rope, chain, etc, for fixing or steadying anything. * *vt* to fix or steady with a guy.

guy[2] *n* an effigy of Guy Fawkes made from old clothes stuffed with newspapers, etc burnt on the anniversary of the Gunpowder Plot (5 November); (*inf*) a man or boy; (*pl*) (*inf*) men or women; a shabby person. * *vt* to tease.

guzzle *vti* to gulp down food or drink greedily.—**guzzler** *n*.

gybe *vti* (*sail, boom*) to swing over from one side to the other; (*yacht*) to alter course in this way.—*also* **jibe**.

gym *n* (*inf*) a gymnasium.

gymkhana *n* a meeting featuring sports contests or athletic skills, esp horse-riding.

gymnasium *n* (*pl* **gymnasiums, gymnasia**) a room or building equipped for physical training and sports.

gymnast *n* a person skilled in gymnastics.

gymnastic *adj* pertaining to gymnastics.—**gymnastically** *adv*.

gymnastics *n sing* training in exercises devised to strengthen the body; (*pl*) gymnastic exercises; (*pl*) feats of dexterity or agility.

gymnosophist *n* one of a class of ancient Hindu philosophers who lived bare-footed and lightly clothed or naked.

gymnosperm *n* a plant whose seeds are not enclosed in a covering; a conifer or a conifer-like plant.—**gymnospermous** *adj*.

gynaecocracy, gynecocracy *n* (*pl* **gynaecocracies, gynecocracies**) female rule or supremacy.—**gynaecocratic, gynecocratic** *adj*.

gynaecology, gynecology *n* the branch of medicine that deals with the diseases and disorders of the female reproductive system.—**gynaecological, gynecological, gynaecologic, gynecologic** *adj*.—**gynaecologist, gynecologist** *n*.

gynarchy *n* (*pl* **gynarchies**) gynaecocracy.

gynoecium *n* (*pl* **gynoecia**) (*bot*) the female organs of a flower.

gynopathy *n* the condition of feeling threatened by women.—**gynopathic** *adj*.

gynophore *n* the long stalk on which the pistil is situated, as in the passion flower.—**gynophoric** *adj*.

gyp *vt* (**gypping, gypped**) (*sl*) to cheat (someone). * *n* a swindle; a swindler; a college servant at Cambridge University; (*sl*) acute pain.—*also* **gip**.

gypsum *n* a chalk-like mineral used to make plaster of Paris and fertilizer.—**gypseous, gypsiferous** *adj*.

Gypsy *n* (*pl* **Gypsies**) a member of a travelling people, orig from India, now spread throughout Europe and North America; (*without cap*) a person who looks or lives like a Gypsy.—*also* **Gipsy** (*pl* **Gipsies**).

gyral *adj* rotatory, whirling; pertaining to a gyrus.

gyrate *vi* to revolve; to whirl or spiral.—**gyration** *n*.—**gyratory** *adj*.

gyre *vt* (*poet*) to gyrate. * (*poet*) a gyration.

gyrfalcon *n* a large northern falcon, often used for hunting.—*also* **gerfalcon**.

gyro *n* (*pl* **gyros**) (*inf*) a gyroscope; a gyrocompass.

gyrocompass *n* a compass mounted on a gyroscope to keep it stable.

gyroscope *n* a wheel mounted in a ring so that its axis is free to turn in any direction, so that when spinning rapidly it keeps its original plane of rotation.—**gyroscopic** *adj*.

gyrose *adj* (*bot*) turned round like a crook.

gyrostabilizer *n* a device of two or more gyroscopes to prevent rolling of a ship or aircraft.

gyrostat *n* a gyrostabilizer.

gyrus *n* (*pl* **gyri**) a convolution (of the brain).

gyve *vt* to fetter * *n* (*usu pl*) shackles.

H

H (*chem symbol*) hydrogen.

ha *interj* used to express surprise, triumph, etc.—*also* **hah.**

ha. *abbr* = hectare(s).

Habakkuk *n* (*Bible*) one of the minor Old Testament book of prophets.

habeas corpus *n* a writ requiring that a prisoner be brought before a court, esp to ascertain the legality of his or her detention.

haberdasher *n* a dealer in sewing accessories; a dealer in men's clothing.—**haberdashery** *n.*

habergeon *n* a sleeveless coat of chain mail covering the neck and breast.

habile *adj* skillful.

habiliment *n* (*often pl*) clothing, attire.

habilitate *vi* to qualify for a post. * *vt* to provide working capital for a mine.—**habilitation** *n.*—**habilitator** *n.*

habit *n* a distinctive costume, as of a nun, etc; a thing done often and hence easily; a usual way of doing things; an addiction, esp to narcotics. * *vt* to clothe.

habitable *adj* capable of being lived in.—**habitability** *n.*—**habitably** *adv.*

habitat *n* the normal environment of an animal or plant.

habitation *n* the act of inhabiting; a dwelling or residence.—**habitational** *adj.*

habited *adj* wearing a habit or a dress.

habit-forming *adj* addictive.

habitual *adj* having the nature of a habit; regular.—**habitually** *adv.*—**habitualness** *n.*

habituate *vt* to accustom.—**habituation** *n.*

habitude *n* a custom or tendency; familiarity.—**habitudinal** *adj.*

habitué *n* a frequent visitor to a place.

hacienda *n* (in Spanish-speaking countries) a large estate or ranch; the main house on such an estate.

hack[1] *vt* to cut or chop (at) violently; to clear (vegetation) by chopping; (*comput*) to gain illegal access to confidential data. * *n* a gash or notch; a harsh, dry cough.

hack[2] *n* a riding horse for hire; an old worn-out horse; a mediocre or unexceptional writer; a coach for hire; (*inf*) a taxicab. * *vti* to ride a horse cross-country. * *adj* banal, hackneyed.

hackbut *n* a type of arquebus.—*also* **hagbut.**

hacker *n* a person who hacks; (*inf*) (*comput*) a person who uses computers as a hobby, esp one who uses a personal computer to gain illegal access to the computer systems of government departments or large corporations.

hacking *adj* (*cough*) short, dry, spasmodic.

hackles *npl* the hairs on the back of a dog, cat, etc, which stick out when the animal is angry or afraid.

hackney *n* a horse for driving or riding; any of an English breed of high-stepping horses; a carriage or vehicle for hire.

hackneyed *adj* made trite or banal through overuse.

hacksaw *n* a fine-toothed saw for cutting metal.

had *see* **have.**

haddock *n* (*pl* **haddocks, haddock**) an important Atlantic food fish related to the cod.

Hades *n* (*Greek myth*) the home of the dead; (*inf*) hell.—**Hadean** *adj.*

Hadith *n* (*pl* **Hadith, Hadiths**) the traditions surrounding Muhammed and his sayings; an appendix to the Koran

hadj *n* (*pl* **hadjes**) a pilgrimage to Mecca, required of all Muslims.—*also* **hajj** (*pl* **hajjes**).

hadji *n* (*pl* **hadjis**) a Muslim who has made the pilgrimage to Mecca.—*also* **haji, hajji** (*pl* **hajjis, hajis**).

hadn't = had not.

haema-, haemo- *prefix* blood.

haemal *adj* of or relating to the blood, blood vessels or the part of the body that contains the heart.

haematic *adj* of, containing, acting on, or relating to blood. * *n* a drug that increases the level of haemoglobin in blood.

haematite *n* native ferric oxide, an important iron ore.

haematoid *adj* relating to blood; blood-like.

haemoptysis *n* the spitting or coughing up of blood or mucus containing blood.

hafiz *n* a Muslim who knows the Koran by heart; a title of respect; the guardian of the Mosque.

hafnium *n* a silvery metallic element found in zirconium.

haft *n* the handle of a weapon or tool.

hag *n* an ugly or unpleasant old woman; a witch.—**haggish** *adj.*—**haggishness** *n.*

Haggadah *n* (*pl* **Haggadoth**) (*Judaisim*) a parable or illustration of a commentary on Scripture; a book containing the order for the traditional Passover feast; a narrative of the flight from Egypt that is the main part of the Passover feast.

haggard *n adj* having an exhausted, untidy look.—**haggardly** *adv.*—**haggardness** *n.*

haggis *n* (*pl* **haggises, haggis**) a traditional Scottish dish made of minced offal with suet, onions, oatmeal, seasonings, etc.

haggle *vi* to bargain; barter; to dispute over terms; to cavil. * *n* the act of haggling.—**haggler** *n.*

hagiography *n* (*pl* **hagiographies**) the history or legends of the saints; an uncritical biography.—**hagiographer, hagiographist** *n.*—**hagriographic, hagiographical** *adj.*

hah *see* **ha.**

ha-ha[1] *interj* an exclamation of mockery; an outburst of laughter.—*also* **haw-haw.**

ha-ha[2] *n* a fence sunk in the ground as a boundary of a park or garden.

haiku *n* (*pl* **haiku**) a Japanese verse form of three lines.

hail[1] *vt* to greet; to summon by shouting or signalling, as a taxi; to welcome with approval, to acclaim. * vi (with from) to come from. * interj an exclamation of tribute, greeting, etc. * n a shout to gain attention; a distance within which one can be heard calling.—hailer n.

hail² n frozen raindrops; something, as abuse, bullets, etc, sent forcefully in rapid succession. * vti to pour down like hail.

hailstone n a pellet of hail.

hailstorm n a sudden storm of hail.

hair n a threadlike growth from the skin of mammals; a mass of hairs, esp on the human head; a threadlike growth on a plant.

haircut n a shortening and styling of hair by cutting it; the style of cutting.

hairdo n (pl hairdos) a particular style of hair after cutting, etc.

hairdresser n a person who cuts, styles, colours, etc, hair.—hairdressing n.

hairgrip n a clip for holding hair in position; a bobby pin.

hairless adj without hair; having little hair.

hairline n a very thin line; the outline of the hair on the head.

Hail Mary n (RC Church) a prayer to the Virgin Mary beginning with these words.

hairnet n a net used to keep the hair in place

hairpiece n a wig or toupee; an additional piece of hair attached to a person's real hair.

hairpin n U-shaped pin used to hold hair in place.

hairpin bend n a sharply curving bend in a road, etc.

hair-raising adj terrifying, shocking.

hair's-breadth n a very small space or amount.

hairsplitting adj making petty distinctions; quibbling. * n the act of making petty distinctions.—hairsplitter n.

hairspring n a slender, hair-like coil spring, as in a watch.

hairstyle n the way in which hair is arranged.—hairstylist n.

hairweaving n the technique of attaching strands of false hair to the follicles of the head.

hairy adj (hairier, hairiest) covered with hair; (inf) difficult, dangerous.—hairiness n.

haji, hajji see hadji.

hajj see hadj.

hake n (pl hake, hakes) a marine food fish related to the cod.

hakim n a judge, administrator or governor of an Islamic country; a Muslim physician.

Halakah, Halacha n (pl Halakoth, Halachoth) (Judaism) traditional law containing minor precepts in addition to the Mosaic law; legal literature in general.

halal n meat from animals butchered according to Muslim law. * adj of or pertaining to such meat.—also hallal.

halation n (photog, TV) a halo-like appearance round an object, caused by light reflection.

halberd, halbert n a medieval weapon consisting of a long staff to which an axe with a spear-like point was affixed.

halberdier n a soldier armed with a halberd.

halcyon adj calm, gentle, peaceful. * n a fabled bird (probably the kingfisher) that nested at sea and calmed it.

hale adj healthy and strong.

half n (pl halves) either of two equal parts of some-

thing; (inf) a half-price ticket for a bus, etc; (inf) half a pint. * adj being a half; incomplete; partial. * adv to the extent of a half; (inf) partly.

half-and-half n something half one thing and half another, esp a mixture of mild and bitter beer. * adj partly one thing and partly another. * adv in two equal parts.

halfback n (football, hockey) a player occupying a position between the forwards and the fullbacks; a player in this position in other sports.

half-baked adj (inf) poorly planned or thought-out; (inf) stupid.

half-brother n a brother through one parent only.

half-caste n a person whose parents are of different races.

half cock n the middle position of a gun's hammer; at half cock not prepared.—half-cocked adj.

half-hearted adj with little interest, enthusiasm, etc.—half-heartedly adv.—half-heartedness n.

half-hour n 30 minutes; the point 30 minutes after the beginning of an hour.

half-life n the time taken for half the atoms in a radioactive substance to decay.

half-mast n the position to which a flag is lowered as a sign of mourning.

half-measure n (often pl) an inadequate action; a compromise.

half-moon n the moon at its phase when half the disc is illuminated; something shaped like this. * adj in the shape of a half-moon.

half-nelson n a wrestling hold, pinning the arm of an opponent behind the back from behind.

half note n (mus) a note with the time value of half of a semibreve.—also minim.

halfpenny (pl halfpence) n a bronze coin worth two farthings in pre-decimal British currency.

half-sister n a sister through one parent only.

half title n a short title on the page before the title page of a book, a bastard title.

half-term n a short holiday in the middle of a school term.

half-time n (sport) an interval between two halves of a game.

halftone n an illustration printed from a relief plate, showing light and shadow by means of minute dots.

half-track n a (military) vehicle with wheels in front but driven by caterpillar tracks at the rear.

half-truth n a statement that is only partly true.

half volley n (tennis, etc) the striking of the ball the instant it bounces.

halfway adj midway between two points, etc.

halfwit n a stupid or silly person; a mentally retarded person.—halfwitted adj.—halfwittedly adv.—halfwittedness n.

halibut n (pl halibut, halibuts) a large marine flatfish used as food.

halide n a compound containing halogen; a haloid.

halitosis n bad-smelling breath.

hall n a public building with offices, etc; a large room for exhibits, gatherings, etc; the main house on a landed estate; a college building, esp a dining room; a vestibule at the entrance of a building; a hallway.

hallal see halal.

Hallel n (Judaism) Psalms 113-118 chanted as part of morning services during Passover and other festivals.

hallelujah, halleluiah interj an exclamation of praise to

God. * *n* a praising of God; a musical composition having this as its theme.—*also* **alleluia.**

halliard *see* **halyard.**

hallmark *n* a mark used on gold, silver or platinum articles to signify a standard of purity, weight, date of manufacture; a mark or symbol of high quality; a characteristic feature. * *vt* to stamp with a hallmark.

hallo *see* **hello.**

hallow *vt* to make or regard as holy.—**hallowed** *adj.*—**hallowedness** *n.*—**hallower** *n.*

Hallowe'en, Halloween *n* the eve of All Saints' Day, October 31.

Hallowmas *n* (*formerly*) All Saints' Day, November 1.

Hallstatt, Hallstadt *adj* of or denoting the final period of the Bronze Age and the first period of the Iron Age (9th–4th centuries BC).

hallucinate *vti* to have or cause to have hallucinations.—**hallucinator** *n.*

hallucination *n* the apparent perception of sights, sounds, etc, that are not actually present; something perceived in this manner.—**hallucinational, hallucinative** *adj.*—**hallucinatory** *adj.*

hallucinogen *n* a drug that produces hallucinations.—**hallucinogenic** *adj.*

hallux (*pl* **halluces**) the big toe; the first digit on the back foot of an amphibian, bird, mammal, or reptile.

halm *see* **haulm.**

halo *n* (*pl* **haloes, halos**) a circle of light, as around the sun; a symbolic ring of light around the head of a saint in pictures; the aura of glory surrounding an idealized person or thing. * *vt* (**haloing, haloed**) to surround with a halo.

halogen *n* any of the five chemical elements fluorine, chlorine, bromine, iodine and astatine.—**halogenous** *adj.*

halt¹ *n* a temporary interruption or cessation of progress; a minor station on a rail line. * *vti* to stop or come to a stop.

halt² *vi* to falter; to hesitate.—**halting** *adj.*

halter *n* a rope or strap for tying or leading an animal; a style of women's dress top tied behind the neck and waist leaving the back and arms bare. * *vt* to put a halter on (a horse, etc).

halve *vt* to divide equally into two; to reduce by half; (*golf*) to play one hole in the same number of strokes as one's opponent.

halves *see* **half.**

halyard *n* a line for hoisting or lowering a sail, yard, or flag.—*also* **halliard.**

ham *n* the upper part of a pig's hind leg, salted, smoked, etc; the meat from this area; (*inf*) the back of the upper thigh; (*inf*) an actor who overacts; (*inf*) a licensed amateur radio operator. * *vti* (**hamming, hammed**) to speak or move in an exaggerated manner, to overact.

hamadryad *n* (*pl* **hamadryads, hamadryades**) (*Greek myth*) a wood nymph; a giant cobra, the king cobra.

hamadryas *n* a North African baboon, the male of which has a heavy mane of silvery hair.

hamal *n* a porter in several Muslim countries.—*also* **hammal, hammaul.**

Hamburg *n* a rich, black grape; a breed of black domestic fowl.

hamburger *n* ground beef; a cooked patty of such meat, often in a bread roll with pickle, etc.

hame¹ *n* either of two curved bars for the traces on the collar of a draught horse.

hame² *n* (*Scot*) home.

ham-handed, ham-fisted *adj* (*inf*) clumsy.

Hamite *n* a descendant of Ham, son of Noah; a member of the Hamitic race.

Hamitic *adj* relating to Ham, the races descended from him, or the languages they speak. * *n* any of a group of languages spoken in North Africa.

hamlet *n* a very small village.

hammal, hammaul *see* **hamal.**

hammer *n* a tool for pounding, driving nails, etc, having a heavy head and a handle; a thing like this in shape or use, as the part of the gun that strikes the firing pin; a bone of the middle ear; a heavy metal ball attached to a wire thrown in athletic contests; **hammer and tongs** with great force. * *vti* to strike repeatedly, as with a hammer; to drive, force, or shape, as with hammer blows; (*inf*) to defeat utterly.—**hammerer** *n.*

hammerhead *n* a shark with a mallet-shaped head.

hammock *n* a length of strong cloth or netting suspended by the ends and used as a bed.

hammy *adj* (**hammier, hammiest**) (*inf*) overacting; exaggerated.

hamper¹ *vt* to hinder; to interfere with; to encumber.—**hamperer** *n.*

hamper² *n* a large, usu covered, basket for storing or transporting food and crockery, etc.

hamster *n* a small short-tailed rodent with cheek pouches.

hamstring *n* any of the tendons at the back of the thigh that flex and rotate the leg. * *vt* (**hamstringing, hamstrung**) to cripple by severing the hamstring of; to render useless; to thwart.

hamulus (*pl* **hamuli**) *n* a small hook-like projection at the end of the bones or between the fore and hind wings of a bee or bee-like insect.—**hamular** *adj.*

hand *n* the part of the arm below the wrist, used for grasping; a side or direction; possession or care; control; an active part; a promise to marry; skill; one having a special skill; handwriting; applause; help; a hired worker; a source; one of a ship's crew; anything like a hand, as a pointer on a clock; the breadth of a hand, four inches when measuring the height of a horse; the cards held by a player at one time; a round of card play; (*inf*) applause. * *adj* of, for, or controlled by the hand. * *vt* to give as with the hand; to help or conduct with the hand. * *vi* (*with* **on**) to pass to the next.

handbag *n* a woman's small bag for carrying personal items.—*also* **bag, pocket book, purse.**

handbill *n* a small printed notice to be passed out by hand.

handbook *n* a book containing useful instructions.

handcart *n* a small cart pulled or pushed by hand.

handcuff *n* (*usu pl*) either of a pair of connected steel rings for shackling the wrists of a prisoner. * *vt* to manacle.

handed *adj* having or involving (a specified kind or number of) hands.

handfast *vt* (*formerly*) to pledge or betroth; to grip with the hand. * *n* a contract of betrothal.

handful *n* as much as will fill the hand; a few; (*inf*) a person who is difficult to handle or control.

handicap *n* a mental or physical impairment; a contest in which difficulties are imposed on, or advantages given to, contestants to equalize their chances; such a difficulty or advantage; any hindrance. * *vt* (**handi-**

capping, **handicapped**) to give a handicap to; to hinder.—**handicapper** *n*.

handicapped *adj* mentally or physically disabled.

handicraft *n* a skill involving the hands, such as basketwork, pottery, etc; an item of pottery, etc made by hand.

handiwork *n* handmade work; something done by a person or thing.

handkerchief *n* a small cloth for blowing the nose, etc.

handle *vt* to touch, hold, or move with the hand; to manage or operate with the hands; to manage, deal with; to buy and sell (goods). * *vi* to react in a specified way. * *n* a part of anything designed to be held or grasped by the hand.—**handleable** *adj*.—**handling** *n*.

handlebar *n* (*often pl*) the curved metal bar with a grip at each end used to steer a bicycle, etc; a bushy moustache with curved ends.

handler *n* a person who trains or controls animals, such as a police dog.

handless *adj* awkward, clumsy.

handmade *adj* made by hand, carefully crafted.

handmaid(en) *n* a female servant.

hand-out *n* an item of food, clothing, etc, given free to the needy; a statement given to the press to replace or supplement an oral presentation.

hand-picked *adj* carefully selected.

handrail *n* a narrow rail for gripping as a support.

hands-on *adj* involving active participation and operating experience.

handsaw *n* any saw that is used in one hand only.

handsel *n* (*formerly*) a good-luck gift on beginning something; a housewarming present; a New Year gift. * *vt* to give a handsel to; to inaugurate; to be first to use something.

handset *n* a telephone earpiece and mouthpiece as a single unit.

handshake *n* a grasping and shaking of a person's hand as a greeting or when concluding an agreement.

handsome *adj* good-looking; dignified; generous; ample.—**handsomely** *adv*.—**handsomeness** *n*.

handspike *n* an iron-shod bar or pipe used as a lever.

handspring *n* (*gymnastics*) a leaping forwards or backwards from a standing position into a handstand then back onto the feet.

handstand *n* the act of supporting the body on the hands with the feet in the air.

hand-to-hand *adj* (*fighting*) at close quarters.

hand-to-mouth *adj* having barely enough food or money to survive.—*also adv*.

handwriting *n* writing done by hand; a style of such writing.—**handwritten** *adj*.

handy *adj* (**handier, handiest**) convenient, near; easy to use; skilled with the hands.—**handily** *adv*.—**handiness** *n*.

handyman *n* (*pl* **handymen**) a person who does odd jobs.

hang *vb* (**hanging, hung**) *vt* to support from above, esp by a rope, chain, etc, to suspend; (*door, etc*) to attach by hinges to allow to swing freely; to decorate with pictures, or other suspended objects; (*wallpaper*) to stick to a wall; to exhibit (works of art); to prevent (a jury) from coming to a decision; (*pt, pp* **hanged**) to put to execute or kill by suspending by the neck. * *vi* to be suspended, so as to dangle loosely; (*clothing, etc*) to fall or flow in a certain direction; to lean, incline, or protrude; to depend; to remain in the air; to be in suspense; to fall or droop; (*pt, pp* **hanged**) to die by hang-

ing; (*with* **about, around**) to loiter; (*with* **back**) to hesitate, be reluctant; (*with* **out**) to meet regularly at a particular place. * *n* the way in which anything hangs; (*sl*) a damn.

hangar *n* a large shelter where aircraft are built, stored or repaired.—*also vt*.

hangbird *n* the Baltimore oriole; any North American bird that builds a hanging nest.

hangdog *adj* abject or ashamed in appearance or manner.

hanger *n* a device on which something is hung; one who hangs things.

hanger-on *n* (*pl* **hangers-on**) a sycophantic follower.

hang-glider *n* an unpowered aircraft consisting of a metal frame over which a lightweight material is stretched, with a harness for the pilot suspended below.—**hang gliding** *n*.

hanging *n* the act of executing a person by suspending them by the neck; something hung, as a picture; (*pl*) decorative draperies hung on walls. * *adj* suspended in the air; undecided; overhanging; situated on a steep slope.

hangman *n* (*pl* **hangmen**) a person who executes prisoners by hanging them.

hangnail *n* a thin strip of torn skin at the root of a fingernail.

hangout *n* a favourite meeting place.

hangover *n* the unpleasant after-effects of excessive consumption of alcohol; something surviving from an earlier time.

hang-up *n* an emotional preoccupation with something.

hank *n* a coiled or looped bundle of wool, rope, etc.

hanker *vi* (*with* **after, for**) to desire longingly.—**hankerer** *n*.—**hankering** *n*.

hanky, hankie *n* (*pl* **hankies**) (*inf*) a handkerchief.

hanky-panky *n* (*inf*) foolish behaviour; dishonesty; illicit sexual relations.

Hansard *n* the official, printed verbatim reports of British parliamentary proceedings.

hanse *n* a medieval guild of merchants; a fee paid by new members of such a guild; (*with cap*) a town of the Hanseatic League; the Hanseatic League.—**hanseatic** *adj*.

Hanseatic League *n* a confederacy of merchants or commercial towns in northern Germany and elsewhere, which lasted from the 14th–19th centuries.

hansom (cab) *n* a light two-wheeled covered horse-drawn carriage, with the driver's seat raised behind.

hap *vb* (**happing, happed**) *vi* (*arch*) to happen or befall. * *vt* to cover up; to wrap up warmly. * *n* (*arch*) chance; luck; a fortunate accident; a covering of any kind.

haphazard *adj* not planned; random. * *adv* by chance.—**haphazardly** *adv*.—**haphazardness** *n*.

hapless *adj* unfortunate, unlucky.—**haplessness** *n*.

haploid *adj* (*cell nucleus, organism*) possessing only half the normal number of chromosomes. * *n* a single set of unpaired chromosomes.

haply *adv* (*formerly*) by chance.

happen *vi* to take place; to be, occur, or come by chance.

happening *n* an occurrence; an improvization.

happy *adj* (**happier, happiest**) fortunate; having, expressing, or enjoying pleasure or contentment; pleased; appropriate, felicitous.—**happily** *adv*.—**happiness** *n*.

happy-go-lucky *adj* irresponsible; carefree.

happy hour *n* a particular time of day when a bar, hotel, etc, sells drinks at reduced prices

happy medium *n* a middle course between extremes.

hapteron *n* (*pl* **haptera**) the tissue in seaweed and related plants that enables them to attach themselves to a host object.

haptic *adj* of or relating to the sense of touch.

harakiri *n* ritual suicide by disembowelment.—*also* **harikari**.

harangue *n* a tirade; a lengthy, forceful speech. * *vti* to make a harangue, to address vehemently.—**haranguer** *n*.

harass *vt* to annoy, to irritate; to trouble (an enemy) by constant raids and attacks.—**harasser** *n*.—**harassment** *n*.

harbinger *n* a person or thing that announces or presages the arrival of another, a forerunner.

harbour, harbor *n* a protected inlet for anchoring ships; any place of refuge. * *vt* to shelter or house; (*grudge, etc*) to keep in the mind secretly. * *vi* to take shelter.—**harbourer, harborer** *n*.

harbourage, harborage *n* a port or anchorage for ships.

hard *adj* firm, solid, not easily cut or punctured; difficult to comprehend; difficult to accomplish; difficult to bear, painful; severe, unfeeling, ungenerous; indisputable, intractable; (*drugs*) addictive and damaging to health; (*weather*) severe; (*currency*) stable in value; (*news*) definite, not speculative; (*drink*) very alcoholic; (*water*) having a high mineral content that prevents lathering with soap; (*colour, sound*) harsh. * *adv* with great effort or intensity; earnestly, with concentration; so as to cause hardness; with difficulty; with bitterness or grief; close, near by.—**hardness** *n*.

hardback *n* a book bound with a stiff cover.—*also adj*.

hard-bitten *adj* (*inf*) tough, seasoned.

hardboard *n* a stiff board made of compressed wood chips.

hard-boiled *adj* (*eggs*) boiled until solid; (*inf*) unfeeling.

hard cash *n* payment in coins and notes as opposed to cheque, credit card, etc.

hard copy *n* output (as from microfilm or a computer) on paper.

hard core *n* the stubborn inner group in an organization that is resistant to change; the heavy foundation material for a road.

hard-core *adj* of a hard core; utterly entrenched; (*pornography*) showing sexual acts in explicit detail.

hard disk *n* (*comput*) a rigid magnetic disk in a sealed unit capable of much greater storage capacity than a floppy disk.

harden *vti* to make or become hard.—**hardener** *n*.

hard-headed *adj* shrewd and unsentimental; practical.—**hard-headedly** *adv*.—**hard-headedness** *n*.

hardhearted *adj* unfeeling; cruel.—**hardheartedly** *adv*.—**hardheartedness** *n*.

hard-hitting *adj* forcefully effective.

hard line *n* an aggressive, unyielding policy.—**hardline** *adj*.—**hardliner** *n*.

hardly *adv* scarcely; barely; with difficulty; not to be expected.

hardpan *n* a hard, impervious layer of clay below the soil; a solid foundation.

hard sell *n* an aggressive selling technique.

hardship *n* something that causes suffering or privation.

hard shoulder *n* in UK, a raised strip of land alongside a motorway for vehicles to make emergency stops.

hardtack *n* a hard, saltless biscuit formerly eaten by seamen.

hard-up *adj* (*inf*) short of money.

hardware *n* articles made of metal as tools, nails, etc; (*comput*) the mechanical and electronic components that make up a computer system.

hardwood *n* the close-grained wood of deciduous trees.

hardy *adj* (**hardier, hardiest**) bold, resolute; robust; vigorous; able to withstand exposure to physical or emotional hardship.—**hardily** *adv*.—**hardiness** *n*.

hare *n* (*pl* **hare, hares**) any of various timid, swift, long-eared mammals, resembling but larger than the rabbit.

harebell *n* the bluebell; the wild hyacinth.

harebrained *adj* flighty; foolish.

harelip *n* a congenital deformity of the upper lip in the form of a vertical fissure.—**harelipped** *adj*.

harem *n* the usu secluded part of a Muslim household where the women live; the women in a harem.

haricot *n* a type of French bean with an edible light-coloured seed.

harikari *see* **harakiri**.

hark *vi* to listen; (*with* **back**) to retrace a course; to revert (to).

harken *see* **hearken**.

harlequin *n* the performer in a pantomime who wears parti-coloured garments and carries a wand. * *adj* fantastic or full of trickery; colourful.

harlequinade *n* a play or the part of a pantomime in which Harlequin plays a leading role; buffoonery.

harlot *n* (*formerly*) a prostitute.—**harlotry** *n*.

harm *n* hurt; damage; injury. * *vt*. to inflict hurt, damage, or injury upon.—**harmer** *n*.

harmattan *n* a hot dust-laden wind that blows from the interior to the west coast of Africa.

harmful *adj* hurtful.—**harmfully** *adv*.—**harmfulness** *n*.

harmless *adj* not likely to cause harm.—**harmlessly** *adv*.—**harmlessness** *n*.

harmonic *adj* (*mus*) of or in harmony. * *n* an overtone; (*pl*) the science of musical sounds.—**harmonically** *adv*.

harmonica *n* a small wind instrument that produces tones when air is blown or sucked across a series of metal reeds; a mouth-organ.

harmonious *adj* fitting together in an orderly and pleasing manner; agreeing in ideas, interests, etc; melodious.—**harmoniously** *adv*.

harmonium *n* a keyboard musical instrument whose tones are produced by thin metal reeds operated by foot bellows.

harmonize *vi* to be in harmony; to sing in harmony. * *vt* to make harmonious.—**harmonization** *n*.

harmony *n* (*pl* **harmonies**) a pleasing agreement of parts in colour, size, etc; agreement in action, ideas, etc; the pleasing combination of musical tones in a chord; a collation of parallel narratives, esp of the Gospels, with a commentary.

harness *n* the leather straps and metal pieces by which a horse is fastened to a vehicle, plough, etc; any similar fastening or attachment, eg for a parachute, hang-glider. * *vt* to put a harness on; to control so as to use the power of.—**harnesser** *n*.

harp *n* a stringed musical instrument played by plucking. * *vi* (*with* **on** *or* **upon**) to talk persistently (on some subject).—**harpist, harper** *n*.

harpoon *n* a barbed spear with an attached line, for spearing whales, etc. * *vt* to strike with a harpoon.—**harpooner** *n*.

harpsichord *n* a musical instrument resembling a grand

piano whose strings are plucked by a mechanism rather than struck.—**harpsichordist** n.

harpy n (pl **harpies**) a grasping, vicious person.

harquebus see **arquebus**.

harridan n a disreputable, shrewish old woman.

harrier n a small breed of hound used for hunting hares; a cross-country runner.

harrow n a heavy frame with spikes, spring teeth, or disks for breaking up and levelling ploughed ground. * vt to draw a harrow over (land); to cause mental distress to.—**harrower** n.—**harrowing** adj, n.—**harrowment** n.

harry vt (**harrying, harried**) to torment or harass.

harsh adj unpleasantly rough; jarring on the senses or feelings; rigorous; cruel.—**harshly** adv.—**harshness** n.

hart n (pl **hart, harts**) a male deer, especially the red deer, aged five years or more.

hartal n (Hinduism) the closing of shops as a sign of mourning or as a political gesture.

hartebeest, hartbeest n the South African antelope.

hartshorn n the antler of a hart; sal volatile.

harum-scarum adj (inf) rash, reckless. * n a giddy rash person.

haruspex n (pl **haruspices**) in ancient Rome, a sooth-sayer who foretold events by inspecting the entrails of sacrificial animals.

harvest n (the season of) gathering in the ripened crops; the yield of a particular crop; the reward or product of any exertion or action. * vti to gather in (a crop). * vt to win by achievement.—**harvester** n.—**harvesting** n.

harvester n a person who harvests; a harvesting machine esp a combine harvester.

harvest moon n the full moon nearest the time of the September equinox.

has see **have**.

has-been n (inf) a person or thing that has lost its former popularity or celebrity status.

hash[1] n a chopped mixture of reheated cooked meat and vegetables. * vt to chop up (meat or vegetables) for hash; to mix or mess up.

hash[2] n (inf) hashish.

hashish n resin derived from the leaves and shoots of the hemp plant, smoked or chewed as an intoxicant.

hasn't = has not.

hasp n a hinged fastening for a door, etc, esp a metal piece fitted over a staple and fastened as by a bolt or padlock.

hassock n a firm cushion used as a footstool or seat.

hast (arch) the second person sing of **have**, used with **thou**.

hastate adj spear-shaped (of a leaf).

haste n quickness of motion; urgency. * vi (poet) to hasten.

hasten vt to accelerate; to cause to hurry. * vi to move or act with speed.—**hastener** n.

hasty adj (**hastier, hastiest**) done in a hurry; rash, precipitate.—**hastily** adv.—**hastiness** n.

hat n a covering for the head. * vt (**hatting, hatted**) to cover with a hat.

hatband n a band or ribbon around the base of a hat; a black cloth band worn as a token of mourning.

hatbox n a box or case for a hat or hats.

hatch[1] n a small door or opening (as on an aircraft or spaceship); an opening in the deck of a ship or in the floor or roof of a building; a lid for such an opening; a hatchway.

hatch[2] vt to produce (young) from the egg, esp by incu-

bating; to devise (eg a plot). * vi to emerge from the egg; to incubate.—**hatchable** adj.—**hatcher** n.

hatch[3] vt (drawing, engraving) to shade using closely spaced parallel lines or incisions.—**hatching** n.

hatchback n a sloping rear end on a car with a door; a car of this design.

hatchery n (pl **hatcheries**) a place for hatching eggs, esp of fish.

hatchet n a small axe with a short handle.

hatchet job n (inf) devastating or malicious verbal or written criticism.

hatchet man n a person hired to perform unpleasant tasks; a critic specializing in invective.

hatchment n (her) a diamond-shaped tablet bearing a dead person's armorial bearings, placed on a house or tomb.

hatchway n an opening in a ship's deck or in a floor or roof; a passage giving access to an enclosed space (as a cellar).

hate vt to feel intense dislike for. * vi to feel hatred; to wish to avoid. * n a strong feeling of dislike or contempt; the person or thing hated.—**hater** n.

hateful adj deserving or arousing hate.—**hatefully** adv.—**hatefulness** n.

hath (arch) the third person sing of **have**.

hatred n intense dislike or enmity.

hatter n a person who makes or sells hats.

hat trick n (cricket) the taking of three wickets with three successive bowls; the scoring of three successive goals, points, etc in any game.

hauberk n a coat of armour, often sleeveless, formed of chain mail, which reached below the knees.

haugh n (Scot) a small, low-lying riverside meadow.

haughty adj (**haughtier, haughtiest**) having or expressing arrogance.—**haughtily** adv.—**haughtiness** n.

haul vti to move by pulling; to transport by truck, etc. * n the act of hauling; the amount gained, caught, etc, at one time; the distance over which something is transported.

haulage n the transport of commodities; the charge for this.

hauler n a person or business that transports goods by road.

haulm n the stalk of potatoes, peas, etc, esp after the crop has been gathered.—also **halm**.

haunch n the part of the body around the hips; the leg and loin of a deer, sheep, etc.—**haunched** adj.

haunt vt to visit often or continually; to recur repeatedly to. * vi to linger; to appear habitually as a ghost. * n a place often visited.—**haunter** n.

haunted adj supposedly visited by ghosts; obsessed; anxious, worried.

haunting adj constantly recurring in the mind; unforgettable.—**hauntingly** adv.

Hausa n a member of the negroid people of West Africa living chiefly in Nigeria; the language of these people.

haustellum n (pl **haustella**) the tip of the proboscis of the housefly or similar insects used for sucking foods.

hautbois, hautboy n (pl **hautbois, hautboy**) (arch) the oboe.

haute couture n high fashion.

haute cuisine n high-class cooking.

hauteur n arrogance, haughtiness.

Havana (cigar) n a cigar rolled from Cuban tobacco.

have vt (**has, having,** pp **had**) to have in one's possession; to possess as an attribute; to hold in the mind; to experience; to give birth to; to allow, or tolerate; to arrange or hold; to engage in; to cause, compel, or require to be; to to be obliged; (*sl*) to have sexual intercourse with; to be pregnant with; (*inf*) to hold at a disadvantage; (*inf*) to deceive; to accept or receive; to consume food, drink, etc; to show some quality; to perplex.

haven *n* a place where ships can safely anchor; a refuge.

haven't = have not.

haver *vi* (*Scot*) to talk foolishly or in consequently; to dither. * *n* (*pl*) nonsense.

haversack *n* a canvas bag similar to a knapsack but worn over one shoulder.

havoc *n* widespread destruction or disorder. * *vt* (**havocking, havocked**) to lay waste.

haw *n* (the berry of) the hawthorn.

Hawaiian *adj* pertaining to Hawaii, its inhabitants or its language. * *n* an inhabitant of Hawaii; a Polynesian language spoken in Hawaii.

hawfinch *n* a rare European finch with a stout bill, brown plumage and black-and-white wings.

haw-haw *see* **ha-ha**[1].

hawk[1] *n* any of numerous birds of prey; a person who advocates aggressive or intimidatory action. * *vti* to hunt with a hawk; to strike like a hawk.—**hawkish** *adj*.—**hawkishly** *adv*.

hawk[2] *vti* to clear the throat (of) audibly. * *n* the sound of this.

hawk[3] *vt* to offer goods for sale, as in the street; to spread gossip. * *vi* to peddle.

hawker *n* a person who goes about offering goods for sale; a person who hunts with a trained hawk.

hawk-eyed *adj* keen-sighted; vigilant.

hawkweed *n* a yellow-flowered plant of the aster family.

hawse *n* (*naut*) the part of a ship's bows where the hawseholes are situated; the distance from the bow of an anchored ship to the anchor. * *vi* (*naut*) to pitch violently when at anchor.

hawsehole *n* (*naut*) one of the two holes in the upper part of a ship's bows through which the anchor cables pass when the vessel is moored.

hawser *n* (*naut*) a heavy rope for towing, mooring, etc.

hawthorn *n* any of a genus of spring-flowering spiny shrubs or trees with white or pink flowers and red fruit.

hay *n* grass cut and dried for fodder.

haybox *n* an airtight box packed with hay or any other natural insulating material used to keep partially cooked food warm and allow to cook by retained heat.

haycock *n* a conical pile of hay left in the fields to dry out.

hay fever *n* an allergic reaction to pollen, causing irritation of the nose and eyes.

haymaker *n* one who lifts and spreads hay; either of two machines used in haymaking; a wild punch.

haystack, hayrick *n* a pile of stacked hay ready for storing.

haywire *adj* (*inf*) out of order; disorganized.

hazard *n* a risk; a danger; an obstacle on a golf course. * *vt* to risk; to venture.—**hazardable** *adj*.

hazardous *adj* dangerous; risky.—**hazardously** *adv*.—**hazardousness** *n*.

haze *n* a thin vapour of fog, smoke, etc. in the air; slight vagueness of mind. * *vti* to make or become hazy.

hazel *n* a tree with edible nuts; a light-brown colour. * *adj* light-brown.

hazelnut *n* the edible nut of the hazel.

hazy *adj* (**hazier, haziest**) misty; vague.—**hazily** *adv*.—**haziness** *n*.

H-bomb *n* a hydrogen bomb.

HC *abbr* = Holy Communion; House of Commons.

HCF *abbr* = highest common factor.

HDTV *abbr* = high-definition television.

HE *abbr* = high explosive; His Eminence; His (or Her) Excellency.

He (*chem symbol*) helium.

he *pron* the male person or animal named before; a person (male or female). * *n* a male person or animal.

head *n* the part of an animal or human body containing the brain, eyes, ears, nose and mouth; the top part of anything; the foremost part; the chief person; (*pl*) a unit of counting; the striking part of a tool; mind; understanding; the topic of a chapter, etc; crisis, conclusion; pressure of water, steam, etc; the source of a river, etc; froth, as on beer. * *adj* at the head, top or front; coming from in front; chief, leading. * *vt* to command; to lead; to cause to go in a specified direction; to set out; to travel (in a particular direction); to strike (a football) with the head.—**headless** *adj*.

headache *n* a continuous pain in the head; (*inf*) a cause of worry or trouble.—**headachy** *adj*.

headband *n* a ribbon or band worn around the head; a narrow strip of cloth stitched to the top of the spine of a book for protection or decoration.

headboard *n* a board that forms the head of a bed, etc.

headdress *n* a decorative covering for the head.

headed *adj* having (a specified kind of) head; having a heading.

header *n* a dive with the head first; (*scoccer*) the action of striking the ball with the head.

headfirst *adj* with the head in front; recklessly.—*also adv*.

headgear *n* a covering for the head, a hat, cap, etc.

head-hunt *vt* to cut off and preserve the heads of enemies as trophies; a person who recruits executive personnel.—**head-hunter** *n*.—**head-hunting** *n*.

heading *n* something forming the head, top, or front; the title, topic, etc of a chapter, etc; the direction in which a vehicle is moving.

headland *n* a promontory; unploughed land at the ends of a furrow.

headless *adj* being without a head; leaderless.

headlamp, headlight *n* a light at the front of a vehicle.

headline *n* printed lines at the top of a newspaper article giving the topic; a brief news summary. * *vt* to give featured billing or publicity to.

headlong *adj*, *adv* with the head first; with uncontrolled speed or force; rashly.

headman *n* (*pl* **headmen**) the chieftain or leader of a tribe; a foreman or overseer.

headmaster, headmistress *n* the principal of a school.—**headmastership, headmistress-ship** *n*.

headmost *adj* foremost

head-on *adj*, *adv* with the head or front foremost; without compromise.

head over heels *adv* as if somersaulting; completely, utterly, deeply.

headphone *n* one of two radio receivers held to the head by a band.

headquarters *n* the centre of operations of one in command, as in an army; the main office in any organization.

headrest *n* a support for the head.

headroom *n* space overhead, as in a doorway or tunnel.

heads-up *adj* self-assured and excellent.

headset *n* a set of headphones, usu with a microphone.

headshrinker *n* (*sl*) a psychiatrist.

headstall *n* the part of a bridle that fits round a horse's head.

head start *n* an early start; any other competitive advantage.

headstone *n* a marker placed at the head of a grave.

headstrong *adj* determined to do as one pleases; obstinate.

head waiter *n* the head of the dining-room staff in a restaurant.

headwaters *npl* the small streams that are the source of a river.

headway *n* forward motion; progress.

headwind *n* a wind blowing against the direction of a ship or aircraft.

headword *n* a term placed at the beginning (as of an entry in a dictionary).

headwork *n* mental work; the decoration on the keystone of an arch.

heady *adj* (**headier, headiest**) (*alcoholic drinks*) intoxicating; invigorating, exciting; impetuous.—**headily** *adv*.—**headiness** *n*.

heal *vti* to make or become healthy; to cure; (*wound, etc*) to repair by natural processes.—**healable** *adj*.—**healer** *n*.—**healingly** *adv*.

health *n* physical and mental well-being; freedom from disease, etc; the condition of body or mind; a wish for one's health and happiness, as in a toast.

health farm *n* a residential establishment for improving health through a strict regime of diet and exercise.

health foods *npl* foods that are organically grown, unprocessed and additive-free.

healthful *adj* healthy.—**healthfully** *adv*.—**healthfulness** *n*.

healthy *adj* (**healthier, healthiest**) having or producing good health; beneficial; sound.—**healthily** *adv*.—**healthiness** *n*.

heap *n* a mass or pile of jumbled things; (*pl*) (*inf*) a large amount. * *vt* to throw in a heap; to pile high; to fill (a plate, etc) full or to overflowing.—**heaper** *n*.

hear *vb* (**hearing, heard**) *vt* to perceive by the ear; to listen to; to conduct a hearing of (a law case, etc); to be informed of; to learn. * *vi* to be able to hear sounds; (*with* of *or* about) to be told.—**hearable** *adj*.—**hearer** *n*.

hearing *n* the sense by which sound is perceived by the ear; an opportunity to be heard; the distance over which something can be heard, earshot.

hearing aid *n* a small electronic amplifier worn behind the ear to improve hearing.

hearken *vi* to listen to.—*also* **harken**.—**hearkener** *n*.

hearsay *n* rumour, gossip.

hearse *n* a vehicle for transporting a coffin to a funeral.

heart *n* the hollow, muscular organ that circulates the blood; the central, vital, or main part; the human heart as the centre of emotions, esp sympathy, courage, etc; a conventional design representing a heart; one of a suit of playing cards marked with such a symbol in red.

heartache *n* sorrow or grief.

heart attack *n* a sudden instance of abnormal heart functioning, esp coronary thrombosis.

heartbeat *n* the rhythmic contraction and dilation of the heart.

heartbreak *n* overwhelming sorrow or grief.—**heartbreaker** *n*.

heartbreaking *adj* causing heartbreak; pitiful.—**heartbreakingly** *adv*.

heartbroken *adj* overcome by sorrow or grief.—**heartbrokenly** *adv*.—**heartbrokenness** *n*.

heartburn *n* a burning sensation in the lower chest.

hearten *vt* to encourage; to cheer up.—**hearteningly** *adv*.

heart failure *n* the inability of the heart to supply enough blood to the body; a cessation of heart activity leading to death.

heartfelt *adj* deeply felt; sincere.

hearth *n* the floor of a fireplace and surrounding area; this as symbolic of house and home.

hearthstone *n* a stone forming a hearth; soft stone used to whiten hearths, floors, steps, etc.

heartily *adv* in a vigorous or enthusiastic way; sincerely.

heartland *n* the central or most vital part of an area, region, etc.

heartless *adj* lacking compassion; unfeeling.—**heartlessly** *adv*.—**heartlessness** *n*.

heart-rending *adj* causing much mental anguish.

heartsease *n* the wild pansy

heartsick *adj* extremely unhappy, despondent.—**heartsickness** *n*.

heartstrings *npl* deepest feelings.

heart-throb *n* (*inf*) the object of a person's infatuation; a heartbeat.

heart-to-heart *n* an intimate conversation. * *adj* intimate; candid.

heartwood *n* the central older wood of a tree, usu harder and darker than the outer rings.—*also* **duramen**.

hearty *adj* (**heartier, heartiest**) warm and friendly; (*laughter, etc*) unrestrained; strong and healthy; nourishing and plentiful.—**heartiness** *n*.

heat *n* energy produced by molecular agitation; the quality of being hot; the perception of hotness; hot weather or climate; strong feeling, esp ardour, anger, etc; a single bout, round, or trial in sports; the period of sexual excitement and readiness for mating in female animals; (*sl*) coercion. * *vti* to make or become warm or hot; to make or become excited.

heated *adj* made hot; excited, impassioned.—**heatedly** *adv*.—**heatedness** *n*.

heater *n* a device that provides heat; (*sl*) a pistol.

heath *n* an area of uncultivated land with scrubby vegetation; any of various shrubby plants that thrive on sandy soil, eg heather.

heathen *n* (*pl* **heathens, heathen**) anyone not acknowledging the God of Christian, Jew, or Muslim belief; a person regarded as irreligious, uncivilized, etc. * *adj* of or denoting a heathen; irreligious; pagan.—**heathendom** *n*.

heathenish *adj* relating to or resembling a heathen or heathenish culture; rude, ignorant or uncultured.—**heathenishly** *adv*.—**heathenishness** *n*.

heathenism *n* ignorance of God; paganism; idolatry.

heather *n* a common evergreen shrub of northern and alpine regions with small sessile leaves and tiny usu purplish pink flowers.—**heathery** *adj*.

heating *n* a system of providing heat, as central heating; the warmth provided.

heat wave *n* a prolonged period of unusually hot weather.

heave *vb* (**heaving, heaved**) *vt* to lift or move, esp with great effort; to utter (a sigh, etc) with effort; (*inf*) to throw. * *vi* to rise and fall rhythmically; to vomit; to pant; to gasp; to haul; (**heaving, hove**) (*with* **to**) (*ship*) to come to a stop. * *n* the act or effort of heaving.—**heaver** *n*.

heaven *n* (*usu pl*) the visible sky; (*sometimes cap*) the dwelling place of God and his angels where the blessed go after death; any place or state of great happiness; (*pl*) *interj* an exclamation of surprise.

heavenly *adj* of or relating to heaven or heavens; divine; (*inf*) excellent, delightful.—**heavenliness** *n*.

heavy *adj* (**heavier, heaviest**) hard to lift or carry; of more than the usual, expected, or defined weight; to an unusual extent; hard to do; stodgy, hard to digest; cloudy; (*industry*) using massive machinery to produce basic materials, as chemicals and steel; (*ground*) difficult to make fast progress on; clumsy; dull, serious. * *n* (*pl* **heavies**) (*theatre*) a villain; (*sl*) a person hired to threaten violence, a thug.—**heavily** *adv*.—**heaviness** *n*.

heavy duty *adj* made to withstand heavy strain or rough usage.

heavy-handed *adj* clumsy; tactless; oppressive.—**heavy-handedly** *adv*.—**heavy-handedness** *n*.

heavy metal *n* a type of rock music characterized by a heavy beat and reliance on loudly amplified instruments.

heavy spar *see* **barium sulphate**.

heavy water *n* deuterium oxide, water in which the normal hydrogen content has been replaced by deuterium.

heavyweight *n* a professional boxer weighing more than 175 pounds (79 kg) or wrestler weighing over 209 pounds (95 kg); (*inf*) a very influential or important individual.

hebdomad *n* (*formerly*) seven; a group of seven; a week.

hebdomadal *adj* weekly.—**hebdomadally** *adv*.

Hebe *n* (*Greek myth*) the goddess of youth.

hebetate *vti* to make or become dull. * *adj* (*plant*) having a blunt or soft point.—**hebetation** *n*.

hebetude *n* mental dullness or lethargy.—**hebetudinous** *adj*.

Hebraic, Hebraical *adj* of or pertaining to the Hebrews, Jewish language or literature.—**Hebraically** *adv*.

Hebraism *n* a linguistic usage, custom or idiom borrowed from and characteristic of the Hebrew language, or to the Jewish people or culture.

Hebraist *n* one who studies or is learned in the Hebrew language and culture.—**Hebraistic, Hebraistical** *adj*.—**Hebraistically** *adv*.

Hebrew *n* a member of an ancient Semitic people; an Israelite; a Jew; the ancient Semitic language of the Hebrews; its modern form. * *adj* pertaining to the Hebrew people; Jewish.

Hecate *n* (*Greek myth*) a goddess of the underworld.

hecatomb *n* in ancient Greece, the ritual sacrifice of 100 oxen; any large sacrifice or slaughter.

heck *interj* an expression of surprise or grief.

heckle *vti* to harass (a speaker) with questions or taunts.—**heckler** *n*.

hect-, hecto- *prefix* hundred.

hectare *n* a metric measure of area, equivalent to 10,000 square metres (2.47 acres).

hectic *adj* involving intense excitement or activity.—**hectically** *adv*.

hectogram *n* a metric unit of mass equivalent to 100 grams (3.527 ounces).

hectograph *n* a process for copying a manuscript by transferring it onto a layer of gelatin coated with glycerin; the machine that uses this process. * *vt* to copy in this way.—**hectographic** *adj*.—**hectographically** *adv*.

hector *vt* to bully; to annoy. * *n* a bully.

he'd = he had, he would.

hedge *n* a fence consisting of a dense line of bushes or small trees; a barrier or means of protection against something, esp financial loss; an evasive or noncommittal answer or statement. * *vt* to surround or enclose with a hedge; to place secondary bets as a precaution. * *vi* to avoid giving a direct answer in an argument or debate.—**hedger** *n*.—**hedgy** *adj*.

hedgehog *n* a small insectivorous mammal with sharp spines on the back.

hedgerow *n* a line of shrubs or trees separating or enclosing fields.

hedonism *n* the doctrine that personal pleasure is the chief good.—**hedonistic** *adj*.—**hedonist** *n*.

heebie-jeebies *npl* (*sl*) nervousness, jitters.

heed *vt* to pay close attention (to). * *n* careful attention.—**heeder** *n*.

heedful *adj* paying attention; mindful.—**heedfully** *adv*.—**heedfulness** *n*.

heedless *adj* inattentive; thoughtless.—**heedlessly** *adv*.—**heedlessness** *n*.

heehaw *n* (an imitation of) the bray of a donkey, a crude laugh. * *vi* to bray like a donkey.

heel[1] *n* the back part of the foot, under the ankle; the part covering or supporting the heel in stockings, socks, etc, or shoes; a solid attachment forming the back of the sole of a shoe; (*inf*) a despicable person. * *vt* to furnish with a heel; to follow closely; (*inf*) to provide with money, etc. * *vi* to follow along at the heels of someone.—**heelless** *adj*.

heel[2] *vti* to tilt or become tilted to one side, as a ship.

heelball *n* a black, waxy substance used to blacken the heels and soles of shoes; a waxy substance used in brass rubbing.

heeler *n* a person who works for a local political organization, esp a ward heeler; (*Austral*) a dog that herds cattle by snapping at their heels.

heeltap *n* a small layer of leather in the heel of a shoe; the dregs of an alcoholic drink left at the bottom of a glass.

heft *vt* to asses the weight of an object by holding it in the hand; to lift; to become used to. * *n* weight; the main part.

hefty *adj* (**heftier, heftiest**) (*inf*) heavy; large and strong; big.—**heftily** *adv*.—**heftiness** *n*.

Hegelian *adj* relating to or pertaining to the German philosopher Georg Hegel (1770–1831) or his theories.—**Hegelianism** *n*.

hegemony *n* (*pl* **hegemonies**) leadership, domination, esp of one nation over others.—**hegemonic** *adj*.

Hegira *n* the flight of Mohammed from Mecca in AD 622, marking the start of the Muslim era.—*also* **Hejira**.

heifer *n* a young cow that has not calved.

height *n* the topmost point; the highest limit; the distance from the bottom to the top; altitude; a relatively great distance above a given level; an eminence; a hill.

heighten *vti* to make or come higher or more intense.—**heightener** *n*.

heinous *adj* outrageously evil; wicked.—**heinously** *adj*.—**heinousness** *n*.

heir *n* a person who inherits or is entitled to inherit another's property, title, etc.—**heirless** *adj*.

heirdom *n* succession by right of blood; inheritance.

heiress *n* a woman or girl who is an heir, esp to great wealth.

heirloom *n* any possession handed down from generation to generation.

heist *n* (*sl*) a robbery. * *vt* (*sl*) to steal.—**heister** *n*.

Hejira *see* **Hegira**.

held *see* **hold**[1].

heliacal *adj* emerging from or passing into the light of the sun.

helianthus *n* any of a genus of plants with large yellow flowers, including the sunflower and Jerusalem artichoke.

helical *adj* like a helix, spiral.—**helically** *adv*.

helicoid *adj* resembling a flattened spiral. * *n*. a spirally curved geometrical figure.

helicopter *n* a kind of aircraft lifted and moved, or kept hovering, by large rotary blades mounted horizontally.

heliculture *n* the rearing of snails for food.

helio- *prefix* sun.

heliocentric *adj* having the sun as the centre; measured or viewed from the sun's centre.—**heliocentrically** *adv*.—**heliocentricity, heliocentricism** *n*.

heliochrome *n* a photograph in natural colours.

heliograph *n* a signalling device using the sun's rays reflected by a mirror.—**heliographer** *n*.—**heliographic** *adj*.—**heliography** *n*.

heliogravure *n* photogravure, the process of photo-engraving or etching.

heliolatry *n* sun worship.

heliometer *n* a refracting telescope used to measure small angular distances between celestial bodies.

heli-skiing *n* the use of helicopters to take skiers to high, uncrowded off-piste slopes.

heliostat *n* an instrument that sends signals by reflecting the light of the sun in a constant direction.

heliotrope *n* a genus of plants whose flowers follow the course of the sun; a green-hued variety of chalcedony with small red spots; a bloodstone; the bluish-pink colour of the flower heliotrope; an instrument used in geodetic surveying.—**heliotropic** *adj*

heliotropism *n* the movement of flowers or leaves towards the sun.—**heliotropic** *adj*.

heliport, helipad *n* a landing and takeoff place for a helicopter.

helium *n* a light nonflammable gaseous element.

helix *n* (*pl* **helices, helixes**) a spiral line, as a line coiled round; (*zool*) a snail or its shell; (*anat*) the folded rim of the external ear; (*archit*) a small volute on a capital.

hell *n* (*Christianity*) the place of punishment of the wicked after death; the home of devils and demons; any place or state of supreme misery or discomfort; (*inf*) a cause of this. * *interj* (*inf*) an exclamation of anger, surprise, etc.

he'll = he will.

hellbent *adj* (*inf*) rashly determined.

hellebore *n* any of a genus of mostly poisonous plants, including the Christmas rose.

Hellene, Hellenian *n* a Greek.

Hellenic *adj* of or relating to classical Greece and the Greeks; relating to classical and modern Greeks and their language. * *n* a branch of the Indo-European family of languages made up of Greek and its dialects.

Hellenism *n* the national character of the Greeks; the ideals and principles of classical Greece; the love of Greek culture and art.

Hellenist *n* a non-Greek, especially a Jew, who spoke Greek in classical times; a student of Greek culture and language.

Hellenistic *adj* relating to or characteristic of classical Greece; relating to Greeks or to Hellenism.

Hellenize *vt* to adopt classical Greek culture or customs; to use or study the Greek language.—**Hellenization** *n*.—**Hellenizer** *n*.

hellish *adj* of, pertaining to, or resembling hell; very wicked; (*inf*) very unpleasant.—**hellishly** *adv*.—**hellishness** *n*.

hello *interj* an expression of greeting. * *n* (*pl* **hellos**) the act of saying "hello."—*also* **hallo, hullo** (*pl* **hallos, hullos**).

helm[1] *n* (*naut*) the tiller or wheel used to steer a ship; any position of control or direction, authority. * *vt* to steer; to control.

helm[2] *n* (*arch*) a helmet. * *vt* to provide or cover with a helmet.

helmet *n* protective headgear worn by soldiers, policemen, divers, etc.—**helmeted** *adj*.

helminth *n* a worm, esp an intestinal one, a fluke.

helminthic *adj* pertaining to worms. * *n* a drug used to treat intestinal worms.

helminthoid *adj* worm-shaped.

helminthology *n* the study of parasitic worms

helmsman *n* (*pl* **helmsmen**) a person who steers.—**helmswoman** *nf* (*pl* **helmswomen**).

helot *n* a serf or slave; (*with cap*) in ancient Sparta, a state-owned slave.

helotry *n* slavery or serfdom; the class of slaves or serfs.

help *vt* to make things better or easier for; to aid; to assist; to remedy; to keep from; to serve or wait on. * *vi* to give aid; to be useful.—*interj* used to ask for assistance. * *n* the action of helping; aid; assistance; a remedy; a person that helps, esp a hired person.—**helper** *n*.

helpful *adj* giving help; useful.—**helpfully** *adv*.—**helpfulness** *n*.

helping *n* a single portion of food.

helpless *adj* unable to manage alone, dependent on others; weak and defenceless.—**helplessly** *adv*.—**helplessness** *n*.

helpmate, helpmeet *n* a helpful companion, esp a wife or husband.

helter-skelter *adv* in confused haste. * *adj* disorderly. * *n* a tall spiral slide usu found in an amusement park.

helve *n* the handle of a tool.

Helvetia *n* the Latin name for Switzerland.

Helvetian *adj* of or relating to Helvetia; Swiss. * *n* a native or citizen of Switzerland.

hem *n* the edge of a garment, etc, turned back and stitched or fixed. * *vt* (**hemming, hemmed**) to finish (a garment) with a hem; (*with* **in**) to enclose, confine.—**hemmer** *n*.

he-man *n* (*pl* **he-men**) (*inf*) an excessively masculine or strongly built male.

hematite *n* native ferric oxide, an important iron ore.—*also* **haematite**.

hematology *n* the branch of medicine dealing with blood and its diseases.—**hematologic, hematological** *adj*.—**hematologist** *n*.

hemi- *prefix* half; partial.

hemicycle *n* a half-circle, semicircle.—**hemicyclic** *adj*.

hemidemisemiquaver n (mus) a sixty-fourth note.

hemihedral adj (crystal) having only half the normal number of faces.

hemiplegia n paralysis of one side.—**hemiplegic** adj, n.

hemisphere n half of a sphere or globe; any of the halves (northern, southern, eastern, or western) of the earth.—**hemispheric, hemispherical** adj.—**hemispherically** adv.

hemistitch n half of a line of verse.

hemline n the bottom edge of a skirt or dress.

hemlock n a poisonous plant with small white flowers; a poison made from this plant.

hemmer n one who stitches hems; a machine for hemming.

hemoglobin n the oxygen-carrying red colouring matter of the red blood corpuscles.

hemophilia n a hereditary condition in which the blood fails to clot normally.—**hemophiliac, hemophile** n.—**hemophilic** adj.

hemorrhage n the escape of blood from a blood vessel; heavy bleeding. * vi to bleed heavily.—**hemorrhagic** adj.

hemorrhoids npl swollen or bleeding veins around the anus.—also **piles**.—**hemorrhoidal** adj.

hemp n a widely cultivated Asian herb of the mulberry family; its fibre, used to make rope, sailcloth, etc; a narcotic drug obtained from different varieties of this plant (—also **cannabis, marijuana**).—**hempen** adj.

hemstitch n an ornamental stitch.—**hemstitcher** n.

hen n the female of many birds, esp the chicken.

henbane n a poisonous, sticky, hairy plant of the nightshade family.

hence adv from here; from this time; from this reason.

henceforth, henceforward adv from now on.

henchman n (pl **henchmen**) a trusted helper or follower.

hendecagon n an eleven-sided plane figure.—**hendecagonal** adj.

hendecasyllable n a verse of eleven syllables.—**hendecasyllabic** adj.

hendiadys n the use of two connected words to express one idea, as "with might and main."

henna n a tropical plant; a reddish-brown dye extracted from its leaves used to tint the hair or skin. * vt to dye with henna.

hennery n (pl **henneries**) a poultry farm.

henotheism n the worship of one god while recognizing the existence of others.—**henotheist** n, adj.—**henotheistic** adj.

henpeck vt to nag and domineer over (one's husband).—**henpecked** adj.

henry n (pl **henries, henrys**) a unit of electrical inductance.

hent vt (arch) to seize; to grasp. * n (arch) a clutching; intention; anything that has been gasped by the mind.

hepat-, hepato- prefix liver.

hepatic adj of, like, or pertaining to the liver. * n a drug for treating the liver.

hepatitis n inflammation of the liver.

heptad n a group of seven; the number seven; an atom or element with the valency of seven.

heptagon n a polygon of seven angles and seven sides.—**heptagonal** adj.

heptahedron n (pl **heptahedrons, heptahedra**) a solid figure with seven plane faces.—**heptahedral** adj.

heptameter n a verse line of seven metrical feet.

heptarchy n (pl **heptarchies**) government by seven rulers; a state divided into seven regions each with its own ruler; the seven kingdoms of Anglo-Saxon England.

Heptateuch n (Bible) the first seven books of the Old Testament.

her pron the objective and possessive case of the personal pronoun she. * adj of or belonging to a female.

herald n a person who conveys news or messages; a forerunner, harbinger; (Middle Ages) an official at a tournament. * vt to usher in; to proclaim.

heraldic adj of a herald or heraldry.—**heraldically** adv.

heraldry n (pl **heraldries**) the study of genealogies and coats of arms; ceremony; pomp.—**heraldist** n.

herb n any seed plant whose stem withers away annually; any plant used as a medicine, seasoning, etc.

herbaceous adj of or like herbs; green and leafy.

herbage n pasturage; the succulent parts of herbs.

herbal adj of herbs. * n a book listing and describing plants with medicinal properties.

herbalist n a person who practises healing by using herbs; a person who grows or deals in herbs.

herbarium n (pl **herbariums, herbaria**) a (place or container for a) systematic collection of dried plants.—**herbarial** adj.

herb Christopher see **baneberry**.

herbicide n a substance for destroying plants.—**herbicidal** adj.

herbivore n a plant-eating animal.

herbivorous adj herb-eating; (animals) plant-eating.—**herbivorousness** n.

herby adj (**herbier, herbiest**) herb-like; rich in herbs.

herculean adj of extraordinary strength, size, or difficulty; (with cap) of or like the Roman god Hercules.

herd n a large number of animals, esp cattle, living and feeding together. * vi to assemble or move animals together. * vt to gather together and move as if a herd; to tend, as a herdsman.—**herder** n.

herdsman n (pl **herdsmen**) a person who tends a herd of animals.

here adv at or in this place; to or into this place; now; on earth.

hereabout, hereabouts adv in this area.

hereafter adv after this, in some future time or state. * n (with **the**) the future, life after death.

hereat adv (arch) because of this.

hereby adv by this means.

hereditable adj that may be inherited, heritable.—**hereditability** n.—**hereditably** adv.

hereditament n (law) property capable of being inherited.

hereditary adj descending by inheritance; transmitted to offspring.—**hereditarily** adv.—**hereditariness** n.

heredity n (pl **heredities**) the transmission of genetic material that determines physical and mental characteristics from one generation to another.

herein adv (formal) in this place, document, etc.

hereinafter adv (formerly) afterwards of this.

hereof adv of this.

heresiarch n the leader or fonder of a heretical movement or sect.

heresy n (pl **heresies**) a religious belief regarded as contrary to the orthodox doctrine of a church; any belief or opinion contrary to established or accepted theory.

heretic n a dissenter from an established belief or doctrine.—**heretical** adj.—**heretically** adv.

hereto adv (formal) to this matter, document, etc.

heretofore adv (formal) until now.

hereunder *adv* (*formal*) below.

hereupon *adv* (*formal*) on this matter, issue, etc; immediately after this.

herewith *adv* (*formal*) with this.

heriot *n* a tribute, usu cattle, paid to a feudal lord on the death of a tenant by his heir.

heritable *adj* able to be inherited, hereditable.—**heritably** *adv*.

heritage *n* something inherited at birth; anything deriving from the past or tradition; historical sites, traditions, practices, etc regarded as the valuable inheritance of contemporary society.

heritor *n* (*law*) one who inherits; a proprietor.

hermaphrodite *n* an animal or organism with both male and female reproductive organs; a plant with stamens and pistils in the same floral envelope.—**hermaphroditic** *adj*.—**hermaphroditically** *adv*.

hermaphrodite brig *n* a brig square-rigged forward and schooner-rigged aft.

hermaphroditism, hermaphrodism *n* the state of being an hermaphrodite.

hermeneutics *n sing* the science of interpretation, esp of the Bible.—**hermeneutic, hermeneutical** *adj*.—**hermeneutically** *adv*

hermetic, hermetical *adj* perfectly closed and airtight; of alchemy, magical.—**hermetically** *adv*.

hermit *n* a person who lives in complete solitude, esp for religious reasons; a recluse.—**hermitic, hermitical** *adj*.—**hermitically** *adv*.

hermitage *n* the dwelling place of a hermit; a secluded retreat.

hern *n* (*arch*) the heron.

hernia *n* (*pl* **hernias, herniae**) the protrusion of an organ, esp part of the intestine, through an opening in the wall of the cavity in which it sits; a rupture.—**hernial** *adj*.—**herniated** *adj*.

hero *n* (*pl* **heroes**) a person of exceptional bravery; a person admired for superior qualities and achievements; the central male character in a novel, play, etc.

heroic *adj* of, worthy of, or like a hero; having the qualities of a hero; daring, risky; (*poetry*) of or about heroes and their deeds, epic; (*language*) grand, high-flown. * *n* heroic verse; (*pl*) melodramatic talk or behaviour.—**heroically** *adv*.

heroic age *n* the age in which the legendary heroes of a nation, esp ancient Greece and Rome, are fabled to have lived in.

heroic couplet *n* a rhyming couplet in iambic pentameter, used in English heroic verse.

heroic verse *n* a verse form used in epic poetry, ie the hexameter in Greek and Latin poetry, the iambic pentameter in English, and the Alexandrine in French.

heroin *n* a powerfully addictive drug derived from morphine.

heroine *n* a woman with the attributes of a hero; the leading female character in a novel, film or play.

heroism *n* the qualities or conduct of a hero; bravery.

heron *n* a slim wading bird with long legs and neck.

heronry *n* (*pl* **heronries**) a heron rookery; a breeding place for herons.

herpes *n* any of several virus diseases marked by small blisters on the skin or mucous membranes.—**herpetic** *adj*.

herpetology *n* the study of snakes and amphibians.—**herpetologist** *n*.

Herr *n* (*pl* **Herren**) a title, the German equivalent of Mister or Sir.

herring *n* (*pl* **herrings, herring**) a small food fish of commercial importance.

herringbone *n* a kind of cross-stitch; a zigzag pattern used in brickwork; (*skiing*) a method of walking uphill with the skis pointing outwards. * *vt* to work in cross-stitch; to decorate with a herringbone pattern. * *vi* to ascend a ski slope in herringbone fashion.

hers *pron* something or someone belonging to her.

herself *pron* the reflexive form of **she** or **her**.

hertz *n* (*pl* **hertz**) the unit of frequency equal to one cycle per second.

he's = he is; he has.

Hesiodic *adj* pertaining to or in the style of Hesiod, a Greek didactic poet of the 8th century BC.

hesitancy *n* (*pl* **hesitancies**) an act of hesitating; the state of being hesitant; indecision.

hesitant *adj* hesitating; indecisive; reluctant; shy.—**hesitantly** *adv*.

hesitate *vi* to be slow in acting due to uncertainty or indecision; to be reluctant (to); to falter or stammer when speaking.—**hesitater** *n*.—**hesitatingly** *adv*.

hesitation *n* the act of hesitating; a pause in speech.

Hesperian *adj* of or relating to the Hesperides; western. * *n* a native or inhabitant of a western land.

Hesperides *n* (*Greek myth*) (*pl*) the nymphs who guarded the golden apples given by Gaia to Hera on her marriage to Zeus; (*sing*) the garden containing the golden apples.

Hesperus *n* the evening star, esp Venus.

Hessian *adj* pertaining to the German state of Hesse. * *n* a native or inhabitant of Hesse; a mercenary soldier.

hessian *n* a coarse cloth made of jute.

hest *n* (*arch*) a behest; a command.

hetaera, hetaira *n* (*pl* **hetaerae, hetaeras, hetairai**) a female prostitute or courtesan, esp in ancient Greece.—**hetaeric, hetairic** *adj*.

heter-, hetero- *prefix* another; abnormal; different, other; unequal.

heterocercal *adj* (*fish*) having the upper lobe of the tail longer than the lower lobe.

heterochromatic *adj* of different colours.

heteroclite *n* an irregularly inflected or unusual word; an unusual person or thing. * *adj* irregular; deviating from the ordinary (—*also* **heteroclitic**).

heterodox *adj* contrary to established beliefs or opinions; unorthodox; heterical.

heterodoxy *n* (*pl* **heterodoxies**) the state of being heterodox; an unorthodox doctrine or opinion; heresy.

heterodyne *vt* to impose (a radio frequency wave) on a transmitting wave to produce pulsations of audible frequency. * *adj* having or produced by combining waves of different lengths.

heterogamous *adj* (*bot*) bearing two kinds of flowers that differ sexually.

heterogeneous *adj* opposite or dissimilar in character, quality structure, etc; not homogeneous; disparate.—**heterogeneity** *n*.—**heterogeneously** *adv*.

heterogenesis *n* the production by certain organisms of offspring differing in structure and habit from the parent, but reverting in subsequent generations to the original type.—**heterogenetic** *adj*.

heterogenous *adj* (*biol*) originating outside the body; foreign.—**heterogeny** *n*.

heterologous *adj* (*biol*) abnormal in type or structure; derived from a different species; consisting of the same elements in varying proportions.—**heterology** *n*.

heteromorphism *n* (*biol*) deviation from the natural form or structure.—**heteromorphic** *adj*.

heteronomous *adj* differing from the normal type; subject to external law, rule or authority.—**heteronomously** *adv*.

heteronym *n* a word spelled in the same way as another or others but having a different meaning, as *brake* (in a vehicle) and *brake* (fern).—**heteronymous** *adj*.

heterophyllous *adj* (*plants*) having leaves of different forms on the same stem.—**heterophylly** *n*.

heterosexual *adj* sexually attracted to the opposite sex. * *n* a heterosexual person.—**heterosexuality** *n*.—**heterosexually** *adv*.

hetman *n* (*pl* **hetmen**) (*formerly*) a Cossack prince or general.

het-up *adj* (*inf*) agitated, annoyed.

heulandite *n* a vitreous transparent brittle mineral.

heuristic *adj* assisting or leading to discovery or invention.—**heuristically** *adv*.

hew *vb* (**hewing, hewed**, *pp* **hewed, hewn**) *vt* to strike or cut with blows using an axe, etc; to shape with such blows. * *vi* to conform (to a rule, principle, etc).—**hewer** *n*.

hex *vt* to bewitch; to bring bad luck. * *n* a magic spell; a curse; a witch.

hex-, hexa- *prefix* six.

hexachord *n* (*mus*) a diatonic series of six notes with a semitone between third and fourth.

hexad *n* a group or series of six; the number or sum of six; a chemical element, atom, or radical that can be combined with, or replaced by, six atoms of hydrogen.—**hexadic** *adj*.

hexagon *n* a polygon having six sides and six angles.—**hexagonal** *adj*.—**hexagonally** *adv*.

hexagram *n* a plane figure having six angles and six sides; a six-pointed star formed by two intersecting triangles; a group of six lines which may be combined into 64 different patterns in I Ching.

hexahedron *n* a solid bounded by six plane faces.—**hexahedral** *adj*

hexameter *n* a line of Greek or Latin verse consisting of six feet the last usually being a spondee; a verse line consisting of six metric feet.—**hexametric, hexametrical** *adj*.

hexapod *n* any of a large class of anthropods; an animal with six legs; an insect. * *adj* having six legs (—*also* **hexapodous**).

Hexateuch *n* (*Bible*) the first six books of the Old Testament.

hey *interj* an expression of joy, surprise or to call attention.

heyday *n* a period of greatest success, happiness, etc.

HF *abbr* = high frequency.

Hf (*chem symbol*) = hafnium.

Hg (*chem symbol*) = mercury.

HGV *abbr* = heavy goods vehicle.

hi *interj* an exclamation of greeting.

hiatus *n* (*pl* **hiatuses, hiatus**) a break in continuity; a lacuna; (*med*) an aperture; (*phonetics*) the concurrence of two vowels in two successive syllables.—**hiatal** *adj*.

hibernaculum *n* (*pl* **hibernacula**) the winter quarters of a hibernating animal; the bud-scales of a winter bud.

hibernal *adj* of or happening in winter; wintry.

hibernate *vi* to spend the winter in a dormant condition like deep sleep; to be inactive.—**hibernation** *n*.—**hibernator** *n*.

Hibernian *adj* relating to Ireland. * *n* a native or inhabitant of Ireland.

hibiscus *n* any plant of a tropical or subtropical genus of plants with large showy flowers.

hiccup, hiccough *n* a sudden involuntary spasm of the diaphragm followed by inhalation and closure of the glottis producing a characteristic sound; (*inf*) a minor setback. * *vt* (**hiccuping, hiccuped** *or* **hiccupping, hiccupped**) to have hiccups.

hic jacet *n* (*Latin* here lies) an inscription on tombstones.

hick *n* (*inf*) an unsophisticated person, esp from a rural area.

hickory *n* (*pl* **hickories**) a North American tree of the walnut family; its wood; its smooth-shelled edible nut.

hid *see* **hide**[1].

hidalgo *n* (*pl* **hidalgoes**) a low-ranking Spanish nobleman.

hidden *adj* concealed or obscured.

hide[1] *vb* (**hiding, hid**, *pp* **hidden, hid**) *vt* to conceal, put out of sight; to keep secret; to screen or obscure from view. * *vi* to conceal oneself. * *n* a camouflaged place of concealment used by hunters, bird-watchers, etc.—**hider** *n*.

hide[2] *n* the raw or dressed skin of an animal; (*inf*) the human skin.

hide[3] *n* an ancient English measure of land.

hide-and-seek *n* a children's game in which one player must find the others, who have hidden themselves.

hidebound *adj* obstinately conservative and narrow-minded; (*animals*) having a tight or contracted hide that impedes movement; (*trees*) having a tight bark that restricts growth.

hideous *adj* visually repulsive; horrifying.—**hideously** *adv*.—**hideousness** *n*.

hiding[1] *n* (*inf*) a thrashing, a beating.

hiding[2] *n* concealment.

hiding place *n* a place of concealment.

hidrosis *n* perspiration; any skin disease affecting the sweat glands.

hidrotic *adj* of or promoting perspiration. * *n* a drug that stimulates sweating.

hie *vti* (**hieing** *or* **hying, hied**) (*poet*) to speed; to hasten.

hier-, hiero- *prefix* sacred.

hierarch *n* the chief ruler of an ecclesiastical body; a person at a high level of hierarchy.

hierarchism *n* hierarchical principles; government by a hierarchy.—**hierarchist** *n*.

hierarchy *n* (*pl* **hierarchies**) a group of persons or things arranged in order of rank, grade, etc.—**hierarchical, hierarchic** *adj*.—**hierarchically** *adv*.

hieratic *adj* of or relating to priests; sacred; consecrated; of or relating to a cursive form of hieroglyphics used by priests in ancient Egypt. * *n* the Egyptian hieratic script.—**hieratically** *adv*.

hierocracy *n* (*pl* **hierocrocies**) government by priests or ecclesiastics.

hieroglyph *n* a character used in a system of hieroglyphic writing.

hieroglyphic *n* a sacred character or symbol; (*pl*) the picture writings of the ancient Egyptians and others. * *adj* pertaining to hieroglyphs; emblematic.—**hieroglyphically** *adv*.

hierology (*pl* **hierologies**) the sacred literature of people; a biography of a saint.

hierophant *n* in ancient Greece, a priest who initiated novices into the sacred mysteries; a person who explains arcane mysteries.

hifalutin *see* **highfalutin**.

hi-fi *n* (*inf*) high fidelity; equipment for reproducing high quality musical sound.

higgle *vi* to dispute over trifling matters; to haggle.

higgledy-piggledy *adj, adv* (*inf*) in confusion; jumbled up.

high *adj* lofty, tall; extending upward a (specified) distance; situated at or done from a height; above others in rank, position, etc; greater in size, amount, cost, etc than usual; raised or acute in pitch; (*meat*) slightly bad; (*inf*) intoxicated; (*inf*) under the influence of drugs. * *adv* in or to a high degree, rank, etc. * *n* a high level, place, etc; an area of high barometric pressure; (*inf*) a euphoric condition induced by alcohol or drugs.

high and dry *adj* helpless; stranded; (*ship*) out of the water.

high and mighty *adj* (*inf*) arrogant.

highball *n* a cool drink with spirits, soda, etc, served in a tall glass.

highborn *adj* of noble birth.

highboy *n* (*US*) a chest of drawers on legs; a tallboy.

highbrow *n* (*inf*) an intellectual. * *adj* (*inf*) interested in things requiring learning.

High Church *n* the part of the Anglican Church that attaches great importance to the authority of the Church, its sacraments and priesthood.—**High-Church** *adj*.

high-class *adj* of good quality; of or appropriate to the upper social classes.

higher *adj* more high. * *adv* in or to a higher position.

higher education *n* education at college or university level.

higher-up *n* (*inf*) a person of higher rank.

high explosive *n* a very powerful chemical explosive, such as gelignite.

highfalutin, highfaluting *adj* (*inf*) pretentious; pompous.—*also* **hifalutin**.

high fidelity *n* the high quality reproduction of sound.

high-five *n* a form of greeting or congratulation when the hands of two people are joined, palms together, above their heads.

high-flown *adj* extravagantly ambitious; bombastic.

high-flyer, high-flier *n* an ambitious person; a person of great ability in any profession.—**high-flying** *adj*.

high frequency *n* any radio frequency between 3 and 30 megahertz.

high-handed *adj* overbearing, arbitrary.—**high-handedly** *adv*.—**high-handedness** *n*.

high-hat *vti* (**high-hatting, high-hatted**) to affect superiority; to treat patronizingly. * *n* a person who behaves in this way.

highjack, highjacker *see* **hijack**.

high jinks *npl* (*inf*) mischievous sport or tricks.

high jump *n* an athletic event in which a competitor jumps over a high bar; (*inf*) (*with* **the**) a severe reprimand.

highland *adj* of or in mountains. * *n* a region with many hills or mountains; (*pl*) mountainous country; (*with cap*) the mountainous region occupying most of northern Scotland.

highlander *n* a person who lives in a highland area; (*with cap*) an inhabitant of the Scottish Highlands.

Highland fling *n* a lively Scottish dance by one person.

highlife *n* (*W Africa*) a style of jazz music combining American and African elements.

high life *n* fashionable society; its manner of living.—**high-life** *adj*.

highlight *n* the lightest area of a painting, etc; the most interesting or important feature; (*pl*) a lightening of areas of the hair using a bleaching agent. * *vt* to bring to special attention; to give highlights to.

highly *adv* highly, very much; favourably; at a high level, wage, rank, etc.

highly strung *adj* nervous and tense; excitable; highstrung.

High Mass *n* (*RC Church*) a ceremonial mass, usu at the high altar, at which a deacon or subdeacon assist the celebrant.

high-minded *adj* having high ideals, etc.—**high-mindedness** *n*.

highness *n* the state or quality of being high; (*with cap and poss pron*) a title used in speaking to or of royalty.

high-pitched *adj* (*sound*) shrill; (*roof*) steep.

high-powered, high-power *adj* (*lens, etc*) producing great magnification; energetic; powerful; highly competent.

high priest *n* a chief priest, esp the principal priest of the Jewish hierarchy; an unofficial leader of fashion, etc.

high-rise *adj* (*building*) having multiple storeys.* *n* a building of this kind.

highroad *n* a chief road, a highway; an easy course or method.

high roller *n* a gambler; an extravagant person; a leader of fashion.—**high rolling** *adj, n*.

high school *n* a secondary school.

high seas *npl* open ocean waters outside the territorial limits of any nation.

high season *n* the busiest time of the year for a holiday resort, etc.

high-sounding *adj* imposing, pompous.

high-spirited *adj* courageous; lively.—**high-spiritedness** *n*.

high-strung *adj* strung to a high pitch; extremely sensitive; highly strung.

hightail *vi* to leave in a great rush.

high tide *n* the tide at its highest level; the time of this; an acme.

high time *adv* (*inf*) fully time. * *n* an especially good or enjoyable time.

high treason *n* treason against the ruler or state.

high-up *n* (*inf*) a person of high status or position.

high water *n* high tide.—**highwater** *adj*.

highwater mark *n* the highest point reached by a high tide; any maximum.

highway *n* a public road; a main thoroughfare.

highwayman *n* (*pl* **highwaymen**) one who robs travellers on a highway.

high wire *n* a high tightrope.

hijack *vt* to steal (goods in transit) by force; to force (an aircraft) to make an unscheduled flight. * *n* an act of hijacking.—*also* **highjack**.—**hijacker, highjacker** *n*.

hike *vi* to take a long walk. * *vt* (*inf*) to pull up, to increase. * *n* a long walk; a tramp.—**hiker** *n*.

hilarious *adj* highly amusing.—**hilariously** *adv*.—**hilariousness** *n*.—**hilarity** *n*.

hilarity *n* mirth; merriment; cheerfulness.

hill *n* a natural rise of land lower than a mountain; a heap or mound; an slope in a road, etc. *vt* to bank up; to draw earth around (plants) in mounds.

hillbilly *n* (*pl* **hillbillies**) (*inf*) a person from the mountainous areas of southeastern US; country music.—*also adj.*

hillock *n* a small hill.—**hillocked, hillocky** *adj.*

hilly *adj* (**hillier, hilliest**) abounding with or characterized by hills; rugged.—**hilliness** *n.*

hilt *n* the handle of a sword, dagger, tool, etc.

hilum *n* (*pl* **hila**) a scar on the surface of a seed indicating where it was attached to the seed grain; the nucleus of a starch grain.

him *pron* the objective case of **he.**

himation *n* (*pl* **himatia**) in ancient Greece, a square-shaped cloak draped around the body.

himself *pron the reflexive* (he killed himself) *or emphatic* (he himself was lucky) *form of* **he, him.**

Himyaritic *n* an extinct language of the Semitic family of the Afro-Asian family; an Arabian dialect. * *adj* of or relating to the Hymarite people of Arabia or their language.

hind[1] *adj* (**hinder, hindmost** *or* **hindermost**) situated at the back; rear.

hind[2] *n* (*pl* **hinds, hind**) a female deer.

hinder *vt* to obstruct, delay or impede. * *vi* to impose instructions or impediments. * *adj* belonging to or constituting the back or rear of anything.—**hinderer** *n.*

Hindi *n* the official language of India; a group of dialects of northern India.

hindmost, hindermost *adj* farthest behind.

hindquarters *npl* the hind legs and accompanying parts of a quadruped.

hindrance *n* the act of hindering; an obstacle, impediment.

hindsight *n* understanding an event after it has occurred.

Hindu *n* (*pl* **Hindus**) any of several peoples of India; a follower of Hinduism.

Hinduism *n* the dominant religion of India, characterized by an emphasis on religious law, a caste system and belief in reincarnation.

hinge *n* a joint or flexible part on which a door, lid, etc turns; a natural joint, as of a clam; a small piece of gummed paper for sticking stamps in an album. * *vti* to attach or hang by a hinge; to depend.

hinny *n* (*pl* **hinnies**) the sterile offspring of a male horse and a female donkey or ass. * *vi* to neigh.

hint *n* an indirect or subtle suggestion; a slight mention; a little piece of practical or helpful advice. * *vt* to suggest or indicate indirectly. * *vi* to give a hint.—**hinter** *n.*

hinterland *n* the land behind that bordering a coast or river; a remote area.

hip[1] *n* either side of the body below the waist and above the thigh.

hip[2] *n* the fruit of the wild rose.

hip[3] *interj* used as part of a cheer (*hip, hip, hurrah*).

hip[4] *adj* (*sl*) stylish, up-to-date.

hippie, hippy *n* (*pl* **hippies**) (*sl*) a person who adopts an alternative lifestyle, eg involving mysticism, psychedelic drugs, or communal living, to express alienation from conventional society.

hippo *n* (*pl* **hippos**) (*inf*) a hippopotamus.

hippocras *n* an old English cordial of spiced wine.

Hippocratic oath *n* an oath taken by a doctor to observe the code of medical ethics derived from Hippocrates, a Greek physician of the 5th century BC.

hippodrome *n* a dance hall, music hall, etc; in ancient Greece, a stadium for horse and chariot races.

hippogriff *n* (*Greek myth*) a monster with a griffin's head, wings and claws, and the body of a horse.

hippopotamus *n* (*pl* **hippopotamuses, hippopotami**) a large African water-loving mammal with thick dark skin, short legs, and a very large head and muzzle.

hircine *adj* of or resembling a goat; smelling like a goat.

hire *vt* to pay for the services of (a person) or the use of (a thing). * *n* the payment for the temporary use of anything; the fact or state of being hired.—**hirable, hireable** *adj.*—**hirer** *n.*

hireling *n* a person who works only for money, esp for doing something unpleasant.

hire-purchase *n* a system by which a person takes possession of an article after paying a deposit and then becomes the owner only after payment of a series of instalments is completed.

hirsute *adj* covered in hair; of or pertaining to hair.—**hirsuteness** *n.*

his *poss pron* of or belonging to *him*.—*also adj.*

Hispanic *adj* of or derived from Spain, Spanish or Spanish-speaking countries. * *n* a person of Hispanic descent, esp in the US.

Hispanicism *n* a word or expression borrowed from Spanish.

hispid *adj* bristly; covered with stiff hairs.—**hispidity** *n.*

hiss *vi* to make a sound resembling a prolonged *s*; to show disapproval by hissing. * *vt* to say or indicate by hissing. * *n* the act or sound of hissing.—**hisser** *n.*

hist. *abbr* = history; historian; historical.

hist-, histo- *prefix* tissue.

histamine *n* a substance released by the tissues in allergic reactions, acting as an irritant.—**histaminic** *adj.*

histogenesis *n* the formation of organic tissue.—**histogenetic** *adj.*—**histogenetically** *adv.*

histogram *n* a statistical diagram representing frequency distribution in terms of columns.

histology *n* the study of the microscopic structure of animal and plant tissues.—**histologic, histological** *adj.*—**histologically** *adv.*—**histologist** *n.*

historian *n* a person who writes or studies history.

historic *adj* (potentially) important or famous in history.

historical *adj* belonging to or involving history or historical methods; concerning actual events as opposed to myth or legend; based on history.—**historically** *adv.*—**historicalness** *n.*

historicity *n* historical authenticity; genuineness.

historiography *n* the principles of historical writing, esp that based on the use of primary sources and techniques of research; the study of methods of historical research and writing.—**historiographic, historiographical** *adj.*—**historiographically** *adv.*

historiographer *n* a writer of history, esp an official historian.

history *n* (*pl* **histories**) a record or account of past events; the study and analysis of past events; past events in total; the past events or experiences of a specific person or thing; an unusual or significant past.

histrionic, histrionical *adj* of actors or the theatre; melodramatic.—**histrionically** *adv.*

histrionics *n* (*used as sing or pl*) the art of theatrical representation; melodramatic behaviour or tantrums to attract attention.

hit *vti* (**hitting, hit**) to come against (something) with force; to give a blow (to), to strike; to strike with a missile; to affect strongly; to arrive at; (*with on*) to discover by accident or unexpectedly. * *n* a blow that strikes its mark; a collision; a successful and popular song, book, etc; (*inf*) an underworld killing; (*sl*) a dose of a drug.

hit-and-run *n* a motor vehicle accident in which the driver leaves the scene without stopping or informing the authorities.

hitch *vt* to move, pull, etc with jerks; to fasten with a hook, knot, etc; to obtain a ride by hitchhiking. * *vi* to hitchhike. * *n* a tug; a hindrance, obstruction; a kind of knot used for temporary fastening; (*inf*) a ride obtained from hitchhiking.—**hitcher** *n*.

hitchhike *vt* to travel by asking for free lifts from motorists along the way.—**hitchhiker** *n*.

hither *adv* (*formal*) to or towards this place.

hitherto *adv* (*formal*) until this time.

hit list *n* (*sl*) a list of people to be eliminated, etc.

hit man *n* a hired assassin.

Hittite *n* a member of an ancient people of Asia Minor; the language of these people. * *adj* of or pertaining to the Hittite people or their language or inscriptions.

HIV *abbr* = human immunodeficiency virus, the virus that causes Aids.

hive *n* a shelter for a colony of bees; a beehive; the bees of a hive; a crowd of busy people; a place of great activity. * *vt* to gather (bees) into a hive. * *vi* to enter a hive; (*with* **off**) to separate from a group.

hives *n* (*used as sing or pl*) a rash on the skin often caused by an allergy; nettle rash.

hiya *interj* an exclamation of greeting.

HM *abbr* = Her (or His) Majesty('s).

HMS *abbr* = Her (or His) Majesty's Ship.

Ho (*chem symbol*) = holmium.

ho *interj* an exclamation used to attract attention.

hoard *n* an accumulation of food, money, etc, stored away for future use. * *vti* to accumulate and store away.—**hoarder** *n*.

hoarding *n* a temporary screen of boards erected around a construction site; a billboard.

hoarfrost *n* a covering of minute ice crystals.—*also* **white frost**.

hoarse *adj* (*voice*) rough, as from a cold; (*person*) having a hoarse voice.—**hoarsely** *adv*.—**hoarseness** *n*.

hoary *adj* (**hoarier, hoariest**) white or grey with age; having whitish or greyish hairs; (*joke, etc*) ancient, hackneyed.—**hoarily** *adv*.

hoax *n* a deception; a practical joke. * *vt* to deceive by a hoax.—**hoaxer** *n*.

hob *n* a ledge near a fireplace for keeping kettles, etc hot; a flat surface on a cooker incorporating hot plates or burners.

hobble *vi* to walk unsteadily, to limp. * *vt* to fasten the legs of (horses, etc) loosely together to prevent straying. * *n* a limp; a rope, etc, used to hobble a horse.—**hobbler** *n*.

hobbledehoy *n* (*arch*) (*pl* **hobbledehoys**) an inexperienced and awkward young person.

hobby *n* (*pl* **hobbies**) a spare-time activity carried out for personal amusement; (*arch*) a hobbyhorse.—**hobbyist** *n*.

hobbyhorse *n* a child's toy comprising a stick with a horse's head; a rocking horse; a favourite topic for discussion.

hobgoblin *n* a mischievous goblin.

hobnail *n* a short nail with a wide head, used on the soles of heavy shoes.—**hobnailed** *adj*.

hobnob *vi* (**hobnobbing, hobnobbed**) to spend time with in a friendly manner.

hobo *n* (*pl* **hoboes, hobos**) a migrant labourer; a tramp.—**hoboism** *n*.

hock¹ *vt* (*sl*) to give something in security for a loan.—**hocker** *n*.

hock² *n* the joint bending backward on the hind leg of a horse, etc.

hock³ *n* a variety of German white wine.

hockey *n* an outdoor game played by two teams of 11 players with a ball and clubs curved at one end (—*also* **field hockey**); ice hockey.

hockshop *n* (*inf*) a pawnshop.

hocus *vt* (**hocusses, hocussing, hocussed** *or* **hocuses, hocusing, hocused**) to cheat or trick; to dupe; to doctor alcohol in order to stupefy a person so as to cheat him or her; to stupefy with a drug. * *n* a trick; drugged alcohol.

hocus-pocus *n* meaningless words used by a conjurer; sleight of hand; deception. * *vti* (**hocus-pocuses, hocus-pocusing, hocus-pocused** *or* **hocus-pocusses, hocus-pocussing, hocus-pocussed**) to play tricks (on).

hod *n* a trough on a pole for carrying bricks or mortar on the shoulder; a coal scuttle.

hodgepodge *n* a jumble.

hoe *n* a long-handled tool for weeding, loosening the earth, etc. * *vti* (**hoeing, hoed**) to dig, weed, till, etc, with a hoe.

hog *n* a domesticated male pig raised for its meat; (*inf*) a selfish, greedy, or filthy person. * *vt* (**hogging, hogged**) to take more than one's due; to hoard greedily.

hogfish *n* (*pl* **hogfish, hogfishes**) a fish with a bristled head of warm Atlantic waters; the wrasse.

Hogmanay *n* (*Scot*) New Year's Eve.

hogshead *n* a large cask or barrel; one of several measures of liquid capacity, esp one of 63 gallons (238.5 litres).

hogwash *n* swill fed to pigs; rubbishy or nonsensical writing or speech.

hoi polloi *n* (*often derog*) the common people; the masses.

hoist *vt* to raise aloft, esp with a pulley, crane, etc. * *n* a hoisting; an apparatus for lifting to a higher flower; a lift, elevator.—**hoister** *n*.

hoity-toity *adj* arrogant or haughty. * *interj* an exclamation of surprise.

hokey-pokey *n* hocus-pocus; a cheap ice cream sold in slabs.

hol-, holo- *prefix* whole.

hold¹ *vb* (**holding, held**) *vt* to take and keep in one's possession; to grasp; to maintain in a certain position or condition; to retain; to contain; to own, to occupy; to support, sustain; to remain firm; to carry on, as a meeting; to regard; to believe, to consider; to bear or carry oneself; (*with* **back**) to withhold; to restrain; (*with* **down**) to restrain; (*inf*) to manage to retain one's job, etc; (*with* **forth**) to offer (eg an inducement); (*with* **off**) to keep apart; (*with* **up**) to delay; to hinder; to commit an armed robbery. * *vi* to go on being firm, loyal, etc; to remain unbroken or unyielding; to be true or valid; to continue; (*with* **back**) to refrain; (*with* **forth**) to speak at length; (*with* **off**) to wait, to refrain; (*with* **on**) to maintain a grip on; to persist; (*inf*) to keep a telephone line open. * *n* the act or manner of holding; grip; a dominating force on a person.—**holdable** *adj*.—**holder** *n*.

hold² *n* the storage space in a ship or aircraft used for cargo.

holdall *n* a portable container for miscellaneous articles.—*also* **carryall**.

holder *n* one who holds; a device for holding things; a person who has control of something; one who is in possession of a financial document.

holdfast *n* a hook or clamp; the act of gripping strongly; the organ by which seaweed and related plants attach themselves to a host object.

holding *n* (*often pl*) legally held property, esp land, stocks, and bonds.

hold-up *n* a delay; an armed robbery.

hole *n* a hollow place; a cavity; a pit; an animal's burrow; an aperture; a perforation; a small, squalid, dingy place; (*inf*) a difficult situation; (*golf*) a small cavity into which the ball is hit; the tee, the fairway, etc leading to this. * *vti* to make a hole in (something); to drive into a hole; (*with* **up**) to hibernate; (*inf*) to hide oneself.

holey *adj* full of holes.

holiday *n* a period away from work, school, etc for travel, rest or recreation; a day of freedom from work, etc, esp one set aside by law. * *vi* to spend a holiday.—*also* **vacation**.

holiday-maker *n* a vacationer.

holily *adv* in a holy manner.

holiness *n* sanctity; (*with cap and poss pron*) the title of the Pope.

holism *n* (*philos*) the creation by creative evolution of wholes that are greater than the sum of the parts; (*med*) consideration of the whole body in the treatment of disease.—**holistic** *adj.*—**holistically** *adv.*

holland *n* an unbleached linen either glazed or unglazed used for furnishing.

hollandaise sauce *n* a rich sauce of egg yolks, lemon juice, butter, etc.

Hollands *n* a kind of Dutch gin sold in stone bottles.

hollow *adj* having a cavity within or below; recessed, concave; empty or worthless. * *n* a hole, cavity; a depression, a valley.* *vti* to make or become hollow.—**hollowly** *adv.*—**hollowness** *n.*

hollow-eyed *adj* with the eyes deep-set or sunken from tiredness, etc.

holly *n* (*pl* **hollies**) an evergreen shrub with prickly leaves and red berries.

hollyhock *n* a tall-stemmed plant with spikes of large flowers.

holmium *n* a malleable white metallic element.

holoblastic *adj* wholly germinal.

holocaust *n* a great destruction of life, esp by fire; (*with cap and* **the**) the mass extermination of European Jews by the Nazis 1939–45.—**holocaustal, holocaustic** *adj.*

hologram *n* an image made without the use of a lens on photographic film by means of interference between two parts of a laser beam, the result appearing as a meaningless pattern until suitably illuminated, when it shows as a three-dimensional image.

holograph *n* a document wholly in the handwriting of the author.

holography *n* the technique of making or using holograms.—**holographic** *adj.*—**holographically** *adv.*

holohedral *adj* showing all the planes necessary for the perfect symmetry of the crystal system.

holophrastic *adj* (*linguistics*) describing the stage in language development where most utterances are single words; having the force of a whole phrase; polysynthetic.

holothurian *n* any echinoderm of the class that contains the sea cumcumber. * *adj* of, related or belonging to the holothurians.

holpen *vb* (*arch*) a past participle of *help*.

holster *n* a leather case attached to a belt for a pistol.—**holstered** *adj.*

holt *n* an otter's den; the burrowed lair of any animal; (*poet*) a wood; a wooded hill.

holus-bolus *adv* (*inf*) at a gulp, all at once.

holy *adj* (**holier, holiest**) dedicated to religious use; without sin; deserving reverence. * *n* (*pl* **holies**) a holy place, innermost shrine.

Holy Communion *n* the celebration of the Eucharist.

Holy Ghost *n* (*Christianity*) the third person of the Trinity.

Holy Grail *n* in medieval legend, the dish or chalice that was used by Christ at the Last Supper, and the object of many knights' quests.

Holy Land *n* Palestine.

Holy Spirit *n* the Holy Spirit.

holystone *n* sandstone used by sailors to scour ships' decks. * *vt* to scrub a ship's deck with holystone.

Holy Thursday *see* **Ascension Day**.

Holy Week *n* the week before Easter Sunday.

hom-, homo- *prefix* same; like.

homage *n* a public demonstration of respect or honour towards someone or something.

hombre *n* (*sl*) a man.

homburg *n* a man's soft felt hat with a dented crown.

home *n* the place where one lives; the city, etc where one was born or reared; a place thought of as home; a household and its affairs; an institution for the aged, orphans, etc. * *adj* of one's home or country; domestic. * *adv* at, to, or in the direction of home; to the point aimed at. * *vi* (*birds*) to return home; to be guided onto a target; to head for a destination; to send or go home.

home economics *n* (*sing or pl*) the art and science of household management, nutrition, etc.

home-grown *adj* grown or produced at home or nearby; characteristic of a particular locale.

homeland *n* the country where a person was born.

homely *adj* (**homelier, homeliest**) simple, everyday; crude; not good-looking.—**homeliness** *n.*

home-made *adj* made, or as if made, at home.

homeopathy *n* the system of treating disease by small quantities of drugs that cause symptoms similar to those of the disease.—**homeopath, homeopathist** *n.*—**homeopathic** *adj.*—**homeopathically** *adv.*

homer *n* (*baseball*) a home run; a homing pigeon; (*inf*) work done on an informal basis, without declaring the earnings.

Homeric *adj* pertaining to the poet Homer, or his works; heroic.—**Homerically** *adv.*

home run *n* (*baseball*) a hit that allows the batter to touch all bases and score a run.

homesick *adj* longing for home.—**homesickness** *n.*

homespun *adj* cloth made of yarn spun at home; coarse cloth like this.

homestead *n* a farmhouse with land and buildings.—**homesteader** *n*

home stretch, home straight *n* the part of a race track between the last turn and the finish line; the final part.

home truth *n* an unpleasant fact that a person has to face about himself or herself.

homeward *adj* going towards home. * *adv* homewards.

homewards *adv* towards home.

homework *n* work, esp piecework, done at home; schoolwork to be done outside the classroom; preliminary study for a project.

homey, homeyness *see* **homy**.

homicidal *adj* characterized by homicide; likely to commit suicide.

homicide *n* the killing of a person by another; a person who kills another.—**homicidal** *adj.*—**homicidally** *adv.*

homiletic, homiletical *adj* of or relating to a homily or sermon; of or relating to homiletics.—**homiletically** *adv.*

homiletics *n sing* the art of writing or preaching sermons.

homily *n* (*pl* **homilies**) a sermon; moralizing talk or writing.—**homilist** *n.*

homing *adj* (*pigeon*) trained to fly home after being transported long distances; (*missile, etc*) designed to guide itself onto a target.

hominid *adj* of or relating to the zoological species that includes present-day man and his ancestors. * *n* a member of this species.

hominoid *adj* resembling man; of or belonging to primates.

hominy (grits) *n* ground maize boiled in water to make a thin porridge.

homo¹ *n* any member of the genus *Homo* that includes modern man.

homo² *n* (*pl* **homos**) (*inf*) a male homosexual.

homocentric *adj* concentric; having the same centre.

homogeneous *adj* composed of parts that are of identical or a similar kind or nature; of uniform structure.—**homogeneity, homogeneousness** *n.*

homogenize *vt* to break up the fat particles (in milk or cream) so they do not separate; to make or become homogeneous.—**homogenization** *n.*—**homogenizer** *n.*

homograph *n* a word spelled the same as another word but with a different meaning and derived from a different root.

homologous *adj* corresponding in relative position, structure, and descent.

homologue, homolog *n* something that exhibits homology.

homology *n* (*pl* **homologies**) a similarity often attributed to a common origin; affinity of structure.—**homological** *adj.*—**homologically** *adv.*

homonym *n* a word with the same spelling or pronunciation as another, but a different meaning.—**homonymic** *adj.*—**homonymy** *n.*

Homoousian *n* a Christian who believes that Jesus is of the same essence as God.

homophobia *n* fear and hatred of homosexuals; persecution of homosexuals.—**homophobe** *n.*—**homophobic** *adj.*

homophone *n* a letter or group of letters having the same sound as another letter or group of letters; one of a group of words with identical pronunciations but with different meanings or spellings or both.—**homophony** *n.*

homophonous *adj* alike in sound but different in meaning; relating to or denoting a homophone.

homoplastic *adj* similar in structure; derived from a donating individual of a tissue graft of the same species as the recipient.

Homo sapiens *n* the species designating mankind.

homosexual *adj* sexually attracted towards a person of the same sex. * *n* a homosexual person.—**homosexuality** *n.*—**homosexually** *adv.*

homunculus *n* (*pl* **homunculi**) a dwarf; a miniature man.

homy *adj* (**homier, homiest**) cosy, home-like.—*also* **homey**.—**hominess, homeyness** *n.*

Hon. *abbr* = Honourable.

hon. *abbr* = honorary; honourable.

hone *n* a stone for sharpening cutting tools. * *vt* to sharpen (as if) on a hone.

honest *adj* truthful; trustworthy; sincere or genuine; gained by fair means; frank, open.—**honestness** *n.*

honestly *adv* in an honest manner; really.

honesty *n* (*pl* **honesties**) the quality of being honest; a European plant with purple flowers that forms transparent seed pods.

honey *n* (*pl* **honeys**) a sweet sticky yellowish substance that bees make as food from the nectar of flowers; sweetness; its colour; (*inf*) darling. * *adj* of, resembling honey; much loved.

honeybee *n* the common bee of the genus that produces honey.

honeycomb *n* the structure of six-sided wax cells made by bees to hold their honey, eggs, etc; anything arranged like this. * *vt* to fill with holes like a honeycomb.

honeydew *n* a sugary deposit on leaves secreted by aphids; a variety of melon with yellowish skin and pale green flesh.—**honeydewed** *adj.*

honeyed, honied *adj* flattering; of, containing, or resembling honey.—**honeyedly, honiedly** *adv.*

honeymoon *n* the vacation spent together by a newly married couple.—*also vi.*—**honeymooner** *n.*

honeysuckle *n* a climbing shrub with small fragrant flowers.

hong *n* (*formerly*) in China, a factory or warehouse, or a commercial establishment owned by a foreigner.

honk *n* (a sound resembling) the call of the wild goose; the sound made by an old-fashioned motor horn. * *vti* to cry like a goose; to sound (a motor horn); (*sl*) to be sick.

honky, honkie *n* (*pl* **honkies**) (*offens*) a white person.

honky-tonk *n* a style of ragtime piano playing.

honorarium *n* (*pl* **honorariums, honoraria**) a voluntary payment for professional services for which no fees are nominally due.

honorary *adj* given as an honour; (*office*) voluntary, unpaid.

honorific *adj* conferring honour.—**honorifically** *adv.*

honour, honor *n* high regard or respect; glory; fame; good reputation; integrity; chastity; high rank; distinction; (*with cap*) the title of certain officials, as judges; cards of the highest value in certain card games. * *vt* to respect greatly; to do or give something in honour of; to accept and pay (a cheque when due, etc).—**honourer, honorer** *n.*

honourable, honorable *adj* worthy of being honoured; honest; upright; bringing honour; (*with cap*) a title of respect for certain officials, as Members of Parliament, when addressing each other.—**honourably, honorably** *adv.*

hooch *n* (*US sl*) alcoholic liquor, esp when illicitly distilled or obtained.

hood¹ *n* a loose covering to protect the head and back of the neck; any hood-like thing as the (folding) top of a car, etc; (*US*) the hinged metal covering over an automobile engine—*see* **bonnet**.

hood² *n* (*inf*) a hoodlum.

hoodlum *n* a gangster; a young hooligan.—**hoodlumism** *n*.

hoodoo *n* (*pl* **hoodoos**) voodoo; a person or thing thought to bring bad luck. * *vt* (**hoodooing, hoodooed**) to bring ill luck to.—**hoodooism** *n*.

hoodwink *vt* to mislead by trickery.—**hoodwinker** *n*.

hooey *n* nonsense; humbug. * *interj* conveying disbelief.

hoof *n* (*pl* **hoofs, hooves**) the horny covering on the ends of the feet of certain animals, as horses, cows, etc.

hook *n* a piece of bent or curved metal to catch or hold anything; a fishhook; something shaped like a hook; a strike, blow, etc, in which a curving motion is involved. * *vt* to seize, fasten, hold, as with a hook; (*rugby*) to pass the ball backwards from a scrum.

hookah *n* an oriental tobacco-pipe with a long tube connected to a container of water, which cools the smoke as it is drawn through.

hooked *adj* shaped like a hook; (*sl*) addicted.—**hookedness** *n*.

hooker *n* (*sl*) a prostitute; (*rugby football*) a player in the scrum whose task is to hook the ball.

hookworm *n* a parasitic worm with hooked mouthparts that can bore through the skin and cause disease.

hooky *n* truancy from school.

hooligan *n* a lawless young person.—**hooliganism** *n*.

hoop *n* a circular band of metal or wood; an iron band for holding together the staves of barrels; anything like this, as a child's toy or ring in a hoop skirt. * *vt* to bind (as if) with hoops.—**hooped** *adj*.

hooper *n* a cooper; the wild swan.

hoopla *n*. (*inf*) noise; bustle; (*inf*) misleading publicity.

hoopoe *n* a bird with a fanlike crest and pinky brown plumage.

hooray, hoorah *see* **hurrah**.

hoosegow *n* (*sl*) jail.

Hoosier *n* the nickname used for a native or resident of Indiana.

hoot *n* the sound that an owl makes; a similar sound, as made by a train whistle; a shout of scorn; (*inf*) laughter; (*inf*) an amusing person or thing. * *vi* to utter a hoot; to blow a whistle, etc. * *vt* to express (scorn) of (someone) by hooting.—**hooter** *n*.

hooves *see* **hoof**.

hop[1] *vi* (**hopping, hopped**) to jump up on one leg; to leap with all feet at once, as a frog, etc; (*inf*) to make a quick trip. * *n* a hopping movement; (*inf*) an informal dance; a trip, esp in an aircraft.

hop[2] *n* a climbing plant with small cone-shaped flowers; (*pl*) the dried ripe cones, used for flavouring beer.

hope *n* a feeling that what is wanted will happen; the object of this; a person or thing on which one may base some hope. * *vt* to want and expect. * *vi* to have hope (for).—**hoper** *n*.

hopeful *adj* filled with hope; inspiring hope or promise of success. * *n* a person who hopes to or looks likely to be a success.—**hopefulness** *n*.

hopefully *adv* in a hopeful manner; it is hoped.

hopeless *adj* without hope; offering no grounds for hope or promise of success; impossible to solve; (*inf*) incompetent.—**hopelessly** *adv*.—**hopelessness** *n*.

hoplite *n* in ancient Greece, a heavily armed foot soldier.

hopper *n* a hopping insect; a funnel-shaped container with an opening at the bottom from which its con-

tents can be discharged into a receptacle.

hopscotch *n* a children's game in which the players hop through a sequence of squares drawn on the ground.

horary *adj* of or pertaining to or lasting an hour; noting the hours; hourly.

Horatian *adj* of or pertaining to the Roman poet Horace (658 BC) or his works.

horde *n* a crowd or throng; a swarm.

horizon *n* the apparent line along which the earth and sky meet; the limit of a person's knowledge, interest, etc.

horizontal *adj* level; parallel to the plane of the horizon.—**horizontally** *adv*.—**horizontalness** *n*.

hormone *n* a product of living cells formed in one part of the organism and carried to another part, where it takes effect; a synthetic compound having the same purpose.—**hormonal** *adj*.

horn *n* a bony outgrowth on the head of certain animals; the hard substance of which this is made; any projection like a horn; a wind instrument, esp the French horn or trumpet; a device to sound a warning. * *vt* to wound with a horn; (*with* in) to intrude.

hornbeam *n* a tree of the birch family.

hornbill *n* a tropical bird with a horny protuberance on its large beak.

hornblende *n* a dark mineral of silica with magnesium, lime or iron.

hornbook *n* a framed child's primer made of a thin slab of wood or paper on which numbers, the alphabet and the Lord's Prayer were printed and protected with a covering of transparent horn; any elementary primer.

horned *adj* having horns.

hornet *n* a large wasp with a severe sting.

hornpipe *n* a lively dance, formerly associated with British sailors; the music for such a dance; an obsolete wind instrument.

hornswoggle *vt* to deceive; to swindle.

horny *adj* (**hornier, horniest**) like horn; hard; callous; (*sl*) sexually aroused.—**hornily** *adv*.—**horniness** *n*.

horologe *n* any instrument that tells the time; a timepiece.

horology *n* the science of measuring time; the art of making clocks, watches, etc.—**horologic, horological** *adj*.—**horologist, horologer** *n*.

horoscope *n* a chart of the zodiacal signs and positions of planets, etc, by which astrologers profess to predict future events, esp in the life of an individual.

horrendous *adj* horrific; (*inf*) disagreeable.—**horrendously** *adv*.

horrible *adj* arousing horror; (*inf*) very bad, unpleasant, etc.—**horribleness** *n*.—**horribly** *adv*.

horrid *adj* terrible; horrible.—**horridly** *adv*.—**horridness** *n*.

horrific *adj* arousing horror; horrible.—**horrifically** *adv*.

horrify *vt* (**horrifying, horrified**) to fill with horror; to shock.—**horrification** *n*.—**horrifyingly** *adv*.

horripilation *n* gooseflesh; the bristling of the skin caused by chill or fright.

horror *n* the strong feeling caused by something frightful or shocking; strong dislike; a person or thing inspiring horror. * *adj* (*film, story, etc*) designed to frighten.

hors de combat *adj* excluded from competition; unrivalled; unequalled; disabled.

hors d'oeuvre *n* (*pl* **hors d'oeuvre, hors d'oeuvres**) an appetizer served at the beginning of a meal.

horse *n* a four-legged, solid-hoofed herbivorous mammal with a flowing mane and a tail, domesticated for carrying loads or riders, etc; cavalry; a vaulting horse; a frame with legs to support something.

horsebox *n* a trailer used for transporting a horse.

horse brass *n* a decorative brass ornament attached to a horse's harness.

horse chestnut *n* a large tree with large palmate leaves and erect clusters of flowers.

horseflesh *n* horses; the flesh of a horse, esp for eating.

horsehair *n* hair from the mane or the tail of a horse, used for padding, etc.

horse latitude *n* either of two oceanic regions between 30 degrees north and 30 degrees south latitude, marked by calms.

horse laugh *n* a boisterous, usu derisive laugh.

horseleech *n* a large carnivorous leech; an insatiable person.

horseman *n* (*pl* **horsemen**) a person skilled in the riding or care of horses.—**horsemanship** *n*.

horseplay *n* rough, boisterous fun.

horsepower *n* (*pl* **horsepower**) a unit for measuring the power of engines, etc, equal to 746 watts or 33,000 foot-pounds per minute.

horseradish *n* a tall herb of the mustard family; a sauce or relish made with its pungent root.

horse sense *n* common sense.

horseshoe *n* a flat U-shaped, protective metal plate nailed to a horse's hoof; anything shaped like this.

horsetail *n* a plant with jointed stems and whorls of small dark toothlike leaves; the tail of a horse, esp when used as a symbol of rank or as a standard.

horse-trade *n* a negotiation marked by shrewd bargaining and mutual concessions.—*also vi*.

horsewhip *n* a whip with a long thong used on horses. * *vt* (**horsewhipping, horsewhipped**) to flog with a horsewhip.

horsewoman *n* (*pl* **horsewomen**) a woman skilled at riding.

horsy, horsey *adj* (**horsier, horsiest**) of or resembling a horse; preoccupied with horses, horse racing, etc.—**horsily** *adv*.—**horsiness** *n*.

hortatory, hortative *adj* exhorting; encouraging.—**hortatorily** *adv*.

horticulture *n* the art or science of growing flowers, fruits, and vegetables.—**horticultural** *adj*.—**horticulturally** *adv*.—**horticulturist** *n*.

hosanna, hosannah *interj* an exclamation of praise to God. * *n* the cry of hosanna; a shout of praise.

hose[1] *n* a flexible tube used to convey fluids. * *vt* to spray with a hose.

hose[2] *n* (*pl* **hose, hosen**) stockings, socks, tights collectively.

Hosea *n* (*Bible*) an Old Testament book containing the oracles of Hosea, a Hebrew prophet of the 8th century BC.

hosier *n* a person who sells stockings, socks, etc.

hospice *n* a home for the care of the terminally ill; a place of rest and shelter for travellers.

hospitable *adj* offering a generous welcome to guests or strangers; sociable.—**hospitableness** *n*.—**hospitably** *adv*.

hospital *n* an institution where the sick or injured are given medical treatment.

hospitality *n* (*pl* **hospitalities**) the act, practice, or quality of being hospitable.

hospitalize *vt* to place in a hospital.—**hospitalization** *n*.

hospitaler, hospitaller *n* (*often cap*) a member of a medieval charitable religious order, esp one who worked in a hospital.

host[1] *n* a person who receives or entertains a stranger or guest at his house; an animal or plant on or in which another lives; a compere on a television or radio programme. * *vti* to act as a host (to a party, television programme, etc).

host[2] *n* a very large number of people or things.

host[3] *n* the wafer of bread used in the Eucharist or Holy Communion.

hostage *n* a person given or kept as security until certain conditions are met.

hostel *n* a lodging place for the homeless, travellers, or other groups.—**hosteler, hosteller** *n*.—**hosteling, hostelling** *n*.

hostelry *n* (*pl* **hostelries**) (*formerly*) an inn.

hostess *n* a woman acting as a host; a woman who entertains guests at a nightclub, etc.

hostile *adj* of or being an enemy; unfriendly.—**hostilely** *adv*.

hostility *n* (*pl* **hostilities**) enmity, antagonism; (*pl*) deliberate acts of warfare.

hostler *see* **ostler**.

hot *adj* (**hotter, hottest**) of high temperature; very warm; giving or feeling heat; causing a burning sensation on the tongue; full of intense feeling; following closely; electrically charged; (*inf*) recent, new; (*inf*) radioactive; (*inf*) stolen. * *adv* in a hot manner.—**hotly** *adv*.—**hotness** *n*.

hot air *n* (*sl*) empty talk.

hotbed *n* a bed of heated earth enclosed by low walls and covered by glass for forcing plants; ideal conditions for the growth of something, esp evil.

hot-blooded *adj* easily excited.—**hot-bloodedness** *n*.

hotchpotch *n* a thick meat and vegetable stew; a hodgepodge.

hot dog *n* a sausage, esp a frankfurter, served in a long soft roll.

hotel *n* a commercial establishment providing lodging and meals for travellers, etc.

hotelier *n* the owner or manager of a hotel.

hotfoot *adv* with all speed; quickly.

hothead *n* an impetuous person.—**hot-headed** *adj*.—**hot-headedly** *adv*.—**hot-headedness** *n*.

hothouse *n* a heated greenhouse for raising plants; an environment that encourages rapid growth.

hot line *n* a direct telephone link between heads of government for emergency use.

hotplate *n* a heated surface for cooking or keeping food warm; a small portable heating device.

hotpot *n* a dish of meat cooked with potatoes in a tight-lidded pot.

hot seat *n* (*inf*) a dangerous position; (*sl*) the electric chair.

Hottentot *n* (*pl* **Hottentots, Hottentot**) a member of a people of the Cape of Good Hope region of South Africa, with pale brown skin; any of the languages spoken by these people.

hot water *n* (*inf*) trouble.

houmous, houmus *see* **hummus**.

hound *n* a dog used in hunting; a contemptible person. * *vt* to hunt or chase as with hounds; to urge on by harassment.—**hounder** *n*.

hour *n* a period of 60 minutes, a 24th part of a day; the time for a specific activity; the time; a special point in time; the distance covered in an hour; (pl) the customary period for work, etc.

hourglass n an instrument for measuring time by trickling sand in a specified period.

houri n (pl **houris**) a beautiful woman of the Muslim paradise; a voluptuous young woman.

hourly adj occurring every hour; done during an hour; frequent. * adv at every hour; frequently.

house n a building to live in, esp by one person or family; a household; a family or dynasty including relatives, ancestors and descendants; the audience in a theatre; a business firm; a legislative assembly; house music. * vt to provide accommodation or storage for; to cover, encase.

house arrest n detention in one's own house, as opposed to prison.

houseboat n a boat furnished and used as a home.

housebound adj confined to the house through illness, injury, etc.

housebreaker n a burglar; a person employed to demolish buildings.—**housebreaking** n.

house-broken adj (dogs, cats, etc) trained not to mess in the house; (inf) well-mannered.

housefly n (pl **houseflies**) a common fly found in houses, which is attracted by food and can spread disease.

household n all those people living together in the same house. * adj pertaining to running a house and family; domestic; familiar.

householder n the person who owns or rents a house.

housekeeper n a person who runs a home, esp one hired to do so.

housekeeping n the daily running of a household; (inf) money used for domestic expenses; routine maintenance of equipment, records, etc in an organization.

housel n (formerly) the Eucharist

houseleek n a plant with a rosette of succulent leaves and pink flowers that grows on walls.

housemaid n a female servant employed to do housework.

houseman n (pl **housemen**) an intern.

housemaster n a male teacher at a boarding school responsible for the pupils in his house.

house martin n a type of swallow with a forked tail.

house music n a pop music style, using electronic bass and synthesizers, a fast hypnotic beat and sporadic vocals, that originated in Chicago.

house party n a party, usu in a large house, where the guests stay over for several days; the guests themselves.

house plant n an indoor plant.

houseproud adj concerned with tidiness and cleanliness, often to excess.

house warming n a party given to celebrate moving into a new house.

housewife n (pl **housewives**) the woman who keeps house.—**housewifely** adj.—**housewifeliness** n.—**housewifery** n.

housework n the cooking, cleaning, etc, involved in running a home.—**houseworker** n.

housing n houses collectively; the provision of accommodation; a casing enclosing a piece of machinery, etc; a slot or groove in a piece of wood, etc, to receive an insertion.

hove see **heave**.

hovel n a small miserable dwelling. * vt (**hoveling, hoveled** or **hovelling, hovelled**) to shelter in a hovel.

hover vi (bird, etc) to hang in the air stationary; to hang about; to linger.—**hoverer** n.—**hoveringly** adv.

hovercraft n a land or water vehicle that travels supported on a cushion of air.

how adv in what way or manner; by what means; to what extent; in what condition.

howbeit conj (arch) though; although.

howdah n a seat fixed on the back of an elephant or camel.

how do you do interj a formal greeting, esp when meeting for the first time.

how-do-you-do, how-d'ye-do n (inf) a difficult situation, mess.

howdy n (inf) how do you do; hello.

however adv in whatever way or degree; still, nevertheless.

howitzer n a short cannon that fires shells at a steep trajectory.

howl vi to utter the long, wailing cry of wolves, dogs, etc; to utter a similar cry of anger, pain, etc; to shout or laugh in pain, amusement, etc. * vt to utter with a howl; to drive by howling. * n the wailing cry of a wolf, dog, etc; any similar sound.

howler n (inf) a stupid mistake.

howsoever conj still; nevertheless. * adv by whatever means; in whatever manner.

hoy n a coastal vessel; a freight barge. * interj a cry used to call attention.

hoya n a plant with pink, yellow or white flowers.

hoyden n a tomboy; a wild girl.—**hoydenish** adj.

HP abbr = hire purchase; horsepower; high pressure; Houses of Parliament.

HQ abbr = headquarters.

hr abbr = hour.

HRH abbr = His or Her Royal Highness.

HT abbr = high tension.

hub n the centre part of a wheel; a centre of activity.

hubba n (sl) a piece of the drug crack.

hubba-hubba interj an exclamation of delight.

hubble-bubble n a bubbling noise; confused talk; a hookah.

hubbub n a confused noise of many voices; an uproar.

hubby n (pl **hubbies**) (inf) a husband.

hubcap n a metal cap that fits over the hub of a car wheel.

hubris n arrogance, presumption.—**hubristic** adj.

huckaback n an absorbent linen or cotton fabric used for towels, etc.

huckleberry n (pl **huckleberries**) a North American shrub with dark-blue berries; the fruit of this plant.

huckster n a person using aggressive or questionable methods of selling.—**hucksterism** n.

huddle vti to crowd together in a confined space; to curl (oneself) up. * n a confused crowd or heap.—**huddler** n.

Hudibrastic adj mock-heroic, in the style of Hudibras, a poem by Samuel Butler (161280).

hue n colour; a particular shade or tint of a colour.

hued adj having a colour or hue as specified.

huff n a state of smouldering resentment. * vi to blow; to puff.

huffish adj prone to fits of anger or petulance.

huffy adj (**huffier, huffiest**) disgruntled, moody.—**huffily** adv.—**huffiness** n.

hug vb (**hugging, hugged**) vt to hold or squeeze tightly with the arms; to cling to; to keep close to. * vi to embrace one another. * n a strong embrace.—**huggable** adj.—**hugger** n.

huge *adj* very large, enormous.—**hugely** *adv.*—**hugeness** *n.*

huggermugger *n* secrecy, concealment; confusion. * *adj* secret, clandestine; confused, jumbled. * *adv* in confusion. * *vt* to conceal, to hush up. * *vi* to muddle.

hula, hula-hula *n* a Polynesian dance performed by men or women; the music for this.

hulk *n* the body of a ship, esp if old and dismantled; a large, clumsy person or thing.

hulking, hulky *adj* unwieldy, bulky.

hull *n* the outer covering of a fruit or seed; the framework of a ship. * *vt* to remove the hulls of; to pierce the hull of (a ship, etc).—**huller** *n.*—**hull-less** *adj.*

hullabaloo, hullaballoo *n* (*pl* **hullabaloos, hullaballoos**) a loud commotion, uproar.

hullo *see* **hello**.

hum *vb* (**humming, hummed**) *vi* to make a low continuous vibrating sound; to hesitate in speaking and utter an inarticulate sound; (*inf*) to be lively, busy; (*sl*) to stink. * *vt* to sing with closed lips. * *n* a humming sound; a murmur; (*sl*) a stink.

human *adj* of or relating to human beings; having the qualities of humans as opposed to animals; kind, considerate. * *n* a human being.—**humanness** *n.*

human being *n* a member of the races of *Homo sapiens*; a man, woman or child.

humane *adj* kind, compassionate, merciful.—**humanely** *adv.*—**humaneness** *n.*

human immunodeficiency virus *n* either of two strains of a virus that inhibits the body from developing resistance to diseases and can lead to the development of Aids.

human interest *adj* (*newspaper story, etc*) appealing to the emotions.

humanism *n* belief in the promotion of human interests, intellect and welfare.

humanist *n* one versed in the knowledge of human nature; a student of the humanities.—**humanistic** *adj.*

humanitarian *adj* concerned with promoting human welfare. * *n* a humanitarian person.—**humanitarianism** *n.*—**humanitarianist** *n.*

humanity *n* (*pl* **humanities**) the human race; the state or quality of being human or humane; philanthropy; kindness; (*pl*) the study of literature and the arts, as opposed to the sciences.

humanize *vti* to make or become human.—**humanization** *n.*—**humanizer** *n.*

humankind *n* the human species; humanity.

humanly *adv* in a way characteristic of humans; within the limits of human capabilities.

humanoid *adj* resembling a human being in appearance or character. * *n* a humanoid thing.

humble *adj* having a low estimation of one's abilities; modest, unpretentious; servile. * *vt* to lower in condition or rank; to humiliate.—**humbleness** *n.*—**humbly** *adv.*

humblebee *n* the bumblebee.

humble pie *n* apology, usu under pressure.

humbug *n* fraud, sham, hoax; an insincere person; a peppermint-flavoured sweet. * *vt* (**humbugging, humbugged**) to cheat or impose upon; to hoax.—**humbugger** *n.*—**humbuggery** *n.*

humdinger *n* (*inf*) a remarkable person or thing.

humdrum *adj* dull, ordinary, boring.—**humdrumness** *n.*

humerus *n* (*pl* **humeri**) the bone extending from the shoulder to the elbow in humans.—**humeral** *adj.*

humid *adj* (*air*) moist, damp.—**humidly** *adv.*—**humidness** *n.*

humidifier fever *n* a collection of symptoms, thought to be caused by micro-organisms found in humidifiers and including lethargy, headache and eye irritation, that affect those who work in totally air-conditioned buildings.—*also* **sick building syndrome**.

humidify *vt* (**humidifying, humidified**) to make humid.—**humidification** *n.*—**humidifier** *n.*

humidity *n* (a measure of the amount of) dampness in the air.

humidor *n* a humid cabinet or room where cigars are kept moist.

humiliate *vt* to cause to feel humble; to lower the pride or dignity of.—**humiliatingly** *adv.*—**humiliator** *n.*—**humiliatory** *adj.*

humiliation *n* the act of humiliation; the state of being humiliated; mortification; abasement.

humility *n* (*pl* **humilities**) the state of being humble; modesty.

hummingbird *n* a tiny brightly coloured tropical bird with wings that vibrate rapidly, making a humming sound.

hummock *n* a hillock.—**hummocky** *adj.*

hummus *n* a dip or appetizer of puréed chick peas, sesame seeds and garlic.—*also* **houmous, houmus**.

humoresque *n* a light musical piece.

humorist *n* a person who writes or speaks in a humorous manner.—**humoristic** *adj.*

humorous *adj* funny, amusing; causing laughter.—**humorously** *adv.*—**humorousness** *n.*

humour, humor *n* the ability to appreciate or express what is funny, amusing, etc; the expression of this; temperament, disposition; state of mind; (*formerly*) any of the four fluids of the body (blood, phlegm, yellow and black bile) that were thought to determine temperament. * *vt* to indulge; to gratify by conforming to the wishes of.—**humourful, humorful** *adj.*

humourless, humorless *adj* done or said without humour; lacking a sense of humour.—**humourlessness, humorlessness** *n.*

humourology, humorology *n* the study of humour.

hump *n* a rounded protuberance; a fleshy lump on the back of an animal (as a camel or whale); a deformity causing curvature of the spine. * *vt* to hunch; to arch.

humpback *n* a hunchback.—**humpbacked** *adj.*

humph *interj* expressing annoyance.

humus *n* dark brown or black organic matter in the soil formed from partially decomposed leaves, plants, etc.

Hun *n* one of the ancient Tartar races that overran Europe in the 4th and 5th centuries; a vandal; (*derog*) a German.

hunch *n* a hump; (*inf*) an intuitive feeling. * *vt* to arch into a hump. * *vi* to move forward jerkily.

hunchback *n* a person with curvature of the spine.

hunchbacked *adj* having an abnormal convex curvature of the thoracic spine.

hundred *adj, n* (*pl* **hundreds, hundred**) ten times ten; the symbol for this (100, C, c); the hundredth in a series or set.

hundredfold *adj, adv* one hundred times as great or many.

hundredth *adj* the last of a hundred.

hundredweight *n* (*pl* **hundredweight, hundredweights**) a unit of weight, equal to 110 pounds in US and 112 pounds in the UK.

hung see **hang**.

Hungarian adj pertaining to Hungary, its inhabitants, or language. * n an inhabitant of Hungary; the language spoken in Hungary.

hunger n (a feeling of weakness or emptiness from) a need for food; a strong desire. * vi to feel hunger; to have a strong desire (for).

hunger strike n refusal to take food as a protest.

hung-over adj (sl) suffering from a hangover.

hungry adj (**hungrier, hungriest**) desiring food; craving for something; greedy.—**hungrily** adv.—**hungriness** n.

hunk n (inf) a large piece, lump, etc; (sl) a sexually attractive man.—**hunky** adj.

hunker vi to squat, crouch down. * npl the haunches or buttocks.

hunkydory adj first-rate.

hunt vti to seek out to kill or capture (game) for food or sport; to search (for); to chase. * n a chase; a search; a party organized for hunting.

hunter n a person who hunts; a horse used in hunting.—**huntress** nf.

hunting n the art or practice of one who hunts; a pursuit; a search.

huntsman n (pl **huntsmen**) a person who manages a hunt and looks after the hounds.

hurdle n a portable frame of bars for temporary fences or for jumping over by horses or runners; an obstacle. (pl) a race over hurdles.—**hurdler** n.

hurdy-gurdy n (pl **hurdy-gurdies**) a mechanical instrument such as a barrel organ.

hurl vt to throw violently; to utter vehemently. * n a violent throw; a ride in a car.—**hurler** n.

hurling, hurley n an Irish form of field hockey.

hurly-burly n (pl **hurly-burlies**) uproar; confusion.

hurrah interj an exclamation of approval or joy.—also **hooray, hoorah**.

hurricane n a violent tropical cyclone with winds of at least 74 miles (119 kilometres) per hour.

hurried adj performed with great haste.—**hurriedly** adv.—**hurriedness** n.

hurry n (pl **hurries**) rush; urgency; eagerness to do, go, etc. * vb (**hurrying, hurried**) vt to cause to move or happen more quickly. * vi to move or act with haste.—**hurryingly** adv.

hurt vb (**hurting, hurt**) vt to cause physical pain to; to injure, damage; to offend. * vi to feel pain; to cause pain.—**hurter** n.

hurtful adj causing hurt, mischievous.—**hurtfully** adv.—**hurtfulness** n.

hurtle vti to move or throw with great speed and force.

husband n a man to whom a woman is married. * vt to conserve; to manage economically.—**husbander** n.

husbandman n (pl **husbandmen**) a farmer.

husbandry n management of resources; farming.

hush vti to make or become silent. * n a silence or calm.

hush-hush adj (inf) secret.

hush money n (sl) money paid to a person to keep a discreditable fact secret.

husk n the dry covering of certain fruits and seeds; any dry, rough, or useless covering. * vt to strip the husk from.—**husker** n.

husky[1] adj (**huskier, huskiest**) (voice) hoarse; rough-sounding; hefty, strong.—**huskily** adv.—**huskiness** n.

husky[2] n (pl **huskies**) an Arctic sled dog.

hussar n a member of any of various European light cavalry regiments, usu with an elegant dress uniform.

hussy n (pl **hussies**) a cheeky woman; a promiscuous woman.

hustings n (pl or sing) the process of, or a place for, political campaigning.

hustle vt to jostle or push roughly or hurriedly; to force hurriedly; (sl) to obtain by rough or illegal means. * vi to move hurriedly. * n an instance of hustling.—**hustler** n.

hut n a very plain or crude little house or cabin.

hutch n a pen or coop for small animals; a hut.

huzzah interj (formerly) hurrah.

hyacinth n a plant of the lily family with spikes of bell-shaped flowers; the orange gemstone jacinth; a light violet to moderate purple.—**hyacinthine** adj.

Hyades n (Greek myth) five nymphs, the daughters of Atlas; the five stars in the constellation Taurus.

hyaline adj glassy; transparent.

hybrid n the offspring of two plants or animals of different species; a mongrel. * adj crossbred.—**hybridism** n.—**hybridity** n.

hybridize vti to produce hybrids; to interbreed.—**hybridizable** adj.—**hybridization** n.—**hybridizer** n.

hydatid n a watery cyst in animal tissue; a large bladder containing the larvae of the tapeworm.—also adj.

hydr-, hydro- prefix water, fluids.

hydra n (pl **hydras, hydrae**) (usu with cap) a legendary many-headed water serpent; any of numerous freshwater polyps having a mouth surrounded by tentacles.

hydrangea n a shrub with large heads of white, pink, or blue flowers.

hydrant n a large pipe with a valve for drawing water from a water main; a fireplug.

hydrate n a chemical compound of water with some other substance. * vt to (cause to) combine with or absorb water.—**hydration** n.—**hydrator** n.

hydraulic adj operated by water or other liquid, esp by moving through pipes under pressure; of hydraulics.—**hydraulically** adv.

hydraulics n sing the science dealing with the mechanical properties of liquids, as water, and their application in engineering.

hydric adj of or containing hydrogen; of or containing water.

hydride n any compound of hydrogen and another element.

hydriodic adj composed of hydrogen and iodine.

hydro n (pl **hydros**) a hotel or resort offering hydropathic treatment.

hydrocarbon n any organic compound containing only hydrogen and carbon.

hydrocele n an accumulation of fluid in a body cavity, esp in the scrotum.

hydrocephalus, hydrocephaly n an accumulation of fluid in the brain.—**hydrocephalic** adj.

hydrochloric acid n a strong, highly corrosive acid that is a solution of the gas hydrogen chloride in water.

hydrochloric adj composed of hydrogen and chlorine.

hydrocyanic adj composed of hydrogen and cyanic.

hydrodynamics n sing the science of the mechanical properties of fluids.—**hydrodynamic** adj.—**hydrodynamically** adv.

hydroelectricity n electricity generated by water power.—**hydroelectric** adj.

hydrofluoric adj composed of hydrogen and fluorine.

hydrofoil n a vessel equipped with vanes that lift the hull out of the water to allow fast cruising speeds.

hydrogen *n* a flammable, colourless, odourless, tasteless, gaseous chemical element, the lightest substance known.

hydrogenate *vt* to combine with or treat with hydrogen.—**hydrogenation** *n.*—**hydrogenator** *n.*

hydrogen bomb *n* a powerful bomb that produces explosive energy through the fusion of hydrogen nuclei.

hydrography *n* the study, surveying and mapping of the oceans, seas, lakes, and rivers as on a chart.—**hydrographer** *n.*—**hydrographic, hydrographical** *adj.*

hydrokinetics *n sing* the branch of physics concerned with the study of fluids in motion.

hydrology *n* the science of the properties of water and its distribution on the earth and in the atmosphere.—**hydrologic, hydrological** *adj.*—**hydrologist** *n.*

hydrolysis *n* the chemical breakdown of organic compounds by interaction with water.

hydrolyze *vti* to decompose by hydrolysis.—**hydrolyzation** *n.*—**hydrolyzer** *n.*

hydromechanics *n sing* the science of the use of fluids as motive- power also called hydrodynamics.

hydromel *n* a mixture of honey and water that is fermented to make mead.

hydrometer *n* a device for measuring the densities of liquids.—**hydrometric, hydrometrical** *adj.*—**hydrometry** *n.*

hydropathy *n* the use of water to treat diseases.—**hydropathic, hydropathical** *adj.*—**hydropathist, hydropath** *n.*

hydrophane *n* a partially opaque, white type of opal that becomes translucent in water.

hydrophobia *n* a morbid fear of water; rabies.—**hydrophobic** *adj.*

hydrophone *n* an instrument that detects sound through water.

hydrophyte *n* a plant that will grow only in water or sodden soil.—**hydrophitic** *adj.*

hydroplane *n* a light motor boat that skims through the water at high speed with its hull raised out of the water; a fin that directs the vertical movement of a submarine; an attachment to an aircraft that enables it to glide along the surface of water. * *vi* (of a boat) to rise out of the water in the manner of a hydroplane.

hydroponics *n sing* the growing of plants in chemical nutrients without soil.—**hydroponically** *adv.*

hydroscope *n* any instrument that makes observations of underwater objects.

hydrosphere *n* the moisture-bearing envelope that surrounds the earth.

hydrostatics *n sing* the branch of physics concerned with the study of fluids at rest.—**hydrostatic** *adj.*

hydrotherapy *n* (*pl* **hydrotherapies**) the treatment of certain diseases and physical conditions by the external application of water.—**hydrotherapist** *n.*

hydrous *adj* containing water.

hyena *n* a nocturnal, carnivorous, scavenging mammal like a wolf.—*also* **hyaena**.

Hygeia *n* (*Greek myth*) the goddess of health.

hygiene *n* the principles and practice of health and cleanliness.—**hygienic** *adj.*—**hygienically** *adv.*

hygienist *n* a person skilled in the practice of hygiene.

hygrometer *n* an instrument for measuring the humidity of the atmosphere.—**hygrometric** *adj.*—**hygrometrically** *adv.*—**hygrometry** *n.*

hygroscope *n* an instrument that shows changes in the humidity of the atmosphere.

hygroscopic *adj* readily absorbing and retaining moisture from the air.—**hygroscopically** *adv.*

hylozoism *n* (*philos*) the doctrine that life is a property of matter; materialism.—**hylozoic** *adj.*—**hylozoist** *n.*

Hymen *n* (*Greek myth*) the god of marriage.

hymen *n* the mucous membrane partly closing the vaginal orifice.—**hymenal** *adj.*

hymeneal *adj* of marriage, nuptial.

hymenopteran *n* (*pl* **hymenopterans, hymenopterana**) any of a large order of insects that have two pairs of membranous wings.—**hymenopterous** *adj.*

hymn *n* a song of praise to God or other object of worship.

hymnal *n* a hymn book.

hymn book *n* a book of hymns.

hymnology *n* the study of the composition of hymns.—**hymnologist** *n.*

hyoid *adj* U-shaped; of or relating to the hyoid bone at the base of the tongue.

hyoscine *see* **scopolamine**.

hyp-, hypo- *prefix* below; slightly.

hype[1] *n* (*sl*) a hypodermic needle. * *vi* (*sl*) to inject a narcotic drug with a needle.

hype[2] *n* (*sl*) deception; aggressive or extravagant publicity. * *vt* to publicize or promote a product, etc in this manner.

hyped-up *adj* aggressively publicized; (*sl*) stimulated as if by injection of a drug.

hyper- *prefix* above; too; exceeding.

hyperactive *adj* abnormally active.—**hyperactivity** *n.*

hyperesthesia, hyperaesthesia *n* increased sensitivity of any of the sense organs.—**hyperaesthetic** *adj.*

hyperbola *n* (*pl* **hyperbolas, hyperbolae**) (*geom*) a curve formed by a plane intersecting a cone at a greater angle to its base than its side.

hyperbole *n* a figure of speech using absurd exaggeration.

hyperbolic, hyperbolical *adj* pertaining to or containing hyperbole, exaggerated; pertaining to or of the nature of a hyperbola.

hyperborean *adj* of or relating to the extreme north. * *n* an inhabitant of the extreme north; (*Greek myth*) (*with cap*) one of the people who lived in the sunny land beyond the north wind.

hypercritical *adj* excessively critical.—**hypercritically** *adv.*—**hypercriticism** *n.*

hypermetric *adj* beyond the normal metre of a line; having one syllable too many

hypersensitive *adj* extremely vulnerable; abnormally sensitive to a drug, pollen, etc.—**hypersensitivity** *n.*

hypersonic *adj* travelling at speeds at least five times faster than sound; of sound frequencies above 1,000 megahertz.—**hypersonics** *n.*

hypertension *n* abnormally high blood pressure.—**hypertensive** *adj.*

hyperthyroidism *n* the overproduction of the thyroid hormone by the thyroid gland.—**hyperthyroid** *adj, n.*

hypertrophy *n* (*pl* **hypertrophies**) abnormal enlargement of an organ or part.—**hypertrophic** *adj.*

hypervitaminosis *n* the pathological condition that results from the excessive intake of vitamins.

hyphen *n* a punctuation mark (-) used to join two syllables or words, or to divide words into parts. * *vt* to hyphenate.

hyphenate *vt* to join by a hyphen.—**hyphenation** *n.*

hypnosis *n* (*pl* **hypnoses**) a relaxed state resembling sleep in which the mind responds to external suggestion.

hypnotherapy *n* the use of hypnosis in treatment of emotional and psychological disorders.

hypnotic *adj* of or producing hypnosis; (*person*) susceptible to hypnosis. * *n* a drug causing sleep; a person susceptible to hypnosis.—**hypnotically** *adv*.

hypnotism *n* the act of inducing hypnosis; the study and use of hypnosis.—**hypnotist** *n*.

hypnotize *vt* to put in a state of hypnosis; to fascinate.—**hypnotizer** *n*.

hypo- *prefix* below; slightly.

hypocaust *n* the hot-air chamber under a Roman bath.

hypochondria *n* chronic anxiety about health, often with imaginary illnesses.

hypochondriac *n* a person suffering from hypochondria. * *adj* pertaining to or affected with hypochrondria.—**hypochondriacally** *adv*.

hypocorism *n* a diminutive pet name; a euphemism.—**hypocoristic, hypocoristical** *adj*.

hypocrisy *n* (*pl* **hypocrisies**) a falsely pretending to possess virtues, beliefs, etc; an example of this.—**hypocritical** *adj*.—**hypocritically** *adv*.

hypocrite *n* a person who pretends to be what he or she is not.

hypocycloid *n* (*geom*) a curve traced by the point on the circumference of a circle, which rolls on to the inside of another circle.

hypodermic *adj* injected under the skin. * *n* a hypodermic needle, syringe or injection.

hypodermic syringe *n* a syringe with a hollow (hypodermic) needle through which blood samples can be drawn.

hypogastrium *n* (*pl* **hypogastria**) the middle part of the lower region of the abdomen.

hypogeal, hypogean, hypogeous *adj* (*bot*) underground; occuring or living underground.

hypogene *adj* (*rocks*) formed under the surface of the ground.

hypostasis *n* (*pl* **hypostates**) the essential personality of a substance; (*Christianity*) any of the three persons of the Godhead which together make up the Holy Trinity; (*med*) an excess of blood in the organs as the result of poor circulation.—**hypostatic** *adj*.

hypostatize *vt* to regard as real; to embody or personify.—**hypostatization** *n*.

hypostyle *n* a roof supported by columns; a covered colonnade; a pillared hall or court.

hypotenuse *n* the side opposite to the right angle in a right-angled triangle .

hypothecate *vt* to pledge (a property) without delivery of title or possession.—**hypothecation** *n*.—**hypothecator** *n*.

hypothermia *n* an abnormally low body temperature.

hypothesis *n* (*pl* **hypotheses**) something assumed for the purpose of argument; a theory to explain some fact that may or may not prove to be true; supposition; conjecture.

hypothesize *vti* to form or assume as a hypothesis.

hypothetical *adj* based on hypothesis, conjectural.—**hypothetically** *adv*.

hypothyroidism *n* deficient activity of the thyroid glands.

hypsometry *n* the science of measuring altitude.—**hypsometric** *adj*

hyrax *n* (*pl* **hyraxes, hyraces**) a small African hamster-like mammal related to the elephant.

hyson *n* Chinese green tea.

hyssop *n* an aromatic plant with blue flowers formerly used in medicine.

hysterectomy *n* (*pl* **hysterectomies**) surgical removal of the womb.

hysteresis *n*. (*pl* **hystereses**) magnetic inertia.—**hysteretic** *adj*.

hysteria *n* a mental disorder marked by excitability, anxiety, imaginary organic disorders, etc; frenzied emotion or excitement.

hysteric *n* a hysterical person; (*pl*) fits of hysteria; (*inf*) uncontrollable laughter.

hysterical *adj* caused by hysteria; suffering from hysteria; (*inf*) extremely funny.—**hysterically** *adv*.

hysterotomy *n* (*pl* **hysterotomies**) a surgical incision into the womb.

Hz *abbr* = hertz.

I

I[1] *pron* the person who is speaking or writing, used in referring to himself or herself.

I[2] (*chem symbol*) iodine.

I. *abbr* = island(s); isle(s).

IAEA *abbr* = International Atomic Energy Authority.

iamb, iambus *n* (*pl* iambi, iambs, iambuses) a metrical foot consisting of two syllables, the first short or unstressed and the second long or stressed.—iambic *adj.*

-iana, -ana *n suffix* sayings of, publications about, as *Shakespeariana*, etc.

-iatric, -iatrical *adj* pertaining to doctors and medicine.

Iberian *adj* pertaining to Spain and Portugal; pertaining to Iberia, the ancient name of the southwest European peninsula now comprising Spain and Portugal.

ibex *n* (*pl* ibexes, ibices, ibex) any of various wild mountain goats with large horns.

ibid *abbr* = ibidem, in, in the same book, page, etc.

ibis *n* (*pl* ibises, ibis) a wading bird with a curved bill.

Ibo *n* (*pl* Ibo, Ibos) a member of a Black people of southern Nigeria; their language.

ICBM *abbr* = intercontinental ballistic missile.

ice *n* water frozen solid; a sheet of this; a portion of ice cream or water ice; (*sl*) diamonds; (*sl*) the drug methamphetamine packaged and sold as a stimulant in smokeable form. * *vti* (*often with* up *or* over) to freeze; to cool with ice; to cover with icing.

ice age *n* a period when much of the earth's surface was covered in glaciers; (with caps) the Pleistocene glacial epoch.

iceberg *n* a great mass of mostly submerged ice floating in the sea.

iceblink *n* a streak of whiteness on the horizon, caused by the reflection of light from masses of ice in the distance.

icebound *adj* (*ship, etc*) surrounded, and immobilized, by ice.

icebox *n* a compartment in a refrigerator for making ice.

icebreaker, iceboat *n* a powerful and reinforced vessel for breaking a channel through ice.

icecap *n* a mass of slowly spreading glacial ice.

ice cream *adj* a sweet frozen food, made from flavoured milk or cream.

ice dance *n* a type of ballroom dancing by skaters on ice.

icefall *n* a steep part of a glacier, resembling a frozen waterfall.

ice field *n* an extensive field of floating ice.

ice floe *n* a sheet of floating ice.

ice hockey *n* an indoor or outdoor hockey game played on ice by two teams of six skaters with curved sticks and a flat disk called a puck.

Icelander *n* a native or inhabitant of Iceland.

Icelandic *adj* of or pertaining to Iceland or its language, literature and people. * *n* the language of Iceland.

ice pack *n* a field of broken and drifting ice, consisting of great masses packed together; a cloth or small bag filled with crushed ice for soothing sores and swellings on the body.

ice pick *n* a pointed awl with a handle for chipping or breaking up ice.

ice plant *n* a type of plant with leaves that glisten as if covered with ice.

ice skate *n* a boot with a steel blade fixed to the sole for skating on ice.—*also vi.*—ice skater *n.*

ichneumon *n* a North African mongoose.

ichneumon fly *n* an insect that lays its eggs in the bodies of other insects.

ichnite, ichnolite *n* a fossil footprint.

ichor *n* (*Greek myth*) the ethereal fluid believed to run, instead of blood, in the veins of the classical gods.—ichorous *adj.*

ichtny-, icthyo- *prefix* fish.

ichthyic *adj* pertaining to fishes.

ichthyoid, ichthyoidal *adj* resembling a fish.

ichthyology *n* the study of fish.—ichthyologic, ichthyological *adj.*—ichthyologist *n.*

ichthyophagous *adj* fish-eating.—ichthyophagy *n.*

ichthyornis *n* an extinct species of toothed fish-eating bird.

ichthyosaur, ichthyosaurus *n* (*pl* ichthyosaurs, ichthosauri) a gigantic, extinct, marine reptile.

ichthyosis *n* a disease in which the skin becomes dry and scaly.

icicle *n* a hanging tapering length of ice formed when dripping water freezes.—icicled *adj.*

icily *adv* in an icy manner, coldly.

iciness *n* the state of being icy, coldness.

icing *n* a semi-solid sugary mixture used to cover cakes, etc.—*also* frosting.

icon *n* an image; (*Eastern Church*) a sacred image, usu on a wooden panel.—*also* ikon.—iconic, iconical *adj.*

iconoclast *n* a person who attacks revered or traditional beliefs, opinions, etc.—iconoclasm *n.*—iconoclastic *adj.*—iconoclastically *adv.*

iconography *n* (*pl* iconographies) the art of representation by means of images (statues), pictures, or engravings; the study of this art.—iconographer *n.*—iconographic, iconographical *adj.*

iconolatry *n* the worship of images.

iconology *n* the study of icons.

icosahedron *n* (*pl* icosahedrons, icosahedra) (*geom*) a solid bounded by 20 plane faces.

icterus *n* jaundice.—icteric *adj.*

ictus *n* (*pl* ictuses, ictus) a stress in verse.

icy *adj* (icier, iciest) full of, made of, or covered with ice; slippery or very cold; cold in manner.

ID *abbr* = identification.

ID card *n* an identity card.

I'd = I had; I should; I would.

id *n* (*psychoanal*) the primitive psychological instincts in the unconscious which are the source of psychic activity.

ide *n* a small European fish.

idea *n* a mental impression of anything; a vague impression, notion; an opinion or belief; a scheme; a supposition; a person's conception of something; a significance or purpose.

ideal *adj* existing in the mind or as an idea; satisfying an ideal, perfect. * *n* the most perfect conception of anything; a person or thing regarded as perfect; a standard for attainment or imitation; an aim or principle.—**ideally** *adv.*—**idealness** *n.*

idealism *n* the pursuit of high ideals; the conception or representation of things in their ideal form as against their reality.—**idealist** *n.*—**idealistic** *adj.*—**idealistically** *adv.*

ideality *n* (*pl* **idealities**) the quality of being ideal; the faculty to form ideals.

idealize *vt* to consider or represent as ideal.—**idealization** *n.*—**idealizer** *n.*

ideate *vti* to imagine.

idée fixe *n* (*pl* **idées fixes**) a fixed idea; an obsession.

identical *adj* exactly the same; having the same origin.—**identically** *adv.*—**identicalness** *n.*

identifiable *adj* able to be identified.—**identifiableness** *n.*

identification *n* the act of identifying; the state of being identified; that which identifies.

identify *vt* (**identifying, identified**) to consider to be the same, equate; to establish the identity of; to associate closely; to regard (oneself) as similar to another.—**identifier** *n.*

identity *n* (*pl* **identities**) the state of being exactly alike; the distinguishing characteristics of a person, personality; the state of being the same as a specified person or thing.

identity card *n* a card carrying personal details, a photograph, etc of an individual as carried by staff of an organization, journalists, etc.

ideogram, ideograph *n* a symbol, as in Chinese writing, used instead of a word to represent an idea or thing; a graphic sign.

ideography *n* the direct representation of ideas by symbols.—**ideographic, ideographical** *adj.*

ideologist, ideologue *n* one occupied with ideals or ideals; a theorist.

ideology *n* (*pl* **ideologies**) the doctrines, beliefs or opinions of an individual, social class, political party, etc.—**ideological, ideologic** *adj.*

ides *n* the 15th day of March, May, July, or October and the 13th day of any other month in the ancient Roman calender.

idiocy *n* (*pl* **idiocies**) mental deficiency; stupidity, imbecility; something stupid or foolish.

idiom *n* an accepted phrase or expression with a different meaning from the literal; the usual way in which the words of a language are used to express thought; the dialect of a people, region, etc; the characteristic style of a school of art, literature, etc—**idiomatic, idiomatical** *adj.*—**idiomatically** *adv.*

idiopathy *n* a disease whose cause is unknown.—**idiopathic** *adj.*

idiosyncrasy *n* (*pl* **idiosyncrasies**) a type of behaviour or characteristic peculiar to a person or group; a quirk, eccentricity.—**idiosyncratic** *adj.*—**idiosyncratically** *adv.*

idiot *n* a severely mentally retarded adult; (*inf*) a foolish or stupid person.

idiot board *n* an autocue.

idiotic *adj* stupid; senseless.—**idiotically** *adv.*

idle *adj* not employed, unoccupied; not in use; averse to work; useless; worthless. * *vt* to waste or spend (time) in idleness. * *vi* to move slowly or aimlessly; (*engine*) to operate without transmitting power.—**idleness** *n.*—**idler** *n.*—**idly** *adv.*

idler *n* someone who idles; a lazy person.

idol *n* an image or object worshipped as a god; a person who is intensely loved, admired or honoured.

idolatry *n* the worship of idols; excessive admiration or devotion.—**idolatrous** *adj.*—**idolater** *n.*

idolize *vt* to make an idol of, for worship; to love to excess.—**idolization** *n.*—**idolizer** *n.*

idyll, idyl *n* a short simple poem, usu evoking the romance and beauty of rural life; a romantic or picturesque event or scene; a romantic or pastoral musical composition.—**idyllist** *n.*

idyllic *adj* pertaining to or of the nature of an idyll, pastoral; romantic, picturesque.—**idyllically** *adv.*

i.e. *abbr* = *id est*, that is.

if *conj* on condition that; in the event that; supposing that; even though; whenever; whether.

iffy *adj* (*inf*) uncertain, unreliable.

igloo *n* (*pl* **igloos**) an Eskimo house built of blocks of snow and ice.

igneous *adj* of fire; (*rocks*) produced by volcanic action or intense heat beneath the earth's surface.

ignite *vti* to set fire to; to catch fire; to burn or cause to burn.—**ignitable** *adj.*

ignition *n* an act or instance of igniting; the starting of an internal combustion engine; the mechanism that ignites an internal combustion engine.

ignoble *adj* dishonourable, despicable; base, of low birth.—**ignobly** *adv.*

ignominious *adj* bringing disgrace or shame; humiliating, degrading.—**ignominiously** *adv.*

ignominy *n* (*pl* **ignominies**) disgrace, dishonour; a cause of ignominy, a disgraceful act.

ignoramus *n* (*pl* **ignoramuses**) an ignorant person.

ignorance *n* the state of being ignorant; a lack of knowledge.

ignorant *adj* lacking knowledge; uninformed, uneducated; resulting from or showing lack of knowledge.—**ignorance** *n.*—**ignorantly** *adv.*

ignore *vt* to disregard; to deliberately refuse to notice someone.—**ignorable** *adj.*—**ignorer** *n.*

iguana *n* any of a family of large lizards of tropical America.—**iguanian** *adj, n.*

iguanodon *n* a gigantic, extinct, herbivorous lizard.

ihram *n* the distinctive white robes worn by Muslims on pilgrimage to Mecca.

ikebana *n* the Japanese art of flower arranging.

ikon *see* icon.

ileac, ileal *adj* (*anat*) pertaining to the ileum.

ileum *n* (*anat*) the lower part of the small intestine.

ilk *n* a type or sort.

ill *adj* (**worse, worst**) not in good health; harmful; bad; hostile; unfavourable. * *adv* badly, wrongly; hardly, with difficulty. * *n* trouble; harm; evil.

ill. *abbr* = illustrated; illustration.

I'll = I shall; I will.

ill-advised *adj* unwise.

ill at ease *adj* uneasy, embarrassed.

ill-bred *adj* bad-mannered.—**ill-breeding** *n.*

ill-considered *adj* lacking consideration; not thought out properly.

ill-disposed *adj* unfavourably inclined (towards).

illegal *adj* against the law.—**illegally** *adv.*—**illegality** *n.*

illegible *adj* impossible to read.—**illegibility, illegibleness** *n.*—**illegibly** *adv.*

illegitimate *adj* born of parents not married to each other; contrary to law, rules, or logic.—**illegitimacy, illegitimateness** *n.*—**illegitimately** *adv.*

ill-fated *adj* unlucky.

ill-favoured, ill-favored *adj* unattractive; unpleasant.

ill-founded *adj* not based on reliable facts; unsubstantiated.

ill-gotten *adj* illegally or dishonestly acquired.

ill-humoured, ill-humored *adj* bad tempered; sullen.—**ill-humour, ill humor** *n.*

illiberal *adj* narrow-minded; mean.—**illiberality, illiberalness** *n.*—**illiberally** *adv.*

illicit *adj* improper; unlawful.—**illicitly** *adv.*

illimitable *adj* limitless, infinite.—**illimitability** *n.*

illiterate *adj* uneducated, esp not knowing how to read or write. * *n* an illiterate person.—**illiteracy** *n.*—**illiterately** *adv.*

ill-mannered *adj* rude.

ill-natured *adj* spiteful.

illness *n* a state of ill-health; sickness.

illogical *adj* not logical or reasonable.—**illogicality, illogicalness** *n.*—**illogically** *adv.*

ill-starred *adj* unlucky.

ill-timed *adj* occurring or done at an unsuitable time.

ill-treat *vt* to treat unkindly, unfairly, etc.—**ill-treatment** *n.*

illume *vt* (*poet*) to light up, illuminate.

illuminant *n* a substance or device that illuminates.

illuminate *vt* to give light to; to light up; to make clear; to inform; to decorate as with gold or lights.—**illumination** *n.*—**illuminative** *adj.*—**illuminator** *n.*

illuminati *npl* (*sing* **illuminato**) a name given to persons professing special spiritual or intellectual enlightenment.

illumination *n* a supply of light; the act of illuminating; the state of being illuminated; (*Brit, esp pl*) decorative coloured lights used in public places.

illumine *vt* (*poet*) to illuminate.

illuminism *n* the belief in and profession of special spiritual and intellectual enlightenment.

ill-usage *n* ill-use, abuse.

ill-use *vt* to treat badly, etc. * *n* abuse.

illusion *n* a false idea or conception; an unreal or misleading image or appearance.—**illusional, illusionary** *adj.*

illusionism *n* (*philos*) a disbelief in objective existence.

illusionist *n* a magician or conjuror.—**illusionism** *n.*

illusory, illusive *adj* deceptive; based on illusion.—**illusorily** *adv.*—**illusoriness** *n.*

illustrate *vt* to explain, as by examples; to provide (books, etc) with explanatory pictures, charts, etc; to serve as an example.—**illustratable** *adj.*—**illustrative** *adj.*—**illustrator** *n.*

illustration *n* the act of illustrating; the state of being illustrated; an example that explains or corroborates; a picture or diagram in a book, etc.—**illustrational** *adj.*

illustrious *adj* distinguished, famous.—**illustriousness** *n.*

ill-will *n* antagonism, hostility.

I'm = I am.

image *n* a representation of a person or thing; the visual impression of something in a lens, mirror, etc; a copy; a likeness; a mental picture; the concept of a person, product, etc held by the public at large. * *vt* to make a representation of; to reflect; to imagine.

imagery *n* (*pl* **imageries**) the work of the imagination; mental pictures; figures of speech; images in general or collectively.

imaginable *adj* able to be imagined.—**imaginably** *adv.*

imaginal *adj* pertaining to an image; pertaining to an imago.

imaginary *adj* existing only in the imagination.—**imaginarily** *adv.*

imagination *n* the image-forming power of the mind, or the power of the mind that modifies the conceptions, esp the higher form of this power exercised in art and poetry; creative ability; resourcefulness in overcoming practical difficulties, etc.

imaginative *adj* having or showing imagination; produced by imagination.—**imaginatively** *adv.*

imagine *vt* to form a mental image of; to believe falsely; (*inf*) to suppose; to guess. * *vi* to employ the imagination.—**imaginer** *n.*

imagist *n* a member of a group of poets, active between 1912 and 1917, who sought clarity of expression through use of precise images.

imago *n* (*pl* **imagoes, imagines**) an insect in its fully developed state; an idealized mental image of oneself or another.

imam *n* a leader of prayer in a mosque; a title given to various Muslim religious leaders.

imamate *n* a region controlled by an imam; the rank or term of office of an imam.

imaret *n* a hostel in Turkey giving accommodation to pilgrims or travellers.

imbalance *n* a lack of balance, as in proportion, emphasis, etc.

imbecile *n* an adult with a mental age of a three- to eight-year-old child; an idiotic person. * *adj* stupid or foolish.

imbecility *n* (*pl* **imbecilities**) mental or physical weakness.

imbed *vt* (**imbedding, imbedded**) to embed.

imbibe *vti* to drink, esp alcoholic liquor; to absorb mentally.—**imbiber** *n.*

imbibition *n* (*chem*) the process of a gel or solid absorbing a liquid; (*photog*) the process, used in colour printing, of using gelatine to absorb dyes.

imbricate, imbricated *adj* (*tiles, leaves*) overlapping.—**imbrication** *n.*

imbroglio *n* (*pl* **imbroglios**) a complicated, confusing situation; a confused misunderstanding.

imbrue *vt* (**imbruing, imbrued**) to wet or moisten; to soak; to drench, esp in blood.—*also* **embrue.**

IMF *abbr* = International Monetary Fund.

imitable *adj* able to be imitated.—**imitability, imitableness** *n.*

imitate *vt* to try to follow as a pattern or model; to mimic humorously, impersonate; to copy, reproduce.—**imitator** *n.*

imitation *n* an act or instance of imitating; a copy; an act of mimicking or impersonation.—**imitational** *adj.*

imitative *adj* imitating or inclined to imitate; characterized by imitation; copying an original, esp something superior.

immaculate *adj* spotless; flawless; pure, morally unblemished.—**immaculacy, immaculateness** *n.*—**immaculately** *adv.*

Immaculate Conception *n* (*RC Church*) the doctrine that the Virgin Mary was conceived without original sin.

immanent *adj* (*qualities*) inherent; (*God*) pervading the universe.—**immanence, immanency** *n*.

immaterial *adj* spiritual as opposed to physical; unimportant.—**immateriality, immaterialness** *n*.

immaterialism *n* (*philos*) the doctrine that matter has no existence independent of the mind.—**immaterialist** *n*.

immaterialize *vt* to make immaterial.

immature *adj* not mature.—**immaturity, immatureness** *n*.

immeasurable *adj* not able to be measured; immense, limitless.—**immeasurably** *adv*.

immediate *adj* acting or occurring without delay; next, nearest, without intervening agency; next in relationship; in close proximity, near to; directly concerning or touching a person or thing.—**immediacy, immediateness** *n*.

immediately *adv* without delay; directly; near, close by. * *conj* as soon as.

immemorial *adj* existing in the distant past, beyond the reach of memory.—**immemorially** *adv*.

immense *adj* very large in size or extent; limitless; (*inf*) excellent.—**immensely** *adv*.

immensity *n* (*pl* **immensities**) the character of being immense; immeasurableness; infinite space; vastness in extent or bulk.

immensurable *adj* immeasurable.

immerse *vt* to plunge into a liquid; to absorb or engross; to baptize by total submergence.—**immersible** *adj*.

immersion *n* the act of immersing; the state of being immersed; baptism by dipping the whole person into water.

immesh *see* enmesh.

immethodical *adj* without method or order.

immigrant *n* a person who immigrates; a person recently settled in a country but not born there.

immigrate *vi* to come into a new country, esp to settle permanently.—**immigration** *n*.—**immigrator** *n*.—**immigratory** *adj*.

imminent *adj* about to happen; impending.—**imminence** *n*.—**imminently** *adv*.

immiscible *adj* incapable of being mixed.—**immiscbility** *n*.

immobile *adj* not able to be moved; motionless.—**immobility** *n*.

immobilize *vt* to make immobile.—**immobilization** *n*.

immoderate *adj* excessive, unrestrained.—**immoderately** *adv*.—**immoderation, immoderateness** *n*.

immodest *adj* lacking in modesty or decency.—**immodestly** *adv*.—**immodesty** *n*.

immolate *vt* to kill as a sacrifice.—**immolation** *n*.—**immolator** *n*.

immoral *adj* against accepted standards of proper behaviour; sexually degenerate; corrupt; wicked.—**immorally** *adv*.

immorality *n* (*pl* **immoralities**) the quality of being immoral; an immoral act or practice.

immortal *adj* living for ever; enduring; having lasting fame. * *n* an immortal being or person; (*pl*) the gods of classical mythology.—**immortality** *n*.—**immortally** *adv*.

immortalize *vt* to render immortal; to bestow lasting fame upon.—**immortalization** *n*.

immortelle *n* a type of flower that retains its colour when dried.

immovable *adj* firmly fixed; impassive, unyielding; (*property*) land, buildings, etc.—**immovability, immovableness** *n*.—**immovably** *adv*.

immune *adj* not susceptible to a specified disease through inoculation or natural resistance; conferring immunity; exempt from a certain obligation, tax, duty, etc.

immunity *n* (*pl* **immunities**) the state of being immune.

immunize *vt* to make immune, esp against infection.—**immunization** *n*.

immuno- *prefix* immunity.

immunology *n* the branch of medical science dealing with immunity to disease.—**immunologic, immunological** *adj*.—**immunologist** *n*.

immure *vt* to enclose within walls; to shut up (in prison), confine.

immutable *adj* not capable of change; unalterable.—**immutability, immutableness** *n*.—**immutably** *adv*.

imp *n* a mischievous child; a little devil.

impact *n* violent contact; a shocking effect; the force of a body colliding with another. * *vt* to force tightly together. * *vi* to hit with force.—**impaction** *n*.

impacted *adj* (*tooth*) unable to emerge through the gum because of an obstruction, esp proximity to another tooth.

impair *vt* to make worse, less, etc.—**impairer** *n*.—**impairment** *n*.

impala *n* (*pl* **impalas, impala**) a type of African antelope.

impale *vt* to fix on, or pierce through, with something pointed.—**impalement** *n*.—**impaler** *n*.

impalpable *adj* not able to be sensed by touch; difficult to apprehend or grasp with the mind.—**impalpability** *n*.—**impalpably** *adv*.

impanel *see* empanel.

imparity *n* (*pl* **imparities**) inequality; disproportion; disparity.

impart *vt* to give, convey; to reveal, disclose.—**imparter** *n*.

impartial *adj* not favouring one side more than another, unbiased.—**impartiality, impartialness** *n*.—**impartially** *adv*.

impartible *adj* (*law*) which cannot be partitioned.

impassable *adj* (*roads, etc*) incapable of being travelled through or over.—**impassability, impassableness** *n*.—**impassably** *adv*.

impasse *n* a situation from which there is no escape; a deadlock.

impassioned *adj* passionate; ardent.—**impassionedly** *adv*.

impassive *adj* not feeling or showing emotion; imperturbable.—**impassively** *adv*.—**impassiveness, impassivity** *n*.

impaste *vt* (*art*) to paint (onto canvas) in thick layers.—**impastation** *n*.

impasto *n* (*art*) the effect produced by applying thick layers of paint to a canvas; the technique of applying paint in thick layers.

impatiens *n* (*pl* **impatiens**) one of a genus of plants of this name, including balsam and touch-me-not.

impatient *adj* lacking patience; intolerant of delay, etc; restless.—**impatience** *n*.—**impatiently** *adv*.

impeach *vt* to question a person's honesty; to try (a public official) on a charge of wrongdoing.—**impeachable** *adj*.—**impeacher** *n*.—**impeachment** *n*.

impearl *vt* (*arch*) to adorn with pearls; to make like pearls.

impeccable *adj* without defect or error; faultless.—**impeccability** *n.*—**impeccably** *adv.*

impecunious *adj* having little or no money.—**impecuniousness, impecuniosity** *n.*

impedance *n* the total resistance in an electric circuit to the flow of alternating current.

impede *vt* to obstruct or hinder the progress of.—**impeder** *n.*—**impedingly** *adv.*

impediment *n* something that impedes; an obstruction; a physical defect, as a stammer that prevents fluency of speech.—**impedimental** *adj.*

impedimenta *npl* heavy items of baggage, esp military equipment.

impel *vt* (**impelling, impelled**) to urge or force into doing something; to propel.—**impeller** *n.*

impend *vi* to be imminent; to threaten.—**impending** *adj.*

impenetrable *adj* unable to be pierced or penetrated; incomprehensible; unable to be seen through.—**impenetrability** *n.*—**impenetrably** *adv.*

impenitent *adj* not sorry or feeling guilty; unrepentant.—**impenitence, impenitency** *n.*

imperative *adj* urgent, pressing; authoritative; obligatory; designating or of the mood of a verb that expresses a command, entreaty, etc. * *n* a command; (*gram*) the imperative mood of a verb.

imperator *n* (*ancient Rome*) a commander-in-chief; a title given to a victorious general; a title given to the head of state.

imperceptible *adj* not able to be detected by the mind or senses; slight, minute, gradual.—**imperceptibility** *n.*—**imperceptibly** *adv.*

impercipient *adj* lacking perception.

imperfect *adj* having faults, flaws, mistakes, etc; defective; incomplete; (*gram*) designating a verb tense that indicates a past action or state as incomplete or continuous. * (*gram*) an imperfect tense.

imperfection *n* the state or quality of being imperfect; a defect, fault.

imperforate *adj* not perforated; (*anat*) without the normal opening.

imperial *adj* of an empire, emperor, or empress; majestic; of great size or superior quality; of the British non-metric system of weights and measures.—**imperially** *adv.*

imperialism *n* the policy of forming and maintaining an empire, as by subjugating territories, establishing colonies, etc.—**imperialist** *n.*—**imperialistic** *adj.*—**imperialistically** *adv.*

imperil *vt* (**imperiling, imperiled** *or* **imperilling, imperilled**) to put in peril, to endanger.

imperious *adj* tyrannical; arrogant.—**imperiously** *adv*

imperishable *adj* indestructible, not subject to decay; permanently enduring.—**imperishability** *n.*

imperium *n* (*pl* **imperia**) supreme power; an empire.

impermanent *adj* not permanent.—**impermanence, impermanency** *n.*

impermeable *adj* not allowing fluids to pass through; impervious.—**impermeability** *n.*

impermissible *adj* not permissible.

impersonal *adj* not referring to any particular person; cold, unfeeling; not existing as a person; (*verb*) occurring only in the third person singular, usu with "it" as subject.—**impersonality** *n.*—**impersonally** *adv.*

impersonate *vt* to assume the role of another person as entertainment or for fraud.—**impersonation** *n.*—**impersonator** *n.*

impertinent *adj* impudent; insolent; irrelevant.—**impertinence** *n.*—**impertinently** *adv.*

imperturbable *adj* not easily disturbed; calm; impassive.—**imperturbability** *n.*—**imperturbably** *adv.*—**imperturbation** *n.*

impervious *adj* incapable of being penetrated, as by water; not readily receptive (to) or affected (by).

impetigo *n* (*pl* **impetigos**) a contagious bacterial skin disease.—**impetiginous** *adj.*

impetrate *vt* to obtain by supplication, esp by prayer.—**impetration** *n.*

impetuous *adj* acting or done suddenly with impulsive energy.—**impetuosity** *n.*—**impetuously** *adv.*

impetus *n* (*pl* **impetuses**) the force with which a body moves against resistance; driving force or motive.

impiety *n* (*pl* **impieties**) want of piety; ungodliness; an act of irreverence or wickedness.

impinge *vi* (*with* **on, upon**) to have an impact; to encroach.—**impingement** *n.*—**impinger** *n.*

impious *adj* showing lack of reverence; wicked.—**impiously** *adv.*

impish *adj* of or like an imp.—**impishly** *adv.*—**impishness** *n.*

implacable *adj* not able to be appeased or pacified; inflexible, inexorable.—**implacability** *n.*—**implacably** *adv.*

implant *vt* to plant firmly; to fix (ideas, etc) firmly in the mind. * *n* something implanted in tissue surgically.—**implantation** *n.*—**implanter** *n.*

implausible *adj* not plausible.—**implausibility** *n.*—**implausibly** *adv.*

implead *vt* to sue, prosecute.

implement *n* something used in a given activity. * *vt* to carry out, put into effect.—**implemental** *adj.*—**implementation** *n.*—**implementer, implementor** *n.*

implicate *vt* to show to have a part, esp in a crime; to imply.—**implicative** *adj.*

implication *n* an implicating or being implicated; that which is implied; an inference not expressed but understood; deduction.

implicit *adj* implied rather than stated explicitly; unquestioning, absolute.—**implicitly** *adv.*—**implicitness, implicity** *n.*

implode *vi* to collapse inwards.

implore *vt* to request earnestly; to plead, entreat.—**imploration** *n.*—**implorer** *n.*—**imploringly** *adv.*

imply *vt* (**implying, implied**) to hint, suggest indirectly; to indicate or involve as a consequence.

impolite *adj* not polite, rude.—**impolitely** *adv.*—**impoliteness** *n.*

impolitic *adj* contrary to good policy; unwise; injudicious; indiscreet.—**impoliticly** *adv.*

imponderable *adj* not able to be weighed or measured. * *n* something difficult to measure or assess.—**imponderability** *n.*—**imponderably** *adv.*

import *vt* to bring (goods) in from a foreign country for sale or use; to mean; to signify. * *vi* to be of importance, to matter. * *n* something imported; meaning; importance.—**importable** *adj.*—**importer** *n.*

importance *n* the quality of being important; a high place in public estimation; high self-esteem.

important *adj* having great significance or consequence; (*person*) having power, authority, etc.—**importantly** *adv.*

importation *n* the act or business of importing; imported goods.

importunate *adj* persistent in asking or demanding.

importune *vt* to ask urgently and repeatedly.—**importuner** *n.*—**importuning** *n.*

importunity *n* (*pl* **importunities**) persistent solicitation or demand; incessant insistence; urgency.

impose *vt* to put (a burden, tax, punishment) on or upon; to force (oneself) on others; to lay pages of type or film and secure them. * *vi* (*with* **on** *or* **upon**) to take advantage of; to cheat or defraud.—**imposable** *adj.*—**imposer** *n.*

imposing *adj* impressive because of size, appearance, dignity, etc.—**imposingly** *adv.*

imposition *n* the act of imposing; something imposed, as a tax; an unfair burden; (*print*) the arrangement of pages of type or film in the correct order.

impossibility *n* (*pl* **impossibilites**) the character of being impossible; that which cannot be, or be supposed to be, done.

impossible *adj* not capable of existing, being done, or happening; (*inf*) unendurable, outrageous.—**impossibly** *adv.*

impost *n* a tax or duty, esp imposed by customs.

impostor, imposter *n* a person who acts fraudulently by impersonating another.

imposture *n* a fraud, deception.

impotent *adj* lacking in necessary strength, powerless; (*man*) unable to engage in sexual intercourse.—**impotence, impotency** *n.*—**impotently** *adv.*

impound *vt* to take legal possession of; to shut up (an animal) in a pound.—**impoundage, impoundment** *n.*—**impounder** *n.*

impoverish *vt* to make poor; to deprive of strength.—**impoverishment** *n.*

impracticable *adj* not able to be carried out, not feasible.—**impracticability** *n.*—**impracticably** *adv.*

impractical *adj* not practical; not competent in practical skills.—**impracticality** *n.*—**impractically** *adv.*

imprecate *vti* to invoke evil (on); to curse or utter curses.—**imprecatory** *adv.*

imprecation *n* a curse.

imprecise *adj* not precise; ill-defined.—**imprecisely** *adv.*—**imprecision** *n.*

impregnable, impregnatable *adj* secure against attack, unyielding.—**impregnability** *n.*—**impregnably** *adv.*

impregnate *vt* to cause to become pregnant, to fertilize; to saturate, soak (with); to imbue, pervade.—**impregnation** *n.*—**impregnator** *n.*

impresario *n* (*pl* **impresarios**) the manager of an opera, a concert series, etc.

impress[1] *vt* to make a strong, usu favourable, impression on; to fix deeply in the mind; to stamp with a mark; to imprint. * *n* an imprint.—**impresser** *n.*—**impressible** *adj.*

impress[2] *vt* to coerce into military service.—**impressment** *n.*

impression *n* the effect produced in the mind by an experience; a mark produced by imprinting; a vague idea, notion; the act of impressing or being impressed; a notable or strong influence on the mind or senses; the number of copies of a book printed at one go (—*also* **printing**); an impersonation or act of mimicry.—**impressional** *adj.*

impressionable *n* easily impressed or influenced.—**impressionability** *n.*—**impressionably** *adv.*

impressionism *n* painting, writing, etc in which objects are painted or described so as to reproduce only their general effect or impression without selection or elaboration of details.—**impressionist** *adj, n.*—**impressionistic** *adj.*

impressive *adj* tending to impress the mind or emotions; arousing wonder or admiration.—**impressiveness** *n.*

impressment *n* the act of seizing (things) for public use or conscripting (people) into public service.

imprest *n* a sum of money advanced.

imprimatur *n* permission or licence to publish a book, etc; an authoritative mark of approval; sanction.

imprint *vt* to stamp or impress a mark on, etc; to fix firmly in the mind. * *n* a mark made by imprinting; a lasting effect; a note in a book giving the facts of publication.—**imprinter** *n.*

imprison *vt* to put in a prison; to confine, as in a prison.—**imprisoner** *n.*—**imprisonment** *n.*

improbable *adj* unlikely to be true or to happen.—**improbability** *n.*—**improbably** *adv.*

improbity *n* (*pl* **improbities**) wickedness, dishonesty.

impromptu *adj, adv* unrehearsed, unprepared. * *n* something impromptu, as a speech.

improper *adj* lacking propriety, indecent; incorrect; not suitable or appropriate.—**improperly** *adv.*

improper fraction *n* a fraction in which the numerator is greater than or equal to the denominator, as 4/3.

impropriety *n* (*pl* **improprieties**) the quality of being improper; indecency; an improper act, etc.

improve *vt* to make or become better.—**improvable** *adj.*—**improver** *n.*—**improvingly** *adj.*

improvement *n* the act of improving or being improved; an alteration that improves or adds to the value of something.

improvident *adj* lacking foresight or thrift; wanting care to provide for the future; careless.—**improvidence** *n.*

improvisation *n* the act of improvising; the act of composing poetry, music, etc, extemporaneously; an impromptu.—**improvisational** *adj.*

improvise *vti* to compose, perform, recite, etc without preparation; to make or do with whatever is at hand.—**improviser** *n.*

imprudent *adj* rash, lacking discretion; unwise.—**imprudence** *n.*—**imprudently** *adv.*

impudent *adj* disrespectfully bold; impertinent.—**impudence** *n.*—**impudently** *adv.*

impugn *vt* to oppose or challenge as false; to discredit.—**impugnation, impugnent** *n.*—**impugner** *n.*

impuissant *adj* powerless, weak.—**impuissance** *n.*

impulse *n* a sudden push or thrust; a stimulus transmitted through a nerve or a muscle; a sudden instinctive urge to act.

impulsion *n* the act of impelling; the state of being impelled; impetus; an irrational urge, compulsion.

impulsive *adj* tending to act on impulse; forceful, impelling; acting momentarily.—**impulsively** *adv.*—**impulsiveness** *n.*

impunity *n* (*pl* **impunities**) exemption or freedom from punishment or harm.

impure *adj* unclean; adulterated.

impurity *n* (*pl* **impurities**) a being impure; an impure substance or constituent.

impute *vt* to attribute (esp a fault or misbehaviour) to another.—**imputable** *adj.*—**imputation** *n.*—**imputative** *adj.*—**imputer** *n.*

In (*chem symbol*) indium.

in. *abbr* = inch(es).

in *prep* inside; within; at; as contained by; during; at the end of; not beyond; affected by; being a member of; wearing; using; because of; into. * *adv* to or at a certain place; so as to be contained by a certain space, condition, etc; (*games*) batting, in play. * *adj* that is in power; inner; inside; gathered, counted, etc; (*inf*) currently smart, fashionable, etc.

inability *n* (*pl* **inabilities**) lack of ability.

in absentia *adv* in the absence of.

inaccessible *adj* not accessible, unapproachable.—**inaccessibility** *n*.—**inaccessibly** *adv*.

inaccurate *adj* not accurate, imprecise.—**inaccuracy** *n*.—**inaccurately** *adv*.

inaction *n* idleness, inertia.

inactive *adj* not active.—**inactively** *adv*.—**inactivity** *n*.

inadequate *adj* not adequate; not capable.— **inadequacy** *n*.—**inadequately** *adv*.

inadmissible *adj* not admissible, esp as evidence.—**inadmissibility** *n*.—**inadmissibly** *adv*.

inadvertent *adj* not attentive or observant, careless; due to oversight.—**inadvertence, inadvertency** *n*.—**inadvertently** *adv*.

inadvisable *adj* not advisable; inexpedient.—**inadvisability** *n*.—**inadvisably** *adv*.

inalienable *adj* that cannot or should not be surrendered or transferred to another.—**inalienability** *n*.—**inalienably** *adv*.

inalterable *adj* unalterable.—**inalterability** *n*.

inamorata *n* (*pl* **inamoratas**) a woman with whom one is in love; a sweetheart.

inamorato *n* (*pl* **inamoratos**) a man who is in love, a lover.

inane *adj* lacking sense, silly.—**inanely** *adv*.

inanimate *adj* not animate; showing no signs of life; dull.—**inanimately** *adv*.—**inanimateness, inanimation** *n*.

inanition *n* emptiness; exhaustion from lack of nourishment.

inanity *n* (*pl* **inanities**) (*arch*) emptiness; silliness; frivolity; a silly action or remark.

inapplicable *adj* not applicable.—**inapplicability** *n*.

inapposite *adj* not apposite, unsuitable.—**inappositely** *adv*.

inappreciable *adj* not to be appreciated or estimated; of no consequence.

inappreciative *adj* unappreciative.

inapproachable *adj* not approachable, inaccessible.

inappropriate *adj* unsuitable.—**inappropriately** *adv*.—**inappropriateness** *n*.

inapt *adj* inappropriate; unfit, unskilful.—**inaptitude** *n*.

inarticulate *adj* not expressed in words; incapable of being expressed in words; incapable of coherent or effective expression of ideas, feelings, etc.—**inarticulately** *adv*.

inartistic *adj* not artistic; not appreciative of art.—**inartistically** *adv*.

inasmuch *adv* in like degree; (*with* **as**) seeing that; because.

inattentive *adj* not attending; neglectful.—**inattention** *n*.

inaudible *adj* unable to be heard.—**inaudibility** *n*.—**inaudibly** *adv*.

inaugural *n* of or pertaining to an inauguration; a speech made at an inauguration.

inaugurate *vt* to admit ceremonially into office; to open (a building, etc) formally to the public; to cause to begin, initiate.—**inauguration** *n*.—**inaugurator** *n*.

inauspicious *adj* ill-starred; unlucky; unfavourable; unfortunate.

inboard *adv, adj* towards the centre or within an aircraft, ship, etc.

inborn *adj* present from birth; hereditary.

inbred *adj* innate; produced by inbreeding.

inbreed *vti* (**inbreeding, inbred**) to breed by continual mating of individuals of the same or closely related stocks.

in-built *adj* built in.

Inc. *abbr* = Incorporated.

incalculable *adj* beyond calculation; unpredictable.—**incalculability** *n*.—**incalculably** *adv*.

incalescent *adj* (*chem*) increasing in heat.—**incalescence** *n*.

in camera *adv* in private; in a judge's chamber as opposed to open court.

incandesce *vi* to glow with heat.

incandescent *adj* glowing or luminous with intense heat.—**incandescence** *n*.

incantation *n* words chanted in magic spells or rites.—**incantational, incantatory** *adj*.

incapable *adj* lacking capability; not able or fit to perform an activity.—**incapability** *n*.—**incapably** *adv*.

incapacitate *vt* to weaken, to disable; to make ineligible.—**incapacitation** *n*.

incapacity *n* (*pl* **incapacities**) lack of power or strength, inability; ineligibility.

incarcerate *vt* to put in prison, to confine.—**incarceration** *n*.—**incarcerator** *n*.

incarnate *adj* endowed with a human body; personified. * *vt* to give bodily form to; to be the type or embodiment of.—**incarnation** *n*.

incautious *adj* not cautious, reckless.—**incautiously** *adv*.—**incautiousness, incaution** *n*.

incendiarism *n* the act of burning illegally; arson.

incendiary *adj* pertaining to arson; (*bomb*) designed to start fires; tending to stir up or inflame. * *n* (*pl* **incendiaries**) a person that sets fire to a building, etc maliciously, an arsonist; an incendiary substance (as in a bomb); a person who stirs up violence, etc.

incense[1] *vt* to make extremely angry.

incense[2] *n* a substance that gives off a fragrant odour when burned; the fumes so produced; any pleasant odour.

incentive *n* a stimulus; a motive. * *adj* serving as a stimulus to action.

incept *vt* (*biol*) to ingest.

inception *n* the beginning of something.

inceptive *adj* noting a beginning, initial.

incertitude *n* doubt, uncertainty.

incessant *adj* never ceasing; continual, constant.—**incessancy** *n*.—**incessantly** *adv*.

incest *n* sexual intercourse between persons too closely related to marry legally.

incestuous *adj* involving incest; guilty of incest.

inch *n* a measure of length equal to 1/12 foot (2.54 cm); a very small distance or amount. * *vti* to move very slowly, or by degrees.

inchmeal *adv* inch by inch, gradually.

inchoate *adj* just begun; at a very early stage.—**inchoation** *n*.—**inchoative** *adj*.

incidence *n* the degree or range of occurrence or effect.

incident *adj* likely to happen as a result; falling upon or affecting. * *n* something that happens; an event, esp a minor one; a minor conflict.

incidental *adj* happening in connection with something more important; happening by chance. * *npl* miscellaneous items, minor expenses.

incidental music *n* background music for a film, play, etc.

incidentally *adv* in passing, as an aside.

incinerate *vt* to reduce to ashes.—**incineration** *n*.

incinerator *n* a furnace for burning rubbish.

incipient *adj* beginning to be or appear; initial.—**incipience, incipiency** *n*.

incise *vt* to cut or carve into a surface; to engrave.—**incised** *adj*.

incision *n* incising; a cut made into something, esp by a surgeon into a body.

incisive *adj* keen, penetrating; decisive; biting.—**incisively** *adv*.—**incisiveness** *n*.

incisor *n* any of the front cutting teeth at the front of the mouth.

incite *vt* to urge to action; to rouse.—**incitement** *n*.—**inciter** *n*.—**incitingly** *adv*.

incivility *n* (*pl* **incivilities**) lack of civility or courtesy; impoliteness.

incl. *abbr* = including; inclusive.

inclement *adj* (*weather*) rough, stormy; lacking mercy; harsh.—**inclemency** *n*.

inclination *n* a propensity or disposition, esp a liking; a deviation from the horizontal or vertical; a slope; inclining or being inclined; a bending movement, a bow.—**inclinational** *adj*.

incline *vi* to lean, to slope; to be disposed towards an opinion or action. * *vt* to cause to bend (the head or body) forwards; to cause to deviate, esp from the horizontal or vertical. * *n* a slope.—**inclinable** *adj*.—**incliner** *n*.

inclinometer *n* an instrument used to measure the angle made by an aircraft with the horizontal.

include *vt* to enclose, contain; to comprise as part or a larger group, amount, etc.—**includable, includible** *adj*.—**inclusion** *n*.

inclusive *adj* comprehensive; including the limits specified.—**inclusively** *adv*.

incognito *adj, adv* under an assumed name or identity. * *n* (*pl* **incognitos**) a person appearing or living incognito; the name assumed by such a person.—**incognita** *nf* (*pl* **incognitas**).

incognizant *adj* (*usu with* of) unaware.—**incognizance** *n*.

incoherent *adj* lacking organization or clarity; inarticulate in speech or thought.—**incoherence, incoherency** *n*.—**incoherently** *adv*.

incombustible *adj* not able to be burned or ignited. * *n* an incombustible substance.—**incombustibility** *n*.—**incombustibly** *adv*.

income *n* the money etc received for labour or services, or from property, investments, etc.

incomer *n* one who comes in; one who succeeds, as a tenant

income tax *n* a tax levied on the net income of a person or business.

incoming *adj* coming; accruing. * *n* the act of coming in; that which comes in; income.

incommensurable *adj* not able to be measured or judged comparatively.—**incommensurability** *n*.—**incommensurably** *adv*.

incommensurate *adj* not commensurate; disproportionate; inadequate; incommensurable.

incommode *vt* to give inconvenience or trouble to; to disturb.—**incommodious** *adj*.

incommunicable *adj* not capable of being communicated.—**incommunicability** *n*.—**incommunicably** *adv*.

incommunicado *adj* not allowed to communicate with others.

incommunicative *adj* not disposed to give information, reserved.

incommutable *adj* which cannot be exchanged or commuted.

incomparable *adj* beyond comparison, matchless; not amenable to comparison.—**incomparability** *n*.—**incomparably** *adv*.

incompatible *adj* not able to exist together in harmony; antagonistic; inconsistent.—**incompatibility** *n*. —**incompatibly** *adv*.

incompetent *adj* lacking the necessary ability, skill, etc. * *n* an incompetent person.—**incompetence, incompetency** *n*.—**incompetently** *adv*.

incomplete *adj* unfinished; lacking a part or parts.—**incompletely** *adv*.—**incompleteness, incompletion** *n*.

incomprehensible *adj* not to be understood or grasped by the mind; inconceivable.—**incomprehensibility** *n*.—**incomprehensibly** *adv*.

incomprehension *n* failure to understand.

incompressible *adj* incapable of being reduced in volume by pressure; resisting pressure.—**incompressibility** *n*.—**incompressibly** *adv*.

incomputable *adj* incalculable, which cannot be reckoned.

inconceivable *adj* impossible to comprehend; (*inf*) unbelievable.—**inconceivably** *adv*.

inconclusive *adj* leading to no definite result; ineffective; inefficient.—**inconclusively** *adv*.—**inconclusiveness** *n*.

incondensable, incondensible *adj* which cannot be condensed or compressed.

inconformity *n* lack of conformity.

incongruity *n* (*pl* **incongruities**) unsuitableness of one thing to another, inconsistency; absurdity.

incongruous *adj* lacking harmony or agreement of parts; unsuitable; inappropriate.—**incongruously** *adv*.—**incongruousness, incongruence** *n*.

inconsequential, inconsequent *adj* not following logically; irrelevant.—**inconsequence** *n*.—**inconsequentiality** *n*.—**inconsequentially, inconsequently** *adv*.

inconsiderable *adj* trivial.—**inconsiderably** *adv*.

inconsiderate *adj* uncaring about others; thoughtless.—**inconsiderately** *adv*.—**inconsideration** *n*.

inconsistency *n* (*pl* **inconsistencies**) the quality of being inconsisteng; incongruity.—**inconsistently** *adv*.

inconsistent *adj* not compatible with other facts; contradictory; irregular, fickle.

inconsolable *adj* not able to be comforted.—**inconsolability** *n*.—**inconsolably** *adv*.

inconsonant *adj* not in harmony or agreement.—**inconsonance** *n*.

inconspicuous *adj* not conspicuous.—**inconspicuously** *adv*.—**inconspicuousness** *n*.

inconstant *adj* subject to change; unstable; variable; fickle; capricious.—**inconstancy** *n*.

inconsumable *adj* which cannot be consumed or used up.

incontestable *adj* not admitting of question or doubt; incontrovertible.—**incontestability** *n*.—**incontestably** *adv*.

incontinent *adj* unable to control the excretion of bodily wastes; lacking self-restraint.—**incontinence** *n*.

incontrovertible *adj* not admitting of controversy; indisputable.—**incontrovertibility** *n*.—**incontrovertibly** *adv*.

inconvenience *n* want of convenience; unfitness; that which incommodes; disadvantage. * *vt* to put to inconvenience; to annoy.—**inconvenient** *adj*.

inconvertible *adj* incapable of being converted into or exchanged for something else.—**inconvertibility** *n*.—**inconvertibly** *adv*.

inconvincible *adj* unable or unwilling to be convinced.

incoordination *n* lack of coordination.

incorporate *vt* to combine; to include; to embody; to merge; to form into a corporation. * *vi* to unite into one group or substance; to form a corporation. * *adj* united; formed into a corporation.—**incorporation** *n*.—**incorporative** *adj*.—**incorporator** *n*.

incorporeal *adj* not corporeal, without substance; spiritual; (*law*) intangible, and existing only in contemplation of the law.—**incorporeally** *adv*.—**incorporeity, incorporeality** *n*.

incorrect *adj* faulty; inaccurate; improper.—**incorrectly** *adv*.—**incorrectness** *n*.

incorrigible *adj* not able to be corrected, reformed or altered.—**incorrigibility** *n*.—**incorrigibly** *adv*.

incorrupt, incorrupted *adj* free from physical or moral taint; unimpaired; upright, esp above the influence of corruption or bribery; honest.

incorruptible *adj* incapable of physical corruption, decay or dissolution; incapable of being bribed; not liable to moral perversion or contamination.—**incorruptibility** *n*.—**incorruptibly** *adv*.

increase *vti* to make or become greater in size, quality, amount, etc. * *n* increasing or becoming increased; the result or amount by which something increases.—**increasable** *adj*.—**increaser** *n*.—**increasingly** *adv*.

incredible *adj* unbelievable; (*inf*) wonderful.—**incredibility** *n*.—**incredibly** *adv*.

incredulity *n* scepticism; disbelief.

incredulous *adj* not able or willing to accept as true; unbelieving.—**incredulously** *adv*.—**incredulousness** *n*.

increment *n* (the amount of) an increase; an addition.—**incremental** *adj*.

increscent *adj* (*moon*) waxing, growing.

incriminate *vt* to involve in or indicate as involved in a crime or fault.—**incrimination** *n*.—**incriminator** *n*.—**incriminatory** *adj*.

incubate *vti* to sit on and hatch (eggs); to keep (eggs, embryos, etc) in a favourable environment for hatching or developing; to develop, as by planning.—**incubation** *n*.—**incubative, incubatory** *adj*.

incubator *n* an apparatus in which eggs are hatched by artificial heat; an apparatus for nurturing premature babies until they can survive unaided.

incubus *n* (*pl* **incubi, incubuses**) an evil spirit believed in folklore to have intercourse with women as they sleep; something oppressive or disturbing, as a nightmare.

inculcate *vt* to teach by frequent repetition or urging.—**inculcation** *n*.—**inculcator** *n*.

inculpate *vt* to blame, censure; to incriminate.—**inculpation** *n*.—**inculpative, inculpatory** *adj*.

incumbency *n* (*pl* **incumbencies**) a duty or obligation; a term of office.

incumbent *adj* resting (on or upon) one as a duty or obligation; currently in office. * *n* the holder of an office, etc.

incunabulum *n* (*pl* **incunabula**) any book printed before 1500; the early stages of anything.—**incunabular** *adj*.

incur *vt* (**incurring, incurred**) to bring upon oneself (something undesirable).—**incurrable** *adj*.

incurable *adj* incapable of being cured; beyond the power of skill or medicine; lacking remedy; incorrigible. * *n* a person diseased beyond cure.—**incurability** *n*.—**incurably** *adv*.

incurious *adj* indifferent, heedless.—**incuriosity** *n*.

incursion *n* an invasion or raid into another's territory, etc.—**incursive** *adj*.

incurvate *vti* to curve inwards. * *adj* curved or bent inwards.—**incurvation** *n*.

incus *n* (*pl* **incudes**) a bone found in the middle ear.

incuse *n* a design stamped onto a coin.

indebted *adj* in debt; obliged; owing gratitude.—**indebtedness** *n*.

indecency *n* (*pl* **indecencies**) lack of decency, modesty, or good manners; something indecent, vulgar, or obscene.

indecent *adj* offending against accepted standards of decent behaviour.—**indecently** *adv*.

indecent assault *n* a sexual assault not involving rape.

indecent exposure *n* the offence of deliberately exposing one's genitals in public.

indeciduous *adj* (*bot*) not deciduous; evergreen.

indecipherable *adj* which cannot be deciphered; illegible.

indecision *n* not able to make a decision; hesitation.

indecisive *adj* inconclusive; irresolute.—**indecisively** *adv*.—**indecisiveness** *n*.

indeclinable *adj* (*gram*) which cannot be declined, having no inflected forms.

indecorous *adj* violating decorum, or any accepted rule of conduct.—**indecorum** *n*.

indeed *adv* truly, certainly. * *interj* expressing irony, surprise, disbelief, etc.

indefatigable *adj* tireless.—**indefatigability** *n*.—**indefatigably** *adv*.

indefeasible *adj* not to be defeated or made void, as a title.—**indefeasibility** *n*.—**indefeasibly** *adv*.

indefensible *adj* unable to be defended or justified.—**indefensibility** *n*.—**indefensibly** *adv*.

indefinable *adj* that cannot be defined.—**indefinably** *adv*.

indefinite *adj* not certain, undecided; imprecise, vague; having no fixed limits.—**indefinitely** *adv*.—**indefiniteness** *n*.

indefinite article *n* the word "a" or "an."

indehiscent *adj* (*bot*) not opening when mature.—**indehiscence** *n*.

indelible *adj* not able to be removed or erased; (*pen, ink, etc*) making an indelible mark.—**indelibility** *adv*.—**indelibly** *adv*.

indelicacy *n* (*pl* **indelicacies**) lack of delicacy; something offensive to modesty or refined taste.

indelicate *adj* improper; rough, crude; tactless.—**indelicately** *adv*.

indemnify *vt* (**indemnifying, indemnified**) to insure against loss, damage, etc; to repay (for damage, loss, etc).—**indemnification** *n*.—**indemnifier** *n*.

indemnity *n* (*pl* **indemnities**) compensation for damage or loss; insurance against future loss or injury.

indemonstrable *adj* which cannot be demonstrated or proved.

indent *vt* to make notches in; to begin (a line of text) farther in from the margin than the rest. * *vi* to form an indentation. * *n* a dent or notch.—**indentor** *n*.

indentation *n* a being indented; a notch, cut, inlet, etc; a dent; a spacing in from the margin (—*also* **indention, indent**).

indenture *n* a written agreement, a contract binding one person to work for another. * *vt* to bind by indentures.

independence *n* the state of being independent.

Independence Day *n* the anniversary of the adoption of the American Declaration of Independence on 4 July 1776.

independency *n* (*pl* **independencies**) a self-governing political unit.

independent *adj* freedom from the influence or control of others; self-governing; self-determined; not adhering to any political party; not connected with others; not depending on another for financial support. * *n* a person who is independent in thinking, action etc.—**independently** *adv*.

in-depth *adj* detailed, thorough.

indescribable *adj* unable to be described; too beautiful, horrible, intense, etc for words.—**indescribability** *n*.—**indescribably** *adv*.

indestructible *adj* not able to be destroyed.—**indestructibility** *n*.—**indestructibly** *adv*.

indeterminable *adj* which cannot be ascertained, settled or classified.

indeterminate *adj* vague, uncertain; not defined or fixed in value.—**indeterminacy, indetermination** *adv*.—**indeterminately** *adv*.

indeterminism *n* (*philos*) the doctrine that the will has a certain freedom, independent of motives.

index *n* (*pl* **indexes, indices**) an alphabetical list of names, subjects, items, etc mentioned in a printed book, usu listed alphabetically at the end of the text; a figure showing ratio or relative change, as of prices or wages; any indication or sign; a pointer or dial on an instrument; the exponent of a number. * *vt* to make an index of or for.—**indexer** *n*.

index arbitrage *see* **arbitrage**.

index finger *n* the forefinger.

Indiaman *n* (*pl* **Indiamen**) (*formerly*) a commercial sailing vessel involved in trade with India.

Indian *n* a native of India; an American Indian, the original inhabitants of the continent of America.

Indian corn *n* maize.

Indian file *n* single file.

Indian ink *n* a solid black pigment; a black ink made from this.—*also* **India ink**.

Indian summer *n* a period of unusually warm weather in the autumn.

indiarubber *n* an elastic gummy substance obtained from the milky juice of several tropical trees and used for rubbing out pencil marks.

Indic *adj* a term sometimes applied to the Indo-European languages of India, eg Sanskrit, Hindi, Bengali, etc.

indicant *n* something which indicates.

indicate *vt* to point out; to show or demonstrate; to be a sign or symptom of; to state briefly, suggest.—**indicatable** *adj*.—**indication** *n*.—**indicatory** *adj*.

indicative *adj* serving as a sign (of); (*gram*) denoting the mood of the verb that affirms or denies.

indicator *n* a thing that indicates or points; a measuring device with a pointer, etc; an instrument showing the operating condition of a piece of machinery, etc; a device giving updated information, such as a departure board in a railway station or airport; a flashing light used to warn of a change in direction of a vehicle.

indices *see* **index**.

indicia *npl* (*sing* **indicium**) distinguishing markings.

indict *vt* to charge with a crime; to accuse.

indictable *adj* subject to being indicted; making one liable to indictment.

indictment *n* a formal written statement framed by a prosecuting authority charging a person of a crime.

indifferent *adj* showing no concern, uninterested; unimportant; impartial; average; mediocre.—**indifference** *n*. —**indifferently** *adv*.

indifferentism *n* systematic indifference, esp with regard to religion.—**indifferentist** *n*.

indigen, indigene *n* a native (person, animal, etc).

indigenous *adj* existing naturally in a particular country, region, or environment; native.

indigent *adj* poor, needy.—**indigence** *n*.

indigestible *adj* difficult or impossible to digest.—**indigestibility** *n*.

indigestion *n* a pain caused by difficulty in digesting food.

indigestive *adj* pertaining to, or having, indigestion.

indign *adj* (*arch*) unworthy; disgraceful.

indignant *adj* expressing anger, esp at mean or unjust action.—**indignantly** *adv*.

indignation *n* anger at something regarded as unfair, wicked, etc.

indignity *n* (*pl* **indignities**) humiliation; treatment making one feel degraded, undignified.

indigo *n* (*pl* **indigos, indigoes**) a deep blue dye or colour.

indirect *adj* not straight; roundabout; secondary; dishonest.—**indirectly** *adv*.—**indirectness** *n*.

indirect evidence *n* circumstantial or inferential evidence.

indirection *n* indirect means or procedure; lack of direction; deceit.

indirect object *n* (*gram*) a person or thing affected by a verb but less directly than the object.

indirect speech *n* reported speech.

indirect tax *n* a tax levied on goods and services (which increases prices) rather than directly on individuals or companies.

indiscernible *adj* not discernible.—**indiscernibly** *adv*.

indiscipline *n* lack of discipline.

indiscreet *adj* not discreet; tactless.—**indiscreetly** *adv*.

indiscrete *adj* not separated into distinct parts.

indiscretion *n* an indiscreet act; rashness.—**indiscretionary** *adj*.

indiscriminate *adj* not making a careful choice; confused; random; making no distinctions.—**indiscriminately** *adv*.—**indiscrimination** *n*.—**indiscriminative** *adj*.

indispensable *adj* absolutely essential.—**indispensability** *n*.—**indispensably** *adv*.

indispose *vt* to make unfit or unwell; to disincline.

indisposed *adj* ill or sick; reluctant; disinclined.

indisposition *n* disinclination; a slight illness.

indisputable *adj* unquestionable; certain.—**indisputability** *n*.—**indisputably** *adv*.

indissoluble *adj* permanent; not able to be dissolved or destroyed.—**indissolubility** *n*.—**indissolubly** *adv*.

indistinct *adj* not clearly marked; dim; not distinct.—**indistinctly** *adv*.—**indistinctness** *n*.

indistinctive *adj* not capable of making distinctions; lacking distinctive characteristics.—**indistinctiveness** *n*.

indistinguishable *adj* not distinguishable; lacking

identifying characteristics.—**indistinguishability** *n*.—**indistinguishably** *adv*.

indite *vt* (*arch*) to write.

indium *n* a soft metallic element used in alloys and electronic circuitry.

individual *adj* existing as a separate thing or being; of, by, for, or relating to a single person or thing. * *n* a single thing or being; a person.

individualist *n* a person who thinks or behaves with marked independence.—**individualism** *n*.—**individualistic** *adj*.—**individualistically** *adv*.

individuality *n* (*pl* **individualities**) the condition of being individual; separate or distinct existence; distinctive character.

individualize *vt* to mark as distinct, particularize; to distinguish individually.—**individualization** *n*.

individually *adv* in a distinctive manner; one by one; separately; personally.

individuate *vt* to individualize.—**individuation** *n*.

indivisible *adj* not divisible.—**indivisibility** *n*.—**indivisibly** *adv*.

indocile *adj* unteachable; intractable.—**indocility** *n*.

indoctrinate *vt* to systematically instruct in doctrines, ideas, beliefs, etc.—**indoctrination** *n*.—**indoctrinator** *n*.

Indo-European *adj* of a family of languages (including English) spoken in most of Europe and Asia as far east as northern India. —*also n*.

indolent *adj* idle; lazy.—**indolence** *n*.—**indolently** *adv*.

indomitable *adj* not easily discouraged or defeated.—**indomitability** *n*.—**indomitably** *adv*.

indoor *adj* done, used, or situated within a building.

indoors *adv* in or into a building.

indorse *see* **endorse**.

indraft *n* an inlet or inward current.

indubitable *adj* not capable of being doubted.—**indubitability** *n*.—**indubitably** *adv*.

induce *vt* to persuade; to bring on; to draw (a conclusion) from particular facts; to bring about (an electric or magnetic effect) in a body by placing it within a field of force.—**inducer** *n*.—**inducible** *adj*.

inducement *n* something that induces; a stimulus; a motive.

induct *vt* to place formally in an office, a society, etc; to enrol (esp a draftee) in the armed forces.

inductance *n* the property of an electric circuit by which an electromotive force is produced by a variation in the current in the same or a neighbouring circuit; the measure of inductance in an electric circuit.

inductile *adj* not ductile, not pliant.

induction *n* the act or an instance of inducting, eg into office; reasoning from particular premises to general conclusions; the inducing of an electric or magnetic effect by a field of force.—**inductional** *adj*.

inductive *adj* proceeding by or producing induction; operating by induction; susceptible to being acted on by induction.

inductor *n* one who inducts; (*elect*) that part of an apparatus that acts inductively.

indue *see* **endue**.

indulge *vt* to satisfy (a desire); to gratify the wishes of; to humour. * *vi* to give way to one's desire.—**indulger** *n*.

indulgence *n* indulging or being indulged; a thing indulged in; a favour or privilege; (*RC Church*) a remission of punishment still due for a sin after the guilt has been forgiven.

indulgent *adj* indulging or characterized by indulgence; lenient.—**indulgently** *adv*.

induline, indulin *n* a dark blue dye.

indult *n* (*RC Church*) a licence from the Pope authorizing something not sanctioned by Church law.

induplicate, induplicated *adj* (*bot*) bent inwards.

indurate *vt* to make hard or callous. * *vi* to grow hard or callous.—**induration** *n*.—**indurative** *adj*.

indusium *n* (*pl* **indusia**) (*bot*) the covering of the growing spores in many ferns.—**indusial** *adj*.

industrial *adj* relating to or engaged in industry; used in industry; having many highly developed industries.—**industrially** *adv*.

industrialism *n* social and economic organization characterized by large industries, machine production, urban workers, etc.

industrialist *n* a person who owns or manages an industrial enterprise.

industrialize *vti* to make or become industrial.—**industrialization** *n*.

industrial relations *n* the relations between employees and employers.

industrious *adj* hard-working.—**industriously** *adv*.—**industriousness** *n*.

industry *n* (*pl* **industries**) organized production or manufacture of goods; manufacturing enterprises collectively; a branch of commercial enterprise producing a particular product; any large-scale business activity; the owners and managers of industry; diligence.

indwelling *vti* (**indwelling, indwelt**) to dwell (in).

inebriate *vt* to intoxicate, esp with alcoholic drink. * *n* a drunkard. * *adj* inebriated.—**inebriation** *n*.

inebriated *adj* drunken.

inedible *adj* not fit to be eaten.—**inedibility** *n*.

inedited *adj* unpublished; not edited.

ineducable *adj* impossible to educate, esp due to mental deficiency.

ineffable *adj* too intense or great to be spoken; unutterable; too sacred to be spoken.—**ineffability** *n*.—**ineffably** *adv*.

ineffaceable *adj* which cannot be effaced.—**ineffaceability** *n*.

ineffective *adj* not effective.—**ineffectively** *adv*.—**ineffectiveness** *n*.

ineffectual *adj* not effectual; futile.—**ineffectuality** *n*.—**ineffectually** *adv*.

inefficacious *adj* not having the power to produce a desired effect.—**inefficacy** *n*.

inefficiency *n* (*pl* **inefficiencies**) the quality or condition of being inefficient; an instance of inefficiency or incompetence.

inefficient *adj* not efficient.—**inefficiently** *adv*.

inelastic *adj* not elastic; inflexible, unyielding.—**inelastically** *adv*.—**inelasticity** *n*.

inelegant *adj* ungraceful; lacking refinement or polish.—**inelegance** *n*.

ineligible *adj* not eligible.—**ineligibility** *n*.

ineluctable *adj* not possible to escape from or avoid.—**ineluctably** *adv*.

inept *adj* unsuitable; unfit; foolish; awkward; clumsy.—**ineptitude** *n*.—**ineptly** *adv*.

inequality *n* (*pl* **inequalities**) lack of equality in size, status, etc; unevenness.

inequitable *adj* unjust, unfair.—**inequitably** *adv*.

inequity *n* (*pl* **inequities**) lack of equity; injustice.

ineradicable *adj* which cannot be eradicated.

inert *adj* without power to move or to resist; inactive; dull; slow; with few or no active properties.—**inertly** *adv.*—**inertness** *n.*

inertia *n* (*physics*) the tendency of matter to remain at rest (or continue in a fixed direction) unless acted on by an outside force; disinclination to act.

inertial *adj* of, or pertaining to, inertia.

inescapable *adj* which cannot be escaped, inevitable.

inessential *adj* not essential.

inestimable *adj* not to be estimated; beyond measure or price; incalculable; invaluable.—**inestimably** *adv.*

inevitable *adj* sure to happen; unavoidable. * *n* something that is inevitable.—**inevitability** *n.*—**inevitably** *adv.*

inexact *adj* not strictly true or correct.—**inexactitude** *n.*—**inexactly** *adv.*

inexcusable *adj* without excuse; unpardonable.—**inexcusably** *adv.*

inexhaustible *adj* not to be exhausted or spent; unfailing; unwearied.—**inexhaustibility** *n.*—**inexhaustibly** *adv.*

inexorable *adj* unable to be persuaded by persuasion or entreaty, relentless.—**inexorability** *n.*—**inexorably** *adv.*

inexpedient *adj* unsuitable to circumstances; inadvisable.—**inexpedience, inexpediency** *n.*

inexpensive *adj* cheap.—**inexpensively** *adv.*

inexperience *n* want of experience or of the knowledge that comes by experience.

inexperienced *adj* lacking experience; unpractised; unskilled; unversed.

inexpert *adj* unskilled; lacking the knowledge or dexterity derived from practice.

inexpiable *adj* which cannot be expiated.

inexplicable *adj* not to be explained, made plain, or intelligible; not to be interpreted or accounted for.—**inexplicability** *n.*—**inexplicably** *adv.*

inexplicit *adj* not clear.

inexpressible *adj* incapable of being expressed, uttered, or described.—**inexpressibly** *adv.*

inexpressive *adj* lacking expression or distinct significance.

inextensible *adj* which cannot be extended.—**inextensibility** *n.*

inextinguishable *adj* which cannot be extinguished, unquenchable.

in extremis *adv* close to death; in a very difficult situation.

inextricable *adj* that cannot be disentangled, solved, or escaped from.—**inextricably** *adv.*

infallible *adj* incapable of being wrong; dependable; reliable.—**infallibility** *n.*—**infallibly** *adv.*

infamous *adj* having a bad reputation; notorious; causing a bad reputation; scandalous.

infamy *n* (*pl* **infamies**) ill fame; public disgrace; ignominy.

infancy *n* (*pl* **infancies**) early childhood; the beginning or early existence of anything.

infant *n* a very young child; a baby.

infanta *n* a title for a Spanish princess, not the heir apparent.

infante *n* a title for a Spanish prince, not the heir apparent.

infanticide *n* the killing of an infant; a person who does this.—**infanticidal** *adj.*

infantile *adj* of infants; like an infant, babyish.

infantile paralysis *n* poliomyletis.

infantry *n* (*pl* **infantries**) soldiers trained to fight on foot.

infatuate *vt* to inspire with intense, foolish, or short-lived passion.—**infatuated** *adj.*—**infatuatedly** *adv.*

infatuation *n* an extravagant passion.

infect *vt* to contaminate with disease-causing microorganisms; to taint; to affect, esp so as to harm.—**infective** *adj.*

infection *n* an infecting or being infected; an infectious disease; a diseased condition.

infectious *adj* (*disease*) able to be transmitted; causing or transmitted by infection; tending to spread to others.—**infectiousness** *n.*

infectious hepatitis *n* an infectious disease which causes inflammation of the liver.

infectious mononucleosis *n* an infectious disease characterized by inflammation of the lymph glands.—*also* **glandular fever.**

infelicitous *adj* unfortunate; unhappy; inappropriate; ill-timed.

infelicity *n* (*pl* **infelicities**) misfortune; unhappiness; inapproriateness; an infelicitous act or expression.

infer *vt* (**inferring, inferred**) to conclude by reasoning from facts or premises; to accept as a fact or consequence.—**inferable** *adj.*—**inferrer** *n.*

inference *n* an inferring; something inferred or deduced; a reasoning from premises to a conclusion.—**inferential** *adj.*

inferior *adj* lower in position, rank, degree, or quality. * *n* an inferior person.—**inferiority** *n.*

inferiority complex *n* (*psychol*) an acute sense of inferiority expressed by a lack of confidence or in exaggerated aggression.

infernal *adj* of hell; hellish; fiendish; (*inf*) irritating, detestable.—**infernally** *adv.*

inferno *n* (*pl* **infernos**) hell; intense heat; a devastating fire.

infertile *adj* not fertile.—**infertility** *n.*

infest *vt* to overrun in large numbers, usu so as to be harmful; to be parasitic in or on.—**infestation** *n.*—**infester** *n.*

infidel *n* a person who does not believe in a certain religion; a person who has no religion.

infidelity *n* (*pl* **infidelities**) unfaithfulness, esp in marriage.

infield *n* (*cricket*) the area of the ground near the wicket; (*baseball*) the area of the field enclosed by the baselines.

infielder *n* (*baseball, cricket*) a player in an infield position.

infighting *n* (*boxing*) exchanging punches at close quarters; intense competition within an organization.—**infighter** *n.*

infiltrate *vti* to filter or pass gradually through or into; to permeate; to penetrate (enemy lines, etc) gradually or stealthily, eg as spies.—**infiltration** *n.*—**infiltrator** *n.*

infinite *adj* endless, limitless; very great; vast.—**infinitely** *adv.*

infinitesimal *adj* immeasurably small.—**infinitesimally** *adv.*

infinitive *n* (*gram*) the form of a verb without reference to person, number or tense.—**infinitival** *adj.*

infinitude *n* the condition or quality of being infinite; infinity.

infinity *n* (*pl* **infinities**) the condition or quality of being infinite; an unlimited number, quantity, or time period.

infirm *adj* physically weak, esp from old age or illness; irresolute.

infirmary *n* (*pl* **infirmaries**) a hospital or place for the treatment of the sick.

infirmity *n* (*pl* **infirmities**) being infirm; a physical weakness.

infix *vt* to fix or insert in.

in flagrante delicto *adv* in the very act of commiting the crime, red-handed.—*also* **flagrante delicto**.

inflame *vti* to arouse, excite, etc, or to become aroused, excited, etc; to undergo or cause to undergo inflammation.—**inflamingly** *adv*.

inflammable *adj* able to catch fire, flammable; easily excited.—**inflammability** *n*.

inflammation *n* an inflaming or being inflamed; redness, pain, heat, and swelling in the body, due to injury or disease.

inflammatory *adj* rousing excitement, anger, etc; of or caused by inflammation.—**inflammatorily** *adv*.

inflatable *adj* able to be inflated.

inflate *vti* to fill or become filled with air or gas; to puff up with pride; to increase beyond what is normal, esp the supply of money or credit.—**inflatedly** *adv*.—**inflater, inflator** *n*.

inflation *n* an inflating or being inflated; an increase in the currency in circulation or a marked expansion of credit, resulting in a fall in currency value and a sharp rise in prices.

inflationary *adj* pertaining to or causing inflation.

inflationist *n, adj* (someone) in favour of a policy of an increased issue of money and availability of credit, with inflation as a consequence.

inflect *vt* to change the form (of a word) by inflection; to vary the tone of (the voice).—**inflective** *adj*.—**inflector** *n*.

inflection *n* a bend; the change in the form of a word to indicate number, case, tense, etc; a change in the tone of the voice.—**inflectional** *adj*.

inflexible *adj* not flexible; stiff, rigid; fixed; unyielding.—**inflexibility** *n*.—**inflexibly** *adv*.

inflict *vt* to impose (pain, a penalty, etc) on a person or thing.—**inflicter, inflictor** *n*.—**infliction** *n*.

inflorescence *n* the producing of blossoms; the arrangement of flowers on a stem; a flower cluster; flowers collectively.—**inflorescent** *adj*.

inflow *n* something which flows in.

influence *n* the power to affect others; the power to produce effects by having wealth, position, ability, etc; a person with influence. * *vt* to have influence on.—**influenceable** *adj*.

influent *adj* flowing in.

influential *adj* having or exerting great influence.—**influentially** *adv*.

influenza *n* a contagious feverish virus disease marked by muscular pain and inflammation of the respiratory system.—**influenzal** *adj*.

influx *n* a sudden inflow of people or things to a place.

info *n* (*sl*) information.

inform *vt* to provide knowledge of something to. * *vi* to give information to the police, etc, esp in accusing another.

informal *adj* not formal; not according to fixed rules or ceremony, etc; casual.—**informally** *adv*.

informality *n* (*pl* **informalities**) the lack of regular, customary, or legal form; an informal act.

informant *n* a person who gives information.

information *n* something told or facts learned; news; knowledge; data stored in or retrieved from a computer.—**informational** *adj*.

information technology *n* (the study of) the collection, retrieval, use, storage and communication of information using computers and microelectronic systems.

information theory *n* mathematical and statistical analysis of information communication systems.

informative, informatory *adj* conveying information, instructive.—**informatively** *adv*.

informer *n* a person who informs on another, esp to the police for a reward.

infra- *prefix* below; within; beneath; after.

infraction *n* a violation of a law, pact, etc.

infra dig *adj* (*inf*) beneath one's dignity.

infrangible *adj* unbreakable; inviolable.—**infrangibility** *n*.

infrared *n* (*radiation*) having a wavelength longer than light but shorter than radio waves; of, pertaining to, or using such radiation.

infrasonic *adj* (*soundwaves*) having a frequency below the audible range.—**infrasound** *n*.

infrastructure *n* the basic structure of any system or organization; the basic installations, such as roads, railways, factories, etc that determine the economic power of a country.

infrequent *adj* seldom occurring; rare.—**infrequence, infrequency** *n*.—**infrequently** *adv*.

infringe *vt* to break or violate, esp an agreement or a law.—**infringement** *n*.

infundibular, infundibulate *adj* funnel-shaped.

infuriate *vt* to enrage; to make furious.—**infuriating** *adj*.—**infuriatingly** *adv*.

infuse *vt* to instil or impart (qualities, etc); to inspire; to steep (tea leaves, etc) to extract the essence.—**infuser** *n*.

infusible[1] *adj* incapable of being fused or melted.—**infusibility** *n*.

infusible[2] *adj* capable of being infused.—**infusibility** *n*.

infusion *n* the act of infusing; something obtained by infusing.

infusorial earth *n* a silicious deposit composed chiefly of the shells of microscopic vegetable organisms called diatoms, used as a polishing powder and in the manufacture of dynamite.

ingenious *adj* clever, resourceful, etc; made or done in an original or clever way.—**ingeniously** *adv*.—**ingeniousness** *n*.

ingénue *n* a naive young woman.

ingenuity *n* (*pl* **ingenuities**) skill in contriving or inventing; resourcefulness.

ingenuous *adj* naive, innocent; candid.—**ingenuously** *adv*.—**ingenuousness** *n*.

ingest *vt* to take (as food) into the body.—**ingestion** *n*.—**ingestive** *adj*.

ingle *n* (*arch*) a fireplace.

inglenook *n* (a seat in) a recess by a large open fireplace.

inglorious *adj* disgraceful, shameful; obscure.

ingot *n* a brick-shaped mass of cast metal, esp gold or silver.

ingrain *vt* to make a deep impression upon; (*arch*) to dye.—*also* **engrain**.

ingrained *adj* (*habits, feelings, etc*) firmly established; (*dirt*) deeply embedded.—*also* **engrained**.

ingrate *adj* (*arch*) ungrateful. * *n* an ungrateful person.

ingratiate *vt* to bring oneself into another's favour.—**in-**

gratiating, **ingratiatory** adj.—**ingratiation** n.

ingratitude n absence of gratitude; insensibility to kindness.

ingredient n something included in a mixture; a component.

ingress n entrance.

in-group n a group favouring its own members at the expense of members of other groups.

ingrowing adj (toe nail, etc) growing abnormally into the flesh.

ingrowth n the process of growing inwards; something which grows inwards.

inguinal adj of the groin or its vicinity.

ingurgitate vt to swallow greedily.—**ingurgitation** n.

inhabit vt to live in; to occupy; to reside.

inhabitable adj fit for habitation.—**inhabitability** n.—**inhabitation** n.

inhabitant n a person or animal inhabiting a specified place.—**inhabitancy, inhabitance** n.

inhalant n a medicine, etc that is inhaled.

inhalation n the act of inhaling.

inhale vti to breathe in.

inhaler n a device that dispenses medicines in a fine spray for inhalation.

inharmonic, inharmonious adj lacking harmony; discordant.

inhere vi to be inherent.

inherent adj existing as an inseparable part of something.—**inherence, inherency** n.—**inherently** adv.

inherit vt to receive (property, a title, etc) under a will or by right of legal succession; to possess by genetic transmission. * vi to receive by inheritance; to succeed as heir.—**inheritor** n.

inheritable adj capable of being inherited.

inheritance n the action of inheriting; something inherited.

inhibit vt to restrain; to prohibit.—**inhibitor, inhibiter** n.

inhibition n an inhibiting or being inhibited; a mental process that restrains or represses an action, emotion, or thought.

inhospitable adj not hospitable; affording no shelter; barren; cheerless.—**inhospitably** adv.—**inhospitality** n.

in-house adj within an organization.

inhuman adj lacking in the human qualities of kindness, pity, etc; cruel, brutal, unfeeling; not human.

inhumane adj not humane; inhuman.

inhumanity n (pl **inhumanites**) the quality of being inhuman; cruelty.

inhume vt to bury, inter.—**inhumation** n.—**injumer** n.

inimical adj hostile; adverse, unfavourable.—**inimically** adv.

inimitable adj impossible to imitate; matchless.—**inimitably** adv.

iniquitous adj marked by iniquity.

iniquity n (pl **iniquities**) wickedness; great injustice.

initial adj of or at the beginning. * n the first letter of each word in a name; a large letter at the beginning of a chapter, etc. * vt (**initialing, initialed** or **initialling, initialled**) to sign with initials.—**initialer, initialler** n.—**initially** adv.

initialize vt (comput) to format (a disk) to suit a particular processor.—**initialization** n.

initiate vt to bring (something) into practice or use; to teach the fundamentals of a subject to; to admit as a member into a club, etc, esp with a secret ceremony.

* n an initiated person.—**initiator** n.—**initiatory** adj.

initiation n the act of initiating; a formal, often secret, ceremony of admission.

initiative n the action of taking the first step; ability to originate new ideas or methods.

inject vt to force (a fluid) into a vein, tissue, etc, esp with a syringe; to introduce (a remark, quality, etc), to interject.—**injectable** adj.

injection n an injecting; a substance that is injected.—**injective** adj.

injector n someone who, or something which, injects; a device for injecting fuel into an internal combustion engine; a device for filling the boiler of a steam engine with water.

injudicious adj not judicious; indiscreet; unwise.

injunction n a command; an order; a court order prohibiting or ordering a given action.—**injunctive** adj.

injure vt to harm physically or mentally; to hurt, do wrong to.—**injurer** n.

injurious adj causing injury.

injury n (pl **injuries**) physical damage; harm.

injury time n (sport) time added to compensate for stoppages through injuries to players.

injustice n the state or practice of being unfair; an unjust act.

ink n a coloured liquid used for writing, printing, etc; the dark protective secretion of an octopus, etc. * vt to cover, mark, or colour with ink.

inkhorn n (formerly) a container for ink.

inkling n a hint; a vague notion.

inkstand n a stand for an ink bottle.

inkwell n a container for ink.

inky adj (**inkier, inkiest**) like very dark ink in colour; black; covered with ink.—**inkiness** n.

inlaid see **inlay**.

inland adj of or in the interior of a country. * n an inland region. * adv into or toward this region.—**inlander** n.

in-law n a relative by marriage.

inlay vt (**inlaying, inlaid**) to decorate a surface by inserting pieces of metal, wood, etc. * n inlaid work; material inlaid.—**inlaid** adj.

inlet n a narrow strip of water extending into a body of land; an opening; a passage, pipe, etc for liquid to enter a machine, etc. * vt (**inletting, inletted**) to inlay; to insert.

in loco parentis (Latin) in the place of a parent.

inmate n a person confined with others in a prison or institution.

in memoriam (Latin) in memory of.

inmost adj farthest within; most secret.

inn n a small hotel; a restaurant or tavern, esp in the countryside.

innards npl (inf) the stomach and intestines, internal organs.

innate adj existing from birth; inherent; instinctive.—**innately** adv.

inner adj further within; inside, internal; private, exclusive. * n (archery) the innermost ring on a target.

inner city n the central area of a city, esp as affected by overcrowding and poverty.

innermost adj furthest within.

inner tube n the separate inflatable tube within a pneumatic tire.

innervation n the arrangement of nerve filaments in the body; special activity or stimulus in any part of the nervous system.

inning n (baseball) a team's turn at bat

innings n (pl **innings**) (cricket) a turn at bat for a batsman or side; the number of runs scored at this time; an opportunity to demonstrate one's abilities.

innkeeper n a person who owns or manages an inn.

innocence n the condition or quality of being innocent.

innocent adj not guilty of a particular crime; free from sin; blameless; harmless; inoffensive; simple, credulous, naive. * n an innocent person, as a child.—**innocence** n.—**innocently** adv.

innocuous adj harmless.—**innocuously** adv.—**innocuousness** n.

innominate adj without a name.

innovate vi to introduce new methods, ideas, etc; to make changes.—**innovation** n.—**innovative, innovatory** adv.

innovator n one who introduces, or seeks to introduce, new things.

innoxious adj harmless.

innuendo n (pl **innuendos, innuendoes**) a hint or sly remark, usu derogatory; an insinuation.

Innuit see **Inuit**.

innumerable, innumerous adj too many to be counted; very numerous.—**innumerability** n.—**innumerably** adv.

innumerate adj lacking knowledge or understanding of mathematics and science; not numerate.—also n.

inobservance n inattention; failure to observe (law, etc).—**inobservant** adj.

inoculate vt to inject a serum or a vaccine into, esp in order to create immunity; to protect as if by inoculation.—**inoculation** n.—**inoculative** adj.

inodorous adj without odour.

inoffensive adj harmless, not offensive.

inofficious adj contrary to moral duty.

inoperable adj not suitable for surgery.—**inoperability** n.

inoperative adj not working; producing no effect.

inopportune adj unseasonable; untimely.—**inopportuneness, inopportunity** n.

inordinate adj excessive.—**inordinately** adv.

inorganic adj not having the structure or characteristics of living organisms; denoting a chemical compound not containing carbon.—**inorganically** adv.

inorganic chemistry n the chemistry of all substances except those containing carbon.

inosculate vti (anat, of blood vessels, fibres, etc) to join closely, be closely joined.—**inosculation** n.

inpatient n a patient being treated while remaining in hospital.

in perpetuum adv perpetually, forever.

in posse adj, adv having a possible but not an actual existence, potential.

input n what is put in, as power into a machine, data into a computer, etc. * vt (**inputting, input** or **inputted**) to put in; to enter (data) into a computer.

inquest n a judicial inquiry held by a coroner, esp into a case of violent or unexplained death; (inf) any detailed inquiry or investigation.

inquietude n unease, disquiet.

inquiline n (zool) an animal which lives in the abode of another but does not harm it, eg a hermit crab.—**inquilinous** adj.

inquire vi to request information about; (usu with **into**) to investigate. * vt to ask about.—also **enquire**.—**inquirer, enquirer** n.

inquiry n (pl **inquiries**) the act of inquiring; a search by questioning; an investigation; a question; research.—also **enquiry**.

inquisition n a detailed examination or investigation; (with cap and **the**) (RC Church) formerly the tribunal for suppressing heresy.—**inquisitional** adj.

inquisitive adj eager for knowledge; unnecessarily curious; prying.—**inquisitively** adv.—**inquisitiveness** n.

inquisitor n a person who questions searchingly or forcefully; (often cap) a member of the Inquisition.

inquisitorial adj of or resembling an inquisitor; prying.—**inquisitorially** adv.

in re prep in the matter of.

inroad n a raid into enemy territory; an encroachment or advance.

inrush n a sudden inward flow or influx.

insalivate vt to mix (food) with saliva while chewing.—**insalivation** n.

insalubrious adj (climate, place) unhealthy.—**insalubrity** n.

insane adj not sane, mentally ill; of or for insane people; very foolish.—**insanely** adv.

insanitary adj unclean, likely to cause infection or ill-health.—**insanitariness, insanitation** n.

insanity n (pl **insanities**) derangement of the mind or intellect; lunacy; madness.

insatiable adj not easily satisfied; greedy.—**insatiability** n.—**insatiability** adv.—**insatiably** adv.

insatiate adj insatiable.

inscribe vt to mark or engrave (words, etc) on (a surface); to add (a person's name) to a list; to dedicate (a book) to someone; to autograph; to fix in the mind.—**inscribable** adj.

inscription n an inscribing; words, etc inscribed on a tomb, coin, stone, etc.—**inscriptional** adj.

inscrutable adj hard to understand, incomprehensible; enigmatic.—**inscrutability** n.—**inscrutably** adv.

insect n any of a class of small arthropods with three pairs of legs, a head, thorax, and abdomen and two or four wings.

insectary n (pl **insectaries**) a place for keeping insects.

insecticide n a substance for killing insects.—**insecticidal** adj.

insectivore n an order of mammals that are small, nocturnal, and feed on insects or other invertebrates; any insect-eating plant or animal.—**insectivorous** adj.

insecure adj not safe; feeling anxiety; not dependable.—**insecurely** adv.

insecurity n (pl **insecurities**) the condition of being insecure; lack of confidence or sureness; instability; something insecure.

inseminate vt to fertilize; to impregnate.—**insemination** n.—**inseminator** n.

insensate adj not feeling sensation; stupid; without regard or feeling; cold.

insensible adj unconscious; unaware; indifferent; imperceptible.—**insensibility** n.—**insensibly** adv.

insensitive adj not sensitive, unfeeling.

insentient adj inert; inanimate.

inseparable adj not able to be separated; closely attached, as romantically.—**inseparability** n.—**inseparably** adv.

insert vt to put or fit (something) into something else. * n something inserted.—**insertion** n.

insertion n the act of inserting; something which is inserted.

in-service adj (training) given during employment.

insessorial adj (ornithology) adapted for perching.

inset n something inserted within something larger; an

insert. * vt (insetting, inset) to set in, insert.—insetter n.

inshore adj, adv near or towards the shore.

inshrine see enshrine.

inside n the inner side, surface, or part; (pl: inf) the internal organs, stomach, bowels. * adj internal; known only to insiders; secret. * adv on or in the inside; within; indoors; (sl) in prison. * prep in or within.

inside job n (inf) a crime committed with the help of someone connected with the victim or premises involved.

inside out adj reversed; with the inner surface facing the outside.

insider n a person within a place or group; a person with access to confidential information.

insidious adj marked by slyness or treachery; more dangerous than seems evident.—insidiously adv.—insidiousness n.

insight n the ability to see and understand clearly the inner nature of things, esp by intuition; an instance of such understanding.—insightful adj.

insignia n (pl insignias, insignia) a mark or badge of authority; a distinguishing characteristic.

insignificant adj having little or no importance; trivial; worthless; small, inadequate.—insignificance, insignificancy n.—insignificantly adv.

insincere adj not sincere; hypocritical.—insincerely adv.—insincerity n.

insinuate vt to introduce or work in slowly, indirectly, etc; to hint.—insinuator n.

insinuation n the act of insinuating; an indirect or sly hint.

insipid adj lacking any distinctive flavour; uninteresting, dull.—insipidity, insipidness n.—insipidly adv.

insist vi (often with on or upon) to take and maintain a stand. * vt to demand strongly; to declare firmly.—insister n.

insistent adj insisting or demanding.—insistence, insistency n.—insistently adv.

in situ adj in the original or natural place or position.

insobriety n drunkenness.

in so far, insofar adv to such a degree or extent.

insole n the innser sole of a shoe, etc; a thickness of material used as a inner sole.

insolent adj disrespectful; impudent, arrogant; rude.—insolence n.—insolently adv.

insoluble adj incapable of being dissolved; impossible to solve or explain.—insolubility n.—insolubly adv.

insolvent adj unable to pay one's debts; bankrupt.—insolvency n.

insomnia n abnormal inability to sleep.

insomniac n a person who suffers from insomnia.

insomuch adv (with as or that) to such an extent; (with as) inasmuch.

insouciant adj calm and unconcerned, carefree.—insouciance n.

inspect vt to look at carefully; to examine or review officially.—inspection n.—inspectional adj.—inspective adj.

inspector n an official who inspects in order to ensure compliance with regulations, etc; a police officer ranking below a superintendent.—inspectorate n.—inspectoral, inspectorial adj.—inspectorship n.

inspectorate n the office, district or rank of an inspector; a body of inspectors.

inspiration n an inspiring; any stimulus to creative thought; an inspired idea, action, etc.—inspirational adj.

inspiratory adj pertaining to inhalation.

inspire vt to stimulate, as to some creative effort; to motivate by divine influence; to arouse (a thought or feeling) in (someone); to cause.—inspiring adj.—inspiringly adv.

inspirit vt to put life into, invigorate; to animate, cheer.

inst. abbr = instant (this month).

instability n (pl instabilities) lack of stability; inconstancy.

install, instal vt (installs or instals, installing, installed) to formally place in an office, rank, etc; to establish in a place; to settle in a position or state.—installer n.

installation n the act of installing or being installed; machinery, equipment, etc that has been installed.

installment, instalment n a sum of money to be paid at regular specified times; any of several parts, as of a magazine story or television serial.

instance n an example; a step in proceeding; an occasion. * vt to give as an example.

instant adj immediate; (food) concentrated or precooked for quick preparation. * n a moment; a particular moment.

instantaneous adj happening or done very quickly.—instantaneously adv.—instantaneousness, instantaneity n.

instanter adv (law) immediately.

instantly adv immediately.

instate vt to install in an office or rank.

instead adv in place of the one mentioned.

instep n the upper part of the arch of the foot, between the ankle and the toes.

instigate vt to urge on, goad; to initiate.—instigation n.—instigator n.

instill, instil vt (instills or instils, instilling, instilled) to put (an idea, etc) in or into (the mind) gradually.—instillation n.—instiller n.

instinct n the inborn tendency to behave in a way characteristic of a species; a natural or acquired tendency; a knack.

instinctive, instinctual adj of, relating to, or prompted by instinct.—instinctively, instinctually adv.

institute vt to organize, establish; to start, initiate. * n an organization for the promotion of science, art, etc; a school, college, or department of a university specializing in some field.—institutor, instituter n.

institution n an established law, custom, etc; an organization having a social, educational, or religious purpose; the building housing it; (inf) a long-established person or thing.

institutional adj of or resembling an institution; dull, routine.

institutionalize vt to make or become an institution; to place in an institution; to make a person dependent on an institutional routine and unable to cope on their own.—institutionalization n.

instruct vt to provide with information; to teach; to give instructions to; to authorize.—instructible adj.—instructor n.—instructress nf.

instruction n an order, direction; the act or process of teaching or training; knowledge imparted; (comput) a command in a program to perform a particular operation; (pl) orders, directions; detailed guidance.—instructional adj.

instructive adj issuing or containing instructions; giving information, educational.—instructively adv.

instructor n someone who instructs; a teacher.

instrument *n* a thing by means of which something is done; a tool or implement; any of various devices for indicating, measuring, controlling, etc; any of various devices producing musical sound; a formal document. * *vt* to orchestrate.

instrument panel *n* a panel in a vehicle or machine in which instruments monitoring speed, engine status, etc are mounted.

instrumental *adj* serving as a means of doing something; helpful; of, performed on, or written for a musical instrument or instruments.—**instrumentality** *n*.—**instrumentally** *adv*.

instrumentalist *n* a person who plays a musical instrument.

instrumentation *n* the arrangement of a musical composition for different instruments; the use or provision of tools or instruments.

insubordinate *adj* not submitting to authority; rebellious.—**insubordination** *n*.

insubstantial *adj* unreal, imaginary; weak or flimsy.—**insubstantiality** *n*.—**insubstantially** *adv*.

insufferable *adj* intolerable; unbearable.—**insufferably** *adv*.

insufficient *adj* not sufficient.—**insufficiency, insufficience** *n*.—**insufficiently** *adv*.

insufflate *vt* to blow (air, powder) into or onto.—**insufflation** *n*.—**insufflator** *n*.

insular *adj* of or like an island or islanders; narrowminded; illiberal.—**insularity, insularism** *n*.

insulate *vt* to set apart; to isolate; to cover with a nonconducting material in order to prevent the escape of electricity, heat, sound, etc.—**insulation** *n*.—**insulator** *n*.

insulation *n* the act of insulating; the material used for insulating.

insulator *n* something which insulates; a non-conductor of electricity, heat or sound.

insulin *n* a hormone that controls absorption of sugar by the body, secreted by islets of tissue in the pancreas.

insult *vt* to treat with indignity or contempt; to offend. * *n* an insulting remark or act.—**insulter** *n*.

insuperable *adj* unable to be overcome.—**insuperability** *n*.—**insuperably** *adv*.

insupportable *adj* unbearable, intolerable

insurable *adj* able to be insured.

insurance *n* insuring or being insured; a contract purchased to guarantee compensation for a specified loss by fire, death, etc; the amount for which something is insured; the business of insuring against loss.

insure *vt* to take out or issue insurance on; to ensure. * *vi* to contract to give or take insurance.

insurer *n* someone who insures, an underwriter; a company which sells insurance.

insurgent *adj* rebellious, rising in revolt. * *n* a person who fights against established authority, a rebel.—**insurgence** *n*.—**insurgency** *n*.

insurmountable *adj* which cannot be overcome, insuperable.

insurrection *adj* a rising or revolt against established authority.—**insurrectional** *adj*.—**insurrectionary** *n, adj*.—**insurrectionism** *n*.—**insurrectionist** *n*.

intact *adj* unimpaired; whole.

intaglio *n* (*pl* **intaglios**) a design carved or engraved below the surface; a printing technique using engraved surfaces.—**intagliated** *adj*.

intake *n* the place in a pipe, etc where a liquid or gas is taken in; a thing or quantity taken in, as students, etc; the process of taking in.

intangible *adj* that cannot be touched, incorporeal; representing value but without material being, as good will; indefinable. * *n* something that is intangible.—**intangibility** *n*.—**intangibly** *adv*.

integer *n* any member of the set consisting of the positive and negative whole numbers and zero, such as -5, 0, 5.

integral *adj* necessary for completeness; whole or complete; made up of parts forming a whole. * *n* the result of a mathematical integration.—**integrally** *adv*.

integral calculus *n* (*maths*) the determination of definite and indefinite integrals and their use in the solution of differential equations.

integrant *adj* component, making part of a whole.

integrate *vti* to make whole or become complete; to bring (parts) together into a whole; to remove barriers imposing segregation upon (racial groups); to abolish segregation; (*math*) to find the integral of.—**integration** *n*.—**integrative** *adj*.

integrated circuit *n* a small electronic circuit assembled from microcomponents mounted on chips of semiconducting material.

integrator *n* someone who, or something which, integrates.

integrity *n* honesty, sincerity; completeness, wholeness; an unimpaired condition.

integument *n* a natural covering as skin, a rind, a husk, etc.—**integumental, integumentary** *adj*.

intellect *n* the ability to reason or understand; high intelligence; a very intelligent person.—**intellective** *adj*.

intellection *n* thought.

intellectual *adj* of, involving, or appealing to the intellect; requiring intelligence. * *n* an intellectual person.—**intellectuality** *n*.—**intellectually** *adv*.

intellectualism *n* the use of the intellect; (*philos*) the theory that all knowledge is derived from the intellect; (*derog*) excessive emphasis on the value of the intellect.—**intellectualist** *n*.

intellectualize *vt* to make intellectual; to use the intellect on. * *vi* to become intellectual; to use the intellect.—**intellectualization** *n*.

intelligence *n* the ability to learn or understand; the ability to cope with a new situation; news or information; those engaged in gathering secret, esp military, information.

intelligence quotient *n* a measure of a person's intelligence, calculated by dividing mental age by actual age and multiplying by 100.

intelligent *adj* having or showing intelligence; clever, wise, etc.—**intelligently** *adv*.

intelligentsia *n* intellectuals collectively.

intelligible *adj* able to be understood; clear.—**intelligibility** *n*.—**intelligibly** *adv*.

intemperate *adj* indulging excessively in alcoholic drink; unrestrained; (*climate*) extreme.—**intemperance** *n*.—**intemperately** *adv*.

intend *vt* to mean, to signify; to propose, have in mind as an aim or purpose.—**intender** *n*.

intendancy *n* (*pl* **intendancies**) the rank or office of an intendant.

intendant *n* a superintendent or manager (esp under a monarch in France, Spain and Portugal).

intended *adj* planned. * *n* (*inf*) a fiancé or fiancée.

intendment *n* the true meaning of something, as fixed by law.

intense *adj* very strong, concentrated; passionate, emotional.—**intensely** *adv*.

intensify *vti* (**intensifying, intensified**) to make or become more intense.—**intensification** *n*.

intensity *n* (*pl* **intensities**) the state or quality of being intense; density, as of a negative plate; the force or energy of any physical agent.

intensive *adj* of or characterized by intensity; thorough; denoting careful attention given to patients right after surgery, etc.—**intensively** *adv*.

intensive care *n* 24-hour monitoring and treatment of acutely ill patients in hospital; the specialized unit administering this.

intent *adj* firmly directed; having one's attention or purpose firmly fixed. * *n* intention; something intended; purpose or meaning —**intently** *adv*.—**intentness** *n*.

intention *n* a determination to act in a specified way; anything intended.

intentional *adj* done purposely.—**intentionality** *n*.—**intentionally** *adv*.

inter *vt* (**interring, interred**) to bury.

inter- *prefix* between, among.

interact *vi* to act upon each other.—**interaction** *n*.—**interactional** *adj*.

interactive *adj* interacting; allowing two-way communication between a device, such as a computer or compact video disc, and its user.—**interactivity** *n*.

inter alia *adv* among other things.

interbreed *vti* (**interbreeding, interbred**) to breed within the same breed or family; to breed by crossing one species with another.

intercalary *adj* inserted into the calendar to harmonize it with the solar year, eg February 29 as inserted in the leap year.

intercalate *vt* to insert (an intercalary day) into the calendar.—**intercalation** *n*.

intercede *vi* to intervene on another's behalf; to mediate.—**interceder** *n*.

intercellular *adj* lying between cells.

intercept *vt* to stop or catch in its course. * *n* a point of intersection of two geometric figures; interception by an interceptor.—**interception** *n*.—**interceptive** *adj*.

interceptor, intercepter *n* a high-speed fighter aircraft used to intercept and destroy enemy aircraft.

intercession *n* the act of interceding, esp by prayer; mediation.—**intercessional, intercessory** *adj*.—**intercessor** *n*.—**intercessorial** *adj*.

interchange *vt* to give and receive one thing for another; to exchange, to put (each of two things) in the place of the other; to alternate. * *n* an interchanging; a junction on a motorway designed to prevent traffic intersecting.

interchangeable *adj* able to be interchanged.—**interchangeability** *n*.—**interchangeably** *adv*.

intercollegiate *adj* between or among colleges or universities.

intercolumniation *n* the distance between pillars; the spacing between pillars.—**intercolumniar** *adj*.

intercom *n* (*inf*) a system of intercommunicating, as in an aircraft.

intercommunicate *vi* to have mutual communication; to have passage to each other.—**intercommunicable** *adj*.—**intercommunication** *n*.

interconnect *vti* to connect by reciprocal links.—**interconnection** *n*.

intercontinental *adj* between continents.

intercostal *adj* (*anat*) lying between the ribs.

intercourse *n* a connection by dealings or communication between individuals or groups; sexual intercourse, copulation.

intercross *vti* to crossbreed.

intercurrent *adj* occurring at the same time; (*disease*) occurring during the course of another.—**intercurrence** *n*.

interdependence, interdependency *n* dependence on each other.—**interdependent** *adj*.

interdict *vt* to prohibit (an action); to restrain from doing or using something. * *n* an official prohibition.—**interdiction** *n*. —**interdictory** *adj*.

interdisciplinary *adj* involving two or more different branches of knowledge.

interest *n* a feeling of curiosity about something; the power of causing this feeling; a share in, or a right to, something; anything in which one has a share; benefit; money paid for the use of money; the rate of such payment. * *vt* to excite the attention of; to cause to have a share in; to concern oneself with.

interested *adj* having or expressing an interest; affected by personal interest, not impartial.—**interestedly** *adv*.

interesting *n* engaging the attention.

interface *n* a surface that forms the common boundary between two things; an electrical connection between one device and another, esp a computer. * *vt* (*elect*) to modify the input and output configurations of (devices) so that they may connect and communicate with each other; to connect using an interface; to be interactive (with).—**interfacial** *adj*.—**interfacially** *adv*.

interfacing *n* a layer of fabric between the neck, etc of a garment and its facing to give body.

interfere *vi* to clash; to come between; to intervene; to meddle; to obstruct.—**interfering** *adj*.

interference *n* an interfering; (*radio, TV*) the interruption of reception by atmospherics or by unwanted signals.

interferometer *n* (*physics*) an instrument used to measure the length of light waves by interference phenomena.

interferon *n* a protein, produced by cells in response to a virus, which then prevents the virus from growing.

interfuse *vti* to mix, blend.—**interfusion** *n*.

intergalactic *adj* occurring or existing between galaxies.

interglacial *adj* occurring between two glacial periods.

intergrade *vi* (*usu biol*) to change form gradually.—**intergradation** *n*.

interim *n* an intervening period of time. * *adj* provisional, temporary. * *adv* meanwhile.

interior *adj* situated within; inner; inland; private. * *n* the interior part, as of a room, country, etc.

interior angle *n* the angle between two adjacent sides of a polygon.

interior design *n* the art or business of an interior designer—*also* **interior decoration.**

interior designer *n* a person whose profession is the planning of the decor and furnishings of the interiors of houses, offices, etc.—*also* **interior decorator.**

interj. *abbr* = interjection.

interject *vt* to throw in between; to interrupt with.—**interjector** *n*.—**interjectory** *adj*.

interjection *n* an interjecting; an interruption; an exclamation.—**interjectional** *adj*.—**interjectionally** *adv*.

interlace *vti* to combine (as if) by lacing or weaving together.—**interlacement** *n*.

interlard vt to insert something foreign into.

interleaf n (pl **interleaves**) an additional, blank leaf inserted into a book.

interleave vti to insert an extra page (usu blank) in a book.

interline vt to write between lines.—**interlinear** adj.—**interlineation** n.

interlining n an extra lining between the lining and the outer fabric of a garment, etc; the material for this.

interlink vt to link together.

interlock vti to lock or become locked together; to join with one another.

interlocution n dialogue, discussion.

interlocutor n a person who takes part in a conversation.—**interlocutress, interlocutrix** nf.

interlocutory adj conversational; (law) pronounced during legal proceedings.

interlope vi to intrude in a matter in which one has no real concern.

interloper n a person who meddles; an intruder.

interlude n anything that fills time between two events, as music between acts of a play.

interlunar adj coming between the old and the new moon.

intermarry vi (**intermarrying, intermarried**) (different races, religions, etc) to become connected by marriage; to marry within one's close family.—**intermarriage** n.

intermediary n (pl **intermediaries**) a mediator. * adj acting as a mediator; intermediate.

intermediate adj in the middle; in between.

interment n burial.

intermezzo n (pl **intermezzos, intermezzi**) a short musical composition between parts of an opera, play, etc; a movement between sections of an extended instrumental work; a similar composition intended as an independent work.

interminable adj lasting or seeming to last forever; endless.—**interminably** adv.

intermingle vti to mingle or mix together.

intermission n an interval of time between parts of a performance.

intermit vb (**intermitting, intermitted**) vt to cause to cease for a time; to suspend. * vi to cease for a time; to be suspended.

intermittent adj stopping and starting again at intervals; periodic.—**intermittence, intermittency** n.—**intermittently** adv.

intermix vti to mix together.

intermixture n the act of mixing together; a mixture.

intern[1] vt to detain and confine within an area, esp during wartime.—**internment** n.

intern[2] n a doctor serving in a hospital, usu just after graduation from medical school, a houseman.

intern[3], **interne** n an apprentice journalist, teacher, etc.

internal adj of or on the inside; of or inside the body; intrinsic; domestic.—**internality** n.—**internally** adv.

internal combustion engine n an engine producing power by the explosion of a fuel-and-air mixture within the cylinders.

international adj between or among nations; concerned with the relations between nations; for the use of all nations; of or for people in various nations. * n a sporting competition between teams from different countries; a member of an international team of players.—**internationality** n.—**internationally** adv.

International Date Line n the line running north to south along the 180-degree meridian, east of which is one day earlier than west of it.

internationalism n an attitude, belief, or policy favouring the promotion of cooperation and understanding between nations.—**internationalist** n.

interne see **intern**[3].

internecine adj extremely destructive to both sides.

internee n a person who is interned.

internist n a physician who specializes in internal diseases.

internode n (bot) the space on a plant stem between two nodes or leaf joints.—**internodal** adj.

internuncial adj pertaining to an internuncio; (anat) transmitting nervous signals.

internuncio n a representative of the Pope.

interpellate vt to question (an official) about government policy or about personal conduct.—**interpellation** n.—**interpellator** n.

interpenetrate vt to penetrate thoroughly. * vi to penetrate each other.—**interpenetration** n.—**interpenetrative** adj.

interplanetary adj between or among planets.

interplay n the action of two things on each other, interaction.

interplead vi (**interpleading, interpleaded, interplead, interpled**) (law) to discuss a point incidentally arising, or concerning a third party.

interpleader n (law) the discussion of a point incidentally arising or concerning a third party.

Interpol (acronym) International Criminal Police Organization.

interpolate vt to change (a text) by inserting new material; to insert between or among others; (math) to estimate a value between two known values.—**interpolator** n.—**interpolation** n.

interpose vti to place or come between; to intervene (with); to interrupt (with).—**interposer** n.—**interposition** n.

interpret vt to explain; to translate; to construe; to give one's own conception of, as in a play or musical composition. * vi to translate between speakers of different languages.—**interpretational** adj.

interpretation n an act or instance of interpreting; an explanation; a rendering (of a piece of music, theatre, etc).

interpreter n a person who translates orally for persons speaking in different languages; (comput) a program that translates an instruction into machine code.

interracial adj between or among races.

interregnum n (pl **interregnums, interregna**) the period between two reigns, governments, etc; a suspension of normal government; a pause in a continuous series.

interrelate vti to be or place in a mutually dependant or reciprocal relationship.—**interrelation** n.—**interrelationship** n.

interrogate vti to question, esp formally.—**interrogation** n.—**interrogational** adj.—**interrogator** n.

interrogative adj asking a question. * n a word used in asking a question.—**interrogatively** adv.

interrogatory adj questioning. * n (pl **interrogatories**) examination by questions.—**interrogatorily** adv.

interrupt vt to break into (a discussion, etc) or break in upon (a speaker, worker, etc); to make a break in the continuity of. * vi to interrupt an action, talk, etc.—**interrupter** n.—**interruptive** adj.

interruption n the act of interrupting; a hindrance; a remark interposed in a conversation, etc.

intersect *vti* to cut or divide by passing through or crossing; (*lines, roads, etc*) to meet and cross each other.

intersection *n* an intersecting; the place where two lines, roads, etc meet or cross.—**intersectional** *adj.*

interspace *n* a space between things.

intersperse *vt* to scatter or insert among other things; to diversify with other things scattered here and there.—**interspersion** *n.*

interstate *adj* between or among different states of a federation.

interstellar *adj* between or among stars.

interstice *n* a crack; a crevice; a minute space.

interstitial *adj* occurring in interstices.

intertexture *n* the act or product of interweaving.

intertribal *adj* between or among tribes.

intertwine *vti* to twine or twist closely together.

interval *n* a space between things; the time between events; (*mus*) the difference of pitch between two notes.

intervene *vi* to occur or come between; to occur between two events, etc; to come in to modify, settle, or hinder some action, etc.—**intervener, intervenor** *n.*—**intervention** *n.*—**interventional** *adj.*

interventionist *n* a person who favours intervention. * *adj* of or in favour of intervention.—**interventionism** *n.*

interview *n* a meeting in which a person is asked about his or her views, etc, as by a newspaper or television reporter; a published account of this; a formal meeting at which a candidate for a job is questioned and assessed by a prospective employer. * *vt* to have an interview with.—**interviewer** *n.*

interviewee *n* a person who is interviewed.

interweave *vti* (**interweaving, interwove** or **interweaved,** *pp* **interwoven** or **interweaved**) to weave together, interlace; to intermingle.

interwind *vt* (**interwinding, interwound**) to wind together.

intestate *adj* having made no will. * *n* a person who dies intestate.— **intestacy** *n.*

intestine *n* the lower part of the alimentary canal between the stomach and the anus.—**intestinal** *adj.*

intifada *n* the Arabic word for "uprising," esp the uprising in Israel in 1987 of Palestinian inhabitants.

intimacy *n* (*pl* **intimacies**) close or confidential friendship; familiarity; sexual relations.

intimate *adj* most private or personal; very close or familiar, esp sexually; deep and thorough. * *n* an intimate friend. * *vt* to indicate; to make known; to hint or imply.—**intimately** *adv.*

intimation *n* the act of intimating; a notice, announcement.

intimidate *vt* to frighten; to discourage, silence, etc esp by threats.—**intimidation** *n.*—**intimidator** *n.*

intinction *n* (*Eastern Church*) the practice of administering both parts of Holy Communion at the same time by dipping the bread into the wine.

into *prep* to the interior or inner parts of; to the middle; to a particular condition; (*inf*) deeply interested or involved in.

intolerable *adj* unbearable.—**intolerably** *adv.*

intolerance *n* lack of toleration of the opinions or practices of others; inability to bear or endure.—**intolerant** *adj.*

intonate *vti* to recite in a singing voice, chant.

intonation *n* intoning; variations in pitch of the speaking voice; an accent.—**intonational** *adj.*

intone *vti* to speak or recite in a singing tone; to chant.—**intoner** *n.*

in toto *adv* completely; as a whole; entirely.

intoxicant *n* something that intoxicates, esp a drug or an alcoholic drink.—*also adj.*

intoxicate *vt* to make drunken; to elate; to poison.—**intoxicatingly** *adv.*

intoxication *n* drunkenness; great excitement; poisoning.

intra- *prefix* within.

intracranial *adj* within the skull.

intractable *adj* unmanageable, uncontrollable; (*problem, illness, etc*) difficult to solve, alleviate, or cure.—**intractability** *n.*—**intractably** *adv.*

intrados *n* (*pl* **intrados, intradoses**) the inner and lower curve of an arch.

intramural *adj* (*education*) within an institution or organization;

intransigent *adj* unwilling to compromise, irreconcilable.—**intransigence** *n.*—**intransigently** *adv.*

intransitive *adj* (*gram*) denoting a verb that does not take a direct object.—**intransitively** *adv.*

intrauterine *adj* inside the uterus.

intrauterine device *n* a small loop or coil inserted into the uterus as a contraceptive.

intravenous *adj* into a vein.—**intravenously** *adv.*

in-tray *n* a tray holding documents, etc, awaiting attention.

intrench *see* **entrench.**

intrepid *adj* bold; fearless; brave.—**intrepidity** *n.*—**intrepidly** *adv.*

intricate *adj* difficult to understand; complex, complicated; involved, detailed.—**intricacy** *n.*—**intricately** *adv.*

intrigue *n* a secret or underhand plotting; a secret or underhanded plot or scheme; a secret love affair. * *vb* (**intriguing, intrigued**) *vi* to carry on an intrigue. * *vt* to excite the interest or curiosity of.—**intriguer** *n.*

intrinsic *adj* belonging to the real nature of a person or thing; inherent.—**intrinsically** *adv.*

intro- *prefix* within, into.

intro *n* (*pl* **intros**) (*inf*) introduction.

introduce *vt* to make (a person) acquainted by name (with other persons); to bring into use or establish; to present (legislation, etc) for consideration or approval; to present a radio or television programme; to bring into or insert.—**introducer** *n.*

introduction *n* an introducing or being introduced; the presentation of one person to another; preliminary text in a book; a preliminary passage in a musical composition.

introductory *adj* serving as an introduction; preliminary.—**introductorily** *adv.*

introit *n* (*RC Church, Church of England*) a psalm or passage of scripture sung by the choir as the priest approaches the altar before Mass or Holy Communion.

intromission *n* insertion; introduction.

intromit *vt* to insert.—**intromittent** *adj.*

introspect *vi* to examine one's own thoughts and feelings.

introspection *n* examination of one's own mind and feelings, etc.—**introspectional, introspective** *adj.*

introversion *n* the act of introverting; the state of being introverted; the direction of, or tendency to direct, one's thoughts and concerns inward.

introvert *vt* to turn or direct inward. * *vi* to produce introversion in. * *n* a person who is more interested in his or her own thoughts, feelings, etc than in external objects or events. * *adj* characterized by introversion.—**introversive** *adj*.

intrude *vti* to force (oneself) upon others unasked.—**intruder** *n*.—**intrudingly** *adj*.

intrusion *n* the act or an instance of intruding; the forcible entry of molten rock into and between existing rocks.—**intrusional** *adj*.

intrusive *adj* intruding; tending to intrude; (*rocks*) formed by intrusion.—**intrusively** *adv*.

intrust *see* **entrust**.

intubate *vt* (*med*) to insert a tube into (the larynx, etc).—**intubation** *n*.

intuit *vt* to know by intuition.

intuition *n* a perceiving of the truth of something immediately without reasoning or analysis; a hunch, an insight.—**intuitional** *adj*.—**intutionally** *adv*.

intuitive *adj* perceiving or perceived by intuition.—**intuitively** *adv*.

intuitivism *n* the doctrine that ethical principles are matters of intuition.—**intuitivist** *n*.

intuitonism, intuitionalism *n* the doctrine that the immediate perception of truth is by intuition.—**intuitionist, intuitionalist** *n*.

intumescence, intumescency *n* a swelling up; a tumid state.—**intumescent** *adj*.

intussusception *n* (*med*) the protrusion of the upper part of the intestinal canal into the lower part; (*biol*) the expansion of a cell.

intwine *see* **entwine**.

Inuit *n* (*pl* **Inuit, Inuits**) an Eskimo from Greenland or North America.—*also* **Innuit**.

inulin *n* a starchy constituent of many plants.

inunction *n* the act of applying ointment; the act of anointing or smearing with oil.

inundate *vt* to cover as with a flood; to deluge.—**inundation** *n*.—**inundator** *n*.

inure *vt* to accustom to, esp to something unpleasant.—*also* **enure**.—**inurement, enurement** *n*.

inurn *vt* to put (ashes) in an urn.

inutile *adj* useless.

invade *vt* to enter (a country) with hostile intentions; to encroach upon; to penetrate; to crowd into as if invading.—**invader** *n*.

in vacuo *adv* in a vacuum.

invaginate *vt* (*anat*) to fold back a part of a tubular organ on itself so that it is sheathed.

invagination *n* the process of invaginating; the state of being invaginated.

invalid[1] *adj* not valid.

invalid[2] *n* a person who is ill or disabled. * *vt* to cause to become an invalid; to disable; to cause to retire from the armed forces because of ill-health or injury.

invalidate *vt* to render not valid; to deprive of legal force.—**invalidation** *n*.

invalidity *n* (*pl* **invalidities**) a lack of validity; a state of illness or disability.

invaluable *adj* too valuable to be measured in money.—**invaluably** *adv*.

Invar *n* (*trademark*) an alloy of nickel and steel, used in scientific instruments because of its invariability.

invariable *adj* never changing; constant.—**invariability** *n*.—**invariably** *adv*.

invasion *n* the act of invading with military forces; an encroachment, intrusion.

invasive *adj* marked by military aggression; tending to spread; tending to infringe.

invective *n* the use of violent or abusive language or writing.

inveigh *vi* to speak violently or bitterly (against).—**inveigher** *n*.

inveigle *vt* to entice or trick into doing something.—**inveiglement** *n*.—**inveigler** *n*.

invent *vt* to think up; to think out or produce (a new device, process, etc); to originate; to fabricate (a lie, etc).—**inventible, inventable** *adj*.—**inventor** *n*.

invention *n* something invented; inventiveness.—**inventional** *adj*.

inventive *adj* pertaining to invention; skilled in inventing.—**inventiveness** *n*.

inventory *n* (*pl* **inventories**) an itemized list of goods, property, etc, as of a business; the store of such goods for such a listing; a list of the property of an individual or an estate. * *vt* (**inventorying, inventoried**) to make an inventory of; to enter in an inventory.—**inventoriable** *adj*.—**inventorial** *adj*.

inveracity *n* (*pl* **inveracities**) untruthfulness.

inverse *adj* reversed in order or position; opposite, contrary. * *n* an inverse state or thing.—**inversely** *adv*.

inversion *n* an inverting or being inverted; something inverted.—**inversive** *adj*.

invert *vt* to turn upside down or inside out; to reverse in order, position or relationship.—**invertible** *adj*.

invertebrate *adj* without a backbone (—*also* **invertebral**). * *n* an animal without a backbone.

inverted comma *n* a quotation mark.

invest *vt* to commit (money) to property, stocks and shares, etc for profit; to devote effort, time, etc on a particular activity; to install in office with ceremony; to furnish with power, authority, etc. * *vi* to invest money.

investigate *vti* to search (into); to inquire, examine.—**investigative, investigatory** *adj*.

investigation *n* the act of investigating; an inquiry; a search to uncover facts, etc.—**investigational** *adj*.

investigator *n* one who investigates, esp a private detective.

investiture *n* the act or right of giving legal possession; the ceremony of investing a person with an office, robes, title, etc.

investment *n* the act of investing money productively; the amount invested; an activity in which time, effort or money has been invested.

investor *n* a person who invests money.

inveterate *adj* firmly established, ingrained; habitual.—**inveteracy** *n*.—**inveterately** *adv*.

invidious *adj* tending to provoke ill-will, resentment or envy; (*decisions, etc*) unfairly discriminating.—**invidiously** *adv*.—**invidiousness** *n*.

invigorate *vt* to fill with vigour and energy; to refresh.—**invigorating** *adj*.—**invigoration** *n*.—**invigorative** *adj*.—**invigorator** *n*.

invincible *adj* unconquerable.—**invincibility** *n*.—**invincibly** *adv*.

inviolable *adj* not to be broken or harmed.—**inviolability** *n*.—**inviolably** *adv*.

inviolate *adj* not violated; unbroken, unharmed.—**inviolacy** *n*.

invisible *adj* unable to be seen; hidden.—**invisibility** *n*.—**invisibly** *adv*.

invitation *n* a message used in inviting.

invite *vt* to ask to come somewhere or do something; to ask for; to give occasion for; to tempt; to entice. * *n* (*inf*) an invitation.

inviting *adj* attractive, enticing.—**invitingly** *adv*.

in vitro *adv, adj* (*biological experiments, etc*) occurring outside the living body and in an artificial environment.

in vivo *adv, adj* (*biological processes, etc*) occurring inside the living body.

invocation *n* the act of invoking; a formula used in invoking.—**invocatory** *adj*.

invoice *n* a document listing goods dispatched, usu with particulars of their price and quantity; to demand due settlement. * *vt* to submit an invoice for or to.

invoke *vt* to call on (God, etc) for help, blessing, etc; to resort to (a law, etc) as pertinent; to implore.

involucel *n* (*bot*) a bract around part of a flower head.

involucre *n* (*bot*) a ring of bracts around the base of a flower cluster.

involuntary *adj* not done by choice; not consciously controlled.—**involuntarily** *adv*.—**involuntariness** *n*.

involute, involuted *adj* intricate; (*bot*) folded or rolled inwards (eg leaves, flowers); curled spirally.

involution *n* something which is involute; the act of involving; involvement, complication; (*anat*) the return of an organ or tissue to its normal size after distension; (*math*) the process of raising an arithmetical or algebraic quantity to a given power.

involve *vt* to affect or include; to require; to occupy, to make busy; to complicate; to implicate.—**involvement** *n*.

invulnerable *adj* not capable of being wounded or hurt in any way.—**invulnerability** *n*.—**invulnerable** *adj*.

inward *adj* situated within or directed to the inside; relating to or in the mind or spirit. * *adv* inwards.

inwardly *adv* within; in the mind or spirit; towards the inside or centre.

inwards *adv* towards the inside or interior; in the mind or spirit.

inweave *vt* (**inweaving, inwove** or **inweaved,** *pp* **inwoven** or **inweaved**) to weave in.

inwrought *adj* worked into or onto (fabric, etc); adorned with figures or patterns.

Io (*chem symbol*) ionium.

iodic *adj* pertaining to, or containing, iodine.

iodide *n* a compound of iodine.

iodine *n* a nonmetallic element, found in seawater and seaweed, whose compounds are used in medicine and photography.

iodism *n* poisoning caused by overdoses of iodine.

iodize *vt* to treat or combine with iodine.

iodoform *n* a compound of iodine, used as an antiseptic.

ion *n* an electrically charged atom or group of atoms formed through the gain or loss of one or more electrons.

Ionic *adj* of a Greek style of architecture that is characterized by ornamental scrolls on the tops of columns.

ionic *adj* of or occurring in the form of ions.

ionize *vti* to change or become changed into ions.—**ionization** *n*.

ionosphere *n* the series of ionized layers high in the stratosphere from which radio waves are reflected.—**ionospheric** *adj*.

iota *n* the ninth letter of the Greek alphabet; a very small quantity; a jot.

IOU *n* (*pl* **IOUs**) a written note promising to pay a sum of money to the holder.

IPA *abbr* = International Phonetic Alphabet.

ipecac, ipecacuanha *n* a South American plant, the root of which is made into a medicine used as an emetic and purgative.

ipso facto *adv* by the fact or act itself.

IQ *abbr* = Intelligence Quotient.

Ir (*chem symbol*) iridium.

IRA *abbr* = Irish Republican Army.

Iranian *n* a native or inhabitant of Iran; a branch of the Indo-European group of languages including Persian; modern Persian.—*also adj*.

irascible *adj* easily angered; hot-tempered.—**irascibility** *n*.—**irascibly** *adv*.

irate *adj* enraged, furious.—**irately** *adv*.

ire *n* anger; wrath.

irenic, ironical *adj* aiming at peace.

iridaceous *adj* (*bot*) of, or pertaining to, the iris family.

iridescent *adj* exhibiting a spectrum of shimmering colours, which change as the position is altered.—**iridescence** *n*.

iridium *n* a metallic element that is extraordinarily resistant to corrosion.

iris¹ *n* (*pl* **irises, irides**) the round, pigmented membrane surrounding the pupil of the eye.

iris² *n* (*pl* **irises**) a perennial herbaceous plant with sword-shaped leaves and brightly coloured flowers.

Irish *adj* of Ireland or its people. * *n* the Celtic language of Ireland.

Irish bull *see* **bull**³.

Irish coffee *n* coffee mixed with Irish whiskey and topped with fresh cream.

Irish moss *see* **carragee.**

Irish stew *n* a stew of mutton, onions and potatoes.

iritis *n* (*med*) inflammation of the iris.

irk *vt* to annoy, irritate.

irksome *adj* tedious; tiresome.

iron *n* a metallic element, the most common of all metals; a tool, etc of this metal; a heavy implement with a heated flat underface for pressing cloth; (*pl*) shackles of iron; firm strength; power; any of certain golf clubs with angled metal heads. * *adj* of iron; like iron, strong and firm. * *vti* to press with a hot iron; (*with* **out**) to correct or settle a problem through negotiation or similar means.—**ironer** *n*.

Iron Age *n* the period when most tools and weapons were made of iron, following the Bronze Age in around 1100BC.

ironbark *n* a type of eucalyptus tree.

ironbound *adj* bound with iron; unyielding.

ironclad *adj* covered in iron; difficult to change or break.

iron curtain *n* the name of the physical and ideological barrier which once separated the former Soviet Union and Communist Eastern Europe from the rest of Europe.

iron gray *adj* a slightly greenish dark grey.

ironic, ironical *adj* of or using irony.—**ironically** *adv*.

ironing *n* the act of ironing; items of clothing, etc, for ironing.

ironing-board *n* a narrow flat surface to iron clothes on.

iron lung *n* a large respirator that encloses all of the body but the head.

iron maiden *n* a medieval instrument of torture consisting of a hinged coffin-like box fitted with spikes which was closed around the victim.

ironmonger *n* a dealer in metal utensils, tools, etc; a hardware shop.—**ironmongery** *n*.

iron rations *npl* emergency food rations for military use.

ironstone *n* a type of iron ore; a type of hardwearing earthenware.

ironwood *n* a name given to the timber of certain trees, which is of exceptional hardness and durability.

ironwork *n* articles made of iron, esp decorative railings, etc.

ironworks *n* (*pl or sing*) a factory where iron is smelted, cast, or wrought.

irony *n* (*pl* **ironies**) an expression in which the intended meaning of the words is the opposite of their usual sense; an event or result that is the opposite of what is expected.

irradiance *n* the act of emitting rays of light; lustre.

irradiant *adj* emitting rays of light; shining brightly.

irradiate *vt* to shine upon; to light up; to enlighten; to radiate; to expose to X-rays or other radiation. * *vi* to emit rays; to shine.—**irradiative** *adj*.—**irradiator** *n*.

irradiation *n* the act of irradiating; the condition of being irradiated; the apparent extension of the edges of an illuminated object seen against a dark background; the use of radiation in medicine.

irrational *adj* not rational, lacking the power of reason; senseless; unreasonable; absurd.—**irrationality** *n*.—**irrationally** *adv*.

irrational number *n* a real number (eg π) that cannot be expressed as the result of dividing one integer by another.

irreclaimable *adj* which cannot be reclaimed.

irreconcilable *adj* not able to be brought into agreement; incompatible.—**irreconcilability** *n*.—**irreconcilably** *adv*.

irrecoverable *adj* beyond recovery.—**irrecoverably** *adv*.

irrecusable *adj* which must be accepted.

irredeemable *adj* not able to be redeemed.—**irredeemably** *adv*.

irredentist *n* an advocate of the return of a country of neighbouring regions claimed by another on language and other grounds.—**irredentism** *n*.

irreducible *adj* unable to be reduced from one form, state, degree, etc to another.—**irreducibility** *n*.—**irreducibly** *adv*.

irrefragable *adj* irrefutable, unanswerable.

irrefrangible *adj* inviolable; (*physics*) which cannot be refracted.

irrefutable *adj* unable to deny or disprove; indisputable.—**irrefutability** *adv*.—**irrefutably** *adv*.

irregular *adj* not regular, straight or even; not conforming to the rules; imperfect; (*troops*) not part of the regular armed forces.—**irregularly** *adv*.

irregularity *n* (*pl* **irregularities**) departure from a rule, order or method; crookedness.

irrelative *adj* unconnected, unrelated.

irrelevant *adj* not pertinent; not to the point.—**irrelevance, irrelevancy** *n*.—**irrelevantly** *adv*.

irreligion *n* lack of religious belief; disregard for, or hostility towards, religion.

irreligious *adj* impious, irreverent.

irremediable *adj* which cannot be remedied.

irremissible *adj* unpardonable; (*obligation*) binding.

irremovable *adj* not removable.—**irremovability** *adv*.—**irremovably** *adv*.

irreparable *adj* that cannot be repaired, rectified or made good.—**irreparably** *adv*.

irreplaceable *adj* unable to be replaced.—**irreplaceability** *n*.

irrepressible *adj* unable to be controlled or restrained.—**irrepressibly** *adv*.

irreproachable *adj* blameless; faultless.—**irreproachability** *adv*.—**irreproachably** *adv*.

irresistible *adj* not able to be resisted; overpowering; fascinating; very charming, alluring.—**irresistibility** *adv*.—**irresistibly** *adv*.

irresolute *adj* lacking resolution, uncertain, hesitating.—**irresolutely** *adv*.—**irresoluteness, irresolution** *n*.

irresolvable *adj* which cannot be resolved or solved.

irrespective *adj* (*with* **of**) regardless.—**irrespectively** *adv*.

irresponsible *adj* not showing a proper sense of the consequences of one's actions; unable to bear responsibility.—**irresponsibility** *n*.—**irresponsibly** *adv*.

irresponsive *adj* not responsive.

irretentive *adj* not retentive.

irretrievable *adj* that cannot be recovered; irreparable.—**irretrievability** *n*.—**irretrievably** *adj*.

irreverent, irreverential *adj* not reverent, disrespectful.—**irreverence** *n*.—**irreverently** *adv*.

irreversible *adj* not able to be reversed; unable to be revoked or altered.—**irreversibility** *n*.—**irreversibly** *adv*.

irrevocable *adj* unable to be revoked, unalterable.—**irrevocability** *n*.—**irrevocably** *adv*.

irrigate *vt* to supply (land) with water as by means of artificial ditches, pipes, etc; (*med*) to wash out (a cavity, wound, etc).—**irrigable** *adj*.—**irrigation** *n*.—**irrigative** *adj*.—**irrigator** *n*.

irritable *adj* easily annoyed, irritated, or provoked; (*med*) excessively sensitive to a stimulus.—**irritability** *n*.—**irritably** *adv*.

irritant *adj* irritating; causing irritation. * *n* something that causes irritation.

irritate *vt* to provoke to anger; to annoy; to make inflamed or sore.—**irritative** *adj*.—**irritator** *n*.

irritation *n* the act of irritating; the state of being irritated; someone who, or something which, irritates.

irrupt *vi* to enter forcibly or suddenly.—**irruption** *n*.

is *see* **be**.

ISBN *abbr* = international standard book number.

isinglass *n* a gelatin prepared from fish bladders; mica, esp in thin sheets.

Islam *n* the Muslim religion, a monotheistic religion founded by Mohammed; the Muslim world.—**Islamic** *adj*.

island *n* a land mass smaller than a continent and surrounded by water; anything like this in position or isolation.

islander *n* a native or inhabitant of an island.

isle *n* an island, esp a small one.

islet *n* a small island.

-ism *n suffix* indicating a system or doctrine, as *Protestantism*; a state or condition, as *barbarism*; action, as *criticism*; a peculiarity or idiom, as *archaism, gallicism*; a morbid condition caused by abuse of drugs, as *alcoholism*.

isn't = is not.

isobar *n* a line on a map connecting places of equal barometric pressure.—**isobaric** *adj*.—**isobarism** *n*.

isochromatic *adj* of the same colour; (*photog*) giving equal intensity to different colours.

isochronal, isochronous *adj*

isoclinal, isoclinic *adj* having the same dip or inclination.

isodynamic *adj* having equal force.

isogon *n* (*geom*) a figure with equal angles.

isohel *n* a line on a map, linking places with the same hours of sunshine.

isohyet *n* a line on a map, linking places with the same rainfall.

isolate *vt* to set apart from others; to place alone; to quarantine a person or animal with a contagious disease; to separate a constituent substance from a compound.—**isolator** *n*.

isolation *n* the state of being isolated; the act of isolating.

isolationism *n* a policy of refraining from involvement in international affairs.—**isolationist** *adj, n*.

isomer *n* any of two or more chemical compounds whose molecules contain the same atoms but in different arrangements.—**isomeric** *adj*.—**isomerism** *n*.

isometric, isometrical *adj* having equality of measure; relating to muscular contraction involving little shortening of the muscle; (*drawing*) projecting an image to scale in three dimensions with the axis equally inclined.—**isometrically** *adv*.

isometrics *n* (*sing or pl*) physical exercises in which muscles are contracted against each other or in opposition to fixed objects.

isomorphism *n* (*biol*) similarity in form; (*chem*) the quality of having the same crystalline form despite being formed of different elements.—**isomorphic, isomorphous** *adj*.

isopod *n* a type of crustacean with seven pairs of equal legs, eg the woodlouse.

isosceles *adj* denoting a triangle with two equal sides.

isoseismic, isoseismal *adj* pertaining to points at which earthquake shock is of the same intensity. * *n* a line on a map, linking these points.

isotherm *n* a line on a map connecting points of the same temperature.—**isothermal** *adj*.

isotope *n* any of two or more forms of an element having the same atomic number but different atomic weights.—**isotopic** *adj*.—**isotopically** *adv*.

Israelite *n* (*Bible*) a descendant of the Hebrew patriarch Jacob.

issuable *adj* which can be issued.

issuance *n* the act of issuing.

issue *n* an outgoing; an outlet; a result; offspring; a point under dispute; a sending or giving out; all that is put forth at one time (an issue of bonds, a periodical, etc). * *vb* (**issuing, issued**) *vi* to go or flow out; to result (from) or end (in); to be published. * *vt* to let out; to discharge; to give or deal out, as supplies; to publish.

isthmian *adj* of or pertaining to an isthmus.

isthmus *n* (*pl* **isthmuses, isthmi**) a narrow strip of land having water at each side and connecting two larger bodies of land.—**isthmoid** *adj*.

istle *n* a tough fibre made from a species of Mexican agave, used to make cord.—*also* **ixtle**.

it *pron* the thing mentioned; the subject of an impersonal verb; a subject or object of indefinite sense in various constructions. * *n* the player, as in tag, who must catch another.

it'll = it will; it shall.

it's = it is; it has.

Italian *adj* of Italy or its people. * a native of Italy; the Italian language.

Italianate *adj* Italian in style or character.

Italic *adj* (*language*) of ancient Italy.

italic *adj* denoting a type in which the letters slant upward to the right (*this is italic type*). * *n* (*usu pl*) italic type or handwriting.

italicize *vi* to write in italics. * *vt* to underline a word to indicate italics.—**italicization** *n*.

itch *n* an irritating sensation on the surface of the skin causing a need to scratch; an insistent desire. * *vi* to have or feel an irritating sensation in the skin; to feel a restless desire.

itchy *adj* (**itchier, itchiest**) pertaining to or affected with an itch.—**itchiness** *n*.

item *n* an article; a unit; a separate thing; a bit of news or information.

itemize *vt* to specify the items of; to set down by items.—**itemization** *n*.

iterate *vt* to say or do again or repetitively.—**iteration** *n*.—**iterative** *adj*.

ithyphallic *adj* (*poet*) in the manner of the rites or hymns to Bacchus.

itinerancy, itineracy *n* (*pl* **itinerancies, itineracies**) the act of travelling from place to place, esp to carry out an official duty.

itinerant *adj* travelling from place to place. * *n* a traveller.

itinerary *n* (*pl* **itineraries**) a route; a record of a journey; a detailed plan of a journey.

its *poss pron* relating to or belonging to **it**.

itself *pron* the reflexive and emphatic form of **it**.

IUD *abbr* = intrauterine device.

I've = I have

IVF *abbr* = in vitro fertilization: a technique for helping infertile couples to have children, in which a woman's eggs are fertilized by the father's sperm in a laboratory and then re-implanted in the womb.

ivory *n* (*pl* **ivories**) the hard, creamy-white substance forming the tusks of elephants, etc; any substance like ivory; creamy white. * *adj* of or like ivory; creamy white.

ivory tower *n* a place or situation which excludes the realities of everyday life.—**ivory towered** *adj*.

ivy *n* (*pl* **ivies**) a climbing or creeping vine with a woody stem and evergreen leaves.—**ivied** *adj*.

ixtle *see* **istle**.

J

J *abbr* = joule(s).

jab *vti* (**jabbing, jabbed**) to poke or thrust roughly; to punch with short, straight blows. * *n* a sudden thrust or stab; (*inf*) an injection with a hypodermic needle.

jabber *vti* to speak or say rapidly, incoherently, or foolishly. * *n* such talk.—**jabberer** *n*.

jabiru *n* a stork-like bird of tropical America; an Australian stork.

jaborandi *n* a tropical American plant that yields an alkoloid used to stimulate perspiration and as a diuretic.

jabot *n* an ornamental frill worn down the front of a blouse or shirt.

jacamar *n* a South American bird similar to a kingfisher.

jacana, jaçana *n* a small tropical wading bird.

jacaranda *n* a South American tree with hard, heavy wood; any one of several similar trees; the fragrant wood from such trees.

jacinth *n* a reddish-orange gem, a variety of zircon.

jack *n* any of various mechanical or hydraulic devices used to lift something heavy; a playing card with a knave's picture on it, ranking below the queen; a small flag flown on a ship's bow as a signal or to show nationality; (*bowls*) a small white ball used as a target. * *vt* (*with* **in**) (*sl*) to abandon (an attempt at something); (*with* **up**) to raise (a vehicle) by means of a jack; to increase (prices, etc); (*sl*) to inject a narcotic drug.

jackal *n* (*pl* **jackals, jackal**) any of various wild dogs of Africa and Asia.

jackanapes *n* a conceited or upstart person; a pert child; (*arch*) a monkey.

jackass *n* a male donkey; a fool.

jackboot *n* a leather military boot extending above the knee; authoritarian rule, oppression.

jackdaw *n* a black bird like the crow but smaller.

jackeroo, jackaroo (*pl* **jackeroos, jackaroos**) (*Austral sl*) a young person training to be a manager on a sheep or cattle station.

jacket *n* a short coat; an outer covering, as the removable paper cover of a book. * *vt* to cover with a jacket or cover.—**jacketed** *adj*.

jackfruit *n* an East Indian tree or its fruit, which is similar to breadfruit.

jack-in-the-box *n* a toy consisting of a box from which a figure on a spring pops out when the lid is lifted.

jackknife *n* (*pl* **jackknives**) a pocket-knife; a dive in which the diver touches his feet with knees straight and then straightens out. * *vi* to dive in this way; (*articulated truck*) to lose control so that the trailer and cab swing against each other.

jack-of-all-trades *n* (*pl* **jacks-of-all-trades**) a person who does many different types of work.

jack-o'-lantern *n* a lantern made from a hollowed-out pumpkin with holes cut in it to resemble a face; a will-o'-the-wisp.

jackpot *n* the accumulated stakes in certain games, as poker; **hit the jackpot** (*sl*) to win; to gain an enormous amount.

jack rabbit *n* a large hare with long ears, common in North America.

jacksnipe *n* (*pl* **jacksnipes, jacksnipe**) a kind of small snipe; a sandpiper.

jack-tar *n* (*inf*) a sailor.

Jacobean *adj* pertaining to the time or reign of James I of England and VI of Scotland. * *n* a person of this period, esp a poet.

Jacobin *n* a French Dominican friar; a member of a violent democratic faction that exercised a powerful influence in the French Revolution; an extreme revolutionary.—**Jacobinic, Jacobinical** *adj*.—**Jacobinism** *n*.

Jacobite *n* a supporter of James II of England and VII of Scotland after his abdication or of his descendants.—*also adj*.—**Jacobitism** *n*.

jaconet *n* a fine soft white cotton material resembling cambric.

jacquard *n* a loom for weaving patterns; a pattern woven on a jacquard loom.

jactitation *n* boasting; (*med*) a restless, feverish tossing of the body in illness; (*law*) a false pretence of being married to another, or likely to harm another person.

Jacuzzi *n* (*trademark*) a device that swirls water in a bath; a bath containing such a device.

jade *n* a hard, ornamental semiprecious stone; its light green colour.

jaded *adj* tired, exhausted; satiated.—**jadedly** *adv*.—**jadedness** *n*.

jadeite *n* a form of jade found in Burma.

jag^1 *n* a sharp, tooth-like notch or projection. * *vt* (**jagging, jagged**) to cut into notches; to prick.

jag^2 *n* (*sl*) intoxication from drugs or alcohol; (*sl*) a drinking spree.

jagged *adj* having sharp notches or projecting points; notched or ragged.—**jaggedly** *adv*.—**jaggedness** *n*.

jaggery, jaggary, jagghery *n* a coarse East Indian sugar made from palm sap.

jaggy *adj* (**jaggier, jaggiest**) jagged.

jaguar *n* (*pl* **jaguars, jaguar**) a large American black-spotted yellow wild cat similar to the leopard.

jail *n* a prison; imprisonment. * *vt* to send to or confine in prison.

jailbird *n* a person who is or has been confined in jail.

jailer, jailor *n* a person in charge of prisoners in a jail.

Jain *n* an adherent of Jainism. * *adj* pertaining to the Jains or their religious system (—*also* **Jaina, Jainist**).

Jainism *n* a Hindu religion of India similar to Buddhism.

jalap, jalop *n* the root of a Mexican plant used formerly as a purgative; the plant itself or similar plants; the resin from the plant.—**jalapic** *adj*.

jalopy n (pl **jalopies**) an old battered vehicle.

jalousie n a blind with slats like a Venetian blind or a louvred shutter; a louvre window.

jam[1] n a preserve made from fruit boiled with sugar until thickened; (inf) something easy or desirable.

jam[2] vb (**jamming, jammed**) vt to press or squeeze into a confined space; to crowd full with people or things; to cause (machinery) to become wedged and inoperable; to cause interference to a radio signal rendering it unintelligible. * vi to become stuck or blocked; (sl) to play in a jam session. * n a crowded mass or congestion in a confined space; a blockage caused by jamming; (inf) a difficult situation.—**jammer** n.

jamb n the straight vertical side-post of a door, fireplace, etc.

jamboree n a large party or spree; a large, usu international, gathering of Scouts.

jam-packed adj filled to capacity.

jam session n (sl) an unrehearsed performance by jazz, rock or other musicians, usu for their own enjoyment.

Jan. abbr = January.

jangle vi to make a harsh or discordant sound, as bells. * vt to cause to jangle; to irritate.—also n.

janitor n a person who looks after a building, doing routine maintenance, etc.—**janitorial** adj.

janizary, janissary (pl **janizaries, janissaries**) n (formerly) a foot-guard of the Turkish sultans; a Turkish infantryman.

Jansenism n the doctrine of sovereign and irresistible grace, promulgated in the 17th century in opposition to the Jesuits; the religion based on these doctrines.—**Jansenist** n, adj.—**Jansenistic** adj.

January n (pl **Januaries**) the first month of the year, having 31 days.

Jap n (sl) a Japanese.

japan vt (**japanning, japanned**) to cover with a hard black glossy lacquer.

Japanese adj of Japan, its people or language. * n the language of Japan; an inhabitant of Japan.

jape n a joke, jest.—**japer** n.—**japery** n.

japonica n any of various species of Japanese plants, Japanese quince, pear, etc; the camellia.

jar[1] vb (**jarring, jarred**) vi to make a harsh, discordant noise; to have an irritating effect (on one); to vibrate from an impact; to clash. * vt to jolt. * n a grating sound; a vibration due to impact; a jolt.

jar[2] n a short cylindrical glass vessel with a wide mouth; (inf) a pint of beer.

jardiniere n an ornamental flower-stand of porcelain or metal; mixed diced vegetables stewed in a sauce and served around a meat dish.

jargon[1] n the specialized or technical vocabulary of a science, profession, etc; obscure and usu pretentious language. * vi to talk in jargon.—**jargonistic** adj.

jargon[2], **jargoon** n a translucent, colourless, yellowish, or smoky kind of zircon.

jargonize vti to put into or talk in jargon.—**jargonization** n.

jarl n an Old Norse chief, a noble.

jasmine, jasmin n any of a genus of climbing shrubs with fragrant white or yellow flowers.

jasper n an opaque, many-shaded variety of quartz that, when polished, is made into a variety of ornamental articles and jewellery; a style of porcelain with a dull surface of green or blue.

jaundice n a condition characterized by yellowing of the skin, caused by excess of bile in the bloodstream; bitterness; resentment; prejudice.

jaundiced adj affected with jaundice; jealous, envious, disillusioned.

jaunt n a short journey, usu for pleasure. * vi to make such a journey.

jaunty adj (**jauntier, jauntiest**) sprightly or self-confident in manner.—**jauntily** adv.—**jauntiness** n.

Javanese n (pl **Javanese**) a native or inhabitant of Java; the language of Java.—also adj.

javelin n a light spear, esp one thrown some distance in a contest.

jaw n one of the bones in which teeth are set; either of two movable parts that grasp or crush something, as in a vice; (sl) a friendly chat, gossip; argument. * vi (sl) to talk boringly and at length.

jawbone n a bone of the jaw, esp of the lower jaw.

jawbreaker n a machine for crushing rocks, etc; (inf) a word that is difficult to pronounce.

jay n any of several birds of the crow family with raucous voices, roving habits, and destructive behaviour to other birds.

jaycee n a young member of a Junior Chamber of Commerce.

jaywalk vi to walk across a street carelessly without obeying traffic rules or signals.—**jaywalker** n.

jazz n a general term for American popular music, characterized by syncopated rhythms and embracing ragtime, blues, swing, jive, and bebop; (sl) pretentious or nonsensical talk or actions. * vt (with **up**) (inf) to play (a piece of music) in a jazz style; to enliven, add colour to.

jazzerati npl famous or accomplished jazz musicians.

jazzy adj (**jazzier, jazziest**) of or like jazz; (sl) lively.—**jazzily** adj.—**jazziness** n.

jealous adj apprehensive of or hostile toward someone thought of as a rival; envious of, resentful; anxiously vigilant or protective.—**jealously** adv.—**jealousness** n.

jealousy n (pl **jealousies**) suspicious fear or watchfulness, esp the fear of being supplanted by a rival.

jean n a hardwearing twilled cotton cloth; (pl) trousers made from this or denim.

jeep n a small robust vehicle with heavy duty tires and four-wheel drive for use on rough terrain, esp by the military.

jeer vt to laugh derisively. * vi to scoff (at). * n a jeering remark.—**jeerer** n.—**jeeringly** adv.

jehad see **jihad**.

Jehovah n (Bible) God.

jejune adj lacking significance, dull; naive; lacking in nourishment.—**jejunely** adv.—**jejuneness** n.

jell vti to become or make into jelly; to crystallize, as a plan.—also **gel**.

jello n (US) a sweet edible gelatin; jelly, jam.

jelly n (pl **jellies**) a soft, gelatinous food made from fruit syrup or meat juice; any substance like this. * vt (**jellying, jellied**) to turn into jelly, to congeal.—**jellied** adj.

jellyfish n (pl **jellyfish, jellyfishes**) a sea creature with a nearly transparent body and long tentacles.

jennet n a small Spanish horse; a female donkey.

jenny n (pl **jennies**) a machine for spinning; a female of some animals, as a wren or donkey.

jeopardize vt to endanger, put at risk.

jeopardy n (pl **jeopardies**) great danger or risk.

jequirity n (pl **jequirities**) an Indian shrub with parti-coloured seeds.

jerbil *see* **gerbil**.

jerboa *n* a small desert rodent with long hind legs and a long tail.

jeremiad *n* a long mournful lament or complaint.

jerk[1] *n* a sudden sharp pull or twist; a sudden muscular contraction or reflex; (*inf*) a stupid person. * *vti* to move with a jerk; to pull sharply; to twitch.

jerk[2] *vt* to preserve (meat) by cutting it into long strips and drying it in the sun. * *n* jerked meat (—*also* **jerky**).

jerkin *n* a close-fitting sleeveless jacket. **jerkiness** *n*.

jerky[1] *see* **jerk**[2].

jerky[2] *adj* (**jerkier, jerkiest**) moving with jerks.—**jerkily** *adv*.—**jerkiness** *n*.

jeroboam *n* a huge bottle four times ordinary size, esp for champagne.

jerry-built *adj* cheaply and flimsily constructed.—**jerry-builder** *n*.—**jerry-building** *n*.

jerry can *n* a flat-sided container for liquids, esp fuel or water, with a capacity of about five gallons (25 litres).

jersey *n* (*pl* **jerseys**) any plain machine-knitted fabric of natural or artificial fibres; a knitted sweater.

Jerusalem artichoke *n* (the edible tuber of) the North American sunflower.

jess, jesse *n* a short leather strap fixed to the leg of a hawk or falcon.

jest *n* a joke; a thing to be laughed at. * *vi* to jeer; to joke.

jester *n* a person who makes jokes, esp an entertainer employed in a royal household in the Middle Ages.

Jesuit *n* a member of the Catholic Society of Jesus, founded by Ignatius Loyola in 1534; an insidious, crafty intriguer.—**Jesuitic, Jesuitical** *adj*.

Jesuitism, Jesuitry *n* (a following of) the principles, system, or practices of the Jesuits; subtle duplicity; disingenuousness.

Jesus (Christ) *n* the Jewish religious teacher and founder of Christianity.

Jesus freak *n* (*sl*) a fervent Christian, esp a young member of an evangelical group.

jet[1] *n* a hard black compact mineral that can be polished and is used in jewellery; a lustrous black.—**jet-black** *adj*.

jet[2] *n* a stream of liquid or gas suddenly emitted; a spout for emitting a jet; a jet-propelled aircraft. * *vti* (**jetting, jetted**) to gush out in a stream; (*inf*) to travel or convey by jet.

jet engine *n* an engine, such as a gas turbine, producing jet propulsion.

jet lag *n* fatigue caused by disruption of the daily bodily rhythms, associated with crossing time zones at high speed.—**jet-lagged** *adj*.

jet propulsion *n* propulsion of aircraft, boats, etc, by the discharge of gases from a rear vent.—**jet-propelled** *adj*.

jetsam *n* cargo thrown overboard from a ship in distress to lighten it, esp such cargo when washed up on the shore.

jet set *n* the wealthy and fashionable social elite who travel widely for pleasure.—**jetsetter** *n*.

jet stream *n* the jet of exhaust gases from a jet engine; high-altitude winds.

jettison *vt* to abandon, to throw overboard.

jetty *n* (*pl* **jetties**) a wharf; a small pier.

Jew *n* a person descended, or regarded as descended, from the ancient Israelites; a person whose religion is Judaism.

jewel *n* a precious stone; a gem; a piece of jewellery; someone or something highly esteemed; a small gem used as a bearing in a watch. * *vt* (**jewelling, jewelled** *or* **jeweling, jeweled**) to adorn or provide with jewels.

jeweller, jeweler *n* a person who makes, repairs or deals in jewellery, watches, etc.

jewellery, jewelry *n* jewels such as rings, brooches, etc, worn for decoration.

Jewish *adj* of or like Jews.

Jewry *n* (*pl* **Jewries**) the Jewish people.

jew's harp *n* a small metal musical instrument that makes a twanging sound when held between the lips and plucked.

Jezebel *n* a woman of abandoned or licentious demeanour.

jib[1] *n* a triangular sail extending from the foremast in a ship. * *vti* (**jibbing, jibbed**) to pull (a sail) round to the other side; (*sail*) to swing round.—**jibber** *n*.

jib[2] *n* the projecting arm of a crane.

jib[3] *vi* to refuse to go on; to balk.

jibe *see* **gybe**.

jiffy, jiff *n* (*pl* **jiffies, jiffs**) (*inf*) a very short time.

jig *n* a lively springing dance; the music for this; a device used to guide a tool. * *vt* (**jigging, jigged**) to dance in lively manner, as in a jig; to jerk up and down rapidly.

jigger[1] *see* **chigoe**.

jigger[2] *n* any of various mechanical devices that operate with a jigging motion; a small glass for spirits; a person or thing that jigs; (*naut*) small tackle, a small sail.

jiggermast *n* the stern mast in a two-masted sailing vessel; a small aftermost mast in a four-master.

jiggery-pokery *n* (*inf*) underhand work; trickery.

jiggle *vt* to jerk; to move (something) up and down lightly. * *n* a jerky movement.

jigsaw *n* a saw with a narrow fine-toothed blade for cutting irregular shapes. * *vt* to cut with a jigsaw.

jigsaw (puzzle) *n* a picture mounted on wood or stiff cardboard and then cut up into irregular pieces, which are then assembled for amusement.

jihad *n* a holy war waged by Muslims against nonbelievers; a crusade for or against a cause.—*also* **jehad**.

jilt *vt* to discard (a lover) unfeelingly, esp without warning.—**jilter** *n*.

jimjams *npl* (*sl*) delirium tremens; nervous jitters.

jingle *n* a metallic tinkling sound like a bunch of keys being shaken together; a catchy verse or song with easy rhythm, simple rhymes, etc. * *vti* (to cause) to make a light tinkling sound.—**jingler** *n*.

jingly *adj* (**jinglier, jingliest**) tinkling.

jingo *n* (*pl* **jingoes**) a blustering patriot, a warmonger.

jingoism *n* advocacy of an aggressive foreign policy.—**jingoist** *adj, n*.—**jingoistic** *adj*.—**jingoistically** *adv*.

jink *n* a rapid swerve from side to side in order to dodge; (*pl*) high spirits. * *vti* to move nimbly; to dodge.

jinni (*pl* **jinn**) (*fairy tales*) a spirit with supernatural powers that can fulfil your wishes.—*also* **genie**.

jinx *n* (*inf*) someone or something thought to bring bad luck.

JIT *abbr* = just-in-time.

jitter *vi* (*inf*) to feel nervous or to act nervously. * *npl* (*inf*) (*with* **the**) an uneasy nervous feeling; fidgets.

jitterbug *n* a fast acrobatic dance for couples, esp popular in the 1940s. * *vi* (**jitterbugging, jitterbugged**) to dance the jitterbug.

jittery *adj* (*inf*) nervous.—**jitteriness** *n*.

jive *n* improvised jazz played at a fast tempo; dancing to this music; (*sl*) foolish, exaggerated, or insincere talk. * *vti* to dance the jive.

Jnr, jnr *abbr* = Junior.

job *n* a piece of work done for pay; a task; a duty; the thing or material being worked on; work; employment; (*sl*) a criminal enterprise; (*inf*) a difficult task. * *adj* hired or done by the job. * *vti* (**jobbing, jobbed**) to deal in (goods) as a jobber; to sublet (work, etc).

jobber *n* a person who jobs; a person who buys and sells goods as a middleman; in UK, a broker.

jobbery n profiting personally from a public office.

jobless *adj* unemployed. * *n* unemployed people collectively.—**joblessness** *n*.

job lot *n* a miscellaneous collection of items sold as one lot; any miscellaneous collection of cheap items.

jock *n* (*inf*) a jockey; a jockstrap; a male athlete; a disc jockey.

jockey *n* (*pl* **jockeys**) a person whose job is riding horses in races. * *vti* (**jockeying, jockeyed**) to act as a jockey; to manœuvre for a more advantageous position; to swindle or cheat.

jockstrap *n* a support for the genitals worn by men participating in sport, an athletic supporter.

jocose *adj* playful, humorous.—**jocosely** *adv*.—**jocoseness** *n*.

jocosity *n* (*pl* **jocosities**) a being jocose; a playful action; a humorous remark.

jocular *adj* joking; full of jokes.—**jocularity** *n*.—**jocularly** *adv*.

jocund *adj* merry, cheerful; jovial.—**jocundity** *n*.—**jocundly** *adv*.

jodhpurs *npl* riding breeches cut loose at the hips but close-fitting from knee to ankle.

joey *n* (*pl* **joeys**) (*Austral inf*) a young kangaroo; any young animal or a small child.

jog *vb* (**jogging, jogged**) *vt* to give a slight shake or nudge to; to rouse, as the memory. * *vi* to move up and down with an unsteady motion; to run at a relaxed trot for exercise; (*horse*) to run at a jogtrot. * *n* a slight shake or push; a nudge; a slow walk or trot.—**jogger** *n*.

joggle *vti* to move or shake slightly. * *n* a slight jolt.

jogtrot *n* a slow even-paced trot. * *vi* (**jogtrotting, jogtrotted**) to move at a slow even-paced trot.

john *n* (*sl*) a toilet; a prostitute's male customer; an easy prey.

John Barleycorn *n* a personification of malt liquor.

John Dory *n* an edible yellow seafish, the dory.

joie de vivre *n* great enjoyment of life.

join *vti* to bring and come together (with); to connect; to unite; to become a part or member of (a club, etc); to participate (in a conversation, etc); (*with* up) to enlist in the armed forces; to unite, connect. * *n* a joining; a place of joining.

joinder *n* the act of joining; (*law*) the coupling of two or more causes of action into the same declaration; the coupling of two issues or two parties.

joiner *n* a carpenter, esp one who finishes interior woodwork; (*inf*) a person who is involved in many clubs and activities, etc.

joinery *n* the trade of a joiner; the work of a joiner.

joint *n* a place where, or way in which, two things are joined; any of the parts of a jointed whole; the parts where two bones move on one another in an animal; a division of an animal carcass made by a butcher; (*sl*) a cheap bar or restaurant; (*sl*) a gambling or drinking den; (*sl*) a cannabis cigarette. * *adj* common to two or more; sharing with another. * *vt* to connect by a joint or joints; to divide (an animal carcass) into parts for cooking.

joint account *n* a bank account accessible to two or more people, for deposting or withdrawing funds.

jointer *n* a tool for pointing; a kind of plane; someone or something that forms joints.

jointly *adv* in common; together.

joint stock *n* capital held in common and distributed as shares among the owners.

joint-stock company *n* a company whose capital is owned jointly by stockholders who may sell their individual shares.

jointure *n* landed estate or other property settled on a woman in consideration of her marriage, to be enjoyed by her after the death of her husband; the provision made to enable this; (*arch*) a joining or being joined.

joint venture *n* the sharing of expertise or commercial risk by two or more businesses, etc.

joist *n* any of the parallel beams supporting floorboards or the laths of a ceiling.

jojoba *n* a broad-leaved evergreen shrub with edible seeds yielding a valuable oil.

joke *n* something said or done to cause laughter; a thing done or said merely in fun; a person or thing to be laughed at. * *vi* to make jokes.—**jokingly** *adv*.

joker *n* a person who jokes; (*sl*) a person; an extra playing card made use of in certain games.

jokey, joky *adj* (**jokier, jokiest**) full, or fond, of jokes.

jollify *vti* (**jollifying, jollified**) to make merry, esp with drink; to make jolly.—**jollification** *n*.

jollity *n* (*pl* **jollities**) the state of being jolly.

jolly *adj* (**jollier, jolliest**) merry; full of fun; delightful; (*inf*) enjoyable. * *vti* (**jollying, jollied**) (*inf*) to try to make (a person) feel good; to make fun of (someone).

Jolly Roger *n* a pirate's flag with a white skull and crossbones on a black background.

jolt *vt* to give a sudden shake or knock to; to move along jerkily; to surprise or shock suddenly. * *n* a sudden jar or knock; an emotional shock.—**joltingly** *adv*.—**jolty** *adj*.

jonquil *n* a species of narcissus.

jooal *see* joual.

jorum *n* a large drinking vessel; its contents, esp punch.

josh *vi* (*sl*) to tease gently. * *n* (*sl*) friendly teasing; a teasing joke.—**josher** *n*.—**joshingly** *adv*.

joss *n* a Chinese god or idol.

joss stick *n* a stick of incense.

jostle *vti* to shake or knock roughly; to collide or come into contact (with); to elbow for position. * *n* a jostling; a push.

jot *n* a very small amount. * *vt* (**jotting, jotted**) to note (down) briefly.—**jotter** *n*.

jotting *n* something noted down, esp a memorandum.

joual *n* a French Canadian dialect also spoken in Maine that has nonstandard French grammar and pronunciation with English syntax and a substantial English vocabulary.—*also* jooal.

joule *n* (*physics*) a unit of energy equal to work done when a force of one newton acts over a distance of one metre.

jounce *vti* to bump; to jolt (someone or something). * *n* a bump, a jolt.

journal *n* a daily record of happenings, as a diary; a

newspaper or periodical; (*bookkeeping*) a book of original entry for recording transactions; that part of a shaft or axle that turns in a bearing.

journalese *n* a facile style of writing found in many magazines, newspapers, etc.

journalism *n* the work of gathering news for or producing a newspaper, magazine or news broadcast.

journalist *n* a person who writes for or edits a newspaper, etc; one who keeps a diary.—**journalistic** *adj*.—**journalistically** *adv*.

journalize *vt* to enter in a journal; to keep a daily record.—**journalization** *n*.—**journalizer** n.

journey *n* (*pl* **journeys**) a travelling or going from one place to another; the distance covered when travelling. * *vi* (**journeying, journeyed**) to make a journey.—**journeyer** *n*.

journeyman *n* (*pl* **journeymen**) a person whose apprenticeship is completed and who is employed by another; a reliable workman.

joust *n* a fight on horseback between two knights with lances. * *vi* to engage in a joust, to run at the tilt.—**jouster** *n*.

Jove *n* the Roman god Jupiter; **by Jove** a mild oath; an exclamation of surprise.

jovial *adj* full of cheerful good humour.—**joviality** *n*.—**jovially** *adv*.

Jovian *adj* (*Roman myth*) of or like Jove or Jupiter.

jowl[1] *n* the lower jaw; (*usu pl*) the cheek.

jowl[2] n the loose flesh around the throat; the similar flesh in an animal, as a dewlap.

jowly *adj* (**jowlier, jowliest**) having heavy jowls.—**jowliness** *n*.

joy *n* intense happiness; something that causes this; its expression.

joyful *adj* filled with, expressing, or causing joy, glad.—**joyfully** *adv*.—**joyfulness** *n*.

joyless *adj* not occasioning joy, unhappy; bleak.—**joylessly** *adv*.—**joylessness** *n*.

joyous *adj* joyful, very happy.—**joyously** *adv*.—**joyousness** *n*.

joyride *n* (*inf*) a car ride, often in a stolen vehicle and at reckless speed, just for pleasure.—**joy-rider** *n*.—**joyriding** *n*.

joystick *n* (*inf*) the control lever of an aircraft; (*comput*) a device for controlling cursor movement on a monitor usu for computer games.

JP *abbr* = Justice of the Peace.

Jr., jr *abbr* = Junior.

jt *abbr* = joint.

jubilant *adj* triumphant; expressing joy; rejoicing.—**jubilance** *n*.—**jubilantly** *adv*.

Jubilate *n* (*Bible*) the 100th psalm, esp as a canticle in morning service; (*mus*) a setting of the 100th psalm.

jubilate *vi* to exult, to show joy.—**jubilation** *n*.

jubilee *n* a 50th or 25th anniversary; a time of rejoicing.

Judaic, Judaical *adj* of the Jews or Judaism.—**Judaically** *adv*

Judaism *n* the religion of the Jews, based on the Old Testament and the Talmud.—**Judaist** *n*.—**Judaistic** *adj*.

Judaize *vi, vt* to make or become Judaistic in belief, customs, precepts, etc.—**Judaization** *n*.

Judas *n* a traitor who pretends to be a friend; (*without cap*) a peephole, as in a cell door.

judder *vi* to vibrate violently. * *n* a spasmodic or rapid shaking.

Judean *adj* of, pertaining to, or from, the ancient region of Judaea.

judge *n* a public official with authority to hear and decide cases in a court of law; a person chosen to settle a dispute or decide who wins; a person qualified to decide on the relative worth of anything. * *vti* to hear and pass judgment (on) in a court of law; to determine the winner of (a contest) or settle (a dispute); to form an opinion about; to criticize or censure; to suppose, think.—**judgeable** *adj*.—**judgingly** *adv*.

judgeship *n* the office of a judge; his or her jurisdiction.

judgment, judgement *n* a judging; a deciding; a legal decision; an opinion; the ability to come to a wise decision; censure.

judgmental, judgemental *adj* of or depending on judgment; tending to make moral or personal judgments.—**judgmentally, judgementally** *adv*.

Judgment Day *n* (*Christianity*) the time of God's final judgment of mankind; (*without cap*) a final judgment; a day of reckoning.

judicable *adj* that may be judged; liable to be judged.

judicator *n* one who judges.

judicatory *n* (*pl* **judicatories**) a system of courts, a judiciary. * *adj* of or pertaining to the administration of justice.

judicature *n* a court or courts of justice; the power of dispensing justice by legal trial and judgment; jurisdiction; a body of judges; a tribunal.

judicial *adj* of judges, courts, or their functions.—**judicially** *adv*.

judiciary *adj* of judges or courts. * *n* (*pl* **judiciaries**) the part of government that administers justice; a system of courts in a country; judges collectively.

judicious *adj* possessing or characterized by sound judgment.—**judiciously** *adv*.—**judiciousness** *n*.

judo *n* a Japanese system of unarmed combat, adapted as a competitive sport from jujitsu.—**judoist** *n*.

jug *n* a vessel for holding and pouring liquids, with a handle and curved lip; a pitcher; (*sl*) prison. * *vt* (**jugging, jugged**) to stew meat (esp hare) in an earthenware pot; (*sl*) to put into prison.—**jugful** *n*.

jugate *adj* coupled together; (*bot*) having leaflets in pairs.

juggernaut *n* a terrible, irresistible force; a large heavy truck; (*with cap*) a Hindu god; his idol, dragged annually in processional car, under whose wheels devotees formerly threw themselves.

juggle *vi* to toss up balls, etc and keep them in the air. * *vt* to manipulate skilfully; to manipulate so as to deceive. * *n* the act of juggling; manipulation.—**jugglery** *n*.

juggler *n* one who juggles, a conjurer; a manipulator, a cheat.

jugular *adj* (*anat*) of the neck or throat. * *n* a jugular vein.

jugular vein *n* (*anat*) any of the large veins in the neck carrying blood from the head.

juice *n* the liquid part of fruit, vegetables or meat; liquid secreted by a bodily organ; (*inf*) vitality; (*inf*) electric current; (*inf*) engine fuel.

juicer *n* a mechanical or electrical device for extracting juice from fruit and vegetables; (*sl*) a person who drinks to excess.

juicy *adj* (**juicier, juiciest**) full of juice; (*inf*) very interesting; (*inf*) highly profitable.—**juicily** *adv*.—**juiciness** *n*.

jujitsu *n* a traditional Japanese system of unarmed defence in which an opponent's strength is used against him.

juju *n* an object of superstitious worship in West Africa used as a fetish or charm; the magic attributed to this.—**jujuism** *n*.

jujube *n* a gelatinous, fruit-flavoured lozenge; the fruit of any of several small trees of the buckthorn family; the trees themselves.

jukebox *n* a coin-operated automatic record or CD player.

Jul. *abbr* = July.

julep *n* a tall drink of bourbon or brandy and sugar over crushed ice, garnished with mint.

Julian *adj* of or pertaining to Julius Caesar or to the Julian calendar.

Julian calendar *n* a calendar introduced in 46BC by Julius Caesar, in which the year was made to consist of 365 days with a leap year of 366 days every fourth year.

julienne *adj* (*vegetables*) cut into very thin strips. * *n* a clear soup containing such vegetable.

July *n* (*pl* **Julies**) the seventh month of the year, having 31 days.

jumble *vt* (*often with* **up**) to mix together in a disordered mass. * *n* items mixed together in a confused mass; articles for a jumble sale.—**jumbly** *adj*.

jumbo *n* (*pl* **jumbos**) something very large of its kind. * *adj* very large.

jumbo jet *n* a very large jet airliner.

jumbuck *n* (*Austral*) a sheep.

jump *vi* to spring or leap from the ground, a height, etc; to jerk; to pass suddenly, as to a new topic; to rise suddenly, as prices; (*sl*) to be lively; (*often with* **at**) to act swiftly and eagerly; (*with* **at**) to accept or agree too eagerly; (*with* **on**) (*inf*) to reprimand or criticize harshly. * *vt* to leap or pass over (something); to leap upon; to cause (prices, etc) to rise; to fail to turn up (for trial when out on bail); (*inf*) to attack suddenly; (*inf*) to react to prematurely; (*sl*) to leave suddenly; * *n* a jumping; a distance jumped; a sudden transition; an obstacle; a nervous start.

jumper *n* a knitted garment for the upper body; a sleeveless dress for wearing over a blouse, etc.

jumper cable, jump lead *n* one of two cables for transferring electric charge from one battery to another, used to start a car with a flat battery by using the battery of another vehicle.

jump jet *n* (*inf*) a jet aircraft that can take off and land vertically.

jump-start *vt* to start a motor vehicle by pushing it in low gear so the engine turns over or by using jump leads; (*inf*) to set (a sluggish system, etc) in motion.

jumpsuit *n* a one-piece garment, as worn by paratroopers.

jumpy *adj* (**jumpier, jumpiest**) moving in jerks, etc; apprehensive; easily startled.—**jumpily** *adv*.—**jumpiness** *n*.

Jun. *abbr* = June.

jun., Jun. *abbr* = junior.

junction *n* a place or point where things join; a place where roads or railway lines, etc meet, link or cross each other.—**junctional** *adj*.

juncture *n* a junction; a point of time; a crisis.

June *n* the sixth month of the year, having 30 days.

jungle *n* an area overgrown with dense tropical trees and other vegetation, etc; any scene of wild confusion, disorder, or of ruthless competition for survival.

jungly *adj* (**junglier, jungliest**) pertaining to or covered with jungle.

junior *adj* younger in age; of more recent or lower status; of juniors. * *n* a person who is younger, of lower rank, etc; a young person employed in minor capacity in an office; a student in the third year of college or school; (*US inf*) (*with cap*) the younger son, often used after the name if the same as the father's.

junior miss *n* a girl in her teens; a clothes size for girls and slim women.

juniper *n* an evergreen shrub that yields purple berries.

junk[1] *n* a flat-bottomed sailing vessel prevalent in the China Seas.

junk[2] *n* discarded useless objects; (*inf*) rubbish, trash; (*sl*) any narcotic drug, such as heroin. * *vt* (*inf*) to scrap. * *adj* cheap, worthless; showy but without substance.

junk bond *n* an interest-bearing certificate held without security, used in junk debt.

junk debt *n* a method of funding takeovers by lending money unsecured in return for a higher yield and other benefits.—*also* **mezzanine debt**.

Junker *n* (*formerly*) a member of the Prussian aristocracy known for its political conservatism and militarism.

junker *n* (*sl*) a jalopy.

junket *n* curdled milk, sweetened and flavoured; a picnic; an excursion, esp one by an official at public expense. * *vi* to go on a junket.

junketeer *n* to make a practice of going on free trips. * *vi* someone who does this.

junk food *n* a snack or fast food with little nutritional value.

junkie, junky *n* (*pl* **junkies**) (*sl*) an addict of a particular activity, food, etc; a drug addict.

junk mail *n* unsolicited mail, eg advertising leaflets.

Juno *n* (*Roman myth*) the queen of the gods, sister and wife of Jupiter; a queenly woman.—**Junoesque** *adj*.

junta *n* a group of people, esp military, who assume responsibility for the government of a country following a coup d'état or revolution.

Jupiter *n* (*Roman myth*) the king of the gods, Jove; (*astron*) the largest planet in the solar system.

jural *adj* of law; of moral rights and obligations.—**jurally** *adv*.

Jurassic *adj* (geol) of or pertaining to the middle system of the Mesozoic Era marked by the existence of dinosaurs and the appearance of birds and mammals. * *n* the Jurassic period.

jurat *n* (law) a record of the time, place, etc, of an affidavit.

juridical, juridic *adj* of judicial proceedings or law.—**juridically** *adv*.

jurisconsult *n* one learned in law, a jurist.

jurisdiction *n* the right or authority to apply the law; the exercise of such authority; the limits of territory over which such authority extends.—**jurisdictional** *adj*.—**jurisdictionally** *adv*.

jurisprudence *n* the science or philosophy of law; a division of law.—**jurisprudential** *adj*.—**jurisprudentially** *adv*.

jurisprudent *adj*, *n* (a person) skilled in law.

jurist *n* an expert on law; a judge.—**juristic** *adj*.—**juristically** *adv*.

juror *n* a member of a jury; a person who takes an oath.

jury[1] *n* (*pl* **juries**) a body of usu 12 people sworn to hear evidence and to deliver a verdict on a case; a committee or panel that decides winners in a contest.

jury[2] *adj* (naut) makeshift, temporary.

juryman *n* (*pl* **jurymen**) a male juror.

jury-rigged *adj* (*yacht, etc*) rigged in a temporary or makeshift way.

jurywoman *n* (*pl* **jurywomen**) a female juror.

jussive *adj* (*gram*) imperative, expressing command. * *n* (*gram*) a jussive word, mood or form.

just *adj* fair, impartial; deserved, merited; proper, exact; conforming strictly with the facts. * *adv* exactly; nearly; only; barely; a very short time ago; immediately; (*inf*) really; justly, equitably; by right.—**justly** *adv*.—**justness** *n*.

justice *n* justness, fairness; the use of authority to maintain what is just; the administration of law; a judge.

justice of the peace *n* a magistrate who summarily tries minor cases within his or her jurisdiction.

justiciable *adj* subject to trial; able to be settled by law.—**justiciability** *n*.

justiciar *n* (*formerly*) in England, the administrator of justice, chief justice.

justiciary *n* (*pl* **justiciaries**) an officer who administers justice; a justiciar. * *adj* of or pertaining to the administration of justice.

justifiable *adj* capable of being justified or defended.—**justifiability** *n*.—**justifiably** *adv*.

justification *n* the act of justifying; vindication or defence; a showing adequate reason; absolution; (*print*) the spacing out of type to the full length of a line.

justify *vt* (**justifying, justified**) to prove or show to be just or right; to vindicate; to space out (a line of type) so that it fills the required length.

just-in-time *adj* pertaining to a method of inventory control in production industries, where components are delivered just before they are needed.

jut *vti* (**jutting, jutted**) to project; to stick out. * *n* a part that projects.

jute *n* the fibre of either of two tropical plants used for making sacking, etc.

juvenescent *adj* becoming young.—**juvenescence** *n*.

juvenile *adj* young; immature; of or for young persons. * *n* a young person.

juvenile delinquency *n* (*pl* **delinquencies**) antisocial or illegal behaviour by young people usu under 18.—**juvenile delinquent** *n*.

juvenilia *npl* works produced in an artist's or author's youth.

juvenility *n* (*pl* **juvenilities**) the state of being juvinile; youthfulness; a childish act.

juxtapose *vt* to place side by side, esp for comparison.—**juxtaposition** *n*.

K

K *abbr* = kelvin(s); one thousand; (*comput*) 1024 words, bits or bytes; (*chem symbol*) potassium.

kabbala, kabala *see* **cabbala**.

kabuki *n* classical Japanese theatre.

Kabyle *n* (*pl* **Kabyles, Kabyle**) an Algerian Berber, or his dialect.

Kaddish *n* (*pl* **Kaddishim**) a Jewish daily prayer, used by mourners for the year following, and on the anniversary of, someone's death.

Kaffir, Kafir *n* (*pl* **Kaffirs, Kaffir, Kafirs, Kafir**) (*S Africa*) (*offensive*) any black native African; a native of Kafiristan in Asia; (*pl*) South African mine shares; the language of a Southern African people chiefly found in Cape Province of the Republic of South Africa; (*offensive*) among Muslims, an infidel; a type of sorghum.

kaftan *see* **caftan**.

kaiak *see* **kayak**.

kainite *n* a mineral fertilizer.

Kaiser *n* (*formerly*) the title of the emperors of Germany and Austria.

kaka *n* a New Zealand parrot with a long beak.

kakapo *n* an owl-like parrot, a flightless nocturnal bird nesting in burrows in New Zealand.

kakemono *n* a Japanese hanging picture of paper or silk, mounted on rollers.

kaki *n* (*pl* **kakis**) *n* the Japanese persimmon.

kale, kail *n* a variety of cabbage with crinkled leaves.

kaleidoscope *n* a small tube containing bits of coloured glass reflected by mirrors to form symmetrical patterns as the tube is rotated; anything that constantly changes.—**kaleidoscopic** *adj*.—**kaleidoscopically** *adv*.

kalends *see* **calends**.

kaleyard, kailyard *n* (*Scot*) a kitchen garden.

Kali *n* (*Hindu myth*) the goddess of destruction.

kalif, khalif *see* **caliph**.

kalmia *n* the American mountain laurel.

Kalmuck, Kalmyk *n* (*pl* **Kalmucks, Kalmuck, Kalmyks, Kalmyk**) *n* a member of a Mongolian Buddhist people; the variety of the Mongolian language. * *adj* of or pertaining to the Kalmuck or their language.

kalong *n* a large Indonesian or tropical fruitbat; a flying fox.

kalpak *see* **calpac**.

kalsomine *see* **calcimine**.

Kamasutra *n* an ancient Hindu manual on erotic love.

kame *n* (*Scot*) an elongated gravel or sand mound or hill of glacial origin; a comb.

kami *n* (*pl* **kami**) a divinity or demigod in the Shinto religion of Japan, from whom the Japanese emperors were supposed to have been descended.

kamikaze *n* (*World War II*) a Japanese aircraft packed with explosives for making a suicidal crashing attack; the pilot of such an aircraft.

kamseen, kamsin *see* **khamsin**.

kangaroo *n* (*pl* **kangaroos**) an Australian marsupial with short forelegs and strong, large hind legs for jumping

kangaroo court *n* an illegal court operated by an unauthorized body, which perverts the proper course of justice.

Kantian *adj* of the German philosopher Immanuel Kant (1724–1804) or his philosophy.

kaolin *n* a white clay used in porcelain, etc.

kapellmeister *n* (*pl* **kapellmeister**) the musical director of an orchestra etc, esp in an 18th-century aristocratic household.

kapok *n* the silky fibres around the seeds of a tropical tree, used for stuffing cushions, etc.

kappa *n* the tenth letter of the Greek alphabet.

kaput *adj* (*sl*) broken, ruined.

karabiner *n* (*mountaineering*) a spring-loaded hook for securing ropes.

karakul n (the black fur of) a breed of sheep from the Bukhara region of central Asia.

karaoke *n* a CD music system that plays recordings of popular songs with the vocal part removed to allow amateurs to sing along.

karat *n* a measure of weight for precious stones; a measure of the purity of gold.—*also* **carat**.

karate *n* a Japanese system of unarmed combat using sharp blows of the feet and hands.

Karen *n* (*pl* **Karens, Karen**) *n* a member of a Thai people in Burma, or their language.

karma *n* (*Buddhism, Hinduism*) the sum of a person's actions during one of their existences, held to determine their destiny in the next; (*inf*) a certain aura that a person or place is felt to possess.—**karmic** *adj*.

karoo, karroo *n* (*pl* **karoos, karroos**) (*S Africa*) (*sometimes with a cap*) a series of clayey tablelands, usu barren except in the wet season; a system of rocks in , or a period; of this period.

kart *n* a small motorized vehicle used in racing.—*also* **go-kart**.

karting *n* kart racing.

karyo- *prefix* = nucleus.

katydid *n* a large green North American insect like a grasshopper.

kauri (*pl* **kauris**) a New Zealand pine with oval leaves from which a resinous gum is extracted; the wood or gum from this tree.

kava *n* a Polynesian shrub; an intoxicating and narcotic drink made from it.

kayak *n* an Eskimo canoe made of skins on a wooden frame.—*also* **kaiak**.

kazoo *n* (*pl* **kazoos**) a small tube-shaped musical instrument through which one hums to vibrate a membrane-covered hole at the end or side

KB *abbr* = kilobyte

KBE *abbr* = Knight Commander of the Order of the British Empire.

kc *abbr* = kilocycle.

kcal *abbr* = kilocalorie.

KCB *abbr* = Knight Commander of the Order of the Bath.

KE *abbr* = kinetic energy.

kebab *n* small cubes of grilled meat and vegetables, usu served on a skewer.

keck *vi* to make a sound as if about to vomit; to feel or express loathing.

keddah *n* in India and Burma, an enclosure for catching wild elephants.

kedge *n* a small anchor for kedging a ship. * *vt* to move (a ship) by hauling on a cable attached to a kedge.

kedgeree *n* a dish containing fish, rice and hard-boiled eggs.

keef *see* **kif.**

keek *vt* (*Scot*) to peep cheekily.

keel *n* one of the main structural members of a ship extending along the bottom from stem to stern to which the frame is attached; any structure resembling this. * *vti* (to cause) to turn over.

keelhaul *vt* (*formerly*) to drag under water beneath the bottom of a ship from one side to the other; to reprimand sternly.

keelson n a beam of timber laid on the middle of the floor timbers over the keel of a vessel to strengthen it.—*also* **kelson.**

keen[1] *adj* eager, enthusiastic; intellectually acute, shrewd; having a sharp point or fine edge; (*senses*) perceptive, penetrating; extremely cold and piercing; intense; (*prices*) very low so as to be competitive.—**keenly** *adv.*—**keenness** *n.*

keen[2] *n* a dirge or lament for the dead. * *vi* to lament the dead.

keep *vb* (**keeping, kept**) *vt* to celebrate, observe; to fulfil; to protect, guard; to take care of; to preserve; to provide for; to make regular entries in; to maintain in a specified state; to hold for the future; to hold and not let go; (*with* **at**) to harass (a person) into continuing (some task, etc); (*with* **back**) to refuse to disclose; to restrain; (*with* **down**) to repress; to subdue; (*with* **from**) to abstain or restrain from; to preserve as a secret (from someone); (*with* **to**) to cause to adhere strictly to; (*with* **up**) to persist in; to continue; to maintain in good condition. * *vi* to stay in a specified condition; to continue, go on; to refrain or restrain oneself; to stay fresh, not spoil; (*with* **at**) to persist; (*with* **away**) to prevent from approaching; (*with* **down**) to stay hidden; (*with* **on**) to talk or nag continuously; (*with* **to**) to (cause to) adhere strictly to; (*with* **up**) to maintain the same pace, level of knowledge, etc as another; to stay informed; to continue relentlessly. * *n* food and shelter; care and custody; the inner stronghold of a castle.

keeper *n* one who guards, watches, or takes care of persons or things.

keeping *n* care, charge; observance; agreement, conformity.

keepsake *n* something kept in memory of the giver.

kef *see* **kif.**

keg *n* a small barrel.

kelp *n* a large brown seaweed.

kelpie (*pl* **kelpies**) *n* in Scottish folklore, a malevolent water sprite, supposed to take the form of a horse.

Keltic *see* **Celtic.**

kelvin *n* a unit of temperature of the Kelvin scale.

Kelvin scale *n* temperature on a scale where absolute zero (-273.15° Celsius) is taken as zero degrees.

ken *n* understanding; view; sight. * *vt* (**kenning, kenned** *or* **kent**) to know; to recognize at sight.

kendo *n* a Japanese style of fencing with bamboo staves.

kennel *n* a small shelter for a dog, a doghouse; (*often pl*) a place where dogs are bred or kept. * *vt* (**kennelling, kennelled** *or* **kenneling, kenneled**) to keep in a kennel.

keno *n* a game of chance, similar to bingo, played with numbered balls and cards.

kenosis *n* (*theology*) the self-limitation of Christ in laying aside his divinity and becoming man.—**kenotic** *adj.*

kentledge *n* (*naut*) ballast of scrap metal.

kepi *n* (*pl* **kepis**) a French military peaked cap.

kept *see* **keep.**

keratin *n* a tough, fibrous protein, the substance of hair, nails, feathers, etc.

keratitis *n* inflammation of the cornea.

keratose *adj* (*sponges*) having a horn-like skeleton.

kerb *n* a line of raised stone forming the edge of a pavement; a curb.

kerbing *n* kerbstones collectively; material for kerbstones, curbing.

kerbstone *n* the stone edge of a path, curbstone.

kerchief *n* a piece of square cloth worn on the head.

kerf *n* a cut or slit made by a saw, etc.

kermes *n* the dried bodies of female scale insects from which a dye of a deep cherry red colour is obtained; an oak tree found in Europe and Asia, on which these insects live.

kermis *n* an open-air festival or fair.

kern[1], **kerne** *n* (*formerly*) a lightly armed Irish or Scottish medieval foot-soldier; a troop of these; (*arch*) a peasant.

kern[2] *n* (*print*) the part of a type or character that overhangs the following piece of type or character.

kernel *n* the inner edible part of a fruit or nut; the essential part of anything.

kerosene, kerosine *n* a fuel oil distilled from petroleum, paraffin.

kersey *n* a coarse smooth-faced woollen cloth.

kerseymere *n* a twilled cloth of fine wool.

kestrel **n** a type of small falcon.

ketch *n* a small two-masted sailing vessel.

ketchup *n* any of various thick sauces, esp one made from puréed tomato, for meat, fish, etc.—*also* **catchup, catsup**

ketone *n* a class of chemical compounds, the simplest being acetone.

kettle *n* a container with a handle and spout for boiling water.

kettledrum *n* a musical instrument consisting of a hollow metal body with a parchment head, the tension of which controls the pitch and is adjusted by screws.

kevel *n* (*naut*) a cleat for belaying ropes.

key[1] *n* a device for locking and unlocking something; a thing that explains or solves, as the legend of a map, a code, etc; a controlling position, person, or thing; one of a set of parts or levers pressed in a keyboard or typewriter, etc; (*mus*) a system of related tones based on a keynote and forming a given scale; style or mood of expression; a roughened surface for improved adhesion of plaster, etc; an electric circuit breaker. * *vt* to furnish with a key; to bring into harmony. * *adj* controlling; important.

key² *n* a low island or reef.

keyboard *n* a set of keys in a piano, organ, microcomputer, etc.

keyhole *n* an opening (in a lock) into which a key is inserted.

keyhole surgery *n* surgery performed through small incisions in the body using fibre-optic tubes both for internal examination and as conduits for tiny surgical instruments.

Keynesianism *n* the economic theories based on the works of the English economist John Maynard Keynes (1883–1946).—**Keynesian** *adj*.

keynote *n* the basic note of a musical scale; the basic idea or ruling principle. * *vt* to give the keynote of; to give the keynote speech at.

keypad *n* a small usu hand-held keyboard of numbered buttons used to tap in a telephone number, operate a calculator, etc.

key signature *n* the sharps or flats at the beginning of a musical stave to indicate the key.

keystone *n* the middle stone at the top of an arch, holding the stones or other pieces in place.

keystroke *n* the depressing of a key on a typewriter, computer keyboard, etc.

kg *abbr* = kilogram(s).

KGB *abbr* = (*formerly*) the secret police of the USSR.

khaddar, khadi *n* an Indian homespun cotton cloth.

khaki *adj* dull yellowish-brown. * *n* (*pl* **khakis**) strong, twilled cloth of this colour; (*often pl*) a khaki uniform or trousers.

khamsin *n* a hot southerly wind, esp in Egypt, that blows for about 50 days in spring.—**kamseen, kamsin**.

khan *n* the title of a ruler, prince, or governor in Asia.

khanate *n* the rule or jurisdiction of a khan.

khedive *n* the title of the viceroy of Egypt (1867–1914).

khoraschot *n* the policy in the former USSR, initiated by President Gorbachev, of the decentralized economic accountability of managers in industrial production and other enterprises.

kHz *abbr* = kilohertz.

kiang *n* a wild ass of Tibet.

kibble *vt* to grind coarsely. * *n* a raiseable bucket used in wells, mines etc.

kibbutz *n* (*pl* **kibbutzim**) an agricultural commune in Israel.

kibbutznik *n* a person who lives in a kibbutz.

kibe *n* ulcerated chilblain, esp one on the heel.

kiblah, kibla *n* the point to which Muslims turn at prayer, Mecca.

kibosh *n* (*sl*) nonsense.

kick *vt* to strike with the foot; to drive, force, etc as by kicking; to score (a goal, etc) by kicking; (*with* **about, around**) (*inf*) to abuse physically or mentally; to discuss or analyse (a problem, etc) in a relaxed unsystematic manner; (*with* **out**) (*inf*) to eject, dismiss; (*with* **up**) (*inf*) to cause (trouble, etc). * *vi* to strike out with the foot; to recoil, as a gun; (*inf*) to complain; (*with* **about, around**) (*inf*) to wander idly; to be unused or forgotten; (*with* **off**) (*football*) to give the ball the first kick to start play; (*inf*) to start. * *n* an act or method of kicking; a sudden recoil; (*inf*) a thrill; (*inf*) an intoxicating effect.—**kicker** *n*.

kickback *n* a recoil; (*inf*) a returning of part of a sum of money received in payment.

kickoff *n* (*football*) a kick putting the ball into play; the beginning or start of proceedings, eg a discussion.

kickshaw *n* a trifle, trinket; (*arch*) a small, light, fancy dish, a delicacy.

kickstand *n* a retractable stand for parking a bicycle or motorbike.

kid *n* a young goat; soft leather made from its skin; (*inf*) a child. * *vti* (**kidding, kidded**) (*inf*) to tease or fool playfully; (*goat*) to bring forth young.—**kidder** *n*.

kiddy, kiddie *n* (*pl* **kiddies**) (*inf*) a child.

kidnap *vt* (**kidnapping, kidnapped** *or* **kidnaping, kidnaped**) to seize and hold to ransom, as of a person.—**kidnapper, kidnaper** *n*.

kidney *n* (*pl* **kidneys**) either of a pair of glandular organs excreting waste products from the blood as urine; an animal's kidney used as food.

kidney bean *n* any of various cultivated beans, esp a large dark red bean seed.

kidney stone *n* a hard mineral deposit in the kidney.

kidskin *n* a soft leather made from the skin of a young goat.

kief *see* **kif**.

kier *n* a vat in which cloth is boiled for bleaching.

kieselguhr *n* mineral remains of algae, used for filtering and insulation purposes etc.

kif *n* a drowsy state of well-being produced by marijuana; marijuana itself; any drug producing a similar state.—*also* **keef, kef, kief**.

kill *vt* to cause the death of; to destroy; to neutralize (a colour); to spend (time) on trivial matters; to turn off (an engine, etc); (*inf*) to cause severe discomfort or pain to. * *n* the act of killing; an animal or animals killed.—**killer** *n*.

killer whale *n* a carnivorous black-and-white toothed whale.

killick, killock *n* (*naut*) a heavy stone used as an anchor; a small anchor.

killing *adj* (*inf*) tiring; very amusing; causing death, deadly. * *n* the act of killing, murder; (*inf*) a sudden (financial) success.—**killingly** *adv*.

killjoy *n* a person who spoils other people's enjoyment.

kiln *n* a furnace or large oven for baking or drying (lime, bricks, etc).

kilo *n* (*pl* **kilos**) kilogram; kilometre.

kilo- *prefix* one thousand.

kilobyte *n* 1024 bytes.

kilocalorie *n* a Calorie.

kilocycle *n* a kilohertz.

kilogram *n* a unit of weight and mass, equal to 1000 grams or 2.2046 pounds.

kilohertz *n* one thousand cycles per second, 1000 hertz.

kilolitre, kiloliter *n* one thousand litres.

kilometre, kilometer *n* a unit of length equal to 1000 metres or 0.62 mile.—**kilometric** *adj*.

kiloton *n* a unit of explosive force equal to 1000 tons of TNT.

kilowatt *n* a unit of electrical power, equal to 1000 watts.

kilowatt-hour *n* a unit of energy equal to work done by one kilowatt in one hour.

kilt *n* a knee-length skirt made from tartan material pleated at the sides, worn as part of the Scottish Highland dress for men and women.

kilter *n* good working order; good condition (*out of kilter*).

kimono *n* (*pl* **kimonos**) a loose Japanese robe.

kin *n* relatives; family.—*see* **kith**.

kind¹ *n* sort; variety; class; a natural group or division; essential character.

kind² *adj* sympathetic; friendly; gentle; benevolent.—**kindness** *n*.

kindergarten *n* a class or school for very young children.

kind-hearted *adj* benevolent; kind, warm.—**kind-heartedly** *adv*.

kindle *vt* to set on fire; to excite (feelings, interest, etc). * *vi* to catch fire; to become aroused or excited.

kindling *n* material, such as bits of dry wood, for starting a fire.

kindly *adj* (**kindlier, kindliest**) kind; gracious; agreeable; pleasant. * *adv* in a kindly manner; favourably.—**kindliness** *n*.

kindred *n* a person's family or relatives; family relationship; resemblance. * *adj* related; like, similar.

kine *n* (*pl*) (*arch*) cattle.

kinematic *adj* of pure motion, without reference to force etc.

kinematics *n* (*sing*) the science of pure motion.

kinetic *adj* of or produced by movement.—**kinetically** *adv*.

kinetic art *n* sculpture, etc that moves or has moving parts.

kinetic energy *n* energy derived from motion.

kinetics *n* (*used as sing*) the science of the effects of forces in producing or changing motion; the study of the mechanisms and rates of chemical reactions.

king *n* the man who rules a country and its people; a man with the title of ruler, but with limited power to rule; man supreme in a certain sphere; something best in its class; the chief piece in chess; a playing card with a picture of a king on it, ranking above a queen; (*draughts*) a piece that has been crowned.

King Charles spaniel *n* a small breed of spaniel with black and brown markings.

kingcup n the marsh marigold; any of various yellow-flowered, five-petalled plants, such as the buttercup or clematis.

kingdom *n* a country headed by a king or queen; a realm, domain; any of the three divisions of the natural world: animal: vegetable, mineral.

kingfisher *n* a short-tailed diving bird that feeds chiefly on fish.

King James Bible, King James Version *n* the version of the Bible published by the sanction of James I of England and VI of Scotland in 1611 and appointed to be read in churches.—*also* **Authorized Version**.

kinglet *n* a minor king; a small bird with a yellow crown found throughout North America.

kingly *adj* (**kinglier, kingliest**) of, resembling, or fit for a king.—**kingliness** *n*.

king-of-arms *n* (*pl* **kings-of-arms**) chief officer of the Heralds' College.

kingpin *n* (*sl*) the chief person in a company, group, etc; the pin in a car, etc that attaches the stub axle to the axle beam and allows limited movement to the stub axle; the foremost pin in tenpin bowling; the central pin in ninepins; the crux of an argument.

kingship *n* the office or authority of a king; the art of ruling as king.

king-size, king-sized *adj* larger than standard size.

kink *n* a tight twist or curl in a piece of string, rope, hair, etc; a painful cramp in the neck, back, etc; a minor problem in some course of action; a personality quirk; (*Brit sl*) a sexual deviation; (*pl*) (*Scot*) a convul-

sive fit of laughter; (*US*) a bright, original idea. * *vt* to form kinks.

kinkajou *n* nocturnal long-tailed quadruped of Central and Southern America similar to a racoon(—*also* **honeybear**); a short-tailed primate with spiny protrusions from the neck (—*also* **potto**).

kinky *adj* (**kinkier, kinkiest**) full of kinks; (*inf*) eccentric; (*inf*) sexually bizarre.—**kinkiness** *n*.

kinnikinnick, kinnikinic *n* a mixture of dried leaves and bark smoked by American Indians; any of the plants used for this.

kino (gum) *n* an astringent vegetable gum of a dark red colour, used in medicine, tanning etc.

kinsfolk *n* blood relations.

kinship *n* blood relationship; close connection.

kinsman, kinswoman *n* (*pl* **kinsmen, kinswomen**) a relative, esp by blood.

kiosk *n* a small open structure used for selling newspapers, confectionery, etc; a public telephone booth.

kip *vi* (**kipping, kipped**) (*sl*) to sleep. * *n* (*sl*) sleep, a lodging.

kipper *n* a kippered herring, etc. * *vt* to cure (fish) by salting and drying or smoking.

kirk *n* (*Scot*) a church.

kirsch, kirschwasser *n* a type of brandy made from cherries.

kismet *n* fate, destiny.

kiss *vti* to touch with the lips as an expression of love, affection or in greeting; to touch the lips with those of another person as a sign of love or desire; to touch lightly. * *n* an act of kissing; a light, gentle touch.—**kissable** *adj*.

kissagram *n* a celebratory telegram or message delivered with a kiss.

kiss-and-tell *adj* (*inf*) pertaining to the publication of memoirs that reveal hitherto secret details.

kisser n one who kisses; (*sl*) the mouth or face.

kiss of life *n* mouth-to-mouth resuscitation.

kist n (*Scot*) a chest or box; (*arch*) a cist; (*S Africa*) a large chest or box used for storing linen, esp for a trousseau.

kit *n* clothing and personal equipment, etc; tools and equipment for a specific purpose; a set of parts with instructions ready to be assembled. * *vt* (**kitting, kitted**) (*usu with* **out** *or* **up**) to provide with kit.

kitchen *n* a place where food is prepared and cooked.

kitchenette *n* a small kitchen.

kitchen garden *n* a garden where vegetables are grown for domestic use.

kite *n* a bird of prey with long narrow wings and a forked tail; a light frame covered with a thin covering for flying in the wind.

kith *n* friends and relations, now only in **kith and kin**.

kithara *see* **cithara**.

kitsch *n* art, literature, etc regarded as pretentious, inferior, or in poor taste.—*also adj*.—**kitschy** *adj*.

kitten *n* a young cat; the young of other small mammals. * *vti* to give birth to kittens.

kittenish *adj* like a kitten, playful; (*woman*) flirtatious.

kittiwake *n* either of two types of gull with black-tipped wings.

kittle *adj* (*Scot*) difficult to manage, capricious. * *vt* (*Scot*) to tickle; to cause (someone) to be puzzled or to bother someone.

kitty *n* (*pl* **kitties**) the stakes in a game of poker or other gambling game; a shared fund of money; affectionate name for a cat or kitten.

kiwi *n* (*pl* **kiwis**) a flightless bird of New Zealand; (*inf*) a New Zealander.

kiwi fruit *n* a fruit of an Asian vine.—*also* **Chinese gooseberry**.

KKK *abbr* = Ku Klux Klan.

kl *abbr* = kiloliter.

klaxon *n* a type of old-fashioned motor horn.

kleptomania *n* an uncontrollable impulse to steal.— **kleptomaniac** *n*.

klipspringer *n* a small antelope of South Africa.

kloof *n* a ravine, a deep narrow valley, in South Africa.

klystron *n* an electronic device that generates and amplifies microwaves.

km *abbr* = kilometre(s).

knack *n* an ability to do something easily; a trick; a habit.

knacker *n* one who buys worn-out horses or old houses, ships, etc, for destruction.

knackwurst *n* a type of spicy German sausage.

knap (**knapping, knapped**) *vt* to break, snap or hit something.

knapsack *n* a bag for carrying equipment or supplies on the back.

knapweed *n* a purple-flowered weed.

knar *see* **knur**.

knave *n* (*formerly*) a tricky or dishonest man; the jack in a pack of playing cards.—**knavish** *adj*.—**knavishly** *adv*.

knavery *n* (*pl* **knaveries**) dishonesty; fraud; deceit.

knead *vt* to squeeze and press together (dough, clay, etc) into a uniform lump with the hands; to make (bread, etc) by kneading; to squeeze and press with the hands.—**kneader** *n*.

knee *n* the joint between the thigh and the lower part of the human leg; anything shaped like a bent knee. * *vt* (**kneeing, kneed**) to hit or touch with the knee.

kneecap *n* the small bone covering and protecting the front part of the knee-joint. * *vt* (**kneecapping, kneecapped**) to maim by shooting into the kneecap.

knee-deep *adj* deep enough to cover the knees; deeply involved.

knee jerk *n* an involuntary jerk when the tendon below the knee is tapped.

kneejerk *adj* responding automatically.

kneel *vi* (**kneeling, kneeled** *or* **knelt**) to go down on one's knee or knees; to remain in this position.— **kneeler** *n*.

knell *n* the sound of a bell rung slowly and solemnly at a death or funeral; a warning of death, failure, etc. * *vi* (*bell*) to ring a knell; to summon, announce, etc (as if) by a knell.

knelt *see* **kneel**.

knew *see* **know**.

Knickerbocker *n* a New Yorker; a descendant of the founders of the original city.

knickerbockers *npl* baggy breeches fastened by a band at the knee.

knickers *npl* an undergarment covering the lower body and having separate leg holes, worn by women and girls.

knickknack *n* a small ornament or trinket.—*also* **nicknack**.

knife *n* (*pl* **knives**) a flat piece of steel, etc, with a sharp edge set in a handle, used to cut or as a weapon; a sharp blade forming part of a tool or machine. * *vt* to cut or stab with a knife.

knife edge *n* the sharp edge of a knife; anything resem- bling this, such as the blade of an ice skate; a sharp wedge used as a pivot for a balance; a critical or precarious situation.

knight *n* (*Middle Ages*) a medieval mounted soldier; a man who for some achievement is given honorary rank entitling him to use "Sir" before his given name; a chessman shaped like a horse's head. * *vt* to make (a man) a knight.—**knightly** *adj*.—**knightliness** *n*.

knight-errant *n* (*pl* **knights-errant**) a quixotic person; (*Middle Ages*) a knight who went in quest of adventure, to show his prowess, chivalry etc.

knight-errantry *n* the practices or customs of knights-errant; quixotic behaviour.

knighthood *n* the character, rank, or dignity of a knight; the order of knights.

knit *vb* (**knitting, knitted** *or* **knit**) *vt* to form (fabric or a garment) by interlooping yarn using knitting needles or a machine; to cause (eg broken bones) to grow together; to link or join together closely; to draw (the brows) together. * *vi* to make knitted fabric from yarn by means of needles; to grow together; to become joined or united. * *n* a knitted garment or fabric.— **knitter** *n*.

knitting *n* work being knitted.

knitting needle *n* a long thin eyeless needle, usu made of plastic or steel, used in knitting.

knitwear *n* knitted clothing.

knives *see* **knife**.

knob *n* a rounded lump or protuberance; a handle, usu round, of a door, drawer, etc.

knobby *adj* (**knobbier, knobbiest**) full of knobs.

knobkerrie *n* a round-headed stick used as a weapon in South Africa.

knock *vi* to strike with a sharp blow; to rap on a door; to bump, collide; (*engine*) to make a thumping noise; (*with* **off**) (*inf*) to finish work; (*with* **up**) (*tennis, etc*) to practise before a match. * *vt* to strike; (*inf*) to criticize; (*with* **about, around**) to wander around aimlessly; to treat roughly; (*with* **back**) (*inf*) to drink, swallow quickly; to reject, refuse; (*with* **down**) to indicate a sale at an auction; (*with* **down** *or* **off**) to hit so as to cause to fall; (*with* **off**) (*inf*) to do or make hastily and without effort; to reduce in price; to discontinue, esp work; (*sl*) to kill; (*sl*) to steal; (*with* **out**) to make unconscious or exhausted; to eliminate in a knockout competition; (*inf*) to amaze; (*with* **up**) (*inf*) to make or arrange hastily; (*cricket*) to score a certain number of runs; to rouse; (*sl*) to make pregnant. * *n* a knocking, a hit, a rap.

knockabout *adj* rough, boisterous.

knockdown *adj* cheap; (*furniture*) easy to dismantle.

knocker *n* a device hinged against a door for use in knocking; (*sl: usu pl*) a woman's breasts.

knock-kneed *adj* having inward-curving legs.

knockout *n* a punch or blow that produces unconsciousness; a contest in which competitors are eliminated at each round; (*inf*) an attractive or extremely impressive person or thing.

knoll *n* a small round hill.

knot *n* a lump in a thread, etc formed by a tightened loop or tangling; a fastening made by tying lengths of rope, etc; an ornamental bow; a small group, cluster; a hard mass of wood where a branch grows out from a tree, which shows as a roundish, cross-grained piece in a board; a unit of speed of one nautical mile per hour; something that ties closely, esp the bond of marriage. * *vti* (**knotting, knotted**) to make or form a knot (in); to entangle or become entangled.—**knotter** *n*.

knotgrass *n* a weed with a jointed stem and green flowers; any of various similar plants.

knothole *n* a hole in wood once filled by a knot.

knotting *n* a kind of lace work made with knots; a sealer applied to knots before priming wood as protection from sap.

knotty *adj* (**knottier, knottiest**) full of knots; hard to solve; puzzling.—**knottiness** *n*.

know *vt* (**knowing, knew**, *pp* **known**) to be well informed about; to be aware of; to be acquainted with; to recognize or distinguish.—**knowable** *adj*.

know-all *n* a know-it-all.

know-how *n* practical skill, experience.

knowing *adj* having knowledge; shrewd; clever; implying a secret understanding.—**knowingly** *adv*.—**knowingness** *n*.

know-it-all *n* a person who acts as if they know about everything.

knowledge *n* what one knows; the body of facts, etc accumulated over time; fact of knowing; range of information or understanding; the act of knowing.

knowledgeable *adj* having knowledge or intelligence; well-informed.—**knowledgeably** *adv*.

known *see* **know**.

knuckle *n* a joint of the finger, esp at the roots of the fingers; the knee of an animal used as food. * *vi* (*with* **down**) (*inf*) to apply oneself in earnest (to some task, duty, etc); (*with* **under**) to submit, to give in.

knuckle-duster *n* a metal device that fits over the knuckles, used for inflicting severe injury by punching.

knur, knurr *n* a knot either in a tree trunk or in wood; a hard lump.—*also* **knar**.

knurl *n* a small ridge, esp one of a series on a metal surface to prevent slippage.

KO *abbr* = knockout.

koa *n* a Hawaiian tree; the hard wood it produces used in making furniture.

koala *n* an Australian tree-dwelling marsupial with thick, grey fur.

koan *n* an insoluble riddle used as a meditation exercise in Zen Buddhism.

kob *n* a South African water antelope.

kobold *n* a household goblin or elf; a spirit of mines and other underground places.

Kohinoor, Koh-i-nor *n* a famous, very large Indian diamond, which has belonged to the British Crown since 1849.

kohl *n* a fine powder, as of antimony, used for darkening the eyelids.

kohlrabi *n* (*pl* **kohlrabies**) a variety of cabbage with a thick stem, used as a vegetable.

kola nut *n* the seed of either of two tropical trees which has stimulant properties and is chewed or used in making sweet drinks.—*also* **cola nut**.

kolinsky *n* (*pl* **kolinskies**) *n* an Asian mink; its fur.

kolkhoz *n* a collective farm in Russia.

koodoo *n* an African striped antelope with long spiral horns.—*also* **kudu**.

kook *n* (*inf*) a person regarded as silly, eccentric, etc.

kookaburra *n* an Australian kingfisher with a harsh cry like loud laughter.

kooky, kookie *adj* (**kookier, kookiest**) (*inf*) crazy; eccentric.

kop *n* (*S Africa*) an isolated hill.

kopeck, kopek *n* a Russian coin, one hundred of which comprise one ruble.

kopje n (*S Africa*) a hillock or small hill.

Koran *n* the sacred book of the Muslims.—**Koranic** *adj*.

Korean *n* a native or inhabitant of Korea; the language spoken in North and South Korea.* *adj* of or pertaining to Korea, its language or people.

kosher *adj* (*Judaism*) clean or fit to eat according to dietary laws; (*inf*) acceptable, genuine. * *n* kosher food.

koto *n* (*pl* **kotos**) *n* a Japanese musical instrument with silk strings, similar to a zither.

kowtow *vi* to show exaggerated respect (to) by bowing.

kph *abbr* = kilometres per hour.

Kr (*chem symbol*) krypton.

kraal *n* an African village consisting of a group of huts surrounded by a pallisade; a sheepfold, or cattle pen. * to pen sheep or cattle in a kraal.

krait *n* a deadly Asian rock snake.

kraken *n* a gigantic fabled sea monster supposed to live in the sea off Norway.

kremlin *n* a Russian citadel; (*with cap and* **the**) the citadel in Moscow, housing the former palace, cathedrals, and the Russian government; (*with cap*) the central government of Russia.

kriegspiel *n* (*sometimes with cap*) (*mil*) a game with blocks or models representing the various sections of an army as if in actual warfare, used in training; a chess game for two players, each playing on their own board with their own pieces, unseen by the other, with the moves regulated by a third person also with a board unseen by either player.

krill *n* (*pl* **krill**) the tiny shrimp-like plankton eaten by many whales.

kris *n* a Malaysian or Indonesian knife or dagger with a wavy blade.—*also* **crease, creese**.

Krishna *n* a great deity of later Hinduism.—**Krishnaism** *n*.

krona *n* (*pl* **kronor**) the monetary unit of Sweden.

króna *n* (*pl* **krónur**) the monetary unit of Iceland.

krone *n* (*pl* **kroner**) the monetary unit of Denmark and Norway.

krypton *n* a colourless, odourless gas used in fluorescent lights and lasers.

Kt *abbr* = Knight.

kudos *n* (*used as sing*) (*inf*) fame, glory, prestige.

kudu *see* **koodoo**.

Kufic *see* **Cufic**.

Ku Klux Klan *n* an American secret society hostile to Blacks, Jews, Catholics, etc.

kulak *n* an independent well-to-do peasant in Russia.

kumiss *n* a spirit made in central Asia from fermented mare's milk and sometimes used as a medicine.

kümmel *n* a liqueur flavoured with caraway seeds.

kumquat *n* a small fruit like an orange with a sweet rind.

kung fu *n* a Chinese system of unarmed combat.

Kurd *n* a native of Kurdistan, an area of plateaus and mountains covering eastern Turkey, northern Iraq, western Iran, and Armenia.

Kurdish *adj* pertaining to the Kurds or to their language. * *n* the language of the Kurds.

kvass, kvas *n* a Russian rye beer that has stale bread as one of its ingredients.—*also* **quass**.

kw. *abbr* = kilowatt(s).

kwashiorkor *n* a disease, esp of children, caused by protein deficiency and characterized by a distended stomach and changes in skin pigmentation.

kwh *abbr* = kilowatt-hour(s).

kyanize vt to preserve wood from dry rot by injecting corrosive sublimate.—**kyanization** n.

kymograph *n* an instrument for recording pressure, oscillations, sound waves, etc, eg an apparatus for determining the pressure of blood, by means of a stylus on a continually rotating drum of paper; (*phonetics*) an instrument to measure muscular strength in the tongue, lips, etc; an instrument that records the angular oscillations of an aircraft in the air.—*also* **cymograph**.

Kyrie (eleison) *n* a prayer, part of a mass; a musical setting of this; the response in an Anglican communion service.

L

l *abbr* = litre(s).

L, l *n* the 12th letter of the English alphabet; something shaped like an L.

La (*chem symbol*) lanthanum.

la *n* the name given to the sixth note of the diatonic scale in solmization.

laager *n* (*S Africa*) a camp in a circle of wagons.—*also* **lager**.

lab *n* (*inf*) laboratory.

labarum *n* (*pl* **labara**) a banner used in Christian processions.

label *n* a slip of paper, cloth, metal, etc attached to anything to provide information about its nature, contents, ownership, etc; a term of generalized classification. * *vt* (**labelling, labelled** *or* **labeling, labeled**) to attach a label to; to designate or classify (as).—**labeller, labeler** *n*.

labellum *n* (*pl* **labella**) the lower petal of an orchid.

labia *npl* (*sing* **labium**) the lips of the female genitals, comprising the outer pair (*labia majora*) and the inner pair (*labia minora*).

labial *adj* of the lips or labia.

labialize *vt* (*phonetics*) to pronounce (a sound) by rounding one's lips.—**labialization** *n*.

labiate *adj, n* (*bot*) (a plant) with the corolla or calyx divided into two parts, resembling lips.

labile *adj* (*chem*) unstable.

labiodental *adj* (*phonetics*) (*sound*) formed by the lips and teeth.

labionasal *adj* (*phonetics*) (*sound*) formed by the lips and nose.

labium *see* **labia**.

labor *see* **labour**.

Labor Day *n* the first Monday in September in US and Canada, a legal holiday honouring labour.

laboratory *n* (*pl* **laboratories**) a room or building where scientific work and research is carried out.

laborious *adj* requiring much work; hard-working; laboured.—**laboriously** *adv*.—**laboriousness** *n*.

labour, labor *n* work, physical or mental exertion; a specific task; all wage-earning workers; workers collectively; the process of childbirth. * *vi* to work; to work hard; to move with difficulty; to suffer (delusions, etc); to be in childbirth. * *vt* to develop in unnecessary detail.

laboured, labored *adj* done with effort; strained.—**labouredly, laboredly** *adv*.

labourer, laborer *n* a person who labours, esp a person whose work requires strength rather than skill.

labour or labor union *n* an organized association of employees of any trade or industry for the protection of their income and working conditions.

Labrador retriever *n* a breed of large, smooth-coated sporting dog.

labradorite *n* a type of feldspar.

labret *n* a shell, etc, worn as an ornament in the lip.

labrum *n* (*pl* **labra**) the liplike shield of an insect's mouth.

laburnum *n* a small tree or shrub with hanging yellow flowers.

labyrinth *n* a structure containing winding passages through which it is hard to find one's way; a maze.—**labyrinthine** *adj*.

lac[1] *n* a resinous substance secreted by certain insects.

lac[2] *see* **lakh**.

lace *n* a cord, etc used to draw together and fasten parts of a shoe, a corset, etc; a delicate ornamental fabric of openwork design using fine cotton, silk, etc. * *vt* to fasten with a lace or laces; to intertwine, weave; to fortify (a drink, etc) with a dash of spirits.

lacerate *vt* to tear jaggedly; to wound (feelings, etc).—**laceration** *n*.

laches *n* (*law*) undue delay in claiming one's rights, etc.

lachrimatory *n* (*pl* **lachrimatories**) a vessel used to hold tears, found in ancient Roman tombs.

lachrymal *adj* of tears; relating to the glands that secrete tears.—*also* **lacrimal**.

lachrymose *adj* tending to shed tears; sad.—**lachrymosity** *n*.

laciniate, laciniated *adj* (*biol*) cut into narrow lobes, fringed.

lack *n* the fact or state of not having any or not having enough; the thing that is needed. * *vti* to be deficient in or entirely without.

lackadaisical *adj* showing lack of energy or interest; listless.—**lackadaisically** *adv*.

lackey *n* a male servant of low rank; a servile hanger-on.

lackluster, lacklustre *adj* lacking in brightness or vigour; dull.

laconic *adj* using few words; concise.—**laconically** *adv*.—**laconicism** *n*.

lacquer *n* a glossy varnish. * *vt* to coat with lacquer, to make glossy.

lacrimal *see* **lachrymal**.

lacrosse *n* a game played by two teams of 10 players with the aim of throwing a ball through the opponents' goal using a long stick topped with a netted pouch for catching and carrying the ball.

lact-, lacto- *prefix* milk.

lactate *vi* (*mammals*) to secrete milk.

lactation *n* the secretion of milk.—**lactational** *adj*.

lacteal *adj* pertaining to, or resembling, milk; (*anat*) conveying chyle.

lactescent *adj* milky; (*plant, insect*) yielding a milky juice.—**lactescence** *n*.

lactic *adj* of or relating to milk; obtained from sour milk or whey; involving the production of lactic acid.

lactic acid *n* an organic acid normally present in sour milk.

lactiferous *adj* producing milk, or a milky juice.

lacto-, lact- *prefix* milk.

lactometer *n* an instrument used for determining the quality of milk.

lactose *n* a sugar present in milk.

lacuna *n* (*pl* **lacunas, lacunae**) a gap, esp a missing portion in a text.—**lacunary** *adj*.

lacustrine *adj* pertaining to lakes; growing by lakesides.

lacy *adj* (**lacier, laciest**) resembling lace.—**lacily** *adv*.—**laciness** *n*.

lad *n* a boy; a young man; a fellow, chap.

ladder *n* a portable metal or wooden framework with rungs between two vertical supports for climbing up and down; something that resembles a ladder in form or use.

ladder back chair *n* a type of chair with a tall slatted back.

laddie *n* a boy; a young lad.

lade *vt* (**lading, laded,** *pp* **laden** *or* **laded**) (*ship*) to load (with cargo); (*with* **with**) to burden; to spoon up (liquid), eg with a ladle.

laden *adj* loaded with cargo; burdened.

la-di-da, la-de-da *adj* (*inf*) affected; foppish. * *n* an affected or foppish person.

ladies' room *n* a public lavatory for women.

lading *n* the act of loading; that which is loaded; cargo; freight.

ladle *n* a long-handled, cup-like spoon for scooping liquids; a device like a ladle in shape or use. * (*with* **out**) (*inf*) to give (money, etc) generously.—**ladleful** *n*.

lady *n* (*pl* **ladies**) a polite term for any woman; (*with* *cap*) a title of honour given to various ranks of women in the British peerage.

Lady Day *n* 25 March, the feast of the Annunciation.

ladybug, ladybird *n* a small, usu brightly coloured beetle.

lady-in-waiting *n* (*pl* **ladies-in-waiting**) a female member of a royal household, who attends upon a queen or princess.

lady-killer *n* (*inf*) a man who is or thinks he is particularly attractive to women.

ladylike *adj* like or suitable for a lady; refined, polite.

ladylove *n* (*arch*) a sweetheart.

ladyship *n* a title used in speaking to or of a woman with the rank of Lady.

lady-slipper *n* an orchid with flowers resembling slippers.

lady's-smock *n* a flowering plant, also known as the cuckooflower.

laevorotation *see* **levorotation**.

laevulose *see* **levulose**.

lag[1] *vi* (**lagging, lagged**) to fall behind, hang back; to fail to keep pace in movement or development; to weaken in strength or intensity. * *n* a falling behind; a delay.

lag[2] *vt* (**lagging, lagged**) to insulate (pipes, etc) with lagging.

lag[3] *n* (*sl*) a convict; a term of imprisonment.

lagan *n* goods, or wreckage, lying on the seabed.—*also* **ligan**.

lager[1] *n* a light beer that has been aged for a certain period.

lager[2] *see* **laager**.

laggard *n* a person who lags behind; a loiterer. * *adj* backward, slow.—**laggardly** *adv*.

lagging *n* insulating material used to lag pipes, boilers, etc.

lagoon *n* a shallow lake or pond, esp one connected with a larger body of water; the water enclosed by a circular coral reef.

laic, laical *adj* non-clerical, lay; secular.

laicize *vt* to make non-clerical or lay; to open to lay persons.—**laicization** *n*.

laid *see* **lay**[2].

laid-back *adj* relaxed, easy-going.

laid paper *n* paper impressed with fine lines from the wires on which the pulp is laid.

lain *see* **lie**[2].

lair *n* the dwelling or resting place of a wild animal; (*inf*) a secluded place, a retreat.

laird *n* (*Scot*) a landowner.

laissez-faire, laisser-faire *n* the policy of non-interference with individual freedom, esp in economic affairs.—**laissez-faireism, laisser-faireism** *n*.

laity *n* laymen, as opposed to clergymen.

lake[1] *n* a large inland body of water.

lake[2] *n* a purplish-red pigment, originally made from lac.

Lake Wobegon effect *n* a propensity to attribute quality to the average, from the novel by Garrison Keillor.

lakh *n* (*India*) 100,000, esp rupees.

lam[1] *vt* (**lamming, lammed**) (*inf*) to beat or thrash.

lam[2] *n* a sudden flight, esp to evade capture by the authorities.

lama *n* a monk or priest of Lamaism.

Lamaism *n* a form of Buddhism in Tibet and Mongolia.—**lamaist** *n*.—**Lamaistic** *adj*.

lamasery *n* (*pl* **lamaseries**) a monastery of lamas.

lamb *n* a young sheep; its flesh as food; (*inf*) an innocent or gentle person. * *vi* to give birth to a lamb; to tend (ewes) at lambing time.

lambada *n* (the music for) a lively erotic dance of Brazilian origin, in which couples dance with their stomachs touching.

lambast, lambaste *vt* (*inf*) to beat or censure severely.

lambda *n* the Greek letter L.

lambdoid *adj* shaped like lambda.

lambent *adj* (*flame*) playing lightly over a surface; marked by radiance; brilliant.—**lambency** *n*.

lambert *n* a measure of brightness, the brightness of a surface radiating one lumen per square centimetre.

lambkin *n* a little lamb.

lambrequin *n* a short hanging over a door, mantelpiece, etc.

lambrusco *n* a sparkling red Italian wine.

lambskin *n* the skin of a lamb with the wool on or as leather, for making clothes, etc.

lame *adj* disabled or crippled, esp in the feet or legs; stiff and painful; weak, ineffectual. * *vt* to make lame.—**lamely** *adv*.—**lameness** *n*.

lamé *n* a fabric interwoven with metallic threads.

lame duck *n* a weak, ineffectual person; an elected official serving between the end of his or her term and the inauguration of a successor.

lamella (*pl* **lamellae, lamellas**) a thin plate, scale, or film.—**lamellar, lamellate, lamellose** *adj*.

lamelliform *adj* lamella-shaped.

lament *vti* to feel or express deep sorrow (for); to mourn. * *n* a lamenting; an elegy, dirge, etc mourning some loss or death.—**lamenter** *n*.

lamentable *adj* distressing, deplorable.—**lamentably** *adv*.

lamentation *n* a lamenting; a lament, expression of grief.

lamented adj grieved for.

lamia n (pl **lamias, lamiae**) (myth) a monster, half snake, half woman.

lamina n (pl **laminae, laminas**) a thin plate, scale or layer; the expanded part of a foliage leaf.—**laminose** adj.

laminate vt to cover with one or more thin layers; to make by building up in layers. * n a product made by laminating. * adj laminated.—**laminator** n.

laminated adj built in thin sheets or layers; covered by a thin film of plastic, etc.

lamination n divisibility, or division, into thin plates.

Lammas n (RC Church) a feast held on August 1; (formerly) a harvest festival celebrated on August 1.

lammergeier, lammergeyer n a vulture found in southern Europe, Africa and Asia, the bearded vulture.

lamp n any device producing light, either by electricity, gas, or by burning oil, etc; a holder or base for such a device; any device for producing therapeutic rays.

lampas n a disease of horses, which causes swelling in the roof of the mouth; a type of flowered silk.

lampblack n fine charcoal or soot.

lampion n a small lamp.

lamplighter n (formerly) someone who lit street lamps.

lampoon n a piece of satirical writing attacking someone. * vt to ridicule maliciously in a lampoon.—**lampooner** n.—**lampoonery** n.

lamppost n a post supporting a street lamp.

lamprey n (pl **lamprey, lampreys**) an animal resembling an eel but having a jawless, round sucking mouth.

LAN (acronym) local area network: a number of computers in close proximity linked together in order to transfer information and share peripherals such as printers.

lanate adj woolly.

lance n a long wooden spear with a sharp iron or steel head. * vt to pierce (as if) with a lance; to open a boil, etc with a lancet.

lance corporal n a noncommissioned officer of the lowest rank in the British army.

lanceolate adj (bot) tapering to a point at either end.

lancer n a cavalry soldier formerly armed with a lance; (pl) a kind of dance, a quadrille.

lancet n a small, usu two-edged, pointed surgical knife.

lancet arch n a sharply pointed arch.

lanceted adj (archit) with one or more lancet arches or windows.

lancet window n a tall narrow window with a lancet arch.

lancewood n a tough, elastic wood.

land n the solid part of the earth's surface; ground, soil; a country and its people; property in land. * vt to set (an aircraft) down on land or water; to put on shore from a ship; to bring to a particular place; to catch (a fish); to get or secure (a job, prize, etc); to deliver (a blow). * vi to go ashore from a ship; to come to port; to arrive at a specified place; to come to rest.

landamman n (Switzerland) the chief official in some cantons.

landau n a four-wheeled horse-drawn carriage with a roof that folds down.

landaulet, landaulette n a small landau.

landed adj consisting of land; owning land.

landfall n a sighting of land, esp from a ship at sea; the land sighted.

landfill n a large pit in which refuse is buried between layers of soil.—also adj.

landgrave n (formerly) a title given to certain counts in Germany.

landgravine n the wife of a landgrave; the title given to a woman landgrave.

landing n the act of coming to shore or to the ground; the place where persons or goods are loaded or unloaded from a ship; a platform at the end of a flight of stairs.

landing craft n a small military vessel designed for landing troops and equipment ashore.

landing gear n the undercarriage of an aircraft.

landing stage n a platform for landing goods or people from a ship.

landing strip n an airstrip.

landlady n (pl **landladies**) a woman who owns and rents property; a woman who owns and runs a boarding house, pub, etc.

landlocked adj surrounded by land.

landlord n a man who owns and rents property; a man who owns and runs a boarding house, pub, etc.

landlubber n a person who has had little experience of the sea.

landmark n any prominent feature of the landscape distinguishing a locality; an important event or turning point.

landmass n a large expanse of land.

land mine n an explosive charge shallowly buried in the ground, usu detonated by stepping or driving on it.

landowner n a person who owns land.—**landowning** adj, n.

landscape n an expanse of natural scenery seen in one view; a picture of natural, inland scenery. * vt to make (a plot of ground) more attractive, as by adding lawns, bushes, trees, etc.

landscape gardening n the decorative design and planting of gardens and grounds in imitation of natural scenery.—**landscape gardener** n.

landscapist n an artist who paints landscapes.

landslide n the sliding of a mass of soil or rocks down a slope; an overwhelming victory, esp in an election.

landsman n (pl **landsmen**) a person who resides and works on land, as opposed to the sea.

Landtag n (Germany, Austria) the parliament of an individual state.

landward adv, adj towards the land.—**landwards** adv.

lane n a narrow road, path, etc; a path or strip specifically designated for ships, aircraft, cars, etc; one of the narrow strips dividing a running track, swimming pool, etc for athletes and swimmers; one of the narrow passages along which balls are bowled in a bowling alley.

langlauf n cross-country skiing.—**langläufer** n.

langouste n the spiny lobster.

langoustine n a large prawn or small lobster.

langsyne adv (Scot) long ago.

language n human speech or the written symbols for speech; any means of communicating; a special set of symbols used for programming a computer; the speech of a particular nation, etc; the particular style of verbal expression characteristic of a person, group, profession, etc.

langue d'oc n a form of medieval French spoken in the South of France.

languid adj lacking energy or vitality; apathetic; drooping, sluggish.—**languidly** adv.—**languidness** n.

languish vi to lose strength and vitality; to pine; to suffer neglect or hardship; to assume a pleading or melancholic expression.—**languisher** *n*.—**languishment** *n*.

languor *n* physical or mental fatigue or apathy; dreaminess; oppressive stillness.—**languorous** *adj*.

langur *n* a long-tailed monkey, found in South Asia.

laniard *n see* **lanyard**.

laniary *n* (*pl* **laniaries**) a canine tooth.

laniferous, lanigerous *adj* wool-bearing.

lank *adj* tall and thin; long and limp.—**lankly** *adv*.—**lankness** *n*.

lanky *adj* (**lankier, lankiest**) lean, tall, and ungainly.—**lankily** *adv*.—**lankiness** *n*.

lanner *n* a falcon found in Mediterranean countries, North Africa and South Asia; the female of this species.

lanneret *n* the male lanner falcon.

lanolin, lanoline *n* wool grease used in cosmetics, ointments, etc.

lantern *n* a portable transparent case for holding a light; a structure with windows on top of a door or roof to provide light and ventilation; the light-chamber of a lighthouse.

lantern jaw *n* a long thin jaw.

lanthanide *n* any of a series of related chemical elements with atomic numbers from 57 (lanthanum) to 71 (lutetium).

lanthanum *n* a metallic element.

lanyard *n* a rope used for fastening things on board a ship; a cord worn round the neck to hold a knife, whistle, etc.

laodicean *adj* indifferent, esp towards religion.

lap[1] *vti* (**lapping, lapped**) to take in (liquid) with the tongue; (*waves*) to flow gently with a splashing sound.

lap[2] *n* the flat area from waist to knees formed by a person sitting; the part of the clothing covering this.

lap[3] *n* an overlapping; a part that overlaps; one complete circuit of a race track. * *vb* (**lapping, lapped**) *vt* to fold (over or on); to wrap. * *vi* to overlap; to extend over something in space or time.

laparotomy *n* (*pl* **laparotomies**) (*med*) the operation of cutting the abdominal wall.

lapdog *n* a dog small and docile enough to be held on the lap.

lapel *n* a part of a suit, coat, jacket, etc folded back and continuous with the collar.—**lapelled** *adj*.

lapidary *adj* of or relating to stones; inscribed on stone; concise, like an inscription. * *n* (*pl* **lapidaries**) a cutter or engraver of gems.—**lapidarian** *adj*.

lapidate *vt* to stone (to death).—**lapidation** *n*.

lapidify *vti* (**lapidifying, lapidified**) to turn to stone.

lapis lazuli *n* an azure, opaque, semi-precious stone.

lap of honour *n* a ceremonial circuit of the field by a winning person or team.

lappet *n* a small, loose flap.

lapse *n* a small error; a decline or drop to a lower condition, degree, or state; a moral decline; a period of time elapsed; the termination of a legal right or privilege through disuse. * *vi* to depart from the usual or accepted standard, esp in morals; to pass out of existence or use; to become void or discontinued; (*time*) to slip away.—**lapsable, lapsible** *adj*.—**lapser** *n*.

lapsus *n* (*pl* **lapsus**) a slip or error.

laptop *n* a small portable computer that can comfortably be used on the lap.

lapwing *n* a crested plover.

larboard *n* (*naut*) (*formerly*) the port or left side of a ship.

larceny *n* (*pl* **larcenies**) the theft of someone else's property.—**larcenist, larcener** *n*.—**larcenous** *adj*.

larch *n* a cone-bearing tree of the pine family.

lard *n* melted and clarified pig fat. * *vt* to insert strips of bacon or pork fat (in meat) before cooking; to embellish.

larder *n* a room or cupboard where food is stored.

lares *npl* (*Roman myth*) the household gods.

large *adj* great in size, amount, or number; bulky; big; spacious; bigger than others of its kind; operating on a big scale.—**largeness** *n*.

large intestine *n* the section of the digestive system comprising the caecum, colon and rectum.

largely *adv* much, in great amounts; mainly, for the most part.

largen *vt* to make larger, to enlarge.

large-scale *adj* drawn on a big scale to reveal much detail; extensive.

largess, largesse *n* the generous distribution of money, gifts, favours, etc; generosity.

larghetto *adv* (*mus*) slowly. * *n* (*pl* **larghettos**) a passage of music played in this way.

largish *adj* quite large.

largo *adv* (*mus*) slow and dignified. * *n* (*pl* **largos**) a passage of music played in this way.

lariat *n* a rope for tethering grazing horses; a lasso.

lark[1] *n* any of a family of songbirds.

lark[2] *n* a playful or amusing adventure; a harmless prank. * *vi* (*usu with* **about**) to have fun, frolic.—**larky** *adj*.

larkspur *n* an annual delphinium.

larrigan *n* a knee-high leather boot worn by trappers.

larrikin *n* (*Austral sl*) a hooligan.

larrup *vt* (*dial*) to thrash, flog.

larva *n* (*pl* **larvae**) the immature form of many animals after emerging from an egg before transformation into the adult state, eg a caterpillar.—**larval** *adj*.

laryngeal *adj* pertaining to, or situated near, the larynx.

laryngitis *n* inflammation of the larynx.—**laryngitic** *adj*.

laryngo-, laryng- *prefix* larynx.

laryngology *n* the medical study of the larynx.—**laryngologist** *n*.

laryngoscope *n* a medical instrument for examining the larynx.—**laryngoscopy** *n*.

laryngotomy *n* (*pl* **laryngotomies**) (*med*) the operation of cutting into the larynx.

larynx *n* (*pl* **larynxes, larynges**) the structure at the upper end of the windpipe, containing the vocal cords.

lasagna, lasagne *n* pasta formed in thin wide strips; a dish of lasagne baked in layers with cheese, minced meat and tomato sauce.

lascar *n* an East Indian sailor.—*also* **lashkar**.

lascivious *adj* lecherous, lustful; arousing sexual desire.—**lasciviously** *adv*.—**lasciviousness** *n*.

lase *vi* (*gem, gas*) able to act as a laser.

laser *n* a device that produces an intense monochromatic beam of coherent light or other electromagnetic radiation.

laser printer *n* a computer printer that uses a laser beam and photoconductive drum to produce high quality text output.

lasertripsy *n* a medical procedure for removing kidney stones, etc, by the use of laser beams.

lash *vt* to strike forcefully (as if) with a lash; to fasten or secure with a cord, etc; to attack with criticism or ridicule. * *vi* to move quickly and violently; (*rain, waves, etc*) to beat violently against; (*with* out) to attack suddenly either physically or verbally; (*inf*) to spend extravagantly (on). * *n* the flexible part of a whip; an eyelash; a stroke (as if) with a whip.—**lasher** *n*.

lashkar *see* **lascar**.

lass, lassie *n* a young woman or girl.

Lassa fever *n* an infectious viral disease of Africa.

lassitude *n* weariness.

lasso *n* (*pl* **lassos, lassoes**) a long rope or leather thong with a running noose for catching horses, cattle, etc. * *vt* (**lassoes** *or* **lassos, lassoing, lassoed**) to catch (as if) with a lasso.—**lassoer** *n*.

last[1] *n* a shoemaker's model of the foot on which boots and shoes are made or repaired. * *vt* to shape with a last.

last[2] *vi* to remain in existence, use, etc; to endure. * *vt* to continue during; to be enough for.

last[3] *adj* being or coming after all the others in time or place; only remaining; the most recent; least likely; conclusive. * *adv* after all the others; most recently; finally. * *n* the one coming last.

last-ditch *adj* being a final effort to avoid disaster.

last hurrah *n* a final appearance; a swan song.

lasting *adj* enduring.—**lastingly** *adv*.

lastly *adv* at the end, in the last place, finally.

last-minute *adj* at the last possible time when something can be done.

last rites *npl* the sacraments prescribed for a person near death.

last straw *n* a final addition to one's burdens that results in collapse or defeat.

last word *n* the final remark in an argument; a definitive statement; the latest fashion.

Lat. *abbr* = Latin.

lat. *abbr* = latitude.

latch *n* a fastening for a door, gate, or window, esp a bar, etc that fits into a notch. * *vti* to fasten with a latch.

latchet *n* (*arch*) a strap or lace for fastening a shoe.

latchkey *n* the key of an outer door.

late *adj*, *adv* after the usual or expected time; at an advanced stage or age; near the end; far on in the day or evening; just prior to the present; deceased; not long past; until lately; out of office.—**lateness** *n*.

latecomer *n* a person or thing that arrives late.

lateen *n* a triangular sail used on boats in the Mediterranean.—**lateenrigged** *adj*.

lately *adv* recently, in recent times.

latent *adj* existing but not yet visible or developed.—**latency** *n*.—**latently** *adv*.

later *adv* subsequently; afterwards.—*also compar of* **late**.

lateral *adj* of, at, from, towards the side.—**laterally** *adv*.

lateral thinking *n* a solving of problems by employing unorthodox thought processes.

latest *adj* most recent or fashionable. * *n* (*inf*: *with* **the**) the most up-to-date fashion, news, etc.—*also superl of* **late**.

latex *n* (*pl* **latexes, latices**) the milky juice produced by certain plants, used in the manufacture of rubber.

lath *n* (*pl* **laths**) a thin narrow strip of wood used in constructing a framework for plaster, etc.

lathe *n* a machine that rotates wood, metal, etc for shaping.

lather *n* a foam made by soap or detergent mixed with water; frothy sweat; a state of excitement or agitation.

* *vti* to cover with or form lather.—**lathery** *adj*.

lathi *n* a long, heavy stick, carried by policemen in India.

Latin *adj* of ancient Rome, its people, their language, etc; denoting or of the languages derived from Latin (Italian, Spanish, etc), the peoples who speak them, their countries, etc. * *n* a native or inhabitant of ancient Rome; the language of ancient Rome; a person, as a Spaniard or Italian, whose language is derived from Latin.

Latinate *adj* of, resembling or derived from Latin.

Latinist *n* a Latin scholar.

Latinity *n* Latin style.

Latinize *vt* to translate into Latin; to give Latin characteristics to.—**Latinization** *n*.—**Latinizer** *n*.

Latino *n* a person of Latin American origin living in the US.

latish *adj* somewhat late.

latitude *n* the distance from north or south of the equator, measured in degrees; a region with reference to this distance; extent; scope; freedom from restrictions on actions or opinions.—**latitudinal** *adj*.—**latitudinally** *adv*.

latitudinarian *adj* claiming or showing freedom of thought, esp regarding religion. * *n* a person with such an outlook.—**latitudinarianism** *n*.

latria *n* (*RC Church*) supreme worship, offered to God alone.

latrine *n* a lavatory, as in a military camp.

-latry *n suffix* worship, esp excessively.

latter *adj* later; more recent; nearer the end; being the last mentioned of two.

latter-day *adj* present-day; modern.

latterly *adv* recently.

lattice *n* a network of crossed laths or bars.—**latticed** *adj*.

laud *vt* to praise; to extol.

laudable *adj* praiseworthy.—**laudability** *n*.—**laudably** *adv*.

laudanum *n* (*formerly*) any of various opium preparations; a solution of opium in alcohol.

laudation *n* praise.

laudatory, laudative *adj* expressing praise.

laugh *vi* to emit explosive inarticulate vocal sounds expressive of amusement, joy or derision. * *vt* to utter or express with laughter; (*with* off) to dismiss as of little importance, make a joke of. * *n* the act or sound of laughing; (*inf*) an amusing person or thing.—**laugher** *n*.—**laughing** *adj*, *n*.—**laughingly** *adv*.

laughable *adj* causing laughter; ridiculous.—**laughably** *adv*.

laughing gas *n* nitrous oxide.

laughing stock *n* an object of ridicule.

laughter *n* the act or sound of laughing.

launch[1] *vt* to throw, hurl or propel forward; to cause (a vessel) to slide into the water; (*rocket, missile*) to set off; to put into action; to put a new product onto the market. * *vi* to involve oneself enthusiastically. * *n* the act or occasion of launching.

launch[2] *n* an open, or partly enclosed, motor boat.

launch pad, launching pad *n* a platform from which a spacecraft is launched.

launder *vti* to wash and iron clothes. * *vt* to legitimize (money) obtained from criminal activity by passing it through foreign banks, or investing in legitimate businesses, etc.—**launderer** *n*.

launderette *n* an establishment equipped with coin-operated washing machines and driers for public use.

laundress *n* a woman who earns her living by doing laundry.

Laundromat *n* (*trademark*) a launderette.

laundry *n* (*pl* **laundries**) a place where clothes are washed and ironed; clothes sent to be washed and ironed.

laureate *adj* crowned with laurel leaves as a mark of honour. * *n* the recipient of an honour or distinction; a poet laureate.—**laureateship** *n*.

laurel *n* an evergreen shrub with large, glossy leaves; the leaves used by the ancient Greeks as a symbol of achievement.

lava *n* molten rock flowing from a volcano; the solid substance formed as this cools.

lavabo *n* (*pl* **lavaboes**, **lavabos**) (*RC Church*) the ritual washing of the celebrant's hands at the Eucharist; a washbasin.

lavation *n* the act of washing.

lavatory *n* (*pl* **lavatories**) a sanitary device for the disposal or faeces and urine; a room equipped with this.—*also* **bathroom, toilet.**

lavender *n* the fragrant flowers of a perennial shrub dried and used in sachets; a pale purple.

laver *n* an edible seaweed.

lavish *vt* to give or spend freely. * *adj* abundant, profuse; generous; extravagant.—**lavishly** *adv*.—**lavishness** *n*.

law *n* all the rules of conduct in an organized community as upheld by authority; any one of such rules; obedience to such rules; the study of such rules, jurisprudence; the seeking of justice in courts under such rules; the profession of lawyers, judges, etc; (*inf*) the police; a sequence of events occurring with unvarying uniformity under the same conditions; any rule expected to be observed.

law-abiding *adj* obeying the law.

lawbreaker *n* a person who violates the law.—**lawbreaking** *adj, n*.

lawful *adj* in conformity with the law; recognized by law.—**lawfully** *adv*.—**lawfulness** *n*.

lawgiver *n* a maker of a code of laws.

lawless *adj* not regulated by law; not in conformity with law, illegal.—**lawlessly** *adv*.—**lawlessness** *n*.

lawmaker *n* a maker of laws, a legislator.

lawn[1] *n* a fine sheer cloth of linen or cotton.—**lawny** *adj*.

lawn[2] *n* land covered with closely cut grass, esp around a house.

lawn darts *n* an outdoor game of darts using a lawn as a board, at which are fired foot-long metal darts.

lawn mower *n* a hand-propelled or power-driven machine to cut lawn grass.

lawn tennis *n* tennis played on a grass court.

lawrencium *n* a radioactive metallic element.

lawsuit *n* a suit between private parties in a law court.

lawyer *n* a person whose profession is advising others in matters of law or representing them in a court of law.

lax *adj* slack, loose; not tight; not strict or exact.—**laxly** *adv*.—**laxness** *n*.

laxative *n* a substance that promotes emptying of the bowels.—*also adj*.

laxity *n* the state or quality of being lax, laxness.

lay[1] *see* **lie**[2].

lay[2] *vt* (**laying, laid**) to put down; to allay or suppress; to place in a resting position; to place or set; to place in a correct position; to produce (an egg); (*sl*) to have sexual intercourse with; to devise; to present or assert; to stake a bet; (*with* **down**) to put down; to surrender, relinquish; to begin to build; to establish (guidelines, rules, etc); to store, esp wine; to record tracks in a music studio; (*with* **in**) to store, to stockpile; (*with* **off**) to suspend from work temporarily or permanently; (*with* **on**) to supply, provide; to install (electricity, etc); (*with* **out**) to plan in detail; to arrange for display; to prepare (a corpse) for viewing; (*inf*) to spend money, esp lavishly; (*with* **up**) to store for future use; to disable or confine through illness. * *vi* (*inf*) to leave (a person or thing) alone; (*with* **into**) to attack physically or verbally. * *n* a way or position in which something is situated; (*sl*) an act of sexual intercourse; a sexual partner.

lay[3] *n* a simple narrative poem, esp as intended to be oung, a ballad.

lay[4] *adj* of or pertaining to those who are not members of the clergy; not belonging to a profession.

layabout *n* a loafer, lazy person.

lay-by *n* (*Austral*) a deposit payment system that reserves an article for a purchaser until full settlement; (*Brit*) a pull-in place for motorists to stop at the side of a main road.—**lay by** *vt* to set aside or save for future needs.

layer *n* a single thickness, fold, etc; the runner of a plant fastened down to take root; a hen that lays. * *vti* to separate into layers; to form by superimposing layers; to (cause to) take root by propagating a plant shoot still attached to its parent.

layette *n* a complete set of clothes, equipment and accessories for a newborn baby

lay figure *n* a jointed model of the human body used by artists for hanging drapery on; a person regarded as a puppet or nonentity.

laying *n* a sitting of eggs; the first coat of plaster.

layman *n* (*pl* **laymen**) a person who is not a member of the clergy; a non-specialist, someone who does not possess professional knowledge.—**laywoman** *nf* (*pl* **laywomen**).

layoff *n* a period of involuntary unemployment.

layout *n* the manner in which anything is laid out, esp arrangement of text and pictures on the pages of a newspaper or magazine, etc; the thing laid out.

layover *n* (*US*) a stop on a journey.

lazar *n* (*arch*) a leper.

lazaretto, lazaret, lazarette *n* (*pl* **lazarettos, lazarets, lazarettes**) (*naut*) a part of a ship's hold; (*formerly*) a hospital for people suffering from infectious diseases.

laze *vti* to idle or loaf.

lazulite *n* an azure blue mineral.

lazy *adj* (**lazier, laziest**) disinclined to work or exertion; encouraging or causing indolence; sluggishly moving.—**lazily** *adv*.—**laziness** *n*.

lazybones *n* a lazy person.

lb *abbr* = pound(s) weight.

lbw *abbr* = (*cricket*) leg before wicket.

LCD *abbr* = liquid-crystal display; (*also without cap*) lowest common denominator.

lea[1] *n* (*poet*) a meadow, grassland.

lea[2] *n* a measure of yarn, varying from 80 yards (approx 73 metres) for wool to 300 yards (approx 274 metres) for linen.

leach *vt* to wash (soil, ore, etc) with a filtering liquid; to extract (a soluble substance) from some material. * *vi* to lose soluble matter through a filtering liquid.—**leacher** *n*.

lead¹ *vb* (**leading, led**) *vt* to show the way, esp by going first; to direct or guide on a course; to direct by influence; to be head of (an expedition, orchestra, etc); to be ahead of in a contest; to live, spend (one's life); (*with* **on**) to lure or entice, esp into mischief. * *vi* to show the way, as by going first; (*with* **to**) to tend in a certain direction; to be or go first. * *n* the role of a leader; first place; the amount or distance ahead; anything that leads, as a clue; the leading role in a play, etc; the right of playing first in cards or the card played.

lead² *n* a heavy, soft, bluish-grey, metallic element; a weight for sounding depths at sea, etc; bullets; a stick of graphite, used in pencils; (*print*) a thin strip of metal used to space lines of type. * *adj* of or containing lead. * *vt* (**leading, leaded**) to cover, weight, or space out with lead.

leaden *adj* made of lead; very heavy; dull grey; gloomy.—**leadenly** *adv*.

leader *n* the person who goes first; the principle first violin-player in an orchestra; the director of an orchestra; the inspiration or head of a movement, such as a political party; a person whose example is followed; the leading editorial in a newspaper; the leading article.

leadership *n* the act of leading; the ability to be a leader; the leaders of an organization or movement collectively.

lead glass *n* flint glass.

lead-in *n* introductory material; the connection between a radio transmitter or receiver with an aerial or transmission cable.

leading¹ *adj* capable of guiding or influencing; principal; in first position.

leading² *n* a covering of lead; (*print*) the body of a type, larger than the size, giving space.

leading article *n* an article in a newspaper stating editorial opinion on a given subject; the leader.

leading light *n* the most important member of a group or organization.

leading question *n* a question worded so as to suggest the desired answer.

leadsman *n* (*pl* **leadsmen**) a sailor who heaves the lead.

lead time *n* the period between the design of a product and its manufacture.

leaf *n* (*pl* **leaves**) any of the flat, thin (usu green) parts growing from the stem of a plant; a sheet of paper; a very thin sheet of metal; a hinged or removable part of a table top. * *vi* to bear leaves; (*with* **through**) to turn the pages of.

leafage *n* foliage.

leafless *adj* without leaves.

leaflet *n* a small or young leaf; a sheet of printed information (often folded), esp advertising matter distributed free. * *vi* to distribute leaflets (to).

leaf mold *n* compost or soil composed of decaying leaves and other vegetable matter; any of various fungal diseases of plants.

leafy *adj* (**leafier, leafiest**) having many or broad leaves; resembling leaves.—**leafiness** *n*.

league¹ *n* an association of nations, groups, etc for promoting common interests; an association of sports clubs that organizes matches between members; any class or category. * *vti* (**leaguing, leagued**) to form into a league.

league² *n* (*formerly*) a varying measure of distance, averaging about three miles (5km).

leak *n* a crack or hole through which liquid or gas may accidentally pass; the liquid or gas passing through such an opening; confidential information made public deliberately or accidentally. * *vi* to (let) escape though an opening; to disclose information surreptitiously.—**leaker** *n*.

leakage *n* the act of leaking; that which enters or escapes by leaking.

leaky *adj* (**leakier, leakiest**) leaking or likely to leak.—**leakiness** *n*.

leal *adj* (*Scot*) loyal.

lean¹ *adj* thin, with little flesh or fat; spare; meagre. * *n* meat with little or no fat.—**leanness** *n*.

lean² *vb* (**leaning, leaned** *or* **leant**) *vi* to bend or slant from an upright position; to rest supported (on or against); to rely or depend for help (on). * *vt* to cause to lean.

leaning *n* inclination, tendency.

leant *see* **lean¹**.

lean-to *n* (*pl* **lean-tos**) a building whose rafters rest on another building.

leap *vb* (**leaping, leaped** *or* **leapt**) *vi* to jump; (*with* **at**) to accept something offered eagerly. * *vt* to pass over by a jump; to cause to leap. * *n* an act of leaping; bound; space passed by leaping; an abrupt transition.—**leaper** *n*.

leapfrog *n* a game in which one player vaults over another's bent back. * *vi* (**leapfrogging, leapfrogged**) to vault in this manner; to advance in alternate jumps.

leap year *n* a year with an extra day (29 February) occurring every fourth year.

learn *vti* (**learning, learned** *or* **learnt**) to gain knowledge of or skill in; to memorize; to become aware of, realize.—**learner** *n*.

learned *adj* having learning; erudite; acquired by study, experience, etc.—**learnedly** *adv*.

learning *n* a gaining of knowledge; the acquiring of knowledge or skill through study.

lease *n* a contract by which an owner lets land, property, etc to another person for a specified period. * *vt* to grant by or hold under lease.—**leaseable** *adj*.—**leaser** *n*.

lease-back *n* the process of selling an asset, esp a building, and then renting it.

leasehold *n* the act of holding by lease; the land, buildings, etc held by lease.—**leaseholder** *n*.

leash *n* a cord, strap, etc by which a dog or animal is held in check. * *vt* to hold or restrain on a leash.

least *adj* smallest in size, degree, etc; slightest. * *adv* to the smallest degree. * *n* the smallest in amount.

leastways *adv* at least.

leather *n* material made from the skin of an animal prepared by removing the hair and tanning; something made of leather. * *vt* to cover with leather; to thrash.

leatherback *n* the largest existing sea turtle, having a flexible shell.

Leatherette *n* (*trademark*) an imitation leather.

leatherjacket *n* a tropical fish with a leathery skin; the larva of the cranefly.

leathern *adj* (*arch*) made of, or resembling, leather.

leatherneck *n* (*sl*) a member of the US Marine Corps.

leathery *adj* like leather; tough and flexible.

leave¹ *n* permission to do something; official authorization to be absent; the period covered by this.

leave² *vb* (**leaving, left**) *vt* to depart from; to cause or allow to remain in a specified state; to cause to remain behind; to refrain from consuming or dealing with; to

have remaining at death, to bequeath; to have as a remainder; to allow to stay or or continue doing without interference; to entrust or commit to another; to
abandon. * *vi* to depart; (*with* off) to stop, desist.—
leaver *n*.

leaved *adj* having leaves.

leaven *n* a substance to make dough rise, esp yeast;
something that changes or enlivens. * *vt* to raise with
leaven; to modify, to enliven.—**leavening** *n*.

leaves *see* **leaf**.

leave-taking *n* a departure, farewell.

leavings *npl* leftovers; remnants; refuse.

leben *n* a food made from soured milk, eaten in North
Africa and the Levant.

Lebensraum *n* a piece of territory claimed by another
country on the basis that it is needed to accommodate
the country's expanding population.

lech *vt* (*sl*) to lust after.

lecher *n* a lecherous man.

lecherous *adj* characterized by or encouraging lechery.

lechery *n* (*pl* **lecheries**) unrestrained sexuality; debauchery.

lecithin *n* any of a group of fatty compounds found in
plant and animal tissues, used as an emulsifier and
antioxidant.

lectern *n* a reading stand in a church; any similar reading support.

lection *n* a reading from scripture for a particular day; a
variant reading of a text.

lectionary *n* (*pl* **lectionaries**) a book listing lessons from
scripture to be read at religious services on particular
days.

lector *n* a lecturer or reader at a university.

lecture *n* an informative talk to a class, etc; a lengthy
reprimand. * *vti* to give a lecture (to); to reprimand.—
lecturer *n*.

lectureship *n* the position of lecturer.

LED *abbr* = light-emitting diode.

led *see* **lead**[1].

lederhosen *npl* leather shorts with braces worn by men
in Austria and Bavaria.

ledge *n* a narrow horizontal surface resembling a shelf
projecting from a wall, rock face, etc; an underwater
ridge of rocks; a rock layer containing ore.—**ledgy**,
adj.

ledger *n* a book in which a record of debits, credits, etc
is kept.

ledger line *n* a short line added above or below a musical staff to extend its range.—*also* **leger line**.

lee *n* a shelter; the side or part away from the wind.

leech *n* a blood-sucking worm; a person who clings to
or exploits another.

leek *n* a vegetable that resembles a greatly elongated
green onion.

leer *n* a sly, oblique or lascivious look. * *vi* to look with a
leer.—**leeringly** *adv*.

leery *adj* (**leerier, leeriest**) (*with* of) suspicious, wary.

lees *npl* sediment in the bottom of a wine bottle, etc.

leeward *adj, n* (*naut*) (in) the quarter towards which the
wind blows.

leeway *n* the distance a ship or aircraft has strayed sideways of its course; freedom of action as regards expenditure of time, money, etc.

left[1] *see* **leave**[2].

left[2] *adj* of or on the side that is towards the west when
one faces north; worn on the left hand, foot, etc. * *n*
the left side; (*often cap*) of or relating to the left in poli-

tics; the left hand; (*boxing*) a blow with the left hand.

left-hand *adj* of or towards the left side of a person or
thing; for use by the left hand.

left-handed *adj* using the left hand in preference to the
right; done or made for use with the left hand; ambiguous, backhanded. * *adv* with the left hand.—**left-
handedly** *adv*.—**left-handedness** *n*.

left-hander *n* a left-handed person; a blow delivered
with the left fist.

left-luggage office *n* (*Brit*) a place at an airport, railway
station, etc., where luggage may be left for a small
charge with an attendant for safekeeping; a
checkroom in the US.

leftist *adj* tending to the left in politics. * *n* a person
tending towards the political left.—**leftism** *n*.

leftovers *npl* unused portions of something, esp
uneaten food.

leftward *adj, adv* on or toward the left.—**leftwards** *adv*.

left-wing *adj* of or relating to the liberal faction of a political party, organization, etc.—**left-winger** *n*.

lefty *n* (*pl* **lefties**) (*inf*) a left-winger; (*US sl*) a left-
handed person.

leg *n* one of the limbs on which humans and animals
support themselves and walk; the part of a garment
covering the leg; anything shaped or used like a leg; a
branch or limb of a forked object; a section, as of a
trip; any of a series of games or matches in a competition.

legacy *n* (*pl* **legacies**) money, property, etc left to someone in a will; something passed on by an ancestor or
remaining from the past.

legal *adj* of or based on law; permitted by law; of or for
lawyers.—**legally** *adv*.

legalese *n* legal language as used in documents.

legalism *n* observance of the letter rather than the spirit
of the law, red tape.—**legalist** *n*.—**legalistic** *adj*.—**le-
galistically** *adv*.

legality *n* (*pl* **legalities**) conformity with the law.

legalize *vt* to make lawful.—**legalization** *n*.

legal tender *n* a currency which a creditor is legally
bound to accept in payment of a debt.

legate *n* an envoy, esp from the Pope; an official emissary.—**legatine** *adj*.

legatee *n* a person to whom a legacy is bequeathed.

legation *n* a diplomatic minister and staff; the headquarters of a diplomatic minister.—**legationary** *adj*.

legato *adj, adv* (*mus*) smoothly and evenly.

leg before wicket *n* (*cricket*) the dismissal of a batsman
for illegally preventing the ball from hitting the
wicket by obstructing it with his or her leg.

leg bye *n* (*cricket*) a run made when the ball touches any
part of the batsman except the hand.

legend *n* a story handed down from the past; a notable
person or the stories of his or her exploits; an inscription on a coin, etc; a caption; an explanation of the
symbols used on a map.—**legendry** *n*.

legendary *adj* of, based on, or presented in legends; famous, notorious.

legerdemain *n* trickery, sleight of hand.

leger line *see* **ledger line**.

legged *adj* having legs.

leggings *npl* protective outer coverings for the lower
legs; a leg-hugging fashion garment for women.

leggy *adj* (**leggier, leggiest**) having long and shapely
legs.—**legginess** *n*.

leghorn *n* fine plaited straw; a hat made of this; (*with
cap*) a breed of domestic fowl.

legible *adj* able to be read.—**legibility** *n*.—**legibly** *adv*.

legion *n* an infantry unit of the ancient Roman army; a large body of soldiers; a large number, a multitude.

legionary *adj* of a legion. * *n* (*pl* **legionaries**) a member of a legion; a soldier in a legion of the ancient Roman army.

legionnaire *n* a member of certain military forces or associations.

Legionnaire's disease *n* a serious and sometimes fatal bacterial infection which causes symptoms like pneumonia (first identified after an outbreak at an American Legion convention in 1976).

legislate *vi* to make or pass laws * *vt* to bring about by legislation.

legislation *n* the act or process of law-making; the laws themselves.

legislative *adj* of legislation or a legislature; having the power to make laws.

legislator *n* a member of a legislative body.

legislature *n* the body of people who have the power of making laws.

legist *n* someone versed in the law.

legit *adj* (*sl*) legitimate.

legitimate *adj* lawful; reasonable, justifiable; conforming to accepted rules, standards, etc; (*child*) born of parents married to each other.—**legitimacy** *n*.—**legitimately** *adv*.

legitimatize *vt* to legitimize.

legitimist *n* a supporter of a hereditary title to a monarchy.—**legitimism** *n*.

legitimize *vt* to make or declare legitimate.—**legitimization** *n*.

legume *n* any of a large family of plants having seeds growing in pods, including beans, peas, etc; the pod or seed of such a plant used as food.

leguminous *adj* (*bot*) belonging to a family of flowering and pod-bearing plants.

legwork *n* (*inf*) work that involves a lot of walking.

lei *n* a garland of flowers worn around the neck, given as a token of affection in Hawaii.

leister *n* a pronged spear used for catching salmon.

leisure *n* ease, relaxation, esp freedom from employment or duties. * *adj* free and unoccupied.—**leisured** *adj*.

leisurely *adj* relaxed, without hurry.

leitmotif, leitmotiv *n* a dominant theme.

lemma *n* (*pl* **lemmas, lemmata**) (*logic*) a premise believed to be true.

lemming *n* a small arctic rodent; one of a group wilfully heading on a course for destruction.

lemon *n* (a tree bearing) a small yellow oval fruit with an acid pulp; pale yellow; (*sl*) a person or thing considered disappointing or useless.—**lemony** *adj*.

lemonade *n* a lemon-flavoured drink.

lemon grass *n* a tropical grass with lemon-scented leaves used in cooking and which yields an aromatic oil.

lemur *n* a Madagascan arboreal primate related to the monkey.

lemuroid, lemurine *adj* pertaining to, or resembling, a lemur.

lend *vb* (**lending, lent**) *vt* to give the use of something temporarily in expectation of its return; to provide (money) at interest; to give, impart. * *vi* to make loans.—**lender** *n*.

length *n* the extent of something from end to end, usu the longest dimension; a specified distance or period of time; something of a certain length taken from a larger piece; a long expanse; (*often pl*) the degree of effort put into some action.

lengthen *vti* to make or become longer.

lengthwise, lengthways *adv* in the direction of the length.

lengthy *adj* (**lengthier, lengthiest**) long, esp too long.—**lengthily** *adv*.—**lengthiness** *n*.

lenient *adj* not harsh or severe; merciful.—**leniency, lenience** *n*.—**leniently** *adv*.

lenitive *adj* easing pain.

lenity *n* (*pl* **lenities**) clemency, mercy; leniency.

leno *n* (*pl* **lenos**) a way of weaving fabric; a fabric woven in this way.

lens *n* a curved piece of transparent glass, plastic, etc used in optical instruments to form an image; any device used to focus electromagnetic rays, sound waves, etc; a similar transparent part of the eye that focuses light rays on the retina.

Lent *n* the forty weekdays from Ash Wednesday to Easter, observed by Christians as a period of fasting and penitence.—**Lenten** *adj*.

lent *see* **lend**.

lentamente *adv* (*mus*) slowly.

lenticular *adj* doubly convex.

lentigo *n* (*pl* **lentigines**) a freckle.

lentil *n* any of several leguminous plants with edible seeds; their seed used for food.

lento *adj, adv* (*mus*) slow, slowly. * *n* (*pl* **lentos**) a piece of music played in this way.

Leo *n* (*astrol*) the fifth sign of the zodiac, in astrology operative July 22–August 21; (*astron*) the Lion, a constellation in the northern hemisphere.

Leonid *n* (*pl* **Leonids, Leonides**) (*astron*) one of the meteors that fall in showers during the November of certain years, their chief point being in the constellation of Leo.

leonine *adj* of or like a lion.

leopard *n* a large tawny feline with black spots found in Africa and Asia.—*also* **panther**.—**leopardess** *nf*.

leotard *n* a skintight one-piece garment worn by dancers and others engaged in strenuous exercise.

leper *n* a person with leprosy.

lepidopteran *n* (*pl* **lepidopterans, lepidoptera**) any of a large order of insects, such as moths or butterflies, that as adults have four wings covered with minute, often coloured, scales and that as larvae are caterpillars.—**lepidopterous** *adj*.

lepidopterist *n* an expert on moths and butterflies.

lepidosiren *n* an eel-like mudfish found in South America

leporine *adj* pertaining to hares; hare-like.

leprechaun *n* (*Irish folklore*) a fairy.

leprosy *n* a chronic infectious bacterial disease of the skin, often resulting in disfigurement.—**leprous** *adj*.

lepton *n* (*phys*) any of various elementary particles, such as electrons and muons, that participate in weak interactions with other elementary particles.

lesbian *n* a female homosexual. * *adj* of or characteristic of lesbians.—**lesbianism** *n*.

lèse-majesté, lese-majesty *n* high treason; a crime against royalty.

lesion *n* any change in an organ or tissue caused by injury or disease; an injury.

less *adj* not so much, not so great, etc; fewer; smaller. * *adv* to a smaller extent. * *n* a smaller amount. * *prep* minus.

lessee *n* a person who holds property under a lease.

lessen *vti* to make or become less.

lesser *adj* less in size, quality or importance.

lesson *n* something to be learned or studied; something that has been learned or studied; a unit of learning or teaching; (*pl*) a course of instruction; a selection from the Bible, read as a part of a church service.

lessor *n* a person who lets property on a lease.

lest *conj* in order, or for fear, that not; that.

let[1] *n* a stoppage; (*tennis*) a minor obstruction of the ball that requires a point to be replayed.

let[2] *vb* (**letting, let**) *vt* to allow, permit; to rent; to assign (a contract); to cause to run out, as blood; as an auxiliary in giving suggestions or commands (*let us go*); (*with* **down**) to lower; to deflate; to disappoint; to untie; to lengthen; (*with* **off**) to allow to leave (a ship, etc); to cause to explode or fire; to release, excuse from (work, etc); to deal leniently with, refrain from punishing; to allow (gas, etc) to escape; (*with* **out**) to release; to reveal; to rent out; to make a garment larger; (*with* **up**) to relax; to cease. * *vi* to be rented; (*with* **on**) (*inf*) to pretend; (*inf*) to reveal (a secret, etc); to pretend. * *n* the letting of property or accommodation.

let-down *n* a disappointment.

lethal *adj* deadly.—**lethality** *n*.—**lethally** *adv*.

lethargy *n* (*pl* **lethargies**) an abnormal drowsiness; sluggishness; apathy.—**lethargic** *adj*.—**lethargically** *adv*.

let's = let us.

letter *n* a symbol representing a phonetic value in a written language; a character of the alphabet; a written or printed message; (*pl*) literature; learning; knowledge; literal meaning. * *vt* to mark with letters.

letter bomb *n* an explosive device concealed in an envelope and sent through the post.

letter box *n* a slit in the doorway of a house or building through which letters are delivered; a postbox.

lettered *adj* literate; highly educated; marked with letters.

letterhead *n* a name, address, etc printed as a heading on stationery; stationery printed with a heading.

lettering *n* the act or process of inscribing with letters; letters collectively; a title; an inscription.

letterpress *n* a method of printing; the printed matter of a book, as opposed to the illustrations.

lettuce *n* a plant with succulent leaves used in salads.

letup *n* a relaxation of effort.

leukemia, leukaemia *n* a chronic disease characterized by an abnormal increase in the number of white blood cells in body tissues and the blood.

leukocyte *n* a white blood cell.

leukoma *n* a white, opaque scar on the cornea of the eye.

leukorrhea *n* a mucous discharge from the vagina.

leukotomy *n* (*pl* **leukotomies**) the severing of nerve fibres in the frontal lobes of the brain formerly used to relieve certain severe mental disorders.

lev *n* (*pl* **leva**) the monetary unit of Bulgaria.

levanter *n* an easterly wind in the Mediterranean.

levantine *n* a kind of reversible silk cloth.

levator *n* (*anat*) a muscle that serves to raise a part of the body.

levee[1] *n* a reception of visitors formerly held by a sovereign or other important person on rising from bed; a reception usu in honour of a particular person.

levee[2] *n* an embankment beside a river.

level *n* a horizontal line or plane; a position in a scale of values; a flat area or surface; an instrument for determining the horizontal. * *adj* horizontal; having a flat surface; at the same height, rank, position, etc; steady. * *vti* (**leveling, leveled** *or* **levelling, levelled**) to make or become level; to demolish; to raise and aim (a gun, criticism, etc).—**levelly** *adv*.

level crossing *n* (*Brit*) a place where a road crosses a railway line on the same level esp where gates or barriers close the road to allow trains to pass; a grade crossing in the US.

leveler, leveller *n* one who levels; an advocate of social equality.

level-headed *adj* having an even temper and sound judgment.—**level-headedly** *adv*.

lever *n* a bar used for prising or moving something; a means to an end; a device consisting of a bar turning about a fixed point; any device used in the same way, eg to operate machinery. * *vt* to raise or move (as with) a lever.

leverage *n* the action of a lever; the mechanical advantage gained by the use of a lever; power, influence.

leveret *n* a hare less than a year old.

leviable *adj* subject to a levy; (*goods*) which may be levied upon or seized.

leviathan *n* something huge.

levigate *vt* to grind to a fine powder.

Levis *n* (*trademark*) jeans made from (blue or black) denim.

levitate *vti* to rise or cause to rise into the air and float without support.—**levitation** *n*.

levity *n* (*pl* **levities**) excessive frivolity; lack of necessary seriousness.

levorotation *n* left-handed or counterclockwise rotation.—*also* **laevorotation.-levorotatory** *adj*.

levulose *n* a fruit found in sugar.—*also* **laevulose**.

levy *vt* (**levying, levied**) to collect by force or authority, as a tax, fine, etc; an amount levied; to enrol or conscript troops; to prepare for or wage war. * *n* (*pl* **levies**) a levying; the amount levied.—**levier** *n*.

lewd *adj* indecent; lustful; obscene.—**lewdly** *adv*.—**lewdness** *n*.

lewis *n* an appliance for lifting heavy blocks of stone.

lewisite *n* a blistering liquid obtained from arsenic and acetylene, used in gas form in chemical warfare.

lexical *adj* of or pertaining to words in a language; of a lexicon or dictionary.—**lexically** *adv*.

lexicographer *n* a person skilled in lexicography.

lexicography *n* the process of writing or compiling a dictionary; the principles and practices of dictionary making.—**lexicographic, lexicographical** *adj*.—**lexicographically** *adv*.

lexicology *n* the branch of linguistics dealing with the meaning and use of words.—**lexicological** *adj*.—**lexicologist** *n*.

lexicon *n* a dictionary; a special vocabulary, as of a specific language, branch of knowledge, etc.

lexis *n* the total of words or vocabulary in a language.

ley, ley-line *n* a straight line joining two landmarks, supposedly of prehistoric origin.

LF *abbr* = low frequency.

Li (*chem symbol*) lithium.

li *n* the Chinese equivalent of a mile, equivalent to approximately 590 yards.

liability *n* (*pl* **liabilities**) a being liable; something for which one is liable; (*inf*) a handicap, disadvantage; (*pl*) debts, obligations, disadvantages.

liable *adj* legally bound or responsible; subject to; likely (to).

liaise *vi* to form a connection and retain contact with.

liaison *n* intercommunication as between units of a military force; an illicit love affair; a thickening for sauces, soups, etc, as egg yolks or cream.

liana, liane *n* a climbing plant found in tropical forests.

liar *n* a person who tells lies.

Lias *n* (*geol*) the lowest division of rocks of the Jurassic system.—Liassic *adj*.

lib *n* (*inf*) liberation.

libation *n* the act of pouring wine or oil on the ground, as a sacrifi e; the liquod so poured out; a drink.

libel *n* any written or printed matter tending to injure a person's reputation unjustly; (*inf*) any defamatory or damaging assertion about a person. * *vt* (libeling, libeled *or* libelling, libelled) to utter or publish a libel against.— libeler, libeller *n*.—libelous, libellous *adj*.

liberal *adj* ample, abundant; not literal or strict; tolerant; (*education*) contributing to a general broadening of the mind, non-specialist; favouring reform or progress. * *n* a person who favours reform or progress.—liberally *adv*.

liberalism *n* liberal opinions, principles or politics.

liberality *n* (*pl* liberalities) generosity; breadth of mind.

liberalize *vti* to make or become less strict.—liberalization *n*.

liberate *vt* to set free from foreign occupation, slavery, etc.—liberator *n*.

liberation *n* the act of liberating; the state of being liberated; the pursuit of social, political or economic equality by or on behalf of those being discriminated against.

liberation priest *n* a priest who is active in working for social and political justice.

liberation theology *n* the belief that Christianity requires commitment to social and political change, as well as faith, esp in South America.

libertarian *n* a person who advocates liberty, esp in conduct or thought; a believer in free will.—libertarianism *n*.

liberticide *n* a destroyer of liberty; the destruction of liberty.

libertine *n* a dissolute person; a freethinker. * *adj* unrestrained, morally or socially; licentious.—libertinism, libertinage *n*.

liberty *n* (*pl* liberties) freedom from slavery, captivity, etc; the right to do as one pleases, freedom; a particular right, freedom, etc granted by authority; an impertinent attitude; authorized leave granted to a sailor.

libidinous *adj* lustful, lascivious.

libido *n* (*pl* libidos) the sexual urge.—libidinal *adj*.

Libra *n* (*astrol*) the 7th sign of the zodiac, operative 24 September–23 October; a constellation represented as a pair of scales.—Libran *n*, *adj*.

librarian *n* a person in charge of a library or trained in librarianship.

librarianship, library science *n* the profession of organizing collections of books, etc for reference by others.

library *n* (*pl* libraries) a collection of books, tapes, records, photographs, etc for reference or borrowing; a room, building or institution containing such a collection; (*comput*) a set of, usu general purpose, programs or subroutines for use in programming.

librate *vi* to waver; to balance.—libratory *adj*.

libration *n* the act of oscillating; the act of balancing; an apparent irregularity in the motion of the moon or a satellite.

librettist *n* a writer of a libretto.

libretto *n* (*pl* libretti, librettos) the text to which an opera, oratorio, etc is set.—librettist *n*.

Libyan *n* a native or inhabitant of Libya.—*also adj*.

lice *see* louse.

license *n* a formal or legal permission to do something specified; a document granting such permission; freedom to deviate from rule, practice, etc; excessive freedom, an abuse of liberty (—*also* licence). *vt* to grant a license to or for; to permit.—licenser, licensor *n*..

license plate *n* (*US*) a plate on the front or rear of a motor vehicle that displays its registration number.—*also* numberplate.

licensee *n* a person who is granted a licence.

licentiate *n* a person holding a certificate of competence in a profession; a degree between that of bachelor and doctor in some universities; one licensed to preach.—licentiateship *n*.

licentious *adj* morally unrestrained; lascivious.—licentiousness *n*.

lichee *see* litchi.

lichen *n* any of various small plants consisting of an alga and a fungus living in symbiotic association, growing on stones, trees, etc.

lichenology *n* the study of lichens.

lich gate *n* (*Brit*) a roofed gate of a churchyard, under which a coffin can be rested.—*also* lych gate.

lichi *see* litchi.

licit *adj* lawful.—licitly *adv*.

lick *vt* to draw the tongue over, esp to taste or clean; (*flames, etc*) to flicker around or touch lightly; (*inf*) to thrash; (*inf*) to defeat. * *vi* (*sl*) to take the drug crack. * *n* a licking with the tongue; (*inf*) a sharp blow; (*inf*) a short, rapid burst of activity.

lickerish *adj* (*arch*) lustful; greedy.

lickety-split *adv* very fast.

licking *n* (*inf*) a severe beating; a defeat.

lickspittle *n* a servile flatterer.

licorice *n* a black extract made from the root of a European plant, used in medicine and confectionery; a licorice-flavoured sweet.—*also* liquorice.

lictor *n* an official serving a magistrate in ancient Rome.

lid *n* a removable cover as for a box, etc; an eyelid.—lidded *adj*.

lido *n* (*pl* lidos) an open air swimming pool and recreational complex for public use.

lie[1] *n* an untrue statement made with intent to deceive; something that deceives or misleads. * *vi* (lying, lied) to speak untruthfully with an intention to deceive; to create a false impression.

lie[2] *vi* (lying, lay, *pp* lain) to be or put oneself in a reclining or horizontal position; to rest on a support in a horizontal position; to be in a specified condition; to be situated; to exist. * *n* the way in which something is situated.

lied *n* (*pl* lieder) a German song or ballad.

lie detector *n* a polygraph device used by police and security services that monitors sharp fluctuations in involuntary physiological responses as evidence of stress, guilt, etc when deliberately lying.

lief *adv* (*arch*) willingly.

liege *n* (*feudalism*) a lord or sovereign (—*also* **liege lord**); a subject or vassal.

lien *n* (*law*) a right to keep another's property pending payment of a debt due to the holder.

lierne *n* (*archit*) a cross-rib or branch rib in vaulting.

lieu *n* place; stead (esp *in lieu of*, in place of, instead of).

lieutenant *n* a commissioned army officer ranking below a captain; a naval officer next below a lieutenant commander; a deputy, a chief assistant to a superior.—**lieutenancy** *n*.

life *n* (*pl* **lives**) that property of plants and animals (ending at death) that enables them to use food, grow, reproduce, etc; the state of having this property; living things collectively; the time a person or thing exists; one's manner of living; one's animate existence, vigour, liveliness, (*inf*) a life sentence; a biography. * *adj* of animate being; lifelong; using a living model; of or relating to or provided by life insurance.

life-belt *n* an inflatable ring to support a person in the water; a safety belt.

lifeblood *n* the blood necessary to life; a vital element.

lifeboat *n* a small rescue boat carried by a ship; a specially designed and equipped rescue vessel that helps those in distress along the coastline.

life buoy *n* a ring-shaped buoyant device to keep a person afloat.

life cycle *n* a sequence of stages through which a living being passes during its lifetime

lifeguard *n* an expert swimmer employed to prevent drownings.

life jacket *n* a sleeveless jacket or vest of buoyant material to keep a person afloat.

lifeless *adj* dead; unconscious; dull.—**lifelessly** *adv.*—**lifelessness** *n*.

lifelike *adj* resembling a real life person or thing.

lifeline *n* a rope for raising or lowering a diver; a rope for rescuing a person, eg as attached to a lifebelt; a vitally important channel of communication or transport.

lifelong *adj* lasting one's whole life.

life peer *n* a British peer whose title lapses with death.

life preserver *n* a club used as a weapon of self-defence; a lifebelt or life jacket.

lifer *n* (*sl*) a person sentenced to prison for life.

life raft *n* a raft kept on board ship for use in emergencies.

lifesaving *adj* something (as drugs) designed to save lives. * *n* the skill or practice of saving lives, esp from drowning.—**lifesaver** *n*.

life science *n* a science dealing with living organisms and life processes, such as biology, zoology, etc.

life sentence *n* imprisonment for life, or a long period, as punishment for a grave offence.

life-size, life-sized *adj* of the size of the original.

lifestyle *n* the particular attitudes, living habits, etc of a person.

lifetime *n* the length of time that a person lives or something lasts.

lift *vt* to bring to a higher position, raise; to raise in rank, condition, etc; (*sl*) to steal; to revoke. * *vi* to exert oneself in raising something; to rise; to go up; (*fog, etc*) to disperse; (*with* off) (*rocket, etc*) to take off. * *n* act or fact of lifting; distance through which a thing is lifted; elevation of mood, etc; elevated position or carriage; a ride in the direction in which one is going; help of any kind; (*Brit*) a cage or platform for moving something from one level to another (—*also* **elevator**); upward air pressure maintaining an aircraft in flight.—**lifter** *n*.

liftoff *n* the vertical thrust of a spacecraft, etc at launching; the time of this.

ligament *n* a band of tissue connecting bones; a unifying bond.

ligan *see* **lagan**.

ligate *vt* to tie up (with a ligature).—**ligation** *n*.

ligature *n* a tying or binding together; a tie, bond, etc; two or more printed letters joined together, as œ; a thread used to suture a blood vessel, etc in surgery.

light[1] *n* the agent of illumination that stimulates the sense of sight; electromagnetic radiation such as ultraviolet, infrared or X-rays; brightness, illumination; a source of light, as the sun, a lamp, etc; daylight; a thing used to ignite something; a window; knowledge, enlightenment; aspect or appearance. * *adj* having light; bright; pale in colour. * *adv* palely. * *vt* (**lighting, lit** *or* **lighted**) to ignite; to cause to give off light; to furnish with light; to brighten, animate.

light[2] *adj* having little weight; not heavy; less than usual in weight, amount, force, etc; of little importance; easy to bear; easy to digest; happy; dizzy, giddy; not serious; moderate; moving with ease; producing small products. * *adv* lightly. * *vi* (**lighting, lit** *or* **lighted**) to come to rest after travelling through the air; to dismount, to alight; to come or happen on or upon; to strike suddenly, as a blow.—**lightly** *adv.*—**lightness** *n*.

lighten[1] *vti* to make or become light or lighter; to shine, flash.—**lightener** *n*.

lighten[2] *vti* to make or become lighter in weight; to make or become more cheerful; to mitigate.—**lightener** *n*.

lighter[1] *n* a small device that produces a naked flame to light cigarettes.

lighter[2] *n* a large barge used in loading or unloading larger ships.

lighterage *n* the transport of goods by lighter; the price paid for the service; lighters collectively.

light-fingered *adj* thievish.

light-headed *adj* dizzy; delirious.—**light-headedly** *adv*.

light-hearted *adj* carefree.—**light-heartedly** *adv*.

lighthouse *n* a tower with a bright light to guide ships.

lighting *n* the process of giving light; equipment for illuminating a stage, television set, etc; the distribution of light on an object, as in a work of art.

lightning *n* a discharge or flash of electricity in the sky. * *adv* fast, sudden.

lightning conductor or **rod** *n* a metal rod placed high on a building and grounded to divert lightning from the structure.

light opera *n* an operetta.

light pen *n* a pen-shaped photoelectric device used to communicate with a computer by pointing at the monitor; a similar device used for reading bar codes.

lightship *n* a ship equipped with a warning beacon and moored at a place dangerous to navigation.

lightsome *adj* (*arch, poet*) carefree; graceful, nimble.

lights out *n* (a signal indicating) the time prescribed for retiring to bed, as in a military barracks.

lightweight *adj* of less than average weight; trivial, unimportant. * *n* a person or thing of less than average weight; a professional boxer weighing 130-135 pounds (59-61 kg); a person of little importance or influence.

light-year *n* the distance light travels in one year.

lignaloes *see* **eaglewood**.

ligneous *adj* of or like wood.

ligniform *adj* resembling wood.

lignify *vti* (**lignifies, lignifying, lignified**) (*bot*) to make or become wood, or woody.—**lignification** *n*.

lignin *n* a woody fibre.

lignite *n* a soft brownish-black coal with the texture of the original wood.—**lignitic** *adj*.

lignum vitae *n* the heavy hard wood of the South American guaiacum tree.

ligroin *n* a solvent distilled from petroleum.

ligulate *adj* (*bot*) strap-shaped.

ligule *n* (*bot*) a membranous appendage at the top of a sheathing petiole in grasses; one of the rays of a composite plant.

likable, likeable *adj* attractive, pleasant, genial, etc.—**likably, likeably** *adv*.

like¹ *adj* having the same characteristics; similar; equal. * *adv* (*inf*) likely. * *prep* similar to; characteristic of; in the mood for; indicative of; as for example. * *conj* (*inf*) as; as if. * *n* an equal; counterpart.

like² *vt* to be pleased with; to wish. * *vi* to be so inclined.

likelihood *n* probability.

likely *adj* (**likelier, likeliest**) reasonably to be expected; suitable; showing promise of success.* *adv* probably.—**likeliness** *n*.

like-minded *adj* sharing the same tastes, ideas, etc.—**likemindedness** *n*.

liken *vt* to compare.

likeness *n* a being like; something that is like, as a copy, portrait, etc; appearance, semblance.

likewise *adv* the same; also.

liking *n* fondness; affection; preference.

lilac *n* a shrub with large clusters of tiny, fragrant flowers; a pale purple. * *adj* lilac coloured.

Lilliputian *adj* tiny; petty. * *n* a tiny person, a midget.

Li-Lo *n* (*pl* **Li-Los**) (*trademark*) an inflatable rubber or plastic mattress.

lilt *n* a light rhythmic song or tune; a springy motion. * *vi* (*music, song*) to have a lilt; to move buoyantly.—**lilting** *adj*.

lily *n* (*pl* **lilies**) a bulbous plant having typically trumpet-shaped flowers; its flower.

lily-livered *adj* cowardly.

lily of the valley *n* a small plant of the lily family with white bell-shaped flowers.

lily-white *adj* pure white; (*inf*) pure, incorruptible.

lima bean *n* a kind of bean that produces flat, edible pale green seeds; its edible seed.

limb *n* a projecting appendage of an animal body, as an arm, leg, or wing; a large branch of a tree; a participating member, agent; an arm of a cross.—**limbless** *adj*.

limbate *adj* (*bot*) with a border of a different colour.

limber¹ *adj* flexible, able to bend the body easily. * *vt* to make limber. * *vi* to become limber; (*with* **up**) to stretch and warm the muscles in readiness for physical exercise.

limber² *n* the detachable wheeled section of a gun carriage.

limbo¹ *n* (*pl* **limbos**) (*Christianity*) the abode after death assigned to unbaptized souls; a place for lost, unwanted, or neglected persons or things; an intermediate stage or condition between extremes.

limbo² *n* (*pl* **limbos**) a West Indian dance that involves bending over backwards and passing under a hori-zontal bar that is progressively lowered.

lime¹ *n* a white calcium compound used for making cement and in agriculture. * *vt* to treat or cover with lime.

lime² *n* a small yellowish-green fruit with a juicy, sour pulp; the tree that bears it; its colour.

lime³ *n* the linden tree.

limekiln *n* a furnace for making lime.

limelight *n* intense publicity; a type of lamp, formerly used in stage lighting, in which lime was heated to produce a brilliant flame.

limen *n* (*pl* **limens, limina**) (*psychol*) the point at which the effect of a stimulus is just discernible.

limerick *n* a type of humorous verse consisting of five lines.

limestone *n* a type of rock composed mainly of calcium carbonate.

limey *n* (*pl* **limeys**) (*US sl*) a British person.

limit *n* a boundary; (*pl*) bounds; the greatest amount allowed; (*inf*) as much as one can tolerate. * *vt* to set a limit to; to restrict.—**limitable** *adj*.

limitary *adj* restrictive; restricted.

limitation *n* the act of limiting or being limited; a hindrance to ability or achievement.

limited *adj* confined within bounds; lacking imagination or originality.

limited liability *n* in UK, responsibility for the debts of a company only to the extent of the amount of capital stock held.

limitless *adj* boundless, immense.—**limitlessly** *adv*.—**limitlessness** *n*.

limn *vt* to paint or draw.—**limner** *n*.

limnology *n* the scientific study of freshwater bodies (e.g. lakes and ponds) in terms of their support for plant and animal life, physical geography, chemical composition, etc.

limo *n* (*inf*) **limousine**.

limousine *n* (*sl*) a large luxury car.

limp¹ *vi* to walk with or as with a lame leg. * *n* a lameness in walking.—**limper** *n*.—**limpingly** *adv*.

limp² *adj* not firm; lethargic; wilted; flexible.—**limply** *adv*.—**limpness** *n*.

limpet *n* a mollusc with a low conical shell that clings to rocks.

limpid *adj* perfectly clear; transparent.—**limpidity** *n*.

limpkin *n* a kind of American wading bird.

limy *adj* (**limier, limiest**) containing, or resembling, lime.

linage *n* the number of written or printed lines on a page.

linchpin *n* a pin passed through an axle to keep a wheel in position; a person or thing regarded as vital to an organization, project, etc.

linden *n* a tree with deciduous heart-shaped leaves and small fragrant yellow flowers.

line¹ *vt* (**lining, lined**) to put, or serve as, a lining in.

line² *n* a length of cord, rope, or wire; a cord for measuring, making level; a system of conducting fluid, electricity, etc; a thin threadlike mark; anything resembling such a mark, as a wrinkle; edge, limit, boundary; border, outline, contour; a row of persons or things, as printed letters across a page; a succession of persons, lineage; a connected series of things; the course a moving thing takes; a course of conduct, actions, etc; a whole system of transportation; a person's trade or occupation; a field of experience or interest; (*inf*) glib, persuasive talk; a verse; the forward combat position in warfare; fortifications, trenches or other defences used in war; a stock of goods; a piece of information; a short letter, note; (*pl*) all the speeches of a character in a play; (*sl*) a measure of the drug cocaine laid in a strip, ready for sniffing. * *vb* (**lining, lined**) *vt* to mark with lines; to form a line along; to cover with lines; to arrange in a line. * *vi* to align.

lineage *n* direct descent from an ancestor; ancestry.

lineal *adj* hereditary; direct; linear.—**lineally** *adv*.

lineament *n* (*usu pl*) a facial feature.

linear *adj* of, made of, or using a line or lines; narrow and long; in relation to length only.—**linearity** *n*.—**linearly** *adv*.

linear accelerator *n* a device for accelerating elementary particles in a straight line by successively activating electric fields at regular intervals along their path.

lineate *adj* marked with lines.

lineation *n* the drawing, or arrangement, of lines.

line drawing *n* a drawing made with solid lines.

lineengraving *n* an engraving with fine lines; the art of this type of engraving.

linen *n* thread or cloth made of flax; household articles (sheets, cloths, etc) made of linen or cotton cloth.

line-out *n* (*Rugby Union*) the method of restarting a game after the ball has been put into touch, the forwards forming two opposing parallel lines at right angles to the touch-line and jumping for the ball that is thrown in.

line printer *n* a high-speed computer printer that prints each line as a single unit instead of character by character.

liner *n* a large passenger ship or aircraft travelling a regular route.

linesman *n* (*pl* **linesmen**) an official in certain games who assists the referee in deciding when the ball is out of play, etc.

lineup *n* an arrangement of persons or things in a line, eg for inspection.

ling. *abbr* = linguistics.

ling[1] *n* a type of heather.

ling[2] *n* (*pl* **ling, lings**) a sea fish of northern waters used as food.

linger *vi* to stay a long time; to delay departure; to dawdle or loiter; to dwell on in the mind; to remain alive though on the point of death.—**lingerer** *n*.—**lingering** *adj*.—**lingeringly** *adv*.

lingerie *n* women's underwear and nightclothes.

lingo *n* (*pl* **lingoes**) (*inf*) a dialect, jargon, etc.

lingua franca *n* (*pl* **lingua francas, linguae francae**) a language used for communication between speakers of different languages.

lingual *adj* of, or pronounced with, the tongue.—**lingually** *adv*.

linguiform *adj* tongue-shaped.

linguist *n* a person who is skilled in speaking foreign languages.

linguistic *adj* of or pertaining to language or linguistics.—**linguistically** *adv*.

linguistics *n* (*used as sing*) the science of language.

lingulate *adj* tongue-shaped.

liniment *n* a soothing medication, usu applied to the skin.

lining *n* a material used to cover the inner surface of a garment, etc; any material covering an inner surface.

link *n* a single loop or ring of a chain; something resembling a loop or ring or connecting piece; a person or thing acting as a connection, as in a communication system, machine or organization. * *vti* to connect or become connected.

linkage *n* a linking; a series or system of links.

linkboy *n* (*formerly*) someone who guided others through dark streets with a torch.

linkman *n* (*pl* **linkmen**) (*radio, TV*) a presenter who links items, reports, etc, esp on a sports programme.

links *npl* (*also used as sing*) flat sandy soil; a golf course, esp by the sea.

linkup *n* a linking together.

linn *n* (*Scot*) a waterfall; the pool beneath a waterfall; a ravine.

Linnaean, Linnean *adj* pertaining to the Swedish naturalist Linnaeus or to his system of classification.

linnet *n* a small brown or grey songbird.

lino *n* (*inf*) (*pl* **linos**) linoleum.

linocut *n* a design cut in relief on a piece of linoleum; a print made from this.

linoleum *n* a floor covering of coarse fabric backing with a smooth, hard decorative coating.

Linotype *n* (*trademark*) a typesetting machine that casts lines in one piece.

linsang *n* a type of civet, found in Indonesia and Borneo.

linseed *n* the seed of flax, from which linseed oil is made.

linseed oil *n* oil made from flax seeds, used in paint and varnish.

linsey-woolsey *n* a sturdy coarse fabric of linen or cotton and wool mixed.

linstock *n* (*formerly*) a staff holding a match, used to light a cannon.

lint *n* scraped and softened linen used to dress wounds; fluff.

lintel *n* the horizontal crosspiece spanning a doorway or window.

lintwhite *n* (*Scot, arch*) a linnet.

lion *n* a large, flesh-eating feline mammal with a shaggy mane in the adult male; a person of great courage or strength.—**lioness** *nf*.

lionhearted *adj* extremely brave.

lionize *vt* to treat as or make famous.—**lionization** *n*.—**lionizer** *n*.

lip *n* either of the two fleshy flaps that surround the mouth; anything like a lip, as the rim of a jug; (*sl*) insolent talk. * *vt* (**lipping, lipped**) to touch with the lips; to kiss; to utter.

lipid *n* an organic compound in fats, which is soluble in solvents but insoluble in water.

lipo-, lip- *prefix* fat, fatty.

lipoid, lipoidal *adj* fatty, resembling fat. * *n* a fat-like substance.

liposuction *n* cosmetic surgery involving the removal of fat from under the skin of the thighs, stomach, etc using a suction device inserted through an incision.

lipped *adj* having lips or rounded edges.

lip-read *vt* (**lip-reading, lip-read**) to understand another's speech by watching their lip movements.

lip service *n* support expressed but not acted upon.

lipstick *n* a small stick of cosmetic for colouring the lips; the cosmetic itself.

lip-sync, lip-synch *vt* to move the lips in time with a prerecorded soundtrack (of dialogue or music) on film or television.

liquate *vt* to melt (metals) to separate or purify them.—**liquation** *n*.

liquefacient *adj* serving to liquefy. * *n* something that liquefies.

liquefy *vti* (**liquefying, liquefied**) to change to a liquid.—**liquefaction** *n*.—**liquefier** *n*.

liquescent *adj* becoming liquid.

liqueur *n* a sweet and variously flavoured alcoholic drink.

liquid *n* a substance that, unlike a gas, does not expand indefinitely and, unlike a solid, flows readily. * *adj* in liquid form; clear; limpid; flowing smoothly and musically, as verse; (*assets*) readily convertible into cash.—**liquidity** *n*.

liquidate *vt* to settle the accounts of; to close a (bankrupt) business and distribute its assets among its creditors; to convert into cash; to eliminate, kill.

liquidation *n* the act of liquidating or paying off; the settlement of the affairs of a bankrupt person or business.

liquidator *n* an official who winds up a business.

liquidize *vt* to make liquid.

liquidizer *n* a domestic appliance for liquidizing and blending foods.

liquid paraffin *n* an oily distillate of petroleum used as a laxative.—*also* **mineral oil**.

liquor *n* an alcoholic drink; any liquid, esp that in which food has been cooked.

liquorice *n see* **licorice**.

liquor store *n* a place where alcohol is sold for consumption off the premises.—*also* **off-licence, package store**.

lira *n* (*pl* **lire, liras**) the monetary unit of Italy and Turkey.

lisle *n* a fine tightly-twisted cotton thread.

lisp *vi* to substitute the sounds *th* (as in *thin*) for *s* or *th* (as in *then*) for *z*; a speech defect or habit involving such pronunciation; to utter imperfectly. * *vt* to speak or utter with a lisp.—*also n*.—**lisper** *n*.

lissom *adj* lithe; supple; agile, etc.—**lissomeness** *n*.

list[1] *n* a series of names, numbers, words, etc written or printed in order. * *vt* to make a list of; to enter in a directory, etc.

list[2] *vti* to tilt to one side, as a ship. * *n* such a tilting.

listed *adj* (*company, etc*) having its shares quoted on a stock exchange; (*building*) of architectural interest and protected from demolition or alteration without permission.

listed building *n* in UK, a building officially designated as of historic or architectural interest and protected from alteration or demolition.

listen *vi* to try to hear; to pay attention, take heed; (*with in*) to intercept radio or telephone communications; to tune into a radio broadcast; to eavesdrop.

listener *n* a person who listens; a person listening to a radio broadcast.

listeriosis *n* chronic food poisoning caused by the bacteria *Listeria*.

listing *n* a list, or an individual entry therein; the act of making a list; (*pl*) a guide giving details of events, eg music, theatre, taking place in a particular area, published in a newspaper or magazine.

listless *adj* lacking energy or enthusiasm because of illness, dejection, etc; languid.—**listlessly** *adv*.—**listlessness** *n*.

lit *see* **light**[1], **light**[2].

lit. *abbr* = literal; literary; literature; litre.

litany *n* (*pl* **litanies**) a type of prayer in which petitions to God are recited by a priest and elicit set responses

by the congregation; any tedious or automatic recital.

litchi *n* a fruit consisting of a soft, sweet white pulp in a thin brown shell; the tree that bears this fruit.—*also* **lichee, lichi**.

-lite *n suffix* stone; mineral; fossil.

liter *see* **litre**.

literacy *n* the ability to read and write.

literal *adj* in accordance with the exact meaning of a word or text; in a basic or strict sense; prosaic, unimaginative; real.—**literalness, literality** *n*.—**literally** *adv*.

literalism *n* adherence to the literal sense of a word or saying.—**literalist** *n*.

literary *adj* of or dealing with literature; knowing much about literature.—**literarily** *adv*.—**literarilness** *n*.

literate *adj* able to read and write; educated.—*also n*.

literati *npl* educated people.

literatim *adv* letter for letter.

literature *n* the writings of a period or of a country, esp those valued for their excellence; of style or form; all the books and articles on a subject; (*inf*) any printed matter.

-lith *n suffix* stone or rock.

litharge *n* an oxide of lead.

lithe *adj* supple, flexible.—**litheness** *n*.

lithesome *adj* lithe, supple.

lithia *n* an oxide of lithium.

lithic *adj* of or pertaining to stone.

lithium *n* the lightest metallic element.

litho *n* (*pl* **lithos**) a lithograph; lithography.

lithograph *n* a print, etc made by lithography.—**lithographic** *adj*.—**lithographically** *adv*

lithography *n* printing from a flat stone or metal plate, parts of which have been treated to repel ink.—**lithographer** *n*.

lithoid, lithoidal *adj* stonelike.

lithology *n* the study of rocks and their physical characteristics.—**lithologic, lithological** *adj*.

lithophyte *n* a stony polyp; a plant which grows on a rocky surface.

lithosphere *n* the solid outer part of the earth.

lithotomy *n* (*pl* **lithotomies**) (*med*) the operation of cutting into the bladder to remove a stone.—**lithotomic** *adj*.

lithotripter, lithotriptor *n* an instrument that fragments kidney or bladder stones, etc by ultrasound without the need for invasive surgery.

lithotrity *n* (*pl* **lithotrities**) (*med*) the operation of crushing a stone in the bladder.

litigant *n* a person engaged in a lawsuit.

litigate *vti* to bring or contest in a lawsuit.—**litigator** *n*.

litigation *n* the act or processs of carrying on a lawsuit; a judicial contest.

litigious *adj* of or causing lawsuits; fond of engaging in lawsuits; contentious.—**litigiousness** *n*.

litmus *n* a colouring material obtained from certain lichens that turns red in acid solutions and blue in alkaline solutions.

litotes *n* (*pl* **litotes**) (*rhetoric*) understatement for effect.

litre, liter *n* a measure of liquid capacity in the metric system, equivalent to 1.76 pints.—*also* **litre**.

Litt.D, Lit.D *abbr* = Doctor of Letters; Doctor of Literature.

litter *n* rubbish scattered about; young animals produced at one time; straw, hay, etc used as bedding for animals; a stretcher for carrying a sick or wounded person. * *vt* to make untidy; to scatter about carelessly.

littérateur *n* a writer.

litterbug *n* a person who drops refuse in public places.

little *adj* not great or big, small in size, amount, degree, etc; short in duration; small in importance or power; narrow-minded. * *n* small in amount, degree, etc. * *adv* less, least, slightly; not much; not in the least.

little people *npl* (*folklore*) supernatural beings such as fairies, elves and leprechauns.

littoral *adj* of or along the seashore.

liturgics *n* (*sing*) the study of liturgies.

liturgist *n* someone who studies or composes liturgies.

liturgy *n* (*pl* **liturgies**) the prescribed form of service of a church.—**liturgical** *adj.*—**liturgically** *adv.*

livable *adj* worth living; suitable for living in.

live[1] *vi* to have life; to remain alive; to endure; to pass life in a specified manner; to enjoy a full life; to reside; (*with* **in, out**) (*employee*) to reside at (or away from) one's place of work; (*with* **together**) (*unmarried couple*) to cohabit. * *vt* to carry out in one's life; to spend; pass; (*with* **down**) to survive or efface the effects of (a crime or mistake) by waiting until it is forgotten or forgiven.

live[2] *adj* having life; of the living state or living beings; of present interest; still burning; unexploded; carrying electric current; broadcast during the actual performance.

liveable *see* **livable**.

livelihood *n* employment; a means of living.

livelong *adj* of the whole length of (the day).

lively *adj* (**livelier, liveliest**) full of life; spirited; exciting; vivid; keen. * *adv* in a lively manner.—**liveliness** *n.*

liven *vti* to make or become lively.—**livener** *n.*

liver *n* the largest glandular organ in vertebrate animals, which secretes bile, etc and is important in metabolism; the liver of an animal used as food; a reddish-brown colour.

liveried *adj* wearing a livery.

liverish *adj* suffering from liver disorder; peevish.

liverwort *n* a cryptogamous plant, found in wet places.

liverwurst *n* sausage made with liver.

livery *n* (*pl* **liveries**) an identifying uniform, as that worn by a servant.

liveryman *n* (*pl* **liverymen**) a keeper of a livery stable; a member of a livery company.

lives *see* **life**.

livestock *n* (*farm*) animals raised for use or sale.

live wire *n* (*inf*) a lively, energetic person.

livid *adj* (*skin*) discoloured, as from bruising; greyish in colour; (*inf*) extremely angry.—**lividly** *adv.*—**lividness, lividity** *n.*

living *adj* having life; still in use; true to life, vivid; of life, for living in. * *n* a being alive; livelihood; manner of existence.

living room *n* a room in a house used for general entertainment and relaxation.

living wage *n* a wage sufficient to maintain a reasonable standard of comfort.

lixiviate *vt* to wash (soil, ore, etc) with a filtering liquid; to extract (a soluble substance) from some material.—**lixiviation** *n.*

lizard *n* a reptile with a slender body, four legs, and a tapering tail.

llama *n* a South American animal, related to the camel, used for carrying loads and as a source of wool.

llano *n* (*pl* **llanos**) one of the vast, level plains of South America.

LLB *abbr* = Bachelor of Laws.

LLD *abbr* = Doctor of Laws.

LLM *abbr* = Master of Laws.

lm *abbr* = lumen.

LNG *abbr* = liquefied natural gas.

lo *interj* behold!, see!

loach *n* an edible freshwater fish.

load *n* an amount carried at one time; something borne with difficulty; a burden; (*often pl*) (*inf*) a great amount. * *vt* to put into or upon; to burden; to oppress; to supply in large quantities; to alter, as by adding a weight to dice or an adulterant to alcoholic drink; to put a charge of ammunition into (a firearm); to put film into (a camera); (*comput*) to install a program in memory. * *vi* to take on a load.—**loader** *n.*

loaded *adj* (*sl*) having plenty of money, drunk, under the influence of drugs.

loadstar *see* **lodestar**.

loadstone *see* **lodestone**.

loaf[1] *n* (*pl* **loaves**) a mass of bread of regular shape and standard weight; food shaped like this; (*sl*) the head.

loaf[2] *vi* to pass time in idleness.—**loafer** *n.*

loam *n* rich and fertile soil.

loamy *adj* (**loamier, loamiest**) consisting of or full of loam.—**loaminess** *n.*

loan *n* the act of lending; something lent, esp money. * *vti* to lend.—**loanable** *adj.*—**loaner** *n.*

loath *adj* unwilling.—*also* **loth**.—**loathly** *adv.*

loathe *vt* to dislike intensely; to detest.—**loather** *n.*—**loathing** *n.*

loathsome *adj* giving rise to loathing; detestable.—**loathsomeness** *n.*

loaves *see* **loaf**[1].

lob *vti* (**lobbing. lobbed**) to toss or hit (a ball) in a high curve. * *n* a high-arching throw or kick.

lobar *adj* of or relating to a lobe.

lobate *adj* having lobes; lobelike.

lobby *n* (*pl* **lobbies**) an entrance hall of a public building; a person or group that tries to influence legislators. * *vti* (**lobbying, lobbied**) to try to influence (legislators) to support a particular cause or take certain action.

lobbyist *n* someone employed to lobby.

lobe *n* a rounded projection, as the lower end of the ear; any of the divisions of the lungs or brain.

lobelia *n* a genus of garden plants, usually with blue flowers.

loblolly *n* (*pl* **loblollies**) a type of American pine tree; (*naut*) gruel.

lobotomy *n* (*pl* **lobotomies**) surgical incision into the lobe of an organ; a leukotomy.

lobscouse *n* a sailor's dish of meat, vegetables and ship's biscuit.

lobster *n* (*pl* **lobsters, lobster**) any of a family of edible sea crustaceans with four pairs of legs and a pair of large pincers.

lobule *n* a small lobe.—**lobular, lobulate**adj.

local *adj* of or belonging to a particular place; serving the needs of a specific district; of or for a particular part of the body. * *n* an inhabitant of a specific place; (*inf*) a pub serving a particular district.—**locally** *adv.*—**localness** *n.*

locale *n* a place or area, esp in regard to the position or scene of some event.

localism *n* a word, idiom or custom restricted to a particular locality; narrowness of outlook.

locality *n* (*pl* **localities**) a neighbourhood or a district; a particular scene, position, or place; the fact or condition of having a location in space and time.

localize *vt* to limit, confine, or trace to a particular place.—**localization** *n*.

locate *vt* to determine or indicate the position of something; to set in or assign to a particular position.

location *n* a specific position or place; a locating or being located; a place outside a studio where a film is (partly) shot; (*comput*) an area in memory where a single item of data is stored.

locative *adj, n* (a grammatical case) indicating place.

loc. cit. *abbr* = loco citato (Latin *in the place cited*).

loch *n* (*Scot*) a lake.

loci *see* **locus**.

lock[1] *n* a fastening device on doors, etc, operated by a key or combination; part of a canal, dock, etc in which the level of the water can be changed by the operation of gates; the part of a gun by which the charge is fired; a controlling hold, as used in wrestling. * *vt* to fasten with a lock; to shut; to fit, link; to jam together so as to make immovable. * *vi* to become locked; to interlock.—**lockable** *adj*.

lock[2] *n* a curl of hair; a tuft of wool, etc.

lockage *n* a system of canal locks; the act of going through a lock; the fee paid for so doing.

locker *n* a small cupboard, chest, etc that can be locked, esp one for storing possessions in a public place.

locker room *n* room equipped with lockers for storing possessions in a public place.

locket *n* a small ornamental case, usu holding a lock of hair, photograph or other memento, hung from the neck.

lockjaw *n* tetanus.

lockout *n* the exclusion of employees from a workplace by an employer, as a means of coercion during an industrial dispute.

locksmith *n* a person who makes and repairs locks and keys.

lockup *n* a jail; a garage or storage room.

loco *adj* (*sl*) crazy.

locomotion *n* motion, or the power of moving, from one place to another.

locomotive *n* an electric, steam, or diesel engine on wheels, designed to move a railway train. * *adj* of locomotion.

locomotor *adj* of or pertaining to locomotion. locomotive.

locular, loculate *adj* (*biol*) split into compartments.

loculus, locule *n* (*pl* **loculi, locules**) (*biol*) a small cavity or cell.

locum *n* (*inf*) a locum tenens.

locum tenens *n* (*pl* **locum tenentes**) a person who stands in for a professional colleague, esp for a doctor, chemist or clergyman.

locus *n* (*pl* **loci**) a place; (*math*) the path of a point or curve, moving according to some specific rule; the aggregate of all possible positions of a moving or generating element.

locust *n* a type of large grasshopper often travelling in swarms and destroying crops; a type of hard-wooded leguminous tree.

locution *n* a word, phrase or expression; an act or mode of speaking.

lode *n* an ore deposit.

lodestar *n* a star, usu the North Star, used to guide navigation.—*also* **loadstar**.

lodestone *n* a magnetic oxide of iron; a piece of this ox-

ide, used as a magnet or a crude compass.—*also* **loadstone**.

lodge *n* a small house at the entrance to a park or stately home; a country house for seasonal leisure activities; a resort hotel or motel; the local chapter or hall of a fraternal society; a beaver's lair. * *vt* to house temporarily; to shoot, thrust, etc firmly (in); to bring before legal authorities; to confer upon. * *vi* to live in a place for a time; to live as a paying guest; to come to rest and stick firmly (in).

lodger *n* a person who lives in a rented room in another's home.

lodging *n* a temporary residence; (*pl*) accommodation rented in another's house.

lodgment, lodgement *n* the act of lodging; the state of being lodged; an accumulation of something deposited; (*mil*) a foothold in enemy territory.

loess *n* a light brown deposit of fine silt and clay found in Asia, Europe and America.—**loessial, loessal** *adj*,

loft *n* a space under a roof; a storage area under the roof of a barn or stable; a gallery in a church or hall. * *vt* to send into a high curve.

lofty *adj* (**loftier, loftiest**) (*objects*) of a great height, elevated; (*person*) noble, haughty, superior in manner.—**loftily** *adv*.—**loftiness** *n*.

log[1] *n* a section of a felled tree; a device for ascertaining the speed of a ship; a record of speed, progress, etc, esp one kept on a ship's voyage or aircraft's flight. * *vb* (**logging, logged**) *vt* to record in a log; to sail or fly (a specified distance). * *vi* (*with* **on, off**) (*comput*) to establish or disestablish communication with a mainframe computer from a remote terminal in a multiuser system.—**logger** *n*.

log[2] *n* a logarithm.

loganberry *n* (*pl* **loganberries**) a hybrid developed from the blackberry and the red raspberry.

logarithm *n* the exponent of the power to which a fixed number (the base) is to be raised to produce a given number, used to avoid multiplying and dividing when solving mathematical problems.—**logarithmic** *adj*.—**logarithmically** *adv*.

logbook *n* an official record of a ship's or aircraft's voyage or flight; an official document containing details of a vehicle's registration.

loge *n* a box in a theatre.

loggerhead *n* (*arch*) a blockhead; (*pl*) a dispute, confrontation (*to be at loggerheads with someone*); (*zool*) a type of turtle.

loggia *n* (*pl* **loggias, loggie**) a covered open gallery or balcony on the side of a building.

logging *n* the business of cutting down timber.

logic *n* correct reasoning, or the science of this; way of reasoning; what is expected by the working of cause and effect.—**logician** *n*.

logical *adj* conforming to the rules of logic; capable of reasoning according to logic.—**logically** *adv*.—**logicality** *n*.

logician *n* someone versed in logic.

logistics *n* (*used as sing*) the science of the organization, transport and supply of military forces; the planning and organization of any complex activity.—**logistic** *adj*.—**logistically** *adv*.

log jam *n* a blockage of logs floating in a watercourse; a deadlock, standstill.

logo *n* (*pl* **logos**) (*inf*) a logotype.

logo- *prefix* word, speech.

logogram, logograph n a sign or letter representing a word or phrase.

logographer n an annalist or writer of speeches in ancient Greece.

logography n a method of printing in which a type represents a word instead of a letter.

logogriph n a word puzzle based on an anagram.

logomachy n (pl **logomachies**) a dispute over words.

logorrhea n excessive or incoherent talkativeness.

Logos n (Christianity) the Divine Word; the second person of the Trinity, Jesus Christ.

logotype n a printed symbol representing a corporation, product, etc; a trademark, emblem.

logrolling n in US, the undemocratic trading of votes between politicians to ensure the passage of legislation of mutual interest.

-logue, -log n suffix indicating a particular type of speech or writing, as in monologue, travelogue.

logwood n a wood of a deep-red colour, used in dyeing.

-logy n suffix science, theory or doctrine of, eg astrology; type of writing or discourse, eg phraseology.

logy adj (**logier, logiest**) dull, sluggish.

loin n (usu pl) the lower part of the back between the hipbones and the ribs; the front part of the hindquarters of an animal used for food.

loincloth n a cloth worn around the loins.

loiter vi to linger or stand about aimlessly.—**loiterer** n.

loll vi to lean or recline in a lazy manner, to lounge; (tongue) to hang loosely.—**loller** n.

lollapalooza, lollapaloosa n (sl) something or someone exceptional.

Lollard n (hist) a follower of the 14th-century English religious reformer, John Wycliff.

lollipop n a flat boiled sweet at the end of a stick.

lollop vi to run or walk with an ungainly, bouncing rhythm.

lolly n (pl **lollies**) (inf) a lollipop; (Brit sl) money.

loment n a plant pod that breaks at maturity into single-seeded joints.

London Pride n a type of saxifrage plant with pink flowers.

lone adj by oneself; isolated; without companions, solitary.—**loneness** n.

lonely adj (**lonelier, loneliest**) isolated; unhappy at being alone; (places) remote, rarely visited.—**loneliness** n.

loner n a person who avoids the company of others.

lonesome adj having or causing a lonely feeling.—**lonesomely** adv.

long. abbr = longitude.

long[1] adj measuring much in space or time; having a greater than usual length, quantity, etc; tedious, slow; far-reaching; well-supplied. * adv for a long time; from start to finish; at a remote time.

long[2] vi to desire earnestly, esp for something not likely to be attained.

longanimity n long-suffering, forbearance.

longboat n the largest boat carried aboard a ship.

longbow n a large hand-drawn bow.

longcloth n a fine cotton fabric.

long-distance adj travelling or communicating over long distances.

longe see **lunge**[2].

longeron n the principal longitudinal spar of an aircraft's fuselage.

longevity n long life.

longhand n ordinary handwriting, as opposed to shorthand.

long-headed adj shrewd.

longhorn n a breed of long-horned cattle.

longicorn n a type of beetle with long antennae.

longing n an intense desire.—**longingly** adv.

longitude n distance east or west of the prime meridian, expressed in degrees or time.

longitudinal adj of or in length; running or placed lengthways; of longitude.—**longitudinally** adv.

long johns npl (inf) warm underpants with long legs.

long jump n an athletic event consisting of a horizontal running jump.

long-lived adj having or tending to live a long time.

long-playing adj of or relating to an LP record.

long-range adj reaching over a long distance or period of time.

longshore adj found on, or pertaining to, the shore.

longshoreman n (pl **longshoremen**) a person who loads and unloads ships at a port.

long shot n a wild guess; a competitor, etc who is unlikely to win; a project that has little chance of success.

long-sighted adj only seeing distant objects clearly.—**long-sightedly** adv.

long-standing adj having continued for a long time.

long-suffering adj enduring pain, provocation, etc patiently.

long-term adj of or extending over a long time.

longueur n a tedious period of time.

long wave n a radio wave of a frequency less than 300 kHz.

longways, longwise adv in the direction of the length (of something), lengthways.

long-winded adj speaking or writing at great length; tiresome.—**long-windedly** adv.—**long-windedness** n.

loo n (pl **loos**) (Brit inf) a lavatory, a toilet.

looby n (pl **loobies**) a clumsy, stupid person.

loofah n the fibrous skeleton of a type of gourd used as a sponge for scrubbing.—also **luffa**.

look vi to try to see; to see; to search; to appear, seem; to be facing in a specified direction; (with **in**) to pay a brief visit; (with **up**) to improve in prospects. * vt to direct one's eyes on; to have an appearance befitting. * n the act of looking; a gaze, glance; appearance; aspect; (with **after**) to take care of; (with **over**) to examine; (with **up**) to research (for information, etc) in book; to visit.

look-alike n a person that looks like another.

looker n (inf) an attractive woman.

looker-on n (pl **lookers-on**) a spectator.

look-in n a brief visit.

looking glass n a mirror.

lookout n a place for keeping watch; a person assigned to watch.

look-see n (inf) a brief inspection.

loom[1] n a machine or frame for weaving yarn or thread. * vt to weave on a loom.

loom[2] vi to come into view indistinctly and often threateningly; to come ominously close, as an impending event.

loon[1] n a large fish-eating diving bird.

loon[2] n (sl) a clumsy or stupid person; a crazy person.

loony, looney n (pl **loonies**) (sl) a lunatic. * adj (**loonier, looniest**) (sl) crazy, demented.—**looniness** n.

loop n a figure made by a curved line crossing itself; a similar rounded shape in cord, rope, etc crossed on itself; anything forming this figure; (comput) a set of instructions in a program that are executed repeatedly; an intrauterine contraceptive device; a segment of film or magnetic tape. * *vt* to make a loop of; to fasten with a loop. * *vi* to form a loop or loops.

looper *n* a caterpillar that crawls by arching itself into loops.

loophole *n* a means of evading an obligation, etc; a slit in a wall for looking or shooting through.

loopy *adj* (**loopier, loopiest**) (*inf*) slightly mad, cracked.

loose *adj* free from confinement or restraint; not firmly fastened; not tight or compact; not precise; inexact; (*inf*) relaxed. * *vt* to release; to unfasten; to untie; to detach; (*bullet*) to discharge. * *vi* to become loose.—**loosely** *adv*.—**looseness** *n*.

loose cannon *n* a person who acts independently and often obstreperously.

loose-leaf *adj* having pages or sheets that can easily be replaced or removed.

loosen *vti* to make or become loose or looser.—**loosener** *n*.

loosestrife *n* a kind of plant with golden or purple flowers.

loot *n* goods taken during warfare, civil unrest, etc; (*sl*) money. * *vti* to plunder, pillage.—**looter** *n*.

lop *vt* (**lopping, lopped**) to sever the branches or twigs from a tree; to cut off or out as superfluous.

lope *vi* to move or run with a long bounding stride.— *also n*.—**loper** *n*.

lop-eared *adj* having drooping ears.

lophobranchiate *adj* (*fish*) with gills arranged in tufts.

lopsided *adj* having one side larger in weight, height, or size than the other; badly balanced.—**lopsidedly** *adv*.—**lopsidedness** *n*.

loquacious *adj* talkative.—**loquaciously** *adv*.—**loquacity** *n*.

loquat *n* an evergreen tree found in China and Japan; its edible fruit.

loquitur (*theatre*) (*formerly*) he or she speaks (as a stage direction).

lord *n* a ruler, master or monarch; a male member of the nobility; (*with cap and* **the**) God; a form of address used to certain peers, bishops and judges.

lordling *n* a young or minor lord.

lordly *adj* (**lordlier, lordliest**) noble; haughty; arrogant.—**lordliness** *n*.

Lord Mayor *n* the mayor of the City of London and certain other UK boroughs and towns—*also* **Lord Provost** in Scotland.

lordosis *n* forward curvature of the spine.

Lord Privy Seal *n* a British cabinet minister without specific responsibilities.

Lord Provost *see* **Lord Mayor**.

Lord's Day *n* (*with* **the**) Sunday.

lordship *n* the rank or authority of a lord; rule, dominion; (*with* **his** *or* **your**) a title used in speaking of or to a lord.

Lord's Prayer *n* (*with* **the**) the prayer taught by Jesus to His disciples beginning 'Our Father'.

lords spiritual *npl* the bishops and archbishops who are members of the British House of Lords.

lords temporal *npl* the peers other than bishops and archbishops in the British House of Lords.

lore *n* knowledge; learning, esp of a traditional nature; a particular body of tradition.

lorgnette *n* a long-handled opera glass; a pair of spectacles fixed to a long handle, into which they fold.

lorica *n* (*pl* **loricae**) the hard outer shell of certain animals.—**loricate, loricated** *adj*.

lorikeet *n* a small, brightly coloured parrot.

loris *n* (*pl* **loris**) a small, nocturnal, climbing primate, found in South and South-East Asia.

lorn *adj* (*poet*) forsaken; forlorn.

lorry *n* (*pl* **lorries**) (*esp Brit*) a large motor vehicle for transporting heavy loads.—*also* **truck**.

lory *n* (*pl* **lories**) a small parrot with brilliant plumage.

lose *vb* (**losing, lost**) *vt* to have taken from one by death, accident, removal, etc; to be unable to find; to fail to keep, as one's temper; to fail to see, hear, or understand; to fail to have, get, etc; to fail to win; to cause the loss of; to wander from (one's way, etc); to squander. * *vi* to suffer (a) loss.—**losable** *adj*.—**loser** *n*.

losel *n* (*dial*) a worthless person.

loss *n* a losing or being lost; the damage, trouble caused by losing; the person, thing, or amount lost.

loss leader *n* an item sold at a price below its value in order to attract customers.

lost *adj* no longer possessed; missing; not won; destroyed or ruined; having wandered astray; wasted.

lot *n* an object, such as a straw, slip of paper, etc drawn from others at random to reach a decision by chance; the decision thus arrived at; one's share by lot; fortune; a plot of ground; a group of persons or things; an item or set of items put up for auction; (*often pl*) (*inf*) a great amount; much; (*inf*) sort. * *vt* (**lotting, lotted**) to divide into lots.

lota, lotah *n* a brass or copper water pot.

loth *see* **loath**.

Lothario *n* (*pl* **Lotharios**) a libertine.

lotion *n* a liquid for cosmetic or external medical use.

lottery *n* (*pl* **lotteries**) a system of raising money by selling numbered tickets that offer the chance of winning a prize; an enterprise, etc which may or may not succeed.

lotto *n* a game of chance based on the drawing of prize numbers.

lotus *n* a type of waterlily; (*Greek legend*) a plant whose fruit induced contented forgetfulness.

lotus-eater *n* a person dedicated to a life of idle pleasure.

lotus position *n* an erect sitting position in yoga with the legs crossed close to the body.

louche *adj* untrustworthy, shady.

loud *adj* characterized by or producing great noise; emphatic; (*inf*) obtrusive or flashy.—**loudly** *adv*.—**loudness** *n*.

louden *vi* to grow louder. * *vt* to make louder.

loudspeaker *n* a device for converting electrical energy into sound.

lough *n* (*Irish*) a lake; an arm of the sea.

louis, louis d'or *n* (*pl* **louis, louis d'or**) (*formerly*) a French gold coin, with a value of 20 francs.

lounge *vi* to move, sit, lie, etc in a relaxed way; to spend time idly. * *n* a room with comfortable furniture for sitting, as a waiting room at an airport, etc; a comfortable sitting room in a hotel or private house.

lounger *n* a comfortable couch or chair for relaxing on; a person who lounges.

lour *vi* to look sullen; to become dark, gloomy, threatening.—*also* **lower**.—**louringly, loweringly** *adv*.

louse *n* (*pl* **lice**) any of various small wingless insects that are parasitic on humans and animals; any similar but unrelated insects that are parasitic on plants; (*inf*) (*pl* **louses**) a mean, contemptible person.

lousy *adj* (**lousier, lousiest**) infested with lice; (*sl*) disgusting, of poor quality, or inferior; (*sl*) well supplied (with).—**lousily** *adv*,—**lousiness** *n*.

lout *n* a clumsy, rude person.—**loutish** *adj*.

louver, louvre *n* one of a set of slats in a door or window set parallel and slanted to admit air but not rain.—**louvered, louvred** *adj*.

lovable *adj* easy to love or feel affection for.—**lovability** *n*.—**lovably** *adv*.

lovage *n* a European herb used as a seasoning in food.

love *n* a strong liking for someone or something; a passionate affection for another person; the object of such affection; (*tennis*) a score of zero. * *vti* to feel love (for).

love affair *n* a romantic or sexual relationship between two people.

lovebird *n* any of various small parrots.

love child *n* an illegitimate child.

love-in-a-mist *n* a flowering garden plant, fennelflower.

loveless *adj* without love; not feeling or receiving love.—**lovelessly** *adv*.

lovelock *n* a curl worn on the forehead.

lovelorn *adj* pining from love.

lovely *adj* (**lovelier, loveliest**) beautiful; (*inf*) highly enjoyable. * *n* (*pl* **lovelies**) a lovely person.—**loveliness** *n*.

lovemaking *n* sexual activity, esp intercourse, between lovers.

lover *n* a person in love with another person; a person, esp a man, having an extramarital sexual relationship; (*pl*) a couple in love with each other; someone who loves a specific person or thing.

lovesick *adj* languishing through love.—**lovesickness** *n*.

lovey-dovey *adj* (*sl*) displaying affection in an excessive or exaggerated manner.

loving *adj* affectionate.—**lovingly** *adv*.—**lovingness** *n*.

loving cup *n* a large cup with two or more handles passed round a group for all to drink from.

low[1] *n* the sound a cow makes, a moo. * *vi* to make this sound.

low[2] *adj* not high or tall; below the normal level; less in size, degree, amount, etc than usual; deep in pitch; depressed in spirits; humble, of low rank; vulgar, coarse; not loud. * *adv* in or to a low degree, level, etc. * *n* a low level, degree, etc; a region of low barometric pressure.

lowborn, lowbred *adj* of humble birth.

lowboy *n* a table with drawers.

lowbrow *n* (*inf*) a person regarded as uncultivated and lacking in taste.—*also adj*.

low comedy *n* comedy reliant on farce or physical slapstick.

lowdown *n* (*sl: with* **the**) the true, pertinent facts

low-down *adj* (*inf*) mean, contemptible.

lower case *n* small letters (not capitals) used for printing.

lower class *n* the class of people having the lowest status in society.

lower house, lower chamber *n* one of the two chambers in a bicameral legislature, such as the US House of Representatives or the British House of Commons.

lower[1] *adj* below in place, rank, etc; less in amount, degree, etc. * *vt* to let or put down; to reduce in height, amount, etc; to bring down in respect, etc. * *vi* to become lower.—**lowerable** *adj*.

lower[2] *see* **lour**.

lowermost *adj* lowest.

low frequency *n* a radio frequency between 300 and 30 kilohertz.

low-key, low-keyed *adj* of low intensity, subdued.

lowland *n* low-lying land; (*pl*) a flat region. * *adj* of or pertaining to lowlands.—**lowlander** *n*.

low-level language *n* (*comput*) a programming language that corresponds more to machine language than human language.

lowlife *n* (*pl* **lowlifes**) (*sl*) a criminal.

lowly *adj* (**lowlier, lowliest**) humble, of low status; meek.—**lowliness** *n*.

Low Mass *n* a Mass without music or elaborate ritual.

low-rise *adj* (*building*) having only one or two storeys.—*also n*.

low spirited *adj* unhappy, depressed.

low-tech *adj* of or involving low technology.

low technology *n* unsophisticated technology limited to the provision of basic human needs.

low tension *adj* using, conveying, or operating at a low voltage.

low tide *n* (the time of) the tide when it is at its lowest level; a low point.

low water *n* low tide.

lox[1] *n* a type of smoked salmon.

lox[2] *n* liquid oxygen.

loyal *adj* firm in allegiance to a person, cause, country, etc, faithful; demonstrating unswerving allegiance.—**loyally** *adv*.—**loyalty** *n*.

loyalist *n* a person who supports the established government, esp during a revolt.—**loyalism** *n*.

lozenge *n* a four-sided diamond-shaped figure; a cough drop, sweet, etc, originally diamond-shaped.

LP *n* a long-playing record, usu 12 inches (30.5 cm) in diameter and played at a speed of 33 1/3 revolutions per minute.

LPG *abbr* = liquefied petroleum gas.

Lr (*chem symbol*) lawrencium.

LSD *n* a powerful hallucinatory drug (lysergic acid diethylamide).

Lt *abbr* = lieutenant.

Ltd *abbr* = limited liability (used by private companies only).

LU (*chem symbol*) lutetium.

luau *n* a sumptuous feast in Hawaii; a warm welcome; an unexpected source of wealth; a bonanza.

lubber *n* a clumsy person.

lubricant *n* a substance that lubricates.

lubricate *vt* to coat or treat (machinery, etc) with oil or grease to lessen friction; to make smooth, slippery, or greasy. * *vi* to act as a lubricant.—**lubrication** *n*.

lubricator *n* person who or thing that lubricates; a device used for oiling machines.

lubricity *n* slipperiness; evasiveness; lewdness.

lucarne *n* a dormer window, esp in a spire.

lucent *adj* bright, shining.—**lucency** *n*.

lucerne *see* alfalfa.

lucid *adj* easily understood; sane.—**lucidly** *adv*.—**lucidity** *n*.

Lucifer *n* Satan.

luck *n* chance; good fortune.

luckless *n* unfortunate, unlucky.—**lucklessly** *adv*.—**lucklessness** *n*.

lucky *adj* (**luckier, luckiest**) having or bringing good luck.—**luckily** *adv*.—**luckiness** *n*.

lucrative *adj* producing wealth or profit; profitable.—**lucratively** *adv*.—**lucrativeness** *n*.

lucre *n* (*derog*) riches, money.

lucubrate *vi* to study, esp by night.—**lucubrator** *n*.

lucubration *n* study, esp nocturnal; (*often pl*) a literary compositon produced as the result of protracted study.

ludicrous *adj* absurd, laughable.—**ludicrously** *adv*.

luff *n* (*naut*) the part of ship towards the wind. * *vti* (*naut*) to turn (a ship) into the wind.

luffa *see* **loofah**.

Luftwaffe *n* the German Air Force.

lug[1] *vt* (**lugging, lugged**) to pull or drag along with effort.

lug[2] *n* an ear-like projection by which a thing is held or supported.

luge *n* a small one-person toboggan.

luggage *n* the suitcases and other baggage containing the possessions of a traveller.

lugger *n* a small vessel rigged with one or more lugsails.

lugsail *n* a square sail, with no boom or lower yard, which hangs nearly at right angles to the mast.

lugubrious *adj* mournful, dismal.—**lugubriously** *adv*.

lugworm *n* a marine worm used as bait.

lukewarm *adj* barely warm, tepid; lacking enthusiasm.

lull *vt* to soothe, to calm; to calm the suspicions of, esp by deception. * *n* a short period of calm.

lullaby *n* (*pl* **lullabies**) a song to lull children to sleep.

lulu *n* (*inf*) a wonderful or remarkable person or thing.

lumbago *n* rheumatic pain in the lower back.

lumbar *adj* of or in the loins.

lumber[1] *n* timber, logs, beams, boards, etc, roughly cut and prepared for use; articles of unused household furniture that are stored away; any useless articles. * *vi* to cut down timber and saw it into lumber. * *vt* to clutter with lumber; to heap in disorder.

lumber[2] *vi* to move heavily or clumsily.—**lumberer** *n*.

lumbering[1] *adj* moving clumsily and heavily.—**lumberingly** *adv*.

lumbering[2] *n* the cutting down and sawing of trees into timber as a business.

lumberjack *n* a person employed to fell trees and transport and prepare timber.

lumbrical *adj* wormlike.

lumen *n* (*pl* **lumina, lumens**) the SI unit of light flux; (*anat*) a duct within a tubular organ.

luminary *n* (*pl* **luminaries**) a body that gives off light, such as the sun; a famous or notable person.

luminescent *adj* emitting light but not heat.—**luminescence** *n*.

luminosity *n* (*pl* **luminosities**) the quality of being luminous; something luminous; (*astron*) the degree of light emitted by a star when compared with the sun.

luminous *adj* emitting light; glowing in the dark; clear, easily understood.—**luminously** *adv*.

lump *n* a small, compact mass of something, usu without definite shape; an abnormal swelling; a dull or stupid person. * *adj* in a lump or lumps. * *vt* to treat or deal with in a mass. * *vi* to become lumpy.

lumper *n* a docker.

lumpfish *n* (*pl* **lumpfish, lumpfishes**) a sea fish found in the North Atlantic, with horny spines and a sucker with which it clings to objects.

lumpish *adj* like a lump; heavy; dull, stupid.

lump sum *n* a sum of money (esp cash) paid as a whole and not in instalments.

lumpy *adj* (**lumpier, lumpiest**) filled or covered with lumps.—**lumpily** *adv*.—**lumpiness** *n*.

lunacy *n* (*pl* **lunacies**) insanity; utter folly.

lunar *adj* of or like the moon.

lunar eclipse *n* an eclipse when the earth passes between the sun and the moon.

lunar month *n* a month measured by the complete revolution of the moon, 29.5 days.

lunar year *n* a year of twelve lunar months, 354.33 days.

lunate, lunated *adj* crescent-shaped.

lunatic *adj* insane; utterly foolish. * *n* an insane person.

lunatic fringe *n* the members of an organization regarded as being fanatical or extreme.

lunation *n* a lunar month, the time taken for the moon to revolve once around the earth.

lunch *n* a light meal, esp between breakfast and dinner; **out to lunch** (*sl*) crazy; eccentric. * *vi* to eat lunch.—**luncher** *n*.

luncheon *n* lunch, esp a formal lunch.

luncheon meat *n* processed meat in tins ready to eat.

lune *n* (*geom*) a figure formed on a plane or sphere by two intersecting arcs of circles.

lunette *n* anything shaped like a crescent; an arched opening in a vaulted roof to admit light.

lung *n* either of the two sponge-like breathing organs in the chest of vertebrates.

lunge[1] *n* a sudden forceful thrust, as with a sword; a sudden plunge forward. * *vti* to move, or cause to move, with a lunge.—**lunger** *n*.

lunge[2] *n* a long halter for training a horse; the use of this in training horses. * *vt* to train with a lunge.—*also* **longe**.

lungfish *n* (*pl* **lungfish, lungfishes**) a freshwater fish with lungs as well as gills.

lungi *n* a long piece of cloth worn as a skirt or loincloth by Indian men.

lungwort *n* a Eurasian plant with dark-coloured leaves spotted with white.

lunisolar *adj* pertaining to the sun and moon; produced by the sun and moon in unison.

lunula, lunule *n* (*pl* **lunulae, lunules**) the white crescent-shaped part near the root of the fingernail.

lupine[1] *n* a garden plant of the pea family.

lupine[2] *adj* of or resembling a wolf.

lupulin *n* a powder, obtained from hops, used as a sedative.

lupus *n* any of several diseases marked by lesions of the skin.

lurch *vi* to lean or pitch suddenly to the side. * *n* a sudden roll to one side.—**lurchingly** *adv*.

lurdan *adj* (*arch*) stupid. * *n* a stupid person.

lure *n* something that attracts, tempts or entices; a brightly coloured fishing bait; a device used to recall a trained hawk; a decoy for wild animals. * *vt* to entice, attract, or tempt.—**luringly** *adv*.

lurid *adj* vivid, glaring; shocking; sensational.—**luridly** *adv*.—**luridness** *n*.

lurk *vi* to lie hidden in wait; to loiter furtively.—**lurker** *n*.

luscious *adj* delicious; richly sweet; delighting any of the senses.—**lusciously** *adv*.—**lusciousness** *n*.

lush[1] *adj* tender and juicy; of or showing abundant growth.—**lushly** *adv*.—**lushness** *n*.

lush[2] *n* (*sl*) an alcoholic.

lust *n* strong sexual desire (for); an intense longing for something. * *vi* to feel lust.—**lustful** *adj*.—**lustfully** *adv*.

lustral *adj* of or relating to ceremonial purification; of or relating to a lustrum.

lustrate *vt* to purify by sacrifice or ceremonial washing.—**lustration** *n*.

lustre, luster *n* gloss; sheen; brightness; radiance; brilliant beauty or fame; glory; a chandelier with pendants of cut glass; a fabric with a lustrous surface; a substance used to give lustre to an object; a metallic glaze on pottery; the quality and intensity of light reflected from the surface of minerals.—**lusterless** *adj*.—**lustrous** *adj*.

lustreware, lusterware *n* earthenware decorated with luster.

lustrum *n* (*pl* **lustrums, lustra**) a period of five years.

lusty *adj* (**lustier, lustiest**) strong; vigorous; healthy.—**lustily** *adv*.—**lustiness** *n*.

lute[1] *n* an old, round-backed stringed musical instrument plucked with the fingers.

lute[2] *n* clay or cement used to make joints airtight, etc.

lutenist, lutist *n* a lute player.

luteous *adj* greenish-yellow.

lutetium *n* a metallic element.

Lutheran *adj* pertaining to Martin Luther 1483-1546), the German religious reformer, or to the Lutheran Church and its doctrines. * *n* a follower of Martin Luther; a member of the Lutheran Church.—**Lutheranism** *n*.

Lutheran Church *n* the Protestant church founded by Martin Luther in Germany in the 16th century.

lux *n* (*pl* **lux**) a unit of illumination.

luxate *vt* to put out of joint.—**luxation** *n*.

luxuriant *adj* profuse, abundant; ornate; fertile.—**luxuriance** *n*.

luxuriate *vi* to enjoy immensely, to revel (in).—**luxuriation** *n*.

luxurious *adj* constituting luxury; indulging in luxury; rich, comfortable.—**luxuriously** *adv*.—**luxuriousness** *n*.

luxury *n* (*pl* **luxuries**) indulgence and pleasure in sumptuous and expensive food, accommodation, clothes, etc; (*often pl*) something that is costly and enjoyable but not indispensable. * *adj* relating to or supplying luxury.

lx *abbr* = lux.

lycanthrope *n* a werewolf; (*med*) a sufferer from lycanthropy.

lycanthropy *n* the supposed power of changing from a human being into a werewolf; (*med*) a form of mental illness in which the sufferer believes himself or herself to be a wolf.

lycée *n* (*pl* **lycées**) a state secondary school in France.

lyceum *n* a public lecture hall.

lychee *see* **lichee**.

lych gate *see* **lich gate**.

lychnis *n* a genus of flowering plants, including the ragged robin and campion.

lycopod *n* a kind of moss, also known as the club moss.

lycopodium *n* any of a genus of perennial plants, the club mosses; an inflammable yellow powder in the spore cases of certain species, used in fireworks.

Lycra *n* (*trademark*) an elastic synthetic material used for tight-fitting garments, such as bicycle shorts and swimwear.

lyddite *n* a powerful explosive, composed chiefly of picric acid.

lye *n* an alkaline solution.

lying *see* **lie**[1], **lie**[2].

lying-in *n* (*pl* **lyings-in, lying-ins**) childbirth.

Lyme disease *n* an infectious disease, carried by ticks, that produces fever, pains in the joints and a rash, and can result in paralysis or chronic fatigue, and, rarely, death.

lymph *n* a clear, yellowish body fluid, found in intercellular spaces and the lymphatic vessels.

lymphatic *adj* of, relating to, or containing lymph; sluggish. * *n* a vessel that contains or conveys lymph.

lymph node *n* any of numerous nodules of tissue distributed along the course of lymphatic vessels that produce lymphocytes.

lympho- *prefix* lymph; lymph tissue; lymphatic system.

lymphocyte *n* a white blood cell formed in the lymph nodes, which helps to protect against infection —**lymphocytic** *adj*.

lymphoid *adj* relating to lymph glands; resembling lymph.

lymphoma *n* (*pl* **lymphomata**) a tumour of the lymphoid tissue.

lyncean *adj* pertaining to or resembling the lynx; sharp-eyed.

lynch *vt* to murder (an accused person) by mob action, without lawful trial, as by hanging.—**lyncher** *n*.—**lynching** *n*.

lynx *n* (*pl* **lynxes, lynx**) a wild feline of Europe and North America with spotted fur.

lynx-eyed *adj* keen-sighted.

lyonnaise *adj* (*cooking*) with onions.

lyrate, lyrated *adj* lyre-shaped.

lyre *n* an ancient musical instrument of the harp family.

lyrebird *n* an Australian bird with a tail shaped like a lyre.

lyric *adj* denoting or of poetry expressing the writer's emotion; of, or having a high voice with a light, flexible quality. * *n* a lyric poem; (*pl*) the words of a popular song.

lyrical *adj* lyric; (*inf*) expressing rapture or enthusiasm.—**lyrically** *adv*.

lyricism *n* lyrical quality or expression.

lyricist *n* a person who writes lyrics, esp for popular songs.

lyrist *n* a lyric poet; a lyre player.

lysergic acid *see* **LSD**.

lysin *n* a specific antibody in blood that can destroy cells.

lysin *n* a substance, esp an antibody, that kills living cells or bacteria.

lysine *n* an amino acid formed by the digestion of dietary protein.

-lysis *n suffix* disintegration; decomposition.

lysis *n* (*pl* **lyses**) (*biol*) the process of destroying cells with a lysin; (*med*) the gradual abatement of an acute disease.

-lyte *n suffix* denoting a substance able to be disintegrated or decomposed.

-lytic *adj suffix* indicating a disintegration or decomposition.

M

M *abbr* = mega-; medium; motorway.

M. *abbr* = Master; Monsieur

m *abbr* = metre(s); mile(s); million(s).

MA *abbr* = Master of Arts; Massachusetts.

ma *n* (*inf*) mother.

ma'am *n* madam (used as a title of respect, esp when addressing royalty).

macabre *adj* gruesome; grim; of death.

macaco *n* (*pl* **macacos**) one of various lemurs, esp the ruffled lemur and the ring-tailed lemur.

macadam *n* a road surface composed of successive layers of small stones compacted into a solid mass.

macadamia *n* an Australian tree bearing white flowers and an edible seed (**macadamia nut**).

macadamize *vt* to surface (a road) with macadam.—**macadamization** *n*.

macaque *n* a short-tailed monkey of Asia and Africa.

macaroni *n* (*pl* **macaronis**, **macaronies**) a pasta made chiefly of fine wheat flour and made into tubes; an 18th-century dandy who copied continental mannerisms etc.

macaronic *adj* (*verse*) using words from more than one language, or a mixture of everyday words and Latin words or words with Latin endings. * *n* (*often pl*) macaronic verse.

macaroon *n* a small cake or biscuit made with sugar, egg whites and ground almonds or coconut.

macaw *n* a large parrot with brightly coloured plumage.

Maccabean *adj* pertaining to the Maccabees, a family of Jewish patriots who led a successful revolt against the Syrians, or to its most famous member, Judas Maccabaeus.

maccaboy *n* a kind of snuff, usu rose-scented.

mace[1] *n* a staff used as a symbol of authority by certain institutions.

mace[2] *n* an aromatic spice made from the external covering of the nutmeg.

macédoine *n* a dish of mixed fruits, served hot or cold; a dish of diced vegetables, usu in jelly or syrup; any mixture.

macerate *vti* to soften or become soft or separated through soaking; to make or become thin.—**maceration** *n*.—**macerator** *n*.

Mach *see* **Mach number**.

machete *n* a large knife used for cutting, or as a weapon.

Machiavellian *adj* cunning; deceitful.

machicolation *n* (*arch*) a projecting parapet, usu found on medieval castles, with openings for dropping stones, etc, on assailants; such an opening.—**machicolated** *adj*.

machinate *vti* to scheme, plan, esp to do harm.—**machinator** *n*.

machination *n* (*usu pl*) an artifice; an intrigue; a plot; the act of plotting or intriguing.

machine *n* a structure of fixed and moving parts, for doing useful work; an organization functioning like a machine; the controlling group in a political party; a device, as the lever, etc that transmits, or changes the application of energy. * *vt* to shape or finish by machine-operated tools. * *adj* of machines; done by machinery.

machine code, machine language *n* (*comput*) programming instructions in binary or hexadecimal code.

machine gun *n* an automatic gun, firing a rapid stream of bullets.—*also vt*.

machine-readable *adj* directly usable by a computer.

machinery *n* machines collectively; the parts of a machine; the framework for keeping something going.

machine tool *n* a mechanized tool for cutting or shaping metals, wood, etc.

machinist *n* one who makes, repairs, or operates machinery.

machismo *n* strong or assertive masculinity; virility.—**macho** *adj*.

Mach number *n* the ratio of the speed of a body in a particular medium to the speed of sound in the same medium. Mach 1 is equal to the speed of sound.

mackerel *n* (*pl* **mackerel**, **mackerels**) a common oily food fish.

Mackinaw (coat) *n* a short, double-breasted coat made of a heavy woollen plaid material.

mackintosh *n* a waterproof raincoat.

mackle *n* (*printing*) a blurred or imprecise impression, which produces the effect of a double printing.—*also* **macule**.

macle *n* a type of crystal in two parts, containing carbon impurities, sometimes used as a gemstone.

macramé *n* (the art of) knotting or weaving coarse thread to produce ornamental work.

macro- *prefix* = long, large.

macrobiotic *adj* (*diet*) composed of an extremely restricted range of foods, usu vegetables and whole grains.

macrocephalic *adj* having an unusually large skull.—*also* **megacephalic** *adj*.—**macrocephaly** *n*.

macrocosm *n* the universe; any complex system.—**macrocosmic** *adj*.

macroeconomics *n* (*used as sing*) the study of the economy in terms of total national income, production and investment.—**macroeconomic** *adj*.

macron *n* a mark placed over a letter to indicate a stressed or long vowel (·).

macropterous *adj* (*zool*) large-winged.

macroscopic *adj* visible to the naked eye; regarded in terms of large elements.

macrospore *see* **megaspore**.

macula *n* (*pl* **maculae**) a spot or mark on the skin; a coloured area near the retina, where vision is esp sharp.—**macular** *adj*.—**maculation** *n*.

macule` see mackle.

mad adj (madder, maddest) insane; frantic; foolish and rash; infatuated; (inf) angry.

madam n a polite term of address to a woman; a woman in charge of a brothel; (inf) a precocious little girl.

madame n (pl mesdames) the title of a married French woman; used as a title equivalent to Mrs.

madcap adj reckless, impulsive.—also n.

madden vti to make or become insane, angry, or wildly excited.—maddening adj.—maddeningly adv.

madder¹ see mad.

madder² n a plant of the genus from whose root a red dye and pigment are extracted; the red dye so obtained; a synthetic pigment used in paints and inks.

madding adj (arch) raging; furious; causing (someone or oomething) to be raging.

made see make.

Madeira n a rich, strong, white wine made in the North Atlantic island of Madeira.

madeleine n a small sponge cake with a coating of red jam covered with coconut.

mademoiselle n (pl mesdemoiselles) the title of an unmarried French girl or woman; used as a title equivalent to Miss; a French teacher or governess.

made-to-order adj produced to a customer's specifications; being ideally suited for a particular purpose.

madhouse n (inf) as mental institution; a state of uproar or confusion.

madly adv in an insane manner; at great speed, force; (inf) excessively.

madman n (pl madmen) an insane person.

madness n insanity; foolishness; excitability.

Madonna n the Virgin Mary, esp as seen in pictures or statues.

madras n a strong cotton or silk material, usu striped.

madrepore n any of several corals, often forming tropical coral reefs.—madreporic adj.

madrigal n a 16th-century love song or pastoral poem in the form of an unaccompanied part-song; 14th-century Italian song derived from a pastoral poem.—madrigalist n.

maduro adj (cigar) dark and full-flavoured. * n (pl maduros) such a cigar.

madwoman n (pl madwomen) an insane person.

madwort n a small herb with yellow or white flowers, formerly reputed to cure madness; a type of small, low-growing, flowering plant with hairy leaves and blue flowers.

maelstrom n a whirlpool; a state of turbulence or confusion.

maenad n (maenads, maenades) (Greek myth) a female adherent of Dionysus; a frantic, agitated woman.—also menad.

maestoso adj, adv (mus) in a majestic manner.

maestro n (pl maestros) a master of an art, esp a musical composer, conductor, or teacher.

mae west n (inf) an inflatable life jacket.

Mafia n a secret society composed chiefly of criminal elements, originating in Sicily.

mafioso n (pl mafiosos, mafiosi) a member of the Mafia.

mag. abbr = magazine.

magazine n a military store; a space where explosives are stored, as in a fort; a supply chamber, as in a camera, a rifle, etc; a periodical publication containing articles, fiction, photographs, etc.

magdalen, magdalene n a reformed prostitute; (rare) an institution for housing and reforming prostitutes.

magenta n a purplish-red dye; purplish red.—also adj.

maggot n a wormlike larva, as of the housefly.—maggoty adj.—maggotiness n.

magi, magian see magus.

magic n the use of charms, spells, etc to supposedly influence events by supernatural means; any mysterious power; the art of producing illusions by sleight of hand, etc. * adj of or relating to magic; possessing supposedly supernatural powers; (inf) wonderful. * vt (magicking, magicked) to influence, produce or take (away) by or as if by magic.—magical adj.—magically adv.

magician n one skilled in magic; a conjurer.

magisterial adj of, or suitable for a magistrate; authoritative.—magisterially adv.

magistracy n (pl magistracies) the office, jurisdiction or dignity of a magistrate; magistrates collectively.

magistral adj or or pertaining to a master or teacher, magisterial; (med) specially prescribed; (fortification) in a strategic position.

magistrate n a public officer empowered to administer the law.—magistrateship, magistrature n.

magma n (pl magmas, magmata) a stratum of hot molten rock within the earth's crust, which solidifies on the surface as lava.

Magna Carta, Magna Charta n in England, the Great Charter, forming the basis of civil liberty, granted by King John to the barons, church and freemen in 1215.

magnanimity n (pl magnanimities) generosity.

magnanimous adj noble and generous in conduct or spirit, not petty.—magnanimously adv.

magnate n a very wealthy or influential person.

magnesia n a magnesium compound used as a mild laxative.

magnesium n a white metallic element that burns very brightly.

magnet n any piece of iron or steel that has the property of attracting iron; anything that attracts.

magnetic adj of magnetism or a magnet; producing or acting by magnetism; having the ability to attract or charm people.—magnetically adv.

magnetic declination n deviation of the magnetic needle from true north; the measure of this.

magnetic equator n the imaginary point near the equator where the magnetic needle has no dip, the aclinic line.

magnetic field n any space in which there is an appreciable magnetic force.

magnetic needle n a thin piece of magnetized iron, steel, etc, used in a compass and other instruments, that indicates the direction of a magnetic field.

magnetic north n the northerly direction of the earth's magnetic field, as pointed to by a compass needle.

magnetic pole n either of the two variable points in the regions of the earth's northern and southern poles to which a magnetic needle points.

magnetic resonance imaging n a method of viewing the body's internal organs by the use of radio waves.

magnetics n sing the science of magnetism.

magnetic tape n a thin plastic ribbon with a magnetized coating for recording sound, video signals, computer data, etc.

magnetism n the property, quality, or condition of being magnetic; the force to which this is due; personal charm.

magnetize vt to make magnetic; to attract strongly.—magnetization n.—magnetizer n.

magneto n (pl **magnetos**) a small generator with permanent magnets for generating high voltages, esp the ignition spark in an internal combustion engine.

magnetoelectricity n electric phenomena produced by magnetism.

magnetometer n an instrument for measuring and comparing magnetic fields.

magneton n one of two units of magnetic moment.

magnet school n a school in which resources are devoted to developing excellence in one particular field, eg science.

Magnificat n the hymn of the Virgin Mary (Luke 1:46-55); a musical setting of this; (without cap) any hymn of praise.

magnification n magnifying or being magnified; the degree of enlargement of something by a lens, microscope, etc.

magnificence n grandeur of appearance; splendour; pomp.

magnificent adj splendid, stately or sumptuous in appearance; superb, of very high quality.—**magnificently** adv.

magnifico n (pl **magnificoes**) a person of importance or high rank; (formerly) a title of a Venetian nobleman.

magnify vt (**magnifying, magnified**) to exaggerate; to increase the apparent size of (an object) as (with) a lens.—**magnifiable** adj.—**magnifier** n.

magniloquent adj pompous in style or speech, bombastic.—**magniloquence** n.—**magniloquently** adv.

magnitude n greatness of size, extent, etc; importance; (astron) the apparent brightness of a star.

magnolia n a spring-flowering shrub or tree with evergreen or deciduous leaves and showy flowers.

magnum n (pl **magnums**) a wine bottle that holds twice the normal quantity.

magnum opus in (pl **magna opera**) the great or chief work of an artist or author.

magpie n a black and white bird of the crow family; a person who chatters; an acquisitive person.

maguey n any of several species of a tropical American plant, esp one from which fibre is obtained or that is used in the production of alcoholic drinks; the fibre from such a plant.

magus n (pl **magi**) a Zoroastrian priest; (with cap) any of the three wise men who paid homage to Christ at His birth; a magician, sorcerer.—**magian** adj, n.

Magyar adj pertaining to the Hungarian or Magyar race or language; (sleeve) cut as part of the bodice, with no armhole seam.

Mahabharata n a great Hindu epic that narrates the dynastic wars of ancient India.

maharajah, maharaja n the former title of an Indian prince.

maharani, maharanee n the wife of a maharajah.

mahatma n (Hinduism, Buddhism) a wise man, a sage; (with cap) (Hinduism) a title or respect for a man of great spirituality.

mahi-mahi n either of two dolphin fish (genus Coryphaena) of the Pacific Ocean, a food fish.

mahjong, mah-jongg n an orig Chinese game for four people played with decorative tiles.

mahlstick see **maulstick**.

mahogany n (pl **mahoganies**) the hard, reddish-brown wood of a tropical tree; a reddish-brown colour.

Mahometan see **Muhammedan**.

mahout n (India) an elephant driver.

maid n a maiden; a woman servant.

maiden n a girl or young unmarried woman. * adj unmarried or virgin; untried; first.—**maidenhood** n.

maidenhair (fern) n a delicate-leafed fern with small light green leaflets.

maidenhead n the hymen.

maidenly adj like or suitable to a maiden; modest; gentle.—**maidenliness** n.

maiden name n the surname of a woman before marriage.

maiden over n (cricket) an over during which no runs are scored.

maid of honour n the principal unmarried attendant of a bride; a small almond-flavoured tart.

maidservant n a female servant.

maieutic adj of the Socratic method of teaching by means of questions.

mail[1] n a body armour made of small metal rings or links.

mail[2] n letters, packages, etc transported and delivered by the post office; a postal system. * vt to send by mail.—**mailable** adj.

mailman n (pl **mailmen**) a person who collects or delivers mail.—also **postman**.

mail order n an order for goods to be sent by post.

maim vt to cripple; to mutilate.

main adj chief in size, importance, etc; principal. * n (often pl but used a sing) a principal pipe in a distribution system for water, gas, etc; the essential point.

mainframe n a large computer that can handle multiple tasks concurrently.

mainland n the principal land mass of a continent, as distinguished from nearby islands.

mainline n the principal road, course, etc. * vt (sl) (drugs) to inject directly into a vein.

mainly adv chiefly, principally.

mainmast n (naut) the principal mast of a sailing ship with more than one mast.

mainsail n (naut) the principal lowermost sail on the mainmast.

mainsheet n (naut) one of the ropes by which the mainsail is extended and fastened, controlling its angle.

mainspring n the principal spring in a clock, watch, etc; the chief incentive, motive, etc.

mainstay n a chief support.

mainstream n a major trend, line of thought, etc.—also adj.

maintain vt to preserve; to support, to sustain; to keep in good condition; to affirm.—**maintainable** adj.—**maintainer** n.

maintenance n upkeep; (financial) support, esp of a spouse after a divorce.

maintop n (naut) the platform on top of the mainmast.

maisonette n a small house; self-contained living quarters, usu on two floors with its own entrance, as part of a larger house.

maître d'hôtel n (pl **maîtres d'hôtel**) n a head waiter; a hotel manager or owner; a house steward.

maize n corn; a light yellow colour.

Maj abbr (mil) = major.

majestic adj dignified; imposing.—**majestically** adv.

majesty n (pl **majesties**) grandeur; (with cap) a title used in speaking to or of a sovereign.

majolica n a fine, soft, enamelled kind of pottery of Italian origin, with a glaze of bright metallic oxides.

major adj greater in size, importance, amount, etc; (surgery) very serious, life-threatening; (mus) higher than the corresponding minor by half a tone. * vi to specialize (in a field of study). * n in US, an officer ranking just above a captain, in UK, a lieutenant-colonel; (mus) a major key, chord or scale.

major-domo n (pl **major-domos**) a head steward; a butler.

majority n (pl **majorities**) the greater number or part of; the excess of the larger number of votes cast for a candidate in an election; full legal age; the military rank of a major.

majuscule n a capital letter used in printing or in writing. * adj of, pertaining to or written in such letters.— **majuscular** adj.

make vb (**making, made**) vt to cause to exist, occur, or appear; to build, create, produce, manufacture, etc; to prepare for use; to amount to; to have the qualities of; to acquire, earn; to understand; to do, execute; to cause or force; to arrive at, reach; (with **believe**) to imagine, pretend; (with **good**) to make up for, pay compensation; (with **out**) to write out; to complete (a form, etc) in writing; to attempt to understand; to discern, identify; (with **up**) to invent, fabricate, esp to deceive; to prepare; to make complete; to put together; to settle differences between. * vi (with **do**) to manage with what is available; (with **for**) to go in the direction of; to bring about; (with **good**) to become successful or wealthy; (with **off**) to leave in haste; (with **out**) to pretend; to fare, manage; (with **up**) to become reconciled; to compensate for; to put on make-up for the stage. * n style, brand, or origin; manner of production.—**maker** n.

make-believe adj imagined, pretended.—also n.

makeshift adj being a temporary substitute.—also n.

make-up n the cosmetics, etc used by an actor; cosmetics generally; the way something is put together, composition; nature, disposition.

makeweight n something added to make up the required weight; anything of little value added to fill a lack.

making n the act or process of making, creation; (pl) earnings; (pl) potential; (pl) (sl) the materials for rolling a cigarette.

Makkah see **mecca**.

mal- prefix = bad or badly, wrong, ill.

malacca n the tough stem of a species of climbing palm, rattan; a brown walking stick made of this (also **malacca cane**).

malachite n copper carbonate occurring as a green mineral, used as an ore and for making ornaments.

malacology n the science of molluscs.—**malacological** adj.—**malacologist** n.

malacostracan adj (crustacean) soft-shelled.

maladjusted adj poorly adjusted, esp to the social environment.—**maladjustment** n.

maladministration n corrupt or incompetent management of public affairs.—**maladminister** vb.

maladroit adj clumsy.—**maladroitness** n.

malady n (pl **maladies**) a disease, illness.

Malaga n a sweet, white dessert wine from the Spanish port of Malaga.

Malagasy n (pl **Malagasy, Malagasies**) a native of Madagascar; the language of Madagascar.* adj pertaining to Madagascar, its language or people.

malaise n a feeling of discomfort or of uneasiness.

malamute n a powerful Alaskan dog with a dense grey coat used to pull sledges.—also **malemute**.

malanders n sing a disease in horses, the main symptom of which is an eczema-like patch on the horse's leg.

malapert adj (arch) impudent; pert; saucy.

malapropism n a ludicrous misuse of words.— **malapropian** adj.

malapropos adj out of place, ill-timed. * adv in an inapproriate way; unseasonably.

malar adj of or relating to the cheek or cheekbone. * n the cheekbone.

malaria n an infectious disease caused by mosquito bites, and characterized by recurring attacks of fevers and chills.—**malarial** adj.

malcontent adj discontented and potentially rebellious.—also n.

mal de mer n seasickness.

male adj denoting or of the sex that fertilizes the ovum; of, like, or suitable for men and boys; masculine. * n a male person, animal or plant.—**maleness** n.

malediction n a curse, an imprecation; a denunciation of evil; a slander.—**maledictory** adj.

malefactor n a criminal, an evildoer.—**malefaction** n.

maleficent adj harmful, causing evil; mischief-making.—**maleficently** adv.—**maleficence** n.

malemute see **malamute**.

malevolent adj ill-disposed toward others; spiteful, malicious.—**malevolence** n.—**malevolently** adv.

malfeasance n (law) an illegal action, official misconduct.—**malfeasant** adj, n.

malformation n faulty or abnormal formation of a body or part.—**malformed** adj.

malfunction n faulty functioning. * vi to function wrongly.

malgré lui adv (French) against one's wishes, despite oneself.

malic acid adj a colourless crystalline acid derived from fruit, esp apples.

malice n active ill will, intention to inflict injury upon another.—**malicious** adj.—**maliciously** adv.—**maliciousness** n.

malign adj harmful; evil. * vt to slander; to defame.— **malignity** n.—**malignly** adv.

malignant adj having a wish to harm others; injurious; (disease) rapidly spreading, resistant to treatment, esp of a tumour.—**malignancy** n.—**malignantly** adv.

malignity n (pl **malignities**) the state of being malignant or deadly; (often pl) (an act of) malice; virulence.

malinger vi to feign illness in order to evade work, duty.—**malingerer** n.

malison n (arch) a curse, execration.

mall n a shaded avenue, open to the public; a shopping street for pedestrians only; an enclosed shopping centre.

mallard n (pl **mallard, mallards**) a common wild duck, the ancestor of domestic breeds of duck.

malleable adj pliable; capable of being shaped.—**malleability** n.

mallee n a dwarf eucalyptus found in Australia; (with **the**) a sparsely populated area in Australia, the bush.

mallemuck n any of various sea birds, incl the fulmar and petrel.

malleolar adj pertaining to the ankle.

mallet n a small, usu wooden-headed, short-handled hammer; a long-handled version for striking the ball in the games of polo and croquet.

mallow n any of a widely found genus of plants with pink flowers and palm-shaped leaves; a similar plant, eg marshmallow.

malm n soft friable limestone rock; a loamy soil derived from this; a clay and chalk mixture used as an ingredient in brickmaking.

malmsey *n* (*pl* **malmseys**) a strong, full-flavoured sweet wine orig from Greece but now also made in Madeira, Spain, etc.

malnutrition *n* lack of nutrition.

malodorous *adj* having a foul smell, bad-smelling.—**malodorously** *adv.*—**malodorousness** *n.*

Malpighian *adj* (*anat*) pertaining to various structures, such as the capillary system, discovered by the Italian anatomist Marcello Malpighi (1628-94).

malpractice *n* professional misconduct, esp by a medical practitioner.

malt *n* a cereal grain, such as barley, which is soaked and dried and used in brewing; (*inf*) malt liquor, malt whisky.—**malty** *adj.*

maltha *n* a natural black bitumen; a mineral wax.

Malthusian *adj* of or pertaining to the British political economist Thomas Malthus (1766-1834) or his theory, which maintains that population tends to outgrow its means of subsistence and should be checked by means of birth control. * *n* an advocate of this theory.—**Malthusianism** *n.*

maltose *n* a sugar obtained from starch by the action of diatase or malt and used in bacteriological cultures and baby foods.

maltreat *vt* to treat roughly or badly.—**maltreatment** *n.*

maltster *n* a maker of or dealer in malt.

malvoisie *n* a French dessert wine similar to malmsey.

mama *n* (*inf*) mother.—*also* **mamma**.

mamba *n* a partly tree-living green or black poisonous snake of tropical and southern Africa.

Mameluke *n* (*formerly*) a member of the ruling class in Egypt.

mamma[1] *see* **mama**.

mamma[2] *n* (*pl* **mammae**) the milk-secreting organ of female mammals, such as the udder of a cow, or breast of a woman.—**mammary** *adj.*

mammal *n* any member of a class of warm-blooded vertebrates that suckle their young with milk.—**mammalian** *adj.*

mammalogy *n* the branch of zoology involving the study of mammals.—**mammalogical** *adj.*—**mammalogist** *n.*

mammee *n* a tropical American tree with edible fruit; the large red-skinned fruit from this tree (—*also* **mamee apple**).

mammiferous *adj* having breasts.

mammilla *n* (*pl* **mamillae**) *n* a nipple; a nipple-shaped thing.

mammillary *adj* of or like the breast or a nipple.

mammock *vt* (*inf*) to break in pieces; to shred. * *n* a small piece.

mammon *n* riches regarded as an object of worship and greedy pursuit; (*with cap*) (*Bible*) the pursuit of wealth personified as a false god.—**mammonism** *n.*—**mammonist** *n.*

mammoth *n* an extinct elephant with long, curved tusks. * *adj* enormous.

mammy (*pl* **mammies**) *n* (*inf*) mother, as used by a child; (*offensive*) a black nurse to white children.

man *n* (*pl* **men**) a human being, esp an adult male; the human race; an adult male with manly qualities, eg courage, virility; a male servant; an individual person; a person with specific qualities for a task, etc; an ordinary soldier, as opposed to an officer; a member of a team, etc; a piece in games such as chess,

draughts, etc; a husband. * *vt* (**manning, manned**) to provide with men for work, defence, etc.

manacle *n* (*usu pl*) a handcuff. * *vt* to handcuff; to restrain.

manage *vt* to control the movement or behaviour of; to have charge of; to direct; to succeed in accomplishing. * *vi* to carry on business; to contrive to get along.—**manageable** *adj.*

management *n* those carrying out the administration of a business; the managers collectively; the technique of managing or controlling.

manager *n* a person who manages a company, organization, etc; an agent who looks after the business affairs of an actor, writer, etc; a person who organizes the training of a sports team; a person who manages efficiently.

manageress *n* a woman who manages a business, shop, etc.

managerial *adj* of or pertaining to a manager or management.—**managerially** *adv.*

manakin *n* any of a genus of small South American birds with bright plumage and short beaks; a manikin.

mañana *adv* tomorrow; by and by. * *n* an unspecified time in the future.

man-at-arms *n* (*pl* **men-at-arms**) *n* an armed soldier, esp of medieval times.

manatee *n* a large aquatic animal resembling a whale found in tropical seas, the sea cow.

manchineel *n* a poisonous tropical American tree.

manciple *n* in UK, a catering official or steward, esp in a monastery, college, or Inn of Court.

Mancunian *adj* of Manchester. * *n* a citizen of Manchester.

mandamus *n* (*pl* **mandamuses**) (*law*) (*formerly*) a writ issued by a superior court directing the person or inferior court to whom it is issued to perform some specified act or public duty.

mandarin *n* (*formerly*) a high-ranking bureaucrat of the Chinese empire; any high-ranking official, esp one given to pedantic sometimes obscure public pronouncements; (*with cap*) the Beijing dialect that is the official pronunciation of the Chinese language; the fruit of a small spiny Chinese tree that has been developed in cultivation (—*also* **tangerine**).

mandarin collar *n* a narrow, stand-up collar, open in front.

mandatary *n* (*pl* **mandataries**) a person or nation to whom a mandate is given.

mandate *n* an order or command; the authority to act on the behalf of another, esp the will of constituents expressed to their representatives in legislatures. * *vt* to entrust by mandate.

mandatory *adj* of, containing, or having the nature of a mandate; required by mandate; compulsory; (*nation*) holding a mandate. * *n* a mandatary.—**mandatorily** *adv.*

mandible *n* the lower jaw of a vertebrate; the mouth parts of an insect; either jaw of a beaked animal.—**mandibular** *adj.*

mandolin *n* a stringed instrument similar to a lute, with four or five pairs of strings.

mandragora *n* (*poet*) mandrake; a narcotic obtained from it.

mandrake *n* a plant of the nightshade family with narcotic properties that, in folklore, shrieked when uprooted; the May apple.

mandrel, mandril n the shank of a lathe, to which work is fixed while turned; the revolving arbor of a circular saw or other machine tool; the spindle that drives the headstock of a lathe.

mandrill n a large baboon of West Africa, the male having a red and blue backside.

manducate vt (poet) to chew, eat.

mane n long hair that grows on the back of the neck of the horse, lion, etc.

man-eater n an animal that eats human flesh.

manège, manege n a school for training horses and teaching horsemanship; the movements of a trained horse.

manes n (pl:often cap) in Ancient Rome, ancestral spirits, shades; gods of the lower world; (sing) the spirit of a dead person.

maneuver n a planned and controlled movement of troops, warships, etc; a skilful or shrewd move; a stratagem. * vti to perform or cause to perform manoeuvres; to manage or plan skilfully; to move, get, make, etc by some scheme.—also **manoeuvre.**— **maneuverable, manoeuvrable** adj.—**maneuverer, manoeuvrer** n.

manful adj showing courage and resolution.—**manfully** adv.

mangabey n (pl **mangabeys**) a large, slender, arboreal, African monkey.

manganate n a salt of manganic acid.

manganese n a hard brittle metallic element; its oxide.

manganic adj pertaining to, resembling, or containing manganese in the trivalent state.

mange n a skin disease affecting mainly domestic animals, which causes itching.

mangel-wurzel n a variety of beet used as cattle-fodder.

manger n a trough in a barn or stable for livestock fodder.

mangle[1] vt to crush, mutilate; to spoil, ruin.

mangle[2] n a machine for drying and pressing sheets, etc between rollers. * vt to smooth through a mangle.

mango n (pl **mangoes**) a yellow-red fleshy tropical fruit with a firm central stone.

mangonel n an ancient military engine for hurling stones.

mangosteen n a tropical Indian tree; its red-brown, sweet, juicy fruit about the size of an orange.

mangrove n a tropical tree or shrub with root-forming branches.

mangy adj (**mangier, mangiest**) having mange; scruffy, shabby.—**manginess** n.

manhandle vt to handle roughly; to move by human force.

manhole n a hole through which one can enter a sewer, drain, etc.

manhood n the state or time of being a man; virility; courage, etc.

man-hour n the time unit equal to one hour of work done by one person.

manhunt n a hunt for a fugitive.—**manhunter** n.

mania n a mental disorder displaying sometimes violent behaviour and great excitement; great excitement or enthusiasm; a craze.

maniac n a madman; a person with wild behaviour; a person with great enthusiasm for something.—**maniacal** adj.

manic adj affected with, characterized by, or relating to mania.

manic-depressive adj of a mental disorder characterized by alternating periods of mania and deep depression. * n a person suffering from this.

Manichaeism, Manicheism the doctrine of the Manicheans, who held the dualistic theory of two eternal equal beings or principles, light (God), the author of all good, and darkness (Evil or Satan), the author of all evil, locked in a constant struggle for ascendancy; any similar doctrine.—**Manichaean, Manichean** n, adj.

Manichee n one of the sect of Manicheans.

manicure n trimming, polishing etc of fingernails.—also vt.—**manicurist** n.

manifest adj obvious, clearly evident. * vt to make clear; to display, to reveal. * n a list of a ship's or aircraft's cargo; a list of passengers on an aircraft.—**manifestation** n.—**manifestly** adv.

manifestation n the act of manifesting; the state of being manifested; the demonstration of the reality or existence of a quality, person, etc; the form of revelation of an idea, divine being, etc.

manifesto n (pl **manifestoes, manifestos**) a public printed declaration of intent and policy issued by a government or political party.

manifold adj having many forms, parts, etc; of many sorts. * n a pipe (eg in an engine) with many inlets and outlets. * vt to make copies of.—**manifolder** n.

manikin n a little man, a dwarf; an anatomical model of the body; a mannequin.—also **mannikin.**

manila, manilla n a strong, buff-coloured paper originally made from hemp from the Philippines.

manioc n cassava, a tropical plant from the roots of which tapioca and cassava are prepared.

maniple n (formerly) a band worn on the left arm by a priest at mass; a company of a Roman legion.

manipulate vt to work or handle skilfully; to manage shrewdly or artfully, often in an unfair way.—**manipulation** n.—**manipulative** adj.—**manipulator** n.

manipulation n the act or process of manipulating; the state of being manipulated; the movement of bones, etc, by a physiotherapist; shrewd or knowing management of others for one's own ends.—**manipulatory** adj.

manitou, manitu (pl **manitous, manitus, manitou, manitu**) n an American Indian spirit of good or evil.

mankind n the human race.

manly adj (**manlier, manliest**) appropriate in character to a man; strong; virile.—**manliness** n.

man-made adj manufactured or created by man; artificial, synthetic.

manna n (Bible) the food miraculously given to the ancient Israelites in the wilderness; any help that comes unexpectedly.

manned adj performed by a person; (spacecraft, etc) having a human crew.

mannequin n a model in a fashion show; a life-size model of the human body, used to fit or display clothes.

manner n a method of way of doing something; behaviour; type or kind; habit; (pl) polite social behaviour.

mannered adj full of mannerisms; artificial, stylized, etc.

mannerism n an idiosyncracy; an affected habit or style in dress, behaviour or gesture; (with cap) a post-Reformation movement in art that held that beauty should be represented as an ideal and used exaggeration and distortion of naturalistic forms to attain this.—**mannerist** adj, n.

mannerless *n* rude, bad-mannered.

mannerly *adj* polite; respectful. * *adv* politely; respectfully.—**mannerliness** *n*.

mannikin *see* **manikin**.

mannish *adj* like or pertaining to a man; (*woman*) masculine, aping men.—**mannishly** *adv*.—**mannishness** *n*.

manoeuvre *see* **maneuver**.

man-of-war *n* (*pl* **men-of-war**) a (sailing) warship.

manometer *n* an instrument for measuring the pressure of gases and liquids.—**manometric, manometrical** *adj*.

manor *n* a landed estate; the main house on such an estate; (*sl*) a police district.—**manorial** *adj*.

manpower *n* power furnish ed by human str ength; the collective availability for work of people in a given area.

manqué *adj* potential; unsuccessful, failed.

mansard (roof) *n* a roof with a break in its slope, the lower part being steeper than the upper.

manse *n* a nonconformist clergyman's house; (*Scot*) the house of a minister, esp a Church of Scotland parish minister; (*arch*) a large house.

manservant *n* (*pl* **menservants**) a male servant, esp a valet.

mansion *n* a large, imposing house.

manslaughter *n* the killing of a human being by another, esp when unlawful but without malice.

mansuetude *n* (*arch*) gentleness, mildness.

manta (ray) *n* a very large fish with a flattened body and wing-like fins.

mantel *n* the facing above a fireplace; the shelf above a fireplace.—*also* **mantelpiece**.

mantelet *n* a woman's short cape of the mid-19th century; a movable, protective screen, formerly used by besiegers, gunners, pioneers, etc (—*also* **mantlet**).

mantic *adj* of, having the power of, or pertaining to divination.

manticore *n* a fabulous beast with a human head, the body of a lion, and the tail of a scorpion.

mantilla *n* a scarf, usu of lace, worn as a headdress in Spain and South America; a woman's light cloak or hood.

mantis *n* (*pl* **mantises, mantes**) an insect that preys on other insects.—*also* **praying mantis**.

mantissa *n* (*math*) the decimal part of a logarithm.

mantle *n* a loose cloak; anything that envelops or conceals; a fine mesh cover on a gas or oil lamp that emits light by incandescence. * *vt* to cover as with a mantle. * *vi* to be or become covered.

mantlet *see* **mantelet**.

mantra *n* (*Hinduism, Buddhism*) a devotional incantation used in prayer, meditation and in certain forms of yoga.

mantua *n* a woman's loose gown of the 17th and 18th centuries, worn with the front of the skirt caught up or back to show an underskirt.

manual *adj* of the hands; operated, done, or used by the hand; involving physical skill or hard work rather than the mind. * *n* a handy book for use as a guide, reference, etc; a book of instructions.—**manually** *adv*.

manufactory *n* (*pl* **manufactories**) *n* (*obs*) a factory, workshop.

manufacture *vt* to make, esp on a large scale, using machinery; to invent, fabricate. * *n* the production of goods by manufacturing.—**manufacturer** *n*.

manumit *vt* (**manumitting, manumitted**) to release

from slavery; to free.—**manumission** *n*.—**manumitter** *n*.

manure *n* animal dung used to fertilize soil. * *vt* to spread manure on.

manus *n* (*pl* **manus**) (*zool*) the hand or that part of the anatomy corresponding to the hand; in ancient Roman law, the fact of a woman's legal subjugation to her husband.

manuscript *n* a book or document that is handwritten or typewritten as opposed to printed; an author's original handwritten or typewritten copy as submitted to a publisher before typesetting and printing.

many *adj* (**more, most**) numerous. * *n* a large number of persons or things.

manyplies *n sing* a ruminant's third stomach, the omasum.

many-sided *adj* with many aspects; versatile.—**many-sidedness** *n*.

Maori *n* (*pl* **Maoris, Maori**) a member of the indigenous peoples of New Zealand; their language.—*also adj*.

map *n* a representation of all or part of the earth's surface, showing either natural features as continents and seas, etc or man-made features as roads, railways etc. * *vt* (**mapping, mapped**) to make a map of.

maple *n* a tree with two-winged fruits, grown for shade, wood, or sap; its hard light-coloured wood; the flavour of the syrup or sugar made from the sap of the sugar maple.

Mar. *abbr* = March.

mar *vt* (**marring, marred**) to blemish, to spoil, to impair.

marabout[1], **marabou** *n* a large African stork with handsome feathers and a short neck; its down, used as trimming, etc; a material produced from a fine raw silk.

marabout[2] *n* in North Africa, a Muslim hermit or saint; the shrine or burial place of a marabout.

maraca *n* a dried gourd or plastic shell filled with beans, pebbles, etc and shaken as a rhythm instrument.

maraschino *n* a strong sweet liqueur made from a type of wild cherry.

maraschino cherry *n* a cherry preserved in maraschino.

marasmus *n* emaciation or atrophy, esp in babies.—**marasmic** *adj*.

marathon *n* a foot race of 26 miles, 385 yards (42.195 km); any endurance contest.

maraud *vi* to roam in search of plunder.—**marauder** *n*.—**marauding** *adj*.

marble *n* a hard limestone rock that takes a high polish; a block or work of art made of marble; a little ball of stone, glass, etc; (*pl*) a children's game played with such balls; (*pl*) (*sl*) wits. * *adj* of or like marble.—**marbly** *adj*.

marbled *adj* veined or mottled like marble; (*meat*) streaked with fat.

marc *n* (*winemaking*) the refuse from pressed fruit; a brandy derived from this.

marcasite *n* white iron pyrites; a white metal, esp steel, cut and polished for use in jewellery.

marcel (wave) *n* a style of artificially waving the hair, popular in the 1920s and 1930s. * *vt* (**marcelling, marcelled**) to style in regular waves.

marcescent *adj* (*bot*) withering without falling off.—**marcescence** *n*.

March *n* the third month of the year having 31 days.

march *vi* to walk with regular steps, as in military formation; to advance steadily. * *vt* to make a person or group march. * n a steady advance; a regular, steady step; the distance covered in marching; a piece of music for marching.—**marcher** n.

marching orders npl official orders for infantry to move to a particular destination; (inf) a notice of dismissal.

marchioness n the wife or widow of a marquess; a woman of the rank of marquess.

Mardi gras n the last day before Lent, Shrove Tuesday, a day of carnival in some cities, esp New Orleans.

mare n a mature female horse, mule, donkey.

mare clausum n (law) a body of water under one country's jurisdiction and closed to foreign ships.

mare liberum n (law) a body of water open to ships of all countries.

maremma (pl **maremme**) n an unhealthy marshy coastal district, esp in Italy.

mare's-tail n an aquatic plant with tiny flowers and tapering leaves; a wisp of trailing alto-cirrus cloud indicating strong winds at high altitude.

margaric adj pertaining to, or like, a pearl.

margarine n a butter substitute made from vegetable and animal fats, etc.

margarite n a pearly translucent mineral related to mica; a bead-like rock formation.

margay n a South American tiger cat.

margin n a border, edge; the blank border of a printed or written page; an amount beyond what is needed; provision for increase, error, etc; (commerce) the difference between cost and selling price.

marginal adj written in the margin; situated at the margin or border; close to the lower limit of acceptability; very slight, insignificant; (Brit politics) denoting a constituency where the sitting MP has only a small majority. * n a marginal constituency.—**marginally** adv.

marginalia npl notes written in the margin of a book, etc.

marginalize vt to transfer someone away from the centre of affairs in order to render them powerless.

marginate adj (biol) having a margin. * vt to border something with a margin.—**margination** n.

margrave n (formerly) a German nobleman, one rank above a count.

margraviate, margravate n the domain or jurisdiction of a margrave.

margravine a female margrave; a margrave's wife or widow.

marguerite n a large daisy with white or yellow flowers.

Marian adj pertaining to the Virgin Mary, or to Mary, Queen of England, or to Mary, Queen of Scots. * n one who worships the Virgin Mary; a partisan of Mary, Queen of England or Mary, Queen of Scots.

marigold n a plant with a yellow or orange flower.

marijuana, marihuana n a narcotic obtained by smoking the dried flowers and leaves of the hemp plant.—also **cannabis, pot**.

marimba n a South American xylophone.

marina n a small harbour with pontoons, docks, services, etc for yachts and pleasure craft.

marinade n a seasoning liquid in which meat, fish, etc is soaked to enhance flavour or to tenderize it before cooking. * vt to soak in a marinade.—also **marinate**.

marine adj of, in, near, or relating to the sea; maritime; nautical; naval. * n a soldier trained for service on land or sea; naval or merchant ships.

mariner n a seaman, sailor.

Mariolatry n the exaggerated worship of the Virgin Mary.

marionette n a little jointed doll or puppet moved by strings or wires.

marital adj of marriage, matrimonial.

maritime adj on, near, or living near the sea; of navigation, shipping, etc.

marjoram n a fragrant herb used in cooking and salads.

mark¹ n a spot, scratch, etc on a surface; a distinguishing sign or characteristic; a cross made instead of a signature; a printed or written symbol, as a punctuation mark; a brand or label on an article showing the maker, etc; an indication of some quality, character, etc; a grade for academic work; a standard of quality; impression, influence, etc; a target; (sl) a potential victim for a swindle.* vt to make a mark or marks on; to identify as by a mark; to show plainly; to heed; to grade, rate; (Brit football) to stay close to an opponent so as to hinder his play.

mark² n the basic monetary unit of Germany.

marked adj having a mark or marks; noticeable; obvious.—**markedly** adv.

marker n one that marks; something used for marking.

market n a meeting of people for buying and selling merchandise; a space or building in which a market is held; the chance to sell or buy; demand for (goods, etc); a region where goods can be sold; a section of the community offering demand for goods. * vti to offer for sale; to sell, buy domestic provisions.—**marketability** n.—**marketable** adj.

marketing n act of buying or selling; all the processes involved in moving goods from the producer to the consumer.

market-making n the activity of buying and selling stocks, shares, bonds, securities, etc.—**market-maker** n.

marketplace n a market in a public square; the world of economic trade and activity; a sphere in which ideas, opinions, etc compete for acceptance.

market research n the gathering of factual information from consumers concerning their preferences for goods and services.

marking n the conferring of a mark or marks; the characteristic arrangement of marks, as on fur or feathers.

marksman n (pl **marksmen**) one who is skilled at shooting.—**marksmanship** n.

markup n a selling at an increased price; the amount of increase.—also vt.

marl¹ n a mixture of clay and carbonate of lime, used as a manure. * vt to manure with marl.—**marly** adj.

marl² vt (naut) to wind with marlines, securing with a hitch at each turn.

marline, marlin, marling n (naut) a two-stranded cord, often tarred, used for winding round ropes, splicing, etc.

marlinespike, marlinspike, marlingspike n a pointed piece of iron used for opening the strands of a rope in splicing, etc.

marmalade n a jam-like preserve made from oranges, sugar and water.

marmoreal, marmorean adj of or like marble.

marmoset n a small monkey of South and Central America.

marmot n a widely distributed rodent with rough fur, a bushy tail and short legs.

maroon¹ n a dark brownish red (—also adj); a type of distress rocket.

maroon² *vt* to abandon alone, esp on a desolate island; to leave helpless and alone.

marque *n* a brand of a product, esp a car.

marquee *n* a large tent used for entertainment; a canopy over an entrance, as to a theatre.

marquess *n* In UK, a title of nobility ranking between a duke and an earl.

marquetry, marqueterie *n* (*pl* **marquetries, marqueteries**) decorative inlaid veneers of wood, ivory, etc used esp in furniture.

marquis *n* (*pl* **marquises, marquis**) (*Europe*) a nobleman equivalent in rank to a British marquess.

marquisate *n* the estate, dignity, or lordship of a marquis.

marquise *n* a marchioness; a gemstone or ring setting cut in an oval pointed form.

marriage *n* the legal contract by which a woman and man become wife and husband; a wedding, either religious or civil; a close union.

marriageable *adj* of an age to marry.—**marriageability** *n*.

marron glacé *n* (*pl* **marrons glacés**) *n* a cooked chestnut coated with sugar.

marrow *n* the fatty tissue in the cavities of bones; the best part or essence of anything; a widely grown green fruit eaten as a vegetable.

marrowbone *n* a bone containing marrow used in cooking.

marrowfat, marrow pea *n* a late variety of pe.. that has large seeds; the seed of one of these.

marry¹ *vb* (**marrying, married**) *vt* to join as wife and husband; to take in marriage; to unite. * *vi* to get married.

marry² *interj* (*arch*) indeed, forsooth.

Mars *n* the Roman god of war; the planet next to Earth, further away from the sun; (*alchemy*) iron.

Marsala *n* a sweet fortified wine from Sicily.

Marseillaise *adj* pertaining to the city of Marseilles in France or to its inhabitants. * *n* the French national anthem, orig a well-known song of the French Revolution, composed in 1792.

marsh *n* an area of boggy, poorly drained land.—**marshiness** *n*.—**marshy** *adj*.

marshal *n* in some armies, a general officer of the highest rank; an official in charge of ceremonies, parades, etc. * *vt* (**marshalling, marshalled** *or* **marshaling, marshaled**) (*ideas, troops*) to arrange in order; to guide.—**marshaller** *n*.

marsh mallow *n* a perennial plant with a pink flower and a mucilaginous root used in confectionery and medicine.

marshmallow *n* a soft spongy confection made of sugar, gelatin, etc; (*formerly*) a sweet paste made from the root of the marsh mallow.

marsupial *adj* of an order of mammals that carry their young in a pouch. * *n* an animal of this kind, as a kangaroo, opossum.

marsupium *n* (*pl* **marsupia**) in female marsupials, an external pouch for carrying and nurturing young.

mart *n* a market.

martagon *n* a variety of lily with purple-red flowers found in Europe and Asia; a Turk's-cap lily.

Martello tower *n* (*formerly*) a small round fort used for coastal defence.

marten *n* (*pl* **martens, marten**) a carnivorous tree-dwelling weasel-like mammal.

martial *adj* warlike; military.—**martially** *adv*.

martial arts *npl* systems of self-defence, usu from the Orient, practised as sports, as karate or judo.

martial law *n* rule by military authorities over civilians, as during a war or political emergency.

Martian *adj* of or relating to the planet Mars. * *n* an inhabitant of Mars.

martin *n* one of various types of bird similar to the swallow, with a characteristic shape of tail; the house martin.

martinet *n* one who exerts strong discipline.—**martinetish, martinettish** *adj*.

martingale, martingal *n* a broad strap passing from the noseband to the girth of a horse between its forelegs to keep its head down and prevent it from rearing; a gambling system of doubling successive stakes; (*naut*) a short spar under the bowsprit used as a lower stay for the jib boom or flying jib boom.

martini *n* (*trademark*) (*often with cap*) Italian vermouth; a cocktail of gin and vermouth

Martinmas *n* St Martin's Day, November 11, a Christian festival; one of the Scottish quarter days.

martlet *n* (*arch*) a martin; (*her*) a bird without legs or beak.

martyr *n* a person tortured for a belief or cause; a person who suffers from an illness. * *vt* to kill as a martyr; to make a martyr of.—**martyrdom** *n*.

martyrize *vt* to martyr.

martyrology *n* (*pl* **martyrologies**) *n* a register or history of martyrs; the study of the lives of the martyrs.—**martyrological, martyrologic** *adj*.—**martyrologist** *n*.

martyry *n* (*pl* **martyries**) *n* a shrine in honour of a martyr.

marvel *n* anything wonderful; a miracle. * *vti* (**marvelling, marvelled** *or* **marveling, marveled**) to become filled with wonder, surprise, etc.—**marvellous, marvelous** *adj*.

Marxian *n* a student or advocate of Marxism.—*also adj*.

Marxism *n* the theory and practice developed by Karl Marx and Friedrich Engels advocating public ownership of the means of production and the dictatorship of the proletariat until the establishment of a classless society.—**Marxist** *adj, n*.

marzipan *n* a paste made from ground almonds, sugar and egg white, used to coat cakes or make confectionery.

mascara *n* a cosmetic for darkening the eyelashes.

mascle *n* (*her*) a lozenge perforated with a lozenge shape; a voided lozenge.

mascot *n* a person, animal or thing thought to bring good luck.

masculine *adj* having characteristics of or appropriate to the male sex; (*gram*) of the male gender.—**masculinity** *n*.

MASH *abbr* = mobile army surgical hospital.

mash *n* any soft, pulpy mass; crushed malt and hot water for brewing; (*inf*) mashed potatoes. * *vt* to crush into a mash.

mashie *n* (*formerly*) an iron golf club with a deep, short blade, more or less lofted.

mask¹ *n* a covering to conceal or protect the face; a moulded likeness of the face; anything that conceals or disguises; a respirator placed over the nose and mouth to aid or prevent inhalation of a gas; (*surgery*) a protective gauze placed over the nose and mouth to prevent the spread of germs; (*photog*) a screen used to cover part of a sensitive surface to prevent exposure by light. * *vt* to cover or conceal as with a mask; to disguise one's intentions or character.—**masked** *adj*.

mask² *see* **masque.**

masker *n* a masked person; a participant in a masque or masquerade.—*also* **masquer.**

masochism *n* abnormal pleasure, esp sexual, obtained from having physical or mental pain inflicted on one by another person.—**masochist** *n.*—**masochistic** *adj.*

mason *n* a person skilled in working or building with stone; (*with cap*) a Freemason.

masonic *adj* (*often cap*) relating to Freemasonry.

masonry *n* (*pl* **masonries**) stonework.

Masora, Masorah *n* a critical work in Hebrew by the rabbis of the 6-10th cents., indicating how the verbal text of the Bible is to be written in accordance with ancient rules; the critical notes and commentaries of this.—**Masoretic** *adj.*

masque *n* a poetic drama with pageantry, pantomime, dance, song, etc, popular in 16th and 17th-century England; the words and music for one of these; a masquerade.—*also* **mask.**

masquer *see* **masker.**

masquerade *n* a ball or party at which fancy dress and masks are worn; a pretence, false show. * *vi* to take part in a masquerade; to pretend to be what one is not.—**masquerader** *n.*

Mass. *abbr* = Massachusetts.

Mass *n* (*RC Church*) the celebration of the Eucharist.

mass *n* (*pl* **masses**) a quantity of matter of indefinite shape and size; a large quantity or number; bulk; size; the main part; (*physics*) the property of a body expressed as a measure of the amount of material contained in it; (*pl*) the common people, esp the lower social classes. * *adj* of or for the masses or for a large number. * *vti* to gather or form into a mass.

massacre *n* the cruel and indiscriminate killing of many people or animals. * *vt* to kill in large numbers.

massage *n* a kneading and rubbing of the muscles to stimulate the circulation of the blood. * *vt* to give a massage to.

massé shot *n* in billiards, a stroke with the cue held upright, usu to cause the ball to curve round another ball before it hits the intended ball.

masseur *n* a man who gives a massage professionally.—**masseuse** *nf.*

massif *n* a central mountain mass; a large plateau with distinct edges.

massive *adj* big, solid, or heavy; large and imposing; relatively large in comparison to normal; extensive.—**massively** *adv.*—**massiveness** *n.*

mass media *npl* newspapers, radio, television, and other means of communication with large numbers of people.

mass production *n* quantity production of goods, esp by machinery and division of labour.

massy *adj* (**massier massiest**) (*arch*) massive.

mast *n* a tall vertical pole used to support the sails on a ship; a vertical pole from which a flag is flown; a tall structure supporting a television or radio aerial.

mastaba, mastabah *n* an early Egyptian tomb with a flat roof, the prototype of the pyramids.

mast cell *n* a large blood-borne cell that has a fast-acting role in the body's immune system in fighting inflammation.

mastectomy *n* (*pl* **mastectomies**) the removal of a breast by surgery.

master *n* a man who rules others or has control over something, esp the head of a household; an employer; an owner of an animal or slave; the captain of a merchant ship; a male teacher in a private school; an expert craftsman; a writer or painter regarded as great; an original from which a copy can be made, esp a phonograph record or magnetic tape; (*with cap*) a title for a boy; one holding an advanced academic degree. * *adj* being a master; chief; main; controlling. * *vt* to be for become master of; (*in art, etc*) to become expert.—**mastership** *n.*

master-at-arms *n* (*pl* **masters-at-arms**) a ship's chief petty officer with responsibility for policing, administration, etc.

masterful *adj* acting the part of a master; domineering; expert; skilful.—**masterfully** *adv.*—**masterfulness** *n.*

masterly *adj* expert; skilful.—**masterliness** *n.*

mastermind *n* a very clever person, esp one who plans or directs a project. * *vt* to be the mastermind of.

masterpiece *n* a work done with extraordinary skill; the greatest work of a person or group.

masterstroke *n* brilliant stroke of policy, skill, etc.

masterwork *n* a masterpiece.

mastery *n* control as by a master; victory; expertise.

masthead *n* the top of a mast; the title and ownership details, etc of a newspaper or periodical printed on the front page.

mastic *n* an aromatic resin from mastic trees used chiefly in varnishes; a type of putty used for sealing wood, plaster, etc.

masticate *vt* to chew food before swallowing; to reduce to a pulp.—**mastication** *n.*—**masticator** *n.*

masticatory *adj* adapted for, or pertaining to, chewing. * *n* (*pl* **masticatories**) (*med*) something chewed in order to promote the flow of saliva.

mastiff *n* a breed of large, thickset dogs used chiefly as watchdogs.

mastitis *n* an inflammation of a female breast or an udder.

mastodon *n* any of an extinct genus of mammals allied to the elephant.—**mastodonic** *adj.*

mastoid *n* the bony prominence behind the ear.

masturbate *vi* to manually stimulate one's sexual organs to achieve orgasm without sexual intercourse.—**masturbation** *n.*

mat¹ *n* a piece of material of woven fibres, etc, used for protection, as under a vase, etc, or on the floor; a thick pad used in wrestling, gymnastics, etc; anything interwoven or tangled into a thick mass. * *vti* (**matting, matted**) to cover as with a mat; to interweave or tangle into a thick mass.

mat² *adj* without lustre, dull.—*also* **matt.**

matador *n* the bullfighter who kills the bull with a sword.

match¹ *n* a thin strip of wood or cardboard tipped with a chemical that ignites under friction.

match² *n* any person or thing equal or similar to another; two persons or things that go well together; a contest or game; a mating or marriage. * *vt* to join in marriage; to put in opposition (*with, against*); to be equal or similar to; (*one thing*) to suit to another. * *vi* to be equal, similar, suitable, etc.

matchboard *n* one of a number of thin planks tongued and grooved to fit together, used for panelling, etc.

matchbox *n* a small box for holding matches.

matchless *adj* unequalled.—**matchlessly** *adv.*

matchmaker *n* a person who arranges marriages for people; one who schemes to bring about the marriage of two others; a maker of matches.

match play *n* (*golf*) scoring by the number of holes won as opposed to strokes played.

match point n (*tennis, badminton, etc*) the situation where the winner of the next point wins the match.

matchwood n wood suitable for making matches; wood splinters or fragments.

maté n an evergreen South American shrub, related to holly; an infusion of its dried leaves which makes a mildly stimulating tea,.—*also* **Paraguay tea.**

mate[1] n an associate or colleague; (*inf*) a friend; one of a matched pair; a marriage partner; the male or female of paired animals; an officer of a merchant ship, ranking below the master. * vti to join as a pair; to couple in marriage or sexual union.

mate[2] vt to checkmate.

matelote n a stew of fish cooked with wine, etc.

mater n (*sl*) mother.

materfamilias n (*pl* **matresfamilias**) the mother of a family or mistress of a household.

material adj of, derived from, or composed of matter, physical; of the body or bodily needs, comfort, etc, not spiritual; important, essential, etc. * n what a thing is, or may be made of; elements or parts; cloth, fabric; (*pl*) tools, etc needed to make or do something; a person regarded as fit for a particular task, position, etc.

materialism n concern with money and possessions rather than spiritual values; the doctrine that everything in the world, including thought, can be explained only in terms of matter.—**materialist** n.—**materialistic** adj.

materiality n (*pl* **materialities**) the quality or state of being material; material existence; substance.

materialize vt to give material form to. * vi to become fact; to make an unexpected appearance.—**materialization** n.

materially adv physically; to a great extent; substantially.

materia medica n the science of substances used in medicine incl pharmacology, pharmacy, etc; a substance employed as a medicine or in making drugs.

materiel, matériel n the baggage, munitions, and provisions of an army or of any other organization.

maternal adj of, like, or from a mother; related through the mother's side of the family.—**maternally** adv.

maternity n motherhood; motherliness. * adj relating to pregnancy.

matey n a crony or companion (often used when directly addressing such). * adj (**matier, matiest**) (*inf*) friendly, sociable.—**mateyness, matiness** n.—**matily** adv.

math n (*inf*) mathematics.

mathematical, mathematic adj of, like or concerned with mathematics; exact and precise.—**mathematically** adv.

mathematics n (*used as sing*) the science dealing with quantities, forms, space, etc and their relationships by the use of numbers and symbols; (*sing or pl*) the mathematical operations or processes used in a particular problem, discipline, etc. —**mathematician** n.

maths n (*inf*) mathematics.

matin, matinal adj of or pertaining to the morning or to matins.

matinée n a daytime, esp an afternoon performance of a play, etc.

matins n sing or pl (*Anglican Church*) a morning prayer; (*RC Church*) one of the canonical hours of prayer; (*poet*) a bird's morning song.

matriarch n a woman who heads or rules her family or tribe.—**matriarchal, matriarchic** adj.

matriarchy n (*pl* **matriarchies**) form of social organization in which the mother is the ruler of the family or tribe and in which descent is traced through the mother.

matrices see **matrix.**

matricide n a person who kills his (her) mother; the killing of one's mother.—**matricidal** adj.

matriculate vti to enrol, esp as a student.—**matriculation** n.

matrimony n (*pl* **matrimonies**) the act or rite of marriage; the married state.—**matrimonial** adj.—**matrimonially** adv.

matrix n (*pl* **matrices, matrixes**) the place, substance, etc from which something originates; a mould; the connective intercellular substance in bone, cartilage, or other tissue; (*math*) a rectangular grid of quantities in rows and columns used in solving certain problems.

matron n a wife or widow, esp one of mature appearance and manner; a woman in charge of domestic and nursing arrangements in a school, hospital or other institution.—**matronal** adj.

matronly adj pertaining to or suitable for a matron; sedate, dignified; (*figure*) plump.—**matronliness** n.

matronymic see **metronymic.**

matt see **mat**[2].

matter n what a thing is made of; material; whatever occupies space and is perceptible to the senses; any specified substance; content of thought or expression; a quantity; a thing or affair; significance; trouble, difficulty; pus. * vi to be of importance.

matter-of-fact adj relating to facts, not opinions, imagination, etc.

matting n a coarse material, such as woven straw or hemp, used for making mats.

mattock n a pick with one head like an axe, the other like an adze.

mattress n a casing of strong cloth filled with cotton, foam rubber, coiled springs, etc, used on a bed.

maturate vti (*med*) to discharge pus, to fester; (*arch*) to bring or come to maturation.—**maturative** adj.

maturation n the process of ripening or coming to maturity; (*biol*) the progressive generation of cells already present in the ovary and testis, mitosis; (*rare*) the act of discharging pus, suppuration.

mature adj mentally and physically well-developed, grown-up; (*fruit, cheese, etc*) ripe; (*bill*) due; (*plan*) completely worked out. * vti to make or become mature; to become due.—**maturely** adv.—**matureness** n.

maturity n the state of being mature; full development; the date a loan becomes due.

matutinal adj of, happening during, or pertaining to the morning; early.—**matutinally** adv.

maud n (*Scot*) a grey-striped woollen plaid worn by shepherds.

maudlin adj foolishly sentimental; tearfully drunk.

maul vt to bruise or lacerate; to paw.

maulstick n a long stick used by painters as a rest for the hand while painting.—*also* **mahlstick.**

maund n any of various Asian units of weight, varying from 25 pounds (11 kilograms) to 82 pounds (37 kilograms), according to locality.

maunder vi to speak, act or move listlessly or purposelessly.—**maunderer** n.

Maundy Thursday the Thursday before Good Friday, in remembrance of the Last Supper.

mausoleum n (*pl* **mausoleums, mausolea**) a large tomb.

mauve *n* any of several shades of pale purple. * *adj* of this colour.

maverick *n* an independent-minded or unorthodox individual; an unbranded animal, eg a stray calf.

mavis *n* the song thrush.

mavourneen, mavournin *n* (*Irish*) my darling.

maw *n* the stomach, crop or throat of animals, esp those who require large quantities of food; (*inf*) the throat and stomach of a person who eats food indiscriminately and in large quantities.

mawkish *adj* maudlin; insipid.—**mawkishly** *adv.*—**mawkishness** *n*.

max. *abbr* = maximum.

maxilla *n* (*pl* **maxillae, maxillas**) the upper jawbone; in some insects, any of several parts of the mouth used as a secondary jaw.—**maxillar, maxillary** *adj*.

maxim *n* a concise rule of conduct; a precept.

maxima *see* **maximum**.

maximal *adj* of, consisting of, or pertaining to a maximum; (*math*) last in order. * *n* (*math*) in an ordered set, the member last in order.—**maximally** *adv*.

maximalist *n* one who insists on maximum demands without compromise; (*often with cap*) one who advocates direct action as a means of accomplishing something, esp social and political ends.

maximize *vt* to increase to a maximum.—**maximization** *n*.

maximum *n* (*pl* **maxima, maximums**) the greatest quantity, number, etc. * *adj* highest; greatest possible reached.

maxixe *n* a Brazilian round dance similar to the tango, and like the two-step in rhythm.

maxwell *n* a unit of magnetic flux in the cgs system.

May *n* the fifth month of the year having 31 days.

may *vb aux* (*past* **might**) expressing possibility; permission; wish or hope.

maya *n* (*Hinduism*) illusion, esp that of the world as experienced by the senses as non-material.

May apple *n* an American plant with an egg-shaped edible fruit; its fruit.

maybe *adv* perhaps.

May Day *n* the first day of May, celebrated as a traditional spring festival; observed in many countries as a labour holiday.

Mayday *n* the international radio-telephone signal indicating a ship or aircraft in distress.

mayhem *n* violent destruction, confusion.

mayn't = may not.

mayonnaise *n* a salad dressing made from egg yolks whisked with oil and lemon juice or vinegar.

mayor *n* the chief administrative officer of a municipality.—**mayoral** *adj.*—**mayorship** *n*.

mayoralty *n* (*pl* **mayoralties**) the office or term of office of a mayor.

mayoress *n* the wife of a mayor; a female mayor.

maypole *n* a flower-decked pole hung with ribbons around which May Day festivities are held.

Mazdaism *n* Zoroastrianism.

maze *n* a confusing, intricate network of pathways, esp one with high hedges in a garden; a labyrinth; a confused state.—*adj* **maze like**.

mazer *n* (*arch*) a large drinking cup of hard wood or metal.

mazuma *n* (*sl*) money.

mazurka, mazourka *n* a Polish folk dance in triple time; a musical composition for or imitating this.

mazy, mazier, maziest *adj* intricate, winding; perplexing.—**mazily** *adv.*—**maziness** *n*.

MB *abbr* = Bachelor of Medicine; megabyte.

MBA *abbr* = Master of Business Administration.

MD *abbr* = Maryland; Doctor of Medicine; Managing Director.

Md (*chem symbol*) mendelevium.

MDMA *abbr* = methylene dioxymethamphetamine, a synthetic drug used as the stimulant Ecstasy.

me *pers pron* the objective case of I.

ME[1] *abbr* = myalgic encephalomyelitis.

ME[2], **Me** *abbr* = Maine.

mead *n* a wine made from a fermented solution of honey and spices.

meadow *n* a piece of land where grass is grown for hay; low, level, moist grassland.

meadowlark *n* one of two North American yellow-breasted songbirds related to the Baltimore oriole; any of several birds of South, Central and North America.

meadowsweet *n* a fragrant white-flowered plant of Europe and Asia.

meagre, meager *adj* thin, emaciated; lacking in quality or quantity.—**meagerly, meagrely** *adv.*—**meagerness, meagreness** *n*.

meal[1] *n* any of the times for eating, as lunch, dinner, etc; the food served at such a time.

meal[2] *n* any coarsely ground edible grain; any substance similarly ground.—**mealiness** *n.*—**mealy** *adj*.

mealy-mouthed *adj* not outspoken and blunt; euphemistic; devious in speech.

mean[1] *adj* selfish, ungenerous; despicable; shabby; bad-tempered; (*sl*) difficult; (*sl*) expert.—**meanly** *adv.*—**meanness** *n*.

mean[2] *adj* halfway between extremes; average. * *n* what is between extremes.

mean[3] *vb* (**meaning, meant**) *vt* to have in mind; to intend; to intend to express; to signify. * *vi* to have a (specified) degree of importance, effect, etc.

meander *n* a winding path esp a labyrinth; a winding of a stream or river. * *vi* (*river*) to wind; to wander aimlessly.—**meandering** *adj*.

meanie *n* (*inf*) one who is mean, selfish, etc.—*also* **meanie** *pl* **meanies**).

meaning *n* sense; significance; import. * *adj* significant.—**meaningful** *adj.*—**meaningless** *adj*.

means *npl* that by which something is done; resources; wealth.

meant *see* **mean**[3].

meantime, meanwhile *adv* in or during the intervening time; at the same time. * *n* the intervening time.

meany *see* **meanie**.

measles *n* (*used as sing*) an acute, contagious viral disease, characterized by small red spots on the skin.

measly *adj* (**measlier, measliest**) (*inf*) slight, worthless; having measles.

measure *n* the extent, dimension, capacity, etc of anything; a determining of this, measurement; a unit of measurement; any standard of valuation; an instrument for measuring; a definite quantity measured out; a course of action; a statute, law; a rhythmical unit. * *vt* to find out the extent, dimensions etc of, esp by a standard; to mark off by measuring; to be a measure of. * *vi* to be of specified measurements.—**measurable** *adj.*—**measurably** *adv*.

measured *adj* set or marked off by a standard; rhythmical, regular; carefully planned or considered.

measureless *adj* infinite, without limit.—**measurelessly** *adv*.

measurement *n* a measuring or being measured; an extent or quantity determined by measuring; a system of measuring or of measures.

meat *n* animal flesh; food as opposed to drink; the essence of something.

meatball *n* a small ball of ground meat usu mixed with breadcrumbs and spices; (*inf*) a stupid or foolish person.

meatus *n* (*pl* **meatuses, meatus**) any passage in the body, eg the ear canal.

meaty *adj* (**meatier, meatiest**) full of meat; full of substance.

mecca *n* a place of pilgrimage or a goal of aspiration; a resort or attraction that is visited by a large number of people; (*with cap*) Islam's holiest city, the birthplace of Muhammed (*c.* AD570) (—*also* **Makkah**).

mechanic *n* a person skilled in maintaining or operating machines, cars, etc.

mechanical *adj* of or using machinery or tools; produced or operated by machinery; done as if by a machine, lacking thought or emotion; of the science of mechanics.—**mechanically** *adv*.

mechanician, *n* a person skilled in mechanics or machinery; a technician; a mechanist.

mechanics *n* (*used as sing*) the science of motion and the action of forces on bodies; knowledge of machinery; (*pl*) the technical aspects of something.

mechanism *n* the working parts of a machine; any system of interrelated parts; any physical or mental process by which a result is produced.

mechanist *n* an expert in mechanics, a mechanician; an advocate of mechanistic philosophy.

mechanistic *adj* of or pertaining to mechanics; of or relating to mechanism; attributing phenomena to physical or biological causes.—**mechanistically** *adv*.

mechanize *vt* to make mechanical; to equip with machinery or motor vehicles.—**mechanization** *n*.—**mechanized** *adj*.

meconium *n* the first faeces of a baby; the juice of the poppy; opium.

MEd *abbr* = Master of Education.

medal *n* a small, flat piece of inscribed metal, commemorating some event or person or awarded for some distinction.—**medallic** *adj*.

medallion *n* a large medal; a design, portrait, etc shaped like a medal; a medal worn on a chain around the neck.

medallist, medalist *n* one awarded a medal.

meddle *vi* to interfere in another's affairs.—**meddler** *n*.—**meddlesome** *adj*.

Mede *n* an inhabitant of Media, an ancient country in southwest Asia to the south of the Caspian Sea.—**Median** *n, adj*.

media *see* **medium**.

mediaeval *see* **medieval**.

mediaevalism, mediaevalist *see* **medievalism**.

medial *adj* of or in the middle; mean, average; (*math*) pertaining to or denoting an average; median; (*phonetics*) denoting a sound made by using an average amount of muscular tension, neither strongly vocalized nor gently pronounced.

median *adj* middle; intermediate. * *n* a median number, point, line, etc.

mediant *n* (*mus*) the third of any scale.—*also adj*.

mediastinum *n* (*pl* **mediastina**) (*anat*) a membranous partition, esp that between the lungs; the part of the body between the lungs containing the heart and associated valves, etc.—**mediastinal** *adj*.

mediate *vt* to intervene (in a dispute); to bring about agreement. * *vi* to be in an intermediate position; to be an intermediary. * *adj* involving an intermediary, not direct or immediate.—**mediately** *adv*.—**mediative** *adj*.

mediation *n* the act of mediating; reconciliation; intervention, esp by a neutral nation seeking a settlement between warring nations.

mediatize *vt* to annex (a state) while leaving its ruler his title.—**mediatization** *n*.

mediator *n* one who or that which mediates; a person who acts as an intermediary; an intercessor.—**mediatory** *adj*.

medic *n* (*inf*) a medical student; (*inf*) a physician or surgeon.

medicable *adj* potentially curable.

medical *adj* relating to the practice or study of medicine. * *n* (*inf*) a medical examination.—**medically** *adv*.

medicament *n* a medicine or healing application.

medicate *vt* to treat with medicine; to impregnate (soap, shampoo, etc) with medication.—**medicative** *adj*.

medication *n* treatment with drugs, medicines, etc; a drug, medicine, or remedy.

medicine *n* any substance used to treat or prevent disease; the science of preventing, treating or curing disease.—**medicinal** *adj*.—**medicinally** *adv*.

medico *n* (*inf*) a doctor or medical student.

medieval *adj* of or like the Middle Ages.—*also* **mediaeval**.

medievalism *n* the spirit, esp in religion and art, customs, etc, characteristic of the Middle Ages; a study of these; any one of these extant since the Middle Ages, or a contemporary imitation of it.—*also* **mediaevalism**.—**medievalist, mediaevalist** *n*.

medigap *n* health insurance taken out by an individual to pay for treatment excluded by government schemes.

mediocre *adj* average; ordinary; inferior.—**mediocrity** *n*.

meditate *vi* to think deeply; to reflect; to empty the mind in order to concentrate on nothing or on one thing, esp as a religious exercise.—**meditator** *n*.

meditation *n* the act of meditating; contemplation of spiritual or religious matters.

meditative *adj* expressing or characterized by meditation; thoughtful.—**meditatively** *adv*.—**meditativeness** *n*.

Mediterranean *n* the Mediterranean Sea. * *adj* of, or relating to (the area around) the Mediterranean Sea; denoting a subdivision of the Caucasian race characterized by a slender build and dark complexion; (*climate*) characterized by hot, dry summers and warm, wet winters.

medium *n* (*pl* **media, mediums**) the middle state or condition; a substance for transmitting an effect; any intervening means, instrument, or agency; (*pl* **media**) a means of communicating information (eg newspapers, television, radio); (*pl* **mediums**) a person claiming to act as an intermediary between the living and the dead. * *adj* midway; average.

medlar *n* a small fruit tree of Europe and Asia; its apple-like fruit; any one of several trees similar to this; the fruit from one of these.

medley *n* (*pl* **medleys**) a miscellany; a musical piece made up of various tunes or passages.

Médoc *n* a red wine from the Bordeaux region of France.

medulla *n* (*pl* **medullas, medullae**) (*anat*) the marrow of bones; inner tissue; (*bot*) the pith of plants.—**medular, medullary** *adj.*

medulla oblongata *n* (*pl* **medulla oblongatas, medullae oblongatae**0 the nervous tissue of the lower part of the cranium, which governs respiration, the action of the heart, etc.

medusa *n* (*pl* **medusas, medusae**) a jellyfish; one of two coelenterate life cycles, when it has a sac-like, umbrella-shaped body that is capable of moving freely in water (—*also* **medusan, medusoid**).—**medusan** *adj.*

meed *n* (*poet*) recompense, reward.

meek *adj* patient, long-suffering; submissive.—**meekly** *adv.*—**meekness** *n.*

meerschaum *n* a creamy claylike silicate of magnesium from which pipe bowls and building stones are made; a tobacco pipe with a bowl made of this.

meet[1] *vb* (**meeting, met**) *vt* to encounter, to come together; to make the acquaintance of; to contend with, deal with; to experience; to be perceived by (the eye, etc); (*demand, etc*) to satisfy; (*bill, etc*) to pay. * *vi* to come into contact with; to be introduced. * *n* a meeting to hunt or for an athletics competition.

meet[2] *adj* (*arch*) fit, suitable.

meeting *n* a coming together; a gathering.

mega- *prefix* great, large; a million of; (*inf*) greatest.

megabyte *n* (*comput*) a unit of information, approximately equal to one million bytes.

megacephalic *see* **macrocephalic.**

megacycle *n* a megahertz.

megahertz *n* a unit of frequency equal to one million hertz.

megalith *n* a huge stone, esp part of a prehistoric monument.—**megalithic** *adj.*

megalomania *n* a mental illness characterized by delusions of grandeur; (*inf*) a lust for power.—**megalomaniac** *n, adj.*—**megalomaniacal** *adj.*

megaphone *n* a device to amplify and direct the voice.

megapode any of a family of birds of Australia and the South Pacific that builds mounds of sand, etc, to incubate its eggs.

megaspore *n* the protective covering containing the embryo in flowering plants (—*also* **macrospore**); the larger spore of certain mosses, ferns and fungi, which forms the female gametophyte.

megass, megasse *n* a type of paper produced from the residue left after the extraction of sugar from cane.

megathere *n* a huge extinct animal allied to the sloth.—**megatherian** *adj.*

megaton *n* a unit of explosive force equivalent to one million tons of TNT.

megavolt *n* a million volts.

megawatt *n* one million watts.

megilp *n* a mixture of linseed oil and mastic varnish or turpentine, used as a base in oil colours.

megohm *n* a million ohms.

megrim *n* (*arch*) a sick or neuralgic headache, usu of one side of the head, a migraine; a whim, caprice; (*pl*) a disease of horses or cattle, characterized by vertigo, the staggers.

meiosis *n* (*pl* **meioses**) *n* (*biol*) the process of cell division where a nucleus splits into four, each new nucleus having half the number of chromosomes that the orig one had; a rhetorical understatement, esp one where a negative is used instead of its opposite, eg "a not inconsiderable amount" instead of "a large amount"; litotes; (*rare*) any division or separation.—**meiotic** *adj.*—**meiotically** *adv.*

Meistersinger *n* (*pl* **Meistersinger, Meistersingers**) a member of one of the various guilds in German cities of the 14th-16th cents., which instituted the development of poetry and music by establishing competitive standards.

melamine *n* a resinous material used for adhesives, coatings, and laminated products.

melancholy *n* gloominess or depression; sadness. * *adj* sad; depressed.—**melancholia** *n.*—**melancholic** *adj.*

mélange *n* a (confused) mixture; a medley; (*geol*) a hotchpotch of variously shaped rocks of different periods and sizes.

melanin *n* a dark brown pigment in the skin, hair, and eyes of humans and animals.

melanism, melanosis *n* dark coloration of the skin in pale-skinned people or dark-coloured feathers, etc, in birds and animals, caused by abnormal deposits of black or dark pigment in skin tissue, the opposite of albinism.—**melanistic, melanotic** *adj.*

melanoma *n* (*pl* **melanomas, melanomata**) a skin tumour composed of darkly pigmented cells.

melee, mêlée *n* a confused, noisy struggle.

melic *adj* (*poem*) meant to be sung, often used of ancient Greek lyric poetry.

melilot *n* a species of sweet-scented trefoil or clover, with clusters of small yellow or white flowers.—*also* **sweet clover.**

melinite *n* a high explosive similar to lyddite.

meliorate *vti* to improve; to grow better; to make (something) better.—**meliorable** *adj.*—**meliorative** *adj, n.*—**meliorator** *n.*

melioration *n* the process of improving; the state of being improved; an improvement.

meliorism *n* the doctrine that in nature there is a tendency to gradual improvement and this may be accelerated by human effort.

melliferous *adj* forming or yielding honey.

mellifluous, mellifluent *adj* (*voice, sounds*) sweetly flowing, smooth. **mellifluously** *adv.* **mellifluousness** *n.*

mellow *adj* (*fruit*) sweet and ripe; (*wine*) matured; (*colour, light, sound*) soft, not harsh; kind-hearted and understanding. * *vti* to soften through age; to mature.—**mellowness** *n.*

melodeon *n* a kind of accordion; a small reed organ.

melodic *adj* pertaining to or having melody.—**melodically** *adv.*

melodious *adj* full of melody, tuneful, musical; sweet-sounding.—**melodiously** *adv.*—**melodiousness** *n.*

melodist *n* a singer; a composer of melodies.

melodize *vti* to make (something) melodious; to compose a melody (for something); to sing a melody.

melodrama *n* a play, film, etc filled with overdramatic emotion and action; drama of this genre; sensational events or emotions.—**melodramatic** *adj.*—**melodramatically** *adv.*—**melodramatist** *n.*

melody *n* (*pl* **melodies**) a tune; a pleasing series of sounds.—**melodic** *adj.*—**melodious** *adj.*

melon *n* the large juicy many-seeded fruit of trailing plants, as the watermelon, cantaloupe.

melt *vti* (**melting, melted**, *pp* **molten**) to make or become liquid; to dissolve; to fade or disappear; to soften or be softened emotionally.—**melting** *adj.*—**meltingly** *adv.*

meltdown *n* the melting of the fuel core of a nuclear reactor; the drastic collapse of almost anything.

melting point *n* the temperature at which a solid melts.

melting pot *n* a place, situation, or product of mixing many different races, traditions, cultures, etc.

melton *n* a kind of thick woollen cloth, with a surface nap, often used for overcoats.

meltwater *n* water derived from the melting of snow or ice.

member *n* a person belonging to a society or club; a part of a body, such as a limb; a representative in a legislative body; a distinct part of a complex whole.

membership *n* the state of being a member; the number of members of a body; the members collectively.

membrane *n* a thin pliable sheet or film; the fibrous tissue that covers or lines animal organs.—**membranous, membranaceous** *adj*.

memento *n* (*pl* **mementos, mementoes**) a reminder, esp a souvenir.

memento mori *n* (*pl* **memente mori**) (an object that serves as) a reminder of death.

memo *n* (*pl* **memos**) a memorandum.

memoir *n* an historical account based on personal experience; (*pl*) an autobiographical record.

memorabilia *npl* (*sing* **memorabile**) things worthy of remembrance or record; clothing, letters, manuscripts, notes, etc, once belonging to or written by famous people or connected with famous events and thought worthy of collection.

memorable *adj* worth remembering; easy to remember.—**memorably** *adv*.

memorandum *n* (*pl* **memorandums**) an informal written communication as within an office; (*pl* **memoranda**) a note to help the memory.

memorial *adj* serving to preserve the memory of the dead. * *n* a remembrance; a monument.

memorialist *n* one who prepares, signs or presents a memorial; one who writes memoirs.

memorialize *vt* to commemorate; to honour by means of a memorial.—**memorialization** *n*.—**memorializer** *n*.

memorize *vt* to learn by heart, to commit to memory.—**memorization** *n*.

memory *n* (*pl* **memories**) the process of retaining and reproducing past thoughts and sensations; the sum of things remembered; an individual recollection; commemoration; remembrance; the part of a computer that stores information (—*also* **store**).

memsahib *n* (*formerly*) a form of address for a European married woman in India.

men *see* **man**.

menace *n* a threat; (*inf*) a nuisance. * *vt* to threaten.—**menacing** *adj*.—**menacingly** *adv*.

menad *see* **maenad**.

ménage *n* a household.

ménage à trois *n* (*pl* **ménages à trois**) a relationship in which a married couple and a lover of one of them live together.

menagerie *n* a place where wild animals are kept for exhibition; a collection of wild animals.

mend *vt* to repair; (*manners, etc*) to reform, improve. * *vi* to become better. * *n* the act of mending; a repaired area in a garment, etc.

mendacity *n* (*pl* **mendacities**) telling lies; a falsehood.—**mendacious** *adj*.—**mendaciously** *adv*.

mendelevium *n* an artificially produced radioactive metallic element.

Mendelism *n* the theories of the Austrian monk and geneticist Gregor Mendel (1822–84) respecting heredity, as set out in Mendel's laws with later modifications.—**Mendelian** *adj*.

mendicant *adj* begging; (*religious orders*) reliant on alms. * *n* a mendicant friar.—**mendicancy, mendicity** *n*.

mending *n* garments requiring to be repaired.

menhaden *n* (*pl* **menhadens, menhaden**)*n* an inedible American fish , yielding a valuable oil.

menhir *n* a tall, monolithic obelisk, sometimes crudely carved, dating from the Bronze Age in the UK or the Neolithic Age in Europe.

menial *adj* consisting of work of little skill; servile. * *n* a domestic servant; a servile person.

meninges *npl* (*sing* **meninx**) the three membranes covering and protecting the brain and the spinal cord.—**meningeal** *adj*.

meningitis *n* inflammation of the membranes enveloping the brain or spinal cord.

meniscus *n* (*pl* **menisci, meniscuses**) a crescent; the crescent-shaped surface of a liquid contained in a tube; a lens convex on one side and concave on the other; (*anat*) the cartilage between the bones of joints, esp at the knee.

menology *n* (*pl* **menologies**) an ecclesiastical calendar; a calendar of saints, esp in the Orthodox Church.

menopause *n* the time of life during which a woman's menstrual cycle ceases permanently.—**menopausal** *adj*.

menorrhagia *n* an excessive menstrual flow.

menses *n* (*pl* **menses**) menstruation; the monthly discharge of blood, etc, from the uterus; the days during which this occurs.

Menshevik *n* (*pl* **Mensheviks, Mensheviki**) (*hist*) a member of the more moderate Russian socialist party (1903-17) or of a liberal opposition party set up after the Revolution.—**Menshevism** *n*.—**Menshevist** *adj*, *n*.

menstruation *n* the monthly discharge of blood from the uterus.—**menstrual** *adj*.—**menstruate** *vi*.

menstruum *n* (*pl* **menstruums, menstrua**) a solvent, esp if used in making drugs.

mensurable *adj* measurable; (*mus*) of a fixed rhythm.—**mensurability** *n*.

mensuration *n* the science of measurement; the act or process of measuring or taking the dimensions of anything; measurement.

mental *adj* of, or relating to the mind; occurring or performed in the mind; having a psychiatric disorder; (*inf*) crazy, stupid.—**mentally** *adv*.

mentality *n* (*pl* **mentalities**) intellectual power; disposition, character.

menthol *n* peppermint oil.—**mentholated** *adj*.

mention *n* a brief reference to something in speech or writing; an official recognition or citation. * *vt* to refer to briefly; to remark; to honour officially.—**mentionable** *adj*.

mentor *n* a wise and trusted adviser.

menu *n* the list of dishes served in a restaurant; a list of options on a computer display.

meow *n* the cry of a cat; a spiteful remark.—*also vi*.

Mephistophelean, Mephistophelian *adj* pertaining to or like Mephistopheles, the devil of the Faust legend; fiendish, cynical; diabolic.

mephitis *n* a noxious gas emitted from the ground; a foul stench.—**mephitic, mephitical** *adj*.

mercantile *adj* of merchants or trade.

mercantilism *n* a theory popular in 17th and 18th century Europe suggesting that the wealth of a nation increases in proportion to the level of the foreign trade surplus, therefore trade and commerce with other countries, the founding of colonies, a merchant navy etc should be encouraged; (*rare*) commercialism—**mercantilist** *n, adj.*

mercenary *adj* working or done for money only. * *n* (*pl* **mercenaries**) a soldier hired to fight for a foreign army.—**mercenarily** *adv.*—**mercenariness** *n.*

mercer *n* a dealer in textiles, esp silk and velvet.

mercerize *vt* to treat cotton thread so as to strengthen it and make it resemble silk.—**mercerization** *n.*

merchandise *n* commercial goods. * *vti* to sell, to trade; to promote sales by display or advertising.—**merchandiser** *n.*

merchandising *n* the display of goods in a store, etc; the exploitation of a fictional character, pop group, etc, by the production of goods with their image, name, etc.

merchant *n* a trader; a retailer; (*sl*) a person fond of a particular activity.

merchantable *adj* marketable.

merchantman *n* (*pl* **merchantmen**) a trading ship.

merchant marine, merchant navy *n* commercial shipping.

merciful *adj* compassionate, humane.—**mercifulness** *n.*

mercifully *adv* in a merciful way; (*inf*) thank goodness.

merciless *adj* cruel, pitiless; without mercy.—**mercilessly** *adv.*—**mercilessness** *n.*

mercurial *adj* of, containing, or caused by mercury; lively, sprightly; volatile.—**mercurially** *adv.*

mercuric *adj* (*chem*) of or containing bivalent mercury.

mercurous *adj* (*chem*) of or containing monovalent mercury.

Mercury *n* the innermost planet, and the smallest; the Roman god of thieves, traders etc; in ancient Rome, the messenger of the gods.

mercury *n* a heavy silvery liquid metallic element used in thermometers etc.

mercy *n* clemency; compassion; kindness; pity.

mere *adj* nothing more than; simple, unmixed.

merely *adv* simply; solely.

meretricious *adj* tawdry, superficially attractive; insincere.

merganser *n* (*pl* **mergansers, merganser**) *n* a large, diving fish-eating duck with a long narrow bill with serrated edges; a sawbill.

merge *vti* to blend or cause to fuse together gradually; to (cause to) combine, unite.

merger *n* a combining together, esp of two or more commercial organizations.

meridian *n* the imaginary circle on the surface of the earth passing through the north and south poles.

meridional *adj* of a meridian; of the south.—**meridionally** *adv.*

meringue *n* a mixture of egg whites beaten with sugar and baked; a small cake or shell made from this, usu filled with cream.

merino *n* (*pl* **merinos**) a breed of sheep with fine silky wool; the wool or the cloth made from it.

merit *n* excellence; worth; (*pl*) (*of a case*) rights and wrongs; a deserving act. * *vt* to be worthy of, to deserve.

meritocracy *n* (*pl* **meritocracies**) rule by those most skilled or talented; a social system or government based on this; the most talented group in a society.

meritorious *adj* deserving of merit or honour.—**meritoriously** *adv.*—**meritoriousness** *n.*

merle *n* (*Scot*) a blackbird. * *adj* (*dog, esp a collie*) having blue-grey fur with black tinges or streaks.

merlin *n* a small dark-coloured falcon, often used in falconry.

merlon *n* the part of a parapet or battlement between two embrasures.

mermaid *n* (*legend*) a woman with a fish's tail.—**merman** *nm* (*pl* **mermen**).

meroblastic *adj* (*biol*) (*fertilized egg*) of or pertaining to the splitting of cells in the white only and not the entire ovum.

Merovingian *adj* pertaining to the first Frankish dynasty of French kings (*c.*500-751). * *n* a member or adherent of this dynasty.

merry *adj* (**merrier, merriest**) cheerful; causing laughter; lively; (*inf*) slightly drunk.—**merrily** *adv.*—**merriment** *n.*

merry-go-round *n* a revolving platform of hobbyhorses, etc, a carousel.

merrymaking *n* festivity, fun.—**merrymaker** *n.*

merrythought *n* (*rare*) the forked bone of a chicken's breast, the wishbone.

mes-, meso- *prefix* middle.

mesa *n* a rocky plateau with steep sides usu found in arid regions.

mésalliance *n* a misalliance; a marriage with one of lower social position.

mescaline *n* a hallucinogenic drug derived from the mescal cactus.

mesdames *see* **madame.**

mesdemoiselles *see* **mademoiselle.**

mesembryanthemum *n* one of a genus of flowering, succulent plants with thick and fleshy leaves and showy flowers.

mesentery *n* (*pl* **mesenteries**) the membrane attaching the small intestines to the abdominal wall.—**mesenteric** *adj.*

mesh *n* an opening between cords of a net, wires of a screen, etc; a net; a network; a snare; (*geared wheels, etc*) engagement. * *vt* to entangle, ensnare. * *vi* to become entangled or interlocked.

mesial *adj* (*anat*) in or toward the middle line of the body.—**mesially** *adv.*

mesmerism *n* hypnotism.—**mesmerist** *n.*

mesmerize *vt* to hypnotize; to fascinate.—**mesmeric** *adj.*—**mesmerizer** *n.*

mesne *adj* (*law*) intervening, intermediate.

meso-, mes- *prefix* middle.

mesoblast *n* (*biol*) the middle germinal layer of an ovum, the basis of muscles, bones, blood etc.—*also* **mesoderm.**

mesocarp *n* the middle layer of the seed vessel of a fruit.

mesocephalic *adj, n* (*person*) with a head or skull of medium proportions.

mesoderm *see* **mesoblast.**

mesogastrium *n* the membrane that supports the embryonic stomach.—**mesogastric** *adj.*

Mesolithic *n, adj* of or pertaining to the archaeological era between the Palaeolithic and Neolithic (*c.*12000-3000BC).

meson *n* an unstable elementary particle having a mass between that of proton and an electron.

mesophyll *n* the internal tissues of a leaf that are between the upper and lower epidermal layers and contain chlorophyll.—**mesophyllic, mesophyllous** *adj.*

mesophyte *n* a plant requiring an average water supply.—**mesophytic** *adj.*

mesothorax *n* (*pl* **mesothoraxes, mesothoraces**) *n* the middle ring of an insect's thorax, with the second pair of walking legs and the front pair of wings.

Mesozoic *adj* pertaining to the era of geological time lasting from about 248 to 65 million years ago. * *n* this era.

mesquite, mesquit *n* a small pod-bearing tree of the southwest US whose pods are used as fodder.

mess *n* a state of disorder or untidiness, esp if dirty; a muddle; an unsightly or disagreeable mixture; a portion of soft and pulpy or semi-liquid food; a building where service personnel dine; a communal meal. * *vti* to make a mess (of), bungle; to eat in company; to potter (about).

message *n* any spoken, written, or other form of communication; the chief idea that the writer, artist, etc seeks to communicate in a work.

messenger *n* a person who carries a message.

Messiah *n* the promised saviour of the Jews; Jesus Christ.—**Messianic** *adj.*

messieurs *see* **monsieur.**

Messrs *pl* of Mr.

messuage *n* (*law*) a dwelling house with its adjacent buildings and land for the use of the household.

messy *adj* (**messier, messiest**) dirty; confused; untidy.—**messily** *adv.*—**messiness** *n.*

mestizo *n* (*pl* **mestizos, mestizoes**) a person of mixed parentage, esp the child of a Spanish American and an American Indian.

met *see* **meet.**

meta-, met- *prefix* after, with, or implying change.

metabolism *n* the total processes in living organisms by which tissue is formed, energy produced and waste products eliminated.—**metabolic** *adj.*

metabolize *vt* to process by metabolism; to assimilate.

metacarpal *adj* pertaining to the metacarpus. * *n* a bone of the metacarpus.

metacarpus *n* (*pl* **metacarpi**) the bones of that part of the hand that is between the wrist and the fingers, or the corresponding part in other animals.

metacenter, metacentre *n* the point in a floating body where the verticals intersect when the body is tilted and on the position of which its equilibrium or stability depends.—**metacentric** *adj.*

metage *n* the official weighing or measuring of the contents of something; the fee paid for this.

metagenesis *n* the alternation of sexual and asexual generations.—**metagenetic** *adj.*—**metagenetically** *adv.*

metal *n* any of a class of chemical elements which are often lustrous, ductile solids, and are good conductors of heat, electricity, etc, such as gold, iron, copper, etc; any alloy of such elements as brass, bronze, etc; anything consisting of metal.—**metalled** *adj.*

metallic *adj* of, relating to, or made of metal; similar to metal.

metalliferous *adj* yielding metal or metallic ores.

metalline *adj* metallic; impregnated with or yielding metal.

metallize, metalize *vt* to give metallic qualities to; to coat or treat with metal.

metallography *n* the science or description of the structure of metals and alloys; (*print*) lithography using metal plates to print an image.

metalloid *n* a nonmetallic element that possesses some of the chemical properties associated with metals. * *adj* of or having the properties of a metalloid; resembling a metal (—*also* **metalloidal**).

metallurgy *n* the science of separating metals from their ores and preparing them for use by smelting, refining, etc.—**metallurgical** *adj.*—**metallurgist** *n.*

metamere *n* a segment of a body, as in earthworms, crayfish, etc.

metameric *adj* (*zool*) of or having metameres; (*chem*) having the same elements and molecular weight but different properties.—**metamerism** *n.*

metamorphism *n* the change in the structure of rocks through heat, pressure, etc.

metamorphosis *n* (*pl* **metamorphoses**) a complete change of form, structure, substance, character, appearance, etc; transformation; the marked change in some animals at a stage in their growth, eg chrysalis to butterfly.—**metamorphic** *adj.*—**metamorphose** *vi.*

metaphor *n* a figure of speech in which a word or phrase is used for another of which it is an image.—**metaphoric, metaphorical** *adj.*—**metaphorically** *adv.*

metaphrase *n* a word-for-word translation, the opposite of paraphrase. * *vt* to alter the wording of something, esp to alter the meaning; to translate literally.

metaphrast *n* one who alters text, esp one who changes the form, as from verse to prose.—**metaphrastic, metaphrastical** *adj.*

metaphysical *adj* of or pertaining to metaphysics; abstruse, abstract; supernatural; (*poetry*) fantastic or over-subtle in style.—**metaphysically** *adv.*

metaphysics *n sing* the branch of philosophy that seeks to explain the nature of being and reality; speculative philosophy in general.—**metaphysician** *n.*

metaplasm *n* (*biol*) that part of the contents of a cell consisting of inert matter; (*gram*) a change in a word by the adding or dropping of a letter.—**metaplasmic** *adj.*

metastasis *n* (*pl* **metastases**) *n* a change or shift in the location of a disease, often used of the spreading of cancer cells; a transformation or change; (*rare*) metabolism.—**metastatic** *adj.*

metatarsal *adj* pertaining to the metatarsus. * *n* one of the bones of the metatarsus.

metatarsus *n* (*pl* **metatarsi**) (*anat*) in humans, the instep, the middle part of the foot between the tarsus and the toes; in other animals, the part corresponding to this.

metathesis *n* (*pl* **metatheses**) the transposition of the letters or syllables of a word; (*chem*) a reaction between two compounds in which the first and second parts of one unite with the second and first parts of the other.—**metathetic, metathetical** *adj.*

metathorax *n* (*pl* **metathoraxes, metathoraces**) *n* the hindmost segment of an insect's thorax, with the third pair of walking legs and the second pair of wings.

metazoan *n* an animal belonging to a division of the animal kingdom in which the body is made up of a large number of cells, ie all animals except sponges and protozoans.

mete *vt* to allot; to portion (out).

metempsychosis *n* (*pl* **metempsychoses**) the transmigration of the soul after the death of the body to another body or form.

meteor *n* a small particle of matter which travels at great speed through space and becomes luminous through friction as it enters the earth's atmosphere; a shooting star.

meteoric *adj* of or relating to a meteor; dazzling, transitory.

meteorite *n* a meteor that has fallen to earth without being completely vaporized.—**meteoritic** *adj*.

meteorograph *n* an instrument for recording various meteorological conditions simultaneously.

meteoroid *n* a small body moving through space, often orbiting the sun which can be seen as a meteor if it enters the earth's atmosphere.

meteorology *n* a study of the earth's atmosphere, particularly weather and climate.—**meteorological** *adj*.—**meteorologist** *n*.

-meter *suffix* denoting a device for measuring; metre(s) in length.

meter[1] *n* a device for measuring and recording a quantity of gas, water, time, etc supplied; a parking meter. * *vt* to measure using a meter.

meter[2] *see* **metre**[1], **metre**[2].

methane *n* a colourless, odourless, flammable gas formed by the decomposition of vegetable matter, as in marshes.

methinks *vb* (*pt* **methought**) (*arch*) it appears or seems to me.

method *n* the mode or procedure of accomplishing something; orderliness of thought; an orderly arrangement or system.

methodical *adj* orderly, systematic.—**methodically** *adv*.

Methodist *n* a member of a Christian denomination founded by John Wesley.—**Methodism** *n*.

methodize *vt* to reduce to method; systematize.

methodology *n* (*pl* **methodologies**) the methods and procedures used by a science or discipline; the philosophical analysis of method and procedure.

methought *see* **methinks**.

meths *n* (*inf*) methylated spirit.

Methuselah *n* a wine bottle eight times the size of an ordinary bottle; (*Old Testament*) a patriarch reputed to have been 969 years old when he died; a very old person.

methyl *n* a compound composed of organic material and metals in which metal groups are bound directly to a metal atom.

methylated spirit *n* a form of alcohol, adulterated to render it undrinkable, used as a solvent.

methylene *n* a bivalent organic radical found in unsaturated hydrocarbons; an inflammable liquid obtained from the distillation of wood.

meticulous *adj* very precise about small details.—**meticulously** *adv*.—**meticulousness** *n*.

métier *n* a person's calling or trade, esp if that person has a natural leaning toward it; a strong point, forte.

métis *n* (*pl* **métis**) *n* (*often cap*) an offspring of mixed parentage; in Canada, one who is the child or a descendant of a French Canadian and an American Indian; one of a group of such people forming a political and national entity, who settled in Manitoba and Saskatchewan.—**métisse** *nf*.

Metol *n* (*trademark*) a colourless, soluble organic substance used as a photographic developer.

metonymy *n* (**metonymies**) a figure of speech in which a thing is replaced by its attribute, eg "the pen is mightier than the sword."—**metonym** *n*.—**metonymical, metonymic** *adj*.

metope *n* (*archit*) the space between two triglyphs of a Doric frieze.

metre[1] *n* rhythmic pattern in verse, the measured arrangement of syllables according to stress; rhythmic pattern in music.—*also* **meter**.

metre[2] *n* the basic unit of length in the metric system, consisting of 100 centimetres and equal to 39.37 inches.—*also* **meter**.

metric *adj* based on the metre as a standard of measurement; of, relating to, or using the metric system.

metrical *adj* of, relating to, or composed in rhythmic metre.—**metrically** *adv*.

metrication *n* conversion of an existent system of units into the metric system.

metrics *n sing* the study of verse form; the art of composing verse.

metric system *n* a decimal system of weights and measures based on the metre, litre and the kilogram.

metro *n* (*pl* **metros**) an urban underground railway system, such as in Paris and other cities.

metrology *n* (*pl* **metrologies**) *n* the science of weights and measures or units of measurement; any of the various systems of units.

metronome *n* an instrument that beats musical tempo.—**metronomic** *adj*.

metronymic *adj* (*name*) derived from one's mother or a female ancestor. * *n* such a name.—*also* **matronymic**.

metropolis *n* the main city, often a capital of a country, state, etc; any large and important city.—**metropolitan** *adj*.

mettle *n* courage, spirit.

mettled *adj* mettlesome.

mettlesome *adj* high-spirited, full of courage.

meunière *adj* (*fish*) coated with flour, cooked in butter and served with parsley and lemon juice.

mew[1] *vi* (*cat*) to emit a high-pitched cry. * *n* the cry of a cat.

mew[2] *n* a gull found in northern areas.

mew[3] *n* a cage for hawks. * *vti* (*hawk*) to shed (feathers), to moult; to put in a mew, to confine.

mewl *vi* (*baby*) to cry feebly, to whimper; to mew. * *n* a whimper.

mews *n sing or pl* a yard or road lined with buildings formerly used stables and later converted into living accommodation.

mezzanine *n* an intermediate storey between others; a theatre balcony.

mezzanine debt *see* **junk debt**.

mezzo *adv* (*mus*) moderately; quite. * *n* (*pl* **mezzos**) a mezzo-soprano.

mezzo-relievo *n* (*pl* **mezzo-relievos**) a carving in half-relief, where the figures project in neither high relief nor low relief from the background.

mezzo-soprano *n* (*pl* **mezzo-sopranos**) (*mus*) a singer, or a part, between soprano and contralto.

mezzotint *n* a method of engraving on copper in which lights are made by scraping a roughened surface; a print so made. * *vt* to engrave a copper plate using this method.

mfr *abbr* = manufacture; manufacturer.

Mg (*chem symbol*) magnesium.

mg *abbr* = milligram.

Mgr *abbr* = manager.

MHR *abbr* = Member of the House of Representatives.

MHz *abbr* = megahertz.

MI *abbr* = Michigan; military intelligence; myocardial infarction.

mi. *abbr* = mile; mill.

MIA *abbr* = missing in action.

miasma *n* (*pl* **miasmas, miasmata**) an unwholesome, foreboding atmosphere; an unpleasant vapour, as from decaying swamp matter.—**miasmal, miasmatic, miasmic** *adj*.

mica *n* a mineral that crystallizes in thin, flexible layers, resistant to heat.—**micaceous** *adj*.

mice *see* **mouse**.

Mich. *abbr* = Michigan.

Michaelmas *n* a church festival commemorating the archangel Michael, celebrated on September 29.

micra *see* **micron**.

micro *n* (*pl* **micros**) a microwave oven; (*comput*) a microcomputer, a microprocessor.

micro-, micr- *prefix* small.

microbe *n* a microscopic organism, esp a disease-causing bacterium.—**microbial, microbic** *adj*.

microbiology *n* the biology of bacteria and other microorganisms and their effects.—**microbiological, microbiologic** *adj*.—**microbiologically** *adv*.—**microbiologist** *n*.

microbus *n* (*pl* **microbuses, microbusses**) a station wagon that resembles a small bus.

microcephalic, microcephalous *adj* having an unusually small head.—**microcephaly** *n*.

microchip *n* a small wafer of silicon, etc, containing electronic circuits.—*also* **chip**.

microcircuit *n* a miniature electronic circuit, esp an integrated circuit.—**microcircuitry** *n*.

microclimate *n* the climate of a restricted specific place within an area as opposed to the climate of the area.—**microclimatic** *adj*.

micrococcus *n* (**micrococci**) a round bacterium, a source of fermentation and of zymotic disease.—**micrococcal** *adj*.

microcomputer *n* a computer in which the central processing unit is contained in one or more microprocessors.

microcosm *n* a miniature universe or world.—**microcosmic, microcosmical** *adj*.—**microcosmically** *adv*.

microcyte *n* an unusually small red blood corpuscle, often present in disease.—**microcytic** *adj*.

microdot *n* a photographic reproduction of a document, plan, etc reduced to a tiny dot, esp for reasons of espionage.

microeconomics *n sing* the branch of economics concerned with the activities of consumers, firms, and commodities.—**microeconomic** *adj*.

microfiche *n* (*pl* **microfiche, microfiches**) a sheet of microfilm containing pages of printed matter.—*also* **film card**.

microfilm *n* film on which documents, etc, are recorded in reduced scale. * *vt* to record on microfilm.

microfloppy *n* (*pl* **microfloppies**) a floppy disk of 3.5 inches diameter contained in a hard covering.

micrograph *n* a photograph of something as seen through a microscope; a device for executing minute engraving or writing.

micrography *n* the description, study or representation of microscopic objects; the process of writing in miniature.—**micrographic** *adj*.

micrometer[1] *n* any of various instruments for measuring minute distances, angles, thicknesses, or apparent diameters, sometimes used with a microscope.

micrometer[2], **micrometre** *n* a unit of length of one thousandth of a millimetre, a micron.

micrometry *n* the measurement of tiny objects, distances, etc, by a micrometer.—**micrometric,** **micrometrical** *adj*.—**micrometrically** *adv*.

micron *n* (*pl* **microns, micra**) one millionth of a metre, a micrometer.

microorganism *n* an organism visible only through a microscope.

microphone *n* an instrument for transforming sound waves into electric signals, esp for transmission, or recording.—**microphonic** *adj*.

microphotograph *n* a photograph taken through a microscope or of microscopic size, in which the details cannot be distinguished by the naked eye; a photomicrograph.—**microphotographic** *adj*.—**microphotography** *n*.

microphyte *n* a microscopic vegetable growth, esp a parasitic one.—**microphytic** *adj*.

microprocessor *n* a computer processor contained on one or more integrated circuits.

microscope *n* an optical instrument for making magnified images of minute objects by means of a lens or lenses.

microscopic *adj* of, with, like, a microscope; visible only through a microscope; very small.—**microscopically** *adv*.

microscopy *n* (*pl* **microscopies**) the use of microscopes; microscopic investigation.—**microscopist** *n*.

microseism *n* a faint earth tremor, probably not related to earthquakes.—**microseismic** *adj*.

microtome *n* an instrument for cutting thin sections for microscopic examination, used particularly in biology.

microwave *n* an electromagnetic wave between 1 and 100 centimetres in length; (*inf*) a microwave oven. * *vt* to cook (food) in a microwave oven.—**microwavable, microwaveable** *adj*.

microwave oven *n* a cooker in which food is cooked or heated by microwaves.

micturate *vi* to urinate.—**micturition** *n*.

mid *adj* middle. * *prep* amid.

mid. *abbr* = middle.

mid- *prefix* middle.

midday *n* the middle of the day, noon.

midden *n* a dunghill, a refuse heap.

middle *adj* halfway between two given points, times, etc; intermediate; central. * *n* the point halfway between two extremes; something intermediate; the waist. * *vt* to put in the middle; (*naut*) to fold (a sail) in the middle.

middle age *n* the time between youth and old age, *c.*40-60.—**middle-aged** *adj*.

Middle Ages *npl* the period of European history between about AD 500 and 1500.

middle class *n* the class between the lower and upper classes, mostly composed of professional and business people.—**middle-class** *adj*.

Middle East *n* a general term applied currently to an area extending from the eastern Mediterranean to the Gulf of Arabia; (formerly) that part of Southern Asia from the Tigris and Euphrates to Burma.

middleman *n* (*pl* **middlemen**) a dealer between producer and consumer; an intermediary.

middle-of-the-road *adj* avoiding extremes, esp political extremes.—**middle-of-the-roader** *n*.

middleweight *n* a professional boxer weighing 154-160 pounds (70-72.5 kilograms); a wrestler weighing usu 172-192 pounds (78-87 kilograms).

middling *adj* of medium quality, size, etc; second-rate. * *adv* moderately.—**middlingly** *adv*.

middy *n* (*pl* **middies**) *n* (*inf*) a midshipman; a middy blouse; (*Austral*) a glass of beer, usu containing half a pint.

middy blouse *n* a loose blouse with a sailor collar.

midge *n* a small gnat-like insect with a painful bite.

midget *n* a very small person, a dwarf; something small of its kind.—*also adj.*

midi *n* a coat or skirt that reaches to mid calf.

midland *n* the middle part of a country; (*pl*) (*with cap*) central England; the industrial and manufacturing area of that part of England. * *adj* of or in midland; inland.

midlife *n* (*pl* **midlives**) middle age.—*also adj.*

midmost *adj* in or nearest the middle. * *adv* in the middle.

midnight *n* twelve o'clock at night.

Midrash *n* (*pl* **Midrashim**) a critical exposition of or a sermon on the Jewish scriptural law or some portion of it; one of the various collections of these originating between AD400 and 1200.

midrib *n* the principal central vein of a leaf.

midriff *n* the middle part of the torso between the abdomen and the chest.—*also adj.*

midship *adj* (*naut*) of or pertaining to the middle part of a ship.

midshipman *n* (*pl* **midshipmen**) in some navies, a noncommissioned officer ranking immediately below a sublieutenant; this naval rank; (*formerly*) a naval cadet officer; an American fish with light-producing organs.

midships *adv* (*naut*) at, near or toward the middle of a ship, amidships.

midst *n* middle. * *prep* amidst, among.

midsummer *n* the middle of summer.—*also adj.*

Midsummer Day *n* June 24, celebrated as the summer solstice or in commemoration of the birth of St John the Baptist.

Midsummer Eve *n* the day before Midsummer Day, June 23.

midway *adv* halfway. * *n* a middle course of action; the area of a carnival where the sideshows are.

midwife *n* (*pl* **midwives**) a person trained to assist women before, during, and after childbirth.—**midwifery** *n.*

mien *n* the expression of the face; demeanour.

miff *n* (*inf*) a petty quarrel, a tiff; a sulky mood. * *vti* to take offence; to offend.

miffy *adj* (**miffier**, **miffiest**) (*inf*) touchy, huffy; oversensitive.—**miffiness** *n.*

might[1] *see* **may**.

might[2] *n* power, bodily strength.

mightn't = might not.

mighty *adj* (**mightier**, **mightiest**) powerful, strong; massive; (*inf*) very.—**mightily** *adv.*—**mightiness** *n.*

mignonette *n* a sweet-scented plant with spikes of small green- white flowers; a greyish-green colour; a delicate bobbin lace.

migraine *n* an intense, periodic headache, usu limited to one side of the head.

migrant *n* a person or animal that moves from one region or country to another; an itinerant agricultural labourer. * *adj* migrating.

migrate *vi* to settle in another country or region; (*birds, animals*) to move to another region with the change in season.—**migration** *n.*—**migratory** *adj.*

mikado *n* (*sl* **mikados**) (*arch*) (*often with cap*) the Japanese emperor.

mike *n* (*inf*) a microphone. * *vt* to provide with a microphone; to transmit by microphone.

mil *n* a unit of length of one thousandth of an inch; (*gunnery*) an angle of one sixty-four-hundredth of a circumference; a milliliter.

mil. *abbr* = military; militia.

milady *n* (*pl* **miladies**) *n* (*formerly*) a word used in Europe for an aristocratic Englishwoman.

milage *see* **mileage**.

milch *adj* yielding milk, used esp of cattle.

milch cow *n* a cow from which milk is obtained for human consumption; a ready source of gain.

mild *adj* (*temper*) gentle; (*weather*) temperate; bland; feeble.—**mildly** *adv.*—**mildness** *n.*

mildew *n* a fungus that attacks some plants or appears on damp cloth, etc as a whitish coating. * *vti* to affect or be affected with mildew.—**mildewy** *adj.*

mile *n* a unit of linear measure equal to 5,280 feet (1.61 km); the nautical mile is 6,075 feet (1.85 km).

mileage *n* total miles travelled; an allowance per mile for travelling expenses; the average number of miles that can be travelled, as per litre of fuel.—*also* **milage**.

milestone *n* a stone marking the number of miles to a place; an important event in life, history, etc.

milfoil *n* a yarrow plant; one of various pond plants with feather-like leaves and small flowers.

miliaria *n* a skin disease resulting from blocked sweat glands and characterized by an acute itchiness, heat rash.—**miliarial** *adj.*

miliary *adj* (*growth, lesion*) very small; (*skin disease*) marked by small lesions resembling millet seeds.

milieu *n* (*pl* **milieus**, **milieux**) environment, esp social setting.

militant *adj* ready to fight, esp for some cause; combative.—*also* *n.*—**militance, militancy** *n.*—**militantly** *adv.*

militarism *n* military spirit; a policy of aggressive military preparedness.

militarist *n* a believer in militarism; a student of military science.—**militaristic** *adj.*—**militaristically** *adv.*

militarize *vt* to equip and prepare for war.—**militarization** *n.*

military *adj* relating to soldiers or to war; warlike. * *n* (*pl* **militaries**) the armed forces.

militate *vt* to have influence or force; to produce an effect or change.

militia *n* an army composed of civilians called out in time of emergency.—**militiaman** *n* (*pl* **militiamen**).

milk *n* a white nutritious liquid secreted by female mammals for feeding their young. * *vt* to draw milk from; to extract money, etc, from; to exploit.—**milker** *n.*

milkmaid *n* a girl or woman who milks cows or works in a dairy.

milkman *n* (*pl* **milkmen**) a person who sells or delivers milk to homes.

milk run *n* (*sl*) a routine journey.

milksop *n* a weak cowardly man or boy.—**milksoppy** *adj.*

milk toast *n* toasted bread soaked in warm milk, often eaten by babies and invalids.

milk tooth *n* any of the first teeth of a mammal.

milkweed *n* a plant found mainly in North America yielding a milky sap and with pointed pods containing tufted seeds; any plant with a milky sap.—*also* **silkweed**.

milkwort *n* a kind of plant with small blue, pink or white flowers.

milky *adj* (**milkier**, **milkiest**) of, filled with, consisting of, yielding, or resembling milk; timid.—**milkily** *adv.*—**milkiness** *n.*

Milky Way *n* (*with* the) the galaxy to which the Earth belongs; the system of stars, nebulae, etc, that can be seen in the night sky as a trailing ribbon of light and forms part of the Galaxy.

mill[1] *n* an apparatus for grinding by crushing between rough surfaces; a building where grain is ground into flour; a factory. * *vt* to produce or grind in a mill; (*coins*) to put a raised edge on. * *vi* to move around confusedly.—**miller** *n.*

mill[2] *n* a unit of money equal to one tenth of a cent.

millboard *n* a thick pasteboard, often black or grey, that forms the front and back covers and spine of a book, usu covered by the book binding.

millenarian *adj* consisting of or pertaining to a thousand years; pertaining to the millennium or to millenarianism. * *n* a believer in the millennium; an advocate of millenarianism.

millenarianism *n* (*Christianity*) the belief that the Second Coming of Christ will be preceded or followed by a thousand years of holiness.

millenary *adj* of or pertaining to a thousand; millenarian. * *n* (*pl* **millenaries**) a thousandth anniversary; one thousand as a total, esp one thousand years; a millenarian.

millennium *n* (*pl* **millennia**, **millenniums**) a period of a thousand years; (*Christianity*) a period of a thousand years of holiness preceding or following the Second Coming of Christ; a coming time of happiness.—**millennial** *adj.*—**millennially** *adv.*

millepede *see* **millipede**.

millepore *n* a tropical coelenterate resembling a coral, with a smooth surface perforated with very small pores.

miller *n* one who or that which mills; an owner of a mill; a moth with a floury appearance.

millesimal *adj* pertaining to a thousandth. * *n* a thousandth.

millet *n* a cereal grass used for grain and fodder.

milli- *prefix* a thousandth part.

milligram *n* a thousandth of a gramme.

milliliter, **millilitre** *n* a thousandth (.001) of a litre.

millimetre, **millimeter** *n* a thousandth (.001) of a metre.

milliner *n* a designer or seller of women's hats.—**millinery** *n.*

milling *n* the act of grinding in or passing through a dressing mill; the process of making a serrated edge on a coin, etc; the serrated edge of such a coin; a stratagem to stop cattle stampeding.

million *n* (*pl* **million**, **millions**) a thousand thousands, the number one followed by six zeros: 1,000,000; (*inf*) a very large number.—**millionth** *adj.*

millionaire *n* a person who owns at least a million of money; one who is extremely rich.

millipede *n* a wormlike arthropod with many legs and a segmented body.—*also* **millepede**.

millpond *n* a reservoir of water for driving a mill; any stretch of calm water.

millrace *n* a current of water that drives a mill; the channel in which this flows.

millstone *n* a stone used for grinding corn; a heavy burden.

millwright *n* a person who designs, builds, and repairs mills or mill parts.

milord *n* (*formerly*) a word used in Europe for an aristocratic or rich Englishman.

milt *n* the sperm of a male fish; its reproductive glands when filled with this; the spleen of some animals. * *vt* to fertilize (the roe of female fish), esp artificially.

milter *n* a male fish in the breeding season.

Miltonic, **Miltonian** *adj* pertaining to, characteristic of, or resembling the writings of the English poet John Milton (1608–74).

mime *n* a theatrical technique using action without words; a mimic. * *vi* to act or express using gestures alone; (*singers*, *musicians*) to perform as if singing or playing live to what is actually a prerecorded piece of music.—**mimer** *n.*

mimeograph *n* a machine for making multiple copies of a letter, drawing, etc, by means of a stencil fixed to an inked drum, and masking the non-printing areas; a copy produced from this machine; * *vti* to produce copies (of something) by using this machine.

mimesis *n* (*art*, *literature*, *etc*) the realistic representation of objects, people, everyday life, etc; (*biol*) mimicry; (*med*) a condition characterized by symptoms that occur in other diseases but that cannot be found by objective medical testing; a disease that mimics the symptoms of another disease.

mimetic *adj* of or given to imitation or mimicry; (*biol*) pertaining to or having the ability to mimic.—**mimetically** *adv.*

mimic *n* a person who imitates, esp an actor skilled in mimicry. * *adj* related to mimicry; make-believe; sham. * *vt* (**mimicking**, **mimicked**) to imitate or ridicule.—**mimicker** *n.*

mimicry *n* (*pl* **mimicries**) practice, art, or way of mimicking; (*biol*) the resemblance of an animal to its environment, another animal, etc, to provide protection from predators, mimesis.

mimosa *n* any of a genus of leguminous plants, usu with clustered yellow flowers, whose leaves and stems fold when touched or when exposed to light; the sensitive plant; any of several related or similar plants.

Min. *abbr* = Minister; Ministry.

min. *abbr* = minimum; minute(s).

mina[1] *n* (*pl* **minas**, **minae**) a weight and coin, current in ancient Anatolia, equal to one sixtieth of a talent.

mina[2] *see* **myna**.

minaret *n* a high, slender tower on a mosque from which the call to prayer is made.

minatory, **minatorial** *adj* threatening.—**minatorily** *adv.*

mince *vt* to chop or cut up into small pieces; to diminish or moderate one's words. * *vi* to speak or walk with affected daintiness.—**mincer** *n.*—**mincing** *adj.*—**mincingly** *adv.*

mincemeat *n* a mixture of chopped apples, raisins, etc, used as a pie filling; finely chopped meat.

mind *n* the faculty responsible for intellect, thought, feelings, speech; memory; intellect; reason; opinion; sanity. * *vt* to object to, take offence to; to pay attention to; to obey; to take care of; to be careful about; to care about. * *vi* to pay attention; to be obedient; to be careful; to object.

mind-bending *adj* (*inf*) (*drugs*, *etc*) unbalancing the mind; (*inf*) stretching credibility to the limits.—**mind-bender** *n.*—**mind-bendingly** *adv.*

mind-blowing *adj* (*inf*) (*drugs*) hallucinatory.

mind-boggling *adj* (*inf*) astonishing, bewildering.—**mind-boggler** *n.*

minded *adj* disposed, inclined; (in compounds) having

a mind as described, eg small-minded.—**mindedness** n.

minder n a person who looks after or protects another.

mind-expanding adj producing awareness; psychedelic, distorting.

mindful adj heedful, not forgetful.—**mindfully** adv.—**mindfulness** n.

mindless adj unthinking, stupid; requiring little intellectual effort.—**mindlessly** adv.—**mindlessness** n.

mindset n attitude, esp when fixed or rigid; a habit.

mind's eye n the visual memory or imagination.

mine[1] poss pron belonging to me.

mine[2] n an excavation from which minerals are dug; an explosive device concealed in the water or ground to destroy enemy ships, personnel, or vehicles that pass over or near them; a rich supply or source. * vt to excavate; to lay explosive mines in an area. * vi to dig or work a mine.

mine detector n a device for indicating the whereabouts of explosive mines.—**mine detection** n.

minefield n an area sown with explosive mines; a situation containing hidden problems.

minelayer n a ship or aircraft for laying mines.

miner n a person who works in a mine.

mineral n an inorganic substance, found naturally in the earth; any substance neither vegetable nor animal. * adj relating to or containing minerals.

mineralize vt to convert (something) into a mineral; to impregnate (something) with mineral matter; to change something into a fossil-like object. * vi (gases, etc, in molten rock) to transform a metal into an ore.—**mineralization** n.

mineral kingdom n the group of natural substances that consist of only inorganic matter.

mineralogy n the science of minerals.—**mineralogical** adj.—**mineralogically** adv.—**mineralogist** n.

mineral water n water containing mineral salts or gases, often with medicinal properties.

minestrone n a soup of vegetables with pieces of pasta.

minesweeper n a ship for clearing away explosive mines.—**minesweeping** n.

mingle vti to mix; to combine.—**mingler** n.

mingy adj (**mingier, mingiest**) (inf) meagre in quantity; miserly, mean.

mini n (pl **minis**) something smaller than others of its type; a miniskirt.

mini- prefix small.

miniature adj minute, on a small scale. * n a painting or reproduction on a very small scale.—**miniaturist** n.

miniaturize vt to greatly reduce the size of.—**miniaturization** n.

minibar n a small refrigerator in a hotel bedroom, stocked with alcoholic drinks.

minibus n (pl **minibuses, minibusses**) a small bus for carrying up to twelve passengers.

minicab n a saloon car used as a taxi, which can be booked by telephone but not hailed.

minicar n a very small car.

minicomputer n a computer intermediate in size and processing power between a mainframe and a microcomputer.

minim n a unit of fluid measure of one sixtieth of a fluid dram (0.0616ml) in the US and one twentieth of a scruple (0.592ml) in the UK; (mus) a half note.

minima see **minimum**.

minimal adj very minute; least possible.—**minimality** n.—**minimally** adv.

minimalism n a style in the creation of art, music, etc, that uses the fewest possible elements to achieve the greatest effect.—**minimalist** n, adj.

minimize vt to reduce to or estimate at a minimum.—**minimization** n.

minimum n (pl **minimums, minima**) the least possible amount; the lowest degree or point reached.

mining n the act, process, or industry of excavating from the earth; (mil) the laying of explosive mines.

minion n a servile flatterer or dependant; an obsequious person acting on behalf of or carrying out the wishes of another. * adj dainty, graceful.

miniseries n (pl **miniseries**) (TV) the dramatization of a novel, etc, shown in several episodes; (sport) a short series.

miniskirt n a very short skirt.

minister n a clergyman serving a church; an official heading a government department; a diplomat. * vi to serve as a minister in a church; to give help (to).—**ministerial** adj.—**ministerially** adv.

ministrant adj serving as a minister. * n a person who ministers.

ministration n the act or process of giving aid; the act of ministering religiously.

ministry n (pl **ministries**) the act of ministering; the clergy; the profession of a clergyman; a government department headed by a minister; the building housing a government department.

minium n red oxide of lead, used as a pigment in paints; red lead.

miniver n a white fur, orig from the Siberian squirrel, used as a trimming on ceremonial robes, etc.

mink n (pl **mink, minks**) any of several carnivorous weasel-like mammals valued for its durable soft fur.

Minn. abbr = Minnesota.

minnesinger n any of the German lyric poets and musicians of the 12th-14th centuries who sang about love and beauty.

minnow n (pl **minnow, minnows**) a small, slender freshwater fish.

minor adj lesser in size, importance, degree, extent, etc; (mus) lower than the corresponding major by a half step. * n (law) a person under full legal age; (education) a secondary area of study requiring fewer credits; (mus) a minor key, interval, or scale; (sport) a minor league, esp in baseball. * vi (with in) to take a subject requiring fewer credits.

Minorite, Minorist n a Franciscan friar, esp one of the order of Friars Minor.

minority n (pl **minorities**) the smaller part or number; a political or racial group smaller than the majority group; the state of being under age.

Minotaur n (Greek myth) a monster with the head of a bull and the body of a man, which ate human flesh.

minster n a large and important church, often with cathedral status.

minstrel n a travelling entertainer and musician in the Middle Ages; a performer in a minstrel show.

minstrel show n a variety show with performers singing and dancing wearing black face make-up.

minstrelsy n (pl **minstrelsies**) the art or occupation of minstrels; minstrels collectively; a collection of ballad poetry.

mint[1] n the place where money is coined; a large amount of money; a source of supply. * adj unused, in perfect condition. * vt (coins) to imprint; to invent.—**minter** n.

mint² n an aromatic plant whose leaves are used for flavouring.—**minty** adj.

mintage n a coin, etc, produced in a mint; the process of producing coins, etc, in a mint; the fee paid to a mint for coining gold or silver; an official mark on a coin.

mint julep n a tall drink of bourbon or brandy and sugar over crushed ice, garnished with mint.

minuend n (math) the number from which another number is to be subtracted.

minuet n (the music for) a slow, graceful dance in triple time.

minus prep less; (inf) without. * adj involving subtraction; negative; less than. * n a sign (-), indicating subtraction or negative quantity.

minute¹ n the sixtieth part of an hour or a degree; a moment; (pl) an official record of a meeting. * vt to record or summarize the proceedings (of).

minute² adj tiny; detailed; exact.—**minuteness** n.

minutely¹ adj occurring every minute. * adv every minute.

minutely² adv in a minute manner; precisely.

minuteman n (pl **minutemen**) (sometimes cap) a member of the militia in the War of American Independence, ready to fight at a minute's notice.

minutiae npl (sing **minutia**) small or unimportant details.

minx n a pert, forward girl; (arch) a prostitute.—**minxish** adj.

Miocene adj pertaining to the middle division of the Tertiary formation after the Olicene and before the Pliocene eras, marked by the appearance of grasses and grazing mammals. * n this division or rock formation.

miosis n abnormal contraction of the pupil of the eye.—also **myosis**.—**miotic** adj, n.

miracle n an extraordinary event attributed to the supernatural; an unusual or astounding event; a remarkable example of something.

miraculous adj supernatural; wonderful; able to work miracles.—**miraculously** adv.—**miraculousness** n.

mirage n an optical illusion in which a distant object or expanse of water seems to be nearby, caused by light reflection from hot air; anything illusory or fanciful.

mire n an area of wet, soggy, or muddy ground. * vt to sink in mire; to dirty; to embroil in difficulties.

mirk see **murk**.

mirky see **murky**.

mirror n a smooth surface that reflects images; a faithful depiction. * vt (**mirroring, mirrored**) to reflect or depict faithfully.

mirth n merriment, esp with laughter.

mirthful adj full of merriment.—**mirthfully** adv.—**mirthfulness** n.

mirthless adj lacking laughter; miserable.—**mirthlessly** adv.—**mirthlessness** n.

mis-¹ prefix wrong(ly); bad(ly); no, not.

mis-² see **miso-**.

misadventure n an unlucky accident; bad luck.

misalliance n an unsuitable alliance, usu by marriage with a person of lower social status; a mésalliance.

misanthrope, misanthropist n a person who hates or distrusts mankind.

misanthropic adj of or characterized by hatred of his or her fellow human beings.—**misanthropically** adv.—**misanthropy** n.

misogynist n a hater or distruster of women. * —**misogynistic** adj.

misapprehend vt to misunderstand; to misconceive.—**misapprehension** n.

misappropriate vt to appropriate wrongly or dishonestly; to use illegally; to embezzle.—**misappropriation** n.

misbehave vi to behave badly. * vt to behave (oneself) badly.—**misbehavior, misbehaviour** n.

misc. abbr = miscellaneous.

miscalculate vti to calculate wrongly.—**miscalculation** n.

miscarriage n the spontaneous expulsion of a foetus prematurely; mismanagement or failure.

miscarry vi (**miscarrying, miscarried**) to spontaneously expel a foetus from the uterus; to be unsuccessful; to fail.

miscellaneous adj consisting of various kinds; mixed.—**miscellaneously** adv.—**miscellaneousness** n.

miscellany n (pl **miscellanies**) a mixed collection; a book comprising miscellaneous writings, etc.

mischance n bad luck; an unlucky event.

mischief n wayward behaviour; damage.

mischievous adj harmful, prankish.—**mischievously** adv.—**mischievousness** n.

miscible adj (chem) (liquids) capable of being mixed.—**miscibility** n.

misconceive vt to conceive wrongly; to misjudge; to misapprehend; to misunderstand.—**misconceiver** n.

misconception n a mistaken idea; misunderstanding.

misconduct n dishonest management; improper behaviour. * vt to conduct (oneself) badly; to manage dishonestly.

misconstrue vt (**misconstruing, misconstrued**) to misinterpret.—**misconstruction** n.

miscreant n an unscrupulous villain; (arch) a heretic. * adj unscrupulous; (arch) heretical.

misdeed n a wrong or wicked act; crime; sin; etc.

misdemeanour, misdemeanor n (law) a minor offence, a misdeed.

miser n a greedy, stingy person who hoards money for its own sake.

miserable adj wretched; unhappy; causing misery; bad, inadequate; pitiable.—**miserableness** n.—**miserably** adv.

Miserere n the 51st Psalm, appointed for penitential acts; a musical setting of this psalm; (without cap) a misericord in a choir stall.

misericord, misericorde n a small ledge, often carved, on the underside of a folding seat in the stall of a church against which a worshipper can lean when standing; in the Middle Ages, a small dagger for giving a death thrust to a seriously wounded person, esp a knight; (Christianity) the relaxation of monastic rules for elderly or infirm monks or nuns; a room in a monastery for those with such a dispensation.

miserly adj like a miser; tending to hoard; very mean.—**miserliness** n.

misery n (pl **miseries**) extreme pain, unhappiness, or poverty; a cause of such suffering.

misfeasance n (law) the wrong performance of something that is itself legal.—**misfeasor** n.

misfire vi (engine, etc) to fail to ignite, start; to fail to succeed.—also n.

misfit n something that fits badly; a maladjusted person.

misfortune n ill luck; trouble; a mishap; bad luck.

misgiving n a feeling of misapprehension, mistrust.

misguided adj foolish; mistaken.—**misguidedly** adv.

mishap *n* an unfortunate accident.

mishmash *n* a confused mixture, hotchpotch.

Mishnah, Mishna *n* (*Judaism*) the oral law; the written form of this, which was collected in the 2nd century and forms the text of the earlier part of the Talmud.

misinform *vt* to supply with wrong information.—**misinformant, misinformer** *n*.—**misinformation** *n*.

misjudge *vt* to judge wrongly, to form a wrong opinion.—**misjudgment** *n*.

mislay *vt* (**mislaying, mislaid**) to lose something temporarily; to put down or install improperly.—**mislayer** *n*.

mislead *vt* (**misleading, misled**) to deceive; to give wrong information to; to lead into wrongdoing.—**misleader** *n*.

misleading *adj* deceptive; confusing.—**misleadingly** *adv*.

misnomer *n* an incorrect or unsuitable name or description.—**misnomered** *adj*.

miso-, mis- *prefix* hatred of.

misogamy *n* hatred of marriage.—**misogamic** *adj*.—**misogamist** *n*.

misogynist *n* a hater or distruster of women. * *adj* of or characterized by hatred of women.—**misogynistic** *adj*.

misogyny *n* hatred of women.—**misogynic** *adj*.

misplace *vt* to put in a wrong place; (*trust, etc*) to place unwisely.—**misplacement** *n*.

misprint *vt* to print incorrectly. * *n* an error in printing.

misprision *n* (*law*) the concealment of a seriously criminal act; the knowledge of the commission of treason and the failure to report this; (*arch*) contempt; the disparagement or undervaluing of something

mispronounce *vt* to pronounce wrongly.—**mispronunciation** *n*.

misquote *vt* to quote wrongly.—**misquotation** *n*.

misread *vt* (**misreading, misread**) to read or to interpret wrongly.

misrepresent *vt* to represent falsely; to give an untrue idea of.—**misrepresentation** *n*.—**misrepresentative** *adj*.

misrule *n* bad government. * *vt* to govern badly; to govern in an inhumane manner or with injustice.

miss[1] *n* (*pl* **misses**) a girl; (*with cap*) a title used before the surname of an unmarried woman or girl.

miss[2] *vt* to fail to reach, hit, find, meet, hear; to omit; to fail to take advantage of; to regret or discover the absence or loss of. * *vi* to fail to hit; to fail to be successful; to misfire, as an engine. * *n* a failure to hit, reach, obtain, etc.

Miss. *abbr* = Mississippi.

missal *n* a book containing the prayers for Mass.

misshapen *adj* badly shaped; deformed.

missile *n* an object, as a rock, spear, rocket, etc, to be thrown, fired, or launched.

missing *adj* absent; lost; lacking.

missing link *n* something required to complete a series; a hypothetical animal supposedly intermediate between the anthropoid apes and man.

mission *n* a group of people sent by a church, government, etc to carry out a special duty or task; the sending of an aircraft or spacecraft on a special assignment; a vocation. * *adj* of a mission; (*archit*) of a style of church building established by Spanish missioners in the southwest USA.

missionary *n* (*pl* **missionaries**) a person who tries to convert unbelievers to his or her religious faith, esp abroad; one sent on a mission. * *adj* of a religious mission; tending to propagandize.

missionary position *n* (*inf*) a position for sexual intercourse with the partners face to face and the man on top.

mission control *n* a command centre that controls space flights from the ground.

missioner *n* a missionary; a person in charge of a parochial mission.

missis *n* (*inf*) (*usu with* **the**) one's wife; (*inf*) a name used when directly addressing a woman.—*also* **missus**.

missive *n* (*formal*) a letter or message, often official. * *adj* (*rare*) sent specially, or intended to be sent.

misspent *adj* wasted, frittered away.

missus *see* **missis**.

mist *n* a large mass of water vapour, less dense than a fog; something that dims or obscures. * *vti* to cover or be covered, as with mist.

mistake *vb* (**mistaking, mistook,** *pp* **mistaken**) * *vt* to misunderstand; to misinterpret; * *vi* to make a mistake. * *n* a wrong idea, answer, etc; an error of judgment; a blunder; a misunderstanding.—**mistakable** *adj*.—**mistakably** *adv*.

mistaken *adj* erroneous, ill-judged.—**mistakenly** *adv*.

mister *n* (*inf*) sir; (*with cap*) the title used before a man's surname.

mistime *vt* to do or say at the wrong time; to time wrongly.

mistletoe *n* an evergreen parasitic plant with white berries used as a Christmas decoration.

mistreat *vt* to treat wrongly or badly.—**mistreatment** *n*.

mistress *n* a woman who is head of a household; a woman with whom a man is having a prolonged affair; a female schoolteacher; (*with cap*) the title used before a married woman's surname.

mistrust *n* lack of trust. * *vti* to doubt; to suspect.—**mistrustful** *adj*. —**mistrustfully** *adv*

misty *adj* (**mistier, mistiest**) full of mist; dim, obscure.—**mistily** *adv*.—**mistiness** *n*.

misunderstand *vt* (**misunderstanding, misunderstood**) to fail to understand correctly.

misunderstanding *n* a mistake as to sense; a quarrel or disagreement.

misunderstood *adj* not fully understood; not appreciated properly.

misuse *vt* to use for the wrong purpose or in the wrong way; to ill-treat, abuse. * *n* improper or incorrect use.

mite *n* any of numerous very small parasitic or free-living insects; (*money, etc*) a very small amount.

miter *see* **mitre**.

mitigate *vti* to become or make less severe.—**mitigable** *adj*.—**mitigation** *n*.—**mitigator** *n*.

mitosis *n* (*pl* **mitoses**) *n* a process by which plant or animal cells divide, in which the nucleus of a somatic cell splits into nuclei, each with the same number of chromosomes as there were in the orig cell.—**mitotic** *adj, adv*.

mitral *adj* of or like a mitre; (*anat*) pertaining to the mitral valve.

mitral valve *n* a valve of the heart between the left atrium and the left ventricle.

mitre, miter *n* the headdress of a bishop; a diagonal joint between two pieces of wood to form a corner. * *vt* to join with a mitre corner.—**miterer** *n*.

mitt *n* a glove covering the hand but only the base of

the fingers; (*sl*) a hand; a boxing glove; a baseball glove.

mitten *n* a glove with a thumb but no separate fingers.

mix *vt* to blend together in a single mass; to make by blending ingredients, as a cake; to combine; (*with* **up**) to make into a mixture; to make disordered; to confuse or mistake. * *vi* to be mixed or blended; to get along together. * *n* a mixture.—**mixable** *adj*.

mixed *adj* blended; made up of different parts, classes, races, etc; confused.

mixed bag *n* (*inf*) a collection of diverse things or people.

mixed economy *n* an economic system containing both state-owned industries and private enterprise.

mixed-up *adj* (*inf*) perplexed, mentally confused.

mixer *n* a device that blends or mixes; a person considered in terms of their ability (good or bad) to get on with others; a soft drink added to an alcoholic beverage.

mixture *n* the process of mixing; a blend made by mixing.

mix-up *n* a mistake; confusion, muddle; (*inf*) a fight.

mizzen, mizen *n* (*naut*) the lowest sail on the mizzenmast of a vessel; the mizzenmast. * *adj* pertaining to something used with the mizzenmast.

mizzenmast, mizenmast *n* (*naut*) the aftermost mast when there are three masts on a ship; the aftermast on other ships.

mizzle *vi* to rain in very minute drops, to drizzle. * *n* a very fine rain.

mkt *abbr* = market.

ml *abbr* = mile; milliliter.

Mlle(s) *abbr* = mademoiselle, mesdemoiselles.

MM *abbr* = Messieurs.

mm *abbr* = millimeter.

MN *abbr* = Minnesota.

Mn (*chem symbol*) manganese.

mnemonic *adj* of or aiding memory.—*n* a device to aid the memory.—**mnemonically** *adv*.

mnemonics *n sing* a technique of assisting the memory by using formulae to remember things.

Mnemosyne *n* (*Greek myth*) the goddess of memory.

MO *abbr* = Missouri.

Mo (*chem symbol*) molybdenum.

moa *n* any one of several extinct species of large, wingless birds of New Zealand.

Moabite *adj* pertaining to the ancient kingdom of Moab, now part of Jordan. * *n* an inhabitant of Moab.

moan *n* a low mournful sound as of sorrow or pain. * *vti* to utter a moan; to complain.—**moaner** *n*.—**moaningly** *adv*.

moat *n* a deep ditch surrounding a fortification or castle, usu filled with water.

mob *n* a disorderly or riotous crowd; a contemptuous term for the masses; (*sl*) a gang of criminals. * *vt* (**mobbing, mobbed**) to attack in a disorderly group; to surround.—**mobbish** *adj*.

mobcap *n* a plain cap, usu surrounded with a frill, worn indoors by women in the 18th century.

mobile *adj* movable, not fixed; easily changing; characterized by ease in change of social status; capable of moving freely and quickly; (*inf*) having transport. * *n* a suspended structure of wood, metal, etc with parts that move in air currents.—**mobility** *n*.

mobilize *vt* to prepare for action, esp war by readying troops for active service; to organize for a particular reason; to put to use.—**mobilization** *n*.

mobocracy *n* (*pl* **mobocracies**) political rule or ascendancy of the mob; a ruling mob.—**mobocrat** *n*.—**mobocratic** *adj*.—**mobocratically** *adv*.

mobster *n* (*sl*) a gangster.

moccasin *n* a flat shoe based on Amerindian footwear; any soft, flexible shoe resembling this.

mocha *n* a type of coffee, orig from Arabia; a flavouring made from coffee and chocolate.—*also adj*.

mock *vt* to imitate or ridicule; to behave with scorn; to defy; (*with* **up**) to make a model of. * *n* ridicule; an object of scorn. * *adj* false, sham, counterfeit.—**mocker** *n*.—**mockingly** *adv*.

mockery *n* (*pl* **mockeries**) derision, ridicule, or contempt; imitation, esp derisive; someone or something that is mocked; an inadequate person, thing, or action.

mock-heroic *adj* parodying the heroic style of literature or, particularly, poetry, esp when the subject matter is unheroic. * *n* a burlesque imitation of an epic poem or of the heroic style in general.—**mock-heroically** *adv*.

mockingbird *n* a grey American bird with the ability to imitate with exactness the call of other birds.

mockup, mock-up *n* a full-scale working model of a machine, etc.

mod *n* (*often with cap*) a member of a British youth group of the mid-1960s who wore highly fashionable clothes and opposed the rockers, another youth group; a member of a revival of this group, in the late 1970s and early 1980s, whose opposition was to skinheads.

mod. *abbr* = moderate, moderato, modern.

modal *adj* of mode or form, not substance; (*gram*) expressing mood; (*philos*) asserting with qualification; (*mus*) of or composed in a mode.—**modality** *n*.—**modally** *adv*.

mode *n* a way of acting, doing or existing; a style or fashion; form; (*mus*) any of the scales used in composition; (*statistics*) the predominant item in a series of items; (*gram*) mood.

model *n* a pattern; an ideal; a standard worth imitating; a representation on a smaller scale, usu three-dimensional; a person who sits for an artist or photographer; a person who displays clothes by wearing them. * *adj* serving as a model; representative of others of the same style. * *vb* (**modelling, modelled** *or* **modeling, modeled**) *vt* (*with* **after, on**) to create by following a model; to display clothes by wearing. * *vi* to serve as a model for an artist, etc.—**modeler, modeller** *n*.

modem *n* a device that links two computers via the telephone network for transmitting data.

moderate *vti* to make or become moderate; to preside over. * *adj* having reasonable limits; avoiding extremes; mild, calm; of medium quality, amount, etc. * *n* a person who holds moderate views.—**moderately** *adv*.—**moderateness** *n*.

moderation *n* moderateness; freedom from excess; equanimity.

moderato *adv* (*mus*) moderately.

moderator *n* a mediator; (*physics*) a substance that slows the speed of neutrons in a nuclear reactor; (*Presbyterian Church*) a minister who presides at a court, assembly, synod, etc.

modern *adj* of the present or recent times; up-to-date.—**modernity** *n*.—**modernly** *adv*.

modernism *n* modern view, methods or usage; the theory or practice of modern art, literature, etc;

(*Christianity*) rationalistic theology.—**modernist** *adj*, *n*.—**modernistic** *adj*.—**modernistically** *adv*.

modernize *vti* to make or become modern.—**modernization** *n*.

modest *adj* moderate; having a humble opinion of oneself; unpretentious.—**modestly** *adv*.

modesty *n* (*pl* **modesties**) the quality or state of being modest; propriety of behaviour or manner; diffidence; moderation.

modicum *n* (*pl* **modicums, modica**) a small quantity.

modification *n* a modifying or being modified; the result of this; a modified form; an adjustment, alteration; (*biol*) a change in an organism caused by environmental factors but not passed on.—**modificator** *n*.—**modificatory, modificative** *adj*.

modifier *n* one who or that which modifies; (*gram*) a word, clause or phrase that qualifies or limits the meaning of another word, etc, a qualifier.

modify *vt* (**modifying, modified**) to lessen the severity of; to change or alter slightly; (*gram*) to limit in meaning, to qualify.—**modifiable** *adj*.—**modifiability** *n*.

modillion *n* (*archit*) an ornamental bracket under a cornice in the Corinthian order.

modiolus (*pl* **modioli**) *n* (*anat*) the pillar of the cochlea of the internal ear.

modish *adj* fashionable, stylish.—**modishly** *adv*.—**modishness** *n*.

modiste *n* a person who makes fashionable dresses or hats.

modulate *vti* to adjust; to regulate; to vary the pitch, intensity, frequency, etc, of.—**modulator** *n*.—**modulatory** *adj*.

modulation *n* a modulating or being modulated; a change in pitch or intensity of the voice; (*gram*) inflection, esp to change meaning; (*mus*) a transition from one key to another by progression; (*electronics*) the variation of amplitude, frequency or phase of a signal or wave in response to another signal or wave, esp in the transfer to carrier waves.

module *n* a unit of measurement; a self-contained unit, esp in a spacecraft; (*archit*) a semi-diameter of a shaft, etc, used as a standard for regulating other proportions; (*education*) one of a set of learning units making up a course of study.—**modular** *adj*.

modulus *n* (*pl* **moduli**) a quantity expressing the measure of some function or property, eg elasticity.

modus operandi *n* (*pl* **modi operandi**) a method of operating, procedure.

modus vivendi *n* (*pl* **modi vivendi**) a compromise, as between two parties in dispute; a way of living.

mofette, moffette *n* a fissure in an almost extinct volcano from which carbon dioxide and other gases issue; the gases.

mogul, moghul *n* (*inf*) an important person, a magnate; (*with cap*) a ruler of the former Moghul Empire in India.

mohair *n* the long, fine hair of the Angora goat; the silk cloth made from it.

Mohammedan *n, adj* a former word for Muslim.

Mohave *n* (*pl* **Mohaves, Mohave**) one of a North American Indian people who occupied the land along the Colorado river.—*also* **Mojave**.

Mohawk *n* (*pl* **Mohawks, Mohawk**) one of a North American Indian people who occupied the area from the St Lawrence to the Mohawk river. * *n* the language of the Mohawk people.

Mohican *see* **Mahican**.

mohican *n* a hairstyle in which the sides of the head are shaved, leaving a central band of hair, often dyed or in spikes, from the forehead to the nape of the neck.

moidore *n* an ancient Portuguese gold coin.

moiety *n* (*pl* **moieties**) one of two parts or shares; a half.

moiré *n* a fabric, usu silk, that has a surface pattern suggesting rippling water; such a pattern impressed on a fabric.

moiré effect *n* a pattern created when the same pattern is superimposed on another version of itself.

moist *adj* damp; slightly wet.—**moistly** *adv*.—**moistness** *n*.

moisten *vti* to make or become moist.—**moistener** *n*.

moisture *n* liquid in a diffused, absorbed, or condensed state.

moisturize *vt* (*skin, air, etc*) to add moisture to.—**moisturizer** *n*.

Mojave *see* **Mohave**.

moke *n* (*sl*) a boring person; (*Br*) a donkey; (*Austral*) a horse not of the top class.

molar[1] *n* a back tooth, used for grinding food.

molar[2] *adj* of or in the whole mass of matter as distinguished from the properties or motions of atoms or molecules.

molasses *n* (*pl* **molasses**) the thick brown sugar that is produced during the refining of sugar; treacle.

mold[1] *n* a fungus producing a furry growth on the surface of organic matter. * *vi* to become moldy.—*also* **mould**.

mold[2] *n* a hollow form in which something is cast; a pattern; something made in a mold; distinctive character. * *vt* to make in or on a mold; to form, shape, guide.—*also* **mould**.—**moldable** *adj*.—**molder** *n*.

molder *vi* to decay to rot, to crumble to dust.

molding *n* anything made in a mould; a shaped strip of wood or plaster, as around the upper walls of a room.—*also* **moulding**.

moldy *adj* (**moldier, moldiest**) containing or covered with mould; musty, stale; antiquated; (*sl*) dull, boring.—*also* **mouldy**.—**moldiness** *n*.

mole[1] *n* a spot on the skin, usu dark-coloured and raised.

mole[2] *n* a small burrowing insectivore with soft dark fur; a spy within an organization.

mole[3] *n* a large breakwater.

mole[4] *n* the basic SI unit of substance.

molecular *adj* of or inherent in molecules.

molecular biology *n* the branch of biology dealing with the molecular basis of heredity and of protein synthesis.

molecular formula the chemical formula that indicates both the number and type of any atom present in a molecular substance.

molecular weight *n* the total of the atomic weights of all the atoms present in a molecule; the average mass per molecule of any substance relative to one-twelfth the mass of an atom of carbon-12.

molecule *n* the simplest unit of a substance, retaining the chemical properties of that substance; a small particle.

molehill *n* a mound of earth thrown up by a burrowing mole.

moleskin *n* the fur of a mole; a twilled cotton cloth with a soft surface resembling a mole's fur, used for work clothes; (*pl*) trousers made of moleskin.

molest *vt* to annoy; to attack or assault, esp sexually.—**molestation** *n*.—**molester** *n*.

moll *adj* (*sl*) a female partner of a thief or other criminal; a prostitute.

mollify *vt* (**mollifying, mollified**) to make less severe or violent; to soften.—**mollification** *n.*—**mollifier** *n.*—**mollifyingly** *adv.*

mollusk, mollusc *n* an invertebrate animal usu enclosed in a shell, as oysters, etc.—**molluscan, molluskan** *adj, n.*

mollycoddle *vti* to care for someone in an indulgent way; to coddle, pamper. * *n* someone so treated.—**mollycoddler** *n.*

moloch *n* a spiny Australian lizard with a horned head, found in desert areas; (*with cap*) (*Old Testament*) an ancient Semitic fire god to whom children were offered as a sacrifice.

molt *vi* to shed hair, skin, horns, etc prior to replacement of new growth. * *n* a moulting.—*also* **moult.**—**molter** *n.*

molten *adj* melted by heat.

molto *adj* (*mus*) very (modifying another musical direction).

moly *n* (*pl* **molies**) (*Greek myth*) a herb with a black root and a white flower with the power of counteracting the spells of Circe.

molybdenum *n* a metallic element used in alloys, esp strengthening steel.—**molybdous, molybdic** *adj.*

mom, mom (*inf*) mother.

moment *n* an indefinitely brief period of time; a definite point in time; a brief time of importance.

momenta *see* **momentum.**

momentarily *adv* for a short time; in an instant; at any moment.

momentary *adj* lasting only for a moment.—**momentariness** *n.*

momentous *adj* very important.—**momentously** *adv.*—**momentousness** *n.*

momentum *n* (*pl* **momenta, momentums**) the impetus of a moving object, equal to the product of its mass and its velocity.

momma *n* mama.

mommy *n* (*pl* **mommies**) (*inf*) mother.

Mon. *abbr* = Monday.

mon-, mono- *prefix* alone, sole, single.

monachism *n* monasticism; the monastic life or system.—**monachal** *adj.*

monad *n* a unit, number one; (*philos*) the ultimate unit of being or evolution in Leibniz's theory; (*chem*) a radical or atom with a valency of one; (*biol*) a single-celled organism.—**monadic, monadical** *adj.*—**monadically** *adv.*

monadelphous *adj* (*bot*) having stamens in one bundle of filaments wrapped around the style.

monadism *n* (*philos*) the theory, esp as propounded by Leibniz, that the real universe is composed of monads.

monandrous *adj* having only one husband or male partner at a time; (*flowers*) having one stamen only; (*plants*) having flowers with only one stamen.

monandry *n* the custom of having only one husband at a time; (*bot*) a being monandrous.

monarch *n* a sovereign who rules by hereditary right; a powerful or dominant thing or person.—**monarchal, monarchic, monarchical** *adj.*—**monarchically** *adv.*

monarchism *n* the principles of, or devotion to, monarchy.—**monarchist** *n, adj.*—**monarchistic** *adj.*

monarchy *n* (*pl* **monarchies**) a government headed by a monarch; a kingdom.

monastery *n* (*pl* **monasteries**) the residence of a group of monks, or nuns.—**monasterial** *adj.*

monastic, monastical *adj* of monks or monasteries. * *n* a monk; a recluse.—**monastically** *adv.*—**monasticism** *n.*

Monday *n* the second day of the week.

monecious *see* **monoecious.**

monetarism *n* (*economics*) the theory that control of the money supply is the key to achieving low inflation and economic growth.—**monetarist** *n, adj.*

monetary *adj* of the coinage or currency of a country; of or relating to money.—**monetarily** *adv.*

monetize *vt* to convert into money; to give a standard of current value to.—**monetization** *n.*

money *n* (*pl* **moneys, monies**) coins or paper notes authorized by a government as a medium of exchange; property; wealth.

moneychanger *n* one who changes money into other coinage at fixed rate; a machine that dispenses coins.

moneyed *adj* rich.—*also* **monied.**

moneylender *n* a person who lends money for interest, esp as a business.—**moneylending** *n.*

monger *n* a dealer.

mongoose *n* (*pl* **mongooses**) a small predatory mammal of Africa and Asia.

mongrel *n* an animal or plant of mixed or unknown breed, esp a dog. * *adj* of mixed breed or origin.—**mongrelism** *n.*—**mongrelly** *adj.*

mongrelize *vt* to render mongrel.—**mongrelization** *n.*

monied *see* **moneyed.**

monies *see* **money.**

moniker, monicker *n* (*sl*) a name; a nickname.

moniliform *adj* (*biol*) shaped like a necklace.

monism *n* (*philos*) the theory that there is only one kind of being and that matter and mind are ultimately identical.—**monist** *n, adj.*—**monistic** *adj.*—**monistically** *adv.*

monition *n* an admonition; a formal notice from an ecclesiastical court to an offender; a summons; a warning.

monitor *n* a student chosen to help the teacher; any device for regulating the performance of a machine, aircraft, etc; a screen for viewing the image being produced by a television camera; a display screen connected to a computer. * *vti* (*TV or radio transmissions, etc*) to observe or listen to for political or technical reasons; to watch or check on; to regulate or control, a machine, etc.—**monitorial** *adj.*

monitory *adj* conveying a warning. * *n* (*pl* **monitories**) a letter containing an admonition or warning, esp a papal letter.

monk *n* a male member of a religious order living in a monastery.

monkey *n* any of the primates except man and the lemurs, esp the smaller, long-tailed primates; a mischievous child; (*sl*) £500 or $500. * *vi* (**monkeying, monkeyed**) (*inf*) to play, trifle, or meddle.

monkey business *n* (*inf*) mischief; underhand dealings.

monkey wrench *n* a large wrench with an adjustable jaw.

monkfish *n* (*pl* **monkfish, monkfishes**) an angelfish.

monkhood *n* the character or condition of a monk; monks collectively.

monkish *adj* pertaining to or resembling a monk; monastic.—**monkishly** *adv.*—**monkishness** *n.*

monkshood, monk's-hood *n* a poisonous plant, aconite.

mono *adj* (*inf*) monophonic. * *n* (*pl* **monos**) (*inf*) monophonic sound.

mono-, mon- *prefix* alone, sole, single.

monobasic *adj* (*chem*) having one base or atom of a base.

monocarp *n* a monocarpic plant.

monocarpic, monocarpous *adj* (*bot*) bearing fruit only once.

monochord *n* a one-stringed musical instrument with a sound box for determining musical intervals.

monochromatic *adj* consisting of one colour.—**monochromatically** *adv*.

monochrome *n* a painting, drawing, or print in a single colour. * *adj* in one colour or shades of one colour; black and white—**monochromic** *adj*.

monocle *n* a single eyeglass held in place by the face muscles.—**monocled** *adj*.

monocline *n* a geological formation in which the strata are tilted one way only.—**monoclinal** *adj*.

monocotyledon *n* any plant with one seed leaf and three-part flowers, incl grasses, lilies and orchids.—**monocotyledonous** *adj*.

monocrat *n* one who governs alone; an advocate of autocracy or monarchy.—**monocracy** *n*.

monocular *adj* pertaining to, for, or with one eye only; adapted for use with one eye.

monodrama *n* a dramatic piece for one actor.—**monodramatic** *adj*.

monody *n* (*pl* **monodies**) in Greek tragedy, a lyrical poem sung by one actor alone; a plaintive poem or song for one voice, a dirge, an elegy; (*mus*) a composition for one voice, usu accompanied.—**monodic, monodical** *adj*.—**monodist** *n*.

monoecious *adj* (*bot*) having stamens and pistils on the same plant but on different flowers; (*zool*) hermaphroditic.—*also* **monecious**.—**monoeciously** *adv*.

monogamy *n* the practice of being married to only one person at a time.—**monogamist** *n*.—**monogamous** *adj*.

monogenesis *n* derivation from a single cell, resulting in an organism like the adult of the species; asexual reproduction from a single cell; the supposed descent of all organisms from one orig cell; the supposed descent of all human beings from one orig pair.—**monogenous** *adj*.

monogenetic *adj* pertaining to or having the property of monogenesis; (*animals*) born, living and dying on a single host; (*rocks*) originating from a single source or by a single process.

monogram *n* the embroidered or printed initials of one's name on clothing, stationery, etc.—**monogrammed** *adj*.—**monogrammatic** *adj*.

monograph *n* a learned paper written on one particular subject. * *vt* to write such a paper on.—**monographer** *n*.—**monographic** *adj*.—**monographically** *adv*.

monolith *n* a single large block of stone; any massive, unyielding structure.—**monolithic** *adj*.—**monolithically** *adv*.

monologue, monolog *n* a long speech; a soliloquy, a skit, etc for one actor only.—**monologuist, monologist** *n*.

monomania *n* an irrational obsession with a single subject, object, idea, etc.—**monomaniac** *n*.—**monomaniacal** *adj*.

monometallic *adj* containing only one metal; of monometallism.

monometallism *n* the use of a single metal, often gold or silver, as a standard of currency; the economic system underpinning such a standard.—**monometallist** *n*.

monomial *n* (*math*) an expression consisting of one term; (*biol*) a taxonomic classification consisting of one term.—*also adj*.

monomorphic, monomorphous *adj* (*species*) of one type or structure or with parts that have only one type or structure; (*individual organism*) unchanging in shape throughout its life cycle; (*chem*) denoting a chemical compound with a single crystalline form.

monopetalous *adj* (*bot*) (*flowers*) having the corolla in one piece; possessing a single petal.

monophobia *n* an overwhelming fear of being alone.—**monophobic** *adj*.

monophonic *adj* (*sound reproduction*) using one channel only for transmission.—**monophonically** *adv*.

monophthong *n* a simple single vowel sound; two different written vowels pronounced as a single sound.—**monophthongal** *adj*.

monoplane *n* an aeroplane with a single pair of wings.

monoplegia *n* paralysis affecting one limb or one group of muscles only.—**monoplegic** *adj, n*.

monopolize *vt* to get, have, or exploit a monopoly of; to get full control of.—**monopolization** *n*.—**monopolizer** *n*.

monopoly *n* (*pl* **monopolies**) exclusive control in dealing in a particular commodity or supplying a service; exclusive use or possession; that which is exclusively controlled; such control granted by a government.—**monopolism** *n*.—**monopolist** *n*.—**monopolistic** *adj*.—**monopolistically** *adv*.

monorail *n* a single track railway, often with suspended carriages.

monosepalous *adj* (*bot*) (*flowers*) having the calyx undivided; possessing a single sepal.

monosodium glutamate *n* a chemical additive used to give food a meaty taste.

monospermous, monospermal *adj* (*plants*) one-seeded.

monostich *n* a poem in one line.—**monostichic** *adj*.

monosyllabic *adj* (*word*) having one syllable; characterized by or made up of one syllable; terse; curt.—**monosyllabically** *adv*.

monosyllable *n* a word of one syllable.

monotheism *n* the doctrine of or belief in the existence of only one God.—**monotheist** *n*.—**monotheistic** *adj*.—**monotheistically** *adv*.

monotone *n* an utterance or musical tone without a change in pitch; a tiresome sameness of style, colour, etc.—**monotonic** *adj*.—**monotonically** *adv*.

monotonous *adj* unvarying in tone; with dull uniformity, wearisome.—**monotonously** *adv*.—**monotonousness** *n*.

monotony *n* (*pl* **monotonies**) lack of variety; irksome sameness.

monotreme *n* one of a primitive order of Australian egg-laying mammals, with a single vent for digestive, urinary and genital organs.—**monotrematous** *adj*.

Monotype *n* (*trademark*) a hot-metal typesetting machine that casts each character separately; type so cast.

monotype *n* (*print*) one print from a metal or glass plate with a painted image; (*biol*) a genus or species that has only a single type.—**monotypic** *adj*.

monovalent *adj* (*chem*) with a valency of one; univalent.—**monovalence, monovalency** *n*.

monoxide *n* an oxide with one oxygen atom in each molecule.

Monseigneur *n* (*pl* **Messeigneurs**) a French title given to princes, prelates and bishops.

monsieur *n* (*pl* **messieurs**) the French equivalent of sir in address and of Mr with a name.

Monsignor *n* (*pl* **Monsignors, Monsignore**) (*RC Church*) a title given, usu by the Pope, to some prelates or offices.

monsoon *n* a seasonal wind of southern Asia; the rainy season.

monster *n* any greatly malformed plant or animal; an imaginary beast; a very wicked person; a very large animal or thing. * *adj* very large, huge.

monstrance *n* (*RC Church*) a transparent vessel, usu set in a gold or silver frame, in which the consecrated Host is carried in procession or exhibited.

monstrosity *n* (*pl* **monstrosities**) the state or quality of being monstrous; an ugly, unnatural or monstrous thing or person.

monstrous *adj* abnormally developed; enormous; horrible.—**monstrously** *adv*.—**monstrousness** *n*.

montage *n* a rapid sequence of film shots, often superimposed; the art or technique of assembling various elements, esp pictures or photographs; such an assemblage.

montane *adj* of or inhabiting mountains or mountainous terrain.

monte (bank) *n* a gambling card game orig played with dice or cards in Spain.

Montessori method *n* a system of educating very young children, through play, based on free discipline, with each child developing at his own pace.

month *n* any of the twelve divisions of the year; a calendar month.

monthly *adj* continuing for a month; done, happening, payable, etc every month. * *n* a monthly periodical. * *adv* once a month; every month.

monticule *n* a hillock; a small mound resulting from a volcanic eruption.

monument *n* an obelisk, statue or building that commemorates a person or an event; an exceptional example.

monumental *adj* of, like, or serving as a monument; colossal; lasting.—**monumentality** *n*.—**monumentally** *adv*.

moo *n* the long deep sound made by a cow. * *vi* (*cattle*) to low; to make a deep long noise like a cow.

mooch *vt* (*sl*) to wander around aimlessly; (*sl*) to cadge, steal.—**moocher** *n*.

mood *n* a temporary state of mind or temper; a gloomy feeling; a predominant feeling or spirit; (*gram*) that form of a verb indicating mode of action; (*mus*) mode.

moody *adj* (**moodier, moodiest**) gloomy; temperamental.—**moodily** *adv*.—**moodiness** *n*.

moon *n* the natural satellite that revolves around the earth and shines by reflected sunlight; any natural satellite of another planet; something shaped like the moon. * *vi* to behave in an idle or abstracted way.

moonbeam *n* a ray of moonlight.

mooncalf *n* (*pl* **mooncalves**) a born fool; an idler; (*arch*) a monster.

moonflower *n* any of a family of climbing or creeping plants with trumpet-shaped flowers that bloom at night; a tropical plant, orig found in Mexico, with white flowers that bloom at night.

moonlight *n* the light of the moon. * *vi* (*inf*) to have a secondary (usu night-time) job.—**moonlighter** *n*.

moonlit *adj* lit by the moon.

moonraker, moonsail *n* (*naut*) a small sail carried above a skysail.

moonshine *n* moonlight; (*inf*) nonsense, foolish talk; (*sl*) illegally distilled spirits.

moonshiner *n* (*sl*) a distiller of illicit whiskey; a whiskey smuggler.

moonstone *n* a translucent yellowish or yellowish-white stone that exhibits pearly blue-tinged reflections, used as a gemstone.

moonstruck, moonstricken *adj* besotted with love or sentiment; demented.

moonwort *n* a fern with crescent-shaped fronds, grape fern; honesty.

moony *adj* (**moonier, mooniest**) of or like the moon; crescent-shaped; round; listless, dreamy; absent-minded.

Moor *n* a North African Muslim of mixed Arab and Berber ancestry.

moor[1] *n* a tract of open wasteland, usu covered with heather and often marshy.

moor[2] *vti* (*a ship*) to secure or be secured by cable or anchor.

moorage *n* the act of mooring a vessel; a place or charge for mooring.

moorcock *n* the male red grouse.

moorfowl *n* (*arch*) red grouse collectively.

moorhen *n* an aquatic dark-coloured bird with a red bill and a characteristic red mark above the bill, found in ponds and lakes; the female red grouse.

mooring *n* the act of mooring; the place where a ship is moored; (*pl*) the lines, cables, etc by which a ship is moored.

Moorish *adj* pertaining to the Moors; denoting a Spanish architectural style of the 13th-16th centuries, one of the distinguishing features of which is the horseshoe arch.

moorland *n* a stretch of moors.

moose *n* (*pl* **moose**) the largest member of the deer family, native to North America.

moot *adj* debatable; hypothetical. * *vt* (**mooting, mooted**) to propose for discussion.

mop *n* a rag, sponge, etc fixed to a handle for washing floors or dishes; a thick or tangled head of hair. * *vt* (**mopping, mopped**) to wash with a mop.

mope *vi* to be gloomy and apathetic. * *n* a person who mopes, a moper.—**moper** *n*.—**mopey** *adj*.—**mopingly** *adv*.

moped *n* a light, motor-assisted bicycle.

moppet *n* a pet name for a small child, esp a girl; (*arch*) a rag doll.

moquette *n* a material with short velvety pile used for carpets and upholstery.

MOR *abbr* = middle-of-the-road.

moraine *n* a mass of earth, stones, etc, deposited by a glacier.—**morainal, morainic** *adj*.

moral *adj* of or relating to character and human behaviour, particularly as regards right and wrong; virtuous, esp in sexual conduct; capable of distinguishing right from wrong; probable, although not certain; psychological, emotional. * *n* a moral lesson taught by a fable, event, etc; (*pl*) principles; ethics.

morale *n* moral or mental condition with respect to courage, discipline, confidence, etc.

moralism *n* moralizing; a moral attitude or maxim; the practice of or belief in a system of morals independent of religion.

moralist *n* a teacher or student of morals; one for whom morality needs no religious sanction; one concerned with the morals of others.—**moralistic** *adj.*—**moralistically** *adv.*

morality *n* (*pl* **moralities**) virtue; moral principles; a particular system of moral principles.

morality play *n* a medieval allegorical play.

moralize, moralise *vt* to explain or interpret morally; to give a moral direction to. * *vi* to make moral pronouncements.—**moralization, moralisation** *n.*—**moralizer, moraliser** *n.*

morally *adv* in a moral manner, ethically; virtually, practically.

moral philosophy *n* ethics.

Moral Rearmament *n* an international evangelical movement, founded in the US by Frank Buchman (1938), that seeks moral and spiritual revival following conservative Christian principles.—*also* **Buchmanism.**

morass *n* a bog, marsh.

moratorium *n* (*pl* **moratoria, moratoriums**) a legally authorized delay in the payment of money due; an authorized delay or suspension of any activity.—**moratory** *adj.*

morbid *adj* diseased, resulting as from a diseased state of mind; gruesome.—**morbidly** *adv.*—**morbidness** *n.*

morbidity *n* the state of being morbid; the relative incidence of disease.

morbific *adj* causing or producing disease.

morceau *n* (*pl* **morceaux**) a small piece, a morsel; a short work, usu a musical one.

mordacious *adj* biting; sarcastic; cutting.—**mordaciously** *adv.*—**mordacity** *n.*

mordant *adj* biting, caustic; corrosive. * *n* a chemical fixative; a corrosive substance.—**mordancy** *n.*—**mordantly** *adv.*

mordent *n* (*mus*) a trill created by one note rapidly alternating with another one degree below it, used as an ornament

more *adj* (*superl* **most**) greater; further; additional (— *also compar of* **many, much**). * *adv* to a greater extent or degree; again; further.

moreen *n* a stout woollen fabric used esp for furnishings, often embossed or figured with a watered pattern.

morel[1] *n* an edible mushroom with a brownish cap.

morel[2] *n* a nightshade, esp the black nightshade.

morello *n* (*pl* **morellos**) a small dark-red cherry with a tart flavour.

moreover *adv* in addition to what has been said before; besides.

mores *npl* customs so fundamentally established that they have the force of law.

Moresque *adj* (*archit*) Moorish style. * *n* an example of such decoration or architecture; a design in this style.

morganatic *adj* (*marriage*) between a royal person and one of lower rank the children of which are legitimate but neither they nor the morganatic wife or husband share royal rank or property.—**morganatically** *adv.*

morgue *n* a place where the bodies of unknown dead or those dead of unknown causes are temporarily kept prior to burial; a collection of reference materials, eg newspaper clippings.

MORI *abbr* = Market and Opinion Research Institute.

moribund *adj* in a dying state; near death.—**moribundity** *n.*

morion *n* a 16th-century hat-shaped helmet without beaver or visor.

Mormon *n* a member of the Church of Latter-Day Saints whose authority is the Bible and the Book of Mormon, revelations to Joseph Smith in 1827.—**Mormonism** *n.*

morn *n* (*poet*) dawn, morning; (*Scot*) tomorrow.

mornay *n* a white sauce flavoured with cheese. * *adj* (*eggs, etc*) cooked with this sauce.

morning *n* the part of the day from midnight or dawn until noon; the early part of anything. * *adj* of or in the morning.

morning coat *n* a tailcoat, usu grey, with a cutaway front.

morning-glory *n* (*pl* **morning-glories**) any of various twining plants with showy blue bell-shaped flowers.

morning sickness *n* a period of nausea and vomiting in the early stages of pregnancy.

morning star *n* a planet, esp Venus, rising before the sun.

morning suit *n* a man's formal suit of a morning coat and striped trousers.

morning watch *n* (*naut*) a watch on board ship from 4 am to 8 am.

morocco *n* (*pl* **moroccos**) a fine kind of grained leather of goatskin or sheepskin, used in bookbinding and for shoes.

moron *n* an adult mentally equal to a 8 to 12-year-old child; (*inf*) a very stupid person.—**moronic** *adj.*—**moronically** *adv.*—**moronism, moronity** *n.*

morose *adj* sullen, surly; gloomy.—**morosely** *adv.*—**moroseness** *n.*

morpheme *n* the smallest meaningful unit of language as a base, prefix or suffix.—**morphemic** *adj.*—**morphemically** *adv.*

Morpheus *n* (*Greek myth*) the god of dreams and of sleep.

morphine, morphia *n* an alkaloid derived from opium, used as an anaesthetic and sedative.—**morphinic** *adj.*

morphinism *n* addiction to morphine; poisoning caused by the excessive use of morphine.

morphogen *n* that substance in an embryo that determines what the structure will become.

morphology *n* a branch of biology dealing with the form and structure of organisms; the study of word formation in a language.—**morphological** *adj.*—**morphologist** *n.*

morris (dance) *n* a traditional English dance accompanied by tambourines, bells, castanets, violin, concertina, etc, and usu performed by men in costumes representing the Robin Hood legend or other characters from English folklore.

morrow *n* (*arch, poet*) morning; the following day.

morse *n* a jewelled clasp on a cope.

Morse code *n* a code in which letters are represented by dots and dashes or long and short sounds, and are transmitted by visual or audible signals.

morsel *n* a small quantity of food; a small piece of anything.

mort[1] *n* a note or notes sounded on a hunting horn to notify a kill.

mort[2] *n* (*dial*) a great amount or number (of).

mort[3] *n* a salmon in its third year.

mortal *adj* subject to death; causing death, fatal; hostile; very intense. * *n* a human being.—**mortally** *adv.*

mortality *n* (*pl* **mortalities**) state of being mortal; death on a large scale, as from war; number or frequency of deaths in a given period relative to population.

mortality rate *n* the yearly proportion of deaths to population.—*also* **death rate**.

mortar *n* a mixture of cement or lime with sand and water used in building; an artillery piece that fires shells at low velocities and high trajectories; a bowl in which substances are pounded with a pestle.

mortarboard *n* a small square board for holding mortar; a square black college or university cap with a tassel.

mortgage *n* a transfer of rights to a piece of property usu as security for the payment of a loan or debt that becomes void when the debt is paid. * *vt* to make over as a security or pledge; to put an advance claim on.

mortgagee *n* one to whom a mortgage is made or given.

mortgagor, mortgager *n* one who grants a mortgage.

mortician *n* a person who manages funerals.

mortification *n* the act of mortifying; gangrene; (*Christianity*) subjugation of passions and appetite by abstinence; humiliation; vexation, chagrin caused by something that injures one's pride; (*Scots law*) a charitable bequest of lands.

mortify *vti* (**mortifying, mortified**) to subdue by repression or penance; to humiliate or shame; to become gangrenous.—**mortifier** *n*.—**mortifyingly** *adv*.

mortise, mortice *n* a hole in a piece of wood to receive a projection of another piece made to fit.

mortise lock *n* a lock fitted into a mortise in the frame of a door.

mortmain *n* (*law*) a tenure of land held by a corporation, ecclesiastical or other, which cannot transfer ownership.

mortuary *n* (*pl* **mortuaries**) a place of temporary storage for dead bodies.

morula *n* (*pl* **morulas, morulae**) the spherical mass of cells produced by the splitting of the ovum in its primary stage.—**morular** *adj*.

Mosaic, Mosaical *adj* pertaining to Moses, the lawgiver of the Bible, or to the law, institutions, etc, given through him, or to his writings.

mosaic *n* a surface decoration made by inlaying small pieces (of glass, stone, etc) to form figures or patterns; a design made in mosaic. * *adj* of or made of mosaic. * *vt* (**mosaicking, mosaicked**) to adorn with or make into mosaic.—**mosaicist** *n*.

moschatel *n* a plant with a pale-green flower and a musky smell.

Moselle, Mosel *n* a German dry white wine from the Moselle valley.

mosey *vi* (*inf*) (*often with* **along, on down**) to go, to saunter, to amble.

Moslem *see* **Muslim**.

mosque *n* a place of worship for Muslims.

mosquito *n* (*pl* **mosquitoes, mosquitos**) a small two-winged bloodsucking insect.

moss *n* a very small green plant that grows in clusters on rocks, moist ground, etc.

mossback *n* (*sl*) a turtle or a crab, lobster, oyster, etc, that is so old that it has moss growing on its back; (*inf*) an out-of-date or provincial person.

mosstrooper *n* one of a gang of marauders that ravaged the borderland of England and Scotland in the mid-17th century.

mossy *adj* (**mossier, mossiest**) overgrown with, or like, moss.—**mossiness** *n*.

most *adj* (*compar* **more**) greatest in number; greatest in amount or degree; in the greatest number of instances (—*also superl of* **many, much**). * *adv* in or to the greatest degree or extent. * *n* the greatest amount or degree; (*with pl*) the greatest number (of).

-most *adj suffix* forming a superlative, eg *hindmost*.

mostly *adv* for the most part; mainly, usually.

mot juste *n* (*pl* **mots justes**) exactly the right word.

mote[1] *n* a very small particle, a speck (of dust); a mite.

mote[2] *vi* (*arch*) might, must.

motel *n* an hotel for motorists with adjacent parking.

motet *n* (*mus*) (*RC Church*) a short sacred vocal composition, an anthem, usu unaccompanied.

moth *n* a four-winged chiefly night-flying insect related to the butterfly.

mothball *n* a small ball of camphor or naphthalene used to protect stored clothes from moths.

moth-eaten *adj* eaten into by moths; dilapidated; outmoded.

mother *n* a female who has given birth to offspring; an origin or source. * *adj* of or like a mother; native. * *vt* to be the mother of or a mother to.

motherhood *n* the state of being a mother; the qualities of feelings of being a mother; mothers collectively.

mother-in-law *n* (*pl* **mothers-in-law**) the mother of one's spouse.

motherland *n* a person's native land or the country of a person's forebears.

motherly *adj* of, proper to a mother; like a mother.—**motherliness** *n*.

mother-of-pearl *n* the iridescent lining of the shell of the pearl oyster.

motif *n* a recurrent theme in a musical composition — *also* **motive**.

motile *adj* (*biol*) able to move without outside aid; exhibiting movement. * *n* (*psychol*) a person whose perception of the material world comprises, to a very strong degree, the imagery of movement, esp his own.—**motility** *n*.

motion *n* activity, movement; a formal suggestion made in a meeting, law court, or legislative assembly; evacuation of the bowels. * *vti* to signal or direct by a gesture.

motionless *adj* not moving, still.—**motionlessness** *n*.

motion picture *n* a film, movie.

motivate *vt* to supply a motive to; to instigate.—**motivator** *n*.

motivation *n* a motivating or being motivated; incentive; (*psychol*) the mental function or instinct that produces, sustains and regulates behaviour in humans and animals.—**motivational** *adj* .

motive *n* something (as a need or desire) that causes a person to act; a motif in music. * *adj* moving to action; of or relating to motion.—**motiveless** *adj*.—**motivity** *n*.

motley *adj* multicoloured; composed of diverse elements.

motmot *n* any of various tropical American blue and brownish-green, long-tailed birds similar to the jay, of the same family as the kingfisher.

motor *n* anything that produces motion; a machine for converting electrical energy into mechanical energy; a motor car. * *adj* producing motion; of or powered by a motor; of, by or for motor vehicles; of or involving muscular movements. * *vi* to travel by car.

motorbike *n* a motorcycle.

motorboat *n* a boat propelled by an engine or motor.

motorbus *n* (*pl* **motorbuses, motorbusses**) a bus driven by a motor engine.

motorcade *n* a procession of motor vehicles.

motorcar *n* a usu four-wheeled vehicle powered by an internal combustion engine.—*also* **automobile**.

motorcycle *n* a two-wheeled motor vehicle.—**motorcyclist** *n*.

motorist *n* a person who drives a car.

motorize *vt* to equip with a motor; to equip with motor vehicles.—**motorization** *n*.

motorman *n* (*pl* **motormen**) the driver of a tram or an underground train, or other vehicle powered by electricity; a person who operates a motor.

motor scooter *n* a small-wheeled motorcycle with an enclosed engine.

motorway *n* a road with controlled access for fast-moving traffic.—*also* **freeway**.

mottle *vt* to mark with coloured blotches or spots, to variegate. * *n* a pattern of coloured blotches of spots, as on marble; one of the coloured blotches in such a pattern.

mottled *adj* marked with blotches of various colours.

motto *n* (*pl* **mottoes, mottos**) a short saying adopted as a maxim or ideal; a slogan on a heraldic crest; a quotation prefixed to a book, etc; verses, etc, in a Christmas cracker.

mouflon, moufflon *n* (*pl* **mouflons, mouflon, moufflons, moufflon**) a wild large-horned sheep with a short fleece, found in Corsica and Sardinia.

mouillé *adj* softened in sound, palatalized, eg *gl* in *seraglio*.

moujik *see* **muzhik**.

mould *see* **mold[1], mold[2]**.

moulder *see* **molder**.

moulding *see* **molding**.

mouldy *see* **moldy**.

moulin *n* a deep crack in a glacier through which water and debris drain.

moult *see* **molt**.

mound *n* an artificial bank of earth or stones; a heap or bank of earth. * *vt* to form into a mound.

mount[1] *n* a high hill.

mount[2] *vi* to increase. * *vt* to climb, ascend; to get up on (a horse, platform, etc); to provide with horses; (*a jewel*) to fix on a support; (*a picture*) to frame. * *n* a horse for riding; (*for a picture*) a backing.—**mountable** *adj*.—**mounter** *n*.

mountain *n* a land mass higher than a hill; a vast number or quantity. * *adj* of or in mountains.

mountaineer *n* one who climbs mountains.

mountaineering *n* the technique of climbing mountains.

mountainous *adj* having many mountains; very high; huge.—**mountainously** *adv*.—**mountainousness** *n*.

mountebank *n* (*formerly*) an itinerant quack doctor; a boastful pretender, a charlatan, an impostor.

mounted *adj* seated on horseback or on a bicycle, etc; serving on horseback, as a policeman; placed on a suitable support.

mourn *vti* (*someone dead*) to grieve for; (*something regrettable*) to feel or express sorrow for.—**mourner** *n*.

mournful *adj* expressing grief or sorrow; causing sorrow.—**mournfully** *adv*.—**mournfulness** *n*.

mourning *adj* grieving. * *n* the expression of grief; dark clothes worn by mourners.

mousaka *see* **moussaka**.

mouse *n* (*pl* **mice**) a small rodent with a pointed snout, long body and slender tail; a timid person; a hand-held device used to position the cursor and control software on a computer screen.

mouser *n* an animal that is skilled at catching mice, esp a cat.

moussaka, mousaka *n* a Greek dish comprising aubergines, minced lamb and tomatoes topped with a cheese or white sauce.

mousse *n* a chilled dessert made of fruit, eggs, and whipped cream; a similar savoury dish made with meat or fish; a foamy substance applied to the hair to help it keep its style.

mousseline *n* a sheer fabric resembling muslin, made of rayon or silk; mousseline sauce.

mousseline sauce *n* a white sauce to which whipped cream or the white of an egg has been added.

moustache *see* **mustache**.

mousy, mousey *adj* (**mousier, mousiest**) mouse-like; grey-brown in colour; quiet, stealthy; timid, retiring.—**mousily** *adv*.—**mousiness** *n*.

mouth *n* (*pl* **mouths**) the opening in the head through which food is eaten, sound uttered or words spoken; the lips; opening, entrance, as of a bottle, etc. * *vt* to say, esp insincerely; to form words with the mouth without uttering sound. * *vi* to utter pompously; to grimace.—**mouther** *n*.

mouthful *n* (*pl* **mouthfuls**) as much (food) as fills the mouth; a word or phrase that is difficult to say correctly; (*sl*) a pertinent remark.

mouth organ *n* a harmonica.

mouthpiece *n* the part of a musical instrument placed in the mouth; a person, periodical, etc that expresses the views of others.

mouth-to-mouth resuscitation *n* a method of artificial respiration in which air is forced into the victim's lungs by blowing into the mouth.

mouthwash *n* a flavoured, often antiseptic liquid for rinsing the mouth.

mouthwatering *adj* appetizing; tasty.

movable, moveable *adj* that may be moved. * *npl* personal property.—**movably** *adv*.—**movability** *n*.

move *vt* (**moving, moved**) to shift or change place; to set in motion; to rouse the emotions; to put (a motion) formally. * *vi* to go from one place to another; to walk, to carry oneself; to change place; to evacuate the bowels; to propose a motion as in a meeting; to change residence; (*chess, draughts, etc*) to change the position of a piece on the board. * *n* the act of moving; a movement, esp in board games; one's turn to move; a premeditated action.

movement *n* act of moving; the moving part of a machine, esp a clock; the policy and activities of a group; a trend, eg in prices; a division of a musical work; tempo.

mover *n* one who moves; (*inf*) a driving force, an innovator; a proposer of a motion.

movie *n* a cinema film, motion picture; (*pl*) the showing of a motion picture; the motion-picture medium or industry.

moving *adj* arousing the emotions; changing position; causing motion.—**movingly** *adv*.

mow *vti* (**mowing, mowed**, *pp* **mowed** *or* **mown**) (*grass, etc*) to cut from with a sickle or lawn mower; (*with* **down**) to cause to fall like cut grass.—**mower** *n*.

moxa *n* down obtained from plants, used in Oriental medicine as a counterirritant or for cauterizing by burning on the skin; any plant that yields such down.

mozzarella *n* a moist curd cheese noted for its elasticity when melted.

MP *abbr* = Member of Parliament; Military Police.

mpg *abbr* = miles per gallon.

mph *abbr* = miles per hour.

Mr *n* (*pl* **Messrs**) used as a title before a man's name or an office he holds.

MRI *abbr* = magnetic resonance imaging.

MRM *abbr* = mechanically removed meat.

Mrs *n* (*pl* **Mrs** *or* **Mesdames**) used as a title before a married woman's name.

MS *abbr* = (*pl* **MSS**) manuscript; multiple sclerosis.

Ms *n* the title used before a woman's name instead of Miss or Mrs.

MSc *abbr* = Master of Science.

MSG *abbr* = monosodium glutamate.

MT *abbr* = Montana.

Mt *abbr* = mount.

much *adj* (*compar* **more**, *superl* **most**) plenty. * *adv* considerably; to a great extent.

muchness *n* (*arch*) bulk, greatness; **much of a muchness** just about the same.

mucilage *n* a adhesive prepared for use; a sticky substance obtained from some plants.—**mucilaginous** *adj*.

muck *n* moist manure; black earth with decaying matter; mud, dirt, filth. * *vt* to spread manure; to make dirty; (*with* **out**) to clear of muck. * *vi* to move or load muck; (*with* **about, around**) to engage in useless activity.

mucker *n* (*mining*) a person who clears broken rocks or other waste; (*Br sl*) a friend; (*US sl*) a coarse person.

muckworm *n* a grub or larva bred in manure or mud; (*inf*) a skinflint, a hoarder.

mucky *adj* (**muckier, muckiest**) of or like muck; muddy; filthy.—**muckily** *adv*.—**muckiness** *n*.

mucous *adj* slimy, sticky; like mucus.—**mucosity** *n*.

mucous membrane *n* the mucus-secreting lining of body cavities.

mucus *n* the slimy secretion that keeps mucous membranes moist.

mud *n* soft, wet earth. * *vt* (**muds, mudding, mudded**) to muddy; to throw mud at; to vilify.

muddle *vt* to confuse; to mix up. * *n* confusion, mess.

muddleheaded *adj* silly; confused; absent-minded.—**muddleheadedness** *n*.

muddy *adj* (**muddier, muddiest**) like or covered with mud; not bright or clear; confused. * *vti* (**muddying, muddied**) to make or become dirty or unclear.—**muddily** *adv*.—**muddiness** *n*.

mudguard *n* a screen on a wheel to catch mud splashes.

mudlark *n* (*formerly*) a person who worked or dabbled in mud, esp a scavenger on the banks of tidal rivers; (*arch sl*) a mischievous, poorly dressed child who frequented city streets.(*Austral sl*) a horse that performs well on wet, muddy ground.

muesli *n* a mixture of rolled oats, dried fruit, nuts, etc eaten with milk.

muezzin *n* a Muslim official who proclaims from the minaret of a mosque the hour of prayer, and summons the faithful to worship.

muff[1] *n* a warm soft fur cover for warming the hands.

muff[2] *n* a bungling performance; failure to hold a ball when trying to catch it. * *vti* to bungle.

muffin *n* baked yeast roll.

muffle *vt* to wrap up for warmth or to hide; (*sound*) to deaden by wrapping up.

muffler *n* a long scarf; any means of deadening sound; a device for reducing the noise of a vehicle exhaust.

Mufti *n* (*pl* **Muftis**) an official expounder of Muslim law.

mufti *n* civilian dress worn by a naval or military officer when off duty.

mug *n* a cylindrical drinking cup, usu of metal or earthenware; its contents; (*sl*) the face; (*sl*) a fool. * *vb* (**mugging, mugged**) *vt* to assault, usu with intent to rob.

mugger[1] *n* a person who assaults with intent to rob.

mugger[2], **muggar**, **muggur** *n* a broad-snouted Asian crocodile that lives in marshes and pools.

muggins *n* (*sl*) an idiot. * *pron* oneself (used deprecatingl).

muggy *adj* (**muggier, muggiest**) (*weather*) warm, damp and close.—**mugginess** *n*.

mugwump *n* an independent in politics; (*formerly*) a chief, a bigwig.

mujik *see* **muzhik**.

mulatto *n* (*pl* **mulattos, mulattoes**) a person with one black parent and one white parent.

mulberry *n* (*pl* **mulberries**) a tree on whose leaves silkworms feed; its berry.

mulch *n* loose, organic, strawy dung providing a protective covering around the roots of plants. * *vt* to spread mulch.

mulct *vt* to punish with a fine; to acquire money, etc, by fraud or deception. * *n* a fine, esp for some misdemeanour.

mule[1] *n* the offspring of a male donkey and a female horse; a machine for spinning cotton; an obstinate person; (*sl*) a person used to smuggle drugs.

mule[2] *n* a slipper without a heel.

muleteer *n* a mule driver.

muliebrity *n* (*formal*) womanhood; the qualities of womanhood.

mulish *adj* like a mule; stubborn, intractable, wilful.—**mulishly** *adv*.—**mulishness** *n*.

mull[1] *vti* (*inf*) to ponder (over).

mull[2] *vt* (*wine, etc*) to heat, sweeten and spice.—**mulled** *adj*.

mullah, mulla (*formerly*) a Muslim theologian or teacher; a Muslim title of respect.

muller *n* a flat-bottomed pestle for grinding (drugs, paints) on a slab.

mullet *n* (*pl* **mullets, mullet**) any of various types of food fish.

mulligatawny *n* a curry-flavoured meat soup.

mullion *n* an upright bar or division between the panes of a window or the panels of a screen, etc, esp in a Gothic arch; a projecting ridge on a rock face. * *vt* to provide with or divide by mullions.

mullock *n* (*Austral*) a rock containing no gold or from which gold has been extracted, rubbish; (*dial*) disorder.

mult-, multi- *prefix* much, many.

multangular, multiangular *adj* many-angled.

multeity *n* multiplicity.

multicolored, multicoloured *adj* many-coloured.

multifarious *adj* multiform; diversified, of great variety; manifold.—**multifariously** *adv*.—**multifariousness** *n*.

multifid, multifidous *adj* (*bot*) cleft into many parts or lobe-like elements.

multifoil *n* (*archit*) an ornament with over five leaf-like divisions.—*also adj*.

multiform *adj* having many shapes; of many kinds.—**multiformity** *n*.

multilateral *adj* having many sides; with several nations or participants.—**multilaterally** *adv*.

multilingual *adj* speaking or in more than two languages.—**multilingually** *adv*.

multimillionaire *n* a person with two or more millions of money.

multinational *n* a business operating in several countries.—*also adj*.

multinomial *n* (*math*) an expression that consists of the sum of several terms, a polynomial.—*also adj*.

multiplane *n* an aeroplane with two or more pairs of wings.

multiple *adj* of many parts; manifold; various; complex. * *n* (*math*) a number exactly divisible by another.

multiple sclerosis *n* a disease of the nervous system with loss of muscular coordination, etc.

multiplex *adj* (*radio, telecommunications*) the use of a single channel of communication to transmit more than one signal; in map-making, the use of three or more cameras so that the end product appears to be rendered in three dimensions; manifold, multiple. * *vi* to transmit messages or send signals in a multiplex system. * *vt* to send (several signals) simultaneously on one frequency.

multipliable, multiplicable *adj* able to be multiplied.

multiplicand *n* a number to be multiplied by another.

multiplicate *adj* (*rare*) consisting of many.

multiplication *n* the act of multiplying; the process of repeatedly adding a quantity to itself a certain number of times, or any other process which has the same result.—**multiplicational** *adj*.

multiplicative *adj* relating to the mathematical operation of mutiplication; tending to multiply; able to multiply.

multiplicity *n* (*pl* **multiplicities**) a great number or variety (of).

multiplier *n* a thing or person that multiplies; the number by which another is to be multiplied.

multiply *vti* (**multiplying, multiplied**) to increase in number, degree, etc; to find the product (of) by multiplication.

multitude *n* a large number (of people).

multitudinous *adj* of a multitude; very many; having innumerable elements.—**multitudinously** *adv*.—**multitudinousness** *n*.

mum[1] *n* (*inf*) mother.

mum[2] *adj* silent, not speaking. * *n* silence, * *vi* (**mumming, mummed**) to act as a mummer (—*also* **mumm**).

mumble *vti* to speak indistinctly, mutter. * *n* a mumbled utterance.—**mumbler** *n*.—**mumblingly** *adv*.

mumbo jumbo *n* (*pl* **mumbo jumbos**) meaningless ritual, talk, etc.

mumchance *adj* (*arch*) silent; tongue-tied.

mumm *see* **mum**[2].

mummer *n* a person who acts in a play without words; an actor.

mummery *n* (*pl* **mummeries**) performance by mummers; ridiculous ceremonial, pretentious display.

mummify *vt* (**mummifying, mummified**) to embalm (a body) as a mummy; to shrivel, to desiccate.—**mummification** *n*.

mummy[1] *n* (*pl* **mummies**) (*inf*) mother.

mummy[2] *n* (*pl* **mummies**) a carefully preserved dead body, esp an embalmed corpse of ancient Egypt.

mumps *n sing or pl* an acute contagious virus disease characterized by swelling of the salivary glands.

munch *vti* to chew steadily.—**muncher** *n*.

muncipalize *vt* to bring under municipal control; to constitute a place as a municipality.—**municipalization** *n*.

mundane *adj* routine, everyday; banal; worldly.—**mundanely** *adv*.

mungo *n* (*pl* **mungos**) a cheap woollen material made from cloth waste.

municipal *adj* of or concerning a city, town, etc or its local government.—**municipally** *adv*.

municipality *n* (*pl* **municipalities**) a city or town having corporate status and powers of self-government; the governing body of a municipality.

munificent *adj* extremely generous, bountiful.—**munificence** *n*.—**munificently** *adv*.

muniment *n* (*rare*) a defence, a fortification; (*pl*) (*law*) deeds, charters, and other papers for proving title to land.

munition *vt* to equip with arms. * *n* (*pl*) war supplies, esp weapons and ammunition.

muntjac, muntjak *n* any of various small, brown Asian deer with small antlers and a cry similar to that of a dog.

mural *adj* relating to a wall. * *n* a picture or design painted directly onto a wall.—**muralist** *n*.

murder *n* the intentional and unlawful killing of one person by another; (*inf*) something unusually difficult or dangerous to do or deal with. * *vti* to commit murder (upon), to kill; to mangle, to mar.—**murderer** *n*.—**murderess** *nf*.

murderous *adj* capable of or bent on murder; deadly.—**murderously** *adv*.—**murderousness** *n*.

murex *n* (*pl* **murices, murexes**) any of a genus of marine gasteropods, one species of which yields a purple dye used in ancient Greece and Rome.

murine *adj* pertaining to or resembling a mouse or rat; affected, caused or transmitted by rats or mice. * *n* any animal belonging to the same family as rats and mice.

murk *n* indistinct gloom, darkness. * *adj* (*arch*) dark, obscured by fog or mist.—*also* **mirk**.

murky *adj* (**murkier, murkiest**) dark, gloomy; darkly vague or obscure.—*also* **mirky**.—**murkily** *adv*.—**murkiness** *n*.

murmur *n* a continuous low, indistinct sound; a mumbled complaint; (*med*) an abnormal sound made by the heart. * *vti* to make a murmur; to say in a murmur.—**murmurer** *n*.—**murmurous** *adj*.

murphy *n* (*pl* **murphies**) (*inf*) a potato.

murrain *n* any infectious disease of cattle, such as foot-and-mouth disease; (*arch*) a plague.

murrhine, murrine *n* of or pertaining to an unknown substance (possibly jade or porcelain) used to make delicate pottery in ancient Rome. * *n* this substance (—*also* **murra**).

murther *n* (*arch*) murder.—**murtherer** *n*.

muscadine *n* a type of woody plant that produces a grape used to make wine.

muscat *n* any of various types of sweet white grapes used to make wine; muscatel.

muscatel, muscadel *n* a sweet wine made from muscat grapes.

muscle *n* fibrous tissue that contracts and relaxes, producing bodily movement; strength; brawn; power. * *vi* (*inf*) to force one's way (in).

muscle-bound *adj* having some of the muscles abnormally enlarged and lacking in elasticity as from too much exercise; inflexible, rigid.

muscovado, muscavado *n* raw sugar left after the molasses has evaporated from sugar cane.

Muscovite *n* a person who lives in, or originates from, Moscow; (*arch*) a Russian. * *adj* (*arch*) Russian.

muscovite *n* a type of mica often found in granite and sedimentary rocks.

Muscovy (duck) *n* a green-brown duck with white markings and a characteristic red fleshy growth on its beak.—*also* **musk duck**.

muscular *adj* of or done by a muscle; having well-developed muscles; strong, brawny.—**muscularity** *n*.—**muscularly** *adv*.

musculature *n* the entire system of muscles in a living thing; the system of muscles in an organ or a part of this system.

muse *vti* to ponder, meditate; to be lost in thought. * *n* a fit of abstraction.—**muser** *n*.

museum *n* a building for exhibiting objects of artistic, historic or scientific interest.

mush *n* a thick porridge of boiled meal; any thick, soft mass; (*inf*) sentimentality.

mushroom *n* a fleshy fungus with a capped stalk, some varieties of which are edible. * *vi* to gather mushrooms; to spread rapidly, to increase.

mushy *adj* (**mushier, mushiest**) soft, pulpy; (*sl*) sentimental, soppy.—**mushily** *adv*.—**mushiness** *n*.

music *n* the art of combining tones into a composition having structure and continuity; vocal or instrumental sounds having rhythm, melody or harmony; an agreeable sound.

musical *adj* of or relating to music or musicians; having the pleasant tonal qualities of music; having an interest in or talent for music. * *n* a play or film incorporating dialogue, singing and dancing.—**musicality** *n*.—**musically** *adv*.

musicale *n* a musical party.

musician *n* one skilled in music, esp a performer.—**musicianly** *adj*.—**musicianship** *n*.

musicology *n* the study of the history, forms, etc of music.—**musicological** *adj*.—**musicologist** *n*.

musing *adj* meditative; lost in thought.—**musingly** *adv*.

musk *n* an animal secretion with a strong odour, used in perfumes; the odour of musk; a plant with a similar odour.

musk duck *see* **Muscovy**.

muskellunge *n* (*pl* **muskellunges, muskellunge**) a large North American game fish similar to the pike.

musket *n* a long-barrelled, smoothbore shoulder gun formerly used by infantrymen.

musketeer *n* (*formerly*) a soldier armed with a musket.

musketry *n* small-arm fire; practice in this; muskets or musketeers collectively.

muskmelon *n* any of several varieties of widely cultivated melon with a netted or ribbed skin and sweet light-coloured or green flesh and a musky smell; any one of several types of melon related to the honeydew and cantaloupe.

muskrat *n* (*pl* **muskrats, muskrat**) a large North American aquatic rodent, related to the vole, that emits a musky secretion; the fur from this.—*also* **musquash**.

musky *adj* (**muskier, muskiest**) like or smelling of musk; sweet-smelling.—**muskiness** *n*.

Muslim *n* an adherent of Islam. * *adj* of Islam, its adherents and culture.—*also* **Moslem**.

muslin *n* a fine cotton cloth.

musquash *n* the fur of the muskrat; the muskrat.

muss *vt* (*often with up*) (*inf*) to disarrange, to rumple. * *n* a state of disorder.

mussel *n* an edible marine bivalve shellfish.

must[1] *aux vb expressing*: necessity; probability; certainty. * *n* (*inf*) something that must be done, had, etc.

must[2] *n* newly pressed grape juice, unfermented or partially fermented wine; the pulp and skin of crushed grapes.

must[3] *see* **musth**.

must[4] *see* **musty**.

mustache *n* the hair on the upper lip.—*also* **moustache**.

mustachio *n* (*pl* **mustachios**) (*often pl*) a moustache, usu bushy or shaped.

mustang *n* a small hardy semi-wild horse of the American prairies.

mustard *n* the powdered seeds of the mustard plant used as a condiment; a brownish-yellow colour; (*sl*) zest.

muster *vt* to assemble or call together, as troops for inspection or duty; to gather. * *vi* to be assembled, as troops. * *n* gathering; review; assembly.

musth, must *n* a state of sexual frenzy in the males of elephants and certain other large mammals. * *adj* denoting an animal in musth.

musty *adj* (**mustier, mustiest**) mouldy, damp; stale.—**mustily** *adv*.—**mustiness, must** *n*.

mutable *adj* able or tending to change or be changed; fickle, inconstant.—**mutability** *n*.—**mutably** *adv*.

mutant *n* a mutation; an organism whose structure has undergone mutation. * *adj* mutating.

mutate *vti* to experience or cause to experience change or alteration.

mutation *n* the act or process of mutating; alteration; (*biol*) a sudden change in some inheritable characteristic of a species; (*linguistics*) a change in a vowel sound when assimilated with another, esp an umlaut.—**mutational** *adj*.

mutatis mutandis (*Latin*) with the necessary changes.

mute *adj* silent; dumb; (*colour*) subdued. * *n* a person who is unable to speak; a device that softens the sound of a musical instrument. * *vt* to lessen the sound of a musical instrument.—**mutely** *adv*.—**muteness** *n*.

mutilate *vt* to maim; to damage by removing an essential part of.—**mutilation** *n*.—**mutilative** *adj*.—**mutilator** *n*.

mutineer *n* a person who takes part in a mutiny.

mutinous *adj* threatening mutiny, rebellious; taking part in a mutiny.—**mutinously** *adv*.

mutiny *vi* (**mutinying, mutinied**) to revolt against authority, esp in military service. * *n* (*pl* **mutines**) a rebellion against authority, esp by soldiers and sailors against officers.

mutism *n* the inability to speak; dumbness; silence; (*psychiatry*) a state in which a person remains silent although there is no physical cause for this.

mutt *n* (*sl*) a fool; a mongrel dog.

mutter *vti* to utter in a low tone or indistinctly; to grumble.—**mutterer** *n*.—**mutteringly** *adv*.

mutton *n* the edible flesh of sheep.

muttonchops *n* whiskers on the side of the face, narrow at the top, broad at the bottom.

mutual *adj* given and received in equal amount; having the same feelings one for the other; shared in common.—**mutuality** *n*.—**mutually** *adv*.

mutule *n* (*archit*) a projecting block under the corona of the Doric cornice.

muzhik *n* a peasant in pre-Revolutionary Russia.—*also* **mujik, moujik**.

muzz *vt* (*inf*) to make (anything) muzzy.

muzzle n the projecting nose or mouth of an animal; a strap fitted over the jaws to prevent biting; the open end of a gun barrel. * vt to put a muzzle on; to silence or gag.—**muzzler** n.

muzzy adj (**muzzier, muzziest**) confused, dazed; dizzy; blurred; dull.—**muzzily** adv.—**muzziness** n.

MW abbr = medium wave; megawatt.

Mx abbr = maxwell.

my poss adj of or belonging to me.

myalgia n pain, stiffness or cramp in the voluntary muscles or in one muscle.

myalgic encephalomyelitis n a viral condition affecting the nervous system, characterized by fatigue and muscle pains.—also **post-viral syndrome**.

mycelium n (pl **mycelia**) a cellular spawn of fungi.

mycetoma n (pl **mycetomas, mycetomata**) a fungoid disease, usu of feet, often caused by a wound.

mycology n the science of fungi or mushrooms; the fungi found in a particular area.—**mycologist** n.

mycosis n (pl **mycoses**) the presence of, or a disease caused by, a parasitic fungus.

mydriasis n excessive dilatation of the pupil of the eye.

mydriatic adj causing mydriasis. * n a drug that induces mydriasis.

myelitis n inflammation of the spinal cord or of bone marrow.

myna (bird) n any of severalAsian birds resembling the starling, some species of which can imitate speech.—also **mina (bird)**.

Mynheer n a Dutch title used before a name, as "Mister" as a term of respect.

myocarditis n an inflammation of the myocardium.

myocardium n (pl **myocardia**) the muscular parts of the heart.—**myocardial** adj.

myology n a branch of medicine concerned with studying the muscles or the diseases affecting them.

myope n a short-sighted person.

myopia n short-sightedness.—**myopic** adj.—**myopically** adv.

myosis see **miosis**.

myosotis, myosote n any of various small plants with blue, pink, or white flowers, incl the forget-me-not.

myriad n a great number of persons or things. * adj innumerable.

myriapod n an arthropod with many legs and a segmented body, incl millipedes and centipedes.—**myriapodan** adj, n.—**myriapodous** adj.

myrica n the root bark of the candleberry or wax myrtle.

myrmecology n the scientific study of ants.—**myrmecological** adj.—**myrmecologist** n.

myrmecophagous adj feeding on ants; (jaws, etc) adapted for eating ants.

Myrmidon n (pl **Myrmidons, Myrmidones**) (Greek myth) one of a tribe of Thracian warriors formed by Zeus from an anthill who accompanied Achilles to the Trojan war; a brutal, unprincipled or unquestioning follower or subordinate.—also adj.

myrobalan n any of several tropical trees containing tannin and bearing a fruit that when dried was used medicinally and in dyeing and tanning; the dye from such a fruit.

myrrh n a fragrant gum resin used in perfume, incense, etc.

myrtaceous adj of the myrtle family, incl eucalyptus, clove and guava, with leaves that secrete oil.

myrtle n an evergreen shrub with fragrant leaves; a trailing periwinkle.

myself pron emphatic and reflexive form of I; in my normal state.

mystagogue n an initiator into or interpreter of mysteries—**mystagogic** adj.—**mystagogy** n.

mysterious adj difficult to understand or explain, obscure; delighting in mystery.—**mysteriously** adv.—**mysteriousness** n.

mystery n (pl **mysteries**) something unexplained and secret; a story about a secret crime, etc; secrecy.

mystic n one who seeks direct knowledge of God or spiritual truths by self-surrender. * adj mystical.

mystical adj having a meaning beyond normal human understanding; magical.—**mystically** adv.

mysticism n the beliefs or practices of a mystic; belief in a reality accessible by intuition, not the intellect; obscurity of thought or doctrine.

mystify vt (**mystifying, mystified**) to puzzle, bewilder, to confuse.—**mystification** n.—**mistifier** n.—**mistifyingly** adv.

myth n a fable; a fictitious event; a traditional story of gods and heroes, taken to be true.—**mythic** adj.

mythical adj imaginary, unreal, untrue; having to do with myths, mythic.—**mythically** adv.

mythicize vt to treat as myth; to interpret mythically; to turn (something) into myth.

mythologist n a student of myths; a writer of myths.

mythology n (pl **mythologies**) myths collectively; the study of myths.—**mythological** adj.

mythopoeic adj producing or creating myths.—**mythopoeia, mythopoeisis** n.

myxedema, myxoedema n an illness leading to physical and mental degeneration due to underactivity of the thyroid gland and thus severe thyroxine deficiency

myxomycete n any of various organisms forming a network of creamy filaments on decaying wood, leaves, etc, and displaying characteristics of both plants and animals.

N

N (*chem symbol*) nitrogen. * *abbr* = North.

N, n *n* the 14th letter of the English alphabet; an indefinite number.

n/a *abbr* (*in commerce*) = no account.

NA *abbr* = North America.

Na (*chem symbol*) sodium.

nab *vt* (**nabbing, nabbed**) (*sl*) to catch, arrest.

nabob *n* in India, a deputy or administrator under the Mogul Empire; one who has amassed wealth in India; a very wealthy man.

nacelle *n* the car of an aircraft.

nacho *n* a Mexican snack consisting of a tortilla chip often served grilled with melted cheese, chilli, etc.

nacre *n* mother-of-pearl; the shellfish that yields it.

nacreous *adj* having an iridescent lustre; resembling mother of pearl.

nadir *n* the point opposite the zenith; the lowest point; the depths of despair.

naevus *see* **nevus**.

nag[1] *vti* (**nagging, nagged**) to scold constantly; to harass; to be felt persistently. * *n* a person who nags.

nag[2] (*inf*) a horse.

Naga *n* (*pl* **Nagas, Naga**) (*Hindu myth*) a deified serpent, esp the cobra; a member of the Naga tribes; a class of mendicant Hindus. * *adj* pertaining to an ancient race who invaded India about the 6th century BC, or to certain Burmese border tribes.

nagana *n* a disease caused by the tsetse-fly.

Nagari *n* the name of the Sanskrit alphabet.

nagelflue *n* a peculiar alpine conglomerate rock, interspersed with nail-like pebbles.

nagor *n* a Senegal antelope.

Nahum *n* one of the prophetical books of the Old Testament.

naiad *n* (*pl* **naiads, naiades**) a water nymph; (*pl*) an order of aquatic plants; a family of freshwater bivalves.

naiant *adj* (*her*) representing fishes swimming in a horizontal position.

naif, naïf *adj* naive.

nail *n* a horny plate covering the end of a human finger or toe; a thin pointed metal spike for driving into wood as a fastening or hanging device. * *vt* to fasten with nails; to fix, secure; (*inf*) to catch or hit; (*inf*) to arrest.

nailfile *n* a small metal file or strip of cardboard coated with emery used for trimming and shaping the nails.

nail polish *n* a lacquer for giving a clear or coloured shiny surface to nails.

nainsook *n* a kind of closely woven muslin originally Indian.

naissant *adj* (*her*) issuing forth or rising from some ordinary, and showing only the foreparts of the body.

naive, naïve *adj* inexperienced; unsophisticated; (*argument*) simple.—**naively, naïvely** *adv*.

naiveté, naïveté, naivety, *n* natural, unaffected simplicity or ingenuousness.

naked *adj* bare, without clothes; without a covering; without addition or ornament; (*eye*) without optical aid.—**nakedness** *n*.

namby-pamby *adj* weakly sentimental or affectedly pretty or fine. * *n* (*pl* **namby-pambies**) an affected person.

name *n* a word or term by which a person or thing is called; a title; reputation; authority. * *vt* to give a name to; to call by name; to designate; to appoint to an office; (*a date, price, etc*) to specify.

name-calling *n* verbal abuse, esp in place of reasoned debate.

name-dropping *n* the practice of mentioning the names of famous or important people as if they were friends, in order to impress others.—**name-dropper** *n*.

nameless *adj* without a name; obscure; anonymous; unnamed; indefinable; too distressing or horrifying to be described.

namely *adv* that is to say.

nameplate *n* a small plate on a door of a room, house, etc displaying the name of the occupant.

namesake *n* a person or thing with the same name as another.

nan bread, naan bread *n* a type of slightly leavened Indian bread in a flattened oval shape.

nance *n* (*derog*) an effeminate man.

nankeen, nankin *n* a buff-coloured cotton cloth, originally from China.

nanny *n* (*pl* **nannies**) a child's nurse.

nanny goat *n* a female domestic goat.

nano- *prefix* one thousand millionth (10^{-9}) part of, eg *nanosecond*.

nap[1] *n* a short sleep, doze. * *vi* (**napping, napped**) to take a nap.

nap[2] *n* a hairy surface on cloth or leather; such a surface.

napalm *n* a substance added to petrol to form a jelly-like compound used in firebombs and flame-throwers. * *vt* to attack or burn with napalm.

nape *n* the back of the neck.

napery *n* household linen, esp for the table.

naphtha *n* a clear, volatile, inflammable bituminous liquid hydrocarbon exuding from the earth or distilled from coal tar, etc; rock oil.

naphthalene *n* a white crystalline hydrocarbon distilled from coal tar, used in making dyes, explosives and in mothballs.

napiform *adj* turnip-shaped.

napkin *n* a square of cloth or paper for wiping fingers or mouth or protecting clothes at table, a serviette.

napoleon *n* a gold coin formerly current in France, value 20 francs.

Napoleonic adj of or like Emperor Napoleon I.

nappy[1] adj (**nappier, nappiest**) covered with nap or pile.

nappy[2] n (pl **nappies**) a diaper.

narceine n an alkaloid obtained from opium and used as a sedative.

narcissism n excessive interest in one's own body or self.—**narcissistic** adj.

narcissus n (pl **narcissi, narcissuses**) a spring-flowering bulb plant, esp the daffodil.

narco- prefix indicating torpor or narcotics.

narcodollars npl (sl) US dollars earned by a country by the export of illegal drugs.

narcosis n (pl **narcoses**) a state of unconsciousness or drowsiness produced by narcotics.

narcotic adj inducing sleep. * n a drug, often addictive, used to relieve pain and induce sleep.

narcotism n a morbid dependence on narcotics.

narcotize vt to use a narcotic upon.—**narcotization**.

nard n spikenard, an aromatic plant; an aromatic unguent prepared from it.

nardoo n a genus of Australian acotyledonous aquatic plants, Australian pillwort, the spore cases of which are used as bread.

narghile n a small hookah pipe.

narrate vt (a story) to tell, relate; to give an account of; (film, TV) to provide a spoken commentary for.

narration n the act of narrating; a statement, written or verbal.

narrative n a spoken or written account of a sequence of events, experiences, etc; the art or process of narration.—also adj.

narrator n one who narrates.

narrow adj small in width; limited; with little margin; (views) prejudiced or bigoted. * n (usu pl) the narrow part of a pass, street, or channel. * vti to make or grow narrow; to decrease; to contract.—**narrowly** adv.—**narrowness** n.

narrow gauge adj denoting the distance of less than standard gauge (4 feet, 8.5 inches/1.44 metres) between rail metals.

narrow-minded adj prejudiced, bigoted; illiberal.—**narrow-mindedness** n.

narthex n in Early Christian churches the western portico, railed off for catechumens and penitents

narwhal n an Arctic whale, the male of which has a long spiral tusk.

nary = never a, ne'er a.

NASA abbr = National Aeronautics and Space Administration.

nasal adj of the nose; sounded through the nose. * n a sound made through the nose.—**nasally** adv.

nascent adj just starting to grow or develop.

naseberry n (pl **naseberries**) sapodilla plum tree.

naso- prefix nose.

nasturtium n an ornamental garden plant with bright flowers, a pungent odour, and edible leaves.

nasty adj (**nastier, nastiest**) unpleasant; offensive; ill-natured; disagreeable; (problem) hard to deal with; (illness) serious or dangerous.—**nastily** adv.—**nastiness** n.

nat. abbr = national; native; natural.

natal adj pertaining to one's birth or birthday; indigenous.—**natality** n.

natant adj swimming; (her) (fish) floating on the surface.

natation n the act or art of swimming.—**natational** adj.

natatorial, natatory adj swimming or adapted for swimming.

nates npl (sing **natis**) the buttocks.

nation n people of common territory, descent, culture, language, or history; people united under a single government.

national adj of a nation; common to a whole nation, general. * n a citizen or subject of a specific country.—**nationally** adv.

national anthem n a patriotic song or hymn adopted officially by a nation for ceremonial and public occasions.

national debt n the total money currently on loan to the government of a nation.

National Guard n in US, state militia that can be called into federal service.

nationalism n patriotic sentiments, principles, etc; a policy of national independence or self-government; fanatical patriotism, chauvinism.—**nationalist** n.—**nationalistic** adj.

nationality n (pl **nationalities**) the status of belonging to a nation by birth or naturalization; a nation or national group.

nationalize vt to make national; to convert into public or government property.—**nationalization** n.

national park n an area designated by a government as of important scenic, historical, or environmental value.

native adj inborn; natural to a person; innate; (language, etc) of one's place of birth; relating to the indigenous inhabitants of a country or area; occurring naturally. * n a person born in the place indicated; a local inhabitant; an indigenous plant or animal; an indigenous inhabitant, esp a non-White under colonial rule.

nativism n (philos) the doctrine of innate ideas; in US, the advocacy of the claim of native as opposed to that of naturalized Americans.—**nativist** adj, n.—**nativistic** adj.

nativity n (pl **nativities**) birth; a horoscope at the time of one's birth; (with cap) the birth of Christ.

NATO abbr = North Atlantic Treaty Organization.

natrolite n a hydrated silicate of aluminium and soda.

natron n a native carbonate of soda.

natter vi (inf) to chat, talk aimlessly. also n.

natty adj (**nattier, nattiest**) tidy, neat, smart.—**nattily** adv.—**nattiness** n.

natural adj of or produced by nature; not artificial; innate, not acquired; true to nature; lifelike; normal; at ease; (mus) not flat or sharp. * n (inf) a person or thing considered to have a natural aptitude (for) or to be an obvious choice (for); (inf) a certainty; (mus) a natural note or a sign indicating one.—**naturalness** n.

natural childbirth n giving birth using techniques of relaxation, controlled breathing, etc rather than with anaesthetics.

natural gas n gas trapped in the earth's crust, a combustible mixture of methane and hydrocarbons extracted for fuel.

natural history n the study of nature, esp the animal, mineral, and vegetable world.

naturalism n (art, literature) the theory or practice of describing nature, character, etc in realistic detail; (philos) a theory of the world based on scientific as opposed to spiritual or supernatural explanations.—**naturalistic** adj.

naturalist n a person who studies natural history; a person who advocates or practises naturalism.

naturalization n the act of investing a foreigner with the rights and privileges of a natural-born citizen.

naturalize *vt* to confer citizenship upon (a person of foreign birth); (*plants*) to become established in a different climate. * *vi* to become established as if native.

natural law *n* law based on innate moral sense.

naturally *adv* in a natural manner, by nature; of course.

natural number *n* any of the whole numbers starting with 1.

natural philosophy *n* physics.

natural resource *n* a naturally occurring source of wealth as in land, oil, coal, water power, etc.

natural science *n* the study of material things.

natural selection *n* the principle that evolution is determined by the survival of the fittest.

nature *n* the phenomena of physical life not dominated by man; the entire material world as a whole, or forces observable in it; the essential character of anything; the innate character of a person, temperament; kind, class; vital force or functions; natural scenery.

nature worship *n* the worship of the deified forces of nature.

naught *see* **nought**.

naughty *adj* (**naughtier, naughtiest**) mischievous or disobedient; titillating.—**naughtily** *adv*.—**naughtiness** *n*.

naumachia, naumachy *n* (*pl* **naumachias**or **naumachiae, naumachies**) a sea fight; a show representing a sea fight.

nausea *n* a desire to vomit; disgust.

nauseate *vti* to arouse feelings of disgust; to feel nausea or revulsion.—**nauseating** *adj*.

nauseous *adj* causing nausea; disgusting.—**nauseously** *adv*.—**nauseousness** *n*.

nautch *n* in India, a dance performed by girls; a dancing exhibition.

nautical *adj* of ships, sailors, or navigation.

nautically *adv* in a nautical manner.

nautical mile *n* an international unit of measure for air and sea navigation equal to 6,075 feet (1.85 km).

nautilus *n* (*pl* **nautiluses, nautili**) a genus of cephalopods, including those furnished with a chambered spinal univalve shell / a shellfish with webbed arms once supposed to sail upon the sea; a kind of diving bell.

naval *adj* of the navy; of ships.

nave[1] *n* the central space of a church, distinct from the chancel and aisles.

nave[2] *n* the central block of a wheel, the hub.

navel *n* the small scar in the abdomen caused by severance of the umbilical cord; a central point.

navigability *n* the quality or state of being navigable.

navigable *adj* (*rivers, seas*) that can be sailed upon or steered through.—**navigably** *adv*.

navigate *vti* to steer or direct a ship, aircraft, etc; to travel through or over (*water, air, etc*) in a ship or aircraft; to find a way through, over, etc, and to keep to a course.

navigation *n* the act, art or science of navigating; the method of calculating the position of a ship, aircraft, etc.—**navigational** *adj*.

navigator *n* one who navigates; one skilled in the science of navigation.

navvy *n* (*pl* **navvies**) (*Brit*) a labourer, esp one who works on roads or railways.

navy *n* (*pl* **navies**) (*often with cap*) the warships of a nation; a nation's entire sea force, including ships, men, stores, etc; navy blue.

navy blue *n* an almost black blue.

nawab *n* an Indian viceroy; a nabob.

nay *adv* (*arch*) no; not only so; yet more; or rather, and even. * *n* a refusal or denial.

Nazarene *n* a native of Nazareth, applied to Jesus Christ, his followers, and the early Christians as a term of contempt; in the early Church, one of a sect of Judaising Christians.

Nazarite, Nazirite *n* a native of Nazareth; a Jew devoted by vow to God to a life of abstinence and purity (Numbers 6).

Nazi *n* (*pl* **Nazis**) a member of the German National Socialist party (1930s).—*also adj*.

NB *abbr* = nota bene (note well); New Brunswick.

Nb (*chem symbol*) niobium.

NBC *abbr* = National Broadcasting Company.

NC *abbr* = North Carolina.

NCO *abbr* = noncommissioned officer.

ND *abbr* = North Dakota.

Nd (*chem symbol*) neodymium.

NE *abbr* = Nebraska; northeast, northeastern.

Ne (*chem symbol*) neon.

Neanderthal *adj* denoting or characteristic of Neanderthal man; primitive.

Neanderthal man *n* a type of primitive human inhabiting Europe in Palaeolithic times.

neap *adj* of either of the lowest high tides in the month. * *n* a neap tide.

Neapolitan *adj* pertaining to Naples or to its inhabitants.

Neapolitan ice cream *n* brick ice cream in layers of different colours and flavours.

near *adj* (**nearer, nearest**) close, not distant in space or time; closely related, intimate; approximate, (*escape, etc*) narrow. * *adv* to or at a little distance; close by; almost. * *prep* close to. * *vti* to approach; to draw close to.—**nearness** *n*.

nearby *adj* neighbouring; close by in position.

Near East *n* Southeast Europe; (formerly) included Turkey, the Balkans and the area of the Ottoman Empire.

nearly *adv* almost, closely.

near miss *n* a bomb, mortar, etc that just fails to hit the target; any type of shot that misses its target; a situation in which two aircraft narrowly avoid a midair collision.

near-sighted *adj* short-sighted, myopic.—**near-sightedness** *n*.

neat[1] *adj* clean and tidy; skilful; efficiently done; well made; (*alcoholic drink*) undiluted; (*sl*) nice, pleasing, etc.—**neatly** *adv*.—**neatness** *n*.

neat[2] *n* cattle of the bovine genus. * *adj* pertaining to bovine animals.

neaten *vt* to make tidy and neat.

neath *prep* (*poet*) beneath.

neb *n* (*Scot*) a bird's beak; a mouth; a nose or snout; a projecting part, a point.

nebula *n* (*pl* **nebulae, nebulas**) a gaseous mass or star cluster in the sky appearing as a hazy patch of light.—**nebular** *adj*.

nebular hypothesis *n* the theory that the solar system in its primal condition existed in the form of a nebula, from which the sun, planets, and satellites were produced by condensation.

nebulosity *n* (*pl* **nebulosities**) the state or quality of being nebulous.

nebulous *adj* indistinct; formless.

necessarily *adv* as a natural consequence.

necessary *adj* indispensable; required; inevitable. * *n* (*pl* necessaries) something necessary; (pl) essential needs.

necessitarianism n (philos) the doctrine of necessity, or that man cannot control his actions by his own free will; fatalism.—**necessitarian** n.

necessitate vt to make necessary; to compel.

necessitous adj urgent; pressing; needy.

necessity n (pl **necessities**) a prerequisite; something that cannot be done without; compulsion; need.

neck n the part of the body that connects the head and shoulders; that part of a garment nearest the neck; a neck-like part, esp a narrow strip of land; the narrowest part of a bottle; a strait. * vti (sl) to kiss and caress.

neckerchief n a cloth square worn around the neck.

necklace n a string or band, often of precious stones, beads, or pearls, worn around the neck.

neckline n the line traced by the upper edge of a garment below the neck.

necktie n a man's tie.

necro-, necr- prefix corpse.

necrobiosis n the decay of living tissue.—**necrobiotic** adj.

necrology n (pl **necrologies**) a register or account of the dead.—**necrological** adj.

necromancer n one who practises necromancy; a conjurer; a wizard.

necromancy n predicting the future by alleged communication with the dead; sorcery.—**necromantic** adj.

necrophagous adj (animal) feeding on carrion.

necrophilia n erotic interest in or copulation with corpses.—also **necromania**.—**necrophile** n.— **necrophiliac** n.

necropolis n (pl **necropolises, necropoleis**) a cemetery.

necropsy n (pl **necropsies**) a post-mortem examination.

necrosis n mortification and death of a bone; gangrene; a disease in plants, characterized by small black spots.—**necrotic** adj.

nectar n a sweetish liquid in many flowers, used by bees to make honey; any delicious drink.

nectareous, nectarous adj producing, or sweet, like nectar.

nectarine n a smooth-skinned peach.

nectary n (pl **nectaries**) that part of a flower which secretes a saccharine fluid.

nee, née adj (literally) born: indicating the maiden name of a married woman.

need n necessity; a lack of something; a requirement; poverty. * vt to have a need for; to require; to be obliged.

needful adj necessary, required, vital. * n (inf) what is required, esp money.—**needfulness** n.

needle n a small pointed piece of steel for sewing; a larger pointed rod for knitting or crocheting; a stylus; the pointer of a compass, gauge, etc; the thin, short leaf of the pine, spruce, etc; the sharp, slender metal tube at the end of a hypodermic syringe. * vt to goad, prod, or tease.

needlepoint n a type of embroidery worked on canvas; point lace.

needless adj not needed, unnecessary; uncalled for, pointless.—**needlessly** adv.—**needlessness** n.

needlework n sewing, embroidery.

needn't = need not.

needs adv necessarily; indispensably.

needy adj (**needier, neediest**) in need, very poor.

neep n (Scot) a turnip.

ne'er (poet) never.

ne'er-do-well adj good-for-nothing; improvident; lazy. * n an irresponsible person.

nefarious adj wicked, evil.

neg. abbr = negative(ly).

negate vt to nullify; to deny.

negation n a negative statement, denial; the opposite or absence of something; a contradiction.

negative adj expressing or meaning denial or refusal; lacking positive attributes; (math) denoting a quantity less than zero, or one to be subtracted; (photog) reversing the light and shade of the original subject, or having the colours replaced by complementary ones; (elect) of the charge carried by electrons; producing such a charge. * n a negative word, reply, etc; refusal; something that is the opposite or negation of something else; (in debate, etc) the side that votes or argues for the opposition; (photog) a negative image on transparent film or a plate. * vt to refuse assent, contradict; to veto.—**negatively** adv.

neglect vt to pay little or no attention to; to disregard; to leave uncared for; to fail to do something. * n disregard; lack of attention or care.

neglectful adj. careless; heedless; slighting.—**neglectfully** adv.

negligee n a woman's loosely fitting dressing gown.

negligence n lack of attention or care; an act of carelessness; a carelessly easy manner.

negligent adj careless, heedless.—**negligently** adv.

negligible adj that need not be regarded; unimportant; trifling.

negotiable adj able to be legally negotiated; (bills, drafts, etc) transferable.—**negotiability** n.

negotiate vti to discuss, bargain in order to reach an agreement or settlement; to settle by agreement; (fin) to obtain or give money value for (a bill); (obstacle, etc) to overcome.

negotiation n the act of negotiating or transacting business; a treaty.

negotiator n one who negotiates.

Negrillo n (pl **Negrillos, Negrilloes**) one of a pigmy Negroid race found in Africa.

Negrito n (pl **Negritos, Negritoes**) one of a diminutive Negroid race of the Philippines and Polynesia.

Negro n (pl **Negroes**) a member of the dark-skinned, indigenous peoples of Africa; a member of the Negroid group; a person with some Negro ancestors.—also adj.—**Negress** nf.

Negroid adj denoting, or of, one of the major groups of humankind, including most of the peoples of Africa south of the Sahara.

Negus n (pl **Neguses**) a title of the ruler of Ethiopia.

negus n (pl **neguses**) a beverage of hot water and wine, sweetened and spiced.

neigh vi (**neighing, neighed**) to whinny; to make a sound like the cry of a horse. * n the cry of a horse; a whinny.

neighbour, neighbor n a person who lives near another; a person or thing situated next to another; a fellow human being. * vt to be near, to adjoin.

neighbourhood, neighborhood n a particular community, area, or district; the people in an area.

neighbouring, neighboring adj adjoining, nearby.

neighbourly, neighborly adj characteristic of a neighbour, friendly. * adv in a neighbourly or social manner.—**neighbourliness, neighborliness** n.

neither adj, pron not one or the other (of two); not either. * conj not either; also not.

nek *n* (*S Africa*) a depression or pass in a mountain range.

nekton *n* a collective term for minute forms of organic life found at various depths in seas and lakes.— **nektonic** *adj.*

nelson *n* (*wrestling*) a type of hold in which the arms are placed under an opponent's arms from behind so that pressure can be exerted by the palms on the back of the opponent's neck.

nemato-, nemat- *prefix* thread, fibre.

nematode *adj* thread-like * *n* a threadworm.

nem. con. *adv* no one contradicting.

nem. diss. *adv* no one dissenting.

Nemean *adj* pertaining to the Nemea valley of ancient Greece or to the games held there.

nemesis *n* (*pl* **nemeses**) retribution; just punishment; an agent of defeat.

neo- *prefix* new, newly.

neodymium *n* a silvery-white metallic element used in alloys, etc.

Neolithic *adj* of the later Stone Age, marked by the use of polished stone implements.

neologism *n* a new word; the coining of new words, neology; the introduction of new doctrines.— **neologistic, neologistical** *adj.*

neologist *n* an innovator in language or religion, esp one who holds doctrinal views opposed to the orthodox interpretation of revealed religion.

neologize *vt* to introduce new words, phrases, or religious doctrines.

neology *n* neologism; doctrines or rationalistic theological interpretation at variance with orthodox belief.

neon *n* an inert gaseous element that gives off a bright orange glow, used in lighting and advertisements.

neophyte *n* a novice; one recently baptised; a convert. * *adj* recently entered.

neoplasm *n* tissue growth more or less distinct from that in which it occurs.

neoplastic *adj* newly formed.

neoplasty *n* the restoration of tissue by plastic surgery.

NeoPlatonism *n* a system of eclectic philosophy combining the doctrines of Plato with Oriental mysticism in the 3rd century AD.—**NeoPlatonist** *n.*

neoteric *adj* recent in origin; newfangled, modern.— **neoterically** *adv.*

Neotropical *adj* of tropical or South America.

Neozoic *adj* noting rocks from the Trias to the present time.

Nepalese *n, adj* (a) Nepali.

Nepali *n* (*pl* **Nepali, Nepalis**) a native or inhabitant of Nepal; the language of Nepal.—*also adj.*

nepenthe *n* a drug supposed by the ancient Greeks to have the power of causing forgetfulness of sorrow.— **nepenthean** *adj.*

nephew *n* the son of a brother or sister.

nephology *n* the study of clouds.—**nephological** *adj.*— **nephologist** *n.*

nephralgia *n* pain or disease in the kidneys.— **nephralgic** *adj.*

nephrite *n* jade.

nephritic *adj* of or pertaining to the kidneys or kidney disease; affected with disease of the kidneys.

nephritis *n* inflammation of the kidneys.

nephro- *or* **nephr-** *prefix* kidney; kidneys.

nephrology *n* study of the kidneys.

nephrotomy *n* (*pl* **nephrotomies**) incision into the kidney.

ne plus ultra *n* (*Latin*) the farthest attainable point; the acme, the perfect state.—*also* **non plus ultra.**

nepotism *n* undue favouritism shown to relatives, esp in securing jobs.

Neptune *n* the Roman god of the sea; the sea personified; the 8th planet from the sun.

Neptunian *adj* pertaining to the classical deity Neptune, god of the sea, or to the sea; deposited by the agency of the sea.

neptunium *n* a radioactive metallic element.

nerd *n* (*sl*) a boring, straight-laced person; a creep,

Nereid *n* (*pl* **Nereides**) (*Greek myth*) a sea nymph.

nereis *n* (*zool*) a sea worm.

neroli *n* the essential oil of orange flowers.

nervate *adj* (*bot*) ribbed.

nervation *n* (*bot*) the arrangement of veins, venation.

nerve *n* any of the fibres or bundles of fibres that transmit impulses of sensation or of movement between the brain and spinal cord and all parts of the body; courage, coolness in danger; (*inf*) audacity, boldness; (*pl*) nervousness, anxiety. * *vt* to give strength, courage, or vigour to.

nerve cell *n* a cell transmitting impulses in nerve tissue.—*also* **neuron, neurone.**

nerve centre, nerve center *n* a group of closely connected cells; (*mil, etc*) a centre of control from which instructions are sent out.

nerve gas *n* a poison gas that affects the nervous system.

nerveless *adj* calm, cool; weak, feeble.—**nervelessly** *adv.*

nerve-racking, nerve-wracking *adj* straining the nerves, stressful.

nervous *adj* excitable, highly strung; anxious, apprehensive; affecting or acting on the nerves or nervous system.

nervous breakdown *n* a (usu temporary) period of mental illness resulting from severe emotional strain or anxiety.

nervous system *n* the brain, spinal cord, and nerves collectively.

nervure *n* the veins of leaves; the horny ribs supporting the membranous wings of an insect.

nervy *adj* (**nervier, nerviest**) (*inf*) anxious, agitated; (*inf*) impudent, cheeky.

nescience *n* ignorance; agnosticism.—**nescient** *adj.*

ness *n* a headland or cape, a promontory.

-ness *suffix* state, quality of being.

nest *n* a structure or place where birds, fish, mice, etc, lay eggs or give birth to young; a place where young are nurtured; a swarm or brood; a lair; a cosy place; a set of boxes, tables, etc of different sizes, designed to fit together. * *vi* to make or occupy a nest.

nest egg *n* money put aside as a reserve or to establish a fund.

nestle *vti* to rest snugly; to lie snugly, as in a nest; to lie sheltered or half-hidden.

nestling *n* a young bird that has not left the nest.

Nestor *n* (*Greek myth*) a Greek sage of the Trojan war; a wise old man.

Nestorianism *n* the 5th-century doctrine of Nestorius, Bishop of Constantinople, who taught that there were two natures in Christ, one human and one divine, which did not unit and form one person; also that the Virgin Mary was not the Mother of God.— **Nestorian** *n, adj.*

net¹ *n* an openwork material of string, rope, or twine

knotted into meshes; a piece of this used to catch fish, to divide a tennis court, etc; a snare. * *vti* (**netting, netted**) to snare or enclose as with a net; to hit (a ball) into a net or goal.

net[2], nett *adj* clear of deductions, allowances or charges. * *n* a net amount, price, weight, profit, etc. * *vt* (**netting, netted**) to clear as a profit.

nether *adj* lower or under.

nether world *n* the underworld, hell.

nethermost *adj* lowest.

netsuke *n* a Japanese ornamental toggle for fastening the front of a garment.

netting *n* netted fabric.

nettle *n* a wild plant with stinging hairs. * *vt* to irritate, annoy.

nettle rash *n* a cutaneous skin eruption resembling the effects of a nettle sting.

network *n* an arrangement of intersecting lines; a group of people who co-operate with each other; a chain of interconnected operations, computers, etc; (*radio, TV*) a group of broadcasting stations connected to transmit the same programme simultaneously. * *vt* to broadcast on a network; (*comput*) to interconnect systems so that information, software, and peripheral devices, such as printers, can be shared..

networking *n* the making of contacts and trading information as for career advancement; the interconnection of computer systems.

neur-, neuro- *prefix* nerve.

neural *adj* of or pertaining to the nerves.

neuralgia *n* pain along a nerve.—**neuralgic** *adj*.

neuralgic *adj* pertaining to neuralgia.

neurasthenia *n* brain and nerve exhaustion, as from influenza, etc.

neurectomy *n* (*pl* **neurectomies**) excision of a nerve.

neuritis *n* inflammation of a nerve.

neuro-, neur- *prefix* nerve.

neuroglia *n* the delicate connective tissue between the nerve fibres of the brain and spinal cord.

neurology *n* the branch of medicine studying the nervous system and its diseases.—**neurological** *adj*.—**neurologist** *n*.

neuroma *n* (*pl* **neuromas, neuromata**) a fibrous tumour occuring in nerve tissue.

neuron, neurone *see* **nerve cell**.

neuropathic *adj* pertaining to, or suffering from, nervous disease; affecting the nerves.—**neuropath** *n*.—**neuropathically** *adv*.

neuropathology *n* the study of diseases of the nervous system.—**neuropathologist** *adj*.

neuropathy *n* disease of the nervous system.

neuropteran *n* (*pl* **neuropterans**) any of an order of insects characterized by four transparent, finely reticulated, membranous wings. * *adj* with four wings marked with a network of nerves (—*also* **neuropterous**).

neurosis *n* (*pl* **neuroses**) a mental disorder with symptoms such as anxiety and phobia.

neurosurgery *n* the branch of surgery dealing with the nervous system.—**neurosurgical** *adj*.

neurotic *adj* suffering from neurosis; highly strung; of or acting upon the nerves. * *n* someone with neurosis.

neurotomy *n* (*pl* **neurotomies**) dissection of the nerves.

neurotransmitter *n* a chemical by which nerves cells communicate with each other or with muscles.

neuter *adj* (*gram*) of gender, neither masculine nor feminine; (*biol*) having no sex organs; having undeveloped sex organs in the adult. * *n* a neuter person, word, plant, or animal. * *vt* to castrate or spay.

neutral *adj* nonaligned; not taking sides with either party in a dispute or war; having no distinctive characteristics; (*colour*) dull; (*chem*) neither acid nor alkaline; (*physics*) having zero charge. * *n* a neutral state, person, or colour; a position of a gear mechanism in which power is not transmitted.

neutrality *n* the state of being neutral.

neutralize *vt* to render ineffective; to counterbalance; to declare neutral.—**neutralization** *n*.—**neutralizer** *n*.

neutrally *adv* in a neutral manner.

neutrino *n* (*pl* **neutrinos**) (*phsyics*) a stable elementary particle with almost zero mass and spin 1/2.

neutron *n* an elementary particle with no electric charge and the same mass approximately as a proton.

neutron bomb *n* a nuclear bomb with a small blast that releases neutrons, destroying life but leaving property undamaged.

neutron number *n* the number of neutrons in the nucleus of an atom.

neutron star *n* a star composed solely of densely packed neutrons that has collapsed under its own gravity.

névé *n* the granular compressed snow that forms glacier ice.

never *adv* at no time, not ever; not at all; in no case; (*inf*) surely not.

nevermore *adv* never again.

never-never *adj* imaginary, ideal.

nevertheless *adv* all the same, notwithstanding; in spite of, however.

nevus *n* (*pl* **nevi**) a birthmark, a mole.—*also* **naevus**.—**nevoid** *adj*.

new *adj* recently made, discovered, or invented; seen, known, or used for the first time; different, changed; recently grown, fresh; unused; unaccustomed; unfamiliar; recently begun. * *adv* again; newly; recently.

new blood *n* a recent arrival in an organization expected to bring new ideas and revitalize the system.

newborn *adj* newly born, reborn.

newcomer *n* a recent arrival.

New Deal *n* the economic and social measures introduced into the USA by President Roosevelt in 1933 to combat the great economic crisis that began in 1929.

newel *n* the central pillar of a spiral staircase; the end post of a banister.

New England *n* six northeastern states of the USA.

newfangled *adj* (*contemptuous*) new; novel, very modern.

Newfoundland *n* a large variety of dog, originally from Newfoundland.

newly *adv* recently, lately.

newlywed *n* a recently married person.

new moon *n* the moon when first visible as a crescent.

news *npl* current events; recent happenings; the mass media's coverage of such events; a programme of news on television or radio; information not known before.

newscast *n* radio or television news broadcast.—**newscaster** *n*.

newsdealer, newsagent *n* a retailer of newspapers, magazines, etc.

newsflash *n* an important news item broadcast separately and often interrupting other programmes.

newsletter *n* a bulletin regularly distributed among the members of a group, society, etc, containing information and news of activities, etc.

newspaper *n* a printed periodical containing news published daily or weekly.

newsprint *n* an inexpensive paper on which newspapers are printed.

newsreel *n* a short film presenting news of current events with a commentary.

newsroom *n* the department of a newspaper or broadcasting system that prepares news for publication or broadcasting; a room, etc, where newspapers, magazines, etc, may be read.

New Style calendar *n* the Gregorian or present style of computing the calendar, which replaced the Julian calendar.

newsworthy *adj* timely and important or interesting.

newt *n* any of various small amphibious lizard-like creatures.

New Testament *n* the second part of the Bible including the story of the life and teachings of Christ.

newton *n* the SI unit of force that when acting for 1 second on a mass of 1 kilogram imparts an acceleration of 1 metre per second.

Newtonian *adj* pertaining to, discovered by, or invented by, Sir Isaac Newton, the philosopher, or to his system.

new town *n* in UK, any of various towns built since 1946 as planned units sponsored by government to house overspill population from nearby cities, aid urban redevelopment, etc.

New World *n* the Americas.

New Year's (Day) *n* the first day of a new year; 1 January, a legal holiday in many countries.

New Year's Eve *n* the evening of the last day of the year; 31 December.—*also* **Hogmanay**.

next *adj* nearest; immediately preceding or following; adjacent. * *adv* in the nearest time, place, rank, etc; on the first subsequent occasion.

next of kin *n* the nearest relative of a person.

nexus *n* (*pl* **nexus, nexuses**) a connecting principle or link.

NH *abbr* = New Hampshire.

NI *abbr* = Northern Ireland.

Ni (*chem symbol*) nickel.

nib *n* a pen point. * *vt* (**nibbing, nibbed**) to furnished with a nib; to cut or insert a pen nib.

nibble *vti* to take small bites at (food, etc); to bite (at) lightly and intermittently.—**nibbler** *n*.

Nibelungenlied *n* a medieval German epic poem.

niblick *n* a golf club with a heavy head, used for lofting.

nice *adj* pleasant, attractive, kind, good, etc; particular, fastidious; delicately sensitive.—**nicely** *adv*.

nice-looking *adj* pretty, handsome.

Nicene Creed *n* the creed, one of the three held by the Anglican Church, drawn up by the Ecumenical Council of the Early Christian Church at the Council of Nicaea in Asia Minor in 325AD, with additions made at the Council of Constantinople 381.

niceness *n* the state or quality of being nice; delicacy of perception or touch.

nicety *n* (*pl* **niceties**) a subtle point of distinction; refinement.

niche *n* a shallow recess in a wall for a statue, etc; a place, use, or work for which a person or thing is best suited.

nick *n* a small cut, chip, etc, made on a surface; (*Brit sl*)

a police station, prison. * *vt* to make a nick in; to wound superficially; (*Brit sl*) to steal; (*Brit sl*) to arrest.

nickel *n* a silvery-white metallic element used in alloys and plating; a US or Canadian coin worth five cents.

nickelodeon *n* an early type of jukebox.

nickel silver *n* an alloy of nickel, copper and zinc.—*also* **German silver**.

nicker *vi* to neigh, to snigger.—*also n*.

nicknack *see* **knickknack**.

nickname *n* a substitute name, often descriptive, given in fun; a familiar form of a proper name. * *vt* to give as a nickname.

nicotiana *n* any of the *Nicotiana* genus of plants of Australia and America, eg tobacco.

nicotine *n* a poisonous alkaloid present in tobacco.

nictitate, nictate *vi* to wink.—**nictitation, nictation** *n*.

nictitating membrane *n* a membrane that can be drawn over the eye beneath the eyelid present in many birds, reptiles, fish and some mammals.

nidificate *vi* to build a nest.

nidification *n* the act of building a nest, rearing young, etc.

nidify *vi* (**nidifying, nidified**) to nidificate.

nidus *n* (*pl* **nidi, niduses**) the developing place of spores, seeds, germs, insects' eggs, etc; an accumulation of eggs, tubercles, etc; a nest or hatching place.

niece *n* the daughter of a brother or sister.

niello *n* (*pl* **nielli, niellos**) an ornamental engraving in black on silver, gold, brass, etc; a black alloy used in this. * *vt* (**nielloing, nielloed**) to engrave or decorate with niello.

Niflheim *n* (*Scandinavian myth*) the region of eternal mist and cold.

nifty *adj* (**niftier, niftiest**) (*sl*) neat, stylish.—**niftily** *adv*.—**niftiness** *n*.

niggard *adj* meanly covetous; parsimonious; miserly; niggardly. * *n* one who is meanly covetous; a stingy person, a miser.

niggardliness *n* the state of being niggardly; stinginess.

niggardly *adj* giving grudgingly, ungenerous. * *adv* like a niggard.

nigger *n* (*offensive*) a Negro, Black person; a dark-skinned person.

niggle *vi* to waste time on petty details; to be finicky.

niggler *n* one who trifles at handiwork.

niggling *adj* finicky, fussy; petty; gnawing, irritating.—**nigglingly** *adv*.

nigh *adj, adv, prep* near.

night *n* the period of darkness from sunset to sunrise; nightfall; a specified or appointed evening.

night blindness *n* poor vision in near darkness.

nightcap *n* a cap worn in bed; (*inf*) an alcoholic drink taken just before going to bed.

nightclothes *npl* clothes for wearing in bed, as a nightgown, pyjamas, etc.

nightclub *n* a place of entertainment for drinking, dancing, etc, at night.

nightdress *n* a loose garment worn in bed by women and girls.

nightfall *n* the close of the day.

nightflower *n* a flower that opens at night.

nightglass *n* a short telescope for night use.

nightgown *n* a nightdress.

nightie *n* (*inf*) a nightdress, nightgown.—*also* **nighty**.

nightingale *n* a songbird celebrated for its musical song at night.

nightjar *n* a nocturnal bird with dull mottled plumage.

night life *n* social entertainment at night, esp in towns.

night-light *n* a dim light kept burning at night.

nightlong *adj* lasting through the night.

nightly *adj, adv* done or happening by night or every night.

nightmare *n* a frightening dream; any horrible experience.—**nightmarish** *adj*.

night owl *n* (*inf*) a person who stays up late at night.

night school *n* an educational institution where classes are held in the evening.

nightshade *n* a flowering plant related to the potato and tomato, esp deadly nightshade (belladonna).

nightshirt *n* a long shirt for sleeping in.

nightspot *n* (*inf*) a nightclub.

nightstick *n* (*US*) a short club carried by a policeman or policewoman; a truncheon.

nighttime *n* night.

night watch *n* a watch by night or the person keeping it; (*pl*) night-time.

night watchman *n* the person who guards a building at night.

nighty *n* (*pl* **nighties**) (*inf*) a nightie.

nigrescent *adj* blackish, growing black.—**nigrescence** *n*.

nihil *n* (*Latin*) nothing, nil.

nihil ad rem *adj* (*Latin*) irrelevant.

nihilism *n* the belief that nothing has real existence, scepticism; the rejection of customary beliefs in morality, religion, etc.

nihilist *n* a supporter of nihilism.—**nihilisitic** *adj*.

nihility *n* nonexistence.

nil *n* nothing.

nilgai, nilgau *n* (*pl* **nilgai, nilgais, nilgau, nilgaus**) a large short-horned Indian antelope.

Nilometer *n* a graduated pillar for measuring the rise of water in the river Nile during its floods; a river gauge.

Nilotic *adj* pertaining to the River Nile.

nimble *adj* agile; quick.—**nimbly** *adv*.

nimbus *n* (*pl* **nimbi, nimbuses**) (*art*) the halo or cloud of light surrounding the heads of divinities, saints, and sovereigns; a rain cloud.

nimby *abbr* = not in my back yard.

niminy-piminy *adj* mincing, prim.

Nimrod *n* a distinguished hunter, from Nimrod, "the mighty hunter" (Genesis 10.9).

nincompoop *n* a stupid, silly person.

nine *adj, n* one more than eight. * *n* the symbol for this (9, IX, ix); the ninth in a series or set; something having nine units as members.

ninefold *adj* having nine units or members; being nine times as great or as many.

ninepins *see* **skittles**.

nineteen *adj, n* one more than eighteen. * *n* the symbol for this (19, XIX, xix).—**nineteenth** *adj*.

nineteenth *adj* being one of 19 equal parts. * *n* a nineteenth part.

nineteenth hole *n* (*golf*) (*sl*) the bar in the clubhouse.

ninetieth *adj* next after 89. * *n* a ninetieth part.

ninety *adj, n* nine times ten. * *n* the symbol for this (90, XC, xc); (*in pl*) **nineties**; the numbers from 90 to 99; the same numbers in a life or century.

ninja *n* a Japanese warrior trained in ninjutsu.—*also adj*.

ninjutsu n an ancient Japanese martial art which practises techniques of stealth or invisibility, orig for the purpose of espionage and political assassination.

ninny *n* (*pl* **ninnies**) a person of weak character or mind, a simpleton.

ninon *n* a light silk material.

ninth *adj, n* next after eighth; one of nine equal parts of a thing.

Niobe *n* an inconsolable bereaved woman; (*Greek myth*) a heroine who was turned to stone while weeping for her slain children.—**Niobean** *adj*.

niobic *adj* of or containing pentavalent niobium.

niobium *n* a metallic element used in alloys.

nip[1] *vt* (**nipping, nipped**) to pinch, pinch off; to squeeze between two surfaces; (*dog*) to give a small bite; to prevent the growth of; (*plants*) to have a harmful effect on because of cold. * *n* a pinch; a sharp squeeze; a bite; severe frost or biting coldness.

nip[2] *n* a small drink of spirits. * *vti* (**nipping, nipped**) to drink in nips.

nipa *n* an East Indian palm.

nipper *n* a person or thing that nips; the pincer of a crab or lobster; (*pl*) pliers, pincers, etc; (*Brit inf*) a small child.

nipple *n* the small protuberance on a breast or udder through which the milk passes, a teat; a teat-like rubber part on the cap of a baby's bottle; a projection resembling a nipple.

nippy *adj* (**nippier, nippiest**) (*weather*) frosty; (*Brit inf*) quick, nimble.

nirvana *n* (*Buddhism*) the highest religious state, when all desire of existence and worldly good is extinguished, and the soul is absorbed into the Deity.

nisi *adj* (*decree, order, rule, etc*) valid unless cause is shown be the contrary by a fixed date, at which it is made absolute.

nisi prius *n* (*law*) a writ, beginning with these words, directing a sheriff to empanel a jury; the name of certain courts for the trial of civil actions in the counties. / a trial of civil causes by judges of assize.

nit *n* the egg of a louse or other parasitic insect.

niter *see* **nitre**.

niton *n* a gaseous radioactive element, radon.

nit-picking *n* (*inf*) concern with petty details in order to find fault.—*also adj*.

nitr-, nitro- *prefix* containing nitrogen; made with nitric acid.

nitrate *n* a salt of nitric acid; a fertilizer made of this.—**nitration** *n*.

nitre *n* potassium nitrate, saltpetre.—*also* **niter**.

nitric *adj* containing nitrogen.

nitric acid *n* a corrosive, caustic liquid used to make explosives, fertilizers, etc.

nitride *n* a compound of nitrogen with a metal, also with phosphorus, silicon or boron.

nitrification *n* the process of converting into nitre.

nitrify *vti* (**nitrifying, nitrified**) to make or become nitrous.

nitrite *n* a salt of nitrous acid.

nitro-, nitr- *prefix* containing nitrogen; made with nitric acid.

nitrogen *n* a gaseous element forming nearly 78 per cent of air.

nitrogenize *vt* to impregnate with nitrogen.—**nitrogenization** *n*.

nitrogenous *adj* pertaining to, or containing, nitrogen.

nitroglycerin, nitroglycerine *n* a powerful explosive made by adding glycerine to a mixture of nitric and sulphuric acids.

nitrous *adj* resembling, obtained from, or impregnated with, nitre.

nitrous acid *n* a compound of four volumes of nitrogen and one of oxygen.

nitrous oxide *n* a compound of one volume of oxygen and two volumes of nitrogen; laughing gas.

nitty-gritty *n* (*sl*) basic elements; harsh realities; practical details.

nitwit *n* (*inf*) a stupid person.

nival *adj* of or pertaining to snow.

niveous *adj* resembling snow, snow-like.

nix[1] *n* (*German myth*) a water sprite; (*Scot*) a kelpie.—**nixie** *nf*.

nix[2] *n* (*sl*) nothing. * *interj* (*sl*) look out! be careful!

nizam *n* (*with cap*) a title of the ruler of Hyderabad, India; a Turkish army soldier.

NJ *abbr* = New Jersey.

NLQ *abbr* = (*comput*) near letter quality.

NM *abbr* = New Mexico.

No[1] (*chem symbol*) nobelium.

No[2], **no**[1] *abbr* = number.

No[3], **Noh** *n* (*pl* **No**, **Noh**) Japanese classic dance-drama.

no *adv* (*used to express denial or disagreement*) not so, not at all, by no amount. * *adj* not any; not a; not one; none; not at all; by no means. * *n* (*pl* **noes**, **nos**) a denial; a refusal; a negative vote or voter.

Noachian, **Noachic** *adj* pertaining to the patriarch Noah, the deluge, or his times.

nob[1] *n* a knob; (*sl*) the head.

nob[2] *n* (*at cribbage*) knave of suit of turn-up card.

nob[3] *n* (*Brit sl*) a member of the upper classes; a wealthy person.

nobble *vt* (*Brit sl*) to tamper with (a racehorse) to prevent its winning; to obtain (money) by dishonest means; to suborn (a juror, etc) by bribes or threats; to defeat by underhand methods; to steal; to kidnap.

nobelium *n* a radioactive metallic element.

Nobel prize *n* an annual international prize given for distinction in one of six areas: physics, chemistry, physiology and medicine, economics, literature, and promoting peace.

nobility *n* (*pl* **nobilities**) nobleness of character, mind, birth, or rank; the class of people of noble birth.

noble *adj* famous or renowned; excellent in quality or character; of high rank or birth. * *n* a person of high rank in society.

nobleman *n* (*pl* **noblemen**) a peer.—**noblewoman** *nf* (*pl* **noblewomen**).

nobleness *n* the state of quality of being noble.

noblesse oblige *n* rank has its obligations.

nobly *adv* in a noble manner; of noble rank.

nobody *n* (*pl* **nobodies**) a person of no importance. * *pron* no person.

nock *n* a notch in a bcw or arrow for the string; (*naut*) the forward upper corner of some sails. * *vt* to fit (an arrow) to string.

nocti-, **noct-** *prefix* night.

noctiluca *n* (*pl* **noctilucae**) a phosphorescent animalcule.

noctule *n* the largest British kind of bat.

nocturn *n* (*RC Church*) a part of matins.

nocturnal *adj* of, relating to, night; active by night.—**nocturnally** *adv*.

nocturne *n* a picture of a night scene; a musical composition appropriate to the night; a lullaby.

nocuous *adj* hurtful.

nod *vti* (**nodding**, **nodded**) to incline the head quickly, esp in agreement or greeting; to let the head drop, be drowsy; to indicate by a nod; (*with* **off**) (*inf*) to fall asleep. * *n* a quick bob of the head; a sign of assent or command.

nodal *adj* pertaining to nodes.

noddy *n* (*pl* **noddies**) a simpleton; a tropical sea bird; a four-wheeled carriage with a door at the back

node *n* a knob; a knot; a point of intersection; (*med*) a swelling; (*bot*) the joint of a stem and leaf or leaves; (*astron*) two points at which the orbit of a planet intersects he ecliptic; (*math*) the point at which a curve crosses itself; the point of rest in a vibrating body.

nodical *adj* (*astron*) pertaining to nodes.

nodose *adj* having knots or nodes, knotty, knobbed.—**nodosity** *n*.

nodular, **nodulose**, **nodulous** *adj* pertaining to, or like, a nodule.

nodule *n* a small lump or tumour.—**nodular** *adj*.

nodus *n* (*pl* **nodi**) a knotty point, a complication in the plot of a story, etc.

noel, **noël** *n* Christmas, esp in carols.

noetic *adj* pertaining to, performed by, or originating in, the mind or intellect, intellectual, abstract. * *n* the science of the intellect [(—*also* **noemics**).]

no-fault *adj* (*insurance*) providing damages without blame being fixed; (*divorce*) concluded without blame being charged.

nog[1] *n* a wooden peg or block; a stump. * *vt* (**nogging**, **nogged**) to secure with nogs.

nog[2] *n* an East Anglian strong beer.

nog[3] *n* (*an*) eggnog.

noggin *n* a small quantity of alcoholic drink; (*inf*) the head.

nogging *n* a partition formed of timber scantlings filled up with bricks.

no-go area *n* an area that certain individuals or groups are forbidden to enter.

nohow *adv* in no way, by no means.

noil *n* a short wool-combing.

noise *n* a sound, esp a loud, disturbing or unpleasant one; a din; unwanted fluctuations in a transmitted signal; (*pl*) conventional sounds, words, etc made in reaction, such as sympathy. * *vt* to make public.

noiseless *adj* making no sound, silent.—**noiselessly** *adv*.—**noiselessness** *n*.

noisette *n* a small round piece of meat.

noisome *adj* harmful, noxious; foul-smelling.

noisy *adj* (**noisier**, **noisiest**) making much noise; turbulent, clamorous.—**noisily** *adv*.—**noisiness** *n*.

nolens volens *adv* (*Latin*) willingly or unwillingly, willy-nilly.

noli me tangere *n* (*Latin*) a warning not to meddle; an erosive ulcer, lupus; a wild cucumber; a picture of Christ as he appeared to Mary Magdalen at the sepulchre.

nolle prosequi *n* an English legal term indicating the plaintiff's abandonment of his suit.

nolo episcopari *n* (*Latin*) unwillingness to accept office.

nomad *n* one of a people or tribe who move in search of pasture; a wanderer.—**nomadic** *adj*.

nomadic *adj* wandering; leading a wandering life; pastoral.—**nomadically** *adv*.

no-man's-land *n* an unclaimed piece of land; a strip of land, esp between armies, borders; an ambiguous area, subject, etc.

nombril *n* (*her*) the centre of an escutcheon.

nom de guerre *n* (*pl* **noms de guerre**) a pseudonym, an assumed name.

nom de plume *n* (*pl* **noms de plume**) a pseudonym.

nome *n* a province of modern Greece; a territorial division in ancient Egypt.

nomenclator *n* an ancient Roman slave who named persons met; one who gives names to things, an inventor of names.

nomenclature *n* a system of names, terminology, used in a science, etc, or for parts of a device, etc.

nominal *adj* of or like a name; existing in name only; having minimal real worth, token.

nominalism *n* (*philos*) the doctrine that general notions exist only in the mind or in name, opposite to realism.

nominalist *n* one who holds the doctrine of nominalism.—**nominalistic** *adj*.

nominally *adv* in name only.

nominate *vt* to appoint to an office or position; (*candidate*) to propose for election.—**nominator** *n*.

nomination *n* the act or right of nominating; the state of being nominated.

nominative *adj* (*gram*) denoting the case of the subject of a verb; appointed, not elected. * *n* (*gram*) the nominative case or a word in it.

nominee *n* a person who is nominated.

nomo-, nom- *prefix* law.

nomography *n* (*pl* **nomographies**) the art of drawing up laws.—**nomographic, nomographical** *adj*.

nomology *n* the science of the laws of the mind.—**nomological** *adj*.—**nomologist** *n*.

nomothetic, nomothetical *adj* legislative, founded on a system of laws.

non- *prefix* not, reversing the meaning of a word.

nonage *n* minority, legal infancy; an early stage.

nonagenarian *n* a person who is in his or her nineties.

nonagon *n* a plane figure with 9 sides and 9 angles.—**nonagonal** *adj*.

nonalcoholic *adj* (*drinks, etc*) containing little or no alcohol.

nonaligned *adj* not in alliance with any side, esp in power politics.

nonce *n* **for the nonce** for this time only.

nonce word *n* a word coined for one occasion.

nonchalance *n* coolness; indifference.

nonchalant *adj* calm; cool, unconcerned, indifferent.—**nonchalantly** *adv*.

noncombatant *n* a member of the armed forces whose duties do not include fighting, as a doctor or chaplain; a civilian during wartime.

noncommissioned officer *n* (*mil*) a subordinate officer, as a corporal, sergeant, etc, appointed from the ranks.

noncommittal *adj* not revealing one's opinion.—**noncommittally** *adv*.

non compos mentis *adj* (*Latin*) of unsound mind, not responsible.

nonconductor *n* a substance that will not conduct electricity or heat.

nonconformist *n* a person who does not conform to prevailing attitudes, behaviour, etc; (*with cap*) in Britain, a Protestant who does not belong to the established church.—*also adj*.

nonconformity *n* (*with cap*) refusal to conform to the established church; a want of conformity, irregularity.

noncooperation *n* refusal to cooperate, esp with government decree, etc.—**noncooperative** *adj*.

nondescript *adj* hard to classify, indeterminate; lacking individual characteristics. * *n* a nondescript person or thing.

none *pron* no one; not anyone; (*pl verb*) not any; no one. * *adv* not at all.

noneffective *adj* not effective; (*soldier, sailor*) not qualified for active service.—*also n*.

nonentity *n* (*pl* **nonentities**) a person or thing of no significance.

nones *npl* in the ancient Roman calendar the ninth day before the Ides, reckoned inclusively, ie 7th of March, May, July, October, and the 5th of the other months; (*RC Church*) the devotional office for the ninth hour or 3 p.m.

nonesuch *n* an unrivalled person or thing, a nonpareil; a plant like clover used for fodder.—*also* **nonsuch**.

nonet *n* a group of nine connected objects or people; (*mus*) a piece for nine players.

nonetheless *conj* nevertheless.

nonevent *n* an event or experience that is unexpectedly disappointing.

nonfeasance *n* (*law*) the omission of an obligatory act.

nonferrous *adj* containing no iron.

nonflammable *adj* not easily set on fire.

nonillion *n* in the US and France, tenth power of a thousand (1 followed by 30 ciphers); in Britain, the ninth power of one million (1 followed by 54 ciphers).—**nonillionth** *adj*.

nonintervention *n* the policy of refusing to interfere in the affairs of others, esp nations.—**noninterventionist** *adj*.

nonjuror *n* one who refused to take the oath of allegiance to William and Mary in 1689.

non-lethal *adj* (*international affairs*) pertaining to foreign aid given to provide medicine, clothing or food rather than weapons.

nonmetal *n* a chemical element (eg carbon) that is not a metal.

nonmoral *adj* unconcerned with morality; without moral standards.

nonpareil *adj* without an equal; (*person or thing*) unrivalled, matchless, unsurpassed. * *n* unequalled excellence; (*print*) a 6-point type; a variety of apple; a kind of bird, moth, wheat, etc.

nonpartisan *adj* not aligned to one particular political party.

nonparty *adj* free from party obligations.

nonplus *vt* (**nonplusses, nonplussing, nonplussed** *or* **nonpluses, nonplusing, nonplused**) to cause to be so perplexed that one cannot, go, speak, act further. * *n* (*pl* **nonpluses**) a state of perplexity, a standstill.

non plus ultra *see* **ne plus ultra**.

non-profit *adj* (*organization*) not conducted for the purpose of making money.

nonproliferation *n* , *adj* (*placing*) restriction on the acquisition or production of, esp nuclear weapons.

nonrepresentational *adj* (*art*) abstract.

nonsense *n* words, actions, etc, that are absurd and have no meaning.—*also adj*. * *interj* absurd!

nonsensical *adj* absurd; unmeaning.—**nonsensically** *adv*.

non sequitur *n* a statement that has no relevance to what has preceded it.

nonstarter *n* a person who is unlikely to succeed; (*horse, racing car, etc*) withdrawn at the last moment.

nonstick *adj* (*saucepans*) coated with a surface that prevents food from sticking.

nonstop *adj* (*train, plane, etc*) not making any intermediate stops; not ceasing. * *adv* without stopping or pausing.

nonsuch *see* **nonesuch**.

nonsuit *n* the withdrawal of a suit during trial either voluntarily or by judgment of the court on the discovery of error or defect in the pleadings. * *vt* to pronounce a nonsuit against.

nonunion *adj* not belonging to a trade union.

nonviolence *n* the abstaining from physical force to achieve civil rights.—**nonviolent** *adj*.

noodle[1] *n* (often *pl*) pasta formed into a strip.

noodle[2] *n* (*inf*) a foolish person; (*sl*) the head.

nook *n* a secluded corner, a retreat; a recess.

noon *n* midday; twelve o'clock in the day. * *adj* pertaining to noon.

noonday, noontide, noontime *adj* pertaining to noon, or midday. * *n* noon.

no one *pron* nobody.

noose *n* a loop of rope with a slipknot, used for hanging, snaring, etc. * *vt* to tie in a noose; to make a noose in or of.

nopal *n* an American cactus, the food of the cochineal insect.

nope *adv* (*sl*) no.

nor *conj* and not; not either.

Nor *abbr* = Norman; north; Norway; Norwegian.

Nordic *adj* (*physical type*) characterized by tall stature, long head, light skin and hair, and blue eyes; (skiing) including cross-country runs and jumping.

Norfolk jacket *n* a man's loose jacket with a belt.

noria *n* a water-raising apparatus in Spain, etc, a waterwheel.

norm *n* a standard or model, esp the standard of achievement of a large group.—**normative** *adj*.

normal *adj* regular; usual; stable mentally. * *n* anything normal; the usual state, amount, etc.—**normalcy** *n*.—**normality** *n*.—**normally** *adv*.

normalize *vti* to make or become normal.—**normalization** *n*.

normal school *n* (*US*) a school for the training of teachers for elementary schools.

Norman *n* any of the people of Normandy who conquered England in 1066; a native or inhabitant of Normandy in France. * *adj* pertaining to the Normans or Normandy; (*archit*) of a style introduced into England by the Normans, characterized by rounded arches and massive square towers (—*also* **Normanesque**).

Norn *n* (*Scand myth*) one of the three fates, Urd, Verdande and Skuld, representing the past, the present and the future.

Norse *adj* of ancient Scandinavia or its inhabitants; of Norway. * *n* the language of Norway.

Norseman *n* (*pl* **Norsemen**) any of the ancient Scandinavian people, the Vikings.

north *n* one of the four points of the compass, opposite the sun at noon, to the right of a person facing the sunset; the direction in which a compass needle points; (*often with cap*) the northern part of one's country or the earth. * *adj* in, of, or towards the north; from the north. * *adv* in or towards the north.

northeast *adj, n* (of) the direction midway between north and east.

northeaster *n* a northeast wind.

northeasterly *adj* towards or coming from the northeast. * *n* (*pl* **northeasterlies**) a northeast wind or storm.

northeastern *adj* belonging to the northeast, or in that direction.

northeastward *adj* towards or in the northeast.—*also adv*.—**northeastwards** *adv*.

norther *n* a wind or storm from the north, esp a strong gale that prevails in the Gulf of Mexico from September to March.

northerly *adj* in, from, or towards the north. * *n* (*pl* **northerlies**) a northerly wind.

northern *adj* of or in the north.

northerner *n* a native or inhabitant of the north.

Northern Hemisphere *n* the half of the earth north of the Equator.

northern lights *npl* the aurora borealis.

northernmost *adj* farthest north.

northing *n* distance northward.

North Pole *n* the northern end of the axis of the earth at a latitude of 90 degrees north.

north star *n* the polar star.

northward *adj* towards or in the north.—*also adv*.—**northwards** *adv*.

northwest *adj, n* (of) the direction midway between north and west.

northwester *n* a northwest wind.

northwesterly *adj* towards or coming from the northwest. * *n* (*pl* **northwesterlies**) a northwest wind or storm.

northwestern *adj* belonging to the northwest, or in that direction.

northwestward *adj* towards or in the northwest.—*also adv*.—**northwestwards** *adv*.

Norwegian *adj, n* (of or relating to) the language, people, etc, of Norway.

nose *n* the part of the face above the mouth, used for breathing and smelling, having two nostrils; the sense of smell; anything like a nose in shape or position. * *vt* to discover as by smell; to nuzzle; to push (away, etc) with the front forward. * *vi* to sniff for; to inch forwards; to pry.

nosebag *n* a bag containing fodder hung from a horse's head.

noseband *n* the part of a bridle that covers the horse's nose.

nosebleed *n* a bleeding from the nose.

nose dive *n* a swift downward plunge of an aircraft, nose first; any sudden sharp drop, as in prices.—**nose-dive** *vi*.

nosegay *n* a bouquet.

nose job *n* (*sl*) cosmetic plastic surgery to reshape the nose.

nosey *see* **nosy**.

nosh *n* (*sl*) food, a meal. * *vt* to chew. * *vi* to eat.

nosing *n* the rounded edge of a step, etc, or the metal shield for it.

noso- *prefix* disease.

nosography *n* the systematic description of diseases.

nosology *n* the classification of the diseases of animals and plants.—**nosological** *adj*.—**nosologically** *adv*.—**nosologist** *n*.

nostalgia *n* yearning for past times or places.

nostalgic *adj* feeling or expressing nostalgia; longing for one's youth.—**nostalgically** *adv*.

nostology *n* the study of senility or ageing, gerontology.—**nostologic** *adj*.

nostril *n* one of the two external openings of the nose for breathing and smelling.

nostrum *n* a quack remedy, patent medicine.

nosy *adj* (**nosier, nosiest**) (*inf*) inquisitive, snooping.—**nosily** *adv*.—**nosiness** *n*.—*also* **nosey**.

nosy parker *n* (*inf*) a prying person, busybody.

not *adv* expressing denial, refusal, or negation.

nota bene note this.—*abbr* = **NB**.

notabilia *npl* things worthy of note.

notability *n* (*pl* **notabilities**) the quality of being notable; a notable person or thing.

notable *adj* worthy of being noted or remembered; remarkable, eminent. * *n* an eminent or famous person.—**notably** *adv*.

notandum *n* (*pl* **notanda**) a thing to be noted.

notarial *adj* pertaining to, or done by, a notary.

notary *n* (*pl* **notaries**) a notary public.

notary public *n* (*pl* **notaries public**) a public official authorized to certify deeds, contracts, etc.

notation *n* a system of symbols or signs to represent quantities, etc, esp in mathematics, music, etc.

notch *n* a V-shaped cut in an edge or surface; (*inf*) a step, degree; a narrow pass with steep sides. * *vt* to cut notches in.

note *n* a brief summary or record, written down for future reference; a memorandum; a short letter; notice, attention; an explanation or comment on the text of a book; a musical sound of a particular pitch; a sign representing such a sound; a piano or organ key; the vocal sound of a bird. * *vt* to notice, observe; to write down; to annotate.

notebook *n* a book with blank pages for writing in.

noted *adj* celebrated, well-known.

note paper *n* paper for writing letters.

noteworthy *adj* outstanding; remarkable.

nothing *n* no thing; not anything; nothingness; a zero; a trifle; a person or thing of no importance or value. * *adv* in no way, not at all.

nothingness *n* the state of being nothing; unconsciousness; worthlessness.

notice *n* an announcement; a warning; a placard giving information; a short article about a book, play, etc; attention, heed; a formal warning of intention to end an agreement at a certain time. * *vt* to observe; to remark upon. * *vi* to be aware of.

noticeable *adj* easily noticed or seen.—**noticeably** *adv*.

notice board *n* a board on which notices are posted.

notifiable *adj* (*infectious diseases*) that must be reported to health authorities.

notification *n* the act of notifying; a notice or paper bearing it.

notify *vt* (**notifying, notified**) to inform; to report, give notice of.

notion *n* a general idea; an opinion; a whim;.

notional *adj* hypothetical, abstract; imaginary.

notions *npl* small useful articles, as thread, needles, etc; haberdashery.

noto- *prefix* back.

notochord *n* the rudimentary form of the vertebral column; a band forming the basis of the spinal column.—**notochordal** *adj*.

notoriety *n* the state of being notorious; disrepute, infamy; public exposure.

notorious *adj* widely known, esp unfavourably.—**notoriously** *adv*.

notornis *n* the gigantic short-winged coot of New Zealand.

nototherium *n* (*pl* **nototheria**) an extinct gigantic marsupial of Australia.

notwithstanding *prep* in spite of. * *adv* nevertheless. * *conj* although.

nougat *n* a chewy sweet consisting of sugar paste with nuts.

nought *n* nothing; a zero. * *adv* in no degree.—*also* **naught**.

noughts and crosses *see* **tick-tack-toe**.

noumenon *n* (*pl* **noumena**) an object of purely intellectual intuition; (*philos*) the substance or real existing under the phenomenal.—**noumenal** *adj*.

noun *n* (*gram*) a word that names a person, a living being, an object, action etc; a substantive.

nourish *vt* to feed; to encourage the growth of; to raise, bring up.

nourishing *adj* containing nourishment; health-giving; beneficial.

nourishment *n* food; the act of nourishing.

nous *n* pure intellect; common sense.

nouveau riche *n* (*pl* **nouveaux riches**) the new rich, a parvenu.—*also adj*.

Nov *abbr* = November.

nova *n* (*pl* **novas, novae**) a new star that explodes into bright luminosity before subsiding.

Novatian *adj* pertaining to the doctrines of the Novatians, a 3rd-century sect who held that the Church should not re-admit the lapsed, and that second marriages were of the nature of sin.

novel *n* a relatively long prose narrative that is usually fictitious and in the form of a story. * *adj* new and unusual.

novelette *n* a short novel.—**novelettish** *adj*.

novelist *n* a writer of novels.

novelize *vt* to turn (a play, film, etc) into a novel.—**novelization** *n*.

novella *n* (*pl* **novellas, novelle**) a short novel.

novelty *n* (*pl* **novelties**) a novel thing or occurrence; a new or unusual thing; (*pl*) cheap, small objects for sale.

November *n* the eleventh month, having 30 days.

novena *n* (*pl* **novenae**) (*RC Church*) a prayer made for nine days to obtain a request through intercession of the Virgin or saint.

novice *n* a person on probation in a religious order before taking final vows; a beginner.

novitiate, noviciate *n* a probationary period, initiation; a novice; a place where novices live.

now *adv* at the present time; by this time; at once; nowadays. * *conj* since; seeing that. * *n* the present time. * *adj* of the present time.

nowadays *adv* in these days; at the present time.

noway *adv* not at all. * *interj* (**no way**) used to express emphatic denial or refusal.

nowhere *adv* not in, at, or to anywhere.

nowise *adv* not in any manner or degree.

noxious *adj* harmful, unhealthy.—**noxiously** *adv*.—**noxiousness** *n*.

noyade *n* execution by drowning, esp that system of capital punishment for political offenders employed by the French revolutionists of 1789.

noyau *n* (*pl* **noyaux**) a liqueur flavoured with bruised bitter almonds.

nozzle *n* the spout at the end of a hose, pipe, etc.

Np (*chem symbol*) neptunium.

NT *abbr* = New Testament.

-n't = not.

nth *adj* (*maths*) of or having an unspecified number; (*inf*) utmost, extreme.

nu *n* the 13th letter of the Greek alphabet.

nuance *n* a subtle difference in meaning, colour, etc.

nub *n* a lump or small piece; (*inf*) the central point or gist of a matter.

nubbin *n* a small or imperfect ear of maize; undeveloped fruit.

nubecula *n* (*pl* **nubeculae**) the Magellanic clouds, a small galaxy; cloudy appearance; a light film on the eye.

nubile *adj* (*girl*) marriageable; attractive.

nuclear *adj* of or relating to a nucleus; using nuclear energy; having nuclear weapons.

nuclear bomb *n* a bomb whose explosive power derives from uncontrolled nuclear fusion or fission.

nuclear energy *n* energy released as a result of nuclear fission or fusion.

nuclear family *n* father, mother and children.

nuclear fission *n* the splitting of a nucleus of an atom either spontaneously or by bombarding it with particles.

nuclear fusion *n* the combining of two nuclei into a heavier nucleus, releasing energy in the process.

nuclear power *n* electrical or motive power produced by a nuclear reactor.

nuclear reactor *n* a device in which nuclear fission is maintained and harnessed to produce energy.

nuclear waste *n* radioactive waste.

nucleate *adj* having a nucleus.

nucleic acid *n* DNA, RNA or similar complex acid present in all living cells.

nucleo-, nucle- *prefix* nucleus; nucleic acid.

nucleolus *n* (*pl* **nucleoli**) a minute body inside a nucleus.

nucleonics *n* (*used as sing*) the physics and technology of the applications of nuclear energy.

nucleus *n* (*pl* **nuclei, nucleuses**) the central part of core around which something may develop, or be grouped or concentrated; the centrally positively charged portion of an atom; the part of an animal or plant cell containing genetic material.

nude *adj* naked; bare; undressed. * *n* a naked human figure, esp in a work of art; the state of being nude.—**nudity** *n*.

nudge *vt* to touch gently with the elbow to attract attention or urge into action; to push slightly. * *n* a gentle touch, as with the elbow.

nudibranch *n* any of the order Nudibranchia of shell-less molluscs with naked gills.

nudism *n* the practice of going nude, esp in groups at designated places and times.

nudist *n* one who believes in going nude.—*also adj*.

nudity *n* (*pl* **nudities**) nakedness.

nugatory *adj* trifling, worthless; inoperative, not valid; useless.

nugget *n* a small lump, esp of gold in its natural state.

nuisance *n* a person or thing that annoys or causes trouble.

nuke *vt* (*sl*) to attack and destroy with a nuclear weapon; (*sl*) to cook or heat (food) in microwave oven. * *n* a nuclear weapon.

null *adj* without legal force; invalid.

nullah *n* in the East Indes, a watercourse or canal; a ravine.

nulla-nulla *n* (*Austral*) a hard wooden club.

nullifier *n* one who nullifies.

nullify *vt* (**nullifying, nullified**) to make null, to cancel out.—**nullification** *n*.

nullipara *n* (*pl* **nulliparae**) a woman who has never given birth to a child, esp if not a virgin.

nullipore *n* a marine coral-like plant with calcareous fronds.

nullity *n* (*pl* **nullities**) the state of being null; a legally invalid document or act; something ineffectual, worthless, etc.

num *abbr* = number; numeral.

numb *adj* deadened; having no feeling (due to cold, shock, etc). * *vt* to make numb.—**numbness** *n*.

number *n* a symbol or word indicating how many; a numeral identifying a person or thing by its position in a series; a single issue of a magazine; a song or piece of music, esp as an item in a performance; (*inf*) an object singled out; a total of persons or things; (*gram*) the form of a word indicating singular or plural; a telephone number; (*pl*) arithmetic; (*pl*) numerical superiority. * *vti* to count; to give a number to; to include or be included as one of a group; to limit the number of; to total.

numberless *adj* too many to count.

number one *n* the first in a list, series, etc; (*inf*) oneself or one's own interests; (*inf*) the most important person or thing; (*inf*) a best-selling pop record. * *adj* most important, urgent, etc.

numberplate *n* a license plate.

Number Ten *n* 10 Downing Street, the London residence of the British prime minister.

numbles *npl* humbles, entrails, esp of a deer.

numbskull *see* **numskull**.

numerable *adj* countable.—**numerably** *adv*.

numeral *n* a symbol or group of symbols used to express a number (eg two = 2 or II, etc).

numerate *adj* having a basic understanding of arithmetic. * *vt* to reckon or enumerate; to point or read, as figures.

numerati *npl* people, esp financiers, who are proficient at arithmetic.

numeration *n* the act of numbering; the art of reading in words numbers expressed by symbols.

numerator *n* the number above the line in a fraction.

numerical, numeric *adj* of or relating to numbers; expressed in numbers.

numerology *n* the study of the supposed occult meaning of numbers.

numerous *adj* many, consisting of many items.

numismatics *n* (*used as sing*) the study of coins, medals, etc.—*also* **numismatology**.—**numismatic** *adj*.

numismatist *n* one skilled in numismatics / a student of coins.

nummular *adj* pertaining to, or like, coins.

nummulite *n* a many-chambered fossil foraminifer resembling a coin.—**nummulitic** *adj*.

numskull *n* a dolt, a blockhead.—*also* **numbskull**.

nun *n* a woman belonging to a religious order.

Nunc Dimittis *n* a canticle.

nunciature *n* the office of a nuncio; the tenure of it.

nuncio *n* (*pl* **nuncios**) the pope's ambassador at a foreign court.

nuncupate *vt* to declare, to make a will verbally, not in writing.

nuncupative *adj* (*law*) verbal, not written; nominal.

nunnery *n* (*pl* **nunneries**) a convent of nuns.

nuptial *adj* relating to marriage. * *npl* a wedding ceremony; marriage.

nurse *n* a person trained to care for the sick, injured or aged; a person who looks after another person's child or children. * *vt* to tend, to care for; (*baby*) to feed at the breast; (*hatred*) to foster; to tend with an eye to the future.

nursemaid *n* a woman in charge of children, a nanny.

nursery *n* (*pl* **nurseries**) a room set aside for children; a place where children may be left in temporary care; a place where young trees and plants are raised for transplanting.

nurseryman *n* (*pl* **nurserymen**) a person who owns or works in a plant nursery.

nursery rhyme *n* a short traditional poem or song for children.

nursery school *n* a school for young children, usu under five.

nursery slope *n* a gently inclined slope for novice skiers.

nursing *n* the profession of a nurse.

nursing home *n* an establishment providing care for convalescent, chronically ill, or disabled people.

nursling, nurseling *n* an infant; one who is nursed.

nurture *vt* to feed; to bring up, educate. * *n* the act of bringing up a child; nourishment.

nut *n* a kernel (sometimes edible) enclosed in a hard shell; a usu metallic threaded block screwed on the end of a bolt; (*sl*) a mad person; (*sl*) a devotee, fan. * *vt* (**nutting, nutted**) to gather nuts.

nutant *adj* (*bot*) having the top bent downward.

nutation *n* nodding; the periodic vibratory movement of the axis of the earth; (*bot*) the turning of flowers towards the sun.—**nutational** *adj*.

nut-brown *adj* coloured like a ripe hazelnut.

nut case *n* (*sl*) a crazy or foolish person.

nutcracker *n* (usu *pl*) a tool for cracking nuts; a bird with speckled plumage.

nuthatch *n* a small climbing bird feeding on nuts.

nutmeg *n* the aromatic kernel produced by a tree, grated and used as a spice.

nutria *n* the fur or skin of the coypu, a South American beaver.

nutrient *n* a substance that nourishes. * *adj* promoting growth.

nutriment *n* nourishing food, nourishment.

nutrition *n* the act or process by which plants and animals take in and assimilate food in their systems; the study of the human diet.—**nutritional** *adj*.

nutritionist *n* a specialist who studies and advises on the human diet.

nutritious *adj* efficient as food; health-giving, nourishing.

nutritive *adj* serving as good. * *n* an article of food.—**nutritively** *adv*.

nuts *adj* (*inf*) very keen (on); (*inf*) crazy.

nuts and bolts *npl* (*inf*) the basic facts or details.

nutshell *n* the hard covering of a nut; a tiny receptacle; a compact way of expression.

nutting *n* nut-gathering.

nutty *adj* (**nuttier, nuttiest**) tasting of or containing nuts; (*sl*) very enthusiastic; (*sl*) crazy, mad, etc.

nux vomica *n* the fruit of an East Indian plant (*Strychnos Nux vomica*), which yields the deadly poison strychnine.

nuzzle *vti* to push (against) or rub with the nose or snout; to nestle, snuggle.

NV *abbr* = Nevada.

NW *abbr* = northwest, northwestern.

NWT *abbr* = Northwest Territories (of Canada).

NY *abbr* = New York.

nyctalopia *n* night blindness; the inability to see clearly except at night.

nyctitropism *n* (*bot*) the so-called sleep of plants, turning in certain direction at night.—**nyctitropic** *adj*.

nylon *n* any of numerous strong, tough, elastic, synthetic materials used esp in plastics and textiles; (*pl*) stockings made of nylon.

nymph *n* (*myth*) a spirit of nature envisaged as a maiden; (*poet*) a lovely young maiden; the chrysalis of an insect.—**nymphean** *adj*.

nymphet *n* a sexually desirable pre-adolescent girl.

nympho *n* (*pl* **nymphos**) (*inf*) a nymphomaniac.

nympholepsy *n* (*pl* **nympholepsies**) frenzy caused by desire of the unattainable.

nympholept *n* one inspired by violent enthusiasm for an ideal.—**nympholeptic** *adj*.

nymphomania *n* uncontrollable sexual desire in women.—**nymphomaniac** *adj*, *n*.—**nymphomaniacal** *adj*.

nystagmus *n* a condition of the eye, with spasmodic movement of the eyeballs.—**nystagmic** *adj*.

NZ *abbr* = New Zealand.

O

O, o *n* the 15th letter of the English alphabet; something shaped like the letter O; nought, nothing, zero.

O., o. *abbr* = octavo; old; only.

O (*chem symbol*) oxygen. * *interj* an exclamation of wonder, pain, etc.

O' *prefix* (in *Irish surnames*) descendant of.

o' *prep* (*inf, arch*) short for *of* or *on*.

-o *n, adj suffix* (*inf*) indicating a diminutive, *cheapo;* (*inf*) forming an interjection, *cheerio.*

oaf *n* (*pl* **oafs**) a loutish or stupid person.—**oafish** *adj.*—**oafishly** *adv*

oak *n* a tree with a hard durable wood, having acorns as fruits.

oak apple *n* a spongy excrescence growing on the leaves or young branches of the oak, caused by the gallfly.

oaken *adj* made of or consisting of oak.

oakum *n* a loose fibre obtained by unpicking old rope and used for caulking.

O & M *abbr* = organization and method(s).

OAP *abbr* = (*Brit*) Old age pensioner, senior citizen.

oar *n* a pole with a flat blade for rowing a boat; an oarsman.

oarlock *n* (*US*) a rowlock.

oarsman *n* (*pl* **oarsmen**) a person who rows a boat.—**oarsmanship** *n.*

OAS *abbr* = Organization of American States.

oasis *n* (*pl* **oases**) a fertile place in a desert; a refuge.

oast *n* a kiln for drying hops or barley.

oatcake *n* a thin broad cake of oatmeal.

oaten *adj* made of oats.

oath *n* (*pl* **oaths**) a solemn declaration to a god or a higher authority that one will speak the truth or keep a promise; a swear word; a blasphemous expression.

oatmeal *n* ground oats; a porridge of this; a pale greyish-brown colour.

oats *npl* a cereal grass widely cultivated for its edible grain; the seeds.

OAU *abbr* = Organization of African Unity.

ob. *abbr* = (*Latin*) *obiit,* died.

ob- *prefix* before, against, toward, in front of, reversed.

obbligato *adj* (*mus*) forming an integral part of a musical composition. * *n* (*pl* **obbligatos, obbligati**) an indispensable instrumental part or accompaniment written especially for the instrument named.—*also* **obligato** (*pl* **obligatos, obligati**).

obcordate *adj* (*bot*) inversely cordate.

obdurate *adj* hard-hearted; unyielding, stubborn.—**obduracy** *n.*—**obdurately** *adv.*

OBE *abbr* = Order of the British Empire.

obeah *see* **obi.**

obedience *n* the condition of being obedient; observance of orders, instructions, etc; respect for authority.

obedient *adj* obeying; compliant; submissive to authority, dutiful.—**obediently** *adv.*

obeisance *n* a bow or curtsey; an act of reverence or homage.

obelisk *n* a four-sided tapering pillar usu with a pyramidal top; a reference mark used in printing (†) (— *also* **dagger**).

obelize *vt* to mark with an obelus.

obelus *n* (*pl* **obeli**) a mark (— *or* + *or* †) used in old MSS to indicate a doubtful or spurious reading; in modern writing, a break (—).

obese *adj* very fat.—**obesity** *n.*

obey *vti* (**obeying, obeyed**) to carry out (orders, instructions); to comply (with); to submit (to).

obfuscate *vt* to bewilder or confuse, to darken.—**obfuscation** *n.*

OB-GYN *abbr* = obstetrician and gynaecologist.

obi[1] *n* (*pl* **obis, obi**) a Japanese woman's sash.

obi[2] *n* (*pl* **obis**) in the West Indies and Africa, a system of secret sorcery or magical rites.—*also* **obeah.**

obit *n* (*inf*) an obituary.

obiter dictum *n* (*pl* **obiter dicta**) (*Latin*) a casual remark or opinion expressed incidentally, as by a judge or writer.

obituary *n* (*pl* **obituaries**) an announcement of a person's death, often with a short biography.—**obituarist** *n.*

object *n* something that can be recognized by the senses; a person or thing toward which action, feeling, etc, is directed; a purpose or aim; (*gram*) a noun or part of a sentence governed by a transitive verb or a preposition. * *vti* to state or raise an objection; to oppose; to disapprove.—**objector** *n.*

object ball *n* (*billiards*) the ball meant to be hit by the cue ball.

object glass *n* the lens of a microscope or telescope nearest to the object to be observed and forming the image.

objectify *vt* (**objectifying, objectified**) to render objective; to embody; to materialize.—**objectification** *n.*

objection *n* the act of objecting; a ground for, or expression of, disapproval.

objectionable *adj* causing an objection; disagreeable.—**objectionably** *adv.*

objective *adj* relating to an object; not influenced by opinions or feelings; impartial; having an independent existence of its own, real; (*gram*) of, or appropriate to an object governed by a verb or a preposition. * *n* the thing or placed aimed at; (*gram*) the objective case.—**objectively** *adv.*

objectivism *n* (*philos*) the doctrine that the knowledge of the non-ego is anterior to that of the ego; (*art, literature*) the representation of persons and incidents as they really appear.—**objectivist** *adj, n.*—**objectivistic** *adj.*

objectivity *n* the state or quality of being objective.

object lesson *n* a convincing practical illustration of some principle.

object program n (*comput*) a computer program derived from the conversion of a source program into machine code by a compiler or assembler.

objet d'art n (*pl* **objets d'art**) a small decorative object.

objurgate vt to chide or reprove, to scold.—**objurgation** n.

objurgatory adj containing reproof or censure.

oblanceolate adj (*bot*) lanceolate in the reversed order.

oblate[1] n (*RC Church*)a secular priest who has devoted himself and his property to the monastery he has entered. adj dedicated to a monastic or religious life.

oblate[2] adj (*spheroid*) depressed or flattened at the poles; orange-shaped.

oblation n an offering or sacrifice; anything presented in religious worship, esp the Eucharist.—**oblatory, oblational** adj.

obligate vt to bind by a contract, promise, sense of duty, etc.

obligation n the act of obligating; a moral or legal requirement; a debt; a favour; a commitment to pay a certain amount of money; the amount owed under such an obligation.

obligato *see* **obbligato**.

obligatory adj binding, not optional; compulsory.

oblige vt to compel by moral, legal, or physical force; (*person*) to make grateful for some favour; to do a favour for.

obligee n (*law*) a person in whose favour a bond is made; a creditor.

obliging adj ready to do favours, agreeable.—**obligingly** adv.

obligor n (*law*) a person who is bound by a bond; a debtor.

oblique adj slanting, at an angle; diverging from the straight; indirect, allusive. * n an oblique line.—**obliquely** adv.

oblique angle n an angle greater or less than a right angle.

oblique case n (*gram*) any case except the nominative and vocative.

obliquity n (*pl* **obliquities**) obliqueness; a slanting direction; deviation from a moral code.

obliterate vt to wipe out, to erase, to destroy.—**obliteration** n.

oblivion n a state of forgetting or being forgotten; a state of mental withdrawal.

oblivious adj forgetful, unheeding; unaware (of).

oblong adj rectangular. * n any oblong figure.

obloquy n (*pl* **obloquies**) reproachful language, detraction; calumny; slander, disgrace.

obnoxious adj objectionable; highly offensive.—**obnoxiously** adv.—**obnoxiousness** n.

oboe n an orchestral woodwind instrument having a mouthpiece with a double reed.—**oboist** n.

obolus, obol n (*pl* **oboli, obols**) an ancient Greek silver coin; a modern Greek weight = 1/10th of a gram.

obovate adj (*bot*) inversely ovate.

obs abbr = observation; obsolete.

obscene adj indecent, lewd; offensive to a moral or social standard.—**obscenely** adv.

obscenity n (*pl* **obscenities**) the state or quality of being obscene; an obscene act, word, etc.

obscurant adj, n (a person) opposed to enlightenment, reactionary.—**obscurantism** n.—**obscurantist** adj, n.

obscure adj not clear; dim; indistinct; remote, secret; not easily understood; inconspicuous; unimportant, humble. * vt to make unclear, to confuse; to hide.—**obscurely** adv.

obscurity n (*pl* **obscurities**) the state or quality of being obscure; an obscure thing or person.

obsequies npl (*sing* **obsequy**) funeral rites, a funeral.

obsequious adj subservient; fawning.—**obsequiously** adv.

observable adj worthy of observation; remarkable.—**observably** adv.

observance n the observing of a rule, duty, law, etc; a ceremony or religious rite.

observant adj watchful; attentive, mindful.—**observantly** adv.

observation n the act or faculty of observing; a comment or remark; careful noting of the symptoms of a patient, movements of a suspect, etc prior to diagnosis, analysis or interpretation.—**observational** adj.—**observationally** adv.

observatory n (*pl* **observatories**) a building for astronomical observation; an institution whose primary purpose is making such observations.

observe vt to notice; to perceive; (*a law, etc*) to keep to or adhere to; to arrive at as a conclusion; to examine scientifically. * vi to take notice; to make a comment (on).—**observable** adj.

observer n a person who observes; a delegate who attends a formal meeting but may not take part; an expert analyst and commentator in a particular field.

obsess vt to possess or haunt the mind of; to preoccupy.—**obsessive** adj, n.—**obsessively** adv.

obsession n a fixed idea, often associated with mental illness; a persistent idea or preoccupation; the condition of obsessing or being obsessed.

obsidian n a hard glassy dark-coloured volcanic lava.

obsolescent adj becoming obsolete, going out of date.—**obsolescence** n.

obsolete adj disused, out of date.

obstacle n anything that hinders something; an obstruction.

obstetrics n *sing* the branch of medicine concerned with the care and treatment of women during pregnancy and childbirth.—**obstetric, obstetrical** adj.—**obstetrician** n.

obstinate adj stubborn, self-willed; intractable; persistent.—**obstinacy** n.—**obstinately** adv.

obstreperous adj unruly, turbulent, noisy.

obstruct vt to block with an obstacle; to impede; to prevent, hinder; to keep (light, etc) from.

obstruction n that which obstructs; the act or an example of obstructing; a hindrance, obstacle.

obstructionism n the systematic hindering of political business, etc.—**obstructionist** adj, n.

obstructive adj tending to obstruct; preventing, hindering.—**obstructively** adv.—**obstructiveness** n.

obtain vt to get, to acquire, to gain. * vi to be prevalent, hold good.—**obtainable** adj.—**obtainment** n.

obtect adj (*pupa*) protected by a hard outer case.

obtrude vti to push (an opinion, oneself) on others uninvited; to intrude.—**obtruding** adj.

obtrusion n the act of obtruding; an unwelcome intrusion.

obtrusive adj apt to obtrude, pushy; protruding, sticking out.—**obtrusively** adv.—**obtrusiveness** n.

obtund vt (*med*) to blunt, to deaden.

obturate vt to stop, to block or seal up; (*gun breech*) to close.—**obturation** n.—**obturator** n.

obtuse adj mentally slow; not pointed; dull, stupid; (*geom*) greater than a right angle.—**obtusely** adv.—**obtuseness** n.

obverse *n* the front or top side; (*coin*) the head; a counterpart. * *adj* facing the viewer; with the top wider than the base.—**obversely** *adv*.

obversion *n* (*logic*) the immediate inference by which we deny the opposite of anything affirmed.

obvert *vt* (*logic*) to infer by obversion; to turn toward, to face.

obviate *vt* to make unnecessary; (*danger, difficulty*) to prevent, clear away.—**obviation** *n*.

obvious *adj* easily seen or understood; evident.—**obviously** *adv*.—**obviousness** *n*.

obvolute *adj* arranged so as to overlap, as the margins of an organ or part of a plant.

oc- *prefix* the form of *ob-* before *c*.

ocarina *n* an egg-shaped wind instrument played like a flute.

occasion *n* a special occurrence or event; a time when something happens; an opportunity; reason or grounds; a subsidiary cause. * *vt* to cause; to bring about.

occasional *adj* infrequent, not continuous; intermittent; produced for an occasion; (*a cause*) incidental.

occasionalism *n* (*philos*) the Cartesian theory of occasional causes, that bodily actions are caused and controlled by divine agency and not by the human will / the Cartesian doctrine that apparent action of mind on matter is due to the invervention of God.

occasionally *adv* intermittently; now and then; infrequently.

occident *n* the west; (*with cap*) specifically Europe and America; the countries west of Asia and Turkey in Europe.—**Occidental, occidental** *adj*.

occipital *adj* of or pertaining to the occiput.

occiput *n* (*pl* **occipita, occiputs**) (*anat*) the back part of the skull or head.

occlude *vti* to shut out or in; to stop up, close; (*chem*) to absorb and retain.

occluded front *n* (*meteorol*) the phenomenon formed by a cold front overtaking a warm front and lifting the warm air above the earth's surface.

occlusion *n* the act of occluding; (*dentistry*) the position of the teeth when the jaws are closed; an occluded front.

occult *adj* supernatural, magical; secret.—*also n.*

occultation *n* (*astron*) a temporary disappearance or obscuration, as the eclipse of a star or planet by the moon, etc.

occulted *adj* (*astron*) hidden from the vision, as a star, etc.

occultism *n* mysticism, spiritualism, theosophy, etc.—**occultist** *n*.

occult sciences *npl* magic, alchemy and astrology.

occupancy *n* (*pl* **occupancies**) the act of taking and holding in possession; the time of possession.

occupant *n* a person who occupies, resides in, holds a position or place, etc.

occupation *n* the act of occupying; the state of being occupied; employment or profession; a pursuit.—**occupational** *adj*.

occupational therapy *n* therapy by means of work in the arts and crafts, to aid recovery from disease or injury.—**occupational therapist** *n*.

occupier *n* an occupant.

occupy *vt* (**occupying, occupied**) to live in; (*room, office*) to take up or fill; (*a position*) to hold; to engross (one's mind); (*city, etc*) to take possession of.

occur *vi* (**occurring, occurred**) to happen; to exist; to come into the mind of.

occurrence *n* a happening, an incident, an event; the act or fact of occurring.

ocean *n* a large stretch of sea, esp one of the earth's five oceans; a huge quantity or expanse.

oceangoing *adj* (*vessel*) designed and equipped for travelling on the open ocean.

oceanarium *n* (*pl* **oceanariums, oceanaria**) a large seawater aquarium for displays of marine life.

Oceania *n* the Pacific islands.—**Oceanic** *adj*.

oceanic *adj* of or relating to the ocean; formed or found in the ocean.

Oceanid *n* (*pl* **Oceanids, Oceanides**) (*Greek myth*) a sea nymph.

oceanography *n* the study of the oceans including their physical and chemical make-up, marine biology, and their exploitation.—**oceanographer** *n*.

ocellate, ocellated *adj* marked with small spots or eyes.

ocellus *n* (*pl* **ocelli**) the facet of a compound eye; an eye-like spot, as on a peacock's tail, etc.

ocelot *n* a medium-sized spotted wildcat of North and South America.

och *interj* (*Scot, Irish*) expressing of surprise, contempt, disagreement, disappointment, etc.

ocher, ochre *n* a yellow to orange-coloured clay used as a pigment.

ochlo-, ochl- *prefix* mob.

ochlocracy *n* (*pl* **ochlocracies**) mob rule.—**ochlocrat** *n.*—**ochlocratic** *adj*.

o'clock *adv* indicating the hour; indicating a relative direction or position, twelve o'clock being directly ahead or above.

OCR *abbr* = optical character reader; optical character recognition.

Oct *abbr* = October.

octa- *prefix* eight.

octachord *n* an eight-stringed musical instrument; a series of eight notes, diatonic scale.—**octachordal** *adj*.

octad *n* a group of eight; the number eight; (*chem*) an element or radical with a valency of eight.—**octadic** *adj*.

octagon *n* a plane figure having eight equal sides.—**octagonal** *adj*.

octahedral *adj* having eight equal sides.

octahedron *n* (*pl* **octahedrons, octahedra**) a solid figure contained by eight equal equilateral triangles.

octal *n* (*comput*) a number system with 8 as its base, one digit being equivalent to three bits.

octameter *n* an eight-foot verse.

octane *n* a hydrocarbon found in petrol.

octane number, octane rating *n* a measure of the anti-knock quality of a liquid motor fuel expressed as a percentage.

octant *n* the eighth part of a circle; an instrument for measuring angles; (*astron*) an aspect of two planets, etc, when 45 degrees apart.

octave *n* (*mus*) the eighth full tone above or below a given tone, the interval of eight degrees between a tone and either of its octaves, or the series of tones within this interval.

octavo *n* (*pl* **octavos**) a sheet of printing paper folded in eight leaves or 16 pages (8vo); this size, average 9 1/2 x 6ins). * *adj* having eight leaves or 16 pages to the sheet.

octennial *adj* recurring every eighth year; continuing eight years.—**octennially** *adv*.

octet, octette *n* a group of eight (performers, lines of a sonnet); a composition for eight instruments or voices.

octillion *n* the eighth power of a million (1 with 48 ciphers; in US and France, the ninth power of a thousand (1 with 27 ciphers).—**octillionth** *adj.*

octo- *prefix* eight.

October *n* the tenth month of the year, having 31 days.

octodecimo *adj* consiting of 18 leaves or 36 pages to a sheet. * *n* (*pl* **octodecimos**) a book of such size (18mo).

octogenarian *n* a person who is in his or her eighties.

octopod *n* an animal with eight feet; an eight-armed mollusc.—*also adj.*

octopus *n* (*pl* **octopuses, octopi**) a mollusc having a soft body and eight tentacles covered with suckers.

octoroon *n* the offspring of a white person and a quadroon.

octosyllable *n* a word or verse of eight syllables.—**octosyllabic** *adj.*

octroi *n* in France and Belgium, a tax levied upon articles brought into the gates of a city; duty on goods.

octuple *adj* eight-fold.

ocular *adj* of, by, or relating to the eye; resembling an eye in form or function.

oculist *n* (*formerly*) an opththalmologist.

OD *n* (*inf*) an overdose of a drug, esp a narcotic. * *vi* (**OD'ing, OD'd**) to take an overdose.

od *n* a hypothetical natural force once used to explain magnetism, mesmerism, etc.

odalisque, odalisk *n* a female slave or concubine in the harem of a sultan; (*art*) the depiction of a woman in eastern garments reclining.

odd *adj* eccentric; peculiar; occasional; not divisible by two; with the other of the pair missing; extra or left over. * *npl* probability; balance of advantage in favour of one against another; excess of one number over another, esp in betting; likelihood; disagreement; strife; miscellaneous articles, scraps.—**oddly** *adv.*—**oddness** *n.*

oddball *n* (*sl*) an eccentric person. * *adj* bizarre.

Odd Fellow *n* a member of the order of the benevolent society of the Odd Fellows, a friendly society similar to freemasons.

oddity *n* (*pl* **oddities**) the state of being odd; an odd thing or person; peculiarity.

odd man out *n* a person left when others pair off.

oddment *n* an odd piece left over, esp of fabric.

odds and ends *npl* miscellaneous articles, scraps.

odds-on *adj* (*horse, etc*) (judged to be) having a better than even chance of winning; likely to happen, succeed, win, etc.

ode *n* a lyric poem marked by lofty feeling and dignified style.

odeum *n* (*pl* **odeums, odea**) a hall for musical performances.

odious *adj* causing hatred or offence; disgusting.—**odiously** *adv.*—**odiousness** *n.*

odium *n* general dislike.

odometer *n* an instrument attached to the axle of a vehicle to measure the distance it travels.

odonto-, odont- *prefix* tooth.

odontoglossum *n* a tropical orchid.

odontoid *adj* tooth-shaped, tooth-like.

odontology *n* dental science.—**odontological** *adj.*—**odontologist** *n.*

odor *n* smell; scent; aroma; a characteristic or predominant quality.— *also* **odour.**

odoriferous *adj* diffusing fragrance; (*sl*) smelly.

odorless *adj* without odour.

odorous *adj* having or emitting a scent; smelly; fragrant.

odour *see* **odor.**

odyssey *n* (*pl* **odysseys**) a long adventurous journey; an intellectual or spiritual quest.

Oe (*symbol*) oersted.

OECD *abbr* = Organization for Economic Cooperation and Development.

oecumenical *adj* a rare spelling of **ecumenical**.

OED *abbr* = Oxford English Dictionary.

oedema *n* (*pl* **oedemata**) a swelling in a body or plant caused by excess fluid.—*also* **edema.**—**oedematous** *adj.*

Oedipus complex *n* (*psychoanal*) a complex arising from the relationship of a son to his parents.

oeil de boeuf *n* a small round or oval window in the roof or frieze of a large building.

oeillade *n* a suggestive glance or ogle.

oeno-, oen- *prefix* wine.

oenology *n* the science of wines.—*also* **enology.**—**oenological, enological** *adj.*—**oenologist, enologist** *n.*

o'er *prep, adv* (*poet*) over.

oersted *n* the cgs unit of magnetic field strength.

oesophagus *n* (*pl* **oesophagi**) that part of the alimentary canal that takes food, etc, from the pharynx to the stomach.—*also* **esophagus.**

oestrogen *n* a hormone that develops and maintains female characteristics of the body.—*also* **estrogen.**

oestrus, oestrum *n* violent desire, frenzy; the period of ovulation of mammals, heat.—**oestrous** *adj.*—*also* **estrus, estrum.**

oeuvre *n* (*pl* **oeuvres**) a work of art, literature, music, etc; the life's work of an artist, writer or composer.

of *prep* from; belonging or relating to; concerning; among; by; during; owing to.

of- *prefix* the form of *ob-* before *f.*

off *adv* away, from; detached, gone; unavailable; disconnected; out of condition; entirely. * *prep* away from; not on. * *adj* distant; no longer operating; cancelled; (*food or drink*) having gone bad; on the right-hand side; (*runners, etc*) having started a race.

offal *n* the entrails of an animal eaten as food.

offbeat *adj* unconventional, eccentric.

off-Broadway *adj* denoting a type of small scale, experimental and generally noncommercial theatre situated outside theatrical Broadway in New York.

off-colour *adj* unwell; risqué.

offend *vt* to affront, displease; to insult. * *vi* to break a law.—**offender** *n.*

offense, offence *n* an illegal action, crime; a sin; an affront, insult; a cause of displeasure or anger.

offensive *adj* causing offence; repulsive, disagreeable; insulting; aggressive. * *n* an attack; a forceful campaign for a cause, etc.—**offensively** *adv.*—**offensiveness** *n.*

offer *vt* to present for acceptance or rejection; to show willingness (to do something); to present for consideration; to bid; (*a prayer*) to say. * *vi* to present itself; to declare oneself willing. * *n* something offered; a bid or proposal.

offering *n* a gift, present; a sacrifice.

offertory *n* (*pl* **offertories**) (*Anglican Church*) the sentences read in the Communion service during the collection of the alms; the alms collecting; (*RC Church*) an anthem chanted during Mass while the priest prepares the elements. / a church collection; the part of the service when it is taken.

offhand *adv* impromptu; without thinking. * *adj* inconsiderate; curt, brusque; unceremonious.

office *n* a room or building where business is carried out; the people there; (*with cap*) the location, staff, of authority of a Government department, etc; a task or function; a position of authority; a duty; a religious ceremony, rite.

officer *n* an official; a person holding a position of authority in a government, business, club, military services, etc; a policeman.

official *adj* of an office or its tenure; properly authorized; formal. * *n* a person who holds a public office.—**officially** *adv*.

officialdom *n* a body of officials.

officialese *n* the jargon of official documents or as expressed by officials.

officiant *n* an officiating clergyman.

officiate *vi* to conduct a ceremony; to act in an official capacity; to perform the functions of a priest, minister, rabbi, etc.

officious *adj* interfering, meddlesome; offering unwanted advice.—**officiously** *adv*.—**officiousness** *n*.

offing *n* the near or foreseeable future.

offish *adj* (*inf*) distant, stiff.

off-key *adj* sung or played in the wrong key; out of tune; out of step.

off-licence *n* in UK, a licence to sell alcohol for consumption off the premises; a place so licensed (—*also* **liquor store, package store**).

off-line *adj* (*comput*) not connected to the central processor; disconnected.

off-load *vt* to unload; to get rid off.

off-piste *adj* pertaining to skiing in areas away from the normal runs.

offprint *n* a separately printed copy or part of a publication.

off-putting *adj* discouraging, daunting.

off-roading *n* the sport or hobby of driving on dirt tracks or other rugged terrain.—**off-roader** *n*.

offscourings *npl* refuse, dregs.

offset *vt* (**offsetting, offset**) to compensate for, counterbalance. * *n* compensation; a method of printing in which an image is transferred from a plate to a rubber surface and then to paper; a sloping ledge on the face of a wall.

offset printing *n* printing in which the impression is transferred from a plate to a rubber surface and then to paper.

offshoot *n* a branch or shoot growing from the main stem; something derivative.

offshore *adv* at sea some distance from the shore.

offside *adj, adv* illegally in advance of the ball.

offspring *n* a child, progeny; a result.

offstage *adj, adv* out of sight of the audience; behind the scenes.

off-the-peg *adj* (*clothes*) produced ready to wear in standard sizes.

off-the-wall *adj* (*sl*) innovative, unusual, unexpected.

off-white *n, adj* (a) white tinged with yellow or grey.

oft *adv* (*poet*) often.

often *adv* many times, frequently.

ogdoad *n* eight, a set of eight.

ogee *n* an architectural wave-like moulding shaped like an S.

Ogen melon *n* a type of small melon similar to a canta-

loupe with sweel orange flesh.

ogham, ogam *n* an ancient British alphabet, the letters formed by notches; a character in it.

ogive *n* a diagonal groin of a vault; a pointed arch.—**ogival** *adj*.

ogle *vti* (**ogling, ogled**) to gape at; to make eyes at; to look at lustfully.—**ogler** *n*.

Ogpu *n* the secret police of Soviet Russia (1923–34).

ogre *n* a man-eating giant; a hideous person.

OH *abbr* = Ohio.

oh *interj* expressing surprise, delight, pain, etc.

ohm *n* a unit of electrical resistance.

ohmmeter *n* an instrument for measuring electrical resistance.

oho *interj* an exclamation of surprise.

-oid *suffix* like, as in *spheroid*.

oil *n* any of various greasy, combustible liquid substances obtained from animal, vegetable, and mineral matter; petroleum; an oil painting; (*pl*) paint mixed by grinding a pigment in oil * *vt* to smear with oil, lubricate.—**oiled** *adj*.

oilcake *n* a cattle food of linseed.

oilcan *n* a container with a long spout for releasing oil for lubricating in individual drops.

oilcloth *n* a waterproof fabric impregnated with oil or synthetic resin.

oil color *n* a colour in which oil is used as a vehicle for pigement.

oiler *n* an oilcan; a greaser.

oil field *n* an area on land or under the sea that produces petroleum.

oilman *n* (*pl* **oilmen**) a dealer in oils.

oil painting *n* a painting in oils; the art of painting in oils.

oil palm *n* an African palm whose fruit yields an edible oil.

oil rig *n* a drilling rig for extracting oil or natural gas.

oilskin *n* fabric made waterproof by treatment with oil; a waterproof garment of oilskin or a plastic-coated fabric.

oil slick *n* a mass of oil floating on the surface of water.

oil well *n* a well from which petroleum is extracted.

oily *adj* (**oilier, oiliest**) like or covered with oil; greasy; too suave or smooth, unctuous.—**oiliness** *n*.

oink *n* (*inf*) the grunt of a pig.—*also vi*.

ointment *n* a fatty substance used on the skin for healing or cosmetic purposes; a salve.

Oireachtas *n* the legislature of Ireland, consisting of the president, the Dáil Eireann (the Chamber of Deputies) and the Seanad Eireann (the Senate).

OK[1] *abbr* = Oklahoma.

OK[2], **okay** *adj, adv* (*inf*) all right; correct(ly). * *n* (*pl* **OK's, okays**) approval; * *vt* (**OK'ing, OK'ed** *or* **okaying, okayed**) to approve, sanction as OK.

okapi *n* (*pl* **okapis, okapi**) an African animal allied to the giraffe but smaller and with a shorter neck.

okay *see* **OK**.

okra *n* a tall annual plant yielding long seed-pods used as a vegetable.

old *adj* aged; elderly, not young; having lived or existed for a long time; long used, not new; former; of the past, not modern; experienced; worn out; of long standing.

Old Bailey *n* the central criminal court of England.

old boy *n* a former pupil of a school; (*inf*) a friendly form of address; an old person.—**old girl** *nf*.

old boy network *n* (*inf*) the monopoly of power by a

privileged elite who attended the best public schools and universities.

Old Catholic *n* one of a body of Roman Catholics who refused to accept the dogma of papal infallibility (1870).

old country *n* the birthplace of an immigrant or an immigrant's ancestors.

olden *adj* relating to a bygone era.

Old English *n* the English language during the 7th to the 11th centuries.—*also* Anglo-Saxon.

Old English sheepdog *n* a breed of sheepdog with an extremely long shaggy coat.

old-fashioned *adj* out of date; in a fashion of an older time.

Old French *n* the French language from the 7th to the early 14th centuries.

Old Glory *n* the Stars and Stripes.

old gold *adj* of the colour of tarnished gold.

old guard *n* the (original) conservative elements within a political party or other organization.

old hat *adj* old-fashioned, cliched.

old lady *n* (*inf*) one's wife or mother.

old maid *n* (*derog*) a woman, esp an older woman who has never married; a prim, prudish, fussy person.

old man *n* (*inf*) father, husband; (*inf*) someone in charge, esp the captain of a ship.

old master *n* a painting by one of the best painters working in Europe in ther 16th and 17th centuries; one of these painters.

Old Nick *n* (*inf*) the Devil.

old school *n* supporters of traditional or conservative values and practices.

old school tie *n* a distinctive tie which indicates which school one attended; the elitism and solidarity use associated with British public schools and their products.

Old Style *n* the old mode of reckoning time acording to the Julian year of 365 and a quarter days.

Old Testament *n* the Christian designation for the Holy Scriptures of Judaism, the first of the two general divisions of the Christian Bible.

old-time *adj* of an earlier period; old-fashioned.

old-timer *n* an old man; a veteran; a person who has been in the same job, position, etc, for many years.

old wives' tale *n* a belief sustained by tradition, not accuracy.

Old World *n* Europe, Asia, and Africa.

old-world *adj* traditional, quaint; antiquated.

oleaginous *adj* oily; unctuous.

oleander *n* a poisonous evergreen shrub with handsome fragrant flowers.

oleaster *n* the wild olive; a yellow-flowered shrub like it.

oleate *n* a salt of oleic acid.

olefin, olefine *n* a hydrocarbon containing two atoms of hydrogen and one atom of carbon.—**olefinic** *adj*.

oleic *adj* obtained from oil.

oleic acid *n* an oily acid obtained from the saponiication of linseed and other oils, or in the making of soap.

olein *n* the pure liquid part of oil or fat.

oleo- *prefix* oil.

oleograph *n* a lithograph in oil colours.

olfactory *adj* relating to the sense of smell. * *n* (*pl* **olfactories**) (*usu pl*) an organ of smell.

olibanum *n* a gum resin used in incense; the frankincense of the ancients.

oligarch *n* a member of an oligarchy.

oligarchy *n* (*pl* **oligarchies**) government by a small group of people; the members of such a government; a state ruled in this way.—**oligarchic, oligarchical** *adj*.

oligo-, olig- *prefix* few, small.

Oligocene *n* (*geol*) a term used to denote certain strata intermediate between the Eocene and Miocene.

olio *n* (*pl* **olios**) a hotchpotch, a stew; a miscellany.

olivaceous *adj* olive-green.

olivary *adj* olive-shaped, oval.

olive *n* an evergreen tree cultivated for its edible hard-stoned fruit and oil; its fruit; a yellow-green colour. * *adj* of a yellow-green colour.

olive branch *n* a gesture of reconciliation of desire to make peace.

olive drab *n* the colour of the US service uniform.

olive oil *n* an edible yellow oil obtained from the fruit of the olive by pressing.

olivine *n* a variety of chrysolite.

olla podrida *n* a mixed stew or hash of meat and vegetables, a favourite Spanish dish; any incongruous mixture.

ology *n* (*pl* **ologies**) (*sl*) a branch of knowledge, a science.

Olympiad *n* in ancient Greece, the interval (four years) between the celebration of the Olympic games; a system of chronology reckoning from the first Olympiad, 776 BC.

Olympian *adj* of Olympus, home of the Greek gods; Olympic; stately; condescending. * *n* a great person.

Olympic *adj* pertaining to Olympia in Elis, where the Olympic games were celebrated.

Olympic Games *n sing or pl* an ancient athletic contest revived in 1896 as an international meeting held every four years in a different country.—*also* **Olympics**.

OM *abbr* = Order of Merit.

om *n* (*Hinduism*) the mystic name of the supreme being uttered when invoking Brahma; (*modern occultism*) spiritual essence, supreme truth and virtue.

-oma *n suffix* indicating a tumour.

omasum *n* (*pl* **omasa**) the third stomach of ruminant animals.

omber, ombre *n* an old card game for three players.

ombudsman *n* (*pl* **ombudsmen**) an official appointed to investigate citizens' or consumers' complaints.

omega *n* the last letter of the Greek alphabet.

omelet, omelette *n* eggs beaten and cooked flat in a pan.

omen *n* a sign or warning of impending happiness or disaster.

omentum *n* (*pl* **omenta, omentums**) (*anat*) the caul or adipose membrane attached to the stomach.

omerta *n* a conspiracy of silence, esp as practised by the Mafia.

omicron *n* the 15th letter of the Greek alphabet.

ominous *adj* relating to an omen; foreboding evil; threatening.—**ominously** *adv*.

omission *n* something that has been left out or neglected; the act of omitting.

omit *vt* (**omitting, omitted**) to leave out; to neglect to do, leave undone.

omni- *prefix* all; universally.

omnibus *n* (*pl* **omnibuses**) (*formal*) a bus; a book containing several works usu by one author.

omnifarious *adj* of all kinds.

omnipotent *adj* all-powerful, almighty; having very great power.—**omnipotence** *n*.

omnipresent *adj* present everywhere, uniquitous.—**omnipresence** *n*.

omniscient *adj* knowing all things.—**omnisciently** *adv*.—**omniscience** *n*.

omnium-gatherum *n* a miscellaneous collection of persons or things.

omnivore *n* an omniverous animal or person.

omnivorous *adj* eating any sort of food; taking in everything indiscriminately.

omophagic, omophagous *adj* eating raw flesh.—**omophagia** *n*.

omphalos *n* centre, hub; (*ancient Greece*) a boss on a shield.

on *prep* in contact with the upper surface of; supported by, attached to, or covering; directed toward; at the time of; concerning, about; using as a basis, condition or principle; immediately after; (*sl*) using; addicted to. * *adv* (so as to be) covering or in contact with something; forward; (*device*) switched on; continuously in progress; due to take place; (*actor*) on stage; on duty. * *adj* (*cricket*) designating the part of the field on the batsman's side in front of the wicket. * *n* (*cricket*) the on side.

onager *n* (*pl* **onagri, onagers**) the wild ass.

onanism *n* masturbation; coitus interruptus.—**onanist** *n, adj*.

once *adv* on one occasion only; formerly; at some time. * *conj* as soon as. * *n* one time.

once-over *n* a preliminary survey.

onco- *prefix* swelling, tumour.

oncology *n* the branch of medicine dealing with tumours.—**oncologist** *n*.

oncoming *adj* approaching.

one *adj* single; undivided, united; the same; a certain unspecified (time, etc). * *n* the first and lowest cardinal number; an individual thing or person; (*inf*) a drink; (*inf*) a joke. * *pron* an indefinite person, used to apply to many people; someone.

one-armed bandit *n* (*inf*) a slot machine for gambling, operated by pulling down a lever on its side.

one-horse *adj* (*sl*) paltry.

oneiro- *prefix* dream.

one-liner *n* (*inf*) a brief joke or witty comment.

oneness *n* unity, singleness, concord.

one-night stand *n* a performance given for one night only in a certain place; (*inf*) (a partner in) a sexual liaison that lasts one night only.

one-off *n, adj* (*Brit*) (something) performed or made only once.

onerous *adj* oppressive, burdensome; troublesome.

oneself *pron reflex form of* one.

one-sided *adj* favouring one side; unequal.

one-time *adj* sometime, former.

one-track *adj* with a single line of rails; with room for only one idea at a time.

one-upmanship *n* the skill of being one jump ahead of or going one better than someone or something else.

one-way *adj* (*traffic*) restricted to one direction; requiring no reciprocal action or obligation.

ongoing *adj* progressing, continuing.

onion *n* an edible bulb with a pungent taste and odour.

on-line *adj* referring to equipment that is connected to and controlled by the central processor of a computer.

onlooker *n* a spectator.

only *adj* alone of its kind; single, sole. * *adv* solely, merely; just; not more than. * *conj* except that, but.

onoma- *prefix* name.

onomastic *adj* of or pertaining to a name or names.

onomastics *n sing* the study of proper names.

onomatopoeia *n* the formation of a word to imitate a sound.—**onomatopoeic** *adj*.

onrush *n* a powerful rushing forwards.

onset *n* a beginning; an assault, attack.

onshore *adj, adv* towards the land; on land, not the sea.

onslaught *n* a fierce attack.

onto *prep* to a position on.

onto- *prefix* being.

ontogeny, ontogenesis *n* (*biol*) the history of the evolution of individual organisms.—**ontogenic, ontogenetic** *adj*.

ontology *n* (*philos*) the logic of pure being or reality; metaphysics.—**ontological** *adj*.—**ontologically** *adv*.

onus *n* (*pl* **onuses**) responsibility, duty; burden.

onward *adj* advancing, forward. * *adv* to the front, ahead, forward.

onwards *adv* onward.

onyx *n* a limestone similar to marble with layers of colour.

oo- *prefix* egg.

oodles *npl* (*sl*) an abundance.

oogamous *adj* heterogamous.

oogenesis *n* the formation of an ovum.—**oogenetic** *adj*.

ooh *interj* expressing surprise, delight, pain, etc.

oolite *n* a limestone composed of grains like the roe of a fish.—**oolitic** *adj*.

oology *n* the scientific study of birds' eggs; a treatise on birds' eggs.—**oological** *adj*.—**oologist** *n*.

oolong *n* a Chinese black tea the flavour of which resembles green tea.

oomiak *see* umiak.

oompah *n* an imitation of the deep sound of a brass instrument such as the luba.

oomph *n* (*inf*) energy, verve; sex appeal.

oops *interj* expressing surprise or apology, esp when making a mistake.

oosperm *n* a fertilized ovum.

ootheca *n* (*pl* **oothecae**) the egg case of certain molluscs and insects containing the eggs.—**oothecal** *adj*.

ooze *vti* to flow or leak out slowly; to seep; to exude. * *n* soft mud or slime.

op. *abbr* = opera; operation; operator; optical; opposite; opus.

op- *prefix* form of *ob-* before *p*.

opacity *n* (*pl* **opacities**) the state of being opaque; obscurity.

opah *n* a bright-coloured sea fish like the mackerel, the kingfish.

opal *n* a white or bluish stone with a play of iridescent colours.

opalescent *adj* resembling opal in its reflection of light, iridescent.—**opalescence** *n*.

opaline *adj* pertaining to or resembling the opal.

opaque *adj* not letting light through; neither transparent nor translucent.—**opaquely** *adv*.—**opaqueness** *n*.

op. cit. *abbr* = (*Latin*) in the work cited.

OPEC *abbr* = Organization of Petroleum Exporting Countries.

open *adj* not closed; accessible; uncovered, unprotected; not fenced; free from trees; spread out, unfolded; public; lacking reserve; (*a person*) forthcoming; generous; readily understood; liable (to); unrestricted; (*syl-*

lable) ending with a vowel; (*consonant*) made without stopping the stream of breath. * *vti* to make or become accessible; to unfasten; to begin; to expand, unfold; to come into view. * *n* a wide space; (*sport*) a competition that any player can enter.—**openness** *n*.

open air *n* outdoors.

open-and-shut *adj* easily solved; straightforward.

opencast mining *see* **strip mining**.

open-ended *adj* with no fixed limit of time or amount.

open-eyed *adj* vigilant.

opener *n* a device for opening cans or bottles.

openhanded *adj* generous.—**openhandedness** *n*.

openhearted *adj* responsive to emotional appeal, frank.—**openheartedness** *n*.

open-heart surgery *n* surgery on the heart whilst its function is performed temporarily by a heart lung machine.

opening *n* a gap, aperture; a beginning; a chance; a job opportunity. * *adj* initial.

open letter *n* a letter addressed to an individual but published in a newspaper for all to see.

openly *adv* frankly; publicly.

open-minded *adj* unprejudiced.—**open-mindedness** *n*.

open-mouthed *adj* having the mouth open in surprise; gaping, expectant.

open secret *n* a supposed secret which is actually widely known.

open sesame *n* a way of getting into something usually inaccessible.

openwork *n* a pattern with interstices.

opera *n* a dramatic work represented through music and song; plural form of **opus**.

operable *adj* capable of being put into action, practicable; (*med*) capable of being operated upon.

opera bouffe *n* a comic or farcical opera.

opera glasses *n* a small binocular telescope used in theatres, etc.

opera hat *n* a man's collapsible top hat.

opera house *n* a theatre for opera.

operate *vi* to work, to function; to produce a desired effect; to carry out a surgical operation. * *vt* (*a machine*) to work or control; to carry on, run.

operatic *adj* of or relating to opera; exaggerated, overacting.

operating system *n* the software in a computer which controls basic operations such as accepting keyboard input, printing, file handling and displaying error messages.

operation *n* a method of operating; a procedure; a military action; a surgical procedure.

operational *adj* of or relating to an operation; functioning; ready for use; involved in military activity.—**operationally** *adv*.

operations research, operational research *n* the application of mathematical techniques to the analysis of business methods.

operative *adj* functioning; in force, effective; of, by surgery. * *n* a mechanic; a secret agent; a private detective.

operator *n* a person who operates or works a machine, esp a telephone switchboard; a person who owns or runs a business; a person who manipulates.

operculum *n* (*pl* **opercula, operculums**) (*biol*) a cap, lid, or cover; the plate closing the orifice of a univalve; a shell; the gill cover of a fish.—**opercular, operculate** *adj*.

operetta *n* a light opera.

ophidian *n* any of the Ophidia, an order of reptiles including the snakes.—*also adj*.

ophiology *n* that branch of natural history which treats of snakes.—**ophiological** *adj*.—**ophiologist** *n*.

ophite *n* serpentine marble.

ophthalmia *n* inflammation of the eye.

ophthalmic *adj* of, relating to, or situated near, the eye.

ophthalmo-, ophthalm- *prefix* eye or eyeball.

ophthalmology *n* the branch of medicine dealing with diseases of the eye.—**ophthalmologist** *n*.

ophthalmoscope *n* an instrument for examining the interior of the eye.

ophthalmoscopy *n* examination of the eye.—**ophthalmoscopic** *adj*.

-opia *n suffix* indicating a visual defect.

opiate *n* a narcotic drug that contains opium; something that induces sleep or calms feelings.

opine *vt* to hold or express the opinion (that).

opinicus *n* (*her*) a fabulous winged animal with the head and wings of a griffin, the body of a lion, and the tail of a camel.

opinion *n* a belief that is not based on proof; judgment; estimation, evaluation; a formal expert judgment; professional advice.

opinionated *adj* unduly confident in one's opinions, dogmatic.

opinionative *adj* fond of preconceived ideas; self-conceited.—**opinionatively** *adv*.

opium *n* a narcotic drug produced from an annual Eurasian poppy.

opossum *n* (*pl* **opossums, opossum**) a small nocturnal and arboreal marsupial.

oppidan *adj* urban, town-dwelling.

oppilate *vt* (*med*) to block up, to obstruct.—**oppilation** *n*.

opponent *n* a person who opposes another; an adversary, antagonist. * *adj* opposing.

opportune *adj* well-timed; convenient.—**opportunely** *adv*.

opportuneness *n* seasonableness.

opportunist *n* a person who forms or adapts his or her views or principles to benefit from opportunities; to seize opportunities as they may arise.—**opportunism** *n*.

opportunity *n* (*pl* **opportunities**) chance; a favourable combination of circumstances.

opposable *adj* that may be opposed.—**opposability** *n*.—**opposably** *adv*.

oppose *vt* to put in front of or in the way of; to place in opposition; to resist; to fight against; to balance against.—**opposer** *n*.

opposite *adj* placed on opposed sides of; face to face; diametrically different; contrary. * *n* a person or thing that is opposite; an antithesis. * *prep, adv* across from.

opposite number *n* a person in a corresponding position on the other side; a counterpart.

opposition *n* the act of opposing or the condition of being opposed; resistance; antithesis; hostility; a political party opposing the government; (*astron*) the diametrically opposite position of two heavenly bodies, when 180 degrees apart.

oppress *vt* to treat unjustly; to subjugate; to weigh down in the mind.—**oppressor** *n*.

oppression *n* the act of oppressing; the state of being oppressed; persecution; physical or mental distress.

oppressive *adj* tyrannical; burdensome; (*weather*) sultry, close.—**oppressively** *adv*.—**oppressiveness** *n*.

opprobrious *adj* abusive; infamous.

opprobrium *n* a reproach with disdain or contempt; disgrace, ignominy.

oppugn *vt* to reason against, to controvert; to resist.—**oppugnant** *adj*, *n*.—**oppugner** *n*.

opsonin *n* a chemical agent in blood serum, which makes bacteria vulnerable to phagocytic activity.—**opsonic** *adj*.

opt *vi* to choose, to exercise an option; (*with* **in**) to choose to participate in something; (*with* **out**) to choose not to participate in something.

optative *adj* (*gram*) expressing a desire or wish. * *n* an optative mood or form of a verb.

optic *adj* relating to the eye or sight. * *n* (*inf*) the eye; a device for dispensing a standard measure of spirits, etc.

optical *adj* of or relating to the eye or light; optic; aiding or correcting vision; visual.—**optically** *adv*.

optical character reader *n* a device that allows printed characters, figures, etc to be scanned and input to a computer, by a process of optical character recognition, the identification of printed text by photoelectric means.

optical disc *n* a compact disc used as a high-capacity storage medium for computers.

optical fiber *n* thin glass fiber through which light can be transmitted.

optician *n* a person who makes or sells optical aids.

optics *n sing* the branch of physics dealing with light and vision.

optimal *adj* optimum.—**optimally** *adv*.

optimism *n* a tendency to take the most cheerful view of things; hopefulness; the belief that good must ultimately prevail.—**optimist** *n*.—**optimistic** *adj*.—**optimistically** *adv*.

optimum *n* (*pl* **optima**, **optimums**) the best, most favourable condition.—*also adj*.

option *n* the act of choosing; the power to choose; a choice; the right to buy, sell or lease at a fixed price within a specified time.

optional *adj* left to choice; not compulsory.—**optionally** *adv*.

optometer *n* an instrument for measuring the limits of distinct vision.

opulent *adj* wealthy; luxuriant.—**opulence** *n*.

opuntia *n* any of a genus of cacti; the Indian fig.

opus *n* (*pl* **opuses**, **opera**) an artistic or literary work; a musical composition, esp any of the numbered works of a composer.

OR *abbr* = Oregon.

or[1] *conj denoting* an alternative; the last in a series of choices.

or[2] *n* (*her*) gold, denoted by small engraved dots.

ora *see* **os**[1].

orach, orache *n* mountain spinach.

oracle *n* a place in ancient Greece where a deity was consulted; the response given (often ambiguous); a wise adviser; sage advice.—**oracular** *adj*.

oral *adj* of the mouth; spoken, not written; (*drugs*) taken by mouth. * *n* a spoken examination.—**orally** *adv*.

oral history *n* the history of past events as recorded from interviews with people living at the time.

orange *n* a round, reddish-yellow, juicy, edible citrus fruit; the tree bearing it; its colour. * *adj* orange-coloured.

orangeade *n* a drink made with the juice of oranges.

Orangeman *n* (*pl* **Orangemen**) a member of an Irish protestant political party named after William of Orange.

orangery *n* (*pl* **orangeries**) a hothouse for the cultivation of oranges; an orange garden.

orange stick *n* a small thin pointed stick, orig orangewood, used in manicuring the nails.

orangutan, orangoutang *n* a large, long-armed, herbivorous anthropoid ape.

orate *vi* to make an oration; (*inf*) to hold forth.

oration *n* a formal or public speech.

orator *n* an eloquent public speaker.—**oratorical** *adj*.

oratorio *n* (*pl* **oratorios**) a sacred story set to music for voices and instruments.

oratory *n* (*pl* **oratories**) the art of public speaking; eloquence; a place for prayer.

orb *n* a sphere or globe; an ornamental sphere surmounted by a cross, esp as carried by a sovereign at a coronation.

orbicular, orbiculate, orbiculated *adj* orb-shaped, spherical.—**orbicularity** *n*.

orbit *n* (*astron*) a curved path along which a planet or satellite moves; a field of action or influence; the eye socket; (*physics*) the path of an electron around the nucleus of an atom. * *vti* to put (a satellite, etc) into orbit; to circle round.—**orbital** *adj*.

orc *n* a grampus; the killer whale; a sea monster.

orchard *n* an area of land planted with fruit trees.

orchestra *n* a group of musicians playing together under a conductor; their instruments; the space (or pit) in a theatre where they sit; the stalls of a theatre.—**orchestral** *adj*.

orchestrate *vt* to arrange music for performance by an orchestra; to arrange, organize to best effect.—**orchestration** *n*.—**orchestrator** *n*.

orchestrion *n* a large automatic barrel organ.

orchid *n* a plant with unusually shaped flowers in brilliant colours comprising three petals of uneven size.

orchil *n* a red or violet dye obtained from lichen; the lichen.—*also* **archil**.

orchis *n* a genus of wild orchid with curiously shaped roots and flowers.

orcinol, orcin *n* a substance obtained from lichens yielding dye.

ordain *vti* to confer holy orders upon; to appoint; to decree; to order, to command.—**ordainer** *n*.—**ordainment** *n*.

ordeal *n* a severe trial or test; an exacting experience.

order *n* arrangement; method; relative position; sequence; an undisturbed condition; tidiness; rules of procedure; an efficient state; a class, group, or sort; a religious fraternity; a style of architecture; an honour or decoration; an instruction or command; a rule or regulation; a state or condition, esp with regard to functioning; a request to supply something; the goods supplied; (*zool*) divisions between class and family or genus. * *vti* to put or keep (things) in order; to arrange; to command; to request (something) to be supplied.

ordered *adj* marked by regularity and discipline; being arranged or identifiable according to a rule; being labelled by ordinal numbers.

orderly *adj* in good order; well-behaved; methodical. * *n* (*pl* **orderlies**) a hospital attendant; a soldier attending an officer.—**orderliness** *n*.

ordinal *adj* showing position in a series. * *n* an ordinal number.

ordinal number *n* a number denoting its order in a sequence, as first, second, etc.

ordinance *n* a decree, a law; a rite.

ordinary *adj* normal, usual; common; plain, unexceptional.* *n* (*pl* **ordinaries**) a meal for all comers at fixed charges and a fixed time, an inn providing this; archbishop in province, bishop in diocese; prescribed form of service; an ecclesiastical judge; a prison chaplain; (*her*) that part of the escutcheon contained between straight and other lines / one of the simple charges.—**ordinarily** *adv*.

ordinary seaman *n* a seaman of the lowest rank, below able-bodied seaman

ordinate *n* (*geom*) one of the co-ordinates of a point; a straight line in a curve terminated on both sides by the curve and bisected by the diameter.

ordination *n* the act of ordaining or being ordained; admission to the ministry.

ordnance *n* military stores; artillery.

Ordovician *adj* (*geol*) of the period between the Cambrian and Silurian.

ordure *n* excrement; dung.

ore *n* a substance from which minerals can be extracted.

öre *n* (*pl* **öre**) a monetary unit in Sweden, (Øre) Denmark and Norway.

oread *n* a mountain nymph (Greek).

Oreg. *abbr* = Oregon.

oregano *n* an aromatic herb whose leaves, either fresh of dried, are used to flavour food.

organ *n* a usu large and complex musical wind instrument with pipes, stops, and a keyboard; a part of an animal or plant that performs a vital or natural function; the means by which anything is done; a medium of information or opinion, a periodical.

organdy, organdie *n* (*pl* **organdies**) a light transparent, usu stiffened cotton fabric.

organ grinder *n* the player of a barrel organ.

organic *adj* of or relating to bodily organs; (disease) affecting a bodily organ; of, or derived from, living organisms; systematically arranged; structural; (*chem*) of the class of compounds that are formed from carbon; (vegetables, etc) grown without the use of artificial fertilizers or pesticides.—**organically** *adv*.

organism *n* an animal or plant, any living thing; an organized body.

organist *n* a person who plays an organ.

organization *n* the act or process of organizing; the state of being organized; arrangement, structure; an organized body or association.

organize *vt* to arrange in an orderly way; to establish; to institute; to persuade to join a cause, group, etc; to arrange for.—**organizer** *n*.

organogenesis *n* organic development.—**organogenetic** *adj*.—**organogenetically** *adv*.

organography *n* a scientific description of the organs of animals or plants.—**organographic** *adj*.

organology *n* that branch of physiology which treats of animal organs.—**organological** *adj*.—**organologist** *n*.

organon *n* (*pl* **organa**, **organons**) a body of rules for regulating scientific or philosophical investigation / a method of thought, a logical system.

organotherapy *n* the treatment of disease with organic extracts.

organzine *n* a strong silk thread of a very fine texture; a fabric made from it.

orgasm *n* the climax of sexual excitement.—**orgasmic** *adj*.

orgeat *n* a drink made of barley water flavoured with almonds.

orgy *n* (*pl* **orgies**) a wild party or gathering of people, with excessive drinking and indiscriminate sexual activity; over-indulgence in any activity.—**orgiastic** *adj*.

oriel *n* a projecting angular recess with a window; the window.

Orient *n* the East, or Asia, esp the Far East.

orient, orientate *vti* to adjust (oneself) to a particular situation; to arrange in a direction, esp in relation to the points of the compass; to face or turn in a particular direction.

oriental *adj* (*often cap*) of the Orient, its people or languages.

Orientalism *n* an idiom or custom characteristic of the East.

Orientalist *n* an expert in Oriental languages, history, etc.

orientation *n* arrangement; alignment; position relative to a compass direction; one's way of thinking or direction of interest.

orienteering *n* the sport of racing on foot over difficult country using a map and compass

orifice *n* an opening or mouth of a cavity.

oriflamme *n* the ancient royal standard of France, a red flag split at one end and forming flame-shaped streamers; a party symbol; a blaze of colour.

orig. *abbr* = origin; original(ly).

origami *n* the Japanese art of paper folding to make complicated shapes.

origin *n* the source or beginning of anything; ancestry or parentage.

original *adj* relating to the origin or beginning; earliest, primitive; novel; unusual; inventive, creative. * *n* an original work, as of art or literature; something from which copies are made; a creative person; an eccentric.—**originality** *n*.—**originally** *adv*.

original sin *n* the inherent tendency of mankind to sin, derived from Adam and imputed to his descendants.

originate *vti* to initiate or begin; to bring or come into being.—**origination** *n*.—**originator** *n*.

orinasal *adj* (*vowel*) sounded with both the mouth and nose.—*also n*.

oriole *n* kinds of yellow, black-winged bird.

orison *n* (*arch*) a prayer.

orle *n* (*her*) an ordinary in the form of a fillet round a shield; (*archit*) a fillet under the capital of a column.

Orlon *n* (*trademark*) an acrylic fibre.

orlop *n* the lowest deck of a ship with three or more decks.

ormer *n* a mollusc, sea ear.

ormolu *n* an imitation gold made of copper and tin alloy, used for decoration.

ornament *n* anything that enhances the appearance of a person or thing; a small decorative object. * *vt* to adorn, to decorate with ornaments.

ornamental *adj* serving as an ornament; decorative, not useful.—**ornamentally** *adv*.

ornamentation *n* the act or process of ornamenting; something that decorates.

ornate *adj* richly adorned; (*style*) highly elaborate.—**ornately** *adv*.—**ornateness** *n*.

ornery *adj* (*sl*) of a bad disposition, hard to manage.

ornitho-, ornith- *prefix* bird.

ornithology *n* the study of birds.—**ornithological** *adj*.—**ornithologically** *adv*.—**ornithologist** *n*.

ornithopter *n* an aircraft with flapping wings.

ornithorhynchus *n* an Australian genus of monotremes, including the platypus.

oro- *prefix* mountain.

orogeny, orogenesis *n* the formation of mountains.—**orogenic, orogenetic** *adj*.

orography, orology *n* the geography of mountains and mountain systems, their mapping, etc.—**orographic, orological** *adj*.

oroide *n* a gold-coloured alloy of tin and copper.

orotund *adj* (*voice*) full, resonant; (*style*) pompous, high-flown.

orphan *n* a child whose parents are dead. * *vt* to cause to become an orphan.—*also adj*.

orphanage *n* a residential institution for the care of orphans.

Orphean *adj* of or pertaining to Orpheus, the celebrated bard of Classic mythology, or his music; melodious, enchanting.

Orphic *adj* of Orpheus or his cult; mystical.

orphrey *n* an embroidered band or bands of gold or silver on the front of an ecclesiastical vestment from the neck downward, esp on a cope.

orpiment *n* a yellow compound of arsenic, used as a pigment.

orpine *n* a succulent plant with fleshy leaves and purple flowers.

orrery *n* (*pl* **orreries**) a moving model of the solar system, which illustrates by balls mounted on rods the motions, magnitudes, and positions of the planets.

orris *n* a kind of iris.

orrisroot *n* the dried roots of the Florentine orris, used in perfumery and medicine.

ortho- *prefix* straight, right, true.

orthocephalic, orthocephalous *adj* (*anat*) with a skull of medium proportions, between brachycephalic and dolichocephalic.

orthochromatic *adj* (*photog*) giving the correct relative tones to colours, isochromatic.

orthoclase *n* potash feldspar.

orthodontics *n sing* the branch of dentistry dealing with the correction of irregularities in the teeth.—**orthodontic** *adj*.—**orthodontist** *n*.

orthodox *adj* conforming with established behaviour or opinions; not heretical; generally accepted, conventional; (*with cap*) of or relating to a conservative political or religious group.

orthodoxy *n* (*pl* **orthodoxies**) the state or quality of being orthodox; an orthodox practice or belief.

orthoepy *n* the science of correct pronunciation.—**orthoepic** *adj*.—**orthepist** *n*.

orthogenesis *n* evolution following a definite line, determinate variation.—**orthogenetic** *adj*.

orthognathous *adj* having an upright jaw, neither receding nor protruding.—**orthognathism** *n*.

orthogonal *adj* rectangular.—**orthogonally** *adv*.

orthography *n* (*pl* **orthographies**) the art of spelling and writing words with grammatical correctness; a map projection with a point of sight supposedly infinitely distant.—**orthographer** *n*.—**orthographic, orthographical** *adj*.

orthopedics, orthopaedics *n* the study and surgical treatment of bone and joint disorders.—**orthopedic** *adj*.—**orthopedist** *n*.

orthopteran*n* (*pl* **orthopterans, orthoptera**) any of the Orthoptera order of insects, having their two outer wings overlapping at the top when shut, as in grasshoppers.—**orthopterous** *adj*.

orthoptic *adj* of correct seeing. * *n* the peep-sight of a rifle.

orthotropism *n* vertical growth in plants.—**orthotropic** *adj*.—**orthotropous** *adj*.

ortolan *n* a small bird, allied to the bunting, much esteemed for its flesh.

oryx *n* (*pl* **oryxes, oryx**) a straight-horned African antelope.

OS *abbr* = ordinary seaman; Ordnance Survey (national mapping agency in the UK).

Os (*chem symbol*) osmium.

os[1] *n* (*pl* **ossa**) (*anat*) bone.

os[2] *n* (*pl* **ora**) (*anat*) the mouth.

Oscar *n* any of several small gold statuettes awarded annually by the US Academy of Motion Picture Arts and Sciences for outstanding achievements.

oscillate *vi* to swing back and forth as a pendulum; to waver, vacillate between extremes of opinion, etc.—**oscillation** *n*.

oscillator *n* a device for producing alternating current.

oscillatory *adj* swinging; vibrating.

oscilloscope *n* a device for viewing oscillations on a display screen of a cathode-ray tube.

osculate *vti* (*species*) to have features in common; (*geom*) to make contact (with); (*humorous*) to kiss, to touch.—**osculation** *n*.

osculatory *adj* pertaining to kissing. * *n* a tablet or board on which the picture of Christ or the Virgin Mary are painted for worshippers to kiss.

-ose *suffix* full of.

osier *n* a willow, the twigs of which are used in basket-making.

Osiris *n* the best loved of the Egyptian gods, husband of Iris and father of Horus.

-osis *n suffix* indicating a particular state, esp a diseased condition, *thrombosis*; increase, development of *,fibrosis*.

Osmanli *adj* of or pertaining to the Ottoman Empire.—*also n*.

osmium *n* a hard bluish-white metallic element used in alloys.

osmometry *n* the measurement of smells.

osmosis *n* (*pl* **osmoses**) the percolation and intermixture of fluids separated by a porous membrane.—**osmotic** *adj*.—**osmotically** *adv*.

osmunda, osmund *n* the flowering fern of the genus Osmunda.

osnaburg *n* a coarse linen cloth.

osprey *n* (*pl* **ospreys**) a large fish-eating bird of prey.

ossa *see* **os**[2].

ossein *n* gelatinous tissue in bone.

osseous *adj* pertaining to, consisting of, or like, bone.

ossicle *n* a little bone, esp of the ear; (*pl*) hard structures of small size, as the calcareous plates of the starfish.—**ossicular** *adj*.

ossiferous *adj* producing or containing bone.

ossification *n* conversion of soft animal tissue into bone.

ossifrage *n* an old name for the osprey or lammergeier.

ossify *vb* (**ossifying, ossified**) *vt* to convert into bone or into a bone-like substance; to harden. * *vi* to become bone; to grow rigid and unprogressive.

ossuary *n* (*pl* **ossuaries**) an urn for bones.

osteal *adj* osseous.

osteitis *n* inflammation of the bone.

ostensible *adj* apparent; seeming; pretended.—**ostensibly** *adv*.

ostensive *adj* showing, exhibiting.

ostentation *n* a showy, pretentious display.—**ostentatious** *adj*.—**ostentatiously** *adv*.

osteo-, oste- *prefix* bone.

osteoarthritis n painful inflammation of the joints, esp the hips, knees and olhers that bear weight.—**osteoarthritic** *adj*.

osteology *n* that part of anatomy treating of bones, their structure, etc; a bony structure.—**osteological** *adj*.—**osteologist** *n*.

osteoma *n* (*pl* **osteomas, osteomata**) a bone tumour.

osteomalacia *n* softening of the bones.

osteomyelitis *n* an infectious disease causing inflammation of the bone marrow.

osteopathy *n* the treatment of disease by manipulation of the bones and muscles, often as an adjunct to medical and surgical measures.—**osteopath** *n*.

osteophyte *n* an abnormal growth from a bone.—**osteophytic** *adj*.

osteoplasty *n* (*pl* **osteoplasties**) surgery involving bone replacement and grafting.—**osteoplastic** *adj*.

osteoporosis *n* the development of brittle bones due to a calcium deficiency in the bone matrix.—**osteoporotic** *adj*.

osteotome *n* an instrument used in dissecting bones.—**osteotomy** *n*.

ostiary *n* (*pl* **ostiaries**) (*RC Church*) a church doorkeeper.

ostler *n* (*formerly*) a man who attended to horses at an inn, a hostler.

ostracize *vt* to exclude, banish from a group, society, etc.—**ostracism** *n*.

ostrich *n* (*pl* **ostriches, ostrich**) a large, flightless, swift-running African bird.

Ostrogoth *n* an eastern Goth.

OT *abbr* = Old Testament.

otalgia *n* earache.

other *adj* second; remaining; different; additional. * *pron* the other one; some other one.

other-directed *adj* guided primarily by the influence or example of others.

otherness *n* diversity.

otherwhere *adv* (*arch*) elsewhere.

otherwhile *adv* (*arch*) at another time.

otherwise *adv* if not, or else; differently.

otherworldly *adj* spiritual; unworldly.—**otherworldliness** *n*.

otic *adj* of the ear.

otiose *adj* superfluous, serving no practical purpose; futile; at leisure.—**otiosity** *n*.

otitis *n* inflammation of the ear.

oto- *prefix* ear.

otolith *n* a chalky concretion in the ear.—**otolithic** *adj*.

otology *n* that part of anatomy which treats of the ear, its structure, etc.—**otological** *adj*.—**otologist** *n*.

otoscope *n* an instrument for examining the interior of the ear.

OTT *abbr* = over the top.

ottava rima *n* (*poet*) an Italian stanza of eight lines of five accents each with three rhymes, the seventh and eighth forming a couplet. / a stanza of eight five-foot lines rhyming abababcc.

otter *n* (*pl* **otters, otter**) a fish-eating mammal with smooth fur and a flat tail.

ottoman *n* an upholstered, backless chair or couch. * *adj* (*with cap*) of or relating to a former Turkish dynasty and empire; Turkish.

oubliette *n* an underground dungeon with its entrance in the roof in which prisoners condemned to perpetual imprisonment or secret death were confined.

ouch[1] *interj* an exclamation of pain or annoyance.

ouch[2] *n* a clasp, a jewel; the setting of a gem.

ought[1] *aux vb* expressing obligation or duty; to be bound, to be obliged (to); a variant spelling of **aught**.

ought[2] *see* **aught**.

Ouija *n* (*trademark*) a board with letters and symbols used to obtain messages at seances.

ounce[1] *n* a unit of weight, equal to one sixteenth of a pound or 28.34 grams; one sixteenth of a pint, one fluid ounce.

ounce[2] *n* the snow leopard; (*poet*) the lynx or an animal like it.

our *poss adj, pron* relating or belonging to us.

ours *pron* belonging to us.

ourselves *pron* emphatic and reflexive form of we.

-ous *suffix* full of, as in *joyous*; (*chem*) containing in lower proportion, as in *ferrous* as opposed to *ferric*.

ousel *see* **ouzel**.

oust *vt* to eject, expel, esp by underhand means; to remove forcibly.

out *adv* not in; outside; in the open air; to the full extent; beyond bounds; no longer holding office; ruled out, no longer considered; loudly and clearly; no longer included (in a game, fashion, etc); in error; on strike; at an end; extinguished; into the open; published; revealed; (*radio conversation*) transmission ends. * *prep* out of; out through; outside. * *adj* external; outward. * *n* an exit; means of escape.

out- *prefix* out, outside, away from; external; separate; more, longer.

out-and-out *adj* thoroughgoing; absolute; complete.

outback *n* a remote area inland, esp in Australia.

outbalance *vt* to exceed in weight.

outbid *vt* (**outbidding, outbid,** *pp* **outbidden** *or* **outbid**) to bid higher than.

outboard *adj* (*engine*) outside a ship, etc. * *n* an engine attached to the outside of a boat.

outbrave *vt* to excel in bravery; to defy.

outbreak *n* a sudden eruption (of disease, strife, etc).

outbuilding *n* a detached subsidiary building.

outburst *n* a bursting out; a spurt; an explosion of anger, etc.

outcast *n* a person who is rejected by society.

outcaste *n* one who has lost caste, a pariah. * *vt* to expel from a caste.

outclass *vt* to surpass or excel greatly.

outcome *n* the result, consequence.

outcrop *n* an exposed rock surface. * *vi* (**outcropping, outcropped**) to crop out at the surface.

outcry *n* (*pl* **outcries**) protest; uproar.

outdated *n* obsolete, old-fashioned.

outdistance *vt* to get well ahead of.

outdo *vt* (**outdoing, outdid,** *pp* **outdone**) to surpass, to do more than, to excel.

outdoor *adj* existing, taking place, or used in the open air.

outdoors *adv* in or into the open air; out of doors. * *n* the open air, outside world.

outer *adj* further out or away.

outermost *adj* furthest out; most distant.

outer space *n* any region of space beyond the earth's atmosphere.

outface *vt* to stare down or out of countenance; to defy.

outfall *n* the lower end of a watercourse; a point of discharge.

outfield *n* the outer part of a cricket or baseball field.

outfit *n* the equipment used in an activity; clothes worn together, an ensemble; a group of people associated in an activity. * *vt* (**outfitting, outfitted**) to provide with an outfit or equipment.

outfitter *n* a supplier of equipment or clothes.

outflank *vt* to get round the side of (an enemy); to circumvent.

outflow *n* a flowing out; something that flows out.

outfox *vt* to outwit by superior cunning.

outgeneral *vt* to outdo in strategy.

outgo *vt* (**outgoing, outwent,** *pp* **outgone**) to go beyond; to surpass.

outgoing *adj* departing; retiring; sociable, forthcoming. * *n* an outlay; (*pl*) expenditure.

outgrow *vt* (**outgrowing, outgrew,** *pp* **outgrown**) to become too big for; to grow taller than; to grow out of.

outgrowth *n* an offshoot.

outgun *vt* (**outgunning, outgunned**) to defeat by greater firepower; (*inf*) to surpass.

outhouse *n* a shet, etc, adjoining a main house.

outing *n* a pleasure trip; an excursion.

outlandish *adj* unconventional; strange; fantastic.

outlast *vt* to endure longer than.

outlaw *vt* to declare illegal. * *n* an outlawed person; a habitual or notorious criminal.

outlay *n* a spending (of money); expenditure.

outlet *n* an opening or release; a means of expression; a market for goods or services.

outlier *n* a part of a rock or stratum detached at some distance from the principal mass.

outline *n* a profile; a general indication; a rough sketch or draft.—*also vt.*

outlive *vt* to live longer than, outlast; to live through; to survive.

outlook *n* mental attitude; view; prospect.

outlying *adj* detached; remote, distant.

outmaneuver, outmanoeuvre*vt* to outwit in tactics.

outmatch *vt* to be more than a match for.

outmoded *adj* old-fashioned.

outmost *adj* outermost.

outnumber *vt* to exceed in number.

out-of-date *adj* no longer valid, unfashionable; outmoded.

out-of-pocket *adj* (*expenses*) paid for in cash; having lost money. **outpoint** *vt* to accumulate more points than.

out-of-the-way *adj* uncommon; secluded.

outpatient *n* a person treated at, but not resident in, a hospital.

outpoint *vt* to accumulate more points than.

outport *n* a part of harbour at some distance from the chief port.

outpost *n* (*mil*) a post or detachment at a distance from a main force.

outpouring *n* an effusion, an emotional speech.

output *n* the quantity (of goods, etc) produced, esp over a given period; information delivered by a computer, esp to a printer; (*elect*) the useful voltage, current, or power delivered.—*also vt.*

outrage *n* an extremely vicious or violent act; a grave insult or offence; great anger, etc, aroused by this.—*also vt.*—**outrageous** *adj.*

outrageous *adj* flagrant; atrocious; violent; excessive.—**outrageously** *adv.*—**outrageousness** *n.*

outrank *vt* to be of a higher rank than; to be of a higher priority.

outré *adj* outraging decorum; eccentric, unconventional; extravagant.

outride *vt* (**outriding, outrode,** *pp* **outridden**) to ride faster or farther than; to keep afloat through (a storm).

outrider *n* a mounted escort who goes in advance of a carriage, car, etc.

outrigger *n* a projecting spar for a sail, etc; a projection with a float extending from a canoe to prevent capsizing; a canoe of this type; a projecting frame to support the elevator or tail of an aircraft or the rotor of a helicopter.

outright *adj* complete, downright, direct. * *adv* at once; without restrictions.

outrun *vt* (**outrunning, outran,** *pp* **outran**) to run faster than; to exceed, to go beyond; to escape by running.

outset *n* the start, beginning.

outshine *vt* (**outshining, outshone**) to outdo in brilliance, ability; to shine longer and brighter than.

outside *n* the outer part or surface, the exterior. * *adj* outer; outdoor; (*chance, etc*) slight. * *adv* on or to the outside. * *prep* on or to the exterior of; beyond.

outsider *n* a person or thing not included in a set, group, etc, a non-member; a contestant, esp a horse, not thought to have a chance in a race.

outsize *adj* of a larger than usual size.

outskirts *npl* districts remote from the centre, as of a city.

outsmart *vt* to outwit.

outspan *vt* (**outspanning, outspanned**) (*S Africa*) to unyoke ox teams from a wagon; to encamp. * *n* a halting place.

outspoken *adj* candid in speech, frank, blunt.

outstanding *adj* excellent; distinguished, prominent; unpaid; unresolved, still to be done.

outstation *n* a distant post or station.

outstay *vt* to stay longer than or too long.

outstrip *vt* (**outstripping, outstripped**) to surpass; to go faster than.

outtalk *vt* to talk down.

outvote *vt* to defeat by a higher number of votes.

outward *adj* directed toward the outside; external; clearly apparent. * *adv* toward the outside.

Outward Bound movement *n* (in UK) an educational scheme to promote youth adventure training.

outwardly *adv* externally.

outwards *adv* outward.

outwear *vt* (**outwearing, outwore,** *pp* **outworn**) to outlast; to wear out.

outweigh *vt* to count for more than, to exceed in value, weight, or importance.

outwent *see* **outgo.**

outwit *vt* (**outwitting, outwitted**) to get the better of, defeat, by wit or cunning.

outwork *n* a defence constructed beyond the main body of a fort, etc; work done outside a factory.

ouzel *n* kinds of small bird; a blackbird.—*also* **ousel.**

ouzo *n* a Greek aniseed-flavoured spirit.

ova *see* **ovum.**

oval *adj* egg-shaped; elliptical. * *n* anything oval.

ovariotomy *n* (*pl* **ovariotomies**) the surgical operation of removing a tumour from the ovary.

ovaritis *n* inflammation of the ovary.

ovary *n* (*pl* **ovaries**) one of the two female reproductive organs producing eggs.—**ovarian** *adj.*

ovate *adj* (*bot*) oval, egg-shaped.

ovation *n* enthusiastic applause or public welcome.

oven *n* an enclosed, heated compartment for baking or drying.

ovenbird *n* a kind of bird with a dome-shaped nest; a fowl for cooking.

oven-ready *adj* (*food*) prepared for immediate cooking in the oven.

ovenware *n* attractive heat-resistant dishes in which food can be cooked and served.

over *prep* higher than; on top of; across; to the other side of; above; more than; concerning. * *adv* above; across; in every part; completed; from beginning to end; up and down; in addition; too. * *adj* upper; excessive; surplus; finished; remaining. * *n* (*cricket*) the number of balls bowled before changing ends.

over- *prefix* in excess, too much; above.

overact *vti* to act in an exaggerated manner, to overdo a part.

overactive *adj* abnormally or excessively active.—**overactivity** *n*.

overall *adj* including everything. * *adv* as a whole; generally. * *n* a loose protective garment; (*pl*) a one-piece protective garment covering body and legs.

overarch *vti* to form an arch (over).

overarm *adj, adv* (*sport*) bowled, thrown, performed, etc with the arm raised above the shoulder.

overawe *vt* to restrain by awe, daunt.

overbalance *vti* to fall over; to upset; to outweigh. * *n* a surplus.

overbear *vt* (**overbearing, overbore,** *pp* **overborne**) to dominate, to repress, to bear down.

overbearing *adj* domineering; overriding.—**overbearingly** *adv*.

overblown *adj* excessive, pretentious.

overboard *adv* over the side of a ship, etc; (*inf*) to extremes of enthusiasm.

overbook *vti* to sell tickets (for) in excess of the available seats or space.

overburden *vt* to load too heavily.

overcall *vti* (*bridge*) to bid more on (a hand) than it is worth; to take a bid away from (a partner).

overcame *see* overcome.

overcapitalize *vt* to float (a company) with too great a capital.—**overcapitalization** *n*.

overcast *adj* clouded over.

overcharge *vt* (*battery*) to overload; to fill to excess; to demand too high a price (from). * *n* an excessive or exorbitant charge or load.

overcloud *vti* to cover or become covered with clouds; to make or become dark or depressed.

overcoat *n* a warm, heavy topcoat.

overcome *vti* (**overcoming, overcame,** *pp* **overcome**) to get the better of, to prevail; to render helpless or powerless, as by tears, laughter, emotion, etc; to be victorious; to surmount obstacles, etc.

overcompensation *n* (*psychoanal*) an excess of compensation, often resulting in an overbearing manner.—**overcompensatory** *adj*.

overcrop *vt* (**overcropping, overcropped**) to exhaust (land) by excessive cultivation.

overcrowd *vti* to make or become too crowded.

overdo *vt* (**overdoing, overdid,** *pp* **overdone**) to do to excess; to overact; to cook (food) too much.—**overdone** *adj*.

overdose *n* an excessive dose —*also vti*.

overdraft *n* an overdrawing, an amount overdrawn, at a bank.

overdraw *vti* (**overdrawing, overdrew,** *pp* **overdrawn**) to draw in excess of a credit balance; to exaggerate in describing; to make an overdraft.

overdress *vti* to dress too warmly, too showily, or too formally.

overdrive *n* a high gear in a motor vehicle to reduce wear for travelling at high speed. * *vt* (**overdriving, overdrove,** *pp* **overdriven**) to drive too hard, overtax.

overdue *adj* past the time for payment, return, performance, etc; in arrears; delayed.

overeat *vi* (**overeating, overate,** *pp* **overeaten**) to eat too much.

overestimate *vt* to set too high an estimate on or for. * *n* an excessive estimate.—**overestimation** *n*.

overexpose *vt* (*phot*) to expose (a film) to light for too long.—**overexposure** *n*.

overflow *vti* (**overflowing, overflowed,** *pp* **overflown**) to flow over, flood; to exceed the bounds (of); to abound (with emotion, etc). * *n* that which overflows; surplus, excess; an outlet for surplus water, etc.

overgrow *vti* (**overgrowing, overgrew,** *pp* **overgrown**) to cover with growth; to grow too big or fast (for); to outgrow.—**overgrowth** *n*.

overgrown *adj* grown beyond the normal size; rank; ungainly.

overhand *adj, adv* (*sport*) bowled, thrown, performed, etc with the hand above the shoulder.

overhang *vti* (**overhanging, overhung**) to hang or project over. * *n* a projecting part.

overhaul *vt* to examine for, or make, repairs; to overtake.—*also n*.

overhead *adj, adv* above the head; in the sky. * *n* (often *pl*) the general, continuing costs of a business, as of rent, light, etc.

overhear *vt* (**overhearing, overheard**) to hear without the knowledge of the speaker.

overheat *vti* to make or become excessively hot; to stimulate unduly.

overjoyed *adj* highly delighted.

overkill *n* the capability to employ more weapons, etc than are necessary to destroy an enemy; excess capacity for a task.

overland *adj, adv* by, on, or across land.

overlap *vt* (**overlapping, overlapped**) to extend over (a thing or each other) so as to coincide in part.—*also n*.

overlay *vt* (**overlaying, overlaid**) to cover with a coating, to spread over. * *n* a coating.

overleaf *adv* on the other side of the leaf of a book.

overlie *vt* (**overlying, overlay,** *pp* **overlain**) to lie on top of; to stifle thus.

overload *vt* to put too great a burden on; (*elect*) to charge with too much current.

overlong *adj, adv* too long.

overlook *vt* to fail to notice; to look at from above; to excuse.

overlord *n* a lord ranking above other lords; an absolute or supreme ruler.

overman *vt* (**overmanning, overmanned**) to supply with too many workers.

overmaster *vt* to dominate wholly, to overpower.

overmuch *adj, adv* too much.

overnice *adj* too particular.

overnight *adv* for the night; in the course of the night; suddenly. * *adj* done in the night; lasting the night.

overpass *n* a road crossing another road, path, etc, at a higher level; the upper level of such a crossing. * *vt* (**overpassing, overpassed,** *pp* **overpast**) to pass beyond, to overstep; to surpass.

overplay *vt* to place too much emphasis on; to behave in an exaggerated or aflected manner.

overplus *n* a surplus, an excess.

overpower *vt* to overcome by superior force, to subdue; to overwhelm.

overpowering *adj* overwhelming; compelling; unbearable.

overproduction *n* supply in excess of the demand.

overqualified *adj* having more qualifications or experience that required for a particular job.

overrate *vt* to value or assess too highly.

overreach *vt* to extend beyond; to circumvent, outwit; to fail by trying too much or being too subtle.

overreact *vi* to show an excessive reaction to something.

override *vt* (**overriding, overrode,** *pp* **overridden**) to ride over; to nullify; to prevail.

overrule *vt* to set aside by higher authority; to prevail over.

overrun *vt* (**overrunning, overran,** *pp* **overrun**) to attack and defeat; to swarm over; to exceed (a time limit, etc).

overseas *adj, adv* across or beyond the sea; abroad.

oversee *vt* (**overseeing, oversaw,** *pp* **overseen**) to supervise; to superintend. * *n* **overseer** *n*.

oversell *vt* (**overselling, oversold**) to sell more than can be delivered, esp stocks.

overset *vti* (**oversetting, overset**) to upset, to disturb; to overthrow.

oversew *vt* (**oversewing, oversewed,** *pp* **oversewn**) to stitch over again to reinforce; to stitch over an edge to prevent fraying.

overshadow *vt* to throw a shadow over; to appear more prominent or important than.

overshoe *n* a galosh.

overshoot *vt* (**overshooting, overshot**) to shoot or send beyond (a target, etc); (*aircraft*) to fly or taxi beyond the end of a runway when landing or taking off.—*also n*.

oversight *n* a careless mistake or omission; supervision.

oversize, oversized *adj* of larger than average size.

overslaugh *n* (*mil*) the passing over of an ordinary duty because of a special one.

oversleep *vi* (**oversleeping, overslept**) to sleep beyond the intended time.

overspend *vt* (**overspending, overspent**) to spend more than necessary; to wear out, tire. * *vi* to spend more than one can afford.

overstate *vt* to state too strongly, to exaggerate.—**overstatement** *n*.

overstay *vt* to remain longer than or beyond the limits of.

overstep *vt* (**overstepping, overstepped**) to exceed; (*a limit*) to step beyond.

overstock *vt* to lay in too large a stock of or for, to glut.—*also n*.

overstrung *adj* too highly strung; too sensitive.

oversubscribe *vt* to apply for more shares in (an issue) than can be allotted.

overt *adj* openly done, unconcealed; (*law*) done with evident intent, deliberate.—**overtly** *adv*.

overtake *vt* (**overtaking, overtook,** *pp* **overtaken**) to catch up with and pass; to come upon suddenly.

overtax *vt* to make too great demands on; to tax too heavily.

overthrow *vt* (**overthrowing, overthrew,** *pp* **overthrown**) to throw over, overturn; (*government, etc*) to bring down by force.—*also n*.

overtime *adv* beyond regular working hours. * *n* extra time worked; payment for this.

overtone *n* an additional subtle meaning; an implicit quality; (*mus*) a harmonic; the colour of light reflected (as by a paint).

overtook *see* **overtake**.

overtop *vt* (**overtopping, overtopped**) to be higher than, to tower above.

overtrain *vti* to train too hard.

overtrump *vt* to play a higher trump than (the card that has trumped another).

overture *n* an initiating of negotiations; a formal offer, proposal; (*mus*) an instrumental introduction to an opera, etc.

overturn *vti* to upset, turn over; to overthrow.

overview *n* a general survey.

overweening *adj* arrogant, presumptuous, conceited.

overweight *adj* weighing more than the proper amount. * *n* excess weight.

overwhelm *vt* to overcome totally; to submerge; to crush; to overpower with emotion.

overwhelming *adj* irresistible; uncontrollable; vast; vastly superior; extreme.

overwork *vti* to work or use too hard or too long.

overwrite *vt* (**overwriting, overwrote, overwritten**) to write in an overly elaborate style; to write too much; to write data to a computer disk thereby erasing the existing contents.

overwrought *adj* over-excited; too elaborate.

ovi- *prefix* egg.

oviduct *n* the tube which conducts the ovum from the ovary to the uterus.

oviferous *adj* egg-carrying.

oviform *adj* egg-shaped.

ovine *adj* pertaining to sheep.

oviparous *adj* producing young by eggs.—**oviparity** *n*.

oviposit *vi* to lay or deposit eggs.—**oviposition** *n*.

ovipositor *n* the organ in certain insects by which its eggs are deposited.

ovisac *n* the cavity in the ovary which contains the ovum.

ovoid *adj* egg-shaped.

ovolo *n* (*pl* **ovoli**) (*archit*) a round or convex egg-shaped moulding.

ovoviviparous *adj* producing eggs containing the young in a living state, as certain animals.—**ovoviviparity** *n*.

ovulate *vi* to discharge or produce eggs from an ovary.—**ovulation** *n*.

ovule *n* the germ borne by the placenta of a plant and subsequently developing into a seed.—**ovular** *adj*.

ovum *n* (*pl* **ova**) an unfertilized female egg cell.

owe *vti* to be in debt; to be obliged to pay; to feel the need to give, do, etc, as because of gratitude.

owing *adj* due, to be paid; owed; (*with* **to**) because of, on account of.

owl *n* a nocturnal bird of prey with a large head and eyes; a person of nocturnal habits, solemn appearance, etc.—**owlish** *adj*.

owlet *n* a young owl.

own[1] *vti* to possess; to acknowledge, admit; to confess to.

own[2] *adj* belonging to oneself or itself, often used reflexively (*my own, their own*).

owner *n* one who owns, a possessor, a proprietor.—**ownership** *n*.

ox *n* (*pl* **oxen**) a cud-chewing mammal of the cattle family; a castrated bull.

oxalate *n* a salt of oxalic acid.

oxalic acid *n* a poisonous acid obtained from oxalis.

oxalis *n* wood sorrel.

oxbow *n* a horseshoe loop in a stream; the U-shaped collar of a yoke.

Oxbridge *n, adj* (of) the British universities of Oxford and Cambridge.

oxen *see* ox.

oxeye *n* a kind of flower; a large eye.

Oxfam (*acronym*) the Oxford Committee for Famine Relief.

Oxford Group *n* a former name of Moral Rearmament.

Oxford movement *n* an Anglican high-church movement begun in Oxford in 1833.

oxidation *n* the operation of converting into an oxide.

oxide *n* a compound of oxygen with another element.

oxidize *vti* to cause to undergo a chemical reaction with oxygen; to rust.—**oxidization** *n*.

oxlip *n* a variety of primula; a hybrid between primrose and cowslip.

Oxon. *abbr* = (*degrees, etc*) of Oxford.

Oxonian *adj* pertaining to Oxford. * *n* a graduate or member of Oxford University.

oxtail *n* the tail of an ox, esp skinned and used for stews, soups, etc.

oxy- *prefix* sharp; oxygen.

oxyacetylene *n* a mixture of oxygen with acetylene used in a blowlamp to cut or weld metal.—*also adj*.

oxygen *n* a colourless, odourless, tasteless, highly reactive gaseous element forming part of air, water, etc, and essential to life and combustion.—**oxygenic, oxygenous** *adj*.

oxygenate *vt* to combine or supply with oxygen.—**oxygenation** *n*.

oxygenize *vt* to oxygenate.—**oxygenizer** *n*.

oxygen tent *n* a canopy over a hospital bed, etc, within which a supply of oxygen is maintained.

oxyhemoglobin, oxyhaemoglobin *n* a loose compound of oxygen and haemoglobin.

oxyhydrogen *n* a mixture of oxygen with acetylene and hydrogen, as in a blowlamp, by which an intense heat is produced by the combination of gases.

oxymoron *n* (*pl* **oxymora**) a figure of speech combining contradictory words, e.g. "faith unfaithful kept him falsely true."

oxytone *adj* (*linguistics*) having an acute sound; having the last syllable accented. * *n* an acute sound; a word with the acute accent on the last syllable.

oyez, oyes *interj* the introductory cry of an official or public crier demanding attention or silence.

oyster *n* an edible marine bivalve shellfish.

oystercatcher *n* a wading sea bird.

oz *abbr* = ounce(s).

Oz *n* (Austral sl) Australia.

ozokerite, ozocerite *n* a waxy fossil resin used for candles.

ozone *n* a condensed form of oxygen; (*inf*) bracing seaside air.—**ozonic, ozonous** *adj*.

ozone layer *n* a layer of ozone in the stratosphere that absorbs ultraviolet rays from the sun.

ozonize *vt* to charge with ozone.—**ozonization** *n*.—**ozonizer** *n*.

P

P¹ *abbr* = parking; (*chess*) pawn.

P² (*chem symbol*) phosphorus.

p *abbr* = page; penny, pence.

PA *abbr* = Panama; Pennsylvania; personal assistant; public address (system).

Pa (*chem symbol*) protactinium.

pa *n* (*inf*) father, papa.

p.a. *abbr* = per annum.

paca *n* a burrowing rodent found in Central and South America.

pace¹ *n* a single step; the measure of a single stride; speed of movement. * *vti* to measure by paces; to walk up and down; to determine the pace in a race; to walk with regular steps.—pacer *n*.

pace² *prep* with the permission of; with due respect to.

pacemaker *n* a person who sets the pace in a race; an electronic device inserted in the heart, used to regulate heartbeat.

pacer *n* a horse trained to pace; a pacemaker.

pacha *see* pasha.

pachinko *n* a Japanese variation on pinball.

pachisi *n* an Indian game, similar to backgammon.

pachouli *see* patchouli.

pachyderm *n* any large thick-skinned mammal, esp an elephant.—pachydermatous *adj*.

pacific *adj* promoting peace; mild, conciliatory.—pacifically *adv*.

pacifier *n* a person or thing that pacifies; a baby's dummy.

pacifism *n* opposition to the use of force under any circumstances, specifically the refusal to participate in war.—pacifist *n*.

pacify *vt* (pacifying, pacified) to soothe; to calm; to restore peace to.—pacification *n*.

pack *n* a load or bundle (esp one carried on the back); a set of playing cards; a group or mass; a number of wild animals living together; an organized troop (as of Cub Scouts); a compact mass (as of snow); a small package used as a container for goods for sale. * *vt* to put together in a bundle or pack; (*suitcase*) to fill; to crowd; to press tightly so as to prevent leakage; to carry in a pack; to send (off); (*sl: gun, etc*) to carry; (*sl: punch*) to deliver with force. * *vi* (*snow, ice*) to form into a hard mass; to assemble one's belongings in suitcases or boxes. * *adj* used for carrying packs, loads, etc.—packer *n*.

package *n* a parcel, a wrapped bundle; several items, arrangements, etc offered as a unit. * *vt* to make a parcel of; to group together several items, etc.—packager *n*.

package holiday, package tour *n* a holiday or tour with all the fares, accommodation, food, etc, arranged for an all-inclusive price.

package store *n* (*US*) a place where alcohol is sold for consumption off the premises.—*also* liquor store.

packaging *n* the wrapping round a product offered for sale; the presentation of a product.

pack animal *n* an animal, such as a mule or camel, used for carrying loads.

packed out *adj* (*inf*) crowded.

packet *n* a small box or package; (*sl*) a considerable sum; a vessel carrying mail, etc, between one port and another.

packhorse *n* a horse used for carrying goods.

pack ice *n* sea ice formed into a mass by the crushing together of floes, etc.

packing *n* material for protecting packed goods or for making airtight or watertight; the act of filling a suitcase, box, etc.

packsaddle *n* a saddle for carrying goods.

pact *n* an agreement or treaty.

pad¹ *n* the dull sound of a footstep. * *vi* (padding, padded) to walk, esp with a soft step.

pad² *n* a piece of a soft material or stuffing; several sheets of paper glued together at one edge; the cushioned thickening of an animal's sole; a piece of folded absorbent material used as a surgical dressing; a flat concrete surface; (*sl*) one's own home or room. * *vt* (padding, padded) to stuff with soft material; to fill with irrelevant information.

padding *n* stuffing; anything unimportant or false added to achieve length or amount.

paddle¹ *vi* to wade about or play in shallow water.

paddle² *n* a short oar with a wide blade at one or both ends; a implement shaped like this, used to hit, beat or stir. * *vti* (*canoe, etc*) to propel by a paddle; to beat as with a paddle; to spank.—paddler *n*.

paddock *n* an enclosed field in which horses are exercised.

Paddy *n* (*pl* Paddies) (*derog*) a nickname for an Irishman.

paddy¹ *n* (*pl* paddies) threshed unmilled rice; a rice field.

paddy² *n* (*pl* paddies) (*sl*) rage, a fit of temper.

pademelon, paddymelon *n* (*Austral*) a small wallaby.

padlock *n* a detachable lock used to fasten doors etc. * *vt* to secure with a padlock.

padre *n* a military chaplain.

padrone *n* an innkeeper, esp in Italy.

paduasoy *n* a silk fabric.

paean *n* a song of triumph or thanks; praise.—*also* pean.

paediatrics *n sing* the branch of medicine dealing with children and their diseases.—*also* pediatrics.—paediatric *adj*.—paediatrician *n*.

paedo- *prefix* child.—*also* pedo-.

paedology *n* the study of children.—*also* pedology.—paedologic, paedological *adj*.—paedologically *adv*.—paedologist *n*.

paedophilia *n* sexual attraction towards children.—*also*

pedophilia.—**paedophiliac, paedophilic** adj.—**pae-dophile** n.

paeon n a four-syllabled metrical foot, comprising, in any order, three short and one long syllable.

pagan n a heathen; a person who has no religion.* adj irreligious; heathen, non-Christian.—**paganism** n.—**paganist** adj, n.

paganize vt to make pagan. * vi to become pagan.

page¹ n a boy attendant at a formal function (as a wedding); a uniformed boy employed to run errands. * vt to summon by messenger, loudspeaker, etc.

page² n a sheet of paper in a book, newspaper etc. * vt (a book) to number the pages of (—also **paginate**).

pageant n a spectacular procession or parade; representation in costume of historical events; a mere show.

pageantry n (pl **pageantries**) grand or formal display; pomp.

pageboy n a page; a medium-length hairstyle with the ends of the hair turned under.

pager n a device carried on a person so he or she can be summoned.—also **bleeper**.

paginal adj consisting of pages; page for page.

paginate see **page**².

pagination n the act of numbering the pages of a book; the arrangement and number of pages.

pagoda n an oriental temple in the form of a tower.

Pahlavi n the Persian dialect in which Zoroastrian scriptures were written.

paid see **pay**.

pail n a bucket.

pain n physical or mental suffering; hurting; (pl) trouble, exertion. * vt to cause distress to.

pained adj hurt, offended.

painful adj giving pain, distressing.—**painfully** adv.—**painfulness** n.

painkiller n a drug that relieves pain.

painless adj without pain.—**painlessly** adv.

painstaking adj very careful, laborious.—**painstakingly** adv.

paint vt (a picture) to make using oil pigments, etc; to depict with paints; to cover or decorate with paint; to describe. * vi to make a picture. * n a colouring pigment; a dried coat of paint.

painter¹ n a person who paints, esp an artist.

painter² n a bow rope for tying up a boat.

painting n the act or art of applying paint; a painted picture.

pair n a set of two things that are equal, suited, or used together; any two persons or animals regarded as a unit. * vti to form a pair (of); to mate.

paisley n an intricate pattern of curved shapes; a soft woollen fabric with this design; a shawl made of this material. * adj of this pattern or material.

pajamas see **pyjamas**.

pakeha n (New Zealand) a non-Maori, esp a white person.

pal n a close friend. * vi (**palling, palled**) (with **up**) (inf) to make friends (with).

palace n the official residence of a sovereign, president or bishop; a large stately house or public building.

paladin n a knight-errant, esp of the court of Charlemagne.

palatable adj (taste) pleasant; (fig) pleasant or acceptable.—**palatability** n.—**palatably** adv.

palate n the roof of the mouth; taste; mental relish.

palatial adj of or like a palace.—**palatially** adv.—**palatialness** n.

palaver n idle chatter; flattery; cajolery. * vt to flatter, cajole. * vi to talk idly.

palaeo- prefix old; ancient; prehistoric.

palaeobotany n the study of fossil plants.—also (US) **paleobotany**.

palaeography n the study of ancient writing and manuscripts.—also (US) **paleography**.—**palaeographic, palaeographical** adj.—**palaeographer** n.

Palaeolithic adj pertaining to the early Stone Age.—also (US) **Paleolithic**.

palaeontology n the study of fossils.—also (US) **paleontology**.—**palaeontological** adj.—**palaeontologist** n.

Palaeozoic adj pertaining to the geological period in which fossils of the earliest forms of life appear which began 600 million years ago and ended 225 million years ago.—also (US) **Paleozoic**.

palaeozoology n the study of fossil animals.—also (US) **paleozoology**.—**palaeozoological** adj.—**palaeozoologist** n.

pale¹ n a fence stake; a boundary; (her) a vertical stripe in the middle of a shield.

pale² adj (complexion) with less colour than usual; (colour, light) faint, wan, dim. * vti to make or become pale.—**palely** adv.—**paleness** n.

paleface n (derog) a term for a white person, supposedly used by Native Americans.

paleo- see **palaeo-**.

paleobotany see **palaeobotany**.

paleography see **palaeography**.

Paleolithic see **Palaeolithic**.

Paleozoic see **Palaeozoic**.

paleozoology see **palaeozoology**.

palette n a small, wooden board on which coloured paints are mixed.

palette knife n (pl **palette knives**) a thin knife used for mixing colours; a round-ended, flexible knife used in cookery.

palfrey n (arch) a saddle horse, esp for a woman.

palimony n (inf) the payment of alimony from one partner in a formal long-term sexual relationship to the other.

palimpsest n a manuscript which has been written on more than once, the former writing being still discernible in spite of erasure.

palindrome n a word or sentence reading the same forwards as backwards, eg "Able was I ere I saw Elba".—**palindromic** adj.

paling n a row of stakes in a fence; a railing.

palingenesis n (pl **palingeneses**) (theology) spiritual rebirth through baptism.—**palingenetic** adj.

palinode n a poem retracting a former poem.

palisade n a fence made of pointed stakes driven into the ground; a pointed stake used in a fence of this kind.

palish adj somewhat pale.

pall¹ n a heavy cloth over a coffin; (of smoke) a mantle.

pall² vi to become boring; to become satiated.

Palladian adj (archit) in the pseudo-classical style of the architect Andrea Palladio (1518–80).

palladium n a rare greyish-white metal found with platinum.

pallbearer n someone who carries the coffin at a funeral.

pallet¹ n a portable platform for lifting and stacking goods.

pallet² n a straw bed.

palletize, palletise *vt* to stack, transport or store on pallets.—**palletization, palletisation** *n*.

palliasse *n* a straw mattress.—*also* **paillasse**.

palliate *vt* to extenuate, to excuse; to alleviate without curing.—**palliation** *n*.—**palliator** *n*.

palliative *adj* alleviating without curing; excusing, extenuating. * *n* a thing that palliates.

pallid *adj* wan, pale.—**pallidness** *n*.

pallium *n* (*pl* **pallia, palliums**) a white woollen scarf worn by an archbishop; (*anat*) the cerebral cortex and surrounding matter; (*zool*) a mollusc's outer fold of skin.

pallor *n* paleness, esp of the face.

pally *adj* (**pallier, palliest**) friendly with; intimate.

palm¹ *n* the underside of the hand between fingers and wrist. * *vt* to conceal in or touch with the palm; (*with* **off**) to pass off by fraud, foist.

palm² *n* a tropical branchless tree with fan-shaped leaves; a symbol of victory.

palmaceous *adj* of the palm family.

palmar *adj* of or in the palm of the hand.

palmate, palmated *adj* like an open hand; (*bot*) having leaves with lobes radiating from a common point; (*zool*) web-footed.—**palmation** *n*.

palmer *n* (*formerly*) a pilgrim returning from the Holy Land, carrying a palm branch as a token of the pilgrimage.

palmetto *n* (*pl* **palmettos, palmettoes**) a species of small palm tree.

palmistry *n* foretelling the future from lines of the hand.—**palmist** *n*.

Palm Sunday *n* the Sunday before Easter.

palm-top *n* a portable computer small enough to fit in the palm of the hand.

palmy *adj* (**palmier, palmiest**) abounding in palm trees; (*fig*) flourishing, prosperous.

palmyra *n* a palm found in Asia, the leaves of which are used for matting and thatching.

palomino *n* (*pl* **palominos**) a horse with a golden or cream-coloured coat and a white mane and tail.

palp, palpus *n* (*pl* **palps, palpi**) a jointed feeler attached to the mouth parts of an insect.

palpable *adj* tangible; easily perceived, obvious.—**palpability** *n*.—**palpably** *adj*.

palpate *vt* to examine by touch, esp medically.—**palpation** *n*.

palpebral *adj* of the eyelids.

palpitate *vi* (*heart*) to beat abnormally fast; to tremble, flutter.—**palpitation** *n*.

palsy *n* (*pl* **palsies**) paralysis; a condition marked by an uncontrollable tremor of a part of the body. * *vt* (**palsying, palsied**) to paralyse; to make helpless.

palter *vi* to be insincere.

paltry *adj* (**paltrier, paltriest**) almost worthless; trifling.—**paltrily** *adv*.—**paltriness** *n*.

pampas *npl* the treeless, grassy plains of South America.

pampas grass *n* a tall-stemmed South American grass growing in thick tussocks.

pamper *vt* to overindulge; to coddle, spoil.—**pamperer** *n*.

pampero *n* (*pl* **pamperos**) a cold south or south west wind which blows across the pampas.

pamphlet *n* a thin, unbound booklet, esp one attacking or advocating a cause, etc; a brochure.—**pamphleteer** *n*.

Pan *n* (*Greek myth*) the god of woods and fields.—**Pandean** *adj*.

pan¹ *n* a wide metal container, a saucepan; (*of scales*) a tray; a depression in the earth filled with water; severe criticism; the bowl of a lavatory. * *vb* (**panning, panned**) *vi* (*with* **out**) (*inf*) to turn out, esp to turn out well; to succeed. * *vt* to wash gold-bearing gravel in a pan; (*inf*) to disparage, find fault with.

pan² *n* a betel leaf; a mixture of betel nuts and lime wrapped in a betel leaf used for chewing.

pan³ *vti* (**panning, panned**) (*film camera*) to move horizontally to follow an object or provide a panoramic view.—*also n*.

pan- *prefix* all; general.

panacea *n* a cure-all, universal remedy.—**panacean** *adj*.

panache *n* flair; sense of style.

panada *n* (*cooking*) bread boiled to a pulp and flavoured, used as a sauce base or as stuffing.

panama *n* a hat of a fine, straw-like material.

Pan-American *adj* of or pertaining to North, South and Central America collectively; advocating unity among American countries.

panatella *n* a long, slim cigar.

pancake *n* a round, thin cake made from batter and cooked on a griddle; a thing shaped thus. * *vi* (*aircraft*) to descend vertically in a level position.

panchromatic *adj* (*photog*) sensitive to light of all colours.

pancreas *n* a large gland secreting a digestive juice into the intestine and also producing insulin.—**pancreatic** *adj*.

pancreatin *n* a clear fluid secreted by the pancreas, often extracted from animals and used in medicine.

panda *n* a large black and white bear-like herbivore (*also* **giant panda**); a related reddish-brown raccoon-like animal with a ringed tail (—*also* **lesser panda**).

Pandean *adj* pertaining to the god Pan.

pandemic *adj* epidemic over a large region, universal.

pandemonium *n* (*pl* **pandemoniums**) uproar; chaos.

pander *n* a go-between in sexual liaisons; a pimp. * *vi* (*usu with* **to**) to gratify or exploit a person's desires or weaknesses, etc.—**panderer** *n*.

pandit *see* **pundit**.

P & L *abbr* = profit and loss.

pane *n* a sheet of glass in a frame of a window, door, etc.—**paned** *adj*.

panegyric *n* an ovation or eulogy in praise of a person or event.—**panegyrical** *adj*.—**panegyrist** *n*.

panegyrize *vti* to compose a panegyric (about); to praise highly.

panel *n* a usu rectangular section or division forming part of a wall, door, etc; a board for instruments or controls; a lengthwise strip in a skirt, etc; a group of selected persons for judging, discussing, etc. * *vt* (**panelling, panelled** *or* **paneling, paneled**) to decorate with panels.

panelling, paneling *n* panels collectively; sheets of wood, plastic, etc used for panels.

panellist, panelist *n* a member of a panel.

panelology *n* the collection of comic books as a hobby.

pang *n* a sudden sharp pain or feeling.

pangenesis *n* (*formerly*) the theory that reproductive cells contain particles from all parts of the parents.—**pangenetic** *adj*.

pangolin *n* an insectivorous mammal, also known as the spiny anteater, found in Africa and Asia.

panhandle¹ *n* a narrow, projecting tongue of land.

panhandle² *vi* (*inf*) to beg, esp from passers-by. * *vt* (*inf*) to obtain by begging.

panic *n* a sudden overpowering fright or terror.—*also adj.* * *vti* (**panicking, panicked**) to affect or be affected with panic.—**panicky** *adj.*

panic button *n* a switch for setting off an alarm; (*sl*) a frenzied response.

panicle *n* (*bot*) an irregularly bunched flower cluster.

panic-stricken, panic-struck *adj* affected by panic.

paniculate, paniculated *adj* (*bot*) arranged in panicles.

panjandrum *n* a pompous official.

panne *n* a soft, velvet-like fabric.

pannier *n* a large basket for carrying loads on the back of an animal or the shoulders of a person; a bag or case slung over the rear wheel of a bicycle or motorcycle.

pannikin *n* a small metal drinking-cup.

panoply *n* (*pl* **panoplies**) a complete array; a full suit of armour.—**panoplied** *adj.*

panorama *n* a complete view in all directions; a comprehensive presentation of a subject; a constantly changing scene.—**panoramic** *adj.*—**panoramically** *adv.*

panpipes *npl* a wind instrument consisting of short hollow tubes of different lengths, originally of reed, bound together.

pansy *n* (*pl* **pansies**) a garden flower of the violet family, with velvety petals; (*sl*) an effeminate boy or man.

pant *vi* to breathe noisily, gasp; to yearn (for or after something). * *vt* to speak while gasping.

pantalets, pantalettes *npl* a woman's long ruffled drawers.

pantaloon *n* (*pantomine*) a foolish old man on whom the clown plays tricks.

pantaloons *npl* (*hist*) a man's tight breeches fastened at the calf or the foot; (*inf*) baggy trousers.

pantheism *n* the doctrine that the universe in its totality is God; willingness to worship all, or several gods.—**pantheist** *n.*—**pantheistic, pantheistical** *adj.*

pantheon *n* a temple to all the gods; a building in which the famous dead of a nation are buried or remembered; a group of famous persons.

panther *n* (*pl* **panther, panthers**) a leopard, esp one with a black unspotted coat; a puma.

pantihose *n* women's tights.—*also* **panty hose.**

panties *npl* (*inf*) short underpants.

pantile *n* a roof tile with an S-shaped cross-section.

panto *n* (*pl* **pantos**) (*Brit inf*) a pantomime.

pantograph *n* an instrument for copying drawings, maps, etc, to scale.

pantomime *n* (*Brit*) a Christmas theatrical entertainment with music and jokes; a drama without words, using only actions and gestures; mime. * *vti* to mime.—**pantomimic** *adj.*

pantomimist *n* a person who performs in a pantomime; one who composes a pantomime.

pantoum *n* a verse form of four-lined rhyming stanzas.

pantry *n* (*pl* **pantries**) a small room or cupboard for storing cooking ingredients and utensils, etc.

pants *npl* trousers; underpants.

panty hose *see* **pantihose.**

panzer *adj* (*division*) armoured. * *n* a tank, or other armoured vehicle, from a panzer division; (*pl*) armoured troops.

pap *n* soft, bland food for infants, invalids, etc; any oversimplified or insipid writing, ideas, etc.

papa *n* (*inf*) father.

papacy *n* (*pl* **papacies**) the office or authority of the pope; papal system of government.

papal *adj* of the pope or the papacy.—**papally** *adv.*

paparazzo *n* (*pl* **paparazzi**) a freelance photographer who pursues celebrities for sensational or candid shots for publication in newspapers and magazines.

papaveraceous *adj* (*bot*) pertaining or belonging to the poppy family.

papaw *n* (the small edible fruit of) a North American tree of the custard-apple family.—*also* **pawpaw.**

papaya *n* (a West Indian tree bearing) an elongated melon-like fruit with edible yellow flesh and small black seeds.

paper *n* the thin, flexible material made from pulped rags, wood, etc which is used to write on, wrap in, or cover walls; a single sheet of this; an official document; a newspaper; an essay or lecture; a set of examination questions; (*pl*) personal documents. * *adj* like or made of paper. * *vt* to cover with wallpaper.

paperback *n* a book bound in a flexible paper cover. * *adj* pertaining to such a book or the publication of such books.

papering *n* the process of covering with paper; paper so used.

paperknife *n* (*pl* **paperknives**) a blunt knife for opening letters or cutting folded paper.

paper money *n* banknotes; paper currency authorized by a government as representing value.

paperweight *n* a small heavy object for keeping papers in place.

paperwork *n* clerical work of any kind.

papery *adj* like paper in appearance or consistency.—**paperiness** *n.*

papeterie *n* a case containing paper and writing materials.

papier-mâché *n* a substance made of paper pulp mixed with size, glue, etc and moulded into various objects when moist.

papilla *n* (*pl* **papillae**) a small, nipple-like protuberance.—**papillary, papillate, papillose** *adj.*

papist *n* (*derog*) a Roman Catholic.—**papistic** *adj.*—**papistry** *n.*

papoose *n* an American Indian young child.

pappus *n* (*pl* **pappi**) (*bot*) the feathery substance on the seeds of some plants, eg dandelion, thistle.

pappy *adj* (**pappier, pappiest**) semi-liquid, like pap.

paprika *n* a mild red condiment ground from the fruit of certain peppers.

Pap test, Pap smear *n* a technique for the early detection of cancer by examining specially stained cells from the cervix, etc.

papule, papula *n* (*pl* **papules, papulae**) a small, solid elevation of the skin.—**papular** *adj.*

papyrology *n* the study of papyri.—**papyrologist** *n.*

papyrus *n* (*pl* **papyri, papyruses**) an aquatic plant; paper made from this plant, as used in ancient times.

par *n* the standard or normal level; the established value of a currency in foreign-exchange rates; the face value of stocks, shares, etc; (*golf*) the score for a hole required by an expert player; equality.

par-, para- *prefix* beside; against; irregular; abnormal; associated in a subsidiary or accessory capacity.

para *n* (*pl* **paras**) (*inf*) a paragraph; a paratrooper.

parabasis *n* (*pl* **parabases**) (*classical Greek comedy*) an address to the audience by the chorus.

parable *n* a short story used to illustrate a religious or moral point.—**parabolist** *n.*

parabola *n* (*pl* **parabolas**) (*maths*) the curve formed by the cutting of a cone by a plane parallel to its side.

parabolic[1] adj of or like a parabola; parabolical.

parabolic[2], parabolical adj of or expressed in a parable.—**parabolically** adv.

paraboloid n (geom) a solid formed by the revolution of a parabola on its axis.

parachronism n an error in chronology, esp in postdating an event.

parachute n a fabric umbrella-like canopy used to retard speed of fall from an aircraft. * vti to drop, descend by parachute.—**parachutist** n.

paraclete n a mediator.

parade n a ceremonial procession; an assembly of troops for review; ostentatious display; public walk, promenade. * vti to march or walk through, as for display; to show off; to assemble in military order.

paradigm n a pattern or model; a list of grammatical inflexions of a word.—**paradigmatic** adj.—**paradigmatically** adv.

paradise n heaven; (Bible) the Garden of Eden; any place of perfection.

paradisiacal, paradisiac adj like, or pertaining to, paradise.

paradox n a self-contradictory statement that may be true; an opinion that conflicts with common beliefs; something with seemingly contradictory qualities or phases.—**paradoxical** adj.—**paradoxically** adv.

paraesthesia n (med) an abnormal tickling sensation on the skin.—also **paresthesia**.—**paraesthetic** adj.

paraffin n a white waxy tasteless substance obtained from shale, wood, etc; a distilled oil used as fuel, kerosene.—**paraffinic** adj.

paragenesis, paragenesia n (geol) the sequence of formation of the various minerals in a mass of rock—**paragenetic** adj.

paragoge, paragogue n (linguistics) the addition of a letter or a syllable to a word.

paragon n a model of excellence or perfection.

paragraph n a subdivision in a piece of writing used to separate ideas, marked by the beginning of a new line; a brief mention in a newspaper. * vt to divide into paragraphs.—**paragraphic** adj.—**paragraphically** adv.

Paraguay tea n an infusion of the dried leaves of maté, which makes a mildly stimulating tea.—also **yerba maté**.

parakeet n a small parrot.

paraldehyde n a colourless liquid used as a sedative.

paraleipsis, paralipsis n (pl **paraleipses, paralipses**) (rhetoric) drawing attention to something by deliberately understating it.

parallax n the apparent angular shifting of an object caused by a change in position of the observer; (astron) the difference in the apparent position of a heavenly body and its true place.

parallel adj equidistant at every point and extended in the same direction; side by side; never intersecting; similar, corresponding. * n a parallel line, surface, etc; a likeness, counterpart; comparison; a line of latitude. * vt (**paralleling, paralleled**) to make or be parallel; to compare.

parallelepiped n a regular solid figure bounded by six parallelograms, of which the opposite pairs are equal and parallel.

parallelism n the state or quality of being parallel.

parallelogram n a four-sided plane figure whose opposite sides are parallel.

paralogism n (logic) a fallacy in reasoning made unconsciously by the reasoner.

paralyse, paralyze vt to affect with paralysis; to bring to a stop.—**paralysation** n.

paralysis n (pl **paralyses**) a partial or complete loss of voluntary muscle function or sensation in any part of the body; a condition of helpless inactivity.—**paralytic** adj, n.

paramatta n a light fabric of cotton and wool.—also **parramatta**.

paramedic n a a person trained to provide emergency medical treatment and to support professional medical staff.

paramedical adj (services) supplementing and assisting the work of professional medical staff.

parameter n (math) an arbitrary constant, the value of which influences the content but not the structure of an expression; (inf) a limit or condition affecting action, decision, etc.—**parametric** adj.—**parametrically** adv.

paramilitary adj (forces) organized on a military pattern and ancillary to military forces.

paramo n (pl **paramos**) a high bleak plateau in the Andes.

paramount adj of great importance.

paramour n an illicit lover.

parang n a heavy Malay sheath knife.

paranoia n a mental illness characterized by delusions of grandeur and persecution; (inf) unfounded fear, suspicion.—**paranoiac** adj, n.

paranoid adj of or like paranoia; (inf) highly suspicious or fearful.—also n.

paranormal adj beyond the scope of normal experience or scientific explanation.—**paranormally** adv.

parapet n a low, protective wall along the edge of a roof, balcony, or bridge, etc.—**parapeted** adj.

paraph n a mark or flourish after a signature.

paraphernalia npl personal belongings; accessories; (law) what a wife possesses in her own right.

paraphrase n expression of a passage in other words in order to clarify meaning. * vt to restate.—**paraphrastic** adj.

paraplegia n paralysis of the lower half of the body.—**paraplegic** adj.

parasailing n the sport of gliding through the air attached to an open parachute and towed by a speedboat.—**parasailer, parasailor** n.

parascending n a form of parachuting in which participants wearing open parachutes are towed into the air by a vehicle or speedboat and then released to glide to the ground.—**parascender** n.

paraselene n (pl **paraselenae**) (astron) a bright spot on a lunar halo.

parasite n an organism that lives on and feeds off another without rendering any service in return; a person who sponges off another.—**parasitic** adj.—**parasitically** adv.

parasiticide n a substance which kills parasites.

parasitism n the parasite-host relationship; the state or behaviour of a parasite.

parasitize n to infest with parasites.

parasitology n the study of parasites.—**parasitologist** n.

parasol n a lightweight umbrella used as a sunshade.

parasynthesis n (gram) derivation from a compound plus affix, eg faint-hearted, which is made up from faint + heart + -ed.

parataxis n (gram) use of successive clauses without connecting words.

parathyroid *adj* (*anat*) lying near the thyroid gland. * *n* a gland near the thyroid that secretes a hormone that regulates the body's calcium levels.

paratroops *npl* troops dropped by parachute into the enemy area.—**paratrooper** *n*.

paravane *n* a device shaped like a torpedo, with serrated teeth for destroying the moorings of sea mines.

parboil *vt* to boil briefly as a preliminary cooking procedure.

parbuckle *n* a rope sling for raising or lowering casks.

parcel *n* a tract or plot of land; a wrapped bundle; a package; a collection or group of persons, animals, or things. * *vt* (**parcelling, parcelled** *or* **parceling, parceled**) to wrap up into a parcel; (*with* **out**) to apportion.

parcenary *n* joint heirship.

parcener *n* a coheir.

parch *vti* to make or become hot and dry, thirsty; to scorch, roast.—**parched** *adj*.

parchment *n* the skin of a sheep, etc prepared as a writing material; paper like parchment.

pard *n* (*arch*) a leopard.

pardon *vt* to forgive; to excuse; to release from penalty. * *n* forgiveness; remission of penalty.—**pardonable** *adj*.—**pardonably** *adv*.

pardoner *n* one who pardons; (*hist*) a person licensed to sell papal indulgences.

pare *vt* to cut or shave; to peel; to diminish.

paregoric *n* (*formerly*) an opium-based drug used to treat diarrhoea and coughs.

parenchyma *n* (*bot*) the soft cellular tissue or pith of plants; (*anat*) the soft tissue of the glandular organs of the body.—**parenchymatous, parenchymal** *adj*.

parent *n* a father or a mother; an organism producing another; a source.—**parental** *adj*.—**parentally** *adv*.—**parenthood** *n*.

parentage *n* descent, extraction from parents.

parenthesis *n* (*pl* **parentheses**) an explanatory comment in a sentence contained within brackets and set in a sentence, independently of grammatical sequence; the brackets themselves ().—**parenthetic, parenthetical** *adj*.—**parenthetically** *adv*.

parenthesize, parenthesise *vt* to insert as a parenthesis; to enclose in parentheses.

parenting *n* the act of being a parent; the role of a parent in relation to a child; that role in relation to someone who is not the child of a parent.

paresis *n* partial or slight paralysis.—**paretic** *adj*.

par excellence *adv* pre-eminently; to the highest degree.

parfait *n* a rich iced dessert of whipped cream, eggs, etc served in a tall glass; layers of ice cream served in a tall glass.

parget *n* a type of plaster. * *vt* to cover with parget.

parhelion *n* (*pl* **parhelia**) a bright spot on a solar halo.

pariah *n* a social outcast; a member of a low caste in southern India and Burma.

parietal *adj* (*anat*) pertaining to the wall of a cavity of the body; pertaining to the large lateral bones of the skull.

paring *n* the act of paring; what is pared off, rind.

pari-mutuel *n* (*pl* **pari-mutuels, paris-mutuels**) a mechanical betting system in which the losers' stakes, less a deduction for the management, are divided among the winners.

pari passu *adv* (*law*) with equal pace, together; in equal degree.

parish *n* an ecclesiastical area with its own church and clergy; the inhabitants of a parish.

parishioner *n* an inhabitant of a parish.

parisyllabic *adj* (*inflected noun or verb*) having an equal number of syllables in all or most inflected forms.

parity *n* (*pl* **parities**) equality; equality of value at a given ratio between different kinds of money, etc; being at par.

park *n* land kept as a game preserve or recreation area; a piece of ground in an urban area kept for ornament or recreation; an enclosed stadium, esp for ball games; a large enclosed piece of ground attached to a country house. * *vti* (*vehicle*) to leave in a certain place temporarily; to manoeuvre into a parking space.

parka *n* a warm hooded garment, often of fur, for wear in arctic conditions.

parking lot *n* a car park.

parking meter *n* a coin-operated machine that registers the purchase of parking time for a motor vehicle.

Parkinsonism *n* Parkinson's disease.

Parkinson's disease *n* a progressive nervous disease resulting in tremor, muscular rigidity, partial paralysis and weakness.

Parkinson's Law *n* any of various humorous observations on human behaviour framed as economic laws, esp the notion that work expands to fill the time available for its completion (named after the English writer C. N. Parkinson b.1909).

parlance *n* a manner of speech, idiom.

parley *n* a conference, esp with an enemy. * *vi* to discuss, esp with an enemy with a view to bringing about a peace.

parliament *n* a legislative assembly made up of representatives of a nation or part of a nation; (*with cap*) the supreme governing and legislative body of various countries, esp the UK.

parliamentarian *n* a skilled parliamentary debater; an expert on parliamentary rules; (*with cap*) (*hist*) a supporter of the English Parliament against Charles I.

parliamentary *adj* of, used in, or enacted by a parliament; conforming to the rules of a parliament; having a parliament.

parlour *n* a room in a house used primarily for conversation or receiving guests; a room or a shop used for business.

parlour game *n* a game usually played indoors.

parlous *adj* (*arch*) dangerous; shrewd.—**parlously** *adv*.—**parlousness** *n*.

parmales *n* any of the order Parmales of single-celled algae found in the polar regions.

Parmesan *n* a hard cheese with a sharp flavour used, esp grated, as a garnish.

parochial *adj* of or relating to a parish; narrow; provincial in outlook.—**parochially** *adv*.

parochialism *n* narrow-mindedness.

parody *n* (*pl* **parodies**) a satirical or humorous imitation of a literary or musical work or style. * *vt* (**parodying, parodied**) to make a parody of.—**parodic** *adj*.—**parodist** *n*.

paroicous, paroecious *adj* (*bot*) with the two sexes developing in close proximity.

parole *n* word of honour; the release of a prisoner before his sentence has expired, on condition of future good behaviour. * *vt* to release on parole.

parolee *n* a person on parole.

paronomasia *n* a pun or play on words.

paronym *n* (*gram*) a paronymic word.

paronymic, paronymous *adj* (*gram*) with the same derivation; with the same sound but different spelling and meaning.

parotid *adj* (*anat*) situated near the ear. * *n* a parotid gland.

parotitis, parotiditis *n* mumps.

paroxysm *n* a sudden attack of a disease; a violent convulsion of pain or emotion; an outburst of laughter.—**paroxysmal** *adj.*

parquet *n* an inlaid hard wood flooring; the stalls of a theatre below the balcony. * *vt* to furnish (a room) with a parquet floor.

parquetry *n* mosaic woodwork used to cover floors.

parr *n* (*pl* **parrs, parr**) a young salmon.

parramatta *see* **paramatta**.

parrot *n* a tropical or subtropical bird with brilliant plumage and the ability to mimic human speech; one who repeats another's words without understanding. * *vt* to repeat mechanically.

parrotfish *n* (*pl* **parrotfish, parrotfishes**) a brightly coloured tropical fish, with mouth parts resembling a parrot's beak.

parry *vt* (**parrying, parried**) to ward off, turn aside. * *n* (*pl* **parries**) a defensive movement in fencing.

parse *vti* (*words*) to classify; (*sentences*) to analyse in terms of grammar; to give a grammatical description of a word or group of words.

parsec *n* (*astron*) a unit of measure for stellar distances equal to 3.26 light years, approx 19 million miles.

Parsee *n* an Indian adherent of the Zoroastrian religion.—**Parseeism** *n.*

parsimony *n* extreme frugality; meanness, stinginess.—**parsimonious** *adj.*

parsley *n* a bright green herb used to flavour or garnish some foods.

parsnip *n* a biennial plant cultivated for its long tapered root used as a vegetable.

parson *n* an Anglican clergyman in charge of a parish; (*inf*) any, esp Protestant, clergyman.

parsonage *n* the house provided for a parson by his church.

part *n* a section; a portion (of a whole); an essential, separable component of a piece of equipment or a machine; the role of an actor in a play; a written copy of his/her words; (*mus*) one of the melodies of a harmony; the music for it; duty, share; one of the sides in a conflict; a parting of the hair; (*pl*) qualities, talent; the genitals; a region, land or territory. * *vt* to separate; to comb the hair so as to leave a parting. * *vi* to become separated; to go different ways.

partake *vi* (**partaking, partook**; *pp* **partaken**) to participate (in); (*food or drink*) to have a portion of.

partan *n* (*Scot*) a crab.

parterre *n* an ornamental flower garden; the area of a ground floor of a theatre that lies underneath the balconies.

parthenocarpy *n* (*bot*) the formation of fruit without seeds having been formed or fertilized.

parthenogenesis *n* reproduction without sexual union; virgin birth.—**parthenogenetic** *adj.*

partial *adj* incomplete; biased, prejudiced; (*with* **to**) having a liking or preference for.—**partially** *adv.*

partiality *n* (*pl* **partialities**) biased judgment; (*with* **for**) liking, fondness.

partible *adj* able to be divided or separated.

participant *n* one who participates; a sharer.

participate *vi* to join in or take part with others (in some

activity).—**participator** *n.*—**participatory** *adj.*

participation *n* the act of participating; the state of being related to a larger whole.

participle *n* (*gram*) a verb form used in compound forms or as an adjective.—**participial** *adj.*—**participially** *adv.*

particle *n* a tiny portion of matter; a speck; a very small part; (*gram*) a word that cannot be used alone, a prefix, a suffix.

parti-coloured *adj* differently coloured in different parts, variegated.

particular *adj* referring or belonging to a specific person or thing; distinct; exceptional; careful; fastidious. * *n* a detail, single item; (*pl*) detailed information.

particularism *n* exclusive devotion to one party or sect; the principle of political freedom for each state in a federation; the theological doctrine that salvation is only for the elect.—**particularist** *n.*

particularity *n* (*pl* **particularities**) the quality of being particular, as distinguished from universal; exactness; fastidiousness.

particularize *vt* to describe in detail; to mention one by one.—**particularization** *n.*

particularly *adv* very; especially; in detail.

parting *n* a departure; a breaking or separating; a dividing line in combing hair. * *adj* departing, esp dying; separating; dividing.

partisan, partizan *n* a strong supporter of a person, party, or cause.—*also adj.*—**partisanship, partizanship** *n.*

partite *adj* (*bot*) divided almost to the base.

partition *n* division into parts; that which divides into separate parts; a dividing wall between rooms. * *vt* to divide.

partitive *adj* (*gram*) denoting a part or partition. * *n* a partitive word.

partizan *see* **partisan**.

partly *adv* in part; to some extent.

partner *n* one of two or more persons jointly owning a business who share the risks and profits; one of a pair who dance or play a game together; either member of a married or non-married couple. * *vt* to be a partner (in or of); to associate as partners.

partnership *n* a contract between two or more people involved in a joint business venture; the state of being a partner.

part of speech *n* each of the categories (eg verb, noun, adjective) into which words are divided according to their grammatical and semantic functions.

partook *see* **partake**.

partridge *n* (*pl* **partridge, partridges**) a stout-bodied game bird of the grouse family.

part song *n* a song with two or more voice parts.

part-time *adj* working fewer than the full number of hours.—**part-timer** *n.*—**part time** *adv.*

parturient *adj* pertaining to childbirth; about to give birth, in labour.

parturition *n* the act of childbirth.

party *n* (*pl* **parties**) a group of people united for political or other purpose; a social gathering; a person involved in a contract or lawsuit; a small company, detachment; a person consenting, accessory; (*inf*) an individual. * *vb* (**partying, partied**) *vi* to attend social parties. * *vt* to give a party for. * *adj* of or for a party.

party line *n* a telephone line shared by two or more subscribers; the policies of a political body.

parvenu *n* someone regarded as vulgar or an upstart,

following a rise in his social or economic status.—**parvenue** *nf*.

pas *n* (*pl* **pas**) (*ballet*) a step or series of steps; a dance sequence.

PASCAL *n* a high-level computer programming language used esp for teaching.

pascal *n* the SI unit of pressure.

pas de deux *n* (*pl* **pas de deux**) a ballet sequence for two dancers.

pasha *n* a Turkish title given to a high official; (*formerly*) a provincial governor in the Ottoman Empire.—*also* **pacha**.

pasque-flower *n* a type of anemone which flowers around Easter.

pasquinade *n* a lampoon or rude satire.

pass *vb* (**passing, passed**) *vi* to go past; to go beyond or exceed; to move from one place or state to another; (*time*) to elapse; to go; to die; to happen; (*with* **for**) to be considered as; (*in exam*) to be successful; (*cards*) to decline to make a bid; (*law*) to be approved by a legislative assembly. * *vt* to go past, through, over, etc; (*time*) to spend; to omit; (*law*) to enact; (*judgment*) to pronounce; to excrete; (*in test, etc*) to gain the required marks; to approve. * *n* a narrow passage or road; a permit; (*in a test, etc*) success; transfer of (a ball) to another player; a gesture of the hand; (*inf*) an uninvited sexual approach.

passable *adj* fairly good, tolerable; (*a river, etc*) that can be crossed.—**passably** *adv*.

passage *n* act or right of passing; transit; transition; a corridor; a channel; a route or crossing; a lapse of time; a piece of text or music.

passageway *n* a narrow way, esp flanked by walls, that allows passage; a corridor.

passbook *n* a bankbook.

passé *adj* past its best; outdated.

passementerie *n* a decorative trimming of gold or silver lace, braid, beads, etc.

passenger *n* a traveller in a public or private conveyance; one who does not pull his/her weight.

passe-partout *n* a frame for a picture in which the picture, glass and backing are held together by gummed paper; a master key.

passer-by *n* (*pl* **passers-by**) one who happens to pass or go by.

passerine *adj* pertaining to the order of birds which perch.—*also n*.

passim *adv* here and there; throughout.

passing *adj* transient; casual. * *n* departure, death.

passion *n* compelling emotion, such as love, hate, envy; ardent love, esp sexual desire; (*with cap*) the suffering of Christ on the cross; the object of any strong desire.—**passionless** *adj*.

passional *adj* pertaining to passion; due to passion.

passionate *adj* moved by, showing, strong emotion or desire; intense; sensual.—**passionately** *adv*.

passionflower *n* a chiefly tropical climbing vine.

passion fruit *n* the edible fruit of a passion flower.

Passion play *n* a play representing Christ's Passion.

Passion Sunday *n* the second Sunday before Easter.

passive *adj* acted upon, not acting; submissive; (*gram*) denoting the voice of a verb whose subject receives the action.—**passively** *adv*.—**passivity** *n*.

passive resistance *n* nonviolent noncooperation with the authorities.

passive smoking *n* the involuntary inhalation of smoke from others' cigarettes.

Passover *n* (*Judaism*) a spring holiday, celebrating the liberation of the Israelites from slavery in Egypt.

passport *n* an official document giving the owner the right to travel abroad; something that secures admission or acceptance.

password *n* a secret term by which a person is recognized and allowed to pass; any means of admission; a sequence of characters required to access a computer system.

past *adj* completed; ended; in time already elapsed. * *adv* by. * *prep* beyond (in time, place, or amount). * *n* time that has gone by; the history of a person, group, etc; a personal background that is hidden or questionable.

pasta *n* the flour paste from which spaghetti, noodles, etc is made; any dish of cooked pasta.

paste *n* a soft plastic mixture; flour and water forming dough or adhesive; a fine glass used for artificial gems. * *vt* to attach with paste; (*sl*) to beat, thrash.

pasteboard *n* a stiff board made from sheets of paper pasted together. * *adj* flimsy.

pastel *n* a dried mixture of chalk, pigments and gum used for drawing; a drawing made with such; a soft, pale colour. * *adj* delicately coloured.

pastelist *n* an artist who uses pastels.

pastern *n* the part of a horse's foot between the fetlock and the hoof.

Pasteur treatment *n* (*med*) a method of inoculation against rabies by successive injections of vaccine.

pasteurize *vt* (*milk, etc*) to sterilize by heat or radiation to destroy harmful organisms.—**pasteurization** *n*.

pastiche *n* (*pl* **pastiches**) a literary, musical, or artistic work in imitation of another's style, or consisting of pieces from other sources.—*also* **pasticcio** (*pl* **pasticci**).

pastille, pastil *n* an aromatic or medicated lozenge.

pastime *n* a hobby; recreation, diversion.

pastor *n* a clergyman in charge of a congregation.

pastoral *adj* of shepherds or rural life; pertaining to spiritual care, esp of a congregation.—**pastorally** *adv*.

pastorale *n* a musical composition with a pastoral subject.

pastorate *n* the office or jurisdiction of a pastor; a collective term for pastors.

pastrami *n* highly seasoned smoked beef.

pastry *n* (*pl* **pastries**) dough made of flour, water, and fat used for making pies, tarts, etc; (*pl*) baked foods made with pastry.

pasturage *n* the right to graze animals; pasture.

pasture *n* land covered with grass for grazing livestock; the grass growing on it. * *vt* (*cattle, etc*) to put out to graze in a pasture.

pasty[1] *n* (*pl* **pasties**) meat, etc enclosed in pastry and baked.

pasty[2] *adj* (**pastier, pastiest**) like paste; pallid and unhealthy in appearance.—**pastily** *adv*.—**pastiness** *n*.

pat[1] *vti* (**patting, patted**) to strike gently with the palm of the hand or a flat object; to shape or apply by patting. * *n* a light tap, usu with the palm of the hand; a light sound; a small lump of shaped butter.

pat[2] *adj* apt; exact; glib.—*also adv*.

patagium *n* (*pl* **patagia**) (*zool*) the wing membrane of a bat.

patch *n* a piece of cloth used for mending; a scrap of material; a shield for an injured eye; a black spot of silk, etc worn on the face; an irregular spot on a surface; a plot of ground; a bandage; an area or spot. * vt to repair with a patch; to piece together; to mend in a makeshift way.—**patchable** adj.—**patcher** n.

patchouli, patchouly n an Asian plant which yields an essential oil from which a perfume is made.

patchwork n needlework made of pieces sewn together; something made of various bits.

patchy adj (**patchier, patchiest**) irregular; uneven; covered with patches.—**patchily** adv.—**patchiness** n.

pate n the head.

pâté n a rich spread made of meat, fish, herbs, etc.

pâté de foie gras n (pl **pâtés de foie gras**) a rich paste made from goose liver.

patella n (pl **patellae**) (anat) the kneecap.—**patellar** adj.

paten n (Christian Church) a plate used for the bread at the Eucharist.

patent adj plain; apparent; open to public inspection; protected by a patent. * n a government document, granting the exclusive right to produce and sell an invention, etc for a certain time; the right so granted; the thing protected by such a right. * vt to secure a patent for.—**patentable** adj.

patentee n a holder of a patent.

patent leather n leather with a hard, glossy finish.

patent medicine n a medicine made and sold under patent and available without a prescription.

patent office n an office which issues patents.

patently adv obviously, openly.

patentor n the grantor of a patent.

paterfamilias n (pl **patresfamilias**) the (male) head of a family.

paternal adj fatherly in disposition; related through the father.—**paternally** adv.

paternalism n a system that provides for human needs but allows no individual responsibility.—**paternalist** adj, n.—**paternalistic** adj.—**paternalistically** adv.

paternity n fatherhood; origin or descent from a father.

paternity suit n a lawsuit to determine whether a particular man is the father of a particular child.

paternity test n a blood test to establish whether a man is or is not the father of a particular child.

paternoster n the Lord's Prayer in Latin; every eleventh bead in a rosary; a fishing line with hooks at intervals; an elevator consisting of a continuously revolving belt of linked compartments.

path n (pl **paths**) a way worn by footsteps; a track for people on foot; a direction; a course of conduct.

-path n suffix denoting an expert in a specific area of medicine; denoting a person suffering from a specified disorder.

pathetic adj inspiring pity; (sl) uninteresting, inadequate.—**pathetically** adv.

pathetic fallacy n the attribution of human emotions to inanimate objects.

pathfinder n a person who discovers a way; a person who explores untraversed regions to mark out a new route; a person or thing that marks a spot; a radar device for homing on to a target or navigating.—**pathfinding** n.

patho- prefix disease.

pathogen n an agent, such as a microorganism, that causes disease.—**pathogenic** adj.

pathogenesis, pathogeny n the origin and development of a disease.—**pathogenetic** adj.

pathognomonic adj characteristic of a particular disease.

pathological, pathologic adj of pathology; of the nature of, caused or altered by disease; (inf) compulsive.—**pathologically** adv.

pathologist n a medical specialist who diagnoses by interpreting the changes in tissue and body fluid caused by a disease.

pathology n (pl **pathologies**) the branch of medicine that deals with the nature of disease, esp its functional and structural effects; any abnormal variation from a sound condition.

pathos n a quality that excites pity or sadness; an expression of deep feeling.

pathway n a path; (chem) a sequence of enzyme-catalyzed reactions.

-pathy n suffix feeling; disease; medical treatment.

patience n the capacity to endure or wait calmly; a card game for one (—also **solitaire**).

patient adj even-tempered; able to wait or endure calmly; persevering. * n a person receiving medical, dental, etc treatment.—**patiently** adv.

patina n a green incrustation on old bronze; a surface appearance of something grown beautiful by age or use; a superficial covering or exterior.

patio n (pl **patios**) an inner, usu roofless, courtyard; a paved area adjoining a house, for outdoor lounging, dining, etc.

patisserie n a pastry shop; pastries.

patois n (pl **patois**) a dialect.

patriarch n the father and head of a family or tribe; a man of great age and dignity.—**patriarchal** adj.

patriarchate n the office, rank or jurisdiction of a patriarch; people ruled by a patriarch.

patriarchy n (pl **patriarchies**) government by the head of a family, tribe, etc; a community ruled in this way.

patrician n (ancient Rome) a member of the nobility. * adj aristocratic; oligarchic.

patricide n the unlawful killing of one's father; a person who kills his or her father.—**patricidal** adj.

patrimony n (pl **patrimonies**) an estate or right inherited from a father or one's ancestors; an ecclesiastical endowment or estate.—**patrimonial** adj.

patriot n one who strongly supports and serves his or her country.—**patriotic** adj.—**patriotically** adv.

patriotism n love for or loyalty to one's country.

patristic, patristical adj pertaining to the theology and writings of the fathers of the early Christian church.

patrol vti (**patrolling, patrolled**) to walk around a building or area in order to watch, guard, inspect. * n the act of going the rounds; a unit of persons or vehicles employed for reconnaissance, security, or combat; a subdivision of a Scout or Guide group.—**patroller** n.

patrolman n (pl **patrolmen**) (chiefly US) a policeman who patrols a particular area.

patron n a regular client or customer; a person who sponsors and supports the arts, charities, etc; a protector.—**patronal** adj.

patronage n the support given or custom brought by a patron; clientele; business; trade; the power to grant political favours; such favours.

patronize vt to treat with condescension; to sponsor or support; to be a regular customer of.—**patronization** n.

patronizing adj condescending.—**patronizingly** adv.

patronymic adj derived from the name of an ancestor. * n a name derived from an ancestor.

patsy n (pl **patsies**) (sl) a gullible person; a sucker.

patten n a wooden shoe on a metal ring, worn as a protection from the damp.

patter[1] *vi* to make quick tapping sounds, as if by striking something; to run with light steps. * *n* the sound of tapping or quick steps.

patter[2] *vi* to talk rapidly and glibly; to mumble (prayers, etc) mechanically. * *vt* to repeat speech mechanically, to gabble. * *n* rapid speech, esp that of a salesman, comedian, etc; glib speech; chatter; jargon.

pattern *n* a decorative arrangement; a model to be copied; instructions to be followed to make something; a regular way of acting or doing; a predictable route, movement, etc. * *vt* to make or do in imitation of a pattern.—**patterned** *adj*.

patty *n* (*pl* **patties**) a small pie; a flat cake of ground meat, fish, etc, usu fried.

patulous *adj* (*bot*) spreading, extended.

paucity *n* fewness, lack of, scarcity.

paulownia *n* a member of a Japanese genus of trees, with heart-shaped leaves and purple flowers.

paunch *n* the belly, esp a potbelly.

paunchy *adj* (**paunchier, paunchiest**) having a big belly.—**paunchiness** *n*.

pauper *n* a very poor person; (*formerly*) a person dependent on charity.—**pauperism** *n*.

pauperize, pauperise *vt* to reduce to pauperism.

pause *n* a temporary stop, esp in speech, action or music. * *vi* to cease in action temporarily, wait; to hesitate.

pavage *n* a tax paid for paving streets.

pavane, pavan *n* (the music for) an old stately dance.

pave *vt* (*a road, etc*) to cover with concrete to provide a hard level surface; **pave the way** to prepare a smooth easy way; to facilitate development.—**paving** *n*.

pavement *n* flat slabs, tiles, etc forming a surface, esp on a public thoroughfare.

pavilion *n* an annexe; a temporary building for exhibitions; a large ornate tent.

pavonine *adj* pertaining to peacocks; resembling a peacock.

paw *n* a foot of a mammal with claws; (*sl*) a hand. * *vti* to touch, dig, hit, etc with paws; to maul; to handle clumsily or roughly.

pawky *adj* (**pawkier, pawkiest**) (*Scot*) having a dry sense of humour.

pawn[1] *n* the piece of lowest value in chess; a person used to advance another's purpose.

pawn[2] *vt* to deposit an article as security for a loan; to wager or risk. * *n* a thing pawned; the state of being given as a pawn.—**pawner** *n*.

pawnbroker *n* a person licensed to lend money at interest on personal property left with him as security.—**pawnbroking** *n*.

pawnshop *n* a pawnbroker's shop.

pawpaw *see* **papaw**.

paxwax *n* a strong tendon in an animal's neck.

pay *vti* (**paying, paid**) to give (money) to in payment for a debt, goods or services; to give in compensation; to yield a profit; to bear a cost; to suffer a penalty; (*homage, attention*) to give. * *n* payment for services or goods; salary, wages.—**paying** *adj*.—**payer** *n*.

payable *adj* that must be paid, due; to be paid on a specified date.

pay dirt *n* soil, gravel, etc worth mining for minerals; (*inf*) a source of wealth.

PAYE *abbr* = pay-as-you-earn; the deduction of income tax from wages or salaries at source.

payee *n* one to whom money is paid.

payload *n* cargo that earns revenue; the total load of an aircraft, spacecraft, satellite, etc.

paymaster *n* a person in charge of paying wages and salaries.

payment *n* the act of paying; amount paid; reward.

paynim *n* (*arch*) a heathen; a Muslim.

payola *n* a bribe paid for the clandestine promotion of a product, esp one paid to a disc jockey to play a particular record; a system of such bribes.

payphone *n* a coin-operated telephone.

payroll *n* a list of employees and their wages; the actual money for paying wages.

Pb (*chem symbol*) lead.

PBX *abbr* = private branch exchange.

PBS (*US*) *abbr* = Public Broadcasting System.

PC *abbr* = personal computer; police constable; political correctness, politically correct.

pc, p.c. *abbr* = per cent; postcard.

PCB *abbr* = polychlorinated biphenyl; printed circuit board.

P.D. (*US*) *abbr* = Police Department; postal district.

Pd (*chem symbol*) palladium.

pd *abbr* = paid.

p.d.q. *abbr* = pretty damn quick.

PE *abbr* = Prince Edward Island; physical education.

pea *n* the edible, round, green seed of a climbing leguminous annual plant.

peace *n* tranquillity, stillness; freedom from contention, violence or war; a treaty that ends a war.

peaceable *adj* inclined to peace.—**peaceably** *adv*.—**peaceableness** *n*.

Peace Corps *n* a US government organization that sends volunteers to work on social, educational, agricultural, etc projects in developing countries.

peace dividend *n* the increase in funds for domestic civil expenditure from a reduction in the defence budget.

peaceful *adj* having peace; tranquil; quiet.—**peacefully** *adv*.—**peacefulness** *n*.

peacemaker *n* one who makes or restores peace; one who reconciles enemies.—**peacemaking** *adj, n*.

peace offering *n* a conciliatory gift.

peace pipe *n* a tobacco pipe smoked by American Indians as a sign of peace.

peach *n* a round, sweet, juicy, downy-skinned stonefruit; the tree bearing it; a yellowish pink colour; (*sl*) a well-liked person or thing.

peachy *adj* (**peachier, peachiest**) of or resembling a peach; (*inf*) great, excellent.—**peachily** *adv*.—**peachiness** *n*.

peacock *n* (**peacocks, peacock**) a male peafowl with a large brilliantly coloured fan-like tail; a person who is a show-off.

peafowl *n* (**peafowls, peafowl**) a peacock or a peahen.

pea-green *adj* bright green.

peahen *n* a female peafowl.

peak *n* the summit of a mountain; the highest point; the pointed end of anything; maximum value; the eyeshade of a cap, visor. * *vti* (*politician, actor, etc*) to reach or cause to reach the height of power, popularity; (*prices*) to reach and stay at the highest level.

peaked *adj* pointed; having a peak; peaky.

peaky *adj* (**peakier, peakiest**) drawn, emaciated; sickly; peaked.

peal *n* a reverberating sound as of thunder, laughter, bells, etc; a set of bells, the changes rung on them. * *vti* to sound in peals, ring out.

pean *see* **paean**.

peanut *n* a leguminous plant with underground pods

containing edible seeds; the pod or any of its seeds; (*pl*) (*sl*) a trifling thing or amount.

peanut butter *n* a food paste made by grinding roasted peanuts.

pear *n* a common juicy fruit of tapering oval shape; the tree bearing it.

pearl *n* the lustrous white round gem produced by oysters; mother-of-pearl; anything resembling a pearl intrinsically or physically; one that is choice and precious; a bluish medium grey. * *vti* to fish for pearls; to form drops (on), to bespangle.—**pearler** *n*.—**pearliness** *n*.

pearl button *n* a button covered with mother-of-pearl.

pearl diver *n* a person who dives for pearl oysters.

pearl oyster *n* any of various marine bivalve molluscs that yield pearls.

pearly *adj* (**pearlier, pearliest**) clear, lustrous, like a pearl; covered with pearls; bluish grey. * *n* (*pl* **pearlies**) (*pl*) a London costermonger's dress covered with pearl buttons.

Pearly Gates *npl* (*inf*) the gates of Heaven.

pearmain *n* a variety of apple.

peasant *n* (*inf*) a countryman or countrywoman; an agricultural labourer; (*derog*) a lout.

peasantry *n* peasants as a class.

pease *n* (*arch*) a pea.

peashooter *n* a toy blowpipe through which peas, etc, are blown.

peasouper *n* (*sl*) a thick yellow fog.

peat *n* decayed vegetable matter from bogs, which is dried and cut into blocks for fuel or used as a fertilizer.—**peaty** *adj*.

pebble *n* a small rounded stone; an irregular, grainy surface.—**pebbled** *adj*.—**pebbly** *adj*.

pecan *n* a hickory tree widely grown in the US and Mexico for its edible nuts; its wood; its thin-shelled nut.

peccable *adj* liable to sin.—**peccability** *n*.

peccadillo *n* (*pl* **peccadilloes, peccadillos**) a trifling misdeed, indiscretion.

peccary *n* (*pl* **peccaries, peccary**) an American wild piglike mammal.

peccavi *n* (*pl* **peccavis**) a confession of guilt.

peck *vt* to strike with the beak or a pointed object; to pick at one's food; (*inf*) to kiss lightly; to nag.—*also n*.

pecker *n* something, esp a bird, that pecks; (*sl*) penis.

pecking order *n* a social hierarchy in groups of some birds (eg hens), characterized by the pecking of those lower in the scale and submitting to being pecked by those higher; any social hierarchy.

peckish *adj* (*inf*) hungry; irritable.—**peckishly** *adv*.—**peckishness** *n*.

pecten *n* (*pl* **pectens, pectines**) (*zool*) a comblike membrane on the eyes of birds and some reptiles.

pectin *n* a carbohydrate found in fruits and vegetables, yielding a gel that is used to set jellies.—**pectic** *adj*.

pectoral *adj* of or relating to the breast, chest. * *n* the muscle in the chest; something worn on the breast.

peculate *vt* to appropriate money entrusted to one's care, to embezzle.—**peculation** *n*.—**peculator** *n*.

peculiar *adj* belonging exclusively (to); special; distinct; characteristic; strange.—**peculiarly** *adv*.

peculiarity *n* (*pl* **peculiarities**) an idiosyncrasy; a characteristic; an oddity.

pecuniary *adj* of or consisting of money.—**pecuniarily** *adv*.

pedagogue *n* a schoolteacher.—**pedagogic, pedagogical** *adj*.

pedagogy *n* the art or science of teaching.

pedal[1] *n* a lever operated by the foot. * *vt* (**pedalling, pedalled** *or* **pedaling, pedaled**) to operate or propel by pressing pedals with the foot.—**pedaller, pedaler** *n*.

pedal[2] *adj* (*zool*) pertaining to the foot or feet.

pedalo *n* (*pl* **pedalos**) a small pedal-operated pleasure boat.

pedant *n* a person who attaches too much importance to insignificant details.

pedantic *adj* of, relating to, or being a pedant; narrowly learned.—**pedantically** *adv*.

pedantry *n* (*pl* **pedantries**) an ostentatious display of learning; the state of being a pedant.

pedate *adj* (*bot*) having lateral sections divided into lobes; (*zool*) having, or resembling, feet.

peddle *vt* to go from place to place selling small items; to sell (drugs, etc) illegally.

peddler *n* a person who peddles goods; a person who sells drugs illegally.

pederast *n* a person who practises pederasty.

pederasty *n* sex between a man and a boy.

pedestal *n* the base that supports a column, statue, etc. * *vt* to set on a pedestal; to serve as a pedestal for.

pedestrian *adj* on foot; dull, commonplace. * *n* a person who walks.

pedestrianism *n* walking, or a fondness for walking; the quality of being dull or commonplace.

pedestrianize *vti* to convert (an area) for use by pedestrians only.—**pedestrianization** *n*.

pedicab *n* a pedal-driven rickshaw.

pedicular, pediculous *adj* pertaining to lice; infested with lice.—**pediculosis** *n*.

pedicure *n* cosmetic care of the feet, toes, and nails; a person trained to care for feet in this way.

pediform *adj* foot-shaped.

pedigree *n* a line of descent of an animal; a recorded purity of breed of an individual; a genealogy; lineage; derivation. * *adj* having a known ancestry.—**pedigreed** *adj*.

pediment *n* a triangular ornament crowning the front of a classical building, esp a Greek temple.—**pedimental, pedimented** *adj*.

pedometer *n* an instrument for measuring the distance walked by recording the number of steps taken.

peduncle *n* a flower stalk.—**peduncular** *adj*.

pedunculate, pedunculated *adj* having, or growing upon, a peduncle.

pee *vi* (*sl*) to urinate. * *n* urination; urine.

peek *vi* to look quickly or furtively.—*also n*.

peekaboo *n* a child's game in which one person hides behind his or her hands then peeps out suddenly, shouting, "peekaboo!"

peel *vt* to remove skin or rind from; to bare. * *vi* to flake off, as skin or paint. * *n* rind, esp that of fruit and vegetables.—**peeling** *n*.

peeler *n* a device for peeling; (*sl*) a stripteaser.

peen *n* the pointed or thin end of a hammer-head.

peep[1] *vi* to make shrill noises as a young bird. * *n* a peeping sound.

peep[2] *vi* to look hastily or furtively; to look through a slit or narrow opening; to be just showing. * *n* a furtive or hurried glance, a glimpse; (*of day*) the first appearance.

peeper *n* one who peeps; (*sl*) the eye; (*sl*) a private detective.

440

peephole n a small hole, esp in a door, to spy through.

peeping Tom n a person who peeps furtively, a voyeur.

peepshow n a small show, esp of erotic pictures, viewed through a hole with a lens; a live show with a nude model, viewed from a booth.

peepul n an Indian fig tree, sacred to Buddhists.—also **pipal**.

peer[1] vi to look closely; to look with difficulty; to peep out.

peer[2] n an equal in rank, ability, etc; a nobleman.—**peeress** nf.

peerage n the rank or title of a peer; peers collectively; a book with a list of peers.

peer group n a group of people of the same age, background, education, interests, etc.

peerless adj having no equal, matchless.

peeve vt (inf) to annoy.

peeved adj annoyed, resentful.

peevish adj fretful, irritable.—**peevishly** adv.—**peevishness** n.

peg n a tapered piece (of wood) for securing or hanging things on, for marking position; a predetermined level at which (a price) is fixed; (mus) one of the movable parts for tuning the string of an instrument. * vti (**pegging, pegged**) to fasten or mark with a peg; (a price) to keep steady; (with **away at**) to work steadily, persevere.

Pegasus n (Greek myth) the winged horse ridden by Bellerophon.

peignoir n a woman's dressing gown.

pejorative adj (word, etc) disparaging, derogatory. * n a disparaging word.—**pejoratively** adv.

peke n (sl) a Pekingese dog.

Pekingese, Pekinese n (pl **Pekingese, Pekinese**) a breed of small dog with long, silky hair, short legs, and a pug nose.

pekoe n a scented black Chinese tea.

pelage n the hair, wool or fur of an animal.

pelagian adj (marine life) of or inhabiting the open sea.—also n.—**pelagic** adj.

pelargonium n a member of a widely cultivated genus of flowering plants, including geraniums.

pelf n (derog) money, wealth.

pelican n a large fish-eating waterbird with an expandable pouched bill.

pelisse n a woman's long cloak, usu trimmed with fur.

pellagra n a disease affecting the skin and nervous system caused by a deficiency of nicotinic acid.—**pellagrous** adj.

pellet n a small ball of paper, bread, etc; a pill; a small ball of hair, bones, etc regurgitated by a bird of prey; a piece of shot. * vt to form into pellets.

pellicle n a thin skin or film.—**pellicular** adj.

pellitory n (pl **pellitories**) a European flowering plant, growing in walls.

pell-mell adv, adj in a disorderly rush; confusedly; headlong.

pellucid adj (water, etc) transparent; (speech, writing, etc) clear, lucid.—**pellucidity, pellucidness** n.

pelmet n a canopy for a window frame to hide a curtain rail, etc; a valance.

pelota n a Basque ball game similar to tennis, played with basket-shaped rackets against a wall.

pelt[1] vt to throw missiles, or words, at. * vi (rain) to fall heavily; to hurry, rush. * n a rush.—**pelter** n.

pelt[2] n a usu undressed skin of an animal with its hair, wool, or fur.

peltry n (pl **peltries**) a collective term for the pelts of animals.

pelvis n (pl **pelvises, pelves**) the bony cavity that joins the lower limbs to the body; the bones forming this.—**pelvic** adj.

pemmican, pemican n a cake of dried lean meat formerly used by North American Indians; a mixture of beef and suet used as emergency rations.

pemphigus n a rare skin disease, characterized by watery blisters.—**pemphigoid, pemphigous** adj.

pen[1] n an implement used with ink for writing or drawing. * vt (**penning, penned**) to write, compose.

pen[2] n a small enclosure for cattle, poultry, etc; a small place of confinement. * vt (**penning, penned**) to enclose in a pen, shut up.

pen[3] n a female swan.

pen[4] n (sl) a penitentiary.

penal adj relating to, liable to, or prescribing punishment; punitive.—**penally** adv.

penal code n a code of laws concerning crimes and offences and their punishment.

penalize vt to impose a penalty; to put under a disadvantage.—**penalization** n.

penalty n (pl **penalties**) a punishment attached to an offence; suffering or loss as a result of one's own mistake; a disadvantage imposed for breaking a rule as in sports; a fine.

penalty area n (soccer) the area in front of goal in which a foul by a defending player results in the award of a penalty kick.

penalty box n (ice hockey) an area of the ice where players are sent as a penalty.

penance n voluntary suffering to atone for a sin; a sacramental rite consisting of confession, absolution, and penance. * vt to impose a penance on.

pence see **penny**.

penchant n inclination, strong liking (for).

pencil n a pointed rod-shaped instrument with a core of graphite or crayon for writing, drawing, etc; a set of convergent light rays or straight lines; a fine paintbrush. * vt (**pencilling, pencilled** or **penciling, penciled**) to write, draw, or colour with a pencil; (with **in**) to commit tentatively.—**penciller, penciler** n.

pendant, pendent n a hanging ornament, esp a jewel on a necklace, bracelet, etc; a light-fitting suspended from a ceiling. * adj (usu **pendent**) hanging; projecting; undecided.—**pendency** n.

pendentive n (archit) a portion of a dome supported by a single pillar.

pending adj undecided; unfinished; imminent. * prep during; until, awaiting.

pendragon n (hist) a chief of the ancient Britons or Welsh.

pendulous adj hanging downwards and swinging freely.—**pendulously** adv.

pendulum n a weight suspended from a fixed point so as to swing freely; such a device used to regulate the movement of a clock; something that swings to and fro.

peneplain, peneplane n (geol) a tract of land which is almost a plain.

penetrable adj able to be penetrated.—**penetrability** n.

penetralia npl the inner parts of a temple, etc; mysteries.

penetrant adj penetrating. * n something which, or someone who, penetrates.

penetrate *vti* to thrust, force a way into or through something; to pierce; to permeate; to understand.—**penetrator** *n.*—**penetrative** *adj.*

penetrating *adj* acute, discerning; (*voice*) easily heard through other sounds.—**penetratingly** *adv.*

penetration *n* the capability, act, or action of penetrating; acute insight.

penguin *n* a flightless, marine bird with black and white plumage, usu found in the Antarctic.

penicillate *adj* (*biol*) having, or forming, small tufts.

penicillin *n* an antibiotic produced naturally and synthetically from moulds.

penile *adj* of, like, or affecting the penis.

peninsula *n* a piece of land almost surrounded by sea.—**peninsular** *adj.*

penis *n* (*pl* **penises, penes**) the male copulative and urinary organ in mammals.

penitence *n* sorrow for committing a sin, repentance.

penitent *adj* feeling regret for sin, repentant, contrite. * *n* a person who atones for sin.—**penitently** *adv.*

penitential *adj* of or expressing penance; being penitent.—**penitentially** *adv.*

penitentiary *n* (*pl* **penitentiaries**) (*US*) a state or federal prison. * *adj* pertaining to penance; pertaining to the reformatory treatment of prisoners.

penknife *n* (*pl* **penknives**) a small knife, usu with one or more folding blades, that fits into the pocket.

penman *n* (*pl* **penmen**) a writer.

penmanship *n* the art, or style, of writing.

Penn, Penna *abbr* = Pennsylvania.

pen name *n* a literary pseudonym.—*also* **nom de plume.**

pennant *n* a long tapering flag used for identifying vessels and for signalling; such a flag symbolizing a championship.

penniless *adj* having no money; poor.—**pennilessly** *adv.*—**pennilessness** *n.*

pennon *n* a small, pointed or swallow-tailed flag of a medieval knight; a long tapering streamer on a ship.

penny *n* (*pl* **pence** *denoting sum,* **pennies** *denoting separate coins*) a bronze coin of the UK worth one hundredth of a pound; (*formerly*) a bronze coin of the UK worth one twelfth of a shilling, or one two hundred and fortieth of a pound; (*US*) a one cent coin.

pennyroyal *n* an aromatic plant of the mint family.

pennyweight *n* a weight, equivalent to 24 grains or $1/20$ of an ounce (troy).

pennywort *n* a kind of round-leafed plant, growing variously in walls or in marshes.

pennyworth *n* a penny's worth (of a purchase); a small amount.

penology *n* the study of the punishment and prevention of crime.—*also* **poenology.**—**penological** *adj.*—**penologist** *n.*

pen pal *n* a friend with whom one is in contact only through correspondence.

pensile *adj* suspended; pendulous.

pension *n* a periodic payment to a person beyond retirement age, or widowed, or disabled; a periodic payment in consideration of past services. * *vt* to grant a pension to; (*with* off) to dismiss or retire from service with a pension.—**pensionable** *adj.*

pensionary *adj* by way of pension. * *n* (*pl* **pensionaries**) a pensioner.

pensioner *n* a person who receives a pension; a senior citizen.

pensive *adj* thoughtful, musing; wistful, melancholic.—**pensively** *adv.*—**pensiveness** *n.*

pentacle *see* **pentagram.**

pentad *n* a group of five; the number five.

pentadactyl *adj* (*zool*) having five fingers or toes.

pentagon *n* (*geom*) a polygon with five sides; (*with cap*) the pentagonal headquarters of the US defence establishment; the US military leadership collectively.—**pentagonal** *adj.*

pentagram *n* a five-pointed star, often used as a magic symbol.—*also* **pentacle.**

pentahedron *n* (*pl* **pentahedrons, pentahedra**) a solid figure with five faces.

pentamerous *adj* (*bot, zool*) with five parts.

pentameter *n* a verse of five metrical feet.

pentangle *n* a pentagram.

Pentateuch *n* the collective name for the first five books of the Old Testament.

pentathlon *n* an athletic contest involving participation by each contestant in five different events.—**pentathlete** *n.*

pentatonic *adj* (*mus*) of five notes.

pentavalent *adj* (*chem*) with a valency of five.

Pentecost *n* a Christian festival on the seventh Sunday after Easter; Whit Sunday.

Pentecostal *adj* denoting a mainly Protestant Christian movement, now with various organized forms, emphasizing the immediate presence of God in the Holy Spirit; of Pentecost or the influence of the Holy Spirit. * *n* a member of a Pentecostal church.—**Pentecostalist** *adj, n.*

penthouse *n* an apartment on the roof or in the top floor of a building.

pentstemon *n* a flowering garden plant of the family including the beard-tongues.—*also* (*chiefly US*) **penstemon.**

pent-up *adj* (*emotion*) repressed, confined.

penult *n* the penultimate syllable of a word. * *adj* last but one.

penultimate *adj* last but one.—*also adj.*

penumbra *n* (*pl* **penumbrae, penumbras**) a shaded region around the shadow of an opaque object, esp the shadow of the moon or earth in an eclipse; the lighter outer part of a sunspot; (*art*) the boundary of light and shade in a picture.—**penumbral** *adj.*

penurious *adj* grudging with money, stingy; poor; scanty.—**penuriously** *adv.*—**penuriousness** *n.*

penury *n* (*pl* **penuries**) extreme poverty; want.

peon *n* a Spanish American labourer; (*formerly*) a Spanish American labourer compelled to work to pay off debts.

peonage, peonism *n* the condition of being a peon; the system of compelling someone to work for a creditor to pay off debts.

peony *n* (*pl* **peonies**) a plant with large, showy, red, pink or white flowers.

people *n* the body of enfranchised citizens of a state; a person's family, relatives; the persons of a certain place, group, or class; persons considered indefinitely; human beings; (*pl*) all the persons of a racial or ethnic group, typically having a common language, institutions, homes, and culture. * *vt* to populate with people.

pep *n* (*inf*) energy, vigour; bounce. * *vt* (**pepping, pepped**) (*usu with* up) to enliven by injecting with pep.

pepper *n* a sharp, hot condiment made from the fruit of various plants; the fruit of the pepper plant, which can be red, yellow, or green, sweet or hot, and is eaten as a vegetable. * *vt* to sprinkle or flavour with pepper; to hit with small shot; to pelt; to beat.

peppercorn *n* a dried pepper berry.

pepper mill *n* hand mill for grinding peppercorns.

peppermint *n* a pungent and aromatic mint plant; its oil used for flavouring; a sweet flavoured with peppermint.

pepperoni *n* a spicy beef and pork sausage.

pepperwort *n* a form of aquatic or marsh fern; a type of cress.

peppery *adj* of, like, full of, pepper; fiery; hot-tempered.—**pepperiness** *n*.

peppy *adj* (**peppier, peppiest**) full of bounce; lively.—**peppiness** *n*.

pepsin, pepsine *n* a digestive enzyme contained in gastric juice.

pep talk *n* (*inf*) a vigorous talk made with the intention of arousing enthusiasm, increasing confidence, etc.

peptic *adj* of or promoting digestion; of, producing, or caused by the action of the digestive juices.

peptic ulcer *n* an ulcer of the stomach lining or duodenum.

peptone *n* a product of the action of pepsin on proteins.

peptonize *vt* to convert into peptone.

per *prep* for or in each; through, by, by means of; (*inf*) according to.

peradventure *adv* (*arch*) by chance; perhaps.

perambulate *vti* to walk around.—**perambulation** *n*.—**perambulatory** *adj*.

perambulator *n* one who or that which perambulates; (*Brit formal*) a pram.

per annum *adv* yearly; each year.

percale *n* a cotton fabric, often used for sheets.

per capita *adj, adv* of or for each person.

perceive *vt* to become aware of, apprehend, through the senses; to recognize.—**perceivable** *adj*.—**perceivably** *adv*.

per cent, percent *adv* in, for each hundred. * *n* a percentage.

percentage *n* rate per hundred parts; a proportion; (*inf*) profit, gain.

percept *n* something which is perceived.

perceptible *adj* able to be perceived; discernible.—**perceptibility** *n*.—**perceptibly** *adv*.

perception *n* the act or faculty of perceiving; discernment; insight; a way of perceiving, view.—**perceptional** *adj*.

perceptive *adj* able to perceive; observant.—**perceptively** *adv*.—**perceptivity, perceptiveness** *n*.

perch[1] *n* (*pl* **perch, perches**) a spiny-finned chiefly freshwater edible fish.

perch[2] *n* a pole on which birds roost or alight; an elevated seat or position. * *vti* to alight, rest, on a perch; to balance (oneself) on; to set in a high position.

perchance *adv* (*arch*) by chance; perhaps.

Percheron *n* a sturdy breed of draughthorse.

percipient *adj* perceiving; perceptive. * *n* a person who perceives.—**percipience** *n*.

percolate *vt* (*liquid*) to pass through a filter or pores; to brew coffee. * *vi* to ooze through; to spread gradually.—**percolation** *n*.

percolator *n* a coffeepot in which boiling water is forced through ground coffee beans.

percuss *vt* to tap sharply; (*med*) to tap (the patient's body) gently to find out the condition of an internal organ by sound.

percussion *n* impact, collision; musical instruments played by striking with sticks or hammers, eg cymbals, drums, etc; such instruments regarded as a section of an orchestra; (*med*) tapping the body to discover the condition of an organ by the sounds.—**percussive** *adj*.

percussionist *n* a person who plays a percussion instrument.

percutaneous *adj* (*med*) done through the skin.

per diem *adv, adj* every day. * *n* a daily allowance, as for expenses.

perdition *n* utter loss of the soul; eternal damnation; (*arch*) total destruction, ruin.

peregrinate *vti* to travel, roam about.—**peregrinator** *n*.—**peregrination** *n*.

peregrine *n* a type of falcon common to most areas of the world.

peremptory *adj* urgent; absolute; dogmatic; dictatorial.—**peremptorily** *adv*.—**peremptoriness** *n*.

perennial *adj* perpetual; lasting throughout the year. * *n* (*bot*) a plant lasting more than two years.—**perennially** *adv*.

perestroika *n* the Russian word for "reform, reconstruction," applied to the policy, initiated by President Gorbachev of the former USSR, of dismantling the monolithic state institutions and replacing them with democratic forms of legislation and administration.—**perestroikan** *adj*.

perfect *adj* faultless; exact; excellent; complete. * *n* (*gram*) a verb form expressing completed action or designating a present state that is the result of an action in the past. * *vt* to improve; to finish; to make fully accomplished in anything.—**perfecter** *n*.—**perfectness** *n*.

perfectible *adj* capable of being made perfect.—**perfectibility** *n*.

perfection *n* the act of perfecting; the quality or condition of being perfect; great excellence; faultlessness; the highest degree; a perfect person or thing.

perfectionist *n* one who demands the highest standard.—**perfectionism** *n*.

perfectly *adv* thoroughly, completely; quite well; in a perfect manner.

perfecto *n* (*pl* **perfectos**) a large cigar, tapered at both ends.

perfervid *adj* (*arch*) very fervid, ardent.

perfidious *adj* treacherous, faithless; deceitful.—**perfidiously** *adv*.—**perfidiousness** *n*.

perfidy *n* (*pl* **perfidies**) breach of faith; treachery.

perfoliate *adj* (*bot*) with a stalk which apparently passes through the leaf.

perforate *vt* to pierce; to make a hole or row of holes, by boring through. * *adj* perforated.—**perforatory** *adj*.—**perforator** *n*.

perforation *n* the act of perforating; the condition of being perforated; a hole; a row of holes to facilitate tearing.

perforce *adv* (*arch*) by necessity.

perform *vti* to carry out, do; to put into effect; to act; to execute; to act before an audience; to play a musical instrument.—**performable** *adj*.—**performing** *adj*.

performance *n* the act of performing; a dramatic or musical production; an act or action; (*inf*) a fuss; the capabilities of a vehicle, aircraft, etc. * *adj* high-performance.

performer *n* a person who performs, esp one who entertains an audience.

perfume *n* a pleasing odour; fragrance; a mixture containing fragrant essential oils and a fixative. * *vt* to scent; to put perfume on.—**perfumer** *n*.

perfumery *n* (*pl* **perfumeries**) a place where perfume is sold; perfume in general.

perfunctory *adj* superficial, hasty; done merely as a matter of form, half-hearted; performed carelessly; indifferent.—**perfunctorily** *adv*.—**perfunctoriness** *n*.

perfuse *vt* (*with* **with**) to suffuse, permeate.—**perfusion** *n*.—**perfusive** *adj*.

pergola *n* an arbour or walk arched by a latticework structure supporting climbing plants.

perhaps *adv* possibly, maybe.

peri- *prefix* around; near.

perianth *n* the outer part of a flower, comprising the calyx and corolla together.

periapt *n* an amulet.

pericarditis *n* inflammation of the pericardium.

pericardium *n* (*pl* **pericardia**) the membrane enclosing the heart.—**pericardiac, pericardial** *adj*.

pericarp *n* the part of a fruit developed from the wall of the ovary.—**pericarpial** *adj*.

perichondrium *n* (*pl* **perichondria**) the membrane covering a cartilage.

periclase *n* magnesium oxide as a mineral in crystal or grain form.

pericranium *n* (*pl* **pericrania**) the membrane surrounding the cranium.

peridot *n* a pale green semi-precious form of olivine.

perigee *n* the point of the moon's, or a planet's, orbit, when it is nearest the earth.—**perigean** *adj*.

perihelion *n* (*pl* **perihelia**) the point of a planet's or comet's orbit when it is nearest the sun.

peril *n* danger, jeopardy; risk, hazard.

perilous *adj* dangerous.—**perilously** *adv*.

perimeter *n* a boundary around an area; (*math*) the curve or line bounding a closed figure; the length of this.—**perimetric** *adj*.—**perimetry** *n*.

perineum *n* the area between the genitals and the anus.—**perineal** *adj*.

period *n* a portion of time; menstruation; an interval of time as in an academic day, playing time in a game, etc; an age or era in history, epoch; a stage in life; (*gram*) a full stop (.); (*astron*) a planet's time of revolution. * *interj* an exclamation used for emphasis.

periodic *adj* relating to a period; recurring at regular intervals, cyclic; intermittent.—**periodically** *adv*.—**periodicity** *n*.

periodical *adj* periodic. * *n* a magazine, etc issued at regular intervals.

periodic table *n* a list of chemical elements tabulated by their atomic number.

periodontics *n sing* the branch of dentistry dealing with disorders of the gums and tissues around the teeth.—**periodontal** *adj*.—**periodontist** *n*.

periosteum *n* (*pl* **periostea**) the membrane covering the bones.

periostitis *n* inflammation of the periosteum.

peripatetic *adj* itinerant; (*teacher*) travelling from one school to another.—*also n*.

peripheral *adj* incidental, superficial; relating to a periphery; (*equipment*) for connection to a computer. * *n* a device such as a printer, scanner, etc used with a computer.—**peripherally** *adv*.

periphery *n* (*pl* **peripheries**) the outer surface or boundary of an area; the outside surface of anything.

periphrasis *n* (*pl* **periphrases**) a roundabout way of speech; circumlocution.

periphrastic *adj* using periphrasis; circumlocutory.—**periphrastically** *adv*.

peripteral *adj* (*archit*) with a row of columns on every side.

periscope *n* a device with mirrors that enables the viewer to see objects above or around an obstacle or above water, as from a submarine.

periscopic *adj* (*lens*) with a view around; of a periscope.—**periscopically** *adv*.

perish *vi* to be destroyed or ruined; to die, esp violently; (*rubber, etc*) to deteriorate, rot. * *vt* to cause to rot or perish.

perishable *adj* liable to spoil or decay. * *n* something perishable, esp food.—**perishability** *n*.

peritoneum *n* (*pl* **peritoneums, peritonea**) a membrane that lines the walls of the abdomen.—**peritoneal** *adj*.

peritonitis *n* inflammation of the peritoneum.—**peritonitic** *adj*.

periwinkle[1] *n* any of various edible small marine gastropods with spiralled shells.

periwinkle[2] *n* any of various evergreen trailing plants with blue or white flowers.

perjure *vt* to commit perjury, swear falsely.—**perjurer** *n*.

perjury *n* (*pl* **perjuries**) (*law*) the crime of giving false witness under oath, swearing to what is untrue.

perk[1] *n* (*usu pl*) (*inf*) a perquisite.

perk[2] *vti* (*usu with* **up**) to recover self-confidence; to become lively or cheerful; to prick up, as of a dog's ears; to smarten up.

perky *adj* (**perkier, perkiest**) pert, cheeky; lively, jaunty.—**perkily** *adv*.—**perkiness** *n*.

perm *n* a straightening or curling of hair by use of chemicals or heat lasting through many washings. *vt* (*hair*) to give a perm to.—*also* **permanent wave**.

permafrost *n* subsoil that is permanently frozen.

permanence *n* the condition or quality of being permanent.

permanency *n* (*pl* **permanencies**) permanence; a person or thing that is permanent.—**permanently** *adv*.

permanent *adj* lasting, or intended to last, indefinitely.

permanent wave *n* a perm.

permanganate *n* a salt of an acid of manganese, esp permanganate of potash.

permeable *adj* admitting the passage of a fluid.—**permeability** *n*.—**permeably** *adv*.

permeate *vti* to fill every part of, saturate; to pervade, be diffused (through); to pass through by osmosis.—**permeation** *n*.

permissible *adj* allowable.—**permissibility** *n*.

permission *n* authorization; consent.

permissive *adj* allowing permission; lenient; sexually indulgent.—**permissively** *adv*.—**permissiveness** *n*.

permit *vti* (**permitting, permitted**) to allow to be done; to authorize; to give opportunity. * *n* a licence.—**permitter** *n*.

permutation *n* any radical alteration; a change in the order of a series; any of the total number of groupings within a group; an ordered arrangement of a set of objects.—**permutational** *adj*.

permute *vt* to put into a different order.

pernicious *adj* destructive; very harmful.—**perniciously** *adv*.—**perniciousness** *n*.

pernickety *see* **persnickety**.

perorate *vi* to speak at length.

peroration *n* the final part of a speech or discourse.

peroxide n hydrogen peroxide; a colourless liquid used as an antiseptic and as a bleach.

perpendicular adj upright, vertical; (geom) at right angles (to). * n a perpendicular line, position or style.—**perpendicularity** n.—**perpendicularly** adv.

perpetrate vt (something evil, criminal, etc) to do; (a blunder, etc) to commit.—**perpetration** n.—**perpetrator** n.

perpetual adj continuous; everlasting; (plant) blooming continuously throughout the season.—**perpetually** adv.

perpetuate vt to cause to continue; to make perpetual.—**perpetuation** n.—**perpetuator** n.

perpetuity n (pl **perpetuities**) endless duration, eternity; perpetual continuance; an annuity payable forever.

perplex vt to puzzle, bewilder, confuse; to complicate.

perplexity n (pl **perplexities**) bewilderment, a being at a loss; a perplexing thing, a dilemma.

perquisite n an expected or promised privilege, gain, or profit incidental to regular wages or salary; a tip, gratuity; something claimed as an exclusive right.—also **perk**.

perron n a flight of steps outside a building, leading to the first floor.

perry n (pl **perries**) a cider-like drink made from pears.

per se adv by itself; by its very nature, intrinsically.

persecute vt to harass, oppress, esp for reasons of race, religion, etc; to worry persistently.—**persecutor** n.

persecution n a persecuting or being persecuted; unfair or cruel treatment for reasons of race, religion, etc; a time of persecution.

perseverance n persisting efforts of belief, esp in the face of opposition; steadfastness; (Christianity) continuance in grace.—**perseverant** adj.

persevere vi to persist, maintain effort, steadfastly, esp in face of difficulties.—**perseveringly** adv.

persiennes npl outside window shutters with horizontal louvres.

persiflage n frivolous talk, banter.

persimmon n one of a species of tropical American trees; the fruit of such a tree.

persist vi to continue in spite of obstacles or opposition; to persevere; to last.—**persister** n.

persistence, persistency n a persisting; tenacity of purpose.

persistent adj persevering; stubborn.—**persistently** adv.

persnickety adj (inf) fussy, fastidious; over-attentive to detail.—also **pernickety**.

person n (pl **persons**) a human being, individual; the body (including clothing) of a human being; (in a play) a character; one who is recognized by law as the subject of rights and duties; (gram) one of the three classes of personal pronouns and verb forms, referring to the person(s) speaking, spoken to, or spoken of.

persona n (pl **personae**) a person; a character in a play, etc; (pl) public role or image.

personable adj pleasing in personality and appearance.—**personableness** n.—**personably** adv.

personage n a distinguished person.

persona grata n (pl **personae gratae**) a person who is acceptable or welcome, esp a diplomat to a foreign government.

personal adj concerning a person's private affairs, or his or her character, habits, body, etc; done in person; (law) of property that is movable; (gram) denoting person.

personality n (pl **personalities**) one's individual characteristics; excellence or distinction of social and personal traits; a person with such qualities; a celebrity.

personalize vt to mark with name, initials, etc; to endow with personal characteristics; to take personally; to personify.—**personalization** n.

personally adv in person; in one's own opinion; as though directed to oneself.

personalty n (pl **personalties**) (law) personal property.

persona non grata n (pl **personae non gratae**) a person who is not acceptable or welcome, esp to a foreign government.

personate vt to play the part of (in a play etc); (law) to pretend to be (someone else) for fraudulent purposes.—**personation** n.—**personator** n.

personification n representation of an abstract idea or a thing as a person; an embodiment, a type; a perfect example.

personify vt (**personifying, personified**) to think of, represent, as a person; to typify.—**personifier** n.

personnel n the employees of an organization or company; the department that hires them.

perspective n objectivity; the art of drawing so as to give an impression of relative distance or solidity; a picture so drawn; relation, proportion, between parts of a subject; vista, prospect. * adj of or in perspective.

perspicacious adj of clear understanding; shrewd; discerning.—**perspicaciously** adv.—**perspicacity** n.

perspicuous adj clearly expressed, lucid.—**perspicuity** n.

perspiration n the salty fluid excreted on to the surface of the skin, sweat; the act of perspiring.

perspire vti to excrete (moisture) through the pores of the skin to cool the body, to sweat.—**perspiringly** adv.

persuadable, persuasible adj able to be persuaded.—**persuadability, persuasibility** n.

persuade vt to convince; to induce by argument, reasoning, advice, etc.—**persuader** n.

persuasion n the act of persuading; a conviction or opinion; a system of religious beliefs; a group adhering to such a system.

persuasive adj able to persuade; influencing the mind or emotions.—**persuasively** adv.—**persuasiveness** n.

pert adj impudent, cheeky; sprightly.—**pertly** adv.—**pertness** n.

pertain vi to belong to; to be appropriate to; to have reference to.

pertinacious adj persistent; unyielding; obstinate.—**pertinacity, pertinaciousness** n.

pertinent adj relevant, apposite; to the point.—**pertinence** n.—**pertinently** adv.

perturb vt to trouble; to agitate; to throw into confusion; (astron) to cause to undergo perturbation.—**perturbable** adj.—**perturbably** adv.—**perturbingly** adv.

perturbation n the state of being troubled, mental agitation; (astron) an irregularity or deviation in a regular orbit produced by some additional force.

peruse vt to read carefully, to examine.—**perusal** n.

pervade vt to permeate or spread through; to be rife among.—**pervasion** n.

pervasive adj able or tending to pervade.—**pervasively** adv.—**pervasiveness** n.

perverse adj deviating from right or truth; persisting in error; wayward; contrary.—**perversely** adv.—**perverseness** n.

perversion n an abnormal way of obtaining sexual gratification, eg sadism; a perverted form or usage of something.

perversity n (pl **perversities**) a being perverse; a disposition to thwart or annoy; a perverse act.

pervert vt to corrupt; to misuse; to distort. * n a person who is sexually perverted.—**perverter** n.—**pervertible** adj.

perverted adj wrong; harmful; unnatural; sexually deviant.—**pervertedly** adv.

pervious adj giving passage, permeable; open to new ideas.

pesade n (dressage) a position in which the horse is standing on its hind legs and raises its forelegs.

peseta n the unit of currency in Spain.

pesky adj (**peskier, peskiest**) (inf) troublesome, annoying.

peso n (pl **pesos**) a unit of currency in several Latin American countries and the Philippines.

pessary n (pl **pessaries**) (med) a surgical appliance or suppository inserted into the vagina.

pessimism n a tendency to see in the world what is bad rather than good; a negative outlook that always expects the worst.—**pessimist** n.—**pessimistic** adj.—**pessimistically** adv.

pest n anything destructive, esp a plant or animal detrimental to man as rats, flies, weeds, etc; a person who pesters or annoys.

pester vt to annoy or irritate persistently.—**pesterer** n.

pesticide n any chemical for killing pests.—**pesticidal** adj.

pestiferous adj spreading infection; (fig) physically or morally noxious.

pestilence n an outbreak of a fatal epidemic disease; anything regarded as harmful.

pestilent adj irritating; likely to cause a fatal epidemic.—**pestilently** adv.

pestilential adj of the nature of or conveying pestilence; harmful; annoying.—**pestilentially** adv.

pestle n a usu club-shaped tool for pounding or grinding substances in a mortar. * vt to beat, pound, or pulverize with a pestle.

pet n a domesticated animal kept as a companion; a person treated as a favourite. * adj kept as a pet; spoiled, indulged; favourite; particular. * vti (**petting, petted**) to stroke or pat gently; to caress; (inf) to kiss, embrace, etc in making love.

petal n any of the leaf-like parts of a flower's corolla.—**petaline** adj.—**petalled** adj.

petard n (formerly) a small bomb used to blow in a door, etc.

peter vi (with **out**) to come to an end; to dwindle to nothing.

petersham n a thick corded ribbon used in dressmaking as a stiffening; a thick woollen fabric used for overcoats, etc.

Peter's Pence n (RC Church) voluntary contributions to the papal treasury; (formerly) in England, an annual tax, until its abolishment by Henry VIII, of one penny levied on every house and paid to the Pope.

petiolate adj (bot) growing on a petiole.

petiole n (bot) a leaf stalk.

petit adj (esp law) of lesser importance.

petite adj (woman) small and trim in figure.

petition n a formal application or entreaty to an authority; a written demand for action by a government, etc, signed by a number of people. * vti to present a petition to; to ask humbly.—**petitionary** adj.—**petitioner** n.

petit mal n a mild form of epilepsy.

petit point n a fine stitch used in needlepoint.

petrel n a dark-coloured sea bird capable of flying far from land.

petrifaction, petrification n the process of changing animal or vegetable material into stone.

petrify vti (**petrifying, petrified**) to turn or be turned into stone; to stun or be stunned with fear, horror, etc.

petro- prefix rock, stone; petroleum.

petrochemical n any chemical obtained from natural gas or petroleum.

petrodollar n a notional unit of money earned by the export of petroleum.

petroglyph n a rock carving or drawing.

petrography n the scientific description and classification of rocks.—**petrographer** n.—**petrographic, petrographical** adj.

petrol n fuel obtained from petroleum; (US) gasoline.

petrolatum n a greasy, jelly-like substance obtained from petroleum and used for ointments, etc.

petroleum n a crude oil consisting of hydrocarbons occurring naturally in certain rock strata and distilled to yield petrol, paraffin, etc.

petrology n (pl **petrologies**) the study of rocks and their structure.

petrous adj of, or like, rock.

petticoat n an underskirt; a slip; (inf) woman.

pettifog vi to be, or behave like, a pettifogger.

pettifogger n an inferior or crooked lawyer; someone who quibbles over details.

pettish adj peevish, sulky.

pettitoes npl pig's trotters, esp as food.

petty adj (**pettier, pettiest**) trivial; small-minded; minor.—**pettily** adv.—**pettiness** n.

petty officer n a noncommissioned officer in the navy.

petulant adj showing impatience or irritation; bad-humoured.—**petulance** n.—**petulantly** adv.

petunia n a plant with funnel-shaped purple or white flowers.

petuntse n a fine white clay used with kaolin in the manufacture of porcelain.

pew n a wooden, bench-like seat in a church, often enclosed; (sl) a chair.

pewit n the lapwing.—also **peewit**.

pewter n an alloy of tin and lead with a silvery-grey colour; dishes, etc, made of pewter.—**pewterer** n.

PFC (US) abbr = private first class.

pfennig n (pl **pfennigs, pfennige**) a unit of currency in Germany worth one hundredth of a Deutschmark.

PG abbr = parental guidance: denoting a motion-picture suitable for all ages, but advising parental guidence.

PGA abbr = Professional Golfers' Association.

phaeton n a light, open, four-wheeled horse-drawn carriage.

phagocyte n a white corpuscle which devours harmful micro-organisms and other foreign bodies.

phagocytosis n the process by which a phagocyte devours foreign bodies.

phalange see **phalanx**.

phalangeal adj (anat) of or pertaining to a phalanx.

phalanger n a small tree-living marsupial of Australasia, with a long tail and bushy fur.

phalanx n (pl **phalanxes, phalanges**) a massed body or rank of people; (pl **phalanges**) a bone of a finger or toe.

phalarope n a small wading bird, with a straight bill and webbed feet.

phallic adj pertaining to, or resembling, a phallus.

phallicism, phallism *n* the worship of the phallus as the emblem of the generative power in nature.

phallus *n* (*pl* **phalli, phalluses**) the male reproductive organ.

phanerogam *n* (*bot*) a flowering plant.—**phanerogamic, phanerogamous** *adj*.

phantasm *n* a phantom; a vision of an absent person.

phantasmagoria, phantasmagory *n* a series of shifting images, like those seen in a dream.—**phantasmagoric, phantasmagorical** *adj*.

phantom *n* a spectre or apparition. * *adj* illusionary.

pharaoh *n* (*also with cap*) the title of the kings of ancient Egypt.—**pharaonic** *adj*.

Pharisaic, Pharisaical *adj* pertaining to, or characteristic of, the Pharisees; (*fig*) hypocritical.

Pharisee *n* a member of a Jewish religious sect, characterized by its strict observance of the letter of the law; (*fig*) a self-righteous person, a hypocrite.

pharmaceutical *adj* of, relating to pharmacy or drugs. * *n* a medicinal drug.

pharmaceutics *n sing* the science of pharmacy.

pharmacist *n* one licensed to practise pharmacy.

pharmacology *n* the science dealing with the effects of drugs on living organisms.—**pharmacological** *adj*.—**pharmacologist** *n*.

pharmacopoeia *n* a book containing a list of drugs with directions for their use.—**pharmacopoeial** *adj*.

pharmacy *n* (*pl* **pharmacies**) the preparation and dispensing of drugs and medicines; a drugstore.

pharyngeal, pharyngal *adj* pertaining to, or situated near, the pharynx.

pharyngitis *n* inflammation of the pharynx.

pharyngology *n* the medical study of the pharynx.

pharyngoscope *n* an instrument used for looking at the pharynx.

pharyngotomy *n* (*pl* **pharynotomies**) the surgical operation of making an incision into the pharynx.

pharynx *n* (*pl* **pharynges, pharynxes**) the cavity leading from the mouth and nasal passages to the larynx and oesophagus.

phase *n* (*pl* **phases**) an amount of the moon's or a planet's surface illuminated at a given time; a characteristic period in a regularly recurring sequence of events or stage in a development. * *vt* to do by stages or gradually; (*with* **out**) (*making, using, etc*) to stop gradually.—**phasic** *adj*.

PhD *abbr* = Doctor of Philosophy.

pheasant *n* a richly coloured game bird.

phellem *n* (*bot*) cork.

phenacetin *n* a drug used for the relief of pain and fever.

Phenobarbital *n* (*trademark*) a crystalline barbiturate used as a hypnotic and sedative.

phenol *n* carbolic acid.

phenology *n* the study of the influence of climate on certain recurrent phenomena of animal and plant life.

phenomenal *adj* perceptible through the senses; remarkable; outstanding.—**phenomenally** *adv*.

phenomenalism *n* (*philos*) the doctrine that all knowledge is derived from sense impressions.—**phenomenalist** *n*.

phenomenon *n* (*pl* **phenomena, phenomenons**) anything perceived by the senses as a fact; a fact or event that can be scientifically described; a remarkable thing or person.

phenyl *n* the hydrocarbon radical of phenol.

pheromone *n* a molecule that functions as a chemical communication signal between individuals of the same species.

phew *interj* an exclamation of relief, surprise, etc.

phi *n* the 21st letter of the Greek alphabet.

phial *n* a small glass bottle; a vial.

Phi Beta Kappa *n* (*US*) (a member of) the oldest college fraternity.

phil-, philo- *prefix* loving.

philander *vi* (*man*) to flirt with women for amusement.—**philanderer** *n*.

philanthropist *n* a person who tries to benefit others.

philanthropy *n* (*pl* **philanthropies**) love of mankind, esp as demonstrated by benevolent or charitable actions.—**philanthropic, philanthropical** *adj*.—**philanthropically** *adv*.

philatelist *n* a person who collects or studies stamps

philately *n* the study and collecting of postage and imprinted stamps; stamp collecting.—**philatelic** *adj*.—**philatelically** *adv*.

philharmonic *adj* loving music.

philhellene *n* a lover or supporter of Greece.

philippic *n* a bitter denunciation, an invective.

philistine *n* a person with no feeling for culture; an uncultured, conventional person; (*with cap*) a member of a warlike race hostile to ancient Israel. * *adj* uncultured.—**philistinism** *n*.

philogyny *n* fondness for women.—**phylogynous** *adj*.—**phylogynist** *n*.

philology *n* the study, esp comparative, of languages and their history and structure.—**philological** *adj*.—**philologist, philologer** *n*.

philomel *n* (*poet*) a nightingale.

philosopher *n* a person who studies philosophy; a person who acts calmly and rationally.

philosophical, philosophic *adj* of, relating to, or according to philosophy; serene; temperate; resigned.—**philosophically** *adv*.

philosophize *vi* to reason like a philosopher; to speculate, moralize.—**philosophizer** *n*.

philosophy *n* (*pl* **philosophies**) the study of the principles underlying conduct, thought, and the nature of the universe; general principles of a field of knowledge; a particular system of ethics; composure; calmness.

philtre, philter *n* a love potion.

phlebitis *n* (*med*) an inflammation of a vein.—**phlebitic** *adj*.

phlebotomize *vti* (*med*) to practise phlebotomy (on).

phlebotomy *n* (*pl* **phlebotomies**) a surgical incision into a vein to let blood.—**phlebotomist** *n*.

phlegm *n* a thick mucus discharged from the throat, as during a cold; sluggishness; apathy.

phlegmatic, phlegmatical *adj* unemotional, composed; sluggish.—**phlegmatically** *adv*.

phloem *n* (*bot*) the tissue which carries food around a plant.

phlogiston *n* (*chem*) an inflammable element once believed to exist in all combustible bodies.

phlox *n* (*pl* **phlox, phloxes**) a North American flowering plant.

phobia *n* an irrational, excessive, and persistent fear of some thing or situation.—**phobic** *adj, n*.

phoenix *n* a mythical bird that set fire to itself and rose from its ashes every 500 years; a symbol of immortality.

phon *n* a unit of loudness.

phonate *vi* to utter vocal sounds.—**phonation** *n*.

phone n, vti (*inf*) (to) telephone.

phone book n (*inf*) telephone book.

phone-in n a radio programme in which questions or comments by listeners are broadcast.

phonetic adj relating to, or representing, speech sounds.—**phonetically** adv.

phonetician n a student of, or expert in, phonetics.

phonetics n sing the science concerned with pronunciation and the representation of speech sounds.

phonetist n a phonetician; an advocate of phonetic spelling.

phoney, phony adj (**phonier, phoniest**) (*inf*) not genuine. * n (*pl* **phoneys, phonies**) a fake; an insincere person.—**phoneyness, phoniness** n.

phonics n sing a phonetics-based method of teaching reading.—**phonic** adj.

phonogram n (*phonetics*) a written character representing a particular sound.

phonograph n a device for reproducing sounds from a vinyl disc.

phonography n spelling based on pronunciation; a system of shorthand writing based on sound.

phonology n (*pl* **phonologies**) the study of speech sounds and their development, and of the sound systems of language.—**phonological** adj.—**phonologist** n.

phony see **phoney**.

phosgene n a poisonous gas used in chemical warfare and in industry.

phosphate n a compound of phosphorus.—**phosphatic** adj.

phosphene n the sensation of luminous rings seen when a closed eye is pressed.

phosphide n a compound of phosphorus with another element.

phosphite n a salt of phosphorous acid.

phosphorescence n the property of giving off light without noticeable heat, as phosphorus does; such light.—**phosphorescent** adj.

phosphorous adj containing phosphorus in lower or higher proportions.

phosphorus n a highly reactive, poisonous nonmetallic element; a phosphorescent substance or body, esp one that glows in the dark.

photic adj of, or pertaining to, light.

photo n (*pl* **photos**) a photograph.

photo- prefix light; a photographic process.

photocell n a photoelectric cell.

photochemical adj of or relating to the effect of radiant energy, esp light.

photochemistry n the branch of chemistry concerned with the effect of radiant energy in producing chemical changes; photochemical properties or processes.

photocopy n (*pl* **photocopies**) a photographic reproduction of written or printed work. * vt (**photocopying, photocopied**) to copy in this way.—**photocopier** n.

photoelectric cell n a cell whose electrical properties are affected by light; any device in which light controls an electric circuit that operates a mechanical device, as for opening doors.—*also* **photocell**.

photoengraving n any photomechanical process of making printing plates.

photo finish n the finish of a race where the decision on the winner has to be determined by a photograph as the contestants are so close; any race where the winning margin is small.

photogenic adj likely to look attractive in photographs; (*biol*) generating light.—**photogenically** adv.

photograph n an image produced by photography.—*also* **photo**.

photographic adj of or like a photograph; minutely accurate like a photograph; (*memory*) capable of retaining facts, etc, after reading for only a brief time.—**photographically** adv.

photography n the art or process of recording images permanently and visibly by the chemical action of light on sensitive material, producing prints, slides or film.—**photographer** n.

photogravure n a printing process using an intaglio plate photographically produced; printed matter so produced.

photojournalism n a form of news reporting in which the story is presented mainly through photographs.—**photojournalist** n.

photolithograph n a picture produced by photolithography.

photolithography n (*print*) lithography using plates made from photographs.

photomechanical adj of or relating to a printing process that utilizes photography in plate-making.—**photomechanically** adv.

photometer n an instrument for measuring the intensity of light.

photometry n the area of physics concerned with the measurement of light; the use of a photometer.

photomicrograph n a photograph taken through a microscope.—**photomicrography** n.

photophobia n (*med*) oversensivity (of the eyes) to light; (*psychol*) fear or, or aversion to, sunlight.

photosphere n the surface of a star, esp the sun.

Photostat n (*trademark*) a device for making photographic copies of documents, etc; a copy made in this way. * vt (*often without cap*) to copy in this way.—**Photostatic** adj.

photosynthesis n (*bot*) the process by which a green plant manufactures sugar from carbon dioxide and water in the presence of light.—**photosynthetic** adj.—**photosynthetically** adv.

photosynthesize vti (*plants, etc*) to produce by or carry on photosynthesis.

phototelegraphy n the telegraphic transmission of photographs and drawings.

phrasal adj of or consisting of a phrase or phrases.—**phrasally** adv.

phrasal verb n (*gram*) a usu simple verb that combines with a preposition or adverb, or both, to convey a meaning more than the sum of its parts, eg *come out*.

phrase n a group of words that does not contain a finite verb but which expresses a single idea by itself; a pointed saying; a high-flown expression; (*mus*) a short, distinct musical passage. * vt to express orally, put in words; (*mus*) to divide into melodic phrases.

phrase book n a book containing idiomatic expressions of a foreign language and their translations.

phraseogram n a shorthand symbol representing a phrase.

phraseology n (*pl* **phraseologies**) mode of expression, wording; phrases used by a particular group.—**phraseological** adj.

phrasing n the wording of a speech or a piece of writing; (*mus*) the division of a melodic line, etc, into musical phrases.

phrenetic see **frenetic**.

phrenic adj (anat) of, or pertaining to, the diaphragm.

phrenology n the belief that intelligence and ability may be judged from the shape of a person's skull; study of the shape of the skull based on this belief.—**phrenological** adj.—**phrenologist** n.

phthisis n a wasting disease, esp tuberculosis of the lungs.

phycology n the study of algae.

phylactery n (pl **phylacteries**) (Judaism) a small case containing Hebrew texts, worn by Jewish men during prayers.

phyletic adj relating to the racial development of an animal or plant type.

phyllode n (bot) a flattened petiole with the functions of a leaf.

phyllotaxy, phyllotaxis n (pl **phyllotaxies, phyllotaxes**) (bot) the arrangement of leaves on a stem.

phylloxera n (pl **phylloxeras, phylloxerae**) an insect which attacks vines.

phylogeny, phylogenesis n (pl **phylogenies, phylogeneses**) (biol) the racial evolution of an animal or plant type.—**phylogenic, phylogenetic** adj.

phylum n (pl **phyla**) a major division of the animal or plant kingdom.

physic vt (**physicking, physicked**) (arch) to administer medicine to.

physical adj relating to the world of matter and energy, the human body, or natural science. * n a general medical examination.—**physically** adv.

physical chemistry n the branch of chemistry concerned with the effect of chemical structure on physical properties and of physical changes brought about by chemical reactions.

physical education n education in fitness and cure of the body, stressing athletics and hygiene.

physical therapy n the treatment of disorders and disease by physical and mechanical means (as massage, exercise, water, heat, etc).—**also physiotherapy**.

physician n a doctor of medicine.

physicist n a specialist in physics.

physics n the branch of science concerned with matter and energy and their interactions in the fields of mechanics, acoustics, optics, heat, electricity, magnetism, radiation, atomic structure and nuclear phenomena; the physical processes and phenomena of a particular system.

physio- prefix nature.

physiocrat n a supporter of the doctine of government according to a natural order based on land as the sole form of wealth.

physiognomy n (pl **physiognomies**) the art of judging character from facial features; facial expression, face; physical features generally.—**physiognomic, physiognomical** adj.—**physiognomist** n.

physiography n the study of the earth's natural features, physical geography.—**physiographer** n.

physiology n the science of the functioning and processes of living organisms.—**physiological** adj.—**physiologist** n.

physiotherapy n physical therapy.—**physiotherapist** n.

physique n bodily structure and appearance; build.

phytogenesis, phytogeny n the study of plant evolution.

phyton n (bot) the smallest unit of a plant capable of growing into a new plant.

pi[1] n the 16th letter of the Greek alphabet; (math) the Greek letter (π) used as a symbol for the ratio of the circumference to the diameter of a circle, approx. 3.14159.

pi[2] n (pl **pis**) (print) a jumble of type; any disorder. * vt to mix, disarrange (type). * vi to become mixed up.—also **pie**.

piacular adj expiatory; sinful.

piaffe n (dressage) a slow trot.

pia mater n (anat) the inner membrane enclosing the brain.

pianissimo adv (mus) very softly.

pianist n a person who plays the piano.

piano n (pl **pianos**) a large stringed keyboard instrument in which each key operates a felt-covered hammer that strikes a corresponding steel wire or wires.

pianoforte n (pl **pianofortes**) a piano.

piastre, piaster n a unit of currency in Egypt, Lebanon, Sudan, Syria and South Vietnam.

piazza n in Italy, a public square; a covered walkway or gallery; a veranda.

pibroch n a kind of music composed for Scottish bagpipes.

pica n (print) a standard measurement, equal to 12 points.

picaresque adj pertaining to a genre of fiction describing the exploits of rogues.

picaroon n (arch) a robber, pirate or marauder.

picayune adj (inf) of little value.

piccalilli n a kind of pickle made with cauliflower, onions, etc.

piccaninny n (pl **piccaninnies**) (offensive) a black baby or child.

piccolo n (pl **piccolos**) a small shrill flute.

pick n a heavy tool with a shaft and pointed crossbar for breaking ground; a tool for picking, such as a toothpick or icepick; a plectrum; right of selection; choice; best (of). * vti to break up or remove with a pick; to pluck at; to nibble (at), eat fussily; to contrive; to choose; (fruit, etc) to gather; to steal from a pocket; (lock) to force open; (with up) to lift; to acquire; to call for; to recover; (inf) to make the acquaintance of casually; to learn gradually; to resume; to give a lift to; to increase speed.

pickaback see **piggyback**.

pickaninny n (pl **pickaninnies**) varient (usu US) spelling of **piccaninny**.

pickaxe, pickax n (pl **pickaxes**) a pick with a long pointed head for breaking up hard ground, etc.

pickerel n (pl **pickerel, pickerels**) a North American freshwater fish of the pike family.

picket n a pointed stake; a patrol or group of men selected for a special duty; a person posted by strikes outside a place of work to persuade others not to enter. * vt (**picketing, picketed**) to tether to a picket; to post as a military picket; to place pickets, or serve as a picket (at a factory, etc).

pickings npl gleanings, perquisites.

pickle n vegetables preserved in vinegar; (inf) a plight, mess. * vt to preserve in vinegar.

pickled adj preserved in pickle; (sl) drunk.

picklock n an instrument for picking locks; someone, esp a thief, who picks locks.

pick-me-up n a tonic.

pickpocket n a person who steals from pockets.

pick-up n the act of picking up; a person or thing picked up; (elect) a device for picking up current; the power to accelerate rapidly; the balanced arm of a record player; a pickup truck.

pickup truck n a light truck with an enclosed cab and open body.

picnic n a usu informal meal taken on an excursion and eaten outdoors; an outdoor snack; the food so eaten; an easy or agreeable task. * vi (**picnicking, picnicked**) to have a picnic.—**picnicker** n.

picot n a small loop of thread used as an edging to lace.

picotee n a type of small carnation.

picric acid n a toxic acid used as a dye and an explosive.

pictograph n a picture representing a word or idea.

pictorial adj relating to pictures, painting,or drawing; containing pictures; expressed in pictures; graphic.—**pictorially** adv.

picture n drawing, painting, photography, or other visual representation; a scene; an impression or mental image; a vivid description; a cinema film. * vt to portray, describe in a picture; to visualize.

picturesque adj striking, vivid, usually pleasing; making an effective picture.—**picturesquely** adv.—**picturesqueness** n.

piddle vt to squander. * vi (inf) to idle; to urinate.

piddling adj (inf) trifling, insignificant.

piddock n a bivalve, boring, shellfish.

pidgin n a jargon for trade purposes, using words and grammar from two or more different languages.

pie[1] n a baked dish of fruit, meat, etc, with an under or upper crust of pastry, or both.

pie[2] see **pi**[2].

piebald adj covered with patches of two colours. * n a piebald horse, etc.

piece n a distinct part of anything; a single object; a literary, dramatic, artistic, or musical composition; (sl) a firearm; a man in chess or draughts; an opinion, view; a short distance. * vt to fit together, join.—**piecer** n.

pièce de résistance n (pl **pièces de résistance**) the most important item or dish.

piecemeal adv gradually; bit by bit.

piecework n work paid for according to the quantity produced.

pied adj of mixed colours, mottled

pied-à-terre n (pl **pieds-à-terre**) a flat for occasional use; a second home.

pier n a structure supporting the spans of a bridge; a structure built out over water and supported by pillars, used as a landing place, promenade, etc; a heavy column used to support weight.

pierce vt to cut or make a hole through; to force a way into; (fig) to touch or move. * vi to penetrate.

piercing adj penetrating; keen; (cold, pain) acute.—**piercingly** adv.

Pierrot n (pantomime) a male character, usu in a loose white costume with a whitened face; a clown in such a costume.

pietà n a picture or sculpture of the Virgin mourning over the dead Christ.

piety n (pl **pieties**) religious devoutness; the characteristic of being pious.

piezoelectricity n the production of electricity in certain types of crystal through the application of mechanical stress.—**piezoeletric, piezoelectrical** adj.—**piezoelectrically** adv.

piffle n (inf) silly stuff, nonsense. * vi to talk nonsense.

pig n a domesticated animal with a broad snout and fat body raised for food; a hog; a greedy or filthy person; an oblong casting of metal poured from the smelting furnace; (sl) a policeman. * vi (**pigging, pigged**) (sow) to give birth; (inf) to live in squalor.

pigeon n a bird with a small head and a heavy body; (inf) a person who is easily conned.

pigeonhole n a small compartment for filing papers, etc; a category usu failing to reflect actual complexities. * vt to file, classify; to put aside for consideration, shelve.

pigeon-toed adj having the toes turned inward.

piggery n (pl **piggeries**) a place where pigs are reared; a pigsty.

piggish adj greedy, dirty, selfish, like a pig.—**piggishly** adv.—**piggishness** n.

piggy n (pl **piggies**) a child's name for a young or little pig. * adj (**piggier, piggiest**) piggish.

piggyback n a ride on the shoulders or back of a person. * adv carried on the shoulders or back; transported on top of a larger object.—also **pickaback**.

piggy bank n a container for coins, often shaped like a pig.

pigheaded adj stupidly stubborn.—**pigheadedly** adv.—**pigheadedness** n.

piglet n a young pig.

pigment n paint; a naturally occurring substance used for colouring.—**pigmentary** adj.

pigmentation n (biol) coloration of the tissues of plants and animals caused by pigment; the depositing of pigments by cells.

pigmy see **pygmy**.

pignut n an earthnut.

pigskin n leather made from the skin of a pig.

pigsticker n a person who goes pigsticking.

pigsticking n the hunting of wild boar with a spear, usu on horseback.

pigsty n (pl **pigsties**) a pen for pigs; a dirty hovel.

pigtail n a tight braid of hair.—**pigtailed** adj.

pike[1] n a sharp point or spike; the top of a spear. * vt to pierce or kill with a pike.

pike[2] n (pl **pike, pikes**) a long-snouted fish, important as a food and game fish.

pike perch n (**pike perch, pike perches**) any of various fishes of the perch family resembling the pike.

pikestaff n the shaft of a pike.

pilaf, pilaff n a dish of spiced rice cooked in stock with, optionally, meat or fish.—also **pilau**.

pilaster n a rectangular pillar, usu set in a wall.

pilch n (arch) a triangular flannel wrap for a baby.

pilchard n a fish of the herring family.

pile[1] n a heap or mound of objects; a large amount; a lofty building; a pyre; (sl) a fortune. * vt (with **up, on**) to heap or stack; to load; to accumulate. * vi to become heaped up; (with **up, out, on**) to move confusedly in a mass.

pile[2] n a vertical beam driven into (the ground) as a foundation for a building, etc. * vt to support with piles; to drive piles into.

pile[3] n the nap of a fabric or carpet; soft, fine fur or wool.

pileate, pileated adj (biol) crested.

piledriver n a machine for driving in piles.

piles npl haemorrhoids.

pile-up n an accumulation of tasks, etc; (inf) a collision of several vehicles.

pilfer vti to steal in small quantities.—**pilferage** n.—**pilferer** n.

pilgrim n a person who makes a pilgrimage.

pilgrimage n a journey to a holy place as an act of devotion; any long journey; a life's journey.

piliferous *adj* (*esp bot*) hairy.

piliform *adj* (*bot*) in the form of or like a hair.

pill *n* medicine in round balls or tablet form; (*with cap*) an oral contraceptive.

pillage *n* looting, plunder. * *vti* to plunder, esp during war.—**pillager** *n*.

pillar *n* a slender, vertical structure used as a support or ornament; a column; a strong supporter of a cause.

pillar box *n* in UK, a mailbox in the shape of a pillar.

pillbox *n* a box for pills, esp a decorative one; a small round hat without a brim; (*mil*) a small, fortified, concrete shelter.

pillion *n* a seat behind the driver for a passenger on a motorcycle, etc.

pillory *n* (*pl* **pillories**) (*formerly*) stocks in which criminals were put as punishment. * *vt* (**pillorying, pilloried**) to expose to public scorn and ridicule.

pillow *n* a cushion that supports the head during sleep; something that supports to equalize or distribute pressure. * *vti* to rest on, serve as, a pillow.

pillowcase, pillowslip *n* a removable cover for a pillow.

pilose *adj* (*biol*) hairy.

pilot *n* a person who operates an aircraft; one who directs ships in and out of harbour; a guide; a television show produced as a sample of a proposed series. * *vt* to direct the course of, act as pilot; to lead or guide.

pilotage *n* the work or fee of a pilot.

pilot light *n* a burning gas flame used to light a larger jet; an electric indicator light.

pilule *n* a small pill.—**pilular** *adj*.

pimento *n* (*pl* **pimentos**) allspice; a pimiento.

pimiento *n* a sweet red pepper (capiscum) used in salads and cooked dishes.

pimp *n* a prostitute's agent.—*also vt*.

pimpernel *n* a primulaceous plant with small scarlet, blue or white flowers.

pimple *n* a small, raised, inflamed swelling of the skin.—**pimpled** *adj*.

pimply *adj* (**pimplier, pimpliest**) covered with pimples.

PIN *abbr* = personal identification number (issued by a bank to a customer to validate electronic transactions).

pin *n* a piece of metal or wood used to fasten things together; a small piece of pointed wire with a head; an ornament or badge with a pin or clasp for fastening to clothing; (*bowling*) one of the clubs at which the ball is rolled. * *vt* (**pinning, pinned**) to fasten with a pin; to hold, fix; (*with* **down**) to get (someone) to commit himself or herself as to plans, etc; (*a fact, etc*) to establish.

pinafore *n* a sleeveless garment worn over a dress, blouse, etc.

pinaster *n* a Southern European pine tree.

pince-nez *n* (*pl* **pince-nez**) eyeglasses clipped to the nose by a spring.

pincers *npl* a tool with two handles and jaws used for gripping and drawing out nails, etc; a grasping claw, as of a crab.

pinch *vti* to squeeze or compress painfully; to press between the fingers; to nip; (*sl*) to steal; (*sl*) to arrest. * *n* a squeeze or nip; what can be taken up between the finger and thumb, a small amount; a time of stress; an emergency.

pinchbeck *n* a copper and zinc alloy, used as imitation gold.

pinched *adj* appearing to be squeezed; drawn by cold or stress.

pincushion *n* a pad for holding pins.

Pindaric *adj* (*ode*) associated with the poet Pindar.

pine[1] *n* an evergreen coniferous tree with long needles and well-formed cones; a tree of the pine family; its wood.

pine[2] *vi* to languish, waste away through longing or mental stress; (*with* **for**) to yearn.

pineal gland *n* a pea-sized gland in the brain.

pineapple *n* a tropical plant; its juicy, fleshy, yellow fruit.

pinfold *n* a pound for stray cattle. * *vt* to shut into, or as if into, such a pound.

ping *n* a high-pitched ringing sound. * *vti* to strike with a ping, emit a ping.—**pinger** *n*.

ping-pong *n* a name for table tennis; (*with caps*) (*trademark*) table tennis equipment.

pinion[1] *n* the outer joint of a bird's wing; a wing feather. * *vt* to cut off a pinion; to bind arms to sides, restrain.

pinion[2] *n* a cogwheel.

pink[1] *n* any of various garden plants with a fragrant flower, including carnations; a pale red colour; a huntsman's red coat; the highest type. * *adj* pink-coloured; (*inf*) radical in political views.

pink[2] *vt* to stab, pierce; (*cloth, etc*) to cut a zigzag edge on; to perforate with pinking shears.

pinkeye *n* an inflammation of the conjunctiva, affecting animals and humans.

pinkie, pinky *n* (*pl* **pinkies**) the little finger on the human hand.

pinking shears *npl* shears with notched edges for pinking edges of cloth.

pin money *n* money given to a woman by her husband for personal expenses.

pinna *n* (*pl* **pinnae, pinnas**) (*biol*) the fin of a fish; the feather or wing of a bird; the leaflet of a pinnate leaf.

pinnace *n* (*naut*) a small light schooner-rigged vessel with oars; an eight-oared small boat belonging to a warship.

pinnacle *n* a slender tower crowning a roof, etc; a rocky peak of a mountain; the highest point, climax.

pinnate, pinnated *adj* shaped like a feather; (*leaf*) divided into leaflets.

pinniped *adj* (*zool*) with fin-like feet or flippers.

pinny *n* (*pl* **pinnies**) (*sl*) a pinafore.

pinochle, pinocle *n* a card game.—*also* **pinuchle**.

pinpoint *vt* to locate or identify very exactly.

pinprick *n* a small puncture as made by a pin; a trivial annoyance.

pins and needles *npl* a tingling feeling in the fingers, toes, etc, caused by impeded blood circulation returning to normal; (*with* **on**) in an anxious or expectant state.

pinstripe *n* a very narrow stripe in suit fabrics, etc.

pint *n* a liquid measure equal to half a quart or one eighth of a gallon (0.47 litres); (*inf*) a drink of beer.

pintail *n* (*pl* **pintails, pintail**) a type of duck.

pintle *n* a bolt or pin esp comprising a pivot.

pinto *n* (*pl* **pintos**) a piebald horse.

pinuchle *see* **pinochle**.

pin-up *n* (*sl*) a photograph of a naked or partially naked person; a person who has been so photographed; a photograph of a famous person.

pioneer *n* a person who initiates or explores new areas of enterprise, research, etc; an explorer; an early settler; (*mil*) one who prepares roads, sinks mines, etc. * *vti* to initiate or take part in the development of; to act as a pioneer (to); to explore (a region).

pious *adj* devout; religious; sanctimonious.—**piously** *adv*.—**piousness** *n*.

pip[1] *n* the seed in a fleshy fruit, eg apple, orange.

pip[2] *n* a spot with a numerical value on a playing card, dice, etc; (*inf*) insignia on a uniform showing an officer's rank; a signal on a radar screen.

pip[3] *vi* (**pipping, pipped**) (*bird*) to chirp, to peep; (*hatching bird*) to pierce (its shell).

pipal *see* **peepul**.

pipe *n* a tube of wood, metal etc for making musical sounds; (*pl*) the bagpipes; a stem with a bowl for smoking tobacco; a long tube or hollow body for conveying water, gas, etc. * *vt* to play on a pipe; (*gas, water, etc*) to convey by pipe; to lead, summon with the sound of a pipe(s); to trim with piping. * *vi.*(*sl*) to take the drug crack.

pipeclay *n* a white clay, used to make tobacco pipes and to whiten leather, etc. * *vt* to whiten using pipeclay.

pipeline *n* a pipe (often underground) used to convey oil, gas, etc; a direct channel for information; the processes through which supplies pass from source to user.

piper *n* a person who plays a pipe, esp bagpipes.

pipette, pipet *n* a hollow glass tube into which liquids are sucked for measurement.

piping *n* a length of pipe, pipes collectively; a tube-like fold of material used to trim seams; a strip of icing, cream, for decorating cakes, etc; the art of playing a pipe or bagpipes; a high-pitched sound. * *adj* making a high-pitched sound.

piping hot *adj* very hot.

pipistrelle, pipistrel *n* a small brown bat.

pipit *n* a type of songbird.

pipkin *n* a small earthenware pot.

pippin *n* one of several types of eating apple.

pipsqueak *n* (*inf*) a contemptible or insigificant person.

piquant *adj* strong-tasting; pungent, sharp; stimulating.—**piquancy** *n*.—**piquantly** *adv*.

pique *n* resentment, ill-feeling. * *vt* (**piquing, piqued**) to cause resentment in; to offend.

piqué *n* a corded cotton fabric.

piquet *n* a card game for two.

piracy *n* (*pl* **piracies**) robbery at sea; the hijacking of a ship or aircraft; infringement of copyright; unauthorized use of patented work.

piragua *see* **pirogue**.

piranha *n* a small voracious freshwater fish of tropical America with sharp teeth and a strong jaw.

pirate *n* a person who commits robbery at sea; a hijacker; one who infringes copyright. * *vti* to take by piracy; to publish or reproduce in violation of a copyright.—**piratical, piratic** *adj*.

pirogue *n* a dugout canoe.—*also* **piragua**.

pirouette *n* a spin on the toes in ballet.—*also vi*.

piscatorial, piscatory *adj* of, or pertaining to, fish or fishing.

Pisces *n* the Fishes, in astrology the twelfth sign of the zodiac, operative from 19 February-20 March.—**Piscean** *adj, n*.

pisciculture *n* the controlled rearing and breeding of fish.—**piscicultural** *adj*.—**pisciculturist** *n*.

piscina *n* (*pl* **piscinae, piscinas**) (*RC Church*) a basin with a drain in a church wall, used for rinsing sacred vessels after Mass.

piscine *adj* pertaining to fish.

piscivorous *adj* fish-eating.

pisiform *adj* pea-shaped.

pismire *n* an ant.

piss *vi* (*vulg*) to urinate. * *n* urine.

pistachio *n* (*pl* **pistachios**) a tree found in Mediterranean countries and West Asia; the edible nut of this tree.

piste *n* a ski trail of packed snow; (*fencing*) the rectangular area where a bout takes place.

pistil *n* the seed-bearing part of a flower.

pistillate *adj* (*bot*) having a pistil; with a pistil but no stamens.

pistol *n* a small, short-barrelled handgun. * *vt* (**pistolling, pistolled** *or* **pistoling, pistoled**) to shoot with a pistol.

pistole *n* (*formerly*) a gold coin used in Europe.

piston *n* a disc that slides to and fro in a close-fitting cylinder, as in engines, pumps.

pit *n* a deep hole in the earth; a (coal) mine; a scooped-out place for burning something; a sunken or depressed area below the adjacent floor area; a space at the front of the stage for the orchestra; the area in a securities or commodities exchange in which members do the trading; the scar left by smallpox, etc; the stone of a fruit; a place where racing cars refuel. * *vti* (**pitting, pitted**) to set in competition; to mark or become marked with pits; to make a pit stop.

pit-a-pat *adv* with quick, light steps or beats. * *n* quick, light steps or beats. * *vi* (**pit-a-patting, pit-a-patted**) to make quick, light steps or beats.

pitch[1] *vti* (*tent, etc*) to erect by driving pegs, stakes, etc, into the ground; to set the level of; (*mus*) to set in key; to express in a style; to throw, hurl; to fall heavily, plunge, esp forward. * *n* a throw; height, intensity; a musical tone; a place where a street trader or performer works; distance between threads (of a screw); amount of slope; a sound wave frequency; a sports field; (*cricket*) the area between the wickets; sales talk.

pitch[2] *n* the black, sticky substance from distillation of tar, etc; any of various bituminous substances. * *vt* to smear with pitch.

pitch-black *adj* black, or extremely dark.

pitchblende *n* a black mineral, composed largely of uranium oxide, that also yields radium.

pitch-dark *adj* completely dark.

pitcher *n* a large water jug; (*baseball*) the player who pitches the ball.

pitchfork *n* a long-handled fork for tossing hay, etc. * *vt* to lift with this; to thrust suddenly or willy-nilly into.

pitchy *adj* (**pitchier, pitchiest**) resembling, or smeared with, pitch.

piteous *adj* arousing pity; heart-rending.—**piteously** *adv*.—**piteousness** *n*.

pitfall *n* concealed danger; unexpected difficulty.

pith *n* the soft tissue inside the rind of citrus fruits; the gist, essence; importance.

pithy *adj* (**pithier, pithiest**) like or full of pith; concise and full of meaning.—**pithily** *adv*.—**pithiness** *n*.

pitiable *adj* deserving pity, lamentable, wretched.—**pitiableness** *n*.—**pitiably** *adv*.

pitiful *adj* causing pity, touching; contemptible, paltry.—**pitifully** *adv*.—**pitifulness** *n*.

pitiless *adj* without pity, ruthless.—**pitilessly** *adv*.—**pitilessness** *n*.

pitman *n* (*pl* **pitmen**) a miner.

pittance *n* a very small quantity or allowance of money.

pituitary *adj* of or pertaining to the pituitary gland; (*arch*) of or secreting mucus. * *n* (*pl* **pituitaries**) the pituitary gland.

pituitary gland *n* a ductless gland at the base of the brain that affects growth and sexual development.

pity *n* (*pl* **pities**) sympathy with the distress of others; a cause of grief; a regrettable fact. * *vt* (**pitying, pitied**) to feel pity for.—**pityingly** *adv*.

pityriasis *n* (*pl* **pityriases**) a skin disease characterized by scaly, pink eruptions.

pivot *n* a pin on which a part turns, fulcrum; a key person upon whom progress depends; a cardinal point or factor. * *vt* to turn or hinge (on) a pivot; to attach by a pivot. * *vi* to run on, or as if on, a pivot.—**pivotal** *adj*.

pixel *n* any of the tiny units that form an image (as on a television screen, computer monitor).

pixie, pixy *n* (*pl* **pixies**) a fairy or elf.

pixilated *adj* acting as if influenced by pixies; unconventional, eccentric, whimsical; (*sl*) drunk.

pizza *n* a baked dough crust covered with cheese, tomatoes, etc.

pizzeria *n* a pizza restaurant.

pizzicato *n* (*pl* **pizzicati, pizzicatos**) (*mus*) a note or passage played by plucking the string of a violin or other bowed instrument.—*also adj*.

placable *adj* easily to placate.—**placability** *n*.

placard *n* a poster or notice for public display.

placate *vt* to appease; to pacify.—**placation** *n*.—**placatory** *adj*.

place *n* a locality, spot; a town or village; a building, residence; a short street, a square; space, room; a particular point, part, position, etc; the part of space occupied by a person or thing; a position or job; a seat; rank, precedence; a finishing position in a race. * *vt* to put; to put in a particular place; to find a place or seat for; to identify; to estimate; to rank; (*order*) to request material from a supplier. * *vi* to finish second or among the first three in a race.

placebo *n* (*pl* **placebos, placeboes**) something harmless given by a doctor to fool a patient into thinking he is undergoing treatment.

place mat *n* a small mat serving as an individual table cover for a person at a meal.

placement *n* a placing or being placed; location or arrangement.

place name *n* the name of a geographical locality.

placenta *n* (*pl* **placentas, placentae**) the organ in the uterus of a female mammal that nourishes the foetus.—**placental** *adj*.

placer *n* a deposit containing a valuable mineral found in a river, etc.

placid *adj* calm, tranquil.—**placidity** *n*.—**placidly** *adv*.

placket *n* a slit at the waist of a dress or skirt to make it easy to put on or take off.

placoid *adj* platelike.

plafond *n* a ceiling, esp one of elaborate design; a card game.

plagal *adj* (*musical composition*) having its principal notes between the fifth of the key and its octave.

plagiarism *n* the act of stealing from another author's work, literary theft; that which is plagiarized.—**plagiarist** *n*.—**plagiaristic** *adj*.

plagiarize *vt* to appropriate writings from another author.—**plagiarizer** *n*.

plague *n* a highly contagious and deadly disease; (*inf*) a person who is a nuisance. * *vt* (**plaguing, plagued**) to afflict with a plague; (*inf*) to annoy, harass.

plaguy, plaguey *adj* (*arch*) (*inf*) troublesome, vexatious.

plaice *n* (*pl* **plaice, plaices**) any of various flatfishes, esp a flounder.

plaid *n* a long wide piece of woollen cloth used as a cloak in Highland dress; cloth with a tartan or chequered pattern.

plain *adj* level, flat; understandable; straightforward; manifest, obvious; blunt; unadorned; not elaborate; not coloured or patterned; not beautiful; ugly; pure; unmixed. * *n* a large tract of level country.—**plainness** *n*.

plain clothes *npl* ordinary clothes, not uniform, as worn by a policeman on duty.—*also adj*.

plainly *adv* clearly, intelligibly.

plain sailing *n* easy progress over an unobstructed course.

plainsman *n* (*pl* **plainsmen**) an inhabitant of a plain.

plainsong *n* an old, plain kind of church music chanted in unison.

plain-spoken *adj* frank, outspoken.

plaint *n* (*poet*) lamentation, sad song; (*law*) formal statement of grievance.

plaintiff *n* (*law*) a person who brings a civil action against another.

plaintive *adj* sad, mournful.—**plaintively** *adv*.—**plaintiveness** *n*.

plait *n* intertwined strands of hair, straw, etc; a pigtail. * *vti* (**plaiting, plaited**) to twist strands (of hair) together into a plait.

plan *n* a scheme or idea; a drawing to scale of a building; a diagram, map; any outline or sketch. * *vti* (**planning, planned**) to make a plan of; to design; to arrange beforehand, intend; to make plans.

planar *adj* of or located in a plane; flat.

planarian *n* a type of flatworm.

planchet *n* a plain metal disc from which a coin is made.

planchette *n* a heart-shaped board on wheels, holding a pencil which is supposed to write automatically, giving messages from spirits, when a hand is rested upon it.

plane[1] *n* a tall tree with large broad leaves.

plane[2] *n* a tool with a steel blade for smoothing level wooden surfaces. * *vt* to smooth with a plane.

plane[3] *n* any level or flat surface; a level of attainment; one of the main supporting surfaces of an aeroplane; an aeroplane. * *adj* flat or level. * *vi* to fly while keeping the wings motionless; to skim across the surface of water; to travel by aeroplane.

planet *n* a celestial body that orbits the sun or other star.

planetarium *n* (*pl* **planetariums, planetaria**) a machine used to exhibit the planets, their motions around the sun and their relative distances and magnitudes; a building for housing this instrument; a model of the solar system.

planetary *adj* (*astrol*) under the influence of one of the planets; terrestrial; wandering, erratic.

planetoid *n* an asteroid.

plangent *adj* (*sound*) loud and deep; resounding.—**plangency** *n*.

planimeter *n* an instrument for measuring the area of an irregular plane figure.

planimetry *n* the measurement of plane figures.

planish *vt* (*metal*) to smooth and flatten with a hammer or between rollers.

planisphere *n* a sphere projected on a plane or a map of the heavens.

plank *n* a long, broad, thick board; one of the policies forming the platform of a political party. * *vt* to cover with planks.

planking *n* planks collectively; the act of laying boards.

plankton *n* the microscopic organisms that float on seas, lakes, etc.

planner *n* a person who plans; in UK, an official who plans architectural development and land use.— **planning** *n*.

planoconcave *adj* (*lens*) with one side flat and the other concave.

planoconvex *adj* (*lens*) with one side flat and the other convex.

plant *n* a living organism with cellulose cell walls, which synthesizes its food from carbon dioxide, water and light; a soft-stemmed organism of this kind, as distinguished from a tree or shrub; the machinery, buildings, etc of a factory, etc; (*sl*) an act of planting; (*sl*) something or someone planted. * *vt* (*seeds, cuttings*) to put into the ground to grow; to place firmly in position; to found or establish; (*sl*) to conceal something in another's possession in order to implicate.

plantain¹ *n* a low-growing weed with tough leaves.

plantain² *n* a tropical broad-leaved tree yielding an edible fruit similar to the banana.

plantar *adj* (*anat*) pertaining to the sole of the foot.

plantation *n* a large cultivated planting of trees; an estate where tea, rubber, cotton, etc, is grown, cultivated by local labour.

planter *n* a person who owns or runs a plantation; a machine that plants; a decorative container for plants.

plantigrade *adj* (*zool*) walking on the sole of the foot. * *n* a plantigrade animal.

plaque *n* an ornamental tablet or disc attached to or inserted in a surface; a film of mucus on the teeth that harbours bacteria.

plash *n* a splash; a marshy pool or puddle.—**plashy** *adj* (**plashier, plashiest**).

plasm *n* a kind of protoplasm; plasma.

plasma *n* the colourless liquid part of blood, milk, or lymph; a collection of charged particles resembling gas but conducting electricity and affected by a magnetic field.

plasmodium *n* (*pl* **plasmodia**) (*biol*) a mass of protoplasm formed by the union of single-cell organisms; (*med*) any of a genus of parasitic protozoa which cause malaria.

plasmolysis *n* (*biol*) the shrinkage of the protoplasm of a plant cell occurring as a result of loss of water.

plasmolyze *vt* to subject to plasmolysis.

plaster *n* an adhesive dressing for cuts; a mixture of sand, lime and water that sets hard and is used for covering walls and ceilings. * *vt* to cover as with plaster; to apply like a plaster; to make lie smooth and flat; to load to excess.—**plasterer** *n*.

plasterboard *n* a thin board formed by layers of plaster and paper, used in wide sheets for walls, etc.

plaster cast *n* a rigid dressing of gauze impregnated with plaster of Paris; a sculptor's model in plaster of Paris.

plastered *adj* (*sl*) intoxicated.

plaster of Paris *n* gypsum and water made into a quick-setting paste.

plastic *adj* able to be moulded; pliant; made of plastic; (*art*) relating to modelling or moulding. * *n* any of various nonmetallic compounds, synthetically produced, that can be moulded, cast, squeezed, drawn, or laminated into objects, films, or filaments.— **plastically** *adv*.

plasticity *n* the ability to be moulded or altered; the ability to retain a shape attained by pressure deformation.

plastic surgery *n* surgery to repair deformed or destroyed parts of the body.

plastron *n* a breastplate; a trimming on a dress front; a shirt front; a bony plate on the underside of a tortoise or turtle.

plat *n* (*US*) a small plot of ground; a map, esp of land divided into lots for building. * *vt* (**platting, platted**) to make a map of.

platan *n* a plane tree.

plate *n* a flat sheet of metal on which an engraving is cut; an illustration printed from it; a full-page illustration separate from text; a sheet of metal photographically prepared with text, etc, for printing from; a sheet of glass with sensitized film used as a photographic negative; a trophy as prize at a race; a coating of metal on another metal; utensils plated in silver or gold; plated ware; a flat shallow dish from which food is eaten; a helping of food; the part of a denture that fits the palate; (*inf*) a denture. * *vt* (*a metal*) to coat with a thin film of another metal; to cover with metal plates.

plateau *n* (*pl* **plateaus, plateaux**) a flat, elevated area of land; a stable period; a graphic representation showing this.

plated *adj* coated with metal, esp silver or gold.

plate glass *n* rolled, ground, and polished sheet glass.

platelet *n* a small disc-shaped cell in the blood involved in the process of blood clotting.

platen *n* the roller on a typewriter; (*print*) a plate which presses the paper against the type.

plater *n* someone who, or something which, plates; a mediocre racehorse.

platform *n* a raised floor for speakers, musicians, etc; a stage; a place or opportunity for public discussion; the raised area next to a railway line where passengers board trains; a statement of political aims.

plating *n* the act or process of plating; a thin coating of metal; a coating of metal plates.

platinize *vt* to coat with platinum.

platinum *n* a valuable, silvery-white metal used for jewellery, etc.

platinum-blond *adj* (*hair*) silvery blond. * *n* someone with hair of this colour.—**platinum-blonde** *nf*.

platitude *n* a dull truism; a commonplace remark.— **platitudinous** *adj*.

platitudinize *vi* to utter platitudes.

platonic *adj* (*love*) spiritual and free from physical desire; (*with cap*) relating to Plato, the Greek philosopher, or his teachings.—**platonically** *adv*.

platoon *n* a military unit divided into squads or sections.

platter *n* an oval flat serving dish.

platy- *prefix* flat.

platyhelminth *n* a type of flatworm.

platypus *n* (*pl* **platypuses**) a small aquatic egg-laying mammal of Australia and Tasmania, with webbed feet, a bill like a duck's, dense fur, and a broad flat tail.—*also* **duck-billed platypus**.

platyrrhine, platyrrhinian *adj* (*zool*) broad-nosed.

plaudit *n* (*usu pl*) a commendation; a round of applause.

plausible *adj* apparently truthful or reasonable.—**plausibility** *n*.—**plausibly** *adv*.

play *vi* to amuse oneself (with toys, games, etc); to act carelessly or trifle (with somebody's feelings); to gamble; to act on the stage or perform on a musical instrument; (*light*) to flicker, shimmer; (*water*) to discharge or direct on. * *vt* to participate in a sport; to be somebody's opponent in a game; to perform a dramatic production; (*instrument*) to produce music on; (*hose*) to direct; (*fish*) to give line to; to bet on. * *n* fun, amusement; the playing of, or manner of playing, a game; the duration of a game; a literary work for performance by actors; gambling; scope, freedom to move.—**playable** *adj*.

playact *vi* to behave affectedly or overdramatically; to make believe, pretend; to act in a play.—**playacting** *n*.—**playactor** *n*.

playback *n* the act of reproducing recorded sound or pictures, esp soon after they are made; a mechanism in an audio or video recorder for doing this.—*also vt*.

playbill *n* a poster advertising a theatrical performance.

playboy *n* a person who lives for pleasure.

player *n* a person who plays a specified game or instrument; an actor.

playfellow *see* **playmate**.

playful *adj* full of fun; humorous; sportive; fond of sport or amusement.—**playfully** *adv*.—**playfulness** *n*.

playgoer *n* a person who goes to the theatre, esp one who attends frequently or regularly.—**playgoing** *adj, n*.

playground *n* an area outdoors for children's recreation.

playhouse *n* a theatre.

playing card *n* one of a set of 52 cards used for playing games, each card having an identical pattern on one side and its own symbol on the reverse.

playing field *n* a place for playing sport.

playlet *n* a short play.

playmate *n* a friend in play.—*also* **playfellow**.

playpen *n* a portable usu collapsible enclosure in which a young child may be left to play safely.

plaything *n* a toy; a thing or person treated as a toy.

playtime *n* a time for recreation, esp at a school.

playwright *n* a writer of plays.

plaza *n* a public square in a town or city; (*US*) an area for the parking and servicing of cars.

plea *n* (*law*) an answer to a charge, made by the accused person; a request; an entreaty.

plead *vti* (**pleading, pleaded, plead** *or* **pled**) to beg, implore; to give as an excuse; to answer (guilty or not guilty) to a charge; to argue (a law case).—**pleadable** *adj*.—**pleader** *n*.

pleading *n* advocacy of a cause in a court of law; one of the allegations and counter allegations made alternately, usu in writing, by the parties in a legal action; the act or instance of making a plea; a sincere entreaty. * *adj* begging, imploring.—**pleadingly** *adv*.

pleasant *adj* agreeable; pleasing.—**pleasantly** *adv*.—**pleasantness** *n*.

pleasantry *n* (*pl* **pleasantries**) a polite or amusing remark.

please *vti* to satisfy; to give pleasure to; to be willing; to have the wish. * *adv* as a word to express politeness or emphasis in a request; an expression of polite affirmation.

pleased *adj* gratified.

pleasing *adj* giving pleasure; agreeable.—**pleasingly** *adv*.

pleasurable *adj* gratifying, delightful.—**pleasurably** *adv*.

pleasure *n* enjoyment, recreation; gratification of the senses; preference.

pleat *n* a double fold of cloth, etc pressed or stitched in place. * *vt* to gather into pleats.

pleb *n* a plebeian; (*sl*) a common person.

plebeian *adj* relating to the common people; base, vulgar. * *n* a commoner of ancient Rome; a vulgar, coarse person.—**plebeianism** *n*.

plebiscite *n* a direct vote of the electorate on a political issue such as annexation, independent nationhood, etc.

plectrum *n* (*pl* **plectra, plectrums**) a thin piece of metal, etc for plucking the strings of a guitar, etc.

pledge *n* a solemn promise; security for payment of a debt; a token or sign; a toast. * *vt* to give as security; to pawn; to bind by solemn promise; to drink a toast to.

pledgee *n* someone to whom a pledge is given.

pledget *n* a small pad of lint, etc, used to apply pressure to wounds.

pleiad *n* a brilliant group (of people).

Pleiades *npl* a cluster of seven stars in the constellation Taurus.

plein-air *adj* (*art*) depicting the effects of light and atmosphere outdoors.

Pleistocene *adj* (*geol*) pertaining to the earliest division of the Quaternary Period.

plenary *adj* full, complete; (*assembly, etc*) attended by all the members.—**plenarily** *adv*.

plenipotentiary *adj* possessing full powers. * *n* (*pl* **plenipotentiaries**) an envoy with authority to act at his own discretion.

plenitude *n* abundance.

plenteous *adj* abundant.

plentiful *adj* abundant, copious.—**plentifully** *adv*.—**plentifulness** *n*.

plenty *n* an abundance; more than enough; a great number. * *adv* (*sl*) quite.

plenum *n* (*pl* **plenums, plena**) a full assembly; a space filled with matter.

pleonasm *n* (*rhetoric*) the use of unnecessary words, eg "he is blind and cannot see".—**pleonastic** *adj*.

plesiosaurus, plesiosaur *n* a large, extinct, long-necked swimming reptile.

plessor *see* **plexor**.

plethora *n* overabundance, glut; (*med*) an excess of red corpuscles in the blood.—**plethoric** *adj*.

pleura *n* (*pl* **pleurae**) the membrane enclosing the lungs.—**pleural** *adj*.

pleurisy *n* inflammation of the membranes enclosing the lungs.—**pleuritic** *adj*.

pleuropneumonia *n* an inflammation of both the pleura and the lung.

Plexiglas *n* (*trademark*) a transparent thermoplastic.

plexor *n* (*med*) a small hammer used in percussion and for testing reflexes.—*also* **plessor**.

plexus *n* (*pl* **plexuses, plexus**) a network, esp of nerves or blood vessels.

pliable *adj* easily bent or moulded; easily influenced.—**pliability** *n*. —**pliably** *adv*.

pliant *adj* easily bent or influenced; supple; flexible, yielding.—**pliancy** *n*.—**pliantly** *adv*.

plicate, plicated *adj* pleated; folded in the form of a fan.

pliers *npl* a tool with hinged arms and jaws for cutting, shaping wire.

plight[1] n a dangerous situation; a predicament.

plight[2] vt to pledge, vow solemnly. * n a pledge; an engagement.—plighter n.

Plimsoll line n a system of markings on the hull of ships to ensure there is no overloading and that cargo is balanced.—also load line.

plimsolls, plimsoles npl (Brit) rubber-soled canvas shoes, sneakers.

Pliocene adj (geol) pertaining to the latest division of the Tertiary Period.

PLO abbr = Palestine Liberation Organization.

plod vi (plodding, plodded) to walk heavily and slowly, to trudge; to work or study slowly and laboriously.—plodder n.—ploddingly adv.

plop vti (plopping, plopped) to fall into water without a splash. * n the sound of this. * adv with a plop.

plot n a small piece of land; a secret plan or conspiracy; the story in a play or novel, etc. * vt (plotting, plotted) to conspire; (route) to mark on a map; (points) to mark (on a graph) with coordinates.—plotter n.

plough, plow n a farm implement for turning up soil; any implement like this, as a snowplough. * vt to cut and turn up with a plough; to make a furrow (in), to wrinkle; to force a way through; to work at laboriously; (with into) to run into; (with back) to reinvest; (sl) to fail an examination.—ploughable adj.—plougher n.

ploughman, plowman n (pl ploughmen, plowmen) one who ploughs; a farmworker.

ploughshare, plowshare n the part of a plough which cuts the soil.

plover n a wading bird with a short tail and a straight bill.

ploy n a tactic or manoeuvre to outwit an opponent; an occupation or job; an escapade.

pluck vt to pull off or at; to snatch; to strip off feathers; (fruit, flowers, etc) to pick; (person) to remove from one situation in life and transfer to another. * vi to make a sharp pull or twitch. * n a pull or tug; heart, courage; dogged resolution.—plucker n.

plucky adj (pluckier, pluckiest) brave, spirited.—pluckily adv.—pluckiness n.

plug n a stopper used for filling a hole; a device for connecting an appliance to an electricity supply; a cake of tobacco; a kind of fishing lure; (inf) a free advertisement usu incorporated in other matter. * vti (plugging, plugged) to stop up with a plug; (sl) to shoot or punch; (inf) to seek to advertise by frequent repetition; (with at) (inf) to work doggedly.

plum n an oval smooth-skinned sweet stone-fruit; a tree bearing it; a reddish-purple colour; a choice thing.

plumage n a bird's feathers.

plumb n a lead weight attached to a line, used to determine how deep water is or whether a wall is vertical; any of various weights. * adj perfectly vertical. * adv vertically; in a direct manner; (inf) entirely. * vt to test by a plumb line; to examine minutely and critically; to weight with lead; to seal with lead; to supply with or install as plumbing. * vi to work as a plumber.

plumbago n (pl plumbagos) graphite; one of a genus of flowering plants.

plumber n a person who installs and repairs water or gas pipes.

plumbing n the system of pipes used in water or gas supply, or drainage; the plumber's craft.

plumbism n lead poisoning.

plume n a large or ornamental bird's feather; a feathery ornament or thing; something resembling a feather in structure or density. * vt (feathers) to preen; to adorn with feathers; to indulge (oneself) with an obvious display of self-satisfaction.

plummet n a plumb. * vi (plummeting, plumeted) to fall in a perpendicular manner; to drop sharply and abruptly.

plummy adj (plummier, plummiest) like, full of, plums; (inf) rich, desirable; (inf) (voice) deep, drawling, rich-sounding.

plump[1] adj rounded, chubby. * vti to make or become plump; to swell.—plumply adv.—plumpness n.

plump[2] vti to fall, drop or sink, or come into contact suddenly and heavily; (someone, something) to favour or give support. * n a sudden drop or plunge or the sound of this. * adv straight down, straight ahead; abruptly; bluntly.

plum pudding n a rich boiled or steamed pudding with suet, dried fruit, spices, etc.

plumule n (zool) a down feather; (bot) the embryonic stem of a plant.

plumy adj (plumier, plumiest) feathery; feathered.

plunder vt to steal goods by force, to loot. * n plundering; booty.—plunderer n.

plunge vti to immerse, dive suddenly; to penetrate quickly; to hurl oneself or rush; (horse) to start violently forward.

plunger n a solid cylinder that operates with a plunging motion, as a piston; a larger rubber suction cup used to free clogged drains.

plunk vt (mus) to pluck. * vti to throw or fall heavily. n the sound produced by something being plucked, or falling in this way.

pluperfect adj, n (gram) (a tense) denoting an action completed before a past point of time.

plural adj more than one; consisting of or containing more than one kind or class. * n (gram) the form referring to more than one person or thing.—plurally adv.

pluralism n the simultaneous holding of more than one office or benefice; a theory that reality is composed of a plurality of entities; a theory that there are at least two levels of ultimate reality; the coexistence in society of people of distinct ethnic, cultural or religious groups, each preserving their own traditions; a doctrine or policy advocating this condition.—pluralist n.—pluralistic adj.—pluralistically adv.

plurality n (pl pluralities) being plural; a majority; a large number; another term for pluralism.

plus prep added to; in addition to. * adj indicating addition; positive. * n the sign (+) indicating a value greater than zero; an advantage or benefit; an extra.

plush n a velvet-like fabric with a nap. * adj made of plush; (inf) luxurious.

Pluto n (Greek myth) the god of the underworld; (astron) the planet farthest from the sun, discovered in 1930.

plutocracy n (pl plutocracies) government or rule by the wealthy; a wealthy class.—plutocratic adj.—plutocratically adv.

plutocrat n a person who has power through wealth; a rich person.

Plutonian adj pertaining to Pluto or the underworld; infernal.

plutonic adj (geol) formed from magma cooling beneath the earth's surface.

plutonium n a highly toxic transuranic element used as fuel in nuclear power stations and in nuclear weapons.

pluvial *adj* caused by the action of rain; rainy.

pluviometer *n* an instrument used to measure rainfall.—*also* **rain gauge**.

ply[1] *vti* (**plying, plied**) to work at diligently and energetically; to wield; to subject to persistently; (*goods*) to sell; to go to and fro, run regularly; to keep busy.

ply[2] *n* (*pl* **plies**) a layer or thickness, as of cloth, plywood, etc; any of the twisted strands in a yarn, etc. * *vt* (**plying, plied**) to twist together.

plywood *n* a building material consisting of several thin layers of wood glued together.

PM *abbr* = post-mortem; Prime Minister.

Pm (*chem symbol*) promethium.

p.m. *abbr* = post meridiem.

PMS *abbr* = premenstrual syndrome.

PMT *abbr* = premenstrual tension.

pneumatic *adj* concerning wind, air, or gases; operated by or filled with compressed air.—**pneumatically** *adv*.

pneumatics *n sing* the science dealing with the mechanical properties of air.

pneumatology *n* the theological study of the Holy Spirit.

pneumatometer *n* an instrument for measuring the amount of air exhaled in one breath.

pneumatophore *n* the breathing organ of a marsh plant.

pneumonia *n* acute inflammation of the lungs.—**pneumonic** *adj*.

PO *abbr* = Personnel Officer; Petty Officer; Pilot Officer; post office; postal order.

Po (*chem symbol*) polonium.

poach[1] *vt* to cook (an egg without its shell, fish, etc) in or over boiling water.

poach[2] *vti* to catch game or fish illegally; to trespass for this purpose; to encroach on, usurp another's rights, etc; to steal another's idea, employee, etc.—**poaching** *n*.

poacher[1] *n* a pan with shallow cups for poaching eggs; a dish for poaching fish, etc.

poacher[2] *n* a person who poaches another's property.

pochard *n* (*pl* **pochards, pochard**) a red-headed European duck.

pock *n* an eruptive pustule on the skin, esp as a result of smallpox.

pocket *n* a small bag or pouch, esp in a garment, for carrying small articles; an isolated or enclosed area; a deposit (as of gold, water, or gas). * *adj* small enough to put in a pocket. * *vt* to put in one's pocket, to steal; (*ball*) to put in a pocket; to envelop; to enclose; (*money*) to take dishonestly; to suppress.

pocketbook *n* a small folder or case for letters, money, credit cards, etc; a woman's purse, a handbag; monetary resources; a small esp paperback book.

pocketful *n* (*pl* **pocketfuls**) as much as a pocket holds.

pocketknife *n* (*pl* **pocketknives**) a small knife with one or more blades that fold into the handle.

pocket money *n* money for occasional expenses; a child's allowance.

poco *adv* (*mus*) a little.

pococurante *n, adj* (someone who is) indifferent.

pod *n* a dry fruit or seed vessel, as of peas, beans, etc; a protective container or housing; a detachable compartment on a spacecraft. * *vi* (**podding, podded**) to remove the pod from.

podagra *n* gout, esp in the feet.—**podagral, podagric, podagrous** *adj*.

podgy *adj* (**podgier, podgiest**) short and fat, squat.—*also* **pudgy**.—**podginess** *n*.

podium *n* (*pl* **podiums, podia**) a platform used by lecturers, etc; a low wall around the arena of an amphitheatre.

podophyllin *n* a purgative resin obtained from the root of the May apple and mandrake.

poem *n* an arrangement of words, esp in metre, often rhymed, in a style more imaginative than ordinary speech; a poetic thing.

poesy *n* (*pl* **poesies**) the art of writing poetry.

poet *n* the writer of a poem; a person with imaginative power and a sense of beauty.—**poetess** *nf*.

poetaster *n* an inferior poet.

poetic, poetical *adj* of poets or poetry; written in verse; imaginative, romantic, like poetry.—**poetically** *adv*.

poetic justice *n* an outcome in which vice is punished and virtue rewarded in an appropriate manner.

poetic licence *n* latitude allowed to a poet in grammar, facts, etc.

poetics *n sing* the theory, or study, of poetry.

poetize *vt* to make poetic; to compose poetry about. * *vi* to compose poetry.

poet laureate *n* (*pl* **poets laureate**) a poet officially appointed by the British sovereign to write poems celebrating national events, etc.

poetry *n* the art of writing poems; poems collectively; poetic quality or spirit.

pogo stick *n* a stilt with a powerful spring used to hop along the ground.

pogrom *n* an organized extermination of a minority group.

poignant *adj* piercing; incisive; deeply moving.—**poignancy** *n*.—**poignantly** *adv*.

poinsettia *n* a South American plant, widely cultivated as a house plant for its red bracts, which resemble petals.

point *n* a dot or tiny mark used in writing or printing (eg a decimal point, a full stop); a location; a place in a cycle, course, or scale; a unit in scoring or judging; the sharp end of a knife or pin; a moment of time; one of thirty-two divisions of the compass; a fundamental reason or aim; the tip; a physical characteristic; a railway switch; a unit of size in printing equal to one seventy-second of an inch; a unit used in quoting the prices of stocks, bonds and commodities; a headland or cape. * *vti* to give point to; to sharpen; to aim (at); to extend the finger (at or to); to indicate something; to call attention (to).

point-blank *adj* aimed straight at a mark; direct, blunt.—*also adv*.

pointed *adj* having a point; pertinent; aimed at a particular person or group; conspicuous.—**pointedly** *adv*.—**pointedness** *n*.

pointer *n* a rod or needle for pointing; an indicator; a breed of hunting dog.

pointillism *n* in painting, the practice of applying small strokes or dots of colour to a surface so that from a distance they blend together.—**pointillist** *n, adj*.

pointless *adj* without a point; irrelevant, aimless.—**pointlessly** *adv*.—**pointlessness** *n*.

poise[1] *vt* to balance; to hold supported without motion; (*the head*) to hold in a particular way; to put into readiness. * *vi* to become drawn up into readiness; to hover. * *n* a balanced state; self-possessed assurance of manner; gracious tact; bearing, carriage.

poise[2] *n* a centimetre-gram-second unit of viscosity equivalent to one dyne-second per square metre.

poison *n* a substance that through its chemical action

usu destroys or injures an organism; any corrupt influence; an object of aversion or abhorrence. * *vt* to administer poison in order to kill or injure; to put poison into; to influence wrongfully.—**poisoner** *n*.

poison gas *n* a poisonous gas, or a liquid or solid giving off poisonous vapours, used in warfare.

poison ivy *n* a climbing plant with ivory-coloured berries and an acutely irritating oil that causes an intensely itchy skin rash; the rash caused by poison ivy.

poisonous *adj* being or containing poison; toxic; having a harmful influence; (*inf*) unpleasant.—**poisonously**. *adv*.—**poisonousness** *n*.

poke *vt* to thrust (at), jab or prod; (*hole, etc*) to make by poking; (*sl*) to hit. * *vi* to jab (at); to pry or search (about or around). * *n* a jab; a prod or nudge; a thrust.

poker[1] *n* a metal rod for poking or stirring fire.

poker[2] *n* a card game in which a player bets that the value of his hand is higher than that of the hands held by others.

poker face *n* an expressionless face, concealing a person's thoughts or feelings.—**poker-faced** *adj*.

poky, pokey *adj* (**pokier, pokiest**) small and uncomfortable.—**pokily** *adv*.—**pokiness** *n*.

polar *adj* of or near the North or South Pole; of a pole; having positive and negative electricity; directly opposite.

polar angle *n* the angle between the positive (polar) axis and the radius vector in polar coordinates.

polar bear *n* a large creamy-white bear that inhabits arctic regions.

polar coordinates *npl* either of a pair of coordinates that determine the position of points in space by measuring their distance along a fixed line from the origin or other given point and their angle, which lies between the fixed line and a single axis.

polarimeter *n* an instrument for measuring the polarization of light.

Polaris *n* (*astron*) the brightest star in the Ursa Minor constellation, also known as the Pole Star.

polariscope *n* an instrument used to detect polarized light.

polarity *n* (*pl* **polarities**) the condition of being polar; the magnet's property of pointing north; attraction towards a particular object or in a specific direction; (*elect*) the state, positive or negative, of a body; diametrical opposition; an instance of such opposition.

polarization *n* the production or acquirement of polarity; (*optics*) the process of causing light waves to vibrate in a uniform circular, elliptical or linear pattern; (*elect*) the separation of positive and negative charges; the grouping about opposing factions.

polarize *vt* (*light waves*) to cause to vibrate in a definite pattern; to give physical polarity to; to break up into opposing factions; to concentrate.—**polarizable** *adj*.—**polarizer** *n*.

Polaroid *n* (*trademark*) a transparent material used esp in sunglasses and lamps to prevent glare; a camera that produces a print in seconds.

polder *n* (*Netherlands*) a piece of land reclaimed from the sea.

pole[1] *n* a long slender piece of wood, metal, etc; a flagstaff. * *vt* to propel, support with a pole.

pole[2] *n* either end of an axis, esp of the earth; either of two opposed forces, parts, etc, as the ends of a magnet, terminals of a battery, etc; either of two opposed principles.

poleaxe, poleax *n* a long-handled battle axe; a type of axe used to slaughter cattle. * *vt* to hit or knock down with, or as if with, such an axe.

pole bean *n* a climbing plant that produces long green edible pods, a runner bean.

polecat *n* (*pl* **polecats, polecat**) a small, dark-brown animal, found in Europe, North Africa and Asia, related to the weasel and known for its unpleasant smell.

polemic *n* a controversy or argument over doctrine; strong criticism; a controversialist. * *adj* involving dispute; controversial (—*also* **polemical**).— **polemically** *adv*.—**polemicist** *n*.

polemics *n sing* the art of controversial debate. * *adj* disputatious, controversial.

polenta *n* an Italian porridge of maize, barley or chestnut meal.

pole vault *n* a field event in which competitors jump over a high bar using a long flexible pole.—**polevault** *vi*.—**pole-vaulter** *n*.

police *n* the government department for keeping order, detecting crime, law enforcement, etc; (*pl*) the members of such a department; any similar organization. * *vt* to control, protect, etc with police or a similar force.

policeman *n* (*pl* **policemen**) a member of a police force.—**policewoman** *nf* (*pl* **policewomen**).

police officer *n* a policeman or policewoman.

policy[1] *n* (*pl* **policies**) a written insurance contract.

policy[2] *n* (*pl* **policies**) political wisdom, statecraft; a course of action selected from among alternatives; a high-level overall plan embracing the general principles and aims of an organization, esp a government.

policyholder *n* a person who has an insurance policy.

polio *n* poliomyelitis.

poliomyelitis *n* an acute infectious virus disease marked by inflammation of nerve cells in the spinal cord, causing paralysis.

Polish *adj* of or pertaining to Poland, its inhabitants, language or culture. * *n* the Slavic language of Poland.

polish *vti* to make or become smooth and shiny by rubbing (with a cloth and polish); to give elegance or culture to; (*with off*) (*inf*) to finish completely. * *n* smoothness; elegance of manner; a finish or gloss; a substance, such as wax, used to polish.—**polisher** *n*.

polished *adj* accomplished; smoothly or professionally done or performed; (*rice*) having had the husk removed.

polite *adj* courteous; well-bred; refined.—**politely** *adv*.—**politeness** *n*.

politesse *n* (excessively) formal politeness.

politic *adj* expedient; shrewdly tactful; prudent.

political *adj* relating to politics or government; characteristic of political parties or politicians.—**politically** *adv*.

political correctness *n* a movement aimed at removing discrimination against women, ethnic minorities, gays and lesbians, etc by combating sexist and racist language or policies in education, the arts, media and government.—**politically correct** *adj*.

political economy *n* the former name for the science of economics.

politician *n* a person engaged in politics, often used with implications of seeking personal or partisan gain, scheming, etc.

politico *n* (*sl*) a politician.

politics *n* (*sing or pl*) the science and art of government; political activities, beliefs or affairs; factional scheming for power.

polity *n* (*pl* **polities**) the form or constitution of the government of a state; a constitution.

polka *n* a lively dance; the music for this. * *vi* to dance the polka.

polka dot *n* any of a pattern of small round dots forming a pattern on cloth.

poll *n* a counting, listing, etc of persons, esp of voters; the number of votes recorded; an opinion survey; (*pl*) a place where votes are cast. * *vti* to receive the votes (of); to cast a vote; to canvass or question in a poll.—**poller** *n*.

pollack *n* (*pl* **pollacks**, **pollack**) a type of food fish.—*also* **pollock** (*pl* **pollocks**, **pollock**).

pollan *n* an Irish freshwater fish.

pollard *n* a tree with its branches pruned to encourage growth; an animal which has cast its horns or antlers, or had them removed.

pollen *n* the yellow dust, containing male spores, that is formed in the anthers of flowers.—**pollinic** *adj*.

pollex *n* (*pl* **pollices**) a thumb or similar first digit.

pollinate *vti* to fertilize by uniting pollen with seed.—**pollinator** *n*.

pollination *n* the transfer of pollen from the anthers of a flower to the stigma, esp by insects.

polliwog, **pollywog** *n* a tadpole.

pollock *see* **pollack**.

pollster *n* a person who conducts a poll or compiles data obtained from a poll.

poll tax *n* a tax of a fixed amount per person levied on adults.

pollute *vt* to contaminate with harmful substances; to make corrupt; to profane.—**polluter** *n*.

pollution *n* the act of polluting; the state of being polluted; contamination by chemicals, noise, etc.

polo *n* a game played on horseback by two teams, using a wooden ball and long-handled mallets.

polonaise *n* a slow, stately dance in three-four time; the music for such a dance; an outfit with a one-piece bodice and a skirt looped up at the sides.

polo shirt *n* a sports shirt made of a knitted fabric.

polonium *n* a radioactive element.

poltergeist *n* a spirit believed to move heavy objects about and to make noises.

poltroon *n* (*arch*) a coward.

poly- *prefix* many.

polyandry *n* the practice of a woman having more than one husband at the same time.—**polyandrous** *adj*.

polyanthus *n* (*pl* **polyanthuses**) a hybrid garden primrose; a narcissus with small yellow or white flowers in clusters.

polyatomic *adj* with more than two atoms in the molecule.

polybasic *adj* (*chem*) having more than two bases or atoms of a base.

polychaete, **poltchete** *n* a type of marine worm. * *adj* pertaining to this type of worm (—*also* **polychaetous**).

polychromatic, **polychromic**, **polychromous** *adj* having many colours; exhibiting a play of colours; (*physics*) (*light*, *etc*) having a mixture of wavelengths.—**polychromatism** *n*.

polychrome *adj* made with, or decorated in, many colours. * *n* a work of art in several colours; a painted statue.

polyclinic *n* a general hospital.

polydactyl *n*, *adj* (an animal or person) with more than the normal number of fingers or toes.

polyester *n* any of a number of synthetic polymeric resins used for adhesives, plastics, and textiles.

polyethylene *n* a light, plastic, multipurpose synthetic material resistant to moisture and chemicals.—*also* **polythene**.

polygamist *n* a person who advocates or practises polygamy.

polygamy *n* the practice of being married to more than one person at a time; (*bot*) the condition of having staminate, pistillate and hermaphrodite flowers on one plant; (*zool*) the practice of having more than one mate.—**polygamous** *adj*.—**polygamously** *adv*.

polygenesis *n* the derivation of a species or race from many origins.—**polygenetic** *adj*.

polyglot *adj* having command of many languages; composed of numerous languages; containing matter in several languages; composed of elements from different languages. * *n* a person who speaks several languages.

polygon *n* a closed plane figure bound by three or more straight lines.—**polygonal** *adj*.

polygonum *n* one of a family of flowering plants including knotgrass.

polygraph *n* an instrument for detecting and measuring involuntary changes in blood pressure, breathing, etc, often used as a lie detector.—**polygraphic** *adj*.

polygyny *n* the practice of a man having more than one wife at the same time.—**polygynous** *adj*.

polyhedron *n* (*pl* **polyhedrons**, **polyhedra**) a solid with many (usu more than six) plane faces.—**polyhedral** *adj*.

polymath *n* someone learned in many subjects.

polymer *n* (*chem*) a compound that has large molecules composed of many simpler molecules.—**polymeric** *adj*.—**polymerism** *n*.

polymerize *vti* to (cause to) form a polymer.

polymorph *n* a polymorphous organism.

polymorphous, **polymorphic** *adj* having, or assuming, many different forms.

polynomial *n* (*math*) an expression consisting of a sum of terms each of which is a product of a constant and one or more variables raised to a positive or zero integral power; (*biol*) a species name of more than two terms. * *adj* composed of or expressed as one or more polynomials.

polyp *n* a small water animal with tentacles at the top of a tube-like body; a growth on mucous membrane.—**polypoid** *adj*.

polyphagous *adj* voracious; (*zool*) feeding on various kinds of food.

polyphone *n* (*linguistics*) a polyphonic letter or symbol

polyphonic *adj* many-voiced; (*mus*) contrapuntal; (*phonetics*) representing more than one sound.

polyphony *n* (*pl* **polyphonies**) being polyphonic; using polyphones; (*mus*) counterpoint.

polypod *n*, *adj* (an animal) with many legs.

polypody *n* (*pl* **polypodies**) a type of fern.

polypus *n* (*pl* **polypi**) (*med*) a tumour with branching roots, found in the nose or womb.

polystyrene *n* a rigid plastic material used for packing, insulating, etc.

polysyllable *n* a word of many syllables.—**polysyllabic** *adj*.—**polysyllabically** *adv*.

polytechnic *n* an institution that provides instruction in many applied sciences and technical subjects.

polytheism *n* belief in many gods, or more than one god.—**polytheist** *n*.—**polytheistic** *adj*.

polythene *see* **polyethylene**.

polyunsaturated *adj* denoting any of certain plant and animal fats and oils with a low cholesterol content.

polyurethane *n* any of various polymers that are used esp in flexible and rigid foams, resins, etc.

pomace *n* crushed apples for making cider; the crushed apples left after making cider.

pomaceous *adj* pertaining to pomes.

pomade *n* a scented ointment for the hair.

pomander *n* an aromatic ball or powder formerly carried for its pleasant smell or as protection against infection; a container for this.

pome *n* the stoneless fruit of the apple and related plants.

pomegranate *n* an edible fruit with many seeds; the widely cultivated tropical tree bearing it.

Pomeranian *n* a breed of small dog.

pomiculture *n* fruit growing.

pommel *n* the rounded, upward-projecting front part of a saddle; a knob on the hilt of a sword. * *vt* (**pommelling, pommelled** *or* **pommeling, pommeled**) to pummel.

pommy, pommie *n* (*pl* **pommies**) (*Austral sl*) a British person.

pomology *n* the study of fruit growing.—**pomological** *adj*.—**pomologist** *n*.

Pomona *n* (*Roman myth*) the goddess of fruit trees.

pomp *n* stately ceremony; ostentation.

pompadour *n* an 18th century hairstyle.

pompano *n* (*pl* **pompano, pompanos**) an edible American sea fish.

pom-pom *n* a quick-firing automatic anti-aircraft gun.

pompon, pompom, *n* an ornamental ball or tuft of fabric strands used on clothing as an ornament; a small tufted flower on some varieties of chrysanthemum and dahlia.

pomposity *n* (*pl* **pomposities**) the state of being pompous; self-importance; a pompous utterance or act.

pompous *adj* stately; self-important.—**pompously** *adv*.—**pompousness** *n*.

poncho *n* (*pl* **ponchos**) a blanket-like cloak with a hole in the centre for the head.

pond *n* a body of standing water smaller than a lake.

ponder *vti* to think deeply; to consider carefully.

ponderable *adj* capable of being evaluated; capable of being weighed.—**ponderability** *n*.

ponderous *adj* heavy; awkward; dull; lifeless.—**ponderously** *adv*.—**ponderousness** *n*.

pone *n* (*US*) corn pone; maize bread.

pong *n* (*Brit sl*) an unpleasant smell. * *vi* (*Brit sl*) to stink.

pongee *n* a thin, unbleached, Chinese silk.

pontifex *n* (*pl* **pontifices**) (*ancient Rome*) a pontiff or high priest.

pontiff *n* the Pope; a bishop; a pontifex.

pontifical *adj* of a pontiff; pompous. * *npl* a bishop's robes.—**pontifically** *adv*.

pontificate *vi* to speak sententiously, pompously or dogmatically; to officiate at a pontifical mass.—**pontificator** *n*.

pontoon[1] *n* a boat or cylindrical float forming a support for a bridge.

pontoon[2] *n* a card game.

pony *n* (*pl* **ponies**) a small horse, a bronco, mustang, etc; (*inf*) a racehorse.

ponytail *n* a style of arranging hair to resemble a pony's tail.

poodle *n* a breed of dog of various sizes with a curly coat.

pool[1] *n* a small pond; a puddle; a small collection of liquid; a swimming pool.

pool[2] *n* a game played on a billiards table with six pockets; a combination of resources, funds, supplies, people, etc for some common purpose; the parties forming such a combination. * *vti* to contribute to a common fund, to share.

poop *n* (*naut*) the stern of a ship; the raised deck in the stern of a ship.

poor *adj* having little money, needy; deserving pity, unfortunate; deficient; disappointing; inferior. * *n* those who have little.—**poorness** *n*.

poorhouse *n* (*formerly*) a public institution housing poor people.

poorly *adv* insufficiently, badly. * *adj* not in good health.

pop[1] *n* a short, explosive sound, a shot; any carbonated, nonalcoholic beverage. * *vti* (**popping, popped**) to make or cause a pop; to shoot; to go or come quickly (in, out, up); (*corn, maize*) to roast until it pops; to put suddenly; (*eyes*) to bulge.

pop[2] *adj* in a popular modern style. * *n* pop music; pop art; pop culture.

pop[3] *n* (*inf*) father; (*inf*) a name used to address an old man.

pop art *n* a realistic art style using techniques and subjects from commercial art, comic strips, posters, etc.

popcorn *n* a kind of corn or maize, which when heated pops or puffs up.

pope *n* the bishop of Rome, head of the RC Church.—**popedom** *n*.

popery *n* (*derog*) Roman Catholicism.

pop-eyed *adj* with bulging eyes; (*fig*) astonished.

popgun *n* a toy gun firing pellets with a popping noise.

popinjay *n* a conceited person.

popish *adj* (*derog*) pertaining to Roman Catholicism.

poplar *n* a slender, quick-growing tree of the willow family.

poplin *n* a sturdy corded fabric.

poppet *n* a term of endearment.

poppet valve *n* a valve opened by being lifted from its seat.

poppy *n* (*pl* **poppies**) an annual or perennial plant with showy flowers, one of which yields opium; a strong reddish colour.

poppycock *n* (*inf*) nonsense.

populace *n* the common people; the masses; all the people in a country, region, etc.

popular *adj* of the people; well liked; pleasing to many people; easy to understand.—**popularly** *adv*.

popularity *n* the condition or quality of being popular.

popularize *vt* to make popular; to make generally accepted or understood.—**popularization** *n*.—**popularizer** *n*.

populate *vt* to inhabit; to supply with inhabitants.

population *n* all the inhabitants or the number of people in an area.

populism *n* any movement based on belief in the rights, wisdom, or virtue of the common people.

populist *n* an advocate of populism; one who claims to represent the people; (*with cap*) a member of the Populist or People's Party in the US (1891–1904) aiming at public control of utilities, etc.

populous *adj* densely inhabited.—**populously** *adv.*—**populousness** *n*.

porbeagle *n* a type of shark.

porcelain *n* a hard, white, translucent variety of ceramic ware. * *adj* made of porcelain.—**porcellaneous** *adj*.

porch *n* a covered entrance to a building; an open or enclosed gallery or room on the outside of a building.

porcupine *n* a large rodent covered with protective quills.

pore[1] *n* a tiny opening, as in the skin, plant leaves, stem, etc, for absorbing and discharging fluids.

pore[2] *vti* (*with* **over**) to look with steady attention; to study closely.

porgy *n* (*pl* **porgy, porgies**) an edible sea fish.

pork *n* the flesh of a pig used as food.

porker *n* a pig, esp a fattened one.

porky *adj* (**porkier, porkiest**) of or like pork; (*sl*) impertinent; (*sl*) obese, fat.—**porkiness** *n*.

porno *n* (*sl*) pornography—*also* **porn**. * *adj* pornographic.

pornography *n* writings, pictures, films, etc, intended primarily to arouse sexual desire.—**pornographer** *n*.—**pornographic** *adj*.—**pornographically** *adv*.

porous *adj* having pores; able to absorb air and fluids, etc.—**porously** *adv*.—**porousness** *n*.

porphyry *n* (*pl* **porphyry**) a reddish igneous rock, containing crystals of feldspar.

porpoise *n* (*pl* **porpoise, porpoises**) any of several small whales, esp a black blunt-nosed whale of the north Atlantic and Pacific; any of several bottle-nosed dolphins.

porridge *n* a thick food, usu made by boiling oats or oatmeal in water or milk.

porringer *n* a small dish for porridge, etc.

port[1] *n* a harbour; a town with a harbour where ships load and unload cargo; airport; a place where goods may be cleared through customs.

port[2] *n* a porthole; an opening, as in a valve face, for the passage of steam, etc; a hole in an armoured vehicle for firing a weapon; a circuit in a computer for inputting or outputting data.

port[3] *n* the left of an aircraft or ship looking forward.—*also adj*.

port[4] *n* a strong, sweet, fortified dark red wine.

portable *adj* capable of being carried or moved about easily.—**portability** *n*.

portage *n* a carrying of boats and supplies overland between navigable rivers, lakes, etc; any route over which this is done. * *vti* (*boats, etc*) to carry over a portage.

portal *n* an impressive gate or doorway.

portamento *n* (*mus*) a continuous glide from one note to another.

portcullis *n* a grating that can be lowered to bar entrance to a castle.

portend *vt* to give warning of, to foreshadow.

portent *n* an omen, warning.

portentous *adj* ominous; pompous, self-important.—**portentously** *adv*.—**portentousness** *n*.

porter[1] *n* a doorman or gatekeeper.

porter[2] *n* a person who carries luggage, etc, for hire at a station, airport, etc; a railway attendant for passengers; a dark brown beer.

porterage *n* the hire of a porter; the charge for this.

porterhouse *n* a choice cut of beef steak; (*formerly*) an eating place.

portfolio *n* (*pl* **portfolios**) a flat case for carrying papers, drawings, etc; a collection of work; the office of a cabinet minister or minister of state; a list of stocks, shares, etc.

porthole *n* an opening (as a window) with a cover or closure esp in the side of a ship or aircraft; a port through which to shoot; an opening for intake or exhaust of a fluid.

portico *n* (*pl* **porticoes, porticos**) a covered walkway with columns supporting the roof.

portière *n* a heavy curtain over a door or doorway.

portion *n* a part, a share, esp an allotted part; a helping of food; destiny. * *vt* to share out.

portly *adj* (**portlier, portliest**) dignified; stout.—**portliness** *n*.

portmanteau *n* (*pl* **portmanteaus, portmanteaux**) a large oblong travelling case with two compartments.

portmanteau word *n* a word combining the sound and sense of two other words, eg brunch.

portrait *n* a painting, photograph, etc, of a person, esp of the face; (*of person*) a likeness; a vivid description.

portraitist *n* a maker of portraits by painting, photography, etc.

portraiture *n* the drawing of portraits; a portrait; a description in words; portraits collectively.

portray *vt* to make a portrait of; to depict in words; to play the part of in a play, film, etc.—**portrayable** *adj*.—**portrayer** *n*.

portrayal *n* the act or process of portraying; a description; a representation.

portress *n* a female porter.

pose *n* a position or attitude, esp one held for an artist or photographer; an attitude deliberately adopted for effect. * *vti* to propound, assert; to assume an attitude for effect; to sit for a painting, photograph; to set oneself up (as).

poser *n* a person who poses; a difficult problem.

poseur *n* an affected, insincere person.

posh *adj* (*inf*) elegant; fashionable.

posit *vt* to assume as fact, postulate.

position *n* place, situation; a position occupied; posture; a job; state of affairs; point of view. * *vt* to place or locate.

positional *adj* related to, or fixed by position; involving little movement; dependent on context, environment or position.

positive *adj* affirmative; definite; sure; marked by presence, not absence, of qualities; expressed clearly, or in a confident manner; constructive; empirical; (*elect*) charged with positive electricity; (*math*) greater than zero, plus; (*gram*) of adjective or adverb, denoting the simple form; (*photog*) having light, shade, colour as in the original. * *n* a positive quality or quantity; a photographic print made from a negative.

positively *adv* in a positive way; decidedly.

positiveness *n* the condition or quality of being positive; confidence; certainty.

positivism *n* a philosophy recognizing only matters of fact and experience; the quality of being positive.—**positivist** *n, adj*.—**positivistic** *adj*.—**positivistically** *adv*.

positron *n* (*physics*) a particle of the same size as an electron, but with a positive charge.

posology *n* the area of medicine dealing with evaluation of doses.

posse *n* a body of people summoned by a sheriff to assist in keeping the peace, etc; (*sl*) a group of criminals, usu of Jamaican origin and in New York.

possess *vt* to own, have, keep; to dominate or control the mind of.—**possessor** *n.*—**possessory** *adj.*

possessed *adj* owned; controlled as if by a demon.

possession *n* ownership; something possessed; (*pl*) property.

possessive *adj* of or indicating possession; (*gram*) denoting a case, form or construction expressing possession; having an excessive desire to possess or dominate.—**possessively** *adv.*—**possessiveness** *n.*

posset *n* a hot drink of milk curdled with wine or ale.

possibility *n* (*pl* **possibilities**) the state of being possible; a possible occurrence, a contingency.

possible *adj* that may be or may happen; feasible, practicable.—**possibly** *adv.*

possum *n* (*inf*) an opossum; a phalanger; **play possum** to pretend to be asleep or dead; to remain silent.

post[1] *n* a piece of wood, metal, etc, set upright to support a building, sign, etc; the starting or finishing point of a race. * *vt* (*poster, etc*) to put up; to announce by posting notices; (*name*) to put on a posted or published list.

post[2] *n* a fixed position, esp where a sentry or group of soldiers is stationed; a position or job; a trading post; a settlement. * *vt* to station in a given place.

post[3] *n* the official conveyance of letters and parcels, mail; letters, parcels, etc, so conveyed; collection or delivery of post, mail. * *vt* to send a letter or parcel; to keep informed.—**postal** *adj.*

post- *prefix* after.

postage *n* the charge for sending a letter, etc, as represented by stamps.

postage stamp *n* an adhesive or imprinted stamp issued or authorized by a government and used on mail as evidence of prepayment of postage.

postal card *n* (*US*) a card with a stamp issued by the government for mailing at low rates; a post card.

postcard *n* a card, usu decorative, for sending messages by post; a postal card.

post chaise *n* (*formerly*) a light, closed, horse-drawn carriage used for carrying both post and passengers.

postcode *n* in UK, letters and digits to denote an address and assist sorting.

postdate *vt* to write a future date on a letter or cheque.

postdiluvian, postdiluvial *adj* occurring after the Flood (of the Old Testament).

poster *n* a usu decorative or ornamental printed sheet for advertising.

poste restante *n* the department of a post office that will hold mail until it is called for, general delivery.

posterior *adj* later in time or order; at the rear. * *n* the buttocks.—**posteriorly** *adv.*

posterity *n* future generations; all of a person's descendants.

postern *n* a back or side entrance; a small private door.

postfix *vt* to append as a suffix. * *n* a suffix.

post-free *adj* postpaid.

postglacial *adj* existing after a glacial period.

postgraduate *n* a person pursuing study after graduating from a high school or college. * *adj* (*study*) continued after the taking of a degree.

posthaste *adv* with all possible speed.

posthumous *adj* (*child*) born after its father's death; (*award, etc*) given after one's death.—**posthumously** *adv.*

postiche *adj* artificial; superfluous; inappropriate. * *n* an ornament added, esp inappropriately, to finished work; a wig; an imitation.

postilion, postillion *n* someone who rides one of the horses drawing a carriage and guiding the team.

postimpressionism *n* a 19th-century school of painting which sought to express the artist's conception of things rather than their outward appearance.—**postimpressionist** *n, adj.*

postliminium, postliminy *n* (*law*) the right of a prisoner of war or exile to resume his or her former privileges on return to his or her own country.

postlude *n* (*mus*) a closing movement.

postman *n* (*pl* **postmen**) a mailman.

postmark *n* the post office mark cancelling the stamp on a letter by showing the date, place of posting.

postmaster *n* the manager of a post office.

postmeridian *adj* of or taking place in the afternoon.

post meridiem = p.m. (Latin for *after noon*).

postmortem *n* an examination of a corpse to determine the cause of death; an autopsy.—*also adj.*

postnatal *adj* occurring immediately after birth.

post-obit *adj* (*law*) after death. * *n* a bond in which a borrower undertakes to repay a loan on the death of someone from whom he or she expects to receive a legacy.

post office *n* the building where postage stamps are sold and other postal business conducted; a public department handling the transmission of mail.

postpaid *adj* with a charge for postage, post free.

postpone *vt* to put off, delay to a future date.—**postponable** *adj.*—**postponement** *n.*—**postponer** *n.*

postprandial *adj* after-dinner.

postscript *n* a note added to a letter after completion.

postulant *n* someone making a request; a candidate for admission to a religious order.

postulate *vt* to assume to be true; to demand or claim. * *n* a position taken as self-evident; (*math*) an unproved assumption taken as basic; an axiom.—**postulation** *n.*

posture *n* a pose; a body position; an attitude of mind; an official stand or position. * *vti* to pose in a particular way; to assume a pose.—**postural** *adj.*—**posturer** *n.*

post-viral syndrome *n* the viral condition myalgic encephalomyelitis that affects the nervous system.

posy *n* (*pl* **posies**) a small bunch of flowers.

pot[1] *n* a deep, round cooking vessel; an earthenware or plastic container for plants; a framework for catching fish or lobsters; (*inf*) a large amount (as of money); (*inf*) all the money bet at a single time. * *vb* (**potting, potted**) *vt* to put or preserve in a pot. * *vi* to take a pot shot, shoot.

pot[2] *n* (*sl*) cannabis.

potable *adj* drinkable.

potash *n* potassium carbonate.

potassium *n* a soft silvery-white metallic element.—**potassic** *adj.*

potation *n* the act of drinking; a draught or drink.

potato *n* (*pl* **potatoes**) a starchy, oval tuber eaten as a vegetable.

potbelly *n* (*pl* **potbellies**) a protruding belly.—**potbellied** *adj.*

potboiler *n* an inferior literary or artistic work done simply to earn money.

potboy *n* (*formerly*) in UK, an assistant in a public house.

poteen *n* (*Irish*) illicitly distilled whiskey.

potency *n* (*pl* **potencies**) the quality or condition of being potent; power; strength.

potent *adj* powerful; influential; intoxicating; (*a male*) able to have sexual intercourse.—**potently** *adv*.

potentate *n* a person with great power; a ruler; a monarch.

potential *adj* possible, but not yet actual. * *n* the unrealized ability to do something.—**potentially** *adv*.

potentiality *n* (*pl* **potentialities**) latent capacity for development or growth; something with this.

potentiate *vt* to make possible; to give power to.

potentilla *n* a flowering plant of the rose family.

pother *n* a bustle or turmoil; a turmoil.

pothole *n* a hole worn in a road by traffic; (*geol*) a deep hole or cave in rock caused by the action of water.

pothouse *n* (*formerly*) in UK, a public house.

pothunter *n* someone who hunts for the sake of the game caught, not for the sport.

potion *n* a mixture of liquids, such as poison.

potpourri *n* (*pl* **potpourris**) a mixture of scented, dried flower petals; a collection; a medley or miscellany.

potsherd, potshard *n* a piece of broken earthenware.

pot shot *n* a random or easy shot.

pottage *n* a thick broth.

potted *adj* in a pot; preserved (in a pot); (*version, history*) abridged.

potter[1] *n* a person who makes earthenware vessels.

potter[2] *vi* to busy oneself idly; (*US*) to putter.—**potterer** *n*.

pottery *n* (*pl* **potteries**) earthenware vessels; a workshop where such articles are made.

potto *n* (*pl* **pottos**) a West African lemur; a kinkajou.

potty[1] *adj* (**pottier, pottiest**) (*inf*) slightly crazy; trivial, petty.—**pottiness** *n*.

potty[2] *n* (*pl* **potties**) (*inf*) a chamber pot.

pouch *n* a small bag or sack; a bag for mail; a sacklike structure, as that on the abdomen of a kangaroo, etc, for carrying young.—**pouched** *adj*.

poult *n* a young fowl.

poultice *n* a hot moist dressing applied to a sore part of the body.

poultry *n* domesticated birds kept for meat or eggs.

pounce *vi* to swoop or spring suddenly (upon) in order to seize; to make a sudden assault or approach.—*also n*.

pound[1] *n* a unit of weight equal to 16 ounces; a unit of money in the UK and other countries, symbol £.

pound[2] *vt* to beat into a powder or a pulp; to hit hard. * *vi* to deliver heavy blows repeatedly (at or on); to move with heavy steps; to throb; (*with* away) to work hard and continuously.—**pounder** *n*.

pound[3] *n* a municipal enclosure for stray animals; a depot for holding impounded personal property until claimed; a place or condition of confinement.

poundage *n* a charge per pound of weight; weight in pounds; the act of impounding; the state of being impounded.

poundal *n* a unit of force, giving to a mass of one pound an acceleration of one foot per second per second.

pour *vti* to cause to flow in a stream; to flow continuously; to rain heavily; to serve tea or coffee.—**pourer** *n*.

pourboire *n* a tip or gratuity.

pout *vti* to push out (the lips); to look sulky. * *n* a thrusting out of the lips; (*pl*) a fit of pique.—**poutingly** *adv*.

pouter *n* someone who pouts; a breed of pigeon with a prominent crop.

poverty *n* the condition of being poor; scarcity.

poverty-stricken *adj* very poor, impoverished.

POW *abbr* = prisoner of war.

powder *n* any substance in tiny, loose particles; a specific kind of powder, esp for medicinal or cosmetic use; fine dry light snow. * *vti* to sprinkle or cover with powder; to reduce to powder.—**powderer** *n*.

powdered *adj* sprinkled or covered with powder; reduced to power.

powdered sugar *n* (*US*) icing sugar.

powdery *adj* like powder; easily crumbled.

power *n* ability to do something; political, social or financial control or force; a person or state with influence over others; legal force or authority; physical force; a source of energy; (*math*) the result of continued multiplication of a quantity by itself a specified number of times. * *adj* operated by electricity, a fuel engine, etc; served by an auxiliary system that reduces effort; carrying electricity. * *vt* to supply with a source of power.—**powered** *adj*.

powerful *adj* mighty; strong; influential.—**powerfully** *adv*.—**powerfulness** *n*.

powerhouse *n* a power station; (*inf*) a strong or energetic person, team, etc.

powerless *adj* without power; helpless; feeble.—**powerlessly** *adv*.—**powerlessness** *n*.

power station, power plant *n* a building where electric power is generated.

power-striding *n* brisk walking as a means of improving fitness.

powwow *n* an American Indian ceremony (as for invoking victory in war); (*inf*) any conference or get-together. * *vi* to confer, chat.

pox *n* a virus disease marked by pustules; (*arch*) smallpox; syphilis; a plague; a curse.

pozzuolana, pozzolana *n* volcanic ashes used in hydraulic cement.

pp *abbr* = past participle; (*mus*) pianissimo.

pp. *abbr* = pages.

p.p. *abbr* = per pro.

ppm *abbr* = (*chem*) parts per million.

PPS *abbr* = post (additional) postscript.

PQ *abbr* = Quebec.

PR *abbr* = public relations; proportional representation.

Pr (*chem symbol*) praseodymium.

practicable *adj* able to be practised; possible, feasible.—**practicability** *n*.—**practicably** *adv*.

practical *adj* concerned with action, not theory; workable; suitable; trained by practice; virtual, in effect.

practicality *n* (*pl* **practicalities**) the condition of being practical; a practical feature or aspect.

practical joke *n* a prank intended to embarrass or to cause discomfort.

practically *adv* in a practical manner; virtually.

practice *n* action; habit, custom; repetition and exercise to gain skill; the exercise of a profession.

practise *vti* to repeat an exercise to acquire skill; to put into practice; to do habitually or frequently; (*profession*) to work at.

practised *adj* acquired by practice; proficient; experienced.

practitioner *n* a person who practises a profession.

praedial *adj* pertaining to land or landed property.—*also* **predial**.

praetor *n* (*ancient Rome*) a magistrate, ranking next to a consul.

pragmatic *adj* practical; testing the validity of all concepts by their practical results.—**pragmatically** *adv*.

pragmatics *n sing* the study of the relationship of signs and symbols and their use; (*linguistics*) the study of meaning derived from context.

pragmatism *n* the judging of events or actions by their results, esp in politics; pragmatic behaviour; (*philos*) a theory that judges the truth of a doctrine by the conduct resulting from belief in it.—**pragmatist** *n.*—**pragmatistic** *adj.*

prairie *n* a large area of level or rolling land predominantly in grass; a dry treeless plateau.

prairie dog *n* a burrowing rodent related to the marmot.

prairie wolf *n* the coyote.

praise *vt* to express approval of, to commend; to glorify, to worship. * *vi* to express praise. * *n* commendation; glorification.—**praiser** *n.*

praiseworthy *adj* deserving praise; commendable.—**praiseworthily** *adv.*—**praiseworthiness** *n.*

praline *n* a confection made of nuts and sugar.

prance *vi* (*horse*) to spring on the hind legs, bound; (*person*) to walk or ride in a showy manner; to swagger. * *n* a prancing; a caper.—**prancer** *n.*—**prancingly** *adv.*

prank[1] *n* a mischievous trick or joke; a ludicrous act.—**prankster** *n.*

prank[2] *vti* to adorn, to deck; to dress up showily.

prase *n* a green, transparent form of quartz.

praseodymium *n* a silvery-white metallic element.

prate *vti* to chatter, talk idly.—**prater** *n.*

pratincole *n* a bird resembling a swallow.

prattle *vti* to talk in a childish manner; to babble. * *n* empty chatter.—**prattler** *n.*

prawn *n* an edible marine shrimp-like crustacean. * *vi* to fish for prawns.—**prawner** *n.*

praxis *n* (*pl* **praxises, praxes**) practice; an example, or set of examples, for an exercise.

pray *vti* to offer prayers to God; to implore.

prayer[1] *n* supplication, entreaty, praise or thanks to God; the form of this; the act of praying; (*pl*) devotional services; something prayed for.

prayer[2] *n* one who prays.

prayerful *adj* given to prayer; devout.—**prayerfully** *adv.*

pre- *prefix* before, beforehand; previous to; surpassingly.

preach *vi* to advocate in an earnest or moralizing way. * *vt* to deliver a sermon; (*patience, etc*) to advocate.

preacher *n* one who preaches, esp a Protestant clergyman.

preachify *vi* (*inf*) to hold forth tediously.—**preachification** *n.*

preachy *adj* (**preachier, preachiest**) (*inf*) fond of moralizing or preaching.

preamble *n* an introductory part to a document, speech, or story, stating its purpose.—**preambulary** *adj.*

prearrange *vt* to arrange beforehand.—**prearrangement** *n.*

prebend *n* a stipend granted to a canon or member of the chapter by a cathedral.—**prebendal** *adj.*

prebendary *n* (*pl* **prebendaries**) someone who holds a prebend.

precancerous *adj* likely to become cancerous.

precarious *adj* dependent on chance; insecure; dangerous.—**precariously** *adv.*—**precariousness** *n.*

precatory, precative *adj* suppliant, expresssing a wish.

precaution *n* a preventive measure; care taken beforehand; careful foresight.—**precautionary** *adj.*

precede *vti* to be, come or go before in time, place, order, rank, or importance.

precedence *n* priority; the right of higher rank.

precedent *n* a previous and parallel case serving as an example; (*law*) a decision, etc, serving as a rule. * *adj* preceding; previous.—**precedented** *adj.*—**precedently** *adv.*

precedential *adj* serving as a precedent; having precedence.

preceding *adj* coming or going before; former.

precentor *n* the leader of a choir in a cathedral or church.

precept *n* a rule of moral conduct; a maxim; an order issued by a legally constituted authority to a subordinate.

preceptive *adj* of or using precepts; didactic.—**preceptively** *adv.*

preceptor *n* an instructor or teacher.—**preceptress** *nf.*

precession *n* going before, in advance of—**precessional** *adj.*

precinct *n* (*usu pl*) an enclosure between buildings, walls, etc; a limited area; an urban area where traffic is prohibited; (*pl*) environs; (*US*) a police district or a subdivision of a voting ward.

precious *adj* of great cost or value; beloved; very fastidious; affected; thoroughgoing. * *adv* (*sl*) very.—**preciously** *adv.*—**preciousness** *n.*

precious metal *n* gold, silver, or platinum.

precious stone *n* a diamond, emerald, ruby, sapphire, pearl, and sometimes black opal; a gem.

precipice *n* a cliff or overhanging rock face.

precipitant *adj* falling headlong; hasty, impetuous. * *n* (*chem*) a substance causing precipitation.—**precipitance, precipitancy** *n.*

precipitate *vti* to throw from a height; to cause to happen suddenly or too soon; (*chem*) to separate out; to rain; to fall as rain, snow, dew, etc.—**precipitately** *adv.*—**precipitateness** *n.*—**precipitator** *n.*

precipitation *n* the act of precipitating; undue haste; rain, snow, etc; the amount of this.

precipitous *adj* of or like a precipice; sheer, steep.—**precipitously** *adv.*—**precipitousness** *n.*

précis *n* (*pl* **précis**) a summary or abstract. * *vt* to make a précis of.

precise *adj* clearly defined, exact; accurate; punctilious; particular.—**precisely** *adv.*—**preciseness** *n.*

precision *n* the quality of being precise; accuracy. * *adj* (*machines*) having a high degree of accuracy.

preclude *vt* to rule out in advance; to make impossible.—**preclusion** *n.*—**preclusive** *adj.*

precocious *adj* prematurely ripe or developed.—**precociously** *adv.*—**precociousness** *n.*

precocity *n* the condition of being precocious, precociousness; early development, esp of a child's mind.

precognition *n* the supposed extrasensory perception of a future event; clairvoyance.—**precognitive** *adj.*

pre-Columbian *adj* of or originating in the Americas before their discovery by Christopher Columbus.

preconceive *vt* to form an idea or opinion of before actual experience.

preconception *n* the act of preconceiving; an opinion formed without actual knowledge.

precondition *n* a requirement that must be met beforehand, a prerequisite. * *vt* (*an organism, a patient*) to prepare to behave or react in a certain way under certain conditions.

precursor *n* a predecessor; a substance from which another substance is formed.—**precursory** *adj.*

predacious, predaceous *adj* living on prey.—**predaciousness, predaceousness, predacity** *n.*

predate *vt* to antedate.

predator *n* a person who preys, plunders or devours; a carnivorous animal.

predatory *adj* living on prey, of or relating to a predator; characterized by hunting or plundering.—**predatorily** *adv.*—**predatoriness** *n.*

predecease *vt* to die before (another).

predecessor *n* a former holder of a position or office; an ancestor.

predella *n* (*pl* **predellae**) a platform for, or shelf upon, an altar; a painting, or sculpture, on such a platform or shelf.

predestinarian *adj* pertaining to predestination. * *n* someone who believes in the doctrine of predestination.

predestinate *adj* predestined. * *vt* to predestine.

predestination *n* a predestining or being predestined; destiny; (*theol*) the doctrine that God has from all eternity decreed the salvation or damnation of each soul.

predestine *vt* to foreordain; to destine beforehand.

predeterminate *adj* predetermined.

predetermine *vt* to decide beforehand.—**predetermination** *n.*

predicable *adj* which can be predicated.

predicament *n* a difficult or embarrassing situation.

predicant *adj* pertaining to preaching. * *n* a preaching friar, esp a Dominican.

predicate *vt* to state as a quality or attribute; to base (on facts, conditions etc). * *n* (*gram*) that which is stated about the subject.—**predication** *n.*

predicative *adj* (*gram*) (*adjective, etc*) making a statement about the subject of a verb. * *n* a predicative construction.

predicatory *adj* of or given to preaching.

predict *vt* to foretell; to state (what one believes will happen).—**predictor** *n.*

predictable *adj* able to be predicted or anticipated; lacking originality.—**predictability** *n.*—**predictably** *adv.*

prediction *n* the act of predicting; that which is predicted; a forecast or prophecy.—**predictive** *adj.*—**predictively** *adv.*

predigest *vt* to treat (food) artificially to make easily digestible.

predilection *n* partiality, liking for.

predispose *vt* to incline beforehand; (*disease, etc*) to make susceptible to.—**predisposition** *n.*

predominant *adj* ruling over, controlling; influencing.—**predominance, predominancy** *n.*

predominantly *adv* mainly.

predominate *vt* to rule over; to have influence or control over; to prevail; to be greater in number, intensity, etc.—**predomination** *n.*—**predominator** *n.*

pre-eminent, preeminent *adj* distinguished above others; outstanding.—**pre-eminence, preeminence** *n.*—**pre-eminently, preeminently** *adv.*

pre-empt, preempt *vt* to take action to check other action beforehand; to gain the right to buy (public land) by settling on it; to seize before anyone else can; to replace; (*in bridge*) to bid highly to exclude bids from opponents.—**pre-emptor, preemptor** *n.*—**pre-emptory, preemptory** *adj.*

pre-emption, preemption *n* a pre-empting or being pre-empted; a buying or the right to buy before the opportunity is given to others; such a purchase.

pre-emptive, preemptive *adj* (*bridge*) denoting a high bid to exclude bids from the opposition.—**pre-emptively, preemptively** *adv.*

preen *vti* (*birds*) to clean and trim the feathers; to congratulate (oneself) for achievement; to groom (oneself); to gloat.—**preener** *n.*

prefab *n* (*inf*) a prefabricated part or building.

prefabricate *vt* (*house, etc*) to build in standardized sections for shipment and quick assembly; to produce artificially.—**prefabrication** *n.*—**prefabricator** *n.*

preface *n* an introduction or preliminary explanation; a foreword or introduction to a book; a preamble. * *vt* to serve as a preface; to introduce.—**prefacer** *n.*

prefatory *adj* of or pertaining to a preface; introductory.—**prefatorily** *adv.*

prefect *n* a person placed in authority over others; a student monitor in a school; in some countries, an administrative official.—**prefectorial** *adj.*

prefecture *n* the office, district, residence, or tenure of a prefect.—**prefectural** *adj.*

prefer *vt* (**preferring, preferred**) to like better; to promote, advance; to put before a court, etc, for consideration.—**preferrer** *n.*

preferable *adj* deserving preference; superior; more desirable.—**preferably** *adv.*

preference *n* the act of preferring, choosing, or favouring one above another; that which is chosen or preferred; prior right; advantage given to one person, country, etc, over others.

preferential *adj* giving or receiving preference.—**preferentialism** *n.*—**preferentially** *adv.*

preferment *n* advancement; promotion to a higher post.

prefiguration *n* the act of prefiguring.—**prefigurative** *adj.*

prefigure *vt* to suggest in advance, foreshadow; to imagine beforehand.

prefix *vt* to put at the beginning of or before; to put as an introduction. * *n* a syllable or group of syllables placed at the beginning of a word, affecting its meaning.—**prefixal** *adj.*—**prefixally** *adv.*

preglacial *adj* existing before a glacial period.

pregnable *adj* capable of being attacked and captured.

pregnancy *n* (*pl* **pregnancies**) the state of being pregnant; the period of this.

pregnant *adj* having a foetus in the womb; significant, meaningful; imaginative; filled (with) or rich (in).—**pregnantly** *adv.*

prehensile *adj* capable of grasping, esp by wrapping around.—**prehensility** *n.*

prehension *n* grasping; the ability to grasp.

prehistoric, prehistorical *adj* of the period before written records began; (*inf*) old-fashioned.—**prehistorically** *adv.*

prehistory *n* (*pl* **prehistories**) events that took place before recorded history; the study of prehistoric events; the history of the earlier background of an incident, etc.—**prehistorian** *n.*

prejudge *vt* to pass judgment on before a trial; to form a premature opinion.—**prejudger** *n.*—**prejudgment, prejudgement** *n.*

prejudice *n* a judgment or opinion made without adequate knowledge; bias; intolerance or hatred of other races, etc; (*law*) injury or disadvantage due to another's action. * *vt* to affect or injure through prejudice.—**prejudiced** *adj.*

prejudicial *adj* causing prejudice; detrimental, damaging.—**prejudicially** *adv.*

prelacy *n* (*pl* **prelacies**) the office or status of a prelate; prelates collectively; church government by prelates.

prelate *n* a church dignity with episcopal authority.—**prelatic** *adj.*

prelature *n* the office or status of a prelate.

preliminary *adj* preparatory; introductory. * *n* (*pl* **preliminaries**) an event preceding another; a preliminary step or measure; (*in school*) a preparatory examination.—**preliminarily** *adv*.

prelims *npl* the front matter of a book, before the main text; preliminary university exams.

prelude *n* an introductory act or event; an event preceding another of greater importance; (*mus*) a movement which acts as an introduction. * *vti* to serve as a prelude to, to usher in; to play a prelude.—**preludial** *adj*.—**prelusion** *n*.—**prelusive, prelusory** *adj*.

premarital *adj* (*sex*) taking place before marriage.

premature *adj* occurring before the expected or normal time; too early, hasty.—**prematurely** *adv*.—**prematurity** *n*.

premeditate *vt* (*crime, etc*) to plan in advance.—**premeditatedly** *adv*.—**premeditative** *adj*.—**premeditator** *n*.

premeditation *n* deliberation or thought before doing something; (*law*) the plotting of a crime beforehand, demonstrating intent to commit it.

premier *adj* principal; first. * *n* the head of a government, a prime minister.—**premiership** *n*.

premiere, prèmiere *n* the first public performance of a play, film, etc. * *vt* to give a premiere of. * *vi* to have a first performance; to appear for the first time as a star performer.

premise *n* a proposition on which reasoning is based; something assumed or taken for granted (—*also* **premiss**); (*pl*) a piece of land and its buildings. * *vt* to state as an introduction; to postulate; to base on certain assumptions.

premium *n* a reward, esp an inducement to buy; a periodical payment for insurance; excess over an original price; something given free or at a reduced price with a purchase; a high value or value in excess of expectation. * *adj* (*goods*) high quality.

premonition *n* a foreboding; a feeling of something about to happen.—**premonitory** *adj*.

prenatal *adj* before birth.

preoccupation *n* a concern that prevents thought of other things; mental absorption; business that takes precedence; preoccupancy.

preoccupied *adj* absent-minded, lost in thought; (*with* **with**) having one's attention completely taken up by.

preoccupy *vt* (**preoccupying, preoccupied**) to take possession of beforehand; to engross, fill the thoughts of.

preordain *vt* to ordain beforehand.—**preordination** *n*.

prep *abbr* = preparatory school; preparation; preposition.

prep school *see* **preparatory school**.

prepaid *see* **prepay**.

preparation *n* the act of preparing; a preparatory measure; something prepared, as a medicine, cosmetic, etc.

preparative *adj* preparatory. * *n* something that prepares the way.—**preparatively** *adv*.

preparatory *adj* serving to prepare; introductory. * *adv* by way of preparation; in a preparatory manner.—**preparatorily** *adv*.

preparatory school *n* a private school that prepares students for an advanced school or college.—*also* **prep (school)**.

prepare *vt* to make ready in advance; to fit out, equip; to cook; to instruct, teach; to put together. * *vi* to make oneself ready.—**preparedly** *adv*.

prepared *adj* subjected to a special process or treatment.

preparedness *n* the state of being prepared, esp for waging war.

prepay *vt* (**prepaying, prepaid**) to pay in advance.—**prepayment** *n*.

prepense *adj* premeditated.

preponderant *adj* being greater in number, amount, importance, weight, etc; predominant.—**preponderance, preponderancy** *n*.—**preponderantly** *adv*.

preponderate *vi* to be greater in number, amount, influence, etc; to predominate, prevail; to weigh more.—**preponderation** *n*.

preposition *n* a word used before a noun or pronoun to show its relation to another part of the sentence.—**prepositional** *adj*.

prepositive *adj, n* (*gram*) (a particle or word) which can be attached as a prefix to a word.

prepossess *vt* to impress favourably; to prejudice.

prepossessing *adj* impressing favourably; attractive.—**prepossessingly** *adv*.

prepossession *n* a prepossessed state; a preconceived opinion or judgement.

preposterous *adj* ridiculous; laughable; absurd.—**preposterously** *adv*.—**preposterousness** *n*.

prepotency *n* the state of being prepotent; (*biol*) a dominant hereditary influence.

prepotent *adj* very or more powerful; (*biol*) having a dominant hereditary influence.

prepuce *n* the loose skin at the end of the penis.—*also* **foreskin**.

pre-Raphaelite *adj, n* (a member) of a 19th-century school of artists who imitated the Italian style of painting before Raphael, using brilliant colour and minute detail.

prerecord *vt* (*radio, TV programme*) to record in advance for later broadcasting.—**prerecorded** *adj*.

prerequisite *n* a condition, etc, that must be fulfilled prior to something else. * *adj* required beforehand.

prerogative *n* a privilege or right accorded through office or hereditary rank.

presage *n* a foreboding or presentiment; an omen. * *vt* to foretell; to have a presentiment of.

presbyopia *n* a condition of long-sightedness, usu progressing with age, in which near objects are seen indistinctly, caused by a change in the refractive power of the eye due to the flattening of the lens.

presbyter *n* in the Presbyterian Church, an elder; in the Episcopal Church, a priest or minister.—**presbyterial** *adj*.

presbyterian *adj* of or denoting government by presbyteries; (*with cap*) of a Presbyterian Church. * *n* a member of a Presbyterian Church.—**Presbyterianism** *n*.

presbytery *n* (*pl* **presbyteries**) in a Presbyterian Church a court composed of ministers and one elder from each church within a district; a district so represented; the eastern part of the chancel of a church; a Roman Catholic priest's house.

preschool *adj* of or for a child between infancy and school age.

prescience *n* foreknowledge.—**prescient** *adj*.

prescribe *vt* to designate; to ordain; (*rules*) to lay down; (*medicine, treatment*) to order, advise.—**prescriber** *n*.

prescript *n* an ordnance or decree. * *adj* prescribed, directed.

prescription *n* act of prescribing; (*med*) a written instruction by a physician for the preparation of a drug;

(*law*) establishment of a right or title through long use.

prescriptive *adj* prescribing, ordering, advising; based on long use, traditional.—**prescriptively** *adv*.

preselect *vt* to select beforehand, usu according to a particular criterion.—**preselection** *n*.—**preselective** *adj*.

presence *n* being present; immediate surroundings; personal appearance and bearing; impressive bearing, personality, etc; something (as a spirit) felt or believed to be present.

presence of mind *n* readiness of resource in an emergency, etc; the ability to say the right thing.

present[1] *adj* being at the specified place; existing or happening now; (*gram*) denoting action or state now or action that is always true. * *n* the time being; now; the present tense.

present[2] *n* a gift.

present[3] *vt* to introduce someone, esp socially; (*a play, etc*) to bring before the public, exhibit; to make a gift or award; to show; to perform; (*law*) to lay a charge before a court; (*weapon*) to point in a particular direction. * *vi* to present a weapon; to become manifest; to come forward as a patient.

presentable *adj* of decent appearance; fit to go into company.—**presentability** *n*.—**presentably** *adv*.

presentation *n* act of presenting; a display or exhibition; style of presenting; something offered or given; a description or persuasive account; (*med*) the position of a foetus in the uterus.—**presentational** *adj*.

presentative *adj* (*of benefice*) admitting presentation by patron; (*philos*) able to be apprehended directly by the mind

presenter *n* a person who presents someone or something; (*radio, TV*) a person who introduces a show, an announcer.

presentiment *n* a premonition, apprehension, esp of evil.

presently *adv* in a short while, soon.

presentment *n* the act of presenting; something which is presented; a representation or delineation; the laying of a formal statement before a court or authority.

preservation *n* the act of preserving or securing; a state of being preserved or repaired.

preservationist *n* someone who undertakes or advocates preservation (as of a biological species or a historic landmark).

preservative *adj* preserving. * *n* something that preserves or has the power of preserving, esp an additive.

preserve *vt* to keep safe from danger; to protect; (*food*) to can, pickle, or prepare for future use; to keep or reserve for personal or special use. * *vi* to make preserves; to raise and protect game for sport. * *n* (*usu pl*) fruit preserved by cooking in sugar; an area restricted for the protection of natural resources, esp one used for regulated hunting, etc; something regarded as reserved for certain persons.—**preservable** *adj*.—**preserver** *n*.

preset *vt* (**presetting, preset**) to set (the controls of an electrical device) in advance.

preside *vi* to take the chair or hold the position of authority; to take control or exercise authority.—**presider** *n*.

presidency *n* (*pl* **presidencies**) the office, dignity, term, jurisdiction or residence of a president.

president *n* the head of state of a republic; the highest officer of a company, club, etc.—**presidential** *adj*.—**presidentially** *adv*.

president-elect *n* a president who has been elected to office but has not yet taken up the post.

presidio *n* (*pl* **presidios**) (*Spain*) a fort or military establishment.

presidium *n* (*pl* **presidiums, presidia**) a presiding committee in a communist organization.

press *vt* to act on with steady force or weight; to push against, squeeze, compress, etc; to squeeze the juice, etc from; (*clothes, etc*) to iron; to embrace closely; to force, compel; to entreat; to emphasize; to trouble; to urge on; (*record*) to make from a matrix. * *vi* to weigh down; to crowd closely; to go forward with determination. * *n* pressure, urgency, etc; a crowd; a machine for crushing, stamping, etc; a machine for printing; a printing or publishing establishment; the gathering and distribution of news and those who perform these functions; newspapers collectively; any of various pressure devices; an upright closet for storing clothes.

press conference *n* a group interview given to members of the press by a politician, celebrity, etc.

pressing *adj* urgent; calling for immediate attention; importunate. * *n* a number of records made at one time from a master.—**pressingly** *adv*.

pressman *n* (*pl* **pressmen**) a journalist; an operator of a printing press.

pressmark *n* a number showing a book's place in a library.

press secretary *n* a person officially in charge of relations with the press for a usu prominent public figure.

press-up *n* an exercise involving raising and lowering the body with the arms.

pressure *n* the act of pressing; a compelling force; a moral force; compression; urgency; constraint; (*physics*) force per unit of area. * *vt* to pressurize.

pressure cooker *n* a strong, sealed pan in which food can be cooked quickly by steam under pressure; (*inf*) a situation beset with emotional or social pressure.

pressure group *n* a group of people organized to alert public opinion, legislators, etc, to a particular area of interest.

pressure point *n* a point on the body where a blood vessel can be compressed to check bleeding.

pressurize *vt* to keep nearly normal atmospheric pressure inside an aeroplane, etc, as at high altitudes; to exert pressure on; to attempt to compel, press.—**pressurization** *n*.—**pressurizer** *n*.

prestidigitation *n* sleight of hand.—**prestidigitator** *n*.

prestige *n* standing in the eyes of people; commanding position in people's minds.

prestigious *adj* imparting prestige or distinction.

prestissimo *adj, adv* (*mus*) very fast.

presto *adj, adv* (*mus*) quick; immediately. * *n* (*pl* **prestos**) (*mus*) a lively passage.

presumable *adj* that may be presumed or taken to be true.

presumably *adv* as may be presumed.

presume *vt* to take for granted, suppose. * *vi* to assume to be true; to act without permission; to take liberties; (*with* **on, upon**) to take advantage of.—**presumedly** *adv*.—**presumer** *n*.

presuming *adj* venturing without permission; presumptuous.—**presumingly** *adv*.

presumption *n* a supposition; a thing presumed; a strong probability; effrontery.

presumptive *adj* assumed in the absence of contrary evidence; probable.—**presumptively** *adv*.

presumptuous *adj* tending to presume; bold; forward.—**presumptuously** *adv*.—**presumptuousness** *n*.

presuppose *vt* to assume beforehand; to involve as a necessary prior condition.—**presupposition** *n*.

pretence *n* the act of pretending; a hypocritical show; a fraud, a sham.—*also* **pretense**.

pretend *vti* to claim, represent, or assert falsely; to feign, make believe; to lay claim (to).

pretended *adj* feigned; ostensible; untrue; insincerely asserted or claimed.—**pretendedly** *adv*.

pretender *n* a person who makes a pretence; a claimant to a title.

pretense *see* **pretence**.

pretension *n* a false claim; affectation; assumption of superiority.

pretentious *adj* claiming great importance; ostentatious.—**pretentiously** *adv*.—**pretentiousness** *n*.

preterit, preterite (*gram*) *adj* denoting past action. * *n* the past tense.

preterition *n* omission; (*theology*) the doctrine of the passing over of the non-elect by God.

preternatural *adj* out of the regular course of things, abnormal.

pretext *n* a pretended reason to conceal a true one; an excuse.

prettify *vt* (**prettifying, prettified**) to make pretty.—**prettifaction** *n*.

pretty *adj* (**prettier, prettiest**) attractive in a dainty, graceful way. * *adv* (*inf*) fairly, moderately. * *n* (*pl* **pretties**) (*inf*) a pretty or pleasing person or thing. * *vt* (**prettying, prettied**) (*with* **up**) (*inf*) to make pretty.—**prettily** *adv*.—**prettiness** *n*.

pretzel *n* a hard, brittle, salted biscuit, often formed in a loose knot.

prevail *vi* to overcome; to predominate; to be customary or in force.

prevailing *adj* generally accepted, widespread; predominant.—**prevailingly** *adv*.

prevalent *adj* current; predominant; widely practised or experienced.—**prevalence** *n*.—**prevalently** *adv*.

prevaricate *vi* to make evasive or misleading statements.—**prevarication** *n*.—**prevaricator** *n*.

prevenient *adj* preceding; anticipating; aiming at prevention.

prevent *vt* to keep from happening; to hinder.—**preventable, preventible** *adj*.—**preventably, preventibly** *adv*.—**preventer** *n*.

prevention *n* a preventing or being prevented; a hindrance; a preventive.

preventive, preventative *adj* serving to prevent, precautionary. * *n* something used to prevent disease.—**preventively** *adv*.—**preventiveness** *n*.

preview *n* an advance, restricted showing, as of a film; a showing of scenes from a film to advertise it. * *vt* to view or show in advance of public presentation; to give a preliminary survey.

previous *adj* coming before in time or order; prior, former.—**previously** *adv*.—**previousness** *n*.

prewar *adj* before a war.

prey *n* an animal killed for food by another; a victim. * *vi* (*with* **on, upon**) to seize and devour prey; (*person*) to victimize; to weigh heavily on the mind.

priapism *n* (*med*) abnormally prolonged penile erection.

price *n* the amount, usu in money, paid for anything; the cost of obtaining some benefit; value, worth. * *vt* to set the price of something; to estimate a price; (*with* **out of the market**) to deprive by raising prices excessively.

priceless *adj* very expensive; invaluable; (*inf*) very amusing, odd, or absurd.—**pricelessly** *adv*.

price war *n* a period of commercial competition marked by repeated cutting of prices among competitors.

pricey *adj* (**pricier, priciest**) (*inf*) expensive.—*also* **pricy**.

prick *n* a sharp point; a puncture or piercing made by a sharp point; the wound or sensation inflicted; a qualm (of conscience); (*vulgar*) penis; (*offensive*) a spiteful person usu with authority. * *vti* to affect with anguish, grief, or remorse; to pierce slightly; to cause a sharp pain to; to goad, spur; (*the ears*) to erect; (*with* **out**) to transfer seedlings.

pricker *n* a thing that pricks, esp a prickle or thorn.

pricket *n* a buck in its second year.

prickle *n* a thorn, spine or bristle; a pricking sensation. * *vti* to feel or cause to feel a pricking sensation.

prickly *adj* (**pricklier, prickliest**) having prickles; tingling; irritable.—**prickliness** *n*.

prickly heat *n* a skin eruption caused by inflammation of the sweat glands.

pride *n* feeling of self-worth or esteem; excessive self-esteem; conceit; a sense of one's own importance; a feeling of elation due to success; the cause of this; splendour; a herd (of lions). * *vti* (*reflex*) (*with* **in** *or* **on**)to be proud of; to take credit for.—**prideful** *adj*.

priedieu *n* a desk with a low rest for kneeling upon while working or praying.

prier *n* one who pries.—*also* **pryer**.

priest *n* in various churches, a person authorized to perform sacred rites; an Anglican, Eastern Orthodox, or Roman Catholic clergyman ranking below a bishop.

priestcraft *n* the work of a priest and its related skills; (*derog*) the schemes used by priests to get power and wealth.

priestess *n* a priest who is a woman; a woman regarded as a leader (as of a movement).

priesthood *n* the office of priest; priests collectively.

priestly *adj* (**priestlier, priestliest**) of or befitting a priest.—**priestliness** *n*.

prig *n* a smug, self-righteous person.—**priggery, priggism** *n*.

priggish *adj* tiresomely precise; strait-laced.—**priggishly** *adv*.—**priggishness** *n*.

prim *adj* (**primmer, primmest**) proper, formal and precise in manner; demure. * *vti* (**primming, primmed**) to make prim; to assume a prim expression.—**primly** *adv*.—**primness** *n*.

prima ballerina *n* (*pl* **prima ballerinas**) the principal female dancer in a ballet company.

primacy *n* (*pl* **primacies**) the office of primate; the state of being first.

prima donna *n* (*pl* **prima donnas**) the leading female singer in an opera; (*inf*) a temperamental person.

prima facie *adv* at first sight. * *adj* true, valid, or sufficient at first impression; self-evident; legally sufficient to establish a fact unless disproved.

primal *adj* primeval; original; primitive; fundamental.

primarily *adv* mainly.

primary *adj* first; earliest; original; first in order of time; chief; elementary. * *n* (*pl* **primaries**) a person or thing that is highest in rank, importance, etc; a preliminary election at which candidates are chosen for the final election.

primary colour n one of the three colours from which all others except black can be obtained: red, blue, and yellow.

primary school n a school for children below age 11; a school for children up to the third or fourth grade of elementary school and sometimes kindergarten.

primate[1] n any of the highest order of mammals, including man.—**primatial** adj.

primate[2] n an archbishop or the highest ranking bishop in a province, etc.—**primateship** n.

prime[1] adj first in rank, importance, or quality; chief; (math) of a number, divisible only by itself and 1. * n the best time; the height of perfection; full maturity; full health and strength. **primeness** n.

prime[2] vt to prepare or make something ready; to pour liquid into (a pump) or powder into (a firearm); to paint on a primer.

prime minister n the head of the government in a parliamentary democracy.

primer[1] n a simple book for teaching; a small introductory book on a subject.

primer[2] n a detonating device; a first coat of paint or oil.

prime time n (radio, TV) the hours when the largest audience is available.

primeval adj of the first age of the world; primitive.

priming n a preliminary coating (of paint); a powder used to explode a charge.

primipara n (pl **primiparas, primiparae**) (obstetrics) a woman due to give birth to her first child, or who has given birth to only one child.—**primiparous** adj.

primitive adj of the beginning or the earliest times; crude; simple; basic. * n a primitive person or thing.—**primitively** adv.—**primitiveness** n.

primo n (pl **primos, primi**) (mus) the leading part in a duet or ensemble.

primogenitor n an ancestor or forefather; an earliest ancestor.

primogeniture n the condition of being the first-born child; (law) the right of inheritance of the eldest child.—**primogenitary** adj.

primordial adj earliest; primeval; fundamental; primitive.—**primordially** adv.

primp vti to dress (oneself) up.

primrose n a perennial plant with pale yellow flowers.

primula n any of a genus of plants that includes the primrose, cowslip, etc.

primum mobile n the first movement or cause of motion; (astron) the tenth and outermost of the imaginary spheres in the Ptolemaic system, which was supposed to revolve from East to West once every 24 hours, carrying the other spheres with it.

prince n the son of a sovereign; a ruler ranking below a king; the head of a principality; any pre-eminent person.—**princedom** n.

princeling n a young prince; a petty ruler.

princely adj (**princelier, princeliest**) of or like a prince; lavish, generous; regal.—**princeliness** n.

princess n a daughter of a sovereign; the wife of a prince; one outstanding in a specified respect.

principal adj first in rank or importance; chief. * n a principal person; a person who organizes; the head of a college or school; the leading player in a ballet, opera, etc; (law) the person who commits a crime; a person for whom another acts as agent; a capital sum lent or invested; a main beam or rafter.—**principalship** n.

principality n (pl **principalities**) the position of responsibility of a principal; the rank and territory of a prince.

principally adv mainly.

principle n a basic truth; a law or doctrine used as a basis for others; a moral code of conduct; a chemical constituent with a characteristic quality; a scientific law explaining a natural action; the method of a thing's working.

principled adj having, or acting in line with, moral principles.

prink vti to dress (oneself) up; to preen oneself.

print vti to stamp (a mark, letter, etc) on a surface; to produce (on paper, etc) the impressions of inked type, etc; to produce (a book, etc); to write in letters resembling printed ones; to make (a photographic print). * n a mark made on a surface by pressure; the impression of letters, designs, etc, made from inked type, a plate, or block; an impression made by a photomechanical process; a photographic copy, esp from a negative.

printable adj able or fit to be printed.—**printability** n.

printed circuit n an electronic circuit whose connections are printed on metal-coated board.

printer n a person engaged in printing; a machine for printing from; a device that produces printout.

printing n the activity, skill, or business of producing printed matter; a style of writing using capital letters; the total number of books, etc, printed at one time (— also **impression**).

printout n the printed output of a computer.

prior[1] adj previous; taking precedence (as in importance).

prior[2] n the superior ranking below an abbot in a monastery; the head of a house or group of houses in a religious community.—**prioress** nf.

priorate n the office or status of a prior.

priority n (pl **priorities**) precedence in rank, time, or place; preference; something requiring specified attention.

priory n (pl **priories**) a religious house under a prior or prioress.

prise, prize vt to force (open, up) with a lever, etc.

prism n (geom) a solid whose ends are similar, equal, and parallel plane figures and whose sides are parallelograms; a transparent body of this form usu with triangular ends used for dispersing or reflecting light.

prismatic adj of or like a prism; (colours) formed by a prism; brilliant.—**prismatically** adv.

prison n a building used to house convicted criminals for punishment and suspects remanded in custody while awaiting trial; a penitentiary or jail.

prisoner n a person held in prison or under arrest; a captive; a person confined by a restraint.

prisoner of war n a member of a military force taken prisoner by the enemy during combat.

pristine adj pure; in an original, unspoiled condition.

prithee interj (arch) pray, please (= "I pray thee").

privacy n (pl **privacies**) being private; seclusion; secrecy; one's private life.

private adj of or concerning a particular person or group; not open to or controlled by the public; for an individual person; not holding public office; secret. * n (pl) the genitals; an enlisted man of the lowest military rank in the army.—**privately** adv.

private enterprise n an economic system in which business activity is operated by private individuals or companies under private not state control.

privateer *n* a privately owned ship commissioned by a government to seize and plunder enemy vessels; a captain or crew member of such a ship.

privation *n* being deprived; want of comforts or necessities; hardship.

privative *adj* depriving; denoting the absence of something.

privatize *vt* to restore private ownership by buying back publicly owned stock in a company.

privet *n* a white-flowered evergreen shrub used for hedges.

privilege *n* a right or special benefit enjoyed by a person or a small group; a prerogative. * *vt* to bestow a privilege on.

privileged *adj* having or enjoying privileges; not subject to disclosure in a court of law.

privity *n* (*pl* **privities**) private knowledge; (*law*) a legally recognized relationship.

privy *adj* private; having access to confidential information. * *n* (*pl* **privies**) a latrine; (*law*) a person with an interest in an action.—**privily** *adv*.

prize *n* an award won in competition or a lottery; a reward given for merit; a thing worth striving for. * *adj* given as, rewarded by, a prize. * *vt* to value highly.

prizefight *n* a professional boxing match.—**prizefighter** *n*.

PRO *abbr* = public relations officer.

pro[1] *adv, prep* in favour of. * *n* (*pl* **pros**) an argument for a proposal or motion.

pro[2] *adj* professional. * *n* (*pl* **pros**) a professional.

pro- *prefix* acting; vice-; favouring; before; forth; according to.

proa *n* a long, narrow, Malay boat propelled by oars and sails.

probability *n* (*pl* **probabilities**) that which is probable; likelihood; (*math*) the ratio of the chances in favour of an event to the total number.

probable *adj* likely; to be expected.

probably *adv* without much doubt.

probang *n* (*med*) a flexible rod with a sponge at the end, used to clear obstructions from, or apply medication to, the gullet.

probate *n* the validating of a will; the certified copy of a will.

probation *n* testing of character or skill; release from prison under supervision by a probation officer; the state or period of being on probation.—**probationary, probational** *adj*.

probationer *n* a person (as a newly admitted student nurse or teacher) whose fitness is being tested during a trial period; a convicted offender on probation.

probation officer *n* an official who watches over prisoners on probation.

probe *n* a flexible surgical instrument for exploring a wound; a device, as an unmanned spacecraft, used to obtain information about an environment; an investigation. * *vt* to explore with a probe; to examine closely; to investigate.—**prober** *n*.

probity *n* honesty, integrity, uprightness.

problem *n* a question for solution; a person, thing or matter difficult to cope with; a puzzle; (*math*) a proposition stating something to be done; an intricate unsettled question.

problematical, problematic *adj* presenting a problem; questionable; uncertain.—**problematically** *adv*.

proboscidian, proboscidean *adj* pertaining to the class of mammals which includes the elephant. **n* an animal with a proboscis.

proboscis *n* (*pl* **proboscises, proboscides**) an elephant's trunk; a long snout; an insect's sucking organ; (*humorous*) a (large) nose.

procedure *n* an established mode of conducting business, esp in law or in a meeting; a practice; a prescribed or traditional course; a step taken as part of an established order of steps.—**procedural** *adj*.—**procedurally** *adv*.

proceed *vi* to go on, esp after stopping; to come from; to continue; to carry on; to issue; to take action; to go to law.

proceeding *n* an advance or going forward; (*pl*) steps, action, in a lawsuit; (*pl*) published records of a society, etc.

proceeds *npl* the total amount of money brought in; the net amount received.

process *n* a course or state of going on; a series of events or actions; a method of operation; forward movement; (*law*) a court summons; the whole course of proceedings in a legal action. * *vt* to handle something following set procedures; (*food, etc*) to prepare by a special process; (*law*) to take action; (*film*) to develop.

procession *n* a group of people marching in order, as in a parade.

processional *adj* pertaining to, or used in, processions. * *n* a processional hymn or hymn book.

processor *n* one who or that which processes; (*comput*) a central processing unit.

pro-choice *adj* supporting a woman's right to choose whether or not to have an abortion.

proclaim *vt* to announce publicly and officially; to tell openly; to praise.—**proclaimer** *n*.

proclamation *n* the act of proclaiming; an official notice to the public.—**proclamatory** *adj*.

proclitic *n, adj* (a word) so closely connected with the following word as to lose its accent.

proclivity *n* (*pl* **proclivities**) a tendency or inclination.

proconsul *n* a governor of a colony or province.—**proconsular** *adj*.—**proconsulate, proconsulship** *n*.

procrastinate *vti* to defer action, to delay.—**procrastination** *n*.—**procrastinator** *n*.

procreate *vt* to bring into being, to engender offspring.—**procreation** *n*.—**procreant, procreative** *adj*.—**procreator** *n*.

Procrustean *adj* compelling uniformity by violent means.

proctor *n* a person who supervises dormitories and examinations in a school.—**proctorial** *adj*.

procumbent *adj* lying face down, prone; (*bot*) trailing.

procuration *n* procuring; (*law*) the authorization to act on behalf of someone else.

procurator *n* an agent; (*ancient Rome*) a provincial governor or treasurer.

procuratory *n* (*law*) the authorization to act on another person's behalf.

procure *vt* to obtain by effort; to get and make available for sexual intercourse; to bring about. * *vi* to procure women.—**procurable** *adj*.—**procurement** *n*.

procurer *n* one who procures, esp one who supplies prostitutes.—**procuress** *nf*.

prod *vt* (**prodding, prodded**) to poke or jab, as with a pointed stick; to rouse into activity. * *n* the action of prodding; a sharp object; a stimulus.—**prodder** *n*.

prodigal *adj* wasteful; extravagant; open-handed. * *n* a wastrel; a person who squanders money.—**prodigally** *adv*.

prodigality *n* (*pl* **prodigalities**) the state or quality of being prodigal; extravagance, wastefulness; lavishness.

prodigious *adj* enormous, vast; amazing.—**prodigiously** *adv*.—**prodigiousness** *n*.

prodigy *n* (*pl* **prodigies**) an extraordinary person, thing or act; a gifted child.

produce *vt* to bring about; to bring forward, show; to yield; to cause; to manufacture, make; to give birth to; (*play, film*) to put before the public. * *vi* to yield something. * *n* that which is produced, esp agricultural products.—**producible** *adj*.—**producibility** *n*.

producer *n* someone who produces, esp a farmer or manufacturer; a person who finances or supervises the putting on of a play or making of a film; an apparatus or plant for making gas.

product *n* a thing produced by nature, industry or art; a result; an outgrowth; (*math*) the number obtained by multiplying two or more numbers together.

production *n* the act of producing; a thing produced; a work presented on the stage or screen or over the air.—**productional** *adj*.

productive *adj* producing or capable of producing; fertile.—**productively** *adv*.—**productiveness** *n*.

productivity *n* the state of being productive; the ratio of the output of a manufacturing business to the input of materials, labour, etc.

proem *n* a preface or introduction.

Prof. *abbr* = professor.

profane *adj* secular, not sacred; showing no respect for sacred things; irreverent; blasphemous; not possessing esoteric or expert knowledge. * *vt* to desecrate; to debase by a wrong, unworthy or vulgar use.—**profanation** *n*.—**profanely** *adv*.—**profaneness** *n*.—**profaner** *n*.

profanity *n* (*pl* **profanities**) irreverence; a profane act; blasphemy, swearing.

profess *vt* to affirm publicly, declare; to claim to be expert in; to declare in words or appearance only.

professed *adj* openly acknowledged.—**professedly** *adv*.

profession *n* an act of professing; avowal, esp of religious belief; an occupation requiring specialized knowledge and often long and intensive academic preparation; the people engaged in this; affirmation; entry into a religious order.

professional *adj* of or following a profession; conforming to the technical or ethical standards of a profession; earning a livelihood in an activity or field often engaged in by amateurs; having a specified occupation as a permanent career; engaged in by persons receiving financial return; pursuing a line of conduct as though it were a profession. * *n* one who follows a profession; a professional sportsman; one highly skilled in a particular occupation or field.—**professionally** *adv*.

professionalism *n* the methods of professionals; the pursuit of an activity, eg a sport, for financial gain.

professor *n* a teacher of the highest rank at an institution of higher education; a teacher.—**professorial** *adj*.—**professorship** *n*.

professoriate, professorate *n* a body of professors.

proffer *vt* to offer, usu something intangible.

proficiency *n* (*pl* **proficiencies**) a being proficient; competence; skill.

proficient *adj* skilled, competent.—**proficiently** *adv*.

profile *n* a side view of the head as in a portrait, drawing, etc; a biographical sketch; a graph representing a person's abilities. * *vt* to represent in profile; to produce (as by writing, drawing, etc) a profile of.

profit *n* gain; the excess of returns over expenditure; the compensation to entrepreneurs resulting from the assumption of risk; (*pl*) the excess returns from a business; advantage, benefit. * *vti* to be of advantage (to), benefit; to gain.—**profitless** *adj*.

profitable *adj* yielding profit, lucrative; beneficial; useful.—**profitably** *adv*.—**profitability** *n*.

profit and loss *n* a statement at the end of an accounting period that summarizes the revenue and expenditure of a business and shows the consequent profit or loss.

profiteer *vi* to make exorbitant profits, esp in wartime. * *n* a person who profiteers.—**profiteering** *n*.

profitless *adj* without profit; useless.

profit sharing *n* a system by which employees share in the profits of a business.—**profit-sharing** *adj*.

profligate *adj* dissolute; immoral; extravagant. * *n* a profligate person, a libertine.—**profligacy** *n*.—**profligately** *adv*.

pro forma *adj* made or carried out as a formality; provided in advance to prescribe form or describe items.

profound *adj* at great depth; intellectually deep; abstruse, mysterious.—**profoundly** *adv*.—**profoundness** *n*.

profundity *n* (*pl* **profundities**) great depth of place, knowledge, skill, etc; a profound or abstruse thing.

profuse *adj* abundant; generous; extravagant.—**profusely** *adv*.—**profuseness** *n*.

profusion *n* an abundance.

progenitive *adj* able to bear offspring.

progenitor *n* an ancestor.

progeny *n* (*pl* **progenies**) offspring; descendants; outcome.

prognathous, prognathic *adj* having projecting lower jaw.—**prognathism** *n*.

prognosis *n* (*pl* **prognoses**) a prediction; (*med*) a forecast of the course of a disease.

prognostic *adj* predictive (of); foretelling. * *n* a prediction; an omen; a forewarning symptom.

prognosticate *vt* to predict; to presage.—**prognostication** *n*.—**prognosticator** *n*.

programme *n* (*US and comput*) **program** a printed list containing details of a ceremony, of the actors in a play, etc; a scheduled radio or television broadcast; a curriculum or syllabus for a course of study; a plan or schedule; a sequence of instructions fed into a computer. * *vti* (**programming, programmed** *or* **programing, programed**) to prepare a plan or schedule; to prepare a plan or schedule to feed a program into a computer; to write a programme.—**programmable** *adj*.—**programmer, programer** *adj*.—**programmatic** *adj*.

progress *n* a movement forwards or onwards, advance; satisfactory growth or development; a tour from place to place in stages. * *vi* to move forward, advance; to improve. * *vt* (*project*) to take to completion.

progression *n* progress; advancement by degrees; (*math*) a series of numbers, each differing from the succeeding according to a fixed law; (*mus*) a regular succession of chords.—**progressional** *adj*.

progressive *adj* advancing, improving; proceeding by degrees; continuously increasing; aiming at reforms;

(*with cap*) denoting a broadly liberal Progressive Party. * *n* a person who believes in moderate political change, esp social improvement by government action; (*with cap*) a member of a Progressive Party.—**progressively** *adv*.—**progressiveness** *n*.—**progressivism** *n*.

prohibit *vt* to forbid by law; to prevent.

prohibition *n* the act of forbidding; an order that forbids; a legal ban on the manufacture and sale of alcoholic drinks; (*with cap*) the period (1920–33) when there was a legal ban of alcohol in the US.

prohibitionist *n* an advocate of legally prohibiting the sale of alcohol; (*with cap*) a member of the Prohibition Party in the US.

prohibitive, prohibitory *adj* forbidding; so high as to prevent purchase, use, etc, of something.—**prohibitively** *adv*.

project *n* a plan, scheme; an undertaking; a task carried out by students, etc, involving research. * *vt* to throw forward; (*light, shadow, etc*) to produce an outline of on a distance surface; to make objective or externalize; (*one's voice*) to make heard at a distance; (*feeling, etc*) to attribute to another; to imagine; to estimate, plan, or figure for the future. * *vi* to jut out; to come across vividly; to make oneself heard clearly.

projectile *n* a missile; something propelled by force. * *adj* throwing forward; capable of being thrown forward.

projection *n* the act of projecting or the condition of being projected; a thing projecting; the representation on a plane surface of part of the earth's surface; a projected image; an estimate of future possibilities based on a current trend; a mental image externalized; an unconscious attribution to another of one's own feelings and motives.—**projectional** *adj*.

projectionist *n* a person who operates a projector.

projective *adj* (*geom*) pertaining to projection.

projector *n* an instrument that projects images from transparencies or film; an instrument that projects rays of light; a person who promotes enterprises.

prolapse *vi* (*med*) to fall or slip out of place. * *n* a prolapsed condition.

prolate *adj* extended; (*spheroid*) elongated at the poles.

prolegomenon *n* (*pl* **prolegomena**) a critical introduction to a text.

proletariat *n* the lowest social or economic class of a community; wage earners; the industrial working class.—**proletarian** *adj, n*.

proliferate *vi* to grow or reproduce rapidly.—**proliferation** *n*.—**proliferative** *adj*.

proliferous *adj* reproducing by budding; producing many offshoots.

prolific *adj* producing abundantly; fruitful.—**prolificacy** *n*.—**prolifically** *adv*.

prolix *adj* verbose, long-winded, tedious.—**prolixity, prolixness** *n*.

prolocutor *n* a chairman or speaker at a convocation, esp of the Anglican Church.

prologue, prolog *n* the introductory lines of a play, speech, or poem; the reciter of these; a preface; an introductory event. * *vt* (**prologuing, prologued** *or* **prologing, prologed**) to provide with a prologue; to usher in.

prolong *vt* to extend or lengthen in space or time; to spin out.—**prolonger** *n*.

prolongation *n* the act of prolonging; an extension or continuation.

prolusion *n* a preliminary essay or article.—**prolusory** *adj*.

prom *n* a dance for a high school or college class.

promenade *n* an esplanade; a ball or dance; a leisurely walk. * *vti* to take a promenade (along or through).—**promenader** *n*.

Promethean *adj* (*myth*) pertaining to Prometheus; life-giving.

prominence, prominency *n* the state of being prominent; a projection; relative importance; celebrity, fame.

prominent *adj* jutting, projecting; standing out, conspicuous; widely and favourably known; distinguished.—**prominently** *adv*.

promiscuity *n* (*pl* **promiscuities**) the state of being promiscuous; promiscuous sexual behaviour; an indiscriminate mixture.

promiscuous *adj* indiscriminate, esp in sexual liaisons.—**promiscuously** *adv*.—**promiscuousness** *n*.

promise *n* a pledge; an undertaking to do or not to do something; an indication, as of a successful future. * *vti* to pledge; to undertake; to give reason to expect.—**promiser** *n*.

promisee *n* (*law*) someone to whom a promise is made.

promising *adj* likely to turn out well; hopeful.

promisor *n* (*law*) someone who makes a promise.

promissory *adj* of the nature of or containing a promise.

promontory *n* (*pl* **promontories**) a peak of high land that juts out into a body of water.

promote *vt* to encourage; to advocate; to raise to a higher rank; (*employee, student*) to advance from one grade to the next higher grade; (*product*) to encourage sales by advertising, publicity, or discounting.—**promotable** *adj*.

promoter *n* a person who promotes, esp one who organizes and finances a sporting event or pop concert; a substance that increases the activity of a catalyst.

promotion *n* an elevation in position or rank; the furtherance of the sale of merchandise through advertising, publicity, or discounting.—**promotional** *adj*.

prompt *adj* without delay; quick to respond; immediate; of or relating to prompting actors. * *vt* to urge; to inspire; (*actor*) to remind of forgotten words, etc (as in a play). * *n* something that reminds; a time limit for payment of an account; the contract by which this time is fixed.—**promptly** *adv*.

prompter *n* one that prompts, esp a person who sits off-stage and reminds actors of forgotten lines.

promptitude *n* quickness of decision and action; readiness; alacrity; punctuality.

promptness *n* alacrity in action or decision; quickness; punctuality.

promulgate *vt* to publish, spread abroad; to put (a law) into effect; to proclaim as coming into force.—**promulgation** *n*.—**promulgator** *n*.

pronate *vt* (*hand, arm*) to turn so that the palm is downwards.—**pronation** *n*.

pronator *n* a pronating muscle.

prone *adj* face downwards; lying flat, prostrate; inclined or disposed (to).—**pronely** *adv*.—**proneness** *n*.

prong *n* a spike of a fork or other forked object.—**pronged** *adj*.

pronominal *adj* pertaining to pronouns; acting as a pronoun.

pronoun *n* a word used to represent a noun (eg *I, he, she, it*).

pronounce *vt* to utter, articulate; to speak officially, pass (judgment); to declare formally.—**pronounceable** *adj.*—**pronouncer** *n.*

pronounced *adj* marked, noticeable.—**pronouncedly** *adv.*

pronouncement *n* a formal announcement, declaration; a confident assertion.

pronto *adv* (*inf*) quickly.

pronunciation *n* articulation; the way a word is pronounced.

proof *n* evidence that establishes the truth; the fact, act, or process of validating; test; demonstration; a sample from type, etc, for correction; a trial print from a photographic negative; the relative strength of an alcoholic liquor. * *adj* resistant; impervious, impenetrable. * *vt* to make proof against (water).

proofread *vti* (**proofreading, proofread**) to read and correct (printed proofs).—**proofreader** *n.*

prop[1] *vt* (**propping, propped**) to support by placing something under or against. * *n* a rigid support; a thing or person giving support.

prop[2] *see* **property**.

prop[3] *n* a propeller.

propaedeutic *adj* pertaining to propaedeutics, the preliminary knowledge or instruction necessary for the study of any art or science.

propagable *adj* which can be propagated.

propaganda *n* the organized spread of ideas, doctrines, etc, to promote a cause; the ideas, etc, so spread.—**propagandism** *n.*—**propagandist** *n, adj.*

propagandize *vt* to spread by propaganda; to use propaganda among. * *vi* to spread propaganda; to use propaganda.

propagate *vti* to cause (a plant or animal) to reproduce itself; (*plant or animal*) to reproduce; (*ideas, customs, etc*) to spread.—**propagation** *n.*—**propagative** *adj.*

propagator *n* a device consisting of a box with a ventilated lid, used to regulate growing conditions for seeds and young plants.

propane *n* a colourless flammable gas obtained from petroleum and used as a fuel.

pro patria for one's country.

propel *vt* (**propelling, propelled**) to drive or move forward.

propellant, propellent *n* a thing that propels; an explosive charge; rocket fuel; the gas that activates an aerosol spray.

propeller, propellor *n* a mechanism to impart drive; a device having two or more blades in a revolving hub for propelling a ship or aircraft.

propensity *n* (*pl* **propensities**) a natural inclination; disposition, tendency.

proper *adj* own, individual, peculiar; appropriate, fit; correct, conventional; decent, respectable; in the most restricted sense; (*sl*) thorough.

properly *adv* in the right way; justifiably; (*sl*) thoroughly.

proper noun *n* the name of a particular person, place, etc.

property *n* (*pl* **properties**) a quality or attribute; a distinctive feature or characteristic; one's possessions; real estate, land; a movable article used in a stage setting (—*also* **prop**).

prophecy *n* (*pl* **prophecies**) a message of divine will and purpose; prediction.

prophesy *vti* (**prophesying, prophesied**) to predict with assurance or on the basis of mystic knowledge; to foretell.—**prophesier** *n.*

prophet *n* a religious leader regarded as, or claiming to be, divinely inspired; one who predicts the future.—**prophetess** *nf.*

prophetic, prophetical *adj* of a prophet or prophecy; prophesying events.—**prophetically** *adv.*

prophylactic *adj* guarding against disease. * *n* a medicine which guards against disease; a condom.

prophylaxis *n* preventive treatment.

propinquity *n* nearness of time, place or relationship.

propitiate *vt* to appease, conciliate.—**propitiation** *n.*—**propitiator** *n.*

propitious *adj* favourable, encouraging; auspicious, opportune.—**propitiously** *adv.*—**propitiousness** *n.*

propolis *n* a resin from tree buds, collected by bees.

proponent *n* someone who makes a proposal, or proposition.

proportion *n* the relationship between things in size, quantity, or degree; ratio; symmetry, balance; comparative part or share; (*math*) the equality of two ratios; a share or quota; (*pl*) dimensions. * *vt* to put in proper relation with something else; to make proportionate (to).—**proportionment** *n.*—**proportionable** *adj.*

proportional *adj* of proportion; aiming at due proportion; proportionate.—**proportionality** *n.*—**proportionally** *adv.*

proportional representation *n* an electoral system arranged so that minorities are represented in proportion to their strength.

proportionate *adj* in due proportion, corresponding in amount. * *vt* to make proportionate.—**proportionately** *adv.*

proposal *n* a scheme, plan, or suggestion; an offer of marriage.

propose *vt* to present for consideration; to suggest; to intend; to announce the drinking of a toast to; (*person*) to nominate; to move as a resolution. * *vi* to make an offer (of marriage).—**proposer** *n.*

proposition *n* a proposal for consideration; a plan; a request for sexual intercourse; (*inf*) a proposed deal, as in business; (*inf*) an undertaking to be dealt with; (*math*) a problem to be solved.—**propositional** *adj.*

propound *vt* to put forward (a question, suggestion, etc).

proprietary *adj* characteristic of a proprietor; privately owned and managed and run as a profit-making organization; (*drug*) made and distributed under a tradename. * *n* (*pl* **proprietaries**) proprietors collectively; a drug protected by secrecy, patent, or copyright against free competition.

proprietor *n* one with legal title to something; an owner.—**proprietorial** *adj.*—**proprietorially** *adv.*

propriety *n* (*pl* **proprieties**) correctness of conduct or taste; fear of offending against rules of behaviour, esp between the sexes; (*pl*) the customs and manners of polite society.

proptosis *n* (*pl* **proptoses**) (*med*) a prolapse, esp of the eyeball.

propulsion *n* the act of propelling; something that propels.—**propulsive, propulsory** *adj.*

propylaeum, propylon *n* (*pl* **propylaea, propylons** *or* **propyla**) a porch or entrance to a temple.

pro rata *adj, adv* in proportion.

prorogue *vt* to terminate a session (of a parliament, etc) without dissolving it.

prosaic *adj* commonplace, matter-of-fact, dull.—**prosaically** *adv.*—**prosaicness** *n.*

prosaism *n* the quality of being prosaic; a word, saying, etc demonstrating this.

proscenium *n* (*pl* **prosceniums**) the part of a stage in front of the curtain.

proscribe *vt* to outlaw; to denounce; to prohibit the use of.—**proscriber** *n*.

proscription *n* the act of proscribing; the condition of being proscribed; outlawry; interdiction.—**proscriptive** *adj*.—**proscriptively** *adv*.

prose *n* ordinary language, as opposed to verse. * *adj* in prose; humdrum, dull. * *vti* to talk tediously; to turn into prose.

prosecute *vt* to bring legal action against; to pursue. * *vi* to institute and carry on a legal suit or prosecution.—**prosecutable** *adj*.

prosecution *n* the act of prosecuting, esp by law; the prosecuting party in a legal case.

prosecutor *n* a person who prosecutes, esp in a criminal court.

proselyte *n* a convert, esp to Judaism. * *vti* to proselytize.

proselytize *vti* to try to make a convert (of).—**proselytizer** *n*.

prosenchyma *n* (*bot*) tissue of elongated cells with little protoplasm.—**prosenchymatous** *adj*.

prose poem *n* a prose work of poetic style.

prosody *n* the study of verse forms and metrical structure; a particular style, system, or theory of versification.—**prosodic** *adj*.—**prosodically** *adv*.—**prosodist** *n*.

prosopopoeia, prosopopeia *n* (*rhetoric*) a figure of speech in which an absent, dead or inanimate figure is represented as present and speaking.

prospect *n* a wide view, a vista; (*pl*) measure of future success; future outlook; expectation; a likely customer, candidate, etc. * *vti* to explore or search (for).

prospective *adj* likely; anticipated, expected.—**prospectively** *adv*.

prospector *n* one who prospects for gold, etc.

prospectus *n* (*pl* **prospectuses**) a printed statement of the features of a new work, enterprise, etc; something (as a condition or statement) that forecasts the course or nature of a situation.

prosper *vi* to thrive; to flourish; to succeed.

prosperity *n* (*pl* **prosperities**) success; wealth.

prosperous *adj* successful, fortunate, thriving; favourable.—**prosperously** *adv*.

prostate *n* (*also* **prostate gland**) a gland situated around the neck of a man's bladder.—**prostatic** *adj*.

prosthesis *n* (*pl* **prostheses**) (*med*) the replacement of a lost limb, tooth, etc with an artificial one; (*gram*) the addition of a letter or syllable at the beginning of a word.—**prosthetic** *adj*.

prostitute *n* a person who has sexual intercourse for money; (*fig*) one who deliberately debases his or her talents (as for money). * *vt* to offer indiscriminately for sexual intercourse, esp for money; to devote to corrupt or unworthy purposes.—**prostitutor** *n*.

prostitution *n* the act or activity of being a prostitute; sexual intercourse for money, etc.

prostrate *adj* lying face downwards; helpless; overcome; lying prone or supine. * *vt* to throw oneself down; to lie flat; to humble oneself.—**prostration** *n*.

prostyle *adj* (*archit*) with columns in front. * *n* a building, esp a temple, with columns in front.

prosy *adj* (**prosier, prosiest**) like prose; dull, dry, tedious.—**prosily** *adv*.—**prosiness** *n*.

protactinium *n* a rare radioactive element similar to uranium.

protagonist *n* the main character in a drama, novel, etc; a supporter of a cause.

protasis *n* (*pl* **protases**) (*gram*) an introductory clause of a conditional sentence.

protean *adj* able to assume many shapes, versatile; variable.

protect *vt* to defend from danger or harm; to guard; to maintain the status and integrity of, esp through financial guarantees; to foster or shield from infringement or restriction; to restrict competition through tariffs and trade controls.

protection *n* the act of protecting; the condition of being protected; something that protects; shelter; defence; patronage; the taxing of competing imports to foster home industry; the advocacy or theory of this (—*also* **protectionism**); immunity from prosecution or attack obtained by the payment of money.

protectionist *n* a person who advocates the protection of home trade by taxing competitive imports. * *adj* serving to protect.—**protectionism** *n*.

protective *adj* serving to protect, defend, shelter.—**protectively** *adv*.—**protectiveness** *n*.

protector *n* a person or thing that protects; (*with cap*) (*formerly*) a regent who ruled during the minority, absence or illness of a monarch.

protectorate *n* the administration of a weaker state by a powerful one; a state so controlled; a regency; (*with cap*) the English government under Oliver and Richard Cromwell (1653–9).

protégé *n* a person guided and helped in his career by another person.—**protégée** *nf*.

protein *n* a complex organic compound containing nitrogen that is an essential constituent of food.

pro tem, pro tempore *adv* for the time being.

proteolysis *n* the disintegration of protein, esp during digestion.—**proteolytic** *adj*.

proteose *n* a compound substance formed by proteolysis.

protest *vi* to object to; to remonstrate. * *vt* to assert or affirm; to execute or have executed a formal protest against; to make a statement or gesture in objection to. * *n* public dissent; an objection; a complaint; a formal statement of objection.—**protester, protestor** *n*.—**protestingly** *adv*.

Protestant *n* a member or adherent of one of the Christian churches deriving from the Reformation; a Christian not of the Orthodox or Roman Catholic Church, who adheres to the principles of the Reformation.—**Protestantism** *n*.

protestation *n* a solemn declaration; a strong protest.

prothalamion *n* (*pl* **prothalamia**) a bridal song, sung before a marriage ceremony.

prothonotary *n* (*pl* **prothonotaries**) (*formerly*) the principal clerk in certain courts.—*also* **protonotary** (*pl* **protonotaries**).

prothorax *n* (*pl* **prothoraxes, prothoraces**) the first segment of an insect's thorax.

protist *n* a single-celled organism, neither animal nor plant.

protocol *n* a note, minute or draft of an agreement or transaction; the ceremonial etiquette accepted as correct in official dealings, as between heads of state or diplomatic officials; the formatting of data in an electronic communications system; the plan of a scientific experiment or treatment.

proton *n* an elementary particle in the nucleus of all atoms, carrying a unit positive charge of electricity.

protonotary *see* **prothonotary**.

protoplasm *n* a semi-fluid viscous colloid, the essential living matter of all plant and animal cells.—**protoplasmic** *adj*.

prototype *n* an original model or type from which copies are made.—**prototypal, prototypic, prototypical** *adj*.

protozoan, protozoon *n* (*pl* **protozoans, protozoa**) a microscopic animal consisting of a single cell or a group of cells. .

protozoology *n* the study of protozoans.

protract *vt* to draw out or prolong; to lay down the lines and angles of with scale and protractor; to extend forwards and outwards.—**protractible** *adj*.—**protraction** *n*.

protracted *adj* extended, prolonged; long-drawn-out.—**protractedly** *adv*.—**protractedness** *n*.

protractile *adj* (*zool*) able to be extended.—**protractility** *n*.

protractive *adj* delaying; protracted.

protractor *n* an instrument for measuring and drawing angles; a muscle that extends a limb.

protrude *vti* to thrust outwards or forwards; to obtrude; to jut out, project.

protrusile *adj* (*zool*) which can be thrust forward.

protrusion *n* the act of protruding; something that protrudes; a bulge, a lump; a projection.

protrusive *adj* tending to protrude; bulging out; unduly conspicuous; obtrusive; (*arch*) thrusting or impelling forward.—**protrusively** *adv*.—**protrusiveness** *n*.

protuberance, protuberancy *n* (*pl* **protuberance, protuberancies**) something that protrudes; a swelling, prominence.

protuberant *adj* bulging out, prominent.—**protuberantly** *adv*.

proud *adj* having too high an opinion of oneself; arrogant, haughty; having proper self-respect; satisfied with one's achievements.—**proudly** *adv*.—**proudness** *n*.

prove *vti* (**proving, proved** *or* **proven**) to try out, test, by experiment; to establish or demonstrate as true using accepted procedures; to show (oneself) to be worthy or capable; to turn out (to be), esp after trial or test; to rise.—**provable** *adj*.—**provably** *adv*.—**prover** *n*.

provenance *n* place of origin, source.

provender *n* dry fodder for cattle; any food.

proverb *n* a short traditional saying expressing a truth or moral instruction; an adage.

proverbial *adj* of or like, a proverb; generally known.—**proverbially** *adv*.

provide *vti* to arrange for; to supply; to prepare; to afford (an opportunity); to make provision for (financially).—**provider** *n*.

provided, providing *conj* on condition (that).

providence *n* foresight, prudence; God's care and protection.

provident *adj* providing for the future; far-seeing; thrifty.—**providently** *adv*.

providential *adj* arranged by providence; very opportune or lucky.—**providentially** *adv*.

province *n* an administrative district or division of a country; the jurisdiction of an archbishop; (*pl*) the parts of a country removed from the main cities; a department of knowledge or activity.

provincial *adj* of a province or provinces; having the way, speech, etc of a certain province; country-like; rustic; unsophisticated. * *n* an inhabitant of the provinces or country areas; a person lacking sophistication.—**provinciality** *n*.—**provincially** *adv*.

provincialism *n* provincial speech, phrases, or point of view; narrowness.

provision *n* a requirement; something provided for the future; a stipulation, condition; (*pl*) supplies of food, stores. * *vt* to supply with stores.—**provisioner** *n*.

provisional, provisionary *adj* temporary; conditional.—**provisionally** *adv*.

proviso *n* (*pl* **provisos, provisoes**) a condition, stipulation; a limiting clause in an agreement, etc.

provisory *adj* conditional; making provision; temporary.—**provisorily** *adv*.

provocation *n* the act of provoking or inciting; a cause of anger, resentment, etc.

provocative *adj* intentionally provoking, esp to anger or sexual desire; (*remark*) stimulating argument or discussion.—**provocatively** *adv*.—**provocativeness** *n*.

provoke *vt* to anger, infuriate; to incite, to arouse; to give rise to; to irritate, exasperate.

provoking *adj* annoying, exasperating.—**provokingly** *adv*.

provost *n* a high executive official, as in some churches, colleges, or universities; in Scotland, a mayor.

prow *n* the forward part of a ship, bow.

prowess *n* bravery, gallantry; skill.

prowl *vi* to move stealthily, esp in search of prey.—*also* *n*.

prowler *n* one that moves stealthily, esp an opportunist thief.

proximal *adj* (*anat*) at the inner end, towards the centre of the body.

proximate *adj* nearest, next; approximate.

proximity *n* nearness in place, time, series, etc.

proximo *adv* next month.

proxy *n* (*pl* **proxies**) the authority to vote or act for another; a person so authorized.—*also adj*.

prude *n* a person who is overly modest or proper in behaviour, speech, attitudes to sex, etc.—**prudery** *n*.

prudence *n* the quality of being prudent; caution; discretion; common sense.

prudent *adj* cautious; sensible; managing carefully; circumspect.—**prudently** *adv*.

prudential *adj* marked by prudence.—**prudentially** *adv*.

prudish *adj* over-correct in behaviour.—**prudishly** *adv*.—**prudishness** *n*.

pruinose *adj* (*bot*) covered with a whitish dust or bloom.

prune[1] *n* a dried plum.

prune[2] *vti* (*plant*) to remove dead or living parts from; to cut away what is unwanted or superfluous.—**pruner** *n*.

prunella *n* a strong silk or worsted fabric, used in shoes.

prurient *adj* tending to excite lust; having lewd thoughts.—**prurience** *n*.—**pruriently** *adv*.

prurigo *n* a skin disease causing violent itching.

pruritus *n* a strong sensation of itching.

Prussian blue *n* a deep blue.

prussic acid *n* a solution of hydrogen and cyanide that makes a deadly poison.

pry[1] *vi* (**prying, pried**) to snoop into other people's affairs; to inquire impertinently. * *n* (*pl* **pries**) close inspection; impertinent peeping; a highly inquisitive person.

pry[2] *vt* (**prying, pried**) to raise with a lever, to prise.

pryer *see* **prier**.

PS *abbr* = postscript.

psalm n a sacred song or hymn, esp one from the Book of Psalms in the Bible.

psalmist n a writer of psalms.

psalmody n (pl **psalmodies**) the art or practice of singing psalms or hymns.—**psalmodic** adj.—**psalmodist** n.

Psalter, psalter n the Book of Psalms, esp as found in a prayer book.

psaltery n (pl **psalteries**) an ancient stringed musical instrument.

Pseudepigrapha npl spurious writings falsely ascribed to Biblical figures or times; Jewish writings of the first century BC and first century AD, allegedly by various prophets and kings of the Hebrew scriptures.

pseudo adj false, pretended.

pseudocarp n (bot) a fruit formed from parts other than the ovary.

pseudomorph n (geol) a mineral with the crystalline shape of another mineral.—**pseudomorphic, pseudomorphous** adj.—**pseudomorphism** n.

pseudonym n a false name adopted as by an author.—**pseudonymity** n.

pseudonymous adj written or writing under an assumed name.—**pseudonymously** adv.

pshaw interj an exclamation of disgust, disbelief, etc.

psittacine n pertaining to parrots.

psittacosis n a contagious parrot disease transmissible to humans, in whom it causes pneumonia.

psoas n a muscle in the loin.

psoriasis n a chronic skin disease marked by red scaly patches.—**psoriatic** adj.

psyche n the spirit, soul; the mind, esp as a functional entity governing the total organism and its interactions with the environment.

psychedelic adj of or causing extreme changes in the conscious mind; of or like the auditory or visual effects produced by drugs (as LSD). * n a psychedelic drug.—**psychedelically** adv.

psychiatrist n a specialist in psychiatric medicine.

psychiatry n the branch of medicine dealing with disorders of the mind, including psychoses and neuroses.—**psychiatric** adj.—**psychiatrically** adv.

psychic adj of the soul or spirit; of the mind; having sensitivity to, or contact with, forces that cannot be explained by natural laws (—also **psychical**). * n a person apparently sensitive to nonphysical forces; a medium; psychic phenomena.

psychoanalyse, psychoanalyze vt to analyse and treat by psychoanalysis.

psychoanalysis n a method of treating neuroses, phobias, and some other mental disorders by analysing emotional conflicts, repressions, etc.—**psychoanalytic, psychoanalytical** adj.

psychoanalyst n a specialist in psychoanalysis.

psychodynamics n sing the study of interaction of thoughts, motives, etc within an individual.—**psychodynamic** adj.

psychological adj of or relating to psychology; of, relating to or coming from the mind or emotions; able to affect the mind or emotions.—**psychologically** adv.

psychologist n a person trained in psychology.

psychology n (pl **psychologies**) the science that studies the human mind and behaviour; mental state.

psychometrics n sing the scientific measurement and testing of mental powers.—**psychometric, psychometrical** adj.—**psychometrician, psychometrist** n.

psychomotor adj denoting a physical action induced by a mental condition.

psychoneurosis n (pl **psychoneuroses**) neurosis.

psychopath n a person suffering from a mental disorder that results in antisocial behaviour and lack of guilt.—**psychopathic** adj.

psychopathology n the study of mental disorders.

psychopathy n mental disorder or disease.

psychophysiology n the study of the relation between psychological and physiological processes.—**psychophysiological** adj.—**psychophysiologist** n.

psychosis n (pl **psychoses**) a mental disorder in which the personality is very seriously disorganized and contact with reality is usu impaired.

psychosomatic adj of physical disorders that have a psychological or emotional origin.—**psychosomatically** adv.

psychotherapy n the treatment of mental disorders by psychological methods.—**psychotherapeutic** adj.—**psychotherapist** n.

psychotic adj of or like a psychosis; having a psychosis. * n a person suffering from a psychosis.—**psychotically** adv.

psychrometer n a type of hygrometer with both a wet and a dry bulb.

psychrophilic adj (biol) thriving in the cold.

PT abbr = physical training.

Pt (chem symbol) platinum.

Pt. abbr = point (in place names).

pt abbr = pint.

PTA abbr = Parent-Teacher Association.

ptarmigan n (pl **ptarmigans, ptarmigan**) a species of grouse.

pteridology n the study of ferns.

pterodactyl n an extinct flying reptile with batlike wings.

pteropod n a small swimming mollusc with winglike lobes on its foot.

pterosaur n an extinct flying reptile.

pterygoid adj (anat) of or pertaining to either of the two processes in the skull attached like wings to the spheroid bone.

PTO abbr = please turn over.

ptomaine, ptomain n a kind of alkaloid, often poisonous, found in decaying matter.

ptosis n (pl **ptoses**) drooping of the eyelid.

ptyalin n an enzyme found in saliva.

ptyalism n excessive salivation.

pub n a public house, an inn.

puberty n the stage at which the reproductive organs become functional.—**pubertal** adj.

pubescent adj arriving at or having reached puberty; of or relating to puberty; covered with fine soft short hairs.—**pubescence** n.

pubic adj related to or situated near the pubis.

pubis n (pl **pubes**) the front part of the bones composing either half of the pelvis.

public adj of, for, or by the people generally; performed in front of people; for the use of all people; open or known to all; acting officially for the people. * n the people in general; a particular section of the people, such as an audience, body of readers, etc; open observation.

public-address system n a system using microphones and loudspeakers to enable groups of people to hear clearly in an auditorium or out of doors.

publican n a person who keeps a public house; in ancient Rome, a collector of taxes.

publication n public notification; the printing and distribution of books, magazines, etc; something published as a periodical, book, etc.

public health *n* the practice and science of protecting and improving community health by organized effort including sanitation, preventive medicine, etc.

publicist *n* a person who publicizes, esp one whose business it is; a political journalist.

publicity *n* any information or action that brings a person or cause to public notice; work concerned with such promotional matter; notice by the public.

publicize *vt* to give publicity to.

publicly *adv* in a public manner; openly; by the public; with the consent of the public.

public relations *n* relations with the general public of a company, institution, etc, as through publicity.

public school *n* a school maintained by public money and supervised by local authorities; in England, a private secondary school, usu boarding.

public service *n* the supply of a commodity (gas, water, etc) or a service (transport, etc) to the community; a service in the public interest; employment in a government department, esp the civil service.

publish *vt* to make generally known; to announce formally; (*book*) to issue for sale to the public. * *vi* to put out an edition; to have one's work accepted for publication.—**publishable** *adj*.

publisher *n* a person or company that prints and issues books, magazines, etc.

publishing *n* the business of the production and distribution of books, magazines, recordings, etc.

puce *n, adj* (a) purplish brown.

puck *n* a hard rubber disc used in ice hockey.

pucker *vti* to draw together in creases, to wrinkle; (*with up*) to contract the lips ready to kiss. * *n* a wrinkle or fold.

puckish *adj* impish, irresponsible.—**puckishly** *adv*.—**puckishness** *n*.

pudding *n* a dessert; a steamed or baked dessert; a suet pie.

puddle *n* a small pool of water, esp stagnant, spilled, or muddy water; a rough cement of kneaded clay. * *vti* to dabble in mud, to make muddy; to make or line with puddle; to stir (molten iron) to free it from carbon.—**puddler** *n*.

pudency *n* modesty, sense of shame.

pudendum *n* (*pl* **pudenda**) (*usu pl*) the external reproductive organs, esp of a woman.—**pudendal** *adj*.

pudgy *adj* (**pudgier, pudgiest**) short and fat, squat.—**pudginess** *n*.

pueblo *n* an Indian settlement in Mexico and the South West United States.

puerile *adj* juvenile; childish.—**puerilely** *adv*.—**puerility** *n*.

puerilism *n* a psychiatric condition of adults characterized by infantile or childish behaviour.

puerperal *adj* pertaining to, or following, childbirth.

puff *n* a sudden short blast or gust; an exhalation of air or smoke; a light pastry; a pad for applying powder; a flattering notice, advertisement. * *vti* to emit a puff; to breathe hard, pant; to put out of breath; to praise with exaggeration; to swell; to blow, smoke, etc, with puffs.

puffball *n* a round fungus which emits dustlike spores when broken.

puffer *n* someone who, or something which puffs; a tropical fish with a spiny body which can be puffed up to form a globe.

puffin *n* a sea bird that has a short neck and a brightly coloured laterally compressed bill.

puffiness *n* the state of being puffy or swollen.

puffy *adj* (**puffier, puffiest**) inflated, swollen; panting.—**puffily** *adv*.

pug *n* a breed of small dog with a face and nose like a bulldog. * *vt* (**pugging, pugged**) to mix (clay) for making bricks; to fill (a space) with clay or mortar.

pug nose *n* a nose having a slightly concave bridge and flattened nostrils.—**pug-nosed** *adj*.

pugilism *n* the practice of fighting with the fists; boxing; skill in doing this.

pugilist *n* a boxer; a prizefighter.—**pugilistic** *adj*.—**pugilistically** *adv*.

pugnacious *adj* fond of fighting, belligerent.—**pugnacity, pugnaciousness** *n*.

puisne *adj* (*judge*) lower in rank.

puissance *n* (*arch*) power; (*showjumping*) an event in which a horse attempts particularly large jumps.—**puissant** *adj*.

puke *vti* (*inf*) to vomit.—*also n*.

pukka *adj* (*Anglo-Indian*) genuine, real; reliable, sound.

pulchritude *n* beauty.

pule *vi* to whine, whimper.

pull *vt* to tug at; to pluck; to move or draw towards oneself; to drag; to rip; to tear; (*muscle*) to strain; (*inf*) to carry out, perform; (*inf*) to restrain; (*inf: gun, etc*) to draw out; (*inf*) to attract. * *vi* to carry out the action of pulling something; to be capable of being pulled; to move (away, ahead, etc). * *n* the act of pulling or being pulled; a tug; a device for pulling; (*inf*) influence; (*inf*) drawing power.

pullet *n* a young hen.

pulley *n* a wheel with a grooved rim for a cord, etc, used to raise weights by downward pull or change of direction of the pull; a group of these used to increase applied force; a wheel driven by a belt.

Pullman *n* (*pl* **Pullmans**) a railway carriage offering luxury accommodation, usu with sleeping berths.

pullover *n* a buttonless garment with or without sleeves pulled on over the head.

pullulate *vi* to sprout, grow; to multiply quickly; to spring up.—**pullulation** *n*.

pulmonary *adj* of, relating to or affecting the lungs; having lungs; denoting the artery that conveys deoxygenated blood directly to the lungs from the right ventricle of the heart.

pulp *n* a soft, moist, sticky mass; the soft, juicy part of a fruit or soft pith of a plant stem; ground-up, moistened fibres of wood, rags, etc, used to make paper; a book or magazine printed on cheap paper and often dealing with sensational material. * *vti* to make or become pulp or pulpy; to produce or reproduce (written matter) in pulp form.

pulpit *n* a raised enclosed platform, esp in a church, from which a clergyman preaches; preachers as a group.

pulpy *adj* (**pulpier, pulpiest**) consisting of or like pulp; soft.—**pulpiness** *n*.

pulque *n* a Mexican alcoholic drink made from the fermented juice of the agave.

pulsar *n* any of several very small stars that emit radio pulses at regular intervals.

pulsate *vi* to beat or throb rhythmically; to vibrate, quiver.—**pulsative** *adj*.

pulsation *n* a pulsating; a single beat or throb; rhythmic throbbing.

pulsatory *adj* pertaining to pulsation; pulsating.

pulse[1] *n* a rhythmic beat or throb, as of the heart; a place where this is felt; an underlying opinion or sentiment or an indication of it; a short radio signal. * *vti* to throb, pulsate.

pulse[2] *n* the edible seeds of several leguminous plants, such as beans, peas and lentils; the plants producing them.

pulsimeter, pulsometer *n* (*med*) an instrument used to measure pulse rate and strength.

pulverize *vti* to reduce to a fine powder; to demolish, smash; to crumble.—**pulverization** *n*.—**pulverizer** *n*.

pulverulent *adj* covered with dust; powdery; crumbling to dust.

pulvinate, pulvinated *adj* (*archit*) curved convexly; (*bot*) having a cushionlike pad or swelling.

puma *n* a mountain lion.

pumice *n* a light, porous volcanic rock, used for scrubbing, polishing, etc.—**pumiceous** *adj*.

pummel *vt* (**pummelling, pummelled** *or* **pummeling, pummeled**) to strike repeatedly with the fists, to thump.

pump[1] *n* a device that forces a liquid or gas into, or draws it out of, something. * *vti* to move (fluids) with a pump; to remove water, etc, from; to drive air into with a pump; to draw out, move up and down, pour forth, etc, as a pump does; (*inf*) to obtain information through questioning.

pump[2] *n* a light low shoe or slipper; a rubber-soled shoe.

pumpernickel *n* a coarse rye bread.

pumpkin *n* a large, round, orange fruit of the gourd family widely cultivated as food.

pun *n* a play on words of the same sound but different meanings, usu humorous. * *vi* (**punning, punned**) to make a pun.—**punningly** *adv*.

punch[1] *vt* to strike with the fist; to prod or poke; to stamp, perforate with a tool; (*US*) (*cattle*) to herd. * *n* a blow with the fist; (*inf*) vigour; a machine or tool for punching.

punch[2] *n* a hot, sweet drink made with fruit juices, often mixed with wine or spirits.

punchbowl *n* a bowl for mixing punch; a bowl-shaped hollow.

punch card, punched card *n* in data processing, a card with a series of holes representing data.

puncheon *n* a large cask holding between 70 and 120 gallons.

Punchinello *n* the figure of the clown in Italian puppet theatre; a grotesque character.

punch line *n* the last line of a joke or story, that conveys its humour or point.

punctate, punctated *adj* marked with dots or points.—**punctation** *n*.

punctilio *n* (*pl* **punctilios**) a fine point of etiquette; petty formality.

punctilious *adj* very formal in conduct; scrupulously exact.

punctual *adj* being on time; prompt.—**punctuality** *n*.—**punctually** *adv*.

punctuate *vt* to use certain standardized marks in (written matter) to clarify meaning; to interrupt; to emphasize. * *vi* to use punctuation marks.—**punctuator** *n*.

punctuation *n* the act of punctuating; the state of being punctuated; a system of punctuation.

punctuation mark *n* one of the standardized symbols used in punctuation, as the period, colon, semicolon, comma, etc.

puncture *n* a small hole made by a sharp object; the deflation of a tyre caused by a puncture. * *vt* to make useless or ineffective as if by a puncture; to deflate. * *vi* to become punctured.—**puncturable** *adj*.

pundit *n* a learned person; an expert; a critic, esp one who writes in a daily newspaper.—*also* **pandit**.

pung *n* (*US*) a horse-drawn sleigh.

pungent *adj* having an acrid smell or a sharp taste; caustic; bitter.—**pungency** *n*.—**pungently** *adv*.

punish *vt* to subject a person to a penalty for a crime or misdemeanour; to chastise; to handle roughly.—**punisher** *n*.

punishable *adj* liable to legal punishment.—**punishability** *n*.

punishing *adj* causing retribution; (*inf*) arduous, gruelling, exhausting.—**punishingly** *adv*.

punishment *n* a penalty for a crime or misdemeanour; rough treatment; the act of punishing or being punished.

punitive, punitory *adj* involving the inflicting of punishment.—**punitively** *adv*.—**punitiveness** *n*.

punk *adj* (*sl*) inferior, of low quality. * *n* (*US*) a young gangster; a follower of punk rock.

punka, punkah *n* a palm-leaf fan; (*Anglo-Indian*) a large swinging fan suspended from the ceiling of a room and worked by an attendant.

punk rock *n* an aggressive form of rock music usu performed in a coarse, offensive way.

punster, punner *n* a person who makes puns.

punt[1] *n* a long flat-bottomed square-ended river boat usu propelled with a pole. * *vti* to propel or convey in a punt.

punt[2] *vt* to kick a dropped ball before it reaches the ground. * *n* such a kick.

punter *n* a person who gambles; (*sl*) a consumer; a customer.

punty *n* (*pl* **punties**) an iron rod used in glass-blowing.

puny *adj* (**punier, puniest**) of inferior size, strength, or importance; feeble.—**puniness** *n*.

pup *n* a young dog, a puppy; a young fox, seal, rat, etc. * *vi* (**pupping, pupped**) to give birth to pups.

pupa *n* (*pl* **pupae, pupas**) an insect at the quiescent stage between the larva and the adult.—**pupal** *adj*.

pupate *vi* (*entomology*) to become a pupa.—**pupation** *n*.

pupil[1] *n* a child or young person taught under the supervision of a teacher or tutor; a person who has been taught or influenced by a famous or distinguished person.

pupil[2] *n* the round, dark opening in the centre of the iris of the eye through which light passes.

pupillage, pupilage *n* the state of being a pupil; the period of time during which someone is a pupil.

pupillary *adj* pertaining to a pupil, or to a legal ward.

pupiparous *adj* (*entomology*) producing young in the pupal state.

puppet *n* a doll moved by strings attached to its limbs or by a hand inserted in its body; a person controlled by another. * *adj* of or relating to puppets; acting in response to the controls of another while appearing independent.

puppeteer *n* a person who controls and entertains with puppets.

puppetry *n* the art of making and entertaining with puppets; stilted presentation.

puppy *n* (*pl* **puppies**) a young domestic dog less than a year old.—**puppyhood** *n*.—**puppyish** *adj*.

Purana *n* a book of Hindu scriptures, written in Sanskrit.

purblind *adj* half-blind; (*fig*) obtuse, dull.

purchase *vt* to buy; to obtain by effort or suffering. * *n* the act of purchasing; an object bought; leverage for raising or moving loads; means of achieving advantage.—**purchasable** *adj*.—**purchaser** *n*.

purdah *n* the custom among Muslims and some Hindus of secluding women from public observation.

pure *adj* clean; not contaminated; not mixed; chaste, innocent; free from taint or defilement; mere; that and that only; abstract and theoretical; (*mus*) not discordant, perfectly in tune.—**pureness** *n*.

purée *n* cooked food sieved or pulped in a blender; a thick soup of this. * *vt* (**puréeing, puréed**) to prepare food in this way.

purely *adv* in a pure way; solely, entirely.

purgation *n* a purging or purifying.

purgative *adj* purging, cleansing; * *n* a drug or agent that purges the bowels.

purgatorial *adj* of, relating to or like purgatory; serving to purify of sin.

purgatory *n* a place of suffering or purification; (*with cap: RC church*) the intermediate place between death and heaven, where venial sins are purged.

purge *vt* to cleanse, purify; (*nation, party, etc*) to rid of troublesome people; to clear (oneself) of a charge; to clear out the bowels of. * *n* the act or process of purging; a purgative; the removal of persons believed to be disloyal from an organization, esp a political party.—**purger** *n*.

purificator *n* (*Christian Church*) a cloth used to wipe the chalice during Holy Communion.

purify *vti* (**purifying, purified**) to make or become pure; to cleanse; to make ceremonially clean; to free from harmful matter.—**purification** *n*.—**purificatory** *adj*.—**purifier** *n*.

Purim *n* a Jewish holiday celebrated yearly in February or March, to commemorate the deliverance of the Jews from massacre at the hands of Haman.

purine *n* a white crystalline compound found in uric acid.

purism *n* insistence on correctness in language, form, style, etc.

purist *n* someone who is a stickler for correctness in language, style, etc.—**purism** *n*.—**puristic** *adj*.—**puristically** *adv*.

puritan *adj* a person who is extremely strict in religion or morals; (*with cap*) an extreme English Protestant of Elizabethan or Stuart times. * *adj* of or like a puritan; (*with cap*) of the Puritans.—**puritanism, Puritanism** *n*.

puritanical *adj* rigorously strict in religious or moral matters; (*with cap*) of the Puritans or Puritanism.—**puritanically** *adv*.—**puritanicalness** *n*.

purity *n* the state of being pure.

purl *vt* to knit a stitch by drawing its base loop from front to back of the fabric. * *n* a stitch made in this way.

purlieu *n* (*usu pl*) adjacent or outlying areas.

purlin, purline *n* a piece of timber lying horizontally to support rafters.

purloin *vt* to steal.—**purloiner** *n*.

purple *n* a dark, bluish red; crimson cloth or clothing, esp as a former emblem of royalty. * *adj* purple-coloured; royal; (*writing style*) over-elaborate. * *vti* to make or become purple.

purport *vt* to claim to be true; to imply; to be intended to seem. * *n* significance; apparent meaning.—**purportedly** *adv*.

purpose *n* objective; intention; aim; function; resolution, determination. * *vti* to intend, design.

purposeful *adj* determined, resolute; intentional.—**purposefully** *adv*.—**purposefulness** *n*.

purposeless *adj* lacking purpose; pointless.—**purposelessly** *adv*.—**purposelessness** *n*.

purposely *adv* deliberately; on purpose.

purposive *adj* having or serving a purpose.—**purposively** *adv*.

purpura *n* a blood disease causing the eruption of small purple spots.

purr *vi* (*cat*) to make a low, murmuring sound of pleasure.—**purring** *n*.

purse *n* a small pouch or bag for money; finances, money; a sum of money for a present or a prize; (*US*) a woman's handbag. * *vt* to pucker, wrinkle up.

purser *n* an officer on a passenger ship in charge of accounts, tickets, etc; an airline official responsible for the comfort and welfare of passengers.

purslane *n* a flowering plant with fleshy leaves, used in salads.

pursuance *n* the pursuing or performance of an action.

pursuant *adj* (*law*) according; (*arch*) pursuing.

pursue *vb* (**pursuing, pursued**) *vt* to follow; to chase; to strive for; to seek to attain; to engage in; to proceed with. * *vi* to follow in order to capture.—**pursuer** *n*.

pursuit *n* the act of pursuing; an occupation; a pastime.

pursuivant *n* a low-ranking officer of the British College of Heralds; (*formerly*) an attendant or state messenger.

purulent *adj* pertaining to pus.—**purulence, purulency** *adj*.—**purulently** *adv*.

purvey *vti* to procure and supply (provisions).

purveyance *n* the procuring of provisions; the provisions provided; (*formerly*) the right accorded to royalty to buy up provisions without the owner's consent.

purveyor *n* a person who, or an organization which, supplies provisions.

pus *n* a yellowish fluid produced by infected sores.

push *vti* to exert pressure so as to move; to press against or forward; to impel forward, shove; to urge the use, sale, etc, of; (*inf*) to approach an age; (*inf*) to sell drugs illegally; to make an effort * *n* a thrust, shove; an effort; an advance against opposition; (*inf*) energy and drive.

push button *n* a knob that activates an electrical switch which opens or closes a circuit to operate a radio, bell, etc.

pushchair *n* a wheeled metal and canvas chair for a small child.—*also* **stroller**.

pusher *n* that which pushes; (*inf*) a person who sells illegal drugs.

pushing *adj* go-ahead, energetic; ambitious; assertive.

pushover *n* (*inf*) something easily done, as a victory over an opposing team; (*inf*) a person easily taken advantage of.

pushy *adj* (**pushier, pushiest**) (*inf*) assertive; forceful; aggressively ambitious.—**pushily** *adv*.—**pushiness** *n*.

pusillanimous *adj* faint-hearted, cowardly.—**pusillanimity** *n*.

puss¹ *n* (*inf*) a cat; (*sl*) a girl.

479

puss² *n* (*sl*) the mouth; the face.

pussy¹ *n* (*pl* **pussies**) (*inf*) a cat, a pussycat; (*vulg sl*) the female genitalia; a contemptuous term for a woman; sex with a woman.

pussy² *adj* (*pl* **pussier, pussiest**) like or containing pus.

pussycat *n* (*inf*) a cat; an amiable person.

pussyfoot *vi* to move stealthily; to be evasive.—**pussyfooter** *n*.

pustule *n* a blister or swelling containing pus.—**pustular** *adj*.—**pustulation** *n*.

put *vti* (**putting, put**) to place, set; to cast, throw; to apply, direct; to bring into a specified state; to add (to); to subject to; to submit; to estimate; to stake; to express; to translate; to propose; (*a weight*) to hurl; (*with* **about**) to change the course of (a ship); to worry; (*with* **across**) to effect successfully; (*with* **away**) to remove; to lay by; (*sl*) to consume; (*arch*) to divorce; (*with* **back**) to replace; to return to land; (*with* **by**) to thrust aside; to store up; (*with* **down**) to suppress; to silence; to kill or have killed; to write or enter; to reckon; to assign; (*with* **forth**) to exert; to bud or shoot; to set out; (*with* **in**) to interpose; to spend (time); to apply (for); to call (at); (*with* **off**) to doff, discard; to postpone; to evade; to get rid of; to discourage, repel; to foist (upon); to leave shore; (*with* **on**) to don; to assume, pretend; to increase; to add; to advance; (*with* **out**) to eject; to extend; to exert; to dislocate; to quench; to publish; to place (money) at interest; to disconcert, to anger; to leave shore; (*with* **over**) to succeed in, to carry through; (*with* **up**) to rouse; to offer (prayer); to propose as a candidate; to pack; to sheathe; to lodge; (*with* **up with**) to endure, to tolerate; (*with* **upon**) to impose upon; (*with* **wise**) to disabuse, to enlighten. * *adj* fixed.

putative *adj* reputed, supposed.—**putatively** *adv*.

putrefy *vti* (**putrefying, putrefied**) to make or become putrid; to rot, decompose.—**putrefaction** *n*.—**putrefactive** *adj*.—**putrefier** *n*.

putrescent *adj* decaying, rotting.—**putrescence** *n*.

putrid *adj* rotten or decayed and foul-smelling.—**putridity** *n*.—**putridly** *adv*.

Putsch *n* an uprising or revolt.

putt *vti* (*golf*) to hit (a ball) with a putter. * *n* in golf, a stroke to make the ball roll into the hole.

puttee *n* a legging made from a strip of cloth wound spirally from the ankle to the knee.

putter¹ *n* (*golf*) a straight-faced club used in putting.

putter² *vi* (*US*) to busy oneself idly; to spend time, to potter.—**putterer** *n*.

putter³ *n* one who or that which puts; an athlete who puts the shot.

putto *n* (*pl* **putti**) (*art*) a figure of cupid and representations of children.—*also* **amoretto, amorino**.

putty *n* (*pl* **putties**) a soft, plastic mixture of powdered chalk and linseed oil used to fill small cracks, fix glass in window frames, etc. * *vt* (**puttying, puttied**) to fix or fill with putty.

puzzle *vt* to bewilder; to perplex. * *vi* to be perplexed; to exercise one's mind, as over a problem. * *n* bewilderment; a difficult problem; a toy or problem for testing skill or ingenuity; a conundrum.—**puzzlement** *n*.—**puzzler** *n*.

puzzling *adj* perplexing, bewildering, inexplicable.—**puzzlingly** *adv*.

PVC *abbr* = polyvinyl chloride.

PWA *abbr* = person with AIDS.

pyaemia, pyemia *n* blood poisoning.—**pyaemic** *adj*.

pycnometer *n* an instrument for measuring densities or specific gravities.

pygmy *n* (*pl* **pygmies**) an undersized person.—*also* **pigmy** (*pl* **pigmies**).

pyjamas *npl* a loosely fitting sleeping suit of jacket and trousers.—*also* (*US*) **pajamas**.

pylon *n* a tower-like structure supporting electric power lines.

pylorus *n* (*pl* **pylori**) (*anat*) the opening from the stomach into the intestine.

pyorrhoea, pyorrhea *n* inflammation of the gums and tooth sockets.

pyracantha *n* a small, flowering, evergreen shrub.

pyramid *n* (*geom*) a solid figure having a polygon as base, and whose sides are triangles sharing a common vertex; a huge structure of this shape, as a royal tomb of ancient Egypt; an immaterial structure built on a broad supporting base and narrowing gradually to an apex.—**pyramidal, pyramidical, pyramidic** *adj*.—**pyramidally, pyramidically** *adv*.

pyre *n* a pile of wood for cremating a dead body.

pyrethrum *n* a type of chrysanthemum with showy flowers; an insecticide made from this plant.

pyretic *adj* pertaining to, or causing, fever.

Pyrex *n* (*trademark*) heat-resistant glassware.

pyrexia *n* fever.—**pyrexial, pyrexic** *adj*.

pyrheliometer *n* an instrument for measuring the sun's heat.

pyrites *n* (*pl* **pyrites**) a sulphide of a metal, esp iron.

pyroelectric *adj* becoming electric as a result of heat.

pyrogenic, pyrogenous *adj* caused by, or causing, heat, or fever.

pyrolisis *n* decomposition by heat.

pyromania *n* (*psychol*) an uncontrollable urge to set things on fire.

pyrometer *n* an instrument used to measure very high temperatures.—**pyrometry** *n*.

pyrope *n* a deep red variety of garnet.

pyrophoric *adj* igniting when exposed to air.

pyrosis *n* heartburn.

pyrotechnics *n sing* the art of making or setting off fireworks; (*sing or pl*) a fireworks display; a brilliant display of virtuosity.—**pyrotechnic, pyrotechnical** *adj*.

pyroxylin, pyroxyline *n* a substance derived from cellulose, used in making plastics.

Pyrrhic *adj* (*victory*) so costly as to be equal to defeat.

pyrrhic *n* a metrical foot of two syllables.

Pythagorean *adj* pertaining to, or characteristic of, the Greek philosopher Pythagoras.

python *n* a large, nonpoisonous snake that kills by constriction.—**pythonic** *adj*.

pythoness *n* a priestess in the temple of Apollo at Delphi, in ancient Greece; a (female) soothsayer; a witch.

pyuria *n* (*med*) the discharge of pus into the urine.

pyx *n* (*Christian Church*) a container in which consecrated bread is kept.

pyxidium *n* (*pl* **pyxidia**) (*bot*) a pyxis.

pyxis *n* (*pl* **pyxides**) a seed capsule with a lid that falls off to release the seeds..

Q

QC *abbr* = Queen's Counsel.

QED *abb* = quod erat demonstratum.

q.t. *abbr* = (*inf*) quiet.

qt *abbr* = quart.

qty *abbr* = quantity.

qua *prep* as, in the character of, because.

quack[1] *n* the cry of a duck. * *vi* to make a sound like a duck.

quack[2] *n* an untrained person who practises medicine fraudulently; a person who pretends to have knowledge and skill he does not have.—*also adj.*

quackery *n* (*pl* quackeries) pretence of medical or other skill; imposture.

quacksalver *n* (*arch*) a quack who deals in ointments, etc; a charlatan.

quad *n* quadrangle; quadruplet.

quadr-, quadri-, quadru- *prefix* four.

quadragenarian *n adj* (a person) forty to forty-nine years old.

Quadragesima (Sunday) *n* the first Sunday in Lent.

Quadragesimal *adj* pertaining to, or used in, Lent.

quadrangle *n* (*geom*) a plane figure with four sides and four angles, a rectangle; a court enclosed by buildings.—quadrangular *adj.*

quadrant *n* (*geom*) a quarter of the circumference of a circle; an arc of 90 degrees; an instrument with such an arc for measuring angles, altitudes, or elevations; a curved street.—quadrantal *adj.*

quadraphonic *adj* using four channels to record and reproduce sound.—quadraphonics, quadraphony *n.*

quadrate *adj* (*zool*) of or pertaining to one of a pair of bones found in the skulls of fishes, reptiles and some birds; (*anat*) of or pertaining to the middle bone of the middle ear in mammals; (*arch*) square or rectangular. * *vt* to square or make rectangular; (*often with* with) to cause to conform; to correspond. * *n* a quadrate bone; a square or cube.

quadratic *adj* square; (*math*) involving the square but no higher power * *n* a quadratic equation.

quadratic equation *n* an equation in which the highest power of the unknown is the square.

quadratics *n* (*sing*) the branch of algebra dealing with quadratic equations.

quadrature *n* the act of squaring; the reduction of a figure to a square, exactly or approximately; (*astron*) the position of a heavenly body when distant 90 degrees from another, usually the earth, said esp of the position of the moon from the sun; (*math*) the finding of square with an area exactly equal to a circle or other figure or a surface; (*electronics*) the state between two waves of being 90 degrees out of phase.

quadrennial *adj* lasting or occurring every four years.—quadrennially *adv.*

quadricentennial *n* a four hundredth anniversary.—*also adj.*

quadrifid *adj* with four parts, four-cleft.

quadriga *n* (*pl* quadrigas, quadrigae) an ancient Roman two-wheeled chariot drawn by four horses abreast.

quadrilateral *adj* having four sides. * *n* (*geom*) a plane figure of four sides; a combination or group that involves four parts or individuals.

quadrille *n* a square dance for four or more couples; the music for this.

quadrillion *n* in Europe, the fourth power of a million, ie 1 with 24 zeros; in US, the fifth power of a thousand, ie, 1 with 15 zeros.—*also adj.*—quadrillionth *adj.*

quadrinomial *n* an algebraic expression consisting of four terms.

quadripartite *adj* of four parts; shared by four.

quadriplegia *n* paralysis of all four limbs.—quadriplegic *adj, n.*

quadrivalent *adj* (*chem*) with four valencies; with a valency of four, tetravalent.— quadrivalency, quadrivalence

quadrivial *adj* pertaining to a quadrivium; (*roads, etc*) leading in four ways; coming from four directions and meeting at the same point.

quadrivium *n* (*pl* quadrivia) a medieval course of study comprising arithmetic, geometry, astronomy, and music.

quadroon *n* the child of one white and one half Negro parent, a person one quarter black.

quadrumanous, quadrumanal *adj* (*monkeys, apes*) having four hands that can grasp.

quadruped *n* a four-footed animal.—quadrupedal *adj.*

quadruple *adj* four times as much or as many; made up of or consisting of four; having four divisions or parts. * *vti* to make or become four times as many.

quadruplet *n* one of four children born at one birth.

quadruplicate *vt* to multiply by four; to make four copies of. * *adj* fourfold.—quadruplication *n.*

quadruplicity *n* (*pl* quadruplicities) four-fold nature.

quaestor, questor *n* in ancient Rome, the public treasurer, or sometimes one of the other public officials.

quaff *vti* to take large drinks (of), drain.—quaffer *n.*

quagga *n* (*pl* quaggas, quagga) an extinct striped South African animal like a sand-coloured zebra.

quaggy *adj* (quaggier, quaggiest) of or like a bog or marsh.

quagmire *n* soft, wet ground; a difficult situation.

quahog *n* an edible North American clam, found on the Atlantic coast.

quail[1] *vi* to cower, to shrink back with fear.

quail[2] *n* (*pl* quails, quail) a small American game bird.

quaint *adj* attractive or pleasant in an odd or old-fashioned style.—quaintly *adv.*—quaintness *n.*

quake *vi* to tremble or shiver, esp with fear or cold; to quiver. * *n* a shaking or tremor; (*inf*) an earthquake.

Quaker *n* a popular name for a member of the Society of Friends, a religious sect advocating peace and simplicity.—**Quakerism** *n.*

quaky *adj* (**quakier, quakiest**) shaky; trembling; unstable.—**quakily** *adv.*—**quakiness** *n.*

qualifiable *adj* that may be qualified.

qualification *n* qualifying; a thing that qualifies; a quality or acquirement that makes a person fit for a post, etc; modification; limitation; (*pl*) academic achievements.

qualifier *n* one that qualifies; an adjective or adverb.

qualify *vti* (**qualifying, qualified**) to restrict; to describe; to moderate; to modify, limit; to make or become capable or suitable; to fulfil conditions; to pass a final examination; (*gram*) to limit the meaning of.—**qualificatory** *adj.*—**qualifyingly** *adv.*

qualitative *adj* of or depending on quality; determining the nature, not the quality, of components.—**qualitatively** *adv.*

quality *n* (*pl* **qualities**) a characteristic or attribute; degree of excellence; high standard. * *adj* of high quality.

qualm *n* a doubt; a misgiving; a scruple; a sudden feeling of faintness or nausea.—**qualmish** *adj.*

quandary *n* (*pl* **quandaries**) a predicament; a dilemma.

quango *n* (*pl* **quangos**) (*acronym*) quasi-autonomous non-governmental organization.

quant *n* a long pole, used in punting, with a disc on the end to prevent it from sinking when pushed into mud etc in a river. * *vt, vi* to punt with a quant.

quantify *vt* (**quantifying, quantified**) to express as a quantity; to determine the amount of.—**quantifiable** *adj.* —**quantification** *n.*

quantitative adj capable of being measured; relating to size or amount.—**quantitatively** adv.

quantity *n* (*pl* **quantities**) an amount that can be measured, counted or weighed; a large amount; the property by which a thing can be measured; a number or symbol expressing this property.

quantum *n* (*pl* **quanta**) a quantity, share or portion; a fixed, elemental unit of energy. * *adj* large, significant.

quantum leap *n* an abrupt transition from one energy state to another; a sudden or noticeable change or increase.—*also* **quantum jump**.

quaquaversal *adj* (*geol*) pointing in every direction.

quarantine *n* a period of isolation imposed to prevent the spread of disease; the time or place of this. * *vt* to put or keep in quarantine.

quark *n* (*physics*) a hypothetical elementary particle.

quarrel *n* an argument; an angry dispute; a cause of dispute. * *vi* (**quarrelling, quarrelled** *or* **quarreling, quarreled**) to argue violently; to fall out (with); to find fault (with).—**quarreller, quarreler** *n.*

quarrelsome *adj* contentious; apt to quarrel.

quarrier, quarryman *n* (*pl* **quarriers, quarrymen**) one who works in a quarry.

quarry[1] *n* (*pl* **quarries**) an excavation for the extraction of stone, slate, etc; a place from which stone is excavated; a source of information, etc. * *vti* (**quarrying, quarried**) to excavate (from) a quarry; to research.

quarry[2] *n* (*pl* **quarries**) a hunted animal, prey.

quart *n* a liquid measure equal to a quarter of a gallon or two pints; a dry measure equal to two pints.

quartan *adj* recurring every third day, said of a fever, esp malaria.

quarter *n* a fourth of something; one fourth of a year; one fourth of an hour; (*US*) 25 cents, or a coin of this value; any leg of a four-legged animal with the adjoining parts; a particular district or section; (pl) lodgings; a particular source; an unspecified person or group; a compass point other than the cardinal points; mercy; (*her*) any of four quadrants of a shield. * *vti* to share or divide into four; to provide with lodgings; to lodge; to range over (an area) in search (of). * *adj* constituting a quarter.

quarterage *n* a quarterly payment; (*rare*) a shelter.

quarterback *n* (*American football*) a player directly behind forwards and the centre, who directs play. * *vt* to direct the attacking play of (a football team); to manage, direct. * *vi* to play quarterback.

quarterbound *adj* a book bound on the spine only in leather, or another material more expensive than the rest of the binding.

quarterdeck *n* the stern area of the upper deck of a ship.

quartered *adj* divided into four quarters, sawn along two diameters, said of logs; (*her*) a shield divided into four parts, each with different arms, or with two sets of arms repeated at diagonally opposite corners; stationed or billeted, said especially of soldiers in civilian lodgings.

quarterfinal *n* one of four matches held before the semifinals in a tournament.—*also adj.*

quartering *n* the assignment of quarters to soldiers etc; (*her*) the division of a shield that contains several coats, often denoting family's alliances and intermarriages; any coat of arms so treated.

quarterlight *n* a usu triangular section within the window of a car.

quarterly *adj* occurring, issued, or spaced at three-month intervals; (*her*) divided into quarters. * *adv* once every three months; (*her*) in quarters. * *n* (*pl* **quarterlies**) a publication issued four times a year.

quartermaster *n* (*mil*) an officer in charge of stores; (*naut*) a petty officer in charge of steering, etc.

quarter note *n* (*mus*) a note having one fourth the duration of a whole note.

quarters *npl* lodgings, esp for soldiers; action stations, esp used in reference to each member of the crew of a battleship; in India, accommodation provided by an employer or by the government; (*sl used by soldiers*) (*sing*) a quartermaster.

quarterstaff (*pl* **quarterstaves**) *n* a staff 6 to 8 feet long and shod with iron, formerly used as a two-handed weapon of defence; the use of one of these.

quartet, quartette *n* a set or group of four; a piece of music composed for four instruments or voices; a group of four instrumentalists or voices.

quartic *adj* (*math*) pertaining to the fourth power, biquadratic. * *n* the fourth power, arising from the multiplication of a square number or quantity by itself, biquadratic.

quartile *n* (*astrol*) (*statistics*) one of three values of a variable that separates its distribution into four sets with equal frequencies. * *adj* (*statistics*) pertaining, or referring, to a quartile; (*astrol*) referring to an aspect of planets separated by 90 degree longitude.

quarto *n* (*pl* **quartos**) a page size, approx 9 by 12 inches; a book of this size of page.

quartz *n* a crystalline mineral, a form of silica, usu colourless and transparent.

quartzite *n* a very hard quartz rock; a light-coloured quartz sandstone.

quasar *n* a distant, starlike, celestial object that emits much light and powerful radio waves.

quash *vt* (*rebellion etc*) to put down; to suppress; to make void.

quasi *adv* seemingly; as if. * *prefix* almost, apparently.

quassia *n* a South American tree yielding bark and wood of excessive bitterness; the bark and wood from a tree of the same family, used to make furniture; formerly a bitter tonic drug obtained from this, which is now used as an ingredient in insecticides.

quatercentenary *n* (*pl* **quatercentenaries**) a 400th anniversary, or the entire year of celebrations etc of a 400th anniversary.

quaternary *adj* consisting of, arranged in, or by, fours; of the number 4; (*chem*) an atom bound to four other atoms or groups, or containing such an atom; (*math*) with four variables. (*with cap*) denoting strata more recent than the Upper Tertiary, ie the most recent geological period, of less than 1 million years ago. * *n* (*pl* **quaternaries**) (*with* **the**) this geological rock system, consisting of Pleistocene and Holocene (recent) epochs.

quaternion *n* the number 4; a set of 4; (*maths*) a calculus or method of mathematical investigation using a generalized complex number with four components.

quaternity *n* (*pl* **quaternities**) four persons regarded as one, esp in relation to God.

quatrain *n* a four-line stanza, rhymed alternately.

quatrefoil *n* a four-leaved plant, such as certain clovers; an ornamental figure in architectural tracery divided by cusps into four leaves.

quattrocento *n* the fifteenth century, esp in connection with Italian art and literature.

quaver *vi* to tremble, vibrate; to speak or sing with a quivering voice. * *n* a trembling sound or note; (*mus*) an eighth note.—**quaveringly** *adv.*—**quavery** *adj.*

quay *n* a loading wharf or landing place for vessels.

quayage *n* an interconnected network of quays; quay dues.

queasy *adj* (**queasier, queasiest**) nauseous; easily upset; over-scrupulous.—**queasily** *adv.*—**queasiness** *n.*

quebracho *n* (*pl* **quebrachos**) one of two types of South American tree with a hard timber rich in tannin, and used in tanning and dyeing; the medicinal bark of a South American tree, the alkaloids from the bark of which are also used in tanning; the wood or bark from any of these trees; any South American tree yielding a hard wood.

queen *n* a female sovereign and head of state; the wife or widow of a king; a woman considered pre-eminent; the egg-laying female of bees, wasps, etc; a playing card with a picture of a queen; (*chess*) the most powerful piece; (*sl*) a male homosexual, esp one who ostentatiously takes a feminine role. * *vi* (*with* **it**) to act like a queen, esp to put on airs. * *vt* (a pawn) to promote to a queen in chess.—**queendom** *n.*

queencake *n* a small currant cake.

queenly *adj* (**queenlier, queenliest**) like or having the character or attributes of a queen; regal.—**queenliness** *n.*

queen mother *n* a queen dowager who is the mother of a ruling sovereign.

queer *adj* strange, odd, curious; (*inf*) eccentric; (*sl*) homosexual. * *n* a (male) homosexual. *vt* (*sl*) to spoil the success of.—**queerness** *n.*

quell *vt* to suppress; to allay.—**queller** *n.*

quench *vt* (*thirst*) to satisfy or slake; (*fire*) to put out, extinguish; (*steel*) to cool; to suppress.—**quenchable** *adj.*—**quencher** *n.*

quenelle *n* a ball of savoury cooked meat, formed into various shapes and boiled in stock or fried.

quercine *adj* of the oak.

querist *n* one who asks questions.

quern *n* a kind of stone handmill for grinding corn.

querulous *adj* complaining, fretful, peevish.—**querulously** *adv.*

query *n* (*pl* **queries**) a question; a question mark; doubt. * *vti* (**querying, queried**) to question; to doubt the accuracy of.

quest *n* a search, seeking, esp involving a journey. * *vti* to search (about) for, seek.—**quester** *n.*—**questingly** *adv.*

question *n* an interrogative sentence; an inquiry; a problem; a doubtful or controversial point; a subject of debate before an assembly; a part of a test or examination. * *vti* to ask questions (of); to interrogate intensively; to dispute; to subject to analysis.—**questioner** *n.*

questionable *adj* doubtful; not clearly true or honest.—**questionability** *n.*—**questionably** *adv.*

question mark *n* a punctuation mark (?) used at the end of a sentence to indicate a question, or to express doubt about something; something unknown.

questionnaire *n* a series of questions designed to collect statistical information; a survey made by the use of questionnaire.

quetzal *n* a large brilliantly coloured Central or Southern American bird, the male having long tail feathers; a Guatemalan coin.

queue *n* a line of people, vehicles, etc awaiting a turn. * *vi* (**queuing, queued**) to wait in turn.

quibble *n* a minor objection or criticism. * *vi* to argue about trifling matters.—**quibbler** *n.*—**quibblingly** *adv.*

quiche *n* a savoury tart filled with onions and a cheese and egg custard.

quick *adj* rapid, speedy; nimble; prompt; responsive; alert; eager to learn. * *adv* (*inf*) in a quick manner. * *n* the sensitive flesh below a fingernail or toenail; the inmost sensibilities.—**quickly** *adv.*—**quickness** *n.*

quicken *vti* to speed up or accelerate; to make alive; to come to life; to invigorate.—**quickener** *n.*

quickie *n* (*inf*) anything done rapidly or in haste.

quicklime *n* calcium oxide.

quicksand *n* loose wet sand easily yielding to pressure in which persons, animals, etc may be swallowed up.

quicksilver *n* mercury.

quickstep *n* a ballroom dance in quick time; the music for this. * *vi* (**quickstepping, quickstepped**) to do this dance.

quick-tempered *adj* easily angered.

quick-witted *adj* mentally alert; quick in repartee.—**quick-wittedness** *n.*

quid *n* (*pl* **quid**) (*sl*) a pound (sterling).

quiddity *n* (*pl* **quiddities**) (*philos*) the essence of a thing; captious subtlety, a quibble.

quidnunc *n* one who is curious to know everything that happens; a gossip, a busybody.

quid pro quo *n* (*pl* **quid pro quos**) something equivalent given in exchange for something else.

quiescent *adj* dormant, inactive, inert; silent.—**quiescence** *n.*

quiet *adj* silent, not noisy; still, not moving; gentle, not boisterous; unobtrusive, not showy; placid, calm; monotonous, uneventful; undisturbed. * *n* stillness, peace, repose; an undisturbed state. * *vti* to quieten.—**quietly** *adv.*—**quietness** *n.*

quieten *vti* to make or become quiet; to calm, soothe.

quietism *n* a mental tranquillity and passive attitude towards life; a form of religious mysticism, founded in 17th–century Spain, in which the cultivation of this attitude with reference to God's will is to be attained.

quietize, quietise *vt* to insulate something from sound; to soundproof.

quietness *n* repose.

quietude *n* repose; tranquillity.

quietus *n* (*pl* **quietuses**) death; the final settlement or discharge of debts etc; anything that results in death or annihilation.

quiff *n* (*Brit*) a curl plastered up above the forehead.

quill *n* the hollow stem of a feather; anything made of this, as a pen; a stiff, hollow spine of a hedgehog or porcupine.

quilt *n* a thick, warm bedcover; a bedspread; a coverlet of two cloths sewn together with padding between. * *vti* to stitch together like a quilt; to make a quilt.—**quilter** *n.*—**quilting** *n.*

quin *n* a quintuplet.

quinary (*pl* **quinaries**) *adj* consisting of, or arranged in, fives; a number system with a base of the number 5; having five parts; the fifth member of something.

quinate *adj* (*bot*) with five leaflets on a petiole; said of a digitate leaf.

quince *n* a hard-fleshed yellow Asian fruit used in preserves; the tree it grows on.

quincentenary *n* (*pl* **quincentenaries**) a 500th anniversary, or the entire year of celebration, etc, of the 500th anniversary.

quincunx *n* an arrangement of five things in form of four corners and centre of a square; (*bot*) such an arrangement of petals or sepals in bud; (*astrol*) two planets with an aspect of 150 degrees.

quindecagon *n* a plane figure with 15 angles and 15 sides.

quinine *n* a bitter crystalline alkaloid used in medicine; one of its salts used esp as an antimalarial and a bitter tonic.

quinqu-, quinque- *prefix* five.

quinquagenarian *adj n* (a person) fifty to fifty-nine years old; relating to such a person.

Quinquagesima (Sunday) *n* the Sunday before Lent.

quinquennial *adj* lasting five years or occurring every five years.—**quinquennially** *adv.*

quinquennium *n* (*pl* **quinquennia**) a period of five years.

quinquepartite *adj* of five parts; shared by five.

quinquereme *n* in ancient Rome, a galley with five banks of oars on each side.

quinquevalent *adj* (*chem*) having a valency of five, pentavalent.—**quinquevalency, quinquevalence** *n.*

quinsy *n* a severe infection of the throat or adjacent parts causing swelling and fever.

quint *n* (*US*) a quintuplet.

quintain n a post with a sandbag on a pivot, or other object, used for practising the medieval sport of tilting; tilting at this.

quintal *n* a measure of weight, 100 lb; a measure of weight of 100 kilograms.

quintan *adj* said of an intermittent fever which recurs every fourth day.

quintessence *n* the purest form or most typical representation of anything, the embodiment.

quintessential *adj* most typical; fundamental.—**quintessentially** *adv.*

quintet, quintette *n* a set or group of five; a piece of music composed for five instruments or voices; a group of five instrumentalists or voices.

quintillion *n* (*pl* **quintillions, quintillion**) in Western Europe, a million raised to the fifth power $(1,000,000^5)$, known in North America as a nonillion; in North America the sixth power of thousand, known as a trillion in Britain.—**quintillionth** *adj.*

quintuple *adj* fivefold; having five divisions or parts; five times as much or as many. * *vti* to multiply by five. * *n* a number five times greater than another.

quintuplet *n* one of five offspring produced at one birth.

quintuplicate *vt* to multiply by five; to make five copies of.* *adj* five-fold. * *n* a set of five objects.—**quintuplication** *n.*

quip *n* a witty remark; a gibe. * *vt* (**quipping, quipped**) to make a clever or sarcastic remark.—**quipster** *n.*

quire *n* a set of 24 sheets of paper; one twentieth of a ream; a section of folded sheets sewn together in bookbinding.

quirk *n* an unexpected turn or twist; a peculiarity of character or mannerism.

quirky *adj* (**quirkier, quirkiest**) odd or unusual in character, behaviour or appearance.—**quirkily** *adv.*—**quirkiness** *n.*

quirt *n* a riding whip of plaited leather with a leather thong at the end. * *vt* to lash with this.

quisling *n* a traitor who aids an invading enemy to regularize their conquest of his country; a collaborator.

quit *vti* (**quitting, quitted** *or* **quit**) to leave; to stop or cease; to resign; to free from obligation; to admit defeat. * *adj* free from; released from.

quitch (grass) *n* couchgrass.

quite *adv* completely; somewhat, fairly; really.

quits *adj* even; on equal terms by payment or revenge.

quittance *n* a release from debt or obligation.

quitter *n* a person who gives up easily.

quiver[1] *vi* to shake; to tremble, shiver. * *n* a shiver, vibration.—**quiveringly** *adv.*—**quivery** *adj.*

quiver[2] *n* a case for holding arrows.—**quiverful** *n.*

qui vive *n* **on the qui vive** on the alert.

quixotic, quixotical *adj* chivalrous or romantic to extravagance; unrealistically idealistic.—**quixotically** *adv.*

quixotism, quixotry *n* romantic or extravagant notions or schemes; quixotic conduct or ideals.

quiz *n* (*pl* **quizzes**) a form of entertainment where players are asked questions of general knowledge; a short written or oral test. * *vt* (**quizzing, quizzed**) to interrogate; to make fun of.—**quizzer** *n.*

quizmaster *n* a person who puts the questions to a contestant in a quiz show.

quiz show *n* an entertainment programme on television or radio in which contestants answer questions to win prizes.

quizzical *adj* humorous and questioning.—**quizzicality** *n.*—**quizzically** *adv.*

quod erat demonstrandum (*Latin*) that which was to be proved.

quodlibet *n* a subtle or moot point, esp as part of a theological argument; (*mus*) a light musical medley.—**quodlibetical** *adj* **quodlibetically** *adv.*

quoin *n* a wedge of wood or metal used to support and steady something (esp formerly a gun or cannon); a keystone; an external angle of a building; the stone forming this, the cornerstone; a wedge-shaped wooden block to tighten the pages of type within a chase.

quoit *n* a ring of metal, plastic, etc thrown in quoits; (*pl*) a game in which rings are thrown at or over a peg.

quondam *adj* that was, former.

quorum *n* the minimum number that must be present at a meeting or assembly to make its proceedings valid.

quota *n* a proportional share; a prescribed amount; a part to be contributed.

quotable *adj* worthy or fit to be quoted.—**quotability** *n*.

quotation *n* the act of quoting; the words quoted; an estimated price.

quotation mark *n* a punctuation mark to indicate the beginning (' *or* ") and the end (' *or* ") of a quoted passage.

quote *vt* to cite; to refer to; to repeat the words of a novel, play, poem, speech, etc exactly; to adduce by way of authority; to set off by quotation marks; to state the price of (something). * *n* (*inf*) something quoted; a quotation mark.

quoth *vt* (*arch*) said, used with nouns and all pronouns except thou and you.

quotidian *adj* daily; recurring every day, occurring every day; belonging to each day; commonplace, routine, everyday, trivial. * *n* a fever, esp malaria, recurring every day.

quotient *n* (*math*) the result obtained when one number is divided by another.

quo warranto *n* (*law*) a proceeding set in motion to determine the authority by which someone claims an office or privilege; (*formerly*) the title of a writ issued to a person to try the question of title to any public office or privilege.

qwerty, QWERTY *n* (*inf*) a standard typewriter or computer keyboard.

R

R. *abbr* = rabbi; Regiment; Regina (*Latin* Queen); Republican; Rex (Latin *King*); River; Royal.

R, r *n* the 18th letter of the English alphabet.

RA *abbr* = (UK) Royal Academy or Royal Academician.

Ra (*chem symbol*) radium.

RAAF *abbr* = Royal Australian Air Force.

rabbet, rebate *n* a recess or groove cut in a surface (eg wood) to receive another piece. * *vt* to cut a rabbet in; to join (pieces of wood, etc) using a rabbet.

rabbi *n* (*pl* **rabbis**) the religious and spiritual leader of a Jewish congregation.

rabbinate *n* the position or tenure of a rabbi; rabbis collectively.

rabbinical *adj* of or pertaining to rabbis, their office, writings, etc.—**rabbinically** *adv*.

rabbit *n* a small burrowing mammal of the hare family with long ears, a short tail, and long hind legs; their flesh as food; their fur.

rabbit punch *n* a sharp blow to the back of the neck.

rabble *n* a disorderly crowd, a mob; the common herd.

rabble-rouser *n* a person who excites a mob to violent action; a demagogue.

Rabelasian *adj* of, pertaining to, or resembling the coarse, satirical humour of the French writer François Rabelais (?1494–1553).

rabid *adj* infected with rabies; raging; fanatical.

rabies *n* an acute, infectious, viral disease transmitted by the bite of an infected animal.—*also* **hydrophobia**.

raccoon *n* a small nocturnal carnivore of North America that lives in trees; its yellowish grey fur.

race[1] *n* any of the divisions of humankind distinguished esp by colour of skin; any geographical, national, or tribal ethnic grouping; a subspecies of plants or animals; distinctive flavour or taste.

race[2] *n* a contest of speed, as in running, swimming, cycling, etc; a rapid current or channel of water. * *vi* to run at top speed or out of control; to compete in a race; (*engine*) to run without a working load or with the transmission disengaged. * *vt* to cause to race; to contest against.

racecourse *n* a track over which races are run, esp an oval track for racing horses.—*also* **racetrack**.

racehorse *n* a horse bred and trained for racing.

raceme *n* (*bot*) an arrangement of flowers directly on a main stem, as in the lily of the valley.

racer *n* a person who races; a machine used for racing, esp a bicycle; a kind of American snake.

race relations *npl* the relationship between different races in a community or nation; the sociological study of such relations.

racetrack *see* **racecourse**

rachis, rhachis *n* (*pl* **rachises, rhachises** *or* **rachides, rhachides**) the main stem of a plant's flower-head; the shaft of a feather; the spinal column.

rachitis *n* rickets.

racial *adj* of or relating to any of the divisions of humankind distinguished by colour, etc.

racism, racialism *n* a belief in the superiority of some races over others; prejudice against or hatred of other races; discriminating behaviour towards people of another race.—**racist** *n*.

rack *n* a framework for holding or displaying articles; an instrument for torture by stretching; the triangular frame for setting up balls in snooker; a toothed bar to engage with the teeth of a wheel pinion or worm gear; extreme pain or anxiety. * *vt* (*person*) to stretch on a rack; to arrange in or on a rack; to torture, torment; to move parts of machinery with a toothed rack.

racket[1] *n* a bat strung with nylon, for playing tennis, etc. (*pl*) a game for two or four players played in a four-walled court (—*also* **racquet**).

racket[2] *n* noisy confusion; din; an obtaining of money illegally; any fraudulent business.

racketeer *n* a person who extorts money by threat or engages in an illegal profit-making enterprise.

rack railway *n* a railway on a steep incline that has a rack or cog between the rails to engage with a pinion on a locomotive.

rack-rent *n* an extortionate rent.—*also vt.*—**rack-renter** *n*.

raconteur *n* a person who excels in relating anecdotes.

racquet *see* **racket**[1].

racy *adj* (**racier, raciest**) lively, spirited; risqué.—**racily** *adv*.

rad[1] *n* a unit of absorbed dose of ionizing radiation.

rad[2] (*symbol*) radian.

radar *n* a system or device for detecting objects such as aircraft by using the reflection of radio waves.

radar beacon *n* a fixed radio transmitter that sends out a signal which allows a ship or an aircraft to determine its own position.

radarscope *n* a cathode-ray oscilloscope which displays radar signals.

radial *adj* like a radius; branching from a common centre.

radial ply *adj* (*tyre*) having the fabric cords of the outer casing lying radial to the hub for greater flexibility.

radial symmetry *n* the state of having similar parts arranged symmetrically around a common axis.

radian *n* the SI unit of plane angle, equal to the angle at the centre of a circle formed by radii of an arc equal in length to the radius.

radiance *n* the condition of being radiant; brilliant light; dazzling beauty.

radiant *adj* shining; beaming with happiness; sending out rays; transmitted by radiation.—**radiantly** *adv*.

radiant energy *n* energy in the form of electromagnetic radiation, such as heat or light.

radiant heat *n* heat conveyed by electromagnetic radiation rather than conduction or convection.

radiate *vt* (*light, heat, etc*) to emit in rays; (*happiness, love, etc*) to give forth. * *vi* to spread out as if from a centre; to shine; to emit rays.

radiation *n* radiant particles emitted as energy; rays emitted in nuclear decay; (*med*) treatment using a radioactive substance.

radiation sickness *n* an illness caused by excessive exposure to radiation from radioactive materials.

radiator *n* an apparatus for heating a room; a cooling device for a vehicle engine.

radical *adj* of or relating to the root or origin; fundamental; favouring basic change. * *n* a person who advocates fundamental political or social change.—**radicalism** *n*.

radically *adv* fundamentally.

radical sign *n* the symbol √ placed before a number to show that the square root (or a higher root denoted by an index number over the sign) is to be extracted.

radicchio *n* (*pl* **radicchios**) a type of Italian chicory with white-veined purple leaves eaten raw in salads.

radices *see* **radix**.

radicle *n* the part of a seed that develops into a root; a root-like subdivision of a nerve or vein.

radii *see* **radius**.

radio- *prefix* radial; radio; using radiant energy.

radio *n* the transmission of sounds or signals by electromagnetic waves through space, without wires, to a receiving set; such a set; broadcasting by radio as an industry, entertainment, etc. * *adj* of, using, used in, or sent by radio. * *vti* to transmit, or communicate with, by radio.

radioactive *adj* giving off radiant energy in the form of particles or rays caused by the disintegration of atomic nuclei.—**radioactivity** *n*.

radioactive decay *n* the disintegration of a nucleus as the result of electron capture.

radioactive waste *n* any waste products that contain radioactive materials.—*also* **nuclear waste**.

radio astronomy *n* astronomy dealing with radio waves in space in order to obtain information about the universe.

radio beacon *n* a radio transmitter that sends out signals as an aid to navigation.

radiocarbon *n* a radioisotope of carbon used in carbon dating.

radiocarbon dating *n* carbon dating.

radio compass *n* a navigational device which can determine the direction of radio waves from a specific radio beacon.

radio control *n* remote control using radio signals.—**radio-controlled** *adj*.

radioelement *n* a radioactive chemical element.

radio frequency *n* a frequency intermediate between audio frequencies and infrared frequencies used esp in radio and television transmission.

radiogram *n* a combined radio and record player.

radiograph *n* an image produced on sensitive photographic film or plate by radiation other than light, esp X-rays.

radiography *n* the production of X-ray photographs for use in medicine, industry, etc.—**radiographer** *n*.

radioisotope *n* a radioactive isotope.

radiology *n* a branch of medicine concerned with the use of radiant energy (as X-rays and radium) in the diagnosis and treatment of disease.—**radiologist** *n*.

radiometer *n* an instrument for measuring radiant energy.—**radiometric** *adj*.

radiopaging *n* a system for alerting a person using a small radio transmitter which beeps in response to a signal from a distance.

radiosonde *n* a small radio transmitter carried by a probe for sending back data on atmospheric conditions.

radio source *n* any celestial object, such as a supernova, that emits radio waves.

radio spectrum *n* that range of frequencies, between 10 kHz and 300,000 MHz, used in radio transmission.

radiotelegraphy *n* telegraphy that uses radio waves to transmit messages.—**radiotelegraph** *n*.—**radiotelegraphic** *adj*.

radiotelephone *n* a device for transmitting telephone messages using radio waves. * *vt* to transmit by radiotelephone. * *vi* to operate a radiotelephone —**radiotelephony** *n*.

radio telescope *n* an instrument used in radio astronomy to receive and analyse radio waves.

radiotherapy *n* the medical treatment of disease, esp cancer, by X-rays or other radioactive substances.—**radiotherapist** *n*.

radio wave *n* an electromagnetic wave having radio frequency.

radish *n* a pungent root eaten raw as a salad vegetable.

radium *n* a highly radioactive metallic element.

radium therapy *n* the treatment of cancer by exposure to radiation from radium.

radius *n* (*pl* **radii**) (*geom*) a straight line joining the centre of a circle or sphere to its circumference; a thing like this, a spoke; a sphere of activity; (*anat*) the thicker of the two bones of the forearm.

radix *n* (*pl* **radices, radixes**) (*maths*) a number that is the base of a number system or for computation of logarithms.

radome *n* a protective housing for a radar antenna constructed from material which is transparent to radio waves.

radon *n* a gaseous radioactive element.—*also* **niton**.

radula *n* (*pl* **radulae**) a horny strip covered with minute teeth on the tongue of certain molluscs.

RAF *abbr* = Royal Air Force.

raffia *n* a kind of palm; fibre from its leaves used in basket-making, etc.

raffish *adj* untidy, disreputable, rakish; vulgarly flashy.

raffle *n* a lottery with prizes. * *vt* to offer as a prize in a raffle.

raft *n* a platform of logs, planks, etc strapped together to float on water.

rafter *n* one of the inclined, parallel beams that support a roof.

rag[1] *n* a torn or waste scrap of cloth; a shred; (*inf*) a sensationalist newspaper; (*pl*) tattered or shabby clothing.

rag[2] *vt* (**ragging, ragged**) to tease; to play practical jokes on. * *n* a practical joke; a series of boisterous stunts staged by British students to raise money for charity.

rag[3] *n* ragtime music.

raga *n* (a composition based on) any of various conventional melodic or rhythmic patterns in Indian music used as the basis for improvisation.

ragamuffin *n* an unkempt dirty person, esp a child.

rag and bone man *n* a junkman.

ragbag *n* a bag for scraps; a miscellaneous collection, jumble.

rage *n* violent anger; passion; frenzy; fashion, craze. * *vi* to behave with violent anger; to storm; to spread rapidly; to be prevalent.

ragged *adj* jagged; uneven; irregular; worn into rags; tattered.—**raggedly** *adv.*—**raggedness** *n.*

ragged robin *n* a Eurasian plant of the pink family with tattered looking pink or white flowers.

raggedy *adj* (*inf*) tattered.

ragi, raggee *n* a cereal grass cultivated in Asia and Africa.

raging *adj* violent; intense.

raglan *n* a type of loose sleeve cut in one piece with the shoulder of a garment.

ragout *n* a stew of meat and vegetables, highly seasoned.

ragtime *n* quick tempo jazz piano music.

ragwort *n* a European composite plant with yellow flowers.

rah *interj* hurrah.

raid *n* a sudden attack to assault or seize. * *vt* to make a raid on; to steal from.—**raider** *n.*

rail¹ *n* a horizontal bar extending from one post to another, as in a fence, etc; one of a pair of parallel steel lines forming a track for the wheels of a train; a railroad.

rail² *vi* to speak angrily.

railhead *n* the furthest point reached by the tracks of an uncompleted railway; a terminus.

railing *n* a fence of rails and posts; rails collectively.

raillery *n* (*pl* **railleries**) good-humoured banter, mockery.

railroad *n* railway. * *vt* to force unduly; (*bill, etc*) to push forward fast; to imprison hastily, esp unjustly.

railway *n* a track of parallel steel rails along which carriages are drawn by locomotive engines; a complete system of such tracks.

raiment *n* (*poet*) clothing.

rain *n* water that falls from the clouds in the form of drops; a shower; a large quantity of anything falling like rain; (*pl*) the rainy season in the tropics. * *vti* (*of rain*) to fall; to fall like rain; (*rain, etc*) to pour down.

rainbow *n* the arc containing the colours of the spectrum formed in the sky by the refraction of the sun's rays in falling rain or in mist. * *adj* many-coloured.

rainbow trout *n* a large freshwater trout of Europe and North America with bright markings.

rain check *n* a ticket stub allowing future admission to an event in the case of it being rained off; the postponement of acceptance of an offer or invitation.

raincoat *n* a waterproof coat.

raindrop *n* a drop of rain.

rainfall *n* a fall of rain; the amount of rain that falls on a given area in a specified time.

rain forest *n* a dense, evergreen forest in a tropical area with much rainfall.

rain gauge *n* an instrument for measuring rainfall.

rainproof *adj* rain-resisting.

rain shadow the leeward side of a hill or mountain where the rain is relatively lighter.

rainy *adj* (**rainier, rainiest**) full of rain; wet.

rainy day *n* a future need, esp financial.

raise *vt* to elevate; to lift up; to set or place upright; to stir up, rouse; to increase in size, amount, degree, intensity, etc; to breed, bring up; (*question, etc*) to put forward; to collect or levy; (*siege*) to abandon. * *n* a rise in wages.

raisin *n* a sweet, dried grape.

raison d'être *n* (*pl* **raisons d'être**) reason for existence; justification.

Raj, the *n* the period of British rule in India.

rajah, raja *n* (*formerly*) an Indian ruler; an Indian or Malayan chief or prince.

rake¹ *n* a tool with a row of teeth and a handle for gathering together, scraping (leaves, hay, etc) or for smoothing gravel, etc. * *vt* to scrape, gather as with a rake; to sweep with gaze or gunshot; (*with in*: *money, etc*) to gather a great amount rapidly; (*with up*: *past misdemeanours, etc*) to bring to light.

rake² *n* the incline or slope of a mast, stern, etc.

rake³ *n* a dissolute, debauched man, a libertine.

raki, rakee *n* a strong aromatic spirit distilled from grain in Turkey.

rakish *adj* jaunty, dashing; dissolute.—**rakishly** *adv.*—**rakishness** *n.*

rale *n* a wheezing rattle detectable with a stethoscope in the chest of patients with lung disorders.

rallentando *adv* (*mus*) gradually slower.

rally *vti* (**rallying, rallied**) to bring or come together; to recover strength, revive; to take part in a motor rally; (*with* **round**) to help (a person); to support financially or morally. * *n* (*pl* **rallies**) a large assembly of people for a political purpose; a recovery (after illness); (*stock exchange*) a sharp increase in price after a decline; (*tennis*) a lengthy exchange of shots; a competitive test of driving and navigational skills.

RAM *abbr* = random-access memory.

ram *n* a male sheep; a battering device; a piston; (*with cap*) Aries, the first sign of the zodiac. * *vt* (**ramming, rammed**) to force or drive; to crash; to cram; to thrust violently.

Ramadan *n* the ninth month of the Islamic year; the great fast during it.

ramble *vi* to wander or stroll about for pleasure; (*plant*) to straggle; to write or talk aimlessly. * *n* a leisurely walk in the countryside.

rambler *n* a person who rambles; a climbing rose.

rambling *adj* spread out, straggling; circuitous; disconnected; disjointed.

Ramboesque *adj* in the aggressive, mindless style of the fictional character Rambo, an indestructible one-man army who featured in several violent action films in the 1980s.

rambunctious *adj* (*inf*) boisterous, unruly.—**rambunctiously** *adv.*—**rambunctiousness** *n.*

rambutan *n* (a Malaysian tree bearing) a hairy red edible fruit.

ramekin *n* a baked dish of cheese, breadcrumbs, etc; the small pot in which this is cooked.

ramification *n* a branching out; an offshoot; a consequence.

ramify *vti* to (cause to) divide into branches or constituent parts.

ramjet *n* (an aircraft having) a type of jet engine that uses compressed air from the forward movement to burn the fuel.

ramose *adj* composed of or having branches.—**ramosely** *adv.*

ramp *n* a sloping walk or runway joining different levels; a wheeled staircase for boarding a plane; a sloping runway for launching boats, as from trailers.

rampage *n* angry or violent behaviour. * *vi* to rush about in an angry or violent manner.

rampant *adj* dominant; luxuriant, unrestrained; violent; rife, prevalent; (*her*) (of a beast) standing on its hind legs.

rampart *n* an embankment surrounding a fortification; a protective wall.

rampion n a Eurasian plant with bell-shaped red or purple flowers whose root is sometimes used in salads.

ramrod n a rod for ramming home a charge in a muzzle-loading gun. * adj denoting a stiff, inflexible person.

ramshackle adj dilapidated.

RAN abbr = Royal Australian Navy.

ran see **run**.

ranch n a large farm for raising cattle, horses, or sheep; a style of house with all the rooms on one floor. * vi to own, manage, or work on a ranch.—**rancher** n.

rancherie n a settlement of North American Indians in a reserve in British Columbia, Canada.

rancid adj having an unpleasant smell and taste, as stale fats or oil.—**rancidity**, **rancidness** n.

rancour, rancor n bitter hate or spite.—**rancorous** adj.—**rancorously** adv.

rand n a unit of money in South Africa, divided into 100 cents.

R & B abbr = rhythm and blues.

R & D abbr = research and development.

random adj haphazard; left to chance.

random-access adj (comput) direct access to data in any desired order.

randomize vt to arrange (eg a survey, samples) in a random way to obtain unbiased statistical results.—**randomization** n.—**randomizer** n.

R and R abbr = rest and recreation.

randy adj (**randier**, **randiest**) (sl) lustful, sexually aroused.

ranee see **rani**.

rang see **ring²**.

range n a row; a series of mountains, etc; scope, compass; the distance a ship, aircraft, or motor vehicle can travel without refuelling; the distance a gun, etc can fire, a projectile can be thrown, or from gun to target; fluctuation; a large open area for grazing livestock; a place for testing rockets in flight; a place for shooting or golf practice; a cooking stove. * vt to place in order or a row; to establish the range of; (live stock) to graze on a range. * vi to be situated in a line; to rank or classify; (gun) to point or aim; to vary (inside limits).

range finder n an instrument for determining the range of a target.

ranger n a forest or park warden.

rangy adj (**rangier**, **rangiest**) tall and slim; long-limbed.—**ranginess** n.

rani, ranee n in India, a queen or princess; the wife of a rajah.

rank¹ n a line of objects; a line of soldiers standing abreast; high standing or position; status; (pl) ordinary members of the armed forces. * vti to arrange in a line; to have a specific position in an organization or on a scale; to outrank; (with **with**) to be counted among.

rank² adj growing uncontrollably; utter, flagrant; offensive in odour or flavour.

rank and file n ordinary soldiers; ordinary members, as distinguished from their leaders.

ranking n a listing of things or people in order of importance. * adj of the highest rank; outstanding.

rankle vi to fester; to cause continuous resentmen· or irritation.

ransack vt to plunder; to search thoroughly.

ransom n the release of a captured person or thing; the price paid for this. * vt to secure release of by payment.

rant vi to speak loudly or violently; to preach noisily. * n loud, pompous talk.

ranunculus n (pl **ranunculuses**, **ranunculi**) a common genus of usu yellow-flowered plants including the buttercup.

rap¹ n a sharp blow; a knock; (inf) talk, conversation; (sl) arrest for a crime; (sl) rap music. * vti (**rapping**, **rapped**) to strike lightly or sharply; to knock; (sl) to criticize sharply; (with **out**) to utter abruptly; (sl) to speak in a fast and rhythmic manner to a musical backing.

rap² n a style of popular music in which (usu rhyming) words and phrases are spoken in a rhythmic chant over an instrumental backing.—**rapper** n.

rapacious adj grasping; extortionate.—**rapaciously** adv.—**rapacity** n.

rape¹ n the act of forcing a person to have sexual intercourse against his or her will; the plundering (of a city, etc) as in warfare. * vti to commit rape (upon).

rape² n a bright yellow plant of the mustard family grown for its leaves and oily seeds.

rapid adj at great speed; fast; sudden; steep. * npl a part of a river where the current flows swiftly.—**rapidity** n.—**rapidly** adv.

rapid eye movement n the rapid jerky movements of the eyeballs associated with dreaming while asleep.

rapier n a straight, two-edged sword with a narrow pointed blade.

rapine n plunder, pillage.

rapist n a person who commits rape.

rap music n a song that is rapidly spoken and accompanied by an insistent electronic rhythm.

rappel vi to abseil.

rapport n a sympathetic relationship; accord.

rapprochement n re-establishment of cordial relations; reconciliation.

rapscallion n a rascal.

rapt adj carried away, enraptured; absorbed, intent.

raptor n a bird of prey.

raptorial adj of or pertaining to birds of prey; (birds' feet) adapted for seizing prey.

rapture n the state of being carried away with love, joy, etc; intense delight, ecstasy.—**rapturous** adj.—**rapturously** adv.

rara avis n a rare or unique person or thing.

rare¹ adj unusual; seldom seen; exceptionally good; (gas) of low density, thin. adv.—**rareness** n.

rare² adj not completely cooked, partly raw; underdone.

rare earth n (an oxide of) any of the lanthanide series of chemical elements.

rarefy vti (**rarefying**, **rarefied**) to make or become less dense; to thin out; to expand without the addition of matter; to make more spiritual, abstruse or refined.—**rarefied** adj.

rare gas n an inert gas.

rarely adv almost never, seldom; exceptionally, unusually.

raring adj (inf) eager, enthusiastic.

rarity n (pl **rarities**) rareness; a rare person or thing.

rasbora n any of various small brightly-coloured tropical fishes popular for aquariums.

rascal n a rogue; a villain; a mischievous person.

rase see **raze**.

rash¹ adj reckless; impetuous.—**rashly** adv.—**rashness** n.

rash² n a skin eruption of spots, etc.

rasher *n* a thin slice of bacon or ham.

rasp *n* a coarse file; a grating sound. * *vt* to scrape with a rasp. * *vi* to produce a grating sound.

raspberry *n* (*pl* **raspberries**) a shrub with white flowers and red berry-like fruits; the fruit produced; (*inf*) a sound of dislike or derision.

Rastafarian, Rasta *n* a member of a largely Jamaican religious and political movement that worships Ras Tafari, the former Emperor of Ethiopia, Haile Selassie, as God.—*also adj.*

raster *n* a grid of lines scanned by an electron beam to make up an image, esp on a television screen.

rat *n* a long-tailed rodent similar to a mouse but larger; (*sl*) a sneaky, contemptible person, esp an informer; a scab. * *vi* (**ratting, ratted**) to hunt or catch rats; to betray or inform on someone; to work as a scab.

ratafia *n* a liqueur flavoured with fruit kernels, such as cherry, peach or almond; a sweet biscuit flavoured with coconut and almond.

ratatouille *n* a dish consisting of a thick stew of roughly chopped vegetables such as onions, peppers, courgettes, aubergine, and tomatoes.

ratchet *n* a device with a toothed wheel that moves in one direction only.

rate *n* the amount, degree, etc of something in relation to units of something else; price, esp per unit; degree. * *vt* to fix the value of; to rank; to regard or consider; (*sl*) to think highly of. * *vi* to have value or status.

ratel *n* a carnivorous nocturnal mammal of Africa and Asia resembling the badger.

ratepayer *n* a person who pays rates, a householder.

rather *adv* more willingly; preferably; somewhat; more accurately; on the contrary; (*inf*) yes, certainly.

ratify *vt* (**ratifying, ratified**) to approve formally; to confirm.

rating *n* an assessment; an evaluation, an appraisal, as of credit worthiness; classification by grade, as of military personnel; (*radio, TV*) the relative popularity of a programme according to sample polls.

ratio *n* (*pl* **ratios**) the number of times one thing contains another; the quantitative relationship between two classes of objects; proportion.

ratiocinate *vi* to reason or argue systematically.—**ratiocination** *n*.

ration *n* (*food, petrol*) a fixed amount or portion; (*pl*) food supply. * *vt* to supply with rations; (*food, petrol*) to restrict the supply of.

rational *adj* of or based on reason; reasonable; sane.—**rationally** *adv*.

rationale *n* the reason for a course of action; an explanation of principles.

rationalism *n* dependence on reason and rejection of intuition or the supernatural to justify ideas and beliefs, esp with regard to religion; the belief that reason can supply knowledge independently of personal experience.

rationality *n* (*pl* **rationalities**) the condition of being rational; the practice of being reasonable.

rationalize *vti* to make rational; to justify one's reasons for an action; to cut down on personnel or equipment; to substitute a natural for a supernatural explanation.—**rationalization** *n*.

rational number *n* a number that can be expressed as the ratio of two integers.

ratline *n* any of the short ropes fastened between the shrouds of a sailing ship to form rungs.

ratoon, rattoon *n* a new shoot sprouting from the root of a perennial plant, esp sugarcane, after it has been cut back. * *vt* to encourage growth in this way.

rat race *n* continual hectic competitive activity.

rattan *n* a climbing palm with a jointed stem; cane made of this.

rattle *vi* to clatter. * *vt* to make a series of sharp, quick noises; to clatter; to recite rapidly; to chatter; (*inf*) to disconcert, fluster. * *n* a rattling sound; a baby's toy that makes a rattling sound; a voluble talker; the rings on the tail of a rattlesnake.

rattler *n* a rattlesnake.

rattlesnake *n* a venomous American snake with a rattle in its tail.

rattling *adj* brisk, vigorous; first-rate. * *adv* to an extreme degree; very.

ratty *adj* (**rattier, rattiest**) like or full of rats; (*sl*) angry, irritable, snappish.

raucous *adj* hoarse and harsh-sounding; loud and rowdy.

raunchy *adj* (**raunchier, raunchiest**) (*sl*) coarse, earthy; careless, slovenly; cheap, inferior.

rauwolfia *n* a tropical flowering shrub of Southeast Asia; an extract from the root of this used in various drugs.

ravage *vt* to ruin, destroy; to plunder, lay waste. * *n* destruction; ruin; (*pl*) the effects of this.

rave *vi* to speak wildly or as if delirious; (*inf*) to enthuse. * *n* enthusiastic praise.—**raving** *adj*.

ravel *vti* (**ravelling, ravelled** *or* **raveling, raveled**) to entangle or disentangle; to fray; to unwind; to make or become complicated.

raven *n* a large crow-like bird with glossy black feathers. * *adj* of the colour or sheen of a raven.

ravenous *adj* famished; voracious.—**ravenously** *adv*.

ravine *n* a deep, narrow gorge, a large gully.

ravioli *n* small cases of pasta filled with highly seasoned chopped meat or vegetables.

ravish *vt* to violate; to rape; to enrapture.

ravishing *adj* charming, captivating.

raw *adj* uncooked; unrefined; in a natural state, crude; untrained, inexperienced; sore, skinned; damp, chilly; (*inf*) harsh or unfair.—**rawness** *n*.

rawhide *n* (a whip made from strips of) untanned leather.

raw material *n* something out of which a finished article is made; something with a potential for development, improvement, etc.

ray[1] *n* a beam of light that comes from a bright source; any of several lines radiating from a centre; a beam of radiant energy, radioactive particles, etc; a tiny amount.

ray[2] *n* any of various fishes with a flattened body and the eyes on the upper surface.

rayon *n* a textile fibre made from a cellulose solution; a fabric of such fibres.

raze *vt* to demolish; to erase; to level to the ground.—*also* **rase**.

razor *n* a sharp-edged instrument for shaving.

razorbill *n* a North Atlantic auk with a flattened sharp-edged bill.

razor clam, razor-shell *n* any of various bivalve marine molluscs with curved sharp shells.

razz *vt* (*inf*) to deride, heckle.

razzle-dazzle, razzmatazz *n* (*inf*) exciting, exuberant or colourful activity or atmosphere.

Rb (*chem symbol*) rubidium.

RC *abbr* = Roman Catholic.

RCCh *abbr* = Roman Catholic Church.

RCA *abbr* = Radio Corporation of America.

RCAF *abbr* = Royal Canadian Air Force.

RCMP *abbr* = Royal Canadian Mounted Police.

RCN *abbr* = Royal Canadian Navy.

RCP *abbr* = Royal College of Physicians.

RCS *abbr* = Royal College of Surgeons.

Rd *abbr* = road.

Re (*chem symbol*) rhenium.

re- *prefix* again, anew; back.

re¹ *prep* concerning, with reference to.

re² *n* the second note of a major scale in solmization.

reach *vti* to arrive at; to extend as far as; to make contact with; to pass, hand over; to attain, realize; to stretch out the hand; to extend in influence, space, etc; to carry, as sight, sound, etc; to try to get. * *n* the act or power of reaching; extent; mental range; scope; a continuous extent, esp of water.

react *vi* to act in response to a person or stimulus; to have a mutual or reverse effect; to revolt; (*chem*) to undergo a chemical reaction.

reaction *n* an action in response to a stimulus; a revulsion of feeling; exhaustion after excitement, etc; opposition to new ideas; (*chem*) an action set up by one substance in another.

reactionary *adj, n* (a person) opposed to political or social change.

reactive *adj* of or relating to reaction; reacting to stimuli; caused by stress.

reactor *n* a person or substance that undergoes a reaction; (*chem*) a vessel in which a reaction occurs; a nuclear reactor.

read *vti* (**reading, read**) to understand something written; to speak aloud (from a book); to study by reading; to interpret, divine; to register, as a gauge; to foretell; (of a computer) to obtain (information) from; (*sl*) to hear and understand (a radio communication, etc); (*with* **about, of**) to learn by reading; to be phrased in certain words. * *adj* well-informed.

readable *adj* legible; pleasantly written.

readdress *vt* to address again; (*letter*) to change the address when forwarding.

reader *n* a person who reads; one who reads aloud to others; a proofreader; a person who evaluates manuscripts; a textbook, esp on reading; a unit that scans material for computation or storage; a senior lecturer.

readership *n* all the readers of a certain publication, author, etc.

readily *adv* in a ready manner; willingly, easily.

reading *n* the act of one who reads; any material to be read; the amount measured by a barometer, meter, etc; a particular interpretation of a play, etc.

readjust *vt* to adjust again.

read-only memory *n* a small computer memory that cannot be changed by the computer and that contains a special-purpose program.

read-out *n* the retrieval of information from a computer memory; the information retrieved.

read-write head *n* (*comput*) an electromagnetic head that can read and write data on a magnetic disc.

ready *adj* (**readier, readiest**) prepared; fit for use; willing; inclined, apt; prompt, quick; handy. * *n* the state of being ready, esp the position of a firearm aimed for firing. * *vt* (**readying, readied**) to make ready.— **readiness** *n*.

ready-made *adj* made in standard sizes, not to measure.

reagent *n* (*chem*) a substance used to detect, measure, or react with other substances.

real *adj* existing, actual, not imaginary; true, genuine, not artificial; (*law*) immovable, consisting of land or houses. * *adv* (*sl*) very; really.

real estate *n* property; land.

realgar *n* a reddish mineral composed of arsenic sulphide.

realign *vti* to align again; (*politics, diplomacy*) to readjust alliances, policies, etc.—**realignment** *n*.

realism *n* practical outlook; (*art, literature*) the ability to represent things as they really are without concealment; (*philos*) the doctrine that the physical world has an objective existence; the doctrine that general ideas have an objective existence.—**realist** *n*.

realistic *adj* matter-of-fact, not visionary; lifelike; of or relating to realism.—**realistically** *adv*.

reality *n* (*pl* **realities**) the fact or condition of being real; an actual fact or thing; truth.

realization *n* the action of realizing; something comprehended or achieved.

realize *vt* to become fully aware of; (*ambition, etc*) to make happen; to cause to appear real; to convert into money, be sold for.

really *adv* in fact, in reality; positively, very. * *interj* indeed.

realm *n* a kingdom, country; domain, region; sphere.

real number *n* any rational or irrational number.

real tennis *n* an early form of tennis played in a walled indoor court.

real-time *adj* involving the continual processing, manipulation and presentation of data by a computer as it is generated.

realtor *n* a person whose business is selling and leasing property, an estate agent.

realty *n* real estate.

ream *n* a quantity of paper varying from 480 to 516 sheets; (*pl: inf*) a great amount.

reap *vti* to harvest; to gain (a benefit).

reaper *n* a person who or a machine that reaps.

rear¹ *n* the back part or position, esp of an army; (*sl*) the rump. * *adj* of, at, or in the rear.

rear² *vt* to raise; (*children*) to bring up; to educate, nourish, etc. * *vi* (*horse*) to stand on the hind legs.

rear guard *n* a military detachment assigned to guard the rear of a body of troops. * *adj* relating to determined defensive resistance.

rear admiral *n* a naval officer next below in rank to a vice admiral.

rear light, rear lamp *n* a taillight.

rearm *vti* to arm or become armed again, esp with better weapons.—**rearmament** *n*.

rearview mirror *n* a mirror in a motor vehicle that allows the driver to see following traffic.

rearward *adj, adv* at or towards the rear.—**rearwards** *adv*.

reason *n* motive or justification (of an action or belief); the mental power to draw conclusions and determine truth; a cause; moderation; sanity; intelligence. * *vti* to think logically (about); to analyse; to argue or infer.

reasonable *adj* able to reason or listen to reason; rational; sensible; not expensive; moderate, fair.—**reasonableness** *n*.—**reasonably** *adv*.

reasoned *adj* convincingly argued.

reassure *vt* to hearten; to give confidence to; to free from anxiety.—**reassurance** *n*.

rebate¹ *n* a refund of part of an amount paid; discount.

rebate² see **rabbet**.

rebec, rebeck *n* a medieval stringed instrument shaped like a lute and played with a bow.

rebel *n* a person who refuses to conform with convention. * *vi* (**rebelling, rebelled** *or* **rebeling, rebeled**) (*army*) to rise up against the authorities or the government; to dissent.

rebellion *n* armed resistance to an established government, insurrection; defiance of authority.

rebellious *adj* of or engaged in rebellion; tending to rebel; stubborn.—**rebelliously** *adv.*

rebirth *n* a second or new birth; a revival, renaissance; spiritual regeneration.

rebound *vi* to spring back after impact; to bounce back; to recover. * *n* a recoil; an emotional reaction.

rebounder *n* a small trampoline used for keep-fit exercises.

rebuff *vt* to snub, repulse; to refuse unexpectedly.—*also* *n.*

rebuke *vt* to reprimand, chide. * *n* a reproof, reprimand.

rebus *n* (*pl* **rebuses**) a puzzle using images to represent the sound of words or syllables.

rebut *vt* (**rebutting, rebutted**) to disprove or refute by argument, etc.—**rebuttal** *n.*

rec *abbr* = receipt; recipe; record.

recalcitrant *adj* refusing to obey authority, etc; actively disobedient.—**recalcitrance** *n.*

recall *vt* to call back; to bring back to mind, remember; to revoke. * *n* remembrance; a summons to return; the removal from office by popular vote.

recant *vti* to repudiate or retract a former opinion, declaration, or belief.—**recantation** *n.*

recap *vti* (**recapping, recapped**) to recapitulate. * *n* (*inf*) recapitulation.

recapitulate *vt* to restate the main points of, to summarize.—**recapitulation** *n.*

recapture *vt* to capture again; (*a lost feeling, etc*) to discover anew, regain. * *n* the act of recapturing; a thing or feeling recaptured.

recd, rec'd *abbr* = received.

recede *vi* to move back; to withdraw, retreat; to slope backwards; to grow less; to decline in value.

receding *adj* sloping backwards; disappearing from view; (*hair*) ceasing to grow at the temples.

receipt *n* the act of receiving; a written proof of this; (*pl*) amount received from business. * *vt* to acknowledge and mark as paid; to write a receipt for.

receive *vt* to acquire, be given; to experience, be subjected to; to admit, allow; to greet on arrival; to accept as true; (*stolen goods*) to take in; to transfer electrical signals. * *vi* to be a recipient; to convert radio waves into perceptible signals.

received *adj* accepted, recognized.

Received Pronunciation *n* the unlocalized accent of British English, regarded as standard.

receiver *n* a person who receives; equipment that receives electronic signals, esp on a telephone; (*law*) a person appointed to manage or hold in trust property in bankruptcy or pending a lawsuit.

receivership *n* the status of a business in the hands of a receiver.

recent *adj* happening lately, fresh; not long established, modern.—**recently** *adv.*

receptacle *n* a container.

reception *n* the act of receiving or being received; a welcome; a social gathering, often to extend a formal welcome; a response, reaction; the quality of the sound or image produced by a radio or television set.

receptionist *n* a person employed to receive visitors to an office, hotel, hospital, etc.

receptive *adj* able or quick to take in ideas or impressions.

recess *n* a temporary halting of work, a vacation; a hidden or inner place; an alcove or niche. * *vti* to place in a recess; to form a recess in; to take a recess.

recession *n* the act of receding; a downturn in economic activity; an indentation.

recharge *vi* to renew the electric charge in (a battery, etc); to recover one's energies.

recherché *adj* uncommon, choice; refined, precious.

recidivism *n* inevitable relapse into crime.—**recidivist** *n.*

recipe *n* a list of ingredients and directions for preparing food; a method for achieving an end.

recipient *n* a person who receives.

reciprocal *adj* done by each to the other; mutual; complementary; interchangeable; (*gram*) expressing a mutual relationship. * *n* (*math*) an expression so related to another that their product is 1.—**reciprocally** *adv.*—**reciprocity** *n.*

reciprocate *vti* to give in return; to repay; (*mech*) to move alternately backwards and forwards.—**reciprocating** *adj.*—**reciprocation** *n.*

recital *n* the act of reciting; a detailed account, narrative; a statement of facts; (*mus*) a performance given by an individual musician.

recitation *n* the act of reciting; something recited, as a poem, etc.

recitative *n* a narrative part of an opera sung in the rhythms of ordinary speech.

recite *vti* to repeat aloud from memory, declaim; to recount, enumerate; to repeat (a lesson).

reckless *adj* rash, careless, incautious.—**recklessly** *adv.*—**recklessness** *n.*

reckon *vti* to count; to regard or consider; to think; to calculate; (*with* **with**) to take into account.

reckoning *n* a calculation; the settlement of an account.

reclaim *vt* to recover, win back from a wild state or vice; (*wasteland*) to convert into land fit for cultivation; (*plastics, etc*) to obtain from waste materials.—**reclaimable** *adj.*—**reclamation** *n.*

recline *vti* to cause or permit to lean or bend backwards; to lie down on the back or side.—**reclinable** *adj.*

recluse *n* a person who lives in solitude; a hermit.

recognition *n* the act of recognizing; identification; acknowledgment, admission; the sensing and encoding of printed and written data by a machine.

recognizance *n* (*law*) a bond by which a person undertakes before a court to observe some condition; the sum pledged as surety for this.

recognize *vt* to know again, identify; to greet; to acknowledge formally; to accept, admit.—**recognizable** *adj.*

recoil *vti* to spring back, kick, as a gun; to shrink or flinch. * *n* the act of recoiling, a rebound.

recollect *vti* to recall; to remind (oneself) of something temporarily forgotten; to call something to mind.

recollection *n* the act of recalling to mind; a memory, impression; something remembered; tranquillity of mind; religious contemplation.

recombinant DNA *n* molecules of DNA from different sources spliced together in the laboratory.

recombination *n* the combination of genetic material from different sources.

recommend *vt* to counsel or advise; to commend or praise; to introduce favourably.—**recommendable** *adj*.—**recommendation** *n*.

recompense *n* to reward or pay an equivalent; to compensate. * *n* reward; repayment; compensation.

reconcile *vt* to re-establish friendly relations; to bring to agreement; to make compatible; to resolve; to settle; to make resigned (to); (*financial account*) to check with another account for accuracy.—**reconcilable** *adj*.—**reconciliation** *n*.

recondite *adj* needing specialized training or knowledge; complex, obscure.

recondition *vt* to repair and restore to good working order.

reconnaissance *n* a survey of an area, esp for obtaining military information about an enemy.

reconnoitre, reconnoiter *vti* to make a reconnaisance (of).

reconsider *vt* to consider afresh, review; to modify.—**reconsideration** *n*.

reconstitute *vt* (*a dried or condensed substance*) to constitute again, esp to restore to its original form by adding water.—**reconstitution** *n*.

reconstruct *vt* to build again; to build up, as from remains, an image of the original; to supply missing parts by conjecture.—**reconstruction** *n*.

record *vt* to preserve evidence of; to write down; to chart; to register, enrol; to register permanently by mechanical means; (*sound or visual images*) to register on a disc, tape, etc for later reproduction; to celebrate; to make a recording. * *vi* to record something. * *adj* being the best, largest, etc. * *n* a written account; a register; a report of proceedings; the known facts about anything or anyone; an outstanding performance or achievement that surpasses others previously recorded; a grooved vinyl disc for playing on a record player; (*comput*) data in machine-readable form.

recorder *n* an official who keeps records; a machine or device that records; a tape recorder; a wind instrument of the flute family.

recording *n* what is recorded, as on a disc or tape; the record.

recordist *n* a person who records sound.

record player *n* an instrument for playing records through a loudspeaker.

recount[1] *vt* to narrate the details of; to narrate.

recount[2] *vt* to count again * *n* a second counting of votes at an election.

recoup *vti* to make good (financial losses); to regain; to make up for something lost.

recourse *n* a resort for help or protection when in danger; that to which one turns when seeking help.

re-cover *vt* to put a new cover on.

recover *vti* to regain after losing; to reclaim; to regain health or after losing emotional control.—**recoverable** *adj*.

recovery *n* (*pl* **recoveries**) the act or process of recovering; the condition of having recovered; reclamation; restoration; a retrieval of a capsule, etc after a space flight.

recovery room *n* a hospital room where patients are kept for close observation or care following surgery.

recreate *vt* to create over again, esp mentally.

recreation *n* relaxation of the body or mind; a sport, pastime or amusement.—**recreational** *adj*.

recreational vehicle *n* a vehicle for camping out such as a motor home, camper, etc.

recreation room *n* a room used for relaxation, recreation, or social activities, esp in a hospital, etc.

recriminate *vi* to return an accusation, make a countercharge.—**recrimination** *n*.—**recriminatory** *adj*.

recrudesce *vi* (*esp disease*) to reappear again.—**recrudescence** *n*.

recruit *n* a soldier newly enlisted; a member newly joined; a beginner. * *vti* to enlist (military personnel); to enlist (new members) for an organization; to increase or maintain the numbers of; to restore, reinvigorate.—**recruitment** *n*.

rectal *adj* of, for, or near the rectum.

rectangle *n* a parallelogram with all its angles right angles.

rectangular *adj* having the shape of a rectangle; crossing, meeting, or lying at a right angle; having faces or surfaces shaped like right angles.

rectifier *n* a device that converts alternating current to direct current.

rectify *vt* (**rectifying, rectified**) to put right, correct; to amend; (*chem*) to refine by repeated distillation; (*elect*) to convert to direct current.—**rectifiable** *adj*.

rectilinear, rectilineal *adj* of or bounded by straight lines; straight.

rectitude *n* moral uprightness; probity; a being correct in judgment or procedure.

recto *n* (*pl* **rectos**) the right-hand page of an open book.

rector *n* in some churches, a clergyman in charge of a parish; the head of certain schools, colleges, etc.—**rectorial** *adj*.

rectory *n* (*pl* **rectories**) the house of a minister or priest.

rectrix *n* (*pl* **rectrices**) any of the tail feathers of a bird, used for controlling the direction of flight.

rectum *n* (*pl* **rectums, recta**) the part of the large intestine leading to the anus.

rectus *n* (*pl* **recti**) any of various straight muscles, esp of the abdomen.

recumbent *adj* leaning, resting; lying down.

recuperate *vti* to get well again; to recover (losses, etc).—**recuperation** *n*.

recur *vi* (**recurring, recurred**) to be repeated in thought, talk, etc; to occur again or at intervals.—**recurrence** *n*.—**recurrent** *adj*.

recycle *vti* (*a substance*) to pass through a process again; (*used matter*) to process to regain re-usable material; to save from loss and restore to usefulness.—**recyclable** *adj*.

red *adj* (**redder, reddest**) of the colour of blood; politically left-wing. * *n* the colour of blood; any red pigment; a communist.

redact *vt* to edit (a manuscript, etc) for publication.—**redaction** *n*.—**redactor** *n*.

red admiral *n* a common butterfly of Europe and North America with black and red markings.

redback *n* (*Austral*) a poisonous spider with red spots on its back.

red blood cell *n* any blood cell containing haemoglobin that conveys oxygen to the tissues.

red-blooded *adj* (*inf*) vigorous, virile.

redbreast *n* a robin.

redbrick *adj, n* (a British university) founded after 1945.

redcap *n* in US, a porter at a railway station or airport; in UK, a military policeman.

red card *n* (*soccer*) a red card held up by the referee indicating that a player is to be sent off.

red carpet *n* a strip of red carpet for dignitaries to walk on; a grand or impressive welcome or entertainment.

red cedar *n* (the reddish wood of) a North American juniper tree.

red cent *n* (*inf*) a trivial quantity of money.

red corpuscle *n* a red blood cell.

Red Crescent *n* the Red Cross in Muslim countries.

Red Cross *n* a red cross on a white ground, the symbol of the International Red Cross, a society for the relief of suffering in time of war and disaster.

red deer *n* a large deer with a reddish brown coat.

redden *vti* to make or become red; to blush.

reddish *adj* tinged with red.—**reddishness** *n*.

red dwarf *n* a star with a relatively small mass and low luminosity.

redeem *vt* to recover by payment; to regain; to deliver from sin; to pay off; to restore to favour; to make amends for.—**redeemable** *adj*.—**redeemer** *n*.

redemption *n* the act of redeeming or the state of being redeemed; recovery; repurchase; salvation.

redeploy *vt* (*troops, workers*) to assign to new positions or activities.—**redeployment** *n*.

redeye *n* (*sl*) cheap whiskey.

red flag *n* a symbol of communism or revolution; a sign of danger.

red fox *n* the common European fox with reddish fur.

red giant *n* a giant star with a relatively low surface temperature that emits a red glow.

red-handed *adj* caught in the act of committing a crime.

redhead *n* a person having red hair.—**redheaded** *adj*.

red herring *n* a herring cured to a dark brown colour; something that diverts attention from the real issue.

red-hot *adj* glowing with heat; extremely hot; very excited, angry, etc; very new.

redirect *vt* to change the direction or course of; to readdress.—**redirection** *n*.

red lead *n* a poisonous red oxide of lead used as a pigment.

red-letter *adj* of special significance.

red light *n* a warning signal, a cautionary sign; a deterrent.

red-light *adj* (*of a district*) containing brothels.

red mullet *n* a food fish of European waters, a goatfish.

redneck *n* (*derog*) a poor white farm labourer in the US South. * *adj* racist, reactionary.

redo *vt* (**redoing, redid,** *pp* **redone**) to do again; to redecorate.

red ochre *n* any of several types of reddish earth used as pigments.

redolent *adj* having a strong scent, fragrant; reminiscent (of).—**redolence** *n*.

redouble *vti* to double again; to make or become twice as much.

redoubt *n* a detached outpost of a fortification.

redoubtable *adj* formidable.

redound *vi* to have a directly positive or negative effect (on); to rebound (on or upon).

red pepper *n* a variety of pepper grown for its spicy red fruit, capsicum; its fruit; the fruit of the sweet pepper when ripe and red; cayenne pepper.

redress *vt* to put right, adjust; to compensate, make up for. * *n* remedy; compensation.

red salmon *n* any salmon with pinkish flesh, esp the sockeye.

redshank *n* a type of large European sandpiper.

red squirrel *n* a squirrel with reddish-brown fur of Europe, North America and Asia.

red tape *n* rigid adherence to bureaucratic routine and regulations, causing delay.

reduce *vt* to diminish or make smaller in size, amount, extent, or number; to lower in price; to simplify; to make thin; to subdue; to bring or convert (to another state or form).—**reducible** *adj*.

reductio ad absurdum *n* a proof of the falsity of a proposition by demonstrating the absurdity of its logical consequences.

reduction *n* the act or process of reducing or being reduced; something reduced; the amount by which a thing is reduced; (*math*) the conversion of a fraction into decimal form.—**reductional** *adj*.—**reductive** *adj*.

redundant *adj* surplus to requirements; (*Brit person*) deprived of one's job as being no longer necessary; excessive, wordy; (*words*) unnecessary to the meaning.—**redundancy** *n*.

reduplicate *vt* to make double, to repeat; (*gram*) to repeat (syllable or letter), to form (word) thus. * *adj* doubled, repeated.—**reduplication** *n*.—**reduplicative** *adj*.

red wine *n* wine made from black grapes with the skins left on.

redwood *n* an important timber tree of California that can reach a height of 360 feet; any of various trees yielding a red dye or reddish wood.

reed *n* a tall grass found in marshes; a thin piece of cane in the mouthpiece of a musical instrument; a person or thing too weak to rely on; one easily swayed or overcome.

reedbird *see* **bobolink**.

re-educate, reeducate *vt* to educate again in order to adapt to changing circumstances.—**re-education, reeducation** *n*.

reedy *adj* (**reedier, reediest**) filled with reeds; resembling a reed; shrill, piping, as in the sound of a reed.—**reedily** *adv*.—**reediness** *n*.

reef *n* a ridge of rocks, sand, or coral at or just below the surface of water; a hazardous obstruction; a lode or vein of ore.

reefer *n* a thick double-breasted jacket, formerly worn by sailors; (*inf*) a cigarette containing cannabis.

reef knot *n* a symmetrical double knot.

reek *n* a strong smell. * *vi* to give off smoke, fumes or a strong or offensive smell.

reel[1] *n* a winding device; a spool or bobbin; thread wound on this; a length of film, about 300m (1,000ft). * *vt* to wind on to a reel; (*with* **in**) to draw in by means of a reel; (*with* **off**) to tell, write, etc with fluency; (*with* **out**) to unwind from a reel.

reel[2] *vi* to stagger or sway about; to be dizzy or in a whirl. * *n* a staggering motion.

reel[3] *n* a lively Scottish or Irish dance; the music for it. * *vi* to dance a reel.

re-enter *vti* to enter again.

re-entry *n* (*pl* **re-entries**) the act of entering or possessing again; the return of a spacecraft to the earth's atmosphere.

ref *n* (*inf*) a referee.

ref. *abbr* = with reference to.

refectory *n* (*pl* **refectories**) the dining hall of a monastery, college, etc.

refer *vti* (**referring, referred**) to attribute, assign (to); (*with* **to**) to direct, have recourse (to); to relate to; to mention or allude to; to direct attention (to).—**referable** *adj*.

referee *n* an adjudicator, arbitrator; an umpire; a judge.

reference *n* the act of referring; a mention or allusion; a testimonial; a person who gives a testimonial; a direction to a passage in a book; a passage in a book referred to.

reference book *n* a book for reference rather than general reading, eg a yearbook, directory.

reference library *n* a library whose books may be consulted but not borrowed.

referendum *n* (*pl* **referendums, referenda**) the submission of an issue directly to the vote of the electorate, a plebiscite.

referral *n* the act of referring or instance of being referred.

refill *vt* to fill again. * *n* a replacement pack for an empty permanent container; a providing again.

refine *vti* to purify; to make free from impurities or coarseness; to make or become cultured.

refined *adj* polished, cultured; affected.

refinement *n* fineness of manners or taste; an improvement; a fine distinction.

refinery *n* (*pl* **refineries**) a plant where raw materials, eg sugar, oil, are refined.

refit *vti* (**refitting, refitted**) to make or become functional again by repairing, re-equipping, etc.—*also n.*

reflation *n* the restoration of deflated prices to a desirable level.—**reflationary** *adj.*

reflect *vt* (*light, heat, etc*) to throw back; to bend aside or back; to show an image of, as a mirror; to express. * *vi* to reproduce to the eye or mind; to mirror; to meditate; (*with* **upon**) to ponder; (*with* **on**) to discredit, disparage.

reflected *adj* thrown or cast back; mirrored; bent or folded back.

reflecting telescope *n* a telescope operated by a series of mirrors.

reflection *n* a reflecting back, turning aside; the action of changing direction when a ray strikes and is thrown back; reflected heat, light or colour; a reflected image; meditation, thought; reconsideration; reproach.—*also* **reflexion.**

reflective *adj* meditative; concerned with ideas.—**reflectively** *adv.*—**reflectiveness** *n.*

reflector *n* a disc, instrument, strip or other surface that reflects light or heat.

reflex *n* an involuntary response to a stimulus. * *adj* (*angle*) of more than 180 degrees; (*camera*) with a full-size viewfinder using the main lens.

reflex camera *n* a camera in which the image from the lens is conveyed by an angled mirror to a viewfinder for composition and focusing.

reflexion *see* **reflection.**

reflexive *adj* (*pron, verb*) referring back to the subject.—**reflexively** *adv.*

reflexology *n* (*alternative medicine*) a technique of applying pressure to specific points on the hands and feet to stimulate the blood supply to other areas of the body and help relieve stress.—**reflexologist** *n.*

reform *vti* to improve; to make or become better by the removal of faults; to amend; to abolish abuse. * *n* improvement or transformation, esp of an institution; removal of social ills.—**reformed** *adj.*

re-form *vti* to form again.

reformation *n* the act of reforming or the state of being reformed; improvement; (*with cap*) the 16th-century religious revolt that resulted in the formation of Protestant churches.

reformatory *adj* reforming; * *n* (*pl* **reformatories**) an institution for reforming young criminals; a prison for women.

reformer *n* a person who advocates or works for reform; an apparatus for changing the molecular structure of a hydrocarbon to form specialized products.

reform school *n* a reformatory for young people.

refract *vt* to cause (a ray of light, etc) to undergo refraction.

refracting telescope *n* a type of telescope in which the image is formed by a series of lenses.

refraction *n* the bending of a ray or wave of light, heat, or sound as it passes from one medium into another.

refractory *adj* obstinate; (*disease, etc*) resistant to treatment; (*muscle*) unresponsive to stimuli; able to withstand high temperatures. * *n* (*pl* **refractories**) a heat-resistant material.

refrain[1] *vi* to abstain (from).

refrain[2] *n* recurring words in a song or poem, esp at the end of a stanza; a chorus.

refrangible *adj* able to be refracted.

refresh *vt* to revive; to give new energy to; to make cool; to take a drink.

refresher *n* something that refreshes, esp a drink; a reminder; a training course to renew one's skill or knowledge.

refresher course *n* a course designed to keep professionals informed of recent developments in their field of knowledge or expertise.

refreshing *adj* invigorating, reviving; pleasing because unsophisticated.

refreshment *n* the act of refreshing; a restorative; (*pl*) food and drink; a light meal.

refrigerate *vti* to make, become, or keep, cold; to preserve by keeping cold.—**refrigeration** *n.*

refrigerator *n* something that refrigerates; a chamber for keeping food, etc, cool; an apparatus for cooling.—*also* **fridge, icebox.**

refuel *vti* (**refuelling, refuelled** *or* **refueling, refueled**) to supply with or take on fresh fuel.

refuge *n* a protection or shelter from danger; a retreat, sanctuary.

refugee *n* a person who flees to another country to escape political or religious persecution.

refund *vti* to repay; to reimburse. * *n* a refunding or the amount refunded.

refurbish *vt* to renovate or re-equip.—**refurbishment** *n.*

refusal *n* the act or process of refusing; the choice of refusing or accepting.

refuse[1] *n* garbage, waste, rubbish.

refuse[2] *vt* to decline, reject; to withhold, deny. * *vi* (*horse*) to decline to jump.

refute *vt* to rebut; to disprove.—**refutable** *adj.*—**refutably** *adv.*—**refutation** *n.*

regain *vt* to get back, recover; to reach again.

regal *adj* royal; relating to a king or queen.

regale *vt* to entertain, as with a feast; to delight.

regalia *npl* royal insignia or prerogatives; the insignia of an order, office, or membership; finery.

regard *vt* to gaze at, observe; to hold in respect; to consider; to heed, take into account. * *n* a look; attention; reference; respect, esteem; (*pl*) good wishes, greetings.

regarding *prep* with reference to, about.

regardless *adj* having no regard to. * *adv* (*inf*) in spite of everything; without heeding the cost, consequences, etc.

regatta *n* a meeting for yacht or boat races.

regency *n* (*pl* **regencies**) the status or authority of a regent; a regent's period of office; a body entrusted with the duties of a regent; rule; (*with cap*) in British history, the period 1810-20.

regenerate *vti* to renew, give new life to; to be reborn spiritually; to reorganize; to produce anew.—**regeneration** *n*.

regent *n* a person who rules or administers a country during the sovereign's minority, absence, or incapacity; a member of a governing board (as of a university).

reggae *n* a strongly accented West Indian musical form with four beats to the bar.

regicide *n* the killer or the killing or a king.

regime, régime *n* a political or ruling system.

regimen *n* a system of diet, exercise, etc, for improving the health; a regular course of training.

regiment *n* a military unit, smaller than a division, consisting usu of a number of battalions. * *vt* to organize in a strict manner; to subject to order or conformity.—**regimental** *adj*.

regimentation *n* the act of regimenting; excessive orderliness.

Regina *n* a reigning queen.

region *n* a large, indefinite part of the earth's surface; one of the zones into which the atmosphere is divided; an administrative area of a country; a part of the body.—**regional** *adj*.

register *n* an official list; a written record, as for attendance; the book containing such a record or list; a tone of voice; a variety of language appropriate to a subject or occasion; (*comput*) a device in which data can be stored and operated on; (*print*) exact alignment; a device for indicating speed, etc; a plate regulating draught. * *vti* to record; to enter in or sign a register; to correspond exactly; to entrust a letter to the post with special precautions for safety; to express emotion facially; to make or convey an impression.

registered *adj* recorded officially; qualified formally or officially.

registrar *n* a person who keeps records, esp one in an educational institution in charge of student records; a hospital doctor below a specialist in rank.

registration *n* the act of registering; the condition of having registered.

registry *n* (*pl* **registries**) registration; a place where records are kept; an official record book.

regius professor *n* in UK, a person appointed to a university chair founded by the Crown.

regnal *adj* pertaining to a sovereign or reign, esp designating a year of a reign calculated from the date of accession.

regress *vi* to move backwards; to revert to a former condition.—**regressive** *adj*.—**regressively** *adv*.

regression *n* the act of regressing; a relapse, reversion; a return to an earlier time or stage; (*psychoanal*) a retreat of the personality.

regret *vt* (**regretting, regretted**) to feel sorrow, grief, or loss; to remember with longing; (*with* that) to repent of. * *n* disappointment; sorrow; grief; (*pl*) polite refusal.—**regretful** *adj*.—**regretfully** *adv*.

regrettable *adj* to be regretted; deserving reproof.—**regrettably** *adv*.

regroup *vti* to group again; (*mil*) to reorganize (troops, etc) following action.

regular *adj* normal; habitual, not casual; at fixed intervals; according to rule, custom, or the accepted practice; uniform, consistent; symmetrical; fully quali-

fied; belonging to a standing army; (*inf*) thorough, complete; (*inf*) pleasant, friendly. * *n* a professional soldier; (*inf*) a person who attends regularly.—**regularity** *n*.—**regularly** *adv*.

regular army *n* a permanent army; (*with caps*) the United States army.

regularize *vt* to make regular or correct.—**regularization** *n*.

regulate *vt* to control according to a rule; to cause to conform to a standard or needs; to adjust so as to put in good order.—**regulatory** *adj*.

regulation *n* the act of regulating or state of being regulated; a prescribed rule, ordinance. * *adj* normal, standard.

regulator *n* one who or that which regulates; a regulating device; a lever in a watch that adjusts its speed.

regurgitate *vti* to pour back, cast up again, esp from the stomach to the mouth.—**regurgitation** *n*.

rehabilitate *vt* (*prisoner etc*) to help adapt to society after a stay in an institution; to put back in good condition; to restore to rights or privileges; (*sick person etc*) to help to adjust to normal conditions after illness.—**rehabilitation** *n*.

rehash *n* old materials put in a new form. * *vt* to dish up again.

rehearse *vti* to practise repeatedly before public performance; to recount, narrate in detail.—**rehearsal** *n*.

rehoboam *n* a wine bottle that holds six times the amount of a standard bottle.

reify *vt* (**reifying, reified**) to make (something abstract) real or concrete.

reign *n* the rule of a sovereign; the period of this; influence; domination. * *vi* to rule; to prevail.

reimburse *vt* to repay; to refund (for expense or loss).—**reimbursable** *adj*.—**reimbursement** *n*.

rein *n* the strap of a bridle for guiding or restraining a horse; (*pl*) a means of control or restraint. * *vt* to control with the rein; to restrain.

reincarnation *n* the incarnation of the soul after death in another body.—**reincarnate** *adj*, *vt*.

reindeer *n* a large deer with branched antlers found in northern regions.

reindeer moss *n* a lichen of northern regions that provides food for reindeer.

reinforce *vt* (*army etc*) to strengthen with fresh troops; (*a material*) to add to the strength of.

reinforced concrete *n* concrete with metal bars, wire, etc inserted in it for strength.

reinforcement *n* the act of reinforcing; additional support; (*pl*) additional troops.

reinstate *vt* to restore to a former position, rank, or condition.—**reinstatement** *n*.

reinterpret *vt* to interpret again; to give a new explanation of.—**reinterpretation** *n*.

reissue *vt* to issue again; to republish. * *n* a new issue; a reprint.

reiterate *vt* to repeat; to say or do again or many times.—**reiteration** *n*.

reject *vt* to throw away, to discard; to refuse to accept, to decline; to rebuff. * *n* a thing or person rejected.—**rejection** *n*.

rejoice *vi* to feel joyful or happy.

rejoin *vt* to join again; to return to.

rejoinder *n* a retort, a reply.

rejuvenate *vt* to give youthful vigour to.—**rejuvenation** *n*.

relapse *vi* to fall back into a worse state after improvement; to return to a former vice, to backslide. * *n* the recurrence of illness after apparent recovery.

relate *vt* to narrate, recount; to show a connection (between two or more things). * *vi* to have a formal relationship (with).

related *adj* connected, allied; akin.

relation *n* the way in which one thing stands in respect to another, footing; reference, regard; connection by blood or marriage; a relative; a narration, a narrative; (*pl*) the connections between or among persons, nations, etc; (*pl*) one's family and in-laws.

relationship *n* the tie or degree of kinship or intimacy; affinity; (*inf*) an affair.

relative *adj* having or expressing a relation; corresponding; pertinent; comparative, conditional; respective; meaningful only in relationship; (*gram*) referring to an antecedent. * *n* a person related by blood or marriage.—**relatively** *adv*.

relative molecular mass *n* the total of the atomic weights of all the atoms present in a molecule; the average mass per molecule of any substance relative to one-twelfth the mass of an atom of carbon-12.—*also* **molecular weight**.

relative pronoun *n* a pronoun that is used to connect a dependent clause to a main clause and that refers to a noun in the main clause.

relativity *n* the state of being relative; the relation between one thing and another; (*physics*) the theory of the relative, rather than absolute, character of motion, velocity, mass, etc, and the interdependence of time, matter, and space.

relax *vti* to slacken; to make or become less severe or strict; to make (the muscles) less rigid; to take a rest.

relaxant *n* a drug that relieves muscular tension.

relaxation *n* the act of relaxing; the condition of being relaxed; recreation.

relay *n* a team of fresh horses, men, etc to relieve others; a race between teams, each member of which goes a part of the distance; (*elect*) a device for enabling a weak current to control others; a relayed broadcast. * *vt* (**relaying, relayed**) (*news, etc*) to spread in stages; to broadcast signals.

relay race *n* a race between teams in which each member does part of the distance.

release *vt* to set free; to let go; to relinquish; (*film, etc*) to issue for public exhibition; (*information*) to make available; (*law*) to make over to another. * *n* a releasing, as from prison, work, etc; a device to hold or release a mechanism; a news item, etc, released to the public; (*law*) a written surrender of a claim.

relegate *vt* to move to an inferior position; to demote; to banish.—**relegation** *n*.

relent *vi* to soften in attitude; to become less harsh or severe.

relentless *adj* pitiless; unremitting.

relevant *adj* applying to the matter in hand, pertinent; to the point.—**relevance, relevancy** *n*.

reliable *adj* dependable, trustworthy.—**reliability** *n*.— **reliably** *adv*.

reliance *n* trust; dependence; a thing relied on.—**reliant** *adj*.

relic *n* an object, fragment, or custom that has survived from the past; part of a saint's body or belongings; (*pl*) remains of the dead.

relief *n* the sensation following the easing or lifting of discomfort or stress; release from a duty by another person; a person who takes the place of another on duty; that which relieves; aid; assistance to the needy or victims of a disaster; the projection of a carved design from its ground; distinctness, vividness. * *adj* providing relief in disasters etc.

relief map *n* a map in which topographic relief is represented by shading, colours, etc.

relieve *vt* to bring relief or assistance to; to release from obligation or duty; to ease; (*with* **oneself**) to empty the bladder or bowels. * *vi* to give relief; to break the monotony of; to bring into relief, to stand out.

relieved *adj* having or showing relief, esp from anxiety or repressed emotions.

religion *n* a belief in God or gods; a system of worship and faith; a formalized expression of belief.

religiosity *n* the condition of being religious, esp excessively or sentimentally so.—**religiose** *adj*.

religious *adj* of or conforming to religion; devout, pious; scrupulously and conscientiously faithful.—**religiously** *adv*.

relinquish *vt* to give up; to renounce or surrender.—**relinquishment** *n*.

reliquary *n* (*pl* **reliquaries**) a container or shrine for sacred relics.

relish *n* an appetizing flavour; a distinctive taste; enjoyment of food or an experience; a spicy accompaniment to food; gusto, zest. * *vt* to like the flavour of; to enjoy, appreciate.

relocate *vti* to set up in a new place; to place (an employee) in a different job; (*business*) to move to a new location.—**relocation** *n*.

reluctant *adj* unwilling, loath; offering resistance.—**reluctance** *n*.—**reluctantly** *adv*.

rely *vi* (**relying, relied**) to depend on; to trust.

REM *abbr* = rapid eye movement.

remain *vi* to stay behind or in the same place; to continue to be; to survive, to last; to be left over. * *npl* anything left after use; a corpse.

remainder *n* what is left, the rest; (*math*) the result of subtraction; the quantity left over after division; unsold stock, esp of books; (*law*) the residual interest in an estate.

remake *vt* (**remaking, remade**) to make again. * *n* a new version of an old film.

remand *vt* to send back into custody for further evidence.—*also n*.

remark *vti* to notice; to observe; to pass a comment (upon). * *n* a brief comment.

remarkable *adj* unusual; extraordinary; worthy of comment.—**remarkably** *adv*.

remaster *vt* to make a new (digital) master recording from an original (analogue) recording to provide improved sound quality on vinyl records or compact discs.

remedial *adj* providing a remedy; corrective; relating to the teaching of people with learning difficulties.

remedy *n* a medicine or any means to cure a disease; anything that puts something else to rights. * *vt* (**remedying, remedied**) to cure; to put right.

remember *vti* to recall; to bear in mind; to mention (a person) to another as sending regards; to exercise or have the power of memory.

remembrance *n* a reminiscence; a greeting or gift recalling or expressing friendship or affection; the extent of memory; an honouring of the dead or a past event.

Remembrance Day *n* in Canada, a day, November 11, on which the dead of the two World Wars are commemorated.

Remembrance Sunday *n* in UK, the Sunday nearest November 11, on which the dead of the two World Wars are commemorated.

remind *vt* to cause to remember.

reminder *n* a thing that reminds, esp a letter from a creditor.

reminisce *vi* to think, talk, or write about past events.

reminiscence *n* the recalling of a past experience; (*pl*) memoirs.

reminiscent *adj* reminding, suggestive (of); recalling the past.

remiss *adj* negligent, slack.

remission *n* the act of remitting; the reduction in length of a prison term; the lessening of the symptoms of a disease; pardon, forgiveness.

remit *vti* (**remitting, remitted**) to forgive; to refrain from inflicting (a punishment) or exacting (a debt); to abate, moderate; to send payment (by post); (*law*) to refer to a lower court for reconsideration. * *n* the act of referring; an area of authority.

remittance *n* the sending of money or a payment (by post); the payment or money sent.

remix *vt* to adjust the balance and separation of a recording.—*also n.*

remnant *n* a small remaining fragment or number; an oddment or scrap; a trace; an unsold or unused end of piece goods.

remodel *vt* (**remodelling, remodelled** *or* **remodeling, remodeled**) to fashion afresh; to recast.

remonstrate *vi* to protest, to make a complaint (against).—**remonstrance** *n.*

remorse *n* regret and guilt for a misdemeanour; compassion.—**remorseful** *adj.*—**remorsefully** *adv.*

remorseless *adj* ruthless, cruel; relentless.—**remorselessly** *adv.*—**remorselessness** *n.*

remote *adj* far apart or distant in time or place; out of the way; not closely related; secluded; aloof; vague, faint.—**remotely** *adv.*

remote control *n* the control of a device or activity from a distance, usu by means of an electric circuit or the making or breaking of radio waves.

removal *n* the act of removing; a change of home or office; dismissal.

remove *vti* to take away and put elsewhere; to dismiss, as from office; to get rid of; to kill; to go away. * *n* a stage in gradation; a degree in relationship.—**removable** *adj.*

removed *adj* remote; separated by a specified degree, as of relationship; of a younger or older relationship.

remunerate *vt* to pay for a service; to reward.—**remuneration** *n.*

renaissance *n* a rebirth or revival; (*with cap*) the revival of European art and literature under the influence of classical study during the 14th-16th centuries.—*also adj.*

renal *adj* relating to or near the kidneys.

renascent *adj* becoming active again, reviving.

rend *vti* (**rending, rent**) to tear, to wrench (apart); to be torn apart.

render *vt* (*payments, accounts, etc*) to submit, as for approval; to give back; to pay back; to perform; to represent as by drawing; to translate, interpret; to cause to be; (*fat*) to melt down.

rendering *n* interpretation, translation.

rendezvous *n* (*pl* **rendezvous**) an arranged meeting; a place to meet; a popular haunt; the process of bringing two spacecraft together. * *vi* to meet by appointment.

rendition *n* an interpretation; performance.

renegade *n* a deserter; a person who is faithless to a principle, party, religion, or cause.

renege *vti* to go back on, or fail to keep, a promise or agreement.

renegotiate *vti* to negotiate again, esp to improve the terms of a contract.—**renegotiable** *adj.*—**renegotiation** *n.*

renew *vti* to restore to freshness or vigour; to begin again; to make or get anew; to replace; to grant or obtain an extension of.—**renewable** *adj.*—**renewal** *n.*

rennet *n* an extract from the stomach of calves, etc, used to curdle milk.

renounce *vt* to abandon formally; to give up; to disown.

renovate *vt* to renew; to restore to good condition; to do up, repair.—**renovation** *n.*—**renovator** *n.*

renown *n* fame, celebrity.

renowned *adj* famous, illustrious.

rent[1] *see* **rend.**

rent[2] *n* regular payment to another for the use of a house, machinery, etc. * *vti* to occupy as a tenant; to hire; to let for rent.

rental *n* an amount paid or received as rent; a house, car, etc, for rent; an act of renting; a business that rents something.

rent boy *n* a young male prostitute.

renunciation *n* the act of renouncing; formal abandonment; repudiation.

reopen *vti* to open again; to resume.

reorganize *vti* to organize again; to bring about a reorganization.—**reorganization** *n.*

Rep. *abbr* = Representative; Republic; Republican.

rep *abbr* = repeat; report; reporter.

repair *vt* to mend; to restore to good working order; to make amends for. * *n* the act of repairing; a place repaired; condition as to soundness.

reparable *adj* capable of being repaired.

reparation *n* amends; (*pl*) compensation, as for war damage.

repartee *n* a witty reply; skill in making such replies.

repast *n* a meal.

repatriate *vt* to send back or restore to one's country of origin or citizenship.—**repatriation** *n.*

repay *vt* (**repaying, repaid**) to pay back; to refund.—**repayable** *adj.*—**repayment** *n.*

repeal *vt* to annul, to rescind; to revoke.—*also n.*

repeat *vti* to say, write, or do again; to reiterate; to recite after another or from memory; to reproduce; to recur. * *n* a repetition, encore; anything said or done again, as a re-broadcast of a television programme; (*mus*) a passage to be repeated; the sign for this.—**repeatable** *adj.*

repeated *adj* frequent; done, seen, etc, again.

repeatedly *adv* many times, over and over again.

repeater *n* a clock or watch with a striking mechanism; a device for receiving and amplifying electronic communication signals; a firearm that has a repeating mechanism for reloading; a habitual violator of the laws.

repeating firearm *n* a firearm designed to load cartridges from a magazine.

repel *vt* (**repelling, repelled**) to drive back; to beat off, repulse; to reject; to hold off; to cause distaste; (*water, dirt*) to be resistant to.

repellent *adj* distasteful, unattractive; capable of repelling; impermeable. * *n* a substance that repels, esp a spray for protection against insects.

repent *vi* to wish one had not done something; to feel remorse or regret (for); to regret and change from evil ways.—**repentant** *adj*.

repentance *n* penitence; contrition.

repercussion *n* a rebound; a reverberation; a far-reaching, often indirect reaction to an event.

repertoire *n* the stock of plays, songs, etc, that a company, singer, etc, can perform.

repertory *n* (*pl* **repertories**) a repertoire; the system of alternating several plays through a season with a permanent acting group.

repetition *n* the act of repeating; something repeated, a copy.—**repetitive** *adj*.

repetitious *adj* full of repetition; boring.—**repetitiously** *adv*.—**repetitiousness** *n*.

rephrase *vt* to phrase (a statement) in a different way.

replace *vt* to put back; to take the place of, to substitute for; to supersede.—**replaceable** *adj*.

replacement *n* the act or process of replacing; a person or thing that replaces another.

replenish *vt* to stock again, refill.—**replenishment** *n*.

replete *adj* filled, well provided; stuffed, gorged.

repletion *n* complete fullness; satisfaction.

replica *n* an exact copy; a reproduction.

reply *vti* (**replying, replied**) to answer, respond; to give as an answer. * *n* an answer.

repo-man *n* (*pl* **repo-men**) (*sl*) a person who repossesses (eg a motor car).

report *vti* to give an account of; to tell as news; to take down and describe for publication; to make a formal statement of; to complain about or against; to inform against; to present oneself (for duty). * *n* an account of facts; the formal statement of the findings of an investigation; a newspaper, radio or television account of an event; a rumour; a sharp, loud noise, as of a gun.

reportage *n* the art of reporting on current events; an accurate, observant and well-written account of an event.

report card *n* a report on a pupil or student that is periodically given to his or her parent; an evaluation of performance.

reportedly *adv* as reported, not directly.

reporter *n* a person who gathers and reports news for a newspaper, radio or television; a person authorized to make statements concerning law decisions or legislative proceedings.

repose *n* rest, sleep; stillness, peace; composure, serenity. * *vti* to lie down or lay at rest; to place (trust, etc) in someone; to rest; to lie dead.

reposition *vt* to place in a different or new position.

repository *n* (*pl* **repositories**) a receptacle; a storehouse, warehouse; a confidant.

repossess *vt* to possess again; to restore possession of (property), esp for nonpayment of debt.—**repossession** *n*.

reprehend *vt* to rebuke, to find fault with, to criticize.

reprehensible *adj* blameworthy, culpable.

reprehension *n* blame, censure.

re-present *vt* to present again.

represent *vt* to portray; to describe; to typify; to stand for, symbolize; to point out; to perform on the stage; to act as an agent for; to deputize for; to serve as a specimen, example, etc, of.—**representable** *adj*.

representation *n* the act of representing or being represented, as in a parliamentary assembly; a portrait, reproduction; (*pl*) a presentation of claims, protests, views, etc.

representative *adj* typical; portraying; consisting of or based on representation of the electorate by delegates. * *n* an example or type; a person who acts for another; a delegate, agent, salesman, etc.

repress *vt* to suppress, restrain; (*emotions*) to keep under control; to exclude involuntarily from the conscious mind.—**repressive** *adj*.—**represser, repressor** *n*.

repression *n* the act of repressing; the condition of being repressed; domination, tyranny.

reprieve *vt* to postpone or commute the punishment of; to give respite to.—*also n*.

reprimand *n* a formal rebuke. * *vt* to reprove formally.

reprint *vt* to print again. * *n* a book or article that has appeared in print before.

reprisal *n* an act of retaliation for an injury done.

reprise *n* (*mus*) the repetition of an earlier theme or passage.—*also vt*.

reproach *vt* to accuse of a fault; to blame. * *n* a reproof; a source of shame or disgrace.—**reproachful** *adj*.

reprobate *n* a depraved person; a hardened sinner; a scoundrel.

reproduce *vti* to make a copy, duplicate, or likeness of; to propagate; to produce offspring; to multiply.

reproduction *n* the act of reproducing; the process by which plants and animals breed; a copy or likeness; a representation.—**reproductive** *adj*.

reprography *n* the process of reproducing printed material, as by photocopying.—**reprographic** *adj*.

reproof *n* a rebuke, blame.

reprove *vt* to rebuke, censure.—**reprovingly** *adv*.

reptile *n* any of a class of cold-blooded, air-breathing vertebrates with horny scales or plates, as turtles, crocodiles, snakes, lizards, etc; a grovelling or despised person.—**reptilian** *adj*.

Repub *abbr* = Republican.

republic *n* a government in which the people elect the head of state, usu called president, and in which the people and their elected representatives have supreme power; a country governed in this way; a body of persons freely engaged in a specified activity.

republican *adj* of, characteristic of, or supporting a republic. * *n* an advocate of republican government; (*with cap*) a member of the US Republican party.—**republicanism** *n*.

republish *vt* to publish again; to issue a new edition of (a book).—**republication** *n*.

repudiate *vt* to reject, disown; to refuse to acknowledge or pay; to deny; (a treaty, etc) to disavow.—**repudiation** *n*.

repugnant *adj* distasteful, offensive; contradictory; incompatible.—**repugnance** *n*.

repulse *vt* to drive back; to repel; to reject. * *n* a rebuff, rejection; a defeat, check.

repulsion *n* a feeling of disgust; aversion; (*physics*) the tendency of bodies to repel each other.

repulsive *adj* disgusting; loathsome; exercising repulsion.—**repulsively** *adv*.

reputable *adj* of good repute, respectable.—**reputably** *adv*.

reputation *n* the estimation in which a person or thing is held; good name, honour.

repute *vt* to consider to be, to deem. * *n* reputation.

reputed *adj* generally reported; supposed, putative.

reputedly *adv* in common estimation; by repute.

request *n* an asking for something; a petition; a demand; the thing asked for. * *vt* to ask for earnestly.

request stop *n* a place where a bus, etc stops only if signalled to do so.—*also* **flag stop**.

requiem n a mass for the dead; music for this.

require vt to demand; to need, call for; to order, command.

requirement n a need or want; an essential condition.

requisite adj needed; essential, indispensable. * n something required or indispensable.

requisition n a formal request, demand, or order, as for military supplies; the taking over of private property, etc, for military use. * vt to order; to take by requisition.

reredos n a screen or partition separating the altar from the choir.

rerun vt to run (a race, etc) again; to show a television programme, film, etc again.—also n.

resale n the selling again (of something) usu to a new buyer; a repeat sale to a customer; a second-hand sale.

reschedule vt (debt) to postpone or extend repayment terms.

rescind vt to annul, cancel.

rescue vt to save (a person, thing) from captivity, danger, or harm; to free forcibly from legal custody.—also n.—**rescuer** n.

research n a diligent search; a systematic and careful investigation of a particular subject; a scientific study. * vi to carry out an investigation; to study.—**researcher** n.

resemble vt to be like, to have a similarity to.—**resemblance** n.

resent vt to be indignant about; to begrudge; to take badly.—**resentful** adj.—**resentfully** adv.—**resentment** n.

reserpine n an alkaloid extracted from the roots of a rauwolfia, used to treat high blood pressure and as a sedative.

reservation n the act of reserving; (of tickets, accommodation, etc) a holding until called for; a limitation or proviso; (pl) doubt, scepticism; land set aside for a special purpose.

reserve vt to hold back for future use; to retain; to have set aside; (tickets, hotel room, etc) to book. * n something put aside for future use; land set aside for wild animals; (sport) a substitute; (mil) a force supplementary to a regular army; a restriction or qualification; reticence of feelings; caution.

reserved adj set apart, booked; uncommunicative, lacking cordiality.—**reservedly** adv.

reservist n a member of a military reserve force.

reservoir n a tank or artificial lake for storing water; an extra supply or store.

reset[1] vt (**resetting, reset**) to set (a bone, gem, type) over again; to place in a new setting; to change the reading of.

reset[2] vt (**resetting, reset**) (Scots law) to receive (stolen goods).—also n.

reshape vti to shape anew.

reside vi to live in a place permanently; to be vested or present in.

residence n the act of living in a place; the period of residing; the house where one lives permanently; the status of a legal resident; a building used as a home.

residency n (pl **residencies**) a usu official place of residence, eg of a governor; a period of advanced training in medicine.

resident adj residing; domiciled; living at one's place of work. * n a permanent inhabitant; a doctor who is serving a residency.

residential adj of or relating to residence; used for private homes.

residual adj left over; remaining as a residue.

residuary adj of or relating to the residue of an estate.

residue n a remainder; a part left over; what is left of an estate after payment of debts and legacies.

resign vti to give up (employment, etc); to relinquish; to yield to; to reconcile (oneself).

resignation n the resigning of office, etc; the written proof of this; patient endurance.

resigned adj submissive, acquiescent; accepting the inevitable.

resilience, resiliency n the quality of being resilient; physical or mental stamina.

resilient adj elastic, springing back; buoyant; (person) capable of carrying on after suffering hardship.

resin n a sticky substance exuded in the sap of trees and plants and used in medicines, varnishes, etc; rosin; a similar synthetic substance used in plastics.—**resinous** adj.

resist vti to fight against; to be proof against; to oppose or withstand.

resistance n the act of resisting; the power to resist, as to ward off disease; opposition, esp to an occupying force; hindrance; (elect) non-conductivity, opposition to a steady current.

resistant adj capable of resisting; (with **to**) immune to.

resistor n an electrical device that resists current in a circuit.

resolute adj determined; firm of purpose, steadfast.—**resolutely** adv.—**resoluteness** n.

resolution n the act of resolving or the state of being resolved; determination; a fixed intention; the formal decision or opinion of a meeting; analysis, disintegration; (med) the dispersion of a tumour, etc; the picture definition in a TV; (mus) the relieving of a discord by a following concord; (physics) the process or capability of making distinguishable closely adjacent optical images or sources of light.

resolve vt to break into component parts, dissolve; to convert or be converted (into); to analyse; to determine, make up one's mind; to solve, settle; to vote by resolution; to dispel (doubt); to explain; to conclude; (med: tumour) to disperse; (mus: discord) to convert into concord. * n a fixed intention; resolution; courage.

resolving power n the ability of a microscope or telescope to produce distinct images of objects in close proximity.

resonance n resounding quality; vibration.

resonant adj ringing; resounding, echoing.

resonator n a device that produces or increases sound by resonance.

resort n a popular holiday location; a source of help, support, etc; recourse. * vi to have recourse to; to turn (to) for help, etc.

resound vti to echo; to reverberate; to go on sounding; to be much talked of; to spread (fame).

resounding adj echoing; notable; thorough.

resource n source of help; an expedient; the ability to cope with a situation; a means of diversion; (pl) wealth; assets; raw materials.

resourceful adj able to cope in difficult situations; ingenious.—**resourcefulness** n.

respect n esteem; consideration; regard; (pl) good wishes; reference; relation. * vt to feel or show esteem or regard to; to treat considerately.

respectable adj worthy of esteem; well-behaved; proper, correct, well-conducted; of moderate quality or size.—**respectability** n.—**respectably** adv.

respectful adj deferential.—**respectfully** adv.

respecting prep concerning.

respective adj proper to each, several.

respectively adv in the indicated order.

respiration n the act or process of breathing.

respirator n an apparatus to maintain breathing by artificial means; a device or mask to prevent the inhalation of harmful substances.

respiratory adj of or for respiration.

respire vti to breathe.

respite n a temporary delay; a period of rest or relief; a reprieve.

resplendent adj dazzling, shining brilliantly; magnificent.

respond vti to answer; to reply; to show a favourable reaction; to be answerable; (with to) to react.

respondent n a defendant, esp in a divorce suit; one who answers.

response n an answer; a reaction to stimulation.

responsibility n (pl **responsibilities**) being responsible; a moral obligation or duty; a charge or trust; a thing one is responsible for.

responsible adj having control (over); (with **for**) accountable (for); capable of rational conduct; trustworthy; involving responsibility.—**responsibly** adv.

responsive adj responding; sensitive to influence or stimulus; sympathetic.

rest[1] n stillness, repose, sleep; inactivity; the state of not moving; relaxation; tranquillity; a support or prop; a pause in music, metre, etc; a place of quiet. * vti to take a rest; to give rest to; to be still; to lie down; to relax; to be fixed (on); to lean, support or be supported; to put one's trust (in).

rest[2] n the remainder; the others. * vi to remain.

restate vt to state over again; to put differently.—**restatement** n.

restaurant n a place where meals can be bought and eaten.

restaurateur n the keeper of a restaurant.

restful adj peaceful.—**restfully** adv.—**restfulness** n.

rest home n an old people's home; a convalescent home.

restitution n the restoring of something to its owner; a reimbursement, as for loss.

restive adj impatient; fidgety.

restless adj unsettled; agitated.—**restlessly** adv.—**restlessness** n.

restoration n the act of restoring; reconstruction; renovation; (with cap) the re-establishment of the monarchy in Britain in 1660 under Charles II.

restorative adj tending to restore health and strength. * n a medicine or food that reinvigorates.

restore vt to give or put back; to re-establish; to repair; to renovate; to bring back to the original condition.—**restorer** n.

restrain vt to hold back; to restrict; (person) to deprive of freedom.

restrained adj moderate; self-controlled; without exuberance.

restraint n the ability to hold back; something that restrains; control of emotions, impulses, etc.

restrict vt to keep within limits, circumscribe.

restricted adj affected by restriction; limited; not generally available.

restriction n restraint; limitation; a limiting regulation.—**restrictive** adj.

restroom n a room equipped with toilets, washbowls, etc for the use of the public.

result vi to have as a consequence; to terminate in. * n a consequence; an outcome; a value obtained by mathematical calculation; (sport) the final score; (pl) a desired effect.

resultant adj derived from or resulting from something else.

resume vti to begin again; to continue after a stop or pause; to proceed after interruption.—**resumption** n.

résumé n a summary, esp of employment experience; a curriculum vitae.

resurgence n a revival; a renewal of activity.—**resurgent** adj.

resurrect vt to bring back into use; (a custom) to revive; to restore to life.

resurrection n a revival; a rising from the dead; (with cap) the rising of Christ from the dead.

resuscitate vti to revive when apparently dead or unconscious.—**resuscitation** n.

resuscitator n an apparatus for forcing oxygen into the lungs; a person who resuscitates.

retable n a step or ledge behind the altar of a church, slightly raised above it for the reception of lights, flowers, and other symbolical ornaments.

retail n selling directly to the consumer in small quantities. * adv at a retail price. * vti to sell or be sold by retail.—also adj.—**retailer** n.

retain vt to keep possession of; to keep in the mind, to remember; to keep in place, support; to hire the services of.

retainer n that which returns; (formerly) a servant to a family, a dependant; a fee to retain the services of.

retaining wall n a wall built to hold back earth or water.

retake vt (**retaking**, **retook**, pp **retaken**) to capture again; to shoot a film scene again. * n a scene that has been reshot.

retaliate vti to revenge oneself, usu by returning like for like; to strike back; to cast back (an accusation).—**retaliation** n.—**retaliatory** adj.

retard vti to slow down, to delay; to make slow or late.—**retardation** n.

retardant n a substance that retards, esp a chemical reaction. * adj retarding.

retarded adj slow in physical or mental development.

retch vi to heave as if to vomit.

retention n the act of retaining; the capacity to retain; memory; (med) the abnormal retaining of fluid in a body cavity.

retentive adj capable of retaining; keeping, holding. * n one who retains.—**retentiveness** n.

rethink vt (**rethinking**, **rethought**) to consider or think about again, esp with a change in mind.

reticent adj reserved in speech; uncommunicative.—**reticence** n.

reticle n a network of fine wires, threads, etc placed in the focal plane of an optical instrument.

reticulate adj resembling a network (—also **reticular**). * vti to arrange or be arranged into a network.—**reticulation** n.

retina n (pl **retinas**, **retinae**) the innermost part of the eye, on which the image is formed.

retinue n a body of attendants.

retire vi to give up one's work when pensionable age is reached; to withdraw; to retreat; to go to bed. * vt (*troops*) to withdraw from use; to compel to retire from a position, work, etc.

retirement *n* the act of retiring or the state of being retired; seclusion; privacy.

retiring *adj* unobtrusive; shy.

retort *vi* to reply sharply or wittily. * *n* a sharp or witty reply; a vessel with a funnel bent downwards used in distilling; a receptacle used in making gas and steel.

retouch *vt* (*photograph, etc*) to improve or change by touching up; (*new growth of hair*) to colour to match other hair.

retrace *vt* to go back over; to trace back to a source.—**retraceable** *adj*.

retract *vti* to draw in or back; to withdraw (a statement, opinion, etc); to recant.—**retractable** *adj*.—**retraction** *n*.

retreat *vi* to withdraw, retire; to recede. * *n* a withdrawal, esp of troops; a sign for retiring; a quiet or secluded place, refuge; seclusion for religious devotion.

retrench *vti* to cut down (esp expenses); to economize.—**retrenchment** *n*.

retrial *n* a second trial.

retribution *n* deserved reward; something given or exacted in compensation, esp punishment.

retrieve *vt* to recover; to revive; (*a loss*) to make good; (*comput*) to obtain information from data stored in a computer. * *vi* (*dogs*) to retrieve game.—**retrievable** *adj*.—**retrieval** *n*.

retriever *n* any of several breeds of dogs capable of being trained for retrieving.

retro *n* (*pl* **retros**) a retrorocket. * *adj* denoting a fashion or style (in music, clothes, etc) that pays homage to the past.

retro- *prefix* backwards; behind.

retroactive *adj* having an effect on things that are already past.

retrograde *adj* going backwards; passing from better to worse.

retrogression *n* going backwards, usu a return to a former, less complex, level of development.

retrorocket *n* a small rocket on an aircraft or spacecraft that produces thrust in the opposite direction to the line of flight to slow it down.

retrospect *n* a looking back; a mental review of the past.—**retrospection** *n*.

retrospective *adj* looking backwards; relating to the past. * *n* an exhibition of an artist's lifetime work.—**retrospectively** *adv*.

retroussé *adj* turned upwards (esp of the nose).

retroversion *n* the act of turning or state of being turned backwards.—**retroverted** *adj*.

Retrovir *n* (*trademark*) AZT.

retrovirus *n* any of various viruses that use RNA to synthesize DNA, reversing the normal process in cells of transcription from DNA to RNA, which includes HIV.

retsina *n* a Greek white wine flavoured with resin.

return *vi* to come or go back; to reply; to recur. * *vt* to give or send back; to repay; to yield; to answer; to elect. * *n* something returned; a recurrence; recompense; (*pl*) yield, revenue; a form for computing (income) tax.

returnable *adj* required to be returned; capable of being returned (for reuse).

return ticket *n* (*Brit etc*) a ticket whose price includes the cost of the journey to and back from a destination.

reunion *n* a meeting following separation; a social gathering of former colleagues.

reunite *vt* to unite again; to reconcile. * *vi* to become reunited.

reusable *adj* able to be used again; renewable.

Rev. *abbr* = Reverend.

rev *vt* (**revving, revved**) (*inf*) (*with* **up**) to increase the speed of an engine. * *n* revolution per minute.

revaluate *vt* to reassess the value of; to change (esp increase) the exchange value of (a currency).

revamp *vt* to renovate, to rework, remodel; to transform. * *n* the process of revamping; something revamped.

revanchism *n* (support for) a policy aimed at regaining lost territory or possessions.—**revanchist** *n, adj*.

reveal *vt* (*something hidden or secret*) to make known; to expose; to make visible.

reveille *n* a morning bugle call to wake soldiers.

revel *vi* (**reveling, revelled** *or* **reveling, reveled**) (*with* **in**) to take pleasure or delight in; to make merry. * *n* (*pl*) merrymaking; entertainment.—**reveler, reveller** *n*.

revelry *n* (*pl* **revelries**) the act of revelling; noisty festivity.

revelation *n* the act of revealing; the disclosure of something secret; a communication from God to man; an illuminating experience.

revenge *vt* to inflict punishment in return for; to satisfy oneself by retaliation; to avenge. * *n* the act of revenging; retaliation; a vindictive feeling.—**revenger** *n*.

revengeful *adj* keen for revenge; vindictive.

revenue *n* the total income produced by taxation; gross income from a business or investment.

reverb *n* (*mus*) an electronic device for producing an artificial echo.

reverberate *vi* to rebound, recoil; to be reflected in; to resound, to echo.—**reverberation** *n*.

revere *vt* to regard with great respect or awe; to venerate.

reverence *n* profound respect; devotion; a gesture of respect (such as a bow). * *vt* to hold in respect.

reverend *adj* worthy of reverence; of or relating to the clergy; (*with cap*) a title for a member of the clergy.

reverent *adj* feeling or expressing reverence.—**reverently** *adv*.

reverie *n* a daydream; (*mus*) a dreamy piece.—*also* **revery** (*pl* **reveries**).

revers *n* (*pl* **revers**) a lapel, esp on a woman's garment.

reversal *n* the act or process of reversing.

reverse *vti* to turn in the opposite direction; to turn outside in, upside down, etc; to move backwards; (*law*) to revoke or annul. * *n* the contrary or opposite of something; the back, esp of a coin; a setback; a mechanism for reversing. * *adj* opposite, contrary; causing movement in the opposite direction.

reverse video *n* a technique for highlighting on a computer monitor by reversing the normal text and background colours.

reversible *adj* with both sides usable; wearable with either side out; able to undergo a series of changes either backwards or forwards. * *n* a reversible cloth or article of clothing.

reversion *n* return to a former condition or type; right to future possession; the return of an estate to the grantor or his heirs.—**reversionary** *adj*.

revert *vi* to go back (to a former state); to take up again (a former subject); (*biol*) to return to a former or primitive type; (*law*) to go back to a former owner or his heirs.—**revertible** *adj*.

revery *see* **reverie**.

review *n* an evaluation; a survey; a reconsideration; a critical assessment, a critique; a periodical containing critical essays; an official inspection of ships or troops. * *vt* to re-examine; to inspect formally; to write a critique on.

reviewer *n* a person who writes a review, esp for a newspaper, a critic.

revile *vti* to use abusive language (to or about).

revise *vt* to correct and amend; to prepare a new, improved version of; to study again (for an examination).—**revision** *n*.

revitalize *vt* to put new life into.—**revitalization** *n*.

revival *n* the act of reviving; recovery from a neglected or depressed state; renewed performance (of a play); renewed interest in; religious awakening.

revivalist *n* a person who encourages religious practice.—**revivalism** *n*.

revive *vti* to return to life; to make active again; to take up again.—**reviver** *n*.

revivify *vt* to put new life into; to reanimate; to revive.—**revification** *n*.—**revivifier** *n*.

revoke *vt* to cancel; to rescind. * *vi* (*cards*) to fail to follow suit.—**revocable** *adj*.—**revocation** *n*.

revolt *vt* to rebel; to overturn; to shock. * *vi* to feel great disgust. * *n* rebellion; uprising; loathing.

revolting *adj* extremely offensive.—**revoltingly** *adv*.

revolution *n* the act of revolting; a motion round a centre or axis; a single completion of an orbit or rotation; a great change; an overthrow of a government, social system, etc.

revolutionary *adj* of or advocating revolution; radically new. * *n* a person who takes part in, or favours, revolution.

revolutionize *vt* to cause a complete change in.

revolve *vt* to travel or cause to travel in a circle or orbit; to rotate.

revolver *n* a handgun with a magazine that revolves to reload.

revolving door *n* a door of two or four panels rotating around a central axis within a round chamber and operated electrically or manually.

revue *n* a musical show with skits, dances, etc, often satirizing recent events.

revulsion *n* disgust; aversion; a sudden change or reversal of feeling, esp withdrawal with a sense of utter distaste.

reward *n* something that is given in return for something done; money offered, as for the capture of a criminal. * *vt* to give a reward.

rewarding *adj* (*experience, activity, etc*) pleasing, profitable.

rewind *vt* to wind again; to wind (an audiotape, etc) back to the beginning. * *n* the act of rewinding.

rewire *vt* to put new wiring into an electrical system.

reword *vt* to change the wording of.

rework *vt* to use again in a different form; to rewrite; to remodel.

rewrite *vt* to write again; to revise. * *n* something rewritten; revision.

Rex *n* a reigning king.

rf *abbr* = radio frequency.

Rh *abbr* = rhesus.

rhachis *see* **rachis**.

rhapsodize *vi* to speak or write (about) with enthusiasm or emotion.—**rhapsodist** *n*.

rhapsody *n* (*pl* **rhapsodies**) an enthusiastic speech or writing; (*mus*) an irregular instrumental composition of an epic, heroic or national character.

rhea *n* any of several large flightless birds of South America resembling ostriches but smaller.

rhenium *n* a hard heat-resistant metallic element.

rheo- *prefix* flow, current.

rheology *n* the physics of the flow and deformation of matter.—**rheologist** *n*.—**rheological** *adj*.

rheostat *n* a device that regulates electric current by varying the resistance to it.—**rheostatic** *adj*.

rhesus factor *n* a substance usually present in the red blood cells of humans and higher animals.

rhesus monkey *n* a type of southern Asian macaque with light brown fur.

rhesus negative *adj* lacking the rhesus factor in the blood.

rhesus positive *adj* containing the rhesus factor in the blood.

rhetoric *n* the art of effective speaking and writing; skill in using speech; insincere language.

rhetorical *adj* of or relating to rhetoric; high-flown, bombastic.—**rhetorically** *adv*.

rhetorical question *n* a question asked for effect, to which no answer is expected.

rheum *n* a watery discharge from the mucous membranes of the nose, eyes, etc.—**rheumy** *adj*.

rheumatic *adj* of, relating to or suffering from rheumatism. * *n* a person who has rheumatism.

rheumatic fever *n* a disease characterized by inflammation and pain in the joints.

rheumatism *n* a disorder causing pain in muscles and joints.

rheumatoid *adj* of or like rheumatism.

rheumatoid arthritis *n* a usu chronic disease characterized by inflammation, pain, and swelling of the joints.

rheumatology *n* the study of rheumatic diseases.—**rheumatologist** *n*.

rhinal *adj* of or pertaining to the nose.

rhinestone *n* a colourless imitation precious stone made from paste, glass, or quartz.

Rhine wine *n* any of several wines from the valley of the River Rhine in Germany; a light dry wine from the Rhine valley or elsewhere.

rhinitis *n* inflammation of the mucous membrane of the nose.

rhino-, rhin- *prefix* nose.

rhino *n* (*pl* **rhinos, rhino**) (*inf*) a rhinoceros.

rhinoceros *n* (*pl* **rhinoceroses, rhinoceros**) a large, thick-skinned mammal with one or two horns on the nose.

rhinology *n* the branch of medicine dealing with the nose.—**rhinologist** *n*.

rhinoplasty *n* plastic surgery of the nose.—**rhinoplastic** *adj*.

rhizo-, rhiz- *prefix* root.

rhizome *n* a stem on or below ground that produces roots below and shoots above; a rootstock.

rho *n* (*pl* **rhos**) the 17th letter of the Greek alphabet.

Rhode Island Red *n* an American breed of domestic fowl with reddish-brown plumage.

rhodium *n* a hard white metallic element similar to platinum.

rhododendron *n* an evergreen shrub with large flowers.

rhomb *n* a rhombus.

rhombohedron *n* (*pl* **rhombohedrons, rhombohedra**) a

six-sided solid figure whose sides are rhombuses.—
rhombohedral *adj*.

rhomboid *n* a parallelogram whose adjacent sides are
unequal and whose angles are not right angles.—*also
adj*.

rhombus *n* (*pl* **rhombuses, rhombi**) a diamond shape.

rhubarb *n* a plant with large leaves and edible (when
cooked) pink stalks; (*inf*) a noisy quarrel.

rhumb *n* an imaginary line crossing all meridians at the
same angle; a course navigated by a ship or aircraft
that maintains a fixed compass bearing.—*also* **rhumb
line**.

rhyme *n* the repetition of sounds usu at the ends of
lines in verse; such poetry or verse; a word corresponding with another in end sound. * *vti* to form a
rhyme (with); to versify, put into rhyme.

rhyming slang *n* a type of slang that substitutes the
original (often indecent) word with a word or phrase
that rhymes with it, eg *loaf of bread* = *head*.

rhythm *n* a regular recurrence of beat, accent or silence
in the flow of sound, esp of words and music; a measured flow; cadence.—**rhythmic, rhythmical** *adj*.—
rhythmically *adv*.

rhythm and blues *n* a type of music that fuses elements
of folk, blues and rock.

rhythm method *n* a method of contraception that relies
on abstinence from sexual intercourse during the period when ovulation is most likely to occur.

rhythm section *n* those instruments in a band or group
whose main role is to supply the rhythm, such as the
double bass and drums.

RI *abbr* = Rhode Island.

rib *n* one of the curved bones of the chest attached to
the spine; any rib-like structure; a leaf vein; a vein of
an insect's wing; a ridge or raised strip, as of knitting;
a ridge of a mountain. * *vt* (**ribbing, ribbed**) to provide with ribs; to form vertical ridges in knitting; (*inf*)
to tease or ridicule.

ribald *adj* irreverent; humorously vulgar.

riband *n* a ribbon.

ribbon *n* silk, satin, velvet, etc, woven into a narrow
band; a piece of this; a strip of cloth, etc, inked for
use, as in a typewriter; (*pl*) torn shreds.

rib cage *n* the bony framework of ribs enclosing the
wall of the chest.

riboflavin *n* a factor of the vitamin B complex found in
milk, eggs, fruits, etc.

ribonuclease *n* any of several enzymes that act as catalytic triggers of RNA hydrolosis.

ribonucleic acid *n* any of a group of nucleic acids found
in all living cells, where they are essential to protein
development.—**RNA** *abbr*.

ribose *n* a sugar occurring in RNA and riboflavin.

ribosome *n* any of the tiny particles containing RNA
and protein in cells where protein synthesis takes
place.—**ribosomal** *adj*.

rice *n* an annual cereal grass cultivated in warm climates; its starchy food grain.

ricebird *see* **bobolink**.

rice paper *n* a delicate paper prepared from pith.

rich *adj* having much money, wealthy; abounding in
natural resources, fertile; costly, fine; (*food*) sweet or
oily, highly flavoured; deep in colour; (*inf*) full of humour. * *n* wealthy people collectively; (*pl* **riches**)
wealth, abundance.—**richly** *adv*.—**richness** *n*.

Richter scale *n* a scale ranging from 1 to 10 for measuring the intensity of an earthquake.

rick¹ *n* a stack or large pile of hay, etc, in the open.

rick² *vt* (*Brit etc*) to sprain or strain slightly. * *n* such an
injury.—*also* **wrick**.

rickets *n* a children's disease marked by softening of
the bones, caused by vitamin D deficiency.

rickettsia *n* (*pl* **rickettsiae, rickettsias**) any of a genus of
microorganisms that inhabit mites, ticks, etc and
cause serious diseases, such as typhus.—**rickettsial**
adj.

rickety *adj* shaky, unsteady.

rickrack *n* a zigzag braid for trimming clothing.

rickshaw, ricksha *n* a light, two-wheeled man-drawn
vehicle, orig used in Japan.

ricochet *vi* (**ricocheting, ricocheted** *or* **ricochetting,
ricochetted**) (*bullet*) to rebound or skip along ground
or water. * *n* a rebound or glancing off; (*bullet*) a hit
made after ricocheting.

ricotta *n* a mildly-flavoured soft white cheese made
from sheep's milk.

rictus *n* (*pl* **rictus, rictuses**) the gap in an open mouth or
beak; a fixed grimace, esp in horror.—**rictal** *adj*.

rid *vt* (**ridding, rid** *or* **ridded**) to free from; to dispose
(of).

riddance *n* clearance; disposal.

ridden¹ *see* **ride**.

ridden² *adj* oppressed by; full of.

riddle¹ *n* a puzzling question; an enigma; a mysterious
person or thing.

riddle² *n* a coarse sieve. * *vt* to sieve or sift; to perforate
with holes; to spread through, permeate.

ride *vb* (**riding, rode,** *pp* **ridden**) *vti* to be carried along
or travel in a vehicle or on an animal, bicycle, etc; to
be supported or move on the water; to lie at anchor;
to travel over a surface; to move on the body; (*inf*) to
continue undisturbed. * *vt* (*horse, bicycle etc*); to sit on
and control; to oppress, dominate; (*inf*) to torment.
* *n* a trip or journey in a vehicle or on horseback, on a
bicycle, etc; a thing to ride at a fairground.

rider *n* a person who rides; an addition to a document,
amending a clause; an additional statement; something used to move along another piece.

ridge *n* a narrow crest or top; the ploughed earth
thrown up between the furrows; a line where two
slopes meet; (*of land etc*) a raised strip or elevation; a
range of hills. * *vti* to form into ridges, wrinkle.—
ridged *adj*.

ridgepole *n* the horizontal pole along the top of a tent.

ridicule *n* mockery, derision. * *vt* to make fun of, to
mock.

ridiculous *adj* deserving ridicule; preposterous, silly.—
ridiculously *adv*.—**ridiculousness** *n*.

riesling *n* (the grape that produces) a dry white wine.

rife *adj* widespread; prevalent.

riff *n* (*jazz, rock*) a musical phrase played repeatedly,
esp as the background to an extended solo improvisation.—*also vi*.

riffle *vt* to leaf or flick rapidly through (pages, files,
etc); to shuffle cards by dividing the deck and then
flicking the corners together with the thumbs. * *vi* to
flick cursorily (through). * *n* (the sound of) an act or
instance of riffling; a ripple in a stream or the small
obstruction causing this; grooves, etc at the bottom of
a sluice to trap gold particles.

riffraff *n* disreputable persons; refuse, rubbish.

rifle¹ *n* a shoulder gun with a spirally grooved bore.

rifle² *vti* to steal; to look through (a person's papers or
belongings).

rifling n (the cutting of) spiral grooves in the bore of a firearm that spin the projectile.

rift n a split; a cleft; a fissure. * vti to split.

rift valley n a narrow valley caused by land subsiding between two parallel faults.

rig vt (**rigging, rigged**) (*naut*) to equip with sails and tackle; to set up in working order; to manipulate fraudulently. * n the way sails, etc, are rigged; equipment or gear for a special purpose, such as oil drilling; a type of truck.

rigging n the ropes for supporting masts and sails; (*in theatre*) a network of ropes and pulleys to support and maintain scenery.

right adj correct, true; just or good; appropriate; fit, recovered; opposite to left; conservative; designating the side meant to be seen. * adv straight; directly; completely, exactly; correctly, properly; to or on the right side. * n that which is just or correct; truth; fairness; justice; privilege; just or legal claim; (*pl*) the correct condition. * vti to set or become upright; to correct; to redress.—**rightness** n.

right angle n an angle of 90 degrees.

righteous adj moral, virtuous.—**righteously** adv.—**righteousness** n.

rightful adj legitimate; having a just claim.—**rightfully** adv.—**rightfulness** n.

right-hand adj of or towards the right side of a person or thing; for use by the right hand.

right-handed adj using the right hand; done or made for use with the right hand. * adv with the right hand.

rightist adj politically conservative. * n a person belonging to or supporting a conservative political party.

rightly adv in truth; in the right; with good reason; properly.

right-minded adj having principles in accordance with standard notions of what is right.

right of way n a public path over private ground; the right to use this; precedence over other traffic.

right-on adj (*inf*) fashionable, trendy.

right-thinking adj holding generally acceptable views.

right-wing adj of or relating to the conservative faction of a political party, organization, etc.—**right-winger** n.

rigid adj stiff, inflexible; severe, strict.—**rigidity** n.—**rigidly** adv.—**rigidness** n.

rigmarole n nonsense; a foolishly involved procedure.

rigor n harsh inflexibility; severity; strictness.—*also* **rigour**.

rigor mortis n the stiffening of the body after death.

rigorous adj stern, severe, strict.—**rigorously** adv.—**rigorousness** n.

rigour *see* **rigor**.

rile vt (*inf*) to irritate, to annoy, to anger.

rill n a small brook or stream.

rim n a border or raised edge, esp of something circular; the outer part of a wheel. * vt (**rimming, rimmed**) to supply or surround with a rim; to form a rim.

rimless adj lacking a rim; (*glasses*) without a frame.

rind n crust; peel; bark.

rinderpest n an acute viral disease of cattle.

ring[1] n a circular band, esp of metal, worn on the finger, in the ear, etc; a hollow circle; a round enclosure; an arena for boxing, etc; a group of people engaged in secret or criminal activity to control a market, etc. * vt (**ringing, ringed**) to encircle, surround; to fit with a ring.

ring[2] vti (**ringing, rang** *or* **rung**, *pp* **rung**) to emit a bell-like sound; to resound; to peal; to sound a bell; to telephone; (*with* up) to total and record esp by means of a cash register; to achieve. * n a ringing sound; a resonant note; a set of church bells.

ringdove n a wood pigeon.

ringed adj wearing rings; forming rings; having ring-like markings; surrounded by.

ringer n a person that rings bells; (*sl*) a person or thing closely resembling another; a horse entered into a race under a false name, weight, etc.

ring finger n the third finger, esp of the left hand, on which a wedding ring is traditionally worn.

ringhals n a poisonous African snake that spits venom at its victims.

ringleader n a person who takes the lead in mischievous or unlawful behaviour.

ringlet n a curling lock of hair.

ringmaster n a master of ceremonies in a circus.

ringworm n a contagious skin infection.

rink n an expanse of ice for skating; a smooth floor for roller skating; an alley for bowling.

rinse vt to wash lightly; to flush under clean water to remove soap. * n the act of rinsing; a preparation for tinting the hair.

rioja n a type of Spanish red or white wine.

riot n violent public disorder; uproar; unrestrained profusion; (*inf*) something very funny. * vi to participate in a riot.—**rioter** n.—**rioting** n.

riotous adj disorderly, tumultuous, seditious; luxurious, wanton.—**riotously** adv.—**riotousness** n.

RIP abbr = rest in peace.

rip[1] vti (**ripping, ripped**) to cut or tear apart roughly; to split; (*with* off, out) to remove in a violent or rough manner; (*inf*) to rush, speed; (*with* into) to attack, esp verbally. * n a tear; a split.

rip[2] n a stretch of broken water caused by currents and tides.

rip cord n a cord for releasing a parachute.

ripe adj ready to be eaten or harvested; fully developed; mature.—**ripely** adv.—**ripeness** n.

ripen vt to grow or make ripe.

rip-off n (*sl*) the act or a means of stealing; plagiarizing, cheating, etc.

riposte, ripost n a counterstroke; a retort; a retaliatory manoeuvre. * vi to make a riposte.

ripple n a little wave or undulation on the surface of water; the sound of this. * vti to have or form little waves on the surface (of).

rip-roaring adj (*inf*) exuberant, boisterous, thrilling.

ripsaw n a handsaw for cutting wood in the direction of the grain.

riptide n a powerful current flowing outwards from the shore.

RISC (*acronym*) reduced instruction set computer: a computer with advanced yet simplified internal circuitry that allows a significant increase in processing speed over standard designs.

rise vi (**rising, rose**, *pp* **risen**) to get up; to stand up; to ascend; to increase in value or size; to swell; to revolt; to be provoked; to originate; to tower; to slope up; (*voice*) to reach a higher pitch; to ascend from the grave; (*fish*) to come to the surface. * n an ascent; origin; an increase in price, salary, etc; an upward slope.

risible adj tending to laugh; provoking laughter, derisory.—**risibility** n.

rising n a revolt, insurrection. * adj ascending; approaching.

risk *n* chance of loss or injury; hazard; danger, peril. * *vt* to expose to possible danger or loss; to take the chance of.

risk capital *n* venture capital.

risky *adj* (**riskier, riskiest**) dangerous; uncertain; not secure.

risotto *n* (*pl* **risottos**) a dish of onions, rice, butter, etc, cooked in meat stock.

risqué *adj* verging on indecency; slightly offensive.

rissole *n* a fried cake of minced meat, egg, and breadcrumbs.

rite *n* a ceremonial practice or procedure, esp religious.

rite of passage *n* a ritual indicating a change in an individual's status, as at puberty or marriage.

ritual *adj* relating to rites or ceremonies. * *n* a fixed (religious) ceremony.—**ritually** *adv*.

ritzy *adj* (**ritzier, ritziest**) (*sl*) luxurious, smart.

rival *n* one of two or more people, organizations or teams competing with each other for the same goal. * *adj* competing; having comparable merit or claim. * *vt* (**rivalling, rivalled**) to strive to equal or excel; to be comparable to; to compete.

rivalry *n* (*pl* **rivalries**) emulation; competition.

river *n* a large natural stream of fresh water flowing into an ocean, lake, etc; a copious flow.

river basin *n* land drained by a river and its tributaries.

riverbed *n* the channel formed by a river.

riverfront *n* the land or an area along a river.

riverine *adj* of, like, or produced by a river; living or located on the banks of a river.

riverside *n* the bank of a river.

rivet *n* a short, metal bolt for holding metal plates together, the headless end being hammered flat. * *vt* to join with rivets; to fix one's eyes upon immovably; to engross one's attention.

riveter *n* a person who rivets; a machine that rivets.

Riviera *n* the coast of the northern Mediterranean from southeast France to northwest Italy.

rivulet *n* a little stream.

riyal *n* the standard currency unit of Saudi Arabia, Yemen, Qatar, or Dubai.

RMA *abbr* = Royal Military Academy.

rms *abbr* = root mean square.

RN *abbr* = Registered Nurse; Royal Navy.

Rn (*chem symbol*) radon.

RNA *abbr* = ribonucleic acid.

roach *n* a small silvery freshwater fish.

road *n* a track, surfaced with tarmac or concrete, made for travelling; a highway; a street; a way or route; an anchorage for ships.

road block *n* a barrier erected across a road to halt traffic.

road hog *n* a car driver who obstructs other vehicles by encroaching on the others' traffic lane.

roadhouse *n* a tavern usu outside city limits providing meals, etc.

roadie *n* (*inf*) a person with responsibility for transporting and setting up stage equipment for a rock group, etc on tour.

road map *n* a map for motorists that gives information on the roads of a particular area.

road metal *n* broken stone and cinders used in making road and railway foundations.

road movie *n* a film genre in which the main characters are on a journey, both in a real and figurative sense.

road runner *n* a long-tailed, swift-running, terrestrial North American cuckoo.

roadshow *n* a group of touring entertainers; a radio or television show presented from a touring outside-broadcasting unit.

roadside *n* the border of a road.—*also adj*.

road-test *vt* to test (a vehicle) under practical operating conditions.—**road test** *n*.

roadway *n* the strip of land over which a road passes; the main part of a road, used by vehicles.

roadwork *n* conditioning for an athletic contest consisting mainly of long runs.

roam *vti* to wander about, to rove.

roan *adj* having a base colour thickly sprinkled with white or grey. * *n* a horse with a roan coat, esp when the base colour is red.

roar *vti* to make a loud, full, growling sound, as a lion, wind, fire, the sea; to utter loudly, as in a rage; to bellow; to guffaw.—*also n*.

roaring *adj* boisterous, noisy; brisk.

roast *vti* (*meat, etc*) to cook with little or no moisture, as before a fire or in an oven; (*coffee, etc*) to process by exposure to heat; to expose to great heat; (*inf*) to criticize severely; to undergo roasting. * *n* roasted meat; a cut of meat for roasting; a picnic at which food is roasted.

rob *vb* (**robbing, robbed**) *vt* to seize forcibly; to steal from; to plunder. * *vi* to commit robbery.—**robber** *n*.

robbery *n* (*pl* **robberies**) theft from a person by intimidation or by violence.

robe *n* a long flowing outer garment; the official dress of a judge, academic, etc; a bathrobe or dressing gown; a covering or wrap; (*pl*) ceremonial vestments. * *vti* to put on or dress in robes.

robin *n* a songbird with a dull red breast.

robot *n* a mechanical device that acts in a seemingly human way; a mechanism guided by automatic controls.

robotics *n* (*used as sing*) the science of designing and using robots.

robust *adj* strong, sturdy; vigorous.—**robustly** *adv*.—**robustness** *n*.

roc *n* (*Arabian legend*) a giant bird of enormous strength.

rock[1] *n* a large stone or boulder; a person or thing providing foundation or support; (*geol*) a natural mineral deposit including sand, clay, etc; a hard sweet; (*inf*) a diamond, ice; (*sl*) the drug crack.

rock[2] *vti* to move to and fro, or from side to side; to sway strongly; to shake. * *n* a rocking motion; rock and roll.

rockabilly *n* a type of fast-paced rock and country music originating in the US South in the 1950s.

rock-and-roll *n* popular music that incorporates country and blues elements and is usu played on electronic instruments with a heavily accented beat.

rock bottom *n* the lowest or most fundamental part or level. * *adj* very lowest.

rock crystal *n* transparent colourless quartz used in electronic and optical equipment.

rocker *n* a rocking chair; a curved support on which a cradle, etc, rocks.

rockery *n* (*pl* **rockeries**) a garden among rocks for alpine plants.—*also* **rock garden**.

rocket *n* any device driven forward by gases escaping through a rear vent, such as a firework, distress signal, or the propulsion mechanism of a spacecraft. * *vi* to move in or like a rocket; to soar.

rocket launcher *n* a device for launching rockets; an aircraft or motor vehicle equipped to launch rockets.

rocketry *n* the science of building and launching rockets.

rock garden *see* **rockery**.

rock house *n* (*sl*) a place where the drug crack is made available by dealers.

rocking chair *n* a chair mounted on rockers.

rocking horse *n* a toy horse fixed on rockers or springs.

rock salt *n* common salt in solid form or in large crystals.

rocky *adj* (**rockier, rockiest**) having many rocks; like rock; rugged, hard; shaky, unstable.

rococo *adj* elaborately ornate, as in an architectural style of 18th-century Europe.—*also n*.

rod *n* a stick; a thin bar of metal or wood; a staff of office; a wand; a fishing rod; (*sl*) a pistol.

rode *see* **ride**.

rodent *n* any of several relatively small gnawing animals with two strong front teeth.

rodeo *n* (*pl* **rodeos**) the rounding up of cattle; a display of cowboy skill.

roe[1] *n* the eggs of fish.

roe[2] *n* a small reddish brown deer (—*also* **roe deer**); the female red deer.

roebuck *n* the male roe deer.

roe deer *n* a small graceful deer of European and Asian woodlands.

roentgen *n* the unit of measuring X-rays or gamma rays.—*also* **röntgen**.

roger *interj* used in radio communications, etc to indicate message received and understood.

rogue *n* a scoundrel; a rascal; a mischievous person; a wild animal that lives apart from the herd.—**roguish** *adj*.—**roguishly** *adv*.

role, rôle *n* a part in a film or play taken by an actor; a function.

role model *n* a person who inspires others to emulate him or her.

role-playing *n* (*psychol*) a technique in which participants take on and act out roles in order to rehearse a situation or resolve a conflict.

roll *n* a scroll; anything wound into cylindrical form; a list or register; a turned-over edge; a rolling movement; a small cake of bread; a trill of some birds; an undulation; the sound of thunder; the beating of drumsticks. * *vi* to move by turning over or from side to side; to move like a wheel; to curl; to move in like waves; to flow. * *vt* to cause to roll; to turn on its axis; to move on wheels; to press with a roller; (*dice*) to throw; to beat rapidly, as a drum.

roll bar *n* a bar that reinforces the frame of a racing or sports car to protect the driver should the vehicle overturn.

roll call *n* the reading aloud of a list of names to check attendance.

roller *n* a revolving cylinder used for spreading paint, flattening surfaces, moving paper, etc; a large wave.

roller coaster *n* an elevated amusement ride in which small cars move on tracks that curve and dip sharply.—*also* **big dipper**.

roller skate *n* a four-wheeled skate strapped on to shoes.—**roller skating** *n*.

roller towel *n* a towel without ends on a roller.

rolling pin *n* a wooden, plastic or stone cylinder for rolling out pastry.

rolling stock *n* all the vehicles of a railway.

rolling stone *n* a person who cannot settle in one place; a free spirit.

rollmop *n* a fillet of herring rolled up and pickled in brine or spiced vinegar.

roll-on/roll-off *adj* pertaining to a cargo ship or passenger ferry designed so that vehicles can be driven straight on and off.

roll-top desk *n* a writing desk with a flexible sliding cover of slats.

roly-poly *n* (*pl* **roly-polies**) a pudding of pastry covered with jam and rolled up; a round and plump person.

ROM *abbr* (*comput*) = read-only memory.

Roman *adj* of or relating to the city of Rome or its ancient empire, or the Latin alphabet; Roman Catholic. * *n* an inhabitant or citizen of Rome; a Roman Catholic.

roman *adj* ordinary type, not italic.

Roman candle *n* a type of cylindrical firework that emits coloured sparks.

Roman Catholic *adj* belonging to the Christian church that is headed by the Pope.—*also n*.

romance *n* a prose narrative; a medieval tale of chivalry; a series of unusual adventures; a novel dealing with this; an atmosphere of awe or wonder; a love story; a love affair; a picturesque falsehood. * *vi* to write romantic fiction; to exaggerate.

Romanesque *adj, n* (in) the style of round-arched and vaulted architecture prevalent between the Classical and Gothic periods.

Roman holiday *n* a holiday or entertainment at the expense of others' suffering.

Roman nose *n* a nose with a slender prominent ridge.

Roman numerals *n* the letters I, V, X, L, C, D, and M used to represent numbers in the manner of the ancient Romans.

romantic *adj* of or given to romance; strange and picturesque; imaginative; sentimental; (*art, literature*) preferring passion and imagination to proportion and finish, subordinating form to content.—**romantically** *adv*.

romanticism *n* a 19th-century philosophical and cultural movement characterized by the desire to bring nature and man into unity through the shaping power of the imagination; romantic approach, quality, or ideals.

romanticize *vt* to imbue (a person, concept, etc) with a romantic character. * *vi* to have romantic ideas.—**romanticization** *n*.

Romany *n* a Gypsy; the Indic language of Gypsies.

romp *vi* to play boisterously. * *n* a noisy game; a frolic; an easy win.

rompers *npl* a child's one-piece garment; a jumpsuit.

rondo *n* (*pl* **rondos**) a musical form with a leading theme to which return is made.

röntgen *see* **roentgen**.

roof *n* (*pl* **roofs**) the upper covering of a building; the top of a vehicle; an upper limit. * *vt* to provide with a roof, to cover.

roof garden *n* a garden on a flat roof or balcony; a top floor decorated as a garden, esp if used as a restaurant.

roofing *n* materials for a roof.

rook[1] *n* a crow-like bird.

rook[2] *n* (*chess*) a piece with the power to move horizontally or vertically, a castle.

rookery *n* (*pl* **rookeries**) a colony of rooks; a breeding ground or haunt of other birds or mammals; a crowded place.

rookie *n* (*sl*) an inexperienced army recruit; any novice.—*also adj*.

room *n* space; unoccupied space; adequate space; a division of a house, a chamber; scope or opportunity; those in a room; (*pl*) lodgings. * *vi* to lodge.

room clerk *n* a receptionist in a hotel who books in guests and allocates rooms, etc.

rooming house *n* a house with individual rooms to let.

roommate *n* a person with whom one shares a room or rooms.

roomy *adj* (**roomier, roomiest**) having ample space; wide.—**roominess** *n*.

roost *n* a bird's perch or sleeping-place; a place for resting. * *vi* to rest or sleep on a roost; to settle down, as for the night.

rooster *n* an adult male domestic fowl, a cockerel.

root[1] *n* the part of a plant, usu underground, that anchors the plant, draws water from the soil, etc; the embedded part of a tooth, a hair, etc; a supporting or essential part; something that is an origin or source; (*math*) the factor of a quantity which multiplied by itself gives the quantity; (*mus*) the fundamental note of a chord; (*pl*) plants with edible roots. * *vti* to take root; to become established; (*with* **out**) to tear up, to eradicate.

root[2] *vti* to dig up with the snout; to search about, rummage; (*with* **for**) (*inf*) to encourage a team by cheering.

root beer *n* a carbonated drink flavored with extracts of certain roots and barks.

root crop *n* a crop, such as turnips, sugar beet, cultivated for its edible roots.

rooted *adj* firmly fixed; planted.

root mean square *n* the square root of the average of the squares of a set of numbers.

rootstock *n* an underground stem, rhizome; a stock for grafting, having a root or a piece of root.

rope *n* a thick cord or thin cable made of twisted fibres or wires; a string or row of things braided, intertwined or threaded together; a viscous thickening in a liquid. * *vt* to tie, bind, divide or enclose with a rope; to lasso; (*liquid*) to become ropy.—**ropy** *adj*.

Roquefort *n* a French blue-veined cheese with a strong flavour.

rorqual *n* any of several large whalebone whales with dorsal fins and deep furrows on the skin of the throat and chest.—*also* **finback**.

rosaceous *adj* of or belonging to the large family of plants that includes the rose; resembling a rose; rose-coloured.

rosary *n* (*pl* **rosaries**) a string of beads for keeping count of prayers; a series of prayers.

rose[1] *see* **rise**.

rose[2] *n* a prickly-stemmed plant with fragrant flowers of many delicate colours; its flower; a rosette; a perforated nozzle; a pinkish red or purplish red.

rosé *n* a pink wine made from skinless red grapes or by mixing white and red wine.

rose-coloured *adj* rosy; overly optimistic.

rosemary *n* a fragrant shrubby mint used in cookery and perfumery.

rosette *n* a rose-shaped bunch of ribbon; a carving, etc, in the shape of a rose.

rosewater *n* water scented with rose petals.

rose window *n* a circular window filled with tracery.

rosewood *n* (any of various tropical trees yielding) a fragrant dark wood used in making furniture.

rosin *n* a pine-wood resin, esp in solid form, used in varnishes, etc, and for waxing the bows of stringed instruments.

roster *n* a list or roll, as of military personnel; a list of duties.

rostrum *n* (*pl* **rostrums, rostra**) a platform or stage for public speaking.

rosy *adj* (**rosier, rosiest**) of the colour of roses; having pink, healthy cheeks; optimistic, hopeful.

rot *vti* (**rotting, rotted**) to decompose; to decay; to become degenerate. * *n* decay; corruption; several different diseases affecting timber or sheep; (*inf*) nonsense.

rota *n* a turn in succession; a list or roster of duties.

rotary *adj* revolving; turning like a wheel.

Rotary Club *n* a club belonging to an international organization of business people for promoting community service.—**Rotarian** *n*.

rotate *vti* to turn around an axis like a wheel; to follow a sequence.

rotation *n* the action of rotating; a regular succession, as of crops to avoid exhausting the soil.

rote *n* a fixed, mechanical way of doing something.

rotgut *n* (*sl*) a cheap or inferior whiskey or other spirit.

rotisserie *n* a large rotating spit on which poultry is roasted; a place where such food is prepared.

rotor *n* a rotating part of a machine or engine.

rotten *adj* decayed, decomposed; corrupt; (*inf*) bad, nasty.—**rottenness** *n*.

rotund *adj* rounded; spherical; plump.

rotunda *n* a circular, esp domed, building or chamber.

rouble *n* a coin and monetary unit of Russia.—*also* **ruble**.

rouge *n* a red cosmetic for colouring the cheeks; a red powder for polishing jewellery, etc. * *vti* to colour (the face) with rouge.

rough *adj* uneven; not smooth; ill-mannered; violent; rude, unpolished; shaggy; coarse in texture; unrefined; violent, boisterous; stormy; wild; harsh, discordant; crude, unfinished; approximate; (*inf*) difficult. * *n* rough ground; (*golf*) any part of a course with grass, etc, left uncut; a first sketch. * *vt* to make rough; to sketch roughly; (*with* **up**) (*inf*) to injure violently, beat up. * *adv* in a rough manner.—**roughly** *adv*.—**roughness** *n*.

roughage *n* rough or coarse food or fodder, as bran, etc.

rough-and-ready *adj* unfinished but sufficient; prepared hastily.

rough-and-tumble *n* a scuffle; confusion.

roughcast *n* a mixture of lime and gravel for coating buildings; a rough surface finish. * *vt* (**roughcasting, roughcast**) to coat with roughcast.

rough-cut *n* an early version of a film with the scenes edited together in sequence and a soundtrack added.

roughen *vti* to make or become rough.

roughhouse *n* (*sl*) (an instance of) noisy, boisterous or violent behaviour.

roughneck *n* (*sl*) a coarse person.

roughshod *adj* marked by force without consideration.

rough stuff *n* (*inf*) violent behaviour.

rough trade *n* (*sl*) a homosexual partner who is tough and possibly violent.

roulade *n* food in the shape of a roll, such as cheese or meat; (*mus*) a run of notes on one syllable.

roulette *n* a gambling game played with a revolving disc and a ball; a toothed wheel for making dots or perforations.

round *adj* circular, spherical, or cylindrical in form; curved; plump; (*math*) expressed to the nearest ten, hundred, etc, not fractional; considerable; candid;

(*style*) flowing, balanced; (*vowel*) pronounced with rounded lips. * *adv* circularly; on all sides; from one side to another; in a ring; by indirect way; through a recurring period of time; in circumference; in a roundabout way; about; near; here and there; with a rotating movement; in the opposite direction; around. * *prep* encircling; on every side of; in the vicinity of; in a circuit through; around. * *n* anything round; a circuit; (*shots*) a volley; a unit of ammunition; a series or sequence; a bout, turn; (*golf*) a circuit of a course; a stage of a contest; (*mus*) a kind of canon. * *vt* to make or become round or plump; (*math*) to express as a round number; to complete; to go or pass around. * *vi* to make a circuit; to turn; to reverse direction.—**roundly** *adv*.—**roundness** *n*.

roundabout *adj* indirect, circuitous. * *n* a circuitous route; a merry-go-round; (*Brit*) a traffic circle.

rounded *adj* curved or round; flowing, not angular.

roundhouse *n* a circular building for repairing and servicing railway locomotives.

round robin *n* a document with signatures in a circle to conceal their order.

round-shouldered *adj* with bent shoulders; stooping.

round-table conference *n* a conference with all the parties on an equal footing.

round trip *n* a journey to a place and back again.

round-trip ticket *n* a ticket whose price includes the cost of the journey to and back from a destination.

roundup *n* a driving together of livestock; (*inf*) the detention of several prisoners; a summary, as of news.

roundworm *n* a nematode parasitic in people and pigs.

rouse *vti* to provoke; to stir up; to awaken; to wake up; to become active.

rousing *adj* stirring; vigorous.

rout¹ *n* a noisy crowd, a rabble; a disorderly retreat. * *vt* to defeat and put to flight.

rout² *vti* to grub up, as a pig; to search haphazardly; to gouge out or make a furrow in (as wood or metal); to cause to emerge, esp from bed; to come up with; to uncover.

route *n* a course to be taken; the roads travelled on a journey. * *vt* to plan the route of; to send (by a specified route).

routine *n* a procedure that is regular and unvarying; a sequence of set movements, as in a dance, skating, etc.—*also adj*.

roux *n* a mixture of equal quantities of flour and melted fat used as the basis for sauces.

rove *vti* to wander about, roam (over).

rover *n* a wanderer; a fickle person; a senior Scout.

row¹ *n* a line of persons or things; a line of seats (in a theatre, etc).

row² *vti* to propel with oars; to transport by rowing. * *n* an act or instance of rowing.—**rower** *n*.

row³ *n* a noisy quarrel or dispute; a scolding; noise, disturbance. * *vi* to quarrel; to scold.

rowan *n* a tree producing white flowers followed by small red berries.

rowboat, rowing boat *n* a small boat made for rowing.

rowdy *adj* (**rowdier, rowdiest**) rough and noisy, disorderly. * *n* (*pl* **rowdies**) a rowdy person, a hooligan.—**rowdiness, rowdyism** *n*.

rowel *n* a spiked revolving disc at the end of a spur.

rowing machine *n* an exercise machine with oars and a sliding seat that simulates a rowing action.

rowlock *n* a fitting on the side of a boat that holds an oar in place and serves as its fulcrum.

royal *adj* relating to or fit for a king or queen; regal; under the patronage of a king or queen; founded by a king or queen; of a kingdom, its government, etc. * *n* a type of topsail; a stag with a head of twelve points; (*inf*) a member of a royal family.—**royally** *adv*.

royal blue *n*, *adj* deep blue.

royal flush *n* (*poker*) a straight flush headed by an ace.

royalist *n* a person who advocates monarchy.

royal jelly *n* a nutritious secretion of the honeybee which is fed to larvae, esp those destined to become queens; a preparation of this sold as a health product.

royalty *n* (*pl* **royalties**) the rank or power of a king or queen; a royal person or persons; a share of the proceeds from a patent, book, song, etc, paid to the owner, author, composer, etc.

rpm *abbr* = revolutions per minute.

-rrhagia *n suffix* denoting an abnormal discharge.

-rrhoea, -rrhea *n suffix* a flow.

RSVP *abbr* = répondez s'il vous plaît.

Ru (*chem symbol*) ruthenium.

rub *vti* (**rubbing, rubbed**) to move (a hand, cloth, etc) over the surface of with pressure; to wipe, scour; to clean or polish; (*with* **away, off, out**) to remove or erase by friction; to chafe, grate; to fret; to take a rubbing of; (*with* **along**) to manage somehow; (*with* **down**) to rub vigorously with a towel; to smooth down. * *n* the act or process of rubbing; a drawback, difficulty.

rubber¹ *n* an elastic substance made synthetically or from the sap of various tropical plants; an eraser; (*pl*) galoshes.

rubber² *n* a group of three games at whist, bridge, etc; the deciding game.

rubberize *vt* to coat with rubber to make waterproof.

rubberneck *n* (*sl*) a person who gapes, esp intrusively; a sightseer.—*also vi*.

rubber plant *n* an Asian plant related to the fig with shiny leaves, popular as a houseplant.

rubber-stamp *vt* (*inf*) to give automatic approval without investigation.

rubber tree *n* a tree native to South America and widely cultivated in the tropics as a source of latex to make rubber.

rubbing *n* an impression of an inscribed brass plate, etc, obtained by rubbing a wax substance on paper laid over it.

rubbish *n* refuse; garbage, trash; nonsense. —**rubbishy** *adj*.

rubble *n* rough broken stone or rock; builders' rubbish.

rubella *n* a mild contagious viral disease that may cause damage to an unborn child; German measles.

Rubenesque *adj* of, like or pertaining to the art of the Florentine painter Peter Paul Rubens (1577-1640); opulent, colourful; (*woman's figure*) full-breasted and shapely.

rubidium *n* a soft radioactive metallic element.

ruble *see* **rouble**.

rubric *n* a heading or line marked out in red; any rule, explanatory comment, etc.

ruby *n* (*pl* **rubies**) a deep red, transparent, valuable precious stone. * *adj* of the colour of a ruby.

ruby orange *n* an orange with red juice.

ruche *vt* to pleat, gather, or flute fabric for use as a trimming. * *n* ruched fabric.

rucksack *n* a bag worn on the back by hikers, used to carry camping or climbing equipment.

ruction *n* (*inf*) a disturbance, a row, uproar.

rudder *n* a flat vertical piece of wood or metal hinged to the stern of a ship or boat or the rear of an aircraft to steer by; a guiding principle.

ruddy *adj* (**ruddier, ruddiest**) reddish pink; (*complexion*) of a healthy, red colour.

rude *adj* uncivil, ill-mannered; uncultured, coarse; harsh, brutal; crude, roughly made; in a natural state, primitive; vigorous, hearty.—**rudely** *adv.*—**rudeness** *n.*

rudiment *n* a first stage; a first slight beginning of something; an imperfectly developed organ; (*pl*) elements, first principles.

rudimentary *adj* elementary; imperfectly developed or represented only by a vestige.

rue *vti* (**rueing, rued**) to feel remorse for (a sin, fault, etc); to regret (an act, etc). * *n* (*arch*) sorrow.

rueful *adj* regretful; dejected; showing good-humoured self-pity.—**ruefully** *adv.*

ruff *n* a pleated collar or frill worn round the neck; a fringe of feathers or fur round the neck of a bird or animal.

ruffian *n* a brutal lawless person; a villain.

ruffle *vti* to disturb the smoothness of, disarrange; to irritate; to agitate; to upset; to swagger about; to be quarrelsome; to flutter. * *n* pleated material used as a trim; a frill; a bird's ruff; a dispute, quarrel.

rug *n* a thick heavy fabric used as a floor covering; a thick woollen wrap or coverlet.

rugby *n* a football game for two teams of 15 players played with an oval ball.

rugged *adj* rocky; rough, uneven; strong, stern; robust.—**ruggedly** *adv.*—**ruggedness** *n.*

rugger *n* (*Brit inf*) rugby.

ruin *n* destruction; downfall, wrecked state; the cause of this; a loss of fortune; (*pl*) the remains of something destroyed, decayed, etc. * *vti* to destroy; to spoil; to bankrupt; to come to ruin.

ruinous *adj* in ruins, tumbledown; causing ruin, disastrous.

rule *n* a straight-edged instrument for drawing lines and measuring; government; the exercise of authority; a regulation, an order; a principle, a standard; habitual practice; the code of a religious order; a straight line. * *vti* to govern, to exercise authority over; to manage; to draw (lines) with a ruler; (*with* **out**) to exclude, to eliminate; to make impossible.

rule of thumb *n* a rough commonsense approach as opposed to a precise or theoretical one.

ruler *n* a person who governs; a strip of wood, metal, etc, with a straight edge, used in drawing lines, measuring, etc.

ruling *adj* governing; reigning; dominant. * *n* an authoritative pronouncement.

rum *n* a spirit made from sugar cane.

rumba *n* a dance of Cuban origin with a complex rhythm. * *vi* to dance the rumba.

rumble *vti* to make a low heavy rolling noise (as thunder); to move with such a sound; (*sl*) to see through, find out. * *n* the dull deep vibrant noise of thunder, etc.

rumbustious *adj* unruly, boisterous.

rumen *n* (*pl* **rumens, rumina**) the first compartment of the stomach of a ruminant mammal.

ruminant *n* a cud-chewing animal, such as cattle, deer, camels, etc. * *adj* chewing the cud; thoughtful.

ruminate *vi* to regurgitate food after it has been swallowed, chew cud; to ponder deeply, muse (on).

rummage *n* odds and ends; a search by ransacking. * *vti* to search thoroughly; to ransack; to fish (out).

rummage sale *n* a sale of second-hand clothes, books, etc to raise money for charity.—*also* **jumble sale**.

rummy *n* a card game whose object is to form sets and sequences.

rumour, rumor *n* hearsay, gossip; common talk not based on definite knowledge; an unconfirmed report, story. * *vt* to report by way of rumour.

rump *n* the hindquarters of an animal's body; the buttocks; the back end.

rumple *n* a crease or wrinkle. * *vti* to crease; to disarrange, tousle.

rumpus *n* (*pl* **rumpuses**) a commotion; a din.

run *vi* (**running, ran** *or* **run**, *pp* **run**) to go by moving the legs faster than in walking; to hurry; to flee; to flow; to operate; to be valid; to compete in a race, election, etc; (*colours*), to merge; (*with* **across**) to meet by accident; (*with* **around** *vi* (*inf*) to associate (with); to behave evasively or promiscuously; (*with* **away** *vi* to take flight, escape; to go out of control; (*with* **away with**) to abscond, elope; to steal; to win easily; (*with* **down**) (*engine, etc*) to cease to operate through lack of power; to become tired or exhausted; (*with* **off**) to leave hastily; to decide (a race) with a run-off; (*with* **through**) to use up (money, etc) completely; to read quickly. * *vt* (*a car, etc*) to drive; (*a business, etc*) to manage; (*a story*) to publish in a newspaper; (*temperature*) to suffer from a fever; (*with* **down**) to knock down with a moving vehicle; to collide with and cause to sink; to chase and capture; to tire, exhaust; to investigate, find; to criticize persistently; (*engine, etc*) to allow to gradually lose power; to reduce in quantity; (*with* **in**) to run a new car engine gently to start with; (*inf*) to arrest; (*with* **off**) to compose and talk glibly; to produce quickly, as copies on a photocopier; (*liquid*) to drain off; (*with* **out**) to exhaust a supply; (*inf*) to desert; (*with* **over**) (*vehicle*) to knock down a person or animal; to overflow; to exceed a limit; to rehearse quickly; (*with* **through**) to pierce with a sword or knife; to rehearse; (*with* **up**) to incur or amass. * *n* an act of running; a trip; a flow; a series; prevalence; a trend; an enclosure for chickens, etc; free and unrestricted access to all parts; (*in tights, etc*) a hole, a ladder.

run-around *n* deceitful or evasive behaviour towards someone.

runaway *n* a person or thing that runs away; a fugitive. * *adj* out of control; (*inflation*) rising uncontrollably; (*race, etc*) easily won.

run-down *adj* dilapidated; ill; tired.

rundown *n* a brief summary; the process of going into a decline.

rune *n* a letter of a primitive Teutonic alphabet; a magic mark or sign.—**runic** *adj.*

run-in *n* (*inf*) a quarrel.

rung[1] *see* **ring**[2].

rung[2] *n* the step of a ladder; the crossbar of a chair.

runner *n* an athlete; a person who runs; a smuggler; a groove or strip on which something glides.

runner bean *n* (*Brit*) a climbing plant that produces long green edible pods.

runner-up *n* (*pl* **runners-up**) the competitor who finishes second in a race, contest, etc.

running *n* the act of moving swiftly; that which runs or flows; a racing, managing, etc. * *adj* moving swiftly; kept for a race; being in motion; continuous; discharing pus. * *adv* in succession.

running commentary *n* a verbal description on TV or radio of an event as it happens, esp sport.

running mate *n* the candidate in a US election standing for the less important of two positions in a linked office.

runny *adj* (**runnier, runniest**) tending to flow.

run-off *n* a final deciding race, contest, etc.

run-of-the-mill *adj* average, mediocre.

runt *n* an unusually small animal, esp the smallest of a litter of pigs; a person of small stature.

run-through *n* a rehearsal; a cursory reading.

run-up *n* a preliminary period.

runway *n* a landing strip for aircraft.

rupee *n* a unit of money in India, Pakistan, Sri Lanka, Seychelles, Mauritius, and Nepal.

rupiah *n* (*pl* **rupiah, rupiahs**) the standard currency unit of Indonesia.

rupture *n* a breach; a severance, quarrel; the act of bursting or breaking; hernia. * *vti* to cause or suffer a rupture.

rural *adj* relating to the country or agriculture, rustic.—**rurally** *adv*.

ruse *n* a trick or stratagem.

rush[1] *vti* to move, push, drive, etc, swiftly or impetuously; to make a sudden attack (on); to do with unusual haste; to hurry. * *adj* marked by or needing extra speed or urgency. * *n* a sudden surge; a sudden demand; a press, as of business, requiring unusual haste; an unedited film print.

rush[2] *n* a marsh plant; its slender pithy stem; a worthless thing.

rush hour *n* the time at the beginning and end of the working day when traffic is at its heaviest.

rusk *n* a sweet or plain bread sliced and rebaked until dry and crisp.

russet *adj* reddish-brown. * *n* a russet colour; a winter apple with a rough russet skin; a homespun russet cloth.

Russian *n* a native or inhabitant of Russia; the Slavonic language of Russians.—*also adj*.

Russian roulette *n* an act of bravado in which the cylinder of a revolver loaded with a single bullet is spun and the muzzle then pointed at the head and fired.

Russo- *prefix* Russia; Russian.

rust *n* a reddish oxide coating formed on iron or steel when exposed to moisture; a reddish brown colour; a red mould on plants; the fungus causing this. * *vti* to form rust (on); to deteriorate, as through disuse.

rustic *n* pertaining to or characteristic of the country; rural; simple, unsophisticated. * *n* a person from the country; a simple country dweller.

rustle *n* a crisp, rubbing sound as of dry leaves, paper, etc. * *vti* to make or move with a rustle; to hustle; to steal (cattle); (*with* **up**) (*inf*) to collect or get together.

rustler *n* a person who steals livestock, esp cattle; a hustler.

rusty *adj* (**rustier, rustiest**) coated with rust; rust-coloured, faded; out of practice; antiquated.—**rustiness** *n*.

rut[1] *n* a track worn by wheels; an undeviating mechanical routine. * *vt* (**rutting, rutted**) to mark with ruts.

rut[2] *n* the seasonal period of sexual excitement in male ruminants, such as deer. * *vi* (**rutting, rutted**) to be in rut.

rutabaga *n* a swede.

ruthenium *n* a rare metallic element of the platinum group.

ruthless *adj* cruel; merciless.—**ruthlessly** *adv*.—**ruthlessness** *n*.

RV *abbr* = recreational vehicle.

rye *n* a hardy annual grass; its grain, used for making flour and whiskey; a whiskey made from rye.

S

S *abbr* = Saint; siemens; small; South, Southern; (*chem symbol*) sulphur.

S, s *n* the 19th letter of the English alphabet; something shaped like an S.

SA *abbr* = South Africa; South America; Salvation Army.

Sabbatarian *n* a strict observer of the sabbath.—Sabbatarianism *n*.

Sabbath *n* a day of rest and worship observed on a Saturday by Jews, Sunday by Christians and Friday by Muslims.

Sabbatical *adj* of, pertaining to, or resembling the Sabbath.

sabbatical *n* a year's leave from a teaching post, often paid, for research or travel.

SABC *abbr* = South African Broadcasting Corporation.

saber *see* sabre.

sabin *n* (*physics*) a unit of acoustic absorption.

Sabine *n* a member of an ancient people who lived in the central Apennines in Italy.—*also adj*.

sable *n* a carnivorous mammal of arctic regions valued for its luxuriant dark brown fur; its fur.

sabot *n* a shoe made from a single piece of wood; a shoe with a wooden sole and cloth upper.

sabotage *n* deliberate damage of machinery, or disruption of public services, by enemy agents, disgruntled employees, etc, to prevent their effective operation. * *vt* to practise sabotage on; to spoil, disrupt.

saboteur *n* a person who engages in sabotage.

sabra *n* a Jew born in Israel.

sabre *n* a cavalry sword with a curved blade; a light fencing sword.—*also* saber.

sabre-rattling *n* (*inf*) a conspicuous display of military power or aggression.

sabre-toothed tiger *n* an extinct species of large cat with long curved upper canine teeth.

sac *n* a bag-like part or cavity in a plant or animal.

saccate *adj* in the shape of a sac or pouch.

saccharide *n* a sugar.

saccharimeter *n* an instrument for measuring the concentration of sugar solutions.

saccharin *n* a non-fattening sugar substitute.

saccharine *adj* containing sugar; excessively sweet.

saccharo-, sacchar- *prefix* sugar.

sacerdotal *adj* relating to priests or the priesthood.—sacerdotalism *n*.—sacerdotally *adv*.

sachem *n* an American Indian chief of certain tribes; a political boss.

sachet *n* a sealed envelope or packet; a small perfumed bag or pad used to perfume clothes.

sack[1] *n* a large bag made of coarse cloth used as a container; the contents of this; a loose-fitting dress or coat; (*baseball*) a bag serving as a base; (*sl: with* the) dismissal. * *vt* to put into sacks; (*sl*) to dismiss.

sack[2] *n* the plunder or destruction of a place. * *vt* to plunder or loot.

sackbut *n* a type of medieval trombone.

sackcloth *n* a coarse fabric for sacks, etc; penitential clothing.

sacking *n* the coarse cloth used for sacks; the storming and plundering of a place.

sack race *n* a jumping race in which the participants' legs and lower bodies are enclosed in sacks.

sacra *see* sacrum.

sacrament *n* a religious ceremony forming outward and visible sign of inward and spiritual grace, esp baptism and the Eucharist; the consecrated elements in the Eucharist, esp the bread; a sacred symbol or pledge.

sacramental *adj* of, pertaining to, or like a sacrament. * *n* (*RC Church*) a rite recognized as similar to a sacrament, eg the use of holy water.—sacramentally *adv*.

sacred *adj* regarded as holy; consecrated to a god or God; connected with religion; worthy of or regarded with reverence, sacrosanct.

sacred cow *n* (*inf*) a person or thing regarded as above criticism.

sacrifice *n* the act of offering ceremonially to a deity; the slaughter of an animal (or person) to please a deity; the surrender of something valuable for the sake of something more important or worthy; loss without return; something sacrificed, an offering. * *vt* to slaughter or give up as a sacrifice; to give up for a higher good; to sell at a loss.—sacrificial *adj*.

sacrilege *n* violation of anything holy or sacred.

sacrilegious *adj* guilty of sacrilege; irreverent.—sacrilegiously *adv*.—sacrilegiousness *n*.

sacristan *n* a person in charge of the contents of a church; a sexton.

sacristy *n* (*pl* sacristies) a room in a church where the sacred vessels, etc are kept

sacrosanct *adj* inviolable; very holy.

sacrum *n* (*pl* sacra) a compound bone at the base of the spine forming the back of the pelvis.

sad *adj* (sadder, saddest) expressing grief or unhappiness; sorrowful; deplorable.—sadly *adv*.—sadness *n*.

sadden *vti* to make or become sad.

saddle *n* a seat, usu of leather, for a rider on a horse, bicycle, etc; a ridge connecting two mountain peaks; a joint of mutton or venison consisting of the two loins; in the saddle mounted on a saddle; in control. * *vt* to put a saddle on; to burden, encumber.

saddlebag *n* a bag hung from the saddle of a horse or bicycle.

saddlebow *n* the arched front of a saddle.

saddlecloth *n* a piece of cloth placed under a horse's saddle to prevent chafing.

saddler *n* a person who makes or sells saddles, harness, etc.

saddlery *n* (*pl* saddleries) articles made by a saddler; the business or premises of a saddler.

saddle soap *n* an oily soap for cleaning and preserving leather.

saddletree n the frame of a saddle.

sadhu, saddhu *n* a Hindu holy man.

sadism *n* sexual pleasure obtained from inflicting cruelty upon another; extreme cruelty.—**sadist** *n*.—**sadistic** *adj*.—**sadistically** *adv*.

sadomasochism *n* sexual pleasure obtained from inflicting cruelty upon oneself and receiving it from another.—**sadomasochist** *n*.—**sadomasochistic** *adj*.

s.a.e. *abbr* = stamped addressed envelope.

safari *n* (*pl* **safaris**) a journey or hunting expedition, esp in Africa.

safari jacket *n* a belted shirt jacket with pleated pockets.

safari suit *n* a safari jacket and matching trousers or skirt made from denim or similar hard-wearing material.

safe *adj* unhurt; out of danger; reliable; secure; involving no risk; trustworthy; giving protection; prudent; sure; incapable of doing harm. * *n* a locking metal box or compartment for valuables.—**safely** *adv*.

safe-conduct *n* written permission for the holder to travel safely through hostile country.

safecracker *n* a person who opens and robs safes.—*also* **safe-breaker**.—**safecracking** *n*.

safe-deposit *adj* (*box, room, etc*) designed for the protective storage of valuables, deeds, etc. * *n* a building with safes for renting—*also* **safety deposit**.

safeguard *n* anything that protects against injury or danger; a proviso against foreseen risks. * *vt* to protect.

safe house *n* a refuge for victims of domestic violence, sexual abuse, etc run by social welfare organizations; a clandestine place used by intelligence services, terrorists, etc as a refuge.

safekeeping *n* the act or process of keeping safely; protection.

safe period *n* the time in a woman's menstrual cycle when she is least likely to conceive.

safe seat *n* a parliamentary constituency in which the sitting MP enjoys a substantial majority and can be assured of re-election.

safe sex *n* sex in which precautions are taken to lessen the risk of catching AIDS or other sexually transmitted diseases.

safety *n* (*pl* **safeties**) freedom from danger; the state of being safe.

safety belt *n* a belt worn by a person working at a great height to prevent falling; a seatbelt in a car.

safety curtain *n* a fireproof curtain that can be lowered to separate a theatre stage from the auditorium.

safety deposit *see* **safe-deposit**.

safety glass *n* shatterproof glass.

safety lamp *n* a miner's lamp in which the flame is enclosed by a protective gauze to prevent it igniting combustible gases.

safety match *n* a match that will only ignite on a particular surface.

safety net *n* a net suspended beneath acrobats, etc; any protection against loss.

safety pin *n* a pin with a guard to cover the point.

safety razor *n* a razor with a guard that covers the blade to protect the skin from accidental cuts.

safety valve *n* an automatic valve for relieving excess pressure of steam, etc; a harmless outlet for emotion.

saffian *n* a brightly dyed leather made from the skin of goats or sheep.

safflower *n* (a red dye and oil derived from) a thistle-like plant with large orange or red flowers.

saffron *n* a crocus whose bright yellow stigmas are used as a food colouring and flavouring; an orange-yellow colour.

sag *vi* (**sagging, sagged**) to droop downward in the middle; to sink or hang down unevenly under pressure.

saga *n* a long story of heroic deeds.

sagacious *adj* mentally acute, shrewd; wise.—**sagaciously** *adv*.—**sagaciousness** *n*.

sagacity *n* (*pl* **sagacities**) readiness of apprehension; discriminating intelligence; acute practical judgment.

sagamore *n* an American Indian chief of certain tribes.

sage[1] *adj* wise through reflection and experience. * *n* a person of profound wisdom.—**sagely** *adv*.—**sagely** *adv*.

sage[2] *n* a herb with leaves used for flavouring food; sagebrush.

sagebrush *n* a low shrub of the alkaline plains of North America.

sagger, saggar *n* a fireproof clay case in which procelain is put for baking.

sagittate *adj* (*leaf*) shaped like an arrowhead.

Sagittarius *n* the Archer, ninth sign of the zodiac; in astrology, operative November 22–December 20.—**Sagittarian** *adj, n*.

sago *n* (*pl* **sagos**) a type of Asian palm; its starchy pith used in puddings.

saguaro *n* (*pl* **saguaros**) a large cactus of North American and Mexican desert areas bearing white flowers and edible fruit.

sahib *n* a form of polite address formerly used by Indians to European men.

said *see* **say**.

saiga *n* a stocky antelope of the Russian steppes.

sail *n* a piece of canvas used to catch the wind to propel or steer a vessel; sails collectively; anything like a sail; an arm of a windmill; a voyage in a sailing vessel; **under sail** with the sails set; under way. * *vt* to navigate a vessel; to manage (a vessel); **to set sail** to spread the sails; to begin a voyage. * *vi* to be moved by sails; to travel by water; to glide or pass smoothly; to walk in a stately manner.

sailboard *n* a type of large surfboard with a sail used in windfsurfing.

sailboat *n* a sailing boat.

sailcloth *n* canvas used for sails; a strong, durable fabric for clothing.

sailer *n* a sailing vessel.

sailfish *n* (*pl* **sailfish, sailfishes**) a large game fish of tropical waters with a long sail-like dorsal fin.

sailing *n* the act of sailing; the motion or direction of a ship, etc on water; a departure from a port.

sailing boat *n* a boat that is propelled by a sail or sails.

sailor *n* a person who sails; one of a ship's crew.

sailoring *n* a sailor's life.

sailplane *n* a type of light glider. * *vi* to fly a sailplane.

sain *vt* (*arch*) to make the sign of the cross on; to bless in order to protect from evil.

sainfoin *n* a Eurasian leguminous plant with pink flowers, grown for fodder.

saint *n* a person who is very patient, charitable, etc; a person who is canonized by the Roman Catholic Church; one of the blessed in heaven.—**sainthood** *n*.

Saint Bernard *n* a breed of large dog with a reddish brown coat, often used as a rescue dog.

sainted *adj* canonized; holy; dead; much admired.

saintly *adj* (**saintlier, saintliest**) of, like, or relating to a saint.—**saintliness** *n*.

Saint Patrick's Day *n* March 17, observed by the Irish in honour of the patron saint of Ireland.

saint's day *n* a day in the church calender which is devoted to the commemoration of a particular saint.

sake[1] *n* behalf; purpose; benefit; interest.

sake[2], **saké, saki** *n* a Japanese alcoholic drink made from fermented rice and drunk warm.

sal *n* (*chem*) a salt.

salaam *n* a form of ceremonial greeting in Muslim countries. * *vti* to make a salaam (to).

salable *adj* marketable; in good demand.—*also* **saleable**.

salacious *adj* lustful; obscene.—**salaciously** *adv*.—**salaciousness** *n*.

salad *n* a dish, usu cold, of vegetables, fruits, meat, eggs, etc; lettuce, etc, used for this.

salad bar *n* a buffet in a restaurant at which diners choose their own salads.

salad days *npl* a time of youth and inexperience.

salad dressing *n* a cooked or uncooked sauce of oil, vinegar, spices, etc, to put on a salad.

salade niçoise *n* a salad of various ingredients, including tomatoes, hard-boiled eggs, and anchovy fillets or tuna fish.

salamander *n* any of various lizard-like amphibians; a mythical lizard-like creature that was supposedly impervious to fire.

salami *n* a highly seasoned Italian sausage.

salaried *adj* receiving a salary.

salary *n* (*pl* **salaries**) fixed, regular payment for non-manual work, usu paid monthly.

salchow *n* (*ice-skating*) a jump incorporating turns in the air.

sale *n* the act of selling; the exchange of goods or services for money; the market or opportunity of selling; an auction; the disposal of goods at reduced prices; the period of this.

saleable *see* **salable**.

salep *n* (food made from) the starchy dried roots of various orchidaceous plants.

saleratus *n* sodium bicarbonate used in cooking.

saleroom *n* a salesroom; an auction room.

salesclerk *n* a person who sells goods in a store.

salesman *n* (*pl* **salesmen**) a person who sells either in a given territory or in a store.—**saleswoman** *nf* (*pl* **saleswomen**).

salesmanship *n* the art or skill of selling.

salesperson *n* (pl **salespeople**) a salesman or saleswoman.

sales representative *n* a person who travels to sell within a given territory.

salesroom *n* a place where goods are displayed for sale; a saleroom.

sales talk *n* talk aimed at selling something; any talk to persuade.

sales tax *n* a tax levied (usu as a percentage) on the price of an object bought by a consumer.

Salic *adj* of or pertaining to the Franks; relating to the Salic law.

Salic law *n* the law of the Franks excluding females from the succession to the French throne.

salicin *n* a bitter compound obtained from the bark of willows and poplars, used in medicine.

salient *adj* projecting outward; conspicuous; noteworthy; leaping, gushing.—**salience, saliency** *n*.—**saliently** *adv*.

salify *vt* to make salty; (*chem*) to convert into a salt.—**salification** *n*.

salimeter *n* a device for measuring the amount of salt in a solution.

saline *adj* of or impregnated with salt or salts; salty. * *n* a solution of salt and water.—**salinity** *n*.

saliva *n* the liquid secreted by glands in the mouth that aids digestion.—**salivary** *adj*.

salivate *vi* to secrete saliva, esp excessively.—**salivation** *n*.

sallenders *npl* an eczematous rash on a horse's hock.

sallet *n* a light helmet of the 15th century.

sallow *adj* (*complexion*) an unhealthy yellow colour, a pale brown colour.—**sallowness** *n*.

sally *n* (pl **sallies**) a sudden attack; an outburst; a lively remark, quip. * *vi* (**sallying, sallied**) to make a sally; to go (forth).

salmagundi *n* a mixed dish of chopped meat, anchovies, eggs, vegetables, etc; a miscellany.

salmi *n* (*pl* **salmis**) a casserole of game-birds in a rich wine sauce.

salmon *n* (*pl* **salmon, salmons**) a large silvery edible fish that lives in salt water and spawns in fresh water; salmon pink.

salmonella *n* (*pl* **salmonellae, salmonella, salmonellas**) any of a genus of bacteria that causes food poisoning and diseases of the genital tract.

salmon ladder *n* a series of steps (eg in a waterfall or dam) to allow salmon to swim upstream to their breeding grounds.

salmon pink *adj* a yellowish pink colour.

salmon trout *n* a large trout resembling a salmon.

salon *n* a large reception hall or drawing room for receiving guests; the shop of a hairdresser, beautician, or couturier; an art gallery.

saloon *n* a large reception room; a large cabin for the social use of a ship's passengers; a four-seater car with a boot; a place where alcoholic drinks are sold and consumed.

saloon bar *n* a comfortably furnished bar.

salopettes *npl* thick quilted trousers with shoulder straps, worn for skiing.

salsa *n* (the music for) a type of Puerto Rican dance.

salsify *n* (*pl* **salsifies**) a purple-flowered plant with an edible root.

SALT *abbr* = Strategic Arms Limitation Talks *or* Treaty.

salt *n* a white crystalline substance (sodium chloride) used as a seasoning or preservative; piquancy, wit; (*chem*) a compound of an acid and a base; (*pl*) mineral salt as an aperient. * *adj* containing or tasting of salt; preserved with salt; pungent. * *vt* to flavour, pickle or sprinkle with salt; to give flavour or piquancy to (as a story); (*with* **away**) to hoard; to keep for the future.

saltbush *n* a shrub-like plant which provides grazing in dry regions.

salt cellar *n* a vessel for salt at the table; a saltshaker.

saltire *n* an X-shaped cross dividing a shield, flag, etc, into four compartments.

salt lick *n* an area where animals go to lick salt residue; a block of salt for animals to lick.

salt marsh *n* an area regularly flooded by seawater.

saltpan *n* a hollow or depression where salt is deposited by evaporating seawater.

saltpetre, saltpeter *n* a white powder (potassium nitrate) used in making gunpowder, etc.

saltshaker *n* a container for salt with a perforated top.

saltwater *adj* of or living in salt water or the sea.

salty *adj* (**saltier, saltiest**) of, containing or tasting of salt; witty; earthy, coarse.

salubrious *adj* health-giving; wholesome.—**salubriously** *adv.*—**salubriousness** *n.*

saluki *n* a breed of tall, slender hounds with long silky coats.

salutary *adj* beneficial, wholesome.—**salutarily** *adv.*—**salutariness** *n.*

salutation *n* a greeting; the words used in it.

salute *n* a gesture of respect or greeting; (*mil*) a motion of the right hand to the head, or to a rifle; a discharge of guns, etc, as a military mark of honour. * *vti* to make a salute (to); to greet; to kiss; to praise or honour.

salvable *adj* able to be salvaged.

salvage *n* the rescuing of a ship or property from loss at sea, by fire, etc; the reward paid for this; the thing salvaged; waste material intended for further use. * *vt* to save from loss or danger.—**salvageable** *adj.*—**salvager** *n.*

salvation *n* the act of saving or the state of being saved; in Christianity, the deliverance from evil; a means of preservation.—**salvational** *adj.*

Salvation Army *n* an international religious and charitable group organized on military lines founded by William Booth in 1865.—**Salvationist** *n.*

salve[1] *n* a healing ointment or balm; a soothing influence. * *vt* to apply ointment to; to smooth over; to soothe.

salve[2] *vt* to salvage; (*arch*) to save.

salver *n* a small tray.

salvia *n* any of a genus of plants or small shrubs with red or purple flowers.

salvo[1] *n* (**salvoes, salvos**) a firing of several guns or missiles simultaneously; a sudden burst; a spirited verbal attack.

salvo[2] *n* (*pl* **salvos**) an exception or reservation.

sal volatile *n* a solution of ammonium carbonate in alcohol used as a remedy for faintness.

salvor *n* a person or vessel effecting a salvage at sea.

SAM (*acronym*) surface-to-air missile.

samara *n* a dry winged single-seeded fruit produced by the ash, elm, etc.

Samaritan *n* a native or inhabitant of Samaria in ancient Palestine; a compassionate person; a Good Samaritan; a member of a voluntary organization that helps people in distress or despair.

samarium *n* a silvery metallic element used in lasers and alloys.

samba *n* a Brazilian dance of African origin; the music for this. * *vi* to dance the samba.

same *adj* identical; exactly similar; unchanged; uniform, monotonous; previously mentioned. * *pron* the same person or thing. * *adv* in like manner.

sameness *n* the state of being the same; monotony.

Samian *n* a native or inhabitant of the Aegean island of Samos in Greece. * *adj* of or pertaining to Samos or its people.

Samian ware *n* a type of red or black pottery from Samos.

samisen *n* a Japanese guitar-like instrument with three strings.

samite *n* a medieval heavy silken fabric.

samizdat *n* in the former Soviet Union, a system for the clandestine printing and distribution of banned literature.

Samoan *n* a native or inhabitant of Samoa, a group of islands in the South Pacific; the Polynesian language of Samoa.* *adj* of or pertaining to Samoa, its people or language.

samosa *n* (*pl* **samosas, samosa**) an Indian savoury pasty with a spicy meat or vegetable filling.

samovar *n* a metal urn with an internal element used for boiling water for tea, esp in Russia.

Samoyed *n* a member of a people of the northern Urals; the language of these people; a breed of sledge-dog with a thick creamy coat and a tightly curled tail.—**Samoyedic** *adj.*

sampan *n* a small flat-bottomed Chinese river boat.

samphire *n* a Eurasian coastal rock plant with edible fleshy leaves.

sample *n* a specimen; a small part representative of the whole; an instance. * *vt* (*food, drink*) to taste a small quantity of; to test by taking a sample.

sampler *n* a person who takes samples; something containing a representative selection (as a record, book); an assortment; a piece of ornamental embroidery showing different stitches and patterns as an example of skill.

sampling *n* (*mus industry*) the practice of extracting phrases from several recorded songs and putting them together electronically to make a new one.

samurai *n* (*pl* **samurai**) a member of an ancient Japanese warrior caste.

samurai bond *n* a financial bond issued in yen by a non-Japanese company.

-san *n suffix* a Japanese title of respect similar to Mr, Mrs, etc.

sanatorium *see* **sanitarium**.

sancta *see* **sanctum**.

sanctified *adj* hallowed; consecrated; sanctimonious.

sanctify *vt* (**sanctifying, sanctified**) to make holy; to purify from sin or evil; (*the Church*) to give official approval.—**sanctification** *n.*—**sanctifier** n.

sanctimonious *adj* pretending to be holy; hypocritically pious or righteous.—**sanctimoniously** *adv.*—**sanctimoniousness** *n.*

sanctimony *n* self-righteousness; hypocrisy.

sanction *n* express permission, authorization; a binding influence; a penalty by which a law is enforced, esp a prohibition on trade with a country that has violated international law. * *vt* to permit; to give authority.—**sanctionable** *adj.*

sanctity *n* (*pl* **sanctities**) the condition of being holy or sacred; inviolability.

sanctuary *n* (*pl* **sanctuaries**) a sacred place; the part of a church around the altar; a place where one is free from arrest or violence, an asylum; a refuge; an animal reserve.

sanctum *n* (*pl* **sanctums, sancta**) a holy place; a private room where one is not to be disturbed.

Sanctus *n* (*Christianity*) the hymn "Holy, holy, holy" used in communion; an orchestral setting of this.

sand *n* very fine rock particles; (*pl*) a desert; a sandy beach. * *vt* to smooth or polish with sand or sandpaper; to sprinkle with sand. * *adj* reddish yellow.

sandal[1] *n* a shoe consisting of a sole strapped to the foot; a low slipper or shoe.—**sandalled, sandaled** *adj.*

sandal[2] *n* sandalwood.

sandalwood *n* the yellow, scented wood of an Asian tree; the tree.

sandbag n a bag of sand used for ballast or to protect against floodwater. * vt (**sandbagging, sandbagged**) to protect by laying sandbags; to hit with a sandbag; (inf) to coerce; (sl) to deceive.—**sandbagger** n.

sandbank n a sand bar; a large deposit of sand forming a hill or mound.

sand bar n a ridge of sand built up in a river, a lake, or coastal waters by currents.

sandblast vt (a building) to clean by blasting with sand at high velocity.—also n.

sand box n a small enclosure filled with sand for children to play in.—also **sandpit**.

sand castle n a model of a castle moulded from damp sand, as made at the seaside by children.

sander n a power-driven tool for sanding wood or other surfaces.

sanderling n a small wading bird.

sandglass n an instrument that measures time by the running of sand through a narrow aperture.

S & L abbr = savings and loan association.

S & M abbr = sadomasochism.

sandman n (pl **sandmen**) (folklore) an imaginary being who sends children to sleep by sprinkling sand in their eyes.

sand martin n a small European songbird that nests in holes in sandy riverbanks, etc.

sandpaper n a paper coated on one side with sand or another abrasive, used to smooth or polish. * vt to rub with sandpaper.

sandpiper n any of numerous small wading birds.

sandpit see **sand box**.

sandstone n a sedimentary rock of compacted sand.

sandstorm n a windstorm in a desert carrying clouds of sand.

sand trap n (golf) a pit of sand forming an obstacle on a golf course, a bunker.

sand wedge n (golf) a club for hitting the ball out of a sand trap.

sandwich n two slices of bread with meat, cheese, or other filling between; anything in a sandwich-like arrangement. * vt to place between two things or two layers; to make such a place for.

sandwich board n two usu hinged boards hanging from the shoulders, one in front and one at the back, carried by a sandwich man.

sandwich man n a person who advertises by wearing a sandwich board.

sandy adj (**sandier, sandiest**) of, like, or sprinkled with sand; yellowish grey.—**sandiness** n.

sane adj mentally sound, not mad; reasonable, sensible.—**sanely** adv.—**saneness** n.

sang see **sing**.

sangfroid n coolness in danger, imperturbability.

Sangreal n the Holy Grail.

sangria n a Spanish drink made with red wine, orange juice and fresh fruit laced with brandy.

sanguinary adj accompanied by bloodshed; bloodthirsty.—**sanguinarily** adv.

sanguine adj confident, hopeful; blood-red; (complexion) ruddy.—**sanguineness** n.

sanguinely adv confidently, hopefully.

sanguineous adj of or relating to blood; full-blooded; blood-red; sanguinary; sanguine.

sanies n a watery mixture of blood and pus discharged from a sore or wound.—**sanious** adj.

sanitarian adj hygienic. * n a specialist in matters of public health.

sanitarium n (pl **sanitariums, sanitaria**) an establishment for the treatment of convalescents or the chronically ill.—also **sanatorium**.

sanitary adj relating to the promotion and protection of health; relating to the supply of water, drainage, and sewage disposal; hygienic.—**sanitarily** adv.—**sanitariness** n.

sanitary cordon n a cordon sanitaire.

sanitary engineering n the design, construction and installation of water and sewage systems.—**sanitary engineer** n.

sanitary napkin, sanitary towel n an absorbent pad worn externally during menstruation.

sanitation n the science and practice of achieving hygienic conditions; drainage and disposal of sewage.

sanitize vt to clean or sterilize; to make (language, etc) more respectable or acceptable.

sanity n the condition of being sane; mental health; common sense.

sank see **sink**.

Sanka n (trademark) a decaffeinated coffee.

sannup n an American Indian warrior, a brave.

Sans. abbr = Sanskrit.

sans prep without.

sansculotte n in the French Revolution, a man without breeches, a term of contempt applied to a revolutionary who wore pantaloons instead of knee breeches; any revolutionary.

sans doute (French) doubtless; certainly.

Sansk. abbr = Sanskrit.

Sanskrit n the ancient language used in Indian and Hindu sacred literature.—**Sanskrit** adj.—**Sanskritic** adj.

sans-serif, sanserif n (print) a character or typeface with no serifs.

sans souci (French) free from care.

Santa n Santa Claus. * adj sainted, holy.

Santa Claus n a legendary fat, white-bearded old man who brings presents to children at Christmas.—also **Father Christmas**.

sap[1] n the vital juice of plants; energy and health; (inf) a fool. * vt (**sapping, sapped**) to drain of sap; to exhaust the energy of..

sap[2] n a narrow or covered siege trench; the digging of this, undermining. * vti (**sapping, sapped**) to attack by or dig a sap; to undermine insidiously.

saphead n (sl) a fool, a stupid person.

sapid adj having a pleasing flavour; agreeable.—**sapidity** n.

sapient adj (often ironical) wise, discerning.—**sapience** n.—**sapiently** adv.

sapling n a young tree; a youth.

saponify vt (**saponifying, saponified**) (chem) to convert (fat, oil, etc) into soap by combination with an alkali. * vi to undergo this process.—**saponification** n.—**saponifier** n.

sapor n taste, flavour.

sapper n one who or that which saps; a soldier who lays, detects or disarms mines.

sapphire n a transparent blue precious stone; a deep pure blue.—also adj.

sapro-, sapr- prefix dead or decaying matter.

saprogenic, saprogenous adj producing or caused by putrefaction.

saprophagous adj feeding on decaying matter.

saprophyte n a plant or fungus that grows on dead organic matter.—**saprophytic** adj.

Saracen *n* a member of a nomadic people of the Syrian desert; a Muslim at the time of the Crusades. * *adj* of or pertaining to Saracens.—**Saracenic** *adj*.

sarcasm *n* a scornful or ironic remark; the use of this.—**sarcastic** *adj*.—**sarcastically** *adv*.

sarco-, sarc- *prefix* flesh.

sarcoma *n* (*pl* **sarcomas, sarcomata**) a malignant tumour of connective tissue.—**sarcomatous** *adj*.

sarcophagus *n* (*pl* **sarcophagi, sarcophaguses**) a large stone coffin or tomb.

sard *n* an orange-red variety of chalcedony.

sardine *n* (pl **sardines, sardine**) a small, edible seafish.

sardonic *adj* (*smile, etc*) derisive, mocking, maliciously jocular.—**sardonically** *adv*.

sardonyx *n* an onyx with alternate layers of white chalcedony and orange sard.

sargasso *n* (*pl* **sargassos**) a large mass of floating sargassum.

sargassum *n* any of a genus of tropical seaweed with air bladders that form to float in large masses.

sarge *n* (*sl*) sergeant.

sari, saree *n* a Hindu woman's principal garment, consisting of a long piece of cloth wrapped around the waist and across the shoulder.

sark *n* (*Scot*) a shirt.

sarong *n* a long strip of cloth wrapped around the lower body, worn esp in the Malay archipelago and the Pacific Islands.

sarsaparilla *n* any of various tropical American trailing plants; the dried roots of these used as a flavouring and (formerly) in medicine; a soft drink flavoured with these roots.

sartorial *adj* of or relating to the making of men's clothing.—**sartorially** *adv*.

sartorius *n* (*pl* **sartorii**) a muscle that helps flex the knee.

SASE *abbr* = self-addressed stamped envelope.

sash[1] *n* a band of satin or ribbon worn around the waist or over the shoulder, often as a badge of honour.

sash[2] *n* a frame for holding the glass of a window, esp one that slides vertically.

sashay *n* (*inf*) to walk in a casual manner, saunter; to swagger.

sash cord *n* a cord used to attach a sash weight to a sash.

sashimi *n* a Japanese dish of thin strips of raw fish.

sash weight *n* a weight used to balance a sliding sash in an open position.

sash window *n* a window with sliding sashes.

sass *n* (*inf*) rudeness, impudence. * *vt* to talk rudely or impudently to.

sassafras *n* a North American tree of the laurel family; the aromatic dried root of this used as a flavouring.

Sassenach *n* (*Scot, Irish*) an English person.

sassy *adj* (**sassier, sassiest**) (*sl*) rude; cheeky.

Sat *abbr* = Saturday; Saturn.

sat *see* **sit**.

Satan *n* the devil, the adversary of God.

satanic, satanical *adj* of or relating to Satan, devilish; marked by viciousness or cruelty.—**satanically** *adv*.

Satanism *n* the worship of Satan; the perversion of Christian ceremonial forms associated with this.—**Satanist** *n*.

satay, saté *n* an Indonesian dish of cubed chicken, beef, etc served with a piquant peanut sauce.

satchel *n* a bag with shoulder straps for carrying school books, etc.

sate *vt* to satisfy to repletion, to satiate.

sateen *n* a closely woven fabric with a glossy surface made in imitation of satin.

satellite *n* a planet orbiting another; a man-made object orbiting the earth, moon, etc, to gather scientific information or for communication; a nation economically dependent on a more powerful one.

satellite broadcasting, satellite television *n* the transmission of television programmes via an orbiting satellite to subscribers in possession of a receiving satellite dish aerial.

sati *see* **suttee**.

satiable *adj* able to be satiated or sated.—**satiability** *n*.—**satiably** *adv*.

satiate *vt* to provide with more than enough so as to weary or disgust; to gorge.—**satiation** *n*.

satiety *n* the state of being sated; a feeling of having had too much.

satin *n* a fabric of woven silk with a smooth, shiny surface on one side. * *adj* of or resembling satin.

satinwood *n* a smooth yellowish brown hard wood; a tree that yields such wood.

satiny *adj* smooth and lustrous, like satin.

satire *n* a literary work in which folly or evil in people's behaviour are held up to ridicule; trenchant wit, sarcasm.—**satirical** *adj*.—**satirically** *adv*.

satirist *n* a writer of satires.

satirize *vt* to attack with satire.—**satirizer** *n*.

satisfaction *n* the act of satisfying or the condition of being satisfied; that which satisfies; comfort; atonement, reparation.

satisfactory *adj* giving satisfaction; adequate; acceptable; convincing.—**satisfactorily** *adv*.—**satisfactoriness** *n*.

satisfy *vb* (**satisfying, satisfied**) *vi* to be enough for; to fulfil the needs or desires of. * *vt* to give enough to; (*hunger, desire etc.*) to appease; to please; to gratify; to comply with; (*creditor*) to discharge, to pay in full; to convince; to make reparation to; (*guilt, etc*) to atone for.

satori *n* (*Zen Buddhism*) a state of intuitive enlightenment.

satsuma *n* a loose-skinned, seedless, small orange; (*with cap*) a glazed yellow Japanese pottery.

saturate *vt* to soak thoroughly; to fill completely.—**saturator** *n*.

saturated *adj* (*chem*) absorbing the maximum amount possible of a substance; pure in colour.

saturation *n* the act of saturating or the condition of being saturated; the supplying of a market with all the goods it will absorb; an overwhelming concentration of military power.

Saturday *n* the seventh and last day of the week.

Saturn *n* (*Roman myth*) the god of agriculture; (*astron*) the second largest planet in the solar system, with three rings revolving about it.—**Saturnian** *adj*.

Saturnalia *n* (*pl* **Saturnalias, Saturnalia**) in ancient Rome, a festival held in December in honour of Saturn; (*without cap*) a wild, unrestrained celebration.—**Saturnalian** *n*.

saturnine *adj* sullen, morose.—**saturninely** *adv*.

satyagraha *n* the principle and practice of passive resistance as adopted by Mahatma Gandhi in opposition to British colonial rule in India.

satyr *n* (*Greek myth*) a woodland god in human form but with goat's ears, tail, and legs; a man with strong sexual appetites; a man with satyriasis.—**satyric** *adj*.

satyriasis *n* excessive sexual desire in men.

sauce *n* a liquid or dressing served with food to enhance its flavour; stewed or preserved fruit eaten with other food or as a dessert; (*inf*) impudence. * *vt* to season with sauce; to make piquant; (*sl*) to cheek.

saucepan *n* a deep cooking pan with a handle and lid.

saucer *n* a round shallow dish placed under a cup; a shallow depression; a thing shaped like a saucer.

saucy *adj* (**saucier, sauciest**) rude, impertinent; sprightly.—**saucily** *adv.*—**sauciness** *n*.

sauerkraut *n* a German dish of chopped pickled cabbage.

sauna *n* exposure of the body to hot steam, followed by cold water; the room where this is done.

saunter *vi* to walk in a leisurely or idle way. * *n* a stroll.—**saunterer** *n*.

-saur *n suffix* (*scientific*) reptiles.

saurian *adj* of or resembling a lizard. * *n* (*formerly*) lizard.

sauro- *prefix* lizard.

saury *n* (*pl* **sauries**) an Atlantic fish with a long body and elongated jaws.

sausage *n* minced seasoned meat, esp pork, packed into animal gut or other casing.

sauté *adj* fried quickly and lightly. * *vt* (**sautéing, sautéed**) to fry in a small amount of oil or fat. * *n* a sautéed dish.

sauve qui peut *n* a precipitate flight, a general stampede.

savage *adj* fierce; wild; untamed; uncivilized; ferocious; primitive. * *n* a member of a primitive society; a brutal, fierce person or animal.—**savagely** *adv.*—**savageness** *n*.

savagery *n* (*pl* **savageries**) the state of being a savage; an act of violence or cruelty; an uncivilized state.

savanna, savannah *n* a treeless plain; an area of tropical or subtropical grassland.

savant *n* (pl **savants**) a person with extensive knowledge, esp in a certain discipline.

savate *n* a form of boxing using both the fists and the feet.

save[1] *vt* to rescue from harm or danger; to keep, to accumulate; to set aside for future use; to avoid the necessity of; (*energy etc*) to prevent waste of; (*theol*) to deliver from sin. * *vi* to avoid waste, expense, etc; to economize; to store up money or goods; (*sports*) to keep an opponent from scoring or winning. * *n* (*sports*) the act of preventing one's opponent from scoring.—**savable, saveable** *adj*.

save[2] *conj, prep* except, but.

saveloy *n* a type of highly-seasoned smoked sausage.

saver *n* a person who saves money in a bank or building society.

savin, savine *n* a small Eurasian juniper bush with dark fruit the oil from which was once used medicinally.

saving[1] *adj* thrifty, economical; (*clause*) containing a reservation; redeeming. * *n* what is saved; (*pl*) money saved for future use.

saving[2] *prep* except; with apology to.

savings and loan association *n* a company that pays interest on deposits and issues loans to enable people to buy their own houses, a building society.

savings account *n* a bank account that earns interest.

savings bank *n* a bank receiving small deposits and holding them in interest-bearing accounts.

saviour, savior *n* a person who saves another from harm or danger; (*with cap*) Jesus Christ.

savory *n* (*pl* **savories**) any of various Mediterranean aromatic plants used as herbs for flavouring.

savoir-faire *n* the skill of knowing the right thing to do; tact.

savour, savor *n* the flavour or smell of something; a distinctive quality. * *vti* to season; to enjoy; to have a specified taste or smell; to smack (of); to appreciate critically.—**savourer, savorer** n.

savoury, savory *adj* having a good taste or smell; spicy, not sweet; reputable. * *n* (*pl* **savouries, savories**) a savoury dish at the beginning or end of dinner; (*pl*) snacks served with drinks.—**savourily, savorily** *adv.*—**savouriness, savoriness** *n*.

savoy (cabbage) *n* a variety of cabbage with wrinkled leaves.

savvy *vti* (**savvying, savvied**) (*sl*) to understand. * *n* (*sl*) understanding, know-how. * *adj* (**savvier, savviest**) (*sl*) shrewd.

saw[1] *see* **see**[1]

saw[2] *n* a tool with a toothed edge for cutting wood, etc. * *vti* (**sawing, sawed**, *pp* **sawed** *or* **sawn**) to cut or shape with a saw; to use a saw; to make a to-and-fro motion.—**sawer** *n*.

saw[3] *n* a wise saying, a proverb.

sawbill *n* a large, diving, fish-eating duck with a long narrow bill with serrated edges.

sawbones *n* (*sl*) a doctor or surgeon.

sawbuck *n* a sawhorse.

sawdust *n* fine particles of wood caused by sawing.

sawed-off *see* **sawn-off.**

sawfish *n* (*pl* **sawfish, sawfishes**) a large ray with a serrated snout.

sawfly *n* (*pl* **sawflies**) any of various insects with a saw-like ovipositor.

sawhorse *n* a trestle, etc on which wood is laid for sawing.

sawmill *n* a mill where timber is cut into logs or planks.

sawn *see* **saw**[2].

sawn-off *adj* (*shotgun*) having the barrel shortened to aid concealment; (*person*) (*sl*) small.—*also* **sawed-off.**

saw set *n* an instrument for setting the teeth of a saw by bending each tooth to the left or right alternately.

sawyer *n* a person employed to saw timber.

sax *n* saxophone.

saxatile *adj* saxicolous.

saxe blue *n* a light greyish-blue.—*also adj*.

saxhorn *n* a brass musical instrument resembling a tuba.

saxicolous, saxicoline *adj* living among or on rocks.

saxifrage *n* any of a genus of plants with small flowers and tufted leaves, popular in rock gardens.

Saxon *adj, n* (of) a member of a North German people that settled the southern part of Britain in the 5th-6th century.

saxony *n* a fine wool; cloth made from it.

saxophone *n* a brass wind instrument with a single reed and about twenty finger-keys.—**saxophonic** *adj.*—**saxophonist** *n*.

say *vb* (**says, saying, said**) *vt* to speak, to utter; to state in words; to affirm, declare; to recite; to estimate; to assume. * *vi* to tell; to express in words. * *n* (*pl* **says**) the act of uttering; the right or opportunity to speak; a share in a decision. * *adv* for example. * *interj* expressing admiration, surprise, etc.

saying *n* a common remark; a proverb or adage.

say-so *n* (*inf*) an unfounded assertion; an authorization; the right to authorize.

sayyid, sayid *n* a Muslim title of respect applied to descendants of Mohammed's daughter Fatima.

Sb (*chem symbol*) antimony.

SBKKV *abbr* = space-based kinetic kill vehicle, a system of missiles launched from a satellite.

'sblood *interj* (*obs*) God's blood.

SC *abbr* = South Carolina; Supreme Court.

Sc (*chem symbol*) scandium.

sc. *abbr* = scene; science; scilicet; (*weight*) scruple; (*print*) small capitals.

scab *n* a dry crust on a wound or sore; a plant disease characterized by crustaceous spots; a worker who refuses to join a strike or who replaces a striking worker. * *vi* (**scabbing, scabbed**) to form a scab; to be covered with scabs; to work as a scab.—**scabby** *adj*.

scabbard *n* a sheath for a sword or dagger. * *vt* to sheathe.

scabies *n* a contagious, itching skin disease.

scabiosa *n* any of a genus of Mediterranean plants with tightly clustered blue, red or white flowers.—*also* **scabious**.

scabious[1] *adj* covered with scabs; of or resembling scabies.

scabious[2] *n* a scabiosa.

scabrous *adj* (*surface*) rough, scaly; indecent, offensive; intractable, difficult to manage.—**scabrously** *adv*.—**scabrousness** *n*.

scaffold *n* a raised platform for the execution of a criminal; capital punishment; scaffolding.

scaffolding *n* a temporary framework of wood and metal for use by workmen constructing a building, etc; materials for a scaffold.

scalable *adj* able to be scaled or climbed.

scalar *adj* (*math*) having magnitude but not direction. * *n* a scalar quantity, eg time, mass.

scalar product *n* a scalar produced by multiplying together the magnitudes of two vectors and the cosine of the angle between them.

scalawag *n* (*inf*) a rascal; a scamp; a Southern white who supported the Republicans after the American Civil War.—*also* **scallawag, scallywag**.

scald *vt* to burn with hot liquid or steam; to heat almost to boiling point; to immerse in boiling water (to sterilize). * *n* an injury caused by hot liquid or steam.

scale[1] *n* (*pl*) a machine or instrument for weighing; one of the pans or the tray of a set of scales; (*pl*) (*with cap*) Libra, the seventh sign of the zodiac. * *vti* to weigh in a set of scales; to have a specified weight on a set of scales.

scale[2] *n* one of the thin plates covering a fish or reptile; a flake (of dry skin); an incrustation on teeth, etc. * *vti* to remove the scales from; to flake off.

scale[3] *n* a graduated measure; an instrument so marked; (*math*) the basis for a numerical system, 10 being that in general use; (*mus*) a series of tones from the keynote to its octave, in order of pitch; the proportion that a map, etc, bears to what it represents; a series of degrees classified by size, amount, etc; relative scope or size. * *vt* (*wall*) to go up or over; (*model*) to make or draw to scale; to increase or decrease in size.

scaled *adj* (*reptile, etc*) covered with or having scales.

scale insect *n* any of various small insects that feed on host plants and secrete a waxy covering for protection.

scalene *adj* (*geom*) having three sides of unequal length. * *n* a scalene triangle.

scallawag, scallywag *see* **scalawag**.

scallion *n* a young onion with a small bulb and long shoots eaten raw in salads, a spring onion or shallot.

scallop *n* an edible shellfish with two fluted, fan-shaped shells; one of a series of curves in an edging. * *vt* to cut into scallops.—**scalloped** *adj*.

scalp *n* the skin covering the skull, usu covered with hair. * *vti* to cut the scalp from; to criticize sharply; (*inf*) (*tickets, etc*) to buy and resell at higher prices.

scalpel *n* a short, thin, very sharp knife used esp for surgery.

scaly *adj* (**scalier, scaliest**) (*reptile etc*) like or covered with scales.—**scaliness** *n*.

scaly anteater *n* a pangolin.

scamp *n* a rascal; a mischievous child.

scamper *vi* to run away quickly or playfully. * *n* a brisk or playful run or movement.

scampi *n* a dish of large shrimps or prawns cooked in breadcrumbs or prepared with a flavoured dressing.

scan *vb* (**scanning, scanned**) *vt* (*page etc*) to look through quickly; to scrutinize; (*med*) to examine with a radiological device; (*TV*) to pass an electronic beam over; (*radar*) to detect with an electronic beam; (*poem*) to conform to a rhythmical pattern; to check for recorded data by means of a mechanical or electronic device; (*human body*) to make a scan of in a scanner. * *vi* to analyse the pattern of verse. * *n* the act of scanning or an instance of being scanned.

scandal *n* a disgraceful event or action; talk arising from immoral behaviour; a feeling of moral outrage; the thing or person causing this; disgrace; malicious gossip.

scandalize *vt* to shock the moral feelings of; to defame.—**scandalization** *n*.—**scandalizer** *n*.

scandalmonger *n* a person who spreads scandal or malicious gossip.—**scandalmongering** *n*.

scandalous *adj* causing scandal; shameful; spreading slander.—**scandalously** *adv*.—**scandalousness** *n*.

Scandinavian *adj* of or pertaining to Scandinavia, the region comprising Norway, Sweden, and Denmark, and sometimes Iceland, or its people. * *n* a native or inhabitant of Scandinavia.

scandium *n* a rare metallic element present in small quantities in various minerals.

scanner *n* a person or thing that scans; an electronic device that monitors or scans; a device for receiving or transmitting radar signals; a device for scanning the human body to obtain an image of an internal part.

scanning electron microscope *n* an electron microscope which scans an object to produce a three-dimensional image.

scansion *n* the analysis of verse to show its metre.

scant *adj* limited; meagre; insufficient; scanty; grudging.

scantling *n* a small piece of timber; the dimensions of timber and stone for a building or of a component for a ship or aircraft; a small quantity.

scanty *adj* (**scantier, scantiest**) barely adequate; insufficient; small.—**scantily** *adv*.—**scantiness** *n*.

scapegoat *n* a person who bears the blame for others; one who is the object of irrational hostility.

scapegrace *n* a graceless, hare-brained person; an incorrigible scamp.

scapula *n* (*pl* **scapulae**) the shoulder blade.

scapular *adj* of or relating to the scapula. * *n* a monastic robe worn in various Christian religious orders, consisting of a wide piece of cloth worn over the shoulders and hanging down at the front and back; any of the feathers along the base of a bird's wing.

scar[1] *n* a mark left after the healing of a wound or sore; a blemish resulting from damage or wear. * *vti* (**scarring, scarred**) to mark with or form a scar.

scar[2] *n* a protruding or isolated rock; a precipitous crag; a rocky part of a hillside.

scarab *n* a dung-beetle held to be sacred in ancient Egypt; a gem or seal in the shape of this.

scarabaeid *n* any of a family of beetles including the dung beetle.—*also adj.*

scarce *adj* not in abundance; hard to find; rare.—**scarceness** *n.*

scarcely *adv* hardly, only just; probably not or certainly not.

scarcity *n* (**scarcities**) the state of being scarce; a dearth, deficiency.

scare *vti* to startle; to frighten or become frightened; to drive away by frightening. * *n* a sudden fear; a period of general fear; a false alarm.

scarecrow *n* a wooden figure dressed in clothes for scaring birds from crops; a thin or tattered person; something frightening but harmless.

scaremonger *n* a person who causes fear or panic by spreading rumours; an alarmist.

scarf *n* (*pl* **scarves**) a rectangular or square piece of cloth worn around the neck, shoulders or head for warmth or decoration.

scarfskin *n* the outer layer of skin; cuticle.

scarify *vt* (**scarifying, scarified**) to make cuts in, to scratch; to criticize savagely; to loosen the surface of (soil); to hasten germination by softening the wall (of a hard seed).—**scarification** *n.*

scarlatina *n* scarlet fever.

scarlet *n* a bright red with a tinge of orange; scarlet cloth or clothes. * *adj* scarlet coloured; immoral or sinful.

scarlet fever *n* an acute contagious disease marked by a sore throat, fever, and a scarlet rash.

scarlet pimpernel *n* a plant with red, purple or white flowers that close in dull weather.

scarlet runner *n* a climbing bean plant with scarlet flowers and elongated edible pods.—*also* **runner bean**.

scarlet woman *n* (*arch*) a prostitute.

scarp *n* a low steep slope; the inner face of a ditch in a fortification.

scarper *vi* (*inf*) to run away.

scarves *see* **scarf**.

scary *adj* (**scarier, scariest**) frightening, alarming.—**scariness** *n.*

scat[1] *vi* (**scatting, scatted**) (*inf*) to leave hastily.

scat[2] *n* (*jazz*) a form of improvised singing without words. * *vi* (**scatting, scatted**) to sing in this way.

scathing *adj* bitterly critical; cutting, withering.—**scathingly** *adv.*

scatology *n* the scientific study of fossil and human excrement; a preoccupation with excrement or obscenity.—**scatological** *adj.*

scatter *vti* to throw loosely about; to sprinkle; to dissipate; to put or take to flight; to disperse; to occur at random. * *n* a scattering or sprinkling.

scatterbrain *n* a frivolous, heedless person.—**scatterbrained** *adj.*

scattered *adj* dispersed widely, spaced out; straggling.

scattering *n* a small amount spread over a large area; a dispersion.

scatty *adj* (**scattier, scattiest**) (*inf*) thoughtless, absentminded, crazy.—**scattily** *adv.*—**scattiness** *n.*

scaup (duck) *n* a diving duck of Europe and America.

scavenge *vi* to gather things discarded by others; (*animal*) to eat decaying matter.—**scavenger** *n.*

ScB *abbr* = Bachelor of Science.

ScD *abbr* = Doctor of Science.

scenario *n* (*pl* **scenarios**) an outline of events, real or imagined; the plot or script of a film, etc.

scene *n* the place in which anything occurs; the place in which the action of a play or a story occurs; a section of a play, a division of an act; the stage of a theatre; a painted screen, etc, used on this; an unseemly display of strong emotion; a landscape; surroundings; a place of action; (*inf*) an area of interest or activity (eg *the music scene*).

scene dock *n* (*theatre*) a storage area for scenery near the stage.

scenery *n* (*pl* **sceneries**) painted screens, etc, used to represent places, as in a play, film, etc; an aspect of a landscape, esp of beautiful or impressive countryside.

scenic *adj* relating to natural scenery; picturesque; of or used on the stage.—**scenically** *adv.*

scenic railway *n* a miniature railway at an amusement park, etc.

scent *n* a perfume; an odour left by an animal, by which it can be tracked; the sense of smell; a line of pursuit or discovery. * *vt* to recognize by the sense of smell; to track by smell; to impart an odour to, to perfume; to get wind of, to detect.

scented *adj* perfumed.

sceptic *n* a person who questions opinions generally accepted; a person who doubts religious doctrines, an agnostic; an adherent of scepticism.—*also* **skeptic**.

sceptical *adj* doubting; questioning.—*also* **skeptical**.—**sceptically, skeptically** *adv.*

scepticism *n* an attitude of questioning criticism, doubt; (*philos*) the doctrine that absolute knowledge is unattainable.—*also* **skepticism**.

sceptre, scepter *n* the staff of office held by a monarch on a ceremonial occasion; sovereignty.

schedule *n* a timetable; a list, inventory or tabulated statement; a timed plan for a project. * *vt* to make a schedule; to plan.

scheelite *n* a mineral consisting of calcium tungstate.

schema *n* (*pl* **schemata**) a plan or diagram.

schematic *adj* of or like a scheme or diagram.—**schematically** *adv.*

schematize *vt* to form into or express as a scheme.—**schematization** *n.*

scheme *n* a plan; a project; a systematic arrangement; a diagram; an underhand plot. * *vti* to devise or plot.—**schemer** *n.*

scheming *adj* cunning; intriguing.

scherzando *adj, adv* (*mus*) to be performed lightheartedly. * *n* (*pl* **scherzandi**) a piece of music played in this manner.

scherzo *n* (*pl* **scherzos, scherzi**) a lively musical passage or movement, usu in triple time.

schilling *n* the standard monetary unit of Austria.

schism *n* a division or separation into two parties, esp of a church; the sin of this; discord, disharmony.

schismatic, schismatical *adj* of or creating schism. * *n* a person who creates schism or supports schism.—**schismatically** *adv.*

schist *n* a type of crystalline rock in thin layers.—**schistose** *adj.*

schistosome *n* any of a genus of parasitic worms that infest the blood vessels of humans and animals.

schistosomiasis *n* a disease caused by infestation with schistosomes.

schizo *n* (*pl* **schizos**) (*inf*) a schizophrenic person. * *adj* schizophrenic.

schizo-, schiz- *prefix* split, division.

schizocarp *n* a dry fruit that splits into single-seeded parts.

schizoid *adj* mildly schizophrenic.—*also n.*

schizomycete *n* any microscopic organism such as a bacterium.

schizophrenia *n* a mental disorder characterized by withdrawal from reality and deterioration of the personality; the presence of mutually contradictory qualities or parts.—**schizophrenic** *adj, n.*

schlieren *n* (*physics*) visible streaks in a transparent medium caused by variations in its density.

schmaltz, schmalz *n* overly sentimental music, art, film, etc.—**schmaltzy, schmalzy** *adj.*

schnapps *n* (*pl* **schnapps**) a Dutch spirit distilled from potatoes; (*Germany*) any strong spirit.

schnauzer *n* an orig German breed of terrier with a short wiry coat.

schnitzel *n* a cutlet of veal.

schnorkle *see* **snorkel**.

schnozzle *n* (*sl*) nose.

scholar *n* a pupil, a student; a learned person; the holder of a scholarship.

scholarly *adj* learned, erudite, academic.

scholarship *n* an annual grant to a scholar or student, usu won by competitive examination; learning, academic achievement.

scholastic *adj* of or relating to schools, scholars, or education; academic.—**scholastically** *adv.*

school[1] *n* a shoal of porpoises, whales, or other aquatic animals of one kind swimming together.

school[2] *n* an educational establishment; its teachers and students; a regular session of teaching; formal education, schooling; a particular division of a university; a place or means of discipline; a group of thinkers, artists, writers, holding similar principles. * *vt* to train; to teach; to control or discipline.

schoolboy *n* a boy who attends school.

schoolchild *n* (*pl* **schoolchildren**) a child who attends school.

schoolgirl *n* a girl who attends school.

schoolhouse *n* a building used as a school.

schooling *n* instruction in school.

schoolmaster *n* a man who teaches in school.

schoolmate *n* a companion at school.—*also* **schoolfellow**.

schoolmistress *n* a woman who teaches in school.

schoolroom *n* a room in which pupils are taught, as in a school.

schoolteacher *n* a person who teaches in school.

schooner *n* a sailing ship with two or more masts rigged with fore-and-aft sails; a large drinking glass for sherry or beer.

schottische *n* (music for) a type of slow dance resembling a polka.

schuss *n* (*skiing*) a fast straight downhill run. * *vi* to ski down this.

sci. *abbr* = science; scientific.

sciatic *adj* of the hip.

sciatica *n* pain along the sciatic nerve, esp in the back of the thigh; (*loosely*) pain in the lower back or adjacent parts.

sciatic nerve *n* a long nerve running from the pelvic region to the back of the thigh.

science *n* knowledge gained by systematic experimentation and analysis, and the formulation of general principles; a branch of this; skill or technique.

science fiction *n* highly imaginative fiction typically involving actual or projected scientific phenomena.

science park *n* an area where scientific discoveries are translated into commercial products and applications.

scientific *adj* of or concerned with science; based on or using the principles and methods of science; systematic and exact; having or showing expert skill.—**scientifically** *adv.*

scientism *n* the use of scientific methods; the inappropriate use of or reliance on scientific methods.

scientist *n* a specialist in a branch of science, as in chemistry, etc.

Scientology *n* (*trademark*) a cult movement founded in 1951.

sci-fi *n* science fiction.

scilicet *adv* namely, that is to say.

scilla *n* any of a genus of plants with small pink, blue or white flowers grown from bulbs.

scimitar *n* an Oriental curved sword, broadest near the point.

scintigraphy *n* the production of images of internal body parts by detecting high-energy particles from a radioactive tracer administered to a patient.

scintilla *n* an iota, tiny amount.

scintillate *vti* to give off sparks; to sparkle.—**scintillation** *n.*

scintillating *adj* sparkling; amusing.

scintillation counter *n* an instrument for registering the intensity of a radioactive source by recording the flashes of light produced by the impact of emitted photons on a phospor.

scion *n* a shoot for grafting; a young member of a family, a descendant.

scirrhus *n* (*pl* **scirrhi, scirrhuses**) a cancerous tumour consisting of fibrous tissue.

scission *n* the act of cutting or dividing; a cut, divide, or split.

scissor *vt* to cut with scissors, to clip. * *npl* a tool for cutting paper, hair, etc, consisting of two fastened pivoted blades whose edges slide past each other; a gymnastic feat in which the leg movements resemble the opening and closing of scissors.

scissors kick *n* (*swimming*) a kick in which the legs move from the hip in a scissoring motion.

sciurine *adj* of or resembling a family of rodents which include squirrels and marmots.

SCLC *abbr* = Southern Christian Leadership Conference.

sclera *n* the opaque outer covering of the eyeball excluding the cornea.

sclerenchyma *n* a tissue forming the hard fibrous parts of plants.

sclero-, scler- *prefix* hardness.

scleroderma *n* (*med*) a chronic disease in women causing thickening and hardening of the skin.

sclerodermatous *adj* (*zool*) covered with a hard layer of tissue, eg scales.

sclerosis *n* a pathological hardening of body tissue; a disease marked by this.

sclerotic *adj* pertaining to the sclera; of or affected by sclerosis. * *n* the sclera.

sclerous *adj* hard, bony.

scoff[1] vti to jeer (at) or mock. * n an expression or object of derision; mocking words, a taunt.

scoff[2] vt (sl) to eat quickly and greedily.

scold vi to reprove angrily; to tell off.

scolding n a harsh reprimand.

scoliosis n (med) lateral curvature of the spine.

scollop see scallop.

scombroid n any member of a suborder of spiny-finned marine fishes used for food, such as the mackerel and tuna.—also adj.

sconce[1] n a bracket on a wall for holding candles or electric lights.

sconce[2] n a defensive fortification, a bulwark.

scone n a small, round cake made from flour and fat which is baked and spread with butter, etc.

scoop n a small shovel-like utensil as for taking up flour, ice cream, etc; the bucket of a dredge, etc; the act of scooping or the amount scooped up at one time; (inf) a piece of exclusive news; (inf) the advantage gained in being the first to publish or broadcast this. * vt to shovel, lift or hollow out with a scoop; (inf) to obtain as a scoop; (inf: rival newspaper etc) to forestall with a news item.

scoot vti to run quickly; to hurry (off).

scooter n a child's two-wheeled vehicle with a footboard and steering handle; a motor scooter.

scope n the opportunity to use one's abilities; extent; range; an instrument for viewing.

scopolamine n an alkaloid extracted from certain plants, used as a sedative and for travel sickness.—also hyoscine.

scorbutic adj of, suffering from, or resembling scurvy.—scorbutically adv.

scorch vti to burn or be burned on the surface; to wither from over-exposure to heat; to singe; (inf) to drive or cycle furiously.

scorcher n (inf) a very hot day.

scorching adj (inf: weather) very hot; scathing.

score n the total number of points made in a game or examination; a notch or scratch; a line indicating deletion or position; a group of twenty; a written copy of a musical composition showing the different parts; the music composed for a film; a grievance for settling; a reason or motive; (inf) the real facts; a bill or reckoning; (pl) an indefinite, large number. * vt to mark with cuts; (mus) to arrange in a score, to orchestrate; to gain or record points, as in a game; to evaluate in testing. * vi to make points, as in a game; to keep the score of a game; to gain an advantage, a success, etc; (sl) to be successful in seduction; (with off) to get the better of someone.—scorer n.

scoreboard n a large manually or electronically operated board showing the score in a game or match.

scorecard n (golf, etc) a card on which scores are recorded.

scorn n extreme contempt or disdain; the object of this. * vt to treat with contempt, to despise; to reject or refuse as unworthy.—scornful adj.—scornfully adv.

Scorpio n the eighth sign of the zodiac in astrology, operative October 23-November 21.—Scorpionic adj.

scorpion n a small, tropical, insect-like animal with pincers and a jointed tail with a poisonous sting.

scorpion fish n any of a genus of fish with poisonous spines on the dorsal fins.

Scot n a native or inhabitant of Scotland; a member of a Celtic people from Ireland who settled in northern Britain in the 5th-6th centuries.

scotch vt (a rumour) to stamp out.

Scotch n whisky made in Scotland.

Scotch broth n a thick soup made from beef or mutton with vegetables and pearl barley.

Scotch egg n a hard-boiled egg enclosed in sausagemeat, coated in breadcrumbs, and fried.

Scotchman n (pl Scotchmen) a Scotsman.—Scotchwoman (pl Scotchwomen) nf.

Scotch mist n a dense, wet mist; fine drizzle.

Scotch terrier n a Scottish terrier.

scoter n (pl scoters, scoter) a large sea duck with black plumage.

scot-free adj without penalty or injury.

Scotland Yard n the headquarters of the London metropolitan police force.

scotoma n (pl scotomas, scotomata) a blind spot in the visual field.

Scots adj of or pertaining to Scotland, its law, money, and people, and the Scots language. * n the dialect of English developed in Lowland Scotland.

Scotsman n (pl Scotsmen) a native or inhabitant of Scotland.—Scotswoman n (pl Scotswomen) nf.

Scots pine n (the wood of) a European pine with needle-like leaves.

Scotticism n a Scottish word or idiom.

Scottie n (inf) a Scotsman; a Scottish terrier.

Scottish adj of or relating to Scotland and its people.

Scottish deerhound n a large rough-haired greyhound, a deerhound.

Scottish National Party n a political party seeking independence for Scotland.

Scottish terrier n a small terrier with short legs and a wiry coat.

scoundrel n a rascal; a dishonest person.

scour[1] vt to clean by rubbing with an abrasive cloth; to flush out with a current of water; to purge. * n the act or process of scouring; a place scoured by running water; scouring action (as of a glacier); damage done by scouring action.

scour[2] vt to hasten over or along, to range over, esp in search or pursuit.

scourge n a whip; a means of inflicting punishment; a person who harasses and causes widespread and great affliction; a pest. * vt to flog; to punish harshly.

Scouse n (inf) a person from Liverpool; the dialect of Liverpool.—also adj.

scout n a person, plane, etc, sent to observe the enemy's strength, etc; a person employed to find new talent or survey a competitor, etc; (with cap) a member of the Scouting Association, an organization for young people. * vti to reconnoitre; to go in search of (something).

scouting n the act of one who scouts; (with cap) the activities of the Scouting Association.

Scouting Association n (formerly Boy Scouts, Girl Guides) an organization to develop in young people self-reliance and initiative, moral and physical courage and a courteous spirit.

scoutmaster n (formerly) the adult leader of a troop of Scouts.

scow n an unpowered flat-bottomed boat for carrying freight, refuse, etc.

scowl n a contraction of the brows in an angry or threatening manner; a sullen expression. * vi to make a scowl; to look sullen.

Scrabble n (trademark) a game in which words are formed from individual lettered tiles on a grid.

scrabble vi to scratch or grope about; to struggle; to scramble. * n a repeated scratching or clawing; a scramble; a scribble.

scrag n a scrawny person or animal; the lean end of a neck of mutton or veal; (loosely) neck.

scraggly adj (scragglier, scraggliest) untidy, uneven.

scraggy adj (scraggier, scraggiest) thin and bony, gaunt.

scram vi (scramming, scrammed) (sl) to get out, to go away at once.

scramble vi to move or climb hastily on all fours; to scuffle or struggle for something; to move with urgency or panic. * vt to mix haphazardly; to stir (slightly beaten eggs) while cooking; (transmitted signals) to make unintelligible in transit. * n a hard climb or advance; a disorderly struggle; a rapid emergency take-off of fighter planes; a motorcycle rally over rough ground.—scrambler n.

scrap[1] n a small piece; a fragment of discarded material; (pl) bits of food. * adj in the form of pieces, leftovers, etc; used and discarded. * vt (scrapping, scrapped) to discard; to make into scraps.

scrap[2] n (inf) a fight or quarrel. * vi (scrapping, scrapped) to have a scrap.

scrapbook n a book for pasting clippings, etc, in.

scrape vt to rub with a sharp or abrasive object so as to clean, smooth or remove; to eke out or to be economical; to amass in small portions; to draw along with a grating or vibration; to get narrowly past, to graze; to draw back the foot in making a bow; (with together) to save or collect with difficulty. * vi (with through) to manage or succeed with difficulty or by a slim margin. * n the act of scraping; a grating sound; an abrasion, scratch; an awkward predicament.

scraper n an instrument for scraping; a grating or edge for scraping mud from boots.

scraperboard n a board with a black surface which can be scraped off with a special tool to form a design.

scrapheap n a pile of discarded material or things.

scraping n a piece scraped off.

scrappy adj (scrappier, scrappiest) disjointed; fragmentary; full of gaps.—scrappily adv.—scrappiness n.

scratch vt to mark with a sharp point; to scrape with the nails or claws; to rub to relieve an itch; to chafe; to write awkwardly; (writing etc) to strike out; to withdraw from a race, etc. * vi to use nails or claws to tear or dig. * n the act of scratching; a mark or sound made by this; a slight injury; a starting line for a race; a scribble. * adj taken at random, haphazard, impromptu; without a handicap.

scratch pad n a notebook.

scratch video n a collage of images from existing television or cinema film.

scratchy adj (scratchier, scratchiest) making a scratching noise; uneven, ragged.—scratchily adv.—scratchiness n.

scrawl n careless or illegible handwriting; a scribble. * vti to draw or write carelessly.

scrawny adj (scrawnier, scrawniest) skinny; bony.—scrawniness n.

scream vti to utter a piercing cry, as of pain, fear, etc; to shout; to shriek. * n a sharp, piercing cry; (inf) a very funny person or thing.

scree n loose shifting stones; a slope covered with these.

screech n a harsh, high-pitched cry. * vti to utter a screech, to shriek.

screed n a long, tedious letter or speech; an informal piece of writing.

screen n a movable partition or framework to conceal, divide, or protect; a shelter or shield from heat, danger or view; an electronic display (as in a television set, computer terminal, etc); a surface on which films, slides, etc are projected; the motion picture industry; a coarse wire mesh over a window or door to keep out insects; a sieve. * vt to conceal or shelter; to grade by passing through a screen; to separate according to skill, etc; (a film) to show on a screen.

screening n a showing of a film; a metal or plastic mesh, as for window screens; the refuse matter after sieving.

screenplay n a story written in a form suitable for a film.

screenwriter n a person who writes screenplays.

screw n a metal cylinder or cone with a spiral thread around it for fastening things by being turned; any spiral thing like this; a twist or turn of a screw; a twist of paper; pressure; a propeller with revolving blades on a shaft. * vt to fasten, tighten etc with a screw; to oppress; to extort, to cheat out of something due; (sl, vulg) to have sexual intercourse with; (with up) to gather (courage, etc). * vi to go together or come apart by being turned like a screw; to twist or turn with a writhing movement; (sl, vulg) to have sexual intercourse; (with up) to bungle.

screwball n (sl) an odd or eccentric person. * adj whimsical, zany.

screwdriver n a tool like a blunt chisel for turning screws; a drink of vodka and orange juice.

screwed adj (sl) drunk.

screw eye n a metal screw with a ring instead of a slotted head.

screw pine n any of various tropical plants with slender stems and clusters of spiral leaves.

screw propeller n an early form of propeller based on the Archimedes screw.

screw top n a cap that screws onto the top of a bottle or other container; a bottle, etc having this.

screwy adj (screwier, screwiest) (sl) eccentric, odd.—screwiness n.

scribble vti to draw or write hastily or carelessly, to scrawl; to be a writer. * n hasty writing, a scrawl.—scribbler n.

scribe n a person who copies (documents); an author or journalist; (Bible) an expounder of Jewish law. * vt to draw a line on by cutting with a pointed instrument.

scriber n a pointed tool used to score or mark lines (e.g on metal) as guides for cutting.

scrim n a light open-weave fabric used in upholstery, lining, and theatre sets.

scrimmage n a confused struggle; a skirmish; (football) the period between the ball entering play and it being declared dead. * vi to engage in a scrimmage.

scrimp vti to be sparing or frugal (with); to make too small, to skimp.

scrimshank vi (inf) to shirk work, esp military duties.

scrimshaw n carvings made from shells, whalebone, ivory, etc, usu by sailors; the art of producing such carvings.

scrip n a written list; a certificate entitling the holder to a share of company stock.

Script. abbr = Scripture(s).

script n handwriting; a style of writing; the text of a stage play, screenplay or broadcast; a plan of action; (print) type that resembles handwriting. * vt to write a script (for).

scriptural *adj* of or based on the Bible or Scripture.

scripture *n* any sacred writing; (*with cap, often pl*) the Jewish Bible or Old Testament; the Christian Bible or Old and New Testaments. * *adj* contained in or quoted from the Bible.

scriptwriter *n* a writer of screenplays for films, TV, etc; a screenwriter —**scriptwriting** *n*.

scrofula *n* tuberculosis of the lymph glands in the neck.—**scrofulous** *adj*.

scroll *n* a roll of parchment or paper with writing on it; an ornament like this; (*her*) a ribbon with a motto; a list. * *vti* (*comput*) to move text across a screen; to decorate with scrolls.

scroll saw *n* a thin saw for cutting intricate designs.

Scrooge *n* (*also without cap*) a miserly, miserable person (after the character in *A Christmas Carol* by Charles Dickens).

scrotum *n* (*pl* **scrota, scrotums**) the pouch of skin containing the testicles.

scrounge *vti* (*inf*) to seek or obtain (something) for nothing.—**scrounger** *n*.

scrub[1] *n* an arid area of stunted trees and shrubs; such vegetation; anything small or mean. * *adj* small, stunted, inferior, etc.

scrub[2] *vti* (**scrubbing, scrubbed**) to clean vigorously, to scour; to rub hard; (*inf*) to remove, to cancel. * *n* the act of scrubbing.

scrubber *n* a person or thing that scrubs; (*sl*) a promiscuous woman.

scrubby *adj* (**scrubbier, scrubbiest**) stunted; paltry; unkempt.—**scrubbily** *adv*.—**scrubbiness** *n*.

scruff[1] *n* the back of the neck, the nape.

scruff[2] *n* (*inf*) a shabbily dressed person.

scruffy *adj* (**scruffier, scruffiest**) shabby; unkempt.—**scruffily** *adv*.—**scruffiness** *n*.

scrum *n* a scrummage.

scrum half *n* (*rugby*) (the position held by) the player who puts the ball into the scrum.

scrummage *n* (*Rugby football*) a play consisting of a tussle between rival forwards in a compact mass for possession of the ball. * *vi* to form a scrum(mage).

scrump *vt* (*dial*) to steal apples from an orchard or garden.

scrumptious *adj* (*inf*) delicious; very pleasing.—**scrumptiously** *adv*.—**scrumptiousness** *n*.

scrunch *vti* to crumple, esp the hair when drying; to crunch; to be crumpled or crunched. * *n* a crunching sound; the act of scrunching.

scruple *n* (*usu pl*) a moral principle or belief causing one to doubt or hesitate about a course of action. * *vti* to hesitate owing to scruples.

scrupulous *adj* careful; conscientious; thorough.—**scrupulously** *adv*.—**scrupulousness** *n*.

scrutineer *n* a person who scrutinizes, esp an inspector of ballot papers.

scrutinize *vti* to look closely at, to examine narrowly; to make a scrutiny.—**scrutinizer** *n*.

scrutiny *n* (*pl* **scrutinies**) a careful examination; a critical gaze; an official inspection of votes cast in an election.

scuba *n* a diver's apparatus with compressed-air tanks for breathing underwater.

scud *vti* (**scudding, scudded**) to go along swiftly; to be driven before the wind. * *n* an act of scudding; light clouds, etc, driven by wind; a type of missile.

scuff *vti* to drag the feet, to shuffle; to wear or mark the surface of by doing this.

scuffle *n* a confused fight; the sound of shuffling. * *vi* to fight confusedly; to move by shuffling.

scull *n* an oar worked from side to side over the stern of a boat; a light rowing boat for racing. * *vti* to propel with a scull.

scullery *n* (*pl* **sculleries**) a room for storage or kitchen work, such as washing dishes, etc.

sculpt *vt* to carve, to sculpture.

sculptor *n* a person skilled in sculpture.

sculptress *n* a woman skilled in sculpture.

sculpture *n* the art of carving wood or forming clay, stone, etc, into figures, statues, etc; a three-dimensional work of art; a sculptor's work. * *vt* to carve, adorn or portray with sculptures; to shape, mould or form like sculpture.—**sculptural** *adj*.

scum *n* a thin layer of impurities on top of a liquid; refuse; despicable people.

scumbag *n* (*sl*) a disgusting or despicable person.

scumble *vt* (*drawing and painting*) to soften lines or colours by applying a thin coat of opaque colour. * *n* the upper layer of colour applied for this purpose.

scunner *n* (*Scot*) disgust. * *vti* to feel or cause to feel disgust.—**scunnered** *adj*

scupper *n* a hole in a ship's side that lets water run from the deck into the sea. * *vt* (*sl*) to sink deliberately; to disable.

scurf *n* small flakes of dead skin (as dandruff); any scaly coating.

scurrilous *adj* abusive; grossly offensive.

scurry *vi* (**scurrying, scurried**) to hurry with quick, short steps, to scamper. * *n* (*pl* **scurries**) a bustle; a flurry (as of snow).

scurvy *n* a disease caused by a deficiency of vitamin C. * *adj* base; contemptible.

scut *n* the short tail of certain animals, such as the deer or hare.

scute, scutum *n* an external scales or plate on the bodies of animals such as the armadillo, turtle, etc.

scutellum *n* (*pl* **scutella**) any of the small horny scales or plates on a plant or animal.

scuttle[1] *vi* to run quickly; to hurry away. * *n* a short swift run; a hurried pace.

scuttle[2] *n* a bucket with a lip for storing coal.

scuttle[3] *n* (*naut*) a hatchway, a hole with a cover in a ship's deck or side. * *vt* to sink a ship by making holes in the bottom.

scuttlebut *n* (*formerly*) a cask containing drinking water on the deck of a ship; (*sl*) gossip.

scuzzy *adj* (**scuzzier, scuzziest**) (*sl*) filthy, squalid.

scythe *n* a two-handed implement with a large curved blade for cutting grass, etc. * *vti* to cut with a scythe; to mow down.

SD *abbr* = South Dakota.

SDI *abbr* = Strategic Defense Initiative.

SE *abbr* = southeast(ern).

Se (*chem symbol*) selenium.

sea *n* the ocean; a section of this; a vast expanse of water; a heavy wave, the swell of the ocean; something like the sea in size; the seafaring life. * *adj* marine, of the sea.

sea anchor *n* a device dragged behind a vessel to slow the rate of drifting or keep it heading into the wind.

sea anemone *n* any of various solitary brightly coloured polyps with a ring of petal-like tentacles surrounding the mouth.

sea bass *n* any of numerous American marine fishes with a long body and a spiny dorsal fin.

seaboard *n, adj* (land) bordering on the sea.

seaborne *adj* conveyed by the sea; carried on a ship.

sea bream *n* any of numerous marine food fishes of European seas.

sea breeze *n* a wind that blows from the sea to the land.

sea change *n* a radical transformation.

seacock *n* a valve in the hull of a vessel through which water can pass in or out.

sea cow *see* **dugong**.

sea cucumber *n* an echinoderm with an elongated body, leathery skin and an oral ring of tentacles at one end.

sea dog *n* an old sailor.

sea eagle *n* any of various fish-eating eagles.

seafarer *n* a sailor; a person who travels by sea.

seafaring *n* travelling by sea, esp the work of a sailor.— *also adj.*

seafood *n* edible fish or shellfish from the sea.

sea front *n* the waterfront of a seaside place.

sea-green *adj, n* (a) pale bluish green.

seagoing *adj* (*ship*) made for use on the open sea.

seagull *n* a gull.

sea holly *n* a European coastal plant with blue flowers.

sea horse *n* a small bony-plated fish with a horselike head and neck and a long tail, that swims in an upright position; in fable, a horse with the tail of a fish.

sea kale *n* a European coastal plant with fleshy leaves and edible shoots.

seal[1] *n* an engraved stamp for impressing wax, lead, etc; wax, lead, etc, so impressed; that which authenticates or pledges; a device for closing or securing tightly. * *vt* to fix a seal to; to close tightly or securely; to shut up; to mark as settled, to confirm.

seal[2] *n* an aquatic mammal with four webbed flippers; the fur of some seals; a dark brown. * *vi* to hunt seals.

sea lane *n* a route for ships.

sealant *n* a thing that seals, as wax, etc; a substance for stopping a leak, making watertight, etc.

sea lavender *n* any of a genus of coastal plants with white, pink or purple flowers.

sealed-beam *adj* (*car headlight*) having the reflector incorporated in the lamp.

sea legs *npl* (*inf*) the ability to walk steadily on a moving ship and to be free from seasickness.

sealer *n* a person or a ship whose business is hunting seals.

sea level *n* the level of the surface of the sea in relation to the land.

sea lily *n* an echinoderm with a thin elongated body topped by petal-like tentacles.

sealing wax *n* a resinous compound that is plastic when warm and used for sealing letters, etc.

sea lion *n* a large seal of the Pacific Ocean that has a loud roar and, in the male, a mane.

sealskin *n* the fur of a seal; a coat of this.

Sealyham terrier *n* a breed of wire-haired terrier with short legs and a longish, usu white, coat.

seam *n* the line where two pieces of cloth are stitched together; (*geol*) a stratum of coal, oil, etc, between thicker ones; a line or wrinkle. * *vt* to join with a seam; to furrow.

seaman *n* (*pl* **seamen**) a sailor; a naval rank.

seamanship *n* the skill of handling, working and navigating a ship.

sea mile *n* a nautical mile.

sea mouse *n* a marine worm with a broad body covered in hairlike bristles.

seamstress *n* a woman who sews for a living.

seamy *adj* (**seamier, seamiest**) unpleasant or sordid.

seance, séance *n* a meeting of spiritualists to try to communicate with the dead.

sea otter *n* a large marine otter of North Pacific coasts that feeds on shellfish.

sea pink *n* the plant thrift.

seaplane *n* an aeroplane with floats that allow it to take off from and land on water.

seaport *n* a port, harbour or town accessible to oceangoing ships.

sear *vt* to burn or scorch the surface of; to brand with a heated iron; to wither up.

search *vi* to look around to find something; to explore. * *vt* to examine or inspect closely; to probe into. * *n* the act of searching; an investigation; a quest.— **searcher** *n.*

searching *adj* keen, piercing; examining thoroughly.— **searchingly** *adv.*

searchlight *n* a powerful ray of light projected by an apparatus on a swivel; the apparatus.

search party *n* a group of people organized to locate a missing person or thing.

search warrant *n* a legal document that authorizes a police search.

seascape *n* a picture of a scene at sea.

Sea Scout *n* a member of a Scout troop specializing in sailing, canoeing, diving, etc.

sea serpent *n* a legendary sea-dwelling monster resembling a snake or dragon.

seashell *n* the discarded or empty shell of a marine mollusc.

seashore *n* land beside the sea or between high and low water marks; the beach.

seasick *adj* affected with nausea brought on by the motion of a ship.—**seasickness** *n.*

seaside *n* seashore.

sea snail *n* a spiral-shelled marine mollusc, such as a whelk; a small slimy fish with pelvic fins formed into a sucker.

sea snake *n* a venomous snake of tropical waters with an oar-shaped tail.

season *n* one of the four equal parts into which the year is divided: spring, summer, autumn, or winter; a period of time; a time when something is plentiful or in use; a suitable time; (*inf*) a season ticket. * *vt* (*food*) to flavour by adding salt, spices, etc; to make mature or experienced; (*wood*) to dry until ready for use. * *vi* to become experienced.

seasonable *adj* suitable for the season; timely, opportune.—**seasonableness** *n.*—**seasonably** *adv.*

seasonal *adj* of or relating to a particular season.—**seasonally** *adv.*

seasonal affective disorder *n* a state of depression that affects some people in the winter months, thought to be caused by a lack of sunlight.

seasoning *n* salt, spices, etc, used to enhance the flavour of food; the process of making something fit for use.

season ticket *n* a ticket or set of tickets valid for a number of concerts, games, journeys, etc, during a specified period.

seat *n* a piece of furniture for sitting on, such as a chair, bench, etc; the part of a chair on which one sits; the buttocks, the part of the trousers covering them; a way of sitting (on a horse, etc); the chief location, or centre; a part at or forming a base; the right to sit as a member; a parliamentary constituency; a large country house. * *vt* to place on a seat; to provide with seats; to settle.

seatbelt *n* an anchored strap worn in a car or aeroplane to secure a person to a seat.

seated *adj* provided with a seat or seats; fixed, confirmed; located.

seating *n* the arrangement or provision of seats.

SEATO *abbr* = South East Asia Treaty Organization.

sea trout *n* a marine variety of brown trout that migrates to fresh water to spawn.

sea urchin *n* a small marine animal with a round body enclosed in a shell covered with sharp spines.

sea wall *n* a barrier or embankment to prevent erosion by the sea.

seaward *adj* toward the sea. * *adv* toward or in the direction of the sea.—**seawards** *adv*.

seaway *n* an ocean traffic lane; a waterway for seagoing traffic to an inland port.

seaweed *n* a mass of plants growing in or under water; a sea plant, esp a marine alga.

seaworthy *adj* fit to go to sea; able to withstand sea water, watertight.—**seaworthiness** *n*.

sebaceous *adj* of, secreting, containing, or producing oily or fatty matter.

sebaceous glands *npl* the small skin glands that secrete sebum onto the skin surface.

seborrhoea, seborrhea *n* the excessive secretion of sebum.—**seborrhoeic, seborrheic** *adj*.

sebum *n* a fatty substance secreted by the sebaceous glands to lubricate the hair and skin.

SEC *abbr* = Securities and Exchange Commission.

sec¹ *adj* (*wine*) dry; (*champagne*) medium sweet.

sec² *n* (*inf*) a second.

sec³ *abbr* = secant.

sec. *abbr* = second.

secant *n* a trigonometrical function that is the reciprocal of the cosine; a straight line that intersects a curve.

secateurs *npl* a pair of small shears with curved blades for pruning, etc.

secede *vi* to withdraw formally one's membership from a society or organization.—**seceder** *n*.

secession *n* the act or an instance of seceding; a breaking away.—**secessional** *adj*.

seclude *vt* to keep (a person, etc) separate from others; to remove or screen from view.

secluded *adj* private; sheltered; kept from contact with other people.

seclusion *n* the state of being secluded; privacy, solitude.

second *adj* next after first; alternate; another of the same kind; next below the first in rank, value, etc. * *n* a person or thing coming second; another; an article of merchandise not of first quality; an aid or assistant, as to a boxer, duellist; the gear after low gear; one sixtieth of a minute of time or of an angular degree; (*pl*) (*inf*) another helping of food. * *adv* in the second place, group, etc. * *vt* to act as a second (to); (*a motion, resolution, etc*) to support; (*mil*) to place on temporary service elsewhere.

secondary *adj* subordinate; second in rank or importance; in the second stage; derived, not primary; relating to secondary school. * *n* (*pl* **secondaries**) that which is secondary; a delegate, a deputy.—**secondarily** *adv*.

secondary cell *n* a battery that can convert chemical energy to electrical energy by reversible chemical reactions and so be recharged.

secondary colour *n* a colour formed by mixing two primary colours.

secondary emission *n* (*physics*) the emission of secondary electrons from a solid surface due to bombardment by a beam of primary electrons or other elementary particles.

secondary school *n* a school between elementary or primary school and college or university.

secondary sexual characteristic *n* an attribute of a human being or animal that is characteristic of a particular sex but is not directly concerned with reproduction.

second best *adj* next to the best; inferior. * *adv* in second place. * *n* next to the best; an inferior alternative.

second chamber *n* the upper house in a legislative assembly with two chambers.

second childhood *n* dotage, senility.

second class *n* the class next to the first in a classification. * *adj* (second-class) relating to a second class; inferior, mediocre; (*seating, accommodation*) next in price and quality to first class; (*mail*) less expensive and handled more slowly (than first class).

Second Coming *n* (*Christianity*) the return to earth of Christ at the Last Judgment as prophesied.

second cousin *n* a child of the first cousin of one's parent.

second-degree burn *n* a burn which causes blistering of the skin.

second fiddle *n* (the musical part for) a second violin in an orchestra or string quartet; (*inf*) a person of secondary importance.

second hand *n* the moving pointer in a clock or watch that indicates the seconds.

second-hand *adj* bought after use by another; derived, not original.—*also adv*.

secondly *adv* in the second place.

second nature *n* a long-established habit, etc, deeply fixed in a person's nature.

second person *n* that form of a pronoun (as *you*) or verb (as *are*) that refers to the person spoken to.

second-rate *adj* of inferior quality.

second sight *n* the supposed faculty of seeing events before they occur.

second string *n* a reserve or substitute player in a team.

second thought *n* a change in thought or decision after consideration.

second wind *n* a return to regular breathing after a bout of exercise; renewed energy or enthusiasm.

secrecy *n* (*pl* **secrecies**) the state of being secret; the ability to keep secret.

secret *adj* not made public; concealed from others; hidden; private; remote. * *n* something hidden; a mystery; a hidden cause.

secret agent *n* a spy.

secretaire *n* a writing desk with an upper section for books and documents.

secretariat *n* an administrative office or staff, as in a government.

secretary *n* (*pl* **secretaries**) a person employed to deal with correspondence, filing, telephone calls of another or of an association; the head of a state department.—**secretarial** *adj*.

secretary bird *n* a large long-legged African bird of prey that eats mostly snakes.

secretary-general *n* (*pl* **secretaries-general**) the chief administrator of a large organization (eg the United Nations).

secretary of state *n* in the UK, any of various ministers in charge of government departments; (*with caps*) in the US, the minister in charge of foreign affairs.

secrete *vt* to conceal; to hide; (*cell, gland, etc*) to produce and release (a substance) out of blood or sap.

secretion *n* the process of secreting; a substance secreted by an animal or plant.

secretive *adj* given to secrecy; uncommunicative, reticent.—**secretively** *adv.*—**secretiveness** *n.*

secretly *adv* in a secret way; unknown to others.

secretory *adj* having the function of secreting, as a gland.

secret police *n* a police force that operates covertly to suppress political dissent rather than criminal activity.

secret service *n* a government agency that gathers intelligence, infiltrates terrorist or subversive organizations, conducts espionage, etc in the interests of national security.

sect *n* a religious denomination; a group of people united by a common interest or belief; a faction.

sectarian *adj* of or confined to a religious sect; bigoted. * *n* a member or adherent of a sect.

sectarianism *n* devotion to a sect; religious narrowness.

section *n* the act of cutting; a severed or separable part; a division; a distinct portion; a slice; a representation of anything cut through to show its interior; (*geom*) the cutting of a solid by a plane; a plane figure formed by this. * *vti* to cut or separate into sections; to represent in sections; to become separated or cut into parts.

sectional *adj* of a section; made up of several sections; local rather than general in character.—**sectionally** *adv.*

sector *n* (*geom*) a space enclosed by two radii of a circle and the arc they cut off; a distinctive part (as of an economy); a subdivision; (*mil*) an area of activity .

secular *adj* having no connection with religion or the church; worldly.—**secularly** *adv.*

secularize *vt* to change from religious to civil use or control.—**secularization** *n.*

secure *adj* free from danger, safe; stable; firmly held or fixed; confident, assured (of); reliable. * *vt* to make safe; to fasten firmly; to protect; to confine; to fortify; to guarantee; to gain possession of, to obtain.—**securely** *adv.*

security *n* (*pl* **securities**) the state of being secure; a financial guarantee, surety; a pledge for repayment, etc; a protection or safeguard; a certificate of shares or bonds.

Security Council *n* the principal council of the United Nations charged with maintaining world peace.

security guard *n* a person employed to protect public buildings, banks, offices, etc and to transport large sums of money.

security police *n* a police force whose function is to prevent espionage; the military police of an air force.

security risk *n* a person or thing regarded as a potential threat to security.

sedan *n* a car with no division between driver and passengers; a covered chair for one person with poles carried by two bearers.

sedate¹ *adj* calm; composed; serious and unemotional.—**sedately** *adv.*—**sedateness** *n.*

sedate² *vti* to calm or become calm by the administration of a sedative.

sedation *n* the act of calming or the condition of being calmed, esp by sedatives; the administration of sedatives to calm a patient.

sedative *n* a drug with a soothing, calming effect. * *adj* having a soothing, calming effect.

sedentary *adj* requiring a sitting position; inactive; not migratory.

Seder *n* a Jewish ceremonial meal held on the first night of Passover.

sedge *n* a grass-like plant that grows in marshes or beside water.

sedge warbler *n* a European songbird that inhabits marshy areas.

sediment *n* matter that settles at the bottom of a liquid; (*geol*) matter deposited by water or wind.

sedimentary *adj* relating to or formed by sediment.

sedition *n* incitement to rebel against the government.—**seditious** *adj.*—**seditiously** *adv.*

seduce *vt* to lead astray; to corrupt; to entice into unlawful sexual intercourse.—**seducer** *n.*

seduction *n* the act of seducing; temptations; attraction.

seductive *adj* tending to seduce; enticing, alluring.—**seductively** *adv.*—**seductiveness** *n.*

sedulous *adj* diligent; persevering.—**sedulously** *adv.*—**sedulousness** *n.*

see¹ *vt* (**seeing, saw,** *pp* **seen**) to perceive with the eyes; to observe; to grasp with the intelligence; to ascertain; to take care (that); to accompany; to visit; to meet; to consult; (*guests*) to receive; (*with* **through**) to persist or endure to the end; to assist (eg a friend) during a crisis, difficulty, etc. * *vi* to have the faculty of sight; to make inquiry; to consider, to reflect; to understand; (*with* **about**) to deal with; to consider in detail; (*with* **off**) to be present when someone leaves on a journey, etc; (*inf*) to repel, get rid of; (*with* **through**) *vi* to recognize the true character of.

see² *n* the diocese of a bishop.

seed *n* the small, hard part (ovule) of a plant from which a new plant grows; such seeds collectively; the source of anything; sperm or semen; descendants; (*tennis*) a seeded tournament player. * *vti* to sow (seed); to produce or shed seed; to remove seeds from; (*tennis*) to arrange (a tournament) so that the best players cannot meet until later rounds.

seedbed *n* a nursery bed for a plant; a place or source of growth or development.

seed cake *n* a sweet cake flavoured with aromatic (usu caraway) seeds.

seed coral *n* small pieces of coral used in jewellery.

seed corn *n* corn reserved for sowing; assets promising future earning potential.

seedless *adj* without seeds.

seedling *n* a young plant raised from seed, not from a cutting; a young tree before it is a sapling.

seed money *n* money used to start a new project or enterprise.

seed oyster *n* a young oyster ready for transplantation to a new bed.

seed pearl *n* a very small pearl.

seed potato *n* a potato tuber ready for planting.

seed vessel *n* a pericarp.

seedy *adj* (**seedier, seediest**) full of seeds; out of sorts, indisposed; shabby; rundown.—**seedily** *adv.*—**seediness** *n.*

seeing *n* vision, sight. * *adj* having sight; observant. * *conj* in view of the fact that; since.

seek *vti* (**seeking, sought**) to search for; to try to find, obtain, or achieve; to resort to; (*with* **to**) to try to, to endeavour; (*with* **out**) to search for and locate a person or thing; to try to secure the society of.—**seeker** *n*.

seem *vi* to appear (to be); to give the impression of; to appear to oneself.

seeming *adj* that seems real, true; ostensible, apparent.—**seemingly** *adv*.

seemly *adj* (**seemlier, seemliest**) proper, fitting.—**seemliness** *n*.

seen *see* **see**[1].

seep *vi* to ooze gently, to leak through.

seepage *n* the act of seeping; the liquid that has seeped.

seer *n* a person who sees visions, a prophet.

seersucker *n* a light, usu cotton, fabric with a puckered surface.

seesaw *n* a plank balanced across a central support so that it is tilted up and down by a person sitting on each end; an up-and-down movement like this; vacillation. * *vi* to move up and down; to fluctuate. * *adj, adv* alternately rising and falling.

seethe *vi* to be very angry inwardly; to swarm (with people).

segment *n* a section; a portion; one of the two parts of a circle or sphere when a line is drawn through it. * *vti* to cut or separate into segments.—**segmentation** *n*.

segregate *vti* to set apart from others, to isolate; to separate racial or minority groups.

segregation *n* the act of segregating or the condition of being segregated; the policy of compelling racial groups to live apart.

seguidilla *n* (the music for) a lively Spanish dance in triple time.

seiche *n* an undulation of the surface of a lake, caused by earth tremors or changes in barometric pressure.

seigneur *n* a feudal lord.

seigneury *n* (*pl* **seigneuries**) the estate or authority of a seigneur.

seine *n* a large fishing net that hangs vertically by means of floats along the top and weights along the bottom. * *vi* to catch fish with this.

seismic *adj* of or caused by earthquakes.—**seismically** *adv*.

seismo-, seism- *prefix* earthquake.

seismograph *n* an instrument for recording the direction, intensity, and time of an earthquake.—**seismographer** *n*.—**seismographic** *adj*.—**seismography** *n*.

seismology *n* the scientific study of earthquakes.—**seismologic, seismological** *adj*.—**seismologist** *n*.

seize *vt* to grasp; to capture; to take hold of suddenly or forcibly; to attack or afflict suddenly. * *vi* (*machinery*) to become jammed.—**seizable** *adj*.

seizure *n* the act of seizing; what is seized; a sudden attack of illness, an apoplectic stroke.

seldom *adv* not often, rarely.

select *vti* to choose or pick out. * *adj* excellent; choice; limited (eg in membership); exclusive.

select committee *n* a parliamentary committee established to investigate and report on a particular subject.

selection *n* the act of selecting; what is or are selected; the process by which certain animals or plants survive while others are eliminated, natural selection.

selective *adj* having the power of selection; highly specific in activity or effect.—**selectively** *adv*.—**selectiveness** *n*.

selenium *n* a nonmetallic solid chemical element with semiconductive and photoconductive properties that has various uses in electronics.

seleno-, selen- *prefix* the moon.

selenography *n* the study and mapping of the physical features of the moon.—**selenographer** *n*.—**selenographic** *adj*.

self- *prefix* of itself or oneself; by, for, in relation to, itself or oneself; automatic.

self *n* (*pl* **selves**) the identity, character, etc, of any person or thing; one's own person as distinct from all others; one's own interests or advantage. * *adj* (*colour*) matching, uniform.

self-abnegation *n* denial of one's own interests or desires in favour of those of others.

self-absorption *n* preoccupation with one's own interests and welfare.

self-abuse *n* masturbation.

self-acting *adj* automatic.

self-addressed *adj* addressed to return to the sender; intended for oneself.

self-aggrandizement *n* acting to increase one's own power and importance at the expense of others.—**self-aggrandizing** *adj*.

self-approbation *n* satisfaction with one's own actions or accomplishments, esp to excess.

self-assertion *n* the act of asserting one's own opinions, ideas, or rights, esp determinedly.—**self-assertive** *adj*.

self-assured *adj* confident.—**self-assurance** *n*.

self-catering *adj* catering for oneself.

self-centred, self-centered *adj* preoccupied with one's own affairs.—**self-centerdly, self-centeredly** *adv*.—**self-centredness, self-centeredness** *n*.

self-coloured, self-colored *adj* of a single colour.

self-confessed *adj* according to one's own testimony.

self-confident *adj* sure of one's own powers.—**self-confidence** *n*.—**self-confidently** *adv*.

self-conscious *adj* embarrassed or awkward in the presence of others, ill at ease.—**self-consciously** *adv*.—**self-consciousness** *n*.

self-contained *adj* complete in itself; showing self-control; uncommunicative.—**self-containment** *n*.

self-control *n* control of one's emotions, desires, etc, by the will.—**self-controlled** *adj*.

self-deception *n* the act or state of deceiving oneself.

self-defence, self-defense *n* the act of defending oneself; (*law*) a plea for the justification for the use of force.

self-denial *n* abstention from pleasure, etc; unselfishness.

self-determination *n* free will; the choice of action without compulsion; the right of a nation to choose its own form of government.

self-drive *adj* (*hired vehicle*) driven by the hirer.

self-educated *adj* educated without benefit of formal instruction; educated at one's own expense.

self-effacement *n* the act of making oneself or one's actions inconspicuous, due to modesty or timidity.

self-employed *adj* earning one's living in one's own business or profession, not employed by another; working freelance.

self-esteem *n* confidence and respect for oneself; an exaggerated opinion of oneself.

self-evident *adj* evident without proof or explanation.—**self-evidently** *adv*.

self-explanatory *adj* easily understood without explanation.

self-expression *n* the expression of one's own personality, as in creative art.

self-governing *adj* autonomous; (*colony, etc*) having an elective legislation.—**self-government** *n*.

self-help *n* the provision of means to help oneself, instead of relying on others.

self-image *n* one's sense of oneself or one's importance.

self-importance *n* an exaggerated estimate of one's own worth; pompousness.—**self-important** *adj*.

self-induced *adj* brought on by oneself or itself.

self-induction *n* the production of an electromotive force in a circuit by a variation in the electric current in the same circuit.

self-indulgence *n* undue gratification of one's desires, appetites, or whims.—**self-indulgent** *adj*.

self-inflicted *adj* (*wound, etc*) caused to a person by himself.

self-interest *n* regard to one's own advantage.

selfish *adj* chiefly concerned with oneself; lacking in consideration for others.—**selfishly** *adv*.—**selfishness** *n*.

self-justification *n* the act or instance of making excuses for one's actions, etc.

selfless *adj* with no thought of self, unselfish.—**selflessly** *adv*.—**selflessness** *n*.

self-loading *n* (*firearm*) semiautomatic.—**self-loader** *n*.

self-love *n* conceit; selfishness.

self-made *adj* having achieved status or wealth by one's own efforts.

self-opinionated *adj* conceited; stubborn.

self-pity *n* pity for oneself.—**self-pitying** *adj*.

self-pollination *n* the transfer of pollen from the anther to the stigma in the same flower.

self-portrait *n* an artist or author's painting or account of himself or herself.

self-possessed *adj* cool and collected.

self-preservation *n* the instinct to protect oneself from injury or death.

self-propelled *adj* (*vehicle*) moving under its own power.

self-raising *adj* (*flour*) self-rising.

self-realization *n* the understanding or achievement of one's own potential or desires.

self-regard *n* concern for one's own interests; respect for oneself.

self-reliant *adj* relying on one's own powers; confident.—**self-reliance** *n*.

self-reproach *n* the act of blaming oneself.

self-respect *n* proper respect for oneself, one's standing and dignity.—**self-respecting** *adj*.

self-righteous *adj* thinking oneself better than others; priggish.—**self-righteousness** *n*.

self-rising *adj* (*flour*) containing a raising agent, self-raising.

self-rule *n* self-government.

self-sacrifice *n* the sacrifice of one's own interests, welfare, etc, to secure that of others.

selfsame *adj* identical, the very same.

self-satisfied *adj* smugly conceited.

self-seeking *adj* preoccupied with securing one's own well-being or interest; selfish.—**self-seeker** *n*.

self-service *adj* serving oneself in a cafe, shop, filling station, etc.

self-serving *adj* always seeking to protect or further one's own interests.

self-sown *adj* (*plants*) grown from seeds that were planted or deposited naturally without intervention by humans or animals.

self-starter *n* an electric device for starting an engine; a motivated employee who requires little supervision.

self-styled *adj* called by oneself; pretended.

self-sufficient *adj* independent; supporting oneself (eg in growing food) without the help of others.—**self-sufficiency** *n*.

self-supporting *adj* able to manage without help from others; able to stand unaided.

self-will *n* fixed adherence to one's own desires, intentions, etc; obstinacy.

self-winding *adj* (*watch*) wound automatically by an internal mechanism.

sell *vb* (**selling, sold**) *vt* to exchange (goods, services, etc) for money or other equivalent; to offer for sale; to promote; to deal in; (*with* **up**) to sell all the goods of (a debtor) to clear the debt. * *vi* (*with* **off**) to clear out (stock) at bargain prices; (*with* **out**) to sell off, to betray for money or reward; (*inf*) to disappoint, to trick; to make sales; to attract buyers; (*with* **up**) to sell one's house, business, etc. * *n* an act or instance of selling; (*inf*) a disappointment, a trick, a fraud.—**seller** *n*.

Sellotape *n* (*trademark*) a transparent adhesive tape. * *vt* to seal or stick (something) using adhesive tape.

sellout *n* a show, game, etc, for which all the tickets are sold; (*inf*) a betrayal.

selvage, selvedge *n* the edge of cloth so finished as to prevent unravelling.

selves *see* self.

Sem *abbr* = Seminary; Semitic.

sem *abbr* = semester; semicolon.

semantic *adj* relating to the meaning of words. * *npl* the study of word meanings and changes.

semaphore *n* a system of visual signalling using the operator's arms, flags, etc; a signalling device consisting of a post with movable arms.

sematic *adj* (*animal colouration*) warning of danger.

semblance *n* likeness, resemblance; an outward, sometimes deceptive appearance.

semen *n* the fluid that carries sperm in men and male animals.

semester *n* an academic or school half-year.

semi *n* (*pl* **semis**) (*inf*) a semidetached house; a semifinal.

semi- *prefix* half; not fully; twice in a (specified period).

semiannual *adj* happening twice a year, or lasting for six months.—*also* **semiyearly**.

semiautomatic *adj* partly automatic; (*firearm*) self-loading but discharging in single shots only as the trigger is pulled.

semibreve *n* (*mus*) a note equal to two minims.—*also* **whole note**.

semicircle *n* half of a circle.—**semicircular** *adj*.

semicircular canal *n* any of the three fluid-filled tubes in the inner ear concerned with maintaining balance.

semicolon *n* the punctuation mark (;) of intermediate value between a comma and a full stop.

semiconductor *n* a substance in a transmitter, as silicon, used to control the flow of current.

semiconscious *adj* not fully conscious.—**semiconsciousness** *n*.

semi-detached *adj* (*house*) with another joined to it on one side.—*also n*.

semifinal *adj, n* (the match or round) before the final in a knockout tournament.—**semifinalist** *n*.

semifluid *adj* having qualities between those of a fluid and a solid; viscous.

semiliterate *adj* barely able to read or write.

semilunar *adj* in the shape of a crescent.

semilunar valve *n* either one of the two crescent-shaped valves in the heart.

seminal *adj* of, relating to, or containing semen; promising or contributing to further development; original, influential.—**seminally** *adv*.

seminar *n* a group of students engaged in study or research under supervision; any group meeting to pool and discuss ideas.

seminary *n* (*pl* **seminaries**) a training college for priests, ministers, etc; a school for young women.

seminiferous *adj* producing or containing semen; (*plants*) bearing seeds.

semiology *n* the study of signs and symbols.—**semiologic, semiological** *adj*.—**semiologist** *n*.

semiotics *n* *sing* the study of signs and symbols, esp their use in language and relationship to the world of things and ideas; the study of the symptoms of disease.—**semiotic, semiotical** *adj*.—**semiotician** *n*.

semiprecious *adj* denoting gems of lower value than precious stones.

semiprofessional *adj* taking part in sport for pay, but not on a fulltime basis.—**semiprofessionally** *adv*.

semiquaver *n* (*mus*) a sixteenth note.

semirigid *adj* (*airship*) having a flexible gas container attached to a rigid keel.

semiskilled *adj* partly skilled or trained.

semiskimmed *adj* (*milk*) having the cream partially removed.

semisolid *adj* having the properties between that of a liquid and a solid; extremely viscous.

Semite *n* a member of the group of peoples including Arabs and Jews.

Semitic *adj* of or belonging to Semites; Jewish.

Semitism *n* any political or economic policy relating to Jews.

semitone *n* (*mus*) an interval equal to half a tone.

semitrailer *n* a trailer that has wheels at the back but is supported at the front by the towing vehicle.

semivowel *n* (*phon*) a consonant that sound like a vowel (eg *y* or *j*), a glide.

semiyearly *see* **semiannual**.

semolina *n* coarse particles of grain left after the sifting of wheat.

sempre *adv* (*mus*) always.

Sen *abbr* = senator; senior.

senate *n* a legislative or governing body; (*with cap*) the upper branch of a two-body legislature in France, the US, etc; the governing body of some universities.

senator *n* a member of a senate.—**senatorial** *adj*.

send *vti* (**sending, sent**) to cause or enable to go; to have conveyed, to dispatch (a message or messenger); to cause to move, to propel; to grant; to cause to be; (*sl*) to move (a person) to ecstasy; (*with* **down**) to expel from university; (*with* **for**) to order to be brought, to summon; (*with* **up**) (*inf*) to send to prison; to imitate or make fun of.—**sender** *n*.

send-off *n* a friendly demonstration at a departure; a start given to someone or something.

senescent *adj* growing old.—**senescence** *n*.

seneschal *n* (*hist*) a steward in the house of a feudal lord.

senile *adj* of or relating to old age; weakened, esp mentally, by old age.—**senility** *n*.

senior *adj* higher in rank; of or for seniors; longer in service; older (when used to distinguish between father and son with the same first name). * *n* one's elder or superior in standing; a person of advanced age; a student in the last year of college or high school.

senior citizen *n* an elderly person, esp a retired one.

senior common room *n* a staffroom in a British college or university.

seniority *n* (*pl* **seniorities**) the condition of being senior; status, priority, etc, in a given job.

sensation *n* awareness due to stimulation of the senses; an effect on the senses; a thrill; a state of excited interest; the cause of this.

sensational *adj* of or relating to sensation; exciting violent emotions; melodramatic.—**sensationally** *adv*.

sensationalism *n* the use of sensational writing, language, etc; the doctrine that all knowledge is obtained from sense impressions.—**sensationalist** *adj*.

sense *n* one of the five human and animal faculties by which objects are perceived: sight, hearing, smell, taste, and touch; awareness; moral discernment; soundness of judgment; meaning, intelligibility; (*pl*) conscious awareness. * *vt* to perceive; to become aware of; to understand; to detect.

senseless *adj* stupid, foolish; meaningless, purposeless; unconscious.—**senselessly** *adv*.—**senselessness** *n*.

sense organ *n* a bodily structure that reacts to stimuli and transmits them to the brain as nerve impulses.

sensibility *n* (*pl* **sensibilities**) the capacity to feel; oversensitiveness; susceptibility; (*pl*) sensitive awareness or feelings.

sensible *adj* having good sense or judgment; reasonable; practical; perceptible by the senses, appreciable; conscious (of); sensitive.—**sensibleness** *n*.—**sensibly** *adv*.

sensitive *adj* having the power of sensation; feeling readily and acutely, keenly perceptive; (*skin*) delicate, easily irritated; (*wound etc*) still in a painful condition; easily hurt or shocked, tender, touchy; highly responsive to slight changes; sensory; (*photog*) reacting to light.—**sensitively** *adj*.—**sensitiveness** *n*.

sensitive plant *n* a tropical American plant whose leaves and stems fold when touched.

sensitivity *n* (*pl* **sensitivities**) the condition of being sensitive; awareness of changes or differences; responsiveness to stimuli or feelings, esp to excess.

sensitize *vt* to make or become sensitive; (*person*) to render sensitive to an antigen, etc; (*photog: paper etc*) to render sensitive to light.—**sensitization** *n*.—**sensitizer** *n*.

sensitometer *n* a device for measuring the sensitivity to light of a photographic medium.

sensor *n* a device for detecting, recording, or measuring physical phenomena, as heat, pulse, etc; a sense organ.

sensorium *n* (*pl* **sensoriums, sensoria**) the area of the brain regarded as responsible for receiving and processing external stimulii; the body's entire sensory apparatus.

sensory *adj* of or relating to the senses, sensation, or the sense organs; conveying nerve impulses to the brain.

sensual *adj* bodily, relating to the senses rather than the mind; arousing sexual desire.—**sensuality** *n*.—**sensually** *adv*.

sensuous *adj* giving pleasure to the mind or body through the senses.—**sensuously** *adv*.—**sensuousness** *n*.

sent *see* **send**.

sentence *n* a court judgment; the punishment imposed; (*gram*) a series of words conveying a complete thought. * *vt* (*a convicted person*) to pronounce punishment upon; to condemn (to).

sententious *adj* terse, pithy; making frequent use of axioms and maxims; exhibiting a pompous, moralizing tone.—**sententiously** *adv.*—**sententiousness** *n.*

sentient *adj* making use of the senses, conscious.—**sentiently** *adv.*

sentiment *n* a feeling, awareness, or emotion; the thought behind something; an attitude of mind; a tendency to be swayed by feeling rather than reason; an exaggerated emotion.

sentimental *adj* of or arising from feelings; foolishly emotional; nostalgic.—**sentimentally** *adv.*

sentimentality *n* (*pl* **sentimentalities**) the quality or state of being sentimental; an affected or extreme tenderness.

sentinel *n* a sentry or guard.

sentry *n* (*pl* **sentries**) a soldier on guard to give warning of danger and to prevent unauthorized access.

sentry box *n* a shelter for a sentry.

senza *prep* (*mus*) without.

señor *n* (*pl* **señors, señores**) the title of a Spanish-speaking man, equivalent to Mr or sir.

señora *n* (*pl* **señoras**) the title of a Spanish-speaking married woman, equivalent to Mrs or madam.

señorita *n* (*pl* **señoritas**) the title of a Spanish-speaking unmarried woman, equivalent to Miss or madam.

Sep. *abbr* = September; Septuagint.

sepal *n* any of the individual parts of the calyx of a flower.

separable *adj* able to be separated or parted.—**separability** *n.*—**separably** *adv.*

separate *vt* to divide or part; to sever; to set or keep apart; to sort into different sizes. * *vi* to go different ways; to cease to live together as man and wife. * *adj* divided; distinct, individual; not shared. * *n* (*pl*) articles of clothing designed to be interchangeable with others to form various outfits.—**separately** *adv.*—**separateness** *n.*

separation *n* the act of separating or the state of being separate; a formal arrangement of husband and wife to live apart.

separatist *n* a person who advocates or practises separation from an organization, church, or government; a person who advocates racial or political separation.—*also adj.*—**separatism** *n.*

separator *n* one who separates; a machine that separates liquids from solids or liquids of different specific gravities.

Sephardi *n* (*pl* **Sephardim**) a Jew of Spanish, Portuguese or North African descent.—**Sephardic** *adj.*

sepia *adj, n* (a) dark reddish brown.

sepoy *n* (*formerly*) an Indian soldier employed by the British.

seppuku *n* harakiri.

sepsis *n* a septic state or agency; blood poisoning.

Sept. *abbr* = September.

septa *see* **septum**.

September *n* the ninth month of the year, having 30 days.

septennial *adj* occuring every, or lasting, seven years. * *n* a seven-year period.—**septennially** *adv.*

septet *n* a set of seven singers or players; a musical composition for seven instruments or voices.

septic *adj* infected by microorganisms; causing or caused by putrefaction.—**septically** *adv.*—**septicity** *n.*

septicaemia, septicemia *n* a disease caused by poisonous bacteria in the blood.—**septicaemic, septicemic** *adj.*

septic tank *n* an underground tank in which sewage is decomposed by the action of bacteria.

septuagenarian *n* a person in his or her seventies.

Septuagesima *n* the third Sunday before Lent.

Septuagint *n* the Greek version of the Old Testament including the Apocrypha (said to have been translated by 70 scholars).

septum *n* (*pl* **septa**) a dividing membrane between two bodily cavities or parts.—**septal** *adj.*

septuplet *n* one of seven offspring produced at one birth.

sepulchral *adj* of or like a sepulchre; dismal, funereal; (*sound*) deep and hollow.

sepulchre, sepulcher *n* a tomb, a burial vault.

sequel *n* something that follows, the succeeding part; a consequence; the continuation of a story begun in an earlier literary work, film, etc.

sequela *n* (*pl* **sequelae**) (*med*) a condition arising from an existing disease; any complication of a disease or injury.

sequence *n* order of succession; a series of succeeding things; a single, uninterrupted episode, as in a film.

sequential *adj* arranged in a sequence; following in sequence; consecutive.—**sequentially** *adv.*

sequester *vt* to place apart; to retire in seclusion; (*law*) to remove from one's possession until the claims of one's creditors are satisfied.

sequestrate *vt* to sequester.—**sequestration** *n.*

sequin *n* a shiny round piece of metal or foil sewn on clothes for decoration.

sequoia *n* a lofty coniferous Californian tree.

sera *see* **serum**.

sérac *n* a pinnacle or tower-shaped mass of ice among the crevasses of a glacier.

seraglio *n* (*pl* **seraglios**) a harem in a Muslim household or palace.

seraph *n* (*pl* **seraphs, seraphim**) (*theol*) a member of the highest order of angels.—**seraphic** *adj.*

Serb, Serbian *n* a native or inhabitant of Serbia; the Serbo-Croatian language of Serbia.—*also adj.*

Serbo-Croatian, Serbo-Croat *n* the Slavonic language of the Serbs and Croatians.—*also adj.*

serenade *n* music sung or played at night beneath a person's window, esp by a lover. * *vt* to entertain with a serenade.

serendipity *n* the faculty of making fortunate finds by chance.

serene *adj* calm; untroubled; tranquil; clear and unclouded; (*with cap*) honoured (used as part of certain royal titles).—**serenely** *adv.*—**serenity** *n.*

serf *n* (*pl* **serfs**) a labourer in feudal service who was bound to, and could be sold with, the land he worked; a drudge.—**serfdom** *n.*

serge *n* a hard-wearing twilled woollen fabric.

sergeant *n* a noncommissioned officer ranking above a corporal in the army, air force, and marine corps; a police officer ranking above a constable.

sergeant-at-arms *n* (*pl* **sergeants-at-arms**) an official in various legislative assemblies responsible for enforcing discipline.

sergeant major *n* a noncommissioned officer in the army, air force, marine corps serving as chief administrative assistant in a headquarters.

Sergt. *abbr* = Sergeant.

serial *adj* of or forming a series; published, shown or broadcast by instalments at regular intervals. * *n* a story presented in regular instalments with a connected plot.

serialism n (mus) the use of the twelve notes of the chromatic scale in a fixed order in a composition.

serialize vt to arrange, publish or broadcast in serial form.—**serialization** n.

serial killer n a person who murders people one at a time over a period of time.

serial number n one of a series of numbers given for identification.

seriatim adv consecutively.

sericeous adj (bot) covered in fine hairs

sericulture n the breeding of silkworms to produce raw silk.—**sericultural** adj.—**sericulturist** n.

series n sing, pl a succession of items or events; a succession of things connected by some likeness; a sequence, a set; a radio or television serial whose episodes have self-contained plots; a set of books issued by one publisher; (math) a progression of numbers or quantities according to a certain law.

serif n (print) a small line at the top or the bottom of the main stroke of a letter.

serigraph n a print made using the silk-screen technique.—**serigraphy** n.

serin n any of various small European finches related to the canary.

seriocomic adj combining humour and seriousness.—**seriocomically** adv.

serious adj grave, solemn, not frivolous; meaning what one says, sincere, earnest; requiring close attention or thought; important; critical.—**seriously** adv.—**seriousness** n.

sermon n a speech on religion or morals, esp by a clergyman; a long, serious talk of reproof, esp a tedious one.

sermonize vti to compose sermons; to preach at or to at length.—**sermonizer** n.

sero- prefix serum.

serology n the scientific study of serums.—**serological** adj.—**serologist** n.

seropositive adj having a particular disease (eg AIDS) for which one's blood has been tested.

serotinin n a substance occurring in various body tissues that induces vasoconstriction.

serous n of or producing serum.

serous membrane n a thin membrane lining a body cavity that secretes a thin lubricant.

serpent n a snake; a venomous or treacherous person.

serpentine adj like a serpent; twisting, tortuous; crooked, treacherous.

serpigo n a spreading skin complaint such as ringworm or herpes.

SERPS (acronym) state earnings-related pension scheme.

serrate adj (leaves, etc) having toothed edges; notched like a saw. * vt to make serrate.

serrated adj having an edge notched like the teeth of a saw.

serration n the state of being serrated; a saw-like edge; a single notch in a serrated edge.

serried adj packed closely, in compact order.

serum n (pl serums, sera) the watery part of bodily fluid, esp liquid that separates out from the blood when it coagulates; such fluid taken from the blood of an animal immune to a disease, used as an antitoxin.

serum albumin n the principal blood protein.

serum hepatitis n a viral disease, characterized by acute inflammation of the liver and jaundice, transmitted by contact with infected blood.

serval n (pl servals. serval) an African cat with long legs and a tawny coat with black spots.

servant n a personal or domestic attendant; one in the service of another.

serve vt to work for; to do military or naval service (for); to be useful to; to meet the needs (of), to suffice; (a customer) to wait upon; (food, etc) to hand round; (a sentence) to undergo; to be a soldier, sailor, etc; (of a male animal) to copulate with; (law) to deliver (a summons, etc); (naut) to bind (a rope) with thin cord to prevent fraying; (tennis) to put (the ball) into play. * vi to be employed as a servant; to be enough. * n the act of serving in tennis, etc.

server n one who serves, esp at tennis; something used in serving food and drink; a person who serves legal processes on another; the celebrant's assistant at mass.

service n the act of serving; the state of being a servant; domestic employment; a department of state employ; the people engaged in it; military employment or duty; work done for others; use, assistance; attendance in a hotel, etc; a facility providing a regular supply of trains, etc; a set of dishes; any religious ceremony; an overhaul of a vehicle; (tennis) the act or manner of seving; (pl) friendly help or professional aid; a system of providing a utility, as water, gas, etc. * vt to provide with assistance; to overhaul.

serviceable adj useful; durable.—**serviceably** adv.—**serviceableness** n.

service area n a place offering a range of services such as restaurants, toilet facilities, and petrol.

service charge n a sum added to a restaurant or hotel bill, etc for service.

serviceman n (pl servicemen) a member of the armed services; a person whose work is repairing something.—**servicewoman** nf (pl servicewomen).

service road n a minor road beside a main route that provides access to local shops, housing, etc.

service station n a place selling fuel, etc, for motor vehicles; a place at which some service is offered.

serviette n a small napkin.

servile adj of or like a slave; subservient; submissive; menial.—**servilely** adv.—**servility** n.

serving n a portion of food or drink.

servitude n slavery, bondage; work imposed as punishment for a crime.

servo n (pl servos) (inf) a servomotor or servomechanism. * adj activated by a servomechanism.

servomechanism n an automatic device which uses small amounts of power to control a system of much greater power.

servomotor n a motor that supplies power to a servomechanism.

sesame n an Asian plant that yields oil-bearing seeds; its seeds, also used for flavouring.

sesamoid adj of or pertaining to the small bones or lumps of cartilage in a tendon.

sesqui- prefix one and a half; (chem) a ratio of two to three.

sesquicentenniel n a period of 150 years; (the celebration of) a 150th anniversary.—also adj.

sessile adj (leaves) without a stalk; permanently attached.

session n the meeting of a court, legislature, etc; a series of such meetings; a period of these; a period of study, classes, etc; a university year; a period of time passed in an activity.

sesterce, sestertius *n* in ancient Rome, a coin worth a quarter of a denarius.

sestet *n* a poem or stanza of six lines, esp the last six lines of a sonnet.

set *vb* (**setting, set**) *vt* to put in a specified place, condition, etc; (*trap for animals*) to fix; (*clock etc*) to adjust; (*table*) to arrange for a meal; (*hair*) to fix in a desired style; (*bone*)to put into normal position, etc; to make settled, rigid, or fixed; (*gems*) to mount; to direct; to furnish (an example) for others; to fit (words to music or music to words); (*type*) to arrange for printing; (*with* **against**) to weigh up, compare; to cause to be opposed to; (*with* **aside**) to discard; to reserve for a particular reason; (*with* **down**) to place (something) on a surface; to record, put in writing; to regard; to attribute (to); to allow to alight from (a vehicle); (*with* **out**) to present or display; to explain in detail; to plan, lay out. * *vi* to become firm, hard or fixed; to begin to move (out, forth, off, etc); (*sun*) to sink below the horizon; (*with* **about**) to begin; to abuse physically or verbally; (*with* **in**) to stitch (a sleeve) within a garment; to become established; (*with* **off**) to show up by contrast; to set in motion; to cause to explode; (*with* **on**) to urge (as a dog) to attack or pursue; to go on, advance; (*with* **out**) to begin a journey, career, etc; (*with* **to**) to start working, esp eagerly; to start fighting; (*with* **up**) to erect; to establish, to found; (*with* **upon**) to attack, usu with violence. * *adj* fixed, established; intentional; rigid, firm; obstinate; ready. * *n* a number of persons or things classed or belonging together; a group, a clique; the way in which a thing is set; direction; the scenery for a play, film, etc; assembled equipment for radio or television reception, etc; (*math*) the totality of points, numbers, or objects that satisfy a given condition; (*tennis*) a series of games forming a unit of a match; a rooted cutting of a plant ready for transplanting; a badger's burrow (—*also* **sett**).

seta *n* (*pl* **setae**) a bristle or similar appendage of an animal or plant.

setback *n* misfortune; a reversal.

setline *n* a long fishing line with hooked shorter lines attached at regular intervals.

set piece *n* a formal or elaborate performance, esp of a work of art, music, etc; an elaborate fireworks display; (*sport*) a carefully rehearsed team move usu aimed at gaining the ball when play resumes.

setscrew *n* a screw which when tightened prevents parts of a machine from moving relative to one another.

set-square *n* a flat triangular instrument for drawing angles.

settee *n* a sofa for two people.

setter *n* a large breed of gundog trained to stand rigid when spotting game.

set theory *n* the branch of mathematics concerned with the relations and properties of sets.

setting *n* a background, scene, surroundings, environment; a mounting, as for a gem; the music for a song, etc.

settle *vti* to put in order; to pay (an account); to clarify; to decide, to come to an agreement; to make or become quiet or calm; to make or become firm; to establish or become established in a place, business, home, etc; to colonize (a country); to take up residence; to come to rest; (*dregs*) to fall to the bottom; to stabilize; to make or become comfortable (for resting); (*bird*) to

alight; to bestow legally for life; (*with* **for**) to be content with.

settlement *n* the act of settling; a sum settled, esp on a woman at her marriage; an arrangement; a small village; a newly established colony; subsidence (of buildings).

settler *n* a person who settles; an early colonist.

set-to *n* (*inf*) a squabble, fight.

set-up *n* the plan, makeup, etc, of equipment used in an organization; the details of a situation, plan, etc; (*inf*) a contest, etc, arranged to result in an easy win.

seven *adj, n* one more than six. * *n* the symbol for this (7, VII, vii); the seventh in a series or set; something having seven units as members.

sevenfold *adj* having seven units or members; being seven times as great or as many.

seven seas *npl* all the world's oceans.

seventeen *adj, n* one more than sixteen. * *n* the symbol for this (17, XVII, xvii).—**seventeenth** *adj*.

seventh *adj, n* next after sixth; one of seven equal parts of a thing. * *n* (*mus*) an interval of seven diatonic degrees; the leading note.

seventh heaven *n* perfect happiness.

seventy *adj, n* seven times ten. * *n* the symbol for this (70, LXX, lxx); (*in pl*) **seventies** (70s) the numbers for 70 to 79; the same numbers in a life or century.—**seventieth** *adj*.

sever *vti* to separate, to divide into parts; to break off.—**severance** *n*.

several *adj* more than two but not very many; various; separate, distinct; respective. * *pron* (*with pl vb*) a few. * *n* (*with pl vb*) a small number (of).

severe *adj* harsh, not lenient; very strict; stern; censorious; exacting, difficult; violent, not slight; (*illness*) critical; (*art*) plain, not florid.—**severely** *adv*.—**severity** *n*.

Seville orange *n* (an orange tree bearing) a fruit with bitter flesh used to make marmalade.

Sèvres *n* a type of fine porcelain made in France.

sew *vti* (**sewing, sewn** *or* **sewed**) to join or stitch together with needle and thread; to make, mend, etc, by sewing; (*with* **up**) to get full control of; (*inf*) to make sure of success in.—**sewing** *n*.

sewage *n* waste matter carried away in a sewer.

sewage farm *n* a place where sewage is treated for use as manure.

sewer[1] *n* one who sews.

sewer[2] *n* an underground pipe or drain for carrying off liquid waste matter, etc; a main drain.

sewerage *n* a system of drainage by sewers; sewage.

sewing machine *n* a machine for sewing or stitching usu driven by an electric motor.

sewn *see* **sew**.

sex *n* the characteristics that distinguish male and female organisms on the basis of their reproductive function; either of the two categories (male and female) so distinguished; males or females collectively; the state of being male or female; the attraction between the sexes; (*inf*) sexual intercourse.

sex- *prefix* six.

sexagenarian *n* a person in the age range 60–69.—*also adj*.

Sexagesima *n* the second Sunday before Lent.

sexagesimal *adj* of or based on the number 60.

sex appeal *n* what makes a person sexually desirable.

sex chromosome *n* a chromosome that determines the sex of an animal.

sexed *adj* having a certain amount of sex or sexuality.

sex hormone *n* a hormone affecting the development of sexual organs and characteristics.

sexism *n* exploitation and domination of one sex by the other, esp of women by men.—**sexist** *adj, n*.

sexless *adj* without sexual intercourse; sexually unappealing.—**sexlessly** *adv*.—**sexlessness** *n*.

sex object *n* a person regarded solely in terms of their sexual attractiveness.

sexology *n* the study of human sexuality.—**sexologist** *n*.—**sexological** *adj*.

sex shop *n* a shop specializing in sex aids, pornographic magazines, etc.

sextant *n* a navigator's instrument for measuring the altitude of the sun, etc, to determine position at sea.

sextet *n* a set of six singers or players; a musical composition for six instruments or voices.

sexton *n* an officer in charge of the maintenance of church property.

sextuple *adj* having six units or members; being six times as much or as many.—*also n*.

sextuplet *n* one of six offspring produced at one birth.

sexual *adj* of sex or the sexes; having sex.—**sexually** *adj*.

sexual harassment *n* frequent unwelcome attention from the opposite sex in the form of suggestive remarks, fondling, etc.

sexual intercourse *n* the act of copulating.

sexuality *n* sexual activity; expression of sexual interest, esp when excessive.

sexually transmitted disease *n* any of various diseases, such as syphilis or AIDS, transmitted by sexual contact.—*also* **venereal disease**.

sexy *adj* (**sexier, sexiest**) (*inf*) exciting, or intending to excite, sexual desire; attractive, entertaining; fashionable or stylish and as a result worthwhile.—**sexily** *adv*.—**sexiness** *n*.

SF *abbr* = science fiction.

sf, sfz *abbr* = sforzando.

sforzando, sforzato *adv* (*mus*) with vigour at the start. * *n* a notation indicating this.

sgd *abbr* = signed.

SGM abbr = Sergeant Major.

sgraffito *n* (*pl* **sgraffiti**) (an example of) a technique in ceramic or mural design in which the surface layer (of glaze, plaster, etc) is scraped away to expose a contrasting background.

Sgt *abbr* = sergeant

Sgt Maj *abbr* = sergeant major.

sh *interj* used to command silence.

shabby *adj* (**shabbier, shabbiest**) (*clothes*) threadbare, worn, or dirty; run-down, dilapidated; (*act, trick*) mean, shameful.—**shabbily** *adv*.—**shabbiness** *n*.

shack *n* a small, crudely built house or cabin; a shanty. * *vi* (*with* **up**) (*sl*) to cohabit (with); to spend the night (with), esp a person of the opposite sex.

shackle *n* a metal fastening, usu in pairs, for the wrists or ankles of a prisoner; a staple; anything that restrains freedom; (*pl*) fetters. * *vt* to fasten or join by a shackle; to hamper, to impede.

shad *n* (*pl* **shad, shads**) any of various fishes of the herring family used as food.

shade *n* relative darkness; dimness; the darker parts of anything; shadow; a shield or screen protecting from bright light; a ghost; a place sheltered from the sun; degree of darkness of a colour, esp when made by the addition of black; a minute difference; a blind; (*pl*) the darkness of approaching night; (*pl: sl*) sunglasses.

* *vti* to screen from light; to overshadow; to make dark; to pass by degrees into another colour; to change slightly or by degrees.

shading *n* the fine gradations of colour, line, tone, etc, creating light and dark in a painting, etc; a shielding against light; nuances.

shadow *n* a patch of shade; darkness, obscurity; the dark parts of a painting, etc; shelter, protection; the dark shape of an object produced on a surface by intercepted light; an inseparable companion; a person (as a detective, etc) who shadows; an unsubstantial thing, a phantom; a mere remnant, a slight trace; gloom, affliction. * *vt* to cast a shadow over; to cloud; to follow and watch, esp in secret. * *adj* having an indistinct pattern or darker section; (*opposition party*) matching a function or position of the party in power.

shadow-box *vi* (*boxing*) to practice blows against an invisible opponent.

shadowy *adj* full of shadows; dim, indistinct; unsubstantial.

shady *adj* (**shadier, shadiest**) giving or full of shade; sheltered from the sun; (*inf*) of doubtful honesty, disreputable.

SHAEF (*acronym*) Supreme Headquarters Allied Expeditionary Forces.

shaft *n* a straight rod, a pole; a stem, a shank; the main part of a column; an arrow or spear, or its stem; anything hurled like a missile; a ray of light, a stroke of lightning; a revolving rod for transmitting power, an axle; one of the poles between which a horse is harnessed; a hole giving access to a mine; a vertical opening through a building, as for a lift; a critical remark or attack; (*sl*) harsh or unfair treatment.

shag *n* a coarse tobacco cut into long pieces; a rough mop of hair, etc; a crested cormorant. * *adj* (*carpet*) having long, thick, woollen threads.

shaggy *adj* (**shaggier, shaggiest**) (*hair, fur, etc*) long and unkempt; rough; untidy.—**shagginess** *n*.

shaggy-dog story *n* (*inf*) a long joke with a punch line that is a deliberate anticlimax.

shagreen *n* the rough skin of certain sharks and rays; a type of leather with a gritty surface made from the hides of certain animals.

shah *n* the title of the former ruler of Iran.

shake *vti* (**shaking, shook**, *pp* **shaken**) to move to and fro with quick short motions, to agitate; to tremble or vibrate; to jar or jolt; to brandish; to make or become unsteady; to weaken; to unsettle; to unnerve or become unnerved; to clasp (another's hand) as in greeting; (*with* **down**) to cause to subside by shaking; to obtain makeshift accommodation; (*sl*) to extort money from; (*with* **off**) to get rid of; (*with* **out**) to empty by shaking; to spread (a sail); (*with* **up**) to shake together, to mix; to upset. * *n* the act of shaking or being shaken; a jolt; a shock; a milkshake; (*inf*) a deal; (*pl inf*) a convulsive trembling.

shakedown *n* a makeshift or improvised bed; (*sl*) an extortion of money, as by blackmail; a thorough search.

shaker *n* a container for holding condiments; a container in which cocktail ingredients are mixed.

shakers *see* **movers and shakers**.

Shakespearean, Shakespearian *adj* of, pertaining to, or characteristic of William Shakespeare (1564-1616) or his works.

shako *n* (*pl* **shakos, shakoes**) a cylindrical military cap with a high crown and tall plume.

shake-up *n* an extensive reorganization.

shaky *adj* (**shakier, shakiest**) unsteady; infirm; unreliable.—**shakily** *adv.*—**shakiness** *n.*

shale *n* a kind of clay rock like slate but softer.

shall *vb aux* (*pt* **should**) used formally to express the future in the 1st person and determination, obligation or necessity in the 2nd and 3rd person; the more common form is **will**.

shallot *n* a small onion.

shallow *adj* having little depth; superficial, trivial. * *n* a shallow area in otherwise deep water.—**shallowness** *n.*

shalt (*arch*) *the 2nd person sing of* **shall**.

sham *n* a pretence; a person or thing that is a fraud. * *adj* counterfeit; fake.

shaman *n* a priest of shamanism believed to possess magical powers which allow him to communicate with and influence the spirit world.

shamanism *n* a religion of northern Asia which views the world as dominated by good and evil spirits that can be influenced only by the shamans.

shamateur *n* (*sport*) a player, athlete, etc who is officially classed as an amateur but who accepts payment.

shamble *vi* to walk with an ungainly stumbling gait.—*also n.*

shambles *npl* a scene of great disorder; a slaughterhouse.

shambolic *adj* (*inf*) disorganized; utterly confused.

shame *n* a painful emotion arising from guilt or impropriety; modesty; disgrace, dishonour; the cause of this; (*sl*) a piece of unfairness. * *vti* to cause to feel shame; to bring disgrace on; to force by shame (into); to humiliate by showing superior qualities.

shamefaced *adj* bashful or modest; sheepish; showing shame; ashamed.—**shamefacedly** *adv.*—**shamefacedness** *n.*

shameful *adj* disgraceful; outrageous.—**shamefully** *adv.*—**shamefulness** *n.*

shameless *adj* immodest; impudent, brazen.—**shamelessly** *adv.*—**shamelessness** *n.*

shammy (leather) *see* **chamois leather**.

shampoo *n* a liquid cleansing agent for washing the hair; the process of washing the hair or a carpet, etc. * *vt* to wash with shampoo.—**shampooer** *n.*

shamrock *n* a three-leaved cloverlike plant, the national emblem of Ireland.

shan't = shall not.

shandy *n* (*pl* **shandies**) beer diluted with a non-alcoholic drink (as lemonade).

shanghai *vt* (**shanghaiing, shanghaied**) to force (a sailor, etc) to join a ship's crew, esp by kidnapping or drugging; to trick or force (a person) into doing something.—**shanghaier** *n.*

Shangri-la *n* an imaginary utopia.

shank *n* the leg from the knee to the ankle, the shin; a shaft, stem, or handle.

shanks's pony, shanks's mare *n* one's own legs as used for walking.

shantung *n* a coarse kind of silk.

shanty¹ *n* (*pl* **shanties**) a crude hut built from corrugated iron or cardboard.

shanty² *n* (*pl* **shanties**) (*formerly*) a song sung by sailors in the rhythm of their work, a chantey.

shantytown *n* a community of poor people living in shanties.

SHAPE (*acronym*) Supreme Headquarters Allied Powers Europe.

shape *n* the external appearance, outline or contour of a thing; a figure; a definite form; an orderly arrangement; a mould or pattern; (*inf*) condition. * *vt* to give shape to; to form; to model, to mould; to determine; (*with* up) to develop to a definite or satisfactory form.

shapeless *adj* lacking definite form; baggy.—**shapelessly** *adv.*—**shapelessness** *n.*

shapely *adj* (**shapelier, shapeliest**) well-proportioned.—**shapeliness** *n.*

shard *n* a fragment or broken piece, esp of pottery.

share *n* an allotted portion, a part; one of the parts into which a company's capital stock is divided, entitling the holder to a share of profits. * *vti* to distribute, to apportion (out); to have or experience in common with others; to divide into portions; to contribute or receive a share of; to use jointly.

sharecropper *n* a tenant farmer who hands over a portion of the crop as rent.—**sharecrop** *vi.*

shareholder *n* a holder of shares in a property, esp a company.

share option *n* an option open to employees to buy shares in the company they work for.

shark *n* a large voracious marine fish; an extortioner, a swindler; (*sl*) an expert in a given activity.

sharkskin *n* a rayon fabric with a smooth shiny finish.

sharp *adj* having a keen edge or fine point; pointed, not rounded; clear-cut; distinct; intense, piercing; cutting, severe; keen, biting; clever, artful; alert, mentally acute; (*mus*) raised a semitone in pitch; out of tune by being too high; (*sl*) smartly dressed. * *adv* punctually; quickly; (*mus*) above the right pitch. * *n* (*mus*) a note that is a semitone higher than the note denoted by the same letter; the symbol for this (#).—**sharply** *adv.*—**sharpness** *n.*

sharpen *vti* to make or become sharp or sharper.

sharpener *n* something that sharpens.

sharpshooter *n* a marksman.

sharp-tongued *adj* sarcastic; quick to criticize.

sharp-witted *adj* thinking quickly and effectively.—**sharp-wittedly** *adv.*—**sharp-wittedness** *n.*

shatter *vti* to reduce to fragments suddenly; to smash; to damage or be damaged severely.

shatterproof *adj* resistant to shattering.

shave *vti* to remove facial or body hair with a razor; to cut away thin slices, to pare; to miss narrowly, to graze. * *n* the act or process of shaving; a narrow escape or miss; a paring.

shaven *adj* shaved.

shaver *n* one who shaves; an instrument for shaving, esp an electrical one.

Shavian *adj* of, relating to, or resembling the works of the writer George Bernard Shaw (1856–1950).

shaving *n* the act of using a razor or scraping; a thin slice of wood, metal, etc, shaved off.

shawl *n* a large square or oblong cloth worn as a covering for the head or shoulders or as a wrapping for a baby.

shawm *n* a medieval woodwind instrument resembling an oboe.

she *pron* (*obj* **her**, *poss* **her, hers**) the female person or thing named before or in question. * *n* a female person or animal.

shea *n* a tropical African tree with seeds that yield a butter-like fat used as food.

sheaf *n* (*pl* **sheaves**) a bundle of reaped corn bound together; a collection of papers, etc, tied in a bundle.

shear *vti* (**shearing, sheared** *or* **shorn**) to clip or cut (through); to remove (a sheep's fleece) by clipping; to divest; (*metal*) to break off because of a heavy force or twist. * *n* a stress acting sideways on a rivet and causing a break, etc; a machine for cutting metal; (*pl*) large scissors; (*pl*) a tool for cutting hedges, etc.

shearling *n* (the fleece of) a sheep after its first shearing.

shearwater *n* any of various seabirds that often glide close to the water.

sheath *n* (*pl* **sheaths**) a close-fitting cover, esp for a blade; a condom; a closefitting dress usu worn without a belt.

sheathe *vt* to put into a sheath; to encase, to protect with a casing; (*cat*) to withdraw its claws.

sheath-knife *n* a knife with a fixed blade covered by a sheath.

sheave[1] *vt* to gather into sheaves.

sheave[2] *n* a grooved wheel, esp in a pulley.

sheaves *see* **sheaf.**

shebang *n* (*inf*) affair, business.

shebeen *n* an unlicensed or illegal drinking den.

she'd = she had; she would.

shed[1] *n* a hut for storing garden tools; a large roofed shelter often with one or more sides open; a warehouse.

shed[2] *vt* (**shedding, shed**) (*tears*) to let fall; (*skin, etc*) to lose or cast off; to allow or cause to flow; to diffuse, radiate. * *n* a parting in the hair.

sheen *n* a gloss, lustre; brightness.

sheep *n* (*pl* **sheep**) a cud-chewing four-footed animal with a fleece and edible flesh called mutton; a bashful, submissive person.

sheepcote *n* a sheepfold.

sheep-dip *n* a liquid disinfectant or insecticide into which sheep are plunged to destroy parasites.

sheepdog *n* a dog trained to tend, drive, or guard sheep.

sheepfold *n* an enclosure for sheep.

sheepish *adj* bashful, embarrassed.—**sheepishly** *adv.*—**sheepishness** *n.*

sheep's eyes *npl* (*arch*) amorous glances.

sheepshank *n* a knot in a rope to shorten it temporarily.

sheepskin *n* the skin of a sheep, esp with the fleece; a rug, parchment, or leather made from it; a garment made of or lined with sheepskin.

sheepwalk *n* an area of pasture for sheep.

sheer[1] *adj* pure, unmixed; downright, utter; perpendicular, extremely steep; (*fabric*) delicately fine, transparent. * *adv* outright; perpendicularly, steeply.

sheer[2] *vti* to deviate or cause to deviate from a course; to swerve. * *n* the act of sheering; the upward curve of a deck toward bow or stern; a change in a ship's course.

sheerlegs *n sing* a hoisting device comprising two or more upright poles crossed at the top from which lifting gear is suspended.

sheet[1] *n* a broad thin piece of any material, as glass, plywood, metal, etc; a large rectangular piece of cloth used as inner bed clothes; a single piece of paper; (*inf*) a newspaper; a broad, flat expanse; a suspended or moving expanse (as of fire or rain).

sheet[2] *n* a rope that controls the angle of a sail in relation to the wind.

sheet anchor *n* a large anchor used only in emergencies; a support in extremity.

sheet bend *n* a knot for joining ropes of different thicknesses.

sheet glass *n* glass made in large sheets directly from the furnace or by making a cylinder and then flattening it.

sheeting *n* fabric for sheets.

sheet lightning *n* lightning that has the appearance of a broad sheet due to reflection and diffusion by the clouds and sky.

sheet metal *n* metal rolled out in the form of a thin sheet.

sheet music *n* music printed on unbound sheets of paper.

sheikh *n* an Arab chief.

sheila *n* (*Austral, NZ sl*) a girl or woman.

shekel *n* the unit of money in Israel; an old Jewish weight or silver coin; (*pl*) (*sl*) money.

shelduck, sheldrake *n* any of several Old World brightly plumaged ducks.

shelf *n* (*pl* **shelves**) a board fixed horizontally on a wall or in a cupboard for holding articles; a ledge on a cliff face; a reef, a shoal.

shelf life *n* the length of time for which something may be stored without deterioration.

shell *n* a hard outside covering of a nut, egg, shellfish, etc; an explosive projectile; an external framework; a light racing boat; outward show; a cartridge. * *vt* to remove the shell from; to bombard (with shells); (*with out*) (*inf*) to pay out (money).

she'll = she will; she shall.

shellac, shellack *n* a resin usu produced in thin, flaky layers or shells; a thin varnish containing this and alcohol.

shellfish *n* an aquatic animal, esp an edible one, with a shell.

shellproof *adj* impervious to artillery shells, rockets and bombs.

shell shock *n* a nervous disorder caused by the shock of being under fire.—**shell-shocked** *adj.*

shelter *n* a structure that protects, esp against weather; a place giving protection, a refuge; protection. * *vti* to give shelter to, to shield, to cover; to take shelter.

sheltie, shelty *n* (*pl* **shelties**) a Shetland pony or Shetland sheepdog.

shelve *vti* to place on a shelf; to defer consideration, to put aside; to slope gently, to incline.

shelves *see* **shelf.**

shelving *n* material for making shelves; shelves collectively.

shemozzle *n* (*inf*) a scene of confusion; a brawl.

shenanigan *n* (*often pl*) trickery, deception; mischief, boisterous high spirits.

shepherd *n* a person who looks after sheep; a pastor. * *vt* to look after, as a shepherd; to manoeuvre or marshal in a particular direction.—**shepherdess** *nf.*

shepherd dog *n* a sheepdog.

shepherd's pie *n* a dish of minced meat covered with a mashed potato crust.

shepherd's purse *n* an annual plant with small white flowers and heart-shaped seed pods.

sherbet *n* a fruit-flavoured powder that can be used to make a slightly sparkling drink; a sorbet.

sheriff *n* in US, the chief law enforcement officer of a county; in Scotland, a judge in an intermediate law court; in England and Wales, the chief officer of the Crown, a ceremonial post.

sheriff court *n* (*Scot*) the court dealing with the majority of criminal and civil cases.

Sherpa *n* (*pl* **Sherpas, Sherpa**) a member of a people living on the southern slopes of the Himalayas on the borders of Nepal and Tibet.

sherry *n* (*pl* **sherries**) a fortified wine originally made in Spain.

she's = she is; she has.

Shetland pony *n* a breed of small sturdy pony with a shaggy mane.

Shetland sheepdog *n* a breed of dog resembling a collie but smaller.

SHF, shf *abbr* = superhigh frequency.

Shiah, Shia *n* a member of the main branch of Islam who acknowledge Muhammad's cousin Ali and his successors as the true imams.—*also adj.*

shibboleth *n* a slogan or catchword, esp that regarded as outmoded or identified with a particular group or culture; a custom or linguistic usage which identifies members of a particular group, party, class, etc.

shied *see* **shy**[1], **shy**[2].

shield *n* a broad piece of armour carried for defence, usu on the left arm; a protective covering or guard; a thing or person that protects; a trophy in the shape of a shield. * *vti* to defend; to protect; to screen.

shier, shiest *see* **shy**[1].

shift *vti* to change position (of); to contrive, to manage; to remove, to transfer; to replace by another or others; (*gears*) to change the arrangement of. * *n* a change in position; an expedient; a group of people working in relay with others; the time worked by them; a change or transfer; a straight dress.

shiftless *adj* incapable; feckless.—**shiftlessly** *adv.*—**shiftlessness** *n.*

shifty *adj* (**shiftier, shiftiest**) artful, tricky; evasive.—**shiftily** *adv.*—**shiftiness** *n.*

shigella *n* any of a genus of rod-shaped bacteria causing dysentery in humans and animals.

Shiite, Shiah *n* a follower of Shiah.—*also adj.*

shillelagh *n* an Irish club or cudgel.

shilling *n* a former unit of currency of the UK and other countries, worth one twentieth of a pound.

shillyshally *vi* (**shillyshallying, shillyshallied**) to vacillate, to hesitate. * *n* (*pl* **shillyshallies**) the inability to make up one's mind.

shim *n* a thin washer or spacer used to tighten or space out joints, etc. * *vt* (**shimming, shimmed**) to space out, etc using shims.

shimmer *vi* to glisten softly, to glimmer.—*also n.*—**shimmery** *adj.*

shimmy *n* (*pl* **shimmies**) a jazz dance involving rapid movements of the upper body; an abnormal vibration in a vehicle or aircraft. * *vi* (**shimmying, shimmied**) to dance a shimmy; to vibrate.

shin *n* the front part of the leg from the knee to the ankle; the shank. * *vi* (*with* **up**) to climb (a pole, etc) by gripping with legs and hands.

shinbone *n* the tibia.

shindig *n* (*inf*) a lively, noisy celebration; an uproar.

shine *vti* (**shining, shone**) to emit light; to be bright, to glow; to be brilliant or conspicuous; to direct the light of; to cause to gleam by polishing; * *n* a lustre, a gloss; (*sl*) a liking.

shiner *n* (*inf*) a black eye.

shingle[1] *n* a thin wedge-shaped roof tile; a small signboard.

shingle[2] *n* waterworn pebbles as on a beach; an area covered with these.—**shingly** *adj.*

shingles *npl* a virus disease marked by a painful rash of red spots on the skin.

Shinto *n* the indigenous religion of Japan, involving veneration of the emperor, and the worship of ancestors and various natural deities.—**Shintoism** *n.*—**Shintoist** *n.*

shinty *n* a game similar to hockey and hurling, played with a ball and curved sticks.

shiny *adj* (**shinier, shiniest**) glossy, polished; worn smooth.

ship *n* a large vessel navigating deep water; its officers and crew; a spacecraft. * *vti* (**shipping, shipped**) to transport by any carrier; to take in (water) over the side; to lay (oars) inside a boat; to go on board; to go or travel by ship.

shipboard *n* the side of a ship.

shipbuilder *n* a person or company that designs or constructs ships.—**shipbuilding** *n.*

ship chandler *n* an individual or business that provides essential supplies for ships.

shipload *n* as much as a ship can carry.

shipmaster *n* the captain or master of a ship.

shipmate *n* a fellow sailor.

shipment *n* goods shipped; a consignment.

ship of the line *n* (*formerly*) a warship large enough to fight in the first line of battle.

shipowner *n* a person who owns (or has shares in) a ship.

shipper *n* an individual or company that ships goods.

shipping *n* the business of transporting goods; ships collectively.

ship's biscuit *n* a type of hard biscuit that was formerly part of a sailor's diet.

shipshape *adj* in good order, tidy.

shipworm *n* any of a genus of worm-like molluscs that burrow in submerged wood.

shipwreck *n* the loss of a vessel at sea; the remains of a wrecked ship; ruin, destruction. * *vti* to destroy by or suffer shipwreck; to ruin.

shipwright *n* a person skilled in constructing and repairing ships.

shipyard *n* a yard or shed where ships are built or repaired.

shire *n* in the UK, a county; a large powerful breed of draught horse.

shirk *vti* to neglect or avoid work; to refuse to face (duty, danger, etc).—**shirker** *n.*

shirr *vt* to gather (fabric) with parallel threads run through it; to bake (eggs) in buttered dishes.

shirring *n* a gathering made in cloth by drawing the material up on parallel rows of short stitches.

shirt *n* a sleeved garment of cotton, etc, for the upper body, typically having a fitted collar and cuffs and front buttons; (*inf*) one's money or resources.

shirtdress *n* a long shirt worn as a dress.

shirting *n* a fabric suitable for men's shirts.

shirtsleeve *n* the sleeve of a shirt.

shirt-tail *n* the flap of material at the back of a shirt below the waist.

shirtwaister, shirtwaist *n* a woman's dress tailored in front in style similar to a shirt.

shirty *adj* (**shirtier, shirtiest**) (*sl*) irritable, rude.

shish kebab *n* a kebab.

shit[1], **shite** *n* (*vulg*) waste matter from humans or animals; excrement; heroin. * *vti* to defecate (on). * *interj* (*sl*) an expression of strong disgust or disapproval.

shit[2] *n* (*sl*) something that is good.

shivaree *see* **charivari**.

shiver[1] *n* a small fragment, a splinter.

shiver² *vi* to shake or tremble, as with cold or fear, to shudder.—*also n.*—**shivery** *adj.*

shoal¹ *n* a large number of fish swimming together; a large crowd. * *vi* to form shoals.

shoal² *n* a submerged sandbank, esp one that shows at low tide; a shallow place; a hidden danger. * *vti* to come to a less deep part; to become shallower.

shock¹ *n* a shaggy mass of hair.

shock² *n* a violent jolt or impact; a sudden disturbance to the emotions; the event or experience causing this; the nerve sensation caused by an electrical charge through the body; a disorder of the blood circulation, produced by displacement of body fluids (due to injury); (*sl*) a paralytic stroke. * *vt* to outrage, horrify. * *vi* to experience extreme horror, outrage, etc.

shock absorber *n* a device, as on the springs of a car, that absorbs the force of bumps and jars.

shocker *n* a sensational novel, play, etc; anything that shocks; (*sl*) a very bad specimen.

shocking *adj* revolting; scandalous, improper; very bad.—**shockingly** *adv.*

shockproof *adj* capable of withstanding shock without damage.

shock therapy, shock treatment *n* the treatment of certain mental illnesses by inducing convulsions using drugs or by passing electricity through the brain.

shock troops *npl* a highly disciplined force trained to lead an attack.

shock wave *n* the violent effect in the vicinity of an explosion caused by the change in atmospheric pressure; the compressed wave built up when the speed of a body or fluid exceeds that at which sound can be transmitted in the medium in which it is travelling.

shod, shodden *see* **shoe.**

shoddy *adj* (**shoddier, shoddiest**) made of inferior material; cheap and nasty, trashy.—**shoddily** *adv.*—**shoddiness** *n.*

shoe *n* an outer covering for the foot not enclosing the ankle; a thing like a shoe, a partial casing; a horseshoe; a drag for a wheel; a device to guide movement, provide contact, or protect against wear or slipping; a dealing box that holds several decks of cards. * *vt* (**shoeing, shod** *or* **shoed,** *pp* **shod, shoed** *or* **shodden**) to provide with shoes; to cover for strength or protection.

shoehorn *n* a curved piece of plastic, metal, or horn used for easing the heel into a shoe.

shoelace *n* a cord that passes through eyelets in a shoe and is tied to keep the shoe on the foot.

shoemaker *n* a person who makes or mends shoes.

shoestring *n* a shoelace; (*inf*) a small amount of money.

shoetree *n* a block of wood, plastic or metal for preserving the shape of a shoe.

shogun *n* the hereditary commander of the army in feudal Japan.

shone *see* **shine.**

shoo *interj* used to frighten (animals, people) away. * *vt* (**shooing, shooed**) to frighten away (as if) by shouting "shoo". * *vi* to cry "shoo".

shoo-in *n* (*inf*) a person or thing certain to win or succeed.

shook *see* **shake.**

shoot *vb* (**shooting, shot**) *vt* to discharge or fire (a gun etc); to hit or kill with a bullet, etc; (*rapids*) to be carried swiftly over; to propel quickly; to thrust out; (*bolt*) to slide home; to variegate (with another colour, etc); (*a film scene*) to photograph; (*sport*) to kick or drive (a ball, etc) at goal; (*with* **down**) to disprove (an argument); (*with* **up**) to grow rapidly, to rise abruptly. * *vi* to move swiftly, to dart; to emit; to put forth buds, to sprout; to attack or kill indiscriminately; (*sl*) to inject a narcotic into a vein. * *n* a contest, a shooting trip, etc; a new growth or sprout.

shooting *n* the act of firing a gun or letting off an arrow.

shooting star *n* a meteor.

shooting stick *n* a spiked stick with a handle that folds out into a small seat.

shop *n* a building where retail goods are sold or services provided; a factory; a workshop; the details and technicalities of one's own work, and talk about these. * *vti* (**shopping, shopped**) to visit shops to examine or buy; (*sl*) to inform on (a person) to the police; (*with* **around**) to hunt for the best buy.

shop assistant *n* a person who serves customers in a retail shop.

shop floor *n* the part of a factory where goods are manufactured; the work force employed there, usu unionized.

shopkeeper *n* a person who owns or runs a shop.—**shopkeeping** *n.*

shoplifter *n* a person who steals goods from shops.

shoplifting *n* stealing from a shop during shopping hours.—**shoplifter** *n.*

shopper *n* a person who shops; a bag for carrying shopping.

shopping *n* the act of shopping; the goods bought.—*also adj.*

shopping centre *n* a complex of shops, restaurants, and service establishments with a common parking area.—*also* **shopping plaza.**

shopping mall *n* a large enclosed shopping centre.

shopsoiled *adj* shopworn.

shoptalk n the specialized vocabulary of those in the same line of work or sharing an area of interest; talk about work after hours.

shopwalker *n* a person employed in large shop who oversees shop assistants, helps customers, etc.

shopworn *adj* faded, etc, from being on display in a shop.

shore¹ *n* land beside the sea or a large body of water; beach.

shore² *n* a prop or beam used for support. * *vt* to prop (up), to support with a shore.

shoreline *n* the edge of an expanse of water.

shorn *see* **shear.**

short *adj* not measuring much; not long or tall; not great in range or scope; brief; concise; not retentive; curt; abrupt; less than the correct amount; below standard; deficient, lacking; (*pastry*) crisp or flaky; (*vowel*) not prolonged, unstressed; (*drink*) undiluted, neat. * *n* something short; (*pl*) trousers not covering the knee; (*pl*) an undergarment like these; a short circuit. * *adv* abruptly; concisely; without reaching the end. * *vti* to give less than what is needed; to short-change; to short-circuit.—**shortness** *n.*

shortage *n* a deficiency.

shortbread *n* a rich, crumbly cake or biscuit made with much shortening.

short-change *vt* to give back less than the correct change; (*sl*) to cheat.

short-circuit *n* the deviation of an electric current by a path of small resistance; an interrupted electric current. * *vti* to establish a short-circuit in; to cut off electric current; to provide with a short cut.

shortcoming *n* a defect or inadequacy.

shortcrust pastry *n* a firm but crumbly pastry made with half as much fat as flour.

short cut *n* a shorter route; any way of saving time, effort, etc.

shorten *vt* to make or become short or shorter; to reduce the amount of (sail) spread; to make (pastry, etc) crisp and flaky by adding fat.

shortening *n* the act of shortening; the state of becoming shortened; a fat used for making pastry, etc, crisp and flaky.

shortfall *n* (the amount or degree of) a deficit or deficiency.

shorthand *n* a method of rapid writing using signs or contractions.—*also adj.*

short-handed *adj* not having the usual number of assistants.

shorthand typist *n* a person who produces typewritten documents from shorthand notes.—*also* **stenographer**.

short head *n* (*horse racing*) a distance less than a horse's head.

shorthorn *n* one of a breed of large heavy cattle with short curved horns.

short list *n* a selected list of qualified applicants from which a choice must be made.

short-list *vt* to place (a person) on a short list.

short-lived *adj* not lasting or living for long.

shortly *adv* soon, in a short time; briefly; rudely.

short-range *adj* having a limited range in time or distance.

short shrift *n* curt, dismissive treatment.

short-sighted *adj* not able to see well at a distance; lacking foresight.—**short-sightedly** *adv.*—**short-sightedness** *n*.

short-tempered *adj* easily annoyed.

short-term *adj* of or for a limited time.

short time *n* a reduction in working hours due to recession, etc.

short-winded *adj* easily becoming breathless; (*speech, writing*) brief, to the point.

shortwave *n* a radio wave 60 metres or less in length.

shot[1] *see* **shoot**.

shot[2] *n* the act of shooting; range, scope; an attempt; a solid projectile for a gun; projectiles collectively; small lead pellets for a shotgun; a marksman; a photograph or a continuous film sequence; a hypodermic injection, as of vaccine; a drink of alcohol.

shotgun *n* a smooth-bore gun for firing small shot at close range.

shotgun wedding *n* (*inf*) an enforced wedding, usu because the woman is pregnant.

shot put *n* a field event in which a heavy metal ball is proepelled with an overhand thrust from the shoulder.—**shot-putter** *n*.

shotten *adj* (*fish*) having spawned recently.

should *vb aux* used to express obligation, duty, expectation or probability, or a future condition.—*also pt of* **shall**.

shoulder *n* the joint connecting the arm with the trunk; a part like a shoulder; (*pl*) the upper part of the back; (*pl*) the capacity to bear a task or blame; a projecting part; the strip of land bordering a road. * *vti* to place on the shoulder to carry; to assume responsibility; to push with the shoulder, to jostle.

shoulder blade *n* the large flat triangular bone on either side of the back part of the human shoulder.

shoulder strap *n* a strap over the shoulders to hold up a garment, bag, etc.

shouldn't = should not.

shout *n* a loud call; a yell. * *vti* to call loudly, to yell; (*with* **down**) to drown out or silence (a person speaking) by shouting.

shove *vti* to drive forward; to push; to jostle; (*with* **off**) to push (a boat) off from the shore; (*inf*) to depart, leave. * *n* a forceful push.

shove-halfpenny *n* a game in which coins or discs are slid across a board marked with a scoring grid.

shovel *n* a broad tool like a scoop with a long handle for moving loose material. * *vt* (**shovelling, shovelled** *or* **shoveling, shoveled**) to move or lift with a shovel.

shoveller, shoveler *n* any of several pond and marsh ducks with a broad beak.

shovelhead *n* a breed of shark with a shovel-shaped head.

show *vti* (**showing, showed** *or* **shown**) to present to view, to exhibit; to demonstrate, to make clear; to prove; to manifest, to disclose; to direct, to guide; to appear, to be visible; to finish third in a horse race; (*inf*) to arrive; (*with* **off**) to display to advantage; to try to attract admiration; to behave pretentiously; (*with* **up**) to put in an appearance, to arrive; to expose to ridicule. * *n* a display, an exhibition; an entertainment; a theatrical performance; a radio or television programme; third place at the finish (as a horse race).

show business, show biz *n* the entertainment industry.

showcase *n* a glass case or cabinet for displaying items in a shop or museum; a setting or situation designed to exhibit something to best advantage.—*also vt.*

showdown *n* (*inf*) a final conflict; a disclosure of cards at poker.

shower *n* a brief period of rain, hail, or snow; a similar fall, as of tears, meteors, arrows, etc; a great number; a method of cleansing in which the body is sprayed with water from above; a wash in this; a party for the presentation of gifts, esp to a bride. * *vt* to pour copiously; to sprinkle; to bestow (with gifts). * *vi* to cleanse in a shower.

showgirl *n* a girl who appears in a chorus line, variety act, etc.

show house *n* a house on a new housing estate used as a sample for prospective buyers.

showjumping *n* the competitive riding of horses to demonstrate their skill in jumping.

showman *n* (*pl* **showmen**) a man who manages or presents a theatrical show, circus, etc; a person skilled in presentation.

shown *see* **show**.

showpiece *n* an exhibit; a perfect example of something.

showplace *n* a place (eg tourist attraction, historic site) regarded as of exemplary interest or beauty.

showroom *n* a room where goods for sale are displayed.

showy *adj* (**showier, showiest**) bright, colourful; ostentatious.—**showily** *adv.*—**showiness** *n*.

shrank *see* **shrink**.

shrapnel *n* an artillery shell filled with small pieces of metal that scatter on impact.

shred *n* a strip cut or torn off; a fragment, a scrap. * *vt* (**shredding, shredded**) to cut or tear into small pieces.

shrew *n* a small, brown, nocturnal mouse-like animal with a long snout; a bad-tempered, nagging woman.

shrewd *adj* astute, having common sense; keen, penetrating.—shrewdly *adv*.—shrewdness *n*.

shrewish *adj* sharp-tongued, nagging.

shriek *n* a loud, shrill cry, a scream. * *vti* to screech, to scream.

shrieval *adj* of or pertaining to a sheriff.

shrievalty *n* (*pl* shrievalties) the office, term of office or jurisdiction of a sheriff.

shrike *n* a bird with a hooked beak that impales its prey, mainly insects and small animals, on thorns.

shrill *adj* high-pitched and piercing in sound; strident.

shrimp *n* a small edible shellfish with a long tail; (*sl*) a small or unimportant person. * *vt* to fish for shrimp.

shrine *n* a container for sacred relics; a saint's tomb; a place of worship; a hallowed place.

shrink *vti* (shrinking, shrank *or* shrunk, *pp* shrunk *or* shrunken) to become smaller, to contract as from cold, wetting, etc; to recoil (from), to flinch; to cause (cloth, etc) to contract by soaking. * *n* (*sl*) a psychiatrist.—shrinkable *adj*.

shrinkage *n* contraction; diminution.

shrinking violet *n* a very shy or unassuming person.

shrink-wrap *vt* (shrink-wrapping, shrink-wrapped) (*book etc*) to wrap in plastic film that is then shrunk by heat to form a tightly fitting package.

shrive *vb* (shriving, shrived *or* shrove, *pp* shriven *or* shrived) *vt* (*arch*) to hear the confession of; to impose penance on and absolve. * *vi* to confess, do penance and receive absolution.

shrivel *vti* (shrivelling, shrivelled *or* shriveling, shriveled) to dry up or wither and become wrinkled; to curl up with heat, etc.

shroud *n* a burial cloth; anything that envelops or conceals; (*naut*) a supporting rope for a mast. * *vt* to wrap in a shroud; to envelop or conceal.

shrove *see* shrive.

Shrovetide *n* the three days before Ash Wednesday.

Shrove Tuesday *n* the last day before Lent.

shrub *n* a woody plant smaller than a tree with several stems rising from the same root; a bush.—shrubby *adj*.

shrubbery *n* (*pl* shrubberies) an area of land planted with shrubs.

shrug *vti* (shrugging, shrugged) to draw up and contract (the shoulders) as a sign of doubt, indifference, etc; (*with* off) to brush aside; to shake off; (*a garment*) to remove by wriggling out. * *n* the act of shrugging.

shrunk *see* shrink.

shrunken *adj* shrivelled, pinched; reduced.

shtoom *n* (*sl*) silent, dumb.

shuck *n* a husk, pod or shell. * *vt* to remove the shucks from.

shucks *interj* used to express disappointment, irritation, etc.

shudder *vi* to tremble violently, to shiver; to feel strong repugnance. * *n* a convulsive shiver of the body; a vibration.

shuffle *vt* to scrape (the feet) along the ground; to walk with dragging steps; (*playing cards*) to change the order of, to mix; to intermingle, to mix up; (*with* off) to get rid of.—*also n*.

shuffleboard *n* a game in which players propel plastic or wooden discs into numbered scoring areas marked on a large flat surface.

shufty, shufti *n* (*pl* shufties) (*sl*) a peek, a glance.

shun *vt* (shunning, shunned) to avoid scrupulously; to keep away from.

shunt *vti* to move to a different place; to put aside, to shelve; (*trains*) to switch from one track to another; (*sl*) to collide.—*also n*.

shush *interj* used to demand silence; peace, silence. * *vt* to demand silence (as if) by saying "shush".

shut *vti* (shutting, shut) to close; to lock, to fasten; to close up parts of, to fold together; to bar; (*with* down) to (cause to) stop working or operating; (*with* in) to confine; to enclose; to block the view from; (*with* off) to check the flow of; to debar; (*with* out) to exclude; (*with* up) to confine; (*inf*) to stop talking; (*inf*) to silence.

shutdown *n* a stoppage of work or activity, as in a factory.

shuteye *n* (*inf*) sleep.

shutter *n* a movable cover for a window; a flap device for regulating the exposure of light to a camera lens.

shuttle *n* a device in a loom for holding the weft thread and carrying it between the warp threads; a bus, aircraft, etc, making back-and-forth trips over a short route. * *vti* to move back and forth rapidly.

shuttlecock[1] *n* a cork stuck with feathers, or a plastic imitation, hit with a racket in badminton.

shuttlecock[2] *see* battledore.

shy[1] *adj* (shyer, shyest *or* shier, shiest) very self-conscious, timid; bashful; wary, suspicious (of); (*sl*) lacking. * *vi* (shying, shied) to move suddenly, as when startled; to be or become cautious, etc. * *n* (*pl* shies) a sudden movement.—shyly *adv*.—shyness *n*.

shy[2] *vt* (shying, shied) to throw (something). * *n* (*pl* shies) a throw; (*inf*) an attempt, try.

shyster *n* (*inf*) a person, esp a lawyer, who is manipulative and disreputable.

SI *n* (Système International d'Unités) the universally used system of units based on the metre, second, kilogram, ampere, kelvin, candela, siemens, tesla, weber and mole.

Si (*chem symbol*) silicon.

si *n* (*mus*) ti.

sial *n* the outer layer of the earth's crust composed mostly of rock rich in silicon and aluminium.

Siamese cat *n* a breed of domestic shorthaired cat with a fawn or grey coat, darker ears, paws, tail and face, and blue eyes.

Siamese fighting fish *n* an aggressive brightly coloured freshwater fish.

Siamese twins *npl* twin babies born with the bodies joined together at some point, esp the hip.

sib *n* a sibling.

sibilant *adj* hissing. * *n* a sibilant letter, eg *s*, *z*.—sibilance *n*.

sibling *n* a brother or sister.

sibyl *n* in ancient Greece and Rome, a female prophet or oracle.

sic *adv* as written (used in text to indicate that an error or doubtful usage is reproduced from the original).

sick *adj* unhealthy, ill; having nausea, vomiting; thoroughly tired (of); disgusted by or suffering from an excess; (*inf*) of humour, sadistic, gruesome.—sickness *n*.

sick bay *n* an area in a ship used as a hospital or dispensary; a room used for the treatment of the sick.

sickbed *n* the bed where one lies sick.

sick building syndrome *n* a collection of symptoms, thought to be caused by micro-organisms found in humidifiers and including lethargy, headache and eye irritation, that affect those who work in totally air-conditioned buildings.—*also* **humidifier fever.**

sicken *vti* to make or become sick or nauseated; to show signs of illness; to nauseate.

sickening *adj* disgusting.—**sickeningly** *adv.*

sickle *n* a tool with a crescent-shaped blade for cutting tall grasses; anything shaped like this.

sick leave *n* absence from work due to illness.

sickle cell anaemia *n* a form of anaemia that is hereditary and marked by the presence of sickle-shaped red blood cells.

sick list *n* a list of employees, soldiers, etc who are absent due to illness.

sickly *adj* (**sicklier, sickliest**) inclined to be ill; unhealthy; causing nausea; mawkish; pale, feeble.—**sickliness** *n.*

sick-making *adj* (*inf*) nauseating, galling.

sick pay *n* wages or salaries paid to an employee while he or she is off sick.

sickroom *n* the room to which a patient is confined while sick.

side *n* a line or surface bounding anything; the left or right part of the body; the top or underneath surface; the slope of a hill; an aspect, a direction; a party or faction; a cause; a team; a line of descent; (*sl*) conceit. * *adj* toward or at the side, lateral; incidental. * *vi* to associate with a particular faction.

side arms *n* weapons (eg a pistol, dagger) worn in a belt or holster at the side of the waist.

sideboard *n* a long table or cabinet for holding cutlery, crockery, etc; (*pl*) two strips of hair growing down a man's cheeks.—*also* **sideburns.**

sidecar *n* a small car attached to the side of a motor cycle; a cocktail of brandy, liqueur, and lemon juice.

sided *adj* having sides of a specified number or kind.

side dish *n* food accompanying a main course at a meal.

side drum *n* a small double-headed drum with snares, carried and played at the side.

side effect *n* a secondary and usu adverse effect, as of a drug or medical treatment.

side-glance *n* a look directed to one side; a slight reference.

sidekick *n* (*sl*) a confederate; a partner; a close friend.

sidelight *n* light coming from the side; a light on the side of a car, etc; incidental information.

sideline *n* a line marking the side limit of a playing area; a minor branch of business; a subsidiary interest.

sidelong *adj* oblique, not direct. * *adv* obliquely.

sidereal *adj* of or by reference to stars and constellations.

siderite *n* a mineral composed mainly of ferrous carbonate used as a source of iron.

sidero-, sider- *prefix* iron.

siderosis *n* a lung disease caused by inhalation of iron or other types of metallic particles.

side-saddle *n* a saddle that enables a rider to sit with both feet on the same side of a horse. * *adv* as if sitting on a side-saddle.

sideshow *n* a minor attraction at a fair, etc; a subsidiary event.

sidesman *n* (*pl* **sidesmen**) (*Anglican Church*) an officer assisting the churchwardens.

side-splitting *adj* uproariously funny.

sidestep *vti* to take a step to one side; to avoid or dodge.—*also n.*

sidestroke *n* (*swimming*) a stroke used while swimming on one's side.

sideswipe *n* a glancing blow; (*inf*) an incidental jibe or criticism.

sidetrack *vt* to prevent action by diversionary tactics; to shunt aside, to shelve. * *n* a railroad siding.

sidewalk *n* a path, usu paved, at the side of a street.

sidewall *n* either of the sides of a pneumatic tyre.

sideward, sidewards *adj*, *adv* sideways.

sideways, sideway *adj*, *adv* toward or from one side; facing to the side.

side whiskers *n* sideboards or sideburns.

sidewinder *n* a North American rattlesnake that moves in a twisting sideways motion.

sidewise *adv* sideways.

siding *n* a short line beside a main railway track for use in shunting; a covering as of boards for the outside of a frame building.

sidle *vi* to move sideways, esp to edge along.

SIDS *abbr* = sudden infant death syndrome.

siege *n* the surrounding of a fortified place to cut off supplies and compel its surrender; the act of besieging; a continued attempt to gain something.

siemens *n* (*pl* **siemens**) the SI unit of electrical conductance.

sienna *n* an earthy pigment, either yellowish brown (raw sienna) or reddish brown (burnt sienna).

sierra *n* a range of mountains with jagged peaks.

siesta *n* a midday nap, esp in hot countries.

sieve *n* a utensil with a meshed wire bottom for sifting and straining; a person who cannot keep secrets. * *vt* to put through a sieve, to sift.

sift *vti* to separate coarser parts from finer with a sieve; to sort out; to examine critically; to pass as through a sieve.

sigh *vti* to draw deep audible breath as a sign of weariness, relief, etc; to make a sound like this; to pine or lament (for); to utter with a sigh.—*also n.*

sight *n* the act or faculty of seeing; what is seen or is worth seeing, a spectacle; a view or glimpse; range of vision; a device on a gun etc to guide the eye in aiming it; aim taken with this; (*inf*) anything that looks unpleasant, odd, etc. * *vti* to catch sight of; to aim through a sight.

sighted *adj* having sight, esp of a particular character, eg shortsighted.

sightless *adj* without sight, blind.—**sightlessly** *adv.*—**sightlessness** *n.*

sightly *adj* (**sightlier, sightliest**) pleasing to the eye; comely.—**sightliness** *n.*

sight-read *vt* (**sight-reading, sight-read**) to play or sing from a piece of printed music without previous preparation. * *vi* to read at sight.

sightseeing *n* the viewing or visiting of places of interest.—**sightseer** *n.*

sigma *n* the 18th letter of the Greek alphabet; (*math*) the symbol S indicating summation.

sigmoid, sigmoidal *adj* curved like the letter S.

sign *n* a mark or symbol; a gesture; an indication, token, trace, or symptom (of); an omen; (*math*) a conventional mark used to indicate an operation to be performed; a board or placard with publicly displayed information. * *vi* to append one's signature; to ratify thus. * *vt* to engage by written contract; to write one's name on; to make or indicate by a sign; to signal; to communicate by sign language; (*with* **away**) to relinquish by signing a deed, etc; (*with* **on**) to accept employment; to register; (*with* **off**) to complete a broadcast.

signal *n* a sign, device or gesture to intimate a warning or to give information, esp at a distance; a message so conveyed; a semaphore system used by railways; in radio, etc, the electrical impulses transmitted or received; a sign or event that initiates action. * *vti* (**signalling, signalled** *or* **signaling, signaled**) to make a signal or signals (to); to communicate by signals. * *adj* striking, notable.—**signaller, signaler** *n*.

signalize *vt* to point out; distinguish.—**signalization** *n*.

signally *adv* remarkably; notably.

signalman *n* (*pl* **signalmen**) a person who works signals or transmits signals.

signatory *n* (*pl* **signatories**) a party or state that has signed an agreement or treaty; the person who signs on behalf of their government.

signature *n* a person's name written by himself or herself; the act of signing one's own name; a characteristic mark; (*mus*) the flats and sharps after the clef showing the key; (*print*) a mark on the first pages of each sheet of a book as a guide to the binder; such a sheet when folded.

signature tune *n* a tune associated with a performer or a TV, radio programme, etc.

signboard *n* a board with a sign or inscription in front of a business, shop, etc.

signet *n* a small seal, esp one set in a ring; an official seal used in lieu of a signature in authenticating documents; the impression made by this.

signet ring *n* a ring with a seal set in it.

significant *adj* full of meaning, esp a special or hidden one; momentous, important; highly expressive; indicative (of).—**significance** *n*.—**significantly** *adv*.

signify *vti* (**signifying, signified**) to mean; to be a sign of; to indicate; to represent; to matter, to be important; to make a sign.—**signification** *n*.

sign language *n* a system of manual signs and gestures for conveying meaning, used esp by the deaf.

signor, signior *n* (*pl* **signors, signori**) an Italian man—equivalent to Mr.

signora *n* (*pl* **signoras, signore**) a married Italian woman—equivalent to Mrs or madam.

signore *n* (*pl* **signori**) an Italian man—equivalent to sir.

signorina *n* (*pl* **signorinas, signorine**) an unmarried Italian woman—equivalent to Miss.

signpost *n* a post with signs on it to direct travellers; a beacon, a guide.—*also vt*.

Sikh *n* a member of an Indian sect, founded in the 16th century, that teaches monotheism and rejects idolatry and caste. * *adj* of or pertaining to the Sikhs or their beliefs.

silage *n* green fodder preserved for the winter in a silo.

sild *n* (*pl* **silds, sild**) a young herring, esp when canned in Norway.

silence *n* absence of sound; the time this lasts; refusal to speak or make a sound; secrecy. * *vt* to cause to be silent. * *interj* be silent!

silencer *n* a device for reducing the noise of a vehicle exhaust or gun, a muffler.

silent *adj* not speaking; taciturn; noiseless; still.—**silently** *adv*.

silent majority *n* those who rarely assert their views but are presumed to be moderates.

silhouette *n* the outline of a shape against light or a lighter background; a solid outline drawing, usu in solid black on white, esp of a profile. * *vt* to show up in outline; to depict in silhouette.

silica *n* a hard mineral, a compound of oxygen and sili-con, found in quartz and flint.

silicate *n* a salt containing silicon.

siliceous, silicious *adj* of or containing silica.

silicon *n* a metalloid element occurring in silica and used extensively in transistors, etc, and as a compound in glass, etc. * *adj* of an area in which there are a number of computer software and hardware companies.

silicon chip *n* a microchip.

silicone *n* an organic polymer compound with good lubricating and insulating properties, used widely as a repellent, resin, etc.

silicosis *n* a disease of the lungs caused by prolonged inhalation of silica particles.

silk *n* a fibre produced by silkworms; lustrous textile cloth, thread or a garment made of silk; (*pl*) silk garments; (*pl*) the colours of a racing stable, worn by a jockey, etc. *adj* of, relating to or made of silk.

silk cotton *n* kapok.

silken *adj* made of or like silk; silky.

silk hat *n* a top hat covered in silk.

silk screen *n* a stencil method of printing a colour design through the meshes of a fabric, as silk; a print so produced.—**silk-screen** *vt*.

silkweed *see* **milkweed**.

silkworm *n* a caterpillar of various moths that feeds on mulberry leaves and produces a strong fibre to construct its cocoon.

silky *adj* (**silkier, silkiest**) soft and smooth like silk; glossy; suave.—**silkiness** *n*.

sill *n* a heavy, horizontal slab of wood or stone at the bottom of a window frame or door.

sillabub *see* **syllabub**.

silly *adj* (**sillier, silliest**) foolish, stupid; frivolous; lacking in sense or judgment; being stunned or dazed. * *n* (pl **sillies**) a silly person.—**silliness** *n*.

silo *n* (pl **silos**) an airtight pit or tower for storing fodder in a green compressed state; a deep pit for storing cement, coal, etc; an underground structure from which a missile can be fired.

silt *n* a fine-grained sandy sediment carried or deposited by water. * *vti* to fill or choke up with silt.

Silurian *adj* (*geol*) of or pertaining to the division of Palaeozoic rocks between Ordovician and Devonian. * *n* this period.

silver *n* a ductile, malleable, greyish-white metallic element used in jewellery, cutlery, tableware, coins, etc; a lustrous, greyish white. * *adj* made of or plated with silver; silvery; (*hair*) grey; marking the 25th in a series * *vt* to coat with silver or a substance resembling silver; to make or become silvery or grey.

silver birch *n* a Eurasian birch tree with silvery bark.

silver fox *n* (the pelt of) a red fox in a colour phase when its fur is black with silver-tipped hairs.

silver-gilt *n* gilded silver.

silver lining *n* a more favourable aspect of an otherwise hopeless situation.

silver paper *n* a metallic paper coated or laminated to resemble silver, tinfoil.

silver plate *n* a plating of silver; domestic utensils made of silver or of silver-plated metal.—**silver-plate** *vt*.

silver screen *n* (*inf*) (*with* **the**) the film industry; the screen on which a film is projected.

silver service *n* (*in restaurants*) a manner of serving food using a spoon and fork in one hand.

silverside *n* a joint of beef cut from the upper haunch.

silversmith *n* a worker in silver.

silver-tongued *adj* plausible, eloquent.

silverware *n* items, such as serving plates, cutlery, etc made from silver or silver plate.

silver wedding *n* the 25th anniversary of a marriage.

silverweed *n* any of various plants with silvery leaves or hairs.

silvery *adj* white and lustrous like silver; covered with silver; resembling silver in colour; (*sound*) soft and clear.

silviculture *n* the branch of forestry dealing with the care and development of forests.

simian *adj* of or like an ape or monkey.

simian immunodeficiency virus *n* a virus, similar to human immunodeficiency virus, that interferes with the ability of the immune system of monkeys to resist disease.

similar *adj* having a resemblance to, like; nearly corresponding; (*geom*) corresponding exactly in shape if not size.—**similarity** *n*.—**similarly** *adv*.

simile *n* a figure of speech likening one thing to another by the use of like, as, etc.

similitude *n* the state of being similar; guise, likeness.

simmer *vti* to boil gently; to be or keep on the point of boiling; to be in a state of suppressed rage or laughter; (*with* **down**) to abate. * *n* the state of simmering.

simnel cake *n* a rich fruit cake with marzipan and decorations traditionally eaten during Lent or Easter.

simony *n* the buying and selling of ecclesiastical offices.

simoom, simoon *n* a strong, hot, dry wind of the Arabian and North African deserts.

simpatico *adj* (*inf*) agreeable, sympathetic.

simper *vi* to smile in a silly or self-conscious way.—*also n*.

simple *adj* single, uncompounded; plain, not elaborate; clear, not complicated; easy to do, understand, or solve; artless, not sophisticated; weak in intellect; unsuspecting, credulous; sheer, mere.—**simpleness** *n*.

simple fraction *n* a fraction in which both the numerator and denominator are whole numbers.

simple-hearted *adj* sincere, honest.

simple interest *n* interest paid on the principal of a loan only.

simple-minded *adj* foolish; mentally retarded.

simpleton *n* a foolish, weak-minded person.

simplicity *n* (*pl* simplicities) the quality or state of being simple; absence of complications; easiness; lack of ornament, plainness, restraint; artlessness; directness; guilelessness, openness, naivety.

simplification *n* the act or result of making less complicated.

simplify *vt* (**simplifying, simplified**) to make simple or easy to understand.

simplistic *adj* oversimplified; uncomplicated.—**simplistically** *adv*.

simply *adv* in a simple way; plainly; merely; absolutely.

simulacrum *n* (*pl* simulacra) a likeness or representation, esp a superficial one.

simulate *vt* to pretend to have or feel, to feign; (*conditions*) to reproduce in order to conduct an experiment; to imitate.—**simulation** *n*.

simulator *n* a device that simulates specific conditions in order to test actions or reactions.

simulcast *n* a simultaneous radio and television broadcast.—*also vt*.

simultaneous *adj* done or occurring at the same time.—**simultaneity** *n*.—**simultaneously** *adv*.

sin[1] *n* an offence against a religious or moral principle; transgression of the law of God; a wicked act, an offence; a misdeed, a fault. * *vi* (**sinning, sinned**) to commit a sin; to offend (against).

sin[2] *abbr* = sine.

sin bin *n* (*ice hockey, etc*) (*sl*) an enclosure off the playing area where players guilty of fouls are temporarily sent.

since *adv* from then until now; subsequently; ago. * *prep* during, or continously from (then) until now; after. * *conj* from the time that; because, seeing that.

sincere *adj* genuine, real, not pretended; honest, straightforward.—**sincerely** *adv*.

sincerity *n* the quality or state of being sincere; genuineness, honesty, seriousness.

sinciput *n* (*pl* sinciputs, sincipita) the front part of the skull; forehead.

sine *n* (*trig*) a function that in a right-angled triangle is equal to the ratio of the length of the side opposite the angle to that of the hypoteneuse.

sinecure *n* a position or office that provides an income without involving duties.

sine die *adv* without a date, indefinitely.

sine qua non *n* an essential condition, a necessity.

sinew *n* a cord of fibrous tissue, a tendon; (*usu pl*) the chief supporting force, a mainstay; (*pl*) muscles, brawn.

sinewy *adj* having a lean body and strong muscles; tough, stringy.

sinfonia *n* (*pl* sinfonie, sinfonias) a symphony.

sinfonietta *n* a short symphony; a small orchestra.

sinful *adj* guilty of sin, wicked.—**sinfully** *adv*.—**sinfulness** *n*.

sing *vti* (**singing, sang,** *pp* **sung**) to utter (words) with musical modulations; (*a song*) to perform; to hum, to ring; to write poetry (about), to praise; (*with* **out**) to shout, call out.—**singer** *n*.—**singing** *n*.

sing. *abbr* = singular.

singe *vt* (**singeing, singed**) to burn slightly; to scorch, esp to remove feathers, etc.—*also n*.

Singhalese *see* **Sinhalese**.

singing *n* the art or an act of singing.

singing telegram *n* (a service that provides) a greetings message delivered in song, usu by a person in fancy dress.

single *adj* one only, not double; individual; composed of one part; alone, sole; separate; unmarried; for one; with one contestant on each side; simple; whole, unbroken; (*tennis*) played between two persons only; (*ticket*) for the outward journey only. * *n* a single ticket; a game between two players; a hit scoring one; a record with one tune on each side. * *vt* (*with* **out**) to pick out, to select.

single blessedness *n* the unmarried state.

single-breasted *adj* (*suit, etc*) fastening in the centre with a single row of buttons.

single cream *n* cream with a low fat content.

single-decker *n* a bus with only one level of passenger accommodation.

single entry *n* (*book-keeping*) a system in which transactions are kept in one account only.

single figures *npl* the numbers less than 10, ie 1 to 9.

single file *n* a single column of persons or things, one behind the other.

single-handed *adj, adv* without assistance, unaided.—**single-handedly** *adv*.—**single-handedness** *n*.

single-lens reflex *n* a camera whose lens allows the photographer to see the same image as it exposes.

single-minded *adj* having only one aim in mind.—**single-mindedly** *adv*.—**single-mindedness** *n*.

singles bar *n* a bar or social club for single people only.

singlestick *n* fencing with wooden sticks instead of swords; the stick used for this.

singlet *n* an undervest.

single ticket *n* a ticket for a one-way journey only.

singleton *n* a playing card that is the only one of its suit in a hand.

singly *adv* alone; one by one.

singsong *n* a droning monotonous utterance; a verse with a regular, marked rhythm and rhyme; (*inf*) a party where everyone sings. * *adj* having a regular or monotonous rhythm.

singular *adj* remarkable; exceptional; unusual; eccentric, odd; (*gram*) referring to only one person or thing. * *n* (*gram*) the singular number or form of a word.

singularity *n* (*pl* **singularities**) the state of being singular; uniqueness; an odd trait, a peculiarity.

singularly *adv* unusually; exceptionally.

Sinhalese *n* a member of a people who form the largest community in Sri Lanka; the language of these people.—*also adj*.—*also* **Singhalese**.

sinister *adj* inauspicious; ominous; ill-omened; evil-looking; malignant; wicked; left; (*her*) on the left side of the shield.

sinistral *adj* of or on the left; left-handed.—**sinistrally** *adv*.

sink *vti* (**sinking, sank** *or* **sunk,** *pp* **sunk**) to go under the surface or to the bottom (of a liquid); to submerge in water; to go down slowly; (*wind*) to subside; to pass to a lower state; to droop, to decline; to grow weaker; to become hollow; to lower, to degrade; to cause to sink; to make by digging out; to invest; (*with* **in**) to penetrate; to thrust into; (*inf*) to be understood in full. * *n* a basin with an outflow pipe, usu in a kitchen; a cesspool; an area of sunken land.—**sinking** *n*.

sinker *n* a weight used to submerge a fishing line.

sinkhole *n* a hole in rock strata, esp limestone, though which water sinks or runs underground; a hole into which foul waste matter is discharged.

sinking fund *n* money put aside for gradual payment of a debt.

Sinn Fein *n* a republican party in Ireland which is the political wing of the IRA.

sinner *n* a person who sins.

Sino- *prefix* Chinese.

Sino-Tebetan *n* a family of languages that includes all the Chinese languages, Burmese and Tibetan.—*also adj*.

Sinology *n* the study of Chinese language, history, society, etc.—**Sinologist** *n*.—**Sinological** *adj*.

sinsemilla *n* (a plant which produces) a highly potent type of marijuana.

sinter *n* a white silicious deposit formed by the evaporation of hot mineral waters. * *vt* to form (metal or glass powder) into lumps by the application of heat and pressure.

sinuate *adj* (*leaf*) having a wavy edge.—**sinuately** *adv*.

sinuous *adj* curving; winding; tortuous.—**sinuously** *adv*.—**sinuousness** *n*.

sinus *n* (*pl* **sinuses**) an air cavity in the skull that opens in the nasal cavities.

sinusitis *n* inflammation of a sinus.

Siouan *n* a family of North American Indian languages.

Sioux *n* (*pl* **Sioux**) a member of various North American Indian peoples who speak Siouan.

sip *vti* (**sipping, sipped**) to drink in small mouthfuls. * *n* the act of sipping; the quantity sipped.

siphon *n* a bent tube for drawing off liquids from a higher to a lower level by atmospheric pressure; a bottle with an internal tube and tap at the top for aerated water. * *vti* to draw off, or be drawn off, with a siphon.—*also* **syphon**.

siphon bottle *n* a soda siphon.

sir *n* a title of respect used to address a man in speech or correspondence; (*with cap*) a title preceding the first name of a knight or baronet. * *vt* to address as "sir".

sire *n* a father; a male ancestor; the male parent of an animal; a form of address to a king. * *vt* (*animal*) to beget.

siren *n* a device producing a loud wailing sound as a warning signal; a fabled sea nymph who lured sailors to destruction with a sweet song; a seductive or alluring woman.

sirenian *n* a member of an order of plant-eating mammals that live in water, comprising the dugong and the manatee.—*also adj*.

sirloin *n* the upper part of a loin of beef.

sirocco *n* a hot, oppressive wind that blows across southern Europe from North Africa.

sirree *interj* (*inf*) sir – used for emphasis, esp after *yes* or *no*.

sis *n* (*inf*) sister.

sisal *n* (a tropical agave plant whose leaves yield) a tough fibre used to make rope.

siskin *n* a Eurasian songbird with greenish plumage related to the goldfinch.

sissy *n* (*pl* **sissies**) an effeminate, feeble or cowardly boy or man.—*also adj*.

sister *n* a female sibling, a daughter of the same parents; a female member or associate of the same race, creed, trade union, etc; a member of a religious sisterhood; one of the same kind, model, etc; a senior nurse. * *adj* (*ship, etc*) belonging to the same type.

sisterhood *n* a female religious or charitable order; the state of being a sister.

sister-in-law *n* (*pl* **sisters-in-law**) the sister of a husband or wife; the wife of a brother.

sisterly *adj* like a sister, kind, affectionate.

sistrum *n* (*pl* **sistra**) an ancient Egyptian metal rattle used as a percussion instrument.

sit *vti* (**sitting, sat**) to rest oneself on the buttocks, as on a chair; (*bird*) to perch; (*hen*) to cover eggs for hatching; (*legislator, etc*) to occupy a seat; (*court*) to be in session; to pose, as for a portrait; to ride (a horse); to press or weigh (upon); to be located; to rest or lie; to take an examination; to take care of a child, pet, etc, while the parents or owners are away; to cause to sit; to provide seats or seating room for; (*with* **down**) to take a seat; (*with* **for**) to represent in parliament; (*with* **in**) to attend a discussion or a musical session; to participate in a sit-in; (*with* **on**) to hold a meeting to discuss; to delay action on something; (*inf*) to suppress; to rebuke; (*with* **out**) to sit through the whole; to abstain from dancing; (*with* **up**) to straighten the back while sitting; not to go to bed; (*inf*) to be astonished.

sitar *n* an Indian musical instrument similar to a lute with a long neck.

sitcom *see* **situation comedy**.

site *n* a space occupied or to be occupied by a building; a situation; the place or scene of something. * *vt* to locate, to place.

sit-in *n* a strike in which the strikers refuse to leave the premises; civil disobedience in which demonstrators occupy a public place and refuse to leave voluntarily.

sitka spruce *n* a tall North American spruce tree.

sitter *n* a person who looks after a child, dog, house, etc, while the parents or owners are away.

sitting *n* the state of being seated; a period of being seated, as for a meal, a portrait; a session, as of a court; a clutch of eggs. * *adj* that is sitting; being in a judicial or legislative seat; used in or for sitting; performed while sitting.

sitting duck, sitting target *n* (*inf*) a person or thing that is an easy target for attack, criticism, etc.

sitting room *n* a room other than a bedroom or kitchen; a parlour.

sitting tenant *n* a tenant in occupation of a property.

situate *vt* to place in a site, situation, or category.

situated *adj* having a site, located; placed; provided with money, etc.

situation *n* a place, a position; a state of affairs, circumstances; a job or post.

situation comedy *n* a comic television or radio series made up of episodes involving the same group of characters.—*also* **sitcom**.

sit-up *n* an exercise of sitting up from a prone position without using hands or legs.

SIV *abbr* = simian immunodeficiency virus.

six *adj*, *n* one more than five. * *n* the symbol for this (6, VI, vi); the sixth in a series or set; something having six units as members.

sixer *n* a leader of a group of six Brownies or Cub Scouts.

sixfold *adj* having six units or members; being six times as great or as many.

six-pack *n* a pack of six units, as of cans of beer, etc, sold together.

sixpence *n* (*formerly*) a British coin worth six old pennies.

six-shooter *n* (*inf*) a six-chambered revolver.

sixteen *adj*, *n* one more than fifteen. * *n* the symbol for this (16, XVI, xvi).—**sixteenth** *adj*, *n*.

sixteenth note *n* a musical note with a sixteenth the time value of a whole note, a semiquaver.

sixth *n* one of six equal parts of a thing; (*mus*) an interval of six diatonic degrees; the sixth tone of a diatonic scale.—*also adv*. * *adj* next after fifth.—**sixthly** *adv*.

sixth sense *n* intuitive power.

sixty *n* six times ten. * *n* (*pl* **sixties**) the symbol for this (60, LX, lx); (in *pl*) sixties (60s), the numbers for 60 to 69; the same numbers in a life or century.—**sixtieth** *adj*, *adv*.

sixty-fourth note. *n* a musical note with the time value of one sixty-fourth of a whole note; a hemidemisemiquaver.

sixty-nine n soixante-neuf.

sizable, sizeable *adj* of some size; large.—**sizably, sizeably** *adv*.—**sizableness, sizeableness** *n*.

size[1] *n* magnitude; the dimensions or proportions of something; a graduated measurement, as of clothing or shoes. * *vt* to sort according to size; to measure; (*with* **up**) (*inf*) to make an estimate or judgment of; to meet requirements.

size[2] *n* a thin pasty substance used to glaze paper, stiffen cloth, etc. * *vt* to treat with size.

sized *adj* having a specified size.

sizzle *vti* to make a hissing spluttering noise, as of frying; to be extremely hot; to be very angry; to scorch, sear or fry with a sizzling sound. * *n* a hissing sound.

SJ *abbr* = Society of Jesus.

sjambok *n* (*in S Africa*) a heavy whip made from rhinoceros hide.

SK *abbr* = Saskatchewan.

ska *n* a form of West Indian pop music, a precursor of reggae.

skate[1] *n* a steel blade attached to a boot for gliding on ice; a boot with such a runner; a roller skate. * *vi* to move on skates; (*with* **over**) to avoid dealing with (an issue, problem, etc) directly.—**skater** *n*.

skate[2] *n* an edible fish of the ray family with a broad, flat body and short, spineless tail.

skateboard *n* a short, oblong board with two wheels at each end for standing on and riding.—*also vi*.

skean-dhu *n* (*Scot*) a dagger worn in the stocking as part of Highland dress.

skedaddle *vi* (*inf*) to run away.—*also n*.

skeet *n* a type of clay-pigeon shooting in which clay targets are hurled into range at varying speeds and trajectories from two traps.

skein *n* a folded coil of yarn, thread, etc; a tangle; a flight of wild fowl, esp geese.

skeleton *n* the bony framework of the body of a human, an animal or plant; the bones separated from flesh and preserved in their natural position; a supporting structure, a framework; an outline, an abstract; a very thin person; something shameful kept secret. * *adj* (*staff, crew, etc*) reduced to the lowest possible level.— **skeletal** *adj*.

skeleton key *n* a key with a slender bit that can open many simple locks.

skeptic *see* **sceptic**.

skeptical *see* **sceptical**.

skepticism *see* **scepticism**.

skerry *n* (*pl* **skerries**) a rocky isle or reef.

sketch *n* a rough drawing, quickly made; a preliminary draft; a short literary piece or essay; a short humorous item for a revue, etc; a brief outline. * *vti* to make a sketch (of); to plan roughly.

sketchy *adj* (**sketchier, sketchiest**) incomplete; vague; inadequate.—**sketchily** *adv*.—**sketchiness** *n*.

skew *adj* slanting, oblique, set at an angle. * *adv* at a slant. * *vti* to slant or set at a slant; to swerve.

skewbald *adj* marked with patches of white and another colour except black. * *n* an animal, esp a horse, with such markings.

skewer *n* a long wooden or metal pin on which pieces of meat and vegetables are cooked. * *vt* to pierce and fasten on a skewer; to transfix.

skewwhiff *adj* (*inf*) askew, not straight.

ski *n* (*pl* **skis**) a long narrow runner of wood, metal or plastic that is fastened to a boot for moving across snow; a water-ski. * *vi* (**skiing, skied**) to travel on skis.—**skier** *n*.

skibob *n* a snow vehicle similar to a bicycle with a low seat and steering handle mounted on two skis instead of wheels.

skid *vti* (**skidding, skidded**) to slide without rotating; to slip sideways; (*vehicle*) to slide sideways out of control; to cause (a vehicle) to skid. * *n* the act of skidding; a drag to reduce speed; a ship's fender; a movable support for a heavy object; a runner on an aircraft's landing gear.

skid row, skid road *n* (*sl*) a shabby district where vagrants, etc, live.

skied *see* **ski**.

skiff *n* a small light boat for rowing.

skiffle *n* a type of music using guitars and makeshift instruments (eg washboards) which became popular in the 1950s.

ski jump *n* a long ramp surmounting a slope from which skiers jump in competition.—**ski-jump** *vi*.

skilful, skillful *adj* having skill; proficient, adroit.—**skilfully, skillfully** *adv*.—**skilfulness, skillfulness** *n*.

ski lift *n* any of various devices for conveying skiers up a slope, such as a chair lift.

skill *n* proficiency; expertness, dexterity; a developed aptitude or ability; a type of work or craft requiring specialist training.

skilled *adj* fully trained, expert.

skillet *n* a frying pan.

skim *vti* (**skimming, skimmed**) to remove (cream, scum) from the surface of; to glide lightly over, to brush the surface of; to read superficially.

skimmer *n* that which skims, esp a perforated utensil for skimming milk.

skimmia *n* any of a genus of evergreen shrubs with red berries.

skim milk, skimmed milk *n* milk from which the cream has been removed.

skimp *vti* to give scant measure (of), to stint; to be sparing or frugal (with).

skimpy *adj* (**skimpier, skimpiest**) small in size; inadequate, scant, meagre.—**skimpily** *adv*.—**skimpiness** *n*.

skin *n* the tissue forming the outer covering of the body; a hide; the rind of a fruit; an outer layer or casing; a film on the surface of a liquid; a vessel for water, etc, made of hide. * *vti* (**skinning, skinned**) to remove the skin from, to peel; to injure by scraping (the knee, etc); to cover or become covered with skin; (*inf*) to swindle.

skin-deep *adj* superficial.

skin diving *n* the sport of swimming underwater with scuba equipment.—**skin-diver** *n*.

skinflick *n* (*sl*) a pornographic film.

skinflint *n* a stingy person.

skinful *n* (*pl* **skinfuls**) (*sl*) as much alcoholic drink as one can take.

skin graft *n* a piece of skin taken from one part of the body to replace damaged skin elsewhere.

skinhead *n* a British youth with cropped hair, large boots and braces, often belonging to an aggressive gang.

skink *n* a small lizard of tropical Asia and Africa.

skinned *adj* having skin of a specified kind.

skinny *adj* (**skinnier, skinniest**) very thin; emaciated.—**skinniness** *n*.

skint *adj* (*sl*) having no money.

skintight *adj* (*clothing*) fitting tightly; clinging.

skip[1] *vti* (**skipping, skipped**) to leap or hop lightly over; to keep jumping over a rope as it is swung under one; to make omissions, to pass over, esp in reading; (*inf*) to leave (town) hurriedly, to make off; (*inf*) to miss deliberately. * *n* a skipping movement; a light jump.

skip[2] *n* a large metal container for holding building debris; a cage or bucket for hoisting workers or materials in a mine, quarry, etc.

ski pants *npl* fashion trousers worn tight with a strap that fits under the foot.

skipjack *n* (*pl* **skipjack, skipjacks**) any of various food fishes including two varieties of tuna, one striped (skipjack) and the other spotted (black skipjack).

skiplane *n* a light aircraft fitted with skis for taking off and landing on snow.

ski pole *n* one of a pair of pointed metal sticks used by skiers to provide forward thrust and to aid stability.—*also* **ski stick**.

skipper *n* the captain of a boat, aircraft, or team. * *vt* to act as skipper; to captain.

skipping rope *n* a light rope, usu with a handle at each end, that is swung over the head and under the feet while jumping.

skirl *n* (*Scot*) the shrill wailing sound characteristic of bagpipes.—*also vi*.

skirmish *n* a minor fight in a war; a conflict or clash. * *vi* to take part in a skirmish.

skirt *n* a woman's garment that hangs from the waist; the lower part of a dress or coat; an outer edge, a border; (*sl*) a woman. * *vti* to border; to move along the edge (of); to evade.

skirting *n* a border, an edging; fabric for skirts.

skirting board *n* a narrow panel of wood at the foot of an interior wall.

ski stick *see ski* **pole**.

skit *n* a short humorous sketch, as in the theatre.

ski tow *n* a motor-driven device that pulls skiers uphill.

skitter *vti* to move or cause to move quickly or to skim across a surface.

skittish *adj* (*animal*) frisky, easily frightened; (*person*) playful, frivolous, lively.—**skittishly** *adv*.—**skittishness** *n*.

skittles *n* a game in which a wooden or plastic bottle-shaped pin is knocked down by a ball.—*also* **ninepins**.

skive *vi* (*inf*) to avoid work or duties because of laziness.

skivvy *n* (*pl* **skivvies**) a female domestic servant. * *vi* (**skivvying, skivvied**) to perform menial domestic duties.

skol, skoal *interj* good health, cheers (*used in a toast*).

skua *n* any of various large predatory seabirds with dark plumage.

skulduggery, skullduggery *n* (*inf*) deceit, underhand dealing.

skulk *vi* to move in a stealthy manner; to lurk.

skull *n* the bony casing enclosing the brain; the cranium.

skunk *n* a small black-and-white mammal that emits a foul-smelling liquid when frightened; its fur; (*sl*) obnoxious or mean person.

sky *n* (*pl* **skies**) the apparent vault over the earth; heaven; the upper atmosphere; weather, climate.

skull and crossbones *n* (*pl* **skulls and crossbones**) an image of a human skull and crossed thighbones used as a warning of danger.

sky-blue *adj, n* (of) a bright pure blue, azure.

sky-diving *n* the sport of parachute jumping involving free-fall manoeuvres.—**sky-diver** *n*.

Skye terrier *n* a breed of short-legged terrier with long hair and a long body.

sky-high *adj, adv* very high; in an enthusiastic manner; extremely expensive.

skyjack *vt* to hijack an aircraft.

skylark *n* a lark famous for its song as it soars.

skylight *n* a window in the roof or ceiling.

skyline *n* the visible horizon; the outline, as of mountains, buildings, etc, seen against the sky.

skyrocket *n* a rocket. * *vi* to rise rapidly (eg in price, status, etc).

skyscraper *n* a very tall building.

skyward *adj, adv* toward the sky.—**skywards** *adv*.

skywriting *n* (the act of creating) writing in the sky formed by smoke or vapour emitted from an aircraft.

slab *n* a flat, broad, thick piece (as of stone, wood, or bread, etc); something resembling this. * *vt* to cut or form into slabs; to cover or support with slabs; to put on thickly.

slack *adj* loose, relaxed, not tight; (*business*) slow, not brisk; sluggish; inattentive, careless. * *n* the part (of a rope, etc) that hangs loose; a dull period; a lull; (*pl*) trousers for casual wear. * *vti* to neglect (one's work, etc), to be lazy; (*with* off) to slacken (a rope, etc).—**slackness** *n*.

slacken *vti* to make or become less active, brisk, etc; to loosen or relax, as a rope; to diminish, to abate.—**slackening** *n, adj*.

slacker *n* a lazy person; a person who shirks.

slack water *n* the turn of the tide; a slow-moving stretch of water.

slag *n* the waste product from the smelting of metals; volcanic lava.

slain *see* **slay**.

slake *vt* to quench or satisfy (thirst, etc); to mix (lime) with water.

slalom *n* downhill skiing in a zigzag course between upright markers; (*skiing, canoeing, etc*) a timed race over a slalom course. * *vi* to move over a zigzag course.

slam *vti* (**slamming, slammed**) to shut with a loud noise, to bang; to throw (down) violently; (*inf*) to criticize severely. * *n* a sound or the act of slamming, a bang; (*inf*) severe criticism; (*bridge*) the taking of 12 or 13 tricks.

slammer *n* (*sl*) a prison or jail.

slander *n* a false and malicious statement about another; the uttering of this. * *vt* to utter a slander about, to defame.—**slanderous** *adj*.

slang *n* words or expressions used in familiar speech but not regarded as standard English; jargon of a particular social class, age group, etc. * *adj* relating to slang.

slant *vti* to incline, to slope; to tell in such a way as to have a bias. * *n* a slope; an oblique position; a bias, a point of view. * *adj* sloping.—**slantly** *adv*.

slanted *adj* prejudiced, biased; sloping.

slantwise *adv* at a slant.

slap *n* a smack with the open hand; an insult; a rebuff. * *vt* (**slapping, slapped**) to strike with something flat; to put, hit, etc, with force. * *adv* directly, full.

slapdash *adj* impetuous; hurried; careless; haphazard. * *adv* carelessly.

slaphappy *adj* (**slaphappier, slaphappiest**) casually or cheerfully irresponsible; giddy, punch-drunk.

slapstick *n* boisterous humour of a knockabout kind.

slap-up *adj* (*inf*) (*meals, entertainment*) lavish, luxury.

slash *vti* to cut gashes in, to slit; to strike fiercely (at) with a sword, etc; to reduce (prices) sharply. * *n* a cutting blow; a long slit, a gash.

slat *n* a thin, flat, narrow strip of wood, etc.

slate[1] *vt* to criticize or punish severely.

slate[2] *n* a fine-grained rock easily split into thin layers; a flat plate of this or other material used in roofing; a tablet (as of slate) for writing on; a list of proposed candidates. * *adj* the colour of slate, a deep bluish-grey colour; made of slate. * *vt* to cover with slates; to suggest as a political candidate.

slater *n* a person trained in roofing with slates; a wood louse.

slatted *adj* having slats.

slattern *n* a slovenly woman; a slut.

slaughter *n* the butchering of animals for food; a wholesale killing, a massacre.—*also vt*.—**slaughterer** *n*.

slaughterhouse *n* a place where animals are slaughtered, an abattoir.

Slav *n* any person who speaks a Slavonic language.

slave *n* a person without freedom or personal rights, who is legally owned by another; a person under domination, esp of a habit or vice; a person who works like a slave, a drudge. * *vti* to toil hard, as a slave.

slave driver *n* a supervisor of slaves at work; a hard taskmaster.

slaveholder *n* a person who owns slaves.

slaver[1] *n* a person engaged in the buying and selling of slaves.

slaver[2] *vti* to dribble, to cover with saliva; to fawn upon, to flatter.

slavery *n* the condition of being a slave; bondage; drudgery; slave-owning as an institution.

slave ship *n* a ship used in the slave trade.

Slave State *n* (*hist*) any of the Southern states of the US where slavery was legal until the Civil War.

slave trade *n* commercial traffic in slaves, esp the transport of Black Africans to Europe and America in the 16th to 19th centuries.

Slavic *see* **Slavonic**.

slavish *adj* servile, abject; unoriginal.—**slavishly** *adv*.—**slavishness** *n*.

Slavonic, Slavic *adj* of or characteristic of the Slavs. * *n* a branch of the Indo-European family of languages, including Russian, Bulgarian, Polish and Czech.

slaw *n* coleslaw.

slay *vti* (**slaying, slew**, *pp* **slain**) to kill in great numbers; to murder; (*sl*) to overwhelm, to affect in a powerful way.—**slayer** *n*.

sleaze *n* (*inf*) sleaziness.

sleazy *adj* (**sleazier, sleaziest**) disreputable, squalid.—**sleaziness** *n*.

sled, sledge *n* a framework on runners for travelling over snow or ice; a toboggan; a sleigh. * *vti* to go or convey by sledge.

sledgehammer *n* a large, heavy hammer for two hands.

sleek *adj* smooth, glossy; having a prosperous or well-groomed appearance; plausible.

sleep *n* a natural, regularly recurring rest for the body, with little or no consciousness; a period spent sleeping; a state of numbness followed by tingling. * *vti* (**sleeping, slept**) to rest in a state of sleep; to be inactive; to provide beds for; (*with* **around**) (*inf*) to be sexually promiscuous; (*with* **in**) to sleep on the premises; to sleep too long in the morning; (*with* **on**) to have a night's rest before making a decision; (*with* **off**) to get rid of by sleeping; (*with* **over**) to pass the night in someone else's house; (*with* **with**) to have sexual relations with.

sleeper *n* a person or thing that sleeps; a horizontal beam that carries and spreads a weight; a sleeping car; something that suddenly attains prominence or value.

sleeping bag *n* a padded bag for sleeping in, esp outdoors.

sleeping car *n* a railway carriage with berths.

sleeping partner *n* a partner in a business who takes no part in its management.

sleeping pill *n* a pill that induces sleep.

sleeping sickness *n* a serious infectious disease marked by lethargy, coma.

sleepless *adj* without sleep; unable to sleep.

sleepwalker *n* a person who walks while asleep, a somnambulist.—**sleepwalking** *n*.

sleepy *adj* (**sleepier, sleepiest**) drowsy; tired; lazy, not alert.—**sleepily** *adv*.—**sleepiness** *n*.

sleepyhead *n* a tired or lazy person.

sleet *n* snow or hail mixed with rain. * *vi* to rain in the form of sleet.

sleeve *n* the part of a garment enclosing the arm; (*mech*) a tube that fits over a part; an open-ended cover, esp a paperboard envelope for a record.

sleeveless *adj* (*garment*) without sleeves.

sleigh *n* a light vehicle on runners for travelling over snow; a sledge.

sleight of hand *n* manual dexterity, such as in conjuring or juggling; a deception.

slender *adj* thin; slim; slight; scanty.—**slenderly** *adv*.—**slenderness** *n*.

slept *see* **sleep**.

sleuth *n* (*inf*) a detective.

sleuthhound *n* a bloodhound; (*inf*) a detective.

slew[1] *see* **slay**.

slew[2], **slue** *vti* to twist or be twisted sideways.

slew[3], **slue** *n* (*inf*) a great quantity.

slice *n* a thin flat piece cut from something (as bread, etc); a wedge-shaped piece (of cake, pie, etc); a portion, a share; a broad knife for serving fish, cheese, etc; (*golf*) a stroke that makes the ball curl to the right. * *vti* to divide into parts; to cut into slices; to strike (a ball) so that it curves.—**slicer** *n* —**slicing** *adj, n*.

slick *adj* clever, deft; smart but unsound; insincere; wily; (*inf*) smooth but superficial, tricky, etc. * *n* a patch or area of oil floating on water. * *vt* to make glossy; (*with* **up**) (*inf*) to make smart, neat, etc.

slicker *n* a loose waterproof coat.

slide *vti* (**sliding, slid**) to move along in constant contact with a smooth surface, as on ice, to glide; to coast over snow and ice; to pass gradually (into); to move (an object) unobtrusively. * *n* the act of sliding, a glide; a strip of smooth ice for sliding on; a chute; the glass plate of a microscope; a photographic transparency; a landslide.

slide rule *n* a ruler with a graduated sliding part for making calculations.

sliding scale *n* a schedule for automatically varying one thing (eg wages) according to the fluctuations of another thing (eg cost of living); a flexible scale.

slier, sliest *see* **sly**.

slight *adj* small, inconsiderable; trifling; slim; frail, flimsy. * *vt* to disregard as insignificant; to treat with disrespect, to snub. * *n* intentional indifference or neglect, discourtesy.

slighting *adj* disparaging; hurtful.

slightly *adv* to a small degree; slenderly.

slightness *n* frailness or slenderness; lack of weight, solidity, importance, or thoroughness.

slim[1] *adj* slender, not stout; small in amount, degree, etc; slight. * *vti* (**slimming, slimmed**) to make or become slim; to reduce one's weight by diet, etc.—**slimness** *n*.

slim[2] *n* the name used in Africa for AIDS.

slime *n* a sticky, slippery, half-liquid substance; a glutinous mud; mucus secreted by various animals (eg slugs).

slimmer *n* a person who controls their diet to lose weight.

slimming *n* the process of losing weight by dieting.

slimy *adj* (**slimier, slimiest**) like or covered with slime; repulsive; fawning.—**sliminess** *n*.

sling[1] *n* a loop of leather with a string attached for hurling stones; a rope for lifting or hoisting weights; a bandage suspended from the neck for supporting an injured arm. * *vt* (**slinging, slung**) to throw, lift, or suspend (as) with a sling; to hurl.

sling[2] *n* a drink of sweetened water mixed with a spirit such as gin.

slingback *n* a shoe whose back consists of a strap.

slingshot *n* a contraption with elastic for shooting small stones, a catapult.

slink *vi* (**slinking, slinked** *or* **slunk**) to move stealthily or furtively, to sneak.

slinky *adj* (**slinkier, slinkiest**) (*inf*) sinuous in line or movement; (*clothes*) hugging the figure.

slip[1] *vti* (**slipping, slipped**) to slide, to glide; to lose one's foothold and slide; to go or put quietly or quickly; to let go, to release; to escape from; (*with* **up**) to make a slight mistake. * *n* the act of slipping; a mistake, a lapse; a woman's undergarment; a pillowcase; a slipway.

slip[2] *n* a small piece of paper; a young, slim person; a long seat or narrow pew; a shoot for grafting, a cutting; a descendant, an offspring.

slip[3] *n* a mixture of watery clay used for coating or decorating pottery.

slipcase *n* a protective case for one or more books with an open end to reveal the spines.

slipknot *n* a knot that slips along the rope around which it is tied; a knot that can be undone at a pull.

slip-on *adj* (*garment or shoe*) easy to put on or take off.—*also n*.

slippage *n* a slipping, as of one gear past another.

slipped disc *n* a ruptured cartilaginous disc between vertebrae.

slipper *n* a light, soft, shoe worn in the house.

slippery *adj* so smooth as to cause slipping; difficult to hold or catch; evasive, unreliable, shifty.

slippy *adj* (**slippier, slippiest**) slippery.

slip road *n* a road that gives access to a main road or motorway.

slipshod *adj* having the shoes down at heel; slovenly, careless.

slip stitch *n* a concealed stitch used for hemming; an unworked stitch in knitting.—**slipstitch** *vt*.

slipstream *n* a stream of air driven astern by the engine of an aircraft; an area of forward suction immediately behind a rapidly moving racing car.

slip-up *n* (*inf*) an error, a lapse.

slipway *n* an inclined surface for launching or repairing ships; a sloped landing stage.

slit *vt* (**slitting, slit**) to cut open or tear lengthways; to slash or tear into strips. * *n* a long cut, a slash; a narrow opening.—**slitter** *n*.

slither *vi* to slide, as on a loose or wet surface; to slip or slide like a snake.—**slithery** *adj*.

slit trench *n* a narrow trench to provide shelter during battle.

sliver *n* a small narrow piece torn off, a splinter; a thin slice.

slivovitz, slivowitz *n* plum brandy.

slob *n* (*sl*) a coarse or sloppy person.

slobber *vti* to drool; to run at the mouth; to smear with dribbling saliva or food. * *n* dribbling saliva; maudlin talk.

sloe *n* (the dark fruit of the) blackthorn.

sloe-eyed *adj* having almond-shaped dark or black eyes.

sloe gin *n* a gin flavoured with sloes.

slog *vti* (slogging, slogged) to hit hard and wildly; to work laboriously; to trudge doggedly. * *n* a hard, boring spell of work; a strenuous walk or hike; a hard, random hit.—**slogger** *n*.

slogan *n* a catchy phrase used in advertising or as a motto by a political party, etc.

sloop *n* a small sailing vessel with one mast and a jib.

slop *n* a puddle of spilled liquid; unappetizing semi-liquid food; (*pl*) liquid kitchen refuse. * *vti* (**slopping, slopped**) to spill or be spilled; (*with* **out**) (*prisoners*) to empty slop from chamber pots in the morning.

slope *n* rising or falling ground; an inclined line or surface; the amount or degree of this. * *vti* to incline, to slant; (*inf*) to make off, to go.

sloppy *adj* (**sloppier, sloppiest**) slushy; (*inf*) maudlin, sentimental; (*inf*) careless, untidy.—**sloppily** *adv*.—**sloppiness** *n*.

slosh *n* watery snow, slush; (*inf*) a heavy blow; the sound of liquid splashing. * *vi* to walk (through) or splash (around) in liquid, mud, etc; (*of liquid*) to splash. * *vt* to throw or splash liquid, etc at someone or something; (*inf*) to hit somebody.

sloshed *adj* (*inf*) drunk.

slot *n* a long narrow opening in a mechanism for inserting a coin, a slit. * *vt* (**slotting, slotted**) to fit into a slot; to provide with a slot; (*inf*) to place in a series.

sloth *n* laziness, indolence; a slow-moving South American animal.—**slothful** *adj*.

slot machine *n* a machine operated by the insertion of a coin, used for gambling or dispensing drinks, etc.

slouch *vti* to sit, stand or move in a drooping, slovenly way. * *n* a drooping slovenly posture or gait; the downward droop of a hat brim; (*inf*) a poor performer, a lazy or incompetent person.

slouch hat *n* a hat with a soft wide brim that can be pulled down to cover the ears.

slough[1] *n* a bog; deep, hopeless dejection.

slough[2] *n* the dead, outer skin of a snake. * *vti* to cast off, as a dead skin.

Slovak *n* a native or inhabitant of Slovakia in Czechoslovakia; the language of Slovakia.—*also adj*.

Slovene *n* a native or inhabitant of Slovenia, formerly part of Yugoslavia; the Slavonic language of Slovenia.—*also adj*.

slovenly *adj* untidy, dirty; careless.—**slovenliness** *n*.

slow *adj* moving at low speed, not fast; gradual; not quick in understanding; reluctant, backward; dull, sluggish; not progressive; (*clock*) behind in time; tedious, boring; (*surface*) causing slowness. * *vti* (*also with* **up, down**) to reduce the speed (of).—**slowly** *adv*.—**slowness** *n*.

slowcoach *n* (*inf*) a person who moves, works or thinks slowly.

slow handclap *n* slow regular clapping expressive of audience dissatisfaction.

slow match, slow fuse *n* a slow-burning match or fuse for igniting explosives.

slow-motion *adj* moving slowly; denoting a filmed or taped scene with the original action slowed down.

slowpoke *see* **slowcoach**.

slowworm *n* a legless European lizard with a greyish elongated body and very small eyes.

SLR *abbr* = single-lens reflex.

slub *n* a lump in a piece of yarn or thread.

sludge *n* soft mud or snow; sediment; sewage.

slue *see* **slew**[2].

slug[1] *n* a mollusc resembling a snail but with no outer shell.

slug[2] *n* a small bullet; a disc for inserting into a slot machine; a line of type; (*inf*) a hard blow; a drink of spirits. * *vt* (**slugging, slugged**) (*inf*) to hit hard with a fist or a bat.

sluggard *n* a lazy person. * *adj* lazy.

sluggish *adj* slow, inactive; unresponsive.—**sluggishly** *adv*.—**sluggishness** *n*.

sluice *n* a gate regulating a flow of water; the water passing through this; an artificial water channel. * *vti* to draw off through a sluice; to wash with a stream of water; to stream out as from a sluice.

slum *n* a squalid, rundown house; (*usu pl*) an overcrowded area characterized by poverty, etc. * *vi* (**slumming, slummed**) to make do with less comfort.

slumber *vi* to sleep. * *n* a light sleep.

slump *n* a sudden fall in value or slackening in demand; (*sport*) a period of poor play. * *vi* to fall or decline suddenly; to sink down heavily; to collapse; to slouch.

slung *see* **sling**.

slunk *see* **slink**.

slur *vti* (**slurring, slurred**) to pronounce or speak indistinctly; (*letters, words*) to run together; (*mus*) to produce by gliding without a break; to make disparaging remarks. * *n* the act of slurring; a stigma, an imputation of disgrace; (*mus*) a curved line over notes to be slurred.

slurp *vti* (*sl*) to drink or eat noisily. * *n* a loud sipping or sucking sound.

slurry *n* (*pl* **slurries**) a liquid mixture of insoluble matter (as mud, lime, etc).

slush *n* liquid mud; melting snow; (*inf*) sentimental language.—**slushy** *adj*.

slush fund *n* a fund of money used secretly to bribe, etc.

slut *n* a slovenly or immoral woman.—**sluttish** *adj*.

sly *adj* (**slyer, slyest** *or* **slier, sliest**) secretively cunning, wily; underhand; knowing.—**slyly** *adv*.—**slyness** *n*.

SM *abbr* = master of science; sergeant major.

Sm (*chem symbol*) samarium.

S/M, S-M *abbr* = sadomasochism.

smack[1] *n* a taste; a distinctive smell or flavour; small quantity, a trace. * *vi* to have a smell or taste (of); to have a slight trace of something.

smack[2] *vt* to strike or slap with the open hand; to kiss noisily; to make a sharp noise with the lips.—*also n*.

smack[3] *n* a small fishing vessel used in coastal waters.

smacker *n* (*sl*) a noisy kiss; (*sl*) a pound note or dollar bill.

small *adj* little in size, number, importance, etc; modest, humble; operating on a minor scale; young; petty. * *adv* in small pieces. * *n* the narrow, curving part of the back.

small arms *npl* portable firearms, such as handguns.

small beer *n* (*inf*) people or things regarded as trivial.

small change *n* coins of low value.

small fry *npl* people or things of little significance.

smallholding *n* in UK, a small piece of agricultural land, usu between one and fifty acres.—**smallholder** *n*.

small hours *npl* the period between midnight and dawn.

small intestine *n* the section of the alimentary canal between the stomach and the colon.

small-minded *adj* intolerant, narrow-minded; mean, vindictive.—**small-mindedly** *adv.*—**small-mindedness** *n*.

smallpox *n* an acute contagious viral disease, now rare, causing the eruption of pustules which leave the skin scarred and pitted.

small print *n* small type that is difficult to read in a contract or other document, esp conditions and limitations made deliberately inconspicuous.

small-scale *adj* small in size or scope.

small screen *n* a television.

small talk *n* light, social conversation.

small-time *adj* (*inf*) unimportant.

smalt *n* a blue pigment used in colouring glass and ceramics.

smarmy *adj* (**smarmier, smarmiest**) (*inf*) obsequious, unpleasantly smooth and flattering.

smart *n* a sudden, stinging pain. * *vi* to have or cause a sharp, stinging pain (as by a slap); to feel distress. * *adj* stinging; astute; clever, witty; fashionable; neatly dressed; (*equipment, etc*) capable of seemingly intelligent action through computer control; (*bombs, missiles*) guided to the target by lasers ensuring pinpoint accuracy.—**smartly** *adv.*—**smartness** *n*.

smart aleck *n* (*inf*) an annoyingly clever person, a know-all.

smart card *n* a credit card containing a memory chip that records transactions made with the card.

smarten *vti* to make or become smart.

smart money *n* money invested or bet by experienced gamblers or financiers; money paid to secure release from an unpleasant situation, or obligation, esp military service.

smart set *n sing or pl* fashionable people or society.

smash *vti* to break into pieces with noise or violence; to hit, collide, or move with force; to destroy or be destroyed. * *n* a hard, heavy hit; a violent, noisy breaking; a violent collision; total failure, esp in business; (*inf*) a popular success.

smashed *adj* (*sl*) drunk or under the influence of drugs.

smasher *n* (*inf*) an attractive or excellent person or thing.

smashing *n* (*inf*) excellent.

smash-up *n* (*inf*) a serious collision, a crash.

smattering *n* a slight superficial knowledge; a small number.

smear *vt* to cover with anything greasy or sticky; to make a smudge; to slander. * *n* a smudge; a slanderous attack; a deposit of blood, secretion, etc on a glass slide for examination under a microscope.

smear test *n* microscopic analysis of a smear of bodily cells, esp from the cervix, for cancer.

smegma *n* a sebaceous secretion which accumulates as solid matter in the folds of the skin, esp under the foreskin.

smell *n* the sense by which odours are perceived with the nose; a scent, odour, or stench; a trace. * *vti* (**smelling, smelt** *or* **smelled**) to have or perceive an odour.—**smelly** *adj*.

smelling salts *npl* a preparation of ammonia used as a stimulant in cases of faintness, etc.

smelt[1] *vt* to extract ore from metal by melting.

smelt[2] *n* any of various small marine or freshwater food fishes related to the salmon.

smelt[3] *see* **smell**.

smidgen, smidgin *n* (*inf*) a small amount.

smilax *n* any of a genus of climbing plants bearing red berries that includes the sarsaparilla; an African vine cultivated for its decorative green leaves.

smile *vti* to express amusement, friendship, pleasure, etc, by a slight turning up of the corners of the mouth. * *n* the act of smiling; a bright aspect.—**smilingly** *adv*.

smirch *vt* to dishonour; to soil, stain, or sully. * *n* a stain on reputation; a smudge, smear.

smirk *vi* to smile in an expression of smugness or scorn. * *n* a smug or scornful smile.—**smirkingly** *adv*.

smite *vb* (**smiting, smote,** *pp* **smitten** *or* **smote**) *vt* (*arch*) to strike hard; to kill or injure; to have a powerful affect on. * *vi* to strike, beat or come down (on) with force.—**smiter** *n*.

smith *n* a person who works in metal; a blacksmith.

smithereens *npl* (*inf*) fragments.

smithery *n* the trade of a blacksmith.

smithy *n* (*pl* **smithies**) a blacksmith's workshop.

smitten *see* **smite**.

smock *n* a loose shirtlike outer garment to protect the clothes.

smocking *n* ornamental stitching in a honeycomb pattern.

smog *n* a mixture of fog and smoke; polluted air.—**smoggy** *adj*.

smoke *n* a cloud or plume of gas and small particles emitted from a burning substance; any similar vapour; an act of smoking tobacco, etc; (*inf*) a cigar or cigarette. * *vi* to give off smoke; to (habitually) draw in and exhale the smoke of tobacco, etc. * *vt* to fumigate; to cure food by treating with smoke; to darken (eg glass) using smoke; (*with* **out**) to flush out using smoke; to bring into public view.—**smokable, smokeable** *adj*.

smoke detector *n* an electrical device that sets off an alarm when smoke is detected.

smokeless *adj* giving off little or no smoke.

smoker *n* a person who habitually smokes tobacco; a smoking car; (*formerly*) a gathering of men to smoke.

smoke screen *n* dense smoke used to conceal military movements, etc; something designed to obscure, conceal, or disguise the truth.

smokestack *n* a tall chimney or funnel which discharges smoke or exhaust gases into the air.

smoking car *n* a train compartment where smoking is permitted.

smoky *adj* (**smokier, smokiest**) emitting smoke, esp excessively; filled with smoke; resembling smoke in appearance, flavour, smell, colour, etc.—**smokily** *adv.*—**smokiness** *n*.

smoky quartz *n* cairngorm.

smolder *see* **smoulder**.

smolt *n* a young salmon, about two years old, at the stage where it migrates to the sea for the first time.

smooch *vi* (*sl*) to kiss and cuddle, esp while dancing as a couple. * *n* (*sl*) a long kiss, an embrace.—**smoochy** *adj*.

smooth *adj* having an even or flat surface; silky; not rough or lumpy; hairless; of even consistency; calm, unruffled; gently flowing in rhythm or sound. * *vti* to make smooth; to calm; to make easier.—**smoothly** *adv.*—**smoothness** *n*.

smoothbore *n* (*firearm*) not rifled. * *n* such a gun.

smoothen *vti* to make or become smooth.

smooth-faced *adj* shaven; having a smooth surface; hypocritical.

smoothie *n* (*sl*) a person, esp a man, who is excessively suave and self-assured in speech and appearance.

smooth muscle *n* a muscle capable of regular involuntary contractions, as in the walls of the stomach and gut.

smooth-tongued *adj* persuasive in speech.

smoothy *n* (*pl* **smoothies**) (*sl*) a smoothie.

smorgasbord, smörgåsbord *n* a type of buffet or hors d'œuvres of various cold dishes of cheese, fish, salads, etc, served in Scandinavia; a restaurant specializing in this.

smote *see* **smite**.

smother *vt* to stifle, to suffocate; to put out a fire by covering it to remove the air supply; to cover over thickly; to hold back, suppress. * *vi* to undergo suffocation.—*also n*.

smoulder *vi* to burn slowly or without flame; (*feelings*) to linger on in a suppressed state; to have concealed feelings of anger, jealousy, etc.—*also* **smolder**.

smudge *n* a dirty or blurred spot or area; a fire made to produce dense smoke. * *vt* to make a smudge; to smear; to blur; to produce smoke to protect against insects, etc. * *vi* to become smudged.

smudgy *adj* blurred or dirty, smeared.—**smudgily** *adv*.—**smudginess** *n*.

smug *adj* (**smugger, smuggest**) complacent, self-satisfied.—**smugly** *adv*.—**smugness** *n*.

smuggle *vt* to import or export (goods) secretly without paying customs duties; to convey or introduce secretly.—**smuggler** *n*.

smut *n* a speck or smudge of dirt, soot, etc; indecent talk, writing, or pictures; a fungal disease of crop plants that covers the leaves in sooty spores. * *vti* (**smutting, smutted**) to stain or become stained with smut; (*crops, etc*) to infect or become infected with smut.

smut disease *n* a disease of wheat caused by fungi.

smutty *adj* (**smuttier, smuttiest**) soiled with smuts; obscene, filthy.—**smuttily** *adv*.—**smuttiness** *n*.

Sn (*chem symbol*) tin.

snack *n* a light meal between regular meals.

snaffle *n* a jointed bit for a bridle (—*also* **snaffle bit**). * *vt* (*inf*) to snatch or steal for oneself.

snafu *n* (*sl*) (situation normal all fucked up) a state of utter confusion. * *adj* confused, chaotic. * *vt* (**snafuing, snafued**) to cause a state of confusion or chaos.

snag *n* a sharp point or projection; a tear, as in cloth, made by a snag, etc; an unexpected or hidden difficulty. * *vti* (**snagging, snagged**) to tear, etc, on a snag; to clear of snags.

snail *n* a mollusc having a wormlike body and a spiral protective shell; a slow-moving or sluggish person or thing.

snail-paced *adj* moving very slowly.

snail's pace *n* a very slow speed or rate of progress.

snake *n* a limbless, scaly reptile with a long, tapering body and with salivary glands often modified to produce venom; a sly, treacherous person. * *vt* to twist along like a snake. * *vi* to crawl silently and stealthily.

snake charmer *n* a person who entertains by appearing to mesmerize venomous snakes by playing music.

snakeroot *n* any of various North American plants whose roots have been used to treat snakebites.

snakes and ladders *n* a British board game in which counters are moved on a grid of squares, some of which have ladders leading nearer the finish, and others snakes leading back toward the start.

snakeskin *n* the skin of a snake as used to make handbags, shoes, etc.

snakestone *n* an ammonite twisted like a ram's horn.

snakeweed *n* a herb with twisted roots, bistort.

snaky *adj* (**snakier, snakiest**) like or full of snakes; treacherous looking.—**snakily** *adv*.—**snakiness** *n*.

snap *vti* (**snapping, snapped**) to break suddenly; to make or cause to make a sudden, cracking sound; to close, fasten, etc with this sound; (*with* at) to bite or grasp suddenly; to speak or utter sharply. * *adj* sudden. * *n* a sharp, cracking sound; a fastener that closes with a snapping sound; a crisp biscuit; a snapshot; a sudden spell of cold weather; (*inf*) vigour, energy.

snapdragon *n* any of several plants of the figwort family with showy white, red or yellow flowers shaped like small jaws.

snap fastener *n* a press stud.

snapper *n* one who or that which snaps; (*pl* **snapper, snappers**) any of various sea fishes used as food; a snapping turtle.

snapping turtle *n* a large North American turtle with powerful jaws, a snapper.

snappy *adj* (**snappier, snappiest**) speaking sharply; brisk; lively; smart, fashionable.—**snappily** *adv*.—**snappiness** *n*.

snapshot *n* a photograph taken casually with a simple camera.

snare *n* a loop of string or wire for trapping birds or animals; something that catches one unawares, a trap; a loop of gut wound with wire stretched around a snare drum that produces a rattling sound. * *vt* to trap using a snare.

snare drum *n* a double-headed drum with snares.

snarl[1] *vi* to growl with bared teeth; to speak in a rough, angry manner. * *vt* to express in a snarling manner. * *n* the act of snarling; the sound of this.

snarl[2] *vti* to make or become entangled or complicated. * *n* a tangle; disorder.

snarl-up *n* (*inf*) an instance or state of blockage or disorder, esp a traffic jam.

snatch *vt* to seize or grasp suddenly; to take as opportunity occurs. * *n* the act of snatching; a brief period; a fragment; (*inf*) a robbery.

snazzy *adj* (**snazzier, snazziest**) (*inf*) stylish, fashionable; flashy.

sneak *vti* (**sneaking, sneaked**, *pp* (*sl*) **snuck**) to move, act, give, put, take, etc, secretly or stealthily. * *n* a person who acts secretly or stealthily; (*inf*) a person who tells or informs on others. * *adj* without warning.

sneaker *n* one who or that which sneaks; a shoe with a cloth upper and soft rubber sole, worn informally.

sneaking *adj* underhand; secret; (*suspicion, admiration, etc*) felt or thought, but not openly expressed.—**sneakingly** *adv*.

sneaky *adj* (**sneakier, sneakiest**) like a sneak; furtive; underhand.—**sneakily** *adv*.—**sneakiness** *n*.

sneer *vi* to show scorn or contempt by curling up the upper lip. * *n* a derisive look or remark.—**sneerer** *n*.—**sneeringly** *adv*.

sneeze *vi* to expel air through the nose violently and audibly. * *n* the act of sneezing.—**sneezy** *adj*.

snick *n* a tiny cut or notch; (*cricket*) a stroke of the edge of the bat. * *vt* to make a tiny cut or notch in something; to hit (a ball) with a snick.

snicker *vi* to laugh furtively and slyly, to snigger; to neigh, to whinny. * *n* a half-suppressed laugh, a giggle.—**snickeringly** *adv*.

snide *adj* malicious; superior in attitude; sneering.—**snidely** *adv*.—**snideness** *n*.

sniff *vti* to inhale through the nose audibly; to smell by sniffing; to scoff; (*with* **at**) to express dislike or contempt for. * *n* the act of sniffing; the sound of this; a smell.—**sniffer** *n*.

sniffer dog *n* a police dog trained to locate hidden drugs or explosives by smell.

sniffle *vi* to sniff repeatedly. * *n* the act or sound of sniffling.

sniffy *adj* (**sniffier, sniffiest**) (*inf*) disdainful, dismissive.—**sniffily** *adv*.—**sniffiness** *n*.

snifter *n* a glass with a wide body and narrow top to preserve the aroma of brandy or other spirits; (*inf*) a small amount of alcoholic drink.

snigger *vti* to laugh disrespectfully, to snicker.—*also n*.

snip *vti* (**snipping, snipped**) to cut or clip with a single stroke of the scissors, etc. * *n* a small piece cut off; the act or sound of snipping; (*inf*) a bargain; (*inf*) a certainty, cinch.

snipe *n* (*pl* **snipes, snipe**) any of various birds with long straight flexible bills. * *vi* to shoot snipe; to shoot at individuals from a hidden position; to make sly criticisms of.—**sniper** *n*.

snippet *n* a scrap of information.

snitch *vi* (*sl*) to inform, betray. * *vt* (*sl*) to steal, pilfer. * *n* (*sl*) an informer; the nose.—**snitcher** *n*.

snivel *vi* (**snivelling, snivelled** *or* **sniveling, sniveled**) to whine or whimper; to have a runny nose.—**sniveler, sniveller** *n*.

Sno-cat *n* (*trademark*) a vehicle designed for travelling on snow.

snob *n* a person who wishes to be associated with those of a higher social status, whilst acting condescendingly to those whom he or she regards as inferior.

snobbery *n* (*pl* **snobberies**) snobbish behaviour or attitude; a snobbish act.

snobbish *adj* pertaining to, characteristic of, or like a snob.—**snobbishly** *adv*.—**snobbishness** *n*.

SNOBOL *n* (*comput*) String Orientated Symbolic Language: a programming language used for text (ie strings of characters) retrieval and manipulation

snog *vi* (**snogging, snogged**) (*sl*) to kiss and cuddle.—*also n*.

snood *n* a small net or fabric pouch for holding a woman's hair at the back of the head; (*Scot*) a ribbon around the hair formerly worn by unmarried girls.

snook *n* (*sl*) a gesture of contempt with the thumb to the nose and fingers spread.

snooker *n* a game played on a billiard table with 15 red balls, 6 variously coloured balls, and a white cue ball; a position in the game where a ball lies directly between the cue ball and target ball. * *vt* to place in a snooker; (*inf*) to obstruct, thwart.

snoop *vi* (*inf*) to pry about in a sneaking way. * *n* an act of snooping; a person who pries into other people's business.—**snooper** *n*.

snooperscope *n* an infrared night-vision device used by the police and military services.

snoot *n* (*sl*) the nose.

snooty *adj* (**snootier, snootiest**) haughty, snobbish.—**snootily** *adv*.—**snootiness** *n*.

snooze *vi* (*inf*) to sleep lightly. * *n* (*inf*) a nap.

snore *vi* to breathe roughly and noisily while asleep. * *n* the act or sound of snoring.

snorkel *n* a breathing tube extending above the water, used in swimming just below the surface. * *vi* (**snorkeling, snorkeled**) to swim using a snorkel.—**snorkeler** *n*.

snort *vi* to exhale noisily through the nostrils, esp as an expression of contempt or scorn. * *vt* to inhale (a drug) through the nose.

snorter *n* (*sl*) something remarkable for its size, strength, difficulty, etc.

snot *n* (*sl*) nasal mucus; (*sl*) a snotty person.

snotty *adj* (**snottier, snottiest**) covered with snot; (*sl*) irritatingly unpleasant; snobbish.—**snottily** *adv*.—**snottiness** *n*.

snout *n* the nose or muzzle of an animal.

snow *n* frozen water vapour in the form of white flakes; a snowfall; a mass of snow; (*sl*) cocaine or heroin. * *vi* to fall as snow; to deceive with smooth talk.

snowball *n* snow pressed together in a ball for throwing; a drink made with advocaat and lemonade. * *vi* to throw snowballs; to increase rapidly in size.

snowberry *n* (*pl* **snowberries**) any of various shrubs bearing white berries.

snow-blind *adj* temporarily blinded or dazzled by the intense glare of sunlight reflected from snow.—**snow-blindness** *n*.

snowblower *n* a machine for clearing snow from roads by sucking it up and blowing it off to the side.

snowbound *adj* trapped by or covered in snow.

snowcap *n* a covering of snow, as on a mountain peak.—**snowcapped** *adj*.

snowdrift *n* a bank of drifted snow.

snowdrop *n* a Eurasian plant of the daffodil family with white flowers that appears in early spring.

snowfall *n* a fall of snow; the amount of snow in a given time or area.

snowflake *n* a fragile cluster of ice crystals.

snow goose *n* a large white North American goose with black-tipped wings.

snow leopard *n* a large cat of the central Asian mountains with a tawny coat that becomes white in winter.

snow line, snow limit *n* the lowest limit in altitude of permanent snow.

snowman *n* (*pl* **snowmen**) snow piled into the shape of a human figure.

snowmobile *n* a motor vehicle for travelling at speed over snow.

snowplough, snowplow *n* a vehicle designed for clearing away snow.

snowshoe *n* footwear in the shape of a racket-like frame with thongs for walking on soft snow. * *vi* (**snowshoeing, snowshoed**) to walk on snow using snowshoes.

snowstorm *n* a storm with heavy snow.

snow tyre *n* a heavy tyre with deep treads for improved traction on snow and ice.

snow-white *adj* pure white.

snowy *adj* (**snowier, snowiest**) covered with snow; white or pure, like snow.—**snowily** *adv*.—**snowiness** *n*.

snowy owl *n* a large owl with white plumage of northern regions.

Snr, snr *abbr* = senior.

snub *vt* (**snubbing, snubbed**) to insult by ignoring or making a cutting remark. * *n* the act of snubbing; an intentional slight.

snub-nosed *adj* having a short upturned nose; (*pistol*) having a very short barrel.

snuck *see* **sneak**.

snuff[1] *n* a powdered preparation of tobacco inhaled through the nostrils.

snuff[2] *n* the charred portion of a wick. * *vt* to extinguish (a candle flame).

snuffbox *n* a small box for snuff.

snuffer *n* a cone-shaped device for putting out a candle.

snuffle *vi* to make sniffing noises, as when suffering from a cold or crying. * *n* the act of snuffling; (*pl*) a form of catarrh.

snuff movie *n* a pornographic film which ends by depicting the brutal murder of an unsuspecting participant.

snug *adj* (**snugger**, **snuggest**) cosy; warm; close-fitting.—**snugly** *adv.*—**snugness** *n*.

snuggle *vi* to nestle, cuddle. * *vt* to cuddle.

so[1] *adv* in this way; as shown; as stated; to such an extent; very; (*inf*) very much; therefore; more or less; also, likewise; then.

so[2] *see* **sol**.

soak *vt* to submerge in a liquid; to take in, absorb; (*sl*) to extract large amounts of money from. * *vi* to become saturated; to penetrate. * *n* the act or process of soaking.

so-and-so *n* (*pl* **so-and-sos**) an unspecified person or thing; (*inf*) (*euphemism*) an unpleasant or disliked person or thing.

soap *n* a substance used with water to produce suds for washing; (*inf*) a soap opera. * *vt* to rub with soap.—**soapy** *adj*.

soapberry *n* (*pl* **soapberries**) any of various tropical American trees bearing fruit which are rich in saponin.

soapbox *n* a temporary platform from which to deliver informal speeches.

soap opera *n* (*inf*) a daytime radio or television serial melodrama.

soapstone *n* a type of soft grey-green stone with a soapy texture.—*also* **steatite**.

soapwort *n* a Eurasian herbaceous plant of the pink family whose leaves form a soapy lather with water.

soapy *adj* (**soapier**, **soapiest**) like or full of soap; flattering, unctuous.—**soapily** *adv.*—**soapiness** *n*.

soar *vi* to rise high in the air; to glide along high in the air; to increase; to rise in status.—**soarer** *n*.

sob *vb* (**sobbing**, **sobbed**) *vi* to weep with convulsive gasps. * *vt* to speak while sobbing.

sober *adj* not drunk; serious and thoughtful; realistic, rational; subdued in colour. * *vt* (*often with* **up** *or* **down**) to make or become sober.—**soberly** *adv.*—**soberness** *n*.

sobriety *n* soberness; temperance; seriousness.

sobriquet *n* a nickname.—*also* **soubriquet**.

sob story *n* (*inf*) a tale of distress intended to arouse sympathy.

Soc., soc. *abbr* = socialist; society.

so-called *adj* commonly named or known as.

soccer *n* a football game played on a field by two teams of 11 players with a round inflated ball, association football.

sociable *adj* friendly; companionable.—**sociability** *n*.—**sociably** *adv*.

social *adj* living or organized in a community, not solitary; relating to human beings living in society; of or intended for communal activities; sociable. * *n* an in-

formal gathering of people, such as a party.—**socially** *adv*.

social anthropology *n* the branch of anthropology that studies social and cultural systems and beliefs.

social climber *n* a person who strives to attain a higher social position.

social contract, social compact *n* a tacit agreement between individuals in society and between individuals and the government which defines the rights and duties of each.

Social Democratic Party *n* a political party that advocates the transition from capitalism to socialism in a gradual manner.—**Social Democrat** *n.*—**Social Democratic** *adj*.

social disease *n* venereal disease.

socialism *n* (a system based on) a political and economic theory advocating state ownership of the means of production and distribution.—**socialist** *n*, *adj.*—**socialistic** *adj.*—**socialistically** *adv*.

socialite *n* a person active or prominent in fashionable society.

socialize *vt* to meet other people socially.—**socialization** *n.*—**socializer** *n*.

social science *n* the study of human social organization and relationships using scientific methods.

social security *n* financial assistance for the unemployed, the disabled, etc to alleviate economic distress.

social service *n* a welfare service provided by the state, such as housing, education, and health.—**social-service** *adj*.

social work *n* any of various professional welfare services to aid the underprivileged in society.—**social worker** *n*.

society *n* (*pl* **societies**) the social relationships between human beings or animals organized collectively; the system of human institutional organization; a community with the same language and customs; an interest group or organization; the fashionable or privileged members of a community; companionship.—**societal** *adj*.

Society of Friends *n* the official name for the Quakers.

Society of Jesus *n* the Roman Catholic religious order of the Jesuits.

socio- *prefix* society; social.

sociobiology *n* the study of human and animal social behaviour.—**sociobiological** *adj.*—**sociobiologist** *n*.

socioeconomic *adj* of or involving social and economic aspects.

sociolinguistics *n sing* the study of the social and cultural context of language.—**sociolinguist** *n*.

sociology *n* the study of the development and structure of society and social relationships.—**sociological** *adj.*—**sociologically** *adv.*—**sociologist** *n*.

sociometry *n* the study of social relations within small groups.—**sociometric** *adj*.

sociopath *n* a person suffering from a mental disorder that results in antisocial behaviour and lack of guilt.—**sociopathic** *adj*.

sociopolitical *adj* of or involving social and political aspects.

sock[1] *n* a kind of short stocking covering the foot and lower leg.

sock[2] *vt* (*sl*) to punch hard. * *n* a blow.

socket *n* a hollow part into which something is inserted, such as an eye, a bone, a tooth, an electric plug, etc.

sockeye *n* a Pacific salmon valued as a food fish.—*also* **red salmon**.

Socratic *adj* of or relating to Socrates (*c.*470-399BC), the Greek philosopher, or his methods. * *n* an adherent of Socrates or his philosophy.

Socratic irony *n* feigning ignorance when posing questions to expose the real ignorance of the person responding.

Socratic method *n* philosophical instruction by means of question and answer.

sod[1] *n* a lump of earth covered with grass; turf. * *vt* (**sodding, sodded**) to cover with turf.

sod[2] *n* (*sl*) an obnoxious person; (*loosely*) a person, man. * *vi* (**sodding, sodded**) (*Brit sl*) to damn; (*with off*) (*sl*) to go away.—*also interj*.

soda *n* sodium bicarbonate; sodium carbonate; soda water.

soda bread *n* bread made with baking soda instead of yeast.

soda fountain *n* a counter selling soft drinks, ice cream, snacks, etc; a device that dispenses soda water.

soda siphon *n* a pressurized container that dispenses soda water.

soda water *n* a fizzy drink made by charging water with carbon dioxide under pressure.

sodden *adj* completely soaked through.—**soddenly** *adv*.

sodium *n* a metallic element.

sodium bicarbonate *n* a white soluble alkaline powder used in baking powder, fire extinguishers and in antacid medicines.

sodium chloride *n* salt.

sodium hydroxide *n* a white alkaline solid used in the manufacture of soap, paper and rayon.

sodium nitrate *n* a white crystalline compound used in fertilizers, matches and explosives, and as a food preservative.

sodium-vapour lamp *n* an electric lamp using sodium vapour through which a current is passed to produce an orange light, esp used for street lighting.

Sodom *n* (*Bible*) a wicked city destroyed by God; a wicked and depraved place.

sodomite *n* a person who practises sodomy.

sodomy *n* anal sexual intercourse between males or between a man and woman.

sofa *n* an upholstered couch or settee with fixed back and arms.

soffit *n* the underside of a structural element, such as an arch, stairway, balcony, etc.

soft *adj* malleable; easily cut, shaped, etc; not as hard as normal, desirable, etc; smooth to the touch; (*drinks*) nonalcoholic; mild, as a breeze; lenient; (*sl*) easy, comfortable; (*colour, light*) not bright; (*sound*) gentle, low; (*drugs*) non-addictive.—**softly** *adv*.—**softness** *n*.

softball *n* a game similar to baseball, but played with a larger, softer ball.

soft-boiled *adj* (*egg*) boiled so that the white hardens while the yolk remains soft.

soft-core *adj* (*pornography*) not sexually explicit.

softcover *adj* paperback. * *n* a paperback book.

soft drink *n* a nonalcoholic drink.

soften *vti* to make or become soft or softer.—**softener** *n*.

soft-focus *adj* (*lens*) designed to produce a slightly blurred image.

soft furnishings *npl* items such as curtains, carpets, rugs, etc.

soft goods *npl* textile and clothing products.

softheaded *adj* stupid, feeble-minded.—**softheadedly** *adv*.—**softheadedness** *n*.

softhearted *adj* kind; sentimental.—**softheartedly** *adv*.—**softheartedness** *n*.

soft landing *n* a landing by a spacecraft which leaves the vehicle and occupants undamaged.

soft option *n* the easiest choice in a range of alternatives.

soft palate *n* the fleshy area at the back of the roof of the mouth.

soft paste *n* a type of translucent porcelain made from refined clay, ground glass, bone ash, etc.

soft-pedal *n* a pedal on a piano for muting the tone. * *vt* (*inf*) (**soft-pedalling, soft-pedalled** *or* **soft-pedaling, soft-pedaled**) to avoid direct reference to, esp something embarrassing or unpleasant.

soft porn *n* (*inf*) soft-core pornography.

soft sell *n* selling by gentle persuasion.—**soft-sell** *adj*.

soft soap *n* a type of semisolid or liquid soap; (*inf*) flattery.

soft-soap *vt* (*inf*) to flatter.—**soft-soaper** *n*.

soft spot *n* a sentimental fondness (for).

soft touch *n* (*inf*) a person who is easily persuaded or exploited.

software *n* the programs used in computers.

softwood *n* the wood of any coniferous tree.

softy *n* (*pl* **softies**) (*inf*) a person regarded as sentimental or physically weak.

soggy *adj* (**soggier, soggiest**) soaked with water; moist and heavy.—**soggily** *adv*.—**sogginess** *n*.

soi-disant *adj* self-styled.

soigné, soignée *adj* well-groomed; elegant.

soil[1] *n* the ground or earth in which plants grow; territory.

soil[2] *vt* to make or become dirty or stained.

soil pipe *n* a sewage or waste-water pipe.

soiree, soirée *n* an evening party of music in a private house.

soixante-neuf *n* a sexual position that facilitates mutual cunnilingus and fellatio; sixty-nine.

sojourn *n* a temporary stay. * *vi* to stay for a short time.—**sojourner** *n*.

sol[1] *n* (*mus*) the name for the fifth note of the diatonic scale —*also* **so**.

sol[2] *n* liquid in which a colloid is dissolved or suspended.

sol. *abbr* = soluble; solution.

solace *n* comfort in misery; consolation. * *vt* to bring solace to.

solar *adj* of or from the sun; powered by light or heat from the sun; reckoned by the sun.

solar cell *n* a cell that converts the sun's rays into electricity.

solar constant *n* the quantity of sun's energy radiated onto a given area of the earth's surface in a prescribed period.

solar day *n* the period of time during which the earth makes a complete revolution relative to the sun.

solar flare *n* a sudden brief eruption of intense energy from the sun's surface.

solarium *n* (*pl* **solariums, solaria**) a glass-enclosed room for sunbathing or exposure to the sun for medical treatment.

solar month *n* the period of time taken for the moon to make one complete revolution around the earth (approx. 27 days).

solar panel *n* a large thin panel that absorbs energy from sunlight and regenerates it.

solar plexus *n* the network of nerves behind the stomach; (*inf*) the pit of the stomach.

solar pond *n* a shallow artificial pond of salt water covered by fresh water, which absorbs heat from the sun's rays and converts it to electricity.

solar system *n* the sun and those bodies moving about it under the attraction of gravity.

solar wind *n* the constant flow of charged particles from the sun into outer space.

solar year *n* the period of time taken for the earth to make one revolution around the sun.

sold *see* sell.

solder *n* a metal alloy used when melted to join or patch metal parts, etc. * *vti* to join or be joined with solder.

soldering iron *n* an electrically heated tool for melting and applying solder.

soldier *n* a person who serves in an army, esp a non-commissioned officer or private. * *vi* to serve as a soldier; (*with* on) to continue regardless of difficulties or dangers.—**soldierly** *adj*.

soldier of fortune *n* a man in constant search of military adventure; a mercenary.

soldiery *n* (*pl* **soldieries**) soldiers collectively; a body of soldiers; the profession of being a soldier.

sole[1] *n* the underside of the foot or shoe. * *vt* to put a new sole on (a shoe).

sole[2] *n* (*pl* **sole, soles**) a type of flatfish used as food.

sole[3] *adj* only, being the only one; exclusive.—**solely** *adv*.

solecism *n* an error in speech or writing; a breach of etiquette or good manners.

solemn *adj* serious; formal; sacred; performed with religious ceremony.—**solemnly** *adv*.—**solemnness** *n*.

solemnity *n* (*pl* **solemnities**) solemness; a formal rite.

solenoid *n* a coil of wire that produces a magnetic field when an electric current is passed through it.—**solenoidal** *adj*.

sol-fa *see* tonic sol-fa.

sol-fa syllable *n* any of the syllables (*do, re, mi,* etc) used to represent the notes of the musical scale in tonic sol-fa or solmization.

solfatara *n* a volcanic outlet that emits only (sulphurous) gases and (water) vapours.

solfeggio *n* (*pl* **solfeggi, solfeggios**) (*singing using*) the application of the sol-fa syllables to musical scales or melody.

solicit *vti* to make a request or application to (a person for something); (*prostitute*) to offer sexual services for money.—**solicitation** *n*.

solicitor *n* a lawyer.

solicitous *adj* showing concern or attention.—**solicitously** *adv*.—**solicitousness** *n*.

solicitude *n* the state of being solicitous; concern; anxiety; carefulness.

solid *adj* firm; compact; not hollow; strongly constructed; having three dimensions; neither liquid nor gaseous; unanimous. * *n* a solid substance (not liquid or gas); a three-dimensional figure.—**solidly** *adv*.—**solidness** *n*.

solidarity *n* (*pl* **solidarities**) unity of interest and action.

solid geometry *n* geometry of three-dimensional figures.

solidi *see* solidus.

solidify *vti* (**solidifying, solidified**) to make or become solid, compact, hard, etc.—**solidification** *n*.

solidity *n* the state of being solid; density; compactness; stability; truth; moral firmness.

solid-state *adj* (*electronic devices*) using components, such as transistors, in which the current flow is through solid materials as opposed to a vacuum; of or relating to solids or their properties and characteristics.

solid-state physics *n sing* the physics of the properties of solids.

solidus *n* (*pl* **solidi**) an oblique stroke (/) used to separate items of text as in dates, alternative words, lists, or the terms of fractions.

soliloquize *vt* to utter a soliloquy. * *vi* to talk to oneself.—**soliloquist** *n*.

soliloquy *n* (*pl* **soliloquies**) the act of talking to oneself; an act or speech in a play that takes this form.

solipsism *n* (*philos*) the theory that the only possible true knowledge is of self-existence.—**solipsistic** *adj*.—**solipsist** *n*.

solitaire *n* a single gemstone, esp a diamond; a card game for one, patience.

solitary *adj* alone; only; single; living alone; lonely. * *n* (*pl* **solitaries**) a recluse.—**solitarily** *adv*.—**solitariness** *n*.

solitude *n* the state of being alone; lack of company; a lonely place.—**solitudinous** *adj*.

solmization *n* (*mus*) the use of syllables to name the notes or degrees of a musical scale.

solo *n* (*pl* **solos**) a musical composition for one voice or instrument; a flight by a single person in an aircraft, esp a first flight. * *vi* to perform by oneself. * *adv* alone. * *adj* unaccompanied.—**soloist** *n*.

so long *interj* (*inf*) goodbye, farewell.

solo whist *n* a form of whist in which any player may bid independently to win or lose a prescribed number of tricks.

solstice *n* either of the two times in the year at which the sun is farthest from the equator (June 21 and December 21).—**solsticial** *adj*.

soluble *adj* capable of being dissolved (usu in water); capable of being solved or answered.—**solubility** *n*.—**solubly** *adv*.

solute *n* a dissolved substance in a solution.

solution *n* the act or process of answering a problem; the answer found; the dispersion of one substance in another, usu a liquid, so as to form a homogeneous mixture.

solvable *adj* capable of being solved.—**solvability** *n*.

solve *vt* to work out the answer to; to clear up, resolve.

solvent *adj* capable of dissolving a substance; able to pay all debts. * *n* a liquid that dissolves substances.—**solvency** *n*.

solvent abuse *n* the deliberate inhalation of fumes from solvents (such as in glue and polish) to become intoxicated.

soma *n* (*pl* **somatas, somas**) all of an organism except the germ cells.

Somali *n* (*pl* **Somalis, Somali**) a native or inhabitant of Somalia; the Somali language.—*also adj*.—**Somalian** *adj*.

somatic *adj* of or relating to the body, as opposed to the mind.—**somatically** *adv*.

somato-, somat- *prefix* body.

somatotype *n* physical build, body type.

sombre, somber *adj* dark, gloomy or dull; dismal; sad.—**sombrely, somberly** *adv*.—**sombreness, somberness** *n*.

sombrero *n* (*pl* **sombreros**) a wide-brimmed hat with a high crown, worn esp in Spanish-speaking countries.

some *adj* certain but not specified or known; of a certain unspecified quantity, degree, etc; a little; (*inf*) remarkable, striking, etc. * *pron* a certain unspecified quantity, number, etc.

-some *adj suffix* apt to, eg *tiresome*. * *n suffix* a group of, eg *foursome*.

somebody *n* (*pl* **somebodies**) an unspecified person; an important person. * *pron* someone.

someday *adv* at some future day or time.

somehow *adv* in a way or by a method not known or stated.

someone *n* somebody.—*also pron*.

someplace *adv* somewhere.

somersault *n* a forward or backward roll head over heels along the ground or in mid-air.—*also vi*.

something *n*, *pron* a thing not definitely known, understood, etc; an important or notable thing. * *adv* to some degree.

sometime *adj* former. * *adv* at some unspecified future date. * *adj* having been formerly; being so occasionally or in only some respects.

sometimes *adv* at times, now and then.

someway *adv* in a certain unspecified manner.

somewhat *adv* to some extent, degree, etc; a little.

somewhere, somewheres *adv* in, to or at some place not known or specified.

sommelier *n* a wine waiter.

somnambulate *vi* to get up and walk while asleep.—**somnambulant** *adj*.—**somnambulation** *n*.

somnambulism *n* the practice of walking in one's sleep.—**somnambulist** *n*.—**somnambulistic** *adj*.

somnolent *adj* sleepy, drowsy.—**somnolence, somnolency** *n*.

son *n* a male offspring or descendant.

sonar *n* an apparatus that detects underwater objects by means of reflecting sound waves.

sonata *n* (*mus*) a composition for a solo instrument, usu the piano.

sondage *n* (*archaeol*) a deep inspection trench.

sonde *n* a device for collecting scientific data in the upper atmosphere.

sone *n* a unit of loudness equivalent to 40 phons.

son et lumière *n* an evening entertainment staged at historical sites and buildings using lighting displays, music and recorded speech to illuminate the history of the place.

song *n* a piece of music composed for the voice; the act or process of singing; the call of certain birds.

song and dance *n* (*inf*) a fuss; a long involved story.

songbird *n* a bird with a musical call.

songster *n* a singer; a songbird—**songstress** *nf*.

sonic *adj* of, producing, or involving sound waves.—**sonically** *adv*.

sonic barrier *n* the increase in air resistance experienced by objects travelling close to the speed of sound, the sound barrier.

sonic boom *n* an explosive sound produced by the shockwave when an aircraft, etc reaches supersonic speed.

son-in-law *n* (*pl* **sons-in-law**) a daughter's husband.

sonnet *n* a rhyming poem in a single stanza of fourteen lines.

sonneteer *n* a composer of sonnets.

sonny *n* (*pl* **sonnies**) a patronizing form of address to a boy.

sonobuoy *n* a buoy used to detect underwater sounds and transmit them by radio to surface vessels.

sonorous *adj* giving out sound; full, rich, or deep in sound.—**sonorously** *adv*.—**sonorousness** *n*.

soon *adv* in a short time; before long; **sooner or later** at some future unspecified time, eventually.

soot *n* a black powder produced from flames.—**sooty** *adj*.

soothe *vt* to calm or comfort; to alleviate; to relieve (pain, etc).—**soothing** *adj*.—**soothingly** *adv*.

soothsayer *n* a person who predicts events.

SOP *abbr* = standard operating procedure.

sop *n* a piece of bread or other food dipped in liquid before being eaten; a concession, bribe offered to appease or cajole. * *vt* (**sopping, sopped**) to dip (bread, etc) into liquid. * *vi* to be soaked.

sop. *abbr* = soprano.

soph *abbr* = sophomore.

sophism *n* a clever but fallacious argument.—**sophistry** *n*.—**sophist** *n*.—**sophistic, sophistical** *adj*.

sophisticated *adj* refined; worldly-wise; intelligent; complex.—**sophistication** *n*.

sophomore *n* in US, a second-year student at college or high school.—**sophomoric** *adj*.

soporific *adj* inducing sleep; sleepy.

sopping *adj* wet through.

soppy *adj* (**soppier, soppiest**) wet; (*inf*) sickly sentimental.—**soppily** *adv*.—**soppiness** *n*.

sopranino *n* (*pl* **sopraninos**) a musical instrument of the highest pitch in its class.

soprano *n* (*pl* **sopranos, soprani**) the highest singing voice of females or boys; a person who sings soprano.

sorbet *n* a flavoured water ice; sherbet.

sorcerer *n* person who uses magic powers; a magician or wizard.—**sorceress** *nf*.

sorcery *n* (*pl* **sorceries**) the practice of magic, esp with the assistance of evil spirits.

sordid *adj* filthy, squalid; vile; base; selfish.—**sordidly** *adv*.—**sordidness** *n*.

sordino *n* (*pl* **sordini**) a mute for a stringed or brass musical instrument.

sore *n* a painful or tender injury or wound; an ulcer or boil; grief; a cause of distress. * *adj* painful; tender; distressed.—**soreness** *n*.

sorehead *n* (*inf*) an angry, disgruntled person.

sorely *adv* seriously, urgently.

sorghum *n* any of a genus of tropical cereal grasses grown for fodder.

sorority *n* (*pl* **sororities**) a society of women university students.

sorrel[1] *n* a colour between orange-brown and light brown; an animal, esp a horse, of this colour.

sorrel[2] *n* a herb with bitter leaves used in salads.

sorrow *n* sadness; regret; an expression of grief. * *vi* to mourn, to grieve.

sorrowful *adj* full of, showing or causing sorrow.—**sorrowfully** *adv*.—**sorrowfulness** *n*.

sorry *adj* (**sorrier, sorriest**) feeling pity, sympathy, remorse or regret; pitiful; poor.—**sorrily** *adv*.—**sorriness** *n*.

sort *n* a class, kind, or variety; quality or type. * *vt* to arrange according to kind; to classify; (*with* **out**) to find a solution to, resolve; to disentangle; to organize, discipline; (*inf*) to punish, to attack violently.—**sorter** *n*.

sortie *n* a sudden attack by troops from a besieged position; one mission by a single military plane.

SOS *n* an international signal code of distress; an urgent call for help or rescue.

so-so *adj* not good but not bad, middling. * *adv* average, indifferently.

sot *n* a habitual drunkard.

soteriology *n* (*theol*) the doctrine of salvation, esp through Jesus Christ.—**soteriological** *adj*.

sotto voce *adv* in an undertone.

sou *n* (*pl* **sous**) (*formerly*) a French coin of little value; a very small sum of money.

soubrette *n* a minor female role in a comedy, esp a pert lady's maid; a saucy girl.

soubriquet *see* **sobriquet**.

soufflé *n* a baked dish made light and puffy by adding beaten egg whites before baking.—*also adj*.

sough *vi* to make a moaning sound like the wind.—*also n*.

sought *see* **seek**.

souk *n* an open-air market in Muslim countries.

soul *n* a person's spirit; the seat of the emotions, desires; essence; character; a human being. * *adj* characteristic of American Blacks.

soul-destroying *adj* extremely boring, depressing.

soul food *n* (*inf*) traditional food (eg yams, chitterlings) eaten by Blacks of the Southern US.

soulful *adj* expressing profound sentiment.—**soulfully** *adv*.—**soulfulness** *n*.

soulless *adj* devoid of emotion; bleak; dull.

soul mate *n* a person, such as a lover or close friend, with whom one bonds deeply.

soul music *n* music derived from Afro-American gospel singing marked by intensity of feeling and closely related to rhythm and blues.

soul-searching *n* close examination of one's conscience, motives, etc.

sound[1] *adj* healthy; free from injury or damage; substantial; stable; deep (as sleep) solid; thorough.—**soundly** *adv*.—**soundness** *n*.

sound[2] *n* a narrow channel of water connecting two seas or between a mainland and an island.

sound[3] *n* vibrations transmitted through the air and detected by the ear; the sensation of hearing; any audible noise; the impression given by something. * *vi* to make a sound; to give a summons by sound. * *vt* to cause to make a sound; to voice; to make a signal or order by sound; (*with* **off**) (*inf*) to complain loudly.

sound[4] *vt* to measure the depth of; (*often with* **out**) to attempt to discover the opinions and intentions of (someone).

sound barrier *n* the increase in air resistance experienced by objects travelling close to the speed of sound, the sonic barrier.

sound board *n* a thin board in certain musical instruments that resonates to enhance the sound; a sounding board.

soundbox *n* the hollow resonating cavity of a musical instrument such as a guitar or violin.

sound effects *npl* artificial sounds used for dramatic purposes in plays, television programmes, films, etc.

sounding[1] *n* measurement of the depth of water; a test, sampling, eg of public opinion.

sounding[2] *adj* resounding.

sounding board *n* a thin board placed behind a platform to direct the sound at the audience; a sound board; a person or thing used to test reaction to a new idea or plan.

sounding line *n* a line marked at regular intervals for sounding.

soundproof *adj* unable to be penetrated by sound. * *vt* to make soundproof by insulation, etc.

soundtrack *n* the sound accompanying a film; the area on cinema film that carries the sound recording.

soup *n* a liquid food made from boiling meat, fish, vegetables, etc, in water; (*inf*) a difficult or embarrassing situation. * *vt* (*with* **up**) (*inf*) to increase the power and performance of an engine.—**soupy** *adj*.

soupçon *n* a slight flavour; a trace.

soup kitchen *n* a place where soup and other food is dispensed to the homeless and destitute.

sour *adj* having a sharp, biting taste; spoiled by fermentation; cross; bad-tempered; distasteful or unpleasant; (*soil*) acid in reaction. * *vti* to make or become sour.—**sourly** *adv*.—**sourness** *n*.

source *n* a spring forming the head of a stream; an origin or cause; a person, book, etc, that provides information. * *vti* (*inf*) to find a supplier; to identify a source.

source program *n* (*comput*) an original program that has been translated into machine code.

sour cream *n* cream deliberately soured by bacteria and used in sauces, dressings, etc.

sourdough *n* dough used in more than one baking to save on fresh yeast; a prospector in North America who lived on bread made from sourdough.

sour grapes *n sing* pretending to dislike something because it cannot be obtained or achieved by oneself.

sourpuss *n* (*inf*) a gloomy person.

souse *vt* to immerse in water or other liquid; to saturate; to pickle or steep in a marinade; (*sl*) to make drunk. * *vi* to become saturated or immersed. * *n* the act of sousing; something pickled; pickling liquid; (*sl*) a drunkard.

soutane *n* a cassock.

south *n* the direction to one's right when facing the direction of the rising sun; the region, country, continent, etc, lying relatively in that direction. * *adj, adv* facing toward or situated in the south.

Southdown *n* a breed of hornless sheep that yields wool and esp meat.

southeast *n* the point on a compass midway between south and east. * *adj, adv* at, toward, or from the southeast.

southeasterly *adj, adv* toward or from the southeast. * *n* (*pl* **southeasterlies**) a wind from the southeast.

southeastern *adj* in, toward, or from the southeast; inhabiting or characteristic of the southeast.—**southeasterner** *n*.

southerly *adj* in, toward, or from the south. * *n* (*pl* **southerlies**) a wind from the south.

southern *adj* in, toward, or from the south; inhabiting or characteristic of the south.—**southernmost** *adj*.

southerner *n* an inhabitant of the south.

southern lights *npl* the aurora australis.

southpaw *n* (*inf*) a left-handed boxer; a left-handed person.—*also adj*.

South Pole *n* the most southerly point on the earth's axis; the most southerly point on the celestial sphere; (*without caps*) the pole of a magnet that points south.

southward *adj* toward the south.—**southwards** *adv*.

southwest *n* the point on a compass midway between south and west. * *adj, adv* at, toward, or from the southwest.

southwester *n* a strong wind from the southwest.

southwesterly *adj, adv* toward or from the southwest. * *n* (*pl* **southwesterlies**) a wind from the southwest.

southwestern *adj* in, toward, or from the southwest; inhabiting or characteristic of the southwest.—**southwesterner** *n*.

souvenir n a keepsake, a memento.

sou'wester n a waterproof hat with a wide brim at the back worn by sailors.

sovereign adj supreme in authority or rank; (country, state, etc) independent. * n a supreme ruler; a monarch.—**sovereignty** n.

soviet n a workers' council in the former USSR.

sovietism n a political system of which the soviet is the unit.

sow[1] n an adult female pig.

sow[2] vt (**sowing, sowed,** pp **sown** or **sowed**) to plant or scatter seed on or in the ground; to disseminate; to implant.—**sower** n.

soya bean, soybean n a type of bean (orig from Asia) used as a source of food and oil.

soy sauce, soya sauce n a dark, salty sauce made from fermented soybeans.

sozzled adj (inf) drunk.

sp abbr = species.

Sp. abbr = Spain; Spaniard; Spanish.

spa n a mineral spring; a resort where there is a mineral spring.

space n the limitless three-dimensional expanse within which all objects exist; outer space; a specific area; an interval, empty area; room; an unoccupied area or seat. * vt to arrange at intervals.

Space Age n the era when space exploration has become possible.

space-age adj of or pertaining to the Space Age; modern.

space bar n the long bar on a typewriter or computer keyboard for inserting spaces.

spacecraft n a vehicle for travel in outer space.

spaced-out, spaced adj (sl) high on drugs.

spaceman n (pl **spacemen**) a person who travels in outer space; an alien.—**spacewoman** (pl **spacewomen**) nf.

space probe n an unmanned rocket equipped for exploring outer space.

spaceship n a crewed spacecraft.

space shuttle n a manned spacecraft designed as a reusable ferry between the earth and a space station.

space station, space platform n a manned artificial satellite designed to orbit the earth and serve as a permanent base for space exploration.

spacesuit n a sealed and pressurized suit worn by astronauts in space.

space-time (continuum) n (physics) the four-dimensional coordinate system comprising the three spatial and one temporal coordinates which together define a continuum in which any particle or event may be located.

spacewalk n a period of time spent by an astronaut floating in space outside a spacecraft. * vi to walk in space.—**spacewalker** n.

spacious adj large in extent; roomy.—**spaciously** adv.—**spaciousness** n.

spade[1] n a tool with a broad blade and a handle, used for digging.

spade[2] n a black symbol resembling a stylized spearhead marking one of the four suits of playing cards; a card of this suit.

spadework n routine preliminary work.

spadix n (pl **spadixes, spadices**) a spike of flowers clustered around a fleshy stem and enclosed in a spathe.

spaghetti n pasta made in thin, solid strings.

spaghetti western n a type of violent cowboy film, usu shot on location in Italy or Spain, which became popular in the 1960s.

spake (arch) pt of **speak.**

Spam n (trademark) tinned pork luncheon meat.

span n a unit of length equal to a hand's breadth (about 9 inches/23 cm); the full extent between any two limits, such as the ends of a bridge or arch. * vt (**spanning, spanned**) to extend across.

Span. abbr = Spanish.

spandrel n the space between the right or left shoulder of an arch and the rectangular wall or moulding enclosing it.

spangle n a sequin or other small piece of shiny decoration; any small glittering particle. * vt to decorate with spangles. * vi to sparkle with or like spangles.—**spangly** adj.

Spaniard n a native or inhabitant of Spain.

spaniel n any of various breeds of dog with large drooping ears and a long silky coat.

Spanish adj of or pertaining to Spain. * n the language of Spain and Spanish Americans; the people of Spain.

Spanish-American adj of or pertaining to the countries in America where Spanish is spoken. * n a native or inhabitant of a Spanish-American country.

Spanish fly n a European blister beetle; a substance prepared from dried Spanish fly (cantharides) which purportedly acts as an aphrodisiac.

Spanish guitar n a type of classical acoustic guitar music; the guitar used to play this.

Spanish omelette n an omelette containing chopped vegetables such as onions, tomatoes, pimentoes, etc.

spank vt to slap with the flat of the hand, esp on the buttocks.—also n.

spanking adj (inf) very impressive, large, smart, etc; (inf) brisk, lively.—also adv.

spanner n a tool with a hole or (often adjustable) jaws to grip and turn nuts or bolts, a wrench.

spar[1] n a pole supporting the rigging of a ship; one of the main structural members of the wing of an airplane.

spar[2] vi to box using gentle blows, as in training; to argue.—also n.

spare vt to refrain from harming or killing; to afford; to make (something) available (eg time). * adj kept as an extra, additional; scanty. * n a spare part; a spare tyre—**sparely** adv.—**spareness** n.

sparerib n a pork rib with most of the meat cut away.

spare tyre n (inf) a roll of excess fat around the waist.

sparing adj frugal, economical.—**sparingly** adv.—**sparingness** n.

spark n a fiery or glowing particle thrown off by burning material or by friction; a flash of light from an electrical discharge; a trace. * vt to stir up; to activate. * vi to give off sparks.

sparking plug n a spark plug.

sparkle n a spark; vivacity. * vi to shine; to glitter; (water, wine) to effervesce; to be lively or witty.

sparkler n a handheld firework that throws off brilliant sparks; (inf) a diamond.

spark plug n a device that produces a spark to ignite the explosive mixture in an internal combustion engine.—also **sparking plug.**

sparring partner n (boxing) a partner who stands in as an opponent for training purposes; a person with whom one regularly argues.

sparrow n any of various small brownish songbirds related to the finch.

sparse *adj* spread out thinly; scanty.—**sparsely** *adv.*—**sparseness, sparsity** *n.*

Spartan *adj* of or pertaining to Sparta in ancient Greece; rigourously severe.

spasm *n* a sudden, involuntary muscular contraction; any sudden burst (of emotion or activity).—**spasmodic** *adj* intermittent; of or like a spasm.—**spasmodically** *adv.*

spastic *n* a person who suffers from cerebral palsy. * *adj* affected by muscle spasm.—**spasticity** *n.*

spat[1] *see* **spit**[2].

spat[2] *n* a gaiter covering the ankle and instep and fastening under the shoe.

spat[3] *n* a young oyster or other bivalve mollusc.

spat[4] *n* a petty argument, or quarrel. * *vi* to have a petty argument.

spate *n* a large amount; a sudden outburst (as of words); a sudden flood.

spathe *n* a leafy part that encloses the floral spikes of certain flowers.

spatial *adj* relating to space.—**spatially** *adv.*

spatiotemporal *adj* of, involving, or occurring in both space and time; of or pertaining to space-time.

spatter *vti* to scatter or spurt out in drops; to splash.—*also n.*

spatula *n* a tool with a broad, flexible blade for spreading or mixing foods, paints, etc.

spatulate *adj* shaped like a spatula.

spawn *n* a mass of eggs deposited by fish, frogs, or amphibians; offspring. * *vti* to lay eggs; to produce, esp in great quantity.

spay *vt* (*female animals*) to sterilize by removing the ovaries from.

SPCA *abbr* = Society for the Prevention of Cruelty to Animals.

SPCC *abbr* = Society for the Prevention of Cruelty to Children.

speak *vi* (**speaking, spoke,** *pp* **spoken**) to utter words; to talk; to converse with; to deliver a speech; to be suggestive of something; to produce a characteristic sound; (*with* **out, up**) to speak loudly; to express an opinion frankly.—**speakable** *adj.*

speakeasy *n* (*pl* **speakeasies**) a club where alcoholic drink was sold illegally during the Prohibition era in the US in the 1920s.

speaker *n* a person who speaks, esp before an audience; the presiding official in a legislative assembly; a loudspeaker.

speaking clock *n* a recorded telephone message which gives the time.

spear *n* a weapon with a long shaft and a sharp point; a blade or shoot (of grass, broccoli, etc). * *vt* to pierce with a spear.

spearhead *n* the pointed head of a spear; the leading person or group in an attack or other action. * *vt* to serve as a leader of.

spearmint *n* a common mint plant which yields an oil used for flavouring.

special *adj* distinguished; uncommon; designed for a particular purpose; peculiar to one person or thing.—**specially** *adv.*

Special Branch *n* the division of the British police force that deals with political security.

specialist n a person who concentrates on a particular area of study or activity, esp in medicine.

speciality *n* (*pl* **specialities**) a special skill or interest; a special product.—*also* **specialty.**

specialize *vi* to concentrate on a particular area of study or activity. * *vt* to adapt to a particular use or purpose.—**specialization** *n.*

special licence *n* in the UK, a licence allowing a marriage to take place without regard to the normal legal requirements.

special pleading *n* (*law*) the allegation of new facts in an action as opposed to a direct denial or admission of the opposition evidence; arguments that concentrate on the positive as opposed to the negative aspects of a case.

specialty *see* **speciality.**

speciation *n* the evolution of a species.—**speciate** *vi.*

specie *n* money in coin.

species *n* (*pl* **species**) a class of plants or animals with the same main characteristics, enabling interbreeding; a distinct kind or sort.

specific *adj* explicit; definite; of a particular kind. * *n* a characteristic quality or influence; a drug effective in treating a particular disease.—**specifically** *adv.*—**specificity** *n.*

specification *n* a requirement; (*pl*) detailed description of dimensions, materials, etc of something.

specific gravity *n* the ratio of the density of a substance to that of the same volume of water.

specific heat capacity *n* the heat required to raise the temperature of a unit of mass of a given substance by one degree.

specify *vt* (**specifying, specified**) to state specifically; to set down as a condition.—**specifier** *n.*

specimen *n* (*plant, animal, etc*) an example of a particular species; a sample; (*inf*) a person.

specious *adj* apparently true, but in fact false.—**speciously** *adv.*—**speciousness** *n.*

speck *n* a small spot; a fleck.

speckle *n* a small mark of a different colour. * *vt* to mark with speckles.

specs *npl* specifications; (*inf*) spectacles.

spectacle *n* an unusual or interesting scene; a large public show; an object of derision or ridicule; (*pl*) a pair of glasses.—**spectacled** *adj.*

spectacular *adj* impressive; astonishing.—**spectacularly** *adv.*

spectate *vi* to be a spectator.

spectator *n* an onlooker.

specter *see* **spectre.**

spectra *see* **spectrum.**

spectral *adj* of or like a spectre; of or produced by a spectrum.—**spectrality** *adv.*—**spectrally** *adv.*

spectre *n* an apparition or ghost; a haunting mental image.—*also* **specter.**

spectro- *prefix* spectrum.

spectrograph *n* a device for producing and recording spectra.—**spectrographic** *adj.*

spectrometer *n* a spectroscope used to measure spectra.—**spectrometric** *adj.*—**spectrometry** *n.*

spectroscope *n* an instrument for generating and examining spectra.—**spectroscopic** *adj.*—**spectroscopically** *adv.*—**spectroscopy** *n.*

spectrum *n* (*pl* **spectra**) the range of colour which is produced when a white light is passed through a prism; any similar distribution of wave frequencies; a broad range.

speculate *vi* to theorize, to conjecture; to make investments in the hope of making a profit.—**speculation** *n.*—**speculator** *n.*

speculative *adj* of or based on speculation; engaging in speculation in finance, etc.—**speculatively** *adv*.

speculum *n* (*pl* **specula, speculums**) a medical instrument for dilating and examining a bodily passage or cavity; a mirror used as a reflector in an optical instrument such as a telescope.

sped *see* **speed**.

speech *n* the action or power of speaking; a public address or talk; language, dialect.

speechify *vi* (**speechifying, speechified**) to make a speech or speeches, esp in a dull or pompous manner.—**speechifier** *n*.

speechless *adj* unable to speak; silent, as from shock; impossible to express in words.—**speechlessly** *adv*.—**speechlessness** *n*.

speed *n* quickness; rapidity or rate of motion; (*photog*) the sensitivity of film to light; (*sl*) an amphetamine drug. * *vi* (**speeding, sped** *or* **speeded**) to go quickly, to hurry; to drive (a vehicle) at an illegally high speed.

speedball *n* (*sl*) a mixture of heroin and cocaine or amphetamines.

speeding n the driving of a vehicle at an illegally high or dangerous speed.

speedometer *n* an instrument in a motor vehicle for measuring its speed.

speedway *n* the sport of racing light motorcycles around dirt or cinder tracks; a stadium for motorcycle racing; in US, a road reserved for fast traffic.

speedwell *n* any of various plants of the figwort family with small blue or white flowers.

speedy *adj* (**speedier, speediest**) quick; prompt.—**speedily** *adv*.—**speediness** *n*.

speleology *n* the scientific study of caves.—**speleological** *adj*.—**speleologist** *n*.

spell[1] *n* a sequence of words used to perform magic; fascination.

spell[2] *vb* (**spelling, spelt** *or* **spelled**) *vt* to name or write down in correct order the letters to form a word; (*letters*) to form a word when placed in the correct order; to indicate; (*with* **out**) to read slowly and painstakingly; to explain in detail; to discern, realize the meaning of. * *vi* to spell words.

spell[3] *n* a usu indefinite period of time; a period of duty in a certain occupation or activity. * *vt* to relieve, stand in for.

spellbound *adj* entranced, enthralled.

spelling bee *n* a spelling contest.

spelt *see* **spell**[2].

spelunker *n* a person whose hobby is exploring caves.—**spelunking** *n*.

spend *vb* (**spending, spent**) *vt* to pay out (money); to concentrate (one's time or energy) on an activity; to pass, as time; to use up. * *vi* to pay out money.—**spender** *n*.

spendthrift *n* a person who spends money wastefully or extravagantly.

spent[1] *see* **spend**.

spent[2] *adj* consumed, used up; physically drained, exhausted.

sperm *n* semen; the male reproductive cell.

spermaceti *n* a waxy substance derived from the oil in the head of a sperm whale.

spermat(o)-, sperm(o)- *prefix* sperm.

spermatic *adj* pertaining to, consisting of, or conveying, sperm.

spermatid *n* any of the four male gametes that form into a spermatozoon.

spermatocyte *n* a cell that develops into a male germ cell.

spermatogenesis *n* the formation and development of spermatozoa in the testis.—**spermatogenetic** *adj*.

spermatogonium *n* (*pl* **spermatogonia**) an immature male germ cell.

spermatophyte *n* a plant that produces seeds.—**spermatophytic** *adj*.

spermatozoon *n* (*pl* **spermatozoa**) any of the male reproductive cells present in the semen.

spermicide *n* a substance that destroys sperm.—**spermicidal** *adj*.

sperm oil *n* oil obtained from the head of the sperm whale.

sperm whale *n* a large whale with a blunt head which is hunted for its oil and spermaceti.

spew *vti* to vomit; to flow or gush forth. * *n* something spewed.

sphagnum *n* a genus of moss which grows in bogs and is a major constituent of peat.

sphalerite *see* **blende**.

sphenoid *adj* wedge-shaped; of or pertaining to the sphenoid bone. * *n* a sphenoid bone.

sphenoid bone *n* a wedge-shaped bone at the base of the skull.

sphere *n* a ball, globe or other perfectly round object; a field of activity or interest; a social class.—**spherical, spheric** *adj*.—**spherically** *adv*.

spheroid *n* a figure that is nearly a sphere.

spherometer *n* an instrument for measuring the curvature of spherical surfaces.

spherule *n* a small sphere.

sphincter *n* a ring-shaped muscle controlling the opening and closing of an orifice.

sphinx *n* (*with cap*) (*Greek myth*) a monster with a lion's body and human head which killed travellers who gave the wrong answer to a riddle; (*without cap*) any of various massive statues with a lion's body and human head erected by the ancient Egyptians; a mysterious or enigmatic person.

sphygmograph *n* a device that records variations in blood pressure and pulse.—**sphygmographic** *adj*.—**sphygmography** *n*.

sphygmomanometer *n* a device for measuring arterial blood pressure.

spicate *adj* (*flowers, leaves*) spiked, pointed.

spicatto *n* (*pl* **spicattos**) (*mus*) (a musical piece or passage played using) a technique in which the bow is made to rebound lightly off the strings of an instrument.—*also adj*.

spice *n* an aromatic vegetable substance used for flavouring and seasoning food; these substances collectively; something that adds zest or interest. * *vt* to flavour with spice; to add zest to.

spicebush *n* an aromatic North American plant.

spick-and-span *adj* scrupulously clean and tidy.

spicule *n* a small needle-like body in the skeleton of sponges, corals, etc; a jet of hot gas erupting from the surface of the sun.

spicy *adj* (**spicier, spiciest**) flavoured with spice; pungent; (*inf*) somewhat scandalous or indecent.—**spicily** *adv*.—**spiciness** *n*.

spider *n* a small wingless creature (arachnid) with eight legs, and abdominal spinnerets for spinning silk threads to make webs.

spider crab *n* any of various crabs with triangular bodies and very long legs.

spider monkey *n* a monkey of South and Central America with a slender body and long limbs.

spiderwort *n* tradescantia.

spidery *adj* thin, and angular, like a spider's legs.

spied *see* **spy**.

spiel *n* glib talk intended to cajole or persuade.—*also vi*.

spiffing *n* (*sl*) (*arch*) excellent.

spiffy *adj* (**spiffier, spiffiest**) smart, elegant.

spigot *n* a small stopper or tap for a cask; a tap.

spike n long heavy nail; a sharp-pointed projection, as on a shoe to prevent slipping; an ear of corn, etc; a cluster of stalkless flowers arranged on a long stem. * *vt* to pierce with a spike.—**spiky** *adj*.

spilikin *see* **spillikin**.

spikenard *n* (a fragrant oil derived from) an Indian aromatic plant.

spill[1] *vti* (**spilling, spilled** *or* **spilt**) to cause, esp unintentionally, to flow out of a container; to shed (blood). * *n* something spilled.—**spillage** *n*.

spill[2] *n* a splinter or thin strip of wood or twisted paper for lighting a fire, etc.

spillikin *n* a sliver of wood, cardboard or plastic.—*also* **spilikin**.

spillway n a channel for surplus water from a dam, etc.

spilt *see* **spill**[1].

spin *vb* (**spinning, spun**) *vt* to rotate rapidly; to draw out and twist fibres into thread or yarn; (*spiders, silkworm, etc*) to make a web or cocoon; to draw out (a story) to a great length; (*with* **out**) to prolong, extend; to cause to last longer, eg money. * *vi* to seem to be spinning from dizziness; (*wheels*) to turn rapidly without imparting forward motion. * *n* a swift rotation; (*inf*) a brief, fast ride in a vehicle; an emphasis or slant imparted to information, proposals or policies.

spina bifida *n* a congenital abnormality in the formation of the spine causing the meninges to protrude, and associated with partial paralysis.

spinach *n* a plant with large, green edible leaves.

spinal *adj* of or relating to the spine or spinal cord.—**spinally** *adv*.

spinal column *n* the skeleton of jointed vertebrae and interconnecting cartilaginous tissue that surrounds and protects the spinal cord.—*also* **spine, backbone**.

spinal cord *n* the cord of nerves enclosed by the spinal column.

spindle *n* the notched rod by which thread is twisted in spinning; a pin around which machinery turns.

spindly *adj* (**spindlier, spindliest**) tall and slender; frail.

spindrift *n* sea spray.

spine *n* a sharp, stiff projection, as a thorn of the cactus or quill of a porcupine; a spinal column; the backbone of a book.

spine-chiller *n* a book, film, etc that inspires terror.—**spine-chilling** *adj*.

spineless *adj* lacking a spine; weak-willed; irresolute.—**spinelessly** *adv*.—**spinelessness** *n*.

spinet *n* a type of small harpsichord.

spinifex *n* any of several coarse Australian grasses with spiny seed heads or spiked leaves.

spinnaker *n* a large triangular sail sometimes carried by racing yachts.

spinner *n* a revolving fishing lure; (*cricket*) a ball bowled with a spin, or a bowler who does this.

spinneret *n* an organ in spiders and other insects for producing silk threads.

spinning wheel *n* a small household machine with a wheel-driven spindle for spinning yarn from fibre.

spin-off *n* a product or benefit derived incidentally from existing research and development.

spinose *adj* (*plants*) spiny.

spinster *n* an unmarried woman.

spiny *adj* (**spinier, spiniest**) covered with spines or thorns; troublesome.

spiny anteater *n* the echidna.

spiny lobster *n* any of several large edible crustaceans with a spiny shell.

spiracle *n* a respiratory aperture in various insects and some fishes; the blowhole in whales.

spiraea, spirea *n* any of various plants of the rose family having clusters of small white or pink flowers.

spiral *adj* winding round in a continuous curve up or down a centre or pole. * *n* a helix; a spiral line or shape; a continuous expansion or decrease, eg in inflation. * *vi* (**spiralling, spiralled** *or* **spiraling, spiraled**) to move up or down in a spiral curve; to increase or decrease steadily.

spiral galaxy *n* a galaxy in which two arms consisting of new stars spiral outward from an ellipsoidal nucleus of old stars.

spire *n* the tapering point of a steeple.

spirillum *n* (*pl* **spirilla**) a bacterium with a curved or spiral body.

spirit *n* soul; a supernatural being, as a ghost, angel, etc; (*pl*) disposition; mood; vivacity, courage, etc; real meaning; essential quality; (*usu pl*) distilled alcoholic liquor. * *vt* to carry (away, off, etc) secretly and swiftly.

spirited *adj* full of life; animated.—**spiritedly** *adv*.—**spiritedness** *n*.

spirit level *n* a glass tube filled with liquid containing an air bubble and mounted in a frame, used for testing whether a surface is level.

spiritual *adj* of the soul; religious; sacred. * *n* an emotional religious song, originating among the Black slaves in the American South.—**spirituality** *n*.—**spiritually** *adv*.

spiritualism *n* the belief that the spirits of the dead can communicate with the living, as through mediums.—**spiritualist** *n*.

spirochaete, spirochete *n* any of a genus of slender spiral-shaped bacteria that includes those causing syphilis.

spirograph *n* a device that records respiratory movements.—**spirographic** *adj*.

spirt *see* **spurt**.

spit[1] *n* a pointed iron rod on which meat is roasted; a long narrow strip of land projecting into the water. * *vt* (**spitting, spitted**) to fix as on a spit, impale.

spit[2] *vb* (**spitting, spat** *or* **spit**) *vt* to eject from the mouth; to utter with scorn. * *vi* to expel saliva from the mouth; (*hot fat*) to splutter; to rain lightly. * *n* saliva.

spit and polish *n* (*inf*) obsession with neatness and cleanliness, esp in the military services.

spite *n* ill will; malice. * *vt* to annoy spitefully, to vex.—**spiteful** *adj*.

spitting image *n* (*inf*) a person who almost exactly resembles another.

spittle *n* saliva ejected from the mouth.

spittoon *n* a usu metal pan for spitting into, a cuspidor.

spiv *n* (*sl*) a person of smart appearance who lives by shady dealings, esp on the black market.

splanchnic *adj* of or pertaining to the viscera.

splash *vti* to spatter with liquid; to move with a splash; to display prominently; (*with* **down**) to land (a spacecraft) on water. * *n* something splashed; a patch of colour; a small amount, esp of a mixer added to an alcoholic drink.—**splashy** *adj*.

splashdown *n* (the scheduled time of) the landing of a spacecraft on the ocean.

splatter *vti* to splash, spatter.—*also n*.

splay *vti* to turn out at an angle; to spread out.

spleen *n* a large lymphatic organ in the upper left part of the abdomen which modifies the blood structure; spitefulness; ill humour.

splendid *adj* brilliant; magnificent; (*inf*) very good.—**splendidly** *adv*.—**splendidness** *n*.

splendiferous *adj* (*inf*) splendid.

splendour, splendor *n* brilliance; magnificence; grandeur.—**splendorous, splendrous** *adj*.

splenetic *adj* of or pertaining to the spleen; spiteful, irritable.—**splenetically** *adv*.

splenic *n* of, pertaining to, or in the spleen.

splenius *n* (*pl* **splenii**) either of the two muscles at either side of the back of the neck that move the head.—**splenial** *adj*.

splenomegaly *n* distension of the spleen.

splice *vt* to unite (two ends of a rope) by intertwining the strands; to connect (two pieces of timber) by overlapping.—*also n*.

spline *n* a key or slot in a shaft that fits into grooves in a surrounding sleeve and locks the two together.

splint *n* a rigid structure used to immobilize and support a fractured limb; a splinter of wood for lighting fires. * *vt* to put in splints.

splinter *n* a thin, sharp piece of wood, glass, or metal broken off. * *vti* to break off into splinters.—**splintery** *adj*.

splinter group *n* a small group that has split off from the main body.

split *vti* (**splitting, split**) to break apart (usu into two pieces); to separate into factions; to divide into shares; to burst or tear. * *n* the act or process of splitting; a narrow gap made (as if) by splitting; a dessert consisting of sliced fruit, esp banana, with ice cream, nuts, etc; (*often pl*) the act of extending the legs in opposite directions and lowering the the body to the floor. * *adj* divided; torn; fractured.

split infinitive *n* (*gram*) an infinitive with another word between *to* and the verb.

split-level *adj* (*building*) having rooms or areas in one part less than a full story higher than another that adjoins them.

split personality *n* unstable in mood or behaviour; having two or more distinct personalities.

split-screen *n* (*cinema, television*) a technique involving the simultaneous projection of different images onto separate areas of the screen.

split second *n* a very brief moment, an instant.—**split-second** *adj*.

split shift *n* a shift in which the working hours are divided into two distinct periods.

splodge, splotch *n* a large irregular spot, stain or smear. * *vt* to mark with a splodge or splotch.—**splodgy, splotchy** *adj*.

splurge *vi* to spend lavishly (on); to show off. * *n* an extravagant display, esp of wealth.

splutter *vi* to spit out food or drops of liquid noisily; to utter words confusedly and hurriedly.—*also n*.

spoil *vb* (**spoiling, spoiled** *or* **spoilt**) *vt* to damage as to make useless, etc; to impair the enjoyment, etc, of; to overindulge (a child). * *vi* to become spoiled; to decay, etc, as food. * *npl* booty, valuables seized in war; the opportunities for financial gain from holding public office.

spoiler *n* a projecting structure on an aircraft wing that increases drag to reduce lift; any similar structure for increasing the stability of vehicles at high speed.

spoil-sport *n* (*inf*) a person who spoils the fun of others.

spoilt *see* **spoil**.

spoke[1], **spoken** *see* **speak**.

spoke[2] *n* any of the braces extending from the hub to the rim of a wheel.

spokeshave *n* a small two-handled plane used for smoothing curved surfaces.

spokesman *n* (*pl* **spokesmen**) a person authorized to speak on behalf of others.—**spokeswoman** *nf* (*pl* **spokeswomen**).

spondylitis *n* inflammation of the vertebrae.

sponge *n* a plantlike marine animal with an internal skeleton of elastic interlacing horny fibres; a piece of natural or manmade sponge for washing or cleaning. * *vt* to wipe with a sponge. * *vi* (*inf*) to scrounge.—**sponginess** *n*.—**spongy** *adj*.

sponge bag *n* a small waterproof bag for toilet articles, a washbag.

sponge cake *n* a sweet cake with a light porous texture.

sponson *n* a projecting gun-mounting on a ship or tank, etc to allow forward fire; an air-filled projection on the hull of a seaplane to provide stability.

sponsor *n* a person or organization that pays the expenses connected with an artistic production or sports event in return for advertising; in US, a business firm, etc that pays for a radio or TV programme advertising its product. * *vt* to act as sponsor for.—**sponsorship** *n*.

spontaneity *n* (*pl* **spontaneities**) the quality of being spontaneous; a spontaneous action, etc.

spontaneous *adj* arising naturally; unpremeditated.—**spontaneously** *adv*.—**spontaneousness** *n*.

spontaneous combustion *n* the self-igniting of a substance through internal chemical processes such as oxidation.

spontaneous generation *n* abiogenesis.

spoof *n* (*sl*) a hoax or joke; a light satire.—*also vti*.

spook *n* (*inf*) a ghost; (*inf*) a spy. * *vt* to frighten.—**spooky** *adj*.

spool *n* a cylinder, bobbin, or reel, upon which thread, photographic film, etc, are wound. * *vt* to wind on a spool.

spoon *n* utensil with a shallow bowl and a handle, for eating, stirring, etc.—**spoonful** *n*.

spoonbill *n* any of various wading birds with flattened bills.

spoonerism *n* the accidental transposition of the initial letters or opening syllables of two or more words with amusing results, e.g *half-warmed fish* for *half-formed wish*.

spoor *n* a trail, esp of a wild animal. * *vti* to track (something) by a spoor.

sporadic *adj* occurring here and there; intermittent.—**sporadically** *adv*.

sporangium *n* (*pl* **sporangia**) (*in fungi, etc*) an organ or part in which asexual spores are produced.

spore *n* an asexual reproductive body produced by algae, fungae and ferns capable of giving rise to new individuals.

sporogenesis *n* the formation of spores in plants and animals.—**sporogenous** *adj*.

sporozoan *n* any of a group of spore-producing parasitic protozoans that includes the malaria parasite.

sporran *n* an ornamental pouch worn in front of the kilt as part of traditional Highland dress in Scotland.

sport *n* an athletic game or pastime, often competitive and involving physical capability; good-humoured joking; (*inf*) a person regarded as fair and abiding by the rules. * *vi* to play, to frolic. * *vt* (*inf*) to display, flaunt.

sporting *adj* interested in, concerned with, or suitable for sport; exhibiting sportsmanship; willing to take a risk.—**sportingly** *adv*.

sportive *adj* playful.—**sportively** *adv*.—**sportiveness** *n*.

sportscast *n* a sports broadcast.—**sportscaster** *n*.

sportsman *n* (*pl* **sportsmen**) a person engaged in sport; a person who plays by the rules, is fair, is a good loser, etc.—**sportswoman** *nf* (*pl* **sportswomen**).—**sportsmanlike**, **sportsmanly** *adj*.— **sportsmanship** *n*.

sports medicine *n* the branch of medicine dealing with sports injuries.

sporty *adj* (**sportier**, **sportiest**) (*inf*) fond of sport; flashy, ostentatious.—**sportily** *adv*.—**sportiness** *n*.

sporule *n* a tiny spore.

spot *n* a small area differing in colour, etc, from the surrounding area; a stain, speck, etc; a taint on character or reputation; a small quantity or amount; a locality; (*inf*) a difficult or embarrassing situation; a place on an entertainment programme; a spotlight. * *vt* (**spotting**, **spotted**) to mark with spots; (*inf*) to identify or recognise; to glimpse.

spot check *n* a sudden random examination.—**spot-check** *vt*.

spotless *adj* immaculate.—**spotlessly** *adv*.—**spotlessness** *n*.

spotlight *n* a powerful light used to illuminate a small area; intense public attention. * *vt* (**spotlighting**, **spotlighted** *or* **spotlit**) to illuminate with a spotlight; to focus attention on.

spot on *adj* (*inf*) absolutely right.

spotted dick *n* a steamed pudding made with suet and currants.

spotty *adj* (**spottier**, **spottiest**) marked with spots, esp on the skin; intermittent, uneven.—**spottily** *adv*.—**spottiness** *n*.

spot-weld *vt* to join two pieces of metal with circular welds.—**spot-welder** *n*.—**spot welding** *n*.

spouse *n* (one's) husband or wife.

spout *vti* to eject in a strong jet or spurts; (*inf*) to drone on boringly. * *n* a projecting lip or tube for pouring out liquids.

spp *abbr* = species (*pl*).

SPQR *abbr* = *Senatus Populusque Romanus* (the Senate and People of Rome).

sprain *n* a wrenching of a joint by sudden twisting or tearing of ligaments.—*also vt*.

sprang *see* **spring**.

sprat *n* a small food fish related to the herring; a small or young herring.

sprawl *vi* to lie down with the limbs stretched out in an untidy manner; to spread out in a straggling way. * *n* a sprawling position.

spray[1] *n* fine particles of a liquid; mist; an aerosol or atomizer. * *vti* to direct a spray (on); to apply as a spray.

spray[2] *n* a number of flowers on one branch; a decorative flower arrangement; an ornament resembling this.

spray gun *n* a device for applying paint, varnish, etc in the form of a spray.

spread *vt* (**spreading**, **spread**) to extend; to unfold or open; to disseminate; to distribute; to apply a coating (eg butter). * *vi* to expand in all directions. * *n* an expanse; (*inf*) a feast; food which can be spread on bread; a bed cover.

spread eagle *n* an emblem of an eagle with wings and legs stretched out.

spread-eagle *vt* to stand or lie with the limbs outstretched.—**spread-eagled** *adj*.

spreadsheet *n* a computer program that allows easy entry and manipulation of text and figures, used for accounting and financial planning.

spree *n* (*inf*) excessive indulgence, eg in spending money, alcohol consumption, etc.

sprier *see* **spry**.

sprig *n* a twig with leaves on it.

sprightly *adj* (**sprightlier**, **sprightliest**) full of life or energy.—**sprightliness** *n*.

spring *vb* (**springing**, **sprang** *or* **sprung**, *pp* **sprung**) *vi* to move suddenly, as by elastic force; to arise suddenly; to originate. * *vt* to cause to spring up, to cause to operate suddenly. * *n* a leap; the season between winter and summer; a coiled piece of wire that springs back to its original shape when stretched; the source of a stream.

spring balance *n* a device that measures weight by the tension of a spring linked to a pointer on a calibrated scale.—*also* **spring scale**.

springboard *n* a flexible board used by divers and in gymnastics to provided added height or impetus.

springbok *n* a South African gazelle.

spring chicken *n* a young chicken from two to ten months old; (*inf*) a young inexperienced person.

spring-clean *vi* to clean (a house, etc) thoroughly.— **spring clean** *n*.

springe *n* a snare for catching small animals.

spring onion *n* a scallion.

spring roll *n* a Chinese savoury snack comprising a mixture of beansprouts, chopped meat, etc rolled in a thin pancake and fried.

spring scale *see* **spring balance**.

springtail *n* any of various small wingless leaping insects.

spring tide *n* a high tide that occurs at the full or new moon.

springtime *n* the season of spring; the earliest and most promising period in the life of something or someone.

springy *adj* (**springier**, **springiest**) elastic, resilient; light, spongy.—**springily** *adv*.—**springiness** *n*.

sprinkle *vt* to scatter in droplets or particles (on something).—*also n*.

sprinkler *n* a nozzle for spraying water; a fire-extinguishing system that operates automatically on detection of smoke or heat.

sprinkling *n* a small quantity scattered randomly.

sprint *n* a short run or race at full speed. * *vi* to go at top speed.—**sprinter** *n*.

sprit *n* a small spar which runs from the mast to the outer upper corner of a sail.

sprite *n* an elf or imp; a dainty person.

spritsail *n* a sail extended by a sprit.

spritzer *n* a drink made with wine, usu white, and soda water.

sprocket *n* a wheel with a row of teeth which engage the holes in a chain, or a reel of film, in order to turn it.

sprout *n* a new shoot on a plant; a small cabbage-like vegetable. * *vt* to put forth (shoots). * *vi* to begin to grow.

spruce[1] *adj* smart, neat, trim. * *vt* to smarten.

spruce[2] *n* an evergreen tree of the pine family with a conical head and soft light wood.

sprung *see* **spring**.

spry *adj* (**sprier, spriest** *or* **spryer, spryest**) vigorous, agile.—**spryly** *av.*—**spryness** *n.*

spud *n* a small narrow digging tool; (*inf*) a potato. * *vt* (**spudding, spudded**) to dig with a spud.—**spudder** *n.*

spume *n* foam; surf; froth.

spun *see* **spin**.

spunk *n* a spark, a match; (*sl*) pluck, courage.

spunky *adj* (**spunkier, spunkiest**) full of courage; spirited.—**spunkily** *adv.*—**spunkiness** *n.*

spun silk *n* a shiny material made from silk waste.

spur *n* a small metal wheel on a rider's heel, with sharp points for urging on the horse; encouragement, stimulus; a hard sharp projection. * *vt* (**spurring, spurred**) to urge on.

spurge *n* any of various plants that produce a bitter milky juice.

spurious *adj* not legitimate or genuine; false.—**spuriously** *adv.*—**spuriousness** *n.*

spurn *vt* to reject with disdain. * *n* disdainful rejection.

spurt *vt* to gush forth in a sudden stream or jet. * *n* a sudden stream or jet; a burst of activity.—*also* **spirt**.

sputnik *n* the name used for series of artificial satellites launched by the former Soviet Union in the 1950s and 1960s (Russian for *travelling companion*).

sputter *vi* to splutter.—*also n.*

sputum *n* (*pl* **sputa**) saliva and mucus.

spy *n* (*pl* **spies**) a secret agent employed to collect information on rivals. * *vb* (**spying, spied**) *vi* to keep under secret surveillance, act as a spy (*usu with* **on**). * *vt* to catch sight of.

spyglass *n* a small telescope.

sq *abbr* = sequence; squadron; square.

squab *n* (*pl* **squabs, squab**) a young bird, esp a pigeon; a stuffed cushion; a short fat person. * *adj* (*birds*) unfledged; short and fat.

squabble *vi* to quarrel noisily. * *n* a noisy, petty quarrel.—*also n.*

squad *n* a small group of soldiers which form a working unit; a section of a police force; (*sport*) a group of players from which a team is selected.

squadron *n* a unit of warships, cavalry, military aircraft, etc.

squalid *adj* filthy; neglected, sordid; degrading.—**squalidly** *adv.*—**squalidness** *n.*

squall *vi* to cry out loudly (like a baby). * *n* a loud cry; a violent gust of wind.

squalor *n* foulness; dirt, filth.

squama *n* (*pl* **squamae**) (*biol*) (something resembling) a scale.

squander *vt* to spend extravagantly or wastefully.

square *n* a shape with four sides of equal length and four right angles; an open space in a town, surrounded by buildings; (*inf*) an old-fashioned person; an instrument for drawing right angles; the product of a number multiplied by itself. * *adj* square-shaped; forming a square; forming a right angle (with); (*finan-*

cial account) settled; fair, honest; equal in score; (*inf*) old-fashioned. * *vt* to make square; to multiply (a quantity) by itself; (*with* **away**) (*inf*) to put in order, tidy up. * *vi* to agree.—**squarely** *adv.*—**squareness** *n.*

square bracket *n* either of a pair of written or printed characters [ ] used to enclose text or in mathematical expressions.

square dance *n* any of various dances in which the participants join hands to form squares.—**square-dance** *vi.*

square meal *n* a meal of satisfying quantity.

square measure *n* the measure of an area; the square of a lineal measure.

square root *n* a number that when multiplied by itself produces a given number (2 *is the square root of* 4).

squash[1] *vt* to squeeze, press, or crush; to suppress. * *vi* to squelch; to crowd. * *n* a crushed mass; a crowd of people pressed together; a fruit-flavoured drink; a game played in a walled court with rackets and rubber ball.—**squashy** *adj.*

squash[2] *n* (*pl* **squashes, squash**) a marrow or gourd eaten as a vegetable.

squat *vi* (**squatting, squatted**) to crouch down upon the heels; to occupy land or property, without permission or title. * *adj* short and dumpy. * *n* the act of squatting; a house that is occupied by squatters.

squatter *n* a person who squats.

squaw *n* a North American Indian woman.

squawk *n* a loud, raucous call or cry, as of a bird; (*inf*) a loud protest.—*also vi.*

squeak *vi* to make a high-pitched cry. * *n* a squeaky noise.—**squeaker** *n.*—**squeaky** *adj.*

squeaky-clean *adj* spotless; above reproach.

squeal *vi* to make a shrill and prolonged cry or sound; (*sl*) to be an informer; to protest.

squeamish *adj* easily nauseated; easily shocked or disgusted.—**squeamishly** *adv.*—**squeamishness** *n.*

squeegee *n* a tool with a rubber-edged blade for scraping away excess water from a surface, esp a window. * *vt* (**squeegeeing, squeegeed**) to wipe clean with a squeegee.

squeeze *vt* to press firmly, compress; to grasp tightly; to hug; to force (through, into) by pressing; to extract liquid, juice, from by pressure; to obtain (money, etc) by force, to harass. * *n* squeezing or being squeezed; a hug; a small amount squeezed from something; a crowding together; financial pressure or hardship.—**squeezable** *adj.*

squelch *vi* to walk through soft, wet ground, making a sucking noise. * *vt* to crush or squash completely. * *n* a squelching sound.

squib *n* a small firework that fizzes then explodes; a short, witty attack in speech or writing, a lampoon.

squid *n* (*pl* **squids, squid**) an edible mollusc, related to the cuttlefish, with a long body and ten arms.

squiffy *adj* (**squiffier, squiffiest**) slightly drunk.

squiggle *n* a short wavy line, esp handwritten. * *vi* to squirm; to wriggle.—**squiggly** *adj.*

squill *n* a Mediterranean plant of the lilly family; a seashore variety of this whose bulbs were formerly used medicinally.

squint *vi* to half close or cross the eyes; to glance sideways. * *n* crossed eyes, as caused by a visual disorder; a glance sideways; (*inf*) a look. * *adj* squinting; (*inf*) crooked.

squire *n* a country gentleman, esp the leading landowner in a district.

squirm *vi* to writhe; to wriggle; to feel embarrassed or ashamed.

squirrel *n* (*pl* **squirrels, squirrel**) a bushy tailed rodent with grey or reddish fur which lives in trees and feeds on nuts. * *vt* (**squirrelling, squirrelled** *or* **squirreling, squirreled**) (*usu with* **away**) to hoard.

squirrel cage *n* a small cylindrical cage which is rotated by a small animal running inside; the rotor of an induction motor with cylindrically arranged copper bars.

squirt *vt* to eject liquid in a jet. * *vi* to spurt. * *n* a jet of liquid; (*inf*) an insignificant person.

squish *vt* to crush, esp so as to produce a squelching sound. * *vi* to make or move with a squelching sound. * *n* a soft squelching sound.—**squishy** *adj*.

Sr¹ (*chem symbol*) strontium.

Sr² *abbr* = Senior; Señor.

SRO *abbr* = standing room only.

SS¹ *abbr* = Saints; steamship;

SS² *abbr* = *Schutzstaffel*, the Nazi paramilitary police force elite guard.

St *abbr* = Saint.

St. *abbr* = Street.

stab *vt* (**stabbing, stabbed**) to injure with a knife or pointed weapon; to pain suddenly and sharply. * *vi* to thrust at (as if) with a pointed weapon. * *n* an act or instance of stabbing; a wound made by stabbing; a sudden sensation, as of emotion, pain, etc; (*inf*) an attempt.

stabile *n* an abstract sculpture resembling a mobile but stationary.

stabilize *vti* to make or become stable or steady.—**stabilization** *n*.

stabilizer *n* a device for stabilizing (an aircraft, ship, bicycle, etc).

stable¹ *adj* steady or firm; firmly established; permanent; not decomposing readily.—**stability** *n*.

stable² *n* a building where horses or cattle are kept; a group of racehorses belonging to one owner; a group of people working for or trained by a specific establishment, as writers, performers, etc. * *vti* to put, keep, or live in a stable.

staccato *adj* (*musical notes*) short, abrupt; (*speech*) sharp, abrupt, disconnected. * *adv* in a staccato manner.

stack *n* a large neatly arranged pile (of hay, papers, records, etc); a chimney stack; (*inf*) a large amount of; a number of aircraft circling an airport waiting for permission to land. * *vt* to pile, arrange in a stack.

stadia *see* **stadium**.

stadium *n* (*pl* **stadium, stadia**) a sports ground surrounded by tiers of seats.

staff *n* (*pl* **staves**) a strong stick or pole; (*mus*) one of the five horizontal lines upon which music is written (— *also* **stave**); (*pl* **staffs**) a body of officers who help a commanding officer, or perform special duties; the workers employed in an establishment; the teachers or lecturers of an educational institution. * *vt* to provide with staff.

stag *n* a full-grown male deer. * *adj* (*party*) for men only.

stag beetle *n* any of various beetles with large pincerlike mandibles.

stage *n* a degree or step in a process; a raised platform, esp for acting on; (*with* **the**) the theatre, the theatrical calling; any field of action or setting; a portion of a journey; a propulsion unit of a space rocket discarded when its fuel is spent. * *vt* to perform a play on the stage; to plan, organize (an event).

stagecoach *n* a four-wheeled vehicle drawn by horses, that formerly carried passengers or mail.

stagecraft *n* skill in writing or staging plays.

stage direction *n* an instruction in the text of a play (regarding characterization, movement, lighting, etc) for an actor or director.

stage door *n* the back entrance to a theatre used by the staff and players.

stage fright *n* nervousness at appearing before an audience.

stage left *n* the area of a stage to the left of an actor facing the audience.

stage-manage *vt* to act as a stage-manager; to organize or direct from behind the scenes.

stage manager *n* a person responsible for the stage arrangements prior to and during the performance of a play.

stage right *n* the area of a stage to the right of an actor facing the audience.

stage-struck *adj* obsessed with theatre and the idea of becoming an actor.

stage whisper *n* a loud whisper made by an actor and intentionally audible to the audience.

stagflation *n* an economic situation characterized by a combination of high inflation and stagnant or declining output and employment.

stagger *vi* to walk unsteadily, to totter. * *vt* to astound; to give a shock to; to arrange so as not to overlap; to alternate.

staggering *adj* astounding.—**staggeringly** *adv*.

staging *n* a temporary platform, esp horizontal planking supported by scaffolding.

staging area *n* an assembly point for troops in transit.

staging post *n* a regular stopover point on a long route.

stagnant *adj* (*water*) not flowing, standing still with a revolting smell; unchanging, dull.—**stagnancy** *n*.

stagnate *vi* to be, or become, stagnant.—**stagnation** *n*.

stag party *n* a party for men only, usu given for one who is due to be married shortly.

stagy, stagey *adj* (**stagier, stagiest**) theatrical, dramatic.

staid *adj* sober; sedate; old-fashioned.—**staidly** *adv*.—**staidness** *n*.

stain *vt* to dye; to discolour with spots of something which cannot be removed. * *vi* to become stained; to produce stains. * *n* a discoloured mark; a moral blemish; a dye or liquid for staining materials, eg wood.

stained glass *n* coloured glass used in windows.

stainless *adj* free from stain; (materials) resistant to staining.—**stainlessly** *adv*.

stainless steel *n* a type of steel resistant to tarnishing and corrosion.

stair *n* a flight of stairs; a single step; (*pl*) a stairway.

staircase *n* a flight of stairs with banisters.

stairway *n* a staircase.

stairwell *n* the vertical shaft for a staircase.

stake¹ *n* a sharpened metal or wooden post driven into the ground, as a marker or fence post; a post to which persons were tied for execution by burning; this form of execution. * *vt* to support with, tie or tether to a stake; to mark out (land) with stakes; (*with* **out**) to put under surveillance.

stake² *vt* to bet; (*inf*) to provide with money or resources. * *n* a bet; a financial interest; (*pl*) money risked on a race; (*pl*) the prize in a race

stakeout *n* surveillance, esp by police; premises under surveillance.

stalactite *n* an icicle-like calcium deposit hanging from the roof of a cave.

stalag *n* a German prisoner-of-war camp in World War II.

stalagmite *n* a cylindrical deposit projecting upward from the floor of a cave, caused by the dripping of water and lime from the roof.

stale *adj* deteriorated from age; tainted; musty; stagnant; jaded.—**staleness** *n*.

stalemate *n* (*chess*) a situation in which a king can only be moved in and out of check, thus causing a draw; a deadlock.—*also vt*.

Stalinism *n* the theory and practice of authoritarian rule associated with the Soviet dictator Joseph Stalin (1879–1953).—**Stalinist** *n, adj*.

stalk[1] *n* the stem of a plant.

stalk[2] *vi* to stride in a stiff or angry way; to hunt (game, prey) stealthily.—**stalker** *n*.

stalking-horse *n* a means of concealing true intentions; a candidate standing in an election to confuse the opposition or test the amount of prospective support for the real candidate in whose favour the stand-in then withdraws.

stall[1] *n* a compartment for one animal in a stable; a table or stand for the display or sale of goods; a stalling of an engine; (*aircraft*) a loss of lift and downward plunge due to an excessive decrease in airspeed; (*pl*) the seats on the ground floor of a theatre. * *vti* (*car engine*) to stop or cause to stop suddenly, eg by misuse of the clutch; (*aircraft*) to lose or cause to lose lift because of an excessive reduction in airspeed.

stall[2] *vti* to play for time; to postpone or delay. * *n* (*inf*) any action used in stalling.

stallion *n* an uncastrated male horse, esp one kept for breeding.

stalwart *adj* strong, sturdy; resolute; dependable. * *n* a loyal, hardworking supporter.

stamen *n* (*pl* **stamens, stamina**) the pollen-bearing part of a flower.

stamina *n* strength; staying power.

staminate *adj* (*plants*) having or producing stamens.

stammer *vti* to pause or falter in speaking; to stutter.—*also n*.—**stammerer** *n*.

stamp *vt* to put a mark on; to imprint with an official seal; to affix a postage stamp; (*with* **out**) to extinguish by stamping; to suppress, eradicate, by force. * *vi* to bring the foot down heavily (on); * *n* a postage stamp; the mark cancelling a postage stamp; a block for imprinting.

stamp duty, stamp tax *n* a tax on some types of legal documents.

stampede *n* an impulsive rush of a panic-stricken herd; a rush of a crowd.—*also vti*.

stamping ground *n* (*inf*) a favourite or habitual meeting place.

stance *n* posture; the attitude taken in a given situation.

stanch see **staunch**[2].

stanchion *n* an upright post, pillar, rod or similar support. * *vt* to provide with a stanchion.

stand *vb* (**standing, stood**) *vi* to be in an upright position; to be on, or rise to one's feet; to make resistance; to remain unchanged; to endure, tolerate; to reach a deadlock; (*with* **by**) to look on without interfering; to be available for use if required; (*with* **down**) to withdraw, resign; to leave a witness box after testifying in court; (*soldier*) to go off duty; (*with* **off**) to remain at a distance; to reach a stalemate; (*with* **up**) to rise to one's feet. * *vt* to put upright; to endure, tolerate; (*with* **by**) to remain loyal to, to defend; (*with* **off**) to (cause to) keep at a distance; to lay off (employees) temporarily; (*with* **up**) to resist; to withstand criticism, close examination, etc; (*inf*) to fail to keep an appointment with. * *n* a strong opinion; a standing position; a standstill; a place for taxis awaiting hire; (*pl*) a structure for spectators; the place taken by a witness for testifying in court; a piece of furniture for hanging things from; a stall or booth for a small retail business.

standard *n* a flag, banner, or emblem; an upright pole, pillar; an authorized weight or measure; a criterion; an established or accepted level of achievement; (*pl*) moral principles. * *adj* serving as a standard; typical.

standard-bearer *n* a person who carries a standard; the leader of a particular cause or party.

standardize *vt* to make standard; to reduce to a standard.—**standardization** *n*.—**standardizer** *n*.

standard of living *n* the level of material comforts enjoyed by an individual, family, group or community.

stand-by *n* (*pl* **stand-bys**) a person or thing held in readiness for use in an emergency, etc.—*also adj*.

stand-in *n* a substitute; a person who takes the place of an actor during the preparation of a scene or in stunts.—*also vi*.

standing *n* status or reputation; length of service, duration. * *adj* upright; permanent; (*jump*) performed from a stationary position.

standing army *n* a permanent body of paid soldiers as maintained by a nation.

standing order *n* an instruction to a bank by a depositor to pay fixed amounts at regular intervals (for bills, etc); a regulation governing conduct, procedure, etc in an organization or assembly.

standoff *n* a deadlock, stalemate.

standoffish *adj* aloof, reserved.

standpipe *n* a vertical pipe with a tap providing an external water supply.

standpoint *n* a point of view, opinion.

stand-up *adj* (*collar*) upright; (*fight*) furious; (*comedian*) telling jokes standing alone in front of an audience.

standstill *n* a complete halt.

stank see **stink**.

stannic *adj* of or containing (tetravalent) tin.

stannous *adj* of or containing (bivalent) tin.

stanza *n* a group of lines which form a division of a poem.

staple[1] *n* a principal commodity of trade or industry of a region or nation; a main constituent. * *adj* chief.

staple[2] *n* a U-shaped thin piece of wire for fastening. * *vt* to fasten with a staple.

star *n* any one of the celestial bodies, esp those visible by night which appear as small points of light, including planets, comets, meteors, and less commonly the sun and moon; a figure with five points; an exceptionally successful or skilful person; a famous actor, actress, musician, etc. * *vti* (**starring, starred**) to feature or be featured as a star.

starboard *n* the right side of a ship or aircraft when facing the bow.

starch *n* a white, tasteless, food substance found in potatoes, cereal, etc; a fabric stiffener based on this. * *vt* to stiffen with starch.—**starchy** *adj*.

star-crossed *adj* ill-fated; unfortunate.

stardom n the fame and status enjoyed by celebrities or stars.

stardust n a large cluster of distant stars appearing as dust; a feeling of romance.

stare vi to gaze fixedly, as in horror, astonishment, etc; to glare. * n a fixed gaze.

starfish n (pl **starfish, starfishes**) an echinoderm consisting of a central disc from which five arms radiate outward.

stargaze vi to look at the stars; to daydream.

stark adj bare; plain; blunt; utter. * adv completely.— **starkly** adv.—**starkness** n.

starkers adj (inf) completely naked.

starlet n a young actress regarded as a potential star.

starling n any of a family of small songbirds, esp a common European bird with black plumage tinged with green that congregates in large groups.

Star of David a six-pointed star formed by two intersecting triangles, a hexagram.

starry-eyed adj dreamy, impractical, overly optimistic.

Stars and Stripes n sing (with **the**) the national flag of the USA consisting of 13 alternate red and white stripes and a blue square filled with white stars representing the individual states.—also **Star-Spangled Banner**.

Star Spangled Banner n (with **the**) the national anthem of the USA; the Stars and Stripes.

star-studded adj featuring many celebrities.

start vi to commence, begin; to jump involuntarily, from fright. * vt to begin. * n a beginning; a slight involuntary body movement; a career opening.

starter n a person who starts something, esp an official who signals the beginning of a race; a competitor in a race; the first course of a meal; a small electric motor used to start an internal combustion engine (—also **self-starter**).

starting block n one of a pair of angled wooden or metal pads or blocks against which a sprinter braces the feet in crouch starts.

starting gate n (horseracing) a removable barrier holding each horse in line and which is raised to start a race.

starting grid n (motor racing) the numbered grid where drivers line up at the start of a race, position being determined by the times gained in practice laps.

starting price n (esp horseracing) the final odds on a horse offered by bookmakers at the start of a race.

starting stalls npl the metal enclosures for horses at the starting line with gates that spring open simultaneously to start the race.

startle vti to be, or cause to be, frightened or surprised.—**startling** adj.

starve vi to die or suffer from a lack of food. * vt deprive (a person) of food; to deprive (of) anything necessary.—**starvation** n.

star warrior n one who advocates the US's Strategic Defense Initiative.

Star Wars n sing the popular name for the Strategic Defense Initiative.

stash vt to hide (money, etc) for future use. * n a hiding place; something hidden; (sl) drugs hidden for personal consumption.

state n condition; frame of mind; position in society; ceremonious style; (with cap) an area or community with its own government, or forming a federation under a sovereign government. * adj of the state or State; public; ceremonial. * vt to express in words; to specify, declare officially.

statecraft n the art of government; statesmanship.

state department n the government department that handles foreign affairs; foreign office.

statehouse n the building which houses a state legislature in the US.

stateless adj not having a nationality.—**statelessness** n.

stately adj (**statelier, stateliest**) dignified; majestic.— **stateliness** n.

stately home n a large country mansion, usu of historical interest, which is open to the public.

statement n a formal announcement; a declaration; a document showing one's bank balance.

state-of-the-art adj using the most advanced technology yet possible.

stateroom n a luxury private cabin in a ship; a large room in a palace used for state occasions.

States n sing or pl the USA.

state school n any school funded by the state which provides free education.

stateside adj of, in, or to the US.—also adv.

statesman n (pl **statesmen**) a well-known and experienced politician.—**statesmanship** n.

static adj fixed; stationary; at rest. * n electrical interference causing noise on radio or TV.

statics n sing the branch of mechanics dealing with the forces that produce a state of equilibrium.

static electricity n electricity which is stationary as opposed to flowing in a current.

station n a railway or bus terminal or stop; headquarters (of the emergency services); military headquarters; (inf) a TV channel; position in society, standing. * vt to assign to a post, place, office.

stationary adj not moving.

stationer n a dealer in stationery, office supplies, etc.

stationery n writing materials, esp paper and envelopes.

station house n a building that houses police or fire services.

stationmaster n the senior official in charge of a railway station.

station wagon n a car with extra carrying space reached through a rear door.

statism n the concentration of economic and political power in the state.—**statist** n.

statistic n a fact obtained from analysing information expressed in numbers.

statistics n sing the branch of mathematics dealing with the collection, analysis and presentation of numerical data.—**statistical** adj.—**statistician** n.

stator n the stationary part of a motor or generator.

statoscope n a sensitive aneroid barometer for indicating minute fluctuations in pressure, used in altimeters in aircraft.

statuary n (pl **statuaries**) statues collectively.

statue n a representation of a human or animal form that is carved or moulded.

statuesque adj like a statue.—**statuesquely** adv.—**statuesqueness** n.

statuette n a small statue, figurine.

stature n the standing height of a person; level of attainment.

status n (pl **statuses**) social or professional position or standing; prestige; condition or standing from the point of view of the law, position of affairs.

status quo n the existing state of affairs.

status symbol n a possession that indicates high social standing, wealth, etc.

statute *n* a law enacted by a legislature; a regulation.

statute book *n* a register of statutes enacted by a legislature.

statute law *n* law enacted by a legislature.

statute mile *n* (*formal*) a mile.

statute of limitations *n* a statute that restricts the period of time in which proceedings may be brought to enforce a right or punish an offence.

statutory *adj* established, regulated, or required by statute.

staunch[1] *adj* loyal; dependable.—**staunchly** *adv*.—**staunchness** *n*.

staunch[2] *vt* to stem the flow of, as blood. * *vi* to cease to flow.—*also* **stanch**.

stave *n* a piece of wood of a cask or barrel; (*mus*) a staff. * *vt* (**staving, staved** *or* **stove**) (*usu with* **in**) to smash or dent inward.

staves *see* **staff**.

stay[1] *n* a rope supporting a mast

stay[2] *vi* to remain in a place; to wait; to reside temporarily. * *vt* to support; to endure; to stop, restrain. * *n* a suspension of legal proceedings; a short time spent as a visitor or guest.

stay-at-home *n* a quiet, placid, unadventurous person.—*also adj*.

staying power *n* stamina.

St Bernard *n* a Saint Bernard dog.

STD *abbr* = sexually transmitted disease; subscriber trunk dialling.

steadfast *adj* firm, fixed; resolute.—**steadfastly** *adv*.—**steadfastness** *n*.

steady *adj* (**steadier, steadiest**) firm, stable; regular, constant; calm, unexcitable. * *n* (*pl* **steadies**) (*inf*) a regular boyfriend or girlfriend. * *vti* (**steadying, steadied**) to make or become steady.—**steadily** *adv*.—**steadiness** *n*.

steady-state theory *n* the theory that the universe remains in a steady equilibrium as matter is continuously created as it expands.

steak *n* a slice of meat, esp beef or fish, for grilling or frying.

steakhouse *n* a restaurant that specializes in steaks.

steal *vt* (**stealing, stole,** *pp* **stolen**) to take (from someone) dishonestly; to obtain secretly. * *n* (*inf*) an unbelievable bargain.

stealth *n* a manner of moving quietly and secretly.

Stealth technology *n* the development, in great secrecy, of a new type of military aircraft.

stealthy *adj* (**stealthier, stealthiest**) acting or performed in a quiet, secret manner; unobtrusive, furtive.—**stealthily** *adv*.—**stealthiness** *n*.

steam *n* the hot mist or vapour created by boiling water. * *vi* to give off steam; to move by steam power; to cook with steam; (*sl*) to take part in illegal steaming; (*with* **up**) (*glasses, windows*) to become covered in condensation. * *adj* driven by steam.

steamboat *n* a boat powered by steam.

steam engine *n* a stationary or locomotive engine powered by steam.

steamer *n* a pan with a perforated bottom for cooking by steam; a ship propelled by steam engines; (*sl*) one who takes part in steaming.

steaming *n* (*sl*) the practice of multiple mugging by a gang of youths who move rapidly down a street, mugging and shiplifting.

steam iron *n* an electric iron that can heat water to use as steam which is emitted through the face to improve pressing.

steamroller *n* a vehicle with heavy rollers for pressing down road surfaces; an overpowering person or thing. * *vt* to crush (as if) with a steamroller; to obtain or influence by overpowering force.

steamy *adj* (**steamier, steamiest**) full of steam; (*inf*) erotic.—**steamily** *adv*.—**steaminess** *n*.

stearic acid *n* a fatty acid derived from solid fats and used for making candles and soap.

steatite *n* soapstone.

steato- *prefix* fat.

steed *n* (*arch, poet*) a horse.

steel *n* an alloy of iron and carbon; strength or courage. * *adj* of, or like, steel. * *vt* to cover with steel; to harden; to nerve (oneself).

steel band *n* a band that uses percussion instruments made from oil drums.

steel grey *n* a bluish-grey colour.

steel wool *n* a compact mass of steel fibres used for scouring and polishing.

steely *adj* (**steelier, steeliest**) of or like steel; hard, relentless.—**steeliness** *n*.

steelyard *n* a balance using a pivoted graduated arm along which a weight slides.

steenbok *n* (*pl* **steenboks, steenbok**) any of a genus of small antelopes of central and southern Africa.

steep[1] *adj* sloping sharply; (*inf*) excessive, exorbitant.—**steeply** *adv*.—**steepness** *n*.

steep[2] *vti* to soak or be soaked in a liquid; to saturate; to imbue.—*also n*.

steepen *vti* to make or become steeper.

steeple *n* a tower of a church, with or without a spire; the spire alone.

steeplechase *n* a horse race across country or on a course over jumps; a track race over hurdles and water jumps.—**steeplechaser** *n*.

steeplejack *n* a person who climbs and repairs tall chimneys.

steer[1] *n* a castrated male of the cattle family.

steer[2] *vti* to direct (a vehicle, ship, bicycle, etc) in the correct direction of travel.

steerage *n* the cheapest berths on a passenger ship.

steerageway *n* a rate of forward motion that allows a vessel to be steered.

steering *n* the mechanism that controls the direction of a ship, vehicle, etc; the practice of manoeuvring non-white house buyers or tenants away from white areas.

steering committee *n* a committee that organizes the content and order of business for a legislative assembly.

stegosaur, stegosaurus *n* (*pl* **stegosaurs, stegosauri**) any of various plant-eating dinosaurs with armoured body plates.

stein *n* an earthenware beer mug, often with a hinged lid.

stele *n* (*pl* **stelae, steles**) an upright slab of stone with inscriptions dating from prehistoric times; an inscribed commemorative slab placed on the front of a building; the vascular tissue in the stems and roots of plants.

stellar *adj* of, or composed of stars.

stellate, stellated *adj* of, resembling or composed of stars.

stellular *adj* filled with or composed of small stars; star-shaped.

St Elmo's fire *n* a flame-like electric discharge from a ship's mast and rigging in thundery weather, St Elmo's fire.—*also* **corposant**.

stem¹ *n* a plant stalk; the upright slender part of anything, such as a wineglass; the root of a word. * *vi* (**stemming, stemmed**) to originate (from).

stem² *vt* (**stemming, stemmed**) to stop, check (the flow or tide).

stench *n* a foul odour.

stencil *n* a pierced sheet of card or metal for reproducing letters by applying paint; a design so made. * *vti* (**stencilling, stencilled** *or* **stenciling, stenciled**) to produce (letters, etc) or designs using a stencil.—**stenciller, stenciler** *n*.

Sten gun *n* a light sub-machine gun.

stenography *n* shorthand.—**stenographer** *n*.

stenosis *n* (*pl* **stenoses**) an abnormal narrowing of a bodily passage or orifice.—**stenotic** *adj*.

stentorian *adj* (*voice*) loud, booming.

step *n* one movement of the foot ahead in walking, running, or dancing; a pace; a grade or degree; a stage toward a goal; one tread of a stair, rung of a ladder. * *vti* (**stepping, stepped**) to take a step or a number of paces.

step- *prefix* related by remarriage of a spouse or parent.

stepbrother *n* a son of one's step-parent from a former marriage.

stepchild *n* (*pl* **stepchildren**) a stepson or stepdaughter.

stepdaughter *n* the daughter of one's spouse from a former marriage.

stepfather *n* the husband of one's remarried mother.

stephanotis *n* a tropical climbing plant with fragrant white flowers.

stepladder *n* a short portable ladder with flat steps fixed within a frame.

stepmother *n* the wife of one's remarried father.

step-parent *n* stepfather or stepmother.

steppe *n* a vast grassy treeless plain.

stepping stone *n* a stone or stones allowing a stream, puddle, etc to be crossed by foot; a means of advancing toward some end.

stepsister *n* the daughter of one's step-parent from a former marriage

stepson *n* the son of one's spouse from a former marriage

steradian *n* a unit of solid angular measurement.

stere *n* a unit equal to one cubic metre (35.3 cubic feet), used for measuring timber.

stereo *n* (*pl* **stereos**) a hi-fi or record player with two loudspeakers; stereophonic sound. * *adj* stereophonic.

stereochemistry *n* the study of the composition and properties of matter in relation to the spatial arrangement of atoms in molecules.

stereograph *n* two almost identical images that when superimposed and viewed through a stereoscope produce a three-dimensional picture.

stereophonic *adj* (*sound reproduction system*) using two separate channels for recording and transmission to create a spatial effect.—**stereophonically** *adv*.—**stereophony** *n*.

stereoscope *n* an optical device which blends two images viewed from a slightly different aspect into a single three-dimensional picture.—**stereoscopic** *adj*.

stereoscopy *n* viewing objects in three dimensions.

stereotype *n* a fixed, general image of a person or thing shared by many people.—*also vt*.

steric *adj* of or pertaining to the spatial arrangement of atoms in a molecule.

sterile *adj* unable to produce offspring, fruit, seeds, or spores; fruitless; free from germs.—**sterility** *n*.

sterilize *vt* to render incapable of reproduction; to free from germs.—**sterilization** *n*.—**sterilizer** *n*.

sterling *n* the British system of money. * *adj* of excellent character.

stern¹ *adj* severe; austere, harsh.—**sternly** *adv*.—**sternness** *n*.

stern² *n* the rear part of a boat or ship

sternum *n* (*pl* **sterna, sternums**) the breastbone.

sternutation *n* sneezing.

sternutator *n* a substance that induces sneezing, tears, etc, such as a gas used in riot control.

steroid *n* any of a large number of compounds sharing the same chemical structure, including sterols and many hormones.

sterol *n* any of various solid steroid alcohols, such as cholesterol, found in plants and animals.

stertorous *adj* characterized by heavy breathing or snoring sounds.—**stertorously** *adv*.—**stertorousness** *n*.

stet *vt* a proofreading direction meaning that deleted matter marked by a row of dots should remain. * *vt* (**stetting, stetted**) to mark (text) in this way.

stethoscope *n* an instrument used to detect body sounds.—**stethoscopic** *adj*.

stetson *n* a man's felt hat with a broad brim and high crown.

stevedore *n* a labourer who loads and unloads ships.

stew *n* a meal of cooked meat with vegetables. * *vt* to cook slowly.

steward *n* a manager (of property); a race organizer; a person who serves food on an aircraft or ship and looks after passengers.

stewardess *n* a woman steward on an aircraft or ship.

stick¹ *vb* (**sticking, stuck**) *vt* to pierce or stab; to attach with glue, adhesive tape, etc; (*with* **up**) (*inf*) to rob at gunpoint. * *vi* to cling to, to adhere; to stay close to; to be held up; (*with* **around**) (*inf*) to wait in the vicinity, to linger; (*with* **by**) to remain faithful to; to stay close to.

stick² *n* a broken off shoot or branch of a tree; a walking stick; a hockey stick; a rod.

sticker *n* an adhesive label or poster.

sticking plaster *n* a thin strip of cloth with an adhesive backing for covering small cuts and abrasions.

stick insect *n* a wingless insect with a long thin body resembling a twig.

stick-in-the-mud *n* (*inf*) a person who feels threatened by new ideas or situations.

stickleback *n* any of various small freshwater fishes with sharp spines on the back.

stickler *n* a person who is scrupulous or obstinate about something.

stick-up *n* (*inf*) a robbery at gunpoint.

sticky *adj* (**stickier, stickiest**) covered with adhesive or something sweet; (*weather*) warm and humid; (*inf*) difficult.—**stickily** *adv*.—**stickiness** *n*.

sticky end *n* (*inf*) an unpleasant death.

sticky wicket *n* (*cricket*) a damp wicket that is difficult to bat on; (*inf*) an awkward or unpleasant situation.

stiff *adj* not flexible or supple; rigid; firm; moving with difficulty; having aching joints and muscles; formal, unfriendly; (*drink*) potent; (*breeze*) strong; (*penalty*) severe. * *n* (*sl*) a corpse. * *adv* utterly.—**stiffly** *adv*.—**stiffness** *n*.

stiffen *vti* to make or become stiff.—**stiffener** *n*.

stiff-necked *adj* stubborn, aloof.

stifle *vt* to suffocate; to smother; to suppress, hold back.

stifling *adj* excessively hot and stuffy.

stigma *n* (*pl* **stigmas, stigmata**) a social disgrace; the part of a flower that receives pollen; (*Christianity*) marks resembling the wounds of Christ thought to appear on the bodies of saintly people.

stigmatize *vt* to brand as bad or disgraceful.—**stigmatization** *n*.

stile *n* a step, or set of steps, for climbing over a wall or fence.

stiletto *n* (*pl* **stilettos**) a small slender dagger; a pointed tool for piercing holes in leather, etc; a high heel tapering to a point on a woman's shoe. * *vt* (**stilettoeing, stilettoed**) to stab with a stiletto.

still[1] *adj* motionless; calm; silent; (*drink*) not carbonated. * *n* a single photograph taken from a cinema film. * *vti* to make or become still. * *adv* continuously; nevertheless.—**stillness** *n*.

still[2] *n* an apparatus for distilling liquids, esp spirits.

stillborn *adj* born dead; (*idea, project, etc*) a failure from the start, abortive.

still life *n* (*pl* **still lives**) a painting of inanimate objects, such as flowers, fruit, etc.

stilt *n* either of a pair of poles with footrests on which one can walk, as in a circus; a supporting column.

stilted *adj* (*speech, writing*) pompous, unnaturally formal; (*conversation*) forced, intermittent.

Stilton *n* a blue-veined cheese with a strong flavour.

stimulant *n* a drug, drink, or food that increases one's heart rate and body activity.

stimulate *vt* to excite, arouse.—**stimulation** *n*.

stimulus *n* (*pl* **stimuli**) something that acts as an incentive; an agent that arouses or provokes a response in a living organism.

sting *n* a sharp pointed organ of a bee, wasp, etc, or hair on a plant, used for injecting poison; a skin wound caused by injected poison from an insect or plant; (*sl*) a swindle. * *vt* to wound with a sting; to cause to suffer mentally; to goad, incite; (*sl*) to cheat by overcharging. * *vi* to feel a sharp pain.

stingray *n* any of various rays with a whiplike tail bearing sharp venomous spines.

stingy *adj* (**stingier, stingiest**) miserly, mean.—**stingily** *adv*.—**stinginess** *n*.

stink *vi* (**stinking, stank** *or* **stunk**, *pp* **stunk**) to give out an offensive smell; (*sl*) to possess something in an excessive amount; (*sl*) to be extremely bad in quality. * *n* a foul smell.

stink bomb *n* a small glass capsule which releases a foul smell when broken, used for practical jokes.

stinker *n* (*inf*) an offensive person or thing; (*inf*) something difficult or unpleasant.

stinkhorn *n* a type of foul-smelling fungus.

stinko *adj* (*sl*) drunk.

stinkweed *n* any of various plants with pungent scents.

stint *vt* to be frugal in the supply or allowance of something. * *vi* to be frugal, miserly. * *n* a fixed period or quantity of work; a limitation, restriction.

stipe *n* a short stalk or stem of a plant, esp of a mushroom.

stipend *n* a regular payment of money as wages or for expenses, esp to a clergyman.

stipendiary *adj* of or receiving a stipend. * *n* (*pl* **stipendiaries**) a person who receives a stipend.

stipple *vt* to engrave, paint, draw, etc, in tiny dots.

stipulate *vt* to specify as a condition of an agreement.—**stipulation** *n*.

stir[1] *vb* (**stirring, stirred**) *vt* to mix, as with a spoon; to rouse; to stimulate or excite; (*with* **up**) to agitate, instigate. * *vi* to be disturbed; to move oneself; to be active. * *n* a stirring movement; tumult.

stir[2] *n* (*sl*) prison.

stir-fry *vt* to cook (chopped vegetables, etc) by stirring rapidly in hot oil in a wok or frying pan.

stirring *adj* rousing, exciting.—**stirringly** *adv*.

stirrup *n* a strap and flat-bottomed ring hanging from a saddle, for a rider's foot.

stirrup cup *n* a farewell drink, orig given to a rider on horseback before departure.

stirrup pump *n* a small portable water pump held steady by a stirrup-shaped foot bracket, used for firefighting.

stitch *n* a single in-and-out movement of a threaded needle in sewing; a single loop of a yarn in knitting or crocheting; a sudden, sharp pain, esp in the side. * *vti* to sew.

stoat *n* a small European mammal related to the weasel.

stochastic *adj* random; involving chance or probability.

stock *n* raw material; goods on hand; shares of corporate capital, or the certificates showing such ownership; lineage, family, race; a store; the cattle, horses, etc, kept on a farm; the broth obtained by boiling meat, bones, and vegetables as a foundation for soup, etc. * *vt* to supply; to keep in store. * *adj* standard; hackneyed.

stockade *n* a defensive enclosure or barrier of stakes fixed in the ground.

stockbroker *n* a person who deals in stocks.

stock car *n* a standard production saloon car modified for racing.

stockholder *n* an owner of corporate stock.

stocking filler *n* a gift suitable for a Christmas stocking.

stocking *n* a sock; a nylon covering for a woman's leg, supported by suspenders.

stock market, stock exchange *n* the market for dealing in stocks and shares.

stockpile *n* a reserve supply of essentials.—*also vt*.

stock-still *adv* motionless.

stocktaking *n* making an inventory of goods on hand (in a shop, warehouse, etc); evaluating one's present condition, resources, etc.

stocky *adj* (**stockier, stockiest**) short and sturdy.—**stockily** *adv*.—**stockiness** *n*.

stockyard *n* a yard for holding cattle, sheep, pigs, etc before they are sold, transported, or slaughtered.

stodge *n* (*inf*) heavy, starchy food.

stodgy *adj* (**stodgier, stodgiest**) (*food*) thick, heavy and indigestible; uninteresting.—**stodgily** *adv*.—**stodginess** *n*.

stoic *n* a person who suffers hardship without showing emotion.—**stoical** *adj*.—**stoically** *adv*.—**stoicism** *n*.

stoke *vt* to stir and feed (a fire) with fuel.

STOL *abbr* = short take-off and landing, a system that allows an aircraft to take off and land within a short distance.

stole[1] *see* **steal**.

stole[2] *n* a long scarf or piece of fur worn on the shoulders.

stolen *see* **steal**.

stolid *adj* impassive; unemotional.—**stolidity** *n*.—**stolidly** *adv*.

stoma *n* (*pl* **stomata**) a minute aperture in the epidermis of a plant for the passage of gases; an orifice or mouthlike opening; a permanent surgical opening, esp in the abdominal wall.

stomach *n* the organ where food is digested; the belly. * *vt* to put up with.

stomach pump *n* a suction pump that empties the contents of the stomach through a long tube inserted orally.

stomata *see* **stoma**.

stomatitis *n* inflammation of the mouth.

stomatology *n* the branch of medicine concerned with the mouth.—**stomatological** *adj*.

stomp *vti* to walk with heavy steps; to stamp. * *n* an early jazz dance.

stone *n* a small lump of rock; a precious stone or gem; the hard seed of a fruit; (*pl* **stone**) a unit of weight (14 lb./6.35 kg). * *vt* to throw stones at; to remove stones from (fruit).

Stone Age *n* the prehistoric age of human culture characterized by the use of stone tools and weapons.

stoned *adj* (*inf*) under the influence of drink or drugs.

stonefish *n* (*pl* **stonefish, stonefishes**) a venomous tropical fish with markings that resemble a stone on the seabed.

stone's throw *n* a short distance.

stonewall *vi* to obstruct or hinder, esp in politics and government.

stonewashed *adj* (*clothes*) made to appear worn and faded by the abrasive action of pumice particles.

stony, stoney *adj* (**stonier, stoniest**) of, like, or full of stones; unfeeling, heartless.—**stonily** *adv*.—**stoniness** *n*.

stony-broke *adj* (*inf*) completely without money.

stony-hearted *adj* unfeeling, cruel.—**stony-heartedness** *n*.

stood *see* **stand**.

stooge *n* (*sl*) a performer who feeds lines to a comedian; a person subordinate to or dominated by another; a stool pigeon. * *vi* to act as a stooge.

stool *n* a seat or a support for the back when sitting, with no back or arms; matter evacuated from the bowels.

stool pigeon *n* a police informer.

stoop[1] *vti* to bend the body forward and downward; to degrade oneself; to deign.—*also n*.

stoop[2] *n* a porch or small landing with stairs at the entrance to a house or building.

stooped *adj* hunched.

stop *vb* (**stopping, stopped**) *vt* to halt; to prevent; to intercept; to plug or block. * *vi* to cease; to come to an end; to stay. * *n* an act or instance of stopping; an impediment; (a knob controlling) a set of organ pipes; any of the standard settings of the aperture in a camera lens, f-stop; a regular stopping place for a bus or train; a punctuation mark, esp full stop.

stop bath *n* a mildy acidic solution used to halt the development of a negative print, plate, etc.

stopcock *n* a device for regulating the flow of liquid in a pipe.

stopgap *n* a temporary substitute, expedient.

stoplight *n* a red light on a traffic signal warning vehicles to halt; a brake light.

stopover *n* a short break in a journey.

stoppage *n* stopping or being stopped; an obstruction; a deduction from pay; a concerted cessation of work by employees, as during a strike.

stopper *n* a cork or bung.

stop press *n* (the space reserved for) an item of last minute news added to a newspaper after printing has begun.

stopwatch *n* a watch that can be started and stopped, used for timing sporting events.

storage *n* storing or being stored; an area reserved for storing; (*comput*) the storing of data in a computer memory or on disk, tape, etc.

storage battery *n* an accumulator.

storage capacity *n* the maximum amount of information that can be held in computer memory or a storage device.

storage device *n* a piece of computer equipment, such as a hard disk, used to store data.

storage heater *n* a radiator which accumulates heat during periods of off-peak electricity.

store *n* a large supply of goods for future use; a warehouse; a shop. * *vt* to set aside; to put in a warehouse, etc; (*comput*) to put (data) into a computer memory or onto a storage device.

store card *n* a charge card issued by a store or chain of stores for the purchase of goods there only.

storehouse *n* a place for storing things; a rich source or supply.

storey *n* (*pl* **storeys**) a horizontal division of a building, a story.

stork *n* a long-necked and long-legged wading bird.

storksbill *n* any of several plants of the geranium family with pink or purple flowers.

storm *n* a heavy fall of rain, snow, etc with strong winds; a violent commotion; a furore; (*mil*) an attack on a fortified place. * *vt* to rush, invade. * *vi* to be angry; to rain, snow hard.—**stormy** *adj*.

stormbound *adj* affected or confined by storms.

storm trooper *n* a member of the Sturmabteilung, a semi-military group of the German Nazi party (1924-45) notorious for its violence; a member of a shock troop.

Storting, Storthing *n* the parliament of Norway.

story[1] *n* (*pl* **stories**) a narrative of real or imaginary events; a plot of a literary work; an anecdote; an account; (*inf*) a lie; a news article.

story[2] *n* (*pl* **stories**) a horizontal division of a building, a storey; a set of rooms occupying this space.

storyboard *n* (*films, television*) a sequence of drawings or photographs showing the images to be shot to film for a particular story.

stout *adj* strong; short and plump; sturdy. * *n* strong dark beer.—**stoutly** *adv*.—**stoutness** *n*.

stouthearted *adj* brave.—**stoutheartedly** *adv*.

stove[1] *n* a cooker; heating apparatus.

stove[2] *see* **stave**.

stow *vt* to store, pack, in an orderly way.

stowage *n* stowing or being stowed; goods in storage; a place for storage or the charge for this.

stowaway *n* a person who hides on a ship, car, aircraft, etc to avoid paying the fare.

St Patrick's Day *abbr* – Saint Patrick's Day.

strabismus *n* a squint.

straddle *vt* to have one leg or support on either side of something.

strafe *vt* to machine-gun (troops, vehicles, etc) from the air.—*also n*.

straggle *vi* to stray; to wander.—**straggler** *n*.—**straggly** *adj*.

straight *adj* (*line*) continuing in one direction, not curved or bent; direct; honest; (*sl*) heterosexual; (*alcoholic drinks*) neat, not diluted. * *adv* directly; without delay. * *n* being straight; a straight line, form, or position; a straight part of a racetrack; (*poker*) a hand containing five cards in sequence.—**straightness** n.

straight and narrow n (inf) the honest and virtuous way of life.

straight angle n an angle of 180°.

straightaway adv without delay.

straightedge n a length of wood, metal, etc used to rule or test for accurate straight lines.

straighten vti to make or become straight; (with out) to make or become less confused or entangled; to resolve.

straight face n a face betraying no signs of emotion, esp amusement.—**straight-faced** adj.

straight fight n a contest between only two candidates.

straight flush n (poker) five cards of the same suit in sequence.

straightforward adj honest, open; simple; easy.—**straightforwardly** adv.—**straightforwardness** n.

straightjacket see **straitjacket**.

straight-laced see **strait-laced**.

straight man n a person who acts as a stooge to a comedian.

straight-out adj (inf) honest, direct; thorough.

strain[1] vt to tax; to stretch; to overexert; to stress; to injure (a muscle) by overstretching; (food) to drain or sieve. * n overexertion; tension; an injury from straining.

strain[2] n a plant or animal within a species having a common characteristic; a trait; a trace.

strained adj (action, behaviour) produced by excessive effort; (mood, atmosphere) tense, worried.

strainer n a sieve or colander used for straining liquids, pasta, tea, etc.

strait n a channel of sea linking two larger seas; (usu pl) difficulty, distress.

straitjacket n a coatlike device for restraining violent people; something that restricts or limits.—also vt. — also **straightjacket**.

strait-laced adj prim, morally strict.—also **straight-laced**.

strand[1] vt to run aground; to leave helpless, without transport or money.

strand[2] n a single piece of thread or wire twisted together to make a rope or cable; a tress of hair.—also vt.

strange adj peculiar; odd; unknown; unfamiliar.—**strangely** adv.—**strangeness** n.

stranger n a person who is unknown; a new arrival to a place, town, social gathering, etc; a person who is unfamiliar with or ignorant of something.

strangle vt to kill by compressing the windpipe, to choke; to stifle, suppress.—**strangler** n.

stranglehold n (wrestling) a grip that presses an opponent's windpipe; a powerful restrictive force or influence.

strangles n sing an infectious bacterial disease of horses that inflames the respiratory tract, equine distemper.

strangulate vt to strangle; to compress (eg a blood vessel or the intestine) so as to cause a blockage. * vi to become strangulated.—**strangulatation** n.

strangury n slow, painful urination.

strap n a narrow strip of leather or cloth for carrying or holding (a bag, etc); a fastening, as on a shoe, wristwatch. * vti (**strapping, strapped**) to fasten with a strap; to beat with a strap.

straphanger n (inf) a standing passenger in a bus or train, etc.

strapping adj tall, well-built.

strata see **stratum**.

stratagem n a clever action planned to deceive or outwit an enemy.

strategic, strategical adj of, relating to, or important in strategy; (weapons) designed to strike at the enemy's homeland, not for use on the battlefield.—**strategically** adv.

Strategic Defense Initiative n the US government's proposed deployment of satellites armed with laser devices to destroy enemy missiles.

strategy n (pl **strategies**) the planning and conduct of war; a political, economic, or business policy.—**strategist** n.

strath n (Scot) a wide, flat river valley.

strathspey n (the music for) a type of Scottish dance with slow gliding steps.

straticulate n (rocks) having thin strata.

stratified adj arranged or deposited in strata or layers.—**stratification** n.

stratigraphy n (the scientific study of) the composition and order of rock strata.—**stratigraphic** adj.

stratocumulus n (pl **stratocumuli**) layers of dark cloud in dense round masses.

stratosphere n a layer of the earth's atmosphere above 10 km (6 miles) in which temperature increases with height.—**stratospheric** adj.

stratum n (pl **strata, stratums**) a layer of sedimentary rock; a level (of society).

stratus n (pl **strati**) a continuous horizontal layer of cloud.

straw n the stalks of threshed grain; a tube for sucking up a drink.

strawberry n (pl **strawberries**) a soft red fruit used in desserts and jam.

strawberry blonde adj (hair) reddish blonde. * n a woman with hair of this colour.

strawberry mark n an irregular blood-coloured birth mark.

strawberry tree n a European evergreen tree bearing fruit resembling strawberries.

straw poll n an unofficial poll to assess public opinion.

stray vi to wander; to deviate; to digress. * n a domestic animal that has become lost. * adj random.

streak n a line or long mark of contrasting colour; a flash of lightning; a characteristic, a trace. * vti to mark with or form streaks; to run naked in public as a prank.—**streaker** n.

streaky adj (**streakier, streakiest**) marked with streaks; (bacon) having alternate layers of fat and lean.

stream n a small river, brook, etc; a flow of liquid; anything flowing and continuous. * vi to flow, gush.

streamer n a banner; a long decorative ribbon.

streamline vt to shape (a car, boat, etc) in a way that lessens resistance through air or water; to make more efficient, to simplify.—**streamlined** adj.

street n a public road in a town or city lined with houses; such a road with its buildings and pavements; the people living, working, etc, along a given street. * adj pertaining to urban youth culture.

streetcar n an electrically powered vehicle for public transport, which travels along rails set into the ground, a tram.

street cred, street credibility n the mastery of the style and ways or urban culture.

street fighter n (sl) a person who is tough and combative.

street value n the value of a commodity, esp an illegal drug, in terms of the price charged to the ultimate users.

streetwalker *n* a prostitute who solicits in the streets.

streetwise *adj* (*inf*) experienced in surviving or avoiding the potential dangers of urban life.

strength *n* the state or quality of being physically or mentally strong; power of exerting or withstanding pressure, stress, force; potency; effectiveness.

strengthen *vti* to make or become stronger.

strenuous *adj* vigorous; requiring exertion.—**strenuously** *adv*.—**strenuousness** *n*.

strep *n* (*inf*) a streptococcus.

strepitoso *adv* (*mus*) in a boisterous manner.

streptococcus *n* (*pl* **streptococci**) any of a genus of spherical bacteria occurring in chains of different length.

streptomycin *n* an antibiotic derived from a soil bacterium, used in the treatment of infections such as tuberculosis.

stress *n* pressure; mental or physical tension or strain; emphasis; (*physics*) a system of forces producing or sustaining a strain. * *vt* to exert pressure on; to emphasize.

stretch *vt* to extend, to draw out. * *vi* to extend, spread; to extend (the limbs, body); to be capable of expanding, as in elastic material. * *n* the act of stretching or instance of being stretched; the capacity for being stretched; an expanse of time or space; (*sl*) a period of imprisonment.—**stretchy** *adj*.

stretcher *n* a portable frame for carrying the sick or injured.

strew *vt* (**strewing, strewed,** *pp* **strewn** *or* **strewed**) to scatter; to spread.

strewth *interj* used to express surprise or alarm.

striation *n* any of a series of parallel grooves, scratches, ridges or lines on a surface.—**striated** *adj*.

stricken *adj* suffering (from an illness); afflicted, as by something painful.

strict *adj* harsh, firm; enforcing rules rigorously; rigid.—**strictly** *adv*.—**strictness** *n*.

stricture *n* harsh criticism, censure.

stride *vi* (**striding, strode,** *pp* **stridden**) to walk with long steps. * *vt* to straddle.—*also n*.

strident *adj* loud and harsh.—**stridency** *n*.—**stridently** *adv*.

stridulate *vi* (of insects) to make a chirping or scraping sound.

strife *n* a fight, quarrel; struggle.

strike *vb* (**striking, struck**) *vt* to hit; to crash into; (*mil*) to attack; to ignite (a match) by friction; (*disease, etc*) to afflict suddenly; to come upon, esp unexpectedly; to delete; (*clock*) to indicate by sounding; to assume (eg an attitude); to occur to; (*medal, coin*) to produce by stamping; (*flag, tent*) to lower, take down; to come upon (oil, ore, etc) by drilling or excavation; (*with* **down**) to afflict or cause to die suddenly; (*with* **off**) to delete or erase from (a list, etc); to prevent from continuing in a profession, esp due to malpractice; to sever or separate from (as if) with a blow; (*with* **out**) to erase or delete; (*with* **up**) to cause to begin, to bring about. * *vi* to cease work to enforce a demand (for higher wages or better working conditions); (*with* **out**) to begin on a journey; (*baseball*) to be put out on strikes; (*inf*) to be completely unsuccessful; (*with* **up**) (*orchestra, band*) to begin to play or sing. * *n* a stoppage of work; a military attack.

strikebound *adj* (*factory, etc*) closed or paralysed by striking workers.

strikebreaker *n* a person who continues work whilst colleagues are on strike; a person hired to replace a striking worker.—**strikebreaking** *n, adj*.

strike pay *n* money paid to workers on strike from trade union funds.

striker *n* a worker who is on strike; a mechanism that strikes, as in a clock; (*soccer*) a forward player whose primary role is to score goals.

striking *adj* impressive.—**strikingly** *adv*.

Strine *n* Australian English (a humorous rendering of the Australian for *Australian*).

string *n* a thin length of cord or twine used for tying, fastening, etc; a stretched length of catgut, wire, or other material in a musical instrument; (*pl*) the stringed instruments in an orchestra; their players; a line or series of things. * *vt* (**stringing, strung**) to thread on a string; (*with* **up**) (*sl*) to kill by hanging. * *vi* (*with* **along**) (*inf*) to appear to agree (with); to accompany; to deceive, esp to gain time.

stringed *adj* (*musical instruments*) having strings.

stringent *adj* strict.—**stringently** *adv*.—**stringency** *n*.

stringer *n* a horizontal support in a structure; a long horizontal brace to strengthen a framework, as in an aircraft fuselage; a journalist or photographer temporarily employed by a newspaper, magazine or news service to cover a particular area.

string quartet *n* (a piece of music written for) a musical ensemble comprising two violins, one viola, and one cello.

string tie *n* a narrow tie.

stringy *adj* (**stringier, stringiest**) of or resembling string; (*meat, etc*) fibrous, chewy; (*physique*) sinewy.

strip *vb* (**stripping, stripped**) *vt* to peel off; to divest; to take away removable parts. * *vi* to undress. * *n* a long, narrow piece (of cloth, land, etc); an airstrip or runway.

strip cartoon *n* a series of drawings in a newspaper, etc which tell a story.

strip club *n* a nightclub which features striptease artists.

stripe *n* a narrow band of a different colour from the background; a chevron worn on a military uniform to indicate rank. * *vt* to mark with a stripe.—**striped** *adj*.—**stripy** *adj*.

strip lighting *n* lighting using long fluorescent tubes.

stripling *n* a youth, boy.

strip mining *n* mining by surface excavation, opencast mining.

stripper *n* a striptease artist; a device or solvent that removes paint.

striptease *n* an erotic show where a person removes their clothes slowly and seductively to music.

strive *vi* (**striving, strove,** *pp* **striven**) to endeavour earnestly, labour hard, to struggle, contend.

strobe *n* (*inf*) a stroboscope.

strobe lighting *n* (the equipment used to produce) high-intensity flashing light.

stroboscope *n* a device for observing motion by making the subject visible at prescribed intervals using a synchronized flashing light.

strode *see* **stride**.

stroganoff *n* sliced beef cooked with mushrooms and onions in a sour cream sauce.

stroke¹ *n* a blow or hit; (*med*) a seizure; the sound of a clock; (*sport*) an act of hitting a ball; a manner of swimming; the sweep of an oar in rowing; a movement of a pen, pencil, or paintbrush.

stroke² *vt* to caress; to do so as a sign of affection.

stroke play n (golf) scoring by the number of strokes taken.

stroll vi to walk leisurely, to saunter. * n a leisurely walk for pleasure.

stroller n a wheeled metal and canvas chair for a small child, a pushchair.

strong adj physically or mentally powerful; potent; intense; healthy; convincing; powerfully affecting the sense of smell or taste, pungent. * adv effectively, vigorously.—**strongly** adv.

strong-arm adj using unwarranted physical force.

strongbox n a solid, secure container for valuables.

strong drink n alcoholic drink.

stronghold n a fortress; a centre of strength or support.

strong-minded adj resolute, determined.—**strong-mindedly** adv.—**strong-mindedness** n.

strong point n something at which one excels.

strongroom n a room specially designed to keep money and valuables secure from theft or fire, etc.

strontium n a soft metallic element.

strop n a strip of leather for sharpening a razor. * vt (**stropping, stropped**) to sharpen using a strop.

strophe n a stanza or movement of a Greek chorus alternating with the antistrophe sung when moving to the left.—**strophic** adj.

stroppy adj (**stroppier, stroppiest**) (inf) surly, angry; quarrelsome.

strove see **strive**.

struck see **strike**.

structuralism n a view of the social sciences, literature, linguistics, etc, which stresses the importance of inherent underlying hierarchical structures, interrelationships and patterns of organization.—**structuralist** n.

structure n organization; construction; arrangement of parts in an organism, or of atoms in a molecule of a substance; system, framework; order. * vt to organize, to arrange; to build up.—**structural** adj.—**structurally** adv.

strudel n very thin pastry rolled up with a fruit filling and baked.

struggle vi to move strenuously so as to escape; to strive; to fight; to exert strength; to make one's way (along, through, up, etc) with difficulty. * n a violent effort; a fight.

strum vt (**strumming, strummed**) to play on (a guitar, etc), by moving the thumb across the strings.

struma n (pl **strumae**) enlargement of the thyroid gland; goitre.

strumpet n (arch) a prostitute.

strung see **string**.

strung-up adj (inf) tense, anxious.

strut[1] vi (**strutting, strutted**) to walk in a proud or pompous manner.

strut[2] n a brace or structural support. * vt to brace.

struthious adj (birds) related to or resembling the ostrich.

strychnine n a poison used in very small quantities as a stimulant.

stub n a short piece left after the larger part has been removed or used; the counterfoil of a cheque, receipt, etc. * vt (**stubbing, stubbed**) to knock (one's toe or foot) painfully; to extinguish (a cigarette).

stubble n the stubs or stumps left in the ground when a crop has been harvested; any short, bristly growth, as of beard.—**stubbly** adj.

stubborn adj obstinate; persevering; determined, in-

flexible.—**stubbornly** adv.—**stubbornness** n.

stubby adj (**stubbier, stubbiest**) short and thick; (Austral sl) a small bottle of beer.

stucco n (pl **stuccoes, stuccos**) a type of cement or plaster used to coat and decorate outside surfaces of walls. * vt (**stuccoing, stuccoed**) to decorate or finish with stucco.

stuck see **stick**.

stuck-up adj (inf) conceited; proud; snobbish.

stud[1] n a male animal, esp a horse, kept for breeding; a collection of horses and mares for breeding; a farm or stable for stud animals.

stud[2] n a large-headed nail; an ornamental fastener. * vt (**studding, studded**) to cover with studs.

studbook n a written record of the pedigree of a thoroughbred horse, dog, etc.

student n a person who studies or investigates a particular subject; a person who is enrolled for study at a school, college, university, etc.

studied adj carefully planned.—**studiedly** adv.—**studiedness** n.

studio n (pl **studios**) the workshop of an artist, photographer or musician; (pl) a building where motion pictures are made; a room where television or radio programmes are recorded.

studio couch n a couch resembling a divan that can be converted into a bed.

studio flat n a small flat with one main room, a kitchen and a bathroom.

studious adj given to study; careful.—**studiously** adv.—**studiousness** n.

study vt (**studying, studied**) to observe and investigate (eg phenomena) closely; to learn (eg a language); to scrutinize; to follow a course (at college, etc). * n (pl **studies**) the process of studying; a detailed investigation and analysis of a subject; the written report of a study of something; a room for studying.

stuff n material; matter; textile fabrics; cloth, esp when woollen; personal possessions generally. * vt to cram or fill.

stuffed shirt n (inf) a pretentious or pompous person.

stuffing n material used to stuff or fill anything; a seasoned mixture put inside poultry, meat, vegetables etc before cooking.

stuffy adj (**stuffier, stuffiest**) badly ventilated; lacking in fresh air; dull, uninspired.—**stuffily** adv.—**stuffiness** n.

stultify vt (**stultifying, stultified**) to make ineffectual or futile.—**stultification** n.

stumble vi to trip up or lose balance when walking; to falter; to discover by chance (with **across** or **on**). * n a trip; a blunder.

stumbling block n an obstacle to further progress.

stump n the part of a tree remaining in the ground after the trunk has been felled; the part of a limb, tooth, that remains after the larger part is cut off or destroyed. * vt (inf) to confuse, baffle; to campaign for an election.

stumpy adj (**stumpier, stumpiest**) short and thick.—**stumpiness** n.

stun vt (**stunning, stunned**) to render unconscious due to a fall or heavy blow; to surprise completely; to shock.

stung see **sting**.

stun gun n a type of gun that emits high-voltage electricity to stun victims.

stunk see **stink**.

stunner n (inf) a strikingly attractive or impressive person or thing.

stunning adj (inf) strikingly attractive.—**stunningly** adv.

stunt[1] vt to prevent the growth of, to dwarf.

stunt[2] n a daring or spectacular feat; a project designed to attract attention. * vi to carry out stunts.

stupa n a domed shrine holding Buddhist relics.

stupefy vt (**stupefying, stupefied**) to dull the senses of.—**stupefaction** n.

stupendous adj wonderful, astonishing.—**stupendously** adv.

stupid adj lacking in understanding or common sense; silly; foolish; stunned.—**stupidity** n.—**stupidly** adv.

stupor n extreme lethargy; mental dullness.

sturdy adj (**sturdier, sturdiest**) firm, strong, robust.—**sturdily** adv.—**sturdiness** n.

sturgeon n any of various large food fishes whose roe is also eaten as caviare.

Sturmabteilung see **storm trooper**.

stutter vi to stammer.—also n.

sty[1], **stye** n (pl **sties**) an inflamed swelling on the eyelid.

sty[2] n (pl **sties**) a pen for pigs; any filthy place.

style n the manner of writing, painting, composing music peculiar to an individual or group; fashion, elegance. * vt to design or shape (eg hair).—**styler** n.

stylish adj having style; fashionable.—**stylishly** adv.—**stylishness** n.

stylist n a person who writes, paints, etc, with attention to style; a designer; a hairdresser.

stylistic adj of literary or artistic style.—**stylistically** adv.

stylize vt to give a conventional style to.—**stylization** n.—**stylizer** n.

stylus n (pl **styluses, styli**) the device attached to the cartridge on the arm of a record-player that rests in the groove of a record and transmits the vibrations that are converted to sound.

stymie n (pl **stymies**) (golf) a situation in which a ball is obstructed by another ball between it and the hole. * vt (**stymieing, stymied**) to obstruct, hinder.

styptic adj acting to stop bleeding by contracting the blood vessels. * n a styptic drug.

styrene n a liquid hydrocarbon used in making rubber and plastics.

suave adj charming, polite.—**suavely** adv.—**suaveness** n.

suavity n (pl **suavities**) politeness; urbanity; a suave action, comment, etc.

sub n (inf) a submarine; a substitute; a subscription; a subeditor.

sub- prefix under, below; subordinate, next in rank to.

subaltern n a commissioned officer in the British army ranking below captain. * adj inferior in rank or status.

subaqua adj of or pertaining to underwater sports.

subatomic adj smaller than an atom; occurring within an atom.

subconscious adj happening without one's awareness. * n the part of the mind that is active without one's conscious awareness.—**subconsciously** adv.—**subconsciousness** n.

subcontinent n a land mass having great size but smaller than any of the usu recognized continents.

subcontract n a secondary contract, under which work or supply of materials is let out to a firm other than the main party of the contract.—also vt.—**subcontractor** n.

subculture n a distinct group with its own customs, language, dress, etc within an existing culture.

subcutaneous adj under the skin.—**subcutaneously** adv.

subdivide vt to further divide what has already been divided. * vi to divide or be divided into parts.—**subdivision** n.

subdue vt to dominate; to render submissive; to repress (eg a desire, impulse); to soften, tone down (eg colour, etc).

subeditor n a person who checks and corrects newspaper articles.—**subedit** vt.

subhead, subheading n a heading associated with a subdivision of a text.

subhuman adj (animals) lower down the evolutionary scale than mankind; less than human.

subject adj under the power of; liable. * n a person under the power of another; a citizen; a topic; a theme; the scheme or idea of a work of art. * vt to bring under control; to make liable; to cause to undergo something.—**subjection** n.

subjective adj determined by one's own mind or consciousness; relating to reality as perceived and not independent of the mind; arising from one's own thoughts and emotions, personal.—**subjectively** adv.—**subjectivity** n.

sub judice adv being decided by a court.

subjugate vt to overpower, to conquer.—**subjugation** n.

subjunctive adv denoting that mood of a verb which expresses doubt, condition, wish, or hope. * n the subjunctive mood.

sublet vt (**subletting, sublet**) to let (a property which one is renting) to another.

sublime adj noble; exalted.—**sublimely** adv.—**sublimity** n.

subliminal adj beneath or beyond the conscious awareness.—**subliminally** adv.

subliminal advertising n advertising using subliminal images to influence the viewer unconsciously.

sub-machine gun n a light automatic or semiautomatic gun designed to be fired from the hip or shoulder.

submarine adj underwater, esp under the sea. * n a naval vessel capable of being propelled under water, esp for firing torpedoes or missiles.

submerge, submerse vt to plunge or sink under water; to cover, hide.—**submergence, submersion** n.

submersible adj capable of being submerged. * n an underwater vessel used for exploration or construction work.

submission n an act of submitting; something submitted, as an idea or proposal; the state of being submissive, compliant; the act of referring something for another's consideration, criticism, etc.—**submissively** adv.—**submissiveness** n.

submit vb (**submitting, submitted**) vt to surrender (oneself) to another person or force; to refer to another for consideration or judgment; to offer as an opinion. * vi to yield, to surrender.

subnormal adj less than normal; having low intelligence.—**subnormality** n.—**subnormally** adv.

subordinate adj secondary; lower in order, rank. * n a subordinate person. * vt to put in a lower position or rank.—**subordination** n.

suborn vt to persuade to commit perjury or some other illegal act.

subpoena n a written legal order requiring the attendance of a person in court. * vt (subpoenaing, subpoenaed) to serve with a subpoena.

sub rosa adv in secret.

subroutine n a self-contained section of a computer program that performs a particular task as many times as required by the main program.

subscribe vt to pay to receive regular copies (of a magazine, etc); to donate money (to a charity, campaign); to support or agree with (an opinion, faith).—subscriber n.—subscription n.

subscriber trunk dialling n a service that allows users to dial long-distance calls directly.

subscript n a character written or printed below another character.—also adj.

subsequent adj occurring or following after.—subsequently adv.

subservient adj obsequious; servile; subordinate.—subservience n.—subserviently adv.

subside vi to sink or fall to the bottom; to settle; to diminish; to abate.—subsidence n.

subsidiarity n the devolution of decision making or control to the lowest effective level.

subsidiary adj secondary; supplementary; (company) owned or controlled by another. * n (pl subsidiaries) an accessory, an auxiliary; a business owned by another.—subsidiarily adv.

subsidize vt to aid or support with a subsidy.—subsidization n.—subsidizer n.

subsidy n (pl subsidies) government financial aid to a private person or company to assist an enterprise.

subsist vi to exist; to continue; to manage to keep oneself alive (on).

subsistence n existence; livelihood.—subsistent adj.

subsoil n the layer of soil lying immediately beneath the surface soil.

subsonic adj travelling at a speed less than that of sound.

substance n matter (such as powder, liquid); the essential nature or part; significance.

substantial adj of considerable value or size; important; strongly built.—substantiality n.—substantially adv.

substantiate vt to prove, to verify.—substantiation n.

substitute vt to put or act in place of another person or thing (with for); to replace (by). * n a person or thing that serves in place of another.—also adj.—substitution n.

substructure n a foundation or supporting framework.

subsume vt to include in a larger group or category.

subterfuge n a trick employed to conceal something.

subterranean adj below the surface of the earth; concealed.

subtitle n an explanatory, usu secondary, title to a book; a printed translation superimposed on a foreign language film.—also vt.

subtle adj delicate; slight; not noticeable; difficult to define, put into words; ingenious.—subtleness n.—subtly adv.

subtlety n (pl subtleties) subtleness; a fine distinction.

subtotal n the sum of part of a series of figures. * vt (subtotalling, subtotalled or subtotaling, subtotaled) to sum in part.

subtract vti to take away or deduct, as one quantity from another.—subtraction n.

subtropical adj of, characteristic of, the regions bordering on the tropics.

suburb n a residential district on the outskirts of a large town or city.—suburban adj.—suburbia n.

suburbanite n a person who lives in a suburb.

subversion n the act of undermining the authority of a government, institution, etc; collapse, ruin.

subversive adj liable to subvert established authority. * n a person who engages in subversive activities.—subversively adv.—subversiveness n.

subvert vt to overthrow, to ruin (something established); to corrupt, as in morals.

subway n a passage under a street; an underground metropolitan electric railway.

succeed vt to come after, to follow; to take the place of. * vi to accomplish what is attempted; to prosper.

success n the gaining of wealth, fame, etc; the favourable outcome (of anything attempted); a successful person or action.

successful adj having success.—successfully adv.—successfulness n.

succession n following in sequence; a number of persons or things following in order; the act or process of succeeding to a title, throne, etc; the line of descent to succeed to something.

successive adj following in sequence.—successively adv.—successiveness n.

successor n a person who succeeds another, as to an office.

succinct adj clear, concise.—succinctly adv.—succinctness n.

succotash n a cooked mixture of sweetcorn and lima beans.

succour, succor n (a person or thing that provides) help, support, esp in time of need. * vt to provide such help.

succubus, succuba n (pl succubi, succubae) a female demon thought to have sexual intercourse with sleeping men.

succulent adj juicy; moist and tasty; (plant) having fleshy tissue. * n a succulent plant (as a cactus).—succulence, succulency n.—succulently adv.

succumb vi to yield to superior strength or overpowering desire; to die.

such adj of a specified kind (eg such people, such a film); so great. * adv so; very.

suchlike adj of similar kind.

suck vt to draw (a liquid, air) into the mouth; to dissolve or roll about in the mouth (as a sweet); to draw in as if by sucking (with in, up, etc).—also n.

sucker n (sl) a person who is easily taken in or deceived; a cup-shaped piece of rubber that adheres to surfaces.

suckle vt to feed at the breast or udder.

suckling n a young animal that is not yet weaned.

sucks interj (sl) used to express disappointment.

sucre n the monetary unit of Ecuador.

sucrose n sugar.

suction n the act or process of sucking; the exertion of a force to form a vacuum.

sudden adj happening quickly and unexpectedly, abrupt.—suddenly adv.—suddenness n.

sudden death n (sport) extra time in a tied match, the winner being the next to score or take a point.

suds npl the bubbles or foam on the surface of soapy water.—sudsy adj.

sue vt (suing, sued) to bring a legal action against.

suede, suède n leather finished with a soft nap.

suet n white, solid fat in animal tissue, used in cooking.

suffer vt to undergo; to endure; to experience. * vi to feel pain or distress.—sufferer n.—suffering n.

sufferable *adj* endurable.—**sufferably** *adv*.

sufferance *n* reluctant tolerance, tacit permission; endurance.

suffice *vi* to be sufficient, adequate (for some purpose).

sufficient *adj* enough; adequate.—**sufficiency** *n*.—**sufficiently** *adv*.

suffix *n* (*pl* **suffixes**) a letter, syllable, or syllables added to the end of a word to modify its meaning or to form a new derivative.

suffocate *vti* to kill or be killed by depriving of oxygen, or by inhaling a poisonous gas; to feel hot and uncomfortable due to lack of air; to prevent from developing.—**suffocation** *n*.

suffrage *n* the right to vote.

suffuse *vt* to spread over or fill, as with colour or light.—**suffusion** *n*.

sugar *n* a sweet white, crystalline substance obtained from sugar cane and sugar beet * *vi* to sweeten.

sugar beet *n* a type of beet from which sugar is extracted.

sugar cane *n* a tall grass with stout canes grown as a source of sugar.

sugar daddy *n* a wealthy and usu elderly man who lavishes gifts on an attractive young woman.

sugary *adj* resembling or containing sugar; cloyingly sweet in manner, content, etc.—**sugariness** *n*.

suggest *vt* to put forward for consideration; to bring to one's mind; to evoke.—**suggestion** *n*.

suggestible *adj* easily influenced by others.—**suggestibility** *n*.

suggestive *adj* evocative; rather indecent, risqué.—**suggestively** *adv*.—**suggestiveness** *n*.

suicidal *adj* of, pertaining to, suicide; liable to commit suicide; destructive of one's own interests.—**suicidally** *adv*.

suicide *n* a person who kills himself intentionally; the act or instance of killing oneself intentionally; ruin of one's own interests.

suicide gene *n* a gene having bacteria that end its life cycle.

sui generis *adj* unique.

suit *n* a set of matching garments, such as a jacket and trousers or skirt; one of the four sets of thirteen playing cards; a lawsuit. * *vt* to be appropriate; to be convenient or acceptable to.

suitable *adj* fitting; convenient (to, for).—**suitably** *adv*.—**suitability** *n*.

suitcase *n* a portable, oblong travelling case.

suite *n* a number of followers or attendants; a set, esp of rooms, furniture, pieces of music.

suitor *n* a man who courts a woman; (*law*) a person who brings a lawsuit.

sukiyaki *n* a Japanese dish of thinly sliced beef, vegetables and seafood cooked rapidly in soy sauce, saké, etc, at the table.

sulf-, sulpf- *see* sulphur.

sulfa *see* sulpha.

sulfate *see* sulphate.

sulfonamide *see* sulphonamide.

sulfur *see* sulphur.

sulfuric *see* sulphuric.

sulk *vi* to be sullen.

sulky *adj* (**sulkier, sulkiest**) bad-tempered, quiet and sullen, because of resentment.—**sulkily** *adv*.—**sulkiness** *n*.

sullen *adj* moody and silent; gloomy, dull.—**sullenly** *adv*.—**sullenness** *n*.

sully *vt* (**sullying , sullied**) to blemish, to defile the purity of. * *n* (*pl* **sullies**) a tarnish or stain.

sulph-, sulf- *prefix* sulphur.

sulpha drug *n* any of various sulphonamide drugs used for treating bacterial infections.

sulphate *n* a salt of sulphuric acid.—*also* **sulfate**.

sulphonamide *n* any of a group of compounds that are amides of sulphonic acid, such as the sulfa drugs.—*also* **sulfonamide**.

sulphonic acid *n* any of a group strong organic acids used in the manufacture of drugs, dyes and detergents.

sulphur *n* a yellow nonmetallic element that is inflammable and has a strong odour.—*also* **sulfur**.—**sulphuric, sulfuric** *adj*.

sulphur dioxide *n* a pungent toxic gas used in various industrial processes that is a major air pollutant.

sulphuric acid *n* a powerfully corrosive acid.

sultan *n* a ruler, esp of a Muslim state.

sultana *n* a dried, white grape used in cooking; the wife or female relative of a sultan.

sultanate *n* a country or region ruled by a sultan; the office or authority of a sultan.

sultry *adj* (**sultrier, sultriest**) (*weather*) very hot, humid and close; sensual; passionate.—**sultrily** *adv*.—**sultriness** *n*.

sum *n* the result of two or more things added together; the total, aggregate; a quantity of money; essence, gist. * *vt* (**summing, summed**) to add (*usu with* **up**); to encapsulate; to summarize.

summarize *vt* to make or be a summary of.—**summarization** *n*.—**summarizer** *n*.

summary *adj* concise; performed quickly, without formality. * *n* (*pl* **summaries**) a brief account of the main points of something.—**summarily** *adv*.—**summariness** *n*.

summation *n* the act of finding a sum or total; the result of summation; a summary; the summing up of an argument, esp by a lawyer before a jury.

summer *n* the warmest season of the year, between spring and autumn.—**summery** *adj*.

summerhouse *n* a small building in a garden used as a shady retreat in summer.

summer school *n* an academic course held during the summer.

summing-up *n* a concluding summary of the points in a speech, argument, etc; a review of the main evidence made by a judge to the jury before it considers its verdict.

summit *n* the highest point, the peak; a meeting of world leaders.

summitry *n* the practice of convening, or style of conducting, summit conferences.

summon *vt* to order to appear, esp in court; to convene; to gather (strength, enthusiasm, etc).

summons *n* (*pl* **summonses**) a call to appear (in court). * *vt* to serve with a summons.

sumo *n* traditional Japanese wrestling.

sump *n* a section of the crankcase under an engine for the oil to drain into to form a reservoir.

sumptuous *adj* lavish; luxurious.—**sumptuously** *adv*.—**sumptuousness** *n*.

sun *n* the star around which the earth and other planets revolve which gives light and heat to the solar system; the sunshine. * *vi* (**sunning, sunned**) to expose oneself to the sun's rays.

Sun. *abbr* = Sunday.

sunbaked *adj* baked hard by exposure to the sun.

sunbathe *vi* to lie in the rays of the sun or a sun lamp to get a suntan.—**sunbather** *n*.

sunbeam *n* a ray of sunlight.

sunburn *n* inflammation of the skin from exposure to sunlight.—*also vti*.

sunburst *n* a sudden flash of sunlight; a pattern resembling the sun surrounded by rays; a brooch with a design resembling this.

sundae *n* a serving of ice cream covered with a topping of fruit, syrup, nuts, etc.

Sunday *n* the day of the week after Saturday, regarded as a day of worship by Christians; a newspaper published on a Sunday.

Sunday best *n* best clothes kept for wearing on Sundays.

Sunday school *n* a class for religious instruction held on Sundays.

sundew *n* any of various bog plants with sticky hairs that trap insects.

sundial *n* a device that shows the time by casting a shadow on a graduated dial.

sundown *n* sunset.

sundry *adj* miscellaneous, various. * *n* (*pl* **sundries**) (*pl*) miscellaneous small things.

sunflower *n* a tall plant with large yellow flowers whose seeds yield oil.

sung *see* **sing**.

sunglasses *npl* tinted glasses to protect the eyes from sunlight.

sunk *see* **sink**.

sunlamp *n* an electric lamp that produces ultra-violet rays for tanning the skin.

Sunna *n* the body of Islamic doctrine accepted by orthodox Muslims as based on the life and teachings of Mohammed.

Sunni *n* the branch of Islam that accepts the orthodoxy of the Sunna.—**Sunnite** *n*.

sunny *adj* (**sunnier, sunniest**) (*weather*) bright with sunshine; (*person, mood*) cheerful.—**sunnily** *adv*.—**sunniness** *n*.

sunrise *n* dawn.

sunrise industry *n* a high-technology industry with a bright future.

sunroof *n* a panel in the roof of a car that slides open.

sunset *n* dusk.

sunshine *n* the light and heat from the sun.

sunspot *n* a dark patch sometimes visible on the sun's surface; (*inf*) a holiday resort with guaranteed sunshine.

sunstroke *n* illness caused by exposure to the sun.

suntan *n* browning of the skin by the sun.—**suntanned** *adj*.

suntrap *n* a sunny sheltered spot.

super *adj* (*inf*) fantastic, excellent; (*inf*) a superintendent, as in the police. * *n* a variety of high-octane petrol.

super- *prefix* above, on the top of; extremely, excessively; greater in size, quality, etc.

superable *adj* able to be overcome.—**superably** *adv*.

superannuate *vt* to pension off on account of old age or illness.

superannuation *n* regular contributions from employees' wages toward a pension scheme.

superb *adj* grand; excellent; of the highest quality.—**superbly** *adv*.

supercharge *vt* to increase the power of an engine by using a device that supplies air or fuel in increased quantities by raising the intake pressure; to charge (the atmosphere, a conversation, etc) with excess tension or emotion.—**supercharger** *n*.

supercilious *adj* arrogant; haughty, disdainful.—**superciliously** *adv*.—**superciliousness** *n*.

superconductivity *n* (*physics*) the complete loss of electrical resistance exhibited by certain materials at very low temperatures.—**superconducting, superconductive** *adj*.—**superconduction** *n*.—**superconductor** *n*.

supercool *vt* to cool (a liquid, etc) below freezing without solidification or crystallization.

superdelegate *n* in US, a delegate to a Democratic party convention, appointed rather than elected.

superego *n* (*pl* **superegos**) (*psychol*) the division of the unconscious mind that functions as a conscience.

superficial *adj* near the surface; slight, not profound; (*person*) shallow in nature.—**superficiality** *n*.—**superficially** *adv*.

superfluous *adj* exceeding what is required; unnecessary.—**superfluity** *n*.

supergiant *n* a star of enormous size and brightness with a low density.

superglue *n* an adhesive that forms strong bonds instantly.

supergrass *n* an informer who incriminates a large number of people.

superheat *vt* to heat above boiling point without vaporization; to heat a vapour above boiling point without boiling occurring.

superhigh frequency *n* a radio frequency between 30 000 and 3000 megahertz.

superhuman *adj* surpassing normal human strength or abilities; divine.

superimpose *vt* to put or lay upon something else.

superintend *vt* to have the charge and direction of; to control, manage.

superintendent *n* a person who manages or supervises; a director; a British police officer next above the rank of inspector.

superior *adj* higher in place, quality, rank, excellence; greater in number, power. * *n* a person of higher rank.—**superiority** *n*.

superiority complex *n* an inflated opinion of one's own abilities and merits.

superl. *abbr* = superlative.

superlative *adj* of outstanding quality; (*gram*) denoting the extreme degree of comparison of adjectives and adverbs.—**superlatively** *adv*.

superman *n* (*pl* **supermen**) a person of outstanding abilities and achievements.

supermarket *n* a large self-service, shop selling food and household goods.

supernatural *adj* relating to things that cannot be explained by nature; involving ghosts, spirits, etc.—**supernaturally** *adv*.

supernova *n* (*pl* **supernovae, supernovas**) a star that explodes temporarily burning with an intensity one hundred million times that of the sun.

supernumerary *adj* extra; beyond the usual number. * *n* (*pl* **supernumeraries**) an extra person or thing.

superpose *vt* to place (a geometric figure) on top of another so that their outlines coincide; to lay on top of.—**superposition** *n*.

superpower *n* a nation with great economic and military strength.

superscript *n* a character written or printed above another character.—*also adj*.

supersede *vt* to take the place of, replace.

supersmart card *n* a smart card equipped with a screen and a keyboard, allowing interaction with the user.

supersonic *adj* faster than the speed of sound.—**supersonically** *adv*.

superstar *n* (*inf*) a sporting celebrity; a famous film actor or musician.

superstition *n* irrational belief based on ignorance or fear.—**superstitious** *adj*.

superstore *n* a very large supermarket.

superstructure *n* a structure above or on something else, as above the base or foundation, as above the main deck of a ship.

Super Tuesday *n* the Tuesday, usu in March, on which a number of states, with over half of all the delegates, hold primary elections for the selection of Presidential candidates.

supervise *vti* to have charge of, direct, to superintend.—**supervision** *n*.

supervisor *n* one who supervises; an overseer, an inspector.—**supervisory** *adj*.

supine *adj* lying on the back; lazy, indigent.—**supinely** *adv*.

supper *n* a meal taken in the evening, esp when dinner is eaten at midday; an evening social event; the food served at a supper; a light meal served late in the evening.

supplant *vt* to replace; to remove in order to replace with something else.

supple *adj* flexible, easily bent; lithe; (*mind*) adaptable.—**suppleness** *n*.

supplement *n* an addition or extra amount (usu of money); an additional section of a book, periodical or newspaper. * *vt* to add to.—**supplemental** *adj*.

supply *vt* (**supplying, supplied**) to provide, meet (a deficiency, a need); to fill (a vacant place). * *n* (*pl* **supplies**) a stock; (*pl*) provisions.—**supplier** *n*.

support *vt* to hold up, bear; to tolerate, withstand; to assist; to advocate (a cause, policy); to provide for (financially). * *n* a means of support; maintenance.

supporter *n* a person who backs a political party, sports team, etc.

suppose *vt* to assume; to presume as true without definite knowledge; to think probable; to expect. * *vi* to conjecture.

supposed *adj* believed to be on available evidence.

supposedly *adv* allegedly.

supposition *n* an assumption, hypothesis.

supposititious *adj* hypothetical.

suppository *n* (*pl* **suppositories**) a cone or cylinder of medicated soluble material for insertion into the rectum or vagina.

suppress *vt* to crush, put an end to (eg a rebellion); to restrain (a person); to subdue.—**suppression** *n*.—**suppressor** *n*.

suppurate *vi* to form or discharge pus.—**suppuration** *n*.—**suppurative** *adj*.

supra *prefix* above, situated above; over; beyond.

supranational *adj* transcending national boundaries or interests.

supremacist *n* a person who advocates the supremacy of a particular group.

supreme *adj* of highest power; greatest; final; ultimate.—**supremacy** *n*.

Supreme Court *n* the highest judicial body in a nation or state.

supremo *n* (*pl* **supremos**) (*inf*) the person in overall charge, a boss.

Supt *abbr* = superintendent.

surcharge *vt* to overcharge (a person); to charge an additional sum; to overload. * *n* an additional tax or charge; an additional or excessive load.

surd *n* (*math*) a number containing an irrational root; an irrational number.

sure *adj* certain; without doubt; reliable, inevitable; secure; safe; dependable. * *adv* certainly.

sure-fire *adj* (*inf*) certain to succeed.

sure-footed *adj* not liable to slip or fall; unlikely to make a mistake.

surely *adv* certainly; securely; it is to be hoped or expected that.

sure thing *n* (*inf*) something assured of success. * *interj* yes, of course.

surety *n* (*pl* **sureties**) a person who undertakes responsibility for the fulfilment of another's debt; security given as a guarantee of payment of a debt.

surf *n* the waves of the sea breaking on the shore or a reef.

surface *n* the exterior face of an object; any of the faces of a solid; the uppermost level of sea or land; a flat area, such as the top of a table; superficial features. * *adj* superficial; external. * *vt* to cover with a surface, as in paving. * *vi* to rise to the surface of water.

surfboard *n* a long, narrow board used in the sport of surfing.

surfeit *n* an excessive amount.

surfing *n* the sport of riding in toward shore on the crest of a wave, esp on a surfboard.

surg. *abbr* = surgeon; surgery; surgical.

surge *n* the rolling of the sea, as after a large wave; a sudden, strong increase, as of power.—*also vi*.

surgeon *n* a medical specialist who practises surgery.

surgery *n* (*pl* **surgeries**) the treatment of diseases or injuries by manual or instrumental operations; the consulting room of a doctor or dentist; the daily period when a doctor is available for consultation; the regular period when an MP, lawyer, etc is available for consultation.—**surgical** *adj*.—**surgically** *adv*.

surgical spirit *n* methylated spirit used for sterilizing.

surly *adj* (**surlier, surliest**) ill-tempered or rude.—**surlily** *adv*.—**surliness** *n*.

surmise *n* guess, conjecture. * *vt* to infer the existence of from partial evidence.

surmount *vt* to overcome; to rise above.

surname *n* the family name. * *vt* to give a surname to.

surpass *vt* to outdo, to outshine; to excel; to exceed.

surpassing *adj* exceptional; greatly exceeding others.—**surpassingly** *adv*.

surplice *n* a loose, white, wide-sleeved clerical garment worn by clergymen and choristers.

surplus *n* (*pl* **surpluses**) an amount in excess of what is required; an excess of revenues over expenditure in a financial year.

surprise *n* the act of catching unawares; an unexpected gift, event; astonishment. * *vt* to cause to feel astonished; to attack unexpectedly; to take unawares.—**surprising** *adj*.—**surprisingly** *adv*.

surreal *adj* bizarre.

surrealism *n* a movement in art characterized by the expression of the activities of the unconscious mind and dream elements.—**surrealist** *n*.—**surrealistic** *adj*.

surrender *vt* to relinquish or give up possession or power. * *vi* to give oneself up (to an enemy).—*also n*.

surreptitious *adj* done by stealth; clandestine, secret.—**surreptitiously** *adv*.

surrogacy, surrogate motherhood *n* a practice in which a woman bears a child for a childless couple.—**surrogate mother** *n*.

surrogate *n* a person or thing acting as a substitute for another person or thing.—*also adj*.

surrogate mother *n* a woman who bears a child on behalf of a childless couple.

surround *vt* to encircle on all or nearly all sides; (*mil*) to encircle. * *n* a border around the edge of something.

surroundings *npl* the conditions, objects, etc around a person or thing; the environment.

surtax *n* an additional tax, esp on income above a prescribed level.—*also vt*.

surtitle *n* a caption projected onto a screen above the stage during an opera as a translation of the libretto or to explain some detail of the action.—*also vt*.

surveillance *n* a secret watch kept over a person, esp a suspect.

survey *vt* (**surveying, surveyed**) to take a general view of; to appraise; to examine carefully; to measure and make a map of an area. * *n* (*pl* **surveys**) a detailed study, as by gathering information and analysing it, a general view; the process of surveying an area or a house.

surveyor *n* a person who surveys land or buildings.

survival *n* surviving; a person or thing that survives; a relic.

survive *vt* to live after the death of another person; to continue, endure; to come through alive. * *vi* to remain alive (after experiencing a dangerous situation).—**survivor** *n*.

susceptible *adj* ready or liable to be affected by; impressionable.—**susceptibility** *n*.—**susceptibly** *adv*.

sushi *n* a Japanese dish of small cakes of cold rice with various toppings, esp raw fish.

suspect *vt* to mistrust; to believe to be guilty; to think probable. * *n* a person under suspicion. * *adj* open to suspicion.

suspend *vt* to hang; to discontinue, or cease temporarily; to postpone; to debar temporarily from a privilege, etc.

suspended animation *n* a cessation of the vital functions in an organism, esp though freezing.

suspended sentence *n* a sentence that does not come into force unless a further offence is committed.

suspender *n* a fastener for holding up stockings; (*pl*) braces.

suspender belt *n* a belt with suspenders to hold up a woman's stockings.

suspense *n* mental anxiety or uncertainty; excitement.

suspension *n* suspending or being suspended; a temporary interruption or postponement; a temporary removal from office, privileges, etc; the system of springs, shock absorbers, etc that support a vehicle on its axles; (*chem*) a dispersion of fine particles in a liquid.

suspension bridge *n* a bridge carrying a roadway suspended by cables anchored to towers at either end.

suspicion *n* act of suspecting; a belief formed or held without sure proof; mistrust; a trace.—**suspicious** *adj*.—**suspiciously** *adv*.

sustain *vt* hold up, support; to maintain; to suffer (eg an injury); to nourish.

sustenance *n* nourishment.

suttee *n* (*Hinduism*) (*formerly*) the practice of a widow throwing herself on her husband's funeral pyre; this custom.—*also* **sati**.

suture *n* a stitch holding together a wound after surgery.—*also vt*.

svelte *adj* slim and elegant.

SW *abbr* = southwest(ern); short wave.

swab *n* a wad of absorbent material, usu cotton, used to clean wounds, take specimens, etc; a mop.—*also vt*.

swaddle *vt* to bind tightly, envelop; to wrap a baby in swaddling clothes.

swaddling clothes *npl* narrow strips of cloth used to wrap and restrain an infant.

swag *n* (*sl*) loot.

swagger *vi* to strut; to brag loudly. * *n* boastfulness; swinging gait.

Swahili *n* a language spoken in Kenya, Tanzania and other parts of east Africa; (*pl* **Swahilis, Swahili**) a member of a people speaking this language who live mainly in Zanzibar.

swain *n* (*poet*) a male suitor or lover.

swallow[1] *n* a small migratory bird with long wings and a forked tail.

swallow[2] *vt* to cause food and drink to move from the mouth to the stomach; to endure; to engulf; (*inf*) to accept gullibly; (*emotion, etc*) to repress.—*also n*.

swallow dive *n* a dive executed with the back arched and arms outstretched at the start.

swam *see* **swim**.

swami *n* (*pl* **swamies, swamis**) a Hindu religious teacher.

swamp *n* wet, spongy land; bog. * *vt* to overwhelm; to flood as with water.—**swampy** *adj*.

swan *n* a large, usu white, bird with a very long neck that lives on rivers and lakes. * *vi* (**swanning, swanned**) (*inf*) to wander aimlessly.

swan dive *n* a swallow dive.

swank *vi* (*inf*) to show off.—*also n*.—**swanky** *adj*.

swan song *n* a final appearance, performance, etc by a person facing retirement or death.

swap *vti* (**swapping, swapped**) (*inf*) to trade, barter. * *n* (*inf*) the act of exchanging one thing for another.—*also* **swop**.

SWAPO, Swapo (*acronym*) South West Africa People's Organization.

sward *n* (an area of land with) a surface of short grass.

swarm *n* a colony of migrating bees; a moving mass, crowd or throng. * *vi* to move in great numbers; to teem.

swarthy *adj* (**swarthier, swarthiest**) dark-complexioned.—**swarthiness** *n*.

swashbuckling *adj* swaggering; exciting, adventurous.—**swashbuckler** *n*.

swastika *n* an ancient symbol formed by a cross with the ends of the arms bent at right-angles, used by Nazi Germany.

swat *vt* (**swatting, swatted**) (*inf*) to hit with a sharp blow; to swipe.—*also n*.—**swatter** *n*.

swath *n* the width of one sweep of a scythe or other mowing device; a strip, row, etc, mowed; a broad strip.

swathe *vt* to bind or wrap round, as with a bandage; to envelop, enclose.

sway *vi* to swing or move from one side to the other or to and fro; to lean to one side; to vacillate in judgment or opinion. * *n* influence; control.

swear *vi* (**swearing, swore,** *pp* **sworn**) to make a solemn affirmation, promise, etc, calling God as a witness; to give evidence on oath; to curse, blaspheme or use obscene language; to vow; (*with* **off**) to promise abstinence from. * vt (with in to appoint to an office by the administration of an oath.

swearword n a profane or obscene expression.

sweat n perspiration; (inf) hard work; (inf) a state of eagerness, anxiety.—also vti.—**sweaty** adj.

sweatband n a strip of material in a hat, or worn on the wrist or around the forehead, to absorb sweat.

sweater n a knitted pullover.

sweatshirt n a loose, collarless, heavy cotton jersey.

sweatshop n a small factory or workshop where employees work long hours at low wages in poor conditions.

Swede n a native of Sweden.

swede n a round root vegetable with yellow flesh.

Swedish adj pertaining to Sweden, its people or language. * n the language of Sweden.

sweep vb (sweeping, swept) vt to clean with a broom; to remove (rubbish, dirt) with a brush. * vi to pass by swiftly. * n a movement, esp in an arc; a stroke; scope, range; a sweepstake.

sweeper n a person who sweeps, esp the roads; (soccer) (inf) a player positioned before the goalkeeper to collect loose balls, tackle attacking players, etc.

sweeping adj wide-ranging; indiscriminate.—**sweepingly** adv.

sweepstake, sweepstakes n a lottery in which the prize constitutes all the money staked; a horserace, etc in which the winner receives the entire prize.

sweet adj having a taste like sugar; pleasing to other senses; gentle; kind. * n a small piece of confectionery; a dessert.—**sweetly** adv.—**sweetness** n.

sweet-and-sour adj (food) cooked in a sauce containing sugar and vinegar or lemon juice.

sweet brier n a Eurasian rose with pink flowers.

sweetbread n the pancreas or thymus gland of an animal, cooked as food.

sweet cicely n an aromatic European plant with small white flowers; the aniseed-flavoured leaves of this once used in cookery.

sweet clover n a species of sweet-scented trefoil or clover, with clusters of small yellow or white flowers; melilot.

sweetcorn n maize, corn on the cob.

sweeten vti to make or become sweet or sweeter; to mollify.

sweetener n a sweetening substance that contains no sugar; (sl) a bribe.

sweetheart n a lover.

sweetie n (inf) a sweet; (inf) sweetheart, darling; a kindly, pleasant person.

sweetmeat n a sweet, preserve, small cake, or other sugary delicacy.

sweet pea n a climbing garden plant cultivated for its large fragrant blooms.

sweet pepper n (a plant bearing) a large fruit with thick fleshy walls eaten ripe (red) or unripe (green).

sweet potato n (a tropical climbing plant with) a large edible tuberous root.

sweet-talk vt (inf) to flatter, cajole.—**sweet talk** n.

sweet william n a widely grown Eurasian plant with clusters of white, red, pink, or purple flowers.

swell vi (swelling, swelled, pp swollen or swelled) to increase in size or volume; to rise into waves; to bulge out. * n the movement of the sea; a bulge; a gradual increase in the loudness of a musical note; (inf) a socially prominent person. * adj excellent.

swelling n inflammation.

swelter vi to suffer from heat. * n humid, oppressive heat.

sweltering adj uncomfortably hot.

swept see **sweep**.

sweptback adj (aircraft wing) slanting backward.

sweptwing adj (aircraft) having sweptback wings.

swerve vi to turn aside suddenly from a line or course; to veer.—also n.

swift adj moving with great speed; rapid. * n a swallow-like bird.—**swiftly** adv.—**swiftness** n.

swig vt (inf) to take a long drink, esp from a bottle.—also n.

swill vti to drink greedily; to guzzle; to rinse with a large amount of water. * n liquid refuse fed to pigs.

swim vi (swimming, swam, pp swum) to move through water by using limbs or fins; to be dizzy; to be flooded with. * n the act of swimming.—**swimmer** n.

swimming costume, swimsuit n a one-piece garment for swimming in.

swimmingly adv (inf) easily, without effort.

swindle vti to cheat (someone) of money or property.—also n.—**swindler** n.

swindle sheet n (sl) an expenses form.

swine n (pl swine) a pig; (inf) an contemptible person; (inf) an unpleasant thing.

swine fever n a viral infection of pigs.

swineherd n a person who looks after pigs.

swing vb (swinging, swung) vi to sway or move to and fro, as an object hanging in the air; to pivot; to shift from one mood or opinion to another; (music) to have a lively rhythm; (sl) to be hanged. * vt to whirl; to play swing music; to influence; to achieve, bring about. * n a swinging, curving or rhythmic movement; a suspended seat for swinging in; a shift from one condition to another; a type of popular jazz played by a large band and characterized by a lively, steady rhythm.

swingeing adj drastic, severe.

swinging adj (inf) up-to-date; lively.

swing-wing adj of or pertaining to an aircraft with movable wings that are swept back at high speeds and moved forward for approach and landing.—also n.

swipe n (inf) a hard, sweeping blow. * vt (inf) to hit with a swipe; (sl) to steal.

swirl vti to turn with a whirling motion.—also n.

swish vi to move with a soft, whistling, hissing sound. * n a swishing sound. * adj (inf) smart, fashionable.

Swiss adj of or belonging to Switzerland. * n (pl Swiss) a native of Switzerland.

swiss roll n a thin sponge cake spread with a layer of jam and rolled up.

switch n a control for turning on and off an electrical device; a sudden change; a swap. * vt to shift, change, swap; to turn on or off (as of an electrical device).

switchback n a zigzag road in a mountain region; a roller coaster.

switchblade n a flick knife.

switchboard n an installation in a building where telephone calls are connected.

swivel n a coupling that permits parts to rotate. * vi (swivelling, swivelled or swiveling, swiveled) to turn (as if) on a pin or pivot.

swollen see **swell**.

swoon vt to faint.—also n.

swoop vt to carry off abruptly. * vi to make a sudden attack (usu with down) as a bird in hunting.—also n.

swop *see* **swap**.

sword *n* a weapon with a long blade and a handle at one end.

sword dance *n* a dance in which swords are brandished or placed on the ground and stepped between.

swordfish *n* a large marine fish with a sword-like upper jaw.

swordplay *n* fighting with swords; verbal combat.

swordsman *n* (*pl* **swordsmen**) a person skilled in the use of a sword.

swordstick *n* a walking stick concealing a sword.

swore, sworn *see* **swear**.

sworn *see* **swear**.

swot *vi* (*inf*) to study hard for an examination. * *n* (*inf*) a person who studies hard.

swum *see* **swim**.

swung *see* **swing**.

sycamore *n* a Eurasian maple tree; an American plane tree; a tree of Africa and Asia bearing a fruit resembling a fig.

sycophant *n* a person who flatters and praises powerful people to win their favour.—**sycophancy** *n*.—**sycophantic** *adj*.

syllabi *see* **syllabus**.

syllabic *adj* consisting of syllables; articulated in syllables.

syllable *n* word or part of a word uttered in a single sound; one or more letters written to represent a spoken syllable.

syllabub, sillabub *n* a cold dessert made with sweetened whipped cream flavoured with sherry, wine, lemon juice, etc.

syllabus *n* (*pl* **syllabuses, syllabi**) a summary or outline of a course of study or of examination requirements; the subjects studied for a particular course.

syllogism *n* a form of reasoning consisting of a major premise, a minor premise and a conclusion, eg *All men must die; I am a man; therefore I must die*.

sylph *n* a slim girl or woman.

symbiosis *n* a mutually advantageous partnership between two interdependent plant or animal species.—**symbiotic** *adj*.

symbol *n* a representation; an object used to represent something abstract; an arbitrary or conventional sign standing for a quality, process, relation, etc as in music, chemistry, mathematics, etc.

symbolic, symbolical *adj* of, using, or constituting a symbol.—**symbolically** *adv*.

symbolism *n* the use of symbols; a system of symbolic representation.—**symbolist** *n*.

symbolize *vt* to be a symbol; to represent by a symbol.—**symbolization** *n*.—**symbolizer** *n*.

symmetrical, symmetric *adj* having symmetry.—**symmetrically** *adv*.

symmetry *n* (*pl* **symmetries**) the corresponding arrangement of one part to another in size, shape and position; balance or harmony of form resulting from this.

sympathetic *adj* having sympathy; compassionate.—**sympathetically** *adv*.

sympathize *vi* feel sympathy for; to commiserate; to be in sympathy (with).—**sympathizer** *n*.—**sympathizingly** *adv*.

sympathy *n* (*pl* **sympathies**) agreement of ideas and opinions; compassion; (*pl*) support for an action or cause.

symphony *n* (*pl* **symphonies**) an orchestral composi-

tion in several movements; a large orchestra for playing symphonic works.—**symphonic** *adj*.—**symphonically** *adv*.

symposium *n* (*pl* **symposiums, symposia**) a conference at which several specialists deliver short addresses on a topic; an anthology of scholarly essays.

symptom *n* a bodily sensation experienced by a patient indicative of a particular disease; an indication.

symptomatic *adj* of, being, or relating to symptoms; indicative.—**symptomatically** *adv*.

syn- *prefix* together.

synagogue *n* the building where Jews assemble for worship and religious study.

synapse *n* the point at which a nerve impulse is transmitted between neurons.

sync, synch *n* (*inf*) synchronization. * *vti* (*inf*) to synchronize.

synchromesh *adj* (*gear system*) incorporating a device that regulates the revolving parts in a gear so that they are at the same speed when brought into contact. * *n* a gear system using this.

synchronize *vti* to occur at the same time and speed; (*watches*) to adjust to show the same time.—**synchronization** *n*.—**synchronizer** *n*.

synchronous *adj* occurring at the same time.—**synchronously** *adv*.—**synchronousness** *n*.

syncopate *vt* (*mus*) to modify beats (in a musical piece) by displacing the rhythmical accents from strong beats to weak ones and vice versa.—**syncopation** *n*.

syndicate *n* an association of individuals or corporations formed for a project requiring much capital; any group, as of criminals, organized for some undertaking; an organization selling articles or features to many newspapers, etc. * *vt* to manage as or form into a syndicate; to sell (an article, etc) through a syndicate. * *vi* to form a syndicate.—**syndication** *n*.

syndrome *n* a characteristic pattern of signs and symptoms of a disease.

synergist *n* a muscle that works in conjunction with another muscle; a drug that combines with another drug, the two having a greater effect when taken together than separately.—**synergism** *n*.—**synergistic** *adj*.

synergy *n* synergism; in business, the possibility that the merger of two individual companies will produce a combined operation of greater productivity and efficiency.—**synergetic, synergistic** *adj*.

synesis *n* (*gram*) a construction in harmony with its sense rather than with strict syntax, eg "a large number were present."

synod *n* a council of members of a church that meets to discuss religious issues.

synonym *n* a word that has the same, or similar, meaning as another or others in the same language.

synonymous *adj* having the same meaning; equivalent.—**synonymously** *adv*.

synonymy *n* (*pl* **synonymies**) the condition of being synonymous; a system or collection of synonyms; the use of synonyms for emphasis, eg "in any shape or form".

synopsis *n* (*pl* **synopses**) a summary or brief review of a subject.

synovia *n* a thick fluid that lubricates the joints and tendons.—**synovial** *adj*.

synovitis *n* inflammation of the membrane around a joint.

syntax *n* (*gram*) the arrangement of words in the sentences and phrases of language; the rules governing this.—**syntactic** *adj*.—**syntactically** *adv*.

synth *n* a synthesizer.

synthesis *n* (*pl* **syntheses**) the process of combining separate elements of thought into a whole; the production of a compound by a chemical reaction.

synthesize *vti* to combine into a whole.

synthesizer *n* an electronic device producing music and sounds by using a computer to combine individual sounds previously recorded.

synthetic *adj* produced by chemical synthesis; artificial.—**synthetically** *adv*.

syphilis *n* a contagious, infectious venereal disease.—**syphilitic** *adj*.

syphon *see* **siphon**.

Syrian *n* a native or inhabitant of Syria; the Arabic dialect spoken there.—*also adj*.

syringe *n* a hollow tube with a plunger at one end and a sharp needle at the other by which liquids are injected or withdrawn, esp in medicine. * *vt* to inject or cleanse with a syringe.

syrinx *n* (*pl* **syringes**) the vocal organ in birds.

syrup *n* a thick sweet substance made by boiling sugar with water; the concentrated juice of a fruit or plant.—**syrupy** *adj*.

systaltic *adj* (*heart, etc*) alternately expanding and contracting; pulsating.

system *n* a method of working or organizing by following a set of rules; routine; organization; structure; a political regime; an arrangement of parts fitting together.

systematic *adj* constituting or based on a system; according to a system.—**systematically** *adv*.

systematize *vt* to arrange according to a system.—**systematization** *n*.—**systematizer** *n*.

systemic *adj* (*poison, infection, etc*) of or affecting the entire body; (*insecticide, etc*) designed to be taken up into the plant tissues.—**systemically** *adv*.

systemize *vt* to systematize.—**systemization** *n*.

systems analysis *n* analysis of a particular task or operation to determine how computer hardware and software may best perform it.—**systems analyst** *n*.

systole *n* the regular contractions of the chambers of the heart by which the circulation of blood is maintained.—**systolic** *adj*.

T

T (*chem symbol*) tritium.

T, t *n* the 20th letter of the English alphabet; something shaped like a T.

t *abbr* = ton.

TA *abbr* = teaching assistant.

Ta (*chem symbol*) tantalum.

tab[1] *n* tabulator; tablet. * *vt* (**tabbing, tabbed**) to tabulate.

tab[2] *n* a small tag, label or flap; (*inf*) a bill, as for expenses. * *vt* (**tabbing, tabbed**) to fix a tab on.

tabard *n* a short armless tunic, esp one bearing a coat of arms and worn by a herald or by a knight over his armour; a sleeveless garment shaped like this worn by women.

Tabasco *n* (*trademark*) a very hot red pepper sauce.

tabbouleh *n* an Arabic salad made with vegetables, spices, lemon juice and cracked wheat.

tabby *n* (*pl* **tabbies**) a domestic cat with a striped coat, esp a female; a heavy watered silk. * *adj* striped in brown or grey. * *vt* (**tabbying, tabbied**) to pattern (silk) with a wavy pattern.

tabernacle *n* (*Bible*) the portable tent carried by Jews through the desert containing their sacred writings; a place of worship.—**tabernacular** *adj*.

tabes *n* (*pl* **tabes**) wasting caused by chronic disease.—**tabetic** *adj, n*.

tabes dorsalis *n* paralysis caused by syphilis at an advanced stage when it attacks the spinal cord.

tablature *n* musical notation indicating the strings, frets, fingering, rhythm, etc, to be used, esp for the lute.

table *n* a piece of furniture consisting of a slab or board on legs; the people seated round a table; supply of food; a flat surface; a level area; a slab or tablet in a wall; an inscription on this; a list of facts and figures arranged in columns for reference or comparison; a folding leaf of a backgammon board; **at table** having a meal; **on the table** (*legislative bill, etc*) postponed, often indefinitely; **to turn the tables on** to put (an opponent) in a position of disadvantage previously held by oneself. * *vt* to submit, to put forward; to postpone indefinitely; to lay on a table. * *adj* of, on or at a table.

tableau *n* (*pl* **tableaux, tableaus**) a dramatic or graphic representation of a group or scene; a tableau vivant.

tableau vivant *n* (*pl* **tableaux vivants**) a representation of an historical scene by people in costume posed silently and motionless.

tablecloth *n* a cloth for covering a table.

table d'hôte *n* (*pl* **tables d'hôte**) a meal at a fixed price for a set number of courses.—*also adj*.

tableland *n* an expanse of flat elevated land, a plateau.

tablespoon *n* a large serving spoon; a unit of measure in cooking.

tablespoonful *n* (**tablespoonfuls**) the amount a tablespoon holds.

tablet *n* a pad of paper; a medicinal pill; a cake of solid substance, such as soap; a slab of stone.

table tennis *n* a game like tennis played on a table with small bats and a ball.

tableware *n* dishes, cutlery, etc for use at mealtimes.

tabloid *n* a small-format newspaper characterized by emphasis on photographs and news in condensed form.

taboo, tabu *n* (*pl* **taboos, tabus**) a religious or social prohibition of the use or practice of something; the thing prohibited. * *adj* forbidden from use, mention, etc. * *vt* (**tabooing, tabooed** *or* **tabuing, tabued**) to forbid by social or personal influence the use, practice or mention of something or contact with someone.

tabor, tabour *n* a small drum formerly used to accompany a pipe, both instruments being played by the same person.

tabular *adj* like a table, flat; arranged in the form of a table; calculated with a table.—**tabularly** *adv*.

tabula rasa *n* (*pl* **tabulae rasae**) the mind when regarded as in its original state and clear of impressions; a fresh start.

tabulate *vt* to arrange (written material) in tabular form.—**tabulation** *n*

tabulator *n* a device that sets stops to locate columns on a typewriter or word processor.

TAC *abbr* = Tactical Air Command.

tacamahac *n* (any tree yielding) any of various pungent gum resins used esp in incense.

tacet *vi* a direction on a musical score indicating that from this point a particular instrument is not to play.

tachism *n* a form of action painting using random blobs of colour.

tachistoscope *n* a device for projecting visual information onto a screen for a split second only, used in the study of perception and learning.

tacho- *prefix* speed.

tachograph *n* a device in motor vehicles, esp lorries, to record speed and time of travel.

tachometer *n* an instrument for measuring the speed of rotation of a shaft, as in a vehicle engine.

tachy- *prefix* rapid or accelerated.

tachycardia *n* an abnormally fast heartbeat.

tachygraphy *n* shorthand, esp as used in ancient Greece and Rome.

tachymeter *n* a surveying instrument for measuring long distances rapidly.

tachyon *n* (*physics*) a theoretical elementary particle that can travel faster than light.

tacit *adj* implied without really being spoken; understood.—**tacitly** *adv*.—**tacitness** *n*.

taciturn *adj* habitually silent and reserved.—**taciturnity** *n*.

tack[1] *n* a short, flat-headed nail; the course of a sailing ship; a course of action, approach; adhesiveness. * *vt* to fasten with tacks. * *vi* to change direction.

tack² *n* (*inf*) food.

tackle *n* a system of ropes and pulleys for lifting; equipment; rigging; (*sport*) an act of grabbing and stopping an opponent. * *vt* (*task, etc*) to attend to, undertake; (*a person*) to confront; (*sport*) to challenge with a tackle.

tacky¹ *adj* (**tackier, tackiest**) (*paint, etc*) sticky.

tacky² *adj* (**tackier, tackiest**) (*inf*) shabby; ostentatious and vulgar; seedy.—**tackiness** *n*.

tact *n* discretion in managing the feelings of others.—**tactful** *adj*.—**tactless** *adj*.

tactical voting *n* the strategy in elections of voting for the candidate most likely to defeat the favourite, rather than voting for one's preferred choice.

tactics *n sing* stratagem; ploy; the science or art of manoeuvring troops in the presence of the enemy.—**tactical** *adj*.—**tactician** *n*.

tactile *adj* relating to, or having a sense of touch.

tad *n* (*inf*) a small boy; (*inf*) a tiny quantity; a bit.

tadpole *n* the larva of a frog or toad, esp at the stage when the head and tail have developed.

taeniasis *n* infestation with tapeworms.—*also* **teniasis**.

taffeta *n* a thin glossy fabric with a silky lustre.

taffrail *n* the rail at the stern of a ship.

tag¹ *n* a strip or label for identification. * *vt* to attach a tag; to mark with a tag. * *vi* (*with* **onto, after, along**) to trail along (behind).

tag² *n* a children's chasing game; (*baseball*) the putting out of a runner by touching him with the ball. * *vt* (**tagging, tagged**) to touch another player in a game of tag; to put a runner out by touching him with the ball.

tag end *n* the final part of something.

tagliatelle *n* pasta in narrow ribbons.

tahini *n* a thick paste of ground sesame seeds.

tahr *n* a type of Himalayan wild goat.

Tahitian *adj* of or pertaining to the South Pacific island of Tahiti, its people or language. * *n* a native of Tahiti; the Polynesian language spoken in Tahiti.

t'ai chi ch'uan *n* a Chinese form of exercise using movements designed to improve balance and coordination.—*also* **t'ai chi**.

taiga *n* coniferous forests dominated by spruces and firs extending across the subarctic regions of Eurasia and North America.

tail *n* the appendage of an animal growing from the rear, generally hanging loose; the rear part of anything; (*pl*) the side of a coin without a head on it; (*inf*) a person who keeps another under surveillance, esp a detective. * *vti* to follow closely, to shadow; (*with* **off, away**) to (cause to) dwindle.

tailback *n* a long queue of traffic behind an obstruction; (*football*) the offensive back farthest from the line of scrimmage.

tailboard *n* a hinged or removable section at the rear of a motor vehicle.

tail coat *n* a man's black or grey coat cut horizontally just below the waist at the front with two long tails at the back.

tail-end *adj* tardy; being the last in line. * *n* the last.

tailgate *n* the hinged board at the rear of a truck which can be let down or removed. * *vti* to drive dangerously close behind (another vehicle).—**tailgater** *n*.

taillight *n* a red warning light at the rear of a motor vehicle.

tailor *n* a person who makes and repairs outer garments, esp. men's suits. * *vi* to work as a tailor. * *vt* to adapt to fit a particular requirement.

tailor-made *adj* specially designed for a particular purpose or person.

tailpipe *n* a pipe at the rear of jet engine or motor vehicle for discharging exhaust gases.

tailplane *n* a small stabilizing wing at the rear of an aircraft, a horizontal stabilizer.

tail rotor *n* the small propeller at the rear of a helicopter that counteracts the tendency of the body to spin in the opposite direction to the main rotor blades.

tailspin *n* a spiralling nose dive; (*inf*) a state of chaos.

tailstock *n* the adjustable part of a lathe that supports the free end of a workpiece.

tailwind *n* a wind in the same direction as a ship or aircraft is travelling.

taint *vt* to contaminate; to infect. * *vi* to be corrupted or disgraced. * *n* a stain; corruption.

taipan¹ *n* a powerful businessman operating in Hong Kong or China.

taipan² *n* a venomous Australian snake.

take *vb* (**taking, took**, *pp* **taken**) *vt* to lay hold of; to grasp or seize; to gain, win; to choose, select; (*attitude, pose*) to adopt; to understand; to consume; to accept or agree to; to lead or carry with one; to use as a means of travel; (*math*) to subtract (from); to use; to steal; (*gram*) to be used with; to endure calmly; (*with* **apart**) to dismantle; to criticize; (*with* **back**) to retract, withdraw (a promise, etc); (*with* **down**) to write down; to dismantle; to humiliate; (*with* **for**) (*inf*) to mistakenly believe to be; (*with* **in**) to understand, perceive; to include; to make a garment smaller by altering seams, etc; to offer accommodation to; (*inf*) to swindle, deceive; (*with* **on**) to employ as labour; to assume or acquire; to agree to do (something); to fight against; (*with* **out**) to extract; to obtain, procure; to escort; (*sl*) to kill; (*with* **up**) to begin as a business or hobby; to accept an offer or invitation; to occupy (time or space); to act as a patron to; to shorten (a garment); to interrupt or criticize; to absorb. * *vi* (*plant, etc*) to start growing successfully; to become effective; to catch on; to have recourse to; to go to; (*with* **after**) to resemble in appearance, character, etc; (*with* **on**) (*inf*) to become upset or distraught; (*with* **to**) to escape to as a refuge; to acquire a liking for; to adopt as a habit; (*with* **up**) to resume, continue further. * *n* (*film, TV*) the amount of film used without stopping the camera when shooting.

takeaway *n* a takeout.

take-home pay *n* pay remaining after all deductions, such as income tax, have been made.

taken *see* **take**.

takeoff *n* the process of an aircraft becoming airborne; (*inf*) an amusing impression or caricature of another person.

takeout, take-out *n* a cooked meal that is sold for consumption outside the premises; a shop or restaurant that provides such meals.—*also adj*.

takeover *n* the taking over of control, as in business.—*also adj*.

taking *adj* attractive, charming; (*inf*) catching, contagious. * *n* the act of one that takes; (*pl*) earnings; profits.

talc *n* a type of smooth mineral used in ceramics and talcum powder; talcum powder.

talcum powder *n* perfumed powdered talc for the skin.

tale *n* a narrative or story; a fictitious account, a lie; idle or malicious gossip.

talent *n* any innate or special aptitude.—**talented** *adj*.

talent scout *n* a person employed to recruit talented people for professional careers in sport, entertainment, etc.

talent show *n* a show which gives amateurs a chance to perform in the hope of attracting interest from professionals for permanent engagements.

talipot *n* a palm tree of the East Indies with large leaves used for roofing, umbrellas, etc.

talisman *n* (*pl* **talismans**) an object or charm supposed to ward off evil and bring good luck; an amulet.

talk *vt* to speak; to know how to speak (a language); to discuss or speak of (something); to influence by talking; (*with* **down**) to silence or override (a speaker, argument, etc) by talking loudly; to radio instructions to (an aircraft) so that it may land safely; (*with* **into**) to persuade by argument or talking; (*with* **out**) to resolve by discussion; (*with* **round**) to persuade by talking. * *vi* to converse; to discuss; to gossip; to divulge information; (*with* **back**) to reply impudently; (*with* **down**) to speak in a condescending manner (to); (*with* **round**) to discuss (a subject) without reaching any conclusion; (*with* **shop**) to discuss work, esp after working hours. * *n* a discussion; a lecture; gossip; (*pl*) negotiations.

talkative *adj* given to talking a great deal.

talkie *n* (*inf*) an early motion-picture film with sound.

talking book *n* a recording of a book for the blind.

talking head *n* the head and shoulders of a person on television talking directly to the camera without using visual material.

talking picture *n* a talkie.

talking point *n* a subject for conversation or discussion; something that lends support to an argument.

talking-to *n* a reprimand, lecture.

talk show *n* a television or radio programme with informal interviews and conversation, a chat show.

tall *adj* above average in height; (*inf*) (*story*) exaggerated.—**tallness** *n*.

tallboy *n* a high chest of drawers on legs, a highboy.

tallith *n* (*pl* **tallithim**) a fringed shawl worn by Jewish men during religious services.

tall order *n* (*inf*) a request that is difficult to fulfil.

tallow *n* solid animal fat used to make soap, candles, etc.

tall ship *n* a square-rigged sailing vessel.

tall story *n* (*inf*) an exaggerated or unbelievable account

tally *n* (*pl* **tallies**) reckoning, account; one score in a game. * *vi* (**tallying, tallied**) to correspond; to keep score.

tally-ho *n* the cry of a person at a fox hunt when sighting the quarry.—*also vti*.

Talmud *n* the body of Jewish law.—**Talmudic** *adj*.

talon *n* a claw of an animal, esp a bird of prey.

talus[1] *n* (*pl* **tali**) the anklebone.

talus[2] *n* (*pl* **taluses**) scree; the sloping side of a wall.

tamale *n* a Mexican dish of minced meat with crushed maize and seasonings.

tamandua *n* a small tree-dwelling anteater of Central and South America.

tamarack *n* (the wood of) any of various North American larches.

tamarin *n* any of numerous small monkeys of South America resembling marmosets.

tamarind *n* a tropical evergreen tree bearing a pulpy fruit used for food, in beverages and in laxative preparations.

tamarisk *n* any of a genus of evergreen trees and shrubs of Mediterranean and tropical regions with tiny leaves and numerous clusters of pink or white flowers.

tambour *n* a drum; (an embroidery produced on) a circular frame for holding fabric taut during embroidery; a rolling top on a desk or cabinet made from thin strips of wood on a canvas backing. * *vt* to embroider using a tambour.

tamboura, tambura *n* an Indian stringed instrument used to provide a drone as accompaniment to singing.

tambourin *n* a dance of Provence in France; the music for this; a long drum used in Provence.

tambourine *n* a percussion hand instrument made of skin stretched over a circular frame with small jingling metal discs around the edge.

tambura *see* **tamboura**.

tame *adj* (*animal*) not wild, domesticated; compliant; dull, uninteresting. * *vt* (*animal*) to domesticate; to subdue; to soften.

Tamil *n* a member of a people inhabiting southeastern India and Sri Lanka; the language they speak.—*also adj*.

tam-o'-shanter *n* a tight-fitting Scottish woollen or cloth beret with a full crown and a pompom on top.

tamp *vt* to pack down firmly with a series of blows; to pack (a blast-hole) with sand or earth above the explosive charge.

tamper *vi* to meddle (with); to interfere (with).

tampion *n* a plug for the muzzle of a gun.

tampon *n* a firm plug of cotton wool inserted in the vagina during menstruation.

tam-tam *n* a gong.

tan[1] *n* a yellowish-brown colour; suntan. * *vti* (**tanning, tanned**) to acquire a suntan through sunbathing; (*skin, hide*) to convert into leather using tannin; (*inf*) to thrash.

tan[2] *abbr* = tangent.

tanager *n* any of numerous American woodland songbirds, the male of which has vividly coloured plumage.

tanbark *n* bark, esp from the oak, used as a source of tannin.

tandem *n* a bicycle for two riders, sitting one behind the other.

tandoori *n* an Indian method of cooking meat, vegetables and bread using a large clay oven.

tang *n* sharp smell or a strong taste.—**tangy** *adj*.

tangent *n* a line that touches a curve or circle at one point, without crossing it. * *adj* touching at one point.

tangential *adj* of superficial relevance; digressive.

tangerine *n* a small, sweet orange with a loose skin; the colour of this.—*also adj*.

tangible *adj* capable of being felt, seen or noticed; substantial; real.—**tangibility** *n*.

tangle *n* a mass of hair, string or wire knotted together confusedly; a complication. * *vt* to intertwine in a mass, to snarl; to entangle, complicate. * *vi* to become tangled or complicated; (*with* **with**) to become involved in argument with.

tango *n* (*pl* **tangos**) a Latin American ballroom dance. * *vi* (**tangoing, tangoed**) to dance the tango.

tangram *n* a Chinese puzzle made from a square cut into a rhomboid, a square and five triangles, which can be combined to produce different figures.

tank *n* a large container for storing liquids or gases; an armoured combat vehicle, mounted with guns and having caterpillar tracks.

tanka *n* (*pl* **tankas, tanka**) a Japanese verse form with five lines.

tankage *n* the capacity of a tank; the storing of oil, etc in tanks.

tankard *n* a tall, one-handled drinking mug, often with a hinged lid.

tanked *adj* (*sl*) extremely drunk.

tank engine *n* a steam locomotive that carries its own water supplies instead of using a tender.

tanker *n* a large ship or truck for transporting oil and other liquids.

tank top *n* a sleeveless pullover with a low neck.

tanner *n* a person who tans skins.

tannery *n* (*pl* **tanneries**) a place where hides are tanned.

tannic *adj* of, resembling, or derived from tan or tannin.

tannic acid *n* tannin.

tannin *n* a yellow or brown chemical found in plants or tea, used in tanning.

tansy *n* (*pl* **tansies**) any of numerous aromatic plants with yellow flowers and finely-divided leaves, once used for seasoning and as a medicine.

tantalize *vt* to tease or torment by presenting something greatly desired, but keeping it inaccessible.

tantalum *n* a hard metallic element of the vanadium family, esp used for hardening alloys.

tantalus *n* a cabinet or case where bottles of spirit may be locked up yet remain visible.

tantamount *adj* equivalent (to) in effect; as good as.

tantara *n* the sound of a horn or trumpet playing a fanfare.

tantrum *n* a childish fit of bad temper.

Tao *n* (*Taoism*) the spirit of creative harmony in the universe; the path of virtuous conduct in harmony with the natural order.

Taoiseach *n* the prime minister of the Republic of Ireland.

Taoism *n* a Chinese religious and philosophical system advocating a simple passive life in harmony with the natural order.

tap[1] *n* a quick, light blow or touch; a piece of metal attached to the heel or toe of a shoe for reinforcement or to tap-dance. * *vti* (**tapping, tapped**) to strike lightly; to make a tapping sound.

tap[2] *n* a device controlling the flow of liquid through a pipe or from a container, a faucet. * *vt* (**tapping, tapped**) to pierce in order to draw fluid from; to connect a secret listening device to a telephone; (*inf*) to ask for money from; (*resources, etc*) to draw on.

tap-dance *vi* to perform a step dance in shoes with taps.—**tap-dancer** *n*.—**tap-dancing** *n*.

tape *n* a strong, narrow strip of cloth, paper, etc, used for tying, binding, etc; tape measure; magnetic tape, as in a cassette or videotape. * *vt* to wrap with tape; to record on magnetic tape.

tape deck *n* a tape recorder in a hi-fi system.

tape measure *n* a tape marked in inches or centimetres for measuring.

tape player *n* a self-contained tape recorder.

tape recorder *n* a machine used for recording and reproducing sounds or music on magnetic tape, esp as part of a hi-fi system, a tape deck.

tape recording *n* a recording made on magnetic tape.

taper *n* a long thin candle. * *vti* to make or become gradually narrower toward one end.—**tapering** *adj*.

tapestry *n* (*pl* **tapestries**) a heavy fabric woven with patterns or figures, used for wall hangings and furnishings.

tapeworm *n* a tape-like, parasitic, intestinal worm.

tapioca *n* a glutinous starch extracted from the root of the cassava and used in puddings, etc.

tapir *n* (*pl* **tapirs, tapir**) a South American hoofed mammal with a short flexible proboscis.

tappet *n* a projecting arm or lever (eg a cam) that moves or is moved by another part in a machine.

taproom *n* a bar.

taps *n sing* a call on a bugle at a military camp signalling lights out; any similar signal, as at a military funeral.

tar[1] *n* a thick, dark, viscous substance obtained from wood, coal, peat, etc., used for surfacing roads. * *vt* to coat with tar.—**tarry** *adj*.

tar[2] *n* a (*inf*) a sailor.

taramasalata *n* a pale pink fish-roe paste served as a starter.

tarantella *n* (the music for) a lively peasant dance of southern Italy.

tarantula *n* (*pl* **tarantulas, tarantulae**) a large, hairy spider with a poisonous bite that is painful but not deadly.

tarboosh, tarbush *n* a brimless red cap resembling a fez worn by Muslim men.

tardy *adj* (**tardier, tardiest**) slow; later than expected.—**tardily** *adv*.—**tardiness** *n*.

tare[1] *n* (the seed of) a type of vetch plant.

tare[2] *n* (an allowance for) the weight of the wrapping or container in which goods are packed; the weight of an unloaded goods vehicle. * *vt* to weigh in order to calculate the tare.

target *n* a mark to aim at, esp in shooting; an objective or ambition.

tariff *n* a tax on imports or exports; (*in a hotel*) a list of prices; the rate of charge for public services, such as gas or electricity.

tarlatan, tarletan *n* a type of thin stiff cotton fabric.

Tarmac, Tarmacadam *n* a material for surfacing roads made from crushed stones and tar; an airport runway. * *vti* (**tarmacking, tarmacked**) to lay down a tarmac surface.

tarn *n* a small mountain lake.

tarnish *vi* (*metal*) to lose its lustre or discolour due to exposure to the air. * *vt* (*reputation*) to taint.—*also n*.

taro *n* (*pl* **taros**) (the edible root of) a tropical Asian plant.

tarot *n* a game played with 22 pictorial cards, which are also used for fortune-telling.

tarpaulin *n* canvas cloth coated with a waterproof substance.

tarragon *n* an aromatic herb used for flavouring.

tarry *vi* (**tarrying, tarried**) to delay or dawdle; to linger; to wait briefly.

tarsus *n* (*pl* **tarsi**) the small bones of the ankle and the heel in vertebrates; the plate of tissue that stiffens the eyelid.—**tarsal** *adj, n*.

tart[1] *adj* having a sour, sharp taste; (*speech*) sharp, severe. —**tartly** *adv*.—**tartness** *n*.

tart[2] *n* an open pastry case containing fruit, jam or custard; (*inf*) a prostitute. * *vt* (*with* **up**) (*inf*) to dress cheaply and gaudily; to decorate, esp cheaply.

tartan *n* a woollen cloth with a chequered pattern, having a distinctive design for each Scottish clan.

tartar *n* a hard, yellow, crusty deposit which forms on the teeth; a salty deposit on the sides of wine casks.

tartaric acid *n* an organic acid obtained from grapes and many other fruits.

tartar sauce *n* a mayonnaise sauce with chopped capers, herbs, etc, eaten esp with fish.

task *n* a specific amount of work to be done; a chore.

task force *n* a small unit with a specific mission, usu military.

taskmaster *n* a person who demands constant hard work.

Tasmanian devil *n* a burrowing flesh-eating marsupial of Tasmania with a black coat and long tail.

tassel *n* an ornamental tuft of silken threads decorating soft furnishings, clothes, etc; a growth that looks like this, esp on corn. * *vb* (**tasselling, tasselled** *or* **tasseling, tasseled**) *vt* to decorate with tassels. * *vi* (*plant*) to grow tassels.

taste *vt* to perceive (a flavour) by taking into the mouth; to try by eating and drinking a little; to sample; to experience. * *vi* to try by the mouth; to have a specific flavour. * *n* the sense by which flavours are perceived; a small portion; the ability to recognize what is beautiful, attractive, etc; liking; a brief experience.

taste bud *n* any of the small projecting sensory organs on the tongue's surface by which taste is perceived.

tasteful *adj* showing good taste.—**tastefully** *adv.*—**tastefulness** *n.*

tasteless *adj* without taste, bland; in bad taste.—**tastelessly** *adv.*

taster *n* a person skilled in determining the balance of flavours in a product, esp tea, wine; a device for tasting or sampling; (*formerly*) a person who tasted food before it was served to a king, etc.

tasty *adj* (**tastier, tastiest**) savoury; having a pleasant flavour.

ta-ta *interj* (*Brit inf*) goodbye.

tatami *n* (*pl* **tatamis, tatami**) straw matting used as a floor covering, esp in Japan.

tatter *n* a torn or ragged piece of cloth.—**tattered** *adj.*

tatterdemalion *n* a person wearing ragged clothes, a ragamuffin.—*also adj.*

tatting *n* (the process of making) a type of delicate handmade lace.

tattle *vi* to gossip. * *vt* to reveal (secrets, etc) by gossiping. * *n* (a) gossip.

tattletale *n* a gossip. * *adj* telltale.

tattoo[1] *n* (*pl* **tattoos**) a continuous beating of a drum; a military display of exercises and music.

tattoo[2] *vt* (**tattooing, tattooed**) to make permanent patterns or pictures on the skin by pricking and marking with dyes. * *n* (*pl* **tattoos**) marks made on the skin in this way.

tatty *adj* (**tattier, tattiest**) shabby, ragged.

tau *n* the 19th letter of the Greek alphabet.

taught *see* **teach.**

taunt *vt* to provoke with mockery or contempt; to tease. * *n* an insult.

taupe *n, adj* (a) brownish-grey.

taurine *n* of or like a bull.

tauromachy *n* the art or practice of bullfighting.

Taurus *n* the Bull, the second sign of the zodiac.—**Taurean** *adj.*

taut *adj* stretched tight; tense; stressed.

tauten *vti* to make or become taut.

tauto-, taut- *prefix* same.

tautog *n* a large North American food fish related to the wrasse.

tautology *n* (*pl* **tautologies**) a statement which uses different words to repeat the same thing.—**tautological, tautologous** *adj.*

tavern *n* a place licensed to sell alcoholic drinks; an inn.

taverna *n* a Greek hotel with its own bar; a Greek restaurant.

tawdry *adj* (**tawdrier, tawdriest**) showy, cheap, and of poor quality.

tawny *adj* yellowish brown.

tawny owl *n* a European owl with brown plumage.

tawse *n* (*Scot*) a leather strap with a slit end formerly used for punishing schoolchildren.

tax *n* a rate imposed by the government on property or persons to raise revenues; a strain. * *vt* to impose a tax (upon); to strain.

taxa *see* **taxon.**

taxable *adj* able or liable to be taxed.

taxation *n* the act of levying taxes; the amount raised as tax.

tax avoidance *n* avoiding paying tax using legal means.

tax-deductible *adj* (*expenses, etc*) legitimately deducted from income before tax assessment.

tax evasion *n* avoiding paying tax using illegal methods.

tax exile *n* a person who lives abroad to avoid paying high taxes.

tax haven *n* a place where taxes are lower than average.

taxi *n* (*pl* **taxis**) a taxicab. * *vi* (**taxiing** *or* **taxying, taxied**) (*aircraft*) to move along the runway before takeoff or after landing.

taxicab *n* a car, usu fitted with a taximeter, that may be hired to transport passengers.

taxidermy *n* the art of preparing and stuffing the skins of animals ready for exhibiting.—**taxidermist** *n.*

taximeter *n* a meter fitted into a taxi to record the time taken for a journey.

taxis *n* a movement in a simple organism (eg a bacterium) in response to certain external stimulii; (*surgery*) the restoration of a displaced part by manual pressure.

taxiway *n* a marked route from a terminal to a runway along which an aircraft taxis.

taxon *n* (*pl* **taxa**) any taxonomic group or category.

taxonomy *n* (the science of) the classification of living things into groups based on similarities of biological origin, design, function, etc.

taxpayer *n* a person who or an organization that pays taxes.

tax return *n* a statement of a person's income for the purposes of tax assessment.

tax shelter *n* a financial arrangement to minimize tax liability.

tax therapist *n* a tax adviser who helps with the completion of income tax forms.

TB *abbr* = tuberculosis.

Tb (*chem symbol*) terbium.

T-bone steak *n* a large sirloin steak containing a T-shaped bone.

tbs., tbsp. *abbr* = tablespoon; tablespoonful.

Tc (*chem symbol*) technetium.

T-cell *n* a lymphocyte that kills cells infected with a virus.—*also* **T-lymphocyte.**

Te (*chem symbol*) tellurium.

tea *n* a shrub growing in China, India, Sri Lanka, etc; its dried, shredded leaves, which are infused in boiling water for a beverage; in UK, a light meal taken in mid-afternoon; a main meal taken in the early evening.

tea bag n a small porous bag containing tea leaves for infusing.

tea ball n a perforated metal ball which holds tea leaves to make tea.

tea caddy n an airtight container for storing tea.

teach vb (**teaching, taught**) vt to impart knowledge to; to give lessons (to); to train; to help to learn. * vi to give instruction, esp as a profession.—**teachable** adj.

tea chest n a large wooden box used to transport tea.

teacher n a person who instructs others, esp as an occupation.

teach-in n an informal conference at a university or college with lectures and discussions on a topical issue.

teaching n the profession or practice of being a teacher; the act of giving instruction.

tea cloth n a tea towel for drying dishes; a dishtowel.

tea cosy n a cover for a teapot to keep the contents warm.

teacup n a small cup for drinking tea.

teak n a type of hard wood from an East Indian tree.

teal n (pl **teal, teals**) a small freshwater duck; a dark greenish blue.

team n a group of people participating in a sport together; a group of people working together; two or more animals pulling a vehicle. * vi (with **up**) to join in cooperative activity.

team-mate n a colleague, a fellow team member.

team spirit n willingness to work harmoniously within a group.

teamster n a truck driver.

teamwork n cooperation of individuals for the benefit of the team; the ability of a team to work together.

teapot n a vessel in which tea is made.

teapoy n a three-legged stand or table.

tear[1] n a drop of salty liquid appearing in the eyes when crying or when the eyes are smarting; anything tear-shaped.

tear[2] vb (**tearing, tore,** pp **torn**) vt to pull apart by force; to split; to lacerate; (with **down**) to destroy, demolish. * vi to move with speed; (with **into**) (inf) to attack physically or verbally. * n a hole or split.

tearaway n an impetuous, violent person.

tearful adj weeping; sad.—**tearfully** adv.

tear gas n gas that irritates the eyes and nasal passages, used in riot control.

tearing adj overwhelming, violent.

tear-jerker n a strongly sentimental book, film, play, etc.

tearoom, teashop n a restaurant where tea and light refreshments are served.

tea rose n any of numerous garden bush roses descended from a Chinese rose and valued for their large tea-scented blooms.

tease vt to separate the fibres of; to torment or irritate; to taunt playfully. * n a person who teases or torments; (inf) a flirt.—**teaser** n.

teasel, teazel, teazle n any of various plants with prickly leaves and flower heads formerly dried and used to raise a nap on woollen cloth; an implement used for this purpose.

tea service, tea set n the set of cups and saucers, etc for serving tea.

teashop n a tearoom.

teaspoon n a small spoon for use with a teacup or as a measure; the amount measured by this.—**teaspoonful** n.

teat n the nipple on a breast or udder; the mouthpiece of a baby's feeding bottle.

tea towel, tea cloth n a towel for drying dishes; a dishtowel.

tech. abbr = technical; technology.

technetium n an artificially produced metallic element whose radioisotope is used in radiotherapy.

technical adj relating to, or specializing in practical, industrial, mechanical or applied sciences; (expression, etc) belonging to or peculiar to a particular field of activity.—**technically** adv.

technicality n (pl **technicalities**) a petty formality or technical point.

technical knockout n (boxing) a decision by a referee to end a fight because a boxer is too badly hurt to continue.

technician n a person skilled in the practice of any art, esp in practical work with scientific equipment.

Technicolor n (trademark) the production of colour film by combining identical scenes with different primary colours into a single print.

technique n method of performing a particular task; knack.

techno- prefix technical; technological.

technocracy n (pl **technocracies**) government by technical experts.—**technocrat** n.—**technocratic** adj.

technology n (pl **technologies**) the application of mechanical and applied sciences to industrial use.—**technological** adj.—**technologist** n.

techy see **tetchy.**

tectonic adj of or relating to building or construction; (geological structures or forces) resulting from deformation of the earth's crust.

tectonics n sing the art or science of constructing buildings, etc; the study of the forces which shape the earth's geological structure.

teddy n (pl **teddies**) a woman's one-piece undergarment.

teddy bear n a stuffed toy bear.

Te Deum n a Latin hymn used in services of thanksgiving to God.

tedious adj monotonous; boring.—**tediously** adv.—**tedium** n.

tee n (golf) the place from where the first stroke is played at each hole; a small peg from which the ball is driven. * vti to position (the ball) on the tee; (with **off**) to hit a golf ball from a tee.

teem[1] vi (with **with**) to be prolific or abundant in.

teem[2] vi to pour (with rain).

teen n a teenager. * adj teenage.

teenager n (inf) a person who is in his or her teens.

teens npl the years of one's life from thirteen to nineteen.—**teenage, teenaged** adj.

teeny adj (**teenier, teeniest**) (inf) tiny.

teenybopper n a young girl who avidly follows the latest fashions in clothes and pop music.

teepee see **tepee.**

tee-shirt see **T-shirt.**

teeter vi to move or stand unsteadily.

teeth see **tooth.**

teethe vi to cut one's first teeth.

teething n the condition in babies of the first growth of teeth.

teething ring n a hard ring for a teething baby to chew on.

teething troubles npl problems encountered in the early stages of a project, etc; pain caused by growing teeth.

teetotaller, teetotaler n a person who abstains from alcoholic drinks.—**teetotal** adj.

TEFL *abbr* = Teaching English as a Foreign Language.

Teflon *n* (*trademark*) polytetrafluoroethylene, a coating for pots and pans that prevents food sticking. * *adj* (*inf*) able to avoid (political) scandal by claiming ignorance or blaming others.

tegument *n* an outer covering; an integument.

tektite *n* a spherical glassy object found in various parts of the world and thought to be of meteoric origin.

tel. *abbr* = telephone.

tel-, tele- *prefix* at a distance; television.

telaesthesia *n* supposed perception of objects or events beyond the normal range of the senses.—*also* **telesthesia.**—**telaesthetic, telesthetic** *adj*.

telamon *n* (*archit*) a figure or half-figure of a man, used in place of a column or pilaster to support an entablature, an atlas.

telecast *vt* to broadcast by television. * *n* a television broadcast.—**telecaster** *n*.

telecom, telecoms *n* short for telecommunications.

telecommunication *n* communication of information over long distances by telephone and radio; (*pl*) the technology of telephone and radio communication.

teledu *n* a mammal of Java and Sumatra resembling the badger and related to the skunk, which releases a foul-smelling liquid when threatened.

telefilm *n* a motion picture produced for television.

telegenic *adj* suitable for television in content or appearance.

telegram *n* a message sent by telegraph.

telegraph *n* a system for transmitting messages over long distances using electricity, wires and a code. * *vt* to transmit by telegraph.—**telegraphic** *adj*.—**telegraphy** *n*.

telekinesis *n* the movement of objects using pure thought without the application of physical force.—**telekinetic** *adj*.

telemark *n* (*skiing*) a turn in which one ski is placed ahead of the other and then angled gradually inward.

telemeter *n* any instrument that measures or records events and transmits the data to a distant receiver; (*surveying*) a device for measuring distances. * *vt* to gather and transmit data from a distance.

telemetry *n* the use of radio waves to transmit, register and record the readings of an instrument at a distance.

telencephalon *n* the frontal brain including the cerebrum, parts of the hypothalamus and the third ventricle.—**telencephalic** *adj*.

teleology *n* the philosophical doctrine that explains nature or natural processes in terms of purpose or design.—**teleological** *adj*.—**teleologist** *n*.

telepathy *n* the communication between people's minds of thoughts and feelings, without the need for speech or proximity.—**telepathic** *adj*.

telephone *n* an instrument for transmitting speech at a distance, esp by means of electricity. * *vt* (*someone*) to call by telephone.

telephone book *n* a book listing the names, addresses and telephone numbers of subscribers in a given area.

telephone booth *n* a cubicle for paid public use of a telephone.

telephone directory *n* a telephone book.

telephone operator, telephonist *n* a person who operates a telephone switchboard.

telephony *n* the system by which sounds are transmitted by telephone.—**telephonic** *adj*.

telephotography *n* the use of a telephoto lens to photograph distant objects.

telephoto lens *n* a camera lens that magnifies distant objects.

teleprinter *n* a teletypewriter.

TelePrompTer *n* (*trademark*) a prompting device used in TV, etc, which provides speakers with a script that remains invisible to the audience, an autocue.

telesales *npl* selling products and services by telephone.

telescope *n* a tubular optical instrument for viewing objects at a distance.

telescopic *adj* of or like a telescope; that can be viewed by through a telescope.—**telescopically** *adv*.

telesthesia *see* **telaesthesia.**

Teletext *n* (*trademark*) written information transmitted non-interactively to television viewers.

telethon *n* a long television extravaganza which encourages viewers to send in money for a charitable cause.

Teletype *n* (*trademark*) a teleprinter.

teletypewriter *n* a telegraph apparatus with a keyboard that transmits and a printer that receives messages over a distance.

televangelist *n* a person, usu a minister of the Christian Pentecostal church, who conducts television shows to preach the church's message and seek donations.

televise *vt* (*a programme*) to transmit by television.

television *n* the transmission of visual images and accompanying sound through electrical and sound waves; a television receiving set; television broadcasting.

telex *n* a communication system whereby subscribers hire teletypewriters for transmitting messages. * *vt* to transmit by telex.

tell *vb* (**telling, told**) *vt* to narrate; to disclose; to inform; to notify; to instruct; to distinguish; (*with* **off**) (*inf*) to reprimand; to count off and assign to a duty. * *vi* to tell tales, to inform on; to produce a marked effect.

teller *n* a bank clerk; a person appointed to count votes in an election.

telling *adj* having great impact.

telltale *n* a person who tells tales about others. * *adj* revealing what is meant to be hidden.

tellurian *adj* of the earth. * *n* an inhabitant of the earth.

telluric *adj* of or in the earth or soil; of or containing (high valency) tellurium.

tellurium *n* a brittle nonmetallic element related to sulphur and selenium.

tellurometer *n* (*surveying*) an electronic instrument for measuring distances using microwaves.

telly *n* (*pl* **tellies**) (*Brit inf*) television.

telo-, tel- *prefix* end.

temerity *n* rashness.

temp *n* (*inf*) a temporary employee.

temp. *abbr* = temperature.

temper *n* a frame of mind; a fit of anger. * *vt* to tone down, moderate; (*steel*) to heat and cool repeatedly to bring to the correct hardness.

tempera *n* (a method of painting using) powdered pigments mixed with an emulsion, esp egg yolk and water; a painting done in tempera; opaque watercolour used for posters.

temperament *n* one's disposition.

temperamental *adj* easily irritated; erratic.—**temperamentally** *adv*.

temperance *n* moderation; abstinence from alcohol.

temperate *adj* mild or moderate in temperature; (*behaviour*) moderate, self-controlled.

temperature *n* degree of heat or cold; body heat above the normal.

tempest *n* a violent storm.

tempestuous *adj* stormy; violent; passionate.

tempi *see* tempo.

template *n* a pattern, gauge or mould used as a guide esp in cutting metal, stone or plastic.

temple[1] *n* a place of worship.

temple[2] *n* the region on either side of the head above the cheekbone.

tempo *n* (*pl* **tempos, tempi**) (*mus*) the speed at which music is meant to be played; rate of any activity.

temporal[1] *adj* relating to time; secular, civil.

temporal[2] *adj* of or relating to the temples of the head.

temporality *n* (*pl* **temporalities**) the state or condition of being temporal; a secular or civil authority or power.

temporal lobe *n* a lobe on each side of the cerebral hemisphere associated with hearing and speech.

temporary *adj* lasting or used for a limited time only; not permanent.—**temporarily** *adv*.

temporize *vi* to delay in order to gain time; to act to fit the occasion.—**temporization** *n*.—**temporizer** *n*.

tempt *vt* to entice to do wrong; to invite, attract, induce.—**tempter** *n*.—**temptress** *nf*.

temptation *n* the act of tempting or the state of being tempted; something or someone that tempts.

tempting *adj* attractive, inviting.

tempura *n* a Japanese dish of seafood or vegetables fried in batter.

ten *adj*, *n* the cardinal number next above nine. * *n* the symbol for this (10, X, x).

tenable *adj* capable of being believed, held, or defended.

tenacious *adj* grasping firmly; persistent; retentive; adhesive.

tenacity *n* the state or quality of being tenacious; doggedness, obstinacy; adhesiveness, stickiness.

tenaculum *n* (*pl* **tenacula**) a hooked surgical instrument for seizing and holding parts, such as arteries.

tenancy *n* (*pl* **tenancies**) the temporary possession by a tenant of another's property; the period of this.

tenant *n* a person who pays rent to occupy a house or flat or for the use of land or buildings; an occupant.

tenant farmer *n* a farmer who works land owned by someone else to whom he pays rent.

tench *n* (*pl* **tench**) a freshwater fish of the carp family.

tend[1] *vt* to take care of; to attend (to).

tend[2] *vi* to be inclined; to move in a specific direction.

tendency *n* (*pl* **tendencies**) an inclination or leaning.

tendentious, tendencious *adj* showing bias, not impartial.—**tendentiousness, tendenciousness** *n*.

tender[1] *n* a railroad car attached to locomotives to carry fuel and water; a small ship that brings stores to a larger one.

tender[2] *vt* to present for acceptance; to offer as payment. * *vi* to make an offer. * *n* an offer to provide goods or services at a fixed price.

tender[3] *adj* soft, delicate; fragile; painful, sore; sensitive; sympathetic.—**tenderly** *adv*.—**tenderness** *n*.

tenderfoot *n* a newcomer to rough, outdoor life; an inexperienced beginner.

tenderhearted *n* having a compassionate, loving or sensitive disposition.—**tenderheartedly** *adv*.—**tenderheartedness** *n*.

tenderize *vt* (*meat*) to make more tender by pounding or by adding a substance that softens.—**tenderization** *n*.—**tenderizer** *n*.

tenderloin *n* a cut of meat from between the ribs and sirloin.

tendon *n* fibrous tissue attaching a muscle to a bone.

tendril *n* a thread-like shoot of a climbing plant by which it attaches itself for support.

tenement *n* a building divided into flats, each occupied by a separate owner or tenant.

tenesmus *n* (*med*) an urgent but ineffectual attempt to urinate or void the bowels.

tenet *n* any belief or doctrine.

tenfold *adj*, *adv* 10 times as much or as many; composed of 10 parts.

ten-gallon hat *n* a wide-brimmed hat with a high crown, esp worn by cowboys.

teniasis *see* taeniasis.

Tenn. *abbr* = Tennessee.

tenner *n* (*inf*) a ten-pound note; a ten-dollar bill.

tennis *n* a game for two or four people, played by hitting a ball over a net with a racket.

tennis court *n* a court surfaced with clay, asphalt or grass on which tennis is played.

tennis elbow *n* stiffness and pain in the elbow joint due to excessive exercise, such as playing tennis.

tenon *n* a projection on the end of a piece of wood for connecting with a mortise. * *vt* to form a tenon; to connect using a tenon and mortise.

tenon saw *n* a fine-toothed saw with a sturdy back used for cutting tenons, etc.

tenor *n* a general purpose or intent; the highest regular adult male voice, higher than a baritone and lower than an alto; a man who sings tenor.

tenor clef *n* a C clef placed so as to designate the fourth line of the staff as middle C.

tenosynovitis *n* inflammation of the tendons in a joint through repetitive movements of the joint concerned.

tenpin *n* a bowling pin used in tenpins.

tenpin bowling *n* in UK, tenpins.

tenpins *n sing* a bowling game involving the rolling of a large bowl along a lane to knock over as many as possible of tenpins.

tenrec *n* any of various related mammals of Madagascar resembling shrews.

tense[1] *n* (*gram*) the verb form that indicates the time of an action or the existence of a state.

tense[2] *adj* stretched, taut; apprehensive; nervous and highly strung. * *vti* to make or become tense.—**tensely** *adv*.—**tenseness** *n*.

tensile *adj* of or relating to tension; stretchable.

tensile strength *n* the greatest stress a material can bear without breaking.

tensimeter *n* an instrument that measures differences in vapour pressures.

tensiometer *n* an instrument for measuring tensile strength; an instrument for comparing vapour pressures in different liquids; an instrument for measuring the surface tension of a liquid; an instrument for measuring the moisture content of soil.

tension *n* the act of stretching; the state of being stretched; (*between forces, etc*) opposition; stress; mental strain.

tensor *n* any muscle that stretches or tightens a body part.

tent *n* a portable shelter of canvas, plastic or other waterproof fabric, which is erected on poles and fixed to the ground by ropes and pegs.

tentacle *n* a long, slender, flexible growth near the mouth of invertebrates, used for feeling, grasping or handling.

tentative *adj* provisional; not definite.—**tentatively** *adv*.—**tentativeness** *n*.

tenterhook *n* one of a series of hooks on which cloth is stretched to dry; (*pl*) (*with* **on**) in a tense or anxious state.

tenth *adj* the last of ten; being one of ten equal parts. * *n* one of ten equal parts.

tenuous *adj* slight, flimsy, insubstantial.—**tenuousness** *n*.

tenure *n* the holding of property or a position; the period of time which a position lasts; a permanent position, usu granted after holding a job for a number of years.—**tenured** *adj*.

tenuto *adv, adj* (*mus*) (*note*) sustained for its full time value.

teocalli *n* (*pl* **teocallis**) the pyramid-shaped bases supporting Aztec temples.

tepee *n* a cone-shaped, North American Indian tent formed of skins; a wigwam.—*also* **teepee**.

tepid *adj* slightly warm, lukewarm.

tequila *n* a spirit distilled from a Mexican agave plant; the plant itself.

ter. *abbr* = terrace; territory.

ter- *prefix* three times; third; three.

tera- *prefix* ten to the power of 12.

terbium *n* a metallic element of the rare earth group.

tercel *see* **tiercel**.

tercentenary *n* (*pl* **tercentenaries**) a three hundredth anniversary.—*also adj*.

terebene *n* a liquid hydrocarbon derived from oil of turpentine and sulphuric acid used in making varnishes, as an antiseptic and in medicines.

terebinth *n* a European tree that yields a resinous liquid.

terebinthine *n* or or pertaining to the terebinth; of or like turpentine.

teredo *n* (*pl* **teredos, teredines**) a burrowing mollusc, the shipworm.

terete *adj* (*plant, animal part*) having a smooth cylindrical shape.

tergiversate *vi* to switch allegiances; to be evasive, to equivocate.

term *n* a limit; any prescribed period of time; a division of an academic year; a word or expression, esp in a specialized field of knowledge; (*pl*) mutual relationship between people; (*pl*) conditions of a contract, etc. * *vt* to call, designate.

termagant *n* (*arch*) a shrewish, nagging woman.

terminal *adj* being or situated at the end or extremity; (*disease*) fatal, incurable. * *n* a bus, coach or railroad station at the end of the line; the point at which an electrical current enters or leaves a device; a device with a keyboard and monitor for inputting or viewing data from a computer.—**terminally** *adv*.

terminate *vti* to bring or come to an end.—**termination** *n*.

terminology *n* (*pl* **terminologies**) the terms used in any specialized subject.

terminus *n* (*pl* **termini, terminuses**) the final part; a limit; end of a transportation line.

termitarium *n* (*pl* **termitaria**) a termites' nest.

termite *n* a wood-eating, white, ant-like insect.

tern *n* a small, black and white sea bird.

ternary *adj* in three parts; (*number system*) using three as a base.

terpene *n* any of various hydrocarbons present in the essential oils of plants, esp conifers.

Terpsichorean *adj* pertaining to dancing, or to Terpsichore, the Muse of dancing and choral song in classical myth.

terrace *n* a raised level area of earth, often part of a slope; an unroofed paved area adjoining a house; a row of houses; a patio or balcony. * *vt* to make into a terrace.

terracotta *n* a brownish-red clay used for making flower pots and statues, which is baked but not glazed; a brown-red colour.

terra firma *n* solid ground; the earth.

terrain *n* the surface features of a tract of land; (*fig*) field of activity.

terra incognita *n* an unexplored or unknown area or country.

terrapin *n* an aquatic North American turtle.

terrarium *n* (*pl* **terraria, terrariums**) an enclosure for small land animals; a glass container for plants.

terrazzo *n* mosaic flooring in the form of marble chips set in mortar and highly polished.

terrestrial *adj* relating to, or existing on, the earth; earthly; representing the earth.

terrible *adj* causing great fear; dreadful; (*inf*) very unpleasant.

terribly *adv* frighteningly; (*inf*) very.

terrier *n* a type of small, active dog.

terrific *adj* of great size; (*inf*) excellent.

terrify *vt* (**terrifying, terrified**) to fill with terror, to frighten greatly.

terrine *n* an earthenware dish for pâté; pâté or similar food served in this.

territorial *adj* relating to or owned by a territory. * *n* (*with cap*) a member of the Territorial Army, a British volunteer reserve force.

territorial waters *npl* the coastal and inland waters under the jurisdiction of a nation.

territory *n* (*pl* **territories**) an area under the jurisdiction of a city or state; a wide tract of land; an area assigned to a salesman; an area of knowledge.

terror *n* great fear; an object or person inspiring fear or dread.

terrorism *n* the use of terror and violence to intimidate.— **terrorist** *n*.

terrorize *vt* to terrify; to control by terror.—**terrorization** *n*.

terry *n* (*pl* **terries**) a cloth with an uncut pile made of looped threads.

terse *adj* abrupt, to the point, concise.—**tersely** *adv*.

tertian *adj* (*fever*) occurring on alternate days.

tertiary *adj* third.

TESOL *abbr* = Teachers of English to Speakers of Other Languages.

tesla *n* the SI unit of magnetic flux density.

tessellated *adj* resembling mosaic.

tessera *n* (*pl* **tesserae**) a piece of marble, glass, etc used in a mosaic.

tessitura *n* (*mus*) the natural pitch of a voice or instrument.

test *n* an examination; trial; a chemical reaction to test a substance or to test for an illness; a series of questions or exercises. * *vt* to examine critically.

testament *n* a will; proof; tribute; (*arch*) a covenant made by God with men; (*with cap*) one of the two main parts of the Bible.

testate *adj* having made and left a will.

testator *n* a person who leaves a will.

test ban *n* an agreement between nations to limit or abandon tests of nuclear weapons.

test-bed *n* an area designed for testing machinery.

test case *n* a legal action that establishes a precedent.

testes *see* **testis**.

testicle *n* either of the two male reproductive glands that produce sperm, a testis.

testify *vb* (**testifying, testified**) *vi* to give evidence under oath; to serve as witness (to); (*with* **to**) to be evidence of. * *vt* to be evidence of.

testimonial *adj* relating to a testimony. * *n* a recommendation of one's character or abilities.

testimony *n* (*pl* **testimonies**) evidence; declaration of truth or fact.

testis *n* (*pl* **testes**) a testicle.

test match *n* one of a series of international cricket or Rugby football matches.

testosterone *n* a steroid hormone secreted by the testes.

test pilot *n* someone who flies new types of aircraft to test their performance and characteristics.

test tube *n* a cylinder of thin glass closed at one end, used in scientific experiments.

test-tube baby *n* a baby which develops from an ovum fertilized outside the mother's body and replaced in the womb.

testy *adj* (**testier, testiest**) touchy, irritable.

tetanus *n* an intense and painful spasm of muscles, caused by the infection of a wound by bacteria; lockjaw.

tetchy *adj* (**tetchier, tetchiest**) irritable, touchy.—*also* **techy.**—**tetchily** *adv.*—**tetchiness** *n.*

tête-à-tête *n* (*pl* **tête-à-têtes, tête-à-tête**) a private conversation between two people.

tether *n* a rope or chain for tying an animal; the limit of one's endurance. * *vt* to fasten with a tether; to limit.

tetra-, tetr- *prefix* four.

tetrahedron *n* (*pl* **tetrahedrons, tetrahedra**) a solid figure enclosed by four plane faces of triangular shape.

tetrahydroamino-acridine *n* a drug currently being tried out for use in the treatment of Alzheimer's disease.

tetrahydrocannabinol *n* a natural compound that is the main intoxicant in cannabis and can also be produced synthetically.

tetralogy *n* (*pl* **tetralogies**) a series of four related works, such as novels or plays.

tetravalent *adj* (*chem*) having a valency of four.

Teutonic *adj* of Germanic peoples or their language.

Tex. *abbr* = Texas.

Tex-Mex *adj* of or pertaining to a Texan version of something Mexican, such as food or music.

text *n* the main part of a printed work; the original or exact wording; a passage from the Bible forming the basis of a sermon; a subject or topic; a textbook.

textbook *n* a book used as a basis for instruction.

textile *n* a woven fabric or cloth. * *adj* relating to the making of fabrics.

textual *adj* of or relating to a text; contained in or based on a text; (*operation, etc*) exactly as planned according to theory or calculation.

textual criticism *n* the study of a written work (eg the Bible) to establish the original text; the close reading and analysis of any literary work.

texture *n* the characteristic appearance, arrangement or feel of a thing; the way in which threads in a material are interwoven.—**textural** *adj.*

TGIF *abbr* = thank God it's Friday.

Th (*chem symbol*) thorium.

Th. *abbr* = Thursday.

THA *abbr* = tetrahydroamino-acridine.

Thai *n* (*pl* **Thais, Thai**) a native or inhabitant of Thailand; the language of Thailand.—*also adj.*

thalamus *n* (*pl* **thalami**) either of the two masses of tissue which sit close together at the base of the brain.

thalidomide *n* a sedative drug withdrawn from use when it was discovered to cause malformation in unborn babies.

thallium *n* a soft white poisonous metallic element.

than *conj* introducing the second element of a comparison.

thanatology *n* the scientific study of death.

thank *vt* to express gratitude to or appreciation for. * *npl* an expression of gratitude.—**thankful** *adj.*—**thankfully** *adv.*

thankless *adj* without thanks; unappreciated; fruitless, unrewarding.—**thanklessness** *n.*

thanksgiving *n* the act of giving thanks; a prayer of gratitude to God; (*with cap*) Thanksgiving Day.

Thanksgiving Day *n* a legal holiday observed on the fourth Thursday of November in the US, and on the second Monday of October in Canada.

thank-you *n* an expression of gratitude.

that *demons adj, pron* (*pl* **those**) the (one) there or then, esp the latter or more distant thing. * *rel pron* who or which. * *conj* introducing noun clause or adverbial clause of purpose or consequence; because; in order that; (*preceded by* **so, such**) as a result.

thatch *n* roofing straw. * *vt* to cover a roof with thatch.

thaumatology *n* (*pl* **thaumatologies**) the study of miracles; a discourse on miracles.

thaumaturge, thaumaturgist *n* a miracle-worker; a magician.—**thaumaturgy** *n.*

thaw *vi* to melt or grow liquid; to become friendly. *vt* to cause to melt. * *n* the melting of ice or snow by warm weather.

THC *abbr* = tetrahydrocannabinol.

the *demons adj* denoting a particular person or thing. * *adv* used before comparative adjectives or adverbs for emphasis.

theatre, theater *n* a building where plays and operas are performed; the theatrical world as a whole; a setting for important events; field of operations.

theatre-in-the-round *n* a theatre with seats arranged in a circle around the stage area.

theatrical *adj* relating to the theatre; melodramatic, affected.—**theatrically** *adv.*

theatricals *npl* performances of drama, esp by amateurs.

thee *pron* the objective case of **thou**.

theft *n* act or crime of stealing.

theine *n* caffeine.

their *poss adj* of or belonging to them; his, hers, its.

theirs *poss pron* of or belonging to them; his, hers, its.

theism *n* belief in the existence of a God or gods, esp God as the supernatural Creator of the universe.—**theist** *n.*—**theistic** *adj.*

them *pron* the objective case of **they**.

theme *n* the main subject of a discussion; an idea or motif in a work; a short essay; a leading melody; a style adopted for an exhibition, activity, etc.—**thematic** *adj.*

theme park *n* a leisure area in which the buildings and settings follow a particular theme, eg a period in history.

theme song *n* a recurring melody in a film score or musical that is associated with the work or a particular character; a signature tune.

themselves *pron* the reflexive form of **they** or **them**.

then *adv* at that time; afterward; immediately; next in time. * *conj* for that reason; in that case.

thenar *n* the ball of the thumb; the palm of the hand.

thence *adv* from that time or place; for that reason.

thenceforth *adv* from that time on; thereafter.

thenceforward, thenceforwards *adv* thenceforth.

theo-, the- *prefix* god.

theobromine *n* an alkaloid similar to caffeine present in cacao beans and tea, used in treating heart disease.

theocracy *n* (*pl* **theocracies**) (a state having) government by a deity or priesthood.—**theocrat** *n*.—**theocratic** *adj*.

theodolite *n* a surveying instrument for measuring angles.

theol. *abbr* = theologian; theological; theology.

theologian *n* a person who studies and interprets religious texts, etc; a teacher of theology.

theology *n* (*pl* **theologies**) the study of God and of religious doctrine and matters of divinity.—**theological, theologic** *adj*.—**theologically** *adv*.

theorem *n* a proposition that can be proved from accepted principles; law or principle.

theoretical, theoretic *adj* of or based on theory, not practical application; hypothetical; conjectural.—**theoretically** *adv*.

theoretician *n* a person who concentrates on the theoretical basis of a subject.

theoretics *npl* the speculative parts of a science.

theorize *vi* to form theories; to speculate.—**theorist, theorizer** *n*.—**theorization** *n*.

theory *n* (*pl* **theories**) an explanation or system of anything; ideas and abstract principles of a science or art; speculation; a hypothesis.

therapeutic, therapeutical *adj* relating to the treatment of disease; beneficial.—**therapeutically** *adv*.

therapeutics *npl* the curative branch of medicine.

therapy *n* (*pl* **therapies**) the treatment of physical or mental illness.—**therapist** *n*.

there *adv* in, at or to, that place or point; in that respect; in that matter.

thereabout, thereabouts *adv* at or near that place or number.

thereafter *adv* after that; according to that.

thereagainst *adv* in opposition to; contrary to.

thereat *adv* at that place; at such time.

thereby *adv* by that means.

therefore *adv* for that or this reason; consequently.

therein *adv* in that place or respect.

thereof *adv* of this or that; because of that.

thereon *adv* on that or it; immediately following that.

thereupon *adv* immediately after that.

therm *n* a measurement of heat.

thermal, thermic *adj* generating heat; hot; warm; (*underwear*) of a knitted material with air spaces for insulation. * *n* a rising current of warm air.

thermion *n* an electron emitted by a material at high temperature.

thermionic *adj* of, pertaining to, or worked by thermions, esp a tube.

thermistor *n* a semiconductor device whose resistance varies inversely with a change in temperature.

thermo-, therm- *prefix* heat.

thermocouple *n* a device which generates a thermoelectric effect between two dissimilar semiconductors, used in measuring temperature differences.

thermodynamics *n sing* the branch of physics concerned with the relationship between heat and other forms of energy.

thermoelectric, thermoelectrical *adj* of or derived from electricity generated by difference of temperature.—**thermoelectricity** *n*.

thermometer *n* an instrument for measuring temperature.

thermonuclear *adj* of or relating to nuclear fusion or nuclear weapons that utilize fusion reactions.

thermoplastic *adj* becoming soft and malleable when heated. * *n* a resin or synthetic plastic that can be heated, moulded and cooled without appreciable change of its properties.

Thermos *n* (*trademark*) a brand of vacuum bottle.

thermostat *n* an automatic device for regulating temperatures.

thesaurus *n* (*pl* **thesauri, thesauruses**) a reference book of synonyms and antonyms.

these *see* **this**.

thesis *n* (*pl* **theses**) a dissertation written as part of an academic degree; a theory expressed as a statement for discussion.

thespian *adj* of or pertaining to drama. * *n* an actor or actress.

theta *n* the eighth letter of the Greek alphabet.

they *pers pron, pl of* **he, she** *or* **it**.

they'd = they would; they had.

they'll = they will; they shall.

they're = they are.

they've = they have.

thiamine, thiamin *n* vitamin B, present in a wide variety of plants and animals and essential for normal metabolism and nerve function.

thick *adj* dense; viscous; fat, broad; abundant, closely set; in quick succession; crowded; (*inf*) stupid. * *adv* closely; frequently.

thicken *vti* to make or become thick.—**thickener** *n*.

thicket *n* a small group of trees or shrubs growing thickly and closely together.

thickhead *n* (*inf*) an ignorant person, an idiot.—**thickheaded** *adj*.

thickness *n* being thick; the dimension other than length or width; a layer.

thickset *adj* having a short, stocky body.

thick-skinned *adj* not sensitive; not easily offended.

thick-witted *adj* stupid.

thief *n* (*pl* **thieves**) a person who steals.

thieve *vti* to steal.

thigh *n* the thick fleshy part of the leg from the hip to the knee.

thighbone *n* the femur.

thimble *n* a cap or cover worn to protect the finger when sewing.

thimbleful *n* what a thimble contains, a tiny amount.

thin *adj* (**thinner, thinnest**) narrow; slim; lean; sparse, weak, watery; (*material*) fine; not dense. * *vt* to make thin; to make less crowded; to water down.—**thinly** *adv*.—**thinness** *n*.

thine *pron* an old-fashioned word for **yours**.

thing *n* an inanimate object; an event; an action; (*pl*) possessions; (*inf*) an obsession.

thingamabob, thingumabob *n* (*inf*) something or someone the name of which has been forgotten, is unknown or is hard to categorize, etc.—*also* **thingamajig, thingumajig, thingummy, thingie**.

think *vb* (**thinking, thought**) *vi* to exercise the mind in order to make a decision; to revolve ideas in the mind, to ponder; to remember; to consider; * *vt* to judge, to believe or consider; (*with* **up**) to concoct, devise; (*with* **over**) to ponder, to consider the costs and benefits of.—**thinker** *n*.

thinking *adj* capable of using thought, rational; intelligent. * *n* the process of using thought; opinion, reasoning.

think-tank *n* (*inf*) a group of experts convened to analyse and advise on ways of handling a particular problem.

thinner *n* a substance, such as turpentine, added to paint, varnish, etc, to thin it.

thin-skinned *adj* overly sensitive to criticism; easily offended.

third *adj* the last of three; being one of three equal parts. * *n* one of three equal parts.

third class *n* a class of mail in the US and Canadian postal systems that includes all printed matter, except periodicals, weighing below a certain amount and unsealed; the cheapest accommodation on a ship, aircraft, etc.—**third-class** *adj*, *adv*.

third degree *n* the use of torture, bullying or rough questioning to obtain information.

third-degree burn *n* a severe burn which destroys surface and underlying tissue and may involve loss of fluid and shock.

thirdly *adv* in the third place; as a third point.

third person *n* grammatical forms, such as pronouns and verbs, used when referring to the person or thing spoken or written of, not to the person speaking or writing or to the person or persons addressed.

third-rate *adj* inferior.

Third World *n* the underdeveloped countries of the world (usu refers to Africa, Asia and South America).

thirst *n* a craving for drink; a longing. * *vi* to feel thirst; to have a longing.

thirsty *adj* (**thirstier, thirstiest**) having a desire to drink; dry, arid; longing or craving for.—**thirstily** *adv*.—**thirstiness** *n*.

thirteen *adj*, *n* three and ten.—**thirteenth** *adj*, *n*.

thirty *adj*, *n* (*pl* **thirties**) three times ten.—**thirtieth** *adj*, *n*.

thirty-second note *n* (*mus*) a note with a time value of one thirty-secondth of a whole note, a demisemiquaver.

this *demons pron* (*pl* **these**) *or adj* denoting a person or thing near, just mentioned, or about to be mentioned.

thistle *n* a wild plant with prickly leaves and a purple flower.

thistledown *n* the feathery cluster of seeds produced by the thistle.

thither *adv* (*arch*) to or toward that place.

tho, tho' *conj*, *adv* (*inf*) though.

thong *n* a piece or strap of leather to lash things together; the lash of a whip; a sandal held on the foot by a thong passing between the toes and fixed to a strap passing over the top of the foot.

Thor *n* (*Norse myth*) the god of thunder.

thorax *n* (*pl* **thoraxes, thoraces**) the part of the body enclosed by the ribs; the chest; (*in insects*) the middle one of the three chief divisions of the body.—**thoracic** *adj*.

thorium *n* a radioactive metallic element used in industry and as a nuclear fuel.

thorn *n* a shrub or small tree having thorns, esp hawthorn; a sharp point or prickle on the stem of a plant or the branch of a tree.

thorny *adj* (**thornier, thorniest**) prickly; (*problem*) knotty.

thoron *n* a gas that is a radioactive isotope of radon.

thorough *adj* complete, very detailed and painstaking, exhaustive.—**thoroughness** *n*.

thoroughbred *adj* bred from pure stock. * *n* a pedigree animal, esp a horse.

thoroughfare *n* a way through; a public highway, road; right of passing through.

thoroughgoing *adj* very thorough; out-and-out.

thoroughly *adv* completely, fully; entirely, absolutely.

those *adj*, *pron* plural of **that**.

thou[1] *pron* an old-fashioned word for **you**.

thou[2] *n* (*pl* **thous, thou**) (*inf*) a thousand; a thousandth of an inch.

though *conj* yet, even if; * *adv* however; nevertheless.

thought *n* the act of thinking; reasoning; serious consideration; an idea; opinions collectively; design, intention. * *pt*, *pp* of **think**.

thoughtful *adj* pensive; considerate.

thoughtless *adj* without thought; inconsiderate.

thousand *adj* ten times one hundred; (*pl*) denoting any large but unspecified number. * *n* the number 1000.—**thousandth** *adj*, *n*.

thrash *vt* to beat soundly; to defeat; (*with* **out**) to discuss thoroughly, until agreement is reached. * *vi* to thresh grain; to writhe.

thrashing *n* a beating or flogging; punishment.

thread *n* a fine strand or filament; a long thin piece of cotton, silk or nylon for sewing; the spiral part of a screw; (*of reasoning*) a line. * *vt* to pass a thread through the eye of a needle; to make one's way (through).

threadbare *adj* worn, shabby.

threadworm *n* a long slender worm, parasitic in humans and pigs.

threat *n* a declaration of an intention to inflict harm or punishment upon another.

threaten *vti* to utter threats to; to portend.

threatening *adj* menacing, intimidating; warning; ominous, sinister.—**threateningly** *adv*.

three *adj*, *n* the cardinal number next above two. * *n* the symbol (3, III, iii) expressing this.

three-D, 3-D *n* a three-dimensional effect.

three-dimensional *adj* having three dimensions.

threefold *adj*, *adv* three times as much or as many; composed of three parts.

three-quarter *adj* being three quarters of the normal size or length. * *n* (*Rugby football*) one of usu four attacking players used particularly for running with the ball.

three Rs *npl* reading, writing and arithmetic, regarded as the basis of learning.

threescore *n* (*arch*) sixty.—*also adj*.

threesome *n* a group of three; a game for three people.

threnody, threnode *n* (*pl* **threnodies, threnodes**) a song or speech of lamentation, esp on a person's death.

thresh *vti* to beat out (grain) from (husks).

threshold *n* the sill at the door of a building; doorway, entrance; the starting point, beginning.

threw *see* **throw**.

thrice *adv* three times.

thrift *n* careful management of money.—**thrifty** *adj*.

thrift shop *n* a shop that sells used clothing and other items to raise money for charity.

thrill *vti* to tingle with pleasure or excitement. * *n* a sensation of pleasure and excitement; a trembling or quiver.

thriller *n* a novel, film or play depicting an exciting story of mystery and suspense.

thrilling *adj* exciting, gripping.

thrips *n* (*pl* **thrips**) any of various small insects with sucking mouthparts that feed on and damage plants.

thrive *vi* (**thriving, thrived** *or* **throve**, *pp* **thrived** *or* **thriven**) to prosper, to be successful; to grow vigorously.—**thriving** *adj*.

thro', thro *prep, adv* (*inf*) through.

throat *n* the front part of the neck; the passage from the back of the mouth to the top part of the tubes into the lungs and stomach; an entrance.

throaty *adj* (**throatier, throatiest**) hoarse; guttural; deep, husky.—**throatily** *adv*.

throb *vi* (**throbbing, throbbed**) to beat or pulsate rhythmically, with more than usual force; to vibrate, beat.—*also n*.

throes *npl* violent pangs or pain.

thrombin *n* an enzyme that contributes to blood clotting.

thrombocyte *n* a blood platelet.

thrombosis *n* (*pl* **thromboses**) the forming of a blood clot in the heart or in a blood-vessel.

thrombus *n* (*pl* **thrombi**) the blood clot that blocks a vessel in thrombosis.

throne *n* a chair of state occupied by a monarch; sovereign power. * *vt* to place on a throne.

throng *n* a crowd. * *vti* to crowd, congregate.

throstle *n* any of various Old World thrushes.

throttle *n* a valve controlling the flow of fuel or steam to an engine. * *vt* to regulate the speed of (an engine) using a throttle; to choke or strangle.

through *prep* from one side or end to the other; into and then out of; covering all parts; from beginning to end of; by means of; in consequence of; up to and including. * *adv* from one end or side to the other; completely. * *adj* going without interruption; unobstructed.

throughout *prep* in every part of; from beginning to end. * *adv* everywhere; at every moment.

throughput *n* the amount of material processed in a particular period, esp by a computer.

throughway *see* **thruway**.

throve *see* **thrive**.

throw *vb* (**throwing, threw**, *pp* **thrown**) *vt* to hurl, to fling; to cast off; (*party*) to hold; (*inf*) to confuse or disconcert; (*with* **off**) to cast off, discard, abandon; to distract, elude; to produce in a casual manner; to confuse, disconcert; (*with* **out**) to discard, reject; to dismiss or eject, esp forcibly; to emit, give forth; to construct out from a main section; to confuse, distract; (*with* **over**) to abandon, jilt; (*with* **together**) to assemble hurriedly or carelessly; to bring (people) into casual contact; (*with* **up**) to raise quickly; to resign from, abandon; to build hurriedly; to produce; (*inf*) to vomit. * *vi* to cast or hurl through the air (with the arm and wrist); to cast dice; (*with* **up**) (*inf*) to vomit. * *n* the act of throwing; the distance to which anything can be thrown; a cast of dice.

throwaway *adj* disposable.

throwback *n* a reversion to an earlier or more primitive type.

throw-in *n* (*soccer*) a throw from touch to resume play.

thrown *see* **throw**.

thru *prep* (*sl*) through.

thrum *vi* (**thrumming, thrummed**) to strum; to beat incessantly.

thrush[1] *n* a songbird with a brown back and spotted breast.

thrush[2] *n* a fungal disease occurring in the mouths of babies or in women's vaginas.

thrust *vti* (**thrusting, thrust**) to push with force; to stab, pierce; to force into a situation. * *n* a forceful push or stab; pressure; the driving force of a propeller; forward movement; the point or basic meaning.

thruway *n* an expressway.—*also* **throughway**.

thud *n* a dull, heavy sound, caused by a blow or a heavy object falling. * *vi* (**thudding, thudded**) to make such a sound.

thug *n* a violent and rough person, esp a criminal.

thuggery *n* rough and violent behaviour.

thulium *n* a malleable metallic element of the rare-earth group.

thumb *n* the first, short, thick finger of the human hand. * *vt* (*book*) to turn (the pages) idly.

thumbed *adj* worn by use.

thumb index *n* a series of semicircular notches cut in the edge of a book for easier reference to particular parts.

thumbnail *n* the nail of the thumb. * *adj* concise.

thumbnut *n* a wing nut.

thumbscrew *n* an instrument of torture that crushes the thumbs; a screw with a modified head for tightening with the finger and thumb.

thumbtack *n* a flat-headed pin used for fastening paper, drawings, etc, a drawing pin.

thump *n* a heavy blow; a thud. * *vt* to strike with something heavy. * *vi* to throb or beat violently.

thumping *adj* (*inf*) very great.

thunder *n* the deep rumbling or loud cracking sound after a flash of lightning; any similar sound. * *vi* to sound as thunder. * *vt* (*words*) to utter loudly.

thunderbolt *n* a flash of lightning accompanied by thunder; anything sudden and shocking.

thunderclap *n* a loud bang of thunder.

thundering *adj* (*inf*) unusually great, excessive.

thunderous *adj* very loud; producing thunder.

thunderstorm *n* a storm with thunder and lightning.

thunderstruck *adj* astonished.

thundery *adj* indicating thunder.

Thur., Thurs. *abbr* = Thursday.

thurible *n* a censer.

Thursday *n* the fifth day of the week.

thus *adv* in this or that way; to this degree or extent; so; therefore.

thwack *vti* to hit hard, whack. * *n* a heavy blow, whack; the sound of this.

thwart *vt* to prevent, to frustrate.

thy *poss adj* an old-fashioned word for **your**.

thyme *n* a herb with small leaves used for flavouring savoury food.

thymol *n* a substance obtained from thyme and used as a fungicide and antiseptic.

thymus *n* (*pl* **thymuses, thymi**) a gland near the base of the neck that shrivels after puberty.

thyristor *n* any of various semiconductor devices that act as switches or rectifiers.

thyroid *n* the gland in the neck affecting growth and metabolism.

thyrotropin, thyrotrophin *n* a hormone secreted by the pituitary gland that stimulates the thyroid gland.

thyroxin, thyroxine *n* the main hormone produced by the thyroid gland.

TI (*chem symbol*) thallium.

Ti (*chem symbol*) titanium.

ti *n* the seventh note of the scale in solmization.

tiara *n* a semicircular crown decorated with jewels.

tibia *n* (*pl* **tibiae, tibias**) the inner and thicker of the two bones between the knee and the ankle; the shinbone.

tic *n* any involuntary, regularly repeated, spasmodic contraction of a muscle.

tick[1] *n* a small bloodsucking insect that lives on people and animals.

tick[2] *vi* to make a regular series of short sounds; to beat, as a clock; (*inf*) to work, function; (*with* **over**) (*engine*) to idle; to function routinely. * *n* the sound of a clock; (*sl*) a moment.

tick[3] *vt* (*often with* **off**) to check off, as items in a list. * *n* a check mark (√) to check off items on a list or to indicate correctness.

ticker *n* a telegraphic device that receives and outputs stock-market prices on a paper tape; any similar device operated electronically and outputting to a display monitor; (*inf*) the heart; (*inf*) a watch.

ticker tape *n* a continuous length of paper tape output from a telegraphic ticker.

ticket *n* a printed card, etc, that gives one a right of travel or entry; a label on merchandise giving size, price, etc.

tickle *vt* to touch lightly to provoke pleasure or laughter; to please or delight.

ticklish, tickly *adj* sensitive to being tickled; easily offended; difficult or delicate.

tick-tack-toe *n sing* a game in which two players place noughts and crosses into squares on a grid with nine spaces, the winner being the first to form a row of three noughts or crosses, noughts and crosses.

ticktock *n* a ticking sound, esp of a clock. * *vi* to make such a sound.

tidal *adj* relating to, or having, tides.

tidal wave *n* a large wave as a result of high winds with spring tides; a huge destructive wave caused by earthquakes; something overwhelming.

tidbit *see* **titbit**.

tiddly *adj* (**tiddlier, tiddliest**) (*inf*) very small; (*inf*) slightly drunk.

tiddlywinks, tiddledywinks *npl* a game whose object is to flick small plastic discs into a container by snapping them with a larger disc.

tide *n* the regular rise and fall of the seas, oceans, etc usu twice a day; a current of water; a tendency; a flood. * *vt* (*with* **over**) to help along temporarily.

tidemark *n* the highest or lowest point reached by the sea.

tide rip *n* a rip current.

tidewater *n* water overflowing land at flood tide; water that is affected by the tide.

tidings *npl* news, information.

tidy *adj* (**tidier, tidiest**) neat; orderly. * *vt* to make neat; to put things in order.—**tidily** *adv*.—**tidiness** *n*.

tie *vb* (**tying, tied**) *vt* to bind; to fasten with a string or thread; to make a bow or knot in; to restrict; (*with* **in**) to link with something; (*with* **up**) to fasten tightly (as if) with cord, string, etc; to connect, link; to invest

money, etc, so as to make it unavailable for alternative uses; to preoccupy, distract. * *vi* to score the same number of points (as an opponent); (*with* **in**) to be linked in a certain way; (*with* **up**) to dock (a vessel). * *n* a knot, bow, etc; a bond; a long narrow piece of cloth worn with a shirt; necktie; an equality in score.

tiebreaker, tiebreak *n* any means of deciding a contest which has ended in a draw, such as an extra game, hole, question, etc.

tie-dyeing, tie-dye *n* a method of producing patterns on textiles by tying or knotting parts of the fabric to limit the amount of dye absorbed.

tie-in *n* a link or connection; a book linked to a film or TV series.

tie line *n* a telephone link between two private branch exchanges.

tiepin *n* a decorative pin used to secure the ends of a tie to a shirt.

tier *n* a row or rank in a series when several rows are placed one above another.

tiercel *n* a male of various hawks, esp as used in falconry.—*also* **tercel**.

tie-up *n* a link, connection; a standstill.

tiff *n* a petty quarrel or disagreement. * *vi* to quarrel; to be in a huff.

tiger *n* a large, fierce carnivorous animal of the cat family, having orange and black stripes.—**tigress** *nf*.

tiger beetle *n* any of numerous predatory beetles with powerful mandibles and spotted wing cases.

tiger cat *n* an ocelot or similar medium-sized wildcat with a striped coat.

tiger lily *n* a lily of China and Japan cultivated for its dark-spotted orange flowers.

tiger moth *n* any of various large moths marked with stripes or spots.

tiger's eye, tigereye *n* a brownish-yellow gemstone.

tiger shark *n* a large shark of warm waters with a striped or spotted skin.

tiger snake *n* an aggressive poisonous Australian snake with striped markings.

tight *adj* taut; fitting closely; not leaky; constricted; miserly; difficult; providing little space or time for variance; (*contest*) close; (*inf*) drunk.

tighten *vti* to make or grow tight or tighter.

tightfisted *adj* miserly.

tightknit *adj* tightly integrated.

tight-lipped *adj* having the lips firmly pressed together, as from annoyance; taciturn.

tightrope *n* a taut rope on which acrobats walk.

tights *npl* a one-piece garment covering the legs and lower body; panty hose.

tigon, tiglon *n* the hybrid offspring of a tiger and a lioness.

tike *see* **tyke**.

tilde *n* a sign ~ placed above a letter to indicate a nasal sound, as in Spanish *señor*.

tile *n* a thin slab of baked clay used for covering roofs, floors, etc. * *vt* to cover with tiles.

till[1] *n* a drawer inside a cash register for keeping money.

till[2] *prep* until. * *conj* until.

till[3] *vt* (*land*) to cultivate for raising crops, as by ploughing.

tiller *n* the handle or lever for turning a rudder in order to steer a boat.

tilt *vi* to slope, incline, slant. * *vt* to raise one end of. * *n* a slope or angle.

timbale *n* a mixture of meat or fish with cream cooked in a mould lined with vegetables or pastry.

timber *n* wood when used as building material; a beam; trees collectively. * *vt* to provide with timber or beams.

timbered *adj* (*building*) having wooden beams on the exterior.

timber hitch *n* a knot used to tie a rope, etc to a log or spar.

timber line *see* **tree line**.

timber wolf *n* a type of large grey North American wolf.

timbre *n* the quality of sound of a voice or musical instrument.

time *n* the past, present and future; a particular moment; hour of the day; an opportunity; the right moment; duration; occasion; musical beat. * *vt* to regulate as to time; to measure or record the duration of.

time and motion study *n* the study of working procedures to improve efficiency.

time bomb *n* a bomb designed to explode at a predetermined time; something with a potentially delayed reaction.

time clock *n* a device that records the times of arrival and departure of an employee on a card.

time-consuming *adj* using up or taking a lot of time.

time exposure *n* exposure of a photographic film for usu several seconds; a photograph taken in this way.

time-honoured *adj* traditional, in accordance with venerable customs.

time immemorial *n* the far distant past beyond memory or record.

timekeeper *n* a person or instrument that records or keeps time; an employee who records the hours worked by others.—**timekeeping** *n*.

time lag *n* the interval between two connected events.

time-lapse photography *n* a technique of filming very slow action, such as plant growth, by taking single frames at fixed intervals and then running them at normal speed.

timeless *adj* eternal; ageless.

timely *adj* at the right time, opportune.—**timeliness** *n*.

time-out *n* (*sport*) a suspension of play to rest, discuss tactics, etc; a brief rest period.

timepiece *n* a clock or watch.

timer *n* a device for measuring, recording or controlling time; a device for controlling lights, heating, etc by setting an electrical clock to regulate their operations.

timeserver *n* a person whose opinions, behaviour, etc, follow current fashions.—**timeserving** *adj, n*.

timeshare *n* joint ownership of holiday accommodation by several people with each occupying the same premises in turn for short periods.

time signature *n* a sign on a musical staff indicating the number of beats per bar and time value of each beat.

timetable *n* a list of times of arrivals and departures of trains, aeroplanes, etc; a schedule showing a planned order or sequence.

timeworn *adj* dilapidated; old-fashioned, hackneyed.

time zone *n* a geographical region throughout which the same standard time is used.

timid *adj* shy; lacking confidence.—**timidity** *n*.—**timidly** *adv*.

timing *n* the control and expression of speech or actions to create the best effect, esp in the theatre, etc.

timocracy *n* (*pl* **timocracies**) a form of government in which ownership of property is required to hold office.

timorous *adj* timid, fearful.—**timorously** *adv*.—**timorousness** *n*.

timpani *npl* a set of kettledrums.—**timpanist** *n*.—*also* **tympani, tympany**.

tin *n* a malleable metallic element; a container of tin, a can. * *adj* made of tin or tin plate. * *vt* (**tinning, tinned**) to put food into a tin.

tinctorial *adj* pertaining to colouring, dyeing or staining.

tincture *n* an extract of a substance in a solution of alcohol for medicinal use; a colour, hue, tint; a hint of flavour or aroma; an heraldic colour. * *vt* to tint with a colour.

tinder *n* dry wood for lighting a fire from a spark.

tinderbox *n* a metal box with tinder, flint and steel for making a spark; an unstable or potentially explosive person, thing or situation.

tine *n* a slender projecting point, as the prong of a fork or point of an antler.

tinea *n* a fungal skin condition, esp ringworm.

tinfoil *n* baking foil for wrapping food; silver paper.

ting *n* a high sharp ringing sound. * *vi* to make this sound.

tinge *vt* to tint or colour. * *n* a slight tint, colour or flavour.

tingle *vi* to feel a prickling, itching or stinging sensation. * *n* a prickling sensation; a thrill.—**tinglingly** *adv*.—**tingly** *adj*.

tin god *n* a self-important person; a person who is undeservedly venerated.

tinker *n* (*formerly*) a travelling mender of pots and pans. * *vi* to fiddle with; to attempt to repair.

tinkle *vi* to make a sound like a small bell ringing; to clink, to jingle; to clink repeatedly. * *n* a tinkling sound; (*inf*) a telephone call.

tinnitus *n* a continuous ringing or roaring sound in the ears caused by an infection, etc.

tinny *adj* (**tinnier, tinniest**) of or resembling tin; flimsy in construction or appearance; (*food*) having a metallic taste; having a high metallic sound.

tin plate *n* thin sheets of iron or steel plated with tin.—**tin-plate** *adj*.

tinsel *n* a shiny Christmas decoration made of long pieces of thread wound round with thin strips of metal or plastic foil; something showy but of low value. * *adj* cheaply showy, flashy. * *vt* (**tinselling, tinselled** *or* **tinseling, tinseled**) to adorn with tinsel.

Tinseltown *n* (*inf*) Hollywood.

tint *n* a shade of any colour, esp a pale one; a tinge; a hair dye. * *vt* to colour or tinge.

tintinnabulation *n* (the sound of) a ringing of bells.

tiny *adj* (**tinier, tiniest**) very small.

tip[1] *n* the pointed end of anything; the end, as of a billiard cue, etc. * *vt* (**tipping, tipped**) to put a tip on.

tip[2] *vti* (**tipping, tipped**) to tilt or cause to tilt; to overturn; to empty (out, into, etc); to give a gratuity to, as a waiter, etc; (*rubbish*) to dump; to give a helpful hint or inside information to. * *n* a light tap; a gratuity; a rubbish dump; an inside piece of information; a helpful hint.

tip-off *n* a warning based on inside information.

tipple *vi* to drink alcohol regularly in small quantities. * *n* an alcoholic drink.

tipster *n* a person who gives horse-racing tips.

tipsy *adj* (**tipsier, tipsiest**) slightly drunk.

tiptoe *vi* (**tiptoeing, tiptoed**) to walk very quietly or carefully.

tiptop *adj* excellent. * *adv* at the peak of condition. * *n* the best; the highest point.

tirade *n* a long angry speech of censure or criticism.

tire[1] *vt* to exhaust the strength of, to weary. * *vi* to become weary; to lose patience; to become bored.

tire[2] *see* **tyre**.

tired *adj* weary, sleepy; hackneyed, conventional, flat; (*with* of) exasperated by, bored with.

tireless *adj* never wearying.—**tirelessly** *adv*.—**tirelessness** *n*.

tiresome *adj* tedious.

tiro *see* **tyro**.

'tis (*poet*) = it is.

tissue *n* thin, absorbent paper used as a disposable handkerchief, etc; a very finely woven fabric; a mass of organic cells of a similar structure and function.

tit[1] *n* a songbird such as a blue tit or great tit.

tit[2] *n* (*vulg*) a woman's breast.

titan *n* a person of enormous strength, size or ability.

titanic *adj* monumental; huge.

titanium *n* a strong metallic element used to make lightweight alloys.

titanium dioxide *n* a white powder used chiefly as a pigment.

titbit *n* a tasty morsel of food; a choice item of information.—*also* **tidbit**.

titer *see* **titre**.

tit for tat *n* an equivalent given in retaliation.

tithe *n* a tenth part of agricultural produce, formerly allotted for the maintenance of the clergy and other church purposes. * *vti* to pay a tithe.

titillate *vt* to tickle; to arouse or excite pleasurably.

titillation *n* the act of titillating; the condition of being titillated; a pleasurable feeling, esp sexual.

titivate, tittivate *vti* to smarten up.

title *n* the name of a book, play, piece of music, work of art, etc; the heading of a section of a book; a name denoting nobility or rank or office held, or attached to a personal name; (*law*) that which gives a legal right (to possession).

titled *adj* having a title.

title deed *n* a deed or document proving a title or right to possession.

title page *n* the page of a book containing its title and usually the author's and publisher's names.

title role *n* the character in a play, film, etc after whom it is named.

titrate *vt* to measure by titration.

titration *n* a method of determining the amount of a constituent in a solution by adding a known quantity of a reagent.

titre *n* the concentration of a substance in a solution as determined by titration.

titter *vi* to giggle, snigger. * *n* a suppressed laugh.

tittle-tattle *n* idle chat, empty gossip.

titular *adj* having, or relating to, a title; existing in name or title only.

tizzy *n* (*inf*) a state of confusion or agitation.

TKO *abbr* = technical knockout.

TLC *abbr* = tender loving care.

T-lymphocyte *see* **T-cell**.

TM *abbr* = trademark; transcendental meditation.

Tm (*chem symbol*) thulium.

TN *abbr* = Tennessee.

TNT *abbr* = trinitrotoluene.

to *prep* in the direction of; toward; as far as; expressing the purpose of an action; indicating the infinitive; introducing the indirect object; in comparison with. * *adv* toward.

toad *n* an amphibious reptile, like a frog, but having a drier skin and spending less time in water.

toadflax *n* a common perennial plant with yellow and orange flowers.

toadstool *n* a mushroom, esp a poisonous or inedible one.

toady *n* (*pl* **toadies**) a person who flatters insincerely, a sycophant. * *vi* (**toadying, toadied**) (*with* to) to act in a servile manner.

to and fro *adj* forward and backward; here and there.— **toing and froing** *n*.

toast *vt* to brown over a fire or in a toaster; to warm; to drink to the health of. * *n* toasted bread; the sentiment or person to which one drinks.

toaster *n* a person who toasts; a thing that toasts, esp an electrical appliance for toasting.

toastmaster *n* the proposer of toasts at public dinners.—**toastmistress** *nf*.

tobacco *n* (*pl* **tobaccos, tobaccoes**) a plant whose dried leaves are used for smoking, chewing or snuff.

tobacconist *n* a person or shop that sells cigarettes, etc.

toboggan *n* a sledge, sled.

toby (jug) *n* (*pl* **tobies, toby jugs**) a mug in the shape of a man with a three-cornered hat.

toccata *n* a piece of music for keyboard in a free style with rapid runs.

tocopherol *n* vitamin E, present in wheat-germ oil, egg yolk, etc.

tocsin *n* an alarm bell; a warning signal.

today *n* this day; the present age. * *adv* on this day; nowadays.

toddle *vi* to walk with short, unsteady, steps, as a child who is learning to walk.

toddler *n* a young child.

toddy *n* (*pl* **toddies**) a drink of whisky or brandy, sugar, and hot water.

to-do *n* (*pl* **to-dos**) (*inf*) a fuss, commotion, quarrel.

toe *n* one of the five digits on the foot; the part of the shoe or sock that covers the toes.

toe cap *n* a reinforced covering on the toe of a shoe or boot.

toehold *n* a small ledge, crack, etc used in climbing; any slight means of support or access; (*wrestling*) a hold in which an opponent's foot is twisted.

toenail *n* the thin, hard covering on the end of the toes.

toffee, toffy *n* (*pl* **toffees, toffies**) a sweet of brittle but tender texture made by boiling sugar and butter together.

toffee apple *n* an apple coated with toffee and eaten from a stick.

toffee-nosed *adj* (*inf*) pretentious, patronizing, arrogant.

tofu *n* unfermented soya bean curd, used in cooking.

tog[1] *n* (*pl*) (*inf*) clothes. * *vt* (**togging, togged**) (*inf*) to dress.

tog[2] *n* in UK, an official measurement of the warmth of a quilt, etc.

toga *n* a piece of cloth draped around the body, as worn by citizens in ancient Rome.

together *adv* in one place or group; in cooperation with; in unison; jointly.

toggle *n* a peg attached to a rope to prevent it from passing through a loop or knot; a button of this form; (*comput*) a software instruction for starting or stopping a style, etc. * *vt* to fasten with a toggle.

toggle switch n an electrical device for opening or closing a circuit.

toil vi to work strenuously; to move with great effort. * n hard work.

toilet n a lavatory; the room containing a lavatory; the act of washing and dressing oneself.

toilet paper, toilet tissue n an absorbent paper for cleansing after urination, etc, usu wound around a cardboard cylinder.

toiletry n (pl **toiletries**) a lotion, perfume, etc used in washing and dressing oneself.

toilet water n a diluted perfume.

token n a symbol, sign; an indication; a metal disc for a slot machine; a souvenir; a gift voucher. * adj nominal; symbolic.

tokenism n the making of only a token effort.

tolbooth n (Scot) a town hall; a jail.

told see **tell**.

tolerable adj bearable; fairly good.—**tolerably** adv.

tolerance n open-mindedness; forbearance; (med) ability to resist the action of a drug, etc; ability of a substance to endure heat, stress, etc without damage.

tolerant adj able to put up with the beliefs, actions, etc of others; broad-minded; showing tolerance to a drug, etc; capable of enduring stress, etc.

tolerate vt to endure, put up with, suffer.

toll[1] n money levied for passing over a bridge or road; a charge for a service, such as a long-distance telephone call; the number of people killed in an accident or disaster.

toll[2] vt (bell) to ring slowly and repeatedly, as a funeral bell. * vi to sound, as a bell. * n the sound of a bell when tolling.

tollbooth n a booth where money is paid to pass over a bridge, road, etc.—also **tolbooth**.

toll call n a telephone call charged at higher than the standard or local rate.

tollgate n a gate where money is paid to pass over a bridge, road, etc.

toluene n a flammable hydrocarbon derived from petroleum and coal tar used as a solvent and in organic synthesis.

tom n a male animal, esp a cat.

tomahawk n a light axe used by North American Indians.

tomato n (pl **tomatoes**) a plant with red pulpy fruit used as a vegetable.

tomb n a vault in the earth for the burial of the dead.

tomboy n a girl who likes rough outdoor activities.

tombstone n a memorial stone over a grave.

tomcat n a male cat.

Tom, Dick and Harry n an ordinary person, anybody taken at random.

tome n a large, heavy book, esp a scholarly one.

-tome n suffix a cutting instrument.

tomfool n a fool.

tomfoolery n (pl **tomfooleries**) foolish behaviour; nonsense.

Tommy n (pl **Tommies**) (inf) a private in the British army.

tommy gun n a (Thompson) sub-machine gun.

tommyrot n complete nonsense.

tomography n a process which produces an x-ray photograph of a plane section of the body or other object.

tomorrow n the day after today; the future.—also adv.

tomtit n any of various small tits, esp a blue tit.

tom-tom n a long small-headed drum usually beaten with the hands.

-tomy n suffix surgical incision.

ton n a unit of weight equivalent to 2,000 pounds in US or 2,240 pounds in UK; (pl) (inf) a great quantity.

tonal n of or pertaining to tone; having a key.

tonality n (pl **tonalities**) the character of a musical composition in relation to scale or key; a system of tones; the scheme of colours and tones in a painting.

tone n the quality of a sound; pitch or inflection of the voice; colour, shade; body condition. * vti to give tone to; to harmonize (with); (with **down**) to (become) moderate in tone; (with **up**) to make or become healthier, tighter, etc.

tone arm n the tracking arm in a record player that holds the cartridge and stylus.

tone-deaf adj insensitive to differences in musical pitch.

tone poem n a symphonic poem.

toner n a cosmetic used on the skin for various effects; a chemical used to alter the tone of a photograph; the ink particles used in various reprographic devices such as laser printers and photocopiers.

tong n a Chinese-American secret society.

tongs npl an instrument consisting of two arms that are hinged, used for grasping and lifting.

tongue n the soft, moveable organ in the mouth, used in tasting, swallowing, and speech; the ability to speak; a language; (shoe) a piece of leather under the laces; a jet of flame; the tongue of an animal served as food; the catch of a buckle.

tongue-lash vt to scold, rebuke severely.—**tongue lashing** n.

tongue-tied adj speechless.

tongue-twister n a sequence of words that it is difficult to pronounce quickly and clearly.

tonic n a medicine that improves physical well-being; something that imparts vigour; a carbonated mineral water with a bitter taste. * adj relating to tones or sounds.

tonic sol-fa n the system of sol-fa or solmization syllables used to represent the notes of the musical scale.

tonight n this night; the night or evening of the present day.—also adv.

tonnage n a merchant ship's capacity measured in tons; the weight of its cargo; the amount of shipping of a country or port; merchant ships collectively; a duty levied on ships based on tonnage or capacity.

tonne n metric ton, 1,000 kg.

tonometer n a device, such as a tuning fork, for measuring the pitch of tones.

tonsil n one of the two oval organs of soft tissue situated one on each side of the throat.

tonsillectomy n (pl **tonsillectomies**) a surgical operation to remove the tonsils.

tonsillitis n inflammation of the tonsils.

tonsure n shaving part of the head to denote a clerical state in certain churches and religious orders; the shaved area itself. * vt to give a tonsure to (a monk, etc).—**tonsured** adj.

Tony n (pl **Tonys, Tonies**) an annual award for excellence in the theatre.

too adv in addition; also, likewise; extremely; very.

took see **take**.

tool n an implement that is used by hand; a means for achieving any purpose.

tooling n a design or decoration made with a tool, as on leather.

tool-maker n a person who repairs and maintains precision machine tools.

toolroom n an area in a factory, machine shop, etc where tools are kept or repaired.

toot vi to hoot a car horn, whistle, etc in short blasts. * n a hoot.—also vt.

tooth n (pl **teeth**) one of the white, bone-like structures arranged in rows in the mouth, used in biting and chewing; the palate; a tooth-like projection on a comb, saw, or wheel.

toothache n a pain in a tooth.

toothbrush n a small brush for cleaning teeth.

toothed whale n any of various whales with simple teeth, such as dolphins.

toothpaste n a paste for cleaning teeth, used with a toothbrush.

toothpick n a sliver of wood or plastic for removing food particles from between the teeth.

tooth powder n a powder used for cleaning the teeth.

toothsome adj appetizing.

toothy adj (**toothier, toothiest**) having or revealing prominent teeth.

top[1] n the highest, or uppermost, part or surface of anything; the highest in rank; the crown of the head; the lid. * adj highest; greatest. * vt to cover on the top; to remove the top of or from; to rise above; to surpass; (with **up**) to raise up to the full capacity or amount.

top[2] n a child's toy, which is spun on its pointed base.

topaz n any of various yellow gems.

top brass npl (inf) the highest-ranking military or other officials.

topcoat n an overcoat.

top dog n (inf) the leader, the most important person.

top drawer n the most prominent people in society.

tope[1] vi to consume alcoholic drink in excessive quantities.—**toper** n.

tope[2] n a small grey European shark.

topee n a pith helmet.—also **topi**.

top flight adj excellent, of the highest quality.

topgallant n a mast or sail above a topmast.—also adj.

top gear n the highest gear in a motor vehicle; maximum speed or activity.

top hat n a man's tall, silk hat.

top-heavy adj having an upper part too heavy for the lower, causing instability.

topi see **topee**.

topiary adj pertaining to the art or practice of trimming bushes and trees into ornamental shapes. * n (**topiaries**) a tree or bush shaped in this way.

topic n a subject for discussion; the theme of a speech or writing.

topical adj of current interest.

topknot n a tuft of hair or knot of ribbons on the head.

topless adj lacking a top; (garment) revealing the breasts; wearing such a garment.

topmast n a mast next above the lowest mast.

topmost adj nearest the top, highest.

topnotch adj (inf) excellent.

topo-, top- prefix place; locality.

topography n (pl **topographies**) the study or description of surface features of a place on maps or charts.—**topographer** n.—**topographical** adj.

topology n the study of the properties of geometric figures that are unaffected by distortion.—**topological** adj.—**topologist** n.

topping n a top layer, esp a sauce for food.

topple vi to fall over. * vt to cause to overbalance and fall; (government) to overthrow.

topsail n a square sail next above the lowest sail on a mast.

top secret adj highly confidential.

topside n the upper side; a boneless cut of beef; the open or upper decks of a ship. * adv on top.

topsoil n the surface layer of soil.

topspin n a spin imparted to a ball that makes it travel faster or higher.

topsy-turvy adj, adv turned upside down; in confusion.

tor n a high, rocky hill.

Torah n (a scroll containing) the Pentateuch; Jewish sacred writings and teachings collectively.

torch n a flashlight; a device for giving off a hot flame.—**torchlight** n.

torchbearer n a person carrying a torch; a leader, source of inspiration.

torch song n a sentimental song about the sufferings of love —**torch singer** n

tore see **tear**.

toreador n a bullfighter, esp on horseback.

torero n (pl **toreros**) a bullfighter, esp one who fights on foot.

torii n (pl **torii**) a gateway to a Japanese Shinto temple.

torment n torture, anguish; a source of pain. * vt to afflict with extreme pain, physical or mental.—**tormentor, tormenter** n.

torn see **tear**[2].

tornado n (pl **tornadoes, tornados**) a violently whirling column of air seen as a funnel-shaped cloud that usu destroys everything in its narrow path.

toroid n (a solid enclosed by) a surface generated by a circle rotated about a line in the same plane as but not intersecting the circle.—**toroidal** adj.

torpedo n (pl **torpedoes**) a self-propelled submarine offensive weapon, carrying an explosive charge. * vt to attack, hit, or destroy with torpedo(es).

torpedo boat n a small high-speed warship from which torpedoes are launched.

torpid adj lethargic, sluggish.—**torpidity** n.

torpor n a state of lethargy.

torque n (physics) a force that causes rotation around a central point, such as an axle.

torr n (pl **torr**) a unit of pressure equal to 133.322 newtons per square metre.

torrent n a rushing stream; a flood of words.—**torrential** adj.

torrid adj burning, parched or scorched with heat; passionate.—**torridity, torridness** n.

torsi see **torso**.

torsion n a twisting effect on an object when equal forces are applied at both ends but in opposite directions.

torsk n (pl **torsk, torsks**) a large marine food fish related to the cod.

torso n (pl **torsos, torsi**) the trunk of the human body.

tort n (law) a private or civil wrong.

torte n a rich cake or tart filled with cream, fruit, etc.

tortellini n small stuffed pasta shapes.

tortilla n a round thin maize pancake usually eaten hot with a topping or filling.

tortoise n a slow-moving reptile with a dome-shaped shell into which it can withdraw.

tortoiseshell n a brown and yellow colour.

tortricid n any of a family of moths whose larvae live in nests of rolled-up leaves.

tortuous adj full of twists, involved.—**tortuously** adv.

torture n subjection to severe physical or mental pain to extort a confession, or as a punishment. —also vt. —**torturer** n.

torus *n* a convex semicircular moulding, esp at the base of a column; a toroid.—**toric** *adj*.

Tory *n* (*pl* **Tories**) a member of the Conservative Party in UK politics; an American supporter of the British during the American Revolution.—*also adj*.

tosh *n* (*sl*) nonsense.

toss *vt* to throw up; to pitch; to fling; (*head*) to throw back; (*with* **off**) to produce, write, perform, etc, quickly and easily; to drink in one gulp. . * *vi* to be tossed about; to move restlessly; (*with* **up**) to spin a coin to decide a question by the side that falls uppermost. * *n* the act of tossing or being tossed; a pitch; a fall.

toss-up *n* the throwing of a coin to decide a question; an even chance.

tot[1] *n* anything little, esp a child; a small measure of spirits.

tot[2] *vt* (**totting, totted**) (*with* **up**) to add up or total.

total *adj* whole, complete; absolute. * *n* the whole sum; the entire amount. * *vt* (**totalling, totalled** *or* **totaling, totaled**) to add up.—**totally** *adv*.

totalitarian *adj* relating to a system of government in which one political group maintains complete control, esp under a dictator. —**totalitarianism** *n*.

totality *n* (*pl* **totalities**) the whole amount.

totalizator *n* a machine for registering bets and computing the odds and payoff, as at a racetrack.

tote[1] *n* (*inf*) totalizator.

tote[2] *vt* to carry.

tote bag *n* (*inf*) a large bag for shopping or other items.

totem *n* an object regarded as a symbol and treated with respect by a particular group of people.

totem pole *n* a large pole carved with totemic symbols used in rituals by certain North American Indian tribes.

totter *vi* to walk unsteadily; to shake or sway as if about to fall.—**tottery** *adj*.

toucan *n* a fruit-eating South American bird with an immense, brightly coloured beak.

touch *vt* to come in contact with, esp with the hand or fingers; to reach; to affect with emotion; to tinge or tint; to border on; (*sl*) to ask for money (from); (*with* **off**) to cause to explode, as with a lighted match; to cause (violence, a riot, etc) to start; (*with* **up**) to improve by making minor alterations or additions to. * *vi* to be in contact; to be adjacent; to allude to. * *n* the act of touching; the sense by which something is perceived through contact; a trace; understanding; a special quality or skill.

touch-and-go *adj* precarious, risky.

touchdown *n* the moment when an aircraft or spaceship lands; (*Rugby football, American football*) a placing of the ball on the ground to score.

touché *interj* (*fencing*) used to acknowledge an opponent's hit; an acknowledgement of a valid or accomplished reply, remark, witty comment, etc.

touched *adj* emotionally affected; mentally disturbed.

touching *adj* affecting, moving.

touch judge *n* a linesman in Rugby football.

touchline *n* (*football, etc*) the side boundary of a pitch.

touchmark *n* a maker's distinguishing mark on pewter.

touchpaper *n* paper impregnated with a slow-burning substance used to ignite fireworks.

touchstone *n* a siliceous stone used to test gold and silver from the marks they make on it; any test or standard of genuineness.

touch-type *vi* to type quickly and accurately without looking at the keyboard.—**touch-typist** *n*.

touchwood *n* dry rotten wood useful for tinder.

touchy *adj* (**touchier, touchiest**) irritable; very risky.

tough *adj* strong; durable; hardy; rough and violent; difficult; (*inf*) unlucky.—**toughen** *vti*.—**toughness** *n*.

tough-minded *adj* realistic; unsentimental.

toupee *n* a wig or section of hair to cover a bald spot, esp worn by men.

tour *n* a turn, period, etc as of military duty; a long trip, as for sightseeing. * *vti* to go on a tour (through).

touraco *n* (*pl* **touracos**) any of a family of brightly coloured crested birds native to Africa.

tour de force *n* (*pl* **tours de force**) an outstanding achievement or performance.

tourism *n* travelling for pleasure; the business of catering for people who do this; the encouragement of touring.

tourist *n* one who makes a tour, a sightseer, travelling for pleasure.—*also adj*.

tourist class *n* economy accommodation, as on a ship, aircraft, etc.

touristy *adj* (*inf*) full of or designed for tourists.

tourmaline *n* a silicate mineral of various colours used in jewellery and electronic equipment.

tournament *n* a sporting event involving a number of competitors and a series of games.

tournedos *n* (*pl* **tournedos**) a thick round fillet of beef steak.

tourniquet *n* a device for compressing a blood vessel to stop bleeding.

tour operator *n* a company that specializes in offering package tours.

tousle *vt* to make untidy, ruffle, make tangled (esp hair).

tout *vti* (*inf*) to praise highly; (*inf*) to sell betting tips on (race horses); (*inf*) to solicit business in a brazen way. * *n* (*inf*) a person who does so.

tovarish, tovarich *n* a comrade.

tow *vt* to pull or drag with a rope. * *n* the act of towing; a towrope.

towage *n* the act of towing; the charge made for it.

toward, towards *prep* in the direction of; concerning; just before; as a contribution to.

towel *n* an absorbent cloth for drying the skin after it is washed, and for other purposes; **to throw in the towel** to admit defeat. * *vti* (**towelling, towelled** *or* **toweling, toweled**) to rub (oneself) with a towel.

towelette *n* a small moistened tissue for cleaning the face, etc.

towelling, toweling *n* cloth for towels; a rubbing with a towel.

tower *n* a tall, narrow building, standing alone or forming part of another; a fortress. * *vi* (*with* **over**) to rise above; to loom.

tower block *n* a skyscraper.

towering *adj* immensely tall; powerful, impressive; intense.

town *n* a densely populated urban centre, smaller than a city and larger than a village; the people of a town.

townie *n* (*pl* **townies**) a person who lives in a city or town as opposed to the countryside.—*also* **towny**.

town hall *n* a large building housing the offices of the town council, often with a hall for public meetings.

town house *n* a two or three-story house with a garage below, usu one of a row; a house in a fashionable area; one's house in town.

township *n* a division of a county in many US states,

constituting a unit of local government; in South Africa, an urban area reserved for Blacks.

towny *see* **townie**.

towpath *n* the footpath beside a river or canal.

towrope, towline *n* a strong rope or cable for towing a wheeled vehicle, ship, etc.

tox-, toxic-, toxico- *prefix* poison.

toxaemia, toxemia *n* a type of blood poisoning.—**toxaemic, toxemic** *adj*.

toxic *adj* poisonous; harmful; deadly.—**toxicity** *n*.

toxicant *n* a poison. * *adj* poisonous.

toxicology *n* the scientific study of poisons, their effects and antidotes.—**toxicologic, toxicological** *adj*.—**toxicologist** *n*.

toxin *n* a poison produced by microorganisms and causing certain diseases.

toxocariasis *n* a disease in humans caused by the larvae of a parasitic roundworm found in dogs and cats.

toxoid *n* a toxin of reduced power used in vaccines to stimulate the production of antitoxins.

toxoplasmosis *n* a disease affecting the central nervous system caused by a parasitic worm.

toy *n* an object for children to play with; a replica; a miniature. * *vi* to trifle; to flirt.

toyboy *n* the younger male lover of an older woman.

trace *n* a mark etc left by a person, animal or thing; a barely perceptible footprint; a small quantity. * *vt* to follow by tracks; to discover the whereabouts of; (*map, etc*) to copy by following the lines on transparent paper.

traceable *adj* able to be traced.—**traceably** *adv*.

trace element *n* a chemical element, as copper, zinc, etc, essential in nutrition but only in minute amounts.

tracer *n* a projectile which glows or leaves a smoke trail allowing its flight to be observed; a radioisotope introduced into the body whose course can be traced by a detector for diagnostic purposes.

trachea *n* (*pl* **tracheae**) the air passage from the mouth to the lungs, the windpipe.

tracheo-, trache- *prefix* trachea.

tracheotomy *n* (*pl* **tracheotomies**) an incision into the trachea, esp to bypass a blockage in the air passage.

trachoma *n* an infectious eye disease caused by a virus that leads to scarring and eventual blindness.—**trachomatous** *adj*.

trachyte *n* a type of light-coloured volcanic rock.

tracing *n* a copy of a drawing, etc made by tracing.

tracing paper *n* transparent paper used for tracing.

track *vt* to follow the tracks of; (*satellite, etc*) to follow by radar and record position; (*with* **down**) to find by tracking. * *n* a mark left; a footprint; parallel steel rails on which trains run; a course for running or racing; sports performed on a track, as running, hurdling; the band on which the wheels of a tractor or tank run; one piece of music on a record; a sound track.

track-and-field *adj* denoting various competitive athletic events (as running, jumping, weight-throwing) performed on a track and adjacent field.

tracker *n* a person who follows by tracking footprints, etc; a dog that follows a scent.

track event *n* an athletic event that takes place on a running track.

tracking station *n* a place that uses radio or radar antennae to follow the course of objects in space or the atmosphere.

tracklaying *adj* (*vehicle*) having an endless loop of metal track around the wheels.

track record *n* (*inf*) a record of the past achievements or failures of someone or something.

track shoe *n* a spiked running shoe.

tracksuit *n* a loose suit worn by athletes to keep warm.

tract[1] *n* an expanse of land or water; a part of a bodily system or organ.

tract[2] *n* a treatise.

tractable *adj* easily worked; easily taught; docile.

traction *n* act or state of drawing and pulling; (*med*) the using of weights to pull on a muscle, etc, to correct an abnormal condition.

tractor *n* a motor vehicle for pulling heavy loads and farming machinery.

trad *adj* (*inf*) traditional. * *n* traditional jazz.

trade *n* buying and selling (of commodities); commerce; occupation; customers; business. * *vi* to buy and sell; to exchange; (*with* **on**) to take advantage of.—**trader** *n*.

trade cycle *n* a recurrent fluctuation in economic activity between boom and slump.

trade gap *n* the amount by which the value of a country's visible imports exceeds its visible exports.

trade-in *n* a used item given in part payment when buying a replacement.

trade-off *n* the exchange or substitution of one thing or priority for another, often as a compromise.

trademark *n* a name used on a product by a manufacturer to distinguish it from its competitors, esp when legally protected.—*also vt*.

tradescantia *n* any of a genus of common houseplants cultivated for their variegated foliage.

tradesman *n* (*pl* **tradesmen**) a shopkeeper; a skilled worker.

trade union, trades union *n* an organized association of employees of any trade or industry for the protection of their income and working conditions.

trade wind *n* a wind that blows toward the equator at either side of it.

trading *n* the act of buying and selling (goods, etc).—*also adj*.

tradition *n* the handing down from generation to generation of opinions and practices; the belief or practice thus passed on; custom.—**traditional** *adj*.—**traditionally** *adv*.

traduce *vt* to speak badly of; to misrepresent.

traffic *n* trade; the movement or number of vehicles, pedestrians, etc, along a street, etc. * *vi* (**trafficking, trafficked**) to do business (esp. in illegal drugs).

traffic circle *n* a junction of thoroughfares where traffic circulates one way to ease progress, a roundabout.

traffic island *n* a raised area in the centre of a road to guide traffic and provide refuge for pedestrians crossing.

traffic light *n* one of a set of coloured lights used to control traffic at street crossings, etc.

traffic pattern *n* a network of airlanes above an airport to which aircraft are restricted.

tragacanth *n* a gum obtained from a species of spiny leguminous plants used in pharmacy and in calico printing.

tragedian *n* an actor who plays mainly tragic roles.—**tragedienne** *nf*.

tragedy *n* (*pl* **tragedies**) a play or drama that is serious and sad, and the climax a catastrophe; an accident or situation involving death or suffering.—**tragic** *adj*.—**tragically** *adv*.

tragicomedy *n* a dramatic or literary work which combines tragic and comic elements; a situation or event with tragic and comic aspects.

trail *vt* to drag along the ground; to have in its wake; to follow behind; to advertise a film, event or programme beforehand. * *vi* to hang or drag loosely behind; (*plant*) to climb; (*with* **off** *or* **away**) to grow weaker or dimmer. * *n* a path or track; the scent of an animal; something left in the wake (eg *a trail of smoke*).

trailblazer *n* a person who blazes a trail; a pioneer in a particular field.

trailer *n* a large vehicle designed to be towed by a truck, etc; a motor home; an advertisement for a film or television programme.

trailer park *n* an area available for rent to motor homes, caravans, etc, usu with electricity, water, etc, piped in.

trailing edge *n* the rear edge of an aerofoil.

train *vt* to teach, to guide; to tame for use, as animals; to prepare for racing, etc; (*gun, etc*) to aim. * *vi* to do exercise or preparation. * *n* a series of railroad cars pulled by a locomotive; a sequence; the back part of a dress that trails along the floor; a retinue.

trained *adj* skilled.

trainee *n* a person who is being trained.

trainer *n* a coach or instructor in sports; a person who prepares horses for racing.

training *n* practical instruction; a course of physical exercises.

training school *n* an institution for training in vocational subjects, eg teaching, nursing.

training ship *n* a moored vessel on which people are taught seamanship.

train oil *n* oil obtained from whale blubber.

train surfing *n* the practice of clinging onto the outside of a moving train for kicks.—**train surfer** *n*.

traipse *vi* to walk wearily, trudge about. * *n* a tiring walk, a trudge.

trait *n* a characteristic feature.

traitor *n* a person who commits treason or betrays his country, friends, etc.—**traitorous** *adj*.

trajectory *n* (*pl* **trajectories**) the path of an object, such as a bullet, moving through space.

tram[1] *n* a small wagon running on rails in a mine; a streetcar; a cable car.

tram[2] *n* a double twisted thread used in some silks.

trammel *n* a type of net for catching birds or fish; (*often pl*) a hindrance to freedom of movement or action; an instrument for drawing ellipses. * *vt* (**trammelling, trammelled** *or* **trammeling, trammeled**) to trap, catch; to hinder, restrict.

tramp *vti* to walk heavily; to tread or trample; to wander about as a tramp. * *n* a vagrant; (*sl*) a prostitute.

trample *vti* to tread under foot.

trampoline *n* a sheet of strong canvas stretched tightly on a frame, used in acrobatic tumbling.

trance *n* a state of unconsciousness, induced by hypnosis, in which some of the powers of the waking body, such as response to commands, may be retained.

tranche *n* a portion of something, esp a sum of money or issue of shares.

tranquil *adj* quiet, calm, peaceful.—**tranquilly** *adv*.

tranquillize, tranquilize *vt* to make tranquil, esp by administering a drug.—**tranquillization, tranquilization** *n*.

tranquillizer, tranquilizer *n* a drug that calms.

tranquility, tranquillity *n* the state of being tranquil; calmness.

trans. *abbr* = transitive; translated; translation; translator.

trans- *prefix* through; across; on the other side of.

transact *vt* (*business*) to conduct or carry out.

transaction *n* the act of transacting; something transacted, esp a business deal; (*pl*) a record of the proceedings of a society.

transalpine *adj* beyond (usu north) of the Alps.

transatlantic *adj* crossing the Atlantic Ocean; across, beyond the Atlantic.

transceiver *n* a combined radio transmitter and receiver.

transcend *vt* to rise above or beyond; to surpass.—**transcendent** *adj*.

transcendental *adj* beyond physical experience; surpassing; supernatural.—**transcendentally** *adv*.

transcendental meditation *n* a technique for emptying and refreshing the mind by repeating a mantra.

transcontinental *adj* extending or travelling across a continent.—**transcontinentally** *adv*.

transcribe *vt* to write out fully from notes or a tape recording; to make a phonetic transcription; to arrange a piece of music for an instrument other than the one it was written for.

transcript *n* a written or printed copy made by transcribing; an official copy of proceedings, etc.

transcription *n* the act of transcribing; something transcribed, esp a piece of music; a transcript; a recording made for broadcasting.

transducer *n* a device that converts energy from one form into another.

transept *n* one of the two wings of a church, at right angles to the nave.

transfer *vb* (**transferring, transferred**) *vt* to carry, convey, from one place to another; (*law*) to make over (property) to another; (*money*) to move from the control of one institution to another. * *vi* to change to another bus, etc. * *n* the act of transferring; the state of being transferred; someone or something that is transferred; a design that can be moved from one surface to another.—**transferable** *adj*.

transference *n* the act of transferring; the state of being transferred; (*psychoanal*) the redirection of emotion under analysis, usu toward the analyst.

transfer RNA *n* a form of RNA that carries an amino acid to a ribosome in protein synthesis.

transfiguration *n* a change in appearance, esp to a more spiritual or exalted form; (*with cap*) (the festival commemorating) the change in the appearance of Christ as described in the Gospels.

transfigure *vt* to transform or become transformed in appearance, esp for the better.

transfix *vt* to impale with a sharp weapon; to paralyse with shock or horror.

transform *vti* to change the shape, appearance, or condition of; to convert.—**transformation** *n*.

transformer *n* a device for changing alternating current with an increase or decrease of voltage.

transfusion *n* the injection of blood into the veins of a sick or injured person.—**transfuse** *vt*.

transgress *vti* to break or violate (a moral law or code of behaviour); to overstep (a limit).—**transgressor** *n*.

transgression *n* the act of transgressing; infringement of a rule, etc; a sin.

transhumance *n* the seasonal movement of livestock to new grazing areas.

transient *adj* temporary; of short duration, momentary.—**transience** *n*.

transistor *n* a device using a semiconductor to amplify sound, as in a radio or television; a small portable radio.

transit *n* a passing over or through; conveyance of people or goods.

transit camp *n* temporary accommodation for soldiers, refugees, etc.

transition *n* passage from one place or state to another; change.—**transitional** *adj*.

transitive *adj* (*gram*) denoting a verb that requires a direct object; of or relating to transition.—**transitively** *adv*.—**transitivity** *n*.

transitory *adj* lasting only a short time.—**transitorily** *adv*.——**transitoriness** *n*.

translate *vti* to express in another language; to explain, interpret.—**translator** *n*.

translation *n* the act of translating; something translated into another language or state; an interpretation.

transliterate *vt* to convert a word, etc into the corresponding characters of another alphabet.—**transliteration** *n*.

translucent *adj* allowing light to pass through, but not transparent.—**translucence** *n*.

transmigrate *vi* (*soul*) to pass into the body of another person after death; to migrate.

transmission *n* the act of transmitting; something transmitted; a system using gears, etc, to transfer power from an engine to a moving part, esp wheels of a vehicle; a radio or television broadcast.

transmit *vt* (**transmitting, transmitted**) to send from one place or person to another; to communicate; to convey; (*radio or television signals*) to send out.

transmitter *n* an apparatus for broadcasting television or radio programmes.

transmogrify *vt* (**transmogrifying, transmogrified**) to change shape, esp in a bizarre or comic manner.—**transmogrification** *n*.

transmute *vt* to change into a different form or substance.—**transmutation** *n*.

transnational *n* extending beyond national boundaries.

transoceanic *adj* on or from the other side of ocean; crossing the ocean.

transom *n* a horizontal bar across a window or between a door and a window over it; a fanlight; any of several transverse beams supporting and strengthening the stern of a vessel.

transparency *n* (*pl* **transparencies**) the state of being transparent; (*photog*) a slide.

transparent *adj* that may be easily seen through; clear, easily understood.—**transparently** *adv*.—**transparentness** *n*.

transpire *vti* to emit, to pass off through the pores of the skin; to exhale (moisture); (*news*) to become known, to leak out; (*inf*) to happen.—**transpiration** *n*.

transplant *vt* (*plant*) to remove and plant in another place; (*med*) to remove an organ from one person and transfer it to another.—*also n*.

transport *vt* to convey from one place to another; to enrapture. * *n* the system of transporting goods or passengers; the conveyance of troops and their equipment by sea or land; a vehicle for this purpose.—**transportable** *adj*.—**transportation** *n*.

transpose *vt* to put into a different order; to interchange; (*mus*) to change the key of.—**transposition** *n*.

transputer *n* (*comput*) a fast microchip comprising a 32-bit microprocessor which is used as a component in compact supercomputers.

transsexual *n* a person born of one sex who identifies psychologically with the opposite sex.—**transsexualism** *n*.

transubstantiation *n* (*esp in RC Church*) the doctrine that the bread and wine of the communion are wholly transformed into the body and blood of Christ when consecrated, although their appearance remains unchanged.

transuranic *adj* (*element*) having an atomic number greater than that of uranium.

transverse *adj* crosswise.—**transversely** *adv*.

transvestite *n* a person who gains sexual pleasure from wearing the clothes of the opposite sex.—**transvestism** *n*.

trap *n* a mechanical device or pit for snaring animals; an ambush; a trick to catch someone out; a two-wheeled horsedrawn carriage. * *vt* (**trapping, trapped**) to catch in a trap; to trick.

trapdoor *n* a hinged or sliding door in a roof, ceiling or floor.

trapeze *n* a gymnastic apparatus consisting of a horizontal bar suspended by two parallel ropes.

trapezium *n* (*pl* **trapeziums, trapezia**) a quadrilateral in which two of the sides are parallel; in US, a quadrilateral in which none of the sides are parallel.—**trapezial** *adj*.

trapezoid *n* a quadrilateral in which none of the sides are parallel. In US, a quadrilateral with two sides parallel.

trapper *n* a person who traps animals, esp for their skins.

trappings *npl* trimmings; additions; ornaments.

trash *n* nonsense; refuse; rubbish.

trash can *n* a container for household refuse, a dustbin, garbage can.

trashy *adj* (**trashier, trashiest**) of poor quality.—**trashiness** *n*.

trattoria *n* (*pl* **trattorias, trattorie**) an Italian restaurant.

trauma *n* an emotional shock that may cause long-term psychological damage; an upsetting experience.—**traumatic** *adj*.

travel *vb* (**travelling, travelled** *or* **traveling, traveled**) *vi* to journey or move from one place to another. * *vt* to journey across, through. * *n* journey.

travel agency *n* an agency through which one can book travel.—**travel agent** *n*.

traveller, traveler *n* a person who travels; a salesman who travels for a company.

traveller's cheque *n* a draft purchased from a bank, etc signed at the time of purchase and signed again at the time of cashing.

travelogue, travelog *n* a film or illustrated lecture on travel.

traverse *n* a horizontal move in rock climbing, skiing, etc. * *vt* to cross.

travertine *n* a mineral comprising mostly calcium carbonate, used for building.

travesty *n* (*pl* **travesties**) a misrepresentation; a poor imitation; a parody.

trawl *vti* to fish by dragging a large net behind a fishing boat.

trawler *n* a boat used for trawling.

tray *n* a flat board, or sheet of metal or plastic, surrounded by a rim, used for carrying food or drink.

treacherous adj untrustworthy, disloyal; unstable, dangerous.

treachery n (pl **treacheries**) disloyalty, betrayal of trust.

treacle n a thick sticky substance obtained during the refining of sugar.—**treacly** adj.

tread vti (**treading, trod**, pp **trodden**) to step or walk on, along, in, over or across; to crush or squash (with the feet); to trample (on). * n a step, way of walking; the part of a shoe, wheel, or tyre that touches the ground.

treadle n a foot lever or pedal on a machine.

treadmill n a grind; a monotonous routine.

treas. abbr = treasurer, treasury.

treason n the crime of betraying one's government or attempting to overthrow it; treachery.—**treasonable** adj.

treasure n wealth and riches hoarded up; a person or thing much valued. * vt to hoard up; to prize greatly.

treasurer n a person appointed to take charge of the finances of a society, government or city.

treasure hunt n a game in which players follow clues to locate a hidden object.

treasure-trove n (law) valuable items such as gold and silver found buried and of unknown ownership; any valuable find.

treasury n (pl **treasuries**) a place where valuable objects are deposited; the funds or revenues of a government.

treat vt to deal with or regard; to subject to the action of a chemical; to apply medical treatment to; to pay for another person's entertainment; to deal with in speech or writing. * n an entertainment paid for by another person; a pleasure seldom indulged; a unusual cause of enjoyment.

treatise n a formal essay in which a subject is treated systematically.

treatment n the application of drugs, etc, to a patient; the manner of dealing with a person or thing, esp in a novel or painting; behaviour toward someone.

treaty n (pl **treaties**) a formal agreement between states.

treble adj triple, threefold; (mus) denoting the treble. * n the highest range of musical notes in singing. * vti to make or become three times as much.

treble clef n (mus) a clef that places G above middle C on the second line of the staff.

trebuchet n a type of medieval military catapult used in sieges.

trecento n the 14th century, esp in reference to Italian art and literature.

tree n a tall, woody, perennial plant having a single trunk, branches and leaves.

tree creeper n any of various small songbirds with curved beaks for prising insects from tree trunks.

tree fern n a large tropical fern with a woody stem.

tree frog n any of various frogs that inhabit trees.

tree line n the height or latitude beyond which no trees grow on mountains or in cold regions.—also **timber line**.

tree surgeon n a person skilled in saving diseased or damaged trees.—**tree surgery** n.

tree toad n a tree frog.

trefoil n any of various plants with three leaflets; an ornament or design resembling this.

trek vi (**trekking, trekked**) to travel slowly or laboriously; (inf) to go on foot (to). * n a long and difficult journey; a migration.

trellis n a structure of latticework, for supporting climbing plants, etc.—**trelliswork** n.

tremble vi to shake, shiver from cold or fear; to quiver.—also n.

trembler n a device that makes or breaks an electric circuit when subject to vibration.

tremendous adj awe-inspiring; very large or great; (inf) wonderful; marvellous.

tremolo n (pl **tremolos**) a tremulous effect in playing or singing; a device that produces this effect, as in an organ.

tremor n a vibration; an involuntary shaking.

tremulous adj quivering; agitated.

trench n a long narrow channel in the earth, used for drainage; such an excavation made for military purposes.

trenchant adj keen; incisive; effective.

trench coat n a waterproof coat.

trencher n a wooden board formerly used for serving food.

trencherman n a person who eats heartily.

trench fever n an infectious disease characterized by fever and muscular pains that is transmitted by lice.

trench foot n a degenerative condition of the feet caused by prolonged immersion in cold water.

trend n tendency; a current style or fashion.

trendsetter n a person who starts a new fashion.

trendy adj (**trendier, trendiest**) (inf) fashionable. * n (pl **trendies**) (inf) a person who tries to be fashionable.—**trendily** adv.—**trendiness** n.

trepan n a primitive form of trephine. * vt (**trepanning, trepanned**) to cut with a trepan.

trepang n a type of large sea cucumber dried and used in Chinese cookery, bêche-de-mer

trephine n a surgical saw for removing circular sections of bone, esp from the skull. * vt to cut with a trephine.

trepidation n a state of fear or anxiety.

trespass vi to intrude upon another person's property without their permission; to encroach upon, or infringe, another's rights. * n act of trespassing.—**trespasser** n.

tress n a lock, braid, or plait of hair.

trestle n a wooden framework for supporting a table top or scaffold boards.

trews npl tight-fitting tartan trousers.

trey n three spots or the number three on a dice, domino or playing card.

tri- prefix having, made up of, or containing three or three parts; every third.

triad n a group or set of three, a trio.

triage n the sorting and treatment of the wounded according to chance of survival.

trial n a test or experiment; judicial examination; an attempt; a preliminary race, game in a competition; suffering; hardship; a person causing annoyance.

trial and error n solving problems through trying various solutions and rejecting the least successful.

trial run n an opportunity to test something before purchase, as a vehicle; a rehearsal.

triangle n (math) a plane figure with three angles and three sides; a percussion instrument consisting of a triangular metal bar beaten with a metal stick.—**triangular** adj.

triangulate vt to divide into triangles; to make triangular; to survey by dividing an area into a network of triangles.—**triangulation** n.

triathlon n an athletic event in which all contestants compete in swimming, cycling and running.

triatomic adj (chem) having three atoms in the molecule.

tribadism *n* simulated heterosexual intercourse by lesbians, with one partner lying on top of the other.

tribe *n* a group of people of the same race, sharing the same customs, religion, language or land.—**tribal** *adj*.—**tribesman** *n*.

tribo- *prefix* friction.

triboelectricity *n* electricity generated by friction.

tribology *n* the study of friction, wear and lubrication between moving surfaces, as gearing systems.

triboluminescence *n* luminescence caused by friction.—**triboluminescent** *adj*.

tribulation *n* distress, difficulty, hardship.

tribunal *n* a court of justice; a committee that investigates and decides on a particular problem.

tribune[1] *n* in ancient Rome, a magistrate appointed to protect the rights of common people; a champion of the people.

tribune[2] *n* a raised platform or dais from which speeches are delivered.

tributary *n* (*pl* **tributaries**) a stream or river flowing into a larger one.

tribute *n* a speech, gift or action to show one's respect or thanks to someone; a payment made at certain intervals by one nation to another in return for peace.

tricentenary *n* (*pl* **tricentenaries**) a tricentennial.—*also adj*.

tricentennial *adj* lasting, or happening every, 300 years. * *n* an anniversary of 300 years; a period of 300 years.

triceps *n* (*pl* **tricepses, triceps**) any three-headed muscle, esp the large muscle that extends the forearm.

trichiasis *n* a condition of having in-growing eyelashes which irritate the eyeball.

trichina *n* (*pl* **trichinae**) a hair-like parasitic worm that infests the intestines and muscles of pigs and humans.

trichinosis *n* a disease in humans caused by infestation of muscular tissues by trichinae.

tricho-, trich- *prefix* hair; filament.

trichology *n* the medical study and treatment of hair diseases.—**trichologist** *n*.

trichosis *n* any disease of the hair.

trichotomy *n* (*pl* **trichotomies**) a division into three parts or categories.—**trichotomous** *adj*.

trichromatic of, involving, or combining three colours; of or having normal colour vision.—**trichromatism** *n*.

trick *n* fraud; deception; a mischievous plan or joke; a magical illusion; a clever feat; skill, knack; the playing cards won in a round. * *adj* using fraud or clever contrivance to deceive. * *vt* to deceive, cheat.—**trickster** *n*.

trickery *n* (*pl* **trickeries**) the practice or an act of using underhand methods to achieve an aim; deception.

trickle *vti* to flow or cause to flow in drops or in a small stream.—*also n*.

trickle-down *adj* denoting a theory in economics that financial incentives to big business will percolate through to small businesses and individuals.

trick or treat *n* a Halloween tradition in which children dress in costumes, call on their neighbours and threaten to do mischief if refused presents of sweets, apples, nuts, money, etc.

tricky *adj* (**trickier, trickiest**) complicated, difficult to handle; risky; cunning, deceitful.—**trickily** *adv*.—**trickiness** *n*.

tricolour, tricolor *n* a flag with three stripes of different colours.

tricorn *adj* having three horns or corners. * *n* a three-cornered hat.

tricuspid *adj* having three cusps, flaps, points, or segments. * *n* a tooth with three cusps.

tricycle *n* a three-wheeled pedal cycle, esp for children.

trident *n* three-pronged spear.

tridentate, tridental *adj* having three teeth or prongs.

tried[1] *see* **try**.

tried[2] *adj* tested; trustworthy.

triennial *adj* happening every third year; lasting for three years.

triennium *n* (*pl* **trienniums, triennia**) a period of three years.

trier *n* one who tries.

trifle *vi* to treat lightly; to dally. * *n* anything of little value; a dessert of whipped cream, custard, sponge cake, sherry, etc.

trifling *adj* insignificant.

trifocal *adj* having three focuses or focal lengths. * *npl* glasses with trifocal lenses.

trifurcate, trifurcated *adj* having three branches or forks.

trig. *abbr* = trigonometrical; trigonometry.

trigeminal *adj* pertaining to the trigeminal nerve.

trigeminal nerve *n* either of a pair of cranial nerves that supply various facial muscles.

trigger *n* a catch that when pulled activates the firing mechanism of a gun. * *vt* (*with* **off**) to initiate; to set (off).

trigger-happy *adj* too eager to resort to firearms or violence; rash, aggressive.

trigonometric function *n* any of various functions (eg sine, cosine, tangent) expressed as ratios of the sides of a right-angled triangle.

trigonometry *n* the branch of mathematics concerned with calculating the angles of triangles or the lengths of their sides.

trike *n* (*inf*) a tricycle.

trilateral *adj* having three sides.

trilby *n* (*pl* **trilbies**) a soft felt hat with a fold in the crown.

trilingual *adj* speaking three languages; written in three languages.—**trilingualism** *n*.

trill *vti* to sing or play with a tremulous tone; (*a bird*) to make a shrill, warbling sound.—*also n*.

trillion *n* a million million (10^{12}); (*formerly*) in UK, a million million million (10^{18}); (*inf*) (*pl*) a very large number.

trilobite *n* any of a group of extinct Palaeozoic marine arthropods with a body in three sections.

trilogy *n* (*pl* **trilogies**) any series of three related literary or operatic works.

trim *adj* (**trimmer, trimmest**) in good condition; tidy, neat; slim. * *vt* to neaten; to cut or prune; to decorate; (*ship, aircraft*) to balance the weight of cargo in. * *n* a decorative edging; a haircut that tidies.

trimaran *n* a boat with three hulls.

trimester *n* a period of three months; a division of the academic year in certain North American colleges and universities.

trimming *n* decorative part of clothing; (*pl*) accompaniments.

trinitrotoluene *n* a solid yellow chemical substance used as a high explosive.

trinity *n* (*pl* **trinities**) a group of three; (*with cap*) in Christianity, the union of Father, Son and Holy Spirit in one God.

trinket *n* a small or worthless ornament.

trinomial *adj* having three terms. * *n* (*math*) a polynomial consisting of three terms.

trio n (pl **trios**) a set of three; (mus) a group of three singers or instrumentalists.

triode n an electronic valve or semiconductor device with three electrodes.

trip vb (**tripping, tripped**) vi to move or tread lightly; to stumble and fall; to make a blunder. * vt (often with **up**) to cause to stumble; to activate a trip. * n a stumble; a journey, tour, or voyage; a slip; a mistake; a light step; a mechanical switch; (sl) a hallucinatory experience under the influence of a drug.

tripartite adj made up of or divided into three parts; involving or binding three parties.

tripe n the stomach lining of a ruminant, prepared for cooking; (inf) rubbish, nonsense.

triplane n an aircraft with three wings positioned one above the other.

triple adj threefold; three times as many. * vti to treble.

triple jump n an athletic event in which a competitor makes a hop, step and jump in succession.

triplet n one of three children born at one birth.

triplicate adj threefold.

tripod n a three-legged stand, as for supporting a camera.

tripper n a tourist; a trip switch.

triptych n a picture consisting of three panels fixed or hinged side by side.

tripwire n a concealed wire that sets off a bomb, booby trap, etc when tripped over.

trireme n an ancient Greek galley with three banks of oars.

trisect vt to divide into three (equal) parts.—**trisection** n.

trishaw n a rickshaw.

triskelion n (pl **triskelia**) a symbol consisting of three bent limbs or branches radiating from a centre.

trismus n lockjaw.

trisyllable n a word of three syllables.

trite adj dull; hackneyed.

tritium n a radioactive isotope of hydrogen.

triton n any of various marine gastropod molluscs having a heavy spiral shell; (with cap) (Greek myth) a seagod depicted as half man and half fish blowing a spiral shell.

triturate vt to crush or grind into a fine powder.—**trituration** n.

triumph n a victory; success; a great achievement. * vi to win a victory or success; to rejoice over a victory.—**triumphal** adj.

triumphant adj feeling or showing triumph; celebratory; victorious.—**triumphantly** adv.

triumvir n (pl **triumvirs, triumviri**) a member of a ruling body of three persons.

triumvirate n the office of a triumvir; joint rule by three persons.

trivalent adj having a valency of three.

trivet n a three-legged metal stand for supporting hot dishes.

trivia npl unimportant details.

trivial adj unimportant; commonplace.

triviality n (pl **trivialities**) a trifle, detail; the state of being trivial.

-trix n suffix female.

t-RNA abbr = transfer RNA.

trocar n a pointed instrument for inserting drainage tubes into bodily cavities.

trochal adj wheel-shaped.

troche n a medicinal lozenge.

trochee n a metrical foot comprising one long syllable followed by one short syllable.

trod, trodden see **tread**.

troglodyte n a cave dweller.

troika n (a Russian vehicle drawn by) three horses harnessed abreast; a triumvirate.

troll n a supernatural creature, dwelling in a cave, hill, etc.

trolley n (pl **trolleys**) a table on wheels for carrying or serving food; a cart for transporting luggage; a cart for carrying shopping in a supermarket; a device that transmits electric current from an overhead wire to a motor vehicle, such as a trolleybus.

trolleybus, trolley car n a bus that sometimes runs on rails and is powered by electricity from overhead wires.

trollop n a slovenly woman; a prostitute.—**trollopy** adj.

trombone n brass musical wind instrument whose length is varied with a U-shaped sliding section.

troop n a crowd of people; a group of soldiers within a cavalry regiment; (pl) armed forces; soldiers. * vi to go in a crowd.

trooper n a cavalryman; a mounted policeman or a state policeman.

troopship n a ship used to transport military forces.

trope n a word or phrase used in a figurative sense.

-trope n suffix turning, being attracted toward.

trophic adj pertaining to nutrition.

tropho-, troph- prefix nutrition.

trophy n (pl **trophies**) a cup or shield won as a prize in a competition or contest; a memento, as taken in battle or hunting.

-trophy n suffix growth, nutrition.

tropic n one of the two parallel lines of latitude north and south of the equator; (pl) the regions lying between these lines.

-tropic adj suffix turning to or responding to an external stimulus.

tropical adj relating to the tropics; (weather) hot and humid.

tropism n the involuntary direction of growth of a plant due to an external stimulus.

-tropism, -tropy n suffix turning or developing in response to an external stimulus.

tropo- prefix turning or changing.

-tropous adj suffix turning away.

tropopause n the region between the troposphere and stratosphere.

troposphere n the region of the atmosphere below the stratosphere which varies in temperature and in which clouds form.

trot vb (**trotting, trotted**) vi (horse) to go, lifting the feet higher than in walking and moving at a faster rate. * vt (with **out**) (inf) to produce or display repeatedly, esp for others' approval; to produce in a trite or careless manner. * n the gait of a horse; a brisk pace.

trotter n a horse trained for fast trotting; the foot of an animal, esp a pig.

troubadour n a minstrel; a poet or singer.

trouble vti to cause trouble to; to worry; to pain; to upset; to cause inconvenience; to take pains (to). * n an anxiety; a medical condition causing pain; a problem; unrest or disturbance.—**troublesome** adj.

troubleshooter n a person whose work is to locate and eliminate a source of trouble or conflict.—**troubleshooting** n.

trough n a long, narrow container for water or animal

feed; a channel in the ground; an elongated area of low barometric pressure.

trounce *vt* to defeat completely.

troupe *n* a travelling company, esp of actors, dancers or acrobats.—**trouper** *n*.

trousers *npl* an item of clothing covering the body from waist to ankle, with two tubes of material for the legs; pants.

trousseau *n* (*pl* **trousseaux, trousseaus**) the clothes and linen a bride collects for her marriage.

trout *n* (*pl* **trout**) a game fish of the salmon family living in fresh water.

trove *see* **treasure trove**.

trowel *n* a hand tool for gardening; a flat-bladed tool for spreading cement, etc.

troy (weight) *n* a system for weighing precious stones and metals, in which one pound = 12 ounces and one ounce = 20 pennyweights or 480 grains.

truant *n* a pupil who is absent from school without permission. * *vi* to play truant.—*also adj.*—**truancy** *n*.

truce *n* an agreement between two armies or states to suspend hostilities.

truck *n* a heavy motor vehicle for transporting goods; a vehicle open at the back for moving goods or animals. * *vt* (*goods*) to convey by truck. * *vi* to drive a truck.

trucker *n* a truck driver.

truculent *adj* sullen; aggressive.—**truculence** *n*.—**truculently** *adv*.

trudge *vti* to travel on foot, heavily or wearily. * *n* a tiring walk.

true *adj* (**truer, truest**) conforming with fact; correct, accurate; genuine; loyal; perfectly in tune. * *adv* truthfully; rightly.

true-blue *adj* staunchly loyal or committed.—**true blue** *n*.

truelove *n* a sweetheart.

truffle *n* a round, edible underground fungus; a sweet made with chocolate, butter and sugar.

truism *n* a self-evident truth.

truly *adv* completely; genuinely; to a great degree.

trump *n* (*cards*) the suit that is chosen to have the highest value in one game. * *vt* to play a trump card on; (*with* **up**) to invent maliciously, fabricate (an accusation, etc).

trumpery *adj* worthless. * *n* (*pl* **trumperies**) foolish talk, nonsense; a worthless article.

trumpet *n* a brass wind instrument consisting of a long tube with a flared end and three buttons. * *vti* to proclaim loudly.—**trumpeter** *n*.

trumpeter swan *n* a rare wild North American swan with a black bill.

truncate *vt* to cut the top end off; to shorten.—**truncation** *n*.

truncheon *n* a short, thick club carried by a policeman.

trundle *vt* (*an object*) to push or pull on wheels. * *vi* to move along slowly.

trunk *n* the main stem of a tree; the torso; the main body of anything; the proboscis of an elephant; a strong box or chest for clothes, etc, esp on a journey; storage space at the rear of an automobile; (*pl*) a man's short, light pants for swimming.

trunk line *n* a transportation system handling through traffic; a communications system.

trunk road *n* a main road.

truss *n* a supporting framework for a roof or bridge; a hernia brace. * *vt* to bind (up).

trust *n* firm belief in the truth of anything, faith in a person; confidence in; custody; a financial arrangement of investing money for another person; a business syndicate. * *adj* held in trust. * *vti* to have confidence in; to believe.—**trustful** *adj*.

trustee *n* a person who has legal control of money or property that they are keeping or investing for another person, or for an organization or institution.—**trusteeship** *n*.

trustworthy *adj* reliable, dependable.

trusty *adj* (**trustier, trustiest**) trustworthy, faithful. * *n* a prisoner granted special privileges as a trustworthy person.—**trustily** *adv*.—**trustiness** *n*.

truth *n* that which is true, factual or genuine; agreement with reality.

truthful *adj* telling the truth; accurate, realistic; honest, frank.—**truthfulness** *n*.

try *vb* (**trying, tried**) *vt* to test the result or effect by experiment; to determine judicially; to put strain on; (*with* **on**) to put (a garment) on to check the fit, etc; (*inf*) to attempt to deceive somebody; (*with* **out**) to test (someone) for a job, etc. * *vi* to attempt; to make an effort; (*with* **out**) to undergo a test (for a job, team, etc). * *n* (*pl* **tries**) an attempt, an effort; (*Rugby football*) a score made with a touchdown.

trying *adj* causing annoyance, exasperating.—**tryingly** *adv*.—**tryingness** *n*.

try-on *n* (*inf*) a trying on of clothes to check the fit; an attempt to deceive.

tryout *n* an experimental test; an audition for a theatrical part; (*sports, etc*) a test for a position in a team.

trypanosome *n* any of genus of parasitic worms that infest the blood of animals and humans and can cause sleeping sickness.

trypanosomiasis *n* (a disease caused by) infection with trypanosomes.

trypsin *n* an enzyme in the pancreas involved in digestion.—**tryptic** *adj*.

tryptophan, tryptophane *n* an amino acid found in proteins which is essential to life.

try square *n* an L-shaped instrument for drawing and testing right angles.

tryst *n* an appointment to meet secretly.

tsar *n* (*formerly*) the title of the emperors of Russia (until 1917) and sovereigns of certain other Slav nations; a powerful person.—*also* **czar**.

tsarevitch *n* the eldest son of a tsar.—*also* **czarevitch**.

tsarina, tsaritsa *n* the wife of a tsar; an empress.—*also* **czarina**.

tsetse fly *n* a fly that feeds on blood and transmits diseases.

T-shirt *n* a short-sleeved casual cotton top.—*also* **tee-shirt**.

tsp. *abbr* = teaspoon.

T-square *n* a T-shaped instrument for drawing and determining right angles.

Tu. *abbr* = Tuesday.

tub *n* a circular container, made of staves and hoops; a bathtub.

tuba *n* a large brass instrument of bass pitch.

tubby *adj* (**tubbier, tubbiest**) plump.

tube *n* a long, thin, hollow pipe; a soft metal or plastic cylinder in which thick liquids or pastes, such as toothpaste, are stored; (*inf*) in UK, the underground railway system.—**tubular** *adj*.

tubeless tyre *n* a tyre that remains airtight without requiring an inner tube.

tuber n the swollen, fleshy root of a plant where reserves of food are stored up, as a potato.

tubercle n a small round swelling or nodule, esp on bone, skin or a plant; an abnormal lump, esp one characteristic of tuberculosis.

tubercle bacillus n a bacterium that causes tuberculosis.

tuberculate adj affected with tubercles.—**tuberculation** n.

tuberculin n a sterile liquid prepared with weakened tubercle bacillus and used in the diagnosis of tuberculosis.

tuberculosis n an infectious disease of the lungs.—**tubercular** adj.

tuberose n a bulbous Mexican plant with fragrant white flowers.

tuberous adj (plants) forming or resembling tubers.

tubing n tubes collectively; a length of tube; the material from which tubes are made; a circular fabric.

tub-thumper n a passionate or aggressive public speaker.

tubular bells npl an orchestral percussion instrument consisting of a set of long metal tubes played with a mallet to simulate the sounds of bells.

tuck vt to draw or gather together in a fold; (with **up**) to wrap snugly. * vi (inf) (with **into**) to eat greedily. * n a fold in a garment.

tucker vt (inf) to exhaust, tire (out).

Tue., Tues. abbr = Tuesday.

Tuesday n the third day of the week.

tufa n a type of porous rock deposited from springs.

tuff n a type of volcanic rock composed of fused lava ash.

tuffet n a small low seat; a clump of grass.

tuft n a bunch of grass, hair or feathers held together at the base; a clump.

tug vti (**tugging, tugged**) to pull with effort or to drag along. * n a strong pull; a tugboat.

tugboat n a small powerful boat for towing ships.

tug of love n a conflict over the custody of a child between separated parents, etc.

tug of war n a contest in which two teams tug on opposite ends of a rope to pull the opposing team over a central line; a struggle for supremacy between two opponents.

tuition n teaching, instruction.

tulip n a highly-coloured cup-shaped flower grown from bulbs.

tulip tree n a North American tree with large tulip-shaped flowers.

tulipwood n the soft white wood of the tulip tree used in making furniture.

tulle n a delicate semi-transparent fabric of rayon, silk, etc, used for scarfs and veils.

tumble vi to fall over; to roll or to twist the body, as an acrobat; (with **to**) (inf) to discover (a secret, etc); to understand. * vt to push or cause to fall. * n a fall; a somersault.

tumbledown adj dilapidated, crumbling.

tumble-dry vt (clothes) to dry by rotating with warm air in a machine.—**tumble dryer** n.

tumbler n a large drinking glass without a handle or stem; an acrobat.

tumbler switch n a simple electrical switch used in lighting.

tumbleweed n a plant that detaches from its roots and is blown around by the wind.

tumbrel, tumbril n a farm cart that tips up to deposit its load; a cart of similar design used to carry prisoners to the guillotine during the French Revolution.

tumescent adj swollen or beginning to swell.

tumid adj swollen, distended; pompous, bombastic.—**tumidly** adv.—**tumidity** n.

tummy n (pl **tummies**) (inf) stomach.

tumour, tumor n an abnormal growth of tissue in any part of the body.

tumult n a commotion; an uproar.

tumultuous adj disorderly; rowdy, noisy; restless.—**tumultuously** adv.—**tumultuousness** n.

tun n a large wine or beer cask; a unit of capacity equal to about 252 wine gallons (954 litres).

tuna n (pl **tuna, tunas**) a large ocean fish of the mackerel group.

tundra n a vast treeless arctic plain.

tune n a melody; correct musical pitch; harmony. * vt (musical instrument) to adjust the notes of; (radio, TV etc) to adjust the resonant frequency, etc, to a particular value; (with **up**) to adjust an engine to improve its performance. * vi (with **up**) to adjust (musical instruments) to a common pitch before playing.—**tuneful** adj.—**tunefully** adv.

tune-up n an adjustment of a musical instrument to correct pitch or of an engine to improve its performance.

tungsten n a hard malleable greyish white metallic element used in lamps, etc, and in alloys with steel.

tunic n a hip or knee-length loose, usu belted blouse-like garment; a close-fitting jacket worn by soldiers and policemen.

tunicate n any of a group of small primitive marine animals with sac-shaped bodies enclosed in a thick membrane. * adj having or enclosed in a membrane; (bulbs) made up from concentric layers of tissue.

tuning fork n a two-pronged steel fork that produces a fixed note when struck and is used to tune musical instruments or set a pitch for singing.

tunnel n an underground passage, esp one for cars or trains underneath a river or town centre. * vb (**tunnelling, tunnelled** or **tunneling, tunneled**) vt to make a way through. * vi to make a tunnel.

tunnel vision n a condition in which peripheral vision is impaired; a narrowness of viewpoint due to preoccupation with a single idea, plan, etc.

tunny n (pl **tunnies, tunny**) tuna.

tuppence n twopence.

turban n a headdress consisting of cloth wound in folds around the head worn by men; a woman's hat of this shape.

turbid adj muddy; dense; thick.—**turbidity** n.—**turbidly** adv.

turbine n a machine in which power is produced when the forced passage of steam, water, etc causes the blades to rotate.

turbo- prefix of, driven or powered by a turbine.

turbofan n a jet engine with a large fan that forces air out with the exhaust gases to increase thrust; an aircraft with such engines; the fan in such an engine.

turbojet n (an aircraft with) a turbojet engine.

turbojet engine n a gas turbine that provides propulsive power from a jet of hot exhaust gases.

turboprop n a jet aircraft engine that also operates a turbine-driven air compressor.

turbot n (pl **turbot, turbots**) a large, flat, round edible fish.

turbulence n a state of confusion and disorder; (weather) instability causing gusty air currents.

turbulent *adj* disturbed, in violent commotion.

turd *n* (*vulg*) a piece of excrement; (*vulg sl*) a despicable person.

tureen *n* a large dish for serving soup, etc.

turf *n* (*pl* **turfs, turves**) the surface layer of grass and its roots; (*with* **the**) horse racing; a racetrack. * *vt* to cover with turf; (*with* **out**) (*inf*) to eject forcibly, throw out.

turgid *adj* swollen; pompous, bombastic.—**turgidity** *n*.—**turgidly** *adv*.

Turk *n* a native or inhabitant of Turkey; any speaker of a Turkic language.

Turk. *abbr* = Turkey; Turkish.

turkey *n* (*pl* **turkeys, turkey**) a large bird farmed for its meat.

turkey buzzard *n* an American vulture.

turkey cock *n* a male turkey.

Turkey red *n* (a cotton fabric of) a bright red colour.

Turki *adj* of, being or pertaining to the Turkic languages or speakers of these languages; the Turkic languages collectively.

Turkic *n* a branch of the Altaic family of languages including Turkish, Tartar, etc.

Turkish *adj* pertaining to Turkey, its people or their language. * *n* the official language of Turkey.

Turkish bath *n* a bath with steam rooms, showers, massage, etc.

Turkish coffee *n* strong black (usu sweetened) coffee.

Turkish delight *n* a jelly-like flower-flavoured sweet covered with icing sugar.

Turk's-cap lily *n* a variety of lily with purple-red flowers found in Europe and Asia, martagon lily.

turmeric *n* a tropical Indian plant; the powdered stem of this plant used as a yellow colouring agent and curry spice.

turmoil *n* agitation; disturbance, confusion.

turn *vi* to revolve; to go in the opposite direction; to depend on; to appeal (to) for help; to direct (thought or attention) away from; to change in character; to be shaped on the lathe; (*with* **off**) to leave or deviate from a road, etc; (*with* **in**) (*inf*) to retire to bed for the night; (*with* **on**) to depend on; (*sl*) to take drugs; (*with* **to**) to begin a task; (*with* **up**) to appear, arrive; to find unexpectedly; to happen without warning. * *vt* to change the position or direction of by revolving; to reverse; to transform; (*age, etc*) to have just passed; to change or convert; to invert; (*with* **off**) to cause to cease operating (as if) by flicking a switch, turning a knob, etc; (*inf*) to cause a person to lose interest in or develop a dislike for something; (*with* **down**) to reduce the volume or intensity of (sound, brightness, etc); to refuse, decline; to fold down (sheets, a collar, etc); (*with* **in**) to deliver; to produce, record (a performance, score, etc); (*with* **on**) to cause to begin operating (as if) by flicking a switch, turning a knob, etc; (*sl*) to arouse or excite, esp sexually; (*sl*) to introduce (a person) to drugs; (*with* **up**) to discover, uncover; to increase the volume or intensity of (sound, brightness, etc). * *n* a rotation; new direction or tendency; a place in sequence; a turning point, crisis; performer's act; an act of kindness or malice; a bend.

turnabout *n* a reversal of position, opinion, attitude, etc.

turncoat *n* a deserter, renegade.

turner *n* a person who operates a lathe.

turning *n* a road, path, etc that leads off from a main way; the point where it leads off; a bend; the art of shaping objects on a lathe; an object so made; (*pl*) waste produced on a lathe.

turning point *n* the point at which a significant change occurs.

turnip *n* a plant with a large white or yellow root, cultivated as a vegetable.

turnout *n* a gathering of people.

turnover *n* the volume of business transacted in a given period; a fruit or meat pasty; the rate of replacement of workers.

turnpike *n* a toll road, esp one that is an expressway.

turnround *n* (the time required to complete) the unloading and reloading of a ship, aircraft, etc.

turnstile *n* a mechanical gate across a footpath or entrance which admits only one person at a time.

turntable *n* a circular, horizontal revolving platform, as in a record player.

turn-up *n* the cuff of a trouser; (*inf*) a surprise.

turpentine *n* an oily resin secreted by coniferous trees, used as a solvent and thinner for paints.—*also* **turps**.

turpentine tree *n* a terebinth or related tree that yields a turpentine.

turpitude *n* depravity; wickedness.

turps *n sing* (*inf*) turpentine.

turquoise *n* an opaque greenish-blue mineral, valued as a gem; the colour of turquoise.—*also adj*.

turret *n* a small tower on a building rising above it; a dome or revolving structure for guns, as on a warship, tank or aeroplane.—**turreted** *adj*.

turtle *n* any of an order of land, freshwater or marine reptiles having a soft body encased in a hard shell; **to turn turtle** to turn upside down.

turtledove *n* a brown dove with speckled wings and a dark tail, noted for its cooing and its care for its partner and young.

turtleneck *n* a high close-fitting neckline on a sweater.

turves *see* **turf**.

tusk *n* a long, projecting tooth on either side of the mouth, as of the elephant.—**tusked** *adj*.

tusker *n* an animal with tusks.

tussle *n* a scuffle.

tussock *n* a dense tuft of grass.

tutelage *n* guardianship; guidance by a tutor.

tutor *n* a private teacher who instructs pupils individually; a member of staff responsible for the supervision and teaching of students in a British university. * *vt* to instruct; to act as a tutor.

tutorial *n* a period of tuition by a tutor to an individual or a small group. * *adj* of or pertaining to a tutor.

tutti *adj, adv* (*mus*) all together, to be performed by the whole orchestra. * *n* a musical piece or passage so performed.

tutti-frutti *n* (*pl* **tutti-fruttis**) a type of ice cream containing pieces of chopped candied fruits.

tut-tut *interj* an exclamation of impatience or mild disapproval. * *vi* (**tut-tutting, tut-tutted**) to express disapproval or impatience by uttering "tut-tut".

tutu *n* a short, projecting, layered skirt worn by a ballerina.

tu-whit tu-whoo *interj* an imitation of the cry of an owl.

tuxedo *n* a man's semi-formal suit with a tailless jacket.—*also* **dinner jacket**.

TV *abbr* = television.

TVA *abbr* = Tennessee Valley Authority.

TVP *abbr* = textured vegetable protein; a meat substitute used in vegetarian dishes.

twaddle *n* utter rubbish in speech or writing. * *vi* to speak or write twaddle.

twain *adj, n* (*arch*) two.

twang *n* a sharp, vibrant sound, as of a taut string when plucked; a nasal tone of voice. * *vt* to make a twanging sound.

'twas (*poet*) = it was.

twat *n* an idiot; (*vulg*) the female genitals.

tweak *vt* to twist, pinch or pull with sudden jerks. * *n* a sharp pinch or twist.

twee *adj* (*inf*) excessively quaint, affected.

tweed *n* a twilled woollen fabric used in making clothes.

'tween *prep* (*arch*) between.

tweet *interj* an imitation of the chirp of a small bird. * *vi* to make this sound.

tweeter *n* a small loudspeaker for reproducing high-frequency sounds.

tweezers *n sing* small pincers used for plucking.

twelfth *adj* the last of twelve; being one of twelve equal parts.

Twelfth Day *n* Epiphany.

twelfth man *n* the reserve member of a cricket team.

Twelfth Night *n* the evening of Epiphany, the twelfth day after Christmas, 6 January; the eve of Epiphany, 5th January.

twelve *adj* the cardinal number next after eleven. * *n* the symbol for this (12, XII, xii).

twelve-tone *adj* pertaining to a type of serial music using only the twelve semitones of the chromatic scale as a tone row for compositions.

twelvemo *n* a book of sheets folded into twelve leaves; this book size.—*also* **duodecimo**.

twenty *adj, n* two times ten. * *n* (*pl* **twenties**) the symbol for this (20, XX, xx). —**twentieth** *adj*.

twenty-one *n* pontoon (card game); blackjack.

twenty-twenty, 20/20 *adj* (*vision*) normal.

'twere (*poet*) = it were.

twerp *n* (*inf*) a foolish or contemptible person.—*also* **twirp**.

twice *adv* two times; two times as much; doubly.

twiddle *vt* to twirl or fiddle with idly.

twig[1] *n* a small branch or shoot of a tree.—**twiggy** *adj*.

twig[2] *vti* (**twigging, twigged**) (*inf*) to grasp the meaning of.

twilight *n* the dim light just after sunset and before sunrise; the final stages of something.

twilit *adj* lit by twilight.

twill *n* a cloth woven in such a way as to produce diagonal lines across it.—**twilled** *adj*.

twin *n* either of two persons or animals born at the same birth; one thing resembling another. * *adj* double; very like another; consisting of two parts nearly alike. * *vt* (**twinning, twinned**) to pair together.

twin bed *n* one of a pair of single beds.

twine *n* a string of twisted fibres or hemp. * *vti* to twist together; to wind around.

twin-engined *adj* (*aircraft*) having two engines.

twinge *n* a sudden, stabbing pain; an emotional pang.

twinkle *vi* to sparkle; to flicker.

twinkling *n* a wink; an instant; the shining of the stars.

twin-screw *adj* (*vessel*) having two propellers.

twinset *n* a jumper and cardigan designed to be worn together.

twin-tub *n* a washing machine with two drums, one for washing and the other for spin-drying.

twirl *vt* to whirl; to rotate; to wind or twist. * *vi* to turn around rapidly.

twirp *see* **twerp**.

twist *vt* to unite by winding together; to coil; to confuse or distort (the meaning of); to bend. * *vi* to revolve; to writhe. * *n* the act or result of twisting; a twist of thread; a curve or bend; an unexpected event; a wrench.

twister *n* a tornado; (*inf*) a dishonest person, a swindler.

twisty *adj* (**twistier, twistiest**) winding.

twit[1] *vt* (**twitting, twitted**) to tease or reproach. * *n* a nervous state.

twit[2] *n* (*Brit inf*) a silly or foolish person.

twitch *vt* to pull with a sudden jerk. * *vi* to be suddenly jerked. * *n* a sudden muscular spasm.

twitter *n* a chirp, as of a bird. * *vi* to chirp.

two *adj, n* the cardinal number next above one. * *n* the symbol for this (2, II, ii).

two-cycle *see* **two-stroke**.

two-dimensional *adj* of or having two dimensions; lacking (the illusion of) depth.

two-edged *adj* having two cutting edges; (*remark, etc*) double-edged.

two-faced *adj* deceitful, hypocritical.

twofold *adj* multiplied by two; double. * *adv* doubly.

two-handed *adj* having or needing two hands; ambidextrous; requiring two people.

twopence *n* the sum of two pence; in UK, a coin of this value; something of little value.—*also* **tuppence**.

two-piece *n* a garment consisting of two separate matching bits.—*also adj*.

two-ply *adj* made of two thicknesses or strands.

twosome *n* a group of two; a game for two people.

two-step *n* (the music for) a ballroom dance in duple time.

two-stroke *n, adj* (an internal combustion engine) having a piston which makes two strokes for every explosion.—*also* **two-cycle**.

two-time *vti* (*sl*) to be unfaithful to (a lover, etc); to double-cross.—**two-timer** *n*.

two-tone *adj* of two colours or shades of the same colour; (*sirens, etc*) having two notes.

two-way *adj* allowing movement or operation in two (opposite) directions; involving two participants; involving mutual obligation; (*radio, telephone*) capable of transmitting and receiving messages.

two-way mirror *n* a sheet of glass that reflects as a mirror on one side but can be seen through from the other.

'twould (*poet*) = it would.

TX *abbr* = Texas.

tycoon *n* a powerful industrialist, etc.

tyke *n* a (mongrel) dog; (*inf*) a cheeky child.—*also* **tike**.

tympani, tympany *see* **timpani**.

tympanic bone *n* a bone enclosing part of the middle ear and supporting the tympanic membrane.

tympanic membrane *n* the eardrum.

tympanites *n* distension of the abdomen caused by the accumulation of gas in the intestine.—**tympanitic** *adj*.

tympanitis *n* inflammation of the eardrum.

tympanum *n* (*pl* **tympanums, tympana**) the cavity of the middle ear; the tympanic membrane, eardrum; the space between the lintel of a doorway and the enclosing arch; the (recessed) triangular face of a pediment.

type *n* a kind, class or group; sort; model; a block of metal for printing letters; style of print. * *vt* to write by means of a typewriter; to classify.

-type *n suffix* of the form specified; printing process.

typecast *vt* (**typecasting, typecast**) (*actor*) to cast in the same role repeatedly because of physical appearance, etc.

typeface *n* the printing surface of a type character; a particular design of a set of type characters.

typescript *n* a typed copy of a book, document, etc.

typeset *vt* (**typesetting, typeset**) to set in type.—**typesetter** *n*.

typewriter *n* a keyboard machine for printing characters.

typhoid *n* typhoid fever. * *adj* of or pertaining to typhoid fever (—*also* **typhoidal**).

typhoid fever *n* an acute infectious disease acquired by ingesting contaminated food or water.

typhoon *n* a violent tropical cyclone originating in the western Pacific.

typhus *n* a highly contagious acute disease spread by body lice and characterized by fever, a rash and headache.—**typhous** *adj*.

typical *adj* representative of a particular type; characteristic.—**typicality** *n*.—**typically** *adv*.

typify *vt* (**typifying, typified**) to characterize.—**typification** *n*.

typist *n* a person who uses a typewriter, esp as a job.

typo *n* (*pl* **typos**) (*inf*) a typographical error.

typography *n* the way in which printed material is designed or set for printing.—**typographic, typographical** *adj*.

tyrannicide *n* (a person responsible for) the killing of a tyrant.

tyrannize *vi* to exercise power (over) in a vicious and oppressive manner. * *vt* to crush, oppress.—**tyrannizer** *n*.

tyrannosaur, tyrannosaurus *n* a large carnivorous dinosaur of the Cretaceous period which stood on powerful hind legs.

tyranny *n* (*pl* **tyrannies**) the government or authority of a tyrant; harshness; oppression.

tyrant *n* a person who uses his or her power arbitrarily and oppressively; a despot.—**tyrannical** *adj*.

tyre *n* a protective, usu rubber, covering around the rim of a wheel.—*also* **tire**.

tyro *n* (*pl* **tyros**) a novice, a beginner.—*also* **tiro**.

tzar *n* a czar.—**tzarevitch** *n*.—**tzarina** *n*.

tzatsiki *n* a Greek dip made from plain yogurt, shredded cucumber, and mint.

U

U *abbr* = uranium; (*cinema*) universal (suitable for all age groups).

U, u *n* the 21st letter of the English alphabet; something shaped like a U.

UAE *abbr* = United Arab Emirates.

ubiety *n* the state of being in a specific place.

ubiquitous *adj* existing, or seeming to exist everywhere at once.—**ubiquity** *n*.

U-boat *n* a German submarine.

uc *abbr* = upper case.

udder *n* a milk-secreting organ containing two or more teats, as in cows.

UFO *abbr* = unidentified flying object.

ufology *n* the study of UFOs.—**ufologist** *n*.

ugh *interj* an expression of disgust, dislike or horror.

ugli, ugli fruit *n* (*pl* uglis, uglies) a citrus fruit that is a cross between a grapefruit and a tangerine.

ugly *adj* (**uglier, ugliest**) unsightly; unattractive; repulsive; ill tempered.—**ugliness** *n*.

ugly duckling *n* an initially unpromising person or thing that turns out successfully.

UHF *abbr* = ultrahigh frequency.

uh-huh *interj* used to indicate assent or agreement.

UHT *abbr* = ultra-heat treated (milk or cream).

UK *abbr* = United Kingdom.

ukelele, ukulele *n* a small, four-stringed guitar.

ulcer *n* an open sore on the surface of the skin or a mucous membrane.—**ulcerous** *adj*

ulcerate *vti* to make or become ulcerous.

-ule *n suffix* smallness.

ulema *n* (a member of) a body of Muslim theologians and religious scholars.

-ulent *adj suffix* abundant.

ullage *n* the amount by which a container (e.g. a barrel) is less than full.

ulna *n* (*pl* ulnas, ulnae) the longer and thinner of the two bones in the human forearm; the corresponding bone in the forelimb of other vertebrates.—**ulnar** *adj*.

ulnar nerve *n* a nerve in the forearm that passes close to the skin surface at the elbow.

ulotrichous *adj* having woolly or curly hair.

ulster *n* a long heavy double-breasted overcoat with a belt.

Ulsterman *n* (*pl* Ulstermen) a native or inhabitant of Ulster (a former province of Ireland now divided between Northern Ireland and the Republic of Ireland).—**Ulsterwoman** (*pl* Ulsterwomen) *nf*.

ulterior *adj* (*motives*) hidden, not evident; subsequent.

ultima *n* the last syllable of a word.

ultimate *adj* last; final; most significant; essential. * *n* the most significant thing.—**ultimately** *adv*.

ultimatum *n* (*pl* ultimatums, ultimata) the final proposal, condition or terms in negotiations.

ultimogeniture *n* (*law*) inheritance by the youngest son.

ultra *adj* extreme, uncompromising. * *n* an extremist.

ultra- *prefix* beyond.

ultraconservative *adj* deeply conservative or reactionary. * *n* a reactionary person.

ultrafiche *n* a type of high-density microfiche containing a very large number of microcopies.

ultrahigh frequency *n* a radio frequency in the range between 300 megahertz and 3000 megahertz.

ultraism *n* the advocacy of extreme action.—**ultraist** *n*.

ultramarine *adj* deep blue. * *n* a blue pigment; a vivid, deep blue.

ultramicroscope *n* an optical device for viewing tiny particles undetectable by a conventional microscope.—**ultramicroscopic** *adj*.

ultrashort *adj* (*radio wave*) having a wavelength less than 10 metres.

ultrasonic *adj* (*waves, vibrations*) having a frequency beyond the human ear's audible range.

ultrasound *n* ultrasonic waves used in medical diagnosis and therapy.

ultraviolet *adj* of light waves, shorter than the wavelengths of visible light and longer than X-rays.

ultraviolet light *n* ultraviolet radiation.

ultravirus *n* a virus small enough to pass through the finest filter.

ululate *vi* to howl or wail, as with pain or grief.—**ululant** *adj*.—**ululation** *n*.

umbel *n* a flower-cluster characteristic of plants of the carrot family, in which the stalks grow from the same place on the main stem producing an umbrella effect.—**umbellate** *adj*.

umbelliferous *adj* of or pertaining to a family of plants and shrubs bearing umbels, including carrots, parsley and fennel.—**umbellifer** *n*.

umber *n* a brown pigment. * *adj* dark brown.

umbilical *n* of, pertaining to, near, or resembling the navel.

umbilical cord *n* the vascular tube connecting a foetus with the placenta through which oxygen and nutrients are passed.

umbilicate, umbilicated *n* depressed or shaped like a navel; having an umbilicus.—**umbilication** *n*.

umbilicus *n* (*pl* umbilici) the navel; a navel-shaped depression on a plant or animal.

umbo *n* (*pl* umbones, umbos) the boss in the centre of a shield; a rounded anatomical protrusion.

umbra *n* (*pl* umbrae, umbras) an area of total shadow, esp during an eclipse; the dark centre of a sunspot.—**umbral** *adj*.

umbrage *n* resentment; offence.

umbrella *n* a cloth-covered collapsible frame carried in the hand for protection from rain or sun; a general protection.

umiak *n* an Eskimo boat made from hide stretched over a wooden frame.—*also* **oomiak**.

umlaut *n* the mark (¨) placed over a vowel in German

and other languages to modify its sound; the change of a vowel brought about by its assimilation to another vowel.

umpire *n* an official who enforces the rules in sport; an arbitrator.—*also vti.*

umpteen *adj* (*inf*) an undetermined large number.— **umpteenth** *adj.*

UN *abbr* = United Nations.

un- *prefix* not; opposite of; contrary to; reversal of an action or state.

'un, un *pron* (*dial*) one.

unable *adj* not able; lacking the strength, skill, power or opportunity (to do something).

unaccountable *adj* inexplicable, puzzling; not to be called to account for one's actions.

unaccustomed *adj* (*with* **to**) not used (to); not usual or familiar.

una corda *adj, adv* (*mus*) (*piano*) to be played with the soft pedal depressed.

unadulterated *adj* pure, unmixed.

unadvised *adj* unwise, imprudent; not advised.— **unadvisedly** *adv.*

unaffected *adj* sincere, frank, without pretension; not influenced or affected.—**unaffectedly** *adv.*

un-American *adj* contrary to US customs, ideals or interests.—**un-Americanism** *n.*

unanimous *adj* showing complete agreement.—**unanimity** *n.*—**unanimously** *adv.*

unapproachable *adj* aloof, unfriendly; impossible to reach; not to be equalled or rivalled.

unarmed *adj* not in possession of weapons; defenceless.

unasked *adj* not asked or asked for; not invited or requested; spontaneous. * *adv* of one's own accord; without prompting.

unassailable *adj* not open to attack; not open to criticism or doubt.

unassuming *adj* unpretentious; modest.

unattached *adj* unmarried, not engaged to be married; not belonging to a particular group, organization, etc.

unattended *adj* not supervised; not accompanied.

unauthorized *adj* not endorsed by authority.

unavailing *adj* futile, hopeless.—**unavailingly** *adv.*

unavoidable *adj* bound to happen, inevitable; necessary, compulsory.—**unavoidably** *adv.*

unaware *adj* not conscious or aware (of); ignorant (of).

unawares *adv* by surprise; unexpectedly, without warning.

unbalanced *adj* mentally unstable; having bias or over-representing a particular view, group, interest, etc; (*bookkeeping*) not having equal debit and credit totals.

unbearable *adj* intolerable, not able to be endured.— **unbearably** *adv.*

unbeatable *adj* impossible to beat; outstanding, excellent.

unbeaten *adj* not beaten, unsurpassed.

unbecoming *adj* (*clothes, make-up, etc*) not enhancing the wearer's appearance; (*behaviour*) not suitable or seemly.

unbeknown *adj* (*with* **to**) happening without (a person's) knowledge.

unbelief *n* disbelief, scepticism, esp in religious matters.

unbelievable *adj* not able to be believed; incredible.— **unbelievably** *adv.*

unbeliever *n* a person who does not believe, esp in a religion.

unbelieving *adj* lacking belief; sceptical.— **unbelievingly** *adv.*

unbend *vb* (**unbending, unbent**) *vt* to straighten from a bent shape; to release or untie (eg a rope). * *vi* to become more relaxed, affable or informal in manner.

unbending *adj* severe, stern; inflexible, unchanging; rigid in behaviour or attitude.

unbiased, unbiassed *adj* without prejudice or bias; impartial, even-handed, disinterested.

unbidden *adj* not commanded, asked for or invited.

unblushing *adj* shameless, impudent.—**unblushingly** *adv.*

unborn *adj* not yet born; still to appear or happen in the future.

unbosom *vt* to reveal the thoughts or feelings of (oneself).

unbounded *adj* without limits.

unbowed *adj* not bowed; not subdued, free.

unbridled *adj* unrestrained; (*horse*) having no bridle.

unbroken *adj* whole, in one piece; continuous, uninterrupted; (*record*) not yet beaten; (*horses, etc*) wild, untamed; organized, disciplined.

unburden *vt* to reveal or confess one's troubles, secrets, etc to another in order to relieve the mind; to take off a burden.

unbutton *vt* to unfasten the buttons of (a garment).

unbuttoned *adj* unfastened; (*inf*) free, uninhibited.

uncalled-for *adj* unnecessary, unwanted, unwarranted.

uncanny *adj* (**uncannier, uncanniest**) odd; unexpected; suggestive of supernatural powers; unearthly.

unceremonious *adj* without ceremony, informal; abrupt, rude.—**unceremoniously** *adv.*

uncertain *adj* not knowing accurately, doubtful; (*with* **of**) not confident or sure; not fixed, variable, changeable.—**uncertainty** *n.*

uncertainty principle *n* (*phys*) the principle that it is impossible to determine accurately both the position and momentum of an elementary particle simultaneously.—*also* **Heisenberg uncertainty principle**.

uncharted *adj* not marked on a map; unsurveyed, unexplored.

unchristian *adj* contrary to Christian belief or principle; savage, pagan.

uncial *adj* written in or resembling large rounded capital letters as used in early medieval Greek and Latin manuscripts. * *n* an uncial character or manuscript.

uncinate *adj* (*plant, animal*) having a hook-shaped part.

uncircumcised *adj* not circumcised; not Jewish; impure.—**uncircumcision** *n.*

uncivil *adj* lacking in manners, impolite.—**uncivility** *n.*

uncivilized *adj* not civilized, unsophisticated; remote, wild.

uncle *n* the brother of one's father or mother; the husband of one's aunt.

unclean *adj* not clean, contaminated; ceremonially defiled.

Uncle Sam *n* the government of the US personified.

Uncle Tom *n* (*derog*) a Black person who acts in a servile manner to white people.

unclothe *vt* (**unclothing, unclothed** *or* **unclad**) to remove the clothes from; to uncover.

uncoil *vti* to (cause to) unwind.

uncomfortable *adj* causing discomfort; feeling discomfort or unease.

uncommitted *adj* not bound to a particular cause, belief or course of action.

uncommon *adj* rare, unusual; extraordinary.

uncommonly *adv* hardly ever; exceptionally, particularly.

uncommunicative *adj* not willing to talk or express an opinion, etc; reserved.

uncompromising *adj* not prepared to compromise; inflexible, obstinate.

unconcern *n* indifference.

unconcerned *adj* not involved in or concerned with; not troubled.

unconditional *adj* without restrictions or conditions, absolute.

unconscionable *adj* unscrupulous; unreasonable.—**unconscionably** *adv*.

unconscious *adj* not aware (of); lacking normal perception by the senses, insensible; unintentional. * *n* the deepest level of mind containing feelings and emotions of which one is unaware and unable to control.—**unconsciously** *adv*.

unconsciousness *n* the state of being without the senses, as when knocked out.

unconstitutional *adj* contrary to the constitution of a country.—**unconstitutionality** *n*.

unconventional *adj* not bound by social rules or conventions.—**unconventionally** *adv*.

uncork *vt* to pull the cork from a bottle; (*emotions, desires, etc*) to unleash, give vent to.

uncouple *vti* to disconnect or become disconnected.

uncouth *adj* lacking in manners; rough; rude.—**uncouthness** *n*.

uncover *vt* to remove the cover from; to reveal or expose; to remove one's hat in greeting or out of respect.

uncovered *adj* not having a cover; revealed; not having any insurance or security; with one's hat removed out of respect, etc.

UNCTAD *abbr* = United Nations Conference on Trade and Development.

unction *n* an anointing, as for medical or religious purposes; anything that soothes or comforts; affected sincerity.

unctuous *adj* oily; smarmy; too suave; insincerely charming.—**unctuously** *adv*.—**unctuousness** *n*.

uncurl *vti* to straighten; to straighten up, relax.

uncut *adj* not cut; (*book*) not having the folds of the leaves trimmed or slit; (*gemstone*) not cut into shape; not abridged.

undaunted *adj* fearless; not discouraged.—**undauntedly** *adv*.

undecagon *n* a polygon with eleven sides.

undeceive *vt* to free from deception or error.

undecided *adj* doubtful, hesitant; (*solution, etc*) not determined.—**undecidedly** *adv*.

undeniable *adj* readily apparent, obviously true; unquestionably excellent.

under *prep* lower than; beneath the surface of; below; covered by; subject to; less than, falling short of. * *adv* beneath, below, lower down. * *adj* lower in position, degree or rank; subordinate.

under- *prefix* beneath, below.

underachieve *vi* to perform less well than expected given one's potential.—**underachiever** *n*.

underact *vt* to perform (a dramatic role) without proper conviction or emphasis.

underage *adj* below the normal or legal age.

underarm *adj* of, for, in, or used on the area under the arm, or armpit; done with the hand below the level of the elbow or shoulder.

underbelly *n* (*pl* **underbellies**) the underside of an animal, etc; the most vulnerable part of something.

underbid *vb* (**underbidding, underbid**) *vt* to bid a lower amount than (rivals); (*bridge, etc*) to bid less than the strength of the hand merits. * *vi* to bid too low.

undercapitalized *adj* (*business*) having insufficient capital to operate efficiently.

undercarriage *n* the landing gear of an aeroplane; a car's supporting framework.

undercharge *vt* to charge below the fair price.

underclass *n* those least privileged people in society who fall outside the normal social scale, characterized by poverty, unemployment, poor education, social instability, etc.

underclothes *npl* underwear.—*also* **underclothing**.

undercoat *n* a coat of paint, etc, applied as a base below another; a growth of hair or fur under another; a coat worn under an overcoat.

undercover *adj* done or operating secretly.

undercurrent *n* a hidden current under water; an emotion, opinion, etc, not apparent.

undercut *vt* (**undercutting, undercut**) to charge less than a competitor; to undermine.

underdeveloped *adj* not fully grown, immature; (*societies*) having an inadequate social and political infrastructure for sustained economic growth; (*film*) not processed long enough to form a proper image.

underdog *n* the loser in an encounter, contest, etc; a person in an inferior position.

underdone *adj* not sufficiently or completely cooked.

underdressed *adj* wearing clothes that are too informal for a particular occasion.

underemployed *adj* not fully or most efficiently employed.

underestimate *vti* to set too low an estimate on or for. * *n* too low an estimate.

underexpose *vt* (*photog*) to fail to expose (film) to light sufficiently long to produce a good image.—**underexposed** *adj*.—**underexposure** *n*.

underfelt *n* a layer of thick felt between a carpet and floor.

underfoot *adv* underneath the foot or feet; on the ground.

undergarment *n* a piece of underwear or clothing worn beneath other outer clothing.

undergo *vt* (**undergoing, underwent,** *pp* **undergone**) to experience, suffer, endure.

undergraduate *n* a student at a college or university studying for a first degree.

underground *adj* situated under the surface of the ground; secret; of noncommercial newspapers, movies, etc that are unconventional, radical, etc. * *n* a secret group working for the overthrow of the government or the expulsion of occupying forces; an underground railway system; a subway.

undergrowth *n* shrubs, plants, etc growing beneath trees.

underhand *adv* (*sport*) with an underarm motion; underhandedly.

underhanded *adj* sly, secret, deceptive.—**underhandedly** *adv*.

underlay *n* a material, lining laid beneath another for support; felt or rubber laid beneath a carpet for insulation, etc.

underlie *vt* (**underlying, underlay,** *pp* **underlain**) to be situated under; to form the basis of.

underline vt to put a line underneath; to emphasize.

underling n a person of inferior rank or status to someone else; a subordinate.

underlying adj existing, but hard to detect; fundamental, supporting.

undermentioned adj mentioned below or later in the text.

undermine vt to wear away, or weaken; to injure or weaken, esp by subtle or insidious means.

underneath adv under. * adj lower. * n the underside.—also prep.

undernourished adj consuming or supplied with less than the minimum quantity of food necessary for normal health and growth.

underpants npl pants worn as an undergarment by men and boys.

underpass n a section of road running beneath another road, a railway, etc.

underpin vt to strengthen or support from beneath.

underpinning n the material used to support a structure, the foundation.

underplay vt to perform (a dramatic role) with restraint; to play down the importance of.

underprivileged adj lacking the basic rights of other members of society; poor.

underproof adj containing less alcohol per volume than proof spirit.

underrate vt to undervalue, to underestimate.

underscore vt to draw a line under; to emphasize.

undersea adj, adv below the surface of the sea.

underseal n a protective layer of tar, etc applied to the underside of a vehicle. * vt to apply this protective layer.

undersecretary n (pl **undersecretaries**) a senior civil servant in Great Britain; in US, a secretary immediately subordinate to a principal.

undersell vt (**underselling, undersold**) to sell at a reduced price; to sell at a price lower than (someone else); to promote with moderation.

undersexed adj having a weaker than normal sex drive.

undershirt n a vest.

undershoot vti (**undershooting, undershot**) to (cause to) land short of a runway; to shoot short of a target.

underside n the lower surface.

undersigned adj signed at the end. * n a person who signs his or her name at the end of a document.

undersized adj less than usual size.

underskirt n a woman's undergarment worn beneath the skirt, a petticoat.

underslung adj suspended from above; (vehicle chassis) suspended below the axles

understand vb (**understanding, understood**) vt to comprehend; to realize; to believe; to assume; to know thoroughly (eg a language); to accept; to be sympathetic with. * vi to comprehend; to believe.—**understandable** adj.

understanding n comprehension; compassion, sympathy; personal opinion, viewpoint; mutual agreement. * adj sympathetic.

understate vt to state something in restrained terms; to represent as less than is the case.—**understatement** n.

understudy vti (**understudying, understudied**) to learn a role or part so as to be able to replace (the actor playing it); to act as an understudy (to).—also n.

undertake vt (**undertaking, undertook,** pp **undertaken**) to attempt to; to agree to; to commit oneself; to promise; to guarantee.

undertaker n a funeral director.

undertaking n enterprise; task; promise; obligation.

underthings npl underwear.

undertone n a hushed tone of voice; an undercurrent of feeling; a pale colour.

undertow n the backwash from a breaking wave; an undercurrent moving in a different direction from the surface current.

undervalue vt (**undervaluing, undervalued**) to put too low a price or value on.—**undervaluation** n.

underwater adj being carried on under the surface of the water, esp the sea; submerged; below the water line of a vessel.—also adv.

under way adv in or into motion or progress.

underwear n garments worn underneath one's outer clothes, next to the skin.

underweight adj weighing less than normal or necessary.

underwent see **undergo.**

underwhelm vt to disappoint.

underworld n criminals as an organized group; (myth) Hades.

underwrite vt to agree to finance (an undertaking, etc); to sign one's name to (an insurance policy), thus assuming liability. * vi to work as an underwriter.—**underwriter** n.

undesirable adj not desirable; not pleasant; objectionable.—**undesirability** n.—**undesirably** adv.

undetermined adj not yet decided; not discovered.

undies npl (inf) women's underwear.

undo vt (**undoing, undid,** pp **undone**) to untie or unwrap; to reverse (what has been done); to bring ruin on.

undone adj not done; not fastened or tied.

undoubted adj without doubt; definite, certain.—**undoubtedly** adv.

undreamed, undreamt n (with **of**) not thought of or imagined.

undress vt to remove the clothes from. * vi to take off one's clothes.

undressed adj not dressed, partially or informally clothed; (wound) not bandaged; (food) not prepared for serving; (hides) not processed.

undue adj improper; excessive.

undulate vti to move or cause to move like waves; to have or cause to have a wavy form or surface.

undulation n a wavelike form or motion.

unduly adv too; excessively; improperly.

undying adj eternal.

unearned adj (income) not earned by labour or skill; undeserved.

unearth vt to dig up from the earth; to discover; to reveal.

unearthly adj mysterious; eerie; supernatural; absurd, unreasonable.

uneasy adj uncomfortable; restless; anxious; disquieting.—**uneasily** adv.—**uneasiness** n.

uneatable adj (food) not edible, esp because of its condition or appearance.

uneconomic adj wasteful; unprofitable.

unemployable adj not fit or acceptable for work.

unemployed adj not having a job, out of work.—**unemployment** n.

unequal adj not equal; not regular or uniform; not sufficiently strong or able.—**unequally** adv.

unequalled, unequaled adj not equalled; supreme.

unequivocal adj unambiguous; plain; clear.—**unequivocally** adv.

unerring *adj* sure, unfailing.

UNESCO *abbr* = United Nations Educational, Scientific and Cultural Organization.

uneven *adj* not level or smooth; variable; not divisible by two without leaving a remainder.—**unevenness** *n.*

uneventful *adj* ordinary, routine.—**uneventfully** *adv.*

unexampled *adj* without precedent or comparison.

unexceptionable *adj* irreproachable.

unexceptional *adj* ordinary, normal.

unexpected *adj* not looked for, unforeseen.—**unexpectedly** *adv.*

unfailing *adj* not failing or giving up; persistent; constant, dependable.—**unfailingly** *adv.*

unfair *adj* unjust; unequal; against the rules.—**unfairly** *adv.*—**unfairness** *n.*

unfaithful *adj* disloyal; not abiding by a promise; adulterous.—**unfaithfully** *adv.*—**unfaithfulness** *n.*

unfamiliar *adj* not known, strange; (*with* **with**) not familiar.

unfasten *vt* to open or become opened; to undo or become undone; to loose, loosen.

unfathomable *adj* not able to be measured; incomprehensible.

unfavourable, unfavorable *adj* negative, disapproving; adverse.

unfeeling *adj* callous, hardhearted.—**unfeelingly** *adv.*

unfinished *adj* not finished, incomplete; in the making; crude, sketchy.

unfit *adj* unsuitable; in bad physical condition.

unflappable *adj* (*inf*) calm, not easily agitated.

unflinching *adj* calm, steadfast.—**unflinchingly** *adv.*

unfold *vti* to open or spread out; to become revealed; to develop.

unforeseen *adj* unsuspected.

unforgettable *adj* never to be forgotten; fixed in the mind; impressive, exceptional.—**unforgettably** *adv.*

unfortunate *adj* unlucky; disastrous; regrettable. * *n* an unlucky person.

unfortunately *adv* regrettably, unluckily, unhappily.

unfounded *adj* groundless; baseless.

unfreeze *vti* (**unfreezing, unfroze, unfrozen**) to (cause to) thaw; to remove restrictions on (wage or price rises, etc).

unfrock *vt* to remove (a person in holy orders) from ecclesiastical office.

unfurl *vti* to open; to unfold.

ungainly *adj* (**ungainlier, ungainliest**) awkward; clumsy.—**ungainliness** *n.*

ungodly *adj* (**ungoldier, ungodliest**) not religious; sinful; wicked; (*inf*) outrageous.

ungovernable *adj* not able to be controlled or restrained.

unguarded *adj* without protection, vulnerable; open to attack; careless; candid, frank.—**unguardedly** *adv.*

unguent *n* a lubricant or ointment.

ungulate *n, adj* (an animal) having hooves.

unhallowed *adj* not consecrated; sinful.

unhappy *adj* (**unhappier, unhappiest**) not happy or fortunate; sad; wretched; not suitable.—**unhappily** *adv.*—**unhappiness** *n.*

unhealthy *adj* (**unhealthier, unhealthiest**) not healthy or fit, sick; encouraging or resulting from poor health; harmful, degrading; dangerous.—**unhealthily** *adv.*—**unhealthiness** *n.*

unheard *adj* not heard; not listened to.

unheard-of *adj* not known before; without precedent.

unhinge *vt* to make crazy, derange.

unholy *adj* (**unholier, unholiest**) wicked; (*inf*) outrageous, enormous.

unhook *vt* to remove from a hook; to unfasten the hooks of (a garment).

uni *n* (*inf*) university.

uni- *prefix* one; single.

unicameral *adj* of or having only one legislative chamber.—**unicamerally** *adv.*

UNICEF *abbr* = United Nations International Children's Emergency Fund, now United Nations Children's Fund.

unicellular *adj* (*microorganisms, etc*) consisting of a single cell.—**unicellularity** *n.*

unicorn *n* an imaginary creature with a body like a horse and a single horn on the forehead.

unicycle *n* a pedal-driven cycle with a single wheel, used by circus and street entertainers.

unidirectional *adj* involving, going in, or operating in one direction only.

uniform *adj* unchanging in form; consistent; identical. * *n* the distinctive clothes worn by members of the same organization, such as soldiers, schoolchildren.—**uniformly** *adv.*

uniformity *n* (*pl* **uniformities**) the state of being consistent or the same; dullness, monotony.

unify *vt* (**unifying, unified**) to make into one; to unite.—**unification** *n.*

unilateral *adj* involving one only of several parties; not reciprocal.—**unilateralism** *n.*—**unilaterally** *adv.*

unimpeachable *adj* completely honest, truthful, etc; irreproachable.—**unimpeachably** *adv.*

uninhibited *adj* not repressed or restrained; relaxed, spontaneous.—**uninhibitedly** *adv.*

uninterested *adj* lacking interest; not concerned, indifferent.—**uninterestedly** *adv.*

union *n* the act of uniting; a combination of several things; a confederation of individuals or groups; marriage; a trades union.

unionist *n* an advocate or supporter of union or unionism.—**unionism** *n.*

unionize *vt* to organize (employees) into a trade union.—**unionization** *n.*

Union Jack *n* the national flag of the UK.

unipolar *adj* of, produced by, or having a single electric or magnetic pole.—**unipolarity** *n.*

unique *adj* without equal; the only one of its kind.—**uniquely** *adv.*

unisex *adj* of a style that can be worn by both sexes.

unisexual *adj* of one sex only; having male or female sex organs but not both.—**unisexually** *adv.*—**unisexuality** *n.*

unison *n* accordance of sound, concord, harmony; **in unison** simultaneously, in agreement, in harmony.

unit *n* the smallest whole number, one; a single or whole entity; (*measurement*) a standard amount; an establishment or group of people who carry out a specific function; a piece of furniture fitting together with other pieces.—**unitary** *adj.*

unite *vti* to join into one, to combine; to be unified in purpose.

United Kingdom *n* Great Britain and Northern Ireland.

United Nations *n sing or pl* an international organization of nations for world peace and security formed in 1945.

United States *n* a federation of states, esp the United States of America.

unit trust *n* a company that manages a range of investments on behalf of members of the public whose interests are looked after by an independent trust.

unity n (pl **unities**) oneness; harmony; concord.

Univ. abbr = university.

universal adj widespread; general; relating to all the world or the universe; relating to or applicable to all mankind.—**universally** adv.—**universality** n (pl **universalities**).

universe n all existing things; (astron) the totality of space, stars, planets and other forms of matter and energy; the world.

university n (pl **universities**) an institution of higher education which confers bachelors' and higher degrees; the campus or staff of a university.

unjust adj not characterized by justice; not fair.—**unjustly** adv.—**unjustness** n.

unkempt adj uncombed; slovenly, dishevelled.

unkind adj lacking in kindness or sympathy; harsh; cruel.—**unkindly** adv.—**unkindness** n.

unknown adj not known; not famous; not understood; with an unknown value. * n an unknown person or thing.

unleaded adj (petrol) not mixed with tetraethyl lead.

unleash vt to release from a leash; to free from restraint.

unleavened adj (bread, etc) made without yeast or other raising agent.

unless conj if not; except that.

unlettered adj illiterate.

unlike adj not the same, dissimilar. * prep not like; not characteristic of.—**unlikeness** n.

unlikely adj improbable; unpromising.

unlimited adj without limits; boundless; not restricted.—**unlimitedly** adv.

unlisted adj not on a list; ex-directory.

unload vti to remove a load, discharge freight from a truck, ship, etc; to relieve of or express troubles, etc; to dispose of, dump; to empty, esp a gun.

unlock vt (door, lock, etc) to unfasten; to let loose; to reveal; to release.

unloose, unloosen vt to relax (a grip, etc); to release, free; to untie.

unlovely n ugly, unpleasant.—**unloveliness** n.

unlucky adj (**unluckier, unluckiest**) not lucky, not fortunate; likely to bring misfortune; regrettable.

unman vt (**unmanning, unmanned**) to weaken the nerve or courage of; to make effeminate.

unmanly adj weak, cowardly; effeminate.—**unmanliness** n.

unmanned adj (spacecraft, etc) not manned, operated by remote control.

unmannerly adj lacking good manners; rude.—**unmannerliness** n.

unmask vti to remove the mask from; to expose, show up.

unmentionable adj too bad, shocking, embarrassing, etc to be mentioned.

unmentionables npl underwear.

unmistakable, unmistakeable adj obvious, clear.—**unmistakably, unmistakeably** adv.

unmitigated adj unqualified, absolute.

unmoved adj not touched by emotion, calm.

unnatural adj abnormal; contrary to nature; artificial; affected; strange; wicked.—**unnaturally** adv.

unnecessary adj not necessary.—**unnecessarily** adv.—**unnecessariness** n.

unnerve vt to cause to lose courage, strength, confidence; to frighten.

unnumbered adj countless; not having a number.

UNO abbr = United Nations Organization.

unobtrusive adj modest, staying in the background.

unoccupied adj not occupied, empty; unemployed.

unpack vti (suitcase, etc) to remove the contents of; (container, etc) to take things out of; to unload.

unparalleled adj having no equal, unmatched.

unparliamentary adj contrary to parliamentary procedure or practice.

unperson n a person (e.g. a political dissident) whose existence is officially ignored or denied.

unpick vt to undo the stitching of.

unplaced adj not placed; not among the first three at the end of a race.

unpleasant adj not pleasing or agreeable; nasty; objectionable.—**unpleasantly** adv.—**unpleasantness** n.

unplumbed adj not plumbed; not fully investigated or explored.

unpopular adj disliked; lacking general approval.—**unpopularity** n.

unprecedented adj having no precedent; unparalleled.

unprejudiced adj not prejudiced, impartial.

unprepossessing adj unattractive, repellent.

unpretentious adj modest, not boasting.

unprincipled adj lacking scruples.

unprintable adj too bad, libellous, obscene, etc to be printed.

unprofessional adj contrary to professional etiquette.—**unprofessionally** adv.

unputdownable adj (book) grippingly readable.

unqualified adj lacking recognized qualifications; not equal to; not restricted, complete.

unquestionable adj certain, not disputed.—**unquestionably** adv.

unquestioned adj not called into question; indisputable.

unquiet adj turbulent, disordered; nervous, agitated.—**unquietly** adv.—**unquietness** n.

unquote interj used when speaking to indicate the end of a direct quotation.

unravel vt (**unravelling, unravelled** or **unraveling, unraveled**) to disentangle; to solve.

unread adj not read (yet); unfamiliar with a specified subject; illiterate.

unreadable adj illegible; not worth reading.

unreal adj not real; imaginary, fanciful; false, insincere.

unreason n absence of reason in thought or action.

unreasonable adj contrary to reason; lacking reason; immoderate; excessive.—**unreasonably** adv.

unreasoning adj lacking reason, irrational

unrelenting adj relentless; continuous.—**unrelentingly** adv.

unremitting adj incessant.

unrequited adj not reciprocated, not returned.

unreserved adj not reserved; frank, demonstrative; absolute, entire; not booked.

unreservedly adv without conditions; openly.

unrest n uneasiness; anxiety; angry discontent verging on revolt.

unrighteous adj sinful, wicked.

unrivalled, unrivaled adj without equal, peerless.

unroll vti to open out or down from a roll; to unfold; to straighten out; to reveal or become revealed.

unruffled adj cool and calm; still, smooth.

unruly adj (**unrulier, unruliest**) hard to control, restrain, or keep in order; disobedient.

unsaddle vt to take the saddle from; to unseat. * vi to remove the saddle from a horse.

unsaid *adj* not said or expressed.

unsaturated *adj* (*chemical substance*) having double or triple bonds and therefore able to form products by chemical addition; (*vegetable fats*) containing fatty acids with double bonds.—**unsaturation** *n*.

unsavoury, unsavory *adj* distasteful; disagreeable; offensive.

unscathed *adj* unharmed.

unscramble *vt* to disentangle; (*a scrambled message*) to make intelligible.

unscrew *vti* to remove a screw from; (*lid, etc*) to loosen by turning.

unscrupulous *adj* without principles.

unseasonable *n* (*weather*) unusual for the season of the year; untimely.—**unseasonableness** *n*.—**unseasonably** *adv*.

unseat *vt* to dislodge from a seat, saddle, etc; to remove from office.

unseeded *adj* (*tennis players, etc*) not ranked among the top players in the preliminary rounds of a competition.

unseemly *adj* unbecoming; inappropriate.

unseen *adj* concealed, hidden; not seen or read beforehand.

unselfish *adj* not selfish; thinking of others before oneself.—**unselfishly** *adv*.—**unselfishness** *n*.

unsettle *vti* to disturb, disrupt, or disorder.

unsettled *adj* changeable; lacking stability; unpredictable; not concluded.

unsheathe *vt* to draw (a weapon) from a sheath.

unsightly *adj* unattractive; ugly.

unskilful, unskillful *adj* clumsy, awkward.

unskilled *adj* without special skill or training.

unsociable *n* antisocial; reserved.

unsocial *n* averse to social activities; (*working hours*) outwith the normal working day.

unsolicited *adj* not asked for.

unsophisticated *adj* naïve, inexperienced; simple; pure, unadulterated.

unsound *adj* flimsy, not stable; defective, flawed; in poor health; not sane.—**unsoundly** *adv*.—**unsoundness** *n*.

unsparing *adj* profuse, lavish; severe.

unspeakable *adj* bad beyond words, indescribable.

unstable *adj* easily upset; mentally unbalanced; irresolute.

unsteady *adj* (**unsteadier, unsteadiest**) shaky, reeling; vacillating.—**unsteadily** *adv*.

unstop *vt* (**unstopping, unstopped**) to remove the stopper from; to free from an obstruction.

unstrung *adj* emotionally distressed.

unstudied *adj* natural; unaffected in manner.

unsubstantial *adj* lacking weight, flimsy; of doubtful factual validity.

unsullied *adj* not stained, pure.

unsung *adj* not acclaimed or celebrated.

unswerving *adj* not deviating; constant, unchanging.

untangle *vt* to rid of tangles, unravel; to sort out.

untaught *adj* not educated or trained; not acquired by teaching.

untenable *adj* not able to be justified or defended.—**untenability** *n*.

unthinkable *adj* inconceivable; out of the question; improbable.—**unthinkably** *adv*.

unthinking *adj* unable to think; thoughtless, inconsiderate.—**unthinkingly** *adv*.

untidy *adj* (**untidier, untidiest**) not neat, disordered.

* *vt* (**untidying, untidied**) to make untidy.—**untidily** *adv*.

untie *vt* (**untying, untied**) to undo a knot in, unfasten.

until *prep* up to the time of; before. * *conj* up to the time when or that; to the point, degree, etc that; before.

untimely *adj* premature; inopportune.

unto *prep* (*arch*) to.

untold *adj* not told; too great to be counted; immeasurable.

untouchable *adj* unable to be touched or handled; exempt from criticism or control; lying beyond reach.

untoward *adj* unseemly; unfavourable; adverse.

untrue *adj* incorrect, false; not faithful, disloyal; inaccurate.

untruth *n* falsehood; a lie.

untruthful *adj* telling lies; false.

untutored *adj* lacking (refined) education.

unused *adj* not (yet) used; (*with to*) not accustomed (to something).

unusual *adj* uncommon; rare.

unutterable *adj* impossible to express in words.—**unutterably** *adv*.

unvarnished *adj* not varnished; plain, direct; not embellished.

unveil *vt* to reveal; to disclose.

unwaged *adj* not paid a wage; unemployed.

unwarrantable *adj* indefensible.

unwarranted *adj* not authorized.

unwary *adj* lacking caution; heedless, gullible; unguarded.—**unwarily** *adv*.

unwelcome *adj* not welcome, not invited; disagreeable; unpleasant.

unwell *adj* ill, not well; (*inf*) suffering from a hangover.

unwholesome *adj* harmful to physical, mental or moral health and well-being; ill-looking; (*food*) of poor quality.—**unwholesomeness** *n*.

unwieldy *adj* not easily moved or handled, as because of large size; awkward.—**unwieldily** *adv*.—**unwieldiness** *n*.

unwilling *adj* not willing, reluctant; said or done with reluctance.—**unwillingly** *adv*.—**unwillingness** *n*.

unwind *vt* to untangle; to undo. * *vi* to relax.

unwise *adj* lacking wisdom; imprudent.—**unwisely** *adv*.

unwitting *adj* not knowing; unintentional.—**unwittingly** *adv*.

unworldly *adj* spiritual, not concerned with the material world.

unworthy *adj* (**unworthier, unworthiest**) not deserving.

unwritten *adj* not written or printed; traditional; oral.

unwritten law *n* law based on custom or mores rather than legislative enactment.

up *adv* to, toward, in or on a higher place; to a later period; so as to be even with in time, degree, etc. * *prep* from a lower to a higher point on or along. * *adj* moving or directed upward; at an end; (*inf*) well-informed. * *vt* (**upping, upped**) to raise; to increase; to take up. * *n* ascent; high point.

up-and-coming *adj* promising for the future; likely to succeed.

upas *n* a Javanese tree that yields a poisonous sap.

upbeat *n* (*mus*) an unaccented beat in the last bar. * *adj* (*inf*) cheerful, optimistic.

upbraid *vt* to rebuke severely; to reproach.

upbringing *n* the process of educating and nurturing (a child).

upcountry *adv* towards the interior of a country, inland.

update *vt* to bring up to date.

updraught, updraft *n* a upward flow of air or other gas.

upend *vti* to turn or become turned on end; to upset or transform completely.

upfront *adj* honest, open. * *adv* (*money*) paid in advance.

upgrade *vt* to improve, raise to a higher grade.

upheaval *n* radical or violent change.

uphill *adj* ascending, rising; difficult, arduous. * *adv* up a slope or hill; against difficulties.

uphold *vt* (**upholding, upheld**) to support, sustain; to defend.

upholster *vt* (*furniture*) to fit with stuffing, springs, covering, etc.—**upholsterer** *n*.

upholstery *n* (*pl* **upholsteries**) materials used to make a soft covering esp for a seat.

upkeep *n* maintenance; the cost of it.

upland *n* an area of high ground. * *adj* of or pertaining to uplands.

uplift *vt* to raise, lift up; to improve the moral, cultural, spiritual, etc standard or condition of. * *n* a moral, cultural, spiritual, etc improvement.

upmarket *adj* of or appealing to wealthier buyers.

upmost *see* **uppermost**.

upon *prep* on, on top of.

upper *adj* farther up; higher in position, rank, status. * *n* the part of a boot or shoe above the sole; (*sl*) a drug used as a stimulant.

upper case *n* capital letters.—**upper-case** *adj*.

upper class *n* people occupying the highest social rank.—*also adj*.

upper crust *n* (*inf*) the aristocracy.

uppercut *n* an upward swinging punch to the chin.—*also vb*.

upper hand *n* the position of control, advantage.

upper house, chamber *n* one of the two houses of a bicameral legislature, such as the British House of Lords or US Senate.

uppermost *adj* at the top; highest in importance. * *adv* into the highest position, etc.—*also* **upmost**.

uppity *adj* (*inf*) snobbish, arrogant.

upright *adj* vertical, in an erect position; righteous, honest, just. * *n* a vertical post or support. * *adv* vertically.

uprising *n* a revolt; a rebellion.

uproar *n* a noisy disturbance; a commotion; an outcry.

uproarious *adj* making or marked by an uproar; extremely funny; (*laughter*) boisterous.—**uproariously** *adv*.

uproot *vt* to tear out by the roots; to remove from established surroundings.

upset[1] *vt* (**upsetting, upset**) to overturn; to spill; to disturb; to put out of order; to distress; to overthrow; to make physically sick.

upset[2] *n* an unexpected defeat; distress or its cause. * *adj* distressed; confused; defeated.

upshot *n* the conclusion; the result.

upside down *adj* inverted; the wrong way up; (*inf*) topsy turvy.

upsilon *n* the 20th letter of the Greek alphabet.

upstage *vt* to draw attention to oneself. * *adv* to the rear of the stage.

upstairs *adv* up the stairs; to an upper level or storey. * *n* an upper floor.

upstanding *adj* honest; of good character; in a standing position.

upstart *n* a person who has suddenly risen to a position of wealth and power; an arrogant person.

upstate *n* the mostly northern areas of a US state. * *adv, adj* towards, in, or pertaining to this area of a US state.

upstream *adv, adj* in the direction from which a stream is flowing.

upstroke *n* an upward stroke, as of a pen, paintbrush, piston, etc.

upsurge *n* a sudden rise or swell.

upswing *n* an upward swing or movement; an improvement, esp in the state of the economy.

uptake *n* a taking up; a shaft or pipe for carrying smoke upwards; (*inf*) understanding.

uptight *adj* (*inf*) very tense, nervous, etc.

up-to-date *adj* modern; fashionable.

upturn *n* an upward trend; an (economic) improvement. * *vt* to turn upside down.

upward, upwards *adj* from a lower to a higher place.—*also adv*.

upwardly-mobile *adj* aspiring to improve one's social and economic status.—**upward mobility** *n*.

upwind *adj, adv* in the direction from which the wind is blowing.

uraemia, uremia *n* the accumulation of waste products in the blood that are normally passed in the urine.

uranium *n* a metallic element used as a source of nuclear energy.

urano- *prefix* sky; the heavens.

uranography *n* the description and mapping of the stars, etc by astronomers.—**uranographer** *n*.—**uranographic** *adj*.

Uranus *n* the seventh planet from the sun.

urate *n* a salt or ester of uric acid.—**uratic** *adj*.

urban *adj* of or relating to a city.—**urbanization, urbanisation** *n*.

urbane *adj* sophisticated; refined.—**urbanity** *n*.

urban guerrilla *n* a terrorist who operates in a town or city.

urbanite *n* a person who lives in a town or city.

urban renewal *n* rehabilitation of dilapidated city areas, as by housing construction and slum clearance.

urchin *n* a raggedly dressed mischievous child; a sea urchin.

urea *n* a soluble crystalline compound present in urine produced by protein metabolism.

ureter *n* a tube that carries urine from the kidney to the bladder or cloaca.

urethra *n* the duct carrying urine out of the bladder.

urethritis *n* inflammation of the urethra.

uretic *adj* of or pertaining to the urine.

urge *vt* to drive forward; to press, plead with. * *n* an impulse, yearning.

urgency *n* (*pl* **urgencies**) the quality or condition of being urgent; compelling need; importance.

urgent *adj* impelling; persistent; calling for immediate attention.—**urgently** *adv*.

-urgy *n suffix* technology; technique.

-uria *n suffix* diseased condition of the urine.

uric *adj* of, present in, or derived from urine.

uric acid *n* a white odourless substance found in the urine of birds, reptiles and some mammals.

urinal *n* a bowl or trough for urination in public lavatories.

urinalysis *n* (*pl* **urinalyses**) the chemical analysis of urine for signs of disease.

urinate *vi* to pass urine.

urine *n* a yellowish fluid excreted by the kidneys and conveyed to the bladder.—**urinary** *adj*.

urinogenital *adj* urogenital.

urn *n* a vase or large vessel; a receptacle for preserving the ashes of the dead; a large metal container for boiling water for tea or coffee.

uro-, ur- *prefix* urine; urinary tract.

urogenital, urinogenital *adj* of or pertaining to the urinary and reproductive organs.—*also* **genitourinary**.

urology *n* the medical study and treatment of urogenital diseases.—**urologist** *n*.—**urological** *adj*.

uroscopy *n* the diagnosis of diseases by the examination of the patient's urine.

ursine *adj* of or resembling a bear.

urticaria *n* an allergic reaction which produces raised itchy whitish patches on the skin.—*also* **hives, nettle rash**.

US *abbr* = United States.

us *pron* the objective case of **we**.

USA *abbr* = United States of America.

USAF *abbr* = United States Air Force.

usage *n* customary use; practice, custom; use of language.

use[1] *vt* to put to some purpose; to utilize; to exploit (a person); to partake of (drink, drugs, tobacco, etc).—**usable, useable** *adj*.

use[2] *n* act of using or putting to a purpose; usage; usefulness; need (for); advantage; practice, custom.

used *adj* not new; second-hand.

useful *adj* able to be used to good effect; (*inf*) capable, commendable.—**usefully** *adv*.

useless *adj* having no use.—**uselessly** *adv*.—**uselessness** *n*.

user *n* one who uses; (*inf*) a drug addict.

user-friendly *adj* easy to understand and operate.

usher *n* one who shows people to their seats in a theatre, church, etc; a doorkeeper in a law court. * *vt* to escort to seats, etc.

usherette *nf* a woman who directs people to their seats in a cinema.

USN *abbr* = United States Navy.

USSR *abbr* = (*formerly*) Union of Soviet Socialist Republics.

usual *adj* customary; ordinary; normal.—**usually** *adv*.

usurer *n* a person who lends money at an excessively high rate of interest.

usurp *vt* to seize or appropriate unlawfully.—**usurper** *n*.

usury *n* (*pl* **usuries**) the practice of taking excessive interest on a loan; an excessive interest rate.

UT *abbr* = Utah.

utensil *n* an implement or container, esp one for use in the kitchen.

uterus *n* (*pl* **uteri**) the female organ in which offspring are developed until birth, the womb.—**uterine** *adj*.

utilitarian *adj* designed to be of practical use.

utility *n* (*pl* **utilities**) usefulness; a public service, such as telephone, electricity, etc; a company providing such a service.

utility room *n* a room containing laundry appliances, heating equipment, etc.

utilize *vt* to make practical use of.—**utilization** *n*.

utmost *adj* of the greatest degree or amount; furthest. * *n* the most possible.

utopia *n* a imaginary society or place considered to be ideal or perfect.—**utopian** *adj, n*.

utter[1] *adj* absolute; complete.

utter[2] *vt* to say; to speak.—**utterance** *n*.

utterly *adv* completely.

UV *abbr* = ultraviolet.

uvula *n* (*pl* **uvulas, uvulae**) the fleshy tissue suspended in the back of the throat over the back part of the tongue.

uxorious *adj* excessively fond of one's wife; doting.—**uxoriously** *adv*.—**uxoriousness** *n*.

V

V *abbr* = volt(s).

V, v *n* the 22nd letter of the English alphabet; something shaped like a V.

v *abbr* = velocity; *versus* against; *vide* see; verb.

VA *abbr* = Veterans Administration; Virginia.

vac *abbr* = vacuum.

vac *n* (*inf*) a vacation.

vacancy *n* (*pl* **vacancies**) emptiness; an unoccupied job or position.

vacant *adj* empty; unoccupied; (*expression*) blank.—**vacantly** *adv.*—**vacantness** *n*.

vacate *vt* to leave empty; to give up possession of.

vacation *n* a holiday; a period of the year when universities, colleges and law courts are closed. * *vi* to go on holiday.

vacationer, vacationist *n* a person on vacation, a holiday-maker.

vaccinal *adj* pertaining to or caused by a vaccine or vaccination.

vaccinate *vt* to inoculate with vaccine as a protection against a disease.—**vaccinator** *n*.

vaccination *n* inoculation with a vaccine; the resulting scar.

vaccine *n* a modified and hence harmless virus or other microorganism used for inoculation to give immunity from certain diseases by stimulating antibody production; cowpox virus used in this way against smallpox.

vaccinia *n* (*med*) cowpox.—**vaccinial** *adj*.

vacillate *vi* to waver, to show indecision; to fluctuate.—**vacillation** *n.*—**vacillator** *n*.

vacuity *n* (*pl* **vacuities**) emptiness; a vacant state of mind or expression; absence of matter; a vacuum; idleness; lack; an inane remark.

vacuole *n* (*biol*) a small cell or cavity filled with fluid in the interior of organic cells or protoplasm.—**vacuolate, vacuolated** *adj*.

vacuous *adj* empty; lacking intelligence, mindless.—**vacuously** *adv.*—**vacuousness** *n*.

vacuum *n* (*pl* **vacuums, vacua**) a region devoid of all matter; a region in which gas is present at low pressure; a vacuum cleaner. * *vt* to clean with a vacuum cleaner. * *adj* of, having or creating a vacuum; working by suction or maintenance of a partial vacuum.

vacuum cleaner *n* an electrical appliance for removing dust from carpets, etc, by suction.—**vacuum-clean** *vt*.

vacuum bottle, vacuum flask *n* a container for keeping liquids hot or cold.

vacuum-packed *adj* sealed in an airtight packet from which the air has been removed.

vade mecum *n* (*pl* **vade mecums**) a handbook or manual, etc, for ready reference, usu of a size to fit in a pocket.

vagabond *n* a vagrant; a wandering, homeless person.—**vagabondage** *n.*—**vagabondism** *n*.

vagal *adj* of, pertaining to, affected or controlled by the vagus nerve.

vagary *n* (*pl* **vagaries**) unpredictable or erratic behaviour or actions; a whim.—**vagarious** *adj*.

vagina *n* (**vaginas, vaginae**) in female mammals and humans, the canal connecting the uterus and the external sex organs.—**vaginal** *adj*.

vaginate, vaginated *adj* (*bot*) (*plant parts*) sheathed; with a vagina or sheath.

vagrancy (*pl* **vagrancies**) the habits and life of a vagrant; a wandering without a settled home.

vagrant *n* a person who has no settled home, a tramp. * *adj* wandering, roaming; wayward.—**vagrantly** *adv*.

vague *adj* unclear; indistinct, imprecise; (*person*) absentminded.—**vaguely** *adv.*—**vagueness** *n*.

vagus *n* (*pl* **vagi**) vagus nerve.

vagus nerve *n* either of a pair of cranial nerves supplying the larynx, heart, lungs, etc.

vail[1] *vti* (*arch*) to lower, to let fall; to take off (a hat) in respect.

vail[2] *n* (*arch*) a gratuity, a tip.

vain *adj* conceited; excessively concerned with one's appearance; senseless; futile; worthless; **in vain** to no purpose.—**vainly** *adv.*—**vainness** *n*.

vainglorious *adj* elated by one's achievements; boastful; showy.—**vaingloriously** *adv.*—**vaingloriousness** *n*.

vainglory *n* (*pl* **vainglories**) excessive vanity; boastfulness; showiness.

vair *n* a fur trimming on medieval robes, probably of Russian squirrel; (*her*) fur represented by small shields, coloured white and blue alternately.

valance *n* a decorative cover for the base of a bed; a canopy for a window frame to hide rods, etc; a pelmet.—**valanced** *adj*.

vale[1] *n* a valley.

vale[2] *interj, n* (*arch*) farewell.

valediction *n* a saying farewell; a taking leave; an instance of this; a speech made at this time.

valedictorian *n* a college student appointed on grounds of merit to deliver the valedictory oration on Commencement day.

valedictory *adj* uttered or bestowed on saying farewell; shown, performed or done by way of valediction. * *n* (*pl* **valedictories**) a valedictory oration; a statement or speech made on leaving a position, etc.

valence, valency *n* (*pl* **valences, valencies**) (*chem*) the power of elements to combine; the number of atoms of hydrogen that an atom or group can combine with to form a compound.

valence electron, valency electron *n* (*chem*) one of the electrons present in the outermost shell of an atom of a corresponding element.

Valenciennes (lace) *n* an ornate type of bobbin lace, formerly made of linen, now usu of cotton.

-valent *adj suffix* having a specified number of valences, eg *univalent*.

valentine *n* a lover or sweetheart chosen on St Valentine's Day, February 14; a card or gift sent on that day.

valerian *n* a herb with a root formerly used for medicinal purposes; the root of this used as a sedative.

valet *n* a manservant; a steward in a hotel or on board ship. * *vt* to attend (someone) as a valet. * *vi* to work as a valet.

valetudinarian, valetudinary *n* (*pl* valetudinarians, valetudinaries) a person who is overly preoccupied with his or her own health, a hypochondriac; a chronic invalid. * *adj* of ill health; sickly; seeking to recover health—valetudinarianism *n*.

valgus *adj* (*med*) deviating outwards from the vertical middle line of the body. * *n* (*pl* valguses) a deformity caused by a twisting from the middle line of the body, eg bow-legs.

Valhalla *n* (*Scandinavian myth*) the palace or hall of immortality in which the souls of heroes slain in battle dwell.—*also* Walhalla.

valiant *adj* courageous; brave.—valiance, valiancy *n*.— valiantly *adv*.

valid *adj* based on facts; (*objection, etc*) sound; legally acceptable; binding.—validity *n*.—validly *adv*.

validate *vt* to corroborate; to legalize.—validation *n*.

valine *n* an amino acid formed by the digestion of protein.

valise *n* a small case, usu of a size large enough to carry what is needed for an overnight visit.

Valkyrie *n* (*Scandinavian myth*) one of the twelve Norse war goddesses, handmaidens of Odin, who selected those who were worthy to be slain in battle and led them to Valhalla.—*also* Walkyrie.

vallation *n* a defensive wall; a rampart; the act of building this.

vallecula *n* (*pl* valleculae) (*anat*) a cleft or depressed area; (*bot*) a groove, a deep wrinkle.—vallecular, valleculate *adj*.

valley *n* (*pl* valleys) low land between hills or mountains usu with a river or stream flowing along its bottom; something resembling a valley, eg the angle where two sloping sides of a roof meet.

valonia *n* a large, dried acorn cup, or unripened acorn, from a particular kind of oak tree, used in tanning, dyeing, ink-making, etc.

valor *see* valour.

valorize *vt* to give an arbitrary price to (something) under government control.—valorization *n*.

valorous *adj* (*person*) valiant, courageous; (*action*) characterized by valour.—valorously *adv*.—valorousness *n*.

valour *n* courage; bravery (in battle).—*also* valor.

valse *n* a waltz, often used in the titles of musical compositions.

valuable *adj* having considerable importance or monetary worth. * *n* a personal possession of value, esp jewellery; (*pl*) valuable possessions.—valuably *adv*.

valuate *vt* to estimate the worth of, to value.—valuator *n*.

valuation *n* the act of valuing or valuating; an estimated price or worth; an estimation.—valuational *adj*.

value *n* worth, merit, importance; market value; purchasing power; relative worth; (*pl*) moral principles. * *vt* (valuing, valued) to estimate the worth of; to regard highly; to prize.—valuer *n*.

value-added tax *n* a tax levied on the difference between the production cost of an item and its selling price.

valued *adj* estimated; esteemed, prized.

value judgment *n* a subjective or unwarranted judgment.

valueless *adj* without value; worthless.—valuelessness *n*.

valuta *n* the value of one currency in terms of another.

valvar *see* valvular.

valvate *adj* having, resembling, or operating by means of a valve or valves; (*bot*) (*petals*) meeting at the edges without overlapping.

valve *n* a device for controlling the flow of a gas or liquid through a pipe; (*anat*) a tube allowing blood to flow in one direction only; (*mus*) a device on a brass instrument for increasing the length of the tube and thus altering the pitch being played.

valvular *adj* of, affecting a valve or valves, esp of the heart; acting like a valve; shaped like a valve; operating by means of a valve or valves.

valvule, valvelet *n* a little valve; anything resembling this.

valvulitis *n* inflammation of the valves, esp of the heart.

vambrace *n* plate armour for the forearm.

vamoose, vamose *vi* (*sl*) to make off quickly, to decamp.

vamp[1] *n* the part of a sock, boot or shoe covering the front of the foot; anything patched up or refurbished; an improvised musical accompaniment made up of chords. * *vt* to provide with a (new) vamp; to mend or repair; (*with* up) to renovate; (*mus*) to improvise.— vamper *n*.

vamp[2] *n* a seductive woman. * *vt* to fascinate or exploit by seducing. * *vi* to act as a vamp.

vampire *n* (*folklore*) a dead creature that by night leaves its grave to suck the blood of living people; a person who preys on others, an extortioner; a vampire bat.— vampiric *adj*.

vampire bat *n* a tropical American blood-sucking bat.

vampirism *n* belief in vampires; bloodsucking, or other acts associated with vampires.

van[1] *n* a covered motor vehicle for transporting goods, etc.

van[2] *n* the vanguard.

vanadium *n* a rare soft white metallic element used in steel alloys.—vanadic *adj*.

vandal *n* a person who wilfully or ignorantly damages property; (*with cap*) a member of a Germanic tribe that sacked Rome (455AD). * *adj* of of acting like a vandal; characterized by vandalism or lack of culture.

vandalism *n* the ruthless destruction or spoiling of anything beautiful or venerable; barbarous, ignorant or inartistic treatment.—vandalistic *adj*.

vandalize *vt* to carry out an act of vandalism.— vandalization *n*.

Van de Graaf generator *n* a machine that continuously separates electrostatic charges and in so doing produces a very high voltage.

van der Waals' force *n* a weak attractive force between two neighbouring atoms.

Vandyke beard *n* a small pointed beard.

Vandyke collar *n* a wide, white collar of lace or sewed work, with a deeply indented edge.

vane *n* a blade at the top of a spire, etc to show wind direction; a weather vane; a blade on a windmill or propeller.

vang n (naut) a guy rope from the end of a gaff to the deck, used for steadying the extremity of the peak of a gaff to the side of a ship; a rope running from the boom of a mainsail to the deck, used to keep the boom lowered.

vanguard n the front part of an army; the leading position of any movement.

vanilla n extract from the orchid pod used as a flavouring.—**vanillic** adj from vanilla.

vanish vi to disappear from sight, to become invisible, esp in a rapid and mysterious manner; to fade away; to cease to exist; (math) (numbers, quantities) to become zero.—**vanisher** n.

vanishing cream n a cleansing or foundation cream for make-up that is colourless when applied to the face.

vanity n (pl **vanities**) a fruitless endeavour; worthlessness; empty pride or conceit; love of indiscriminate admiration; an idle matter or show; a worthless or unfounded idea or statement; emptiness, lightness.

vanity case, vanity box n a small case used for carrying cosmetics, etc.

vanquish vt to conquer; to defeat; to overcome, to subdue.—**vanquisher** n.—**vanquishment** n.

vantage n a favourable position; a position allowing a clear view or understanding.

vanward adj towards the front, in the van. * adv forward, towards the front.

vapid adj flavourless, flat, insipid; dull, lifeless.—**vapidity** n.—**vapidly** adv.

vapor see **vapour**.

vaporish see **vapourish**.

vaporize vt to change into vapour.—**vaporization** n.—**vaporizer** n.

vaporous adj in the form of or like vapour; foggy, steamy; unreal, fanciful.—**vaporously** adv.—**vaporosity** n.

vapour n the gaseous state of a substance normally liquid or solid; particles of water or smoke in the air; (pl) hysteria. * vi to pass off in vapour, vaporize; to boast.—also **vapor**.

vapourish adj like vapour; full of vapour; (arch) in a state of depression and lethargy.—also **vaporish**.—**vapourishness, vapurishness** n.

vapour trail n condensed vapour left in the wake of an aircraft exhaust appearing as a white trail in the sky.

varec n the ash left after burning kelp.

variable adj liable to change; not constant. * n (math) a changing quantity that can have different values, as opposed to a constant.—**variability** n.—**variably** adv.

variance n disagreement, dissension; variation; tendency to vary; (law) a discrepancy between two statements or documents; **at variance** in conflict.

variant adj different; differing from an accepted or normal type, text, etc. * n a variant form or reading.

variation n a varying or being varied; alteration; deviation from a standard or type; diversity; deviation of the magnetic needle from true north; the measure of this; (gram) inflexion; (mus) repetition of a theme or melody with modifications.—**variational** adj.

varicella n (med) chickenpox.—**varicelloid** adj.

varices see **varix**.

varicocele n a swelling of the veins of the scrotum or of the spermatic cord.

varicoloured, varicolored) adj variegated, particoloured; of several colours.

varicose adj (veins) abnormally swollen and dilated.—**varicosis** n.—**varicosity** n.

varied adj showing variety, changing; partially changed; various; variegated.—**variedly** adv.

variegate vt to mark with different colours or tints; to dapple, streak; to cause to diversify.

variegated adj marked with different colours.

variegation n the condition of being variegated; diversity of colours.

variety n (pl **varieties**) diversity; an assortment.—**varietal** adj.

variety show n an entertainment made up of various acts, such as songs, comedy turns, etc.

variform adj having various forms.

variola n (med) smallpox.—**variolar** adj.

variolate adj having shallow, pitted depressions similar to those left on the skin after smallpox. * vt to inoculate with smallpox virus.—**variolation** n.

variole n a whitish spot or round mass consisting of radiating threads of crystal.

variolite n a kind of igneous rock with whitish spots, made up of clustered varioles.—**variolitic** adj.

varioloid n smallpox modified by vaccination or other means of acquired partial immunity. * adj like smallpox.

variorum n an edition of the works of an author with notes by various commentators.—also adj.

various adj varied, different; several.—**variously** adv.

varix n (pl **varices**) (med) a varicose vein; a twisted, dilated artery.

varlet n a scoundrel; (arch) a servant, attendant, or page of a knight.

varmint n (dial) a rascal; an offensive or trying person or animal; (hunting sl) the fox.

varnish n a sticky liquid which dries and forms a hard, glossy coating. * vt to coat with varnish.—**varnisher** n.

varsity n (pl **varsities**) (Brit, NZ inf) university.

varus n (pl **varuses**) a deformity caused by a turning in towards the vertical midline of the body, eg pigeon toes.

vary vti (**varying, varied**) to change, to diversify, modify; to become altered.—**varyingly** adv.

vascular adj (biol) of, consisting of, or containing vessels as part of a structure of animal and vegetable organisms for conveying blood, sap, etc.—**vascularity** n.

vasculum n (pl **vascula, vasculums**) a botanist's specimen box.

vas deferens n (pl **vasa deferentia**) the spermatic duct.

vase n a vessel for displaying flowers.

vasectomy n (pl **vasectomies**) male sterilization involving the cutting of the sperm-carrying tube.

Vaseline n (trademark) petroleum jelly used as a lubricant.

vasoconstrictor n a nerve, drug, etc, that constricts blood vessels.—**vasoconstrictive** adj.

vasodilator n a nerve, drug etc that dilates blood vessels.—**vasodilative** adj.

vasomotor adj (nerve, drug, etc) pertaining to or controlling the diameter of blood vessels.

vassal n a servant, dependant; subordinate.

vassalage n the state of being a vassal; the obligations associated with such a state; servitude; dependence; (rare) vassals collectively.

vast adj immense.—**vastly** adv.—n **vastness**.

vasty (**vastier, vastiest**) adj (arch) vast.

VAT abbr = value added tax.

vat n a large barrel or tank. * vt (**vatting, vatted**) to put in a vat; to treat in a vat.

vatic, vatical *adj* of or relating to a prophet or prophecy.

Vatican *n* the residence of the pope in Rome; papal authority.

Vaticanism *n* (*often derog*) the doctrine of Papal supremacy and infallibility.

vatication *n* a prophecy.

vaudeville *n* a stage show consisting of various acts, such as singing, dancing and comedy.

vault[1] *n* an arched ceiling or roof; a burial chamber; a strongroom for valuables; a cellar.—**vaulted** *adj*.

vault[2] *vti* to leap or jump over an obstacle. * *n* a leap.—**vaulter** *n*.

vaulting[1] *n* (*arch*) arched work in a building, etc.

vaulting[2] *adj* overly confident; to an exaggerated degree; used in the act of leaping over.

vaunt *vti* to display boastfully; to brag. * *n* a boast.—**vaunter** *n*.—**vauntingly** *adv*.

vavasour, vavasor, vavassor *n* (*feudalism*) the tenant of a baron or lord who is that lord's vassal and who in turn has other vassals under him.

VC *abbr* = Victoria Cross; vice-chairman; Vietcong.

VCR *abbr* = video cassette recorder.

VD *abbr* = venereal disease.

VDU *abbr* = video display unit.

veal *n* the edible flesh of a calf.

vector *n* (*physics*) a physical quantity having both direction and magnitude, eg displacement, acceleration, etc; an aircraft's or missile's course; (*biol*) a piece of DNA that transmits a parasitic disease.—**vectorial** *adj*.

Veda *n* (any of) the oldest sacred books or collection of hymns of the Hindus, written in old Sanskrit and of great antiquity.—**Vedic** *adj*.

Vedanta *n* a Hindu philosophy based on the Veda, postulating that the world of the senses is based on an illusion.—**Vedantic** *adj*.

vedette *n* a small patrol boat (—*also* **vedette boat**); a mounted sentry in advance of an outpost (—*also* **vidette**).

Vedic *adj* pertaining to the Veda, or to the old Sanskrit in which these were written; pertaining to the original Indo-Europeans of India.

veer *vi* (*wind*) to change direction; to swing around; to change from one mood or opinion to another.—**veeringly** *adv*.

veery *n* (*pl* **veeries**) a tawny North American thrush.

veg. *abbr* = vegetable(s).

vegan *n* a strict vegetarian who consumes no animal or dairy products.

vegetable *n* a herbaceous plant grown for food; (*inf*) a person who has suffered brain damage. * *adj* of, relating to or derived from plants.

vegetal *adj* of growth and vital functions; vegetable.

vegetarian *n* a person who consumes a diet that excludes meat and fish. * *adj* of vegetarians; consisting wholly of vegetables.

vegetarianism *n* the doctrine or practice of vegetarians; abstention from meating meat, fish, or other animal products.

vegetate *vi* to grow like a plant; to sprout; to lead a mentally inactive, aimless life.

vegetation *n* vegetable growth; plants in general.—**vegetational** *adj*.

vegetative, vegetive *adj* (*plants*) growing or having the power of growing, or producing growth in; (*way of life*) dull, passive, uneventful; (*reproduction*) asexual; referring to functions other than sexual reproduction.

vehement *adj* passionate; forceful; furious.—**vehemence, vehemency** *n*.—**vehemently** *adv*.

vehicle *n* a conveyance, such as a car, bus or truck, for carrying people or goods on land; a means of transmission for ideas, impressions, etc, a medium; (*med*) a substance in which a strong medicine can be administered palatably.—**vehicular** *adj*.

veil *n* a thin fabric worn over the head or face of a woman; a nun's headdress; anything that conceals; a velum. * *vt* to put on a veil; to cover; to conceal, dissemble.

veiled *adj* covered with or wearing a veil; shrouded in a veil; concealed, hidden; covert; not openly declared; (*sound, voice*) indistinct, muffled.

vein *n* (*anat*) one of the vessels that convey the blood back to the heart; (*geol*) a seam of a mineral within a rock; (*bot*) a branching rib in a leaf; a streak of different colour, as in marble, cheese, etc; a style or mood (*serious vein*). * *vt* to streak.—**veiny** *adj*.

veinlet *n* a small vein.

veinprint *n* the pattern of veins on the back of the hand, which is unique to an individual.

velamen *n* (*pl* **velamina**) (*anat*) an outer membrane or epidermis; a velum; (*bot*) a thick, moisture-absorbing aerial root, consisting of dead cells, found on some plants.

velar *adj* of the velum or soft palate; (*phonetics*) pronounced with the back of the tongue touching the soft palate. * *n* a velar sound.

velarium *n* (*pl* **velaria**) in ancient Rome, the great awning that stretched over open theatres.

Velcro *n* (*trademark*) a nylon material made of matching strips of tiny hooks and pile that are easily pressed together or pulled apart.

veld, veldt *n* in South Africa, open grass country.

velites *n* in ancient Rome, a lightly armed soldier, usu from the poorer section of society.

velleity *n* (*pl* **velleities**) (*arch*) the lowest degree of desire, mere inclination.

vellum *n* fine parchment; a good quality writing paper.

veloce *adv* (*mus*) very quickly.

velocipede *n* an early form of bicycle, propelled by striking the toes on the road; any early form of bicycle or tricycle.

velocity *n* (*pl* **velocities**) the rate of change of position of any object; speed.

velour, velours *n* a velvet-like fabric.

velouté *n* a rich white sauce or soup, with a basis of egg yolks, cream and stock.

velum *n* (*pl* **vela**) (*anat*) the soft palate; any body structure resembling a veil; (*bot, zool*) a membranous covering or organ, such as the membranous covering of certain molluscs or that covering a developing mushroom.

velure *n* a kind of plush or velvet-like material; a velvet pad for smoothing a silk hat.

velutinous *adj* (*bot*) thickly covered with short hairs, velvety.

velvet *n* a fabric made from silk, rayon, etc with a soft, thick pile; anything like velvet in texture.

velveteen *n* a cotton cloth with a pile like velvet.

velvety *adj* soft to the touch; mellow.

vena *n* (*pl* **venae**) (*anat*) a vein.

vena cava *n* (*pl* **venae cavae**) one of the two major veins that empty blood into the right chamber of the heart in air-breathing vertebrates.

venal *adj* corrupt; willing to accept bribes.—**venality** *n*.—**venally** *adv*.

venatic, venatical *adj* of or pertaining to hunting; (*people*) likely to engage in hunting.

venation *n* the arrangement of veins in a leaf or an insect's wing; these veins collectively.—**venational** *adj*.

vend *vt* to sell, to offer for sale; to peddle; (*rare*) to state or disseminate (an opinion, etc).

vendace *n* (*pl* **vendaces, vendace**) either of two types of small European freshwater fish.

vendee *n* (*law*) a buyer; someone to whom something has been sold.

vendetta *n* the taking of private vengeance; a feud.—**vendettist** *n*.

vendible *adj* saleable; (*arch*) venal. * *n* (*usu pl*) something that is saleable.

vending machine *n* a coin-operated machine which dispenses goods.

vendor, vender *n* a seller; a machine that ejects goods, etc, after a required amount of coins has been inserted.

veneer *n* an overlay of fine wood or plastic; a superficial appearance. * *vt* to cover with veneer.

venerable *adj* worthy of reverence or respect.—**venerability** *n*.—**venerably** *adv*.

venerate *vt* to revere; to respect.—**venerator** *n*.

veneration *n* a venerating or being venerated; respect mingled with awe, deep reverence.

venereal *adj* (*disease*) resulting from sexual intercourse.

venereal disease *n* any of various diseases, such as syphilis or AIDS, transmitted by sexual contact.—*also* **sexually transmitted disease**.

venery[1] *n* (*arch*) hunting, usu with hounds, the chase.

venery[2] *n* (*arch*) sexual indulgence, the pursuit of sexual gratification.

venesection *n* the operation of opening a vein; phlebotomy.

Venetian blind *n* a window blind formed of long thin horizontal slips of wood that can be pivoted.

vengeance *n* the act of taking revenge; retribution; **with a vengeance** to a high degree; and no mistake.

vengeful *adj* bent on vengeance; vindictive.—**vengefully** *adv* **vengefulness** *n*.

venial *adj* (*sin*) forgivable, excusable, not very wrong; (*sin*) not entailing damnation.—**veniality** *n*.—**venially** *adv*.

venison *n* the edible flesh of the deer.

Venite *n* (*Anglican church*) the 95th Psalm, used as a canticle at Matins; the music for this.

venom *n* the poison of a snake, wasp, etc; spite, malice, rancour.

venomous *adj* secreting venom; malicious, spiteful.—**venomously** *adv*.—**venomousness** *n*.

venose *adj* having many veins, veiny; venous; (*plant*) with a surface of vein-like ridges.

venosity *n* the state of being abnormally venose; (*blood vessels, organs*) the condition of containing too much blood.

venous *adj* pertaining to, contained in, or consisting of veins or blood.—**venously** *adv*.—**venousness** *n*.

vent[1] *n* a small opening or slit; an outlet or flue for the escape of fumes. * *vt* to release; (*temper*) to give expression to.—**venter** *n*

vent[2] *n* a slit in the back of a coat, often forming a flap; an opening in a battlemented wall.

ventage *n* a finger-hole of a flute or similar instrument; a small opening, an outlet.

ventail *n* the part of a helmet protecting the lower part of the face.

venter *n* (*anat, zool*) the belly or abdomen of vertebrates; the part of a muscle that swells outwards; (*bot*) the swollen base of that part of some plants containing the egg cell; (*law*) the womb.

ventilate *vt* to supply with fresh air; to oxygenate (the blood); to make public, to submit to discussion.—**ventilative** *adj*.

ventilation *n* the act of ventilating; the state of being ventilated; free discussion.

ventilator *n* an appliance for ventilating a room, etc; (*med*) a device for enabling a patient to breathe normally.

ventral *adj* (*anat*) of or on the belly, abdominal; (*bot*) of, pertaining to, or located on that part of a plant facing towards the stem, esp a leaf.

ventricle *n* a small cavity; one of the lower chambers of the heart, which pumps blood; one of the four cavities of the brain.—**ventricular** *adj*.

ventricose, ventricous *adj* (*biol*) swelling, esp on one side only.—**ventricosity** *n*.

ventriloquism, ventriloquy *n* the act or art of speaking so that the sounds appear to come from a source other than the actual speaker.—**ventriloquial** *adj*.—**ventriloquist** *n*.—**ventriloquistic** *adj*.

ventriloquize *vi* to practise ventriloquism.

venture *n* a dangerous expedition; a risky undertaking. * *vti* to risk; to dare.—**venturer** *n*.

venture capital *n* capital available for investment in risky but potentially very profitable enterprises and repayable at higher than normal interest rates, risk capital.

venturesome *adj* daring, rash; risky, hazardous.—**venturesomely** *adv*.—**venturesomeness** *n*.

venue *n* the place of an action or event.

Venus *n* (*Roman myth*) the goddess of love; (*astron*) the planet second from the sun, that can sometimes be seen as a bright star in the morning or evening; a beautiful woman.

veracious *adj* observant of the truth, truthful; honest; true, accurate.—**veraciously** *adv*.—**veraciousness** *n*.

veracity *n* (*pl* **veracities**) habitual observance of the truth; correspondence with the truth or facts; a truthful statement, a truth.

veranda, verandah *n* a roofed porch, supported by light pillars.

veratrine *n* a poisonous mixture of alkaloids from plants of the hellebore family, formerly used medically, to relieve neuralgia or as a counter-irritant.

verb *n* (*gram*) the part of speech that expresses an action, a process, state or condition or mode of being.

verbal *adj* of, concerned with or expressed in words; spoken, not written; literal; (*gram*) of, pertaining to or characteristic of a verb.—**verbally** *adv*.

verbalism *n* something expressed in words; a word or phrase; excessive attention to wording rather than content; meaningless phrases or sentences resulting from this.

verbalist *n* one skilled with words; one who concentrates on words rather than content.—**verbalistic** *adj*.

verbalize *vt* to put into words; to make into a verb.—**verbalization** *n*.

verbatim *adj, adv* word for word.

verbena *n* any of various kinds of ornamental fragrant plant, usu found in America, with red, white or purple flowers; any similar type of plant.

verbiage *n* more words than are needed for clarity, wordiness; the use of too many words.

verbify *vti* (**verbifying, verbified**) to convert (a noun, etc) into a verb; to be verbose.

verbose *adj* using more words than are necessary; overloaded with words.—**verbosely** *adv*.—**verbosity** *n*.

verdant *adj* (*grass, foliage*) green and fresh; covered with grass; inexperienced, gullible.—**verdancy** *n*.—**verdantly** *adv*.

verderer *n* (*formerly*) in England, an official who had charge of the royal forests and was responsible for maintaining peace in them.

verdict *n* the decision of a jury at the end of a trial; decision, judgment.

verdigris *n* a greenish deposit that forms on copper or brass.

verdure *n* green vegetation; greenness; freshness; the freshness and healthy growth of vegetation.—**verdurous** *adj*.—**verdurousness** *n*.

verge[1] *n* the brink; the extreme edge or margin; a grass border beside a road; a staff or wand as an emblem of office; the spindle of a watch balance; (*archit*) a projecting edge of roof tiles or slates.

verge[2] *vi* to incline, descend; (*with* **on**) to border on, to be on the verge of.

verger *n* an official who has care of the interior of a church; a staff bearer of a bishop, etc.

veridical *adj* truthful, veracious; (*psychol*) of or pertaining to events in dreams that in retrospect appear to have foretold the future.

verifiable *adj* capable of being verified.—**verifiability** *n*.

verification *n* the act of proving to be true; confirmation; the state of being verified; a marshalling of facts, etc that proves the truth of, eg a theory; (*law*) (*formerly*) a short affidavit at the end of a pleading indicating that the pleader is willing to supply proof.

verify *vt* (**verifying, verified**) to confirm the truth of, to check; to substantiate, to bear out; (*law*) to authenticate or support by proofs.—**verifiable** *adj*.—**verification** *n*.—**verifier** *n*.

verily *adv* (*arch*) in truth, certainly.

verisimilitude *n* the appearance of truth, probability.—**verisimilar** *adj*.

verismo *n* a type of opera concerned with representing contemporary life of ordinary people in an honest and realistic way.

veritable *adj* real, genuine.—**veritably** *adv*.

verity *n* (*pl* **verities**) the quality or state of being true; a truth; a true fact, reality.

verjuice *n* an acidic liquor expressed from unripe grapes, apples, etc, formerly used in sauces; sourness, tartness.

vermeil *n* silver-gilt, or any other metal gilded; (*poet*) vermilion. * *adj* of a bright red colour.

vermicelli *n* a pasta similar to spaghetti but in finer strings.

vermicide *n* a substance for killing worms.—**vermicidal** *adj*.

vermicular *adj* vermiform; vermiculate; worm-like; pertaining to or caused by worms.

vermiculate *adj* moving like a worm; worm-eaten; adorned with wavy lines; (*thoughts*) constantly recurring, casuistic. * *vt* to mark with close wavy lines.—**vermiculation** *n*.

vermiform *adj* worm-shaped.

vermiform appendix *n* the worm-shaped structure attached to the caecum vestigially in humans and certain other mammals, the appendix.

vermifuge *n* a drug, etc, that expels intestinal worms.

vermilion, vermillion *n* a bright scarlet colour. * *adj* of this colour.

vermin *n* (*used as pl*) pests, such as insects and rodents; persons dangerous to society.

vermination *n* the breeding or spread of vermin, worms or larvae; infestation with vermin, worms or larvae.

verminous *adj* infested with, caused by, or like vermin.

vermouth *n* a white wine flavoured with herbs, used in cocktails and as an aperitif.

vernacular *n* the commonly spoken language or dialect of a country or region. * *adj* native.—**vernacularly** *adv*.

vernacularism *n* vernacular usage; a vernacular word or expression.

vernal *adj* of, appearing in, relating to, or suggestive of the spring.—**vernally** *adv*.

vernation *n* (*bot*) the arrangement of leaves within a bud.

vernier *n* a small sliding scale attached to a larger fixed scale, with gradations to indicate minute subdivisions of the smallest divisions on the main fixed scale; an additional apparatus used to finetune or adjust an instrument. * *adj* of, pertaining to, or having a vernier.

Veronal (*trademark*) *n* a sedative or hypnotic drug; barbitone.

veronica[1] *n* any of several plants with blue, pink or white flowers, incl speedwell.

veronica[2] *n* (*RC Church*) the image of Christ's face that in legend appeared on a handkerchief given to him by St Veronica as he went to his crucifixion; this handkerchief; any similar image of Christ's face on a cloth.

veronica[3] *n* (*bullfighting*) a manoeuvre by a matador in which he swings the cape slowly before the bull while standing still.

verruca *n* (*pl* **verrucae, verrucas**) a wart on the hand or foot; (*biol*) a wart-like excrescence.—**verrucose, verrucous** *adj*.

versatile *adj* turning readily from one occupation to another, adaptable; talented in many different ways; variable, fickle, changeable; (*biol*) able to move or turn freely.—**versatilely** *adv*.—**versatility** *n*.

verse *n* a line of poetry; a stanza of a poem; a metrical composition, esp of a light nature; a short section of a chapter in the Bible. * *vti* to make verses (about).

versed *adj* skilled or learned in a subject.

versicle *n* a short verse or text sung by priest and congregation alternately in a liturgical service.

versicolour, versicolor *adj* parti-coloured; changeable in colour, iridescent.

versification *n* verse-making; the metre or verses of a poem; the conversion of prose into verse.

versify *vti* (**versifying, versified**) to write poetry or verse; to turn into verse.—**versifier** *n*.

version *n* a translation from one language into another; a particular account or description.—**versional** *adj*.

vers libre *n* verse with no regular metrical system; free verse.

verso *n* (*pl* **versos**) a left-hand, even-numbered page of a book, the back of the recto; the back of a printed sheet; the reverse of a coin.

versus *prep* against; in contrast to.

vert *n* (*English law*) (*formerly*) the right to collect whatever grows and bears a green leaf in a forest; green vegetation; (*her*) green.

vert. *abbr* = vertical.

vertebra *n* (*pl* **vertebrae, vertebras**) one of the interconnecting bones of the spinal column.—**vertebral** *adj*.

vertebrate *n* an animal with a backbone. * *adj* having a backbone; of the vertebrates.

vertebration *n* division into vertebrae or vertebrae-like segments.

vertex *n* (*pl* **vertexes, vertices**) the topmost point; apex; (*anat*) the crown of the head; (*geom*) the point at which two sides of a polygon or the planes of a solid intersect.

vertical *adj* perpendicular to the horizon; upright. * *n* a vertical line or plane.—**verticality** *n*.—**vertically** *adv*.

verticil *n* a whorl-like arrangement of leaves or flowers around a stem

verticillate *adj* (*biol*) arranged in a whorl-like pattern.—**verticillately** *adv*.—**verticillation** *n*.

vertiginous *adj* revolving, rotary; giddy; causing giddiness; whirling.—**vertiginously** *adv*.—**vertiginousness** *n*.

vertigo *n* (*pl* **vertigoes, vertigines**) a sensation of dizziness and sickness caused by a disorder of the sense of balance.—**vertiginous** *adj*.

vertu *see* **virtu**.

vervain *n* a perennial European with clusters of tiny bluish-purple flowers.

verve *n* enthusiasm; liveliness; energy.

vervet *n* a small African monkey with dark hands and feet and yellowish or greenish coat.

very *adj* complete; absolute; same. * *adv* extremely; truly; really.

Very light *n* a coloured flare fired from a Very pistol as a signal at sea or to give temporary light.

vesica *n* (*pl* **vesicae**) (*anat*) the bladder, esp the urinary bladder; (*art*) a pointed oval halo used as an aureole in medieval sculpture or painting.—**vesical** *adj*.

vesicant, vesicatory *n* (*pl* **vesicants, vesicatories**) a substance (eg mustard gas) that causes blistering, with applications in chemical warfare. * *adj* raising blisters.

vesicate *vt* to raise blisters on. * *vi* to become blistered.—**vesication** *n*.

vesicle *n* a small blister; a small cyst or sac; (*anat*) a bladder-like vessel or cavity, esp one filled with serous fluid; (*geol*) a cavity in rock formed by gases during solidification; (*bot*) a small sac found in some seaweeds and aquatic plants.—**vesicular** *adj*.

vesper *n* (*arch*) evening; (*with cap*) the evening star; (*Anglican Church*) evensong; (*RC Church*) the sixth of the canonical hours. * *adj* pertaining to evening or vespers.

vespertine, vespertinal *adj* of evening; (*bot*) opening in the evening; (*zool*) active in the evening; (*astron*) setting about sunset.

vespiary *n* (*pl* **vespiaries**) a nest of wasps or hornets.

vespine *adj* of, pertaining to, or like a wasp or wasps.

vessel *n* a container; a ship or boat; a tube in the body along which fluids pass.

vest *n* a sleeveless undergarment worn next to the skin, a singlet; a waistcoat. * *vt* to place or settle (power, authority, etc.); (*with* **in**) to confer or be conferred on; to invest with a right to.

Vesta *n* (*astron*) a bright asteroid; (*Roman myth*) the goddess of the hearth and the household fire.

vesta *n* a short match of wax or wood, lit by friction.

vestal *adj* pertaining to or sacred to the goddess Vesta; vowed to chastity, pure. * *n* a vestal virgin; a virgin.

vestal virgin *n* one of the six virgin priestesses who tended the sacred fire on the altar of the temple of Vesta, in ancient Rome.

vested *adj* (*law*) having permanent entitlement to the possession or use of property, now and in the future, ratified by law or custom; (*priest, etc*) clothed in ecclesiastical vestments.

vested interest *n* (*law*) a permanent entitlement to the possession and use of property, now and in the future; a strong reason for acting in a certain way, usu for personal gain; (*usu pl*) people in such a state.

vestibule *n* an entrance hall or lobby; a covered entrance at the end of a rail carriage; (*anat*) a communicating channel.—**vestibular** *adj*.

vestige *n* a hint; a trace; a rudimentary survival of a former organ; a particle.—**vestigial** *adj*.—**vestigially** *adv*.

vestment *n* a garment or robe, esp that worn by a priest or official.—**vestmental** *adj*.

vestry *n* (*pl* **vestries**) a room in a church where vestments, etc, are kept and parochial meetings held; a meeting for parish business.—**vestral** *adj*.

vestryman *n* (*pl* **vestrymen**) a member of a vestry elected by the parishioners.

vesture *n* (*arch*) clothing; something that clothes, a covering; (*law*) everything growing on someone's land apart from trees; something obtained from land, such as wheat. * (*arch*) *vt* to clothe.

vesuvianite *n* a mineral of a green, brown or yellow colour, similar to the garnet, idocrase.

vet *n* a veterinary surgeon. * *vt* (**vetting, vetted**) to examine, check for errors, etc.

vetch *n* a common leguminous climbing plant with blue or purple flowers and a stem with tendrils, found in temperate climates and used for green fodder; any similar plant.

vetchling *n* a climbing plant like a vetch mainly found in northern temperate regions with angled or winged stems with tendrils and gaudy flowers.

veteran *adj* old, experienced; having served in the armed forces. * *n* a person who has served in the armed forces; a person who has given long service in a particular activity.

veterinary *adj* of or dealing with diseases of domestic animals.

veterinarian, veterinary surgeon *n* a person trained in treating sick or injured animals.

veto *n* (*pl* **vetoes**) the right of a person or group to prohibit an action or legislation; a prohibition. * *vt* (**vetoing, vetoed**) to refuse to agree to; to prohibit.—**vetoer** *n*.

vex *vt* to annoy; to puzzle, confuse.—**vexer** *n*.—**vexingly** *adv*.

vexation *n* a vexing or being vexed; an annoying thing; irritation, distress.

vexatious *adj* causing vexation; annoying; troublesome; harassing; (*litigation*) designed merely to annoy.—**vexatiously** *adv*.

vexed *adj* annoyed; (*question*) much debated.—**vexedly** *adv*.—**vexedness** *n*.

vexillum *n* (*pl* **vexilla**) (*bot*) the largest petal found on flowers of the plant family to which the sweet pea and similar plants belong; (*zool*) the vane of a feather.

VHF *abbr* = very high frequency.

via *prep* by way of.

viable *adj* capable of growing or developing; workable; practicable.—**viability** *n*.—**viably** *adv*.

viaduct *n* a road or railway carried by a bridge with arches over a valley, river, etc.

vial *n* a small bottle for medicines, etc; a phial.

via media *n* a middle course between extremes; a compromise.

viand *n* an article of food. (*pl*) meat ready to be cooked; food.

viaticum *n* (*pl* **viatica, viaticums**) (*RC Church*) the Eucharist administered to someone whose death is or might be imminent; (*rare*) an allowance or provisions given to a person setting out on a journey.

vibes *npl* (*sl*) vibrations; vibraphone.

vibraculum *n* (*pl* **vibracula**) (*zool*) a whip-like appendage by which some polyzoans ward off parasites.

vibrant *adj* vibrating; resonant; bright; lively.—**vibrancy** *n*.—**vibrantly** *adv*.

vibraphone *n* a percussion instrument that produces a vibrato by resonating metal bars.—**vibraphonist** *n*.

vibrate *vti* to shake; to move quickly backwards and forwards; to quiver; to oscillate; to resound.—**vibratingly** *adv*.

vibratile *adj* capable of or characterized by vibrating.—**vibratility** *n*.

vibration *n* a vibrating or being vibrated; oscillation; resonance; vacillation; (*usu pl*) an emotional reaction instinctively sensed; (*physics*) the rapid alternating of particles caused by the disturbance of equilibrium.—**vibrational** *adj*.

vibrative *adj* vibratory.

vibrato *n* (*pl* **vibratos**) (*mus*) a pulsating effect obtained by rapid variation of emphasis on the same tone.

vibrator *n* the vibrating part in various instruments; a dildo.

vibratory *adj* vibrating; consisting of or causing vibrations.

vibrio *n* (*pl* **vibrios**) a spiral or curved, rod-like bacillus.—**vibrioid** *adj*.

vibrissa *n* (*pl* **vibrissae**) a sensitive whisker on an animal's face; any of the bristle-like feathers found in the beak area of certain insect-eating birds.

viburnum *n* any of several shrubs or trees, incl the guelder rose, with red or black berry-like fruits, found in various temperate and sub-tropical regions; the dried bark from some of these, sometimes used medicinally.

vicar *n* a parish priest; a clergyman in charge of a chapel.

vicarage *n* the residence of a vicar.

vicarial *adj* of, pertaining to, or acting as a vicar, vicars or a vicariate; (*ecclesiastical functions*) delegated, vicarious.

vicariate, vicarate *n* the rank, office, or district of a vicar.

vicarious *adj* substitute; obtained second-hand by listening to or watching another person's experiences.—**vicariously** *adv*.—**vicariousness** *n*.

vice[1] *n* an evil action or habit; a grave moral fault; great wickedness; a serious defect, a blemish.

vice[2] *n* a clamping device with jaws, used for holding objects firmly.—*also* **vise**.

vice- *prefix* one who acts in place of or as a deputy to another.

vice admiral *n* a rank of naval officer next below admiral.

vice-chairman *n* (*pl* **vice-chairmen**) one who takes the chair in a chairman's absence.

vice chancellor *n* the chief executive officer of a university.

vice consul *n* a person who acts in place of a consul in a subordinate district, etc.

vicegerent *n adj* a person holding delegated power or ruling as another's deputy.—*also adj*.—**vicegerency** *n*.

vicennial *adj* lasting twenty years; happening every twenty years.

vice president *n* a deputy or assistant president.

viceregal *adj* of or relating to a viceroy; (*Austral, NZ*) of or relating to a governor general.

vicereine *n* a viceroy's wife.

viceroy *n* one who rules a country or province as a representative of a king or queen.

viceroyalty, viceroyship *n* (*pl* **viceroyalties, viceroyships**) the office or term of a viceroy.

vice versa *adv* conversely; the other way round.

vichyssoise *n* leek and potato soup consumed cold.

Vichy water *n* a mineral water from Vichy in France.

vicinage *n* a surrounding district, a neighbourhood; the people of a neighbourhood; proximity.

vicinal *adj* neighbouring; adjacent; (*chem*) resembling or substituting for a crystal face or form; denoting substituted atoms on adjacent atoms in a molecule.

vicinity *n* (*pl* **vicinities**) a nearby area; proximity.

vicious *adj* cruel; violent; malicious; ferocious.—**viciously** *adv*.—**viciousness** *n*.

vicissitude *n* a change of circumstances or fortune; (*pl*) ups and downs.—**vicissitudinary, vicissitudinous** *adj*.

victim *n* a person who has been killed or injured by an action beyond his or her control; a dupe.

victimize *vt* to make a victim of, to cause to suffer.—**victimization** *n*.—**victimizer** *n*.

victor *n* a winner; a conqueror.

victoria *n* a light, open, four-wheeled, two-seater carriage; a giant South American water-lily; a victoria plum.

Victorian *adj* of or living in the reign of Queen Victoria; old-fashioned, prudish.

victoria plum *n* a large purplish-red sweet variety of plum.

victorious *adj* having won in battle or contest; emblematic of victory; triumphant.—**victoriously** *adv*.

victory *n* (*pl* **victories**) triumph in battle; success; achievement.

victual *n* (*usu pl*) food, provisions. * *vt* (**victualling, victualled** *or* **victualing, victualed**) to supply with food; to take in provisions.

victualler, victualer *n* (*formerly*) a supplier of provisions, esp to an army; a provision ship; an innkeeper.

vicuña, vicuna *n* a South American animal similar to the llama with a fine, long, reddish silky fleece; cloth made from this fleece.

vide (*Latin*) see.

vide infra (*Latin*) see later (in this book).

videlicet *adv* that is to say, namely.

video *n* (*pl* **videos**) the transmission or recording of television programmes or films, using a television set and a video recorder and tape. * *vt* (**videoing, videoed**) to record on video tape.

video cassette *n* a cassette containing video tape.

video recorder *n* the machine on which video cassettes are played or recorded.

video tape *n* a magnetic tape on which images and sounds can be recorded for reproduction on television.—**video-tape** *vt*.

vide supra (*Latin*) see earlier (in this book).

vidette *see* vedette.

vidkid *n* a child who is addicted to watching television or video.

vie *vi* (vying, vied) to contend or strive for superiority.—vier *n*.

view *n* sight; range of vision; inspection, examination; intention; scene; opinion. * *vt* to see; to consider; to examine intellectually.

viewer *n* a person who views, esp television; an optical device used in viewing.

viewfinder *n* a device in a camera showing the view to be photographed.

viewless *adj* without a view; (*poet*) invisible, unseen.

viewpoint *n* opinion; a place from which something can be viewed, esp a scenic panorama.

vigil *n* keeping watch at night.

vigilance *n* a being vigilant; watchfulness; alertness.

vigilant *adj* on the watch to discover and avoid danger, watchful; alert; cautious.—vigilantly *adv*.

vigilante *n* a self-appointed law enforcer.

vignette *n* a small picture or design in a book without a line framing it; a picture, the edges of which shade off gradually into the background; a short word sketch. * *vt* to depict in vignette; to shade off into the background.—vignettist *n*.

vigor *see* vigour.

vigoroso *adv* (*mus*) with vigour.

vigorous *adj* full of vigour; powerful; lusty.—vigorously *adv*.—vigorousness *n*.

vigour *n* physical or mental strength; vitality.—*also* vigor.

Viking *n* one of the Norse pirates who ravaged the coasts of Europe from the 8th–10th centuries.

vilayet *n* a province of Turkey.

vile *adj* wicked; evil; offensive; very bad.—vilely *adv*.—vileness *n*.

vilify *vt* (vilifying, vilified) to malign.—vilification *n*.—vilifier *n*.

villa *n* a large country or suburban house.

village *n* a collection of houses smaller than a town.

villager *n* an inhabitant of a village.

villain *n* a scoundrel; the main evil character in a play, film or novel; (*arch*) a boor.

villainous *adj* depraved, evil, wicked; very bad, wretched.—villainously *adv*.—villainousness *n*.

villainy *n* (*pl* villainies) great wickedness; an atrocious crime.

villanella *n* (*pl* villanelle) a popular part-song of 17th-century Italy.

villanelle *n* a poem of 19 lines in six stanzas rhymed aba aba aba aba aba abaa, the 6th, 12th and 18th lines being the same as the first, and the 9th, 15th and 19th the same as the third.

villein *n* (*hist*) a feudal tenant of the lowest class, a serf.

villi *see* villus.

villous, villose *adj* covered with villi; (*bot*) covered with long, thin, soft hairs.

villus *n* (*pl* villi) (*biol*) the velvety fibre of the mucous membrane of the intestine; (*bot*) the soft hair covering a fruit or flower.—villosity *n*.

vim (*sl*) energy, force.

vimineous *adj* (*bot*) of or producing long flexible shoots.

vina *n* a seven-stringed Indian musical instrument.

vinaceous *adj* of the colour of wine; wine-red.

vinaigrette *n* a salad dressing made from oil, vinegar and seasoning.

vincible *adj* capable of being conquered or overcome.—vincibility *n*.

vinculum *n* (*pl* vincula) (*anat*) a ligament; (*math*) a horizontal line over quantities having the effect of a parenthesis; (*print*) a brace; a bond of union, a tie.

vindicate *vt* to establish the existence or truth of, to justify; to clear of charges, to absolve from blame.—vindicable *adj*.—vindicator *n*.—vindicatory *adj*.

vindication *n* a vindicating or being vindicated; an event, fact, evidence, etc, that justifies a deed or claim.

vindictive *adj* vengeful; spiteful; (*damages*) exemplary, punitive.—vindictively *adv*.—vindictiveness *n*.

vine *n* any climbing plant, or its stem; a grapevine; a sphere of activity, esp spiritual or mental endeavour.

vinedresser *n* a person who cultivates vines.

vinegar *n* a sour-tasting liquid containing acetic acid, used as a condiment and preservative.

vinegary *adj* of or like vinegar; sour; ill-tempered.

vinery *n* (*pl* vineries) a place where grapes are grown or wine is made.

vineyard *n* a plantation of grapevines.

vingt-et-un *n* a gambling game with cards in which players try to obtain points better than the banker's but not more than 21.—*also* blackjack, pontoon, twenty-one.

vinic *adj* contained in or obtained from wine.

viniculture *n* the cultivation of vines and manufacture of wine, viticulture.—vinicultural *adj*.—viniculturist *n*.

viniferous *adj* wine-producing.

vinificator *n* in winemaking, an apparatus for collecting alcoholic vapours.

vin ordinaire *n* (*pl* vins ordinaires) the ordinary table wine of France.

vinous *adj* of, pertaining to, or having the qualities of wine; like wine; wine-coloured; inspired by wine.—vinosity *n*.

vintage *n* the grape harvest of one season; wine, esp of good quality, made in a particular year; wine of a particular region; the product of a particular period. * *adj* (*cars*) classic; (*wine*) of a specified year and of good quality; (*play*) characteristic of the best.

vintager *n* a gatherer of grapes in a wine harvest.

vintner *n* a wine merchant.

vinyl *n* a strong plastic used in floor coverings, furniture and records, etc.

viol *n* a family of medieval six-stringed instruments played with a bow, similar to a violin but with a softer sound.

viola¹ *n* a stringed instrument of the violin family, and tuned a fifth below it.

viola² *n* any of several plants of the genus that includes violets and pansies.

violable *adj* capable of being violated or broken.

violaceous *adj* of violet colour or family.

viola da gamba *n* the bass viol.

viola d'amore *n* a tenor viol with seven strings and a sweet tone.

violate *vt* to break or infringe (an agreement); to rape; to disturb (one's privacy).—violative *adj*.—violator *n*.

violation *n* the act of violating, infringing, or injuring; rape; outrage; an act of irreverence or profanation.

violence *n* physical force intended to cause injury or destruction; natural force; passion, intensity.

violent *adj* urged or driven by force; vehement; impetuous; forcible; furious; severe.—violently *adv*.

violet *n* a small plant with bluish-purple flowers; a bluish-purple colour.

violin *n* a four-stringed musical instrument, played with a bow.

violinist *n* a person who plays the violin.

violist *n* a player of a viol or viola.

violoncellist *n* a performer on the violoncello.

violoncello *n* (*pl* **violoncellos**) the full name for a **cello**.

violone *n* the largest type of viol, corresponding to the double-bass.

VIP *abbr* = Very Important Person.

viper *n* a common European venomous snake.—**viperine** *adj*.

viperous, viperish *adj* viper-like; malignant.

virago *n* (*pl* **viragoes, viragos**) a bad-tempered woman.

viral *adj* of or caused by a virus.

virelay, virelai *n* an old French form of poem with short lines and two rhymes variously arranged.

vireo *n* (*pl* **vireos**) a small greenish American singing bird.

virescence *n* the state of being virescent, esp in place of the normal colour of petals.

virescent *adj* beginning to be green; greenish.

virgate[1] *adj* (*bot*) slim and straight.

virgate[2] *n* an old English unit of land equal to approx 30 acres.

virgin *n* a person (esp a woman) who has never had sexual intercourse; (*with cap*) Mary, the mother of Christ; a painting or statue of her. * *adj* chaste; pure; untouched.

virginal[1] *adj* of or pertaining to a virgin or virginity; befitting a virgin; chaste, pure, innocent; fresh, unsullied, untouched.

virginal[2] *n* a small rectangular keyed musical instrument resembling a harpsichord but without legs.

virginity *n* the state of being a virgin; the state of being chaste, untouched, etc.

Virgo *n* the Virgin, the 6th sign of the zodiac.—**Virgoan** *adj*.

virgo intacta *n* (*pl* **virgines intactae**) (*law*) a girl or woman who is a virgin.

virgulate *adj* rod-shaped.

virgule *n* a small rod; a slanting punctuation mark (/), a solidus.

viridescent *adj* greenish; turning green.— **viridescence** *n*.

viridity *n* greenness; freshness.

virile *adj* of a mature man, manly; strong, forceful; sexually potent.—**virility** *n*.

virtu *n* a love or knowledge of the fine arts, connoisseurship; artistic excellence, fine workmanship; the quality of appealing to a collector; artistic objects, antiques, curios, etc, collectively.—*also* **vertu**.

virtual *adj* in effect or essence, though not in fact or strict definition; (*comput*) denoting memory, making use of an external memory to increase capacity.

virtually *adv* to all intents and purposes, practically.

virtue *n* moral excellence; any admirable quality; chastity; merit.

virtuoso *n* (*pl* **virtuosos, virtuosi**) a person highly skilled in an activity, esp in playing a musical instrument. * *adj* skilled, masterly in technique.—**virtuosic** *adj*.—**virtuosity** *n*.

virtuous *adj* righteous; upright; pure.—**virtuously** *adv*.—**virtuousness** *n*.

virulent *adj* (*disease*) deadly; extremely poisonous; hostile; vicious.—**virulence** *n*.—**virulently** *adv*.

virus *n* (*pl* **viruses**) a very simple microorganism capable of replicating within living cells, producing disease; the disease caused by a virus; a harmful influence.

visa *n* an endorsement on a passport allowing the bearer to travel in the country of the government issuing it. * *vt* (**visaing, visaed**) to mark with a visa; to grant a visa to.

visage *n* the face; the countenance; appearance.

visard *see* **vizard**.

vis-à-vis *prep* opposite to; in face of. * *adj, adv* facing. * *n* the person opposite; a counterpart.

viscacha *n* a South American burrowing rodent, that looks like a large chinchilla.—*also* **vizcacha**.

viscera *npl* (*sing* **viscus**) the large internal organs of the animal body, the entrails.

visceral *adj* of, pertaining to, or affecting the viscera; pertaining to or touching deeply inward feelings.—**viscerally** *adv*.

viscid *adj* (*leaves*) covered with a sticky layer; (*fluids*) thick, glutinous.—**viscidity** *n* —**viscidly** *adv*.

viscometer, viscosimeter *n* an instrument for measuring viscosity.

viscose *n* a form of cellulose used in making artificial silk.

viscosity *n* (*pl* **viscosities**) the property or state of being sticky or glutinous; (*physics*) a property of fluids that indicates their resistance to flow.

viscount *n* in Britain, a title of nobility next below an earl.—**viscountess** *nf*.

viscountcy *n* (*pl* **viscountcies**) the rank of a viscount.

viscous *adj* sticky, thick; having viscosity.—**viscously** *adv*.—**viscousness** *n*.

viscus *see* **viscera**.

vise *see* **vice**.

visibility *n* (*pl* **visibilities**) clearness of seeing or being seen; the degree of clearness of the atmosphere.

visible *adj* able to be seen, perceptible; apparent, evident.—**visibleness** *n*.—**visibly** *adv*.

visible speech *n* a phonetic alphabet representing the actual movements of the vocal organs and used in teaching the deaf.

vision *n* the power of seeing, sight; a supernatural appearance; a revelation; foresight; imagination; a mental concept; a person, scene, etc of unusual beauty; something seen in a dream or trance.—**visional** *adj*.

visionary *adj* imaginative; having foresight; existing in imagination only, not real. * *n* (*pl* **visionaries**) an imaginative person; a dreamer; an idealist, a mystic.

visit *vt* to go to see; to pay a call upon a person or place; to stay with or at; to punish or reward with. * *vi* to see or meet someone regularly. * *n* the act of going to see, a call.—**visitable** *adj*.

visitant *n* a migratory bird; a visitor, esp a pilgrim; a ghost. * *adj* (*arch*) visiting.

visitation *n* a visit by a superior; a punitive act of God; an official visit; right of access of a divorced parent to his or her children; a large migration of animals; (*with cap*) the visit paid by the Virgin Mary to Elizabeth (Luke 1:39*ff*); a picture representing the event; the day on which this is commemorated, 2 July.—**visitational** *adj*.

visiting card *n* a small card with a person's name on it, left when paying visits.

visitor *n* a person who visits; a caller; a tourist; a migratory bird pausing in transit; an official acting as an inspector and adviser.

visor *n* a movable part of a helmet protecting the face; the peak of a cap.—*also* **vizor**.—**visored** *adj*.

vista *n* a view, as from a high place; a mental picture.—**vistaed, vista'd** *adj*.

visual *adj* having, producing, or relating to vision or sight; perceptible, visible; (*knowledge*) attained by sight or vision; (*impressions, etc*) based upon something seen; of the nature of, producing or conveying a picture in the mind; (*physics*) optical. * *n* a piece of graphic material used for display or to convey a concept, etc; (*pl*) the visual aspect of a film, etc.—**visually** *adv*.

visual aid *n* a film, slide or overhead projector, etc used to aid teaching.

visualize *vt* to form a mental picture of; to make visible to the mind or imagination. * *vi* to construct a visual image in the mind.—**visualization** *n*.—**visualizer** *n*.

vital *adj* of, connected with or necessary to life; essential; lively, animated; fundamental; (*wound, error*) fatal. * *n* (*pl*) the bodily organs essential for life.—**vitally** *adv*.

vitalism *n* the belief that life cannot be explained as resulting wholly from physical and chemical processes, but must include some other vital non-material force or process.—**vitalist** *n*.—**vitalistic** *adj*.

vitality *n* (*pl* **vitalities**) vigour, hold on life; spirits; animation; capacity to last, durability.

vitalize *vt* to give life to; to animate; to make vigorous.—**vitalization** *n*.

vital statistics *npl* data recording births, deaths, marriages, etc used in compiling population statistics; (*inf*) the measurements of a woman's figure.

vitamin *n* one of several organic substances occurring naturally in foods, which are essential for good health.—**vitaminic** *adj*.

vitellin *n* a protein forming the major component in the yolk of birds' eggs.

vitelline *adj* of or pertaining to egg yolk; of a yellow colour close to the shade of egg yolk.

vitiate *vt* to make faulty or ineffective; to taint; to deprave; to invalidate or annul (a legal document, etc).—**vitiation** *n*.—**vitiator** *n*.

viticulture *n* the science of grapes and grape-growing.—**viticulturer, viticulturist** *n*.—**viticultural** *adj*.

vitreous *adj* of like or obtained from glass; of the vitreous body.—**vitreousness** *n*.

vitreous body, vitreous humour *n* the transparent tissue of the eyeball.

vitrescence *n* the quality of being vitrescent; the process of changing something, such as a crystalline material, into glass.

vitrescent *adj* capable of being made into or becoming like glass.

vitric *adj* glass-like.

vitrify *vt* (**vitrifying, vitrified**) to convert into glass or a glass-like substance.—**vitrifiable** *adj*.—**vitrification, vitrifaction** *n*.

vitriol *n* sulphuric acid; savage criticism. * *vt* (**vitrioling, vitrioled** *or* **vitriolling, vitriolled**) to throw vitriol over, to poison with vitriol.

vitriolic *adj* of or relating to vitriol; scathing, bitter.

vitriolize *vt* to harm by throwing vitriol over; to change into vitriol; to use vitriol in or as a part of the processing of something.—**vitriolization** *n*.

vitta *n* (*pl* **vittae**) (*bot*) an oil tube in the fruit of some plants, eg parsley; (*zool*) a coloured stripe.—**vittate** *adj*.

vituline *adj* of, like, calves or veal.

vituperate *vt* to berate; to abuse verbally.—**vituperative** *adj*.—**vituperator** *n*.

vituperation *n* the act of vituperating; blame, censure, reproof; the expression of this in abusive or violent language.

viva *interj* long live, hurrah for.

viva *n* in UK, an oral examination, a viva voce. * *vt* (**vivas** *or* **viva's, vivaing, vivaed** *or* **viva'd**) to examine orally.

vivace *adv* (*mus*) in a lively manner; with spirit.

vivacious *adj* lively; animated; spirited.—**vivaciously** *adv*.—**vivaciousness** *n*.

vivacity *n* (*pl* **vivacities**) vivaciousness; animation of the mind or disposition; liveliness of conception or perception; spirited conduct, manner or speech; brilliancy of light or colour.

vivarium *n* (*pl* **vivariums, vivaria**) a place for keeping animals in their natural state for research or observation.

viva voce *adj, adv* orally, by word of mouth. * *n* an oral examination, a viva.

vivid *adj* brightly coloured; graphic; lively; intense.—**vividly** *adv*.—**vividness** *n*.

vivify *vt* (**vivifying, vivified**) to give life to; to make more lively or more vivid.—**vivification** *n*.—**vivifier** *n*.

viviparous *adj* (*zool*) giving birth to young that have developed inside the body, as do most mammals.—**viviparity** *n*.—**viviparously** *adv*.

vivisect *vt* to subject to vivisection.—**vivisector** *n*.

vivisection *n* the practice of performing surgical operations on living animals for scientific research.—**vivisectional** *adj*.

vivisectionist *n* a person who practises or approves of vivisection.

vixen *n* a female fox; a malicious or shrewish woman.—**vixenish** *adj*.

viz *abbr* = *videlicet* namely.

vizard *n* (*arch*) a mask or other object that disguises; a visor.—*also* **visard**.

vizcacha *see* **vischacha**.

vizier, vizir *n* a minister of state or high official in Muslim countries, esp in the Ottoman Empire.

vizierate *n* the status, authority or (term of) office of a vizier.

vizor *see* **visor**.

vocable *n* (*linguistics*) a word looked on as a pattern of characters or sounds with no regard to meaning; a sound; a vowel. * *adj* able to be spoken.

vocabulary *n* (*pl* **vocabularies**) an alphabetical list of words with their meanings; the words of a language; an individual's command or use of particular words.

vocal *adj* of, for, endowed with, relating to, or produced by the voice; outspoken, noisy; (*phonetics*) having a vowel function. * *n* a vowel; (*pl*) music for the voice, not another instrument.—**vocally** *adv*.

vocal chords *npl* either of two pairs of elastic membranous folds in the larynx, esp the lower pair, which vibrate and produce sound.

vocalic *adj* of, like or containing vowels.

vocalise *n* a vocal exercise to improve flexibility and control of the voice in which a singer sings to one vowel sound.

vocalist *n* a singer.

vocalize *vti* to express with the voice; to articulate, utter distinctly; to use the singing voice; to sing to vowel sounds; to write with vowels or vowel points.—**vocalization** *n*.—**vocalizer** *n*.

vocation n a calling to a particular career or occupation, esp to a religious life; a sense of fitness for a particular career.

vocational adj of or relating to a vocation or occupation; providing special training for a particular career.—**vocationally** adv.

vocative adj used, involved in or pertaining to loud utterances to attract attention; (gram) denoting the case of a noun, adjective, or pronoun used in addressing a person in some inflected languages, eg Latin. * n (gram) a vocative case or form.

vociferant adj clamorous, noisy. * n a clamorous, noisy person.

vociferate vti to speak loudly and insistently, to clamour; to shout, to bawl.—**vociferation** n.—**vociferator** n.

vociferous adj clamorous, noisy.—**vociferously** adv.—**vociferousness** n.

vodka n a spirit distilled from rye, potatoes, etc.

vogue n the fashion at a specified time; popularity. * adj fashionable, in vogue.—**voguish** adj.

voice n sound from the mouth; sound produced by speaking or singing; the quality of this; the power of speech; utterance; expressed opinion, vote; (gram) the forms of a verb showing the relation of subject to action; (phonetics) a sound uttered with vibration of the vocal chords not with mere breath. * vt to express; to speak; (mus) to regulate so as to give the correct tone; (phonetics) to utter with the voice, to make sonant.—**voicer** n.

voiced adj having a voice, esp of a specified kind, quality or tone; (phonetics) uttered with the voice or vibration of the vocal chords, sonant.

voiceful adj (poet) having a voice; sonorous.

voiceless adj speechless, dumb; (phonetics) not voiced.—**voicelessly** adv.—**voicelessness** n.

voice-over n the voice of an unseen narrator, esp in a film, TV commercial, etc.

void adj unoccupied, empty; not legally binding; having no cards of a particular suit. * n an empty space, a vacuum; vacancy, sense of loss. * vt to discharge, to emit; empty; to make invalid.—**voidable** adj.—**voider** n.

voidance n the act of voiding or evacuating; emptiness; the annulment of a legal deed.

voided adj (her) having the inner part of a figure cut away, leaving only the outer edges; being, or having been caused to be, empty.

voile n a light, sheer fabric of silk, rayon, etc, used for dresses, scarves, etc.

volant adj flying; able to fly; (her) appearing to fly; (poet) nimble.

Volapuk, Volapük n an artificial language taking elements from English, French, German, Latin. etc, invented in 1880 and intended for international commercial use.—**Volapukist, Volapükist** n.

volar adj (anat) of the palm of the hand or sole of the foot.

volatile adj evaporating very quickly; changeable, fickle; unstable; light-hearted, mercurial; flighty; (comput) having a memory that loses data when power is disconnected.—**volatility** n.

volatilize vti to turn into vapour, to (cause to) evaporate. —**volatilization** n.

vol-au-vent n a case of light puff pastry filled with a savoury sauce.

volcanic adj of, like or due to the action of a volcano; violent, intense.—**volcanically** adv.

volcanism n volcanic action.—also **vulcanism**.

volcanize vt to subject to volcanic heat; to cause to change by means of volcanic heat.—**volcanization** n.

volcano n (pl **volcanoes, volcanos**) a hill or mountain formed by ejection of lava, ashes, etc through an opening in the earth's crust.

volcanology n the science of volcanoes and the occurrences associated with them.—also **vulcanology**.—**volcanological, vulcanological** adj.—**volcanologist, vulcanologist** n.

vole[1] n a small rat-like rodent with a short tail.

vole[2] vt to win all the tricks in a deal. * n a slam.

volitant adj able to fly, volant; flying, or otherwise moving about, in a rapid, nimble fashion.

volition n the exercise of the will; choice.—**volitional** adj.

volitive adj pertaining to or having the power of will; (gram) desiderative; expressing a wish or intention.

volley n (pl **volleys**) the multiple discharge of many missiles or small arms; a barrage; (tennis, volleyball) the return of the ball before it reaches the ground. * vt (**volleying, volleyed**) to return (a ball) before it hits the ground.—**volleyer** n.

volleyball n a team game played by hitting a large inflated ball over a net with the hands; the ball used.

volt[1] n the circular gait of a horse in dressage; (fencing) a leap to avoid a thrust.

volt[2] n the unit of measure of the force of an electrical current.

volta n (pl **volte**) a lively 16th-century Italian dance; (mus) music in triple time, originally written to accompany such a dance; (mus) a particular time as specified.

voltage n electrical energy that moves a charge around a circuit, measured in volts.

voltaic adj pertaining to electricity generated by chemical action or galvanism; galvanic.

voltaism n galvanism; electricity generated by chemical action.

voltameter n an instrument for measuring an electric charge; a coulombmeter.

volte-face n (pl **volte-faces, volte-face**) a change to an opposite opinion or direction.

voltmeter n an instrument for measuring voltage.

voluble adj speaking with a great flow of words, fluent; (arch) revolving, rotating; (bot) twining.—**volubility** n.—**volubly** adv.

volubleness n excessive fluency of speech.

volume n the amount of space occupied by an object; quantity, amount; intensity of sound; a book; one book of a series.—**volumed** adj.

volumeter n an instrument for measuring the volume of a gas, liquid, or solid.

volumetric adj of or relating to measurement by volume.—**volumetrically** adv.

voluminous adj of great size or bulk; (writings) capable of filling many volumes; (clothes) ample, loose.—**voluminosity** n.—**voluminously** adv.

voluntarism n the theory that the will is dominant over the intellect; a belief in voluntary participation not compulsion in a course of action; voluntaryism.—**voluntaryist** n.

voluntary adj spontaneous, deliberate; without remuneration; supported by voluntary effort; having free will; (law) acting gratuitously or from choice, not because of any legal compulsion or argument; (muscles) controlled by conscious effort; designed; pertaining to voluntaryism.* n (pl voluntaries) an organ solo, often improvised, played before or after a church service; (arch) a volunteer.—voluntarily adv.—voluntariness n.

voluntaryism n the theory that churches, schools, etc, should depend on voluntary contributions, not state aid.—voluntarist n.—voluntaristic adj.

volunteer n a person who carries out work voluntarily; a person who freely undertakes military service. * vti to offer unasked; to come forward, enlist or serve voluntarily.

voluptuary n (pl voluptuaries) a person given up to bodily pleasures or the enjoyment of luxury, a sensualist. * adj exciting sensual desire; devoted to pleasures of the senses; voluptuous; luxurious.

voluptuous adj excessively fond of pleasure, having an attractive figure; luxurious; exciting sensual desire.—voluptuously adv.—voluptuousness n.

volute n a spiral; a whorl; anything shaped to resemble a spiral or otherwise convoluted form; a spiral, scroll-shaped ornament, esp on an Ionic capital, a helix; a tropical shellfish with a spiral shell; any of the whorls found on the shells of snails; an auxiliary curved part of an engine that collects waste gases or liquids from that engine. * adj spiral-shaped; (machinery) moving spirally; (bot) rolled up (—also voluted).

volution n a spiral; a convoluted or turning shape or movement; any of the whorls of a shell.

volvox n a genus of round, hollow microscopic plants having a rotatory motion, found in ponds, etc.

vomer n the flat, slender bone separating the nostrils in mammals.

vomit vi to eject the contents of the stomach through the mouth, to spew. * n matter ejected from the stomach when vomiting.—vomiter n.

vomitive adj of or causing vomiting. * n an emetic.

vomitory adj vomitive. * n (pl vomitories) an emetic; an aperture for vomited matter; any opening through which something is ejected; in ancient Rome, a corridor from a street entrance to a tier of seats in an amphitheatre (—also vomitorium).

vomiturition n violent retching; repeated vomiting.

voodoo n (pl voodoos) a religious cult in the West Indies, based on a belief in sorcery, etc; one who practises voodoo. * vt (voodooing, voodooed) to affect by voodoo.

voodooism n the beliefs and practices of voodoo.—voodooist n.—voodooistic adj.

voracious adj eager to devour (food, literature etc); very greedy.—voraciously adv.—voracity n.

vortex n (pl vortexes, vortices) a whirlpool; a powerful eddy; a whirlwind; a whirling motion or mass.—vortical adj.—vortically adv.

vorticella n (pl vorticellae) any of a genus of ciliated, bell-shaped animalcules.

vorticism n an art movement in which cubist techniques were amalgamated with that aspect of futurism expressing reservations about the quality of contemporary life, and its reliance on machines, so that objects were presented so as to give the effect of an assemblage of vortices.—vorticist n.

vortiginous adj whirling, vortical; vortex-like.

votary n (pl votaries) a person vowed to religious service or worship; an ardent follower, a devotee of a person, religion, occupation, idea, etc (—also votarist). * adj ardently devoted to a deity or saint.

vote n an indication of a choice or opinion as to a matter on which one has a right to be consulted; a ballot; decision by a majority; the right to vote; franchise. * vi to cast one's vote. * vt to elect (to office).—votable, voteable adj.

voter n a person with a right to vote, esp one who uses it.

votive adj given, consecrated, or promised by vow; (RC Church) voluntary, given by free will not by prescription.

vouch vt to provide evidence or proof of. * vi to give assurance; to guarantee.

voucher n a written record of a transaction; a receipt; a token that can be exchanged for something else.

vouchsafe vt to give, to grant; to condescend (to).—vouchsafement n.

voussoir n any of the wedge-shaped stones forming the arch of a bridge or vault.

vow n a solemn or binding promise. * vt to promise; to resolve.—vower n.

vowel n an open speech sound produced by continuous passage of the breath; a letter representing such a sound, as a, e, i, o, u. * adj of or constituting a vowel.—vowelless adj.

vowelize vt to insert vowel points in (usu something written in Hebrew).—vowelization n.

vowel point n a diacritical mark indicating a vowel in Hebrew, Arabic, etc.

vox n (pl voces) a voice; a sound.

vox humana n an organ stop with tones like the human voice.

vox populi n popular opinion; the voice of the people.

voyage n a long journey, esp by ship or spacecraft. * vi to journey.—voyager n.

voyageur n a Canadian boatman working for a fur-trading company, esp if covering an area inland; any boatman, trapper or guide, esp in Northern Canada.

voyeur n a person who is sexually gratified from watching sexual acts or objects; a peeping Tom.—voyeurism n.—voyeuristic adj.

VP abbr = vice-president.

vraisemblance n an appearance of truth, verisimilitude.

vs abbr = versus against.

VSO abbr = Voluntary Service Overseas.

VT abbr = Vermont.

vug, vugh n (mining) a small cavity, often crystal-lined, in a lode or rock.

Vulcan n (Roman myth) the god of fire and smiths; (arch) a planet once thought to orbit Mercury.

vulcanism see volcanism.

vulcanite n a hard, vulcanized rubber, which is resistant to the effects of chemicals, ebonite.

vulcanize vt to treat (rubber) with sulphur, white lead and other substances at high temperatures under pressure to improve its strength and elasticity or render it hard and non-elastic; to change the properties of (any material) in a similar way.—vulcanization n.

vulcanology see volcanology.

vulgar adj of the common people; vernacular; unrefined, in bad taste; coarse; offensive, indecent.—vulgarly adv.—vulgarness n.

vulgarian n a vulgar pretentious person, esp one who shows of his or her wealth.

vulgarism n a crude expression; coarseness.

vulgarity n (pl vulgarities) coarseness of manners or language; a vulgar phrase, expression, act, etc.

vulgarize *vt* to debase; to popularize.—**vulgarization** *n*.—**vulgarizer** *n*.

Vulgate *n* a 4th–century Latin version of the Bible made by St Jerome, by combining text from the original language material and an earlier Latin text derived from the Greek; (*RC Church*) a revised form of this used as the authorized version. * *adj* pertaining to, or contained in, the Vulgate.

vulnerable *adj* capable of being wounded physically or mentally; open to persuasion; easily influenced; open to attack, assailable; (*contract bridge*) having won one game and liable to doubled penalties.—**vulnerability** *n*.—**vulnerably** *adv*.

vulnerary *adj* used for healing wounds. * *n* (*pl* **vulneraries**) a drug, ointment, etc, used in this way.

vulpine, vulpecular *adj* pertaining to, like, or characteristic of a fox; cunning.

vulture *n* a large bird of prey having no feathers on the neck or head and feeding chiefly on carrion; a rapacious person.

vulturine, vulturous *adj* vulture-like.

vulva *n* (*pl* **vulvae, vulvas**) the external genitals of human females.—**vulval, vulvar, vulvate** *adj*.

vulviform *adj* like a cleft with projecting edges.

vulvitis *n* inflammation of the vulva.

vying *see* **vie**.

W

W (*chem symbol*) tungsten.

w *abbr* = watt(s); west.

W, w *n* the 23rd letter of the English alphabet.

WA *abbr* = Washington.

WAC *abbr* = Women's Army Corps.

wacky *adj* (**wackier, wackiest**) (*sl*) crazy, eccentric.—
wackily *adv*.—**wackiness** *n*.

wad *n* a small, soft mass, as of cotton or paper; a bundle
of paper money.

wadding *n* any soft material for use in padding, packing, etc.

waddle *vi* to walk with short steps and sway from side
to side, as a duck.—*also n*.

waddy *n* (*pl* **waddies**) a club with a thickened head
used as a weapon by Australian Aborigines. * *vt*
(**waddying, waddied**) to hit with a waddy.

wade *vti* to walk through water; to pass (through) with
difficulty.

wader *n* a bird that wades, eg the heron; (*pl*) high waterproof boots worn by anglers.

wadi, wady *n* a channel of a stream in North Africa
which is dry except in the rainy season.

WAF *abbr* = Women in the Air Force.

wafer *n* a thin crisp cracker or biscuit; (*Christianity*) the
disc of unleavened bread used in the Eucharist.

waffle[1] *n* a thick, crisp pancake baked in a waffle iron.

waffle[2] *vi* (*esp Brit inf*) to speak or write at length without saying anything substantial.

waffle iron *n* a metal cooking utensil with two hinged
metal parts that close and impress a square pattern
on a waffle.

waft *vt* to drift or float through the air. * *n* a breath,
scent or sound carried through the air.

wag[1] *vti* (**wagging, wagged**) to move rapidly from side
to side or up and down (as of a finger, tail).—*also n*.

wag[2] *n* a joker, a wit.

wage *vt* to carry on, esp war. * *n* (*often pl*) payment for
work or services.

wage earner *n* a person who works for wages.

wager *n* a bet. * *vti* to bet.

waggle *vti* to wag.—*also n*.

Wagnerian *n* of or resembling the music of Richard
Wagner (1813–83), characterized by dramatic grandeur and emotional intensity.

wagon *n* a four-wheeled vehicle pulled by a horse or
tractor, for carrying heavy goods.

wagoner *n* a driver of a wagon.

wagon-lit *n* (*pl* **wagons-lits**) a sleeping-car on a European train.

wagtail *n* any of numerous small birds with tails that
jerk constantly.

wah-wah *n* the sound of a trumpet, etc when alternately muted and unmuted; a pedal or lever used
with an electric guitar, etc to imitate this sound.

waif *n* a homeless, neglected child.

wail *vi* to make a long, loud cry of sorrow or grief; to
howl, to moan.—*also n*.

wain *n* (*poet*) a farm wagon.

wainscot *n* wooden panelling on the interior of a wall (—
also **wainscoting**). * *vt* to line (a wall) with a wainscot.

wainwright *n* a person who builds wagons.

waist *n* the narrowest part of the human trunk, between
the ribs and the hips; the narrow part of anything that
is wider at the ends; the part of a garment covering
the waist.

waistband *n* a band of material (on a skirt, trousers, etc)
that strengthens and completes the waist.

waistcoat *n* a waist-length, sleeveless garment worn
immediately under a suit jacket; a vest.

waistline *n* the narrowest part of the waist; its measurement; the seam that joins the bodice and skirt of a
dress, etc; the level of this.

wait *vti* to stay, or to be, in expectation or readiness; to
defer or to be postponed; to remain; (*with* **at** *or* **on**) to
serve food at a meal. * *n* act or period of waiting.

waiter *n* a man or woman who serves at table, as in a
restaurant.—**waitress** *nf*.

waiting *n* the act of remaining inactive or stationary; a
period of waiting. * *adj* of or pertaining to a wait; in
attendance.

waiting game *n* a delay in acting or deciding in order to
benefit from more favourable circumstances later.

waiting list *n* a list of people applying for or waiting to
obtain something.

waiting room *n* a room for people to wait in at a station,
hospital, etc.

waive *vt* to refrain from enforcing; to relinquish voluntarily.

waiver *n* (*law*) a waiving of a right, claim etc.

wake[1] *vb* (**waking, woke**, *pp* **woken**) *vi* to emerge from
sleep; to become awake. * *vt* to rouse from sleep. * *n* a
watch or vigil beside a corpse, on the eve of the
burial.—**wakeful** *adj*.—**waken** *vti*.

wake[2] *n* the waves or foamy water left in the track of a
ship; a trail.

wale *n* a ridge or mark on the body, a weal; a ridge on a
ribbed material such as corduroy; a heavy plank
along a ship's side.

Walhalla *see* Valhalla.

walk *vi* to travel on foot with alternate steps; (*with* **out**)
to leave suddenly; to go on strike; (*with* **on**) to abandon,
jilt. * *vt* to pass through or over; (*a dog*) to exercise; to escort on foot. * *n* the act of walking; distance walked
over; gait; a ramble or stroll; a profession.—**walker** *n*.

walkabout *n* a ceremonial wander through the Australian
bush made periodically by an Aborigine; an informal
stroll through a crowd by a politician, celebrity, etc.

walkie-talkie, walky-talky *n* (*pl* **walkie-talkies**,
walky-talkies) a portable two-way radio transmitter
and receiver.

walk-in *adj* (*cupboard*) large enough to enter and move
around in.

walking *adj* able to walk; appearing to walk; ambulatory; marked by travelling on foot (*walking holiday*); intended for walkers (*walking boots*); in animate form (*walking bomb*). * *n* the act of walking; gait; the condition of a track, etc.

walking papers *n* (*sl*) notice of dismissal.

walking stick *n* a stick used in walking, a cane.

Walkman *n* (*trademark*) a small portable cassette player (and sometimes radio) used with earphones.

walk-on *n* a small (esp non-speaking) part in a play.

walkout *n* a strike; a sudden departure.

walkover *n* an unopposed or easy victory; a horse race with only one starter.

walk-through *n* a rehearsal.

walkway *n* road, path, etc, for pedestrians only.

Walkyrie *see* **Valkyrie**.

wall *n* a vertical structure of brick, stone, etc for enclosing, dividing or protecting. * *vt* to enclose with a wall; to close up with a wall.

wallaby *n* (*pl* **wallabies, wallaby**) a small kangaroo-like animal.

wallah, walla *n* (*inf*) a person with a specified job or responsibility.

wallaroo *n* (*pl* **wallaroos, wallaroo**) a type of large kangaroo.

walled *adj* having walls; surrounded or protected as if by walls; fortified.

wallet *n* a flat pocketbook for paper money, cards etc.

walleye *n* an eye with an opaque cornea; any eye with a pale or white iris; a squint in which an eye turns outward.

wallflower *n* a fragrant plant with red or yellow flowers; a person who does not dance for lack of a partner.

Walloon *n* a member of a French-speaking people of southern Belgium and adjacent areas of France; the French dialect of Walloons.—*also adj*.

wallop *vt* (*inf*) to beat or defeat soundly; (*inf*) to strike hard. * *n* (*inf*) a hard blow.

walloping *adj* (*inf*) large, massive. * *n* (*inf*) a thrashing, a defeat.

wallow *vi* (*animal*) to roll about in mud; to indulge oneself in emotion.—*also n*.

wallpaper *n* decorated paper for covering the walls of a room.

Wall Street *n* a street in New York where the Stock Exchange is situated; the centre of American finance.

wall-to-wall *adj* (*carpet*) covering the whole area of a room; (*inf*) nonstop, continuous.

wally *n* (*pl* **wallies**) (*Brit sl*) an idiot.

walnut *n* a tree producing an edible nut with a round shell and wrinkled seed; its nut; its wood used for furniture.

walrus *n* (*pl* **walruses, walrus**) a large, thick-skinned aquatic animal, related to the seals, having long canine teeth and coarse whiskers.

walrus moustache *n* a thick drooping moustache.

waltz *n* a piece of music with three beats to the bar; a whirling or slowly circling dance. * *vi* to dance a waltz.

wampum *n* polished shells strung like beads formerly used as money by North American Indians.

wan *adj* (**wanner, wannest**) pale and sickly; feeble or weak.—**wanly** *adv*.—**wanness** *n*.

wand *n* a magician's rod.

wander *vi* to ramble with no definite destination; to go astray; to lose concentration.—*also n*.

wandering Jew *n* any of various trailing or climbing plants; (*with cap*) a legendary figure condemned by Christ to roam the world until the Day of Judgement as punishment for an insult.

wanderlust *n* a compelling desire for travel.

wane *vi* to decrease, esp of the moon; to decline. * *n* decrease, decline.

wangle *vti* (*inf*) to achieve (something) by devious means.

wank *vi* (*Brit vulg*) to masturbate.—*also n*.

wanker *n* (*Brit vulg*) a person who masturbates; (*derog*) a stupid, contemptible or worthless person.

wannabee *n* (*sl*) a person who wants to be someone or something else.

want *n* lack; poverty. * *vt* to need; to require; to lack; to wish (for).

want ad *n* (*inf*) a newspaper or magazine advertisement requesting an item, job, etc.

wanted *adj* sought after.

wanting *adj* lacking.

wanton *adj* malicious; wilful; sexually provocative.

wapiti *n* (*pl* **wapitis**) a large deer of North America.

war *n* military conflict between nations or parties; a conflict; a contest. * *vi* (**warring, warred**) to make war.

warble *vi* to sing with trills and runs; to sing like a bird.

warble fly *n* a species of fly the larvae of which burrow under the skin of cattle causing painful lumps.

warbler *n* any of a family of small Old World songbirds which includes the nightingale and robin.

war crime *n* a crime committed in wartime (such as mistreatment of prisoners) which violates conventional notions of decency.

war cry *n* a rallying call in battle; a party catchword.

ward *n* a section of a hospital; an electoral district; a division of a prison; a child placed under the supervision of a court. * *vt* (*with* **off**) to repel; to fend off.—**wardship** *n*.

-ward, -wards *adj suffix* indicating a certain direction.

war dance *n* a ritual dance before or after battle as practised by certain North American Indian tribes.

warden *n* an official; a person in charge of a building or home; a prison governor;

warder *n* (*Brit*) a prison officer.

ward heeler *n* (*sl*) a local political hanger-on for a politician.

wardrobe *n* a cupboard for clothes; one's clothes.

wardroom *n* a room in a warship for use by officers with the exception of the captain.

ware *n* (*pl*) merchandise, goods for sale; pottery.

warehouse *n* a building for storing goods.

warfare *n* armed hostilities; conflict.

warfarin *n* a crystalline substance used in medicine as an anticoagulant and also as a poison to kill rodents.

war game *n* a simulated battle or tactical exercise using models or computers for military training; a re-enactment of a battle using model soldiers.

warhead *n* the section of a missile containing the explosive.

warhorse *n* a horse used in battle; (*inf*) a veteran of military or political conflict.

warlike *adj* hostile.

warlock *n* a sorcerer, a magician.

warlord *n* a military leader or ruler of (part of) a country.

warm *adj* moderately hot; friendly, kind; (*colours*) rich; enthusiastic. * *vt* to make warm. * *vi* to become enthusiastic (about). —**warmly** *adv*.—**warmth** *n*.

warm-blooded *adj* having a constant and relatively high temperature; passionate.

warm front *n* the edge of an advancing mass of warm air.

warm-hearted *adj* kind, sympathetic; affectionate.

warming pan *n* a long-handled (usu copper) pan filled with hot coals and formerly used to warm a bed.

warmonger *n* a person who incites war, esp for personal gain; warrior, a fighting soldier.

warm-up *n* a period of exercise or practice before a race, etc.

warn *vt* to notify of danger; to caution or advise (against).—**warning** *n*.

warp *vti* to twist out of shape; to distort; to corrupt. * *n* the threads arranged lengthwise on a loom across which other threads are passed.

war paint *n* paint smeared on the face and body by North American Indians before entering battle; (*inf*) formal or ceremonial dress, regalia; (*inf*) cosmetics.

warpath *n* the route used by a war party of North American Indians; (*with* **on the**) on a hostile expedition; (*with* **on the**) (*inf*) angry.

warped *adj* distorted, twisted; embittered.

warplane *n* an aircraft for use in combat.

warrant *vt* to guarantee; to justify. * *n* a document giving authorization; a writ for arrest.

warrantee *n* somebody to whom a warrant is given.

warrant officer *n* a person in the armed services holding a rank between commissioned officers and NCOs.

warrantor *n* a person or company that offers a warranty.

warranty *n* (*pl* **warranties**) a pledge to replace something if it is not as represented, a guarantee.

warren *n* an area in which rabbits breed.

warring *adj* engaged in war.

warrior *n* a soldier, fighter.

warship *n* a ship equipped for war.

wart *n* a small, hard projection on the skin.—**warty** *adj*.

wart hog *n* an African wild pig with warty lumps on the face, large tusks and thick course hair.

wartime *adj*, *n* (of) a period or time of war.

wary *adj* (**warier, wariest**) watchful; cautious.—**warily** *adv*.—**wariness** *n*.

was *see* **be**.

wash *vti* to cleanse with water and soap; to flow against or over; to sweep along by the action of water; to separate gold, etc, from earth by washing; to cover with a thin coat of metal or paint; (*with* **down**) to wash thoroughly from top to bottom; to take a drink of liquid to help in swallowing food. * *n* a washing; the break of waves on the shore; the waves left behind by a boat; a liquid used for washing.

washable *adj* able to be washed without damage.—**washability** *n*.

washboard *n* a corrugated board used (esp formerly) for scrubbing clothes.

washbowl, washbasin *n* a basin or bowl, esp a bathroom fixture, for use in washing one's hands, etc.—*also* **wash-hand basin**.

washcloth *n* a flannel.

washed-out *adj* faded in colour; fatigued.

washed-up *adj* unsuccessful, ineffective; unpromising.

washer *n* a flat ring of metal, rubber, etc, to give tightness to joints; a washing machine.

washing *n* the act of cleansing with water; a number of items washed together.

washing machine *n* a device for washing clothes.

washing powder *n* a powdered detergent formulated for washing fabrics.

washing soda *n* sodium carbonate dissolved in water used for washing and cleaning.

washing-up *n* (*Brit*) the washing of dishes and cutlery after a meal; the dishes and cutlery waiting to be washed.

washout *n* (*sl*) a failure.

washroom *n* cloakroom, lavatory.

washstand *n* a piece of furniture for holding a bowl and jug of water used for washing.

washtub *n* a large tub used for washing clothes.

washy *adj* (**washier, washiest**) weak, watery; pale; lacking in strength or vigour.—**washiness** *n*.

wasn't = was not.

wasp *n* a winged insect with a black and yellow striped body, which can sting.

Wasp, WASP *n* an American of northern European, esp British, descent and Protestant upbringing, regarded as belonging to the most privileged group in American society (White Anglo-Saxon Protestant).

waspish *adj* sharp in speech or manner, irritable.

wasp waist *n* a very slender waist.

wassail *n* (*formerly*) a toast made at festivities; a festive celebration with a lot of drinking and merriment; spiced ale or mulled wine served (esp formerly) at Christmas or other festive occasions. * *vi* to make merry.

Wassermann test *n* a blood test used to diagnose syphilis.

wastage *n* anything lost by use or natural decay; wasteful or avoidable loss of something valuable.

waste *adj* useless; left over; uncultivated or uninhabited. * *vt* to ravage; to squander; to use foolishly; to fail to use. * *vi* to lose strength, etc as by disease. * *n* uncultivated or uninhabited land; discarded material, garbage, excrement.—**wasteful** *adj*.—**wastefully** *adv*.—**wastefulness** *n*.

wasted *adj* ravaged, devastated; not used to best advantage; weak, emaciated; (*sl*) dead, killed; (*sl*) showing the effects of alcohol or drug abuse.

wasteland *n* a piece of barren or uncultivated land; a desolate region; something (eg a period of time, relationship) lacking in moral, spiritual, emotional, etc vitality.

wastepaper *n* paper discarded as waste.

wastepipe *n* a pipe carrying off used water from sinks, baths, etc.

waster *n* a wasteful person or thing; a good-for-nothing.

wasting asset *n* a non-renewable resource such as a coal mine.

wastrel *n* a vagabond; a waster, idler.

watch *n* surveillance; close observation; vigil; guard; a small timepiece worn on the wrist, etc; a period of duty on a ship * *vi* to look with attention; to wait for; to keep vigil. * *vt* to keep one's eyes fixed on; to guard; to tend; to observe closely; (*chance, etc*) to wait for.—**watcher** *n*.—**watchful** *adj*.—**watchfully** *adv*.—**watchfulness** *n*.

watchband *n* a strap of leather, etc, for securing a watch to the wrist.

watchcase *n* a protective metal casing for a watch mechanism.

watchdog *n* a dog that guards property; a person or group that monitors safety, standards, etc.

watchmaker *n* a person who makes and repairs watches.

watchman *n* (*pl* **watchmen**) a person who guards a building or other property.

watch night *n* a religious service on New Year's Eve.

watchtower *n* a tower for a sentry to keep watch from.

watchword *n* a password.

water *n* the substance H_2O, a clear, thin liquid, lacking taste or smell, and essential for life; any body of it, as the ocean, a lake, river, etc; bodily secretions such as tears, urine. * *vt* to moisten with water; to irrigate; to dilute with water; (*with* **down**) to dilute; to reduce in strength or effectiveness. * *vi* (*eyes*) to smart; to salivate; to take in water.

water bed *n* a bed with a water-filled mattress.

water bird *n* any swimming or wading bird.

water biscuit *n* a thin, crisp biscuit, usu served with cheese.

water blister *n* a blister on the skin filled with watery fluid instead of blood.

water boatman *n* any of various aquatic bugs adapted for swimming.

waterborne *adj* floating on or travelling by water.

waterbuck *n* an African antelope which lives in swampy areas.

water buffalo *n* a common domesticated Asian buffalo.

water cannon *n* an apparatus for pumping water at high pressure to disperse crowds.

water chestnut *n* an Asian aquatic plant with edible nutlike fruit; (the edible tuber of) a Chinese plant with a succulent root.

water clock *n* a clock with a mechanism operated by flowing or dripping water.

water-closet *n* a lavatory.

watercolour, watercolor *n* a water-soluble paint; a picture painted with watercolours.

water-cooled *adj* (*engine etc*) cooled by the circulation of water.

watercourse *n* (a channel for) a stream, river or canal.

watercraft *n* skill in handling boats and other vessels; a vessel travelling by water.

watercress *n* a plant growing in ponds and streams, used in a salad.

water cure *n* hydropathy.

water diviner *n* a person who searches for water using a divining rod.

waterfall *n* a fall of water over a precipice or down a hill.

water flea *n* any of numerous tiny freshwater crustaceans.

waterfowl *n* (*pl* **waterfowl**) a bird that frequents lakes, rivers, etc, esp a duck.

waterfront *n* an area alongside a body of water, esp a docks.

water gas *n* a toxic inflammable mixture of carbon monoxide and hydrogen produced by passing steam over hot carbon, used as a fuel.

water glass *n* a solution of sodium or potassium silicate in water used as a protective coating and to preserve eggs.

water hammer *n* (the sound of) the concussion of water in a pipe when a blockage is suddenly dislodged.

water hole *n* a water-filled hollow where animals drink.

water hyacinth *n* a floating aquatic plant of tropical America that often blocks waterways with its dense growth.

water ice *n* an iced dessert made from frozen water, sugar and a flavouring.

watering can *n* a container with a spout for watering plants.

watering hole *n* (*inf*) a bar or pub.

watering place *n* a place where animals or people can obtain water; a spa resort.

water jacket *n* a casing filled with water used for cooling machinery.

water jump *n* a ditch filled with water used as an obstacle in a steeplechase and other sporting contests.

water level *n* the surface level of water in a reservoir, etc.

water lily *n* any of a family of plants with large floating leaves and showy flowers.

waterline *n* a line up to which a ship's hull is submerged.

waterlogged *adj* soaked or saturated with water.

water main *n* a main pipe or conduit for carrying water.

watermark *n* a line marking the height to which water has risen; a mark impressed on paper which can only be seen when held up to the light.

watermelon *n* a large fruit with a hard green rind and edible red watery flesh.

water mill *n* a mill operated by a water wheel.

water pistol *n* a toy gun that shoots a stream of water.

water polo *n* a game played in water by two teams of seven swimmers with the aim of scoring by hitting a ball into the opponents' goal.

water power *n* the power of falling or moving water used to operate machinery or generate electricity.

waterproof *adj* impervious to water; watertight.—*also vt.*

water-repellent *adj* (*fabrics, etc*) treated with a substance that prevents penetration by water.

water-resistant *adj* (*fabrics, etc*) designed to resist water penetration as long as possible.

watershed *n* a turning point.

waterside *n* the edge of a body of water.

water-skiing *n* the sport of planing on water by being towed by a motorboat—**water-skier** *n*.

water softener *n* a device or chemical designed to counteract chemicals that cause hardness in water.

water-soluble *adj* capable of dissolving in water.

water spaniel *n* a breed of large curly-coated spaniel used in hunting waterfowl.

waterspout *n* a pipe for draining water; a tall column of water formed by a whirlwind and reaching from the sea to the clouds.

water table *n* the level below which the ground is saturated with water.

watertight *adj* not allowing water to pass through; foolproof.

water tower *n* an elevated tank or reservoir to allow water to be supplied under pressure.

waterway *n* a navigable channel of water.

water wheel *n* a wheel designed to be turned by running water and used to drive machinery; a wheel used for raising water.

water wings *npl* inflatable rubber floats worn on the arms of those learning to swim.

waterworks *n* (*as sing*) an establishment that supplies water to a district; (*pl: inf*) the urinary system; (*inf*) tears.

waterworn *adj* rubbed smooth by the action of water.

watery *adj* thin, diluted.

watt *n* a unit of electrical power.

wattage *n* amount of electrical power.

wattle *n* (material for) a framework of stakes or poles interwoven with thin branches, twigs, etc formerly used for fencing and building; a loose flap of skin hanging from the necks of certain birds and lizards; an Australian acacia tree with small brightly-coloured flowers. * *vt* to build of or with wattle; to interweave or interlace (with sticks, etc) to make a light frame.

wave *n* an undulation travelling on the surface of water; the form in which light and sound are thought to travel; an increase or upsurge (eg of crime); a hair curl; a movement of the hand in greeting or farewell. * *vti* to move freely backward and forward; to flutter; to undulate; to move the hand to and fro in greeting, farewell, etc; (*with* **down**) to signal (a vehicle, etc) to stop with a wave.—**wavy** *adj*.

wave band *n* a range of radio frequencies or wavelengths.

waveguide *n* a metal tube used to guide microwaves along a particular path.

wavelength *n* the distance between the crests of successive waves of light or sound; radio frequency.

wavelet *n* a small wave.

wave mechanics *n sing* (*physics*) the theory in quantum mechanics that describes the behaviour of elementary particles in terms of their wave properties.

waver *vi* to hesitate; to falter.—**waverer** *n*.

wax[1] *n* beeswax; an oily substance used to make candles, polish, etc * *vt* to rub, polish, cover or treat with wax.

wax[2] *vi* to increase in strength, size, etc.

waxen *adj* made of wax; pale and smooth like wax.

wax paper *n* paper that has been rendered moistureproof by treating with wax.

waxwork *n* a figure or model formed of wax; (*pl*) an exhibition of such figures.

waxy *adj* (**waxier, waxiest**) consisting of or like wax; adhesive.—**waxily** *adv*.—**waxiness** *n*.

way *n* path, route; road; distance; room to advance; direction; state; means; possibility; manner of living; (*pl*) habits.

waybill *n* a document with list of goods and shipping instructions accompanying a shipment.

wayfarer *n* a traveller.

waylay *vt* (**waylaying, waylaid**) to lie in wait for; to accost.

way-out *adj* (*inf*) unconventional, unusual; amazing.

-ways *adv suffix* indicating a certain direction or manner.

ways and means *npl* the methods used to accomplish something; the revenues and means of raising revenues for the use of government.

wayside *n* the side of or land adjacent to a road.

wayward *adj* wilful, stubborn; unpredictable.—**waywardness** *n*.

WBA *abbr* = World Boxing Association.

WBC *abbr* = World Boxing Council.

WC *abbr* = (*Brit*) water-closet.

we *pron pl* of I; I and others.

weak *adj* lacking power or strength; feeble; ineffectual.—**weakness** *n*.

weaken *vti* to make or grow weaker.

weak interaction *n* (*physics*) an interaction between elementary particles that is responsible for certain particle decay processes.

weak-kneed *adj* (*inf*) submissive, easily intimidated.

weakling *n* a person who lacks strength of character.

weakly *adj* (**weaklier, weakliest**) not robust; sickly. * *adv* in a weak manner, feebly.

weak-minded *adj* lacking in determination; feebleminded.

weal *n* a raised mark on the skin left by a blow with a lash.

wealth *n* a large amount of possessions or money; affluence; an abundance (of).—**wealthy** *adj*.

wean *vt* (*baby, animal*) to replace the mother's milk with other nourishment; to dissuade (from indulging a habit).

weapon *n* any instrument used in fighting.

weaponry *n* weapons collectively.

wear *vb* (**wearing, wore,** *pp* **worn**) *vt* to have on the body as clothing; (*hair, etc*) to arrange in a particular way; to display; to rub away; to impair by use; to exhaust, tire; (*with* **down**) to overcome gradually through persistent pressure; (*with* **out**) to tire or exhaust. * *vi* to be impaired by use or time; to be spent tediously; (*with* **off**) to become gradually weaker in effect; (*with* **out**) to make or become worthless through prolonged use. * *n* deterioration from frequent use; articles worn.—**wearer** *n*.

wearable *adj* suitable to be worn.

wear and tear *n* deterioration or depreciation from everyday use.

wearing *adj* exhausting, tiresome, oppressive.

weary *adj* (**wearier, weariest**) tired; bored. * *vti* (**wearying, wearied**) to make or become tired.—**weariness** *n*.—**wearisome** *adj*.

weasel *n* a small carnivorous animal with a long slender body and reddish fur.

weasel words *npl* (*inf*) evasive or misleading talk.

weather *n* atmospheric conditions, such as temperature, rainfall, cloudiness, etc * *vt* to expose to the action of the weather; to survive. * *vi* to withstand the weather.

weather-beaten *adj* worn or damaged by the weather; hardened or bronzed through exposure to the weather.

weatherboard *n* a sloping, usu overlapping, timber board used as external cladding for a wall or roof.—**weatherboarding** *n*.

weather-bound *adj* delayed or postponed due to bad weather.

weathercock *n* a weather vane in the form of a cock to show the wind direction.

weathered *adj* affected or seasoned by exposure to the weather; (*rocks*) altered in shape by erosion; (*roof*) having a sloped surface to allow rainwater to escape.

weather eye *n* an eye trained to observe changes in the weather; (*inf*) an alert or watchful gaze.

weatherglass *n* a barometer.

weathering *n* the erosion of rocks through the action of the wind, rain, frost, etc.

weatherman *n* (*pl* **weathermen**) a weather forecaster on radio or television who is usually also a professional meteorologist.

weather map *n* a chart showing weather conditions over a particular area for a specified period.

weatherproof *adj* designed to withstand exposure to weather without damage or deterioration.—*also vt*.

weather station *n* a meteorological post for collecting, recording and transmitting data on weather conditions.

weather vane *n* a device attached to a tall structure to indicate wind direction.

weave *vb* (**weaving, wove,** *pp* **woven**) *vt* to interlace threads in a loom to form fabric; to construct. * *vi* to make a way through (eg a crowd), to zigzag.—**weaver** *n*.

weaverbird *n* any of various Old World songbirds that build nests of interwoven grass, twigs, etc, including the house sparrow.

web *n* a woven fabric; the fine threads spun by a spider; the membrane joining the digits of birds, animals.

webbed *adj* (*ducks, etc*) having the digits connected by a fold of skin.

webbing *n* a strong narrow woven fabric of jute, cotton, etc, used for straps and belts; anything forming a web.

weber *n* the SI unit of magnetic flux.

wed *vti* (**wedding, wedded** *or* **wed**) to marry; to join closely.

Wed *abbr* = Wednesday.

we'd = we had; we would.

wedded *adj* of or resulting from marriage; devoted (to art, etc).

wedding *n* marriage; the ceremony of marriage.

wedding cake *n* an ornately decorated rich fruit cake, usu in three tiers, served at a wedding.

wedding ring *n* a band of gold or platinum used at a wedding and worn to show marital status.

wedge *n* a v-shaped block of wood or metal for splitting or fastening; a wedge-shaped object. * *vti* to split or secure with a wedge; to thrust (in) tightly; to become fixed tightly.

wedlock *n* marriage.

Wednesday *n* fourth day of the week, between Tuesday and Thursday.

wee[1] *adj* (*Scot*) small, tiny.

wee[2] *n* (*inf*) the act of passing urine; urine. * *vt* (*inf*) to pass urine.—*also* **wee-wee**.

weed *n* any undesired plant, esp one that crowds out desired plants; (*sl*) marijuana; (*pl*) a widow's black mourning clothes. * *vt* to remove weeds; (*with* **out**) to remove or eliminate (something superfluous or harmful).

weedkiller *n* a chemical or hormonal substance used to kill weeds.

weedy *adj* (**weedier, weediest**) full of weeds; (*inf*) thin and scrawny.

week *n* the period of seven consecutive days, esp from Sunday to Sunday.

weekday *n* a day of the week other than Saturday or Sunday.

weekend, week-end *n* the period from Friday night to Sunday night—*also adj.*

weekly *adj* happening once a week or every week.

weeknight *n* the evening or night of a weekday.

weeny *adj* (**weenier, weeniest**) (*inf*) tiny, minute.

weep *vti* (**weeping, wept**) to shed tears, to cry; (*wound*) to ooze.

weepie *n* (*inf*) a sentimental film.

weeping *n* the act of weeping. * *adj* shedding tears; exuding moisture; (*tree*) with drooping branches.—**weepingly** *adv.*

weeping willow *n* a Chinese willow tree with slender drooping branches.

weepy *adj* (**weepier, weepiest**) tearful; prone to crying.—**weepily** *adv.*—**weepiness** *n.*

weevil *n* a beetle which feeds on plants and crops.

wee-wee *see* **wee**[2].

weft *n* the yarn woven across the lengthwise threads in a loom.—*also* **woof**.

weigh *vt* to measure the weight of; to consider carefully; (*with* **down**) to weight; to oppress; (*with* **up**) to assess, make a judgment about (a person, thing, etc). * *vi* to have weight; to be burdensome; (*with* **in**) (*boxer, wrestler*) to be weighed before a bout; (*jockey*) to be weighed after a race; (*inf*) to make a contribu-

tion to (eg an argument).

weighbridge *n* a large scale consisting of a metal plate set into the road onto which vehicles are driven to be weighed.

weigh-in *n* (*sports*) the checking of the weight of a contestant, esp of a jockey after a race or of a boxer before a bout.

weight *n* the amount which anything weighs; influence; any unit of heaviness. * *vt* to attach a weight to.

weightlessness *n* the state of having no or little reaction to gravity, esp in space travel.

weight lifting *n* the sport of lifting weights of a specific amount in a particular way.—**weight lifter** *n.*

weight training *n* physical exercise involving lifting heavy weights.

weight watcher *n* a person on a diet to lose weight.

weighty *adj* (**weightier, weightiest**) heavy; serious.—**weightily** *adv.*

weir *n* a low dam across a river which controls the flow of water.

weird *adj* unearthly, mysterious; eerie; bizarre.—**weirdly** *adv.*

weirdo, weirdie *n* (*pl* **weirdos, weirdies**) (*inf*) an eccentric person.

welch *see* **welsh**.

welcome *adj* gladly received; pleasing. * *n* reception of a person or thing. * *vt* to greet kindly.

weld *vt* to unite, as metal by heating until fused or soft enough to hammer together; to join closely. * *n* a welded joint.

welfare *n* wellbeing; health; assistance or financial aid granted to the poor, the unemployed, etc.

welfare state *n* a state in which the government assumes responsibility for the health and social security of its citizens.

well[1] *n* a spring; a hole bored in the ground to provide a source of water, oil, gas, etc; the open space in the middle of a staircase * *vi* to pour forth.

well[2] *adj* (**better, best**) agreeable; comfortable; in good health. * *adv* in a proper, satisfactory, or excellent manner; thoroughly; prosperously; with good reason; to a considerable degree; fully. * *interj* an expression of surprise, etc.

we'll = we will; we shall.

well-advised *adj* acting with good sense; carefully thought out.

well-appointed *adj* fully equipped or furnished.

well-balanced *adj* sensible, sane.

well-being *n* condition of being well or contented; welfare.

well-bred *adj* well brought up; of good stock.

well-connected *adj* having powerful friends or relatives.

well-disposed *adj* favourable, feeling kindly (toward).

well-done *adj* performed with skill; thoroughly cooked, as meat.

well-favoured, well-favored *adj* attractive.

well-found *adj* fully equipped.

well-founded *adj* borne out by facts.

well-groomed *adj* clean and tidy in dress and appearance.

well-grounded *adj* well instructed in a subject.

wellhead *n* the source of a stream, spring, etc; a source, origin.

well-heeled *adj* (*inf*) wealthy.

wellies *npl* (*Brit inf*) wellingtons.

well-informed *adj* knowledgeable on a wide range of

subjects; possessing reliable information on a specific matter.

wellington (boot) n a rubber, waterproof boot.

well-intentioned adj having good intentions (but often without producing good results).

well-knit adj firm, compact.

well-known adj widely known, famous; known fully.

well-mannered adj having or showing good manners; polite.

well-meaning adj having good intentions (but often without producing good results).

well-nigh adv almost.

well-off adj in comfortable circumstances; prosperous.

well-preserved adj well looked after; remaining youthful in appearance.

well-read adj having read widely and deeply.

well-rounded adj having a pleasantly curved or rounded shape; full, complete.

well-spoken adj spoken clearly and eloquently; spoken in a pleasing manner.

well-thought-of adj having a good reputation.

well-thumbed adj (book) marked by frequent handling.

well-to-do adj prosperous.

well-wisher n a person who is sympathetic to another person, cause, etc.

well-worn adj showing signs of wear; (phrase, etc) trite, hackneyed.

Welsh adj relating to the people of Wales or their language.—also n.

welsh vti to avoid paying a gambling debt; to run off without paying.—also **welch**.—**welsher, welcher** n.

Welsh corgi n a corgi.

Welsh dresser n a dresser with drawers and cupboards below and open shelves above.

Welsh rabbit, Welsh rarebit n melted cheese on toast.

welt n a band or strip to strengthen a seam; a weal.

welter vi to roll or wallow. * n a jumble.

welterweight n a professional boxer weighing 140–147 pounds; a wrestler weighing 154–172 pounds.

wench n (used facetiously) a girl or young woman.

wend vt to amble, to saunter.

Wendy house n (Brit) a toy house for children to play in.

Wensleydale n a mild crumbly English cheese.

went see **go**.

wept see **weep**.

were see **be**.

we're = we are.

weren't = were not.

werewolf n (pl **werewolves**) an imaginary person able to transform himself for a time into a wolf.

west n the direction of the sun at sunset; one of the four points of the compass; the region in the west of any country; (with cap) Europe and the Western Hemisphere. * adj situated in, or toward the west. * adv in or to the west.

westerly adj toward the west; blowing from the west. * n (pl **westerlies**) a wind blowing from the west.—also adv.

western adj of or in the west. * n a film, novel, etc about the usu pre-20th century American West.

westerner n a person from the west.

Western Hemisphere n that half of the earth containing North and South America.

westernize vti to make or become familiar with the ideas, institutions, customs, etc of the West.—**westernization** n.

westernmost adj farthest west.

westward adj toward the west.—also adv.—**westwards** adv.

wet adj (**wetter, wettest**) covered or saturated with water or other liquid; rainy; misty; not yet dry. * n water or other liquid; rain or rainy weather. * vti (**wetting, wet** or **wetted**) to soak; to moisten.—**wetness** n.

wet blanket n (inf) a person who dampens the enthusiasm of others.

wet dream n an erotic dream causing orgasm.

wet nurse n a woman employed to care for or suckle another's child.

wet-nurse vt to act as a wet nurse; (inf) to devote constant attention to (a person).

wet rot n (Brit) decay in timber caused by a fungus; any of various fungi that cause rot in damp timber.

wet suit n a close-fitting suit worn by divers, etc, to retain body heat.

we've = we have.

whack vti (inf) to strike sharply, esp making a sound. * n (inf) a sharp blow.

whacking adj (Brit inf) enormous. * adv (inf) very, extremely.

whale n a very large sea mammal that breathes through a blowhole, and resembles a fish in shape. * vi to hunt whales.

whalebone n a horny substance forming plates in the upper jaws of toothless whales; a piece of this formerly used for stiffening undergarments.

whalebone whale n any of various large whales that have whalebone plates instead of teeth which are used to filter plankton for food.

whaler n a person or a ship employed in hunting whales.

whaling n the practice of hunting whales for food, oil, etc.

wham n (the sound of) a heavy blow. * vti (**whamming, whammed**) to hit or cause to hit with a loud noise.

whang n (the sound of) a forceful blow. * vti to hit or cause to hit with force.

wharf n (pl **wharfs, wharves**) a platform for loading and unloading ships in harbour.

wharfage n (the charge for) the use of a wharf; wharves collectively.

wharfinger n the owner or manager of a wharf.

what adj of what sort, how much, how great. * relative pron that which; as much or many as. * interj used as an expression of surprise or astonishment.

whatever pron anything that; no matter what.

whatnot n (inf) something or someone the name of which has been forgotten, is unknown or is hard to categorize; a set of open shelves for ornaments, photographs, etc.

whatsit n (inf) something or someone the name of which has been forgotten, is unknown or is hard to categorize.

whatsoever adj whatever.

wheat n a cereal grain usu ground into flour for bread.

wheatear n a small grey and white migratory thrush.

wheaten adj made from the grain or flour of wheat; pale yellow in colour.

wheat germ n the kernel of a grain of wheat, high in nutritive value.

wheatmeal adj, n (made from) brown flour with a high proportion of wheat grain.

whee interj used to express joy or delight.

wheedle vt to persuade, to cajole (into); to coax with flattery.

wheel *n* a solid disc or circular rim turning on an axle; a steering wheel; (*pl*) the moving forces. * *vt* to transport on wheels. * *vi* to turn round or on an axis; to move in a circular direction, as a bird.

wheelbarrow *n* a cart with one wheel in front and two handles and legs at the rear.

wheelbase *n* the distance between the front and rear axles of a vehicle.

wheelchair *n* a chair with large wheels for invalids.

wheel clamp *n* (*Brit*) a device that prevents an illegally parked car from being driven away until a fine is paid to release it.—*also vt*.

wheeler-dealer *n* (*inf*) a shrewd operator in business, politics, etc.

wheelie *n* a stunt in which a bicycle or motorcycle is ridden for a distance with the front wheel off the ground.

wheelwright *n* a person who makes and repairs wheels for a living.

wheeze *vi* to breathe with a rasping sound; to breathe with difficulty.—*also n*.

wheezy *adj* (**wheezier, wheeziest**) making a wheezing sound.—**wheezily** *adv*.—**wheeziness** *n*.

whelk *n* a shellfish with a snail-like shell.

whelp *n* the young of various animals, esp a dog; an impudent child. * *vt* to give birth to (a puppy, etc). * *vi* (*bitch*) to bring forth young.

when *adv* at what or which time * *conj* at the time at which; although; *relative pron* at which.

whence *adv* from what place.—*also conj*.

whenever *adv, conj* at whatever time.

whensoever *conj, adv* whenever.

where *adv* at which or what place; to which place; from what source; *relative pron* in or to which.

whereabouts *adv* near or at what place; about where. * *n* approximate location.

whereas *conj* since; on the contrary.

whereby *adv* by which.—*also conj*.

wherein *adv* (*formal*) in what; how. * *conj* in which; where.

whereof *adv, conj* (*arch*) of what or which.

whereon *adv, conj* (*arch*) on what or which.

wheresoever *adv* (*emphatic*) wherever.

whereto *adv, conj* (*formal*) to what or which.

whereupon *adv* at which point; upon which.

wherever *adv* at or to whatever place.

wherewithal *n* the means or resources.

whet *vt* (**whetting, whetted**) to sharpen by rubbing, to stimulate.

whether *conj* introducing an alternative possibility or condition.

whetstone *n* a stone for sharpening the edges of tools; something that sharpens or stimulates.

whew *interj* an exclamation of astonishment, amazement, relief, etc.

whey *n* the watery part of milk that is separated from the curds in sour milk.

which *adj* what one (of) * *pron* which person or thing; that. * *relative pron* person or thing referred to.

whichever *pron* whatever one that; whether one or the other; no matter which.—*also adj*.

whichsoever *adj, pron* (*arch*) whichever.

whiff *n* a sudden puff of air, smoke or odour.

while *n* a period of time. * *conj* during the time that; whereas; although. * *vt* to pass (the time) pleasantly.

whilst *conj* (*esp Brit*) while.

whim *n* a fancy; an irrational thought.

whimper *vi* to make a low, unhappy cry.—*also n*.

whimsical *adj* unusual, odd, fantastic.—**whimsicality** *n*.

whimsy, whimsey *n* (*pl* **whimsies, whimseys**) a fanciful notion, a whim.

whine *vi* (*dog*) to make a long, high-pitched cry; (*person*) to complain childishly. * *n* a plaintive cry.

whinge *vi* to moan, complain.—*also n*.

whinny *vi* (**whinnying, whinnied**) to neigh softly.—*also n*.

whip *n* a piece of leather attached to a handle used for punishing people or driving on animals; an officer in parliament who maintains party discipline. * *vb* (**whipping, whipped**) *vt* to move, pull, throw, etc suddenly; to strike, as with a lash; (*eggs, etc*) to beat into a froth; (*with* **up**) to stir into action, excite; (*inf*) to produce in a hurry. * *vi* to move rapidly.

whipcord *n* a strong cord of tightly twisted strands used for whips; a cotton or worsted fabric with diagonal ridges.

whip hand *n* (*usu with* **the**) the dominant position.

whiplash *n* a stroke with a whip; a neck injury when the head is jerked forward and backward.

whipped cream *n* cream that has been stiffened by beating, used as a topping for desserts, etc.

whippersnapper *n* an insignificant but impudent young person.

whippet *n* a small racing dog like a greyhound.

whipping boy *n* a person who is constantly punished for the mistakes of others, a scapegoat.

whippoorwill *n* a nocturnal American bird with a distinctive call.

whip-round *n* (*Brit inf*) an appeal among friends for contributions.

whipsaw *n* any of various types of saw with a long flexible blade.

whipstock *n* the handle of a whip.

whir, whirr *n* a humming or buzzing sound. * *vti* (**whirring, whirred**) to revolve with a buzzing noise.

whirl *n* a swift turning; confusion, commotion; (*inf*) an attempt or try. * *vti* to turn around rapidly; to spin.

whirligig *n* a spinning top.

whirlpool *n* a circular current or vortex of water.

whirlpool bath *n* a bath with a device that swirls water.

whirlwind *n* a whirling column of air; rapid activity.

whisk *vt* to make a quick sweeping movement; (*eggs, cream*) to beat, whip. * *vi* to move nimbly and efficiently. * *n* a kitchen utensil for whisking; (*inf*) a small amount.

whisker *n* any of the sensory bristles on the face of a cat, etc; (*pl*) the hair growing on a man's face, esp the cheeks.—**whiskered** *adj*.

whiskey *n* whisky distilled in the US or Ireland.

whisky *n* (*pl* **whiskies**) a spirit distilled from barley or rye.

whisper *vti* to speak softly; to spread a rumour. * *n* a hushed tone; a hint, trace.

whist *n* a card game for four players in two sides, each side attempting to win the greater number of the 13 tricks.

whistle *vti* to make a shrill sound by forcing the breath through the lips; to make a similar sound with a whistle; (*wind*) to move with a shrill sound; (*with* **for**) (*inf*) to demand or hope for in vain. * *n* a whistling sound; a musical instrument; a metal tube that is blown to make a shrill warning sound.

whistle stop *n* a minor railroad station where trains stop only on signal; a brief appearance by a candidate on tour during an election campaign.

Whit *see* **Whitsuntide.**

whit *n* the tiniest possible amount.

white *adj* of the colour of snow; pure; bright; (*skin*) light-coloured. * *n* the colour white; the white part of an egg or the eye.

white ant *n* a termite.

whitebait *n* (*pl* **whitebait**) the edible young of the herring and sprat.

white blood cell *n* a leucocyte.

whitecap *n* a wave with a white foamy crest.

white-collar *adj* of office and professional workers.

white dwarf *n* a small faint star of high density.

white elephant *n* a thing of little use.

white feather *n* a symbol of cowardice.

white flag *n* a flag of plain white material used to signify surrender or arrange a truce.

whitefly *n* (*pl* **whiteflies**) any of various small insects that feed on and injure plants.

white gold *n* a pale alloy of gold chiefly with platinum and palladium.

white goods *npl* household appliances, as refrigerators, etc; household linen, as sheets, towels, etc.

Whitehall *n* the British government; departmental government.

white heat *n* an intense heat accompanied by the emission of white light from a substance; (*inf*) intense excitement or emotion.

white hope *n* (*inf*) a person who is expected to win fame for his or her community, country, etc.

white-hot *adj* of a temperature so hot that white light is emitted; intensely passionate.

White House *n* the official residence of the president of the US; the US presidency.

white lead *n* a white solid of mostly lead carbonate, esp used in pigments.

white lie *n* a harmless lie, esp as uttered out of politeness.

white light *n* light, eg sunlight, that contains approximately equal proportions of the whole spectrum of visible radiation.

white matter *n* whitish tissue in the brain and spinal cord composed of nerve fibres.

white meat *n* a light-coloured meat such as poultry or veal.

white metal *n* an alloy, esp of tin, used in bearings, domestic utensils, etc.

whiten *vti* to make or become white; to bleach.

white noise *n* sound that contains approximately equal proportions of all the audible frequencies.

whiteout *n* a weather condition when heavy cloud and snow reflect most of the available light and greatly reduce visibility.

white paper *n* a government document detailing proposed legislation.

white sauce *n* a sauce made with butter, flour and seasonings mixed with milk, cream or stock.

white slave *n* a woman or girl held against her will and forced into prostitution.

white spirit *n* (*Brit*) a colourless inflammable liquid distilled from petroleum and used as a solvent and thinner for paint.

white tie *n* a white bow tie worn as part of a man's formal evening dress.—**white-tie** *adj*.

whitewash *n* a mixture of lime and water, used for whitening walls; concealment of the truth.—*also vt.*

white water *n* water with a foaming surface, as in rapids.

white whale *n* the beluga.

white wine *n* wine made from green grapes or from skinned black grapes.

whitewood *n* (any of various trees yielding) a light-coloured wood.

whitey *n* (*pl* **whities**) (*derog*) in US, a Black person's term for a white person.

whither *adv* to what or which place.

whiting *n* (*pl* **whitings, whiting**) an edible saltwater fish of the cod family.

whitlow *n* a painful inflammation at the end of a finger or toe.

Whitsun *adj* (*Christianity*) of, observed on, or pertaining to Whit Sunday or Whitsuntide. * *n* Whitsuntide.

Whit Sunday *n* (*Christianity*) the seventh Sunday after Easter, Pentecost.

Whitsuntide *n* (*Christianity*) the week beginning with Whit Sunday.—*also* **Whit.**

whittle *vt* to pare or cut thin shavings from (wood); (*with* **away** *or* **down**) to reduce.

whiz, whizz *vi* (**whizzing, whizzed**) to make a humming sound. * *n* (*pl* **whizzes**) a humming sound; (*inf*) an expert.

whiz kid, whizz kid *n* (*inf*) a person of extraordinary achievements given their relatively young age.

WHO *abbr* = World Health Organization.

who *pron* what or which person; that.

whoa *interj* a command given, esp to a horse, to slow down or come to a halt.

who'd = who would.

whodunit, whodunnit *n* (*inf*) a detective novel, play, etc.

whoever *pron* anyone who; whatever person.

whole *adj* not broken, intact; containing the total amount, number, etc.; complete. * *n* the entire amount; a thing complete in itself.

wholefood *n* unrefined food, free from additives.

wholehearted *adj* sincere, single-minded, enthusiastic.—**wholeheartedly** *adv.*

whole hog *n* (*inf*) the complete amount or extent.

wholemeal *adj* (*Brit*) *see* **wholewheat.**

whole note *n* (*mus*) a note with a time value equal to two half notes.—*also* **semibreve**

whole number *n* a number without fractions; an integer.

wholesale *n* selling of goods, usu at lower prices and in quantity, to a retailer.

wholesome *adj* healthy; mentally beneficial.—**wholesomeness** *n.*

wholewheat *adj* (*esp US flour*) made from the entire wheat kernel.—*also* **wholemeal.**

who'll = who will; who shall.

wholly *adv* completely.

whom *pron* objective case of **who.**

whomever *pron* the objective form of **whoever.**

whoop *n* a loud cry of excitement.

whoopee *interj* used to express wild excitement. * *n* boisterous fun.

whoopee cushion *n* a joke cushion that emits a rude noise when sat on.

whooping cough *n* an infectious disease, esp of children, causing coughing spasms.

whoops *interj* (*inf*) an exclamation of surprise or apology.

whoosh *n* a rushing or hissing sound. * *vi* to make or move with such a sound.

whop *vt* (**whopping, whopped**) to beat, thrash; to defeat completely.

whopper n (inf) a large specimen.—**whopping** adj.

whore n a prostitute.

whorehouse n a brothel.

whoremonger n a person who uses the services of whores.—also **whoremaster**.

whorl n a ring of leaves or petals round a stem; a single turn of a spiral; something shaped like a spiral; the central ridges of a fingerprint forming a complete circle.

whortleberry n a bilberry.

who's = who is.

whose pron the possessive case of **who** or **which**.

whosoever pron (arch) whoever.

who's who n a reference book containing the names and brief biographical details of famous or important people.

why adv for what cause or reason? * interj exclamation of surprise. * n (pl **whys**) a cause.

whydah n any of various African weaverbirds with black and white plumage.

WI abbr = Wisconsin; West Indies; (esp Brit) Women's Institute.

wick n a cord, as in a candle or lamp, that supplies fuel to the flame.

wicked adj evil, immoral, sinful.—**wickedly** adv.—**wickedness** n.

wicker n a long, thin, flexible twig; such twigs woven together, as in making baskets.—**wickerwork** n.

wicket n a small door or gate; (croquet) any of the small wire arches through which the balls must be hit; (cricket) the stumps at which the bowler aims the ball; the area between the bowler and the batsman; a batsman's innings.

wicketkeeper n (cricket) the fielder standing immediately behind the wicket.

widdershins see **withershins**.

wide adj broad; extensive; of a definite distance from side to side; (with of) far from the aim; open fully. * n (cricket) a ball bowled beyond the reach of the batsman.—**widely** adv.

wide-angle adj (photog) with an angle of view of 60 degrees or more.

wide-awake adj fully awake; ready, alert.

wide-eyed adj astonished; innocent.

widen vti to make or grow wide or wider.

widespread adj widely extended; general.

widget n (inf) a small device or gadget the name of which is lost or forgotten; a whatsit.

widow n a woman whose husband has died. * vt to cause to become a widow.—**widowhood** n.

widower n a man whose wife has died.

widow's peak n a pointed growth of hair in the middle of the forehead.

width n breadth.

wield vt (a weapon, etc) to brandish; to exercise power.

wife n (pl **wives**) a married woman.

wig n an artificial covering of real or synthetic hair for the head.

wigeon, widgeon n a Eurasian wild duck the male of which has a gingery head.

wigging n (Brit inf) a severe reprimand.

wiggle vti to move from side to side with jerky movements.

wigwag vb (**wigwagging, wigwagged**) vi to move back and forth; to send a signal by means of flag semaphore. * vt to signal by wigwagging; to cause (something) to move back and forth. * n (the message sent using) a system of signalling with flags.

wigwam n a North American Indian conical shelter.

wilco interj used in telecommunications to indicate that a message is received and being acted upon.

wild adj in its natural state; not tamed or cultivated; uncivilized; lacking control; disorderly; furious.—**wildly** adv.—**wildness** n.

wild boar n a wild pig with tusks, of Europe and Asia.

wild card n (card games) a card with an arbitrary value determined by the holder; (sport) a team that has not qualified for a competition but is allowed to take part; (sl) an unpredictable element.

wildcat adj (strike) unofficial. * n a fierce, undomesticated cat.

wildebeest n (pl **wildebeests, wildebeest**) a gnu.

wilderness n an uncultivated and desolate place.

wild-eyed adj staring angrily or crazily.

wildfire n a fire that spreads fast and is hard to put out.

wildfowl n any bird that is hunted for game, esp waterbirds such as ducks and geese.

wild-goose chase n a futile pursuit of something.

wilding n (the fruit of) any uncultivated plant; a wild animal; (sl) a violent rampage though the streets by a teenage gang.

wildlife n animals in the wild.

wild oat n (usu pl) a Eurasian grass related to cultivated oats; (pl) youthful excesses.

wild rice n a North American grass that bears edible grains; its grain.

Wild West n the western US during the lawless period of early settlement.

wile n a trick, craftiness.

wilful adj stubborn; done intentionally.—also **willful**.—**wilfully, willfully** adv.—**wilfulness, willfulness** n.

will[1] n power of choosing or determining; desire; determination; attitude, disposition; a legal document directing the disposal of one's property after death. * vt to bequeath; to command.

will[2] aux vb used in constructions with 2nd and 3rd persons; used to show futurity, determination, obligation.

willful see **wilful**.

willies npl (with the) nervousness, jumpiness.

willing adj ready, inclined; eager.—**willingly** adv.—**willingness** n.

will-o'-the-wisp n a pale phosphorescent glow sometimes seen over marshy areas and thought to be caused by combustion of gas from decaying organic matter; an elusive person or thing.

willow n a tree or shrub with slender, flexible branches; the wood of the willow.

willowherb n any of various plants of the evening-primrose family with pink or white flowers.

willow pattern n a traditional oriental-style design on china tableware consisting of a scene with figures and a willow tree, usu in blue on a white background.

willowy adj flexible, graceful.

willpower n the ability to control one's emotions and actions.

willy-nilly adv whether desired or not.

wilt vi to become limp, as from heat; (plant) to droop; to become weak or faint.

wily adj (**wilier, wiliest**) crafty; sly.—**wiliness** n.

WIMP, Wimp (acronym) (comput) a graphical interface using Windows, Icons, Mice and Pull-down menus that makes a computer easier to use.

wimp n (inf) a weak or ineffectual person.

wimple n a linen or silk cloth draped round the head

and neck but leaving the face uncovered, worn by women in medieval times and still used by some nuns.

win *vti* (**winning, won**) to gain with effort; to succeed in a contest; to gain eg by luck; to achieve influence over; (*with* **over**) to gain the support or affection of (someone). * *n* a success.

wince *vi* to shrink back; to flinch (as in pain).—*also n*.

winch *n* a hoisting machine. * *vt* to hoist or lower with a winch.

wind[1] *n* a current of air; breath; scent of game; (*inf*) flatulence; tendency; (*mus*) wind instrument(s). * *vt* (**winding, winded**) to cause to be short of breath; to perceive by scent.

wind[2] *vb* (**winding, wound**) *vt* to turn by cranking; to tighten the spring of a clock; to coil around something else; to encircle or cover, as with a bandage; (*with* **down**) to lower by winding a handle, etc. * *vi* to turn, to twist, to meander; (*with* **down**) to diminish in power or intensity; to slacken; to relax.

windage *n* the difference between the bore of a gun and the diameter of the projectile; (an allowance for) the deflection of a projectile caused by the wind.

windbag *n* (*inf*) a person who talks a lot of rubbish.

windblown *adj* blown or shaped by the wind.

windbreak *n* a shelter that breaks the force of the wind, as a line of trees.

windburn *n* redness and soreness of the skin due to the wind.

windcheater *n* a warm hooded jacket of windproof material.

wind-chill *n* a measure of the effect of low temperature combined with wind.

winded *adj* out of breath.

winder *n* one who or that which winds; a winding apparatus; a key for winding a spring-driven mechanism; a step in a spiral staircase.

windfall *n* fruit blown off a tree; any unexpected gain, esp financial.

winding *adj* meandering.

winding sheet *n* a sheet used to wrap a body for burial.

wind instrument *n* a musical instrument played by blowing into it or passing an air current through it.

windjammer *n* a large fast merchant sailing vessel.

windlass *n* any of various devices for hoisting, hauling or lifting using a rope or chain wound round a motorized drum. * *vt* to hoist, etc using a windlass.

wind machine *n* a device used in film and theatre to produce realistic wind effects.

windmill *n* a machine operated by the force of the wind turning a set of sails.

window *n* a framework containing glass in the opening in a wall of a building, or in a vehicle, etc, for air and light.

window box *n* a narrow box on a windowsill for growing flowers, etc.

windowdressing *n* the arrangement of goods in a shop window; ornamentation intended to disguise the true nature of something.

windowpane *n* the glass in a window.

window-shopping *n* the occupation of looking at goods for sale without buying them.—**window-shopper** *n*.

windowsill *n* a sill beneath a window.

windpipe *n* the air passage from the mouth to the lungs, the trachea.

windscreen, windshield *n* a protective shield of glass in the front of a vehicle.

windscreen wiper, windshield wiper *n* a metal blade with a rubber edge that removes rain, etc, from a windscreen.

windsock *n* a canvas cylinder flown from an airport mast to show the direction of the wind.—*also* **drogue**.

windsurfing *n* the sport of skimming along the surface of the water standing on a surfboard fitted with a sail.

windswept *adj* exposed to the wind; dishevelled.

wind tunnel *n* an apparatus for maintaining a constant force of air current to test the aerodynamics of an aircraft, etc.

wind-up *n* the conclusion.

windward *adv, adj* toward the direction where the wind blows from.

windy *adj* (**windier, windiest**) exposed to the winds; stormy; verbose.

wine *n* fermented grape juice used as an alcoholic beverage; the fermented juice of other fruits or plants.

wine bar *n* a bar that serves wine and food.

wine box *n* wine sold in a box with a small tap for pouring.

wine cellar *n* a place for storing wines, ideally a cool cellar; a stock of stored wines.

wine-coloured *adj* dark purplish-red.

wine cooler *n* a vessel that is filled with ice for cooling wine bottles.

wineglass *n* a glass, usu with a stem, for drinking wine.

winegrower *n* a person who grows vines and makes wine.

wine press *n* (a place containing) equipment for squeezing juice from grapes to make wine.

winery *n* (*pl* **wineries**) a place where wine is made.

wineskin *n* the skin of an animal, esp a goat, sewn into a bag for holding wine.

wing *n* the forelimb of a bird, bat or insect, by which it flies; the main lateral surface of an aeroplane; a projecting part of a building; the side of a stage; a section of a political party. * *vti* to make one's way swiftly; to wound without killing.

wing chair *n* an armchair with high sides for excluding draughts.

wing collar *n* a stiff upturned shirt collar with the points turned down.

wingding *n* (*inf*) a wild party; a real or pretended fit.

wing nut *n* a nut that is tightened manually using flat wings that project on each side.

wingspan, wingspread *n* the width of a bird or aeroplane between the tips of the wings.

wink *vi* to quickly open and close one's eye; to give a hint by winking; (*with* **at**) to disregard; to allow (something normally prohibited) to happen. * *n* the act of winking; an instant.

winkle[1] *n* a periwinkle.

winkle[2] *n* an edible sea snail. * *vt* (*with* **out**) (*inf*) to extract, prise out; to uncover, disclose.

winkle-pickers *npl* shoes or boots with sharp pointed toes.

winner *n* one that wins; (*inf*) a person or thing that is assured of success.

winning *n* a victory; (*pl*) money won in gambling. * *adj* charming.

winnow *vt* to separate out the chaff from (the grain) by blowing air across it; to analyze.

wino *n* (*pl* **winos**) (*inf*) a down-and-out addicted to cheap wine.

winsome *adj* charming, pleasing.

winter *n* the coldest season of the year: in the northern hemisphere from November or December to January or February. * *vi* to spend the winter.

wintergreen *n* any of various evergreen plants or shrubs; an aromatic essential oil from these formerly used in medicine.

winterize *vt* to prepare something (eg a car) to withstand winter weather.—**winterization** *n*.

winter sports *npl* sports that take place on ice or snow, such as skiing.

wintry, wintery *adj* (**wintrier, wintriest**) typical of winter, cold, stormy, snowy; unfriendly, frigid.

winy *adj* (**winier, winiest**) tasting like or resembling wine.

wipe *vt* to rub a surface with a cloth in order to clean or dry it; (*with* out) to remove; to erase; to kill off; to destroy. * *n* a wiping.

wiper *n* a person or thing that wipes; a windscreen wiper.

wire *n* a flexible thread of metal; a length of this; (*horse racing*) the finish line of a race; a telegram. * *adj* formed of wire. * *vt* to fasten, furnish, connect, etc, with wire; to send a telegram.

wired *adj* (*sl*) wearing a hidden electronic recording or listening device; (*sl*) nervous or edgy, esp as a result of taking a stimulating drug.

wire-haired *adj* (*dogs, etc*) having a coat of stiff hairs.

wireless *n* (*formerly*) a radio.

wire service *n* in US, a news agency that sends out news to television and radio stations.

wiretap *vb* (**wiretapping, wiretapped**) *vi* to connect to a telephone wire in order to listen in to a private conversation. * *vt* to tap (a telephone).—**wiretapper** *n*.

wireworm *n* the filament-like larva of certain beetles which infest and destroy plant roots.

wiring *n* a system of wires used in an electrical device or circuit.

wiry *adj* (**wirier, wiriest**) lean, supple and sinewy.—**wiriness** *n*.

wisdom *n* the ability to use knowledge; sound judgment.

wisdom tooth *n* one of four teeth set at the end of each side of the upper and lower jaw in humans and grown last.

wise *adj* having knowledge or common sense; learned; prudent. * *vti* (*with* up) (*inf*) (to cause) to become informed or aware.— **wisely** *adv*.

-wise *adv suffix* direction or manner; concerning.

wiseacre *n* a person who pretends to be clever or wise, a know-all.

wisecrack *n* (*inf*) a witty or sarcastic remark.—*also vi*.

wise guy *n* (*inf*) a person who is always making critical or sarcastic comments.

wish *vti* to long for; to express a desire. * *n* desire; thing desired.

wishbone *n* the forked bone at the front of the breastbone of a bird consisting of the fused clavicles.

wishful *adj* having a wish; hopeful.

wishful thinking *n* the mistaken belief that one's wishes correspond to reality.

wishy-washy *adj* weak, thin, feeble.

wisp *n* a thin strand; a small bunch, as of hay; anything slender.—**wispy** *adj*.

wisteria, wistaria *n* a purple-flowered climbing plant.

wistful *adj* pensive; sad; yearning.—**wistfully** *adv*.—**wistfulness** *n*.

wit *n* (*speech, writing*) the facility of combining ideas with humorous effect; a person with this ability; (*pl*) ability to think quickly.

witch *n* a woman who practises magic and is considered to a have dealings with the devil.

witchcraft *n* the practice of magic.

witch doctor *n* a man in certain tribes who appears to be able to cure sickness or cause harm to people.

witchery *n* (*pl* **witcheries**) witchcraft; fascination.

witch hazel *n* any of a genus of North American shrubs with yellow flowers; a soothing lotion made from the bark of this applied to lumps, bruises, skin rashes, etc.

witch hunt *n* a campaign of harassment of those with dissenting opinions; the search for and persecution of those accused of witchcraft.

witching *adj* of or suitable for witchcraft.

with *prep* denoting nearness or agreement; in the company of; in the same direction as; among; by means of; possessing.

withal *adv* (*arch*) as well; moreover.

withdraw *vb* (**withdrawing, withdrew,** *pp* **withdrawn**) *vt* to draw back or away; to remove; to retract. * *vi* to retire; to retreat.—**withdrawal** *n*.

withdrawn *adj* introverted, reserved; remote.

wither *vi* to fade or become limp or dry, as of a plant. * *vt* to cause to dry up or fade.

withers *npl* the ridge between the shoulder blades of a horse.

withershins *adv* counter-clockwise.—*also* **widdershins**.

withhold *vt* (**withholding, withheld**) to hold back; to deduct; to restrain; to refuse to grant.

within *prep* inside; not exceeding; not beyond.

without *prep* outside or out of, beyond; not having, lacking. * *adv* outside.

withstand *vt* (**withstanding, withstood**) to oppose or resist, esp successfully; to endure.

witless *adj* foolish, stupid; not witty.

witness *n* a person who gives evidence or attests a signing; testimony (of a fact). * *vt* to have first-hand knowledge of; to see; to be the scene of; to serve as evidence of; to attest a signing. * *vi* to testify.

witness stand, witness box *n* an enclosure for witnesses in a court of law.

witticism *n* a witty remark.

wittingly *adv* knowingly.

witty *adj* (**wittier, wittiest**) full of wit.—**wittily** *adv*.—**wittiness** *n*.

wives *see* **wife**.

wizard *n* a magician; a man who practises witchcraft or magic; an expert.—**wizardry** *n*.

wizened *adj* dried up, wrinkled, shrivelled.

wk *abbr* = week.

woad *n* (a blue dye obtained from the leaves of) a European plant of the mustard family.

wobble *vi* to sway unsteadily from side to side; to waver, to hesitate.—**wobbly** *adj*.

wodge *n* (*Brit inf*) a thick slice or chunk of something.

woe *n* grief, misery; (*pl*) misfortune.—**woeful** *adj*.—**woefully** *adv*.

woebegone *adj* sorrowful.

wog *n* (*Brit offensive*) a non-white person.

wok *n* a large, metal, hemispherical pan used for Chinese-style cooking.

woke, woken *see* **wake**[1].

wolf *n* (*pl* **wolves**) a wild animal of the dog family that hunts in packs; a flirtatious man.

wolfcall *n* a whistle made by a man when seeing an attractive woman.—*also* **wolf whistle**.

wolfhound *n* any of several types of large dog formerly used to hunt wolves.

wolfram *n* tungsten; wolframite.

wolframite *n* a mineral that is the chief ore of tungsten and also contains iron and manganese.

wolf whistle *see* **wolf call.**

wolverine *n* a voracious carnivorous animal of northern forests of Europe, North America and Asia with thick black fur.

wolves *see* **wolf.**

woman *n* (*pl* **women**) an adult human female; the female sex.

womanhood *n* the state of being a woman.

womanish *adj* resembling a woman; suitable for women.

womanize *vi* to pursue women for sex.—**womanizer** *n*.

womankind *n* female human beings, women collectively, esp as distinct from men.

womanly *adj* having the qualities of a woman.

womb *n* the female organ in which offspring are developed until birth, the uterus; any womb-like cavity; a place where something is produced.

wombat *n* an Australian marsupial mammal resembling a small bear.

women *see* **woman.**

womenfolk *npl* women collectively; the female members of a family, group or community.

Women's Institute *n* (*esp Brit*) an organization for women which engages in various social and cultural activities.

Women's Movement *n* a feminist movement seeking to end male domination of women in society.

won *see* **win.**

wonder *n* a feeling of surprise or astonishment; something that excites such a feeling; a prodigy. * *vi* to feel wonder; to be curious; to speculate; to marvel.

wonderful *adj* marvellous.—**wonderfully** *adv*.

wonderland *n* a land full of marvels.

wonderment *n* astonishment, awe; curiosity.

wondrous *adj* (*poet*) wonderful, marvellous.

wonky *adj* (**wonkier, wonkiest**) (*sl*) crooked, unsteady.

wont *adj* accustomed; inclined. * *n* habit.

won't = will not.

woo *vt* (**wooing, wooed**) to seek to attract with a view to marriage; to court; to solicit eagerly.—**wooer** *n*.

wood *n* the hard fibrous substance under the bark of trees; trees cut or sawn, timber; a thick growth of trees.

wood alcohol *n* methanol.

woodbine *n* wild honeysuckle.

woodchuck *n* a North American marmot with thick reddish-brown fur.—*also* **groundhog.**

woodcock *n* a game bird related to the snipe.

woodcraft *n* skill in living and surviving in the forest, esp hunting; skill at woodwork.

woodcut *n* an engraving made on wood; a print made from this.

woodcutter *n* a person whose job is to cut down trees.

wooded *adj* covered with trees.

wooden *adj* made of wood; stiff.

wood engraving *n* the art of engraving illustrations on wood; (a print taken from) a piece of engraved wood.

woodenhead *n* (*inf*) a foolish person.

woodland *n* land covered with trees.

woodlouse *n* (*pl* **woodlice**) a small ground-dwelling wingless crustacean with a segmented body that can roll itself into a ball.

woodman *n* (*pl* **woodmen**) a forester or woodcutter.

wood nymph *n* (*Greek myth*) a nymph of the woods, a dryad.

woodpecker *n* a bird that pecks holes in trees to extract insects.

wood pigeon *n* a large European wild pigeon with white patches of feathers on the body and neck.

woodpile *n* a pile of wood, esp firewood.

wood pulp *n* wood that has been pulped and treated for papermaking.

wood screw *n* a pointed metal screw with an external thread and slotted head designed to be driven into wood with a screwdriver.

woodshed *n* a small shed for storing wood (eg firewood), tools, gardening equipment, etc.

woodsman *n* (*pl* **woodsmen**) a person who lives and works in a wood, a woodman.

woodwind *n* section of an orchestra in which wind instruments, originally made of wood, are played.

woodwork *n* carpentry.

woodworm *n* (*esp Brit*) an insect larva that bores into wood; the damage in furniture so caused.

woody *adj* (**woodier, woodiest**) covered in trees.

woof[1] *n* the horizontal threads crossing the warp in a woven fabric.

woof[2] *interj* a noise like the bark of a dog. * *vi* to make this sound.

woofer *n* a loudspeaker.

wool *n* the fleece of sheep and other animals; thread or yarn spun from the coats of sheep; cloth made from this yarn.

woollen, woolen *adj* made of wool.

woolly bear *n* a large furry caterpillar produced by the tiger moth.

woolly, wooly *adj* (**woollier, woolliest** *or* **woolier, wooliest**) of, like or covered with wool; indistinct, blurred; muddled. * *n* (*pl* **woollies**) (*inf*) a woollen garment.—**woolliness, wooliness** *n*.

woolsack *n* the official seat of the Lord Chancellor in the British House of Lords (formerly made from a large sack of wool).

woozy *adj* (**woozier, wooziest**) (*inf*) mentally confused, dazed; dizzy, nauseous.

wop *n* (*derog*) an Italian.

word *n* a single unit of language in speech or writing; talk, discussion; a message; a promise; a command; information; a password; (*pl*) lyrics; (*pl*) a quarrel. * *vt* to put into words, to phrase; to flatter.

word blindness *n* alexia or dyslexia.

word for word *adj*, *adv* (*a translation, etc*) using exactly the same words, verbatim.

wording *n* the way in which words are used, esp in written form; a choice of words.

word-perfect *adj* able to repeat something without mistake.—*also* **letter-perfect.**

wordplay *n* verbal wit or repartee.

word processor *n* computer software that allows the input, formatting, storage and printing of text electronically; the hardware, including microprocessor, monitor, keyboard and printer, required to operate word-processing software.

wordy *adj* (**wordier, wordiest**) verbose.

wore *see* **wear.**

work *n* employment, occupation; a task; the product of work; manner of working; place of work; a literary composition; (*pl*) a factory, plant. * *vi* to be employed, to have a job; to operate (a machine, etc); to produce effects; (*with* **on**) to (attempt to) persuade by persistent effort; (*with* **out**) to undertake a regular, planned series of exercises. * *vt* to effect, to achieve; (*with* **off**) to eliminate though effort; (*with* **over**) to examine closely; (*inf*) to assault violently. —**workable** *adj*.— **worker** *n*.

workaday *adj* suited for working days; ordinary, mundane.

workaholic *n* a person with a compulsive need to work.

workbench *n* a bench designed for woodworking, metalworking, etc.

workbook *n* an exercise book with spaces for answers to set questions.

workbox *n* a box for holding material and tools for work.

workday *see* **working day.**

work force *n* the number of workers who are engaged in a particular industry; the total number of workers who are potentially available.

workhorse *n* a horse used for work on a farm; (*inf*) a person or thing that works the hardest in an organization, business, etc.

workhouse *n* (*formerly*) in UK, a public institution for paupers; in US, a prison for petty offenders whose sentences are served by manual labour.

working *adj* spent in or used for work; functioning. * *n* operation; mode of operation; (*pl*) the manner of functioning or operating; (*pl*) the parts of a mine that are worked.

working capital *n* liquid capital available for the daily operation of a business.

working class *n* people who work for wages, esp manual workers; proletariat.—*also adj.*

working day, workday *n* a day for working as opposed to a holiday; the number of hours spent working during the day.

working drawing *n* a plan or drawing used to guide a builder, engineer, etc during the actual construction.

working party *n* (*esp Brit*) a committee established to investigate a particular problem.

workload *n* the amount of work done or required to be done in a particular period.

workman *n* (*pl* **workmen**) a person employed in manual labour; a person who works in a particular manner.

workmanlike *adj* skilful.

workmanship *n* technical skill; the way a thing is made, style.

workmate *n* (*Brit*) a colleague with whom one works.

work of art *n* a fine painting, sculpture, building, etc; something that has the aesthetic qualities of a work of art.

work-out *n* a session of strenuous physical exercises.

workroom *n* a room for work, a workshop.

workshop *n* a room or building where work is done; a seminar for specified intensive study, work, etc.

workshy *adj* (*Brit*) disinclined to work.

work station *n* a place in an office, esp a desk equipped with a computer terminal, where a single person works.

work-to-rule *n* (*Brit*) industrial action in which employees adhere strictly to rules and regulations in the workplace with the aim of slowing production.— **work to rule** *vi*.

worktop *n* (*Brit*) an area in a kitchen, usu with a laminated surface, where food is prepared.

world *n* the planet earth and its inhabitants; mankind; the universe; a sphere of existence; the public.

worldbeater *n* someone or something surpassing all others, a champion.—**worldbeating** *adj*.

world-class *adj* of the highest quality in the world.

worldly *adj* (**worldlier, worldliest**) earthly, rather than spiritual; material; experienced.

world music *n* popular music of or combining ethnic styles from various different countries around the world.

world power *n* a country that is powerful enough to influence international politics.

World Series *n* an annual competition (best of seven games) between the winning teams of the two major North American baseball leagues.

world-shaking *adj* of momentous significance.

World War I *n* a war (1914–18) in which Belgium, France, Italy, Japan, Russia, UK, US, and other allies defeated Germany, Austria, Bulgaria, and Turkey.

World War II *n* a war (1939–45) in which France, UK, US, USSR, and other allies defeated Germany, Italy, and Japan.

world-weary *adj* tired of life.

worldwide *adj* universal.

WORM (*acronym*) (*comput*) write once read many times: an optical disk that stores information which cannot then be overwritten, used for data archiving and backup.

worm *n* an earthworm; an insect larva; the thread of a screw. * *vt* to work (oneself into a position) slowly or secretly; to extract information by slow and persistent means.

worm-eaten *adj* eaten into (as if) by worms; decayed; antiquated.

worms *n sing* any disease or condition caused by infestation with parasitic worms.

worm's-eye view *n* the view from the very bottom or humblest position.

wormwood *n* a European plant that yields a bitter oil used in making absinthe; (something causing) bitterness.

wormy *adj* (**wormier, wormiest**) infested with or eaten by worms; resembling a worm; full of holes caused by burrowing worms.

worn *see* **wear.**

worn-out *adj* (*machine, etc*) past its useful life; (*person*) depressed, tired.

worriment *n* (*inf*) worry, anxiety.

worrisome *adj* causing worry; prone to anxiety.

worry *vb* (**worrying, worried**) *vt* to bother, pester, harass. * *vi* to be uneasy or anxious; to fret. * *n* (*pl* **worries**) a cause or feeling of anxiety.—**worrier** *n*.

worry beads *npl* a string of beads fiddled with for comfort or to relieve tension.

worse *adj* (*compar of* **bad** *and* **ill**) less favourable; not so well as before. * *adv* with great severity.—**worsen** *vti*.

worship *n* religious adoration; a religious ritual, eg prayers; devotion. * *vb* (**worshipping, worshipped** *or* **worshiping, worshiped**) *vt* to adore or idolize. * *vi* to participate in a religious service.—**worshipper, worshiper** *n*.

worshipful *adj* feeling or displaying worship or respect; (*with cap*) in UK, used as a title of respect for various high-ranking officials.

worst *adj* (*superl of* **bad** *or* **ill**; *see also* **worse**) bad or ill in the highest degree; of the lowest quality. * *adv* to the worst degree. * *n* the least good part.

worst-case *adj* being, or taking account of, the worst possible situation or outcome (*worst-case scenario*).

worsted *n* twisted thread or yarn made from long, combed wool.

worth *n* value; price; excellence; importance. * *adj* equal in value to; meriting.

worthless *adj* valueless; useless; of bad character.—**worthlessness** *n*.

worthwhile *adj* important or rewarding enough to justify the effort.

worthy *adj* (**worthier, worthiest**) virtuous; deserving. * *n* (*pl* **worthies**) a worthy person, a local celebrity.—**worthily** *adv*.

would *see* **will²**.

would-be *adj* aspiring or professing to be.

wouldn't = would not.

wound¹ *n* any cut, bruise, hurt, or injury caused to the skin; hurt feelings. * *vt* to injure.

wound² *see* **wind²**.

wove, woven *see* **weave**.

wow *interj* exclamation of astonishment. * *n* (*sl*) a success.

wp, WP *abbr* = word processing; word processor.

wpm *abbr* = words per minute.

wrack¹ *n* destruction; **wrack and ruin** (the remains of) something destroyed.

wrack² *n* seaweed deposited on the shore.

wraith *n* an apparition of a living person, supposedly a sign of impending death; any ghost.

wrangle *vi* to argue; to dispute noisily. * *n* a noisy argument.

wrap *vt* (**wrapping, wrapped**) to fold (paper) around (a present, purchase etc); to wind (around); to enfold; (*with* **up**) to enclose in paper; (*inf*) to make the final arrangements for. * *vi* (*with* **up**) to put warm clothes on; (*inf*) to be quiet. * *n* a shawl.

wrapper *n* one who or that which wraps; a book jacket; a light dressing gown.

wrasse *n* a marine food fish with thick lips and brilliant colouration.

wrath *n* intense anger; rage.—**wrathful** *adj*.

wreak *vt* to inflict or exact (eg vengeance, havoc).

wreath *n* (*pl* **wreaths**) a twisted ring of leaves, flowers, etc; something like this in shape.

wreathe *vti* to form into a wreath; to decorate with wreaths; to move or coil in wreaths.

wreck *n* accidental destruction of a ship; a badly damaged ship; a run-down person or thing. * *vt* to destroy; to ruin.

wreckage *n* the process of wrecking; remnants from a wreck.

wrecked *adj* (*sl*) intoxicated by alcohol or drugs; exhausted.

wrecker *n* a person who causes a wreck; a demolition worker; a breakdown van.

wren *n* small brownish songbird, with a short erect tail.

wrench *vt* to give something a violent pull or twist; to injure with a twist, to sprain; to distort. * *n* a forceful twist; a sprain; a spanner; emotional upset caused by parting.

wrest *vt* to take with force (from); to seize; to obtain by toil.

wrestle *vti* to fight by holding and trying to throw one's opponent down; to struggle. * *n* a contest in which the opponents wrestle.—**wrestler** *n*.

wrestling *n* the skill or sport of fighting by grappling and trying to throw each other to the ground.

wretch *n* a miserable or pitied person; a despised and scorned person.

wretched *adj* very miserable; in poor circumstances; despicable.—**wretchedly** *adv*.—**wretchedness** *n*.

wrier, wriest *see* **wry**.

wriggle *vi* to move with a twisting motion; to squirm, to writhe; to use evasive tricks.—*also n*.—**wriggler** *n*.—**wriggly** *adj*.

wright *n* a maker (eg *playwright*), a builder (eg *shipwright*).

wring *vt* (**wringing, wrung**) to twist; to compress by twisting in order to squeeze water from; to pain; to obtain forcibly.

wrinkle *n* a small crease or fold on a surface. * *vti* to make or become wrinkled.

wrist *n* the joint connecting the hand with the forearm.

wristband *n* the cuff of a sleeve that covers the wrist; a band round the wrist that absorbs sweat.

wristwatch *n* a watch worn on a bracelet or strap around the wrist.

writ *n* (*law*) a written court order.

write *vb* (**writing, wrote,** *pp* **written**) *vt* to form letters on paper with a pen or pencil; to express in writing; to compose (a letter, music, literary work, etc); to communicate by letter; (*with* **off**) to cancel a bad debt as a loss; (*inf*) to damage (a vehicle) beyond repair; (*with* **down**) *vt* to put in writing; to harm or demean (a person) in writing; (*with* **up**) to describe, update, or put into finished form by writing; to praise or publicize in writing. * *vi* to be a writer; (*with* **down to** *or* **for**) to write in a simplified style for a less educated taste.

write-off *n* a debt cancelled as a loss; (*inf*) a badly damaged car.

writer *n* an author; a scribe or clerk.

writer's cramp *n* painful spasms or paralysis in the thumb and fingers from excessive writing.

write-up *n* a published report or review, esp a favourable one.

writhe *vi* to twist the body violently, as in pain; to squirm (under, at).

writing *n* the act of forming letters on paper, etc; a written document; authorship; (*pl*) literary works.

writing paper *n* paper treated to accept ink and used esp for letters.

written *see* **write**.

wrong *adj* not right, incorrect; mistaken, misinformed; immoral. * *n* harm; injury done to another. * *adv* incorrectly. * *vt* to do wrong to.—**wrongly** *adv*.

wrongdoer *n* a person who breaks (moral) laws.—**wrongdoing** *n*.

wrongful *adj* unwarranted, unjust.—**wrongfully** *adv*.

wrong-headed *adj* stubborn; of poor judgment.

wrote *see* **write**.

wrought *adj* formed; made; (*metals*) shaped by hammering, etc.

wrought iron *n* iron that is forged or rolled, not cast.

wrung *see* **wring**.

wry *adj* (**wryer, wryest** *or* **wrier, wriest**) twisted, contorted; ironic.—**wryly** *adv*.—**wryness** *n*.

wt *abbr* = weight.

wunderkind *n* (*pl* **wunderkinder, wunderkinds**) a child prodigy; a whizz kid.

wurst *n* any of various types of spicy sausage from Germany or Austria.

WWI *abbr* = World War I.

WWII abbr = World War II.

WWF *abbr* = World Wildlife Fund for Nature.

WY *abbr* = Wyoming.

WYSIWYG *adj* (*acronym*) (*comput*) *what you see is what you get*: meaning that the layout and style of text, etc, on screen will be exactly as printed out.

X

X, x *n* the 24th letter of the English alphabet; something shaped like an X; the mark used by an illiterate person to represent a signature; a mark (on a map) to show a particular spot.

X, x *symbol* (*math*) unknown quantity; the figure 10. * *n* an unknown or mysterious factor.

xanth-, xantho- *prefix* yellow.

xanthein *n* a soluble yellow pigment found in plant tissue.

xanthic *adj* yellowish; of or relating to xanthine.

xanthine *n* an insoluble yellow pigment found in plant tissue; a yellowish-white crystalline compound allied to uric acid; a derivative of this.

Xanthippe *n* the wife of Socrates (*fl* 5th century BC); a quarrelsome scolding wife.

xantho-, xanth- *prefix* yellow.

xanthochroid *adj* blond and blue-eyed with fair white skin. * *n* an xanthochroid person.

xanthoma *n* (*pl* xanthomas, xanthomata) a small yellow tumour in the skin caused by deposits of lipids.—**xanthomatous** *adj*.

xanthophyll *n* (*bot*) an orange or yellow pigment in autumn leaves.—**xanthophyllous** *adj*.

xanthopsia *n* a disturbance in vision causing everthing to appear yellow.

xanthosis *n* a yellow pigmentation of the skin in diabetes, etc.

xanthous *adj* yellow.

x-axis *n* (*pl* x-axes) the reference axis of a graph along which the x coordinate is measured.

X-chromosome *n* one of the pair (with the Y-chromosome) of sex chromosomes that occur in females.

Xe (*chem symbol*) xenon.

xebec *n* a small three-masted Mediterranean sailing vessel with lateen sails.

xeno-, xen- *prefix* strange; foreign.

xenolith *n* (*geol*) a rock occuring in a system of rocks to which it does not belong.

xenomorphic *adj* (*mineral grain*) abnormal in shape owing to the pressure of adjacent minerals in rock.

xenon *n* a heavy inert colourless odourless gaseous element found in tiny quantities in the atmosphere.

xenophobia *n* fear or dislike of strangers or foreigners.—**xenophobe** *n*.—**xenophobic** *adj*.

xer-, xero- *prefix* dryness.

xeroderma, xerodermia *n* dryness of the skin caused by a deficiency in secretions from the sebaceous glands.

xerography *n* photocopying by using light to form an electrostatic image on a photoconductive plate to which toner powder adheres, the particles then being fused by heat and the image transferred onto paper.—**xerographic** *adj*.—**xerographically** *adv*.

xerophilous *adj* (*plant*) drought-loving; adapted to a dry climate.—**xerophily** *n*.

xerophthalmia *n* a disease of the eye with dryness and ulceration of the cornea, caused by vitamin deficiency.—**xerophthalmic** *adj*.

xerophyte *n* a xerophilous plant, eg cactus, that has adapted for growth with a limited water supply.—**xerophytic** *adj*.

xerostomia *n* abnormal dryness of the mouth caused by failure of the salivary glands.

Xerox *n* (*trademark*) a photocopying process using xerography; the copy produced by this. * *vt* to produce a copy in this way.

x-height *n* (*print*) the height of the letter x in lowercase.

xi *n* (*pl* xis) the 14th letter of the Greek alphabet.

xiphisternum *n* (*pl* xiphisterna) (*anat, zool*) the lowest part of the breastbone, the xiphoid process.—**xiphisternal** *adj*.

xiphoid *adj* sword-shaped. * *n* the xiphoid process.

xiphoid process *n* the xiphisternum.

Xmas *abbr* = Christmas.

X-ray, x-ray *n* radiation of very short wavelengths, capable of penetrating solid bodies, and printing on a photographic plate a shadow picture of objects not permeable by light rays. * *vt* to photograph by x-rays.

XST *abbr* = experimental Stealth technology.

xylem *n* the woody vegetable tissue in plants that conducts water and gives support.

xylo-, xyl- *prefix* wood.

xylograph *n* a wood engraving; an impression made from a wood block.

xylography *n* the art of making wood engravings or making woodcuts; the art of printing from wood blocks.—**xylographer** *n*.—**xylographic** *adj*.—**xylographically** *adv*.

xyloid *adj* like wood.

xylophagous *adj* (*insects*) wood-eating.

xylophone *n* a percussion instrument consisting of a series of wooden bars which are struck with small hammers.—**xylophonic** *adj*.

xylophonist *n* a performer on a xylophone.

xylotomous *adj* (*insects*) boring into or cutting wood.

Y

Y (*chem symbol*) yttrium.

Y *abbr* = yen (Japanese currency).

Y, y *n* the 25th letter of the English alphabet; something shaped like a Y.

Y, y *symbol* (*math*) the second unknown quantity.

y *abbr* = year; yard.

yabber *n* (*Austral sl*) talk, esp in broken English. * *vti* to talk.

yacht *n* a sailing or mechanically driven vessel, used for pleasure cruises or racing. * *vi* to race or cruise in a yacht.—**yachting** *n.*—**yachtsman** *n* (*pl* **yachtsmen**).—**yachtswoman** *nf* (*pl* **yachtswomen**).

yackety-yak *n* (*sl*) persistent trivial chatter.

yah *interj* expressing derision.

yahoo *n* (*pl* **yahoos**) a crude, vicious person.

Yahweh, Yahveh *n* Jehovah.

yak[1] *n* a domesticated species of ox found in Tibet having horns and long hair.

yak[2] *n* (*sl*) persistent trivial talk or chatter. * *vi* (**yakking, yakked**) to talk in this way.

Yale lock *n* (*trademark*) a type of cylinder lock for doors.

yam *n* the edible, starchy tuberous root of a tropical climbing plant; sweet potato.

yamen *n* (*formerly*) the official residence of a Chinese madarin.

yammer *vi* (*inf*) to whimper or whine constantly; (*inf*) to complain loudly and persistently. * *n* (*inf*) a whining or complaining sound.

Yank *n* (*inf*) a Yankee.

yank *vti* to pull suddenly, to jerk. * *n* a sudden sharp pull.

Yankee *n* (*inf*) a citizen of the US, an American.

yap *vi* (**yapping, yapped**) to yelp, bark; (*sl*) to talk constantly, esp in a noisy or irritating manner.

yapok, yapock *n* a tropical American aquatic marsupial with webbed hind feet, thick fur, and a long tail.

yard[1] *n* a unit of measure of three feet and equivalent to 0.9144 metres; (*naut*) a spar hung across a mast to support a sail.

yard[2] *n* an enclosed concrete area, esp near a building; an enclosure for a commercial activity (eg a shipyard); an area of ground for growing herbs, fruits, flowers, or vegetables, usu attached to a house, a garden; an area with tracks for the making up of trains, servicing of locomotives, etc.

yardage[1] *n* a length measured in yards.

yardage[2] *n* the use of a yard; the charge made for this.

yardarm *n* (*naut*) either half of a yard.

yardman *n* (*pl* **yardmen**) a worker in a railroad yard.

yardmaster *n* the manager of a railroad yard.

yardstick *n* a standard used in judging.

yare *adj* ready; active, brisk; (*yacht, etc*) easily handled.

yarmulke *n* a skullcap worn by Jewish men at prayer and by Orthodox male Jews at all times.

yarn *n* fibres of wool, cotton etc spun into strands for weaving, knitting, etc; (*inf*) a tale or story. * *vi* to tell a yarn; to talk at length.

yarrow *n* a strongly scented astringent herb with clusters of small flowers.

yashmak, yashmac *n* a veil worn by Muslim women, showing only the eyes.

yataghan, yatagan *n* a short curved Turkish sword without a guard.

yatter *vi* (*sl*) to gabble, to chatter.—*also n.*

yauld *adj* (*Scot*) active; alert.

yaupon *n* an American evergreen shrub of the holly family.

yaw *vi* (*ship, aircraft*) to deviate from a course; (*aircraft*) to turn from side to side about the vertical axis. * *vt* to cause to yaw. * *n* a yawing movement or course.

yawl *n* a two-masted sailing vessel with its aftermast at the stern.

yawn *vi* to open the jaws involuntarily and inhale, as from drowsiness; to gape.—*also n.*

yawning *adj* gaping; wide-open; drowsy.—**yawningly** *adv.*

yawp *vi* to cry harshly, to scream; (*sl*) to speak foolishly. * *n* such a cry or talk.

yaws *n sing* a tropical disease causing ulceration of the skin, framboesia.

y-axis *n* (pl **y-axes**) the reference axis of a graph along which the y coordinate is measured.

Yb (*chem symbol*) ytterbium.

Y-chromosome *n* one of the pair (with the X-chromosome) of sex chromosomes that occur in males.

yclept *adj* (*arch*) named.

yd., yds *abbr* = yard(s).

ye[1] *pron* (*arch*) you (the person addressed and others) the old method of printing the.

ye[2] *definite article* (*arch*) the.

yea *adv, n* (*arch*) yes.

yeah *adv* (*inf*) yes.

yean *vi* (*sheep, goat*) to bring forth (a lamb or kid).

yeanling *n* a lamb or kid.

year *n* a period of twelve months, or 365 or 366 days, beginning with 1 January and ending with 31 December; a period of approximately twelve months.

yearbook *n* an annual publication reviewing the events of the previous year or bringing information up to date.

yearling *n* an animal a year old or in its second year.

yearlong *adj* lasting a year.

yearly *adj* occurring every year; lasting a year. * *adv* once a year; from year to year.

yearn *vi* to feel desire (for); to long for.—**yearning** *n.*

yeast *n* a fungus that causes alcoholic fermentation, used in brewing and baking.

yeasty *adj* (**yeastier, yeastiest**) smelling of or containing yeast.—**yeastiness** *n.*

yegg, yegman *n* (*pl* **yeggs, yegmen**) (*sl*) a safecracker, a criminal.

yeld *adj* (*Scot*) barren, giving no milk.

yell *vti* to shout loudly; to scream; to emit a yell. * *n* a loud shout; a concerted cheer by supporters, students, etc, at a game.

yellow *adj* of the colour of lemons, egg yolk, etc; having a yellowish skin; (*inf*) cowardly. * *n* the colour yellow. * *vi* to become or turn yellow.

yellow-belly *n* (*pl* **yellow-bellies**) (*sl*) a coward.—**yellow-bellied** *adj*.

yellow fever *n* an infectious tropical fever caused by a virus transmitted by certain mosquitoes.

yellowhammer *n* a small European bird with a yellow head, neck, and breast.

yellow jacket *n* an American hornet or wasp with yellow markings.

yellow pages *npl* (part of) a telephone directory that lists business subscribers under different categories according to the type of service offered.

yellow spot n (*anat*) the point of acutest vision in the retina.

yellow streak *n* (*inf*) a cowardly nature.

yellowwood *n* an American tree; its wood, which yields a yellow dye.

yelp *vti* to utter a sharp, shrill cry or bark.—*also n*.

yen[1] *n* (*pl* **yen**) the monetary unit of Japan.

yen[2] *n* (*inf*) a yearning, an ambition.

yeoman *n* (*pl* **yeomen**) (*formerly*) a farmer who cultivated his own land; a non-commissioned officer in the navy, marines.

yeomanly *adj* of or like a yeoman; workmanlike.—*also adv*.

yeoman of the guard *n* a member of the British sovereign's veteran bodyguard.

yeomanry *n* yeomen collectively; in UK, a volunteer cavalry force raised from country districts as a home guard (1761–1907) now part of the Territorial Army.

yeoman service *n* effective assistance.

yep *adv* (*inf*) yes.

yerba (maté) *n* an infusion of dried leaves of the maté, which makes a mildly stimulating tea.

yes *adv* a word of affirmation or consent.

yes man *n* a servile, fawning, sycophantic person.

yester *adv* (*rare*) of yesterday.

yesterday *n* the day before today; the recent past. * *adv* on the day before today; recently.

yet *adv* still; so far; even. * *conj* nevertheless; however; still.

yeti *n* a mysterious animal thought to live high in the Himalayan mountains but never seen.—*also* **abominable snowman**.

yew *n* an evergreen tree or shrub with thin, sharp leaves and red berries.

Y-fronts *npl* (*trademark*) men's underpants with an inverted Y-shaped opening at the front.

Ygdrasil, Yggdrasil *n* (*Norse myth*) an ash tree whose roots and branches bind together earth, heaven, and hell.

yid *n* (*derog*) a Jew.

Yiddish *n* a mixed German and Hebrew dialect spoken by European Jews.

yield *vt* to resign; to give forth, to produce, as a crop, result, profit, etc. * *vi* to submit; to give way to physical force, to surrender. * *n* the amount yielded; the profit or return on a financial investment.

yip *n* a cry, an exclamation. * *vi* (**yipping, yipped**) to utter a yip.

yippee *interj* used to express exuberant delight.

ylang-ylang *n* a Malaysian tree with fragrant flowers; a perfume made from the flowers.

YMCA *abbr* = Young Men's Christian Association.

YMHA *abbr* = Young Men's Hebrew Association.

yob, yobbo *n* (*pl* **yobs, yobbos**) (*sl*) a young lout, a hooligan.

yodel *vti* (**yodelling, yodelled** *or* **yodeling, yodeled**) to sing, alternating from the ordinary voice to falsetto.—**yodeller, yodeler** *n*.

yoga *n* a system of exercises for attaining bodily and mental control and well-being.—**yogic** *adj*.

yogurt, yoghurt *n* a semi-liquid food made from milk curdled by bacteria.

yogi *n* (*pl* **yogis, yogin**) a person skilled in yoga.

yo-heave-ho *interj* (*formerly*) a cry made by sailors while heaving anchor, etc.

yoicks *interj* a foxhunting cry urging on the hounds.

yoke *n* a bond or tie; slavery; the wooden frame joining oxen to make them pull together; part of a garment that is fitted below the neck. * *vt* to put a yoke on; to join together.

yokel *n* (*derog*) country people who are regarded as unsophisticated and simple-minded.

yolk *n* the yellow part of an egg.

yolk sac *n* the membrane enclosing an egg yolk.

Yom Kippur *n* an annual Jewish holiday marked by fasting and prayer.—*also* **Day of Atonement**.

yomp *vi* to march laboriously carrying heavy equipment, esp over rough terrain.

yon *adj, adv* (*dial*) yonder, over there.

yonder *adv* over there.

yore *n* time long past.

Yorkist *n* an adherent of the royal house of York in England, esp during the Wars of the Roses (1455-85).—*also adj*.

Yorkshire pudding *n* a baked pudding made from batter and traditionally eaten with roast beef.

Yorkshire terrier *n* a small shaggy breed of terrier with a long coat of bluish grey and tan hair.

you *pron* (*gram*) 2nd person singular or plural; the person or persons spoken to.

you'd = you would; you had.

you'll = you will; you shall.

young *adj* in the early period of life; in the first part of growth; new; inexperienced. * *n* young people; offspring.

youngling *n* (*poet*) a young child or animal.

youngster *n* a young person; a youth.

your *poss adj* of or belonging to or done by you.

you're = you are.

yours *poss pron* of or belonging to you.

yourself *pron* (*pl* **yourselves**) the emphatic and reflexive form of **you**.

youth *n* the period between childhood and adulthood; young people collectively; the early stages of something; a young man or boy.—**youthful** *adj*.—**youthfully** *adv*.

youth hostel *n* a supervised lodging for usu young travellers.

you've = you have.

yowl *n* a loud mournful cry, esp from pain.—*also vi*.

yo-yo *n* (*pl* **yo-yos**) a hand-held toy made of a flat spool which can be made to wind up and down a piece of string.

yr *abbr* = year; younger; your.

yrs *abbr* = years; yours.

YT *abbr* = Yukon Territory.

ytterbium *n* a soft metallic element of the lanthanide series.

yttrium *n* a metallic element used in alloys and lasers.

yuan *n* (*pl* **yuan**) the monetary unit of the People's Republic of China.

yucca *n* a plant with stiff, spear-like leaves and white flowers.

yuck *interj* (*sl*) expressing disgust.

yucky *adj* (**yuckier, yuckiest**) (*sl*) disgusting.

yule *n* Christmas.

Yule log *n* a large log traditionally burnt in the fire on Christmas Eve.

yuletide *n* the Christmas festival or season.

yummy *adj* (**yummier, yummiest**) (*inf*) tasty, pleasing. * *interj* yum-yum.

yum-yum *interj* used to express pleasure, esp when eating.

yup *adv* (*inf*) yes.

yuppie *n* (*inf*) any young professional regarded as affluent, ambitious, materialistic, etc.

yurt *n* a circular portable tent of skins used by the Mongolian nomads of Siberia.

YWCA *abbr* = Young Women's Christian Association.

YWHA *abbr* = Young Women's Hebrew Association.

Z

Z (*symbol*) (*physics*) impedance; (*chem*) atomic number.

z (*symbol*) (*math*) an algebraic variable; the z-axis.

Z, z *n* the 26th letter of the English alphabet; something shaped like a Z; (*math*) the third unknown quantity.

z. *abbr* = zero; zone.

zabaglione *n* a dessert of whipped egg yolks, sugar and marsala wine.

Zaïrese *n* a native or inhabitant of the African republic of Zaïre.—*also adj.*

zamindar *n* (*hist*) in India, a district tax collector under the Mogul empire; a landowner paying land tax.—*also* **zemindar.**

zany *adj* (**zanier, zaniest**) comical; eccentric.—**zanily** *adv.*—**zaniness** *n.*

zap *vb* (**zapping, zapped**) *vt* to attack; to kill; to bombard; (*comput*) to get rid of data. * *vi* to rush around.

zappy *adj* (**zappier, zappiest**) (*sl*) energetic, snappy.

zareba, zariba *n* in northern East Africa, a stockade made of thorn hedges as a protection against wild animals or enemies; a place so protected.

zarf *n* an ornamental holder for a coffee cup used in Arab countries.

zarzuela *n* a traditional Spanish one-act comic opera with a satirical theme and including dialogue.

z-axis *n* the reference axis of a three-dimensional coordinate system, along which the z-coordinate is measured.

zeal *n* fervent devotion; fanaticism.

zealot *n* an extreme partisan, a fanatic.

zealous *adj* full of zeal; ardent.—**zealously** *adv.*—**zealousness** *n.*

zebra *n* (*pl* **zebras, zebra**) a black and white striped wild animal related to the horse.—**zebrine** *adj.*

zebra crossing *n* a street crossing for pedestrians marked by black and white strips on the road.

zebu *n* (*pl* **zebus, zebu**) an Asian and African ox with a prominent hump and a large dewlap.

zed *n* in UK, the letter z.

zedoary *n* an aromatic substance like ginger made from the root stock of an Indian plant.

zee *n* (*pl* **zees**) in US, the letter z.

Zeitgeist *n* the spirit of the time; the beliefs, attitudes, tastes, etc, of a particular period.

zemindar *see* **zamindar.**

zemstvo *n* (*pl* **zemstvos, zemstva**) a local elective assembly in the old Russian empire.

Zen *n* a Japanese Buddhist sect that emphasizes self-awareness and self-mastery as the means to enlightenment.

zenana *n* the part of the house reserved for women and girls in a Muslim household.

Zend-Avesta *n* the sacred writings of the Zoroastrians.

zenith *n* the point at which the sun or moon appears to be exactly overhead; peak, summit (of ambition, etc).

zephyr *n* a soft, gentle breeze; a very thin woollen material; a garment made of this.

zeppelin *n* a rigid, cigar-shaped airship.

zero *n* (*pl* **zeros, zeroes**) the symbol 0; nothing; the lowest point; freezing point, 0 degrees Celsius. * *vi* (*with* **in**) (*inf*) to focus attention on (a problem, subject, etc); (*inf*) to converge upon; (*with* **in on**) to concentrate fire (from a weapon) on a specific target.

zero gravity *n* weightlessness.

zero hour *n* the time at which something is scheduled to begin.

zest *n* the outer part of the skin of an orange or lemon used to give flavour; enthusiasm; excitement.—**zestful** *adj.*—**zestfully** *adv.*—**zestfulness** *n.*

zeta *n* the sixth letter of the Greek alphabet.

zeugma *n* a figure of speech in which a word is used with two others, to only one of which it properly applies.—**zeugmatic** *adj.*

Zeus *n* (*Greek myth*) the king of the gods.

zigzag *n* a series of short, sharp angles in alternate directions. * *adj* having sharp turns. * *vti* (**zigzagging, zigzagged**) to move or form in a zigzag.

zilch, zilcho *n* (*sl*) nothing.

zillah *n* (*hist*) an administrative district in India during British rule.

zillion *n* (*pl* **zillion, zillions**) (*inf*) an indefinitely large number or quantity.

Zimb *abbr* = Zimbabwe.

Zimbabwean *n* a native or inhabitant of the African republic of Zimbabwe.—*also adj.*

Zimmer *n* (*trademark*) a frame of tubular metal used by the infirm as a walking aid.

zinc *n* a bluish-white metallic element used in alloys and batteries. * *vt* (**zinking, zinked** *or* **zincking, zincked**) to coat with zinc.—**zincic** *adj.*

zincograph *n* a design in relief on a zinc plate; a print made from this. * *vti* to etch on zinc; to reproduce in this way.—**zincographer** *n.*—**zincographic** *adj.*—**zincography** *n.*

zing *n* (*inf*) a high-pitched buzz; (*inf*) vitality, exuberance. * *vi* (*inf*) to move with a zinging sound.

zinnia *n* a tropical American plant with showy flowers.

Zionism *n* a movement formerly to resettle Jews in Palestine as their national home, now concerned with the development of Israel.—**Zionist** *n, adj.*—**Zionistic** *adj.*

zip *n* a light whizzing sound of a bullet, etc; (*sl*) brisk energy; a slide fastener on clothing, bags, etc with interlocking teeth, a zipper. * *vb* (**zipping, zipped**) *vi* to move at high speed, to dart. * *vt* to fasten with a zip.

ZIP Code *n* (*trademark*) a postcode that uses digits to denote an area.

zipper *n* a zip.

zippy *adj* (**zippier, zippiest**) speedy; energetic.

zircon *n* a variously coloured hard translucent mineral, some varieties of which are cut as gemstones.

zirconium *n* a metallic element found in zircon and used in alloys.

zit *n* (*sl*) a pimple, spot.

zither *n* a musical instrument with 30–45 strings over a shallow sounding box played by plucking.—**zitherist** *n*.

zloty *n* (*pl* **zlotys, zloty**) the monetary unit of Poland.

Zn (*chem symbol*) zinc.

zodiac *n* an imaginary belt in the heavens along which the sun, moon, and chief planets appear to move, divided crosswise into twelve equal areas, called "signs of the zodiac," each named after a constellation; a diagram representing this.—**zodiacal** *adj*.

zodiacal light *n* a luminous triangular tract of sky sometimes seen before dawn or after dusk, esp in the tropics.

zoetrope *n* a toy with a revolving cylinder showing a series of pictures in apparent motion.

-zoic *adj suffix* (*animal*) having a specified kind of existence; (*geol*) belonging to an era with a particular form of life.

Zollverein *n* in 19th century, a union of German states with common customs tariffs against outside countries and free trade among themselves; any customs union.

zombie, zombi *n* (*pl* **zombies**) a person who is lifeless and apathetic; an automaton.

zonate, zonated *adj* (*bot, zool*) marked with bands.

zone *n* a region, area; a subdivision; any area with a specified use or restriction. * *vt* to divide or mark off into zones; to designate as a zone; to encircle with a zone.—**zonal** *adj*.

zonked *adj* (*sl*) intoxicated by drugs or alcohol; (*sl*) exhausted.

zoo *n* (*pl* **zoos**) a place where a collection of living wild animals is kept for public showing.

zoo-, zo- *prefix* animals.

zoochemistry *n* the chemistry of the constituents of animal bodies.—**zoochemical** *adj*.

zoogeography *n* the science of the geographical distribution of animals.—**zoogeographer** *n*.—**zoogeographic, zoogeographical** *adj*.

zoography *n* descriptive zoology.—**zoographic, zoographical** *adj*.

zooid *adj* resembling but not completely being an animal or plant. * *n* a zooid organism; an animal organism produced by fission; (*corals, etc*) a member of a compound organism.

zool. *abbr* = zoological; zoology.

zoological garden *n* a zoo.

zoologist *n* a person who studies animals and animal behaviour.

zoology *n* (*pl* **zoologies**) the study of animals with regard to their classification, structure and habits.—**zoological** *adj*.—**zoologically** *adv*.

zoom *vi* to go quickly, to speed; to climb upward sharply in an aeroplane; to rise rapidly; (*photog*) to focus in on an object using a zoom lens. * *n* the act of zooming; a zoom lens.

zoom lens *n* (*photog*) a camera lens that makes distant objects appear closer without moving the camera.

zoomorphism *n* the representation (esp of a deity) in the form of or with the attributes of an animal.—**zoomorphic** *adj*.

zoophyte *n* any animal (eg coral, a sponge) that resembles a plant.—**zoophytic** *adj*.

zootomy *n* animal anatomy; the dissection of animals.—**zootomical** *adj*.—**zootomist** *n*.

zorille, zoril *n* a small African mammal that resembles and smells like a skunk.

Zoroastrianism n a religious system founded by the Persian prophet Zoroaster (*c.*628-551BC), based on the recognition of the dual principle of good and evil.—**Zoroastrian** *n, adj*.

Zouave *n* (*formerly*) a soldier in a French-Algerian infantry unit characterized by a colourful eastern-style uniform; a soldier in a similiar unit, esp a Union Army unit of the American Civil War.

zounds *interj* (*arch*) expressing anger and astonishment.

Zr (*chem symbol*) zirconium.

zucchetto *n* (*pl* **zucchettos**) a skullcap worn by Roman Catholic ecclesiastics, which varies in colour according to rank (black for a priest, purple for a bishop, red for a cardinal, white for the Pope).

zucchini *npl* n a type of small vegetable marrow.—*also* **courgette**.

Zulu *n* (*pl* **Zulus, Zulu**) a member of a Negroid people of South Africa, or their language.—*also adj*.

zwieback *n* a thin rusk.

zyg-, zygo- *prefix* yoked, paired.

zygodactyl *adj* (*bird*) with the toes in pairs, two pointing forward and two backward. * *n* a zygodactyl bird, eg the parrot.—**zygodactylous** *adj*.

zygomorphic, zygomorphous *adj* (*flowers*) bilaterally symmetrical.—**zygomorphism, zygomorphy** *n*.

zygospore *n* a spore formed from the fusion of gametes.—**zygosporic** *adj*.

zygote *n* the cell formed by the union of an ovum and a sperm; the developing organism from such a cell.

zymosis *n* (*pl* **zymoses**) an infectious disease caused by a virus or organism that acts like a ferment; fermentation.

zymotic *adj* caused by or relating to an infection or an infectious disease; producing fermentation.

zymurgy *n* the chemistry of fermentation in brewing, etc.

Thesaurus

A

aback *adv* back, backward, rearward, regressively.

abaft *prep* (*naut*) aft, astern, back of, behind.

abandon *vb* abdicate, abjure, desert, drop, evacuate, forsake, forswear, leave, quit, relinquish, yield; cede, forgo, give up, let go, renounce, resign, surrender, vacate, waive. * *n* careless freedom, dash, impetuosity, impulse, wildness.

abandoned *adj* depraved, derelict, deserted, discarded, dropped, forsaken, left, outcast, rejected, relinquished; corrupt, demoralized, depraved, dissolute, graceless, impenitent, irreclaimable, lost, obdurate, profligate, reprobate, shameless, sinful, unprincipled, vicious, wicked.

abandonment *n* desertion, dereliction, giving up, leaving, relinquishment, renunciation, surrender.

abase *vb* depress, drop, lower, reduce, sink; debase, degrade, disgrace, humble, humiliate.

abasement *n* abjection, debasement, degradation, disgrace, humbleness, humiliation, shame.

abash *vb* affront, bewilder, confound, confuse, dash, discompose, disconcert, embarrass, humiliate, humble, shame, snub.

abashment *n* confusion, embarrassment, humiliation, mortification, shame.

abate *vb* diminish, decrease, lessen, lower, moderate, reduce, relax, remove, slacken; allow, bate, deduct, mitigate, rebate, remit; allay, alleviate, appease, assuage, blunt, calm, compose, dull, mitigate, moderate, mollify, pacify, qualify, quiet, quell, soften, soothe, tranquillize.

abatement *n* alleviation, assuagement, decrement, decrease, extenuation, mitigation, moderation, remission; cessation, decline, diminution, ebb, fading, lowering, sinking, settlement; allowance, deduction, rebate, reduction.

abbey *n* convent, monastery, priory.

abbreviate *vb* abridge, compress, condense, contract, cut, curtail, epitomize, reduce, retrench, shorten.

abbreviation *n* abridgment, compression, condensation, contraction, curtailment, cutting, reduction, shortening.

abdicate *vb* abandon, cede, forgo, forsake, give up, quit, relinquish, renounce, resign, retire, surrender.

abdication *n* abandonment, abdicating, relinquishment, renunciation, resignation, surrender.

abdomen *n* belly, gut, paunch, stomach.

abduct *vb* carry off, kidnap, spirit away, take away.

abduction *n* carrying off, kidnapping, removal, seizure, withdrawal.

aberrant *adj* deviating, devious, divergent, diverging, erratic, rambling, wandering; abnormal, anomalistic, anomalous, disconnected, eccentric, erratic, exceptional, inconsequent, peculiar, irregular, preternatural, singular, strange, unnatural, unusual.

aberration *n* departure, deviation, divergence, rambling, wandering; abnormality, anomaly, eccentricity, irregularity, peculiarity, singularity, unconformity; delusion, disorder, hallucination, illusion, instability.

abet *vb* aid, assist, back, help, support, sustain, uphold, advocate, condone, countenance, encourage, favour, incite, sanction.

abettor *n* ally, assistant; adviser, advocate, promoter; accessory, accomplice, associate, confederate.

abeyance *n* anticipation, calculation, expectancy, waiting; dormancy, inactivity, intermission, quiescence, remission, reservation, suppression, suspension.

abhor *vb* abominate, detest, dislike intensely, execrate, hate, loathe, nauseate, view with horror.

abhorrence *n* abomination, antipathy, aversion, detestation, disgust, hatred, horror, loathing.

abhorrent *adj* abominating, detesting, hating, loathing; hateful, horrifying, horrible, loathsome, nauseating, odious, offensive, repellent, repugnant, repulsive, revolting, shocking.

abide *vb* lodge, rest, sojourn, stay, wait; dwell, inhabit, live, reside; bear, continue, persevere, persist, remain; endure, last, suffer, tolerate; (*with* **by**) act up to, conform to, discharge, fulfil, keep, persist in.

abiding *adj* changeless, constant, continuing, durable, enduring, immutable, lasting, permanent, stable, unchangeable.

ability *n* ableness, adroitness, aptitude, aptness, cleverness, dexterity, efficacy, efficiency, facility, might, ingenuity, knack, power, readiness, skill, strength, talent, vigour; competency, qualification; calibre, capability, capacity, expertness, faculty, gift, parts.

abject *adj* base, beggarly, contemptible, cringing, degraded, despicable, dirty, grovelling, ignoble, low, mean, menial, miserable, paltry, pitiful, poor, servile, sneaking, slavish, vile, worthless, wretched.

abjectness *n* abasement, abjection, baseness, contemptibleness, meanness, pitifulness, servility, vileness.

abjuration *n* abandonment, abnegation, discarding, disowning, rejection, relinquishment, renunciation, repudiation; disavowal, disclaimer, disclaiming, recall, recantation, repeal, retraction, reversal, revocation.

abjure *vb* abandon, discard, disclaim, disown, forgo, forswear, give up, reject, relinquish, renounce, repudiate; disavow, disclaim, recall, recant, renounce, repeal, retract, revoke, withdraw.

able *adj* accomplished, adroit, apt, clever, expert, ingenious, practical, proficient, qualified, quick, skilful, talented, versed; competent, effective, efficient, fitted, quick; capable, gifted, mighty, powerful, talented; athletic, brawny, muscular, robust, stalwart, strong, vigorous.

ablution *n* baptism, bathing, cleansing, lavation, purification, washing.

abnegation *n* abandonment, denial, renunciation, surrender.

abnormal *adj* aberrant, anomalous, divergent, eccentric, exceptional, peculiar, odd, singular, strange, uncomfortable, unnatural, unusual, weird.

abnormality *n* abnormity, anomaly, deformity, idiosyncrasy, irregularity, monstrosity, peculiarity, oddity, singularity, unconformity.

aboard *adv* inside, within, on.

abode *n* domicile, dwelling, habitation, home, house, lodging, quarters, residence, residency, seat.

abolish *vb* abrogate, annul, cancel, eliminate, invalidate, nullify, quash, repeal, rescind, revoke; annihilate, destroy, end, eradicate, extirpate, extinguish, obliterate, overthrow, suppress, terminate.

abolition *n* abrogation, annulling, annulment, cancellation, cancelling, nullification, repeal, rescinding, rescission, revocation; annihilation, destruction, eradication, extinction, extinguishment, extirpation, obliteration, overthrow, subversion, suppression

abominable *adj* accursed, contemptible, cursed, damnable, detestable, execrable, hellish, horrid, nefarious, odious; abhorrent, detestable, disgusting, foul, hateful, loathsome, nauseous, obnoxious, shocking, revolting, repugnant, repulsive; shabby, vile, wretched.

abominate *vb* abhor, detest, execrate, hate, loathe, recoil from, revolt at, shrink from, shudder at.

abomination *n* abhorrence, antipathy, aversion, detestation, disgust, execration, hatred, loathing; nauseation; contamination, corruption, corruptness, defilement, foulness, impurity, loathsomeness, odiousness, pollution, taint, uncleanness; annoyance, curse, evil, infliction, nuisance, plague, torment.

aboriginal *adj* autochthonal, autochthonous, first, indigenous, native, original, primary, prime, primeval, primitive, pristine.

abortion *n* miscarriage, premature labour; disappointment, failure.

abortive *adj* immature, incomplete, rudimental, rudimentary, stunted, untimely; futile, fruitless, idle, ineffectual, inoperative, nugatory, profitless, unavailing, unsuccessful, useless, vain.

abound *vb* flow, flourish, increase, swarm, swell; exuberate, luxuriate, overflow, proliferate, swarm, teem.

about *prep* around, encircling, surrounding, round; near; concerning, referring to, regarding, relating to, relative to, respecting, touching, with regard to, with respect to; all over, over, through. * *adv* around, before; approximately, near, nearly.

above *adj* above-mentioned, aforementioned, aforesaid, foregoing, preceding, previous, prior. * *adv* aloft, overhead; before, previously; of a higher rank. * *prep* higher than, on top of; exceeding, greater than, more than, over; beyond, superior to.

above-board *adj* candid, frank, honest, open, straightforward, truthful, upright. * *adv* candidly, fairly, openly, sincerely.

abrade *vb* erase, erode, rub off, scrape out, wear away.

abrasion *n* attrition, disintegration, friction, wearing down; scrape, scratch.

abreast *adv* aligned, alongside.

abridge *vb* abbreviate, condense, compress, shorten, summarize; contract, diminish, lessen, reduce.

abridgment *n* compression, condensation, contraction, curtailment, diminution, epitomizing, reduction, shortening; abstract, brief, compendium, digest, epitome, outline, précis, summary, syllabus, synopsis; deprivation, limitation, restriction.

abroad *adv* expansively, unrestrainedly, ubiquitously, widely; forth, out of doors; overseas; extensively, publicly.

abrogate *vb* abolish, annul, cancel, invalidate, nullify, overrule, quash, repeal, rescind, revoke, set aside, vacate, void.

abrogation *n* abolition, annulling, annulment, cancellation, cancelling, repeal rescinding, rescission, revocation, voidance, voiding.

abrupt *adj* broken, craggy, jagged, rough, rugged; acclivous, acclivitous, precipitous, steep; hasty, illtimed, precipitate, sudden, unanticipated, unexpected; blunt, brusque, curt, discourteous; cramped, harsh, jerky, stiff.

abscess *n* boil, fester, pustule, sore, ulcer.

abscond *vb* bolt, decamp, elope, escape, flee, fly, retreat, run off, sneak away, steal away, withdraw.

absence *n* nonappearance, nonattendance; abstraction, distraction, inattention, musing, preoccupation, reverie; default, defect, deficiency, lack, privation.

absent *adj* abroad, away, elsewhere, gone, not present, otherwhere; abstracted, dreaming, inattentive, lost, musing, napping, preoccupied.

absolute *adj* complete, ideal, independent, perfect, supreme, unconditional, unconditioned, unlimited, unqualified, unrestricted; arbitrary, authoritative, autocratic, despotic, dictatorial, imperious, irresponsible, tyrannical, tyrannous; actual, categorical, certain, decided, determinate, genuine, positive, real, unequivocal, unquestionable, veritable.

absolutely *adv* completely, definitely, unconditionally; actually, downright, indeed, indubitably, infallibly, positively, really, truly, unquestionably.

absoluteness *n* actuality, completeness, ideality, perfection, positiveness, reality, supremeness; absolutism, arbitrariness, despotism, tyranny.

absolution *n* acquittal, clearance, deliverance, discharge, forgiveness, liberation, pardon, release, remission, shrift, shriving.

absolutism *n* absoluteness, arbitrariness, autocracy, despotism, tyranny.

absolve *vb* acquit, clear, deliver, discharge, exculpate, excuse, exonerate, forgive, free, liberate, loose, pardon, release, set free, shrive.

absorb *vb* appropriate, assimilate, drink in, imbibe, soak up; consume, destroy, devour, engorge, engulf, exhaust, swallow up, take up; arrest, engage, engross, fix, immerse, occupy, rivet.

absorbent *adj* absorbing, imbibing, penetrable, porous, receptive.

absorption *adj* appropriation, assimilation, imbibing, osmosis, soaking up; consumption, destroying, devouring, engorgement, engulfing, exhaustion, swallowing up; concentration, engagement, engrossment, immersion, occupation, preoccupation.

abstain *vb* avoid, cease, deny oneself, desist, forbear, refrain, refuse, stop, withhold.

abstemious *adj* abstinent, frugal, moderate, self-denying, sober, temperate.

abstinence *n* abstemiousness, avoidance, forbearance, moderation, self-restraint, soberness, sobriety, teetotalism, temperance.

abstinent *adj* abstaining, fasting; abstemious, restraining, self-denying, self-restraining, sober, temperate.

abstract *vb* detach, disengage, disjoin, dissociate, disunite, isolate, separate; appropriate, purloin, seize, steal, take; abbreviate, abridge, epitomize. * *adj* isolated, separate, simple, unrelated; abstracted, occult, recondite, refined, subtle, vague; nonobjective, nonrepresentational. * *n* abridgment, condensation, digest, excerpt, extract, précis, selection, summary, synopsis.

abstracted *adj* absent, absent-minded, dreaming, inattentive, lost, musing, preoccupied; abstruse, refined, subtle.

abstraction *n* absence, absent-mindedness, brown study, inattention, muse, musing, preoccupation, reverie; disconnection, disjunction, isolation, separation; abduction, appropriation, pilfering, purloining, seizure, stealing, taking.

abstruse *adj* abstract, attenuated, dark, difficult, enigmatic, hidden, indefinite, mysterious, mystic, mystical, obscure, occult, profound, recondite, remote, subtle, transcendental, vague.

absurd *adj* egregious, fantastic, foolish, incongruous, ill-advised, ill-judged, irrational, ludicrous, nonsensical, nugatory, preposterous, ridiculous, self-annulling, senseless, silly, stupid, unreasonable.

absurdity *n* drivel, extravagance, fatuity, folly, foolery, foolishness, idiocy, nonsense.

abundance *n* affluence, amplitude, ampleness, copiousness, exuberance, fertility, flow, flood, largeness, luxuriance, opulence, overflow, plenitude, profusion, richness, store, wealth.

abundant *adj* abounding, ample, bountiful, copious, exuberant, flowing, full, good, large, lavish, rich, liberal, much, overflowing, plentiful, plenteous, replete, teeming, thick.

abuse *vb* betray, cajole, deceive, desecrate, dishonour, misapply, misemploy, misuse, pervert, pollute, profane, prostitute, violate, wrong; harm, hurt, ill-use, ill-treat, injure, maltreat, mishandle; asperse, berate, blacken, calumniate, defame, disparage, lampoon, lash, malign, revile, reproach, satirize, slander, traduce, upbraid, vilify. * *n* desecration, dishonour, illuse, misuse, perversion, pollution, profanation; illtreatment, maltreatment, outrage; malfeasance, malversation; aspersion, defamation, disparagement, insult, invective, obloquy, opprobrium, railing, rating, reviling, ribaldry, rudeness, scurrility, upbraiding, vilification, vituperation.

abusive *adj* calumnious, carping, condemnatory, contumelious, damnatory, denunciatory, injurious, insolent, insulting, offensive, opprobrious, reproachful, reviling, ribald, rude, scurrilous, vilificatory, vituperative.

abut *vb* adjoin, border, impinge, meet, project.

abutment *n* bank, bulwark, buttress, embankment, fortification; abutting, abuttal, adjacency, contiguity, juxtaposition.

abuttal *n* adjacency, boundary, contiguity, juxtaposition, nearness, next, terminus.

abyss *n* abysm, chasm, gorge, gulf, pit.

academic *adj* collegiate, lettered, scholastic. * *n* academician, classicist, doctor, fellow, pundit, savant, scholar, student, teacher.

academy *n* college, high school, institute, school.

accede *vb* accept, acquiesce, agree, assent to, comply with, concur, consent, yield.

accelerate *vb* dispatch, expedite, forward, hasten, hurry, precipitate, press on, quicken, speed, urge on.

acceleration *n* expedition, hastening, hurrying, quickening, pickup, precipitation, speeding up, stepping up.

accent *vb* accentuate, emphasize, stress. * *n* cadence, inflection, intonation, tone; beat, emphasis, ictus.

accentuate *vb* accent, emphasize, mark, point up, punctuate, stress; highlight, overemphasize, overstress, underline, underscore.

accept *vb* acquire, derive, get, gain, obtain, receive, take; accede to, acknowledge, acquiesce in, admit, agree to, approve, assent to, avow, embrace; estimate, construe, interpret, regard, value.

acceptable *adj* agreeable, gratifying, pleasant, pleasing, pleasurable, welcome.

acceptance *n* accepting, acknowledgment, receipt, reception, taking; approbation, approval, gratification, satisfaction.

acceptation *n* construction, import, interpretation, meaning, sense, significance, signification, understanding; adoption, approval, currency, vogue.

access *vb* broach, enter, open, open up. * *n* approach, avenue, entrance, entry, passage, way; admission, admittance, audience, interview; addition, accession, aggrandizement, enlargement, gain, increase, increment; (*med*) attack, fit, onset, recurrence.

accession *n* addition, augmentation, enlargement, extension, increase; succession.

accessory *adj* abetting, additional, additive, adjunct, aiding, ancillary, assisting, contributory, helping, subsidiary, subordinate, supplemental. * *n* abettor, accomplice, assistant, associate, confederate, helper; accompaniment, attendant, concomitant, detail, subsidiary.

accident *n* calamity, casualty, condition, contingency, disaster, fortuity, incident, misadventure, miscarriage, mischance, misfortune, mishap; affection, alteration, chance, contingency, mode, modification, property, quality, state.

accidental *adj* casual, chance, contingent, fortuitous, undesigned, unintended; adventitious, dispensable, immaterial, incidental, nonessential.

acclamation *n* acclaim, applause, cheer, cry, plaudit, outcry, salutation, shouting.

acclimatization, acclimation *n* adaptation, adjustment, conditioning, familiarization, habituation, inurement, naturalization.

acclimatize, acclimate *vb* accustom, adapt, adjust, condition, familiarize, habituate, inure, naturalize, season.

acclivity *n* ascent, height, hill, rising ground, steep, upward slope.

accommodate *vb* contain, furnish, hold, oblige, serve, supply; adapt, fit, suit; adjust, compose, harmonize, reconcile, settle.

accommodation *n* advantage, convenience, privilege; adaptation, agreement, conformity, fitness, suitableness; adjustment, harmonization, harmony, pacification, reconciliation, settlement.

accompaniment *n* adjunct, appendage, attachment, attendant, concomitant.

accompany *vb* attend, chaperon, convoy, escort, follow, go with.

accomplice *n* abettor, accessory, ally, assistant, associate, confederate, partner.

accomplish *vb* achieve, bring about, carry, carry through, complete, compass, consummate, do, effect, execute, perform, perfect; conclude, end, finish, terminate.

accomplished *adj* achieved, completed, done, effected, executed, finished, fulfilled, realized; able, adroit, apt, consummate, educated, experienced, expert, finished, instructed, practised, proficient, qualified, ripe, skilful, versed; elegant, fashionable, fine, polished, polite, refined.

accomplishment *n* achievement, acquirement, attainment, qualification; completion, fulfilment.

accord *vb* admit, allow, concede, deign, give, grant, vouchsafe, yield; agree, assent, concur, correspond, harmonize, quadrate, tally. * *n* accordance, agreement, concord, concurrence, conformity, consensus, harmony, unanimity, unison.

accordant *adj* agreeable, agreeing, congruous, consonant, harmonious, suitable, symphonious.

accordingly *adv* agreeably, conformably, consistently, suitably; consequently, hence, so, thence, therefore, thus, whence, wherefore.

accost *vb* address, confront, greet, hail, salute, speak to, stop.

account *vb* assess, appraise, estimate, evaluate, judge, rate; (*with* **for**) assign, attribute, explain, expound, justify, rationalize, vindicate. * *n* inventory, record, register, score; bill, book, charge; calculation, computation, count, reckoning, score, tale, tally; chronicle, detail, description, narration, narrative, portrayal, recital, rehearsal, relation, report, statement, tidings, word; elucidation, explanation, exposition; consideration, ground, motive, reason, regard, sake; consequence, consideration, dignity, distinction, importance, note, repute, reputation, worth.

accountable *adj* amenable, answerable, duty-bound, liable, responsible.

start here

accoutre *vb* arm, dress, equip, fit out, furnish.

accredit *vb* authorize, depute, empower, entrust.

accrue *vb* arise, come, follow, flow, inure, issue, proceed, result.

accumulate *vb* agglomerate, aggregate, amass, bring together, collect, gather, grow, hoard, increase, pile, store.

accumulation *n* agglomeration, aggregation, collection, heap, hoard, mass, pile, store.

accuracy *n* carefulness, correctness, exactness, fidelity, precision, strictness.

accurate *adj* close, correct, exact, faithful, nice, precise, regular, strict, true, truthful.

accusation *n* arraignment, charge, incrimination, impeachment, indictment.

accuse *vb* arraign, charge, censure, impeach, indict, tax.

accustom *vb* discipline, drill, familiarize, habituate, harden, inure, train, use.

ace *n* (*cards, dice*) one spot, single pip, single point; atom, bit, grain, iota, jot, particle, single, unit, whit; expert, master, virtuoso. * *adj* best, expert, fine, outstanding, superb.

acerbity *n* acidity, acridity, acridness, astringency, bitterness, roughness, sourness, tartness; acrimony, bitterness, harshness, severity, venom.

achieve *vb* accomplish, attain, complete, do, effect, execute, finish, fulfil, perform, realize; acquire, gain, get, obtain, win.

achievement *n* accomplishment, acquirement, attainment, completion, consummation, performance, realization; deed, exploit, feat, work.

acid *adj* pungent, sharp, sour, stinging, tart, vinegary.

acknowledge *vb* recognize; accept, admit, accept, allow, concede, grant; avow, confess, own, profess.

acme *n* apex, climax, height, peak, pinnacle, summit, top, vertex, zenith.

acquaint *vb* familiarize; announce, apprise, communicate, enlighten, disclose, inform, make aware, make known, notify, tell.

acquaintance *n* companionship, familiarity, fellowship, intimacy, knowledge; associate, companion, comrade, friend.

acquiesce *vb* bow, comply, consent, give way, rest, submit, yield; agree, assent, concur, consent.

acquire *vb* achieve, attain, earn, gain, get, have, obtain, procure, realize, secure, win; learn thoroughly, master.

acquirement *n* acquiring, gaining, gathering, mastery; acquisition, accomplishment, attainment.

acquit *vb* absolve, clear, discharge, exculpate, excuse, exonerate, forgive, liberate, pardon, pay, quit, release, set free, settle.

acquittal *n* absolution, acquittance, clearance, deliverance, discharge, exoneration, liberation, release.

acquittance *n* discharge; quittance, receipt.

acrid *adj* biting, bitter, caustic, pungent, sharp.

acrimonious *adj* acrid, bitter, caustic, censorious, crabbed, harsh, malignant, petulant, sarcastic, severe, testy, virulent.

acrimony *n* causticity, causticness, corrosiveness, sharpness; abusiveness, acridity, asperity, bitterness, churlishness, harshness, rancour, severity, spite, venom.

act *vb* do, execute, function, make, operate, work; enact, feign, perform, play. * *n* achievement, deed, exploit, feat, performance, proceeding, turn; bill, decree, enactment, law, ordinance, statute; actuality, existence, fact, reality.

acting *adj* interim, provisional, substitute, temporary. * *n* enacting, impersonation, performance, portrayal, theatre; counterfeiting, dissimulation, imitation, pretence.

action *n* achievement, activity, agency, deed, exertion, exploit, feat; battle, combat, conflict, contest, encounter, engagement, operation; lawsuit, prosecution.

active *adj* effective, efficient, influential, living, operative; assiduous, bustling, busy, diligent, industrious, restless; agile, alert, brisk, energetic, lively, nimble, prompt, quick, smart, spirited, sprightly, supple; animated, ebullient, fervent, vigorous.

actual *adj* certain, decided, genuine, objective, real, substantial, tangible, true, veritable; perceptible, present, sensible, tangible; absolute, categorical, positive.

actuate *vb* impel, incite, induce, instigate, move, persuade, prompt.

acumen *n* acuteness, astuteness, discernment, ingenuity, keenness, penetration, sagacity, sharpness, shrewdness.

acute *adj* pointed, sharp; astute, bright, discerning, ingenious, intelligent, keen, quick, penetrating, piercing, sagacious, sage, sharp, shrewd, smart, subtle; distressing, fierce, intense, piercing, pungent, poignant, severe, violent; high, high-toned, sharp, shrill; (*med*) sudden, temporary, violent.

adage *n* aphorism, dictum, maxim, proverb, saw, saying.

adapt *vb* accommodate, adjust, conform, coordinate, fit, qualify, proportion, suit, temper.

add *vb* adjoin, affix, annex, append, attach, join, tag; sum, sum up, total.

addict *vb* accustom, apply, dedicate, devote, habituate. * *n* devotee, enthusiast, fan; head, junkie, user.

addicted *adj* attached, devoted, given up to, inclined, prone, wedded.

addition *n* augmentation, accession, enlargement, extension, increase, supplement; adjunct, appendage, appendix, extra.

address *vb* accost, apply to, court, direct. * *n* appeal, application, entreaty, invocation, memorial, petition, request, solicitation, suit; discourse, oration, lecture, sermon, speech; ability, adroitness, art, dexterity, expertness, skill; courtesy, deportment, demeanour, tact.

adduce *vb* advance, allege, assign, offer, present; cite, mention, name.

adept *adj* accomplished, experienced, practised, proficient, skilled. * *n* expert, master, virtuoso.

adequate *adj* able, adapted, capable, competent, equal, fit, requisite, satisfactory, sufficient, suitable.

adhere *vb* cling, cleave, cohere, hold, stick; appertain, belong, pertain.

adherent *adj* adhering, clinging, sticking. * *n* acolyte, dependant, disciple, follower, partisan, supporter, vassal.

adhesion *n* adherence, attachment, clinging, coherence, sticking.

adhesive *adj* clinging, sticking; glutinous, gummy, sticky, tenacious, viscous. * *n* binder, cement, glue, paste.

adieu *n* farewell, goodbye, parting, valediction.

adipose *adj* fat, fatty, greasy, oily, oleaginous, sebaceous.

adjacent *adj* adjoining, bordering, conterminous, contiguous, near, near to, neighbouring, touching.

adjoin *vb* abut, add, annex, append, border, combine, neighbour, unite, verge.

adjourn *vb* defer, delay, postpone, procrastinate; close, dissolve, end, interrupt, prorogue, suspend.

adjudge *vb* allot, assign, award; decide, decree, determine, settle.

adjunct *n* addition, advantage, appendage, appurtenance, attachment, attribute, auxiliary, dependency, help.

adjure *vb* beg, beseech, entreat, pray, supplicate.

adjust *vb* adapt, arrange, dispose, rectify; regulate, set right, settle, suit; compose, harmonize, pacify, reconcile, settle; accommodate, adapt, fit, suit.

administer *vb* contribute, deal out, dispense, supply; conduct, control, direct, govern, manage, oversee, superintend; conduce, contribute.

admirable *adj* astonishing, striking, surprising, wonderful; excellent, fine, rare, superb.

admiration *n* affection, approbation, approval, astonishment, delight, esteem, pleasure, regard.

admirer *n* beau, gallant, suitor, sweetheart; fan, follower, supporter.

admissible *adj* allowable, lawful, permissible, possible.

admission *n* access, admittance, entrance, introduction; acceptance, acknowledgement, allowance, assent, avowal, concession.

admit *vb* give access to, let in, receive; agree to, accept, acknowledge, concede, confess; allow, bear, permit, suffer, tolerate.

admonish *vb* censure, rebuke, reprove; advise caution, counsel, enjoin, forewarn, warn; acquaint, apprise, inform, instruct, notify, remind.

admonition *n* censure, rebuke, remonstrance; advice, caution, chiding, counsel, instruction, monition.

adolescence *n* minority, nonage, teens, youth.

adolescent *adj* juvenile, young, youthful. * *n* minor, teenager, youth.

adopt *vb* appropriate, assume; accept, approve, avow, espouse, maintain, support; affiliate, father, foster.

adore *vb* worship; esteem, honour, idolize, love, revere, venerate.

adorn *vb* beautify, decorate, embellish, enrich, garnish, gild, grace, ornament.

adroit *adj* apt, dextrous, expert, handy, ingenious, ready, skilful.

adulation *n* blandishment, cajolery, fawning, flattery, flummery, praise, sycophancy.

adult *adj* grown-up, mature, ripe, ripened. * *n* grown-up person.

adulterate *vb* alloy, contaminate, corrupt, debase, deteriorate, vitiate.

advance *adj* beforehand, forward, leading. * *vb* propel, push, send forward; aggrandize, dignify, elevate, exalt, promote; benefit, forward, further, improve, promote; adduce, allege, assign, offer, propose, propound; augment, increase; proceed, progress; grow, improve, prosper, thrive. * *n* march, progress; advancement, enhancement, growth, promotion, rise; offer, overture, proffering, proposal, proposition, tender; appreciation, rise.

advancement *n* advance, benefit, gain, growth, improvement, profit.

advantage *n* ascendancy, precedence, pre-eminence, superiority, upper-hand; benefit, blessing, emolument, gain, profit, return; account, behalf, interest; accommodation, convenience, prerogative, privilege.

advantageous *adj* beneficial, favourable, profitable.

advent *n* accession, approach, arrival, coming, visitation.

adventitious *adj* accidental, extraneous, extrinsic, foreign, fortuitous, nonessential.

adventure *vb* dare, hazard, imperil, peril, risk, venture. * *n* chance, contingency, experiment, fortuity, hazard, risk, venture; crisis, contingency, event, incident, occurrence, transaction.

adventurous *adj* bold, chivalrous, courageous, daring, doughty; foolhardy, headlong, precipitate, rash, reckless; dangerous, hazardous, perilous.

adversary *n* antagonist, enemy, foe, opponent.

adverse *adj* conflicting, contrary, opposing; antagonistic, harmful, hostile, hurtful, inimical, unfavourable, unpropitious; calamitous, disastrous, unfortunate, unlucky, untoward.

adversity *n* affliction, calamity, disaster, distress, misery, misfortune, sorrow, suffering, woe.

advertise *vb* advise, announce, declare, inform, placard, proclaim, publish.

advertisement *n* announcement, information, notice, proclamation.

advice *n* admonition, caution, counsel, exhortation, persuasion, suggestion, recommendation; information, intelligence, notice, notification; care, counsel, deliberation, forethought.

advisable *adj* advantageous, desirable, expedient, prudent.

advise *vb* admonish, counsel, commend, recommend, suggest, urge; acquaint, apprise, inform, notify; confer, consult, deliberate.

adviser *n* counsellor, director, guide, instructor.

advocate *vb* countenance, defend, favour, justify, maintain, support, uphold, vindicate. * *n* apologist, counsellor, defender, maintainer, patron, pleader, supporter; attorney, barrister, counsel, lawyer, solicitor.

aegis *n* defence, protection, safeguard, shelter.

aesthetic *adj* appropriate, beautiful, tasteful.

affable *adj* accessible, approachable, communicative, conversable, cordial, easy, familiar, frank, free, sociable, social; complaisant, courteous, civil, obliging, polite, urbane.

affair *n* business, circumstance, concern, matter, office, question; event, incident, occurrence, performance, proceeding, transaction; battle, combat, conflict, encounter, engagement, skirmish.

affairs *npl* administration, relations; business, estate, finances, property.

affect *vb* act upon, alter, change, influence, modify, transform; concern, interest, regard, relate; improve, melt, move, overcome, subdue, touch; aim at, aspire to, crave, yearn for; adopt, assume, feign.

affectation *n* affectedness, airs, artificiality, foppery, pretension, simulation.

affected *adj* artificial, assumed, feigned, insincere, theatrical; assuming, conceited, foppish, vain.

affection *n* bent, bias, feeling, inclination, passion, proclivity, propensity; accident, attribute, character, mark, modification, mode, note, property; attachment, endearment, fondness, goodwill, kindness, partiality, love.

affectionate *adj* attached, devoted, fond, kind, loving, sympathetic, tender.

affiliate *vb* ally, annex, associate, connect, incorporate, join, unite. * *n* ally, associate, confederate.

affinity *n* connection, propinquity, relationship; analogy, attraction, correspondence, likeness, relation, resemblance, similarity, sympathy.

affirm *vb* allege, assert, asseverate, aver, declare, state; approve, confirm, establish, ratify.

affix *vb* annex, attach, connect, fasten, join, subjoin, tack.

afflict *vb* agonize, distress, grieve, pain, persecute, plague, torment, trouble, try, wound.

affliction *n* adversity, calamity, disaster, misfortune, stroke, visitation; bitterness, depression, distress, grief, misery, plague, scourge, sorrow, trial, tribulation, wretchedness, woe.

affluent *adj* abounding, abundant, bounteous, plenteous; moneyed, opulent, rich, wealthy.

afford *vb* furnish, produce, supply, yield; bestow, communicate, confer, give, grant, impart, offer; bear, endure, support.

affray *n* brawl, conflict, disturbance, feud, fight, quarrel, scuffle, struggle.

affright *vb* affray, alarm, appal, confound, dismay, shock, startle. * *n* alarm, consternation, fear, fright, panic, terror.

affront *vb* abuse, insult, outrage; annoy, chafe, displease, fret, irritate, offend, pique, provoke, vex. * *n* abuse, contumely, insult, outrage, vexation, wrong.

afraid *adj* aghast, alarmed, anxious, apprehensive, frightened, scared, timid.

after *prep* later than, subsequent to; behind, following; about, according to; because of, in imitation of. * *adj* behind, consecutive, ensuing, following, later, succeeding, successive, subsequent; aft, back, hind, rear, rearmost, tail.* *adv* afterwards, later, next, since, subsequently, then, thereafter.

again *adv* afresh, anew, another time, once more; besides, further, in addition, moreover.

against *prep* adverse to, contrary to, in opposition to, resisting; abutting, close up to, facing, fronting, off, opposite to, over; in anticipation of, for, in expectation of; in compensation for, to counterbalance, to match.

age *vb* decline, grow old, mature. * *n* aeon, date, epoch, period, time; decline, old age, senility; antiquity, oldness.

agency *n* action, force, intervention, means, mediation, operation, procurement; charge, direction, management, superintendence, supervision.

agent *n* actor, doer, executor, operator, performer; active element, cause, force; attorney, broker, commissioner, deputy, factor, intermediary, manager, middleman.

agglomeration *n* accumulation, aggregation, conglomeration, heap, lump, pile.

agglutinate *vb* cement, fasten, glue, unite.

aggrandize *vb* advance, dignify, elevate, enrich, exalt, promote.

aggravate *vb* heighten, increase, worsen; colour, exaggerate, magnify, overstate; enrage, irritate, provoke, tease.

aggravation *n* exaggeration, heightening, irritation.

aggregate *vb* accumulate, amass, collect, heap, pile. * *adj* collected, total. * *n* amount, gross, total, whole.

aggressive *adj* assailing, assailant, assaulting, attacking, invading, offensive; pushing, self-assertive.

aggressor *n* assailant, assaulter, attacker, invader.

aggrieve *vb* afflict, grieve, pain; abuse, ill-treat, impose, injure, oppress, wrong.

aghast *adj* appalled, dismayed, frightened, horrified, horror-struck, panic-stricken, terrified; amazed, astonished, startled, thunderstruck.

agile *adj* active, alert, brisk, lively, nimble, prompt, smart, ready.

agitate *vb* disturb, jar, rock, shake, trouble; disquiet, excite, ferment, rouse, trouble; confuse, discontent, flurry, fluster, flutter; canvass, debate, discuss, dispute, investigate.

agitation *n* concussion, shake, shaking; commotion, convulsion, disturbance, ferment, jarring, storm, tumult, turmoil; discomposure, distraction, emotion, excitement, flutter, perturbation, ruffle, tremor, trepidation; controversy, debate, discussion.

agnostic *n* doubter, empiricist, sceptic.

agonize *vb* distress, excruciate, rack, torment, torture.

agony *n* anguish, distress, pangs.

agree *vb* accord, concur, harmonize, unite; accede, acquiesce, assent, comply, concur, subscribe; bargain, contract, covenant, engage, promise, undertake; compound, compromise; chime, cohere, conform, correspond, match, suit, tally.

agreeable *adj* charming, pleasant, pleasing.

agreement *n* accordance, compliance, concord, harmony, union; bargain, compact, contract, pact, treaty.

agriculture *n* cultivation, culture, farming, geoponics, husbandry, tillage.

aid *vb* assist, help, serve, support; relieve, succour; advance, facilitate, further, promote. * *n* assistance, cooperation, help, patronage; alms, subsidy, succour, relief.

ailment *n* disease, illness, sickness.

aim *vb* direct, level, point, train; design, intend, mean, purpose, seek. * *n* bearing, course, direction, tendency; design, object, view, reason.

air *vb* expose, display, ventilate. * *n* atmosphere, breeze;

appearance, aspect, manner; melody, tune.

aisle *n* passage, walk.

akin *adj* allied, kin, related; analogous, cognate, congenial, connected.

alacrity *n* agility, alertness, activity, eagerness, promptitude; cheerfulness, gaiety, hilarity, liveliness, vivacity.

alarm *vb* daunt, frighten, scare, startle, terrify. * *n* alarm-bell, tocsin, warning; apprehension, fear, fright, terror.

alert *adj* awake, circumspect, vigilant, watchful, wary; active, brisk, lively, nimble, quick, prompt, ready, sprightly. * *vb* alarm, arouse, caution, forewarn, signal, warn. * *n* alarm, signal, warning.

alertness *n* circumspection, vigilance, watchfulness, wariness; activity, briskness, nimbleness, promptness, readiness, spryness.

alien *adj* foreign, not native; differing, estranged, inappropriate, remote, unallied, separated. * *n* foreigner, stranger.

alienate *vb* (*legal*) assign, demise, transfer; disaffect, estrange, wean, withdraw.

alienation *n* (*legal*) assignment, conveyance, transfer; breach, disaffection, division, estrangement, rupture; (*med*) aberration, delusion, derangement, hallucination, insanity, madness.

alike *adj* akin, analogous, duplicate, identical, resembling, similar. * *adv* equally.

aliment *n* diet, fare, meat, nutriment, provision, rations, sustenance.

alive *adj* animate, breathing, live; aware, responsive, sensitive, susceptible; brisk, cheerful, lively, sprightly.

allay *vb* appease, calm, check, compose; alleviate, assuage, lessen, moderate, solace, temper.

allege *vb* affirm, assert, declare, maintain, say; adduce, advance, assign, cite, plead, produce, quote.

allegiance *n* duty, homage, fealty, fidelity, loyalty, obligation.

allegory *n* apologue, fable, myth, parable, story, tale.

alleviate *vb* assuage, lighten, mitigate, mollify, moderate, quell, quiet, quieten, soften, soothe.

alliance *n* affinity, intermarriage, relation; coalition, combination, confederacy, league, treaty, union; affiliation, connection, relationship, similarity.

allot *vb* divide, dispense, distribute; assign, fix, prescribe, specify.

allow *vb* acknowledge, admit, concede, confess, grant, own; authorize, grant, let, permit; bear, endure, suffer, tolerate; grant, yield, relinquish, spare; approve, justify, sanction; abate, bate, deduct, remit.

allude *vb* glance, hint, mention, imply, insinuate, intimate, refer, suggest, touch.

allure *vb* attract, beguile, cajole, coax, entice, lure, persuade, seduce, tempt. * *n* appeal, attraction, lure, temptation.

allusion *n* hint, implication, intimation, insinuation, mention, reference, suggestion.

ally *vb* combine, connect, join, league, marry, unite. * *n* aider, assistant, associate, coadjutor, colleague, friend, partner.

almighty *adj* all-powerful, omnipotent.

alms *npl* benefaction, bounty, charity, dole, gift, gratuity.

alone *adj* companionless, deserted, forsaken, isolated, lonely, only, single, sole, solitary.

along *adv* lengthways, lengthwise; forward, onward; beside, together, simultaneously.

aloud *adv* audibly, loudly, sonorously, vociferously.

alter *vb* change, conform, modify, shift, turn, transform, transmit, vary.

altercation *n* bickering, contention, controversy, dispute, dissension, strife, wrangling.

alternating *adj* intermittent, interrupted.

alternative *adj* another, different, second, substitute. * *n* choice, option, preference.

although *conj* albeit, even if, for all that, notwithstanding, though.

altitude *n* elevation, height, loftiness.

altogether *adv* completely, entirely, totally, utterly.

always *adv* continually, eternally, ever, evermore, perpetually, unceasingly.

amalgamate *vb* blend, combine, commingle, compound, incorporate, mix.

amass *vb* accumulate, aggregate, collect, gather, heap, scrape together.

amateur *n* dilettante, nonprofessional.

amaze *vb* astonish, astound, bewilder, confound, confuse, dumbfound, perplex, stagger, stupefy.

amazement *n* astonishment, bewilderment, confusion, marvel, surprise, wonder.

ambassador *n* deputy, envoy, legate, minister, plenipotentiary.

ambiguous *adj* dubious, doubtful, enigmatic, equivocal, uncertain, indefinite, indistinct, obscure, vague.

ambition *n* aspiration, emulation, longing, yearning.

ambitious *adj* aspiring, avid, eager, intent.

ameliorate *vb* amend, benefit, better, elevate, improve, mend.

amenability *n* amenableness, responsiveness; accountability, liability, responsibility.

amenable *adj* acquiescent, agreeable, persuadable, responsive, susceptible; accountable, liable, responsible.

amend *vb* better, correct, improve, mend, redress, reform.

amends *npl* atonement, compensation, expiation, indemnification, recompense, reparation, restitution.

amenity *n* agreeableness, mildness, pleasantness, softness; affability, civility, courtesy, geniality, graciousness, urbanity.

amiable *adj* attractive, benign, charming, genial, goodnatured, harmonious, kind, lovable, lovely, pleasant, pleasing, sweet, winning, winsome.

amicable *adj* amiable, cordial, friendly, harmonious, kind, kindly, peaceable.

amiss *adj* erroneous, inaccurate, incorrect, faulty, improper, wrong. * *adv* erroneously, inaccurately, incorrectly, wrongly.

amnesty *n* absolution, condonation, dispensation, forgiveness, oblivion.

amorous *adj* ardent, enamoured, fond, longing, loving, passionate, tender; erotic, impassioned.

amorphous *adj* formless, irregular, shapeless, unshapen; noncrystalline, structureless; chaotic, characterless, clumsy, disorganized, misshapen, unorganized, vague.

amount *n* aggregate, sum, total.

ample *adj* broad, capacious, extended, extensive, great, large, roomy, spacious; abounding, abundant, copious, generous, liberal, plentiful; diffusive, unrestricted.

amputate *vb* clip, curtail, prune, lop, remove, separate, sever.

amuse *vb* charm, cheer, divert, enliven, entertain, gladden, relax, solace; beguile, cheat, deceive, delude, mislead.

amusement *n* diversion, entertainment, frolic, fun, merriment, pleasure.

analeptic *adj* comforting, invigorating, restorative.

analogy *n* correspondence, likeness, parallelism, parity, resemblance, similarity.

analysis *n* decomposition, dissection, resolution, separation.

anarchy *n* chaos, confusion, disorder, misrule, lawlessness, riot.

anathema *n* ban, curse, denunciation, excommunication, execration, malediction, proscription.

anatomy *n* dissection; form, skeleton, structure.

ancestor *n* father, forebear, forefather, progenitor.

ancestry *n* family, house, line, lineage; descent, genealogy, parentage, pedigree, stock.

anchor *vb* fasten, fix, secure; cast anchor, take firm hold. * *n* (*naut*) ground tackle; defence, hold, security, stay.

ancient *adj* old, primitive, pristine; antiquated, antique, archaic, obsolete.

ancillary *adj* accessory, auxiliary, contributory, helpful, instrumental.

angelic *adj* adorable, celestial, cherubic, heavenly, saintly, seraphic; entrancing, enrapturing, rapturous, ravishing.

anger *vb* chafe, displease, enrage, gall, infuriate, irritate, madden. * *n* choler, exasperation, fury, gall, indignation, ire, passion, rage, resentment, spleen, wrath.

angle *vb* fish. * *n* divergence, flare, opening; bend, corner, crotch, cusp, point; fish-hook, hook.

angry *adj* chafed, exasperated, furious, galled, incensed, irritated, nettled, piqued, provoked, resentful.

anguish *n* agony, distress, grief, pang, rack, torment, torture.

anile *adj* aged, decrepit, doting, imbecile, senile.

animadversion *n* comment, notice, observation, remark; blame, censure, condemnation, reproof, stricture.

animate *vb* inform, quicken, vitalize, vivify; fortify, invigorate, revive; activate, enliven, excite, heat, impel, kindle, rouse, stimulate, stir, waken; elate, embolden, encourage, exhilarate, gladden, hearten. * *adj* alive, breathing, live, living, organic, quick.

animosity *n* bitterness, enmity, grudge, hatred, hostility, rancour, rankling, spleen, virulence.

annals *npl* archives, chronicles, records, registers, rolls.

annex *vb* affix, append, attach, subjoin, tag, tack; connect, join, unite.

annihilate *vb* abolish, annul, destroy, dissolve, exterminate, extinguish, kill, obliterate, raze, ruin.

annotation *n* comment, explanation, illustration, note, observation, remark.

announce *vb* advertise, communicate, declare, disclose, proclaim, promulgate, publish, report, reveal, trumpet.

announcement *n* advertisement, annunciation, bulletin, declaration, manifesto, notice, notification, proclamation.

annoy *vb* badger, chafe, disquiet, disturb, fret, hector, irk, irritate, molest, pain, pester, plague, trouble, vex, worry, wound.

annul *vb* abolish, abrogate, cancel, countermand, nullify, overrule, quash, repeal, recall, reverse, revoke.

anoint *vb* consecrate, oil, sanctify, smear.

anonymous *adj* nameless, unacknowledged, unsigned.

answer *vb* fulfil, rejoin, reply, respond, satisfy. * *n* rejoinder, reply, response, retort; confutation, rebuttal, refutation.

answerable *adj* accountable, amenable, correspondent, liable, responsible, suited.

antagonism *n* contradiction, discordance, disharmony, dissonant, incompatibility, opposition.

antecedent *adj* anterior, foregoing, forerunning, precedent, preceding, previous. * *n* forerunner, precursor.

anterior *adj* antecedent, foregoing, preceding, previous, prior; fore, front.

anticipate *vb* antedate, forestall, foretaste, prevent; count upon, expect, forecast, foresee.

anticipation *n* apprehension, contemplation, expectation, hope, prospect, trust; expectancy, forecast, foresight, foretaste, preconception, presentiment.

antidote *n* corrective, counteractive, counter-poison; cure, remedy, restorative, specific.

antipathy *n* abhorrence, aversion, disgust, detestation, hate, hatred, horror, loathing, repugnance.

antique *adj* ancient, archaic, bygone, old, old-fashioned.

anxiety *n* apprehension, care, concern, disquiet, fear, foreboding, misgiving, perplexity, trouble, uneasiness, vexation, worry.

anxious *adj* apprehensive, restless, solicitous, uneasy, unquiet, worried.

apart *adv* aloof, aside, separately; asunder.

apathetic *adj* cold, dull, impassive, inert, listless, obtuse, passionless, sluggish, torpid, unfeeling.

ape *vb* counterfeit, imitate, mimic; affect. * *n* simian, troglodyte; imitator, mimic; image, imitation, likeness, type.

aperture *n* chasm, cleft, eye, gap, opening, hole, orifice, passage.

aphorism *n* adage, apothegm, byword, maxim, proverb, saw, saying.

apish *adj* imitative, mimicking; affected, foppish, trifling.

aplomb *n* composure, confidence, equanimity, self-confidence.

apocryphal *adj* doubtful, fabulous, false, legendary, spurious, uncanonical.

apologetic *adj* exculpatory, excusatory; defensive, vindictive.

apology *n* defence, justification, vindication; acknowledgement, excuse, explanation, plea, reparation.

apostate *adj* backsliding, disloyal, faithless, false, perfidious, recreant, traitorous, untrue. * *n* backslider, deserter, pervert, renegade, turncoat.

apostle *n* angel, herald, messenger, missionary, preacher; advocate, follower, supporter.

apothegm *n* aphorism, byword, dictum, maxim, proverb, saw, saying.

appal *vb* affright, alarm, daunt, dismay, frighten, horrify, scare, shock.

apparel *n* attire, array, clothes, clothing, dress, garments, habit, raiment, robes, suit, trappings, vestments.

apparent *adj* discernible, perceptible, visible; conspicuous, evident, legible, manifest, obvious, open, patent, plain, unmistakable; external, ostensible, seeming, superficial.

apparition *n* appearance, appearing, epiphany, manifestation; being, form; ghost, phantom, spectre, spirit, vision.

appeal *vb* address, entreat, implore, invoke, refer, request, solicit. * *n* application, entreaty, invocation, solicitation, suit.

appear *vb* emerge, loom; break, open; arise, occur, offer; look, seem, show.

appearance *n* advent, arrival, apparition, coming; form, shape; colour, face, fashion, feature, guise, pretence, pretext; air, aspect, complexion, demeanour, manner, mien.

appease *vb* abate, allay, assuage, calm, ease, lessen, mitigate, pacify, placate, quell, soothe, temper, tranquillize.

appellation *n* address, cognomen, denomination, epithet, style, title.

append *vb* attach, fasten, hang; add, annex, subjoin, tack, tag.

appendix *n* addition, adjunct, appurtenance, codicil; excursus, supplement.

appetite *n* craving, desire, longing, lust, passion; gusto, relish, stomach, zest; hunger.

applaud *vb* acclaim, cheer, clap, compliment, encourage, extol, magnify.

applause *n* acclamation, approval, cheers, commendation, plaudit.

applicable *adj* adapted, appropriate, apt, befitting, fitting, germane, pertinent, proper, relevant.

application *n* emollient, lotion, ointment, poultice, wash; appliance, exercise, practice, use; appeal, petition, request, solicitation, suit; assiduity, constancy, diligence, effort, industry.

apply *vb* bestow, lay upon; appropriate, convert, employ, exercise, use; addict, address, dedicate, devote, direct, engage.

appoint *vb* determine, establish, fix, prescribe; bid, command, decree, direct, order, require; allot, assign, delegate, depute, detail, destine, settle; constitute, create, name, nominate; equip, furnish, supply.

apportion *vb* allocate, allot, allow, assign, deal, dispense, divide, share.

apposite *adj* apt, fit, germane, pertinent, relevant, suitable, pertinent.

appraise *vb* appreciate, estimate, prize, rate, value.

appreciate *vb* appreciate, esteem, estimate, rate, realize, value.

apprehend *vb* arrest, catch, detain, seize, take; conceive, imagine, regard, view; appreciate, perceive, realize, see, take in; fear, forebode; conceive, fancy, hold, imagine, presume, understand.

apprehension *n* arrest, capture, seizure; intellect, intelligence, mind, reason; discernment, intellect, knowledge, perception, sense; belief, fancy, idea, notion, sentiment, view; alarm, care, dread, distrust, fear, misgiving, suspicion.

apprise *vb* acquaint, inform, notify, tell.

approach *vb* advance, approximate, come close; broach; resemble. * *n* advance, advent; approximation, convergence, nearing, tendency; entrance, path, way.

approbation *n* approval, commendation, liking, praise; assent, concurrence, consent, endorsement, ratification, sanction.

appropriate *vb* adopt, arrogate, assume, set apart; allot, apportion, assign, devote; apply, convert, employ, use. * *adj* adapted, apt, befitting, fit, opportune, seemly, suitable.

approve *vb* appreciate, commend, like, praise, recommend, value; confirm, countenance, justify, ratify, sustain, uphold.

approximate *vb* approach, resemble. * *adj* approaching, proximate; almost exact, inexact, rough.

apt *adj* applicable, apposite, appropriate, befitting, fit, felicitous, germane; disposed, inclined, liable, prone, subject; able, adroit, clever, dextrous, expert, handy, happy, prompt, ready, skilful.

aptitude *n* applicability, appropriateness, felicity, fitness, pertinence, suitability; inclination, tendency, turn; ability, address, adroitness, quickness, readiness, tact.

arbitrary *adj* absolute, autocratic, despotic, domineering, imperious, overbearing, unlimited; capricious, discretionary, fanciful, voluntary, whimsical.

arcade *n* colonnade, loggia.

arch¹ *adj* cunning, knowing, frolicsome, merry, mirthful, playful, roguish, shrewd, sly; consummate, chief, leading, pre-eminent, prime, primary, principal.

arch² *vb* span, vault; bend, curve. * *n* archway, span, vault.

archaic *adj* ancient, antiquated, antique, bygone, obsolete, old.

archives *npl* documents, muniments, records, registers, rolls.

ardent *adj* burning, fiery, hot; eager, earnest, fervent, impassioned, keen, passionate, warm, zealous.

ardour *n* glow, heat, warmth; eagerness, enthusiasm, fervour, heat, passion, soul, spirit, warmth, zeal.

arduous *adj* high, lofty, steep, uphill; difficult, fatiguing, hard, laborious, onerous, tiresome, toilsome, wearisome.

area *n* circle, circuit, district, domain, field, range, realm, region, tract.

argue *vb* plead, reason upon; debate, dispute; denote, evince, imply, indicate, mean, prove; contest, debate, discuss, sift.

arid *adj* barren, dry, parched, sterile, unfertile; dry, dull, jejune, pointless, uninteresting.

aright *adv* correctly, justly, rightly, truly.

arise *vb* ascend, mount, soar, tower; appear, emerge, rise, spring; begin, originate; rebel, revolt, rise; accrue, come, emanate, ensue, flow, issue, originate, proceed, result.

aristocracy *n* gentry, nobility, noblesse, peerage.

arm¹ *n* bough, branch, limb, protection; cove, creek, estuary, firth, fjord, frith, inlet.

arm² *vb* array, equip, furnish; clothe, cover, fortify, guard, protect, strengthen.

arms *npl* accoutrements, armour, array, harness, mail, panoply, weapons; crest, escutcheon.

army *n* battalions, force, host, legions, troops; host, multitude, throng, vast assemblage.

around *prep* about, encircling, encompassing, round, surrounding. * *adv* about, approximately, generally, near, nearly, practically, round, thereabouts.

arouse *vb* animate, awaken, excite, incite, kindle, provoke, rouse, stimulate, warm, whet.

arraign *vb* accuse, censure, charge, denounce, impeach, indict, prosecute, tax.

arrange *vb* array, class, classify, dispose, distribute, group, range, rank; adjust, determine, fix upon, settle; concoct, construct, devise, plan, prepare, project.

arrant *adj* bad, consummate, downright, gross, notorious, rank, utter.

array *vb* arrange, dispose, place, range, rank; accoutre, adorn, attire, decorate, dress, enrobe, embellish, equip, garnish, habit, invest. * *n* arrangement, collection, disposition, marshalling, order; apparel, attire, clothes, dress, garments; army, battalions, soldiery, troops.

arrest *vb* check, delay, detain, hinder, hold, interrupt, obstruct, restrain, stay, stop, withhold; apprehend, capture, catch, seize, take; catch, engage, engross, fix, occupy, secure, rivet. * *n* check, checking, detention, hindrance, interruption, obstruction, restraining, stay, staying, stopping; apprehension, capture, detention, seizure.

arrive *vb* attain, come, get to, reach.

arrogance *n* assumption, assurance, disdain, effrontery, haughtiness, loftiness, lordliness, presumption, pride, scornfulness, superciliousness.

arrogate *vb* assume, claim unduly, demand, usurp.

arrow *n* bolt, dart, reed, shaft.

art *n* business, craft, employment, trade; address, adroitness, aptitude, dexterity, ingenuity, knack, readiness, sagacity, skill; artfulness, artifice, astuteness, craft, deceit, duplicity, finesse, subtlety.

artful *adj* crafty, cunning, disingenuous, insincere, sly, tricky, wily.

article *n* branch, clause, division, head, item, member, paragraph, part, point, portion; essay, paper, piece; commodity, substance, thing.

artifice *n* art, chicanery, contrivance, cunning, deception, deceit, duplicity, effort, finesse, fraud, imposture, invention, stratagem, subterfuge, trick, trickery.

artificial *adj* counterfeit, sham, spurious; assumed, affected, constrained, fictitious, forced, laboured, strained.

artless *adj* ignorant, rude, unskilful, untaught; natural, plain, simple; candid, fair, frank, guileless, honest, plain, unaffected, simple, sincere, truthful, unsuspicious.

ascend *vb* arise, aspire, climb, mount, soar, tower.

ascendancy, ascendency *n* authority, control, domination, mastery, power, predominance, sovereignty, superiority, sway.

ascertain *vb* certify, define, determine, establish, fix, settle, verify; discover, find out, get at.

ashamed *adj* abashed, confused.

ask *vb* interrogate, inquire, question; adjure, beg, conjure, crave, desire, dun, entreat, implore, invite, inquire, petition, request, solicit, supplicate, seek, sue.

aspect *n* air, bearing, countenance, expression, feature, look, mien, visage; appearance, attitude, condition, light, phase, position, posture, situation, state, view; angle, direction, outlook, prospect.

asperity *n* ruggedness, roughness, unevenness; acrimony, causticity, corrosiveness, sharpness, sourness, tartness; acerbity, bitterness, churlishness, harshness, sternness, sullenness, severity, virulence.

aspersion *n* abuse, backbiting, calumny, censure, defamation, detraction, slander, vituperation, reflection, reproach.

aspiration *n* aim, ambition, craving, hankering, hope, longing.

aspire *vb* desire, hope, long, yearn; ascend, mount, rise, soar, tower.

assail *vb* assault, attack, invade, oppugn; impugn, malign, maltreat; ply, storm.

assassinate *vb* dispatch, kill, murder, slay.

assault *vb* assail, attack, charge, invade. * *n* aggression, attack, charge, incursion, invasion, onset, onslaught; storm.

assemble *vb* call, collect, congregate, convene, convoke, gather, levy, muster; converge, forgather.

assembly *n* company, collection, concourse, congregation, gathering, meeting, rout, throng; caucus, congress, conclave, convention, convocation, diet, legislature, meeting, parliament, synod.

assent *vb* accede, acquiesce, agree, concur, subscribe, yield. * *n* accord, acquiescence, allowance, approval, approbation, consent.

assert *vb* affirm, allege, aver, asseverate, declare, express, maintain, predicate, pronounce, protest; claim, defend, emphasize, maintain, press, uphold, vindicate.

assertion *n* affirmation, allegation, asseveration, averment, declaration, position, predication, remark, statement, word; defence, emphasis, maintenance, pressing, support, vindication.

assess *vb* appraise, compute, estimate, rate, value; assign, determine, fix, impose, levy.

asseverate *vb* affirm, aver, avow, declare, maintain, protest.

assiduous *adj* active, busy, careful, constant, diligent, devoted, indefatigable, industrious, sedulous, unremitting, untiring.

assign *vb* allot, appoint, apportion, appropriate; fix, designate, determine, specify; adduce, advance, allege, give, grant, offer, present, show.

assist *vb* abet, aid, befriend, further, help, patronize, promote, second, speed, support, sustain; aid, relieve, succour; alternate with, relieve, spell.

associate *vb* affiliate, combine, conjoin, couple, join, link, relate, yoke; consort, fraternize, mingle, sort. * *n* chum, companion, comrade, familiar, follower, mate; ally, confederate, friend, partner, fellow.

association *n* combination, company, confederation, connection, partnership, society.

assort *vb* arrange, class, classify, distribute, group, rank, sort; agree, be adapted, consort, suit.

assuage *vb* allay, alleviate, appease, calm, ease, lessen, mitigate, moderate, mollify, pacify, quell, relieve, soothe, tranquillize.

assume *vb* take, undertake; affect, counterfeit, feign, pretend, sham; arrogate, usurp; beg, hypothesize, imply, postulate, posit, presuppose, suppose, simulate.

assurance *n* assuredness, certainty, conviction, persuasion, pledge, security, surety, warrant; engagement, pledge, promise; averment, assertion, protestation; audacity, confidence, courage, firmness, intrepidity; arrogance, brass, boldness, effrontery, face, front, impudence.

assure *vb* encourage, embolden, hearten; certify, insure, secure against loss, vouch for.

astonish *vb* amaze, astound, confound, daze, dumbfound, overwhelm, startle, stun, stupefy, surprise.

astute *adj* acute, cunning, deep, discerning, ingenious, intelligent, penetrating, perspicacious, quick, sagacious, sharp, shrewd.

asylum *n* refuge, retreat, sanctuary, shelter.

athletic *adj* brawny, lusty, muscular, powerful, robust, sinewy, stalwart, stout, strapping, strong, sturdy.

athletics *npl* aerobics, eurythmics, exercise, exercising, gymnastics, sports, track and field, workout.

atom *n* bit, molecule, monad, particle, scintilla.

atone *vb* answer, compensate, expiate, satisfy.

atonement *n* amends, expiation, propitiation, reparation, satisfaction.

atrocity *n* depravity, enormity, flagrancy, ferocity, savagery, villainy.

attach *vb* affix, annex, connect, fasten, join, hitch, tie;

charm, captivate, enamour, endear, engage, win; (*legal*) distress, distrain, seize, take.

attack *vb* assail, assault, charge, encounter, invade, set upon, storm, tackle; censure, criticise, impugn. * *n* aggression, assault, charge, offence, onset, onslaught, raid, thrust.

attain *vb* accomplish, achieve, acquire, get, obtain, secure; arrive at, come to, reach.

attempt *vb* assail, assault, attack; aim, endeavour, seek, strive, try. * *n* effort, endeavour, enterprise, experiment, undertaking, venture; assault, attack, onset.

attend *vb* accompany, escort, follow; guard, protect, watch; minister to, serve, wait on; give heed, hear, harken, listen; be attendant, serve, tend, wait.

attention *n* care, circumspection, heed, mindfulness, observation, regard, watch, watchfulness; application, reflection, study; civility, courtesy, deference, politeness, regard, respect; addresses, courtship, devotion, suit, wooing.

attentive *adj* alive, awake, careful, civil, considerate, courteous, heedful, mindful, observant, watchful.

attenuate *vb* contract, dilute, diminish, elongate, lengthen, lessen, rarefy, reduce, slim, thin, weaken.

attest *vb* authenticate, certify, corroborate, confirm, ratify, seal, vouch; adjure, call to witness, invoke; confess, display, exhibit, manifest, prove, show, witness.

attic *n* garret, loft, upper storey.

Attic *adj* delicate, subtle, penetrating, pointed, pungent; chaste, classic, correct, elegant, polished, pure.

attire *vb* accoutre, apparel, array, clothe, dress, enrobe, equip, rig, robe. * *n* clothes, clothing, costume, dress, garb, gear, habiliment, outfit, toilet, trapping, vestment, vesture, wardrobe.

attitude *n* pose, position, posture; aspect, conjuncture, condition, phase, prediction, situation, standing, state.

attract *vb* draw, pull; allure, captivate, charm, decoy, enamour, endear, entice, engage, fascinate, invite, win.

attraction *n* affinity, drawing, pull; allurement, charm, enticement, fascination, magnetism, lure, seduction, witchery.

attribute *vb* ascribe, assign, impute, refer. * *n* characteristic, mark, note, peculiarity, predicate, property, quality.

attrition *n* abrasion, friction, rubbing.

attune *vb* accord, harmonize, modulate, tune; accommodate, adapt, adjust, attempt.

audacity *n* boldness, courage, daring, fearlessness, intrepidity; assurance, brass, effrontery, face, front, impudence, insolence, presumption, sauciness.

audience *n* assemblage, congregation; hearing, interview, reception.

augment *vb* add to, enhance, enlarge, increase, magnify, multiply, swell.

augmentation *n* accession, addition, enlargement, extension, increase.

augury *n* prediction, prognostication, prophecy, soothsaying; auspice, forerunner, harbinger, herald, omen, precursor, portent, sign.

august *adj* awe-inspiring, awful, dignified, grand, imposing, kingly, majestic, noble, princely, regal, solemn, stately, venerable.

auspicious *adj* fortunate, happy, lucky, prosperous, successful; bright, favourable, golden, opportune, promising, prosperous.

austere *adj* ascetic, difficult, formal, hard, harsh, morose, relentless, rigid, rigorous, severe, stern, stiff, strict, uncompromising, unrelenting.

authentic *adj* genuine, pure, real, true, unadulterated, uncorrupted, veritable; accurate, authoritative, reliable, true, trustworthy.

authority *n* dominion, empire, government, jurisdiction, power, sovereignty; ascendency, control, influence, rule, supremacy, sway; authorization, liberty, order, permit, precept, sanction, warranty; testimony, witness; connoisseur, expert, master.

authorize *vb* empower, enable, entitle; allow, approve, confirm, countenance, permit, ratify, sanction.

auxiliary *adj* aiding, ancillary, assisting, helpful, subsidiary. * *n* ally, assistant, confederate, help.

avail *vb* assist, benefit, help, profit, use, service.

available *adj* accessible, advantageous, applicable, beneficial, profitable, serviceable, useful.

avarice *n* acquisitiveness, covetousness, greediness, penuriousness, rapacity.

avaricious *adj* grasping, miserly, niggardly, parsimonious.

avenge *vb* punish, retaliate, revenge, vindicate.

avenue *n* access, entrance, entry, passage; alley, path, road, street, walk; channel, pass, route, way.

aver *vb* allege, assert, asseverate, avouch, declare, pronounce, protest, say.

averse *adj* adverse, backward, disinclined, indisposed, opposed, unwilling.

aversion *n* abhorrence, antipathy, disgust, dislike, hate, hatred, loathing, reluctance, repugnance.

avid *adj* eager, greedy, voracious.

avocation *n* business, calling, employment, occupation, trade, vocation; distraction, hindrance, interruption.

avoid *vb* dodge, elude, escape, eschew, shun; forebear, refrain from.

avouch *vb* allege, assert, declare, maintain, say.

avow *vb* admit, acknowledge, confess, own.

awaken *vb* arouse, excite, incite, kindle, provoke, spur, stimulate; wake, waken; begin, be excited.

award *vb* adjudge, allot, assign, bestow, decree, grant. * *n* adjudication, allotment, assignment, decision, decree, determination, gift, judgement.

aware *adj* acquainted, apprised, conscious, conversant, informed, knowing, mindful, sensible.

away *adv* absent, not present. * *adj* at a distance; elsewhere; out of the way.

awe *vb* cow, daunt, intimidate, overawe. * *n* abashment, fear, reverence; dread, fear, fearfulness, terror.

awful *adj* august, awesome, dread, grand, inspired; abashed, alarming, appalled, dire, frightful, portentous, tremendous.

awkward *adj* bungling, clumsy, inept, maladroit, unskilful; lumbering, unfit, ungainly, unmanageable; boorish; inconvenient, unsuitable.

axiom *n* adage, aphorism, apothegm, maxim, postulation, truism.

axis *n* axle, shaft, spindle.

azure *adj* blue, cerulean, sky-coloured.

B

babble *vb* blather, chatter, gibber, jabber, prate, prattle. * *n* chat, gossip, palaver, prate, tattle.

babel *n* clamour, confusion, din, discord, disorder, hubbub, jargon, pother.

baby *vb* coddle, cosset, indulge, mollycoddle, pamper, spoil. * *adj* babyish, childish, infantile, puerile; diminutive, doll-like, miniature, pocket, pocket-sized, small-scale. * *n* babe, brat, child, infant, suckling, nursling; chicken, coward, milksop, namby-pamby, sad sack, weakling; miniature; innocent.

bacchanal *n* carouse, debauchery, drunkenness, revelry, roisterousness.

back *vb* abet, aid, countenance, favour, second, support, sustain; go back, move back, retreat, withdraw. * *adj* hindmost. * *adv* in return, in consideration; ago, gone, since; aside, away, behind, by; abaft, astern, backwards, hindwards, rearwards. * *n* end, hind part, posterior, rear.

backbite *vb* abuse, asperse, blacken, defame, libel, malign, revile, scandalize, slander, traduce, vilify.

backbone *n* chine, spine; constancy, courage, decision, firmness, nerve, pluck, resolution, steadfastness.

backslider *n* apostate, deserter, renegade.

backward *adj* disinclined, hesitating, indisposed, loath, reluctant, unwilling, wavering; dull, slow, sluggish, stolid, stupid. * *adv* aback, behind, rearward.

bad *adj* baleful, baneful, detrimental, evil, harmful, hurtful, injurious, noxious, pernicious, unwholesome, vicious; abandoned, corrupt, depraved, immoral, sinful, unfair, unprincipled, wicked; unfortunate, unhappy, unlucky, miserable; disappointing, discouraging, distressing, sad, unwelcoming; abominable, mean, shabby, scurvy, vile, wretched; defective, inferior, imperfect, incompetent, poor, unsuitable; hard, heavy, serious, severe.

badge *n* brand, emblem, mark, sign, symbol, token.

badger *vb* annoy, bait, bother, hector, harry, pester, persecute, tease, torment, trouble, vex, worry.

baffle *vb* balk, block, check, circumvent, defeat, foil, frustrate, mar, thwart, undermine, upset; bewilder, confound, disconcert, perplex.

bait *vb* harry, tease, worry. * *n* allurement, decoy, enticement, lure, temptation.

balance *vb* equilibrate, pose, (*naut*) trim; compare, weigh; compensate, counteract, estimate; adjust, clear, equalize, square. * *n* equilibrium, liberation; excess, remainder, residue, surplus.

bald *adj* bare, naked, uncovered, treeless; dull, inelegant, meagre, prosaic, tame, unadorned, vapid.

baleful *adj* baneful, deadly, calamitous, hurtful, injurious, mischievous, noxious, pernicious, ruinous.

balk *vb* baffle, defeat, disappoint, disconcert, foil, frustrate, thwart.

ball *n* drop, globe, orb, pellet, marble, sphere; bullet, missile, projectile, shot; assembly, dance.

balmy *adj* aromatic, fragrant, healing, odorous, perfumed.

ban *vb* anathematize, curse, execrate; interdict, outlaw. * *n* edict, proclamation; anathema, curse, denunciation, execration; interdiction, outlawry, penalty, prohibition

band[1] *vb* belt, bind, cinch, encircle, gird, girdle; ally, associate, combine, connect, join, league; bar, marble, streak, stripe, striate, vein. * *n* crew, gang, horde, society, troop; ensemble, group, orchestra.

band[2] *n* ligament, ligature, tie; bond, chain, cord, fetter, manacle, shackle, trammel; bandage, belt, binding, cincture, girth, tourniquet.

bandit *n* brigand, freebooter, footpad, gangster, highwayman, outlaw, robber.

baneful *adj* poisonous, venomous; deadly, destructive, hurtful, mischievous, noxious, pernicious.

bang *vb* beat, knock, maul, pommel, pound, strike, thrash, thump; slam; clatter, rattle, resound, ring. * *n* clang, clangour, whang; blow, knock, lick, thump, thwack, whack.

banish *vb* exile, expatriate, ostracize; dismiss, exclude, expel.

bank[1] *vb* incline, slope, tilt; embank. * *n* dike, embankment, escarpment, heap, knoll, mound; border, bound, brim, brink, margin, rim, strand; course, row, tier.

bank[2] *vb* deposit, keep, save. * *n* depository, fund, reserve, savings, stockpile.

banner *n* colours, ensign, flag, standard, pennon, standard, streamer.

banter *vb* chaff, deride, jeer, joke, mock, quiz, rally, ridicule. * *n* badinage, chaff, derision, jesting, joking, mockery, quizzing, raillery, ridicule.

bar *vb* exclude, hinder, obstruct, prevent, prohibit, restrain, stop. * *n* grating, pole, rail, rod; barricade, hindrance, impediment, obstacle, obstruction, stop; bank, sand bar, shallow, shoal, spit; (*legal*) barristers, counsel, court, judgement, tribunal.

barbarian *adj* brutal, cruel, ferocious, fierce, fell, inhuman, ruthless, savage, truculent, unfeeling. * *n* brute, ruffian, savage.

barbaric *adj* barbarous, rude, savage, uncivilized, untamed; capricious, coarse, gaudy, riotous, showy, outlandish, uncouth, untamed, wild.

bare *vb* denude, depilate, divest, strip, unsheathe; disclose, manifest, open, reveal, show. * *adj* denuded, exposed, naked, nude, stripped, unclothed, uncovered, undressed, unsheltered; alone, mere, sheer, simple; bald, meagre, plain, unadorned, uncovered, unfurnished; empty, destitute, indigent, poor.

bargain *vb* agree, contract, covenant, stipulate; convey, sell, transfer. * *n* agreement, compact, contract, covenant, convention, indenture, transaction, stipulation, treaty; proceeds, purchase, result.

barren *adj* childless, infecund, sterile; (*bot*) acarpous, sterile; bare, infertile, poor, sterile, unproductive; ineffectual, unfruitful, uninstructive.

barricade *vb* block up, fortify, protect, obstruct. * *n* barrier, obstruction, palisade, stockade.

barrier *n* bar, barricade, hindrance, impediment, obstacle, obstruction, stop.

barter *vb* bargain, exchange, sell, trade, traffic.

base[1] *adj* cheap, inferior, worthless; counterfeit, debased, false, spurious; baseborn, humble, lowly, mean, nameless, plebeian, unknown, untitled, vulgar; abject, beggarly, contemptible, degraded, despicable, low, menial, pitiful, servile, sordid, sorry, worthless.

base[2] *vb* establish, found, ground. * *n* foundation, fundament, substructure, underpinning; pedestal, plinth, stand; centre, headquarters, HQ, seat; starting point; basis, cause, grounds, reason, standpoint; bottom, foot, foundation, ground.

bashful *adj* coy, diffident, shy, timid.

basis n base, bottom, foundation, fundament, ground, groundwork.

bastard *adj* adulterated, baseborn, counterfeit, false, illegitimate, sham. * *n* love child.

batch *vb* assemble, bunch, bundle, collect, gather, group. * *n* amount, collection, crowd, lot, quantity.

bathe *vb* immerse, lave, wash; cover, enfold, enwrap, drench, flood, infold, suffuse. * *n* bath, shower, swim.

batter[1] *vb* beat, pelt, smite; break, bruise, demolish, destroy, shatter, shiver, smash; abrade, deface, disfigure, indent, mar; incline, recede, retreat, slope. * *n* batsman, striker.

batter[2] *n* dough, goo, goop, gunk, paste, pulp.

battle *vb* contend, contest, engage, fight, strive, struggle. * *n* action, affair, brush, combat, conflict, contest, engagement, fight, fray.

bauble *n* gewgaw, gimcrack, knick-knack, plaything, toy, trifle, trinket.

bawdy *adj* obscene, filthy, impure, indecent, lascivious, lewd, smutty, unchaste.

bawl *vb* clamour, cry, hoot, howl, roar, shout, squall, vociferate, yell.

bay[1] *vb* bark, howl, wail, yell, yelp.

bay[2] *n* alcove, compartment, niche, nook, opening, recess.

bay[3] *n* bight, cove, gulf, inlet.

bays *npl* applause, chaplet, fame, garland, glory, honour, plaudits, praise, renown.

beach *vb* ground, maroon, strand. * *n* coast, margin, rim, sands, seashore, seaside, shore, shoreline, strand, waterfront.

beacon *vb* brighten, flame, shine, signal; enlighten, illuminate, illumine, guide, light, signal. * *n* lighthouse, pharos, watchtower; sign, signal.

beadle *n* apparitor, church officer, crier, servitor, summoner.

beak *n* bill, mandible, (*sl*) nose; (*naut*) bow, prow, stem.

beam *vb* beacon, gleam, glisten, glitter, shine. * *n* balk, girder, joist, scantling, stud; gleam, pencil, ray, streak.

bear *vb* support, sustain, uphold; carry, convey, deport, transport, waft; abide, brook, endure, stand, suffer, tolerate, undergo; carry on, keep up, maintain; cherish, entertain, harbour; produce; cast, drop, sustain; endure, submit, suffer; act, operate, work. * *n* growler, grumbler, moaner, snarler; speculator.

bearable *adj* endurable, sufferable, supportable, tolerable.

bearing *n* air, behaviour, demeanour, deportment, conduct, carriage, conduct, mien, port; connection, dependency, relation; endurance, patience, suffering; aim, course, direction; bringing forth, producing; bed, receptacle, socket.

beastly *adj* abominable, brutish, ignoble, low, sensual, vile.

beat *vb* bang, baste, belabour, buffet, cane, cudgel, drub, hammer, hit, knock, maul, pound, pummel, punch, strike, thrash, thump, thwack, whack, whip; bray, bruise, pound, pulverize; batter, pelt; conquer, defeat, overcome, rout, subdue, surpass, vanquish; pulsate, throb; dash, strike. * *adj* baffled, bamboozled, confounded, mystified, nonplused, perplexed, puzzled, stumped; done, dog-tired, exhausted, tired out, worn out; beaten, defeated, licked, worsted. * *n* blow, striking, stroke; beating, pulsation, throb; accent, metre, rhythm; circuit, course, round.

beatific *adj* ecstatic, enchanting, enraptured, ravishing, rapt.

beatitude *n* blessing, ecstasy, felicity, happiness.

beau *n* coxcomb, dandy, exquisite, fop, popinjay; admirer, lover, suitor, sweetheart.

beautiful *adj* charming, comely, fair, fine, exquisite, handsome, lovely, pretty.

beautify *vb* adorn, array, bedeck, deck, decorate, embellish, emblazon, garnish, gild, grace, ornament, set.

beauty *n* elegance, grace, symmetry; attractiveness, comeliness, fairness, loveliness, seemliness; belle.

become *vb* change to, get, go, wax; adorn, befit, set off, suit.

becoming *adj* appropriate, apt, congruous, decent, decorous, due, fit, proper, right, seemly, suitable; comely, graceful, neat, pretty.

bed *vb* embed, establish, imbed, implant, infix, inset, plant; harbour, house, lodge. * *n* berth, bunk, cot, couch; channel, depression, hollow; base, foundation, receptacle, support, underlay; accumulation, layer, seam, stratum, vein.

bedim *vb* cloud, darken, dim, obscure.

befall *vb* betide, overtake; chance, happen, occur, supervene.

befitting *adj* appropriate, apt, becoming, decorous, fit, proper, right, suitable, seemly.

befool *vb* bamboozle, beguile, cheat, circumvent, delude, deceive, dupe, fool, hoax, hoodwink, infatuate, stupefy, trick.

befriend *vb* aid, benefit, countenance, encourage, favour, help, patronize.

beg *vb* adjure, ask, beseech, conjure, crave, entreat, implore, importune, petition, pray, request, solicit, supplicate.

beggarly *adj* destitute, needy, poor; abject, base, despicable, grovelling, low, mean, miserable, miserly, paltry, pitiful, scant, servile, shabby, sorry, stingy, vile, wretched.

begin *vb* arise, commence, enter, open; inaugurate, institute, originate, start.

beginning *n* arising, commencement, dawn, emergence, inauguration, inception, initiation, opening, outset, start, rise; origin, source.

beguile *vb* cheat, deceive, delude; amuse, cheer, divert, entertain, solace.

behaviour *n* air, bearing, carriage, comportment, conduct, demeanour, deportment, manner, manners, mien.

behest *n* bidding, charge, command, commandment,

direction, hest, injunction, mandate, order, precept.

behind *prep* abaft, after, following. * *adv* abaft, aft, astern, rearward. * *adj* arrested, backward, checked, detained, retarded; after, behind. * *n* afterpart, rear, stern, tail; back, back side, reverse; bottom, buttocks, posterior, rump.

behold *vb* consider, contemplate, eye, observe, regard, see, survey, view.

behoove *vb* become, befit, suit; be binding, be obligatory.

being *n* actuality, existence, reality, subsistence; core, essence, heart, root.

beleaguer *vb* besiege, blockade, invest; beset, block, encumber, encompass, encounter, obstruct, surround.

belief *n* assurance, confidence, conviction, persuasion, trust; acceptance, assent, credence, credit, currency; creed, doctrine, dogma, faith, opinion, tenet.

bellow *vb* bawl, clamour, cry, howl, vociferate, yell.

belt *n* band, cincture, girdle, girth, zone; region, stretch, strip.

bemoan *vb* bewail, deplore, lament, mourn.

bemused *adj* bewildered, confused, fuddled, muddled, muzzy, stupefied, tipsy.

bend *vb* bow, crook, curve, deflect, draw; direct, incline, turn; bend, dispose, influence, mould, persuade, subdue; (*naut*) fasten, make fast; crook, deflect, deviate, diverge, swerve; bow, lower, stoop; condescend, deign. * *n* angle, arc, arcuation, crook, curvature, curve, elbow, flexure, turn.

beneath *prep* below, under, underneath; unbecoming, unbefitting, unworthy. * *adv* below, underneath.

benediction *n* beatitude, benefit, benison, blessing, boon, grace, favour.

benefaction *n* alms, boon, charity, contribution, donation, favour, gift, grant, gratuity, offering, present.

beneficent *adj* benevolent, bounteous, bountiful, charitable, generous, kind, liberal.

beneficial *adj* advantageous, favourable, helpful, profitable, salutary, serviceable, useful, wholesome.

benefit *vb* befriend, help, serve; advantage, avail, profit. * *n* favour, good turn, kindness, service; account, advantage, behalf, gain, good, interest, profit, utility.

benevolence *n* beneficence, benignity, generosity, goodwill, humanity, kindliness, kindness.

benevolent *adj* altruistic, benign, charitable, generous, humane, kind, kind-hearted, liberal, obliging, philanthropic, tender, unselfish.

benign *adj* amiable, amicable, beneficent, benevolent, complaisant, friendly, gentle, good, gracious, humane, kind, kindly, obliging.

bent *adj* angled, angular, bowed, crooked, curved, deflected, embowed, flexed, hooked, twisted; disposed, inclined, prone, minded; (*with* **on**) determined, fixed on, resolved, set on. * *n* bias, inclination, leaning, partiality, penchant, predilection, prepossession, proclivity, propensity

bequeath *vb* devise, give, grant, leave, will; impart, transmit.

berate *vb* chide, rate, reprimand, reprove, scold.

bereave *vb* afflict, deprive of, despoil, dispossess, divest, rob, spoil, strip.

beseech *vb* beg, conjure, entreat, implore, importune, petition, supplicate; ask, beg, crave, solicit.

beset *vb* besiege, encompass, enclose, environ, encircle, hem in, surround; decorate, embarrass, embellish, entangle, garnish, ornament, perplex, set.

beside[1] *prep* at the side of, by the side of, close to, near; aside from, not according to, out of the course of, out of the way of; not in possession of, out of.

besides[1] *prep* barring, distinct from, excluding, except, excepting, in addition to, other than, over and above, save.

beside[2], **besides**[2] *adv* additionally, also, further, furthermore, in addition, more, moreover, over and above, too, yet.

besiege *vb* beset, blockade, encircle, encompass, environ, invest, surround.

besot *vb* drench, intoxicate, soak, steep; befool, delude, infatuate, stultify, stupefy.

bespatter *vb* bedaub, befoul, besmirch, smear, spatter.

bespeak *vb* accost, address, declare, evince, forestall, imply, indicate, prearrange, predict, proclaim, solicit.

best *vb* better, exceed, excel, predominate, rival, surpass; beat, defeat, outdo, worst. * *adj* chief, first, foremost, highest, leading, utmost. * *adv* advantageously, excellently; extremely, greatly. * *n* choice, cream, flower, pick.

bestial *adj* beast-like, beastly, brutal, degraded, depraved, irrational, low, vile; sensual.

bestow *vb* deposit, dispose, put, place, store, stow; accord, give, grant, impart.

bet *vb* gamble, hazard, lay, pledge, stake, wage, wager. * *n* gamble, hazard, stake, wager.

bethink *vb* cogitate, consider, ponder, recall, recollect, reflect, remember.

betide *vb* befall, happen, occur, overtake.

betimes *adv* beforehand, early, forward, soon.

betoken *vb* argue, betray, denote, evince, imply, indicate, prove, represent, show, signify, typify.

betray *vb* be false to, break, violate; blab, discover, divulge, expose, reveal, show, tell; argue, betoken, display, evince, expose, exhibit, imply, indicate, manifest, reveal; beguile, delude, ensnare, lure, mislead; corrupt, ruin, seduce, undo.

betroth *vb* affiance, engage to marry, pledge in marriage, plight.

better *vb* advance, amend, correct, exceed, improve, promote, rectify, reform. * *adj* bigger, fitter, greater, larger, less ill, preferable. * *n* advantage, superiority, upper hand, victory; improvement, greater good.

between *prep* amidst, among, betwixt.

bewail *vb* bemoan, deplore, express, lament, mourn over, rue, sorrow.

beware *vb* avoid, heed, look out, mind.

bewilder *vb* confound, confuse, daze, distract, embarrass, entangle, muddle, mystify, nonplus, perplex, pose, puzzle, stagger.

bewitch *vb* captivate, charm, enchant, enrapture, entrance, fascinate, spellbind, transport.

beyond *prep* above, before, farther, over, past, remote, yonder.

bias *vb* bend, dispose, incline, influence, predispose, prejudice. * *n* bent, inclination, leaning, partiality, penchant, predilection, prepossession, proclivity, propensity, slant, tendency, turn.

bicker *vb* argue, dispute, jangle, quarrel, spar, spat, squabble, wrangle.

bid *vb* charge, command, direct, enjoin, order, require, summon; ask, call, invite, pray, request, solicit; offer, propose, proffer, tender. * *n* bidding, offer, proposal.

big *adj* bumper, bulking, bulky, great, huge, large, massive, monstrous; important, imposing; distended, inflated, full, swollen, tumid; fecund, fruitful, productive, teeming.

bigoted *adj* dogmatic, hidebound, intolerant, obstinate, narrow-minded, opinionated, prejudiced.

bill[1] *vb* charge, dun, invoice; programme, schedule; advertise, boost, plug, promote, publicize. * *n* account, charges, reckoning, score; advertisement, banner, hoarding, placard, poster; playbill, programme, schedule; bill of exchange, certificate, money; account, reckoning, statement.

bill[2] *n* beak, mandible, (*sl*) nose; billhook, brush-cutter, hedge-bill, hedging knife; caress, fondle, kiss, toy.

billet *vb* allot, apportion, assign, distribute, quarter, station. * *n* accommodation, lodgings, quarters.

billow *vb* surge, wave; heave, roll; bag, baloon, bulge, dilate, swell. * *n* roller, surge, swell, wave.

bin *n* box, bunker, crib, frame, receptacle.

bind *vb* confine, enchain, fetter, restrain, restrict; bandage, tie up, wrap; fasten, lash, pinion, secure, tie, truss; engage, hold, oblige, obligate, pledge; contract, harden, shrink, stiffen.

birth *n* ancestry, blood, descent, extraction, lineage, race; being, creation, creature, offspring, production, progeny.

bit *n* crumb, fragment, morsel, mouthful, piece, scrap; atom, grain, jot, mite, particle, tittle, whit; instant, minute, moment, second.

bite *vb* champ, chew, crunch, gnaw; burn, make smart, sting; catch, clutch, grapple, grasp, grip; bamboozle, cheat, cozen, deceive, defraud, dupe, gull, mislead, outwit, overreach, trick. * *n* grasp, hold; punch, relish, spice, pungency, tang, zest; lick, morsel, sip, taste; crick, nip, pain, pang, prick, sting.

bitter *adj* acrid; dire, fell, merciless, relentless, ruthless; harsh, severe, stern; afflictive, calamitous, distressing, galling, grievous, painful, poignant, sore, sorrowful.

black *adj* dark, ebony, inky, jet, sable, swarthy; dingy, dusky, lowering, murky, pitchy; calamitous, dark, depressing, disastrous, dismal, doleful, forbidding, gloomy, melancholy, mournful, sombre, sullen.

blacken *vb* darken; deface, defile, soil, stain, sully; asperse, besmirch, calumniate, defame, malign, revile, slander, traduce, vilify.

blamable *adj* blameable, blameworthy, censurable, culpable, delinquent. faulty, remiss, reprehensible.

blame *vb* accuse, censure, condemn, disapprove, reflect upon, reprehend, reproach, reprove, upbraid. * *n* animadversion, censure, condemnation, disapproval, dispraise, disapprobation, reprehension, reproach, reproof; defect, demerit, fault, guilt, misdeed, shortcoming, sin, wrong.

blameless *adj* faultless, guiltless, inculpable, innocent, irreproachable, unblemished, undefiled, unimpeachable, unspotted, unsullied, spotless, stainless.

blanch *vb* bleach, fade, etiolate, whiten.

bland *adj* balmy, demulcent, gentle, mild, soothing, soft; affable, amiable, complaisant, kindly, mild, suave.

blandishment *n* cajolery, coaxing, compliment, fascination, fawning, flattery, wheedling

blank *adj* bare, empty, vacuous, void; amazed, astonished, confounded, confused, dumbfounded, nonplussed; absolute, complete, entire, mere, perfect, pure, simple, unabated, unadulterated, unmitigated, unmixed, utter, perfect.

blare *vb* blazon, blow, peal, proclaim, trumpet. * *n* blast, clang, clangour, peal.

blasphemy *n* impiousness, sacrilege; cursing, profanity, swearing.

blast *vb* annihilate, blight, destroy, kill, ruin, shrivel, wither; burst, explode, kill. * *n* blow, gust, squall; blare, clang, peal; burst, discharge, explosion.

blaze *vb* blazon, proclaim, publish; burn, flame, glow. * *n* flame, flare, flash, glow, light.

bleach *vb* blanch, etiolate, render white, whiten.

bleak *adj* bare, exposed, unprotected, unsheltered, storm-beaten, windswept; biting, chill, cold, piercing, raw; cheerless, comfortless, desolate, dreary, uncongenial,

blemish *vb* blur, injure, mar, spot, stain, sully, taint, tarnish; asperse, calumniate, defame, malign, revile, slander, traduce, vilify. * *n* blot, blur, defect, disfigurement, fault, flaw, imperfection, soil, speck, spot, stain, tarnish; disgrace, dishonour, reproach, stain, taint.

blend *vb* amalgamate, coalesce, combine, commingle, fuse, mingle, mix, unite. * *n* amalgamation, combination, compound, fusion, mix, mixture, union.

bless *vb* beatify, delight, gladden; adore, celebrate, exalt, extol, glorify, magnify, praise.

blessedness *n* beatitude, bliss, blissfulness, felicity, happiness, joy.

blight *vb* blast, destroy, kill, ruin, shrivel, wither; annihilate, annul, crush, disappoint, frustrate. * *n* blast, mildew, pestilence.

blind *vb* blear, darken, deprive of sight; blindfold, hoodwink. * *adj* eyeless, sightless, stone-blind, unseeing; benighted, ignorant, injudicious, purblind, undiscerning, unenlightened; concealed, confused, dark, dim, hidden, intricate, involved, labyrinthine, obscure, private, remote; careless, headlong, heedless, inconsiderate, indiscriminate, thoughtless; blank, closed, shut. * *n* cover, curtain, screen, shade, shutter; blinker; concealment, disguise, feint, pretence, pretext, ruse, stratagem, subterfuge.

blink *vb* nictate, nictitate, wink; flicker, flutter, gleam, glitter, intermit, twinkle; avoid, disregard, evade, gloss over, ignore, overlook, pass over. * *n* glance, glimpse, sight, view, wink; gleam, glimmer, sheen, shimmer, twinkle.

bliss *n* beatification, beatitude, blessedness, blissfulness, ecstasy, felicity, happiness, heaven, joy, rapture, transport.

blithe *adj* airy, animated, blithesome, buoyant, cheerful, debonair, elated, happy, jocund, joyful, joyous, lively, mirthful, sprightly, vivacious.

bloat *vb* dilate, distend, inflate, swell.

block *vb* arrest, bar, blockade, check, choke, close, hinder, impede, jam, obstruct, stop; form, mould, shape; brace, stiffen. * *n* lump, mass; blockhead, dunce, fool, simpleton; pulley, tackle; execution, scaffold; jam, obstruction, pack, stoppage.

blood *n* children, descendants, offspring, posterity, progeny; family, house, kin, kindred, line, relations; consanguinity, descent, kinship, lineage, relationship; courage, disposition, feelings, mettle, passion, spirit, temper.

bloom *vb* blossom, blow, flower; thrive, prosper. * *n* blossom, blossoming, blow, efflorescence, florescence, flowering; delicacy, delicateness, flush, freshness, heyday, prime, vigour; flush, glow, rose.

blossom *vb* bloom, blow, flower. * *n* bloom, blow, efflorescence, flower.

blot *vb* cancel, efface, erase, expunge, obliterate, rub out; blur, deface, disfigure, obscure, spot, stain, sully; disgrace, dishonour, tarnish. * *n* blemish, blur, erasure, spot, obliteration, stain; disgrace, dishonour, stigma.

blow¹ *n* bang, beat, buffet, dab, impact, knock, pat, punch, rap, slam, stroke, thump, wallop, buffet, impact; affliction, calamity, disaster, misfortune, setback.

blow² *vb* breathe, gasp, pant, puff; flow, move, scud, stream, waft. * *n* blast, gale, gust, squall, storm, wind.

blue *adj* azure, cerulean, cobalt, indigo, sapphire, ultramarine; ghastly, livid, pallid; dejected, depressed, dispirited, downcast, gloomy, glum, mopey, melancholic, melancholy, sad.

bluff¹ *adj* abrupt, blunt, blustering, coarse, frank, good-natured, open, outspoken; abrupt, precipitous, sheer, steep. * *n* cliff, headland, height.

bluff² *vb* deceive, defraud, lie, mislead. * *n* deceit, deception, feint, fraud, lie.

blunder *vb* err, flounder, mistake: stumble. * *n* error, fault, howler, mistake, solecism.

blunt *adj* dull, edgeless, obtuse, pointless, unsharpened; insensible, stolid, thick-witted; abrupt, bluff, downright, plain-spoken, outspoken, unceremonious, uncourtly. * *vb* deaden, dull, numb, weaken.

blur *vb* bedim, darken, dim, obscure; blemish, blot, spot, stain, sully, tarnish. * *n* blemish, blot, soil, spot, stain, tarnish; disgrace, smear.

blush *vb* colour, flush, glow, redden. * *n* bloom, flush, glow, colour, reddening, suffusion.

bluster *vb* boast, brag, bully, domineer, roar, swagger, swell, vaunt. * *n* boisterousness, noise, tumult, turbulence; braggadocio, bravado, boasting, gasconade, swaggering.

board *n* deal, panel, plank; diet, entertainment, fare, food, meals, provision, victuals; cabinet, conclave, committee, council; directorate; panel.

boast *vb* bluster, brag, crack, flourish, crow, vaunt. * *n* blustering, boasting, bombast, brag, braggadocio, bravado, bombast, swaggering, vaunt.

bode *vb* augur, betoken, forebode, foreshadow, foretell, portend, predict, prefigure, presage, prophesy.

bodily *adj* carnal, corporeal, fleshly, physical. * *adv* altogether, completely, entirely, wholly.

body *n* carcass, corpse, remains; stem, torso, trunk; aggregate, bulk, corpus, mass; being, individual, mortal creature, person; assemblage, association, band, company, corporation, corps, coterie, force, party, society, troop; consistency, substance, thickness.

boggle *vb* demur, falter, hang fire, hesitate, shrink, vacillate, waver.

boil¹ *vb* agitate, bubble, foam, froth, rage, seethe, simmer. * *n* ebullience, ebullition.

boil² (*med*) gathering, pimple, pustule, swelling, tumour.

boisterous *adj* loud, roaring, stormy; clamouring, loud, noisy, obstreperous, tumultuous, turbulent.

bold *adj* adventurous, audacious, courageous; brave, daring, dauntless, doughty, fearless, gallant, hardy, heroic, intrepid, mettlesome, manful, manly, spirited, stouthearted, undaunted, valiant, valorous; assured, confident, self-reliant; assuming, forward, impertinent, impudent, insolent, push, rude, saucy; conspicuous, projecting, prominent, striking; abrupt, precipitous, prominent, steep.

bolster *vb* aid, assist, defend, help, maintain, prop, stay, support. * *n* cushion, pillow; prop, support.

bolt *vb* abscond, flee, fly. * *n* arrow, dart, missile, shaft; thunderbolt.

bombast *n* bluster, brag, braggadocio, fustian, gasconade, mouthing, pomposity, rant.

bond *vb* bind, connect, fuse, glue, join. * *adj* captive, enslaved, enthralled, subjugated. * *n* band, cord, fastening, ligament, ligature, link, nexus; bondage, captivity, chains, constraint, fetters, prison, shackle; attachment, attraction, connection, coupling, link, tie, union; compact, obligation, pledge, promise.

bondage *n* captivity, confinement, enslavement, enthralment, peonage, serfdom, servitude, slavery, thraldom, vassalage.

bonny *adj* beautiful, handsome, fair, fine, pretty; airy, blithe, buoyant, buxom, cheerful, jolly, joyous, merry. playful, sporty, sprightly, winsome.

bonus *n* gift, honorarium, premium, reward, subsidy.

booby *n* blockhead, dunce, fool, idiot, simpleton.

book *vb* bespeak, engage, reserve; programme, schedule; list, log, record, register. * *n* booklet, brochure, compendium, handbook, manual, monograph, pamphlet, textbook, tract, treatise, volume, work.

bookish *adj* erudite, learned, literary, scholarly, studious.

boon *adj* convivial, jolly, jovial, hearty; close, intimate. * *n* benefaction, favour, grant, gift, present; advantage, benefit, blessing, good, privilege.

boor *n* bumpkin, clodhopper, clown, lout, lubber, peasant, rustic, swain.

boorish *adj* awkward, bearish, clownish, course, gruff, ill-bred, loutish, lubberly, rude, rustic, uncivilized, uncouth, uneducated.

bootless *adj* abortive, fruitless, futile, profitless, vain, worthless, useless.

booty *n* loot, pillage, plunder, spoil.

border *vb* bound, edge, fringe, line, march, rim, skirt, verge; abut, adjoin, butt, conjoin, connect, neighbour. * *n* brim, brink, edge, fringe, hem, margin, rim, skirt, verge; boundary, confine, frontier, limit, march, outskirts.

bore¹ *vb* annoy, fatigue, plague, tire, trouble, vex, weary, worry. * *n* bother, nuisance, pest, worry.

bore² *vb* drill, perforate, pierce, sink, tunnel. * *n* calibre, hole, shaft, tunnel.

borrow *vb* take and return, use temporarily; adopt, appropriate, imitate; dissemble, feign, simulate.

boss¹ *vb* emboss, stud; * *n* knob, protuberance, stud.

boss² *vb* command, direct, employ, run. * *n* employer, foreman, master, overseer, superintendent.

botch *vb* blunder, bungle, cobble, mar, mend, mess, patch, spoil. * *n* blotch, pustule, sore; failure, miscarriage.

bother *vb* annoy, disturb, harass, molest, perplex, pester, plague, tease, trouble, vex, worry. * *n* annoyance, perplexity, plague, trouble, vexation.

bottom *vb* build, establish, found. * *adj* base, basic, ground, lowermost, lowest, nethermost, undermost. * *n* base, basis, foot, foundation, groundwork; dale, meadow, valley; buttocks, fundament, seat; dregs, grounds, lees, sediment.

bounce *vb* bound, jump, leap, rebound, recoil, spring. * *n* knock, thump; bound, jump, leap, spring, vault.

bound¹ *adj* assured, certain, decided, determined, resolute, resolved; confined, hampered, restricted, restrained; committed, contracted, engaged, pledged, promised; beholden, duty-bound, obligated, obliged.

bound² *vb* border, delimit, circumscribe, confine, demarcate, limit, restrict, terminate. * *n* boundary, confine, edge, limit, march, margin, periphery, term, verge.

bound³ *vb* jump, leap, spring. * *n* bounce, jump, leap, spring, vault.

boundary *n* border, bourn, circuit, circumference, confine, limit, march, periphery, term, verge.

boundless *adj* endless, immeasurable, infinite, limitless, unbounded, unconfined, undefined, unlimited, vast.

bountiful *adj* beneficent, bounteous, generous, liberal, munificent, princely.

bounty *n* beneficence, benevolence, charity, donation, generosity, gift, kindness, premium, present, reward.

bourn *n* border, boundary, confine, limit; brook, burn, rill, rivulet, stream, torrent.

bow¹ *n* (*naut*) beak, prow, stem.

bow² *vb* arc, bend, buckle, crook, curve, droop, flex, yield; crush, depress, subdue; curtsy, genuflect, kowtow, submit. * *n* arc, bend, bilge, bulge, convex, curve, flexion; bob, curtsy, genuflection, greeting, homage, obeisance; coming out, debut, introduction; curtain call, encore.

bowels *npl* entrails, guts, insides, viscera; compassion, mercy, pity, sympathy, tenderness.

box¹ *vb* fight, hit, mill, spar. * *n* blow, buffet, fight, hit, spar.

box² *vb* barrel, crate, pack, parcel. * *n* case, chest, container, crate, portmanteau, trunk.

boy *n* lad, stripling, youth.

brace *vb* make tight, tighten; buttress, fortify, reinforce, shore, strengthen, support, truss. * *n* couple, pair; clamp, girder, prop, shore, stay, support, tie, truss.

brag *vb* bluster, boast, flourish, gasconade, vaunt.

branch *vb* diverge, fork, bifurcate, ramify, spread. * *n* bough, offset, limb, shoot, sprig, twig; arm, fork, ramification, spur; article, department, member, part, portion, section, subdivision.

brand *vb* denounce, stigmatize, mark. * *n* firebrand, torch; bolt, lightning flash; cachet, mark, stamp, tally; blot, reproach, stain, stigma.

brave *vb* dare, defy. * *adj* bold, courageous, fearless, heroic, intrepid, stalwart.

bravery *n* courage, daring, fearlessness, gallantry, valour.

brawl *vb* bicker, dispute, jangle, quarrel, squabble. * *n* broil, dispute, feud, fracas, fray, jangle, quarrel, row, scuffle, squabble, uproar, wrangle.

brawny *adj* athletic, lusty, muscular, powerful, robust, sinewy, stalwart, strapping, strong, sturdy.

bray *vb* clamour, hoot, roar, trumpet, vociferate. * *n* blare, crash, roar, shout.

breach *n* break, chasm, crack, disruption, fissure, flaw, fracture, opening, rent, rift, rupture; alienation, difference, disaffection, disagreement, split.

bread *n* aliment, diet, fare, food, nourishment, nutriment, provisions, regimen, victuals.

break *vb* crack, disrupt, fracture, part, rend, rive, sever; batter, burst, crush, shatter, smash, splinter; cashier, degrade, discard, discharge, dismiss; disobey, infringe, transgress, violate; intermit, interrupt, stop; disclose, open, unfold. * *n* aperture, breach, chasm, fissure, gap, rent, rip, rupture; break-up, crash, debacle.

breast *vb* face, oppose, resist, stem, withstand. * *n* bosom, chest, thorax; affections, conscience, heart; mammary gland, mammary organ, pap, udder.

breath *n* exhaling, inhaling, pant, sigh, respiration, whiff; animation, existence, life; pause, respite, rest; breathing space, instant, moment.

breathe *vb* live, exist; emit, exhale, give out; diffuse, express, indicate, manifest, show.

breed *vb* bear, beget, engender, hatch, produce; bring up, foster, nourish, nurture, raise, rear; discipline, educate, instruct, nurture, rear, school, teach, train; generate, originate. * *n* extraction, family, lineage, pedigree, progeny, race, strain.

brevity *n* briefness, compression, conciseness, curtness, pithiness, shortness, terseness, transiency.

brew *vb* concoct, contrive, devise, excite, foment, instigate, plot. * *n* beverage, concoction, drink, liquor, mixture, potation.

bribe *vb* buy, corrupt, influence, pay off, suborn. * *n* allurement, corruption, enticement, graft, pay-off, subornation.

bridle *vb* check, curb, control, govern, restrain. * *n* check, control, curb.

brief *vb* direct, give directions, instruct; capsulate, summarize, delineate, describe, draft, outline, sketch; (*law*) retain. * *adj* concise, curt, inconsiderable, laconic, pithy, short, succinct, terse; fleeting, momentary, short, temporary, transient. * *n* abstract, breviary, briefing, epitome, compendium, summary, syllabus; (*law*) precept, writ.

brigand *n* bandit, footpad, freebooter, gangster, highwayman, marauder, outlaw, robber, thug.

bright *adj* blazing, brilliant, dazzling, gleaming, glowing, light, luminous, radiant, shining, sparkling, sunny; clear, cloudless, lambent, lucid, transparent; famous, glorious, illustrious; acute, discerning, ingenious, intelligent, keen; auspicious, cheering, encouraging, exhilarating, favourable, inspiring, promising, propitious; cheerful, genial, happy, lively, merry, pleasant, smiling, vivacious.

brilliant *adj* beaming, bright, effulgent, gleaming, glistening, glittering, lustrous, radiant, resplendent, shining, sparkling splendid; admirable, celebrated, distinguished, famous, glorious, illustrious, renowned; dazzling, decided, prominent, signal, striking, unusual.

brim *n* border, brink, edge, rim, margin, skirt, verge; bank, border, coast, margin, shore.

bring *vb* bear, convey, fetch; accompany, attend, conduct, convey, convoy, guide, lead; gain, get, obtain, procure, produce.

brisk *adj* active, alert, agile, lively, nimble, perky, quick, smart, spirited, spry.

brittle *adj* brash, breakable, crisp, crumbling, fragile, frangible, frail, shivery.

broach *vb* open, pierce, set; approach, break, hint, suggest; proclaim, publish, utter.

broad *adj* ample, expansive, extensive, large, spacious, sweeping, vast, wide; enlarged, hospitable, liberal, tolerant; diffused, open, spread; coarse, gross, indecent, indelicate, unrefined, vulgar.

broaden *vb* augment, enlarge, expand, extend, increase, spread, stretch, widen.

broken *adj* fractured, rent, ruptured, separated, severed, shattered, shivered, torn; exhausted, feeble, impaired, shaken, shattered, spent, wasted; defective, halting, hesitating, imperfect, stammering, stumbling; contrite, humble, lowly, penitent; abrupt, craggy, precipitous, rough.

broker *n* agent, factor, go-between, middleman.

brood *vb* incubate, sit. * *n* issue, offspring, progeny; breed, kind, line, lineage, sort, strain.

brook *vb* abide, bear, endure, suffer, tolerate. * *n* burn, beck, creek, rill, rivulet, run, streamlet.

brotherhood *n* association, clan, clique, coterie, fraternity, junta, society.

brotherly *adj* affectionate, amicable, cordial, friendly, kind.

browbeat *vb* bully, intimidate, overawe, overbear.

bruise *vb* contuse, crunch, squeeze; batter, break, maul, pound, pulverize; batter, deface, indent. * *n* blemish, contusion, swelling.

brush[1] *n* brushwood, bush, scrub, scrubwood, shrubs, thicket, wilderness.

brush[2] *vb* buff, clean, polish, swab, sweep, wipe; curry, groom, rub down; caress, flick, glance, graze, scrape, skim, touch. * *n* besom, broom; action, affair, collision, contest, conflict, encounter, engagement, fight, skirmish.

brutal *adj* barbaric, barbarous, brutish, cruel, ferocious, inhuman, ruthless, savage; bearish, brusque, churlish, gruff, impolite, harsh, rude, rough, truculent, uncivil.

brute *n* barbarian, beast, monster, ogre, savage; animal, beast, creature. * *adj* carnal, mindless, physical; bestial, coarse, gross.

bubble *vb* boil, effervesce, foam. * *n* bead, blob, fluid, globule; bagatelle, trifle; cheat, delusion, hoax.

buccaneer *n* corsair, freebooter, pirate.

buck *vb* jump, leap. * *n* beau, blade, blood, dandy, fop, gallant, spark; male.

bud *vb* burgeon, germinate, push, shoot, sprout, vegetate. * *n* burgeon, gem, germ, gemmule, shoot, sprout.

budget *vb* allocate, cost, estimate. * *n* account, estimate, financial statement; assets, finances, funds, means, resources; bag, bundle, pack, packet, parcel, roll; assortment, batch, collection, lot, set, store.

buffet[1] *vb* beat, box, cuff, slap, smite, strike; resist, struggle against, * *n* blow, box, cuff, slap, strike;

buffet[2] *n* cupboard, sideboard; refreshment counter.

buffoon *n* antic, clown, droll, fool, harlequin, jester, mountebank.

build *vb* construct, erect, establish, fabricate, fashion, model, raise, rear. * *n* body, figure, form, frame, physique; construction, shape, structure.

building *n* construction, erection, fabrication; edifice, fabric, house, pile, substructure, structure,

bulk *n* dimension, magnitude, mass, size, volume; amplitude, bulkiness, massiveness; body, majority, mass.

bully *vb* browbeat, bulldoze, domineer, haze, hector, intimidate, overbear. * *n* blusterer, browbeater, bulldozer, hector, swaggerer, roisterer, tyrant.

bulwark *n* barrier, fortification, parapet, rampart, wall; palladium, safeguard, security.

bump *vb* collide, knock, strike, thump. * *n* blow, jar, jolt, knock, shock, thump; lump, protuberance, swelling.

bunch *vb* assemble, collect, crowd, group, herd, pack. * *n* bulge, bump, bundle, hump, knob, lump, protuberance; cluster, hand, fascicle; assortment, batch, collection, group, lot, parcel, set; knot, tuft.

bundle *vb* bale, pack, package, parcel, truss, wrap. * *n* bale, batch, bunch, collection, heap, pack, package, packet, parcel, pile, roll, truss.

bungler *n* botcher, duffer, fumbler, lout, lubber, mismanager, muddler.

burden *vb* encumber, grieve, load, oppress, overlay, overload, saddle, surcharge, try. * *n* capacity, cargo, freight, lading, load, tonnage, weight; affliction, charge, clog, encumbrance, impediment, grievance, sorrow, trial, trouble; drift, point, substance, tenor, surcharge.

bureau *n* chest of drawers, dresser; counting room, office.

burial *n* burying, entombment, inhumation, interment, sepulture.

burlesque *vb* ape, imitate, lampoon, mock, ridicule, satirize. * *n* caricature, extravaganza, parody, send-up, take-off, travesty.

burn[1] *n* beck, brook, gill, rill, rivulet, runnel, runlet, stream. water

burn[2] *vb* blaze, conflagrate, enflame, fire, flame, ignite, kindle, light, smoulder; cremate, incinerate; scald, scorch, singe; boil, broil, cook, roast, seethe, simmer, stew, swelter, toast; bronze, brown, sunburn, suntan, tan; bake, desiccate, dry, parch, sear, shrivel, wither; glow, incandesce, tingle, warm. * *n* scald, scorch, singe; sunburn.

burning *adj* aflame, fiery, hot, scorching; ardent, earnest, fervent, fervid, impassioned, intense.

burnish *vb* brighten, buff, furbish, polish, shine. * *n* glaze, gloss, patina, polish, shine.

burst *vb* break open, be rent, explode, shatter, split open. * *adj* broken, kaput, punctured, ruptured, shattered, split. * *n* break, breakage, breach, fracture, rupture; blast, blowout, blowup, discharge, detonation, explosion; spurt; blaze, flare, flash; cloudburst, downpour; bang, crack, crash, report, sound; fusillade, salvo, spray, volley, outburst, outbreak flare-up, blaze, eruption.

bury *vb* entomb, inearth, inhume, inter; conceal, hide, secrete, shroud.

business *n* calling, employment, occupation, profession, pursuit, vocation; commerce, dealing, trade, traffic; affair, concern, engagement, matter, transaction, undertaking; duty, function, office, task, work.

bustle *vb* fuss, hurry, scurry. * *n* ado, commotion, flurry, fuss, hurry, hustle, pother, stir, tumult.

busy *vb* devote, employ, engage, occupy, spend, work. * *adj* employed, engaged, occupied; active, assiduous, diligent, engrossed, industrious, sedulous, working; agile, brisk, nimble, spry, stirring; meddling, officious.

but *conj* except, excepting, further, howbeit, moreover, still, unless, yet. * *adv* all the same, even, notwithstanding, still, yet.

butchery *n* massacre, murder, slaughter.

butt[1] *vb* bunt, push, shove, shunt, strike; encroach, impose, interfere, intrude, invade, obtrude. * *n* buck, bunt, push, shove, shunt, thrust.

butt[2] *n* barrel, cask.

butt[3] *n* aim, goal, mark, object, point, target; dupe, gull, victim.

butt[4] *vb* abut, adjoin, conjoin, connect, neighbour. * *n* end, piece, remainder, stub, stump; buttocks, posterior, rump.

buttonhole *vb* bore, catch, detain in conversation, importune.

buttress *vb* brace, prop, shore, stay, support. * *n* brace, bulwark, prop, stay, support.

buxom *adj* comely, fresh, healthy, hearty, plump, rosy, ruddy, vigorous.

byword *n* adage, aphorism, apothegm, dictum, maxim, proverb, saying, saw.

C

cabal *vb* conspire, intrigue, machinate, plot. * *n* clique, combination, confederacy, coterie, faction, gang, junta, league, party, set; conspiracy, intrigue, machination, plot.

cabbalistic, cabalistic *adj* dark, fanciful, mysterious, mystic, occult, secret.

cabaret *n* tavern, inn, public house, wine shop.

cabin *n* berth, bunk, cot, cottage, crib, dwelling, hovel, hut, shack, shanty, shed.

cabinet *n* apartment, boudoir, chamber, closet; case, davenport, desk, escritoire; council, ministry.

cachinnation *n* guffaw, laugh, laughter.

cackle *vb* giggle, laugh, snicker, titter; babble, chatter, gabble, palaver, prate, prattle, titter. * *n* babble, chatter, giggle, prate, prattle, snigger, titter.

cacophonous *adj* discordant, grating, harsh, inharmonious, jarring, raucous.

cadaverous *adj* bloodless, deathlike, ghastly, pale, pallid, wan.

cage *vb* confine, immure, imprison, incarcerate. * *n* coop, pen, pound.

caitiff *adj* base, craven, pusillanimous, rascally, recreant. * *n* coward, knave, miscreant, rascal, rogue, scoundrel, sneak, traitor, vagabond, villain, wretch.

cajole *vb* blandish, coax, flatter, jolly, wheedle; beguile, deceive, delude, entrap, inveigle, tempt.

calamity *n* adversity, affliction, blow, casualty, cataclysm, catastrophe, disaster, distress, downfall, evil, hardship, mischance, misery, misfortune, mishap, reverse, ruin, stroke, trial, visitation.

calculate *vb* cast, compute, count, estimate, figure, rate, reckon, weigh; tell.

calculating *adj* crafty, designing, scheming, selfish; careful, cautious, circumspect, far-sighted, politic, sagacious, wary.

calefaction *n* heating, warming; hotness, incandescence, warmth.

calendar *n* almanac, ephemeris, register; catalogue, list, schedule.

calibre *n* bore, capacity, diameter, gauge; ability, capacity, endowment, faculty, gifts, parts, scope, talent.

call *vb* christen, denominate, designate, dub, entitle, name, phrase, style, term; bid, invite, summons; assemble, convene, convoke, muster; cry, exclaim; arouse, awaken, proclaim, rouse, shout, waken; appoint, elect, ordain. * *n* cry, outcry, voice; appeal, invitation, summons; claim, demand, summons; appointment, election, invitation.

calling *n* business, craft, employment, occupation, profession, pursuit, trade.

callous *adj* hard, hardened, indurated; apathetic, dull, indifferent, insensible, inured, obdurate, obtuse, sluggish, torpid, unfeeling, unsusceptible.

callow *adj* naked, unfeathered, unfledged; green, immature, inexperienced, sappy, silly, soft, unfledged,

unsophisticated.

calm *vb* allay, becalm, compose, hush, lull, smooth, still, tranquillize; alleviate, appease, assuage, moderate, mollify, pacify, quiet, soften, soothe, tranquillize. * *adj* halcyon, mild, peaceful, placid, quiet, reposeful, serene, smooth, still, tranquil, unruffled; collected, cool, composed, controlled, impassive, imperturbable, sedate, self-possessed, undisturbed, unperturbed, unruffled, untroubled. * *n* lull; equanimity, peace, placidity, quiet, repose, serenity, stillness, tranquillity.

calorific *adj* heat, heat-producing.

calumniate *vb* abuse, asperse, backbite, blacken, blemish, defame, discredit, disparage, lampoon, libel, malign, revile, slander, traduce, vilify.

calumny *n* abuses, aspersion, backbiting, defamation, detraction, evil-speaking, insult, libel, lying, obloquy, slander, vilification, vituperation.

camarilla *n* cabal, clique, junta, ring.

camber *vb* arch, bend, curve. * *n* arch, arching, convexity.

camp[1] *vb* bivouac, encamp, lodge, pitch, tent. * *n* bivouac, cantonment, encampment, laager; cabal, circle, clique, coterie, faction, group, junta, party, ring, set.

camp[2] *adj* affected, artificial, effeminate, exaggerated, mannered, theatrical.

canaille *n* mob, populace, proletariat, rabble, ragbag, riffraff, scum.

canal *n* channel, duct, pipe, tube.

cancel *vb* blot, efface, erase, expunge, obliterate; abrogate, annul, countermand, nullify, quash, repeal, rescind, revoke.

candelabrum *n* candlestick, chandelier, lustre.

candid *adj* fair, impartial, just, unbiased, unprejudiced; artless, frank, free, guileless, honest, honourable, ingenuous, naive, open, plain, sincere, straightforward.

candidate *n* applicant, aspirant, claimant, competitor, probationer.

candour *n* fairness, impartiality, justice; artlessness, frankness, guilelessness, honesty, ingenuousness, openness, simplicity, sincerity, straightforwardness, truthfulness.

canker *vb* corrode, erode, rot, rust, waste; blight, consume, corrupt, embitter, envenom, infect, poison, sour. * *n* gangrene, rot; bale, bane, blight, corruption, infection, irritation.

canon *n* catalogue, criterion, formula, formulary, law, regulation, rule, standard, statute.

canorous *adj* musical, tuneful.

cant[1] *vb* whine. * *adj* current, partisan, popular, rote, routine, set; argotic, slangy. * *n* hypocrisy; argot, jargon, lingo, slang.

cant[2] *vb* bevel, incline, list, slant, tilt, turn. * *n* bevel, inclination, leaning, list, pitch, slant, tilt, turn.

cantankerous *adj* contumacious, crabbed, cross-grained, dogged, headstrong, heady, intractable, obdurate, obstinate, perverse, refractory, stiff, stubborn, wilful, unyielding.

canting *adj* affected, pious, sanctimonious, whining.

canvas *n* burlap, scrim, tarpaulin.

canvass *vb* discuss, dispute; analyze, consider, examine, investigate, review, scrutinize, sift, study; campaign, electioneer, solicit votes. * *n* debate, discussion, dispute; examination, scrutiny, sifting.

canyon *n* gorge, gulch, ravine.

cap *vb* cover, surmount; complete, crown, finish; exceed, overtop, surpass, transcend; match, parallel, pattern. * *n* beret, head-cover, head-dress; acme, chief, crown, head, peak, perfection, pitch, summit, top.

capability *n* ability, brains, calibre, capableness, capacity, competency, efficiency, faculty, force, power, scope, skill.

capable *adj* adapted, fitted, qualified, suited; able, accomplished, clever, competent, efficient, gifted, ingenious, intelligent, sagacious, skilful.

capacious *adj* ample, broad, comprehensive, expanded, extensive, large, roomy, spacious, wide.

capacitate *vb* enable, qualify.

capacity *n* amplitude, dimensions, magnitude, volume; aptitude, aptness, brains, calibre, discernment, faculty, forte, genius, gift, parts, power, talent, turn, wit; ability, capability, calibre, cleverness, competency, efficiency, skill; character, charge, function, office, position, post, province, service, sphere.

caparison *vb* accoutre, costume, equip, outfit, rig out. * *n* accoutrements, armour, get-up, harness, housing, livery, outfit, panoply, tack, tackle, trappings, turnout .

caper *vb* bound, caracole, frisk, gambol, hop, leap, prank, romp, skip, spring. * *n* bound, dance, gambol, frisk, hop, jump, leap, prance, romp, skip.

capillary *adj* delicate, fine, minute, slender.

capital *adj* cardinal, chief, essential, important, leading, main, major, pre-eminent, principal, prominent; fatal; excellent, first-class, first-rate, good, prime, splendid. * *n* chief city, metropolis, seat; money, estate, investments, shares, stock.

caprice *n* crotchet, fancy, fickleness, freak, humour, inconstancy, maggot, phantasy, quirk, vagary, whim, whimsy.

capricious *adj* changeable, crotchety, fanciful, fantastical, fickle, fitful, freakish, humoursome, odd, puckish, queer, uncertain, variable, wayward, whimsical.

capsize *vb* overturn, upset.

capsule *n* case, covering, envelope, sheath, shell, wrapper: pericarp, pod, seed-vessel.

captain *vb* command, direct, head, lead, manage, officer, preside. * *n* chief, chieftain, commander, leader, master, officer, soldier, warrior.

captious *adj* carping, caviling, censorious, critical, fault-finding, hypercritical; acrimonious, cantankerous, contentious, crabbed, cross, snappish, snarling, splenetic, testy, touchy, waspish; ensnaring, insidious.

captivate *vb* allure, attract, bewitch, catch, capture, charm, enamour, enchant, enthral, fascinate, gain, hypnotize, infatuate, win.

captivity *n* confinement, durance, duress, imprisonment; bondage, enthralment, servitude, slavery, subjection, thraldom, vassalage.

capture *vb* apprehend, arrest, catch, seize. * *n* apprehension, arrest, catch, catching, imprisonment, seizure; bag, prize.

carcass *n* body, cadaver, corpse, corse, remains.

cardinal *adj* capital, central, chief, essential, first, important, leading, main, pre-eminent, primary, principal, vital.

care *n* anxiety, concern, perplexity, trouble, solicitude, worry; attention, carefulness, caution, circumspection, heed, regard, vigilance, wariness, watchfulness; charge, custody, guardianship, keep, oversight, superintendence, ward; burden, charge, concern, responsibility.

careful *adj* anxious, solicitous, concerned, troubled, uneasy; attentive, heedful, mindful, regardful, thoughtful; cautious, canny, circumspect, discreet, leery, vigilant, watchful.

careless *adj* carefree, nonchalant, unapprehensive, undisturbed, unperplexed, unsolicitous, untroubled; disregardful, heedless, inattentive, incautious, inconsiderate, neglectful, negligent, regardless, remiss, thoughtless, unobservant, unconcerned, unconsidered, unmindful, unthinking.

carelessness *n* heedlessness, inadvertence, inattention, inconsiderateness, neglect, negligence, remissness, slackness, thoughtlessness, unconcern.

caress *vb* coddle, cuddle, cosset, embrace, fondle, hug, kiss, pet. * *n* cuddle, embrace, fondling, hug, kiss.

caressing *n* blandishment, dalliance, endearment, fondling.

cargo *n* freight, lading. load.

caricature *vb* burlesque, parody, send-up, take-off, travesty. * *n* burlesque, farce, ludicrous, parody, representation, take-off, travesty.

carious *adj* decayed, mortified, putrid, rotten, ulcerated.

cark *vb* annoy, fret, grieve, harass, perplex, worry.

carnage *n* bloodshed, butchery, havoc, massacre, murder, slaughter.

carnal *adj* animal, concupiscent, fleshly, lascivious, lecherous, lewd, libidinous, lubricous, lustful, salacious, sensual, voluptuous; bodily, earthy, mundane. natural, secular, temporal, unregenerate, unspiritual.

carol *vb* chant, hum, sing, warble. * *n* canticle, chorus, ditty, hymn, lay, song, warble.

carousal *n* banquet, entertainment, feast, festival, merry-making, regale; bacchanal, carouse, debauch, jamboree, jollification, orgy, revel, revelling, revelry, saturnalia, spree, wassail.

carp *vb* cavil, censure, criticize, fault.

carping *adj* captious, cavilling, censorious, hypercritical. * *n* cavil, censure, fault-finding, hypercriticism.

carriage *n* conveyance, vehicle; air, bearing, behaviour, conduct, demeanour, deportment, front, mien, port.

carry *vb* bear, convey, transfer, transmit, transport; impel, push forward, urge; accomplish, compass, effect, gain, secure; bear up, support, sustain; infer, involve, imply, import, signify.

cart *n* conveyance, tumbril, van, vehicle, wagon.

carte-blanche *n* authority, power.

carve *vb* chisel, cut, divide, engrave, grave, hack, hew, indent, incise, sculpt, sculpture; fashion, form, mould, shape.

cascade *vb* cataract, descend, drop, engulf, fall, inundate, overflow, plunge, tumble. * *n* cataract, fall, falls, force, linn, waterfall.

case¹ *vb* cover, encase, enclose, envelop, protect, wrap; box, pack. * *n* capsule, covering, sheathe; box, cabinet, container, holder, receptacle.

case² *n* condition, plight, predicament, situation, state;

example, instance, occurrence; circumstance, condition, contingency, event; action, argument, cause, lawsuit, process, suit, trial.

case-hardened *adj* hardened, indurated, steeled; brazen, brazen-faced, obdurate, reprobate.

cash *n* banknotes, bullion, coin, currency, money, payment, specie.

cashier *vb* break, discard, discharge, dismiss.

cast *vb* fling, hurl, pitch, send, shy, sling, throw, toss; drive, force, impel, thrust; lay aside, put off, shed; calculate, compute, reckon; communicate, diffuse, impart, shed, throw. * *n* fling, throw, toss; shade, tinge, tint, touch; air, character, look, manner, mien, style, tone, turn; form, mould.

castaway *adj* abandoned, cast-off, discarded, rejected. * *n* derelict, outcast, reprobate, vagabond.

caste *n* class, grade, lineage, order, race, rank, species, status.

castigate *vb* beat, chastise, flog, lambaste, lash, thrash, whip; chaste, correct, discipline, punish; criticize, flagellate, upbraid.

castle *n* citadel, fortress, stronghold.

castrate *vb* caponize, emasculate, geld; mortify, subdue, suppress, weaken.

casual *adj* accidental, contingent, fortuitous, incidental, irregular, occasional, random, uncertain, unforeseen, unintentional, unpremeditated; informal, relaxed.

casualty *n* chance, contingency, fortuity, mishap; accident, catastrophe, disaster, mischance, misfortune.

cat *n* grimalkin, kitten, puss, tabby, tomcat.

cataclysm *n* deluge, flood, inundation; disaster, upheaval.

catacomb *n* crypt, tomb, vault.

catalogue *vb* alphabetize, categorize, chronicle, class, classify, codify, file, index, list, record, tabulate. * *n* enumeration, index, inventory, invoice, list, record, register, roll, schedule.

cataract *n* cascade, fall, waterfall.

catastrophe *n* conclusion, consummation, denouement, end, finale, issue, termination, upshot; adversity, blow, calamity, cataclysm, debacle, disaster, ill, misfortune, mischance, mishap, trial, trouble.

catch *vb* clutch, grasp, gripe, nab, seize, snatch; apprehend, arrest, capture; overtake; enmesh, ensnare, entangle, entrap, lime, net; bewitch, captivate, charm, enchant, fascinate, win; surprise, take unawares. * *n* arrest, capture, seizure; bag, find, haul, plum, prize; drawback, fault, hitch, obstacle, rub, snag; captive, conquest.

catching *adj* communicable, contagious, infectious, pestiferous, pestilential; attractive, captivating, charming, enchanting, fascinating, taking, winning, winsome.

catechize *adj* examine, interrogate, question, quiz.

catechumen *n* convert, disciple, learner, neophyte, novice, proselyte, pupil, tyro.

categorical *adj* absolute, direct, downright, emphatic, explicit, express, positive, unconditional, unqualified, unreserved, utter.

category *n* class, division, head, heading, list, order, rank, sort.

catenation *n* conjunction, connection, union.

cater *vb* feed, provide, purvey.

cathartic *adj* abstergent, aperient, cleansing, evacuant, laxative, purgative. * *n* aperient, laxative, physic, purgative, purge.

catholic *adj* general, universal, world-wide; charitable, liberal, tolerant, unbigoted, unexclusive, unsectarian.

cause *vb* breed, create, originate, produce; effect, effectuate, occasion, produce. * *n* agent, creator, mainspring, origin, original, producer, source, spring; account, agency, consideration, ground, incentive, incitement, inducement, motive, reason; aim, end, object, purpose; action, case, suit, trial.

caustic *adj* acrid, cathartic, consuming, corroding, corrosive, eating, erosive, mordant, virulent; biting, bitter, burning, cutting, sarcastic, satirical, scalding, scathing, severe, sharp, stinging.

caution *vb* admonish, forewarn, warn. * *n* care, carefulness, circumspection, discretion, forethought, heed, heedfulness, providence, prudence, wariness, vigilance, watchfulness; admonition, advice, counsel, injunction, warning.

cautious *adj* careful, chary, circumspect, discreet, heedful, prudent, wary, vigilant, wary, watchful.

cavalier *adj* arrogant, curt, disdainful, haughty, insolent, scornful, supercilious; debonair, gallant, gay. * *n* chevalier, equestrian, horseman, horse-soldier, knight.

cave *n* cavern, cavity, den, grot, grotto.

cavil *vb* carp, censure, hypercriticize, object.

cavilling *adj* captious, carping, censorious, critical, hypercritical.

cavity *n* hollow, pocket, vacuole, void.

cease *vb* desist, intermit, pause, refrain, stay, stop; fail; discontinue, end, quit, terminate.

ceaseless *adj* continual, continuous, incessant, unceasing, unintermitting, uninterrupted, unremitting; endless, eternal, everlasting, perpetual.

cede *vb* abandon, abdicate, relinquish, resign, surrender, transfer, yield; convey, grant.

celebrate *vb* applaud, bless, commend, emblazon, extol, glorify, laud, magnify, praise, trumpet; commemorate, honour, keep, observe; solemnize.

celebrated *adj* distinguished, eminent, famed, famous, glorious, illustrious, notable, renowned.

celebrity *n* credit, distinction, eminence, fame, glory, honour, renown, reputation, repute; lion, notable, star.

celerity *n* fleetness, haste, quickness, rapidity, speed, swiftness, velocity.

celestial *adj* empyreal, empyrean; angelic, divine, godlike, heavenly, seraphic, supernal, supernatural.

celibate *adj* single, unmarried. * *n* bachelor, single, virgin.

cellular *adj* alveolate, honeycombed.

cement *vb* attach, bind, join, combine, connect, solder, unite, weld; cohere, stick. * *n* glue, paste, mortar, solder.

cemetery *n* burial-ground, burying-ground, churchyard, god's acre, graveyard, necropolis.

censor *vb* blue-pencil, bowdlerize, cut, edit, expurgate; classify, kill, quash, squash, suppress. * *n* caviller, censurer, faultfinder.

censorious *adj* captious, carping, caviling, condemnatory, faultfinding, hypercritical, severe.

censure *vb* abuse, blame, chide, condemn, rebuke, reprehend, reprimand, reproach, reprobate, reprove, scold, upbraid. *n* animadversion, blame, condemnation, criticism, disapprobation, disapproval, rebuke, remonstrance, reprehension, reproach, reproof, stricture.

ceremonious *adj* civil, courtly, lofty, stately; formal, studied; exact, formal, punctilious, precise, starched, stiff.

ceremony *n* ceremonial, etiquette, form, formality, observance, solemnity, rite; parade, pomp, show, stateliness.

certain *adj* absolute, incontestable, incontrovertible, indisputable, indubitable, positive, undeniable, undisputed, unquestionable, unquestioned; assured, confident, sure, undoubting; infallible, never-failing, unfailing; actual, existing, real; constant, determinate, fixed, settled, stated.

certainty *n* indubitability, indubitableness, inevitableness, inevitability, surety, unquestionability, unquestionableness; assurance, assuredness, certitude, confidence, conviction, surety.

certify *vb* attest, notify, testify, vouch; ascertain, determine, verify, show.

cerulean *adj* azure, blue, sky-blue.

cessation *n* ceasing, discontinuance, intermission, pause, remission, respite, rest, stop, stoppage, suspension.

cession *n* abandonment, capitulation, ceding, concession, conveyance, grant, relinquishement, renunciation, surrender, yielding.

chafe *vb* rub; anger, annoy, chagrin, enrage, exasperate, fret, gall, incense, irritate, nettle, offend, provoke, ruffle, tease, vex; fret, fume, rage.

chaff *vb* banter, deride, jeer, mock, rally, ridicule. scoff. * *n* glumes, hulls, husks; refuse, rubbish, trash, waste.

chaffer *n* bargain, haggle, higgle, negotiate.

chagrin *vb* annoy, chafe, displease, irritate, mortify, provoke, vex. * *n* annoyance, displeasure, disquiet, dissatisfaction, fretfulness, humiliation, ill-humour, irritation, mortification, spleen, vexation.

chain *vb* bind, confine, fetter, manacle, restrain, shackle, trammel; enslave. * *n* bond, fetter, manacle, shackle, union.

chalice *n* bowl, cup, goblet.

challenge *vb* brave, call out, dare, defy, dispute; demand, require. * *n* defiance, interrogation, question; exception, objection.

chamber *n* apartment, hall, room; cavity, hollow.

champion *vb* advocate, defend, uphold. * *n* defender, promoter, protector, vindicator; belt-holder, hero, victor, warrior, winner.

chance *vb* befall, betide, happen, occur. * *adj* accidental, adventitious, casual, fortuitous, incidental, unexpected, unforeseen. * *n* accident, cast, fortuity, fortune, hap, luck; contingency, possibility; occasion, opening, opportunity; contingency, fortuity, gamble, peradventure, uncertainty; hazard, jeopardy, peril, risk.

change *vb* alter, fluctuate, modify, vary; displace, remove, replace, shift, substitute; barter, commute, exchange. * *n* alteration, mutation, revolution, transition, transmutation, turning, variance, variation; innovation, novelty, variety, vicissitude.

changeable *adj* alterable, inconstant, modifiable, mutable, uncertain, unsettled, unstable, unsteadfast, unsteady, variable, variant; capricious, fickle, fitful, flighty, giddy, mercurial, vacillating, volatile, wavering.

changeless *adj* abiding, consistent, constant, fixed, immutable, permanent, regular, reliable, resolute, settled, stationary, unalterable, unchanging.

channel *vb* chamfer, cut, flute, groove. * *n* canal, conduit, duct, passage; aqueduct, canal, chute, drain, flume, furrow; chamfer, groove, fluting, furrow, gutter.

chant *vb* carol, sing, warble; intone, recite; canticle, song.

chaos *n* anarchy, confusion, disorder.

chapfallen *adj* blue, crest-fallen, dejected, depressed, despondent, discouraged, disheartened, dispirited, downcast, downhearted, low-spirited, melancholy, sad.

chaplet *n* coronal, garland, wreath.

char *vb* burn, scorch.

character *n* emblem, figure, hieroglyph, ideograph, letter, mark, sign, symbol; bent, constitution, cast, disposition, nature, quality; individual, original, person, personage; reputation, repute; nature, traits; eccentric, trait.

characteristic *adj* distinctive, peculiar, singular, special, specific, typical. * *n* attribute, feature, idiosyncrasy, lineament, mark, peculiarity, quality, trait.

charge *vb* burden, encumber, freight, lade, load; entrust; ascribe, impute, lay; accuse, arraign, blame, criminate, impeach, inculpate, indict, involve; bid, command, exhort, enjoin, order, require, tax; assault, attack bear down. * *n* burden, cargo, freight, lading, load; care, custody, keeping, management, ward; commission, duty, employment, office, trust; responsibility, trust; command, direction, injunction, mandate, order, precept; exhortation, instruction; cost, debit, expense, expenditure, outlay; price, sum; assault, attack, encounter, onset, onslaught.

charger *n* dish, platter; mount, steed, war-horse.

charily *adv* carefully, cautiously, distrustfully, prudently, sparingly, suspiciously, warily.

charitable *adj* beneficial, beneficent, benignant, bountiful, generous, kind, liberal, open-handed; candid, considerate, lenient, mild.

charity *n* benevolence, benignity, fellow-feeling, good-nature, goodwill, kind-heartedness, kindness, tenderheartedness; beneficence, bounty, generosity, humanity, philanthropy. liberality.

charlatan *n* cheat, empiric, impostor, mountebank, pretender, quack.

charm *vb* allure, attract, becharm, bewitch, captivate, catch, delight, enamour, enchain, enchant, enrapture, enravish, fascinate, transport, win. * *n* enchantment, incantation, magic, necromancy, sorcery, spell, witchery; amulet, talisman; allurement, attraction, attractiveness, fascination.

charming *adj* bewitching, captivating, delightful, enchanting, enrapturing, fascinating, lovely.

charter *vb* incorporate; hire, let. * *n* franchise, immunity, liberty, prerogation, privilege, right; bond, deed, indenture, instrument, prerogative.

chary *adj* careful, cautious, circumspect, shy, wary; abstemious, careful, choice, economical, frugal, provident, saving, sparing, temperate, thrifty, unwasteful.

chase *vb* follow, hunt, pursue, track; emboss. * *n* course, field-sport, hunt, hunting.

chasm *n* cavity, cleft, fissure, gap, hollow, hiatus, opening.

chaste *adj* clean, continent, innocent, modest, pure, pure-minded, undefiled, virtuous; chastened, pure, simple, unaffected, uncorrupt.

chasten *vb* correct, humble; purify, refine, render, subdue.

chastening *n* chastisement, correction, discipline, humbling.

chastise *vb* castigate, correct, flog, lash, punish, whip; chasten, correct, discipline, humble, punish, subdue.

chastity *n* abstinence, celibacy, continence, innocence, modesty, pure-mindedness, purity, virtue; cleanness, decency; chasteness, refinement, restrainedness, simplicity, sobriety, unaffectedness.

chat *vb* babble, chatter, confabulate, gossip, prate, prattle. * *n* chit-chat, confabulation, conversation, gossip, prattle.

chatter *vb* babble, chat, confabulate, gossip, prate, prattle. * *n* babble, chat, gabble, jabber, patter, prattle.

cheap *adj* inexpensive, low-priced; common, indifferent, inferior, mean, meretricious, paltry, poor.

cheapen *vb* belittle, depreciate.

cheat *vb* cozen, deceive, dissemble, juggle, shuffle; bamboozle, befool, beguile, cajole, circumvent, deceive, defraud, chouse, delude, dupe, ensnare, entrap, fool, gammon, gull, hoax, hoodwink, inveigle, jockey, mislead, outwit, overreach, trick. * *n* artifice, beguilement, blind, catch, chouse, deceit, deception, fraud, imposition, imposture, juggle, pitfall, snare, stratagem, swindle, trap, trick, wile; counterfeit, deception, delusion, illusion, mockery, paste, sham, tinsel; beguiler, charlatan, cheater, cozener, impostor, jockey, knave, mountebank, trickster, rogue, render, sharper, seizer, shuffler, swindler, taker, tearer.

check *vb* block, bridle, control, counteract, curb, hinder, obstruct, repress, restrain; chide, rebuke, reprimand, reprove. * *n* bar, barrier, block, brake, bridle, clog, control, curb, damper, hindrance, impediment, interference, obstacle, obstruction, rebuff, repression, restraint, stop, stopper.

cheep *vb* chirp, creak, peep, pipe, squeak.

cheer *vb* animate, encourage, enliven, exhilarate, gladden, incite, inspirit; comfort, console, solace; applaud, clap. * *n* cheerfulness, gaiety, gladness, glee, hilarity, jollity, joy, merriment, mirth; entertainment, food, provision, repast, viands, victuals; acclamation, hurrah, huzza.

cheerful *adj* animated, airy, blithe, buoyant, cheery, gay, glad, gleeful, happy, joyful, jocund, jolly, joyous, light-hearted, lightsome, lively, merry, mirthful, sprightly, sunny; animating, cheering, cheery, encouraging, enlivening, glad, gladdening, gladsome, grateful, inspiriting, jocund, pleasant.

cheerless *adj* dark, dejected, desolate, despondent, disconsolate, discouraged, dismal, doleful, dreary, forlorn, gloomy, joyless, low-spirited, lugubrious, melancholy, mournful, rueful, sad, sombre, spiritless, woe-begone.

cherish *vb* comfort, foster, nourish, nurse, nurture, support, sustain; treasure; encourage, entertain, indulge, harbour.

chest *n* box, case, coffer; breast, thorax, trunk.

chew *vb* crunch, manducate, masticate, munch; bite, champ, gnaw; meditate, ruminate.

chicanery *n* chicane, deception, duplicity, intrigue, intriguing, sophistication, sophistry, stratagems, tergiversation, trickery, wiles, wire-pulling.

chide *vb* admonish, blame, censure, rebuke, reprimand, reprove, scold, upbraid; chafe, clamour, fret, fume, scold.

chief *adj* first, foremost, headmost, leading, master, supereminent, supreme, top; capital, cardinal, especial, essential, grand, great, main, master, paramount, prime, principal, supreme, vital. * *n* chieftain, commander; head, leader.

chiffonier *n* cabinet, sideboard.

child *n* babe, baby, bairn, bantling, brat, chit, infant,

nursling, suckling, wean; issue, offspring, progeny.

childbirth *n* child-bearing, delivery, labour, parturition, travail.

childish *adj* infantile, juvenile, puerile, tender, young; foolish, frivolous, silly, trifling, weak.

childlike *adj* docile, dutiful, gentle, meek, obedient, submissive; confiding, guileless, ingenuous, innocent, simple, trustful, uncrafty.

chill *vb* dampen, depress, deject, discourage, dishearten. * *adj* bleak, chilly, cold, frigid, gelid. * *n* chilliness, cold, coldness, frigidity; ague, rigour, shiver; damp, depression.

chime *vb* accord, harmonize. * *n* accord, consonance.

chimera *n* crochet, delusion, dream, fantasy, hallucination, illusion, phantom.

chimerical *adj* delusive, fanciful, fantastic, illusory, imaginary, quixotic, shadowy, unfounded, visionary, wild.

chink[1] *vb* cleave, crack, fissure, crevasse, incise, split, slit. * *n* aperture, cleft, crack, cranny, crevice, fissure, gap, opening, slit.

chink[2] *vb, n* jingle, clink, ring, ting, tink, tinkle.

chip *vb* flake, fragment, hew, pare, scrape. * *n* flake, fragment, paring, scrap.

chirp *vb* cheep, chirrup, peep, twitter.

chirrup *vb* animate, cheer, encourage, inspirit.

chisel *vb* carve, cut, gouge, sculpt, sculpture.

chivalrous *adj* adventurous, bold, brave, chivalric, gallant, knightly, valiant, warlike; gallant, generous, high-minded, magnanimous.

chivalry *n* knighthood, knight-errantry; courtesy, gallantry, politeness; courage, valour.

choice *adj* excellent, exquisite, precious, rare, select, superior, uncommon, unusual, valuable; careful, chary, frugal, sparing. * *n* alternative, election, option, selection; favourite, pick, preference.

choke *vb* gag, smother, stifle, strangle, suffocate, throttle; overcome, overpower, smother, suppress; bar, block, close, obstruct, stop.

choleric *adj* angry, fiery, hasty, hot, fiery, irascible, irritable, passionate, petulant, testy, touchy, waspish.

choose *vb* adopt, co-opt, cull, designate, elect, pick, predestine, prefer, select.

chop *vb* cut, hack, hew; mince; shift, veer. * *n* slice; brand, quality; chap, jaw.

chouse *vb* bamboozle, beguile, cheat, circumvent, cozen, deceive, defraud, delude, dupe, gull, hoodwink, overreach, swindle, trick, victimize. * *n* cully, dupe, gull, simpleton, tool; artifice, cheat, circumvention, deceit, deception, delusion, double-dealing, fraud, imposition, imposture, ruse, stratagem, trick, wile.

christen *vb* baptize; call, dub, denominate, designate, entitle, name, style, term, title.

chronic *adj* confirmed, continuing, deep-seated, inveterate, rooted.

chronicle *vb* narrate, record, register. * *n* diary, journal, register; account, annals, history, narration, recital, record.

chuckle *vb* crow, exult, giggle, laugh, snigger, titter. * *n* giggle, laughter, snigger, titter.

chum *n* buddy, companion, comrade, crony, friend, mate, pal.

churl *n* boor, bumpkin, clodhopper, clown, countryman, lout, peasant, ploughman, rustic; curmudgeon, hunks, miser, niggard, scrimp, skinflint.

churlish *adj* brusque, brutish, cynical, harsh, impolite, rough, rude, snappish, snarling, surly, uncivil, waspish; crabbed, ill-tempered, morose, sullen; close, close-fisted, illiberal, mean, miserly, niggardly, penurious, stingy.

churn *vb* agitate, jostle.

cicatrice *n* cicatrix, mark, scar, seam.

cicesbeo *n* beau, escort, gallant, gigolo.

cincture *n* band, belt, cestos, cestus, girdle.

cipher *n* naught, nothing, zero; character, device, monogram, symbol; nobody, nonentity.

circle *vb* compass, encircle, encompass, gird, girdle, ring; gyrate, revolve, rotate, round, turn. * *n* circlet, corona, gyre, hoop, ring, rondure; circumference, cordon, periphery; ball, globe, orb, sphere; compass, enclosure; class, clique, company, coterie, fraternity, set, society; bounds, circuit, compass, field, province, range, region, sphere.

circuit *n* ambit, circumambience, circumambiency, cycle, revolution, turn; bounds, district, field, province, range, region, space, sphere, tract; boundary, compass; course, detour, perambulation, round, tour.

circuitous *adj* ambiguous, devious, indirect, roundabout, tortuous, turning, winding.

circulate *vb* diffuse, disseminate, promulgate, propagate, publish, spread.

circumference *n* bound, boundary, circuit, girth, outline, perimeter, periphery.

circumlocution *n* circuitousness, obliqueness, periphrase, periphrasis, verbosity, wordiness.

circumscribe *vb* bound, define, encircle, enclose, encompass, limit, surround; confine, restrict.

circumspect *adj* attentive, careful, cautious, considerate, discreet, heedful, judicious, observant, prudent, vigilant, wary, watchful.

circumstance *n* accident, incident; condition, detail, event, fact, happening, occurrence, position, situation.

circumstantial *adj* detailed, particular; indirect, inferential, presumptive.

circumvent *vb* check, checkmate, outgeneral, thwart; bamboozle, beguile, cheat, chouse, cozen, deceive, defraud, delude, dupe, gull, hoodwink, inveigle, mislead, outwit, overreach, trick.

circumvention *n* cheat, cheating, chicanery, deceit, deception, duplicity, fraud, guile, imposition, imposture, indirection, trickery, wiles.

cistern *n* basin, pond, reservoir, tank.

citation *n* excerpt, extract, quotation; enumeration, mention, quotation, quoting.

cite *vb* adduce, enumerate, extract, mention, name, quote; call, summon.

citizen *n* burgess, burgher, denizen, dweller, freeman, inhabitant, resident, subject, townsman.

civil *adj* civic, municipal, political; domestic; accommodating, affable, civilized, complaisant, courteous, courtly, debonair, easy, gracious, obliging, polished, polite, refined, suave, urbane, well-bred, well-mannered.

civility *n* affability, amiability, complaisance, courteousness, courtesy, good-breeding, politeness, suavity, urbanity.

civilize *vb* cultivate, educate, enlighten, humanize, improve, polish, refine.

claim *vb* ask, assert, challenge, demand, exact, require. * *n* call, demand, lien, requisition; pretension, privilege, right, title.

clammy *adj* adhesive, dauby, glutinous, gummy, ropy, smeary, sticky, viscid, viscous; close, damp, dank, moist, sticky, sweaty.

clamour *vb* shout, vociferate. * *n* blare, din, exclamation, hullabaloo, noise, outcry, uproar, vociferation.

clan *n* family, phratry, race, sect, tribe; band, brotherhood, clique, coterie, fraternity, gang, set, society, sodality.

clandestine *adj* concealed, covert, fraudulent, furtive, hidden, private, secret, sly, stealthy, surreptitious, underhand.

clap *vb* pat, slap, strike; force, slam; applaud, cheer. * *n* blow, knock, slap; bang, burst, explosion, peal, slam.

clarify *vb* cleanse, clear, depurate, purify, strain.

clash *vb* collide, crash, strike; clang, clank, clatter, crash, rattle; contend, disagree, interfere. * *n* collision; clang, clangour, clank, clashing, clatter, crash, rattle; contradiction, disagreement, interference, jar, jarring, opposition.

clasp *vb* clutch, entwine, grasp, grapple, grip, seize; embrace, enfold, fold, hug. * *n* buckle, catch, hasp, hook; embrace, hug.

class *vb* arrange, classify, dispose, distribute, range, rank. * *n* form, grade, order, rank, status; group, seminar; breed, kind, sort; category, collection, denomination, division, group, head.

classical *adj* first-rate, master, masterly, model, standard; Greek, Latin, Roman; Attic, chaste, elegant, polished, pure, refined.

classify *vb* arrange, assort, categorize, class, dispose, distribute, group, pigeonhole, rank, systematize, tabulate.

clatter *vb* clash, rattle; babble, clack, gabble, jabber, prate, prattle. * *n* clattering, clutter, rattling.

clause *n* article, condition, provision, stipulation.

claw *vb* lacerate, scratch, tear. * *n* talon, ungula.

clean *vb* cleanse, clear, purge, purify, rinse, scour, scrub, wash, wipe. * *adj* immaculate, spotless, unsmirched, unsoiled, unspotted, unstained, unsullied, white; clarified, pure, purified, unadulterated, unmixed; adroit, delicate, dextrous, graceful, light, neat, shapely; complete, entire, flawless, faultless, perfect, unabated, unblemished, unimpaired, whole; chaste, innocent, moral, pure, undefiled. * *adv* altogether, completely, entirely, perfectly, quite, thoroughly, wholly.

cleanse *vb* clean, clear, elutriate, purge, purify, rinse, scour, scrub, wash, wipe.

clear *vb* clarify, cleanse, purify, refine; emancipate, disenthral, free, liberate, loose; absolve, acquit, discharge, exonerate, justify, vindicate; disembarrass, disengage, disentangle, extricate, loosen, rid; clean up, scour, sweep; balance; emancipate, free, liberate. * *adj* bright, crystalline, light, limpid, luminous, pellucid, transparent; pure, unadulterated, unmixed; free, open, unencumbered, unobstructed; cloudless, fair, serene, sunny, unclouded, undimmed, unobscured; net; distinct, intelligible, lucid, luminous, perspicuous; apparent, conspicuous, distinct, evident, indisputable, manifest, obvious, palpable, unambiguous, undeniable, unequivocal, unmistakable, unquestionable, visible; clean, guiltless, immaculate, innocent, irreproachable, sinless, spotless, unblemished, undefiled, unspotted, unsullied; unhampered, unimpeded, unobstructed; euphonious, fluty, liquid, mellifluous, musical, silvery, sonorous.

cleave[1] *vb* crack, divide, open, part, rend, rive, sever, split, sunder.

cleave[2] vb adhere, cling, cohere, hold, stick.

cleft adj bifurcated, cloven, forked. * n breach, break, chasm, chink, cranny, crevice, fissure, fracture, gap, interstice, opening, rent, rift.

clemency n mildness, softness; compassion, fellow-feeling, forgivingness, gentleness, kindness, lenience, leniency, lenity, mercifulness, mercy, mildness, tenderness.

clement adj compassionate, forgiving, gentle, humane, indulgent, kind, kind-hearted, lenient, merciful, mild, tender, tender-hearted.

clench vb close tightly, grip; fasten, fix, rivet, secure.

clergy n clergymen, the cloth, ministers.

clever adj able, apt, gifted, talented; adroit, capable, dextrous, discerning, expert, handy, ingenious, knowing, quick, ready, skilful, smart, talented.

click vb beat, clack, clink, tick. * n beat, clack, clink, tick; catch, detent, pawl, ratchet.

cliff n crag, palisade, precipice, scar, steep.

climate n clime, temperature, weather; country, region.

climax vb consummate, crown, culminate, peak. * n acme, consummation, crown, culmination, head, peak, summit, top, zenith.

clinch vb clasp, clench, clutch, grapple, grasp, grip; fasten, secure; confirm, establish, fix. * n catch, clutch, grasp, grip; clincher, clamp, cramp, holdfast.

cling vb adhere, clear, stick; clasp, embrace, entwine.

clink vb, n chink, jingle, ring, tinkle; chime, rhyme.

clip vb cut, shear, snip; curtail, cut, dock, pare, prune, trim. * n cutting, shearing; blow, knock, lick, rap, thump, thwack, thump.

clique n association, brotherhood, cabal, camarilla, clan, club, coterie, gang, junta, party, ring, set, sodality.

cloak vb conceal, cover, dissemble, hide, mask, veil. * n mantle, surcoat; blind, cover, mask, pretext, veil.

clock vb mark time, measure, stopwatch; clock up, record, register. * n chronometer, horologue, time-keeper, timepiece, timer, watch.

clog vb fetter, hamper, shackle, trammel; choke, obstruct; burden, cumber, embarrass, encumber, hamper, hinder, impede, load, restrain, trammel. * n dead-weight, drag-weight, fetter, shackle, trammel; check, drawback, encumbrance, hindrance, impediment, obstacle, obstruction.

cloister n abbey, convent, monastery, nunnery, priory; arcade, colonnade, piazza.

close[1] adj closed, confined, snug, tight; hidden, private, secret; incommunicative, reserved, reticent, secretive, taciturn; concealed, retired, secluded, withdrawn; confined, motionless, stagnant; airless, oppressive, stale, stifling, stuffy, sultry; compact, compressed, dense, form, solid, thick; adjacent, adjoining, approaching, immediately, near, nearly, neighbouring; attached, dear, confidential, devoted, intimate; assiduous, earnest, fixed, intense, intent, unremitting; accurate, exact, faithful, nice, precise, strict; churlish, close-fisted, curmudgeonly, mean, illiberal, miserly, niggardly, parsimonious, penurious, stingy, ungenerous. * n courtyard, enclosure, grounds, precinct, yard.

close[2] vb occlude, seal, shut; choke, clog, estop, obstruct, stop; cease, complete, concede, end, finish, terminate; coalesce, unite; cease, conclude, finish, terminate; clinch, grapple; agree. * n cessation, conclusion, end, finish, termination.

closet n cabinet, retiring-room; press, store-room.

clot vb coagulate, concrete. * n coagulation, concretion, lump.

clothe vb array, attire, deck, dress, rig; cover, endow, envelop, enwrap, invest with, swathe.

clothes n apparel, array, attire, clothing, costume, dress, garb, garments, gear, habiliments, habits, raiment, rig, vestments, vesture.

cloud vb becloud, obnubilate, overcast, overspread; befog, darken, dim, obscure, shade, shadow. * n cirrus, cumulus, fog, haze, mist, nebulosity, scud, stratus, vapour; army, crowd, horde, host, multitude, swarm, throng; darkness, eclipse, gloom, obscuration, obscurity.

cloudy adj clouded, filmy, foggy, hazy, lowering, lurid, murky, overcast; confused, dark, dim, obscure; depressing, dismal, gloomy, sullen; clouded, mottled; blurred, dimmed, lustreless, muddy.

clown n churl, clod-breaker, clodhopper, hind, husbandman, lubber; boor, bumpkin, churl, fellow, lout; blockhead, dolt, clodpoll, dunce, dunderhead, numbskull, simpleton, thickhead; buffoon, droll, farceur, fool, harlequin, jack-a-dandy, jack-pudding, jester, merry-andrew, mime, pantaloon, pickle-herring, punch, scaramouch, zany.

clownish adj awkward, boorish, clumsy, coarse, loutish, ungainly, rough, rustic; churlish, ill-bred, ill-mannered, impolite, rude, uncivil.

cloy vb glut, pall, sate, satiate, surfeit.

club vb combine, unite; beat, bludgeon, cudgel. * n bat, bludgeon, cosh, cudgel, hickory, shillelagh, stick, truncheon; association, company, coterie, fraternity, set, society, sodality.

clump vb assemble, batch, bunch, cluster, group, lump; lumber, stamp, stomp, stump, trudge. * n assemblage, bunch, cluster, collection, group, patch, tuft.

clumsy adj botched, cumbrous, heavy, ill-made, ill-shaped, lumbering, ponderous, unwieldy; awkward, blundering, bungling, elephantine, heavy-handed, inapt, mal adroit, unhandy, unskilled.

cluster vb assemble, batch, bunch, clump, collect, gather, group, lump, throng. * n agglomeration, assemblage, batch, bunch, clump, collection, gathering, group, throng.

clutch[1] vb catch, clasp, clench, clinch, grab, grapple, grasp, grip, hold, seize, snatch, squeeze. * n clasp, clench, clinch, grasp, grip, hold, seizure, squeeze.

clutch[2] n aerie, brood, hatching, nest.

clutches npl claws, paws, talons; hands, power.

clutter vb confuse, disarrange, disarray, disorder, jumble, litter, mess, muss; clatter. * n bustle, clatter, clattering, racket; confusion, disarray, disorder, jumble, litter, mess, muss.

coadjutor n abettor, accomplice, aider, ally, assistant, associate, auxiliary, collaborator, colleague, cooperator, fellow-helper, helper, helpmate, partner.

coagulate vb clot, congeal, concrete, curdle, thicken.

coalesce vb amalgamate, blend, cohere, combine, commix, incorporate, mix, unite; concur, fraternize.

coalition n alliance, association, combination, compact, confederacy, confederation, conjunction, conspiracy, co-partnership, federation, league, union.

coarse adj crude, impure, rough, unpurified; broad, gross, indecent, indelicate, ribald, vulgar; bearish, bluff, boorish, brutish, churlish, clownish, gruff, impolite, loutish, rude, unpolished; crass, inelegant.

coast vb flow, glide, roll, skim, sail, slide, sweep. * n littoral, seaboard, sea-coast, seaside, shore, strand; border.

coat *vb* cover, spread. * *n* cut-away, frock, jacket; coating, cover, covering; layer.

coax *vb* allure, beguile, cajole, cog, entice, flatter, persuade, soothe, wheedle.

cobble *vb* botch, bungle; mend, patch, repair, tinker.

cobweb *adj* flimsy, gauzy, slight, thin, worthless. * *n* entanglement, meshes, snare, toils.

cochleate *adj* cochlear, cochleary, cochleous, cochleated, spiral, spiry.

cockle *vb* corrugate, pucker, wrinkle.

coddle *vb* caress, cocker, fondle, humour, indulge, nurse, pamper, pet.

codger *n* churl, curmudgeon, hunks, lick-penny, miser, niggard, screw, scrimp, skinflint.

codify *vb* condense, digest, summarize, systematize, tabulate.

coerce *vb* check, curb, repress, restrain, subdue; compel, constrain, drive, force, urge.

coercion *n* check, curb, repression, restraint; compulsion, constraint, force.

coeval *adj* coetaneous, coexistent, contemporaneous, contemporary, synchronous.

coexistent *adj* coetaneous, coeval, simultaneous, synchronous.

coffer *n* box, casket, chest, trunk; money-chest, safe, strongbox; caisson.

cogent *adj* compelling, conclusive, convincing, effective, forcible, influential, irresistible, persuasive, potent, powerful, resistless, strong, trenchant, urgent.

cogitate *vb* consider, deliberate, meditate, ponder, reflect, ruminate, muse, think, weigh.

cognate *adj* affiliated, affined, akin, allied, alike, analogous, connected, kindred, related, similar.

cognizance *n* cognition, knowing, knowledge, notice, observation.

cohere *vb* agree, coincide, conform, fit, square, suit.

coherence *n* coalition, cohesion, connection, dependence, union; agreement, congruity, consistency, correspondence, harmony, intelligibility, intelligible, meaning, rationality, unity.

coherent *adj* adherent, connected, united; congruous, consistent, intelligible, logical.

cohort *n* band, battalion, line, squadron.

coil *vb* curl, twine, twirl, twist, wind. * *n* convolution, curlicue, helix, knot, roll, spiral, tendril, twirl, volute, whorl; bustle, care, clamour, confusion, entanglements, perplexities, tumult, turmoil, uproar.

coin *vb* counterfeit, create, devise, fabricate, forge, form, invent, mint, originate, mould, stamp. * *n* coign, corner, quoin; key, plug, prop, wedge; cash, money, specie.

coincide *vb* cohere, correspond, square, tally; acquiesce, agree, harmonize, concur.

coincidence *n* corresponding, squaring, tallying; agreeing, concurrent, concurring.

cold *adj* arctic, biting, bleak, boreal, chill, chilly, cutting, frosty, gelid, glacial, icy, nipping, polar, raw, wintry; frost-bitten, shivering; apathetic, cold-blooded, dead, freezing, frigid, indifferent, lukewarm, passionless, phlegmatic, sluggish, stoical, stony, torpid, unconcerned, unfeeling, unimpressible, unresponsive, unsusceptible, unsympathetic; dead, dull, spiritless, unaffecting, uninspiring, uninteresting. * *n* chill, chilliness, coldness.

collapse *vb* break down, fail, fall. * *n* depression, exhaustion, failure, faint, prostration, sinking, subsidence.

collar *vb* apprehend, arrest, capture, grab, nab, seize. * *n* collarette, gorget, neckband, ruff, torque; band, belt, fillet, guard, ring, yoke.

collate *vb* adduce, collect, compare, compose.

collateral *adj* contingent, indirect, secondary, subordinate; concurrent, parallel; confirmatory, corroborative; accessory, accompanying, additional, ancillary, auxiliary, concomitant, contributory, simultaneous, supernumerary; consanguineous, related. * *n* guarantee, guaranty, security, surety, warranty; accessory, extra, nonessential, unessential; consanguinean, relative.

collation *n* luncheon, repast, meal.

colleague *n* aider, ally, assistant, associate, auxiliary, coadjutor, collaborator, companion, confederate, confrere, cooperator, helper, partner.

collect *vb* assemble, compile, gather, muster; accumulate, aggregate, amass, garner.

collected *adj* calm, composed, cool, placid, self-possessed, serene, unperturbed.

collection *n* aggregation, assemblage, cluster, crowd, drove, gathering, group, pack; accumulation, congeries, conglomeration, heap, hoard, lot, mass, pile, store; alms, contribution, offering, offertory.

colligate *vb* bind, combine, fasten, unite.

collision *n* clash, concussion, crash, encounter, impact, impingement, shock; conflict, crashing, interference, opposition.

collocate *vb* arrange, dispose, place, set.

colloquy *n* conference, conversation, dialogue, discourse, talk.

collude *vb* concert, connive, conspire.

collusion *n* connivance, conspiracy, coven, craft, deceit.

collusive *adj* conniving, conspiratorial, , dishonest, deceitful, deceptive, fraudulent.

colossal *adj* Cyclopean, enormous, gigantic, Herculean, huge, immense, monstrous, prodigious, vast.

colour *vb* discolour, dye, paint, stain, tinge, tint; disguise, varnish; disguise, distort, garble, misrepresent, pervert; blush, flush, redden, show. * *n* hue, shade, tinge, tint, tone; paint, pigment, stain; redness, rosiness, ruddiness; complexion; appearance, disguise, excuse, guise, plea, pretence, pretext, semblance.

colourless *adj* achromatic, uncoloured, untinged; blanched, hueless, livid, pale, pallid; blank, characterless, dull, expressionless, inexpressive, monotonous.

colours *n* banner, ensign, flag, standard.

column *n* pillar, pilaster; file, line, row.

coma *n* drowsiness, lethargy, somnolence, stupor, torpor; bunch, clump, cluster, tuft.

comatose *adj* drowsy, lethargic, sleepy, somnolent, stupefied.

comb *vb* card, curry, dress, groom, rake, unknot, untangle; rake, ransack, rummage, scour, search. * *n* card, hatchel, ripple; harrow, rake.

combat *vb* contend, contest, fight, struggle, war; battle, oppose, resist, struggle, withstand. * *n* action, affair, battle, brush, conflict, contest, encounter, fight, skirmish.

combative *adj* belligerent, contentious, militant, pugnacious, quarrelsome.

combination *n* association, conjunction, connection, union; alliance, cartel, coalition, confederacy, consolidation, league, merger, syndicate; cabal, clique, conspiracy, faction, junta, ring; amalgamation, compound, mixture.

combine *vb* cooperate, merge, pool, unite; amalgamate, blend, incorporate, mix.

combustible *adj* consumable, inflammable.

come *vb* advance, approach; arise, ensue, flow, follow, issue, originate, proceed, result; befall, betide, happen, occur.

comely *adj* becoming, decent, decorous, fitting, seemly, suitable; beautiful, fair, graceful, handsome, personable, pretty, symmetrical.

comfort *vb* alleviate, animate, cheer, console, encourage, enliven, gladden, inspirit, invigorate, refresh, revive, solace, soothe, strengthen. * *n* aid, assistance, countenance, help, support, succour; consolation, solace, encouragement, relief; ease, enjoyment, peace, satisfaction.

comfortable *adj* acceptable, agreeable, delightful, enjoyable, grateful, gratifying, happy, pleasant, pleasurable, welcome; commodious, convenient, easeful, snug; painless.

comfortless *adj* bleak, cheerless, desolate, drear, dreary, forlorn, miserable, wretched; broken-hearted, desolate, disconsolate, forlorn, heart-broken, inconsolable, miserable, woe-begone, wretched.

comical *adj* amusing, burlesque, comic, diverting, droll, farcical, funny, humorous, laughable, ludicrous, sportive, whimsical.

coming *adj* approaching, arising, arriving, ensuing, eventual, expected, forthcoming, future, imminent, issuing, looming, nearing, prospective, ultimate; emergent, emerging, successful; due, owed, owing. * *n* advent, approach, arrival; imminence, imminency, nearness; apparition, appearance, disclosure, emergence, manifestation, materialization, occurrence, presentation, revelation, rising.

comity *n* affability, amenity, civility, courtesy, politeness, suavity, urbanity.

command *vb* bid, charge, direct, enjoin, order, require; control, dominate, govern, lead, rule, sway; claim, challenge, compel, demand, exact. * *n* behest, bidding, charge, commandment, direction, hest, injunction, mandate, order, requirement, requisition; ascendency, authority, dominion, control, government, power, rule, sway, supremacy.

commander *n* captain, chief, chieftain, commandment, head, leader.

commemorate *vb* celebrate, keep, observe, solemnize.

commence *vb* begin, inaugurate, initiate, institute, open, originate, start.

commend *vb* assign, bespeak, confide, recommend, remit; commit, entrust, yield; applaud, approve, eulogize, extol, laud, praise.

commendation *n* approbation, approval, good opinion, recommendation; praise, encomium, eulogy, panegyric.

commensurate *adj* commeasurable, commensurable; co-extensive, conterminous, equal; adequate, appropriate, corresponding, due, proportionate, proportioned, sufficient.

comment *vb* animadvert, annotate, criticize, explain, interpret, note, remark. * *n* annotation, elucidation, explanation, exposition, illustration, commentary, note, gloss; animadversion, observation, remark.

commentator *n* annotator, commentator, critic, expositor, expounder, interpreter.

commerce *n* business, exchange, dealing, trade, traffic; communication, communion, intercourse.

commercial *adj* mercantile, trading.

commination *n* denunciation, menace, threat, threatening.

commingle *vb* amalgamate, blend, combine, commix, intermingle, intermix, join, mingle, mix, unite.

comminute *vb* bray, bruise, grind, levigate, powder, pulverize, triturate.

commiserate *vb* compassionate, condole, pity, sympathize.

commiseration *n* compassion, pitying; condolence, pity, sympathy.

commission *vb* authorize, empower; delegate, depute. * *n* doing, perpetration; care, charge, duty, employment, errand, office, task, trust; allowance, compensation, fee, rake-off.

commissioner *n* agent, delegate, deputy.

commit *vb* confide, consign, delegate, entrust, remand; consign, deposit, lay, place, put, relegate, resign; do, enact, perform, perpetrate; imprison; engage, implicate, pledge.

commix *vb* amalgamate, blend, combine, commingle, compound, intermingle, mingle, mix, unite.

commodious *adj* advantageous, ample, comfortable, convenient, fit, proper, roomy, spacious, suitable, useful.

commodity *n* goods, merchandise, produce, wares.

common *adj* collective, public; general, useful; common-place, customary, everyday, familiar, frequent, habitual, usual; banal, hackneyed, stale, threadbare, trite; indifferent, inferior, low, ordinary, plebeian, popular, undistinguished, vulgar.

commonplace *adj* common, hackneyed, ordinary, stale, threadbare, trite. * *n* banality, cliché, platitude; jotting, memoir, memorandum, note, reminder.

common-sense, common-sensical *adj* practical, sagacious, sensible, sober.

commotion *n* agitation, disturbance, ferment, perturbation, welter; ado, bustle, disorder, disturbance, hurlyburly, pother, tumult, turbulence, turmoil.

communicate *vb* bestow, confer, convey, give, impart, transmit; acquaint, announce, declare, disclose, divulge, publish, reveal, unfold; commune, converse, correspond.

communication *n* conveyance, disclosure, giving, imparting, transmittal; commence, conference, conversation, converse, correspondence, intercourse; announcement, dispatch, information, message, news.

communicative *adj* affable, chatty, conversable, free, open, sociable, unreserved.

communion *n* converse, fellowship, intercourse, participation; Eucharist, holy communion, Lord's Supper, sacrament.

community *n* commonwealth, people, public, society; association, brotherhood, college, society; likeness, participancy, sameness, similarity.

compact[1] *n* agreement, arrangement, bargain, concordant, contract, covenant, convention, pact, stipulation, treaty.

compact[2] *vb* compress, condense, pack, press; bind, consolidate, unite. * *adj* close, compressed, condensed, dense, firm, solid; brief, compendious, concise, laconic, pithy, pointed, sententious, short, succinct, terse.

companion *n* accomplice, ally, associate, comrade, compeer, confederate, consort, crony, friend, fellow, mate; partaker, participant, participator, partner, sharer.

companionable *adj* affable, conversable, familiar, friendly, genial, neighbourly, sociable.

companionship *n* association, fellowship, friendship, intercourse, society.

company *n* assemblage, assembly, band, bevy, body, circle, collection, communication, concourse, congregation, coterie, crew, crowd, flock, gang, gathering, group, herd, rout, set, syndicate, troop; party; companionship, fellowship, guests, society, visitor, visitors; association, copartnership, corporation, firm, house, partnership.

compare *vb* assimilate, balance, collate, parallel; liken, resemble.

comparison *n* collation, compare, estimate; simile, similitude.

compartment *n* bay, cell, division, pigeonhole, section.

compass *vb* embrace, encompass, enclose, encircle, environ, surround; beleaguer, beset, besiege, block, blockade, invest; accomplish, achieve, attain, carry, consummate, effect, obtain, perform, procure, realize; contrive, devise, intend, meditate, plot, purpose. * *n* bound, boundary, extent, gamut, limit, range, reach, register, scope, stretch; circuit, round.

compassion *n* clemency, commiseration, condolence, fellow-feeling, heart, humanity, kind-heartedness, kindness, kindliness, mercy, pity, rue, ruth, sorrow, sympathy, tenderheartedness, tenderness.

compassionate *adj* benignant, clement, commiserative, gracious, kind, merciful, pitying, ruthful, sympathetic, tender.

compatible *adj* accordant, agreeable to, congruous, consistent, consonant, reconcilable, suitable.

compeer *n* associate, comrade, companion, equal, fellow, mate, peer.

compel *vb* constrain, force, coerce, drive, necessitate, oblige; bend, bow, subdue, subject.

compend *n* abbreviation, abridgement, abstract, breviary, brief, compendium, conspectus, digest, epitome, précis, summary, syllabus, synopsis.

compendious *adj* abbreviated, abridged, brief, comprehensive, concise, short, succinct, summary.

compensate *vb* counterbalance, counterpoise, countervail; guerdon, recompense, reimburse, remunerate, reward; indemnify, reimburse, repay, requite; atone.

compensation *n* pay, payment, recompense, remuneration, reward, salary; amends, atonement, indemnification, indemnity, reparation, requital, satisfaction; balance, counterpoise, equalization, offset.

compete *vb* contend, contest, cope, emulate, rival, strive, struggle, vie.

competence *n* ability, capability, capacity, fitness, qualification, suitableness; adequacy, adequateness, enough, sufficiency.

competent *adj* able, capable, clever, equal, endowed, qualified; adapted, adequate, convenient, fit, sufficient, suitable.

competition *n* contest, emulation, rivalry, rivals.

competitor *n* adversary, antagonist, contestant, emulator, opponent.

compile *vb* compose, prepare, write; arrange, collect, select.

complacency *n* content, contentment, gratification, pleasure, satisfaction; affability, civility, complaisance, courtesy, politeness.

complacent *adj* contented, gratified, pleased, satisfied; affable, civil, complaisant, courteous, easy, gracious, grateful, obliging, polite, urbane.

complain *vb* bemoan, bewail, deplore, grieve, groan, grouch, grumble, lament, moan, murmur, repine, whine.

complainant *n* accuser, plaintiff.

complaining *adj* fault-finding, murmuring, querulous.

complaint *n* grievance, gripe, grumble, lament, lamentation, plaint, murmur, wail; ail, ailment, annoyance, disease, disorder, illness, indisposition, malady, sickness; accusation, charge, information

complete *vb* accomplish, achieve, conclude, consummate, do, effect, effectuate, end, execute, finish, fulfil, perfect, perform, realize, terminate. * *adj* clean, consummate, faultless, full, perfect, perform, thorough; all, entire, integral, total, unbroken, undiminished, undivided, unimpaired, whole; accomplished, achieved, completed, concluded, consummated, ended, finished.

completion *n* accomplishing, accomplishment, achieving, conclusion, consummation, effecting, effectuation, ending, execution, finishing, perfecting, performance, termination.

complex *adj* composite, compound, compounded, manifold, mingled, mixed; complicate, complicated, entangled, intricate, involved, knotty, mazy, tangled. * *n* complexus, complication, involute, skein, tangle; entirety, integration, network, totality, whole; compulsion, fixation, obsession, preoccupation, prepossession; prejudice.

complexion *n* colour, hue, tint.

complexity *n* complication, entanglement, intricacy, involution.

compliance *n* concession, obedience, submission; acquiescence, agreement, assent, concurrence, consent; compliancy, yieldingness.

complicate *vb* confuse, entangle, interweave, involve.

complication *n* complexity, confusion, entanglement, intricacy; combination, complexus, mixture.

compliment *vb* commend, congratulate, eulogize, extol, flatter, laud, praise. * *n* admiration, commendation, courtesy, encomium, eulogy, favour, flattery, honour, laudation, praise, tribute.

complimentary *adj* commendatory, congratulatory, encomiastic, eulogistic, flattering, laudatory, panegyrical.

comply *vb* adhere to, complete, discharge, fulfil, meet, observe, perform, satisfy; accede, accord, acquiesce, agree to, assent, consent to, yield.

component *adj* composing, constituent, constituting. * *n* constituent, element, ingredient, part.

comport *vb* accord, agree, coincide, correspond, fit, harmonize, square, suit, tally.

compose *vb* build, compact, compound, constitute, form, make, synthesize; contrive, create, frame, imagine, indite, invent, write; adjust, arrange, regulate, settle; appease, assuage, calm, pacify, quell, quiet, soothe, still, tranquillize.

composed *adj* calm, collected, cool, imperturbable, placid, quiet, sedate, self-possessed, tranquil, undisturbed, unmoved, unruffled.

composite *adj* amalgamated, combined, complex, compounded, mixed; integrated, unitary. * *n* admixture, amalgam, blend, combination, composition, compound, mixture, unification.

composition *n* constitution, construction, formation, framing, making; compound, mixture; arrangement, combination, conjunction, make-up, synthesize, union; invention, opus, piece, production, writing; agreement, arrangement, compromise.

compost n fertilizer, fertilizing, manure, mixture.

composure n calmness, coolness, equanimity, placidity, sedateness, quiet, self-possession, serenity, tranquillity.

compotation n conviviality, frolicking, jollification, revelling, revelry, rousing, wassailling; bacchanal, carousal, carouse, debauch, orgy, revel, saturnalia, wassail.

compound[1] vb amalgamate, blend, combine, intermingle, intermix, mingle, mix, unite; adjust, arrange, compose, compromise, settle. * adj complex, composite. * n combination, composition, mixture; farrago, hodgepodge, jumble, medley, mess, olio.

compound[2] n enclosure, garden, yard.

comprehend vb comprise, contain, embrace, embody, enclose, include, involve; apprehend, conceive, discern, grasp, know, imagine, master, perceive, see, understand.

comprehension n comprising, embracing, inclusion; compass, domain, embrace, field, limits, province, range, reach, scope, sphere, sweep; connotation, depth, force, intention; conception, grasp, intelligence, understanding; intellect, intelligence, mind, reason, understanding.

comprehensive adj all-embracing, ample, broad, capacious, compendious, extensive, full, inclusive, large, sweeping, wide.

compress vb abbreviate, condense, constrict, contract, crowd, press, shorten, squeeze, summarize.

compression n condensation, confining, pinching, pressing, squeezing; brevity, pithiness, succinctness, terseness.

comprise vb comprehend, contain, embody, embrace, enclose, include, involve.

compromise vb adjust, arbitrate, arrange, compose, compound, settle; imperil, jeopardize, prejudice; commit, engage, implicate, pledge; agree, compound. * n adjustment, agreement, composition, settlement.

compulsion n coercion, constraint, force, forcing, pressure, urgency.

compulsory adj coercive, compelling, constraining; binding, enforced, imperative, necessary, obligatory, unavoidable.

compunction n contrition, misgiving, penitence, qualm, regret, reluctance, remorse, repentance, sorrow.

computable adj calculable, numerable, reckonable.

computation n account, calculation, estimate, reckoning, score, tally.

compute vb calculate, count, enumerate, estimate, figure, measure, number, rate, reckon, sum.

comrade n accomplice, ally, associate, chum, companion, compatriot, compeer, crony, fellow, mate, pal.

concatenate vb connect, join, link, unite.

concatenation n connection; chain, congeries, linking, series, sequence, succession.

concave adj depressed, excavated, hollow, hollowed, scooped.

conceal vb bury, cover, screen, secrete; disguise, dissemble, mask.

concede vb grant, surrender, yield; acknowledge, admit, allow, confess, grant.

conceit n belief, conception, fancy, idea, image, imagination, notion, thought; caprice, illusion, vagary, whim; estimate, estimation, impression, judgement, opinion; conceitedness, egoism, self-complacency, priggishness, priggery, self-conceit, self-esteem, self-

sufficiency, vanity; crotchet, point, quip, quirk.

conceited adj egotistical, opinionated, opinionative, overweening, self-conceited, vain,

conceivable adj imaginable, picturable; cogitable, comprehensible, intelligible, rational, thinkable.

conceive vb create, contrive, devise, form, plan, purpose; fancy, imagine; comprehend, fathom, think, understand; assume, imagine, suppose; bear, become pregnant.

concern vb affect, belong to, interest, pertain to, regard, relate to, touch; disquiet, disturb, trouble. * n affair, business, matter, transaction; concernment, consequence, importance, interest, moment, weight; anxiety, care, carefulness, solicitude, worry; business, company, establishment, firm, house.

concert vb combine, concoct, contrive, design, devise, invent, plan, plot, project. * n agreement, concord, concordance, cooperation, harmony, union, unison.

concession n acquiescence, assent, cessation, compliance, surrender, yielding; acknowledgement, allowance, boon, confession, grant, privilege.

conciliate vb appease, pacify, placate, propitiate, reconcile; engage, gain, secure, win, win over.

concise adj brief, compact, compendious, comprehensive, compressed, condensed, crisp, laconic, pithy, pointed, pregnant, sententious, short, succinct, summary, terse.

conclave n assembly, cabinet, council.

conclude vb close, end, finish, terminate; deduce, gather, infer, judge; decide, determine, judge; arrange, complete, settle; bar, hinder, restrain, stop; decide, determine, resolve.

conclusion n deduction, inference; decision, determination, judgement; close, completion, end, event, finale; issue, termination, upshot; arrangement, closing, effecting, establishing, settlement.

conclusive adj clinching, convincing, decisive, irrefutable, unanswerable; final, ultimate.

concoct vb brew, contrive, design, devise, frame, hatch, invent, mature, plan, plot, prepare, project.

concomitant adj accessory, accompanying, attendant, attending, coincident, concurrent, conjoined. * n accessory, accompaniment, attendant.

concord n agreement, amity, friendship, harmony, peace, unanimity, union, unison, unity; accord, adaptation, concordance, consonance, harmony.

concordant adj accordant, agreeable, agreeing, harmonious.

concordat n agreement, bargain, compact, convention, covenant, stipulation, treaty.

concourse n confluence, conflux, congress; assemblage, assembly, collection, crowd, gathering, meeting, multitude, throng.

concrete vb cake, congeal, coagulate, harden, solidify, thicken. * adj compact, consolidated, firm, solid, solidified; agglomerated, complex, conglomerated, compound, concreted; completely, entire, individualized, total. * n compound, concretion, mixture; cement.

concubine n hetaera, hetaira, mistress, paramour.

concupiscence n lasciviousness, lechery, lewdness, lust, pruriency.

concupiscent adj carnal, lascivious, lecherous, lewd, libidinous, lustful, prurient, rampant, salacious, sensual.

concur vb accede, acquiesce, agree, approve, assent, coincide, consent, harmonize; combine, conspire, cooperate, help.

concurrent *adj* agreeing, coincident, harmonizing, meeting, uniting; associate, associated, attendant, concomitant, conjoined, united.

concussion *n* agitation, shaking; clash, crash, shock.

condemn *vb* adjudge, convict, doom, sentence; disapprove, proscribe, reprobate; blame, censure, damn, deprecate, disapprove, reprehend, reprove, upbraid.

condemnation *n* conviction, doom, judgement, penalty, sentence; banning, disapproval, proscription; guilt, sin, wrong; blame, censure, disapprobation, disapproval, reprobation, reproof.

condemnatory *adj* blaming, censuring, damnatory, deprecatory, disapproving, reproachful.

condense *vb* compress, concentrate, consolidate, densify, thicken; abbreviate, abridge, contract, curtail, diminish, epitomize, reduce, shorten, summarize; liquefy.

condescend *vb* deign, vouchsafe; descend, stoop, submit.

condescension *n* affability, civility, courtesy, deference, favour, graciousness, obeisance.

condign *adj* adequate, deserved, just, merited, suitable.

condiment *n* appetizer, relish, sauce, seasoning.

condition *vb* postulate, specify, stipulate; groom, prepare, qualify, ready, train; acclimatize, accustom, adapt, adjust, familiarize, habituate, naturalize; attune, commission, fix, overhaul, prepare, recondition, repair, service, tune. * *n* case, circumstances, plight, predicament, situation, state; class, estate, grade, rank, station; arrangement, consideration, provision, proviso, stipulation; attendant, necessity, postulate, precondition, prerequisite.

condole *vb* commiserate, compassionate, console, sympathize.

condonation *n* forgiveness, overlooking, pardon.

condone *vb* excuse, forgive, pardon.

conduce *vb* contribute, lead, tend; advance, aid.

conducive *adj* conducting, contributing, instrumental, promotive, subservient, subsidiary.

conduct *vb* convoy, direct, escort, lead; administer, command, govern, lead, preside, superintend; manage, operate, regulate; direct, lead. * *n* administration, direction, guidance, leadership, management; convoy, escort, guard; actions, bearing, behaviour, career, carriage, demeanour, deportment, manners.

conductor *n* guide, lead; director, leader, manager; propagator, transmitter.

conduit *n* canal, channel, duct, passage, pipe, tube.

confederacy *n* alliance, coalition, compact, confederation, covenant, federation, league, union.

confer *vb* advise, consult, converse, deliberate, discourse, parley, talk; bestow, give, grant, vouchsafe.

confess *vb* acknowledge, admit, avow, own; admit, concede, grant, recognize; attest, exhibit, manifest, prove, show; shrive.

confession *n* acknowledgement, admission, avowal.

confide *vb* commit, consign, entrust, trust.

confidence *n* belief, certitude, dependence, faith, reliance, trust; aplomb, assurance, boldness, cocksureness, courage, firmness, intrepidity, self-reliance; secrecy.

confident *adj* assured, certain, cocksure, positive, sure: bold, presumptuous. sanguine, undaunted.

confidential *adj* intimate, private, secret; faithful, trustworthy.

configuration *n* conformation, contour, figure, form, gestalt, outline, shape.

confine *vb* restrain, shut in, shut up; immure, imprison, incarcerate, impound, jail, mew; bound, circumscribe, limit, restrict. * *n* border, boundary, frontier, limit.

confinement *n* restraint; captivity, duress, durance, immurement, imprisonment, incarceration; childbed, childbirth, delivery, lying-in, parturition.

confines *npl* borders, boundaries, edges, frontiers, limits, marches, precincts.

confirm *vb* assure, establish, fix, settle; strengthen; authenticate, avouch, corroborate, countersign, endorse, substantiate, verify; bind, ratify, sanction.

confirmation *n* establishment, settlement; corroboration, proof, substantiation, verification.

confiscate *vb* appropriate, forfeit, seize.

conflict *vb* clash, combat, contend, contest, disagree, fight, interfere, strive, struggle. * *n* battle, collision, combat, contention, contest, encounter, fight, struggle; antagonism, clashing, disagreement, discord, disharmony, inconsistency, interference, opposition.

confluence *n* conflux, junction, meeting, union; army, assemblage, assembly, concourse, crowd, collection, horde, host, multitude, swarm.

confluent *adj* blending, concurring, flowing, joining, meeting, merging, uniting.

conform *vb* accommodate, adapt, adjust; agree, comport, correspond, harmonize, square, tally.

conformation *n* accordance, agreement, compliance, conformity; configuration, figure, form, manner, shape, structure.

confound *vb* confuse; baffle, bewilder, embarrass, flurry, mystify, nonplus, perplex, pose; amaze, astonish, astound, bewilder, dumfound, paralyse, petrify, startle, stun, stupefy, surprise; annihilate, demolish, destroy, overthrow, overwhelm, ruin; abash, confuse, discompose, disconcert, mortify, shame.

confront *vb* face; challenge, contrapose, encounter, oppose, threaten.

confuse *vb* blend, confound, intermingle, mingle, mix; derange, disarrange, disorder, jumble, mess, muddle; darken, obscure, perplex; befuddle, bewilder, embarrass, flabbergast, flurry, fluster, mystify, nonplus, pose; abash, confound, discompose, disconcert, mortify, shame.

confusion *n* anarchy, chaos, clutter, confusedness, derangement, disarrangement, disarray, disorder, jumble, muddle; agitation, commotion, ferment, stir, tumult, turmoil; astonishment, bewilderment, distraction, embarrassment, fluster, fuddle, perplexity; abashment, discomfiture, mortification, shame; annihilation, defeat, demolition, destruction, overthrow, ruin.

confute *vb* disprove, oppugn, overthrow, refute, silence.

congeal *vb* benumb, condense, curdle, freeze, stiffen, thicken.

congenial *adj* kindred, similar, sympathetic; adapted, agreeable, natural, suitable, suited; agreeable, favourable, genial.

congenital *adj* connate, connatural, inborn.

congeries *n* accumulation, agglomeration, aggregate, aggregation, collection, conglomeration, crowd, cluster, heap, mass.

congratulate *vb* compliment, felicitate, gratulate, greet, hail, salute.

congregate *vb* assemble, collect, convene, convoke, gather, muster; gather, meet, swarm, throng.

congregation *n* assemblage, assembly, collection, gathering, meeting.

congress *n* assembly, conclave, conference, convention, convocation, council, diet, meeting.

congruity *n* agreement, conformity, consistency, fitness, suitableness.

congruous *adj* accordant, agreeing, compatible, consistent, consonant, suitable; appropriate, befitting, fit, meet, proper, seemly.

conjecture *vb* assume, guess, hypothesize, imagine, suppose. surmise, suspect; dare say, fancy, presume. * *n* assumption, guess, hypothesis, supposition, surmise, theory.

conjoin *vb* associate, combine, connect, join, unite.

conjugal *adj* bridal, connubial, hymeneal, matrimonial, nuptial.

conjuncture *n* combination, concurrence, connection; crisis, emergency, exigency, juncture.

conjure *vb* adjure, beg, beseech, crave, entreat, implore, invoke, pray, supplicate; bewitch, charm, enchant, fascinate; juggle.

connect *vb* associate, conjoin, combine, couple, hyphenate, interlink, join, link, unite; cohere, interlock.

connected *adj* associated, coupled, joined, united; akin, allied, related; communicating.

connection *n* alliance, association, dependence, junction, union; commerce, communication, intercourse; affinity, relationship; kindred, kinsman, relation, relative.

connive *vb* collude, conspire, plot, scheme.

connoisseur *n* critic, expert, virtuoso.

connotation *n* comprehension, depth, force, intent, intention, meaning.

connubial *adj* bridal, conjugal, hymeneal, matrimonial, nuptial.

conquer *vb* beat, checkmate, crush, defeat, discomfit, humble, master, overcome, overpower, overthrow, prevail, quell, reduce, rout, subdue, subjugate, vanquish; overcome, surmount.

conqueror *n* humbler, subduer, subjugator, vanquisher; superior, victor, winner.

conquest *n* defeat, discomfiture, mastery, overthrow, reduction, subjection, subjugation; triumph, victor; winning.

consanguinity *n* affinity, kinship, blood-relationship, kin, kindred, relationship.

conscientious *adj* careful, exact, fair, faithful, high-principled, honest, honourable, incorruptible, just, scrupulous, straightforward, uncorrupt, upright.

conscious *adj* intelligent, knowing, percipient, sentient; intellectual, rational, reasoning, reflecting, self-conscious, thinking; apprised, awake, aware, cognizant, percipient, sensible; self-admitted, self-accusing.

consecrate *vb* dedicate, devote, ordain; hallow, sanctify, venerate.

consecutive *adj* following, succeeding.

consent *vb* agree, allow, assent, concur, permit, yield; accede, acquiesce, comply. * *n* approval, assent, concurrence, permission; accord, agreement, consensus, concord, cooperation, harmony, unison; acquiescence, compliance.

consequence *n* effect, end, event, issue, result; conclusion, deduction, inference; concatenation, connection, consecution; concern, distinction, importance, influence, interest, moment, standing, weight.

consequential *adj* consequent, following, resulting, sequential; arrogant, conceited, inflated, pompous, pretentious, self-important, self-sufficient, vainglorious.

conservation *n* guardianship, maintenance, preservation, protection.

conservative *adj* conservatory, moderate, moderationist; preservative; reactionary, unprogressive. * *n* die-hard, reactionary, redneck, rightist, right-winger; moderate; preservative.

conserve *vb* keep, maintain, preserve, protect, save, sustain, uphold. * *n* confit, confection, jam, preserve, sweetmeat.

consider *vb* attend, brood, contemplate, examine, heed, mark, mind, ponder, reflect, revolve, study, weigh; care for, consult, envisage, regard, respect; cogitate, deliberate, mediate, muse, ponder, reflect, ruminate, think; account, believe, deem, hold, judge, opine.

considerate *adj* circumspect, deliberate, discrete, judicious, provident, prudent, serious, sober, staid, thoughtful; charitable, forbearing, patient.

consideration *n* attention, cogitation, contemplation, deliberation, notice, heed, meditation, pondering, reflection, regard; consequence, importance, important, moment, significant, weight; account, cause, ground, motive, reason, sake, score.

consign *vb* deliver, hand over, remand, resign, transfer, transmit; commit, entrust; ship.

consignor *n* sender, shipper, transmitter.

consistency *n* compactness, consistence, density, thickness; agreement, compatibility, conformableness, congruity, consonance, correspondence, harmony.

consistent *adj* accordant, agreeing, comfortable, compatible, congruous, consonant, correspondent, harmonious, logical.

consolation *n* alleviation, comfort, condolence, encouragement, relief, solace.

console *vb* assuage, calm, cheer, comfort, encourage, solace, relieve, soothe.

consolidate *vb* cement, compact, compress, condense, conduce, harden, solidify, thicken; combine, conjoin, fuse, unite.

consolidation *n* solidification; combination, union.

consonance *n* accord, concord, conformity, harmony; accord, accordance, agreement, congruence, congruity, consistency, unison.

consonant *adj* accordant, according, harmonious; compatible, congruous, consistent. * *n* articulation, letter-sound.

consort *vb* associate, fraternize. * *n* associate, companion, fellow, husband, spouse, partner.

conspectus *n* abstract, brief, breviary, compend, compendium, digest, epitome, outline, precis, summary, syllabus, synopsis.

conspicuous *adj* apparent, clear, discernible, glaring, manifest, noticeable, perceptible, plain, striking, visible; celebrated, distinguished, eminent, famed, famous, illustrious, marked, noted, outstanding. pre-eminent, prominent, remarkable, signal.

conspiracy *n* cabal, collusion, confederation, intrigue, league, machination, plot, scheme.

conspire *vb* concur, conduce, cooperate; combine, compass, contrive, devise, project; confederate, contrive, hatch, plot, scheme.

constancy *n* immutability, permanence, stability, unchangeableness; regularity, unchangeableness; decision, determination, firmness, inflexibility, resolution, steadfastness, steadiness; devotion, faithfulness, fidelity, loyalty, trustiness, truth.

constant *adj* abiding, enduring, fixed, immutable, invariable, invariant, permanent, perpetual, stable, unalterable, unchanging, unvaried; certain, regular, stated, uniform; determined, firm, resolute, stanch, steadfast, steady, unanswering, undeviating, unmoved, unshaken, unwavering; assiduous, diligent, persevering, sedulous, tenacious, unremitting; continual, continuous, incessant, perpetual, sustained, unbroken, uninterrupted; devoted, faithful, loyal, true, trusty.

consternation n alarm, amazement, awe, bewilderment, dread, fear, fright, horror, panic, terror.

constituent adj component, composing, constituting, forming; appointing, electoral. * n component, element, ingredient, principal; elector, voter.

constitute vb compose, form, make; appoint, delegate, depute, empower; enact, establish, fix, set up.

constitution n establishment, formation, make-up, organization, structure; character, characteristic, disposition, form, habit, humour, peculiarity, physique, quality, spirit, temper, temperament.

constitutional adj congenital, connate, inborn, inbred, inherent, innate, natural, organic; lawful, legal, legitimate. * n airing, exercise, promenade, stretch, walk.

constrain vb coerce, compel, drive, force; chain, confine, curb, enthral, hold, restrain; draw, impel, urge.

constriction n compression, constraint, contraction.

construct vb build, fabricate, erect, raise, set up; arrange, establish, form, found, frame, institute, invent, make, organize, originate.

construction n building, erection, fabrication; configuration, conformation, figure, form, formation, made, shape, structure; explanation, interpretation, rendering, version.

construe vb analyse, explain, expound, interpret, parse, render, translate.

consult vb advise, ask, confer, counsel, deliberate, interrogate, question; consider, regard.

consume vb absorb, decay, destroy, devour, dissipate, exhaust, expend, lavish, lessen, spend, squander, vanish, waste.

consummate[1] vb accomplish, achieve, compass, complete, conclude, crown, effect, effectuate, end, execute, finish, perfect, perform.

consummate[2] adj complete, done, effected, finished, fulfilled, perfect, supreme.

consumption n decay, decline, decrease, destruction, diminution, expenditure, use, waste; atrophy, emaciation.

contact vb hit, impinge, touch; approach, be heard, communicate with, reach. * n approximation, contiguity, junction, juxtaposition, taction, tangency, touch.

contagion n infection; contamination, corruption, infection, taint.

contagious adj catching, epidemic, infectious; deadly, pestiferous, pestilential, poisonous.

contain vb accommodate, comprehend, comprise, embody, embrace, enclose, include; check, restrain.

contaminate vb corrupt, defile, deprave, infect, poison, pollute, soil, stain, sully, taint, tarnish, vitiate.

contamination n contaminating, defilement, defiling, polluting, pollution; abomination, defilement, impurity, foulness, infection, pollution, stain, taint, uncleanness.

contemn vb despise, disdain, disregard, neglect, scorn, scout, slight, spurn.

contemplate vb behold, gaze upon, observe, survey; consider, dwell on, meditate on, muse on, ponder, reflect upon, study, survey, think about; design, intend, mean, plan, purpose.

contemplation n cogitation, deliberation, meditation, pondering, reflection, speculation, study, thought; prospect, prospective, view; expectation.

contemporaneous adj coetaneous, coeval, coexistent, coexisting, coincident, concomitant, contemporary, simultaneous, synchronous.

contemporary adj coetaneous, coeval, coexistent, coexisting, coincident, concomitant, concurrent, contemporaneous, current, present, simultaneous, synchronous; advanced, modern, modernistic, progressive, up-to-date. * n coeval, coexistent, compeer, fellow.

contempt n contumely, derision, despite, disdain, disregard, misprision, mockery, scorn, slight.

contemptible adj abject, base, despicable, haughty, insolent, insulting, low, mean, paltry, pitiful, scurvy, sorry, supercilious, vile, worthless.

contemptuous adj arrogant, contumelious, disdainful, haughty, insolent, insulting, scornful, sneering, supercilious.

contend vb battle, combat, compete, contest, fight, strive, struggle, vie; argue, debate, dispute, litigate; affirm, assert, contest, maintain.

content[1] n essence, gist, meaning, meat, stuff, substance; capacity, measure, space, volume.

content[2] vb appease, delight, gladden, gratify, humour, indulge, please, satisfy, suffice. * adj agreeable, contented, happy, pleased, satisfied. * n contentment, ease, peace, satisfaction.

contention n discord, dissension, feud, squabble, strife, quarrel, rapture, wrangle, wrangling; altercation, bickering, contest, controversy, debate, dispute, litigation, logomachy.

contentious adj belligerent, cross, litigious, peevish, perverse, petulant, pugnacious, quarrelsome, wrangling; captious, caviling, disputatious.

conterminous adj adjacent, adjoining, contiguous; coextensive, coincident, commensurate.

contest vb argue, contend, controvert, debate, dispute, litigate, question; strive, struggle; compete, cope, fight, vie. * n altercation, contention, controversy, difference, dispute, debate, quarrel; affray, battle, bout, combat, conflict, encounter, fight, match, scrimmage, struggle, tussle; competition, contention, rivalry.

contexture n composition, constitution, framework, structure, texture.

contiguous adj abutting, adjacent, adjoining, beside, bordering, conterminous, meeting, near, neighbouring, touching.

continent[1] n mainland, mass, tract.

continent[2] adj abstemious, abstinent, chaste, restrained, self-commanding, self-controlled, moderate, sober, temperate.

contingency n accidentalness, chance, fortuity, uncertainty; accident, casualty, event, incident, occurrence.

contingent adj accidental, adventitious, casual, fortuitous, incidental; conditional, dependent, uncertain. * n proportion, quota, share.

continual adj constant, constant, perpetual, unceasing, uninterrupted, unremitting; endless, eternal, everlasting, interminable, perennial, permanent, perpetual, unending; constant, oft-repeated.

continuance n abiding, continuation, duration, endurance, lasting, persistence, stay; continuation, extension, perpetuation, prolongation, protraction;

concatenation, connection, sequence, succession; constancy, endurance, perseverance, persistence.

continue *vb* endure, last, remain; abide, linger, remain, stay, tarry; endure, persevere, persist, stick; extend, prolong, perpetuate, protract.

continuous *adj* connected, continued, extended, prolonged, unbroken, unintermitted, uninterrupted.

contour *n* outline, profile.

contraband *adj* banned, forbidden, illegal, illicit, interdicted, prohibited, smuggled, unlawful.

contract *vb* abbreviate, abridge, condense, confine, curtail, diminish, epitomize, lessen, narrow, reduce, shorten; absorb, catch, incur, get, make, take; constrict, shrink, shrivel, wrinkle; agree, bargain, covenant, engage, pledge, stipulate. * *n* agreement, arrangement, bargain, bond, compact, concordat, covenant, convention, engagement, pact, stipulation, treaty.

contradict *vb* assail, challenge, controvert, deny, dispute, gainsay, impugn, traverse; abrogate, annul, belie, counter, disallow, negative, contravene, counteract, oppose, thwart.

contradiction *n* controversion, denial, gainsaying; antinomy, clashing, contrariety, incongruity, opposition.

contradictory *adj* antagonistic, contrary, incompatible, inconsistent, negating, opposed, opposite, repugnant.

contrariety *n* antagonism, clashing, contradiction, contrast, opposition, repugnance.

contrary *adj* adverse, counter, discordant, opposed, opposing, opposite; antagonistic, conflicting, contradictory, repugnant, retroactive; forward, headstrong, obstinate, refractory, stubborn, unruly, wayward, perverse. * *n* antithesis, converse, obverse, opposite, reverse.

contrast *vb* compare, differentiate, distinguish, oppose. * *n* contrariety, difference, opposition; comparison, distinction.

contravene *vb* abrogate, annul, contradict, counteract, countervail, cross, go against, hinder, interfere, nullify, oppose, set aside, thwart.

contravention *n* abrogation, contradiction, interference, opposition, transgression, traversal, violation.

contretemps *n* accident, mischance, mishap.

contribute *vb* bestow, donate, give, grant, subscribe; afford, aid, furnish, supply; concur, conduce, conspire, cooperate, minister, serve, tend.

contribution *n* bestowal, bestowment, grant; donation, gift, offering, subscription.

contrite *adj* humble, penitent, repentant, sorrowful.

contrition *n* compunction, humiliation, penitence, regret, remorse, repentance, self-condemnation, self-reproach, sorrow.

contrivance *n* design, inventive, inventiveness; contraption, device, gadget, invention, machine; artifice, device, fabrication, machination, plan, plot, scheme, shift, stratagem.

contrive *vb* arrange, brew, concoct, design, devise, effect, form, frame, hatch, invent, plan, project; consider, plan, plot, scheme; manage, make out.

control *vb* command, direct, dominate, govern, manage, oversee, sway, regulate, rule, superintend; bridle, check, counteract, curb, check, hinder, repress, restrain. * *n* ascendency, command, direction, disposition, dominion, government, guidance, mastery, oversight, regiment, regulation, rule, superintendence, supremacy, sway.

controversy *n* altercation, argument, contention, debate, discussion, disputation, dispute, logomachy, polemics, quarrel, strife; lawsuit.

contumacious *adj* disobedient, cross-grained, disrespectful, haughty, headstrong, intractable, obdurate, obstinate, pertinacious, perverse, rebellious, refractory, stiff-necked, stubborn.

contumacy *n* doggedness, haughtiness, headiness, obduracy, obstinacy, pertinacity, perverseness, stubbornness; contempt, disobedience, disrespect, insolence, insubordination, rebelliousness.

contumelious *adj* abusive, arrogant, calumnious, contemptuous, disdainful, insolent, insulting, opprobrious, overbearing, rude, scornful, supercilious.

contumely *n* abuse, affront, arrogance, contempt, contemptuousness, disdain, indignity, insolence, insult, obloquy, opprobrium, reproach, rudeness, scorn, superciliousness.

contuse *vb* bruise, crush, injure, knock, squeeze, wound.

contusion *n* bruise, crush, injury, knock, squeeze, wound.

convalescence *n* recovery, recuperation.

convene *vb* assemble, congregate, gather, meet, muster; assemble, call, collect, convoke, muster, summon.

convenience *n* fitness, propriety, suitableness; accessibility, accommodation, comfort, commodiousness, ease, handiness, satisfaction, serviceability, serviceableness.

convenient *adj* adapted, appropriate, fit, fitted, proper, suitable, suited; advantageous, beneficial, comfortable, commodious, favourable, handy, helpful, serviceable, timely, useful.

convent *n* abbey, cloister, monastery, priory.

convention *n* assembly, congress, convocation, meeting; agreement, bargain, compact, contract, pact, stipulation, treaty; custom, formality, usage.

conventional *adj* agreed on, bargained for, stipulated; accustomed, approved, common, customary, everyday, habitual, ordinary, orthodox, regular, standard, traditional, usual, wonted.

conversable *adj* affable, communicative, free, open, sociable, social, unreversed.

conversation *n* chat, colloquy, communion, confabulation, conference, converse, dialogue, discourse, intercourse, interlocution, parley, talk.

converse[1] *vb* commune; chat, confabulate, discourse, gossip, parley, talk. * *n* commerce, communication, intercourse; colloquy, conversation, talk.

converse[2] *adj* adverse, contradictory, contrary, counter, opposed, opposing, opposite; *n* antithesis, contrary, opposite, reverse.

conversion *n* change, reduction, resolution, transformation, transmutation; interchange, reversal, transposition.

convert *vb* alter, change, transform, transmute; interchange, reverse, transpose; apply, appropriate, convince. * *n* catechumen, disciple, neophyte, proselyte.

convey *vb* bear, bring, carry, fetch, transmit, transport, waft; abalienate, alienate, cede, consign, deliver, demise, devise, devolve, grant, sell, transfer.

conveyance *n* alienation, cession, transfer, transference, transmission; carriage, carrying, conveying, transfer, transmission.

convict *vb* condemn, confute, convince, imprison, sentence. * *n* criminal, culprit, felon, malefactor, prisoner.

convivial *adj* festal, festive, gay, jolly, jovial, merry, mirthful, social.

convocation *n* assembling, convening, convoking, gathering, summoning; assembly, congress, convention, council, diet, meeting, synod.

convoke *vb* assemble, convene, muster, summon.

convoy *vb* accompany, attend, escort, guard, protect. * *n* attendance, attendant, escort, guard, protection.

convulse *vb* agitate, derange, disorder, disturb, shake, shatter.

convulsion *n* cramp, fit, spasm; agitation, commotion, disturbance, shaking, tumult.

cook *vb* bake, boil, broil, fry, grill, microwave, roast, spit-roast, steam, stir-fry; falsify, garble.

cool *vb* chill, ice, refrigerate; abate, allay, calm, damp, moderate, quiet, temper. * *adj* calm, collected, composed, dispassionate, placid, sedate, self-possessed, quiet, staid, unexcited, unimpassioned, undisturbed, unruffled; cold-blooded, indifferent, lukewarm, unconcerned; apathetic, chilling, freezing, frigid, repellent; bold, impertinent, impudent, self-possessed, shameless. * *n* chill, chilliness, coolness; calmness, composure, coolheadedness, countenance, equanimity, poise, self-possession, self-restraint.

coop *vb* cage, confine, encage, immure, imprison. * *n* barrel, box, cage, pen.

cooperate *vb* abet, aid, assist, co-act, collaborate, combine, concur, conduce, conspire, contribute, help, unite.

cooperation *n* aid, assistance, co-action, concert, concurrence, collaboration, synergy.

coordinate *vb* accord, agree, arrange, equalize, harmonize, integrate, methodize, organize, regulate, synchronize, systematize. * *adj* coequal, equal, equivalent, tantamount; coincident, synchronous. * *n* complement, counterpart, like, pendant; companion, fellow, match, mate.

copartnership *n* association, fraternity, partnership; company, concern, establishment, firm, house.

cope *vb* combat, compete, contend, encounter, engage, strive, struggle, vie.

copious *adj* abundant, ample, exuberant, full, overflowing, plenteous, plentiful, profuse, rich.

copiousness *n* abundance, exuberance, fullness, plenty, profusion, richness.

copse *n* coppice, grove, thicket.

copulation *n* coition, congress, coupling.

copy *vb* duplicate, reproduce, trace, transcribe; follow, imitate, pattern. * *n* counterscript, duplicate, facsimile, off-print, replica, reproduction, transcript; archetype, model, original, pattern; manuscript, typescript.

cord *n* braid, gimp, line, string.

cordate *adj* cordiform, heart-shaped.

cordial *adj* affectionate, ardent, earnest, heartfelt, hearty, sincere, warm, warm-hearted; grateful, invigorating, restorative, pleasant, refreshing. * *n* balm, balsam, elixir, tisane, tonic; liqueur.

core *n* centre, essence, heart, kernel.

corner *vb* confound, confuse, nonplus, perplex, pose, puzzle. * *n* angle, bend, crutch, cusp, elbow, joint, knee; niche, nook, recess, retreat.

corollary *n* conclusion, consequence, deduction, induction, inference.

coronal *n* bays, chaplet, crown, garland, laurel, wreath.

corporal *adj* bodily; corporeal, material, physical.

corporeal *adj* bodily, fleshly, substantial; corporal, material, nonspiritual, physical.

corps *n* band, body, company, contingent, division, platoon, regiment, squad, squadron, troop.

corpse *n* body, carcass, corse, remains; ashes, dust.

corpulent *adj* big, burly, fat, fleshy, large, lusty, obese, plump, portly, pursy, rotund, stout.

corpuscle *n* atom, bit, grain, iota, jot, mite, molecule, monad, particle, scintilla, scrap, whit.

correct *vb* adjust, amend, cure, improve, mend, reclaim, rectify, redress, reform, regulate, remedy; chasten, discipline, punish. * *adj* accurate, equitable, exact, faultless, just, precise, proper, regular, right, true, upright.

correction *n* amendment, improvement, redress; chastening, discipline, punishment.

corrective *adj* alternative, correctory, counteractive, emendatory, improving, modifying, rectifying, reformative, reformatory.

correctness *n* accuracy, exactness, faultlessness, nicety, precision, propriety, rectitude, regularity, rightness, truth.

correlate *n* complement, correlative, counterpart.

correspond *vb* accord, agree, answer, comport, conform, fit, harmonize, match, square, suit, tally; answer, belong, correlate; communicate.

correspondence *n* accord, agreement, coincidence, concurrence, conformity, congruity, fitness, harmony, match; correlation, counterposition; communication, letters, writing.

corroborate *vb* confirm, establish, ratify, substantiate, support, sustain, strengthen.

corrode *vb* canker, erode, gnaw; consume, deteriorate, rust, waste; blight, embitter, envenom, poison.

corrosive *adj* acrid, biting, consuming, cathartic, caustic, corroding, eroding, erosive, violent; consuming, corroding, gnawing, mordant, wasting, wearing; blighting, cankerous, carking, embittering, envenoming, poisoning.

corrugate *vb* cockle, crease, furrow, groove, pucker, rumple, wrinkle.

corrupt *vb* putrefy, putrid, render; contaminate, defile, infect, pollute, spoil, taint, vitiate; degrade, demoralize, deprave, pervert; adulterate, debase, falsify, sophisticate; bribe, entice. * *adj* contaminated, corrupted, impure, infected, putrid, rotten, spoiled, tainted, unsound; abandoned, debauched, depraved, dissolute, profligate, reprobate, vicious, wicked; bribable, buyable.

corruption *n* putrefaction, putrescence, rottenness; adulteration, contamination, debasement, defilement, infection, perversion, pollution, vitiation; demoralization, depravation, depravity, immorality, laxity, sinfulness, wickedness; bribery, dishonesty.

corsair *n* buccaneer, picaroon, pirate, rover, sea-robber, sea-rover.

corset *n* bodice, girdle, stays.

cosmonaut *n* astronaut, spaceman.

cosmos *n* creation, macrocosm, universe, world; harmony, order, structure.

cost *vb* absorb, consume, require. * *n* amount, charge, expenditure, expense, outlay, price; costliness, preciousness, richness, splendour, sumptuousness; damage, detriment, loss, pain, sacrifice, suffering.

costly *adj* dear, expensive, high-priced; gorgeous, luxurious, precious, rich, splendid, sumptuous, valuable.

costume *n* apparel, attire, dress, robes, uniform.

cosy, cozy *adj* comfortable, easy, snug; chatty, conversable, social, talkative.

coterie n association, brotherhood, circle, club, set, society, sodality.

cottage n cabin, chalet, cot, hut, lodge, shack, shanty.

couch vb lie, recline; crouch, squat; bend down, stoop; conceal, cover up, hide; lay, level. * n bed, davenport, divan, lounge, seat, settee, settle, sofa.

council n advisers, cabinet, ministry; assembly, congress, conclave, convention, convocation, diet, husting, meeting, parliament, synod.

counsel vb admonish, advise, caution, recommend, warm. * n admonition, advice, caution, instruction, opinion, recommendation, suggestion; deliberation, forethought; advocate, barrister, counsellor, lawyer.

count vb enumerate, number, score; calculate, cast, compute, estimate, reckon; account, consider, deem, esteem, hold, judge, regard, think; tell. * n reckoning, tally.

countenance vb abet, aid, approve, assist, befriend, encourage, favour, patronize, sanction, support. * n aspect, look, men; aid, approbation, approval, assistance, encouragement, favour, patronage, sanction, support.

counter¹ n abacus, calculator, computer, meter, reckoner, tabulator, totalizator; bar, buffet, shopboard, table; (naut) end, poop, stern, tail; chip, token.

counter² vb contradict, contravene, counteract, oppose, retaliate. * adj adverse, against, contrary, opposed, opposite. * adv contrariwise, contrary. * n antithesis, contrary, converse, opposite, reverse; counterblast, counterblow, retaliation.

counteract vb check, contrapose, contravene, cross, counter, counterpose, defeat, foil, frustrate, hinder, oppose, resist, thwart, traverse; annul, countervail, counterbalance, destroy, neutralize, offset.

counteractive adj antidote, corrective, counteragent, medicine, remedy, restorative.

counterbalance vb balance, counterpoise; compensate, countervail.

counterfeit vb forge, imitate; fake, feign, pretend, sham, simulate; copy, imitate. * adj fake, forged, fraudulent, spurious, supposititious; false, feigned, hypocritical, mock, sham, simulated, spurious; copied, imitated, resembling. * n copy, fake, forgery, sham.

countermand vb abrogate, annul, cancel, recall, repeal, rescind, revoke.

counterpane n coverlet, duvet, quilt.

counterpart n copy, duplicate; complement, correlate, correlative, reverse, supplement; fellow, mate, match, tally, twin.

counterpoise vb balance, counteract, countervail, counterbalance, equilibrate, offset. * n balance, counterweight.

countersign n password, watchword.

countervail vb balance, compensate, counterbalance.

country n land, region; countryside; fatherland, home, kingdom, state, territory; nation, people, population. * adj rural, rustic; countrified, rough, rude, uncultivated, unpolished, unrefined.

countryman n compatriot, fellow-citizen; boor, clown, farmer, hind, husbandman, peasant, rustic, swain.

couple vb pair, unite; copulate, embrace; buckle, clasp, conjoin, connect, join, link, pair, yoke. * n brace, pair, twain, two; bond, coupling, lea, link, tie.

courage n audaciousness, audacity, boldness, bravery, daring, derring-do, dauntlessness, fearlessness, firmness, fortitude, gallantry, hardihood, heroism, intrepidity, manhood, mettle, nerve, pluck, prowess, resolution, spirit, spunk, valorousness, valour.

courageous adj audacious, brave, bold, chivalrous, daring, dauntless, fearless, gallant, hardy, heroic, intrepid, lion-hearted, mettlesome, plucky, resolute, reliant, staunch, stout, undismayed, valiant, valorous.

course vb chase, follow, hunt, pursue, race, run. * n career, circuit, race, run; road, route, track, way; bearing, direction, path, tremor, track; ambit, beat, orbit, round; process, progress, sequence; order, regularity, succession, turn; behaviour, conduct, deportment; arrangement, series, system.

court vb coddle, fawn, flatter, ingratiate; address, woo; seek; invite, solicit. * n area, courtyard, patio, quadrangle; addresses, civilities, homage, respects, solicitations; retinue, palace, tribunal.

courteous adj affable, attentive, ceremonious, civil, complaisant, courtly, debonair, elegant, gracious, obliging, polished, polite, refined, respected, urbane, well-bred, well-mannered.

courtesan n harlot, prostitute, strumpet, vamp, wanton, wench, whore.

courtesy n affability, civility, complaisance, courteousness, elegance, good-breeding, graciousness, polish, politeness, refine, urbanity.

courtly adj affable, ceremonious, civil, elegant, flattering, lordly, obliging, polished, polite, refined, urbane.

courtyard n area, court, patio, quadrangle, yard.

cove¹ n anchorage, bay, bight, creek, firth, fjord, inlet.

cove² n bloke, chap, character, customer, fellow, type.

covenant vb agree, bargain, contract, stipulate. * n bond, deed; arrangement, bargain, compact, concordat, contract, convention, pact, stipulation, treaty.

cover vb overlay, overspread; cloak, conceal, curtain, disguise, hide, mask, screen, secrete, shroud, veil; defend, guard, protect, shelter, shield; case, clothe, envelop, invest, jacket, sheathe; comprehend, comprise, contain, embody, embrace, include. * n capsule, case, covering, integument, tegument, top; cloak, disguise, screen, veil; guard, defence, protection, safeguard, shelter, shield; shrubbery, thicket, underbrush, undergrowth, underwood, woods.

covert adj clandestine, concealed, disguised, hidden, insidious, private, secret, sly, stealthy, underhand. * n coppice, shade, shrubbery, thicket, underwood; asylum; defence, harbour, hiding-place, refuge, retreat, sanctuary, shelter.

covet vb aim after, desire, long for, yearn for; hanker after, lust after.

covetous adj acquisitive, avaricious, close-fisted, grasping, greedy, miserly, niggardly, parsimonious, penurious, rapacious.

cow¹ n bovine, heifer.

cow² vb abash, break, daunt, discourage, dishearten, frighten, intimidate, overawe, subdue.

coward adj cowardly, timid. * n caitiff, craven, dastard, milksop, poltroon, recreant, skulker, sneak, wheyface.

cowardly adj base, chicken-hearted, coward, craven, dastardly, faint-hearted, fearful, lily-livered, mean, pusillanimous, timid, timorous, white-livered, yellow.

cower vb bend, cringe, crouch, fawn, shrink, squat, stoop.

coxcomb n beau, dandy, dude, exquisite, fop, jackanapes, popinjay, prig.

coy adj backward, bashful, demure, diffident, distant,

modest, reserved, retiring, self-effacing, shrinking, shy, timid.

coyness n affectation, archness, backwardness, bashfulness, coquettishness, demureness, diffidence, evasiveness, modesty, primness, reserve, shrinking, shyness, timidity.

cozen vb beguile, cheat, chouse, circumvent, deceive, defraud, diddle, dupe, gull, overreach, swindle, trick, victimize.

cozy see cosy.

crabbed adj acrid, rough, sore, tart; acrimonious, cantankerous, captious, caustic, censorious, churlish, cross, growling, harsh, ill-tempered, morose, peevish, petulant, snappish, snarling, splenetic, surly, testy, touchy, waspish; difficult, intractable, perplexing, tough, trying, unmanageable.

crabbedness n acridity, acridness, roughness, sourness, tartness; acerbity, acrimonious, asperity, churlishness, harshness, ill-tempered, moodiness, moroseness, sullenness; difficulty, intractability, perplexity.

crack vb break; chop, cleave, split; snap; craze, madden; boast, brag, bluster, crow, gasconade, vapour, vaunt. * adj capital, excellent, first-class, first-rate, tip-top. * n breach, break, chink, cleft, cranny, crevice, fissure, fracture, opening, rent, rift, split; burst, clap, explosion, pop, report; snap.

cracked adj broken, crackled, split; crack-brained, crazed, crazy, demented, deranged, flighty, insane.

crackle vb crepitate, decrepitate, snap.

craft n ability, aptitude, cleverness, dexterity, expertness, power, readiness, skill, tact, talent; artifice, artfulness, cunning, craftiness, deceitfulness, deception, guile, shrewdness, subtlety; art, avocation, business, calling, employment, handicraft, trade, vocation; vessel.

crafty adj arch, artful, astute, cunning, crooked, deceitful, designing, fraudulent, guileful, insidious, intriguing, scheming, shrewd, sly, subtle, tricky, wily.

crag n rock; neck, throat.

craggy adj broken, cragged, jagged, rough, rugged, scraggy, uneven.

cram vb fill, glut, gorge, satiate, stuff; compress, crowd, overcrowd, press, squeeze; coach, grind.

cramp vb convulse; check, clog, confine, hamper, hinder, impede, obstruct, restrain, restrict. * n convulsion, crick, spasm; check, restraint, restriction, obstruction

crank vb bend, crankle, crinkle, turn, twist, wind. * n bend, quirk, turn, twist, winding.

cranny n breach, break, chink, cleft, crack, crevice, fissure, gap, hole, interstice, nook, opening, rift.

crapulous adj crapulent, drunk, drunken, inebriated, intoxicated, tipsy.

crash vb break, shatter, shiver, smash, splinter. * adj emergency, fast, intensive, rushed, speeded-up. * n clang, clash, collision concussion, jar.

crass adj coarse, gross, raw, thick, unabated, unrefined.

cravat n neckcloth, neckerchief, necktie.

crave vb ask, beg, beseech, entreat, implore, petition, solicit, supplicate; desire, hanker after, long for, need, want, yearn for.

craven n coward, dastard, milk-sop, poltroon, recreant. *adj cowardly, chicken-hearted, lily-livered, pusillanimous, yellow.

craving n hankering, hungering, longing, yearning.

craw n crop, gullet, stomach, throat.

craze vb bewilder, confuse, dement, derange, madden;

disorder, impair, weaken. * n fashion, mania, mode, novelty.

crazy adj broken, crank, rickety, shaky, shattered, tottering; crack-brained, delirious, demented, deranged, distracted, idiotic, insane, lunatic, mad, silly.

create vb originate, procreate; cause, design, fashion, form, invent, occasion, produce; appoint, constitute, make.

creation n formation, invention, origination, production; cosmos, universe; appointment, constitution, establishment, nomination.

creator n author, designer, inventor, fashioner, maker, originator; god.

creature n animal, beast, being, body, brute, man, person; dependant, hanger-on, minion, parasite, retainer, vassal; miscreant, wretch.

credence n acceptance, belief, confidence, credit, faith, reliance, trust.

credentials npl certificate, diploma, missive, passport, recommendation, testament, testimonial, title, voucher, warrant.

credibility n believability, plausibility, tenability, trustworthiness.

credit vb accept, believe, trust; loan, trust. * n belief, confidence, credence, faith, reliance, trust; esteem, regard, reputableness, reputation; influence, power; honour, merit; loan, trust.

creditable adj estimable, honourable, meritorious, praiseworthy, reputable, respectable.

credulity n credulousness, gullibility, silliness, simplicity, stupidity.

credulous adj dupable, green, gullible, naive, overtrusting, trustful, uncritical, unsuspecting, unsuspicious.

creed n belief, confession, doctrine, dogma, opinion, profession, tenet.

creek n bay, bight, cove, fjord, inlet; rivulet, streamlet.

creep vb crawl; steal upon; cringe, fawn, grovel, insinuate. * n crawl, scrabble, scramble; fawner, groveller, sycophant, toady.

crenate adj indented, notched, scalloped.

crepitate vb crack, crackle, decrepitate, snap.

crest n comb, plume, topknot, tuft; apex, crown, head, ridge, summit, top; arms, badge, bearings.

crestfallen adj chap-fallen, dejected, depressed, despondent, discouraged, disheartened, dispirited, downcast, down-hearted, low-spirited, melancholy, sad.

crevice n chink, cleft, crack, cranny, fissure, fracture, gap, hole, interstice, opening, rent, rift.

crew n company, complement, hands; company, corps, gang, horde, mob, party, posse, set, squad, team, throng.

crib vb cage, confine, encage, enclose, imprison; pilfer, purloin. * n manger, rack; bin, bunker; plagiarism, plunder, theft.

crick vb jar, rick, wrench, wrick. * n convulsion, cramp, jarring, spasm, rick, wrench, wrick.

crime n felony, misdeed, misdemeanour, offence, violation; delinquency, fault, guilt, iniquity, sin, transgression, unrighteousness, wickedness, wrong.

criminal adj culpable, felonious, flagitious, guilty, illegal, immoral, iniquitous, nefarious, unlawful, vicious, wicked, wrong. * n convict, culprit, delinquent, felon, malefactor, offender, sinner, transgressor.

criminate vb accuse, arraign, charge, convict, impeach, indict; implicate, involve.

crimp vb crisp, curl.

cringe *vb* bend, bow, cower, crouch, fawn, grovel, kneel, sneak, stoop, truckle.

cripple *vb* cramp, destroy, disable, enfeeble, impair, lame, maim, mutilate, paralyse, ruin, weaken.

crisis *n* acme, climax, height; conjuncture, emergency, exigency, juncture, pass, pinch, push, rub, strait, urgency.

crisp *adj* brittle, curled, friable, frizzled.

criterion *n* canon, gauge, measure, principle, proof, rule, standard, test, touchstone.

critic *n* arbiter, caviller, censor, connoisseur, judge, nitpicker, reviewer.

critical *adj* accurate, exact, nice; captious, carping, caviling, censorious, exacting; crucial, decisive, determining, important, turning: dangerous, dubious, exigent, hazardous, imminent, momentous, precarious, ticklish.

criticism *n* analysis, animadversion, appreciation, comment, critique, evaluation, judgement, review, strictures.

criticize *vb* appraise, evaluate, examine, judge.

croak *vb* complain, groan, grumble, moan, mumble, repine; die.

crone *n* hag, witch.

crony *n* ally, associate, chum, friend, mate, mucker, pal.

crook *vb* bend, bow, curve, incurvate, turn, wind. * *n* bend, curvature, flexion, turn; artifice, machination, trick; criminal, thief, villain

crooked *adj* angular, bent, bowed, curved, winding, zigzag; askew, aslant, awry, deformed, disfigured, distorted, twisted, wry; crafty, deceitful, devious, dishonest, dishonourable, fraudulent, insidious, intriguing, knavish, tricky, underhanded, unfair, unscrupulous.

crop *vb* gather, mow, pick, pluck, reap; browse, nibble; clip, curtail, lop, reduce, shorten. * *n* harvest, produce, yield.

cross *vb* intersect, pass over, traverse; hinder, interfere, obstruct, thwart; interbred, intermix. * *adj* transverse; cantankerous, captious, crabbed, churlish, crusty, cynical, fractious, fretful, grouchy, ill-natured, ill-tempered, irascible, irritable, morose, peevish, pettish, petulant, snappish, snarling, sour, spleeny, splenetic, sulky, sullen, surly, testy, touchy, waspish. * *n* crucifix, gibbet, rood; affliction, misfortune, trial, trouble, vexation; cross-breeding, hybrid, intermixture.

cross-grained *adj* cantankerous, headstrong, obdurate, peevish, perverse, refractory, stubborn, untractable, wayward.

crossing *n* intersection, overpass, traversing, underpass.

crossways, crosswise *adv* across, over, transversely.

crotchet *n* caprice, fad, fancy, freak, quirk, vagary, whim, whimsy.

crouch *vb* cower, cringe, fawn, truckle; crouch, kneel, stoop, squat; bow, curtsy, genuflect.

croup *n* buttocks, crupper, rump.

crow *vb* bluster, boast, brag, chuckle, exult, flourish, gasconade, swagger, triumph, vapour, vaunt.

crowd *vb* compress, cram, jam, pack, press; collect, congregate, flock, herd, huddle, swarm. * *n* assembly, company, concourse, flock, herd, horde, host, jam, multitude, press, throng; mob, pack, populace, rabble, rout.

crown *vb* adorn, dignify, honour; recompense, requite, reward; cap, complete, consummate, finish, perfect.

* *n* bays, chaplet, coronal, coronet, garland, diadem, laurel, wreath; monarchy, royalty, sovereignty; diadem; dignity, honour, recompense, reward; apex, crest, summit, top.

crowning *adj* completing, consummating, dignifying, finishing, perfecting.

crucial *adj* intersecting, transverse; critical, decisive, searching, severe, testing, trying.

crude *adj* raw, uncooked, undressed, unworked; harsh, immature, rough, unripe; crass, coarse, unrefined; awkward, immature, indigestible, rude, uncouth, unpolished, unpremeditated.

cruel *adj* barbarous, blood-thirsty, dire, fell, ferocious, inexorable, hard-hearted, inhuman, merciless, pitiless, relentless, ruthless, sanguinary, savage, truculent, uncompassionate, unfeeling, unmerciful, unrelenting; bitter, cold, hard, severe, sharp, unfeeling.

crumble *vb* bruise, crush, decay, disintegrate, perish, pound, pulverize, triturate.

crumple *vb* rumple, wrinkle.

crush *vb* bruise, compress, contuse, squash, squeeze; bray, comminute, crumble, disintegrate, mash; demolish, raze, shatter; conquer, overcome, overpower, overwhelm, quell, subdue.

crust *n* coat, coating, incrustation, outside, shell, surface.

crusty *adj* churlish, crabbed, cross, cynical, fretful, forward, morose, peevish, pettish, petulant, snappish, snarling, surly, testy, touchy, waspish; friable, hard, short.

cry *vb* call, clamour, exclaim; blubber, snivel, sob, wail, weep, whimper; bawl, bellow, hoot, roar, shout, vociferate, scream, screech, squawk, squall, squeal, yell; announce, blazon, proclaim, publish. * *n* acclamation, clamour, ejaculation, exclamation, outcry; crying, lament, lamentation, plaint, weeping; bawl, bellow, howl, roar, scream, screech, shriek, yell; announcement, proclamation, publication.

crypt *n* catacomb, tomb, vault.

cuddle *vb* cosset, nestle, snuggle, squat; caress, embrace, fondle, hug, pet. * *n* caress, embrace, hug.

cudgel *vb* bang, baste, batter, beat, cane, drub, thrash, thump. * *n* bastinado, baton, bludgeon, club, shillelagh, stick, truncheon.

cue *vb* intimate, prompt, remind, sign, signal. * *n* catchword, hint, intimation, nod, prompting, sign, signal, suggestion.

cuff *vb* beat, box, buffet, knock, pummel, punch, slap, smack, strike, thump. * *n* blow, box, punch, slap, smack, strike, thump.

cul-de-sac *n* alley, dead end, impasse, pocket.

cull *vb* choose, elect, pick, select; collect, gather, glean, pluck.

culmination *n* acme, apex, climax, completion, consummation, crown, summit, top, zenith.

culpability *n* blame, blameworthiness, criminality, culpableness, guilt, remissness, sinfulness.

culpable *adj* blameable, blameworthy, censurable, faulty, guilty, reprehensible, sinful, transgressive, wrong.

culprit *n* delinquent, criminal, evil-doer, felon, malefactor, offender.

cultivate *vb* farm, fertilize, till, work; civilize, develop, discipline, elevate, improve, meliorate, refine, train; investigate, prosecute, pursue, search, study; cherish, foster, nourish, patronize, promote.

culture *n* agriculture, cultivation, farming, husbandry, tillage; cultivation, elevation, improvement, refinement.

cumber *vb* burden, clog, encumber, hamper, impede, obstruct, oppress, overload; annoy, distract, embarrass, harass, perplex, plague, torment, trouble, worry.

cumbersome *adj* burdensome, clumsy, cumbrous, embarrassing, heavy, inconvenient, oppressive, troublesome, unmanageable, unwieldy, vexatious.

cuneiform *adj* cuneate, wedge-shaped.

cunning *adj* artful, astute, crafty, crooked, deceitful, designing, diplomatic, foxy, guileful, intriguing, machiavellian, sharp, shrewd, sly, subtle, tricky, wily; curious, ingenious. * *n* art, artfulness, artifice, astuteness, craft, shrewdness, subtlety; craftiness, chicane, chicanery, deceit, deception, intrigue, slyness.

cup *n* beaker, bowl, chalice, goblet, mug; cupful, draught, potion.

cupboard *n* buffet, cabinet, closet.

cupidity *n* avidity, greed, hankering, longing, lust; acquisitiveness, avarice, covetousness, greediness, stinginess.

curative *adj* healing, medicinal, remedial, restorative.

curator *n* custodian, guardian, keeper, superintendent.

curb *vb* bridle, check, control, hinder, moderate, repress, restrain. * *n* bridle, check, control, hindrance, rein, restraint.

cure *vb* alleviate, correct, heal, mend, remedy, restore; kipper, pickle, preserve. * *n* antidote, corrective, help, remedy, reparative, restorative, specific; alleviation, healing, restorative.

curiosity *n* interest, inquiringness, inquisitiveness; celebrity, curio, marvel, novelty, oddity, phenomenon, rarity, sight, spectacle, wonder.

curious *adj* interested, inquiring, inquisitive, meddling, peering, prying, scrutinizing; extraordinary, marvellous, novel, queer, rare, singular, strange, unique, unusual; cunning, elegant, fine, finished, neat, skilful, well-wrought.

curl *vb* coil, twist, wind, writhe; bend, buckle, ripple, wave. * *n* curlicue, lovelock, ringlet; flexure, sinuosity, undulation, wave, waving, winding.

curmudgeon *n* churl, lick-penny, miser, niggard, screw, scrimp, skinflint.

currency *n* publicity; acceptance, circulation, transmission; bills, coins, money, notes.

current *adj* common, general, popular, rife; circulating, passing; existing, instant, present, prevalent, widespread. * *n* course, progression, river, stream, tide, undertow. * *adv* commonly, generally, popularly, publicly.

curry *vb* comb, dress; beat, cudgel, drub, thrash.

curse *vb* anathematize, damn, denounce, execrate, imprecate, invoke, maledict; blast, blight, destroy, doom; afflict, annoy, harass, injure, plague, scourge, torment, vex; blaspheme, swear. * *n* anathema, ban, denunciation, execration, fulmination, imprecation, malediction, malison; affliction, annoyance, plague, scourge, torment, trouble, vexation; ban, condemnation, penalty, sentence.

cursed *adj* accursed, banned, blighted, curse-laden, unholy; abominable, detestable, execrable, hateful, villainous; annoying, confounded, plaguing, scourging, tormenting, troublesome, vexatious.

cursory *adj* brief, careless, desultory, hasty, passing, rapid, slight, summary, superficial, transient, transitory.

curt *adj* brief, concise, laconic, short, terse; crusty, rude, snappish, tart.

curtail *vb* abridge, dock, lop, retrench, shorten; abbreviate, contract, decrease, diminish, lessen.

curtain *vb* cloak, cover, drape, mantle, screen, shade, shield, veil. * *n* arras, drape, drop, portière, screen, shade.

curvature *n* arcuation, bend, bending, camber, crook, curve, flexure, incurvation.

curve *vb* bend, crook, inflect, turn, twist, wind. * *n* arcuation, bend, bending, camber, crook, flexure, incurvation.

curvet *vb* bound, leap, vault; caper, frisk.

cushion *vb* absorb, damp, dampen, deaden, dull, muffle, mute, soften, subdue, suppress; cradle, pillow, support. * *n* bolster, hassock, pad, pillow, woolsack.

cusp *n* angle, horn, point.

custodian *n* curator, guardian, keeper, sacristan, superintendent, warden.

custody *n* care, charge, guardianship, keeping, safekeeping, protection, watch, ward; confinement, durance, duress, imprisonment, prison.

custom *n* consuetude, convention, fashion, habit, manner, mode, practice, rule, usage, use, way; form, formality, observation; patronage; duty, impost, tax, toll, tribute.

customary *adj* accustomed, common, consuetudinary, conventional, familiar, fashionable, general, habitual, gnomic, prescriptive, regular, usual, wonted.

cut *vb* chop, cleave, divide, gash, incise, lance, sever, slice, slit, wound; carve, chisel, sculpture; hurt, move, pierce, touch; ignore, slight; abbreviate, abridge, curtail, shorten. * *n* gash, groove, incision, nick, slash, slice, slit; channel, passage; piece, slice; fling, sarcasm, taunt; fashion, form, mode, shape, style.

cutthroat *adj* barbarous, cruel, ferocious, murderous; competitive, exacting, exorbitant, extortionate, rivalling, ruthless, usurious, vying.* *n* assassin, murderer, ruffian.

cutting *adj* keen, sharp; acid, biting, bitter, caustic, piercing, sarcastic, sardonic, satirical, severe, trenchant, wounding.

cycle *n* age, circle, era, period, revolution, round.

Cyclopean *adj* colossal, enormous, gigantic, Herculean, immense, vast.

cynical *adj* captious, carping, censorious, churlish, crabbed, cross, crusty, fretful, ill-natured, ill-tempered, morose, peevish, pettish, petulant, sarcastic, satirical, snappish, snarling, surly, testy, touchy, waspish; contemptuous, derisive, misanthropic, pessimistic, scornful.

cynosure *n* attraction, centre.

cyst *n* pouch, sac.

D

dab vb box, rap, slap, strike, tap touch; coat, daub, smear. * adj adept, expert, proficient; pat. * n lump, mass, pat.

dabble vb dip, moisten, soak, spatter, splash, sprinkle, wet; meddle, tamper, trifle.

daft adj absurd, delirious, foolish, giddy, idiotic, insane, silly, simple, stupid, witless; frolicsome, merry, mirthful, playful, sportive.

dagger n bayonet, dirk, poniard, stiletto.

dainty adj delicate, delicious, luscious, nice, palatable, savoury, tender, toothsome; beautiful, charming, choice, delicate, elegant, exquisite, fine, neat; fastidious, finical, finicky, over-nice, particular, scrupulous, squeamish. * n delicacy, titbit, treat.

dale n bottom, dell, dingle, glen, vale, valley.

dalliance n caressing, endearments, flirtation, fondling.

dally vb dawdle, fritter, idle, trifle, waste time; flirt, fondle, toy.

damage vb harm, hurt, impair, injure, mar. * n detriment, harm, hurt, injury, loss, mischief.

damages npl compensation, fine, forfeiture, indemnity, reparation, satisfaction.

dame n babe, baby, broad, doll, girl; lady, madam, matron, mistress.

damn vb condemn, doom, kill, ruin. * n bean, curse, fig, hoot, rap, sou, straw, whit.

damnable adj abominable, accursed, atrocious, cursed, detestable, hateful, execrable, odious, outrageous.

damp vb dampen, moisten; allay, abate, check, discourage, moderate, repress, restrain; chill, cool, deaden, deject, depress, dispirit. * adj dank, humid, moist, wet. * n dampness, dank, fog, mist, moisture, vapour; chill, dejection, depression.

damper n check, hindrance, impediment, obstacle; damp, depression, discouragement, wet blanket.

dandle vb amuse, caress, fondle, pet, toss; dance.

danger n jeopardy, insecurity, hazard, peril, risk, venture.

dangerous adj critical, hazardous, insecure, perilous, risky, ticklish, unsafe.

dangle vb drape, hang, pend, sway, swing; fawn.

dank adj damp, humid, moist, wet.

dapper adj active, agile, alert, brisk, lively, nimble, quick, ready, smart, spry; neat, nice, pretty, spruce, trim.

dapple vb diversify, spot, variegate. * adj dappled, spotted, variegated.

dare vb challenge, defy, endanger, hazard, provoke, risk. * n challenge, defiance, gage.

daring adj adventurous, bold, brave, chivalrous, courageous, dauntless, doughty, fearless, gallant, heroic, intrepid, valiant, valorous. * n adventurousness, boldness, bravery, courage, dauntlessness, doughtiness, fearlessness, intrepidity, undauntedness, valour.

dark adj black, cloudy, darksome, dusky, ebon, inky, lightless, lurid, moonless, murky, opaque, overcast, pitchy, rayless, shady, shadowy, starless, sunless, swart, tenebrous, umbrageous, unenlightened, unilluminated; abstruse, cabbalistic, enigmatical, incomprehensible, mysterious, mystic, mystical, obscure, occult, opaque, recondite, transcendental, unillumined, unintelligible; cheerless, discouraging, dismal, disheartening, funereal, gloomy; benighted, darkened, ignorant, rude, unlettered, untaught; atrocious, damnable, infamous, flagitious, foul, horrible, infernal, nefarious, vile, wicked. * n darkness, dusk, murkiness, obscurity; concealment, privacy, secrecy; blindness, ignorance.

darken vb cloud, dim, eclipse, obscure, shade, shadow; chill, damp, depress, gloom, sadden; benight, stultify, stupefy; obscure, perplex; defile, dim, dull, stain, sully.

darkness n blackness, dimness, gloom, obscurity; blindness, ignorance; cheerlessness, despondency, gloom, joylessness; privacy, secrecy.

darling adj beloved, cherished, dear, loved, precious, treasured. * n dear, favourite, idol, love, sweetheart.

dart vb ejaculate, hurl, launch, propel, sling, throw; emit, shoot; dash, rush, scoot, spring.

dash vb break, destroy, disappoint, frustrate, ruin, shatter, spoil, thwart; abash, confound, disappoint, surprise; bolt, dart, fly, run, speed, rush. * n blow, stroke; advance, onset, rush; infusion, smack, spice, sprinkling, tincture, tinge, touch; flourish, show.

dashing adj headlong, impetuous, precipitate, rushing; brilliant, gay, showy, spirited.

dastardly adj base, cowardly, coward, cowering, craven, pusillanimous, recreant. * n coward, craven, milksop, poltroon, recreant.

data npl conditions, facts, information, premises.

date n age, cycle, day, generation, time; epoch, era, period; appointment, arrangement, assignation, engagement, interview, rendezvous, tryst; catch, steady, sweetheart.

daub vb bedaub, begrime, besmear, blur, cover, deface, defile, grime, plaster, smear, smudge, soil, sully. * n smear, smirch, smudge.

daunt vb alarm, appal, check, cow, deter, discourage, frighten, intimate, scare, subdue, tame, terrify, thwart.

dauntless adj bold, brave, chivalrous, courageous, daring, doughty, gallant, heroic, indomitable, intrepid, unaffrighted, unconquerable, undaunted, undismayed, valiant, valorous.

dawdle vb dally, delay, fiddle, idle, lag, loiter, potter, trifle.

dawn vb appear, begin, break, gleam, glimmer, open, rise. * n daybreak, dawning, cockcrow, sunrise, sunup.

day *n* daylight, sunlight, sunshine; age, epoch, generation, lifetime, time.

daze *vb* blind, dazzle; bewilder, confound, confuse, perplex, stun, stupefy. * *n* bewilderment, confusion, discomposure, perturbation, pother; coma, stupor, swoon, trance.

dazzle *vb* blind, daze; astonish, confound, overpower, surprise. * *n* brightness, brilliance, splendour.

dead *adj* breathless, deceased, defunct, departed, gone, inanimate, lifeless; apathetic, callous, cold, dull, frigid, indifferent, inert, lukewarm, numb, obtuse, spiritless, torpid, unfeeling; flat, insipid, stagnant, tasteless, vapid; barren, inactive, sterile, unemployed, unprofitable, useless. * *adv* absolutely, completely, downright, fundamentally, quite; direct, directly, due, exactly, just, right, squarely, straight. * *n* depth, midst; hush, peace, quietude, silence, stillness.

deaden *vb* abate, damp, dampen, dull, impair, muffle, mute, restrain, retard, smother, weaken; benumb, blunt, hebetate, obtund, paralyse.

deadly *adj* deleterious, destructive, fatal, lethal, malignant, mortal, murderous, noxious, pernicious, poisonous, venomous; implacable, mortal, rancorous, sanguinary.

deal *vb* allot, apportion, assign, bestow, dispense, distribute, divide, give, reward, share; bargain, trade, traffic, treat with. * *n* amount, degree, distribution, extent, lot, portion, quantity, share; bargain, transaction.

dear *adj* costly, expensive, high-priced; beloved, cherished, darling, esteemed, precious, treasured. * *n* beloved, darling, deary, honey, love, precious, sweet, sweetie, sweetheart.

dearth *n* deficiency, insufficiency, scarcity; famine, lack, need, shortage, want.

death *n* cessation, decease, demise, departure, destruction, dissolution, dying, end, exit, mortality, passing.

deathless *adj* eternal, everlasting, immortal, imperishable, undying; boring, dull, turgid.

debacle *n* breakdown, cataclysm, collapse; rout, stampede.

debar *vb* blackball, deny, exclude, hinder, prevent, prohibit, restrain, shut out, stop, withhold.

debase *vb* adulterate, alloy, depress, deteriorate, impair, injure, lower, pervert, reduce, vitiate; abase, degrade, disgrace, dishonour, humble, humiliate, mortify, shame; befoul, contaminate, corrupt, defile, foul, pollute, soil, taint.

debate *vb* argue, canvass, contest, discuss, dispute; contend, deliberate, wrangle. * *n* controversy, discussion, disputation; altercation, contention, contest, dispute, logomachy.

debauch *vb* corrupt, deprave, pollute, vitiate; deflower, ravish, seduce, violate. * *n* carousal, orgy, revel, saturnalia.

debauchery *n* dissipation, dissoluteness, excesses, intemperance; debauch, excess, intemperance, lewdness, licentiousness, lust; bacchanal, carousal, compotation, indulgence, orgies, potation, revelry, revels, saturnalia, spree.

debilitate *vb* enervate, enfeeble, exhaust, prostrate, relax, weaken.

debility *n* enervation, exhaustion, faintness, feebleness, frailty, imbecility, infirmity, languor, prostration, weakness.

debonair *adj* affable, civil, complaisant, courteous, easy, gracious, kind, obliging, polite, refined, urbane, well-bred.

debris *n* detritus, fragments, remains, rubbish, rubble, ruins, wreck, wreckage.

debt *n* arrears, debit, due, liability, obligation; fault, misdoing, offence, shortcoming, sin, transgression, trespass.

decadence *n* caducity, decay, declension, decline, degeneracy, degeneration, deterioration, fall, retrogression.

decamp *vb* abscond, bolt, escape, flee, fly.

decapitate *vb* behead, decollate, guillotine.

decay *vb* decline, deteriorate, disintegrate, fail, perish, wane, waste, wither; decompose, putrefy, rot. * *n* caducity, decadence, declension, decline, decomposition, decrepitude, degeneracy, degeneration, deterioration, dilapidation, disintegration, fading, failing, perishing, putrefaction, ruin, wasting, withering.

deceased *adj* dead, defunct, departed, gone, late, lost.

deceit *n* artifice, cheating, chicanery, cozenage, craftiness, deceitfulness, deception, double-dealing, duplicity, finesse, fraud, guile, hypocrisy, imposition, imposture, pretence, sham, treachery, tricky, underhandedness, wile.

deceitful *adj* counterfeit, deceptive, delusive, fallacious, hollow, illusive, illusory, insidious, misleading; circumventive, cunning, designing, dissembling, dodgy, double-dealing, evasive, false, fraudulent, guileful, hypocritical, insincere, tricky, underhanded, wily.

deceive *vb* befool, beguile, betray, cheat, chouse, circumvent, cozen, defraud, delude, disappoint, double-cross, dupe, ensnare, entrap, fool, gull, hoax, hoodwink, humbug, mislead, outwit, overreach, trick.

deceiver *n* charlatan, cheat, humbug, hypocrite, knave, impostor, pretender, rogue, sharper, trickster.

decent *adj* appropriate, becoming, befitting, comely, seemly, decorous, fit, proper, seemly; chaste, delicate, modest, pure; moderate, passable, respectable, tolerable.

deception *n* artifice, cheating, chicanery, cozenage, craftiness, deceitfulness, deception, double-dealing, duplicity, finesse, fraud, guile, hoax, hypocrisy, imposition, imposture, pretence, sham, treachery, trick, underhandedness, wile; cheat, chouse, ruse, stratagem, wile.

deceptive *adj* deceitful, deceiving, delusive, disingenuous, fallacious, false, illusive, illusory, misleading.

decide *vb* close, conclude, determine, end, settle, terminate; resolve; adjudge, adjudicate, award.

decided *adj* determined, firm, resolute, unhesitating, unwavering; absolute, categorical, positive, unequivocal; certain, clear, indisputable, undeniable, unmistakable, unquestionable.

deciduous *adj* caducous, nonperennial, temporary.

decipher *vb* explain, expound, interpret, reveal, solve, unfold, unravel; read.

decision *n* conclusion, determination, judgement, settlement; adjudication, award, decree, pronouncement, sentence; firmness, resolution.

decisive *adj* conclusive, determinative, final.

deck *vb* adorn, array, beautify, decorate, embellish, grace, ornament; apparel, attire, bedeck, clothe, dress, robe.

declaim *vb* harangue, mouth, rant, speak, spout.

declamation *n* declaiming, haranguing, mouthing, ranting, spouting.

declamatory *adj* bombastic, discursive, fustian, grandiloquent, high-flown, high-sounding, incoherent, inflated, pompous, pretentious, rhetorical, swelling, turgid.

declaration *n* affirmation, assertion, asseveration, averment, avowal, protestation, statement; announcement, proclamation, publication.

declaratory *adj* affirmative, annunciatory, assertive, declarative, definite, enunciative, enunciatory, expressive; explanatory, expository.

declare *vb* advertise, affirm, announce, assert, asseverate, aver, blazon, bruit, proclaim, promulgate, pronounce, publish, state, utter.

declension *n* decadence, decay, decline, degeneracy, deterioration, diminution; inflection, variation; declination, nonacceptance, refusal.

declination *n* bending, descent, inclination; decadence, decay, decline, degeneracy, degeneration, degradation, deterioration, diminution; aberration, departure, deviation, digression, divagation, divergence; declinature, nonacceptance, refusal.

decline *vb* incline, lean, slope; decay, decline, fail, flag, languish, pine, sink; degenerate, depreciate, deteriorate; decrease, diminish, dwindle, fade, ebb, lapse, lessen, wane; avoid, refuse, reject; inflect, vary. * *n* decadence, decay, declension, declination, degeneracy, deterioration, diminution, wane; atrophy, consumption, marasmus, phthisis; declivity, hill, incline, slope.

declivity *n* declination, descent, incline, slope.

decompose *vb* analyse, disintegrate, dissolve, distil, resolve, separate; corrupt, decay, putrefy, rot.

decomposition *n* analysis, break-up, disintegration, resolution; caries, corruption, crumbling, decay, disintegration, dissolution, putrescence, rotting.

decorate *vb* adorn, beautify, bedeck, deck, embellish, enrich, garnish, grace, ornament.

decoration *n* adorning, beautifying, bedecking, decking, enriching, garnishing, ornamentation, ornamenting; adornment, enrichment, embellishment, ornament.

decorous *adj* appropriate, becoming, befitting, comely, decent, fit, suitable, proper, sedate, seemly, staid.

decorum *n* appropriate behaviour, courtliness, decency, deportment, dignity, gravity, politeness, propriety, sedateness, seemliness.

decoy *vb* allure, deceive, ensnare, entice, entrap, inveigle, lure, seduce, tempt. * *n* allurement, lure, enticement.

decrease *vb* abate, contract, decline, diminish, dwindle, ebb, lessen, subside, wane; curtail, diminish, lessen, lower, reduce, retrench. * *n* abatement, contraction, declension, decline, decrement, diminishing, diminution, ebb, ebbing, lessening, reduction, subsidence, waning.

decree *vb* adjudge, appoint, command, decide, determine, enact, enjoin, order, ordain. * *n* act, command, edict, enactment, fiat, law, mandate, order, ordinance, precept, regulation, statute.

decrement *n* decrease, diminution, lessening, loss, waste.

decrepit *adj* feeble, effete, shattered, wasted, weak; aged, crippled, superannuated.

decry *vb* abuse, belittle, blame, condemn, denounce, depreciate, detract, discredit, disparage, run down, traduce, underrate, undervalue.

dedicate *vb* consecrate, devote, hallow, sanctify; address, inscribe.

deduce *vb* conclude, derive, draw, gather, infer.

deducible *adj* derivable, inferable.

deduct *vb* remove, subtract, withdraw; abate, detract.

deduction *n* removal, subtraction, withdrawal; abatement, allowance, defalcation, discount, rebate, reduction, reprise; conclusion, consequence, corollary, inference.

deed *n* achievement, act, action, derring-do, exploit, feat, performance; fact, truth, reality; charter, contract, document, indenture, instrument, transfer.

deem *vb* account, believe, conceive, consider, count, estimate, hold, imagine, judge, regard, suppose, think; fancy, opine.

deep *adj* abysmal, extensive, great, profound; abstruse, difficult, hard, intricate, knotty, mysterious, recondite, unfathomable; astute, cunning, designing, discerning, intelligent, insidious, penetrating, sagacious, shrewd; absorbed, engrossed; bass, grave, low; entire, great, heartfelt, thorough. * *n* main, ocean, water, sea; abyss, depth, profundity; enigma, mystery, riddle; silence, stillness.

deeply *adv* profoundly; completely, entirely, extensively, greatly, thoroughly; affectingly, distressingly, feelingly, mournfully, sadly.

deface *vb* blotch, deform, disfigure, injure, mar, mutilate, obliterate, soil, spoil, sully, tarnish.

de facto *adj* actual, real. * *adv* actually, in effect, in fact, really, truly.

defalcate *vb* abate, curtail, retrench, lop.

defalcation *n* abatement, deduction, diminution, discount, reduction; default, deficiency, deficit, shortage, shortcoming; embezzlement, fraud.

defamation *n* abuse, aspersion, back-biting, calumny, detraction, disparagement, libel, obloquy, opprobrium, scandal, slander.

defamatory *adj* abusive, calumnious, libellous, slanderous.

defame *vb* abuse, asperse, blacken, belie, besmirch, blemish, calumniate, detract, disgrace, dishonour, libel, malign, revile, slander, smirch, traduce, vilify.

default *vb* defalcate, dishonour, fail, repudiate, welsh. * *n* defalcation, failure, lapse, neglect, offence, omission, oversight, shortcoming ; defect, deficiency, deficit, delinquency, destitution, fault, lack, want.

defaulter *n* delinquent, embezzler, offender, peculator.

defeat *vb* beat, checkmate, conquer, discomfit, overcome, overpower, overthrow, repulse, rout, ruin, vanquish; baffle, balk, block, disappoint, disconcert, foil, frustrate, thwart. * *n* discomfiture, downfall, overthrow, repulse, rout, vanquishment; bafflement, checkmate, frustration.

defect *vb* abandon, desert, rebel, revolt. * *n* default, deficiency, destitution, lack, shortcoming, spot, taint, want; blemish, blotch, error, flaw, imperfection, mistake; failing, fault, foible.

defection *n* abandonment, desertion, rebellion, revolt; apostasy, backsliding, dereliction.

defective *adj* deficient, inadequate, incomplete, insufficient, scant, short; faulty, imperfect, marred.

defence *n* defending, guarding, holding, maintaining, maintenance, protection; buckler, bulwark, fortification, guard, protection, rampart, resistance, shield; apology, excuse, justification, plea, vindication.

defenceless *adj* exposed, helpless, unarmed, unprotected, unguarded, unshielded, weak.

defend *vb* cover, fortify, guard, preserve, protect, safeguard, screen, secure, shelter, shield; assert, espouse, justify, maintain, plead, uphold, vindicate.

defender *n* asserter, maintainer, pleader, upholder; champion, protector, vindicator.

defer[1] *vb* adjourn, delay, pigeonhole, procrastinate, postpone, prorogue, protract, shelve, table.

defer[2] *vb* abide by, acknowledge, bow to, give way, submit, yield; admire, esteem, honour, regard, respect.

deference *n* esteem, homage, honour, obeisance, regard, respect, reverence, veneration; complaisance, consideration; obedience, submission.

deferential *adj* respectful, reverential.

defiance *n* challenge, daring; contempt, despite, disobedience, disregard, opposition, spite.

defiant *adj* contumacious, recalcitrant, resistant; bold, courageous, resistant.

deficiency *n* dearth, default, deficit, insufficiency, lack, meagreness, scantiness, scarcity, shortage, shortness, want; defect, error, failing, falling, fault, foible, frailty, imperfection, infirmity, weakness.

deficient *adj* defective, faulty, imperfect, inadequate, incomplete, insufficient, lacking, scant, scanty, scarce, short, unsatisfactory, wanting.

deficit *n* deficiency, lack, scarcity, shortage, shortness.

defile[1] *vb* dirty, foul, soil, stain, tarnish; contaminate, debase, poison, pollute, sully, taint, vitiate; corrupt, debauch, deflower, ravish, seduce, violate.

defile[2] *vb* file, march, parade, promenade. * *n* col, gorge, pass, passage, ravine, strait.

define *vb* bound, circumscribe, designate, delimit, demarcate, determine, explain, limit, specify.

definite *adj* defined, determinate, determined, fixed, restricted; assured, certain, clear, exact, explicit, positive, precise, specific, unequivocal.

definitive *adj* categorical, determinate, explicit, express, positive, unconditional; conclusive, decisive, final.

deflect *vb* bend, deviate, diverge, swerve, turn, twist, waver, wind.

deflower *vb* corrupt, debauch, defile, seduce.

deform *vb* deface, disfigure, distort, injure, mar, misshape, ruin, spoil.

deformity *n* abnormality, crookedness, defect, disfigurement, distortion, inelegance, irregularity, malformation, misproportion, misshapenness, monstrosity, ugliness.

defraud *vb* beguile, cheat, chouse, circumvent, cozen, deceive, delude, diddle, dupe, embezzle, gull, overreach, outwit, pilfer, rob, swindle, trick.

defray *vb* bear, discharge, liquidate, meet, pay, settle.

deft *adj* adroit, apt, clever, dab, dextrous, expert, handy, ready, skilful.

defunct *adj* dead, deceased, departed, extinct, gone; abrogated, annulled, cancelled, inoperative.

defy *vb* challenge, dare; brave, contemn, despise, disregard, face, flout, provoke, scorn, slight, spurn.

degeneracy *n* abasement, caducity, corruption, debasement, decadence, decay, declension, decline, decrease, degenerateness, degeneration, degradation, depravation, deterioration; inferiority, meanness, poorness.

degenerate *vb* decay, decline, decrease, deteriorate, retrograde, sink. * *adj* base, corrupt, decayed, degenerated, deteriorated, fallen, inferior, low, mean, perverted.

degeneration *n* debasement, decline, degeneracy, deterioration.

degradation *n* deposition, disgrace, dishonour, humiliation, ignominy; abasement, caducity, corruption, debasement, decadence, decline, degeneracy, degeneration, deterioration, perversion, vitiation.

degrade *vb* abase, alloy, break, cashier, corrupt, debase, demote, discredit, disgrace, dishonour, disparage, downgrade, humiliate, humble, lower, pervert, vitiate; deteriorate, impair, lower, sink.

degree *n* stage, step; class, grade, order, quality, rank, standing, station; extent, measure; division, interval, space.

deify *vb* apotheosize, idolize, glorify, revere; elevate, ennoble, exalt.

deign *vb* accord, condescend, grant, vouchsafe.

deject *vb* depress, discourage, dishearten, dispirit, sadden.

dejected *adj* blue, chapfallen, crestfallen, depressed, despondent, disheartened, dispirited, doleful, downcast, down-hearted, gloomy, low-spirited, miserable, sad, wretched.

delay *vb* defer, postpone, procrastinate; arrest, detain, check, hinder, impede, retard, stay, stop; prolong, protract; dawdle, linger, loiter, tarry. * *n* deferment, postponement, procrastination; check, detention, hindrance, impediment, retardation, stoppage; prolonging, protraction; dallying, dawdling, lingering, tarrying, stay, stop.

delectable *adj* agreeable, charming, delightful, enjoyable, gratifying, pleasant, pleasing.

delectation *n* delight, ecstasy, gladness, joy, rapture, ravishment, transport.

delegate *vb* appoint, authorize, mission, depute, deputize, transfer; commit, entrust. * *n* ambassador, commissioner, delegate, deputy, envoy, representative.

delete *vb* cancel, efface, erase, expunge, obliterate, remove.

deleterious *adj* deadly, destructive, lethal, noxious, poisonous; harmful, hurtful, injurious, pernicious, unwholesome.

deliberate *vb* cogitate, consider, consult, meditate, muse, ponder, reflect, ruminate, think, weigh. * *adj* careful, cautious, circumspect, considerate, heedful, purposeful, methodical, thoughtful, wary; well-advised, well-considered; aforethought, intentional, premeditated, purposed, studied.

deliberation *n* caution, circumspection, cogitation, consideration, coolness, meditation, prudence, reflection, thought, thoughtfulness, wariness; purpose.

delicacy *n* agreeableness, daintiness, deliciousness, pleasantness, relish, savouriness; bonne bouche, dainty, tidbit; elegance, fitness, lightness, niceness, nicety, smoothness, softness, tenderness; fragility, frailty, slenderness, slightness, tenderness, weakness; carefulness, discrimination, fastidiousness, finesse, nicety, scrupulousness, sensitivity, subtlety, tact; purity, refinement, sensibility.

delicate *adj* agreeable, delicious, pleasant, pleasing, palatable, savoury; elegant, exquisite, fine, nice; careful, dainty, discriminating, fastidious, scrupulous; fragile, frail, slender, slight, tender, delicate; pure, refined.

delicious *adj* dainty, delicate, luscious, nice, palatable, savory; agreeable, charming, choice, delightful, exquisite, grateful, pleasant.

delight *vb* charm, enchant, enrapture, gratify, please, ravish, rejoice, satisfy, transport. * *n* charm, delectation, ecstasy, enjoyment, gladness, gratification, happiness, joy, pleasure, rapture, ravishment, satisfaction, transport.

delightful *adj* agreeable, captivating, charming, delectable, enchanting, enjoyable, enrapturing, rapturous, ravishing, transporting.

delineate *vb* design, draw, figure, paint, sketch, trace; depict, describe, picture, portray.

delineation *n* design, draught, drawing, figure, outline, sketch; account, description, picture, portrayal.

delinquency *n* crime, fault, misdeed, misdemeanour, offence, wrong-doing.

delinquent *adj* negligent, offending. * *n* criminal, culprit, defaulter, malefactor, miscreant, misdoer, offender, transgressor, wrong-doer.

delirious *adj* crazy, demented, deranged, frantic, frenzied, light-headed, mad, insane, raving, wandering.

delirium *n* aberration, derangement, frenzy, hallucination, incoherence, insanity, lunacy, madness, raving, wandering.

deliver *vb* emancipate, free, liberate, release; extricate, redeem, rescue, save; commit, give, impart, transfer; cede, grant, relinquish, resign, yield; declare, emit, promulgate, pronounce, speak, utter; deal, discharge.

deliverance *n* emancipation, escape, liberation, redemption, release.

delivery *n* conveyance, surrender; commitment, giving, rendering, transference, transferral, transmission; elocution, enunciation, pronunciation, speech, utterance; childbirth, confinement, labour, parturition, travail.

dell *n* dale, dingle, glen, valley, ravine.

delude *vb* beguile, cheat, chouse, circumvent, cozen, deceive, dupe, gull, misguide, mislead, overreach, trick.

deluge *vb* drown, inundate, overflow, overwhelm, submerge. * *n* cataclysm, downpour, flood, inundation, overflow, rush.

delusion *n* artifice, cheat, clap-trap, deceit, dodge, fetch, fraud, imposition, imposture, ruse, snare, trick, wile; deception, error, fallacy, fancy, hallucination, illusion, mistake, mockery, phantasm.

delusive *adj* deceitful, deceiving, deceptive, fallacious, illusional, illusionary, illusive.

demand *vb* challenge, exact, require; claim, necessitate, require; ask, inquire. * *n* claim, draft, exaction, requirement, requisition; call, want; inquiry, interrogation, question.

demarcation *n* bound, boundary, confine, distinction, division, enclosure, limit, separation.

demeanour *n* air, bearing, behaviour, carriage, deportment, manner, mien.

demented *adj* crack-brained, crazed, crazy, daft, deranged, dotty, foolish, idiotic, infatuated, insane, lunatic.

dementia *n* idiocy, insanity, lunacy.

demerit *n* delinquency, fault, ill-desert.

demise *vb* alienate, consign, convey, devolve, grant, transfer; bequeath, devise, leave, will. * *n* alienation, conveyance, transfer, transference, transmission; death, decease.

demolish *vb* annihilate, destroy, dismantle, level, overthrow, overturn, pulverize, raze, ruin.

demon *n* devil, fiend, kelpie, goblin, troll.

demoniac, demoniacal *adj* demonic, demonical, devilish, diabolic, diabolical, fiendish, hellish, infernal, Mephistophelean, Mephistophelian, satanic; delirious, distracted, frantic, frenzied, feverish, hysterical, mad, overwrought, rabid.

demonstrate *vb* establish, exhibit, illustrate, indicate, manifest, prove, show.

demonstration *n* display, exhibition, manifestation, show.

demonstrative *adj* affectionate, communicative, effusive, emotional, expansive, expressive, extroverted, open, outgoing, passionate, sentimental, suggestive, talkative, unreserved; absolute, apodictic, certain, conclusive, probative; exemplificative, illustrative.

demoralize *vb* corrupt, debase, debauch, deprave, vitiate; depress, discourage, dishearten, weaken.

demulcent *adj* emollient, lenitive, mild, mollifying, sedative, soothing.

demur *vb* halt, hesitate, pause, stop, waver; doubt, object, scruple. * *n* demurral, hesitance, hesitancy, hesitation, objection, pause, qualm, scruple.

demure *adj* prudish; coy, decorous, grave, modest, priggish, prudish, sedate, sober, staid.

den *n* cavern, cave; haunt, lair, resort, retreat.

denial *n* contradiction, controverting, negation; abjuration, disavowal, disclaimer, disowning; disallowance, refusal, rejection.

denizen *n* citizen, dweller, inhabitant, resident.

denominate *vb* call, christen, designate, dub, entitle, name, phrase, style, term.

denomination *n* appellation, designation, name, style, term, title; class, kind, sort; body, persuasion, school, sect.

denote *vb* betoken, connote, designate, imply, indicate, mark, mean, note, show, signify, typify.

dénouement *n* catastrophe, unravelling; consummation, issue, finale, upshot, conclusion, termination.

denounce *vb* menace, threaten; arraign, attack, brand, censure, condemn, proscribe, stigmatize, upbraid; accuse, inform, denunciate.

dense *adj* close, compact, compressed, condensed, thick; dull, slow, stupid.

dent *vb* depress, dint, indent, pit. * *n* depression, dint, indentation, nick, notch.

dentate *adj* notched, serrate, toothed.

denude *vb* bare, divest, strip.

denunciation *n* menace, threat; arraignment, censure, fulmination, invective; exposure.

deny *vb* contradict, gainsay, oppose, refute, traverse; abjure, abnegate, disavow, disclaim, disown, renounce; disallow, refuse, reject, withhold.

depart *vb* absent, disappear, vanish; abandon, decamp, go, leave, migrate, quit, remove, withdraw; decease, die; deviate, diverge, vary.

department *n* district, division, part, portion, province; bureau, function, office, province, sphere, station; branch, division, subdivision.

departure *n* exit, leaving, parting, removal, recession, removal, retirement, withdrawal; abandonment, forsaking; death, decease, demise, deviation, exit.

depend *vb* hang, hinge, turn.

dependant *n* client, hanger-on, henchman, minion, retainer, subordinate, vassal; attendant, circumstance, concomitant, consequence, corollary.

dependence *n* concatenation, connection, interdependence; confidence, reliance, trust; buttress, prop, staff, stay, support, supporter; contingency, need, subjection, subordination.

dependency *n* adjunct, appurtenance; colony, province.

dependent *adj* hanging, pendant; conditioned, contingent, relying, subject, subordinate.

depict *vb* delineate, limn, outline, paint, pencil, portray, sketch; describe, render, represent.

deplete *vb* drain, empty, evacuate, exhaust, reduce.

deplorable *adj* calamitous, distressful, distressing, grievous, lamentable, melancholy, miserable, mournful, pitiable, regrettable, sad, wretched.

deplore *vb* bemoan, bewail, grieve for, lament, mourn, regret.

deploy *vb* display, expand, extend, open, unfold.

deportment *n* air, bearing, behaviour, breeding, carriage, comportment, conduct, demeanour, manner, mien, port.

depose *vb* break, cashier, degrade, dethrone, dismiss, displace, oust, reduce; avouch, declare, depone, testify.

deposit *vb* drop, dump, precipitate; lay, put; bank, hoard, lodge, put, save, store; commit, entrust. * *n* diluvium, dregs, lees, precipitate, precipitation, sediment, settlement, settlings, silt; money, pawn, pledge, security, stake.

depositary *n* fiduciary, guardian, trustee.

deposition *n* affidavit, evidence, testimony; deposit, precipitation, settlement; dethroning, displacement, removal.

depository *n* deposit, depot, storehouse, warehouse.

depot *n* depository, magazine, storehouse, warehouse.

depravation *n* abasement, corruption, deterioration, impairing, injury, vitiation; debasement, degeneracy, degeneration, depravity, impairment.

depraved *adj* abandoned, corrupt, corrupted, debased, debauched, degenerate, dissolute, evil, graceless, hardened, immoral, lascivious, lewd, licentious, lost, perverted, profligate, reprobate, shameless, sinful, vicious, wicked.

depravity *n* corruption, degeneracy, depravedness; baseness, contamination, corruption, corruptness, criminality, demoralization, immorality, iniquity, license, perversion, vice, viciousness, wickedness.

depreciate *vb* underestimate, undervalue, underrate; belittle, censure, decry, degrade, disparage, malign, traduce.

depreciation *n* belittling, censure, derogation, detraction, disparagement, maligning, traducing.

depredation *n* despoiling, devastation, pilfering, pillage, plunder, rapine, robbery, spoliation, theft.

depress *vb* bow, detrude, drop, lower, reduce, sink; abase, abash, degrade, debase, disgrace, humble, humiliate; chill, damp, dampen, deject, discourage, dishearten, dispirit, sadden; deaden, lower.

depression *n* cavity, concavity, dent, dimple, dint, excavation, hollow, hollowness, indentation, pit; blues, cheerlessness, dejection, dejectedness, despondency, disconsolateness, disheartenment, dispiritedness, dole, dolefulness, downheartedness, dumps, gloom, gloominess, hypochondria, melancholy, sadness, vapours; inactivity, lowness, stagnation; abasement, debasement, degradation, humiliation.

deprivation *n* bereavement, dispossession, loss, privation, spoliation, stripping.

deprive *vb* bereave, denude, despoil, dispossess, divest, rob, strip.

depth *n* abyss, deepness, drop, profundity; extent, measure; middle, midst, stillness; astuteness, discernment, penetration, perspicacity, profoundness, profundity, sagacity, shrewdness.

deputation *n* commission, delegation; commissioners, deputies, delegates, delegation, embassies, envoys, legation.

depute *vb* accredit, appoint, authorize, charge, commission, delegate, empower, entrust.

deputy *adj* acting, assistant, vice, subordinate. * *n* agent, commissioner, delegate, envoy, factor, legate, lieutenant, proxy, representative, substitute, viceregent.

derange *vb* confound, confuse, disarrange, disconcert, disorder, displace, madden, perturb, unsettle; discompose, disconcert, disturb, perturb, ruffle, upset; craze, madden, unbalance, unhinge.

derangement *n* confusion, disarrangement, disorder, irregularity; discomposure, disturbance, perturbation; aberration, alienation, delirium, dementia, hallucination, insanity, lunacy, madness, mania.

derelict *adj* abandoned, forsaken, left, relinquished; delinquent, faithless, guilty, neglectful, negligent, unfaithful. * *n* castaway, castoff, outcast, tramp, vagrant, wreck, wretch.

dereliction *n* abandonment, desertion, relinquishement, renunciation; delinquency, failure, faithlessness, fault, neglect, negligence.

deride *vb* chaff, flout, gibe, insult, jeer, lampoon, mock, ridicule, satirize, scoff, scorn, sneer, taunt.

derision *n* contempt, disrespect, insult, laughter, mockery, ridicule, scorn.

derisive *adj* contemptuous, contumelious, mocking, ridiculing, scoffing, scornful.

derivation *n* descent, extraction, genealogy; etymology; deducing, deriving, drawing, getting, obtaining; beginning, foundation, origination, source.

derive *vb* draw, get, obtain, receive; deduce, follow, infer, trace.

derogate *vb* compromise, depreciate, detract, diminish, disparage, lessen.

derogatory *adj* belittling, depreciative, deprecatory, detracting, dishonouring, disparaging, injurious.

descant *vb* amplify, animadvert, dilate, discourse, discuss, enlarge, expatiate. * *n* melody, soprano, treble; animadversion, commentary, remarks; discourse, discussion.

descend *vb* drop, fall, pitch, plunge, sink, swoop; alight, dismount; go, pass, proceed, devolve; derive, issue, originate.

descendants *npl* offspring, issue, posterity, progeny.

descent *n* downrush, drop, fall; descending; decline, declivity, dip, pitch, slope; ancestry, derivation, extraction, genealogy, lineage, parentage, pedigree; assault, attack, foray, incursion, invasion, raid.

describe *vb* define, delineate, draw, illustrate, limn, sketch, specify, trace; detail; depict, explain, narrate, portray, recount, relate, represent; characterize.

description *n* delineation, tracing; account, depiction, explanation, narration, narrative, portrayal, recital, relation, report, representation; class, kind, sort, species.

descry *vb* behold, discover, discern, distinguish, espy, observe, perceive, see; detect, recognize.

desecrate *vb* abuse, pervert, defile, pollute, profane, violate.

desert[1] *n* due, excellence, merit, worth; punishment, reward.

desert[2] *vb* abandon, abscond, forsake, leave, quit, relinquish, renounce, resign, quit, vacate.

desert[3] *adj* barren, desolate, forsaken, lonely, solitary, uncultivated, uninhabited, unproductive, untilled, waste, wild.

deserted *adj* abandoned, forsaken, relinquished.

deserter *n* abandoner, forsaker, quitter, runaway; apostate, backslider, fugitive, recreant, renegade, revolter, traitor, turncoat.

desertion n abandonment, dereliction, recreancy, relinquishment.

deserve vb earn, gain, merit, procure, win.

desiderate vb desire, lack, miss, need, want.

design vb brew, concoct, contrive, devise, intend, invent, mean, plan, project, scheme; intend, mean, purpose; delineate, describe, draw, outline, sketch, trace. * n aim, device, drift, intent, intention, mark, meaning, object, plan, proposal, project, purport, purpose, scheme, scope; delineation, draught, drawing, outline, plan, sketch; adaptation, artifice, contrivance, invention, inventiveness.

designate vb denote, distinguish, indicate, particularize, select, show, specify, stipulate; characterize, define, describe; call, christen, denominate, dub, entitle, name, style; allot, appoint, christen.

designation n indication, particularization, selection, specification; class, description, kind; appellation, denomination, name, style, title.

designing adj artful, astute, crafty, crooked, cunning, deceitful, insidious, intriguing, Machiavellian, scheming, sly, subtle, treacherous, trickish, tricky, unscrupulous, wily.

desirable adj agreeable, beneficial, covetable, eligible, enviable, good, pleasing, preferable.

desire vb covet, crave, desiderate, fancy, hanker after, long for, lust after, want, wish, yearn for; ask, entreat, request, solicit. * n eroticism, lasciviousness, libidinousness, libido, lust, lustfulness, passion; eagerness, fancy, hope, inclination, mind, partiality, penchant, pleasure, volition, want, wish.

desirous adj avid, eager, desiring, longing, solicitous, wishful.

desist vb cease, discontinue, forbear, pause, stay, stop.

desolate vb depopulate, despoil, destroy, devastate, pillage, plunder, ravage, ruin, sack. * adj bare, barren, bleak, desert, forsaken, lonely, solitary, unfrequented, uninhabited, waste, wild; companionable, lonely, lonesome, solitary; desolated, destroyed, devastated, ravaged, ruined; cheerless, comfortless, companionless, disconsolate, dreary, forlorn, forsaken, miserable, wretched.

desolation n destruction, devastation, havoc, ravage, ruin; barrenness, bleakness, desolateness, dreariness, loneliness, solitariness, solitude, wildness; gloom, gloominess, misery, sadness, unhappiness, wretchedness.

despair vb despond, give up, lose hope. * n dejection, desperation, despondency, disheartenment, hopelessness.

despatch see **dispatch**.

desperado n daredevil, gangster, marauder, ruffian, thug, tough.

desperate adj despairing, despondent, desponding, hopeless; forlorn, irretrievable; extreme; audacious, daring, foolhardy, frantic, furious, headstrong, precipitate, rash, reckless, violent, wild, wretched; extreme, great, monstrous, prodigious, supreme.

desperation n despair, hopelessness; fury, rage.

despicable adj abject, base, contemptible, degrading, low, mean, paltry, pitiful, shameful, sordid, vile, worthless.

despise vb contemn, disdain, disregard, neglect, scorn, slight, spurn, undervalue.

despite n malevolence, malice, malignity, spite; contempt, contumacy, defiance. * prep notwithstanding.

despoil vb bereave, denude, deprive, dispossess, divest, strip; devastate, fleece, pillage, plunder, ravage, rifle, rob.

despond vb despair, give up, lose hope, mourn, sorrow.

despondency n blues, dejection, depression, discouragement, gloom, hopelessness, melancholy, sadness.

despondent adj dejected, depressed, discouraged, disheartened, dispirited, low-spirited, melancholy.

despot n autocrat, dictator; oppressor, tyrant.

despotic adj absolute, arrogant, autocratic, dictatorial, imperious; arbitrary, oppressive, tyrannical, tyrannous.

despotism n absolutism, autocracy, dictatorship; oppression, tyranny.

destination n appointment, decree, destiny, doom, fate, foreordainment, foreordination, fortune, lot, ordination, star; aim, design, drift, end, intention, object, purpose, scope; bourne, goal, harbour, haven, journey's end, resting-place, terminus.

destine vb allot, appoint, assign, consecrate, devote, ordain; design, intend, predetermine; decree, doom, foreordain, predestine.

destitute adj distressed, indigent, moneyless, necessitous, needy, penniless, penurious, pinched, poor, reduced, wanting.

destitution n indigence, need, penury, poverty, privation, want.

destroy vb demolish, overthrow, overturn, subvert, raze, ruin; annihilate, dissolve, efface, quench; desolate, devastate, devour, ravage, waste; eradicate, extinguish, extirpate, kill, uproot, slay.

destruction n demolition, havoc, overthrow, ruin, subversion; desolation, devastation, holocaust, ravage; annihilation, eradication, extinction, extirpation; death, massacre, murder, slaughter.

destructive adj baleful, baneful, deadly, deleterious, detrimental, fatal, hurtful, injurious, lethal, mischievous, noxious, pernicious, ruinous; annihilatory, eradicative, exterminative, extirpative.

desultory adj capricious, cursory, discursive, erratic, fitful, inconstant, inexact, irregular, loose, rambling, roving, slight, spasmodic, unconnected, unmethodical, unsettled, unsystematic, vague, wandering.

detach vb disengage, disconnect, disjoin, dissever, disunite, divide, part, separate, sever, unfix; appoint, detail, send.

detail vb delineate, depict, describe, enumerate, narrate, particularize, portray, recount, rehearse, relate, specify; appoint, detach, send. * n account, narration, narrative, recital, relation; appointment, detachment; item, part.

details npl facts, minutiae, particulars, parts.

detain vb arrest, check, delay, hinder, hold, keep, restrain, retain, stay, stop; confine.

detect vb ascertain, catch, descry, disclose, discover, expose, reveal, unmask.

detention n confinement, delay, hindrance, restraint, withholding.

deter vb debar, discourage, frighten, hinder, prevent, restrain, stop, withhold.

deteriorate vb corrupt, debase, degrade, deprave, disgrace, impair, spoil, vitiate; decline, degenerate, depreciate, worsen.

deterioration n corruption, debasement, degradation, depravation, vitiation, perversion; caducity, decadence, decay, decline, degeneracy, degeneration, impairment.

determinate *adj* absolute, certain, definite, determined, established, explicit, express, fixed, limited, positive, settled; conclusive, decided, decisive, definitive.

determination *n* ascertainment, decision, deciding, determining, fixing, settlement, settling; conclusion, judgment, purpose, resolution, resolve, result; direction, leaning, tendency; firmness, constancy, effort, endeavour, exertion, grit, persistence, stamina, resoluteness; definition, limitation, qualification.

determine *vb* adjust, conclude, decide, end, establish, fix, resolve, settle; ascertain, certify, check, verify; impel, incline, induce, influence, lead, turn; decide, resolve; condition, define, limit; compel, necessitate.

detest *vb* abhor, abominate, despise, execrate, hate, loathe, nauseate, recoil from.

detestable *adj* abhorred, abominable, accursed, cursed, damnable, execrable, hateful, odious; disgusting, loathsome, nauseating, offensive, repulsive, sickening, vile.

dethrone *vb* depose, uncrown.

detract *vb* abuse, asperse, belittle, calumniate, debase, decry, defame, depreciate, derogate, disparage, slander, traduce, vilify; deprecate, deteriorate, diminish, lessen.

detraction *n* abuse, aspersion, calumny, censure, defamation, depreciation, derogation, disparagement, slander.

detriment *n* cost, damage, disadvantage, evil, harm, hurt, injury, loss, mischief, prejudice.

detrimental *adj* baleful, deleterious, destructive, harmful, hurtful, injurious, mischievous, pernicious, prejudicial.

devastate *vb* desolate, despoil, destroy, lay waste, harry, pillage, plunder, ravage, sack, spoil, strip, waste.

devastation *n* despoiling, destroying, harrying, pillaging, plundering, ravaging, sacking, spoiling, stripping, wasting; desolation, destruction, havoc, pillage, rapine, ravage, ruin, waste.

develop *vb* disentangle, disclose, evolve, exhibit, explicate, uncover, unfold, unravel; cultivate, grow, mature, open, progress.

development *n* disclosure, disentanglement, exhibition, unfolding, unravelling; growth, increase, maturation, maturing; evolution, growth, progression; elaboration, expansion, explication.

deviate *vb* alter, deflect, digress, diverge, sheer off, slew, tack, turn aside, wheel, wheel about; err, go astray, stray, swerve, wander; differ, vary.

deviation *n* aberration, departure, depression, divarication, divergence, turning; alteration, change, difference, variance, variation.

device *n* contraption, contrivance, gadget, invention; design, expedient, plan, project, resort, resource, scheme, shift; artifice, evasion, fraud, manoeuvre, ruse, stratagem, trick, wile; blazon, emblazonment, emblem, sign, symbol, type.

devil *n* archfiend, demon, fiend, goblin; Apollyon, Belial, Deuce, Evil One, Lucifer, Old Harry, Old Nick, Old Serpent, Prince of Darkness, Satan.

devilish *adj* demon, demonic, demonical, demoniac, demoniacal, diabolic, diabolical, fiendish, hellish, infernal, Mephistophelean, Mephistophelian, satanic; atrocious, barbarous, cruel, malevolent, malicious, malign, malignant, wicked.

devilry *n* devilment, diablerie, mischief; devilishness, fiendishness, wickedness.

devious *adj* deviating, erratic, roundabout, wandering; circuitous, confusing, crooked, labyrinthine, mazy, obscure; crooked, disingenuous, misleading, treacherous.

devise *vb* brew, compass, concert, concoct, contrive, dream up, excogitate, imagine, invent, plan, project, scheme; bequeath, demise, leave, will.

devoid *adj* bare, destitute, empty, vacant, void.

devolve *vb* alienate, consign, convey, deliver over, demise, fall, hand over, make over, pass, transfer.

devote *vb* appropriate, consecrate, dedicate, destine; set apart; addict, apply, give up, resign; consign, doom, give over.

devoted *adj* affectionate, attached, loving; ardent, assiduous, earnest, zealous.

devotee *n* bigot, enthusiast, fan, fanatic, zealot.

devotion *n* consecration, dedication, duty; devotedness, devoutness, fidelity, godliness, holiness, piety, religion, religiousness, saintliness, sanctity; adoration, prayer, worship; affection, attachment, love; ardour, devotedness, eagerness, earnestness, fervour, passion, spirit, zeal.

devotional *adj* devout, godly, pious, religious, saintly.

devour *vb* engorge, gorge, gulp down, raven, swallow eagerly, wolf; annihilate, consume, destroy, expend, spend, swallow up, waste.

devout *adj* devotional, godly, holy, pious, religious, saintlike, saintly; earnest, grave, serious, sincere, solemn.

dexterity *n* ability, address, adroitness, aptitude, aptness, art, cleverness, expertness, facility, knack, quickness, readiness, skilfulness, skill, tact.

dexterous, dextrous *adj* able, adept, adroit, apt, deft, clever, expert, facile, handy, nimble-fingered, quick, ready, skilful.

diabolic, diabolical *adj* atrocious, barbarous, cruel, devilish, fiendish, hellish, impious, infernal, malevolent, malign, malignant, satanic, wicked.

diagram *n* chart, delineation, figure, graph, map, outline, plan, sketch.

dialect *n* idiom, localism, provincialism; jargon, lingo, patois, patter; language, parlance, phraseology, speech, tongue.

dialectal *adj* idiomatic, local, provincial.

dialectic, dialectical *adj* analytical, critical, logical, rational, rationalistic.

dialogue *n* colloquy, communication, conference, conversation, converse, intercourse, interlocution; playbook, script, speech, text, words.

diaphanous *adj* clear, filmy, gossamer, pellucid, sheer, translucent, transparent.

diarrhoea *n* (*med*) flux, looseness, purging, relaxation.

diary *n* chronicle, daybook, journal, register.

diatribe *n* disputation, disquisition, dissertation; abuse, harangue, invective, philippic, reviling, tirade.

dictate *vb* bid, direct, command, decree, enjoin, ordain, order, prescribe, require. * *n* bidding, command, decree, injunction, order; maxim, precept, rule.

dictation *n* direction, order, prescription.

dictator *n* autocrat, despot, tyrant.

dictatorial *adj* absolute, unlimited, unrestricted; authoritative, despotic, dictatory, domineering, imperious, overbearing, peremptory, tyrannical.

dictatorship *n* absolutism, authoritarianism, autocracy, despotism, iron rule, totalitarianism, tyranny.

diction *n* expression, language, phraseology, style, vocabulary, wording.

dictionary *n* glossary, lexicon, thesaurus, vocabulary, wordbook; cyclopedia, encyclopedia.

dictum *n* affirmation, assertion, saying; (*law*) award, arbitrament, decision, opinion.

didactic, didactical *adj* educational, instructive, pedagogic, preceptive.

die *vb* decease, demise, depart, expire, pass on; decay, decline, fade, fade out, perish, wither; cease, disappear, vanish; faint, fall, sink.

diet[1] *vb* eat, feed, nourish; abstain, fast, regulate, slim. * *n* aliment, fare, food, nourishment, nutriment, provision, rations, regimen, subsistence, viands, victuals.

diet[2] *n* assembly, congress, convention, convocation, council, parliament.

differ *vb* deviate, diverge, vary; disagree, dissent; bicker, contend, dispute, quarrel, wrangle.

difference *n* contrariety, contrast, departure, deviation, disagreement, disparity, dissimilarity, dissimilitude, divergence, diversity, heterogeneity, inconformity, nuance, opposition, unlikeness, variation; alienation, altercation, bickering, breach, contention, contest, controversy, debate, disaccord, disagreement, disharmony, dispute, dissension, embroilment, falling out, irreconcilability, jarring, misunderstanding, quarrel, rupture, schism, strife, variance, wrangle; discrimination, distinction.

different *adj* distinct, nonidentical, separate, unlike; contradistinct, contrary, contrasted, deviating, disagreeing, discrepant, dissimilar, divergent, diverse, incompatible, incongruous, unlike, variant, various; divers, heterogeneous, manifold, many, sundry.

difficult *adj* arduous, exacting, hard, Herculean, stiff, tough, uphill; abstruse, complex, intricate, knotty, obscure, perplexing; austere, rigid, unaccommodating, uncompliant, unyielding; dainty, fastidious, squeamish.

difficulty *n* arduousness, laboriousness; bar, barrier, crux, deadlock, dilemma, embarrassment, emergency, exigency, fix, hindrance, impediment, knot, obstacle, obstruction, perplexity, pickle, pinch, predicament, stand, standstill, thwart, trial, trouble; cavil, objection; complication, controversy, difference, embarrassment, embroilment, imbroglio, misunderstanding.

diffidence *n* distrust, doubt, hesitance, hesitancy, hesitation, reluctance; bashfulness, modesty, sheepishness, shyness, timidity.

diffident *adj* distrustful, doubtful, hesitant, hesitating, reluctant; bashful, modest, over-modest, sheepish, shy, timid.

diffuse[1] *vb* circulate, disperse, disseminate, distribute, intermingle, propagate, scatter, spread, strew.

diffuse[2] *adj* broadcast, dispersed, scattered, sparse, sporadic, widespread; broad, extensive, liberal, profuse, wide; copious, loose, prolix, rambling, verbose, wordy.

diffusion *n* circulation, dispersion, dissemination, distribution, extension, propagation, spread, strewing.

diffusive *adj* expansive, permeating, wide-reaching; spreading, dispersive, disseminative, distributive, distributory.

dig *vb* channel, delve, excavate, grub, hollow out, quarry, scoop, tunnel. * *n* poke, punch, thrust.

digest[1] *vb* arrange, classify, codify, dispose, methodize, systemize, tabulate; concoct; assimilate, consider, contemplate, meditate, ponder, reflect upon, study; master; macerate, soak, steep.

digest[2] *n* code, system; abridgement, abstract, brief, breviary, compend, compendium, conspectus, epitome, summary, synopsis.

dignified *adj* august, courtly, decorous, grave, imposing, majestic, noble, stately.

dignify *vb* advance, aggrandize, elevate, ennoble, exalt, promote; adorn, grace, honour.

dignity *n* elevation, eminence, exaltation, excellence, glory, greatness, honour, place, rank, respectability, standing, station; decorum, grandeur, majesty, nobleness, stateliness; preferment; dignitary, magistrate; elevation, height.

digress *vb* depart, deviate, diverge, expatiate, wander.

digression *n* departure, deviation, divergence; episode, excursus.

dilapidate *vb* demolish, destroy, disintegrate, ruin, waste.

dilapidated *adj* decayed, ruined, run down, wasted.

dilapidation *n* decay, demolition, destruction, disintegration, disrepair, dissolution, downfall, ruin, waste.

dilate *vb* distend, enlarge, expand, extend, inflate, swell, tend, widen; amplify, descant, dwell, enlarge, expatiate.

dilation *n* amplification, bloating, distension, enlargement, expanding, expansion, spreading, swelling.

dilatory *adj* backward, behind-hand, delaying, laggard, lagging, lingering, loitering, off-putting, procrastinating, slack, slow, sluggish, tardy.

dilemma *n* difficulty, fix, plight, predicament, problem, quandary, strait.

diligence *n* activity, application, assiduity, assiduousness, attention, care, constancy, earnestness, heedfulness, industry, laboriousness, perseverance, sedulousness.

diligent *adj* active, assiduous, attentive, busy, careful, constant, earnest, hard-working, indefatigable, industrious, laborious, notable, painstaking, persevering, persistent, sedulous, tireless.

dilly-dally *vb* dally, dawdle. delay, lag, linger, loiter, saunter, trifle.

dilute *vb* attenuate, reduce, thin, weaken. * *adj* attenuated, diluted, thin, weak, wishy-washy.

dim *vb* blur, cloud, darken, dull, obscure, sully, tarnish. * *adj* cloudy, dark, dusky, faint, ill-defined, indefinite, indistinct, mysterious, obscure, shadowy; dull, obtuse; clouded, confused, darkened, faint, obscured; blurred, dulled, sullied, tarnished.

dimension *n* extension, extent, measure.

dimensions *npl* amplitude, bigness, bulk, capacity, greatness, largeness, magnitude, mass, massiveness, size, volume; measurements.

diminish *vb* abate, belittle, contract, decrease, lessen, reduce; curtail, cut, dwindle, melt, narrow, shrink, shrivel, subside, taper off, weaken.

diminution *n* abatement, abridgement, attenuation, contraction, curtailment, decrescendo, cut, decay, decrease, deduction, lessening, reduction, retrenchment, weakening.

diminutive *adj* contracted, dwarfish, little, minute, puny, pygmy, small, tiny.

din *vb* beat, boom, clamour, drum, hammer, pound, repeat, ring, thunder. * *n* bruit, clamour, clash, clatter, crash, crashing, hubbub, hullabaloo, hurly-burly, noise, outcry, racket, row, shout, uproar.

dingle *n* dale, dell, glen, vale, valley.

dingy *adj* brown, dun, dusky; bedimmed, colourless, dimmed, dulled, faded, obscure, smirched, soiled, sullied.

dint *n* blow, stroke; dent, indentation, nick, notch; force, power.

diocese *n* bishopric, charge, episcopate, jurisdiction, see.

dip *vb* douse, duck, immerse, plunge, souse; bail, ladle; dive, pitch; bend, incline, slope. * *n* decline, declivity, descent, drop, fall; concavity, depression, hole, hollow, pit, sink; bathe, dipping, ducking, sousing, swim.

diplomat *n* diplomatist, envoy, legate, minister, negotiator.

dire *adj* alarming, awful, calamitous, cruel, destructive, disastrous, dismal, dreadful, fearful, gloomy, horrible, horrid, implacable, inexorable, portentous, shocking, terrible, terrific, tremendous, woeful.

direct *vb* aim. cast, level, point, turn; advise, conduct, control, dispose, guide, govern, manage, regulate, rule; command, bid, enjoin, instruct, order; lead, show; address, superscribe. * *adj* immediate, straight, undeviating; absolute, categorical, express, plain, unambiguous; downright, earnest, frank, ingenuous, open, outspoken, sincere, straightforward, unequivocal.

direction *n* aim; tendency; bearing, course; administration, conduct, control, government, management, oversight, superintendence; guidance, lead; command, order, prescription; address, superscription.

directly *adv* absolutely, expressly, openly, unambiguously; forthwith, immediately, instantly, quickly, presently, promptly, soon, speedily.

director *n* boss, manager, superintendent; adviser, counsellor, guide, instructor, mentor, monitor.

direful *adj* awful, calamitous, dire, dreadful, fearful, gloomy, horrible, shocking, terrible, terrific, tremendous.

dirge *n* coronach, elegy, lament, monody, requiem, threnody.

dirty *vb* befoul, defile, draggle, foul, pollute, soil, sully. * *adj* begrimed. defiled, filthy, foul, mucky, nasty, soiled, unclean; clouded, cloudy, dark, dull, muddy, sullied; base, beggarly, contemptible, despicable, grovelling, low, mean, paltry, pitiful, scurvy, shabby, sneaking, squalid; disagreeable, rainy, sloppy, uncomfortable.

disability *n* disablement, disqualification, impotence, impotency, inability, incapacity, incompetence, incompetency, unfitness, weakness.

disable *vb* cripple, enfeeble, hamstring, impair, paralyse, unman, weaken; disenable, disqualify, incapacitate, unfit.

disabuse *vb* correct, undeceive.

disadvantage *n* disadvantageousness, inconvenience, unfavourableness; damage, detriment, disservice, drawback, harm, hindrance, hurt, injury, loss, prejudice.

disadvantageous *adj* inconvenient, inexpedient, unfavourable; deleterious, detrimental, harmful, hurtful, injurious, prejudicial.

disaffect *vb* alienate, disdain, dislike, disorder, estrange.

disaffected *adj* alienated, disloyal, dissatisfied, estranged.

disaffection *n* alienation, breach, disagreement, dislike, disloyalty, dissatisfaction, estrangement, repugnance, ill will, unfriendliness.

disagree *vb* deviate, differ, diverge, vary; dissent; argue, bicker, clash, debate, dispute, quarrel, wrangle.

disagreeable *adj* contrary, displeasing, distasteful, nasty, offensive, unpleasant, unpleasing, unsuitable.

disagreement *n* deviation, difference, discrepancy, dissimilarity, dissimilitude, divergence, diversity, incongruity, unlikeness; disaccord, dissent; argument, bickering, clashing, conflict, contention, dispute, dissension, disunion, disunity, jarring, misunderstanding, quarrel, strife, variance, wrangle.

disallow *vb* forbid, prohibit; disapprove, reject; deny, disavow, disclaim, dismiss, disown, repudiate.

disappear *vb* depart, fade, vanish; cease, dissolve.

disappoint *vb* baffle, balk, deceive, defeat, delude, disconcert, foil, frustrate, mortify, tantalize, thwart, vex.

disappointment *n* baffling, balk, failure, foiling, frustration, miscarriage, mortification, unfulfilment.

disapprobation *n* blame, censure, condemnation, disapproval, dislike, displeasure, reproof.

disapprove *vb* blame, censure, condemn, deprecate, dislike; disallow, reject.

disarrange *vb* agitate, confuse, derange, disallow, dishevel, dislike, dislocate, disorder, disorganize, disturb, jumble, reject, rumple, tumble, unsettle.

disarray *n* confusion, disorder; dishabille.

disaster *n* accident, adversity, blow, calamity, casualty, catastrophe, misadventure, mischance, misfortune, mishap, reverse, ruin, stroke.

disastrous *adj* adverse, calamitous, catastrophic, destructive, hapless, ill-fated, ill-starred, ruinous, unfortunate, unlucky, unpropitious, unprosperous, untoward.

disavow *vb* deny, disallow, disclaim, disown.

disband *vb* break up, disperse, scatter, separate.

disbelief *n* agnosticism, doubt, nonconviction, rejection, unbelief.

disburden *vb* alleviate, diminish, disburden, discharge, disencumber, ease, free, relieve, rid.

disbursement *n* expenditure, spending.

discard *vb* abandon, cast off, lay aside, reject; banish, break, cashier, discharge, dismiss, remove, repudiate.

discern *vb* differentiate, discriminate, distinguish, judge; behold, descry, discover, espy, notice, observe, perceive, recognize, see.

discernible *adj* detectable, discoverable, perceptible.

discerning *adj* acute, astute, clear-sighted, discriminating, discriminative, eagle-eyed, ingenious, intelligent, judicious, knowing, perspicacious, piercing, sagacious, sharp, shrewd.

discernment *n* acumen, acuteness, astuteness, brightness, cleverness, discrimination, ingenuity, insight, intelligence, judgement, penetration, perspicacity, sagacity, sharpness, shrewdness; beholding, descrying, discerning, discovery, espial, notice, perception.

discharge *vb* disburden, unburden, unload; eject, emit, excrete, expel, void; cash, liquidate, pay; absolve, acquit, clear, exonerate, free, release, relieve; cashier, discard, dismiss, sack; destroy, remove; execute, perform, fulfil, observe; annul, cancel, invalidate, nullify, rescind. * *n* disburdening, unloading; acquittal, dismissal, displacement, ejection, emission, evacuation, excretion, expulsion, vent, voiding; blast, burst, detonation, explosion, firing; execution, fulfilment, observance; annulment, clearance, liquidation, payment, satisfaction, settlement; exemption, liberation, release; flow, flux, execration.

disciple *n* catechumen, learner, pupil, scholar, student; adherent, follower, partisan, supporter.

discipline *vb* breed, drill, educate, exercise, form, instruct, teach, train; control, govern, regulate, school; chasten, chastise, punish. * *n* culture, drill, drilling, education, exercise, instruction, training; control, government, regulation, subjection; chastisement, correction, punishment.

disclaim *vb* abandon, disallow, disown, disavow; reject, renounce, repudiate.

disclose *vb* discover, exhibit, expose, manifest, uncover; bare, betray, blab, communicate, divulge, impart, publish, reveal, show, tell, unfold, unveil, utter.

disclosure *n* betrayal, discovery, exposé, exposure, revelation, uncovering. discolour *vb* stain, tarnish, tinge.

discomfit *vb* beat, checkmate, conquer, defeat, overcome, overpower, overthrow, rout, subdue, vanquish, worst; abash, baffle, balk, confound, disconcert, foil, frustrate, perplex, upset.

discomfiture *n* confusion, defeat, frustration, overthrow, rout, vexation.

discomfort *n* annoyance, disquiet, distress, inquietude, malaise, trouble, uneasiness, unpleasantness, vexation.

discommode *vb* annoy, disquiet, disturb, harass, incommode, inconvenience, molest, trouble.

discompose *vb* confuse, derange, disarrange, disorder, disturb, embroil, jumble, unsettle; agitate, annoy, chafe, displease, disquiet, fret, harass, irritate, nettle, plague, provoke, ruffle, trouble, upset, vex, worry; abash, bewilder, disconcert, embarrass, fluster, perplex.

disconcert *vb* baffle, balk, contravene, defeat, disarrange, frustrate, interrupt, thwart, undo, upset; abash, agitate, bewilder, confuse, demoralize, discompose, disturb, embarrass, faze, perplex, perturb, unbalance, worry.

disconnect *vb* detach, disengage, disjoin, dissociate, disunite, separate, sever, uncouple, unlink.

disconsolate *adj* broken-hearted, cheerless, comfortless, dejected, desolate, forlorn, gloomy, heartbroken, inconsolable, melancholy, miserable, sad, sorrowful, unhappy, woeful, wretched.

discontent *n* discontentment, displeasure, dissatisfaction, inquietude, restlessness, uneasiness.

discontinuance *n* cessation, discontinuation, disjunction, disruption, intermission, interruption, separation, stop, stoppage, stopping, suspension.

discontinue *vb* cease, intermit, interrupt, quit, stop.

discord *n* contention, difference, disagreement, dissension, opposition, quarrelling, rupture, strife, variance, wrangling; cacophony, discordance, dissonance, harshness, jangle, jarring.

discordance *n* conflict, disagreement, incongruity, inconsistency, opposition, repugnance; discord, dissonance.

discordant *adj* contradictory, contrary, disagreeing, incongruous, inconsistent, opposite, repugnant; cacophonous, dissonant, harsh, inharmonious, jangling, jarring.

discount *vb* allow for, deduct, lower, rebate, reduce, subtract; disregard, ignore, overlook. * *n* abatement, drawback; allowance, deduction, rebate, reduction.

discourage *vb* abase, awe, damp, daunt, deject, depress, deject, dismay, dishearten, dispirit, frighten, intimidate; deter, dissuade, hinder; disfavour, discountenance.

discouragement *n* disheartening; dissuasion; damper, deterrent, embarrassment, hindrance, impediment, obstacle, wet blanket.

discourse *vb* expiate, hold forth, lucubrate, sermonize, speak; advise, confer, converse, parley, talk; emit, utter. * *n* address, disquisition, dissertation, homily, lecture, preachment, sermon, speech, treatise; colloquy, conversation, converse, talk.

discourteous *adj* abrupt, brusque, curt, disrespectful, ill-bred, ill-mannered, impolite, inurbane, rude, uncivil, uncourtly, ungentlemanly, unmannerly.

discourtesy *n* abruptness, brusqueness, ill-breeding, impoliteness, incivility, rudeness.

discover *vb* communicate, disclose, exhibit, impart, manifest, show, reveal, tell; ascertain, behold, discern, espy, see; descry, detect, determine, discern; contrive, invent, originate.

discredit *vb* disbelieve, doubt, question; depreciate, disgrace, dishonour, disparage, reproach. * *n* disbelief, distrust; disgrace, dishonour, disrepute, ignominy, notoriety, obloquy, odium, opprobrium, reproach, scandal.

discreditable *adj* derogatory, disgraceful, disreputable, dishonourable, ignominious, infamous, inglorious, scandalous, unworthy.

discreet *adj* careful, cautious, circumspect, considerate, discerning, heedful, judicious, prudent, sagacious, wary, wise.

discrepancy *n* contrariety, difference, disagreement, discordance, dissonance, divergence, incongruity, inconsistency, variance, variation.

discrete *adj* discontinuous, disjunct, distinct, separate; disjunctive.

discretion *n* care, carefulness, caution, circumspection, considerateness, consideration, heedfulness, judgement, judicious, prudence, wariness; discrimination, maturity, responsibility; choice, option, pleasure, will.

discrimination *n* difference, distinction; acumen, acuteness, discernment, in-sight, judgement, penetration, sagacity.

discriminatory *adj* characteristic, characterizing, discriminating, discriminative, distinctive, distinguishing.

discursive *adj* argumentative, reasoning; casual, cursory, desultory, digressive, erratic, excursive, loose, rambling, roving, wandering, wave.

discus *n* disk, quoit.

discuss *vb* agitate, argue, canvass, consider, debate, deliberate, examine, sift, ventilate.

disdain *vb* contemn, deride, despise, disregard, reject, scorn, slight, scout, spurn. * *n* arrogance, contempt, contumely, haughtiness, hauteur, scorn, sneer, superciliousness.

disdainful *adj* cavalier, contemptuous, contumelious, haughty, scornful, supercilious.

disease *n* affection, affliction, ail, ailment, complaint, disorder, distemper, illness, indisposition, infirmity, malady, sickness.

disembarrass *vb* clear, disburden, disencumber, disengage, disentangle, extricate, ease, free, release, rid.

disembodied *adj* bodiless, disincarnate, immaterial, incorporeal, spiritual, unbodied.

disembowel *vb* degut, embowel, eviscerate.

disengage *vb* clear, deliver, discharge, disembarrass, disembroil, disencumber, disentangle, extricate, liberate, release; detach, disjoin, dissociate, disunite, divide, separate; wean, withdraw.

disentangle *vb* loosen, separate, unfold, unravel, untwist; clear, detach, disconnect, disembroil, disengage, extricate, liberate, loose, unloose.

disfavour n disapproval, disesteem, dislike, disrespect; discredit, disregard, disrepute, unacceptableness; disservice, unkindness. * vb disapprove, dislike, object, oppose.

disfigure vb blemish, deface, deform, injure, mar, spoil.

disfigurement n blemishing, defacement, deforming, disfiguration, injury, marring, spoiling; blemish, defect, deformity, scar, spot, stain.

disgorge vb belch, cast up, spew, throw up, vomit; discharge, eject; give up, relinquish, surrender, yield.

disgrace vb degrade, humble, humiliate; abase, debase, defame, discredit, disfavour, dishonour, disparage, reproach, stain, sully, taint, tarnish. * n abomination, disrepute, humiliation, ignominy, infamy, mortification, shame, scandal.

disgraceful adj discreditable, dishonourable, disreputable, ignominious, infamous, opprobrious, scandalous, shameful.

disguise vb cloak, conceal, cover, dissemble, hide, mask, muffle, screen, secrete, shroud, veil. * n concealment, cover, mask, veil; blind, cloak, masquerade, pretence, pretext, veneer.

disguised adj cloaked, masked, veiled.

disgust vb nauseate, sicken; abominate, detest, displease, offend, repel, repulse, revolt. * n disrelish, distaste, loathing, nausea; abhorrence, abomination, antipathy, aversion, detestation, dislike, repugnance, revulsion.

dish vb deal out, give, ladle, serve; blight, dash, frustrate, mar, ruin, spoil. * n bowl, plate, saucer, vessel.

dishearten vb cast down, damp, dampen, daunt, deject, depress, deter, discourage, dispirit.

dished adj baffled, balked, disappointed, disconcerted, foiled, frustrated, upset.

dishevelled adj disarranged, disordered, messed, tousled, tumbled, unkempt, untidy, untrimmed.

dishonest adj cheating, corrupt, crafty, crooked, deceitful, deceiving, deceptive, designing, faithless, false, falsehearted, fraudulent, guileful, knavish, perfidious, slippery, treacherous, unfair, unscrupulous.

dishonesty n deceitfulness, faithlessness, falsehood, fraud, fraudulence, fraudulency, improbity, knavery, perfidious, treachery, trickery.

dishonour vb abase, defame, degrade, discredit, disfavour, dishonour, disgrace, disparage, reproach, shame, taint. * n abasement, basement, contempt, degradation, discredit, disesteem, disfavour, disgrace, dishonour, disparagement, disrepute, ignominy, infamy, obloquy, odium, opprobrium, reproach, scandal, shame.

dishonourable adj discreditable, disgraceful, disreputable, ignominious, infamous, scandalous, shameful; base, false, falsehearted, shameless.

disinclination n alienation, antipathy, aversion, dislike, indisposition, reluctance, repugnance, unwillingness.

disinfect vb cleanse, deodorize, fumigate, purify, sterilize.

disingenuous adj artful, deceitful, dishonest, hollow, insidious, insincere, uncandid, unfair, wily.

disintegrate vb crumble, decompose, dissolve, disunite, pulverize, separate.

disinter vb dig up, disentomb, disinhume, exhume, unbury.

disinterested adj candid, fair, high-minded, impartial, indifferent, unbiased, unselfish, unprejudiced; generous, liberal, magnanimous.

disjoin vb detach, disconnect, dissever, dissociate, disunite, divide, part, separate, sever, sunder.

disjointed adj desultory, disconnected, incoherent, loose.

disjunction n disassociation, disconnection, disunion, isolation, parting, separation, severance.

dislike vb abominate, detest, disapprove, disrelish, hate, loathe. * n antagonism, antipathy, aversion, disapproval, disfavour, disgust, disinclination, displeasure, disrelish, distaste, loathing, repugnance.

dislocate vb disarrange, displace, disturb; disarticulate, disjoint, luxate, slip.

dislodge vb dismount, dispel, displace, eject, expel, oust, remove.

disloyal adj disaffected, faithless, false, perfidious, traitorous, treacherous, treasonable, undutiful, unfaithful, unpatriotic, untrue.

disloyalty n faithlessness, perfidy, treachery, treason, undutifulness, unfaithfulness.

dismal adj cheerless, dark, dreary, dull, gloomy, lonesome; blue, calamitous, doleful, dolorous, funereal, lugubrious, melancholy, mournful, sad, sombre, sorrowful.

dismantle vb divest, strip, unrig.

dismay vb affright, alarm, appal, daunt, discourage, dishearten, frighten, horrify, intimidate, paralyse, scare, terrify. * n affright, alarm, consternation, fear, fright, horror, terror.

dismember vb disjoint, dislimb, dislocate, mutilate; divide, separate, rend, sever.

dismiss vb banish, cashier, discard, discharge, disperse, reject, release, remove.

dismount vb alight, descend, dismantle, unhorse; dislodge, displace.

disobedient adj froward, noncompliant, noncomplying, obstinate, rebellious, refractory, uncomplying, undutiful, unruly, unsubmissive.

disobey vb infringe, transgress, violate.

disobliging adj ill-natured, unaccommodating, unamiable, unfriendly, unkind.

disorder vb confound, confuse, derange, disarrange, discompose, disorganize, disturb, unsettle, upset. * n confusion, derangement, disarrangement, disarray, disorganization, irregularity, jumble, litter, mess, topsy-turvy; brawl, commotion, disturbance, fight, quarrel, riot, tumult; riotousness, tumultuousness, turbulence; ail, ailment, complaint, distemper, illness, indisposition, malady, sickness.

disorderly adj chaotic, confused, intemperate, irregular, unmethodical, unsystematic, untidy; lawless, rebellious, riotous, tumultuous, turbulent, ungovernable, unmanageable, unruly.

disorganization n chaos, confusion, demoralization, derangement, disorder.

disorganize vb confuse, demoralize, derange, disarrange, discompose, disorder, disturb, unsettle, upset.

disown vb disavow, disclaim, reject, renounce, repudiate; abnegate, deny, disallow.

disparage vb belittle, decry, depreciate, derogate from, detract from, doubt, question, run down, underestimate, underpraise, underrate, undervalue; asperse, defame, inveigh against, reflect on, reproach, slur, speak ill of, traduce, vilify.

disparagement n belittlement, depreciation, derogation, detraction, underrating, undervaluing; derogation, detraction, diminution, harm, impairment, injury, lessening, prejudice, worsening; aspersion, calumny, defamation, reflection, reproach, traduction, vilification; blackening, disgrace, dispraise, indignity, reproach.

disparity *n* difference, disproportion, inequality; dissimilarity, dissimilitude, unlikeness.

dispassionate *adj* calm, collected, composed, cool, imperturbable, inexcitable, moderate, quiet, serene, sober, staid, temperate, undisturbed, unexcitable, unexcited, unimpassioned, unruffled; candid, disinterested, fair, impartial, neutral, unbiased.

dispatch, despatch *vb* assassinate, kill, murder, slaughter, slay; accelerate, conclude, dismiss, expedite, finish, forward, hasten, hurry, quicken, speed. * *n* dispatching, sending; diligence, expedition, haste, rapidity, speed; completion, conduct, doing, transaction; communication, document, instruction, letter, message, missive, report.

dispel *vb* banish, disperse, dissipate, scatter.

dispensation *n* allotment, apportioning, apportionment, dispensing, distributing, distribution; administration, stewardship; economy, plan, scheme, system; exemption, immunity, indulgence, licence, privilege.

dispense *vb* allot, apportion, assign, distribute; administer, apply, execute; absolve, excuse, exempt, exonerate, release, relieve.

disperse *vb* dispel, dissipate, dissolve, scatter, separate; diffuse, disseminate, spread; disappear, vanish.

dispirit *vb* damp, dampen, depress, deject, discourage, dishearten.

dispirited *adj* chapfallen, dejected, depressed, discouraged, disheartened, down-cast, down-hearted.

displace *vb* dislocate, mislay, misplace, move; dislodge, remove; cashier, depose, discard, discharge, dismiss, oust, replace, unseat.

display *vb* expand, extend, open, spread, unfold; exhibit, show; flaunt, parade. * *n* exhibition, manifestation, show; flourish, ostentation, pageant, parade, pomp.

displease *vb* disgruntle, disgust, disoblige, dissatisfy, offend; affront, aggravate, anger, annoy, chafe, chagrin, fret, irritate, nettle, pique, provoke, vex.

displeasure *n* disaffection, disapprobation, disapproval, dislike, dissatisfaction, distaste; anger, annoyance, indignation, irritation, pique, resentment, vexation, wrath; injury, offence.

disport *vb* caper, frisk, frolic, gambol, play, sport, wanton; amuse, beguile, cheer, divert, entertain, relax, solace.

disposal *n* arrangement, disposition; conduct, control, direction, disposure, government, management, ordering, regulation; bestowment, dispensation, distribution.

dispose *vb* arrange, distribute, marshal, group, place, range, rank, set; adjust, determine, regulate, settle; bias, incline, induce, lead, move, predispose; control, decide, regulate, rule, settle; arrange, bargain, compound; alienate, convey, demise, sell, transfer.

disposed *adj* apt, inclined, prone, ready, tending.

disposition *n* arrangement, arranging, classification, disposing, grouping, location, placing; adjustment, control, direction, disposure, disposal, management, ordering, regulation; aptitude, bent, bias, inclination, nature, predisposition, proclivity, proneness, propensity, tendency; character, constitution, humour, native, nature, temper, temperament, turn; inclination, willingness; bestowal, bestowment, dispensation, distribution.

dispossess *vb* deprive, divest, expropriate, strip; dislodge, eject, oust; disseise, disseize, evict, oust.

dispraise *n* blame, censure; discredit, disgrace, dishonour, disparagement, opprobrium, reproach, shame.

disproof *n* confutation, rebuttal, refutation.

disproportion *n* disparity, inadequacy, inequality, insufficiency, unsuitableness; incommensurateness.

disprove *vb* confute, rebel, rebut.

disputable *adj* controvertible, debatable, doubtful, questionable.

disputation *n* argumentation, controversy, debate, dispute.

disputatious *adj* argumentative, bickering, captious, caviling, contentious, dissentious, litigious, polemical, pugnacious, quarrelsome.

dispute *vb* altercate, argue, debate, litigate, question; bicker, brawl, jangle, quarrel, spar, spat, squabble, tiff, wrangle; agitate, argue, debate, ventilate; challenge, contradict, controvert, deny, impugn; contest, struggle for. * *n* controversy, debate, discussion, disputation; altercation, argument, bickering, brawl, disagreement, dissension, spat, squabble, tiff, wrangle.

disqualification *n* disability, incapitation.

disqualify *vb* disable, incapacitate, unfit; disenable, preclude, prohibit.

disquiet *vb* agitate, annoy, bother, discompose, disturb, excite, fret, harass, incommode, molest, plague, pester, trouble, vex, worry. * *n* anxiety, discomposure, disquietude, disturbance, restlessness, solicitude, trouble, uneasiness, unrest, vexation, worry.

disquisition *n* dissertation, discourse, essay, paper, thesis, treatise.

disregard *vb* contemn, despise, disdain, disobey, disparage, ignore, neglect, overlook, slight. * *n* contempt, ignoring, inattention, neglect, pretermit, oversight, slight; disesteem, disfavour, indifference.

disrelish *vb* dislike, loathe. * *n* dislike, distaste; flatness, insipidity, insipidness, nauseousness; antipathy, aversion, repugnance.

disreputable *adj* derogatory, discreditable, dishonourable, disgraceful, infamous, opprobrious, scandalous, shameful; base, contemptible, low, mean, vicious, vile, vulgar.

disrepute *n* abasement, degradation, derogation, discredit, disgrace, dishonour, ill-repute, odium.

disrespect *n* disesteem, disregard, irreverence, neglect, slight.

disrespectful *adj* discourteous, impertinent, impolite, rude, uncivil, uncourteous.

dissatisfaction *n* discontent, disquiet, inquietude, uneasiness; disapprobation, disapproval, dislike, displeasure.

dissect *vb* analyze, examine, explore, investigate, scrutinize, sift; cut apart.

dissemble *vb* cloak, conceal, cover, disguise, hide; counterfeit, dissimulate, feign, pretend.

dissembler *n* dissimulator, feigner, hypocrite, pretender, sham.

disseminate *vb* circulate, diffuse, disperse, proclaim, promulgate, propagate, publish, scatter, spread.

dissension *n* contention, difference, disagreement, discord, quarrel, strife, variance.

dissent *vb* decline, differ, disagree, refuse. * *n* difference, disagreement, nonconformity, opposition, recusancy, refusal.

dissentient *adj* disagreeing, dissenting, dissident, factious.

dissertation *n* discourse, disquisition, essay, thesis, treatise.

disservice *n* disadvantage, disfavour, harm, hurt, ill-turn, injury, mischief.

dissidence *n* disagreement, dissent, nonconformity, sectarianism.

dissimilar *adj* different, divergent, diverse, heterogeneous, unlike, various.

dissimilarity *n* dissimilitude, disparity, divergent, diversity, unlikeness, variation.

dissimulation *n* concealment, deceit, dissembling, double-dealing, duplicity, feigning, hypocrisy, pretence.

dissipate *vb* dispel, disperse, scatter; consume, expend, lavish, spend, squander, waste; disappear, vanish.

dissipation *n* dispersion, dissemination, scattering, vanishing; squandering, waste; crapulence, debauchery, dissoluteness, drunkenness, excess, profligacy.

dissociate *vb* disjoin, dissever, disunite, divide, separate, sever, sunder.

dissolute *adj* abandoned, corrupt, debauched, depraved, disorderly, dissipated, graceless, lax, lewd, licentious, loose, profligate, rakish, reprobate, shameless, vicious, wanton, wild.

dissolution *n* liquefaction, melting, solution; decomposition, putrefaction; death, disease; destruction, overthrow, ruin; termination.

dissolve *vb* liquefy, melt; disorganize, disunite, divide, loose, separate, sever; destroy, ruin; disappear, fade, scatter, vanish; crumble, decompose, disintegrate, perish.

dissonance *n* cacophony, discord, discordance, harshness, jarring; disagreement, discrepancy, incongruity, inconsistency.

dissonant *adj* discordant, grating, harsh, jangling, jarring, unharmonious; contradictory, disagreeing, discrepant, incongruous, inconsistent.

distance *vb* excel, outdo, outstrip, surpass. * *n* farness, remoteness; aloofness, coldness, frigidity, reserve, stiffness, offishness; absence, separation, space.

distant *adj* far, far-away, remote; aloof, ceremonious, cold, cool, frigid, haughty, reserved, stiff, uncordial; faint, indirect, obscure, slight.

distaste *n* disgust, disrelish; antipathy, aversion, disinclination, dislike, displeasure, dissatisfaction, repugnance.

distasteful *adj* disgusting, loathsome, nauseating, nauseous, unpalatable, unsavoury; disagreeable, displeasing, offensive, repugnant, repulsive, unpleasant.

distemper *n* ail, ailment, complaint, disease, disorder, illness, indisposition, malady, sickness.

distempered *adj* diseased, disordered; immoderate, inordinate, intemperate, unregulated.

distend *vb* bloat, dilate, enlarge, expand, increase, inflate, puff, stretch, swell, widen.

distil *vb* dribble, drip, drop; extract, separate.

distinct *adj* definite, different, discrete, disjunct, individual, separate, unconnected; clear, defined, manifest, obvious, plain, unconfused, unmistakable, well-defined.

distinction *n* discernment, discrimination, distinguishing; difference; account, celebrity, credit, eminence, fame, name, note, rank, renown, reputation, repute, respectability, superiority.

distinctive *adj* characteristic, differentiating, discriminating, distinguishing.

distinctness *n* difference, separateness; clearness, explicitness, lucidity, lucidness, perspicuity, precision.

distinguish *vb* characterize, mark; differentiate, discern, discriminate, perceive, recognize, see, single out, tell; demarcate, divide, separate; celebrate, honour, signalize.

distinguished *adj* celebrated, eminent, famous, illustrious, noted; conspicuous, extraordinary, laureate, marked, shining, superior, transcendent.

distort *vb* contort, deform, gnarl, screw, twist, warp, wrest; falsify, misrepresent, pervert.

distortion *n* contortion, deformation, deformity, twist, wryness; falsification, misrepresentation, perversion, wresting.

distract *vb* divert, draw away; bewilder, confound, confuse, derange, discompose, disconcert, disturb, embarrass, harass, madden, mystify, perplex, puzzle.

distracted *adj* crazed, crazy, deranged, frantic, furious, insane, mad, raving, wild.

distraction *n* abstraction, bewilderment, confusion, mystification, embarrassment, perplexity; agitation, commotion, discord, disorder, disturbance, division, perturbation, tumult, turmoil; aberration, alienation, delirium, derangement, frenzy, hallucination, incoherence, insanity, lunacy, madness, mania, raving, wandering.

distress *vb* afflict, annoy, grieve, harry, pain, perplex, rack, trouble; distrain, seize, take. * *n* affliction, calamity, disaster, misery, misfortune, adversity, hardship, perplexity, trial, tribulation; agony, anguish, dolour, grief, sorrow, suffering; gnawing, gripe, griping, pain, torment, torture; destitution, indigence, poverty, privation, straits, want.

distribute *vb* allocate, allot, apportion, assign, deal, dispense, divide, dole out, give, mete, partition, prorate, share; administer, arrange, assort, class, classify, dispose.

distribution *n* allocation, allotment, apportionment, assignment, assortment, dispensation, dispensing; arrangement, disposal, disposition, classification, division, dole, grouping, partition, sharing.

district *n* circuit, department, neighbourhood, province, quarter, region, section, territory, tract, ward.

distrust *vb* disbelieve, discredit, doubt, misbelieve, mistrust, question, suspect. * *n* doubt, misgiving, mistrust, question, suspicion.

distrustful *adj* doubting, dubious, suspicious.

disturb *vb* agitate, shake, stir; confuse, derange, disarrange, disorder, unsettle, upset; annoy, discompose, disconcert, disquiet, distract, fuss, incommode, molest, perturb, plague, trouble, ruffle, vex, worry; impede, interrupt, hinder.

disturbance *n* agitation, commotion, confusion, convulsion, derangement, disorder, perturbation, unsettlement; annoyance, discomposure, distraction, excitement, fuss; hindrance, interruption, molestation; brawl, commotion, disorder, excitement, fracas, hubbub, riot, rising, tumult, turmoil, uproar.

disunion *n* disconnection, disjunction, division, separation, severance; breach, feud, rupture, schism.

disunite *vb* detach, disconnect, disjoin, dissever, dissociate, divide, part, rend, separate, segregate, sever, sunder; alienate, estrange.

disuse *n* desuetude, discontinuance, disusage, neglect, nonobservance.

ditch *vb* canalize, dig, excavate, furrow, gouge, trench; abandon, discard, dump, jettison, scrap. * *n* channel, drain, fosse, moat, trench.

divagation *n* deviation, digression, rambling, roaming, straying, wandering.

divan *n* bed, chesterfield, couch, settee, sofa.

divaricate *vb* diverge, fork, part.

dive *vb* explore, fathom, penetrate, plunge, sound. * *n* drop, fall, header, plunge; bar, den, dump, joint, saloon.

diverge *vb* divide, radiate, separate; divaricate, separate; deviate, differ, disagree, vary.

divers *adj* different, manifold, many, numerous, several, sundry, various.

diverse *adj* different, differing, disagreeing, dissimilar, divergent, heterogeneous, multifarious, multiform, separate, unlike, variant, various, varying.

diversion *n* deflection, diverting; amusement, delight, distraction, enjoyment, entertainment, game, gratification, pastime, play, pleasure, recreation, sport; detour, digression.

diversity *n* difference, dissimilarity, dissimilitude, divergence, unlikeness, variation; heterogeneity, manifoldness, multifariousness, multiformity, variety.

divert *vb* deflect, distract, disturb; amuse, beguile, delight, entertain, exhilarate, give pleasure, gratify, recreate, refresh, solace.

divest *vb* denude, disrobe, strip, unclothe, undress; deprive, dispossess, strip.

divide *vb* bisect, cleave, cut, dismember, dissever, disunite, open, part, rend, segregate, separate, sever, shear, split, sunder; allocate, allot, apportion, assign, dispense, distribute, dole, mete, portion, share; compartmentalize, demarcate, partition; alienate, disunite, estrange.

divination *n* augury, divining, foretelling, incantation, magic, sooth-saying, sorcery; prediction, presage, prophecy.

divine *vb* foretell, predict, presage, prognosticate, vaticinate, prophesy; believe, conjecture, fancy, guess, suppose, surmise, suspect, think. * *adj* deiform, godlike, superhuman, supernatural; angelic, celestial, heavenly, holy, sacred, seraphic, spiritual; exalted, exalting, rapturous, supreme, transcendent. * *n* churchman, clergyman, ecclesiastic, minister, parson, pastor, priest.

division *n* compartmentalization, disconnection, disjunction, dismemberment, segmentation, separation, severance; category, class, compartment, head, parcel, portion, section, segment; demarcation, partition; alienation, allotment, apportionment, distribution; breach, difference, disagreement, discord, disunion, estrangement, feud, rupture, variance.

divorce *vb* disconnect, dissolve, disunite, part, put away, separate, sever, split up, sunder, unmarry. * *n* disjunction, dissolution, disunion, division, divorcement, parting, separation, severance.

divulge *vb* communicate, declare, disclose, discover, exhibit, expose, impart, proclaim, promulgate, publish, reveal, tell, uncover.

dizzy *adj* giddy, vertiginous; careless, heedless, thoughtless.

do *vb* accomplish, achieve, act, commit, effect, execute, perform; complete, conclude, end, finish, settle, terminate; conduct, transact; observe, perform, practice; translate, render; cook, prepare; cheat, chouse, cozen, hoax, swindle; serve, suffice. * *n* act, action, adventure, deed, doing, exploit, feat, thing; banquet, event, feast, function, party.

docile *adj* amenable, obedient, pliant, teachable, tractable, yielding.

dock[1] *vb* clip, curtail, cut, deduct, truncate; lessen, shorten.

dock[2] *vb* anchor, moor; join, meet. * *n* anchorage, basin, berth, dockage, dockyard, dry dock, harbour, haven, marina, pier, shipyard, wharf.

doctor *vb* adulterate, alter, cook, falsify, manipulate, tamper with; attend, minister to, cure, heal, remedy, treat; fix, mend, overhaul, repair, service. * *n* general practitioner, GP, healer, leech, medic, physician; adept, savant.

doctrinaire *adj* impractical, theoretical. * *n* ideologist, theorist, thinker.

doctrine *n* article, belief, creed, dogma, opinion, precept, principle, teaching, tenet.

dodge *vb* equivocate, evade, prevaricate, quibble, shuffle. * *n* artifice, cavil, evasion, quibble, subterfuge, trick.

dogged *adj* cantankerous, headstrong, inflexible, intractable, mulish, obstinate, pertinacious, perverse, resolute, stubborn, tenacious, unyielding, wilful; churlish, morose, sour, sullen, surly.

dogma *n* article, belief, creed, doctrine, opinion, precept, principle, tenet.

dogmatic *adj* authoritative, categorical, formal, settled; arrogant, confident, dictatorial, imperious, magisterial, opinionated, oracular, overbearing, peremptory, positive; doctrinal.

dole *vb* allocate, allot, apportion, assign, deal, distribute, divide, share. * *n* allocation, allotment, apportionment, distribution; part, portion, share; alms, donation, gift, gratuity, pittance; affliction, distress, grief, sorrow, woe.

doleful *adj* lugubrious, melancholy, piteous, rueful, sad, sombre, sorrowful, woebegone, woeful; cheerless, dark, dismal, dolorous, dreary, gloomy.

dolorous *adj* cheerless, dark, dismal, gloomy; doleful, lugubrious, mournful, piteous, rueful, sad, sorrowful, woeful.

dolt *n* blockhead, booby, dullard, dunce, fool, ignoramus, simpleton.

domain *n* authority, dominion, jurisdiction, province, sway; empire, realm, territory; lands, estate; branch, department, region.

domestic *n* charwoman, help, home help, maid, servant. * *adj* domiciliary, family, home, household, private; domesticated; internal, intestine.

domesticate *vb* tame; adopt, assimilate, familiarize, naturalize.

domicile *vb* domiciliate, dwell, inhabit, live, remain, reside. * *n* abode, dwelling, habitation, harbour, home, house, residence.

dominant *adj* ascendant, ascending, chief, controlling, governing, influential, outstanding, paramount, predominant, pre-eminent, preponderant, presiding, prevailing, ruling.

dominate *vb* control, rule, sway; command, overlook, overtop, surmount.

domineer *vb* rule, tyrannize; bluster, bully, hector, menace, swagger, swell, threaten.

dominion *n* ascendancy, authority, command, control, domain, domination, government, jurisdiction, mastery, rule, sovereign, sovereignty, supremacy, sway; country, kingdom, realm, region, territory.

donation *n* alms, benefaction, boon, contribution, dole, donative, gift, grant, gratuity, largesse, offering, present, subscription.

done *adj* accomplished, achieved, effected, executed, performed; completed, concluded, ended, finished, terminated; carried on, transacted; rendered, translated; cooked, prepared; cheated, cozened, hoaxed, swindled; (*with* **for**) damned, dished, *hors de combat*, ruined, shelved, spoiled, wound up.

donkey *n* ass, mule; dunce, fool, simpleton.

donor *n* benefactor, bestower, giver; donator.

double *vb* fold, plait; duplicate, geminate, increase, multiply, repeat; return. * *adj* binary, coupled, geminate, paired; dual, twice, twofold; deceitful, dishonest, double-dealing, false, hollow, insincere, knavish, perfidious, treacherous, two-faced. * *adv* doubly, twice, twofold. * *n* doubling, fold, plait; artifice, manoeuvre, ruse, shift, stratagem, trick, wile; copy, counterpart, twin.

doublet *n* jacket, jerkin.

doubt *vb* demur, fluctuate, hesitate, vacillate, waver; distrust, mistrust, query, question, suspect. * *n* dubiety, dubiousness, dubitation, hesitance, hesitancy, hesitation, incertitude, indecision, irresolution, question, suspense, uncertainty, vacillation; distrust, misgiving, mistrust, scepticism, suspicion.

doubtful *adj* dubious, hesitating, sceptical, undecided, undetermined, wavering; ambiguous, dubious, enigmatical, equivocal, hazardous, obscure, problematical, unsure; indeterminate, questionable, undecided, unquestioned.

doubtless *adv* certainly, unquestionably; clearly, indisputably, precisely.

doughty *adj* adventurous, bold, brave, chivalrous, courageous, daring, dauntless, fearless, gallant, heroic, intrepid, redoubtable, valiant, valorous.

douse *see* **dowse**.

dowdy *adj* awkward, dingy, ill-dressed, shabby, slatternly, slovenly; old-fashioned, unfashionable.

dowel *n* peg, pin, pinion, tenon.

dower *n* endowment, gift; dowry; portion, share.

downcast *adj* chapfallen, crestfallen, dejected, depressed, despondent, discouraged, disheartened, dispirited, downhearted, low-spirited, sad, unhappy.

downfall *n* descent, destruction, fall, ruin.

downhearted *adj* chapfallen, crestfallen, dejected, depressed, despondent, discouraged, disheartened, dispirited, downcast, low-spirited, sad, unhappy.

downright *adj* absolute, categorical, clear, explicit, plain, positive, sheer, simple, undisguised, unequivocal, utter; above-board, artless, blunt, direct, frank, honest, ingenuous, open, sincere, straightforward, unceremonious.

downy *adj* lanate, lanated, lanose.

dowse, douse *vb* dip, immerse, plunge, souse, submerge.

doxy *n* mistress, paramour; courtesan, drab, harlot, prostitute, strumpet, streetwalker, whore.

doze *vb* drowse, nap, sleep, slumber. * *n* drowse, forty-winks, nap.

dozy *adj* drowsy, heavy, sleepy, sluggish.

draft *vb* detach, select; commandeer, conscript, impress; delineate, draw, outline, sketch. * *n* conscription, drawing, selection; delineation, outline, sketch; bill, cheque, order.

drag *vb* draw, haul, pull, tow, tug; trail; linger, loiter. * *n* favour, influence, pull; brake, check, curb, lag, resistance, retardation, scotch, skid, slackening, slack-off, slowing.

draggle *vb* befoul, bemire, besmirch, dangle, drabble, trail.

dragoon *vb* compel, drive, force, harass, harry, persecute. * *n* cavalier, equestrian, horse-soldier.

drain *vb* milk, sluice, tap; empty, evacuate, exhaust; dry. * *n* channel, culvert, ditch, sewer, sluice, trench, watercourse; exhaustion, withdrawal.

draught *n* current, drawing, pulling, traction; cup, dose, drench, drink, potion; delineation, design, draft, outline, sketch.

draw *vb* drag, haul, tow, tug, pull; attract; drain, suck, syphon; extract, extort; breathe in, inhale, inspire; allure, engage, entice, induce, influence, lead, move, persuade; extend, protract, stretch; delineate, depict, sketch; deduce, derive, infer; compose, draft, formulate, frame, prepare; blister, vesicate, write.

drawback *n* defect, deficiency, detriment, disadvantage, fault, flaw, imperfection, injury; abatement, allowance, deduction, discount, rebate, reduction.

drawing *n* attracting, draining, inhaling, pulling, traction; delineation, draught, outline, picture, plan, sketch.

dread *vb* apprehend, fear. * *adj* dreadful, frightful, horrible, terrible; awful, venerable. * *n* affright, alarm, apprehension, fear, terror; awe, veneration.

dreadful *adj* alarming, appalling, awesome, dire, direful, fearful, formidable, frightful, horrible, horrid, terrible, terrific, tremendous; awful, venerable.

dream *vb* fancy, imagine, think. * *n* conceit, day-dream, delusion, fancy, fantasy, hallucination, illusion, imagination, reverie, vagary, vision.

dreamer *n* enthusiast, visionary.

dreamy *adj* absent, abstracted, fanciful, ideal, misty, shadowy, speculative, unreal, visionary.

dreary *adj* cheerless, chilling, comfortless, dark, depressing, dismal, drear, gloomy, lonely, lonesome, sad, solitary, sorrowful; boring, dull, monotonous, tedious, tiresome, uninteresting, wearisome.

dregs *npl* feculence, grounds, lees, off-scourings, residuum, scourings, sediment, waste; draff, dross, refuse, scum, trash.

drench *vb* dowse, drown, imbrue, saturate, soak, souse, steep, wet; physic, purge.

dress *vb* align, straighten; adjust, arrange, dispose; fit, prepare; accoutre, apparel, array, attire, clothe, robe, rig; adorn, bedeck, deck, decorate, drape, embellish, trim. * *n* apparel, attire, clothes, clothing, costume, garb, guise, garments, habiliment, habit, raiment, suit, toilet, vesture; bedizenment, bravery; frock, gown, rob.

dressing *n* compost, fertilizer, manure; forcemeat, stuffing.

dressy *adj* flashy, gaudy, showy.

driblet *n* bit, drop, fragment, morsel, piece, scrap.

drift *vb* accumulate, drive, float, wander. * *n* bearing, course, direction; aim, design, intent, intention, mark, object, proposal, purpose, scope, tendency; detritus, deposit, diluvium; gallery, passage, tunnel; current, rush, sweep; heap, pile.

drill[1] *vb* bore, perforate, pierce; discipline, exercise, instruct, teach, train. * *n* borer; discipline, exercise, training.

drill[2] *n* channel, furrow, trench.

drink *vb* imbibe, sip, swill; carouse, indulge, revel, tipple, tope; swallow, quaff; absorb. * *n* beverage, draught, liquid, potation, potion; dram, nip, sip, snifter, refreshment.

drip *vb* dribble, drop, leak, trickle; distil, filter, percolate; ooze, reek, seep, weep. * *n* dribble, drippings, drop, leak, leakage, leaking, trickle, tricklet; bore, nuisance, wet blanket.

drive *vb* hurl, impel, propel, send, shoot, thrust; actuate, incite, press, urge; coerce, compel, constrain, force, harass, oblige, overburden, press, rush; go, guide, ride, travel; aim, intend. * *n* effort, energy, pressure; airing, ride; road.

drivel *vb* babble, blether, dote, drool, slaver, slobber. * *n* balderdash, drivelling, fatuity, nonsense, prating, rubbish, slaver, stuff, twaddle.

drizzle *vb* mizzle, rain, shower, sprinkle. * *n* haar, mist, mizzle, rain, sprinkling.

droll *adj* comic, comical, farcical, funny, jocular, ludicrous, laughable, ridiculous; amusing, diverting, facetious, odd, quaint, queer, waggish. * *n* buffoon, clown, comedian, fool, harlequin, jester, punch, Punchinello, scaramouch, wag, zany.

drollery *n* archness, buffoonery, fun, humour, jocularity, pleasantry, waggishness, whimsicality.

drone *vb* dawdle, drawl, idle, loaf, lounge; hum. * *n* idler, loafer, lounger, sluggard.

drool *vb* drivel, slaver.

droop *vb* fade, wilt, wither; decline, fail, faint, flag, languish, sink, weaken; bend, hang.

drop *vb* distil, drip, shed; decline, depress, descend, dump, lower, sink; abandon, desert, forsake, forswear, leave, omit, relinquish, quit; cease, discontinue, intermit, remit; fall, precipitate. * *n* bead, droplet, globule; earring, pendant.

dross *n* cinder, lees, recrement, scoria, scum, slag; refuse, waste.

drought *n* aridity, drouth, dryness, thirstiness.

drove *n* flock, herd; collection, company, crowd.

drown *vb* deluge, engulf, flood, immerse, inundate, overflow, sink, submerge, swamp; overcome, overpower, overwhelm.

drowse *vb* doze, nap, sleep, slumber, snooze. * *n* doze, forty winks, nap, siesta, sleep, snooze.

drowsy *adj* dozy, sleepy; comatose, lethargic, stupid; lulling, soporific.

drub *vb* bang, beat, cane, cudgel, flog, hit, knock, pommel, pound, strike, thrash, thump, whack.

drubbing *n* beating, caning, cudgelling, flagellation, flogging, pommelling, pounding, thrashing, thumping, whacking.

drudge *vb* grub, grind, plod, slave, toil, work. * *n* grind, hack, hard worker, menial, plodder, scullion, servant, slave, toiler, worker.

drug *vb* dose, medicate; disgust, surfeit. * *n* medicine, physic, remedy; poison.

drunk *adj* boozed, drunken, inebriated, intoxicated, maudlin, soaked, tipsy; ablaze, aflame, delirious, fervent, suffused. * *n* alcoholic, boozer, dipsomaniac, drunkard, inebriate, lush, soak; bacchanal, bender, binge.

drunkard *n* alcoholic, boozer, carouser, dipsomaniac, drinker, drunk, inebriate, reveller, sot, tippler, toper.

dry *vb* dehydrate, desiccate, drain, exsiccate, parch. * *adj* desiccated, dried, juiceless, sapless, unmoistened; arid, droughty, parched; drouthy, thirsty; barren, dull, insipid, jejune, plain, pointless, tame, tedious, tiresome, unembellished, uninteresting, vapid; cutting, keen, sarcastic, severe, sharp, sly.

dub *vb* call, christen, denominate, designate, entitle, name, style, term.

dubious *adj* doubtful, fluctuating, hesitant, irresolute, skeptical, uncertain, undecided, unsettled, wavering; ambiguous, doubtful, equivocal, improbable, questionable, uncertain.

duck *vb* dip, dive, immerse, plunge, submerge, souse; bend, bow, dodge, stoop.

duct *n* canal, channel, conduit, pipe, tube; blood-vessel.

ductile *adj* compliant, docile, facile, tractable, yielding; flexible, malleable, pliant; extensible, tensile.

dudgeon *n* anger, indignation, ill will, ire, malice, resentment, umbrage, wrath.

due *adj* owed, owing; appropriate, becoming, befitting, bounden, fit, proper, suitable, right. * *adv* dead, direct, directly, exactly, just, right, squarely, straight. * *n* claim, debt, desert, right.

dulcet *adj* delicious, honeyed, luscious, sweet; harmonious, melodious; agreeable, charming, delightful, pleasant, pleasing.

dull *vb* blunt; benumb, besot, deaden, hebetate, obtund, paralyse, stupefy; dampen, deject, depress, discourage, dishearten, dispirit; allay, alleviate, assuage, mitigate, moderate, quiet, soften; deaden, dim, sully, tarnish. * *adj* blockish, brutish, doltish, obtuse, stolid, stupid, unintelligent; apathetic, callous, dead, insensible, passionless, phlegmatic, unfeeling, unimpassioned, unresponsive; heavy, inactive, inanimate, inert, languish, lifeless, slow, sluggish, torpid; blunt, dulled, hebetate, obtuse; cheerless, dismal, dreary, gloomy, sad, sombre; dim, lack-lustre, lustreless, matt, obscure, opaque, tarnished; dry, flat, insipid, irksome, jejune, prosy, tedious, tiresome, uninteresting, wearisome.

duly *adv* befittingly, decorously, fitly, properly, rightly; regularly.

dumb *adj* inarticulate, mute, silent, soundless, speechless, voiceless.

dumbfound, dumfound *vb* amaze, astonish, astound, bewilder, confound, confuse, nonplus, pose.

dumps *npl* blues, dejection, depression, despondency, gloom, gloominess, melancholy, sadness.

dun[1] *adj* greyish-brown, brown, drab.

dun[2] *vb* beset, importune, press, urge.

dunce *n* ass, block, blockhead, clodpole, dolt, donkey, dullard, dunderhead, fool, goose, halfwit, ignoramus, jackass, lackwit, loon, nincompoop, numskull, oaf, simpleton, thickhead, witling.

dupe *vb* beguile, cheat, chouse, circumvent, cozen, deceive, delude, gull, hoodwink, outwit, overreach, swindle, trick. * *n* gull, simpleton.

duplicate *vb* copy, double, repeat, replicate, reproduce. * *adj* doubled, twofold. * *n* copy, counterpart, facsimile, replica, transcript.

duplicity *n* artifice, chicanery, circumvention, deceit, deception, dishonesty, dissimulation, double-dealing, falseness, fraud, guile, hypocrisy, perfidy.

durable *adj* abiding, constant, continuing, enduring, firm, lasting, permanent, persistent, stable.

duration *n* continuance, continuation, permanency, perpetuation, prolongation; period, time.

duress *n* captivity, confinement, constraint, durance, hardship, imprisonment, restraint; compulsion.

dusky *adj* cloudy, darkish, dim, murky, obscure, overcast, shady, shadowy; dark, swarthy, tawny.

dutiful *adj* duteous, obedient, submissive; deferential, respectful, reverential.

duty *n* allegiance, devoirs, obligation, responsibility, reverence; business, engagement, function, office, service; custom, excise, impost, tariff, tax, toll.

dwarf *vb* lower, stunt. * *n* bantam, homunculus, manikin, midget, pygmy.

dwarfish *adj* diminutive, dwarfed, little, low, pygmy, small, stunted, tiny, undersized.

dwell *vb* abide, inhabit, live, lodge, remain, reside, rest, sojourn, stay, stop, tarry, tenant.

dwelling *n* abode, cot, domicile, dugout, establishment, habitation, home, house, hutch, lodging, mansion, quarters, residence.

dwindle *vb* decrease, diminish, lessen, shrink; decay, decline, deteriorate, pine, sink, waste away.

dye *vb* colour, stain, tinge. * *n* cast, colour, hue, shade, stain, tinge, tint.

dying *adj* expiring; mortal, perishable. * *n* death, decease, demise, departure, dissolution, exit.

dynasty *n* dominion, empire, government, rule, sovereignty.

dyspepsia *n* indigestion.

E

eager *adj* agog, avid, anxious, desirous, fain, greedy, impatient, keen, longing, yearning; animated, ardent, earnest, enthusiastic, fervent, fervid, forward, glowing, hot, impetuous, sanguine, vehement, zealous.

eagerness *n* ardour, avidity, earnestness, enthusiasm, fervour, greediness, heartiness, hunger, impatience, impetuosity, intentness, keenness, longing, thirst, vehemence, yearning, zeal.

eagle-eyed *adj* discerning, hawk-eyed, sharp-sighted.

ear[1] *n* attention, hearing, heed, regard.

ear[2] *n* head, spike.

early *adj* opportune, seasonable, timely; forward, premature; dawning, matutinal. * *adv* anon, beforehand, betimes, ere, seasonably, shortly, soon.

earn *vb* acquire, gain, get, obtain, procure, realize, reap, win; deserve, merit.

earnest *adj* animated, ardent, eager, cordial, fervent, fervid, glowing, hearty, impassioned, importune, warm, zealous; fixed, intent, steady; sincere, true, truthful; important, momentous, serious, weighty. * *n* reality, seriousness, truth; foretaste, pledge, promise; handsel, payment.

earnings *npl* allowance, emoluments, gains, income, pay, proceeds, profits, remuneration, reward, salary, stipend.

earth *n* globe, orb, planet, world; clay, clod, dirt, glebe, ground, humus, land, loam, sod, soil, turf; mankind, world.

earthborn *adj* abject, base, earthly, grovelling, low, mean, unspiritual.

earthly *adj* terrestrial; base, carnal, earthborn, low, gross, grovelling, sensual, sordid, unspiritual, worldly; bodily, material, mundane, natural, secular, temporal.

earthy *adj* clayey, earth-like, terrene; earthly, terrestrial; coarse, gross, material, unrefined.

ease *vb* disburden, disencumber, pacify, quiet, relieve, still; abate, allay, alleviate, appease, assuage, diminish, mitigate, soothe; loosen, release; facilitate, favour. * *n* leisure, quiescence, repose, rest; calmness, content, contentment, enjoyment, happiness, peace, quiet, quietness, quietude, relief, repose, satisfaction, serenity, tranquillity; easiness, facility, readiness; flexibility, freedom, liberty, lightness, naturalness, unconcern, unconstraint; comfort, elbowroom.

easy *adj* light; careless, comfortable, contented, effortless, painless, quiet, satisfied, tranquil, untroubled; accommodating, complaisant, compliant, complying, facile, indolent, manageable, pliant, submissive, tractable, yielding; graceful, informal, natural, unconstrained; flowing, ready, smooth, unaffected; gentle, lenient, mild, moderate; affluent, loose, unconcerned, unembarrassed.

eat *vb* chew, consume, devour, engorge, ingest, ravage, swallow; corrode, demolish, erode; breakfast, dine, feed, lunch, sup.

eatable *adj* edible, esculent, harmless, wholesome.

ebb *vb* abate, recede, retire, subside; decay, decline, decrease, degenerate, deteriorate, sink, wane. * *n* refluence, reflux, regress, regression, retrocedence, retrocession, retrogression, return; caducity, decay, decline, degeneration, deterioration, wane, waning; abatement, decrease, decrement, diminution.

ebullience *n* ebullition, effervescence; burst, bursting, overenthusiasm, overflow, rush, vigour.

ebullition *n* boiling, bubbling; effervescence, fermentation; burst, fit, outbreak, outburst, paroxysm.

eccentric *adj* decentred, parabolic; aberrant, abnormal, anomalous, cranky, erratic, fantastic, irregular, odd, outlandish, peculiar, singular, strange, uncommon, unnatural, wayward, whimsical. * *n* crank, curiosity, original.

eccentricity *n* ellipticity, flattening, flatness, oblateness; aberration, irregularity, oddity, oddness, peculiarity, singularity, strangeness, waywardness.

ecclesiastic[1], ecclesiastical *adj* churchish, churchly, clerical, ministerial, nonsecular, pastoral, priestly, religious, sacerdotal.

ecclesiastic[2] *n* chaplain, churchman, clergyman, cleric, clerk, divine, minister, parson, pastor, priest, reverend, shepherd.

echo *vb* reply, resound, reverberate, ring; re-echo, repeat. * *n* answer, repetition, reverberation; imitation.

éclat *n* acclamation, applause, brilliancy, effect, glory, lustre, pomp, renown, show, splendour.

eclipse *vb* cloud, darken, dim, obscure, overshadow, veil; annihilate, annul, blot out, extinguish. * *n* clouding, concealment, darkening, dimming, disappearance, hiding, obscuration, occultation, shrouding, vanishing, veiling; annihilation, blotting out, destruction, extinction, extinguishment, obliteration.

eclogue *n* bucolic, idyl, pastoral.

economize *vb* husband, manage, save; retrench.

economy *n* frugality, husbandry, parsimony, providence, retrenchment, saving, skimping, stinginess, thrift, thriftiness; administration, arrangement, management, method, order, plan, regulation, system; dispensation.

ecstasy *n* frenzy, madness, paroxysm, trance; delight, gladness, joy, rhapsody, rapture, ravishment, transport.

eddy *vb* gurgle, surge, spin, swirl, whirl. * *n* countercurrent; swirl, vortex, whirlpool.

edge *vb* sharpen; border, fringe, rim. * *n* border, brim, brink, bound, crest, fringe, hem, lip, margin, rim, verge; animation, intensity, interest, keenness, sharpness, zest; acrimony, bitterness, gall, sharpness, sting.

edging *n* border, frill, fringe, trimming.

edible *adj* eatable, esculent, harmless, wholesome.

edict *n* act, command, constitution, decision, decree, law, mandate, manifesto, notice, order, ordinance, proclamation, regulation, rescript, statute.

edifice *n* building, fabric, habitation, house, structure.

edify *vb* educate, elevate, enlightenment, improve, inform, instruct, nurture, teach, upbuild.

edition *n* impression, issue, number.

educate *vb* breed, cultivate, develop, discipline, drill, edify, exercise, indoctrinate, inform, instruct, mature, nurture, rear, school, teach, train.

educated *adj* cultured, lettered, literate.

education *n* breeding, cultivation, culture, development, discipline, drilling, indoctrination, instruction, nurture, pedagogics, schooling, teaching, training, tuition.

educe *vb* bring out, draw out, elicit, evolve, extract.

eerie *adj* awesome, fearful, frightening, strange, uncanny, weird.

efface *vb* blot, blot out, cancel, delete, destroy, erase, expunge, obliterate, remove, sponge.

effect *vb* cause, create, effectuate, produce; accomplish, achieve, carry, compass, complete, conclude, consummate, contrive, do, execute, force, negotiate, perform, realize, work. * *n* consequence, event, fruit, issue, outcome, result; efficiency, fact, force, power, reality; validity, weight; drift, import, intent, meaning, purport, significance, tenor.

effective *adj* able, active, adequate, competent, convincing, effectual, sufficient; cogent, efficacious, energetic, forcible, potent, powerful.

effects *npl* chattels, furniture, goods, movables, property.

effectual *adj* operative, successful; active, effective, efficacious, efficient.

effectuate *vb* accomplish, achieve, complete, do, effect, execute, fulfil, perform, secure.

effeminate *adj* delicate, feminine, soft, tender, timorous, unmanly, womanish, womanlike, womanly; camp.

effervesce *vb* bubble, ferment, foam, froth.

effete *adj* addle, barren, fruitless, sterile, unfruitful, unproductive, unprolific; decayed, exhausted, spent, wasted.

efficacious *adj* active, adequate, competent, effective, effectual, efficient, energetic, operative, powerful.

efficacy *n* ability, competency, effectiveness, efficiency, energy, force, potency, power, strength, vigour, virtue.

efficient *adj* active, capable, competent, effective, effectual, efficacious, operative, potent; able, energetic, ready, skilful.

effigy *n* figure, image, likeness, portrait, representation, statue.

effloresce *vb* bloom, flower.

efflorescence *n* blooming, blossoming, flowering.

effluence *n* discharge, efflux, effluvium, emanation, emission, flow, outflow, outpouring.

effort *n* application, attempt, endeavour, essay, exertion, pains, spurt, strain, strife, stretch, struggle, trial, trouble.

effrontery *n* assurance, audacity, boldness, brass, disrespect, hardihood, impudence, incivility, insolence, presumption, rudeness, sauciness, shamelessness.

effulgent *adj* burning, beaming, blazing, bright, brilliant, dazzling, flaming, glowing, lustrous, radiant, refulgent, resplendent, shining, splendid.

effusion *n* discharge, efflux, emission, gush, outpour-ing; shedding, spilling, waste; address, speech, talk, utterance.

egg *vb* (*with* on) encourage, incite, instigate, push, stimulate, urge; harass, harry, provoke.

ego *n* id, self, me, subject, superego.

egotism *n* self-admiration, self-assertion, self-commendation, self-conceit, self-esteem, self-importance, self-praise; egoism, selfishness.

egotistic, egotistical *adj* bumptious, conceited, egoistical, opinionated, self-asserting, self-admiring, self-centred, self-conceited, self-important, self-loving, vain.

egregious *adj* conspicuous, enormous, extraordinary, flagrant, great, gross, huge, monstrous, outrageous, prodigious, remarkable, tremendous.

egress *n* departure, emergence, exit, outlet, way out.

eject *vb* belch, discharge, disgorge, emit, evacuate, puke, spew, spit, spout, spurt, void, vomit; bounce, cashier, discharge, dismiss, disposes, eliminate, evict. expel, fire, oust; banish, reject, throw out.

elaborate *vb* develop, improve, mature, produce, refine, ripen. * *adj* complicated, decorated, detailed, dressy, laboured, laborious, ornate, perfected, studied.

elapse *vb* go, lapse, pass.

elastic *adj* rebounding, recoiling, resilient, springy; buoyant, recuperative.

elated *adj* animated, cheered, elate, elevated, excited, exhilarated, exultant, flushed, puffed up, roused.

elbow *vb* crowd, force, hustle, jostle, nudge, push, shoulder. * *n* angle, bend, corner, flexure, joining, turn.

elder *adj* older, senior; ranking; ancient, earlier, older. * *n* ancestor, senior; presbyter, prior, senator.

elect *vb* appoint, choose, cull, designate, pick, prefer, select. * *adj* choice, chosen, picked, selected; appointed, elected; predestinated, redeemed.

election *n* appointment, choice, preference, selection; alternative, freedom, freewill, liberty; predestination.

elector *n* chooser, constituent, selector, voter.

electrify *vb* charge, galvanize; astonish, enchant, excite, rouse, startle, stir, thrill.

elegance, elegancy *n* beauty, grace, propriety, symmetry; courtliness, daintiness, gentility, nicety, polish, politeness, refinement, taste.

elegant *adj* beautiful, chaste, classical, dainty, graceful, fine, handsome, neat, symmetrical, tasteful, trim, well-made, well-proportioned; accomplished, courtly, cultivated, fashionable, genteel, polished, polite, refined.

elegiac *adj* dirgeful, mournful, plaintive, sorrowful.

elegy *n* dirge, epicedium, lament, ode, threnody.

element *n* basis, component, constituent, factor, germ, ingredient, part, principle, rudiment, unit; environment, milieu, sphere.

elementary *adj* primordial, simple, uncombined, uncomplicated, uncompounded; basic, component, fundamental, initial, primary, rudimental, rudimentary.

elevate *vb* erect, hoist, lift, raise; advance, aggrandize, exalt, promote; dignify, ennoble, exalt, greaten, improve, refine; animate, cheer, elate, excite, exhilarate, rouse.

elfin *adj* elflike, elvish, mischievous, weird.

elicit *vb* draw out, educe, evoke, extort, fetch, obtain, pump, wrest, wring; deduce, educe.

eligible *adj* desirable, preferable; qualified, suitable, worthy.

eliminate *vb* disengage, eradicate, exclude, expel, remove, separate; ignore, omit, reject.

ellipsis *n* gap, hiatus, lacuna, omission.

elliptical *adj* oval; defective, incomplete.

elocution *n* declamation, delivery, oratory, rhetoric, speech, utterance.

elongate *vb* draw, draw out, extend, lengthen, protract, stretch.

elope *vb* abscond, bolt, decamp, disappear, leave.

eloquence *n* fluency, oratory, rhetoric.

else *adv* besides, differently, otherwise.

elucidate *vb* clarify, demonstrate, explain, expound, illuminate, illustrate, interpret, unfold.

elucidation *n* annotation, clarification, comment, commentary, elucidating, explaining, explanation, exposition, gloss, scholium.

elude *vb* avoid, escape, evade, shun, slip; baffle, balk, disappoint, disconcert, escape, foil, frustrate, thwart.

elusive *adj* deceptive, deceitful, delusive, evasive, fallacious, fraudulent, illusory; equivocatory, equivocating, shuffling.

Elysian *adj* blissful, celestial, delightful, enchanting, heavenly, ravishing, seraphic.

emaciation *n* attenuation, lankness, leanness, meagreness, tabes, tabescence, thinness.

emanate *vb* arise, come, emerge, flow, issue, originate, proceed, spring.

emancipate *vb* deliver, discharge, disenthral, enfranchise, free, liberate, manumit, release, unchain, unfetter, unshackle.

emancipation *n* deliverance, enfranchisement, deliverance, freedom, liberation, manumission, release.

emasculate *vb* castrate, geld; debilitate, effeminize, enervate, unman, weaken.

embalm *vb* cherish, consecrate, conserve, enshrine, preserve, store, treasure; perfume, scent.

embargo *vb* ban, bar, blockade, debar, exclude, prohibit, proscribe, restrict, stop, withhold. * *n* ban, bar, blockade, exclusion, hindrance, impediment, prohibition, prohibitory, proscription, restraint, restriction, stoppage.

embark *vb* engage, enlist.

embarrass *vb* beset, entangle, perplex; annoy, clog, bother, distress, hamper, harass, involve, plague, trouble, vex; abash, confound, confuse, discomfit, disconcert, dumbfound, mortify, nonplus, pose, shame.

embellish *vb* adorn, beautify, bedeck, deck, decorate, emblazon, enhance, enrich, garnish, grace, ornament.

embellishment *n* adornment, decoration, enrichment, ornament, ornamentation.

embezzle *vb* appropriate, defalcate, filch, misappropriate, peculate, pilfer, purloin, steal.

embitter *vb* aggravate, envenom, exacerbate; anger, enrage, exasperate, madden.

emblem *n* badge, cognizance, device, mark, representation, sign, symbol, token, type.

embody *vb* combine, compact, concentrate, incorporate; comprehend, comprise, contain, embrace, include; codify, methodize, systematize.

embolden *vb* animate, cheer, elate, encourage, gladden, hearten, inspirit, nerve, reassure.

embosom *vb* bury, cherish, clasp, conceal, enfold, envelop, enwrap, foster, hide, nurse, surround.

embrace *vb* clasp; accept, seize, welcome; comprehend, comprise, contain, cover, embody, encircle, enclose, encompass, enfold, hold, include. * *n* clasp, fold, hug.

embroil *vb* commingle, encumber, ensnarl, entangle, implicate, involve; confuse, discompose, disorder, distract, disturb, perplex, trouble.

embryo *n* beginning, germ, nucleus, root, rudiment.

embryonic *adj* incipient, rudimentary, undeveloped.

emendation *n* amendment, correction, improvement, rectification.

emerge *vb* rise; emanate, escape, issue; appear, arise, outcrop.

emergency *n* crisis, difficulty, dilemma, exigency, extremity, necessity, pass, pinch, push, strait, urgency; conjuncture, crisis, juncture, pass.

emigration *n* departure, exodus, migration, removal.

eminence *n* elevation, hill, projection, prominence, protuberance; celebrity, conspicuousness, distinction, exaltation, fame, loftiness, note, preferment, reputation, repute, renown.

eminent *adj* elevated, high, lofty; celebrated, conspicuous, distinguished, exalted, famous, illustrious, notable, prominent, remarkable, renowned.

emissary *n* messenger, scout, secret agent, spy.

emit *vb* breathe out, dart, discharge, eject, emanate, exhale, gust, hurl, jet, outpour, shed, shoot, spurt, squirt.

emollient *adj* relaxing, softening. soothing. * *n* softener.

emolument *n* compensation, gain, hire, income, lucre, pay, pecuniary, profits, salary, stipend, wages; advantage, benefit, profit, perquisites.

emotion *n* agitation, excitement, feeling, passion, perturbation, sentiment, sympathy, trepidation.

emphasis *n* accent, stress; force, importance, impressiveness, moment, significance, weight.

emphatic *adj* decided, distinct, earnest, energetic, expressive, forcible, impressive, intensive, positive, significant, strong, unequivocal.

empire *n* domain, dominion, sovereignty, supremacy; authority, command, control, government, rule, sway.

empirical, empiric *adj* experimental, experiential; hypothetical, provisional, tentative; charlatanic, quackish.

employ *vb* busy, devote, engage, engross, enlist, exercise, occupy, retain; apply, commission, use. * *n* employment, service.

employee *n* agent, clerk, employee, hand, servant, workman.

employment *n* avocation, business, calling, craft, employ, engagement, occupation, profession, pursuit, trade, vocation, work.

emporium *n* market, mart, shop, store.

empower *vb* authorize, commission, permit, qualify, sanction, warrant; enable.

empty *vb* deplete, drain, evacuate, exhaust; discharge, disembogue; flow, embogue. * *adj* blank, hollow, unoccupied, vacant, vacuous, void; deplete, destitute, devoid, hungry; unfilled, unfurnished, unsupplied; unsatisfactory, unsatisfying, unsubstantial, useless, vain; clear, deserted, desolate, exhausted, free, unburdened, unloaded, waste; foolish, frivolous, inane, senseless, silly, stupid, trivial, weak.

empyrean, empyreal *adj* aerial, airy, ethereal, heavenly, refined, sublimated, sublimed.

emulation *n* competition, rivalry, strife, vying; contention, envy, jealousy.

enable *vb* authorize, capacitate, commission, empower, fit, permit, prepare, qualify, sanction, warrant.

enact *vb* authorize, command, decree, establish, legislate, ordain, order, sanction; act, perform, personate, play, represent.

enactment *n* act, decree, law, edict, ordinance.

enamour *vb* bewitch, captivate, charm, enchant, endear, fascinate.

enchain *vb* bind, confine, enslave, fetter, hold, manacle, restrain, shackle.

enchant *vb* beguile, bewitch, charm, delude, fascinate; captivate, catch, enamour, win; beatify, delight, enrapture, rapture, ravish, transport.

enchanting *adj* bewitching, blissful, captivating, charming, delightful, enrapturing, fascinating, rapturous, ravishing.

enchantment *n* charm, conjuration, incantation, magic, necromancy, sorcery, spell, witchery; bliss, delight, fascination, rapture, ravishment, transport.

encase *vb* encircle, enclose, incase, infix, set; chase, emboss, engrave, inlay, ornament.

encage *vb* confine, coop up, impound, imprison, shut up.

encircle *vb* belt, circumscribe, encompass, enclose, engird, enring, environ, gird, ring, span, surround, twine; clasp, embrace, enfold, fold.

enclose, inclose *vb* circumscribe, corral, coop, embosom, encircle, encompass, environ, fence in, hedge, include, pen, shut in, surround; box, cover, encase, envelop, wrap.

encomium *n* applause, commendation, eulogy, laudation, panegyric, praise.

encompass *vb* belt, compass, encircle, enclose, engird, environ, gird, surround; beset, besiege, hem in, include, invest, surround.

encounter *vb* confront, face, meet; attack, combat, contend, engage, strive, struggle. * *n* assault, attack, clash, collision, meeting, onset; action, affair, battle, brush, combat, conflict, contest, dispute, engagement, skirmish.

encourage *vb* animate, assure, cheer, comfort, console, embolden, enhearten, fortify, hearten, incite, inspirit, instigate, reassure, stimulate, strengthen; abet, aid, advance, approve, countenance, favour, foster, further, help, patronize, promote, support.

encroach *vb* infringe, invade, intrude, tench, trespass, usurp.

encumber *vb* burden, clog, hamper, hinder, impede, load, obstruct, overload, oppress, retard; complicate, embarrass, entangle, involve, perplex.

encumbrance *n* burden, clog, deadweight, drag, embarrassment, hampering, hindrance, impediment, incubus, load; claim, debt, liability, lien.

end *vb* abolish, close, conclude, discontinue, dissolve, drop, finish, stop, terminate; annihilate, destroy, kill; cease, terminate. * *n* extremity, tip; cessation, close, denouement, ending, expiration, finale, finis, finish, last, period, stoppage, wind-up; completion, conclusion, consummation; annihilation, catastrophe, destruction, dissolution; bound, limit, termination, terminus; consequence, event, issue, result, settlement, sequel, upshot; fragment, remnant, scrap, stub, tag, tail; aim, design, goal, intent, intention, object, objective, purpose.

endanger *vb* compromise, hazard, imperil, jeopardize, peril, risk.

endear *vb* attach, bind, captivate, charm, win.

endearment *n* attachment, fondness, love, tenderness; caress, blandishment, fondling.

endeavour *vb* aim, attempt, essay, labour, seek, strive, struggle, study, try. * *n* aim, attempt, conatus, effort, essay, exertion, trial, struggle, trial.

endless *adj* boundless, illimitable, immeasurable, indeterminable, infinite, interminable, limitless, unlimited; dateless, eternal, everlasting, never-ending, perpetual, unending; deathless, ever-enduring, ever-living, immortal, imperishable, undying.

endorse, indorse *vb* approve, back, confirm, guarantee, ratify, sanction, superscribe, support, visé, vouch for, warrant; superscribe.

endow *vb* bequeath, clothe, confer, dower, endue, enrich, gift, indue, invest, supply.

endowment *n* bequest, boon, bounty, gift, grant, largesse, present; foundation, fund, property, revenue; ability, aptitude, capability, capacity, faculty, genius, gift, parts, power, qualification, quality, talent.

endurance *n* abiding, bearing, sufferance, suffering, tolerance, toleration; backbone, bottom, forbearance, fortitude, guts, patience, resignation.

endure *vb* bear, support, sustain; experience, suffer, undergo, weather; abide, brook, permit, pocket, swallow, tolerate, stomach, submit, withstand; continue, last, persist, remain, wear.

enemy *n* adversary, foe; antagonist, foeman, opponent, rival.

energetic *adj* active, effective, efficacious, emphatic, enterprising, forceful, forcible, hearty, mettlesome, potent, powerful, strenuous, strong, vigorous.

energy *n* activity, dash, drive, efficacy, efficiency, force, go, impetus, intensity, mettle, might, potency, power, strength, verve, vim; animation, life, manliness, spirit, spiritedness, stamina, vigour, zeal.

enervate *vb* break, debilitate, devitalize, emasculate, enfeeble, exhaust, paralyse, relax, soften, unhinge, unnerve, weaken.

enfeeble *vb* debilitate, devitalize, enervate, exhaust, relax, unhinge, unnerve, weaken.

enfold, infold *vb* enclose, envelop, fold, enwrap, wrap; clasp, embrace.

enforce *vb* compel, constrain, exact, force, oblige, require, urge.

enfranchise *vb* emancipate, free, liberate, manumit, release.

engage *vb* bind, commit, obligate, pledge, promise; affiance, betroth, plight; book, brief, employ, enlist, hire, retain; arrest, allure, attach, draw, entertain, fix, gain, win; busy, commission, contract, engross, occupy; attack, encounter; combat, contend, contest, fight, interlock, struggle; embark, enlist; agree, promise, stipulate, undertake, warrant.

engagement *n* appointment, assurance, contract, obligation, pledge, promise, stipulation; affiancing, betrothment, betrothal, plighting; avocation, business, calling, employment, enterprise, occupation; action, battle, combat, encounter, fight.

engender *vb* bear, beget, breed, create, generate, procreate, propagate; cause, excite, incite, occasion, produce.

engine *n* invention, machine; agency, agent, device, implement, instrument, means, method, tool, weapon.

engorge *vb* bolt, devour, eat, gobble, gorge, gulp, swallow; glut, obstruct, stuff.

engrave *vb* carve, chisel, cut, etch, grave, hatch, incise, sculpt; grave, impress, imprint, infix.

engross *vb* absorb, engage, occupy, take up; buy up, forestall, monopolize.

engrossment *n* absorption, forestalling, monopoly.

engulf, ingulf *vb* absorb, overwhelm, plunge, swallow up.

enhance *vb* advance, aggravate, augment, elevate, heighten, increase, intensify, raise, swell.

enhearten *vb* animate, assure, cheer, comfort, console, embolden, encourage, hearten, incite, inspirit, reassure, stimulate.

enigma *n* conundrum, mystery, problem, puzzle, riddle.

enigmatic, enigmatical *adj* ambiguous, dark, doubtful, equivocal, hidden, incomprehensible, mysterious, mystic, obscure, occult, perplexing, puzzling, recondite, uncertain, unintelligible.

enjoin *vb* admonish, advise, urge; bid, command, direct, order, prescribe, require; prohibit, restrain.

enjoy *vb* like, possess, relish.

enjoyment *n* delight, delectation, gratification, happiness, indulgence, pleasure, satisfaction; possession.

enkindle *vb* inflame, ignite, kindle; excite, incite, instigate, provoke, rouse, stimulate.

enlarge *vb* amplify, augment, broaden, develop, dilate, distend, expand, extend, grow, increase, magnify, widen; aggrandize, engreaten, ennoble, expand, exaggerate, greaten; swell.

enlighten *vb* illume, illuminate, illumine; counsel, educate, civilize, inform, instruct, teach.

enlist *vb* enrol, levy, recruit, register; enrol, list; embark, engage.

enliven *vb* animate, invigorate, quicken, reanimate, rouse, wake; exhilarate, cheer, brighten, delight, elate, gladden, inspire, inspirit, rouse.

enmity *n* animosity, aversion, bitterness, hate, hatred, hostility, ill-will, malevolence, malignity, rancour.

ennoble *vb* aggrandize, dignify, elevate, engreaten, enlarge, exalt, glorify, greaten, raise.

ennui *n* boredom, irksomeness, languor, lassitude, listlessness, tedium, tiresomeness, weariness.

enormity *n* atrociousness, atrocity, depravity, flagitiousness, heinousness, nefariousness, outrageousness, villainy, wickedness.

enormous *adj* abnormal. exceptional, inordinate, irregular; colossal, Cyclopean, elephantine, Herculean, huge, immense, monstrous, vast, gigantic, prodigious, titanic, tremendous.

enough *adj* abundant, adequate, ample, plenty, sufficient. * *adv* satisfactorily, sufficiently. * *n* abundance, plenty, sufficiency.

enquire *see* **inquire.**

enrage *vb* anger, chafe, exasperate, incense, inflame, infuriate, irritate, madden, provoke.

enrapture *vb* beatify, bewitch, delight, enchant, enravish, entrance, surpassingly, transport.

enrich *vb* endow; adorn, deck, decorate, embellish, grace, ornament.

enrobe *vb* clothe, dress, apparel, array, attire, invest, robe.

enrol *vb* catalogue, engage, engross, enlist, list, register; chronicle, record.

ensconce *vb* conceal, cover, harbour, hide, protect, screen, secure, settle, shelter, shield, snugly.

enshrine *vb* embalm, enclose, entomb; cherish, treasure.

ensign *n* banner, colours, eagle, flag, gonfalcon, pennon, standard, streamer; sign, signal, symbol; badge, hatchment.

enslave *vb* captivate, dominate, master, overmaster, overpower, subjugate.

ensnare *vb* catch, entrap; allure, inveigle, seduce; bewilder, confound, embarrass, encumber, entangle, perplex.

ensue *vb* follow, succeed; arise, come, flow, issue, proceed, result, spring.

entangle *vb* catch, ensnare, entrap; confuse, enmesh, intertwine, intertwist, interweave, knot, mat, ravel, tangle; bewilder, embarrass, encumber, ensnare, involve, nonplus, perplex, puzzle.

enterprise *n* adventure, attempt, cause, effort, endeavour, essay, project, undertaking, scheme, venture; activity, adventurousness, daring, dash, energy, initiative, readiness, push.

enterprising *adj* adventurous, audacious, bold, daring, dashing, venturesome, venturous; active, adventurous, alert, efficient, energetic, prompt, resourceful, smart, spirited, stirring, strenuous, zealous.

entertain *vb* fete, receive, regale, treat; cherish, foster, harbour, hold, lodge, shelter; admit, consider; amuse, cheer, divert, please, recreate.

entertainment *n* hospitality; banquet, collation, feast, festival, reception, treat; amusement, diversion, pastime, recreation, sport.

enthusiasm *n* ecstasy, exaltation, fanaticism; ardour, carnestness, devotion, eagerness, fervour, passion, warmth, zeal.

enthusiast *n* bigot, devotee, fan, fanatic, freak, zealot; castle-builder, dreamer, visionary.

entice *vb* allure, attract, bait, cajole, coax, decoy, inveigle, lure, persuade, prevail on, seduce, tempt, wheedle, wile.

enticement *n* allurement, attraction, bait, blandishment, inducement, inveiglement, lure, persuasion, seduction.

entire *adj* complete, integrated, perfect, unbroken, undiminished, undivided, unimpaired, whole; complete, full, plenary, thorough; mere, pure, sheer, unalloyed, unmingled, unmitigated, unmixed.

entitle *vb* call, characterize, christen, denominate, designate, dub, name, style; empower, enable, fit for, qualify for.

entomb *vb* bury, inhume, inter.

entrails *npl* bowels, guts, intestines, inwards, offal, viscera.

entrance[1] *n* access, approach, avenue, incoming, ingress; adit, avenue, aperture, door, doorway, entry, gate, hallway, inlet, lobby, mouth, passage, portal, stile, vestibule; beginning, commencement, debut, initiation, introduction; admission, entrée.

entrance[2] *vb* bewitch, captivate, charm, delight, enchant, enrapture, fascinate, ravish, transport.

entrap *vb* catch, ensnare; allure, entice, inveigle, seduce; embarrass, entangle, involve, nonplus, perplex, pose, stagger.

entreat *vb* adjure, beg, beseech, crave, enjoin, implore, importune, petition, pray, solicit, supplicate.

entreaty *n* adjuration, appeal, importunity, petition, prayer, request, solicitation, suit, supplication.

entrée *n* access, admission, admittance.

entrench, intrench *vb* furrow; circumvallate, fortify; encroach, infringe, invade, trench, trespass.

entrenchment, intrenchment *n* entrenching; earthwork, fortification; defence, protection, shelter; encroachment, inroad, invasion.

entrust *vb* commit, confide, consign.

entwine *vb* entwist, interlace, intertwine, interweave, inweave, twine, twist, weave; embrace, encircle, encumber, interlace, surround.

enumerate *vb* calculate, cite, compute, count, detail, mention, number, numerate, reckon, recount, specify, tell.

enunciate vb articulate, declare, proclaim, promulgate, pronounce, propound, publish, say, speak, utter.

envelop vb encase, enfold, enwrap, fold, pack, wrap; cover, encircle, encompass, enshroud, hide, involve, surround.

envelope n capsule, case, covering, integument, shroud, skin, wrapper, veil, vesture, wrap.

envenom vb poison, taint; embitter, malign; aggravate, enrage, exasperate, incense, inflame, irritate, madden, provoke.

environ n begird, belt, embrace, encircle, encompass, enclose, engird, envelop, gird, hedge, hem, surround; beset, besiege, encompass, invest.

environs npl neighbourhood, vicinage, vicinity.

envoy n ambassador, legate, minister, plenipotentiary; courier, messenger.

envy vb hate; begrudge, grudge; covet, emulate, desire. * n enviousness, hate, hatred, ill-will, jealousy, malice, spite; grudge, grudging.

enwrap vb absorb, cover, encase, engross, envelop, infold, involve, wrap, wrap up.

ephemeral adj brief, diurnal, evanescent, fleeting, flitting, fugacious, fugitive, momentary, occasional, short-lived, transient, transitory.

epic adj Homeric, heroic, narrative.

epicure n gastronome, glutton, gourmand, gourmet; epicurean, sensualist, Sybarite, voluptuary.

epidemic adj general, pandemic, prevailing, prevalent. * n outbreak, pandemia, pestilence, plague, spread, wave.

epidermis n cuticle, scarf-skin.

epigrammatic adj antithetic, concise, laconic, piquant, poignant, pointed, pungent, sharp, terse.

episcopal adj Episcopalian, pontifical, prelatic.

epistle n communication, letter, missive, note.

epithet n appellation, description, designation, name, predicate, title.

epitome n abbreviation, abridgement, abstract, breviary, brief, comment, compendium, condensation, conspectus, digest, summary, syllabus, synopsis.

epitomize vb abbreviate, abridge, abstract, condense, contract, curtail, cut, reduce, shorten, summarize.

epoch n age, date, era, period, time.

equable adj calm, equal, even, even-tempered, regular, steady, uniform, serene, tranquil, unruffled.

equal vb equalize, even, match. * adj alike, coordinate, equivalent, like, tantamount; even, level, equable, regular, uniform; equitable, even-handed, fair, impartial, just, unbiased; co-extensive, commensurate, corresponding, parallel, proportionate; adequate, competent, fit, sufficient. * n compeer, fellow, match, peer; rival.

equanimity n calmness, composure, coolness, peace, regularity, self-possession, serenity, steadiness.

equestrian adj equine, horse-like, horsy. * n horseman, rider; cavalier, cavalryman, chevalier, horse soldier, knight.

equilibrist n acrobat, balancer, funambulist, rope-walker.

equip vb appoint, arm, furnish, provide, rig, supply; accoutre, array, dress.

equipage n accoutrements, apparatus, baggage, effects, equipment, furniture; carriage, turnout, vehicle; attendance, procession, retinue, suite, train.

equipment n accoutrement, apparatus, baggage, equipage, furniture, gear, outfit, rigging.

equipoise n balance, equilibrium.

equitable adj even-handed, candid, honest, impartial, just, unbiased, unprejudiced, upright; adequate, fair, proper, reasonable, right.

equity n just, right; fair play, fairness, impartiality, justice, rectitude, reasonableness, righteousness, uprightness.

equivalent adj commensurate, equal, equipollent, tantamount; interchangeable, synonymous. * n complement, coordinate, counterpart, double, equal, fellow, like, match, parallel, pendant, quid pro quo.

equivocal adj ambiguous; doubtful, dubious, enigmatic, indeterminate, problematical, puzzling, uncertain.

equivocate vb dodge, evade, fence, palter, prevaricate, shuffle, quibble.

equivocation n evasion, paltering, prevarication, quibbling, shuffling; double entendre, double meaning, quibble.

era n age, date, epoch, period, time.

eradicate vb extirpate, root, uproot; abolish, annihilate, destroy, obliterate.

erase vb blot, cancel, delete, efface, expunge, obliterate, scrape out.

erasure n cancellation, cancelling, effacing, expunging, obliteration.

erect vb build, construct, raise, rear; create, establish, form, found, institute, plant. * adj standing, unrecumbent, uplifted, upright; elevated, vertical, perpendicular, straight; bold, firm, undaunted, undismayed, unshaken, unterrified.

erelong adv early, quickly, shortly, soon, speedily.

eremite n anchoret, anchorite, hermit, recluse, solitary.

ergo adv consequently, hence, therefore.

erode vb canker, consume, corrode, destroy, eat away, fret, rub.

erosive adj acrid, cathartic, caustic, corroding, corrosive, eating, virulent.

erotic adj amorous, amatory, arousing, seductive, stimulating, titillating.

err vb deviate, ramble, rove, stray, wander; blunder, misjudge, mistake; fall, lapse, nod, offend, sin, stumble, trespass, trip.

errand n charge, commission, mandate, message, mission, purpose.

errant adj adventurous, rambling, roving, stray, wandering.

erratic adj nomadic, rambling, roving, wandering; moving, planetary; abnormal, capricious, deviating, eccentric, irregular, odd, queer, strange.

erratum n correction, corrigendum, error, misprint, mistake.

erroneous adj false, incorrect, inaccurate, inexact, mistaken untrue, wrong.

error n blunder, fallacy, inaccuracy, misapprehension, mistake, oversight; delinquency, fault, iniquity, misdeed, misdoing, misstep, obliquity, offence, shortcoming, sin, transgression, trespass, wrongdoing.

erudition n knowledge, learning, lore, scholarship.

eruption n explosion, outbreak, outburst; sally; rash.

escape vb avoid, elude, evade, flee from, shun; abscond, bolt, decamp, flee, fly; slip. * n flight; release; passage, passing; leakage.

eschew vb abstain, avoid, elude, flee from, shun.

escort vb convey, guard, protect; accompany, attend, conduct. * n attendant, bodyguard, cavalier, companion, convoy, gallant, guard, squire; protection, safe conduct, safeguard; attendance, company.

esculent *adj* eatable, edible, wholesome.

esoteric *adj* hidden, inmost, inner, mysterious, private, recondite, secret.

especial *adj* absolute, chief, distinct, distinguished, marked, particular, peculiar, principal, singular, special, specific, uncommon, unusual; detailed, minute, noteworthy.

espousal *n* affiancing, betrothing, espousing, plighting; adoption, defence, maintenance, support.

espouse *vb* betroth, plight, promise; marry, wed; adopt, champion, defend, embrace, maintain, support.

espy *vb* descry, detect, discern, discover, observe, perceive, spy, watch.

esquire *n* armiger, attendant, escort, gentleman, squire.

essay[1] *vb* attempt, endeavour, try. * *n* aim, attempt, effort, endeavour, exertion, struggle, trial.

essay[2] *n* article, composition, disquisition, dissertation, paper, thesis.

essence *n* nature, quintessence, substance; extract, part; odour, perfume, scent; being, entity, existence, nature.

essential *adj* fundamental, indispensable, important, inward, intrinsic, necessary, requisite, vital; diffusible, pure, rectified, volatile.

establish *vb* fix, secure, set, settle; decree, enact, ordain; build, constitute, erect, form, found, institute, organize, originate, pitch, plant, raise; ensconce, ground, install, place, plant, root, secure; approve, confirm, ratify, sanction; prove, substantiate, verify.

estate *n* condition, state; position, rank, standing; division, order; effects, fortune, possessions, property; interest.

esteem *vb* appreciate, estimate, rate, reckon, value; admire, honour, like, prize, respect, revere, reverence, value, venerate, worship; account, believe, consider, deem, fancy, hold, imagine, suppose, regard, think. * *n* account, appreciation, consideration, estimate, estimation, judgement, opinion, reckoning, valuation; credit, honour, regard, respect, reverence.

estimable *adj* appreciable, calculable, computable; admirable, credible, deserving, excellent, good, meritorious, precious, respectful, valuable, worthy.

estimate *vb* appraise, appreciate, esteem, prise, rate, value; assess, calculate, compute, count, gauge, judge, reckon. * *n* estimation, judgement, valuation; calculation, computation.

estimation *n* appreciation, estimate, valuation; esteem, estimate, judgement, opinion; honour, reckoning, regard, respect, reverence.

estop *vb* bar, impede, preclude, stop.

estrange *vb* withdraw, withhold; alienate, divert; disaffect, destroy.

estuary *n* creek, inlet, fiord, firth, frith, mouth.

etch *vb* corrode, engrave.

eternal *adj* absolute, inevitable, necessary, self-active, self-existent, self-originated; abiding, ceaseless, endless, ever-enduring, everlasting, incessant, interminable, never-ending, perennial, permanent, perpetual, sempiternal, unceasing, unending; deathless, immortal, imperishable, incorruptible, indestructible, never-dying, undying; immutable, unchangeable; constant, continual, continuous, incessant, persistent, unbroken, uninterrupted.

ethereal *adj* aerial, airy, celestial, empyreal, heavenly, unworldly; attenuated, light, subtle, tenuous, volatile; delicate, fairy, flimsy, fragile, rare, refined, subtle.

eulogize *vb* applaud, commend, extol, laud, magnify, praise.

eulogy *n* discourse, eulogium, panegyric, speech; applause, encomium, commendation, laudation, praise.

euphonious *adj* clear, euphonic, harmonious, mellifluous, mellow, melodious, musical, silvery, smooth, sweet-toned.

evacuant *adj* abstergent, cathartic, cleansing, emetic, purgative. * *n* cathartic, purgative.

evacuate *vb* empty; discharge, clean out, clear out, eject, excrete, expel, purge, void; abandon, desert, forsake, leave, quit, relinquish, withdraw.

evade *vb* elude, escape; avoid, decline, dodge, funk, shun; baffle, elude, foil; dodge, equivocate, fence, palter, prevaricate, quibble, shuffle.

evanescence *n* disappearance, evanishing, evanishment, vanishing; transience, transientness, transitoriness.

evanescent *adj* ephemeral, fleeting, flitting, fugitive, passing, short-lived, transient, transitory, vanishing.

evaporate *vb* distil, volatilize; dehydrate, dry, vaporize; disperse, dissolve, fade, vanish.

evaporation *n* distillation, volatilization; dehydration, drying, vaporization; disappearance, dispersal, dissolution.

evasion *n* artifice, avoidance, bluffing, deceit, dodge, equivocation, escape, excuse, funking, prevarication, quibble, shift, subterfuge, shuffling, sophistical, tergiversation.

evasive *adj* elusive, elusory, equivocating, prevaricating, shuffling, slippery, sophistical.

even *vb* balance, equalize, harmonize, symmetrize, align, flatten, flush, level, smooth, square. * *adj* flat, horizontal, level, plane, smooth; calm, composed, equable, equal, peaceful, placid, regular, steady, uniform, unruffled; direct, equitable, fair, impartial, just, straightforward. * *adv* exactly, just, verily; likewise. * *n* eve, evening, eventide, vesper.

evening *n* dusk, eve, even, eventide, nightfall, sunset, twilight.

event *n* circumstance, episode, fact, happening, incident, occurrence; conclusion, consequence, end, issue, outcome, result, sequel, termination; adventure, affair.

eventful *adj* critical, important, memorable, momentous, remarkable, signal, stirring.

eventual *adj* final, last, ultimate; conditional, contingent, possible. * *adv* always, aye, constantly, continually, eternally, ever evermore, forever, incessantly, perpetually, unceasingly.

everlasting *adj* ceaseless, constant, continual, endless, eternal, ever-during, incessant, interminable, never-ceasing, never-ending, perpetual, unceasing, unending, unintermitting, uninterrupted; deathless, ever-living, immortal, imperishable, never-dying, undying.

evermore *adv* always, constantly, continually, eternally, ever, forever, perpetually.

everyday *adj* accustomed, common, commonplace, customary, habitual, routine, usual, wonted.

evict *vb* dispossess, eject, thrust out.

evidence *vb* evince, make clear, manifest, prove, show, testify, vouch. * *n* affirmation, attestation, averment, confirmation, corroboration, deposition, grounds, indication, proof, testimony, token, trace, voucher, witness.

evident *adj* apparent, bald, clear, conspicuous, distinct, downright, incontestable, indisputable, manifest, obvious, open, overt, palpable, patent, plain, unmistakable.

evil *adj* bad, ill; base, corrupt, malicious, malevolent, malign, nefarious, perverse, sinful, vicious, vile, wicked, wrong; bad, deleterious, baleful, baneful, destructive, harmful, hurtful, injurious, mischievous, noxious, pernicious, profane; adverse, calamitous, diabolic, disastrous, unfortunate, unhappy, unpropitious, woeful. * *n* calamity, disaster, ill, misery, misfortune, pain, reverse, sorrow, suffering, woe; badness, baseness, corruption, depravity, malignity, sin, viciousness, wickedness; bale, bane, blast, canker, curse, harm, injury, mischief, wrong.

evince *vb* establish, evidence, manifest, prove, show; disclose, display, exhibit, indicate, reveal.

eviscerate *vb* disembowel, embowel, gut.

evoke *vb* arouse, elicit, excite, provoke, rouse.

evolve *vb* develop, educe, exhibit, expand, open, unfold, unroll.

exacerbate *vb* aggravate, embitter, enrage, exasperate, excite, inflame, infuriate, irritate, provoke, vex.

exact *vb* elicit, extort, mulch, require, squeeze; ask, claim, compel, demand, enforce, requisition, take. * *adj* rigid, rigorous, scrupulous, severe, strict; diametric, express, faultless, precise, true; accurate, close, correct, definite, faithful, literal, undeviating; accurate, critical, delicate, fine, nice, sensitive; careful, methodical, punctilious, orderly, punctual, regular.

exacting *adj* critical, difficult, exactive, rigid, extortionary.

exaction *n* contribution, extortion, oppression, rapacity, tribute.

exactness *n* accuracy, correctness, exactitude, faithfulness, faultlessness, fidelity, nicety, precision, rigour; carefulness, method, precision, regularity, rigidness, scrupulousity, scrupulousness, strictness.

exaggerate *vb* enlarge, magnify, overcharge, overcolour, overstate, romance, strain, stretch.

exalt *vb* elevate, erect, heighten, lift up, raise; aggrandize, dignify, elevate, ennoble; bless, extol, glorify, magnify, praise.

exalted *adj* elated, elevated, high, highflown, lofty, lordly, magnificent.

examination *n* inspection, observation; exploration, inquiry, inquisition, investigation, perusal, research, search, scrutiny, survey; catechism, probation, review, test, trial.

examine *vb* inspect, observe; canvass, consider, explore, inquire, investigate, scrutinize, study, test; catechize, interrogate.

example *n* archetype, copy, model, pattern, piece, prototype, representative, sample, sampler, specimen, standard; exemplification, illustration, instance, precedent, warning.

exanimate *adj* dead, defunct, inanimate, lifeless; inanimate, inert, sluggish, spiritless, torpid.

exasperate *vb* affront, anger, chafe, enrage, incense, irritate, nettle, offend, provoke, vex; aggravate, exacerbate, inflame, rouse.

exasperation *n* annoyance, exacerbation, irritation, provocation; anger, fury, ire, passion, rage, wrath; aggravation, heightening, increase, worsening.

excavate *vb* burrow, cut, delve, dig, hollow, hollow out, scoop, trench.

exceed *vb* cap, overstep, surpass, transcend; excel, outdo, outstrip, outvie, pass.

excel *vb* beat, eclipse, outdo, outrival, outstrip, outvie, surpass; cap, exceed, transcend.

excellence *n* distinction, eminence, pre-eminence, superiority, transcendence; fineness, fitness, goodness, perfection, purity, quality, superiority; advantage; goodness, probity, uprightness, virtue, worth.

excellent *adj* admirable, choice, crack, eminent, first-rate, prime, sterling, superior, tiptop, transcendent; deserving, estimable, praiseworthy, virtuous, worthy.

except *vb* exclude, leave out, omit, reject. * *conj* unless. * *prep* bar, but, excepting, excluding, save.

exceptional *adj* aberrant, abnormal, anomalous, exceptive, irregular, peculiar, rare, special, strange, superior, uncommon, unnatural, unusual.

excerpt *vb* cite, cull, extract, quote, select, take. * *n* citation, extract, quotation, selection.

excess *adj* excessive, unnecessary, redundant, spare, superfluous, surplus. * *n* disproportion, fulsomeness, glut, oversupply, plethora, redundance, redundancy, surfeit, superabundance, superfluity; overplus, remainder, surplus; debauchery, dissipation, dissoluteness, intemperance, immoderation, overindulgence, unrestraint; extravagance, immoderation, overdoing.

excessive *adj* disproportionate, exuberant, superabundant, superfluous, undue; extravagant, enormous, inordinate, outrageous, unreasonable; extreme, immoderate, intemperate; vehement, violent.

exchange *vb* barter, change, commute, shuffle, substitute, swap, trade, truck; bandy, interchange. * *n* barter, change, commutation, dealing, shuffle, substitution, trade, traffic; interchange, reciprocity; bazaar, bourse, fair, market.

excise[1] *n* capitation, customs, dues, duty, tariff, tax, taxes, toll.

excise[2] *vb* cancel, cut, delete, edit, efface, eradicate, erase, expunge, extirpate, remove, strike out.

excision *n* destruction, eradication, extermination, extirpation.

excitable *adj* impressible, nervous, sensitive, susceptible; choleric, hasty, hot-headed, hot-tempered, irascible, irritable, passionate, quick-tempered.

excite *vb* animate, arouse, awaken, brew, evoke, impel, incite, inflame, instigate, kindle, move, prompt, provoke, rouse, spur, stimulate; create, elicit, evoke, raise; agitate, discompose, disturb, irritate.

excitement *n* excitation, exciting; incitement, motive, stimulus; activity, agitation, bustle, commotion, disturbance, ferment, flutter, perturbation, sensation, stir, tension; choler, heat, irritation, passion, violence, warmth.

exclaim *vb* call, cry, declare, ejaculate, shout, utter, vociferate.

exclude *vb* ban, bar, blackball, debar, ostracize, preclude, reject; hinder, prevent, prohibit, restrain, withhold; except, omit; eject, eliminate, expel, extrude.

exclusive *adj* debarring, excluding; illiberal, narrow, narrow-minded, selfish, uncharitable; aristocratic, choice, clannish, cliquish, fastidious, fashionable, select, snobbish; only, sole, special.

excommunicate *vb* anathematize, ban, curse, denounce, dismiss, eject, exclude, expel, exscind, proscribe, unchurch.

excoriate *vb* abrade, flay, gall, scar, scarify, score, skin, strip.

excrement *n* dejections, dung, faeces, excreta, excretion, ordure, stool.

excrescence n fungus, growth, knob, lump, outgrowth, protuberance, tumour, wart.

excrete vb discharge, eject, eliminate, separate.

excruciate vb agonize, rack, torment, torture.

exculpate vb absolve, acquit, clear, discharge, exonerate, free, justify, release, set right, vindicate.

excursion n drive, expedition, jaunt, journey, ramble, ride, sally, tour, trip, voyage, walk; digression, episode.

excursive adj devious, diffuse, digressive, discursive, erratic, rambling, roaming, roving, wandering.

excusable adj allowable, defensible, forgivable, justifiable, pardonable, venial, warrantable.

excursus n discussion, disquisition, dissertation.

excuse vb absolve, acquit, exculpate, exonerate, forgive, pardon, remit; extenuate, justify; exempt, free, release; overlook. * n absolution, apology, defence, extenuation, justification, plea; colour, disguise, evasion, guise, pretence, pretext, makeshift, semblance, subterfuge.

execrable adj abhorrent, abominable, accursed, cursed, damnable, detestable, hateful, odious; disgusting, loathsome, nauseating, nauseous, obnoxious, offensive, repulsive, revolting, sickening, vile.

execrate vb curse, damn, imprecate; abhor, abominate, detest, hate, loathe.

execute vb accomplish, achieve, carry out, complete, consummate, do, effect, effectuate, finish, perform, perpetrate; administer, enforce, seal, sign; behead, electrocute, guillotine, hang.

execution n accomplishment, achievement, completion, consummation, operation, performance; warrant, writ; beheading, electrocution, hanging.

executive adj administrative, commanding, controlling, directing, managing, ministerial, officiating, presiding, ruling. * n administrator, director, manager.

exegetic, exegetical adj explanatory, explicative, explicatory, expository, hermeneutic, interpretative.

exemplary adj assiduous, close, exact, faithful, punctual, punctilious, rigid, rigorous, scrupulous; commendable, correct, good, estimable, excellent, praiseworthy, virtuous; admonitory, condign, monitory, warning.

exemplify vb evidence, exhibit, illustrate, manifest, show.

exempt vb absolve, except, excuse, exonerate, free, release, relieve. * adj absolved, excepted, excused, exempted, free, immune, liberated, privileged, released.

exemption n absolution, dispensation, exception, immunity, privilege, release.

exercise vb apply, busy, employ, exert, praxis, use; effect, exert, produce, wield; break in, discipline, drill, habituate, school, train; practise, prosecute, pursue; task, test, try; afflict, agitate, annoy, burden, pain, trouble. * n appliance, application, custom, employment, operation, performance, play, plying, practice, usage, use, working; action, activity, effort, exertion, labour, toil, work; discipline, drill, drilling, schooling, training; lesson, praxis, study, task, test, theme.

exert vb employ, endeavour, exercise, labour, strain, strive, struggle, toil, use, work.

exertion n action, exercise, exerting, use; attempt, effort, endeavour, labour, strain, stretch, struggle, toil, trial.

exhalation n emission, evaporation; damp, effluvium, fog, fume, mist, reek, smoke, steam, vapour.

exhale vb breathe, discharge, elect, emanate, emit, evaporate, reek; blow, expire, puff.

exhaust vb drain, draw, empty; consume, destroy, dissipate, expend, impoverish, lavish, spend, squander, waste; cripple, debilitate, deplete, disable, enfeeble, enervate, overtire, prostrate, weaken.

exhaustion n debilitation, enervation, fatigue, lassitude, weariness.

exhibit vb demonstrate, disclose, display, evince, expose, express, indicate, manifest, offer, present, reveal, show; offer, present, propose.

exhibition n demonstration, display, exposition, manifestation, representation, spectacle, show; allowance, benefaction, grant, pension, scholarship.

exhilarate vb animate, cheer, elate, enliven, gladden, inspire, inspirit, rejoice, stimulate.

exhilaration n animating, cheering, elating, enlivening, gladdening, rejoicing, stimulating; animation, cheer, cheerfulness, gaiety, gladness, glee, good spirits, hilarity, joyousness.

exhort vb advise, caution, encourage, incite, persuade, stimulate, urge, warm; preach.

exhume vb disentomb, disinhume, disinter, unbury, unearth.

exigency, exigence n demand, necessity, need, requirement, urgency, want; conjuncture, crisis, difficulty, distress, emergency, extremity, juncture, nonplus, quandary, pass, pinch, pressure, strait.

exiguous adj attenuated, diminutive, fine, small, scanty, slender, tiny.

exile vb banish, expatriate, expel, ostracize, proscribe. * n banishment, expatriation, expulsion, ostracism, proscription, separation; outcast, refugee.

exist vb be, breathe, live; abide, continue, endure, last, remain.

existence n being, subsisting, subsistence; being, creature, entity, essence, thing; animation, continuation, life, living, vitality, vivacity.

exit vb depart, egress, go, leave. * n departure, withdrawal; death, decrease, demise, end; egress, outlet.

exonerate vb absolve, acquit, clear, exculpate, justify, vindicate; absolve, discharge, except, exempt, free, release.

exorbitant adj enormous, excessive, extravagant, inordinate, unreasonable.

exorcise vb cast out, drive away, expel; deliver, purify; address, conjure.

exordium n introduction, opening, preamble, preface, prelude, proem, prologue.

exotic adj extraneous, foreign; extravagant.

expand vb develop, open, spread, unfold, unfurl; diffuse, enlarge, extend, increase, stretch; dilate, distend, enlarge.

expanse n area, expansion, extent, field, stretch.

expansion n expansion, opening, spreading; diastole, dilation, distension, swelling; development, diffusion, enlargement, increase; expanse, extent, stretch.

ex parte adj biased, one-sided, partisan.

expatiate vb amplify, decant, dilate, enlarge, range, rove.

expatriate vb banish, exile, expel, ostracize, proscribe. * adj banished, exiled, refugee. * n displaced person, emigrant, exile.

expect vb anticipate, await, calculate, contemplate, forecast, foresee, hope, reckon, rely.

expectancy n expectance, expectation; abeyance, prospect.

expectation *n* anticipation, expectance, expectancy, hope, prospect; assurance, confidence, presumption, reliance, trust.

expedient *adj* advisable, appropriate, convenient, desirable, fit, proper, politic, suitable; advantageous, profitable, useful. * *n* contrivance, device, means, method, resort, resource, scheme, shift, stopgap, substitute.

expedite *vb* accelerate, advance, dispatch, facilitate, forward, hasten, hurry, precipitate, press, quicken, urge.

expedition *n* alacrity, alertness, celerity, dispatch, haste, promptness, quickness, speed; enterprise, undertaking; campaign, excursion, journey, march, quest, voyage.

expeditious *adj* quick, speedy, swift, rapid; active, alert, diligent, nimble, prompt, punctual, swift.

expel *vb* dislodge, egest, eject, eliminate, excrete; discharge, eject, evacuate, void; bounce, discharge, exclude, exscind, fire, oust, relegate, remove; banish, disown, excommunicate, exile, expatriate, ostracize, proscribe, unchurch.

expend *vb* disburse, spend; consume, employ, exert, use; dissipate, exhaust, scatter, waste.

expenditure *n* disbursement, outlay, outlaying, spending; charge, cost, expenditure, outlay.

expensive *adj* costly, dear, high-priced; extravagant, lavish, wasteful.

experience *vb* endure, suffer; feel, know; encounter, suffer, undergo. * *n* endurance, practice, trial; evidence, knowledge, proof, test, testimony.

experienced *adj* able, accomplished, expert, instructed, knowing, old, practised, qualified, skilful, trained, thoroughbred, versed, veteran, wise.

experiment *vb* examine, investigate, test, try. * *n* assay, examination, investigation, ordeal, practice, proof, test, testimony, touchstone, trial.

expert *adj* able, adroit, apt, clever, dextrous, proficient, prompt, quick, ready, skilful. * *n* adept, authority, connoisseur, crack, master, specialist.

expertise *n* adroitness, aptness, dexterity, facility, promptness, skilfulness, skill.

expiate *vb* atone, redeem, satisfy.

expiration n death, decease, demise, departure, exit; cessation, close, conclusion, end, termination.

expire *vb* cease, close, conclude, end, stop, terminate; emit, exhale; decease, depart, die, perish.

explain *vb* demonstrate, elucidate, expound, illustrate, interpret, resolve, solve, unfold, unravel; account for, justify, warrant.

explanation *n* clarification, description, elucidation, exegesis, explication, exposition, illustration, interpretation; account, answer, deduction, justification, key, meaning, secret, solution, warrant.

explicit *adj* absolute, categorical, clear, definite, determinate, exact, express, plain, positive, precise, unambiguous, unequivocal, unreserved.

explode *vb* burst, detonate, discharge, displode, shatter, shiver; contemn, discard, repudiate, scorn, scout.

exploit *vb* befool, milk, use, utilize. * *n* achievement, act, deed, feat.

explore *vb* examine, fathom, inquire, inspect, investigate, prospect, scrutinize, seek.

explosion *n* blast, burst, bursting, clap, crack, detonation, discharge, displosion, fulmination, pop.

exponent *n* example, illustration, index, indication, specimen, symbol, type; commentator, demonstrator, elucidator, expounder, illustrator, interpreter.

expose *vb* bare, display, uncover; descry, detect, disclose, unearth; denounce, mask; subject; endanger, jeopardize, risk, venture.

exposé *n* exhibit, exposition, manifesto; denouncement, divulgement, exposure, revelation.

exposition *n* disclosure, interpretation; commentary, critique, elucidation, exegesis, explanation, explication, interpretation; display, show.

expound *vb* develop, present, rehearse, reproduce, unfold; clear, elucidate, explain, interpret.

express *vb* air, assert, asseverate, declare, emit, enunciate, manifest, utter, vent, signify, speak, state, voice; betoken, denote, equal, exhibit, indicate, intimate, present, represent, show, symbolize. * *adj* categorical, clear, definite, determinate, explicit, outspoken, plain, positive, unambiguous; accurate, close, exact, faithful, precise, true; particular, special; fast, nonstop, quick, rapid, speedy, swift. * *n* dispatch, message.

expression *n* assertion, asseveration, communication, declaration, emission, statement, utterance, voicing; language, locution, phrase, remark, saying, term, word; air, aspect, look, mien.

expressive *adj* indicative, meaningful, significant; demonstrative, eloquent, emphatic, energetic, forcible, lively, strong, vivid; appropriate, sympathetic, well-modulated.

expulsion *n* discharge, eviction, expelling, ousting; elimination, evacuation, excretion; ejection, excision, excommunication, extrusion, ostracism, separation.

expunge *vb* annihilate, annul, cancel, delete, destroy, efface, erase, obliterate, wipe out.

expurgate *vb* clean, cleanse, purge, purify; bowdlerize, emasculate.

exquisite *adj* accurate, delicate, discriminating, exact, fastidious, nice, refined; choice, elect, excellent, precious, rare, valuable; complete, consummate, matchless, perfect; acute, keen, intense, poignant. * *n* beau, coxcomb, dandy, fop, popinjay.

extant *adj* existent, existing, present, surviving, undestroyed, visible.

extempore *adj* extemporaneous, extemporary, impromptu, improvised. * *adv* offhand, suddenly, unpremeditatedly, unpreparedly.

extend *vb* reach, stretch; continue, elongate, lengthen, prolong, protract, widen; augment, broaden, dilate, distend, enlarge, expand, increase; diffuse, spread; give, impart, offer, yield; lie, range.

extensible *adj* ductile, elastic, extendible, extensile, protractible, protractile.

extension *n* augmentation, continuation, delay, dilatation, dilation, distension, enlargement, expansion, increase, prolongation, protraction.

extensive *adj* broad, capacious, comprehensive, expanded, extended, far-reaching, large, wide, widespread.

extent *n* amplitude, expanse, expansion; amount, bulk, content, degree, magnitude, size, volume; compass, measure, length, proportions, reach, stretch; area, field, latitude, range, scope; breadth, depth, height, width.

extenuate *vb* diminish, lessen, reduce, soften, weaken; excuse, mitigate, palliate, qualify.

exterior *adj* external, outer, outlying, outside, outward, superficial, surface; extrinsic, foreign. * *n* outside, surface; appearance.

exterminate *vb* abolish, annihilate, destroy, eliminate, eradicate, extirpate, uproot.

external *adj* exterior, outer, outside, outward, superficial; extrinsic, foreign; apparent, visible.

extinct *adj* extinguished, quenched; closed, dead, ended, lapsed, terminated, vanished.

extinction *n* death, extinguishment; abolishment, abolition, annihilation, destruction, excision, extermination, extirpation.

extinguish *vb* choke, douse, put out, quell, smother, stifle, suffocate, suppress; destroy, nullify, subdue; eclipse, obscure.

extirpate *vb* abolish, annihilate, deracinate, destroy, eradicate, exterminate, uproot, weed.

extol *vb* celebrate, exalt, glorify, laud, magnify, praise; applaud, commend, eulogize, panegyrize.

extort *vb* elicit, exact, extract, force, squeeze, wrench, wrest, wring.

extortion *n* blackmail, compulsion, demand, exaction, oppression, overcharge, rapacity, tribute; exorbitance.

extortionate *adj* bloodsucking, exacting, hard, harsh, oppressive, rapacious, rigorous, severe; exorbitant, unreasonable.

extra *adj* accessory, additional, auxiliary, collateral; another, farther, fresh, further, more, new, other, plus, ulterior; side, spare, supernumerary, supplemental, supplementary, surplus; extraordinary, extreme, unusual. * *adv* additionally, also, beyond, farthermore, furthermore, more, moreover, plus. * *n* accessory, appendage, collateral, nonessential, special, supernumerary, supplement; bonus, premium; balance, leftover, remainder, spare, surplus.

extract *vb* extort, pull out, remove, withdraw; derive, distil, draw, express, squeeze; cite, determine, derive, quote, select. * *n* citation, excerpt, passage, quotation, selection; decoction, distillation, essence, infusion, juice.

extraction *n* drawing out, derivation, distillation, elicitation, essence, pulling out; birth, descent, genealogy, lineage, origin, parentage.

extraneous *adj* external, extrinsic, foreign; additional, adventitious, external, superfluous, supplementary, unessential.

extraordinary *adj* abnormal, amazing, distinguished, egregious, exceptional, marvellous, monstrous, particular, peculiar, phenomenal, prodigious, rare, remarkable, signal, singular, special, strange, uncommon, unprecedented, unusual, unwonted, wonderful.

extravagance *n* excess, enormity, exorbitance, preposterousness, unreasonableness; absurdity, excess, folly, irregularity, wildness; lavishness, prodigality, profuseness, profusion, superabundance; waste.

extravagant *adj* excessive, exorbitant, inordinate, preposterous, unreasonable; absurd, foolish, irregular, wild; lavish, prodigal, profuse, spendthrift.

extreme *adj* farthest, outermost, remotest, utmost, uttermost; greatest, highest; final, last, ultimate; drastic, egregious, excessive, extravagant, immoderate, intense, outrageous, radical, unreasonable. * *n* end, extremity, limit; acme, climax, degree, height, pink; danger, distress.

extremity *n* border, edge, end, extreme, limb, termination, verge.

extricate *vb* clear, deliver, disembarrass, disengage, disentangle, liberate, release, relieve.

extrinsic *adj* external, extraneous, foreign, outside, outward, superabundance, superfluity.

exuberance *n* abundance, copiousness, flood, luxuriance, plenitude; excess, lavishness, overabundance, overflow, overgrowth, over-luxuriance, profusion, rankness, redundancy, superabundance, superfluity.

exuberant *adj* abounding, abundant, copious, fertile, flowing, luxuriant, prolific, rich; excessive, lavish, overabundant, overflowing, over-luxuriant, profuse, rank, redundant, superabounding, superabundant, wanton.

exude *vb* discharge, excrete, secrete, sweat; infiltrate, ooze, percolate.

exult *vb* gloat, glory, jubilate, rejoice, transport, triumph, taunt, vault.

exultation *n* delight, elation, joy, jubilation, transport, triumph.

eye *vb* contemplate, inspect, ogle, scrutinize, survey, view, watch. * *n* estimate, judgement, look, sight, vision, view; inspection, notice, observation, scrutiny, sight, vigilance, watch; aperture, eyelet, peephole, perforation; bud, shoot.

F

fable *n* allegory, legend, myth, parable, story, tale; fabrication, falsehood, fiction, figment, forgery, untruth.

fabric *n* building, edifice, pile, structure; conformation, make, texture, workmanship; cloth, material, stuff, textile, tissue, web.

fabricate *vb* build, construct, erect, frame; compose, devise, fashion, make, manufacture; coin, fake, feign, forge, invent.

fabrication *n* building, construction, erection; manufacture; fable, fake, falsehood, fiction, figment, forgery, invention, lie.

fabulous *adj* amazing, apocryphal, coined, fabricated, feigned, fictitious, forged, imaginary, invented, legendary, marvellous, mythical, romancing, unbelievable, unreal.

façade *n* elevation, face, front.

face *vb* confront; beard, buck, brave, dare, defy, front, oppose; dress, level, polish, smooth; cover, incrust, veneer. * *n* cover, facet, surface; breast, escarpment, front; countenance, features, grimace, physiognomy, visage; appearance, expression, look, semblance; assurance, audacity, boldness, brass, confidence, effrontery, impudence.

facet *n* cut, face, lozenge, surface.

facetious *adj* amusing, comical, droll, funny, humorous, jocose, jocular, pleasant, waggish, witty; entertaining, gay, lively, merry, sportive, sprightly.

facile *adj* easy; affable, approachable, complaisant, conversable, courteous, mild; compliant, ductile, flexible, fluent, manageable, pliable, pliant, tractable, yielding; dextrous, ready, skilful.

facilitate *vb* expedite, help.

facility *n* ease, easiness; ability, dexterity, expertness, knack, quickness, readiness; ductility, flexibility, pliancy; advantage, appliance, convenience, means, resource; affability, civility, complaisance, politeness.

facsimile *n* copy, duplicate, fax, reproduction.

fact *n* act, circumstance, deed, event, incident, occurrence, performance; actuality, certainty, existence, reality, truth.

faction *n* cabal, clique, combination, division, junta, party, side; disagreement, discord, disorder, dissension, recalcitrance, recalcitrancy, refractoriness, sedition, seditiousness, tumult, turbulence, turbulency.

factious *adj* litigious, malcontent, rebellious, recalcitrant, refractory, seditious, turbulent.

factitious *adj* artful, artificial, conventional, false, unnatural, unreal.

factor *n* agent, bailiff, broker, consignee, go-between, steward, component, element, ingredient; influence, reason.

factory *n* manufactory, mill, work, workshop.

faculty *n* ability, capability, capacity, endowment, power, property, quality; ableness, address, adroitness, aptitude, aptness, clearness, competency, dexterity, efficiency, expertness, facility, forte, ingenuity, knack, qualification, quickness, readiness, skill, skilfulness, talent, turn; body, department, profession; authority, prerogative, license, privilege, right.

fade *vb* disappear, die, evanesce, fall, faint, perish, vanish; decay, decline, droop, fall, languish, wither; bleach, blanch, pale; disperse, dissolve.

faeces *npl* dregs, lees, sediment, settlings; dung, excrement, ordure, settlings.

fag *vb* droop, flag, sink; drudge, toil; fatigue, jade, tire, weary. * *n* drudgery, fatigue, work; drudge, grub, hack; cigarette, smoke.

fail *vb* break, collapse, decay, decline, fade, sicken, sink, wane; cease, disappear; fall, miscarry, miss; neglect, omit; bankrupt, break.

failing *adj* deficient, lacking, needing, wanting; declining, deteriorating, fading, flagging, languishing, sinking, waning, wilting; unsuccessful. * *prep* lacking, needing, wanting. * *n* decay, decline; failure, miscarriage; defect, deficiency, fault, foible, frailty, imperfection, infirmity, shortcoming, vice, weakness; error, lapse, slip; bankruptcy, insolvency.

failure *n* defectiveness, deficiency, delinquency, shortcoming; fail, miscarriage, negligence, neglect, nonobservance, nonperformance, omission, slip; abortion, botch, breakdown, collapse, fiasco, fizzle; bankruptcy, crash, downfall, insolvency, ruin; decay, declension, decline, loss.

fain *adj* anxious, glad, inclined, pleased, rejoiced, well-pleased. * *adv* cheerfully, eagerly, gladly, joyfully, willingly.

faint *vb* swoon; decline, fade, fail, languish, weaken. * *adj* swooning; drooping, exhausted, feeble, languid, listless, sickly, weak; gentle, inconsiderable, little, slight, small, soft, thin; dim, dull, indistinct, perceptible, scarce, slight; cowardly, dastardly, faint-hearted, fearful, timid, timorous; dejected, depressed, discouraged, disheartened, dispirited. * *n* blackout, swoon.

faint-hearted *adj* cowardly, dastardly, faint, fearful, timid, timorous.

fair[1] *adj* spotless, unblemished, unspotted, unstained, untarnished; blond, light, white; beautiful, comely, handsome, shapely; clear, cloudless, pleasant, unclouded; favourable, prosperous; hopeful, promising, propitious; clear, distinct, open, plain, unencumbered, unobstructed; candid, frank, honest, honourable, impartial, ingenuous, just, unbiased, upright; equitable, proper; average, decent, indifferent, mediocre, moderate, ordinary, passable, reasonable, respectful, tolerable.

fair[2] *n* bazaar, carnival, exposition, festival, fete, funfair, gala, kermess.

fairy *n* brownie, elf, demon, fay, sprite.

faith *n* assurance, belief, confidence, credence, credit, dependence, reliance, trust; creed, doctrine, dogma, persuasion, religion, tenet; constancy, faithfulness, fidelity, loyalty, truth, truthfulness.

faithful *adj* constant, devoted, loyal, staunch, steadfast, true; honest, upright, reliable, trustworthy, trusty; reliable, truthful; accurate, close, conscientiousness, exact, nice, strict.

faithless *adj* unbelieving; dishonest, disloyal, false, fickle, fluctuating, inconstant, mercurial, mutable, perfidious, shifting, treacherous, truthless, unsteady, untruthful, vacillating, variable, wavering.

fall *vb* collapse, depend, descend, drop, sink, topple, tumble; abate, decline, decrease, depreciate, ebb, subside; err, lapse, sin, stumble, transgress, trespass, trip; die, perish; befall, chance, come, happen, occur, pass; become, get; come, pass. * *n* collapse, comedown, descent, downcome, dropping, falling, flop, plop, tumble; cascade, cataract, waterfall; death, destruction, downfall, overthrow, ruin, surrender; comeuppance, degradation; apostasy, declension, failure, lapse, slip; decline, decrease, depreciation, diminution, ebb, sinking, subsidence; cadence, close; declivity, inclination, slope.

fallacious *adj* absurd, deceptive, deceiving, delusive, disappointing, erroneous, false, illusive, illusory, misleading; paralogistic, sophistical, worthless.

fallacy *n* aberration, deceit, deception, delusion, error, falsehood, illusion, misapprehension, misconception, mistake, untruth; non sequitur, paralogism, sophism, sophistry.

fallibility *n* frailty, imperfection, uncertainty.

fallible *adj* erring, frail, ignorant, imperfect, uncertain, weak.

fallow *adj* left, neglected, uncultivated, unsowed, untilled; dormant, inactive, inert.

false *adj* lying, mendacious, truthless, untrue, unveracious; dishonest, dishonourable, disingenuous, disloyal, double-faced, double-tongued, faithless, false-hearted, perfidious, treacherous, unfaithful; fictitious, forged, made-up, unreliable, untrustworthy; artificial, bastard, bogus, counterfeit, factitious, feigned, forged, hollow, hypocritical, make-believe, pretended, pseudo, sham, spurious, supposititious; erroneous, improper, incorrect, unfounded, wrong; deceitful, deceiving, deceptive, disappointing, fallacious, misleading.

false-hearted *adj* dishonourable, disloyal, double, double-tongued, faithless, false, perfidious, treacherous.

falsehood *n* falsity; fabrication, fib, fiction, lie, untruth; cheat, counterfeit, imposture, mendacity, treachery.

falsify *vb* alter, adulterate, belie, cook, counterfeit, doctor, fake, falsely, garble, misrepresent, misstate, represent; disprove; violate.

falsity *n* falsehood, untruth, untruthfulness.

falter *vb* halt, hesitate, lisp, quaver, stammer, stutter; fail, stagger, stumble, totter, tremble, waver; dodder.

fame *n* bruit, hearsay, report, rumour; celebrity, credit, eminence, glory, greatness, honour, illustriousness, kudos, lustre, notoriety, renown, reputation, repute.

familiar *adj* acquainted, aware, conversant, well-versed; amicable, close, cordial, domestic, fraternal, friendly, homely, intimate, near; affable, accessible, companionable, conversable, courteous, civil, friendly, kindly, sociable, social; easy, free and easy, unceremonious, unconstrained; common, frequent, well-known. * *n* acquaintance, associate, companion, friend, intimate.

familiarity *n* acquaintance, knowledge, understanding; fellowship, friendship, intimacy; closeness, friendliness, sociability; freedom, informality, liberty; disrespect, overfreedom, presumption; intercourse.

familiarize *vb* accustom, habituate, inure, train, use.

family *n* brood, household, people; ancestors, blood, breed, clan, dynasty, kindred, house, lineage, race, stock, strain, tribe; class, genus, group, kind, subdivision.

famine *n* dearth, destitution, hunger, scarcity, starvation.

famish *vb* distress, exhaust, pinch, starve.

famous *adj* celebrated, conspicuous, distinguished, eminent, excellent, fabled, famed, far-famed, great, glorious, heroic, honoured, illustrious, immortal, notable, noted, notorious, remarkable, renowned, signal.

fan¹ *vb* agitate, beat, move, winnow; blow, cool, refresh, ventilate; excite, fire, increase, rouse, stimulate. * *n* blower, cooler, punkah, ventilator.

fan² *n* admirer, buff, devotee, enthusiast, fancier, follower, pursuer, supporter.

fanatic *n* bigot, devotee, enthusiast, visionary, zealot.

fanatical *adj* bigoted, enthusiastic, frenzied, mad, rabid, visionary, wild, zealous.

fanciful *adj* capricious, crotchety, imaginary, visionary, whimsical; chimerical, fantastical, ideal, imaginary, wild.

fancy *vb* apprehend, believe, conjecture, imagine, suppose, think; conceive, imagine. * *adj* elegant, fine, nice, ornamented; extravagant, fanciful, whimsical. * *n* imagination; apprehension, conceit, conception, impression, idea, image, notion, thought; approval, fondness, inclination, judgement, liking, penchant, taste; caprice, crotchet, fantasy, freak, humour, maggot, quirk, vagary, whim, whimsy; apparition, chimera, daydream, delusion, hallucination, megrim, phantasm, reverie, vision.

fanfaron *n* blatherskite, blusterer, braggadocio, bully, hector, swaggerer, vapourer.

fang *n* claw, nail, talon, tooth; tusk.

fantastic *adj* chimerical, fanciful, imaginary, romantic, unreal, visionary; bizarre, capricious, grotesque, odd, quaint, queer, strange, whimsical, wild.

far *adj* distant, long, protracted, remote; farther, remoter; alienated, estranged, hostile. * *adv* considerably, extremely, greatly, very much; afar, distantly, far away, remotely.

farce *n* burlesque, caricature, parody, travesty; forcemeat, stuffing.

farcical *adj* absurd, comic, droll, funny, laughable, ludicrous, ridiculous.

fardel *n* bundle, burden, load, pack; annoyance, burden, ill, trouble.

fare *vb* go, journey, pass, travel; happen, prosper, prove; feed, live, manage, subsist. * *n* charge, price, ticket money; passenger, traveller; board, commons, food, table, victuals, provisions; condition, experience, fortune, luck, outcome.

farewell *n* adieu, leave-taking, valediction; departure, leave, parting, valedictory.

far-fetched *adj* abstruse, catachrestic, forced, recondite, strained.

farrago *n* gallimaufry, hodgepodge, hotchpotch, jumble, medley, miscellany, mixture, potpourri, salmagundi.

farther *adj* additional; further, remoter, ulterior. * *adv* beyond, further; besides, furthermore, moreover.

farthingale *n* crinoline, hoop, hoop skirt.

fascinate *vb* affect, bewitch, overpower, spellbind, stupefy, transfix; absorb, captivate, catch, charm, delight, enamour, enchant, enrapture, entrance.

fascination *n* absorption, charm, enchantment, magic, sorcery, spell, witchcraft, witchery.

fash *vb* harass, perplex, plague, torment, trouble, vex, worry. * *n* anxiety, care, trouble, vexation.

fashion *vb* contrive, create, design, forge, form, make, mould, pattern, shape; accommodate, adapt, adjust, fit, suit. * *n* appearance, cast, configuration, conformation, cut, figure, form, make, model, mould, pattern, shape, stamp; manner, method, sort, wake; conventionalism, conventionality, custom, fad, mode, style, usage, vogue; breeding, gentility; quality.

fashionable *adj* modish, stylish; current, modern, prevailing, up-to-date; customary, usual; genteel, well-bred.

fast[1] *adj* close, fastened, firm, fixed, immovable, tenacious, tight; constant, faithful, permanent, resolute, staunch, steadfast, unswerving, unwavering; fortified, impregnable, strong; deep, profound, sound; fleet, quick, rapid, swift; dissipated, dissolute, extravagant, giddy, reckless, thoughtless, thriftless, wild. * *adv* firmly, immovably, tightly; quickly, rapidly, swiftly; extravagantly, prodigally, reckless, wildly.

fast[2] *vb* abstain, go hungry, starve. * *n* abstention, abstinence, diet, fasting, starvation.

fasten *vb* attach, bind, bolt, catch, chain, cleat, fix, gird, lace, lock, pin, secure, strap, tether, tie; belay, bend; connect, hold, join, unite.

fastidious *adj* critical, dainty, delicate, difficult, exquisite, finical, hypercritical, meticulous, overdelicate, overnice, particular, precise, precious, punctilious, queasy, squeamish.

fat *adj* adipose, fatty, greasy, oily, oleaginous, unctuous; corpulent, fleshy, gross, obese, paunchy, portly, plump, pudgy, pursy; coarse, dull, heavy, sluggish, stupid; lucrative, profitable, rich; fertile, fruitful, productive, rich. * *n* adipose tissue, ester, grease, oil; best part, cream, flower; corpulence, fatness, fleshiness, obesity, plumpness, stoutness.

fatal *adj* deadly, lethal, mortal; baleful, baneful, calamitous, catastrophic, destructive, mischievous, pernicious, ruinous; destined, doomed, foreordained, inevitable, predestined.

fatality *n* destiny, fate; mortality; calamity, disaster.

fate *n* destination, destiny, fate; cup, die, doom, experience, lot, fortune, portion, weird; death, destruction, ruin.

fated *adj* appointed, destined, doomed, foredoomed, predetermined, predestinated, predestined, preordained.

fatherly *adj* benign, kind, paternal, protecting, tender.

fathom *vb* comprehend, divine, penetrate, reach, understand; estimate, gauge, measure, plumb, probe, sound.

fathomless *adj* abysmal, bottomless, deep, immeasurable, profound; impenetrable, incomprehensible, obscure.

fatigue *vb* exhaust, fag, jade, tire, weaken, weary. * *n* exhaustion, lassitude, tiredness, weariness; hardship, labour, toil.

fatuity *n* foolishness, idiocy, imbecility, stupidity; absurdity, folly, inanity, infatuation, madness.

fatuous *adj* dense, drivelling, dull, foolish, idiotic, stupid, witless; infatuated, mad, senseless, silly, weak.

fault *n* blemish, defect, flaw, foible, frailty, imperfection, infirmity, negligence, obliquity, offence, shortcoming, spot, weakness; delinquency, error, indiscretion, lapse, misdeed, misdemeanour, offence, peccadillo, slip, transgression, trespass, vice, wrong; blame, culpability.

faultless *adj* blameless, guiltless, immaculate, innocent, sinless, spotless, stainless; accurate, correct, perfect, unblemished.

faulty *adj* bad, defective, imperfect, incorrect; blameable, blameworthy, censurable, culpable, reprehensible.

faux pas *n* blunder, indiscretion, mistake.

favour *vb* befriend, countenance, encourage, patronize; approve; ease, facilitate; aid, assist, help, oblige, support; extenuate, humour, indulge, palliate, spare. * *n* approval, benignity, countenance, esteem, friendless, goodwill, grace, kindness; benefaction, benefit, boon, dispensation, kindness; championship, patronage, popularity, support; gift, present, token; badge, decoration, knot, rosette; leave, pardon, permission; advantage, cover, indulgence, protection; bias, partiality, prejudice.

favourable *adj* auspicious, friendly, kind, propitious, well-disposed, willing; conductive, contributing, propitious; adapted, advantage, beneficial, benign, convenient, fair, fit, good, helpful, suitable.

favourite *adj* beloved, darling, dear; choice, fancied, esteemed, pet, preferred.

fawn *vb* bootlick, bow, creep, cringe, crouch, dangle, kneel, stoop, toady, truckle.

fealty *n* allegiance, homage, loyalty, obeisance, submission; devotion, faithfulness, fidelity, honour, loyalty.

fear *vb* apprehend, dread; revere, reverence, venerate. * *n* affright, alarm, apprehension, consternation, dismay, dread, fright, horror, panic, phobia, scare, terror; disquietude, flutter, perturbation, palpitation, quaking, quivering, trembling, tremor, trepidation; anxiety, apprehension, concern, misdoubt, misgiving, qualm, solicitude; awe, dread, reverence, veneration.

fearful *adj* afraid, apprehensive, haunted; chicken-hearted, chicken-livered, cowardly, faint-hearted, lily-livered, nervous, pusillanimous, timid, timorous; dire, direful, dreadful, frightful, ghastly, horrible, shocking, terrible.

fearless *adj* bold, brave, courageous, daring, dauntless, doughty, gallant, heroic, intrepid, unterrified, valiant, valorous.

feasible *adj* achievable, attainable, possible, practicable, suitable.

feast *vb* delight, gladden, gratify, rejoice. * *n* banquet, carousal, entertainment, regale, repast, revels, symposium, treat; celebration, festival, fete, holiday; delight, enjoyment, pleasure.

feat *n* accomplishment, achievement, act, deed, exploit, performance, stunt, trick.

feather *n* plume; kind, nature, species.

featly *adv* adroitly, dextrously, nimbly, skilfully.

feature *vb* envisage, envision, picture, visualize; imagine; specialize; appear in, headline, star. * *n* appearance, aspect, component; conformation, fashion, make; characteristic, item, mark, particularity, peculiarity, property, point, trait; leader, lead item, special; favour, expression, lineament; article, film, motion picture, movie, story; highlight, high spot.

fecund *adj* fruitful, impregnated, productive, prolific, rich.

fecundity *n* fertility, fruitfulness, productiveness.

federation *n* alliance, allying, confederation, federating, federation, leaguing, union, uniting; affiliation, coalition, combination, compact, confederacy, entente, federacy, league, copartnership.

fee *vb* pay, recompense, reward. * *n* account, bill, charge, compensation, honorarium, remuneration, reward, tip; benefice, fief, feud.

feeble *adj* anaemic, debilitated, declining, drooping, enervated, exhausted, frail, infirm, languid, languishing, sickly; dim, faint, imperfect, indistinct.

feed *vb* contribute, provide, supply; cherish, eat, nourish, subsist, sustain. * *n* fodder, food, foodstuff, forage, provender.

feel *vb* apprehend, intuit, perceive, sense; examine, handle, probe, touch; enjoy, experience, suffer; prove, sound, test, try; appear, look, seem; believe, conceive, deem, fancy, infer, opine, suppose, think. * *n* atmosphere, feeling, quality; finish, surface, texture.

feeling *n* consciousness, impression, notion, perception, sensation; atmosphere, sense, sentience, touch; affecting, emotion, heartstrings, impression, passion, soul, sympathy; sensibility, sentiment, susceptibility, tenderness; attitude, impression, opinion.

feign *vb* devise, fabricate, forge, imagine, invent; affect, assume, counterfeit, imitate, pretend, sham, simulate.

feint *n* artifice, blind, expedient, make-believe, pretence, stratagem, trick.

felicitate *vb* complicate, congratulate; beatify, bless, delight.

felicitous *adj* appropriate, apt, fit, happy, ingenious, inspired, opportune, pertinent, seasonable, skilful, well-timed; auspicious, fortunate, prosperous, propitious, successful.

felicity *n* blessedness, bliss, blissfulness, gladness, happiness, joy; appropriateness, aptitude, aptness, felicitousness, fitness, grace, propriety, readiness, suitableness; fortune, luck, success.

fell[1] *vb* beat, knock down, level, prostrate; cut, demolish, hew.

fell[2] *adj* barbarous, bloodthirsty, bloody, cruel, ferocious, fierce, implacable, inhuman, malicious, malign, malignant, pitiless, relentless, ruthless, sanguinary, savage, unrelenting, vandalistic; deadly, destructive.

fellow *adj* affiliated, associated, joint, like, mutual, similar, twin. * *n* associate, companion, comrade; compeer, equal, peer; counterpart, mate, match, partner; member; boy, character, individual, man, person.

fellowship *n* brotherhood, companionship, comradeship, familiarity, intimacy; participation; partnership; communion, converse, intercourse; affability, kindliness, sociability, sociableness.

felon *n* convict, criminal, culprit, delinquent, malefactor, outlaw; inflammation, whitlow.

felonious *adj* atrocious, cruel, felon, heinous, infamous, malicious, malign, malignant, nefarious, perfidious, vicious, villainous.

female *adj* delicate, gentle, ladylike, soft; fertile, pistil-bearing, pistillate.

feminine *adj* affectionate, delicate, gentle, graceful, modest, soft, tender; female, ladylike, maidenly, womanish, womanly; effeminateness, effeminacy, softness, unmanliness, weakness, womanliness.

fen *n* bog, marsh, moor, morass, quagmire, slough, swamp.

fence *vb* defend, enclose, fortify, guard, protect, surround; circumscribe, evade, equivocate, hedge, prevaricate; guard, parry. * *n* barrier, hedge, hoarding, palings, palisade, stockade, wall; defence, protection, guard, security, shield; fencing, swordplay, swordsmanship; receiver.

fenny *adj* boggy, fennish, swampy, marshy.

feral, ferine *adj* ferocious, fierce, rapacious, ravenous, savage, untamed, wild.

ferment *vb* agitate, excite, heat; boil, brew, bubble, concoct, heat, seethe. * *n* barm, leaven, yeast; agitation, commotion, fever, glow, heat, tumult.

ferocious *adj* feral, fierce, rapacious, ravenous, savage, untamed, wild; barbarous, bloody, bloodthirsty, brutal, cruel, fell, inhuman, merciless, murderous, pitiless, remorseless, ruthless, sanguinary, truculent, vandalistic, violent.

ferocity *n* ferociousness, ferocity, fierceness, rapacity, savageness, wildness; barbarity, cruelty, inhumanity.

fertile *adj* bearing, breeding, fecund, prolific; exuberant, fruitful, luxuriant, plenteous, productive, rich, teeming; female, fruit-bearing, pistillate.

fertility *n* fertileness, fertility; abundance, exuberant, fruitfulness, luxuriance, plenteousness, productiveness, richness.

fervent *adj* burning, hot, glowing, melting, seething; animated, ardent, earnest, enthusiastic, fervid, fierce, fiery, glowing, impassioned, intense, passionate, vehement, warm, zealous.

fervour *n* heat, warmth; animation, ardour, eagerness, earnestness, excitement, fervency, intensity, vehemence, zeal.

fester *vb* corrupt, rankle, suppurate, ulcerate; putrefy, rot. * *n* abscess, canker, gathering, pustule, sore, suppination; festering, rankling.

festival *n* anniversary, carnival, feast, fete, gala, holiday, jubilee; banquet, carousal, celebration, entertainment, treat.

festive *adj* carnival, convivial, festal, festival, gay, jolly, jovial, joyful, merry, mirthful, uproarious.

festivity *n* conviviality, festival, gaiety, jollity, joviality, joyfulness, joyousness, merrymaking, mirth.

festoon *vb* adorn, decorate, embellish, garland, hoop, ornament. * *n* decoration, embellishment, garland, hoop, ornament, ornamentation.

fetch *vb* bring, elicit, get; accomplish, achieve, effect, perform; attain, reach. * *n* artifice, dodge, ruse, stratagem, trick.

fetid *adj* foul, malodorous, mephitic, noisome, offensive, rancid, rank, rank-smelling, stinking, strong-smelling.

fetish *n* charm, medicine, talisman.

fetter *vb* clog, hamper, shackle, trammel; bind, chain, confine, encumber, hamper, restrain, tie, trammel. * *n* bond, chain, clog, hamper, shackle.

feud *vb* argue, bicker, clash, contend, dispute, quarrel. * *n* affray, argument, bickering, broil, clashing, contention, contest, discord, dissension, enmity, fray, grudge, hostility, jarring, quarrel, rupture, strife, vendetta.

fever *n* agitation, excitement, ferment, fire, flush, heat, passion.

fey *adj* clairvoyant, ethereal, strange, unusual, whimsical; death-smitten, doomed.

fiasco *n* failure, fizzle.

fiat *n* command, decree, order, ordinance.

fibre *n* filament, pile, staple, strand, texture, thread; stamina, strength, toughness.

fickle *adj* capricious, changeable, faithless, fitful, inconstant, irresolute, mercurial, mutable, shifting, unsettled, unstable, unsteady, vacillating, variable, veering, violate, volatile, wavering.

fiction *n* fancy, fantasy, imagination, invention; novel, romance; fable, fabrication, falsehood, figment, forgery, invention, lie.

fictitious *adj* assumed, fabulous, fanciful, feigned, imaginary, invented, mythical, unreal; artificial, counterfeit, dummy, false, spurious, suppositious.

fiddle *vb* dawdle, fidget, interfere, tinker, trifle; cheat, swindle, tamper. * *n* fraud, swindle; fiddler, violin, violinist.

fiddle-de-dee *interj* fudge, moonshine, nonsense, stuff.

fiddle-faddle *n* frivolity, gabble, gibberish, nonsense, prate, stuff, trifling, trivia, twaddle.

fidelity *n* constancy, devotedness, devotion, dutifulness, faithfulness, fealty, loyalty, true-heartedness, truth; accuracy, closeness, exactness, faithfulness, precision.

fidget *vb* chafe, fret, hitch, twitch, worry. * *n* fidgetiness, impatience, restlessness, uneasiness.

fiduciary *adj* confident, fiducial, firm, steadfast, trustful, undoubting, unwavering; reliable, trustworthy. * *n* depositary, trustee.

field *n* clearing, glebe, meadow; expanse, extent, opportunity, range, room, scope, surface; department, domain, province, realm, region.

fiendish *adj* atrocious, cruel, demoniac, devilish, diabolical, hellish, implacable, infernal, malevolent, malicious, malign, malignant.

fierce *adj* barbarous, brutal, cruel, fell, ferocious, furious, infuriate, ravenous, savage; fiery, impetuous, murderous, passionate, tearing, tigerish, truculent, turbulent, uncurbed, untamed, vehement, violent.

fiery *adj* fervent, fervid, flaming, heated, hot, glowing, lurid; ardent, fierce, impassioned, impetuous, inflamed, passionate, vehement.

fight *vb* battle, combat, war; contend, contest, dispute, feud, oppose, strive, struggle, wrestle; encounter, engage; handle, manage, manoeuvre. * *n* affair, affray, action, battle, brush, combat, conflict, confrontation, contest, duel, encounter, engagement, melée, quarrel, struggle, war; brawl, broil, riot, row, skirmish; fighting, pluck, pugnacity, resistance, spirit, temper.

figment *n* fable, fabrication, falsehood, fiction, invention.

figurative *adj* emblematical, representative, symbolic, representative, typical; metaphorical, tropical; florid, flowery, ornate, poetical.

figure *vb* adorn, diversify, ornament, variegate; delineate, depict, represent, signify, symbolize, typify; conceive, image, imagine, picture; calculate, cipher, compute; act, appear, perform. * *n* configuration, conformation, form, outline, shape; effigy, image, likeness, representative; design, diagram, drawing, pattern; image, metaphor, trope; emblem, symbol, type; character, digit, number, numeral.

filament *n* cirrus, fibre, fibril, gossamer, hair, strand, tendril, thread.

filch *vb* crib, nick, pilfer, purloin, rob, snitch, seal, thieve.

file[1] *vb* order, pigeonhole, record, tidy. * *n* data, dossier, folder, portfolio; column, line, list, range, rank, row, series, tier.

file[2] *vb* burnish, furbish, polish, rasp, refine, smooth.

filibuster *vb* delay, frustrate, obstruct, play for time, stall, temporize. * *n* frustrater, obstructionist, thwarter; adventurer, buccaneer, corsair, freebooter, pirate.

fill *vb* occupy, pervade; dilate, distend, expand, stretch, trim; furnish, replenish, stock, store, supply; cloy, congest, content, cram, glut, gorge, line, pack, pall, sate, satiate, satisfy, saturate, stuff, suffuse, swell; engage, fulfil, hold, occupy, officiate, perform.

film *vb* becloud, cloud, coat, cover, darken, fog, mist, obfuscate, obscure, veil; photograph, shoot, take. * *n* cloud, coating, gauze, membrane, nebula, pellicle, scum, skin, veil; thread.

filter *vb* filtrate, strain; exude, ooze, percolate, transude. * *n* diffuser, colander, riddle, sieve, sifter, strainer.

filth *n* dirt, nastiness, ordure; corruption, defilement, foulness, grossness, impurity, obscenity, pollution, squalor, uncleanness, vileness.

filthy *adj* defiled, dirty, foul, licentious, nasty, obscene, pornographic, squalid, unclean; corrupt, gross, impure, unclean; miry, mucky, muddy.

final *adj* eventual, extreme, last, latest, terminal, ultimate; conclusive, decisive, definitive, irrevocable.

finale *n* conclusion, end, termination.

finances *npl* funds, resources, revenues, treasury; income, property.

find *vb* discover, fall upon; gain, get, obtain, procure; ascertain, notice, observe, perceive, remark; catch, detect; contribute, furnish, provide, supply. * *n* acquisition, catch, discovery, finding, plum, prize, strike.

fine[1] *vb* filter, purify, refine. * *adj* comminuted, little, minute, small; capillary, delicate, small; choice, light; exact, keen, sharp; attenuated, subtle, tenuous, thin; exquisite, fastidious, nice, refined, sensitive, subtle; dandy, excellent, superb, superior; beautiful, elegant, handsome, magnificent, splendid; clean, pure, unadulterated.

fine[2] *vb* amerce, mulct, penalize, punish. * *n* amercement, forfeit, forfeiture, mulct, penalty, punishment.

finery *n* decorations, frippery, gewgaws, ornaments, splendour, showiness, trappings, trimmings, trinkets.

finesse *vb* manipulate, manoeuvre. * *n* artifice, contrivance, cunning, craft, manipulation, manoeuvre, manoeuvring, ruses, stratagems, strategy, wiles.

finger *vb* handle, manipulate, play, purloin.

finical *adj* critical, dainty, dapper, fastidious, foppish, jaunty, overnice, overparticular, scrupulous, spruce, squeamish, trim.

finish *vb* accomplish, achieve, complete, consummate, execute, fulfil, perform; elaborate, perfect, polish; close, conclude, end, terminate. * *n* elaboration, elegance, perfection, polish; close, end, death, termination, wind-up.

finite *adj* bounded, circumscribed, conditioned, contracted, definable, limited, restricted, terminable.

fire *vb* ignite, kindle, light; animate, enliven, excite, inflame, inspirit, invigorate, rouse, stir up; discharge, eject, expel, hurl. * *n* combustion; blaze, conflagration; discharge, firing; animation, ardour, enthusiasm, fervour, fervency, fever, force, heat, impetuosity, inflammation, intensity, passion, spirit, vigour, violence; light, lustre, radiance, splendour; imagination, imaginativeness, inspiration, vivacity; affliction, persecution, torture, trouble.

firm[1] *adj* established, coherent, confirmed, consistent, fast, fixed, immovable, inflexible, rooted, secure, settled, stable; compact, compressed, dense, hard, solid; constant, determined, resolute, staunch, steadfast, steady, unshaken; loyal, robust, sinewy, stanch, stout, sturdy, strong.

firm[2] *n* association, business, company, concern, corporation, house, partnership.

firmament *n* heavens, sky, vault, welkin.

firmness *n* compactness, fixedness, hardness, solidity; stability, strength; constancy, soundness, steadfastness, steadiness.

first *adj* capital, chief, foremost, highest, leading, prime, principal; earliest, eldest, original; maiden; elementary, primary, rudimentary; aboriginal, primal, primeval, primitive, pristine. * *adv* chiefly, firstly, initially, mainly, primarily, principally; before, foremost, headmost; before, rather, rather than, sooner, sooner than. * *n* alpha, initial, prime.

first-rate *adj* excellent, prime, superior.

fissure *n* breach, break, chasm, chink, cleft, crack, cranny, crevice, fracture, gap, hole, interstice, opening, rent, rift.

fit[1] *vb* adapt, adjust, suit; become, conform; accommodate, equip, prepare, provide, qualify. * *adj* capacitated, competent, fitted; adequate, appropriate, apt, becoming, befitting, consonant, convenient, fitting, good, meet, pertinent, proper, seemly, suitable.

fit[2] *n* convulsion, fit, paroxysm, qualm, seizure, spasm, spell; fancy, humour, whim; mood, pet, tantrum; interval, period, spell, turn.

fitful *adj* capricious, changeable, convulsive, fanciful, fantastic, fickle, humoursome, impulsive, intermittent, irregular, odd, spasmodic, unstable, variable, whimsical; checkered, eventful.

fitness *n* adaptation, appropriateness, aptitude, aptness, pertinence, propriety, suitableness; preparation, qualification.

fix *vb* establish, fasten, place, plant, set; adjust, correct, mend, repair; attach, bind, clinch, connect, fasten, lock, rivet, stay, tie; appoint, decide, define, determine, limit, seal, settle; consolidate, harden, solidify; abide, remain, rest; congeal, stiffen. * *n* difficulty, dilemma, quandary, pickle, plight, predicament.

flabbergast *vb* abash, amaze, astonish, astound, confound, confuse, disconcert, dumbfound, nonplus.

flabby *adj* feeble, flaccid, inelastic, limp, soft, week, yielding.

flaccid *adj* baggy, drooping, flabby, inelastic, lax, limber, limp, loose, pendulous, relaxed, soft, weak, yielding.

flag[1] *vb* droop, hang, loose; decline, droop, fail, faint, lag, languish, pine, sink, succumb, weaken, weary; stale, pall.

flag[2] *vb* indicate, mark, semaphore, sign, signal. * *n* banner, colours, ensign, gonfalon, pennant, pennon, standard, streamer.

flagellate *vb* beat, castigate, chastise, cudgel, drub, flog, scourge, thrash, whip.

flagitious *adj* abandoned, atrocious, corrupt, flagrant, heinous, infamous, monstrous, nefarious, profligate, scandalous, villainous, wicked.

flagrant *adj* burning, flaming, glowing, raging; crying, enormous, flagitious, glaring, monstrous, nefarious, notorious, outrageous, shameful, wanton, wicked.

flake *vb* desquamate, scale. * *n* lamina, layer, scale.

flamboyant *adj* bright, gorgeous, ornate, rococo.

flame *vb* blaze, shine; burn, flash, glow, warm. * *n* blaze, brightness, fire, flare, vapour; affection, ardour, enthusiasm, fervency, fervour, keenness, warmth.

flaming *adj* blazing; burning, bursting, exciting, glowing, intense, lambent, vehement, violent.

flap *vb* beat, flutter, shake, vibrate, wave. * *n* apron, fly, lap, lappet, tab; beating, flapping, flop, flutter, slap, shaking, swinging, waving.

flare *vb* blaze, flicker, flutter, waver; dazzle, flame, glare; splay, spread, widen. * *n* blaze, dazzle, flame, glare.

flash *vb* blaze, glance, glare, glisten, light, shimmer, scintillate, sparkle, twinkle. * *n* instant, moment, twinkling.

flashy *adj* flaunting, gaudy, gay, loud, ostentatious, pretentious, showy, tawdry, tinsel.

flat *adj* champaign, horizontal, level; even, plane, smooth, unbroken; low, prostrate, overthrow; dull, frigid, jejune, lifeless, monotonous, pointless, prosaic, spiritless, tame, unanimated, uniform, uninteresting; dead, flashy, insipid, mawkish, stale, tasteless, vapid; absolute, clear, direct, downright, peremptory, positive. * *adv* flatly, flush, horizontally, level. * *n* bar, sandbank, shallow, shoal, strand; champaign, lowland, plain; apartment, floor, lodging, storey.

flatter *vb* compliment, gratify, praise; blandish, blarney, butter up, cajole, coax, coddle, court, entice, fawn, humour, inveigle, wheedle.

flattery *n* adulation, blandishment, blarney, cajolery, fawning, obsequiousness, servility, sycophancy, toadyism.

flaunt *vb* boast, display, disport, flourish, parade, sport, vaunt; brandish.

flaunting *adj* flashy, garish, gaudy, ostentatious, showy, tawdry.

flavour *n* gust, gusto, relish, savour, seasoning, smack, taste, zest; admixture, lacing, seasoning; aroma, essence, soul, spirit.

flaw *n* break, breach, cleft, crack, fissure, fracture, gap, rent, rift; blemish, defect, fault, fleck, imperfection, speck, spot.

flay *vb* excoriate, flay; criticize.

fleck *vb* dapple, mottle, speckle, spot, streak, variegate. * *n* speckle, spot, streak.

flecked *adj* dappled, mottled, piebald, spotted, straked, striped, variegated.

flee *vb* abscond, avoid, decamp, depart, escape, fly, leave, run, skedaddle.

fleece *vb* clip, shear; cheat, despoil, pluck, plunder, rifle, rob, steal, strip.

fleer *vb* mock, jeer, gibe, scoff, sneer.

fleet[1] *n* armada, escadrille, flotilla, navy, squadron; company, group.

fleet[2] *adj* fast, nimble, quick, rapid, speedy, swift.

fleeting *adj* brief, caducous, ephemeral, evanescent, flitting, flying, fugitive, passing, short-lived, temporary, transient, transitory.

fleetness *n* celerity, nimbleness, quickness, rapidity, speed, swiftness, velocity.

flesh *n* food, meat; carnality, desires; kindred, race, stock; man, mankind, world.

fleshly *adj* animal, bodily, carnal, lascivious, lustful, lecherous, sensual.

fleshy *adj* corpulent, fat, obese, plump, stout.

flexibility *n* flexibleness, limbersome, lithesome, pliability, pliancy, suppleness; affability, complaisance, compliance, disposition, ductility, pliancy, tractableness, tractability, yielding.

flexible *adj* flexible, limber, lithe, pliable, pliant, supple, willowy; affable, complaisant, ductile, docile, gentle, tractable, tractile, yielding.

flexose, flexuous *adj* bending, crooked, serpentine, sinuate, sinuous, tortuous, waxy, winding.

flibbertigibbet *n* demon, imp, sprite.

flight[1] *n* flying, mounting, soaring, volition; shower, flight; steps, stairs.

flight[2] *n* departure, fleeing, flying, retreat, rout, stampede; exodus, hegira.

flighty *adj* capricious, deranged, fickle, frivolous, giddy, light-headed, mercurial, unbalanced, volatile, wild, whimsical.

flimsy *adj* slight, thin, unsubstantial; feeble, foolish, frivolous, light, puerile, shallow, superficial, trashy, trifling, trivial, weak; insubstantial, sleazy.

flinch *vb* blench, flee, recoil, retreat, shirk, shrink, swerve, wince, withdraw.

fling *vb* cast, chuck, dart, emit, heave, hurl, pitch, shy, throw, toss; flounce, wince. * *n* cast, throw, toss.

flippancy *n* volubility; assuredness, glibness, pertness.

flippant *adj* fluent, glib, talkative, voluble; bold, forward, frivolous, glib, impertinent, inconsiderate, irreverent, malapert, pert, saucy, trifling.

flirt *vb* chuck, fling, hurl, pitch, shy, throw, toss; flutter, twirl, whirl, whisk; coquet, dally, philander. * *n* coquette, jilt, philanderer; jerk.

flirtation *n* coquetry, dalliance, philandering.

flit *vb* flicker, flutter, hover; depart, hasten, pass.

flitting *adj* brief, ephemeral, evanescent, fleeting, fugitive, passing, short, transient, transitory.

float *vb* drift, glide, hang, ride, sail, soar, swim, waft; launch, support.

flock *vb* collect, congregate, gather, group, herd, swarm, throng. * *n* collection, group, multitude; bevy, company, convoy, drove, flight, gaggle, herd, pack, swarm, team, troupe; congregation.

flog *vb* beat, castigate, chastise, drub, flagellate, lash, scourge, thrash, whip.

flood *vb* deluge, inundate, overflow, submerge, swamp. * *n* deluge, freshet, inundation, overflow, tide; bore, downpour, eagre, flow, outburst, spate, rush; abundance, excess.

floor *vb* deck, pave; beat, confound, conquer, overthrow, prevail, prostrate, puzzle; disconcert, nonplus. * *n* storey; bottom, deck, flooring, pavement, stage.

florid *adj* bright-coloured, flushed, red-faced, rubicund; embellished, figurative, luxuriant, ornate, rhetorical, rococo.

flounce[1] *vb* fling, jerk, spring, throw, toss, wince. * *n* jerk, spring.

flounce[2] *n* frill, furbelow, ruffle.

flounder *vb* blunder, flop, flounce, plunge, struggle, toss, tumble, wallow.

flourish *vb* grow, thrive; boast, bluster, brag, gasconade, show off, vaunt, vapour; brandish, flaunt, swing, wave. * *n* dash, display, ostentation, parade, show; bombast, fustian, grandiloquence; brandishing, shake, waving; blast, fanfare, tantivy.

flout *vb* chaff, deride, fleer, gibe, insult, jeer, mock, ridicule, scoff, sneer, taunt. * *n* gibe, fling, insult, jeer, mock, mockery, mocking, scoff, scoffing, taunt.

flow *vb* pour, run, stream; deliquesce, liquefy, melt; arise, come, emanate, follow, grow, issue, proceed, result, spring; glide; float, undulate, wave, waver;

abound, run. * *n* current, discharge, flood, flux, gush, rush, stream, trickle; abundance, copiousness.

flower *vb* bloom, blossom, effloresce; develop. * *n* bloom, blossom; best, cream, elite, essence, pick; freshness, prime, vigour.

flowery *adj* bloomy, florid; embellished, figurative, florid, ornate, overwrought.

flowing *adj* abundant, copious, fluent, smooth.

fluctuate *vb* oscillate, swing, undulate, vibrate, wave; change, vary; vacillate, waver.

flue *n* chimney, duct; flew, fluff, nap, floss, fur.

fluency *n* liquidness, smoothness; affluence, copiousness; ease, facility, readiness.

fluent *adj* current, flowing, gliding, liquid; smooth; affluent, copious, easy, facile, glib, ready, talkative, voluble.

fluff *vb* blunder, bungle, forget, fumble, mess up, miscue, misremember, muddle, muff. * *n* down, flew, floss, flue, fur, lint, nap; cobweb, feather, gossamer, thistledown; blunder, bungle, fumble, muff.

flume *n* channel, chute, mill race, race.

flummery *n* chaff, frivolity, froth, moonshine, nonsense, trash, trifling; adulation, blandishment, blarney, flattery; brose, porridge, sowens.

flunky, flunkey *n* footman, lackey, livery servant, manservant, valet; snob, toady.

flurry *vb* agitate, confuse, disconcert, disturb, excite, fluster, hurry, perturb. * *n* gust, flaw, squall; agitation, bustle, commotion, confusion, disturbance, excitement, flutter, haste, hurry, hurry-scurry, perturbation, ruffle, scurry.

flush[1] *vb* flow, rush, start; glow, mantle, redden; animate, elate, elevate, erect, excite; cleanse, drench. * *adj* bright, fresh, glowing, vigorous; abundant, affluent, exuberant, fecund, fertile, generous, lavish, liberal, prodigal, prolific, rich, wealthy, well-supplied; even, flat, level, plane. * *adv* evenly, flat, level; full, point-blank, right, square, squarely, straight. * *n* bloom, blush, glow, redness, rosiness, ruddiness; impulse, shock, thrill.

flush[2] *vb* disturb, rouse, start, uncover.

fluster *vb* excite, flush, heat; agitate, disturb, flurry, hurry, perturb, ruffle; confound, confuse, discompose, disconcert. * *n* glow, heat; agitation, flurry, flutter, hurry, hurry-scurry, perturbation, ruffle.

fluted *adj* channelled, corrugated, grooved.

flutter *vb* flap, hover; flirt, flit; beat, palpitate, quiver, tremble; fluctuate, oscillate, vacillate, waver. * *n* agitation, tremor; hurry, commotion, confusion, excitement, flurry, fluster, hurry-scurry, perturbation, quivering, tremble, tumult, twitter.

flux *n* flow, flowing; change, mutation, shifting, transition; diarrhoea, dysentery, looseness; fusing, melting, menstruum, solvent.

fly[1] *vb* aviate, hover, mount, soar; flap, float, flutter, play, sail, soar, undulate, vibrate, wave; burst, explode; abscond, decamp, depart, flee, vanish; elapse, flit, glide, pass, slip.

fly[2] *adj* alert, bright, sharp, smart, wide-awake; astute, cunning, knowing, sly; agile, fleet, nimble, quick, spry.

foal *n* colt, filly.

foam *vb* cream, froth, lather, spume; boil, churn, ferment, fume, seethe, simmer, stew. * *n* bubbles, cream, froth, scum, spray, spume, suds.

fodder *n* feed, food, forage, provender, rations.

foe *n* adversary, antagonist, enemy, foeman, opponent.

fog *vb* bedim, bemist, blear, blur, cloud, dim, enmist, mist; addle, befuddle, confuse, fuddle, muddle. * *n* blear, blur, dimness, film, fogginess, haze, haziness, mist, smog, vapour; befuddlement, confusion, fuddle, maze, muddle.

foggy *adj* blurred, cloudy, dim, dimmed, hazy, indistinct, misty, obscure; befuddled, bewildered, confused, dazed, muddled, muddy, stupid.

foible *n* defect, failing, fault, frailty, imperfection, infirmity, penchant, weakness.

foil[1] *vb* baffle, balk, check, checkmate, circumvent, defeat, disappoint, frustrate, thwart.

foil[2] *n* film, flake, lamina; background, contrast.

foist *vb* impose, insert, interpolate, introduce, palm off, thrust.

fold[1] *vb* bend, cover, double, envelop, wrap; clasp, embrace, enfold, enwrap, gather, infold, interlace; collapse, fail. * *n* double, doubling, gather, plait, plicature.

fold[2] *n* cot, enclosure, pen.

foliaceous *adj* foliate, leafy; flaky, foliated, lamellar, lamellate, lamellated, laminated, scaly, schistose.

folk *n* kindred, nation, people.

follow *vb* ensue, succeed; chase, dog, hound, pursue, run after, trail; accompany, attend; conform, heed, obey, observe; cherish, cultivate, seek; practise, pursue; adopt, copy, imitate; arise, come, flow, issue, proceed, result, spring.

follower *n* acolyte, attendant, associate, companion, dependant, retainer, supporter; adherent, admirer, disciple, partisan, pupil; copier, imitator.

folly *n* doltishness, dullness, imbecility, levity, shallowness; absurdity, extravagance, fatuity, foolishness, imprudence, inanity, indiscretion, ineptitude, nonsense, senselessness; blunder, faux pas, indiscretion, unwisdom.

foment *vb* bathe, embrocate, stupe; abet, brew, encourage, excite, foster, instigate, promote, stimulate.

fond *adj* absurd, baseless, empty, foolish, senseless, silly, vain, weak; affectionate, amorous, doting, loving, overaffectionate, tender.

fondle *vb* blandish, caress, coddle, cosset, dandle, pet.

fondness *n* absurdity, delusion, folly, silliness, weakness; liking, partiality, predilection, preference, propensity; appetite, relish, taste.

food *n* aliment, board, bread, cheer, commons, diet, fare, meat, nourishment, nutriment, nutrition, pabulum, provisions, rations, regimen, subsistence, sustenance, viands, victuals; feed, fodder, forage, provender.

fool *vb* jest, play, toy, trifle; beguile, cheat, circumvent, cozen, deceive, delude, dupe, gull, hoodwink, overreach, trick. * *n* blockhead, dolt, driveller, idiot, imbecile, nincompoop, ninny, nitwit, simpleton; antic, buffoon, clown, droll, harlequin, jester, merryandrew, punch, scaramouch, zany; butt, dupe.

foolery *n* absurdity, folly, foolishness, nonsense; buffoonery, mummery, tomfoolery.

foolhardy *adj* adventurous, bold, desperate, harebrained, headlong, hot-headed, incautious, precipitate, rash, reckless, venturesome, venturous.

foolish *adj* brainless, daft, fatuous, idiotic, inane, inept, insensate, irrational, senseless, shallow, silly, simple, thick-skulled, vain, weak, witless; absurd, ill-judged, imprudent, indiscreet, nonsensical, preposterous, ridiculous, unreasonable, unwise; childish, contemptible, idle, puerile, trifling, trivial, vain.

foolishness *n* doltishness, dullness, fatuity, folly, imbecility, shallowness, silliness, stupidity; absurdity, extravagance, imprudence, indiscretion, nonsense; childishness, puerility, triviality.

footing *n* foothold, purchase; basis, foundation, groundwork, installation; condition, grade, rank, standing, state, status; settlement, establishment.

footman *n* footboy, menial, lackey, runner, servant.

footpad *n* bandit, brigand, freebooter, highwayman, robber.

footpath *n* footway, path, trail.

footprint *n* footfall, footmark, footstep, trace, track.

footstep *n* footmark, footprint, trace, track; footfall, step, tread; mark, sign, token, trace, vestige.

fop *n* beau, coxcomb, dandy, dude, exquisite, macaroni, popinjay, prig, swell.

foppish *adj* coxcombical, dandified, dandyish, dressy, finical, spruce, vain.

forage *vb* feed, graze, provender, provision, victual; hunt for, range, rummage, search, seek; maraud, plunder, raid. * *n* feed, fodder, food, pasturage, provender; hunt, rummage, search.

foray *n* descent, incursion, invasion, inroad, irruption, raid.

forbear *vb* cease, desist, hold, pause, stop, stay; abstain, refrain; endure, tolerate; avoid, decline, shun; abstain, omit, withhold.

forbearance *n* abstinence, avoidance, forbearing, self-restraint, shunning, refraining; indulgence, leniency, long-suffering, mildness, moderation, patience.

forbid *vb* ban, debar, disallow, embargo, enjoin, hinder, inhibit, interdict, prohibit, proscribe, taboo, veto.

forbidding *adj* abhorrent, disagreeable, displeasing, odious, offensive, repellant, repulsive, threatening, unpleasant.

force *vb* coerce, compel, constrain, necessitate, oblige; drive, impel, overcome, press, urge; ravish, violate. * *n* emphasis, energy, head, might, pith, power, strength, stress, vigour, vim; agency, efficacy, efficiency, cogency, potency, validity, virtue; coercion, compulsion, constraint, enforcement, vehemence, violence; army, array, battalion, host, legion, phalanx, posse, soldiery, squadron, troop.

forcible *adj* all-powerful, cogent, impressive, irresistible, mighty, potent, powerful, strong, weighty; impetuous, vehement, violent, unrestrained; coerced, coercive, compulsory; convincing, energetic, effective, efficacious, telling, vigorous.

forcibly *adv* mightily, powerfully; coercively, compulsorily, perforce, violently; effectively, energetically, vigorously.

ford *n* current, flood, stream; crossing, wading place.

fore *adj* anterior, antecedent, first, foregoing, former, forward, preceding, previous, prior; advanced, foremost, head, leading.

forebode *vb* augur, betoken, foreshow, foretell, indicate, portend, predict, prefigure, presage, prognosticate, promise, signify.

foreboding *n* augury, omen, prediction, premonition, presage, presentiment, prognostication.

forecast *vb* anticipate, foresee, predict; calculate, contrive, devise, plan, project, scheme. * *n* anticipation, foresight, forethought, planning, prevision, prophecy, provident.

foreclose *vb* debar, hinder, preclude, prevent, stop.

foredoom *vb* foreordain, predestine, preordain.

forego *see* **forgo**.

foregoing adj antecedent, anterior, fore, former, preceding, previous, prior.

foregone adj bygone, former, past, previous.

foreign adj alien, distant, exotic, exterior, external, outward, outlandish, remote, strange, unnative; adventitious, exterior, extraneous, extrinsic, inappropriate, irrelevant, outside, unnatural, unrelated.

foreknowledge n foresight, prescience, prognostication.

foremost adj first, front, highest, leading, main, principal.

foreordain vb appoint, foredoom, predestinate, predetermine, preordain.

forerunner n avant-courier, foregoer, harbinger, herald, precursor, predecessor; omen, precursor, prelude, premonition, prognosticate, sign.

foresee vb anticipate, forebode, forecast, foreknow, foretell, prognosticate, prophesy.

foreshadow vb forebode, predict, prefigure, presage, presignify, prognosticate, prophesy.

foresight n foreknowledge, prescience, prevision; anticipation, care, caution, forecast, forethought, precaution, providence, prudence.

forest n wood, woods, woodland.

forestall vb hinder, frustrate, intercept, preclude, prevent, thwart; antedate, anticipate, foretaste; engross, monopolize, regrate.

foretaste n anticipation, forestalling, prelibation.

foretell vb predict, prophesy; augur, betoken, forebode, forecast, foreshadow, foreshow, portend, presage, presignify, prognosticate, prophesy.

forethought n anticipation, forecast, foresight, precaution, providence, prudence.

forever adv always, constantly, continually, endlessly, eternally, ever, evermore, everlastingly, perpetually, unceasingly.

forewarn vb admonish, advise, caution, dissuade.

forfeit vb alienate, lose. * n amercement, damages, fine, forfeiture, mulct, penalty.

forfend vb avert, forbid, hinder, prevent, protect.

forge vb beat, fabricate, form, frame, hammer; coin, devise, frame, invent; counterfeit, falsify, feign. * n furnace, ironworks, smithy.

forgery n counterfeit, fake, falsification, imitation.

forgetful adj careless, heedless, inattentive, mindless, neglectful, negligent, oblivious, unmindful.

forgive vb absolve, acquit, condone, excuse, exonerate, pardon, remit.

forgiveness n absolution, acquittal, amnesty, condoning. exoneration, pardon, remission, reprieve.

forgiving adj absolutory, absolvatory, acquitting, clearing, excusing, pardoning, placable, releasing.

forgo vb abandon, cede, relinquish, renounce, resign, surrender, yield.

fork vb bifurcate, branch, divaricate, divide. * n bifurcation, branch, branching, crotch, divarication, division.

forked adj bifurcated, branching, divaricated, furcate, furcated.

forlorn adj abandoned, deserted, forsaken, friendless, helpless, lost, solitary; abject, comfortless, dejected, desolate, destitute, disconsolate, helpless, hopeless, lamentable, pitiable, miserable, woebegone, wretched.

form vb fashion model, mould, shape; build, conceive, construct, create, fabricate, make, produce; contrive, devise, frame, invent; compose, constitute, develop,

organize; discipline, educate, teach, train. * n body, build, cast, configuration, conformation, contour, cut, fashion, figure, format, mould, outline, pattern, shape; formula, formulary, method, mode, practice, ritual; class, kind, manner, model, order, sort, system, type; arrangement, order, regularity, shapeliness; ceremonial, ceremony, conventionality, etiquette, formality, observance, ordinance, punctilio, rite, ritual; bench, seat; class, rank; arrangement, combination, organization.

formal adj explicit, express, official, positive, strict; fixed, methodical, regular, rigid, set, stiff; affected, ceremonious, exact, precise, prim, punctilious, starchy. starched; constitutive, essential; external, outward, perfunctory; formative, innate, organic, primordial.

formality n ceremonial, ceremony, conventionality, etiquette, punctilio, rite, ritual.

formation n creation, genesis, production; composition, constitution; arrangement, combination, disposal, disposition.

formative adj creative, determinative, plastic, shaping; derivative, inflectional, nonradical.

former adj antecedent, anterior, earlier, foregoing, preceding, previous, prior; late, old-time, quondam; by, bygone, foregone, gone, past.

formidable adj appalling, dangerous, difficult, dreadful, fearful, frightful, horrible, menacing, redoubtable, shocking, terrible, terrific, threatening, tremendous.

forsake vb abandon, desert, leave, quit; drop, forgo, forswear, relinquish, renounce, surrender, yield.

forsooth adv certainly, indeed, really, surely, truly.

forswear vb abandon, desert, drop, forsake, leave, quit, reject, renounce; abjure, deny, eschew, perjure, recant, repudiate, retract.

fort n bulwark, castle, citadel, defence, fastness, fortification, fortress, stronghold.

forthwith adv directly, immediately, instantly, quickly, straightaway.

fortification n breastwork, bulwark, castle, citadel, defence, earthwork, fastness, fort, keep, rampart, redoubt, stronghold, tower.

fortify vb brace, encourage, entrench, garrison, protect, reinforce, stiffen, strengthen; confirm, corroborate.

fortitude n braveness, bravery, courage, determination, endurance, firmness, hardiness, patience, pluck, resolution, strength, valour.

fortuitous adj accidental, casual, chance, contingent, incidental.

fortunate adj favoured, happy, lucky, prosperous, providential, successful; advantageous, auspicious, favourable, happy, lucky, propitious, timely.

fortune n accident, casualty, chance, contingency, fortuity, hap, luck; estate, possessions, property, substance; affluence, felicity, opulence, prosperity, riches, wealth; destination, destiny, doom, fate, lot, star; event, issue, result; favour, success.

forward vb advance, aid, encourage, favour, foster, further, help, promote, support; accelerate, dispatch, expedite, hasten, hurry, quicken, speed; dispatch, post, send, ship, transmit. * adj ahead, advanced, onward; anterior, front, fore, head; prompt, eager, earnest, hasty, impulsive, quick, ready, willing, zealous; assuming, bold, brazen, brazen-faced, confident, flippant, impertinent, pert, presumptuous, presuming; advanced, early, premature. * adv ahead, onward.

foster *vb* cosset, feed, nurse, nourish, support, sustain; advance, aid, breed, cherish, cultivate, encourage, favour, foment, forward, further, harbour, patronize, promote, rear, stimulate.

foul *vb* besmirch, defile, dirty, pollute, soil, stain, sully; clog, collide, entangle, jam. * *adj* dirty, fetid, filthy, impure, nasty, polluted, putrid, soiled, stained, squalid, sullied, rank, tarnished, unclean; disgusting, hateful, loathsome, noisome, odious, offensive; dishonourable, underhand, unfair, sinister; abominable, base, dark, detestable, disgraceful, infamous, scandalous, scurvy, shameful, wile, wicked; coarse, low, obscene, vulgar; abusive, foul-mouthed, foul-spoken, insulting, scurrilous; cloudy, rainy, rough, stormy, wet; feculent, muddy, thick, turbid; entangled, tangled.

foul-mouthed *adj* abusive, blackguardy, blasphemous, filthy, foul, indecent, insolent, insulting, obscene, scurrilous.

found *vb* base, fix, ground, place, rest, set; build, construct, erect, raise; colonize, establish, institute, originate, plant; cast, mould.

foundation *n* base, basis, bed, bottom, footing, ground, groundwork, substructure, support; endowment, establishment, settlement.

founder[1] *n* author, builder, establisher, father, institutor, originator, organizer, planter.

founder[2] *n* caster, moulder.

founder[3] *vb* sink, swamp, welter; collapse, fail, miscarry; fall, stumble, trip.

fountain *n* fount, reservoir, spring, well; jet, upswelling; cause, fountainhead, origin, original, source.

foxy *adj* artful, crafty, cunning, sly, subtle, wily.

fracas *n* affray, brawl, disturbance, outbreak, quarrel, riot, row, uproar, tumult,

fractious *adj* captious, cross, fretful, irritable, peevish, pettish, perverse, petulant, querulous, snappish, splenetic, touchy, testy, waspish.

fracture *vb* break, crack, split. * *n* breaking, rupture; breach, break, cleft, crack, fissure, flaw, opening, rift, rent.

fragile *adj* breakable, brittle, delicate, frangible; feeble, frail, infirm, weak.

fragility *n* breakability, breakableness, brittleness, frangibility, frangibleness; feebleness, frailty, infirmity, weakness.

fragment *vb* atomize, break, fracture, pulverize, splinter. * *n* bit, chip, fraction, fracture, morsel, part, piece, remnant, scrap.

fragrance *n* aroma, balminess, bouquet, odour, perfume, redolence, scent, smell.

fragrant *adj* ambrosial, aromatic, balmy, odoriferous, odorous, perfumed, redolent, spicy, sweet, sweet-scented, sweet-smelling.

frail *adj* breakable, brittle, delicate, fragile, frangible, slight; feeble, infirm, weak.

frailty *n* feebleness, frailness, infirmity, weakness; blemish, defect, failing, fault, foible, imperfection, peccability, shortcoming.

frame *vb* build, compose, constitute, construct, erect, form, make, mould, plan, shape; contrive, devise, fabricate, fashion, forge, invest, plan. * *n* body, carcass, framework, framing, shell, skeleton; constitution, fabric, form, structure, scheme, system; condition, humour, mood, state, temper.

franchise *n* privilege, right; suffrage, vote; exemption, immunity.

frangible *adj* breakable, brittle, fragile.

frank *adj* artless, candid, direct, downright, frank-hearted, free, genuine, guileless, ingenuous, naive, open, outspoken, outright, plain, plain-spoken, point-blank, sincere, straightforward, truthful, unequivocal, unreserved, unrestricted.

frankness *n* candour, ingenuousness, openness, outspokenness, plain speaking, truth, straightforwardness.

frantic *adj* crazy, distracted, distraught, frenzied, furious, infuriate, mad. outrageous, phrenetic, rabid, raging, raving, transported, wild.

fraternity *n* association, brotherhood, circle, clan, club, company, fellowship, league, set, society, sodality; brotherliness.

fraternize *vb* associate, coalesce, concur, consort, cooperate, harmonize, sympathize, unite.

fraud *n* artifice, cheat, craft, deception, deceit, duplicity, guile, hoax, humbug, imposition, imposture, sham, stratagem, treachery, trick, trickery, wile.

fraudulent *adj* crafty, deceitful, deceptive, dishonest, false, knavish, treacherous, trickish, tricky, wily.

fraught *adj* abounding, big, burdened, charged, filled, freighted, laden, pregnant, stored, weighted.

fray[1] *n* affray, battle, brawl, broil, combat, fight, quarrel, riot.

fray[2] *vb* chafe, fret, rub, wear; ravel, shred.

freak *adj* bizarre, freakish, grotesque, monstrous, odd, unexpected, unforeseen. * *n* caprice, crotchet, fancy, humour, maggot, quirk, vagary, whim, whimsey; antic, caper, gambol; abnormality, abortion, monstrosity.

freakish *adj* capricious, changeable, eccentric, erratic, fanciful, humoursome, odd, queer, whimsical.

free *vb* deliver, discharge, disenthral, emancipate, enfranchise, enlarge, liberate, manumit, ransom, release, redeem, rescue, save; clear, disencumber, disengage, extricate, rid, unbind, unchain, unfetter, unlock; exempt, immunize, privilege. * *adj* bondless, independent, loose, unattached, unconfined, unentangled, unimpeded, unrestrained, untrammelled; autonomous, delivered, emancipated, freeborn, liberated, manumitted, ransomed, released, self-governing; clear, exempt, immune, privileged; allowed, permitted; devoid, empty, open, unimpeded, unobstructed, unrestricted; affable, artless, candid, frank, ingenuous, sincere, unreserved; bountiful, charitable, free-hearted, generous, hospitable, liberal, munificent, openhanded; immoderate, lavish, prodigal; eager, prompt, ready, willing; available, gratuitous, spontaneous; careless, lax, loose; bold, easy, familiar, informal, overfamiliar, unconstrained. * *adv* openly, outright, unreservedly, unrestrainedly, unstintingly; freely, gratis, gratuitously.

freebooter *n* bandit, brigand, despoiler, footpad, gangster, highwayman, marauder, pillager, plunderer, robber; buccaneer, pirate, rover.

freedom *n* emancipation, independence, liberation, liberty, release; elbowroom, margin, play, range, scope, swing; franchise, immunity, privilege; familiarity, laxity, license, looseness.

freethinker *n* agnostic, deist, doubter, infidel, sceptic, unbeliever.

freeze *vb* congeal, glaciate, harden, stiffen; benumb, chill.

freight *vb* burden, charge, lade, load. * *n* burden, cargo, lading, load.

frenzy *n* aberration, delirium, derangement, distraction, fury, insanity, lunacy, madness, mania, paroxysm, rage, raving, transport.

frequent *vb* attend, haunt, resort, visit. * *adj* iterating, oft-repeated; common, customary, everyday, familiar, habitual, persistent, usual; constant, continual, incessant.

fresh *adj* new, novel, recent; renewed, revived; blooming, flourishing, green, undecayed, unimpaired, unfaded, unobliterated, unwilted, unwithered, well-preserved; sweet; delicate, fair, fresh-coloured, ruddy, rosy; florid, hardy, healthy, vigorous, strong; active, energetic, unexhausted, unfatigued, unwearied, vigorous; keen, lively, unabated, undecayed, unimpaired, vivid; additional, further; uncured, undried, unsalted, unsmoked; bracing, health-giving, invigorating, refreshing, sweet; brink, stiff, strong; inexperienced, raw, uncultivated, unpracticed, unskilled, untrained, unused.

freshen *vb* quicken, receive, refresh, revive.

fret[1] *vb* abrade, chafe, fray, gall, rub, wear; affront, agitate, annoy, gall, harass, irritate, nettle, provoke, ruffle, tease, vex, wear, worry; ripple, roughen; corrode; fume, peeve, rage, stew. * *n* agitation, fretfulness, fretting, irritation, peevishness, vexation.

fret[2] *vb* diversify, interlace, ornament, variegate. * *n* fretwork, interlacing, ornament; ridge, wale, whelk.

fretful *adj* captious, cross, fractious, ill-humoured, ill-tempered, irritable, peevish, pettish, petulant, querulous, short-tempered, snappish, spleeny, splenetic, testy, touchy, uneasy, waspish.

friable *adj* brittle, crisp, crumbling, powdery, pulverable.

friction *n* abrasion, attrition, grating, rubbing; bickering, disagreement, dissension, wrangling.

friend *adj* benefactor, chum, companion, comrade, crony, confidant, intimate; adherent, ally, associate, confrere, partisan; advocate, defender, encourager, favourer, patron, supporter, well-wisher.

friendly *adj* affectionate, amiable, benevolent, favourable, kind, kind-hearted, kindly, well-disposed; amicable, cordial, fraternal, neighbourly; conciliatory, peaceable, unhostile.

friendship *n* affection, attachment, benevolence, fondness, goodness, love, regard; fellowship, intimacy; amicability, amicableness, amity, cordiality, familiarity, fraternization, friendliness, harmony.

fright *n* affright, alarm, consternation, dismay, funk, horror, panic, scare, terror.

frighten *vb* affright, alarm, appal, daunt, dismay, intimidate, scare, stampede, terrify.

frightful *adj* alarming, awful, dire, direful, dread, dreadful, fearful, horrible, horrid, shocking, terrible, terrific; ghastly, grim, grisly, gruesome, hideous.

frigid *adj* cold, cool, gelid; dull, lifeless, spiritless, tame, unanimated, uninterested, uninteresting; chilling, distant, forbidding, formal, freezing, prim, repellent, repelling, repulsive, rigid, stiff.

frill *n* edging, frilling, furbelow, gathering, ruche, ruching, ruffle; affectation, mannerism.

fringe *vb* border, bound, edge, hem, march, rim, skirt, verge. * *n* border, edge, edging, tassel, trimming. * *adj* edging, extra, unofficial.

frisk *vb* caper, dance, frolic, gambol, hop, jump, play, leap, romp, skip, sport, wanton.

frisky *adj* frolicsome, coltish, gay, lively, playful, sportive.

frivolity *n* flummery, folly, fribbling, frippery, frivolousness, levity, puerility, trifling, triviality.

frivolous *adj* childish, empty, flighty, flimsy, flippant, foolish, giddy, idle, light, paltry. petty, puerile, silly, trashy, trifling, trivial, unimportant, vain, worthless.

frolic *vb* caper, frisk, gambol, lark, play, romp, sport. * *n* escapade, gambol, lark, romp, skylark, spree, trick; drollery, fun, play, pleasantry, sport.

frolicsome *adj* coltish, fresh, frolic, gamesome, gay, lively, playful, sportive.

front *vb* confront, encounter, face, oppose. * *adj* anterior, forward; foremost, frontal, headmost. * *n* brow, face, forehead; assurance, boldness, brass, effrontery, impudence; breast, head, van, vanguard; anterior, face, forepart, obverse; facade, frontage.

frontier *n* border, boundary, coast, confine, limits, marches.

frosty *adj* chill, chilly, cold, icy, stinging, wintry; cold, cold-hearted, frigid, indifferent, unaffectionate, uncordial, unimpassioned, unloving; dull-hearted, lifeless, spiritless, unanimated; frosted, grey-hearted, hoary, white.

froth *vb* bubble, cream, foam, lather, spume. * *n* bubbles, foam, lather, spume; balderdash, flummery, nonsense, trash, triviality.

frothy *adj* foamy, spumy; empty, frivolous, light, trifling, trivial, unsubstantial, vain.

froward *adj* captious, contrary, contumacious, cross, defiant, disobedient, fractious, impudent, intractable, obstinate, peevish, perverse, petulant, refractory, stubborn, ungovernable, untoward, unyielding, wayward, wilful.

frown *vb* glower, lower, scowl.

frowzy, frowsy *adj* fetid, musty, noisome, rancid, rank, stale; disordered, disorderly, dowdy, slatternly, slovenly.

frugal *adj* abstemious, careful, chary, choice, economical, provident, saving, sparing, temperate, thrifty, unwasteful.

fruit *n* crop, harvest, produce, production; advantage, consequence, effect, good, outcome, product, profit, result; issue, offspring, young.

fruitful *adj* abounding, productive; fecund, fertile, prolific; abundant, exuberant, plenteous, plentiful, rich, teeming.

fruition *n* completion, fulfilment, perfection; enjoyment.

fruitless *adj* acarpous, barren, sterile, infecund, unfertile, unfruitful, unproductive, unprolific; abortive, bootless, futile, idle, ineffectual, profitless, unavailing, unprofitable, useless, vain.

frumpish, frumpy *adj* cross, cross-grained, cross-tempered, dowdy, grumpy, irritable, shabby, slatternly, snappish.

frustrate *vb* baffle, balk, check, circumvent, defeat, disappoint, disconcert, foil, thwart; cross, hinder, outwit.

frustrated *adj* balked, blighted, dashed, defeated, foiled, thwarted; ineffectual, null, useless, vain.

fuddled *adj* befuddled, boozy, corned, crapulous, drunk, groggy, high, inebriated, intoxicated, muddled, slewed, tight, tipsy.

fugacious *adj* evanescent, fleeting, fugitive, transient, transitory.

fugitive *adj* escaping, fleeing, flying; brief, ephemeral, evanescent, fleeting, flitting, fugacious, momentary, short, short-lived, temporal, temporary, transient, transitory, uncertain, unstable, volatile. * *n* émigré, escapee, evacuee, fleer, outlaw, refugee, runaway.

fulfil *vb* accomplish, complete, consummate, effect, effectuate, execute, realize; adhere, discharge, do, keep, obey, observe, perform; answer, fill, meet, satisfy.

full *adj* brimful, filled, flush, replete; abounding, replete, well-stocked; bagging, flowing, loose, voluminous; chock-full, cloyed, crammed, glutted, gorged, overflowing, packed, sated, satiated, saturated, soaked, stuffed, swollen; adequate, complete, entire, mature, perfect; abundant, ample, copious, plenteous, plentiful, sufficient; clear, deep, distinct, loud, rounded, strong; broad, large, capacious, comprehensive, extensive, plump; circumstantial, detailed, exhaustive. * *adv* completely, fully; directly, exactly, precisely.

fullness *n* abundance, affluence, copiousness, plenitude, plenty, profusion; glut, satiety, sating, repletion; completeness, completion, entireness, perfection; clearness, loudness, resonance, strength; dilation, distension, enlargement, plumpness, rotundity, roundness, swelling.

fully *adv* abundantly, amply, completely, copiously, entirely, largely, plentifully, sufficiently.

fulminate *vb* detonate, explode; curse, denounce, hurl, menace, threaten, thunder.

fulsome *adj* excessive, extravagant, fawning; disgusting, nauseous, nauseating, offensive, repulsive; coarse, gross, lustful, questionable.

fumble *vb* bungle, grope, mismanage, stumble; mumble, stammer, stutter.

fume *vb* reek, smoke, vaporize. * *n* effluvium exhalation, reek, smell, smoke, steam, vapour; agitation, fret, fry, fury, passion, pet, rage, storm.

fun *adj* amusing, diverting, droll, entertaining. * *n* amusement, diversion, drollery, frolic, gaiety, humour, jesting, jocularity, jollity, joy, merriment, mirth, play, pranks, sport, pleasantry, waggishness.

function *vb* act, discharge, go, operate, officiate, perform, run, serve, work. * *n* discharge, execution, exercise, operation, performance, purpose, use; activity, business, capacity, duty, employment, occupation, office, part, province, role; ceremony, rite; dependant, derivative.

fund *vb* afford, endow, finance, invest, provide, subsidise, support; garner, hoard, stock, store. * *n* accumulation, capital, endowment, reserve, stock; store, supply; foundation.

fundament *n* bottom, buttocks, seat.

fundamental *adj* basal, basic, bottom, cardinal, constitutional, elementary, essential, indispensable, organic, principal, primary, radical. * *n* essential, principal, rule.

funeral *n* burial, cremation, exequies, internment, obsequies.

funereal *adj* dark, dismal, gloomy, lugubrious, melancholy, mournful, sad, sepulchral, sombre, woeful.

funk *vb* blanch, shrink, quail. * *n* stench, stink; fear, fright, panic.

funny *adj* amusing, comic, comical, diverting, droll, facetious, farcical, humorous, jocose, jocular, laughable, ludicrous, sportive, witty; curious, odd, queer, strange. * *n* jest, joke; cartoon, comic.

furbish *vb* burnish, brighten, polish, renew, renovate, rub, shine.

furious *adj* angry, fierce, frantic, frenzied, fuming, infuriated, mad, raging, violent, wild; boisterous, fierce, impetuous, stormy, tempestuous, tumultuous, turbulent, vehement.

furnish *vb* appoint, endow, provide, supply; decorate, equip, fit; afford, bestow, contribute, give, offer, present, produce, yield.

furniture *n* chattels, effects, household goods, movables; apparatus, appendages, appliances, equipment, fittings, furnishings; decorations, embellishments, ornaments.

furore *n* commotion, craze, enthusiasm, excitement, fad, fury, madness, mania, rage, vogue.

furrow *vb* chamfer, channel, cleave, corrugate, cut, flute, groove, hollow; pucker, seam, wrinkle. * *n* chamfer, channel, cut, depression, fluting, groove, hollow, line, seam, track, trench, rot, wrinkle.

further *vb* advance, aid, assist, encourage, help, forward, promote, succour, strengthen. * *adj* additional. * *adv* also, besides, farther, furthermore, moreover.

furtive *adj* clandestine, hidden, secret, sly, skulking, sneaking, sneaky, stealthy, stolen, surreptitious.

fury *n* anger, frenzy, fit, furore, ire, madness, passion, rage; fierceness, impetuosity, turbulence, turbulency, vehemence; bacchant, bacchante, bedlam, hag, shrew, termagant, virago, vixen.

fuse *vb* dissolve, melt, liquefy, smelt; amalgamate, blend, coalesce, combine, commingle, intermingle, intermix, merge, unite. * *n* match.

fusion *n* liquefaction, melting; amalgamation, blending, commingling, commixture, intermingling, intermixture, union; coalition, merging.

fuss *vb* bustle, fidget; fret, fume, worry. * *n* ado, agitation, bother, bustle, commotion, disturbance, excitement, fidget, flurry, fluster, fret, hurry, pother, stir, worry.

fustian *n* bombast, claptrap, rant, rodomontade; balderdash, inanity, nonsense, stuff, trash, twaddle.

fusty *adj* ill-smelling, malodorous, mildewed, mouldy, musty, rank.

futile *adj* frivolous, trifling, trivial; bootless, fruitless, idle, ineffectual, profitless, unavailing, unprofitable, useless, vain, valueless, worthless.

futility *n* frivolousness, triviality; bootlessness, fruitlessness, uselessness, vanity, worthlessness.

future *adj* coming, eventual, forthcoming, hereafter, prospective, subsequent. * *n* hereafter, outlook, prospect.

G

gabble vb babble, chatter, clack, gibber, gossip, prate, prattle. * n babble, chatter, clack, gap, gossip, jabber, palaver, prate, prattle, twaddle.

gadabout n idler, loafer, rambler, rover, vagrant; gossip, talebearer, vagrant.

gaffer n boss, foreman, overseer, supervisor.

gag[1] n jape, jest, joke, stunt, wisecrack.

gag[2] vb muffle, muzzle, shackle, silence, stifle, throttle; regurgitate, retch, throw up, vomit; choke, gasp, pant. * n muzzle.

gage n pawn, pledge, security, surety; challenge, defiance, gauntlet, glove.

gaiety n animation, blithesomeness, cheerfulness, glee, hilarity, jollity, joviality, merriment, mirth, vivacity.

gain vb achieve, acquire, earn, get, obtain, procure, reap, secure; conciliate, enlist, persuade, prevail, win; arrive, attain, reach; clear, net, profit. * n accretion, addition, gainings, profits, winnings; acquisition, earnings, emolument, lucre; advantage, benefit, blessing, good, profit.

gainful adj advantageous, beneficial, profitable; lucrative, paying, productive, remunerative.

gainsay vb contradict, controvert, deny, dispute, forbid.

gait n carriage, pace, step, stride, walk.

galaxy n assemblage, assembly, cluster, collection, constellation, group.

gale n blast, hurricane, squall, storm, tempest, tornado, typhoon.

gall[1] n effrontery, impudence; bile; acerbity, bitterness, malice, maliciousness, malignity, rancour, spite.

gall[2] vb chafe, excoriate, fret, hurt; affront, annoy, exasperate, harass, incense, irritate, plague, provoke, sting, tease, vex.

gallant adj fine, magnificent, showy, splendid, well-dressed; bold, brave, chivalrous, courageous, daring, fearless, heroic, high-spirited, intrepid, valiant, valorous; chivalrous, fine, honourable, high-minded, lofty, magnanimous, noble. * n beau, blade, spark; lover, suitor, wooer.

gallantry n boldness, bravery, chivalry, courage, courageousness, fearlessness, heroism, intrepidity, prowess, valour; courtesy, courteousness, elegance, politeness.

galling adj chafing, irritating, vexing.

gallop vb fly, hurry, run, rush, scamper, speed.

gamble vb bet, dice, game, hazard, plunge, speculate, wager. * n chance, risk, speculation; bet, punt, wager.

gambol vb caper, cut, frisk, frolic, hop, jump, leap, romp, skip. * n frolic, hop, jump, skip.

game[1] vb gamble, sport, stake. * n amusement, contest, diversion, pastime, play, sport; adventure, enterprise, measure, plan, project, scheme, stratagem, undertaking; prey, quarry, victim.

game[2] adj brave, courageous, dauntless, fearless, gallant, heroic, intrepid, plucky, unflinching, valorous; enduring, persevering, resolute, undaunted; ready, eager, willing.

game[3] adj crippled, disabled, halt, injured, lame.

gameness n bravery, courage, grit, heart, mettle, nerve, pith, pluck, pluckiness, spirit, stamina.

gamesome adj frisky, frolicsome, lively, merry, playful, sportive, sprightly, vivacious.

gammon vb bamboozle, beguile, cheat, circumvent, deceive, delude, dupe, gull, hoax, humbug, inveigle, mislead, overreach, outwit. * n bosh, hoax, humbug, imposition, nonsense.

gang n band, cabal, clique, company, coterie, crew, horde, party, set, troop.

gaol see **jail**.

gap n breach, break, cavity, chasm, chink, cleft, crack, cranny, crevice, hiatus, hollow, interval, interstice, lacuna, opening, pass, ravine, rift, space, vacancy.

gape vb burst open, dehisce, open, stare, yawn.

garb vb attire, clothe, dress. * n apparel, attire, clothes, costume, dress, garments, habiliment, habit, raiment, robes, uniform, vestment.

garbage n filth, offal, refuse, remains, rubbish, trash, waste.

garble vb corrupt, distort, falsify, misquote, misrepresent, mutilate, pervert.

gargantuan adj big, Brobdingnagian, colossal, enormous, gigantic, huge, prodigious, tremendous.

garish adj bright, dazzling, flashy, flaunting, gaudy, glaring, loud, showy, staring, tawdry.

garland vb adorn, festoon, wreathe. * n chaplet, coronal, crown, festoon, wreath.

garment n clothes, clothing, dress, habit, vestment.

garner vb accumulate, collect, deposit, gather, hoard, husband, reserve, save, store, treasure.

garnish vb adorn, beautify, bedeck, decorate, deck, embellish, grace, ornament, prank, trim. * n decoration, enhancement, ornament, trimming.

garrulous adj babbling, loquacious, prating, prattling, talkative.

gasconade n bluster, boast, brag, bravado, swagger, vaunt, vapouring.

gasp vb blow, choke, pant, puff. * n blow, exclamation, gulp, puff.

gather vb assemble, cluster, collect, convene, group, muster, rally; accumulate, amass, garner, hoard, huddle, lump; bunch, crop, cull, glean, pick, pluck, rake, reap, shock, stack; acquire, gain, get, win; conclude, deduce, derive, infer; fold, plait, pucker, shirr, tuck; condense, grow, increase, thicken.

gathering n acquisition, collecting, earning, gain, heap, pile, procuring; assemblage, assembly, collection, company, concourse, congregation, meeting, muster; abscess, boil, fester, pimple, pustule, sore, suppuration, tumour, ulcer.

gauche *adj* awkward, blundering, bungling, clumsy, inept, tactless, uncouth.

gaudy *adj* bespangled, brilliant, brummagem, cheap, flashy, flaunting, garish, gimcrack, glittering, loud, ostentatious, overdecorated, sham, showy, spurious, tawdry, tinsel.

gauge *vb* calculate, check, determine, weigh; assess, estimate, guess, reckon. * *n* criterion, example, indicator, measure, meter, touchstone, yardstick; bore, depth, height, magnitude, size, thickness, width.

gaunt *adj* angular, attenuated, emaciated, haggard, lank, lean, meagre, scraggy, skinny, slender, spare, thin.

gawky *adj* awkward, boorish, clownish, clumsy, green, loutish, raw, rustic, uncouth, ungainly.

gay *adj* bright, brilliant, dashing, fine, showy; flashy, flaunting, garish, gaudy, glittering, loud, tawdry, tinsel; airy, blithe, blithesome, cheerful, festive, frivolous, frolicsome, gladsome, gleeful, hilarious, jaunty, jolly, jovial, light-hearted, lively, merry, mirthful, sportive, sprightly, vivacious.

gear *vb* adapt, equip, fit, suit, tailor. * *n* apparel, array, clothes, clothing, dress, garb; accoutrements, appliances, appointments, appurtenances, array, harness, goods, movables, subsidiaries; harness, rigging, tackle, trappings; apparatus, machinery, mechanics.

gelid *adj* chill, chilly, cold, freezing, frigid, icy.

gem *n* jewel, stone, treasure.

genealogy *n* ancestry, descent, lineage, pedigree, stock.

general *adj* broad, collective, generic, popular, universal, widespread; catholic, ecumenical; common, current, ordinary, usual; inaccurate, indefinite, inexact, vague.

generally *adv* commonly, extensively, universally, usually.

generate *vb* beget, breed, engender, procreate, propagate, reproduce, spawn; cause, form, make, produce.

generation *n* creation, engendering, formation, procreation, production; age, epoch, era, period, time; breed, children, family, kind, offspring, progeny, race, stock.

generosity *n* disinterestedness, high-mindedness, magnanimity, nobleness; bounteousness, bountifulness, bounty, charity, liberality, openhandedness.

generous *adj* high-minded, honourable, magnanimous, noble; beneficent, bountiful, charitable, free, hospitable, liberal, munificent, open-handed; abundant, ample, copious, plentiful, rich.

genial *adj* cheering, encouraging, enlivening, fostering, inspiring, mild, warm; agreeable, cheerful, cordial, friendly, hearty, jovial, kindly, merry, mirthful, pleasant.

genius *n* aptitude, aptness, bent, capacity, endowment, faculty, flair, gift, talent, turn; brains, creative power, ingenuity, inspiration, intellect, invention, parts, sagacity, wit; adeptness, master, master hand, proficiency; character, disposition, naturalness, nature; deity, demon, spirit.

genteel *adj* aristocratic, courteous, gentlemanly, ladylike, polished, polite, refined, well-bred; elegant, fashionable, graceful, stylish.

gentility *n* civility, courtesy, good breeding, politeness, refinement, urbanity.

gentle *adj* amiable, bland, clement, compassionate, humane, indulgent, kind, kindly, lenient, meek, merciful, mild, moderate, soft, tender, tender-hearted; docile, pacific, peaceable, placid, quiet, tame, temperate,

tractable; bland, easy, gradual, light, slight, soft; high-born, noble, well-born; chivalrous, courteous, cultivated, knightly, polished, refined, well-bred.

gentlemanly *adj* civil, complaisant, courteous, cultivated, delicate, genteel, honourable, polite, refined, urbane, well-bred.

genuine *adj* authentic, honest, proper, pure, real, right, true, unadulterated, unalloyed, uncorrupted, veritable; frank, native, sincere, unaffected.

genus *n* class, group, kind, order, race, sort, type.

germ *n* embryo, nucleus, ovule, ovum, seed, seed-bud; bacterium, microbe, microorganism; beginning, cause, origin, rudiment, source.

germane *adj* akin, allied, cognate, related; apposite, appropriate, fitting, pertinent, relevant, suitable.

germinate *vb* bud, burgeon, develop, generate, grow, pollinate, push, shoot, sprout, vegetate.

gesture *vb* indicate, motion, signal, wave. * *n* action, attitude, gesticulation, gesturing, posture, sign, signal.

get *vb* achieve, acquire, attain, earn, gain, obtain, procure, receive, relieve, secure, win; finish, master, prepare; beget, breed, engender, generate, procreate.

gewgaw *n* bauble, gimcrack, gaud, kickshaw, knickknack, plaything, trifle, toy, trinket.

ghastly *adj* cadaverous, corpse-like, death-like, deathly, ghostly, lurid, pale, pallid, wan; dismal, dreadful, fearful, frightful, grim, grisly, gruesome, hideous, horrible, shocking, terrible.

ghost *n* soul, spirit; apparition, phantom, revenant, shade, spectre, spook, sprite, wraith.

giant *adj* colossal, enormous, Herculean, huge, large, monstrous, prodigious, vast. * *n* colossus, cyclops, Hercules, monster.

gibberish *n* babble, balderdash, drivel, gabble, gobbledygook, jabber, nonsense, prate, prating.

gibe, jibe *vb* deride, fleer, flout, jeer, mock, ridicule, scoff, sneer, taunt. * *n* ridicule, sneer, taunt.

giddiness *n* dizziness, head-spinning, vertigo.

giddy *adj* dizzy, head-spinning, vertiginous; careless, changeable, fickle, flighty, frivolous, hare-brained, headlong, heedless, inconstant, irresolute, lightheaded, thoughtless, unsteady, vacillating, wild.

gift *n* alms, allowance, benefaction, bequest, bonus, boon, bounty, contribution, donation, dowry, endowment, favour, grant, gratuity, honorarium, largesse, legacy, offering, premium, present, prize, subscription, subsidy, tip; faculty, talent.

gifted *adj* able, capable, clever, ingenious, intelligent, inventive, sagacious, talented.

gigantic *adj* colossal, Cyclopean, enormous, giant, herculean, huge, immense, prodigious, titanic, tremendous, vast.

giggle *vb, n* cackle, grin, laugh, snigger, snicker, titter.

gild *vb* adorn, beautify, bedeck, brighten, decorate, embellish, grace, illuminate.

gimcrack *adj* flimsy, frail, puny; base, cheap, paltry, poor. * *n* bauble, knick-knack, toy, trifle.

gird *vb* belt, girdle; begird, encircle, enclose, encompass, engird, environ, surround; brace, support. * *n* band, belt, cincture, girdle, girth, sash, waistband.

gist *n* basis, core, essence, force, ground, marrow, meaning, pith, point, substance.

give *vb* accord, bequeath, bestow, confer, devise, entrust, present; afford, contribute, donate, furnish, grant, proffer, spare, supply; communicate, impart; deliver, exchange, pay, requite; allow, permit, vouchsafe; emit, pronounce, render, utter; produce, yield;

cause, occasion; apply, devote, surrender; bend, sink, recede, retire, retreat, yield.

glad *adj* delighted, gratified, happy, pleased, rejoicing, well-contented; animated, blithe, cheerful, cheery, elated, gladsome, jocund, joyful, joyous, light, light-hearted, merry, playful, radiant; animating, bright, cheering, exhilarating, gladdening, gratifying, pleasing.

gladden *vb* bless, cheer, delight, elate, enliven, exhilarate, gratify, please, rejoice.

gladiator *n* prize-fighter, sword-player, swordsman.

gladness *n* animation, cheerfulness, delight, gratification, happiness, joy, joyfulness, joyousness, pleasure.

gladsome *adj* airy, blithe, blithesome, cheerful, delighted, frolicsome, glad, gleeful, jocund, jolly, jovial, joyful, joyous, light-hearted, lively, merry, pleased, sportive, sprightly, vivacious.

glamour *n* bewitchment, charm, enchantment, fascination, spell, witchery.

glance *vb* coruscate, gleam, glisten, glister, glitter, scintillate, shine; dart, flit; gaze, glimpse, look, view. * *n* gleam, glitter; gleam, look, view.

glare *vb* dazzle, flame, flare, gleam, glisten, glitter, sparkle; frown, gaze, glower. * *n* flare, glitter.

glaring *adj* dazzling, gleaming, glistening, glittering; barefaced, conspicuous, extreme, manifest, notorious, open.

glassy *adj* brilliant, crystal, crystalline, gleaming, lucent, shining, transparent.

glaze *vb* burnish, calender, furbish, gloss, polish. * *n* coat, enamel, finish, glazing, polish, varnish.

gleam *vb* beam, coruscate, flash, glance, glimmer, glitter, shine, sparkle. * *n* beam, flash, glance, glimmer, glimmering, glow, ray; brightness, coruscation, flashing, gleaming, glitter, glittering, lustre, splendour.

glean *vb* collect, cull, gather, get, harvest, pick, select.

glee *n* exhilaration, fun, gaiety, hilarity, jocularity, jollity, joviality, joy, liveliness, merriment, mirth, sportiveness, verve.

glib *adj* slippery, smooth; artful, facile, flippant, fluent, ready, talkative, voluble.

glide *vb* float, glissade, roll on, skate, skim, slide, slip; flow, lapse, run, roll. * *n* gliding, lapse, sliding, slip.

glimmer *vb* flash, flicker, gleam, glitter, shine, twinkle. * *n* beam, gleam, glimmering, ray; glance, glimpse.

glimpse *vb* espy, look, spot, view. * *n* flash, glance, glimmering, glint, look, sight.

glitter *vb* coruscate, flare, flash, glance, glare, gleam, glisten, glister, scintillate, shine, sparkle. * *n* beam, beaming, brightness, brilliancy, coruscation, gleam, glister, lustre, radiance, scintillation, shine, sparkle, splendour.

gloaming *n* dusk, eventide, nightfall, twilight.

gloat *vb* exult, gaze, rejoice, stare, triumph.

globe *n* ball, earth, orb, sphere.

globular *adj* globate, globated, globe-shaped, globose, globous, round, spheral, spheric, spherical.

globule *n* bead, drop, particle, spherule.

gloom *n* cloud, darkness, dimness, gloominess, obscurity, shade, shadow; cheerlessness, dejection, depression, despondency, downheartedness, dullness, melancholy, sadness.

gloomy *adj* dark, dim, dusky, obscure; cheerless, dismal, lowering, lurid; crestfallen, dejected, depressed, despondent, disheartened, dispirited, downcast, downhearted, glum, melancholy, morose, sad, sullen;

depressing, disheartening, dispiriting, heavy, saddening.

glorify *vb* adore, bless, celebrate, exalt, extol, honour, laud, magnify, worship; adorn, brighten, elevate, ennoble, make bright.

glorious *adj* celebrated, conspicuous, distinguished, eminent, excellent, famed, famous, illustrious, preeminent, renowned; brilliant, bright, grand, magnificent, radiant, resplendent, splendid; consummate, exalted, high, lofty, noble, supreme.

glory *vb* boast, exult, vaunt. * *n* celebrity, distinction, eminence, fame, honour, illustriousness, praise, renown; brightness, brilliancy, effulgence, lustre, pride, resplendence, splendour; exaltation, exceeding, gloriousness, greatness, grandeur, nobleness; bliss, happiness.

gloss[1] *vb* coat, colour, disguise, extenuate, glaze, palliate, varnish, veneer, veil. * *n* coating, lustre, polish, sheen, varnish, veneer; pretence, pretext.

gloss[2] *vb* annotate, comment, elucidate, explain, interpret. * *n* annotation, comment, commentary, elucidation, explanation, interpretation, note.

glove *n* gantlet, gauntlet, handwear, mitt, mitten; challenge.

glow *vb* incandesce, radiate, shine; blush, burn, flush, redden. * *n* blaze, brightness, brilliance, burning, incandescence, luminosity, reddening; ardour, bloom, enthusiasm, fervency, fervour, flush, impetuosity, vehemence, warmth.

glower *vb* frown, glare, lower, scowl, stare. * *n* frown, glare, scowl.

glum *adj* churlish, crabbed, crestfallen, cross-grained, crusty, depressed, frowning, gloomy, glowering, moody, morose, sour, spleenish, spleeny, sulky, sullen, surly.

glut *vb* block up, cloy, cram, gorge, satiate, stuff. * *n* excess, saturation, surfeit, surplus.

glutinous *adj* adhesive, clammy, cohesive, gluey, gummy, sticky, tenacious, viscid, viscous.

glutton *n* gobbler, gorger, gourmand, gormandizer, greedy-guts, lurcher, pig.

gnarled *adj* contorted, cross-grained, gnarly, knotted, knotty, snaggy, twisted.

go *vb* advance, move, pass, proceed, progress repair; act, operate; be about, extravagate, fare, journey, roam, rove, travel, walk, wend; depart, disappear, cease; elapse, extend, lead, reach, run; avail, concur, contribute, tend, serve; eventuate, fare, turn out; afford, bet, risk, wager. * *n* action, business, case, chance, circumstance, doings, turn; custom, fad, fashion, mode, vogue; energy, endurance, power, stamina, verve, vivacity.

goad *vb* annoy, badger, harass, irritate, sting, worry; arouse, impel, incite, instigate, prod, spur, stimulate, urge. * *n* incentive, incitement, pressure, stimulation.

goal *n* bound, home, limit, mark, mete, post; end, object; aim, design, destination.

gobble *vb* bolt, devour, gorge, gulp, swallow.

goblin *n* apparition, elf, bogey, demon, gnome, hobgoblin, phantom, spectre, sprite.

god *n* almighty, creator, deity, divinity, idol, Jehovah, omnipotence, providence.

godless *adj* atheistic, impious, irreligious, profane, ungodly, wicked.

godlike *adj* celestial, divine, heavenly, supernal.

godly *adj* devout, holy, pious, religious, righteous, saint-like, saintly.

godsend n fortune, gift, luck, present, windfall.

golden adj aureate, brilliant, bright, gilded, resplendent, shining, splendid; excellent, precious; auspicious, favourable, opportune, propitious; blessed, delightful, glorious, halcyon, happy.

good adj advantageous, beneficial, favourable, profitable, serviceable, useful; adequate, appropriate, becoming, convenient, fit, proper, satisfactory, suitable, well-adapted; decorous, dutiful, honest, just, pious, reliable, religious, righteous, true, upright, virtuous, well-behaved, worthy; admirable, capable, excellent, genuine, healthy, precious, sincere, sound, sterling, valid, valuable; benevolent, favourable, friendly, gracious, humane, kind, merciful, obliging, well-disposed; fair, honourable, immaculate, unblemished, unimpeachable, unimpeached, unsullied, untarnished; cheerful, companionable, lively, genial, social; able, competent, dextrous, expert, qualified, ready, skilful, thorough, well-qualified; credit-worthy; agreeable, cheering, gratifying, pleasant. * n advantage, benefit, boon, favour, gain, profit, utility; interest, prosperity, welfare, weal; excellence, righteousness, virtue, worth.

good breeding n affability, civility, courtesy, good manners, polish, politeness, urbanity.

goodbye n adieu, farewell, parting.

goodly adj beautiful, comely, good-looking, graceful; agreeable, considerate, desirable, happy, pleasant.

good-natured adj amiable, benevolent, friendly, kind, kind-hearted, kindly.

goodness n excellence, quality, value, worth; honesty, integrity, morality, principle, probity, righteousness, uprightness, virtue; benevolence, beneficence, benignity, good-will, humaneness, humanity, kindness.

goods npl belongings, chattels, effects, furniture, movables; commodities, merchandise, stock, wares.

goodwill n benevolence, kindness, good nature; ardour, earnestness, heartiness, willingness, zeal; custom, patronage.

gore vb horn, pierce, stab, wound.

gorge[1] vb bolt, devour, eat, feed, swallow; cram, fill, glut, gormandize, sate, satiate, stuff, surfeit. * n craw, crop, gullet, throat.

gorge[2] n canyon, defile, fissure, notch, ravine.

gorgeous adj bright, brilliant, dazzling, fine, glittering, grand, magnificent, resplendent, rich, shining, showy, splendid, superb.

Gorgon n bugaboo, fright, hobgoblin, hydra, ogre, spectre.

gory adj bloody, ensanguined, sanguinary.

gospel n creed, doctrine, message, news, revelation, tidings.

gossip vb chat, cackle, clack, gabble, prate, prattle, tattle. * n babbler, busybody, chatterer, gossipmonger, newsmonger, quidnunc, tale-bearer, tattler, tell-tale; cackle, chat, chit-chat, prate, prattle, tattle.

gourmet n connoisseur, epicure, epicurean.

govern vb administer, conduct, direct, manage, regulate, reign, rule, superintend, supervise; guide, pilot, steer; bridle, check, command, control, curb, restrain, rule, sway.

government n autonomy, command, conduct, control, direction, discipline, dominion, guidance, management, regulation, restraint, rule, rulership, sway; administration, cabinet, commonwealth, polity, sovereignty, state.

governor n commander, comptroller, director, head, headmaster, manager, overseer, ruler, superintendent, supervisor; chief magistrate, executive; guardian, instructor, tutor.

grab vb capture, clutch, seize, snatch.

grace vb adorn, beautify, deck, decorate, embellish; dignify, honour. * n benignity, condescension, favour, good-will, kindness, love; devotion, efficacy, holiness, love, piety, religion, sanctity, virtue; forgiveness, mercy, pardon, reprieve; accomplishment, attractiveness, charm, elegance, polish, propriety, refinement; beauty, comeliness, ease, gracefulness, symmetry; blessing, petition, thanks.

graceful adj beautiful, becoming, comely, easy, elegant; flowing, natural, rounded, unlaboured; appropriate; felicitous, happy, tactful.

graceless adj abandoned, corrupt, depraved, dissolute, hardened, incorrigible, irreclaimable, lost, obdurate, profligate, reprobate, repugnant, shameless,

gracious adj beneficent, benevolent, benign, benignant, compassionate, condescending, favourable, friendly, gentle, good-natured, kind, kindly, lenient, merciful, mild, tender; affable, civil, courteous, easy, familiar, polite.

grade vb arrange, classify, group, order, rank, sort. * n brand, degree, intensity, stage, step, rank; gradient, incline, slope.

gradual adj approximate, continuous, gentle, progressive, regular, slow, successive.

graduate vb adapt, adjust, proportion, regulate. * n alumna, alumnus, laureate, postgraduate.

graft vb ingraft, inoculate, insert, transplant. * n bud, scion, shoot, slip, sprout; corruption, favouritism, influence, nepotism.

grain n kernel, ovule, seed; cereals, corn, grist; atom, bit, glimmer, jot, particle, scintilla, scrap, shadow, spark, tittle, trace, whit; disposition, fibre, humour, temper, texture; colour, dye, hue, shade, stain, texture, tincture, tinge.

granary n corn-house, garner, grange, store-house.

grand adj august, dignified, elevated, eminent, exalted, great, illustrious, lordly, majestic, princely, stately, sublime; fine, glorious, gorgeous, magnificent, pompous, lofty, noble, splendid, superb; chief, leading, main, pre-eminent, principal, superior.

grandee n lord, noble, nobleman.

grandeur n elevation, greatness, immensity, impressiveness, loftiness, vastness; augustness, dignity, eminence, glory, magnificence, majesty, nobility, pomp, splendour, state, stateliness.

grandiloquent adj bombastic, declamatory, high-minded, high-sounding, inflated, pompous, rhetorical, stilted, swelling, tumid, turgid.

grant vb accord, admit, allow, sanction; cede, concede, give, impart, indulge; bestow, confer, deign, invest, vouchsafe; convey, transfer, yield. * n admission, allowance, benefaction, bestowal, boon, bounty, concession, donation, endowment, gift, indulgence, largesse, present; conveyance, cession.

graphic adj descriptive, diagrammatic, figural, figurative, forcible, lively, pictorial, picturesque, striking, telling, vivid, well-delineated, well-drawn.

grapple vb catch, clutch, grasp, grip, hold, hug, seize, tackle, wrestle.

grasp vb catch, clasp, clinch, clutch, grapple, grip, seize; comprehend, understand. * n clasp, grip, hold; comprehension, power, reach, scope, understanding.

grasping *adj* acquisitive, avaricious, covetous, exacting, greedy, rapacious, sordid, tight-fisted.

grate *vb* abrade, rub, scrape, triturate; comminute, rasp; creak, fret, grind, jar, vex. * *n* bars, grating, lattice-work, screen; basket, fire bed.

grateful *adj* appreciative, beholden, indebted, obliged, sensible, thankful; pleasant, welcome.

gratification *n* gratifying, indulgence, indulging, pleasing, satisfaction, satisfying; delight, enjoyment, fruition, pleasure, reward.

gratify *vb* delight, gladden, please; humour, fulfil, grant, indulge, requite, satisfy.

gratifying *adj* agreeable, delightful, grateful, pleasing, welcome.

grating *adj* disagreeable, displeasing, harsh, irritating, offensive. * *n* grate, partition.

gratis *adv* freely, gratuitously.

gratitude *n* goodwill, gratitude, indebtedness, thankfulness.

gratuitous *adj* free, spontaneous, unrewarded, voluntary; assumed, baseless, groundless, unfounded, unwarranted, wanton.

gratuity *n* benefaction, bounty, charity, donation, endowment, gift, grant, largesse, present.

grave[1] *n* crypt, mausoleum, ossuary, pit, sepulchre, sepulture, tomb, vault.

grave[2] *adj* cogent, heavy, important, momentous, ponderous, pressing, serious, weighty; dignified, sage, sedate, serious, slow, solemn, staid, thoughtful; dull, grim, plain, quiet, sober, sombre, subdued; cruel, hard, harsh, severe; despicable, dire, dismal, gross, heinous, infamous, outrageous, scandalous, shameful, shocking; heavy, hollow, low, low-pitched, sepulchral.

grave[3] *vb* engrave, impress, imprint, infix; carve, chisel, cut, sculpt.

gravel *vb* bewilder, embarrass, nonplus, perplex, pose, puzzle, stagger. * *n* ballast, grit, sand, shingle.

graveyard *n* burial ground, cemetery, churchyard, god's acre, mortuary, necropolis.

gravity *n* heaviness, weight; demureness, sedateness, seriousness, sobriety, thoughtfulness; importance, moment, momentousness, weightiness.

graze *vb* brush, glance, scrape, scratch; abrade, shave, skim; browse, crop, feed, pasture. * *n* abrasion, bruise, scrape, scratch.

great *adj* ample, big, bulky, Cyclopean, enormous, gigantic, Herculean, huge, immense, large, pregnant, vast; decided, excessive, high, much, pronounced; countless, numerous; chief, considerable, grand, important, leading, main, pre-eminent, principal, superior, weighty; celebrated, distinguished, eminent, exalted, excellent, famed, famous, far-famed, illustrious, noted, prominent, renowned; august, dignified, elevated, grand, lofty, majestic, noble, sublime; chivalrous, generous, high-minded, magnanimous; fine, magnificent, rich, sumptuous.

greatness *n* bulk, dimensions, largeness, magnitude, size; distinction, elevation, eminence, fame, importance, renown; augustness, dignity, grandeur, majesty, loftiness, nobility, nobleness, sublimity; chivalry, generosity, magnanimity, spirit.

greed, greediness *n* gluttony, hunger, omnivorousness, ravenousness, voracity; avidity, covetousness, desire, eagerness, longing; avarice, cupidity, graspingness, grasping, rapacity, selfishness.

greedy *adj* devouring, edacious, gluttonous, insatiable, insatiate, rapacious, ravenous, voracious; desirous, eager; avaricious, grasping, selfish.

green *adj* aquamarine, emerald, olive, verdant, verdure, viridescent, viridian; blooming, flourishing, fresh, undecayed; fresh, new, recent; immature, unfledged, unripe; callow, crude, inexpert, ignorant, inexperienced, raw, unskilful, untrained, verdant, young; unseasoned; conservationist, ecological, environmentalist. * *n* common, grass plot, lawn, sward, turf, verdure.

greenhorn *n* beginner, novice, tyro.

greet *vb* accost, address, complement, hail, receive, salute, welcome.

greeting *n* compliment, salutation, salute, welcome.

grief *n* affliction, agony, anguish, bitterness, distress, dole, heartbreak, misery, regret, sadness, sorrow, suffering, tribulation, mourning, woe; grievance, trial; disaster, failure, mishap.

grievance *n* burden, complaint, hardship, injury, oppression, wrong; affliction, distress, grief, sorrow, trial, woe.

grieve *vb* afflict, aggrieve, agonize, discomfort, distress, hurt, oppress, pain, sadden, wound; bewail, deplore, mourn, lament, regret, sorrow, suffer.

grievous *adj* afflicting, afflictive, burdensome, deplorable, distressing, heavy, lamentable, oppressive, painful, sad, sorrowful; baleful, baneful, calamitous, destructive, detrimental, hurtful, injurious, mischievous, noxious, troublesome; aggravated, atrocious, dreadful, flagitious, flagrant, gross, heinous, iniquitous, intense, intolerable, severe, outrageous, wicked.

grill *vb* broil, griddle, roast, toast; sweat; cross-examine, interrogate, question; torment, torture. * *n* grating, gridiron; cross-examination, cross-questioning.

grim *adj* cruel, ferocious, fierce, harsh, relentless, ruthless, savage, stern, unyielding; appalling, dire, dreadful, fearful, frightful, grisly, hideous, horrid, horrible, terrific.

grimace *vb, n* frown, scowl, smirk, sneer.

grime *n* dirt, filth, foulness, smut.

grimy *adj* begrimed, defiled, dirty, filthy, foul, soiled, sullied, unclean.

grind *vb* bruise, crunch, crush, grate, grit, pulverize, rub, triturate; sharpen, whet; afflict, harass, oppress, persecute, plague, trouble. * *n* chore, drudgery, labour, toil.

grip *vb* clasp, clutch, grasp, hold, seize. * *n* clasp, clutch, control, domination, grasp, hold.

grisly *adj* appalling, frightful, dreadful, ghastly, grim, grey, hideous, horrible, horrid, terrible, terrific.

grit *vb* clench, grate, grind. * *n* bran, gravel, pebbles, sand; courage, decision, determination, firmness, perseverance, pluck, resolution, spirit.

groan *vb* complain, lament, moan, whine; creak. * *n* cry, moan, whine; complaint; grouse, grumble.

groom *vb* clean, dress, tidy; brush, tend; coach, educate, nurture, train. * *n* equerry, hostler, manservant, ostler, servant, stable-hand, valet, waiter.

groove *n* channel, cut, furrow, rabbet, rebate, recess, rut, scoring; routine.

gross *vb* accumulate, earn, make. * *adj* big, bulky, burly, fat, great, large; dense, dull, stupid, thick; beastly, broad, carnal, coarse, crass, earthy, impure, indelicate, licentious, low, obscene, unbecoming, unrefined, unseemly, vulgar, rough, sensual; aggravated, brutal, enormous, flagrant, glaring, grievous, manifest, obvious, palpable, plain, outrageous, shameful; aggregate, entire, total, whole. * n aggregate, bulk, total, whole.

grossness n bigness, bulkiness, greatness; density, thickness; coarseness, ill-breeding, rudeness, vulgarity; bestiality, brutality, carnality, coarseness, impurity, indelicacy, licentiousness, sensuality.

grotesque adj bizarre, extravagant, fanciful, fantastic, incongruous, odd, strange, unnatural, whimsical, wild; absurd, antic, burlesque, ludicrous, ridiculous.

ground vb fell, place; base, establish, fix, found, set; instruct, train. * n area, clod, distance, earth, loam, mould, sod, soil, turf; country, domain, land, region, territory; acres, estate, field, property; base, basis, foundation, groundwork, support; account, consideration, excuse, gist, motive, opinion, reason.

groundless adj baseless, causeless, false, gratuitous, idle, unauthorized, unfounded, unjustifiable, unsolicited, unsought, unwarranted.

grounds npl deposit, dregs, grouts, lees, precipitate, sediment, settlings; accounts, arguments, considerations, reasons, support; campus, gardens, lawns, premises, yard.

group vb arrange, assemble, dispose, order. * n aggregation, assemblage, assembly, body, combination, class, clump, cluster, collection, order.

grove n copse, glade, spinney, thicket, wood, woodland.

grovel vb cower, crawl, creep, cringe, fawn, flatter, sneak.

grovelling adj creeping, crouching, squat; abject, base, beggarly, cringing, fawning, low, mean, servile, slavish, sneaking, undignified, unworthy, vile.

grow vb enlarge, expand, extend, increase, swell; arise, burgeon, develop, germinate, shoot, sprout, vegetate; advance, extend, improve, progress, thrive, wax; cultivate, produce, raise.

growl vb complain, croak, find fault, gnarl, groan, grumble, lament, murmur, snarl. * n croak, grown, snarl; complaint.

growth n augmentation, development, expansion, extension, growing, increase; burgeoning, excrescence, formation, germination, pollution, shooting, sprouting, vegetation; cultivation, produce, product, production; advance, advancement, development, improvement, progress; adulthood, maturity.

grub vb clear, dig, eradicate, root. * n caterpillar, larvae, maggot; drudge, plodder.

grudge vb begrudge, envy, repine; complain, grieve, murmur. * n aversion, dislike, enmity, grievance, hate, hatred, ill-will, malevolence, malice, pique, rancour, resentment, spite, venom.

gruff adj bluff, blunt, brusque, churlish, discourteous, grumpy, harsh, impolite, rough, rude, rugged, surly, uncivil, ungracious.

grumble vb croak, complain, murmur, repine; gnarl, growl, snarl; roar, rumble. * n growl, murmur, complaint, roar, rumble.

grumpy adj crabbed, cross, glum, moody, morose, sour, sullen, surly.

guarantee vb assure, insure, pledge, secure, warrant. * n assurance, pledge, security, surety, warrant, warranty.

guard vb defend, keep, patrol, protect, safeguard, save, secure, shelter, shield, watch. * n aegis, bulwark, custody, defence, palladium, protection, rampart, safeguard, security, shield; keeper, guardian, patrol, sentinel, sentry, warden, watch, watchman; conduct, convoy, escort; attention, care, caution, circumspection, heed, watchfulness.

guarded adj careful, cautious, circumspect, reserved, reticent, wary, watchful.

guardian n custodian, defender, guard, keeper, preserver, protector, trustee, warden.

guerdon n recompense, remuneration, requital, reward.

guess vb conjecture, divine, mistrust, surmise, suspect; fathom, find out, penetrate, solve; believe, fancy, hazard, imagine, reckon, suppose, think. * n conjecture, divination, notion, supposition, surmise.

guest n caller, company, visitant.

guidance n conduct, control, direction, escort, government, lead, leadership, pilotage, steering.

guide vb conduct, escort, lead, pilot; control, direct, govern, manage, preside, regulate, rule, steer, superintend, supervise. * n cicerone, conductor, director, monitor, pilot; adviser, counsellor, instructor, mentor; clew, directory, index, key, thread; guidebook, itinerary, landmark.

guild n association, brotherhood, company, corporation, fellowship, fraternity, society, union.

guile n art, artfulness, artifice, craft, cunning, deceit, deception, duplicity, fraud, knavery, ruse, subtlety, treachery, trickery, wiles, wiliness.

guileless adj artless, candid, frank, honest, ingenuous, innocent, open, pure, simple-minded, sincere, straightforward, truthful, undesigning, unsophisticated.

guilt n blame, criminality, culpability, guiltless; ill-desert, iniquity, offensiveness, wickedness, wrong; crime, offence, sin.

guiltless adj blameless, immaculate, innocent, pure, sinless, spotless, unpolluted, unspotted, unsullied, untarnished.

guilty adj criminal, culpable, evil, sinful, wicked, wrong.

guise n appearance, aspect, costume, dress, fashion, figure, form, garb, manner, mode, shape; air, behaviour, demeanour, mien; cover, custom, disguise, habit, pretence, pretext, practice.

gulf n abyss, chasm, opening; bay, inlet; whirlpool.

gull vb beguile, cheat, circumvent, cozen, deceive, dupe, hoax, overreach, swindle, trick. * n cheat, deception, hoax, imposition, fraud, trick; cat's paw, dupe.

gullibility n credulity, naiveness, naivety, overtrustfulness, simplicity, unsophistication.

gullible adj confiding, credulous, naive, overtrustful, simple, unsophisticated, unsuspicious.

gumption n ability, astuteness, cleverness, capacity, common sense, discernment, penetration, power, sagacity, shrewdness, skill; courage, guts, spirit.

gun n blunderbuss, cannon, carbine, firearm, musket, pistol, revolver, rifle, shotgun.

gurgle vb babble, bubble, murmur, purl, ripple. * n babbling, murmur, ripple.

gush vb burst, flood, flow, pour, rush, spout, stream; emotionalize, sentimentalize. * n flow, jet, onrush, rush, spurt, surge; effusion, effusiveness, loquacity, loquaciousness, talkativeness.

gushing adj flowing, issuing, rushing; demonstrative, effusive, sentimental.

gust vb blast, blow, puff. * n blast, blow, squall; burst, fit, outburst, paroxysm.

gusto n enjoyment, gust, liking, pleasure, relish, zest.

gusty *adj* blustering, blustery, puffy, squally, stormy, tempestuous, unsteady, windy.

gut *vb* destroy, disembowel, embowel, eviscerate, paunch. * *n* bowels, entrails, intestines, inwards, viscera.

gutter *n* channel, conduit, kennel, pipe, tube.

guttural *adj* deep, gruff, hoarse, thick, throaty.

guy *vb* caricature, mimic, ridicule. * *n* boy, man, person; dowdy, eccentric, fright, scarecrow.

guzzle *vb* carouse, drink, gorge, gormandize, quaff, swill, tipple, tope.

gyrate *vb* revolve, rotate, spin, whirl.

H

habiliment *n* apparel, attire, clothes, costume, dress, garb, garment, habit, raiment, robes, uniform, vesture, vestment.

habit *vb* accoutre, array, attire, clothe, dress, equip, robe. * *n* condition, constitution, temperament; addiction, custom, habitude, manner, practice, rule, usage, way, wont; apparel, costume, dress, garb, habiliment.

habitation *n* abode, domicile, dwelling, headquarters, home, house, lodging, quarters, residence.

habitual *adj* accustomed, common, confirmed, customary, everyday, familiar, inveterate, ordinary, regular, routine, settled, usual, wonted.

habituate *vb* accustom, familiarize, harden, inure, train, use.

habitude *n* custom, practice, usage, wont.

hack[1] *vb* chop, cut, hew, mangle, mutilate, notch; cough, rasp. * *n* cut, cleft, incision, notch; cough, rasp.

hack[2] *vb* ride. * *adj* hired, mercenary; banal, hackneyed, pedestrian, uninspired, unoriginal. * *n* horse, nag, pony; hireling, mercenary; journalist, scribbler, writer.

hackneyed *adj* banal, common, commonplace, overworked, pedestrian, stale, threadbare, trite.

hag *n* beldame, crone, fury, harridan, jezebel, she-monster, shrew, termagant, virago, vixen, witch.

haggard *adj* intractable, refractory, unruly, untamed, wild, wayward; careworn, emaciated, gaunt, ghastly, lank, lean, meagre, raw, spare, thin, wasted, worn.

haggle *vb* argue, bargain, cavil, chaffer, dispute, higgle, stickle; annoy, badger, bait, fret, harass, tease, worry.

hail[1] *vb* acclaim, greet, salute, welcome; accost, address, call, hallo, signal. * *n* greeting, salute.

hail[2] *vb* assail, bombard, rain, shower, storm, volley. * *n* bombardment, rain, shower, storm, volley.

halcyon *adj* calm, golden, happy, palmy, placid, peaceful, quiet, serene, still, tranquil, unruffled, undisturbed.

hale *adj* hardy, healthy, hearty, robust, sound, strong, vigorous, well.

halfwit *n* blockhead, dunce, moron, simpleton.

halfwitted *adj* doltish, dull, dull-witted, feeble-minded, foolish, sappy, shallow, silly, simple, soft, stolid, stupid, thick.

hall *n* chamber, corridor, entrance, entry, hallway, lobby, passage, vestibule; manor, manor-house; auditorium, lecture-room.

halloo *vb* call, cry, shout. * *n* call, cry, hallo, holla, hollo, shout.

hallow *vb* consecrate, dedicate, devote, revere, sanctify, solemnize; enshrine, honour, respect, reverence, venerate.

hallowed *adj* blessed, holy, honoured, revered, sacred.

hallucination *n* blunder, error, fallacy, mistake; aberration, delusion, illusion, phantasm, phantasy, self-deception, vision.

halo *n* aura, aureole, glory, nimbus.

halt[1] *vb* cease, desist, hold, rest, stand, stop. * *n* end, impasse, pause, standstill, stop.

halt[2] *vb* hesitate, pause, stammer, waver; falter, hobble, limp. * *adj* crippled, disabled, lame. * *n* hobble, limp.

hammer *vb* beat, forge, form, shape; excogitate, contrive, invent.

hammer and tongs *adv* earnestly, energetically, resolutely, strenuously, vigorously, zealously.

hamper *vb* bind, clog, confine, curb, embarrass, encumber, entangle, fetter, hinder, impede, obstruct, prevent, restrain, restrict, shackle, trammel. * *n* basket, box, crate, picnic basket; embarrassment, encumbrance, fetter, handicap, impediment, obstruction, restraint, trammel.

hand *vb* deliver, give, present, transmit; conduct, guide, lead. * *n* direction, part, side; ability, dexterity, faculty, skill, talent; course, inning, management, turn; agency, intervention, participation, share; control, possession, power; artificer, artisan, craftsman, employee, labourer, operative, workman; index, indicator, pointer; chirography, handwriting.

handbook *n* guidebook, manual.

handcuff *vb* bind, fetter, manacle, shackle. * *n* fetter, manacle, shackle.

handful *n* fistful, maniple, smattering.

handicap *vb* encumber, hamper, hinder, restrict. * *n* disadvantage, encumbrance, hampering, hindrance, restriction.

handicraft *n* hand manufacture, handwork, workmanship.

handle *vb* feel, finger, manhandle, paw, touch; direct, manage, manipulate, use, wield; discourse, discuss, treat. * *n* haft, helve, hilt, stock.

handsome *adj* admirable, comely, fine-looking, stately, well-formed, well-proportioned; appropriate, suitable, becoming, easy, graceful; generous, gracious, liberal, magnanimous, noble; ample, large, plentiful, sufficient.

handy *adj* adroit, clever, dextrous, expert, ready, skilful, skilled; close, convenient, near.

hang *vb* attach, swing; execute, truss; decline, drop, droop, incline; adorn, drape; dangle, depend, impend, suspend; rely; cling, loiter, rest, stick; float, hover, pay.

hangdog *adj* ashamed, base, blackguard, low, villainous, scurvy, sneaking.

hanger-on *n* dependant, minion, parasite, vassal.

hanker *vb* covet, crave, desire, hunger, long, lust, want, yearn.

hap *n* accident, chance, fate, fortune, lot.

haphazard *adj* aimless, chance, random.

hapless *adj* ill-fated, ill-starred, luckless, miserable, unfortunate, unhappy, unlucky, wretched.

happen *vb* befall, betide, chance, come, occur.

happily *adv* fortunately, luckily; agreeably, delightfully, prosperously, successfully.

happiness *n* brightness, cheerfulness, delight, gaiety, joy, light-heartedness, merriment, pleasure; beatitude, blessedness, bliss, felicity, enjoyment, welfare, well-being.

happy *adj* blessed, blest, blissful, cheerful, contented, joyful, joyous, light-hearted, merry; charmed, delighted, glad, gladdened, gratified, pleased; fortunate, lucky, prosperous, successful; able, adroit, apt, dextrous, expert, ready, skilful; befitting, felicitous, opportune, pertinent, seasonable, well-timed; auspicious, bright, favourable, propitious.

harangue *vb* address, declaim, spout. * *n* address, bombast, declamation, oration, rant, screed, speech, tirade.

harass *vb* exhaust, fag, fatigue, jade, tire, weary; annoy, badger, distress, gall, heckle, disturb, harry, molest, pester, plague, tantalize, tease, torment, trouble, vex, worry.

harbour *vb* protect, lodge, shelter; cherish, entertain, foster, indulge. * *n* asylum, cover, refuge, resting place, retreat, sanctuary, shelter; anchorage, destination, haven, port.

hard *adj* adamantine, compact, firm, flinty, impenetrable, marble, rigid, solid, resistant, stony, stubborn, unyielding; difficult, intricate, knotty, perplexing, puzzling; arduous, exacting, fatiguing, laborious, toilsome, wearying; austere, callous, cruel, exacting, hard-hearted, incorrigible, inflexible, insensible, insensitive, obdurate, oppressive, reprobate, rigorous, severe, unfeeling, unkind, unsusceptible, unsympathetic, unyielding, untender; calamitous, disagreeable, distressing, grievous, painful, unpleasant; acid, alcoholic, harsh, rough, sour; excessive, intemperate. * *adv* close, near; diligently, earnestly, energetically, incessantly, laboriously; distressfully, painfully, rigorously, severely; forcibly, vehemently, violently.

harden *vb* accustom, discipline, form, habituate, inure, season, train; brace, fortify, indurate, nerve, steel, stiffen, strengthen.

hardened *adj* annealed, case-hardened, tempered, indurated; abandoned, accustomed, benumbed, callous, confirmed, deadened, depraved, habituated, impenitent, incorrigible, inured, insensible, irreclaimable, lost, obdurate, reprobate, seared, seasoned, steeled, trained, unfeeling.

hard-headed *adj* astute, collected, cool, intelligent, sagacious, shrewd, well-balanced, wise.

hardhearted *adj* cruel, fell, implacable, inexorable, merciless, pitiless, relentless, ruthless, unfeeling, uncompassionate, unmerciful, unpitying, unrelenting.

hardihood *n* audacity, boldness, bravery, courage, decision, firmness, fortitude, intrepidity, manhood, mettle, pluck, resolution, stoutness; assurance, audacity, brass, effrontery, impudence.

hardly *adv* barely, scarcely; cruelly, harshly, rigorously, roughly, severely, unkindly.

hardship *n* fatigue, toil, weariness; affliction, burden, calamity, grievance, hardness, injury, misfortune, privation, suffering, trial, trouble.

hardy *adj* enduring, firm, hale, healthy, hearty, inured, lusty, rigorous, robust, rugged, sound, stout, strong, sturdy, tough; bold, brave, courageous, daring, heroic, intrepid, manly, resolute, stout-hearted, valiant.

harebrained *adj* careless, changeable, flighty, giddy, harum-scarum, headlong, heedless, rash, reckless, unsteady, volatile, wild.

hark *interj* attend, hear, hearken, listen.

harlequin *n* antic, buffoon, clown, droll, fool, jester, punch, fool.

harm *vb* damage, hurt, injure, scathe; abuse, desecrate, ill-use, ill-treat, maltreat, molest. * *n* damage, detriment, disadvantage, hurt, injury, mischief, misfortune, prejudice, wrong.

harmful *adj* baneful, detrimental, disadvantageous, hurtful, injurious, mischievous, noxious, pernicious, prejudicial.

harmless *adj* innocent, innocuous, innoxious; inoffensive, safe, unoffending.

harmonious *adj* concordant, consonant, harmonic; dulcet, euphonious, mellifluous, melodious, musical, smooth, tuneful; comfortable, congruent, consistent, correspondent, orderly, symmetrical; agreeable, amicable, brotherly, cordial, fraternal, friendly, neighbourly.

harmonize *vb* adapt, attune, reconcile, unite; accord, agree, blend, chime, comport, conform, correspond, square, sympathize, tally, tune.

harmony *n* euphony, melodiousness, melody; accord, accordance, agreement, chime, concord, concordance, consonance, order, unison; adaptation, congruence, congruity, consistency, correspondence, fairness, smoothness, suitableness; amity, friendship, peace.

harness *vb* hitch, tackle. * *n* equipment, gear, tackle, tackling; accoutrements, armour, array, mail, mounting.

harp *vb* dwell, iterate, reiterate, renew, repeat.

harping *n* dwelling, iteration, reiteration, repetition.

harrow *vb* harass, lacerate, rend, tear, torment, torture, wound.

harry *vb* devastate, pillage, plunder, raid, ravage, rob; annoy, chafe, disturb, fret, gall, harass, harrow, incommode, pester, plague, molest, tease, torment, trouble, vex, worry.

harsh *adj* acid, acrid, astringent, biting, caustic, corrosive, crabbed, rough, sharp, sour, tart; cacophonous, discordant, grating, jarring, metallic, raucous, strident, unmelodious; abusive, austere, crabbed, crabby, cruel, disagreeable, hard, ill-natured, ill-tempered, morose, rigorous, severe, stern, unfeeling; bearish, bluff, blunt, brutal, gruff, rude, uncivil, ungracious.

harshness *n* roughness; acerbity, asperity, austerity, churlishness, crabbedness, hardness, ill-nature, ill-temper, moroseness, rigour, severity, sternness, unkindness; bluffness, bluntness, churlishness, gruffness, incivility, ungraciousness, rudeness.

harum-scarum *adj* hare-brained, precipitate, rash, reckless, volatile, wild.

harvest *vb* gather, glean, reap. * *n* crops, produce, yield; consequence, effect, issue, outcome, produce, result.

haste *n* alacrity, celerity, dispatch, expedition, nimbleness, promptitude, quickness, rapidity, speed, urgency, velocity; flurry, hurry, hustle, impetuosity, precipitateness, precipitation, press, rashness, rush, vehemence.

hasten *vb* haste, hurry; accelerate, dispatch, expedite, precipitate, press, push, quicken, speed, urge.

hasty *adj* brisk, fast, fleet, quick, rapid, speedy, swift; cursory, hurried, passing, slight, superficial; ill-advised, rash, reckless; headlong, helter-skelter, pell-mell, precipitate; abrupt, choleric, excitable, fiery, fretful, hot-headed, irascible, irritable, passionate, peevish, peppery, pettish, petulant, testy, touchy, waspish.

hatch *vb* brew, concoct, contrive, excogitate, design, devise, plan, plot, project, scheme; breed, incubate.

hate *vb* abhor, abominate, detest, dislike, execrate, loathe, nauseate. * *n* abomination, animosity, antipathy, detestation, dislike, enmity, execration, hatred, hostility, loathing.

hateful *adj* malevolent, malicious, malign, malignant, rancorous, spiteful; abhorrent, abominable, accursed, damnable, detestable, execrable, horrid, odious, shocking; disgusting, foul, loathsome, nauseous, obnoxious, offensive, repellent, repugnant, repulsive, revolting, vile.

hatred *n* animosity, enmity, hate, hostility, ill-will, malevolence, malice, malignity, odium, rancour; abhorrence, abomination, antipathy, aversion, detestation, disgust, execration, horror, loathing, repugnance, revulsion.

haughtiness *n* arrogance, contempt, contemptuousness, disdain, hauteur, insolence, loftiness, pride, self-importance, snobbishness, stateliness, superciliousness.

haughty *adj* arrogant, assuming, contemptuous, disdainful, imperious, insolent, lofty, lordly, overbearing, overweening, proud, scornful, snobbish, supercilious.

haul *vb* drag, draw, lug, pull, tow, trail, tug. * *n* heaving, pull, tug; booty, harvest, takings, yield.

haunt *vb* frequent, resort; follow, importune; hover, inhabit, obsess. * *n* den, resort, retreat.

hauteur *n* arrogance, contempt, contemptuousness, disdain, haughtiness, insolence, loftiness, pride, self-importance, stateliness, superciliousness.

have *vb* cherish, exercise, experience, keep, hold, occupy, own, possess; acquire, gain, get, obtain, receive; accept, take.

haven *n* asylum, refuge, retreat, shelter; anchorage, harbour, port.

havoc *n* carnage, damage, desolation, destruction, devastation, ravage, ruin, slaughter, waste, wreck.

hawk-eyed *adj* eagle-eyed, sharp-sighted.

hazard *vb* adventure, risk, venture; endanger, imperil, jeopardize. * *n* accident, casualty, chance, contingency, event, fortuity, stake; danger, jeopardy, peril, risk, venture.

hazardous *adj* dangerous, insecure, perilous, precarious, risky, uncertain, unsafe.

haze *n* fog, har, mist, smog; cloud, dimness, fume, miasma, obscurity, pall.

hazy *adj* foggy, misty; cloudy, dim, nebulous, obscure; confused, indefinite, indistinct, uncertain, vague.

head *vb* command, control, direct, govern, guide, lead, rule; aim, point, tend; beat, excel, outdo, precede, surpass. * *adj* chief, first, grand, highest, leading, main, principal; adverse, contrary. * *n* acme, summit, top; beginning, commencement, origin, rise, source; chief, chieftain, commander, director, leader, master, principal, superintendent, superior; intellect, mind, thought, understanding; branch, category, class, department, division, section, subject, topic; brain, crown, headpiece, intellect, mind, thought, understanding; cape, headland, point, promontory.

headiness *n* hurry, precipitation, rashness; obstinacy, stubbornness.

headless *adj* acephalous, beheaded; leaderless, undirected; headstrong, heady, imprudent, obstinate, rash, senseless, stubborn.

headlong *adj* dangerous, hasty, heady, impulsive, inconsiderate, perilous, precipitate, rash, reckless, ruinous, thoughtless; perpendicular, precipitous, sheer, steep. * *adv* hastily, headfirst, helter-skelter, hurriedly, precipitately, rashly, thoughtlessly.

headstone *n* cornerstone, gravestone.

headstrong *adj* cantankerous, cross-grained, dogged, forward, headless, heady, intractable, obstinate, self-willed, stubborn, ungovernable, unruly, violent, wayward.

heady *adj* hasty, headlong, impetuous, impulsive, inconsiderate, precipitate, rash, reckless, rushing, stubborn, thoughtless; exciting, inebriating, inflaming, intoxicating, spirituous, strong.

heal *vb* amend, cure, remedy, repair, restore; compose, harmonize, reconcile, settle, soothe.

healing *adj* curative, palliative, remedial, restoring, restorative; assuaging, assuasive, comforting, composing, gentle, lenitive, mild, soothing.

health *n* healthfulness, robustness, salubrity, sanity, soundness, strength, tone, vigour.

healthy *adj* active, hale, hearty, lusty, sound, vigorous, well; bracing, healthful, health-giving, hygienic, invigorating, nourishing, salubrious, salutary, wholesome.

heap *vb* accumulate, augment, amass, collect, overfill, pile up, store. * *n* accumulation, collection, cumulus, huddle, lot, mass, mound, pile, stack.

hear *vb* eavesdrop, hearken, heed, listen, overhear; ascertain, discover, gather, learn, understand; examine, judge.

heart *n* bosom, breast; centre, core, essence, interior, kernel, marrow, meaning, pith; affection, benevolence, character, disposition, feeling, inclination, love, mind, passion, purpose, will; affections, ardour, emotion, feeling, love; boldness, courage, fortitude, resolution, spirit.

heartache *n* affliction, anguish, bitterness, distress, dole, grief, heartbreak, sorrow, woe.

heartbroken *adj* broken-hearted, cheerless, comfortless, desolate, disconsolate, forlorn, inconsolable, miserable, woebegone, wretched.

hearten *vb* animate, assure, cheer, comfort, console, embolden, encourage, enhearten, incite, inspire, inspirit, reassure, stimulate.

heartfelt *adj* cordial, deep, deep-felt, hearty, profound, sincere, warm.

hearth *n* fireplace, fireside, forge, hearthstone.

heartily *adv* abundantly, completely, cordially, earnestly, freely, largely, sincerely, vigorously.

heartless *adj* brutal, cold, cruel, hard, harsh, merciless, pitiless, unfeeling, unsympathetic; spiritless, timid, timorous, uncourageous.

heart-rending *adj* affecting, afflicting, anguishing, crushing, distressing.

hearty *adj* cordial, deep, earnest, fervent, heartfelt, profound, sincere, true, unfeigned, warm; active, animated, energetic, fit, vigorous, zealous; convivial, hale, healthy, robust, sound, strong, warm; abundant, full, heavy; nourishing, nutritious, rich.

heat *vb* excite, flush, inflame; animate, rouse, stimulate, stir. * *n* calorie, caloricity, torridity, warmth; excitement, fever, flush, impetuosity, passion, vehemence, violence; ardour, earnestness, fervency, fervour, glow, intensity, zeal; exasperation, fierceness, frenzy, rage.

heath n field, moor, wasteland, plain.

heathen adj animist, animistic; pagan, paganical, paganish, paganistic, unconverted; agnostic, atheist, atheistic, gentile, idolatrous, infidel, irreligious; barbarous, cruel, inhuman, savage. * n atheist, gentile, idolater, idolatress, infidel, pagan, unbeliever; barbarian, philistine, savage.

heave vb elevate, hoist, lift, raise; breathe, exhale; cast, fling, hurl, send, throw, toss; dilate, expand, pant, rise, swell; retch, throw up; strive, struggle.

heaven n empyrean, firmament, sky, welkin; bliss, ecstasy, elysium, felicity, happiness, paradise, rapture, transport.

heavenly adj celestial, empyreal, ethereal; angelic, beatific, beatified, cherubic, divine, elysian, glorious, god-like, sainted, saintly, seraphic; blissful, delightful, divine, ecstatic, enrapturing, enravishing, exquisite, golden, rapturous, ravishing, exquisite, transporting.

heaviness n gravity, heft, ponderousness, weight; grievousness, oppressiveness, severity; dullness, languor, lassitude, sluggishness, stupidity; dejection, depression, despondency, gloom, melancholy, sadness, seriousness.

heavy adj grave, hard, onerous, ponderous, weighty; afflictive, burdensome, crushing, cumbersome, grievous, oppressive, severe, serious; dilatory, dull, inactive, inanimate, indolent, inert, lifeless, listless, sleepy, slow, sluggish, stupid, torpid; chapfallen, crestfallen, crushed, depressed, dejected, despondent, disconsolate, downhearted, gloomy, low-spirited, melancholy, sad, sobered, sorrowful; difficult, laborious; tedious, tiresome, wearisome, weary; burdened, encumbered, loaded; clammy, clayey, cloggy, ill-raised, miry, muddy, soggy; boisterous, deep, energetic, loud, roaring, severe, stormy, strong, tempestuous, violent; cloudy, dark, dense, gloomy, lowering, overcast.

hebetate adj blunt; dull, obtuse, sluggish, stupid, stupefied.

hectic adj animated, excited, fevered, feverish, flushed, heated, hot.

hector vb bluster, boast, bully, menace, threaten; annoy, fret, harass, harry, irritate, provoke, tease, vex, worry. * n blusterer, bully, swaggerer.

hedge vb block, encumber, hinder, obstruct, surround; enclose, fence, fortify, guard, protect; disappear, dodge, evade, hide, skulk, temporize. * n barrier, hedgerow, fence, limit.

heed vb attend, consider, mark, mind, note, notice, observe, regard. * n attention, care, carefulness, caution, circumspection, consideration, heedfulness, mindfulness, notice, observation, regard, wariness, vigilance, watchfulness.

heedful adj attentive, careful, cautious, circumspect, mindful, observant, observing, provident, regardful, watchful, wary.

heedless adj careless, inattentive, neglectful, negligent, precipitate, rash, reckless, thoughtless, unmindful, unminding, unobserving, unobservant.

heft n handle, haft, helve; bulk, weight.

hegemony n ascendancy, authority, headship, leadership, predominance, preponderance, rule.

height n altitude, elevation, tallness; acme, apex, climax, eminence, head, meridian, pinnacle, summit, top, vertex, zenith; eminence, hill, mountain; dignity, exaltation, grandeur, loftiness, perfection.

heighten vb elevate, raise; ennoble, exalt, magnify, make greater; augment, enhance, improve, increase, strengthen; aggravate, intensify.

heinous adj aggravated, atrocious, crying, enormous, excessive, flagitious, flagrant, hateful, infamous, monstrous, nefarious, odious, villainous.

heir n child, inheritor, offspring, product.

helical adj screw-shaped, spiral, winding.

hellish adj abominable, accursed, atrocious, curst, damnable, damned, demoniacal, detestable, devilish, diabolical, execrable, fiendish, infernal, monstrous, nefarious, satanic.

helm n rudder, steering-gear, tiller, wheel; command, control, direction, rein, rule.

help vb relieve, save, succour; abet, aid, assist, back, cooperate, second, serve, support, sustain, wait; alleviate, ameliorate, better, cure, heal, improve, remedy, restore; control, hinder, prevent, repress, resist, withstand; avoid, forbear, control. * n aid, assistance, succour, support; relief, remedy; assistant, helper, servant.

helper adj aider, abettor, ally, assistant, auxiliary, coadjutor, colleague, helpmate, partner, supporter.

helpful adj advantageous, assistant, auxiliary, beneficial, contributory, convenient, favourable, kind, profitable, serviceable, useful.

helpless adj disabled, feeble, imbecile, impotent, infirm, powerless, prostrate, resourceless, weak; abandoned, defenceless, exposed, unprotected; desperate, irremediable, remediless.

helpmate n companion, consort, husband, partner, wife; aider, assistant, associate, helper.

helter-skelter adj disorderly, headlong, irregular, pell-mell, precipitate. * adv confusedly, hastily, headlong, higgledy-piggledy, pell-mell, precipitately, wildly.

hem vb border, edge, skirt; beset, confine, enclose, environ, surround, sew; hesitate. * n border, edge, trim.

henchman n attendant, follower, retainer, servant, supporter.

herald vb announce, proclaim, publish. * n announcer, crier, publisher; harbinger, precursor, proclaimer.

heraldry n blazonry, emblazonry.

herbage n greenery, herb, pasture, plants, vegetation.

herculean adj able-bodied, athletic, brawny, mighty, muscular, powerful, puissant, sinewy, stalwart, strong, sturdy, vigorous; dangerous, difficult, hard, laborious, perilous, toilsome, troublesome; colossal, Cyclopean, gigantic, great, large, strapping.

herd vb drive, gather, lead, tend; assemble, associate, flock. * n drover, herder, herdsman, shepherd; crowd, multitude, populace, rabble; assemblage, assembly, collection, drove, flock, pack.

hereditary adj ancestral, inheritable, inherited, patrimonial, transmitted.

heresy n dissent, error, heterodoxy, impiety, recusancy, unorthodoxy.

heretic n dissenter, dissident, nonconformist, recusant, schismatic, sectarian, sectary, separatist, unbeliever.

heretical adj heterodox, impious, schismatic, schismatical, sectarian, unorthodox.

heritage n estate, inheritance, legacy, patrimony, portion.

hermetic adj airtight, impervious; cabbalistic, emblematic, emblematical, magical, mysterious, mystic, mystical, occult, secret, symbolic, symbolical.

hermit *n* anchoress, anchoret, anchorite, ascetic, eremite, monk, recluse, solitaire, solitary.

heroic *adj* bold, brave, courageous, daring, dauntless, fearless, gallant, illustrious, intrepid, magnanimous, noble, valiant; desperate, extravagant, extreme, violent.

heroism *n* boldness, bravery, courage, daring, endurance, fearlessness, fortitude, gallantry, intrepidity, prowess, valour.

hesitate *vb* boggle, delay, demur, doubt, pause, scruple, shilly-shally, stickle, vacillate, waver; falter, stammer, stutter.

hesitation *n* halting, misgiving, reluctance; delay, doubt, indecision, suspense, uncertainty, vacillation; faltering, stammering, stuttering.

heterodox *adj* heretical, recusant, schismatic, unorthodox, unsound; apocryphal, uncanonical.

heterogeneous *adj* contrasted, contrary, different, dissimilar, diverse, incongruous, indiscriminate, miscellaneous, mixed, opposed, unhomogeneous, unlike.

hew *vb* chop, cut, fell, hack; fashion, form, shape, smooth.

hiatus *n* blank, break, chasm, gap, interval, lacuna, opening, rift.

hidden *adj* blind, clandestine, cloaked, close, concealed, covered, covert, enshrouded, latent, masked, occult, private, secluded, secret, suppressed, undiscovered, veiled; abstruse, cabbalistic, cryptic, dark, esoteric, hermetic, inward, mysterious, mystic, mystical, obscure, oracular, recondite.

hide *vb* bury, conceal, cover, secrete, suppress, withhold; cloak, disguise, eclipse, hoard, mask, screen, shelter, veil.

hideous *adj* abominable, appalling, awful, dreadful, frightful, ghastly, ghoulish, grim, grisly, horrible, horrid, repulsive, revolting, shocking, terrible, terrifying.

hie *vb* hasten, speed.

hieratic *adj* consecrated, devoted, priestly, sacred, sacerdotal.

hieroglyph *n* picture-writing, rebus, sign, symbol.

hieroglyphic *adj* emblematic, emblematical, figurative, obscure, symbolic, symbolical.

higgle *vb* hawk, peddle; bargain, chaffer, haggle, negotiate.

higgledy-piggledy *adj* chaotic, confused, disorderly, jumbled. * *adv* confusedly, in disorder, helter-skelter, pell-mell.

high *adj* elevated, high-reaching, lofty, soaring, tall, towering; distinguished, eminent, pre-eminent, prominent, superior; admirable, dignified, exalted, great, noble; arrogant, haughty, lordly, proud, supercilious; boisterous, strong, tumultuous, turbulent, violent; costly, dear, pricey; acute, high-pitched, high-toned, piercing, sharp, shrill; tainted, malodorous. * *adv* powerfully, profoundly; eminently, loftily; luxuriously, richly.

high-flown *adj* elevated, presumptuous, proud, lofty, swollen; extravagant, high-coloured, lofty, overdrawn, overstrained; bombastic, inflated, pompous, pretentious, strained, swollen, turgid.

high-handed *adj* arbitrary, despotic, dictatorial, domineering, oppressive, overbearing, self-willed, violent, wilful.

highly strung *adj* ardent, excitable, irascible, nervous, quick, tense; high-spirited, sensitive.

high-minded *adj* arrogant, haughty, lofty, proud; elevated, high-toned; generous honourable, magnanimous, noble, spiritual.

highwayman *n* bandit, brigand, footpad, freebooter, marauder, outlaw, robber.

hilarious *adj* boisterous, cheerful, comical, convivial, riotous, uproarious, jovial, joyful, merry, mirthful, noisy.

hilarity *n* cheerfulness, conviviality, exhilarated, gaiety, glee, jollity, joviality, joyousness, merriment, mirth.

hill *n* ascent, ben, elevation, eminence, hillock, knoll, mount, mountain, rise, tor.

hind *adj* back, hinder, hindmost, posterior, rear, rearward.

hinder *vb* bar, check, clog, delay, embarrass, encumber, impede, interrupt, obstruct, oppose, prevent, restrain, retard, stop, thwart.

hindrance *n* check, deterrent, encumbrance, hitch, impediment, interruption, obstacle, obstruction, restraint, stop, stoppage.

hinge *vb* depend, hang, rest, turn.

hint *vb* allude, glance, imply, insinuate, intimate, mention, refer, suggest. * *n* allusion, clue, implication, indication, innuendo, insinuation, intimation, mention, reminder, suggestion, taste, trace.

hire *vb* buy, rent, secure; charter, employ, engage, lease, let. * *n* allowance, bribe, compensation, pay, remuneration, rent, reward, salary, stipend, wages.

hireling *n* employee, mercenary, myrmidon.

hirsute *adj* bristled, bristly, hairy, shaggy; boorish, course, ill-bred, loutish, rough, rude, rustic, uncouth, unmannerly.

hiss *vb* shrill, sibilate, whistle, whir, whiz; condemn, damn, ridicule. * *n* fizzle, hissing, sibilant, sibilation, sizzle.

historian *n* annalist, autobiographer, biographer, chronicler, narrator, recorder.

history *n* account, autobiography, annals, biography, chronicle, genealogy, memoirs, narration, narrative, recital, record, relation, story.

hit *vb* discomfit, hurt, knock, strike; accomplish, achieve, attain, gain, reach, secure, succeed, win; accord, fit, suit; beat, clash, collide, contact, smite. * *n* blow, collision, strike, stroke; chance, fortune, hazard, success, venture.

hitch *vb* catch, impede, stick, stop; attach, connect, fasten, harness, join, tether, tie, unite, yoke. * *n* catch, check, hindrance, impediment, interruption, obstacle; knot, noose.

hoar *adj* ancient, grey, hoary, old, white.

hoard *vb* accumulate, amass, collect, deposit, garner, hive, husband, save, store, treasure. * *n* accumulation, collection, deposit, fund, mass, reserve, savings, stockpile, store.

hoarse *adj* discordant, grating, gruff, guttural, harsh, husky, low, raucous, rough.

hoary *adj* grey, hoar, silvery, white; ancient, old, venerable.

hoax *vb* deceive, dupe, fool, gammon, gull, hoodwink, swindle, trick. * *n* canard, cheat, deception, fraud, humbug, imposition, imposture, joke, trick, swindle.

hobble *vb* falter, halt, hop, limp; fasten, fetter, hopple, shackle, tie. * *n* halt, limp; clog, fetter, shackle; embarrassment, difficulty, perplexity, pickle, strait.

hobgoblin *n* apparition, bogey, bugbear, goblin, imp, spectre, spirit, sprite.

hobnail *n* bumpkin, churl, clodhopper, clown, lout, rustic.

hocus-pocus n cheater, impostor, juggler, sharper, swindler, trickster; artifice, cheat, deceit, deception, delusion, hoax, imposition, juggle, trick.

hodgepodge n farrago, hash, hotchpotch, jumble, medley, miscellany, mixture, ragout, stew.

hog n beast, glutton, pig; grunter, porker, swine.

hoggish adj brutish, filthy, gluttonish, piggish, swinish; grasping, greedy, mean, selfish, sordid.

hoist vb elevate, heave, lift, raise, rear. * n elevator, lift.

hold vb clasp, clinch, clutch, grasp, grip, seize; have, keep, occupy, possess, retain; bind, confine, control, detain, imprison, restrain, restrict; connect, fasten, fix, lock; arrest, check, stay, stop, suspend, withhold; continue, keep up, maintain, manage, prosecute, support, sustain; cherish, embrace, entertain; account, believe, consider, count, deem, entertain, esteem, judge, reckon, regard, think; accommodate, admit, carry, contain, receive, stow; assemble, conduct, convene; endure, last, persist, remain; adhere, cleave, cling, cohere, stick. * n anchor, bite, clasp, control, embrace, foothold, grasp, grip, possession, retention, seizure; prop, stay, support; claim, footing, vantage point; castle, fort, fortification, fortress, stronghold, tower; locker, storage, storehouse.

hole n aperture, opening, perforation; abyss, bore, cave, cavern, cavity, chasm, depression, excavation, eye, hollow, pit, pore, void; burrow, cover, lair, retreat; den, hovel, kennel.

holiday n anniversary, celebration, feast, festival, festivity, fete, gala, recess, vacation.

holiness n blessedness, consecration, devotion, devoutness, godliness, piety, purity, religiousness, righteousness, sacredness, saintliness, sanctity, sinlessness.

hollow vb dig, excavate, groove, scoop. * adj cavernous, concave, depressed, empty, sunken, vacant, void; deceitful, faithless, false, false-hearted, hollow-hearted, hypocritical, insincere, pharisaical, treacherous, unfeeling; deep, low, muffled, reverberating, rumbling, sepulchral. * n basin, bowl, depression; cave, cavern, cavity, concavity, dent, dimple, dint, depression, excavation, hole, pit; canal, channel, cup, dimple, dig, groove, pocket, sag.

holocaust n carnage, destruction, devastation, genocide, massacre.

holy adj blessed, consecrated, dedicated, devoted, hallowed, sacred, sanctified; devout, godly, pious, pure, religious, righteous, saintlike, saintly, sinless, spiritual.

homage n allegiance, devotion, fealty, fidelity, loyalty; court, deference, duty, honour, obeisance, respect, reverence, service; adoration, devotion, worship.

home adj domestic, family; close, direct, effective, penetrating, pointed. * n abode, dwelling, seat, quarters, residence.

homely adj domestic, familiar, house-like; coarse, commonplace, homespun, inelegant, plain, simple, unattractive, uncomely, unpolished, unpretentious.

homespun adj coarse, homely, inelegant, plain, rude, rustic, unpolished.

homicide n manslaughter, murder.

homily n address, discourse, lecture, sermon.

homogeneous adj akin, alike, cognate, kindred, similar, uniform.

honest adj equitable, fair, faithful, honourable, open, straight, straightforward; conscientious, equitable, reliable, sound, square, true, trustworthy, trusty, uncorrupted, upright, virtuous; above-board, faithful, genuine, thorough, unadulterated; creditable, decent, proper, reputable, respectable, suitable; chaste, decent; candid, direct, frank, ingenuous, sincere, unreserved.

honesty n equity, fairness, faithfulness, fidelity, honour, integrity, justice, probity, trustiness, trustworthiness, uprightness; truth, truthfulness, veracity; genuineness, thoroughness; candour, frankness, ingenuousness, openness, sincerity, straightforwardness, unreserve.

honorary adj formal, nominal, titular, unofficial, unpaid.

honour vb dignify, exalt, glorify, grace; respect, revere, reverence, venerate; adore, hallow, worship; celebrate, commemorate, keep, observe. * n civility, deference, esteem, homage, respect, reverence, veneration; dignity, distinction, elevation, nobleness; consideration, credit, fame, glory, reputation; high-mindedness, honesty, integrity, magnanimity, probity, uprightness; chastity, purity, virtue; boast, credit, ornament, pride.

honourable adj elevated, famous, great, illustrious, noble; admirable, conscientious, fair, honest, just, magnanimous, true, trustworthy, upright, virtuous, worshipful; creditable, esteemed, estimable, equitable, proper, respected, reputable, right.

honours npl dignities, distinctions, privilege, titles; adornments, beauties, decorations, glories; civilities.

hood n capuche, coif, cover, cowl, head.

hoodwink vb blind, blindfold; cloak, conceal, cover, hide; cheat, circumvent, cozen, deceive, delete, dupe, fool, gull, impose, overreach, trick.

hook vb catch, ensnare, entrap, hasp, snare; bend, curve. * n catch, clasp, fastener, hasp; snare, trap; cutter, grass-hook, reaper, reaping-hook, sickle.

hooked adj aquiline, bent, crooked, curved, hamate, unciform.

hoop vb clasp, encircle, enclose, surround. * n band, circlet, girdle, ring; crinoline, farthingale.

hoot vb boo, cry, jeer, shout, yell; condemn, decry, denounce, execrate, hiss. * n boo, cry, jeer, shout, yell.

hop vb bound, caper, frisk, jump, leap, skip, spring; dance, trip; halt, hobble, limp. * n bound, caper, dance, jump, leap, skip, spring.

hope vb anticipate, await, desire, expect, long; believe, rely, trust. * n confidence, belief, faith, reliance, sanguineness, sanguinity, trust; anticipation, desire, expectancy, expectation.

hopeful adj anticipatory, confident, expectant, fond, optimistic, sanguine; cheerful, encouraging, promising.

hopeless adj abject, crushed, depressed, despondent, despairing, desperate, disconsolate, downcast, forlorn, pessimistic, woebegone; abandoned, helpless, incurable, irremediable, remediless; impossible, impracticable, unachievable, unattainable.

horde n clan, crew, gang, troop; crowd, multitude, pack, throng.

horn vb gore, pierce. * n trumpet, wind instrument; beaker, drinking cup, cornucopia; spike, spur; cusp, prong, wing.

horrid adj alarming, awful, bristling, dire, dreadful, fearful, frightful, harrowing, hideous, horrible, horrific, horrifying, rough, terrible, terrific; abominable, disagreeable, disgusting, odious, offensive, repulsive, revolting, shocking, unpleasant, vile.

horrify vb affright, alarm, frighten, shock, terrify, terrorise.

horror *n* alarm, awe, consternation, dismay, dread, fear, fright, panic; abhorrence, abomination, antipathy, aversion, detestation, disgust, hatred, loathing, repugnance, revulsion; shuddering.

horse *n* charger, cob, colt, courser, filly, gelding, mare, nag, pad, palfrey, pony, stallion, steed; cavalry, horseman; buck, clotheshorse, frame, sawhorse, stand, support.

horseman *n* cavalier, equestrian, rider; cavalryman, chasseur, dragoon, horse-soldier.

hospitable *adj* attentive, bountiful, kind; bountiful, cordial, generous, liberal, open, receptive, sociable, unconstrained, unreserved.

host[1] *n* entertainer, innkeeper, landlord, master of ceremonies, presenter, proprietor, owner, receptionist.

host[2] *n* array, army, legion; assemblage, assembly, horde, multitude, throng.

host[3] *n* altar bread, bread, consecrated bread, loaf, wafer.

hostile *adj* inimical, unfriendly, warlike; adverse, antagonistic, contrary, opposed, opposite, repugnant.

hostilities *npl* conflict, fighting, war, warfare.

hostility *n* animosity, antagonism, enmity, hatred, ill-will, unfriendliness; contrariness, opposition, repugnance, variance.

hot *adj* burning, fiery, scalding; boiling, flaming, heated, incandescent, parching, roasting, torrid; heated, oppressive, sweltering, warm; angry, choleric, excitable, furious, hasty, impatient, impetuous, irascible, lustful, passionate, touchy, urgent, violent; animated, ardent, eager, fervent, fervid, glowing, passionate, vehement; acrid, biting, highly flavoured, highly seasoned, peppery, piquant, pungent, sharp, stinging.

hotchpotch *n* farrago, jumble, hodgepodge, medley, miscellany, stew.

hotel *n* inn, public house, tavern.

hot-headed *adj* furious, headlong, headstrong, hotbrained, impetuous, inconsiderate, passionate, precipitate, rash, reckless, vehement, violent.

hound *vb* drive, incite, spur, urge; bate, chase, goad, harass, harry, hunt, pursue.

house *vb* harbour, lodge, protect, shelter. * *n* abode, domicile, dwelling, habitation, home, mansion, residence; building, edifice; family, household; kindred, race, lineage, tribe; company, concern, firm, partnership; hotel, inn, public house, tavern.

housing *n* accommodation, dwellings, houses; casing, container, covering, protection, shelter.

hovel *n* cabin, cot, den, hole, hut, shed.

hover *vb* flutter; hang; vacillate, waver.

however *adv* but, however, nevertheless, notwithstanding, still, though, yet.

howl *vb* bawl, cry, lament, ululate, weep, yell, yowl. * *n* cry, yell, ululation.

hoyden *n* romp, tomboy.

hoydenish *adj* bad-mannered, boisterous, bold, ill-behaved, ill-taught, inelegant, romping, rough, rude, rustic, tomboyish, uncouth, ungenteel, unladylike, unruly.

hubbub *n* clamour, confusion, din, disorder, disturbance, hullabaloo, racket, riot, outcry, tumult, uproar.

huckster *n* hawker, peddler, retailer.

huddle *vb* cluster, crowd, gather; crouch, curl up, nestle, snuggle. * *n* confusion, crowd, disorder, disturbance, jumble, tumult.

hue *n* cast, colour, complexion, dye, shade, tinge, tint, tone.

huff *vb* blow, breathe, exhale, pant, puff. * *n* anger, fume, miff, passion, pet, quarrel, rage, temper, tiff.

hug *vb* clasp, cling, cuddle, embrace, grasp, grip, squeeze; cherish, nurse, retain. * *n* clasp, cuddle, embrace, grasp, squeeze.

huge *adj* bulky, colossal, Cyclopean, elephantine, enormous, gigantic, herculean, immense, stupendous, vast,

huggermugger *adj* clandestine, secret, sly; base, contemptible, mean, unfair; confused, disorderly, slovenly.

hull *vb* husk, peel, shell. * *n* covering, husk, rind, shell.

hullabaloo *n* clamour, confusion, din, disturbance, hubbub, outcry, racket, vociferation, uproar.

hum *vb* buzz, drone, murmur; croon, sing.

humane *adj* accommodating, benevolent, benign, charitable, clement, compassionate, gentle, good-hearted, kind, kind-hearted, lenient, merciful, obliging, tender, sympathetic; cultivating, elevating, humanizing, refining, rational, spiritual.

humanity *n* benevolence, benignity, charity, fellow-feeling, humaneness, kind-heartedness, kindness, philanthropy, sympathy, tenderness; humankind, mankind, mortality.

humanize *vb* civilize, cultivate, educate, enlighten, improve, polish, reclaim, refine, soften.

humble *vb* abase, abash, break, crush, debase, degrade, disgrace, humiliate, lower, mortify, reduce, sink, subdue. * *adj* meek, modest, lowly, simple, submissive, unambitious, unassuming, unobtrusive, unostentatious, unpretending; low, obscure, mean, plain, poor, small, undistinguished, unpretentious.

humbug *vb* cheat, cozen, deceive, hoax, swindle, trick. * *n* cheat, dodge, gammon, hoax, imposition, imposture, deception, fraud, trick; cant, charlatanism, charlatanry, hypocrisy, mummery, quackery; charlatan, impostor, fake, quack.

humdrum *adj* boring, dronish, dreary, dry, dull, monotonous, prosy, stupid, tedious, tiresome, wearisome.

humid *adj* damp, dank, moist, wet.

humiliate *vb* abase, abash, debase, degrade, depress, humble, mortify, shame.

humiliation *n* abasement, affront, condescension, crushing, degradation, disgrace, dishonouring, humbling, indignity, mortification, self-abasement, submissiveness, resignation.

humility *n* diffidence, humbleness, lowliness, meekness, modesty, self-abasement, submissiveness.

humorist *n* comic, comedian, droll, jester, joker, wag, wit.

humorous *adj* comic, comical, droll, facetious, funny, humorous, jocose, jocular, laughable, ludicrous, merry, playful, pleasant, sportive, whimsical, witty.

humour *vb* favour, gratify, indulge. * *n* bent, bias, disposition, predilection, prosperity, temper, vein; mood, state; caprice, crotchet, fancy, freak, vagary, whim, whimsy, wrinkle; drollery, facetiousness, fun, jocoseness, jocularity, pleasantry, wit; fluid, moisture, vapour.

hunch *vb* arch, jostle, nudge, punch, push, shove. * *n* bunch, hump, knob, protuberance; nudge, punch, push, shove; feeling, idea, intuition, premonition.

hungry *adj* covetous, craving, desirous, greedy; famished, starved, starving; barren, poor, unfertile, unproductive.

hunk *n* chunk, hunch, lump, slice.

hunt *vb* chase, drive, follow, hound, pursue, stalk, trap, trail; poach, shoot; search, seek. * *n* chase, field-sport, hunting, pursuit.

hurl *vb* cast, dart, fling, pitch, project, send, sling, throw, toss.

hurly-burly *n* bustle, commotion, confusion, disturbance, hurl, hurly, uproar, tumult, turmoil.

hurricane *n* cyclone, gale, storm, tempest, tornado, typhoon.

hurried *adj* cursory, hasty, slight, superficial.

hurry *vb* drive, precipitate; dispatch, expedite, hasten, quicken, speed; haste, scurry. * *n* agitation, bustle, confusion, flurry, flutter, perturbation, precipitation; celerity, haste, dispatch, expedition, promptitude, promptness, quickness.

hurt *vb* damage, disable, disadvantage, harm, impair, injure, mar; bruise, pain, wound; afflict, grieve, offend; ache, smart, throb. * *n* damage, detriment, disadvantage, harm, injury, mischief; ache, bruise, pain, suffering, wound.

hurtful *adj* baleful, baneful, deleterious, destructive, detrimental, disadvantageous, harmful, injurious, mischievous, noxious, pernicious, prejudicial, unwholesome.

husband *vb* economize, hoard, save, store.

husbandry *n* agriculture, cultivation, farming, geoponics, tillage; economy, frugality, thrift.

hush *vb* quiet, repress, silence, still, suppress; appease, assuage, calm, console, quiet, still. * *n* quiet, quietness, silence, stillness.

hypocrite *n* deceiver, dissembler, impostor, pretender.

hypocritical *adj* deceiving, dissembling, false, insincere, spurious, two-faced.

hypothesis *n* assumption, proposition, supposition, theory.

hypothetical *adj* assumed, imaginary, supposed, theoretical.

hysterical *adj* frantic, frenzied, overwrought, uncontrollable; comical, uproarious.

I

ice *vb* chill, congeal, freeze. * *n* crystal; frosting, sugar.

icy *adj* glacial; chilling, cold, frosty; cold-hearted, distant, frigid, indifferent, unemotional.

idea *n* archetype, essence, exemplar, ideal, model, pattern, plan, model; fantasy, fiction, image, imagination; apprehension, conceit, conception, fancy, illusion, impression, thought; belief, judgement, notion, opinion, sentiment, supposition.

ideal *adj* intellectual, mental; chimerical, fancied, fanciful, fantastic, illusory, imaginary, unreal, visionary, shadowy; complete, consummate, excellent, perfect; impractical, unattainable, utopian. * *n* criterion, example, model, standard.

identical *adj* equivalent, same, selfsame, tantamount.

identity *n* existence, individuality, personality, sameness.

ideology *n* belief, creed, dogma, philosophy, principle.

idiocy *n* fatuity, feebleness, foolishness, imbecility, insanity.

idiosyncrasy *n* caprice, eccentricity, fad, peculiarity, singularity.

idiot *n* blockhead, booby, dunce, fool, ignoramus, imbecile, simpleton.

idiotic *adj* fatuous, foolish, imbecile, irrational, senseless, sottish, stupid.

idle *adj* inactive, unemployed, unoccupied, vacant; indolent, inert, lazy, slothful, sluggish; abortive, bootless, fruitless, futile, groundless, ineffectual, unavailing, useless, vain; foolish, frivolous, trashy, trifling, trivial, unimportant, unprofitable. * *vb* dally, dawdle, laze, loiter, potter, waste; drift, shirk, slack.

idler *n* dawdler, doodle, drone, laggard, lazybones, loafer, lounger, slacker, slowcoach, sluggard, trifler.

idol *n* deity, god, icon, image, pagan, simulacrum, symbol; delusion, falsity, pretender, sham; beloved, darling, favourite, pet.

idolater *n* heathen, pagan; admirer, adorer, worshipper.

idolize *vb* canonize, deify; adore, honour, love, reverence, venerate.

idyll *n* eclogue, pastoral.

if *conj* admitting, allowing, granting, provided, supposing, though, whether. * *n* condition, hesitation, uncertainty.

igneous *adj* combustible, combustive, conflagrative, fiery, molten.

ignite *vb* burn, inflame, kindle, light, torch.

ignoble *adj* base-born, low, low-born, mean, peasant, plebeian, rustic, vulgar; contemptible, degraded, insignificant, mean, worthless; disgraceful, dishonourable, infamous, low, unworthy.

ignominious *adj* discreditable, disgraceful, dishonourable, disreputable, infamous, opprobrious, scandalous, shameful; base, contemptible, despicable.

ignominy *n* abasement, contempt, discredit, disgrace, dishonour disrepute, infamy, obloquy, odium, opprobrium, scandal, shame.

ignoramus *n* blockhead, duffer, dunce, fool, greenhorn, novice, numskull, simpleton.

ignorance *n* benightedness, darkness, illiteracy, nescience, rusticity; blindness, unawareness.

ignorant *adj* blind, illiterate, nescient, unaware, unconversant, uneducated, unenlightened, uninformed, uninstructed, unlearned, unread, untaught, untutored, unwitting.

ignore *vb* disregard, neglect, overlook, reject, skip.

ill *adj* bad, evil, faulty, harmful, iniquitous, naughty, unfavourable, unfortunate, unjust, wicked; ailing, diseased, disordered, indisposed, sick, unwell, wrong; crabbed, cross, hateful, malicious, malevolent, peevish, surly, unkind, ill-bred; ill-favoured, ugly, unprepossessing. * *adv* badly, poorly, unfortunately. * *n* badness, depravity, evil, mischief, misfortune, wickedness; affliction, ailment, calamity, harm, misery, pain, trouble.

ill-advised *adj* foolish, ill-judged, imprudent, injudicious, unwise.

ill-bred *adj* discourteous, ill-behaved, ill-mannered, impolite, rude, uncivil, uncourteous, uncourtly, uncouth.

illegal *adj* contraband, forbidden, illegitimate, illicit, prohibited, unauthorized, unlawful, unlicensed.

illegible *adj* indecipherable, obscure, undecipherable, unreadable.

illegitimate *adj* bastard, misbegotten, natural.

ill-fated *adj* ill-starred, luckless, unfortunate, unlucky.

ill-favoured *adj* homely, ugly, offensive, plain, unpleasant.

ill humour *n* fretfulness, ill-temper, peevishness, petulance, testiness.

illiberal *adj* close, close-fisted, covetous, mean, miserly, narrow, niggardly, parsimonious, penurious, selfish, sordid, stingy, ungenerous; bigoted, narrow-minded, uncharitable, ungentlemanly, vulgar.

illicit *adj* illegal, illegitimate, unauthorized, unlawful, unlegalized, unlicensed; criminal, guilty, forbidden, improper, wrong.

illimitable *adj* boundless, endless, immeasurable, immense, infinite, unbounded, unlimited, vast.

illiterate *adj* ignorant, uneducated, uninstructed, unlearned, unlettered, untaught, untutored.

ill-judged *adj* foolish, ill-advised, imprudent, injudicious, unwise.

ill-mannered *adj* discourteous, ill-behaved, ill-bred, impolite, rude, uncivil, uncourteous, uncourtly, uncouth, unpolished.

ill-natured *adj* disobliging, hateful, malevolent, unamiable, unfriendly, unkind; acrimonious, bitter, churlish, crabbed, cross, cross-grained, crusty, ill-tempered, morose, perverse, petulant, sour, spiteful, sulky, sullen, wayward.

illness n ailing, ailment, complaint, disease, disorder, distemper, indisposition, malady, sickness.

illogical adj absurd, fallacious, inconsistent, inconclusive, inconsequent, incorrect, invalid, unreasonable, unsound.

ill-proportioned adj awkward, ill-made, ill-shaped, misshapen, misproportioned, shapeless.

ill-starred adj ill-fated, luckless, unfortunate, unhappy, unlucky.

ill temper n bad temper, crabbedness, crossness, grouchiness, ill nature, moroseness, sulkiness, sullenness.

ill-tempered adj acrimonious, bad-tempered, crabbed, cross, grouchy, ill-natured, morose, sour, sulky, surly.

ill-timed adj inapposite, inopportune, irrelevant, unseasonable, untimely.

ill-treat vb abuse, ill-use, injure, maltreat, mishandle, misuse.

illude vb cheat, deceive, delude, disappoint, mock, swindle, trick.

illuminate vb illume, illumine, light; adorn, brighten, decorate, depict, edify, enlighten, inform, inspire, instruct, make wise.

illusion n chimera, deception, delusion, error, fallacy, false appearance, fantasy, hallucination, mockery, phantasm.

illusive, illusory adj barmecide, deceitful, deceptive, delusive, fallacious, imaginary, make-believe, mock, sham, unsatisfying, unreal, unsubstantial, visionary, tantalizing.

illustrate vb clarify, demonstrate, elucidate, enlighten, exemplify, explain; adorn, depict, draw.

illustration n demonstration, elucidation, enlightenment, exemplification, explanation, interpretation; adornment, decoration, picture.

illustrative adj elucidative, elucidatory, exemplifying.

illustrious adj bright, brilliant, glorious, radiant, splendid; celebrated, conspicuous, distinguished, eminent, famed, famous, noble, noted, remarkable, renowned, signal.

ill will n animosity, dislike, enmity, envy, grudge, hate, hatred, hostility, ill nature, malevolence, malice, malignity, rancour, spleen, spite, uncharitableness, unkindness, venom.

image n idol, statue; copy, effigy, figure, form, imago, likeness, picture, resemblance, representation, shape, similitude, simulacrum, statue, symbol; conception, counterpart, embodiment, idea, reflection.

imagery n dream, phantasm, phantom, vision.

imaginable adj assumable, cogitable, conceivable, conjecturable, plausible, possible, supposable, thinkable.

imaginary adj chimerical, dreamy, fancied, fanciful, fantastic, fictitious, ideal, illusive, illusory, invented, quixotic, shadowy, unreal, utopian, visionary, wild; assumed, conceivable, hypothetical, supposed.

imagination n chimera, conception, fancy, fantasy, invention, unreality; position; contrivance, device, plot, scheme.

imaginative adj creative, dreamy, fanciful, inventive, poetical, plastic, visionary.

imagine vb conceive, dream, fancy, imagine, picture, pretend; contrive, create, devise, frame, invent, mould, project; assume, suppose, hypothesize; apprehend, assume, believe, deem, guess, opine, suppose, think.

imbecile adj cretinous, drivelling, fatuous, feeble, fee-

ble-minded, foolish, helpless, idiotic, imbecilic, inane, infirm, witless. * n dotard, driveller.

imbecility n debility, feebleness, helplessness, infirmity, weakness; foolishness, idiocy, silliness, stupidity, weak-mindedness.

imbibe vb absorb, assimilate, drink, suck, swallow; acquire, gain, gather, get, receive.

imbroglio n complexity, complication, embarrassment, entanglement, misunderstanding.

imbrue vb drench, embrue, gain, moisten, soak, stain, steep, wet.

imbue vb colour, dye, stain, tincture, tinge, tint; bathe, impregnate, infuse, inoculate, permeate, pervade, provide, saturate, steep.

imitate vb copy, counterfeit, duplicate, echo, emulate, follow, forge, mirror, reproduce, simulate; ape, impersonate, mimic, mock, personate; burlesque, parody, travesty.

imitation adj artificial, fake, man-made, mock, reproduction, synthetic. * n aping, copying, imitation, mimicking, parroting; copy, duplicate, likeness, resemblance; mimicry, mocking; burlesque, parody, travesty.

imitative adj copying, emulative, imitating, mimetic, simulative; apeish, aping, mimicking.

imitator n copier, copycat, copyist, echo, impersonator, mimic, mimicker, parrot.

immaculate adj clean, pure, spotless, stainless, unblemished, uncontaminated, undefiled, unpolluted, unspotted, unsullied, untainted, untarnished; faultless, guiltless, holy, innocent, pure, saintly, sinless, stainless.

immanent adj congenital, inborn, indwelling, inherent, innate, internal, intrinsic, subjective.

immaterial adj bodiless, ethereal, extramundane, impalpable, incorporeal, mental, metaphysical, spiritual, unbodied, unfleshly, unsubstantial; inconsequential, insignificant, nonessential, unessential, unimportant.

immature adj crude, green, imperfect, raw, rudimental, rudimentary, unfinished, unformed, unprepared, unripe, unripened, youthful; hasty, premature, unseasonable, untimely.

immaturity n crudeness, crudity, greenness, imperfection, rawness, unpreparedness, unripeness.

immeasurable adj bottomless, boundless, illimitable, immense, infinite, limitless, measureless, unbounded, vast.

immediate adj close, contiguous, near, next, proximate; intuitive, primary, unmeditated; direct, instant, instantaneous, present, pressing, prompt.

immediately adv closely, proximately; directly, forthwith, instantly, presently, presto, pronto.

immemorial adj ancient, hoary, olden.

immense adj boundless, illimitable, infinite, interminable, measureless, unbounded, unlimited; colossal, elephantine, enormous, gigantic, huge, large, monstrous, mountainous, prodigious, stupendous, titanic, tremendous, vast.

immensity n boundlessness, endlessness, limitlessness, infiniteness, infinitude, infinity; amplitude, enormity, greatness, hugeness, magnitude, vastness.

immerse vb baptize, bathe, dip, douse, duck, overwhelm, plunge, sink, souse, submerge; absorb, engage, engross, involve.

immersion n dipping, immersing, plunging; absorption, engagement; disappearance; baptism.

imminent *adj* close, impending, near, overhanging, threatening; alarming, dangerous, perilous.

immobile *adj* fixed, immovable, inflexible, motionless, quiescent, stable, static, stationary, steadfast; dull, expressionless, impassive, rigid, stiff, stolid.

immobility *n* fixedness, fixity, immovability, immovableness, motionlessness, stability, steadfastness, unmovableness; dullness, expressionlessness, inflexibility, rigidity, stiffness, stolidity.

immoderate *adj* excessive, exorbitant, extravagant, extreme, inordinate, intemperate, unreasonable.

immodest *adj* coarse, gross, indecorous, indelicate, lewd, shameless; bold, brazen, forward, impudent, indecent; broad, filthy, impure, indecent, obscene, smutty, unchaste.

immodesty *n* coarseness, grossness, indecorum, indelicacy, shamelessness; impurity, lewdness, obscenity, smuttiness, unchastity; boldness, brass, forwardness, impatience.

immolate *vb* kill, sacrifice.

immoral *adj* antisocial, corrupt, loose, sinful, unethical, vicious, wicked, wrong; bad, depraved, dissolute, profligate, unprincipled; abandoned, indecent, licentious.

immorality *n* corruption, corruptness, criminality, demoralization, depravity, impurity, profligacy, sin, sinfulness, vice, wickedness; wrong.

immortal *adj* deathless, ever-living, imperishable, incorruptible, indestructible, indissoluble, never-dying, undying, unfading; ceaseless, continuing, eternal, endless, everlasting, never-ending, perpetual, sempiternal; abiding, enduring, lasting, permanent. * *n* god, goddess; genius, hero.

immortality *n* deathlessness, incorruptibility, incorruptibleness, indestructibility; perpetuity.

immortalize *vb* apotheosize, enshrine, glorify, perpetuate.

immovable *adj* firm, fixed, immobile, stable, stationary; impassive, steadfast, unalterable, unchangeable, unshaken, unyielding.

immunity *n* exemption, exoneration, freedom, release; charter, franchise, liberty, license, prerogative, privilege, right.

immure *vb* confine, entomb, imprison, incarcerate.

immutability *n* constancy, inflexibility, invariability, invariableness, permanence, stability, unalterableness, unchangeableness.

immutable *adj* constant, fixed, inflexible, invariable, permanent, stable, unalterable, unchangeable, undeviating.

imp *n* demon, devil, elf, flibbertigibbet, hobgoblin, scamp, sprite; graft, scion, shoot.

impact *vb* collide, crash, strike. * *n* brunt, impression, impulse, shock, stroke, touch; collision, contact, impinging, striking.

impair *vb* blemish, damage, deface, deteriorate, injure, mar, ruin, spoil, vitiate; decrease, diminish, lessen, reduce; enervate, enfeeble, weaken.

impale *vb* hole, pierce, puncture, spear, spike, stab, transfix.

impalpable *adj* attenuated, delicate, fine, intangible; imperceptible, inapprehensible, incorporeal, indistinct, shadowy, unsubstantial.

impart *vb* bestow, confer, give, grant; communicate, disclose, discover, divulge, relate, reveal, share, tell.

impartial *adj* candid, disinterested, dispassionate, equal, equitable, even-handed, fair, honourable, just, unbiased, unprejudiced, unwarped.

impassable *adj* blocked, closed, impenetrable, impermeable, impervious, inaccessible, pathless, unattainable, unnavigable, unreachable.

impassioned *adj* animated, ardent, burning, excited, fervent, fervid, fiery, glowing, impetuous, intense, passionate, vehement, warm, zealous.

impassive *adj* calm, passionless; apathetic, callous, indifferent, insensible, insusceptible, unfeeling, unimpressible, unsusceptible.

impassivity *n* calmness, composure, indifference, insensibility, insusceptibility, passionlessness, stolidity.

impatience *n* disquietude, restlessness, uneasiness; eagerness, haste, impetuosity, precipitation, vehemence; heat, irritableness, irritability, violence.

impatient *adj* restless, uneasy, unquiet; eager, hasty, impetuous, precipitate, vehement; abrupt, brusque, choleric, fretful, hot, intolerant, irritable, peevish, sudden, testy, violent.

impeach *vb* accuse, arraign, charge, indict; asperse, censure, denounce, disparage, discredit, impair, impute, incriminate, lessen.

impeachment *n* accusation, arraignment, indictment; aspersion, censure, disparagement, imputation, incrimination, reproach.

impeccable *adj* faultless, immaculate, incorrupt, innocent, perfect, pure, sinless, stainless, uncorrupt.

impede *vb* bar, block, check, clog, curb, delay, encumber, hinder, interrupt, obstruct, restrain, retard, stop, thwart.

impediment *n* bar, barrier, block, check, curb, difficulty, encumbrance, hindrance, obstacle, obstruction, stumbling block.

impel *vb* drive, push, send, urge; actuate, animate, compel, constrain, embolden, incite, induce, influence, instigate, move, persuade, stimulate.

impend *vb* approach, menace, near, threaten.

impending *adj* approaching, imminent, menacing, near, threatening.

impenetrable *adj* impermeable, impervious, inaccessible; cold, dull, impassive, indifferent, obtuse, senseless, stolid, unsympathetic; dense, proof.

impenitence *n* hardheartedness, impenitency, impenitentness, obduracy, stubbornness.

impenitent *adj* hardened, hard-hearted, incorrigible, irreclaimable, obdurate, recusant, relentless, seared, stubborn, uncontrite, unconverted, unrepentant.

imperative *adj* authoritative, commanding, despotic, domineering, imperious, overbearing, peremptory, urgent; binding, obligatory.

imperceptible *adj* inaudible, indiscernible, indistinguishable, invisible; fine, impalpable, inappreciable, gradual, minute.

imperfect *adj* abortive, crude, deficient, garbled, incomplete, poor; defective, faulty, impaired.

imperfection *n* defectiveness, deficiency, faultiness, incompleteness; blemish, defect, fault, flaw, stain, taint; failing, foible, frailty, limitation, vice, weakness.

imperial *adj* kingly, regal, royal, sovereign; august, consummate, exalted, grand, great, kingly, magnificent, majestic, noble, regal, royal, queenly, supreme, sovereign, supreme, consummate.

imperil *vb* endanger, expose, hazard, jeopardize, risk.

imperious *adj* arrogant, authoritative, commanding, compelling, despotic, dictatorial, domineering, haughty, imperative, lordly, magisterial, overbearing, tyrannical, urgent, compelling.

imperishable *adj* eternal, everlasting, immortal, incorruptible, indestructible, never-ending, perennial, unfading.

impermeable *adj* impenetrable, impervious.

impermissible *adj* deniable, insufferable, objectionable, unallowable, unallowed, unlawful.

impersonate *vb* act, ape, enact, imitate, mimic, mock, personate; embody, incarnate, personify, typify.

impersonation *n* incarnation, manifestation, personification; enacting, imitation, impersonating, mimicking, personating, representation.

impertinence *n* irrelevance, irrelevancy, unfitness, impropriety; assurance, boldness, brass, brazenness, effrontery, face, forwardness, impudence, incivility, insolence, intrusiveness, presumption, rudeness, sauciness, pertness.

impertinent *adj* inapplicable, inapposite, irrelevant; bold, forward, impudent, insolent, intrusive, malapert, meddling, officious, pert, rude, saucy, unmannerly.

imperturbability *n* calmness, collectedness, composure, dispassion, placidity, placidness, sedateness, serenity, steadiness, tranquility.

imperturbable *adj* calm, collected, composed, cool, placid, sedate, serene, tranquil, unmoved, undisturbed, unexcitable, unmoved, unruffled.

impervious *adj* impassable, impenetrable, impermeable.

impetuosity *n* force, fury, haste, precipitancy, vehemence, violence.

impetuous *adj* ardent, boisterous, brash, breakneck, fierce, fiery, furious, hasty, headlong, hot, hotheaded, impulsive, overzealous, passionate, precipitate, vehement, violent.

impetus *n* energy, force, momentum, propulsion.

impiety *n* irreverence, profanity, ungodliness; iniquity, sacreligiousness, sin, sinfulness, ungodliness, unholiness, unrighteousness, wickedness.

impinge *vb* clash, dash, encroach, hit, infringe, strike, touch.

impious *adj* blasphemous, godless, iniquitous, irreligious, irreverent, profane, sinful, ungodly, unholy, unrighteous, wicked.

implacable *adj* deadly, inexorable, merciless, pitiless, rancorous, relentless, unappeasable, unforgiving, unpropitiating, unrelenting.

implant *vb* ingraft, infix, insert, introduce, place.

implement *vb* effect, execute, fulfil. * *n* appliance, instrument, tool, utensil.

implicate *vb* entangle, enfold; compromise, concern, entangle, include, involve.

implication *n* entanglement, involvement, involution; connotation, hint, inference, innuendo, intimation; conclusion, meaning, significance.

implicit *adj* implied, inferred, understood; absolute, constant, firm, steadfast, unhesitating, unquestioning, unreserved, unshaken.

implicitly *adv* by implication, silently, tacitly, unspokenly, virtually, wordlessly.

implore *vb* adjure, ask, beg, beseech, entreat, petition, pray, solicit, supplicate.

imply *vb* betoken, connote, denote, import, include, infer, insinuate, involve, mean, presuppose, signify.

impolicy *n* folly, imprudence, ill-judgement, indiscretion, inexpediency.

impolite *adj* bearish, boorish, discourteous, disrespectful, ill-bred, insolent, rough, rude, uncivil, uncourteous, ungentle, ungentlemanly, ungracious, unmannerly, unpolished, unrefined.

impoliteness *n* boorishness, discourteousness, discourtesy, disrespect, ill-breeding, incivility, insolence, rudeness, unmannerliness.

impolitic *adj* ill-advised, imprudent, indiscreet, inexpedient, injudicious, unwise.

import *vb* bring in, introduce, transport; betoken, denote, imply, mean, purport, signify. * *n* goods, importation, merchandise; bearing, drift, gist, intention, interpretation, matter, meaning, purpose, sense, signification, spirit, tenor; consequence, importance, significance, weight.

importance *n* concern, consequence, gravity, import, moment, momentousness, significance, weight, weightiness; consequence, pomposity, self-importance.

important *adj* considerable, grave, material, momentous, notable, pompous, ponderous, serious, significant, urgent, valuable, weighty; esteemed, influential, prominent, substantial; consequential, pompous, self-important.

importunate *adj* busy, earnest, persistent, pertinacious, pressing, teasing, troublesome, urgent.

importune *vb* ask, beset, dun, ply, press, solicit, urge.

importunity *n* appeal, beseechment, entreaty, petition, plying, prayer, pressing, suit, supplication, urging; contention, insistence; urgency.

impose *vb* lay, place, put, set; appoint, charge, dictate, enjoin, force, inflict, obtrude, prescribe, tax; (*with* **on, upon**) abuse, cheat, circumvent, deceive, delude, dupe, exploit, hoax, trick, victimize.

imposing *adj* august, commanding, dignified, exalted, grand, grandiose, impressive, lofty, magnificent, majestic, noble, stately, striking.

imposition *n* imposing, laying, placing, putting; burden, charge, constraint, injunction, levy, oppression, tax; artifice, cheating, deception, dupery, fraud, imposture, trickery.

impossibility *n* hopelessness, impracticability, inability, infeasibility, unattainability; inconceivability.

impossible *adj* hopeless, impracticable, infeasible, unachievable, unattainable; inconceivable, self-contradictory, unthinkable.

impost *n* custom, duty, excise, rate, tax, toil, tribute.

impostor *n* charlatan, cheat, counterfeiter, deceiver, double-dealer, humbug, hypocrite, knave, mountebank, pretender, quack, rogue, trickster.

imposture *n* artifice, cheat, deceit, deception, delusion, dodge, fraud, hoax, imposition, ruse, stratagem, trick, wile.

impotence *n* disability, feebleness, frailty, helplessness, inability, incapability, incapacity, incompetence, inefficaciousness, inefficacy, inefficiency, infirmity, powerlessness, weakness.

impotent *adj* disabled, enfeebled, feeble, frail, helpless, incapable, incapacitated, incompetent, inefficient, infirm, nerveless, powerless, unable, weak; barren, sterile.

impound *vb* confine, coop, engage, imprison.

impoverish *vb* beggar, pauperize; deplete, exhaust, ruin.

impracticability *n* impossibility, impracticableness, impracticality, infeasibility, unpracticability.

impracticable *adj* impossible, infeasible; intractable, obstinate, recalcitrant, stubborn, thorny, unmanageable; impassable, insurmountable.

impracticality *n* impossibility, impracticableness, impractibility, infeasibility, unpracticability; irrationality, unpracticalness, unrealism, unreality, unreasonableness.

imprecate *vb* anathematize, curse, execrate, invoke, maledict.

imprecation *n* anathema, curse, denunciation, execration, invocation, malediction.

imprecatory *adj* appealing, beseeching, entreating, imploratory, imploring, imprecatory, pleading; cursing, damnatory, execrating, maledictory.

impregnable *adj* immovable, impenetrable, indestructible, invincible, inviolable, invulnerable, irrefrangible, secure, unconquerable, unassailable, unyielding.

impregnate *vb* fecundate, fertilize, fructify; dye, fill, imbrue, imbue, infuse, permeate, pervade, saturate, soak, tincture, tinge.

impress *vb* engrave, imprint, print, stamp; affect, move, strike; fix, inculcate; draft, enlist, levy, press, requisition. * *n* impression, imprint, mark, print, seal, stamp; cognizance, device, emblem, motto, symbol.

impressibility *n* affectibility, impressionability, pliancy, receptiveness, responsiveness, sensibility, sensitiveness, susceptibility.

impressible *adj* affectible, excitable, impressionable, pliant, receptive, responsive, sensitive, soft, susceptible, tender.

impression *n* edition, imprinting, printing, stamping; brand, dent, impress, mark, stamp; effect, influence, sensation; fancy, idea, instinct, notion, opinion, recollection.

impressive *adj* affecting, effective, emphatic, exciting, forcible, moving, overpowering, powerful, solemn, speaking, splendid, stirring, striking, telling, touching.

imprint *vb* engrave, mark, print, stamp; impress, inculcate. * *n* impression, mark, print, sign, stamp.

imprison *vb* confine, jail, immure, incarcerate, shut up.

imprisonment *n* captivity, commitment, confinement, constraint, durance, duress, incarceration, restraint.

improbability *n* doubt, uncertainty, unlikelihood.

improbable *adj* doubtful, uncertain, unlikely, unplausible.

improbity *n* dishonesty, faithlessness, fraud, fraudulence, knavery, unfairness.

impromptu *adj* extempore, improvised, offhand, spontaneous, unpremeditated, unprepared, unrehearsed. * *adv* extemporaneously, extemporarily, extempore, offhand, ad-lib.

improper *adj* immodest, inapposite, inappropriate, irregular, unadapted, unapt, unfit, unsuitable, unsuited; indecent, indecorous, indelicate, unbecoming, unseemly; erroneous, inaccurate, incorrect, wrong.

impropriety *n* inappropriateness, unfitness, unsuitability, unsuitableness; indecorousness, indecorum, unseemliness.

improve *vb* ameliorate, amend, better, correct, edify, meliorate, mend, rectify, reform; cultivate; gain, mend, progress; enhance, increase, rise.

improvement *n* ameliorating, amelioration, amendment, bettering, improving, meliorating, melioration; advancement, proficiency, progress.

improvidence *n* imprudence, thriftlessness, unthriftiness.

improvident *adj* careless, heedless, imprudent, incautious, inconsiderate, negligent, prodigal, rash, reck-

less, shiftless, thoughtless, thriftless, unthrifty, wasteful.

improvisation *n* ad-libbing, contrivance, extemporaneousness, extemporariness, extemporization, fabrication, invention; (*mus*) extempore, impromptu.

improvise *vb* ad-lib, contrive, extemporize, fabricate, imagine, invent.

imprudence *n* carelessness, heedlessness, improvidence, incautiousness, inconsideration, indiscretion, rashness.

imprudent *adj* careless, heedless, ill-advised, ill-judged, improvident, incautious, inconsiderate, indiscreet, rash, unadvised, unwise.

impudence *n* assurance, audacity, boldness, brashness, brass, bumptiousness, cheek, cheekiness, effrontery, face, flippancy, forwardness, front, gall, impertinence, insolence, jaw, lip, nerve, pertness, presumption, rudeness, sauciness, shamelessness.

impudent *adj* bold, bold-faced, brazen, brazen-faced, cool, flippant, forward, immodest, impertinent, insolent, insulting, pert, presumptuous, rude, saucy, shameless.

impugn *vb* assail, attack, challenge, contradict, dispute, gainsay, oppose, question, resist.

impulse *n* force, impetus, impelling, momentum, push, thrust; appetite, inclination, instinct, passion, proclivity; incentive, incitement, influence, instigation, motive, instigation.

impulsive *adj* impelling, moving, propulsive; emotional, hasty, heedless, hot, impetuous, mad-cap, passionate, quick, rash, vehement, violent.

impunity *n* exemption, immunity, liberty, licence, permission, security.

impure *adj* defiled, dirty, feculent, filthy, foul, polluted, unclean; bawdy, coarse, immodest, gross, immoral, indelicate, indecent, lewd, licentious, loose, obscene, ribald, smutty, unchaste; adulterated, corrupt, mixed.

impurity *n* defilement, feculence, filth, foulness, pollution, uncleanness; admixture, coarseness, grossness, immodesty, indecency, indelicacy, lewdness, licentiousness, looseness, obscenity, ribaldry, smut, smuttiness, unchastity, vulgarity.

imputable *adj* ascribable, attributable, chargeable, owing, referable, traceable, owing.

imputation *n* attributing, charging, imputing; accusation, blame, censure, charge, reproach.

impute *vb* ascribe, attribute, charge, consider, imply, insinuate, refer.

inability *n* impotence, incapacity, incapability, incompetence, incompetency, inefficiency; disability, disqualification.

inaccessible *adj* unapproachable, unattainable.

inaccuracy *n* erroneousness, impropriety, incorrectness, inexactness; blunder, defect, error, fault, mistake.

inaccurate *adj* defective, erroneous, faulty, incorrect, inexact, mistaken, wrong.

inaccurately *adv* carelessly, cursorily, imprecisely, incorrectly, inexactly, mistakenly, unprecisely, wrongly.

inactive *adj* inactive; dormant, inert, inoperative, peaceful, quiet, quiescent; dilatory, drowsy, dull, idle, inanimate, indolent, inert, lazy, lifeless, lumpish, passive, slothful, sleepy, stagnant, supine.

inactivity *n* dilatoriness, idleness, inaction, indolence, inertness, laziness, sloth, sluggishness, supineness, torpidity, torpor.

inadequacy *n* inadequateness, insufficiency; defectiveness, imperfection, incompetence, incompetency, incompleteness, insufficiency, unfitness, unsuitableness.

inadequate *adj* disproportionate, incapable, insufficient, unequal; defective, imperfect, inapt, incompetent, incomplete.

inadmissible *adj* improper, incompetent, unacceptable, unallowable, unqualified, unreasonable.

inadvertence, inadvertency *n* carelessness, heedlessness, inattention, inconsiderateness, negligence, thoughtlessness; blunder, error, oversight, slip.

inadvertent *adj* careless, heedless, inattentive, inconsiderate, negligent, thoughtless, unobservant.

inadvertently *adv* accidently, carelessly, heedlessly, inconsiderately, negligently, thoughtlessly, unintentionally.

inalienable *adj* undeprivable, unforfeitable, untransferable.

inane *adj* empty, fatuous, vacuous, void; foolish, frivolous, idiotic, puerile, senseless, silly, stupid, trifling, vain, worthless.

inanimate *adj* breathless, dead, extinct; dead, dull, inert, lifeless, soulless, spiritless.

inanition *n* emptiness, inanity, vacuity; exhaustion, hunger, malnutrition, starvation, want.

inanity *n* emptiness, foolishness, inanition, vacuity; folly, frivolousness, puerility, vanity, worthlessness.

inapplicable *adj* inapposite, inappropriate, inapt, irrelevant, unfit, unsuitable, unsuited.

inapposite *adj* impertinent, inapplicable, irrelevant, nonpertinent; inappropriate, unfit, unsuitable.

inappreciable *adj* impalpable, imperceptible, inconsiderable, inconspicuous, indiscernible, infinitesimal, insignificant, negligible, undiscernible, unnoticed.

inappropriate *adj* inapposite, unadapted, unbecoming, unfit, unsuitable, unsullied.

inapt *adj* inapposite, unapt, unfit, unsuitable; awkward, clumsy, dull, slow, stolid, stupid.

inaptitude *n* awkwardness, inapplicability, inappropriateness, inaptness, unfitness, unsuitableness.

inarticulate *adj* blurred, indistinct, thick; dumb, mute.

inartificial *adj* artless, direct, guileless, ingenuous, naive, simple, simple-minded, sincere, single-minded.

inasmuch as *conj* considering that, seeing that, since.

inattention *n* absent-mindedness, carelessness, disregard, heedlessness, inadvertence, inapplication, inconsiderateness, neglect, remissness, slip, thoughtlessness, unmindfulness, unobservance

inattentive *adj* absent-minded, careless, disregarding, heedless, inadvertent, inconsiderate, neglectful, remiss, thoughtless, unmindful, unobservant.

inaudible *adj* faint, indistinct, muffled; mute, noiseless, silent, still.

inaugurate *vb* induct, install, introduce, invest; begin, commence, initiate, institute, originate.

inauguration *n* beginning, commencement, initiation, institution, investiture, installation, opening, origination.

inauspicious *adj* bad, discouraging, ill-omened, ill-starred, ominous, unfavourable, unfortunate, unlucky, unpromising, unpropitious, untoward.

inborn *adj* congenital, inbred, ingrained, inherent, innate, instinctive, native, natural.

incalculable *adj* countless, enormous, immense, incalculable, inestimable, innumerable, sumless, unknown, untold.

incandescence *n* candescence, glow, gleam, luminousness, luminosity.

incandescent *adj* aglow, candent, candescent, gleaming, glowing, luminous, luminant, radiant.

incantation *n* charm, conjuration, enchantment, magic, necromancy, sorcery, spell, witchcraft, witchery.

incapability *n* disability, inability, incapacity, incompetence.

incapable *adj* feeble, impotent, incompetent, insufficient, unable, unfit, unfitted, unqualified, weak.

incapacious *adj* cramped, deficient, incommodious, narrow, scant.

incapacitate *vb* cripple, disable; disqualify, make unfit.

incapacity *n* disability, inability, incapability, incompetence; disqualification, unfitness.

incarcerate *vb* commit, confine, immure, imprison, jail, restrain, restrict.

incarnate *vb* body, embody, incorporate, personify. * *adj* bodied, embodied, incorporated, personified.

incarnation *n* embodiment, exemplification, impersonation, manifestation, personification.

incautious *adj* impolitic, imprudent, indiscreet, uncircumspect, unwary; careless, headlong, heedless, inconsiderate, negligent, rash, reckless, thoughtless.

incendiary *adj* dissentious, factious, inflammatory, seditious. * *n* agitator, firebrand, fire-raiser.

incense[1] *vb* anger, chafe, enkindle, enrage, exasperate, excite, heat, inflame, irritate, madden, provoke.

incense[2] *n* aroma, fragrance, perfume, scent; admiration, adulation, applause, laudation.

incentive *n* cause, encouragement, goad, impulse, incitement, inducement, instigation, mainspring, motive, provocation, spur, stimulus.

inception *n* beginning, commencement, inauguration, initiation, origin, rise, start.

incertitude *n* ambiguity, doubt, doubtfulness, indecision, uncertainty.

incessant *adj* ceaseless, constant, continual, continuous, eternal, everlasting, never-ending, perpetual, unceasing, unending, uninterrupted, unremitting.

inchoate *adj* beginning, commencing, inceptive, incipient, initial.

incident *n* circumstance, episode, event, fact, happening, occurrence. * *adj* happening; belonging, pertaining, appertaining, accessory, relating, natural; falling, impinging.

incidental *adj* accidental, casual, chance, concomitant, contingent, fortuitous, subordinate; adventitious, extraneous, nonessential, occasional.

incinerate *vb* burn, char, conflagrate, cremate, incremate.

incipient *adj* beginning, commencing, inchoate, inceptive, originating, starting.

incised *adj* carved, cut, engraved, gashed, graved, graven.

incision *n* cut, gash, notch, opening, penetration.

incisive *adj* cutting; acute, biting, sarcastic, satirical, sharp; acute, clear, distinct, penetrating, sharp-cut, trenchant.

incite *vb* actuate, animate, arouse, drive, encourage, excite, foment, goad, hound, impel, instigate, prod, prompt, provoke, push, rouse, spur, stimulate, urge.

incitement *n* encouragement, goad, impulse, incentive, inducement, motive, provocative, spur, stimulus.

incivility *n* discourteousness, discourtesy, disrespect, ill-breeding, ill-manners, impoliteness, impudence, inurbanity, rudeness, uncourtliness, unmannerliness.

inclemency *n* boisterousness, cruelty, harshness, rigour, roughness, severity, storminess, tempestuousness, tyranny.

inclement *adj* boisterous, harsh, rigorous, rough, severe, stormy; cruel, unmerciful.

inclination *n* inclining, leaning, slant, slope; trending, verging; aptitude, bent, bias, disposition, penchant, predilection, predisposition, proclivity, proneness, propensity, tendency, turn, twist; desire, fondness, liking, taste, partiality, predilection, wish; bow, nod, obeisance.

incline *vb* lean, slant, slope; bend, nod, verge; tend; bias, dispose, predispose, turn; bow. * *n* ascent, descent, grade, gradient, rise, slope.

inclose *see* **enclose.**

include *vb* contain, hold; comprehend, comprise, contain, cover, embody, embrace, incorporate, involve, take in.

inclusive *adj* comprehending, embracing, encircling, enclosing, including, taking in.

incognito, incognita *adj* camouflaged, concealed, disguised, unknown. * *n* camouflage, concealment, disguise.

incoherent *adj* detached, loose, nonadhesive, noncohesive; disconnected, incongruous, inconsequential, inconsistent, uncoordinated; confused, illogical, irrational, rambling, unintelligible, wild.

income *n* earnings, emolument, gains, interest, pay, perquisite, proceeds, profits, receipts, rents, return, revenue, salary, wages.

incommensurate *adj* disproportionate, inadequate, insufficient, unequal.

incommode *vb* annoy, discommode, disquiet, disturb, embarrass, hinder, inconvenience, molest, plague, trouble, upset, vex.

incommodious *adj* awkward, cumbersome, cumbrous, inconvenient, unhandy, unmanageable, unsuitable, unwieldy; annoying, disadvantageous, harassing, irritating, vexatious.

incommunicative *adj* exclusive, unsociable, unsocial, reserved.

incomparable *adj* matchless, inimitable, peerless, surpassing, transcendent, unequalled, unparalleled, unrivalled.

incompatibility *n* contrariety, contradictoriness, discrepancy, incongruity, inconsistency, irreconcilability, unsuitability, unsuitableness

incompatible *adj* contradictory, incongruous, inconsistent, inharmonious, irreconcilable, unadapted, unsuitable.

incompetence *n* inability, incapability, incapacity, incompetency; inadequacy, insufficiency; disqualification, unfitness.

incompetent *adj* incapable, unable; inadequate, insufficient; disqualified, incapacitated, unconstitutional, unfit, unfitted.

incomplete *adj* defective, deficient, imperfect, partial; inexhaustive, unaccompanied, uncompleted, unexecuted, unfinished.

incomprehensible *adj* inconceivable, inexhaustible, unfathomable, unimaginable; inconceivable, unintelligible, unthinkable.

incomputable *adj* enormous, immense, incalculable, innumerable, prodigious.

inconceivable *adj* incomprehensible, incredible, unbelievable, unimaginable, unthinkable.

inconclusive *adj* inconsequent, inconsequential, indecisive, unconvincing. illogical, unproved, unproven.

incongruity *n* absurdity, contradiction, contradictoriness, contrariety, discordance, discordancy, discrepancy, impropriety, inappropriateness, incoherence, incompatibility, inconsistency, unfitness, unsuitableness.

incongruous *adj* absurd, contradictory, contrary, disagreeing, discrepant, inappropriate, incoherent, incompatible, inconsistent, inharmonious, unfit, unsuitable.

inconsequent *adj* desultory, disconnected, fragmentary, illogical, inconclusive, inconsistent, irrelevant, loose.

inconsiderable *adj* immaterial, insignificant, petty, slight, small, trifling, trivial, unimportant.

inconsiderate *adj* intolerant, uncharitable, unthoughtful; careless, heedless, giddy, harebrained, hasty, headlong, imprudent, inadvertent, inattentive, indifferent, indiscreet, light-headed, negligent, rash, thoughtless.

inconsistency *n* incoherence, incompatibility, incongruity, unsuitableness; contradiction, contrariety; changeableness, inconstancy, instability, vacillation, unsteadiness.

inconsistent *adj* different, discrepant, illogical, incoherent, incompatible, incongruous, inconsequent, inconsonant, irreconcilable, unsuitable; contradictory, contrary; changeable, fickle, inconstant, unstable, unsteady, vacillating, variable.

inconsolable *adj* comfortless, crushed, disconsolate, forlorn, heartbroken, hopeless, woebegone.

inconstancy *n* changeableness, mutability, variability, variation, fluctuation, faithlessness, fickleness, capriciousness, vacillation, uncertainty, unsteadiness, volatility.

inconstant *adj* capricious, changeable, faithless, fickle, fluctuating, mercurial, mutable, unsettled, unsteady, vacillating, variable, varying, volatile, wavering; mutable, uncertain, unstable.

incontestable *adj* certain, incontrovertible, indisputable, indubitable, irrefrangible, sure, undeniable, unquestionable.

incontinence *n* excess, extravagance, indulgence, intemperance, irrepressibility, lasciviousness, lewdness, licentiousness, prodigality, profligacy, riotousness, unrestraint, wantonness, wildness.

incontinent *adj* debauched, lascivious, lewd, licentious, lustful, prodigal, unchaste, uncontrolled, unrestrained.

incontrovertible *adj* certain, incontestable, indisputable, indubitable, irrefutable, sure, undeniable, unquestionable.

inconvenience *vb* discommode; annoy, disturb, molest, trouble, vex. * *n* annoyance, disadvantage, disturbance, molestation, trouble, vexation; awkwardness, cumbersomeness, incommodiousness, unwieldiness; unfitness, unseasonableness, unsuitableness.

inconvenient *adj* annoying, awkward, cumbersome, cumbrous, disadvantageous, incommodious, inopportune, troublesome, uncomfortable, unfit, unhandy, unmanageable, unseasonable, unsuitable, untimely, unwieldy, vexatious.

incorporate *vb* affiliate, amalgamate, associate, blend, combine, consolidate, include, merge, mix, unite; embody, incarnate. * *adj* incorporeal, immaterial, spiritual, supernatural; blended, consolidated, merged, united.

incorporation *n* affiliation, alignment, amalgamation, association, blend, blending, combination, consolidation, fusion, inclusion, merger, mixture, unification, union, embodiment, incarnation, personification.

incorporeal *adj* bodiless, immaterial, impalpable, incorporate, spiritual, supernatural, unsubstantial.

incorrect *adj* erroneous, false, inaccurate, inexact, untrue, wrong; faulty, improper, mistaken, ungrammatical, unbecoming, unsound.

incorrectness *n* error, inaccuracy, inexactness, mistake.

incorrigible *adj* abandoned, graceless, hardened, irreclaimable, lost, obdurate, recreant, reprobate, shameless; helpless, hopeless, irremediable, irrecoverable, irreparable, irretrievable, irreversible, remediless.

incorruptibility *n* unpurchasableness; deathlessness, immortality, imperishableness, incorruptibleness, incorruption, indestructibility.

incorruptible *adj* honest, unbribable; imperishable, indestructible, immortal, undying, deathless, everlasting.

increase *vb* accrue, advance, augment, enlarge, extend, grow, intensify, mount, wax; multiply; enhance, greaten, heighten, raise, reinforce; aggravate, prolong. * *n* accession, accretion, accumulation, addition, augmentation, crescendo, development, enlargement, expansion, extension, growth, heightening, increment, intensification, multiplication, swelling; gain, produce, product, profit; descendants, issue, offspring, progeny.

incredible *adj* absurd, inadmissible, nonsensical, unbelievable.

incredulity *n* distrust, doubt, incredulousness, scepticism, unbelief.

incredulous *adj* distrustful, doubtful, dubious, sceptical, unbelieving.

increment *n* addition, augmentation, enlargement, increase.

incriminate *vb* accuse, blame, charge, criminate, impeach.

incubate *vb* brood, develop, hatch, sit.

inculcate *vb* enforce, implant, impress, infix, infuse, ingraft, inspire, instil.

inculpable *adj* blameless, faultless, innocent, irreprehensible, irreproachable, irreprovable, sinless, unblamable, unblameable.

inculpate *vb* accuse, blame, censure, charge, incriminate, impeach, incriminate.

inculpatory *adj* criminatory, incriminating.

incumbent *adj* binding, devolved, devolving, laid, obligatory; leaning, prone, reclining, resting. * *n* holder, occupant.

incur *vb* acquire, bring, contract.

incurable *adj* cureless, hopeless, irrecoverable, remediless; helpless, incorrigible, irremediable, irreparable, irretrievable, remediless.

incurious *adj* careless, heedless, inattentive, indifferent, uninquisitive, unobservant, uninterested.

incursion *n* descent, foray, raid, inroad, irruption.

incursive *adj* aggressive, hostile, invasive, predatory, raiding.

incurvate *vb* bend, bow, crook, curve. * *adj* (*bot*) aduncous, arcuate, bowed, crooked, curved, hooked.

indebted *adj* beholden, obliged, owing.

indecency *n* impropriety, indecorum, offensiveness, outrageousness, unseemliness; coarseness, filthiness, foulness, grossness, immodesty, impurity, obscenity, vileness.

indecent *adj* bold, improper, indecorous, offensive, outrageous, unbecoming, unseemly; coarse, dirty, filthy, gross, immodest, impure, indelicate, lewd, nasty, obscene, pornographic, salacious, shameless, smutty, unchaste.

indecipherable *adj* illegible, undecipherable, undiscoverable, inexplicable, obscure, unintelligible, unreadable.

indecision *n* changeableness, fickleness, hesitation, inconstancy, irresolution, unsteadiness, vacillation.

indecisive *adj* dubious, hesitating, inconclusive, irresolute, undecided, unsettled, vacillating, wavering.

indecorous *adj* coarse, gross, ill-bred, impolite, improper, indecent, rude, unbecoming, uncivil, unseemly.

indecorum *n* grossness, ill-breeding, ill manners, impoliteness, impropriety, incivility, indecency, indecorousness.

indeed *adv* absolutely, actually, certainly, in fact, in truth, in reality, positively, really, strictly, truly, verily, veritably. * *interj* really! you don't say so! is it possible!

indefatigable *adj* assiduous, never-tiring, persevering, persistent, sedulous, tireless, unflagging, unremitting, untiring, unwearied.

indefeasible *adj* immutable, inalienable, irreversible, irrevocable, unalterable.

indefensible *adj* censurable, defenceless, faulty, unpardonable, untenable; inexcusable, insupportable, unjustifiable, unwarrantable, wrong.

indefinite *adj* confused, doubtful, equivocal, general, imprecise, indefinable, indecisive, indeterminate, indistinct, inexact, inexplicit, lax, loose, nondescript, obscure, uncertain, undefined, undetermined, unfixed, unsettled, vague.

indelible *adj* fast, fixed, ineffaceable, ingrained, permanent.

indelicacy *n* coarseness, grossness, indecorousness, indecorum, impropriety, offensiveness, unseemliness, vulgarity; immodesty, indecency, lewdness, unchastity; foulness, obscenity.

indelicate *adj* broad, coarse, gross, indecorous, intrusive, rude, unbecoming, unseemly; foul, immodest, indecent, lewd, obscene, unchaste, vulgar.

indemnification *n* compensation, reimbursement, remuneration, security.

indemnify *vb* compensate, reimburse, remunerate, requite, secure.

indent *vb* bruise, jag, notch, pink, scallop, serrate; bind, indenture.

indentation *n* bruise, dent, depression, jag, notch.

indenture *vb* bind, indent. * *n* contract, instrument; indentation.

independence *n* freedom, liberty, self-direction; distinctness, nondependence, separation; competence, ease.

independent *adj* absolute, autonomous, free, self-directing, uncoerced, unrestrained, unrestricted, voluntary; (*person*) self-reliant, unconstrained, unconventional.

indescribable *adj* ineffable, inexpressible, nameless, unutterable.

indestructible *adj* abiding, endless, enduring, everlasting, fadeless, imperishable, incorruptible, undecaying.

indeterminate *adj* indefinite, uncertain, undetermined, unfixed.

index *vb* alphabetize, catalogue, codify, earmark, file, list, mark, tabulate. * *n* catalogue, list, register, tally;

indicator, lead, mark, pointer, sign, signal, token; contents, table of contents; forefinger; exponent.

indicate *vb* betoken, denote, designate, evince, exhibit, foreshadow, manifest, mark, point out, prefigure, presage, register, show, signify, specify, tell; hint, imply, intimate, sketch, suggest.

indication *n* hint, index, manifestation, mark, note, sign, suggestion, symptom, token.

indicative *adj* significant, suggestive, symptomatic; (*gram*) affirmative, declarative.

indict *vb* (*law*) accuse, charge, present.

indictment *n* (*law*) indicting, presentment; accusation, arraignment, charge, crimination, impeachment.

indifference *n* apathy, carelessness, coldness, coolness, heedlessness, inattention, insignificance, negligence, unconcern, unconcernedness, uninterestedness; disinterestedness, impartiality, neutrality.

indifferent *adj* apathetic, cold, cool, dead, distant, dull, easy-going, frigid, heedless, inattentive, incurious, insensible, insouciant, listless, lukewarm, nonchalant, perfunctory, regardless, stoical, unconcerned, uninterested, unmindful, unmoved; equal; fair, medium, middling, moderate, ordinary, passable, tolerable; mediocre, so-so; immaterial, unimportant; disinterested, impartial, neutral, unbiased.

indigence *n* destitution, distress, necessity, need, neediness, pauperism, penury, poverty, privation, want.

indigenous *adj* aboriginal, home-grown, inborn, inherent, native.

indigent *adj* destitute, distressed, insolvent, moneyless, necessitous, needy, penniless, pinched, poor, reduced.

indigested *adj* unconcocted, undigested; crude, ill-advised, ill-considered, ill-judged; confused, disorderly, ill-arranged, unmethodical.

indigestion *n* dyspepsia, dyspepsy.

indignant *adj* angry, exasperated, incensed, irate, ireful, provoked, roused, wrathful, wroth.

indignation *n* anger, choler, displeasure, exasperation, fury, ire, rage, resentment, wrath.

indignity *n* abuse, affront, contumely, dishonour, disrespect, ignominy, insult, obloquy, opprobrium, outrage, reproach, slight.

indirect *adj* circuitous, circumlocutory, collateral, devious, oblique, roundabout, sidelong, tortuous; deceitful, dishonest, dishonorable, unfair; mediate, remote, secondary, subordinate.

indiscernible *adj* imperceptible, indistinguishable, invisible, undiscernible, undiscoverable.

indiscipline *n* laxity, insubordination.

indiscreet *adj* foolish, hasty, headlong, heedless, imprudent, incautious, inconsiderate, injudicious, rash, reckless, unwise.

indiscretion *n* folly, imprudence, inconsiderateness, rashness; blunder, faux pas, lapse, mistake, misstep.

indiscriminate *adj* confused, heterogeneous, indistinct, mingled, miscellaneous, mixed, promiscuous, undiscriminating, undistinguishable, undistinguishing.

indispensable *adj* essential, expedient, necessary, needed, needful, requisite.

indisputable *adj* certain, incontestable, indubitable, infallible, sure, undeniable, undoubted, unmistakable, unquestionable.

indisposed *adj* ailing, ill, sick, unwell; averse, backward, disinclined, loath, reluctant, unfriendly, unwilling.

indisposition *n* ailment, illness, sickness; aversion, backwardness, dislike, disinclination, reluctance, unwillingness.

indisputable *adj* certain, incontestable, indutitable, infallible, sure, undeniable, undoubted, unmistakable, unquestionable.

indissoluble *adj* abiding, enduring, firm, imperishable, incorruptible, indestructible, lasting, stable, unbreakable.

indistinct *adj* ambiguous, doubtful, uncertain; blurred, dim, dull, faint, hazy, misty, nebulous, obscure, shadowy, vague; confused, inarticulate, indefinite, indistinguishable, undefined, undistinguishable.

indistinguishable *adj* imperceptible, indiscernible, unnoticeable, unobservable; chaotic, confused, dim, indistinct, obscure, vague.

indite *vb* compose, pen, write.

individual *adj* characteristic, distinct, identical, idiosyncratic, marked, one, particular, personal, respective, separate, single, singular, special, unique; peculiar, proper; decided, definite, independent, positive, self-guided, unconventional. * *n* being, character, party, person, personage, somebody, someone; type, unit.

individuality *n* definiteness, indentity, personality; originality, self-direction, self-determination, singularity, uniqueness.

individualize *vb* individuate, particularize, singularize, specify.

indivisible *adj* incommensurable, indissoluble, inseparable, unbreakable, unpartiable.

indocile *adj* cantankerous, contumacious, dogged, froward, inapt, headstrong, intractable, mulish, obstinate, perverse, refractory, stubborn, ungovernable, unmanageable, unruly, unteachable.

indoctrinate *vb* brainwash, imbue, initiate, instruct, rehabilitate, teach.

indoctrination *n* grounding, initiation, instruction, rehabilitation.

indolence *n* idleness, inactivity, inertia, inertness, laziness, listlessness, sloth, slothfulness, sluggishness.

indolent *adj* easy, easy-going, inactive, inert, lazy, listless, lumpish, otiose, slothful, sluggish, supine.

indomitable *adj* invincible, unconquerable, unyielding.

indorse *see* **endorse**.

indubitable *adj* certain, evident, incontestable, incontrovertible, indisputable, sure, undeniable, unquestionable.

induce *vb* actuate, allure, bring, draw, drive, entice, impel, incite, influence, instigate, move, persuade, prevail, prompt, spur, urge; bring on, cause, effect, motivate, lead, occasion, produce.

inducement *n* allurement, draw, enticement, instigation, persuasion; cause, consideration, impulse, incentive, incitement, influence, motive, reason, spur, stimulus.

induct *vb* inaugurate, initiate, install, institute, introduce, invest.

induction *n* inauguration, initiation, institution, installation, introduction; conclusion, generalization, inference.

indue *vb* assume, endow, clothe, endue, invest, supply.

indulge *vb* gratify, license, revel, satisfy, wallow, yield to; coddle, cosset, favour, humour, pamper, pet, spoil; allow, cherish, foster, harbour, permit, suffer.

indulgence *n* gratification, humouring, pampering; favour, kindness, lenience, lenity, liberality, tenderness; (*theol*) absolution, remission.

indulgent *adj* clement, easy, favouring, forbearing, gentle, humouring, kind, lenient, mild, pampering, tender, tolerant.

indurate *vb* harden, inure, sear, strengthen.

induration *n* hardening, obduracy.

industrious *adj* assiduous, diligent, hard-working, laborious, notable, operose, sedulous; brisk, busy, persevering, persistent.

industry *n* activity, application, assiduousness, assiduity, diligence; perseverance, persistence, sedulousness, vigour; effort, labour, toil.

inebriated *adj* drunk, intoxicated, stupefied.

ineffable *adj* indescribable, inexpressible, unspeakable, unutterable.

ineffaceable *adj* indelible, indestructible, inerasable, inexpungeable, ingrained.

ineffectual *adj* abortive, bootless, fruitless, futile, inadequate, inefficacious, ineffective, inoperative, useless, unavailing, vain; feeble, inefficient, powerless, impotent, weak.

inefficacy *n* ineffectualness, inefficiency.

inefficient *adj* feeble, incapable, ineffectual, ineffective, inefficacious, weak.

inelastic *adj* flabby, flaccid, inductile, inflexible, irresilient.

inelegant *adj* abrupt, awkward, clumsy, coarse, constrained, cramped, crude, graceless, harsh, homely, homespun, rough, rude, stiff, tasteless, uncourtly, uncouth, ungainly, ungraceful, unpolished, unrefined.

ineligible *adj* disqualified, unqualified; inexpedient, objectionable, unadvisable, undesirable.

inept *adj* awkward, improper, inapposite, inappropriate, unapt, unfit, unsuitable; null, useless, void, worthless; foolish, nonsensical, pointless, senseless, silly, stupid.

ineptitude *n* inappositeness, inappropriateness, inaptitude, unfitness, unsuitability, unsuitableness; emptiness, nullity, uselessness, worthlessness; folly, foolishness, nonsense, pointlessness, senselessness, silliness, stupidity.

inequality *n* disproportion, inequitableness, injustice, unfairness; difference, disparity, dissimilarity, diversity, imparity, irregularity, roughness, unevenness; inadequacy, incompetency, insufficiency.

inequitable *adj* unfair, unjust.

inert *adj* comatose, dead, inactive, lifeless, motionless, quiescent, passive; apathetic, dronish, dull, idle, indolent, lazy, lethargic, lumpish, phlegmatic, slothful, sluggish, supine, torpid.

inertia *n* apathy, inertness, lethargy, passiveness, passivity, slothfulness, sluggishness.

inestimable *adj* incalculable, invaluable, precious, priceless, valuable.

inevitable *adj* certain, necessary, unavoidable, undoubted.

inexact *adj* imprecise, inaccurate, incorrect; careless, crude, loose.

inexcusable *adj* indefensible, irremissible, unallowable, unjustifiable, unpardonable.

inexhaustible *adj* boundless, exhaustless, indefatigable, unfailing, unlimited.

inexorable *adj* cruel, firm, hard, immovable, implacable, inflexible, merciless, pitiless, relentless, severe, steadfast, unbending, uncompassionate, unmerciful, unrelenting, unyielding.

inexpedient *adj* disadvantageous, ill-judged, impolitic, imprudent, indiscreet, injudicious, inopportune, unadvisable, unprofitable, unwise.

inexperience *n* greenness, ignorance, rawness.

inexperienced *adj* callow, green, raw, strange, unacquainted, unconversant, undisciplined, uninitiated, unpractised, unschooled, unskilled, untrained, untried, unversed, young.

inexpert *adj* awkward, bungling, clumsy, inapt, maladroit, unhandy, unskilful, unskilled.

inexpiable *adj* implacable, inexorable, irreconcilable, unappeasable; irremissible, unatonable, unpardonable.

inexplicable *adj* enigmatic, enigmatical, incomprehensible, inscrutable, mysterious, strange, unaccountable, unintelligible.

inexpressible *adj* indescribable, ineffable, unspeakable, unutterable; boundless, infinite, surpassing.

inexpressive *adj* blank, characterless, dull, unexpressive.

inextinguishable *adj* unquenchable.

in extremis *adv* moribund.

inextricable *adj* entangled, intricate, perplexed, unsolvable.

infallibility *n* certainty, infallibleness, perfection.

infallible *adj* certain, indubitable, oracular, sure, unerring, unfailing.

infamous *adj* abominable, atrocious, base, damnable, dark, detestable, discreditable, disgraceful, dishonorable, disreputable, heinous, ignominious, nefarious, odious, opprobrious, outrageous, scandalous, shameful, shameless, vile, villainous, wicked.

infamy *n* abasement, discredit, disgrace, dishonour, disrepute, ignominy, obloquy, odium, opprobrium, scandal, shame; atrocity, detestableness, disgracefulness, dishonorableness, odiousness, scandalousness, shamefulness, villainy, wickedness.

infancy *n* beginning, commencement; babyhood, childhood, minority, nonage, pupillage.

infant *n* babe, baby, bairn, bantling, brat, chit, minor, nursling, papoose, suckling, tot.

infantile *adj* childish, infantine, newborn, tender, young; babyish, childish, weak; babylike, childlike.

infatuate *vb* befool, besot, captivate, delude, prepossess, stultify.

infatuation *n* absorption, besottedness, folly, foolishness, prepossession, stupefaction.

infeasible *adj* impractical, unfeasible.

infect *vb* affect, contaminate, corrupt, defile, poison, pollute, taint, vitiate.

infection *n* affection, bane, contagion, contamination, corruption, defilement, pest, poison, pollution, taint, virus, vitiation.

infectious *adj* catching, communicable, contagious, contaminating, corrupting, defiling, demoralizing, pestiferous, pestilential, poisoning, polluting, sympathetic, vitiating.

infecund *adj* barren, infertile, sterile, unfruitful, unproductive, unprolific.

infecundity *n* unfruitfulness.

infelicitous *adj* calamitous, miserable, unfortunate, unhappy, wretched; inauspicious, unfavourable, unpropitious; ill-chosen, inappropriate, unfitting.

infer *vb* collect, conclude, deduce, derive, draw, gather, glean, guess, presume, reason.

inference *n* conclusion, consequence, corollary, deduction, generalization, guess, illation, implication, induction, presumption.

inferior *adj* lower, nether; junior, minor, secondary, subordinate; bad, base, deficient, humble, imperfect, indifferent, mean, mediocre, paltry, poor, second-rate, shabby.

inferiority *n* juniority, subjection, subordination, mediocrity; deficiency, imperfection, inadequacy, shortcoming.

infernal *adj* abominable, accursed, atrocious, damnable, dark, demoniacal, devilish, diabolical, fiendish, fiendlike, hellish, malicious, nefarious, satanic, Stygian.

infertility *n* barrenness, infecundity, sterility, unfruitfulness, unproductivity.

infest *vb* annoy, disturb, harass, haunt, molest, plague, tease, torment, trouble, vex, worry; beset, overrun, possess, swarm, throng.

infidel *n* agnostic, atheist, disbeliever, heathen, heretic, sceptic, unbeliever.

infidelity *n* adultery, disloyalty, faithlessness, treachery, unfaithfulness; disbelief, scepticism, unbelief.

infiltrate *vb* absorb, pervade, soak.

infinite *adj* boundless, endless, illimitable, immeasurable, inexhaustible, interminable, limitless, measureless, perfect, unbounded, unlimited; enormous, immense, stupendous, vast; absolue, eternal, self-determined, self-existent, unconditioned.

infinitesimal *adj* infinitely small; microscopic, miniscule.

infinity *n* absoluteness, boundlessness, endlessness, eternity, immensity, infiniteness, infinitude, interminateness, self-determination, self-existence, vastness.

infirm *adj* ailing, debilitated, enfeebled, feeble, frail, weak, weakened; faltering, irresolute, vacillating, wavering; insecure, precarious, unsound, unstable.

infirmity *n* ailment, debility, feebleness, frailness, frailty, weakness; defect, failing, fault, foible, weakness.

infix *vb* fasten, fix, plant, set; implant, inculcate, infuse, ingraft, instil.

inflame *vb* animate, arouse, excite, enkindle, fire, heat, incite, inspirit, intensify, rouse, stimulate; aggravate, anger, chafe, embitter, enrage, exasperate, incense, infuriate, irritate, madden, nettle, provoke.

inflammability *n* combustibility, combustibleness, inflammableness.

inflammable *adj* combustible, ignitible; excitable.

inflammation *n* burning, conflagration; anger, animosity, excitement, heat, rage, turbulence, violence.

inflammatory *adj* fiery, inflaming; dissentious, incendiary, seditious.

inflate *vb* bloat, blow up, distend, expand, swell, sufflate; elate, puff up; enlarge, increase.

inflated *adj* bloated, distended, puffed-up, swollen; bombastic, declamatory, grandiloquent, high-flown, magniloquent, overblown, pompous, rhetorical, stilted, tumid, turgid.

inflation *n* enlargement, increase, overenlargement, overissue; bloatedness, distension, expansion, sufflation; bombast, conceit, conceitedness, self-conceit, self-complacency, self-importance, self-sufficiency, vaingloriousness, vainglory.

inflect *vb* bend, bow, curve, turn; (*gram*) conjugate, decline, vary.

inflection *n* bend, bending, crook, curvature, curvity, flexure; (*gram*) accidence, conjugation, declension, variation; (*mus*) modulation.

inflexibility *n* inflexibleness, rigidity, stiffness; doggedness, obstinacy, perinacity, stubbornness; firmness, perseverance, resolution, tenacity.

inflexible *adj* rigid, rigorous, stiff, unbending; cantankerous, cross-grained, dogged, headstrong, heady, inexorable, intractable, obdurate, obstinant, pertinacious, refractory, stubborn, unyielding, wilful; firm, immovable, persevering, resolute, steadfast, unbending.

inflict *vb* bring, impose, lay on.

infliction *n* imposition, inflicting; judgment, punishment.

inflorescence *n* blooming, blossoming, flowering.

influence *vb* affect, bias, control, direct, lead, modify, prejudice, prepossess, sway; actuate, arouse, impel, incite, induce, instigate, move, persuade, prevail upon, rouse. * *n* ascendancy, authority, control, mastery, potency, predominance, pull, rule, sway; credit, reputation, weight; inflow, inflowing, influx; magnetism, power, spell.

influential *adj* controlling, effective, effectual, potent, powerful, strong; authoritative, momentous, substantial, weighty.

influx *n* flowing in, introduction.

infold *see* **enfold**.

inform *vb* animate, inspire, quicken; acquaint, advise, apprise, enlighten, instruct, notify, teach, tell, tip, warn.

informal *adj* unceremonious, unconventional, unofficial; easy, familiar, natural, simple; irregular, nonconformist, unusual.

informality *n* unceremoniousness; unconventionality; ease, familiarity, naturalness, simplicity; noncomformity, irregularity, unusualness.

informant *n* advertiser, adviser, informer, intelligencer, newsmonger, notifier, relator; accuser, complainant, informer.

information *n* advice, data, intelligence, knowledge, notice; advertisement, enlightenment, instruction, message, tip, word, warning; accusation, complaint, denunciation.

informer *n* accuser, complainant, informant, snitch.

infraction *n* breach, breaking, disobedience, encroachment, infringement, nonobservance, transgression, violation.

infrangible *adj* inseparable, inviolable, unbreakable.

infrequency *n* rareness, rarity, uncommonness, unusualness.

infrequent *adj* rare, uncommon, unfrequent, unusual; occasional, scant, scarce, sporadic.

infringe *vb* break, contravene, disobey, intrude, invade, transgress, violate.

infringement *n* breach, breaking, disobedience, infraction, nonobservance, transgression, violation.

infuriated *adj* angry, enraged, furious, incensed, maddened, raging, wild.

infuse *vb* breathe into, implant, inculcate, ingraft, insinuate, inspire, instil, introduce; macerate, steep.

infusion *n* inculcation, instillation, introduction; infusing, macerating, steeping.

ingathering *n* harvest.

ingenious *adj* able, adroit, artful, bright, clever, fertile, gifted, inventive, ready, sagacious, shrewd, witty.

ingenuity *n* ability, acuteness, aptitude, aptness, capacity, capableness, cleverness, faculty, genius, gift, ingeniousness, inventiveness, knack, readiness, skill, turn.

ingenuous *adj* artless, candid, childlike, downright, frank, generous, guileless, honest, innocent, naive, open, open-hearted, plain, simple-minded, sincere, single-minded, straightforward, transparent, truthful, unreserved.

ingenuousness *n* artlessness, candour, childlikeness, frankness, guilelessness, honesty, naivety, openheartedness, openness, sincerity, single-mindedness, truthfulness.

inglorious *adj* humble, lowly, mean, nameless, obscure, undistinguished, unhonoured, unknown, unmarked, unnoted; discreditable, disgraceful, humiliating, ignominious, scandalous, shameful.

ingloriousness *n* humbleness, lowliness, meanness, namelessness, obscurity; abasement, discredit, disgrace, dishonour, disrepute, humiliation, infamy, ignominiousness, ignominy, obloquy, odium, opprobrium, shame.

ingraft *vb* graft, implant, inculcate, infix, infuse, instil.

ingrain *vb* dye, imbue, impregnate.

ingratiate *vb* insinuate.

ingratitude *n* thanklessness, ungratefulness, unthankfulness.

ingredient *n* component, constituent, element.

ingress *n* entrance, entré, entry, introgression.

ingulf *see* **engulf.**

inhabit *vb* abide, dwell, live, occupy, people, reside, sojourn.

inhabitable *adj* habitable, livable.

inhabitant *n* citizen, denizen, dweller, inhabiter, resident.

inhalation *n* breath, inhaling, inspiration; sniff, snuff.

inhale *vb* breathe in, draw in, inbreathe, inspire.

inharmonious *adj* discordant, inharmonic, out of tune, unharmonious, unmusical.

inhere *vb* cleave to, stick, stick fast; abide, belong, exist, lie, pertain, reside.

inherent *adj* essential, immanent, inborn, inbred, indwelling, ingrained, innate, inseparable, intrinsic, native, natural, proper; adhering, sticking.

inherit *vb* get, receive.

inheritance *n* heritage, legacy, patrimony; inheriting.

inheritor *n* heir, (*law*) parcener.

inhibit *vb* bar, check, debar, hinder, obstruct, prevent, repress, restrain, stop; forbid, interdict, prohibit.

inhibition *n* check, hindrance, impediment, obstacle, obstruction, restraint; disallowance, embargo, interdict, interdiction, prevention, prohibition.

inhospitable *adj* cool, forbidding, unfriendly, unkind; bigoted, illiberal, intolerant, narrow, prejudiced, ungenerous, unreceptive; barren, wild.

inhospitality *n* inhospitableness, unkindness; illiberality, narrowness.

inhuman *adj* barbarous, brutal, cruel, fell, ferocious, merciless, pitiless, remorseless, ruthless, savage, unfeeling; nonhuman.

inhumanity *n* barbarity, brutality, cruelty, ferocity, savageness; hard-heartedness, unkindness.

inhume *vb* bury, entomb, inter.

inimical *adj* antagonistic, hostile, unfriendly; adverse, contrary, harmful, hurtful, noxious, opposed, pernicious, repugnant, unfavourable.

inimitable *adj* incomparable, matchless, peerless, unequalled, unexampled, unmatched, unparagoned, unparalleled, unrivalled, unsurpassed.

iniquitous *adj* atrocious, criminal, flagitious, heinous, inequitable, nefarious, sinful, wicked, wrong, unfair, unjust, unrighteous.

iniquity *n* injustice, sin, sinfulness, unrighteousness, wickedness, wrong; crime, misdeed, offence.

initial *adj* first; beginning, commencing, incipient, initiatory, introductory, opening, original; elementary, inchoate, rudimentary.

initiate *vb* begin, commence, enter upon, inaugurate, introduce, open; ground, indoctrinate, instruct, prime, teach.

initiation *n* beginning, commencement, inauguration, opening; admission, entrance, introduction; indoctrinate, instruction.

initiative *n* beginning; energy, enterprise.

initiatory *adj* inceptive, initiative.

inject *vb* force in, interject, insert, introduce, intromit.

injudicious *adj* foolish, hasty, ill-advised, ill-judged, imprudent, incautious, inconsiderate, indiscreet, rash, unwise.

injunction *n* admonition, bidding, command, mandate, order, precept.

injure *vb* damage, disfigure, harm, hurt, impair, mar, spoil, sully, wound; abuse, aggrieve, wrong; affront, dishonour, insult.

injurious *adj* baneful, damaging, deadly, deleterious, destructive, detrimental, disadvantageous, evil, fatal, hurtful, mischievous, noxious, pernicious, prejudicial, ruinous; inequitable, iniquitous, unjust, wrongful; contumelious, detractory, libellous, slanderous.

injury *n* evil, ill, injustice, wrong; damage, detriment, harm, hurt, impairment, loss, mischief, prejudice.

injustice *n* inequity, unfairness; grievance, iniquity, injury, wrong.

inkhorn *n* inkbottle, inkstand.

inkling *n* hint, intimation, suggestion, whisper.

inky *adj* atramentous, black, murky.

inland *adj* domestic, hinterland, home, upcountry; interior, internal.

inlet *n* arm, bay, bight, cove, creek; entrance, ingress, passage.

inmate *n* denizen, dweller, guest, intern, occupant.

inmost *adj* deepest, innermost.

inn *n* hostel, hostelry, hotel, pub, public house, tavern.

innate *adj* congenital, constitutional, inborn, inbred, indigenous, inherent, inherited, instinctive, native, natural, organic.

inner *adj* interior, internal.

innermost *adj* deepest, inmost.

innkeeper *n* host, innholder, landlady, landlord, tavernkeeper.

innocence *n* blamelessness, chastity, guilelessness, guiltlessness, purity, simplicity, sinlessness, stainlessness; harmlessness, innocuousness, innoxiousness, inoffensiveness.

innocent *adj* blameless, clean, clear, faultless, guiltless, immaculate, pure, sinless, spotless, unfallen, upright; harmless, innocuous, innoxious, inoffensive; lawful, legitimate, permitted; artless, guileless, ignorant, ingenuous, simple. * *n* babe, child, ingénue, naif, naive, unsophisticate.

innocuous *adj* harmless, innocent, inoffensive, safe.

innovate *vb* change, introduce.

innovation *n* change, introduction; departure, novelty.

innuendo *n* allusion, hint, insinuation, intimation, suggestion.

innumerable *adj* countless, numberless.

inoculate *vb* infect, vaccinate.

inoffensive *adj* harmless, innocent, innocuous, innoxious, unobjectionable, unoffending.

inoperative *adj* inactive, ineffectual, inefficacious, not in force.

inopportune *adj* ill-timed, inexpedient, infelicitous, mistimed, unfortunate, unhappy, unseasonable, untimely.

inordinate *adj* excessive, extravagant, immoderate, intemperate, irregular.

inorganic *adj* inanimate, unorganized; mineral.

inquest *n* inquiry, inquisition, investigation, quest, search.

inquietude *n* anxiety, disquiet, disquietude, disturbance, restlessness, uneasiness.

inquire, enquire *vb* ask, catechize, interpellate, interrogate, investigate, query, question, quiz.

inquiry, enquiry *n* examination, exploration, investigation, research, scrutiny, study; interrogation, query, question, quiz.

inquisition *n* examination, inquest, inquiry, investigation, search.

inquisitive *adj* curious, inquiring, scrutinizing; curious, meddlesome, peeping, peering, prying.

inroad *n* encroachment, foray, incursion, invasion, irruption, raid.

insalubrious *adj* noxious, unhealthful, unhealthy, unwholesome.

insane *adj* abnormal, crazed, crazy, delirious, demented, deranged, distracted, lunatic, mad, maniacal, unhealthy, unsound.

insanity *n* craziness, delirium, dementia, derangement, lunacy, madness, mania, mental aberration, mental alienation.

insatiable *adj* greedy, rapacious, voracious; insatiate, unappeasable.

inscribe *vb* emblaze, endorse, engrave, enroll, impress, imprint, letter, mark, write; address, dedicate.

inscrutable *adj* hidden, impenetrable, incomprehensible, inexplicable, mysterious, undiscoverable, unfathomable, unsearchable.

inscrutableness *n* impenetrability, incomprehensibility, incomprehensibleness, inexplicability, inscrutability, mysteriousness, mystery, unfathomableness, unsearchableness.

insecure *adj* risky, uncertain, unconfident, unsure; exposed, ill-protected, unprotected, unsafe; dangerous, hazardous, perilous; infirm, shaking, shaky, tottering, unstable, weak, wobbly.

insecurity *n* riskiness, uncertainty; danger, hazardousness, peril; instability, shakiness, weakness, wobbliness.

insensate *adj* dull, indifferent, insensible, torpid; brutal, foolish, senseless, unwise; inanimate, insensible, insentient, nonpercipient, unconscious, unperceiving.

insensibility *n* dullness, insentience, lethargy, torpor; apathy, indifference, insusceptibility, unfeelingness, dullness, stupidity; anaesthesia, coma, stupor, unconsciousness.

insensible *adj* imperceivable, imperceptible, undiscoverable; blunted, brutish, deaf, dull, insensate, numb, obtuse, senseless, sluggish, stolid, stupid, torpid, unconscious; apathetic, callous, phlegmatic, impassive, indifferent, insensitive, insentient, unfeeling, unimpressible, unsusceptible.

insensibly *adv* imperceptibly.

insentient *adj* inert, nonsentient, senseless; inanimate, insensible, insensate, nonpercipient, unconscious, unperceiving.

inseparable *adj* close, friendly, intimate, together; indissoluble, indivisible, inseverable.

insert *vb* infix, inject, intercalate, interpolate, introduce, inweave, parenthesize, place, put, set.

inside *adj* inner, interior, internal; confidential, exclusive, internal, private, secret. * *adv* indoors, within. * *n* inner part, interior; nature.

insidious *adj* creeping, deceptive, gradual, secretive; arch, artful, crafty, crooked, cunning, deceitful, designing, diplomatic, foxy, guileful, intriguing, Machiavellian, sly, sneaky, subtle, treacherous, trickish, tricky, wily.

insight *n* discernment, intuition, penetration, perception, perspicuity, understanding.

insignia *npl* badges, marks.

insignificance *n* emptiness, nothingenss, paltriness, triviality, unimportance.

insignificant *adj* contemptible, empty, immaterial, inconsequential, inconsiderable, inferior, meaningless, paltry, petty, small, sorry, trifling, trivial, unessential, unimportant.

insincere *adj* deceitful, dishonest, disingenuous, dissembling, dissimulating, double-faced, double-tongued, duplicitous, empty, faithless, false, hollow, hypocritical, pharisaical, truthless, uncandid, untrue.

insincerity *n* bad faith, deceitfulness, dishonesty, disingenuousness, dissimulation, duplicity, falseness, faithlessness, hypocrisy.

insinuate *vb* hint, inculcate, infuse, ingratiate, instil, intimate, introduce, suggest.

insipid *adj* dead, dull, flat, heavy, inanimate, jejune, lifeless, monotonous, pointless, prosaic, prosy, spiritless, stupid, tame, unentertaining, uninteresting; mawkish, savourless, stale, tasteless, vapid, zestless.

insipidity, insipidness *n* dullness, heaviness, lifelessness, prosiness, stupidity, tameness; flatness, mawkishness, staleness, tastlessness, unsavouriness, vapidness, zestlessness.

insist *vb* demand, maintain, urge.

insistence *n* importunity, solicitousness, urging, urgency.

insnare *see* ensnare.

insolence *n* impertinence, impudence, malapertness, pertness, rudeness, sauciness; contempt, contumacy, contumely, disrespect, frowardness, insubordination.

insolent *adj* abusive, contemptuous, contumelious, disrespectful, domineering, insulting, offensive, overbearing, rude, supercilious; cheeky, impertinent, impudent, malapert, pert, saucy; contumacious, disobedient, froward, insubordinate.

insoluble *adj* indissoluble, indissolvable, irreducible; inexplicable, insolvable.

insolvable *adj* inexplicable.

insolvent *adj* bankrupt, broken, failed, ruined.

insomnia *n* sleeplessness, wakefulness.

inspect *vb* examine, investigate, look into, pry into, scrutinize; oversee, superintend, supervise.

inspection *n* examination, investigation, scrutiny; oversight, superintendence, supervision.

inspector *n* censor, critic, examiner, visitor; boss, overseer, superintendent, supervisor.

inspiration *n* breathing, inhalation; afflatus, fire, inflatus; elevation, exaltation; enthusiasm.

inspire *vb* breathe, inhale; infuse, instil; animate, cheer, enliven, inspirit; elevate, exalt, stimulate; fill, imbue, impart, inform, quicken.

inspirit *vb* animate, arouse, cheer, comfort, embolden, encourage, enhearten, enliven, fire, hearten, incite, invigorate, quicken, rouse, stimulate.

instable *see* unstable.

instability *n* changeableness, fickleness, inconstancy, insecurity, mutability.

install, instal *vb* inaugurate, induct, introduce; establish, place, set up.

installation *n* inauguration, induction, instalment, investiture.

instalment *n* earnest, payment, portion.

instance *vb* adduce, cite, mention, specify. * *n* case, example, exemplification, illustration, occasion; impulse, incitement, instigation, motive, prompting, request, solicitation.

instant *adj* direct, immediate, instantaneous, prompt, quick; current, present; earnest, fast, imperative, importunate, pressing, urgent; ready cooked. * *n* flash, jiffy, moment, second, trice, twinkling; hour, time.

instantaneous *adj* abrupt, immediate, instant, quick, sudden.

instantaneously *adv* forthwith, immediately, presto, quickly, right away.

instauration *n* reconstitution, reconstruction, redintegration, re-establishment, rehabilitation, reinstatement, renewal, renovation, restoration.

instead *adv* in lieu, in place, rather.

instigate *vb* actuate, agitate, encourage, impel, incite, influence, initiate, move, persuade, prevail upon, prompt, provoke, rouse, set on, spur on, stimulate, stir up, tempt, urge.

instigation *n* encouragement, incitement, influence, instance, prompting, solicitation, urgency.

instil, instill *vb* enforce, implant, impress, inculcate, ingraft; impart, infuse, insinuate.

instillation *n* infusion, insinuation, introduction.

instinct *n* natural impulse.

instinctive *adj* automatic, inherent, innate, intuitive, involuntary, natural, spontaneous; impulsive, unreflecting.

institute[1] *n* academy, college, foundation, guild, institution, school; custom, doctrine, dogma, law, maxim, precedent, principle, rule, tenet.

institute[2] *vb* begin, commence, constitute, establish, found, initial, install, introduce, organize, originate, start.

institution *n* enactment, establishment, foundation, institute, society; investiture; custom, law, practice.

instruct *vb* discipline, educate, enlighten, exercise, guide, indoctrinate, inform, initiate, school, teach, train; apprise, bid, command, direct, enjoin, order, prescribe to.

instruction *n* breeding, discipline, education, indoctrination, information, nurture, schooling, teaching, training, tuition; advice, counsel, precept; command, direction, mandate, order.

instructor *n* educator, master, preceptor, schoolteacher, teacher, tutor.

instrument *n* appliance, apparatus, contrivance, device, implement, musical instrument, tool, utensil; agent, means, medium; charter, deed, document, indenture, writing.

instrumental *adj* ancillary, assisting, auxiliary, conducive, contributory, helpful, helping, ministerial, ministrant, serviceable, subservient, subsidiary.

instrumentality *n* agency, intermediary; intervention, means, mediation.

insubordinate *adj* disobedient, disorderly, mutinous, refractory, riotous, seditious, turbulent, ungovernable, unruly.

insubordination *n* disobedience, insurrection, mutiny,

revolt, riotousness, sedition; indiscipline, laxity.

insufferable *adj* intolerable, unbearable, unendurable, insupportable; abominable, detestable, disgusting, execrable, outrageous.

insufficiency *n* dearth, defectiveness, deficiency, lack, inadequacy, inadequateness, incapability, incompetence, paucity, shortage.

insufficient *adj* deficient, inadequate, incommensurate, incompetent, scanty; incapable, incompetent, unfitted, unqualified, unsuited, unsatisfactory.

insular *adj* contracted, illiberal, limited, narrow, petty, prejudiced, restricted; isolated, remote.

insulate *vb* detach, disconnect, disengage, disunite, isolate, separate.

insulation *n* disconnection, disengagement, isolation, separation.

insult *vb* abuse, affront, injure, offend, outrage, slander, slight. * *n* abuse, affront, cheek, contumely, indignity, insolence, offence, outrage, sauce, slight.

insulting *adj* abusive, arrogant, contumelious, impertinent, impolite, insolent, rude, vituperative.

insuperable *adj* impassable, insurmountable.

insupportable *adj* insufferable, intolerable, unbearable, unendurable.

insuppressible *adj* irrepressible, uncontrollable.

insurance *n* assurance, security.

insure *vb* assure, guarantee, indemnify, secure, underwrite.

insurgent *adj* disobedient, insubordinate, mutinous, rebellious, revolting, revolutionary, seditious. * *n* mutineer, rebel, revolter, revolutionary.

insurmountable *adj* impassable, insuperable.

insurrection *n* insurgence, mutiny, rebellion, revolt, revolution, rising, sedition, uprising.

intact *adj* scathless, unharmed, unhurt, unimpaired, uninjured, untouched; complete, entire, integral, sound, unbroken, undiminished, whole.

intangible *adj* dim, impalpable, imperceptible, indefinite, insubstantial, intactile, shadowy, vague; aerial, phantom, spiritous.

intangibility *n* imperceptibility, insubstantiality, intangibleness, shadowiness, vagueness.

integral *adj* complete, component, entire, integrant, total, whole.

integrity *n* goodness, honesty, principle, probity, purity, rectitude, soundness, uprightness, virtue; completeness, entireness, entirety, wholeness.

integument *n* coat, covering, envelope, skin, tegument.

intellect *n* brains, cognitive faculty, intelligence, mind, rational faculty, reason, reasoning, faculty, sense, thought, understanding, wit.

intellectual *adj* cerebral, intelligent, mental, scholarly, thoughtful. * *n* academic, highbrow, pundit, savant, scholar.

intelligence *n* acumen, apprehension, brightness, discernment, imagination, insight, penetration, quickness, sagacity, shrewdness, understanding, wits; information, knowledge; advice, instruction, news, notice, notification, tidings; brains, intellect, mentality, sense, spirit.

intelligent *adj* acute, alert, apt, astute, brainy, bright, clear-headed, clear-sighted, clever, discerning, keen-eyed, keen-sighted, knowing, long-headed, quick, quick-sighted, sagacious, sensible, sharp-sighted, sharp-witted, shrewd, understanding.

intelligibility *n* clarity, comprehensibility, intelligibleness, perspicuity.

intelligible *adj* clear, comprehensible, distinct, evident, lucid, manifest, obvious, patent, perspicuous, plain, transparent, understandable.

intemperate *adj* drunken; excessive, extravagant, extreme, immoderate, inordinate, unbridled, uncontrolled, unrestrained; self-indulgent.

intend *vb* aim at, contemplate, design, determine, drive at, mean, meditate, propose, purpose, think of.

intendant *n* inspector, overseer, superintendent, supervisor.

intense *adj* ardent, earnest, fervid, passionate, vehement; close, intent, severe, strained, stretched, strict; energetic, forcible, keen, potent, powerful, sharp, strong, vigorous, violent; acute, deep, extreme, exquisite, grievous, poignant.

intensify *vb* aggravate, concentrate, deepen, enhance, heighten, quicken, strengthen, whet.

intensity *n* closeness, intenseness, severity, strictness; excess, extremity, violence; activity, energy, force, power, strength, vigour; ardour, earnestness, vehemence.

intensive *adj* emphatic, intensifying.

intent *adj* absorbed, attentive, close, eager, earnest, engrossed, occupied, pre-occupied, zealous; bent, determined, decided, resolved, set. * *n* aim, design, drift, end, import, intention, mark, meaning, object, plan, purport, purpose, purview, scope, view.

intention *n* aim, design, drift, end, import, intent, mark, meaning, object, plan, purport, purpose, purview, scope, view.

intentional *adj* contemplated, deliberate, designed, intended, preconcerted, predetermined, premeditated, purposed, studied, voluntary, wilful.

inter *vb* bury, commit to the earth, entomb, inhume, inurn.

intercalate *vb* insert, interpolate.

intercede *vb* arbitrate, interpose, mediate; entreat, plead, supplicate.

intercept *vb* cut off, interrupt, obstruct, seize.

intercession *n* interposition, intervention, mediation; entreaty, pleading, prayer, supplication.

intercessor *n* interceder, mediator.

interchange *vb* alternate, change, exchange, vary. * *n* alternation.

interchangeableness *n* interchangeability.

interchangeably *adv* alternately.

intercourse *n* commerce, communication, communion, connection, converse, correspondence, dealings, fellowship, truck; acquaintance, intimacy.

interdict *vb* debar, forbid, inhibit, prohibit, prescribe, proscribe, restrain from. * *n* ban, decree, interdiction, prohibition.

interest *vb* affect, concern, touch; absorb, attract, engage, enlist, excite, grip, hold, occupy. * *n* advantage, benefit, good, profit, weal; attention, concern, regard, sympathy; part, participation, portion, share, stake; discount, premium, profit.

interested *adj* attentive, concerned, involved, occupied; biassed, patial, prejudiced; selfish, self-seeking.

interesting *adj* attractive, engaging, entertaining, pleasing.

interfere *vb* intermeddle, interpose, meddle; clash, collide, conflict.

interference *n* intermeddling, interposition; clashing, collision, interfering, opposition.

interim *n* intermediate time, interval, meantime.

interior *adj* inmost, inner, internal, inward; inland, remote; domestic, home. * *n* inner part, inland, inside.

interjacent *adj* intermediate, interposed, intervening, parenthetical.

interject *vb* comment, inject, insert, interpose.

interjection *n* exclamation.

interlace *vb* bind, complicate, entwine, intersperse, intertwine, interweave, inweave, knit, mix, plait, twine, twist, unite.

interlard *vb* difersify, interminate, intersperse, intertwine, mix, vary.

interline *vb* insert, write between.

interlineal *adj* interlinear, interlined.

interlink, interlock *vb* connect, interchain, interrelate, join.

interlocution *n* colloquy, conference, dialogue, interchange.

interlocutor *n* respondent, speaker.

interloper *n* intruder, meddler.

intermeddle *vb* interfere, interpose, meddle.

intermediary *n* go-between, mediator.

intermediate *adj* interjacent, interposed, intervening, mean, median, middle, transitional.

interment *n* burial, entombment, inhumation, sepulture.

interminable *adj* boundless, endless, illimitable, immeasurable, infinite, limitless, unbounded, unlimited; long-drawn-out, tedious, wearisome.

intermingle *vb* blend, commingle, commix, intermix, mingle, mix.

intermission *n* cessation, interruption, interval, lull, pause, remission, respite, rest, stop, stoppage, suspension.

intermit *vb* interrupt, intervene, stop, suspend; discontinue, give over, leave off; abate, subside.

intermittent *adj* broken, capricious, discontinuous, fitful, flickering, intermitting, periodic, recurrent, remittent, spasmodic.

intermix *vb* blend, commingle, commix, intermingle, mingle, mix.

internal *adj* inner, inside, interior, inward; incorporeal, mental, spiritual; deeper, emblematic, hidden, higher, metaphorical, secret, symbolical, under; genuine, inherent, intrinsic, real, true; domestic, home, inland, inside.

international *adj* cosmopolitan, universal.

internecine *adj* deadly, destructive, exterminating, exterminatory, interneciary, internecinal, internecive, mortal.

interpellate *vb* interrogate, question.

interpellation *n* interruption; intercession, interposition; interrogation, questioning.

interplay *n* interaction.

interpolate *vb* add, foist, insert, interpose; (*math*) intercalate, introduce.

interpose *vb* arbitrate, intercede, intervene, mediate; interfere, intermeddle, interrupt, meddle, tamper; insert, interject, put in, remark, sandwich, set between; intrude, thurst in.

interposition *n* intercession, interpellation, intervention, mediation.

interpret *vb* decipher, decode, define, elucidate, explain, expound, solve, unfold, unravel; construe, render, translate.

interpretation *n* meaning, sense, signification; elucidation, explanation, explication, exposition; construction, rendering, rendition, translation, version.

interpreter *n* expositor, expounder, translator.

interrogate *vb* ask, catechize, examine, inquire of, interpellate, question.

interrogation *n* catechizing, examination, examining, interpellation, interrogating, questioning; inquiry, query, question.

interrogative *adj* interrogatory, questioning.

interrupt *vb* break, check, disturb, hinder, intercept, interfere with, obstruct, pretermit, stop; break, cut, disconnect, disjoin, dissever, dissolve, disunite, divide, separate, sever, sunder; break off, cease, discontinue, intermit, leave off, suspend.

interruption *n* hindrance, impediment, obstacle, obstruction, stop, stoppage; cessation, discontinuance, intermission, pause, suspension; break, breaking, disconnecting, disconnection, disjunction, dissolution, disunion, disuniting, division, separation, severing, sundering.

intersect *vb* cross, cut, decussate, divide, interrupt.

intersection *n* crossing.

interspace *n* interlude, interstice, interval.

intersperse *vb* intermingle, scatter, sprinkle; diversify, interlard, mix.

interstice *n* interspace, interval, space; chink, crevice.

interstitial *adj* intermediate, intervening.

intertwine *vb* interlace, intertwine, interweave, inweave, twine.

interval *n* interim, interlude, interregnum, pause, period, recess, season, space, spell, term; interstice, skip.

intervene *vb* come between, interfere, mediate; befall, happen, occur.

intervening *adj* interjacent, intermediate; interstitial.

intervention *n* interference, interposition; agency, mediation.

interview *n* conference, consultation, parley; meeting.

interweave *vb* interlace, intertwine, inweave, weave; intermingle, intermix, mingle, mix.

intestinal *adj* domestic, interior, internal.

intestines *npl* bowels, entrails, guts, insides, inwards, viscera.

intimacy *n* close acquaintance, familiarity, fellowship, friendship; closeness, nearness.

intimate[1] *adj* close, near; familiar, friendly; bosom, chummy, close, dear, homelike, special; confidential, personal, private, secret; detailed, exhaustive, firsthand, immediate, penetrating, profound; cosy, warm. * *n* chum, confidant, companion, crony, friend.

intimate[2] *vb* allude to, express, hint, impart, indicate, insinuate, signify, suggest, tell.

intimately *adv* closely, confidentially, familiarly, nearly, thoroughly.

intimation *n* allusion, hint, innuendo, insinuation, suggestion.

intimidate *vb* abash, affright, alarm, appal, browbeat, bully, cow, daunt, dishearten, dismay, frighten, overawe, scare, subdue, terrify, terrorize.

intimidation *n* fear, intimidating, terror, terrorism.

intolerable *adj* insufferable, insupportable, unbearable, unendurable.

intolerance *n* bigotry, narrowness; impatience, rejection.

intolerant *adj* bigoted, narrow, proscriptive; dictatorial, impatient, imperious, overbearing, supercilious.

intonation *n* cadence, modulation, tone; musical recitation.

in toto *adv* entirely, wholly.

intoxicate *vb* fuddle, inebriate, muddle.

intoxicated *adj* boozy, drunk, drunken, fuddled, inebriated, maudlin, mellow, muddled, stewed, tight, tipsy.

intoxication *n* drunkenness, ebriety, inebriation, inebriety; excitement, exhilaration, infatuation.

intractability *n* cantankerousness, contrariety, inflexibility, intractableness, obduracy, obstinacy, perverseness, perversity, pig-headedness, stubbornness, wilfulness.

intractable *adj* cantankerous, contrary, contumacious, cross-grained, dogged, froward, headstrong, indocile, inflexible, mulish, obdurate, obstinate, perverse, pig-headed, refractory, restive, stubborn, tough, uncontrollable, ungovernable, unmanageable, unruly, unyielding, wilful.

intrench *see* **entrench**.

intrenchment *see* **entrenchment**.

intrepid *adj* bold, brave, chivalrous, courageous, daring, dauntless, doughty, fearless, gallant, heroic, unappalled, unawed, undaunted, undismayed, unterrified, valiant, valorous.

intrepidity *n* boldness, bravery, courage, daring, dauntlessness, fearlessness, gallantry, heroism, intrepidness, prowess, spirit, valour.

intricacy *n* complexity, complication, difficulty, entanglement, intricateness, involution, obscurity, perplexity.

intricate *adj* complicated, difficult, entangled, involved, mazy, obscure, perplexed.

intrigue *vb* connive, conspire, machinate, plot, scheme; beguile, bewitch, captivate, charm, fascinate. * *n* artifice, cabal, conspiracy, deception, finesse, Machiavelianism, machination, manoeuvre, plot, ruse, scheme, stratagem, wile; amour, liaison, love affair.

intriguing *adj* arch, artful, crafty, crooked, cunning, deceitful, designing, diplomatic, foxy, Machiavelian, insidious, politic, sly, sneaky, subtle, tortuous, trickish, tricky, wily.

intrinsic *adj* essential, genuine, real, sterling, true; inborn, inbred, ingrained, inherent, internal, inward, native, natural.

intrinsically *adv* essentially, really, truly; inherently, naturally.

introduce *vb* bring in, conduct, import, induct, inject, insert, lead in, usher in; present; begin, broach, commence, inaugurate, initiate, institute, start.

introduction *n* exordium, preface, prelude, proem; introducing, ushering in; presentation.

introductory *adj* precursory, prefatory, preliminary, proemial.

introspection *n* introversion, self-contemplation.

intrude *vb* encroach, impose, infringe, interfere, interlope, obtrude, trespass.

intruder *n* interloper, intermeddler, meddler, stranger.

intrusion *n* encroachment, infringement, intruding, obtrusion.

intrusive *adj* obtrusive, trespassing.

intuition *n* apprehension, cognition, insight, instinct; clairvoyance, divination, presentiment.

intuitive *adj* instinctive, intuitional, natural; clear, distinct, full, immediate.

intumesce *vb* bubble up, dilate, expand, swell.

intumescence *n* inturgescence, swelling, tumefaction, turgescence.

inundate *vb* deluge, drown, flood, glut, overflow, overwhelm, submerge.

inundation *n* cataclysm, deluge, flood, glut, overflow, superfluity.

inure *vb* accustom, discipline, familiarize, habituate, harden, toughen, train, use.

inutile *adj* bootless, ineffectual, inoperative, unavailing, unprofitable, useless.

invade *vb* encroach upon, infringe, violate; attack, enter in, march into.

invalid[1] *adj* baseless, fallacious, false, inoperative, nugatory, unfounded, unsound, untrue, worthless; (*law*) null, void.

invalid[2] *adj* ailing, bedridden, feeble, frail, ill, infirm, sick, sickly, valetudinary, weak, weakly. * *n* convalescent, patient, valetudinarian.

invalidate *vb* abrogate, annul, cancel, nullify, overthrow, quash, repeal, reverse, undo, unmake, vitiate.

invalidity *n* baselessness, fallaciousness, fallacy, falsity, unsoundness.

invaluable *adj* inestimable, priceless.

invariable *adj* changeless, constant, unchanging, uniform, unvarying; changeless, immutable, unalterable, unchangeable.

invariableness *n* changelessness, constancy, uniformity, unvaryingness; changelessness, immutability, unchangeableness, invariability.

invasion *n* encroachment, incursion, infringement, inroad; aggression, assault, attack, foray, raid.

invective *n* abuse, censure, contumely, denunciation, diatribe, railing, reproach, sarcasm, satire, vituperation.

inveigh *vb* blame, censure, condemn, declaim against, denounce, exclaim against, rail at, reproach, vituperate.

inveigle *vb* contrive, devise; concoct, conceive, create, design, excogitate, frame, imagine, originate; coin, fabricate, forge, spin.

invent *vb* concoct, contrive, design, devise, discover, fabricate, find out, frame, originate.

invention *n* creation, discovery, ingenuity, inventing, origination; contrivance, design, device; coinage, fabrication, fiction, forgery.

inventive *adj* creative, fertile, ingenious.

inventor *n* author, contriver, creator, originator.

inventory *n* account, catalogue, list, record, roll, register, schedule.

inverse *adj* indirect, inverted, opposite, reversed.

inversion *n* inverting, reversing, transposal, transposition.

invert *vb* capsize, overturn; reverse, transpose.

invertebrate *adj* invertebral; spineless.

invest *vb* put money into; confer, endow, endue; (*mil*) beset, besiege, enclose, surround; array, clothe, dress.

investigate *vb* canvass, consider, dissect, examine, explore, follow up, inquire into, look into, overhaul, probe, question, research, scrutinize, search into, search out, sift, study.

investigation *n* examination, exploration, inquiry, inquisition, overhauling, research, scrutiny, search, sifting, study.

investiture *n* habilitation, induction, installation, ordination.

investment *n* money invested; endowment; (*mil*) beleaguerment, siege; clothes, dress, garments, habiliments, robe, vestment.

inveteracy *n* inveterateness, obstinacy.

inveterate *adj* accustomed, besetting, chronic, confirmed, deep-seated, habitual, habituated, hardened, ingrained, long-established, obstinate.

invidious *adj* disagreeable, envious, hateful, odious, offensive, unfair.

invigorate *vb* animate, brace, energize, fortify, harden, nerve, quicken, refresh, stimulate, strengthen, vivify.

invincible *adj* impregnable, indomitable, ineradicable, insuperable, insurmountable, irrepressible, unconquerable, unsubduable, unyielding.

inviolable *adj* hallowed, holy, inviolate, sacramental, sacred, sacrosanct, stainless.

inviolate *adj* unbroken, unviolated; pure, stainless, unblemished, undefiled, unhurt, uninjured, unpolluted, unprofaned, unstained; inviolable, sacred.

invisibility *n* imperceptibility, indistinctness, invisibleness, obscurity.

invisible *adj* impalpable, imperceptible, indistinguishable, intangible, unapparent, undiscernable, unperceivable, unseen.

invitation *n* bidding, call, challenge, solicitation, summons.

invite *vb* ask, bid, call, challenge, request, solicit, summon; allure, attract, draw on, entice, lead, persuade, prevail upon.

inviting *adj* alluring, attractive, bewitching, captivating, engaging, fascinating, pleasing, winning; prepossessing, promising.

invocation *n* conjuration, orison, petition, prayer, summoning, supplication.

invoice *vb* bill, list. * *n* bill, inventory, list, schedule.

invoke *vb* adjure, appeal to, beseech, beg, call upon, conjure, entreat, implore, importune, pray, pray to, solicit, summon, supplicate.

involuntary *adj* automatic, blind, instinctive, mechanical, reflex, spontaneous, unintentional; compulsory, reluctant, unwilling.

involve *vb* comprise, contain, embrace, imply, include, lead to; complicate, compromise, embarrass, entangle, implicate, incriminate, inculpate; cover, envelop, enwrap, surround, wrap; blend, conjoin, connect, join, mingle; entwine, interlace, intertwine, interweave, inweave.

invulnerability *n* invincibility, invulnerableness.

invulnerable *adj* incontrovertible, invincible, unassailable, irrefragable.

inward[1] *adj* incoming, inner, interior, internal; essential, hidden, mental, spiritual; private, secret.

inward[2], **inwards** *adv* inwardly, towards the inside, within.

inweave *vb* entwine, interlace, intertwine, interweave, weave together.

iota *n* atom, bit, glimmer, grain, jot, mite, particle, scintilla, scrap, shadow, spark, tittle, trace, whit.

irascibility *n* hastiness, hot-headedness, impatience, irascibleness, irritability, peevishness, petulance, quickness, spleen, testiness, touchiness.

irascible *adj* choleric, cranky, hasty, hot, hot-headed, impatient, irritable, nettlesome, peevish, peppery, pettish, petulant, quick, splenetic, snappish, testy, touchy, waspish.

irate *adj* angry, incensed, ireful, irritated, piqued.

ire *n* anger, choler, exasperation, fury, indignation, passion, rage, resentment, wrath.

ireful *adj* angry, furious, incensed, irate, raging, passionate.

iridescent *adj* irisated, nacreous, opalescent, pavonine, prismatic, rainbow-like.

iris *n* rainbow; (*bot*) fleur-de-lis, flower-de-luce; diaphragm of the eye.

irksome *adj* annoying, burdensome, humdrum, monotonous, tedious, tiresome, wearisome, weary, wearying.

iron *adj* ferric, ferrous.

ironic, ironical *adj* mocking, sarcastic.

irons *npl* chains, fetters, gyves, hampers, manacles, shackles.

irony *n* mockery, raillery, ridicule, sarcasm, satire.

irradiate *vb* brighten, illume, illuminate, illumine, light up, shine upon.

irrational *adj* absurd, extravagant, foolish, injudicious, preposterous, ridiculous, silly, unwise; unreasonable, unreasoning, unthinking; brute, brutish; aberrant, alienated, brainless, crazy, demented, fantastic, idiotic, imbecilic, insane, lunatic.

irrationality *n* absurdity, folly, foolishness, unreasonableness; brutishness.

irreclaimable *adj* hopeless, incurable, irrecoverable, irreparable, irretrievable, irreversible, remediless; abandoned, graceless, hardened, impenitent, incorrigible, lost, obdurate, profligate, recreant, reprobate, shameless, unrepentant.

irreconcilable *adj* implacable, inexorable, inexpiable, unappeasable; incompatible, incongruous, inconsistent.

irrecoverable *adj* hopeless, incurable, irremediable, irreparable, irretrievable, remediless.

irrefragable *adj* impregnable, incontestable, incontrovertible, indisputable, invincible, irrefutable, irresistible, unanswerable, unassailable, undeniable.

irrefutable *adj* impregnable, incontestable, incontrovertible, indisputable, invincible, irrefragable, irresistible, unanswerable, unassailable, undeniable.

irregular *adj* aberrant, abnormal, anomalistic, anomalous, crooked, devious, eccentric, erratic, exceptional, heteromorphous, raged, tortuous, unconformable, unusual; capricious, changeable, desultory, fitful, spasmodic, uncertain, unpunctual, unsettled, variable; disordered, disorderly, improper, uncanonical, unparliamentary, unsystematic; asymmetric, uneven, unsymmetrical; disorderly, dissolute, immoral, loose, wild. * *n* casual, freelance, hireling, mercenary.

irregularity *n* aberration, abnormality, anomaly, anomalousness, singularity; capriciousness, changeableness, uncertainty, variableness; asymmetry; disorderliness, dissoluteness, immorality, laxity, looseness, wildness.

irrelevance, irrelevancy *n* impertinency, inapplicability, nonpertinency.

irrelevant *adj* extraneous, foreign, illogical, impertinent, inapplicable, inapposite, inappropriate, inconsequent, unessential, unrelated.

irreligion *n* atheism, godlessness, impiety, ungodliness.

irreligious *adj* godless, ungodly, undevout; blasphemous, disrespectful, impious, irreverent, profane, ribald, wicked.

irremediable *adj* hopeless, incurable, immedicable, irrecoverable, irreparable, remediless.

irremissible *adj* binding, inexpiable, obligatory, unatonable, unpardonable.

irreparable *adj* irrecoverable, irremediable, irretrievable, remediless.

irreprehensible *adj* blameless, faultless, inculpable, innocent, irreproachable, irreprovable, unblamable.

irrepressible *adj* insuppressible, uncontrollable, unquenchable, unsmotherable.

irreproachable *adj* blameless, faultless, inculpable, innocent, irreprehensible, irreprovable, unblamable.

irresistible *adj* irrefragable, irrepressible, overpowering, overwhelming, resistless.

irresolute *adj* changeable, faltering, fickle, hesitant, hesitating, inconstant, mutable, spineless, uncertain, undecided, undetermined, unsettled, unstable, unsteady, vacillating, wavering.

irrespective *adj* independent, regardless.

irresponsible *adj* unaccountable; untrustworthy.

irretrievable *adj* incurable, irrecoverable, irremediable, irreparable, remediless.

irreverence *n* blasphemy, impiety, profaneness, profanity; disesteem, disrespect.

irreverent *adj* blasphemous, impious, irreligious, profane; disrespectful, slighting.

irreversible *adj* irrepealable, irrevocable, unalterable, unchangeable; changeless, immutable, invariable.

irrevocable *adj* irrepealable, irreversible, unalterable, unchangeable.

irrigate *vb* moisten, wash, water, wet.

irrigation *n* watering.

irritability *n* excitability, fretfulness, irascibility, peevishness, petulance, snappishness, susceptibility, testiness.

irritable *adj* captious, choleric, excitable, fiery, fretful, hasty, hot, irascible, passionate, peppery, peevish, pettish, petulant, snappish, splenetic, susceptible, testy, touchy, waspish.

irritate *vb* anger, annoy, chafe, enrage, exacerbate, exasperate, fret, incense, jar, nag, nettle, offend, provoke, rasp, rile, ruffle, vex; gall, tease; (*med*) excite, inflame, stimulate.

irritation *n* irritating; anger, exacerbation, exasperation, excitement, indignation, ire, passion, provocation, resentment, wrath; (*med*) excitation, inflammation, stimulation; burn, itch.

irruption *n* breaking in, bursting in; foray, incursion, inroad, invasion, raid.

island *n* atoll, isle, islet, reef.

isochronal *adj* isochronous, uniform.

isolate *vb* detach, dissociate, insulate, quarantine, segregate, separate, set apart.

isolated *adj* detached, separate, single, solitary.

isolation *n* detachment, disconnection, insulation, quarantine, segregation, separation; loneliness, solitariness, solitude.

issue *vb* come out, flow out, flow forth, gush, run, rush out, spout, spring, spurt, well; arise, come, emanate, ensue, flow, follow, originate, proceed, spring; end, eventuate, result, terminate; appear, come out, deliver, depart, debouch, discharge, emerge, emit, put forth, send out; distribute, give out; publish, utter. * *n* conclusion, consequence, consummation, denouement, end, effect, event, finale, outcome, result, termination, upshot; antagonism, contest, controversy; debouchment, delivering, delivery, discharge, emergence, emigration, emission, issuance; flux, outflow, outpouring, stream; copy, edition, number; egress, exit, outlet, passage out, vent, way out; escape, sally, sortie; children, offspring, posterity, progeny.

itch *vb* tingle. * *n* itching; burning, coveting, importunate craving, teasing desire, uneasy hankering.

itching *n* itch; craving, longing, importunate craving, desire, appetite, hankering.

item *adv* also, in like manner. * *n* article, detail, entry, particular, point.

iterate *vb* reiterate, repeat.

itinerant *adj* nomadic, peripatetic, roaming, roving, travelling, unsettled, wandering.

itinerary *n* guide, guidebook; circuit, route.

J

jabber *vb* chatter, gabble, prate, prattle.

jacket *n* casing, cover, sheath; anorak, blazer coat, doublet, jerkin.

jaded *adj* dull, exhausted, fatigued, satiated, tired, weary.

jagged *adj* cleft, divided, indented, notched, serrated, ragged, uneven.

jail, gaol *n* bridewell, (*sl*) clink, dungeon, lockup, (*sl*) nick, penitentiary, prison.

jam *vb* block, crowd, crush, press. * *n* block, crowd, crush, mass, pack, press.

jangle *vb* bicker, chatter, dispute, gossip, jar, quarrel, spar, spat, squabble, tiff, wrangle. * *n* clang, clangour, clash, din, dissonance.

jar[1] *vb* clash, grate, interfere, shake; bicker, contend, jangle, quarrel, spar, spat, squabble, tiff, wrangle; agitate, jolt, jounce, shake. * *n* clash, conflict, disaccord, discord, jangle, dissonance; agitation, jolt, jostle, shake, shaking, shock, start.

jar[2] *n* can, crock, cruse, ewer, flagon.

jarring *adj* conflicting, discordant, inconsistent, inconsonant, wrangling.

jargon *n* gabble, gibberish, nonsense, rigmarole: argot, cant, lingo, slang; chaos, confusion, disarray, disorder, jumble.

jaundiced *adj* biased, envious, prejudiced.

jaunt *n* excursion, ramble, tour, trip.

jaunty *adj* airy, cheery, garish, gay, fine, fluttering, showy, sprightly, unconcerned.

jealous *adj* distrustful, envious, suspicious; anxious, apprehensive, intolerant, solicitous, zealous.

jealousy *n* envy, suspicion, watchfulness.

jeer *vb* deride, despise, flout, gibe, jape, jest, mock, scoff, sneer, spurn, rail, ridicule, taunt. * *n* abuse, derision, mockery, sneer, ridicule, taunt.

jeopardize *vb* endanger, hazard, imperil, risk, venture.

jeopardy *n* danger, hazard, peril, risk, venture.

jerk *vb, n* flip, hitch, pluck, tweak, twitch, yank.

jest *vb* banter, joke, quiz. * *n* fun, joke, pleasantry, raillery, sport.

jester *n* humorist, joker, wag; buffoon, clown, droll, fool, harlequin, punch.

jibe *see* **gibe**.

jiffy *n* instant, moment, second, twinkling, trice.

jilt *vb* break with, deceive, disappoint, discard. * *n* coquette, flirt, light-o'-love.

jingle *vb* chink, clink, jangle, rattle, tinkle. * *n* chink, clink, jangle, rattle, tinkle; chorus, ditty, melody, song.

jocose *adj* comical, droll, facetious, funny, humorous, jesting, jocular, merry, sportive, waggish, witty.

jocund *adj* airy, blithe, cheerful, debonair, frolicsome, jolly, joyful, joyous, lively, merry, playful.

jog *vb* jostle, notify, nudge, push, remind, warn; canter, run, trot. * *n* push, reminder.

join *vb* add, annex, append, attach; cement, combine, conjoin, connect, couple, dovetail, link, unite, yoke; amalgamate, assemble, associate, confederate, consolidate.

joint *vb* fit, join, unite. * *adj* combined, concerted, concurrent, conjoint. * *n* connection, junction, juncture, hinge, splice.

joke *vb* banter, jest, frolic, rally. * *n* crank, jest, quip, quirk, witticism.

jolly *adj* airy, blithe, cheerful, frolicsome, gamesome, facetious, funny, gay, jovial, joyous, merry, mirthful, jocular, jocund, playful, sportive, sprightly, waggish; bouncing, chubby, lusty, plump, portly, stout.

jolt *vb* jar, shake, shock. * *n* jar, jolting, jounce, shaking.

jostle *vb* collide, elbow, hustle, joggle, shake, shoulder, shove.

jot *n* ace, atom, bit, corpuscle, iota, grain, mite, particle, scrap, whit.

journal *n* daybook, diary, log; gazette, magazine, newspapers, periodical.

journey *vb* ramble, roam, rove, travel: fare, go, proceed. * *n* excursion, expedition, jaunt, passage, pilgrimage, tour, travel, trip, voyage.

jovial *adj* airy, convivial, festive, jolly, joyous, merry, mirthful.

joy *n* beatification, beatitude, delight, ecstasy, exultation, gladness, glee, mirth, pleasure, rapture, ravishment, transport; bliss, felicity, happiness.

joyful *adj* blithe, blithesome, buoyant, delighted, elate, elated, exultant, glad, happy, jocund, jolly, joyous, merry, rejoicing.

jubilant *adj* exultant, exulting, rejoicing, triumphant.

judge *vb* conclude, decide, decree, determine, pronounce; adjudicate, arbitrate, condemn, doom, sentence, try, umpire; account, apprehend, believe, consider, deem, esteem, guess, hold, imagine, measure, reckon, regard, suppose, think; appreciate, estimate. * *n* adjudicator, arbiter, arbitrator, bencher, justice, magistrate, moderator, referee, umpire, connoisseur, critic.

judgment, judgement *n* brains, ballast, circumspection, depth, discernment, discretion, discrimination, intelligence, judiciousness, penetration, prudence, sagacity, sense, sensibility, taste, understanding, wisdom, wit; conclusion, consideration, decision, determination, estimation, notion, opinion, thought; adjudication, arbitration, award, censure, condemnation, decree, doom, sentence.

judicious *adj* cautious, considerate, cool, critical, discriminating, discreet, enlightened, provident, politic, prudent, rational, reasonable, sagacious, sensible, sober, solid, sound, staid, wise.

jug *n* cruse, ewer, flagon, pitcher, vessel.

juicy *adj* lush, moist, sappy, succulent, watery; entertaining, exciting, interesting, lively, racy, spicy.

jumble *vb* confound, confuse, disarrange, disorder, mix, muddle. * *n* confusion, disarrangement, disorder, medley, mess, mixture, muddle.

jump *vb* bound, caper, clear, hop, leap, skip, spring, vault. * *n* bound, caper, hop, leak, skip, spring, vault; fence, hurdle, obstacle; break, gap, interruption, space; advance, boost, increase, rise; jar, jolt, shock, start, twitch.

junction *n* combination, connection, coupling, hookup, joining, linking, seam, union; conjunction, joint, juncture.

junta *n* cabal, clique, combination, confederacy, coterie, faction, gang, league, party, set.

just *adj* equitable, lawful, legitimate, reasonable, right, rightful; candid, even-handed, fair, fair-minded, impartial; blameless, conscientious, good, honest, honourable, pure, square, straightforward, virtuous; accurate, correct, exact, normal, proper, regular, true; condign, deserved, due, merited, suitable.

justice *n* accuracy, equitableness, equity, fairness, honesty, impartiality, justness, right; judge, justiciary.

justifiable *adj* defensible, fit, proper, right, vindicable, warrantable.

justification *n* defence, exculpation, excuse, exoneration, reason, vindication, warrant.

justify *vb* approve, defend, exculpate, excuse, exonerate, maintain, vindicate, support, warrant.

justness *n* accuracy, correctness, fitness, justice, precision, propriety.

juvenile *adj* childish, immature, puerile, young, youthful. * *n* boy, child, girl, youth.

juxtaposition *n* adjacency, contiguity, contact, proximity.

K

keen[1] *adj* ardent, eager, earnest, fervid, intense, vehement, vivid; acute, sharp; cutting; acrimonious, biting, bitter, caustic, poignant, pungent, sarcastic, severe; astute, discerning, intelligent, quick, sagacious, sharp-sighted, shrewd.

keen[2] *vb* bemoan, bewail, deplore, grieve, lament, mourn, sorrow, weep. * *n* coronach, dirge, elegy, lament, lamentation, monody, plaint, requiem, threnody.

keenness *n* ardour, eagerness, fervour, vehemence, zest; acuteness, sharpness; rigour, severity, sternness; acrimony, asperity, bitterness, causticity, causticness, pungency; astuteness, sagacity, shrewdness.

keep *vb* detain, hold, retain; continue, preserve; confine, detain, reserve, restrain, withhold; attend, guard, preserve, protect; adhere to, fulfil; celebrate, commemorate, honour, observe, perform, solemnize; maintain, support, sustain; husband, save, store; abide, dwell, lodge, stay, remain; endure, last. * *n* board, maintenance, subsistence, support; donjon, dungeon, stronghold, tower.

keeper *n* caretaker, conservator, curator, custodian, defender, gaoler, governor, guardian, jailer, superintendent, warden, warder, watchman.

keeping *n* care, charge, custody, guard, possession; feed, maintenance, support; agreement, conformity, congruity, consistency, harmony.

keepsake *n* memento, souvenir, token.

ken *n* cognizance, sight, view.

key *adj* basic, crucial, essential, important, major, principal. * *n* lock-opener, opener; clue, elucidation, explanation, guide, solution, translation; (*mus*) keynote, tonic; clamp, lever, wedge.

kick *vb* boot, punt; oppose, rebel, resist, spurn. * *n* force, intensity, power, punch, vitality; excitement, pleasure, thrill.

kidnap *vb* abduct, capture, carry off, remove, steal away.

kill *vb* assassinate, butcher, dispatch, destroy, massacre, murder, slaughter, slay.

kin *adj* akin, allied, cognate, kindred, related. * *n* affinity, consanguinity, relationship; connections, family, kindred, kinsfolk, relations, relatives, siblings.

kind[1] *adj* accommodating, amiable, beneficent, benevolent, benign, bland, bounteous, brotherly, charitable, clement, compassionate, complaisant, gentle, good, good-natured, forbearing, friendly, generous, gracious, humane, indulgent, lenient, mild, obliging, sympathetic, tender, tender-hearted.

kind[2] *n* breed, class, family, genus, race, set, species, type; brand, character, colour, denomination, description, form, make, manner, nature, persuasion, sort, stamp, strain, style,

kindle *vb* fire, ignite, inflame, light; animate, awaken, bestir, exasperate, excite, foment, incite, provoke, rouse, stimulate, stir, thrill, warm.

kindliness *n* amiability, benevolence, benignity, charity, compassion, friendliness, humanity, kindness, sympathy; gentleness, mildness, softness.

kindly *adj* appropriate, congenial, kindred, natural, proper; benevolent, considerate, friendly, gracious, humane, sympathetic, well-disposed. * *adv* agreeably, graciously, humanely, politely, thoughtfully.

kindness *n* benefaction, charity, favour; amiability, beneficence, benevolence, benignity, clemency, generosity, goodness, grace, humanity, kindliness, mildness, philanthropy, sympathy, tenderness.

kindred *adj* akin, allied, congenial, connected, related, sympathetic. * *n* affinity, consanguinity, flesh, relationship; folks, kin, kinsfolk, kinsmen, relations, relatives.

king *n* majesty, monarch, sovereign.

kingdom *n* dominion, empire, monarchy, rule, sovereignty, supremacy; region, tract; division, department, domain, province, realm.

kingly *adj* imperial, kinglike, monarchical, regal, royal, sovereign; august, glorious, grand, imperial, imposing, magnificent, majestic, noble, splendid.

kink *n* cramp, crick, curl, entanglement, knot, loop, twist; crochet, whim, wrinkle.

kinsfolk *n* kin, kindred, kinsmen, relations, relatives.

kit *n* equipment, implements, outfit, set, working.

knack *n* ability, address, adroitness, aptitude, aptness, dexterity, dextrousness, expertness, facility, quickness, readiness, skill.

knave *n* caitiff, cheat, miscreant, rascal, rogue, scamp, scapegrace, scoundrel, sharper, swindler, trickster, villain.

knavery *n* criminality, dishonesty, fraud, knavishness, rascality, scoundrelism, trickery, villainy.

knavish *adj* dishonest, fraudulent, rascally, scoundrelly, unprincipled, roguish, trickish, tricky, villainous.

knell *vb* announce, peal, ring, toll. * *n* chime, peal, ring, toll.

knife *vb* cut, slash, stab. * *n* blade, jackknife, lance.

knit *vb* connect, interlace, join, unite, weave.

knob *n* boss, bunch, hunch, lump, protuberance, stud.

knock *vb* clap, cuff, hit, rap, rattle, slap, strike, thump; beat, blow, box. * *n* blow, slap, smack, thump; blame, criticism, rejection, setback.

knoll *n* hill, hillock, mound.

knot *vb* complicate, entangle, gnarl, kink, tie, weave. * *n* complication, entanglement; connection, tie; joint, node, knag; bunch, rosette, tuft; band, cluster, clique, crew, gang, group, pack, set, squad.

knotty *adj* gnarled, hard, knaggy, knurled, knotted, rough, rugged; complex, difficult, harassing, intricate, involved, perplexing, troublesome.

know *vb* apprehend, comprehend, cognize, discern, perceive, recognize, see, understand; discriminate, distinguish.

knowing *adj* accomplished, competent, experienced, intelligent, proficient, qualified, skilful, well-informed; aware, conscious, percipient, sensible, thinking; cunning, expressive, significant.

knowingly *adv* consciously, intentionally, purposely, wittingly.

knowledge *n* apprehension, command, comprehension, discernment, judgment, perception, understanding, wit; acquaintance, acquirement, attainments, enlightenment, erudition, information, learning, lore, mastery, scholarship, science; cognition, cognizance, consciousness, ken, notice, prescience, recognition.

knowledgeable *adj* aware, conscious, experienced, well-informed; educated, intelligent, learned, scholarly.

knuckle *vb* cringe, crouch, stoop, submit, yield.

L

laborious *adj* assiduous, diligent, hardworking, indefatigable, industrious, painstaking, sedulous, toiling; arduous, difficult, fatiguing, hard, Herculean, irksome, onerous, tiresome, toilsome, wearisome.

labour *vb* drudge, endeavour, exert, strive, toil, travail, work. * *n* drudgery, effort, exertion, industry, pains, toil, work; childbirth, delivery, parturition.

labyrinth *n* entanglement, intricacy, maze, perplexity, windings.

labyrinthine *adj* confused, convoluted, intricate, involved, labyrinthian, labyrinthic, perplexing, winding.

lace *vb* attach, bind, fasten, intertwine, tie, twine. * *n* filigree, lattice, mesh, net, netting, network, openwork, web.

lacerate *vb* claw, cut, lancinate, mangle, rend, rip, sever, slash, tear, wound; afflict, harrow, rend, torture, wound.

lack *vb* need, want. * *n* dearth, default, defectiveness, deficiency, deficit, destitution, insufficiency, need, scantiness, scarcity, shortcoming, shortness, want.

lackadaisical *adj* languishing, sentimental, pensive.

laconic *adj* brief, compact, concise, pithy, sententious, short, succinct, terse.

lad *n* boy, schoolboy, stripling, youngster, youth.

lading *n* burden, cargo, freight, load.

ladylike *adj* courtly, genteel, refined, well-bred.

lag *vb* dawdle, delay, idle, linger, loiter, saunter, tarry.

laggard *n* idler, lingerer, loiterer, lounger, saunterer, sluggard.

lair *n* burrow, couch, den, form, resting place.

lambent *adj* flickering, gliding, gleaming, licking, touching, twinkling.

lame *vb* cripple, disable, hobble. * *adj* crippled, defective, disabled, halt, hobbling, limping; feeble, insufficient, poor, unsatisfactory, weak.

lament *vb* complain, grieve, keen, moan, mourn, sorrow, wail, weep; bemoan, bewail, deplore, regret. * *n* complaint, lamentation, moan, moaning, plaint, wailing; coronach, dirge, elegy, keen, monody, requiem, threnody.

lamentable *adj* deplorable, doleful, grievous, lamented, melancholy, woeful; contemptible, miserable, pitiful, poor, wretched.

lamentation *n* dirge, grief, lament, moan, moaning, mourning, plaint, ululation, sorrow, wailing.

lampoon *vb* calumniate, defame, lash, libel, parody, ridicule, satirize, slander. * *n* calumny, defamation, libel, parody, pasquinade, parody, satire, slander.

land *vb* arrive, debark, disembark. * *n* earth, ground, soil; country, district, province, region, reservation, territory, tract, weald.

landlord *n* owner, proprietor; host, hotelier, innkeeper.

landscape *n* prospect, scene, view.

language *n* dialect, speech, tongue, vernacular; conversation; expression, idiom, jargon, parlance, phraseology, slang, style, terminology; utterance, voice.

languid *adj* drooping, exhausted, faint, feeble, flagging, languishing, pining, weak; dull, heartless, heavy, inactive, listless, lukewarm, slow, sluggish, spiritless, torpid.

languish *vb* decline, droop, fade, fail, faint, pine, sicken, sink, wither.

languor *n* debility, faintness, feebleness, languidness, languishment, weakness; apathy, ennui, heartlessness, heaviness, lethargy, listlessness, torpidness, torpor, weariness.

lank *adj* attenuated, emaciated, gaunt, lean, meagre, scraggy, slender, skinny, slim, starveling, thin.

lap[1] *vb* drink, lick, mouth, tongue; plash, ripple, splash, wash; quaff, sip, sup, swizzle, tipple. * *n* draught, dram, drench, drink, gulp, lick, swig, swill, quaff, sip, sup, suck; plash, splash, wash.

lap[2] *vb* cover, enfold, fold, turn, twist, swaddle, wrap; distance, pass, outdistance, overlap. * *n* fold, flap, lappet, lapel, ply, plait; ambit, beat, circle, circuit, cycle, loop, orbit, revolution, round, tour, turn, walk.

lapse *vb* glide, sink, slide, slip; err, fail, fall. * *n* course, flow, gliding; declension, decline, fall; error, fault, indiscretion, misstep, shortcoming, slip.

larceny *n* pilfering, robbery, stealing, theft, thievery.

large *adj* big, broad, bulky, colossal, elephantine, enormous, heroic, great, huge, immense, vast; broad, expanded, extensive, spacious, wide; abundant, ample, copious, full, liberal, plentiful; capacious, comprehensive.

lascivious *adj* concupiscent, immodest, incontinent, goatish, lecherous, lewd, libidinous, loose, lubricious, lustful, prurient, salacious, sensual, unchaste, voluptuous, wanton.

lash[1] *vb* belay, bind, strap, tie; fasten, join, moor, pinion, secure.

lash[2] *vb* beat, castigate, chastise, flagellate, flail, flay, flog, goad, scourge, swinge, thrash, whip; assail, censure, excoriate, lampoon, satirize, trounce. * *n* scourge, strap, thong, whip; cut, slap, smack, stroke, stripe.

lass *n* damsel, girl, lassie, maiden, miss.

lassitude *n* dullness, exhaustion, fatigue, languor, languidness, prostration, tiredness, weariness.

last[1] *vb* abide, carry on, continue, dwell, endure, extend, maintain, persist, prevail, remain, stand, stay, survive.

last[2] *adj* hindermost, hindmost, latest; conclusive, final, terminal, ultimate; eventual, endmost, extreme, farthest, ultimate; greatest, highest, maximal, maximum, most, supreme, superlative, utmost; latest, newest; aforegoing, foregoing, latter, preceding; departing, farewell, final, leaving, parting, valedictory. * *n* conclusion, consummation, culmination, end, ending, finale, finis, finish, termination.

last[3] n cast, form, matrix, mould, shape, template.

lasting adj abiding, durable, enduring, fixed, perennial, permanent, perpetual, stable.

lastly adv conclusively, eventually, finally, ultimately.

late adj behindhand, delayed, overdue, slow, tardy; deceased, former; recent. * adv lately, recently, sometime; tardily.

latent adj abeyant, concealed, hidden, invisible, occult, secret, unseen, veiled.

latitude n amplitude, breadth, compass, extent, range, room, scope; freedom, indulgence, liberty; laxity.

latter adj last, latest, modern, recent.

lattice n espalier, grating, latticework, trellis.

laud vb approve, celebrate, extol, glorify, magnify, praise.

laudable adj commendable, meritorious, praiseworthy.

laugh vb cackle, chortle, chuckle, giggle, guffaw, snicker, snigger, titter. * n chortle, chuckle, giggle, guffaw, laughter, titter.

laughable adj amusing, comical, diverting, droll, farcical, funny, ludicrous, mirthful, ridiculous.

laughter n cackle, chortle, chuckle, glee, giggle, guffaw, laugh, laughing.

launch vb cast, dart, dispatch, hurl, lance, project, throw; descant, dilate, enlarge, expiate; begin, commence, inaugurate, open, start.

lavish vb dissipate, expend, spend, squander, waste. * adj excessive, extravagant, generous, immoderate, overliberal, prodigal, profuse, thriftless, unrestrained, unstinted, unthrifty, wasteful.

law n act, code, canon, command, commandment, covenant, decree, edict, enactment, order, precept, principle, statute, regulation, rule; jurisprudence; litigation, process, suit.

lawful adj constitutional, constituted, legal, legalized, legitimate; allowable, authorized, permissible, warrantable; equitable, rightful, just, proper, valid.

lawless adj anarchic, anarchical, chaotic, disorderly, insubordinate, rebellious, reckless, riotous, seditious, wild.

lawyer n advocate, attorney, barrister, counsel, counsellor, pettifogger, solicitor.

lax adj loose, relaxed, slow; drooping, flabby, soft; neglectful, negligent, remiss; dissolute, immoral, licentious, seditious, wild.

lay[1] vb deposit, establish, leave, place, plant, posit, put, set, settle, spread; arrange, dispose, locate, organize, position; bear, produce; advance, lodge, offer, submit; allocate, allot, ascribe, assign, attribute, charge, impute; concoct, contrive, design, plan, plot, prepare; apply, burden, encumber, impose, saddle, tax; bet, gamble, hazard, risk, stake, wager; allay, alleviate, appease, assuage, calm, relieve, soothe, still, suppress; disclose, divulge, explain, reveal, show, unveil; acquire, grab, grasp, seize; assault, attack, beat up; discover, find, unearth; bless, confirm, consecrate, ordain. * n arrangement, array, form, formation; attitude, aspect, bearing, demeanour, direction, lie, pose, position, posture, set.

lay[2] adj amateur, inexpert, nonprofessional; civil, laic, laical, nonclerical, nonecclesiastical, nonreligious, secular, temporal, unclerical.

lay[3] n ballad, carol, ditty, lied, lyric, ode, poem, rhyme, round, song, verse.

layer n bed, course, lay, seam, stratum.

laziness n idleness, inactivity, indolence, slackness, sloth, fulness, sluggishness, tardiness.

lazy adj idle, inactive, indolent, inert, slack, slothful, slow, sluggish, supine, torpid.

lead vb conduct, deliver, direct, draw, escort, guide; front, head, precede; advance, excel, outstrip, pass; allure, entice, induce, persuade, prevail; conduce, contribute, serve, tend. * adj chief, first, foremost, main, primary, prime, principal. * n direction, guidance, leadership; advance; precedence, priority.

leader n conductor, director, guide; captain, chief, chieftain, commander, head; superior, dominator, victor.

leading adj governing, ruling; capital, chief, first, foremost, highest, principal, superior.

league vb ally, associate, band, combine, confederate, unite. * n alliance, association, coalition, combination, combine, confederacy, confederation, consortium, union.

leak vb drip, escape, exude, ooze, pass, percolate, spill. * n chink, crack, crevice, hole, fissure, oozing, opening; drip, leakage, leaking, percolation.

lean[1] adj bony, emaciated, gaunt, lank, meagre, poor, skinny, thin; dull, barren, jejune, meagre, tame; inadequate, pitiful, scanty, slender; bare, barren, infertile, unproductive.

lean[2] vb incline, slope; bear, recline, repose, rest; confide, depend, rely, trust.

leaning n aptitude, bent, bias, disposition, inclination, liking, predilection, proneness, propensity, tendency.

leap vb bound, clear, jump, spring, vault; caper, frisk, gambol, hop, skip. * n bound, jump, spring, vault; caper, frisk, gambol, hop, skip.

learn vb acquire, ascertain, attain, collect, gain, gather, hear, memorize.

learned adj erudite, lettered, literate, scholarly, well-read; expert, experienced, knowing, skilled, versed, well-informed.

learner n beginner, novice, pupil, student, tyro.

learning n acquirements, attainments, culture, education, information, knowledge, lore, scholarship, tuition.

least adj meanest, minutest, smallest, tiniest.

leave[1] vb abandon, decamp, go, quit, vacate, withdraw; desert, forsake, relinquish, renounce; commit, consign, refer; cease, desist from, discontinue, refrain, stop; allow, let, let alone, permit; bequeath, demise, desist, will.

leave[2] n allowance, liberty, permission, licence, sufferance; departure, retirement, withdrawal; adieu, farewell, goodbye.

leaven vb ferment, lighten, raise; colour, elevate, imbue, inspire, lift, permeate, tinge; infect, vitiate. * n barm, ferment, yeast; influence, inspiration.

leavings npl bits, dregs, fragments, leftovers, pieces, relics, remains, remnants, scraps.

lecherous adj carnal, concupiscent, incontinent, lascivious, lewd, libidinous, lubricious, lustful, wanton, salacious, unchaste.

lechery n concupiscence, lasciviousness, lewdness, lubriciousness, lubricity, lust, salaciousness, salacity.

lecture vb censure, chide, reprimand, reprove, scold, sermonize; address, harangue, teach. * n censure, lecturing, lesson, reprimand, reproof, scolding; address, discourse, prelection.

ledge n projection, ridge, shelf.

lees npl dregs, precipitate, refuse, sediment, settlings.

leg n limb, prop.

legacy n bequest, gift, heirloom; heritage, inheritance, tradition.

legal *adj* allowable, authorized, constitutional, lawful, legalized, legitimate, proper, sanctioned.

legalize *vb* authorize, legitimate, legitimatize, legitimize, permit, sanction.

legend *n* fable, fiction, myth, narrative, romance, story, tale.

legendary *adj* fabulous, fictitious, mythical, romantic.

legible *adj* clear, decipherable, fair, distinct, plain, readable; apparent, discoverable, recognizable, manifest.

legion *n* army, body, cohort, column, corps, detachment, detail, division, force, maniple, phalanx, platoon; squad; army, horde, host, multitude, number, swarm, throng. * *adj* many, multitudinous, myriad, numerous.

legislate *vb* enact, ordain.

legitimacy *n* lawfulness, legality; genuineness.

legitimate *adj* authorized, lawful, legal, sanctioned; genuine, valid; correct, justifiable, logical, reasonable, warrantable, warranted.

leisure *n* convenience, ease, freedom, liberty, opportunity, recreation, retirement, vacation.

lend *vb* advance, afford, bestow, confer, furnish, give, grant, impart, loan, supply.

lengthen *vb* elongate, extend, produce, prolong, stretch; continue, protract.

lengthy *adj* diffuse, lengthened, long, long-drawn-out, prolix, prolonged, protracted.

lenience, leniency *n* clemency, compassion, forbearance, gentleness, lenity, mercy, mildness, tenderness.

lenient *adj* assuasive, lenitive, mitigating, mitigative, softening, soothing; clement, easy, forbearing, gentle, humouring, indulgent, long-suffering, merciful, mild, tender, tolerant.

lesion *n* derangement, disorder, hurt, injury.

less *adj* baser, inferior, lower, smaller; decreased, fewer, lesser, reduced, smaller, shorter; * *adv* barely, below, least, under; decreasingly. * *prep* excepting, lacking, minus, sans, short of, without.

lessen *vb* abate, abridge, contract, curtail, decrease, diminish, narrow, reduce, shrink; degrade, lower; dwindle, weaken.

lesson *n* exercise, task; instruction, precept; censure, chiding, lecture, lecturing, rebuke, reproof, scolding.

let[1] *vb* admit, allow, authorize, permit, suffer; charter, hire, lease, rent.

let[2] *vb* hinder, impede, instruct, prevent. * *n* hindrance, impediment, interference, obstacle, obstruction, restriction.

lethal *adj* deadly, destructive, fatal, mortal, murderous.

lethargic *adj* apathetic, comatose, drowsy, dull, heavy, inactive, inert, sleepy, stupid, stupefied, torpid.

lethargy *n* apathy, coma, drowsiness, dullness, hypnotism, inactiveness, inactivity, inertia, sleepiness, sluggishness, stupefaction, stupidity, stupor, torpor.

letter *n* epistle, missive, note.

lettered *adj* bookish, educated, erudite, learned, literary, versed, well-read.

levee *n* ceremony, entertainment, reception, party, soiree; embankment.

level *vb* equalize, flatten, horizontalize, smooth; demolish, destroy, raze; aim, direct, point. * *adj* equal, even, flat, flush, horizontal, plain, plane, smooth. * *n* altitude, degree, equality, evenness, plain, plane, smoothness; deck, floor, layer, stage, storey, tier.

levity *n* buoyancy, facetiousness, fickleness, flightiness, flippancy, frivolity, giddiness, inconstancy, levity, volatility.

levy *vb* collect, exact, gather, tax; call, muster, raise, summon. * *n* duty, tax.

lewd *adj* despicable, impure, lascivious, libidinous, licentious, loose, lustful, profligate, unchaste, vile, wanton, wicked.

liability *n* accountableness, accountability, duty, obligation, responsibility, tendency; exposedness; debt, indebtedness, obligation.

liable *adj* accountable, amenable, answerable, bound, responsible; exposed, likely, obnoxious, subject.

liaison *n* amour, intimacy, intrigue; connection, relation, union.

libel *vb* calumniate, defame, lampoon, satirize, slander, vilify. * *n* calumny, defamation, lampoon, satire, slander, vilification, vituperation.

liberal *adj* beneficent, bountiful, charitable, disinterested, free, generous, munificent, open-hearted, princely, unselfish; broad-minded, catholic, chivalrous, enlarged, high-minded, honourable, magnanimous, tolerant, unbiased, unbigoted; abundant, ample, bounteous, full, large, plentiful, unstinted; humanizing, liberalizing, refined, refining.

liberality *n* beneficence, bountifulness, bounty, charity, disinterestedness, generosity, kindness, munificence; benefaction, donation, gift, gratuity, present; broad-mindedness, catholicity, candour, impartiality, large-mindedness, magnanimity, toleration.

liberate *vb* deliver, discharge, disenthral, emancipate, free, manumit, ransom, release.

libertine *adj* corrupt, depraved, dissolute, licentious, profligate, rakish. * *n* debauchee, lecher, profligate, rake, roue, voluptuary.

liberty *n* emancipation, freedom, independence, liberation, self-direction, self-government; franchise, immunity, privilege; leave, licence, permission.

libidinous *adj* carnal, concupiscent, debauched, impure, incontinent, lascivious, lecherous, lewd, loose, lubricious, lustful, salacious, sensual, unchaste, wanton, wicked.

licence *n* authorization, leave, permission, privilege, right; certificate, charter, dispensation, imprimatur, permit, warrant; anarchy, disorder, freedom, lawlessness, laxity, liberty.

license *vb* allow, authorize, grant, permit, warrant; suffer, tolerate.

licentious *adj* disorderly, riotous, uncontrolled, uncurbed, ungovernable, unrestrained, unruly, wanton; debauched, dissolute, lax, libertine, loose, profligate, rakish; immoral, impure, lascivious, lecherous, lewd, libertine, libidinous, lustful, sensual, unchaste, wicked.

lick *vb* beat, flog, spank, thrash; lap, taste. * *n* blow, slap, stroke; salt-spring.

lie[1] *vb* couch, recline, remain, repose, rest; consist, pertain.

lie[2] *vb* equivocate, falsify, fib, prevaricate, romance. * *n* equivocation, falsehood, falsification, fib, misrepresentation, prevarication, untruth; delusion, illusion.

lief *adv* freely, gladly, willingly.

life *n* activity, alertness, animation, briskness, energy, sparkle, spirit, sprightliness, verve, vigour, vivacity; behaviour, conduct, deportment; being, duration, existence, lifetime; autobiography, biography, curriculum vitae, memoirs, story.

lifeless *adj* dead, deceased, defunct, extinct, inanimate; cold, dull, flat, frigid, inert, lethargic, passive, pulseless, slow, sluggish, tame, torpid.

lift *vb* elevate, exalt, hoist, raise, uplift. * *n* aid, assistance, help; elevator.

light¹ *vb* alight, land, perch, settle. * *adj* porous, sandy, spongy, well-leavened; loose, sandy; free, portable, unburdened, unencumbered; inconsiderable, moderate, negligible, slight, small, trifling, trivial, unimportant; ethereal, feathery, flimsy, gossamer, insubstantial, weightless; easy, effortless, facile; fickle, frivolous, unsettled, unsteady, volatile; airy, buoyant, carefree, light-hearted, lightsome; unaccented, unstressed, weak.

light² *vb* conflagrate, fire, ignite, inflame, kindle; brighten, illume, illuminate, illumine, luminate, irradiate, lighten. * *adj* bright, clear, fair, lightsome, luminous, pale, pearly, whitish. * *n* dawn, day, daybreak, sunrise; blaze, brightness, effulgence, gleam, illumination, luminosity, phosphorescence, radiance, ray; candle, lamp, lantern, lighthouse, taper, torch; comprehension, enlightenment, information, insight, instruction, knowledge; elucidation, explanation, illustration; attitude, construction, interpretation, observation, reference, regard, respect, view.

lighten¹ *vb* allay, alleviate, ease, mitigate, palliate; disburden, disencumber, relieve, unburden, unload.

lighten² *vb* brighten, gleam, shine; light, illume, illuminate, illumine, irradiate; enlighten, inform; emit, flash.

light-headed *adj* dizzy, giddy, vertiginous; confused, delirious, wandering; addle-pated, frivolous, giddy, heedless, indiscreet, light, rattle-brained, thoughtless, volatile.

light-hearted *adj* blithe, blithesome, carefree, cheerful, frolicsome, gay, glad, gladsome, gleeful, happy, jocund, jovial, joyful, lightsome, merry.

lightness *n* flightiness, frivolity, giddiness, levity, volatility; agility, buoyancy, facility.

like¹ *vb* approve, please; cherish, enjoy, love, relish; esteem, fancy, regard; choose, desire, elect, list, prefer, select, wish. * *n* liking, partiality, preference.

like² *adj* alike, allied, analogous, cognate, corresponding, parallel, resembling, similar; equal, same; likely, probable. * *adv* likely, probably. * *n* counterpart, equal, match, peer, twin.

likelihood *n* probability, verisimilitude.

likely *adj* credible, liable, possible, probable; agreeable, appropriate, convenient, likable, pleasing, suitable, well-adapted, well-suited. * *adv* doubtlessly, presumably, probably.

likeness *n* appearance, form, parallel, resemblance, semblance, similarity, similitude; copy, counterpart, effigy, facsimile, image, picture, portrait, representation.

liking *n* desire, fondness, partiality, wish; appearance, bent, bias, disposition, inclination, leaning, penchant, predisposition, proneness, propensity, tendency, turn.

limb *n* arm, extremity, leg, member; bough, branch, offshoot.

limit *vb* bound, circumscribe, define; check, condition, hinder, restrain, restrict. * *n* bound, boundary, bourn, confine, frontier, march, precinct, term, termination, terminus; check, hindrance, obstruction, restraint, restriction.

limitation *n* check, constraint, restraint, restriction.

limitless *adj* boundless, endless, eternal, illimitable, immeasurable, infinite, never-ending, unbounded, undefined, unending, unlimited.

limp¹ *vb* halt, hitch, hobble, totter. * *n* hitch, hobble, shamble, shuffle, totter.

limp² *adj* drooping, droopy, floppy, sagging, weak; flabby, flaccid, flexible, limber, pliable, relaxed, slack, soft.

limpid *adj* bright, clear, crystal, crystalline, lucid, pellucid, pure, translucent, transparent.

line *vb* align, line up, range, rank, regiment; border, bound, edge, fringe, hem, interline, march, rim, verge; seam, stripe, streak, striate, trace; carve, chisel, crease, cut, crosshatch; define, delineate, describe. * *n* mark, streak, stripe; cable, cord, rope, string, thread; rank, row; ancestry, family, lineage, race, succession; course, method; business, calling, employment, job, occupation, post, pursuit.

lineage *n* ancestry, birth, breed, descendants, descent, extraction, family, forebears, forefathers, genealogy, house, line, offspring, progeny, race.

lineament *n* feature, line, outline, trait.

linen *n* cloth, fabric, flax, lingerie.

linger *vb* dally, dawdle, delay, idle, lag, loiter, remain, saunter, stay, tarry, wait.

link *vb* bind, conjoin, connect, fasten, join, tie, unite. * *n* bond, connection, connective, copula, coupler, joint, juncture; division, member, part, piece.

liquefy *vb* dissolve, fuse, melt, thaw.

liquid *adj* fluid; clear, dulcet, flowing, mellifluous, mellifluent, melting, soft. * *n* fluid, liquor.

list¹ *vb* alphabetize, catalogue, chronicle, codify, docket, enumerate, file, index, inventory, record, register, tabulate, tally; enlist, enroll; choose, desire, elect, like, please, prefer, wish. * *n* catalogue, enumeration, index, inventory, invoice, register, roll, schedule, scroll, series, table, tally; border, bound, limit; border, edge, selvedge, strip, stripe; fillet, listel.

list² *vb* cant, heel, incline, keel, lean, pitch, tilt, tip. * *n* cant, inclination, incline, leaning, pitch, slope, tilt, tip.

listen *vb* attend, eavesdrop, hark, hear, hearken, heed, obey, observe.

listless *adj* apathetic, careless, heedless, impassive, inattentive, indifferent, indolent, languid, torpid, vacant, supine, thoughtless, vacant.

listlessness *n* apathy, carelessness, heedlessness, impassivity, inattention, indifference, indolence, languidness, languor, supineness, thoughtlessness, torpor, torpidity, vacancy.

literally *adv* actually, really; exactly, precisely, rigorously, strictly.

literary *adj* bookish, book-learned, erudite, instructed, learned, lettered, literate, scholarly, well-read.

literature *n* erudition, learning, letters, lore, writings.

lithe *adj* flexible, flexile, limber, pliable, pliant, supple.

litigation *n* contending, contest, disputing, lawsuit.

litigious *adj* contentious, disputatious, quarrelsome; controvertible, disputable.

litter *vb* derange, disarrange, disorder, scatter, strew; bear. * *n* bedding, couch, palanquin, sedan, stretcher; confusion, disarray, disorder, mess, untidiness; fragments, rubbish, shreds, trash.

little *adj* diminutive, infinitesimal, minute, small, tiny, wee; brief, short, small; feeble, inconsiderable, insignificant, moderate, petty, scanty, slender, slight, trivial, unimportant, weak; contemptible, illiberal, mean, narrow, niggardly, paltry, selfish, stingy. * *n* handful, jot, modicum, pinch, pittance, trifle, whit.

live¹ *vb* be, exist; continue, endure, last, remain, survive; abide, dwell, reside; fare, feed, nourish, subsist, support; continue, lead, pass.

live² *adj* alive, animate, living, quick; burning, hot, ignited; bright, brilliant, glowing, lively, vivid; active, animated, earnest, glowing, wide-awake.

livelihood *n* living, maintenance, subsistence, support, sustenance.

liveliness *n* activity, animation, briskness, gaiety, spirit, sprightliness, vivacity.

lively *adj* active, agile, alert, brisk, energetic, nimble, quick, smart, stirring, supple, vigorous, vivacious; airy, animated, blithe, blithesome, buoyant, frolicsome, gleeful, jocund, jolly, merry, spirited, sportive, sprightly, spry; bright, brilliant, clear, fresh, glowing, strong, vivid; dynamic, forcible, glowing, impassioned, intense, keen, nervous, piquant, racy, sparkling, strenuous, vigorous.

living *adj* alive, breathing, existing, live, organic, quick; active, lively, quickening. ** n* livelihood, maintenance, subsistence, support; estate, keeping; benefice.

load *vb* freight, lade; burden, cumber, encumber, oppress, weigh. ** n* burden, freightage, pack, weight; cargo, freight, lading; clog, deadweight, encumbrance, incubus, oppression, pressure.

loafer *n* (*sl*) bum, idler, lounger, vagabond, vagrant.

loath *adj* averse, backward, disinclined, indisposed, reluctant, unwilling.

loathe *vb* abhor, abominate, detest, dislike, hate, recoil.

loathing *n* abhorrence, abomination, antipathy, aversion, detestation, disgust, hatred, horror, repugnance, revulsion.

loathsome *adj* disgusting, nauseating, nauseous, offensive, palling, repulsive, revolting, sickening; abominable, abhorrent, detestable, execrable, hateful, odious, shocking.

local *adj* limited, neighbouring, provincial, regional, restricted, sectional, territorial, topical.

locality *n* location, neighbourhood, place, position, site, situation, spot.

locate *vb* determine, establish, fix, place, set, settle.

lock¹ *vb* bolt, fasten, padlock, seal; confine; clog, impede, restrain, stop; clasp, embrace, encircle, enclose, grapple, hug, join, press. ** n* bolt, fastening, padlock; embrace, grapple, hug.

lock² *n* curl, ringlet, tress, tuft.

lodge *vb* deposit, fix, settle; fix, place, plant; accommodate, cover, entertain, harbour, quarter, shelter; abide, dwell, inhabit, live, reside, rest; remain, rest, sojourn, stay, stop. ** n* cabin, cot, cottage, hovel, hut, shed; cave, den, haunt, lair; assemblage, assembly, association club, group, society.

lodging *n* abode, apartment, dwelling, habitation, quarters, residence; cover, harbour, protection, refuge, shelter.

loftiness *n* altitude, elevation, height; arrogance, haughtiness, pride, vanity; dignity, grandeur, sublimity.

lofty *adj* elevated, high, tall, towering; arrogant, haughty, proud; eminent, exalted, sublime; dignified, imposing, majestic, stately.

logical *adj* close, coherent, consistent, dialectical, sound, valid; discriminating, rational, reasoned.

loiter *vb* dally, dawdle, delay, dilly-dally, idle, lag, linger, saunter, stroll, tarry.

loneliness *n* isolation, retirement, seclusion, solitariness, solitude; desolation, dreariness, forlornness.

lonely *adj* apart, dreary, isolated, lonesome, remote, retired, secluded, separate, sequestrated, solitary; alone, lone, companionless, friendless, unaccompa-

nied; deserted, desolate, forlorn, forsaken, withdrawn.

lonesome *adj* cheerless, deserted, desolate, dreary, gloomy, lone, lonely.

long¹ *vb* anticipate, await, expect; aspire, covet, crave, desire, hanker, lust, pine, wish, yearn.

long² *adj* drawn-out, extended, extensive, far-reaching, lengthy, prolonged, protracted, stretched; diffuse, long-winded, prolix, tedious, wearisome; backward, behindhand, dilatory, lingering, slack, slow, tardy.

longing *n* aspiration, coveting, craving, desire, hankering, hunger, pining, yearning.

long-suffering *adj* enduring, forbearing, patient. ** n* clemency, endurance, forbearing.

look *vb* behold, examine, notice, see, search; consider, inspect, investigate, observe, study, contemplate, gaze, regard, scan, survey, view; anticipate, await, expect; heed, mind, watch; face, front; appear, seem. ** n* examination, gaze, glance, peep, peer, search; appearance, aspect, complexion; air, aspect, manner, mien.

loophole *n* aperture, crenellation, loop, opening; excuse, plea, pretence, pretext, subterfuge.

loose *vb* free, liberate, release, unbind, undo, unfasten, unlash, unlock, untie; ease, loosen, relax, slacken; detach, disconnect, disengage. ** adj* unbound, unconfined, unfastened, unsewn, untied; disengaged, free, unattached; relaxed; diffuse, diffusive, prolix, rambling, unconnected; ill-defined, indefinite, indeterminate, indistinct, vague; careless, heedless, negligent, lax, slack; debauched, dissolute, immoral, licentious, unchaste, wanton.

loosen *vb* liberate, relax, release, separate, slacken, unbind, unloose, untie.

looseness *n* easiness, slackness; laxity, levity; lewdness, unchastity, wantonness, wickedness; diarrhoea, flux.

loot *vb* pillage, plunder, ransack, rifle, rob, sack. ** n* booty, plunder, spoil.

lop *vb* cut, truncate; crop, curtail, dock, prune; detach, dissever, sever.

loquacious *adj* garrulous, talkative, voluble, wordy; noisy, speaking, talking; babbling, blabbing, tattling, tell-tale.

loquacity *n* babbling, chattering, gabbling, garrulity, loquaciousness, talkativeness, volubility.

lord *n* earl, noble, nobleman, peer, viscount; governor, king, liege, master, monarch, prince, ruler, seigneur, seignior, sovereign, superior; husband, spouse.

lordly *adj* aristocratic, dignified, exalted, grand, lofty, majestic, noble; arrogant, despotic, domineering, haughty, imperious, insolent, masterful, overbearing, proud, tyrannical; large, liberal.

lordship *n* authority, command, control, direction, domination, dominion, empire, government, rule, sovereignty, sway; manor, domain, seigneury, seigniory.

lore *n* erudition, knowledge, learning, letters, scholarship; admonition, advice, counsel, doctrine, instruction, lesson, teaching, wisdom.

lose *vb* deprive, dispossess, forfeit, miss; dislodge, displace, mislay, misspend, squander, waste; decline, fall, succumb, yield.

loss *n* deprivation, failure, forfeiture, privation; casualty, damage, defeat, destruction, detriment, disadvantage, injury, overthrow, ruin; squandering, waste.

lost *adj* astray, missing; forfeited, missed, unredeemed; dissipated, misspent, squandered, wasted; bewildered, confused, distracted, perplexed, puzzled; absent, absent-minded, abstracted, dreamy, napping, preoccupied; abandoned, corrupt, debauched, depraved, dissolute, graceless, hardened, incorrigible, irreclaimable, licentious, profligate, reprobate, shameless, unchaste, wanton; destroyed, ruined.

lot *n* allotment, apportionment, destiny, doom, fate; accident, chance, fate, fortune, hap, haphazard, hazard; division, parcel, part, portion.

loth *adj* averse, disinclined, disliking, reluctant, unwilling

loud *adj* high-sounding, noisy, resounding, sonorous; deafening, stentorian, strong, stunning; boisterous, clamorous, noisy, obstreperous, tumultuous, turbulent, uproarious, vociferous; emphatic, impressive, positive, vehement; flashy, gaudy, glaring, loud, ostentatious, showy, vulgar.

lounge *vb* loll, recline, sprawl; dawdle, idle, loaf, loiter.

love *vb* adore, like, worship. * *n* accord, affection, amity, courtship, delight, fondness, friendship, kindness, regard, tenderness, warmth; adoration, amour, ardour, attachment, passion; devotion, inclination, liking; benevolence, charity, goodwill.

lovely *adj* beautiful, charming, delectable, delightful, enchanting, exquisite, graceful, pleasing, sweet, winning; admirable, adorable, amiable.

loving *adj* affectionate, dear, fond, kind, tender.

low[1] *vb* bellow, moo.

low[2] *adj* basal, depressed, profound; gentle, grave, soft, subdued; cheap, humble, mean, plebeian, vulgar; abject, base, base-minded, degraded, dirty, grovelling, ignoble, low-minded, menial, scurvy, servile, shabby, slavish, vile; derogatory, disgraceful, dishonourable, disreputable, unbecoming, undignified, ungentlemanly, unhandsome, unmanly; exhausted, feeble, reduced, weak; frugal, plain, poor, simple, spare; lowly, reverent, submissive; dejected, depressed, dispirited.

lower[1] *vb* depress, drop, sink, subside; debase, degrade, disgrace, humble, humiliate, reduce; abate, decrease, diminish, lessen. * *adj* baser, inferior, less, lesser, shorter, smaller; subjacent, under.

lower[2] *vb* blacken, darken, frown, glower, threaten.

lowering *adj* dark, clouded, cloudy, lurid, murky, overcast, threatening.

lowliness *n* humbleness, humility, meekness, self-abasement, submissiveness.

lowly *adj* gentle, humble, meek, mild, modest, plain, poor, simple, unassuming, unpretending, unpretentious; low-born, mean, servile.

loyal *adj* constant, devoted, faithful, patriotic, true.

loyalty *n* allegiance, constancy, devotion, faithfulness, fealty, fidelity, patriotism.

lubricious *adj* slippery, smooth; uncertain, unstable, wavering; impure, incontinent, lascivious, lecherous, lewd, libidinous, licentious, lustful, salacious, unchaste, wanton.

lucid *adj* beaming, bright, brilliant, luminous, radiant, resplendent, shining, clear, crystalline, diaphanous, limpid, lucent, pellucid, pure, transparent; clear, distinct, evident, intelligible, obvious, perspicuous, plain; reasonable, sane, sober, sound.

luck *n* accident, casualty, chance, fate, fortune, hap, haphazard, hazard, serendipity, success.

luckless *adj* ill-fated, ill-starred, unfortunate, unhappy, unlucky, unpropitious, unprosperous, unsuccessful.

lucky *adj* blessed, favoured, fortunate, happy, successful; auspicious, favourable, propitious, prosperous.

lucrative *adj* advantageous, gainful, paying, profitable, remunerative.

ludicrous *adj* absurd, burlesque, comic, comical, droll, farcical, funny, laughable, odd, ridiculous, sportive.

lugubrious *adj* complaining, doleful, gloomy, melancholy, mournful, sad, serious, sombre, sorrowful.

lukewarm *adj* blood-warm, tepid, thermal; apathetic, cold, dull, indifferent, listless, unconcerned, torpid.

lull *vb* calm, compose, hush, quiet, still, tranquillize; abate, cease, decrease, diminish, subside. * *n* calm, calmness, cessation.

lumber[1] *vb* rumble, shamble, trudge.

lumber[2] *n* refuse, rubbish, trash, trumpery; wood.

luminous *adj* effulgent, incandescent, radiant, refulgent, resplendent, shining; bright, brilliant, clear; clear, lucid, lucent, perspicuous, plain.

lunacy *n* aberration, craziness, dementia, derangement, insanity, madness, mania.

lunatic *adj* crazy, demented, deranged, insane, mad, psychopathic. * *n* madman, maniac, psychopath.

lurch *vb* appropriate, filch, pilfer, purloin, steal; deceive, defeat, disappoint, evade; ambush, lurk, skulk; contrive, dodge, shift, trick; pitch, sway.

lure *vb* allure, attract, decoy, entice, inveigle, seduce, tempt. * *n* allurement, attraction, bait, decoy, enticement, temptation.

lurid *adj* dismal, ghastly, gloomy, lowering, murky, pale, wan; glaring, sensational, startling, unrestrained.

lurk *vb* hide, prowl, skulk, slink, sneak, snoop.

luscious *adj* delicious, delightful, grateful, palatable, pleasing, savoury, sweet.

lush *adj* fresh, juicy, luxuriant, moist, sappy, succulent, watery.

lust *vb* covet, crave, desire, hanker, need, want, yearn. * *n* cupidity, desire, longing; carnality, concupiscence, lasciviousness, lechery, lewdness, lubricity, salaciousness, salacity, wantonness.

lustful *adj* carnal, concupiscent, hankering, lascivious, lecherous, licentious, libidinous, lubricious, salacious.

lustily *adv* strongly, vigorously.

lustiness *n* hardihood, power, robustness, stoutness, strength, sturdiness, vigour.

lustre *n* brightness, brilliance, brilliancy, splendour.

lusty *adj* healthful, lively, robust, stout, strong, sturdy, vigorous; bulky, burly, corpulent, fat, large, stout.

luxuriance *n* exuberance, profusion, superabundance.

luxuriant *adj* exuberant, plenteous, plentiful, profuse, superabundant.

luxuriate *vb* abound, delight, enjoy, flourish, indulge, revel.

luxurious *adj* epicurean, opulent, pampered, self-indulgent, sensual, sybaritic, voluptuous.

luxury *n* epicureanism, epicurism, luxuriousness, opulence, sensuality, voluptuousness; delight, enjoyment, gratification, indulgence, pleasure; dainty, delicacy, treat.

lying *adj* equivocating, false, mendacious, untruthful, untrue.

lyric *adj* dulcet, euphonious, lyrical, mellifluous, mellifluent, melodic, melodious, musical, poetic, silvery, tuneful.

lyrical *adj* ecstatic, enthusiastic, expressive, impassion; dulcet, lyric, mellifluous, mellifluent, melodic, melodious, musical, poetic.

M

macabre *adj* cadaverous, deathlike, deathly, dreadful, eerie, frightening, frightful, ghoulish, grim, grisly, gruesome, hideous, horrid, morbid, unearthly, weird.

mace *n* baton, staff, truncheon.

macerate *vb* harass, mortify, torture; digest, soak, soften, steep.

Machiavellian *adj* arch, artful, astute, crafty, crooked, cunning, deceitful, designing, diplomatic, insidious, intriguing, shrewd, sly, subtle, tricky, wily.

machination *n* artifice, cabal, conspiracy, contrivance, design, intrigue, plot, scheme, stratagem, trick.

machine *n* instrument, puppet, tool; machinery, organization, system; engine.

mad *adj* crazed, crazy, delirious, demented, deranged, distracted, insane, irrational, lunatic, maniac, maniacal; enraged, furious, rabid, raging, violent; angry, enraged, exasperated, furious, incensed, provoked, wrathful; distracted, infatuated, wild; frantic, frenzied, raving.

madden *vb* annoy, craze, enrage, exasperate, inflame, infuriate, irritate, provoke.

madness *n* aberration, craziness, dementia, derangement, insanity, lunacy, mania; delirium, frenzy, fury, rage.

magazine *n* depository, depot, entrepot, receptacle, repository, storehouse, warehouse; pamphlet, paper, periodical.

magic *adj* bewitching, charming, enchanting, fascinating, magical, miraculous, spellbinding. * *n* conjuring, enchantment, necromancy, sorcery, thaumaturgy, voodoo, witchcraft; char, fascination, witchery.

magician *n* conjurer, enchanter, juggler, magus, necromancer, shaman, sorcerer, wizard.

magisterial *adj* august, dignified, majestic, pompous; authoritative, despotic, domineering, imperious, dictatorial.

magnanimity *n* chivalry, disinterestedness, forbearance, high-mindedness, generosity, nobility.

magnificence *n* brilliance, éclat, grandeur, luxuriousness, luxury, majesty, pomp, splendour.

magnificent *adj* elegant, grand, majestic, noble, splendid, superb; brilliant, gorgeous, imposing, lavish, luxurious, pompous, showy, stately.

magnify *vb* amplify, augment, enlarge; bless, celebrate, elevate, exalt, extol, glorify, laud, praise; exaggerate.

magnitude *n* bulk, dimension, extent, mass, size, volume; consequence, greatness, importance; grandeur, loftiness, sublimity.

maid *n* damsel, girl, lass, lassie, maiden, virgin; maidservant, servant.

maiden *adj* chaste, pure, undefiled, virgin; fresh, new, unused. * *n* girl, maid, virgin.

maidenly *adj* demure, gentle, modest, maidenlike, reserved.

maim *vb* cripple, disable, disfigure, mangle, mar, mutilate. * *n* crippling, disfigurement, mutilation; harm, hurt, injury, mischief.

main[1] *adj* capital, cardinal, chief, leading, principal; essential, important, indispensable, necessary, requisite, vital; enormous, huge, mighty, vast; pure, sheer; absolute, direct, entire, mere. * *n* channel, pipe; force, might, power, strength, violence.

main[2] *n* high seas, ocean; continent, mainland.

maintain *vb* keep, preserve, support, sustain, uphold; hold, possess; defend, vindicate, justify; carry on, continue, keep up; feed, provide, supply; allege, assert, declare; affirm, aver, contend, hold, say.

maintenance *n* defence, justification, preservation, support, sustenance, vindication; bread, food, livelihood, provisions, subsistence, sustenance, victuals.

majestic *adj* august, dignified, imperial, imposing, lofty, noble, pompous, princely, stately, regal, royal; grand, magnificent, splendid, sublime.

majesty *n* augustness, dignity, elevation, grandeur, loftiness, stateliness.

majority *n* bulk, greater, mass, more, most, plurality, preponderance, superiority; adulthood, manhood.

make *vb* create; fashion, figure, form, frame, mould, shape; cause, construct, effect, establish, fabricate, produce; do, execute, perform, practice; acquire, gain, get, raise, secure; cause, compel, constrain, force, occasion; compose, constitute; go, journey, move, proceed, tend, travel; conduce, contribute, effect, favour, operate; estimate, judge, reckon, suppose, think. * *n* brand, build, constitution, construction, form, shape, structure.

maker *n* creator, god; builder, constructor, fabricator, framer, manufacturer; author, composer, poet, writer.

maladministration *n* malversation, misgovernment, misrule.

maladroit *adj* awkward, bungling, clumsy, inept, inexpert, unhandy, unskilful, unskilled.

malady *n* affliction, ailment, complaint, disease, disorder, illness, indisposition, sickness.

malcontent *adj* discontented, dissatisfied, insurgent, rebellious, resentful, uneasy, unsatisfied. * *n* agitator, complainer, fault-finder, grumbler, spoilsport.

malediction *n* anathema, ban, curse, cursing, denunciation, execration, imprecation, malison.

malefactor *n* convict, criminal, culprit, delinquent, evil-doer, felon, offender, outlaw.

malevolence *n* hate, hatred, ill-will, malice, malignity, rancour, spite, spitefulness, vindictiveness.

malevolent *adj* evil-minded, hateful, hostile, ill-natured, malicious, malignant, mischievous, rancorous, spiteful, venomous. vindictive.

malice *n* animosity, bitterness, enmity, grudge, hate, ill-will, malevolence, maliciousness, malignity, pique, rancour, spite, spitefulness, venom, vindictiveness.

malicious *adj* bitter, envious, evil-minded, ill-disposed, ill-natured, invidious, malevolent, malignant, mischievous, rancorous, resentful, spiteful, vicious.

malign vb abuse, asperse, blacken, calumniate, defame, disparage, revile, scandalize, slander, traduce, vilify. * adj malevolent, malicious, malignant, ill-disposed; baneful, injurious, pernicious, unfavourable, unpropitious.

malignant adj bitter, envious, hostile, inimical, malevolent, malicious, malign, spiteful, rancorous, resentful, virulent; heinous, pernicious; ill-boding, unfavourable, unpropitious; dangerous, fatal.

malignity n animosity, hatred, ill-will, malice, malevolence, maliciousness, rancour, spite; deadliness, destructiveness, fatality, harmfulness, malignancy, perniciousness, virulence; enormity, evilness, heinousness.

malpractice n dereliction, malversation, misbehaviour, misconduct, misdeed, misdoing, sin, transgression.

maltreat vb abuse, harm, hurt, ill-treat, ill-use, injure.

mammoth adj colossal, enormous, gigantic, huge, immense, vast.

man vb crew, garrison, furnish; fortify, reinforce, strengthen. * n adult, being, body, human, individual, one, person, personage, somebody, soul; humanity, humankind, mankind; attendant, butler, dependant, liege, servant, subject, valet, vassal; employee, workman.

manacle vb bind, chain, fetter, handcuff, restrain, shackle, tie. * n bond, chain, handcuff, gyve, hand-fetter, shackle.

manage vb administer, conduct, direct, guide, handle, operate, order, regulate, superintend, supervise, transact, treat; control, govern, rule; handle, manipulate, train, wield; contrive, economize, husband, save.

manageable adj controllable, docile, easy, governable, tamable, tractable.

management n administration, care, charge, conduct, control, direction, disposal, economy, government, guidance, superintendence, supervision, surveillance, treatment.

manager n comptroller, conductor, director, executive, governor, impresario, overseer, superintendent, supervisor.

mandate n charge, command, commission, edict, injunction, order, precept, requirement.

manful adj bold, brave, courageous, daring, heroic, honourable, intrepid, noble, stout, strong, undaunted, vigorous.

mangily adv basely, foully, meanly, scabbily, scurvily, vilely.

mangle[1] vb hack, lacerate, mutilate, rend, tear; cripple, crush, destroy, maim, mar, spoil.

mangle[2] vb calender, polish, press, smooth.

manhood n virility; bravery, courage, firmness, fortitude, hardihood, manfulness, manliness, resolution; human nature, humanity; adulthood, maturity.

mania n aberration, craziness, delirium, dementia, derangement, frenzy, insanity, lunacy, madness; craze, desire, enthusiasm, fad, fanaticism.

manifest vb declare, demonstrate, disclose, discover, display, evidence, evince, exhibit, express, reveal, show. * adj apparent, clear, conspicuous, distinct, evident, glaring, indubitable, obvious, open, palpable, patent, plain, unmistakable, visible.

manifestation n disclosure, display, exhibition, exposure, expression, revelation.

manifold adj complex, diverse, many, multifarious, multiplied, multitudinous, numerous, several, sundry, varied, various.

manipulate vb handle, operate, work.

manliness n boldness, bravery, courage, dignity, fearlessness, firmness, heroism, intrepidity, nobleness, resolution, valour.

manly adj bold, brave, courageous, daring, dignified, firm, heroic, intrepid, manful, noble, stout, strong, undaunted, vigorous; male, masculine, virile.

manner n fashion, form, method, mode, style, way; custom, habit, practice; degree, extent, measure; kind, kinds, sort, sorts; air, appearance, aspect, behaviour, carriage, demeanour, deportment, look, mien; mannerism, peculiarity; behaviour, conduct, habits, morals; civility, deportment.

mannerly adj ceremonious, civil, complaisant, courteous, polite, refined, respectful, urbane, well-behaved, well-bred.

manners npl conduct, habits, morals; air, bearing, behaviour, breeding, carriage, comportment, deportment, etiquette.

manoeuvre vb contrive, finesse, intrigue, manage, plan, plot, scheme. * n evolution, exercise, movement, operation; artifice, finesse, intrigue, plan, plot, ruse, scheme, stratagem, trick.

mansion n abode, dwelling, dwelling house, habitation, hall, residence, seat.

mantle vb cloak, cover, discover, obscure; expand, spread; bubble, cream, effervesce, foam, froth, sparkle. * n chasuble, cloak, toga; cover, covering, hood.

manufacture vb build, compose, construct, create, fabricate, forge, form, make, mould, produce, shape. * n constructing, fabrication, making, production.

manumission n deliverance, emancipation, enfranchisement, freedom, liberation, release.

manumit vb deliver, emancipate, enfranchise, free, liberate, release.

manure vb enrich, fertilize. * n compost, dressing, fertilizer, guano, muck.

many adj abundant, diverse, frequent, innumerable, manifold, multifarious, multifold, multiplied, multitudinous, numerous, sundry, varied, various. * n crowd, multitude, people.

map vb chart, draw up, plan, plot, set out, sketch. * n chart, diagram, outline, plot, sketch.

mar vb blot, damage, harm, hurt, impair, injure, ruin, spoil, stain; deface, deform, disfigure, maim, mutilate.

marauder n bandit, brigand, desperado, filibuster, freebooter, outlaw, pillager, plunderer, ravager, robber, rover.

march vb go, pace, parade, step, tramp, walk. * n hike, tramp, walk; parade, procession; gait, step, stride; advance, evolution, progress.

marches npl borders, boundaries, confines, frontiers, limits, precincts.

margin n border, brim, brink, confine, edge, limit, rim, skirt, verge; latitude, room, space, surplus.

marine adj oceanic, pelagic, saltwater, sea; maritime, naval, nautical. * n navy, shipping; sea-dog, sea soldier, soldier; sea piece, seascape.

mariner n navigator, sailor, salt, seafarer, seaman, tar.

marital adj connubial, conjugal, matrimonial.

maritime adj marine, naval, nautical, oceanic, sea, seafaring, seagoing; coastal, seaside.

mark vb distinguish, earmark, label; betoken, brand,

characterize, denote, designate, engrave, impress, imprint, indicate, print, stamp; evince, heed, note, notice, observe, regard, remark, show, spot. * *n* brand, character, characteristic, impression, impress, line, note, print, sign, stamp, symbol, token, race; evidence, indication, proof, symptom, trace, track, vestige; badge; footprint; bull's-eye, butt, object, target; consequence, distinction, eminence, fame, importance, notability, position, preeminence, reputation, significance.

marked *adj* conspicuous, distinguished, eminent, notable, noted, outstanding, prominent, remarkable.

marriage *n* espousals, nuptials, spousals, wedding; matrimony, wedlock; union; alliance, association, confederation.

marrow *n* medulla, pith; cream, essence, quintessence, substance.

marsh *n* bog, fen, mire, morass, quagmire, slough, swamp.

marshal *vb* arrange, array, dispose, gather, muster, range, order, rank; guide, herald, lead. * *n* conductor, director, master of ceremonies, regulator; harbinger, herald, pursuivant.

marshy *adj* boggy, miry, mossy, swampy, wet.

martial *adj* brave, heroic, military, soldier-like, warlike.

marvel *vb* gape, gaze, goggle, wonder. * *n* miracle, prodigy, wonder; admiration, amazement, astonishment, surprise.

marvellous *adj* amazing, astonishing, extraordinary, miraculous, prodigious, strange, stupendous, wonderful, wondrous; improbable, incredible, surprising, unbelievable.

masculine *adj* bold, hardy, manful, manlike, manly, mannish, virile; potent, powerful, robust, strong, vigorous; bold, coarse, forward.

mask *vb* cloak, conceal, cover, disguise, hide, screen, shroud, veil. * *n* blind, cloak, disguise, screen, veil; evasion, pretence, plea, pretext, ruse, shift, subterfuge, trick; masquerade; bustle, mummery.

masquerade *vb* cover, disguise, hide, mask, revel, veil. * *n* mask, mummery, revel, revelry.

Mass *n* communion, Eucharist.

mass *vb* accumulate, amass, assemble, collect, gather, rally, throng. * *adj* extensive, general, large-scale, widespread. * *n* cake, clot, lump; assemblage, collection, combination, congeries, heap; bulk, dimension, magnitude, size; accumulation, aggregate, body, sum, total, totality, whole.

massacre *vb* annihilate, butcher, exterminate, kill, murder, slaughter, slay. * *n* annihilation, butchery, carnage, extermination, killing, murder, pogrom, slaughter.

massive *adj* big, bulky, colossal, enormous, heavy, huge, immense, ponderous, solid, substantial, vast, weighty.

master *vb* conquer, defeat, direct, govern, overcome, overpower, rule, subdue, subjugate, vanquish; acquire, learn. * *adj* cardinal, chief, especial, grand, great, main, leading, prime, principal; adept, expert, proficient. * *n* director, governor, lord, manager, overseer, superintendent, ruler; captain, commander; instructor, pedagogue, preceptor, schoolteacher, teacher, tutor; holder, owner, possessor, proprietor; chief, head, leader, principal.

masterly *adj* adroit, clever, dextrous, excellent, expert, finished, skilful, skilled; arbitrary, despotic, despotical, domineering, imperious.

mastery *n* command, dominion, mastership, power, rule, supremacy, sway; ascendancy, conquest, leadership, preeminence, superiority, upper-hand, victory; acquisition, acquirement, attainment; ability, cleverness, dexterity, proficiency, skill.

masticate *vb* chew, eat, munch.

match *vb* equal, rival; adapt, fit, harmonize, proportion, suit; marry, mate; combine, couple, join, sort; oppose, pit; correspond, suit, tally. * *n* companion, equal, mate, tally; competition, contest, game, trial; marriage, union.

matchless *adj* consummate, excellent, exquisite, incomparable, inimitable, peerless, perfect, surpassing, unequalled, unmatched, unparalleled, unrivalled.

mate *vb* marry, match, wed; compete, equal, vie; appal, confound, crush, enervate, subdue, stupefy. * *n* associate, companion, compeer, consort, crony, friend, fellow, intimate; companion, equal, match; assistant, subordinate; husband, spouse, wife.

material *adj* bodily, corporeal, nonspiritual, physical, temporal; essential, important, momentous, relevant, vital, weighty. * *n* body, element, stuff, substance.

maternal *adj* motherlike, motherly.

matrimonial *adj* conjugal, connubial, espousal, hymeneal, marital, nuptial, spousal.

matrimony *n* marriage, wedlock.

matter *vb* import, signify, weigh. * *n* body, content, sense, substance; difficulty, distress, trouble; material, stuff; question, subject, subject matter, topic; affair, business, concern, event; consequence, import, importance, moment, significance; discharge, purulence, pus.

mature *vb* develop, perfect, ripen. * *adj* complete, fit, full-grown, perfect, ripe; completed, prepared, ready, well-considered, well-digested.

maturity *n* completeness, completion, matureness, perfection, ripeness.

mawkish *adj* disgusting, flat, insipid, nauseous, sickly, stale, tasteless, vapid; emotional, feeble, maudlin, sentimental.

maxim *n* adage, aphorism, apothegm, axiom, byword, dictum, proverb, saw, saying, truism.

maze *vb* amaze, bewilder, confound, confuse, perplex. * *n* intricacy, labyrinth, meander; bewilderment, embarrassment, intricacy, perplexity, puzzle, uncertainty.

mazy *adj* confused, confusing, intricate, labyrinthian, labyrinthic, labyrinthine, perplexing, winding.

meagre *adj* emaciated, gaunt, lank, lean, poor, skinny, starved, spare, thin; barren, poor, sterile, unproductive; bald, barren, dry, dull, mean, poor, prosy, feeble, insignificant, jejune, scanty, small, tame, uninteresting, vapid.

mean¹ *vb* contemplate, design, intend, purpose; connote, denote, express, imply, import, indicate, purport, signify, symbolize.

mean² *adj* average, medium, middle; intermediate, intervening. * *n* measure, mediocrity, medium, moderation; average; agency, instrument, instrumentality, means, measure, method, mode, way.

mean³ *adj* coarse, common, humble, ignoble, low, ordinary, plebeian, vulgar; abject, base, base-minded, beggarly, contemptible, degraded, dirty, dishonourable, disingenuous, grovelling, low-minded, pitiful, rascally, scurvy, servile, shabby, sneaking, sorry, spiritless, unfair, vile; illiberal, mercenary, miserly, narrow, narrow-minded, niggardly, parsimonious, penurious, selfish, sordid, stingy, ungenerous, unhandsome; contemptible, despicable, diminutive, insignificant, paltry, petty, poor, small, wretched.

meaning n acceptation, drift, import, intention, purport, purpose, sense, signification.

means npl instrument, method, mode, way; appliance, expedient, measure, resource, shift, step; estate, income, property, resources, revenue, substance, wealth, wherewithal.

measure vb mete; adjust, gauge, proportion; appraise, appreciate, estimate, gauge, value. * n gauge, meter, rule, standard; degree, extent, length, limit; allotment, share, proportion; means, step; foot, metre, rhythm, tune, verse.

measureless adj boundless, endless, immeasurable, immense, limitless, unbounded, unlimited, vast.

meat n aliment, cheer, diet, fare, feed, flesh, food, nourishment, nutriment, provision, rations, regimen, subsistence, sustenance, viands, victuals.

mechanic n artificer, artisan, craftsman, hand, handicraftsman, machinist, operative, workman.

meddle vb interfere, intermeddle, interpose, intrude.

meddlesome adj interfering, intermeddling, intrusive, officious, prying.

mediate vb arbitrate, intercede, interpose, intervene, settle. * adj interposed, intervening, middle.

mediation n arbitration, intercession, interposition, intervention.

mediator n advocate, arbitrator, interceder, intercessor, propitiator, umpire.

medicine n drug, medicament, medication, physic; therapy.

mediocre adj average, commonplace, indifferent, mean, medium, middling, ordinary.

meditate vb concoct, contrive, design, devise, intend, plan, purpose, scheme; chew, contemplate, ruminate, study; cogitate, muse, ponder, think.

meditation n cogitation, contemplation, musing, pondering, reflection, ruminating, study, thought.

meditative adj contemplative, pensive, reflective, studious, thoughtful.

medium adj average, mean, mediocre, middle. * n agency, channel, intermediary, instrument, instrumentality, means, organ; conditions, environment, influences; average, means.

medley n confusion, farrago, hodgepodge, hotchpotch, jumble, mass, melange, miscellany, mishmash, mixture.

meed n award, guerdon, premium, prize, recompense, remuneration, reward.

meek adj gentle, humble, lowly, mild, modest, pacific, soft, submissive, unassuming, yielding.

meekness n gentleness, humbleness, humility, lowliness, mildness, modesty, submission, submissiveness.

meet vb cross, intersect, transact; confront, encounter, engage; answer, comply, fulfil, gratify, satisfy; converge, join, unite; assemble, collect, convene, congregate, forgather, muster, rally. * adj adapted, appropriate, befitting, convenient, fit, fitting, proper, qualified, suitable, suited.

meeting n encounter, interview; assemblage, assembly, audience, company, concourse, conference, congregation, convention, gathering; assignation, encounter, introduction, rendezvous; confluence, conflux, intersection, joining, junction, union; collision.

melancholy adj blue, dejected, depressed, despondent, desponding, disconsolate, dismal, dispirited, doleful, down, downcast, downhearted, gloomy, glum, hypochondriac, low-spirited, lugubrious, moody, mopish, sad, sombre, sorrowful, unhappy; afflictive, calamitous, unfortunate, unlucky; dark, gloomy, grave, quiet. * n blues, dejection, depression, despondency, dismals, dumps, gloom, gloominess, hypochondria, sadness, vapours.

melee n affray, brawl, broil, contest, fight, fray, scuffle.

mellifluous, mellifluent adj dulcet, euphonic, euphonical, euphonious, mellow, silver-toned, silvery, smooth, soft, sweet.

mellow vb mature, ripen; improve, smooth, soften, tone; pulverize; perfect. * adj mature, ripe; dulcet, mellifluous, mellifluent, rich, silver-toned, silvery, smooth, soft; delicate; genial, good-humoured, jolly, jovial, matured, softened; mellowy, loamy, unctuous; perfected, well-prepared; disguised, fuddled, intoxicated, tipsy.

melodious adj arioso, concordant, dulcet, euphonious, harmonious, mellifluous, mellifluent, musical, silvery, sweet, tuneful.

melody n air, descant, music, plainsong, song, theme, tune.

melt vb dissolve, fuse, liquefy, thaw; mollify, relax, soften, subdue; dissipate, waste; blend, pass, shade.

member n arm, leg, limb, organ; component, constituent, element, part, portion; branch, clause, division, head.

memento n memorial, remembrance, reminder, souvenir.

memoir n account, autobiography, biography, journal, narrative, record, register.

memorable adj celebrated, distinguished, extraordinary, famous, great, illustrious, important, notable, noteworthy, remarkable, signal, significant.

memorandum n minute, note, record.

memorial adj commemorative, monumental. * n cairn, commemoration, memento, monument, plaque, record, souvenir; memorandum, remembrance.

memory n recollection, remembrance, reminiscence; celebrity, fame, renown, reputation; commemoration, memorial.

menace vb alarm, frighten, intimidate, threaten. * n danger, hazard, peril, threat, warning; nuisance, pest, troublemaker.

menage n household, housekeeping, management.

mend vb darn, patch, rectify, refit, repair, restore, retouch; ameliorate, amend, better, correct, emend, improve, meliorate, reconcile, rectify, reform; advance, help; augment, increase.

mendacious adj deceitful, deceptive, fallacious, false, lying, untrue, untruthful.

mendacity n deceit, deceitfulness, deception, duplicity, falsehood, lie, untruth.

mendicant n beggar, pauper, tramp.

menial adj base, low, mean, servile, vile. * n attendant, bondsman, domestic, flunkey, footman, lackey, serf, servant, slave, underling, valet, waiter.

mensuration n measurement, measuring; survey, surveying.

mental adj ideal, immaterial, intellectual, psychiatric, subjective.

mention vb acquaint, allude, cite, communicate, declare, disclose, divulge, impart, inform, name, report, reveal, state, tell. * n allusion, citation, designation, notice, noting, reference.

mentor *n* adviser, counsellor, guide, instructor, monitor.

mephitic *adj* baleful, baneful, fetid, foul, mephitical, noisome, noxious, poisonous, pestilential.

mercantile *adj* commercial, marketable, trading.

mercenary *adj* hired, paid, purchased, venal; avaricious, covetous, grasping, mean, niggardly, parsimonious, penurious, sordid, stingy. * *n* hireling, soldier.

merchandise *n* commodities, goods, wares.

merchant *n* dealer, retailer, shopkeeper, trader, tradesman.

merciful *adj* clement, compassionate, forgiving, gracious, lenient, pitiful; benignant, forbearing, gentle, humane, kind, mild, tender, tender-hearted.

merciless *adj* barbarous, callous, cruel, fell, hard-hearted, inexorable, pitiless, relentless, remorseless, ruthless, savage, severe, uncompassionate, unfeeling, unmerciful, unrelenting, unrepenting, unsparing.

mercurial *adj* active, lively, nimble, prompt, quick, sprightly; cheerful, light-hearted; changeable, fickle, flighty, inconstant, mobile, volatile.

mercy *n* benevolence, clemency, compassion, gentleness, kindness, lenience, leniency, lenity, mildness, pity, tenderness; blessing, favour, grace; discretion, disposal; forgiveness, pardon.

mere *adj* bald, bare, naked, plain, sole, simple; absolute, entire, pure, sheer, unmixed. * *n* lake, pond, pool.

meretricious *adj* deceitful, brummagem, false, gaudy, make-believe, sham, showy, spurious, tawdry.

merge *vb* bury, dip, immerse, involve, lose, plunge, sink, submerge.

meridian *n* acme, apex, climax, culmination, summit, zenith; midday, noon, noontide.

merit *vb* deserve, earn, incur; acquire, gain, profit, value. * *n* claim, right; credit, desert, excellence, goodness, worth, worthiness.

meritorious *adj* commendable, deserving, excellent, good, worthy.

merriment *n* amusement, frolic, gaiety, hilarity, jocularity, jollity, joviality, laughter, liveliness, mirth, sport, sportiveness.

merry *adj* agreeable, brisk, delightful, exhilarating, lively, pleasant, stirring; airy, blithe, blithesome, buxom, cheerful, comical, droll, facetious, frolicsome, gladsome, gleeful, hilarious, jocund, jolly, jovial, joyous, light-hearted, lively, mirthful, sportive, sprightly, vivacious.

mess *n* company, set; farrago, hodgepodge, hotchpotch, jumble, medley, mass, melange, miscellany, mishmash, mixture; confusion, muddle, perplexity, pickle, plight, predicament.

message *n* communication, dispatch, intimation, letter, missive, notice, telegram, wire, word.

messenger *n* carrier, courier, emissary, envoy, express, mercury, nuncio; forerunner, harbinger, herald, precursor.

metamorphic *adj* changeable, mutable, variable.

metamorphose *vb* change, mutate, transfigure, transform, transmute.

metamorphosis *n* change, mutation, transfiguration, transformation, transmutation.

metaphorical *adj* allegorical, figurative, symbolic, symbolical.

metaphysical *adj* abstract, allegorical, figurative, general, intellectual, parabolic, subjective, unreal.

mete *vb* dispense, distribute, divide, measure, ration, share. * *n* bound, boundary, butt, limit, measure, term, terminus.

meteor *n* aerolite, falling star, shooting star.

method *n* course, manner, means, mode, procedure, process, rule, way; arrangement, classification, disposition, order, plan, regularity, scheme, system.

methodical *adj* exact, orderly, regular, systematic, systematical.

metropolis *n* capital, city, conurbation.

mettle *n* constitution, element, material, stuff; character, disposition, spirit, temper; ardour, courage, fire, hardihood, life, nerve, pluck, sprightliness, vigour.

mettlesome *adj* ardent, brisk, courageous, fiery, frisky, high-spirited, lively, spirited, sprightly.

mew *vb* confine, coop, encase, enclose, imprison; cast, change, mould, shed.

microscopic *adj* infinitesimal, minute, tiny.

middle *adj* central, halfway, mean, medial, mid; intermediate, intervening. * *n* centre, halfway, mean, midst.

middleman *n* agent, broker, factor, go-between, intermediary.

mien *n* air, appearance, aspect, bearing, behaviour, carriage, countenance, demeanour, deportment, look, manner.

might *n* ability, capacity, efficacy, efficiency, force, main, power, prowess, puissance, strength.

mighty *adj* able, bold, courageous, potent, powerful, puissant, robust, strong, sturdy, valiant, valorous, vigorous; bulky, enormous, huge, immense, monstrous, stupendous, vast.

migratory *adj* nomadic, roving, shifting, strolling, unsettled, wandering, vagrant.

mild *adj* amiable, clement, compassionate, gentle, good-natured, indulgent, kind, lenient, meek, merciful, pacific, tender; bland, pleasant, soft, suave; calm, kind, placid, temperate, tranquil; assuasive, compliant, demulcent, emollient, lenitive, mollifying, soothing.

mildness *n* amiability, clemency, gentleness, indulgence, kindness, meekness, moderation, softness, tenderness, warmth.

mildew *n* blight, blast, mould, must, mustiness, smut, rust.

milieu *n* background, environment, sphere, surroundings.

militant *adj* belligerent, combative, contending, fighting.

military *adj* martial, soldier, soldierly, warlike. * *n* army, militia, soldiers.

mill *vb* comminute, crush, grate, grind, levigate, powder, pulverize. * *n* factory, manufactory; grinder; crowd, throng.

mimic *vb* ape, counterfeit, imitate, impersonate, mime, mock, parody. * *adj* imitative, mock, simulated. * *n* imitator, impersonator, mime, mocker, parodist, parrot.

mince[1] *vb* chop, cut, hash, shatter. * *n* forcemeat, hash, mash, mincemeat.

mince[2] *vb* attenuate, diminish, extenuate, mitigate, palliate, soften; pose, sashay, simper, smirk.

mind[1] *vb* attend, heed, mark, note, notice, regard, tend, watch; obey, observe, submit; design, incline, intend, mean; recall, recollect, remember, remind; beware, look out, watch out. * *n* soul, spirit; brains, common sense, intellect, reason, sense, understanding; belief, consideration, contemplation, judgement, opinion, reflection, sentiment, thought; memory, recollection, remembrance; bent, desire, disposition, inclination, intention, leaning, purpose, tendency, will.

mind² *vb* balk, begrudge, grudge, object, resent.

mindful *adj* attentive, careful, heedful, observant, regardful, thoughtful.

mindless *adj* dull, heavy, insensible, senseless, sluggish, stupid, unthinking; careless, forgetful, heedless, neglectful, negligent, regardless.

mine *vb* dig, excavate, quarry, unearth; sap, undermine, weaken; destroy, ruin. * *n* colliery, deposit, lode, pit, shaft.

mingle *vb* blend, combine, commingle, compound, intermingle, intermix, join, mix, unite.

miniature *adj* bantam, diminutive, little, small, tiny.

minion *n* creature, dependant, favourite, hanger-on, parasite, sycophant; darling, favourite, flatterer, pet.

minister *vb* administer, afford, furnish, give, supply; aid, assist, contribute, help, succour. * *n* agent, assistant, servant, subordinate, underling; administrator, executive; ambassador, delegate, envoy, plenipotentiary; chaplain, churchman, clergyman, cleric, curate, divine, ecclesiastic, parson, pastor, preacher, priest, rector, vicar.

ministry *n* agency, aid, help, instrumentality, interposition, intervention, ministration, service, support; administration, cabinet, council, government.

minor *adj* less, smaller; inferior, junior, secondary, subordinate, younger; inconsiderable, petty, unimportant, small.

minstrel *n* bard, musician, singer, troubadour.

mint *vb* coin, stamp; fabricate, fashion, forge, invent, make, produce. * *adj* fresh, new, perfect, undamaged. * *n* die, punch, seal, stamp; fortune, (*inf*) heap, million, pile, wad.

minute¹ *adj* diminutive, fine, little, microscopic, miniature, slender, slight, small, tiny; circumstantial, critical, detailed, exact, fussy, meticulous, nice, particular, precise.

minute² *n* account, entry, item, memorandum, note, proceedings, record; instant, moment, second, trice, twinkling.

miracle *n* marvel, prodigy, wonder.

miraculous *adj* supernatural, thaumaturgic, thaumaturgical; amazing, extraordinary, incredible, marvellous, unaccountable, unbelievable, wondrous.

mirror *vb* copy, echo, emulate, reflect, show. * *n* looking-glass, reflector, speculum; archetype, exemplar, example, model, paragon, pattern, prototype.

mirth *n* cheerfulness, festivity, frolic, fun, gaiety, gladness, glee, hilarity, festivity, jollity, joviality, joyousness, laughter, merriment, merry-making, rejoicing, sport.

mirthful *adj* cheery, cheery, festive, frolicsome, hilarious, jocund, jolly, merry, jovial, joyous, lively, playful, sportive, vivacious; comic, droll, humorous, facetious, funny, jocose, jocular, ludicrous, merry, waggish, witty.

misadventure *n* accident, calamity, catastrophe, cross, disaster, failure, ill-luck, infelicity, mischance, misfortune, mishap, reverse.

misanthrope *n* cynic, egoist, egotist, man-hater, misanthropist.

misapply *vb* abuse, misuse, pervert.

misapprehend *vb* misconceive, mistake, misunderstand.

misbehaviour *n* ill-behaviour, ill-conduct, incivility, miscarriage, misconduct, misdemeanour, naughtiness, rudeness.

miscarriage *n* calamity, defeat, disaster, failure, mis-

chance, mishap; misbehaviour, misconduct, ill-behaviour.

miscellaneous *adj* confused, diverse, diversified, heterogeneous, indiscriminate, jumbled, many, mingled, mixed, promiscuous, stromatic, stromatous, various.

miscellany *n* collection, diversity, farrago, gallimaufry, hodgepodge, hotchpotch, jumble, medley, mishmash, melange, miscellaneous, mixture, variety.

mischance *n* accident, calamity, disaster, ill-fortune, ill-luck, infelicity, misadventure, misfortune, mishap.

mischief *n* damage, detriment, disadvantage, evil, harm, hurt, ill, injury, prejudice; ill-consequence, misfortune, trouble; devilry, wrong-doing.

mischievous *adj* destructive, detrimental, harmful, hurtful, injurious, noxious, pernicious; malicious, sinful, vicious, wicked; annoying, impish, naughty, troublesome, vexatious.

misconceive *vb* misapprehend, misjudge, mistake, misunderstand.

misconduct *vb* botch, bungle, misdirect, mismanage. * *n* bad conduct, ill-conduct, misbehaviour, misdemeanour, rudeness, transgression; ill-management, mismanagement.

misconstrue *vb* misread, mistranslate; misapprehend, misinterpret, mistake, misunderstand.

miscreant *adj* corrupt, criminal, evil, rascally, unprincipled, vicious, villainous, wicked. * *n* caitiff, knave, ragamuffin, rascal, rogue, ruffian, scamp, scoundrel, vagabond, villain.

misdemeanour *n* fault, ill-behaviour, misbehaviour, misconduct, misdeed, offence, transgression, trespass.

miser *n* churl, curmudgeon, lickpenny, money-grabber, niggard, penny-pincher, pinch-fist, screw, scrimp, skinflint.

miserable *adj* afflicted, broken-hearted, comfortless, disconsolate, distressed, forlorn, heartbroken, unhappy, wretched; calamitous, hapless, ill-starred, pitiable, unfortunate, unlucky; poor, valueless, worthless; abject, contemptible, despicable, low, mean, worthless.

miserly *adj* avaricious, beggarly, close, close-fisted, covetous, grasping, mean, niggardly, parsimonious, penurious, sordid, stingy, tight-fisted.

misery *n* affliction, agony, anguish, calamity, desolation, distress, grief, heartache, heavy-heartedness, misfortune, sorrow, suffering, torment, torture, tribulation, unhappiness, woe, wretchedness.

misfortune *n* adversity, affliction, bad luck, blow, calamity, casualty, catastrophe, disaster, distress, hardship, harm, ill, infliction, misadventure, mischance, mishap, reverse, scourge, stroke, trial, trouble, visitation.

misgiving *n* apprehension, distrust, doubt, hesitation, suspicion, uncertainty.

mishap *n* accident, calamity, disaster, ill luck, misadventure, mischance, misfortune.

misinterpret *vb* distort, falsify, misapprehend, misconceive, misconstrue, misjudge.

mislead *vb* beguile, deceive, delude, misdirect, misguide.

mismanage *vb* botch, fumble, misconduct, mishandle, misrule.

misprize *vb* slight, underestimate, underrate, undervalue.

misrepresent *vb* belie, caricature, distort, falsify, misinterpret, misstate, pervert.

misrule *n* anarchy, confusion, disorder, maladministration, misgovernment, mismanagement.

miss[1] *vb* blunder, err, fail, fall short, forgo, lack, lose, miscarry, mistake, omit, overlook, trip; avoid, escape, evade, skip, slip; feel the loss of, need, want, wish. * *n* blunder, error, failure, fault, mistake, omission, oversight, slip, trip; loss, want.

miss[2] *n* damsel, girl, lass, maid, maiden.

misshapen *adj* deformed, ill-formed, ill-shaped, ill-proportioned, misformed, ugly, ungainly.

missile *n* projectile, weapon.

mission *n* commission, legation; business, charge, duty, errand, office, trust; delegation, deputation, embassy.

missive *n* communication, epistle, letter, message, note.

mist *vb* cloud, drizzle, mizzle, smog. * *n* cloud, fog, haze; bewilderment, obscurity, perplexity.

mistake *vb* misapprehend, miscalculate, misconceive, misjudge, misunderstand; confound, take; blunder, err. * *n* misapprehension, miscalculation, misconception, mistaking, misunderstanding; blunder, error, fault, inaccuracy, oversight, slip, trip.

mistaken *adj* erroneous, inaccurate, incorrect, misinformed, wrong.

mistrust *vb* distrust, doubt, suspect; apprehend, fear, surmise, suspect. * *n* doubt, distrust, misgiving, suspicion.

misty *adj* cloudy, clouded, dark, dim, foggy, obscure, overcast.

misunderstand *vb* misapprehend, misconceive, misconstrue, mistake.

misunderstanding *n* error, misapprehension, misconception, mistake; difference, difficulty, disagreement, discord, dissension, quarrel.

misuse *vb* desecrate, misapply, misemploy, pervert, profane; abuse, ill-treat, maltreat, ill-use; fritter, squander, waste. * *n* abuse, perversion, profanation, prostitution; ill-treatment, ill-use, ill-usage, misusage; misapplication, solecism.

mitigate *vb* abate, alleviate, assuage, diminish, extenuate, lessen, moderate, palliate, relieve; allay, appease, calm, mollify, pacify, quell, quiet, reduce, soften, soothe; moderate, temper.

mitigation *n* abatement, allaying, alleviation, assuagement, diminution, moderation, palliation, relief.

mix *vb* alloy, amalgamate, blend, commingle, combine, compound, incorporate, interfuse, interlard, mingle, unite; associate, join. * *n* alloy, amalgam, blend, combination, compound, mixture.

mixture *n* admixture, association, intermixture, union; compound, farrago, hash, hodgepodge, hotchpotch, jumble, medley, melange, mishmash; diversity, miscellany, variety.

moan *vb* bemoan, bewail, deplore, grieve, groan, lament, mourn, sigh, weep. * *n* groan, lament, lamentation, sigh, wail.

mob *vb* crowd, jostle, surround, swarm, pack, throng. * *n* assemblage, crowd, rabble, multitude, throng, tumult; dregs, canaille, populace, rabble, riffraff, scum.

mobile *adj* changeable, fickle, expressive, inconstant, sensitive, variable, volatile.

mock *vb* ape, counterfeit, imitate, mimic, take off; deride, flout, gibe, insult, jeer, ridicule, taunt; balk, cheat, deceive, defeat, disappoint, dupe, elude, illude, mislead. * *adj* assumed, clap-trap, counterfeit, fake, false, feigned, make-believe, pretended, spurious. * *n* fake, imitation, phoney, sham; gibe, insult, jeer, scoff, taunt.

mockery *n* contumely, counterfeit, deception, derision, imitation, jeering, mimicry, ridicule, scoffing, scorn, sham, travesty.

mode *n* fashion, manner, method, style, way; accident, affection, degree, graduation, modification, quality, variety.

model *vb* design, fashion, form, mould, plan, shape. * *adj* admirable, archetypal, estimable, exemplary, ideal, meritorious, paradigmatic, perfect, praiseworthy, worthy. * *n* archetype, design, mould, original, pattern, protoplast, prototype, type; dummy, example, form; copy, facsimile, image, imitation, representation.

moderate *vb* abate, allay, appease, assuage, blunt, dull, lessen, soothe, mitigate, mollify, pacify, quell, quiet, reduce, repress, soften, still, subdue, diminish, qualify, slacken, temper; control, govern, regulate. * *adj* abstinent, frugal, sparing, temperate; limited, mediocre; abstemious, sober; calm, cool, judicious, reasonable, steady; gentle, mild, temperate, tolerable.

moderation *n* abstemiousness, forbearance, frugality, restraint, sobriety, temperance; calmness, composure, coolness, deliberateness, equanimity, mildness, sedateness.

modern *adj* fresh, late, latest, new, novel, present, recent, up-to-date.

modest *adj* bashful, coy, diffident, humble, meek, reserved, retiring, shy, unassuming, unobtrusive, unostentatious, unpretending, unpretentious; chaste, proper, pure, virtuous; becoming, decent, moderate.

modesty *n* bashfulness, coyness, diffidence, humility, meekness, propriety, prudishness, reserve, shyness, unobtrusiveness; chastity, purity, virtue; decency, moderation.

modification *n* alteration, change, qualification, reformation, variation; form, manner, mode, state.

modify *vb* alter, change, qualify, reform, shape, vary; lower, moderate, qualify, soften.

modish *adj* fashionable, stylish; ceremonious, conventional, courtly, genteel.

modulate *vb* attune, harmonize, tune; inflict, vary; adapt, adjust, proportion.

moiety *n* half; part, portion, share.

moil *vb* drudge, labour, toil; bespatter, daub, defile, soil, splash, spot, stain; fatigue, weary, tire.

moist *adj* damp, dank, humid, marshy, muggy, swampy, wet.

moisture *n* dampness, dankness, humidity, wetness.

mole *n* breakwater, dike, dyke, jetty, mound, pier, quay.

molecule *n* atom, monad, particle.

molest *vb* annoy, badger, bore, bother, chafe, discommode, disquiet, disturb, harass, harry, fret, gull, hector, incommode, inconvenience, irritate, oppress, pester, plague, tease, torment, trouble, vex, worry.

mollify *vb* soften; appease, calm, compose, pacify, quiet, soothe, tranquillize; abate, allay, assuage, blunt, dull, ease, lessen, mitigate, moderate, relieve, temper; qualify, tone down.

moment *n* flash, instant, jiffy, second, trice, twinkling, wink; avail, consequence, consideration, force, gravity, importance, significance, signification, value, weight; drive, force, impetus, momentum.

momentous *adj* grave, important, serious, significant, vital, weighty.

momentum *n* impetus, moment.

monarch *n* autocrat, despot; chief, dictator, emperor, king, potentate, prince, queen, ruler, sovereign.

monastery *n* abbey, cloister, convent, lamasery, nunnery, priory.

monastic *adj* coenobitic, coenobitical, conventual, monkish, secluded.

money *n* banknotes, cash, coin, currency, riches, specie, wealth.

moneyed, monied *adj* affluent, opulent, rich, well-off, well-to-do.

monitor *vb* check, observe, oversee, supervise, watch. * *n* admonisher, admonitor, adviser, counsellor, instructor, mentor, overseer.

monomania *n* delusion, hallucination, illusion, insanity, self-deception.

monopolize *vb* control, dominate, engross, forestall.

monotonous *adj* boring, dull, tedious, tiresome, undiversified, uniform, unvaried, unvarying, wearisome.

monotony *n* boredom, dullness, sameness, tedium, tiresomeness, uniformity, wearisomeness.

monster *adj* enormous, gigantic, huge, immense, mammoth, monstrous. * *n* enormity, marvel, prodigy, wonder; brute, demon, fiend, miscreant, ruffian, villain, wretch.

monstrous *adj* abnormal, preternatural, prodigious, unnatural; colossal, enormous, extraordinary, huge, immense, stupendous, vast; marvellous, strange, wonderful; bad, base, dreadful, flagrant, frightful, hateful, hideous, horrible, shocking, terrible.

monument *n* memorial, record, remembrance, testimonial; cairn, cenotaph, gravestone, mausoleum, memorial, pillar, tomb, tombstone.

mood *n* disposition, humour, temper, vein.

moody *adj* capricious, humoursome, variable; angry, crabbed, crusty, fretful, ill-tempered, irascible, irritable, passionate, pettish, peevish, petulant, snappish, snarling, sour, testy; cross-grained, dogged, frowning, glowering, glum, intractable, morose, perverse, spleeny, stubborn, sulky, sullen, wayward; abstracted, gloomy, melancholy, pensive, sad, saturnine.

moonshine *n* balderdash, fiction, flummery, fudge, fustian, nonsense, pretence, stuff, trash, twaddle, vanity.

moor[1] *vb* anchor, berth, fasten, fix, secure, tie.

moor[2] *n* bog, common, heath, moorland, morass, moss, wasteland.

moot *vb* agitate, argue, debate, discuss, dispute. * *adj* arguable, debatable, doubtful, unsettled.

mopish *adj* dejected, depressed, desponding, downcast, down-hearted, gloomy, glum, sad.

moral *adj* ethical, good, honest, honourable, just, upright, virtuous; abstract, ideal, intellectual, mental. * *n* intent, meaning, significance.

morals *npl* ethics, morality; behaviour, conduct, habits, manners.

morass *n* bog, fen, marsh, quagmire, slough, swamp.

morbid *adj* ailing, corrupted, diseased, sick, sickly, tainted, unhealthy, unsound, vitiated; depressed, downcast, gloomy, pessimistic, sensitive.

mordacious *adj* acrid, biting, cutting, mordant, pungent, sharp, stinging; caustic, poignant, satirical, sarcastic, scathing, severe.

mordant *adj* biting, caustic, keen, mordacious, nipping, sarcastic.

moreover *adv, conj* also, besides, further, furthermore, likewise, too.

morning *n* aurora, daybreak, dawn, morn, morningtide, sunrise.

morose *adj* austere, churlish, crabbed, crusty, dejected, desponding, downcast, downhearted, gloomy, glum, melancholy, moody, sad, severe, sour, sullen, surly.

morsel *n* bite, mouthful, titbit; bit, fragment, part, piece, scrap.

mortal *adj* deadly, destructive, fatal, final, human, lethal, perishable, vital. * *n* being, earthling, human, man, person, woman.

mortality *n* corruption, death, destruction, fatality.

mortification *n* chagrin, disappointment, discontent, dissatisfaction, displeasure, humiliation, trouble, shame, vexation; humility, penance, self-abasement, self-denial; gangrene, necrosis.

mortify *vb* annoy, chagrin, depress, disappoint, displease, disquiet, dissatisfy, harass, humble, plague, vex, worry; abase, abash, confound, humiliate, restrain, shame, subdue; corrupt, fester, gangrene, putrefy.

mortuary *n* burial place, cemetery, churchyard, graveyard, necropolis; charnel house, morgue.

mostly *adv* chiefly, customarily, especially, generally, mainly, particularly, principally.

mote *n* atom, corpuscle, flaw, mite, particle, speck, spot.

motherly *adj* affectionate, kind, maternal, paternal, tender.

motion *vb* beckon, direct, gesture, signal. * *n* action, change, drift, flux, movement, passage, stir, transit; air, gait, port; gesture, impulse, prompting, suggestion; proposal, proposition.

motionless *adj* fixed, immobile, quiescent, stable, stagnant, standing, stationary, still, torpid, unmoved.

motive *adj* activating, driving, moving, operative. * *n* cause, consideration, ground, impulse, incentive, incitement, inducement, influence, occasion, prompting, purpose, reason, spur, stimulus.

motley *adj* coloured, dappled, mottled, speckled, spotted, variegated; composite, diversified, heterogeneous, mingled, mixed.

mottled *adj* dappled, motley, piebald, speckled, spotted, variegated.

mould[1] *vb* carve, cast, fashion, form, make, model, shape. * *n* cast, character, fashion, form, matrix, pattern, shape; material, matter, substance.

mould[2] *n* blight, mildew, mouldiness, must, mustiness, rot; fungus, lichen, mushroom, puffball, rust, smut, toadstool; earth, loam, soil.

moulder *vb* crumble, decay, perish, waste.

mouldy *adj* decaying, fusty, mildewed, musty.

mound *n* bank, barrow, hill, hillock, knoll, tumulus; bulwark, defence, rampart.

mount[1] *n* hill, mountain, peak.

mount[2] *vb* arise, ascend, climb, rise, soar, tower; escalate, scale; embellish, ornament; bestride, get upon. * *n* charger, horse, ride, steed.

mountain *n* alp, height, hill, mount, peak; abundance, heap, mound, stack.

mountebank *n* charlatan, cheat, impostor, pretender, quack.

mourn *vb* bemoan, bewail, deplore, grieve, lament, sorrow, wail.

mournful *adj* afflicting, afflictive, calamitous, deplorable, distressed, grievous, lamentable, sad, woeful; doleful, heavy, heavy-hearted, lugubrious, melancholy, sorrowful, tearful.

mouth *vb* clamour, declaim, rant, roar, vociferate. * *n* chaps, jaws; aperture, opening, orifice; entrance, inlet; oracle, mouthpiece, speaker, spokesman.

movables *npl* chattels, effects, furniture, goods, property, wares.

move *vb* dislodge, drive, impel, propel, push, shift, start, stir; actuate, incite, instigate, rouse; determine, incline, induce, influence, persuade, prompt; affect, impress, touch, trouble; agitate, awaken, excite, incense, irritate; propose, recommend, suggest; go, march, proceed, walk; act, live; flit, remove. * *n* action, motion, movement.

movement *n* change, move, motion, passage; emotion; crusade, drive.

moving *adj* impelling, influencing, instigating, persuading, persuasive; affecting, impressive, pathetic, touching.

mucous *adj* glutinous, gummy, mucilaginous, ropy, slimy, viscid.

mud *n* dirt, mire, muck, slime.

muddle *vb* confuse, disarrange, disorder; fuddle, inebriate, stupefy; muff, mull, spoil. * *n* confusion, disorder, mess, plight, predicament.

muddy *vb* dirty, foul, smear, soil; confuse, obscure. * *adj* dirty, foul, impure, slimy, soiled, turbid; bothered, confused, dull, heavy, stupid; incoherent, obscure, vague.

muffle *vb* cover, envelop, shroud, wrap; conceal, disguise, involve; deaden, soften, stifle, suppress.

mulish *adj* cross-grained, headstrong, intractable, obstinate, stubborn.

multifarious *adj* different, divers, diverse, diversified, manifold, multiform, multitudinous, various.

multiloquence *n* garrulity, loquacity, loquaciousness, talkativeness.

multiply *vb* augment, extend, increase, spread.

multitude *n* numerousness; host, legion; army, assemblage, assembly, collection, concourse, congregation, crowd, horde, mob, swarm, throng; commonality, herd, mass, mob, pack, populace, rabble.

mundane *adj* earthly, secular, sublunary, temporal, terrene, terrestrial, worldly.

munificence *n* benefice, bounteousness, bountifulness, bounty, generosity, liberality.

munificent *adj* beneficent, bounteous, bountiful, free, generous, liberal, princely.

murder *vb* assassinate, butcher, destroy, dispatch, kill, massacre, slaughter, slay; abuse, mar, spoil. * *n* assassination, butchery, destruction, homicide, killing, manslaughter, massacre.

murderer *n* assassin, butcher, cut-throat, killer, manslaughterer, slaughterer, slayer.

murderous *adj* barbarous, bloodthirsty, bloody, cruel, fell, sanguinary, savage.

murky *adj* cheerless, cloudy, dark, dim, dusky, gloomy, hazy, lowering, lurid, obscure, overcast.

murmur *vb* croak, grumble, mumble, mutter; hum, whisper. * *n* complaint, grumble, mutter, plaint, whimper; hum, undertone, whisper.

muscular *adj* sinewy; athletic, brawny, powerful, lusty, stalwart, stout, strong, sturdy, vigorous.

muse *vb* brood, cogitate, consider, contemplate, deliberate, dream, meditate, ponder, reflect, ruminate, speculate, think. * *n* abstraction, musing, reverie.

music *n* harmony, melody, symphony.

musical *adj* dulcet, harmonious, melodious, sweet, sweet-sounding, symphonious, tuneful.

musing *adj* absent-minded, meditative, preoccupied. * *n* absent-mindedness, abstraction, contemplation, daydreaming, meditation, muse, reflection, reverie, rumination.

muster *vb* assemble, collect, congregate, convene, convoke, gather, marshal, meet, rally, summon. * *n* assemblage, assembly, collection, congregation, convention, convocation, gathering, meeting, rally.

musty *adj* fetid, foul, fusty, mouldy, rank, sour, spoiled; hackneyed, old, stale, threadbare, trite; ill-favoured, insipid, vapid; dull, heavy, rusty, spiritless.

mutable *adj* alterable, changeable; changeful, fickle, inconstant, irresolute, mutational, unsettled, unstable, unsteady, vacillating, variable, wavering.

mutation *n* alteration, change, variation.

mute *vb* dampen, lower, moderate, muffle, soften. * *adj* dumb, voiceless; silent, speechless, still, taciturn.

mutilate *vb* cripple, damage, disable, disfigure, hamstring, injure, maim, mangle, mar.

mutinous *adj* contumacious, insubordinate, rebellious, refractory, riotous, tumultuous, turbulent, unruly; insurgent, seditious.

mutiny *vb* rebel, revolt, rise, resist. * *n* insubordination, insurrection, rebellion, revolt, revolution, riot, rising, sedition, uprising.

mutter *vb* grumble, muffle, mumble, murmur.

mutual *adj* alternate, common, correlative, interchangeable, interchanged, reciprocal, requited.

myopic *adj* near-sighted, purblind, short-sighted.

myriad *adj* innumerable, manifold, multitudinous, uncounted. * *n* host, million(s), multitude, score(s), sea, swarm, thousand(s).

mysterious *adj* abstruse, cabbalistic, concealed, cryptic, dark, dim, enigmatic, enigmatical, hidden, incomprehensible, inexplicable, inscrutable, mystic, mystical, obscure, occult, puzzling, recondite, secret, sphinxlike, unaccountable, unfathomable, unintelligible, unknown.

mystery *n* enigma, puzzle, riddle, secret; art, business, calling, trade.

mystical *adj* abstruse, cabbalistic, dark, enigmatical, esoteric, hidden, inscrutable, mysterious, obscure, occult, recondite, transcendental; allegorical, emblematic, emblematical, symbolic, symbolical.

mystify *vb* befog, bewilder, confound, confuse, dumbfound, embarrass, obfuscate, perplex, pose, puzzle.

myth *n* fable, legend, tradition; allegory, fiction, invention, parable, story; falsehood, fancy, figment, lie, untruth.

mythical *adj* allegorical, fabled, fabulous, fanciful, fictitious, imaginary, legendary, mythological.

N

nab *vb* catch, clutch, grasp, seize.

nag[1] *vb* carp, fuss, hector, henpeck, pester, torment, worry. * *n* nagger, scold, shrew, tartar.

nag[2] *n* bronco, crock, hack, horse, pony, scrag.

naive *adj* artless, candid, ingenuous, natural, plain, simple, unaffected, unsophisticated.

naked *adj* bare, nude, uncovered; denuded, unclad, unclothed, undressed; defenceless, exposed, open, unarmed, unguarded, unprotected; evident, manifest, plain, stark, unconcealed, undisguised; mere, sheer, simple; bare, destitute, rough, rude, unfurnished, unprovided; uncoloured, unexaggerated, unvarnished.

name *vb* call, christen, denounce, dub, entitle, phrase, style, term; mention; denominate, designate, indicate, nominate, specify. * *n* appellation, cognomen, denomination, designation, epithet, nickname, surname, sobriquet, title; character, credit, reputation, repute; celebrity, distinction, eminence, fame, honour, note, praise, renown.

narcotic *adj* stupefacient, stupefactive, stupefying. * *n* anaesthetic, anodyne, dope, opiate, sedative, stupefacient, tranquillizer.

narrate *vb* chronicle, describe, detail, enumerate, recite, recount, rehearse, relate, tell.

narration *n* account, description, chronicle, history, narrative, recital, rehearsal, relation, story, tale.

narrow *vb* confine, contract, cramp, limit, restrict, straiten. * *adj* circumscribed, confined, contracted, cramped, incapacious, limited, pinched, scanty, straitened; bigoted, hidebound, illiberal, ungenerous; close, near.

nastiness *n* defilement, dirtiness, filth, filthiness, foulness, impurity, pollution, squalor, uncleanness; indecency, grossness, obscenity, pornography, ribaldry, smut, smuttiness.

nasty *adj* defiled, dirty, filthy, foul, impure, loathsome, polluted, squalid, unclean; gross, indecent, indelicate, lewd, loose, obscene, smutty, vile; disagreeable, disgusting, nauseous, odious, offensive, repulsive, sickening; aggravating, annoying, pesky, pestering, troublesome.

nation *n* commonwealth, realm, state; community, people, population, race, stock, tribe.

native *adj* aboriginal, autochthonal, autochthonous, domestic, home, indigenous, vernacular; genuine, intrinsic, natural, original, real; congenital, inborn, inbred, inherent, innate, natal. * *n* aborigine, autochthon, inhabitant, national, resident.

natty *adj* dandyish, fine, foppish, jaunty, neat, nice, spruce, tidy.

natural *adj* indigenous, innate, native, original; characteristic, essential; legitimate, normal, regular; artless, authentic, genuine, ingenious, unreal, simple, spontaneous, unaffected; bastard, illegitimate.

nature *n* universe, world; character, constitution, essence; kind, quality, species, sort; disposition, grain, humour, mood, temper; being, intellect, intelligence, mind.

naughty *adj* bad, corrupt, mischievous, perverse, worthless.

nausea *n* queasiness, seasickness; loathing, qualm; aversion, disgust, repugnance.

nauseous *adj* abhorrent, disgusting, distasteful, loathsome, offensive, repulsive, revolting, sickening.

naval *adj* marine, maritime, nautical.

navigate *vb* cruise, direct, guide, pilot, plan, sail, steer.

navy *n* fleet, shipping, vessels.

near *vb* approach, draw close. * *adj* adjacent, approximate, close, contiguous, neighbouring, nigh; approaching, forthcoming, imminent, impending; dear, familiar, friendly, intimate; direct, immediate, short, straight; accurate, literal; narrow, parsimonious.

nearly *adv* almost, approximately, well-nigh; closely, intimately, pressingly; meanly, parsimoniously, penuriously, stingily.

neat *adj* clean, cleanly, orderly, tidy, trim, unsoiled; nice, smart, spruce; chaste, pure, simple; excellent, pure, unadulterated; adroit, clever, exact, finished; dainty, nice.

nebulous *adj* cloudy, hazy, misty.

necessary *adj* inevitable, unavoidable; essential, expedient, indispensable, needful, requisite; compelling, compulsory, involuntary. * *n* essential, necessity, requirement, requisite.

necessitate *vb* compel, constrain, demand, force, impel, oblige.

necessitous *adj* destitute, distressed, indigent, moneyless, needy, penniless, pinched, poor, poverty-stricken; narrow, pinching.

necessity *n* inevitability, inevitableness, unavoidability, unavoidableness; compulsion, destiny, fatality, fate; emergency, urgency; exigency, indigence, indispensability, indispensableness, need, needfulness, poverty, want; essentiality, essentialness, requirement, requisite.

necromancy *n* conjuration, divination, enchantment, magic, sorcery, witchcraft, wizardry.

necropolis *n* burial ground, cemetery, churchyard, crematorium, graveyard, mortuary.

need *vb* demand, lack, require, want. * *n* emergency, exigency, extremity, necessity, strait, urgency, want; destitution, distress, indigence, neediness, penury, poverty, privation.

needful *adj* distressful, necessitous, necessary; essential, indispensable, requisite.

needless *adj* superfluous, unnecessary, useless.

needy *adj* destitute, indigent, necessitous, poor.

nefarious *adj* abominable, atrocious, detestable, dreadful, execrable, flagitious, heinous, horrible, infamous, iniquitous, scandalous, vile, wicked.

negation *n* denial, disavowal, disclaimer, rejection, renunciation.

neglect *vb* condemn, despise, disregard, forget, ignore, omit, overlook, slight. * *n* carelessness, default, failure, heedlessness, inattention, omission, remissness; disregard, disrespect, slight; indifference, negligence.

negligence *n* carelessness, disregard, heedlessness, inadvertency, inattention, indifference, neglect, remissness, slackness, thoughtlessness; defect, fault, inadvertence, omission, shortcoming.

negligent *adj* careless, heedless, inattentive, indifferent, neglectful, regardless, thoughtless.

negotiate *vb* arrange, bargain, deal, debate, sell, settle, transact, treat.

neighbourhood *n* district, environs, locality, vicinage, vicinity; adjacency, nearness, propinquity, proximity.

neighbourly *adj* attentive, civil, friendly, kind, obliging, social.

neophyte *n* beginner, catechumen, convert, novice, pupil, tyro.

nerve *vb* brace, energize, fortify, invigorate, strengthen. * *n* force, might, power, strength, vigour; coolness, courage, endurance, firmness, fortitude, hardihood, manhood, pluck, resolution, self-command, steadiness.

nervous *adj* forcible, powerful, robust, strong, vigorous; irritable, fearful, shaky, timid, timorous, weak, weakly.

nestle *vb* cuddle, harbour, lodge, nuzzle, snug, snuggle.

nettle *vb* chafe, exasperate, fret, harass, incense, irritate, provoke, ruffle, sting, tease, vex.

neutral *adj* impartial, indifferent; colourless, mediocre.

neutralize *vb* cancel, counterbalance, counterpoise, invalidate, offset.

nevertheless *adv* however, nonetheless, notwithstanding, yet.

new *adj* fresh, latest, modern, novel, recent, unused; additional, another, further; reinvigorated, renovated, repaired.

news *n* advice, information, intelligence, report, tidings, word.

nice *adj* accurate, correct, critical, definite, delicate, exact, exquisite, precise, rigorous, strict; dainty, difficult, exacting, fastidious, finical, punctilious, squeamish; discerning, discriminating, particular, precise, scrupulous; neat, tidy, trim; fine, minute, refined, subtle; delicate, delicious, luscious, palatable, savoury, soft, tender; agreeable, delightful, good, pleasant.

nicety *n* accuracy, exactness, niceness, precision, truth, daintiness, fastidiousness, squeamishness; discrimination, subtlety.

niggard *n* churl, curmudgeon, miser, screw, scrimp, skinflint.

niggardly *adj* avaricious, close, close-fisted, illiberal, mean, mercenary, miserly, parsimonious, penurious, skinflint, sordid, stingy.

nigh *adj* adjacent, adjoining, contiguous, near; present, proximate. * *adv* almost, near, nearly.

nimble *adj* active, agile, alert, brisk, lively, prompt, quick, speedy, sprightly, spry, swift, tripping.

nobility *n* aristocracy, dignity, elevation, eminence, grandeur, greatness, loftiness, magnanimity, nobleness, peerage, superiority, worthiness.

noble *adj* dignified, elevated, eminent, exalted, generous, great, honourable, illustrious, magnanimous, superior, worthy; choice, excellent; aristocratic, gentle, high-born, patrician; grand, lofty, lordly, magnificent, splendid, stately. * *n* aristocrat, grandee, lord, nobleman, peer.

noctambulist *n* sleepwalker, somnambulist.

noise *vb* bruit, gossip, repeat, report, rumour. * *n* ado, blare, clamour, clatter, cry, din, fuss, hubbub, hullabaloo, outcry, pandemonium, racket, row, sound, tumult, uproar, vociferation.

noiseless *adj* inaudible, quiet, silent, soundless.

noisome *adj* bad, baneful, deleterious, disgusting, fetid, foul, hurtful, injurious, mischievous, nocuous, noxious, offensive, pernicious, pestiferous, pestilential, poisonous, unhealthy, unwholesome.

noisy *adj* blatant, blustering, boisterous, brawling, clamorous, loud, uproarious, riotous, tumultuous, vociferous.

nomadic *adj* migratory, pastoral, vagrant, wandering.

nominal *adj* formal, inconsiderable, minimal, ostensible, pretended, professed, so-called, titular.

nominate *vb* appoint, choose, designate, name, present, propose.

nonchalant *adj* apathetic, careless, cool, indifferent, unconcerned.

nondescript *adj* amorphous, characterless, commonplace, dull, indescribable, odd, ordinary, unclassifiable, uninteresting, unremarkable.

nonentity *n* cipher, futility, inexistence, inexistency, insignificance, nobody, nonexistence, nothingness.

nonplus *vb* astonish, bewilder, confound, confuse, discomfit, disconcert, embarrass, floor, gravel, perplex, pose, puzzle.

nonsensical *adj* absurd, foolish, irrational, senseless, silly, stupid.

norm *n* model, pattern, rule, standard.

normal *adj* analogical, legitimate, natural, ordinary, regular, usual; erect, perpendicular, vertical.

notable *adj* distinguished, extraordinary, memorable, noted, remarkable, signal; conspicuous, evident, noticeable, observable, plain, prominent, striking; notorious, rare, well-known. * *n* celebrity, dignitary, notability, worthy.

note *vb* heed, mark, notice, observe, regard, remark; record, register; denote, designate. * *n* memorandum, minute, record; annotation, comment, remark, scholium; indication, mark, sign, symbol, token; account, bill, catalogue, reckoning; billet, epistle, letter; consideration, heed, notice, observation; celebrity, consequence, credit, distinction, eminence, fame, notability, notedness, renown, reputation, respectability; banknote, bill, promissory note; song, strain, tune, voice.

noted *adj* celebrated, conspicuous, distinguished, eminent, famed, famous, illustrious, notable, notorious, remarkable, renowned, well-known.

nothing *n* inexistence, nonentity, nonexistence, nothingness, nullity; bagatelle, trifle.

notice *vb* mark, note, observe, perceive, regard, see; comment on, mention, remark; attend to, heed. * *n* cognizance, heed, note, observation, regard; advice, announcement, information, intelligence, mention, news, notification; communication, intimation, premonition, warning; attention, civility, consideration, respect; comments, remarks.

notify *vb* advertise, announce, declare, publish, promulgate; acquaint, apprise, inform.

notion *n* concept, conception, idea; apprehension, belief, conceit, conviction, expectation, estimation, impression, judgement, opinion, sentiment, view.

notoriety *n* celebrity, fame, figure, name, note, publicity, reputation, repute, vogue.

notorious *adj* apparent, egregious, evident, notable, obvious, open, overt, manifest, patent, well-known; celebrated, conspicuous, distinguished, famed, famous, flagrant, infamous, noted, remarkable, renowned.

notwithstanding *conj* despite, however, nevertheless, yet. * *prep* despite.

nourish *vb* feed, nurse, nurture; maintain, supply, support; breed, educate, instruct, train; cherish, encourage, foment, foster, promote, succour.

nourishment *n* aliment, diet, food, nutriment, nutrition, sustenance.

novel *adj* fresh, modern, new, rare, recent, strange, uncommon, unusual. * *n* fiction, romance, story, tale.

novice *n* convert, proselyte; initiate, neophyte, novitiate, probationer; apprentice, beginner, learner, tyro.

noxious *adj* baneful, deadly, deleterious, destructive, detrimental, hurtful, injurious, insalubrious, mischievous, noisome, pernicious, pestilent, poisonous, unfavourable, unwholesome.

nude *adj* bare, denuded, exposed, naked, uncovered, unclothed, undressed.

nugatory *adj* frivolous, insignificant, trifling, trivial, vain, worthless; bootless, ineffectual, inefficacious, inoperative, null, unavailing, useless.

nuisance *n* annoyance, bore, bother, infliction, offence, pest, plague, trouble.

null *adj* ineffectual, invalid, nugatory, useless, void; characterless, colourless.

nullify *vb* abolish, abrogate, annul, cancel, invalidate, negate, quash, repeal, revoke.

numb *vb* benumb, deaden, stupefy. * *adj* benumbed, deadened, dulled, insensible, paralysed.

number *vb* calculate, compute, count, enumerate, numerate, reckon, tell; account, reckon. * *n* digit, figure, numeral; horde, multitude, numerousness, throng; aggregate, collection, sum, total.

numerous *adj* abundant, many, numberless.

nuncio *n* ambassador, legate, messenger.

nunnery *n* abbey, cloister, convent, monastery.

nuptial *adj* bridal, conjugal, connubial, hymeneal, matrimonial.

nuptials *npl* espousal, marriage, wedding.

nurse *vb* nourish, nurture; rear, suckle; cherish, encourage, feed, foment, foster, pamper, promote, succour; economize, manage; caress, dandle, fondle. * *n* auxiliary, orderly, sister; amah, *au pair*, babysitter, nanny, nursemaid, nurserymaid.

nurture *vb* feed, nourish, nurse, tend; breed, discipline, educate, instruct, rear, school, train. * *n* diet, food, nourishment; breeding, discipline, education, instruction, schooling, training, tuition; attention, nourishing, nursing.

nutriment *n* aliment, food, nourishment, nutrition, pabulum, subsistence, sustenance.

nutrition *n* diet, food, nourishment, nutriment.

nutritious *adj* invigorating, nourishing, strengthening, supporting, sustaining.

nymph *n* damsel, dryad, lass, girl, maid, maiden, naiad.

O

oaf *n* blockhead, dolt, dunce, fool, idiot, simpleton.

oath *n* blasphemy, curse, expletive, imprecation, malediction; affirmation, pledge, promise, vow.

obduracy *n* contumacy, doggedness, obstinacy, stubbornness, tenacity; depravity, impenitence.

obdurate *adj* hard, harsh, rough, rugged; callous, cantankerous, dogged, firm, hardened, inflexible, insensible, obstinate, pigheaded, unfeeling, stubborn, unbending, unyielding; depraved, graceless, lost, reprobate, shameless, impenitent, incorrigible, irreclaimable.

obedience *n* acquiescence, agreement, compliance, duty, respect, reverence, submission, submissiveness, subservience.

obedient *adj* acquiescent, compliant, deferential, duteous, dutiful, observant, regardful, respectful, submissive, subservient, yielding.

obeisance *n* bow, courtesy, curtsy, homage, reverence, salutation.

obelisk *n* column, pillar.

obese *adj* corpulent, fat, fleshy, gross, plump, podgy, portly, stout.

obesity *n* corpulence, corpulency, embonpoint, fatness, fleshiness, obeseness, plumpness.

obey *vb* comply, conform, heed, keep, mind, observe, submit, yield.

obfuscate *vb* cloud, darken, obscure; bewilder, confuse, muddle.

object[1] *vb* cavil, contravene, demur, deprecate, disapprove of, except to, impeach, oppose, protest, refuse.

object[2] *n* particular, phenomenon, precept, reality, thing; aim, butt, destination, end, mark, recipient, target; design, drift, goal, intention, motive, purpose, use, view.

objection *n* censure, difficulty, doubt, exception, protest, remonstrance, scruple.

objurgate *vb* chide, reprehend, reprove.

oblation *n* gift, offering, sacrifice.

obligation *n* accountability, accountableness, responsibility; agreement, bond, contract, covenant, engagement, stipulation; debt, indebtedness, liability.

obligatory *adj* binding, coercive, compulsory, enforced, necessary, unavoidable.

oblige *vb* bind, coerce, compel, constrain, force, necessitate, require; accommodate, benefit, convenience, favour, gratify, please; obligate, bind.

obliging *adj* accommodating, civil, complaisant, considerate, kind, friendly, polite.

oblique *adj* aslant, inclined, sidelong, slanting; indirect, obscure.

obliterate *vb* cancel, delete, destroy, efface, eradicate, erase, expunge.

oblivious *adj* careless, forgetful, heedless, inattentive, mindless, negligent, neglectful.

obloquy *n* aspersion, backbiting, blame, calumny, censure, contumely, defamation, detraction, disgrace, odium, reproach, reviling, slander, traducing.

obnoxious *adj* blameworthy, censurable, faulty, reprehensible; hateful, objectionable, obscene, odious, offensive, repellent, repugnant, repulsive, unpleasant, unpleasing.

obscene *adj* broad, coarse, filthy, gross, immodest, impure, indecent, indelicate, ribald, unchaste, lewd, licentious, loose, offensive, pornographic, shameless, smutty; disgusting, dirty, foul.

obscure *vb* becloud, befog, blur, cloud, darken, eclipse, dim, obfuscate, obnubilate, shade; conceal, cover, equivocate, hide. * *adj* dark, darksome, dim, dusky, gloomy, lurid, murky, rayless, shadowy, sombre, unenlightened, unilluminated; abstruse, blind, cabbalistic, difficult, doubtful, enigmatic, high, incomprehensible, indefinite, indistinct, intricate, involved, mysterious, mystic, recondite, undefined, unintelligible, vague; remote, secluded; humble, inglorious, nameless, renownless, undistinguished, unhonoured, unknown, unnoted, unnoticed.

obsequious *adj* cringing, deferential, fawning, flattering, servile, slavish, supple, subservient, sycophantic, truckling.

observant *adj* attentive, heedful, mindful, perceptive, quick, regardful, vigilant, watchful.

observation *n* attention, cognition, notice, observance; annotation, note, remark; experience, knowledge.

observe *vb* eye, mark, note, notice, remark, watch; behold, detect, discover, perceive, see; express, mention, remark, say, utter; comply, conform, follow, fulfil, obey; celebrate, keep, regard, solemnize.

obsolete *adj* ancient, antiquated, antique, archaic, disused, neglected, old, old-fashioned, obsolescent, out-of-date, past, passé, unfashionable.

obstacle *n* barrier, check, difficulty, hindrance, impediment, interference, interruption, obstruction, snag, stumbling block.

obstinacy *n* contumacy, doggedness, headiness, firmness, inflexibility, intractability, obduracy, persistence, perseverance, perversity, resoluteness, stubbornness, tenacity, wilfulness.

obstinate *adj* cross-grained, contumacious, dogged, firm, headstrong, inflexible, immovable, intractable, mulish, obdurate, opinionated, persistent, pertinacious, perverse, resolute, self-willed, stubborn, tenacious, unyielding, wilful.

obstreperous *adj* boisterous, clamorous, loud, noisy, riotous, tumultuous, turbulent, unruly, uproarious, vociferous.

obstruct *vb* bar, barricade, block, blockade, block up, choke, clog, close, glut, jam, obturate, stop; hinder, impede, oppose, prevent; arrest, check, curb, delay, embrace, interrupt, retard, slow.

obstruction *n* bar, barrier, block, blocking, check, difficulty, hindrance, impediment, obstacle, stoppage; check, clog, embarrassment, interruption, obturation.

obtain *vb* achieve, acquire, attain, bring, contrive, earn, elicit, gain, get, induce, procure, secure; hold, prevail, stand, subsist.

obtrude *vb* encroach, infringe, interfere, intrude, trespass.

obtrusive *adj* forward, interfering, intrusive, meddling, officious.

obtuse *adj* blunt; blockish, doltish, dull, dull-witted, heavy, stockish, stolid, stupid, slow, unintellectual, unintelligent.

obviate *vb* anticipate, avert, counteract, preclude, prevent, remove.

obvious *adj* exposed, liable, open, subject; apparent, clear, distinct, evident, manifest, palatable, patent, perceptible, plain, self-evident, unmistakable, visible.

occasion *vb* breed, cause, create, originate, produce; induce, influence, move, persuade. * *n* casualty, event, incident, occurrence; conjuncture, convenience, juncture, opening, opportunity; condition, necessity, need, exigency, requirement, want; cause, ground, reason; inducement, influence; circumstance, exigency.

occasional *adj* accidental, casual, incidental, infrequent, irregular, uncommon; causative, causing.

occasionally *adv* casually, sometimes.

occult *adj* abstruse, cabbalistic, hidden, latent, secret, invisible, mysterious, mystic, mystical, recondite, shrouded, undetected, undiscovered, unknown, unrevealed, veiled. * *n* magic, sorcery, witchcraft.

occupation *n* holding, occupancy, possession, tenure, use; avocation, business, calling, craft, employment, engagement, job, post, profession, trade, vocation.

occupy *vb* capture, hold, keep, possess; cover, fill, garrison, inhabit, take up, tenant; engage, employ, use.

occur *vb* appear, arise, offer; befall, chance, eventuate, happen, result, supervene.

occurrence *n* accident, adventure, affair, casualty, event, happening, incident, proceeding, transaction.

odd *adj* additional, redundant, remaining; casual, incidental; inappropriate, queer, unsuitable; comical, droll, erratic, extravagant, extraordinary, fantastic, grotesque, irregular, peculiar, quaint, singular, strange, uncommon, uncouth, unique, unusual, whimsical.

odds *npl* difference, disparity, inequality; advantage, superiority, supremacy.

odious *adj* abominable, detestable, execrable, hateful, shocking; hated, obnoxious, unpopular; disagreeable, forbidding, loathsome, offensive.

odium *n* abhorrence, detestation, dislike, enmity, hate, hatred; odiousness, repulsiveness; obloquy, opprobrium, reproach, shame.

odorous *adj* aromatic, balmy, fragrant, perfumed, redolent, scented, sweet-scented, sweet-smelling.

odour *n* aroma, fragrance, perfume, redolence, scent, smell.

offal *n* carrion, dregs, garbage, refuse, rubbish, waste.

offence *n* aggression, attack, assault; anger, displeasure, indignation, pique, resentment, umbrage, wrath; affront, harm, injury, injustice, insult, outrage, wrong; crime, delinquency, fault, misdeed, misdemeanour, sin, transgression, trespass.

offend *vb* affront, annoy, chafe, displease, fret, gall, irritate, mortify, nettle, provoke, vex; molest, pain,

shock, wound; fall, sin, stumble, transgress.

offender *n* convict, criminal, culprit, delinquent, felon, malefactor, sinner, transgressor, trespasser.

offensive *adj* aggressive, attacking, invading; disgusting, loathsome, nauseating, nauseous, repulsive, sickening; abominable, detestable, disagreeable, displeasing, execrable, hateful, obnoxious, repugnant, revolting, shocking, unpalatable, unpleasant; abusive, disagreeable, impertinent, insolent, insulting, irritating, opprobrious, rude, saucy, unpleasant. * *n* attack, onslaught.

offer *vb* present, proffer, tender; exhibit; furnish, propose, propound, show; volunteer; dare, essay, endeavour, venture. * *n* overture, proffering, proposal, proposition, tender, overture; attempt, bid, endeavour, essay.

offhand *adj* abrupt, brusque, casual, curt, extempore, impromptu, informal, unpremeditated, unstudied. * *adv* carelessly, casually, clumsily, haphazardly, informally, slapdash; ad-lib, extemporaneously, extemporarily, extempore, impromptu.

office *n* duty, function, service, work; berth, place, position, post, situation; business, capacity, charge, employment, trust; bureau, room.

officiate *vb* act, perform, preside, serve.

officious *adj* busy, dictatorial, forward, impertinent, interfering, intermeddling, meddlesome, meddling, obtrusive, pushing, pushy.

offset *vb* balance, counteract, counterbalance, counterpoise. * *n* branch, offshoot, scion, shoot, slip, sprout, twig; counterbalance, counterpoise, set-off, equivalent.

offspring *n* brood, children, descendants, issue, litter, posterity, progeny; cadet, child, scion.

often *adv* frequently, generally, oftentimes, repeatedly.

ogre *n* bugbear, demon, devil, goblin, hobgoblin, monster, spectre.

old *adj* aged, ancient, antiquated, antique, archaic, elderly, obsolete, olden, old-fashioned, superannuated; decayed, done, senile, worn-out; original, primitive, pristine; former, preceding, pre-existing.

oleaginous *adj* adipose, fat, fatty, greasy, oily, sebaceous, unctuous.

omen *n* augury, auspice, foreboding, portent, presage, prognosis, sign, warning.

ominous *adj* inauspicious, monitory, portentous, premonitory, threatening, unpropitious.

omission *n* default, failure, forgetfulness, neglect, oversight.

omit *vb* disregard, drop, eliminate, exclude, miss, neglect, overlook, skip.

omnipotent *adj* almighty, all-powerful.

omniscient *adj* all-knowing, all-seeing, all-wise.

oneness *n* individuality, singleness, unity.

onerous *adj* burdensome, difficult, hard, heavy, laborious, oppressive, responsible, weighty.

one-sided *adj* partial, prejudiced, unfair, unilateral, unjust.

only *adj* alone, single, sole, solitary. * *adv* barely, merely, simply.

onset *n* assault, attack, charge, onslaught, storm, storming.

onus *n* burden, liability, load, responsibility.

ooze *vb* distil, drip, drop, shed; drain, exude, filter, leak, percolate, stain, transude. * *n* mire, mud, slime.

opaque *adj* dark, dim, hazy, muddy; abstruse, cryptic, enigmatic, enigmatical, obscure, unclear.

open vb expand, spread; begin, commence, initiate; disclose, exhibit, reveal, show; unbar, unclose, uncover, unlock, unseal, untie. * adj expanded, extended, unclosed, spread wide; aboveboard, artless, candid, cordial, fair, frank, guileless, hearty, honest, sincere, openhearted, single-minded, undesigning, undisguised, undissembling, unreserved; bounteous, bountiful, free, generous, liberal, munificent; ajar, uncovered; exposed, undefended, unprotected; clear, unobstructed; accessible, public, unenclosed, unrestricted; mild, moderate; apparent, debatable, evident, obvious, patent, plain, undetermined.

opening adj commencing, first, inaugural, initiatory, introductory. * n aperture, breach, chasm, cleft, fissure, flaw, gap, gulf, hole, interspace, loophole, orifice, perforation, rent, rift; beginning, commencement, dawn; chance, opportunity, vacancy.

openly adv candidly, frankly, honestly, plainly, publicly.

openness n candour, frankness, honesty, ingenuousness, plainness, unreservedness.

operate vb act, function, work; cause, effect, occasion, produce; manipulate, use, run.

operation n manipulation, performance, procedure, proceeding, process; action, affair, manoeuvre, motion, movement.

operative adj active, effective, effectual, efficient, serviceable, vigorous; important, indicative, influential, significant. * n artisan, employee, labourer, mechanic, worker, workman.

opiate adj narcotic, sedative, soporiferous, soporific. * n anodyne, drug, narcotic, sedative, tranquillizer.

opine vb apprehend, believe, conceive, fancy, judge, suppose, presume, surmise, think.

opinion n conception, idea, impression, judgment, notion, sentiment, view; belief, persuasion, tenet; esteem, estimation, judgment.

opinionated adj biased, bigoted, cocksure, conceited, dictatorial, dogmatic, opinionative, prejudiced, stubborn.

opponent adj adverse, antagonistic, contrary, opposing, opposite, repugnant. * n adversary, antagonist, competitor, contestant, counteragent, enemy, foe, opposite, opposer, party, rival.

opportune adj appropriate, auspicious, convenient, favourable, felicitous, fit, fitting, fortunate, lucky, propitious, seasonable, suitable, timely, well-timed.

opportunity n chance, convenience, moment, occasion.

oppose vb combat, contravene, counteract, dispute, obstruct, oppugn, resist, thwart, withstand; check, prevent; confront, counterpoise.

opposite adj facing, fronting; conflicting, contradictory, contrary, different, diverse, incompatible, inconsistent, irreconcilable; adverse, antagonistic, hostile, inimical, opposed, opposing, repugnant. * n contradiction, contrary, converse, reverse.

opposition n antagonism, antinomy, contrariety, inconsistency, repugnance; counteraction, counterinfluence, hostility, resistance; hindrance, obstacle, obstruction, oppression, prevention.

oppress vb burden, crush, depress, harass, load, maltreat, overburden, overpower, overwhelm, persecute, subdue, suppress, tyrannize, wrong.

oppression n abuse, calamity, cruelty, hardship, injury, injustice, misery, persecution, severity, suffering, tyranny; depression, dullness, heaviness, lassitude.

oppressive adj close, muggy, stifling, suffocating, sultry.

opprobrious adj abusive, condemnatory, contemptuous, damnatory, insolent, insulting, offensive, reproachable, scandalous, scurrilous, vituperative; despised, dishonourable, disreputable, hateful, infamous, shameful.

opprobrium n contumely, scurrility; calumny, disgrace, ignominy, infamy, obloquy, odium, reproach.

oppugn vb assail, argue, attack, combat, contravene, oppose, resist, thwart, withstand.

option n choice, discretion, election, preference, selection.

optional adj discretionary, elective, nonobligatory, voluntary.

opulence n affluence, fortune, independence, luxury, riches, wealth.

opulent adj affluent, flush, luxurious, moneyed, plentiful, rich, sumptuous, wealthy.

oracular adj ominous, portentous, prophetic; authoritative, dogmatic, magisterial, positive; aged, grave, wise; ambiguous, blind, dark, equivocal, obscure.

oral adj nuncupative, spoken, verbal, vocal.

oration n address, declamation, discourse, harangue, speech.

orb n ball, globe, sphere; circle, circuit, orbit, ring; disk, wheel.

orbit vb circle, encircle, revolve around. * n course, path, revolution, track.

ordain vb appoint, call, consecrate, elect, experiment, constitute, establish, institute, regulate; decree, enjoin, enact, order, prescribe.

order vb adjust, arrange, methodize, regulate, systematize; carry on, conduct, manage; bid, command, direct, instruct, require. * n arrangement, disposition, method, regularity, symmetry, system; law, regulation, rule; discipline, peace, quiet; command, commission, direction, injunction, instruction, mandate, prescription; class, degree, grade, kind, rank; family, tribe; brotherhood, community, fraternity, society; sequence, succession.

orderly adj methodical, regular, systematic; peaceable, quiet, well-behaved; neat, shipshape, tidy.

ordinance n appointment, command, decree, edict, enactment, law, order, prescript, regulation, rule, statute; ceremony, observance, sacrament, rite, ritual.

ordinary adj accustomed, customary, established, everyday, normal, regular, settled, wonted, everyday, regular; common, frequent, habitual, usual; average, commonplace, indifferent, inferior, mean, mediocre, second-rate, undistinguished; homely, plain.

organization n business, construction, constitution, organism, structure, system.

organize vb adjust, constitute, construct, form, make, shape; arrange, coordinate, correlate, establish, systematize.

orgy n carousal, debauch, debauchery, revel, saturnalia.

orifice n aperture, hole, mouth, perforation, pore, vent.

origin n beginning, birth, commencement, cradle, derivation, foundation, fountain, fountainhead, original, rise, root, source, spring, starting point; cause, occasion; heritage, lineage, parentage.

original adj aboriginal, first, primary, primeval, primitive, primordial, pristine; fresh, inventive, novel; eccentric, odd, peculiar. * n cause, commencement, origin, source, spring; archetype, exemplar, model, pattern, prototype, protoplast, type.

originate vb arise, begin, emanate, flow, proceed, rise, spring; create, discover, form, invent, produce.

originator *n* author, creator, former, inventor, maker, parent.

orison *n* petition, prayer, solicitation, supplication.

ornament *vb* adorn, beautify, bedeck, bedizen, decorate, deck, emblazon, garnish, grace. * *n* adornment, bedizenment, decoration, design, embellishment, garnish, ornamentation.

ornate *adj* beautiful, bedecked, decorated, elaborate, elegant, embellished, florid, flowery, ornamental, ornamented.

orthodox *adj* conventional, correct, sound, true.

oscillate *vb* fluctuate, sway, swing, vacillate, vary, vibrate.

ostensible *adj* apparent, assigned, avowed, declared, exhibited, manifest, presented, visible; plausible, professed, specious.

ostentation *n* dash, display, flourish, pageantry, parade, pomp, pomposity, pompousness, show, vaunting; appearance, semblance, showiness.

ostentatious *adj* boastful, dashing, flaunting, pompous, pretentious, showy, vain, vainglorious; gaudy.

ostracize *vb* banish, boycott, exclude, excommunicate, exile, expatriate, expel, evict.

oust *vb* dislodge, dispossess, eject, evict, expel.

outbreak *n* ebullition, eruption, explosion, outburst; affray, broil, conflict, commotion, fray, riot, row; flare-up, manifestation.

outcast *n* exile, expatriate; castaway, pariah, reprobate, vagabond.

outcome *n* conclusion, consequence, event, issue, result, upshot.

outcry *n* cry, scream, screech, yell; bruit, clamour, noise, tumult, vociferation.

outdo *vb* beat, exceed, excel, outgo, outstrip, outvie, surpass.

outlandish *adj* alien, exotic, foreign, strange; barbarous, bizarre, uncouth.

outlaw *vb* ban, banish, condemn, exclude, forbid, make illegal, prohibit. * *n* bandit, brigand, crook, freebooter, highwayman, lawbreaker, marauder, robber, thief.

outlay *n* disbursement, expenditure, outgoings.

outline *vb* delineate, draft, draw, plan, silhouette, sketch. * *n* contour, profile; delineation, draft, drawing, plan, rough draft, silhouette, sketch.

outlive *vb* last, live longer, survive.

outlook *n* future, prospect, sight, view; lookout, watchtower.

outrage *vb* abuse, injure, insult, maltreat, offend, shock, injure. * *n* abuse, affront, indignity, insult, offence.

outrageous *adj* abusive, frantic, furious, frenzied, mad, raging, turbulent, violent, wild; atrocious, enormous, flagrant, heinous, monstrous, nefarious, villainous; enormous, excessive, extravagant, unwarrantable.

outré *adj* excessive, exorbitant, extravagant, immoderate, inordinate, overstrained, unconventional.

outrun *vb* beat, exceed, outdistance, outgo, outstrip, outspeed, surpass.

outset *n* beginning, commencement, entrance, opening, start, starting point.

outshine *vb* eclipse, outstrip, overshadow, surpass.

outspoken *adj* abrupt, blunt, candid, frank, plain, plainspoken, unceremonious, unreserved.

outstanding *adj* due, owing, uncollected, ungathered, unpaid, unsettled; conspicuous, eminent, prominent, striking.

outward *adj* exterior, external, outer, outside.

outwit *vb* cheat, circumvent, deceive, defraud, diddle, dupe, gull, outmanoeuvre, overreach, swindle, victimize.

overawe *vb* affright, awe, browbeat, cow, daunt, frighten, intimidate, scare, terrify.

overbalance *vb* capsize, overset, overturn, tumble, upset; outweigh, preponderate.

overbearing *adj* oppressive, overpowering; arrogant, dictatorial, dogmatic, domineering, haughty, imperious, overweening, proud, supercilious.

overcast *vb* cloud, darken, overcloud, overshadow, shade, shadow. * *adj* cloudy, darkened, hazy, murky, obscure.

overcharge *vb* burden, oppress, overburden, overload, surcharge; crowd, overfill; exaggerate, overstate, overstrain.

overcome *vb* beat, choke, conquer, crush, defeat, discomfit, overbear, overmaster, overpower, overthrow, overturn, overwhelm, prevail, rout, subdue, subjugate, surmount, vanquish.

overflow *vb* brim over, fall over, pour over, pour out, shower, spill; deluge, inundate, submerge. * *n* deluge, inundation, profusion, superabundance.

overhaul *vb* overtake; check, examine, inspect, repair, survey. * *n* check, examination, inspection.

overlay *vb* cover, spread over; overlie, overpress, smother; crush, overpower, overwhelm; cloud, hide, obscure, overcast. * *n* appliqué, covering, decoration, veneer.

overlook *vb* inspect, oversee, superintend, supervise; disregard, miss, neglect, slight; condone, excuse, forgive, pardon, pass over.

overpower *vb* beat, conquer, crush, defeat, discomfit, overbear, overcome, overmaster, overturn, overwhelm, subdue, subjugate, vanquish.

overreach *vb* exceed, outstrip, overshoot, pass, surpass; cheat, circumvent, deceive, defraud.

override *vb* outride, outweigh, pass, quash, supersede, surpass.

overrule *vb* control, govern, sway; annul, cancel, nullify, recall, reject, repeal, repudiate, rescind, revoke, reject, set aside, supersede, suppress.

oversight *n* care, charge, control, direction, inspection, management, superintendence, supervision, surveillance; blunder, error, fault, inadvertence, inattention, lapse, miss, mistake, neglect, omission, slip, trip.

overt *adj* apparent, glaring, open, manifest, notorious, patent, public, unconcealed.

overthrow *vb* overturn, upset, subvert; demolish, destroy, level; beat, conquer, crush, defeat, discomfit, foil, master, overcome, overpower, overwhelm, rout, subjugate, vanquish, worst. * *n* downfall, fall, prostration, subversion; destruction, demolition, ruin; defeat, discomfiture, dispersion, rout.

overturn *vb* invert, overthrow, reverse, subvert, upset.

overture *n* invitation, offer, proposal, proposition.

overweening *adj* arrogant, conceited, consequential, egotistical, haughty, opinionated, proud, supercilious, vain, vainglorious.

overwhelm *vb* drown, engulf, inundate, overflow, submerge, swallow up, swamp; conquer, crush, defeat, overbear, overcome, overpower, subdue, vanquish.

overwrought *adj* overdone, overelaborate; agitated, excited, overexcited, overworked, stirred.

own[1] *vb* have, hold, possess; avow, confess; acknowledge, admit, allow, concede.

own[2] *adj* particular, personal, private.

owner *n* freeholder, holder, landlord, possessor, proprietor.

P

pace *vb* go, hasten, hurry, move, step, walk. * *n* amble, gait, step, walk.

pacific *adj* appeasing, conciliatory, ironic, mollifying, placating, peacemaking, propitiatory; calm, gentle, peaceable, peaceful, quiet, smooth, tranquil, unruffled.

pacify *vb* appease, conciliate, harmonize, tranquillize; allay, appease, assuage, calm, compose, hush, lay, lull, moderate, mollify, placate, propitiate, quell, quiet, smooth, soften, soothe, still.

pack *vb* compact, compress, crowd, fill; bundle, burden, load, stow. * *n* bale, budget, bundle, package, packet, parcel; burden, load; assemblage, assembly, assortment, collection, set; band, bevy, clan, company, crew, gang, knot, lot, party, squad.

pact *n* agreement, alliance, bargain, bond, compact, concordat, contract, convention, covenant, league, stipulation.

pagan *adj* heathen, heathenish, idolatrous, irreligious, paganist, paganistic. * *n* gentile, heathen, idolater.

pageantry *n* display, flourish, magnificence, parade, pomp, show, splendour, state.

pain *vb* agonize, bite, distress, hurt, rack, sting, torment, torture; afflict, aggrieve, annoy, bore, chafe, displease, disquiet, fret, grieve, harass, incommode, plague, tease, trouble, vex, worry; rankle, smart, shoot, sting, twinge. * *n* ache, agony, anguish, discomfort, distress, gripe, hurt, pang, smart, soreness, sting, suffering, throe, torment, torture, twinge; affliction, anguish, anxiety, bitterness, care, chagrin, disquiet, dolour, grief, heartache, misery, punishment, solicitude, sorrow, trouble, uneasiness, unhappiness, vexation, woe, wretchedness.

painful *adj* agonizing, distressful, excruciating, racking, sharp, tormenting, torturing; afflicting, afflictive, annoying, baleful, disagreeable, displeasing, disquieting, distressing, dolorous, grievous, provoking, troublesome, unpleasant, vexatious; arduous, careful, difficult, hard, severe, sore, toilsome.

pains *npl* care, effort, labour, task, toilsomeness, trouble; childbirth, labour, travail.

painstaking *adj* assiduous, careful, conscientious, diligent, hardworking, industrious, laborious, persevering, plodding, sedulous, strenuous.

paint *vb* delineate, depict, describe, draw, figure, pencil, portray, represent, sketch; adorn, beautify, deck, embellish, ornament. * *n* colouring, dye, pigment, stain; cosmetics, greasepaint, make-up.

pair *vb* couple, marry, mate, match. * *n* brace, couple, double, duo, match, twosome.

pal *n* buddy, chum, companion, comrade, crony, friend, mate, mucker.

palatable *adj* acceptable, agreeable, appetizing, delicate, delicious, enjoyable, flavourful, flavoursome, gustative, gustatory, luscious, nice, pleasant, pleasing, savoury, relishable, tasteful, tasty, toothsome.

palaver *vb* chat, chatter, converse, patter, prattle, say, speak, talk; confer, parley; blandish, cajole, flatter, wheedle. * *n* chat, chatter, conversation, discussion, language, prattle, speech, talk; confab, confabulation, conference, conclave, parley, powwow; balderdash, cajolery, flummery, gibberish.

pale *vb* blanch, lose colour, whiten. * *adj* ashen, ashy, blanched, bloodless, pallid, sickly, wan, white; blank, dim, obscure, spectral. * *n* picket, stake; circuit, enclosure; district, region, territory; boundary, confine, fence, limit.

pall[1] *n* cloak, cover, curtain, mantle, pallium, shield, shroud, veil.

pall[2] *vb* cloy, glut, gorge, satiate, surfeit; deject, depress, discourage, dishearten, dispirit; cloak, cover, drape, invest, overspread, shroud.

palliate *vb* cloak, conceal, cover, excuse, extenuate, hide, gloss, lessen; abate, allay, alleviate, assuage, blunt, diminish, dull, ease, mitigate, moderate, mollify, quell, quiet, relieve, soften, soothe, still.

pallid *adj* ashen, ashy, cadaverous, colourless, pale, sallow, wan, whitish.

palm[1] *vb* foist, impose, obtrude, pass off; handle, touch.

palm[2] *n* bays, crown, laurels, prize, trophy, victory.

palmy *adj* flourishing, fortunate, glorious, golden, halcyon, happy, joyous, prosperous, thriving, victorious.

palpable *adj* corporeal, material, tactile, tangible; evident, glaring, gross, intelligible, manifest, obvious, patent, plain, unmistakable.

palpitate *vb* flutter, pulsate, throb; quiver, shiver, tremble.

palter *vb* dodge, equivocate, evade, haggle, prevaricate, quibble, shift, shuffle, trifle.

paltry *adj* diminutive, feeble, inconsiderable, insignificant, little, miserable, petty, slender, slight, small, sorry, trifling, trivial, unimportant, wretched.

pamper *vb* baby, coddle, fondle, gratify, humour, spoil.

panacea *n* catholicon, cure-all, medicine, remedy.

panegyric *adj* commendatory, encomiastic, encomiastical, eulogistic, eulogistical, laudatory, panegyrical. * *n* eulogy, laudation, praise, paean, tribute.

pang *n* agony, anguish, distress, gripe, pain, throe, twinge.

panic *vb* affright, alarm, scare, startle, terrify; become terrified, overreact. * *n* alarm, consternation, fear, fright, jitters, terror.

pant *vb* blow, gasp, puff; heave, palpitate, pulsate, throb; languish; desire, hunger, long, sigh, thirst, yearn. * *n* blow, gasp, puff.

parable *n* allegory, fable, story.

paraclete *n* advocate, comforter, consoler, intercessor, mediator.

parade *vb* display, flaunt, show, vaunt. * *n* ceremony, display, flaunting, ostentation, pomp, show; array, pageant, review, spectacle; mall, promenade.

paradox *n* absurdity, contradiction, mystery.

paragon *n* flower, ideal, masterpiece, model, nonpareil, pattern, standard.

paragraph *n* clause, item, notice, passage, section, sentence, subdivision.

parallel *vb* be alike, compare, conform, correlate, match. * *adj* abreast, concurrent; allied, analogous, correspondent, equal, like, resembling, similar. * *n* conformity, likeness, resemblance, similarity; analogue, correlative, counterpart.

paramount *adj* chief, dominant, eminent, pre-eminent, principal, superior, supreme.

paraphernalia *n* accoutrements, appendages, appurtenances, baggage, belongings, effects, equipage, equipment, ornaments, trappings.

parasite *n* bloodsucker, fawner, flatterer, flunky, hanger-on, leech, spaniel, sycophant, toady, wheedler.

parcel *vb* allot, apportion, dispense, distribute, divide. * *n* budget, bundle, package; batch, collection, group, lot, set; division, part, patch, pierce, plot, portion, tract.

parched *adj* arid, dry, scorched, shrivelled, thirsty.

pardon *vb* condone, forgive, overlook, remit; absolve, acquit, clear, discharge, excuse, release. * *n* absolution, amnesty, condonation, discharge, excuse, forgiveness, grace, mercy, overlook, release.

parentage *n* ancestry, birth, descent, extraction, family, lineage, origin, parenthood, pedigree, stock.

pariah *n* outcast, wretch.

parish *n* community, congregation, parishioners; district, subdivision.

parity *n* analogy, correspondence, equality, equivalence, likeness, sameness, similarity.

parody *vb* burlesque, caricature, imitate, lampoon, mock, ridicule, satirize, travesty. * *n* burlesque, caricature, imitation, ridicule, satire, travesty.

paroxysm *n* attack, convulsion, exacerbation, fit, outburst, seizure, spasm, throe.

parsimonious *adj* avaricious, close, close-fisted, covetous, frugal, grasping, grudging, illiberal, mean, mercenary, miserly, near, niggardly, penurious, shabby, sordid, sparing, stingy, tightfisted.

parson *n* churchman, clergyman, divine, ecclesiastic, incumbent, minister, pastor, priest, rector.

part *vb* break, dismember, dissever, divide, sever, subdivide, sunder; detach, disconnect, disjoin, dissociate, disunite, separate; allot, apportion, distribute, divide, mete, share; secrete. * *n* crumb, division, fraction, fragment, moiety, parcel, piece, portion, remnant, scrap, section, segment, subdivision; component, constituent, element, ingredient, member, organ; lot, share; concern, interest, participation; allotment, apportionment, dividend; business, charge, duty, function, office, work; faction, party, side; character, cue, lines, role; clause, paragraph, passage.

partake *vb* engage, participate, share; consume, eat, take; evince, evoke, show, suggest.

partial *adj* component, fractional, imperfect, incomplete, limited; biased, influential, interested, one-sided, prejudiced, prepossessed, unfair, unjust, warped; fond, indulgent.

participate *vb* engage in, partake, perform, share.

particle *n* atom, bit, corpuscle, crumb, drop, glimmer, grain, granule, iota, jot, mite, molecule, morsel, mote,

scrap, shred, snip, spark, speck, whit.

particular *adj* especial, special, specific; distinct, individual, respective, separate, single; characteristic, distinctive, peculiar; individual, intimate, own, personal, private; notable, noteworthy; circumstantial, definite, detailed, exact, minute, narrow, precise; careful, close, conscientious, critical, fastidious, nice, scrupulous, strict; marked, odd, singular, strange, uncommon. * *n* case, circumstance, count, detail, feature, instance, item, particularity, point, regard, respect.

parting *adj* breaking, dividing, separating; final, last, valedictory; declining, departing. * *n* breaking, disruption, rupture, severing; detachment, division, separation; death, departure, farewell, leave-taking.

partisan *adj* biased, factional, interested, partial, prejudiced. * *n* adherent, backer, champion, disciple, follower, supporter, votary; baton, halberd, pike, quarterstaff, truncheon, staff.

partition *vb* apportion, distribute, divide, portion, separate, share. * *n* division, separation; barrier, division, screen, wall; allotment, apportionment, distribution.

partner *n* associate, colleague, copartner, partaker, participant, participator; accomplice, ally, coadjutor, confederate; companion, consort, spouse.

partnership *n* association, company, copartnership, firm, house, society; connection, interest, participation, union.

parts *npl* abilities, accomplishments, endowments, faculties, genius, gifts, intellect, intelligence, mind, qualities, powers, talents; districts, regions.

party *n* alliance, association, cabal, circle, clique, combination, confederacy, coterie, faction, group, junta, league, ring, set; body, company, detachment, squad, troop; assembly, gathering; partaker, participant, participator, sharer; defendant, litigant, plaintiff; individual, one, person, somebody; cause, division, interest, side.

pass[1] *vb* devolve, fall, go, move, proceed; change, elapse, flit, glide, lapse, slip; cease, die, fade, expire, vanish; happen, occur; convey, deliver, send, transmit, transfer; disregard, ignore, neglect; exceed, excel, surpass; approve, ratify, sanction; answer, do, succeed, suffice, suit; express, pronounce, utter; beguile, wile.

pass[2] *n* avenue, ford, road, route, way; defile, gorge, passage, ravine; authorization, licence, passport, permission, ticket; condition, conjecture, plight, situation, state; lunge, push, thrust, tilt; transfer, trick.

passable *adj* admissible, allowable, mediocre, middling, moderate, ordinary, so-so, tolerable; acceptable, current, receivable; navigable, traversable.

passage *n* going, passing, progress, transit; evacuation, journey, migration, transit, voyage; avenue, channel, course, pass, path, road, route, thoroughfare, vennel, way; access, currency, entry, reception; act, deed, event, feat, incidence, occurrence, passion; corridor, gallery, gate, hall; clause, paragraph, sentence, text; course, death, decease, departure, expiration, lapse; affair, brush, change, collision, combat, conflict, contest, encounter, exchange, joust, skirmish, tilt.

passenger *n* fare, itinerant, tourist, traveller, voyager, wayfarer.

passionate *adj* animated, ardent, burning, earnest, enthusiastic, excited, fervent, fiery, furious, glowing, hot-blooded, impassioned, impetuous, impulsive, intense, vehement, warm, zealous; hot-headed, irascible, quick-tempered, tempestuous, violent.

passive *adj* inactive, inert, quiescent, receptive; apathetic, enduring, long-suffering, nonresistant, patient, stoical, submissive, suffering, unresisting.

past *adj* accomplished, elapsed, ended, gone, spent; ancient, bygone, former, obsolete, outworn. * *adv* above, extra, beyond, over. * *prep* above, after, beyond, exceeding. * *n* antiquity, heretofore, history, olden times, yesterday.

pastime *n* amusement, diversion, entertainment, hobby, play, recreation, sport.

pastor *n* clergyman, churchman, divine, ecclesiastic, minister, parson, priest, vicar.

pat[1] *vb* dab, hit, rap, tap; caress, chuck, fondle, pet. * *n* dab, hit, pad, rap, tap; caress.

pat[2] *adj* appropriate, apt, fit, pertinent, suitable. * *adv* aptly, conveniently, fitly, opportunely, seasonably.

patch *vb* mend, repair. * *n* repair; parcel, plot, tract.

patent *adj* expanded, open, spreading; apparent, clear, conspicuous, evident, glaring, indisputable, manifest, notorious, obvious, public, open, palpable, plain, unconcealed, unmistakable. * *n* copyright, privilege, right.

paternity *n* derivation, descent, fatherhood, origin.

path *n* access, avenue, course, footway, passage, pathway, road, route, track, trail, way.

pathetic *adj* affecting, melting, moving, pitiable, plaintive, sad, tender, touching.

patience *n* endurance, fortitude, long-sufferance, resignation, submission, sufferance; calmness, composure, quietness; forbearance, indulgence, leniency; assiduity, constancy, diligence, indefatigability, indefatigableness, perseverance, persistence.

patient *adj* meek, passive, resigned, submissive, uncomplaining, unrepining; calm, composed, contented, quiet; indulgent, lenient, long-suffering; assiduous, constant, diligent, indefatigable, persevering, persistent. * *n* case, invalid, subject, sufferer.

patrician *adj* aristocratic, blue-blooded, highborn, noble, senatorial, well-born. * *n* aristocrat, blue blood, nobleman.

patron *n* advocate, defender, favourer, guardian, helper, protector, supporter.

patronize *vb* aid, assist, befriend, countenance, defend, favour, maintain, support; condescend, disparage, scorn.

pattern *vb* copy, follow, imitate. * *n* archetype, exemplar, last, model, original, paradigm, plan, prototype; example, guide, sample, specimen; mirror, paragon; design, figure, shape, style, type.

paucity *n* deficiency, exiguity, insufficiency, lack, poverty, rarity, shortage.

paunch *n* abdomen, belly, gut, stomach.

pauperism *n* beggary, destitution, indigence, mendicancy, mendicity, need, poverty, penury, want.

pause *vb* breathe, cease, delay, desist, rest, stay, stop, wait; delay, forbear, intermit, stay, stop, tarry, wait; deliberate, demur, hesitate, waver. * *n* break, caesura, cessation, halt, intermission, interruption, interval, remission, rest, stop, stoppage, stopping, suspension; hesitation, suspense, uncertainty; paragraph.

pawn[1] *n* cat's-paw, dupe, plaything, puppet, stooge, tool, toy.

pawn[2] *vb* bet, gage, hazard, lay, pledge, risk, stake, wager. * *n* assurance, bond, guarantee, pledge, security.

pay *vb* defray, discharge, discount, foot, honour, liquidate, meet, quit, settle; compensate, recompense, reimburse, requite, reward; punish, revenge; give, offer, render. * *n* allowance, commission, compensation, emolument, hire, recompense, reimbursement, remuneration, requital, reward, salary, wages.

peace *n* calm, calmness, quiet, quietness, repose, stillness; accord, amity, friendliness, harmony; composure, equanimity, imperturbability, placidity, quietude, tranquillity; agreement, armistice.

peaceable *adj* pacific, peaceful; amiable, amicable, friendly, gentle, inoffensive, mild; placid, quiet, serene, still, tranquil, undisturbed, unmoved.

peaceful *adj* quiet, undisturbed; amicable, concordant, friendly, gentle, harmonious, mild, pacific, peaceable; calm, composed, placid, serene, still.

peak *vb* climax, culminate, top; dwindle, thin. * *n* acme, apex, crest, crown, pinnacle, summit, top, zenith.

peaked *adj* piked, pointed, thin.

peasant *n* boor, countryman, clown, hind, labourer, rustic, swain.

peculate *vb* appropriate, defraud, embezzle, misappropriate, pilfer, purloin, rob, steal.

peculiar *adj* appropriate, idiosyncratic, individual, proper; characteristic, eccentric, exceptional, extraordinary, odd, queer, rare, singular, strange, striking, uncommon, unusual; individual, especial, particular, select, special, specific.

peculiarity *n* appropriateness, distinctiveness, individuality, speciality; characteristic, idiosyncrasy, oddity, peculiarity, singularity.

pedantic *adj* conceited, fussy, officious, ostentatious, over-learned, particular, pedagogical, pompous, pragmatical, precise, pretentious, priggish, stilted.

pedlar *n* chapman, costermonger, hawker, packman, vendor.

pedigree *adj* purebred, thoroughbred. * *n* ancestry, breed, descent, extraction, family, genealogy, house, line, lineage, race, stock, strain.

peer[1] *vb* gaze, look, peek, peep, pry, squinny, squint; appear, emerge.

peer[2] *n* associate, co-equal, companion, compeer, equal, equivalent, fellow, like, mate, match; aristocrat, baron, count, duke, earl, grandee, lord, marquis, noble, nobleman, viscount.

peerless *adj* excellent, incomparable, matchless, outstanding, superlative, unequalled, unique, unmatched, unsurpassed.

peevish *adj* acrimonious, captious, churlish, complaining, crabbed, cross, crusty, discontented, fretful, ill-natured, ill-tempered, irascible, irritable, pettish, petulant, querulous, snappish, snarling, splenetic, spleeny, testy, waspish; forward, headstrong, obstinate, self-willed, stubborn; childish, silly, thoughtless, trifling.

pellucid *adj* bright, clear, crystalline, diaphanous, limpid, lucid, transparent.

pelt[1] *vb* assail, batter, beat, belabour, bombard, pepper, stone, strike; cast, hurl, throw; hurry, rush, speed, tear.

pelt[2] *n* coat, hide, skin.

pen[1] *vb* compose, draft, indite, inscribe, write.

pen[2] *vb* confine, coop, encage, enclose, impound, imprison, incarcerate. * *n* cage, coop, corral, crib, hutch, enclosure, paddock, pound, stall, sty.

penalty *n* chastisement, fine, forfeiture, mulct, punishment, retribution.

penance *n* humiliation, maceration, mortification, penalty, punishment.

penchant *n* bent, bias, disposition, fondness, inclination, leaning, liking, predilection, predisposition, proclivity, proneness, propensity, taste, tendency, turn.

penetrate *vb* bore, burrow, cut, enter, invade, penetrate, percolate, perforate, pervade, pierce, soak, stab; affect, sensitize, touch; comprehend, discern, perceive, understand.

penetrating *adj* penetrative, permeating, piercing, sharp, subtle; acute, clear-sighted, discerning, intelligent, keen, quick, sagacious, sharp-witted, shrewd.

penetration *n* acuteness, discernment, insight, sagacity.

penitence *n* compunction, contrition, qualms, regret, remorse, repentance, sorrow.

penitent *adj* compunctious, conscience-stricken, contrite, regretful, remorseful, repentant, sorrowing, sorrowful. * *n* penance-doer, penitentiary, repentant.

penniless *adj* destitute, distressed, impecunious, indigent, moneyless, pinched, poor, necessitous, needy, pensive, poverty-stricken, reduced.

pensive *adj* contemplative, dreamy, meditative, reflective, sober, thoughtful; grave, melancholic, melancholy, mournful, sad, serious, solemn.

penurious *adj* inadequate, ill-provided, insufficient, meagre, niggardly, poor, scanty, stinted; avaricious, close, close-fisted, covetous, illiberal, grasping, grudging, mean, mercenary, miserly, near, niggardly, parsimonious, sordid, stingy, tightfisted.

penury *n* beggary, destitution, indigence, need, poverty, privation, want.

people *vb* colonize, inhabit, populate. * *n* clan, country, family, nation, race, state, tribe; folk, humankind, persons, population, public; commons, community, democracy, populace, proletariat; mob, multitude, rabble.

perceive *vb* behold, descry, detect, discern, discover, discriminate, distinguish, note, notice, observe, recognize, remark, see, spot; appreciate, comprehend, know, understand.

perceptible *adj* apparent, appreciable, cognizable, discernible, noticeable, perceivable, understandable, visible.

perception *n* apprehension, cognition, discernment, perceiving, recognition, seeing; comprehension, conception, consciousness, perceptiveness, perceptivity, understanding, feeling.

perchance *adv* haply, maybe, mayhap, peradventure, perhaps, possibly, probably.

percolate *vb* drain, drip, exude, filter, filtrate, ooze, penetrate, stain, transude.

percussion *n* collision, clash, concussion, crash, encounter, shock.

perdition *n* damnation, demolition, destruction, downfall, hell, overthrow, ruin, wreck.

peremptory *adj* absolute, authoritative, categorical, commanding, decisive, express, imperative, imperious, positive; determined, resolute, resolved; arbitrary, dogmatic, incontrovertible.

perennial *adj* ceaseless, constant, continual, deathless, enduring, immortal, imperishable, lasting, never-failing, permanent, perpetual, unceasing, undying, unfailing, uninterrupted.

perfect *vb* accomplish, complete, consummate, elaborate, finish. * *adj* completed, finished; complete, entire, full, unqualified, utter, whole; capital, consum-

mate, excellent, exquisite, faultless, ideal; accomplished, disciplined, expert, skilled; blameless, faultless, holy, immaculate, pure, spotless, unblemished.

perfection *n* completeness, completion, consummation, correctness, excellence, faultlessness, finish, maturity, perfection, perfectness, wholeness; beauty, quality.

perfidious *adj* deceitful, dishonest, disloyal, double-faced, faithless, false, false-hearted, traitorous, treacherous, unfaithful, untrustworthy, venal.

perfidy *n* defection, disloyalty, faithlessness, infidelity, perfidiousness, traitorousness, treachery, treason.

perforate *vb* bore, drill, penetrate, pierce, pink, prick, punch, riddle, trepan.

perform *vb* accomplish, achieve, compass, consummate, do, effect, transact; complete, discharge, execute, fulfil, meet, observe, satisfy; act, play, represent.

performance *n* accomplishment, achievement, completion, consummation, discharge, doing, execution, fulfilment; act, action, deed, exploit, feat, work; composition, production; acting, entertainment, exhibition, play, representation, hold; execution, playing.

perfume *n* aroma, balminess, bouquet, fragrance, incense, odour, redolence, scent, smell, sweetness.

perfunctory *adj* careless, formal, heedless, indifferent, mechanical, negligent, reckless, slight, slovenly, thoughtless, unmindful.

perhaps *adv* haply, peradventure, perchance, possibly.

peril *vb* endanger, imperil, jeopardize, risk. * *n* danger, hazard, insecurity, jeopardy, pitfall, risk, snare, uncertainty.

perilous *adj* dangerous, hazardous, risky, unsafe.

period *n* aeon, age, cycle, date, eon, epoch, season, span, spell, stage, term, time; continuance, duration; bound, conclusion, determination, end, limit, term, termination; clause, phrase, proposition, sentence.

periodical *adj* cyclical, incidental, intermittent, recurrent, recurring, regular, seasonal, systematic. * *n* magazine, paper, review, serial, weekly.

periphery *n* boundary, circumference, outside, perimeter, superficies, surface.

perish *vb* decay, moulder, shrivel, waste, wither; decease, die, expire, vanish.

perishable *adj* decaying, decomposable, destructible; dying, frail, mortal, temporary.

perjured *adj* false, forsworn, perfidious, traitorous, treacherous, untrue.

permanent *adj* abiding, constant, continuing, durable, enduring, fixed, immutable, invariable, lasting, perpetual, persistent, stable, standing, steadfast, unchangeable, unchanging, unfading, unmovable.

permissible *adj* admissible, allowable, free, lawful, legal, legitimate, proper, sufferable, unprohibited.

permission *n* allowance, authorization, consent, dispensation, leave, liberty, licence, permit, sufferance, toleration, warrant.

permit *vb* agree, allow, endure, let, suffer, tolerate; admit, authorize, consent, empower, license, warrant. * *n* leave, liberty, licence, passport, permission, sanction, warrant.

pernicious *adj* baleful, baneful, damaging, deadly, deleterious, destructive, detrimental, disadvantageous, fatal, harmful, hurtful, injurious, malign, mischievous, noisome, noxious, prejudicial, ruinous; evil-hearted, malevolent, malicious, malignant, mischief-making, wicked.

perpetrate *vb* commit, do, execute, perform.

perpetual *adj* ceaseless, continual, constant, endless, enduring, eternal, ever-enduring, everlasting, incessant, interminable, never-ceasing, never-ending, perennial, permanent, sempiternal, unceasing, unending, unfailing, uninterrupted.

perplex *vb* complicate, encumber, entangle, involve, snarl, tangle; beset, bewilder, confound, confuse, corner, distract, embarrass, fog, mystify, nonplus, pother, puzzle, set; annoy, bother, disturb, harass, molest, pester, plague, tease, trouble, vex, worry.

persecute *vb* afflict, distress, harass, molest, oppress, worry; annoy, beset, importune, pester, solicit, tease.

perseverance *n* constancy, continuance, doggedness, indefatigableness, persistence, persistency, pertinacity, resolution, steadfastness, steadiness, tenacity.

persevere *vb* continue, determine, endure, maintain, persist, remain, resolve, stick.

persist *vb* continue, endure, last, remain; insist, persevere.

persistent *adj* constant, continuing, enduring, fixed, immovable, persevering, persisting, steady, tenacious; contumacious, dogged, indefatigable, obdurate, obstinate, pertinacious, perverse, pigheaded, stubborn.

personable *adj* comely, good-looking, graceful, seemly, well-turned-out.

personal *adj* individual, peculiar, private, special; bodily, corporal, corporeal, exterior, material, physical.

personate *vb* act, impersonate, personify, play, represent; disguise, mast; counterfeit, feign, simulate.

perspective *n* panorama, prospect, view, vista; proportion, relation.

perspicacious *adj* keen-sighted, quick-sighted, sharp-sighted; acute, clever, discerning, keen, penetrating, sagacious, sharp-witted, shrewd.

perspicacity *n* acumen, acuteness, astuteness, discernment, insight, penetration, perspicaciousness, sagacity, sharpness, shrewdness.

perspicuity *n* clearness, distinctness, explicitness, intelligibility, lucidity, lucidness, perspicuousness, plainness, transparency.

perspicuous *adj* clear, distinct, explicit, intelligible, lucid, obvious, plain, transparent, unequivocal.

perspire *vb* exhale, glow, sweat, swelter.

persuade *vb* allure, actuate, entice, impel, incite, induce, influence, lead, move, prevail upon, urge; advise, counsel; convince, satisfy; inculcate, teach.

persuasion *n* exhortation, incitement, inducement, influence; belief, conviction, opinion; creed, doctrine, dogma, tenet; kind, sort, variety.

persuasive *adj* cogent, convincing, inducing, inducible, logical, persuading, plausible, sound, valid, weighty.

pert *adj* brisk, dapper, lively, nimble, smart, sprightly, perky; bold, flippant, forward, free, impertinent, impudent, malapert, presuming, smart, saucy.

pertain *vb* appertain, befit, behove, belong, concern, refer, regard, relate.

pertinacious *adj* constant, determined, firm, obdurate, persevering, resolute, staunch, steadfast, steady; dogged, headstrong, inflexible, mulish, intractable, obstinate, perverse, stubborn, unyielding, wayward, wilful.

pertinent *adj* adapted, applicable, apposite, appropriate, apropos, apt, fit, germane, pat, proper, relevant, suitable; appurtenant, belonging, concerning, pertaining, regarding.

perturb *vb* agitate, disquiet, distress, disturb, excite, trouble, unsettle, upset, vex, worry; confuse.

pervade *vb* affect, animate, diffuse, extend, fill, imbue, impregnate, infiltrate, penetrate, permeate.

perverse *adj* bad, disturbed, oblique, perverted; contrary, dogged, headstrong, mulish, obstinate, pertinacious, perversive, stubborn, ungovernable, intractable, unyielding, wayward, wilful; cantankerous, churlish, crabbed, cross, cross-grained, crusty, cussed, morose, peevish, petulant, snappish, snarling, spiteful, spleeny, surly, testy, touchy, wicked, wrong-headed; inconvenient, troublesome, untoward, vexatious.

perversion *n* abasement, corruption, debasement, impairment, injury, prostitution, vitiation.

perverted *adj* corrupt, debased, distorted, evil, impaired, misguiding, vitiated, wicked.

pessimistic *adj* cynical, dark, dejected, depressed, despondent, downhearted, gloomy, glum, melancholy, melancholic, morose, sad.

pest *n* disease, epidemic, infection, pestilence, plague; annoyance, bane, curse, infliction, nuisance, scourge, trouble.

pestilent *adj* contagious, infectious, malignant, pestilential; deadly, evil, injurious, malign, mischievous, noxious, poisonous; annoying, corrupt, pernicious, troublesome, vexatious.

petition *vb* ask, beg, crave, entreat, pray, solicit, sue, supplicate. * *n* address, appeal, application, entreaty, prayer, request, solicitation, supplication, suit.

petrify *vb* calcify, fossilize, lapidify; benumb, deaden; amaze, appal, astonish, astound, confound, dumbfound, paralyse, stun, stupefy.

petty *adj* diminutive, frivolous, inconsiderable, inferior, insignificant, little, mean, slight, small, trifling, trivial, unimportant.

petulant *adj* acrimonious, captious, cavilling, censorious, choleric, crabbed, cross, crusty, forward, fretful, hasty, ill-humoured, ill-tempered, irascible, irritable, peevish, perverse, pettish, querulous, snappish, snarling, testy, touchy, waspish.

phantom *n* apparition, ghost, illusion, phantasm, spectre, vision, wraith.

pharisaism *n* cant, formalism, hypocrisy, phariseeism, piety, sanctimoniousness, self-righteousness.

phenomenal *adj* marvellous, miraculous, prodigious, wondrous.

philanthropy *n* alms-giving, altruism, benevolence, charity, grace, humanitarianism, humanity, kindness.

philosophical, philosophic *adj* rational, reasonable, sound, wise; calm, collected, composed, cool, imperturbable, sedate, serene, stoical, tranquil, unruffled.

phlegmatic *adj* apathetic, calm, cold, cold-blooded, dull, frigid, heavy, impassive, indifferent, inert, sluggish, stoical, tame, unfeeling.

phobia *n* aversion, detestation, dislike, distaste, dread, fear, hatred.

phrase *vb* call, christen, denominate, designate, describe, dub, entitle, name, style. * *n* diction, expression, phraseology, style.

phraseology *n* diction, expression, language, phrasing, style.

physical *adj* material, natural; bodily, corporeal, external, substantial, tangible, sensible.

physiognomy *n* configuration, countenance, face, look, visage.

picaroon *n* adventurer, cheat, rogue; buccaneer, corsair, freebooter, marauder, pirate, plunderer, sea-rover.

pick *vb* peck, pierce, strike; cut, detach, gather, pluck; choose, cull, select; acquire, collect, get; pilfer, steal. * *n* pickaxe, pike, spike, toothpick.

picture *vb* delineate, draw, imagine, paint, represent. * *n* drawing, engraving, painting, print; copy, counterpart, delineation, embodiment, illustration, image, likeness, portraiture, portrayal, semblance, representation, resemblance, similitude; description.

picturesque *adj* beautiful, charming, colourful, graphic, scenic, striking, vivid.

piece *vb* mend, patch, repair; augment, complete, enlarge, increase; cement, join, unite. * *n* amount, bit, chunk, cut, fragment, hunk, part, quantity, scrap, shred, slice; portion; article, item, object; composition, lucubration, work, writing.

pied *adj* irregular, motley, mottled, particoloured, piebald, spotted, variegated.

pierce *vb* gore, impale, pink, prick, stab, transfix; bore, drill, excite, penetrate, perforate, puncture; affect, move, rouse, strike, thrill, touch.

piety *n* devotion, devoutness, holiness, godliness, grace, religion, sanctity.

pile[1] *vb* accumulate, amass; collect, gather, heap, load. * *n* accumulation, collection, heap, mass, stack; fortune, wad; building, edifice, erection, fabric, pyramid, skyscraper, structure, tower; reactor, nuclear reactor.

pile[2] *n* beam, column, pier, pillar, pole, post.

pile[3] *n* down, feel, finish, fur, fluff, fuzz, grain, nap, pappus, shag, surface, texture.

pilfer *vb* filch, purloin, rob, steal, thieve.

pilgrim *n* journeyer, sojourner, traveller, wanderer, wayfarer; crusader, devotee, palmer.

pilgrimage *n* crusade, excursion, expedition, journey, tour, trip.

pillage *vb* despoil, loot, plunder, rifle, sack, spoil, strip. * *n* depredation, destruction, devastation, plundering, rapine, spoliation; despoliation, plunder, rifling, sack, spoils.

pillar *n* column, pier, pilaster, post, shaft, stanchion; maintainer, prop, support, supporter, upholder.

pilot *vb* conduct, control, direct, guide, navigate, steer. * *adj* experimental, model, trial. * *n* helmsman, navigator, steersman; airman, aviator, conductor, director, flier, guide.

pinch *vb* compress, contract, cramp, gripe, nip, squeeze; afflict, distress, famish, oppress, straiten, stint; frost, nip; apprehend, arrest; economize, spare, stint. * *n* gripe, nip; pang, throe; crisis, difficulty, emergency, exigency, oppression, pressure, push, strait, stress.

pine *vb* decay, decline, droop, fade, flag, languish, waste, wilt, wither; desire, long, yearn.

pinion *vb* bind, chain, fasten, fetter, maim, restrain, shackle. * *n* pennon, wing; feather, quill, pen, plume, wing; fetter.

pinnacle *n* minaret, turret; acme, apex, height, peak, summit, top, zenith.

pious *adj* filial; devout, godly, holy, religious, reverential, righteous, saintly.

piquant *adj* biting, highly flavoured, piercing, prickling, pungent, sharp, stinging; interesting, lively, racy, sparkling, stimulating; cutting, keen, pointed, severe, strong, tart.

pique *vb* goad, incite, instigate, spur, stimulate, urge; affront, chafe, displease, fret, incense, irritate, nettle, offend, provoke, sting, vex, wound. * *n* annoyance,

displeasure, irritation, offence, resentment, vexation.

pirate *vb* copy, crib, plagiarize, reproduce, steal. * *n* buccaneer, corsair, freebooter, marauder, picaroon, privateer, seadog, sea-robber, sea-rover, sea wolf.

pit *vb* match, oppose; dent, gouge, hole, mark, nick, notch, scar. * *n* cavity, hole, hollow; crater, dent, depression, dint, excavation, well; abyss, chasm, gulf; pitfall, snare, trap: auditorium, orchestra.

pitch *vb* fall, lurch, plunge, reel; light, settle, rest; cast, dart, fling, heave, hurl, lance, launch, send, toss, throw; erect, establish, fix, locate, place, plant, set, settle, station. * *n* degree, extent, height, intensity, measure, modulation, rage, rate; declivity, descent, inclination, slope; cast, jerk, plunge, throw, toss; place, position, spot; field, ground; line, patter.

piteous *adj* affecting, distressing, doleful, grievous, mournful, pathetic, rueful, sorrowful, woeful; deplorable, lamentable, miserable, pitiable, wretched; compassionate, tender.

pith *n* chief, core, essence, heart, gist, kernel, marrow, part, quintessence, soul, substance; importance, moment, weight; cogency, force, energy, strength, vigour.

pithy *adj* cogent, energetic, forcible, powerful; compact, concise, brief, laconic, meaty, pointed, short, sententious, substantial, terse; corky, porous.

pitiable *adj* deplorable, lamentable, miserable, pathetic, piteous, pitiable, woeful, wretched; abject, base, contemptible, despicable, disreputable, insignificant, low, paltry, mean, rascally, sorry, vile, worthless.

pitiably *adv* deplorably, distressingly, grievously, lamentably, miserably, pathetically, piteously, woefully, wretchedly.

pitiful *adj* compassionate, kind, lenient, merciful, mild, sympathetic, tender, tenderhearted; deplorable, lamentable, miserable, pathetic, piteous, pitiable, wretched; abject, base, contemptible, despicable, disreputable, insignificant, mean, paltry, rascally, sorry, vile, worthless.

pitiless *adj* cruel, hardhearted, implacable, inexorable, merciless, unmerciful, relentless, remorseless, unfeeling, unpitying, unrelenting, unsympathetic.

pittance *n* allowance, allotment, alms, charity, dole, gift; driblet, drop, insufficiency, mite, modicum, trifle.

pity *vb* commiserate, condole, sympathize. * *n* clemency, commiseration, compassion, condolence, fellow-feeling, grace, humanity, leniency, mercy, quarter, sympathy, tenderheartedness.

pivot *vb* depend, hinge, turn. * *n* axis, axle, centre, focus, hinge, joint.

place *vb* arrange, bestow, commit, deposit, dispose, fix, install, lay, locate, lodge, orient, orientate, pitch, plant, pose, put, seat, set, settle, situate, stand, station, rest; allocate, arrange, class, classify, identify, order, organize, recognize; appoint, assign, commission, establish, induct, nominate. * *n* area, courtyard, square; bounds, district, division, locale, locality, location, part, position, premises, quarter, region, scene, site, situation, spot, station, tract, whereabouts; calling, charge, employment, function, occupation, office, pitch, post; calling, condition, grade, precedence, rank, sphere, stakes, standing; abode, building, dwelling, habitation, mansion, residence, seat; city, town, village; fort, fortress, stronghold; paragraph, part, passage, portion; ground, occasion, opportunity, reason, room; lieu, stead.

placid *adj* calm, collected, composed, cool, equable, gentle, peaceful, quiet, serene, tranquil, undisturbed, unexcitable, unmoved, unruffled; halcyon, mild, serene.

plague *vb* afflict, annoy, badger, bore, bother, pester, chafe, disquiet, distress, disturb, embarrass, harass, fret, gall, harry, hector, incommode, irritate, molest, perplex, tantalize, tease, torment, trouble, vex, worry. * *n* disease, pestilence, pest; affliction, annoyance, curse, molestation, nuisance, thorn, torment, trouble, vexation, worry.

plain *adj* dull, even, flat, level, plane, smooth, uniform; clear, open, unencumbered, uninterrupted; apparent, certain, conspicuous, evident, distinct, glaring, manifest, notable, notorious, obvious, overt, palpable, patent, prominent, pronounced, staring, transparent, unmistakable, visible; explicit, intelligible, perspicuous, unambiguous, unequivocal; homely, ugly; aboveboard, blunt, crude, candid, direct, downright, frank, honest, ingenuous, open, openhearted, sincere, single-minded, straightforward, undesigning, unreserved, unsophisticated: artless, common, natural, simple, unaffected, unlearned; absolute, mere, unmistakable; clear, direct, easy; audible, articulate, definite; frugal, homely; unadorned, unfigured, unornamented, unvariegated. * *n* expanse, flats, grassland, pampas, plateau, prairie, steppe, stretch.

plaint *n* complaint, cry, lament, lamentation, moan, wail.

plaintiff *n* accuser, prosecutor.

plaintive *adj* dirge-like, doleful, grievous, melancholy, mournful, piteous, rueful, sad, sorrowful, woeful.

plan *vb* arrange, calculate, concert, delineate, devise, diagram, figure, premeditate, project, represent, study; concoct, conspire, contrive, design, digest, hatch, invent, manoeuvre, machinate, plot, prepare, scheme. * *n* chart, delineation, diagram, draught, drawing, layout, map, plot, sketch; arrangement, conception, contrivance, design, device, idea, method, programme, project, proposal, proposition, scheme, system; cabal, conspiracy, intrigue, machination; custom, process, way.

plane *vb* even, flatten, level, smooth; float, fly, glide, skate, skim, soar. * *adj* even, flat, horizontal, level, smooth. * *n* degree, evenness, level, levelness, smoothness; aeroplane, aircraft; groover, jointer, rabbet, rebate, scraper.

plant *vb* bed, sow; breed, engender; direct, point, set; colonize, furnish, inhabit, settle; establish, introduce; deposit, establish, fix, found, hide. * *n* herb, organism, vegetable; establishment, equipment, factory, works.

plaster *vb* bedaub, coat, cover, smear, spread. * *n* cement, gypsum, mortar, stucco.

plastic *adj* ductile, flexible, formative, mouldable, pliable, pliant, soft.

platitude *n* dullness, flatness, insipidity, mawkishness; banality, commonplace, truism; balderdash, chatter, flummery, fudge, jargon, moonshine, nonsense, palaver, stuff, trash, twaddle, verbiage.

plaudit *n* acclaim, acclamation, applause, approbation, clapping, commendation, encomium, praise.

plausible *adj* believable, credible, probable, reasonable; bland, fair-spoken, glib, smooth, suave.

play *vb* caper, disport, frisk, frolic, gambol, revel, romp, skip, sport; dally, flirt, idle, toy, trifle, wanton; flutter, hover, wave; act, impersonate, perform, personate, represent; bet, gamble, stake, wager. * *n* amusement, exercise, frolic, gambols, game, jest, pastime, prank, romp, sport; gambling, gaming; act, comedy, drama, farce, performance, tragedy; action, motion, movement; elbowroom, freedom, latitude, movement, opportunity, range, scope, sweep, swing, use.

playful *adj* frisky, frolicsome, gamesome, jolly, kittenish, merry, mirthful, rollicking, sportive; amusing, arch, humorous, lively, mischievous, roguish, skittish, sprightly, vivacious.

plead *vb* answer, appeal, argue, reason; argue, defend, discuss, reason, rejoin; beg, beseech, entreat, implore, petition, sue, supplicate.

pleasant *adj* acceptable, agreeable, delectable, delightful, enjoyable, grateful, gratifying, nice, pleasing, pleasurable, prepossessing, seemly, welcome; cheerful, enlivening, good-humoured, gracious, likable, lively, merry, sportive, sprightly, vivacious; amusing, facetious, humorous, jocose, jocular, sportive, witty.

please *vb* charm, delight, elate, gladden, gratify, pleasure, rejoice; content, oblige, satisfy; choose, like, prefer.

pleasure *n* cheer, comfort, delight, delectation, elation, enjoyment, exhilaration, joy, gladness, gratifying, gusto, relish, satisfaction, solace; amusement, diversion, entertainment, indulgence, refreshment, treat; gratification, luxury, sensuality, voluptuousness; choice, desire, preference, purpose, will, wish; favour, kindness.

plebeian *adj* base, common, ignoble, low, lowborn, mean, obscure, popular, vulgar. * *n* commoner, peasant, proletarian.

pledge *vb* hypothecate, mortgage, pawn, plight; affiance, bind, contract, engage, plight, promise. * *n* collateral, deposit, gage, pawn; earnest, guarantee, security; hostage, security.

plenipotentiary *n* ambassador, envoy, legate, minister.

plenitude *n* abundance, completeness, fullness, plenteousness, plentifulness, plenty, plethora, profusion, repletion.

plentiful *adj* abundant, ample, copious, full, enough, exuberant, fruitful, luxuriant, plenteous, productive, sufficient.

plenty *n* abundance, adequacy, affluence, amplitude, copiousness, enough, exuberance, fertility, fruitfulness, fullness, overflow, plenteousness, plentifulness, plethora, profusion, sufficiency, supply.

pleonastic *adj* circumlocutory, diffuse, redundant, superfluous, tautological, verbose, wordy.

plethora *n* fullness, plenitude, repletion; excess, redundance, redundancy, superabundance, superfluity, surfeit.

pliable *adj* flexible, limber, lithe, lithesome, pliable, pliant, supple; adaptable, compliant, docile, ductile, facile, manageable, obsequious, tractable, yielding.

plight[1] *n* case, category, complication, condition, dilemma, imbroglio, mess, muddle, pass, predicament, scrape, situation, state, strait.

plight[2] *vb* avow, contract, covenant, engage, honour, pledge, promise, propose, swear, vow. * *n* avowal, contract, covenant, oath, pledge, promise, troth, vow, word; affiancing, betrothal, engagement.

plod *vb* drudge, lumber, moil, persevere, persist, toil, trudge.

plot[1] *vb* connive, conspire, intrigue, machinate, scheme; brew, concoct, contrive, devise, frame, hatch, compass, plan, project; chart, map. * *n* blueprint, chart, diagram, draft, outline, plan, scenario, skeleton; cabal, combination, complicity, connivance, conspiracy, intrigue, plan, project, scheme, stratagem; script, story, subject, theme, thread, topic.

plot² *n* field, lot, parcel, patch, piece, plat, section, tract.

pluck¹ *vb* cull, gather, pick; jerk, pull, snatch, tear, tug, twitch.

pluck² *n* backbone, bravery, courage, daring, determination, energy, force, grit, hardihood, heroism, indomitability, indomitableness, manhood, mettle, nerve, resolution, spirit, valour.

plump¹ *adj* bonny, bouncing, buxom, chubby, corpulent, fat, fleshy, full-figured, obese, portly, rotund, round, sleek, stout, well-rounded; distended, full, swollen, tumid.

plump² *vb* dive, drop, plank, plop, plunge, plunk, put; choose, favour, support * *adj* blunt, complete, direct, downright, full, unqualified, unreserved.

plunder *vb* desolate, despoil, devastate, fleece, forage, harry, loot, maraud, pillage, raid, ransack, ravage, rifle, rob, sack, spoil, spoliate, plunge. * *n* freebooting, devastation, harrying, marauding, rapine, robbery, sack; booty, pillage, prey, spoil.

ply¹ *vb* apply, employ, exert, manipulate, wield; exercise, practise; assail, belabour, beset, press; importune, solicit, urge; offer, present.

ply² *n* fold, layer, plait, twist; bent, bias, direction, turn.

pocket *vb* appropriate, steal; bear, endure, suffer, tolerate. * *n* cavity, cul-de-sac, hollow, pouch, receptacle.

poignant *adj* bitter, intense, penetrating, pierce, severe, sharp; acrid, biting, mordacious, piquant, prickling, pungent, sharp, stinging; caustic, irritating, keen, mordant, pointed, satirical, severe.

point *vb* acuminate, sharpen; aim, direct, level; designate indicate, show; punctuate. * *n* apex, needle, nib, pin, prong, spike, stylus, tip; cape, headland, projection, promontory; eve, instant, moment, period, verge; place, site, spot, stage, station; condition, degree, grade, state; aim, design, end, intent, limit, object, purpose; nicety, pique, punctilio, trifle; position, proposition, question, text, theme, thesis; aspect, matter, respect; characteristic, peculiarity, trait; character, mark, stop; dot, jot, speck; epigram, quip, quirk, sally, witticism; poignancy, sting.

point-blank *adj* categorical, direct, downright, explicit, express, plain, straight. * *adv* categorically, directly, flush, full, plainly, right, straight.

pointless *adj* blunt, obtuse; aimless, dull, flat, fruitless, futile, meaningless, vague, vapid, stupid.

poise *vb* balance, float, hang, hover, support, suspend. * *n* aplomb, balance, composure, dignity, equanimity, equilibrium, equipoise, serenity.

poison *vb* adulterate, contaminate, corrupt, defile, embitter, envenom, impair, infect, intoxicate, pollute, taint, vitiate. * *adj* deadly, lethal, poisonous, toxic. * *n* bane, canker, contagion, pest, taint, toxin, venom, virulence, virus.

poisonous *adj* baneful, corruptive, deadly, fatal, noxious, pestiferous, pestilential, toxic, venomous.

poke *vb* jab, jog, punch, push, shove, thrust; interfere, meddle, pry, snoop. * *n* jab, jog, punch, push, shove, thrust; bag, pocket, pouch, sack.

pole¹ *n* caber, mast, post, rod, spar, staff, stick; bar, beam, pile, shaft; oar, paddle, scull.

pole² *n* axis, axle, hub, pivot, spindle.

poles *npl* antipodes, antipoles, counterpoles, opposites.

policy *n* administration, government, management,

rule; plan, plank, platform, role; art, address, cunning, discretion, prudence, shrewdness, skill, stratagem, strategy, tactics; acumen, astuteness, wisdom, wit.

polish *vb* brighten, buff, burnish, furbish, glaze, gloss, scour, shine, smooth; civilize, refine. * *n* brightness, brilliance, brilliancy, lustre, splendour; accomplishment, elegance, finish, grace, refinement.

polished *adj* bright, burnished, glossed, glossy, lustrous, shining, smooth; accomplished, cultivated, elegant, finished, graceful, polite, refined.

polite *adj* attentive, accomplished, affable, chivalrous, civil, complaisant, courtly, courteous, cultivated, elegant, gallant, genteel, gentle, gentlemanly, gracious, mannerly, obliging, polished, refined, suave, urbane, well, well-bred, well-mannered.

politic *adj* civic, civil, political; astute, discreet, judicious, long-headed, noncommittal, provident, prudent, prudential, sagacious, wary, wise; artful, crafty, cunning, diplomatic, expedient, foxy, ingenious, intriguing, Machiavellian, shrewd, skilful, sly, subtle, strategic, timeserving, unscrupulous, wily; well-adapted, well-devised.

political *adj* civic, civil, national, politic, public.

pollute *vb* defile, foul, soil, taint; contaminate, corrupt, debase, demoralize, deprave, impair, infect, pervert, poison, stain, tarnish, vitiate; desecrate, profane; abuse, debauch, defile, deflower, dishonour, ravish, violate.

pollution *n* abomination, contamination, corruption, defilement, foulness, impurity, pollutedness, taint, uncleanness, vitiation.

poltroon *n* coward, crave, dastard, milksop, recreant, skulk, sneak.

pomp *n* display, flourish, grandeur, magnificence, ostentation, pageant, pageantry, parade, pompousness, pride, show, splendour, state, style.

pompous *adj* august, boastful, bombastic, dignified, gorgeous, grand, inflated, lofty, magisterial, ostentatious, pretentious, showy, splendid, stately, sumptuous, superb, vainglorious.

ponder *vb* cogitate, consider, contemplate, deliberate, examine, meditate, muse, reflect, study, weigh.

ponderous *adj* bulky, heavy, massive, weighty; dull, laboured, slow-moving; important, momentous; forcible, mighty.

poniard *n* dagger, dirk, stiletto.

poor *adj* indigent, necessitous, needy, pinched, straitened; destitute, distressed, embarrassed, impecunious, impoverished, insolvent, moneyless, penniless, poverty-stricken, reduced, seedy, unprosperous; emaciated, gaunt, spare, lank, lean, shrunk, skinny, spare, thin; barren, fruitless, sterile, unfertile, unfruitful, unproductive, unprolific; flimsy, inadequate, insignificant, insufficient, paltry, slender, slight, small, trifling, trivial, unimportant, valueless, worthless; decrepit, delicate, feeble, frail, infirm, unsound, weak; inferior, shabby, valueless, worthless; bad, beggarly, contemptible, despicable, humble, inferior, low, mean, pitiful, sorry; bald, cold, dry, dull, feeble, frigid, jejune, languid, meagre, prosaic, prosing, spiritless, tame, vapid, weak; ill-fated, ill-starred, inauspicious, indifferent, luckless, miserable, pitiable, unfavourable, unfortunate, unhappy, unlucky, wretched; deficient, imperfect, inadequate, insufficient, mediocre, scant, scanty; faulty, unsatisfactory; feeble.

populace *n* citizens, crowd, inhabitants, masses, people, public, throng.

popular *adj* lay, plebeian, public; comprehensible, easy, familiar, plain; acceptable, accepted, accredited, admired, approved, favoured, liked, pleasing, praised, received; common, current, prevailing, prevalent; cheap, inexpensive.

pore[1] *n* hole, opening, orifice, spiracle.

pore[2] *vb* brood, consider, dwell, examine, gaze, read, study.

porous *adj* honeycombed, light, loose, open, penetrable, perforated, permeable, pervious, sandy.

porridge *n* broth, gruel, mush, pap, pottage, soup.

port[1] *n* anchorage, harbour, haven, shelter; door, entrance, gate, passageway; embrasure, porthole.

port[2] *n* air, appearance, bearing, behaviour, carriage, demeanour, deportment, mien, presence.

portable *adj* convenient, handy, light, manageable, movable, portative, transmissible.

portend *vb* augur, betoken, bode, forebode, foreshadow, foretoken, indicate, presage, procrastinate, signify, threaten.

portent *n* augury, omen, presage, prognosis, sign, warning; marvel, phenomenon, wonder.

portion *vb* allot, distribute, divide, parcel; endow, supply. * *n* bit, fragment, morsel, part, piece, scrap, section; allotment, contingent, dividend, division, lot, measure, quantity, quota, ration, share; inheritance.

portly *adj* dignified, grand, imposing, magisterial, majestic, stately; bulky, burly, corpulent, fleshy, large, plump, round, stout.

portray *vb* act, draw, depict, delineate, describe, paint, picture, represent, pose, position, sketch.

pose *vb* arrange, place, set; bewilder, confound, dumbfound, embarrass, mystify, nonplus, perplex, place, puzzle, set, stagger; affect, attitudinize. * *n* attitude, posture; affectation, air, facade, mannerism, pretence, role.

position *vb* arrange, array, fix, locate, place, put, set, site, stand. * *n* locality, place, post, site, situation, spot, station; relation; attitude, bearing, posture; affirmation, assertion, doctrine, predication, principle, proposition, thesis; caste, dignity, honour, rank, standing, status; circumstance, condition, phase, place, state; berth, billet, incumbency, place, post, situation.

positive *adj* categorical, clear, defined, definite, direct, determinate, explicit, express, expressed, precise, unequivocal, unmistakable, unqualified; absolute, actual, real, substantial, true, veritable; assured, certain, confident, convinced, sure; decisive, incontrovertible, indisputable, indubitable, inescapable; imperative, unconditional, undeniable; decided, dogmatic, emphatic, obstinate, overbearing, overconfident, peremptory, stubborn, tenacious.

possess *vb* control, have, hold, keep, obsess, obtain, occupy, own, seize.

possession *n* monopoly, ownership, proprietorship; control, occupation, occupancy, retention, tenancy, tenure; bedevilment, lunacy, madness, obsession; (*pl*) assets, effects, estate, property, wealth.

possessor *n* owner, proprietor.

possible *adj* conceivable, contingent, imaginable, potential; accessible, feasible, likely, practical, practicable, workable.

possibly *adv* haply, maybe, mayhap, peradventure, perchance, perhaps.

post[1] *vb* advertise, announce, inform, placard, publish; brand, defame, disgrace, vilify; enter, slate, record, register. * *n* column, picket, pier, pillar, stake, support.

post[2] *vb* establish, fix, place, put, set, station. * *n* billet, employment, office, place, position, quarter, seat, situation, station.

post[3] *vb* drop, dispatch, mail. * *n* carrier, courier, express, mercury, messenger, postman; dispatch, haste, hurry, speed.

posterior *adj* after, ensuing, following, later, latter, postprandial, subsequent. * *n* back, buttocks, hind, hinder, rump.

posterity *n* descendants, offspring, progeny, seed; breed, brood, children, family, heirs, issue.

postpone *vb* adjourn, defer, delay, procrastinate, prorogue, retard.

postscript *n* addition, afterthought, appendix, supplement.

postulate *vb* assume, presuppose; beseech, entreat, solicit, supplicate. * *n* assumption, axiom, conjecture, hypothesis, proposition, speculation, supposition, theory.

posture *vb* attitudinize, pose. * *n* attitude, pose, position; condition, disposition, mood, phase, state.

pot *n* kettle, pan, saucepan, skillet; can, cup, mug, tankard; crock, jar, jug.

potency *n* efficacy, energy, force, intensity, might, power, strength, vigour; authority, control, influence, sway.

potent *adj* efficacious, forceful, forcible, intense, powerful, strong, virile; able, authoritative, capable, efficient, mighty, puissant, strong; cogent, influential.

potentate *n* emperor, king, monarch, prince, sovereign, ruler.

potential *adj* able, capable, inherent, latent, possible. * *n* ability, capability, dynamic, possibility, potentiality, power.

pother *vb* beset, bewilder, confound, confuse, embarrass, harass, perplex, pose, puzzle, tease. * *n* bustle, commotion, confusion, disturbance, flutter, fuss, huddle, hurly-burly, rumpus, tumult, turbulence, turmoil.

pound[1] *vb* beat, strike, thump; bray, bruise, comminute, crush, levigate, pulverize, triturate; confound, coop, enclose, impound.

pound[2] *n* enclosure, fold, pen.

pour *vb* cascade, emerge, flood, flow, gush, issue, rain, shower, stream.

pouting *adj* bad-tempered, cross, ill-humoured, moody, morose, sulky, sullen.

poverty *n* destitution, difficulties, distress, impecuniosity, impecuniousness, indigence, necessity, need, neediness, penury, privation, straits, want; beggary, mendicancy, pauperism, pennilessness; dearth, jejuneness, lack, scantiness, sparingness, meagreness; exiguity, paucity, poorness, smallness; humbleness, inferiority, lowliness; barrenness, sterility, unfruitfulness, unproductiveness.

power *n* ability, ableness, capability, cogency, competency, efficacy, faculty, might, potency, validity, talent; energy, force, strength, virtue; capacity, susceptibility; endowment, faculty, gift, talent; ascendancy, authoritativeness, authority, carte blanche, command, control, domination, dominion, government, influence, omnipotence, predominance, prerogative, pressure, proxy, puissance, rule, sovereignty, sway, warrant; governor, monarch, potentate, ruler, sovereign; army, host, troop.

powerful *adj* mighty, potent, puissant; able-bodied, herculean, muscular, nervous, robust, sinewy, strong, sturdy, vigorous, vivid; able, commanding, dominating, forceful, forcible, overpowering; cogent, effective, effectual, efficacious, efficient, energetic, influential, operative, valid.

practicable *adj* achievable, attainable, bearable, feasible, performable, possible, workable; operative, passable, penetrable.

practical *adj* hardheaded, matter-of-fact, pragmatic, pragmatical; able, experienced, practised, proficient, qualified, trained, skilled, thoroughbred, versed; effective, useful, virtual, workable.

practice *n* custom, habit, manner, method, repetition; procedure, usage, use; application, drill, exercise, pursuit; action, acts, behaviour, conduct, dealing, proceeding.

practise *vb* apply, do, exercise, follow, observe, perform, perpetrate, pursue.

practised *adj* able, accomplished, experienced, instructed, practical, proficient, qualified, skilled, thoroughbred, trained, versed.

pragmatic *adj* impertinent, intermeddling, interfering, intrusive, meddlesome, meddling, obtrusive, officious, over-busy; earthy, hard-headed, matter-of-fact, practical, pragmatical, realistic, sensible, stolid.

praise *vb* approbate, acclaim, applaud, approve, commend; celebrate, compliment, eulogize, extol, flatter, laud; adore, bless, exalt, glorify, magnify, worship. * *n* acclaim, approbation, approval, commendation; encomium, eulogy, glorification, laud, laudation, panegyric; exaltation, extolling, glorification, homage, tribute, worship; celebrity, distinction, fame, glory, honour, renown; desert, merit, praiseworthiness.

praiseworthy *adj* commendable, creditable, good, laudable, meritorious.

prank *n* antic, caper, escapade, frolic, gambol, trick.

prate *vb* babble, chatter, gabble, jabber, palaver, prattle, tattle. * *n* chatter, gabble, nonsense, palaver, prattle, twaddle.

pray *vb* ask, beg, beseech, conjure, entreat, implore, importune, invoke, petition, request, solicit, supplicate.

prayer *n* beseeching, entreaty, imploration, petition, request, solicitation, suit, supplication; adoration, devotion(s), litany, invocation, orison, praise, suffrage.

preach *vb* declare, deliver, proclaim, pronounce, publish; inculcate, press, teach, urge; exhort, lecture, moralize, sermonize.

preamble *n* foreword, introduction, preface, prelude, prologue.

precarious *adj* critical, doubtful, dubious, equivocal, hazardous, insecure, perilous, unassured, riskful, risky, uncertain, unsettled, unstable, unsteady.

precaution *n* care, caution, circumspection, foresight, forethought, providence, prudence, safeguard, wariness; anticipation, premonition, provision.

precautionary *adj* preservative, preventative, provident.

precede *vb* antedate, forerun, head, herald, introduce, lead, utter.

precedence *n* advantage, antecedence, lead, pre-eminence, preference, priority, superiority, supremacy.

precedent *n* antecedent, authority, custom, example, instance, model, pattern, procedure, standard, usage.

precept *n* behest, bidding, canon, charge, command, commandment, decree, dictate, edict, injunction, instruction, law, mandate, ordinance, ordination, order, regulation; direction, doctrine, maxim, principle, teaching, rubric, rule.

preceptor *n* instructor, lecturer, master, pedagogue, professor, schoolteacher, teacher, tutor.

precinct *n* border, bound, boundary, confine, environs, frontier, enclosure, limit, list, march, neighbourhood, purlieus, term, terminus; area, district.

precious *adj* costly, inestimable, invaluable, priceless, prized, valuable; adored, beloved, cherished, darling, dear, idolized, treasured; fastidious, overnice, overrefined, precise.

precipice *n* bluff, cliff, crag, steep.

precipitate *vb* advance, accelerate, dispatch, expedite, forward, further, hasten, hurry, plunge, press, quicken, speed. * *adj* hasty, hurried, headlong, impetuous, indiscreet, overhasty, rash, reckless; abrupt, sudden, violent.

precipitous *adj* abrupt, cliffy, craggy, perpendicular, uphill, sheer, steep.

precise *adj* accurate, correct, definite, distinct, exact, explicit, express, nice, pointed, severe, strict, unequivocal, well-defined; careful, scrupulous; ceremonious, finical, formal, prim, punctilious, rigid, starched, stiff.

precision *n* accuracy, correctness, definiteness, distinctness, exactitude, exactness, nicety, preciseness.

preclude *vb* bar, check, debar, hinder, inhibit, obviate, prevent, prohibit, restrain, stop.

precocious *adj* advanced, forward, overforward, premature.

preconcert *vb* concoct, prearrange, predetermine, premeditate, prepare.

precursor *n* antecedent, cause, forerunner, predecessor; harbinger, herald, messenger, pioneer; omen, presage, sign.

precursory *adj* antecedent, anterior, forerunning, precedent, preceding, previous, prior; initiatory, introductory, precursive, prefatory, preliminary, prelusive, prelusory, premonitory, preparatory, prognosticative.

predatory *adj* greedy, pillaging, plundering, predacious, rapacious, ravaging, ravenous, voracious.

predestination *n* doom, fate, foredoom, foreordainment, foreordination, necessity, predetermination, preordination.

predicament *n* attitude, case, condition, plight, position, posture, situation, state; corner, dilemma, emergency, exigency, fix, hole, impasse, mess, pass, pinch, push, quandary, scrape.

predict *vb* augur, betoken, bode, divine, forebode, forecast, foredoom, foresee, forespeak, foretell, foretoken, forewarn, portend, prognosticate, prophesy, read, signify, soothsay.

predilection *n* bent, bias, desire, fondness, inclination, leaning, liking, love, partiality, predisposition, preference, prejudice, prepossession.

predisposition *n* aptitude, bent, bias, disposition, inclination, leaning, proclivity, proneness, propensity, willingness.

predominant *adj* ascendant, controlling, dominant, overruling, prevailing, prevalent, reigning, ruling, sovereign, supreme.

predominate *vb* dominate, preponderate, prevail, rule.

pre-eminent *adj* chief, conspicuous, consummate, controlling, distinguished, excellent, excelling, paramount, peerless, predominant, renowned, superior, supreme, surpassing, transcendent, unequalled.

preface *vb* begin, introduce, induct, launch, open, precede. * *n* exordium, foreword, induction, introduction, preamble, preliminary, prelude, prelusion, premise, proem, prologue, prolusion.

prefatory *adj* antecedent, initiative, introductory, precursive, precursory, preliminary, prelusive, prelusory, preparatory, proemial.

prefer *vb* address, offer, present, proffer, tender; advance, elevate, promote, raise; adopt, choose, elect, fancy, pick, select, wish.

preference *n* advancement, choice, election, estimation, precedence, priority, selection.

preferment *n* advancement, benefice, dignity, elevation, exaltation, promotion.

pregnant *adj* big, enceinte, parturient; fraught, full, important, replete, significant, weighty; fecund, fertile, fruitful, generative, potential, procreant, procreative, productive, prolific.

prejudice *vb* bias, incline, influence, turn, warp; damage, diminish, hurt, impair, injure. * *n* bias, intolerance, partiality, preconception, predilection, prejudgement, prepossession, unfairness; damage, detriment, disadvantage, harm, hurt, impairment, injury, loss, mischief.

prejudiced *adj* biased, bigoted, influenced, one-sided, partial, partisan, unfair.

preliminary *adj* antecedent, initiatory, introductory, precedent, precursive, precursory, prefatory, prelusive, prelusory, preparatory, previous, prior, proemial. * *n* beginning, initiation, introduction, opening, preamble, preface, prelude, start.

prelude *n* introduction, opening, overture, prelusion, preparation, voluntary; exordium, preamble, preface, preliminary, proem.

premature *adj* hasty, ill-considered, precipitate, unmatured, unprepared, unripe, unseasonable, untimely.

premeditation *n* deliberation, design, forethought, intention, prearrangement, predetermination, purpose.

premise *vb* introduce, preamble, preface, prefix. * *n* affirmation, antecedent, argument, assertion, assumption, basis, foundation, ground, hypothesis, position, premiss, presupposition, proposition, support, thesis, theorem.

premium *n* bonus, bounty, encouragement, fee, gift, guerdon, meed, payment, prize, recompense, remuneration, reward; appreciation, enhancement.

premonition *n* caution, foreboding, foreshadowing, forewarning, indication, omen, portent, presage, presentiment, sign, warning.

preoccupied *adj* absent, absentminded, abstracted, dreaming, engrossed, inadvertent, inattentive, lost, musing, unobservant.

prepare *vb* adapt, adjust, fit, qualify; arrange, concoct, fabricate, make, order, plan, procure, provide.

preponderant *adj* outweighing, overbalancing, preponderating.

prepossessing *adj* alluring, amiable, attractive, bewitching, captivating, charming, engaging, fascinating, inviting, taking, winning.

preposterous *adj* absurd, excessive, exorbitant, extravagant, foolish, improper, irrational, monstrous, nonsensical, perverted, ridiculous, unfit, unreasonable, wrong.

prerogative *n* advantage, birthright, claim, franchise, immunity, liberty, privilege, right.

presage *vb* divine, forebode; augur, betoken, bode, foreshadow, foretell, foretoken, indicate, portend, predict, prognosticate, prophesy, signify, soothsay. * *n* augury, auspice, boding, foreboding, foreshowing, indication, omen, portent, prognostication, sign, token; foreknowledge, precognition, prediction, premonition, presentiment, prophecy.

prescribe *vb* advocate, appoint; command, decree, dictate, direct, enjoin, establish, institute, ordain, order.

presence *n* attendance, company, inhabitance, inhabitancy, nearness, neighbourhood, occupancy, propinquity, proximity, residence, ubiquity, vicinity; air, appearance, carriage, demeanour, mien, personality.

present[1] *adj* near; actual, current, existing, happening, immediate, instant, living; available, quick, ready; attentive, favourable. * *n* now, time being, today.

present[2] *n* benefaction, boon, donation, favour, gift, grant, gratuity, largesse, offering.

present[3] *vb* introduce, nominate; exhibit, offer; bestow, confer, give, grant; deliver, hand; advance, express, prefer, proffer, tender.

presentiment *n* anticipation, apprehension, foreboding, forecast, foretaste, forethought, prescience.

presently *adv* anon, directly, forthwith, immediately, shortly, soon.

preservation *n* cherishing, conservation, curing, maintenance, protection, support; safety, salvation, security; integrity, keeping, soundness.

preserve *vb* defend, guard, keep, protect, rescue, save, secure, shield; maintain, uphold, sustain, support; conserve, economize, husband, retain. * *n* comfit, compote, confection, confiture, conserve, jam, jelly, marmalade, sweetmeat; enclosure, warren.

preside *vb* control, direct, govern, manage, officiate.

press *vb* compress, crowd, crush, squeeze; flatten, iron, smooth; clasp, embrace, hug; force, compel, constrain; emphasize, enforce, enjoin, inculcate, stress, urge; hasten, hurry, push, rush; crowd, throng; entreat, importune, solicit. * *n* crowd, crush, multitude, throng; hurry, pressure, urgency; case, closet, cupboard, repository.

pressing *adj* constraining, critical, distressing, imperative, importunate, persistent, serious, urgent, vital.

pressure *n* compressing, crushing, squeezing; influence, force; compulsion, exigency, hurry, persuasion, press, stress, urgency; affliction, calamity, difficulty, distress, embarrassment, grievance, oppression, straits; impression, stamp.

prestidigitation *n* conjuring, juggling, legerdemain, sleight-of-hand.

prestige *n* credit, distinction, importance, influence, reputation, weight.

presume *vb* anticipate, apprehend, assume, believe, conjecture, deduce, expect, infer, surmise, suppose, think; consider, presuppose; dare, undertake, venture.

presumption *n* anticipation, assumption, belief, concession, conclusion, condition, conjecture, deduction, guess, hypothesis, inference, opinion, supposition, understanding; arrogance, assurance, audacity, boldness, brass, effrontery, forwardness, haughtiness, presumptuousness; probability.

presumptuous *adj* arrogant, assuming, audacious, bold, brash, forward, irreverent, insolent, intrusive, presuming; foolhardy, overconfident, rash.

pretence *n* affectation, cloak, colour, disguise, mask, semblance, show, simulation, veil, window-dressing; excuse, evasion, fabrication, feigning, makeshift, pretext, sham, subterfuge; claim, pretension.

pretend *vb* affect, counterfeit, deem, dissemble, fake, falsify, feign, sham, simulate; act, imagine, lie, profess; aspire, claim.

pretension *n* assertion, assumption, claim, demand, pretence; affectation, airs, conceit, ostentation, pertness, pretentiousness, priggishness, vanity.

pretentious *adj* affected, assuming, conceited, conspicuous, ostentatious, presuming, priggish, showy, tawdry, unnatural, vain.

preternatural *adj* abnormal, anomalous, extraordinary, inexplicable, irregular, miraculous, mysterious, odd, peculiar, strange, unnatural.

pretext *n* affectation, appearance, blind, cloak, colour, guise, mask, pretence, semblance, show, simulation, veil; excuse, justification, plea, vindication.

pretty *adj* attractive, beautiful, bonny, comely, elegant, fair, handsome, neat, pleasing, trim; affected, foppish. * *adv* fairly, moderately, quite, rather, somewhat.

prevail *vb* overcome, succeed, triumph, win; obtain, predominate, preponderate, reign, rule.

prevailing *adj* controlling, dominant, effectual, efficacious, general, influential, operative, overruling, persuading, predominant, preponderant, prevalent, ruling, successful.

prevalent *adj* ascendant, compelling, efficacious, governing, predominant, prevailing, successful, superior; extensive, general, rife, widespread.

prevaricate *vb* cavil, deviate, dodge, equivocate, evade, palter, pettifog, quibble, shift, shuffle, tergiversate.

prevent *vb* bar, check, debar, deter, forestall, help, hinder, impede, inhibit, intercept, interrupt, obstruct, obviate, preclude, prohibit, restrain, save, stop, thwart.

prevention *n* anticipation, determent, deterrence, deterrent, frustration, hindrance, interception, interruption, obstruction, preclusion, prohibition, restriction, stoppage.

previous *adj* antecedent, anterior, earlier, foregoing, foregone, former, precedent, preceding, prior.

prey *vb* devour, eat, feed on, live off; exploit, intimidate, terrorize; burden, distress, haunt, oppress, trouble, worry. * *n* booty, loot, pillage, plunder, prize, rapine, spoil; food, game, kill, quarry, victim; depredation, ravage.

price *vb* assess, estimate, evaluate, rate, value. * *n* amount, cost, expense, outlay, value; appraisal, charge, estimation, excellence, figure, rate, quotation, valuation, value, worth; compensation, guerdon, recompense, return, reward.

priceless *adj* dear, expensive, precious, inestimable, invaluable, valuable; amusing, comic, droll, funny, humorous, killing, rich.

prick *vb* perforate, pierce, puncture, stick; drive, goad, impel, incite, spur, urge; cut, hurt, mark, pain, sting, wound; hasten, post, ride. * *n* mark, perforation, point, puncture; prickle, sting, wound.

pride *vb* boast, brag, crow, preen, revel in. * *n* conceit, egotism, self-complacency, self-esteem, self-exaltation, self-importance, self-sufficiency, vanity; arrogance, assumption, disdain, haughtiness, hauteur, insolence, loftiness, lordliness, pomposity, presumption, superciliousness, vainglory; decorum, dignity,

elevation, self-respect; decoration, glory, ornament, show, splendour.

priest *n* churchman, clergyman, divine, ecclesiastic, minister, pastor, presbyter.

prim *adj* demure, formal, nice, precise, prudish, starch, starched, stiff, strait-laced.

primary *adj* aboriginal, earliest, first, initial, original, prime, primitive, primeval, primordial, pristine; chief, main, principal; basic, elementary, fundamental, preparatory: radical.

prime[1] *adj* aboriginal, basic, first, initial, original, primal, primary, primeval, primitive, primordial, pristine; chief, foremost, highest, leading, main, paramount, principal; blooming, early; capital, cardinal, dominant, predominant; excellent, first-class, first-rate, optimal, optimum, quintessential, superlative; beginning, opening. * *n* beginning, dawn, morning, opening; spring, springtime, youth; bloom, cream, flower, height, heyday, optimum, perfection, quintessence, zenith.

prime[2] *vb* charge, load, prepare, undercoat; coach, groom, train, tutor.

primeval *adj* original, primitive, primordial, pristine.

primitive *adj* aboriginal, first, fundamental, original, primal, primary, prime, primitive, primordial, pristine; ancient, antiquated, crude, old-fashioned, quaint, simple, uncivilized, unsophisticated.

prince *n* monarch, potentate, ruler, sovereign; dauphin, heir apparent, infant; chief, leader, potentate.

princely *adj* imperial, regal, royal; august, generous, grand, liberal, magnanimous, magnificent, majestic, munificent, noble, pompous, splendid, superb, titled; dignified, elevated, high-minded, lofty, noble, stately.

principal *adj* capital, cardinal, chief, essential, first, foremost, highest, leading, main, pre-eminent, prime. * *n* chief, head, leader; head teacher, master.

principally *adv* chiefly, essentially, especially, mainly, particularly.

principle *n* cause, fountain, fountainhead, groundwork, mainspring, nature, origin, source, spring; basis, constituent, element, essence, substratum; assumption, axiom, law, maxim, postulation; doctrine, dogma, impulse, maxim, opinion, precept, rule, tenet, theory; conviction, ground, motive, reason; equity, goodness, honesty, honour, incorruptibility, integrity, justice, probity, rectitude, righteousness, trustiness, truth, uprightness, virtue, worth; faculty, power.

prink *vb* adorn, deck, decorate; preen, primp, spruce.

print *vb* engrave, impress, imprint, mark, stamp; issue, publish. * *n* book, periodical, publication; copy, engraving, photograph, picture; characters, font, fount, lettering, type, typeface.

prior *adj* antecedent, anterior, earlier, foregoing, precedent, preceding, precursory, previous, superior.

priority *n* antecedence, anteriority, precedence, pre-eminence, pre-existence, superiority.

priory *n* abbey, cloister, convent, monastery, nunnery.

prison *n* confinement, dungeon, gaol, jail, keep, lockup, penitentiary, reformatory; can, clink, cooler, jug.

pristine *adj* ancient, earliest, first, former, old, original, primary, primeval, primitive, primordial.

privacy *n* concealment, secrecy; retirement, retreat, seclusion, solitude.

private *adj* retired, secluded, sequestrated, solitary; individual, own, particular, peculiar, personal, special, unofficial; confidential, privy; clandestine, concealed, hidden, secret. * *n* GI, soldier, tommy.

privation *n* bereavement, deprivation, dispossession, loss; destitution, distress, indigence, necessity, need, want; absence, negation; degradation.

privilege *n* advantage, charter, claim, exemption, favour, franchise, immunity, leave, liberty, licence, permission, prerogative, right.

privy *adj* individual, particular, peculiar, personal, private, special; clandestine, secret; retired, sequestrated.

prize[1] *vb* appreciate, cherish, esteem, treasure, value.

prize[2] *adj* best, champion, first-rate, outstanding, winning. * *n* guerdon, honours, meed, premium, reward; cup, decoration, medal, laurels, palm, trophy; booty, capture, lot, plunder, spoil; advantage, gain, privilege.

probability *n* chance, prospect, likelihood, presumption; appearance, credibility, credibleness, likeliness, verisimilitude.

probable *adj* apparent, credible, likely, presumable, reasonable.

probably *adv* apparently, likely, maybe, perchance, perhaps, presumably, possibly, seemingly.

probation *n* essay, examination, ordeal, proof, test, trial; novitiate.

probe *vb* examine, explore, fathom, investigate, measure, prove, scrutinize, search, sift, sound, test, verify. * *n* examination, exploration, inquiry, investigation, scrutiny, study.

probity *n* candour, conscientiousness, equity, fairness, faith, goodness, honesty, honour, incorruptibility, integrity, justice, loyalty, morality, principle, rectitude, righteousness, sincerity, soundness, trustworthiness, truth, truthfulness, uprightness, veracity, virtue, worth.

problem *adj* difficult, intractable, uncontrollable, unruly. * *n* dilemma, dispute, doubt, enigma, exercise, proposition, puzzle, riddle, theorem.

problematic *adj* debatable, disputable, doubtful, dubious, enigmatic, problematical, puzzling, questionable, suspicious, uncertain, unsettled.

procedure *n* conduct, course, custom, management, method, operation, policy, practice, process; act, action, deed, measure, performance, proceeding, step, transaction.

proceed *vb* advance, continue, go, pass, progress; accrue, arise, come, emanate, ensue, flow, follow, issue, originate, result, spring.

proceeds *npl* balance, earnings, effects, gain, income, net, produce, products, profits, receipts, returns, yield.

process *vb* advance, deal with, fulfil, handle, progress; alter, convert, refine, transform. * *n* advance, course, progress, train; action, conduct, management, measure, mode, operation, performance, practice, procedure, proceeding, step, transaction, way; action, case, suit, trial; outgrowth, projection, protuberance.

procession *n* cavalcade, cortege, file, march, parade, retinue, train.

proclaim *vb* advertise, announce, blazon, broach, broadcast, circulate, cry, declare, herald, promulgate, publish, trumpet; ban, outlaw, proscribe.

proclamation *n* advertisement, announcement, blazon, declaration, promulgation, publication; ban, decree, edict, manifesto, ordinance.

proclivity *n* bearing, bent, bias, determination, direction, disposition, drift, inclination, leaning, predispo-

sition, proneness, propensity, tendency, turn; aptitude, facility, readiness.

procrastinate *vb* adjourn, defer, delay, postpone, prolong, protract, retard; neglect, omit; lag, loiter.

procrastination *n* delay, dilatoriness, postponement, protraction, slowness, tardiness.

procreate *vb* beget, breed, engender, generate, produce, propagate.

procurable *adj* acquirable, compassable, obtainable.

procurator *n* agent, attorney, deputy, proctor, proxy, representative, solicitor.

procure *vb* acquire, gain, get, obtain; cause, compass, contrive, effect.

procurer *n* bawd, pander, pimp.

prodigal *adj* abundant, dissipated, excessive, extravagant, generous, improvident, lavish, profuse, reckless, squandering, thriftless, unthrifty, wasteful. * *n* spendthrift, squanderer, waster, wastrel.

prodigality *n* excess, extravagance, lavishness, profusion, squandering, unthriftiness, waste, wastefulness.

prodigious *adj* amazing, astonishing, astounding, extraordinary, marvellous, miraculous, portentous, remarkable, startling, strange, surprising, uncommon, wonderful, wondrous; enormous, huge, immense, monstrous, vast.

prodigy *n* marvel, miracle, phenomenon, portent, sign, wonder; curiosity, monster, monstrosity.

produce *vb* exhibit, show; bear, beget, breed, conceive, engender, furnish, generate, hatch, procreate, yield; accomplish, achieve, cause, create, effect, make, occasion, originate; accrue, afford, give, impart, make, render; extend, lengthen, prolong, protract; fabricate, fashion, manufacture. * *n* crop, fruit, greengrocery, harvest, product, vegetables, yield.

producer *n* creator, inventor, maker, originator; agriculturalist, farmer, greengrocer, husbandman, raiser.

product *n* crops, fruits, harvest, outcome, proceeds, produce, production, returns, yield; consequence, effect, fruit, issue, performance, production, result, work.

production *n* fruit, produce, product; construction, creation, erection, fabrication, making, performance; completion, fruition; birth, breeding, development, growth, propagation; opus, publication, work; continuation, extension, lengthening, prolongation.

productive *adj* copious, fertile, fruitful, luxuriant, plenteous, prolific, teeming; causative, constructive, creative, efficient, life-giving, producing.

proem *n* exordium, foreword, introduction, preface, prelims, prelude, prolegomena.

profane *vb* defile, desecrate, pollute, violate; abuse, debase. * *adj* blasphemous, godless, heathen, idolatrous, impious, impure, pagan, secular, temporal, unconsecrated, unhallowed, unholy, unsanctified, worldly, unspiritual; impure, polluted, unholy.

profanity *n* blasphemy, impiety, irreverence, profaneness, sacrilege.

profess *vb* acknowledge, affirm, allege, aver, avouch, avow, confess, declare, own, proclaim, state; affect, feign, pretend.

profession *n* acknowledgement, assertion, avowal, claim, declaration; avocation, evasion, pretence, pretension, protestation, representation; business, calling, employment, engagement, occupation, office, trade, vocation.

proffer *vb* offer, propose, propound, suggest, tender, volunteer. * *n* offer, proposal, suggestion, tender.

proficiency *n* advancement, forwardness, improvement; accomplishment, aptitude, competency, dexterity, mastery, skill.

proficient *adj* able, accomplished, adept, competent, conversant, dextrous, expert, finished, masterly, practised, skilled, skilful, thoroughbred, trained, qualified, well-versed. * *n* adept, expert, master, master-hand.

profit *vb* advance, benefit, gain, improve. * *n* aid, clearance, earnings, emolument, fruit, gain, lucre, produce, return; advancement, advantage, benefit, interest, perquisite, service, use, utility, weal.

profitable *adj* advantageous, beneficial, desirable, gainful, productive, useful; lucrative, remunerative.

profitless *adj* bootless, fruitless, unprofitable, useless, valueless, worthless.

profligate *adj* abandoned, corrupt, corrupted, degenerate, depraved, dissipated, dissolute, graceless, immoral, shameless, vicious, vitiated, wicked. * *n* debauchee, libertine, rake, reprobate, roué.

profound *adj* abysmal, deep, fathomless; heavy, undisturbed; erudite, learned, penetrating, sagacious, skilled; deeply felt, far-reaching, heartfelt, intense, lively, strong, touching, vivid; low, submissive; abstruse, mysterious, obscure, occult, subtle, recondite; complete, thorough.

profundity *n* deepness, depth, profoundness.

profuse *adj* abundant, bountiful, copious, excessive, extravagant, exuberant, generous, improvident, lavish, overabundant, plentiful, prodigal, wasteful.

profusion *n* abundance, bounty, copiousness, excess, exuberance, extravagance, lavishness, prodigality, profuseness, superabundance, waste.

progenitor *n* ancestor, forebear, forefather.

progeny *n* breed, children, descendants, family, issue, lineage, offshoot, offspring, posterity, race, scion, stock, young.

prognostic *adj* foreshadowing, foreshowing, foretokening. * *n* augury, foreboding, indication, omen, presage, prognostication, sign, symptom, token; foretelling, prediction, prophecy.

prognosticate *vb* foretell, predict, prophesy; augur, betoken, forebode, foreshadow, foreshow, foretoken, indicate, portend, presage.

prognostication *n* foreknowledge, foreshowing, foretelling, prediction, presage; augury, foreboding, foretoken, indication, portent, prophecy.

progress *vb* advance, continue, proceed; better, gain, improve, increase. * *n* advance, advancement, progression; course, headway, ongoing, passage; betterment, development, growth, improvement, increase, reform; circuit, procession.

prohibit *vb* debar, hamper, hinder, preclude, prevent; ban, disallow, forbid, inhibit, interdict.

prohibition *n* ban, bar, disallowance, embargo, forbiddance, inhibition, interdict, interdiction, obstruction, prevention, proscription, taboo, veto.

prohibitive *adj* forbidding, prohibiting, refraining, restrictive.

project *vb* cast, eject, fling, hurl, propel, shoot, throw; brew, concoct, contrive, design, devise, intend, plan, plot, purpose, scheme; delineate, draw, exhibit; bulge, extend, jut, protrude. * *n* contrivance, design, device, intention, plan, proposal, purpose, scheme.

projectile *n* bullet, missile, shell.

projection *n* delivery, ejection, emission, propulsion, throwing; contriving, designing, planning, scheming; bulge, extension, outshoot, process, prominence, protuberance, salience, saliency, salient, spur; delineation, map, plan.

proletarian *adj* mean, plebeian, vile, vulgar. * *n* commoner, plebeian.

proletariat *n* commonality, hoi polloi, masses, mob, plebs, working class.

prolific *adj* abundant, fertile, fruitful, generative, productive, teeming.

prolix *adj* boring, circumlocutory, discursive, diffuse, lengthy, long, long-winded, loose, prolonged, protracted, prosaic, rambling, tedious, tiresome, verbose, wordy.

prologue *n* foreword, introduction, preamble, preface, preliminary, prelude, proem.

prolong *vb* continue, extend, lengthen, protract, sustain; defer, postpone.

promenade *vb* saunter, walk. * *n* dance, stroll, walk; boulevard, esplanade, parade, walkway.

prominent *adj* convex, embossed, jutting, projecting, protuberant, raised, relieved; celebrated, conspicuous, distinguished, eminent, famous, foremost, influential, leading, main, noticeable, outstanding; conspicuous, distinctive, important, manifest, marked, principal, salient.

promiscuous *adj* confused, heterogeneous, indiscriminate, intermingled, mingled, miscellaneous, mixed; abandoned, dissipated, dissolute, immoral, licentious, loose, unchaste, wanton.

promise *vb* covenant, engage, pledge, subscribe, swear, underwrite, vow; assure, attest, guarantee, warrant; agree, bargain, engage, stipulate, undertake. * *n* agreement, assurance, contract, engagement, oath, parole, pledge, profession, undertaking, vow, word.

promising *adj* auspicious, encouraging, hopeful, likely, propitious.

promote *vb* advance, aid, assist, cultivate, encourage, further, help, promote; dignify, elevate, exalt, graduate, honour, pass, prefer, raise.

promotion *n* advancement, encouragement, furtherance; elevation, exaltation, preferment.

prompt *vb* actuate, dispose, impel, incite, incline, induce, instigate, stimulate, urge; remind; dictate, hint, influence, suggest. * *adj* active, alert, apt, quick, ready; forward, hasty; disposed, inclined, prone; early, exact, immediate, instant, precise, punctual, seasonable, timely. * *adv* apace, directly, forthwith, immediately, promptly. * *n* cue, hint, prompter, reminder, stimulus.

promptly *adv* apace, directly, expeditiously, forthwith, immediately, instantly, pronto, punctually, quickly, speedily, straightway, straightaway, summarily, swiftly.

promptness *n* activity, alertness, alacrity, promptitude, readiness, quickness.

promulgate *vb* advertise, announce, broadcast, bruit, circulate, declare, notify, proclaim, publish, spread, trumpet.

prone *adj* flat, horizontal, prostrate, recumbent; declivitous, inclined, inclining, sloping; apt, bent, disposed, inclined, predisposed, tending; eager, prompt, ready.

pronounce *vb* articulate, enunciate, frame, say, speak, utter; affirm, announce, assert, declare, deliver, state.

proof *adj* firm, fixed, impenetrable, stable, steadfast. * *n* essay, examination, ordeal, test, trial; attestation, certification, conclusion, conclusiveness, confirmation, corroboration, demonstration, evidence, ratification, substantiation, testimony, verification.

prop *vb* bolster, brace, buttress, maintain, shore, stay, support, sustain, truss, uphold. * *n* support, stay; buttress, fulcrum, pin, shore, strut.

propaganda *n* inculcation, indoctrination, promotion.

propagate *vb* continue, increase, multiply; circulate, diffuse, disseminate, extend, promote, promulgate, publish, spread, transmit; beget, breed, engender, generate, originate, procreate.

propel *vb* drive, force, impel, push, urge; cast, fling, hurl, project, throw.

propensity *n* aptitude, bent, bias, disposition, inclination, ply, proclivity, proneness, tendency.

proper *adj* individual, inherent, natural, original, particular, peculiar, special, specific; adapted, appropriate, becoming, befitting, convenient, decent, decorous, demure, fit, fitting, legitimate, meet, pertinent, respectable, right, seemly, suitable; accurate, correct, exact, fair, fastidious, formal, just, precise; actual, real.

property *n* attribute, characteristic, disposition, mark, peculiarity, quality, trait, virtue; appurtenance, assets, belongings, chattels, circumstances, effects, estate, goods, possessions, resources, wealth; ownership, possession, proprietorship, tenure; claim, copyright, interest, participation, right, title.

prophecy *n* augury, divination, forecast, foretelling, portent, prediction, premonition, presage, prognostication; exhortation, instruction, preaching.

prophesy *vb* augur, divine, foretell, predict, prognosticate.

propinquity *n* adjacency, contiguity, nearness, neighbourhood, proximity, vicinity; affinity, connection, consanguinity, kindred, relationship.

propitiate *vb* appease, atone, conciliate, intercede, mediate, pacify, reconcile, satisfy.

propitious *adj* benevolent, benign, friendly, gracious, kind, merciful; auspicious, encouraging, favourable, fortunate, happy, lucky, opportune, promising, prosperous, thriving, timely, well-disposed.

proportion *vb* adjust, graduate, regulate; form, shape. * *n* arrangement, relation; adjustment, commensuration, dimension, distribution, symmetry; extent, lot, part, portion, quota, ratio, share.

proposal *n* design, motion, offer, overture, proffer, proposition, recommendation, scheme, statement, suggestion, tender.

propose *vb* move, offer, pose, present, propound, proffer, put, recommend, state, submit, suggest, tender; design, intend, mean, purpose.

proposition *vb* accost, proffer, solicit. * *n* offer, overture, project, proposal, suggestion, tender, undertaking; affirmation, assertion, axiom, declaration, dictum, doctrine, position, postulation, predication, statement, theorem, thesis.

proprietor *n* lord, master, owner, possessor, proprietary.

propriety *n* accuracy, adaptation, appropriation, aptness, becomingness, consonance, correctness, fitness, justness, reasonableness, rightness, seemliness, suitableness; conventionality, decency, decorum, demureness, fastidiousness, formality, modesty, properness, respectability.

prorogation *n* adjournment, continuance, postponement.

prosaic *adj* commonplace, dull, flat, humdrum, matter-of-fact, pedestrian, plain, prolix, prosing, sober, stupid, tame, tedious, tiresome, unentertaining, unimaginative, uninspired, uninteresting, unromantic, vapid.

proscribe *vb* banish, doom, exile, expel, ostracize, outlaw; exclude, forbid, interdict, prohibit; censure, condemn, curse, denounce, reject.

prosecute *vb* conduct, continue, exercise, follow, persist, pursue; arraign, indict, sue, summon.

prospect *vb* explore, search, seek, survey. * *n* display, field, landscape, outlook, perspective, scene, show, sight, spectacle, survey, view, vision, vista; picture, scenery; anticipation, calculation, contemplation, expectance, expectancy, expectation, foreseeing, foresight, hope, presumption, promise, trust; likelihood, probability.

prospectus *n* announcement, conspectus, description, design, outline, plan, programme, sketch, syllabus.

prosper *vb* aid, favour, forward, help; advance, flourish, grow rich, thrive, succeed; batten, increase.

prosperity *n* affluence, blessings, happiness, felicity, good luck, success, thrift, weal, welfare, well-being; boom, heyday.

prosperous *adj* blooming, flourishing, fortunate, golden, halcyon, rich, successful, thriving; auspicious, booming, bright, favourable, good, golden, lucky, promising, propitious, providential, rosy.

prostrate *vb* demolish, destroy, fell, level, overthrow, overturn, ruin; depress, exhaust, overcome, reduce. * *adj* fallen, prostrated, prone, recumbent, supine; helpless, powerless.

prostration *n* demolition, destruction, overthrow; dejection, depression, exhaustion.

prosy *adj* prosaic, unpoetic, unpoetical; dull, flat, jejune, stupid, tedious, tiresome, unentertaining, unimaginative, uninteresting.

protect *vb* cover, defend, guard, shield; fortify, harbour, house, preserve, save, screen, secure, shelter; champion, countenance, foster, patronize.

protector *n* champion, custodian, defender, guardian, patron, warden.

protest *vb* affirm, assert, asseverate, attest, aver, avow, declare, profess, testify; demur, expostulate, object, remonstrate, repudiate. * *n* complaint, declaration, disapproval, objection, protestation.

prototype *n* archetype, copy, exemplar, example, ideal, model, original, paradigm, precedent, protoplast, type.

protract *vb* continue, extend, lengthen, prolong; defer, delay, postpone.

protrude *vb* beetle, bulge, extend, jut, project.

protuberance *n* bulge, bump, elevation, excrescence, hump, lump, process, projection, prominence, roundness, swelling, tumour.

proud *adj* assuming, conceited, contended, egotistical, overweening, self-conscious, self-satisfied, vain; arrogant, boastful, haughty, high-spirited, highly strung, imperious, lofty, lordly, presumptuous, supercilious, uppish, vainglorious.

prove *vb* ascertain, conform, demonstrate, establish, evidence, evince, justify, manifest, show, substantiate, sustain, verify; assay, check, examine, experiment, test, try.

proverb *n* adage, aphorism, apothegm, byword, dictum, maxim, precept, saw, saying.

proverbial *adj* acknowledged, current, notorious, unquestioned.

provide vb arrange, collect, plan, prepare, procure; gather, keep, store; afford, contribute, feed, furnish, produce, stock, supply, yield; cater, purvey; agree, bargain, condition, contract, covenant, engage, stipulate.

provided, providing conj granted, if, supposing.

provident adj careful, cautious, considerate, discreet, farseeing, forecasting, forehanded, foreseeing, prudent; economical, frugal, thrifty.

province n district, domain, region, section, territory, tract; colony, dependency; business, calling, capacity, charge, department, duty, employment, function, office, part, post, sphere; department, division, jurisdiction.

provincial adj annexed, appendant, outlying; bucolic, countrified, rude, rural, rustic, unpolished, unrefined; insular, local, narrow. * n peasant, rustic, yokel.

provision n anticipation, providing; arrangement, care, preparation, readiness; equipment, fund, grist, hoard, reserve, resources, stock, store, supplies, supply; clause, condition, prerequisite, proviso, reservation, stipulation.

provisions npl eatables, fare, food, provender, supplies, viands, victuals.

proviso n clause, condition, provision, stipulation.

provocation n incentive, incitement, provocativeness, stimulant, stimulus; affront, indignity, insult, offence; angering, vexation.

provoke vb animate, arouse, awaken, excite, impel, incite, induce, inflame, instigate, kindle, move, rouse, stimulate; affront, aggravate, anger, annoy, chafe, enrage, exacerbate, exasperate, incense, infuriate, irritate, nettle, offend, pique, vex; cause, elicit, evoke, instigate, occasion, produce, promote.

provoking adj aggravating, annoying, exasperating, irritating, offensive, tormenting, vexatious, vexing.

prowess n bravery, courage, daring, fearlessness, gallantry, heroism, intrepidity, valour; aptitude, dexterity, expertness, facility.

proximity n adjacency, contiguity, nearness, neighbourhood, propinquity, vicinage, vicinity.

proxy n agent, attorney, commissioner, delegate, deputy, lieutenant, representative, substitute.

prudence n carefulness, caution, circumspection, common sense, considerateness, discretion, forecast, foresight, judgment, judiciousness, policy, providence, sense, tact, wariness, wisdom.

prudent adj cautious, careful, circumspect, considerate, discreet, foreseeing, heedful, judicious, politic, provident, prudential, wary, wise.

prudish adj coy, demure, modest, precise, prim, reserved, strait-laced.

prune vb abbreviate, clip, cut, dock, lop, thin, trim; dress, preen.

prurient adj covetous, craving, desiring, hankering, itching, lascivious, libidinous, longing, lustful.

pry vb examine, ferret, inspect, investigate, peep, peer, question, scrutinize, search; force, lever, prise.

public adj civil, common, countrywide, general, national, political, state; known, notorious, open, popular, published, well-known. * n citizens, community, country, everyone, general public, masses, nation, people, population; audience, buyers, following, supporters.

publication n advertisement, announcement, disclosure, divulgement, divulgence, proclamation, promulgation, report; edition, issue, issuance, printing.

publicity n daylight, currency, limelight, notoriety, spotlight; outlet, vent.

publish vb advertise, air, bruit, announce, blaze, blazon, broach, communicate, declare, diffuse, disclose, disseminate, impart, placard, post, proclaim, promulgate, reveal, tell, utter, vent, ventilate.

pucker vb cockle, contract, corrugate, crease, crinkle, furrow, gather, pinch, purse, shirr, wrinkle. * n crease, crinkle, fold, furrow, wrinkle.

puerile adj boyish, childish, infantile, juvenile, youthful; foolish, frivolous, idle, nonsensical, petty, senseless, silly, simple, trifling, trivial, weak.

puffy adj distended, swelled, swollen, tumid, turgid; bombastic, extravagant, inflated, pompous.

pugnacious adj belligerent, bellicose, contentious, fighting, irascible, irritable, petulant, quarrelsome.

puissant adj forcible, mighty, potent, powerful, strong.

pull vb drag, draw, haul, row, tow, tug; cull, extract, gather, pick, pluck; detach, rend, tear, wrest. * n pluck, shake, tug, twitch, wrench; contest, struggle; attraction, gravity, magnetism; graft, influence, power.

pulsate vb beat, palpitate, pant, throb, thump, vibrate.

pulverize vb bruise, comminute, grind, levigate, triturate.

pun vb assonate, alliterate, play on words. * n assonance, alliteration, clinch, conceit, double-meaning, paranomasia, play on words, quip, rhyme, witticism, wordplay.

punctilious adj careful, ceremonious, conscientious, exact, formal, nice, particular, precise, punctual, scrupulous, strict.

punctual adj exact, nice, precise, punctilious; early, prompt, ready, regular, seasonable, timely.

puncture vb bore, penetrate, perforate, pierce, prick. * n bite, hole, sting, wound.

pungent adj acid, acrid, biting, burning, caustic, hot, mordant, penetrating, peppery, piercing, piquant, prickling, racy, salty, seasoned, sharp, smart, sour, spicy, stimulating, stinging; acute, acrimonious, cutting, distressing, irritating, keen, painful, peevish, poignant, pointed, satirical, severe, tart, trenchant, waspish.

punish vb beat, castigate, chasten, chastise, correct, discipline, flog, lash, scourge, torture, whip.

punishment n castigation, chastening, chastisement, correction, discipline, infliction, retribution, scourging, trial; judgment, nemesis, penalty.

puny adj feeble, inferior, weak; dwarf, dwarfish, insignificant, diminutive, little, petty, pygmy, small, stunted, tiny, underdeveloped, undersized.

pupil n beginner, catechumen, disciple, learner, neophyte, novice, scholar, student, tyro.

pupillage n minority, nonage, tutelage, wardship.

puppet n doll, image, manikin, marionette; cat's-paw, pawn, tool.

purchase vb buy, gain, get, obtain, pay for, procure; achieve, attain, earn, win. * n acquisition, buy, gain, possession, property; advantage, foothold, grasp, hold, influence, support.

pure adj clean, clear, fair, immaculate, spotless, stainless, unadulterated, unalloyed, unblemished, uncorrupted, undefiled, unpolluted, unspotted, unstained, unsullied, untainted, untarnished; chaste, continent, guileless, guiltless, holy, honest, incorrupt, innocent, modest, sincere, true, uncorrupt, upright, virgin, virtuous; genuine, perfect, real, simple, true, unadorned; absolute, essential, mere, sheer, thorough; classic, classical.

purge *vb* cleanse, clear, purify; clarify, defecate, evacuate; deterge, scour; absolve, pardon, shrive. * *n* elimination, eradication, expulsion, removal, suppression; cathartic, emetic, enema, laxative, physic.

purify *vb* clean, cleanse, clear, depurate, expurgate, purge, refine, wash; clarify, fine.

puritanical *adj* ascetic, narrow-minded, overscrupulous, prim, prudish, rigid, severe, strait-laced, strict.

purity *n* clearness, fineness; cleanness, correctness, faultlessness, immaculacy, immaculateness; guilelessness, guiltlessness, holiness, honesty, innocence, integrity, piety, simplicity, truth, uprightness, virtue; excellence, genuineness; homogeneity, simpleness; chasteness, chastity, continence, modesty, pudency, virginity.

purlieus *npl* borders, bounds, confines, environs, limits, neighbourhood, outskirts, precincts, suburbs, vicinage, vicinity.

purloin *vb* abstract, crib, filch, pilfer, rob, steal, thieve.

purport *vb* allege, assert, claim, maintain, pretend, profess; denote, express, imply, indicate, mean, signify, suggest. * *n* bearing, current, design, drift, gist, import, intent, meaning, scope, sense, significance, signification, spirit, tendency, tenor.

purpose *vb* contemplate, design, intend, mean, meditate; determine, resolve. * *n* aim, design, drift, end, intent, intention, object, resolution, resolve, view; plan, project; meaning, purport, sense; consequence, effect.

pursue *vb* chase, dog, follow, hound, hunt, shadow, track; conduct, continue, cultivate, maintain, practise, prosecute; seek, strive; accompany, attend.

pursuit *n* chase, hunt, race; conduct, cultivation, practice, prosecution, pursuance; avocation, calling, business, employment, fad, hobby, occupation, vocation.

pursy *adj* corpulent, fat, fleshy, plump, podgy, pudgy, short, thick; short-breathed, short-winded; opulent, rich.

purview *n* body, compass, extent, limit, reach, scope, sphere, view.

push *vb* elbow, crowd, hustle, impel, jostle, shoulder, shove, thrust; advance, drive, hurry, propel, urge; importune, persuade, tease. * *n* pressure, thrust; determination, perseverance; emergency, exigency, extremity, pinch, strait, test, trial; assault, attack, charge, endeavour, onset.

pusillanimous *adj* chicken, chicken-hearted, cowardly, dastardly, faint-hearted, feeble, lily-livered, mean-spirited, spiritless, timid, recreant, timorous, weak.

pustule *n* abscess, blain, blister, blotch, boil, fester, gathering, pimple, sore, ulcer.

put *vb* bring, collocate, deposit, impose, lay, locate, place, set; enjoin, impose, inflict, levy; offer, present, propose, state; compel, constrain, force, oblige; entice, incite, induce, urge; express, utter.

putative *adj* deemed, reckoned, reported, reputed, supposed.

putrefy *vb* corrupt, decay, decompose, fester, rot, stink.

putrid *adj* corrupt, decayed, decomposed, fetid, rank, rotten, stinking.

puzzle *vb* bewilder, confound, confuse, embarrass, gravel, mystify, nonplus, perplex, pose, stagger; complicate, entangle.* *n* conundrum, enigma, labyrinth, maze, paradox, poser, problem, riddle; bewilderment, complication, confusion, difficulty, dilemma, embarrassment, mystification, perplexity, point, quandary, question.

pygmy *adj* diminutive, dwarf, dwarfish, Lilliputian, little, midget, stunted, tiny. * *n* dwarf, Lilliputian, midget.

Q

quack[1] *vb, n* cackle, cry, squeak.

quack[2] *adj* fake, false, sham. * *n* charlatan, empiric, humbug, impostor, mountebank, pretender.

quadruple *adj* fourfold, quadruplicate.

quagmire *n* bog, fen, marsh, morass, slough, swamp; difficulty, impasse, muddle, predicament.

quail *vb* blench, cower, droop, faint, flinch, shrink, tremble.

quaint *adj* antiquated, antique, archaic, curious, droll, extraordinary, fanciful, odd, old-fashioned, queer, singular, uncommon, unique, unusual; affected, fantastic, far-fetched, whimsical; artful, ingenious.

quake *vb* quiver, shake, shiver, shudder; move, vibrate. * *n* earthquake, shake, shudder.

qualification *n* ability, accomplishment, capability, competency, eligibility, fitness, suitability; condition, exception, limitation, modification, proviso, restriction, stipulation; abatement, allowance, diminution, mitigation.

qualified *adj* accomplished, certificated, certified, competent, fitted, equipped, licensed, trained; adapted, circumscribed, conditional, limited, modified, restricted.

qualify *vb* adapt, capacitate, empower, entitle, equip, fit; limit, modify, narrow, restrain, restrict; abate, assuage, ease, mitigate, moderate, reduce, soften; diminish, modulate, temper, regulate, vary.

quality *n* affection, attribute, characteristic, colour, distinction, feature, flavour, mark, nature, peculiarity, property, singularity, timbre, tinge, trait; character, condition, disposition, humour, mood, temper; brand, calibre, capacity, class, description, excellence, grade, kind, rank, sort, stamp, standing, station, status, virtue; aristocracy, gentility, gentry, noblesse, nobility.

qualm *n* agony, pang, throe; nausea, queasiness, sickness; compunction, remorse, uneasiness, twinge.

quandary *n* bewilderment, difficulty, dilemma, doubt, embarrassment, perplexity, pickle, plight, predicament, problem, puzzle, strait, uncertainty.

quantity *n* content, extent, greatness, measure, number, portion, share, size; aggregate, batch, amount, bulk, lot, mass, quantum, store, sum, volume; duration, length.

quarrel *vb* altercate, bicker, brawl, carp, cavil, clash, contend, differ, dispute, fight, jangle, jar, scold, scuffle, spar, spat, squabble, strive, wrangle. * *n* altercation, affray, bickering, brawl, breach, breeze, broil, clash, contention, contest, controversy, difference, disagreement, discord, dispute, dissension, disturbance, feud, fight, fray, imbroglio, jar, miff, misunderstanding, quarrelling, row, rupture, spat, squabble, strife, tiff, tumult, variance, wrangle.

quarrelsome *adj* argumentative, choleric, combative, contentious, cross, discordant, disputatious, dissen-

tious, fiery, irascible, irritable, petulant, pugnacious, ugly, wranglesome.

quarter *vb* billet, lodge, post, station; allot, furnish, share. * *n* abode, billet, dwelling, habitation, lodgings, posts, quarters, stations; direction, district, locality, location, lodge, position, region, territory; clemency, mercy, mildness.

quash *vb* abate, abolish, annul, cancel, invalidate, nullify, overthrow; crush, extinguish, repress, stop, subdue, suppress.

queasy *adj* nauseated, pukish, seasick, sick, squeamish.

queer *vb* botch, harm, impair, mar, spoil. * *adj* curious, droll, extraordinary, fantastic, odd, peculiar, quaint, singular, strange, uncommon, unusual, whimsical; gay, homosexual.

quell *vb* conquer, crush, overcome, overpower, subdue; bridle, check, curb, extinguish, lay, quench, rein in, repress, restrain, stifle; allay, calm, compose, hush, lull, pacify, quiet, quieten, still, tranquillize; alleviate, appease, blunt, deaden, dull, mitigate, mollify, soften, soothe.

quench *vb* extinguish, put out; check, destroy, repress, satiate, stifle, still, suppress; allay, cool, dampen, extinguish, slake.

querulous *adj* bewailing, complaining, cross, discontented, dissatisfied, fretful, fretting, irritable, mourning, murmuring, peevish, petulant, plaintive, touchy, whining.

query *vb* ask, enquire, inquire, question; dispute, doubt. * *n* enquiry, inquiry, interrogatory, issue, problem, question.

quest *n* expedition, journey, search, voyage; pursuit, suit; examination, enquiry, inquiry; demand, desire, invitation, prayer, request, solicitation.

question *vb* ask, catechize, enquire, examine, inquire, interrogate, quiz, sound out; doubt, query; challenge, dispute. * *n* examination, enquiry, inquiry, interpellation, interrogation; enquiry, inquiry, interrogatory, query; debate, discussion, disquisition, examination, investigation, issue, trial; controversy, dispute, doubt; motion, mystery, point, poser, problem, proposition, puzzle, topic.

questionable *adj* ambiguous, controversial, controvertible, debatable, doubtful, disputable, equivocal, problematic, problematical, suspicious, uncertain, undecided.

quibble *vb* cavil, equivocate, evade, prevaricate, shuffle. * *n* equivocation, evasion, pretence, prevarication, quirk, shift, shuffle, sophism, subtlety, subterfuge.

quick *adj* active, agile, alert, animated, brisk, lively, nimble, prompt, ready, smart, sprightly; expeditious, fast, fleet, flying, hurried, rapid, speedy, swift; adroit, apt, clever, dextrous, expert, skilful; choleric, hasty, impetuous, irascible, irritable, passionate, peppery, petulant, precipitate, sharp, unceremonious, testy, touchy, waspish; alive, animate, live, living.

quicken *vb* animate, energize, resuscitate, revivify, vivify; cheer, enliven, invigorate, reinvigorate, revive, whet; accelerate, dispatch, expedite, hasten, hurry, speed; actuate, excite, incite, kindle, refresh, sharpen, stimulate; accelerate, live, take effect.

quickly *adv* apace, fast, immediately, nimbly, quick, rapidly, readily, soon, speedily, swiftly.

quickness *n* celerity, dispatch, expedition, haste, rapidity, speed, swiftness, velocity; agility, alertness, activity, briskness, liveliness, nimbleness, promptness, readiness, smartness; adroitness, aptitude, aptness, dexterity, facility, knack; acumen, acuteness, keenness, penetration, perspicacity, sagacity, sharpness, shrewdness.

quiescent *adj* at rest, hushed, motionless, quiet, resting, still; calm, mute, placid, quiet, serene, still, tranquil, unagitated, undisturbed, unruffled.

quiet *adj* hushed, motionless, quiescent, still, unmoved; calm, contented, gentle, mild, meek, modest, peaceable, peaceful, placid, silent, smooth, tranquil, undemonstrative, unobtrusive, unruffled; patient; retired, secluded. * *n* calmness, peace, repose, rest, silence, stillness.

quieten *vb* arrest, discontinue, intermit, interrupt, still, stop, suspend; allay, appease, calm, compose, lull, pacify, sober, soothe, tranquillize; hush, silence; alleviate, assuage, blunt, dull, mitigate, moderate, mollify, soften.

quip *n* crank, flout, gibe, jeer, mock, quirk, repartee, retort, sarcasm, sally, scoff, sneer, taunt, witticism.

quit *vb* absolve, acquit, deliver, free, release; clear, deliver, discharge from, free, liberate, relieve; acquit, behave, conduct; carry through, perform; discharge, pay, repay, requite; relinquish, renounce, resign, stop, surrender; depart from, leave, withdraw from; abandon, desert, forsake, forswear. * *adj* absolved, acquitted, clear, discharged, free, released.

quite *adv* completely, entirely, exactly, perfectly, positively, precisely, totally, wholly.

quiver *vb* flicker, flutter, oscillate, palpitate, quake, play, shake, shiver, shudder, tremble, twitch, vibrate. * *n* shake, shiver, shudder, trembling.

quixotic *adj* absurd, chimerical, fanciful, fantastic, fantastical, freakish, imaginary, mad, romantic, utopian, visionary, wild.

quiz *vb* examine, question, test; peer at; banter, hoax, puzzle, ridicule. * *n* enigma, hoax, jest, joke, puzzle; jester, joker, hoax.

quota *n* allocation, allotment, apportionment, contingent, portion, proportion, quantity, share.

quotation *n* citation, clipping, cutting, extract, excerpt, reference, selection; estimate, rate, tender.

quote *vb* adduce, cite, excerpt, extract, illustrate, instance, name, repeat, take; estimate, tender.

R

rabble *n* commonality, horde, mob, populace, riffraff, rout, scum, trash.

rabid *adj* frantic, furious, mad, raging, wild; bigoted, fanatical, intolerant, irrational, narrow-minded, rampant.

race[1] *n* ancestry, breed, family, generation, house, kindred, line, lineage, pedigree, stock, strain; clan, folk, nation, people, tribe; breed, children, descendants, issue, offspring, progeny, stock.

race[2] *vb* career, compete, contest, course, hasten, hurry, run, speed. * *n* career, chase, competition, contest, course, dash, heat, match, pursuit, run, sprint; flavour, quality, smack, strength, taste.

rack *vb* agonize, distress, excruciate, rend, torment, torture, wring; exhaust, force, harass, oppress, strain, stretch, wrest. * *n* agony, anguish, pang, torment, torture; crib, manger; neck, crag; dampness, mist, moisture, vapour.

racket *n* clamour, clatter, din, dissipation, disturbance, fracas, frolic, hubbub, noise, outcry, tumult, uproar; game, graft, scheme, understanding.

racy *adj* flavoursome, palatable, piquant, pungent, rich, spicy, strong; forcible, lively, pungent, smart, spirited, stimulating, vigorous, vivacious.

radiance *n* brightness, brilliance, brilliancy, effluence, efflux, emission, glare, glitter, light, lustre, refulgence, resplendence, shine, splendour.

radiant *adj* beaming, brilliant, effulgent, glittering, glorious, luminous, lustrous, resplendent, shining, sparkling, splendid; ecstatic, happy, pleased.

radiate *vb* beam, gleam, glitter, shine; emanate, emit; diffuse, spread.

radical *adj* constitutional, deep-seated, essential, fundamental, ingrained, inherent, innate, native, natural, organic, original, uncompromising; original, primitive, simple, uncompounded, underived; complete, entire, extreme, fanatic, insurgent, perfect, rebellious, thorough, total. * *n* etymon, radix, root; fanatic, revolutionary.

rage *vb* bluster, boil, chafe, foam, fret, fume, ravage, rave. * *n* excitement, frenzy, fury, madness, passion, rampage, raving, vehemence, wrath; craze, fashion, mania, mode, style, vogue.

ragged *adj* rent, tattered, torn; contemptible, mean, poor, shabby; jagged, rough, rugged, shaggy, uneven; discordant, dissonant, inharmonious, unmusical.

raid *vb* assault, forage, invade, pillage, plunder. * *n* attack, foray, invasion, inroad, plunder.

rail *vb* abuse, censure, inveigh, scoff, scold, sneer, upbraid.

raillery *n* banter, chaff, irony, joke, pleasantry, ridicule, satire.

raiment *n* array, apparel, attire, clothes, clothing, costume, dress, garb, garments, habiliment, habit, vestments, vesture.

rain *vb* drizzle, drop, fall, pour, shower, sprinkle, teem; bestow, lavish. * *n* cloudburst, downpour, drizzle, mist, shower, sprinkling.

raise *vb* boost, construct, erect, heave, hoist, lift, uplift, upraise, rear; advance, elevate, ennoble, exalt, promote; aggravate, amplify, augment, enhance, heighten, increase, invigorate; arouse, awake, cause, effect, excite, originate, produce, rouse, stir up, occasion, start; assemble, collect, get, levy, obtain; breed, cultivate, grow, propagate, rear; ferment, leaven, work.

rake[1] *vb* collect, comb, gather, scratch; ransack, scour.

rake[2] *n* debauchee, libertine, profligate, roué.

rakish *adj* debauched, dissipated, dissolute, lewd, licentious; cavalier, jaunty.

ramble *vb* digress, maunder, range, roam, rove, saunter, straggle, stray, stroll, wander. * *n* excursion, rambling, roving, tour, trip, stroll, wandering.

rambling *adj* discursive, irregular; straggling, strolling, wandering.

ramification *n* arborescence, branching, divarication, forking, radiation; branch, division, offshoot, subdivision; consequence, upshot.

ramify *vb* branch, divaricate, extend, separate.

rampant *adj* excessive, exuberant, luxuriant, rank, wanton; boisterous, dominant, headstrong, impetuous, predominant, raging, uncontrollable, unbridled, ungovernable, vehement, violent.

rampart *n* bulwark, circumvallation, defence, fence, fortification, guard, security, wall.

rancid *adj* bad, fetid, foul, fusty, musty, offensive, rank, sour, stinking, tainted.

rancorous *adj* bitter, implacable, malevolent, malicious, malign, malignant, resentful, spiteful, vindictive, virulent.

rancour *n* animosity, antipathy, bitterness, enmity, gall, grudge, hate, hatred, ill-will, malevolence, malice, malignity, spite, venom, vindictiveness.

random *adj* accidental, casual, chance, fortuitous, haphazard, irregular, stray, wandering.

range *vb* course, cruise, extend, ramble, roam, rove, straggle, stray, stroll, wander; bend, lie, run; arrange, class, dispose, rank. * *n* file, line, row, rank, tier; class, kind, order, sort; excursion, expedition, ramble, roving, wandering; amplitude, bound, command, compass, distance, extent, latitude, reach, scope, sweep, view; register.

rank[1] *vb* arrange, class, classify, range. * *n* file, line, order, range, row, tier; class, division, group, order, series; birth, blood, caste, degree, estate, grade, position, quality, sphere, stakes, standing; dignity, distinction, eminence, nobility.

rank[2] *adj* dense, exuberant, luxuriant, overabundant, overgrown, vigorous, wild; excessive, extreme, extravagant, flagrant, gross, rampant, sheer, unmitigated, utter, violent; fetid, foul, fusty, musty, offensive, rancid; fertile, productive, rich; coarse, disgusting.

ransack vb pillage, plunder, ravage, rifle, sack, strip; explore, overhaul, rummage, search thoroughly.

ransom vb deliver, emancipate, free, liberate, redeem, rescue, unfetter. * n money, payment pay-off, price; deliverance, liberation, redemption, release.

rant vb declaim, mouth, spout, vociferate. * n bombast, cant, exaggeration, fustian.

rapacious adj predacious, preying, raptorial; avaricious, grasping, greedy, ravenous, voracious.

rapid adj fast, fleet, quick, swift; brisk, expeditious, hasty, hurried, quick, speedy.

rapine n depredation, pillage, plunder, robbery, spoliation.

rapt adj absorbed, charmed, delighted, ecstatic, engrossed, enraptured, entranced, fascinated, inspired, spellbound.

rapture vb enrapture, ravish, transport. * n delight, exultation, enthusiasm, rhapsody; beatification, beatitude, bliss, ecstasy, felicity, happiness, joy, spell, transport.

rare[1] adj sparse, subtle, thin; extraordinary, infrequent, scarce, singular, strange, uncommon, unique, unusual; choice, excellent, exquisite, fine, incomparable, inimitable.

rare[2] adj bloody, underdone.

rarity n attenuation, ethereality, etherealness, rarefaction, rareness, tenuity, tenuousness, thinness; infrequency, scarcity, singularity, sparseness, uncommonness, unwontedness.

rascal n blackguard, caitiff, knave, miscreant, rogue, reprobate, scallywag, scapegrace, scamp, scoundrel, vagabond, villain.

rash[1] adj adventurous, audacious, careless, foolhardy, hasty, headlong, headstrong, heedless, incautious, inconsiderate, indiscreet, injudicious, impetuous, impulsive, incautious, precipitate, quick, rapid, reckless, temerarious, thoughtless, unguarded, unwary, venturesome.

rash[2] n breaking-out, efflorescence, eruption; epidemic, flood, outbreak, plague, spate.

rashness n carelessness, foolhardiness, hastiness, heedlessness, inconsideration, indiscretion, precipitation, recklessness, temerity, venturesomeness.

rate[1] vb appraise, compute, estimate, value. * n cost, price; class, degree, estimate, rank, value, valuation, worth; proportion, ration; assessment, charge, impost, tax.

rate[2] vb abuse, berate, censure, chide, criticize, find fault, reprimand, reprove, scold.

ratify vb confirm, corroborate, endorse, establish, seal, settle, substantiate; approve, bind, consent, sanction.

ration vb apportion, deal, distribute, dole, restrict. * n allowance, portion, quota, share.

rational adj intellectual, reasoning; equitable, fair, fit, just, moderate, natural, normal, proper, reasonable, right; discreet, enlightened, intelligent, judicious, sagacious, sensible, sound, wise.

raucous adj harsh, hoarse, husky, rough.

ravage vb consume, desolate, despoil, destroy, devastate, harry, overrun, pillage, plunder, ransack, ruin, sack, spoil, strip, waste. * n desolation, despoilment, destruction, devastation, havoc, pillage, plunder, rapine, ruin, spoil, waste.

ravenous adj devouring, ferocious, gluttonous, greedy, insatiable, omnivorous, ravening, rapacious, voracious.

ravine n canyon, cleft, defile, gap, gorge, gulch, gully, pass.

raving adj delirious, deranged, distracted, frantic, frenzied, furious, infuriated, mad, phrenetic, raging. * n delirium, frenzy, fury, madness, rage.

ravish vb abuse, debauch, defile, deflower, force, outrage, violate; captivate, charm, delight, enchant, enrapture, entrance, overjoy, transport; abduct, kidnap, seize, snatch, strip.

raw adj fresh, inexperienced, unpractised, unprepared, unseasoned, untried, unskilled; crude, green, immature, unfinished, unripe; bare, chafed, excoriated, galled, sensitive, sore; bleak, chilly, cold, cutting, damp, piercing, windswept; uncooked.

ray n beam, emanation, gleam, moonbeam, radiance, shaft, streak, sunbeam.

raze vb demolish, destroy, dismantle, extirpate, fell, level, overthrow, ruin, subvert; efface, erase, obliterate.

reach vb extend, stretch; grasp, hit, strike, touch; arrive at, attain, gain, get, obtain, win. * n capability, capacity, grasp.

readily adv easily, promptly, quickly; cheerfully, willingly.

readiness n alacrity, alertness, expedition, quickness, promptitude, promptness; aptitude, aptness, dexterity, easiness, expertness, facility, quickness, skill; preparation, preparedness, ripeness; cheerfulness, disposition, eagerness, ease, willingness.

ready vb arrange, equip, organize, prepare. * adj alert, expeditious, prompt, quick, punctual, speedy; adroit, apt, clever, dextrous, expert, facile, handy, keen, nimble, prepared, prompt, ripe, quick, sharp, skilful, smart; cheerful, disposed, eager, free, inclined, willing; accommodating, available, convenient, near, handy; easy, facile, fluent, offhand, opportune, short, spontaneous.

real adj absolute, actual, certain, literal, positive, practical, substantial, substantive, veritable; authentic, genuine, true; essential, internal, intrinsic.

realize vb accomplish, achieve, discharge, effect, effectuate, perfect, perform; apprehend, comprehend, experience, recognize, understand; externalize, substantiate; acquire, earn, gain, get, net, obtain, produce, sell.

reality n actuality, certainty, fact, truth, verity.

really adv absolutely, actually, certainly, indeed, positively, truly, verily, veritably.

reap vb acquire, crop, gain, gather, get, harvest, obtain, receive.

rear[1] adj aft, back, following, hind, last. * n background, reverse, setting; heel, posterior, rear end, rump, stern, tail; path, trail, train, wake.

rear[2] vb construct, elevate, erect, hoist, lift, raise; cherish, educate, foster, instruct, nourish, nurse, nurture, train; breed, grow; rouse, stir up.

reason vb argue, conclude, debate, deduce, draw from, infer, intellectualize, syllogize, think, trace. * n faculty, intellect, intelligence, judgement, mind, principle, sanity, sense, thinking, understanding; account, argument, basis, cause, consideration, excuse, explanation, gist, ground, motive, occasion, pretence, proof; aim, design, end, object, purpose; argument, reasoning; common sense, reasonableness, wisdom; equity, fairness, justice, right; exposition, rationale, theory.

reasonable *adj* equitable, fair, fit, honest, just, proper, rational, right, suitable; enlightened, intelligent, judicious, sagacious, sensible, wise; considerable, fair, moderate, tolerable; credible, intellectual, plausible, well-founded; sane, sober, sound; cheap, inexpensive, low-priced.

rebate *vb* abate, bate, blunt, deduct, diminish, lessen, reduce; cut, pare, rabbet. * *n* decrease, decrement, diminution, lessening; allowance, deduction, discount, reduction.

rebel *vb* mutiny, resist, revolt, strike. * *adj* insubordinate, insurgent, mutinous, rebellious. * *n* insurgent, mutineer, traitor.

rebellion *n* anarchy, insubordination, insurrection, mutiny, resistance, revolt, revolution, uprising.

rebellious *adj* contumacious, defiant, disloyal, disobedient, insubordinate, intractable, obstinate, mutinous, rebel, refractory, seditious.

rebuff *vb* check, chide, oppose, refuse, reject, repel, reprimand, resist, snub. * *n* check, defeat, discouragement, opposition, rejection, resistance, snub.

rebuke *vb* blame, censure, chide, lecture, upbraid, reprehend, reprimand, reprove, scold, silence. * *n* blame, censure, chiding, expostulation, remonstrance, reprimand, reprehension, reproach, reproof, reproval; affliction, chastisement, punishment.

recall *vb* abjure, abnegate, annul, cancel, countermand, deny, nullify, overrule, recant, repeal, repudiate, rescind, retract, revoke, swallow, withdraw; commemorate, recollect, remember, retrace, review, revive. * *n* abjuration, abnegation, annulment, cancellation, nullification, recantation, repeal, repudiation, rescindment, retraction, revocation, withdrawal; memory, recollection, remembrance, reminiscence.

recant *vb* abjure, annul, disavow, disown, recall, renounce, repudiate, retract, revoke, unsay.

recapitulate *vb* epitomize, recite, rehearse, reiterate, repeat, restate, review, summarize.

recede *vb* desist, ebb, retire, regress, retreat, retrograde, return, withdraw.

receive *vb* accept, acquire, derive, gain, get, obtain, take; admit, shelter, take in; entertain, greet, welcome; allow, permit, tolerate; adopt, approve, believe, credit, embrace, follow, learn, understand; accommodate, carry, contain, hold, include, retain; bear, encounter, endure, experience, meet, suffer, sustain.

recent *adj* fresh, new, novel; latter, modern, young; deceased, foregoing, late, preceding, retiring.

reception *n* acceptance, receipt, receiving; entertainment, greeting, welcome; levee, soiree, party; admission, credence; belief, credence, recognition.

recess *n* alcove, corner, depth, hollow, niche, nook, privacy, retreat, seclusion; break, holiday, intermission, interval, respite, vacation; recession, retirement, retreat, withdrawal.

reciprocal *adj* alternate, commutable, complementary, correlative, correspondent, mutual.

recital *n* rehearsal, repetition, recitation; account, description, detail, explanation, narration, relation, statement, telling.

recite *vb* declaim, deliver, rehearse, repeat; describe, mention, narrate, recount, relate, tell; count, detail, enumerate, number, recapitulate.

reckless *adj* breakneck, careless, desperate, devil-may-care, flighty, foolhardy, giddy, harebrained, headlong, heedless, inattentive, improvident, imprudent,

inconsiderate, indifferent, indiscreet, mindless, negligent, rash, regardless, remiss, thoughtless, temerarious, uncircumspect, unconcerned, unsteady, volatile, wild.

reckon *vb* calculate, cast, compute, consider, count, enumerate, guess, number; account, class, esteem, estimate, regard, repute, value.

reckoning *n* calculation, computation, consideration, counting; account, bill, charge, estimate, register, score; arrangement, settlement.

reclaim *vb* amend, correct, reform; recover, redeem, regenerate, regain, reinstate, restore; civilize, tame.

recline *vb* couch, lean, lie, lounge, repose, rest.

recluse *adj* anchoritic, anchoritical, cloistered, eremitic, eremitical, hermitic, hermitical, reclusive, solitary. * *n* anchorite, ascetic, eremite, hermit, monk, solitary.

reclusive *adj* recluse, retired, secluded, sequestered, sequestrated, solitary.

recognition *n* identification, memory, recollection, remembrance; acknowledgement, appreciation, avowal, comprehension, confession, notice; allowance, concession.

recognize *vb* apprehend, identify, perceive, remember; acknowledge, admit, avow, confess, own; allow, concede, grant; greet, salute.

recoil *vb* react, rebound, reverberate; retire, retreat, withdraw; blench, fail, falter, quail, shrink. * *n* backstroke, boomerang, elasticity, kick, reaction, rebound, repercussion, resilience, revulsion, ricochet, shrinking.

recollect *vb* recall, remember, reminisce.

recollection *n* memory, remembrance, reminiscence.

recommend *vb* approve, commend, endorse, praise, sanction; commit; advise, counsel, prescribe, suggest.

recommendation *n* advocacy, approbation, approval, commendation, counsel, credential, praise, testimonial.

recompense *vb* compensate, remunerate, repay, requite, reward, satisfy; indemnify, redress, reimburse. * *n* amends, compensation, indemnification, indemnity, remuneration, repayment, reward, satisfaction; requital, retribution.

reconcilable *adj* appeasable, forgiving, placable; companionable, congruous, consistent.

reconcile *vb* appease, conciliate, pacify, placate, propitiate, reunite; content, harmonize, regulate; adjust, compose, heal, settle.

recondite *adj* concealed, dark, hidden, mystic, mystical, obscure, occult, secret, transcendental.

record *vb* chronicle, enter, note, register. * *n* account, annals, archive, chronicle, diary, docket, enrolment, entry, file, list, minute, memoir, memorandum, memorial, note, proceedings, register, registry, report, roll, score; mark, memorial, relic, trace, track, trail, vestige; memory, remembrance; achievement, career, history.

recount *vb* describe, detail, enumerate, mention, narrate, particularize, portray, recite, relate, rehearse, report, tell.

recover *vb* recapture, reclaim, regain; rally, recruit, repair, retrieve; cure, heal, restore, revive; redeem, rescue, salvage, save; convalesce, recuperate.

recreant *adj* base, cowardly, craven, dastardly, faint-hearted, mean-spirited, pusillanimous, yielding; apostate, backsliding, faithless, false, perfidious, treacherous, unfaithful, untrue. * *n* coward, dastard; apostate, backslider, renegade.

recreation *n* amusement, cheer, diversion, entertainment, fun, game, leisure, pastime, play, relaxation, sport.

recreational *adj* amusing, diverting, entertaining, refreshing, relaxing, relieving.

recruit *vb* repair, replenish; recover, refresh, regain, reinvigorate, renew, renovate, restore, retrieve, revive, strengthen, supply. * *n* auxiliary, beginner, helper, learner, novice, tyro.

rectify *vb* adjust, amend, better, correct, emend, improve, mend, redress, reform, regulate, straighten.

rectitude *n* conscientiousness, equity, goodness, honesty, integrity, justice, principle, probity, right, righteousness, straightforwardness, uprightness, virtue.

recumbent *adj* leaning, lying, prone, prostrate, reclining; idle, inactive, listless, reposing.

recur *vb* reappear, resort, return, revert.

recusancy *n* dissent, heresy, heterodoxy, nonconformity.

redeem *vb* reform, regain, repurchase, retrieve; free, liberate, ransom, rescue, save; deliver, reclaim, recover, reinstate; atone, compensate for, recompense; discharge, fulfil, keep, perform, satisfy.

redemption *n* buying, compensation, recovery, repurchase, retrieval; deliverance, liberation, ransom, release, rescue, salvation; discharge, fulfilment, performance.

redolent *adj* aromatic, balmy, fragrant, odoriferous, odorous, scented, sweet, sweet-smelling.

redoubtable *adj* awful, doughty, dreadful, formidable, terrible, valiant.

redound *vb* accrue, conduce, contribute, result, tend.

redress *vb* amend, correct, order, rectify, remedy, repair; compensate, ease, relieve. * *n* abatement, amends, atonement, compensation, correction, cure, indemnification, rectification, repair, righting, remedy, relief, reparation, satisfaction.

reduce *vb* bring; form, make, model, mould, remodel, render, resolve, shape; abate, abbreviate, abridge, attenuate, contract, curtail, decimate, decrease, diminish, lessen, minimize, shorten, thin; abase, debase, degrade, depress, dwarf, impair, lower, weaken; capture, conquer, master, overpower, overthrow, subject, subdue, subjugate, vanquish; impoverish, ruin; resolve, solve.

redundant *adj* copious, excessive, exuberant, fulsome, inordinate, lavish, needless, overflowing, overmuch, plentiful, prodigal, superabundant, replete, superfluous, unnecessary, useless; diffuse, periphrastic, pleonastic, tautological, verbose, wordy.

reel[1] *n* capstan, winch, windlass; bobbin, spool.

reel[2] *vb* falter, flounder, heave, lurch, pitch, plunge, rear, rock, roll, stagger, sway, toss, totter, tumble, wallow, welter, vacillate; spin, swing, turn, twirl, wheel, whirl. * *n* gyre, pirouette, spin, turn, twirl, wheel, whirl.

re-establish *vb* re-found, rehabilitate, reinstall, reinstate, renew, renovate, replace, restore.

refer *vb* commit, consign, direct, leave, relegate, send, submit; ascribe, assign, attribute, impute; appertain, belong, concern, pertain, point, relate, respect, touch; appeal, apply, consult; advert, allude, cite, quote.

referee *vb* arbitrate, judge, umpire. * *n* arbiter, arbitrator, judge, umpire.

reference *n* concern, connection, regard, respect; allusion, ascription, citation, hint, intimation, mark, reference, relegation.

refine *vb* clarify, cleanse, defecate, fine, purify; cultivate, humanize, improve, polish, rarefy, spiritualize.

refined *adj* courtly, cultured, genteel, polished, polite; discerning, discriminating, fastidious, sensitive; filtered, processed, purified.

refinement *n* clarification, filtration, purification, sublimation; betterment, improvement; delicacy, cultivation, culture, elegance, elevation, finish, gentility, good breeding, polish, politeness, purity, spirituality, style.

reflect *vb* copy, imitate, mirror, reproduce; cogitate, consider, contemplate, deliberate, meditate, muse, ponder, ruminate, study, think.

reflection *n* echo, shadow; cogitation, consideration, contemplation, deliberation, idea, meditation, musing, opinion, remark, rumination, thinking, thought; aspersion, blame, censure, criticism, disparagement, reproach, slur.

reflective *adj* reflecting, reflexive; cogitating, deliberating, musing, pondering, reasoning, thoughtful.

reform *vb* amend, ameliorate, better, correct, improve, mend, meliorate, rectify, reclaim, redeem, regenerate, repair, restore; reconstruct, remodel, reshape. * *n* amendment, correction, progress, reconstruction, rectification, reformation.

reformation *n* amendment, emendation, improvement, reform; adoption, conversion, redemption; refashioning, regeneration, reproduction, reconstruction.

refractory *adj* cantankerous, contumacious, crossgrained, disobedient, dogged, headstrong, heady, incoercible, intractable, mulish, obstinate, perverse, recalcitrant, self-willed, stiff, stubborn, sullen, ungovernable, unmanageable, unruly, unyielding.

refrain[1] *vb* abstain, cease, desist, forbear, stop, withhold.

refrain[2] *n* chorus, song, undersong.

refresh *vb* air, brace, cheer, cool, enliven, exhilarate, freshen, invigorate, reanimate, recreate, recruit, reinvigorate, revive, regale, slake.

refreshing *adj* comfortable, cooling, grateful, invigorating, pleasant, reanimating, restful, reviving.

refuge *n* asylum, covert, harbour, haven, protection, retreat, safety, sanction, security, shelter.

refulgent *adj* bright, brilliant, effulgent, lustrous, radiant, resplendent, shining.

refund *vb* reimburse, repay, restore, return. * *n* reimbursement, repayment.

refuse[1] *n* chaff, discard, draff, dross, dregs, garbage, junk, leavings, lees, litter, lumber, offal, recrement, remains, rubbish, scoria, scum, sediment, slag, sweepings, trash, waste.

refuse[2] *vb* decline, deny, withhold; disallow, disavow, exclude, rebuff, reject, renege, renounce, repel, repudiate, repulse, revoke, veto.

refute *vb* confute, defeat, disprove, overcome, overthrow, rebut, repel, silence.

regain *vb* recapture, recover, re-obtain, repossess, retrieve.

regal *adj* imposing, imperial, kingly, noble, royal, sovereign.

regale *vb* delight, entertain, gratify, refresh; banquet, feast.

regard *vb* behold, gaze, look, notice, mark, observe, remark, see, view, watch; attend to, consider, heed, mind, respect; esteem, honour, revere, reverence, value; account, believe, estimate, deem, hold, imagine, reckon, suppose, think, treat, use. * *n* aspect, gaze, look, view; attention, attentiveness, care, concern, consideration, heed, notice, observance; account, reference, relation, respect; admiration, affection, attachment, deference, esteem, estimation, favour, honour, interest, liking, love, respect, reverence, sympathy, value; account, eminence, note, reputation, repute; condition, matter, point.

regardful *adj* attentive, careful, considerate, deferential, heedful, mindful, observing, thoughtful, watchful.

regarding *prep* concerning, respecting, touching.

regardless *adj* careless, disregarding, heedless, inattentive, indifferent, mindless, neglectful, negligent, unconcerned, unmindful, unobservant. * *adv* however, irrespectively, nevertheless, nonetheless, notwithstanding.

regenerate *vb* reproduce; renovate, revive; change, convert, renew, sanctify. * *adj* born-again, converted, reformed, regenerated.

regime *n* administration, government, rule.

region *n* climate, clime, country, district, division, latitude, locale, locality, province, quarter, scene, territory, tract; area, neighbourhood, part, place, portion, spot, space, sphere, terrain, vicinity.

register *vb* delineate, portray, record, show. * *n* annals, archive, catalogue, chronicle, list, record, roll, schedule; clerk, registrar, registry; compass, range.

regret *vb* bewail, deplore, grieve, lament, repine, sorrow; bemoan, repent, mourn, rue. * *n* concern, disappointment, grief, lamentation, rue, sorrow, trouble; compunction, contrition, penitence, remorse, repentance, repining, self-condemnation, self-reproach.

regular *adj* conventional, natural, normal, ordinary, typical; correct, customary, cyclic, established, fixed, habitual, periodic, periodical, recurring, reasonable, rhythmic, seasonal, stated, usual; steady, constant, uniform, even; just, methodical, orderly, punctual, systematic, unvarying; complete, genuine, indubitable, out-and-out, perfect, thorough; balanced, consistent, symmetrical.

regulate *vb* adjust, arrange, dispose, methodize, order, organize, settle, standardize, time, systematize; conduct, control, direct, govern, guide, manage, rule.

regulation *adj* customary, mandatory, official, required, standard. * *n* adjustment, arrangement, control, disposal, disposition, law, management, order, ordering, precept, rule, settlement.

rehabilitate *vb* reinstate, re-establish, restore; reconstruct, reconstitute, reintegrate, reinvigorate, renew, renovate.

rehearsal *n* drill, practice, recital, recitation, repetition; account, history, mention, narration, narrative, recounting, relation, statement, story, telling.

rehearse *vb* recite, repeat; delineate, depict, describe, detail, enumerate, narrate, portray, recapitulate, recount, relate, tell.

reign *vb* administer, command, govern, influence, predominate, prevail, rule. * *n* control, dominion, empire, influence, power, royalty, sovereignty, power, rule, sway.

reimburse *vb* refund, repay, restore; compensate, indemnify, requite, satisfy.

rein *vb* bridle, check, control, curb, guide, harness, hold, restrain, restrict. * *n* bridle, check, curb, harness, restraint, restriction.

reinforce *vb* augment, fortify, strengthen.

reinstate *vb* re-establish, rehabilitate, reinstall, replace, restore.

reject *vb* cashier, discard, dismiss, eject, exclude, pluck; decline, deny, disallow, despise, disapprove, disbelieve, rebuff, refuse, renounce, repel, repudiate, scout, slight, spurn, veto. * *n* cast-off, discard, failure, refusal, repudiation.

rejoice *vb* cheer, delight, enliven, enrapture, exhilarate, gladden, gratify, please, transport; crow, exult, delight, gloat, glory, jubilate, triumph, vaunt.

rejoin *vb* answer, rebut, respond, retort.

relate *vb* describe, detail, mention, narrate, recite, recount, rehearse, report, tell; apply, connect, correlate.

relation *n* account, chronicle, description, detail, explanation, history, mention, narration, narrative, recital, rehearsal, report, statement, story, tale; affinity, application, bearing, connection, correlation, dependency, pertinence, relationship; concern, reference, regard, respect; alliance, nearness, propinquity, rapport; blood, consanguinity, cousinship, kin, kindred, kinship, relationship; kinsman, kinswoman, relative.

relax *vb* loose, loosen, slacken, unbrace, unstrain; debilitate, enervate, enfeeble, prostrate, unbrace, unstring, weaken; abate, diminish, lessen, mitigate, reduce, remit; amuse, divert, ease, entertain, recreate, unbend.

release *vb* deliver, discharge, disengage, exempt, extricate, free, liberate, loose, unloose; acquit, discharge, quit, relinquish, remit. * *n* deliverance, discharge, freedom, liberation; absolution, dispensation, excuse, exemption, exoneration; acquaintance, clearance.

relentless *adj* cruel, hard, impenitent, implacable, inexorable, merciless, obdurate, pitiless, rancorous, remorseless, ruthless, unappeasable, uncompassionate, unfeeling, unforgiving, unmerciful, unpitying, unrelenting, unyielding, vindictive.

relevant *adj* applicable, appropriate, apposite, apt, apropos, fit, germane, pertinent, proper, relative, suitable.

reliable *adj* authentic, certain, constant, dependable, sure, trustworthy, trusty, unfailing.

reliance *n* assurance, confidence, credence, dependence, hope, trust.

relic *n* keepsake, memento, memorial, remembrance, souvenir, token, trophy; trace, vestige.

relics *npl* fragments, leavings, remainder, remains, remnants, ruins, scraps; body, cadaver, corpse, remains.

relict *n* dowager, widow.

relief *n* aid, alleviation, amelioration, assistance, assuagement, comfort, deliverance, ease, easement, help, mitigation, reinforcement, respite, rest, succour, softening, support; indemnification, redress, remedy; embossment, projection, prominence, protrusion; clearness, distinction, perspective, vividness.

relieve *vb* aid, comfort, help, spell, succour, support, sustain; abate, allay, alleviate, assuage, cure, diminish, ease, lessen, lighten, mitigate, remedy, remove, soothe; indemnify, redress, right, repair; disengage, free, release, remedy, rescue.

religious *adj* devotional, devout, god-fearing, godly, holy, pious, prayerful, spiritual; conscientious, exact, rigid, scrupulous, strict; canonical, divine, theological.

relinquish *vb* abandon, desert, forsake, forswear, leave, quit, renounce, resign, vacate; abdicate, cede, forbear, forgo, give up, surrender, yield.

relish *vb* appreciate, enjoy, like, prefer; season, flavour, taste. * *n* appetite, appreciation, enjoyment, fondness, gratification, gusto, inclination, liking, partiality, predilection, taste, zest; cast, flavour, manner, quality, savour, seasoning, sort, tang, tinge, touch; appetizer, condiment.

reluctance *n* aversion, backwardness, disinclination, dislike, loathing, repugnance, unwillingness.

reluctant *adj* averse, backward, disinclined, hesitant, indisposed, loath, unwilling.

rely *vb* confide, count, depend, hope, lean, reckon, repose, trust.

remain *vb* abide, continue, endure, last; exceed, persist, survive; abide, continue, dwell, halt, inhabit, rest, sojourn, stay, stop, tarry, wait.

remainder *n* balance, excess, leavings, remains, remnant, residue, rest, surplus.

remark *vb* heed, notice, observe, regard; comment, express, mention, observe, say, state, utter. * *n* consideration, heed, notice, observation, regard; annotation, comment, gloss, note, stricture; assertion, averment, comment, declaration, saying, statement, utterance.

remarkable *adj* conspicuous, distinguished, eminent, extraordinary, famous, notable, noteworthy, noticeable, pre-eminent, rare, singular, strange, striking, uncommon, unusual, wonderful.

remedy *vb* cure, heal, help, palliate, relieve; amend, correct, rectify, redress, repair, restore, retrieve. * *n* antidote, antitoxin, corrective, counteractive, cure, help, medicine, nostrum, panacea, restorative, specific; redress, reparation, restitution, restoration; aid, assistance, relief.

remembrance *n* recollection, reminiscence, retrospection; keepsake, memento, memorial, memory, reminder, souvenir, token; consideration, regard, thought.

reminiscence *n* memory, recollection, remembrance, retrospective.

remiss *adj* backward, behindhand, dilatory, indolent, languid, lax, lazy, slack, slow, tardy; careless, dilatory, heedless, idle, inattentive, neglectful, negligent, shiftless, slothful, thoughtless.

remission *n* abatement, decrease, diminution, lessening, mitigation, moderation, reduction, relaxation; cancellation, discharge, release, relinquishment; intermission, interruption, pause, rest, stop, stoppage, suspense, suspension; absolution, acquittal, excuse, exoneration, forgiveness, indulgence, pardon.

remit *vb* replace, restore, return; abate, bate, diminish, relax; release; absolve, condone, excuse, forgive, overlook, pardon; relinquish, resign, surrender; consign, forward, refer, send, transmit. * *n* authorization, brief, instructions, orders.

remnant *n* remainder, remains, residue, rest, trace; fragment, piece, scrap.

remorse *n* compunction, contrition, penitence, qualm, regret, repentance, reproach, self-reproach, sorrow.

remorseless *adj* cruel, barbarous, hard, harsh, implacable, inexorable, merciless, pitiless, relentless, ruthless, savage, uncompassionate, unmerciful, unrelenting.

remote *adj* distant, far, out-of-the-way; alien, far-fetched, foreign, inappropriate, unconnected, unrelated; abstracted, separated; inconsiderable, slight; isolated, removed, secluded, sequestrated.

removal *n* abstraction, departure, dislodgement, displacement, relegation, remove, shift, transference; elimination, extraction, withdrawal; abatement, destruction; discharge, dismissal, ejection, expulsion.

remove *vb* carry, dislodge, displace, shift, transfer, transport; abstract, extract, withdraw; abate, banish, destroy, suppress; cashier, depose, discharge, dismiss, eject, expel, oust, retire; depart, move.

remunerate *vb* compensate, indemnify, pay, recompense, reimburse, repay, requite, reward, satisfy.

remuneration *n* compensation, earnings, indemnity, pay, payment, recompense, reimbursement, reparation, repayment, reward, salary, wages.

remunerative *adj* gainful, lucrative, paying, profitable; compensatory, recompensing, remuneratory, reparative, requiting, rewarding.

rend *vb* break, burst, cleave, crack, destroy, dismember, dissever, disrupt, divide, fracture, lacerate, rive, rupture, sever, shiver, snap, split, sunder, tear.

render *vb* restore, return, surrender; assign, deliver, give, present; afford, contribute, furnish, supply, yield; construe, interpret, translate.

rendition *n* restitution, return, surrender; delineation, exhibition, interpretation, rendering, representation, reproduction; translation, version.

renegade *adj* apostate, backsliding, disloyal, false, outlawed, rebellious, recreant, unfaithful. * *n* apostate, backslider, recreant, turncoat; deserter, outlaw, rebel, revolter, traitor; vagabond, wretch.

renew *vb* rebuild, recreate, re-establish, refit, refresh, rejuvenate, renovate, repair, replenish, restore, resuscitate, revive; continue, recommence, repeat; iterate, reiterate; regenerate, transform.

renounce *vb* abjure, abnegate, decline, deny, disclaim, disown, forswear, neglect, recant, repudiate, reject, slight; abandon, abdicate, drop, forgo, forsake, desert, leave, quit, relinquish, resign.

renovate *vb* reconstitute, re-establish, refresh, refurbish, renew, restore, revamp; reanimate, recreate, regenerate, reproduce, resuscitate, revive, revivify.

renown *n* celebrity, distinction, eminence, fame, figure, glory, honour, greatness, name, note, notability, notoriety, reputation, repute.

renowned *adj* celebrated, distinguished, eminent, famed, famous, honoured, illustrious, remarkable, wonderful.

rent[1] *n* breach, break, crack, cleft, crevice, fissure, flaw, fracture, gap, laceration, opening, rift, rupture, separation, split, tear; schism.

rent[2] *vb* hire, lease, let. * *n* income, rental, revenue.

repair[1] *vb* mend, patch, piece, refit, retouch, tinker, vamp; correct, recruit, restore, retrieve. * *n* mending, refitting, renewal, reparation, restoration.

repair[2] *vb* betake oneself, go, move, resort, turn.

repairable *adj* curable, recoverable, reparable, restorable, retrievable.

reparable *adj* curable, recoverable, repairable, restorable, retrievable.

reparation *n* renewal, repair, restoration; amends, atonement, compensation, correction, indemnification, recompense, redress, requital, restitution, satisfaction.

repay *vb* refund, reimburse, restore, return; compensate, recompense, remunerate, reward, satisfy; avenge, retaliate, revenge.

repeal *vb* abolish, annul, cancel, recall, rescind, reverse, revoke. * *n* abolition, abrogation, annulment, cancellation, rescission, reversal, revocation.

repeat *vb* double, duplicate, iterate; cite, narrate, quote, recapitulate, recite, rehearse; echo, renew, reproduce. * *n* duplicate, duplication, echo, iteration, recapitulation, reiteration, repetition.

repel *vb* beat, disperse, repulse, scatter; check, confront, oppose, parry, rebuff, resist, withstand; decline, refuse, reject; disgust, revolt, sicken.

repellent *adj* abhorrent, disgusting, forbidding, repelling, repugnant, repulsive, revolting, uninviting.

repent *vb* atone, regret, relent, rue, sorrow.

repentance *n* compunction, contriteness, contrition, penitence, regret, remorse, self-accusation, self-condemnation, self-reproach.

repentant *adj* contrite, penitent, regretful, remorseful, rueful, sorrowful, sorry.

repercussion *n* rebound, recoil, reverberation; backlash, consequence, result.

repetition *n* harping, iteration, recapitulation, reiteration; diffuseness, redundancy, tautology, verbosity; narration, recital, rehearsal, relation, retailing; recurrence, renewal.

repine *vb* croak, complain, fret, grumble, long, mope, murmur.

replace *vb* re-establish, reinstate, reset; refund, repay, restore; succeed, supersede, supplant.

replenish *vb* fill, refill, renew, re-supply; enrich, furnish, provide, store, supply.

replete *adj* abounding, charged, exuberant, fraught, full, glutted, gorged, satiated, well-stocked.

repletion *n* abundance, exuberance, fullness, glut, profusion, satiation, satiety, surfeit.

replica *n* autograph, copy, duplicate, facsimile, reproduction.

reply *vb* answer, echo, rejoin, respond. * *n* acknowledgement, answer, rejoinder, repartee, replication, response, retort.

report *vb* announce, annunciate, communicate, declare; advertise, broadcast, bruit, describe, detail, herald, mention, narrate, noise, promulgate, publish, recite, relate, rumour, state, tell; minute, record. * *n* account, announcement, communication, declaration, statement; advice, description, detail, narration, narrative, news, recital, story, tale, talk, tidings; gossip, hearsay, rumour; clap, detonation, discharge, explosion, noise, repercussion, sound; fame, reputation, repute; account, bulletin, minute, note, record, statement.

repose[1] *vb* compose, recline, rest, settle; couch, lie, recline, sleep, slumber; confide, lean. * *n* quiet, recumbence, recumbency, rest, sleep, slumber; breathing time, inactivity, leisure, respite, relaxation; calm, ease, peace, peacefulness, quietness, quietude, stillness, tranquillity.

repose[2] *vb* place, put, stake; deposit, lodge, reposit, store.

repository *n* conservatory, depository, depot, magazine, museum, receptacle, repertory, storehouse, storeroom, thesaurus, treasury, vault.

reprehend *vb* accuse, blame, censure, chide, rebuke, reprimand, reproach, reprove, upbraid.

reprehensible *adj* blameable, blameworthy, censurable, condemnable, culpable, reprovable.

reprehension *n* admonition, blame, censure, condemnation, rebuke, reprimand, reproof.

represent *vb* exhibit, express, show; delineate, depict, describe, draw, portray, sketch; act, impersonate, mimic, personate, personify; exemplify, illustrate, image, reproduce, symbolize, typify.

representation *n* delineation, exhibition, show; impersonation, personation, simulation; account, description, narration, narrative, relation, statement; image, likeness, model, portraiture, resemblance, sem-

blance; sight, spectacle; expostulation, remonstrance.

representative *adj* figurative, illustrative, symbolic, typical; delegated, deputed, representing. * *n* agent, commissioner, delegate, deputy, emissary, envoy, legate, lieutenant, messenger, proxy, substitute.

repress *vb* choke, crush, dull, overcome, overpower, silence, smother, subdue, suppress, quell; bridle, chasten, chastise, check, control, curb, restrain; appease, calm, quiet.

reprimand *vb* admonish, blame, censure, chide, rebuke, reprehend, reproach, reprove, upbraid. * *n* admonition, blame, censure, rebuke, reprehension, reproach, reprobation, reproof, reproval.

reprint *vb* republish. * *n* reimpression, republication; copy.

reproach *vb* blame, censure, rebuke, reprehend, reprimand, reprove, upbraid; abuse, accuse, asperse, condemn, defame, discredit, disparage, revile, traduce, vilify. * *n* abuse, blame, censure, condemnation, contempt, contumely, disapprobation, disapproval, expostulation, insolence, invective, railing, rebuke, remonstrance, reprobation, reproof, reviling, scorn, scurrility, upbraiding, vilification; abasement, discredit, disgrace, dishonour, disrepute, indignity, ignominy, infamy, insult, obloquy, odium, offence, opprobrium, scandal, shame, slur, stigma.

reproachful *adj* abusive, censorious, condemnatory, contemptuous, contumelious, damnatory, insolent, insulting, offensive, opprobrious, railing, reproving, sacrifice, scolding, scornful, scurrilous, upbraiding, vituperative; base, discreditable, disgraceful, dishonourable, disreputable, infamous, scandalous, shameful, vile.

reprobate *vb* censure, condemn, disapprove, discard, reject, reprehend; disallow; abandon, disown. * *adj* abandoned, base, castaway, corrupt, depraved, graceless, hardened, irredeemable, lost, profligate, shameless, vile, vitiated, wicked. * *n* caitiff, castaway, miscreant, outcast, rascal, scamp, scoundrel, sinner, villain.

reproduce *vb* copy, duplicate, emulate, imitate, print, repeat, represent; breed, generate, procreate, propagate.

reproof *n* admonition, animadversion, blame, castigation, censure, chiding, condemnation, correction, criticism, lecture, monition, objurgation, rating, rebuke, reprehension, reprimand, reproach, reproval, upbraiding.

reprove *vb* admonish, blame, castigate, censure, chide, condemn, correct, criticize, inculpate, lecture, objurgate, rate, rebuke, reprimand, reproach, scold, upbraid.

reptilian *adj* abject, crawling, creeping, grovelling, low, mean, treacherous, vile, vulgar.

repudiate *vb* abjure, deny, disavow, discard, disclaim, disown, nullify, reject, renounce.

repugnance *n* contrariety, contrariness, incompatibility, inconsistency, irreconcilability, irreconcilableness, unsuitability, unsuitableness; contest, opposition, resistance, struggle; antipathy, aversion, detestation, dislike, hatred, hostility, reluctance, repulsion, unwillingness.

repugnant *adj* incompatible, inconsistent, irreconcilable; adverse, antagonistic, contrary, hostile, inimical, opposed, opposing, unfavourable; detestable, distasteful, offensive, repellent, repulsive.

repulse *vb* check, defeat, refuse, reject, repel. * *n* repelling, repulsion; denial, refusal; disappointment, failure.

repulsion *n* abhorrence, antagonism, anticipation, aversion, discard, disgust, dislike, hatred, hostility, loathing, rebuff, rejection, repugnance, repulse, spurning.

repulsive *adj* abhorrent, cold, disagreeable, disgusting, forbidding, frigid, harsh, hateful, loathsome, nauseating, nauseous, odious, offensive, repellent, repugnant, reserved, revolting, sickening, ugly, unpleasant.

reputable *adj* creditable, estimable, excellent, good, honourable, respectable, worthy.

reputation *n* account, character, fame, mark, name, repute; celebrity, credit, distinction, eclat, esteem, estimation, glory, honour, prestige, regard, renown, report, respect; notoriety.

repute *vb* account, consider, deem, esteem, estimate, hold, judge, reckon, regard, think.

request *vb* ask, beg, beseech, call, claim, demand, desire, entreat, pray, solicit, supplicate. * *n* asking, entreaty, importunity, invitation, petition, prayer, requisition, solicitation, suit, supplication.

require *vb* beg, beseech, bid, claim, crave, demand, dun, importune, invite, pray, requisition, request, sue, summon; need, want; direct, enjoin, exact, order, prescribe.

requirement *n* claim, demand, exigency, market, need, needfulness, requisite, requisition, request, urgency, want; behest, bidding, charge, command, decree, exaction, injunction, mandate, order, precept.

requisite *adj* essential, imperative, indispensable, necessary, needful, needed, required. * *n* essential, necessity, need, requirement.

requite *vb* compensate, pay, remunerate, reciprocate, recompense, repay, reward, satisfy; avenge, punish, retaliate, satisfy.

rescind *vb* abolish, abrogate, annul, cancel, countermand, quash, recall, repeal, reverse, revoke, vacate, void.

rescue *vb* deliver, extricate, free, liberate, preserve, ransom, recapture, recover, redeem, release, retake, save. * *n* deliverance, extrication, liberation, redemption, release, salvation.

research *vb* analyse, examine, explore, inquire, investigate, probe, study. * *n* analysis, examination, exploration, inquiry, investigation, scrutiny, study.

resemblance *n* affinity, agreement, analogy, likeness, semblance, similarity, similitude; counterpart, facsimile, image, representation.

resemble *vb* compare, liken; copy, counterfeit, imitate.

resentful *adj* angry, bitter, choleric, huffy, hurt, irascible, irritable, malignant, revengeful, sore, touchy.

resentment *n* acrimony, anger, annoyance, bitterness, choler, displeasure, dudgeon, fury, gall, grudge, heartburning, huff, indignation, ire, irritation, pique, rage, soreness, spleen, sulks, umbrage, vexation, wrath.

reservation *n* reserve, suppression; appropriation, booking, exception, restriction, saving; proviso, salvo; custody, park, reserve, sanctuary.

reserve *vb* hold, husband, keep, retain, store. * *adj* alternate, auxiliary, spare, substitute. * *n* reservation; aloofness, backwardness, closeness, coldness, concealment, constraint, suppression, reservedness, retention, restraint, reticence, uncommunicativeness, unresponsiveness; coyness, demureness, modesty, shyness, taciturnity; park, reservation, sanctuary.

reserved *adj* coy, demure, modest, shy, taciturn; aloof, backward, cautious, cold, distant, incommunicative, restrained, reticent, self-controlled, unsociable, unsocial; bespoken, booked, excepted, held, kept, retained, set apart, taken, withheld.

reside *vb* abide, domicile, domiciliate, dwell, inhabit, live, lodge, remain, room, sojourn, stay.

residence *n* inhabitance, inhabitancy, sojourn, stay, stop, tarrying; abode, domicile, dwelling, habitation, home, house, lodging, mansion.

residue *n* leavings, remainder, remains, remnant, residuum, rest; excess, overplus, surplus.

resign *vb* abandon, abdicate, abjure, cede, commit, disclaim, forego, forsake, leave, quit, relinquish, renounce, surrender, yield.

resignation *n* abandonment, abdication, relinquishment, renunciation, retirement, surrender; acquiescence, compliance, endurance, forbearance, fortitude, long-sufferance, patience, submission, sufferance.

resist *vb* assail, attack, baffle, block, check, confront, counteract, disappoint, frustrate, hinder, impede, impugn, neutralize, obstruct, oppose, rebel, rebuff, stand against, stem, stop, strive, thwart, withstand.

resolute *adj* bold, constant, decided, determined, earnest, firm, fixed, game, hardy, inflexible, persevering, pertinacious, relentless, resolved, staunch, steadfast, steady, stout, stouthearted, sturdy, tenacious, unalterable, unbending, undaunted, unflinching, unshaken, unwavering, unyielding.

resolution *n* boldness, disentanglement, explication, unravelling; backbone, constancy, courage, decision, determination, earnestness, energy, firmness, fortitude, grit, hardihood, inflexibility, intention, manliness, pluck, perseverance, purpose, relentlessness, resolve, resoluteness, stamina, steadfastness, steadiness, tenacity.

resolve *vb* analyse, disperse, scatter, separate, reduce; change, dissolve, liquefy, melt, reduce, transform; decipher, disentangle, elucidate, explain, interpret, unfold, solve, unravel; conclude, decide, determine, fix, intend, purpose, will. * *n* conclusion, decision, determination, intention, will; declaration, resolution.

resonant *adj* booming, clangorous, resounding, reverberating, ringing, roaring, sonorous, thundering, vibrant.

resort *vb* frequent, haunt; assemble, congregate, convene, go, repair. * *n* application, expedient, recourse; haunt, refuge, rendezvous, retreat, spa; assembling, confluence, concourse, meeting; recourse, reference.

resound *vb* echo, re-echo, reverberate, ring; celebrate, extol, praise, sound.

resource *n* dependence, resort; appliance, contrivance, device, expedient, instrumentality, means, resort.

resources *npl* capital, funds, income, money, property, reserve, supplies, wealth.

respect *vb* admire, esteem, honour, prize, regard, revere, reverence, spare, value, venerate; consider, heed, notice, observe. * *n* attention, civility, courtesy, consideration, deference, estimation, homage, honour, notice, politeness, recognition, regard, reverence, veneration; consideration, favour, goodwill, kind; aspect, bearing, connection, feature, matter, particular, point, reference, regard, relation.

respects *npl* compliments, greetings, regards.

respectable *adj* considerable, estimable, honourable, presentable, proper, upright, worthy; adequate, moderate; tolerable.

respectful *adj* ceremonious, civil, complaisant, courteous, decorous, deferential, dutiful, formal, polite.

respire *vb* breathe, exhale, live.

respite *vb* delay, relieve, reprieve. * *n* break, cessation, delay, intermission, interval, pause, recess, rest, stay, stop; forbearance, postponement, reprieve.

resplendent *adj* beaming, bright, brilliant, effulgent, lucid, glittering, glorious, gorgeous, luminous, lustrous, radiant, shining, splendid.

respond *vb* answer, reply, rejoin; accord, correspond, suit.

response *n* answer, replication, rejoinder, reply, retort.

responsible *adj* accountable, amenable, answerable, liable, trustworthy.

rest[1] *vb* cease, desist, halt, hold, pause, repose, stop; breathe, relax, unbend; repose, sleep, slumber; lean, lie, lounge, perch, recline, ride; acquiesce, confide, trust; confide, rely, trust; calm, comfort, ease. * *n* fixity, immobility, inactivity, motionlessness, quiescence, quiet, repose; hush, peace, peacefulness, quietness, relief, security, stillness, tranquillity; cessation, intermission, interval, lull, pause, relaxation, respite, stop, stay; siesta, sleep, slumber; death; brace, stay, support; axis, fulcrum, pivot.

rest[2] *vb* be left, remain. * *n* balance, remainder, remnant, residuum; overplus, surplus.

restaurant *n* bistro, café, cafeteria, chophouse, eatery, eating house, pizzeria, trattoria.

restitution *n* restoration, return; amends, compensation, indemnification, recompense, rehabilitation, remuneration, reparation, repayment, requital, satisfaction.

restive *adj* mulish, obstinate, stopping, stubborn, unwilling; impatient, recalcitrant, restless, uneasy, unquiet.

restless *adj* disquieted, disturbed, restive, sleepless, uneasy, unquiet, unresting; changeable, inconstant, irresolute, unsteady, vacillating; active, astatic, roving, transient, unsettled, unstable, wandering; agitated, fidgety, fretful, turbulent.

restoration *n* recall, recovery, re-establishment, reinstatement, reparation, replacement, restitution, return; reconsideration, redemption, reintegration, renewal, renovation, repair, resuscitation, revival; convalescence, cure, recruitment, recuperation.

restorative *adj* curative, invigorating, recuperative, remedial, restoring, stimulating. * *n* corrective, curative, cure, healing, medicine, remedy, reparative, stimulant.

restore *vb* refund, repay, return; caulk, cobble, emend, heal, mend, patch, reintegrate, re-establish, rehabilitate, reinstate, renew, repair, replace, retrieve; cure, heal, recover, revive; resuscitate.

restrain *vb* bridle, check, coerce, confine, constrain, curb, debar, govern, hamper, hinder, hold, keep, muzzle, picket, prevent, repress, restrict, rule, subdue, tie, withhold; abridge, circumscribe, narrow.

restraint *n* bridle, check, coercion, control, compulsion, constraint, curb, discipline, repression, suppression; arrest, deterrence, hindrance, inhibition, limitation, prevention, prohibition, restriction, stay, stop; confinement, detention, imprisonment, shackles; constraint, stiffness, reserve, unnaturalness.

restrict *vb* bound, circumscribe, confine, limit, qualify, restrain, straiten.

restriction *n* confinement, limitation; constraint, restraint; reservation, reserve.

result *vb* accrue, arise, come, ensue, flow, follow, issue, originate, proceed, spring, rise; end, eventuate, terminate. * *n* conclusion, consequence, deduction, inference, outcome; corollary, effect, end, event, eventuality, fruit, harvest, issue, product, sequel, termination; decision, determination, finding, resolution, resolve, solution, verdict.

resume *vb* continue, recommence, renew, restart, summarize.

résumé *n* abstract, curriculum vitae, epitome, recapitulation, summary, synopsis.

resuscitate *vb* quicken, reanimate, renew, resurrect, restore, revive, revivify.

retain *vb* detain, hold, husband, keep, preserve, recall, recollect, remember, reserve, save, withhold; engage, maintain.

retainer *n* adherent, attendant, dependant, follower, hanger-on, servant.

retaliate *vb* avenge, match, repay, requite, retort, return, turn.

retaliation *n* boomerang, counterstroke, punishment, repayment, requital, retribution, revenge.

retard *vb* check, clog, hinder, impede, obstruct, slacken; adjourn, defer, delay, postpone, procrastinate.

reticent *adj* close, reserved, secretive, silent, taciturn, uncommunicative.

retinue *n* bodyguard, cortege, entourage, escort, followers, household, ménage, suite, tail, train.

retire *vb* discharge, shelve, superannuate, withdraw; depart, leave, resign, retreat.

retired *adj* abstracted, removed, withdrawn; apart, private, secret, sequestrated, solitary.

retirement *n* isolation, loneliness, privacy, retreat, seclusion, solitude, withdrawal.

retiring *adj* coy, demure, diffident, modest, reserved, retreating, shy, withdrawing.

retort *vb* answer, rejoin, reply, respond. * *n* answer, rejoinder, repartee, reply, response; crucible, jar, vessel, vial.

retract *vb* reverse, withdraw; abjure, cancel, disavow, recall, recant, revoke, unsay.

retreat *vb* recoil, retire, withdraw; recede. * *n* departure, recession, recoil, retirement, withdrawal; privacy, seclusion, solitude; asylum, cove, den, habitat, haunt, niche, recess, refuge, resort, shelter.

retrench *vb* clip, curtail, cut, delete, dock, lop, mutilate, pare, prune; abridge, decrease, diminish, lessen; confine, limit; economize, encroach.

retribution *n* compensation, desert, judgement, nemesis, penalty, recompense, repayment, requital, retaliation, return, revenge, reward, vengeance.

retrieve *vb* recall, recover, recoup, recruit, re-establish, regain, repair, restore.

retrograde *vb* decline, degenerate, recede, retire, retrocede. * *adj* backward, inverse, retrogressive, unprogressive.

retrospect *n* recollection, re-examination, reminiscence, re-survey, review, survey.

return *vb* reappear, recoil, recur, revert; answer, reply, respond; recriminate, retort; convey, give, communicate, reciprocate, recompense, refund, remit, repay, report, requite, send, tell, transmit; elect. * *n* payment, reimbursement, remittance, repayment; recompense, recovery, recurrence, renewal, repayment, requital, restitution, restoration, reward; advantage, benefit, interest, profit, rent, yield.

reunion *n* assemblage, assembly, gathering, meeting, re-assembly; rapprochement, reconciliation.

reveal *vb* announce, communicate, confess, declare, disclose, discover, display, divulge, expose, impart, open, publish, tell, uncover, unmask, unseal, unveil.

revel *vb* carouse, disport, riot, roister, tipple; delight, indulge, luxuriate, wanton. * *n* carousal, feast, festival, saturnalia, spree.

revelry *n* bacchanal, carousal, carouse, debauch, festivity, jollification, jollity, orgy, revel, riot, rout, saturnalia, wassail.

revenge *vb* avenge, repay, requite, retaliate, vindicate. * *n* malevolence, rancour, reprisal, requital, retaliation, retribution, vengeance, vindictiveness.

revengeful *adj* implacable, malevolent, malicious, malignant, resentful, rancorous, spiteful, vengeful, vindictive.

revenue *n* fruits, income, produce, proceeds, receipts, return, reward, wealth.

reverberate *vb* echo, re-echo, resound, return.

revere *vb* adore, esteem, hallow, honour, reverence, venerate, worship.

reverence *vb* adore, esteem, hallow, honour, revere, venerate, worship. * *n* adoration, awe, deference, homage, honour, respect, veneration, worship.

reverential *adj* deferential, humble, respectful, reverent, submissive.

reverse *vb* invert, transpose; overset, overthrow, overturn, quash, subvert, undo, unmake; annul, countermand, repeal, rescind, retract, revoke; back, back up, retreat. * *adj* back, converse, contrary, opposite, verso. * *n* back, calamity, check, comedown, contrary, counterpart, defeat, opposite, tail; change, vicissitude; adversity, affliction, hardship, misadventure, mischance, misfortune, mishap, trial.

revert *vb* repel, reverse; backslide, lapse, recur, relapse, return.

review *vb* inspect, overlook, reconsider, re-examine, retrace, revise, survey; analyse, criticize, discuss, edit, judge, scrutinize, study. * *n* reconsideration, re-examination, re-survey, retrospect, survey; analysis, digest, synopsis; commentary, critique, criticism, notice, review, scrutiny, study.

revile *vb* abuse, asperse, backbite, calumniate, defame, execrate, malign, reproach, slander, traduce, upbraid, vilify.

revise *vb* reconsider, re-examine, review; alter, amend, correct, edit, overhaul, polish.

revive *vb* reanimate, reinspire, reinspirit, reinvigorate, resuscitate, revitalize, revivify; animate, cheer, comfort, invigorate, quicken, reawaken, recover, refresh, renew, renovate, rouse, strengthen; reawake, recall.

revocation *n* abjuration, recall, recantation, repeal, retraction, reversal.

revoke *vb* abolish, abrogate, annul, cancel, countermand, invalidate, quash, recall, recant, repeal, repudiate, rescind, retract.

revolt *vb* desert, mutiny, rebel, rise; disgust, nauseate, repel, sicken. * *n* defection, desertion, faithlessness, inconstancy; disobedience, insurrection, mutiny, outbreak, rebellion, sedition, strike, uprising.

revolting *adj* abhorrent, abominable, disgusting, hateful, monstrous, nauseating, nauseous, objectionable, obnoxious, offensive, repulsive, shocking, sickening; insurgent, mutinous, rebellious.

revolution *n* coup, disobedience, insurrection, mutiny, outbreak, rebellion, sedition, strike, uprising; change, innovation, reformation, transformation, upheaval; circle, circuit, cycle, lap, orbit, rotation, spin, turn..

revolve *vb* circle, circulate, rotate, swing, turn, wheel; devolve, return; consider, mediate, ponder, ruminate, study.

revulsion *n* abstraction, shrinking, withdrawal; change, reaction, reversal, transition; abhorrence, disgust, loathing, repugnance.

reward *vb* compensate, gratify, indemnify, pay, punish, recompense, remember, remunerate, requite. * *n* compensation, gratification, guerdon, indemnification, pay, recompense, remuneration, requital; bounty, bonus, fee, gratuity, honorarium, meed, perquisite, premium, remembrance, tip; punishment, retribution.

rhythm *n* cadence, lilt, pulsation, swing; measure, metre, number.

ribald *adj* base, blue, coarse, filthy, gross, indecent, lewd, loose, low, mean, obscene, vile.

rich *adj* affluent, flush, moneyed, opulent, prosperous, wealthy; costly, estimable, gorgeous, luxurious, precious, splendid, sumptuous, superb, valuable; delicious, luscious, savoury; abundant, ample, copious, enough, full, plentiful, plenteous, sufficient; fertile, fruitful, luxuriant, productive, prolific; bright, dark, deep, exuberant, vivid; harmonious, mellow, melodious, soft, sweet; comical, funny, humorous, laughable.

riches *npl* abundance, affluence, fortune, money, opulence, plenty, richness, wealth, wealthiness.

rickety *adj* broken, imperfect, shaky, shattered, tottering, tumbledown, unsteady, weak.

rid *vb* deliver, free, release; clear, disburden, disencumber, scour, sweep; disinherit, dispatch, dissolve, divorce, finish, sever.

riddance *n* deliverance, disencumberment, extrication, escape, freedom, release, relief.

riddle[1] *vb* explain, solve, unriddle. * *n* conundrum, enigma, mystery, puzzle, rebus.

riddle[2] *vb* sieve, sift, perforate, permeate, spread. * *n* colander, sieve, strainer.

ridge *n* chine, hogback, ledge, saddle, spine, rib, watershed, weal, wrinkle.

ridicule *vb* banter, burlesque, chaff, deride, disparage, jeer, mock, lampoon, rally, satirize, scout, taunt. * *n* badinage, banter, burlesque, chaff, derision, game, gibe, irony, jeer, mockery, persiflage, quip, raillery, sarcasm, satire, sneer, squib, wit.

ridiculous *adj* absurd, amusing, comical, droll, eccentric, fantastic, farcical, funny, laughable, ludicrous, nonsensical, odd, outlandish, preposterous, queer, risible, waggish.

rife *adj* abundant, common, current, general, numerous, plentiful, prevailing, prevalent, replete.

riffraff *n* horde, mob, populace, rabble, scum, trash.

rifle *vb* despoil, fleece, pillage, plunder, ransack, rob, strip.

rift *vb* cleave, rive, split. * *n* breach, break, chink, cleft, crack, cranny, crevice, fissure, fracture, gap, opening, reft, rent.

rig *vb* accoutre, clothe, dress. * *n* costume, dress, garb; equipment, team.

right *vb* adjust, correct, regulate, settle, straighten, vindicate. * *adj* direct, rectilinear, straight; erect, perpendicular, plumb, upright; equitable, even-handed, fair, just, justifiable, honest, lawful, legal, legitimate, rightful, square, unswerving; appropriate, becoming, correct, conventional, fit, fitting, meet, orderly, proper, reasonable, seemly, suitable, well-done; actual, genuine, real, true, unquestionable; dexter, dextral, right-handed. * adv equitably, fairly, justly, lawfully, rightfully, rightly; correctly, fitly, properly, suitably, truly; actually, exactly, just, really, truly, well. * n authority, claim, liberty, permission, power, privilege, title; equity, good, honour, justice, lawfulness, legality, propriety, reason, righteousness, truth.

righteous adj devout, godly, good, holy, honest, incorrupt, just, pious, religious, saintly, uncorrupt, upright, virtuous; equitable, fair, right, rightful.

righteousness n equity, faithfulness, godliness, goodness, holiness, honesty, integrity, justice, piety, purity, right, rightfulness, sanctity, uprightness, virtue.

rightful adj lawful, legitimate, true; appropriate, correct, deserved, due, equitable, fair, fitting, honest, just, legal, merited, proper, reasonable, suitable.

rigid adj firm, hard, inflexible, permanent, stiff, stiffened, unbending, unpliant, unyielding; bristling, erect, precipitous, steep; austere, conventional, correct, exact, formal, harsh, meticulous, precise, rigorous, severe, sharp, stern, strict, unmitigated; cruel.

rigmarole n balderdash, flummery, gibberish, gobbledegook, jargon, nonsense, palaver, trash, twaddle, verbiage.

rigour n hardness, inflexibility, rigidity, rigidness, stiffness; asperity, austerity, harshness, severity, sternness; evenness, strictness; inclemency.

rile vb anger, annoy, irritate, upset, vex.

rim n brim, brink, border, confine, curb, edge, flange, girdle, margin, ring, skirt.

ring[1] vb circle, encircle, enclose, girdle, surround. * n circle, circlet, girdle, hoop, round, whorl; cabal, clique, combination, confederacy, coterie, gang, junta, league, set.

ring[2] vb chime, clang, jingle, knell, peal, resound, reverberate, sound, tingle, toll; call, phone, telephone. * n chime, knell, peal, tinkle, toll; call, phone call, telephone call.

riot vb carouse, luxuriate, revel. * n affray, altercation, brawl, broil, commotion, disturbance, fray, outbreak, pandemonium, quarrel, squabble, tumult, uproar; dissipation, excess, luxury, merrymaking, revelry.

riotous adj boisterous, luxurious, merry, revelling, unrestrained, wanton; disorderly, insubordinate, lawless, mutinous, rebellious, refractory, seditious, tumultuous, turbulent, ungovernable, unruly, violent.

ripe adj advanced, grown, mature, mellow, seasoned, soft; fit, prepared, ready; accomplished, complete, consummate, finished, perfect, perfected.

ripen vb burgeon, develop, mature, prepare.

rise vb arise, ascend, clamber, climb, levitate, mount; excel, succeed; enlarge, heighten, increase, swell, thrive; revive; grow, kindle, wax; begin, flow, head, originate, proceed, spring, start; mutiny, rebel, revolt; happen, occur. * n ascension, ascent, rising; elevation, grade, hill, slope; beginning, emergence, flow, origin, source, spring; advance, augmentation, expansion, increase.

risible adj amusing, comical, droll, farcical, funny, laughable, ludicrous, ridiculous.

risk vb bet, endanger, hazard, jeopardize, peril, speculate, stake, venture, wager. * n chance, danger, hazard, jeopardy, peril, venture.

rite n ceremonial, ceremony, form, formulary, ministration, observance, ordinance, ritual, rubric, sacrament, solemnity.

ritual adj ceremonial, conventional, formal, habitual, routine, stereotyped. * n ceremonial, ceremony, liturgy, observance, rite, sacrament, service; convention, form, formality, habit, practice, protocol.

rival vb emulate, match, oppose. * adj competing, contending, emulating, emulous, opposing. * n antagonist, competitor, emulator, opponent.

rive vb cleave, rend, split.

river n affluent, current, reach, stream, tributary.

road n course, highway, lane, passage, path, pathway, roadway, route, street, thoroughfare, track, trail, turnpike, way.

roam vb jaunt, prowl, ramble, range, rove, straggle, stray, stroll, wander.

roar vb bawl, bellow, cry, howl, vociferate, yell; boom, peal, rattle, resound, thunder. * n bellow, roaring; rage, resonance, storm, thunder; cry, outcry, shout; laugh, laughter, shout.

rob vb despoil, fleece, pilfer, pillage, plunder, rook, strip; appropriate, deprive, embezzle, plagiarize.

robber n bandit, brigand, desperado, depredator, despoiler, footpad, freebooter, highwayman, marauder, pillager, pirate, plunderer, rifler, thief.

robbery n depredation, despoilation, embezzlement, freebooting, larceny, peculation, piracy, plagiarism, plundering, spoliation, theft.

robe vb array, clothe, dress, invest. * n attire, costume, dress, garment, gown, habit, vestment; bathrobe, dressing gown, housecoat.

robust adj able-bodied, athletic, brawny, energetic, firm, forceful, hale, hardy, hearty, iron, lusty, muscular, powerful, seasoned, self-assertive, sinewy, sound, stalwart, stout, strong, sturdy, vigorous.

rock[1] n boulder, cliff, crag, reef, stone; asylum, defence, foundation, protection, refuge, strength, support; gneiss, granite, marble, slate, etc.

rock[2] vb calm, cradle, lull, quiet, soothe, still, tranquilize; reel, shake, sway, teeter, totter, wobble.

rogue n beggar, vagabond, vagrant; caitiff, cheat, knave, rascal, scamp, scapegrace, scoundrel, sharper, swindler, trickster, villain.

roguish adj dishonest, fraudulent, knavish, rascally, scoundrelly, trickish, tricky; arch, sportive, mischievous, puckish, waggish, wanton.

role n character, function, impersonation, part, task.

roll vb gyrate, revolve, rotate, turn, wheel; curl, muffle, swathe, wind; bind, involve, enfold, envelop; flatten, level, smooth, spread; bowl, drive; trundle, wheel; gybe, lean, lurch, stagger, sway, yaw; billow, swell, undulate; wallow, welter; flow, glide, run. * n document, scroll, volume; annals, chronicle, history, record, rota; catalogue, inventory, list, register, schedule; booming, resonance, reverberation, thunder; cylinder, roller.

rollicking adj frisky, frolicking, frolicsome, jolly, jovial, lively, swaggering.

romance vb exaggerate, fantasize. * n fantasy, fiction, legend, novel, story, tale; exaggeration, falsehood, lie; ballad, idyll, song.

romantic adj extravagant, fanciful, fantastic, ideal, imaginative, sentimental, wild; chimerical, fabulous, fantastic, fictitious, imaginary, improbable, legendary, picturesque, quixotic, sentimental. * n dreamer, idealist, sentimentalist, visionary.

romp vb caper, gambol, frisk, sport. * n caper, frolic, gambol.

room n accommodation, capacity, compass, elbow-room, expanse, extent, field, latitude, leeway, play, scope, space, swing; place, stead; apartment, chamber, lodging; chance, occasion, opportunity.

roomy *adj* ample, broad, capacious, comfortable, commodious, expansive, extensive, large, spacious, wide.

root[1] *vb* anchor, embed, fasten, implant, place, settle; confirm, establish. * *n* base, bottom, foundation; cause, occasion, motive, origin, reason, source; etymon, radical, radix, stem.

root[2] *vb* destroy, eradicate, extirpate, exterminate, remove, unearth, uproot; burrow, dig, forage, grub, rummage; applaud, cheer, encourage.

rooted *adj* chronic, confirmed, deep, established, fixed, radical.

roseate *adj* blooming, blushing, rose-coloured, rosy, rubicund; hopeful.

rostrum *n* platform, stage, stand, tribune.

rosy *adj* auspicious, blooming, blushing, favourable, flushed, hopeful, roseate, ruddy, sanguine.

rot *vb* corrupt, decay, decompose, degenerate, putrefy, spoil, taint. * *n* corruption, decay, decomposition, putrefaction.

rotary *adj* circular, rotating, revolving, rotatory, turning, whirling.

rotten *adj* carious, corrupt, decomposed, fetid, putrefied, putrescent, putrid, rank, stinking; defective, unsound; corrupt, deceitful, immoral, treacherous, unsound, untrustworthy.

rotund *adj* buxom, chubby, full, globular, obese, plump, round, stout; fluent, grandiloquent.

roué *n* debauchee, libertine, profligate, rake.

rough *vb* coarsen, roughen; manhandle, mishandle, molest. * *adj* bumpy, craggy, irregular, jagged, rugged, scabrous, scraggy, scratchy, stubby, uneven; approximate, cross-grained, crude, formless, incomplete, knotty, rough-hewn, shapeless, sketchy, uncut, unfashioned, unfinished, unhewn, unpolished, unwrought, vague; bristly, bushy, coarse, disordered, hairy, hirsute, ragged, shaggy, unkempt; austere, bearish, bluff, blunt, brusque, burly, churlish, discourteous, gruff, harsh, impolite, indelicate, rude, surly, uncivil, uncourteous, ungracious, unpolished, unrefined; harsh, severe, sharp, violent; astringent, crabbed, hard, sour, tart; discordant, grating, inharmonious, jarring, raucous, scabrous, unmusical; boisterous, foul, inclement, severe, stormy, tempestuous, tumultuous, turbulent, untamed, violent, wild; acrimonious, brutal, cruel, disorderly, riotous, rowdy, severe, uncivil, unfeeling, ungentle. * *n* bully, rowdy, roughneck, ruffian; draft, outline, sketch, suggestion; unevenness.

round *vb* curve; circuit, encircle, encompass, surround. * *adj* bulbous, circular, cylindrical, globular, orbed, orbicular, rotund, spherical; complete, considerable, entire, full, great, large, unbroken, whole; chubby, corpulent, plump, stout, swelling; continuous, flowing, harmonious, smooth; brisk, quick; blunt, candid, fair, frank, honest, open, plain, upright. * *adv* around, circularly, circuitously. * *prep* about, around. * *n* bout, cycle, game, lap, revolution, rotation, succession, turn; canon, catch, dance; ball, circle, circumference, cylinder, globe, sphere; circuit, compass, perambulation, routine, tour, watch.

roundabout *adj* circuitous, circumlocutory, indirect, tortuous; ample, broad, extensive; encircling, encompassing.

rouse *vb* arouse, awaken, raise, shake, wake, waken; animate, bestir, brace, enkindle, excite, inspire, kindle, rally, stimulate, stir, whet; startle, surprise.

rout *vb* beat, conquer, defeat, discomfit, overcome, overpower, overthrow, vanquish; chase away, dispel, disperse, scatter. * *n* defeat, discomfiture, flight, ruin; concourse, multitude, rabble; brawl, disturbance, noise, roar, uproar.

route *vb* direct, forward, send, steer. * *n* course, circuit, direction, itinerary, journey, march, road, passage, path, way.

routine *adj* conventional, familiar, habitual, ordinary, standard, typical, usual; boring, dull, humdrum, predictable, tiresome. * *n* beat, custom, groove, method, order, path, practice, procedure, round, rut.

rove *vb* prowl, ramble, range, roam, stray, struggle, stroll, wander.

row[1] *n* file, line, queue, range, rank, series, string, tier; alley, street, terrace.

row[2] *vb* argue, dispute, fight, quarrel, squabble. * *n* affray, altercation, brawl, broil, commotion, dispute, disturbance, noise, outbreak, quarrel, riot, squabble, tumult, uproar.

royal *adj* august, courtly, dignified, generous, grand, imperial, kingly, kinglike, magnanimous, magnificent, majestic, monarchical, noble, princely, regal, sovereign, splendid, superb.

rub *vb* abrade, chafe, grate, graze, scrape; burnish, clean, massage, polish, scour, wipe; apply, put, smear, spread. * *n* caress, massage, polish, scouring, shine, wipe; catch, difficulty, drawback, impediment, obstacle, problem.

rubbish *n* debris, detritus, fragments, refuse, ruins, waste; dregs, dross, garbage, litter, lumber, scoria, scum, sweepings, trash, trumpery.

rubicund *adj* blushing, erubescent, florid, flushed, red, reddish, ruddy.

rude *adj* coarse, crude, ill-formed, rough, rugged, shapeless, uneven, unfashioned, unformed, unwrought; artless, barbarous, boorish, clownish, ignorant, illiterate, loutish, raw, savage, uncivilized, uncouth, uncultivated, undisciplined, unpolished, ungraceful, unskilful, unskilled, untaught, untrained, untutored, vulgar; awkward, barbarous, bluff, blunt, boorish, brusque, brutal, churlish, gruff, ill-bred, impertinent, impolite, impudent, insolent, insulting, ribald, saucy, uncivil, uncourteous, unrefined; boisterous, fierce, harsh, severe, tumultuous, turbulent, violent; artless, inelegant, rustic, unpolished; hearty, robust.

rudimentary *adj* elementary, embryonic, fundamental, initial, primary, rudimental, undeveloped.

rue *vb* deplore, grieve, lament, regret, repent.

rueful *adj* dismal, doleful, lamentable, lugubrious, melancholic, melancholy, mournful, penitent, regretful, sad, sorrowful, woeful.

ruffian *n* bully, caitiff, cutthroat, hoodlum, miscreant, monster, murderer, rascal, robber, roisterer, rowdy, scoundrel, villain, wretch.

ruffle *vb* damage, derange, disarrange, dishevel, disorder, ripple, roughen, rumple; agitate, confuse, discompose, disquiet, disturb, excite, harass, irritate, molest, plague, perturb, torment, trouble, vex, worry; cockle, flounce, pucker, wrinkle. * *n* edging, frill, ruff; agitation, bustle, commotion, confusion, contention, disturbance, excitement, fight, fluster, flutter, flurry, perturbation, tumult.

rugged *adj* austere, bristly, coarse, crabbed, cragged, craggy, hard, hardy, irregular, ragged, robust, rough, rude, scraggy, severe, seamed, shaggy, uneven, unkempt, wrinkled; boisterous, inclement, stormy, tempestuous, tumultuous, turbulent, violent; grating, harsh, inharmonious, unmusical, scabrous.

ruin *vb* crush, damn, defeat, demolish, desolate, destroy, devastate, overthrow, overturn, overwhelm, seduce, shatter, smash, subvert, wreck; beggar, impoverish. * *n* damnation, decay, defeat, demolition, desolation, destruction, devastation, discomfiture, downfall, fall, loss, perdition, prostration, rack, ruination, shipwreck, subversion, undoing, wrack, wreck; bane, mischief, pest.

ruination *n* demolition, destruction, overthrow, ruin, subversion.

ruinous *adj* decayed, demolished, dilapidated; baneful, calamitous, damnatory, destructive, disastrous, mischievous, noisome, noxious, pernicious, subversive, wasteful.

rule *vb* bridle, command, conduct, control, direct, domineer, govern, judge, lead, manage, reign, restrain; advise, guide, persuade; adjudicate, decide, determine, establish, settle; obtain, prevail, predominate. * *n* authority, command, control, direction, domination, dominion, empire, government, jurisdiction, lordship, mastery, mastership, regency, reign, sway; behaviour, conduct; habit, method, order, regularity, routine, system; aphorism, canon, convention, criterion, formula, guide, law, maxim, model, precedent, precept, standard, system, test, touchstone; decision, order, prescription, regulation, ruling.

ruler *n* chief, governor, king, lord, master, monarch, potentate, regent, sovereign; director, head, manager, president; controller, guide, rule; straight-edge.

ruminate *vb* brood, chew, cogitate, consider, contemplate, meditate, muse, ponder, reflect, think.

rumour *vb* bruit, circulate, report, tell. * *n* bruit, gossip, hearsay, report, talk; news, report, story, tidings; celebrity, fame, reputation, repute.

rumple *vb* crease, crush, corrugate, crumple, disarrange, dishevel, pucker, ruffle, wrinkle. * *n* crease, corrugation, crumple, fold, pucker, wrinkle.

run *vb* bolt, career, course, gallop, haste, hasten, hie, hurry, lope, post, race, scamper, scour, scud, scuttle, speed, trip; flow, glide, go, move, proceed, stream; fuse, liquefy, melt; advance, pass, proceed, vanish; extend, lie, spread, stretch; circulate, pass, press; average, incline, tend; flee; pierce, stab; drive, force, propel, push, thrust, turn; cast, form, mould, shape; follow, perform, pursue, take; discharge, emit; direct, maintain, manage. * *n* race, running; course, current, flow, motion, passage, progress, way, wont; continuance, currency, popularity; excursion, gallop, journey, trip, trot; demand, pressure; brook, burn, flow, rill, rivulet, runlet, runnel, streamlet.

rupture *vb* break, burst, fracture, sever, split. * *n* breach, break, burst, disruption, fracture, split; contention, faction, feud, hostility, quarrel, schism.

rural *adj* agrarian, bucolic, country, pastoral, rustic, sylvan.

ruse *n* artifice, deception, deceit, fraud, hoax, imposture, manoeuvre, sham, stratagem, trick, wile.

rush *vb* attack, career, charge, dash, drive, gush, hurtle, precipitate, surge, sweep, tear. * *n* dash, onrush, onset, plunge, precipitance, precipitancy, rout, stampede, tear.

rust *vb* corrode, decay, degenerate. * *n* blight, corrosion, crust, mildew, must, mould, mustiness.

rustic *adj* country, rural; awkward, boorish, clownish, countrified, loutish, outlandish, rough, rude, uncouth, unpolished, untaught; coarse, countrified, homely, plain, simple, unadorned; artless, honest, unsophisticated. * *n* boor, bumpkin, clown, countryman, peasant, swain, yokel.

ruthless *adj* barbarous, cruel, fell, ferocious, hardhearted, inexorable, inhuman, merciless, pitiless, relentless, remorseless, savage, truculent, uncompassionate, unmerciful, unpitying, unrelenting, unsparing.

S

sable *adj* black, dark, dusky, ebony, sombre.

sabulous *adj* gritty, sabulose, sandy.

sack[1] *n* bag, pouch.

sack[2] *vb* despoil, devastate, pillage, plunder, ravage, spoil. * *n* desolation, despoliation, destruction, devastation, havoc, ravage, sacking, spoliation, waste; booty, plunder, spoil.

sacred *adj* consecrated, dedicated, devoted, divine, hallowed, holy; inviolable, inviolate; sainted, venerable.

sacrifice *vb* forgo, immolate, surrender. * *n* immolation, oblation, offering; destruction, devotion, loss, surrender.

sacrilege *n* desecration, profanation, violation.

sacrilegious *adj* desecrating, impious, irreverent, profane.

sad *adj* grave, pensive, sedate, serious, sober, sombre, staid.

saddle *vb* burden, charge, clog, encumber, load.

sadly *adv* grievously, miserable, mournfully, sorrowfully; afflictively, badly, calamitously; darkly; gravely, seriously, soberly.

sadness *n* dejection, depression, despondency, melancholy, mournful, sorrow, sorrowfulness; dolefulness, gloominess, grief, mournfulness, sorrow; gravity, sedateness, seriousness.

safe *adj* undamaged, unharmed, unhurt, unscathed; guarded, protected, secure, snug, unexposed; certain, dependable, reliable, sure, trustworthy; good, harmless, sound, whole. * *n* chest, coffer, strongbox.

safeguard *vb* guard, protect. * *n* defence, protection, security; convoy, escort, guard, safe-conduct; pass, passport.

sagacious *adj* acute, apt, astute, clear-sighted, discerning, intelligent, judicious, keen, penetrating, perspicacious, rational, sage, sharp-witted, wise, shrewd.

sagacity *n* acuteness, astuteness, discernment, ingenuity, insight, penetration, perspicacity, quickness, readiness, sense, sharpness, shrewdness, wisdom.

sage *adj* acute, discerning, intelligent, prudent, sagacious, sapient, sensible, shrewd, wise; judicious, well-judged; grave, serious, solemn. * *n* philosopher, pundit, savant.

sailor *n* mariner, navigator, salt, seafarer, seaman, tar.

saintly *adj* devout, godly, holy, pious, religious.

sake *n* end, cause, purpose, reason; account, consideration, interest, regard, respect, score.

saleable *adj* marketable, merchantable, vendible.

salacious *adj* carnal, concupiscent, incontinent, lascivious, lecherous, lewd, libidinous, loose, lustful, prurient, unchaste, wanton.

salary *n* allowance, hire, pay, stipend, wages.

salient *adj* bounding, jumping, leaping; beating, springing, throbbing; jutting, projecting, prominent; conspicuous, remarkable, striking.

saline *adj* briny, salty.

sally *vb* issue, rush. * *n* digression, excursion, sortie, run, trip; escapade, frolic; crank, fancy, jest, joke, quip, quirk, sprightly, witticism.

salt *adj* saline, salted, salty; bitter, pungent, sharp. * *n* flavour, savour, seasoning, smack, relish, taste; humour, piquancy, poignancy, sarcasm, smartness, wit, zest; mariner, sailor, seaman, tar.

salubrious *adj* beneficial, benign, healthful, healthy, salutary, sanitary, wholesome.

salutary *adj* healthy, healthful, helpful, safe, salubrious, wholesome; advantageous, beneficial, good, profitable, serviceable, useful.

salute *vb* accost, address, congratulate, greet, hail, welcome. * *n* address, greeting, salutation.

salvation *n* deliverance, escape, preservation, redemption, rescue, saving.

same *adj* ditto, identical, selfsame; corresponding, like, similar.

sample *vb* savour, sip, smack, sup, taste; test, try; demonstrate, exemplify, illustrate, instance. * *adj* exemplary, illustrative, representative. * *n* demonstration, exemplification, illustration, instance, piece, specimen; example, model, pattern.

sanctify *vb* consecrate, hallow, purify; justify, ratify, sanction.

sanctimonious *adj* affected, devout, holy, hypocritical, pharisaical, pious, self-righteous.

sanction *vb* authorize, countenance, encourage, support; confirm, ratify. * *n* approval, authority, authorization, confirmation, countenance, endorsement, ratification, support, warranty; ban, boycott, embargo, penalty.

sanctity *n* devotion, godliness, goodness, grace, holiness, piety, purity, religiousness, saintliness.

sanctuary *n* altar, church, shrine, temple; asylum, protection, refuge, retreat, shelter.

sane *adj* healthy, lucid, rational, reasonable, sober, sound.

sang-froid *n* calmness, composure, coolness, imperturbability, indifference, nonchalance, phlegm, unconcern.

sanguinary *adj* bloody, gory, murderous; barbarous, bloodthirsty, cruel, fell, pitiless, savage, ruthless.

sanguine *adj* crimson, florid, red; animated, ardent, cheerful, lively, warm; buoyant, confident, enthusiastic, hopeful, optimistic; full-blooded.

sanitary *adj* clean, curative, healing, healthy, hygienic, remedial, therapeutic, wholesome.

sanity *n* normality, rationality, reason, saneness, soundness.

sapient *adj* acute, discerning, intelligent, knowing, sagacious, sage, sensible, shrewd, wise.

sarcastic *adj* acrimonious, biting, cutting, mordacious, mordant, sardonic, satirical, sharp, severe, sneering, taunting.

sardonic *adj* bitter, derisive, ironical, malevolent, malicious, malignant, sarcastic.

satanic *adj* devilish, diabolical, evil, false, fiendish, hellish, infernal, malicious.

satellite *adj* dependent, subordinate, tributary, vassal. * *n* attendant, dependant, follower, hanger-on, retainer, vassal.

satiate *vb* fill, sate, satisfy, suffice; cloy, glut, gorge, overfeed, overfill, pall, surfeit.

satire *n* burlesque, diatribe, invective, fling, irony, lampoon, pasquinade, philippic, ridicule, sarcasm, skit, squib.

satirical *adj* abusive, biting, bitter, censorious, cutting, invective, ironical, keen, mordacious, poignant, reproachful, sarcastic, severe, sharp, taunting.

satirize *vb* abuse, censure, lampoon, ridicule.

satisfaction *n* comfort, complacency, contentment, ease, enjoyment, gratification, pleasure, satiety; amends, appeasement, atonement, compensation, indemnification, recompense, redress, remuneration, reparation, requital, reward.

satisfactory *adj* adequate, conclusive, convincing, decisive, sufficient; gratifying, pleasing.

satisfy *vb* appease, content, fill, gratify, please, sate, satiate, suffice; indemnify, compensate, liquidate, pay, recompense, remunerate, requite; discharge, settle; assure, convince, persuade; answer, fulfil, meet.

saturate *vb* drench, fill, fit, imbue, soak, steep, wet.

saturnine *adj* dark, dull, gloomy, grave, heavy, leaden, morose, phlegmatic, sad, sedate, sombre; melancholic, mournful, serious, unhappy; mischievous, naughty, troublesome, vexatious, wicked.

sauce *n* cheekiness, impudence, insolence; appetizer, compound, condiment, relish, seasoning.

saucy *adj* bold, cavalier, disrespectful, flippant, forward, immodest, impertinent, impudent, insolent, pert, rude.

saunter *vb* amble, dawdle, delay, dilly-dally, lag, linger, loiter, lounge, stroll, tarry. * *n* amble, stroll, walk.

savage *vb* attack, lacerate, mangle, maul. * *adj* rough, uncultivated, wild; rude, uncivilized, unpolished, untaught; bloodthirsty, feral, ferine, ferocious, fierce, rapacious, untamed, vicious; beastly, bestial, brutal, brutish, inhuman; atrocious, barbarous, barbaric, bloody, brutal, cruel, fell, fiendish, hardhearted, heathenish, merciless, murderous, pitiless, relentless, ruthless, sanguinary, truculent; native, rough, rugged. * *n* barbarian, brute, heathen, vandal.

save *vb* keep, liberate, preserve, rescue; salvage, recover, redeem; economize, gather, hoard, husband, reserve, store; hinder, obviate, prevent, spare. * *prep* but, deducting, except.

saviour *n* defender, deliverer, guardian, protector, preserver, rescuer, saver.

savour *vb* affect, appreciate, enjoy, like, partake, relish; flavour, season. * *n* flavour, gusto, relish, smack, taste; fragrance, odour, smell, scent.

savoury *adj* agreeable, delicious, flavourful, luscious, nice, palatable, piquant, relishing.

saw *n* adage, aphorism, apothegm, axiom, byword, dictum, maxim, precept, proverb, sententious saying.

say *vb* declare, express, pronounce, speak, tell, utter; affirm, allege, argue; recite, rehearse, repeat; assume, presume, suppose. * *n* affirmation, declaration, speech, statement; decision, voice, vote.

saying *n* declaration, expression, observation, remark, speech, statement; adage, aphorism, byword, dictum, maxim, proverb, saw.

scale¹ *n* basin, dish, pan; balance.

scale² *n* flake, lamina, lamella, layer, plate.

scale³ *vb* ascend, climb, escalate, mount. * *n* graduation.

scamp *n* cheat, knave, rascal, rogue, scapegrace, scoundrel, swindler, trickster, villain.

scamper *vb* haste, hasten, hie, run, scud, speed, trip.

scan *vb* examine, investigate, scrutinize, search, sift.

scandal *vb* asperse, defame, libel, traduce. * *n* aspersion, calumny, defamation, obloquy, reproach; discredit, disgrace, dishonour, disrepute, ignominy, infamy, odium, opprobrium, offence, shame.

scandalize *vb* offend; asperse, backbite, calumniate, decry, defame, disgust, lampoon, libel, reproach, revile, satirize, slander, traduce, vilify.

scandalous *adj* defamatory, libellous, opprobrious, slanderous; atrocious, disgraceful, disreputable, infamous, inglorious, ignominious, odious, shameful.

scanty *adj* insufficient, meagre, narrow, scant, small; hardly, scarce, short, slender; niggardly, parsimonious, penurious, scrimpy, skimpy, sparing.

scar¹ *vb* hurt, mark, wound. * *n* cicatrice, cicatrix, seam; blemish, defect, disfigurement, flaw, injury, mark.

scar² *n* bluff, cliff, crag, precipice.

scarce *adj* deficient, wanting; infrequent, rare, uncommon. * *adv* barely, hardly, scantily.

scarcely *adv* barely, hardly, scantily.

scarcity *n* dearth, deficiency, insufficiency, lack, want; infrequency, rareness, rarity, uncommonness.

scare *vb* affright, alarm, appal, daunt, fright, frighten, intimidate, shock, startle, terrify. * *n* alarm, fright, panic, shock, terror.

scathe *vb* blast, damage, destroy, injure, harm, haste. * *n* damage, harm, injury, mischief, waste.

scatter *vb* broadcast, sprinkle, strew; diffuse, disperse, disseminate, dissipate, distribute, separate, spread; disappoint, dispel, frustrate, overthrow.

scene *n* display, exhibition, pageant, representation, show, sight, spectacle, view; place, situation, spot; arena, stage.

scent *vb* breathe in, inhale, nose, smell, sniff; detect, smell out, sniff out; aromatize, perfume. * *n* aroma, balminess, fragrance, odour, perfume, smell, redolence.

sceptic *n* doubter, freethinker, questioner, unbeliever.

sceptical *adj* doubtful, doubting, dubious, hesitating, incredulous, questioning, unbelieving.

scepticism *n* doubt, dubiety, freethinking, incredulity, unbelief.

schedule *vb* line up, list, plan, programme, tabulate. * *n* document, scroll; catalogue, inventory, list, plan, record, register, roll, table, timetable.

scheme *vb* contrive, design, frame, imagine, plan, plot, project. * *n* plan, system, theory; cabal, conspiracy, contrivance, design, device, intrigue, machination, plan, plot, project, stratagem; arrangement, draught, diagram, outline.

schism *n* division, separation, split; discord, disunion, division, faction, separation.

scholar *n* disciple, learner, pupil, student; don, fellow, intellectual, pedant, savant.

scholarship *n* accomplishments, acquirements, attainments, erudition, knowledge, learning; bursary, exhibition, foundation, grant, maintenance.

scholastic *adj* academic, bookish, lettered, literary; formal, pedantic.

school *vb* drill, educate, exercise, indoctrinate, instruct, teach, train; admonish, control, chide, discipline, govern, reprove, tutor. * *adj* academic, collegiate, institutional, scholastic, schoolish. * *n* academy, college, gymnasium, institute, institution, kindergarten, lyceum, manège, polytechnic, seminary, university; adherents, camarilla, circle, clique, coterie, disciples, followers; body, order, organization, party, sect.

schooling *n* discipline, education, instruction, nurture, teaching, training, tuition.

scintillate *vb* coruscate, flash, gleam, glisten, glitter, sparkle, twinkle.

scoff *vb* deride, flout, jeer, mock, ridicule, taunt; gibe, sneer. * *n* flout, gibe, jeer, sneer, mockery, taunt; derision, ridicule.

scold *vb* berate, blame, censure, chide, rate, reprimand, reprove; brawl, rail, rate, reprimand, upbraid, vituperate. * *n* shrew, termagant, virago, vixen.

scope *n* aim, design, drift, end, intent, intention, mark, object, purpose, tendency, view; amplitude, field, latitude, liberty, margin, opportunity, purview, range, room, space, sphere, vent; extent, length, span, stretch, sweep.

scorch *vb* blister, burn, char, parch, roast, sear, shrivel, singe.

score *vb* cut, furrow, mark, notch, scratch; charge, note, record; impute, note; enter, register. * *n* incision, mark, notch; account, bill, charge, debt, reckoning; consideration, ground, motive, reason.

scorn *vb* condemn, despise, disregard, disdain, scout, slight, spurn. * *n* contempt, derision, disdain, mockery, slight, sneer; scoff.

scornful *adj* contemptuous, defiant, disdainful, contemptuous, regardless.

scot-free *adj* untaxed; clear, unhurt, uninjured, safe.

scoundrel *n* cheat, knave, miscreant, rascal, reprobate, rogue, scamp, swindler, trickster, villain.

scour[1] *vb* brighten, buff, burnish, clean, cleanse, polish, purge, scrape, scrub, rub, wash, whiten; rake; efface, obliterate, overrun.

scour[2] *vb* career, course, range, scamper, scud, scuttle; comb, hunt, rake, ransack, rifle, rummage, search.

scourge *vb* lash, whip; afflict, chasten, chastise, correct, punish; harass, torment. * *n* cord, cowhide, lash, strap, thong, whip; affliction, bane, curse, infliction, nuisance, pest, plague, punishment.

scout *vb* contemn, deride, disdain, despise, ridicule, scoff, scorn, sneer, spurn; investigate, probe, search. * *n* escort, lookout, precursor, vanguard.

scowl *vb* frown, glower, lower. * *n* frown, glower, lower.

scraggy *adj* broken, craggy, rough, rugged, scabrous, scragged, uneven; attenuated, bony, emaciated, gaunt, lank, lean, meagre, scrawny, skinny, thin.

scrap[1] *vb* discard, junk, trash. * *n* bit, fragment, modicum, particle, piece, snippet; bite, crumb, morsel, mouthful; debris, junk, litter, rubbish, rubble, trash, waste.

scrap[2] *vb* altercate, bicker, dispute, clash, fight, hassle, quarrel, row, spat, squabble, tiff, tussle, wrangle. * *n* affray, altercation, bickering, clash, dispute, fight, fray, hassle, melee, quarrel, row, run-in, set-to, spat, squabble, tiff, tussle, wrangle.

scrape *vb* bark, grind, rasp, scuff; accumulate, acquire, collect, gather, save; erase, remove. * *n* difficulty, distress, embarrassment, perplexity, predicament.

scream *vb* screech, shriek, squall, ululate. * *n* cry, outcry, screech, shriek, shrill, ululation.

screen *vb* cloak, conceal, cover, defend, fence, hide, mask, protect, shelter, shroud. * *n* blind, curtain, lattice, partition; defence, guard, protection, shield; cloak, cover, veil, disguise; riddle, sieve.

screw *vb* force, press, pressurize, squeeze, tighten, twist, wrench; oppress, rack; distort. * *n* extortioner, extortionist, miser, scrimp, skinflint; prison guard; sexual intercourse.

scrimmage *n* brawl, melee, riot, scuffle, skirmish.

scrimp *vb* contract, curtail, limit, pinch, reduce, scant, shorten, straiten.

scrimpy *adj* contracted, deficient, narrow, scanty.

scroll *n* inventory, list, parchment, roll, schedule.

scrub[1] *adj* contemptible, inferior, mean, niggardly, scrubby, shabby, small, stunted. * *n* brushwood, underbrush, underwood.

scrub[2] *vb* clean, cleanse, rub, scour, scrape, wash.

scruple *vb* boggle, demur, falter, hesitate, object, pause, stickle, waver. * *n* delicacy, hesitancy, hesitation, nicety, perplexity, qualm.

scrupulous *adj* conscientious, fastidious, nice, precise, punctilious, rigorous, strict; careful, cautious, circumspect, exact, vigilant.

scrutinize *vb* canvass, dissect, examine, explore, investigate, overhaul, probe, search, sift, study.

scrutiny *n* examination, exploration, inquisition, inspection, investigation, search, searching, sifting.

scud *vb* flee, fly, haste, hasten, hie, post, run, scamper, speed, trip.

scuffle *vb* contend, fight, strive, struggle. * *n* altercation, brawl, broil, contest, encounter, fight, fray, quarrel, squabble, struggle, wrangle.

sculpt *vb* carve, chisel, cut, sculpture; engrave, grave.

scurrilous *adj* abusive, blackguardly, contumelious, foul, foul-mouthed, indecent, infamous, insolent, insulting, offensive, opprobrious, reproachful, ribald, vituperative; coarse, gross, low, mean, obscene, vile, vulgar.

scurry *vb* bustle, dash, hasten, hurry, scamper, scud, scutter. * *n* burst, bustle, dash, flurry, haste, hurry, scamper, scud, spurt.

scurvy *adj* scabbed, scabby, scurfy; abject, bad, base, contemptible, despicable, low, mean, pitiful, sorry, vile, vulgar, worthless; malicious, mischievous, offensive.

scuttle[1] *vb* hurry, hustle, run, rush, scamper, scramble, scud, scurry. * *n* dash, drive, flurry, haste, hurry, hustle, race, rush, scamper, scramble, scud, scurry.

scuttle[2] *vb* capsize, founder, go down, sink, overturn, upset. * *n* hatch, hatchway.

seal *vb* close, fasten, secure; attest, authenticate, confirm, establish, ratify, sanction; confine, enclose, imprison. * *n* fastening, stamp, wafer, wax; assurance, attestation, authentication, confirmation, pledge, ratification.

seamy *adj* disreputable, nasty, seedy, sordid, unpleasant.

sear *vb* blight, brand, cauterize, dry, scorch, wither. * *adj* dried up, dry, sere, withered.

search *vb* examine, explore, ferret, inspect, investigate, overhaul, probe, ransack, scrutinize, sift; delve, hunt, forage, inquire, look, rummage. * *n* examination, exploration, hunt, inquiry, inspection, investigation, pursuit, quest, research, seeking, scrutiny.

searching *adj* close, keen, penetrating, trying; examining, exploring, inquiring, investigating, probing, seeking.

seared *adj* callous, graceless, hardened, impenitent, incorrigible, obdurate, shameless, unrepentant.

season *vb* acclimatize, accustom, form, habituate, harden, inure, mature, qualify, temper, train; flavour, spice. * *n* interval, period, spell, term, time, while.

seasonable *adj* appropriate, convenient, fit, opportune, suitable, timely.

seasoning *n* condiment, flavouring, relish, salt, sauce.

seat *vb* establish, fix, locate, place, set, station. * *n* place, site, situation, station; abode, capital, dwelling, house, mansion, residence; bottom, fundament; bench, chair, pew, settle, stall, stool.

secede *vb* apostatize, resign, retire, withdraw.

secluded *adj* close, covert, embowered, isolated, private, removed, retired, screened, sequestrated, withdrawn.

seclusion *n* obscurity, privacy, retirement, secrecy, separation, solitude, withdrawal.

second[1] *n* instant, jiffy, minute, moment, trice.

second[2] *vb* abet, advance, aid, assist, back, encourage, forward, further, help, promote, support, sustain; approve, favour. * *adj* inferior, second-rate, secondary; following, next, subsequent; additional, extra, other; double, duplicate. * *n* another, other; assistant, backer, supporter.

secondary *adj* collateral, inferior, minor, subsidiary, subordinate. * *n* delegate, deputy, proxy.

secrecy *n* clandestineness, concealment, furtiveness, stealth, surreptitiousness.

secret *adj* close, concealed, covered, covert, cryptic, hid, hidden, mysterious, privy, shrouded, veiled, unknown, unrevealed, unseen; cabbalistic, clandestine, furtive, privy, sly, stealthy, surreptitious, underhand; confidential, private, retired, secluded, unseen; abstruse, latent, mysterious, obscure, occult, recondite, unknown. * *n* confidence, enigma, key, mystery.

secretary *n* clerk, scribe, writer; escritoire, writing-desk.

secrete[1] *vb* bury, cache, conceal, disguise, hide, shroud, stash; screen, separate.

secrete[2] *vb* discharge, emit, excrete, exude, release, secern.

secretive *adj* cautious, close, reserved, reticent, taciturn, uncommunicative, wary.

sect *n* denomination, faction, schism, school.

section *n* cutting, division, fraction, part, piece, portion, segment, slice.

secular *adj* civil, laic, laical, lay, profane, temporal, worldly.

secure *vb* guard, protect, safeguard; assure, ensure, guarantee, insure; fasten; acquire, gain, get, obtain, procure. * *adj* assured, certain, confident, sure; insured, protected, safe; fast, firm, fixed, immovable, stable; careless, easy, undisturbed, unsuspecting; heedless, inattentive, incautious, negligent, overconfident.

security *n* bulwark, defence, guard, palladium, protection, safeguard, safety, shelter; bond, collateral, deposit, guarantee, pawn, pledge, stake, surety, warranty; carelessness, heedlessness, overconfidence, negligence; assurance, assuredness, certainty, confidence, ease.

sedate *adj* calm, collected, composed, contemplative, cool, demure, grave, placid, philosophical, quiet, serene, serious, sober, still, thoughtful, tranquil, undisturbed, unemotional, unruffled.

sedative *adj* allaying, anodyne, assuasive, balmy, calming, composing, demulcent, lenient, lenitive, soothing, tranquillizing. * *n* anaesthetic, anodyne, hypnotic, narcotic, opiate.

sedentary *adj* inactive, motionless, sluggish, torpid.

sediment *n* dregs, grounds, lees, precipitate, residue, residuum, settlings.

sedition *n* insurgence, insurrection, mutiny, rebellion, revolt, riot, rising, treason, tumult, uprising, uproar.

seditious *adj* factious, incendiary, insurgent, mutinous, rebellious, refractory, riotous, tumultuous, turbulent.

seduce *vb* allure, attract, betray, corrupt, debauch, deceive, decoy, deprave, ensnare, entice, inveigle, lead, mislead.

seductive *adj* alluring, attractive, enticing, tempting.

sedulous *adj* active, assiduous, busy, diligent, industrious, laborious, notable, painstaking, persevering, unremitting, untiring.

see *vb* behold, contemplate, descry, glimpse, sight, spot, survey; comprehend, conceive, distinguish, espy, know, notice, observe, perceive, recognize, remark, understand; beware, consider, envisage, regard, visualize; experience, feel, suffer; examine, inspire, notice, observe; discern, look; call on, visit.

seed *n* semen, sperm; embryo, grain, kernel, matured ovule; germ, original; children, descendants, offspring, progeny; birth, generation, race.

seedy *adj* faded, old, shabby, worn; destitute, distressed, indigent, needy, penniless, pinched, poor.

seek *vb* hunt, look, search; court, follow, prosecute, pursue, solicit; attempt, endeavour, strive, try.

seem *vb* appear, assume, look, pretend.

seeming *adj* apparent, appearing, ostensible, specious. * *n* appearance, colour, guise, look, semblance.

seemly *adj* appropriate, becoming, befitting, congruous, convenient, decent, decorous, expedient, fit, fitting, meet, proper, right, suitable; beautiful, comely, fair, good-looking, graceful, handsome, pretty, well-favoured.

seer *n* augur, diviner, foreteller, predictor, prophet, soothsayer.

segment *n* bit, division, part, piece, portion, section, sector.

segregate *vb* detach, disconnect, disperse, insulate, part, separate.

segregation *n* apartheid, discrimination, insulation, separation.

seize *vb* capture, catch, clutch, grab, grapple, grasp, grip, snatch; confiscate, impress, impound; apprehend, comprehend; arrest, take.

seldom *adv* infrequently, occasionally, rarely.

select *vb* choose, cull, pick, prefer. * *adj* choice, chosen, excellent, exquisite, good, picked, rare, selected.

selection *n* choice, election, pick, preference.

self-conscious *adj* awkward, diffident, embarrassed, insecure, nervous.

self-control *n* restraint, willpower.

self-important *adj* assuming, consequential, proud, haughty, lordly, overbearing, overweening.

selfish *adj* egoistic, egotistical, greedy, illiberal, mean, narrow, self-seeking, ungenerous.

self-possessed *adj* calm, collected, composed, cool, placid, sedate, undisturbed, unexcited, unruffled.

self-willed *adj* contumacious, dogged, headstrong, obstinate, pig-headed, stubborn, uncompliant, wilful.

sell *vb* barter, exchange, hawk, market, peddle, trade, vend.

semblance *n* likeness, resemblance, similarity; air, appearance, aspect, bearing, exterior, figure, form, mien, seeming, show; image, representation, similitude.

seminal adj important, original; germinal, radical, rudimental, rudimentary, unformed.

seminary n academy, college, gymnasium, high school, institute, school, university.

send vb cast, drive, emit, fling, hurl, impel, lance, launch, project, propel, throw, toss; delegate, depute, dispatch; forward, transmit; bestow, confer, give, grant.

senile adj aged, doddering, superannuated; doting, imbecile.

senior adj elder, older; higher.

seniority n eldership, precedence, priority, superiority.

sensation n feeling, sense, perception; excitement, impression, thrill.

sensational adj exciting, melodramatic, startling, thrilling.

sense vb appraise, appreciate, estimate, notice, observe, perceive, suspect, understand. * n brains, intellect, intelligence, mind, reason, understanding; appreciation, apprehension, discernment, feeling, perception, recognition, tact; connotation, idea, implication, judgment, notion, opinion, sentiment, view; import, interpretation, meaning, purport, significance; sagacity, soundness, substance, wisdom.

senseless adj apathetic, inert, insensate, unfeeling; absurd, foolish, ill-judged, nonsensical, silly, unmeaning, unreasonable, unwise; doltish, foolish, simple, stupid, witless, weak-minded.

sensible adj apprehensible, perceptible; aware, cognizant, conscious, convinced, persuaded, satisfied; discreet, intelligent, judicious, rational, reasonable, sagacious, sage, sober, sound, wise; observant, understanding; impressionable, sensitive.

sensitive adj perceptive, sentient; affected, impressible, impressionable, responsive, susceptible; delicate, tender, touchy.

sensual adj animal, bodily, carnal, voluptuous; gross, lascivious, lewd, licentious, unchaste.

sentence vb condemn, doom, judge. * n decision, determination, judgment, opinion, verdict; doctrine, dogma, opinion, tenet; condemnation, conviction, doom; period, proposition.

sententious adj compendious, compact, concise, didactic, laconic, pithy, pointed, succinct, terse.

sentiment n judgment, notion, opinion; maxim, saying; emotion, tenderness; disposition, feeling, thought.

sentimental adj impressible, impressionable, over-emotional, romantic, tender.

sentinel n guard, guardsman, patrol, picket, sentry, watchman.

separate vb detach, disconnect, disjoin, disunite, dissever, divide, divorce, part, sever, sunder; eliminate, remove, withdraw; cleave, open. * adj detached, disconnected, disjoined, disjointed, dissociated, disunited, divided, parted, severed; discrete, distinct, divorced, unconnected; alone, segregated, withdrawn.

separation n disjunction, disjuncture, dissociation; disconnection, disseverance, disseveration, disunion, division, divorce; analysis, decomposition.

sepulchral adj deep, dismal, funereal, gloomy, grave, hollow, lugubrious, melancholy, mournful, sad, sombre, woeful.

sepulchre n burial place, charnel house, grave, ossuary, sepulture, tomb.

sequel n close, conclusion, denouement, end, termination; consequence, event, issue, result, upshot.

sequence n following, graduation, progression, succession; arrangement, series, train.

sequestrated adj hidden, private, retired, secluded, unfrequented, withdrawn; seized.

seraphic adj angelic, celestial, heavenly, sublime; holy, pure, refined.

serene adj calm, collected, placid, peaceful, quiet, tranquil, sedate, undisturbed, unperturbed, unruffled; bright, calm, clear, fair, unclouded.

serenity n calm, calmness, collectedness, composure, coolness, imperturbability, peace, peacefulness, quiescence, sedateness, tranquillity; brightness, calmness, clearness, fairness, peace, quietness, stillness.

serf n bondman, servant, slave, thrall, villein.

serfdom n bondage, enslavement, enthralment, servitude, slavery, subjection, thraldom.

series n chain, concatenation, course, line, order, progression, sequence, succession, train.

serious adj earnest, grave, demure, pious, resolute, sedate, sober, solemn, staid, thoughtful; dangerous, great, important, momentous, weighty.

sermon n discourse, exhortation, homily, lecture.

serpentine adj anfractuous, convoluted, crooked, meandering, sinuous, spiral, tortuous, twisted, undulating, winding.

servant n attendant, dependant, factotum, helper, henchman, retainer, servitor, subaltern, subordinate, underling; domestic, drudge, flunky, lackey, menial, scullion, slave.

serve vb aid, assist, attend, help, minister, oblige, succour; advance, benefit, forward, promote; content, satisfy, supply; handle, officiate, manage, manipulate, work.

service vb check, maintain, overhaul, repair. * n labour, ministration, work; attendance, business, duty, employ, employment, office; advantage, benefit, good, gain, profit; avail, purpose, use, utility; ceremony, function, observance, rite, worship.

serviceable adj advantageous, available, beneficial, convenient, functional, handy, helpful, operative, profitable, useful.

servile adj dependent, menial; abject, base, beggarly, cringing, fawning, grovelling, low, mean, obsequious, slavish, sneaking, sycophantic, truckling.

servility n bondage, dependence, slavery; abjection, abjectness, baseness, fawning, meanness, obsequiousness, slavishness, sycophancy.

servitor n attendant, dependant, footman, lackey, retainer, servant, squire, valet, waiter.

servitude n bondage, enslavement, enthralment, serfdom, service, slavery, thraldom.

set[1] vb lay, locate, mount, place, put, stand, station; appoint, determine, establish, fix, settle; risk, stake, wager; adapt, adjust, regulate; adorn, stud, variegate; arrange, dispose, pose, post; appoint, assign, predetermine, prescribe; estimate, prize, rate, value; embarrass, perplex, pose; contrive, produce; decline, sink; congeal, concern, consolidate, harden, solidify; flow, incline, run, tend; (with **about**) begin, commence; (with **apart**) appropriate, consecrate, dedicate, devote, reserve, set aside; (with **aside**) abrogate, annul, omit, reject; reserve, set apart; (with **before**) display, exhibit; (with **down**) chronicle, jot down, record, register, state, write down; (with **forth**) display, exhibit, explain, expound, manifest, promulgate, publish, put forward, represent, show; (with **forward**) advance, further, promote; (with **free**) acquit, clear, emancipate, liberate, release; (with **off**) adorn, decorate, embellish; define, portion off; (*with* **on**) actuate, encourage, impel, influence, incite, instigate, prompt, spur, urge; attack, assault, set upon; (*with* **out**) display, issue, publish, proclaim, prove, recommend, show; (*with* **right**) correct, put in order; (*with* **to rights**) adjust, regulate; (*with* **up**) elevate, erect, exalt, raise; establish, found, institute; (*with* **upon**) assail, assault, attack, fly at, rush upon. * *adj* appointed, established, formal, ordained, prescribed, regular, settled; determined, fixed, firm, obstinate, positive, stiff, unyielding; immovable, predetermined; located, placed, put. * *n* attitude, position, posture; scene, scenery, setting.

set² *n* assortment, collection, suit; class, circle, clique, cluster, company, coterie, division, gang, group, knot, party, school, sect.

setback *n* blow, hitch, hold-up, rebuff; defeat, disappointment, reverse.

set-off *n* adornment, decoration, embellishment, ornament; counterbalance, counterclaim, equivalent.

settle *vb* adjust, arrange, compose, regulate; account, balance, close up, conclude, discharge, liquidate, pay, pay up, reckon, satisfy, square; allay, calm, compose, pacify, quiet, repose, rest, still, tranquillize; confirm, decide, determine, make clear; establish, fix, set; fall, gravitate, sink, subside; abide, colonize, domicile, dwell, establish, inhabit, people, place, plant, reside; (*with* **on**) determine on, fix on, fix upon; establish. * *n* bench, seat, stool.

settled *adj* established, fixed, stable; decided, deep-rooted, steady, unchanging; adjusted, arranged; methodical, orderly, quiet; common, customary, everyday, ordinary, usual, wonted.

set-to *n* combat, conflict, contest, fight.

sever *vb* divide, part, rend, separate, sunder; detach, disconnect, disjoin, disunite.

several *adj* individual, single, particular; distinct, exclusive, independent, separate; different, divers, diverse, manifold, many, sundry, various.

severance *n* partition, separation.

severe *adj* austere, bitter, dour, hard, harsh, inexorable, morose, painful, relentless, rigid, rigorous, rough, sharp, stern, stiff, strait-laced, unmitigated, unrelenting, unsparing; accurate, exact, methodical, strict; chaste, plain, restrained, simple, unadorned; biting, caustic, cruel, cutting, harsh, keen, sarcastic, satirical, trenchant; acute, afflictive, distressing, excruciating, extreme, intense, stringent, violent; critical, exact.

severity *n* austerity, gravity, harshness, rigour, seriousness, sternness, strictness; accuracy, exactness, niceness; chasteness, plainness, simplicity; acrimony, causticity, keenness, sharpness; afflictiveness, extremity, keenness, stringency, violence; cruelty.

sew *vb* baste, bind, hem, stitch, tack.

sex *n* gender, femininity, masculinity, sexuality; coitus, copulation, fornication, love-making.

shabby *adj* faded, mean, poor, ragged, seedy, threadbare, worn, worn-out; beggarly, mean, paltry, penurious, stingy, ungentlemanly, unhandsome.

shackle *vb* chain, fetter, gyve, hamper, manacle; bind, clog, confine, cumber, embarrass, encumber, impede, obstruct, restrict, trammel. * *n* chain, fetter, gyve, hamper, manacle.

shade *vb* cloud, darken, dim, eclipse, obfuscate, obscure; cover, ensconce, hide, protect, screen, shelter. * *n* darkness, dusk, duskiness, gloom, obscurity, shadow; cover, protection, shelter; awning, blind,

curtain, screen, shutter, veil; degree, difference, kind, variety; cast, colour, complexion, dye, hue, tinge, tint, tone; apparition, ghost, manes, phantom, shadow, spectre, spirit.

shadow *vb* becloud, cloud, darken, obscure, shade; adumbrate, foreshadow, symbolize, typify; conceal, cover, hide, protect, screen, shroud. * *n* penumbra, shade, umbra, umbrage; darkness, gloom, obscurity; cover, protection, security, shelter; adumbration, foreshadowing, image, prefiguration, representation; apparition, ghost, phantom, shade, spirit; image, portrait, reflection, silhouette.

shadowy *adj* shady, umbrageous; dark, dim, gloomy, murky, obscure; ghostly, imaginary, impalpable, insubstantial, intangible, spectral, unreal, unsubstantial, visionary.

shady *adj* shadowy, umbrageous; crooked.

shaft *n* arrow, missile, weapon; handle, helve; pole, tongue; axis, spindle; pinnacle, spire; stalk, stem, trunk.

shaggy *adj* rough, rugged.

shake *vb* quake, quaver, quiver, shiver, shudder, totter, tremble; agitate, convulse, jar, jolt, stagger; daunt, frighten, intimidate; endanger, move, weaken; oscillate, vibrate, wave; move, put away, remove, throw off. * *n* agitation, concussion, flutter, jar, jolt, quaking, shaking, shivering, shock, trembling, tremor.

shaky *adj* jiggly, quaky, shaking, tottering, trembling.

shallow *adj* flimsy, foolish, frivolous, puerile, trashy, trifling, trivial; empty, ignorant, silly, slight, simple, superficial, unintelligent.

sham *vb* ape, feign, imitate, pretend; cheat, deceive, delude, dupe, impose, trick. * *adj* assumed, counterfeit, false, feigned, mock, make-believe, pretended, spurious. * *n* delusion, feint, fraud, humbug, imposition, imposture, pretence, trick.

shamble *vb* hobble, shuffle.

shambles *npl* abattoir, slaughterhouse; confusion, disorder, mess.

shame *vb* debase, degrade, discredit, disgrace, dishonour, stain, sully, taint, tarnish; abash, confound, confuse, discompose, disconcert, humble, humiliate; deride, flout, jeer, mock, ridicule, sneer. * *n* contempt, degradation, derision, discredit, disgrace, dishonour, disrepute, ignominy, infamy, obloquy, odium, opprobrium; abashment, chagrin, confusion, embarrassment, humiliation, mortification; reproach, scandal; decency, decorousness, decorum, modesty, propriety, seemliness.

shamefaced *adj* bashful, diffident, overmodest.

shameful *adj* atrocious, base, disgraceful, dishonourable, disreputable, heinous, ignominious, infamous, nefarious, opprobrious, outrageous, scandalous, vile, villainous, wicked; degrading, indecent, unbecoming.

shameless *adj* assuming, audacious, bold-faced, brazen, brazen-faced, cool, immodest, impudent, indecent, indelicate, insolent, unabashed, unblushing; abandoned, corrupt, depraved, dissolute, graceless, hardened, incorrigible, irreclaimable, lost, obdurate, profligate, reprobate, sinful, unprincipled, vicious.

shape *vb* create, form, make, produce; fashion, model, mould; adjust, direct, frame, regulate; conceive, conjure up, figure, image, imagine. * *n* appearance, aspect, fashion, figure, form, guise, make; build, cast, cut, model, mould, pattern; apparition, image.

shapeless *adj* amorphous, formless; grotesque, irregular, rude, uncouth, unsymmetrical.

shapely *adj* comely, symmetrical, trim, well-formed.

share *vb* apportion, distribute, divide, parcel out, portion, split; partake, participate; experience, receive. * *n* part, portion, quantum; allotment, allowance, contingent, deal, dividend, division, interest, lot, proportion, quantity, quota.

sharer *n* communicant, partaker, participator.

sharp *adj* acute, cutting, keen, keen-edged, knife-edged, razor-edged, trenchant; acuminate, needle-shaped, peaked, pointed, ridged; apt, astute, canny, clear-sighted, clever, cunning, discerning, discriminating, ingenious, inventive, keen-witted, penetrating, perspicacious, quick, ready, sagacious, sharp-witted, shrewd, smart, subtle, witty; acid, acrid, biting, bitter, burning, high-flavoured, high-seasoned, hot, mordacious, piquant, poignant, pungent, sour, stinging; acrimonious, biting, caustic, cutting, harsh, mordant, sarcastic, severe, tart, trenchant; cruel, hard, rigid; afflicting, distressing, excruciating, intense, painful, piercing, shooting, sore, violent; nipping, pinching, ardent, eager, fervid, fierce, fiery, impetuous, strong; high, screeching, shrill; attentive, vigilant, severe; close, exacting, shrewd, cold, crisp, freezing, icy wintry. * *adv* abruptly, sharply, suddenly; exactly, precisely, punctually.

sharp-cut *adj* clear, distinct, well-defined.

sharpen *vb* edge, intensify, point.

sharper *n* cheat, deceiver, defrauder, knave, rogue, shark, swindler, trickster.

sharply *adv* rigorously, roughly, severely; acutely, keenly; vehemently, violently; accurately, exactly, minutely, trenchantly, wittily; abruptly, steeply.

sharpness *n* acuteness, keenness, trenchancy; acuity, spinosity; acumen, cleverness, discernment, ingenuity, quickness, sagacity, shrewdness, smartness, wit; acidity, acridity, piquancy, pungency, sting, tartness; causticness, incisiveness, pungency, sarcasm, satire, severity; afflictiveness, intensity, painfulness, poignancy; ardour, fierceness, violence; discordance, dissonance, highness, screechiness, squeakiness, shrillness.

sharp-sighted *adj* clear-sighted, keen, keen-eyed, keen-sighted.

sharp-witted *adj* acute, clear-sighted, cunning, discerning, ingenious, intelligent, keen, keen-sighted, long-headed, quick, sagacious, sharp, shrewd.

shatter *vb* break, burst, crack, rend, shiver, smash, splinter, split; break up, derange, disorder, overthrow.

shave *vb* crop, cut off, mow, pare; slice; graze, skim, touch.

shaver *n* boy, child, youngster; bargainer, extortioner, sharper.

shear *vb* clip, cut, fleece, strip; divest; break off.

sheath *n* case, casing, covering, envelope, scabbard, sheathing.

sheathe *vb* case, cover, encase, enclose.

shed[1] *n* cabin, cot, hovel, hut, outhouse, shack, shelter.

shed[2] *vb* effuse, let fall, pour out, spill; diffuse, emit, give out, scatter, spread; cast, let fall, put off, slough, throw off.

sheen *n* brightness, gloss, glossiness, shine, spendour.

sheep *n* ewe, lamb, ram.

sheepish *adj* bashful, diffident, overmodest, shamefaced, timid, timorous.

sheer[1] *adj* perpendicular, precipitous, steep, vertical; clear, downright, mere, pure, simple, unadulterated, unmingled, unmixed, unqualified, utter; clear; fine, transparent. * *adv* outright; perpendicularly, steeply.

sheer[2] *vb* decline, deviate, move aside, swerve. * *n* bow, curve.

shelf *n* bracket, console, ledge, mantelpiece.

shell *vb* exfoliate, fall off, peel off; bombard. * *n* carapace, case, covering, shard; bomb, grenade, sharpnel; framework.

shelter *vb* cover, defend, ensconce, harbour, hide, house, protect, screen, shield, shroud. * *n* asylum, cover, covert, harbour, haven, hideaway, refuge, retreat, sanctuary; defence, protection, safety, screen, security, shield; guardian, protector.

shelve *vb* dismiss, put aside; incline, slope.

shepherd *vb* escort, guide, marshal, usher; direct, drive, drove, herd, lead; guard, tend, watch over. * *n* drover, grazier, herder, herdsman; chaplain, churchman, clergyman, cleric, divine, ecclesiastic, minister, padre, parson, pastor; chaperon, duenna, escort, guide, squire, usher.

shield *vb* cover, defend, guard, protect, shelter; repel, ward off; avert, forbid, forfend. * *n* aegis, buckler, escutcheon, scutcheon, targe; bulwark, cover, defence, guard, palladium, protection, rampart, safeguard, security, shelter.

shift *vb* alter, change, fluctuate, move, vary; chop, dodge, swerve, veer; contrive, devise, manage, plan, scheme, shuffle. * *n* change, substitution, turn; contrivance, expedient, means, resort, resource; artifice, craft, device, dodge, evasion, fraud, mask, ruse, stratagem, subterfuge, trick, wile; chemise, smock.

shiftless *adj* improvident, imprudent, negligent, slack, thriftless, unresourceful.

shifty *adj* tricky, undependable, wily.

shillyshally *vb* hesitate, waver. * *n* hesitation, irresolute, wavering.

shimmer *vb* flash, glimmer, glisten, shine. * *n* blink, glimmer, glitter, twinkle.

shin *vb* climb, swarm. * *n* shinbone, tibia.

shindy *n* disturbance, riot, roughhouse, row, spree, uproar.

shine *vb* beam, blaze, coruscate, flare, give light, glare, gleam, glimmer, glisten, glitter, glow, lighten, radiate, sparkle; excel. * *n* brightness, brilliancy, glaze, gloss, polish, sheen.

shining *adj* beaming, bright, brilliant, effulgent, gleaming, glowing, glistening, glittering, luminous, lustrous, radiant, resplendent, splendid; conspicuous, distinguished, illustrious.

shiny *adj* bright, clear, luminous, sunshiny, unclouded; brilliant, burnished, glassy, glossy, polished.

ship *n* boat, craft, steamer, vessel.

shipshape *adj* neat, orderly, tidy, trim, well-arranged.

shipwreck *vb* cast away, maroon, strand, wreck. * *n* demolition, destruction, miscarriage, overthrow, perdition, ruin, subversion, wreck.

shirk *vb* avoid, dodge, evade, malinger, quit, slack; cheat, shark, trick.

shiver[1] *vb* break, shatter, splinter. * *n* bit, fragment, piece, slice, sliver, splinter.

shiver[2] *vb* quake, quiver, shake, shudder, tremble. * *n* shaking, shivering, shuddering, tremor.

shivery[1] *adj* brittle, crumbly, frangible, friable, shatterable, splintery.

shivery[2] *adj* quaking, quavering, quivering, shaky, trembly, tremulous; chilly, shivering.

shoal[1] *vb* crowd, throng. * *n* crowd, horde, multitude, swarm, throng.

shoal[2] *n* sandbank, shallows; danger.

shock *vb* appall, horrify; disgust, disquiet, disturb, nauseate, offend, outrage, revolt, scandalize, sicken; astound, stagger, stun; collide with, jar, jolt, shake, strike against; encounter, meet. * *n* agitation, blow, offence, stroke, trauma; assault, brunt, conflict; clash, collision, concussion, impact, percussion.

shocking *adj* abominable, detestable, disgraceful, disgusting, execrable, foul, hateful, loathsome, obnoxious, odious, offensive, repugnant, repulsive, revolting; appalling, awful, dire, dreadful, fearful, frightful, ghastly, hideous, horrible, horrid, horrific, monstrous, terrible.

shoot *vb* catapult, expel, hurl, let fly, propel; discharge, fire, let off; dart, fly, pass, pelt; extend, jut, project, protrude, protuberate, push, put forth, send forth, stretch; bud, germinate, sprout; (*with* **up**) grow increase, spring up, run up, start up. * *n* branch, offshoot, scion, sprout, twig.

shop *n* emporium, market, mart, store; workshop.

shore[1] *n* beach, brim, coast, seabord, seaside, strand, waterside.

shore[2] *vb* brace, buttress, prop, stay, support. * *n* beam, brace, buttress, prop, stay, support.

shorn *adj* cut-off; deprived.

short *adj* brief, curtailed; direct, near, straight; compendious, concise, condensed, laconic, pithy, terse, sententious, succinct, summary; abrupt, curt, petulant, pointed, sharp, snappish, uncivil; defective, deficient, inadequate, insufficient, niggardly, scanty, scrimpy; contracted, desitute, lacking, limited, minus, wanting; dwarfish, squat, undersized; brittle, crisp, crumbling, friable. * *adv* abruptly, at once, forthwith, suddenly.

shortcoming *n* defect, deficiency, delinquency, error, failing, failure, fault, imperfection, inadequacy, remissness, slip, weakness.

shorten *vb* abbreviate, abridge, curtail, cut short; abridge, contract, diminish, lessen, retrench, reduce; cut off, dock, lop, trim; confine, hinder, restrain, restrict.

shortening *n* abbreviation, abridgment, contraction, curtailment, diminution, retrenchment, reduction.

shorthand *n* brachygraphy, stenography, tachygraphy.

short-lived *adj* emphemeral, transient, transitory.

shortly *adv* quickly, soon; briefly, concisely, succinctly, tersely.

short-sighted *adj* myopic, nearsighted, purblind; imprudent, indiscreet.

shot[1] *n* discharge; ball, bullet, missile, projectile; marksman, shooter.

shot[2] *adj* chatoyant, iridescent, irisated, moiré, watered; intermingled, interspersed, interwoven.

shoulder *vb* bear, bolster, carry, hump, maintain, pack, support, sustain, tote; crowd, elbow, jostle, press forward, push, thrust. * *n* projection, protuberance.

shoulder blade *n* blade bone, omoplate, scapula, shoulder bone.

shout *vb* bawl, cheer, clamour, exclaim, halloo, roar, vociferate, whoop, yell. * *n* cheer, clamour, exclamation, halloo, hoot, huzza, outcry, roar, vociferation, whoop, yell.

shove *vb* jostle, press against, propel, push, push aside; (*with* **off**) push away, thrust away.

show *vb* blazon, display, exhibit, flaunt, parade, present; indicate, mark, point out; disclose, discover, divulge, explain, make clear, make known, proclaim, publish, reveal, unfold; demonstrate, evidence, manifest, prove, verify; conduct, guide, usher; direct, inform, instruct, teach; expound, elucidate, interpret; (*with* **off**) display, exhibit, make a show, set off; (*with* **up**) expose. * *n* array, exhibition, representation, sight, spectacle; blazonry, bravery, ceremony, dash, demonstration, display, flourish, ostentation, pageant, pageantry, parade, pomp, splendour, splurge; likeness, resemblance, semblance; affectation, appearance, colour, illusion, mask, plausibility, pose, pretence, pretext, simulation, speciousness; entertainment, production.

showy *adj* bedizened, dressy, fine, flashy, flaunting, garish, gaudy, glaring, gorgeous, loud, ornate, smart, swanky, splendid; grand, magnificent, ostentatious, pompous, pretentious, stately, sumptuous.

shred *vb* tear. * *n* bit, fragment, piece, rag, scrap, strip, tatter.

shrew *n* brawler, fury, scold, spitfire, termagant, virago, vixen.

shrewd *adj* arch, artful, astute, crafty, cunning, Machiavellian, sly, subtle, wily; acute, astute, canny, discerning, discriminating, ingenious, keen, knowing, penetrating, sagacious, sharp, sharp-sighted.

shrewdness *n* address, archness, art, artfulness, astuteness, craft, cunning, policy, skill, slyness, subtlety; acumen, acuteness, discernment, ingenuity, keenness, penetration, perspicacity, sagacity, sharpness, wit.

shrewish *adj* brawling, clamorous, froward, peevish, petulant, scolding, vixenish.

shriek *vb* scream, screech, squeal, yell, yelp. * *n* cry, scream, screech, yell.

shrill *adj* acute, high, high-toned, high-pitched, piercing, piping, sharp.

shrine *n* reliquary, sacred tomb; altar, hallowed place, sacred place.

shrink *vb* contract, decrease, dwindle, shrivel, wither; balk, blench, draw back, flinch, give way, quail, recoil, retire, swerve, wince, withdraw.

shrivel *vb* dry, dry up, parch; contract, decrease, dwindle, shrink, wither, wrinkle.

shroud *vb* bury, cloak, conceal, cover, hide, mask, muffle, protect, screen, shelter, veil. * *n* covering, garment; grave clothes, winding sheet.

shrub *n* bush, dwarf tree, low tree.

shrubby *adj* bushy.

shudder *vb* quake, quiver, shake, shiver, tremble. * *n* shaking, shuddering, trembling, tremor.

shuffle *vb* confuse, disorder, intermix, jumble, mix, shift; cavil, dodge, equivocate, evade, prevaricate, quibble, vacillate; struggle. * *n* artifice, cavil, evasion, fraud, pretence, pretext, prevarication, quibble, ruse, shuffling, sophism, subterfuge, trick.

shun *vb* avoid, elude, eschew, escape, evade, get clear of.

shut *vb* close, close up, stop; confine, coop up, enclose, imprison, lock up, shut up; (*with* **in**) confine, enclose; (*with* **off**) bar, exclude, intercept; (*with* **up**) close up, shut; confine, enclose, fasten in, imprison, lock in, lock up.

shy *vb* cast, chuck, fling, hurl, jerk, pitch, sling, throw, toss; boggle, sheer, start aside. * *adj* bashful, coy, diffident, reserved, retiring, sheepish, shrinking, timid; cautious, chary, distrustful, heedful, wary. * *n* start; fling, throw.

sibilant *adj* buzzing, hissing, sibilous.

sick *adj* ailing, ill, indisposed, laid-up, unwell, weak;

nauseated, queasy; disgusted, revolted, tired, weary; diseased, distempered, disordered, feeble, morbid, unhealthy, unsound, weak; languishing, longing, pining.

sicken vb ail, disease, fall sick, make sick; nauseate; disgust, weary; decay, droop, languish, pine.

sickening adj nauseating, nauseous, palling, sickish; disgusting, distasteful, loathsome, offensive, repulsive, revolting.

sickly adj ailing, diseased, faint, feeble, infirm, languid, languishing, morbid, unhealthy, valetudinary, weak, weakly.

sickness n ail, ailment, complaint, disease, disorder, distemper, illness, indisposition, invalidism, malady, morbidity; nausea, qualmishness, queasiness.

side vb border, bound, edge, flank, frontier, march, rim, skirt, verge; avert, turn aside; (with **with**) befriend, favour, flock to, join with, second, support. * adj flanking, later, skirting; indirect, oblique; extra, odd, off, spare. * n border, edge, flank, margin, verge; cause, faction, interest, party, sect.

sideboard n buffet, dresser.

side by side abreast, alongside, by the side.

sidelong adj lateral, oblique. * adv laterally, obliquely; on the side.

sidewalk n footpath, footway, pavement.

sideways, sidewise adv laterally. * adv athwart, crossways, crosswise, laterally, obliquely, sidelong, sidewards.

siesta n doze, nap.

sift vb part, separate; bolt, screen, winnow; analyse, canvass, discuss, examine, fathom, follow up, inquire into, investigate, probe, scrutinze, sound, try.

sigh vb complain, grieve, lament, mourn. * n long breath, sough, suspiration.

sight vb get sight of, perceive, see. * n cognizance, ken, perception, view; beholding, eyesight, seeing, vision; exhibition, prospect, representation, scene, show, spectacle, wonder; consideration, estimation, knowledge; examination, inspection.

sightless adj blind, eyeless, unseeing.

sightly adj beautiful, comely, handsome.

sign vb indicate, signal, signify; countersign, endorse, subscribe. * n emblem, index, indication, manifestation, mark, note, proof, signal, signification, symbol, symptom, token; beacon; augury, auspice, foreboding, miracle, omen, portent, presage, prodigy, prognostic, wonder; type; countersign, password.

signal vb flag, glance, hail, nod, nudge, salute, sign, signalize, sound, speak, touch, wave, wink. * adj conspicuous, eminent, extraordinary, memorable, notable, noteworthy, remarkable. * n cue, indication, mark, sign, token.

signalize vb celebrate, distinguish, make memorable.

signature n mark, sign, stamp; autograph, hand.

significance n implication, import, meaning, purport, sense; consequence, importance, moment, portent, weight; emphasis, energy, expressiveness, force, impressiveness.

significant adj betokening, expressive, indicative, significative, signifying; important, material, momentous, portentous, weighty; forcible, emphatic, expressive, telling.

signification n expression; acceptation, import, meaning, purport, sense.

signify vb betoken, communication, express, indicate, intimate; denote, imply, import, mean, purport, suggest; announce, declare, give notice of, impart, make

known, manifest, proclaim, utter; augur, foreshadow, indicate, portend, represent; matter, weigh.

silence vb hush, muzzle, still; allay, calm, quiet. * interj be silent, be still, hush, soft, tush, tut, whist. * n calm, hush, lull, noiselessness, peace, quiet, quietude, soundlessness, stillness; dumbness, mumness, muteness, reticence, speechlessness, taciturnity.

silent adj calm, hushed, noiseless, quiet, soundless, still; dumb, inarticulate, mum, mute, nonvocal, speechless, tacit; reticent, taciturn, uncommunicative.

silken adj flossy, silky, soft.

silkiness n smoothness, softness.

silly adj brainless, childish, foolish, inept, senseless, shallow, simple, stupid, weak-minded, witless; absurd, extravagant, frivolous, imprudent, indiscreet, nonsensical, preposterous, trifling, unwise. * n ass, duffer, goose, idiot, simpleton.

silt n alluvium, deposit, deposition, residue, settlement, settlings, sediment.

silver adj argent, silvery; bright, silvery, white; clear, mellifluous, soft.

similar adj analogous, duplicate, like, resembling, twin; homogeneous, uniform.

similarity n agreement, analogy, correspondence, likeness, parallelism, parity, resemblance, sameness, semblance, similitude.

simile n comparison, metaphor, similitude.

similitude n image, likeness, resemblance; comparison, metaphor, simile.

simmer vb boil, bubble, seethe, stew.

simper vb smile, smirk.

simple adj bare, elementary, homogeneous, incomplex, mere, single, unalloyed, unblended, uncombined, uncompounded, unmingled, unmixed; chaste, plain, homespun, inornate, natural, neat, unadorned, unaffected, unembellished, unpretentious, unstudied, unvarnished; artless, downright, frank, guileless, inartificial, ingenuous, naive, open, simple-hearted, simple-minded, sincere, single-minded, straightforward, true, unconstrained, undesigning, unsophisticated; credulous, fatuous, foolish, shallow, silly, unwise, weak; clear, intelligible, understandable, uninvolved, unmistakable.

simple-hearted adj artless, frank, ingenuous, open, simple, single-hearted.

simpleton n fool, greenhorn, nincompoop, ninny.

simplicity n chasteness, homeliness, naturalness, neatness, plainness, artlessness, frankness, naivety, openness, simplesse, sincerity; clearness; gullibility, folly, silliness, weakness.

simply adv artlessly, plainly, sincerely, unaffectedly; barely, merely, of itself, solely; absolutely, alone.

simulate vb act, affect, ape, assume, counterfeit, dissemble, feign, mimic, pretend, sham.

simulation n counterfeiting, feigning, personation, pretence.

simultaneous adj coeval, coincident, concomitant, concurrent, contemporaneous, synchronous.

sin vb do wrong, err, transgress, trespass. * n delinquency, depravity, guilt, iniquity, misdeed, offence, transgression, unrighteousness, wickedness, wrong.

since conj as, because, considering, seeing that. * adv ago, before this; from that time. * prep after, from the time of, subsequently to.

sincere adj pure, unmixed; genuine, honest, inartificial, real, true, unaffected, unfeigned, unvarnished; artless, candid, direct, frank, guileless, hearty, honest, ingenuous, open, plain, single, straightforward, truthful, undissembling, upright, whole-hearted.

sincerity *n* artlessness, candour, earnestness, frankness, genuineness, guilelessness, honesty, ingenuousness, probity, truth, truthfulness, unaffectedness, veracity.

sinew *n* ligament, tendon; brawn, muscle, nerve, strength.

sinewy *adj* able-bodied, brawny, firm, Herculean, muscular, nervous, powerful, robust, stalwart, strapping, strong, sturdy, vigorous, wiry.

sinful *adj* bad, criminal, depraved, immoral, iniquitous, mischievous, peccant, transgressive, unholy, unrighteous, wicked, wrong.

sinfulness *n* corruption, criminality, depravity, iniquity, irreligion, ungodliness, unholiness, unrighteousness, wickedness.

sing *vb* cantillate, carol, chant, hum, hymn, intone, lilt, troll, warble, yodel.

singe *vb* burn, scorch, sear.

singer *n* cantor, caroler, chanter, gleeman, prima donna, minstrel, psalmodist, songster, vocalist.

single *vb* (*with* **out**) choose, pick, select, single. * *adj* alone, isolated, one only, sole, solitary; individual, particular, separate; celibate, unmarried, unwedded; pure, simple, uncompounded, unmixed; honest, ingenuous, sincere, unbiased, uncorrupt, upright.

single-handed *adj* alone, by one's self, unaided, unassisted.

single-minded *adj* artless, candid, guileless, ingenuous, sincere.

singleness *n* individuality, unity; purity, simplicity; ingenuousness, integrity, sincerity, uprightness.

singular *adj* eminent, exceptional, extraordinary, rare, remarkable, strange, uncommon, unusual, unwonted; particular, unexampled, unparalleled, unprecedented; unaccountable; bizarre, curious, eccentric, fantastic, odd, peculiar, queer; individual, single; not complex, single, uncompounded, unique.

singularity *n* aberration, abnormality, irregularity, oddness, rareness, rarity, strangeness, uncommonness; characteristic, idiosyncrasy, individuality, particularity, peculiarity; eccentricity, oddity.

sinister *adj* baleful, injurious, untoward; boding ill, inauspicious, ominous, unlucky; left, on the left hand.

sink *vb* droop, drop, fall, founder, go down, submerge, subside; enter, penetrate; collapse, fail; decay, decline, decrease, dwindle, give way, languish, lose strength; engulf, immerse, merge, submerge, submerse; dig, excavate, scoop out; abase, bring down, crush, debase, degrade, depress, diminish, lessen, lower, overbear; destroy, overthrow, overwhelm, reduce, ruin, swamp, waste. * *n* basin, cloaca, drain.

sinless *adj* faultless, guiltless, immaculate, impeccable, innocent, spotless, unblemished, undefiled, unspotted, unsullied, untarnished.

sinner *n* criminal, delinquent, evildoer, offender, reprobate, wrongdoer.

sinuosity *n* crook, curvature, flexure, sinus, tortuosity, winding.

sinuous *adj* bending, crooked, curved, curvilinear, flexuous, serpentine, sinuate, sinuated, tortuous, undulating, wavy, winding.

sip *vb* drink, suck up, sup; absorb, drink in. * *n* small draught, taste.

sire *vb* father, reproduce; author, breed, conceive, create, generate, originate, produce, propagate. * *n* father, male parent, progenitor; man, male person; sir, sirrah; author, begetter, creator, father, generator, originator.

siren *adj* alluring, bewitching, fascinating, seducing, tempting. * *n* mermaid; charmer, Circe, seducer, seductress, tempter, temptress.

sit *vb* be, remain, repose, rest, stay; bear on, lie, rest; abide, dwell, settle; perch; brood, incubate; become, be suited, fit.

site *vb* locate, place, position, situate, station. * *n* ground, locality, location, place, position, seat, situation, spot, station, whereabouts.

sitting *n* meeting, session.

situation *n* ground, locality, location, place, position, seat, site, spot, whereabouts; case, category, circumstances, condition, juncture, plight, predicament, state; employment, office, place, post, station.

size *n* amplitude, bigness, bulk, dimensions, expanse, greatness, largeness, magnitude, mass, volume.

skeleton *n* framework; draft, outline, sketch.

sketch *vb* design, draft, draw out; delineate, depict, paint, portray, represent. * *n* delineation, design, draft, drawing, plan, skeleton.

sketchy *adj* crude, incomplete, unfinished.

skilful *adj* able, accomplished, adept, adroit, apt, clever, competent, conversant, cunning, deft, dexterous, dextrous, expert, handy, ingenious, masterly, practised, proficient, qualified, quick, ready, skilled, trained, versed, well-versed.

skill *n* ability, address, adroitness, aptitude, aptness, art, cleverness, deftness, dexterity, expertise, expertness, facility, ingenuity, knack, quickness, readiness, skilfulness; discernment, discrimination, knowledge, understanding, wit.

skim *vb* brush, glance, graze, kiss, scrape, scratch, sweep, touch lightly; coast, flow, fly, glide, sail, scud, whisk; dip into, glance at, scan, skip, thumb over, touch upon.

skin *vb* pare, peel; decorticate, excoriate, flay. * *n* cuticle, cutis, derm, epidermis, hide, integument, pellicle, pelt; hull, husk, peel, rind.

skinflint *n* churl, curmudgeon, lickpenny, miser, niggard, scrimp.

skinny *adj* emaciated, lank, lean, poor, shrivelled, shrunk, thin.

skip *vb* bound, caper, frisk, gambol, hop, jump, leap, spring; disregard, intermit, miss, neglect, omit, pass over, skim. * *n* bound, caper, frisk, gambol, hop, jump, leap, spring.

skirmish *vb* battle, brush, collide, combat, contest, fight, scuffle, tussle. * *n* affair, affray, battle, brush, collision, combat, conflict, contest, encounter, fight, scuffle, tussle.

skirt *vb* border, bound, edge, fringe, hem, march, rim; circumnavigate, circumvent, flank, go along. * *n* border, boundary, edge, margin, rim, verge; flap, kilt, overskirt, petticoat.

skittish *adj* changeable, fickle, inconstant; hasty, volatile, wanton; shy, timid, timorous.

skulk *vb* hide, lurk, slink, sneak.

skulker *n* lurker, sneak; shirk, slacker, malingerer.

skull *n* brain pan, cranium.

sky *n* empyrean, firmament, heaven, heavens, welkin.

sky-blue *adj* azure, cerulean, sapphire, sky-coloured.

skylarking *n* carousing, frolicking, sporting.

slab *adj* slimy, thick, viscous. * *n* beam, board, layer, panel, plank, slat, table, tablet; mire, mud, puddle, slime.

slabber vb drivel, slaver, slobber; drop, let fall, shed, spill.

slack vb ease off, let up; abate, ease up, relax, slacken; malinger, shirk; choke, damp, extinguish, smother, stifle. * adj backward, careless, inattentive, lax, negligent, remiss; abated, dilatory, diminished, lingering, slow, tardy; loose, relaxed; dull, idle, inactive, quiet, sluggish. * n excess, leeway, looseness, play; coal dust, culm, residue.

slacken vb abate, diminish, lessen, lower, mitigate, moderate, neglect, remit, relieve, retard, slack; loosen, relax; flag, slow down; bridle, check, control, curb, repress, restrain.

slackness n looseness; inattention, negligence, remissness; slowness, tardiness.

slander vb asperse, backbite, belie, brand, calumniate, decry, defame, libel, malign, reproach, scandalize, traduce, vilify; detract from, disparage. * n aspersion, backbiting, calumny, defamation, detraction, libel, obloquy, scandal, vilification.

slanderous adj calumnious, defamatory, false, libellous, malicious, maligning.

slang n argo, cant, jargon, lingo.

slant vb incline, lean, lie obliquely, list, slope. * n inclination, slope, steep, tilt.

slap vb dab, clap, pat, smack, spank, strike. * adv instantly, quickly, plumply. * n blow, clap.

slapdash adv haphazardly, hurriedly, precipitately.

slash vb cut, gash, slit. * n cut, gash, slit.

slashed adj cut, slit; (bot) jagged, laciniate, multifid.

slattern adj slatternly, slovenly, sluttish. * n drab, slut, sloven, trollop.

slatternly adj dirty, slattern, slovenly, sluttish, unclean, untidy. * adv carelessly, negligently, sluttishly.

slaughter vb butcher, kill, massacre, murder, slay. * n bloodshed, butchery, carnage, havoc, killing, massacre, murder, slaying.

slaughterer n assassin, butcher, cutthroat, destroyer, killer, murderer, slayer.

slave vb drudge, moil, toil. * n bondmaid, bondservant, bondslave, bondman, captive, dependant, henchman, helot, peon, serf, thrall, vassal, villein; drudge, menial.

slavery n bondage, bond-service, captivity, enslavement, enthralment, serfdom, servitude, thraldom, vassalage, villeinage; drudgery, mean labour.

slavish adj abject, beggarly, base, cringing, fawning, grovelling, low, mean, obsequious, servile, sycophantic; drudging, laborious, menial, servile.

slay vb assassinate, butcher, dispatch, kill, massacre, murder, slaughter; destroy, ruin.

slayer n assassin, destroyer, killer, murderer, slaughterer.

sledge n drag, sled; cutter, pung, sleigh.

sleek adj glossy, satin, silken, silky, smooth.

sleekly adv evenly, glossily, nicely, smoothly.

sleep vb catnap, doze, drowse, nap, slumber. * n dormancy, hypnosis, lethargy, repose, rest, slumber.

sleeping adj dormant, inactive, quiescent.

sleepwalker n night-walker, noctambulist, somnambulist.

sleepwalking n somnambulism.

sleepy adj comatose, dozy, drowsy, heavy, lethargic, nodding, somnolent; narcotic, opiate, slumberous, somniferous, somnific, soporiferous, soporific; dull, heavy, inactive, lazy, slow, sluggish, torpid.

sleight n adroitness, dexterity, manoeuvring.

sleight of hand n conjuring, hocus-pocus, jugglery, legerdemain, prestdigitation.

slender adj lank, lithe, narrow, skinny, slim, spindly, thin; feeble, fine, flimsy, fragile, slight, tenuous, weak; inconsiderable, moderate, small, trivial; exiguous, inadequate, insufficient, lean, meagre, pitiful, scanty; abstemious, light, simple, spare, sparing.

slice vb cut, divide, part, section; cut off, sever. * n chop, collop, piece.

slick adj glassy, glossy, polished, sleek, smooth; alert, clever, cunning, shrewd, slippery, unctuous. vb burnish, gloss, lacquer, polish, shine, sleek, varnish; grease, lubricate, oil.

slide vb glide, move smoothly, slip. * n glide, glissade, skid, slip.

sliding adj gliding, slippery, uncertain. * n backsliding, falling, fault, lapse, transgression.

slight vb cold-shoulder, disdain, disregard, neglect, snub; overlook; scamp, skimp, slur. * adj inconsiderable, insignificant, little, paltry, petty, small, trifling, trivial, unimportant, unsubstantial; delicate, feeble, frail, gentle, weak; careless, cursory, desultory, hasty, hurried, negligent, scanty, superficial; flimsy, perishable; slender, slim. * n discourtesy, disregard, disrespect, inattention, indignity, neglect.

slightingly adv contemptuously, disrespectfully, scornfully, slightly.

slightly adv inconsiderably, little, somewhat; feebly, slenderly, weakly; cursorily, hastily, negligently, superficially.

slim vb bant, diet, lose weight, reduce, slenderize. * adj gaunt, lank, lithe, narrow, skinny, slender, spare; inconsiderable, paltry, poor, slight, trifling, trivial, unsubstantial, weak; insufficient, meagre.

slime n mire, mud, ooze, sludge.

slimy adj miry, muddy, oozy; clammy, gelatinous, glutinous, gummy, lubricious, mucilaginous, mucous, ropy, slabby, viscid, viscous.

sling vb cast, fling, hurl, throw; hang up, suspend.

slink vb skulk, slip away, sneak, steal away.

slip vb glide, slide; err, mistake, trip; lose, omit; disengage, throw off; escape, let go, loose, loosen, release, . * n glide, slide, slipping; blunder, lapse, misstep, mistake, oversight, peccadillo, trip; backsliding, error, fault, impropriety, indiscretion, transgression; desertion, escape; cord, leash, strap, string; case, covering, wrapper.

slippery adj glib, slithery, smooth; changeable, insecure, mutable, perilous, shaky, uncertain, unsafe, unstable, unsteady; cunning, dishonest, elusive, faithless, false, knavish, perfidious, shifty, treacherous.

slipshod adj careless, shuffling, slovenly, untidy.

slit vb cut; divide, rend, slash, split, sunder. * n cut, gash.

slobber vb drivel, drool, slabber, slaver; daub, obscure, smear, stain.

slobbery adj dank, floody, moist, muddy, sloppy, wet.

slope vb incline, slant, tilt. * n acclivity, cant, declivity, glacis, grade, gradient, incline, inclination, obliquity, pitch, ramp.

sloping adj aslant, bevelled, declivitous, inclining, oblique, shelving, slanting.

sloppy adj muddy, plashy, slabby, slobbery, splashy, wet.

sloth n dilatoriness, slowness, tardiness; idleness, inaction, inactivity, indolence, inertness, laziness, lumpishness, slothfulness, sluggishness, supineness, torpor.

slothful adj dronish, idle, inactive, indolent, inert, lazy, lumpish, slack, sluggish, supine, torpid.

slouch vb droop, loll, slump; shamble, shuffle. * n malingerer, shirker, slacker; shamble, shuffle, stoop.

slouching adj awkward, clownish, loutish, lubberly, uncouth, ungainly.

slough[1] n bog, fen, marsh, morass, quagmire; dejection, depression, despondence, despondency.

slough[2] vb cast, desquamate, excuviate, moult, shed, throw off; cast off, discard, divest, jettison, reject. * n cast, desquamation.

sloven n slattern, slob, slouch, slut.

slovenly adj unclean, untidy; blowsy, disorderly, dowdy, frowsy, loose, slatternly, tacky, unkempt, untidy; careless, heedless, lazy, negligent, perfunctory.

slow vb abate, brake, check, decelerate, diminish, lessen, mitigate, moderate, modulate, reduce, weaken; delay,detain, retard; ease, ease up, relax, slack, slacken, slack off. * adj deliberate, gradual; dead, dull, heavy, inactive, inert, sluggish, stupid; behindhand, late, tardy, unready; delaying, dilatory, lingering, slack.

sludge n mire, mud; slosh, slush.

sluggard n dawdler, drone, idler, laggard, lounger, slug.

sluggish adj dronish, drowsy, idle, inactive, indolent, inert, languid, lazy, listless, lumpish, phlegmatic, slothful, torpid; slow; dull, stupid, supine, tame.

sluice vb drain, drench, flood, flush, irrigate. * n floodgate, opening, vent.

slumber vb catnap, doze, nap, repose, rest, sleep. * n catnap, doze, nap, repose, rest, siesta, sleep.

slumberous adj drowsy, sleepy, somniferous, somnific, soporific.

slump vb droop, drop, fall, flop, founder, sag, sink, sink down; decline, depreciate, deteriorate, ebb, fail, fall away, lose ground, recede, slide, slip, subside, wane. * n droop, drop, fall, flop, lowering, sag, sinkage; decline, depreciation, deterioration, downturn, downtrend, subsidence, ebb, falling off, wane; crash, recession, smash.

slur vb asperse, calumniate, disparage, depreciate, reproach, traduce; conceal, disregard, gloss over, obscure, pass over, slight. * n mark, stain; brand, disgrace, reproach, stain, stigma; innuendo.

slush n slosh, sludge.

slushy vb plashy, sloppy, sloshy, sludgy.

slut n drab, slattern, sloven, trollop.

sluttish adj careless, dirty, disorderly, unclean, untidy.

sly adj artful, crafty, cunning, insidious, subtle, wily; astute, cautious, shrewd; arch, knowing, clandestine, secret, stealthy, underhand.

smack[1] vb smell, taste. * n flavour, savour, tang, taste, tincture; dash, infusion, little, space, soupçon, sprinkling, tinge, touch; smattering.

smack[2] vb slap, strike; crack, slash, snap; buss, kiss. * n crack, slap, slash, snap; buss, kiss.

small adj diminutive, Lilliputian, little, miniature, petite, pygmy, tiny, wee; infinitesimal, microscopic, minute; inappreciable, inconsiderable, insignificant, petty, trifling, trivial, unimportant; moderate, paltry, scanty, slender; faint, feeble, puny, slight, weak; illiberal, mean, narrow, narrow-minded, paltry, selfish, sorded, ungenerous, unworthy.

small talk n chat, conversation, gossip.

smart[1] vb hurt, pain, sting; suffer. * adj keen, painful, poignant, pricking, pungent, severe, sharp, stinging.

smart[2] adj active, agile, brisk, fresh, lively, nimble, quick, spirited, sprightly, spry; effective, efficient, energetic, forcible, vigorous; adroit, alert, clever, dexterous, dextrous, expert, intelligent, stirring; acute, apt, pertinent, ready, witty; chic, dapper, fine, natty, showy, spruce, trim.

smartness n acuteness, keenness, poignancy, pungency, severity, sharpness; efficiency, energy, force, vigour; activity, agility, briskness, liveliness, nimbleness, sprightliness, spryness, vivacity; alertness, cleverness, dexterity, expertise, expertness, intelligence, quickness; acuteness, aptness, pertinency, wit, wittiness; chic, nattiness, spruceness, trimness.

smash vb break, crush, dash, mash, shatter. * n crash, debacle, destruction, ruin; bankruptcy, failure.

smattering n dabbling, smatter, sprinkling.

smear vb bedaub, begrime, besmear, daub, plaster, smudge; contaminate, pollute, smirch, smut, soil, stain, sully, tarnish. * n blot, blotch, daub, patch, smirch, smudge, spot, stain; calumny, defamation, libel, slander.

smell vb scent, sniff, stench, stink. * n aroma, bouquet, fragrance, fume, odour, perfume, redolence, scent, stench, stink; sniff, snuff.

smelt vb fuse, melt.

smile vb grin, laugh, simper, smirk. * n grin, simper, smirk.

smite vb beat, box, collide, cuff, knock, strike, wallop, whack; destroy, kill, slay; afflict, chasten, punish; blast, destroy.

smitten adj attracted, captivated, charmed, enamoured, fascinated, taken; destroyed, killed, slain; smit, struck; afflicted, chastened, punished.

smock n chemise, shift, slip; blouse, gaberdine.

smoke vb emit, exhale, reek, steam; fumigate, smudge; discover, find out, smell out. * n effluvium, exhalation, fume, mist, reek, smother, steam, vapour; fumigation, smudge.

smoky adj fuliginous, fumid, fumy, smudgy; begrimed, blackened, dark, reeky, sooty, tanned.

smooth vb flatten, level, plane; ease, lubricate; extenuate, palliate, soften; allay, alleviate, assuage, calm, mitigate, mollify. * adj even, flat, level, plane, polished, unruffled, unwrinkled; glabrous, glossy, satiny, silky, sleek, soft, velvet; euphonious, flowing, liquid, mellifluent; fluent, glib, voluble; bland, flattering, ingratiating, insinuating, mild, oily, smooth-tongued, soothing, suave, unctuous.

smoothly adv evenly; easily, readily, unobstructedly; blandly, flatteringly, gently, mildly, pleasantly, softly, soothingly.

smooth-tongued adj adulatory, cozening, flattering, plausible, smooth, smooth-spoken.

smother vb choke, stifle, suffocate; conceal, deaden, extinguish, hide, keep down, repress, suppress; smoke, smoulder.

smudge vb besmear, blacken, blur, smear, smut, smutch, soil, spot, stain. * n blur, blot, smear, smut, spot, stain.

smug adj complacent, self-satisfied; neat, nice, spruce, trim.

smuggler n contrabandist, runner.

smut vb blacken, smouch, smudge, soil, stain, sully, taint, tarnish. * n dirt, smudge, smutch, soot; nastiness, obscenity, ribaldry, smuttiness; pornography.

smutty adj coarse, gross, immodest, impure, indecent, indelicate, loose, nasty; dirty, foul, nasty, soiled, stained.

snack *n* bite, light meal, nibble.

snag *vb* catch, enmesh, entangle, hook, snare, sniggle, tangle. * *n* knarl, knob, knot, projection, protuberance, snub; catch, difficulty, drawback, hitch, rub, shortcoming, weakness; obstacle.

snaky *adj* serpentine, snaking, winding; artful, cunning, deceitful, insinuating, sly, subtle.

snap *vb* break, fracture; bite, catch at, seize, snatch at, snip; crack; crackle, crepitate, decrepitate, pop. * *adj* casual, cursory, hasty, offhand, sudden, superficial. * *n* bite, catch, nip, seizure; catch, clasp, fastening, lock; crack, fillip, flick, flip, smack; briskness, energy, verve, vim.

snappish *adj* acrimonious, captious, churlish, crabbed, cross, crusty, froward, irascible, ill-tempered, peevish, perverse, pettish, petulant, snarling, splenetic, surly, tart, testy, touchy, waspish.

snare *vb* catch, ensnare, entangle, entrap. * *n* catch, gin, net, noose, springe, toil, trap, wile.

snarl[1] *vb* girn, gnarl, growl, grumble, murmur. * *n* growl, grumble.

snarl[2] *vb* complicate, disorder, entangle, knot; confuse, embarrass, ensnare. * *n* complication, disorder, entanglement, tangle; difficulty, embarrassment, intricacy.

snatch *vb* catch, clutch, grasp, grip, pluck, pull, seize, snip, twich, wrest, wring. * *n* bit, fragment, part, portion; catch, effort.

sneak *vb* lurk, skulk, slink, steal; crouch, truckle. * *adj* clandestine, concealed, covert, hidden, secret, sly, underhand. * *n* informer, telltale; lurker, shirk.

sneaky *adj* furtive, skulking, slinking; abject, crouching, grovelling, mean; clandestine, concealed, covert, hidden, secret, sly, underhand.

sneer *vb* flout, gibe, jeer, mock, rail, scoff; (*with* **at**) deride, despise, disdain, laugh at, mock, rail at, scoff, spurn. * *n* flouting, gibe, jeer, scoff.

snicker *vb* giggle, laugh, snigger, titter.

sniff *vb* breathe, inhale, snuff; scent, smell.

snip *vb* clip, cut, nip; snap, snatch. * *n* bit, fragment, particle, piece, shred; share, snack.

snivel *vb* blubber, cry, fret, sniffle, snuffle, weep, whimper, whine.

snivelly *adj* snotty; pitiful, whining.

snob *n* climber, toady.

snooze *vb* catnap, doze, drowse, nap, sleep, slumber. * *n* catnap, nap, sleep, slumber.

snout *n* muzzle, nose; nozzle.

snowy *adj* immaculate, pure, spotless, unblemished, unstained, unsullied, white.

snub[1] *vb* abash, cold-shoulder, cut, discomfit, humble, humiliate, mortify, slight, take down. * *n* check, rebuke, slight.

snub[2] *vb* check, clip, cut short, dock, nip, prune, stunt. * *adj* pug, retroussé, snubbed, squashed, squat, stubby, turned-up.

snuff[1] *vb* breathe, inhale, sniff; scent, smell; snort.

snuff[2] *vb* (*with* **out**) annihilate, destroy, efface, extinguish, obliterate.

snuffle *vb* sniffle; snort, snuff.

snug *adj* close, concealed; comfortable, compact, convenient, neat, trim.

snuggle *vb* cuddle, nestle, nuzzle.

so *adv* thus, with equal reason; in such a manner; in this way, likewise; as it is, as it was, such; for this reason, therefore; be it so, thus be it. * *conj* in case that, on condition that, provided that.

soak *vb* drench, moisten, permeate, saturate, wet; absorb, imbibe; imbue, macerate, steep.

soar *vb* ascend, fly aloft, glide, mount, rise, tower.

sob *vb* cry, sigh convulsively, weep.

sober *vb* (*with* **up**) calm down, collect oneself, compose oneself, control oneself, cool off, master, moderate, simmer down. * *adj* abstemious, abstinent, temperate, unintoxicated; rational, reasonable, sane, sound; calm, collected, composed, cool, dispassionate, moderate, rational, reasonabler, regular, restrained, steady, temperate, unimpassioned, unruffled, well-regulated; demure, grave, quiet, sedate, serious, solemn, sombre, staid; dark, drab, dull-looking, quiet, sad, subdued.

sobriety *n* abstemiousness, abstinence, soberness, temperance; calmness, coolness, gravity, sedateness, sober-mindedness, staidness, thoughtfulness; gravity, seriousness, solemnity.

sobriquet *n* appellation, nickname, nom de plume, pseudonym.

sociability *n* companionableness, comradeship, good fellowship, sociality.

sociable *adj* accessible, affable, communicative, companionable, conversable, friendly, genial, neighbourly, social.

social *adj* civic, civil; accessible, affable, communicative, companionable, familiar, friendly, hospitable, neighbourly, sociable; convivial, festive, gregarious. * *n* conversazione, gathering, get-together, party, reception, soiree.

society *n* association, companionship, company, converse, fellowship; the community, populace, the public, the world; élite, *monde*; body, brotherhood, co-partnership, corporation, club, fraternity, partnersnip, sodality, union.

sodden *adj* drenched, saturated, soaked, steeped, wet; boiled, decocted, seethed, stewed.

sofa *n* couch, davenport, divan, ottoman, settee.

soft *adj* impressible, malleable, plastic, pliable, yielding; downy, fleecy, velvety, mushy, pulpy, squashy; compliant, facile, irresolute, submissive, undecided, weak; bland, mild, gentle, kind, lenient, soft-hearted, tender; delicate; easy, even, quiet, smooth-going, steady; effeminate, luxurious, unmanly; dulcet, fluty, mellifluous, melodious, smooth. * *interj* hold, stop.

soften *vb* intenerate, mellow, melt, tenderize; abate, allay, alleviate, appease, assuage, attemper, balm, blunt, calm, dull, ease, lessen, make easy, mitigate, moderate, mollify, milden, qualify, quell, quiet, relent, relieve, soothe, still, temper; extenuate, modify, palliate, qualify; enervate, weaken.

soil[1] *n* earth, ground loam, mould; country, land.

soil[2] *vb* bedaub, begrime, bemire, besmear, bespatter, contaminate, daub, defile, dirty, foul, pollute, smirch, stain, sully, taint, tarnish. * *n* blemish, defilement, dirt, filth, foulness; blot, spot, stain, taint, tarnish.

sojourn *vb* abide, dwell, live, lodge, remain, reside, rest, stay, stop, tarry, visit. * *n* residence, stay.

solace *vb* cheer, comfort, console, soothe; allay, assuage, mitigate, relieve, soften. * *n* alleviation, cheer, comfort, consolation, relief.

soldier *n* fighting man, man-at-arms, warrior; GI, private.

soldierly *adj* martial, military, warlike; brave, courageous, gallant, heroic, honourable, intrepid, valiant.

sole *adj* alone, individual, one, only, single, solitary, unique.

solecism *n* barbarism, blunder, error, faux pas, impropriety, incongruity, mistake, slip.

solemn *adj* ceremonial, formal, ritual; devotional, devout, religious, reverential, sacred; earnest, grave, serious, sober; august, awe-inspiring, awful, grand, imposing, impressive, majestic, stately, venerable.

solemnity *n* celebration, ceremony, observance, office, rite; awfulness, sacredness, sanctity; gravity, impressiveness, seriousness.

solemnize *vb* celebrate, commemorate, honour, keep, observe.

solicit *vb* appeal to, ask, beg, beseech, conjure, crave, entreat, implore, importune, petition, pray, press, request, supplicate, urge; arouse, awaken, entice, excite, invite, summon; canvass, seek.

solicitation *n* address, appeal, asking, entreaty, imploration, importunity, insistence, petition, request, suit, supplication, urgency; bidding, call, invitation, summons.

solicitor *n* attorney, law agent, lawyer; asker, canvasser, drummer, petitioner, solicitant.

solicitous *adj* anxious, apprehensive, careful, concerned, disturbed, eager, troubled, uneasy.

solicitude *n* anxiety, care, carefulness, concern, perplexity, trouble.

solid *adj* congealed, firm, hard, impenetrable, rock-like; compact, dense, impermeable, massed; cubic; sound, stable, stout, strong, substantial; just, real, true, valid, weighty; dependable, faithful, reliable, safe, staunch, steadfast, trustworthy, well established.

solidarity *n* communion of interests, community, consolidation, fellowship, joint interest, mutual responsibility.

solidify *vb* compact, congeal, consolidate, harden, petrify.

solidity *n* compactness, consistency, density, firmness, hardness, solidness; fullness; massiveness, stability, strength; dependability, gravity, justice, reliability, soundness, steadiness, validity, weight; cubic content, volume.

soliloquy *n* monologue.

solitariness *n* isolation, privacy, reclusion, retirement, seclusion; loneliness, solitude.

solitary *adj* alone, companionless, lone, lonely, only, separate, unaccompanied; individual, single, sole; desert, deserted, desolate, isolated, lonely, remote, retired, secluded, unfrequented.

solitude *n* isolation, loneliness, privacy, recluseness, retiredness, retirement, seclusion, solitariness; desert, waste, wilderness.

solution *n* answer, clue, disentanglement, elucidation, explication, explanation, key, resolution, unravelling, unriddling; disintegration, dissolution, liquefaction, melting, resolution, separation; breach, disconnection, discontinuance, disjunction, disruption.

solve *vb* clear, clear up, disentangle, elucidate, explain, expound, interpret, make plain, resolve, unfold.

solvent *n* diluent, dissolvent, menstruum.

somatic *adj* bodily, corporeal.

sombre *adj* cloudy, dark, dismal, dull, dusky, gloomy, murky, overcast, rayless, shady, sombrous, sunless; doleful, funereal, grave, lugubrious, melancholy, mournful, sad, sober.

some *adj* a, an, any, one; about, near; certain, little, moderate, part, several.

somebody *n* one, someone, something; celebrity, VIP.

somehow *adv* in some way.

something *n* part, portion, thing; somebody; affair, event, matter.

sometime *adj* former, late. * *adv* formerly, once; now and then, at one time or other, sometimes.

sometimes *adv* at intervals, at times, now and then, occasionally; at a past period, formerly, once.

somewhat *adv* in some degree, more or less, rather, something. * *n* something, a little, more or less, part.

somewhere *adv* here and there, in one place or another, in some place.

somnambulism *n* sleepwalking, somnambulation.

somnambulist *n* night-walker, noctambulist, sleepwalker, somnambulator, somnambule.

somniferous *adj* narcotic, opiate, slumberous, somnific, soporific, soporiferous.

somnolence *n* doziness, drowsiness, sleepiness, somnolency.

somnolent *adj* dozy, drowsy, sleepy.

son *n* cadet, heir, junior, scion.

song *n* aria, ballad, canticle, canzonet, carol, ditty, glee, lay, lullaby, snatch; descant, melody; anthem, hymn, poem, psalm, strain; poesy, poetry, verse.

sonorous *adj* full-toned, resonant, resounding, ringing, sounding; high-sounding, loud.

soon *adv* anon, before long, by and by, in a short time, presently, shortly; betimes, early, forthwith, promptly, quick; gladly, lief, readily, willingly.

soot *n* carbon, crock, dust.

soothe *vb* cajole, flatter, humour; appease, assuage, balm, calm, compose, lull, mollify, pacify, quiet, soften, still, tranquillize; allay, alleviate, blunt, check, deaden, dull, ease, lessen, mitigate, moderate, palliate, qualify, relieve, repress, soften, subdue, temper.

soothsayer *n* augur, diviner, foreteller, necromancer, predictor, prophet, seer, sorcerer, vaticinator.

sooty *adj* black, dark, dusky, fuliginous, murky, sable.

sophism *n* casuistry, fallacy, paralogism, paralogy, quibble, specious argument.

sophist *n* quibbler.

sophistical *adj* casuistical, fallacious, illogical, quibbling, subtle, unsound.

soporific *adj* dormitive, hypnotic, narcotic, opiate, sleepy, slumberous, somnific, somniferous, soporiferous, soporous.

soppy *adj* drenched, saturated, soaked, sopped; emotional, mawkish, sentimental.

soprano *n* (*mus*) descant, discant, treble.

sorcerer *n* charmer, conjurer, diviner, enchanter, juggler, magician, necromancers, seer, shaman, soothsayer, thaumaturgist, wizard.

sorcery *n* black art, charm, divination, enchantment, necromancy, occultism, shamanism, spell, thaumaturgy, voodoo, witchcraft.

sordid *adj* base, degraded, low, mean, vile; avaricious, close-fisted, covetous, illiberal, miserly, niggardly, penurious, stingy, ungenerous.

sore *adj* irritated, painful, raw, tender, ulcerated; aggrieved, galled, grieved, hurt, irritable, vexed; afflictive, distressing, severe, sharp, violent. * *n* abscess, boil, fester, gathering, imposthume, pustule, ulcer; affliction, grief, pain, sorrow, trouble.

sorely *adv* greatly, grievously, severely, violently.

sorrily *adv* despicably, meanly, pitiably, poorly, wretchedly.

sorrow *vb* bemoan, bewail, grieve, lament, mourn, weep. * *n* affliction, dolour, grief, heartache, mourning, sadness, trouble, woe.

sorrowful *adj* afflicted, dejected, depressed, grieved, grieving, heartsore, sad; baleful, distressing, grievous, lamentable, melancholy, mournful, painful; disconsolate, dismal, doleful, dolorous, drear, dreary, lugubrious, melancholy, piteous, rueful, woebegone, woeful.

sorry *adj* afflicted, dejected, grieved, pained, poor, sorrowful; distressing, pitiful; chagrined, mortified, pained, regretful, remorseful, sad, vexed; abject, base, beggarly, contemptible, despicable, low, mean, paltry, insignificant, miserable, shabby, worthless, wretched.

sort *vb* arrange, assort, class, classify, distribute, order; conjoin, join, put together; choose, elect, pick out, select; associate, consort, fraternize; accord, agree with, fit, suit * *n* character, class, denomination, description, kind, nature, order, race, rank, species, type; manner, way.

sortie *n* attack, foray, raid, sally.

so-so *adj* indifferent, mediocre, middling, ordinary, passable, tolerable.

sot *n* blockhead, dolt, dullard, dunce, fool, simpleton; drunkard, tippler, toper.

sottish *adj* doltish, dull, foolish, senseless, simple, stupid; befuddled, besotted, drunken, insensate, senseless, tipsy.

sotto voce *adv* in a low voice, in an undertone, softly.

sough *n* murmur, sigh; breath, breeze, waft.

soul *n* mind, psyche, spirit; being, person; embodiment, essence, personification, spirit, vital principle; ardour, energy, fervour, inspiration, vitality.

soulless *adj* dead, expressionless, lifeless, unfeeling.

sound[1] *adj* entire, intact, unbroken, unhurt, unimpaired, uninjured, unmutilated, whole; hale, hardy, healthy, hearty, vigorous; good, perfect, undecayed; sane, well-balanced; correct, orthodox, right, solid, valid, well-founded; legal; deep, fast, profound, unbroken, undisturbed; forcible, lusty, severe, stout.

sound[2] *n* channel, narrows, strait.

sound[3] *vb* resound; appear, seem; play on; express, pronounce, utter; announce, celebrate, proclaim, publish, spread. * *n* noise, note, tone, voice, whisper.

sound[4] *vb* fathom, gauge, measure, test; examine, probe, search, test, try.

sounding *adj* audible, resonant, resounding, ringing, sonorous; imposing, significant.

soundless *adj* dumb, noiseless, silent; abysmal, bottomless, deep, profound, unfathomable, unsounded.

soundly *adv* satisfactorily, thoroughly, well; healthily, heartily, forcibly, lustily, severely, smartly, stoutly; correctly, rightly, truly; firmly, strongly; deeply, fast, profoundly.

soundness *n* entireness, entirety, integrity, wholeness; healthiness, vigour, saneness, sanity; correctness, orthodoxy, rectitude, reliability, truth, validity; firmness, solidity, strength, validity.

soup *n* broth, consommé, purée.

sour *vb* acidulate; embitter, envenom. * *adj* acetose, acetous, acid, astringent, pricked, sharp, tart, vinegary; acrimonious, crabbed, cross, crusty, fretful, glum, ill-humoured, ill-natured, ill-tempered, peevish, pettish, petulant, snarling, surly; bitter, disagreeable, unpleasant; austere, dismal, gloomy, morose, sad, sullen; bad, coagulated, curdled, musty, rancid, turned.

source *n* beginning, fountain, fountainhead, head, origin, rise, root, spring, well; cause, original.

sourness *n* acidity, sharpness, tartness; acrimony, asperity, churlishness, crabbedness, crossness, discontent, harshness, moroseness, peevishness.

souse *vb* pickle; dip, douse, immerse, plunge, submerge.

souvenir *n* keepsake, memento, remembrance, reminder.

sovereign *adj* imperial, monarchical, princely, regal, royal, supreme; chief, commanding, excellent, highest, paramount, predominant, principal, supreme, utmost; efficacious, effectual. * *n* autocrat, monarch, suzerain; emperor, empress, king, lord, potentate, prince, princess, queen, ruler.

sovereignty *n* authority, dominion, empire, power, rule, supremacy, sway.

sow *vb* scatter, spread, strew; disperse, disseminate, propagate, spread abroad; plant; besprinkle, scatter.

space *n* expanse, expansion, extension, extent, proportions, spread; accommodation, capacity, room, place; distance, interspace, interval.

spacious *adj* extended, extensive, vast, wide; ample, broad, capacious, commodious, large, roomy, wide.

span *vb* compass, cross, encompass, measure, overlay. * *n* brief period, spell; pair, team, yoke.

spank *vb* slap, strike.

spar[1] *n* beam, boom, pole, sprit, yard.

spar[2] *vb* box, fight; argue, bicker, contend, dispute, quarrel, spat, squabble, wrangle.

spare *vb* lay aside, lay by, reserve, save, set apart, set aside; dispense with, do without, part with; forbear, omit, refrain, withhold; exempt, forgive, keep from; afford, allow, give, grant; save; economize, pinch. * *adj* frugal, scanty, sparing, stinted; chary, parsimonious; emaciated, gaunt, lank, lean, meagre, poor, thin, scraggy, skinny, raw-boned; additional, extra, supernumerary.

sparing *adj* little, scanty, scarce; abstemious, meagre, spare; chary, economical, frugal, parsimonious, saving; compassionate, forgiving, lenient, merciful.

spark *vb* scintillate, sparkle; begin, fire, incite, instigate, kindle, light, set off, start, touch off, trigger. * *n* scintilla, scintillation, sparkle; beginning, element, germ, seed.

sparkle *vb* coruscate, flash, gleam, glisten, glister, glitter, radiate, scintillate, shine, twinkle; bubble, effervesce, foam, froth. * *n* glint, scintillation, spark; luminosity, lustre.

sparkling *adj* brilliant, flashing, glistening, glittering, glittery, twinkling; bubbling, effervescing, eloquent, foaming, frothing, mantling; brilliant, glowing, lively, nervous, piquant, racy, spirited, sprightly, witty.

sparse *adj* dispersed, infrequent, scanty, scattered, sporadic, thin.

spartan *adj* bold, brave, chivalric, courageous, daring, dauntless, doughty, fearless, hardy, heroic, intrepid, lion-hearted, undaunted, valiant, valorous; austere, exacting, hard, severe, tough, unsparing; enduring, long-suffering, self-controlled, stoic.

spasm *n* contraction, cramp, crick, twitch; fit, paroxysm, seizure, throe.

spasmodic *adj* erratic, fitful, intermittent, irregular, sporadic; convulsive, paroxysmal, spasmodical, violent.

spat *vb* argue, bicker, dispute, jangle, quarrel, spar, squabble, wrangle.

spatter *vb* bespatter, besprinkle, plash, splash, sprinkle; spit, sputter.

spawn *vb* bring forth, generate, produce. * *n* eggs, roe; fruit, offspring, product.

speak *vb* articulate, deliver, enunciate, express, pronounce, utter; announce, confer, declare, disclose, mention, say, tell; celebrate, make known, proclaim, speak abroad; accost, address, greet, hail; exhibit; argue, converse, dispute, talk; declaim, discourse, hold forth, harangue, orate, plead, spout, treat.

speaker *n* discourse, elocutionist, orator, prolocutor, spokesman; chairman, presiding officer.

speaking *adj* rhetorical, talking; eloquent, expressive; lifelike. * *n* discourse, talk, utterance; declamation, elocution, oratory.

spear *n* dart, gaff, harpoon, javelin, lance, pike; shoot, spire.

special *adj* specific, specifical; especial, individual, particular, peculiar, unique; exceptional, extraordinary, marked, particular, uncommon; appropriate, express.

speciality, specialty *n* particularity; feature, forte, pet subject.

species *n* assemblage, class, collection, group; description, kind, sort, variety; (*law*) fashion, figure, form, shape.

specific *adj* characteristic, especial, particular, peculiar; definite, limited, precise, specified.

specification *n* characterization, designation; details, particularization.

specify *vb* define, designate, detail, indicate, individualize, name, show, particularize.

specimen *n* copy, example, model, pattern, sample.

specious *adj* manifest, obvious, open, showy; flimsy, illusory, ostensible, plausible, sophistical.

speck *n* blemish, blot, flaw, speckle, spot, stain; atom, bit, corpuscle, mite, mote, particle, scintilla.

spectacle *n* display, exhibition, pageant, parade, representation, review, scene, show, sight; curiosity, marvel, phenomenon, wonder.

spectacles *npl* glasses, goggles, shades.

spectator *n* beholder, bystander, observer, onlooker, witness.

spectral *adj* eerie, ghostlike, ghostly, phantomlike, shadowy, spooky, weird, wraithlike.

spectre, specter *n* apparition, banshee, ghost, goblin, hobgoblin, phantom, shade, shadow, spirit, sprite, wraith.

spectrum *n* appearance, image, representation.

speculate *vb* cogitate, conjecture, contemplate, imagine, meditate, muse, ponder, reflect, ruminate, theorize, think; bet, gamble, hazard, risk, trade, venture.

speculation *n* contemplation, intellectualization; conjecture, hypothesis, scheme, supposition, reasoning, reflection, theory, view.

speculative *adj* contemplative, philosophical, speculatory, unpractical; ideal, imaginary, theoretical; hazardous, risky, unsecured.

speculator *n* speculatist, theorist, theorizer; adventurer, dealer, gambler, trader.

speech *n* articulation, language, words; dialect, idiom, locution, tongue; conversation, oral communication, parlance, talk, verbal intercourse; mention, observation, remark, saying; address, declaration, discourse, harangue, oration, palaver.

speechless *adj* dumb, gagged, inarticulate, mute, silent; dazed, dumbfounded, flabbergasted, shocked.

speed *vb* hasten, hurry, rush, scurry; flourish, prosper, succeed, thrive; accelerate, expedite, hasten, hurry, quicken, press forward, urge on; carry through, dispatch, execute; advance, aid, assist, help; favour. * *n* acceleration, celerity, dispatch, expedition, fleetness, haste, hurry, quickness, rapidity, swiftness, velocity; good fortune, good luck, prosperity, success; impetuosity.

speedy *adj* fast, fleet, flying, hasty, hurried, hurrying, nimble, quick, rapid, swift; expeditious, prompt, quick; approaching, early, near.

spell[1] *n* charm, exorcism, hoodoo, incantation, jinx, witchery; allure, bewitchment, captivation, enchantment, entrancement, fascination.

spell[2] *vb* decipher, interpret, read, unfold, unravel, unriddle.

spell[3] *n* fit, interval, period, round, season, stint, term, turn.

spellbound *adj* bewitched, charmed, enchanted, entranced, enthralled, fascinated.

spend *vb* disburse, dispose of, expend, lay out, part with; consume, dissipate, exhaust, lavish, squander, use up, wear, waste; apply, bestow, devote, employ, pass.

spendthrift *n* prodigal, spender, squanderer, waster.

spent *adj* exhausted, fatigued, played out, used up, wearied, worn out.

spew *vb* cast up, puke, throw up, vomit; cast forth, eject.

spheral *adj* complete, perfect, symmetrical.

sphere *n* ball, globe, orb, spheroid; ambit, beat, bound, circle, circuit, compass, department, function, office, orbit, province, range, walk; order, rank, standing; country, domain, quarter, realm, region.

spherical *adj* bulbous, globated, globous, globular, orbicular, rotund, round, spheroid; planetary.

spice *n* flavour, flavouring, relish, savour, taste; admixture, dash, grain, infusion, particle, smack, soupçon, sprinkling, tincture.

spicily *adv* pungently, wittily.

spicy *adj* aromatic, balmy, fragrant; keen, piquant, pointed, pungent, sharp; indelicate, off-colour, racy, risqué, sensational, suggestive.

spill *vb* effuse, pour out, shed. * *n* accident, fall, tumble.

spin *vb* twist; draw out, extend; lengthen, prolong, protract, spend; pirouette, turn, twirl, whirl. * *n* drive, joyride, ride; autorotation, gyration, loop, revolution, rotation, turning, wheeling; pirouette, reel, turn, wheel, whirl.

spindle *n* axis, shaft.

spine *n* barb, prickle, thorn; backbone; ridge.

spinose *adj* briery, spinous, spiny, thorny.

spiny *adj* briery, prickly, spinose, spinous, thorny; difficult, perplexed, troublesome.

spiracle *n* aperture, blowhole, orifice, pore, vent.

spiral *adj* cochlear, cochleated, curled, helical, screwshaped, spiry, winding. * *n* helix, winding, worm.

spire *n* curl, spiral, twist, wreath; steeple; blade, shoot, spear, stalk; apex, summit.

spirit *vb* animate, encourage, excite, inspirit; carry off, kidnap. * *n* immaterial substance, life, vital essence; person, soul; angel, apparition, demon, elf, fairy, genius, ghost, phantom, shade, spectre, sprite; disposition, frame of mind, humour, mood, temper; spirits; ardour, cheerfulness, courage, earnestness, energy, enterprise, enthusiasm, fire, force, mettle, resolution, vigour, vim, vivacity, zeal; animation, cheerfulness, enterprise, esprit, glow, liveliness, piquancy, spice, spunk, vivacity, warmth; drift, gist, intent, meaning, purport, sense, significance, tenor; character, characteristic, complexion, essence, nature, quality, quintessence; alcohol, liquor; (*with* **the**) Comforter, Holy Ghost, Paraclete.

spirited *adj* active, alert, animated, ardent, bold, brisk, courageous, earnest, frisky, high-mettled, high-spirited, high-strung, lively, mettlesome, sprightly, vivacious.

spiritless *adj* breathless, dead, extinct, lifeless; dejected, depressed, discouraged, dispirited, low-spirited; apathetic, cold, dull, feeble, languid, phlegmatic, sluggish, soulless, torpid, unenterprising; dull, frigid, heavy, insipid, prosaic, prosy, stupid, tame, uninteresting.

spiritual *adj* ethereal, ghostly, immaterial incorporeal, psychical, supersensible; ideal, moral, unwordly; divine, holy, pure, sacred; ecclesiastical.

spiritualize *vb* elevate, etherealize, purify, refine.

spirituous *adj* alcoholic, ardent, spiritous.

spit[1] *vb* impale, thrust through, transfix.

spit[2] *vb* eject, throw out; drivel, drool, expectorate, salivate, slobber, spawl, splutter. * *n* saliva, spawl, spittle, sputum.

spite *vb* injure, mortify, thwart; annoy, offend, vex. * *n* grudge, hate, hatred, ill-nature, ill-will, malevolence, malice, maliciousness, malignity, pique, rancour, spleen, venom, vindictiveness.

spiteful *adj* evil-minded, hateful, ill-disposed, ill-natured, malevolent, malicious, malign, malignant, rancorous.

spittoon *n* cuspidor.

splash *vb* dabble, dash, plash, spatter, splurge, swash, swish. * *n* blot, daub, spot.

splay *adj* broad, spreading out, turned out, wide.

spleen *n* anger, animosity, chagrin, gall, grudge, hatred, ill-humour, irascibility, malevolence, malice, malignity, peevishness, pique, rancour, spite.

spleeny *adj* angry, fretful, ill-tempered, irritable, peevish, spleenish, splenetic.

splendid *adj* beaming, bright, brilliant, effulgent, glowing, lustrous, radiant, refulgent, resplendent, shining; dazzling, gorgeous, imposing, kingly, magnificent, pompous, showy, sumptuous, superb; celebrated, conspicuous, distinguished, eminent, excellent, famous, glorious, illustrious, noble, pre-eminent, remarkable, signal; grand, heroic, lofty, noble, sublime.

splendour *n* brightness, brilliance, brilliancy, lustre, radiance, refulgence; display, éclat, gorgeousness, grandeur, magnificence, parade, pomp, show, showiness, stateliness; celebrity, eminence, fame, glory, grandeur, renown; grandeur, loftiness, nobleness, sublimity.

splenetic *adj* choleric, cross, fretful, irascible, irritable, peevish, pettish, petulant, snappish, testy, touchy, waspish; churlish, crabbed, morose, sour, sulky, sullen; gloomy, jaundiced.

splice *vb* braid, connect, join, knit, mortise.

splinter *vb* rend, shiver, sliver, split. * *n* fragment, piece.

split *vb* cleave, rive; break, burst, rend, splinter; divide, part, separate, sunder. * *n* crack, fissure, rent; breach, division, separation.

splotch *n* blot, daub, smear, spot, stain.

splutter *vb* sputter, stammer, stutter.

spoil *vb* despoil, fleece, loot, pilfer, plunder, ravage, rob, steal, strip, waste; corrupt, damage, destroy, disfigure, harm, impair, injure, mar, ruin, vitiate; decay, decompose. * *n* booty, loot, pillage, plunder, prey; rapine, robbery, spoliation, waste.

spoiler *n* pillager, plunderer, robber; corrupter, destroyer.

spokesman *n* mouthpiece, prolocutor, speaker.

spoliate *vb* despoil, destroy, loot, pillage, plunder, rob, spoil.

spoliation *n* depradation, deprivation, despoliation, destruction, robbery; destruction, devastation, pillage, plundering, rapine, ravagement.

sponge *vb* cleanse, wipe; efface, expunge, obliterate, rub out, wipe out.

sponger *n* hanger-on, parasite.

spongy *adj* absorbent, porous, spongeous; rainy, showery, wet; drenched, marshy, saturated, soaked, wet.

sponsor *vb* back, capitalize, endorse, finance, guarantee, patronize, promote, support, stake, subsidize, take up, underwrite. * *n* angel, backer, guarantor, patron, promoter, supporter, surety, underwriter; godfather, godmother, godparent.

spontaneity *n* improvisation, impulsiveness, spontaneousness.

spontaneous *adj* free, gratuitous, impulsive, improvised, instinctive, self-acting, self-moving, unbidden, uncompelled, unconstrained, voluntary, willing.

sporadic *adj* dispersed, infrequent, isolated, rare, scattered, separate, spasmodic.

sport *vb* caper, disport, frolic, gambol, have fun, make merry, play, romp, skip; trifle; display, exhibit. * *n* amusement, diversion, entertainment, frolic, fun, gambol, game, jollity, joviality, merriment, merry-making, mirth, pastime, pleasantry, prank, recreation; jest, joke; derision, jeer, mockery, ridicule; monstrosity.

sportive *adj* frisky, frolicsome, gamesome, hilarious, lively, merry, playful, prankish, rollicking, sprightly, tricksy; comic, facetious, funny, humorous, jocose, jocular, lively, ludicrous, mirthful, vivacious, waggish.

spot *vb* besprinkle, dapple, dot, speck, stud, variegate; blemish, disgrace, soil, splotch, stain, sully, tarnish; detect, discern, espy, make out, observe, see, sight. * *n* blot, dapple, fleck, freckle, maculation, mark, mottle, patch, pip, speck, speckle; blemish, blotch, flaw, pock, splotch, stain, taint; locality, place, site.

spotless *adj* perfect, undefaced, unspotted; blameless, immaculate, innocent, irreproachable, pure, stainless, unblemished, unstained, untainted, untarnished.

spotted *adj* bespeckled, bespotted, dotted, flecked, freckled, maculated, ocellated, speckled, spotty.

spousal *adj* bridal, conjugal, connubial, hymeneal, marital, matrimonial, nuptial, wedded.

spouse *n* companion, consort, husband, mate, partner, wife.

spout *vb* gush, jet, pour out, spirit, spurt, squirt; declaim, mouth, speak, utter. * *n* conduit, tube; beak, nose, nozzle, waterspout.

sprain *vb* overstrain, rick, strain, twist, wrench, wrick.

spray[1] *vb* atomize, besprinkle, douche, gush, jet, shower, splash, splatter, spout, sprinkle, squirt. * *n* aerosol, atomizer, douche, foam, froth, shower, sprinkler, spume.

spray[2] *n* bough, branch, shoot, sprig, twig.

spread *vb* dilate, expand, extend, mantle, stretch; diffuse, disperse, distribute, radiate, scatter, sprinkle, strew; broadcast, circulate, disseminate, divulge, make known, make public, promulgate, propagate, publish; open, unfold, unfurl; cover, extend over, overspread. * *n* compass, extent, range, reach, scope, stretch; expansion, extension; circulation, dissemination, propagation; cloth, cover; banquet, feast, meal.

spree n bacchanal, carousal, debauch, frolic, jollification, orgy, revel, revelry, saturnalia.

sprig n shoot, spray, twig; lad, youth.

sprightliness n animation, activity, briskness, cheerfulness, frolicsomeness, gaiety, life, liveliness, nimbleness, vigour, vivacity.

sprightly adj airy, animated, blithe, blithesome, brisk, buoyant, cheerful, debonair, frolicsome, joyous, lively, mercurial, vigorous, vivacious.

spring vb bound, hop, jump, leap, prance, vault; arise, emerge, grow, issue, proceed, put forth, shoot forth, stem; derive, descend, emanate, flow, originate, rise, start; fly back, rebound, recoil; bend, warp; grow, thrive, wax. * adj hopping, jumping, resilient, springy. * n bound, hop, jump, leap, vault; elasticity, flexibility, resilience, resiliency, springiness; fount, fountain, fountainhead, geyser, springhead, well; cause, origin, original, principle, source; seed time, springtime.

springe n gin, net, noose, snare, trap.

springiness n elasticity, resilience, spring; sponginess, wetness.

springy adj bouncing, bounding, elastic, rebounding, recoiling, resilient.

sprinkle vb scatter, strew; bedew, besprinkle, dust, powder, sand, spatter; wash, cleanse, purify, shower.

sprinkling n affusion, baptism, bedewing, spattering, splattering, spraying, wetting; dash, scattering, seasoning, smack, soupçon, suggestion, tinge, touch, trace, vestige.

sprite n apparition, elf, fairy, ghost, goblin, hobgoblin, phantom, pixie, shade, spectre, spirit.

sprout vb burgeon, burst forth, germinate, grow, pullulate, push, put forth, ramify, shoot, shoot forth. * n shoot, sprig.

spruce vb preen, prink; adorn, deck, dress, smarten, trim. * adj dandyish, dapper, fine, foppish, jaunty, natty, neat, nice, smart, tidy, trig, trim.

spry adj active, agile, alert, brisk, lively, nimble, prompt, quick, ready, smart, sprightly, stirring, supple.

spume n foam, froth, scum, spray.

spumy adj foamy, frothy, spumous.

spur vb gallop, hasten, press on, prick; animate, arouse, drive, goad, impel, incite, induce, instigate, rouse, stimulate, urge forward. * n goad, point, prick, rowel; fillip, impulse, incentive, incitement, inducement, instigation, motive, provocation, stimulus, whip; gnarl, knob, knot, point, projection, snag.

spurious adj bogus, counterfeit, deceitful, false, feigned, fictitious, make-believe, meretricious, mock, pretended, sham, supposititious, unauthentic.

spurn vb drive away, kick; contemn, despise, disregard, flout, scorn, slight; disdain, reject, repudiate.

spurt vb gush, jet, spirt, spout, spring out, stream out, well. * n gush, jet, spout, squirt; burst, dash, rush.

sputter vb spawl, spit, splutter, stammer.

spy vb behold, discern, espy, see; detect, discover, search out; explore, inspect, scrutinize, search; shadow, trail, watch. * n agent, detective, double agent, mole, scout, undercover agent.

squabble vb brawl, fight, quarrel, scuffle, struggle, wrangle; altercate, bicker, contend, dispute, jangle. * n brawl, dispute, fight, quarrel, rumpus, scrimmage.

squad n band, bevy, crew, gang, knot, lot, relay, set.

squalid adj dirty, filthy, foul, mucky, slovenly, unclean, unkempt.

squalidness n filthiness, foulness, squalidity, squalor.

squall vb bawl, cry, cry out, scream, yell. * n bawl, cry, outcry, scream, yell; blast, flurry, gale, gust, hurricane, storm, tempest.

squally adj blustering, blustery, gusty, stormy, tempestuous, windy.

squander vb dissipate, expend, lavish, lose, misuse, scatter, spend, throw away, waste.

squanderer n lavisher, prodigal, spendthrift, waster.

square vb make square, quadrate; accommodate, adapt, fit, mould, regulate, shape, suit; adjust, balance, close, make even, settle; accord, chime in, cohere, comport, fall in, fit, harmonize, quadrate, suit. * adj four-square, quadrilateral, quadrate; equal, equitable, exact, fair, honest, just, upright; adjusted, balanced, even, settled; true, suitable. * n four-sided figure, quadrate, rectangle, tetragon; open area, parade, piazza, plaza.

squash vb crush, mash.

squashy adj pulpy, soft.

squat vb cower, crouch; occupy, plant, settle. * adj cowering, crouching; dumpy, pudgy, short, stocky, stubby, thickset.

squeal vb creak, cry, howl, scream, screech, shriek, squawk, yell; betray, inform on. * n creak, cry, howl, scream, screech, shriek, squawk, yell.

squeamish adj nauseated, qualmish, queasy, sickish; dainty, delicate, fastidious, finical, hypercritical, nice, over-nice, particular, priggish.

squeeze vb clutch, compress, constrict, grip, nip, pinch, press; drive, force; crush, harass, oppress; crowd, force through; press; (with out) extract. * n congestion, crowd, crush, throng; compression.

squelch vb crush, quash, quell, silence, squash, suppress.

squib n firework, fuse; lampoon, pasquinade, satire.

squint vb look askance, look obliquely, peer. * adj askew, aslant, crooked, oblique, skew, skewed, twisted.

squire vb accompany, attend, escort, wait on.

squirm vb twist, wriggle, writhe.

squirt vb eject, jet, splash, spurt.

stab vb broach, gore, jab, pierce, pink, spear, stick, transfix, transpierce; wound. * n cut, jab, prick, thrust; blow, dagger-stroke, injury, wound.

stability n durability, firmness, fixedness, immovability, permanence, stableness, steadiness; constancy, firmness, reliability.

stable adj established, fixed, immovable, immutable, invariable, permanent, unalterable, unchangeable; constant, firm, staunch, steadfast, steady, unwavering; abiding, durable, enduring, fast, lasting, permanent, perpetual, secure, sure.

staff n baton, cane, pole, rod, stick, wand; bat, bludgeon, club, cudgel, mace; prop, stay, support; employees, personnel, team, workers, work force.

stage vb dramatize, perform, present, produce, put on. * n dais, platform, rostrum, scaffold, staging, stand; arena, field; boards, playhouse, theatre; degree, point, step; diligence, omnibus, stagecoach.

stagey adj bombastic, declamatory, dramatic, melodramatic, ranting, theatrical.

stagger vb reel, sway, totter; alternate, fluctuate, overlap, vacillate, vary; falter, hesitate, waver; amaze, astonish, astound, confound, dumbfound, nonplus, pose, shock, surprise.

stagnant adj close, motionless, quiet, standing; dormant, dull, heavy, inactive, inert, sluggish, torpid.

stagnate *vb* decay, deteriorate, languish, rot, stand still, vegetate.

staid *adj* calm, composed, demure, grave, sedate, serious, settled, sober, solemn, steady, unadventurous.

stain *vb* blemish, blot, blotch, discolour, maculate, smirch, soil, splotch, spot, sully, tarnish; colour, dye, tinge; contaminate, corrupt, debase, defile, deprave, disgrace, dishonour, pollute, taint. * *n* blemish, blot, defect, discoloration, flaw, imperfection, spot, tarnish; contamination, disgrace, dishonour, infamy, pollution, reproach, shame, taint, tarnish.

stainless *adj* spotless, unspotted, untarnished; blameless, faultless, innocent, guiltless, pure, spotless, uncorrupted, unsullied.

stairs *npl* flight of steps, staircase, stairway.

stake[1] *vb* brace, mark, prop, secure, support. * *n* pale, palisade, peg, picket, post, stick.

stake[2] *vb* finance, pledge, wager; hazard, imperil, jeopardize, peril, risk, venture. * *n* bet, pledge, wager; adventure, hazard, risk, venture.

stale *adj* flat, fusty, insipid, mawkish, mouldy, musty, sour, tasteless, vapid; decayed, effete, faded, old, time-worn, worn-out; common, commonplace, hackneyed, stereotyped, threadbare, trite.

stalk[1] *n* culm, pedicel, peduncle, petiole, shaft, spire, stem, stock.

stalk[2] *vb* march, pace, stride, strut, swagger; follow, hunt, shadow, track, walk stealthily.

stall[1] *n* stable; cell, compartment, recess; booth, kiosk, shop, stand.

stall[2] *vb* block, delay, equivocate, filibuster, hinder, postpone, procrastinate, temporize; arrest, check, conk out, die, fail, halt, stick, stop.

stalwart *adj* able-bodied, athletic, brawny, lusty, muscular, powerful, robust, sinewy, stout, strapping, strong, sturdy, vigorous; bold, brave, daring, gallant, indomitable, intrepid, redoubtable, resolute, valiant, valorous. * *n* backer, member, partisan, supporter.

stamina *n* energy, force, lustiness, power, stoutness, strength, sturdiness, vigour.

stammer *vb* falter, hesitate, stutter. * *n* faltering, hesitation, stutter.

stamp *vb* brand, impress, imprint, mark, print. * *n* brand, impress, impression, print; cast, character, complexion, cut, description, fashion, form, kind, make, mould, sort, type.

stampede *vb* charge, flee, panic. * *n* charge, flight, rout, running away, rush.

stanch *see* **staunch**[1].

stanchion *n* prop, shore, stay, support.

stand *vb* be erect, remain upright; abide, be fixed, continue, endure, hold good, remain; halt, pause, stop; be firm, be resolute, stand ground, stay; be valid, have force; depend, have support, rest; bear, brook, endure, suffer, sustain, weather; abide, admit, await, submit, tolerate, yield; fix, place, put, set upright; (*with* **against**) oppose, resist, withstand; (*with* **by**) be near, be present; aid, assist, defend, help, side with, support; defend, make good, justify, maintain, support, vindicate; (*naut*) attend, be ready; (*with* **fast**) be fixed, be immovable; (*with* **for**) mean, represent, signify; aid, defend, help, maintain, side with, support; (*with* **off**) keep aloof, keep off; not to comply; (*with* **out**) be prominent, jut, project, protrude; not comply, not yield, persist; (*with* **up for**) defend, justify, support, sustain, uphold; (*with* **with**) agree. * *n* place, position, post, standing place, station; halt, stay, stop; dais, platform, rostrum; booth, stall; opposition, resistance.

standard[1] *n* banner, colours, ensign, flag, gonfalon, pennon, streamer.

standard[2] *adj* average, conventional, customary, normal, ordinary, regular, usual; accepted, approved, authoritative, orthodox, received; formulary, prescriptive, regulation. * *n* canon, criterion, model, norm, rule, test, type; gauge, measure, model, scale; support, upright.

standing *adj* established, fixed, immovable, settled; durable, lasting, permanent; motionless, stagnant. * *n* position, stand, station; continuance, duration, existence; footing, ground, hold; condition, estimation, rank, reputation, status.

standpoint *n* point of view, viewpoint.

standstill *n* cessation, interruption, stand, stop; deadlock.

stanza *n* measure, staff, stave, strophe, verse.

staple *adj* basic, chief, essential, fundamental, main, primary, principal. * *n* fibre, filament, pile, thread; body, bulk, mass, substance.

star *vb* act, appear, feature, headline, lead, perform, play; emphasize, highlight, stress, underline. * *adj* leading, main, paramount, principal; celebrated, illustrious, well-known. * *n* heavenly body, luminary; asterisk, pentacle, pentagram; destiny, doom, fate, fortune, lot; diva, headliner, hero, heroine, lead, leading lady, leading man, prima ballerina, prima donna, principal, protagonist.

starchy *adj* ceremonious, exact, formal, precise, prim, punctilious, rigid, starched, stiff.

stare *vb* gape, gaze, look intently, watch.

stark *adj* rigid, stiff; absolute, bare, downright, entire, gross, mere, pure, sheer, simple. * *adv* absolutely, completely, entirely, fully, wholly.

starry *adj* astral, sidereal, star-spangled, stellar; bright, brilliant, lustrous, shining, sparkling, twinkling.

start *vb* begin, commence, inaugurate, initiate, institute; discover, invent; flinch, jump, shrink, startle, wince; alarm, disturb, fright, rouse, scare; depart, set off, take off; arise, call forth, evoke, raise; dislocate, move suddenly, spring. * *n* beginning, commencement, inauguration, outset; fit, jump, spasm, twitch; impulse, sally.

startle *vb* flinch, shrink, start, wince; affright, alarm, fright, frighten, scare, shock; amaze, astonish, astound.

startling *adj* abrupt, alarming, astonishing, shocking, sudden, surprising, unexpected, unforeseen, unheard of.

starvation *n* famine, famishment.

starve *vb* famish, perish; be in need, lack, want; kill, subdue.

starveling *adj* attenuated, emaciated, gaunt, hungry, lank, lean, meagre, scraggy, skinny, thin. * *n* beggar, mendicant, pauper.

state *vb* affirm, assert, aver, declare, explain, expound, express, narrate, propound, recite, say, set forth, specify, voice. * *adj* civic, national, public. * *n* case, circumstances, condition, pass, phase, plight, position, posture, predicament, situation, status; condition, guise, mode, quality, rank; dignity, glory, grandeur, magnificence, pageantry, parade, pomp, spendour; body politic, civil community, commonwealth, nation, realm.

statecraft *n* diplomacy, political subtlety, state management, statesmanship.

stated *adj* established, fixed, regular, settled; detailed, set forth, specified.

stately *adj* august, dignified, elevated, grand, imperial, imposing, lofty, magnificent, majestic, noble, princely, royal; ceremonious, formal, magisterial, pompous, solemn.

statement *n* account, allegation, announcement, communiqué, declaration, description, exposition, mention, narration, narrative, recital, relation, report, specification; assertion, predication, proposition, pronouncement, thesis.

statesman *n* politician.

station *vb* establish, fix, locate, place, post, set. * *n* location, place, position, lost, seat, situation; business, employment, function, occupation, office; character, condition, degree, dignity, footing, rank, standing, state, status; depot, stop, terminal.

stationary *adj* fixed, motionless, permanent, quiescent, stable, standing, still.

statuary *n* carving, sculpture, statues.

statue *n* figurine, image, statuette.

stature *n* height, physique, size, tallness; altitude, consequence, elevation, eminence, prominence.

status *n* caste, condition, footing, position, rank, standing, station.

statute *n* act, decree, edict, enactment, law, ordinance, regulation.

staunch[1], **stanch** *vb* arrest, block, check, dam, plug, stem, stop.

staunch[2] *adj* firm, sound, stout, strong; constant, faithful, firm, hearty, loyal, resolute, stable, steadfast, steady, strong, trustworthy, trusty, unwavering, zealous.

stave *vb* break, burst; (*with* **off**) adjourn, defer, delay, postpone, procrastinate, put off, waive.

stay *vb* abide, dwell, lodge, rest, sojourn, tarry; continue, halt, remain, stand still, stop; attend, delay, linger, wait; arrest, check, curb, hold, keep in, prevent, rein in, restrain, withhold; delay, detain, hinder, obstruct; hold up, prop, shore up, support, sustain, uphold. * *n* delay, repose, rest, sojourn; halt, stand, stop; bar, check, curb, hindrance, impediment, interruption, obstacle, obstruction, restraint, stumbling block; buttress, dependence, prop, staff, support, supporter.

stead *n* place, room.

steadfast *adj* established, fast, firm, fixed, stable; constant, faithful, implicit, persevering, pertinacious, resolute, resolved, staunch, steady, unhesitating, unreserved, unshaken, unwavering, wholehearted.

steadiness *n* constancy, firmness, perseverance, persistence, resolution, steadfastness; fixedness, stability.

steady *vb* balance, counterbalance, secure, stabilize, support. * *adj* firm, fixed, stable; constant, equable, regular, undeviating, uniform, unremitting; persevering, resolute, staunch, steadfast, unchangeable, unwavering.

steal *vb* burglarize, burgle, crib, embezzle, filch, peculate, pilfer, plagiarize, poach, purloin, shoplift, thieve; creep, sneak, pass stealthily.

stealing *n* burglary, larceny, peculation, shoplifting, robbery, theft, thievery.

stealth *n* secrecy, slyness, stealthiness.

stealthy *adj* clandestine, furtive, private, secret, skulking, sly, sneaking, surreptitious, underhand.

steam *vb* emit vapour, fume; evaporate, vaporize; coddle, cook, poach; navigate, sail; be hot, sweat. * *n* vapour; effluvium, exhalation, fume, mist, reek, smoke.

steamboat *n* steamer, steamship.

steamy *adj* misty, moist, vaporous; erotic, voluptuous.

steed *n* charger, horse, mount.

steel *vb* case-harden, edge; brace, fortify, harden, make firm, nerve, strengthen.

steep[1] *adj* abrupt, declivitous, precipitous, sheer, sloping, sudden. * *n* declivity, precipice.

steep[2] *vb* digest, drench, imbrue, imbue, macerate, saturate, soak.

steeple *n* belfry, spire, tower, turret.

steer *vb* direct, conduct, govern, guide, pilot, point.

steersman *n* conductor, guide, helmsman, pilot.

stellar *adj* astral, starry, star-spangled, stellary.

stem[1] *vb* (*with* **from**) bud, descend, generate, originate, spring, sprout. * *n* axis, stipe, trunk; pedicel, peduncle, petiole, stalk; branch, descendant, offspring, progeny, scion, shoot; ancestry, descent, family, generation, line, lineage, pedigree, race, stock; (*naut*) beak, bow, cutwater, forepart, prow; helm, lookout; etymon, radical, radix, origin, root.

stem[2] *vb* breast, oppose, resist, withstand; check, dam, oppose, staunch, stay, stop.

stench *n* bad smell, fetor, offensive odour, stink.

stenography *n* brachygraphy, shorthand, tachygraphy.

stentorian *adj* loud-voiced, powerful, sonorous, thundering, trumpet-like.

step *vb* pace, stride, tramp, tread, walk. * *n* footstep, pace, stride; stair, tread; degree, gradation, grade, interval; advance, advancement, progression; act, action, deed, procedure, proceeding; footprint, trace, track, vestige; footfall, gait, pace, walk; expedient, means, measure, method; round, rundle, rung.

steppe *n* pampa, prairie, savannah.

sterile *adj* barren, infecund, unfruitful, unproductive, unprolific; bare, dry, empty, poor; (*bot*) acarpous, male, staminate.

sterility *n* barrenness, fruitlessness, infecundity, unfruitfulness, unproductiveness.

sterling *adj* genuine, positive, pure, real, sound, standard, substantial, true.

stern[1] *adj* austere, dour, forbidding, grim, severe; bitter, cruel, hard, harsh, inflexible, relentless, rigid, rigorous, severe, strict, unrelenting; immovable, incorruptible, steadfast, uncompromising.

stern[2] *n* behind, breach, hind part, posterior, rear, tail; (*naut*) counter, poop, rudderpost, tailpost; butt, buttocks, fundament, rump.

sternness *n* austerity, rigidity, severity; asperity, cruelty, harshness, inflexibility, relentlessness, rigour.

sternum *n* (*anat*) breastbone, sternon.

stertorous *adj* hoarsely breathing, snoring.

stew *vb* boil, seethe, simmer, stive. * *n* ragout; confusion, difficulty, mess, scrape.

steward *n* chamberlain, majordomo, seneschal; maniple, purveyor.

stick[1] *vb* gore, penetrate, pierce, puncture, spear, stab, transfix; infix, insert, thrust; attach, cement, glue, paste; fix in, set; adhere, cleave, cling, hold; abide, persist, remain, stay, stop; doubt, hesitate, scruple, stickle, waver; (*with* **by**) adhere to, be faithful, support. * *n* prick, stab, thrust.

stick[2] *n* birch, rod, switch; bat, bludgeon, club, cudgel, shillelah; cane, staff, walking stick; cue, pole, spar, stake.

stickiness *n* adhesiveness, glutinousness, tenacity, viscosity, viscousness.

stickle *vb* altercate, contend, contest, struggle; doubt, hesitate, scruple, stick, waver.

sticky *adj* adhesive, clinging, gluey, glutinous, gummy, mucilaginous, tenacious, viscid, viscous.

stiff *adj* inflexible, rigid, stark, unbending, unyielding; firm, tenacious, thick; obstinate, pertinacious, strong, stubborn; absolute, austere, dogmatic, inexorable, peremptory, positive, rigorous, severe, straitlaced, strict, stringent, uncompromising; ceremonious, chilling, constrained, formal, frigid, prim, punctilious, stately, starchy, stilted; abrupt, cramped, crude, graceless, harsh, inelegant.

stiff-necked *adj* contumacious, cross-grained, dogged, headstrong, intractable, mulish, obdurate, obstinate, stubborn, unruly.

stiffness *n* hardness, inflexibility, rigidity, rigidness, rigour, starkness; compactness, consistence, denseness, density, thickness; contumaciousness, inflexibility, obstinacy, pertinacity, stubbornness; austerity, harshness, rigorousness, severity, sternness, strictness; constraint, formality, frigidity, precision, primness, tenseness.

stifle *vb* choke, smother, suffocate; check, deaden, destroy, extinguish, quench, repress, stop, suppress; conceal, gag, hush, muffle, muzzle, silence, smother, still.

stigma *n* blot, blur, brand, disgrace, dishonour, reproach, shame, spot, stain, taint, tarnish.

stigmatize *vb* brand, defame, discredit, disgrace, dishonour, post, reproach, slur, villify.

stiletto *n* dagger, dirk, poniard, stylet; bodkin, piercer.

still[1] *vb* hush, muffle, silence, stifle; allay, appease, calm, compose, lull, pacify, quiet, smooth, tranquillize; calm, check, immobilize, restrain, stop, subdue, suppress. * *adj* hushed, mum, mute, noiseless, silent; calm, placid, quiet, serene, stilly, tranquil, unruffled; inert, motionless, quiescent, stagnant, stationary. * *n* hush, lull, peace, quiet, quietness, quietude, silence, stillness, tranquillity; picture, photograph, shot.

still[2] *n* distillery, still-house; distillatory, retort, stillatory.

still[3] *adv, conj* till now, to this time, yet; however, nevertheless, notwithstanding; always, continually, ever, habitually, uniformly; after that, again, in continuance.

stilted *adj* bombastic, fustian, grandiloquent, grandiose, high-flown, high-sounding, inflated, magniloquent, pompous, pretentious, stilty, swelling, tumid, turgid.

stimulant *adj* exciting, stimulating, stimulative. * *n* bracer, cordial, pick-me-up, tonic; fillip, incentive, provocative, spur, stimulus.

stimulate *vb* animate, arouse, awaken, brace, encourage, energize, excite, fire, foment, goad, impel, incite, inflame, inspirit, instigate, kindle, prick, prompt, provoke, rally, rouse, set on, spur, stir up, urge, whet, work up.

stimulus *n* encouragement, fillip, goad, incentive, incitement, motivation, motive, provocation, spur, stimulant.

sting *vb* hurt, nettle, prick, wound; afflict, cut, pain.

stinging *adj* acute, painful, piercing; biting, nipping, pungent, tingling.

stingy *adj* avaricious, close, close-fisted, covetous, grudging, mean, miserly, narrow-hearted, niggardly, parsimonious, penurious.

stink *vb* emit a stench, reek, smell bad. * *n* bad smell, fetor, offensive odour, stench.

stint *vb* bound, confine, limit, restrain; begrudge, pinch, scrimp, skimp, straiten; cease, desist, stop. * *n* bound, limit, restraint; lot, period, project, quota, share, shift, stretch, task, time, turn.

stipend *n* allowance, compensation, emolument, fee, hire, honorarium, pay, remuneration, salary, wages.

stipulate *vb* agree, bargain, condition, contract, covenant, engage, provide, settle terms.

stipulation *n* agreement, bargain, concordat, condition, contract, convention, covenant, engagement, indenture, obligation, pact.

stir *vb* budge, change place, go, move; agitate, bestir, disturb, prod; argue, discuss, moot, raise, start; animate, arouse, awaken, excite, goad, incite, instigate, prompt, provoke, quicken, rouse, spur, stimulate; appear, happen, turn up; get up, rise; (*with* **up**) animate, awaken, incite, instigate, move, provoke, quicken, rouse, stimulate. * *n* activity, ado, agitation, bustle, confusion, excitement, fidget, flurry, fuss, hurry, movement; commotion, disorder, disturbance, tumult, uproar.

stirring *adj* active, brisk, diligent, industrious, lively, smart; animating, arousing, awakening, exciting, quickening, stimulating.

stitch *vb* backstitch, baste, bind, embroider, fell, hem, seam, sew, tack, whip.

stive *vb* stow, stuff; boil, seethe, stew; make close, hot or sultry.

stock *vb* fill, furnish, store, supply; accumulate, garner, hoard, lay in, reposit, reserve, save, treasure up. * *adj* permanent, standard, standing. * *n* assets, capital, commodities, fund, principal, shares; accumulation, hoard, inventory, merchandise, provision, range, reserve, store, supply; ancestry, breed, descent, family, house, line, lineage, parentage, pedigree, race; cravat, neckcloth; butt, haft, hand; block, log, pillar, post, stake; stalk, stem, trunk.

stockholder *n* shareholder.

stocking *n* hose, sock.

stock market *n* stock exchange; cattle market.

stocks *npl* funds, public funds, public securities; shares.

stockstill *adj* dead-still, immobile, motionless, stationary, still, unmoving.

stocky *adj* chubby, chunky, dumpy, plump, short, stout, stubby, thickset.

stoic, stoical *adj* apathetic, cold-blooded, impassive, imperturbable, passionless, patient, philosophic, philosophical, phlegmatic, unimpassioned.

stoicism *n* apathy, coldness, coolness, impassivity, indifference, insensibility, nonchalance, phlegm.

stolen *adj* filched, pilfered, purloined; clandestine, furtive, secret, sly, stealthy, surreptitious.

stolid *adj* blockish, doltish, dull, foolish, heavy, obtuse, slow, stockish, stupid.

stolidity *n* doltishness, dullness, foolishness, obtuseness, stolidness, stupidity.

stomach *vb* abide, bear, brook, endure, put up with, stand, submit to, suffer, swallow, tolerate. * *n* abdomen, belly, gut, paunch, pot, tummy; appetite, desire, inclination, keenness, liking, relish, taste.

stone *vb* cover, face, slate, tile; lapidate, pelt. * *n* boulder, cobble, gravel, pebble, rock; gem, jewel, precious stone; cenotaph, gravestone, monument, tombstone; nut, pit; adamant, agate, flint, gneiss, granite, marble, slate, etc.

stony *adj* gritty, hard, lapidose, lithic, petrous, rocky; adamantine, flinty, hard, inflexible, obdurate; cruel, hard-hearted, inexorable, pitiless, stony-hearted, unfeeling, unrelenting.

stoop *vb* bend forward, bend down, bow, lean, sag, slouch, slump; abase, cower, cringe, give in, submit, succumb, surrender; condescend, deign, descend, vouchsafe; fall, sink. * *n* bend, inclination, sag, slouch, slump; descent, swoop.

stop *vb* block, blockade, close, close up, obstruct, occlude; arrest, check, halt, hold, pause, stall, stay; bar, delay, embargo, hinder, impede, intercept, interrupt, obstruct, preclude, prevent, repress, restrain, staunch, suppress, thwart; break off, cease, desist, discontinue, forbear, give over, leave off, refrain from; intermit, quiet, quieten, terminate; lodge, tarry. * *n* halt, intermission, pause, respite, rest, stoppage, suspension, truce; block, cessation, check, hindrance, interruption, obstruction, repression; bar, impediment, obstacle; full stop, point.

stopcock *n* cock, faucet, tap.

stoppage *n* arrest, block, check, closure, hindrance, interruption, obstruction, prevention.

stopper *n* cork, plug, stopple.

store *vb* accumulate, amass, cache, deposit, garner, hoard, husband, lay by, lay in, lay up, put by, reserve, save, store up, stow away, treasure up; furnish, provide, replenish, stock, supply. * *n* accumulation, cache, deposit, fund, hoard, provision, reserve, stock, supply, treasure, treasury; abundance, plenty; storehouse; emporium, market, shop.

storehouse *n* depository, depot, godown, magazine, repository, store, warehouse.

storm *vb* assail, assault, attack; blow violently; fume, rage, rampage, rant, rave, tear. * *n* blizzard, gale, hurricane, squall, tempest, tornado, typhoon, whirlwind; agitation, clamour, commotion, disturbance, insurrection, outbreak, sedition, tumult, turmoil; adversity, affliction, calamity, distress; assault, attack, brunt, onset, onslaught; violence.

storminess *n* inclemency, roughness, tempestuousness.

stormy *adj* blustering, boisterous, gusty, squally, tempestuous, windy; passionate, riotous, rough, turbulent, violent, wild; agitated, furious.

story *n* annals, chronicle, history, record; account, narration, narrative, recital, record, rehearsal, relation, report, statement, tale; fable, fiction, novel, romance; anecdote, incident, legend, tale; canard, fabrication, falsehood, fib, figure, invention, lie, untruth.

storyteller *n* bard, chronicler, narrator, raconteur.

stout *adj* able-bodied, athletic, brawny, lusty, robust, sinewy, stalwart, strong, sturdy, vigorous; courageous, hardy, indomitable, stouthearted; contumacious, obstinate, proud, resolute, stubborn; compact, firm, solid, staunch; bouncing, bulky, burly, chubby, corpulent, fat, heavy, jolly, large, obese, plump, portly, stocky, strapping, thickset.

stouthearted *adj* fearless, heroic, redoubtable; bold, brave, courageous, dauntless, doughty, firm, gallant, hardy, indomitable, intrepid, resolute, valiant, valorous.

stow *vb* load, pack, put away, store, stuff.

straddle *vb* bestride.

straggle *vb* rove, wander; deviate, digress, ramble, range, roam, stray, stroll.

straggling *adj* rambling, roving, straying, strolling, wandering; scattered.

straight *adj* direct, near, rectilinear, right, short, undeviating, unswerving; erect, perpendicular,

plumb, right, upright, vertical; equitable, fair, honest, honourable, just, square, straightforward. * *adv* at once, directly, forthwith, immediately, straightaway, straightway, without delay.

straightaway, straightway *adv* at once, directly, forthwith, immediately, speedily, straight, suddenly, without delay.

straighten *vb* arrange, make straight, neaten, order, tidy.

straight-laced *see* **strait-laced**.

strain[1] *vb* draw tightly, make tense, stretch, tighten; injure, sprain, wrench; exert, overexert, overtax, rack; embrace, fold, hug, press, squeeze; compel, constrain, force; dilute, distill, drain, filter, filtrate, ooze, percolate, purify, separate; fatigue, overtask, overwork, task, tax, tire. * *n* stress, tenseness, tension, tensity; effort, exertion, force, overexertion; burden, task, tax; sprain, wrech; lay, melody, movement, snatch, song, stave, tune.

strain[2] *n* manner, style, tone, vein; disposition, tendency, trait, turn; descent, extraction, family, lineage, pedigree, race, stock.

strait *adj* close, confined, constrained, constricted, contracted, narrow; rigid, rigorous, severe, strict; difficult, distressful, grievous, straitened. * *n* channel, narrows, pass, sound.

straits *npl* crisis, difficulty, dilemma, distress, embarrassment, emergency, exigency, extremity, hardship, pass, perplexity, pinch, plight, predicament.

straiten *vb* confine, constrain, constrict, contract, limit; narrow; intensify, stretch; distress, embarrass, perplex, pinch, press.

straitened *adj* distressed, embarrassed limited, perplexed, pinched.

strait-laced, straight-laced *adj* austere, formal, prim, rigid, rigorous, stern, stiff, strict, uncompromising.

straitness *n* narrowness, rigour, severity, strictness; difficulty, distress, trouble; insufficiency, narrowness, scarcity, want.

strand[1] *vb* abandon, beach, be wrecked, cast away, go aground, ground, maroon, run aground, wreck. * *n* beach, coast, shore.

strand[2] *n* braid, cord, fibre, filament, line, rope, string, tress.

stranded *adj* aground, ashore, cast away, lost, shipwrecked, wrecked.

strange *adj* alien, exotic, far-fetched, foreign, outlandish, remote; new, novel; curious, exceptional, extraordinary, irregular, odd, particular, peculiar, rare, singular, surprising, uncommon, unusual; abnormal, anomalous, extraordinary, inconceivable, incredible, inexplicable, marvellous, mysterious, preternatural, unaccountable, unbelievable, unheard of, unique, unnatural, wonderful; bizarre, droll, grotesque, quaint, queer; inexperienced, unacquainted, unfamiliar, unknown; bashful, distant, distrustful, reserved, shy, uncommunicative.

strangeness *n* foreignness; bashfulness, coldness, distance, reserve, shyness, uncommunicativeness; eccentricity, grotesqueness, oddness, singularity, uncommonness, uncouthness.

stranger *n* alien, foreigner, newcomer, immigrant, outsider; guest, visitor.

strangle *vb* choke, contract, smother, squeeze, stifle, suffocate, throttle, tighten; keep back, quiet, repress, still, suppress.

strap *vb* beat, thrash, whip; bind, fasten, sharpen, strop.

* *n* thong; band, ligature, strip, tie; razor-strap, strop.

strapping *adj* big, burly, large, lusty, stalwart, stout, strong, tall.

stratagem *n* artifice, cunning, device, dodge, finesse, intrigue, machination, manoeuvre, plan, plot, ruse, scheme, trick, wile.

strategic, strategical *adj* calculated, deliberate, diplomatic, manoeuvering, planned, politic, tactical; critical, decisive, key, vital.

strategy *n* generalship, manoeuvering, plan, policy, stratagem, strategetics, tactics.

stratum *n* band, bed, layer.

straw *n* culm, stalk, stem; button, farthing, fig, penny, pin, rush, snap.

stray *vb* deviate, digress, err, meander, ramble, range, roam, rove, straggle, stroll, swerve, transgress, wander. * *adj* abandoned, lost, strayed, wandering; accidental, erratic, random, scattered.

streak *vb* band, bar, striate, stripe, vein; dart, dash, flash, hurtle, run, speed, sprint, stream, tear. * *n* band, bar, belt, layer, line, strip, stripe, thread, trace, vein; cast, grain, tone, touch, vein; beam, bolt, dart, dash, flare, flash, ray, stream.

streaky *adj* streaked, striped, veined.

stream *vb* course, flow, glide, pour, run, spout; emit, pour out, shed; emanate, go forth, issue, radiate; extend, float, stretch out, wave. * *n* brook, burn, race, rill, rivulet, run, runlet, runnel, trickle; course, current, flow, flux, race, rush, tide, torrent, wake, wash; beam, gleam, patch, radiation, ray, streak.

streamer *n* banner, colours, ensign, flag, pennon, standard.

street *n* avenue, highway, road, way.

strength *n* force, might, main, nerve, potency, power, vigour; hardness, solidity, toughness; impregnability, proof; brawn, grit, healthy, lustiness, muscle, robustness, sinew, stamina, thews, vigorousness; animation, courage, determination, firmness, fortitude, resolution, spirit; cogency, efficacy, soundness, validity; emphasis, energy; security, stay, support; brightness, brilliance, clearness, intensity, vitality, vividness; body, excellence, virtue; impetuosity, vehemence, violence; boldness.

strengthen *vb* buttress, recruit, reinforce; fortify; brace, energize, harden, nerve, steel, stimulate; freshen, invigorate, vitalize; animate, encourage; clench, clinch, confirm, corroborate, establish, fix, justify, sustain, support.

strenuous *adj* active, ardent, eager, earnest, energetic, resolute, vigorous, zealous; bold, determined, doughty, intrepid, resolute, spirited, strong, valiant.

stress *vb* accent, accentuate, emphasize, highlight, point up, underline, underscore; bear, bear upon, press, pressurize; pull, rack, strain, stretch, tense, tug. * *n* accent, accentuation, emphasis; effort, force, pull, strain, tension, tug; boisterousness, severity, violence; pressure, urgency.

stretch *vb* brace, screw, strain, tense, tighten; elongate, extend, lengthen, protract, pull; display, distend, expand, spread, unfold, widen; sprain, strain; distort, exaggerate, misrepresent. * *n* compass, extension, extent, range, reach, scope; effort, exertion, strain, struggle; course, direction.

strict *adj* close, strained, tense, tight; accurate, careful, close, exact, literal, particular, precise, scrupulous; austere, inflexible, harsh, orthodox, puritanical, rigid, rigorous, severe, stern, strait-laced, stringent, uncompromising, unyielding.

stricture *n* animadversion, censure, denunciation, criticism, compression, constriction, contraction.

strife *n* battle, combat, conflict, contention, contest, discord, quarrel, struggle, warfare.

strike *vb* bang, beat, belabour, box, buffet, cudgel, cuff, hit, knock, lash, pound, punch, rap, slap, slug, smite, thump, whip; impress, imprint, stamp; afflict, chastise, deal, give, inflict, punish; affect, astonish, electrify, stun; clash, collide, dash, touch; surrender, yield; mutiny, rebel, rise.

stringent *adj* binding, contracting, rigid, rigorous, severe, strict.

strip[1] *n* piece, ribbon, shred, slip.

strip[2] *vb* denude, hull, skin, uncover; bereave, deprive, deforest, desolate, despoil, devastate, disarm, dismantle, disrobe, divest, expose, fleece, loot, shave; plunder, pillage, ransack, rob, sack, spoil; disrobe, uncover, undress.

strive *vb* aim, attempt, endeavour, exert, labour, strain, struggle, toil; contend, contest, fight, tussle, wrestle; compete, cope.

stroke[1] *n* blow, glance, hit, impact, knock, lash, pat, percussion, rap, shot, switch, thump; attack, paralysis, stroke; affliction, damage, hardship, hurt, injury, misfortune, reverse, visitation; dash, feat, masterstroke, touch.

stroke[2] *vb* caress, feel, palpate, pet, knead, massage, nuzzle, rub, touch.

stroll *vb* loiter, lounge, ramble, range, rove, saunter, straggle, stray, wander. * *n* excursion, promenade, ramble, rambling, roving, tour, trip, walk, wandering.

strong *adj* energetic, forcible, powerful, robust, sturdy; able, enduring; cogent, firm, valid.

structure *vb* arrange, constitute, construct, make, organize. * *n* arrangement, conformation, configuration, constitution, construction, form, formation, make, organization; anatomy, composition, texture; building, edifice, fabric, framework, pile.

struggle *vb* aim, endeavour, exert, labour, strive, toil, try; battle, contend, contest, fight, wrestle; agonize, flounder, writhe. * *n* effort, endeavour, exertion, labour, pains; battle, conflict, contention, contest, fight, strife; agony, contortions, distress.

stubborn *adj* contumacious, dogged, headstrong, heady, inflexible, intractable, mulish, obdurate, obstinate, perverse, positive, refractory, ungovernable, unmanageable, unruly, unyielding, willful; constant, enduring, firm, hardy, persevering, persistent, steady, stoical, uncomplaining, unremitting; firm, hard, inflexible, stiff, strong, tough, unpliant, studied.

studious *adj* contemplative, meditative, reflective, thoughtful; assiduous, attentive, desirous, diligent, eager, lettered, scholarly, zealous.

study *vb* cogitate, lucubrate, meditate, muse, ponder, reflect, think; analyze, contemplate, examine, investigate, ponder, probe, scrutinize, search, sift, weigh. * *n* exercise, inquiry, investigation, reading, research, stumble; cogitation, consideration, contemplation, examination, meditation, reflection, thought; stun; model, object, representation, sketch; den, library, office, studio.

stunning *adj* deafening, stentorian; dumbfounding, stupefying.

stunted *adj* checked, diminutive, dwarfed, dwarfish, lilliputian, little, nipped, small, undersized.

stupendous *adj* amazing, astonishing, astounding, marvellous, overwhelming, surprising, wonderful; enormous, huge, immense, monstrous, prodigious, towering, tremendous, vast.

stupid *adj* brainless, crass, doltish, dull, foolish, idiotic, inane, inept, obtuse, pointless, prosaic, senseless, simple, slow, sluggish, stolid, tedious, tiresome, witless.

stupor *n* coma, confusion, daze, lethargy, narcosis, numbness, stupefaction, torpor.

sturdy *adj* bold, determined, dogged, firm, hardy, obstinate, persevering, pertinacious, resolute, stiff, stubborn, sturdy; athletic, brawny, forcible, lusty, muscular, powerful, robust, stalwart, stout, strong, thickset, vigorous, well-set.

style *vb* address, call, characterize, denominate, designate, dub, entitle, name, term. * *n* dedication, expression, phraseology, turn; cast, character, fashion, form, genre, make, manner, method, mode, model, shape, vogue, way; appellation, denomination, designation, name, title; chic, elegance, smartness; pen, pin, point, stylus.

stylish *adj* chic, courtly, elegant, fashionable, genteel, modish, polished, smart.

suave *adj* affable, agreeable, amiable, bland, courteous, debonair, delightful, glib, gracious, mild, pleasant, smooth, sweet, oily, unctuous, urbane.

subdue *vb* beat, bend, break, bow, conquer, control, crush, defeat, discomfit, foil, master, overbear, overcome, overpower, overwhelm, quell, rout, subject, subjugate, surmount, vanquish, worst; allay, choke, curb, mellow, moderate, mollify, reduce, repress, restrain, soften, suppress, temper.

subject *vb* control, master, overcome, reduce, subdue, subjugate, tame; enslave, enthral; abandon, refer, submit, surrender. * *adj* beneath, subjacent, underneath; dependent, enslaved, inferior, servile, subjected, subordinate, subservient; conditional, obedient, submissive; disposed, exposed to, liable, obnoxious, prone. * *n* dependent, henchman, liegeman, slave, subordinate; matter, point, subject matter, theme, thesis, topic; nominative, premise; case, object, patient, recipient; ego, mind, self, thinking.

subjoin *vb* add, affix, annex, append, join, suffix.

subjugate *vb* conquer, enslave, enthral, master, overcome, overpower, overthrow, subdue, subject, vanquish.

sublimate *vb* alter, change, repress.

sublime *adj aloft, elevated, high,* sacred; eminent, exalted, grand, great, lofty, mighty; august, glorious, magnificent, majestic, noble, stately, solemn, sublunary; elated, elevated, eloquent, exhilarated, raised.

submission *n* capitulation, cession, relinquishment, surrender, yielding; acquiescence, compliance, obedience, resignation; deference, homage, humility, lowliness, obeisance, passiveness, prostration, self-abasement, submissiveness.

submissive *adj* amenable, compliant, docile, pliant, tame, tractable, yielding; acquiescent, long-suffering, obedient, passive, patient, resigned, unassertive, uncomplaining, unrepining; deferential, humble, lowly, meek, obsequious, prostrate, self-abasing.

submit *vb* cede, defer, endure, resign, subject, surrender, yield; commit, propose, refer; offer; acquiesce, bend, capitulate, comply, stoop, succumb.

subordinate *adj* ancillary, dependent, inferior, junior, minor, secondary, subject, subservient, subsidiary. * *n*

assistant, dependant, inferior, subject, underling.

subscribe *vb* accede, approve, agree, assent, consent, yield; contribute, donate, give, offer, promise.

subscription *n* aid, assistance, contribution, donation, gift, offering.

subsequent *adj* after, attendant, ensuing, later, latter, following, posterior, sequent, succeeding.

subservient *adj* inferior, obsequious, servile, subject, subordinate; accessory, aiding, auxiliary, conducive, contributory, helpful, instrumental, serviceable, useful.

subside *vb* settle, sink; abate, decline, decrease, diminish, drop, ebb, fall, intermit, lapse, lessen, lower, lull, wane.

subsidence *n* settling, sinking; abatement, decline, decrease, descent, ebb, diminution, lessening.

subsidiary *adj* adjutant, aiding, assistant, auxiliary, co-operative, corroborative, helping, subordinate, subservient.

subsidize *vb* aid, finance, fund, sponsor, support, underwrite.

subsidy *n* aid, bounty, grant, subvention, support, underwriting.

subsist *vb* be, breathe, consist, exist, inhere, live, prevail; abide, continue, endure, persist, remain; feed, maintain, ration, support.

subsistence *n* aliment, food, livelihood, living, maintenance, meat, nourishment, nutriment, provision, rations, support, sustenance, victuals.

substance *n* actuality, element, groundwork, hypostasis, reality, substratum; burden, content, core, drift, essence, gist, heart, import, meaning, pith, sense, significance, solidity, soul, sum, weight; estate, income, means, property, resources, wealth.

substantial *adj* actual, considerable, essential, existent, hypostatic, pithy, potential, real, subsistent, virtual; concrete, durable, positive, solid, tangible, true; corporeal, bodily, material; bulky, firm, goodly, heavy, large, massive, notable, significant, sizable, solid, sound, stable, stout, strong, well-made; cogent, just, efficient, influential, valid, weighty.

substantially *adv* adequately, essentially, firmly, materially, positively, really, truly.

substantiate *vb* actualize, confirm, corroborate, establish, prove, ratify, verify.

subterfuge *n* artifice, evasion, excuse, expedient, mask, pretence, pretext, quirk, shift, shuffle, sophistry, trick.

subtle *adj* arch, artful, astute, crafty, crooked, cunning, designing, diplomatic, intriguing, insinuating, sly, tricky, wily; clever, ingenious; acute, deep, discerning, discriminating, keen, profound, sagacious, shrewd; airy, delicate, ethereal, light, nice, rare, refined, slender, subtle, thin, volatile.

subtlety *n* artfulness, artifice, astuteness, craft, craftiness, cunning, guile, subtleness; acumen, acuteness, cleverness, discernment, intelligence, keenness, sagacity, sharpness, shrewdness; attenuation, delicacy, fitness, nicety, rareness, refinement.

subtract *vb* deduct, detract, diminish, remove, take, withdraw.

suburbs *npl* environs, confines, neighbourhood, outskirts, precincts, purlieus, vicinage.

subversive *adj* destructive, overthrowing, pervasive, ruining, upsetting. * *n* collaborator, dissident, insurrectionist, saboteur, terrorist, traitor.

subvert *vb* invert, overset, overthrow, overturn, reverse, upset; demolish, destroy, extinguish, raze, ruin; confound, corrupt, injure, pervert.

succeed vb ensue, follow, inherit, replace; flourish, gain, hit, prevail, prosper, thrive, win.

success n attainment, issue, result; fortune, happiness, hit, luck, prosperity, triumph.

successful adj auspicious, booming, felicitous, fortunate, happy, lucky, prosperous, victorious, winning.

succession n chain, concatenation, cycle, consecution, following, procession, progression, rotation, round, sequence, series, suite; descent, entail, inheritance, lineage, race, reversion.

succinct adj brief, compact, compendious, concise, condensed, curt, laconic, pithy, short, summary, terse.

succour vb aid, assist, help, relieve; cherish, comfort, encourage, foster, nurse. * n aid, assistance, help, relief, support.

succulent adj juicy, luscious, lush, nutritive, sappy.

succumb vb capitulate, die, submit, surrender, yield.

sudden adj abrupt, hasty, hurried, immediate, instantaneous, rash, unanticipated, unexpected, unforeseen, unusual; brief, momentary, quick, rapid.

sue vb charge, court, indict, prosecute, solicit, summon, woo; appeal, beg, demand, entreat, implore, petition, plead, pray, supplicate.

suffer vb feel, undergo; bear, endure, sustain, tolerate; admit, allow, indulge, let, permit.

sufferable adj allowable, bearable, endurable, permissible, tolerable.

sufferance n endurance, inconvenience, misery, pain, suffering; long-suffering, moderation, patience, submission; allowance, permission, toleration.

suffice vb avail, content, satisfy, serve.

sufficient adj adequate, ample, commensurate, competent, enough, full, plenteous, satisfactory; able, equal, fit, qualified, responsible.

suffocate vb asphyxiate, choke, smother, stifle, strangle.

suffrage n ballot, franchise, voice, vote; approval, attestation, consent, testimonial, witness.

suggest vb advise, allude, hint, indicate, insinuate, intimate, move, present, prompt, propose, propound, recommend.

suggestion n allusion, hint, indication, insinuation, intimation, presentation, prompting, proposal, recommendation, reminder.

suit vb accommodate, adapt, adjust, fashion, fit, level, match; accord, become, befit, gratify, harmonize, please, satisfy, tally. * n appeal, entreaty, invocation, petition, prayer, request, solicitation, supplication; courtship, wooing; action, case, cause, process, prosecution, trial; clothing, costume, habit.

suitable adj adapted, accordant, agreeable, answerable, apposite, applicable, appropriate, apt, becoming, befitting, conformable, congruous, convenient, consonant, correspondent, decent, due, eligible, expedient, fit, fitting, just, meet, pertinent, proper, relevant, seemly, worthy.

suite n attendants, bodyguard, convoy, cortege, court, escort, followers, staff, retainers, retinue, train; collection, series, set, suit; apartment, rooms.

sulky adj aloof, churlish, cross, cross-grained, dogged, grouchy, ill-humoured, ill-tempered, moody, morose, perverse, sour, spleenish, spleeny, splenetic, sullen, surly, vexatious, wayward.

sullen adj cross, crusty, glum, grumpy, ill-tempered, moody, morose, sore, sour, sulky; cheerless, cloudy, dark, depressing, dismal, foreboding, funereal, gloomy, lowering, melancholy, mournful, sombre; dull, heavy, slow, sluggish; intractable, obstinate,

perverse, refractory, stubborn, vexatious; baleful, evil, inauspicious, malign, malignant, sinister, unlucky, unpropitious.

sully vb blemish, blot, contaminate, deface, defame, dirty, disgrace, dishonour, foul, smirch, soil, slur, spot, stain, tarnish.

sultry adj close, damp, hot, humid, muggy, oppressive, stifling, stuffy, sweltering.

sum vb add, calculate, compute, reckon; collect, comprehend, condense, epitomize, summarize. * n aggregate, amount, total, totality, whole; compendium, substance, summary; acme, completion, height, summit.

summary adj brief, compendious, concise, curt, laconic, pithy, short, succinct, terse; brief, quick, rapid. * n abridgement, abstract, brief, compendium, digest, epitome, precis, résumé, syllabus, synopsis.

summit n acme, apex, cap, climax, crest, crown, pinnacle, top, vertex, zenith.

summon vb arouse, bid, call, cite, invite, invoke, rouse; convene, convoke; charge, indict, prosecute, subpoena, sue.

sumptuous adj costly, dear, expensive, gorgeous, grand, lavish, luxurious, magnificent, munificent, pompous, prodigal, rich, showy, splendid, stately, superb.

sunburnt adj bronzed, brown, ruddy, tanned.

sunder vb break, disconnect, disjoin, dissociate, dissever, disunited, divide, part, separate, sever.

sundry adj different, divers, several, some, various.

sunny adj bright, brilliant, clear, fine, luminous, radiant, shining, unclouded, warm; cheerful, genial, happy, joyful, mild, optimistic, pleasant, smiling.

superannuated adj aged, anile, antiquated, decrepit, disqualified, doting, effete, imbecile, passé, retired, rusty, time-worn, unfit.

superb adj august, beautiful, elegant, exquisite, grand, gorgeous, imposing, magnificent, majestic, noble, pompous, rich, showy, splendid, stately, sumptuous.

supercilious adj arrogant, condescending, contemptuous, dictatorial, domineering, haughty, high, imperious, insolent, intolerant, lofty, lordly, magisterial, overbearing, overweening, proud, scornful, vainglorious.

superficial adj external, flimsy, shallow, untrustworthy.

superfluity n excess, exuberance, redundancy, superabundance, surfeit.

superfluous adj excessive, redundant, unnecessary.

superintend vb administer, conduct, control, direct, inspect, manage, overlook, oversee, supervise.

superintendence n care, charge, control, direction, guidance, government, inspection, management, oversight, supervision, surveillance.

superior adj better, greater, high, higher, finer, paramount, supreme, ultra, upper; chief, foremost, principal; distinguished, matchless, noble, pre-eminent, preferable, sovereign, surpassing, unrivalled, unsurpassed; predominant, prevalent. * n boss, chief, director, head, higher-up, leader, manager, principal, senior, supervisor.

superiority n advantage, ascendency, lead, odds, predominance, pre-eminence, prevalence, transcendence; excellence, nobility, worthiness.

superlative adj consummate, greatest, incomparable, peerless, pre-eminent, supreme, surpassing, transcendent.

supernatural adj abnormal, marvellous, metaphysical, miraculous, otherworldly, preternatural, unearthly.

supernumerary *adj* excessive, odd, redundant, superfluous.

supersede *vb* annul, neutralize, obviate, overrule, suspend; displace, remove, replace, succeed, supplant.

supervise *vb* administer, conduct, control, direct, inspect, manage, overlook, oversee, superintend.

supine *adj* apathetic, careless, drowsy, dull, idle, indifferent, indolent, inert, languid, lethargic, listless, lumpish, lazy, negligent, otiose, prostrate, recumbent, sleepy, slothful, sluggish, spineless, torpid.

supplant *vb* overpower, overthrow, undermine; displace, remove, replace, supersede.

supple *adj* elastic, flexible, limber, lithe, pliable, pliant; compliant, humble, submissive, yielding; adulatory, cringing, fawning, flattering, grovelling, obsequious, oily, parasitical, servile, slavish, sycophantic.

supplement *vb* add, augment, extend, reinforce, supply. * *n* addendum, addition, appendix, codicil, complement, continuation, postscript.

suppliant *adj* begging, beseeching, entreating, imploring, precative, precatory, praying, suing, supplicating. * *n* applicant, petitioner, solicitor, suitor, supplicant.

supplicate *vb* beg, beseech, crave, entreat, implore, importune, petition, pray, solicit.

supplication *n* invocation, orison, petition, prayer; entreaty, petition, prayer, request, solicitation.

supply *vb* endue, equip, furnish, minister, outfit, provide, replenish, stock, store; afford, accommodate, contribute, furnish, give, grant, yield. * *n* hoard, provision, reserve, stock, store.

support *vb* brace, cradle, pillow, prop, sustain, uphold; bear, endure, undergo, suffer, tolerate; cherish, keep, maintain, nourish, nurture; act, assume, carry, perform, play, represent; accredit, confirm, corroborate, substantiate, verify; abet, advocate, aid, approve, assist, back, befriend, champion, countenance, encourage, favour, float, hold, patronize, relieve, reinforce, succour, vindicate. * *n* bolster, brace, buttress, foothold, guy, hold, prop, purchase, shore, stay, substructure, supporter, underpinning; groundwork, mainstay, staff; base, basis, bed, foundation; keeping, living, livelihood, maintenance, subsistence, sustenance; confirmation, evidence; aid, assistance, backing, behalf, championship, comfort, countenance, encouragement, favour, help, patronage, succour.

suppose *vb* apprehend, believe, conceive, conclude, consider, conjecture, deem, imagine, judge, presume, presuppose, think; assume, hypothesize; imply, posit, predicate, think; fancy, opine, speculate, surmise, suspect, theorize, wean.

supposition *n* conjecture, guess, guesswork, presumption, surmise; assumption, hypothesis, postulation, theory, thesis; doubt, uncertainty.

suppress *vb* choke, crush, destroy, overwhelm, overpower, overthrow, quash, quell, quench, smother, stifle, subdue, withhold; arrest, inhibit, obstruct, repress, restrain, stop; conceal, extinguish, keep, retain, secret, silence, stifle, strangle.

supremacy *n* ascendancy, domination, headship, lordship, mastery, predominance, pre-eminence, primacy, sovereignty.

supreme *adj* chief, dominant, first, greatest, highest, leading, paramount, predominant, pre-eminent, principal, sovereign.

sure *adj* assured, certain, confident, positive; accurate, dependable, effective, honest, infallible, precise, reli-

able, trustworthy, undeniable, undoubted, unmistakable, well-proven; guaranteed, inevitable, irrevocable; fast, firm, safe, secure, stable, steady.

surely *adv* assuredly, certainly, infallibly, sure, undoubtedly; firmly, safely, securely, steadily.

surety *n* bail, bond, certainty, guarantee, pledge, safety, security.

surfeit *vb* cram, gorge, overfeed, sate, satiate; cloy, nauseate, pall. * *n* excess, fullness, glut, oppression, plethora, satiation, satiety, superabundance, superfluity.

surge *vb* billow, rise, rush, sweep, swell, swirl, tower. * *n* billow, breaker, roller, wave, white horse.

surly *adj* churlish, crabbed, cross, crusty, discourteous, fretful, gruff, grumpy, harsh, ill-natured, ill-tempered, morose, peevish, perverse, pettish, petulant, rough, rude, snappish, snarling, sour, sullen, testy, touchy, uncivil, ungracious, waspish; dark, tempestuous.

surmise *vb* believe, conclude, conjecture, consider, divine, fancy, guess, imagine, presume, suppose, think, suspect. * *n* conclusion, conjecture, doubt, guess, notion, possibility, supposition, suspicion, thought.

surmount *vb* clear, climb, crown, overtop, scale, top, vault; conquer, master, overcome, overpower, subdue, vanquish; exceed, overpass, pass, surpass, transcend.

surpass *vb* beat, cap, eclipse, exceed, excel, outdo, outmatch, outnumber, outrun, outstrip, override, overshadow, overtop, outshine, surmount, transcend.

surplus *adj* additional, leftover, remaining, spare, superfluous, supernumerary, supplementary. * *n* balance, excess, overplus, remainder, residue, superabundance, surfeit.

surprise *vb* amaze, astonish, astound, bewilder, confuse, disconcert, dumbfound, startle, stun. * *n* amazement, astonishment, blow, shock, wonder.

surprising *adj* amazing, astonishing, astounding, extraordinary, marvellous, unexpected, remarkable, startling, strange, unexpected, wonderful.

surrender *vb* cede, sacrifice, yield; abdicate, abandon, forgo, relinquish, renounce, resign, waive; capitulate, comply, succumb. * *n* abandonment, capitulation, cession, delivery, relinquishment, renunciation, resignation, yielding.

surreptitious *adj* clandestine, fraudulent, furtive, secret, sly, stealthy, unauthorized, underhand.

surround *vb* beset, circumscribe, compass, embrace, encircle, encompass, environ, girdle, hem, invest, loop.

surveillance *n* care, charge, control, direction, inspection, management, oversight, superintendence, supervision, surveyorship, vigilance, watch.

survey *vb* contemplate, observe, overlook, reconnoitre, review, scan, scout, view; examine, inspect, scrutinize; oversee, supervise; estimate, measure, plan, plot, prospect. * *n* prospect, retrospect, sight, view; examination, inspection, reconnaissance, review; estimating, measuring, planning, plotting, prospecting, work-study.

survive *vb* endure, last, outlast, outlive.

susceptible *adj* capable, excitable, impressible, impressionable, inclined, predisposed, receptive, sensitive.

suspect *vb* believe, conclude, conjecture, fancy, guess, imagine, judge, suppose, surmise, think; distrust, doubt, mistrust. * *adj* doubtful, dubious, suspicious.

suspend *vb* append, hang, sling, swing; adjourn, arrest, defer, delay, discontinue, hinder, intermit, interrupt, postpone, stay, withhold; debar, dismiss, rusticate.

suspicion *n* assumption, conjecture, dash, guess, hint, inkling, suggestion, supposition, surmise, trace; apprehension, distrust, doubt, fear, jealousy, misgiving, mistrust.

suspicious *adj* distrustful, jealous, mistrustful, suspect, suspecting; doubtful, questionable.

sustain *vb* bear, bolster, fortify, prop, strengthen, support, uphold; maintain, nourish, perpetuate, preserve; aid, assist, comfort, relieve; brave, endure, suffer, undergo; approve, confirm, ratify, sanction, validate; confirm, establish, justify, prove.

sustenance *n* maintenance, subsistence, support; aliment, bread, food, nourishment, nutriment, nutrition, provisions, supplies, victuals.

swagger *vb* bluster, boast, brag, bully, flourish, hector, ruffle, strut, swell, vapour. * *n* airs, arrogance, bluster, boastfulness, braggadocio, ruffling, strut.

swain *n* clown, countryman, hind, peasant, rustic; adorer, gallant, inamorata, lover, suitor, wooer.

swallow *vb* bolt, devour, drink, eat, englut, engorge, gobble, gorge, gulp, imbibe, ingurgitate, swamp; absorb, appropriate, arrogate, devour, engulf, submerge; consume, employ, occupy; brook, digest, endure, pocket, stomach; recant, renounce, retract. * *n* gullet, oesophagus, throat; inclination, liking, palate, relish, taste; deglutition, draught, gulp, ingurgitation, mouthful, taste.

swamp *vb* engulf, overwhelm, sink; capsize, embarrass, overset, ruin, upset, wreck. * *n* bog, fen, marsh, morass, quagmire, slough.

sward *n* grass, lawn, sod, turf.

swarm *vb* abound, crowd, teem, throng. * *n* cloud, concourse, crowd, drove, flock, hive, horde, host, mass, multitude, press, shoal, throng.

swarthy *adj* black, brown, dark, dark-skinned, dusky, tawny.

sway *vb* balance, brandish, move, poise, rock, roll, swing, wave, wield; bend, bias, influence, persuade, turn, urge; control, dominate, direct, govern, guide, manage, rule; hoist, raise; incline, lean, lurch, yaw. * *n* ascendency, authority, command, control, domination, dominion, empire, government, mastership, mastery, omnipotence, predominance, power, rule, sovereignty; bias, direction, influence, weight; preponderance, preponderation; oscillation, sweep, swing, wag, wave.

swear *vb* affirm, attest, avow, declare, depose, promise, say, state, testify, vow; blaspheme, curse.

sweep *vb* clean, brush; graze, touch; rake, scour, traverse. * *n* amplitude, compass, drive, movement, range, reach, scope; destruction, devastation, havoc, ravage; curvature, curve.

sweeping *adj* broad, comprehensive, exaggerated, extensive, extravagant, general, unqualified, wholesale.

sweet *adj* candied, cloying, honeyed, luscious, nectareous, nectarous, sugary, saccharine; balmy, fragrant, odorous, redolent, spicy; harmonious, dulcet, mellifluous, mellow, melodious, musical, pleasant, soft, tuneful, silver-toned, silvery; beautiful, fair, lovely; agreeable, charming, delightful, grateful, gratifying; affectionate, amiable, attractive, engaging, gentle, mild, lovable, winning; benignant, serene; clean, fresh, pure, sound. * *n* fragrance, perfume, redolence; blessing, delight, enjoyment, gratification, joy, pleasure; candy, treat.

swell *vb* belly, bloat, bulge, dilate, distend, expand, inflate, intumesce, puff, swell, tumefy; augment, enlarge, increase; heave, rise, surge; strut, swagger. * *n* swelling; augmentation, excrescence, protuberance; ascent, elevation, hill, rise; force, intensity, power; billows, surge, undulation, waves; beau, blade, buck, coxcomb, dandy, exquisite, fop, popinjay.

swerve *vb* deflect, depart, deviate, stray, turn, wander; bend, incline, yield; climb, swarm, wind.

swift *adj* expeditious, fast, fleet, flying, quick, rapid, speedy; alert, eager, forward, prompt, ready, zealous; instant, sudden.

swiftness *n* celerity, expedition, fleetness, quickness, rapidity, speed, velocity.

swindle *vb* cheat, con, cozen, deceive, defraud, diddle, dupe, embezzle, forge, gull, hoax, overreach, steal, trick, victimize. * *n* cheat, con, deceit, deception, fraud, hoax, imposition, knavery, roguery, trickery.

swindler *n* blackleg, cheat, defaulter, embezzler, faker, fraud, impostor, jockey, knave, peculator, rogue, sharper, trickster.

swing *vb* oscillate, sway, vibrate, wave; dangle, depend, hang; brandish, flourish, whirl; administer, manage. * *n* fluctuation, oscillation, sway, undulation, vibration; elbow-room, freedom, margin, play, range, scope, sweep; bias, tendency.

swoop *vb* descend, pounce, rush, seize, stoop, sweep. * *n* clutch, pounce, seizure; stoop, descent.

sword *n* brand, broadsword, claymore, cutlass, epee, falchion, foil, hanger, rapier, sabre, scimitar.

sybarite *n* epicure, voluptuary.

sycophancy *n* adulation, cringing, fawning, flattery, grovelling, obsequiousness, servility.

sycophant *n* cringer, fawner, flunky, hanger-on, lickspittle, parasite, spaniel, toady, wheedler.

syllabus *n* abridgement, abstract, breviary, brief, compendium, digest, epitome, outline, summary, synopsis.

symbol *n* badge, emblem, exponent, figure, mark, picture, representation, representative, sign, token, type.

symbolic, symbolical *adj* emblematic, figurative, hieroglyphic, representative, significant, typical.

symmetry *n* balance, congruity, evenness, harmony, order, parallelism, proportion, regularity, shapeliness.

sympathetic *adj* affectionate, commiserating, compassionate, condoling, kind, pitiful, tender.

sympathy *n* accord, affinity, agreement, communion, concert, concord, congeniality, correlation, correspondence, harmony, reciprocity, union; commiseration, compassion, condolence, fellow-feeling, kindliness, pity, tenderness, thoughtfulness.

symptom *n* diagnostic, indication, mark, note, prognostic, sign, token.

symptomatic *adj* characteristic, indicative, symbolic, suggestive.

synonymous *adj* equipollent, equivalent, identical, interchangeable, similar, tantamount.

synopsis *n* abridgement, abstract, compendium, digest, epitome, outline, precis, résumé, summary, syllabus.

system *n* method, order, plan.

systematic *adj* methodic, methodical, orderly, regular.

T

tabernacle *n* pavilion, tent; cathedral, chapel, church, minster, synagogue, temple.

table *vb* enter, move, propose, submit, suggest. * *n* plate, slab, tablet; board, counter, desk, stand; catalogue, chart, compendium, index, list, schedule, syllabus, synopsis, tabulation; diet, fare, food, victuals.

tableau *n* picture, scene, representation.

taboo *vb* forbid, interdict, prohibit, proscribe. * *adj* banned, forbidden, inviolable, outlawed, prohibited, proscribed. * *n* ban, interdict, prohibition, proscription.

tacit *adj* implicit, implied, inferred, silent, understood, unexpressed, unspoken.

taciturn *adj* close, dumb, laconic, mum, reserved, reticent, silent, tight-lipped, uncommunicative.

tack *vb* add, affix, append, attach, fasten, tag; gybe, yaw, zigzag. * *n* nail, pin, staple; bearing, course, direction, heading, path, plan, procedure.

tackle *vb* attach, grapple, seize; attempt, try, undertake. * *n* apparatus, cordage, equipment, furniture, gear, harness, implements, rigging, tackling, tools, weapons.

tact *n* address, adroitness, cleverness, dexterity, diplomacy, discernment, finesse, insight, knack, perception, skill, understanding.

tail *vb* dog, follow, shadow, stalk, track. * *adj* abridged, curtailed, limited, reduced. * *n* appendage, conclusion, end, extremity, stub; flap, skirt; queue, retinue, train.

taint *vb* imbue, impregnate; contaminate, corrupt, defile, inflect, mildew, pollute, poison, spoil, touch; blot, stain, sully, tarnish. * *n* stain, tincture, tinge, touch; contamination, corruption, defilement, depravation, infection, pollution; blemish, defect, fault, flaw, spot.

take *vb* accept, obtain, procure, receive; clasp, clutch, grasp, grip, gripe, seize, snatch; filch, misappropriate, pilfer, purloin, steal; abstract, apprehend, appropriate, arrest, bag, capture, ensnare, entrap; attack, befall, smite; capture, carry off, conquer, gain, win; allure, attract, bewitch, captivate, charm, delight, enchant, engage, fascinate, interest, please; consider, hold, interrupt, suppose, regard, understand; choose, elect, espouse, select; employ, expend, use; claim, demand, necessitate, require; bear, endure, experience, feel, perceive, tolerate; deduce, derive, detect, discover, draw; carry, conduct, convey, lead, transfer; clear, surmount; drink, eat, imbibe, inhale, swallow. * *n* proceeds, profits, return, revenue, takings, yield.

tale *n* account, fable, legend, narration, novel, parable, recital, rehearsal, relation, romance, story, yarn; catalogue, count, enumeration, numbering, reckoning, tally.

talent *n* ableness, ability, aptitude, capacity, cleverness, endowment, faculty, forte, genius, gift, knack, parts, power, turn.

talk *vb* chatter, communicate, confer, confess, converse, declaim, discuss, gossip, pontificate, speak. * *n* chatter, communication, conversation, diction, gossip, jargon, language, rumour, speech, utterance.

talkative *adj* chatty, communicative, garrulous, loquacious, voluble.

tally *vb* accord, agree, conform, coincide, correspond, harmonize, match, square, suit. * *n* match, mate; check, counterpart, muster, roll call; account, reckoning.

tame *vb* domesticate, reclaim, train; conquer, master, overcome, repress, subdue, subjugate. * *adj* docile, domestic, domesticated, gentle, mild, reclaimed; broken, crushed, meek, subdued, unresisting, submissive; barren, commonplace, dull, feeble, flat, insipid, jejune, languid, lean, poor, prosaic, prosy, spiritless, tedious, uninteresting, vapid.

tamper *vb* alter, conquer, dabble, damage, interfere, meddle; intrigue, seduce, suborn.

tang *n* aftertaste, flavour, relish, savour, smack, taste; keenness, nip, sting.

tangible *adj* corporeal, material, palpable, tactile, touchable; actual, certain, embodied, evident, obvious, open, perceptible, plain, positive, real, sensible, solid, stable, substantial.

tangle *vb* complicate, entangle, intertwine, interweave, mat, perplex, snarl; catch, ensnare, entrap, involve, catch; embarrass, embroil, perplex. * *n* complication, disorder, intricacy, jumble, perplexity, snarl; dilemma, embarrassment, quandary, perplexity.

tantalize *vb* balk, disappoint, frustrate, irritate, provoke, tease, torment, vex.

tantamount *adj* equal, equivalent, synonymous.

tantrum *n* fit, ill-humour, outburst, paroxysm, temper, whim.

tap[1] *vb* knock, pat, rap, strike, tip, touch. * *n* pat, tip, rap, touch.

tap[2] *vb* broach, draw off, extract, pierce; draw on, exploit, mine, use, utilize; bug, eavesdrop, listen in. * *n* faucet, plug, spigot, spout, stopcock, valve; bug, listening device, transmitter.

tardiness *n* delay, dilatoriness, lateness, procrastination, slackness, slowness.

tardy *adj* slow, sluggish, snail-like; backward, behindhand, dilatory, late, loitering, overdue, slack.

tarn *n* bog, fen, marsh, morass, swamp.

tarnish *vb* blemish, deface, defame, dim, discolour, dull, slur, smear, soil, stain, sully. * *n* blemish, blot, soiling, spot, stain.

tarry *vb* delay, dally, linger, loiter, remain, stay, stop, wait; defer; abide, lodge, rest, sojourn.

tart *adj* acid, acidulous, acrid, astringent, piquant, pungent, sharp, sour; acrimonious, caustic, crabbed, curt, harsh, ill-humoured, ill-tempered, keen, petulant, sarcastic, severe, snappish, testy.

task *vb* burden, overwork, strain, tax. * *n* drudgery, labour, toil, work; business, charge, chore, duty, employment, enterprise, job, mission, stint, undertaking; assignment, exercise, lesson.

taste *vb* experience, feel, perceive, undergo; relish, savour, sip. * *n* flavour, gusto, relish, savour, smack, piquancy; admixture, bit, dash, fragment, hint, infusion, morsel, mouthful, sample, shade, sprinkling, suggestion, tincture; appetite, desire, fondness, liking, partiality, predilection; acumen, cultivation, culture, delicacy, discernment, discrimination, elegance, fine-feeling, grace, judgement, polish, refinement; manner, style.

tasteful *adj* appetizing, delicious, flavoursome, palatable, savoury, tasty, toothsome; aesthetic, artistic, attractive, elegant.

tasteless *adj* flat, insipid, savourless, stale, watery; dull, mawkish, uninteresting, vapid.

tattle *vb* babble, chat, chatter, jabber, prate, prattle; blab, gossip, inform. * *n* gabble, gossip, prate, prattle, tittle-tattle, twaddle.

taunt *vb* censure, chaff, deride, flout, jeer, mock, scoff, sneer, revile, reproach, ridicule, twit, upbraid. * *n* censure, derision, gibe, insult, jeer, quip, quirk, reproach, ridicule, scoff.

taut *adj* strained, stretched, tense, tight.

tautology *n* iteration, pleonasm, redundancy, reiteration, repetition, verbosity, wordiness.

tavern *n* bar, chophouse, hostelry, inn, pub, public house.

tawdry *adj* flashy, gaudy, garish, glittering, loud, meretricious, ostentatious, showy.

tax *vb* burden, demand, exact, load, overtax, require, strain, task; accuse, charge. * *n* assessment, custom, duty, excise, impost, levy, rate, taxation, toll, tribute; burden, charge, demand, requisition, strain; accusation, censure.

teach *vb* catechize, coach, discipline, drill, edify, educate, enlighten, inform, indoctrinate, initiate, instruct, ground, prime, school, train, tutor; communicate, disseminate, explain, expound, impart, implant, inculcate, infuse, instil, interpret, preach, propagate; admonish, advise, counsel, direct, guide, signify, show.

teacher *n* coach, educator, inculcator, informant, instructor, master, pedagogue, preceptor, schoolteacher, trainer, tutor; adviser, counsellor, guide, mentor; pastor, preacher.

tear *vb* burst, slit, rive, rend, rip; claw, lacerate, mangle, shatter, rend, wound; sever, sunder; fume, rage, rant, rave. * *n* fissure, laceration, rent, rip, wrench.

tease *vb* annoy, badger, beg, bother, chafe, chagrin, disturb, harass, harry, hector, importune, irritate, molest, pester, plague, provoke, tantalize, torment, trouble, vex, worry.

tedious *adj* dull, fatiguing, irksome, monotonous, tiresome, trying, uninteresting, wearisome; dilatory, slow, sluggish, tardy.

teem *vb* abound, bear, produce, swarm; discharge, empty, overflow.

teeming *adj* abounding, fraught, full, overflowing, pregnant, prolific, replete, swarming.

tell *vb* compute, count, enumerate, number, reckon; describe, narrate, recount, rehearse, relate, report; acknowledge, announce, betray, confess, declare, disclose, divulge, inform, own, reveal; acquaint, communicate, instruct, teach; discern, discover, distin-

guish; express, mention, publish, speak, state, utter.

temper *vb* modify, qualify; appease, assuage, calm, mitigate, mollify, moderate, pacify, restrain, soften, soothe; accommodate, adapt, adjust, fit, suit. * *n* character, constitution, nature, organization, quality, structure, temperament, type; disposition, frame, grain, humour, mood, spirits, tone, vein; calmness, composure, equanimity, moderation, tranquillity; anger, ill-temper, irritation, spleen, passion.

temperament *n* character, constitution, disposition, habit, idiosyncrasy, nature, organization, temper.

temperate *adj* abstemious, ascetic, austere, chaste, continent, frugal, moderate, self-controlled, self-denying, sparing; calm, cool, dispassionate, mild, sober, sedate.

tempest *n* cyclone, gale, hurricane, squall, storm, tornado; commotion, disturbance, excitement, perturbation, tumult, turmoil.

temporal *adj* civil, lay, mundane, political, profane, secular, terrestrial, worldly; brief, ephemeral, evanescent, fleeting, momentary, short-lived, temporal, transient, transitory.

temporary *adj* brief, ephemeral, evanescent, fleeting, impermanent, momentary, short-lived, transient, transitory.

tempt *vb* prove, test, try; allure, decoy, entice, induce, inveigle, persuade, seduce; dispose, incite, incline, instigate, lead, prompt, provoke.

tempting *adj* alluring, attractive, enticing, inviting, seductive.

tenable *adj* defensible, maintainable, rational, reasonable, sound.

tenacious *adj* retentive, unforgetful; adhesive, clinging, cohesive, firm, glutinous, gummy, resisting, retentive, sticky, strong, tough, unyielding, viscous; dogged, fast, obstinate, opinionated, opinionative, pertinacious, persistent, resolute, stubborn, unwavering.

tenacity *n* retentiveness, tenaciousness; adhesiveness, cohesiveness, glutinosity, glutinousness, gumminess, toughness, stickiness, strength, viscidity; doggedness, firmness, obstinacy, perseverance, persistency, pertinacity, resolution, stubbornness.

tend[1] *vb* accompany, attend, graze, guard, keep, protect, shepherd, watch.

tend[2] *vb* aim, exert, gravitate, head, incline, influence, lead, lean, point, trend, verge; conduce, contribute.

tendency *n* aim, aptitude, bearing, bent, bias, course, determination, disposition, direction, drift, gravitation, inclination, leaning, liability, predisposition, proclivity, proneness, propensity, scope, set, susceptibility, turn, twist, warp.

tender[1] *vb* bid, offer, present, proffer, propose, suggest, volunteer. * *n* bid, offer, proffer, proposal; currency, money.

tender[2] *adj* callow, delicate, effeminate, feeble, feminine, fragile, immature, infantile, soft, weak, young; affectionate, compassionate, gentle, humane, kind, lenient, loving, merciful, mild, pitiful, sensitive, sympathetic, tender-hearted; affecting, disagreeable, painful, pathetic, touching, unpleasant.

tenebrous *adj* cloudy, dark, darksome, dusky, gloomy, murky, obscure, shadowy, shady, sombre, tenebrious.

tenement *n* abode, apartment, domicile, dwelling, flat, house.

tenet *n* belief, creed, position, dogma, doctrine, notion, opinion, position, principle, view.

tenor n cast, character, cut, fashion, form, manner, mood, nature, stamp, tendency, trend, tone; drift, gist, import, intent, meaning, purport, sense, significance, spirit.

tense vb flex, strain, tauten, tighten. * adj rigid, stiff, strained, stretched, taut, tight; excited, highly strung, intent, nervous, rapt.

tentative adj essaying, experimental, provisional, testing, toying.

tenure n holding, occupancy, occupation, possession, tenancy, tenement, use.

term vb call, christen, denominate, designate, dub, entitle, name, phrase, style. * n bound, boundary, bourn, confine, limit, mete, terminus; duration, period, season, semester, span, spell, termination, time; denomination, expression, locution, name, phrase, word.

termagant n beldam, hag, scold, shrew, spitfire, virago, vixen.

terminal adj bounding, limiting; final, terminating, ultimate. * n end, extremity, termination; bound, limit; airport, depot, station, terminus.

terminate vb bound, limit; end, finish, close, complete, conclude; eventuate, issue, prove.

termination n ending, suffix; bound, extend, limit; end, completion, conclusion, consequence, effect, issue, outcome, result.

terms npl conditions, provisions, stipulations.

terrestrial adj earthly, mundane, subastral, subcelestial, sublunar, sublunary, tellurian, worldly. * n earthling, human.

terrible adj appalling, dire, dreadful, fearful, formidable, frightful, gruesome, hideous, horrible, horrid, shocking, terrific, tremendous; alarming, awe-inspiring, awful, dread; great, excessive, extreme, severe.

terrific adj marvellous, sensational, superb; immense, intense; alarming, dreadful, formidable, frightful, terrible, tremendous.

terrify vb affright, alarm, appal, daunt, dismay, fright, frighten, horrify, scare, shock, startle, terrorize.

territory n country, district, domain, dominion, division, land, place, province, quarter, region, section, tract.

terror n affright, alarm, anxiety, awe, consternation, dismay, dread, fear, fright, horror, intimidation, panic, terrorism.

terse adj brief, compact, concise, laconic, neat, pithy, polished, sententious, short, smooth, succinct.

test vb assay; examine, prove, try. * n attempt, essay, examination, experiment, ordeal, proof, trial; criterion, standard, touchstone; example, exhibition; discrimination, distinction, judgment.

testify vb affirm, assert, asseverate, attest, avow, certify, corroborate, declare, depose, evidence, state, swear.

testimonial n certificate, credential, recommendation, voucher; monument, record.

testimony n affirmation, attestation, confession, confirmation, corroboration, declaration, deposition, profession; evidence, proof, witness.

testy adj captious, choleric, cross, fretful, hasty, irascible, irritable, quick, peevish, peppery, pettish, petulant, snappish, splenetic, touchy, waspish.

tetchy adj crabbed, cross, fretful, irritable, peevish, sullen, touchy.

tether vb chain, fasten, picket, stake, tie. * n chain, fastening, rope.

text n copy, subject, theme, thesis, topic, treatise.

texture n fabric, web, weft; character, coarseness, composition, constitution, fibre, fineness, grain, make-up, nap, organization, structure, tissue.

thankful adj appreciative, beholden, grateful, indebted, obliged.

thankfulness n appreciation, gratefulness, gratitude.

thankless adj profitless, ungracious, ungrateful, unthankful.

thaw vb dissolve, liquefy, melt, soften, unbend.

theatre n opera house, playhouse; arena, scene, seat, stage.

theatrical adj dramatic, dramaturgic, dramaturgical, histrionic, scenic, spectacular; affected, ceremonious, meretricious, ostentatious, pompous, showy, stagy, stilted, unnatural.

theft n depredation, embezzlement, fraud, larceny, peculation, pilfering, purloining, robbery, spoliation, stealing, swindling, thieving.

theme n composition, essay, motif, subject, text, thesis, topic, treatise.

theoretical adj abstract, conjectural, doctrinaire, ideal, hypothetical, pure, speculative, unapplied.

theory n assumption, conjecture, hypothesis, idea, plan, postulation, principle, scheme, speculation, surmise; system; doctrine, philosophy, science; explanation, exposition, philosophy, rationale.

therefore adv accordingly, afterward, consequently, hence, so, subsequently, then, thence, whence.

thesaurus n dictionary, encyclopedia, repository, storehouse, treasure.

thick adj bulky, chunky, dumpy, plump, solid, squab, squat, stubby, thickset; clotted, coagulated, crass, dense, dull, gross, heavy, viscous; blurred, cloudy, dirty, foggy, hazy, indistinguishable, misty, obscure, vaporous; muddy, roiled, turbid; abundant, frequent, multitudinous, numerous; close, compact, crowded, set, thickset; confused, guttural, hoarse, inarticulate, indistinct; dim, dull, weak; familiar, friendly, intimate, neighbourly, well-acquainted. * adv fast, frequently, quick; closely, densely, thickly. * n centre, middle, midst.

thicket n clump, coppice, copse, covert, forest, grove, jungle, shrubbery, underbrush, undergrowth, wood, woodland.

thief n depredator, filcher, pilferer, lifter, marauder, purloiner, robber, shark, stealer; burglar, corsair, defaulter, defrauder, embezzler, footpad, highwayman, housebreaker, kidnapper, pickpocket, pirate, poacher, privateer, sharper, swindler, peculator.

thieve vb cheat, embezzle, peculate, pilfer, plunder, purloin, rob, steal, swindle.

thin vb attenuate, dilute, diminish, prune, reduce, refine, weaken. * adj attenuated, bony, emaciated, fine, fleshless, flimsy, gaunt, haggard, lank, lanky, lean, meagre, peaked, pinched, poor, scanty, scraggy, scrawny, slender, slight, slim, small, sparse, spindly.

thing n being, body, contrivance, creature, entity, object, something, substance; act, action, affair, arrangement, circumstance, concern, deed, event, matter, occurrence, transaction.

think vb cogitate, contemplate, dream, meditate, muse, ponder, reflect, ruminate, speculate; consider, deliberate, reason, undertake; apprehend, believe, conceive, conclude, deem, determine, fancy, hold, imagine, judge, opine, presume, reckon, suppose, surmise; design, intend, mean, purpose; account, count, deem, esteem, hold, regard; compass, design, plan, plot. * n assessment, contemplation, deliberation, meditation, opinion, reasoning, reflection.

thirst *n* appetite, craving, desire, hunger, longing, yearning; aridity, drought, dryness.

thirsty *adj* arid, dry, parched; eager, greedy, hungry, longing, yearning.

thorn *n* prickle, spine; annoyance, bane, care, evil, infliction, nettle, nuisance, plague, torment, trouble, scourge.

thorny *adj* briary, briery, prickly, spinose, spinous, spiny; acuminate, barbed, pointed, prickling, sharp, spiky; annoying, difficult, harassing, perplexing, rugged, troublesome, trying, vexatious.

thorough, thoroughgoing *adj* absolute, arrant, complete, downright, entire, exhaustive, finished, perfect, radical, sweeping, total unmitigated, utter; accurate, correct, reliable, trustworthy.

though *conj* admitting, allowing, although, granted, granting, if, notwithstanding, still. * *adv* however, nevertheless, still, yet.

thought *n* absorption, cogitation, engrossment, meditation, musing, reflection, reverie, rumination; contemplation, intellect, ratiocination, thinking, thoughtfulness; application, conception, consideration, deliberation, idea, pondering, speculation, study; consciousness, imagination, intellect, perception, understanding; conceit, fancy, notion; conclusion, judgment, motion, opinion, sentiment, supposition, view; anxiety, attention, care, concern, provision, regard, solicitude, thoughtfulness; design, expectation, intention, purpose.

thoughtful *adj* absorbed, contemplative, deliberative, dreamy, engrossed, introspective, pensive, philosophic, reflecting, reflective, sedate, speculative; attentive, careful, cautious, circumspect, considerate, discreet, heedful, friendly, kind-hearted, kindly, mindful, neighbourly, provident, prudent, regardful, watchful, wary; quiet, serious, sober, studious.

thoughtless *adj* careless, casual, flighty, heedless, improvident, inattentive, inconsiderate, neglectful, negligent, precipitate, rash, reckless, regardless, remiss, trifling, unmindful, unthinking; blank, blockish, dull, insensate, stupid, vacant, vacuous.

thraldom *n* bondage, enslavement, enthralment, serfdom, servitude, slavery, subjection, thrall, vassalage.

thrash *vb* beat, bruise, conquer, defeat, drub, flog, lash, maul, pommel, punish, thwack, trounce, wallop, whip.

thread *vb* course, direction, drift, tenor; reeve, trace. * *n* cord, fibre, filament, hair, line, twist; pile, staple.

threadbare *adj* napless, old, seedy, worn; common, commonplace, hackneyed, stale, trite, worn-out.

threat *n* commination, defiance, denunciation, fulmination, intimidation, menace, thunder, thunderbolt.

threaten *vb* denounce, endanger, fulminate, intimidate, menace, thunder; augur, forebode, foreshadow, indicate, portend, presage, prognosticate, warn.

threshold *n* doorsill, sill; door, entrance, gate; beginning, commencement, opening, outset, start.

thrift *n* economy, frugality, parsimony, saving, thriftiness; gain, luck, profit, prosperity, success.

thriftless *adj* extravagant, improvident, lavish, profuse, prodigal, shiftless, unthrifty, wasteful.

thrifty *adj* careful, economical, frugal, provident, saving, sparing; flourishing, prosperous, thriving, vigorous.

thrill *vb* affect, agitate, electrify, inspire, move, penetrate, pierce, rouse, stir, touch. * *n* excitement, sensation, shock, tingling, tremor.

thrilling *adj* affecting, exciting, gripping, moving, sensational, touching.

thrive *vb* advance, batten, bloom, boom, flourish, prosper, succeed.

throng *vb* congregate, crowd, fill, flock, pack, press, swarm. * *n* assemblage, concourse, congregation, crowd, horde, host, mob, multitude, swarm.

throttle *vb* choke, silence, strangle, suffocate.

throw *vb* cast, chuck, dart, fling, hurl, lance, launch, overturn, pitch, pitchfork, send, sling, toss, whirl. * *n* cast, fling, hurl, launch, pitch, sling, toss, whirl; chance, gamble, try, venture.

thrust *vb* clap, dig, drive, force, impel, jam, plunge, poke, propel, push, ram, run, shove, stick. * *n* dig, jab, lunge, pass, plunge, poke, propulsion, push, shove, stab, tilt.

thump *vb* bang, batter, beat, belabour, knock, punch, strike, thrash, thwack, whack. * *n* blow, knock, punch, strike, stroke.

thwart *vb* baffle, balk, contravene, counteract, cross, defeat, disconcert, frustrate, hinder, impede, oppose, obstruct, oppugn; cross, intersect, traverse.

tickle *vb* amuse, delight, divert, enliven, gladden, gratify, please, rejoice, titillate.

ticklish *adj* dangerous, precarious, risky, tottering, uncertain, unstable, unsteady; critical, delicate, difficult, nice.

tide *n* course, current, ebb, flow, stream.

tidings *npl* advice, greetings, information, intelligence, news, report, word.

tidy *vb* clean, neaten, order, straighten. * *adj* clean, neat, orderly, shipshape, spruce, trig, trim.

tie *vb* bind, confine, fasten, knot, lock, manacle, secure, shackle, fetter, yoke; complicate, entangle, interlace, knit; connect, hold, join, link, unite; constrain, oblige, restrain, restrict. * *n* band, fastening, knot, ligament, ligature; allegiance, bond, obligation; bow, cravat, necktie.

tier *n* line, rank, row, series.

tiff *n* fit, fume, passion, pet, miff, rage.

tight *adj* close, compact, fast, firm; taut, tense, stretched; impassable, narrow, strait.

till *vb* cultivate, plough, harrow.

tillage *n* agriculture, cultivation, culture, farming, geoponics, husbandry.

tilt *vb* cant, incline, slant, slope, tip; forge, hammer; point, thrust; joust, rush. * *n* awning, canopy, tent; lunge, pass, thrust; cant, inclination, slant, slope, tip.

time *vb* clock, control, count, measure, regulate, schedule. * *n* duration, interim, interval, season, span, spell, tenure, term, while; aeon, age, date, epoch, eon, era; term; cycle, dynasty, reign; confinement, delivery, parturition; measure, rhythm.

timely *adj* acceptable, appropriate, apropos, early, opportune, prompt, punctual, seasonable, well-timed.

timid *adj* afraid, cowardly, faint-hearted, fearful, irresolute, meticulous, nervous, pusillanimous, skittish, timorous, unadventurous; bashful, coy, diffident, modest, shame-faced, shrinking.

tincture *vb* colour, dye, shade, stain, tinge, tint; flavour, season; imbue, impregnate, impress, infuse. * *n* grain, hue, shade, stain, tinge, tint, tone; flavour, smack, spice, taste; admixture, dash, infusion, seasoning, sprinkling, touch.

tinge *vb* colour, dye, stain, tincture, tint; imbue, impregnate, impress, infuse. * *n* cast, colour, dye, hue, shade, stain, tincture, tint; flavour, smack, spice, quality, taste.

tint *n* cast, colour, complexion, dye, hue, shade, tinge, tone.

tiny *adj* diminutive, dwarfish, Lilliputian, little, microscopic, miniature, minute, puny, pygmy, small, wee.

tip[1] *n* apex, cap, end, extremity, peak, pinnacle, point, top, vertex.

tip[2] *vb* incline, overturn, tilt; dispose of, dump. * *n* donation, fee, gift, gratuity, perquisite, reward; inclination, slant; hint, pointer, suggestion; strike, tap.

tirade *n* abuse, denunciation, diatribe, harangue, outburst.

tire *vb* exhaust, fag, fatigue, harass, jade, weary; bore, bother, irk.

tiresome *adj* annoying, arduous, boring, dull, exhausting, fatiguing, fagging, humdrum, irksome, laborious, monotonous, tedious, wearisome, vexatious.

tissue *n* cloth, fabric; membrane, network, structure, texture, web; accumulation, chain, collection, combination, conglomeration, mass, series, set.

titanic *adj* colossal, Cyclopean, enormous, gigantic, herculean, huge, immense, mighty, monstrous, prodigious, stupendous, vast.

title *vb* call, designate, name, style, term. * *n* caption, legend, head, heading; appellation, application, cognomen, completion, denomination, designation, epithet, name; claim, due, ownership, part, possession, prerogative, privilege, right.

tittle *n* atom, bit, grain, iota, jot, mite, particle, scrap, speck, whit.

tittle-tattle *vb, n* babble, cackle, chatter, discourse, gabble, gossip, prattle.

toast *vb* brown, dry, heat; honour, pledge, propose, salute. * *n* compliment, drink, pledge, salutation, salute; favourite, pet.

toil *vb* drudge, labour, strive, work. * *n* drudgery, effort, exertion, exhaustion, grinding, labour, pains, travail, work; gin, net, noose, snare, spring, trap.

toilsome *adj* arduous, difficult, fatiguing, hard, laborious, onerous, painful, severe, tedious, wearisome.

token *adj* nominal, superficial, symbolic. * *n* badge, evidence, index, indication, manifestation, mark, note, sign, symbol, trace, trait; keepsake, memento, memorial, reminder, souvenir.

tolerable *adj* bearable, endurable, sufferable, supportable; fair, indifferent, middling, ordinary, passable, so-so.

tolerance *n* endurance, receptivity, sufferance, toleration.

tolerate *vb* admit, allow, indulge, let, permit, receive; abide, brook, endure, suffer.

toll[1] *n* assessment, charge, customs, demand, dues, duty, fee, impost, levy, rate, tax, tribute; cost, damage, loss.

toll[2] *vb* chime, knell, peal, ring, sound. * *n* chime, knell, peal, ring, ringing, tolling.

tomb *n* catacomb, charnel house, crypt, grave, mausoleum, sepulchre, vault.

tone *vb* blend, harmonize, match, suit. * *n* note, sound; accent, cadence, emphasis, inflection, intonation, modulation; key, mood, strain, temper; elasticity, energy, force, health, strength, tension, vigour; cast, colour, manner, hue, shade, style, tint; drift, tenor.

tongue *n* accent, dialect, language, utterance, vernacular; discourse, parlance, speech, talk; nation, race.

too *adv* additionally, also, further, likewise, moreover, overmuch.

toothsome *adj* agreeable, dainty, delicious, luscious, nice, palatable, savoury.

top *vb* cap, head, tip; ride, surmount; outgo, surpass. * *adj* apical, best, chief, culminating, finest, first, foremost, highest, leading, prime, principal, topmost, uppermost. * *n* acme, apex, crest, crown, head, meridian, pinnacle, summit, surface, vertex, zenith.

topic *n* business, question, subject, text, theme, thesis; division, head, subdivision; commonplace, dictum, maxim, precept, proposition, principle, rule; arrangement, scheme.

topple *vb* fall, overturn, tumble, upset.

torment *vb* annoy, agonize, distress, excruciate, pain, rack, torture; badger, fret, harass, harry, irritate, nettle, plague, provoke, tantalize, tease, trouble, vex, worry. * *n* agony, anguish, pang, rack, torture.

tornado *n* blizzard, cyclone, gale, hurricane, storm, tempest, typhoon, whirlwind.

torpid *adj* benumbed, lethargic, motionless, numb; apathetic, dormant, dull, inactive, indolent, inert, listless, sleepy, slothful, sluggish, stupid.

torpor *n* coma, insensibility, lethargy, numbness, torpidity; inaction, inactivity, inertness, sluggishness, stupidity.

torrid *adj* arid, burnt, dried, parched; burning, fiery, hot, parching, scorching, sultry, tropical, violent.

tortuous *adj* crooked, curved, curvilineal, curvilinear, serpentine, sinuate, sinuated, sinuous, twisted, winding; ambiguous, circuitous, crooked, deceitful, indirect, perverse, roundabout.

torture *vb* agonize, distress, excruciate, pain, rack, torment.* *n* agony, anguish, distress, pain, pang, rack, torment.

toss *vb* cast, fling, hurl, pitch, throw; agitate, rock, shake; disquiet, harass, try; roll, writhe. * *n* cast, fling, pitch, throw.

total *vb* add, amount to, reach, reckon. * *adj* complete, entire, full, whole; integral, undivided. * *n* aggregate, all, gross, lump, mass, sum, totality, whole.

totter *vb* falter, reel, stagger, vacillate; lean, oscillate, reel, rock, shake, sway, tremble, waver; fail, fall, flag.

touch *vb* feel, graze, handle, hit, pat, strike, tap; concern, interest, regard; affect, impress, move, stir; grasp, reach, stretch; melt, mollify, soften; afflict, distress, hurt, injure, molest, sting, wound. * *n* hint, smack, suggestion, suspicion, taste, trace; blow, contract, hit, pat, tap.

touchiness *n* fretfulness, irritability, irascibility, peevishness, pettishness, petulance, snappishness, spleen, testiness.

touching *adj* affecting, heart-rending, impressive, melting, moving, pathetic, pitiable, tender; abutting, adjacent, bordering, tangent.

touchy *adj* choleric, cross, fretful, hot-tempered, irascible, irritable, peevish, petulant, quick-tempered, snappish, splenetic, tetchy, testy, waspish.

tough *adj* adhesive, cohesive, flexible, tenacious; coriaceous, leathery; clammy, ropy, sticky, viscous; inflexible, intractable, rigid, stiff; callous, hard, obdurate, stubborn; difficult, formidable, hard, troublesome. * *n* brute, bully, hooligan, ruffian, thug.

tour *vb* journey, perambulate, travel, visit. * *n* circuit, course, excursion, expedition, journey, perambulation, pilgrimage, round.

tow *vb* drag, draw, haul, pull, tug. * *n* drag, lift, pull.

tower *vb* mount, rise, soar, transcend. * *n* belfry, bell tower, column, minaret, spire, steeple, turret; castle, citadel, fortress, stronghold; pillar, refuge, rock, support.

towering *adj* elevated, lofty; excessive, extreme, prodigious, violent.

toy *vb* dally, play, sport, trifle, wanton. * *n* bauble, doll, gewgaw, gimmick, knick-knack, plaything, puppet, trinket; bagatelle, bubble, trifle; play, sport.

trace *vb* follow, track, train; copy, deduce, delineate, derive, describe, draw, sketch. * *n* evidence, footmark, footprint, footstep, impression, mark, remains, sign, token, track, trail, vestige, wake; memorial, record; bit, dash, flavour, hint, suspicion, streak, tinge.

track *vb* chase, draw, follow, pursue, scent, track, trail. * *n* footmark, footprint, footstep, spoor, trace, vestige; course, pathway, rails, road, runway, trace, trail, wake, way.

trackless *adj* pathless, solitary, unfrequented, unused.

tract[1] *n* area, district, quarter, region, territory; parcel, patch, part, piece, plot, portion.

tract[2] *n* disquisition, dissertation, essay, homily, pamphlet, sermon, thesis, tractate, treatise.

tractable *adj* amenable, docile, governable, manageable, submissive, willing, yielding; adaptable, ductile, malleable, plastic, tractile.

trade *vb* bargain, barter, chaffer, deal, exchange, interchange, sell, traffic. * *n* bargaining, barter, business, commerce, dealing, traffic; avocation, calling, craft, employment, occupation, office, profession, pursuit, vocation.

traditional *adj* accustomed, apocryphal, customary, established, historic, legendary, old, oral, transmitted, uncertain, unverified, unwritten.

traduce *vb* abuse, asperse, blemish, brand, calumniate, decry, defame, depreciate, disparage, revile, malign, slander, vilify.

traducer *n* calumniator, defamer, detractor, slanderer, vilifier.

traffic *vb* bargain, barter, chaffer, deal, exchange, trade. * *n* barter, business, chaffer, commerce, exchange, intercourse, trade, transportation, truck.

tragedy *n* drama, play; adversity, calamity, catastrophe, disaster, misfortune.

tragic *adj* dramatic; calamitous, catastrophic, disastrous, dreadful, fatal, grievous, heart-breaking, mournful, sad, shocking, sorrowful.

trail *vb* follow, hunt, trace, track; drag, draw, float, flow, haul, pull. * *n* footmark, footprint, footstep, mark, trace, track.

train *vb* drag, draw, haul, trail, tug; allure, entice; discipline, drill, educate, exercise, instruct, school, teach; accustom, break in, familiarize, habituate, inure, prepare, rehearse, use. * *n* trail, wake; entourage, cortege, followers, retinue, staff, suite; chain, consecution, sequel, series, set, succession; course, method, order, process; allure, artifice, device, enticement, lure, persuasion, stratagem, trap.

trait *n* line, mark, stroke, touch; characteristic, feature, lineage,particularity, peculiarity, quality.

traitor *n* apostate, betrayer, deceiver, Judas, miscreant, quisling, renegade, turncoat; conspirator, deserter, insurgent, mutineer, rebel, revolutionary.

traitorous *adj* faithless, false, perfidious, recreant, treacherous; insidious, treasonable.

trammel *vb* clog, confine, cramp, cumber, hamper, hinder, fetter, restrain, restrict, shackle, tie. * *n* bond, chain, fetter, hindrance, impediment, net, restraint, shackle.

tramp *vb* hike, march, plod, trudge, walk. * *n* excursion, journey, march, walk; landloper, loafer, stroller, tramper, vagabond, vagrant.

trample *vb* crush, tread; scorn, spurn.

trance *n* dream, ecstasy, hypnosis, rapture; catalepsy, coma.

tranquil *adj* calm, hushed, peaceful, placid, quiet, serene, still, undisturbed, unmoved, unperturbed, unruffled, untroubled.

tranquillity *n* calmness, peace, peacefulness, placidity, placidness, quiet, quietness, serenity, stillness, tranquilness.

tranquillize *vb* allay, appease, assuage, calm, compose, hush, lay, lull, moderate, pacify, quell, quiet, silence, soothe, still.

transact *vb* conduct, dispatch, enact, execute, do, manage, negotiate, perform, treat.

transaction *n* act, action, conduct, doing, management, negotiation, performance; affair, business, deal, dealing, incident, event, job, matter, occurrence, procedure, proceeding.

transcend *vb* exceed, overlap, overstep, pass, transgress; excel, outstrip, outrival, outvie, overtop, surmount, surpass.

transcendent *adj* consummate, inimitable, peerless, pre-eminent, supereminent, surpassing, unequalled, unparalleled, unrivalled, unsurpassed; metempiric, metempirical, noumenal, super-sensible.

transcript *n* duplicate, engrossment, rescript.

transfer *vb* convey, dispatch, move, remove, send, translate, transmit, transplant, transport; abalienate, alienate, assign, cede, confer, convey, consign, deed, devise, displace, forward, grant, pass, relegate. * *n* abalienation, alienation, assignment, bequest, carriage, cession, change, conveyance, copy, demise, devisal, gift, grant, move, relegation, removal, shift, shipment, transference, transferring, transit, transmission, transportation.

transfigure *vb* change, convert, dignify, idealize, metamorphose, transform.

transform *vb* alter, change, metamorphose, transfigure; convert, resolve, translate, transmogrify, transmute.

transgress *vb* exceed, transcend, overpass, overstep; break, contravene, disobey, infringe, violate; err, intrude, offend, sin, slip, trespass.

transgression *n* breach, disobedience, encroachment, infraction, infringement, transgression, violation; crime, delinquency, error, fault, iniquity, misdeed, misdemeanour, misdoing, offence, sin, slip, trespass, wrongdoing.

transient *adj* diurnal, ephemeral, evanescent, fleeting, fugitive, impertinent, meteoric, mortal, passing, perishable, short-lived, temporary, transitory, volatile; hasty, imperfect, momentary, short.

transitory *adj* brief, ephemeral, evanescent, fleeting, flitting, fugacious, momentary, passing, short, temporary, transient.

translate *vb* remove, transfer, transport; construe, decipher, decode, interpret, render, turn.

translucent *adj* diaphanous, hyaline, pellucid, semi-opaque, semi-transparent.

transmit *vb* forward, remit, send; communicate, conduct, radiate; bear, carry, convey.

transparent *adj* bright, clear, diaphanous, limpid, lucid; crystalline, hyaline, pellucid, serene, translucent, transpicuous, unclouded; open, porous, transpicuous; evident, obvious, manifest, patent.

transpire *vb* befall, chance, happen, occur; evaporate, exhale.

transport *vb* bear, carry, cart, conduct, convey, fetch, remove, ship, take, transfer, truck; banish, expel; beatify, delight, enrapture, enravish, entrance, ravish. * n carriage, conveyance, movement, transportation, transporting; beatification, beatitude, bliss, ecstasy, felicity, happiness, rapture, ravishment; frenzy, passion, vehemence, warmth.

transude vb exude, filter, ooze, percolate, strain.

trap vb catch, ensnare, entrap, noose, snare, springe; ambush, deceive, dupe, trick; enmesh, tangle, trepan. * n gin, snare, springe, toil; ambush, artifice, pitfall, stratagem, trepan.

trappings npl adornments, decorations, dress, embellishments, frippery, gear, livery, ornaments, paraphernalia, rigging; accoutrements, caparisons, equipment, gear.

trash n dregs, dross, garbage, refuse, rubbish, trumpery, waste; balderdash, nonsense, twaddle.

travel vb journey, peregrinate, ramble, roam, rove, tour, voyage, walk, wander; go, move, pass. * n excursion, expedition, journey, peregrination, ramble, tour, trip, voyage, walk.

traveller n excursionist, explorer, globe-trotter, itinerant, passenger, pilgrim, rover, sightseer, tourist, trekker, tripper, voyager, wanderer, wayfarer.

traverse vb contravene, counteract, defeat, frustrate, obstruct, oppose, thwart; ford, pass, play, range.

travesty vb imitate, parody, take off. * n burlesque, caricature, imitation, parody, take-off.

treacherous adj deceitful, disloyal, faithless, false, false-hearted, insidious, perfidious, recreant, sly, traitorous, treasonable, unfaithful, unreliable, unsafe, untrustworthy.

treachery n betrayal, deceitfulness, disloyalty, double-dealing, faithlessness, foul play, infidelity, insidiousness, perfidiousness, treason, perfidy.

treason n betrayal, disloyalty, lèse-majesté, lese-majesty, perfidy, sedition, traitorousness, treachery.

treasonable adj disloyal, traitorous, treacherous.

treasure vb accumulate, collect, garner, hoard, husband, save, store; cherish, idolize, prize, value, worship. * n cash, funds, jewels, money, riches, savings, valuables, wealth; abundance, reserve, stock, store.

treasurer n banker, bursar, purser, receiver, trustee.

treat vb entertain, feast, gratify, refresh; attend, doctor, dose, handle, manage, serve; bargain, covenant, negotiate, parley. * n banquet, entertainment, feast; delight, enjoyment, entertainment, gratification, luxury, pleasure, refreshment.

treatise n commentary, discourse, dissertation, disquisition, monograph, tractate.

treatment n usage, use; dealing, handling, management, manipulation; doctoring, therapy.

treaty n agreement, alliance, bargain, compact, concordat, convention, covenant, entente, league, pact.

tremble vb quake, quaver, quiver, shake, shiver, shudder, vibrate, wobble. * n quake, quiver, shake, shiver, shudder, tremor, vibration, wobble.

tremendous adj colossal, enormous, huge, immense; excellent, marvellous, wonderful; alarming, appalling, awful, dreadful, fearful, frightful, horrid, horrible, terrible.

tremor n agitation, quaking, quivering, shaking, trembling, trepidation, tremulousness, vibration.

tremulous adj afraid, fearful, quavering, quivering, shaking, shaky, shivering, timid, trembling, vibrating.

trench vb carve, cut; ditch, channel, entrench, furrow. * n channel, ditch, drain, furrow, gutter, moat, pit, sewer, trough; dugout, entrenchment, fortification.

trenchant adj cutting, keen, sharp; acute, biting, caustic, crisp, incisive, pointed, piquant, pungent, sarcastic, sententious, severe, unsparing, vigorous.

trend vb drift, gravitate, incline, lean, run, stretch, sweep, tend, turn. * n bent, course, direction, drift, inclination, set, leaning, tendency, trending.

trepidation n agitation, quaking, quivering, shaking, trembling, tremor; dismay, excitement, fear, perturbation, tremulousness.

trespass vb encroach, infringe, intrude, trench; offend, sin, transgress. * n encroachment, infringement, injury, intrusion, invasion; crime, delinquency, error, fault, sin, misdeed, misdemeanour, offence, transgression; trespasser.

trial adj experimental, exploratory, testing. * n examination, experiment, test; experience, knowledge; aim, attempt, effort, endeavour, essay, exertion, struggle; assay, criterion, ordeal, prohibition, proof, test, touchstone; affliction, burden, chagrin, dolour, distress, grief, hardship, heartache, inclination, misery, mortification, pain, sorrow, suffering, tribulation, trouble, unhappiness, vexation, woe, wretchedness; action, case, cause, hearing, suit.

tribe n clan, family, lineage, race, sept, stock; class, distinction, division, order.

tribulation n adversity, affliction, distress, grief, misery, pain, sorrow, suffering, trial, trouble, unhappiness, woe, wretchedness.

tribunal n bench, judgement seat; assizes, bar, court, judicature, session.

tribute n subsidy, tax; custom, duty, excise, impost, tax, toll; contribution, grant, offering.

trice n flash, instant, jiffy, moment, second, twinkling.

trick vb cheat, circumvent, cozen, deceive, defraud, delude, diddle, dupe, fob, gull, hoax, overreach. * n artifice, blind, deceit, deception, dodge, fake, feint, fraud, game, hoax, imposture, manoeuvre, shift, ruse, swindle, stratagem, wile; antic, caper, craft, deftness, gambol, sleight; habit, mannerism, peculiarity, practice.

trickle vb distil, dribble, drip, drop, ooze, percolate, seep. * n dribble, drip, percolation, seepage.

tricky adj artful, cunning, deceitful, deceptive, subtle, trickish.

trifle vb dally, dawdle, fool, fribble, palter, play, potter, toy. * n bagatelle, bauble, bean, fig, nothing, triviality; iota, jot, modicum, particle, trace.

trifling adj empty, frippery, frivolous, inconsiderable, insignificant, nugatory, petty, piddling, shallow, slight, small, trivial, unimportant, worthless.

trill vb shake, quaver, warble. * n quaver, shake, tremolo, warbling.

trim vb adjust, arrange, prepare; balance, equalize, fill; adorn, array, bedeck, decorate, dress, embellish, garnish, ornament; clip, curtail, cut, lop, mow, poll, prune, shave, shear; berate, chastise, chide, rebuke, reprimand, reprove, trounce; fluctuate, hedge, shift, shuffle, vacillate. * adj compact, neat, nice, shapely, snug, tidy, well-adjusted, well-ordered; chic, elegant, finical, smart, spruce. * n dress, embellishment, gear, ornaments, trappings, trimmings; case, condition, order, plight, state.

trinket n bagatelle, bauble, bijoux, gewgaw, gimcrack, knick-knack, toy, trifle.

trinkets *npl* bijouterie, jewellery, jewels, ornaments.

trip *vb* caper, dance, frisk, hop, skip; misstep, stumble; bungle, blunder, err, fail, mistake; overthrow, supplant, upset; catch, convict, detect. * *n* hop, skip; lurch, misstep, stumble; blunder, bungle, error, failure, fault, lapse, miss, mistake, oversight, slip; circuit, excursion, expedition, jaunt, journey, ramble, route, stroll, tour.

trite *adj* banal, beaten, common, commonplace, hackneyed, old, ordinary, stale, stereotyped, threadbare, usual, worn.

triturate *vb* beat, bray, bruise, grind, pound, rub, thrash; comminute, levigate, pulverize.

triumph *vb* exult, rejoice; prevail, succeed, win; flourish, prosper, thrive; boast, brag, crow, gloat, swagger, vaunt. * *n* celebration, exultation, joy, jubilation, jubilee, ovation; accomplishment, achievement, conquest, success, victory.

triumphant *adj* boastful, conquering, elated, exultant, exulting, jubilant, rejoicing, successful, victorious.

trivial *adj* frivolous, gimcrack, immaterial, inconsiderable, insignificant, light, little, nugatory, paltry, petty, small, slight, slim, trifling, trumpery, unimportant.

trollop *n* prostitute, slattern, slut, whore.

troop *vb* crowd, flock, muster, throng. * *n* company, crowd, flock, herd, multitude, number, throng; band, body, party, squad, troupe.

trophy *n* laurels, medal, palm, prize.

troth *n* candour, sincerity, truth, veracity, verity; allegiance, belief, faith, fidelity, word; betrothal.

trouble *vb* agitate, confuse, derange, disarrange, disorder, disturb; afflict, ail, annoy, badger, concern, disquiet, distress, fret, grieve, harass, molest, perplex, perturb, pester, plague, torment, vex, worry. * *n* adversity, affliction, calamity, distress, dolour, grief, hardship, misfortune, misery, pain, sorrow, suffering, tribulation, woe; ado, annoyance, anxiety, bother, care, discomfort, embarrassment, fuss, inconvenience, irritation, pains, perplexity, plague, torment, vexation, worry; commotion, disturbance, row; bewilderment, disquietude, embarrassment, perplexity, uneasiness.

troublesome *adj* annoying, distressing, disturbing, galling, grievous, harassing, painful, perplexing, vexatious, worrisome; burdensome, irksome, tiresome, wearisome; importunate, intrusive, teasing; arduous, difficult, hard, inconvenient, trying, unwieldy.

troublous *adj* agitated, disquieted, disturbed, perturbed, tumultuous, turbulent.

trough *n* hutch, manger; channel, depression, hollow, furrow.

truant *vb* be absent, desert, dodge, malinger, shirk, skive. * *n* absentee, deserter, idler, laggard, loiterer, lounger, malingerer, quitter, runaway, shirker, vagabond.

truce *n* armistice, breathing space, cessation, delay, intermission, lull, pause, recess, reprieve, respite, rest.

truck *vb* barter, deal, exchange, trade, traffic. * *n* lorry, van, wagon.

truckle *vb* roll, trundle; cringe, crouch, fawn, knuckle, stoop, submit, yield.

truculent *adj* barbarous, bloodthirsty, ferocious, fierce, savage; cruel, malevolent, relentless; destructive, deadly, fatal, ruthless.

true *adj* actual, unaffected, authentic, genuine, legitimate, pure, real, rightful, sincere, sound, truthful, veritable; substantial, veracious; constant, faithful, loyal, staunch, steady; equitable, honest, honourable, just, upright, trusty, trustworthy, virtuous; accurate, correct, even, exact, right, straight, undeviating. * *adv* good, well.

truism *n* axiom, commonplace, platitude.

trumpery *adj* pinchbeck, rubbishy, trashy, trifling, worthless. * *n* deceit, deception, falsehood, humbug, imposture; frippery, rubbish, stuff, trash, trifles.

truncheon *n* club, cudgel, nightstick, partisan, staff; baton, wand.

trunk *n* body, bole, butt, shaft, stalk, stem, stock, torso; box, chest, coffer.

trundle *vb* bowl, revolve, roll, spin, truckle, wheel.

truss *vb* bind, bundle, close, cram, hang, pack. * *n* bundle, package, packet; apparatus, bandage, support.

trust *vb* confide, depend, expect, hope, rely; believe, credit; commit, entrust. * *n* belief, confidence, credence, faith; credit, tick; charge, deposit; commission, duty, errand; assurance, conviction, expectation, hope, reliance, secutity.

trustful *adj* confiding, trusting, unquestioning, unsuspecting; faithful, trustworthy, trusty.

trustworthy *adj* confidential, constant, credible, dependable, faithful, firm, honest, incorrupt, upright, reliable, responsible, straightforward, staunch, true, trusty, uncorrupt, upright.

truth *n* fact, reality, veracity; actuality, authenticity, realism; canon, law, oracle, principle; right, truthfulness, veracity; candour, fidelity, frankness, honesty, honour, ingenuousness, integrity, probity, sincerity, virtue; constancy, devotion, faith, fealty, loyalty, steadfastness; accuracy, correctness, exactitude, exactness, nicety, precision, regularity, trueness.

truthful *adj* correct, reliable, true, trustworthy, veracious; artless, candid, frank, guileless, honest, ingenuous, open, sincere, straightforward, trusty.

truthless *adj* canting, disingenuous, dishonest, false, faithless, hollow, hypocritical, insincere, pharisaical, treacherous, unfair, untrustworthy.

try *vb* examine, prove, test; attempt, essay; adjudicate, adjudge, examine, hear; purify, refine; sample, sift, smell, taste; aim, attempt, endeavour, seek, strain, strive. * *n* attempt, effort, endeavour, experiment, trial.

trying *adj* difficult, fatiguing, hard, irksome, tiresome, wearisome; afflicting, afflictive, calamitous, deplorable, dire, distressing, grievous, hard, painful, sad, severe.

tryst *n* appointment, assignation, rendezvous.

tube *n* bore, bronchus, cylinder, duct, hollow, hose, pipe, pipette, worm.

tuft *n* brush, bunch, crest, feather, knot, plume, topknot, tussock; clump, cluster, group.

tug *vb* drag, draw, haul, pull, tow, wrench; labour, strive, struggle. * *n* drag, haul, pull, tow, wrench.

tuition *n* education, instruction, schooling, teaching, training.

tumble *vb* heave, pitch, roll, toss, wallow; fall, sprawl, stumble, topple, trip; derange, disarrange, dishevel, disorder, disturb, rumple, tousle. * *n* collapse, drop, fall, plunge, spill, stumble, trip.

tumbler *n* acrobat, juggler; glass.

tumid *adj* bloated, distended, enlarged, puffed-up, swelled, swollen, turgid; bombastic, declamatory, fustian, grandiloquent, grandiose, high-flown, inflated, pompous, puffy, rhetorical, stilted, swelling.

tumour *n* boil, carbuncle, swelling, tumefaction.

tumult n ado, affray, agitation, altercation, bluster, brawl, disturbance, ferment, flurry, feud, fracas, fray, fuss, hubbub, huddle, hurly-burly, melee, noise, perturbation, pother, quarrel, racket, riot, row, squabble, stir, turbulence, turmoil, uproar.

tumultuous adj blustery, breezy, bustling, confused, disorderly, disturbed, riotous, turbulent, unruly.

tune vb accord, attune, harmonize, modulate; adapt, adjust, attune. * n air, aria, melody, strain, tone; agreement, concord, harmony; accord, order.

tuneful adj dulcet, harmonious, melodious, musical.

turbid adj foul, impure, muddy, thick, unsettled.

turbulence n agitation, commotion, confusion, disorder, disturbance, excitement, tumult, tumultuousness, turmoil, unruliness, uproar; insubordination, insurrection, mutiny, rebellion, riot, sedition.

turbulent adj agitated, disturbed, restless, tumultuous, wild; blatant, blustering, boisterous, brawling, disorderly, obstreperous, tumultuous, uproarious, vociferous; factious, insubordinate, insurgent, mutinous, raging, rebellious, refractory, revolutionary, riotous, seditious, stormy, violent.

turf n grass, greensward, sod, sward; horse racing, race-course, race-ground.

turgid adj bloated, distended, protuberant, puffed-up, swelled, swollen, tumid; bombastic, declamatory, diffuse, digressive, fustian, high-flown, inflated, grandiloquent, grandiose, ostentatious, pompous, puffy, rhetorical, stilted.

turmoil n activity, agitation, bustle, commotion, confusion, disorder, disturbance, ferment, flurry, huddle, hubbub, hurly-burly, noise, trouble, tumult, turbulence, uproar.

turn vb revolve, rotate; bend, cast, defect, inflict, round, spin, sway, swivel, twirl, twist, wheel; crank, grind, wind; deflect, divert, transfer, warp; form, mould, shape; adapt, fit, manoeuvre, suit; alter, change, conform, metamorphose, transform, transmute, vary; convert, persuade, prejudice; construe, render, translate; depend, hang, hinge, pivot; eventuate, issue, result, terminate; acidify, curdle, ferment. * n cycle, gyration, revolution, rotation, round; bending, deflection, deviation, diversion, doubling, flection, flexion, flexure, reel, retroversion, slew, spin, sweep, swing, swirl, swivel, turning, twist, twirl, whirl, winding; alteration, change, variation, vicissitude; bend, circuit, drive, ramble, run, round, stroll; bout, hand, innings, opportunity, shift, spell; act, action, deed, office; convenience, occasion, purpose; cast, fashion, form, guise, manner, mould, phase, shape; aptitude, bent, bias, disposition, faculty, genius, gift, inclination, leaning, proclivity, proneness, propensity, talent, tendency.

turncoat n apostate, backslider, deserter, recreant, renegade, traitor, wretch.

turpitude n baseness, degradation, depravity, vileness, wickedness.

turret n cupola, minaret, pinnacle.

tussle vb conflict, contend, contest, scuffle, struggle, wrestle. * n conflict, contest, fight, scuffle, struggle.

tutelage n care, charge, dependence, guardianship, protection, teaching, tutorage, tutorship, wardship.

tutor vb coach, educate, instruct, teach; discipline, train. * n coach, governess, governor, instructor, master, preceptor, schoolteacher, teacher.

twaddle vb chatter, gabble, maunder, prate, prattle. * n balderdash, chatter, flummery, gabble, gibberish, gobbledegook, gossip, jargon, moonshine, nonsense, platitude, prate, prattle, rigmarole, stuff, tattle.

tweak vb, n jerk, pinch, pull, twinge, twitch.

twig[1] n bough, branch, offshoot, shoot, slip, spray, sprig, stick, switch.

twig[2] vb catch on, comprehend, discover, grasp, realize, recognize, see, understand.

twin vb couple, link, match, pair. * adj double, doubled, duplicate, geminate, identical, matched, matching, second, twain. * n corollary, double, duplicate, fellow, likeness, match.

twine vb embrace, encircle, entwine, interlace, surround, wreathe; bend, meander, wind; coil, twist. * n convolution, coil, twist; embrace, twining, winding; cord, string.

twinge vb pinch, tweak, twitch. * n pinch, tweak, twitch; gripe, pang, spasm.

twinkle vb blink, twink, wink; flash, glimmer, scintillate, sparkle. * n blink, flash, gleam, glimmer, scintillation, sparkle; flash, instant, jiffy, moment, second, tick, trice, twinkling.

twinkling n flashing, sparkling, twinkle; flash, instant, jiffy, moment, second, tick, trice.

twirl vb revolve, rotate, spin, turn, twist, twirl. * n convolution, revolution, turn, twist, whirling.

twist vb purl, rotate, spin, twine; complicate, contort, convolute, distort, pervert, screw, wring; coil, writhe; encircle, wind, wreathe. * n coil, curl, spin, twine; braid, roll; change, complication, development, variation; bend, convolution, turn; defect, distortion, flaw, imperfection; jerk, pull, sprain, wrench; aberration, characteristic, eccentricity, oddity, peculiarity, quirk.

twit[1] vb banter, blame, censure, reproach, taunt, tease, upbraid.

twit[2] n blockhead, fool, idiot, nincompoop, nitwit.

twitch vb jerk, pluck, pull, snatch. * n jerk, pull; contraction, pull, quiver, spasm, twitching.

type n emblem, mark, stamp; adumbration, image, representation, representative, shadow, sign, symbol, token; archetype, exemplar, model, original, pattern, prototype, protoplast, standard; character, form, kind, nature, sort; figure, letter, text, typography.

typical adj emblematic, exemplary, figurative, ideal, indicative, model, representative, symbolic, true.

typify vb betoken, denote, embody, exemplify, figure, image, indicate, represent, signify.

tyrannical adj absolute, arbitrary, autocratic, cruel, despotic, dictatorial, domineering, high, imperious, irresponsible, severe, tyrannical, unjust; galling, grinding, inhuman, oppressive, overbearing, severe.

tyranny n absolutism, autocracy, despotism, dictatorship, harshness, oppression.

tyrant n autocrat, despot, dictator, oppressor.

tyro n beginner, learner, neophyte, novice; dabbler, smatterer.

U

ubiquitous *adj* omnipresent, present, universal.

udder *n* nipple, pap, teat.

ugly *adj* crooked, homely, ill-favoured, plain, ordinary, unlovely, unprepossessing, unshapely, unsightly; forbidding, frightful, gruesome, hideous, horrible, horrid, loathsome, monstrous, shocking, terrible, repellent, repulsive; bad-tempered, cantankerous, churlish, cross, quarrelsome, spiteful, surly, spiteful, vicious.

ulcer *n* boil, fester, gathering, pustule, sore.

ulterior *adj* beyond, distant, farther; hidden, personal, secret, selfish, undisclosed.

ultimate *adj* conclusive, decisive, eventual, extreme, farthest, final, last. * *n* acme, consummation, culmination, height, peak, pink, quintessence, summit.

ultra *adj* advanced, beyond, extreme, radical.

umbrage *n* shadow, shade; anger, displeasure, dissatisfaction, dudgeon, injury, offence, pique, resentment.

umpire *vb* adjudicate, arbitrate, judge, referee. * *n* adjudicator, arbiter, arbitrator, judge, referee.

unabashed *adj* bold, brazen, confident, unblushing, undaunted, undismayed.

unable *adj* impotent, incapable, incompetent, powerless, weak.

unacceptable *adj* disagreeable, distasteful, offensive, unpleasant, unsatisfactory, unwelcome.

unaccommodating *adj* disobliging, noncompliant, uncivil, ungracious.

unaccomplished *adj* incomplete, unachieved, undone, unperformed, unexecuted, unfinished; ill-educated, uncultivated, unpolished.

unaccountable *adj* inexplicable, incomprehensible, inscrutable, mysterious, unintelligible; irresponsible, unanswerable.

unaccustomed *adj* uninitiated, unskilled, unused; foreign, new, strange, unfamiliar, unusual.

unaffected *adj* artless, honest, naive, natural, plain, simple, sincere, real, unfeigned; chaste, pure, unadorned; insensible, unchanged, unimpressed, unmoved, unstirred, untouched.

unanimity *n* accord, agreement, concert, concord, harmony, union, unity.

unanimous *adj* agreeing, concordant, harmonious, likeminded, solid, united.

unassuming *adj* humble, modest, reserved, unobtrusive, unpretending, unpretentious.

unattainable *adj* inaccessible, unobtainable.

unavailing *adj* abortive, fruitless, futile, ineffectual, ineffective, inept, nugatory, unsuccessful, useless, vain.

unbalanced *adj* unsound, unsteady; unadjusted, unsettled.

unbearable *adj* insufferable, insupportable, unendurable.

unbecoming *adj* inappropriate, indecent, indecorous, improper, unbefitting, unbeseeming, unseemly, unsuitable.

unbelief *n* disbelief, dissent, distrust, incredulity, incredulousness, miscreance, miscreancy, nonconformity; doubt, freethinking, infidelity, scepticism.

unbeliever *n* agnostic, deist, disbeliever, doubter, heathen, infidel, sceptic.

unbending *adj* inflexible, rigid, stiff, unpliant, unyielding; firm, obstinate, resolute, stubborn.

unbiased *adj* disinterested, impartial, indifferent, neutral, uninfluenced, unprejudiced, unwarped.

unbind *vb* loose, undo, unfasten, unloose, untie; free, unchain, unfetter.

unblemished *adj* faultless, guiltless, immaculate, impeccable, innocent, intact, perfect, pure, sinless, spotless, stainless, undefiled, unspotted, unsullied, untarnished.

unblushing *adj* boldfaced, impudent, shameless.

unbounded *adj* absolute, boundless, endless, immeasurable, immense, infinite, interminable, measureless, unlimited, vast; immoderate, uncontrolled, unrestrained, unrestricted.

unbridled *adj* dissolute, intractable, lax, licensed, licentious, loose, uncontrolled, ungovernable, unrestrained, violent, wanton.

unbroken *adj* complete, entire, even, full, intact, unimpaired; constant, continuous, fast, profound, sound, successive, undisturbed; inviolate, unbetrayed, unviolated.

unbuckle *vb* loose, unfasten, unloose.

uncanny *adj* inopportune, unsafe; eerie, eery, ghostly, unearthly, unnatural, weird.

unceremonious *adj* abrupt, bluff, blunt, brusque, course, curt, gruff, plain, rough, rude, ungracious; casual, familiar, informal, offhand, unconstrained.

uncertain *adj* ambiguous, doubtful, dubious, equivocal, indefinite, indeterminate, indistinct, questionable, unsettled; insecure, precarious, problematical; capricious, changeable, desultory, fitful, fluctuating, irregular, mutable, shaky, slippery, unreliable, variable.

unchaste *adj* dissolute, incontinent, indecent, immoral, lascivious, lecherous, libidinous, lewd, loose, obscene, wanton.

unchecked *adj* uncurbed, unhampered, unhindered, unobstructed, unrestrained, untrammelled.

uncivil *adj* bearish, blunt, boorish, brusque, discourteous, disobliging, disrespectful, gruff, ill-bred, ill-mannered, impolite, irreverent, rough, rude, uncomplaisant, uncourteous, uncouth, ungentle, ungracious, unmannered, unseemly.

unclean *adj* abominable, beastly, dirty, filthy, foul, grimy, grubby, miry, muddy, nasty, offensive, purulent, repulsive, soiled, sullied; improper, indecent, indecorous, obscene, polluted, risqué, sinful, smutty, unholy, uncleanly.

uncomfortable *adj* disagreeable, displeasing, disquieted, distressing, disturbed, uneasy, unpleasant, restless; cheerless, close, oppressive; dismal, miserable, unhappy.

uncommon *adj* choice, exceptional, extraordinary, infrequent, noteworthy, odd, original, queer, rare, remarkable, scarce, singular, strange, unexampled, unfamiliar, unusual, unwonted.

uncommunicative *adj* close, inconversable, reserved, reticent, taciturn, unsociable, unsocial.

uncomplaining *adj* long-suffering, meek, patient, resigned, tolerant.

uncompromising *adj* inflexible, narrow, obstinate, orthodox, rigid, stiff, strict, unyielding.

unconcerned *adj* apathetic, careless, indifferent.

unconditional *adj* absolute, categorical, complete, entire, free, full, positive, unlimited, unqualified, unreserved, unrestricted.

uncongenial *adj* antagonistic, discordant, displeasing, ill-assorted, incompatible, inharmonious, mismatched, unsuited, unsympathetic.

uncouth *adj* awkward, boorish, clownish, clumsy, gawky, inelegant, loutish, lubberly, rough, rude, rustic, uncourtly, ungainly, unpolished, unrefined, unseemly; odd, outlandish, strange, unfamiliar, unusual.

uncover *vb* denude, divest, lay bare, strip; disclose, discover, expose, reveal, unmask, unveil; bare, doff; open, unclose, unseal.

unctuous *adj* adipose, greasy, oily, fat, fatty, oleaginous, pinguid, sebaceous; bland, lubricious, smooth, slippery; bland, fawning, glib, obsequious, plausible, servile, suave, sycophantic; fervid, gushing.

uncultivated *adj* fallow, uncultured, unreclaimed, untilled; homely, ignorant, illiterate, rude, uncivilized, uncultured, uneducated, unfit, unlettered, unpolished, unread, unready, unrefined, untaught; rough, savage, sylvan, uncouth, wild.

undaunted *adj* bold, brave, courageous, dauntless, fearless, intrepid, plucky, resolute, undismayed.

undefiled *adj* clean, immaculate, pure, spotless, stainless, unblemished, unspotted, unsullied, untarnished; honest, innocent, inviolate, pure, uncorrupted, unpolluted, unstained.

undemonstrative *adj* calm, composed, demure, impassive, modest, placid, quiet, reserved, sedate, sober, staid, tranquil.

undeniable *adj* certain, conclusive, evident, incontestable, incontrovertible, indisputable, indubitable, obvious, unquestionable.

under *prep* below, beneath, inferior to, lower than, subordinate to, underneath. * *adv* below, beneath, down, lower.

underestimate *vb* belittle, underrate, undervalue.

undergo *vb* bear, endure, experience, suffer, sustain.

underhand *adj* clandestine, deceitful, disingenuous, fraudulent, hidden, secret, sly, stealthy, underhanded, unfair. * *adv* clandestinely, privately, secretly, slyly, stealthily, surreptitiously; fraudulently, unfairly.

underling *n* agent, inferior, servant, subordinate.

undermine *vb* excavate, mine, sap; demoralize, foil, frustrate, thwart, weaken.

understand *vb* apprehend, catch, comprehend, conceive, discern, grasp, know, penetrate, perceive, see, seize, twig; assume, interpret, take; imply, mean.

understanding *adj* compassionate, considerate, forgiving, kind, kindly, patient, sympathetic, tolerant. * *n*

brains, comprehension, discernment, faculty, intellect, intelligence, judgement, knowledge, mind, reason, sense.

undertake *vb* assume, attempt, begin, embark on, engage in, enter upon, take in hand; agree, bargain, contract, covenant, engage, guarantee, promise, stipulate.

undertaking *n* adventure, affair, attempt, business, effort, endeavour, engagement, enterprise, essay, move, project, task, venture.

undesigned *adj* spontaneous, unintended, unintentional, unplanned, unpremeditated.

undigested *adj* crude, ill-advised, ill-considered, illjudged; confused, disorderly, ill-arranged, unmethodical.

undivided *adj* complete, entire, whole; one, united.

undo *vb* annul, cancel, frustrate, invalidate, neutralize, nullify, offset, reverse; disengage, loose, unfasten, unmake, unravel, untie; crush, destroy, overturn, ruin.

undoubted *adj* incontrovertible, indisputable, indubitable, undisputed, unquestionable, unquestioned.

undress *vb* denude, dismantle, disrobe, unclothe, unrobe, peel, strip. * *n* disarray, nakedness, nudity; mufti, negligee.

undue *adj* illegal, illegitimate, improper, unlawful, excessive, disproportionate, disproportioned, immoderate, unsuitable; unfit.

undulation *n* billowing, fluctuation, pulsation, ripple, wave.

undying *adj* deathless, endless, immortal, imperishable.

unearthly *adj* preternatural, supernatural, uncanny, weird.

uneasy *adj* disquieted, disturbed, fidgety, impatient, perturbed, restless, restive, unquiet, worried; awkward, stiff, ungainly, ungraceful; constraining, cramping, disagreeable, uncomfortable.

unending *adj* endless, eternal, everlasting, interminable, never-ending, perpetual, unceasing.

unequal *adj* disproportionate, disproportioned, illmatched, inferior, irregular, insufficient, not alike, uneven.

unequalled *adj* exceeding, incomparable, inimitable, matchless, new, nonpareil, novel, paramount, peerless, pre-eminent, superlative, surpassing, transcendent, unheard of, unique, unparalleled, unrivalled.

unequivocal *adj* absolute, certain, clear, evident, incontestable, indubitable, positive; explicit, unambiguous, unmistakable.

uneven *adj* hilly, jagged, lumpy, ragged, rough, rugged, stony; motley, unequal, variable, variegated.

uneventful *adj* commonplace, dull, eventless, humdrum, quiet, monotonous, smooth, uninteresting.

unexceptionable *adj* excellent, faultless, good, irreproachable.

unexpected *adj* abrupt, sudden, unforeseen.

unfair *adj* dishonest, dishonourable, faithless, false, hypocritical, inequitable, insincere, oblique, onesided, partial, unequal, unjust, wrongful.

unfaithful *adj* adulterous, derelict, deceitful, dishonest, disloyal, false, faithless, fickle, perfidious, treacherous, unreliable; negligent; changeable, inconstant, untrue.

unfamiliar *adj* bizarre, foreign, new, novel, outlandish, queer, singular, strange, uncommon, unusual.

unfashionable *adj* antiquated, destitute, disused, obsolete, old-fashioned, unconventional.

unfavourable adj adverse, contrary, disadvantageous, discouraging, ill, inauspicious, inimical, inopportune, indisposed, malign, sinister, unfriendly, unlucky, unpropitious, untimely; foul, inclement.

unfeeling adj apathetic, callous, heartless, insensible, numb, obdurate, torpid, unconscious, unimpressionable; adamantine, cold-blooded, cruel, hard, merciless, pitiless, stony, unkind, unsympathetic.

unfit vb disable, disqualify, incapacitate. * adj improper, inappropriate, incompetent, inconsistent, unsuitable; ill-equipped, inadequate, incapable, unqualified, useless; debilitated, feeble, flabby, unhealthy, unsound.

unflagging adj constant, indefatigable, never-ending, persevering, steady, unfaltering, unremitting, untiring, unwearied.

unflinching adj firm, resolute, steady, unshrinking.

unfold vb display, expand, open, separate, unfurl, unroll; declare, disclose, reveal, tell; decipher, develop, disentangle, evolve, explain, illustrate, interpret, resolve, unravel.

unfortunate adj hapless, ill-fated, ill-starred, infelicitous, luckless, unhappy, unlucky, unprosperous, unsuccessful, wretched; calamitous, deplorable, disastrous; inappropriate, inexpedient.

unfrequented adj abandoned, deserted, forsaken, lone, solitary, uninhabited, unoccupied.

unfruitful adj barren, fruitless, sterile; infecund, unprolific; unprofitable, unproductive.

ungainly adj awkward, boorish, clownish, clumsy, gawky, inelegant, loutish, lubberly, lumbering, slouching, stiff, uncourtly, uncouth, ungraceful.

ungentlemanly adj ill-bred, impolite, rude, uncivil, ungentle, ungracious, unmannerly.

unhappy adj afflicted, disastrous, dismal, distressed, drear, evil, inauspicious, miserable, painful, unfortunate, wretched.

unhealthy adj ailing, diseased, feeble, indisposed, infirm, poorly, sickly, toxic, unsanitary, unsound, toxic, venomous.

uniform adj alike, constant, even, equable, equal, smooth, steady, regular, unbroken, unchanged, undeviating, unvaried, unvarying. * n costume, dress, livery, outfit, regalia, suit.

uniformity n constancy, continuity, permanence, regularity, sameness, stability; accordance, agreement, conformity, consistency, unanimity.

unimportant adj immaterial, inappreciable, inconsequent, inconsequential, inconsiderable, indifferent, insignificant, mediocre, minor, paltry, petty, small, slight, trifling, trivial.

unintentional adj accidental, casual, fortuitous, inadvertent, involuntary, spontaneous, undesigned, unmeant, unplanned, unpremeditated, unthinking.

uninterrupted adj continuous, endless, incessant, perpetual, unceasing.

union n coalescence, coalition, combination, conjunction, coupling, fusion, incorporation, joining, junction, unification, uniting; agreement, concert, concord, concurrence, harmony, unanimity, unity; alliance, association, club, confederacy, federation, guild, league.

unique adj choice, exceptional, matchless, only, peculiar, rare, single, sole, singular, uncommon, unexampled, unmatched.

unison n accord, accordance, agreement, concord, harmony.

unite vb amalgamate, attach, blend, centralize, coalesce, confederate, consolidate, embody, fuse, incorporate, merge, weld; associate, conjoin, connect, couple, link, marry; combine, join; harmonize, reconcile; agree, concert, concur, cooperate, fraternize.

universal adj all-reaching, catholic, cosmic, encyclopedic, general, ubiquitous, unlimited; all, complete, entire, total, whole.

unjust adj inequitable, injurious, partial, unequal, unfair, unwarranted, wrong, wrongful; flagitious, heinous, influenced, iniquitous, nefarious, unrighteous, wicked; biased, prejudiced, uncandid.

unjustifiable adj indefensible, unjust, unreasonable, unwarrantable; inexcusable, unpardonable.

unknown adj unappreciated, unascertained; undiscovered, unexplored, uninvestigated; concealed, dark, enigmatic, hidden, mysterious, mystic; anonymous, incognito, inglorious, nameless, obscure, renownless, undistinguished, unheralded, unnoted.

unladylike adj ill-bred, impolite, rude, uncivil, ungentle, ungracious, unmannerly.

unlamented adj unmourned, unregretted.

unlimited adj boundless, infinite, interminable, limitless, measureless, unbounded; absolute, full, unconfined, unconstrained, unrestricted; indefinite, undefined.

unlucky adj baleful, disastrous, ill-fated, ill-starred, luckless, unfortunate, unprosperous, unsuccessful; ill-omened, inauspicious; miserable, unhappy.

unmanageable adj awkward, cumbersome, inconvenient, unwieldy; intractable, unruly, unworkable, vicious; difficult, impractical.

unmatched adj matchless, unequalled, unparalleled, unrivalled.

unmitigated adj absolute, complete, consummate, perfect, sheer, stark, thorough, unqualified, utter.

unnatural adj aberrant, abnormal, anomalous, foreign, irregular, prodigious, uncommon; brutal, cold, heartless, inhuman, unfeeling, unusual; affected, artificial, constrained, forced, insincere, self-conscious, stilted, strained; factitious.

unpleasant adj disagreeable, displeasing, distasteful, obnoxious, offensive, repulsive, unlovely, ungrateful, unacceptable, unpalatable, unwelcome.

unpremeditated adj extempore, impromptu, offhand, spontaneous, undesigned, unintentional, unstudied.

unprincipled adj bad, crooked, dishonest, fraudulent, immoral, iniquitous, knavish, lawless, profligate, rascally, roguish, thievish, trickish, tricky, unscrupulous, vicious, villainous, wicked.

unqualified adj disqualified, incompetent, ineligible, unadapted, unfit; absolute, certain, consummate, decided, direct, downright, full, outright, unconditional, unmeasured, unrestricted, unmitigated; exaggerated, sweeping.

unreal adj chimerical, dreamlike, fanciful, flimsy, ghostly, illusory, insubstantial, nebulous, shadowy, spectral, visionary, unsubstantial.

unreasonable adj absurd, excessive, exorbitant, foolish, ill-judged, illogical, immoderate, impractical, injudicious, irrational, nonsensical, preposterous, senseless, silly, stupid, unfair, unreasoning, unwarrantable, unwise.

unreliable adj fallible, fickle, irresponsible, treacherous, uncertain, undependable, unstable, unsure, untrustworthy.

unremitting adj assiduous, constant, continual, diligent, incessant, indefatigable, persevering, sedulous, unabating, unceasing.

unrepentant *adj* abandoned, callous, graceless, hardened, impenitent, incorrigible, irreclaimable, lost, obdurate, profligate, recreant, seared, shameless.

unrequited *adj* unanswered, unreturned, unrewarded.

unreserved *adj* absolute, entire, full, unlimited; aboveboard, artless, candid, communicative, fair, frank, guileless, honest, ingenuous, open, sincere, single-minded, undesigning, undissembling; demonstrative, emotional, open-hearted.

unresisting *adj* compliant, long-suffering, non-resistant, obedient, passive, patient, submissive, yielding.

unresponsive *adj* irresponsive, unsympathetic.

unrestrained *adj* unbridled, unchecked, uncurbed, unfettered, unhindered, unobstructed, unreserved; broad, dissolute, incontinent, inordinate, lax, lewd, licentious, loose, wanton; lawless, wild.

unrestricted *adj* free, unbridled, unconditional, unconfined, uncurbed, unfettered, unlimited, unqualified, unrestrained; clear, open, public, unobstructed.

unrevealed *adj* hidden, occult, secret, undiscovered, unknown.

unrewarded *adj* unpaid, unrecompensed.

unriddle *vb* explain, expound, solve, unfold, unravel.

unrighteous *adj* evil, sinful, ungodly, unholy, vicious, wicked, wrong; heinous, inequitable, iniquitous, nefarious, unfair, unjust.

unripe *adj* crude, green, hard, immature, premature, sour; incomplete, unfinished.

unrivalled *adj* incomparable, inimitable, matchless, peerless, unequalled, unexampled, unique, unparalleled.

unrobe *vb* disrobe, undress.

unroll *vb* develop, discover, evolve, open, unfold; display, lay open.

unromantic *adj* literal, matter-of-fact, prosaic.

unroot *vb* eradicate, extirpate, root out, uproot.

unruffled *adj* calm, peaceful, placid, quiet, serene, smooth, still, tranquil; collected, composed, cool, imperturbable, peaceful, philosophical, placid, tranquil, undisturbed, unexcited, unmoved.

unruly *adj* disobedient, disorderly, fractious, headstrong, insubordinate, intractable, mutinous, obstreperous, rebellious, refractory, riotous, seditious, turbulent, ungovernable, unmanageable, wanton, wild; lawless, obstinate, rebellious, stubborn, vicious.

unsafe *adj* dangerous, hazardous, insecure, perilous, precarious, risky, treacherous, uncertain, unprotected.

unsaid *adj* tacit, unmentioned, unspoken, unuttered.

unsanctified *adj* profane, unhallowed, unholy.

unsatisfactory *adj* insufficient; disappointing; faulty, feeble, imperfect, poor, weak.

unsatisfied *adj* insatiate, unsated, unsatiated, unstaunched; discontented, displeased, dissatisfied, malcontent; undischarged, unpaid, unperformed, unrendered.

unsavoury *adj* flat, insipid, mawkish, savourless, tasteless, unflavoured, unpalatable, vapid; disagreeable, disgusting, distasteful, nasty, nauseating, nauseous, offensive, rank, revolting, sickening, uninviting, unpleasing.

unsay *vb* recall, recant, retract, take back.

unscathed *adj* unharmed, uninjured.

unschooled *adj* ignorant, uneducated, uninstructed; undisciplined, untrained.

unscrupulous *adj* dishonest, reckless, ruthless, unconscientious, unprincipled, unrestrained.

unsealed *adj* open, unclosed.

unsearchable *adj* hidden, incomprehensible, inscrutable, mysterious.

unseasonable *adj* ill-timed, inappropriate, infelicitous, inopportune, untimely; late, too late; inexpedient, undesireable, unfit, ungrateful, unsuitable, unwelcome; premature, too early.

unseasonably *adv* malapropos, unsuitably, untimely.

unseasoned *adj* inexperienced, unaccustomed, unqualified, untrained; immoderate, inordinate, irregular; green; fresh, unsalted.

unseeing *adj* blind, sightless.

unseemly *adj* improper, indecent, inappropriate, indecorous, unbecoming, uncomely, unfit, unmeet, unsuitable.

unseen *adj* undiscerned, undiscovered, unobserved, unperceived; imperceptible, indiscoverable, invisible, latent.

unselfish *adj* altruistic, devoted, disinterested, generous, high-minded, impersonal, liberal, magnanimous, self-denying, self-forgetful, selfless, self-sacrificing.

unserviceable *adj* ill-conditioned, unsound, useless; profitless, unprofitable.

unsettle *vb* confuse, derange, disarrange, disconcert, disorder, disturb, trouble, unbalance, unfix, unhinge, upset.

unsettled *adj* changeable, fickle, inconstant, restless, transient, unstable, unsteady, vacillating, wavering; inequable, unequal; feculent, muddy, roiled, roily, turbid; adrift, afloat, homeless, unestablished, uninhabited; open, tentative, unadjusted, undecided, undetermined; due, outstanding, owing, unpaid; perturbed, troubled, unnerved.

unshackle *vb* emancipate, liberate, loose, release, set free, unbind, unchain, unfetter.

unshaken *adj* constant, firm, resolute, steadfast, steady, unmoved.

unshapen *adj* deformed, grotesque, ill-formed, illmade, ill-shaped, misshapen, shapeless, ugly, uncouth.

unsheltered *adj* exposed, unprotected.

unshrinking *adj* firm, determined, persisting, resolute, unblenching, unflinching.

unshroud *vb* discover, expose, reveal, uncover.

unsightly *adj* deformed, disagreeable, hideous, repellent, repulsive, ugly.

unskilful, unskillful *adj* awkward, bungling, clumsy, inapt, inexpert, maladroit, rough, rude, unhandy, unskilled, unversed.

unskilled *adj* inexperienced, raw, undisciplined, undrilled, uneducated, unexercised, unpractised, unprepared, unschooled; unskilful.

unslaked *adj* unquenched, unslacked.

unsleeping *adj* unslumbering, vigilant, wakeful, watchful.

unsmirched *adj* undefiled, unpolluted, unspotted.

unsociable *adj* distant, reserved, retiring, segregative, shy, solitary, standoffish, taciturn, uncommunicative, uncompanionable, ungenial, unsocial; inhospitable, misanthropic, morose.

unsoiled *adj* clean, spotless, unspotted, unstained, unsullied, untarnished.

unsophisticated *adj* genuine, pure, unadulterated; good, guileless, innocent, undepraved, unpolluted, invitiated; artless, honest, ingenuous, naive, natural, simple, sincere, straightforward, unaffected, undesigning, unstudied.

unsound *adj* decayed, defective, impaired, imperfect, rotten, thin, wasted, weak; broken, disturbed, light, restless; diseased, feeble, infirm, morbid, poorly, sickly, unhealthy, weak; deceitful, erroneous, fallacious, false, faulty, hollow, illogical, incorrect, invalid, ill-advised, irrational, questionable, sophistical, unreasonable, unsubstantial, untenable, wrong; dishonest, false, insincere, unfaithful, untrustworthy, untrue; insubstantial, unreal; heretical, heterodox, unorthodox.

unsparing *adj* bountiful, generous, lavish, liberal, profuse, ungrudging; harsh, inexorable, relentless, rigorous, ruthless, severe, uncompromising, unforgiving.

unspeakable *adj* indescribable, ineffable, inexpressible, unutterable.

unspiritual *adj* bodily, carnal, fleshly, sensual.

unspotted *adj* clean, spotless, unsoiled, unstained, unsullied, untarnished; faultless, immaculate, innocent, pure, stainless, unblemished, uncorrupted, undefiled, untainted.

unstable *adj* infirm, insecure, precarious, top-heavy, tottering, unbalanced, unballasted, unreliable, unsafe, unsettled, unsteady; changeable, erratic, fickle, inconstant, irresolute, mercurial, mutable, vacillating, variable, wavering, weak, volatile.—*also* **instable**.

unstained *adj* colourless, uncoloured, undyed, untinged; clean, spotless, unspotted.

unsteady *adj* fluctuating, oscillating, unsettled; insecure, precarious, unstable; changeable, desultory, ever-changing, fickle, inconstant, irresolute, mutable, unreliable, variable, wavering; drunken, jumpy, tottering, vacillating, wobbly, tipsy.

unstinted *adj* abundant, ample, bountiful, full, large, lavish, plentiful, prodigal, profuse.

unstrung *adj* overcome, shaken, unnerved, weak.

unstudied *adj* extempore, extemporaneous, impromptu, offhand, spontaneous, unpremeditated; inexpert, unskilled, unversed.

unsubdued *adj* unbowed, unbroken, unconquered, untamed.

unsubmissive *adj* disobedient, contumacious, indocile, insubordinate, obstinate, perverse, refractory, uncomplying, ungovernable, unmanageable, unruly, unyielding.

unsubstantial *adj* airy, flimsy, gaseous, gossamery, light, slight, tenuous, thin, vaporous; apparitional, bodiless, chimerical, cloudbuilt, dreamlike, empty, fantastical, ideal, illusory, imaginary, imponderable, moonshiny, spectral, unreal, vague, visionary; erroneous, fallacious, flimsy, groundless, illogical, unfounded, ungrounded, unsolid, unsound, untenable, weak.

unsuccessful *adj* abortive, bootless, fruitless, futile, ineffectual, profitless, unavailing, vain; ill-fated, ill-starred, luckless, unfortunate, unhappy, unlucky, unprosperous.

unsuitable *adj* ill-adapted, inappropriate, malapropos, unfit, unsatisfactory, unsuited; improper, inapplicable, inapt, incongruous, inexpedient, infelicitous, unbecoming, unbeseeming, unfitting.

unsuited *adj* unadapted, unfitted, unqualified.

unsullied *adj* chaste, clean, spotless, unsoiled, unspotted, unstained, untarnished; immaculate, pure, stainless, unblemished, uncorrupted, undefiled, untainted, untouched, virginal.

unsupplied *adj* destitute, unfurnished, unprovided.

unsupported *adj* unaided, unassisted; unbacked, unseconded, unsustained, unupheld.

unsurpassed *adj* matchless, peerless, unequalled, unexampled, unexcelled, unmatched, unparagoned, unparalleled, unrivalled.

unsusceptible *adj* apathetic, cold, impassive, insusceptible, phlegmatic, stoical, unimpressible, unimpressionable.

unsuspecting *adj* confiding, credulous, trusting, unsuspicious.

unsuspicious *adj* confiding, credulous, gullible, simple, trustful, unsuspecting.

unsustainable *adj* insupportable, intolerable; controvertible, erroneous, unmaintainable, untenable.

unswerving *adj* direct, straight, undeviating; constant, determined, firm, resolute, staunch, steadfast, steady, stable, unwavering.

unsymmetrical *adj* amorphous, asymmetric, disproportionate, formless, irregular, unbalanced.

unsystematic, unsystematical *adj* casual, disorderly, haphazard, irregular, planless, unmethodical.

untainted *adj* chaste, clean, faultless, fresh, healthy, pure, sweet, wholesome; spotless, unsoiled, unstained, unsullied, untarnished; immaculate, stainless, unblemished, uncorrupted, undefiled, unspotted.

untamable *adj* unconquerable.

untamed *adj* fierce, unbroken, wild.

untangle *vb* disentangle, explain, explicate.

untarnished *adj* chaste, clean, spotless, unsoiled, unspotted, unstained, unsullied; immaculate, pure, spotless, stainless, unblemished, uncorrupted, undefiled, unspotted, unsullied, untainted, virginal, virtuous.

untaught *adj* illiterate, unenlightened, uninformed, unlettered; ignorant, inexperienced, undisciplined, undrilled, uneducated, uninitiated, uninstructed, untutored.

untenable *adj* indefensible, unmaintainable, unsound; fallacious, hollow, illogical, indefensible, insupportable, unjustifiable, weak.

untenanted *adj* deserted, empty, tenantless, uninhabited, unoccupied.

unterrified *adj* fearless, unappalled, unawed, undismayed, undaunted, unscared.

unthankful *adj* thankless, ungrateful.

unthinking *adj* careless, heedless, inconsiderate, thoughtless, unreasoning, unreflecting; automatic, mechanical.

unthoughtful *adj* careless, heedless, inconsiderable, thoughtless.

unthrifty *adj* extravagant, improvident, lavish, prodigal, profuse, thriftless, wasteful.

untidy *adj* careless, disorderly, dowdy, frumpy, mussy, slatternly, slovenly, unkempt, unneat.

untie *vb* free, loose, loosen, unbind, unfasten, unknot, unloose; clear, resolve, solve, unfold.

until *adv, conj* till, to the time when; to the place, point, state or degree that; * *prep* till, to.

untimely *adj* ill-timed, immature, inconvenient, inopportune, mistimed, premature, unseasonable, unsuitable; ill-considered, inauspicious, uncalled for, unfortunate. * *adv* unseasonably, unsuitably.

untinged *adj* achromatic, colourless, hueless, uncoloured, undyed, unstained.

untiring *adj* persevering, incessant, indefatigable, patient, tireless, unceasing, unfatiguable, unflagging, unremitting, unwearied, unwearying.

untold *adj* countless, incalculable, innumerable, uncounted, unnumbered; unrelated, unrevealed.

untouched *adj* intact, scatheless, unharmed, unhurt, uninjured, unscathed; insensible, unaffected, unmoved, unstirred.

untoward *adj* adverse, froward, intractable, perverse, refractory, stubborn, unfortunate; annoying, ill-timed, inconvenient, unmanageable, vexatious; awkward, uncouth, ungainly, ungraceful.

untrained *adj* green, ignorant, inexperienced, raw, unbroken, undisciplined, undrilled, uneducated, uninstructed, unpractised, unskilled, untaught, untutored.

untrammelled *adj* free, unhampered.

untried *adj* fresh, inexperienced, maiden, new, unassayed, unattempted, unattested, virgin; undecided.

untrodden *adj* pathless, trackless, unbeaten.

untroubled *adj* calm, careless, composed, peaceful, serene, smooth, tranquil, undisturbed, unvexed.

untrue *adj* contrary, false, inaccurate, wrong; disloyal, faithless, perfidious, recreant, treacherous, unfaithful.

untrustworthy *adj* deceitful, dishonest, inaccurate, rotten, slippery, treacherous, undependable, unreliable; disloyal, false; deceptive, fallible, illusive, questionable.

untruth *n* error, faithlessness, falsehood, falsity, incorrectness, inveracity, treachery; deceit, deception, fabrication, fib, fiction, forgery, imposture, invention, lie, misrepresentation, misstatement, story.

untutored *adj* ignorant, inexperienced, undisciplined, undrilled, uneducated, uninitiated, uninstructed, untaught; artless, natural, simple, unsophisticated.

untwist *vb* disentangle, disentwine, ravel, unravel, unwreathe.

unused *adj* idle, unemployed, untried; new, unaccustomed, unfamiliar.

unusual *adj* abnormal, curious, exceptional, extraordinary, odd, peculiar, queer, rare, recherché, remarkable, singular, strange, unaccustomed, uncommon, unwonted.

unutterable *adj* incommunicable, indescribable, ineffable, inexpressible, unspeakable.

unvarnished *adj* unpolished; candid, plain, simple, true, unadorned, unembellished.

unvarying *adj* constant, invariable, unchanging.

unveil *vb* disclose, expose, reveal, show, uncover, unmask.

unveracious *adj* false, lying, mendacious, untruthful.

unversed *adj* inexperienced, raw, undisciplined, undrilled, uneducated, unexercised, unpractised, unprepared, unschooled; unskilful.

unviolated *adj* inviolate, unbetrayed, unbroken.

unwarlike *adj* pacific, peaceful.

unwarped *adj* impartial, unbiased, undistorted, unprejudiced.

unwarrantable *adj* improper, indefensible, unjustifiable.

unwary *adj* careless, hasty, heedless, imprudent, incautious, indiscreet, precipitate, rash, reckless, remiss, uncircumspect, unguarded.

unwavering *adj* constant, determined, firm, fixed, resolute, settled, staunch, steadfast, steady, unhesitating.

unwearied *adj* unfatigued; constant, continual, incessant, indefatigable, persevering, persistent, unceasing, unremitting, untiring.

unwelcome *adj* disagreeable, unacceptable, ungrateful, unpleasant, unpleasing.

unwell *adj* ailing, delicate, diseased, ill, indisposed, sick.

unwept *adj* unlamented, unmourned, unregretted.

unwholesome *adj* baneful, deleterious, injurious, insalubrious, noisome, noxious, poisonous, unhealthful, unhealthy; injudicious, pernicious, unsound; corrupt, tainted.

unwieldy *adj* bulky, clumsy, cumbersome, cumbrous, elephantine, heavy, hulking, large, massy, ponderous, unmanageable, weighty.

unwilling *adj* averse, backward, disinclined, indisposed, laggard, loath, opposed, recalcitrant, reluctant; forced, grudging.

unwind *vb* unravel, unreel, untwine, wind off; disentangle.

unwise *adj* brainless, foolish, ill-advised, ill-judged, impolitic, imprudent, indiscreet, injudicious, inexpedient, senseless, silly, stupid, unwary, weak.

unwitnessed *adj* unknown, unseen, unspied.

unwittingly *adv* ignorantly, inadvertently, unconsciously, undesignedly, unintentionally, unknowingly.

unwonted *adj* infrequent, rare, uncommon, unusual; unaccustomed, unused.

unworthy *adj* undeserving; bad, base, blameworthy, worthless; shameful, unbecoming, vile; contemptible, derogatory, despicable, discreditable, mean, paltry, reprehensible, shabby.

unwrap *vb* open, unfold.

unwrinkled *adj* smooth, unforrowed.

unwritten *adj* oral, traditional, unrecorded; conventional, customary.

unwrought *adj* crude, rough, rude, unfashioned, unformed.

unyielding *adj* constant, determined, indomitable, inflexible, pertinacious, resolute, staunch, steadfast, steady, tenacious, uncompromising, unwavering; headstrong, intractable, obstinate, perverse, self-willed, stiff, stubborn, wayward, wilful; adamantine, firm, grim, hard, immovable, implastic, inexorable, relentless, rigid, unbending.

unyoke *vb* disconnect, disjoin, part, separate.

unyoked *adj* disconnected, separated; licentious, loose, unrestrained.

upbraid *vb* accuse, blame, chide, condemn, criticize, denounce, fault, reproach, reprove, revile, scold, taunt, twit.

upheaval *n* elevation, upthrow; cataclysm, convulsion, disorder, eruption, explosion, outburst, overthrow.

uphill *adj* ascending, upward; arduous, difficult, hard, laborious, strenuous, toilsome, wearisome.

uphold *vb* elevate, raise; bear up, hold up, support, sustain; advocate, aid, champion, countenance, defend, justify, maintain, vindicate.

upland *n* down, fell, ridge, plateau.

uplift *vb* raise, upraise; animate, elevate, inspire, lift, refine. * *n* ascent, climb, elevation, lift, rise, upthrust; exaltation, inspiration, uplifting; improvement, refinement.

upon *prep* on, on top of, over; about, concerning, on the subject of, relating to; immediately after, with.

upper hand *n* advantage, ascendancy, control, dominion, mastership, mastery, pre-eminence, rule, superiority, supremacy, whip hand.

uppermost *adj* foremost, highest, loftiest, supreme, topmost, upmost.

uppish *adj* arrogant, assuming, haughty, perky, proud, smart.

upright *adj* erect, perpendicular, vertical; conscientious, equitable, fair, faithful, good, honest, honourable, incorruptible, just, pure, righteous, straightforward, true, trustworthy, upstanding, virtuous.

uprightness *n* erectness, perpendicularity, verticality; equity, fairness, goodness, honesty, honour, incorruptibility, integrity, justice, probity, rectitude, righteousness, straightforwardness, trustiness, trustworthiness, virtue, worth.

uproar *n* clamour, commotion, confusion, din, disturbance, fracas, hubbub, hurly-burly, noise, pandemonium, racket, riot, tumult, turmoil, vociferation.

uproarious *adj* boisterous, clamorous, loud, noisy, obstreperous, riotous, tumultuous.

uproot *vb* eradicate, extirpate, root out.

upset *vb* capsize, invert, overthrow, overtumble, overturn, spill, tip over, topple, turn turtle; agitate, confound, confuse, discompose, disconcert, distress, disturb, embarrass, excite, fluster, muddle, overwhelm, perturb, shock, startle, trouble, unnerve, unsettle; checkmate, defeat, overthrow, revolutionize, subvert; foil, frustrate, nonplus, thwart. * *adj* disproved, exposed, overthrown; bothered, confused, disconcerted, flustered, mixed-up, perturbed; shocked, startled, unsettled; beaten, defeated, overcome, overpowered, overthrown; discomfited, distressed, discomposed, overexcited, overwrought, shaken, troubled, unnerved. * *n* confutation, refutation; foiling, frustration, overthrow, revolution, revulsion, ruin, subversdion, thwarting.

upshot *n* conclusion, consummation, effect, end, event, issue, outcome, result, termination.

upside down *adj* bottom side up, bottom up, confused, head over heels, inverted, topsy-turvy.

upstart *n* adventurer, arriviste, parvenu, snob, social cimber, yuppie.

upturned *adj* raised, uplifted; retroussé.

upward *adj* ascending, climbing, mounting, rising, uphill. * *adv* above, aloft, overhead, up; heavenwards, skywards.

urbane *adj* civil, complaisant, courteous, courtly, elegant, mannerly, polished, polite, refined, smooth, suave, well-mannered.

urbanity *n* amenity, civility, complaisance, courtesy, politeness, smoothness, suavity.

urchin *n* brat, child, kid, ragamuffin, rascal, scrap, squirt, tad.

urge *vb* crowd, drive, force on, impel, press, press on, push, push on; beg, beseech, conjure, entreat, exhort, implore, importune, ply, solicit, tease; animate, egg on, encourage, goad, hurry, incite, instigate, quicken, spur, stimulate. * *n* compulsion, desire, drive, impulse, longing, pressure, wish, yearning.

urgency *n* drive, emergency, exigency, haste, necessity, press, pressure, push, stress; clamorousness, entreaty, insistence, importunity, instance, solicitation; goad, incitement, spur, stimulus.

urgent *adj* cogent, critical, crucial, crying, exigent, immediate, imperative, important, importunate, insistent, instant, pertinacious, pressing, serious.

urinal *n* chamber, chamber pot, lavatory, pot, potty, jordan, toilet.

urinate *vb* make water, pee, pee-pee, piddle, piss, stale, wee.

usage *n* treatment; consuetude, custom, fashion, habit, method, mode, practice, prescription, tradition, use.

use *vb* administer, apply, avail oneself of, drive, employ, handle, improve, make use of, manipulate, occupy, operate, ply, put into action, take advantage of, turn to account, wield, work; exercise, exert, exploit, practice, profit by, utilize; absorb, consume, exhaust, expend, swallow up, waste, wear out; accustom, familiarize, habituate, harden, inure, train; act toward, behave toward, deal with, manage, treat; be accustomed, be wont. * *n* appliance, application, consumption, conversion, disposal, exercise, employ, employment, practice, utilization; adaptability, advantage, avail, benefit, convenience, profit, service, usefulness, utility, wear; exigency, necessity, indispensability, need, occasion, requisiteness; custom, habit, handling, method, treatment, usage, way.

useful *adj* active, advantageous, available, availing, beneficial, commodious, conducive, contributory, convenient, effective, good, helpful, instrumental, operative, practical, profitable, remunerative, salutary, suitable, serviceable, utilitarian; available, helpful, serviceable, valuable.

usefulness *n* advantage, profit, serviceableness, utility, value.

useless *adj* abortive, bootless, fruitless, futile, helpless, idle, incapable, incompetent, ineffective, ineffectual, inutile, nugatory, null, profitless, unavailing, unprofitable, unproductive, unserviceable, valueless, worthless; good for nothing, waste.

usher *vb* announce, forerun, herald, induct, introduce, precede; conduct, direct, escort, shepherd, show. * *n* attendant, conductor, escort, shepherd, squire.

usual *adj* accustomed, common, customary, everyday, familiar, frequent, general, habitual, normal, ordinary, prevailing, prevalent, regular, wonted.

usurp *vb* appropriate, arrogate, assume, seize.

usurpation *n* assumption, dispossession, infringement, seizure.

usury *n* interest; exploitation, extortion, profiteering.

utensil *n* device, implement, instrument, tool.

utility *n* advantageousness, avail, benefit, profit, service, use, usefulness; happiness, welfare.

utilize *vb* employ, exploit, make use of, put to use, turn to account, use.

utmost *adj* extreme, farthest, highest, last, main, most distant, remotest; greatest, uttermost. * *n* best, extreme, maximum, most.

Utopian *adj* air-built, air-drawn, chimerical, fanciful, ideal, imaginary, visionary, unreal.

utricle *n* bladder, cyst, sac, vesicle.

utter[1] *adj* complete, entire, perfect, total; absolute, blank, diametric, downright, final, peremptory, sheer, stark, thorough, thoroughgoing, unconditional, unqualified, total.

utter[2] *vb* articulate, breathe, deliver, disclose, divulge, emit, enunciate, express, give forth, pronounce, reveal, speak, talk, tell, voice; announce, circulate, declare, issue, publish.

utterance *n* articulation, delivery, disclosure, emission, expression, pronouncement, pronunciation, publication, speech.

utterly *adv* absolutely, altogether, completely, downright, entirely, quite, totally, unconditionally, wholly.

uttermost *adj* extreme, farthest; greatest, utmost.

V

vacant *adj* blank, empty, unfilled, void; disengaged, free, unemployed, unoccupied, unencumbered; thoughtless, unmeaning, unthinking, unreflective; uninhabited, untenanted.

vacate *vb* abandon, evacuate, relinquish, surrender; abolish, abrogate, annul, cancel, disannul, invalidate, nullify, overrule, quash, rescind.

vacillate *vb* dither, fluctuate, hesitate, oscillate, rock, sway, waver.

vacillation *n* faltering, fluctuation, hesitation, inconstancy, indecision, irresolution, reeling, rocking, staggering, swaying, unsteadiness, wavering.

vacuity *n* emptiness, inanition, vacancy; emptiness, vacancy, vacuum, void; expressionlessness, inanity, nihility.

vacuous *adj* empty, empty-headed, unfilled, vacant, void; inane, unintelligent.

vacuum *n* emptiness, vacuity, void.

vagabond *adj* footloose, idle, meandering, rambling, roving, roaming, strolling, vagrant, wandering. * *n* beggar, castaway, landloper, loafer, lounger, nomad, outcast, tramp, vagrant, wanderer.

vagary *n* caprice, crotchet, fancy, freak, humour, whim.

vagrant *adj* erratic, itinerant, roaming, roving, nomadic, strolling, unsettled, wandering. * *n* beggar, castaway, landloper, loafer, lounger, nomad, outcast, tramp, vagabond, wanderer.

vague *adj* ambiguous, confused, dim, doubtful, indefinite, ill-defined, indistinct, lax, loose, obscure, uncertain, undetermined, unfixed, unsettled.

vain *adj* baseless, delusive, dreamy, empty, false, imaginary, shadowy, suppositional, unsubstantial, unreal, void; abortive, bootless, fruitless, futile, ineffectual, nugatory, profitless, unavailing, unprofitable; trivial, unessential, unimportant, unsatisfactory, unsatisfying, useless, vapid, worthless; arrogant, conceited, egotistical, flushed, high, inflated, opinionated, ostentatious, overweening, proud, self-confident, self-opinionated, vainglorious; gaudy, glittering, gorgeous, showy.

valediction *n* adieu, farewell, goodbye, leave-taking.

valet *n* attendant, flunky, groom, lackey, servant.

valetudinarian *adj* delicate, feeble, frail, infirm, sickly.

valiant *adj* bold, brave, chivalrous, courageous, daring, dauntless, doughty, fearless, gallant, heroic, intrepid, lion-hearted, redoubtable, Spartan, valorous, undaunted.

valid *adj* binding, cogent, conclusive, efficacious, efficient, good, grave, important, just, logical, powerful, solid, sound, strong, substantial, sufficient, weighty.

valley *n* basin, bottom, canyon, dale, dell, dingle, glen, hollow, ravine, strath, vale.

valorous *adj* bold, brave, courageous, dauntless, doughty, intrepid, stout.

valour *n* boldness, bravery, courage, daring, gallantry, heroism, prowess, spirit.

valuable *adj* advantageous, precious, profitable, useful; costly, expensive, rich; admirable, estimable, worthy. * *n* heirloom, treasure.

value *vb* account, appraise, assess, estimate, price, rate, reckon; appreciate, esteem, prize, regard, treasure. * *n* avail, importance, usefulness, utility, worth; cost, equivalent, price, rate; estimation, excellence, importance, merit, valuation.

valueless *adj* miserable, useless, worthless.

vandal *n* barbarian, destroyer, savage.

vandalism *n* barbarism, barbarity, savagery.

vanish *vb* disappear, dissolve, fade, melt.

vanity *n* emptiness, falsity, foolishness, futility, hollowness, insanity, triviality, unreality, worthlessness; arrogance, conceit, egotism, ostentation, self-conceit.

vanquish *vb* conquer, defeat, outwit, overcome, overpower, overthrow, subdue, subjugate; crush, discomfit, foil, master, quell, rout, worst.

vapid *adj* dead, flat, insipid, lifeless, savourless, spiritless, stale, tasteless; dull, feeble, jejune, languid, meagre, prosaic, prosy, tame.

vapour *n* cloud, exhalation, fog, fume, mist, rack, reek, smoke, steam; daydream, dream, fantasy, phantom, vagary, vision, whim, whimsy.

variable *adj* changeable, mutable, shifting; aberrant, alterable, capricious, fickle, fitful, floating, fluctuating, inconstant, mobile, mutable, protean, restless, shifting, unsteady, vacillating, wavering.

variance *n* disagreement, difference, discord, dissension, incompatibility, jarring, strife.

variation *n* alteration, change, modification; departure, deviation, difference, discrepancy, innovation; contrariety, discordance.

variegated *adj* chequered, dappled, diversified, flecked, kaleidoscopic, mottled, multicoloured, pied, spotted, striped.

variety *n* difference, dissimilarity, diversity, diversification, medley, miscellany, mixture, multiplicity, variation; kind, sort.

various *adj* different, diverse, manifold, many, numerous, several, sundry.

varnish *vb* enamel, glaze, japan, lacquer; adorn, decorate, embellish, garnish, gild, polish; disguise, excuse, extenuate, gloss over, palliate. * *n* enamel, lacquer, stain; cover, extenuation, gloss.

vary *vb* alter, metamorphose, transform; alternate, exchange, rotate; diversify, modify, variegate; depart, deviate, swerve.

vassal *n* bondman, liegeman, retainer, serf, slave, subject, thrall.

vassalage *n* bondage, dependence, serfdom, servitude, slavery, subjection.

vast *adj* boundless, infinite, measureless, spacious,

wide; colossal, enormous, gigantic, huge, immense, mighty, monstrous, prodigious, tremendous; extraordinary, remarkable.

vaticination *n* augury, divination, prediction, prognostication, prophecy.

vault[1] *vb* arch, bend, curve, span. * *n* cupola, curve, dome; catacomb, cell, cellar, crypt, dungeon, tomb; depository, strongroom.

vault[2] *vb* bound, jump, leap, spring; tumble, turn. * *n* bound, leap, jump, spring.

vaunt *vb* advertise, boast, brag, display, exult, flaunt, flourish, parade.

veer *vb* change, shift, turn.

vegetate *vb* blossom, develop, flourish, flower, germinate, grow, shoot, sprout, swell; bask, hibernate, idle, stagnate.

vehemence *n* impetuosity, violence; ardour, eagerness, earnestness, enthusiasm, fervency, fervour, heat, keenness, passion, warmth, zeal; force, intensity.

vehement *adj* furious, high, hot, impetuous, passionate, rampant, violent; ardent, burning, eager, earnest, enthusiastic, fervid, fiery, keen, passionate, sanguine, zealous; forcible, mighty, powerful, strong.

veil *vb* cloak, conceal, cover, curtain, envelop, hide, invest, mask, screen, shroud. * *n* cover, curtain, film, shade, screen; blind, cloak, disguise, mask, muffler, visor.

vein *n* course, current, lode, seam, streak, stripe, thread, wave; bent, character, faculty, humour, mood, talent, turn.

velocity *n* acceleration, celerity, expedition, fleetness, haste, quickness, rapidity, speed, swiftness.

velvety *adj* delicate, downy, smooth, soft.

venal *adj* corrupt, mean, purchasable, sordid.

vend *vb* dispose, flog, hawk, retail, sell.

venerable *adj* grave, respected, revered, sage, wise; awful, dread, dreadful; aged, old, patriarchal.

venerate *vb* adore, esteem, honour, respect, revere.

veneration *n* adoration, devotion, esteem, respect, reverence, worship.

vengeance *n* retaliation, retribution, revenge.

venial *adj* allowed, excusable, pardonable, permitted, trivial.

venom *n* poison, virus; acerbity, acrimony, bitterness, gall, hate, ill-will, malevolence, malice, maliciousness, malignity, rancour, spite, virulence.

venomous *adj* deadly, poisonous, septic, toxic, virulent; caustic, malicious, malignant, mischievous, noxious, spiteful.

vent *vb* emit, express, release, utter. * *n* air hole, hole, mouth, opening, orifice; air pipe, air tube, aperture, blowhole, bunghole, hydrant, plug, spiracle, spout, tap, orifice; effusion, emission, escape, outlet, passage; discharge, expression, utterance.

ventilate *vb* aerate, air, freshen, oxygenate, purify; fan, winnow; canvass, comment, discuss, examine, publish, review, scrutinize.

venture *vb* adventure, dare, hazard, imperil, jeopardize, presume, risk, speculate, test, try, undertake. * *n* adventure, chance, hazard, jeopardy, peril, risk, speculation, stake.

venturesome *adj* adventurous, bold, courageous, daring, doughty, enterprising, fearless, foolhardy, intrepid, presumptuous, rash, venturous.

veracious *adj* reliable, straightforward, true, trustworthy, truthful; credible, genuine, honest, unfeigned.

veracity *n* accuracy, candour, correctness, credibility,

exactness, fidelity, frankness, honesty, ingenuousness, probity, sincerity, trueness, truth, truthfulness.

verbal *adj* nuncupative, oral, spoken, unwritten.

verbose *adj* diffusive, long-winded, loquacious, talkative, wordy.

verdant *adj* fresh, green, verdure, verdurous; green, inexperienced, raw, unsophisticated.

verdict *n* answer, decision, finding, judgement, opinion, sentence.

verge *vb* bear, incline, lean, slope, tend; approach, border, skirt. * *n* mace, rod, staff; border, boundary, brink, confine, edge, extreme, limit, margin; edge, eve, point.

verification *n* authentication, attestation, confirmation, corroboration.

verify *vb* attest, authenticate, confirm, corroborate, prove, substantiate.

verily *adv* absolutely, actually, confidently, indeed, positively, really, truly.

verity *n* certainty, reality, truth, truthfulness.

vermicular *adj* convoluted, flexuose, flexuous, meandering, serpentine, sinuous, tortuous, twisting, undulating, waving, winding, wormish, wormlike.

vernacular *adj* common, indigenous, local, mother, native, vulgar. * *n* cant, dialect, jargon, patois, speech.

versatile *adj* capricious, changeable, erratic, mobile, variable; fickle, inconstant, mercurial, unsteady; adaptable, protean, plastic, varied.

versed *adj* able, accomplished, acquainted, clever, conversant, practised, proficient, qualified, skilful, skilled, trained.

version *n* interpretation, reading, rendering, translation.

vertex *n* apex, crown, height, summit, top, zenith.

vertical *adj* erect, perpendicular, plumb, steep, upright.

vertiginous *adj* rotatory, rotary, whirling; dizzy, giddy.

vertigo *n* dizziness, giddiness.

verve *n* animation, ardour, energy, enthusiasm, force, rapture, spirit.

very *adv* absolutely, enormously, excessively, hugely, remarkably, surpassingly. * *adj* actual, exact, identical, precise, same; bare, mere, plain, pure, simple.

vesicle *n* bladder, blister, cell, cyst, follicle.

vest *vb* clothe, cover, dress, envelop; endow, furnish, invest. * *n* dress, garment, robe, vestment, vesture, waistcoat.

vestibule *n* anteroom, entrance hall, lobby, porch.

vestige *n* evidence, footprint, footstep, mark, record, relic, sign, token.

veteran *adj* adept, aged, experienced, disciplined, seasoned, old. * *n* campaigner, old soldier; master, past master, old-timer, old-stager.

veto *vb* ban, embargo, forbid, interdict, negate, prohibit. * *n* ban, embargo, interdict, prohibition, refusal.

vex *vb* annoy, badger, bother, chafe, cross, distress, gall, harass, harry, hector, molest, perplex, pester, plague, tease, torment, trouble, roil, spite, worry; affront, displease, fret, irk, irritate, nettle, offend, provoke; agitate, disquiet, disturb.

vexation *n* affliction, agitation, chagrin, discomfort, displeasure, disquiet, distress, grief, irritation, pique, sorrow, trouble; annoyance, curse, nuisance, plague, torment; damage, troubling, vexing.

vexed *adj* afflicted, agitated, annoyed, bothered, disquieted, harassed, irritated, perplexed, plagued, provoked, troubled, worried.

vibrate *vb* oscillate, sway, swing, undulate, wave; impinge, quiver, sound, thrill; fluctuate, hesitate, vacillate, waver.

vibration *n* nutation, oscillation, vibration.

vicarious *adj* commissioned, delegated, indirect, second-hand, substituted.

vice *n* blemish, defect, failing, fault, imperfection, infirmity; badness, corruption, depravation, depravity, error, evil, immorality, iniquity, laxity, obliquity, sin, viciousness, vileness, wickedness.

vicinity *n* nearness, proximity; locality, neighbourhood, vicinage.

vicious *adj* abandoned, atrocious, bad, corrupt, degenerate, demoralized, depraved, devilish, diabolical, evil, flagrant, hellish, immoral, iniquitous, mischievous, profligate, shameless, sinful, unprincipled, wicked; malicious, spiteful, venomous; foul, impure; debased, faulty; contrary, refractory.

viciousness *n* badness, corruption, depravity, immorality, profligacy.

vicissitude *n* alteration, interchange; change, fluctuation, mutation, revolution, variation.

victim *n* martyr, sacrifice, sufferer; prey; cat's-paw, cull, cully, dupe, gull, gudgeon, puppet.

victimize *vb* bamboozle, befool, beguile, cheat, circumvent, cozen, deceive, defraud, diddle, dupe, fool, gull, hoax, hoodwink, overreach, swindle, trick.

victor *n* champion, conqueror, vanquisher, winner.

victorious *adj* conquering, successful, triumphant, winning.

victory *n* achievement, conquest, mastery, triumph.

victuals *npl* comestibles, eatables, fare, food, meat, provisions, repast, sustenance, viands.

vie *vb* compete, contend, emulate, rival, strive.

view *vb* behold, contemplate, eye, inspect, scan, survey; consider, inspect, regard, study. * *n* inspection, observation, regard, sight; outlook, panorama, perspective, prospect, range, scene, survey, vista; aim, intent, intention, design, drift, object, purpose, scope; belief, conception, impression, idea, judgement, notion, opinion, sentiment, theory; appearance, aspect, show.

vigilance *n* alertness, attentiveness, carefulness, caution, circumspection, observance, watchfulness.

vigilant *adj* alert, attentive, careless, cautious, circumspect, unsleeping, wakeful, watchful.

vigorous *adj* lusty, powerful, strong; active, alert, cordial, energetic, forcible, strenuous, vehement, vivid, virile; brisk, hale, hardy, robust, sound, sturdy, healthy; fresh, flourishing; bold, emphatic, impassioned, lively, nervous, piquant, pointed, severe, sparkling, spirited, trenchant.

vigour *n* activity, efficacy, energy, force, might, potency, power, spirit, strength; bloom, elasticity, haleness, health, heartiness, pep, punch, robustness, soundness, thriftiness, tone, vim, vitality; enthusiasm, freshness, fire, intensity, liveliness, piquancy, strenuousness, vehemence, verve, raciness.

vile *adj* abject, base, beastly, beggarly, brutish, contemptible, despicable, disgusting, grovelling, ignoble, low, odious, paltry, pitiful, repulsive, scurvy, shabby, slavish, sorry, ugly; bad, evil, foul, gross, impure, iniquitous, lewd, obscene, sinful, vicious, wicked; cheap, mean, miserable, valueless, worthless.

vilify *vb* abuse, asperse, backbite, berate, blacken, blemish, brand, calumniate, decry, defame, disparage, lampoon, libel, malign, revile, scandalize, slander, slur, traduce, vituperate.

villain *n* blackguard, knave, miscreant, rascal, reprobate, rogue, ruffian, scamp, scapegrace, scoundrel.

villainous *adj* base, mean, vile; corrupt, depraved, knavish, unprincipled, wicked; atrocious, heinous, outrageous, sinful; mischievous, sorry.

vindicate *vb* defend, justify, uphold; advocate, avenge, assert, maintain, right, support.

vindication *n* apology, excuse, defence, justification.

vindictive *adj* avenging, grudgeful, implacable, malevolent, malicious, malignant, retaliative, revengeful, spiteful, unforgiving, unrelenting, vengeful.

violate *vb* hurt, injure; break, disobey, infringe, invade; desecrate, pollute, profane; abuse, debauch, defile, deflower, outrage, ravish, transgress.

violent *adj* boisterous, demented, forceful, forcible, frenzied, furious, high, hot, impetuous, insane, intense, stormy, tumultuous, turbulent, vehement, wild; fierce, fiery, fuming, heady, heavy, infuriate, passionate, obstreperous, strong, raging, rampant, rank, rapid, raving, refractory, roaring, rough, tearing, towering, ungovernable; accidental, unnatural; desperate, extreme, outrageous, unjust; acute, exquisite, poignant, sharp.

virago *n* amazon, brawler, fury, shrew, tartar, vixen.

virgin *adj* chaste, maidenly, modest, pure, undefiled, stainless, unpolluted, vestal, virginal; fresh, maiden, untouched, unused. * *n* celibate, damsel, girl, lass, maid, maiden.

virile *adj* forceful, manly, masculine, robust, vigorous.

virtual *adj* constructive, equivalent, essential, implicit, implied, indirect, practical, substantial.

virtue *n* chastity, goodness, grace, morality, purity; efficacy, excellence, honesty, integrity, justice, probity, quality, rectitude, worth.

virtuous *adj* blameless, equitable, exemplary, excellent, good, honest, moral, noble, righteous, upright, worthy; chaste, continent, immaculate, innocent, modest, pure, undefiled; efficacious, powerful.

virulent *adj* deadly, malignant, poisonous, toxic, venomous; acrid, acrimonious, bitter, caustic.

visage *n* aspect, countenance, face, guise, physiognomy, semblance.

viscera *n* bowels, entrails, guts, intestines.

viscous *adj* adhesive, clammy, glutinous, ropy, slimy, sticky, tenacious.

visible *adj* observable, perceivable, perceptible, seeable, visual; apparent, clear, conspicuous, discoverable, distinct, evident, manifest, noticeable, obvious, open, palpable, patent, plain, revealed, unhidden, unmistakable.

vision *n* eyesight, seeing, sight; eyeshot, ken; apparition, chimera, dream, ghost, hallucination, illusion, phantom, spectre.

visionary *adj* imaginative, impractical, quixotic, romantic; chimerical, dreamy, fancied, fanciful, fantastic, ideal, illusory, imaginary, romantic, shadowy, unsubstantial, utopian, wild. * *n* dreamer, enthusiast, fanatic, idealist, optimist, theorist, zealot.

vital *adj* basic, cardinal, essential, indispensable, necessary, needful; animate, alive, existing, life-giving, living; paramount.

vitality *n* animation, life, strength, vigour, virility.

vitiate *vb* adulterate, contaminate, corrupt, debase, defile, degrade, deprave, deteriorate, impair, infect, injure, invalidate, poison, pollute, spoil.

vitiation *n* adulteration, corruption, degeneracy, degeneration, degradation, depravation, deterioration, impairment, injury, invalidation, perversion, pollution, prostitution.

vituperate *vb* abuse, berate, blame, censure, denounce, overwhelm, rate, revile, scold, upbraid, vilify.

vituperation *n* abuse, blame, censure, invective, reproach, railing, reviling, scolding, upbraiding.

vivacious *adj* active, animated, breezy, brisk, buxom, cheerful, frolicsome, gay, jocund, light-hearted, lively, merry, mirthful, spirited, sportive, sprightly.

vivacity *n* animation, cheer, cheerfulness, gaiety, liveliness, sprightliness.

vivid *adj* active, animated, bright, brilliant, clear, intense, fresh, lively, living, lucid, quick, sprightly, strong; expressive, graphic, striking, telling.

vivify *vb* animate, arouse, awake, quicken, vitalize.

vixen *n* brawler, scold, shrew, spitfire, tartar, virago.

vocabulary *n* dictionary, glossary, lexicon, wordbook; language, terms, words.

vocation *n* call, citation, injunction, summons; business, calling, employment, occupation, profession, pursuit, trade.

vociferate *vb* bawl, bellow, clamour, cry, exclaim, rant, shout, yell.

vociferous *adj* blatant, clamorous, loud, noisy, obstreperous, ranting, stunning, uproarious.

vogue *adj* fashionable, modish, stylish, trendy. * *n* custom, fashion, favour, mode, practice, repute, style, usage, way.

voice *vb* declare, express, say, utter. * *n* speech, tongue, utterance; noise, notes, sound; opinion, option, preference, suffrage, vote; accent, articulation, enunciation, inflection, intonation, modulation, pronunciation, tone; expression, language, words.

void *vb* clear, eject, emit, empty, evacuate. * *adj* blank, empty, hollow, vacant; clear, destitute, devoid, free, lacking, wanting, without; inept, ineffectual, invalid, nugatory, null; imaginary, unreal, vain. * *n* abyss, blank, chasm, emptiness, hole, vacuum.

volatile *adj* gaseous, incoercible; airy, buoyant, frivolous, gay, jolly, lively, sprightly, vivacious; capricious, changeable, fickle, flighty, flyaway, giddy, harebrained, inconstant, light-headed, mercurial, reckless, unsteady, whimsical, wild.

volition *n* choice, determination, discretion, option, preference, will.

volley *n* fusillade, round, salvo; blast, burst, discharge, emission, explosion, outbreak, report, shower, storm.

voluble *adj* fluent, garrulous, glib, loquacious, talkative.

volume *n* book, tome; amplitude, body, bulk, compass, dimension, size, substance, vastness; fullness, power, quantity.

voluminous *adj* ample, big, bulky, full, great, large; copious, diffuse, discursive, flowing.

voluntary *adj* free, spontaneous, unasked, unbidden, unforced; deliberate, designed, intended, purposed; discretionary, optional, willing.

volunteer *vb* offer, present, proffer, propose, tender.

voluptuary *n* epicure, hedonist, sensualist.

voluptuous *adj* carnal, effeminate, epicurean, fleshy, licentious, luxurious, sensual, sybaritic.

vomit *vb* discharge, eject, emit, puke, regurgitate, spew, throw up.

voracious *adj* devouring, edacious, greedy, hungry, rapacious, ravenous.

vortex *n* eddy, maelstrom, whirl, whirlpool.

votary *adj* devoted, promised. * *n* adherent, devotee, enthusiast, follower, supporter, votarist, zealot.

vote *vb* ballot, elect, opt, return; judge, pronounce, propose, suggest. * *n* ballot, franchise, poll, referendum, suffrage, voice.

vouch *vb* affirm, asseverate, attest, aver, declare, guarantee, support, uphold, verify, warrant.

vouchsafe *vb* accord, cede, deign, grant, stoop, yield.

vow *vb* consecrate, dedicate, devote; asseverate. * *n* oath, pledge, promise.

voyage *vb* cruise, journey, navigate, ply, sail. * *n* crossing, cruise, excursion, journey, passage, sail, trip.

vulgar *adj* base-born, common, ignoble, lowly, plebeian; boorish, cheap, coarse, discourteous, flashy, homespun, garish, gaudy, ill-bred, inelegant, loud, rustic, showy, tawdry, uncultivated, unrefined; general, ordinary, popular, public; base, broad, loose, low, gross, mean, ribald, vile; inelegant, unauthorized.

vulgarity *n* baseness, coarseness, grossness, meanness, rudeness.

vulnerable *adj* accessible, assailable, defenceless, exposed, weak.

W

waddle *vb* toddle, toggle, waggle, wiggle, wobble.

waft *vb* bear, carry, convey, float, transmit, transport. * *n* breath, breeze, draught, puff.

wag[1] *vb* shake, sway, waggle; oscillate, vibrate, waver; advance, move, progress, stir. * *n* flutter, nod, oscillation, vibration.

wag[2] *n* humorist, jester, joker, wit.

wage *vb* bet, hazard, lay, stake, wager; conduct, undertake.

wager *vb* back, bet, gamble, lay, pledge, risk, stake. * *n* bet, gamble, pledge, risk, stake.

wages *npl* allowance, compensation, earnings, emolument, hire, pay, payment, remuneration, salary, stipend.

waggish *adj* frolicsome, gamesome, mischievous, roguish, tricksy; comical, droll, facetious, funny, humorous, jocular, jocose, merry, sportive.

wagon *n* cart, lorry, truck, van, waggon, wain.

wail *vb* bemoan, deplore, lament, mourn; cry, howl, weep. * *n* complaint, cry, lamentation, moan, wailing.

waist *n* bodice, corsage, waistline.

wait *vb* delay, linger, pause, remain, rest, stay, tarry; attend, minister, serve; abide, await, expect, look for. * *n* delay, halt, holdup, pause, respite, rest, stay, stop.

waiter, waitress *n* attendant, lackey, servant, servitor, steward, valet.

waive *vb* defer, forgo, surrender, relinquish, remit, renounce; desert, reject.

wake[1] *vb* arise, awake, awaken; activate, animate, arouse, awaken, excite, kindle, provoke, stimulate. * *n* vigil, watch, watching.

wake[2] *n* course, path, rear, track, trail, wash.

wakeful *adj* awake, sleepless, restless; alert, observant, vigilant, wary, watchful.

wale *n* ridge, streak, stripe, welt, whelk.

walk *vb* advance, depart, go, march, move, pace, saunter, step, stride, stroll, tramp. * *n* amble, carriage, gait, step; beat, career, course, department, field, province; conduct, procedure; alley, avenue, cloister, esplanade, footpath, path, pathway, pavement, promenade, range, sidewalk, way; constitutional, excursion, hike, ramble, saunter, stroll, tramp, turn.

wall *n* escarp, parapet, plane, upright.

wallet *n* bag, knapsack, pocketbook, purse, sack.

wan *adj* ashen, bloodless, cadaverous, colourless, haggard, pale, pallid.

wand *n* baton, mace, truncheon, sceptre.

wander *vb* forage, prowl, ramble, range, roam, rove, stroll; deviate, digress, straggle, stray; moon, rave. * *n* amble, cruise, excursion, ramble, stroll.

wane *vb* abate, decrease, ebb, subside; decline, fail, sink. * *n* decrease, diminution, lessening; decay, declension, decline, failure.

want *vb* crave, desire, need, require, wish; fail, lack, neglect, omit. * *n* absence, defect, default, deficiency, lack; defectiveness, failure, inadequacy, insufficiency, meagreness, paucity, poverty, scantiness, scarcity, shortness; requirement; craving, desire, longing, wish; destitution, distress, indigence, necessity, need, penury, poverty, privation, straits.

wanton *vb* caper, disport, frisk, frolic, play, revel, romp, sport; dally, flirt, toy, trifle. * *adj* free, loose, unchecked, unrestrained, wandering; abounding, exuberant, luxuriant, overgrown, rampant; airy, capricious, coltish, frisky, playful, skittish, sportive; dissolute, irregular, licentious, loose; carnal, immoral, incontinent, lascivious, lecherous, lewd, libidinous, light, lustful, prurient, salacious, unchaste; careless, gratuitous, groundless, heedless, inconsiderate, needless, perverse, reckless, wayward, wilful. * *n* baggage, flirt, harlot, light-o'-love, prostitute, rake, roué, slut, whore.

war *vb* battle, campaign, combat, contend, crusade, engage, fight, strive. * *n* contention, enmity, hostility, strife, warfare.

warble *vb* sing, trill, yodel. * *n* carol, chant, hymn, hum.

ward *vb* guard, watch; defend, fend, parry, protect, repel. * *n* care, charge, guard, guardianship, watch; defender, guardian, keeper, protector, warden; custody; defence, garrison, protection; minor, pupil; district, division, precinct, quarter; apartment, cubicle.

warehouse *n* depot, magazine, repository, store, storehouse.

wares *npl* commodities, goods, merchandise, movables.

warfare *n* battle, conflict, contest, discord, engagement, fray, hostilities, strife, struggle, war.

warily *adv* carefully, cautiously, charily, circumspectly, heedfully, watchfully, vigilantly.

wariness *n* care, caution, circumspection, foresight, thought, vigilance.

warlike *adj* bellicose, belligerent, combative, hostile, inimical, martial, military, soldierly, watchful.

warm *vb* heat, roast, toast; animate, chafe, excite, rouse. * *adj* lukewarm, tepid; genial, mild, pleasant, sunny; close, muggy, oppressive; affectionate, ardent, cordial, eager, earnest, enthusiastic, fervent, fervid, glowing, hearty, hot, zealous; excited, fiery, flushed, furious, hasty, keen, lively, passionate, quick, vehement, violent.

warmth *n* glow, tepidity; ardour, fervency, fervour, zeal; animation, cordiality, eagerness, earnestness, enthusiasm, excitement, fervency, fever, fire, flush, heat, intensity, passion, spirit, vehemence.

warn *vb* caution, forewarn; admonish, advise; apprise, inform, notify; bid, call, summon.

warning *adj* admonitory, cautionary, cautioning, monitory. * *n* admonition, advice, caveat, caution, monition; information, notice; augury, indication, intimation, omen, portent, presage, prognostic, sign, symptom; call, summons; example, lesson, sample.

warp *vb* bend, bias, contort, deviate, distort, pervert, swerve, turn, twist. * *n* bent, bias, cast, crook, distortion, inclination, leaning, quirk, sheer, skew, slant, slew, swerve, twist, turn.

warrant *vb* answer for, certify, guarantee, secure; affirm, assure, attest, avouch, declare, justify, state; authorize, justify, license, maintain, sanction, support, sustain, uphold. * *n* guarantee, pledge, security, surety, warranty; authentication, authority, commission, verification; order, pass, permit, summons, subpoena, voucher, writ.

warrantable *adj* admissible, allowable, defensible, justifiable, lawful, permissible, proper, right, vindicable.

warrior *n* champion, captain, fighter, hero, soldier.

wary *adj* careful, cautious, chary, circumspect, discreet, guarded, heedful, prudent, scrupulous, vigilant, watchful.

wash *vb* purify, purge; moisten, wet; bathe, clean, flush, irrigate, lap, lave, rinse, sluice; colour, stain, tint. * *n* ablution, bathing, cleansing, lavation, washing; bog, fen, marsh, swamp, quagmire; bath, embrocation, lotion; laundry, washing.

washy *adj* damp, diluted, moist, oozy, sloppy, thin, watery, weak; feeble, jejune, pointless, poor, spiritless, trashy, trumpery, unmeaning, vapid, worthless.

waspish *adj* choleric, fretful, irascible, irritable, peevish, petulant, snappish, testy, touchy; slender, slim, small-waisted.

waste *vb* consume, corrode, decrease, diminish, emaciate, wear; absorb, deplete, devour, dissipate, drain, empty, exhaust, expend, lavish, lose, misspend, misuse, scatter, spend, squander; demolish, desolate, destroy, devastate, devour, dilapidate, harry, pillage, plunder, ravage, ruin, scour, strip; damage, impair, injure; decay, dwindle, perish, wither. * *adj* bare, desolated, destroyed, devastated, empty, ravaged, ruined, spoiled, stripped, void; dismal, dreary, forlorn; abandoned, bare, barren, uncultivated, unimproved, uninhabited, untilled, wild; useless, valueless, worthless; exuberant, superfluous. * *n* consumption, decrement, diminution, dissipation, exhaustion, expenditure, loss, wasting; destruction, dispersion, extravagance, loss, squandering, wanton; decay, desolation, destruction, devastation, havoc, pillage, ravage, ruin; chaff, debris, detritus, dross, excrement, husks, junk, matter, offal, refuse, rubbish, trash, wastrel, worthlessness; barrenness, desert, expanse, solitude, wild, wilderness.

wasteful *adj* destructive, ruinous; extravagant, improvident, lavish, prodigal, profuse, squandering, thriftless, unthrifty.

watch *vb* attend, guard, keep, oversee, protect, superintend, tend; eye, mark, observe. * *n* espial, guard, outlook, wakefulness, watchfulness, watching, vigil, ward; alertness, attention, inspection, observation, surveillance; guard, picket, sentinel, sentry, watchman; pocket watch, ticker, timepiece, wristwatch.

watchful *adj* alert, attentive, awake, careful, circumspect, guarded, heedful, observant, vigilant, wakeful, wary.

watchword *n* catchword, cry, motto, password, shibboleth, word.

waterfall *n* cascade, cataract, fall, linn.

watery *adj* diluted, thin, waterish, weak; insipid, spiritless, tasteful, vapid; moist, wet.

wave *vb* float, flutter, heave, shake, sway, undulate, wallow; brandish, flaunt, flourish, swing; beckon, signal. * *n* billow, bore, breaker, flood, flush, ripple, roll, surge, swell, tide, undulation; flourish, gesture, sway; convolution, curl, roll, unevenness.

waver *vb* flicker, float, undulate, wave; reel, totter; falter, fluctuate, flutter, hesitate, oscillate, quiver, vacillate.

wax *vb* become, grow, increase, mount, rise.

way *n* advance, journey, march, progression, transit, trend; access, alley, artery, avenue, beat, channel, course, highroad, highway, passage, path, road, route, street, track, trail; fashion, manner, means, method, mode, system; distance, interval, space, stretch; behaviour, custom, form, guise, habit, habitude, practice, process, style, usage; device, plan, scheme.

wayfarer *n* itinerant, nomad, passenger, pilgrim, rambler, traveller, walker, wanderer.

wayward *adj* capricious, captious, contrary, forward, headstrong, intractable, obstinate, perverse, refractory, stubborn, unruly, wilful.

weak *adj* debilitated, delicate, enfeebled, enervated, exhausted, faint, feeble, fragile, frail, infirm, invalid, languid, languishing, shaky, sickly, spent, strengthless, tender, unhealthy, unsound, wasted, weakly; accessible, defenceless, unprotected, vulnerable; light, soft, unstressed; boneless, cowardly, infirm; compliant, irresolute, pliable, pliant, undecided, undetermined, unsettled, unstable, unsteady, vacillating, wavering, yielding; childish, foolish, imbecile, senseless, shallow, silly, simple, stupid, weak-minded, witless; erring, foolish, indiscreet, injudicious, unwise; gentle, indistinct, low, small; adulterated, attenuated, diluted, insipid, tasteless, thin, watery; flimsy, frivolous, poor, sleazy, slight, trifling; futile, illogical, inconclusive, ineffective, ineffectual, inefficient, lame, unconvincing, unsatisfactory, unsupported, unsustained, vague, vain; unsafe, unsound, unsubstantial, untrustworthy; helpless, impotent, powerless; breakable, brittle, delicate, frangible; inconsiderable, puny, slender, slight, small.

weaken *vb* cramp, cripple, debilitate, devitalize, enervate, enfeeble, invalidate, relax, sap, shake, stagger, undermine, unman, unnerve, unstring; adulterate, attenuate, debase, depress, dilute, exhaust, impair, impoverish, lessen, lower, reduce.

weakness *n* debility, feebleness, fragility, frailty, infirmity, languor, softness; defect, failing, fault, flaw; fondness, inclination, liking.

weal *n* advantage, good, happiness, interest, profit, utility, prosperity, welfare; ridge, streak, stripe.

wealth *n* assets, capital, cash, fortune, funds, goods, money, possessions, property, riches, treasure; abundance, affluence, opulence, plenty, profusion.

wean *vb* alienate, detach, disengage, withdraw.

wear *vb* bear, carry, don; endure, last; consume, impair, rub, use, waste. * *n* corrosion, deterioration, disintegration, erosion, wear and tear; consumption, use; apparel, array, attire, clothes, clothing, dress, garb, gear.

wearied *adj* apathetic, bored, exhausted, fagged, fatigued, jaded, tired, weary, worn.

weariness *n* apathy, boredom, ennui, exhaustion, fatigue, languor, lassitude, monotony, prostration, sameness, tedium.

wearisome *adj* annoying, boring, dull, exhausting, fatiguing, humdrum, irksome, monotonous, prolix, prosaic, slow, tedious, tiresome, troublesome, trying, uninteresting, vexatious.

weary vb debilitate, exhaust, fag, fatigue, harass, jade, tire. * adj apathetic, bored, drowsy, exhausted, jaded, spent, tired, worn; irksome, tiresome, wearisome.

weave vb braid, entwine, interlace, lace, mat, plait, pleat, twine; compose, construct, fabricate, make.

wed vb contract, couple, espouse, marry, unite.

wedding n bridal, espousal, marriage, nuptials.

wedlock n marriage, matrimony.

ween vb fancy, imagine, suppose, think.

weep vb bemoan, bewail, complain, cry, lament, sob.

weigh vb balance, counterbalance, lift, raise; consider, deliberate, esteem, examine, study.

weight vb ballast, burden, fill, freight, load; weigh. * n gravity, heaviness, heft, tonnage; burden, load, pressure; consequence, efficacy, emphasis, importance, impressiveness, influence, moment, pith, power, significance, value.

weighty adj heavy, massive, onerous, ponderous, unwieldy; considerable, efficacious, forcible, grave, important, influential, serious, significant.

weird adj eerie, ghostly, strange, supernatural, uncanny, unearthly, witching.

welcome vb embrace, greet, hail, receive. * adj acceptable, agreeable, grateful, gratifying, pleasant, pleasing, satisfying. * n greeting, reception, salutation.

welfare n advantage, affluence, benefit, happiness, profit, prosperity, success, thrift, weal, wellbeing.

well[1] vb flow, gush, issue, jet, pour, spring. * n fount, fountain, reservoir, spring, wellhead, wellspring; origin, source; hole, pit, shaft.

well[2] adj hale, healthy, hearty, sound; fortunate, good, happy, profitable, satisfactory, useful. * adv accurately, adequately, correctly, efficiently, properly, suitably; abundantly, considerably, fully, thoroughly; agreeably, commendably, favourably, worthily.

wellbeing n comfort, good, happiness, health, prosperity, welfare.

welter vb flounder, roll, toss, wallow. * n confusion, jumble, mess.

wet vb dabble, damp, dampen, dip, drench, moisten, saturate, soak, sprinkle, water. * adj clammy, damp, dank, dewy, dripping, humid, moist; rainy, showery, sprinkly. * n dampness, humidity, moisture, wetness.

whack vb, n bang, beat, rap, strike, thrash, thump, thwack.

wharf n dock, pier, quay.

wheedle vb cajole, coax, flatter, inveigle, lure.

wheel vb gyrate, revolve, roll, rotate, spin, swing, turn, twist, whirl, wind. * n circle, revolution, roll, rotation, spin, turn, twirl.

whet vb grind, sharpen; arouse, awaken, excite, provoke, rouse, stimulate; animate, inspire, kindle, quicken, warm.

whiff vb, n blast, gust, puff.

whim n caprice, crotchet, fancy, freak, frolic, humour, notion, quirk, sport, vagary, whimsy, wish.

whimsical adj capricious, crotchety, eccentric, erratic, fanciful, frolicsome, odd, peculiar, quaint, singular.

whine vb cry, grumble, mewl, moan, snivel, wail, whimper. * n complaint, cry, grumble, moan, sob, wail, whimper.

whip vb beat, lash, strike; flagellate, flog, goad, horsewhip, scourge, slash; hurt, sting; jerk, snap, snatch, whisk. * n bullwhip, cane, crop, horsewhip, knout, lash, scourge, switch, thong.

whipping n beating, castigation, dusting, flagellation, flogging, thrashing.

whirl vb gyrate, pirouette, roll, revolve, rotate, turn, twirl, twist, wheel. * n eddy, flurry, flutter, gyration, rotation, spin, swirl, twirl, vortex.

whit n atom, bit, grain, iota, jot, mite, particle, scrap, speck, tittle.

white adj argent, canescent, chalky, frosty, hoary, ivory, milky, silver, snowy; grey, pale, pallid, wan; candid, clean, chaste, immaculate, innocent, pure, spotless, unblemished.

whole adj all, complete, entire, intact, integral, total, undivided; faultless, firm, good, perfect, strong, unbroken, undivided, uninjured; healthy, sound, well. * adv entire, in one. * n aggregate, all, amount, ensemble, entirety, gross, sum, total, totality.

wholesome adj healthy, healthful, invigorating, nourishing, nutritious, salubrious, salutary; beneficial, good, helpful, improving, salutary; fresh, sound, sweet.

wholly adv altogether, completely, entirely, fully, totally, utterly.

whoop vb halloo, hoot, roar, shout, yell. * n bellow, hoot, roar, shout, yell.

whore n bawd, courtesan, drab, harlot, prostitute, streetwalker, strumpet.

wicked adj abandoned, abominable, depraved, devilish, godless, graceless, immoral, impious, infamous, irreligious, irreverent, profane, sinful, ungodly, unholy, unprincipled, unrighteous, vicious, vile, worthless; atrocious, bad, black, criminal, dark, evil, heinous, ill, iniquitous, monstrous, nefarious, unjust, villainous.

wide adj ample, broad, capacious, comprehensive, distended, expanded, large, spacious, vast; distant, remote; prevalent, rife, widespread. * adv completely, farthest, fully.

wield vb brandish, flourish, handle, manipulate, ply, work; control, manage, sway, use.

wild adj feral, undomesticated, untamed; desert, desolate, native, rough, rude, uncultivated; barbarous, ferocious, fierce, savage, uncivilized; dense, luxuriant, rank; disorderly, distracted, frantic, frenzied, furious, impetuous, irregular, mad, outrageous, raving, turbulent, ungoverned, uncontrolled, violent; dissipated, fast, flighty, foolish, giddy, harebrained, heedless, ill-advised, inconsiderate, reckless, thoughtless, unwise; boisterous, rough, stormy; crazy, extravagant, fanciful, grotesque, imaginary, strange. * n desert, waste, wilderness.

wilderness n desert, waste, wild.

wilful adj cantankerous, contumacious, dogged, headstrong, heady, inflexible, intractable, mulish, obdurate, obstinate, perverse, pig-headed, refractory, self-willed, stubborn, unruly, unyielding; arbitrary, capricious; deliberate, intended, intentional, planned, premeditated.

will vb bid, command, decree, direct, enjoin, ordain; choose, desire, elect, wish; bequeath, convey, demise, devise, leave. * n decision, determination, resoluteness, resolution, self-reliance; desire, disposition, inclination, intent, pleasure, purpose, volition, wish; behest, command, decree, demand, direction, order, request, requirement.

willing adj adaptable, amenable, compliant, desirous, disposed, inclined, minded; deliberate, free, intentional, spontaneous, unasked, unbidden, voluntary; cordial, eager, forward, prompt, ready.

willingly adv cheerfully, gladly, readily, spontaneously, voluntarily.

wily *adj* arch, artful, crafty, crooked, cunning, deceitful, designing, diplomatic, foxy, insidious, intriguing, politic, sly, subtle, treacherous, tricky.

win *vb* accomplish, achieve, acquire, catch, earn, effect, gain, gather, get, make, obtain, procure, reach, realize, reclaim, recover; gain, succeed, surpass, triumph; arrive; allure, attract, convince, influence, persuade. * *n* conquest, success, triumph, victory.

wind[1] *n* air, blast, breeze, draught, gust, hurricane, whiff, zephyr; breath, breathing, expiration, inspiration, respiration; flatulence, gas, windiness.

wind[2] *vb* coil, crank, encircle, involve, reel, roll, turn, twine, twist; bend, curve, meander, zigzag. * *n* bend, curve, meander, twist, zigzag.

winding *adj* circuitous, devious, flexuose, flexuous, meandering, serpentine, tortuous, turning, twisting. * *n* bend, curve, meander, turn, twist.

windy *adj* breezy, blowy, blustering, boisterous, draughty, gusty, squally, stormy, tempestuous; airy, empty, hollow, inflated. **winning** *adj* alluring, attractive, bewitching, brilliant, captivating, charming, dazzling, delightful, enchanting, engaging, fascinating, lovely, persuasive, pleasing, prepossessing; conquering, triumphant, victorious.

winnow *vb* cull, glean, divide, fan, part, select, separate, sift.

winsome *adj* blithe, blithesome, bonny, buoyant, charming, cheerful, debonair, jocund, light-hearted, lively, lovable, merry, pleasant, sportive, winning.

wintry *adj* arctic, boreal, brumal, cold, frosty, icy, snowy.

wipe *vb* clean, dry, mop, rub. * *n* mop, rub, blow, hit, strike; gibe, jeer, sarcasm, sneer, taunt.

wisdom *n* depth, discernment, far-sightedness, foresight, insight, judgement, judiciousness, prescience, profundity, prudence, sagacity, sapience, sense, solidity, understanding, wiseness; attainment, edification, enlightenment, erudition, information, knowledge, learning, lore, scholarship; reason.

wise *adj* deep, discerning, enlightened, intelligent, judicious, penetrating, philosophical, profound, rational, seasonable, sensible, sage, sapient, solid, sound; erudite, informed, knowing, learned, scholarly; crafty, cunning, designing, foxy, politic, sly, subtle, wary, wily.

wish *vb* covet, desire, hanker, list, long; bid, command, desire, direct, intend, mean, order, want. * *n* behest, desire, intention, mind, pleasure, want, will; craving, desire, hankering, inclination, liking, longing, want, yearning.

wistful *adj* contemplative, engrossed, meditative, musing, pensive, reflective, thoughtful; desirous, eager, earnest, longing.

wit *n* genius, intellect, intelligence, reason, sense, understanding; brightness, banter, cleverness, drollery, facetiousness, fun, humour, jocularity, piquancy, point, raillery, satire, sparkle, whim; conceit, epigram, jest, joke, pleasantry, quip, quirk, repartee, sally, witticism; humorist, joker, wag.

witch *n* charmer, enchantress, fascinator, sorceress; crone, hag, sibyl.

witchcraft *n* conjuration, enchantment, magic, necromancy, sorcery, spell.

withdraw *vb* abstract, deduct, remove, retire, separate, sequester, sequestrate, subduct, subtract; disengage, wean; abjure, recall, recant, relinquish, resign, retract, revoke; abdicate, decamp, depart, dissociate, retire, shrink, vacate.

wither *vb* contract, droop, dry, sear, shrivel, wilt, wizen; decay, decline, languish, pine, waste.

withhold *vb* check, detain, hinder, repress, restrain, retain, suppress.

withstand *vb* confront, defy, face, oppose, resist.

witless *adj* daft, dull, foolish, halfwitted, obtuse, senseless, shallow, silly, stupid, unintelligent.

witness *vb* corroborate, mark, note, notice, observe, see. * *n* attestation, conformation, corroboration, evidence, proof, testimony; beholder, bystander, corroborator, deponent, eyewitness, onlooker, spectator, testifier.

witty *adj* bright, clever, droll, facetious, funny, humorous, jocose, jocular, pleasant, waggish; alert, penetrating, quick, sparkling, sprightly.

wizard *n* charmer, diviner, conjurer, enchanter, magician, necromancer, seer, soothsayer, sorcerer.

woe *n* affliction, agony, anguish, bitterness, depression, distress, dole, grief, heartache, melancholy, misery, sorrow, torture, tribulation, trouble, unhappiness, wretchedness.

woeful *adj* afflicted, agonized, anguished, burdened, disconsolate, distressed, melancholy, miserable, mournful, piteous, sad, sorrowful, troubled, unhappy, wretched; afflicting, afflictive, calamitous, deplorable, depressing, disastrous, distressing, dreadful, tragic, tragical, grievous, lamentable, pitiable, saddening.

wonder *vb* admire, gape, marvel; conjecture, ponder, query, question, speculate. * *n* amazement, astonishment, awe, bewilderment, curiosity, marvel, miracle, prodigy, surprise, stupefaction, wonderment.

wonderful *adj* amazing, astonishing, astounding, awe-inspiring, awesome, awful, extraordinary, marvellous, miraculous, portentous, prodigious, startling, stupendous, surprising.

wont *adj* accustomed, customary, familiar, habitual, ordinary, usual. * *n* custom, habit, practice, rule, usage.

wonted *adj* accustomed, common, conventional, customary, everyday, familiar, frequent, habitual, ordinary, regular, usual.

wood *n* coppice, copse, covert, forest, greenwood, grove, spinney, thicket, woodland.

word *vb* express, phrase, put, say, state, term, utter. * *n* expression, name, phrase, term, utterance; account, advice, information, intelligence, message, news, report, tidings; affirmation, assertion, averment, avowal, declaration, statement; conversation, speech; agreement, assurance, engagement, parole, pledge, plight, promise; behest, bidding, command, direction, order, precept; countersign, password, signal, watchword.

wordy *adj* circumlocutory, diffuse, garrulous, inflated, lengthened, long-winded, loquacious, periphrastic, rambling, talkative, tedious, verbose, windy.

work *vb* act, operate; drudge, fag, grind, grub, labour, slave, sweat, toil; move, perform, succeed; aim, attempt, strive, try; effervesce, ferment, leaven, rise; accomplish, beget, cause, effect, engender, manage, originate, produce; exert, strain; embroider, stitch. * *n* exertion, drudgery, grind, labour, pain, toil; business, employment, function, occupation, task; action, accomplishment, achievement, composition, deed, feat, fruit, handiwork, opus, performance, product, production; fabric, manufacture; ferment, leaven; management, treatment.

workman *n* journeyman, employee, labourer, operative, worker, wright; artisan, craftsman, mechanic.

world *n* cosmos, creation, earth, globe, nature, planet, sphere, universe.

worldly *adj* common, earthly, human, mundane, sublunary, terrestrial; carnal, fleshly, profane, secular, temporal; ambitious, grovelling, irreligious, selfish, proud, sordid, unsanctified, unspiritual; sophisticated, worldly-wise.

worry *vb* annoy, badger, bait, beset, bore, bother, chafe, disquiet, disturb, fret, gall, harass, harry, hector, infest, irritate, molest, persecute, pester, plague, tease, torment, trouble, vex. * *n* annoyance, anxiety, apprehensiveness, care, concern, disquiet, fear, misgiving, perplexity, solicitude, trouble, uneasiness, vexation.

worship *vb* adore, esteem, honour, revere, venerate; deify, idolize; aspire, pray. * *n* adoration, devotion, esteem, homage, idolatry, idolizing, respect, reverence; aspiration, exultation, invocation, laud, praise, prayer, supplication.

worst *vb* beat, choke, conquer, crush, defeat, discomfit, foil, master, overpower, overthrow, quell, rout, subdue, subjugate, vanquish.

worth *n* account, character, credit, desert, excellence, importance, integrity, merit, nobleness, worthiness, virtue; cost, estimation, price, value.

worthless *adj* futile, meritless, miserable, nugatory, paltry, poor, trifling, unproductive, unsalable, unserviceable, useless, valueless, wretched; abject, base, corrupt, degraded, ignoble, low, mean, vile.

worthy *adj* deserving, fit, suitable; estimable, excellent, exemplary, good, honest, honourable, reputable, righteous, upright, virtuous. * *n* celebrity, dignitary, luminary, notability, personage, somebody, VIP.

wound *vb* damage, harm, hurt, injure; cut, gall, harrow, irritate, lacerate, pain, prick, stab; annoy, mortify, offend. * *n* blow, hurt, injury; damage, detriment; anguish, grief, pain, pang, torture.

wraith *n* apparition, ghost, phantom, spectre, vision.

wrangle *vb* argue, bicker, brawl, cavil, dispute, jangle, jar, quarrel, squabble, spar, spat. * *n* altercation, argument, bickering, brawl, contest, controversy, jar, quarrel, squabble.

wrap *vb* cloak, cover, encase, envelop, muffle, swathe, wind. * *n* blanket, cape, cloak, cover, overcoat, shawl.

wrath *n* anger, choler, exasperation, fury, heat, resentment, indignation, ire, irritation, offence, passion, rage.

wrathful *adj* angry, enraged, exasperated, furious, hot, indignant, infuriated, irate, mad, passionate, provoked, rageful.

wreak *vb* execute, exercise, indulge, inflict, work.

wreath *n* chaplet, curl, festoon, garland, ring, twine.

wreathe *vb* encircle, festoon, garland, intertwine, surround, twine, twist.

wreck *vb* founder, shipwreck, strand; blast, blight, break, devastate, ruin, spoil. * *n* crash, desolation, destruction, perdition, prostration, ruin, shipwreck, smash, undoing.

wrench *vb* distort, pervert, twist, wrest, wring; sprain, strain; extort, extract. * *n* twist, wring; sprain, strain; monkey wrench, spanner.

wrest *vb* force, pull, strain, twist, wrench, wring.

wrestle *vb* contend, contest, grapple, strive, struggle.

wretch *n* outcast, pariah, pilgarlic, troglodyte, vagabond, victim, sufferer; beggar, criminal, hound, knave, miscreant, rascal, ruffian, rogue, scoundrel, villain.

wretched *adj* afflicted, comfortless, distressed, forlorn, sad, unfortunate, unhappy, woebegone; afflicting, calamitous, deplorable, depressing, pitiable, sad, saddening, shocking, sorrowful; bad, beggarly, contemptible, mean, paltry, pitiful, poor, shabby, sorry, vile, worthless.

wring *vb* contort, twist, wrench; extort, force, wrest; anguish, distress, harass, pain, rack, torture.

wrinkle[1] *vb* cockle, corrugate, crease, gather, pucker, rumple. * *n* cockle, corrugation, crease, crimp, crinkle, crumple, fold, furrow, gather, plait, ridge, rumple.

wrinkle[2] *n* caprice, fancy, notion, quirk, whim; device, tip, trick.

writ *n* decree, order, subpoena, summons.

write *vb* compose, copy, indite, inscribe, pen, scrawl, scribble, transcribe.

writer *n* amanuensis, author, clerk, penman, scribe, secretary.

writhe *vb* contort, distort, squirm, twist, wriggle.

written *adj* composed, indited, inscribed, penned, transcribed.

wrong *vb* abuse, encroach, injure, maltreat, oppress. * *adj* inequitable, unfair, unjust, wrongful; bad, criminal, evil, guilty, immoral, improper, iniquitous, reprehensible, sinful, vicious, wicked; amiss, improper, inappropriate, unfit, unsuitable; erroneous, false, faulty, inaccurate, incorrect, mistaken, untrue. * *adv* amiss, erroneously, falsely, faultily, improperly, inaccurately, incorrectly, wrongly. * *n* foul, grievance, inequity, injury, injustice, trespass, unfairness; blame, crime, dishonesty, evil, guilt, immorality, iniquity, misdeed, misdoing, sin, transgression, unrighteousness, vice, wickedness, wrongdoing; error, falsity.

wroth *adj* angry, enraged, exasperated, furious, incensed, indignant, irate, passionate, provoked, resentful.

wrought *adj* done, effected, performed, worked.

wry *adj* askew, awry, contorted, crooked, distorted, twisted.

XYZ

xanthous *adj* blonde, fair, light-complexioned, xanthic, yellow.

xiphoid *adj* ensiform, gladiate, sword-like, sword-shaped.

Xmas *n* Christmas, Christmastide, Noel, Yule, Yuletide.

X-ray *n* roentgen ray, röntgen ray.

xylograph *n* cut, woodcut, wood engraving.

xylographer *n* wood engraver.

xylophagous *adj* wood-eating, wood-nourished.

yap *vb* bark, cry, yelp. * *n* bark, cry, yelp.

yard *n* close, compound, court, courtyard, enclosure, garden.

yarn *n* anecdote, boasting, fabrication, narrative, story, tale, untruth.

yawn *vb* dehisce, gape, open wide. * *n* gap, gape, gulf.

yearn *vb* crave, desire, hanker after, long for.

yell *vb* bawl, bellow, cry out, howl, roar, scream, screech, shriek, squeal.* *n* cry, howl, roar, scream, screech, shriek.

yellow *adj* aureate, gilded, gilt, gold, golden, lemon, primrose, saffron, xanthic, xanthous.

yelp *vb* bark, howl, yap; complain, bitch, grouse. * *n* bark, sharp cry, howl.

yet *adv* at last, besides, further, however, over and above, so far, still, thus far, ultimately.* *conj* moreover, nevertheless, notwithstanding, now.

yield *vb* afford, bear, bestow, communicate, confer, fetch, furnish, impart, produce, render, supply; accede, accord, acknowledge, acquiesce, allow, assent, comply, concede, give, grant, permit; abandon, abdicate, cede, forgo, give up, let go, quit, relax, relinquish, resign, submit, succumb, surrender, waive. * *n* earnings, income, output, produce, profit, return, revenue.

yielding *adj* accommodating, acquiescent, affable, compliant, complaisant, easy, manageable, obedient, passive, submissive, unresisting; bending, flexible, flexile, plastic, pliant, soft, supple, tractable; fertile, productive.

yoke *vb* associate, bracket, connect, couple, harness, interlink, join, link, unite. * *n* bond, chain, ligature, link, tie, union; bondage, dependence, enslavement, service, servitude, subjection, vassalage; couple, pair.

yokel *n* boor, bumpkin, countryman, peasant, rustic.

yore *adj* ancient, antique, old, olden. * *n* long ago, long since, olden times.

young *adj* green, ignorant, inexperienced, juvenile, new, recent, youthful. * *n* young people, youth; babies, issue, brood, offspring, progeny, spawn.

youngster *n* adolescent, boy, girl, lad, lass, stripling, youth.

youth *n* adolescence, childhood, immaturity, juvenile, juvenility, minority, nonage, pupillage, wardship; boy, girl, lad, lass, schoolboy, schoolgirl, slip, sprig, stripling, youngster.

youthful *adj* boyish, childish, girlish, immature, juvenile, puerile, young.

zany *adj* comic, comical, crazy, droll, eccentric, funny, imaginative, scatterbrained; clownish, foolish, ludicrous, silly. * *n* buffoon, clown, droll, fool, harlequin, jester, punch.

zeal *n* alacrity, ardour, cordiality, devotedness, devotion, earnestness, eagerness, energy, enthusiasm, fervour, glow, heartiness, intensity, jealousness, passion, soul, spirit, warmth.

zealot *n* bigot, devotee, fanatic, freak, partisan.

zealous *adj* ardent, burning, devoted, eager, earnest, enthusiastic, fervent, fiery, forward, glowing, jealous, keen, passionate, prompt, ready, swift, warm.

zenith *n* acme, apex, climax, culmination, heyday, pinnacle, prime, summit, top, utmost, height.

zero *n* cipher, naught, nadir, nil, nothing, nought.

zest *n* appetite, enjoyment, exhilaration, gusto, liking, piquancy, relish, thrill; edge, flavour, salt, savour, tang, taste; appetizer, sauce.

zone *n* band, belt, cincture, girdle, girth; circuit, clime, region.

zymotic *adj* bacterial, fermentative, germinating.

English Grammar

A

a *see* **indefinite article**.

a-, an- is a prefix derived from Greek, meaning 'not', 'without'. Older words using it include agnostic, anarchy, anonymous. Several modern words have been formed using it, as in apolitical, asexual, atypical.

abbreviations are shortened forms of words usually used as a space-saving technique and becoming increasingly common in modern usage. They cause problems with regard to punctuation. The common question asked is whether the letters of an abbreviation should be separated by full stops. In modern usage the tendency is to omit full stops from abbreviations. This is most true of abbreviations involving initial capital letters, as in TUC, BBC, EEC and USA. In such cases full stops should definitely not be used if one or some of the initial letters do not belong to a full word. Thus television is abbreviated to TV and educationally subnormal to ESN.

There are usually no full stops in abbreviations involving the first and last letters of a word (contractions) Dr, Mr, Rd, St, but this is a matter of taste.

Abbreviations involving the first few letters of a word, as in 'Prof' (Professor) are the most likely to have full stops, as in 'Feb.' (February) but again this is now a matter of taste.

These are mostly formed by adding lower-case *s*, as in Drs, JPs, TVs. Note the absence of apostrophes. *See also* ACRONYMS.

ablative refers to a case in Latin grammar that expressed 'by, with or from'. In English this case does not exist, prepositional phrases being used its place.

-able is a suffix meaning 'that can be', as in laughable, readable, washable. *See* **adjective**.

abstract noun is a noun which is the name of a thing that cannot be touched but refers to a quality, concept or idea. Examples of abstract nouns include 'anger', 'beauty', 'courage', 'Christianity', 'danger', 'fear', 'greed', 'hospitality', 'ignorance', 'jealousy', 'kudos', 'loyalty', 'Marxism', 'need', 'obstinacy', 'pain', 'quality', 'resistance', 'safety', 'truth', 'unworthiness', 'vanity', 'wisdom', 'xenophobia', 'youth', 'zeal'. *See also* CONCRETE NOUN.

accent commonly refers to a regional or individual way of speaking or pronouncing words, as in 'a Glasgow accent'. The word is also used to mean emphasis as in 'In hotel the accent is on the second syllable of the word' or 'In fashion this year the accent is on longer skirts'.

Accent also refers to certain symbols used on some foreign words adopted into English. In modern usage, which has a tendency to punctuate less than formerly was the case, accents are frequently omitted. For example an actor's part in a play is now usually spelt role but originally it was spelt rôle, the accent on *o* being called a circumflex. The accent is most likely to be retained if it affects the pronunciation. Thus cliché and divorcé usually retain the acute accent, as it is called, on the *e*. On the other hand, the accent known as the cedilla is frequently omitted from beneath the *c* in words such as façade/facade, although it is there to indicate that the *c* is soft, pronounced like an *s*, rather than a hard sound, pronounced like a *k*. The grave accent is retained in English in some words and phrases derived from French, as *mise en scène*.

accusative refers to a case in Latin grammar, the equivalent of 'objective'. It is sometimes used in English instead of 'objective'.

acronyms, like some **abbreviations**, are formed from the initial letters of several words. Unlike abbreviations, however, **acronyms** are pronounced as words rather than as just a series of letters. For example, OPEC (Organization of Petroleum Producing Countries) is pronounced o-pek and is thus an acronym, unlike USA (United States of America) which is pronounced as a series of letters and not as a word (oo-sa or yoo-sa) and is thus an abbreviation.

Acronyms are written without full stops, as in UNESCO (United Nations Educational, Scientific and Cultural Organization). Mostly **acronyms** are written in capital letters, as in NASA (National Aeronautics and Space Administration). However, very common **acronyms**, such as Aids (Acquired Immune Deficiency Syndrome), are written with just an initial capital, the rest of the letters being lower case.

Acronyms which refer to a piece of scientific or technical equipment are written like ordinary words in lower-case letters as in laser (light amplification by simulated emission of radiation).

active voice is one of two voices that verbs are divided into, the other being PASSIVE VOICE. In verbs in the active voice, commonly called *active verbs*, the subject of the verb performs the action described by the verb. Thus, in the sentence 'The boy threw the ball', 'throw' is in the active voice since the subject of the verb (the boy) is doing the throwing. Similarly, in the sentence 'Her mother was driving the car', 'driving' is in the active voice since it is the subject of the sentence (her mother) that is doing the driving. Similarly, in the sentence 'We saw the cows in the field', 'saw' is the active voice since it is the subject of the sentence (we) that is doing the seeing. *See also* PASSIVE VOICE.

acute accent refers to a mark placed over some letters in certain languages, such as French, to indicate vowel length, vowel quality, pronunciation, etc. It is found in English in some words that have been borrowed from the French, as in 'fiancé' and 'divorcé' to indicate pronunciation.

-ade is a suffix meaning 'fruit drink', as in 'lemonade'.

adjectival clause is a kind of subordinate clause which describes or modifies a noun or pronoun. *See under* RELATIVE CLAUSE, the name by which it is better known.

adjective is a word that describes or gives information about a noun or pronoun. It is said to qualify a noun or pronoun since it limits the word it describes in some way, by making it more specific. Thus, adding the adjective 'red' to 'book' limits 'book', since it means we can forget about books of any other colour. Similarly, adding 'large' to 'book' limits it, since it means we can forget about books of any other size.

Adjectives tell us something about the colour, size, number, quality, or classification of a noun or pronoun, as in 'purple curtains', 'jet-black hair', 'bluish eyes'; 'tiny baby', 'large houses', 'biggish gardens', 'massive estates'; five children', 'twenty questions', 'seventy-five books'; 'sad people', 'joyful occasions', 'delicious food', 'civil engineering', 'nuclear physics', 'modern languages', 'Elizabethan drama'.

Several adjectives may modify one noun or pronoun, as in 'the small, black cat', 'an enormous, red-brick, Victorian house'. The order in which they appear is flexible and can vary according to the emphasis one wishes to place on the various adjectives. However, a common sequence is size, quality, colour and classification, as in 'a small, beautiful, pink wild rose' and 'a large, ugly, grey office building'.

Adjectives do not change their form. They remain the same whether the noun to which they refer is singular or plural, or masculine or feminine.

All the above examples of adjectives come before the noun, but not all adjectives do so. For information on the position of adjectives *see* ATTRIBUTIVE ADJECTIVE, PREDICATIVE ADJECTIVE, POST-MODIFIER.

Many **adjectives** are formed from either the past participles of verbs, and so end in *-ed*, or from the present participles and so end in *-ing*. Examples of adjectives ending in *-ed* include 'annoyed', 'blackened', 'coloured', 'damaged', 'escaped', 'fallen', 'guarded', 'heated', 'identified', 'jailed', 'knotted', 'labelled', 'mixed', 'numbered', 'opened', 'pleated', 'recorded', 'satisfied', 'taped', 'used', 'varied', 'walled', 'zoned'. Examples of adjectives ending in *-ing* include 'amusing', 'boring', 'captivating', 'demanding', 'enchanting', 'fading', 'grating', 'horrifying', 'identifying', 'jarring', 'kneeling', 'labouring', 'manufacturing', 'nursing', 'operating', 'parting', 'quivering', 'racing', 'satisfying', 'telling', 'undermining', 'worrying', 'yielding'.

Several **adjectives** end in *-ical* and are formed by adding *-al* to certain nouns ending in *-ic*. Examples include 'arithmetical', 'comical', 'critical', 'cynical', 'fanatical', 'logical', 'magical', 'musical', 'mystical' and 'sceptical'. Sometimes the adjectives ending in *-ical* are formed from nouns that end in *-ics*. These include 'acoustical', 'ethical', 'hysterical', 'statistical' and 'tropical'. Several adjectives end in *-ic* and are formed from nouns ending in *-ics*. These include 'acoustic', 'acrobatic', 'aerobic', 'athletic', 'economic', 'electronic', 'genetic', 'gymnastic', 'histrionic' and 'linguistic'.

Other common adjectival endings include *-ful*, as in 'beautiful', 'dreadful', 'eventful', 'graceful', 'hateful', 'tearful' and 'youthful'. They also include *-less*, as in 'clueless', 'graceless', 'hatless', 'meaningless' and 'sunless'.

Many adjectives end in *-able* and many end in *-ible*. There are often spelling problems with such adjectives. The following adjectives are likely to be misspelt:

Some adjectives in *-able*:

abominable	disreputable	nameable
acceptable	durable	non-flammable
adaptable	durable	objectionable
adorable	enviable	operable
advisable	excitable	palpable
agreeable	excusable	pleasurable
amiable	expendable	preferable
approachable	foreseeable	readable
available	forgettable	recognizable
bearable	forgivable	regrettable
bearable	healable	renewable
beatable	hearable	reputable
believable	immovable	sizeable
blameable	impassable	stoppable
calculable	impeccable	tenable
capable	implacable	tolerable
changeable	impracticable	transferable
comfortable	impressionable	understandable
commendable	indescribable	unmistakable
conceivable	indispensable	usable
definable	inimitable	variable
delectable	insufferable	viable
demonstrable	lamentable	washable
dependable	manageable	wearable
desirable	measurable	winnable
discreditable	memorable	workable

Some adjectives ending in *-ible*:

accessible	divisible	perceptible
admissible	edible	permissible
audible	exhaustible	possible
collapsible	expressible	repressible
combustible	fallible	reproducible
compatible	feasible	resistible
comprehensible	flexible	responsible
contemptible	forcible	reversible
credible	gullible	risible
defensible	indelible	sensible
destructible	intelligible	susceptible
digestible	irascible	tangible
discernible	negligible	visible

See also COMPARISON OF ADJECTIVES, COMPOUNDS, DEMONSTRATIVE ADJECTIVE, DETERMINER, INTERROGATIVE ADJECTIVE and POSSESSIVE ADJECTIVE.

adverb is a word that adds to our information about a verb, as in 'work rapidly'; about an adjective, as in 'an extremely beautiful young woman'; or about another adverb, as in 'sleeping very soundly'. **Adverbs** are said to modify the words to which they apply since they limit the words in some way and make them more specific. Thus, adding 'slowly' to 'walk', as in 'They walked slowly down the hill', limits the verb 'walk' since all other forms of 'walk', such as 'quickly', 'lazily', etc, have been discarded.

There are several different kinds of **adverbs**, categorized according to the information they provide about the word they modify. They include adverbs of time, adverbs of place, adverbs of manner, adverbs of degree, adverbs of frequency, adverbs of probability, adverbs of duration, and interrogative adverbs.

Adverbs of time tell us when something happened and include such words as 'now', 'then', 'later', 'soon', 'afterwards', 'yesterday', etc, as in 'He is due to arrive now', I will call you later', 'She had a rest and went out afterwards', 'They left yesterday'.

Adverbs of place tell us where something happened and include such words as 'there', 'here', 'somewhere', 'anywhere', 'thereabouts', 'abroad', 'outdoors', 'overhead', 'underground', 'hither and thither', etc, as in 'I haven't been there', 'They couldn't see her anywhere', 'His family live abroad', and 'We heard a noise overhead'.

Adverbs of manner tell us how something happens and include a wide range of possibilities. Frequently adverbs in this category are formed by adding -*ly* to an adjective. Examples of these include:

adjective	adverb	adjective	adverb
anxious	anxiously	mean	meanly
bad	badly	narrow	narrowly
cautious	cautiously	pale	palely
dumb	dumbly	quick	quickly
elegant	elegantly	soothing	soothingly
fearless	fearlessly	tough	toughly
hot	hotly	unwilling	unwillingly
interested	interestedly	vain	vainly
joking	jokingly	weak	weakly
lame	lamely		

Some adjectives have to be modified in some way before the suffix -*ly* is added to form the adverbs. For example, in adjectives ending in -*y*, the *y* changes to *i* before -*ly* is added. Examples of these include:

adjective	adverb	adjective	adverb
angry	angrily	happy	happily
busy	busily	merry	merrily
canny	cannily	pretty	prettily
dry	drily	silly	sillily
easy	easily	tatty	tattily
funny	funnily	weary	wearily

Note the exceptions 'shyly', 'slyly', 'wryly'.
Adjectives ending in -*e* frequently drop the *e* before adding -*ly*. Examples of these include:

adjective	adverb	adjective	adverb
able	ably	peaceable	peaceably
feeble	feebly	true	truly
gentle	gently	unintelligible	unintelligibly

Suffixes other than -*ly* that may be added to adjectives to form **adverbs of manner** include -*wards*, as in 'backwards', 'heavenwards'; -*ways*, as in 'edgeways', 'sideways'; -*wise*, as in 'clockwise', 'moneywise'.

Some **adverbs of manner** may take the same form as the adjectives to which they correspond. These include 'fast', 'hard', 'solo', 'straight', 'wrong', as in 'She took the wrong book' and 'Don't get me wrong'.

Adverbs of degree tells us the degree, extent or intensity of something that happens and include 'hugely', 'immensely', 'moderately', 'adequately', 'greatly', 'strongly', 'tremendously', 'profoundly', 'totally', 'entirely', 'perfectly', 'partially', 'practically', 'virtually', 'almost', as in 'They enjoyed the show hugely', 'The office was not adequately equipped', 'We strongly disapprove of such behaviour', 'He was totally unaware of the facts', 'They are virtually penniless'.

Adverbs of frequency are used to tell us how often something happens and include 'never', 'rarely', 'sel-

dom', 'infrequently', 'occasionally', 'periodically', 'intermittently', 'sometimes', 'often', 'frequently', 'regularly', 'normally', 'always', 'constantly', 'continually', as in 'She never eats breakfast', 'We go to the cinema occasionally', 'He goes to the dentist regularly', 'Normally they travel by bus', 'He is in pain constantly'.

Adverbs of probability tells us how often something happens and include 'probably', 'possibly', 'conceivably', 'perhaps', 'maybe', 'presumably', 'hopefully', 'definitely', 'certainly', 'indubitably', 'doubtless', as in 'You will probably see them there', 'He may conceivably pass the exam this time', 'Presumably they know that she is leaving', 'Hopefully the news will be good', 'I am definitely not going', 'He is indubitably a criminal'.

Adverbs of duration tell us how long something takes or lasts and include 'briefly', 'temporarily', 'long', 'indefinitely', 'always', 'permanently', 'forever', as in 'We stopped briefly for coffee', 'Have you known her long?', 'Her face is permanently disfigured', 'They have parted forever'.

Adverbs of emphasis add emphasis to the action described by the verb and include 'absolutely', 'certainly', 'positively', 'quite', 'really', 'simply', 'just', as in 'They absolutely detest each other', 'He positively adores her', 'She really wants to be forgiven', 'I simply must go now'

Interrogative adverbs ask questions and include 'where', 'when', 'how', and 'why', as in 'Where are you going?', 'When will you be back?', 'How will you get there?', 'Why have they asked you to go?' They are placed at the beginning of sentences, and such sentences always end with a question mark.

adverbial clauses are subordinate clauses that modify the main or principal clause by adding information about time, place, concession, condition, manner, purpose and result. They usually follow the main clause but most of them can be put in front of the main clause for reason of emphasis or style.

Adverbial clauses of time indicate the time of an event and are introduced by conjunctions such as 'after', 'as', 'as soon as', 'before', 'once', 'since', 'the minute', 'the moment', 'till', 'until', 'when', 'whenever', 'while', 'whilst', as in 'He left after the meal was over', 'She arrived as I was leaving', 'Once I recognized him I spoke to him', 'I recognized him the minute I saw him', 'We won't know until tomorrow' and 'The thief ran away when he saw the police'.

Adverbial clauses of place indicate the location of an event and are introduced by conjunctions such as 'where', 'wherever' or 'everywhere', as in 'He was miserable where he was', 'They left it where they found it', 'Wherever I went I saw signs of poverty' and 'Everywhere she goes she causes trouble'.

Adverbial clauses of concession contain a fact that contrasts in some way with the main clause and are introduced by conjunctions such as 'although', 'even though', 'though', 'whereas', 'while', 'whilst', as in 'I have to admire his speech, although I disagree with what he said', 'He does his best at school work even though he is not very good at it' and 'Whilst I myself do not like him I can understand why he is popular'.

Adverbial clauses of condition deal with possible situations and are introduced by the conjunctions 'if', 'only if', 'unless', 'as long as', 'providing', 'provided', as in 'If you had kept quiet they would not have known about the event', 'We cannot go unless we get permission', 'They can leave only if they have finished their work' and 'Provided he is feeling better he can leave hospital'. Inversion can be used in such clauses instead of a conjunction, as in 'Had you been present you would have been most amused' and 'Had he any sense he would leave now'.

Adverbial clauses of manner describe the way that someone behaves or the way in which something is done, and are introduced by conjunctions such as 'as', 'as if', 'as though', 'like', 'the way', as in 'Why does he behave as he does', 'He slurred his speech as though he were drunk' and 'He looked at her as if he hated her'.

Adverbial clauses of purpose indicate the intention someone has when doing something and is introduced by conjunctions such as 'to', 'in order to', 'so as to', 'so', 'so that', as in 'He did that just to upset her', 'They will have to work long hours in order to make that amount of money', 'They started to run so as to get home before it rained' and 'The firm reduced the number of staff in order that they might avoid bankruptcy'.

Adverbial clauses of reason explain why something happens or is done and are introduced by conjunctions such as 'because', 'since', 'as', as in 'We didn't go because the car broke down', 'As it was raining we had the party indoors' and 'since he has broken the school rules he should be punished'.

Adverbial clauses of result indicate the result of an event or situation and are introduced by the conjunctions 'so' or 'so that', as in 'He fell awkwardly so that he broke his leg' and 'She stumbled over her words so that the audience had difficulty understanding her'. *See* COMPARISON OF ADVERBS and COMPOUNDS.

aero- is a prefix meaning 'air', as in 'aerobics', 'aerodynamics', 'aeroplane' and 'aerospace', or 'aircraft', as in as in 'aerodrome', 'aeronaut'.

affix refers to an element that is added to a base or root word to form another word. **Affixes** can be in the form of 'prefixes' or 'suffixes'. 'Prefix' is an **affix** that is added to the beginning of a word. Thus *audio* in 'audiovisual' is both a prefix and an affix. 'Suffix' is an **affix** that is added to the end of a word. Thus *-aholic* in 'workaholic' is a 'suffix' and an **affix.**

agent noun refers to someone that is the 'doer' of the action of a verb. It is usually spelt ending in either *-er*, as 'enquirer', or in *-or*, as in 'investigator' and 'supervisor', but frequently either of these endings is acceptable, as 'adviser/advisor'.

agreement or **concord** refers to the agreeing of two or more elements in a clause or sentence, i.e. they take the same number, person or gender. In English the most common form of **agreement** is that between subject and verb, and this usually involves **number agreement**. This means that singular nouns are usually accompanied by singular verbs, as in 'She looks well', 'He is working late' and 'The boy has passed the exam', and that plural nouns are usually accompanied by plural verbs, as in 'They look well', 'They are working late' and 'The boys have passed the exam'.

Problems arise when the noun in question can be either singular or plural, for example, 'audience', 'committee', 'crowd', 'family', 'government', 'group'. Such nouns take a singular verb if the user is regarding the people or items referred to by the noun as a group, as in 'The family is moving house', or as individuals, as in 'The family are quarrelling over where to go on holiday'.

Compound subjects, that is two or more nouns acting as the subject, whether singular or plural, joined with 'and', are used with a plural noun, as in 'My friend and

I are going to the cinema tonight' and 'James and John are leaving today', unless the two nouns together represent a single concept, as 'brandy and soda', in which case the verb is in the singular, as in 'Brandy and soda is his favourite drink' and 'cheese and pickle' in 'Cheese and pickle is the only sandwich filing available.

In cases where two or more singular nouns acting as the subject are connected with such phrases as 'as well as', 'together with' and 'plus', as in 'His mother, as well as his father, is away from home' and 'The flat, together with the house, is up for sale', the verb is in the singular.

Indefinite pronouns such as 'anyone', 'everyone', 'no one', 'someone', 'either', 'neither' are singular and should be followed by a singular verb, as in 'Each of the flats is self-contained', 'Everyone is welcome', 'No one is allowed in without a ticket' and 'Neither is quite what I am looking for'.

When the subject is a singular noun, which is separated from the verb by a number of plural nouns, as in 'a list of dates and times of the next concerts', the verb is in the singular because 'list' is singular, as in 'A list of dates and times of the next concerts is available'.

Agreement with reference to both number and gender affects pronouns, as in 'She blames herself', 'He could have kicked himself' and 'They asked themselves why they had got involved'. Problems arise when the pronoun is indefinite and so the sex of the person is unspecified. Formerly in such cases the masculine pronouns were assumed to be neutral and so 'Each of the pupils was asked to hand in his work' was considered quite acceptable. The rise of feminism has led to a questioning of this assumption and alternatives have been put forward. These include 'Each of the pupils was asked to hand in his/her (or his or her) work', but some people feel that this is clumsy. Another alternative is 'Each of the pupils was asked to hand in their work'. Although it is ungrammatical, this convention is becoming quite acceptable in modern usage. To avoid both the clumsiness of the former and the ungrammaticalness of the latter, it is possible to cast the whole sentence in the plural, as in 'All the pupils were asked to hand in their work'.

agro-, agri- is a prefix derived from Greek meaning 'field', as in 'agriculture', 'agribusiness', 'agrobiology', 'agrochemicals'.

-aholic is a suffix meaning 'addicted to', formed on analogy with 'alcoholic', as in 'workaholic', 'shopaholic'. It sometimes becomes *-oholic*, as in chocoholic.

allegory is a kind of story which has deeper significance as well as the obvious surface meaning of the story. It is usually used to get a moral message across symbolically. Two of the famous allegories in English literature are *Pilgrim's Progress* by John Bunyan (1628-88) and *The Faerie Queene* by Edmund Spenser (1552-99).

alliteration is a figure of speech in which a sequence of words begin with the same letter or sound as in 'Round and round the rugged rocks the ragged rascal ran' and 'Peter Piper picked a peck of pickled peppers'. The given examples are both tongue twisters but **alliteration** is frequently used by poets for literary effect as in a 'red, red rose'.

also is an adverb and should not be used as a conjunction instead of 'and'. Thus sentences such as 'Please send me some apples, also some pears' are grammatically incorrect.

although is a conjunction used to introduce a 'subordinate adverbial clause of concession', as in 'They are very happy although they are poor', meaning 'Despite the fact they are poor they are happy'. 'Though' or 'even though' can be substituted for 'although', as in 'they are very happy even though they are poor'. *See* ADVERBIAL CLAUSE and CONJUNCTION.

ambi- is a prefix derived from Greek 'two', 'both', as in 'ambidextrous', 'ambivalent'.

an *see* **indefinite article.**

an- *see* **a-.**

-ana is a suffix meaning 'things associated with', as in 'Victoriana', 'Americana'.

anacoluthon is a figure of speech which refers to a change of construction in a sentence before the original structure is complete, as in 'My feeling is—but you must decide for yourself—how long did you say you have?' **Anacoluthon** is usually found in spoken English when someone is thinking aloud. Unlike many figures of speech, it is usually used accidentally rather than for literary or rhetorical effect.

anadiplosis is a figure of speech which refers to the repetition of a word or group at the end of one phrase or sentence and the beginning of the next for literary effect, as in 'sit and think about the past—the past which had been so warm and happy'.

analogy is a figure of speech rather like the simile in which there is an inference of a resemblance between two items that are being compared, as in 'Mary's parties are a bit like Christmas—much looked forward to but often a bit of a disappointment'.

anastrophe is a figure of speech which refers to an inversion of the usual order of words in a sentence or phrase for emphasis, or literary or rhetorical effect, as in 'Many a foreign dawn has he seen'.

and is called a coordinating conjunction because it joins elements of language which are of equal status. The elements may be words, as in 'cows and horses', 'John and James', 'provide wine and beer'; phrases, as in 'working hard and playing hard' and 'trying to look after her children and her elderly parents'; clauses, as in 'John has decided to emigrate and his brother has decided to join him' and 'He has lost his job and he now has no money'. When a coordinating conjunction is used, the subject of the second clause can sometimes be omitted if it is the same as the subject of the first clause, as in 'They have been forced to sell the house and are very sad about it'. *See* CONJUNCTION.

The use of **and** at the beginning of a sentence is disliked by many people. It should be used only for deliberate effect, as in 'And then he saw the monster', or in informal contexts.

Other coordinating conjunctions include 'but', 'or', 'yet', 'both... and', 'either... or', and 'neither.... nor', as in 'poor but honest' and 'the blue dress or the green one'.

Anglo- is a prefix meaning 'English', as in 'Anglo-Irish', 'Anglo-Indian'.

ante- is a prefix derived from Latin meaning 'before', as in 'antedate', 'antenatal', 'anteroom'.

antecedent refers to the noun or noun phrase in a main clause to which a relative pronoun in a relative clause refers back. Thus in the sentence 'People who live dangerously frequently get hurt', 'people' is an antecedent. Similarly, in the sentence 'The child identified the old man who attacked her', 'the old man' is the antecedent'. *See* RELATIVE CLAUSE.

anthropo- is a prefix derived from Greek meaning 'human being', as in anthropoid, anthropology.

anti- is a prefix derived from Greek meaning 'against'. It is used in many words that have been established in the language for a long time, as in 'antidote' and 'antipathy', but it has also been used to form modern words, as 'anti-establishment', 'antifreeze', 'anti-inflationary', 'anti-nuclear', 'anti-warfare'.

anticlimax is a figure of speech in which there is a sudden descent from the lofty to the ridiculous or the trivial, as in 'She went home in a flood of tears and a taxi' and Alexander Pope's 'When husbands or when lapdogs breathe their last'.

antiphrasis is a figure of speech in which a word or phrase is used in a sense that is opposite to the accepted sense. It is often used to achieve an ironic or humorous effect, as in 'His mother is ninety years young today'. Young is usually associated with youth but here it is associated with old age.

antithesis is a figure of speech in contrasting ideas are balanced for effect, as in 'We need money, not advice', 'More haste, less speed' and 'Marry at haste, repent at leisure'. It is a common figure of speech in literature, as in Alexander Pope's 'To err is human, to forgive, divine' and John Milton's 'Better to reign in hell than to serve in heaven'.

antonomasia is a figure of speech indicating the use of a personal name or proper name to anyone belonging to a class or group, as in 'John is such an Einstein that the other members of the class are in awe of him', where the meaning is that 'John has such a brilliant mind that the other members of the class are in awe of him'.

antonym refers to a word that is the opposite of another word. Thus 'black' is an antonym for 'white', 'cowardly' is an antonym for 'courageous' , 'dull' is an antonym for 'bright', and 'fast' is an antonym for 'slow'.

any is a pronoun which may take either a singular or plural verb, depending on the context. When a singular noun is used, a singular verb is used, as in 'Is any of the cloth still usable?' 'Are any of the children coming?' When a plural noun is used, either a plural or a singular verb can be used, the singular verb being more formal, as in 'Did you ask if any of his friends were/was there?'.

anyone should be used with a singular verb, as in 'Has anyone seen my book' and 'Is anyone coming to the lecture'. It should also be followed, where relevant, by a singular, not plural, personal pronoun or possessive adjective, as in 'Has anyone left his/her book'. Because this construction, which avoids the sexist 'his', is considered by many people to be clumsy, there is a growing tendency to use 'their' and be ungrammatical.

aposiopesis is a figure of speech in which words are omitted or there is a sudden breaking off for dramatic effect, as in 'The door slowly opened and....' and 'There was the noise of gunshot and then....'

apostrophe¹ is a figure of speech which takes the form of a rhetorical address to an absent or dead person or to a personified thing, as in 'O Romeo! Romeo! wherefore art thou, Romeo?' and 'Oh Peace, why have you deserted us?'

apostrophe² is a form of punctuation that is mainly used to indicate possession. Many spelling errors centre on the position of the apostrophe in relation to s.

Possessive nouns are usually formed by adding 's to the singular noun, as in 'the girl's mother', and Peter's car'; by adding an apostrophe to plural nouns that end in s, as in 'all the teachers' cars'; by adding 's to irregular plural nouns that do not end in s, as in 'women's shoes'.

In the possessive form of a name or singular noun that ends in s, x or z, the apostrophe may or may not be followed by s. In words of one syllable the final s is usually added, as in 'James's house', 'the fox's lair', 'Roz's dress'. The final s is most frequently omitted in names, particularly in names of three or more syllables, as in 'Euripides' plays'. In many cases the presence or absence of final s is a matter of convention.

The apostrophe is also used to indicate omitted letters in contracted forms of words, as in 'can't' and 'you've'. They are sometimes used to indicate missing century numbers in dates, as in 'the '60s and '70s', but are not used at the end of decades, etc, as in '1960s', not '1960's'.

Generally apostrophes are no longer used to indicate omitted letters in shortened forms that are in common use, as in 'phone' and 'flu'.

Apostrophes are often omitted wrongly in modern usage, particularly in the media and by advertisers, as in 'womens hairdressers', 'childrens helpings'. In addition, apostrophes are frequently added erroneously (as in 'potato's for sale' and 'Beware of the dog's'). This is partly because people are unsure about when and when not to use them and partly because of a modern tendency to punctuate as little as possible.

apposition refers to a noun or a phrase which provides further information about another noun or phrase. Both nouns and phrases refer to the same person or thing. In the phrase 'Peter Jones, our managing director', ' Peter Jones' and 'our managing director' are said to be in **apposition**. Similarly, in the phrase 'his cousin, the chairman of the firm', 'his cousin' and 'the chairman of the firm' are in **apposition.**

arch- is a prefix derived from Greek meaning 'chief', as in 'archbishop', 'archduke', 'arch-enemy'.

-arch is a suffix derived from the Greek meaning 'chief, ruler', as in 'anarchy', 'hierarchy' and 'monarchy'.

-arian is a suffix derived from Latin and means, in one of its senses, 'a supporter of', as in 'vegetarian', or 'one connected with', as in 'antiquarian' and 'librarian'.

article see **definite article** and **indefinite article.**

as is a conjunction which can introduce either a 'subordinate adverbial clause of time', as in 'I caught sight of him as I was leaving', a 'subordinate adverbial clause of manner', as in 'He acted as he promised', and 'a subordinate adverbial clause of reason', as in 'As it's Saturday he doesn't have to work'. it is also used in the **as....as** construction, as in 'She doesn't play as well as her sister does'.

The construction may be followed by a subject pronoun or an object pronoun, according to sense. In the sentence 'He plays as well as she', which is a slightly shortened form of 'She plays as well as he does', 'he' is a subject pronoun. In informal English the subject pronoun often becomes an object pronoun, as in 'She plays as well as him'. In the sentence 'They hate their father as much as her', 'her' is an object and the sentence means 'They hate their father as much as they hate

her', but in the sentence 'They hate their father as much as she', 'she' is a subject and the sentence means 'They hate their father as much as she does'. See ADVERBIAL CLAUSE and CONJUNCTION.

assonance is a figure of speech in which vowel sounds are repeated to give a half-rhyme effect, as in 'with gun, drum, trumpet, blunderbuss and thunder'.

astro- is a prefix derived from Greek meaning 'star', as in 'astrology', 'astronomy', 'astronaut', 'astrophysics'.

asyndeton is a figure of speech referring to the omission of conjunctions for dramatic or literary effect, as in 'I came, I saw, I conquered' and 'He entered, he looked round, he left'.

-athon, -thon is a suffix meaning 'large scale or long-lasting contest or event', as in 'swimathon', 'telethon'. These words are formed on analogy with the Greek derived word 'marathon', and they often refer to events undertaken for charity.

attributive adjective refers to an **adjective** that is placed immediately before the noun which it qualifies. In the phrases 'a red dress', 'the big house' and 'an enjoyable evening', 'red, 'big' and 'enjoyable' are attributive adjectives.

audio- is derived from Latin 'hear'. It is found in several words that have been established in the language for a long time, as in 'auditory', 'audition', but it is also used to form many modern words, as in 'audiotape', 'audiocassette' and 'audiovisual'.

auto- is a prefix derived from Greek meaning 'of or by itself', as in 'autobiography' and 'autograph'. It is also used to refer to things that work by themselves 'automatically', as in 'automobile', 'autocue', 'automaton', and to things that have to do with cars, as in 'automobiles', 'autosport', 'autotheft'.

auxiliary verb refers to a verb which is used in forming tenses, moods and voices of other verbs. These include 'be', 'do' and 'have'.

The verb 'to be' is used as an **auxiliary verb** with the -ing form of the main verb to form the continuous present tense, as in 'They are living abroad just now' and 'We were thinking of going on holiday but we changed our minds'.

The verb 'to be' is used as an **auxiliary verb** with the past participle of the main verb to form the passive voice, as in 'Her hands were covered in blood' and 'These toys are manufactured in China'.

The verb 'to have' is used as an **auxiliary verb** along with the past participle of the main verb to form the perfect tenses, as in 'They have filled the post', 'She had realized her mistake' and 'They wished that they had gone earlier'.

The verb 'to be' is used as an **auxiliary verb** along with the main verb to form negative sentences, as in 'She is not accepting the job'. The verb 'to do' is used as an **auxiliary verb** along with the main verb to form negative sentences, as in 'he does not believe her'. It is also used along with the main verb to form questions, as in 'Does he know that she's gone?' and to form sentences in which the verb is emphasized, as in 'She *does* want to go'. See **modal auxiliary.**

B

back formation refers to the process of forming a new word by removing an element from an existing word. This is the reversal of the usual process since many words are formed by adding an element to a base or root word. Examples of **back formation** include 'burgle' from 'burglary'; 'caretake' from 'caretaker'; 'donate' from 'donation; 'eavesdrop' from 'eavesdropper'; 'enthuse' from 'enthusiasm'; 'intuit' from 'intuition'; 'liaise' from 'liaison'; 'reminisce' from 'reminiscence'; 'televise' from 'television'.

base refers to the basic uninflected form of a verb. It is found as the infinitive form, as in 'to go' and 'to take', and as the imperative form, as in 'Go away!' and 'Take it!' It is also the form that the verb in the present indicative tense takes, except for the third person singular, as in 'I always go there on a Sunday' and 'They go there regularly.' **Base** also refers to the basic element in word formation. In this sense it is also known as 'root' or 'stem'. For example, in 'infectious' 'infect' is the base, in 'indescribable' 'describe' is the base and in 'enthusiastic' 'enthuse' is the base.

bathos is a figure of speech consisting of sudden descent from the lofty or noble to the ridiculous or trivial. This descent can be either intentional for comic or satiric effect, as in Alexander Pope's 'When husbands or when lapdogs breathe their last', or it can be accidental, as in 'She collected her children and her coat'. **Bathos** and 'anticlimax' mean the same. *See* **anticlimax**.

be *see* **auxiliary verb**.

both can be used as determiner, as in 'He broke both his arms' and 'He lost both his sons in the war'; a pronoun, as in 'I don't mind which house we rent. I like them both' and 'Neither of them work here. The boss sacked them both'; a conjunction, as in 'He both likes and admires her' and 'She is both talented and honest'. **Both** can sometimes be followed by 'of'. 'Both their children are grown up' and 'Both of their children are grown up' are both acceptable. Care should be taken to avoid using **both** unnecessarily. In the sentence 'The two items are both identical', **both** is redundant.

because is a conjunction that introduces a subordinate adverbial clause of reason', as in 'They sold the house because they are going abroad' and 'Because she is shy she never goes to parties'. It is often used incorrectly in such constructions as 'The reason they went away is because they were bored'. This should be rephrased as either 'The reason that they went away is that they were bored' or 'They went away because they were bored'.

before can either be a preposition, an adverb or a conjunction. As a preposition it means either 'coming or going in front of in time', as in 'He was the chairman before this one', or coming or going in front of in place, as in 'She went before him into the restaurant'. As an adverb it means 'at a time previously', as in 'I told you before' and 'He has been married before'. As a conjunction it introduces a 'subordinate adverbial clause of time', as in 'The guests arrived before she was ready for them' and 'Before I knew it they had arrived'.

bi- is a prefix derived from Latin meaning 'two', as in 'bicycle', 'bifocal', 'bilingual', 'binoculars', 'bisect'. **Bi-** forms words in English in which it means 'half', and other words in which it means 'twice'. This can give rise to confusion in such words as 'biweekly' and 'bimonthly', where there are two possible sets of meanings. 'Biweekly' can mean either 'every two weeks' or 'twice a week' so that one would not be able to be certain about the frequency of a 'biweekly' publication. Similarly, a 'bimonthly' publication might appear either twice a month or once every two months.

biblio- is a prefix derived from Greek meaning 'book', as in 'bibliophile' (a person who is fond of or collects books) and 'bibliography'.

bio- is a prefix derived from Greek meaning life or living material, as in 'biography', 'biology', 'biochemistry', 'biodegradable', 'biosphere', 'biopsy'.

blend refers to a word formed by the merging of two other words or elements, as in 'brunch' from 'breakfast' and 'lunch'; 'camcorder' from 'camera' and 'recorder'; 'chocoholic' from 'chocolate' and 'alcoholic'; 'motel' from 'motor' and 'hotel'; 'smog' from 'smoke' and 'fog'; 'televangelist' from 'television' and 'evangelist'.

bold or **bold face** refers to a typeface that is thick and black. It is used for emphasis or to highlight certain words. The headwords or entry words in this book are set in bold type.

book titles cause problems as to punctuation. How they are treated in publications, business reports, etc, depends largely on the house style of the firm concerned. However, they are generally written in documents, letters, etc, as they appear on their title pages, that is with the first letter of the first word and of the following main words of the title in capital letters, and those of words of lesser importance, such as the articles, prepositions and coordinate conjunctions, in lowercase letters, as in The Guide to Yoga, Hope for the Best and In the Middle of Life.

Some people, and some house-style manuals, prefer to put the titles in italic, as in *A Room with a View* and *A Guide to Dental Health*. Others prefer to put book titles in quotation marks, as in 'Gardening for Beginners'. Such a convention can make use of either single or double quotation marks. Thus either 'Desserts for the Summer' or "Desserts for the Summer" is possible provided that the writer is consistent throughout any one piece of writing. If the title of a book is mentioned in a piece of direct speech in quotation marks it goes within the opposite style of quotation marks from the piece in direct speech. Thus if the direct speech is within single quotation marks, the book title goes within double quotation marks, as in 'Have you read "Wuthering Heights" or are you not a Bronte fan?' If the direct speech is within double quotation marks, the book title goes between single quotation marks, as in "Would you say that 'Animal Farm' was your favourite Orwell novel?"

It is even quite common for book titles to appear in documents both in italic type and with quotation marks. To some extent the punctuation of book titles is a matter of choice as long as they are consistent, but there is a growing tendency to have as little punctuation as possible and to have as uncluttered a page as possible.

borrowing refers to the taking over of a word from a foreign language and also refers to the word so borrowed. Many words borrowed into English are totally assimilated as to spelling and pronunciation. Others remain obviously different and retain their own identity as to spelling or pronunciation, as 'raison d'être', borrowed from French. Many of them have been so long part of the English language, such as since the Norman Conquest, that they are no longer thought of as being foreign words. However the process goes on, and recent borrowings include 'glasnost' and 'perestroika' from Russian.

French, Latin and Greek have been the main sources of our **borrowings** over the centuries. However, we have borrowed extensively from other languages as well. These include Italian, from which we have borrowed many terms relating to music, art and architecture. These include 'piano', 'libretto', 'opera', 'soprano', 'tempo', 'corridor', 'fresco', 'niche', 'parapet' and 'grotto', as well as many food terms such as 'macaroni', 'pasta', 'semolina' and 'spaghetti'.

From the Dutch we have acquired many words relating to the sea and ships since they were a great sea-faring nation. These include 'cruise', 'deck', 'skipper' and 'yacht'. Through the Dutch/Afrikaans connection we have borrowed 'apartheid', 'boss' and 'trek'.

From German we have borrowed 'dachshund', 'hamster', 'frankfurter', 'kindergarten' and 'waltz', as well as some words relating to World War II, for example, 'blitz', 'flak' and 'strafe'.

From Norse and the Scandinavian languages have come a wide variety of common words, such as 'egg', 'dirt', 'glitter', 'kick', 'law', 'odd', 'skill', 'take', 'they', 'though', as well as some more modern sporting terms such as 'ski' and 'slalom'.

From the Celtic languages have come 'bannock', 'bog', 'brogue', 'cairn', 'clan', 'crag', 'slogan' and 'whisky', and from Arabic have come 'algebra', 'alkali', 'almanac', 'apricot', 'assassin', 'cypher', 'ghoul', 'hazard', 'mohair', 'safari', 'scarlet' and 'talisman'.

The Indian languages have provided us with many words, originally from the significant British presence there in the days of the British Empire. They include 'bungalow', 'chutney', 'dinghy', 'dungarees', 'gymkhana', 'jungle', 'pundit' and 'shampoo'. In modern times there has been an increasing interest in Indian food and cookery, and words such as 'pakora', 'poppadom', 'samosa', etc, have come into the language.

From the South American languages have come 'avocado', 'chocolate', 'chilli', 'potato', 'tobacco' and 'tomato'. From Hebrew have come 'alphabet', 'camel', 'cinnamon' and 'maudlin', as well as more modern borrowings from Yiddish such as 'bagel', 'chutzpah', 'schmaltz' and 'schmuck'.

From the native North American languages have come 'anorak', 'kayak', 'raccoon' and 'toboggan', and from the Aboriginal language of Australia have come 'boomerang' and 'kangaroo'.

'Judo', 'bonsai', and 'tycoon' have come from Japanese, 'rattan' from Malay and 'kung-fu', 'sampan' and 'ginseng' from Chinese.

The borrowing process continues. With Britain becoming more of a cosmopolitan and multi-cultural nation the borrowing is increasing.

-bound is a suffix meaning 'confined or restricted', as in housebound, snowbound and spellbound. It can also mean 'obligated', as in 'duty-bound'.

brackets are used to enclose information that is in some way additional to the main statement. The information so enclosed is called 'parenthesis' and the pair of brackets enclosing it can be known as 'parentheses'. The information that is enclosed in the brackets is purely supplementary or explanatory in nature and could be removed without changing the overall basic meaning or grammatical completeness of the statement. **Brackets**, like 'commas' and 'dashes', interrupt the flow of the main statement but **brackets** indicate a more definite or clear-cut interruption. The fact that they are more visually obvious emphasizes this.

Material within brackets can be one word, as in 'In a local wine bar we had some delicious crepes (pancakes)' and 'They didn't have the chutzpah (nerve) to challenge her'. It can also take the form of dates, as in 'Robert Louis Stevenson (1850-94) wrote *Treasure Island*' and '*Animal Farm* was written by George Orwell (1903-50)'.

The material within brackets can also take the form of a phrase, as in 'They served lasagne (a kind of pasta) and some delicious veal' and 'They were drinking Calvados (a kind of brandy made from apples)' or in the form of a clause, as in 'We were to have supper (or so they called it) later in the evening' and 'They went for a walk round the loch (as a lake is called in Scotland) before taking their departure'.

It can also take the form of a complete sentence, as in 'He was determined (we don't know why) to tackle the problem alone' and 'She made it clear (nothing could be more clear) that she was not interested in the offer'. Sentences that appear in brackets in the middle of a sentence are not usually given an initial capital letter or a full stop, as in 'They very much desired (she had no idea why) to purchase her house'. If the material within brackets comes at the end of a sentence the full stop comes outside the second bracket, as in 'For some reason we agreed to visit her at home (we had no idea where she lived)'.

If the material in the brackets is a sentence which comes between two other sentences it is treated like a normal sentence with an initial capital letter and a closing full stop, as in 'He never seems to do any studying. (He is always either asleep or watching television.) Yet he does brilliantly in his exams.' Punctuation of the main statement is unaffected by the presence of the brackets and their enclosed material except that any punctuation that would have followed the word before the first bracket follows the second bracket, as in 'He lives in a place (I am not sure exactly where), that is miles from anywhere.

There are various shapes of brackets. Round brackets are the most common type. Square brackets are sometimes used to enclose information that is contained inside other information already in brackets, as in '(Christopher Marlowe [1564-93] was a contemporary of Shakespeare)' or in a piece of writing where round brackets have already been used for some other purpose. Thus in a dictionary if round brackets are used to separate off the pronunciation, square brackets are sometimes used to separate off the etymologies.

Square brackets are also used for editorial comments in a scholarly work where the material within brackets is more of an intrusion to the flow of the main statement than is normerly the case with bracketed material. Angle brackets and brace brackets tend to be used in more scholarly or technical contexts.

buildings can cause problems with regard to the style and punctuation of their names. The proper name attached to the building should have an initial capital, as should the common noun that may be part of it, as in The White House, The Saltire Building, The National Portrait Gallery and The Museum of Childhood.

businesses and **organizations** often cause style and punctuation problems with regard to their names or titles. In general the initial letters of the main words of the title should be in capital letters and the words of lesser importance, such as the articles, coordinating conjunctions and prepositions, should be in lower case, except when they are the first word of the title, as in 'The Indian Carpet Company', 'Kitchens for All' and 'Capital Industrial Cleaners'. Obviously, when the names of people are involved these should have initial capital letters, as in 'Jones and Brown'.

but is a conjunction that connects two opposing ideas. It is a 'coordinating conjunction' in that it connects two elements of equal status. The elements may be words, as in 'not James but John'; phrases, as in 'working hard but not getting anywhere' and 'trying to earn a living but not succeeding'; clauses, as in 'He has arrived but his sister is late', 'I know her but I have never met him' and 'He likes reading but she prefers to watch TV'. It should not be used when no element of contrast is present. Thus the following sentence should be rephrased, at least in formal English—'She is not professionally trained but taught herself'. The two clauses are in fact agreeing, not disagreeing, with each other and so, strictly speaking, **but** should not be used.

The use of **but** at the beginning of a sentence is disliked by many people. It should be used only for deliberate effect or in informal contexts.

by- is a prefix meaning 'subordinate', 'secondary', 'incidental', as in by-product, by-road, by-effect. It can also mean 'around', as in by-pass.

C

capital letters are much less common than lower-case letters. They are used as the initial letter of proper nouns. Thus names of countries, rivers, mountains, cities, etc. Thus we find Africa, Mount Everest, River Nile, Paris, etc. The first names and surnames of people have initial capital letters, as in John Black and Mary Brown. Initial capital letters are used for the days of the week, as in Tuesday and Wednesday, for the months of the year, as in May and October, public and religious holidays, as in Easter Sunday, Ramadan and Hanaku. Initial capital letters are used for the books of the Bible.

Points of the compass are spelt with an initial capital letter if they are part of a specific geographical feature or region, as in South Africa.

Initial capital letters are usually used in the titles of books. Only the main words are capitalized. Prepositions, determiners and the articles are left in lower-case, unless they form the first word of the title, as in *A Room with a View* and *For Whom the Bell Tolls*—*see* BOOK TITLES.

Initial capital letters are necessary in tradenames, as in Hoover, Jacuzzi, Xerox and Kodak. Note that verbs formed from trade names are not spelt with an initial capital letter.

The first word in a sentence is spelt with a capital letter, as in 'We heard them come in. They made very little noise. However, we are light sleepers.'.

For capital letters in direct speech see DIRECT SPEECH. For capital letters in abbreviation and acronyms see ABBREVIATIONS and ACRONYMS.

cardi- is a prefix derived from Greek meaning 'heart', as in 'cardiology', 'cardiac'.

cardinal number refers to numbers such as one, two three, etc, as opposed to 'ordinal numbers' which refer to numbers such as first, second, third, etc.

clause refers to a group of words containing a finite verb which forms part of a compound or complex sentence. See MAIN CLAUSE, SUBORDINATE CLAUSES, ADVERBIAL CLAUSES, NOUN CLAUSES and RELATIVE **clauses**.

clerihew is a humorous four-line light verse in which the first two lines rhyme with each other and the last two rhyme with each other. The clerihew was popularized by Edward Clerihew Bentley (1875-1956). It usually deals with a person named in the first line and then describes him in a humorous way, as in

> Mr Michael Foot
> Had lots of loot
> He loved to gloat
> While petting his stoat

cliché is a hackneyed stereotyped expression which is much overused. Examples of clichés include 'unaccustomed as I am to public speaking', 'the light at the end of the tunnel' and 'All's well that ends well'.

collective noun refers to a group of things or people. It is used when the whole group is being considered, as in 'flock of sheep', 'herd of cattle', 'team of oxen', 'shoal of herring', 'covey of partridges', 'unkindness of ravens', 'gaggle of geese', 'pride of lions', 'mutation of thrushes', 'exaltation of larks', 'convocation of eagles'.

colloquial refers to informal language, such as that found in informal conversation.

colon is a punctuation mark (:) which is used within a sentence to explain, interpret, clarify or amplify what has gone before it. 'The standard of school work here is extremely high: it is almost university standard', 'The fuel bills are giving cause for concern: they are almost double last year's'. 'We have some new information: the allies have landed'. A capital letter is not usually used after the colon in this context.

The **colon** is also used to introduce lists or long quotations, as in 'The recipe says we need: tomatoes, peppers, courgettes, garlic, oregano and basil', 'The boy has a huge list of things he needs for school: blazer, trousers, shirts, sweater, ties, shoes, tennis shoes, rugby boots, sports clothes and leisure wear' and 'One of his favourite quotations was: "If music be the food of love play on"'.

The **colon** is sometimes used in numerals, as in '7:30 a.m.', '22:11:72' and 'a ratio of 7:3'. It is used in the titles of some books, for example where there is a subtitle or explanatory title, as in 'The Dark Years: the Economy in the 1930s.

In informal writing, the dash is sometimes used instead of the colon, Indeed the dash tends to be overused for this purpose.

comma is a very common punctuation mark. In modern usage there is a tendency to adopt a system of minimal punctuation and the comma is one of the casualties of this new attitude. Most people use the comma considerably less frequently than was formerly the case.

However there are certain situations in which the comma is still commonly used. One of these concerns lists. The individual items in a series of three or more items are separated by commas. Whether a comma is put before the 'and' which follows the second-last item is now a matter of choice. Some people dislike the use of a comma after 'and' in this situation, and it was formerly considered wrong. Examples of lists include— 'at the sports club we can play tennis, squash, badminton and table tennis', 'We need to buy bread, milk, fruit and sugar', and 'They are studying French, German, Spanish and Russian'. The individual items in a list can be quite long, as in 'We opened the door, let ourselves in, fed the cat and started to cook a meal' and 'They consulted the map, planned the trip, got some foreign currency and were gone before we realized it'. Confusion may arise if the last item in the list contains 'and' in its own right, as in 'In the pub they served ham salad, shepherd's pie, pie and chips and omelette. In such cases it as well to put a comma before the 'and'.

In cases where there is a list of adjectives before a noun, the use of commas is now optional although it was formerly standard practice. Thus both 'She wore a long, red, sequinned dress' and 'She wore a long red sequinned dress' are used. When the adjective immediately before the noun has a closer relationship with it than the other adjectives no comma should be used, as in 'a beautiful old Spanish village'.

The **comma** is used to separate clauses or phrases that are parenthetical or naturally cut off from the rest of a sentence, as in 'My mother, who was of Irish extraction, was very superstitious'. In such a sentence the clause within the commas can be removed without altering the basic meaning. Care should be taken to include both commas. Commas are not normally used to separate main clauses and relative clauses, as in 'The woman whom I met was my friend's sister'. Nor are they usually used to separate main clauses and subordinate clauses, as in 'He left when we arrived' and 'They came to the party although we didn't expect them to'. If the subordinate clause precedes the main clause, it is sometimes followed by a comma, especially if it is a reasonably long clause, as in 'Although we stopped and thought about it, we still made the wrong decision'. If the clause is quite short, or if it is a short phrase, a comma is not usually inserted, as in 'Although it rained we had a good holiday' and 'Although poor they were happy'. The use of commas to separate such words and expression from the rest of the sentence to which they are related is optional. Thus one can write 'However, he could be right' or 'However he could be right'. The longer the expression is, the more likely it is to have a comma after it, as in 'On the other hand, we may decide not to go'.

Commas are always used to separate terms of address, interjections or question tags from the rest of the sentence, as in 'Please come this way, Ms Brown, and make yourself at home', 'Now, ladies, what can I get you?' and 'It's cold today, isn't it?'

Commas may be used to separate main clauses joined by a coordinating conjunction, but this is not usual if the clauses have the same subject or object, as in 'She swept the floor and dusted the table'. In cases where the subjects are different and the clauses are fairly long, it is best to insert a comma, as in 'They took all the furniture with them, and she was left with nothing'.

A **comma** can be inserted to avoid repeating a verb in the second of two clause, as in 'he plays golf and tennis, his brother rugby'.

commands are expressed in the imperative mood, as in 'Be quiet!', 'Stop crying!', 'Go away!'

common nouns are simply the names of ordinary, everyday non-specific things and people, as opposed to proper nouns which refer to the names of particular individuals or specific places. **Common nouns** include 'baby', 'cat', 'girl', 'hat', 'park', 'sofa' and 'table'.

comparison of adjectives is achieved in two different ways. Some adjectives form their comparative by adding -er to the positive or absolute form, as in 'braver', 'louder', 'madder', 'shorter' and 'taller'. Other adjectives form their comparative by using 'more' in conjunction with them, as in 'more beautiful', 'more realistic', 'more suitable', and 'more tactful'. Which is the correct form is largely a matter of length. One-syllable adjectives, such as 'loud', add -er, as 'louder'. Two-syllable adjectives sometimes have both forms as a possibility, as in 'gentler/more gentle', and 'cleverest/most clever'. Adjectives with three or more syllables usually form their comparatives with 'more', as in 'more comfortable', 'more gracious', 'more regular', and 'more understanding'. Some adjectives are irregular in their comparative forms, as in 'good/better', 'bad/worse', 'many/more'. Only if they begin with *un-* are they likely to end in *-er*, as in 'untrustworthier'.

Some adjectives by their very definitions do not normally have a comparative form, for example 'unique'.

complement is the equivalent of 'object' in a clause with a linking or copula verb. In the sentence 'Jack is a policeman', 'a policeman' is the **complement**. In the sentence 'Jane is a good mother', 'a good mother' is the complement, and in the sentence 'His son is an excellent football player', 'an excellent football player' is the complement.

complex sentence refers to a type of sentence in which there is a main clause and one or more subordinate clauses. The sentence 'We went to visit him although he had been unfriendly to us' is a complex sentence since it is composed of a main clause and one subordinate clause ('although he had been unfriendly to us'). The sentence 'We wondered where he had gone and why he was upset' is a complex sentence since it has a main clause and two subordinate clauses ('where he had gone' and 'why he was upset').

compound sentence refers to a type of sentence with more than one clause and linked by a coordinating conjunction, such as 'and' or 'but', as in 'He applied for a new job and got it' and 'I went to the cinema but I didn't enjoy the film'.

concord *see* **number agreement**.

concrete noun refers to something which one can touch, as opposed to an 'abstract noun' which one cannot. **Concrete nouns** include 'bag', 'glass', 'plate', 'pot', 'clothes', 'field', 'garden', 'flower', 'potato', 'foot' and 'shoe'. *See* ABSTRACT NOUN.

conjunctions are of two types. Coordinating conjunctions join units of equal status, as in 'bread and butter', 'We asked for some food and we got it'. A subordinating conjunction joins a dependent or subordinating clause to main verbs: in 'We asked him why he was there', 'why he was there' is a subordinate clause and thus 'why' is a subordinating conjunction.

continuous tenses *see* **tense**.

copula *see* **linking verb**.

copular verb *see* **linking verb**.

count noun is the same as COUNTABLE NOUN.

countable noun is one which can be preceded by 'a' and can take a plural, as in 'hat/hats', 'flower/flowers'. *See also* UNCOUNTABLE NOUN.

D

dangling participle is one that has been misplaced in a sentence. A participle is often used to introduce a phrase which is attached to a subject mentioned later in a sentence, as in 'Worn out by the long walk, she fell to the ground in a faint'. 'Worn out' is the participle and 'she' the subject. Another example is 'Laughing in glee at having won, she ordered some champagne'. In this sentence 'laughing' is the participle and 'she' is the subject. It is a common error for such a participle not to be related to any subject, as in 'Imprisoned in the dark basement, it seemed a long time since she had seen the sun'. This participle is said to be 'dangling'. Another example of a **dangling participle** is contained in 'Living alone, the days seemed long'.

It is also a common error for a participle to be related to the wrong subject in a sentence, as in 'Painting the ceiling, some of the plaster fell on his head', 'Painting' is the participle and should go with a subject 'he'. Instead it goes with 'some of the plaster'. Participles in this situation are more correctly known as 'misrelated participles', although they are also called **dangling participles.**

dash is a punctuation mark in the form of a short line that indicates a short break in the continuity of a sentence, as in 'He has never been any trouble at school—quite the reverse', 'I was amazed when he turned up—I thought he was still abroad'. In such situations it serves the same purpose as brackets, except that it is frequently considered more informal. The dash should be used sparingly. Depending on it too much can lead to careless writing with ideas set down at random rather than turned into a piece of coherent prose.

The **dash** can be used to emphasize a word or phrase, as in 'They said goodbye then—forever'. It can also be used to add a remark to the end of a sentence, as in 'They had absolutely no money—a regular state of affairs towards the end of the month.' The **dash** can also be used to introduce a statement that amplifies or explains what has been said, as in 'The burglars took everything of value—her jewellery, the silver, the TV set, her hi-fi and several hundred pounds.' It can be used to summarize what has gone before, as in 'Disease, poverty, ignorance—these are the problems facing us.' The **dash** is also used to introduce an afterthought, as in 'You can come with me—but you might not want to'. It can also introduce a sharp change of subject, as in 'I'm just making tea—what was that noise?' It can also be used to introduce some kind of balance in a sentence, as in 'It's going to take two of us to get this table out of here—one to move it and one to hold the door open.'

The **dash** is sometimes found in pairs. A pair of dashes acts in much the same way as a set of round brackets. A pair of dashes can be used to indicate a break in a sentence, as in 'We prayed—prayed as we had never prayed before—that the children would be safe', 'It was—on reflection—his best performance yet', and 'He introduced me to his wife—an attractive pleasant woman—before he left'.

Dashes are used to indicate hesitant speech, as in 'I don't—well—maybe—you could be right'. They can be used to indicate the omission of part of a word or name, as in 'It's none of your b—business.', 'He's having an affair with Mrs D—'.

They can also be used between points in time or space, as in 'Edinburgh—London' and '1750—1790.'

dates are usually written in figures, as in 1956, rather than in words, as in nineteen fifty-six, except in formal contexts, such as legal documents. There are various ways of writing dates. The standard form in Britain is becoming day followed by month followed by year, as in '24 February 1970'. In America the standard form of this is 'February 24 1970', and that is a possibility in Britain also. Alternatively, some people write '24th February 1970'. Care should be taken with the writing of dates entirely in numbers, especially if one is corresponding with someone in America. In Britain the day of the month is put first, the month second and the year third, as in '2/3/50', '2 March 1950'. In America the month is put first, followed by the day of the month and the year. Thus in America '2/3/50' would be 3 February 1950.

Centuries may be written either in figures, as in 'the 19th century', or in words, as in 'the nineteenth century'.

Decades and centuries are now usually written without apostrophes. as in '1980s' and '1990s'.

dative case refers to the case which indicates 'to' or 'for'. This is applicable to Latin but not to English, where such meanings are expressed by prepositional phrases. In English the 'indirect object' is equivalent to the **dative case** in some situations.

deca- is a prefix derived from Greek meaning 'ten', as in 'decade', 'decathlon' and 'decahedron'.

deci- is a prefix derived from Latin meaning 'tenth', as in 'decibel', 'decimal', 'decimate' and 'decilitre'.

declarative sentence refers to a sentence which conveys information. The subject precedes the verb in it. Examples include 'They won the battle', 'He has moved to another town', 'Lots of people go there' and 'There is a new person in charge'. **Declarative mood** is the same as **indicative mood.**

declension refers to the variation of the form of a noun, adjective or pronoun to show different cases, such as nominative and accusative. It also refers to the class into which such words are placed, as in first declension, second declension, etc. The term applies to languages such as Latin but is not applicable to English.

definite article is a term for 'the', which is the most frequently used word in the English language. 'The' is used to refer back to a person or thing that has already been mentioned, as in 'Jack and Jill built a model. The model was of a ship' and 'We've bought a car. It was the cheapest car we could find'.

'The' can be used to make a general statement about all things of a particular type, as in 'The computer has lead to the loss of many jobs' and 'The car has caused damage to the environment'. 'The' can be used to refer to a whole class or group, as in 'the Italians', 'the Browns' and 'the younger generation'.

'The' can also be used to refer to services or systems, as in 'They are not on the phone' and 'She prefers going by bus'. It can be used to refer to the name of a musical instrument when someone's ability to play it is being referred to, as in 'Her son is learning to play the violin'.

'The' indicates a person or thing to be the only one, as in the Bible, the King of Spain, the White House, the Palace of Westminster and the President of the United States.

'The' can be used instead of a possessive determiner to refer to parts of the body, as in 'She took him by the arm' and 'The dog bit him on the leg'.

'The' is used in front of superlative adjectives, as in 'the largest amount of money' and 'the most beautiful woman'. It can also be used to indicate that a person or thing is unique or exceptional, as in 'the political debater of his generation'. In this last sense 'the' is pronounced 'thee'.

degree refers to a level of comparison of gradable adjectives. The degrees of comparison comprise 'absolute' or 'positive', as in 'big', 'calm', 'dark', 'fair', 'hot', 'late', 'short' and 'tall'; 'comparative', as in 'bigger', 'calmer', 'darker', 'fairest', 'hotter', 'late', 'shorter' and 'taller'; 'superlative', as in 'biggest', 'calmest', 'darkest', 'fairest', 'hottest', 'latest', 'shortest' and 'tallest'.

Degree can also refer to adverbs. 'Adverbs of degree' include 'extremely', 'very', 'greatly', 'rather', 'really', 'remarkably', 'terribly', as in 'an extremely rare case', 'a very old man', 'He's remarkably brave' and 'We're terribly pleased'.

demi-is a prefix derived from old French meaning 'half', as in 'demigod' and 'demijohn'.

demonstrative determiners are used to indicate things or people in relationship to the speaker or writer in space or time. 'This' and 'these' indicate nearness to the speaker, as in 'Will you take this book home?' and 'These flowers are for you'. 'That' and 'those' indicate distance from the speaker, as in 'Get that creature out of here!' and 'Aren't those flowers over there beautiful!'

demonstrative pronouns are similar to **demonstrative determiners** except that they stand alone in place of a noun rather than preceding a noun, as in 'I'd like to give you this', 'What is that?', 'These are interesting books' and 'Those are not his shoes'.

dependent clause refers to a clause which cannot stand alone and make sense, unlike an independent or main clause. **Dependent clauses** depend on the main clause. The term is the same as 'subordinate clause'. *See* SUBORDINATE CLAUSE.

derivation has two meanings. It can refer to the etymology of a word, as in 'The derivation of the expression is unknown'. It can also refer to the process of forming a new word by adding an affix of some kind to an existing word or base, as in 'helpless' from 'help' and 'maker' from 'make'.

derivative refers to a word formed by **derivation**. For example, 'sweetly' is a derivative of 'sweet', 'peaceful' is a derivative from 'peace', 'clinging' from 'cling' and 'shortest' from 'short'.

derm- is a prefix derived from Greek meaning 'skin', as in 'dermatitis', 'dermatologist' and 'dermatology'.

determiner is a word used in front of a noun or pronoun to tell us something about it. Unlike an adjective, it does not, strictly speaking, 'describe' a noun or pronoun. **Determiners** are divided into the following categories—articles (a, an, the) as in 'a cat', 'an eagle', 'the book'; demonstrative determiners (this, that, these, those), as in 'this girl', 'that boy' and 'those people'; possessive determiners (my, your, his/her/its, our, their), as in 'my dog', 'her house', 'its colour', 'their responsibility'; numbers (one, two, three, four, etc, first, second, third, fourth, etc), as in 'two reasons', 'five ways', 'ten children'; and indefinite or general determiners (all, another, any, both, each, either, enough, every, few, fewer, less, little, many, most, much, neither, no, other, several, some), as in 'both parents', 'enough food', 'several issues'. Many words used as determiners are also pronouns. *See* ADJECTIVE; DEMONSTRATIVE DETERMINER; POSSESSIVE DETERMINER; NUMBERS; INDEFINITE DETERMINER.

di- is a prefix derived from Greek meaning 'two' or 'double', as in 'dioxide', 'dilemma', 'diphthong' and 'disyllabic'.

dia- is a prefix meaning 'through', as in 'diaphanous'; 'apart', as in 'diacritical', 'diaphragm' and 'dialysis'; and 'across', as in 'diameter'.

diacritic refers to a mark placed over, under or through a letter to indicate a sound or stress value different from that of the same letter when it is unmarked. **Diacritics** include the cedilla, as in 'façade', the German umlaut, as in 'mädchen' and diaeresis, as in 'naïve'.

diaeresis refers to a mark that is placed over a vowel to indicate that it is sounded separately from a neighbouring vowel, as in 'naïve', 'Chloë'.

dialect refers to a variety of language that is distinct from other varieties in terms of pronunciation, accent, vocabulary, grammar and sentence structure. The term **dialect** tends to imply a deviation from some standard form of language, usually the dialect used by educated upper-class or upper-middle-class people, known in English as 'standard' English.

Dialects may be regional in nature. Thus in Britain there is a Cornish dialect, a Liverpool dialect, a Glasgow dialect, and so on. Alternatively, they may be based on class differences, when they are sometimes known as 'social dialects'. These include working-class dialect, upper-class dialect, and so on.

At one time regional dialects were looked down on by people who spoke only standard English. People with regional accents, using regional dialects, were unlikely to get jobs in professions such as radio and television, where the use of language was a major consideration. People intent on such careers tried to change their accents to remove all traces of dialect. However, things have changed, and now it is quite common for people using regional accents and dialects to have jobs associated with radio and television.

Note that the word **dialect** is not appropriate if it is a global variety of English that is being referred to. For example, the English spoken in America is known as American English.

diction has two meanings. It can refer to the choice of

words in writing or speech, especially with regard to correctness, clarity or effectiveness, as in 'The content of his essay was very interesting but his diction was poor'. It can also refer to the pronunciation and enunciation of words in speaking and singing, as in 'She has a beautiful natural singing voice but should take lessons in diction'.

dialogue in novels, etc, is placed on a new line, often in a new paragraph, if there is a change of speaker, as in:

'We're going now', said John. 'Do you want to join us? If you do you'd better hurry. We can't wait.'

'Just go on', replied Mary. 'I'm not quite ready. I'll catch you up'.

digraph refers to a group of two letters representing one sound, as in 'ay' in 'hay', 'ey' in 'key', 'oy' in 'boy', 'ph' in 'phone' and 'th' in 'thin'. When the **digraph** consists of two letters physically joined together as 'ae', it is called a 'ligature'.

diminutive refers to something small or a small form or version of something, as in 'booklet', 'droplet', 'flatlet', 'auntie', 'doggy', 'islet', 'piglet', 'poppet', 'snippet', 'starlet', 'kitchenette', 'hillock', 'paddock', 'mannikin', 'lambkin', 'duckling', 'gosling', 'nestling', 'majorette', 'pipette'. Proper names often have diminutive forms. as in 'Alf' for Alfred, 'Annie' for Ann, 'Babs' for Barbara, 'Bill' for William, 'Charlie' for Charles, 'Dot' for Dorothy, 'Jimmy' for James, 'Lizzie' for Elizabeth, 'Meg' for Margaret, 'Nell' for Helen, 'Pat' for Patrick and 'Teddy' for Edward.

diphthong is a speech sound that changes its quality within the same single syllable. The sound begins as for one vowel and moves on as for another. Since the sound glides from one vowel into another, a **diphthong** is sometimes called a 'gliding vowel'. Examples include the vowels sounds in 'rain', 'weigh', 'either', 'voice', 'height', 'aisle', 'road', 'soul', 'know', 'house', 'care', 'pure', 'during', 'here' and 'weird'.

direct object refers to the noun, noun phrase, noun or nominal clause or pronoun which is acted upon by the action of a transitive verb. In the sentence 'She bought milk', 'bought' is a transitive verb and 'milk' is a noun which is the direct object. In the sentence 'She bought loads of clothes', 'bought' is a transitive verb and 'loads of clothes' is the direct object. In the sentence 'He knows what happened', 'knows' is a transitive verb and 'what happened' is a 'noun clause' or 'nominal clause'. A **direct object** is frequently known just as 'object'. *See* INDIRECT OBJECT.

direct speech refers to the reporting of speech by repeating exactly the actual words used by the speaker. In the sentence 'Peter said, "I am tired of this"', "I am tired of this" is a piece of direct speech because it represents exactly what Peter said. Similarly, in the sentence 'Jane asked, "Where are you going?"', "Where are you going" is a piece of direct speech since it represents exactly what Jane said.

Quotation marks, also known as inverted commas or informally as quotes, are used at the beginning and the end of pieces of **direct speech.** Only the words actually spoken are placed within the quotation marks, as in '"If I were you," he said, "I would refuse to go"'. The quotation marks involved can be either single or double, according to preference or house style.

If there is a statement such as 'he said' following the piece of direct speech, a comma is placed before the second inverted comma, as in '"Come along," he said'. If the piece of direct speech is a question or exclama-

tion, a question mark or exclamation mark is put instead of the comma, as in '"What are you doing?" asked John' and '"Get away from me!" she screamed'.

If a statement such as 'he said' is placed within a sentence in direct speech, a comma is placed after 'he said' and the second part of the piece of direct speech does not begin with a capital letter, as in '"I know very well," he said, "that you do not like me."'

If the piece of direct speech includes a complete sentence, the sentence begins with a capital letter, as in '"I am going away," she said, "and I am not coming back. I don't feel that I belong here anymore."' Note that the full stop at the end of a piece of direct speech that is a sentence should go before the closing inverted comma.

If the piece of direct speech quoted takes up more than one paragraph, quotation marks are placed at the beginning of each new paragraph. However, quotation marks are not placed at the end of each paragraph, just at the end of the final one.

When writing a story, etc, which includes dialogue or conversation, each new piece of direct speech should begin on a new line or sometimes in a new paragraph.

Quotation marks are not used only to indicate **direct speech.** For example, they are sometimes used to indicate the title of a book or newspaper. The quotation marks used in this way can be either single or double, according to preference or house style. If a piece of direct speech contains the title of a book, newspaper, etc, it should be put in the opposite type of quotation marks to those used to enclose the piece of direct speech. Thus, if single quotation marks have been used in the direct speech, then double quotation marks should be used for the title within the direct speech, as in '"Have you read "Animal Farm" by George Orwell?' the teacher asked'. If double quotation marks have been used for the direct speech, single quotation marks should be used for the title, as in '"Have you read 'Animal Farm?' by George Orwell?" the teacher asked'.

Sometimes titles are put in italic type instead of quotation marks. This avoids the clumsiness which can occur when both sets of quotation marks end on the same word, as in 'The pupil replied, 'No, I have not read "Animal Farm".'

dis- is a prefix derived from Latin indicating 'opposite', 'not', as in 'disappear', 'disapprove', 'disband', 'disbelieve', 'disclaim', 'disconnect', 'discontinue', 'disenchant', 'disengage', 'disinherit', 'dislike', 'disobey', 'dispossess', 'distrust', and 'disunite'.

distributive pronouns refer to individual members of a class or group. These include 'each', 'either', 'neither', 'none', 'everyone', 'no one'. Such pronouns, where relevant, should be accompanied by singular verbs and singular personal pronouns, as in 'All the men are to be considered for the new posts. Each is to send in his application'. Problems arise when the sex of the noun to which the **distributive pronoun** refers back is either unknown or unspecified. Formerly it was the convention to treat such nouns as masculine and so to make the **distributive pronoun** masculine, as in 'All pupils must obey the rules. Each is to provide his own sports equipment'. Nowadays this convention is frequently considered to be unacceptably sexist and attempts have been made to get round this. One solution is to use 'him/her' (or 'him or her'), etc, as in 'The students have received a directive from the professor. Each is to produce his/her essay by tomorrow.' This convention is considered by many people to be clumsy. They prefer to be ungrammatical and use a plural personal pronoun, as in 'The pupils are being punished. Each is to inform their parents'. Where possible it is preferable to rephrase sentences to avoid being either sexist or ungrammatical, as in 'All of the pupils must tell their parents.'

Each, either, etc, in such contexts is fairly formal. In less formal situations 'each of', 'either of', etc, is more usual, as in 'Each of the boys will have to train really hard to win' and 'Either of the dresses is perfectly suitable'.

disyllabic means having two syllable. For example 'window' is disyllabic, since it consists of the syllable 'win' and the syllable 'dow'. Similarly 'curtain' is disyllabic since it consists of the syllable 'cur' and 'tain'.

do is an auxiliary verb which is used to form negative forms, as in, 'I do not agree with you', 'They do not always win', 'He does not wish to go' and 'She did not approve of their behaviour'. It is also used to form interrogative forms, as in 'Do you agree?', 'Does she know about it?', 'Did you see that?' and 'I prefer to go by train. Don't you?' **Do** is also used for emphasis, as in 'I do believe you're right' and 'They do know, don't they?'

-dom is a suffix meaning 'state, condition', as in 'boredom', 'freedom', 'officialdom', 'martyrdom'. It can also mean 'rank or status', as in 'earldom', 'dukedom', or 'domain, territory' as in 'kingdom'.

double negative refers to the occurrence of two negative words in a single sentence or clause, as in 'He didn't say nothing' and 'We never had no quarrel'. This is usually considered incorrect in standard English, although it is a feature of some social or regional dialects. The use of the **double negative**, if taken literally, often has the opposite meaning to the one intended. Thus 'He didn't say nothing' conveys the idea that 'He said something'.

Some **double negatives** are considered acceptable, as in 'I wouldn't be surprised if they don't turn up', although it is better to restrict such constructions to informal contexts. The sentence quoted conveys the impression that the speaker will be quite surprised if 'they' do 'turn up'. Another example of an acceptable **double negative** is 'I can't not worry about the children. Anything could have happened to them'. Again this type of construction is best restricted to informal contexts.

It is the semi-negative forms, such as 'hardly' and 'scarcely', which cause most problems with regard to **double negatives**, as in 'We didn't have hardly any money to buy food' and 'They didn't have barely enough time to catch the bus'. Such sentences are incorrect.

double passive refers to a clause which contains two verbs in the passive, the second of which is an infinitive, as in 'The goods are expected to be despatched some time this week'. Some examples of **double passives** are clumsy or ungrammatical and should be avoided, as in 'Redundancy notices are proposed to be issued next week'.

doubling of consonants causes spelling problems. There are a few rules which help to solve these problems. These include the following: In words of one syllable ending in a single consonant preceded by a single vowel, the consonant is doubled when an ending starting with a vowel is added, as in 'drop' and 'dropped', 'pat' and 'patting' and 'rub' and 'rubbing'.

In words of more than one syllable that end in a single consonant preceded by a single vowel, the consonant is doubled if the stress is on the last syllable, as in 'begin' and 'beginning', 'occur' and 'occurring', 'prefer' and 'preferred', 'refer' and 'referring' and 'commit' and 'committed'. In similar words where the stress is not on the last syllable, the consonant does not double, as in 'bigot' and 'bigoted' and 'develop' and 'developed'.

Exceptions to this rule include words ending in 'l'. The 'l' doubles even in cases where the last syllable containing it is unstressed, as in 'travel' and 'travelled' and 'appal' and 'appalling'. 'Worship', in which the stress is on the first syllable, is also an exception, as in 'worshipped'.

doubles are words that habitually go together, as in 'out and out', 'neck and neck', 'over and over', 'hale and hearty', 'rant and rave', 'fast and furious', 'hue and cry', 'stuff and nonsense', 'rough and ready', 'might and main', 'give and take', 'ups and downs', 'fair and square', 'high and dry' and 'wear and tear'. **Doubles** are also sometimes called **dyads**.

doublets are pairs of words that have developed from the same original word but now differ somewhat in form and usually in meaning. Examples include 'human' and 'humane', 'shade' and 'shadow', 'hostel' and 'hotel', 'frail' and 'fragile', and 'fashion' and 'faction'.

dramatic irony refers to a situation in which a character in a play, novel, etc, says or does something that has a meaning for the audience or reader, other than the obvious meaning, that he/she does not understand. Its use is common in both comedy and tragedy.

dual gender refers to a category of nouns in which there is no indication of gender. The nouns referred to include a range of words used for people, and occasionally animals, which can be of either gender. Unless the gender is specified we do not know the sex of the person referred to. Such words include 'artist', 'author', 'poet', 'singer', 'child', 'pupil', 'student', 'baby', 'parent', 'teacher', 'dog'. Such words give rise to problems with accompanying singular pronouns. *See* EACH.

dummy subject describes a subject that has no intrinsic meaning but is inserted to maintain a balanced grammatical structure. In the sentences 'It has started to rain' and 'It is nearly midnight', 'it' is a dummy subject. In the sentences 'There is nothing else to say' and 'There is no reason for his behaviour', 'there' is a dummy subject.

dyads see **doubles**.

dynamic verb refers to a verb with a meaning that indicates action, as 'work' in 'They work hard', 'play' in 'The boys play football at the weekend' and 'come' in 'The girls come here every Sunday'.

dys- is a prefix derived from the Greek meaning 'bad', as in 'dyslexia', 'dysgraphia', 'dysmenorrhea', 'dyspepsia'.

E

each can be either a DETERMINER or a DISTRIBUTIVE PRONOUN. **Each** as a determiner is used before a singular noun and is accompanied by a singular verb, as in 'Each candidate is to reapply', 'Each athlete has a place in the final', 'Each country is represented by a head of state' and 'Each chair was covered in chintz'.

Each of can sometimes be used instead of **each**, as in 'each of the candidates'. Again a singular verb is used, as in 'Each of the books has pages missing', 'Each of the chairs has a broken leg' and 'Each of the pupils is to make a contribution to the cost of the outing'. **Each of** can also be used in front of plural pronouns, as in 'each of them'. Once again a singular verb is used, as in 'Each of them wants something different', 'Each of us is supposed to make a contribution' and 'Each of the words has several meanings'. If the user wishes to emphasize the fact that something is true about every member of a group, **each one of** should be used and not 'every', as in 'Each one of them feels guilty', 'Each one of us has a part to play' and 'Each one of the actors has improved'.

As a pronoun **each** also takes a singular verb, as in 'They hate each other. Each is plotting revenge', 'These exercises are not a waste of time. Each provides valuable experience'. For emphasis **each one** can be used, as in 'We cannot leave any of these books behind. Each one of them is necessary' and 'We should not dismiss any of the staff. Each one has a part to play in the new firm'.

Each, where relevant, should be accompanied by a singular personal pronoun, as in 'Each girl has to provide her own sports equipment', 'Each of the men is to take a turn at working night shift', 'The boys are all well off and each can afford the cost of the holiday' and 'There are to be no exceptions among the women staff. Each one has to work full time'.

Problems arise when the noun that **each** refers back to is of unknown or unspecified sex. Formerly nouns in such situations were assumed to be masculine, as in 'Each pupil was required to bring his own tennis racket' and 'Each of the students has to provide himself with a tape recorder'. Nowadays such a convention is regarded as being sexist and the use of 'he/her', 'his/her', etc, is proposed, as in 'Each pupil was required to bring his/her (or 'his or her') own tennis racket' and 'Each student has to provide himself/herself (or 'himself or herself') with a tape recorder'. Even in written English such a convention can be clumsy and it is even more so in spoken English. For this reason many people decide to be ungrammatical and opt for 'Each pupil was required to bring their own tennis racket' and 'Each student has to provide themselves with a tape recorder'.

Both sexism and grammatical error can be avoided by rephrasing such sentences, as in 'All pupils are required to bring their own tennis rackets' and 'All students have to provide themselves with tape recorders'.

Each is used rather than **every** when the user is thinking of the members of a group as individuals.

eco- is a prefix indicating ecology. Following the increased awareness of the importance of the environment, there has been a growing interest in ecology and many words beginning with **eco-** have been added to the English language. Some of these are scientific terms such as 'ecotype', 'ecosystem' or 'ecospecies'. Others are more general terms, such as 'ecocatastrophe' and 'ecopolitics', and some are even slang terms, such as 'ecofreak' and 'econut'.

-ectomy is a suffix of Greek origin which indicates 'surgical removal', as in 'hysterectomy', the surgical removal of the womb, 'mastectomy', the surgical removal of a breast, and 'appendicectomy', the surgical removal of the appendix, the American English version of which is 'appendectomy'.

-ed is a suffix which forms the past tense and past participles of regular verbs, as in 'asked', 'blinded', 'caused', 'darkened', 'escaped', 'frightened', 'guarded', 'hunted', 'injured', 'jilted', 'kicked', 'landed', 'marked', 'noted', 'opened', 'painted', 'quarrelled', 'rattled', 'started', 'tormented', 'unveiled', 'washed', 'yielded'. Some past participles ending in '-ed' can act as adjectives, as in 'darkened room', 'escaped prisoners', 'frightened children', 'hunted animals', 'painted faces' and 'tormented souls'.

In the case of some verbs, the past tense and past participle may end in '-ed' or 't', according to preference. Such verbs include 'burn', 'dream', 'dwell', 'kneel', 'lean', 'leapt', 'smell', 'spell', 'spill' and 'spoil'. Thus 'burned' and 'burnt', 'dreamed' and 'dreamt', 'kneeled' and 'knelt', and 'learned' and 'learnt', etc, are acceptable forms.

-ee is a suffix derived from French and is used as part of nouns that are the recipients of an action, as in 'deportee', a person who has been deported; 'employee', a person who is employed; 'interviewee', a person who is being interviewed; 'licensee', a person who has been licensed; 'trainee', a person who is being trained.

-Ee can also be used as part of a noun indicating a person who acts or behaves in a particular way, as 'absentee', a person who absents himself/herself and 'escapee', a person who escapes.

e.g. is the abbreviation of the Latin phrase *exempli gratia* and means 'for example'. It is used before examples of what has previously been referred to, as in 'The tourists want to visit the historic sites of Edinburgh, e.g. Edinburgh Castle and Holyrood House'. By its very nature e.g. is mostly restricted to written English, becoming 'for example' in speech. Many writers also prefer to use 'for example' rather than use e.g. Both letters of the abbreviation usually have a full stop after them, as e.g., and it is usually preceded by a comma.

either can be used as either a determiner or distributive pronoun. As a determiner it is used with a singular verb, as in 'Either hotel is expensive' and 'In principle they are both against the plan but is either likely to vote for it?'

Either of can be used instead of **either**. It is used before a plural noun, as in 'either of the applicants' and 'either of the houses'. It is accompanied by a singular verb, as in 'Either of the applicants is suitable' and 'Either of the houses is big enough for their family'.

Either can be used as a distributive pronoun and takes a singular verb, as in 'We have looked at both houses and either is suitable' and 'She cannot decide between the two dresses but either is appropriate for the occasion'. This use is rather formal.

In the **either ... or** construction, a singular verb is used if both subjects are singular, as in 'Either Mary or Jane knows what to do' and 'Either my mother or my father plans to be present'. A plural verb is used if both nouns involved are plural, as in 'Either men or women can play' and 'Either houses or flats are available'.

When a combination of singular and plural subjects is involved, the verb traditionally agrees with the subject which is nearer to it, as in 'Either his parents or his sister is going to come' and 'Either his grandmother or his parents are going to come'.

As a pronoun, **either** should be used only of two possibilities.

electro- is a prefix meaning 'electric, electrical' as in 'electrocardiograph', 'electromagnetic', 'electroscope', 'electrotherapy'.

elision refers to the omission of a speech sound or syllable, as in the omission of 'd' in one of the possible pronunciations of 'Wednesday' and in the omission of 'ce' from the pronunciation of 'Gloucester'.

ellipsis indicates omission of some kind. It can refer to the omission of words from a statement because they are thought to be obvious from the context. In many cases it involves using an auxiliary verb on its own rather than a full verb, as in 'Jane won't accept it but Mary will' and 'They would go if they could'. In such cases the full form of 'Jane won't accept it but Mary will accept it' and 'They would go if they could go' would sound unnatural and repetitive. This is common in spoken English. Some sentences containing an ellipsis sound clumsy as well as ungrammatical, as in 'This is as good, or perhaps even better than that', where 'as' is omitted after 'good' and in 'People have and still do express their disapproval about it', where 'expressed' is omitted after 'have'. Care should be taken to avoid ellipsis if the use of it is going to be ambiguous or clumsy.

Ellipsis is often used to indicate an omission from a quoted passage. If part of a passage is quoted and there is a gap before the next piece of the same passage is required to be quoted an **ellipsis** is used in the form of three dots. If the part of the passage quoted does not start at the beginning of a sentence the ellipsis precedes it.

emphasizing adjective is an adjective used for emphasis. 'Very' is an **emphasizing adjective** in the sentence 'His very mother dislikes him' and 'own' is an **emphasizing adjective** in 'He likes to think that he is own master'.

emphasizing adverb is an adverb used for emphasis. 'Really' is an **emphasizing adverb** in the sentence 'She really doesn't care whether she lives or dies' and 'positively' is an **emphasizing adverb** in the sentence 'He positively does not want to know anything about it'.

emphatic pronoun is a reflexive pronoun that is used for emphasis, as in 'He knows himself that he is wrong', 'She admitted herself that she had made a mistake' and 'The teachers themselves say that the headmaster is too strict'.

-en is a suffix with several functions. In one sense it indicates 'causing to be', as in 'broaden', 'darken', 'gladden', 'lighten' and 'sweeten'. It also indicates a diminutive or small version of something, as in 'chicken' and 'maiden'. It also indicates what something is made of, as in 'silken', 'wooden' and 'woollen'. It is also used to form the past participle of many irregular words, as 'broken', 'fallen', 'forgotten' and 'taken'.

en- is a prefix indicating 'causing to be', as in 'enrich' and 'enlarge', and 'putting into', as in 'endanger', 'enrage', 'enslave'.

ending is the final part of a word consisting of an inflection which is added to a base or root word. The '-ren' part of 'children' is an ending, the '-er' of 'poorer' is an ending and the '-ing' of 'falling' is an ending.

epic originally referred to a very long narrative poem dealing with heroic deeds and adventures on a grand scale, as Homer's 'Iliad'. In modern usage it has been extended to include novels or films with some of these qualities.

epigram is a figure of speech consisting of a brief, pointed and witty saying, as in Jonathan Swift's 'Every man desires to live long; but no man would be old' and Oscar Wilde's 'A cynic is a man who knows the price of everything and the value of nothing'. **Epigram** originally referred to a short poem inscribed on a public monument or tomb.

epithet is an adjective that describes a quality of a noun, as in 'a beautiful dress', 'an amazing story' and 'an enjoyable occasion'. It is also used to indicate a term of abuse, as in 'The drunk man let out a stream of epithets at the policeman.'

eponym refers to a person after whom something is named. The name of the thing in question can also be referred to as an eponym, or it can be said to be eponymous, eponymous being the adjective from **eponym**. English has several eponymous words. Some of these are listed below together with their derivations.

Bailey bridge, a type of temporary military bridge that can be assembled very quickly, called after Sir Donald **Bailey** (1901-85), the English engineer who invented it.

Bowie knife, a type of hunting knife with a long curving blade, called after the American soldier and adventurer, James **Bowie** (1799-1836), who made it popular.

cardigan, a knitted jacket fastened with buttons called after the Earl of **Cardigan** (1797-1868) who was fond of wearing such a garment and was the British cavalry officer who led the unsuccessful Charge of the Light Brigade during the Crimean War (1854).

Celsius the temperature scale, called after the Swedish astronomer, Anders **Celsius** (1701-44).

freesia, a type of sweet-smelling flower, called after the German physician, Friedrich Heinrich Theodor **Freese** (died 1876).

garibaldi, a type of biscuit with a layer of currants in it, called after Giuseppe **Garibaldi** (1807-1882), an Italian soldier patriot who is said to have enjoyed such biscuits.

Granny Smith, a variety of hard green apple, called after the Australian gardener, Maria Ann Smith, known as **Granny Smith** (died 1870), who first grew the apple in Sydney in the 1860s.

greengage, a type of greenish plum, called after Sir William **Gage** who introduced it into Britain from France (1777-1864).

leotard, a one-piece, close-fitting garment worn by acrobats and dancers, called after the French acrobat, Jules **Leotard** (1842-70), who introduced the costume as a circus garment.

mackintosh, a type of raincoat, especially one made of rubberized cloth, called after the Scottish chemist, Charles **Mackintosh** (1766-1843), who patented it in the early 1820s.

praline, a type of confectionery made from nuts and sugar, is called after Count Plessis-**Praslin** (1598-1675), a French field marshal, whose chef is said to have been the first person to make the sweet.

plimsoll, a type of light rubber-soled canvas shoe, called after the English shipping reform leader, Samuel **Plimsoll** (1824-98). The shoe is so named because the upper edge of the rubber was thought to resemble the **Plimsoll** Line, the set of markings on the side of a ship which indicate the levels to which the ship may be safely loaded. The Plimsoll Line became law in 1876.

salmonella, the bacteria that causes some diseases such as food poisoning, called after Daniel Elmer **Salmon** (1850-1914), the American veterinary surgeon who identified it.

sandwich, a snack consisting of two pieces of buttered bread with a filling, called after the Earl of **Sandwich** (1718-92) who was such a compulsive gambler that he would not leave the gaming tables to eat, but had some cold beef between two slices of bread brought to him.

saxophone, a type of keyed brass instrument often used in jazz music, called after Adolphe **Sax** (1814-94), the Belgium instrument-maker who invented it.

shrapnel, an explosive projectile that contains bullets or fragments of metal and a charge that is exploded before impact, called after the British army officer, Henry **Shrapnel** (1761-1842), who invented it.

stetson, a type of wide-brimmed, high-crowned felt hat, called after its designer, the American hat-maker, John Batterson **Stetson** (1830-1906).

trilby, a type of soft felt hat with an indented crown, called after '**Trilby**', the dramatized version of the novel by the English writer, George du Maurier. The heroine of the play, Trilby O'Ferrall, wore such a hat.

wellington, a waterproof rubber boot that extends to the knee, called after the Duke of **Wellington** (1769-1852), who defeated Napoleon at Waterloo (1815).

equative indicates that one thing is equal to, or the same as, another. The verb 'to be' is sometimes known as an **equative verb** because it links a subject and complement which are equal to each other, as in 'He is a rogue' ('he' and 'rogue' refer to the same person) and 'His wife is a journalist' ('his wife' and 'journalist' refer to the same person). Other **equative verbs** include 'appear', 'become', 'look', 'remain' and 'seem', as in 'She looks a nasty person' and 'He became a rich man'. Such verbs are more usually known as **copular verbs**.

-er is a suffix with several functions. It can indicate 'a person that does something', as in 'bearer', 'cleaner', 'employer', 'farmer', 'manager'. Some words in this category can also end in '-or', as in 'adviser/advisor'. It can also indicate 'a person who is engaged in something', as in 'lawyer'. It also indicates 'a thing which does something', as in 'blender', 'cooker', 'mower',

'printer' and 'strainer'. It can also indicate the comparative form of an adjective, as in 'darker', 'fairer', 'older', 'shorter' and 'younger'. It can also indicate 'someone that comes from somewhere', as in 'Londoner' and 'Southerner'.

-esque is a prefix of French origin which means 'in the style or fashion of', as in 'Junoesque', 'statuesque', 'Picassoesque', 'Ramboesque'.

-ese is a suffix indicating 'belonging to, coming from' and is used of people and languages, as 'Chinese', 'Japanese' and 'Portuguese'. By extension it refers to words indicating some kind of jargon, as 'computerese', 'journalese' and 'officialese'.

Esq. can be used instead of 'Mr' when addressing an envelope to a man, as in 'John Jones, Esq.'. It is mostly used in formal contexts. Note that Esq. is used instead of 'Mr', not as well as it. It is usually spelt with a full stop.

-ess is a suffix which was formerly widely used to indicate the feminine form of a word, as 'authoress' from 'author', 'poetess' from 'poet', 'editress' from 'editor', and 'sculptress' from 'sculptor'. In many cases the supposed male form, such as 'author', is now considered a neutral form and so is used of both a woman and a man. Thus a woman as well as a man may be an author, a poet, an editor and a sculptor, etc. Some words ending in **-ess** remain, as princess, duchess, heiress and hostess. Actress and waitress are still also fairly widespread.

-est is a suffix which indicates the superlative forms of adjectives, as in 'biggest', 'hardest', 'lowest', 'smallest', 'ugliest'.

etc is the abbreviation of a Latin phrase *et cetera*, meaning 'and the rest, and other things'. It is used at the end of lists to indicate that there exist other examples of the kind of thing that has just been named, as in 'He grows potatoes, carrots, turnips, etc', 'The girls can play tennis, hockey, squash, etc', 'The main branch of the bank can supply francs, marks, lire, kroner, etc'. **Etc** is preceded by a comma and is also spelt with a full stop.

-ette is a suffix indicating a diminutive or smaller version, as 'cigarette', 'kitchenette', 'rosette', 'serviette'. It can also indicate 'imitation', as in 'flannelette', 'leatherette', 'satinette'. It can also indicate 'female', as in 'majorette', 'usherette', 'suffragette'. In this last sense it is sometimes used disparagingly, as in 'jockette' (a derogatory word for a female jockey) and 'hackette' (a derogatory word for a female journalist).

etymology refers to the source of the formation of a word and the development of its meaning, as in 'What is the etymology of the word "biochemistry"?' It also means the branch of language studies that deals with the origin and development of words, as in 'He specializes in etymology'. In addition it refers to an account or statement of the formation of a word or phrase, as in 'Does that dictionary have etymologies?' In larger dictionaries it is usual to include etymologies, often at the end of each entry. These indicate which language the relevant word has been derived from, for example, whether it has come from Old English, Norse, Latin, Greek, French, German, Dutch, Italian, Spanish, etc. Alternatively they indicate which person, place, etc, the word has been named after. Some dictionaries also include the date at which the relevant word entered the English language. *See* BORROWING.

Many words and phrases in the English language are of unknown or uncertain origin. In such cases much guesswork goes on and various suggestions put forward, most of which cannot be proved.

euphemism is a term given to an expression that is a milder, more pleasant, less direct way of saying something that might be thought to be too harsh or direct. English has a great many euphemisms, many of these referring to certain areas of life. Euphemisms range from the high-flown, to the coy, to slang. Some examples of euphemisms and of the areas in which they tend to occur are listed below.

euphemisms for 'die' or 'be dead':
'be in the arms of Jesus', 'be laid to rest', 'be with one's maker', 'be no longer with us', 'be with the Lord', 'be written out of the script', 'bite the dust', 'cash in one's chips', 'croak', 'depart this life', 'go to a better place', 'go the way of all flesh', 'go to one's long home', 'go to the happy hunting grounds', 'have been taken by the grim reaper', 'have bought it', 'have breathed one's last', 'have gone to a better place', 'kick the bucket', 'meet one's end', 'pass away', 'pay the supreme sacrifice', 'pop off', 'push up the daisies', 'rest in peace', 'shuffle off this mortal coil', 'slip one's rope', 'turn up one's toes'.

euphemisms for 'old':
'getting on a bit', 'not as young as one was', 'not in the first flush of youth', 'in the sunset years', 'in the twilight years', 'of advanced years', 'so many years young (as in 90 years young)'.

euphemisms for 'suicide':
'do away with one self', 'die by one's own hand', 'end it all', 'make away with oneself', 'take one's own life', 'take the easy way out', 'top oneself'.

euphemisms for 'to dismiss':
'declare (someone) redundant', 'deselect', 'dispense with (someone's) services', 'give early retirement to', 'give (someone) a golden handshake', 'give (someone) his/her marching orders', 'let (someone) go', 'not to renew (someone's) contract'.

euphemisms for 'drunk':
'blotto', 'feeling no pain ', 'happy', 'half-cut', 'legless', 'merry', 'one over the eight', 'plastered', 'three sheets to the wind', 'tiddly', 'tipsy', 'tired and emotional', 'squiffy', 'well-oiled'.

euphemisms for 'naked':
'in a state of nature', 'in one's birthday suit', 'in the buff', 'in the nuddy', 'in the raw', 'starkers', 'without a stitch', 'wearing only a smile'.

euphemisms for 'pregnant':
'awaiting the patter of tiny feet', 'expecting', 'expecting a happy event', 'in a delicate condition', 'in an interesting condition', 'in the club', 'in the family way', 'in the pudding club', 'up the pole', 'up the spout', 'with a bun in the oven'.

euphemisms for 'to have sexual intercourse':
'be intimate with', 'do it', 'get one's end away', 'go to bed with', 'have it off with', 'make love', 'make out', 'sleep with', 'score'.

euphemisms for 'sexual intercourse':
'hanky panky', 'intimacy', 'nookie', 'roll in the hay', 'rumpy pumpy/rumpty pumpy'.

euphemisms for to go to the toilet:
'answer the call of nature', 'freshen up', 'go somewhere', 'pay a visit', 'powder one's nose', 'spend a penny', 'take a slash', 'wash one's hands'.

euphemisms for 'toilet':
'bathroom', 'bog', 'can', 'john', 'karzy', 'powder room', 'rest room', 'the facilities', 'the conveniences', 'the geography of the house', 'the little boys' room/the little girls' room', 'the littlest room', 'the smallest room', 'the plumbing', 'wash room'.

euphemisms and political correctness:
Many of the expressions advocated by the politically correct movement for viewing physical and mental disabilities in a more positive light are in fact **euphemisms**. These include 'aurally challenged' for 'deaf', 'optically challenged' for 'blind', and 'uniquely abled' for 'physically disabled'.

Euro- is a prefix meaning either 'referring to Europe', as in 'Eurovision', but more commonly now 'referring to the European Community', as in 'Euro-MP', 'Eurocrat', 'Eurocurrency'.

every is used with a singular noun to indicate that all the members of a group are being referred to. It takes a singular verb, as in 'Every soldier must report for duty', 'Every machine is to be inspected' and 'Every house has a different view'. **Every** should also be accompanied, where relevant, by a singular pronoun, as in 'Every boy has his job to do', 'Every girl is to wear a dress' and 'Every machine is to be replaced'. Problems arise when the sex of the noun to which **every** refers is unknown or unspecified. Formerly it was the custom to assume such a noun to be masculine and to use masculine pronouns, as in 'Every pupil is to behave himself properly'. This assumption is now regarded as sexist, and to avoid this 'he/she', 'him/her' and 'his/her' can be used. Many people feel that this convention can become clumsy and prefer to be ungrammatical by using 'they', 'them' and 'their', as in 'Every pupil is to behave themselves properly.' Many sentences of this kind can be rephrased to avoid being either sexist or ungrammatical, as in 'All pupils are to behave themselves properly'. *See* EACH.

everyone is a pronoun which takes a singular verb, as in 'Everyone is welcome' and 'Everyone has the right to a decent standard of living'. In order to be grammatically correct, it should be accompanied, where relevant, by a singular personal pronoun but it is subject to the same kind of treatment as **every**. *See* EVERY.

ex- is a prefix meaning 'former', as in 'ex-chairman', 'ex-president', 'ex-wife'.

exclamation is a word, phrase or sentence called out with strong feeling of some kind. It is marked by an **exclamation mark** which occurs at the end of the **exclamation**, as in 'Get lost!', 'What a nerve!', 'Help!', 'Ouch!' 'Well I never!', 'What a disaster!', 'I'm tired of all this!' and 'Let me out of here!' An **exclamatory question** is a sentence that is interrogative in form but is an **exclamation** in meaning, as in 'Isn't the baby beautiful!' and 'Isn't it lovely!'.

extra- is a prefix meaning 'beyond, outside' as in 'extra-marital', 'extra-terrestrial', 'extra-curricular'.

F

fable is a story that is intended to convey a moral lesson. **Fables** frequently feature animals which speak and act like human beings. Most famous are those of Aesop, a Phrygian slave (620-560 BC), who wrote such fables as 'The Hare and the Tortoise' and 'The Fox and the Grapes'.

false friends refer to words that have the same or similar forms in different languages but have different meanings in each. For example, the French word *abusif* and the English word 'abusive' are **false friends**. *Abusif* does not mean 'abusive' but 'incorrect, illegal, unauthorized, excessive'. Similarly, the French word *actuel* and the English 'actual' are **false friends**. *Actuel* does not mean 'actual' but 'present-day'. Similarly, the French *eventuel* and Italian *eventuale* are false freinds with the English 'eventual'. *Eventuel* and *eventuale* do not mean 'eventual' but 'possible', while *sensible* in French and *sensibile* in Italian do not mean 'sensible, having good sense or judgement' but 'sensitive, tender, touchy'.

feminine refers to the gender that indicates female persons or animals. It is the opposite of 'masculine'. The feminine gender demands the use of the appropriate pronoun, including 'she', 'her', 'hers' and 'herself', as in 'The girl tried to save the dog but *she* was unable to do so', 'The woman hurt *her* leg', 'Mary said that the book is *hers*', and 'The waitress cut *herself*'.

feminine forms of words, formed by adding —*ess*, used to be common but many such forms are now thought to be sexist. Words such as 'author', 'sculptor', 'poet' are now considered to be neutral terms that can be used to refer to a man or a woman. Some -*ess* words are either still being used or are in a state of flux, as in 'actress'. See -ESS.

few and **a few** are not interchangeable. Both expressions mean 'some, but not many', but they convey different impressions. **Few** is the opposite of 'many', as in 'We have few resources' and 'We have few ideas left'. **A few** conveys a more positive impression and is the opposite of 'none', as in 'We have a few pounds set aside for Christmas' and 'We have not reached a definite decision but we have a few ideas in hand'. The sentence 'We have few ideas left' indicates a negative situation, that 'we' are running out of 'ideas', but the sentence 'We have a few ideas in hand' conveys a positive impression.

fewer and **less** are liable to be used wrongly. **Fewer** means 'a smaller number of' and should be used with plural nouns, as in 'fewer problems', 'fewer resources', 'fewer fears', 'fewer boxes', 'fewer books', 'fewer bottles' and 'fewer chairs'. **Less** means 'a smaller amount of' and should be used with singular nouns, as in 'less responsibility', less anxiety', less work', 'less milk', 'less wood' and 'less material'. It is a very common error to use **less** where **fewer** is correct, as in 'less bottles' and 'less queues'.

figurative refers to words that are not used literally. For example, 'mine' in the sense of 'excavation in the earth from which coal, tin, etc, is taken' is a literal use of the word. 'Mine' in the sense of 'He is a mine of information' is a figurative use of the word. There are many figurative expressions in English. These include 'take the bull by the horns', 'put one's shoulder to the wheel', 'hide one's light under a bushel', 'be in seventh heaven', 'count one's chickens', 'change horses in midstream', 'blow hot and cold', 'run with the hare and hunt with the hounds', 'make the feathers fly', 'put the cat among the pigeons', 'cut corners', 'cry over spilt milk', 'jump on the bandwagon', 'let the grass grow under one's feet', 'drop a brick', 'burn the midnight oil', 'show a clean pair of heels', 'turn one's coat', 'drive a coach and horses through' and 'take coals to Newcastle'.

figure of speech is a form of expression used to heighten the effect of a statement. The most commonly known are 'similes' and 'metaphors' but there are many more, such as 'personification'. See the individual entries for further information.

finite verb is a verb that has a tense and has a subject with which it agrees in number and person. For example 'cries' is finite in the sentence 'The child cries most of the time', and 'looks' is finite in the sentence 'The old man looks ill'. However 'go' in the sentence 'He wants to go' is non-finite since it has no variation of tense and does not have a subject. Similarly in the sentence 'Sitting on the river-bank, he was lost in thought', 'sitting' is non-finite.

finite clause is a clause which contains a 'finite verb', as in 'when she sees him', 'after she had defeated him', and 'as they were sitting there'.

first person refers to the person who is speaking or writing when referring to himself or herself. The **first person** pronouns are 'I', 'me', 'myself' and 'mine', with the plural forms being 'we', 'us', 'ourselves' and 'ours'. Examples include 'She said, "*I* am going home"', '"*I* am going shopping," he said', '"*We* have very little money left," she said to her husband' and 'He said, "*We* shall have to leave now if we are to get there on time"'. The first person determiners are 'my' and 'our', as in 'I have forgotten to bring *my* notebook' and 'We must remember to bring *our* books home.'

fixed phrase, also called **set phrase**, refers to a phrase that has no, or virtually no, variants, as in 'from bad to worse', 'to and fro', 'hither and thither', 'horse and cart', 'this and that', 'alas and alack' and 'rough and ready'.

-fold is a suffix meaning 'times, multiplied by', as in fourfold, a hundredfold.

for- is a prefix derived from Old English with several meanings. These include 'prohibition', as in 'forbid'; 'abstention' as in 'forbear', 'forgo' and 'forswear'; 'neglect', as in 'forsake'; 'excess, intensity', as in 'forlorn'; and 'away, off, apart', as in 'forgive'.

fore- is a prefix derived from Old English meaning 'before', as in 'forecast', 'forestall', 'foretell', 'forewarn', 'foregoing' and 'forefathers'. It can also mean 'front', as in 'foreleg', 'forehead', 'forepart'.

foreign plural refers to a plural of a word in English that has retained the plural form of the foreign word from which the English word has been derived. Examples include 'phenomena' from 'phenomenon', 'crises' from 'crisis' and 'criteria' from 'criterion'. There is a modern tendency to anglicize some of the foreign plural forms. In some cases the foreign plural form and the anglicized form exist alongside each other as 'formulae/formulas', 'thesauri/thesauruses', 'radii/radiuses', 'indices/indexes' and 'bureaux/bureaus'.

foreign expressions which have been adopted into English but not 'naturalized' are sometimes written in italic type, as in *bête noire* (a fear or obsession), *rara avis* (a rarity), *en passant* (in passing), *hors de combat*, (out of the contest, disabled), *en route* (on the way), *bon mot* (witty saying), *in toto* (completely), *in flagrante delicto* (in the very act of committing an offence), *enfant terrible* (a person who causes embarrassment by indiscreet or outrageous behaviour), *en famille* (with one's family) and *inter alia* (among other things).

-form is a suffix meaning 'having the form of', as in 'cruciform', or 'having such a number of', as in 'uniform', 'multiform'.

formal refers to speech and writing that is characterized by more complicated and more difficult language and by more complicated grammatical structures. Short forms and contractions are avoided in **formal** speech and writing. *See* INFORMAL.

formula refers to set phrases that are used in certain conventions, as in 'How do you do?', 'Yours faithfully', 'Yours sincerely', 'Kind regards', 'See you later', 'Nice to see you!' and 'Many happy returns'.

form word *see* **function word.**

-free is a suffix used to form adjectives indicating 'absence of, freedom from', as in 'carefree', 'trouble-free', 'anxiety-free', 'tax-free', 'duty-free', 'additive-free', 'lead-free'.

-friendly is a modern suffix formed on analogy with 'user-friendly' to mean 'helpful to, supporting', as in 'child-friendly', 'environment-friendly' and 'ozone-friendly'.

frequentative refers to a verb which expresses frequent repetition of an action. In English the verb endings *-le* and *-el* sometimes indicate the **frequentative** form, as in 'waddle' from 'wade', 'sparkle' from 'spark', 'crackle' from 'crack' and 'dazzle' from 'daze'. The ending *-er* can also indicate the **frequentative** form, as in 'stutter', 'spatter' and 'batter'.

-ful is a suffix indicating 'the amount that fills something', as in 'bucketful', 'basinful', 'handful', 'spoonful', 'bagful' and 'pocketful'. It can also mean 'full of', as in 'beautiful', 'truthful' and 'scornful'. It can also mean 'having the qualities of', as in 'masterful' and 'apt to, able to', as in 'forgetful', 'mournful' and 'useful'.

full stop is a punctuation mark consisting of a small dot. Its principal use is to end a sentence that is not a question or an exclamation, as in 'They spent the money.', 'She is studying hard.', 'He has been declared redundant and is very upset.' and 'Because she is shy, she rarely goes to parties.'

The **full stop** is also used in decimal fractions, as in '4.5 metres', '6.3 miles' and '12.2 litres'. It can also be used in dates, as in '22.2.94', and in times, as in '3.15 tomorrow afternoon'.

In modern usage the tendency is to omit **full stops** from abbreviations. This is most true of abbreviations involving initial capital letters as in TUC, BBC, EEC and USA. In such cases full stops should definitely not be used if one or some of the initial letters do not belong to a full word. Thus, television is abbreviated to TV and educationally subnormal to ESN.

There are usually no full stops in abbreviations involving the first and last letters of a word (contractions) Dr, Mr, Rd, St, but this is a matter of taste.

Abbreviations involving the first few letters of a word, as in 'Prof' (Professor) are the most likely to have full stops, as in 'Feb.' (February), but again this is now a matter of taste.

For the use of the **full stop** in direct speech *see* DIRECT SPEECH. The **full stop** can also be called **point** or **period.**

function word is a word that has very little meaning but is primarily of grammatical significance and merely performs a 'function' in a sentence. **Function words** include determiners, and prepositions, such as in, on and up. Words which are not **function words** are sometimes known as 'content words'.

Function word is also known as **form word** or **structure word.**

future tense describes actions or states that will occur at some future time. It is marked by 'will' and 'shall'. Traditionally 'shall' was used with subjects in the first person, as in 'I shall see you tomorrow' and 'We shall go there next week', and 'will' was used with subjects in the second and third person, as in 'You will find out next week', 'He will recognize her when he sees her' and 'They will be on the next train'. Formerly 'will' was used with the first person and 'shall' with the second and third person to indicate emphasis or insistence, as in 'I *will* go on my own' and 'We *will* be able to afford it'; 'You *shall* pay what you owe' and 'The children *shall* get a holiday'. In modern usage 'shall' is usually used only for emphasis or insistence, whether with the first, second or third person, except in formal contexts. Otherwise 'will' is used, as in 'I will go tomorrow', 'We will have to see', 'You will be surprised', and 'They will be on their way by now'.

The **future tense** can also be marked by 'be about to' plus the infinitive of the relevant verb or 'be going to' plus the infinitive of the relevant verb. Examples include 'We are about to leave for work', 'They are about to go on holiday', 'She is going to be late' and 'They are going to demolish the building'.

future perfect tense is formed by 'will' or 'shall' together with the 'perfect tense', as in 'They will have been married ten years next week', 'You will have finished work by this time tomorrow' and 'By the time Jane arrives here she will have been travelling nonstop for forty-eight hours'.

G

-gate is a modern suffix which is added to a noun to indicate something scandalous. Most of the words so formed are short-lived and forgotten about almost as soon as they are invented. In modern usage they are frequently used to apply to sexual scandals, but originally **-gate** was restricted to some form of political scandal. The suffix is derived from **Watergate**, and refers to a political scandal in the United States during President Richard Nixon's re-election campaign in 1972, when Republican agents were caught breaking into the headquarters of the Democratic Party in Washington, which were in a building called the Watergate Building. The uncovering of the attempts to cover up the break-in led to Richard Nixon's resignation.

gemination refers to the doubling of consonants before a suffix. *See* DOUBLING OF CONSONANTS.

gender in the English language usually refers to the natural distinctions of sex (or absence of sex) that exist, and nouns are classified according to these distinctions—masculine, feminine and neuter. Thus, 'man', 'boy', 'king', 'prince', 'emperor', 'duke', 'heir', 'son', 'brother', 'father', 'nephew', 'husband', 'bridegroom', 'widower', 'hero', 'cock', 'drake', 'fox' and 'lion' are masculine nouns. Similarly, 'girl', 'woman', 'queen', 'princess', 'empress', 'duchess', 'heiress', 'daughter', 'sister', 'mother', 'niece', 'wife', 'bride', 'widow', 'heroine', 'hen', 'duck', 'vixen' and 'lioness' are feminine nouns. Similarly, 'table', 'chair', 'desk', 'carpet', 'window', 'lamp', 'car', 'shop', 'dress', 'tie', 'newspaper', 'book', 'building' and 'town' are all neuter.

Some nouns in English can refer either to a man or a woman, unless the sex is indicated in the context. Such neutral nouns are sometimes said to have **dual gender**. Examples include 'author', 'singer', 'poet', 'sculptor', 'proprietor', 'teacher', 'parent', 'cousin', 'adult' and 'child'. Some words in this category were formerly automatically assumed to be masculine and several of them had feminine forms, such as 'authoress', 'poetess', 'sculptress' and 'proprietrix'. In modern times this was felt to be sexist and many of these feminine forms are now rarely used, for example, 'authoress' and 'poetess'. However some, such as actress and waitress, are still in common use. *See* -ESS.

In many languages **grammatical gender** plays a major part. In French, for example, all nouns are divided into masculine and feminine, and there is no neuter classification. Masculine nouns are preceded by *le* (definite article). Thus 'ceiling' is masculine (*le plafond*), 'hat' is masculine (*le chapeau*) and 'book' is masculine (*le livre*). Feminine nouns are preceded by *la* (definite article). Thus 'door' is feminine (*la porte*), 'dress' is feminine (*la robe*), and 'window' is feminine (*la fenêtre*).

In German there are three grammatical genders—masculine, feminine and neuter. Masculine nouns are preceded by *der* (definite article) as *der Stuhl* (the chair); feminine nouns are preceded by *die* (definite article) as *die Brücke* (the bridge); neuter nouns are preceded by *das*, as *das Brot* (bread).

Grammatical gender in English is not relevant except in the third personal singular pronouns, as 'he/him/his/himself', 'she/her/hers/herself' and 'it/it/its/itself'. Traditionally 'he', etc, was considered an acceptable pronoun not just for nouns of the masculine gender, but also for those of neutral or dual gender as well. Thus 'Every student must check that he has registered for the exam' was considered acceptable, as was 'Each passenger must be responsible for his own luggage'. Nowadays such sentences are considered sexist. In order to avoid this, some people use the 'he/she', 'his/her', etc, convention, as in 'Every employee must supply his/her own transport' and 'Each candidate must hand in his/her application form now'. People who feel this is clumsy sometimes prefer to be ungrammatical and use a plural pronoun, as in 'Every writer was told to collect their manuscripts in person' and 'Every pupil was told that they would have to be back in school by four o'clock'. It is sometimes possible to avoid being both sexist and ungrammatical by rephrasing such sentences in the plural, as in 'All pupils were told that they would have to be back in school by four o'clock'.

genitive case indicates possession or ownership. It is usually marked by *s* and an apostrophe. Many spelling errors centre on the position of the *s* in relation to the apostrophe.

Nouns in the **genitive case** are usually formed by adding *'s* to the singular noun, as in 'the girl's mother', and Peter's car'; by adding an apostrophe to plural nouns that end in *s*, as in 'all the teachers' cars' and 'the doctors' surgeries'; by adding *'s* to irregular plural nouns that do not end in *s*, as in 'women's shoes'.

In the genitive form of a name or singular noun which ends in *s*, *x* or *z*, the apostrophe may or may not be followed by *s*. In words of one syllable the final *s* is usually added, as in 'James's house', 'the fox's lair', 'Roz's dress'.

The final *s* is most frequently omitted in names, particularly in names of three or more syllables, as in 'Euripides' plays'.

In many cases the presence or absence of final *s* is a matter of convention.

Apostrophes are often omitted wrongly in modern usage, particularly in the media and by advertisers, as in 'womens hairdressers', 'childrens helpings'. In addition, apostrophes are frequently added erroneously (as in 'potato's for sale' and 'Beware of the dog's'). This is partly because people are unsure about when and when not to use them and partly because of a modern tendency to punctuate as little as possible.

A group **genitive** occurs when more than one noun is

involved, as in 'Gilbert and Sullivan's operas'. Note there is only one apostrophe s.

The alternative genitive construction involves the use of 'of', as in 'the mother of the girl', 'the uncle of the little girl', 'the pages of the newspaper' and 'the leg of the chair'. In general, proper nouns and animate beings tend to take the apostrophe and s ending and inanimate objects tend to take the 'of' construction.

geo- is a prefix derived from Greek indicating 'earth', as in 'geography', 'geology', 'geomagnetic' and 'geophysics'.

geographical features should be written with initial capital letters. These include the common nouns that are part of the name of the feature, as in 'Niagara Falls', 'Atlantic Ocean', 'River Thames', 'Mount Everest' and 'Devil's Island'.

gerund refers to the *-ing* form of a verb when it functions as a noun. It is sometimes known as a **verbal noun**. It has the same form as the present participle but has a different function. For example, in the sentence 'He was jogging down the road', 'jogging' is the present participle in the verb phrase 'was jogging', but in the sentence 'Running is his idea of relaxation', 'running' is a gerund because it acts as a noun as the subject of the sentence. Similarly, in the sentence 'We were smoking when the teacher found us', 'smoking' is the present participle in the verb phrase 'were smoking', but in the sentence 'We were told that smoking is bad for our health', 'smoking' is a gerund since it acts as a noun as the subject of the clause.

get is sometimes used to form the passive voice instead of the verb 'to be'. The use of the verb 'to **get**' to form the passive, as in 'They get married tomorrow', 'Our team got beaten today' and 'We got swindled by the con man' is sometimes considered to be more informal than the use of 'be'. Often there is more action involved when the **get** construction is used than when 'be' is used, since **get** is a more dynamic verb, as in 'She was late leaving the pub because she got involved in an argument' and in 'It was her own fault that she got arrested by the police. She hit one of the constables'.

Get is frequently overused. Such overuse should be avoided, particularly in formal contexts. **Get** can often be replaced by a synonym such as 'obtain', 'acquire', 'receive', 'get hold of', etc. Thus, 'If you are getting into

money difficulties you should get some financial advice. Perhaps you could get a bank loan' could be rephrased as 'If you are in financial difficulty you should obtain some financial help. Perhaps you could receive a bank loan'.

Got, the past tense of **get**, is often used unnecessarily, as in 'She has got red hair and freckles' and 'We have got enough food to last us the week'. In these sentences 'has' and 'have' are sufficient on their own.

gliding vowel means the same as **diphthong**.

goal can be used to describe the recipient of the action of a verb, the opposite of 'agent' or 'actor'. Thus, in the sentence 'The boy hit the girl', 'boy' is the 'agent' or 'actor' and 'girl' is the **goal**. Similarly, in the sentence 'The dog bit the postman', 'dog' is the 'agent' or 'actor' and 'postman' is the **goal**.

gobbledygook is used informally to refer to pretentious and convoluted language of the type that is found in official documents and reports. It is extremely difficult to understand and should be avoided and 'plain English' used instead.

govern is used of a verb or preposition in relation to a noun or pronoun and indicates that the verb or preposition has a noun or pronoun depending on it. Thus, in the phrase 'on the table', 'on' is said to govern 'table'.

gradable is used of adjectives and adverbs and means that they can take degrees of comparison. Thus 'clean' is a **gradable** adjective since it has a comparative form (cleaner) and a superlative form (cleanest). 'Soon' is a **gradable** adverb since it has a comparative form (sooner) and a superlative form (soonest). Such words as 'supreme', which cannot normally have a comparative or superlative form, are called **non-gradable**.

-gram is a suffix derived from Greek indicating 'writing' or 'drawing', as in 'telegram', 'electrocardiogram' and 'diagram'. It is also used in modern usage to indicate a 'greeting' or 'message', as in 'kissogram'.

-graph is a suffix derived from Greek indicating 'written, recorded, represented', as in 'autograph', 'monograph', 'photograph'. It is also used to indicate 'an instrument that records', as in 'seismograph', 'tachograph' and 'cardiograph'.

group noun means the same as **collective noun**.

gynaec(o)- is a prefix derived from Greek indicating 'female, woman', as in 'gynaecology', 'gynaecium'.

H

habitual refers to the action of a verb that occurs regularly and repeatedly.. The **habitual present** is found in such sentences as 'He goes to bed at ten every night', 'She always walks to work' and 'The old man sleeps all day'. This is in contrast to the 'stative present', which indicates the action of the verb that occurs at all times, as in 'Cows chew the cud', 'Water becomes ice when it freezes', 'Children grow up' and 'We all die'. Examples of the **habitual past** tense include; 'They travelled by train to work all their lives', 'We worked twelve hours a day on that project' and 'She studied night and day for the exams'.

-hand is a suffix meaning 'worker', as in 'deckhand', 'farmhand' and 'cowhand'. It can also mean 'position', as in 'right-hand' and 'left-hand'.

haem(o)- is a prefix derived from Greek meaning 'blood', as in 'haemorrhage', 'haenatology' and 'haematoma'.

haiku refers to a short Japanese poem in three unrhymed lines with an exact number of syllables per line, the syllable pattern being 5-7-5. The traditional subject matter is usually something to do with nature. A master of the form was the 17th-century Japanese poet Basho, and the following is one of his haiku:

The | white | chry|san|themum
Even | when | lif|ted | to | the | eye
Re|mains | im|macu|late.

half and **halve** are liable to be confused. **Half** is a noun and **halve** is a verb. **Half** is followed by a singular noun when it is referring to an amount, as in 'Half of the milk has gone sour' and 'Half the money is hers'. It is followed by a plural verb when it is referring to a number, as in 'Half of the people are still undecided' and 'Half of the sweets are for the younger children'. The plural of **half** is **halves**, as in 'They cut the oranges in two and distributed the halves to the members of the two teams'.

The plural noun **halves** is liable to be confused with the verb **halve**. Examples of the noun **halves** include 'They served halves of grapefruit for breakfast' and 'He split the estate into halves and left it to his son and daughter'. Examples of the verb **halve** include 'halve the grapefruit for breakfast' and 'He decided to halve his estate between his son and daughter'.

hanged and **hung** are both past tense and past participles of the verb 'to hang' but they are not interchangeable. **Hung** is the more usual form, as in 'The children hung their outdoor clothes on pegs outside the classroom', 'They hung the portrait of her father in the dining room', 'Dark clouds of smoke hung over the city' and 'The boy has hung around with the same crowd of friends for years'. **Hanged** is restricted to the meaning 'suspended by the neck until dead', as in 'They hanged him for the murder of his wife in the 1920s', 'The murderer took his own life before he could be hanged',

'They had to break the news to the children that their father had hanged himself' and 'She hanged herself while the balance of her mind was disturbed'

hanging participle *see* **dangling participle**.

have is a verb which has several functions. A major use is its part in forming the 'perfect tense' and 'past perfect tense', or 'pluperfect tense', of other verb tenses. It does this in conjunction with the 'past participle' of the verb in question.

The perfect tense of a verb is formed by the present tense of the verb **have** and the past participle of the verb. Examples include 'We have acted wisely', 'They have beaten the opposition', 'The police have caught the thieves', 'The old man has died', 'The child has eaten all the food', 'The baby has fallen downstairs', 'They have grabbed all the bargains', 'You have hated him for years' and 'He has indicated that he is going to retire'. The past perfect or pluperfect is formed by the past tense of the verb **have** and the past participle of the verb in question, as in 'He had jumped over the fence', 'They had kicked in the door', 'The boy had led the other children to safety', 'His mother had made the cake', 'The headmaster had punished the pupils' and 'They had rushed into buying a new house'. Both perfect tenses and past perfect or pluperfect tenses are often contracted in speech or in informal written English, as in 'We've had enough for today', 'You've damaged the suitcase', 'You've missed the bus', 'He's lost his wallet', 'She's arrived too late', 'They'd left before the news came through', 'She'd married without telling her parents', 'He'd packed the goods himself' and 'You'd locked the door without realizing it'.

Have is often used in the phrase **have to** in the sense that something must be done. In the present tense **have to** can be used instead of 'must', as in 'You have to leave now', 'We have to clear this mess up', 'He has to get the next train' and 'The goods have to be sold today'. If the 'something that must be done' refers to the future the verb **will have to** is used', as in 'He will have to leave now to get there on time', 'The old man will have to go to hospital' and 'They'll have to move out of the house when her parents return'. If the 'something that must be done' refers to the past, **had to** is used, as in 'We had to take the injured man to hospital', 'They had to endure freezing conditions on the mountain', 'They'd to take a reduction in salary' and 'We'd to wait all day for the workman to appear'.

Have is also used in the sense of 'possess' or 'own', as in 'He has a swimming pool behind his house ', 'She has a huge wardrobe', 'We have enough food' and 'They have four cars'. In spoken or in informal English 'have got' is often used, as in 'They've got the largest house in the street', 'We've got problems now', 'They haven't got time'. This use should be avoided in formal English.

Have is also used to indicate suffering from an illness or disease, as in 'The child has measles', 'Her father has flu' and 'She has heart disease'. **Have** can also indicate that an activity is taking place, as in 'She's having a shower', 'We're having a party', 'She is having a baby' and 'They are having a dinner party'.

he is a personal pronoun and is used as the subject of a sentence or clause to refer to a man, boy, etc. It is thus said to be a 'masculine' personal pronoun. Since he refers to a third party and does not refer to the speaker or the person being addressed , it is a 'third-person pronoun'. Examples include 'James is quite nice but he can be boring', 'Bob has got a new job and he is very pleased' and 'He is rich but his parents are very poor'.

He traditionally was used not only to refer to nouns relating to the masculine sex but also to nouns that are now regarded as being neutral or of 'dual gender'. Such nouns include 'architect', 'artist', 'athlete', 'doctor', 'passenger', 'parent', 'pupil', 'singer', 'student'. Without further information from the context it is impossible to know to which sex such nouns are referring. In modern usage it is regarded as sexist to assume such words to be masculine by using **he** to refer to one of them unless the context indicates that the noun in question refers to a man or boy. Formerly it was considered acceptable to write or say 'Send a message to the architect who designed the building that he is to attend the meeting' whether or not the writer or speaker knew that the architect was a man. Similarly it was considered acceptable to write or say 'Please tell the doctor that he is to come straight away' whether or not the speaker or writer knew that the doctor was in fact a man. Nowadays this convention is considered sexist. In order to avoid sexism it is possible to use the convention 'he/she', as in 'Every pupil was told that he/she was to be smartly dressed for the occasion', 'Each passenger was informed that he/she was to arrive ten minutes before the coach was due to leave' and 'Tell the doctor that he/she is required urgently'. However this convention is regarded by some people as being clumsy, particularly in spoken English or in informal written English. Some people prefer to be ungrammatical and use the plural personal pronoun 'they' instead of 'he/she' in certain situations, as in 'Every passenger was told that they had to arrive ten minutes before the coach was due to leave' and 'Every student was advised that they should apply for a college place by March'. In some cases it may be possible to rephrase sentences and avoid being either sexist or ungrammatical, as in 'All the passengers were told that they should arrive ten minutes before the coach was due to leave' and 'All students were advised that they should apply for a college place by March'.

headline is the name given to the title of a newspaper article. From the very nature of headlines they are short, partly because of shortage of space and partly to capture the attention of the would-be reader. In order to achieve this, the definite and indefinite articles and other minor words tend to be omitted, the future tense represented by a to-infinitive, as in 'Prescription charges to rise', and the present tenses used for past events. **Headline** language, particularly that of tabloid newspapers which has to be especially succinct and eye-catching, can have an effect on the general language. Thus expressions such as 'tug-of-love', which describes the state of a child whose custody is being bitterly fought over by both parents, is now quite com-

mon in the general language but started out as a headline term. Other expressions which are typical of the language of the headlines include 'killing spree', which describes someone who loses control and kills, usually by shooting, several people indiscriminately, as in 'Local gunman goes on killing spree'. Another one is 'have-a-go', which describes an attempt by a member of the public to try and catch a criminal, as in 'Pensioner in have-a-go with bank-raider'. The language and style of **headlines** is frequently known as **headlinese**.

heading refers to a word, phrase or sentence put at the top of a page, chapter, section, etc, of a book or other printed document. These are sometimes written with initial capital letters (except for articles or prepositions), as in 'Annual Report', 'Department Budget for the Year', 'The Year Ahead', 'What Went Wrong', 'Company Plans', 'Trading Outlook Overseas', but this is a matter of taste or of house style . Some people prefer to use lower-case letters except for the first word, as in 'Sales targets for the year', 'A review of export markets', and 'The way forward'. Headings can be underlined or placed in italic type or bold type to highlight them on the page.

headword refers to a word which is at the head of an entry in a dictionary or other reference book. It is also known as 'entry word' and is usually written in bold type so that it stands out on the page and is readily identifiable.

helping verb is another name for **auxiliary verb**.

hemi- is a prefix derived from Greek meaning 'half', as in 'hemisphere' and 'hemiplegia'.

hendiadys is a figure of speech in which two nouns joined by 'and' are used to express an idea that would normally be expressed by the use of an adjective and a noun, as in 'through storm and weather' instead of 'through stormy weather'.

he/she *see* **he**.

her is a personal pronoun. It is the third person singular, is feminine in gender and acts as the object in a sentence, as in 'We saw her yesterday', 'I don't know her', 'He hardly ever sees her', 'Please give this book to her', 'Our daughter sometimes plays with her' and 'We do not want her to come to the meeting'. *See* **he**; **she**.

hers is a personal pronoun. It is the third person singular, feminine in gender and is in the poassessive case. 'The car is not hers', 'I have forgotten my book but I don't want to borrow hers', 'This is my seat and that is hers', and 'These clothes are hers'. *See* **his**; **her** and **possessive**.

hetero- is a prefix derived from Greek meaning 'other, another, different', as in 'heterodox' and 'heterosexual'.

hexa- is a prefix derived from Greek meaning 'six', as in 'hexagram' and 'hexagon'.

hiatus refers to a break in pronunciation between two vowels that come together in different syllables, as in 'Goyaesque' and 'cooperate'.

him is the third person masculine personal pronoun when used as the object of a sentence or clause, as in 'She shot him', 'When the police caught the thief they arrested him' and 'His parents punished him after the boy stole the money'. Traditionally **him** was used to apply not only to masculine nouns, such as 'man' and 'boy', but also to nouns that are said to be 'of dual gender'. These include 'architect', 'artist', 'parent', 'passenger', 'pupil' and 'student'. Without further information from the context, it is not possible for the speaker or writer to know the sex of the person referred to by one of these words. Formerly it was acceptable to write or say 'The artist must bring an easel with him' and 'Each pupil must bring food with him'. In modern usage this convention is considered sexist and there is a modern convention that 'him/her' should be used instead to avoid sexism, as in 'The artist must bring an easel with him/her' and 'Each pupil must bring food with 'him/her'. This convention is felt by some people to be clumsy, particularly in spoken and in informal English, and some people prefer to be ungrammatical and use the plural personal pronoun 'them' instead, as in 'The artist must bring an easel with them' and 'Each pupil must bring food with them'. In some situations it is possible to avoid being either sexist or ungrammatical by rephrasing the sentence, as in 'All artists must bring easels with them' and 'All pupils must bring food with them. *See* **he.**

him/her *see* **him.**

his is the third personal masculine pronoun when used to indicate possession, as in 'He has hurt his leg', 'The boy has taken his books home' and 'Where has your father left his tools?' Traditionally **his** was used to refer not only to masculine nouns, such as 'man', 'boy', etc, but to what are known as nouns 'of dual gender'. These include 'architect', 'artist', 'parent', 'passenger', 'pupil' and 'student'. Without further information from the context it is not possible for the speaker or the writer to know the sex of the person referred to by one of these words. Formerly it was considered acceptable to use **his** in such situations, as in 'Every pupil has to supply his own sports equipment' and 'Every passenger is responsible for his own luggage'. In modern usage this is now considered sexist and there is a modern convention that 'his/her' should be used instead to avoid sexism, as in 'Every pupil has to supply his/her own sports equipment' and 'Every passenger is responsible for his/her own luggage'. This convention is felt by some people to be clumsy, particularly when used in spoken or informal written English. Some people prefer to be ungrammatical and use the plural personal pronoun 'their', as in 'Every pupil must supply their own sports equipment' and 'Every passenger is to be responsible for their own luggage'. In some situations it is possible to avoid being sexist, clumsy and ungrammatical by rephrasing the sentence, as in 'All pupils must supply their own sports equipment' and 'All passengers are to be responsible for their own luggage.

his/her *see* **his**

holidays, in the sense of public holidays or festivals, should be written with an initial capital letter, as in 'Christmas Day', 'Easter Sunday', 'New Year' and 'Independence Day'.

holo- is a prefix meaning 'complete, whole', as in 'holistic'.

homo- is a prefix derived from Greek meaning 'same', as in 'homogenous', 'homonym', 'homograph', 'homophone' and 'homosexual'.

homograph refers to a word that is spelt the same as another word but has a different meaning and pronunciation. **Homographs** include:

bow, pronounced to rhyme with 'how', a verb meaning 'to bend the head or body as a sign of respect or in greeting, etc', as in 'The visitors bowed to the emperor'

and 'The mourners bowed their heads as the coffin was lowered into the grave'.

bow, pronounced to rhyme with 'low', a noun meaning 'a looped knot, a ribbon tied in this way', as in 'She tied her hair in a bow' and 'She wears blue bows in her hair'.

lead, pronounced 'leed', a verb meaning 'to show the way', as in 'The guide will lead you down the mountain'.

lead, pronounced 'led', a noun meaning 'a type of greyish metal', as in 'They are going to remove any water pipes made from lead'.

row, pronounced to rhyme with 'low', a noun meaning 'a number of people or things arranged in a line', as in 'The princess sat in the front row'.

row, pronounced to rhyme with 'how', a noun meaning 'a quarrel, a disagreement', as in 'He has had a row with his neighbour over repairs to the garden wall'.

slough, pronounced to rhyme with 'rough', a verb meaning 'to cast off', as in 'The snake had sloughed off its old skin'.

slough, pronounced to rhyme with 'how', a noun meaning 'a swamp', as in 'Get bogged down in a slough' and 'in the Slough of Despond'.

sow, pronounced to rhyme with 'low', a verb meaning 'to scatter seeds in the earth', as in 'In the spring the gardener sowed some flower seeds in the front garden'.

sow, pronounced to rhyme with 'how', a noun meaning 'a female pig', as in 'The sow is in the pigsty with her piglets'.

homonym refers to a word that has the same spelling and the same pronunciation as another word but has a different meaning from it. Examples include:

bill, a noun meaning 'a written statement of money owed', as in 'You must pay the bill for the conversion work immediately', or 'a written or printed advertisement', as in 'We were asked to deliver handbills advertising the play'.

bill, a noun meaning 'a bird's beak', as in 'The seagull has injured its bill'.

fair, an adjective meaning 'attractive', as in 'fair young women'; 'light in colour', as in 'She has fair hair'; 'fine, not raining', as in 'I hope it keeps fair'; 'just, free from prejudice', as in 'We felt that the referee came to a fair decision'.

fair, a noun meaning 'a market held regularly in the same place, often with stalls, entertainments and rides' (now often simply applying to an event with entertainments and rides without the market), as in 'He won a coconut at the fair'; 'a trade exhibition', as in 'the Frankfurt Book Fair'.

pulse, a noun meaning 'the throbbing caused by the contractions of the heart', as in 'The patient has a weak pulse'.

pulse, a noun meaning 'the edible seeds of any of various crops of the pea family, as lentils, peas and beans', as in 'Vegetarians eat a lot of food made with pulses'.

row, a verb meaning 'to propel a boat by means of oars', as in 'He plans to row across the Atlantic single-handed'.

row, a noun meaning 'a number of people or things arranged in a line', as in 'We tried to get into the front row to watch the procession' and 'The gardener has planted rows of cabbages'.

homonym is sometimes used to describe words that are more correctly classified as **homographs** or **homophones.** *See* **homograph; homophone.**

homophone refers to a word that is pronounced in the same way as another but is spelt in a different way and has a different meaning. **Homophones** include:

aisle, a noun meaning 'a passage between rows of seats in a church, theatre, cinema etc', as in 'The bride walked down the aisle on her father's arm'.

isle, a noun meaning 'an island', as in 'the Isle of Wight'.

alter, a verb meaning 'to change', as in 'They have had to alter their plans'.

altar, a noun meaning 'in the Christian church, the table on which the bread and wine are consecrated for Communion and which serves as the centre of worship', as in 'The priest moved to the altar, from where he dispensed Communion', 'There is a holy painting above the altar'; or 'a raised structure on which sacrifices are made or incense burned in worship', as in 'The Druids made human sacrifices on the altar of their gods'.

ail, a verb meaning 'to be ill', as in 'The old woman is ailing'; 'to be the matter, to be wrong', as in 'What ails you?'

ale, a noun meaning 'a kind of beer', as in 'a pint of foaming ale'.

blew, a verb, the past tense of the verb 'blow', as in 'They blew the trumpets loudly'.

blue, a noun and adjective meaning 'a colour of the shade of a clear sky', as in 'She wore a blue dress'.

boar, a noun meaning 'a male pig', as in 'a dish made with wild boar'.

bore, a verb meaning 'to make tired and uninterested', as in 'The audience was obviously bored by the rather academic lecture'.

bore, a verb, the past tense of the verb 'bear', as in 'They bore their troubles lightly'.

cereal, a noun meaning 'a plant yielding grain suitable for food', as in 'countries which grow cereal crops' and 'a prepared food made with grain', as in 'We often have cereal for breakfast'.

serial, a noun meaning 'a story or television play which is published or appears in regular parts, as in 'the final instalment of the magazine serial which she was following'.

cite, a verb meaning 'to quote or mention by way of example or proof', as in 'The lawyer cited a previous case to try and get his client off'.

sight, a noun meaning 'the act of seeing', as in 'They recognized him at first sight'.

site, a noun meaning 'a location, place', as in 'They have found a site for the new factory'.

feat, a noun meaning 'a notable act or deed', as in 'The old man received an award for his courageous feat'.

feet, a noun, the plural form of 'foot', as in 'The child got her feet wet from wading in the puddle'.

none, a pronoun meaning 'not any', as in 'They are demanding money but we have none'.

nun, a noun meaning 'a woman who joins a religious order and takes vows of poverty, chastity and obedience', as in 'She gave up the world to become a nun'.

know, a verb meaning 'to have understanding or knowledge of', as in 'He is the only one who knows the true facts of the situation', and 'to be acquainted with', as in 'I met her once but I don't really know her'.

no, an adjective meaning 'not any', as in 'We have no food left'.

rite, a noun meaning 'a ceremonial act or words,' as in 'rites involving witchcraft'.

right, an adjective meaning 'correct', as in 'Very few people gave the right answer to the question'.

write, a verb meaning 'to form readable characters', as in 'he writes regularly for the newspapers'.

stare, a verb and noun meaning 'to look fixedly' and 'a fixed gaze', as in 'She stared at him in disbelief when he told her the news' and 'He has the stare of a basilisk'.

stair, a noun meaning 'a series of flights of stairs', as in 'The old lady is too feeble to climb the stairs to her bedroom'.

-hood is a suffix meaning 'state, condition', as in 'babyhood', 'childhood', 'manhood', 'priesthood', 'womanhood' and 'widowhood'.

hydro- is a prefix derived from Greek meaning 'water, as in 'hydro-electric' and 'hydrophobia'. It also means 'hydrogen', as in 'hydrochloride'.

hyper- is a prefix derived from Greek meaning 'over, above', as in 'hyperactive', 'hypercritical', 'hyperinflation' and 'hypersensitive'.

hypo- is a prefix derived from Greek meaning 'under', as in 'hypothermia', 'hypodermic'.

hyphen refers to a small stroke used to join two words together or to indicate that a word has been broken at the end of a line because of lack of space. It is used in a variety of situations.

The **hyphen** is used as the prefixed element in a proper noun, as in 'pre-Christian', 'post-Renaissance', 'anti-British', 'anti-Semitic', 'pro-French' and 'pro-Marxism'. It is also used before dates or numbers, as in 'pre-1914', 'pre-1066', 'post-1920', 'post-1745'. It is also used before abbreviations, as in 'pro-BBC', 'anti-EEC' and 'anti-TUC'.

The **hyphen** is used for clarification. Some words are ambiguous without the presence of a hyphen. For example, 're-cover', as in 're-cover a chair', is spelt with a hyphen to differentiate it from 'recover', as in 'The accident victim is likely to recover'. Similarly, it is used in 're-form', meaning 'to form again', as in 'They have decided to re-form the society which closed last year', to differentiate the word from 'reform', meaning 'to improve, to become better behaved', as in 'He was wild as a young man but he has reformed now'. Similarly 're-count' in the sense of 'count again' , as in 're-count the number of votes cast', is spelt with a hyphen to differentiate it from 'recount' in the sense of 'tell', as in 'recount what happened on the night of the accident'.

The **hyphen** was formerly used to separate a prefix from the main element of a word if the main element begins with a vowel, as in 'pre-eminent', but there is a growing tendency in modern usage to omit the **hyphen** in such cases. At the moment both 'pre-eminent' and 'preeminent' are found. However, if the omission of the **hyphen** results in double *i*, the **hyphen** is usually retained, as in 'anti-inflationary' and 'semi-insulated'.

The **hyphen** was formerly used in words formed with the prefix *non-*, as in 'non-functional', 'non-political', 'non-flammable' and 'non-pollutant'. However there is a growing tendency to omit the hyphen in such cases, as in 'nonfunctional' and 'nonpollutant'. At the moment both forms of such words are common.

The **hyphen** is usually used with 'ex-' in the sense of 'former', as in 'ex-wife' and 'ex-president'.

The **hyphen** is usually used when 'self-' is prefixed to words, as in 'self-styled', 'a self-starter' and 'self-evident'.

Use or non-use of the **hyphen** is often a matter of choice, house style or frequency of usage, as in 'drawing-room' or 'drawing room'. and 'dining-room' or 'dining room'. There is a modern tendency to punctuate less frequently than was formerly the case and so in modern usage use of the **hyphen** in such expressions is less frequent. The length of compounds often affects the inclusion or omission of the hyphen. Compounds of two short elements that are well-established words tend not to be hyphenated, as in 'bedroom' and 'toothbrush'. Compound words with longer elements are more likely to be hyphenated, as in 'engine-driver' and 'carpet-layer'.

Some fixed compounds of two or three or more words are always hyphenated, as in 'son-in-law', 'good-for-nothing' and 'devil-may-care'

Some compounds formed from phrasal verbs are sometimes hyphenated and sometimes not. Thus both 'take-over' and 'takeover' are common, and 'rundown' and 'rundown' are both common. Again the use of the hyphen is a matter of choice. However some words formed from phrasal verbs are usually spelt without a hyphen, as in 'breakthrough'.

Compound adjectives consisting of two elements, the second of which ends in -*ed*, are usually hyphenated, as in 'heavy-hearted', 'fair-haired', 'fair-minded' and 'long-legged'.

Compound adjectives when they are used before nouns are usually hyphenated, as in 'gas-fired central heating', 'oil-based paints', 'solar-heated buildings' and 'chocolate-coated biscuits'.

Compounds containing some adverbs are usually hyphenated, sometimes to avoid ambiguity, as in 'his best-known opera', a 'well-known singer', 'an ill-considered venture' and 'a half-planned scheme'.

Generally adjectives and participles preceded by an adverb are not hyphenated if the adverb ends in -*ly*, as in 'a highly talented singer', 'neatly pressed clothes' and 'beautifully dressed young women'.

In the case of two or more compound hyphenated adjectives with the same second element qualifying the same noun, the common element need not be repeated but the **hyphen** should be, as in 'two- and three-bedroom houses' and 'long- and short-haired dogs'.

The **hyphen** is used in compound numerals from 21 to 99 when they are written in full, as in 'thirty-five gallons', 'forty-four years', 'sixty-seven miles' and 'two hundred and forty-five miles'. Compound numbers such as 'three hundred' and 'two thousand' are not hyphenated.

Hyphens are used in fractions, as in 'three-quarters', 'two-thirds', and 'seven-eighths'.

Hyphens are also used in such number phrases as 'a seventeenth-century play', 'a sixteenth-century church', 'a five-gallon pail', 'a five-year contract' and a 'third-year student'.

The other use of **hyphens** is to break words at the ends of lines. Formerly people were more careful about where they broke words. Previously, words were broken up according to etymological principles but there is a growing tendency to break words according to how they are pronounced. Some dictionaries or spelling dictionaries give help with the division and hyphenation of individual words. General points are that one-syllable words should not be divided and words should not be broken after the first letter of a word or before the last letter. Care should be taken not to break up words, for example by forming elements that are words in their own right, in such a way as to mislead the reader. Thus divisions such as 'the-rapist' and 'mans-laughter' should be avoided.

hybrid refers to a word that is formed from words or elements derived from different languages, such as 'television'.

hyperbole is a figure of speech consisting of exaggeration or over-statement, used for emphasis, as in 'I could eat a horse' and in 'I am boiling in this heat'.

I

I and **me** are liable to be confused. They are both parts of the first person singular pronoun, but **I** acts as the subject of a sentence and **me** as the object. People often assume wrongly that **me** is less 'polite' than '**I**'. This is probably because they have been taught that in answer to such questions as 'Who is there?' the grammatically correct reply is 'It is I'. In fact, except in formal contexts, 'It is me' is frequently found in modern usage, especially in spoken contexts. Confusion arises as to whether to use **I** or **me** after 'between'. Since 'between' is followed by an object, **me** is the correct form. Thus it is correct to say 'Just between you and me, I think he is dishonest'. On the other hand, **me**, being an object, should not be used in such sentences as 'You and I have both been invited', 'May Jane and I play?' and 'The children and I are going to join you'. **Me** should, however, be used in such sentences as 'The cake was made by Mary and me', 'They were sitting in front of my son and me at the cinema' and 'My brother and father played against my mother and me', since in all these cases it is the object form of the first person singular that is required.

-ian is a suffix either indicating 'a profession, job or pastime', as in 'comedian', 'musician', 'optician', 'physician', or indicating 'proper names', as in 'Elizabethan', 'Dickensian', 'Orwellian' and 'Shakesperian'.

-iana is a suffix form of -ana, indicating 'memorabilia or collections relating to people or places of note', as in 'Victoriana' and 'Churchilliana'.

-ible *see* **adjectives**.

-ics is a suffix indicating 'science' or 'study', as in 'acoustics', 'electronics', 'genetics', 'obstetrics', 'politics' and 'physics'.

ideogram refers to a written character that symbolizes a word or phrase without indicating the pronunciation, such as £, &, +.

idiolect refers to the speech habits, knowledge and command of language of an individual. This can vary considerably from person to person. For example, one person might have a much more formal **idiolect** than another.

idiom refers to an expression whose meaning cannot be easily deduced from the individual meanings of the words it contains. Thus, in the expression 'know the ropes' one can know what 'know' means and know what 'ropes' means without being able to deduce the meaning of 'know the ropes'. In fact, 'know the ropes' is a nautical idiom. If a sailor was being taught the basics of seamanship in the days of sailing ships, he would have to be taught the mechanics of ropes which were an important part of sailing in those days. Hence, 'know the ropes' has come to mean 'to understand the procedures and details involved in something', as in 'When he first started the job the trainee mechanic felt really awkward and useless, but he when he knew the ropes he felt more confident and happier'.

Similarly, one can easily understand the meanings of the various individual words in the expression 'out on a limb', but it is not at all obvious that it means idiomatically 'in a risky and often lonely position', this being a reference to someone being stuck in an isolated and precarious position on the branch of a tree. This idiom is found in sentences such as 'The young designer has gone out on a limb and produced clothes that his boss says are too experimental for the mass market'. Literally it refers to a person or animal that has crawled so far out on a branch of a tree that he/she is in danger of falling or of not being able to crawl back to the main tree.

Similarly, in the expression 'throw someone to the lions' one can easily understand the meanings of the various individual words without realizing that the expression means 'deliberately to put someone in a difficult or dangerous position', as in 'All the teachers were responsible for the change in policy with regard to school uniform but they threw the deputy head to the lions when they asked him to address a parents' meeting on the subject'. In order to appreciate the meaning of the idiom fully, the reader or listener has to understand that the idiom refers to a supposed form of entertainment in ancient Rome in which prisoners were thrown to hungry wild animals to be attacked and killed (while spectators looked on enthusiastically).

Similarly, in the expression 'throw in the towel' one can easily understand the meanings of the various individual words without realizing that the phrase means 'to give in, to admit defeat', as in 'She tried to stand up to the bullies in her school but finally she threw in the towel and asked her parents to send her to another school'. This idiom comes from the world of boxing in which 'throwing in the towel' indicates a method of conceding defeat.

Similarly, understanding the individual words of the expression 'sell someone down the river' will not help one to understand that it means 'to betray or be disloyal to someone', as in 'The bank robber who was caught by the police refused to sell his associates down the river'. The origin here is slightly more obscure in that it refers historically to slave owners in the Mississippi states of the United States, who sold their slaves to buyers downstream in Louisiana where living and working conditions were much harder.

Such idioms as 'sell someone down the river' are known as 'opaque idioms' since there is no resemblance between the meaning of the individual words of the idiom and the idiom itself. Idioms such as 'keep a straight face' are known as 'transparent idioms' since, although they are not to be interpreted literally, it is reasonably obvious what they mean.

i.e. is the abbreviation of the Latin phrase *id est* and is used before explanations or amplifications of what has just been mentioned, as in 'He was a mercenary in the war, i.e. he fought for money' and 'She is agoraphobic, i.e. she is afraid of open spaces' and 'He is a bibliophile, i.e. he loves books'. It is usually spelt with a full stop after each of the letters.

if is a conjunction which is often used to introduce a subordinate adverbial clause of condition, as in 'If he is talking of leaving he must be unhappy', 'If you tease the dog it will bite you', 'If he had realized that the weather was going to be so bad he would not have gone on the expedition', 'If I had been in charge I would have sacked him' and 'If it were a better organized firm things like that would not happen'.

If can also introduce a 'nominal' or 'noun clause', as in 'He asked if we objected' and 'She inquired if we wanted to go'.

-ify is a suffix indicating 'making or becoming', as in 'beautify', 'clarify', 'dignify', 'purify', 'satisfy' and 'simplify'.

imperative mood is the verb mood that expresses commands. The verbs in the following sentences are in the **imperative mood**. 'Go away!', 'Run faster!', 'Answer me!', 'Sit down!', 'Please get out of here!'. All of these expressions with verbs in the **imperative mood** sound rather imperious or dictatorial and usually end with an exclamation mark, but this is not true of all expressions with verbs in the **imperative mood**. For example, the following sentences all have verbs in the **imperative mood**: 'Have another helping of ice cream', 'Help yourself to more wine', 'Just follow the yellow arrows to the X-ray department', and 'Turn right at the roundabout'. Sentences with verbs in the **imperative mood** are known as **imperative sentences**.

imperfect indicates a tense that denotes an action in progress but not complete. The term derives from the classification in Latin grammar and was traditionally applied to the 'past imperfect', as in 'They were standing there'. The **imperfect** has now been largely superseded by the 'progressive/continuous tense', which is marked by the use of 'be' plus 'present participle'. Continuous tenses are used when talking about temporary situations at a particular point in time, as in 'They were waiting for the bus'.

impersonal refers to a verb which is used with a formal subject, usually 'it', as in 'It is raining' and 'They say it will snow tomorrow'.

indefinite article: **a** and **an** are the forms of the indefinite article. The form **a** is used before words that begin with a consonant sound, as 'a box', 'a garden', 'a road', 'a wall'. The form **an** is used before words that begin with a vowel sound, as 'an apple', 'an easel', 'an ostrich', 'an uncle'. Note that it is the sound of the initial letter that matters and not the spelling. Thus **a** is used before words beginning with a *u* when they are pronounced with a *y* sound as though it were a consonant, as 'a unit', 'a usual occurrence'. Similarly, **an** is used, for example, before words beginning with the letter *h* where this is not pronounced, as in 'an heir', 'an hour', 'an honest man'.

Formerly it was quite common to use **an** before words that begin with an *h* sound and also begin with an unstressed syllable, as in 'an hotel (ho-tel)', 'an historic (his-tor-ik) occasion', 'an hereditary (her-ed-it-ary) disease'. It is now more usual nowadays to use **a** in such cases and ignore the question of the unstressed syllable.

indefinite pronouns refer to people or things without being specific as to exactly who or what they are. They include 'everyone', 'everybody', 'everything', 'anyone', 'anybody', 'anything', 'somebody', 'someone', 'something' and 'nobody', 'no one', 'nothing', as in 'Everyone is to make a contribution', 'Anyone can enter', 'Something will turn up' and 'Nobody cares'.

independent clause refers to a clause which can stand alone and make sense without being dependent on another clause, as in 'The children are safe'. Main clauses are **independent clauses**. Thus in the sentence 'She is tired and she wants to go home', there are two **independent clauses** joined by 'and'. In the sentence 'She will be able to rest when she gets home', 'She will be able to rest' is an **independent clause** and 'when she gets home' is a 'dependent clause'. In the sentence 'Because she is intelligent she thinks for herself', 'she thinks for herself' is an **independent clause** and 'because she is intelligent' is a 'dependent clause'.

indicative mood refers to the mood of a verb which denotes making a statement. The following sentences have verbs in the **indicative mood**: 'We go on holiday tomorrow', 'He was waiting for her husband', 'They have lost the match' and 'She will arrive this afternoon'. The **indicative mood** is sometimes known as the 'declarative mood'. The other moods are IMPERATIVE MOOD and SUBJUNCTIVE MOOD.

indirect object refers to an object which can be preceded by 'to' or 'for'. The **indirect object** usually refers to the person who benefits from an action or receives something as the result of it. In the sentence 'Her father gave the boy food', 'boy' is the **indirect object** and 'food' is the 'direct object'. The sentence could be rephrased as 'Her father gave food to the boy'. In the sentence 'He bought his mother flowers', 'his mother' is the **indirect object** and 'flowers' is the 'direct object'. The sentence could have been rephrased as 'he bought flowers for his mother'. In the sentence 'They offered him a reward', 'him' is the **indirect object** and 'reward' is the 'direct object'. The sentence could be rephrased as 'They offered a reward to him'.

indirect question refers to a question that is reported in indirect speech, as in 'We asked them where they were going', 'They inquired why we had come' and 'They looked at us curiously and asked where we had come from'.

indirect speech is also known as **reported speech** and is a way of reporting what someone has said without using the actual words used by the speaker. There is usually an introductory verb and a subordinate 'that' clause, as in 'He said that he was going away', 'They announced that they were leaving next day' and 'She declared that she had seen him there before'. In direct speech these sentences would become 'He said, "I am going away"', 'They announced, "We are leaving tomorrow"' and 'She declared, "I have seen him there before"'. When the change is made from 'direct speech' to **indirect speech**, the pronouns, adverbs of time and place and tenses are changed to accord with the viewpoint of the person doing the reporting.

infinitive refers to the 'base' form of a verb when used without any indication of person, number or tense. There are two forms of the **infinitive**. One is the 'to infinitive' form, as in 'They wished to leave', 'I plan to go tomorrow', 'We aim to please' and 'They want to emigrate', 'To know all is to forgive all', 'To err is human', 'Pull the lever to open', 'You should bring a book to read', 'The child has nothing to do', 'She is not very nice to know' and 'It is hard to believe that it happened'. The other form of the **infinitive** is called the **bare infinitive**. This form consists of the base form of the verb without 'to', as in 'We saw him fall', 'She watched him go', 'They noticed him enter', 'She heard him sigh', 'They let him go', 'I had better leave' and 'Need we return' and 'we dare not go back'. *See* SPLIT INFINITIVE.

inflect as applied to a word means to change form in order to indicate differences of tense, number, gender, case, etc. Nouns inflect for plural, as in 'ships', 'chairs', 'houses' and 'oxen'; nouns inflect for possessive, as in 'boys'', 'woman's', 'teachers', and 'parents''; some adjectives inflect for the comparative form, as in 'brighter', 'clearer', 'shorter' and 'taller'; verbs inflect for the third person singular present tense, as in 'hears', 'joins', 'touches' and 'kicks'; verbs inflect for the present participle, as in 'hearing', 'joining', 'touching' and 'kicking'; verbs inflect for the past participle, as in 'heard', 'joined', 'touched' and 'kicked'.

inflection refers to the act of inflecting—*see* INFLECT. It also refers to an inflected form of a word or a suffix or other element used to inflect a word.

informal refers to a spoken or style of language that has a simpler grammatical structure and simpler vocabulary often involving vocabulary that is colloquial in nature or even slang.

infra- is a prefix derived from Latin indicating 'below, beneath', as in 'infrared' and 'infrastructure'.

-ing forms of verbs can be either PRESENT PARTICIPLES or GERUNDS. Present participles are used in the formation of the progressive or continuous tenses, as in 'We were looking at the pictures', 'Children were playing in the snow', 'They are waiting for the bus', 'Parents were showing their anger', 'He has been sitting there for hours'. Present participles can also be used in non-finite clauses or phrases, as in 'Walking along, she did not have a care in the world', 'Lying there, he thought about his life', 'Sighing, he left the room' and 'Smiling broadly he congratulated his friend'.

A large number of adjectives end in **-ing**. Many of these have the same form as the present participle of a transitive verb and are similar in meaning. Examples include 'an amazing spectacle', 'a boring show', 'an interesting idea', 'a tiring day', 'an exhausting climb' and 'aching limbs'. Some **-ing** adjectives are related to intransitive verbs, as 'existing problems', 'increasing responsibilities', 'dwindling resources', 'an ageing work force' and 'prevailing circumstances'. Some **-ing** adjectives are related to the forms of verbs but have different meanings from the verbs, as in 'becoming dress', 'an engaging personality', 'a dashing young man' and 'a retiring disposition'. Some **-ing** adjectives are not related to verbs at all. These include 'appetizing', 'enterprising', 'impending' and 'balding'. Some **-ing** adjectives are used informally for emphasis, as in 'a blithering idiot', 'a stinking cold' and 'a flaming cheek'.

Gerunds act as nouns and are sometimes known as 'verbal nouns'. Examples include 'Smoking is bad for one's health', 'Cycling is forbidden in the park' and 'Swimming is his favourite sport'.

intensifier refers to an adverb that affects the degree of intensity of another word. Intensifiers include 'thoroughly' in 'We were thoroughly shocked by the news', 'scarcely' in 'We scarcely recognized them' and 'totally' in 'She was totally amazed'.

inter- is a prefix of Latin origin indicating 'between', as in 'intercity', 'intercontinental' and 'interstate'.

interjections are kinds of 'exclamations'. Sometimes they are formed by actual words and sometimes they simply consist of sounds indicating emotional noises. Examples of **interjections** include 'Oh! I am quite shocked', 'Gosh! I'm surprised to hear that!', 'Phew! It's hot!', 'Ouch! That was my foot!', 'Tut-tut! He shouldn't have done that!' and 'Alas! She is dead.'

International Phonetic Alphabet is a system of written symbols designed to enable the speech sounds of any language to be consistently represented. Some of the symbols are the ordinary letters of the Roman alphabet but some have been specially invented. The alphabet was first published in 1889 and is commonly known as **IPA**.

interrogative adjective or **determiner** is an adjective or determiner that asks for information in relation to the nouns which they qualify, as in 'What dress did you choose in the end?', 'What kind of book are you looking for?', 'Which house do you like best?', 'Which pupil won the prize?', 'Whose bike was stolen?' and 'Whose dog is that?'

interrogative adverb is an adverb that asks a question, as in 'When did they leave?', 'When does the meeting start?', 'Where do they live?', 'Where was the stolen car found?', 'Where did you last see her?', 'Why was she crying?', 'Why have they been asked to leave?', 'How is the invalid?', 'How do you know that she has gone?' and 'Wherever did you find that?'

interrogative pronoun is a pronoun that asks a question, as in 'Who asked you to do that?', 'Who broke the vase?', 'What did he say?, 'What happened next?', 'Whose are those books?', 'Whose is that old car?', 'To whom was that remark addressed?' and 'To whom did you address the package?'

interrogative sentence refers to a sentence that asks a question, as in 'Who is that?', 'Where is he?', 'Why have they appeared?', 'What did they take away?, 'Which do you prefer?' and 'Whose baby is that?'. Sentences which take the form of an **interrogative question** do not always seek information. Sometimes they are exclamations, as in 'Did you ever see anything so beautiful?', 'Isn't she sweet?' and 'Aren't they lovely?'. Sentences which take the form of questions may really be commands or directives, as in 'Could you turn down that radio?', 'Would you make less noise?' and 'Could you get her a chair?'. Sentences which take the form of questions may function as statements, as in 'Isn't there always a reason?' and 'Haven't we all experienced disappointment?'. Some **interrogative sentences** are what are known as 'rhetorical questions', which are asked purely for effect and require no answer, as in 'Do you think I am a fool?', 'What is the point of life?' and 'What is the world coming to?'.

intra- is a prefix of Latin origin indicating 'within', as in 'intramuscular', 'intra-uterine' and 'intravenous'.

intransitive verb refers to a verb that does not take a 'direct object', as in 'Snow fell yesterday', 'The children played in the sand', 'The path climbed steeply', 'Time will tell', 'The situation worsened', 'Things improved' and 'Prices increased'. Many verbs can be either transitive or intransitive, according to the context. Thus 'play' is **intransitive** in the sentence 'The children played in the sand' but 'transitive' in the sentence 'The boy plays the piano'. Similarly 'climb' is intransitive in the sentence 'The path climbs steeply' but transitive in the sentence 'The mountaineers climbed Everest'. Similarly 'tell' is **intransitive** in the sentence 'Time will tell' but 'transitive' in the sentence 'He will tell his life story'.

introductory it refers to the use of 'it' as the subject of a sentence in the absence of a meaningful subject. It is used particularly in sentences about time and the weather, as in 'It is midnight', 'It is dawn', 'It is five o'clock', 'It is twelve noon', 'It is raining', 'It was snowing', 'It was windy' and 'It was blowing a gale'.

intrusive r refers to the pronunciation of the *r* sound between two words or syllables where the first of these ends in a vowel sound and the second begins with a vowel sound and where there is no 'r' in the spelling. It appears in such phrases as 'law and order', which is frequently pronounced as 'lawr and order'.

invariable refers to a word whose form does not vary by inflection. Such words include 'sheep' and 'but'.

inversion refers to the reversal of the usual word order. It particularly refers to subjects and verbs. **Inversion** is used in questions, in some negative sentences, and for literary effect. In questions, an auxiliary verb is usually put in front of the subject and the rest of the verb group is put after the subject, as in 'Are you going to see her?' and 'Have they inspected the goods yet?'. The verb 'to do' is frequently used in **inversion**, as in 'Did he commit the crime?' and 'Do they still believe that?'. Examples of the use of **inversion** in negative sentences include 'Seldom have I witnessed such an act of selfishness', 'Never had she experienced such pain' and 'Rarely do we have time to admire the beauty of the countryside'. This use in negative sentences is rather formal.

Inversion frequently involves adverbial phrases of place, as in 'Beyond the town stretched field after field', 'Above them soared the eagle' and 'Along the driveway grew multitudes of daffodils'.

Inversion is also found in conditional clauses that are not introduced by conjunction, as in 'Had you arrived earlier you would have got a meal' and 'Had we some more money we could do more for the refugees'.

inverted commas, also called **quotation marks** and **quotes**, are used to enclose material that is part of reported speech. *See* REPORTED SPEECH. They can also be used instead of italic type in the titles of books, newspapers, magazines, plays, films, musical works, works of art, etc, as in 'The Times', 'Northanger Abbey' by Jane Austen, 'Two Gentlemen of Verona', 'The Silence of the Lambs' and 'The Mikado'. **Inverted commas** can also be used to emphasize or draw attention to a particular word or phrase, as in 'She wants to know how to spell "picnicked"'. **Inverted** commas can either be single or double. If a word, phrase or passage is already contained within quotes one should use the opposite style of **inverted commas** to the set already in use, as in 'She asked how to pronounce "controversy"' or "She asked how to pronounce 'controversy'".

irony indicates the use of a word or words to convey something that is completely different from the literal meaning, as in 'I don't suppose you'd be interested to hear that your house has been burgled', 'So you've crashed the car. Thanks! That's a great help!'. *See* DRAMATIC IRONY.

irregular plurals refer to the plural form of nouns that do not form their plural in the regular way. Most nouns in English add -*s* to the singular form to form the plural form, as in 'boy' to 'boys'. Some add -*es* to the singular form to form the plural, as in 'church' to 'churches'. Nouns ending in a consonant followed by -*y* have -*ies* as a regular plural ending. Thus 'fairy' becomes 'fairies' and 'berry' becomes 'berries'. The foregoing are all examples of 'regular plurals'.

Irregular plurals include words that are different in form from the singular forms and do not simply add an ending. These include 'men' from 'man', 'women' from 'woman' and 'mice' from 'mouse'. Some irregular plurals are formed by changing the vowel of the singular forms, as in 'feet' from 'foot', 'geese' from 'goose' and 'teeth' from 'tooth'. Some irregular plural forms are formed by adding -*en*, as 'oxen' from 'ox' and 'children' from 'child'. Some nouns ending in -*f* form plurals in -*ves*, as in 'loaf' to 'loaves', 'half' to 'halves', 'wife' to 'wives' and 'wolf' to 'wolves', but some have alternative endings, as 'hoof' to either 'hoofs' or 'hooves', and some form regular plurals unchanged, as 'roof' to 'roofs'. Some irregular plural forms are the original foreign plural forms of words adopted into English, for example 'stimuli' from 'stimulus', 'phenomena' from 'phenomenon', 'criteria' from 'criterion', 'larvae' from 'larva'. In modern usage there is a growing tendency to anglicize the plural forms of foreign words. Many of these co-exist with the plural form, for example 'thesauruses' and 'thesauri', 'formulas' and 'formulae', 'gateaus' and 'gateaux' and 'indexes' and 'indices'. Sometimes the anglicized plural formed according to the regular English rules differs slightly in meaning from the irregular foreign plural. Thus 'indexes' usually applies to guides in books and 'indices' is usually used in mathematics. Some nouns have irregular plurals in that the plural form the singular form are the same. These include 'sheep', 'grouse' (the game-bird) and 'salmon'. Some nouns have a regular plural and an irregular plural form .Thus 'brother' has the plural forms 'brothers' and 'brethren' although 'brethren' is now mainly used in a religious context and is archaic in general English.

irregular adjectives refer to adjectives that do not conform to the usual rules of forming the comparison and superlative. Many adjectives either add -*er* for the comparative and add -*est* for the superlative, as in 'taller', 'shorter' and 'tallest', 'shortest'. Some adjectives form their comparatives with 'more' and their superlatives with 'most', as in 'more beautiful', 'more practical' and 'most beautiful', 'most practical'. **Irregular adjectives** do not form their comparatives and superlatives in either of these ways. Irregular adjectives include:

positive	comparative	superlative
good	better	best
bad	worse	worst
little	less	least
many	more	most

irregular verbs are verbs that do not conform to the usual pattern of verbs in that some of their forms deviate from what one would expect if the pattern of regular verbs was being followed. There are four main forms of a regular verb—the INFINITIVE or 'base' form, as in 'hint', 'halt', 'hate' and 'haul'; the 'third-person singular' form as 'hints', 'halts', 'hates' and 'hauls'; the -ING form or 'present participle', as 'hinting', halting', 'hating' and 'hauling'; the -*ed* form or 'past tense' or 'past participle', as 'hinted', halted', 'hated' and 'hauled'.

Irregular verbs deviate in some way from that pattern, in particular from the pattern of adding -*ed* to the past tense and past participle. They fall into several categories.

One category concerns those which have the same form in the past tense and past participle forms as the infinitive and do not end in *-ed*, like regular verbs. These include:

infinitive	past tense	past participle
bet	bet	bet
burst	burst	burst
cast	cast	cast
cost	cost	cost
cut	cut	cut
hit	hit	hit
hurt	hurt	hurt
let	let	let
put	put	put
run	run	run
set	set	set
shed	shed	shed
shut	shut	shut
slit	slit	slit
split	split	split
spread	spread	spread

Some **irregular verbs** have two past tenses and two past participles which are the same, as in:

infinitive	past tense	past participle
burn	burned, burnt	burned, burnt,
dream	dreamed, dreamt	dreamed, dreamt,
dwell	dwelled, dwelt	dwelled, dwelt,
hang	hanged, hung,	hanged, hung
kneel	kneeled, knelt,	kneeled, knelt
lean	leaned, leant	learned, learnt
leap	leaped, leapt,	leaped, leapt
learn	learned, learnt	learned, learnt
light	lighted, lit	lighted, lit
smell	smelled, smelt	smelled, smelt
speed	speeded, sped	speeded, sped
spill	spilled, spilt	spilled, spilt
spoil	spoiled, spoilt	spoiled, spoilt
weave	weaved, woven	weaved, woven
wet	wetted, wet	wetted, wet,

Some **irregular verbs** have past tenses which do not end in *-ed* and have the same form as the past participle. These include:

infinitive	past tense	past participle
become	became	became
bend	bent	bent
bleed	bled	bled
breed	bred	bred
build	built	built
cling	clung	clung
come	came	came
dig	dug	dug
feel	felt	felt
fight	fought	fought
find	found	found
flee	fled	fled
fling	flung	flung
get	got	got
grind	ground	ground
hear	heard	heard
hold	held	held
keep	kept	kept
lay	laid	laid
lead	led	led
leave	left	left
lend	lent	lent
lose	lost	lost
make	made	made
mean	meant	meant
meet	met	met
pay	paid	paid
rend	rent	rent
say	said	said
seek	sought	sought
sell	sold	sold
send	sent	sent
shine	shone	shone
shoe	shod	shod
sit	sat	sat
sleep	slept	slept
slide	slid	slid
sling	slung	slung
slink	slunk	slunk
spend	spent	spent
spin	spun	spun
stand	stood	stood
stick	stuck	stuck
sting	stung	stung
strike	struck	struck
string	strung	strung
sweep	swept	swept
swing	swung	swung
teach	taught	taught
tell	told	told
think	thought	thought
understand	understood	understood
weep	wept	wept
win	won	won
wring	wrung	wrung

Some **irregular verbs** have regular past tense forms but two possible past participles, one of which is regular. These include:

infinitive	past tense	past participle
mow	mowed	mowed, mown
prove	proved	proved, proven
sew	sewed	sewn, sewed
show	showed	showed, shown
sow	sowed	sowed, sown
swell	swelled	swelled, swollen

Some **irregular verbs** have past tenses and past participles that are different from each other and different from the infinitive. These include:

infinitive	past tense	past participle
arise	arose	arisen
awake	awoke	awoken
bear	bore	borne
begin	began	begun
bid	bade	bidden
bite	bit	bitten
blow	blew	blown
break	broke	broken
choose	chose	chosen
do	did	done
draw	drew	drawn
drink	drank	drunk
drive	drove	driven
eat	ate	eaten
fall	fell	fallen
fly	flew	flown

forbear	forbore	forborne
forbid	forbade	forbidden
forgive	forgave	forgiven
forget	forgot	forgotten
forsake	forsook	forsaken
freeze	froze	frozen
forswear	forswore	forewarn
give	gave	given
go	went	gone
grow	grew	grown
hew	hewed	hewn
hide	hid	hidden
know	knew	known
lie	lay	lain
ride	rode	ridden
ring	rang	rung
saw	sawed	sawn
see	saw	seen
rise	rose	risen
shake	shook	shaken
shrink	shrank	shrunk
slay	slew	slain
speak	spoke	spoken
spring	sprang	sprung
steal	stole	stolen
stink	stank	stunk
strew	strewed	strewn
stride	strode	stridden
strive	strove	striven
swear	swore	sworn
swim	swam	swum
take	took	taken
tear	tore	torn
throw	threw	thrown
tread	trod	trodden
wake	woken	woke
wear	wore	worn
write	written	wrote

-ise and **-ize** are both verb endings. In British English there are many verbs which can be spelt ending in either **-ise** or **-ize**, as 'computerise/ize', 'economise/ize', 'finalist/ize', 'hospitalise/ize', 'modernise/ize', 'organise/ize', 'realise/ize', 'theorise/ize'. There are a few verbs which cannot be spelt **-ize**. These include 'advertise', 'advise', 'comprise', 'despise', 'exercise', 'revise', 'supervise' and 'televise'.

-ish is a suffix indicating 'somewhat', as in 'baldish', 'biggish', 'smallish', 'youngish', and 'nationality', as 'Spanish', 'Turkish' and 'Polish'.

-ism is a suffix indicating 'state, condition', as in 'alcoholism', 'fatalism', 'heroism' and 'plagiarism', or indicating 'doctrine, movement, system, theory', as in 'Catholicism', 'Marxism' and 'Thatcherism'. It now also indicates 'discrimination', as in 'ageism', 'sexism', 'racism'.

iso- is a prefix indicating 'equal', as in 'isobar', 'isotherm' and 'isosceles'.

-ist is a suffix indicating 'believer, supporter, practitioner', as in 'atheist', 'fascist', 'feminist' and 'Methodist'.

italic type refers to a sloping typeface that is used for a variety of purposes. It is used to differentiate a piece of text from the main text, which is usually in Roman type. For example, it is used sometimes for the titles of books, newspapers, magazines, plays, films, musical works and works of art, as in 'he is a regular reader of *The Times*', 'She reads *Private Eye*', 'Have you read *Animal Farm* by George Orwell', 'He has never seen a production of Shakespeare's *Othello*', 'We went to hear Handel's *Messiah*', '*Mona Lisa* is a famous painting'. Sometimes such titles are put in quotation marks rather than in italic.

Italic type is also sometimes used for the names of ships, trains, etc, as in 'the launch of *The Queen Elizabeth II*', 'She once sailed in *The Queen Mary*' and 'Their train was called *The Flying Scotsman*'.

Italic type is also used for the Latin names of plants and animals, as in 'of the genus *Lilium*', 'trees of the genus *Pyrus*, *Panthera pardus* and *Canis lupus*.

Italic type is sometimes used for foreign words that have been adopted into the English language but have never been fully integrated . Examples include *bête noire, raison d'être, inter alia* and *Weltschmerz.*

Italic type can also sometimes be used to draw attention to a particular word, phrase or passage, as in 'How do you pronounce *formidable*?', or to emphasize a word or phrase, as in 'Is he *still* in the same job?'

-ite is a suffix which can indicate 'believer, supporter, practitioner', as in 'Thatcherite' and 'Trotskyite'.

-itis is a suffix indicating 'illness or disease', as in 'bronchitis', 'hepatitis' and 'meningitis'.

its and **it's** are liable to be confused. **Its** is an adjective meaning 'belonging to it', as in 'The house has lost its charm' and 'The dog does not like its kennel'. **It's** means 'it is', as in 'Do you know if it's raining?' and 'It's not fair to expect her to do all the chores'.

-ize *see* **-ise**.

J

jargon refers to the technical or specialist language used among members of a particular profession or area. It is often used as a derogatory term to describe unnecessarily obscure or pretentious language used within a profession and incomprehensible to members of the public who might come into contact with it and require to know what is being talked about. **Jargon** should be avoided in any document or situation involving lay people who have no specialist knowledge of the subject being referred to or of the language associated with it. **Jargon** in some professions easily becomes **goddledegook**.

journalese is a derogatory name for the style of writing and choice of vocabulary supposedly found in newspapers. It is usually the style of writing in tabloid newspapers, such as widespread use of clichés, sensational language and short sentences, that is meant by the term. *See* HEADLINE.

jussive refers to a type of clause or sentence that expresses a command, as in 'Do be quiet! I'm trying to study', 'Let's not bother going to the party. I'm too tired', 'Would you pass me that book' and 'Look at that everybody! The river has broken its banks'.

just is an adverb which indicates that something happened a short time previously. In British English it is usually used with the perfect tense of the verb which it accompanies, as in 'I have just finished work', 'We have just decided to buy a new car', 'You've just missed the bus' and 'She's just passed her driving test'.

In American English **just** usually accompanies the past tense of the verb, and some speakers of British English do also, especially in an informal context, as in 'I just saw a bad accident on the motorway', 'We just noticed that it's snowing' and 'He just left'.

Just has more than meaning. It can also mean 'only' and 'exactly'. In the sense of 'only', care should be taken to position it in the correct place in the sentence. For example, in the sentence 'He drank just two glasses of wine', it means that he drank only two glasses of wine, but in the sentence 'He just drank two glasses of wine' it means that he very recently drank two glasses of wine. To add to the confusion, although people may be careful about the positioning of **just** in formal writing they tend not to be in informal writing or speech. Thus someone could say in reply to the questions 'How much has he had to drink? Is he fit to drive?', 'He just had two glasses of wine', meaning that that was all he had drunk. In speech the meaning is usually obvious from intonation and context.

Just can also be used in the sense of 'only' in such sentences as 'Just Peter went on holiday with his parents. The other children stayed at home' and 'Just one coat was left on the stall. The rest were sold early on'. Again care should be taken to place *just* before the word it refers to in order to avoid ambiguity.

Just can also mean 'exactly', as in 'I see you have a food processor. That's just what I need' and 'Where did you find that cape? That's just what I've been looking for'.

K

kibbutzim is an example of an irregular plural form. Most nouns in English form plurals by adding -*s* or -*es* to the singular form, as in 'book and books' and 'church and churches'. However several words of foreign origin which have been adopted into English but not fully integrated retain the plural form found in the foreign language. **Kibbutz**, meaning a communal settlement in Israel, is one such word. Of Hebrew origin, it retains the plural form **kibbutzim**. In some cases there is a growing tendency for foreign plurals to be anglicized, or to exist alongside an anglicized plural, as in 'thesauruses/thesauri', but this is not yet the case with **kibbutzim**.

kilo- is a prefix indicating 'a thousand', as in 'kilogram', 'kilohertz', 'kilolitre', 'kilometre' and 'kilowatt'.

-kin is a suffix which indicates 'a diminutive or smaller version', as in 'lambkin' and 'mannikin'.

kind as a noun can cause grammatical problems. It is used to refer to a class of people or things. Since it is a 'count' noun, it should take the plural form 'kinds' after words such as 'all' and 'many', as in 'He met all kinds of people when he was travelling round the world', 'We found all kinds of treasure when we were clearing out the attic' and 'We found all kinds of wild flower in the meadows'. A singular noun should follow 'kinds of', as in 'We found all kinds of treasure' but it is quite common for people to use a plural noun instead, as in 'We found all kinds of treasures'. This is best restricted to informal or spoken use.

'These' and 'those' are frequently found preceding **kind of**, as in 'She doesn't like these kind of cakes' and 'My mother used to make those kind of biscuits' but this is incorrect and 'this' and 'that' should be used, as in 'I don't like that kind of joke' and 'My mother prefers this kind of holiday'.

The use of 'kind of' to mean 'somewhat' or 'rather', as in 'I'm kind of hungry', 'She's kind of rude to him' and It's kind of cold in there' should be restricted to informal speech or dialect. This phrase is sometimes written 'kinda', as in 'We're kinda bored'.

Kind is also used as an adjective meaning 'caring' or 'generous', as in 'A kind old lady lent the children money to get a bus home', 'It was kind of you to let them borrow your car' and 'Children should be taught to be kind to animals'.

-kind is a suffix indicating 'a group of people', as in 'humankind', 'mankind', 'womankind'.

kindly looks like an adverb but it can be either an adverb or an adjective. As an adverb it means 'in a kind or caring manner' or 'generously', as in 'They treated us kindly during our stay', 'Her parents kindly treated us to a meal in a restaurant' and 'They very kindly offered us a lift'. The adverb **kindly** is also used in rather an ironic way when the user is annoyed, as in 'Would you kindly stop allowing your dog to foul the pavement'. It is also used in the phrase 'not to take kindly to', meaning 'to be unwilling to accept', as in 'The new pupil doesn't take kindly to discipline', 'He won't take kindly to being kept waiting' and 'The candidate was so confident that he is unlikely to take kindly to being rejected'.

Kindly is more common as an adjective and means 'kind, warm, friendly', as in 'a kindly old lady who was always helping her neighbours' and 'She gave the children a kindly smile'.

kneel is one of several verbs in English which have more than one past participle and past tense form. The past participle and past tense can both be either 'kneeled' or 'knelt', as in 'The child knelt in prayer', 'She kneeled before the altar' and 'She had knelt at her dying husband's bedside every night' and 'They had kneeled in supplication before the emperor but he spurned them'. Although both 'knelt' and 'kneeled' are acceptable forms in British English, 'knelt' is the more common form.

L

laid and lain are liable to be confused. Laid is the past tense and past participle of the verb 'lay', meaning 'to place or put', as in 'She laid the antique vase carefully on the table', 'He laid the new carpet tiles in the hall', 'They have laid the baby on a mat on the floor' and 'We have laid vinyl tiles on the kitchen floor'. Lain is the past participle of the verb 'lie', 'to rest in a horizontal position', as in 'Those letters have lain on his desk all week', 'The dead man had lain in the empty house for several days', and 'They had lain on the beach in the midday sun'.

language refers to the means by which human beings communicate using words, as in 'Children acquire language at different rates. Some speak much earlier than others'. Language can refer either to spoken or written communication. It can also refer to the variety of communication used by a particular nation or state, as in 'He visits France regularly but makes no attempt to understand the French language', 'He won't start to learn a foreign language until he goes to secondary school' and 'People in other parts of Europe tend to speak more languages than the British'. The language that a person speaks from birth is known as his/her 'first language' or 'mother tongue'. He/she is said to be a native speaker of this language.

Language can also be used to refer to the style and vocabulary of a piece of writing, as in 'The language of his novels is very poetic'.

Language can also apply to the particular style and variety of language that is used in a particular profession or among a particular group of people with some common interest, as in 'legal language', 'scientific language', 'technical language', etc. Such technical or specialist language is sometimes referred to rather pejoratively as 'jargon' or as 'legalese', 'medicalese', 'computerese', etc.

A person's own style of language with regard to vocabulary, structure, etc, is known as 'ideolect', as in 'He is the son of academic parents and has rather a formal ideolect'.

The language of a region or community with regard to vocabulary, structure, grammar and pronunciation is known as 'dialect', as in 'the dialect of the North-East of England'.

last can be an adverb or an adjective. As an adjective it can give rise to ambiguity. It can mean 'coming after all others, final', as in 'He was the last runner to hit the finishing tape', 'That was the last novel he wrote before he died', 'He did not die until he was 90 but he wrote his last novel at the age of 40'. Ambiguity arises when last takes on other meanings. For example, it is frequently used as a synonym for 'latest', as in 'I really enjoyed his last novel and I'm looking forward to the next'. In this particular sentence it is clear that last means 'latest' not 'final' but this is not always the case.

For example, in the sentence 'He was 60 when he directed his last film', it is not at all clear from the evidence of the sentence alone whether it is his 'final' or 'latest' film that is being referred to. Thus it is better to use either 'final' or 'latest' rather than 'last' in order to clarify the meaning.

Confusion can arise also between last meaning 'final' and last meaning 'preceding', as in 'I did not quite understand the last chapter'. On the evidence of the sentence alone, it is not clear whether last refers to the preceding chapter or to the final chapter. Again it is best to avoid ambiguity by using a synonym for last.

Yet more confusion can be caused with regard to last when it is used to refer to days of the week. It varies from person to person whether 'last Saturday' refers to the Saturday that has just gone or to the one before that. To some extent it depends which day of the week it is when the statement is made. To avoid ambiguity it is best to specify the date.

Last is also used as an adverb, as in 'They last saw their father when he was going to war', 'When the family go to the dentist my brother always wants to go in last' and 'If you are adding cream to the soup you add it last'. The adverbial use does not suffer from problems of ambiguity.

latest is an adjective that is liable to be confused with last–see LAST. It can also mean 'most up-to-date', 'most fashionable', as in 'the very latest dresses from the Paris designers'. Latest is also found in this meaning in the phrase 'the very latest', as in 'she always dresses in the very latest'. It can also mean 'most late', the superlative of 'late' in the sense of 'far on in the day or night', as in 'The latest train which you can get from that station leaves at ten o' clock'. In this sense latest is also found in the phrase 'at the latest' and in the phrase 'at the very latest', meaning 'most late time', as in 'You must arrive at the station at ten o'clock at the latest' and 'The students' essays must be handed in by Friday at the very latest'.

lay and lie are liable to be confused. This is because lay as well as being a verb in its own right is also one of the principal parts of lie–the past tense as in 'They lay on the beach in the sun', 'The books lay on the table gathering dust' and 'She lay on her bed and wept'.

Lay is a transitive verb meaning 'to place or put', as in 'She asked him to lay new tiles in the kitchen' and 'She had to lay down her shopping to open the door'. The principal parts of lay are 'lays' (third person singular present), as in 'She always lays the baby on the grass to play'; 'laying' (present participle), as in 'Laying her shopping down she put her key in the lock'; 'laid' (past participle and past tense), as in 'She laid the package on the table' and 'He had laid his car keys on the table and forgotten about them'.

Lie is an intransitive verb whose principal parts are

'lies' (third person singular present), as in 'Their house lies to the north of the village'; 'lying' (present participle), as in 'Lying on the grass they looked up at the sky'; 'lay' (past tense), as in 'The climbers lay on the summit exhausted'; 'lain' (past participle), as in 'Those books have lain there for weeks'.

Lie has another totally unrelated meaning. It means 'to say or write something that is untrue', as in 'You didn't have to lie about your part in the affair'. The principal parts of the verb **lie** are 'lies' (third person singular present), as in 'lies about why he arrives home late from work'; 'lying' (present participle), as in 'Lying, he looked her straight in the face'; 'lied' (past participle and past tense), as in 'He lied to his employers about his qualifications' and 'she suddenly realized that he had lied all the time'.

lean is one of several verbs in English which have two forms of the past tense and the past participle, 'leaned' and 'leant', as in 'She leaned over the fence to talk to her neighbour', 'He leaned over his desk to catch the attention of his colleagues', 'They have leaned over backwards to help her' and 'She has leant down to pick something up and hurt her back'. The two forms are interchangeable.

leap is one of several verbs in English which have two forms of the past tense and past participle, 'leaped' and 'leapt', as in 'The children leaped around the park in high spirits', 'She leapt up in surprise when she heard the news', 'She had leaped over a high fence and broken her leg' and 'The child has leapt over the steam and run off'. The two forms are virtually interchangeable but 'leapt' is more common in British English.

learn is one of several verbs in English which have two forms of the past tense and past participle, 'learned' and 'learnt', as in 'They learned French at school', 'She learnt to ski in Austria', 'I think the boys have learned their lesson' and 'He had learnt to be grateful for what he was given'. The forms are interchangeable. 'Learned' as a past tense or past participle should not be confused with 'learned', the adjective meaning 'erudite, well-read, intellectual', as in 'Students filled the lecture hall to listen to the learned professor' and 'The company publishes learned journals'. This adjective is pronounced with two syllables—*ler-nid*—whereas 'learned', the past tense and past participle, is pronounced as one syllable—*lernd*.

length mark is a mark used in phonetics in relation to a vowel to indicate that it is long. This can take the form of a 'macron', a small horizontal stroke placed above a letter, or a symbol resembling a colon placed after a vowel in the IPA pronunciation system.

-less is a suffix meaning 'without, lacking' added to nouns to form adjectives, as in 'characterless', 'clueless', 'expressionless', 'fearless', 'flawless', 'harmless', 'homeless', 'hopeless', 'passionless', 'toothless' and 'useless'. It can also mean 'without being able to be measured', as in 'ageless', 'countless', 'priceless' and 'timeless'.

less and **fewer** are liable to be confused. *See* FEWER.

-let is a suffix indicating a diminutive or smaller form of something, as in 'booklet', 'coverlet', 'droplet', 'islet', 'piglet', 'starlet' and 'streamlet'.

letter-writing has become something of a dying art in view of the widespread use of the telephone. However, all of us from time to time have to write some form of letter and many of these are business letters. There are a few conventions in formal letters that should be observed.

One's own address, including one's postcode, should be placed at the right-hand side of the page. Each line of one's own address should be indented slightly below the one above and the date put below the last line of the address, as in:

> 23 Park Drive
> Raleigh
> Blackshire
> RA14 2TY
>
> 5 June 1993

Whether one puts a comma at the end of the various lines of the address is a matter of taste. It is becoming common in modern usage not to do so.

One's telephone number can either be placed between the postcode and the date or at the other side of the page on the same line as the first line of the address.

If one is writing a business letter one should also put the address of the person to whom one is writing. It should be placed at the other side of the page below one's own address and the lines of this should be placed directly below each other without being indented, as in:

> 23, Park Drive
> Raleigh
> Blackshire
> RA 14 2TY.
>
> 5 June 1993.

The Manager Eastlands Bank
33 West Street
Northlands
Blackshire
NR15 3RJ.

With regard to deciding how to address the person to whom one is writing it is best to find out his/her name. Having done so then one can start the letter off, as in :

Dear Mr White,

If one is writing to a woman the situation is slightly more problematic. Formerly it was considered acceptable to address the person written to as 'Miss' if one knew her to be unmarried or as 'Mrs' if one knew her to be married. If one did not know her marital status one could either use 'Miss' or use the 'Madam' convention. In modern usage 'Ms' is the acceptable term if one does not know the marital status of the woman to whom one is writing. Many people prefer to use this designation even if they do know the person's marital status and many women prefer to be addressed in this way. On the other hand, some women, especially older women, do not like the 'Ms' designation.

In modern usage some people prefer to put the first name and surname of the relevant person instead of the surname preceded by Mr, etc, as in:

Dear John White,

The above style of address is considered rather informal by some people.

If it is not easy to ascertain the name of the person to whom one wishes to write then it is perfectly acceptable to address him/her in terms of their position or job, as in:

Dear manager,

Dear Personnel Manager,

Dear Area Manager,

In formal letters it is also acceptable to use 'Sir' or 'Madam', as in:

Dear Sir,

Dear Madam,

Dear Sir/Madam,

Obviously the above style of address is used in cases where one does not know the sex of the person to whom one is writing.

In ending a formal letter it was traditionally the custom to write 'Yours faithfully' before one's signature, if one had addressed the person written to as 'Dear sir' or 'Dear madam', as in :

Yours faithfully,
Jane Black.

It was also the custom to end the letter with 'Yours sincerely' if the letter was either informal in nature or a formal letter which began with 'Dear Mr White' etc, as in:

Yours sincerely,
Mary Brown.

In modern usage it is now considered acceptable to end a letter with 'Yours sincerely' even if one has begun it with 'Dear sir', etc. 'Yours faithfully' is considered exceptionally formal.

It is common to end even business letters with 'Kind regards', especially if the person written to is known to one.

On the envelope the lines can be indented or not, according to taste. Each line, except the last one, can have a comma after or not. However, in modern usage there is an increasing tendency to punctuate as little as possible and the commas are frequently omitted, as in:

Ms Mary Brown
29 Lower Forth Street
Redwood
Blackshire
RD16 5YP.

The same comments on Mrs, Miss and Ms apply to envelopes as apply to the opening greeting in letters. *See above.* Anything that can be done to make the address as clear as possible should be done. It is important always to put the postcode as failure to do so slows down delivery of the letter. It is also advisable to highlight the town one is sending the letter to, either by putting it in capital letters, or by underlining it, as in:

Mr James Green
45, Park Avenue
BOSTON
Blackshire
BT16 6GH.

In modern usage it is becoming increasingly common to write the full name of the person written to on the envelope, as in:

James Black

36, High Street
BLANKTON
Blankshire
BL13 9T2.

It is considered formal or old-fashioned to use 'Esq.', usually spelt with a full stop at the end and preceded by a comma. If used, 'Esq.' should be placed after the mans's name and there should be no accompmanying 'Mr', as in:
John Brown, Esq
43 Queen Street
Whiteoaks
Blankshire
WH12 TY.

lexicography refers to the art and practice of defining words, selecting them and arranging them in dictionaries and glossaries.

licence and **license** are liable to be confused. **Licence** is a noun referring to 'a document indicating that official permission or authorization has been given to do something', as in 'He does not have a current driving licence', 'You need a trading licence to sell goods there' and 'The pub owner lost his licence'. **Licence** also means 'too great freedom, disregard for rules of behaviour, social acceptability, morals, etc', as in 'The organizers of the concert objected to the licence shown by the young people in their dress'. In this sense the word **licence** is usually used in formal situations.

License is a verb meaning 'to give a licence to, to give official permission or authorization to', as in 'He is licensed to sell alcohol', 'She is not licensed to sell goods in the market' and 'The restaurant is not licensed but you can bring your own wine'. **Licence** is often misspelt as **license**.

The above comments refer to British English. In American English **license** is used for both the noun and the verb.

lie *see* **lay.**

ligature refers to a printed character combining two letters in one, as in æ and œ. It is sometimes called a 'digraph'.

-like is a suffix indicating similarity, as in 'childlike', 'cowlike', 'dreamlike', 'ladylike', 'lifelike' and 'warlike'.

-ling is a suffix indicating a diminutive or smaller version of something, as in 'duckling', 'gosling' and 'nestling'.

-logue is a suffix derived from Greek meaning 'indicating 'conversation, discussion', as in 'dialogue', 'epilogue', 'monologue', 'prologue' and 'travelogue'.

limerick refers to a humorous five-lined piece of light verse, with the first two lines rhyming with each other, the third and fourth lines rhyming with each other, and the fifth line rhyming with the first line. Usually there are three stressed beats in the first, second and fifth lines and two stressed beats on the third and fourth lines. Traditionally the name of a place is mentioned in the first line and may be repeated in the last line. Edward Lear made the form popular in the nineteenth century. Limerick is a town in Ireland but the name of the verse is probably derived from a Victorian custom of singing nonsense songs at parties where 'Will you come up to Limerick' was a common refrain. An example is:

There once was a man from Nantucket
Who kept all his cash in a bucket;
    But his daughter named Nan
    Ran away with a man,
And as for the bucket, Nantucket.

lingua franca refers to 'a language adopted as a common language by speakers whose mother tongues or native languages are different'. This enables people to have a common medium of communication for various purposes, such as trading. Examples include Swahili in East Africa, Hausa in West Africa and Tok Pisin in Papua New Guinea. The term historically referred to 'a language that was a mixture of Italian, French, Greek, Spanish and Arabic, used for trading and military purposes.'

linguistics refers to the systematic, scientific study of language. It describes language and seeks to establish general principles rather than to prescribe rules of correctness.

line-break refers to the division of a word at the end of a line for space purposes. This is marked by a 'hyphen'. *See* HYPHEN.

linking adverbs and **linking adverbials** refer to words and phrases which indicate some kind of connection between one clause or sentence and another. Examples include 'however', as in 'The award had no effect on their financial situation. It did, however, have a marked effect on their morale'; 'moreover', as in 'He is an unruly pupil. Moreover, he is a bad influence on the other pupils'; 'then again', as in 'She does not have very good qualifications. Then again, most of the other candidates have even fewer'; 'in the meantime', as in 'We will not know the planning committee's decision until next week. In the meantime we can only hope'; 'instead', as in 'I thought he would have reigned. Instead he seems determined to stay'.

linking verb is a verb which 'links' a subject with its complement. Unlike other verbs, **linking verbs** do not denote an action but indicate a state. Examples of **linking verbs** include 'He is a fool', 'She appears calm', 'He appeared a sensible man', 'You seemed to become anxious', 'They became Buddhists', 'The child feels unwell', 'It is getting rather warm', 'It is growing colder', 'You look well', 'She remained loyal to her friend', 'She lived in America but remained a British citizen' and 'You seem thoughtful' and 'She seems a nice person'. **Linking verbs** are also called 'copula' or 'copular verbs'.

literary criticism refers to the formal study, discussion and evaluation of a literary work, as in 'The students who are studying literary criticism have been asked to write a critical analysis of *Ulysses* by James Joyce.'

litotes refers to a kind of understatement in which a statement is conveyed by contradicting or denying its opposite, as in 'It will be no easy task to look after their children for a week' (meaning that it will be a difficult task), 'She's not exactly communicative' (meaning she is silent or reserved).

loanword refers to a word that has been taken into another language from another. From the point of view of the language taking the word in, the word is known as a 'borrowing'—*see* BORROWING. Some **loanwords** become naturalized or fully integrated into the language and have a pronunciation and spelling reflecting the conventions of the language which has borrowed it. Other **loanwords** retain the spelling and pronunciation of the language from which they have been borrowed. These include 'Gastarbeiter', borrowed from German and meaning 'a foreign worker'.

localism refers to a word or expression whose use is restricted to a particular place or area. The area in question can be quite small, unlike 'dialect' words or 'regionalism'.

lower-case letter is the opposite of 'capital letter'. It is also known informally as 'small letter'. **Lower-case letters** are used for most words in the language. It is 'capital letters' which are exceptional in their use. *See* CAPITAL LETTER.

-ly is a common adverbial ending. *See* ADVERBS.

M

macro- is a prefix derived from the Greek meaning 'large in size or scope', as in 'macrobiotic', 'macrocosm', 'macroeconomics', 'macromolecular' and 'macrostructure'.

macron *see* **length mark**.

main clause refers to the principal clause in a sentence on which any 'subordinate clauses' depend for their sense. The main clause can stand alone and make some sense but the subordinate clauses cannot. In the sentence 'I left early because I wanted to catch the 6 o'clock train', 'I left early' is the principal clause and 'because I wanted to catch the 6 o'clock train' is the subordinate clause. In the sentence 'When we saw the strange man we were afraid', the main clause is 'we were afraid' and the subordinate clause is 'when we saw the strange man'. In the sentence 'Because it was late we decided to start out for home as soon as we could', the main clause is 'we decided to start out for home' and the subordinate clauses are 'because it was late' and 'as soon as we could'. A **main clause** can also be known as a 'principal clause' or an 'independent clause'.

mal- is a prefix derived from French meaning 'bad, unpleasant', as in 'malodorous', or 'imperfect, faulty', as in 'malabsorption', 'maladjusted', 'maladministration', 'malformation', 'malfunctioning', 'malnutrition', 'malpractice' and 'maltreatment'.

malapropism refers to the incorrect use of a word, often through confusion with a similar-sounding word. It often arises from someone's attempt to impress someone else with a knowledge of long words or of technical language. Examples include 'The doctor says the old man is not in possession of all his facilities'. Here 'facilities' has been wrongly used instead of 'faculties'. Another example is 'My friend lives in a computer belt'. Here 'computer' has been wrongly used instead of 'commuter'. Another example is 'Her husband's had a vivisection'. Here 'vivisection' has been used instead of 'vasectomy'. 'Ah! It's wonderful to be on terracotta again. I hate sailing'. Here 'terracotta' has been wrongly used instead of 'terra firma'. The effect of **malapropism** is often humorous. Sometimes people use it deliberately for a comic effect, as in 'He was under the affluence of incahol'.

　Malapropism is called after Mrs Malaprop, a character in a play called *The Rivals* (1775), a comedy by R. B. Sheridan. Her name is derived from the French *mal à propos*, 'not apposite, inappropriate'. Some of her **malapropisms** in the play include 'She's as headstrong as an allegory on the banks of the Nile'. She has used 'allegory' wrongly instead of 'alligator'. Another of Mrs Malaropism's **malapropisms** is 'Illiterate him quite from your mind'. Here she has used 'illiterate' wrongly instead of 'obliterate'.

major sentence can be used to refer to a sentence that contains at least one subject and a finite verb, as in 'We are going' and 'They won'. They frequently have more elements than this, as in 'They bought a car', 'We lost the match', 'They arrived yesterday' and 'We are going away next week'. They are sometimes described as 'regular' because they divide into certain structural patterns, a subject, finite verb, adverb or adverbial, etc. The opposite of a **major sentence** is called a 'minor sentence', 'irregular sentence' or 'fragmentary sentence'. These include interjections such as 'Ouch!' and 'How terrible'; formula expressions, such as 'Good morning' and 'Well done'; and short forms of longer expressions, as in 'Traffic diverted', 'Shop closed', 'No dogs' and 'Flooding ahead'. Such short forms could be rephrased to become 'major sentences', as in 'Traffic has been diverted because of roadworks', 'The shop is closed on Sundays', 'The owner does not allow dogs in her shop' and 'There was flooding ahead on the motorway'.

-man is used with nouns to form nouns indicating someone's job, as in 'barman', 'chairman', 'clergyman', 'coalman', 'fireman', 'policeman', 'postman', 'salesman'. In modern usage when attempts are being made to remove sexism from the language alternatives have been sought for any words ending in **-man**. Formerly, words ending in **-man** were often used whether or not the person referred to was definitely known to be a man. Different ways have been found to avoid the sexism of **-man**. 'Salesman' has been changed in many cases to 'salesperson', 'chairman' often becomes 'chairperson' or 'chair'. Similarly, 'fireman' has become 'firefighter' and 'policeman' frequently becomes 'police officer'. *See* -PERSON.

-mania is a suffix indicating abnormal or obsessional behaviour, as in 'kleptomania', 'nymphomania' and 'pyromania'.

manner, adverbs of *see* **adverb**.

manner, adverbial clause of *see* **adverbial clause**.

masculine in grammatical terms refers to one of the grammatical genders that nouns are divided into. Nouns in the **masculine** gender include words that obviously belong to the male sex, as in 'man', 'boy', 'king', 'prince' 'bridegroom', 'schoolboy' and 'salesman'. Many words now considered to be 'of dual gender' formerly were assumed to be masculine. These include such words as 'author', 'sculptor' and 'engineer'. *See* GENDER. Gender also applies to personal pronouns and the third personal singular pronoun masculine is 'he' (subject), 'him' (object) and 'his' (possessive). For further information *see* HE; SHE.

mass noun is the same as UNCOUNTABLE NOUN.

-mate is a suffix referring to 'someone who shares something with someone', as in 'bedmate', 'classmate', 'room-mate', 'schoolmate', 'shipmate', 'team-mate' and 'workmate'.

mega- is a prefix derived from Greek meaning 'very large', as in 'megabid', 'megabucks', 'megaproduction' and 'megastar'. Many words using **mega-** in this way are modern and many of them are also informal or slang. In technical language **mega-** means 'a million times bigger than the unit to which it is attached, as in 'megabyte', 'megacycle', 'megahertz' and 'megawatt'.

meiosis is a figure of speech using understatement to emphasize the size or importance of something, as in 'He's a decent enough bloke' and 'He's rather a decent tennis player'.

melted and **molten** are liable to be confused. **Melted** is the past tense and past participle of the verb 'to melt', as in 'The chocolate melted in the heat' and 'The ice cream had melted by the time they got home'. **Melted** is also used as an adjective, as in 'melted chocolate'. **Molten** is used only as an adjective but it is not synonymous with **melted**. It means 'melted or made liquid at high temperatures', as in 'molten lava' and 'molten metal'.

meta- is a prefix derived from Greek indicating 'alteration or transformation', as in 'metamorphosis', 'metaphor' and 'metaphysics'.

metaphor is a figure of speech which compares two things by saying that one thing is another, as in 'He was a lion in the fight' (meaning that he was as brave as a lion), 'She is a mouse whenever he is present' (meaning that she is very timid), 'He is a giant among men' (meaning that he is a great man), 'She was a shining light to us all' (meaning she was a source of inspiration) and 'Life was not a bed of roses' (meaning life was not easy and enjoyable). By extension, **metaphor** refers to a word or phrase used in a sentence where it does not have a literal meaning, as in 'a butter mountain', 'a wine lake', 'My colleague is a snake in the grass', 'She always sits on the fence at committee meetings', 'They walked home with leaden feet' and 'He was rooted to the spot when he saw the man with the gun'. *See* MIXED METAPHOR and SIMILE.

-meter is a suffix indicating 'a measuring instrument', as in 'altimeter', 'barometer', 'pedometer', 'calorimeter', 'speedometer', 'thermometer'.

metonym is a figure of speech in which a word or expression is used to indicate something with which it has a close relationship, as in 'The position of the Crown is more uncertain than it was formerly' (meaning that the position of the monarchy is not as stable as it once was), 'The City is nervously awaiting the announcement of this month's trade figures' (meaning that the people who work in London's financial sector are nervously awaiting the announcement of this month's trade figures) and 'The Kremlin began to adopt a more enlightened approach to foreign visitors' (meaning that the Russian government began to adopt a more enlightened approach to foreign visitors), 'The White house has yet to comment on the proposal' (meaning that the President of the United States has yet to reply to the proposal).

-metre is a suffix indicating 'meter, the unit of length', as in 'centimetre', 'kilometre' and 'millimetre'.

micro- is a prefix derived from Greek meaning 'very small', as in 'microbiology', 'microfiche', 'microfilm', 'microscope', 'microsurgery'.

milli- is a prefix derived from Latin meaning 'thousand', as in 'millisecond'.

mini- is a prefix derived from Latin meaning 'very small, least', as in 'minimum', 'minimal', and 'mini-

ature'. **Mini-** is frequently used to form modern words, as in 'minibus', 'minicab', 'mini-computer', 'mini-cruise', 'mini-golf', 'mini-market' and 'miniskirt'. Modern words beginning with **mini-** can be spelt either with a hyphen or without.

minor sentence *see* **major sentence**.

mis- is a prefix indicating 'badly, wrongly', as in 'misbehave', 'miscalculate', 'misdirect', 'mishandle', 'mishear', 'misjudge', 'mismanage', 'mispronounce', 'misspell', 'mistreat', 'mistrust', 'misunderstanding' and 'misuse'.

mixed metaphor occurs when unrelated metaphors are put in the same sentence. Examples include 'She sailed into the room with both guns blazing'. Here the use of the word 'sail' belongs to nautical metaphors but the 'guns blazing' belongs to cowboy or Wild West metaphors. Another example is 'The company's new flagship did not get off the ground'. Here 'flagship' is a nautical term and 'get off the ground' refers to aircraft'. Another example is 'They were caught red-handed with their trousers down'. Here 'caught red-handed' is a metaphorical reference to a murderer caught with blood on his/her hands but 'caught with one's trousers down' is either a reference to the embarrassing experience of being caught unawares in the toilet or else caught in an embarrassing sexual situation.

modifier refers to a word, or group of words, that 'modifies' or affects the meaning of another word in some way, usually by adding more information about it. **Modifiers** are frequently used with nouns. They can be adjectives, as in 'He works in the *main* building' and 'They need a *larger* house'. **Modifiers** of nouns can be nouns themselves, as in 'the *theatre* profession', 'the *publishing* industry' and '*singing* tuition'. They can also be place names, as in 'the *Edinburgh* train', 'a *Paris* cafe' and 'the *London* underground' or adverbs of place and direction, as in 'a *downstairs* cloakroom' and 'an *upstairs* sitting room.

Adverbs, adjectives and pronouns can be accompanied by **modifiers**. Examples of modifiers with adverbs include 'walking *amazingly* quickly' and 'stopping *incredibly* abruptly'. Examples of modifiers with adjectives include 'a *really* warm day' and 'a *deliriously* happy child'. Examples of modifiers with pronouns include '*almost* no one there' and '*practically* everyone present'.

The examples given above are all 'pre-modifiers'. *See also* POST-MODIFIER.

-monger is a suffix derived from Old English meaning 'dealer, trader', as in 'fishmonger' and 'ironmonger'. As well as being used for occupations in which people sell things, it is used for people who 'trade' in less tangible things, as in 'gossipmonger', 'rumourmonger', 'scaremonger' and 'warmonger'.

mono- is a prefix derived from Greek meaning 'one, single', as in 'monochrome', 'monocracy', 'monogamy', 'monologue', 'monoplane', 'monosyllabic' and 'monoxide'.

months of the year are spelt with initial capital letters, as in January, February, March, April, May, June, July, August, September, October, November and December.

modal verb refers to a type of 'auxiliary verb' that 'helps' the main verb to express a range of meanings including, for example, such meanings as possibility, probability, wants, wishes, necessity, permission, suggestions, etc. The main modal verbs are 'can', 'could'; 'may', 'might'; 'will', 'would'; 'shall', 'should'; 'must'.

Modal verbs have only one form. They have no -*s* form in the third person singular, no infinitive and no participles. Examples of modal verbs include 'He cannot read and write', 'She could go if she wanted to' (expressing ability); 'You can have another biscuit', 'You may answer the question' (expressing permission); 'We may see her on the way to the station', 'We might get there by nightfall' (expressing possibility); 'Will you have some wine?', 'Would you take a seat?' (expressing an offer or invitation); 'We should arrive by dawn', 'That must be a record' (expressing probability and certainty); 'You may prefer to wait', 'You might like to leave instructions' (expressing suggestion); 'Can you find the time to phone him for me?' ,'Could you give him a message?' (expressing instructions and requests), 'They must leave at once', 'We must get there on time' (expressing necessity).

mood refers to one of the categories into which verbs are divided. The verb moods are 'indicative', 'imperative' and 'subjunctive'. The indicative makes a statement, as in 'He lives in France', 'They have two children' and 'It's starting to rain'. The 'imperative' is used for giving orders or making requests, as in 'Shut that door!', 'Sit quietly until the teacher arrives' and 'Please bring me some coffee'. The subjunctive was originally a term in Latin grammar and expressed a wish, supposition, doubt, improbability or other non-factual statement. It is used in English for hypothetical statements and certain formal 'that' clauses, as in 'If I were you I would have nothing to do with it', 'If you were to go now you would arrive on time', 'Someone suggested that we ask for more money' and 'It was his solicitor who suggested that he sue the firm'. The word **mood** arose because it was said to indicate the verb's attitude or viewpoint. *See* SUBJUNCTIVE.

more is an adverb which is added to some adjectives to make the comparative form. In general it is the longer adjectives which have **more** as part of their comparative form, as in 'more abundant', 'more beautiful', 'more catastrophic', 'more dangerous', 'more elegant', 'more frantic', 'more graceful', 'more handsome', 'more intelligent', 'more luxurious', 'more manageable', 'more noteworthy', 'more opulent', 'more precious', 'more ravishing', 'more satisfactory', 'more talented', 'more unusual', 'more valuable'. Examples of adverbs with **more** in their comparative form include 'more elegantly', 'more gracefully', 'more energetically', 'more determinedly'. *See* COMPARISON OF ADJECTIVES.

most is an adverb added to some adjectives and adverbs to make the superlative form. In general it is the longer adjectives which have **most** as part of their superlative form, as in 'most abundant', 'most beautiful', 'most catastrophic', 'most dangerous', 'most elegant', 'most frantic', 'most graceful', 'most handsome', 'most intelligent', 'most luxurious', 'most manageable', 'most noteworthy', 'most opulent', 'most precious', most ravishing', 'most satisfactory', 'most talented', 'most unusual', 'most valuable'. Examples of adverbs with **most** in their superlative form include 'most elegantly', 'most gracefully', 'most energetically', 'most dangerously' and 'most determinedly'.

mother tongue refers to the language that one first learns, the language of which one is a 'native speaker'. It means the same as 'native tongue'.

ms, miss and miss *see* **letter-writing**.

mow has two possible past participles—**mowed and mown**, as in 'He has not yet mowed the grass' and 'We have mown the grass several times this summer'. The two participles are interchangeable. Only **mowed**, however, can be used as the past tense, as in 'They mowed the grass yesterday' and 'If they mowed the grass more often the garden would be tidier'. **Mown** can also be an adjective, as in 'the smell of freshly mown hay'.

multi- is a prefix derived from Latin meaning 'many many', as in 'multiply', 'multitude' and 'multitudinous'. **Multi-** is frequently used to form new modern words, as in 'multi-married', 'multi-media', 'multi-publicized', 'multi-purpose', 'multi-storey ', 'multi-talented' and 'multi-travelled'.

multi-sentence refers to a sentence with more than one clause, as in 'She tripped over a rock and broke her ankle' and 'She was afraid when she saw the strange man'.

N

-naut is a suffix derived from Greek 'sailor' and meaning 'navigator', as in 'astronaut' and 'cosmonaut'.

negative sentence refers to a sentence that is the opposite of 'positive sentence'. 'She has a dog' is an example of a positive sentence. 'She does not have a dog' is an example of a **negative sentence**. The **negative** concept is expressed by an 'auxiliary' verb accompanied by 'not' or 'n't'. Other words used in **negative sentences** include 'never', 'nothing' and 'by no means', as in 'She has never been here' and 'We heard nothing'.

neither as an adjective or a pronoun takes a singular verb, as in 'Neither parent will come' and 'Neither of them wishes to come'. In the **neither ... nor** construction, a singular verb is used if both parts of the construction are singular, as in 'Neither Jane nor Mary was present'. If both parts are plural the verb is plural, as in 'Neither their parents nor their grandparents are willing to look after them'. If the construction involves a mixture of singular and plural, the verb traditionally agrees with the subject that is nearest it, as in 'Neither her mother nor her grandparents are going to come' and 'Neither her grandparents nor her mother is going to come'. If pronouns are used, the nearer one governs the verb as in 'Neither they nor he is at fault' and 'Neither he nor they are at fault'.

neologism refers to a word that has been newly coined or newly introduced into the language, as 'camcorder', 'Jacuzzi' and 'karaoke'.

neuro- is a prefix derived from Greek meaning 'nerve', as in 'neuritis', 'neurology', 'neuron' and 'neurosurgery'.

neuter refers to one of the grammatical genders. The other two grammatical genders are 'masculine' and 'feminine'. Inanimate objects are members of the **neuter** gender. Examples include 'table', 'desk', 'garden', 'spade', 'flower' and 'bottle'.

non-finite clause is a clause which contains a 'non-finite verb'. Thus in the sentence 'He works hard to earn a living', 'to earn a living' is a non-finite clause since 'to earn' is an infinitive and so a non-finite verb. Similarly in the sentence 'Getting there was a problem', 'getting there' is a non-finite clause, 'getting' being a present participle and so a non-finite verb.

non-finite verb is one which shows no variation in tense and which has no subject. The non-finite verb forms include the infinitive form, as in 'go', the present participle and gerund, as in 'going', and the past participle, as in 'gone'.

noun indicates the name of something or someone. Thus 'anchor', 'baker', 'cat', 'elephant', 'foot', 'gate', 'lake', 'pear', 'shoe', 'trunk' and 'wallet' are all nouns. There are various categories of nouns. *See* ABSTRACT NOUN, COMMON NOUN, CONCRETE NOUN, COUNTABLE NOUN, PROPER NOUN and UNCOUNTABLE NOUN.

noun clause refers to a 'subordinate clause' which performs a function in a sentence similar to a noun or noun phrase. It can act as the subject, object or complement of a main clause. In the sentence 'Where he goes is his own business', 'where he goes' is a **noun clause**. In the sentence 'They asked why he objected', 'why he objected' is a **noun clause**. A **noun clause** is also known as a **nominal clause**.

noun phrase refers to a group of words containing a noun as its main word and functioning like a noun in a sentence. Thus it can function as the subject, object or complement of a sentence. In the sentence 'The large black dog bit him', 'the large black dog' is a **noun phrase** and in the sentence 'They bought a house with a garden', 'with a garden' is a **noun phrase**. In the sentence 'She is a complete fool', 'a complete fool' is a noun phrase.

number in grammar is a classification consisting of 'singular' and 'plural'. Thus the **number** of the pronoun 'they' is 'plural' and the **number** of the verb 'carries' is singular. *See* NUMBER AGREEMENT.

number agreement or **concord** refers to the fact that grammatical units should agree in terms of number. Thus a singular subject is followed by a singular verb, as in 'The girl likes flowers', 'He hates work' and 'She was carrying a suitcase'. Similarly a plural subject should be followed by a plural verb, as in 'They have many problems', 'The men work hard' and 'The girls are training hard'.

numbers can be written in either figures or words. It is largely a matter of taste which method is adopted. As long as the method is consistent it does not really matter. Some establishments, such as a publishing house or a newspaper office, will have a house style. For example, some of them prefer to have numbers up to 10 written in words, as in 'They have two boys and three girls'. If this system is adopted, guidance should be sought as to whether a mixture of figures and words in the same sentence is acceptable, as in 'We have 12 cups but only six saucers', or whether the rule should be broken in such situations as 'We have twelve cups but only six saucers'.

numeral is a word for 'number', as in 'print all the numerals in bold type'. **Numeral** is often used to refer to 'one, two, three, etc' in grammar since **number** is used to refer to the singular/plural category.

O

object refers to the part of a sentence that is acted upon or is affected by the verb. It usually follows the verb to which it relates. There are two forms of **object**—the 'direct object' and 'indirect object'. A direct object can be a noun, and in the sentence 'The girl hit the ball', 'ball' is a noun and the object. In the sentence 'They bought a house', 'house' is a noun and the object. In the sentence 'They made an error', 'error' is a noun and the object. A direct object can be a noun phrase, and in the sentence 'He has bought a large house', 'a large house' is a noun phrase and the object. In the sentence 'She loves the little girl', 'the little girl' is a noun phrase and the object. In the sentence 'They both wear black clothes', 'black clothes' is a noun phrase and the object'. A direct object can be a noun clause, and in the sentence 'I know what he means', 'what he means' is a noun phrase and the object. In the sentence 'He denied that he had been involved', 'that he had been involved' is a noun phrase and the object. In the sentence 'I asked when he would return', 'when he would return' is a noun phrase and the object. A direct object can also be a pronoun, and in the sentence 'She hit him', 'him' is a pronoun and the object. In the sentence 'They had a car but they sold it', 'it' is a pronoun and the object. In the sentence 'She loves them', 'them' is a pronoun and the object. *See* INDIRECT OBJECT.

objective case is the case expressing the 'object' . In Latin it is known as the 'accusative' case.

oblique is a diagonal mark / which has various uses. Its principal use is to show alternatives, as in 'he/she', 'Dear Sir/Madam', 'two/three-room flat' and 'the budget for 1993/4'. The **oblique** is used in some abbreviations, as in ' c/o Smith' (meaning 'care of Smith'). The word 'per' is usually shown by means of an **oblique**, as in 60km/hr (60 kilometres per hour).

officialese is a derogatory term for the vocabulary and style of writing often found in official reports and documents and thought of as being pretentious and difficult to understand. It is usually considered to be the prime example of GOBBLEDEGOOK.

-oholic *see* **-aholic**.

-ology is a suffix derived from Greek indicating 'study of', as in 'biology', 'geology' and 'technology'.

omni- is a prefix derived from Latin indicating 'all', as in 'omnipotent' and 'omnivorous'.

onomatopoeia is a figure of speech which uses words whose sound suggests their meaning, as in 'The sausages sizzled in the pan', 'The fire crackled in the grate' and 'The water gurgled in the pipes'.

orthographic refers to spelling, as in 'words which give rise to orthographic problems'.

orthography means the study or science of how words are spelt, as in 'make a survey of the orthography and the pronunciation of Scandinavian languages'.

ordinal numbers refer to 'first', 'second', 'third', etc, as opposed to 'cardinal numbers' which are 'one', 'two', 'three', etc.

-osis is a suffix derived from Greek indicating either 'a disease', as in 'cirrhosis' and 'thrombosis'.

oxymoron is a figure of speech which is based on the linking of incongruous or contradictory words, as in 'and honour rooted in dishonour stood' (Tennyson) and 'the wisest fool in Christendom'.

P

paragraph is a subdivision of a piece of prose. Many people find it difficult to divide their work into paragraphs. Learning to do so can be difficult but it is an area of style that improves with practice.

A **paragraph** should deal with one particular theme or point of the writer's writing or argument. When that has been dealt with, a new paragraph should be started. However, there are other considerations to be taken into account. If the paragraph is very long it can appear offputting visually to the would-be reader and can be difficult to make one's way through. In such cases it is best to sub-divide themes and shorten paragraphs. On the other hand, it is best not to make all one's paragraphs too short as this can create a disjointed effect. It is best to try to aim for a mixture of lengths to create some variety.

Traditionally it was frowned upon to have a one-sentence paragraph but there are no hard and fast rules about this. Usually it takes more than one sentence to develop the theme of the paragraph, unless one is a tabloid journalist or copywriter for an advertising firm, and it is best to avoid long, complex sentences.

The opening paragraph of a piece of writing should introduce the topic about which one is writing. The closing paragraph should sum up what one has been writing about. New paragraphs begin on new lines and they are usually indented from the margin. In the case of dialogue in a work of fiction, each speaker's utterance usually begins on a new line for the clarification of the reader.

parenthesis *see* **brackets**.

passive voice designates the voice of a verb whereby the subject is the recipient of the action of the verb. Thus, in the sentence 'Mary was kicked by her brother', 'Mary' is the receiver of the 'kick' and so 'kick' is in the passive voice. Had it been in the active voice it would have been 'Her brother kicked Mary'. Thus 'the brother' is the subject and not the receiver of the action.

past participles are formed by adding -*ed* or -*d* to the base words of regular verbs, as in 'acted', ' alluded', 'boarded', 'dashed', 'flouted', 'handed', 'loathed', 'tended' and 'wanted', or in various other ways for irregular verbs. *See* IRREGULAR VERBS.

past tense is formed by adding -*ed* or -*d* to the base form of the verb in regular verbs, as in 'added', 'crashed', 'graded', 'smiled', 'rested' and 'yielded', and in various ways for irregular verbs. *See* IRREGULAR VERBS and TENSE.

perfect tense *see* **tense**.

period *see* **full stop**.

personal pronouns are used to refer back to someone or something that has already been mentioned. The personal pronouns are divided into subject pronouns, object , pronouns and possessive pronouns. They are also categorized according to 'person'. *See* FIRST PERSON, SECOND PERSON and THIRD PERSON.

plural noun refers to 'more than one' and is contrasted with 'singular noun'. Singular nouns form plural forms in different ways. Most singular nouns add *s*, as in 'bat/bats', 'monkey/monkeys', 'table/tables', 'umbrella/umbrellas', or add *es*, as in 'church/churches' or 'torch/torches'. Singular nouns ending in a consonant followed by *y* add *ies*, as in 'fairy/fairies' and 'story/stories'. Some plural forms are formed irregularly. *See* IRREGULAR PLURALS.

possessive apostrophe *see* **apostrophe**.

possessive pronoun *see* **personal pronoun, first person, second person** and **third person**.

postmodifiers come after the main word of a noun phrase, as in 'of stone' in 'tablets of stone'.

predicate refers to all the parts of a clause or sentence that are not contained in the subject. Thus in the sentence 'The little girl was exhausted and hungry', 'exhausted and hungry' is the **predicate**. Similarly, in the sentence 'The tired old man slept like a top', 'slept like a top' is the **predicate**.

predicative adjectives help to form the predicate and so come after the verb, as 'tired' in 'She was very tired' and 'mournful' in 'The music was very mournful'.

premodifiers come before the main word of a noun phrase, as 'green' in 'green dress' and 'pretty' in 'pretty houses'.

prepositions are words which relate two elements of a sentence, clause or phrase together. They show how the elements relate in time or space and generally precede the words which they 'govern'. Words governed by **prepositions** are nouns or pronouns. **Prepositions** are often very short words, as 'at', 'in', 'on', 'to', 'before' and 'after'. Some complex prepositions consist of two words, as 'ahead of', 'instead of', 'apart from', and some consist of three, as 'with reference to', 'in accordance with' and 'in addition to'. Examples of **prepositions** in sentences include 'The cat sat on the mat', 'We were at a concert', 'They are in shock', 'We are going to France', 'She arrived before me', 'Apart from you she has no friends' and 'We acted in accordance with your instructions'.

present continuous *see* **tense**.

present participle *see* **-ing words**.

present tense *see* **tense**.

pronoun is a word that takes the place of a noun or a noun phrase. *See* PERSONAL PRONOUNS, HE, HER, HIM and HIS, RECIPROCAL PRONOUNS, REFLEXIVE PRONOUNS, DEMONSTRATIVE PRONOUNS, RELATIVE PRONOUNS, DISTRIBUTIVE PRONOUNS, INDEFINITE PRONOUNS and INTERROGATIVE PRONOUNS.

proper noun is a noun which refers to a particular individual or specific thing. It is the 'name' of someone or something', as in Australia, Vesuvius, John Brown, River Thames, Rome and Atlantic Ocean. *See* CAPITAL LETTERS.

Q

question mark refers to the punctuation mark that is placed at the end of a question or interrogative sentence, as in 'Who is he?', 'Where are they?', 'Why have they gone?', 'Whereabouts are they?', 'When are you going?' and 'What did he say?'. The question mark is sometimes known as the 'query'.

question tag refers to a phrase that is interrogative in form but is not really asking a question. It is added to a statement to seek agreement, etc. Examples include 'That was a lovely meal, wasn't it?', 'You will be able to go, won't you?', 'He's not going to move house, is he?' and 'She doesn't drive, does she?'. Sentences containing question tags have 'question marks' at the end.

query see question mark.

quotation marks, also known as 'inverted commas' or 'quotes', are used in 'direct speech'. For the use of quotation marks in 'direct speech' see DIRECT SPEECH. Quotation marks are also used to enclose titles of newspapers, books, plays, films, musical works and works of art, as in 'The Times', 'Animal Farm', 'Othello', 'My Fair Lady' and 'Portrait of the Artist'. Quotation marks may consist of a set of single inverted commas or a set of double inverted commas. If a title, etc, is to be enclosed in quotation marks and the title is part of a piece of writing already in quotation marks for some other reason, such as being part of direct speech, then the quotation marks round the title should be in the type of quotation marks opposite to the other ones. Thus if the piece of writing is in single quotation marks then the title should be in double quotation marks. If the piece of prose is in double quotation marks the title should be in single quotation marks. Examples include 'Have you read "Wuthering Heights"?' and "Did you go to see 'My Fair Lady'?"

quotes see quotation marks.

R

re- is a common prefix, meaning 'again', in verbs. In most cases it is not followed by a hyphen, as in 'retrace one's footsteps', 'a retrial ordered by the judge' and 'reconsider his decision'. However, it should be followed by a hyphen if its absence is likely to lead to confusion with another word, as in 're-cover a chair'/'recover from an illness', 're-count the votes'/'recount a tale of woe', 'the re-creation of a 17th-century village for a film set'/'play tennis for recreation' and 're-form the group'/'reform the prison system'. In cases where the second element of a word begins with *e*, re- is traditionally followed by a hyphen, as in 're-educate', 're-entry' and 're-echo', but in modern usage the hyphen is frequently omitted.

reciprocal pronoun is used to convey the idea of reciprocity or a two-way relationship. The **reciprocal pronouns** are 'each other' and 'one another'. Examples include 'They don't love each other any more', 'They seem to hate each other', 'We must try to help each other', 'The children were calling one another names', 'The two families were always criticizing one another' and 'The members of the family blame one another for their mother's death'.

reduplication refers to the process by which words are created by repetition or by semi-repetition. These include 'argy-bargy', 'dilly-dally', 'shilly-shally', 'flim-flam', 'heebie-jeebies', 'hocus-pocus', 'hugger-mugger', 'knick-knack', and 'mish-mash'.

reflexive pronoun is one which refers back to a noun or pronoun which has occurred earlier in the same sentence. The **reflexive pronouns** include 'myself', 'ourselves'; 'yourself', 'yourselves'; 'himself', 'herself', 'itself', 'themselves'. Examples include 'The children washed themselves', 'He cut himself shaving', 'Have you hurt yourself?' and 'She has cured herself of the habit'.

  Reflexive pronouns are sometimes used for emphasis, as in 'The town itself was not very interesting' and 'The headmaster himself punished the boys'. They can also be used to indicate that something has been done by somebody by his/her own efforts without any help, as in 'He built the house himself', 'We converted the attic ourselves'. They can also indicate that someone or something is alone, as in 'She lives by herself' and 'The house stands by itself'.

regular verb see **irregular verb**.

relative clause is a subordinate clause which has the function of an adjective. It is introduced by a **relative pronoun**. *See* RELATIVE PRONOUNS.

relative pronouns introduce **relative clauses**. The **relative pronouns** are 'who', 'whom', 'whose', 'which' and 'that'. Examples of **relative clauses** introduced by **relative pronouns** include 'There is the man who stole the money', 'She is the person to whom I gave the money', 'This is the man whose wife won the prize', 'They criticized the work which he had done' and 'That's the house that I would like to buy'. **Relative pronouns** refer back to a noun or noun phrase in the main clause. These nouns and noun phrases are known as 'antecedents'. The antecedents in the example sentences are respectively 'man', 'person', 'man', 'work' and 'house'.

  Sometimes the **relative clause** divides the parts of the main clause, as in 'The woman whose daughter is ill is very upset', 'The people whom we met on holiday were French' and 'The house that we liked best was too expensive'.

reported speech *see* **indirect speech**.

retro- is a prefix derived from Latin meaning 'back, backwards', as in 'retrograde', 'retrospect', 'retrorocket'.

retronym is a word or phrase that has had to be renamed slightly in the light of another invention, etc. For example, an ordinary guitar has become 'acoustic guitar' because of the existence of 'electric guitar'. Leather has sometimes become 'real leather' because of the existence of 'imitation leather'.

rhetorical question is a question which is asked to achieve some kind of effect and requires no answer. Examples include 'What's this country coming to?', 'Did you ever see the like', 'Why do these things happen to me?', 'Where did youth go?', 'Death, where is thy sting?' and 'Where does time go?'.

root means the same as **base**.

S

second person refers to the person or thing to whom one is talking. The term is applied to personal pronouns. The second person singular whether acting as the subject of a sentence is 'you', as in 'I told you so', 'We informed you of our decision' and 'They might have asked you sooner'. The **second person** personal pronoun does not alter its form in the plural in English, unlike in some languages. The possessive form of the **second person** pronoun is 'yours' whether singular or plural, as in "He said to the boys 'These books are not yours'"and 'This pen must be yours'.

semi-colon is a rather formal form of punctuation. It is mainly used between clauses that are not joined by any form of conjunction, as in 'We had a wonderful holiday; sadly they did not', 'She was my sister; she was also my best friend' and 'He was a marvellous friend; he is much missed'. A dash is sometimes used instead of a semi-colon but this more informal.

The **semi-colon** is also used to form subsets in a long list or series of names so that the said list seems less complex, as in 'The young man who wants to be a journalist has applied everywhere. He has applied to *The Times* in London; *The Globe and Mail* in Toronto; *The Age* in Melbourne; *The Tribune* in Chicago.

The **semi-colon** is also sometimes used before 'however', 'nevertheless' 'hence', etc, as in 'We have extra seats for the concert; however you must not feel obliged to come'.

sentence is at the head of the hierarchy of grammar. All the other elements, such as words, phrases and clauses go to make up sentences. It is difficult to define a sentence. In terms of recognizing a sentence visually it can be described as beginning with a capital letter and ending with a full stop, or with an equivalent to the full stop, such as an exclamation mark. It is a unit of grammar that can stand alone and make sense and obeys certain grammatical rules, such as usually having a subject and a predicate, as in 'The girl banged the door', where 'the girl' is the 'subject' and 'the door' is the predicate. *See* MAJOR SENTENCE, SIMPLE SENTENCE, COMPLEX SENTENCE.

simile is a figure of speech in which something is compared with another and said to be like it. This is in contradistinction to 'metaphor' where one thing is said actually to be another. Examples of similes include 'She is like an angel', 'Her hair is like silk', 'The old man's skin is like leather', 'He swims like a fish'.

simple sentence is a sentence which cannot be broken down into other clauses. It generally contains a finite verb. Simple sentences include 'The man stole the car', 'She nudged him' and 'He kicked the ball'. See COMPLEX SENTENCE and COMPOUND SENTENCE.

sexism was formerly widespread in the English language whether this was intentional or not. Efforts are now being made to rectify this situation, although some of the suggestions made are rather extreme. Sensible progress has, however, been made. *See* HE; EACH; -MAN and -PERSON.

singular noun refers to 'one' rather than 'more than one', which is the plural form. *See* PLURAL; IRREGULAR PLURAL.

spelling *see* **Appendix I.**

split infinitive refers to an infinitive which has had another word in the form of an adverb, placed between itself and 'to', as in 'to rudely push' and 'to quietly leave'. This was once considered a a great grammatical sin but the **split infinitive** is becoming acceptable in modern usage. In any case it sometimes makes for a clumsy sentence if one slavishly adheres to the correct form.

spoonerism refers to the accidental or deliberate transposition of the initial letters of two or more words, as in 'the queer old dean' instead of 'the dear old queen', 'a blushing crow' instead of a 'crushing blow' and 'a well-boiled icicle' instead of a 'well-oiled bicycle'. **Spoonerism** is called after the Reverend William Archibald Spooner (1844-1930) of Oxford University.

stative present *see* **tense.**

strong verb is the more common term for 'irregular verb'. *See* IRREGULAR VERB.

subject of a sentence or clause is usually either a noun, as in 'Birds fly' (birds is the noun as subject); a noun phrase, as in 'The people in the town dislike him' (the people in the town' is the subject); a pronoun, as in 'She hit the child' (she is the pronoun as subject); a proper noun, as in 'Paris is the capital of France'. *See* DUMMY SUBJECT.

subjunctive *see* **mood.**

subordinate clause is dependent on another clause, namely the 'main' clause. Unlike the main clause, it cannot stand alone and make sense. **Subordinate clauses** are introduced by conjunctions. Examples of conjunctions which introduce subordinate clauses include 'after', 'before', 'when', 'if', 'because' and 'since'. *See* ADVERBIAL CLAUSE; NOUN CLAUSE.

suffix is an 'affix' which goes at the beginning of a word. 'Pre-' is a suffix in 'prepare' and 'pre-holiday'. *See* AFFIX.

superlative forms of of adjectives and adverbs follow the same rules as comparative forms, except that they end in *-est* instead of *-er* and the longer ones use 'most' instead of 'more'.

syllepsis is another word for **zeugma.**

synecdoche is a figure of speech in which the part is put for the whole. For example 'The power of the Sceptre is fading' where sceptre is used for 'monarch'. 'The country has a fleet of a hundred sail' where 'sail' is used for 'ship'. 'He had a very successful career on the boards' where 'boards' is used for 'stage'.

T

tautology refers to unnecessary repetition, as in 'new innovations', 'a see-through transparent material' and 'one after the other in succession'.

techno- is a prefix derived from Greek meaning 'craft, skill', as in 'technical', 'technology', 'technique', etc.

tele- is a prefix derived from Greek meaning 'distance' as in 'telephone', 'telescope' and 'television', etc.

tense is used to show the time at which the action of a verb takes place. One of the tenses in English is the 'present tense'. It is used to indicate an action now going on or a state now existing. A distinction can be made between the 'habitual present', which marks habitual or repeated actions or recurring events, and the 'stative present', which indicates something that is true at all times. Examples of 'habitual present' include 'He works long hours' and 'She walks to work'. Examples of the 'stative tense' include 'The world is round' and 'Everyone must die eventually'.

The 'progressive present' or 'continuous present' is formed with the verb 'to be' and the 'present participle', as in ,He is walking to the next village', 'They are thinking about leaving' ,'She was driving along the road when she saw him' and 'They were worrying about the state of the economy'

The 'past tense' refers to an action or state which has taken place before the present time. In the case of 'irregular verbs' it is formed by adding -ed to the base form of the verb, as in 'fear/feared', 'look/looked', and 'turn/turned'. For the past tense of 'irregular verbs', *see* IRREGULAR VERBS.

The 'future tense' refers to an action or state that will take place at some time in the future. It is formed with 'will' and 'shall'. Traditionally 'will' was used with the second and third person pronouns ('you', 'he/she/it', 'they') and 'shall' with the first person ('I' and 'we'), as in 'You will be bored', 'He will soon be home', 'They will leave tomorrow', 'I shall buy some bread' and 'We shall go by train'. Also traditionally 'shall' was used with the second and third persons to indicate emphasis, insistence, determination, refusal, etc., as in 'You shall go to the ball' and 'He shall not be admitted'. 'Will' was used with the first person in the same way, as in 'I will get even with him'.

In modern usage 'will' is generally used for the first person as well as for second and third, as in 'I will see you tomorrow' and 'We will be there soon' and 'shall' is used for emphasis, insistence, etc. for first, second and third persons.

The 'future tense' can also be formed with the use of 'be about to' or 'be going to', as in 'We were about to leave' and 'They were going to look for a house.

Other tenses include the 'perfect tense' which is formed using the verb 'to have' and the past participle. In the case of 'regular verbs' the 'past participle' is formed by adding 'ed' to the base form of the verb. For the past participles of 'irregular verbs' see irregular verbs. Examples of the 'perfect tense' include 'He has played his last match','We have travelled all day' and 'They have thought a lot about it'.

The 'past perfect tense' or 'pluperfect tense' is formed using the verb 'to have' and the past participle, as in 'She had no idea that he was dead', and 'They had felt unhappy about the situation'.

The 'future perfect' is formed using the verb 'to have' and the past participle, as in 'He will have arrived by now'.

the usually refers back to something already identified or to something specific, as in 'Where is the key?', 'What have you done with the book which I gave you?' and 'We have found the book which we lost'. It is also used to denote someone or something as being the only one, as in 'the House of Lords', 'the King of Spain' and 'the President of Russia' and to indicate a class or group, as in 'the aristocracy', the cat family' and 'the teaching profession'. The is sometimes pronounced 'thee' when it is used to identify someone or something unique or important, as in 'Is that the John Frame over there?' and She is the fashion designer of the moment'.

they see he.

third person refers to a third party not the speaker or the person or thing being spoken to. Note that 'person' in this context can refer to things as well as people. 'Person' in this sense applies to personal pronouns. The third person singular forms are 'he', 'she' and 'it' when the subject of a sentence or clause, as in 'She will win' and 'It will be fine'. The third person singular forms are 'him', 'her','it' when the object, as in 'His behaviour hurt her' and 'She meant it'. The third person plural is 'they' when the subject, as in 'They have left' and 'They were angry' and 'them' when the object, as in 'His words made them angry' and 'We accompanied them.

The possessive forms of the singular are 'his', 'hers' and 'its', as in 'he played his guitar' and 'The dog hurt its leg' and the the possessive form of the plural is theirs,as in 'That car is theirs' and 'They say that the book is theirs'. See he.

to-infinitive refers to the 'infinitive' form of the verb when it is accompanied by 'to' rather than when it is the 'bare infinitive' without 'to'. Examples of the **to-infinitive** include 'We were told to go' ,'I didn't want to stay' and 'To get there on time we'll have to leave now'.

transitive verb is a verb which takes a 'direct object'. In the sentence 'The boy broke the window' 'window' is a 'direct object' and so 'broke' (breakO is a transitive verb. In the sentence 'She eats fruit' 'fruit' is a 'direct object' and so 'eat' is a transitive verb. In the sentence 'They kill enemy soldiers' 'enemy soldiers' is a 'direct object' and so 'kill' is a transitive verb'. See direct object and intransitive verb.

U

ultra- is a prefix derived from Latin meaning 'beyond', as in 'ultraviolet' and 'ltramodern'.

umlaut refers to the diacritic which indicates a change of vowel sound in German, as in *madchen*.

un- is a prefix with two meanings. It can mean either 'not', as in 'unclean', 'untrue' and 'unwise'. it can also mean 'back, reversal', as in 'undo', 'unfasten', 'unlatch' and 'untie'.

uncount noun see uncountable noun.

uncountable noun refers to a noun that is not usually pluralized or 'counted'. Such a noun is usually preceded by 'some', rather than 'a'. **Uncountable nouns** often refer to substances or commodities or qualities, processes and states. Examples of uncountable nouns include butter, china, luggage, petrol, sugar, heat, information, poverty, richness and warmth.In some situations it is possible to have a countable version of what is usually an **uncountable noun.** Thus 'sugar' is usually considered to be an 'uncountable noun' but it can be used in a 'countable' form in contexts such as 'I take two sugars in my coffee please'. Some nouns exist in an uncountable and 'countable' form. Examples include 'cake', as in 'Have some cake' and 'She ate three cakes' and 'She could not paint for lack of light' and 'the lights went out'.

uni- is a prefix derived from Latin meaning 'one' , as in unicycle, unilateral and unity.

V

verb is often known as a 'doing' word. Although this is rather restrictive ,since it tends to preclude auxiliary verbs, modal verbs, etc. the verb is the word in a sentence that is most concerned with the action and is usually essential to the structure of the sentence. **Verbs** 'inflect' and indicate tense, voice, mood, number, number and person. Most of the information on **Verbs** has been placed under related entries. See active, passive, voice, auxiliary verb, modal verb, mood, finite verb, non-finite verb, transitive verb, intransitive verb, irregular verb, linking verb, -ing forms and phrasal verbs.

verb phrase refers to a group of verb forms which has the same function as a single verb. Examples include 'have been raining', 'must have been lying', should not have been doing and 'has been seen doing'.

virgule is a rare word for oblique.

vocative case is relevant mainly to languages suchas Latin which are based on cases and inflections. In English the vocative is expressed by addressing someons, as 'John, could I se you for a minute' or by some form of greeting, endearment or exclamation.

voice is one of the categories that describes verbs. It involves two different ways of looking at the action of verbs. It is divided into 'active voice' and 'passive voice'. See active and passive.

W

Z

weak verb is a less common term for 'regular verb'. See irregular verb.

who and **whom** take information from Usage Guide See relative clause.

whose and **whose** are liable to be confused because they sound the same. However they are not at all the same. Who's is a contraction of 'who is' and is used in speech and informal written contexts, as in 'Who's going to the cinema?', 'Who's been eating garlic?' and 'Who's afraid of spiders'. **Whose** is a possessive pronoun or possessive adjective, as in 'That's the woman whose house was burgled', 'Whose hat is this?' and 'Whose are they?'.

-ways is prefix which to some extent acts an alternative to 'wise' in its first two meanings, as in crabways and lengthways.

-wise is a prefix with several meanings. It can mean 'indicating manner or way', as in clockwise and crabwise. It can also mean' in the position or direction of' as in lengthwise and breadthwise. It can also mean 'with reference to', as in 'careerwise, familywise. jobwise and salarywise. This last use is very much over-used. -Wise can also mean 'clever, sensible', as in streetwise and worldlywise.

zero plural refers to a plural form that has the same form as the singular. Examples include 'cod', 'deer', 'grouse' (gamebird) and 'sheep'. Some nouns have ordinary plurals and **zero plurals** as alternatives, as 'fish/fishes'. Nouns of measurement often have **zero plurals** , as in 'She is five foot three' and 'Six dozen eggs'.

zeugma is a figure of speech which uses a single word to apply to two words which are not appropriate to each other , as in 'We collected our coats and our baby', 'She left the building and her job' and 'She left in taxi and a fit of hysterics'. **Zeugma** is similar to bathos.

English Usage

A

a *and* an are the forms of the indefinite article. The form a is used before words that begin with a consonant sound, as in *a* box, *a* garden, *a* road, *a* wall. The form an is used before words that begin with a vowel sound, as in *an* apple, *an* easel, *an* ostrich, *an* uncle. Note that it is the *sound* of the initial letter that matters and not the *spelling*. Thus a is used before words beginning with a *u* when they are pronounced with a *y* sound as though it were a consonant, as *a* unit, *a* usual occurrence. Similarly an is used, for example, before words beginning with the letter *h* where this is not pronounced, as in *an* heir, *an* hour, *an* honest man.

Formerly it was quite common to use an before words that begin with an *h* sound and also begin with an unstressed syllable, as in *an* hotel (ho-*tel*), *an* historic (his*tor*-ik) occasion, *an* hereditary (her-*ed*-it-ary) disease. It is more usual nowadays to use a in such cases, ignoring the question of the unstressed syllable.

abbreviations are shortened forms of words, usually used as a space-saving technique and are becoming increasingly common in modern usage. They frequently take the form of the initial letters of several words as, for example, in the title of an organization, person, etc, e.g. TUC (Trade Union Council) or BBC (British Broadcasting Corporation), JP (Justice of the Peace). Note that, unlike acronyms, abbreviations are not pronounced as words even when this would be possible. Thus TUC is not pronounced *tuk*.

Abbreviations may also be formed from the first and last letters of a word (when they are known as contractions), e.g. Dr (Doctor), Rd (Road), St (Street or Saint), pd (paid). Many of these are found mainly in written, rather than spoken, form.

Abbreviations may also be formed from the first few letters of a word, e.g. Feb (February), Prof (Professor), Rev (Reverend).

In modern usage the tendency is to omit full stops from abbreviations. This is most true of abbreviations involving initial capital letters, as in TUC, BBC, EEC and USA. In such cases full stops should definitely not be used if one or some of the initial letters do not belong to a full word. Thus 'television' is abbreviated to TV.

There are usually no full stops in abbreviations involving the first and last letters of a word (contractions), as in Dr, Mr, Rd, St, but this is a matter of taste.

Abbreviations involving the first few letters of a word, as in Prof for 'Professor', are the most likely to have full stops, as Feb. for 'February', but again this is now a matter of taste.

Plurals in abbreviations are mostly formed by adding lower-case *s*, as in Drs, JPs, TVs. Note the absence of apostrophes.

See also acronyms.

abdomen is now usually pronounced with the emphasis on the first syllable (*ab*-do-men).

aberration is frequently misspelt. Note the single *b* and double *r*. It means deviation or departure from what is considered normal, as in 'mental aberration'

-able *and* -ible are both used to form adjectives. It is easy to confuse the spelling of words ending in these, and the best way to get them right is to memorize them, unless you have a good knowledge of Latin. Words ending in -ible are usually formed from Latin words ending in *-ibilis*, and some words ending in -able are formed from Latin words ending in *-abilis*.

In addition, some words ending in -able are derived from French, and words formed from English words end in -able rather than -ible. The form -able is what is known as a 'living suffix' and is the form that is used when coining modern words, as 'a sackable offence', 'washable materials', 'a jailable crime', 'a kickable ball', 'a catchable ball'.

Some words ending in -able:

abominable	healable	manageable	sizeable
acceptable	hearable	measurable	solvable
agreeable	identifiable	memorable	stoppable
bearable	impeccable	nameable	storable
beatable	immutable	nonflammable	tenable
blameable	impracticable	objectionable	tolerable
comfortable	inapplicable	operable	touchable
commendable	inappreciable	palpable	undoable
delectable	incalculable	passable	usable
discreditable	indispensable	purchasable	variable
disreputable	indescribable	rateable	viable
enviable	indisputable	readable	washable
forgettable	lamentable	reviewable	wearable
forgivable	laudable	saleable	winnable
governable	likeable	shakeable	workable

Some words ending in -ible:

accessible	discernible	indelible	repressible
admissible	divisible	intelligible	reproducible
audible	edible	irascible	resistible
collapsible	exhaustible	legible	responsible
combustible	expressible	negligible	reversible
compatible	fallible	ostensible	risible
comprehensible	feasible	perceptible	sensible
contemptible	flexible	permissible	susceptible
credible	forcible	plausible	tangible
defensible	gullible	possible	visible
digestible			

-abled is a suffix meaning 'able-bodied'. It is most usually found in such phrases as 'differently abled', a 'politically correct', more positive way of referring to people with some form of disability, as in 'provide access to the club building for differently abled members'. In common with many politically correct terms, it is disliked by many people, including many disabled people.

ableism *or* ablism means discrimination in favour of able-bodied people as in 'people in wheelchairs unable to get jobs because of ableism'. Also known as **able-bodiedism** and **able-bodism**. Note that the suffix '-ism' is often used to indicate discrimination against the group to which it refers, as in 'ageism'.

Aboriginal rather than **Aborigine** is now the preferred term for an original inhabitant of Australia, especially where the word is in the singular.

abscess, meaning an inflamed swelling with pus in it, is frequently misspelt. Note the *c* after the first *s*.

abuse *and* **misuse** both mean wrong or improper use or treatment. However, **abuse** tends to be a more condemnatory term, suggesting that the wrong use or treatment is morally wrong or illegal. Thus we find 'misuse of the equipment' or 'misuse of one's talents', but 'abuse of a privileged position' or 'abuse of children'. 'Child abuse' is usually used to indicate physical violence or sexual assault.

Abuse is also frequently applied to the use of substances that are dangerous or injurious to health, as in 'drug abuse', 'solvent abuse', or 'alcohol abuse'. In addition, it is used to describe insulting or offensive language, as in 'shout abuse at the referee'.

academic is used to describe scholarly or educational matters, as in 'a child with academic rather than sporting interests'. From this use it has come to mean theoretical rather than actual or practical, as in 'wasting time discussing matters of purely academic concern'. In modern use it is frequently used to mean irrelevant, as in 'Whether you vote for him or not is academic. He is certain of a majority of votes'.

accelerate, meaning 'to go faster', is a common word that is frequently misspelt. Note the double *c* but single *l*.

accent commonly refers to a regional or individual way of speaking or pronouncing words, as in 'a Glasgow accent'. The word is also used to mean emphasis, as in 'In hotel the accent is on the second syllable of the word', or 'In fashion this year the accent is no longer on shirts'.

Accent also refers to certain symbols used on some foreign words adopted into English. In modern usage, which has a tendency to punctuate less than was formerly the case, accents are frequently omitted. For example, an actor's part in a play is now usually spelt 'role' but originally it was spelt 'rôle', the accent on *o* being called a circumflex. The accent is most likely to be retained if it affects the pronunciation. Thus 'cliché' and 'divorcé' usually retain the acute accent, as it is called, on the *e*. On the other hand, the accent known as the cedilla is frequently omitted from beneath the *c* in words such as 'façade/facade', although it is there to indicate that the *c* is soft, pronounced like an *s*, rather than a hard sound pronounced like a *k*.

access is commonly misspelt. Note the double *c* and double *s*. The word is usually a noun meaning 'entry or admission', as in 'try to gain access to the building', or 'the opportunity to use something', as in 'have access to confidential information'. It is also used to refer to the right of a parent to spend time with his or her children, as in 'Father was allowed access to the children at weekends'.

However **access** can also be used as a verb. It is most commonly found in computing, meaning obtaining information from, as in 'accessing details from the computer file relating to the accounts'. In modern usage many technical words become used, and indeed overused, in the general language. Thus the verb **access** can now be found meaning to obtain information not on a

computer, as in 'access the information in the filing cabinet'. It can also be found in the sense of gaining entry to a building, as in 'Their attempts to access the building at night were unsuccessful'.

accessory and **accessary** are interchangeable as regards only one meaning of **accessory**. A person who helps another person to commit a crime is known either as an **accessory** or an **accessary**, although the former is the more modern term. However, only **accessory** is used to describe a useful or decorative extra that is not strictly necessary, as in 'Seat covers are accessories that are included in the price of the car' and 'She wore a red dress with black accessories' ('accessories' in the second example being handbag, shoes and gloves).

accompany can be followed either by the preposition 'with' or 'by'. When it means 'to go somewhere with someone', 'by' is used, as in 'She was accompanied by her parents to church' Similarly, 'by' is used when **accompany** is used in a musical context, as in 'The singer was accompanied on the piano by her brother'. When **accompany** means 'to go along with something' or 'supplement something', either 'by' or 'with' may be used, as in 'The roast turkey was accompanied by all the trimmings', 'His words were accompanied by/with a gesture of dismissal', and 'The speaker accompanied his words with expressive gestures'.

accommodation is one of the most commonly misspelt words. Note the double *c*, and double *m*.

acetic is a common misspelling of **ascetic** although it is a word in its own right. **Acetic** refers to the acid used in vinegar and is used to mean sour. **Ascetic** means 'self-denying' or 'self-disciplined' and is used to refer to a person (or to his/her lifestyle) who abstains from many of life's pleasures and who is often a recluse. A person who has such a lifestyle is known as an **ascetic**.

acknowledgement and **acknowledgment** are both acceptable spellings.

acoustics can take either a singular or plural verb. When it is being thought of as a branch of science it is treated as being singular, as in 'Acoustics deals with the study of sound', but when it is used to describe the qualities of a hall, etc, with regard to its sound-carrying properties, it is treated as being plural, as in 'The acoustics in the school hall are very poor'.

acquaint is often misspelt. It is a common error to omit the *c*. It means 'to become familiar with' or 'to inform'. The same problem arises in the word **acquaintance**, which means 'someone whom one knows slightly'.

acquire, **acquirement** and **acquisition** are all frequently misspelt. It is a common error to omit the *c*.

acronyms, like some **abbreviations**, are formed from the initial letters of several words. Unlike **abbreviations**, however, **acronyms** are pronounced as words rather than as just a series of letters. For example OPEC (Organization of Petroleum Producing Countries) is pronounced *o-pek* and is thus an acronym, unlike USA (United States of America) which is pronounced as a series of letters and *not* as a word (*oo-sa* or *yoo-sa*) and is thus an **abbreviation**.

Acronyms are written without full stops, as in UNESCO (United Nations Educational, Scientific and Cultural Organization). Mostly **acronyms** are written in capital letters, as in NASA (National Aeronautics and Space Administration). However, very common **acronyms**, such as Aids (Acquired Immune Deficiency Syndrome), are written with just an initial capital, the rest of the letters being lower case.

Acronyms that refer to a piece of scientific or technical equipment are written like ordinary words in lower-case letters, as 'laser' (light amplification by simulated emission of radiation).

A fashion originated in the mid 1980s for inventing **acronyms** relating to lifestyles or categories of society. These included 'yuppie', also spelt 'yuppy', which is an acronym of 'young urban (or upwardly mobile) professional'. 'Yuppie' became an established part of the language, as to a certain extent did 'nimby' (not in my back yard), an **acronym** that indicates people's reluctance to have any new developments, such as a hostel for ex-prisoners, in the vicinity of their homes, even if they are in theory in general favour of such developments. The majority of **acronyms** coined at this time were short-lived and are no longer commonly used. These included 'dinky' ('dual or double income, no kids') and 'woopie' ('well-off older person'). The fashion in forming such acronyms became rather silly, resulting in such words as 'pippie' ('person inheriting parents' property') and 'whanny' ('we have a nanny').

acrylic refers to the fibre used in a kind of man-made textile. The word is commonly misspelt. Note the *y*, not *i*, before the *l*.

activate and **actuate** both mean 'make active' but are commonly used in different senses. **Activate** refers to physical or chemical action, as in 'The terrorists activated the explosive device'. **Actuate** means 'to move to action' and 'to serve as a motive', as in 'The murderer was actuated by jealousy'.

acute and **chronic** both refer to disease. **Acute** is used of a disease that is sudden in onset and lasts a relatively short time, as in 'Flu is an acute illness'. **Chronic** is used of a disease that may be slow to develop and lasts a long time, possibly over several years, as in 'Asthma is a chronic condition'.

acumen is now usually pronounced *ak*-yoo-men, with the emphasis on the first syllable, although formerly the stress was usually on the second syllable (yoo). It means 'the ability to make good or shrewd judgements, as in 'a woman of excellent business acumen'.

actress is still widely used as a term for a woman who acts in plays or films, although many people prefer the term 'actor', regarding this as a neutral term rather than simply the masculine form. The -ess suffix, used to indicate the feminine form of a word, is generally becoming less common as these forms are regarded as sexist or belittling. *See also* **-ess.**

AD and **BC** are abbreviations that accompany year numbers. **AD** stands for 'Anno Domini', meaning 'in the year of our Lord' and indicates that the year concerned is one occurring after Jesus Christ was born. Traditionally **AD** is placed before the year number concerned, as in 'Their great-grandfather was born in AD 1801', but in modern usage it sometimes follows the year number, as in 'The house was built in 1780 AD.' **BC** stands for 'Before Christ' and indicates that the year concerned is one occurring before Jesus Christ was born. It follows the year number, as in 'The event took place in Rome in 55 BC'.

adagio is a musical direction indicating that a piece or passage of music should be played slowly. It is an Italian word meaning 'at ease' and is pronounced a-*dah*-jee-o.

adapter and **adaptor** can be used interchangeably, but commonly **adapter** is used to refer to a person who adapts, as in 'the adapter of the stage play for televi-

sion and **adaptor** is used to refer to a thing that adapts, specifically a type of electrical plug.

ad hoc is a Latin phrase commonly used in English to mean 'for a particular purpose only', as in 'An ad hoc committee was formed to deal with the flooding of the town'.

adjourn is commonly misspelt. Note the *d* before the *j*. It means either 'to postpone or stop for a short time', as in 'The meeting will adjourn for lunch', and 'to go', as in 'They adjourned to another room'.

admissible is frequently misspelt. Note the -IBLE ending.

admission and **admittance** both mean 'permission or right to enter'. **Admission** is the more common term, as in 'They refused him admission to their house', and, unlike **admittance**, it can also mean 'the price or fee charged for entry' as in 'Admission to the football match is £3'. **Admittance** is largely used in formal or official situations, as in 'They ignored the notice saying "No Admittance" '. **Admission** also means 'confession' or 'acknowledgement of responsibility', as in 'On her own admission she was the thief'.

admit may be followed either by the preposition 'to' or the preposition 'of', depending on the sense. In the sense of 'to confess', **admit** is usually not followed by a preposition at all, as in 'He admitted his mistake' and 'She admitted stealing the brooch'. However, in this sense **admit** is sometimes followed by 'to', as in 'They have admitted to their error' and 'They have admitted to their part in the theft'.

In the sense of 'to allow to enter', **admit** is followed by 'to', as in 'The doorman admitted the guest to the club'. Also in the rather formal sense of 'give access or entrance to', **admit** is followed by 'to', as in 'the rear door admits straight to the garden'. In the sense of 'to be open to' or 'leave room for', **admit** is followed by 'of', as in 'The situation admits of no other explanation'.

admittance *see* **admission.**

adolescence is frequently misspelt. Note the letters *sc* in the middle of the word. Adolescence refers to the period of life between puberty and adulthood.

adopted and **adoptive** are liable to be confused. **Adopted** is applied to children who have been adopted, as in 'The couple have two adopted daughters'. **Adoptive** is applied to a person or people who adopt a child, as in 'Her biological parents tried to get the girl back from her adoptive parents'.

adult may be pronounced with the emphasis on either of the two syllables. Thus *a*-dult and a-*dult* are both acceptable although the pronunciation with the emphasis on the first syllable (*a*-dult) is the more common. The adjective **adult** means 'mature', as in 'a very adult young man' and 'for adults' as in 'courses in adult education'. However it can also mean 'pornographic', as in 'adult movies'.

adversary is commonly pronounced with the emphasis on the first syllable (*ad*-ver-sar-i) although in modern usage it is also found with the emphasis on the second syllable (ad-*ver*-sar-i).

adverse and **averse** are often confused because they sound and look rather alike, although they are different in meaning. **Adverse** means 'unfavourable' or 'hostile', as in 'Her actions had an adverse effect on her career' and 'The committee's proposals met with an adverse reaction'. **Averse** means 'unwilling' or 'having a dislike', as in 'The staff are not averse to the reconstruction plans', 'Her mother is totally averse to her marrying him'. Note that **averse** is followed by the preposition 'to'.

Adverse is usually pronounced with the emphasis on the first syllable (*ad*-vers) and **averse** is always pronounced with the emphasis on the second syllable (a-*vers*).

advertise is commonly misspelt. It is not one of those verbs that can end in either -*ise* or -*ize*. 'Advertize' is an erroneous spelling.

advice and **advise** are sometimes confused. **Advice** is a noun meaning 'helpful information or guidance', as in 'She asked her sister's advice on clothes' and 'She should seek legal advice'. **Advise** is a verb meaning 'to give advice', as in 'The career's office will advise you about educational qualifications'. It can also mean to 'inform', as in 'The officer advised the men of the change of plan'. It is usually used in a formal or official context. Note that it is wrong to spell advise with a *z*.

adviser and **advisor** are both acceptable spellings. The word is applied to someone who gives advice, usually someone in a professional or official capacity, as in 'He is a financial adviser/advisor'.

aerial is commonly misspelt. Note the *ae* at the beginning of the word. **Aerial** as an adjective means either 'of the air', as in 'aerial changes', or 'from the air or an aircraft', as in 'an aerial view'.

aeroplane is commonly abbreviated to **plane** in modern usage. In American English **aeroplane** becomes **airplane**.

affect and **effect** are often confused. **Affect** is a verb meaning 'to have an effect on', 'to influence or change in some way', as in 'His health was affected by his poor working conditions', 'Their decision was affected by personal prejudice'. It is often confused with **effect**, a noun meaning 'result or consequence' or 'influence', as in 'Their terrible experiences will have an effect on the children'. **Effect** is also a verb used mostly in formal contexts and means 'to bring about', as in 'The company plans to effect major changes'. **Affect** can also mean 'to pretend or feign' as in 'She affected an appearance of poverty although she was very wealthy'.

affinity may be followed by the preposition 'with' or 'between', and means 'close relationship', 'mutual attraction' or similarity, as in 'the affinity which twins have with each other' and 'There was an affinity between the two families who had lost children'. In modern usage it is sometimes followed by 'for' or 'towards', and means 'liking', as in 'She has an affinity for fair-haired men'.

aficionado is frequently misspelt. Note the single *f* and single *n*. It means a fan or supporter as in 'an aficionado of jazz', 'an opera aficionado', and is pronounced a-fiss-eon-*ah*-do. The plural is **aficionados**.

afters *see* **dessert**.

aged has two possible pronunciations depending on the sense. When it means 'very old', as in 'aged men with white beards', it is pronounced *ay*-jid. When it means 'years of age', as in 'a girl aged nine', it is pronounced with one syllable, *ayjd*.

ageing in modern usage may also be spelt **aging**.

ageism means discrimination on the grounds of age, as in 'By giving an age range in their job advert the firm were guilty of ageism'. Usually it refers to discrimination against older or elderly people, but it also refers to discrimination against young people.

agenda in modern usage is a singular noun having the plural **agendas**. It means 'a list of things to be attended to', as in 'The financial situation was the first item on the committee's agenda'. Originally it was a plural noun, derived from Latin, meaning 'things to be done'.

aggravate literally means 'to make worse', as in 'Her remarks simply aggravated the situation'. In modern usage it is frequently found meaning 'to irritate or annoy', as in 'The children were aggravating their mother when she was trying to read'. It is often labelled as 'informal' in dictionaries and is best avoided in formal situations.

agnostic and **atheist** are both words meaning 'disbeliever in God', but there are differences in sense between the two words. **Agnostics** believe that it is not possible to know whether God exists or not. **Atheists** believe that there is no God.

agoraphobia is frequently misspelt. Note the *o*, not *a*, after *g*. The word means 'fear of open spaces'.

alcohol abuse is a modern term for alcoholism. *See* **abuse**.

alibi is derived from the Latin word for 'elsewhere'. It is used to refer to a legal plea that a person accused or under suspicion was somewhere other than the scene of the crime at the time the crime was committed. In modern usage **alibi** is frequently used to mean simply 'excuse' or 'pretext', as in 'He had the perfect alibi for not going to the party—he was ill in hospital'.

align is frequently misspelt. Note the single *l*. The word means either 'to bring into (a straight) line', as in 'align the wheels of a car', or 'to support, be on the side of', as in 'He aligned himself with the rebels'.

all right is frequently misspelt as 'alright'. Although 'alright' is commonly found, it is still regarded as an error.

allude should be used only in the meaning of 'to refer indirectly to', as in 'When he spoke of people who had suffered from mental illness he was alluding to himself'. It should not be used simply to mean 'to refer to', as in 'In his speech he alluded frequently to the fact that he was retiring', although this is commonly found nowadays in informal contexts.

allusion and **illusion** are liable to be confused because of the similarity in their pronunciation, but they are completely different in meaning. **Allusion** means 'an indirect reference', as in 'His remarks on poverty in the area were an allusion to the hardship of his own childhood there'. *See* **allude**. **Illusion** means 'a false or misleading impression', as in 'Putting a screen round her part of the room gave at least the illusion of privacy'.

alternate and **alternative** are liable to be confused. **Alternate** means 'every other' or 'occurring by turns', as in 'They visit her mother on alternate weekends' and 'between alternate layers of meat and cheese sauce'. **Alternative** means 'offering a choice' or 'being an alternative', as in 'If the motorway is busy there is an alternative route'. **Alternative** is found in some cases in modern usage to mean 'not conventional, not traditional', as in 'alternative medicine' and 'alternative comedy'.

Alternative as a noun refers to the choice between two possibilities, as in 'The alternatives are to go by train or by plane'. In modern usage, however, it is becoming common to use it to refer also to the choice among two or more possibilities, as in 'He has to use a college from five alternatives'.

although and **though** are largely interchangeable but **though** is slightly less formal, as in 'We arrived on time although/though we left late'.

all together and **altogether** are not interchangeable. **All together** means 'at the same time' or 'in the same place', as in 'The guests arrived all together' and 'They kept their personal papers all together in a filing cabinet'. **Altogether** means 'in all, in total' or 'completely', as in 'We collected £500 altogether' and 'The work was altogether too much for him'.

a.m. and **p.m.** are liable to be confused. **A.M.**, which is short for Latin 'ante meridiem' meaning 'before noon', is used to indicate that the time given occurs between the hours of midnight and midday, as in 'She asked friends for coffee at 11 a.m'. **P.M.**, which is short for *post meridiem*, meaning 'after noon', is used to indicate that the time given occurs during the hours between midday and midnight, as in 'The shop stays open until 10 p.m.' Full stops are usually used both in **a.m.** and **p.m.**; in the case of **a.m.** to distinguish it from the verb 'am'. Usually both **a.m.** and **p.m.** are spelt with lower-case letters.

amend and **emend** are liable to be confused. Both words mean 'to correct', but **emend** has a more restricted use than **amend**. **Emend** means specifically 'to remove errors from something written or printed', as in 'The editor in the publishing office emended the author's manuscript'. **Amend** means 'to correct', 'to improve' or 'to alter', as in 'We have overcharged you but we shall amend the error', and 'The rules for entry are old-fashioned and have to be amended'.

amiable and **amicable** both refer to friendliness and goodwill. **Amiable** means 'friendly' or 'agreeable and pleasant', and is mostly used of people or their moods, as in 'amiable neighbours', 'amiable travelling companions', 'of an amiable temperament' and 'be in an amiable mood'. **Amicable** means 'characterized by friendliness and goodwill' and is applied mainly to relationships, agreements, documents, etc, as in 'an amicable working relationship', 'reach an amicable settlement at the end of the war' and 'send an amicable letter to his former rival'.

among and **amongst** are interchangeable, as in 'We searched among/amongst the bushes for the ball,' 'Divide the chocolate among/amongst you', and 'You must choose among/amongst the various possibilities'.

among and **between** may be used interchangeably in most contexts. Formerly **between** was used only when referring to the relationship of two things, as in 'Share the chocolate between you and your brother', and **among** was used when referring to the relationship of three or more things, as in 'Share the chocolate among all your friends'. In modern usage **between** may be used when referring to more than two things, as in 'There is agreement between all the countries of the EC' and 'Share the chocolate between all of you'. However, **among** is still used only to describe more than two things.

amoral and **immoral** are not interchangeable. **Amoral** means 'lacking moral standards, devoid of moral sense', indicating that the person so described has no concern with morals, as in 'The child was completely amoral and did not know the difference between right and wrong'. **Immoral** means 'against or breaking moral standards, bad'. 'He knows he's doing wrong but he goes on being completely immoral' and 'commit immoral acts'. Note the spelling of both words. **Amoral** has only one *m* but **immoral** has double *m*.

an *see* **a**.

anaesthetic and **analgesic** are liable to be confused. As an adjective, **anaesthetic** means 'producing a loss of feeling', as in 'inject the patient with an anaesthetic substance', and as a noun it means 'a substance that produces a loss of feeling', as in 'administer an anaesthetic to the patient on the operating table'. A local anaesthetic produces a loss of feeling in only part of the body, as in 'remove the rotten tooth under local anaesthetic'. A **general anaesthetic** produces loss of feeling in the whole body and induces unconsciousness, as in 'The operation on his leg will have to be performed under general anaesthetic'. As an adjective **analgesic** means 'producing a lack of or reduction in, sensitivity to pain, pain-killing', as in 'aspirin has an analgesic effect'. As a noun **analgesic** means 'a substance that produces a lack of, or reduction in, sensitivity to pain', as in 'aspirin, paracetamol, and other analgesics'.

analyse is frequently misspelt. Note that it is not one of those verbs that can end in *-ize*. However, in American English 'analyze' is the accepted spelling.

annex and **annexe** are not interchangeable. Annex is a verb meaning 'to take possession of', as in 'The enemy invaders annexed the country' or 'to add or attach', as in 'She annexed a note to the document'. **Annexe** is a noun meaning 'a building added to, or used as an addition to, another building', as in 'build an annexe to the house as a workshop' and 'some school classes taking place in an annexe'.

antihistamine is sometimes misspelt. Note the *i*, not *y*, after *h*. **Antihistamine** is used to treat allergies.

apostrophe is a form of punctuation that is mainly used to indicate possession. Many spelling errors centre on the position of the apostrophe in relation to *s*.

Possessive nouns are usually formed by adding 's to the singular noun, as in 'the girl's mother', and Peter's car'; by adding an apostrophe to plural nouns that end in *s*, as in 'all the teachers' cars'; by adding 's to irregular plural nouns that do not end in *s*, as in 'women's shoes'.

In the possessive form of a name or singular noun that ends in *s*, *x* or *z*, the apostrophe may or may not be followed by *s*. In words of one syllable the final *s* is usually added, as in 'James's house', 'the fox's lair', 'Roz's dress'. The final *s* is most frequently omitted in names, particularly in names of three or more syllables, as in 'Euripides' plays'. In many cases the presence or absence of final *s* is a matter of convention.

The apostrophe is also used to indicate omitted letters in contracted forms of words, as in 'can't' and 'you've'. They are sometimes used to indicate missing century numbers in dates, as in 'the '60s and '70s', but are not used at the end of decades, etc, as in '1960s', not '1960's'.

Generally apostrophes are no longer used to indicate omitted letters in shortened forms that are in common use, as in 'phone' and 'flu'.

Apostrophes are often omitted wrongly in modern usage, particularly in the media and by advertisers, as in 'womens hairdressers', 'childrens helpings'. In addition, apostrophes are frequently added erroneously (as in 'potato's for sale' and 'Beware of the dog's'). This is partly because people are unsure about when and when not to use them and partly because of a modern tendency to punctuate as little as possible.

appal is very frequently misspelt. Note the double *p* and single *l*. Note also the double *ll* in **appalled** and **appalling**.

arbiter and **arbitrator**, although similar in meaning, are not totally interchangeable. **Arbiter** means 'a person who has absolute power to judge or make decisions', as in 'Parisian designers used to be total arbiters of fashion'. **Arbitrator** is 'a person appointed to settle differences in a dispute', as in 'act as arbitrator between management and workers in the wages dispute'. **Arbiter** is occasionally used with the latter meaning also.

archaeology is liable to be misspelt. Note the order of the three vowels in the middle—*aeo*.

artist and **artiste** are liable to be confused. **Artist** refers to 'a person who paints or draws,' as in 'Renoir was a great artist'. The word may also refer to 'a person who is skilled in something', as in 'The mechanic is a real artist with an engine'. **Artiste** refers to 'an entertainer, such as a singer or a dancer', as in 'a list of the artistes in the musical performances'. The word is becoming a little old-fashioned.

asphyxiate is frequently misspelt. Note that it has *y*, not *i*, before *x*. It means 'to suffocate', as in 'asphyxiate his victim with a pillow'.

assassinate is frequently misspelt. Note the two sets of double *s*. It means 'to murder, especially someone of political importance', as in 'Rebels assassinated the president'. Note also the spelling of **assassin**, 'a person who assassinates someone'.

asthma is frequently misspelt. Note the *th*, which is frequently wrongly omitted. The word refers to 'a chronic breathing disorder'.

atheist *see* **agnostic**.

at this moment in time is an overused phrase meaning simply 'now'. In modern usage there is a tendency to use what are thought to be grander-sounding alternatives for simple words. It is best to avoid such overworked phrases and use the simpler form.

au fait is French in origin but it is commonly used in English to mean 'familiar with' or 'informed about', as in 'not completely au fait with the new office system'. It is pronounced *o fay*.

aural and **oral** are liable to be confused because they sound similar and are both related to parts of the body. **Aural** means 'of the ear' or 'referring to the sense of hearing', as in 'aural faculties affected by the explosion' and 'The children were given an aural comprehension test (that is, one that one was read out to them) in French'. **Oral** means 'of the mouth' or 'referring to speech', as in 'oral hygiene' and 'an oral examination' (that is, one in which questions and answers are spoken, not written).

aurally challenged means 'deaf' or 'hard of hearing'. It is part of the 'politically correct' movement to make a personal problem or disadvantage appear in a positive rather than a negative light. Although the intention behind it is a good one, the phrase, and others like it, have not really caught on, and such phrases are indeed subject to ridicule because they sound rather highflown.

authoress is not used in modern usage since it is considered sexist. **Author** is regarded as a neutral term to describe both male and female authors.

averse *see* **adverse**.

avoid *see* **evade**.

avoidance *see* **evasion**.

B

bachelor is frequently misspelt, it being common, and wrong, to include a *t* before the *c*. Note that the term **bachelor girl** is objected to by many women for the same reason that they object to adding *-ess* to the masculine to make a feminine form, as in 'authoress'.

backward and **backwards** in British English are respectively adjective and adverb. Examples of **backward** include 'take a backward step' and 'The child is rather backward for his age'. Examples of **backwards** include 'take a step backwards'. In American English **backward** is frequently used as a adverb.

bacteria is a plural noun, the singular form being **bacterium**, which is found mainly in scientific or medical texts. Thus it is correct to say 'a stomach infection caused by bacteria in the water' but quite wrong to say 'an infection caused by a bacteria'.

bail and **bale** are liable to be confused. **Bail** as a noun means 'the security money deposited as a guarantee that an arrested person will appear in court', as in 'Her family provided money for her bail' and 'Her brother stood bail for her.' It also has a verb form, as in 'His friends did not have enough money to bail him'. This verb often takes the form **bail out**. **Bale** is a noun meaning 'a bundle', as in 'a bundle of hay'.

    Bail and **bale** are both acceptable forms of the verb meaning 'to scoop', as in 'The fishermen had to bail/bale water out of the bottom of the boat'. Similarly, both forms of the verb are acceptable when they mean 'to make an emergency parachute jump from a plane', as in 'The plane caught fire and the pilot had to bail/bale out'.

baited *see* **bated**.

bale *see* **bail**.

balk and **baulk** are both acceptable spellings of the verb meaning 'to refuse or be reluctant to do something', as in 'She balked/baulked at paying such a high price for a dress' and 'to obstruct or prevent', as in 'She was balked/baulked in her attempt at swimming the Channel by bad weather'.

banal is frequently mispronounced. It should rhyme with 'canal', with the emphasis on the second syllable (ba-*nal*).

banister, meaning 'the handrail supported by posts fixed at the side of a staircase', may be spelt **bannister** but it is a less common form.

barmaid is disliked by many people on the grounds that it sounds a belittling term and is thus sexist. It is also disliked by people who are interested in political correctness. However the word continues to be quite common, along with **barman**, and efforts to insist on **bar assistant** or **barperson** have not yet succeeded.

basis, meaning 'something on which something is founded', as in 'The cost of the project was the basis of his argument against it', has the plural form **bases** although it is not commonly used. It would be more usual to say 'arguments without a firm basis' than 'arguments without firm bases'.

basically means literally 'referring to a base or basis, fundamentally', as in 'The scientist's theory is basically unsound', but it is frequently used almost meaninglessly as a fill-up word at the beginning of a sentence, as in 'Basically he just wants more money'. Overuse of this word should be avoided.

bated, as in 'with bated breath' meaning 'tense and anxious with excitement', is frequently misspelt **baited**. Care should be taken not to confuse the two words.

bath and **bathe** are not interchangeable. **Bath** as a verb means 'to have a bath', as in 'He baths every morning' or 'to wash someone in a bath', as in 'The mother bathed the baby in a small tin bath'. **Bathe**, on the other hand, is used to mean 'to wash (a wound, etc)', as in 'She bathed the boy's grazed knee with warm water' or 'to swim in the sea', as in 'too cold to bathe today'. In American English **bathe** is used in the sense of 'have a bath', as in 'prefer to bathe than take a shower'.

bathroom *see* **toilet**.

baulk *see* **balk**.

BC *see* **AD**.

beat and **beaten** are frequently used wrongly. **Beat** is the past tense of the verb 'to beat', as in 'Our team beat the opposition easily' and 'His father used to beat him when he was a child'. **Beaten** is the past participle of the verb 'to beat', as in 'We should have beaten them easily' and 'He thought the child should have been beaten for his bad behaviour'.

beautiful is frequently misspelt. Note the order of the vowels (*eau*). Note also the single *l*.

because means 'for the reason that', as in 'He left because he was bored', and is sometimes misused. It is wrong to use it in a sentence that also contains 'the reason that', as in 'The reason she doesn't say much is that she is shy'. The correct form of this is 'She doesn't say much because she is shy' or 'The reason she doesn't say much is that she is shy'.

because of *see* **due to**.

beg the question is often used wrongly. It means 'to take for granted the very point that has to be proved', as in 'To say that God must exist because we can see all his wonderful creations in the world around us begs the question'. The statement assumes that these creations have been made by God although this has not been proved and yet this fact is being used as evidence that there is a God. **Beg the question** is often used wrongly to mean 'to evade the question', as in 'The police tried to get him to say where he had been but he begged the question and changed the subject'.

beige, meaning 'a pale brown colour', is frequently misspelt. Note the order of *e* and *i*. The pronunciation of the word may also cause difficulties. It is pronounced *bayzh*.

947

benefit causes problems with the parts of the verb. The past tense is **benefited**, as in 'They benefited from having had an excellent education'. The present participle is **benefiting**, as in 'Benefiting from the will of their late uncle they were able to buy a bigger house'. Note the single *t*.

benign means 'kindly, well-disposed' when applied to people, as in 'fortunate enough to have a benign ruler'. This meaning may also be used of things, as in 'give a benign smile' and 'live in a benign climate'. As a medical term **benign** means 'nonmalignant, non-cancerous'. **Innocent** is another word for **benign** in this sense.

beside and **besides** are not interchangeable. **Beside** is a preposition meaning 'by the side of', as in 'The little girl wants to sit beside her friend' and 'They walked beside each other all the way'. **Beside** is also found in the phrase **'beside oneself'**, meaning 'extremely agitated', as in 'The children were beside themselves with excitement waiting to go on a picnic' and 'He was beside himself with rage when his rival won the prize'.

Besides has several meanings. It means 'moreover, in addition', as in 'The house is overpriced. Besides, it's too far from the village'. It also means 'as well as, in addition to', as in 'We have visited many countries besides France', and 'other than, except for', as in 'They are interested in nothing besides work' and 'I have told no one besides you'.

bet is the common form of the past tense and past participle of the verb 'to bet', as in 'He bet me he could run faster than me' and 'He would have bet hundreds of pounds that the horse he fancied would win'. 'Placed a bet' is an alternative form, as in 'He has never placed a bet in his life' as an alternative to 'He has never bet in his life'. The form **betted** exists but it is rare.

bête noire refers to 'something that one detests or fears', as in 'Loud pop music is her father's bête noire, although she sings with a pop group'. Note the spelling, particularly the accent (circumflex) on **bête** and the *e* at the end of **noire**. The phrase is French in origin and the plural form is **bêtes noires**, as in 'A bearded man is one of her many bêtes noires'.

betted *see* **bet**.

better should be preceded by 'had' when it means 'ought to' or 'should', as in 'You had better leave now if you want to arrive there by nightfall' and 'We had better apologize for upsetting her'. In informal contexts, especially in informal speech as in 'Hey Joe, Mum says you better come now', the 'had' is often omitted but it should be retained in formal contexts. The negative form is 'had better not', as in 'He had better not try to deceive her'.

between *see* **among**.

between is often found in the phrase 'between you and me' as in 'Between you and me I think he stole the money'. Note that 'me' is correct and that 'I' is wrong. This is because prepositions like 'between' are followed by an object, not a subject. 'I' acts as the subject of a sentence, as in 'I know her', and 'me' as the object, as in 'She knows me'.

bi- Of the words beginning with the prefix bi-, biannual and biennial are liable to be confused. **Biannual** means 'twice a year' and **biennial** means 'every two years'.

Bicentenary and **bicentennial** both mean 'a 200th anniversary', as in 'celebrating the bicentenary/bicentennial of the firm'. **Bicentenary** is, however, the more common expression in British English, although

bicentennial is more common in American English.

Biweekly is a confusing word as it has two different meanings. It means both 'twice a week' and 'once every two weeks'. Thus there is no means of knowing without other information whether 'a bi-weekly publication' comes out once a week or every two weeks. The confusion arises because the prefix 'bi-', which means 'two', can refer both to doubling, as in 'bicycle', and halving, as in 'bisection'.

biannual *see* **bi-**.

bias should become **biased** and **biasing** in the past tense and past participle, and the present participle, respectively, as in 'The behaviour of some of the competitors biased the judges against them' and in 'The behaviour of some of the competitors seem to be biasing the judges against them.'. However in modern usage **biassed** and **biassing** respectively are acceptable alternative spellings.

bicentenary and **bicentennial** *see* **bi-**.

biennial *see* **bi-**.

billion traditionally meant 'one million million' in British English, but in modern usage it has increasingly taken on the American English meaning of 'one thousand million'. When the number of million pounds, etc, is specified, the number immediately precedes the word 'million' without the word 'of', as in 'The firm is worth five billion dollars', but if no number is present then 'of' precedes 'dollars, etc', ' as in 'The research project cost the country millions of dollars'. The word **billion** may also be used loosely to mean 'a great but unspecified number', as in 'Billions of people in the world live in poverty'.

birth name is a suggested alternative for **maiden name**, a woman's surname before she married and took the name of her husband. **Maiden name** is considered by some to be inappropriate since maiden in one of its senses is another name for 'virgin' and it is now not at all usual for women to be virgins when they marry. Another possible name alternative is **family name.**

biweekly *see* **bi-**.

bizarre, meaning 'odd, weird', is frequently misspelt. Note the single *z* and double *r*.

black is the word now usually applied to dark-skinned people of Afro-Caribbean origins and is the term preferred by most black-skinned people themselves. **Coloured** is considered by many to be offensive since it groups all non-Caucasians together. In America, African-American is becoming increasingly common as a substitute for **black**.

blackguard, meaning 'a wicked or dishonourable person, a scoundrel', has an unusual pronunciation. It is pronounced *blagg*-ard.

blind is objected to by those concerned with 'political correctness' on the grounds that it concentrates on the negative aspect of being without sight. They suggest 'optically challenged' although this has not become widely used.

bloc and **block** are liable to be confused. **Bloc** refers to 'a group of people, parties or countries that get together for a particular purpose, often a political one', as in 'Those countries were formerly members of the communist bloc'. **Block** has a wide range of meanings, as in 'a block of wood', 'a block of cheese', 'an office block', 'a road block'.

blond and **blonde** are both used to mean 'a fair-haired person', but they are not interchangeable. **Blond** is used to describe a man or boy, **blonde** is used to describe a woman or girl. They are derived from the French adjective, which changes endings according to the gender of the noun.

boat and **ship** are often used interchangeably, but usually **boat** refers to a smaller vessel than a ship.

bona fide is an expression of Latin origin meaning literally 'of good faith'. It means 'genuine, sincere' or 'authentic', as in 'a bona fide member of the group', 'a bona fide excuse for not going', or 'a bona fide agreement'.

born-again was originally applied to an evangelical Christian who had been converted. Although this use still exists, the meaning has extended to refer to a conversion to a belief or cause, especially when this is extremely enthusiastic and fervent, as in 'a born-again nonsmoker', 'a born-again conservationist'.

bottom line is an expression from accountancy that has become commonly used in the general language. In accountancy it refers to the final line of a set of company accounts, which indicates whether the company has made a profit or a loss, obviously a very important line. In general English, **bottom line** has a range of meanings, from 'the final outcome or result', as in 'The bottom line of their discussion was that they decided to sell the company', through 'the most important point of something', as in 'The bottom line was whether they could get there on time or not', to 'the last straw', as in 'His affair with another woman was the bottom line of their stormy relationship and she left him'.

bouquet is frequently misspelt and mispronounced. Note the *ou* and *qu* in the spelling. It is pronounced boo-*kay*.

bourgeois, a word meaning middle-class that is usually derogatory, is frequently misspelt. Note the *our* in the first syllable and the *e* before the *ois*.

boycott, meaning 'to refuse to having anything to do with', is frequently misspelt. Note the double *t* at the end of the word.

brackets may be used to enclose any material of a supplementary or explanatory nature that interrupts the flow of a sentence. The material inside the brackets may be removed without altering the central meaning of the sentence. Commas or dashes may be used to serve the same purpose, when the interruption to the flow of the sentence is not quite so marked. Round brackets are more commonly used than square brackets. Examples of brackets include 'Pablo Picasso (1881-1973) was a famous artist'; 'There are a great many people with her family name (Brown) listed in the tel-

ephone directory'; 'He has a yucca (a kind of plant) in his study'. **Brackets** are also known as **parentheses** (singular **parenthesis**).

breach and **breech** are liable to be confused. **Breach** means 'a break or gap', as in 'cows getting through a breach in the fence', and 'the breaking or violation of', as in 'commit a breach of the peace', 'a breach of the local bye-laws'. **Breech**, on the other hand, means 'the rear part of the body' as in 'It was a breech delivery (i.e. the baby was delivered bottom first)', or 'the part of a gun behind the barrel', as in 'a breech-loading gun'.

broach and **brooch** are liable to be confused. They are pronounced alike but have different meanings. **Broach** is a verb meaning either to 'introduce or mention (a subject)', as in 'She did not like to broach the subject of money at the interview', or 'to open (a bottle)', as in 'broach a bottle of champagne to celebrate the baby's birth'. **Brooch** is a noun that means 'a piece of jewellery that one pins on a blouse, sweater, etc.'

brochure is usually pronounced *bro*-sher, despite the *ch* spelling, rather than bro-*shoor*, which is French-sounding. The word is French in origin.

brooch *see* **broach**.

buffet has two different pronunciations according to sense. In the sense of 'a counter or sideboard from which food is served' and 'self-service food set out on tables', as in 'They are having a buffet rather than a sit-down meal at the wedding', **buffet** is pronounced *boo*-fay. **Buffet** also has the meaning of 'to strike', as in 'ships buffeted by the wind', and 'a blow', as in 'give the boy a buffet across the ear', when it is pronounced buf-fet.

buoyant, meaning either 'able to float', as in 'Rubber is a buoyant substance', or 'cheerful', as in 'in buoyant mood', is frequently misspelt. The most common error is to put the *u* and *o* in the wrong order.

bureaucracy is frequently misspelt. Note the *eau* combination and the *c*, not *s*, before *y*.

burned and **burnt** may be used interchangeably as the past tense and the past participle of the verb 'to burn', as in 'They burned/burnt the rubbish in the back garden' and 'She has burned/burnt her arm on the stove'.

business is frequently misspelt. The most common error is to omit letter *i* since it is not pronounced.

bus was originally an abbreviation for omnibus but it is no longer spelt with an apostrophe before it. Thus **bus**, not **'bus**. The plural is **buses**.

bylaw and **bye-law** are both acceptable spellings. The word means a law or rule applying to a local area.

C

caffeine, a stimulant found in coffee and tea, is frequently misspelt. Note the double *f* and the *ei* combination. Note also the pronunciation (*kaf*-feen).

calendar, calender and colander: calendar is often misspelt as calender, which is the name of 'a machine used to smooth paper or cloth', or as calander, simply an erroneous spelling. Calendar is also sometimes confused with colander, a perforated bowl used for straining.

can and may both mean in one of their senses 'to be permitted'. In this sense can is much less formal than may and is best restricted to informal contexts, as in '"Can I go to the park now?" asked the child'. May is used in more formal contexts, as in 'May I please have your name?' Both can and may have other meanings. Can has the meaning 'to be able', as in 'They thought his legs were permanently damaged but he can still walk'. May has the additional meaning 'to be likely', as in 'You may well be right'.

The past tense of can is could, as in 'The children asked if they could (= be permitted to) go to the park'. 'The old man could (= be unable to) not walk upstairs'. The past tense of may is might, as in 'The child asked if he might have a piece of cake (= be permitted to)'. 'They might (= be likely to) well get here tonight'.

cannon and canon are liable to be confused although they mean completely different things. Cannon means 'a large gun', as in 'large cannons placed on the castle ramparts', or 'a kind of shot in billiards', as in 'His opponent won the match with a superb cannon'. Canon refers to 'a ruling, particularly one laid down by the church', as in 'accused of breaking the canons of his church' and 'refuse to obey the traditional moral canons', or to 'a title given to some clergymen' as in 'one of the cathedral canons'.

cannot, can not, and can't all mean the same thing but they are used in different contexts. Cannot is the most usual form, as in 'The children have been told that they cannot go' and 'We cannot get there by public transport'. Cannot is written as two words only for emphasis, as in 'No, you can not have any more' and 'The invalid certainly can not walk to the ambulance'. Can't is used in less formal contexts and often in speech, as in 'I can't be bothered going out' and 'They can't bear to be apart'.

canvas and canvass are liable to be confused. Canvas is 'a type of heavy cloth', as in 'tents made of canvas', 'trousers made of canvas', and 'paint on canvas'. Canvass is a verb meaning 'to solicit votes, orders, etc, from', as in 'members of various political parties canvassing people in the high street' and 'encyclopedia salesmen canvassing our neighbours', and also meaning 'to find out how people are going to vote in an election, etc', as in 'Party workers canvassed our street the night before the election'. Canvass may also be a noun, as in 'an eve-of-election canvass'.

capital letters are used in a number of different situations. The first word of a sentence or a direct quotation begins with a capital letter, as in 'They left early', 'Why have they gone?' and 'He said weakly, "I don't feel very well"'.

The first letter of a name or proper noun is always a capital letter, as in 'Mary Brown', 'John Smith', 'South America', 'Rome', 'speak Italian', 'Buddhism', 'Marxism'. Capital letters are also used in the titles of people, places or works of art, as in 'Uncle Fred', 'Professor Jones', 'Ely Cathedral', 'Edinburgh University', 'reading *Wuthering Heights*', 'watching *Guys and Dolls*', 'listen to Beethoven's Third Symphony' and 'a copy of *The Potato Eaters* by van Gogh'. They are also used in the titles of wars and historical, cultural and geological periods, as in 'the Wars of the Roses', 'the Renaissance', 'the Ice Age'.

Note that only the major words of titles, etc, are in capital letters, words, such as 'the', 'on', 'of', etc, being in lower-case letters.

A capital letter is used as the first letter of days of the week, months of the year, and religious festivals, as in 'Monday', 'October', 'Easter', 'Yom Kippur'. It is a matter of choice whether the seasons of the year are given capital letters or not, as in 'spring/Spring', 'autumn/Autumn'.

Apart from 'I', pronouns are lower-case except when they refer to God or Christ, when some people capitalize them, as in 'God asks us to trust in Him'.

Trade names should be spelt with an initial capital letter, as in 'Filofax', 'Jacuzzi', 'Xerox', 'Biro', 'Hoover'. When verbs are formed from these, they are spelt with an initial lower-case letter, as 'xerox the letter', 'hoover the carpet'.

carburettor is frequently misspelt. Note the single *r* and double *t*.

carcass and carcase are both acceptable spellings for the word for the body of a dead animal. The dead body of a human is called a corpse.

cardinal and ordinal numbers refer to different aspects of numbers. Cardinal is applied to those numbers that refer to quantity or value without referring to their place in the set, as in 'one', 'two', 'fifty' 'one hundred'. Ordinal is applied to numbers that refer to their order in a series, as in 'first', 'second', 'fortieth', 'hundredth'.

cardigan, jersey, jumper and sweater all refer to knitted garments for the top part of the body. Cardigan refers to a jacket-like garment with buttons down the front. Jersey, jumper and sweater refer to a knitted garment pulled over the head to get it on and off.

carer has recently taken on the meaning of 'a person who looks after a sick, handicapped or old relative or friend', as in 'carers requiring a break from their responsibilities'.

caring has recently been used to apply to professions

such as social workers, nurses and doctors, and others who are professionally involved in the welfare of people, as in 'the members of the caring professions'.

carpet and **rug** both refer to forms of floor covering. Generally a rug is smaller than a carpet, and the fitted variety of fabric floor covering is always known as carpet.

caster and **castor** are mainly interchangeable. Both forms can be applied to 'a swivelling wheel attached to the base of a piece of furniture to enable it to be moved easily' and 'a container with a perforated top from which sugar is sprinkled'. The kind of sugar known as **caster** can also be called **castor**, although this is less usual. The lubricating or medicinal oil known as **castor oil** is never spelt **caster**.

catarrh is frequently misspelt. Note the single *t*, double *r*, and *h*.

Catholic and **catholic** have different meanings. **Catholic** as an adjective refers to the Roman Catholic Church, as in 'The Pope is head of the Catholic Church', or to the universal body of Christians. As a noun it means 'a member of the Catholic Church', as in 'She is a Catholic but he is a Protestant'. Catholic with a lower-case initial letter means 'general, wide-ranging', as in 'a catholic selection of essays', and ' broad-minded, liberal', as in 'a catholic attitude to the tastes of others'.

ceiling is frequently misspelt. Note the *e* before *i*. As well as its literal use, **ceiling** is used to mean 'upper limit', as in 'impose a ceiling on rent increases'.

celibate means 'unmarried' or 'remaining unmarried and chaste, especially for religious reasons', as in 'Roman Catholic priests have to be celibate'. In modern usage, because of its connection with chastity, **celibate** has come to mean 'abstaining from sexual intercourse', as in 'The threat of Aids has made many people celibate'. The word is frequently misspelt. Note the *i* after *l*.

Celsius, centigrade and **Fahrenheit** are all scales of temperature. **Celsius** and **centigrade** mean the same and refer to a scale on which water freezes at O° and boils at 100°. This scale is now the principal unit of temperature. **Celsius** is now the more acceptable term. **Fahrenheit** refers to a scale on which water freezes at 32° and boils at 212°. It is still used, informally at least, of the weather, and statements such as 'The temperature reached the nineties today' are still common.

Note the initial capital letters in **Celsius** and **Fahrenheit**. This is because they are named after people, namely the scientists who devised them.

Celtic is usually pronounced kel-tik. It refers to the 'language, people or culture of Scotland, Ireland, Wales and Brittany', as in 'try to preserve the Celtic tradition'.

censor, censure and **censer** are liable to be confused. **Censor** means 'to examine letters, publications, etc, and remove anything whose inclusion is against official policy, or is obscene or libellous', as in 'In wartime, soldiers' letters were often censored in case the enemy got hold of useful information' and in 'Parts of the film had to be censored in order to make it suitable for children'. **Censure** means 'to blame or criticize severely', as in 'The police were censured by the press for not catching the murderer of the child' and in 'The pupils were censured by the headmaster for bullying younger children'. **Censure** may also be a noun, as in 'They encountered strong censure from their neighbours for reprimanding the children'. The spelling of **censor** is often confused with that of **censer**, 'a vessel used for burning incense'.

centenary and **centennial** are both used to refer to a 'one-hundredth anniversary'. **Centenary** is the more common term in British English, as in 'celebrate the town's centenary', whereas **centennial** is more common in American English. **Centennial** may be used as an adjective, as in 'organize the town's centennial celebrations'.

centigrade *see* **Celsius**.

centre and **middle** mean much the same, but **centre** is used more precisely than **middle** in some cases, as in 'a line through the centre of the circle' and 'She felt faint in the middle of the crowd'.

centre on and **centre around** are often used interchangeably, as in 'Her world centres on/around her children'. **Centre around** is objected to by some people on the grounds that **centre** is too specific to be used with something as vague as **around**. When it is used as a verb with place names, **centre** is used with 'at', as in 'Their business operation is centred at London'.

centuries are calculated from 1001, 1501, 1901, etc, not 1000, 1500, 1900, etc. This is because the years are counted from AD 1, there being no year 0.

cervical has two possible pronunciations. Both ser-vik-al, with the emphasis on the first syllable, and ser-*vik*-al, with the emphasis on the second syllable which has the same sound as in Viking. The word means 'referring to the neck or the constricted part of an organ', e.g. of the uterus, as in 'cervical cancer'.

chair is often used to mean 'a person in charge of a meeting, committee, etc', as in 'The committee has a new chair this year'. Formerly **chairman** was always used in this context, as in 'He was appointed chairman of the fund-raising committee' but this is disapproved of on the grounds that it is sexist. Formerly, **chairman** was sometimes used even if the person in charge of the meeting or committee was a woman, and sometimes **chairwoman** was used in this situation. **Chairperson**, which also avoids sexism, is frequently used instead of **chair**. **Chair** is also a verb meaning 'to be in charge of a meeting, committee, etc'.

-challenged is a modern suffix that is very much part of politically correct language. It is used to convey a disadvantage, problem or disorder in a more positive light. For example, 'visually challenged' is used in politically correct language instead of 'blind' or 'partially sighted', and 'aurally challenged' is used instead of 'deaf' or 'hard of hearing'. **-Challenged** is often used in humorous coinages, as in 'financially challenged', meaning 'penniless', and 'intellectually challenged', meaning 'stupid'.

chamois is frequently both misspelt and mispronounced. In the sense of 'a kind of cloth (made from the skin of the chamois antelope) used for polishing or cleaning' it is pronounced *sham*-mi. In the sense of 'a kind of antelope', it is pronounced *sham*-wa.

changeable is frequently spelt wrongly. Note the *e* after the *g*.

chaperon and **chaperone** are both acceptable spellings. The word means 'an older woman who accompanies or supervises a young unmarried woman on social occasions', as in 'in Victorian times young unmarried women did not go out with young men without a chaperon/chaperone'. The word may also be a verb, as in 'She was asked to chaperon/chaperone her niece to the ball'.

charisma was formerly a theological word used to

mean 'a spiritual gift', such as the gift of healing, etc. In modern usage it is used to describe 'a special quality or power that influences, inspires or stimulates other people, personal magnetism', as in 'The president was elected because of his charisma'. The adjective from **charisma** is **charismatic**, as in 'his charismatic style of leadership'.

charted and **chartered** are liable to be confused. **Charted** is formed from the verb 'to chart', meaning 'to make a chart or map of', as in 'few charted areas of the continent'. It is more common in the negative, as in 'uncharted areas of the interior of the country'. **Chartered** has two meanings. One is formed from the verb 'to charter', meaning 'to hire', as in 'a chartered yacht'. The other is usually found in such phrases as 'chartered accountant/surveyor/engineer, etc', and means 'an accountant, etc, who has passed the examinations of the Institute of Chartered Accountants, etc'. The institutes in question have received a royal charter or 'document granting certain official rights or privileges'.

chauvinism originally meant 'excessive patriotism', being derived from the name of Nicolas Chauvin, a soldier in the army of Napoleon Bonaparte, who was noted for his excessive patriotism. In modern usage **chauvinism** has come to mean 'excessive enthusiasm or devotion to a cause' or, more particularly, 'an irrational and prejudiced belief in the superiority of one's own cause'. When preceded by 'male', it refers specifically to attitudes and actions that assume the superiority of the male sex and thus the inferiority of women, as in 'accused of not giving her the job because of male chauvinism'. **Chauvinism** is frequently used to mean **male chauvinism**, as in 'He shows his chauvinism towards his female staff by never giving any of them senior jobs'. The adjective formed from **chauvinism** is **chauvinistic**.

check and **cheque** are liable to be confused. **Check** as a verb means 'to make sure that something is in order', as in 'check the tread of the tyres', or 'to make sure', as in 'check you locked the windows', or 'to slow down, stop or control', as 'check the growth of drug-related offences'. As a noun **check** means 'an examination to make sure that something is in order, as in 'conduct checks on all tyre treads', or 'a slowing-down or stopping', as in 'ordering a check on public expenditure', or 'a curb, restraint or check', as in 'His common sense acted as a check on their extravagance'. **Cheque** means 'a money order', as in 'pay his bill by cheque'. In American English **check** is used for 'money order' as well as the other meanings.

chemist and **pharmacist** have the same meaning in one sense of **chemist** only. **Chemist** and **pharmacist** are both words for 'one who prepares drugs ordered by medical prescription'. **Chemist** has the additional meaning of 'a scientist who works in the field of chemistry', as in 'He works as an industrial chemist'.

cheque *see* **check**.

chilblain is frequently misspelt. Note the single *l*.

childish and **childlike** both refer to someone being like a child but they are used in completely different contexts. **Childish** is used in a derogatory way about someone to indicate that he or she is acting like a child in an immature way, as in 'Even though she is 20 years old she has childish tantrums when she does not get her own way' and 'childish handwriting for an adult'. **Childlike** is a term of approval or a complimentary

term used to describe something that has some of the attractive qualities of childhood, as in 'She has a child-like enthusiasm for picnics' and 'He has a childlike trust in others'.

chiropodist, meaning 'a person who treats minor disorders of the feet, is usually pronounced kir-*op*-od-ist with an initial *k* sound, but the pronunciation shir-*op*-od-ist with an initial *sh* sound is also possible.

chord and **cord** are liable to be confused because they sound alike. The spelling **chord** is used in the musical sense, as in 'play the wrong chord', and in the mathematical sense, as in 'draw a chord joining the points on the circumference of a circle'. The spelling **cord** is used to mean 'a kind of string', as in 'tie up the bundle with cord' and 'use a piece of nylon cord as a washing line'. Cord is also used with reference to certain parts of the body, as in 'spinal cord', 'vocal cords', umbilical cord'.

Christian name is used to mean someone's first name as opposed to someone's **surname**. It is increasingly being replaced by **first name** or **forename** since Britain has become a multicultural society where there are several religions as well as Christianity.

chronic *see* **acute**.

cirrhosis is liable to be misspelt. Note the *rrh* combination. The word refers to 'a disease of the liver'.

city and **town** in modern usage are usually distinguished on grounds of size and status, a city being larger and more important than a town. Originally in Britain a **city** was a town which had special rights conferred on it by royal charter and which usually had a cathedral.

clandestine, meaning 'secret or furtive', usually has the emphasis on the second syllable, as klan-*des*-tin', but it is acceptable to pronounce it with the emphasis on the first syllable, as *klan*-des-tin.

classism means 'discrimination on the grounds of class, snobbism', as in 'Not letting her children play with the children of her housekeeper was classism'. **Classist** refers to 'a person who practises classism, a snob', as in 'She's such a classist that she is always rude to shop assistants'.

claustrophobia, fear of confined spaces, is frequently misspelt. Note the *au* and the *o* before *p*.

clean and **cleanse** as verbs both mean 'to clean', as in 'clean the house' and 'cleanse the wound'. However, **cleanse** tends to indicate a more thorough cleaning than **clean** and sometimes carries the suggestion of 'to purify', as in 'prayer cleansing the soul'.

cliché is 'a phrase that has been used so often that it has become stale'. Some examples include 'unused to public speaking as I am', 'time heals everything', 'a blessing in disguise', 'keep a low profile', 'conspicuous by their absence', 'part and parcel', 'at death's door'. Sometimes the phrase in question was quite apt when first used but overuse has made it trite and frequently almost meaningless.

client and **customer**, although closely related in meaning, are not interchangeable. **Client** refers to 'a person who pays for the advice or services of a professional person', as in 'They are both clients of the same lawyer', 'a client waiting to see the bank manager' and 'hairdressers who keep their clients waiting'. **Customer** refers to 'a person who purchases goods from a shop, etc', as in 'customers complaining to shopkeepers about faulty goods' and 'a regular customer at the local supermarket'. **Client** is used in the sense of 'customer' by shops who regard it as a more superior word, as in ' clients of an exclusive dress boutique'.

clientele, meaning a group of clients, is frequently both mispronounced and misspelt. It is pronounced klee-on-*tel*. Note the *le*, not double *ll*.

climate no longer refers just to weather, as in 'go to live in a hot climate', 'Britain has a temperate climate'. It has extended its meaning to refer to 'atmosphere', as in 'live in a climate of despair' and to 'the present situation', as in 'businessmen nervous about the financial climate'.

clone originally was a technical word meaning 'one of a group of offspring that are asexually produced and which are genetically identical to the parent and to other members of the group'. In modern usage **clone** is frequently used loosely to mean 'something that is very similar to something else', as in 'In the sixties there were many Beatles' clones', and 'grey-suited businessmen looking like clones of each other'.

collaborate and **cooperate** are not interchangeable in all contexts. They both mean 'to work together for a common purpose', as in 'The two scientists are collaborating/cooperating on cancer research' and 'The rival building firms are collaborating/cooperating on the new shopping complex'. When the work concerned is of an artistic or creative nature **collaborate** is the more commonly used word, as in 'The two directors are collaborating on the film' and 'The composers collaborated on the theme music'. **Collaborate** also has the meaning of 'to work with an enemy, especially an enemy that is occupying one's country', as in 'a Frenchman who collaborated with the Germans when they installed a German government in France'.

coloured *see* **black**.

coloration, meaning 'arrangement or mode of colouring', as in 'the unusual coloration of the bird', is frequently misspelt. Unlike **colour**, it has no *u* before the *r*.

columnist, meaning 'a person who writes a column, or regular feature, in a newspaper or magazine', as in 'a columnist with the *New York Times*', is liable to be mispronounced. The *n* is pronounced, unlike in **column** where the *n* is silent.

commemorate means 'to remember, or mark the memory of, especially with some kind of ceremony', as in 'commemorate the soldiers who died in the war with an annual church service'. When applied to a plaque, piece of sculpture, etc, it means 'to serve as a memorial to', as in 'The statue in the village square commemorates those who gave their lives in World War II.

commence, begin, and **start** mean the same, but **commence** is used in a more formal context than the other two words, as in 'The legal proceedings will commence tomorrow' and 'The memorial service will commence with a hymn'. **Begin** and **start** are used less formally, as 'The match begins at 2 p.m.' and 'The film has already started'.

commensurate is followed by 'with' to form a phrase meaning 'proportionate to, appropriate to', as in 'a salary commensurate with her qualifications' and 'a price commensurate with the quality of the goods'.

commitment, meaning 'dedication or loyalty', as in 'his commitment to the socialist cause' and 'unable to make the commitment that marriage demands', is frequently misspelt. Note the double *m* but single *t*. Note that **committed** has double *t*.

committee is frequently misspelt. Note the double *m*,

double *t* and double *e*. It may be either a singular or plural noun, and so takes either a singular or plural verb, as in 'The committee meets tomorrow' and 'The committee have reached a decision'.

comparable is liable to be mispronounced. The emphasis should be on the first syllable, as in *kom-par-able*. It is often mispronounced with the emphasis on the second syllable.

comparatively means 'relatively, in comparison with a standard', as in 'The house was comparatively inexpensive for that area of the city' and 'In an area of extreme poverty they are comparatively well off'. In modern usage it is often used loosely to mean 'rather' or 'fairly' without any suggestion of reference to a standard, as in 'She has comparatively few friends' and 'It is a comparatively quiet resort'.

compare may take either the preposition 'to' or 'with'. 'To' is used when two things or people are being likened to each other or being declared similar, as in 'He compared her hair to silk' and 'He compared his wife to Helen of Troy'. 'With' is used when two things or people are being considered from the point of view of both similarities and differences, as in 'If you compare the new pupil's work with that of the present class you will find it brilliant', and 'If you compare the prices in the two stores you will find that the local one is the cheaper'. In modern usage the distinction is becoming blurred because the difference is rather subtle.

comparison is usually followed by the preposition 'with', as in 'In comparison with hers his work is brilliant'. However, when it means 'the action of likening something or someone to something or someone else', it is followed by 'to', as in 'the comparison of her beauty to that of Garbo'.

complacent and **complaisant** are liable to be confused because they are pronounced similarly, as kom-*play*-sint and kom-*play*-zint. However, they have slightly different meanings. **Complacent** means 'smug, self-satisfied', as in 'He knows that he has passed the exam and he is very complacent' and 'She gave a complacent smile when she realized that she had won'. **Complaisant** is rather a formal word meaning 'willing to go along with the wishes of others, acquiescent', as in "She will not raise any objections—she is so complaisant'. 'She indicated her agreement with a complaisant gesture'.

complement and **compliment** are liable to be confused since they sound alike. However, they have totally different meanings. **Complement** refers to 'something that makes something complete', as in 'The wine was the perfect complement to the meal' and 'Her hat and shoes were the ideal complement to her outfit'. It also refers to 'the complete number or quantity required or allowed', as in 'We have our full complement of staff' and 'a full complement of passengers'. When trying to distinguish between **complement** and **compliment** it is helpful to remember the connection between complement and complete since both have *ple* in the middle. **Compliment** is 'an expression of praise, admiration, approval, etc', as in 'pay her a compliment on her hair' and 'receive compliments on the high standard of their work'. **Complement** and **compliment** are also verbs, as in 'The wine complemented the meal very well' and 'He complimented her on her musical performance'.

complementary medicine is a term applied to the treatment of illness or disorders by techniques other than conventional medicine. These include homoeopathy, osteopathy, acupuncture, acupressure, iridology, etc. The word **complementary** suggests that the said techniques complement and work alongside conventional medical techniques. **Alternative medicine** means the same as **complementary medicine**, but the term suggests that they are used instead of the techniques of conventional medicine rather than alongside them.

complex in one of its senses is used rather loosely in modern usage. It refers technically to 'an abnormal state caused by unconscious repressed desires or past experiences', as in 'an inferiority complex'. In modern usage it is used loosely to describe 'any obsessive concern or fear', as in 'She has a complex about her weight', 'He has a complex about his poor background'. **Complex** is also used to refer to 'a group of connected or similar things'. It is now used mainly of a group of buildings or units connected in some way, as in 'a shopping complex' or 'a sports complex'.

Complex is also an adjective meaning 'complicated', as in 'His motives in carrying out the crime were complex' and 'The argument was too complex for most people to understand'.

compose, comprise and **constitute** are all similar in meaning but are used differently. **Compose** means 'to come together to make a whole, to make up'. It is most commonly found in the passive, as in 'The team was composed of young players' and 'The group was composed largely of elderly people'. It can be used in the active voice, as in 'the tribes which composed the nation' and 'the members which composed the committee', but this use is rarer. **Constitute** means the same as **compose** but it is usually used in the active voice, as in 'the foodstuffs that constitute a healthy diet' and 'the factors that constitute a healthy environment'. **Comprise** means 'to consist of, to be made up of', as in 'The firm comprises six departments' and 'The team comprises eleven players and two reserve players'. It is frequently used wrongly instead of **compose**, as in 'The team is comprised of eleven players' and instead of **constitute**, as in 'the players that comprise a team'.

compulsory and **compulsive** are liable to be confused. They are both adjectives derived from the verb 'to compel', meaning 'to force', but they are used differently. **Compulsory** means 'obligatory, required by a rule, law, etc', as in 'Foreign languages are not compulsory in that school' and 'It is compulsory to wear school uniform in some schools'. **Compulsive** means 'caused by an obsession or internal urge', as in 'a compulsive gambler' and 'a compulsive eater'. It is also used to mean 'fascinating' in some situations, as in 'A compulsive novel' and 'a compulsive TV series'.

concave and **convex** are liable to be confused. **Concave** means 'curved inwards', as in 'The inside of a spoon would be described as concave'. **Convex** means 'curved outwards, bulging', as in 'The outside or bottom of a spoon would be described as convex'.

conducive, meaning 'leading to, contributing to', is followed by the preposition 'to', as in 'conditions conducive to health growth'.

confidant and **confident** are liable to be confused. They sound alike but have different meanings. **Confidant** is rather a rare formal noun referring to 'a person in whom one confides', as in 'The king used two of his most trusted nobles as confidants'. It is derived from French and adds an *e* at the end if the person being confided in is female, as in 'ladies-in-waiting who were the queen's confidantes'. It has two possible pronunciations. The older pronunciation has the emphasis on the last syllable (kon-fi-*dant*). The more modern pronunciation has the emphasis on the first syllable (*kon*-fi-dant). **Confident** is a common adjective meaning 'self-assured, having confidence', as in 'She looks confident but she is rather an uncertain person', 'give a confident smile', and 'be confident that he will get the job'.

conform may be followed by the preposition 'to' or the preposition 'with'. It is followed by 'to' when it means 'to keep to or comply with', as in 'conform to the conventions' and 'refuse to conform to the company regulations', and with 'with' when it means 'to agree with, to go along with', as in 'His ideas do not conform with those of the rest of the committee'.

conjurer and **conjuror**, meaning a person who does conjuring tricks, are both acceptable spellings.

connection and **connexion** are different forms of the same word, meaning 'a relationship between two things'. In modern usage **connection** is much the commoner spelling, as in 'no connection between the events' and 'a fire caused by a faulty connection'.

connoisseur is liable to be misspelt. Note the double *n* and double *s*, and the *oi*. The word means 'a person having specialized knowledge and judgement on a subject' as in 'a connoisseur of French wines' and 'a connoisseur of Italian opera'.

conscientious, meaning 'diligent and careful', as in 'conscientious pupils doing their home work', is commonly misspelt. Note the *t*, which is frequently wrongly omitted.

connote and **denote** are liable to be confused. **Connote** means 'to suggest something in addition to the main, basic meaning of something', as in 'the fear that the word cancer connotes' and 'The word 'home' connotes security and love'. **Denote** means 'to mean or indicate', as in 'The word cancer denotes a malignant illness' and 'The word "home" denotes the place where one lives'.

consequent and **consequential** are liable to be confused. **Consequent** means 'following as a direct result', as in 'He was badly wounded in the war and never recovered from the consequent lameness'. In one of its senses **consequential** has a meaning similar to that of **consequent** in that it means 'following as a indirect result', as in 'She was injured and suffered a consequential loss of earnings'. In this sense **consequential** is usually used in a legal or formal context. **Consequential** also means 'important', as in 'a grave and consequential meeting' and is sometime applied to people when it means 'self-important', as in 'a pompous, consequential little man'.

consequent and **subsequent** are liable to be confused. **Consequent** means 'following as a direct result', as in 'his accident and consequent injuries', while **subsequent** means simply 'happening or occurring after', as in 'their arrival and subsequent speedy departure'.

Consequent is sometimes followed by the preposition 'on' or 'upon', as in 'The court requires him to prove that his disability was consequent upon his accident at work'. **Subsequent** is sometimes followed by the preposition 'to', as in 'He was a security man subsequent to his retirement from the police'.

conservative when spelt with a lower-case *c* means 'supporting established traditions, institutions, etc, and opposed to great or sudden change', as in 'Some of the members of the amateur dramatics group wanted to stage a modern play this year but the more conservative members opted for a Shakespearian play instead', and 'She would like to go somewhere exotic on holiday but her conservative husband likes to go to the same place every year'. **Conservative** with an initial capital C refers to 'a person who is a member or supporter of the Conservative party', as in 'His wife votes Labour but he is a Conservative'. **Conservative** also means 'cautious, moderate', as in 'At a conservative estimate there must have been a thousand people there'.

consist can be followed either by the preposition 'of' or by the preposition 'in', depending on the meaning. **Consist of** means 'to be made up of, to comprise', as in 'The team consists of eleven players and two reserve players'. **Consist in** means 'to have as the chief or only element or feature, to lie in', as in 'The charm of the village consists in its isolation' and 'The effectiveness of the plan consisted in its simplicity'.

constitute see **compose**.

contagious and **infectious** both refer to diseases that can be passed on to other people but they do not mean the same. **Contagious** means 'passed on by physical contact', as in 'He caught a contagious skin disease while working in the clinic' and 'Venereal diseases are contagious'. **Infectious** means 'caused by airborne or waterborne microorganisms', as in 'The common cold is highly infectious and is spread by people sneezing and coughing'.

contemporary originally meant 'living or happening at the same time', as in 'Shakespeare and Marlowe were contemporary playwrights' and 'Marlowe was contemporary with Shakespeare'. Later it came to mean also 'happening at the present time, current', as in 'What is your impression of the contemporary literary scene?' and 'Contemporary moral values are often compared unfavourably with those of the past'. These two uses of **contemporary** can cause ambiguity. In modern usage it is also used to mean 'modern, up-to-date', as in 'extremely contemporary designs'.

contemptible and **contemptuous** are both adjectives formed from the noun 'contempt', but they are different in meaning. **Contemptible** means 'deserving contempt, despicable', as in 'The contemptible villain robbed the blind man' and 'It was contemptible of her to swindle an old woman'. **Contemptuous** means 'feeling or showing contempt', as in 'their contemptuous attitude to the people they employ' and 'have a contemptuous disregard for the law of the land'.

continual and **continuous** are not interchangeable. **Continual** means 'frequently repeated', as in 'Tired of the continual interruptions he took the telephone off the hook' and 'There were continual complaints from the school about the truancy of their children'. **Continuous** means 'without a break or interruption', as in 'a continuous period of ill health', 'machines giving off a continuous high-pitched whine' and 'a continuous roll of paper'.

contrary has two possible pronunciations. When it means 'opposite', as in 'hold contrary views', 'traffic going in contrary directions' and 'On the contrary, I would like to go very much', it is pronounced with the emphasis on the first syllable (*kon*-trar-i). When it means 'perverse, stubborn', as in 'contrary children' it is pronounced with the emphasis on the second syllable, which is pronounced to rhyme with 'Mary'.

controversy is usually pronounced with the emphasis on the first syllable (*kon*-tro-ver-si). In modern usage there is a growing tendency to place the emphasis on the second syllable (kon-*tro*-ver-si).

convalescence is commonly misspelt. Note the *sc* combination. The word means 'recovery after an illness', as in 'She will have to undergo a long convalescence after her operation'.

convertible is commonly misspelt. Note the *-ible* spelling.

convex see **concave**.

cooperate see **collaborate**.

cord see **chord**.

co-respondent see **correspondent**.

correspondence is frequently misspelt. Note the *ence*. This is often misspelt as *ance*.

correspondent and **co-respondent** are liable to be confused. **Correspondent** refers either to 'a person who communicates by letter', as in 'They were correspondents for years but had never met', or to 'a person who contributes news items to a newspaper or radio or television programme', as in 'the foreign correspondent of the *Times*'. A **co-respondent** is 'a person who has been cited in a divorce case as having committed adultery with one of the partners'.

council and **counsel** sound alike but have different meanings. **Council** refers to 'an assembly of people meeting for discussion, consultation, administrative purposes, etc', as in 'the town council' and 'a community council'. **Counsel** means 'advice', as in 'She received wise counsel from her parents but ignored it'. **Counsel** is also a verb meaning 'to give advice to', as in he counselled him on possible careers', 'She was counselled against leaving school without qualifications'.

councillor and **counsellor** sound alike but have different meanings. **Councillor** is a member of a council, as in 'town councillors'. **Counsellor** refers to 'a person who gives advice, especially professional advice on a social issue', as in 'a debt counsellor' and 'a career counsellor'.

cousin can cause confusion. The children of brothers and sisters are **first cousins** to each other. The children of **first cousins** are **second cousins** to each other. The child of one's **first cousin** and the **first cousin** of one's parents is one's **first cousin first removed**. The grandchild of one's **first cousin** or the **first cousin** of one's grandparent is one's **second cousin twice removed**.

credible, **creditable** and **credulous** are liable to be confused. **Credible** means 'believable', as in 'a scarcely credible story' and 'I do not find her account of the accident credible'. **Creditable** means 'deserving praise', as in 'Despite his injury the athlete gave a very creditable performance'. **Credulous** means 'too ready to believe, gullible', as in 'She was so credulous that she was taken in by the swindler' and 'a credulous young girl believing everything her new boyfriend said'.

crisis literally means 'turning point' and should be used to refer to 'a turning point in an illness', as in 'The fever reached a crisis and she survived' and 'a decisive or crucial moment in a situation, whose outcome will make a definite difference or change for better or worse', as in 'The financial situation has reached a crisis—the firm will either survive or go bankrupt'. In modern usage **crisis** is becoming increasingly used loosely for 'any worrying or troublesome situation', as in 'There's a crisis in the kitchen. The cooker's broken down'. The plural is **crises**.

criterion, meaning 'a standard by which something or someone is judged or evaluated', as 'What criterion is used for deciding which pupils will gain entrance to the school?' and 'The standard of play was the only criterion for entrance to the golf club'. It is a singular noun of which **criteria** is the plural, as in 'They must satisfy all the criteria for entrance to the club or they will be refused'.

critical has two main meanings. It means 'finding fault', as in 'His report on her work was very critical'. It also means 'at a crisis, at a decisive moment, crucial', as in 'It was a critical point in their relationship'. This meaning is often applied to the decisive stage of an illness, as in 'the critical hours after a serious operation', and is used also to describe an ill person who is at a crucial stage of an illness or dangerously ill. **Critical** also means 'involved in making judgements or assessments of artistic or creative works', as in 'give a critical evaluation of the author's latest novel'.

crucial means 'decisive, critical', as in 'His vote is crucial since the rest of the committee is split down the middle'. In modern usage it is used loosely to mean 'very important', as in 'It is crucial that you leave now'. **Crucial** is derived from crux, meaning 'a decisive point', as in 'the crux of the situation'.

cuisine is liable to be misspelt. Note the *u* before the first *i*. It is rather a formal word and means 'cooking' or 'a style of cooking', as in 'The cuisine at the new restaurant is outstanding'; 'She prefers Italian cuisine to French cuisine'. Note that it is pronounced kwee-*zeen*.

curb and **kerb** are not interchangeable although they sound similar. **Curb** is both a noun and a verb. As a noun it means 'control, check, restraint', as in 'act as a curb on his extravagance'. As a verb it means 'to control, to restrain', as in 'She must learn to curb his anger' and 'If he does not learn to curb his expenditure he will become bankrupt'. **Kerb** is a noun meaning 'the edge of a pavement', as in 'The child stood on the kerb waiting to cross the road'. In American English **curb** is used instead of **kerb**.

curriculum is commonly misspelt. Note the double *r* and single *l*. The word means 'a programme of educational courses', as in 'The government is making changes to the primary school curriculum' and 'There is a wide range of options on the sixth form curriculum'. **Curriculum** is derived from Latin and originally took the plural form **curricula**, but in modern usage the plural form **curriculums** is becoming common.

curriculum vitae refers to 'a brief account of a person's qualifications and career to date'. It is often requested by an employer when a candidate is applying for a job. **Vitae** is pronounced *vee*-ti, the second syllable rhyming with my.

curtsy and **curtsey** are both acceptable spellings. The word refers to 'a sign of respect in which a woman puts one foot behind the other and bends her knees, sometimes holding her skirt out'.

customer *see* **client**.

D

dais, meaning 'platform' or 'stage', is now usually pronounced as two syllables, as day-is. Formerly it was pronounced as one syllable, as days.

data was formerly used mainly in a scientific or technical context and was always treated as a plural noun, taking a plural verb, as in 'compare the data which were provided by the two research projects'. The singular form was **datum**, which is now rare. In modern usage the word **data** became used in computing as a collective noun meaning 'body of information' and is frequently used with a singular verb, as in 'The data is essential for our research'. This use has spread into the general language.

dates are usually written in figures rather than in words except in formal contexts, such as legal documents. There are various ways of writing dates. The standard form in Britain is becoming day followed by month followed by year, as in '24 February 1970'. In America the standard form of this is 'February 24 1970' and that is a possibility in Britain also. Alternatively, some people write '24th February 1970'. Care should be taken with the writing of dates entirely in numbers, especially if one is corresponding with someone in America. In Britain the day of the month is put first, the month second and the year third, as in '2/3/50', '2 March 1950'. In America the month is put first, followed by the day of the month and the year. Thus in America '2/3/50', would be 3 February 1950.

Centuries may be written either in figures, as in 'the 19th century' or in words, as in 'the nineteenth century'. Decades and centuries are now usually written without apostrophes, as in '1980s' and '1900s'.

datum *see* **data**.

deadly and **deathly** both refer to death but they have different meanings. **Deadly** means 'likely to cause death, fatal', as in 'His enemy dealt him a deadly blow with his sword' and 'He contracted a deadly disease in the jungle'. **Deathly** means 'referring to death, resembling death', as in 'She was deathly pale with fear'.

decade is pronounced with the emphasis on the first syllable as *dek*-ayd. An alternative but rare pronunciation is dek-*ayd*.

decimate literally means 'to kill one in ten' and is derived from the practice in ancient Rome of killing every tenth soldier as a punishment for mutiny. In modern usage it has come to mean 'to kill or destroy a large part of', as in 'Disease has decimated the population'. It has also come to mean 'to reduce considerably', as in 'the recession has decimated the jobs in the area'.

decry and **descry** are liable to be confused. **Decry** means 'to express criticism or disapproval of, to disparage', as in 'The neighbours decried their treatment of their children' and 'The local people decried the way the police handled the situation'. **Descry** means 'catch sight of', as in 'descry a herd of deer on the horizon'.

defective and **deficient** are similar in meaning but are not interchangeable. **Defective** means 'having a fault, not working properly', as in 'return the defective vacuum cleaner to the shop', 'The second-hand car proved to be defective' and 'He cannot be a pilot as his eyesight is defective'. **Deficient** means 'having a lack, lacking in', as in 'The athlete is very fast but he is deficient in strength' and 'Her diet is deficient in vitamin C.

defence, as in 'soldiers losing their lives in defence of their country' is commonly misspelt. Note the *c*. The word is frequently wrongly spelt with an *s* along the lines of **defensive**. In American English **defence** is spelt **defense**.

deficient *see* **defective**.

definitely is frequently misspelt. Note the *i* before the *t*. It is a common error to put *a* in that position.

delicatessen is liable to be misspelt. Note the single *l*, single *t* and double *s*. It refers to 'a shop selling prepared foods, such as cooked meats, cheeses, etc', as in 'buy some quiche from the local delicatessen'.

deliverance and **delivery** are both nouns formed from the verb 'to deliver' but they are used in different senses. **Deliverance** refers to 'the act of delivering from danger etc, to rescue or save', as in 'thank God for their child's deliverance from the evil kidnappers' and 'pray for their deliverance from evil'. This word is now used only in literary or very formal contexts. **Delivery** has several meanings. It refers to 'the act of delivering letters, goods, etc', as in 'There is no delivery of mail on Sundays' and 'awaiting delivery of a new washing machine'; 'the pro-cess of birth', as in 'Her husband was present at the delivery of their son'; 'manner of speaking', as in 'The lecturer's subject was interesting but his delivery was poor'.

delusion and **illusion** in modern usage are often used interchangeably but they are not quite the same. **Delusion** means 'a false or mistaken idea or belief', as in 'He is under the delusion that he is brilliant' and 'suffer from delusions of grandeur'. It can be part of a mental disorder, as in 'He suffers from the delusion that he is Napoleon. **Illusion** means 'a false or misleading impression', as in 'There was no well in the desert—it was an optical illusion', 'The conjurer's tricks were based on illusion' and 'the happy childhood illusions that everyone lived happy ever after'.

demise is a formal word for death, as in 'He never recovered from the demise of his wife'. In modern usage it applies to the ending of an activity, as in 'The last decade saw the demise of coal-mining in the area'. In modern usage it has come to mean also 'the decline or failure of an activity', as in 'the gradual demise of his business'.

demonstrable is most commonly pronounced di-*mon*-

strabl, with the emphasis on the second syllable, in modern usage. Previously the emphasis was on the first syllable as *dem*-on-strabl.

dénouement is commonly misspelt. Note the *oue* combination. The first *e* was originally always spelt with an acute accent, as *é*, but in modern usage it is frequently written without the acute. The word means 'the final outcome', as in 'The novel had a unexpected denouement'. It is pronounced day-*noo*-mon.

dependant and **dependent** are frequently confused. **Dependant** is a noun meaning 'a person who depends on someone else for financial support', as in 'He has four dependants—his wife and three children'. **Dependent** is an adjective meaning 'reliant on', as in 'dependent on drugs'; 'relying on someone else for financial support', as in 'have several dependent relatives'; 'decided by, affected by', as in 'Success in that exam is dependent on hard work'.

deprecate and **depreciate** are liable to be confused although they have totally different meanings. **Deprecate** means 'to express disapproval of', as in 'It was unsporting of him to deprecate his rival's performance' and 'deprecate their choice of furnishings'. **Depreciate** means 'to reduce in value', as in 'New cars depreciate very quickly'. It also means 'to belittle or disparage', as in 'They made great efforts to help but she depreciated them', 'Management depreciated the role the deputy manager played in the firm'. In modern usage **deprecate** is sometimes used with the second meaning of **depreciate**, as in 'He was always praising his elder son's work and deprecating that of his younger son although the latter was the cleverer pupil'.

deprived means 'having something removed', as in 'The prisoner was punished by being deprived of his privileges' and 'The fire deprived the children of their home'. In modern usage it has come to mean 'not having what are considered to be basic rights, standard of living, etc', as in 'deprived children sent to school in worn-out clothes' and 'deprived people living in substandard accommodation'.

derisive and **derisory** are both adjectives connected with the noun 'derision' but they have different meanings. **Derisive** means 'expressing derision, scornful, mocking' as in 'give a derisive smile' and 'His efforts were met with derisive laughter'. Derisory means 'deserving derision, ridiculous' as in 'Their attempts at playing the game were derisory'. **Derisory** is frequently used to mean 'ridiculously small or inadequate', as in 'The salary offered was derisory'.

descry *see* **decry**.

desert and **dessert** are frequent confused. **Desert** as a noun refers to 'a large area of barren land with very little water or vegetation and often sand-covered', as in 'the Sahara Desert'. **Deserts** is a plural noun meaning 'what someone deserves', as in 'The thief who mugged the old lady got his just deserts when he was sent to prison'. As a verb **desert** means 'to abandon', as in 'desert his wife and children' and 'soldiers deserting their post', or 'to fail', as in 'his courage deserted him'. **Dessert** means the last (and sweet) course of a meal, as in 'She served apple pie and cream for dessert'. *See* **dessert**.

desiccated is frequently misspelt. Note the single *s* and double *c*. It means 'dried', as in 'desiccated coconut', or 'lacking animation', as in 'a desiccated old bachelor'.

despatch and **dispatch** are interchangeable. It is most common as a verb meaning 'to send', as in 'despatch/dispatch an invitation'. It is rarer as a noun. It means 'a message or report, often official', as in 'receive a despatch/dispatch that the soldiers were to move on'. It also means 'rapidity, speed', as in 'carry out the orders with despatch/dispatch'.

desperate is frequently misspelt. Note the *e* before the *r*. It is a common error to put *a* instead.

dessert, **pudding**, **sweet** and **afters** all mean the same thing. They refer to the last and sweet course of a meal. **Dessert** has relatively recently become the most widespread of these terms. **Pudding** was previously regarded by the upper and middle classes as the most acceptable word of these, but it is now thought of by many as being rather old-fashioned or as being more suited to certain types of dessert than others—thus syrup sponge would be a pudding, but not fresh fruit salad. **Sweet** is a less formal word and is regarded by some people as being lower-class or regional. **Afters** is common only in very informal English. *See also* **desert**.

detach is often misspelt. Note that there is no *t* before the *ch*.

detract and **distract** are liable to be confused. **Detract** means 'to take away from', as in 'Nothing he could say could detract from her reputation as a writer'. 'The new high-rise buildings detracted from the old-fashioned charm of the village'. **Distract** means 'to take someone's mind off something, to divert someone's attention', as in 'The golf-player said he lost the match because he was distracted by a dog running on the course'.

device and **devise** are liable to be confused. **Device** is a noun and refers to 'a gadget or tool', as in 'a device for taking stones out of horses' hoofs'. **Devise** is a verb meaning 'to plan, to bring about', as in 'He succeeded in devising a scheme that was certain to succeed'.

devil's advocate is a phrase that is often misunderstood. It means 'someone who points out the possible flaws or faults in an argument etc', as in 'He played the devil's advocate and showed her the weakness in her argument so that she was able to perfect it before presenting it to the committee'. The phrase is sometimes wrongly thought of as meaning 'someone who defends an unpopular point of view or person'.

devise *see* **device**.

diagnosis and **prognosis** are liable to be confused. Both are used with reference to disease but have different meanings. **Diagnosis** refers to 'the identification of a disease or disorder', as in 'She had cancer but the doctor failed to make the correct diagnosis until it was too late'. **Prognosis** refers to 'the prediction of the likely course of a disease or disorder', as in 'According to the doctor's prognosis, the patient will be dead in six months'.

dialect refers to an established form of language confined to an area of a country or to a particular class of people. It includes pronunciation, vocabulary, grammar or sense structure.

dialogue refers to 'a discussion between two or more people'. It usually refers to an exchange of views of people who are involved in a conflict of interest and are trying to reach a compromise, as in 'management and union leaders in dialogue over the factory wages structure' and 'The leaders are engaged in a dialogue to try to prevent a war'.

diarrhoea is frequently misspelt. Note the *rrh* combination and the *oea* combination. The word refers to a very loose bowel movement.

dice was originally the plural form of the singular noun **die**, but **die** is now rarely used. Instead, **dice** is used as both a singular and a plural noun, as in 'throw a wooden dice' and 'use three different dice in the same game'.

dietician and **dietitian** are both acceptable spellings. The word means 'a person who specializes in the principles of nutrition', as in 'hospital dieticians drawing up menus for the patients'.

different is most usually followed by the preposition 'from', as in 'Their style of living is different from ours'. **Different from** is considered to be the most correct construction, particularly in formal English. **Different to** is used in informal situations, as in 'His idea of a good time is different to ours'. **Different than** is used in American English.

differently abled *see* **disabled**.

dilatation and **dilation** are both acceptable forms of the same word formed from the verb 'dilate', meaning 'to expand', as in 'Note the dilatation/dilation of the patient's pupils'.

dilapidated is frequently misspelt. Common errors include putting *t* instead of the middle *d* and substituting *de* at the beginning for *di*.

dilemma is frequently used wrongly. It refers to 'a situation in which one is faced with two or more equally undesirable possibilities', as in 'I can't decide which of the offers to accept. It's a real dilemma'.

dinghy and **dingy** are liable to be confused. **Dinghy** refers to 'a type of small boat', as in 'They went out for a sail in their dinghy'. **Dingy** means 'dirty-looking, gloomy', as in 'colourful curtains to cheer up a dingy room'.

dinner, lunch, supper and **tea** are terms that can cause confusion. Their use can vary according to class, region of the country and personal preference. Generally speaking, people who have their main meal in the evening call it **dinner**. However, people who have their main meal in the middle of the day frequently call this meal **dinner**. People who have **dinner** in the evening usually refer to their midday meal, usually a lighter meal, as **lunch**. A more formal version of this word is **luncheon**, which is now quite a rare word. **Supper** has two meanings, again partly dependent on class and region. It can refer either to the main meal of the day if it is eaten in the evening—when it is virtually a synonym for **dinner**. Alternatively, it can refer to a light snack, such as cocoa and toasted cheese, eaten late in the evening before going to bed. **Tea** again has two meanings when applied to a meal. It either means a light snack-type meal of tea, sandwiches and cakes eaten in the late afternoon. Alternatively, it can refer to a cooked meal, sometimes taken with tea, and also referred to as **high tea**, eaten in the early evening, rather than **dinner** later in the evening.

diphtheria can cause problems both with spelling and pronunciation. Note the *phth* combination in the spelling. The word, which refers to a type of infectious disease, should be pronounced with an *f* at the end of the first syllable (*dif*) but it is often pronounced with a *p* (*dip*).

disabled is objected to by some people on the grounds that it is a negative term, but it is difficult to find an acceptable alternative. In politically correct language **physically challenged** has been suggested as has **differently abled**, but neither of these has gained widespread use. It should be noted that the use of 'the disabled' should be avoided. 'Disabled people' should be used instead.

disablism and **disableism** mean 'discrimination against

disabled people', as in 'He felt his failure to get a job was because of disablism'. **Disablist** and **disableist** are adjectives meaning 'showing or practising disablism', as in 'guilty of disablist attitudes'. They also refer to 'a person who discriminates on the grounds of disability', as in 'That employer is a disablist'.

disadvantaged and **disadvantageous** are both formed from disadvantage but they are used in different senses. **Disadvantaged** means 'not having the standard of living, living conditions or basic rights that others enjoy', as in 'disadvantaged families living in slum conditions'. It means much the same as deprived. **Disadvantageous** means 'causing a disadvantage, unfavourable', as in 'At the end of the first round of the competition the former champion was in a disadvantageous position'.

disappoint is very frequently misspelt. Note the single *s* and double *p*. A common error is to put double *s* and single *p*.

disassociate and **dissociate** are used interchangeably, as in 'She wished to disassociate/dissociate herself from the statement issued by her colleagues', but **dissociate** is the more usual.

disastrous is frequently misspelt. Note that, unlike **disaster** from which it is derived, it has no *e*.

discoloration is frequently misspelt. Note, unlike **colour**, the absence of *u*.

discomfit and **discomfort** are liable to be confused. **Discomfit** is a verb which means 'to disconcert, to embarrass', as in 'They were discomfited by her direct questions', or 'to thwart, to defeat', as in 'He succeeded in discomfiting his opponent'. **Discomfort** is most commonly a noun, although it does exist as a verb. It means 'lack of comfort, lack of ease', as in 'the discomfort of their holiday conditions'.

discover and **invent** are not interchangeable. **Discover** means 'to find something that is already in existence but is generally unknown', as in 'discover a new route to China' and 'discover the perfect place for a holiday'. **Invent** means 'to create something that has never before existed', as in 'invent the telephone' and 'invent a new form of heating system'.

discriminating and **discriminatory** are both formed from **discrimination** but they have different meanings. **Discriminating** means 'able to tell the difference between good and poor quality, etc, having good judgement', as in 'a discriminating collector of antiques' and 'discriminating in their choice of wines'. **Discriminatory** means 'showing or practising discrimination or prejudice', as in 'have a discriminatory attitude towards people of a different race' and 'employers accused of being discriminatory towards women'.

disempowered in modern usage does not mean only 'having one's power removed', as in 'The king was disempowered by the invading general', but also means the same as 'powerless', as in 'We are disempowered to give you any more money'. **Disempowered** is seen in politically correct language as a more positive way of saying **powerless**.

disinterested and **uninterested** are often used interchangeably in modern usage to mean 'not interested, indifferent', as in 'pupils totally *disinterested/uninterested* in school work'. Many people dislike **disinterested** being used in this way and regard it as a wrong use, but it is becoming increasingly common. **Disinterested** also means 'impartial, unbiased', as in 'ask a disinterested party to settle the dispute between them'.

disorient and **disorientate** are used interchangeably. 'The town had changed so much since his last visit that he was completely disoriented/disorientated' and 'After the blow to her head she was slightly disoriented/disorientated'.

distinct and **distinctive** are liable to be confused. **Distinct** means 'definite, easily heard, seen, felt, etc', as in 'I got the distinct impression that I had offended him', or 'different, separate', as in 'an artistic style quite distinct from that of his father'. **Distinctive** means 'distinguishing, characteristic', as in 'The zebra has distinctive markings'.

distract *see* **detract**.

divorcee refers to 'a divorced person', as in 'a club for divorcees'. **Divorcé** refers to 'a divorced man', and **divorcée** to 'a divorced woman'.

doubtful and **dubious** can be used interchangeably in the sense of 'giving rise to doubt, uncertain', as in 'The future of the project is dubious/doubtful', and in the sense of 'having doubts, unsure', as in 'I am doubtful/dubious about the wisdom of going'. **Dubious** also means 'possibly dishonest or bad', as in 'of dubious morals'.

downward and **downwards** are not used interchangeably. **Downward** is an adjective, as in 'a downward slope' and 'in a downward direction'. **Downwards** is an adverb, as in 'look downwards from the top of the hill'.

draft and **draught** are liable to be confused. **Draft** as a noun in British English has several meanings. It can mean 'a preliminary version', as in 'present a rough draft of their proposals'; 'a money order', as in 'a draft drawn on a foreign bank'; 'a group of soldiers or other people chosen for a special purpose', as in 'a draft of new recruits sent to the front' and 'a draft of nurses and doctors despatched to the scene of the disaster'. **Draught** as a noun in British English refers to 'a current of air', as in 'a draught from an ill-fitting window', or to 'a drink, a swallow of liquid', as in 'long for a draught of cool beer'. In American English **draught** is spelt **draft**.

drawing room *see* **sitting room**.

draught *see* **draft**.

draughtsman/woman and **draftsman/woman** are not the same. **Draughtsman/woman** refers to 'a person who draws detailed plans of a building, etc', as in 'study the plans of the bridge prepared by the draughtsman'. **Draftsman/woman** refers to 'a person who prepares a preliminary version of plans, etc', as in 'several draftswomen working on the draft parliamentary bills'.

dreamed and **dreamt** are interchangeable both as the past tense and the past participle of the verb 'dream', as in 'She *dreamed/dreamt* about living in the country' and in 'He has dreamed/dreamt the same dream for several nights'.

drier and **dryer** can both be used to describe 'a machine or appliance that dries', as in 'hair-drier/hair-dryer' and 'tumbler drier/dryer'. As an adjective meaning 'more dry', **drier** is the usual word, as in 'a drier summer than last year'.

drunk and **drunken** both mean 'intoxicated' but they are used rather differently. When someone is temporarily intoxicated **drunk** is used, as in 'The drunk men staggered home'. **Drunken** tends to be used to describe someone who is in the habit of being intoxicated, as in 'drunken creatures who are rarely sober'. Otherwise **drunk** is usually used after a verb, as in 'They were all drunk at the party'. **Drunken** is usually used before a noun as in 'take part in a drunken party'.

dryer *see* **drier**.

dubious *see* **doubtful**.

dual and **duel** are liable to be confused since they sound alike. **Dual** is an adjective meaning 'double, twofold', as in 'He played a dual role in the team as captain and trainer' and 'a dual carriageway'. **Duel** is a noun meaning ' a formal fight between two people, using swords or pistols', as in 'He challenged a fellow officer to a duel because he had called him a liar'. **Duel** can also be a verb. The *l* doubles before '-ing', '-ed', or '-er' is added, as in 'duelling at dawn'.

due to, owing to and **because of** should not be used interchangeably. Strictly speaking, **due to** should be used only adjectivally, as in 'His poor memory is due to brain damage' and 'cancellations due to bad weather'. When a prepositional use is required **owing to** and **because of** should be used, as in 'the firm was forced to close owing to a lack of capital' and 'The train was cancelled because of snow on the line'. In modern usage it is quite common for **due to** to be used instead of **owing to** or **because of** because the distinction is rather difficult to comprehend.

dyeing and **dying** sound alike but are completely different in meaning. **Dyeing** is formed from the verb 'to dye' and is used in such contexts as 'dyeing white dresses blue'. **Dying** is formed from the verb 'to die' and is used in such contexts as 'dying from starvation'.

E

each, when it is the subject of a sentence, should be followed by a singular verb and, where relevant, by a pronoun in the singular, as in 'Each boy brought his own lunch'. In order to avoid sexism in language some people advocate using a plural pronoun instead, as in 'Each pupil had their own books'. Before sexism in language became an issue, the assumption was that words such as pupil, which can indicate members of either sex, should take a male pronoun, as in 'Each pupil had his own books'. People who dislike using a plural pronoun with **each** on the grounds that it is ungrammatical but do not wish to be sexist can use 'his/her', as in 'Each pupil had his/her own books' although this device can be clumsy. It is often possible to avoid the problem by rephrasing the sentence, as in 'All the pupils had their own books'. When **each** follows a plural noun or pronoun, the verb should be plural as in 'The houses each have a red door' and 'They each have black hair'.

each other and **one another** used not to be used interchangeably. It was taught that **each other** should be used when only two people are involved and that **one another** should be used when more than two people are involved, as in 'John and Mary really love each other' and 'All the members of the family love one another'. In modern use this restriction is often ignored.

earthly and **earthy** are both adjectives formed from 'earth' but they have different meanings. **Earthly** is used to refer to this world rather than to heaven or the spiritual world, as in 'He is interested only in earthly pleasures but his brother is interested in spiritual satisfaction'. It is also used informally to mean 'possible', as in 'What earthly reason could she have for leaving?' **Earthy** refers to earth in the sense of 'soil', as in 'the earthy smell of a garden after rain'. It can also mean 'unrefined, coarse', as in 'an earthy sense of humour'.

EC and **EEC** both refer to the same thing, but **EC**, the abbreviation for **Economic Community** has now replaced **EEC**, the abbreviation for **European Economic Community.**

economic and **economical** are both connected with the noun 'economy' but they have different meanings. **Economic** means 'referring to or relating to the economy or economics', as in 'the government's economic policies' and 'studying economic theory'. **Economical** means 'thrifty, avoiding waste', as in 'She is a very economical housekeeper', and 'cheap', as in 'It is more economical for four of us to go by car than by train'. The phrase **economical with the truth** is a less forthright way of saying 'lying', as in 'politicians accused of being economical with the truth'.

ecstasy, meaning 'great joy', is frequently misspelt. Note the *cs* and *as*. Ecstasy, spelt with a capital *E*, is also the name of a non-medicinal drug, associated with raves, professionally organized large-scale parties for young people.

effect *see* **affect**.

effeminate *see* **female**.

e.g. means 'for example' and is an abbreviation of the Latin phrase *exempli gratia*. It is used before examples of something just previously mentioned, as in 'He cannot eat dairy products, e.g. milk, butter and cream'. A comma is usually placed just before it and, unlike some abbreviations, it has full stops.

egoist and **egotist** are frequently used interchangeably in modern usage. Although they are not, strictly speaking, the same, the differences between them are rather subtle. **Egoist** refers to 'a person intent on self-interest, a selfish person', as in 'an egoist who never gave a thought to the needs of others'. **Egotist** refers to 'a person who is totally self-centred and obsessed with his/her own concerns', as in 'a real egotist who was always talking about herself'.

eighth is frequently misspelt. Note the *h* before the *t*.

either should be used only when referring to two people or things, as in 'He hasn't been in touch with either of his parents for several years', but 'He hasn't been in touch with any of his four brothers'.

Either as an adjective or a pronoun takes a singular verb, as in 'Either parent will do' and 'Either of you can come'.

In the **either ... or** construction, a singular verb is used if both parts of the construction are singular, as in 'Either Jane or Mary is in charge'. If both parts are plural the verb is plural, as in 'Either their parents or their grandparents are in charge.' If the construction involves a mixture of singular and plural the verb traditionally agrees with the subject that is nearer it, as in 'Either her mother or her grandparents are in charge' and 'Either her grandparents or her mother is in charge'. If pronouns are used, the nearer one governs the verb, as in 'Either they or he is at fault' and 'Either she or they are at fault'. *See* **neither**.

eke out originally meant 'to make something more adequate by adding to it or supplementing it', as in 'The poor mother eked out the small amount of meat with a lot of vegetables to feed her large family'. It can now also mean 'to make something last longer by using it sparingly', as in 'try to eke out our water supply until we reach a town', and 'to succeed or make with a great deal of effort', as in 'eke out a meagre living from their small farm'.

elder and **older** are not interchangeable. **Elder** is used only of people, as in 'The smaller boy is the elder of the two'. It is frequently used of family relationships, as in 'His elder brother died before him'. **Older** can be used of things as well as people, as in 'The church looks ancient but the castle is the older of the buildings' and 'The smaller girl is the older of the two'. It also can be used of family relationships, as in 'It was his older brother who helped him'. **Elder** used as a noun suggests experience or worthiness as well as age, as in 'Important issues used to be decided by the village elders' and 'Children should respect their elders and betters'.

elderly, as well as meaning 'quite or rather old', as in 'a town full of middle-aged and elderly people', is a more polite term than 'old', no matter how old the person referred to is, as in 'a residential home for elderly people'. **Elderly** is used only of people, except when used humorously, as in 'this cheese is getting rather elderly'.

eldest and **oldest** follow the same pattern as **elder** and **older**, as in 'The smallest boy is the eldest of the three', 'His eldest brother lived longer than any of them', 'The castle is the oldest building in the town' and 'He has four brothers but the oldest one is dead'.

elemental and **elementary** are both connected with the noun 'element' but they are not interchangeable. **Elemental** means 'like the elements (in the sense of forces of nature), powerful, uncontrolled', as in 'give way to elemental passion'. It also means 'basic, essential', as in 'the elemental truths of Buddhism'. **Elementary** means 'basic, introductory', as in 'teaching elementary maths', and 'easy, simple', as in 'He cannot carry out the most elementary of tasks' and 'The test is very elementary'.

embarrass is very frequently misspelt. Note the double *r* and double *s*. Note also **embarrassed** and **embarrassing**. The word means 'to cause to feel self-conscious, confused or ashamed', as in 'His extravagant compliments embarrassed her'.

emigrant and **immigrant** are liable to be confused. **Emigrant** refers to 'a person who leaves his/her native land to go and live elsewhere', as in 'go down to the docks to say farewell to the emigrants on the ship'. **Immigrant** refers to 'a person who arrives to live in another country, having left his/her native land', as in 'go down to the docks to welcome the immigrants arriving on the ship'. Both terms can apply to the same person, viewed from different points of view.

emotional and **emotive** are both connected with the noun 'emotion' but they have different meanings. **Emotional** means 'referring to emotion', as in 'emotional problems', 'expressing emotion or excessive emotion', as in 'an emotional farewell', and 'having emotions that are easily excited', as in 'The rest of the family are very calm but she is so emotional that she is always either in tears or laughing with joy'. **Emotive** means 'causing emotion', as in 'Child abuse is often an emotive subject'.

empathy and **sympathy** are liable to be confused although they are not interchangeable. **Empathy** means 'the ability to imagine and share another's feelings, experiences, etc', as in 'As a single parent herself, the journalist has a real empathy with women bringing up children on their own' and 'The writer felt a certain empathy with the subject of his biography since they both came from a poverty-stricken childhood'. **Sympathy** means 'a feeling of compassion, pity or sorrow towards someone', as in 'feel sympathy for homeless children' and 'show sympathy towards the widow'.

encyclopaedia and **encyclopedia** are now both acceptable spellings in modern British English. **Encyclopaedia** is the traditional spelling in British English but the traditional spelling in American English, **encyclopedia**, is now becoming more and more common in British English.

endemic is usually used to describe a disease and means 'occurring in a particular area', as in 'a disease endemic to the coastal areas of the country' and 'difficult to clear the area of endemic disease'.

enervate is a word that is frequently misused. It means 'to weaken, to lessen in vitality', as in 'she was enervated by the extreme heat' and 'Absence of funding had totally enervated the society'. It is often wrongly used as though it meant the opposite.

enormity and **enormousness** are liable to be confused but mean different things. **Enormity** means 'outrageousness or wickedness', as in 'The whole village was shocked by the enormity of his crime'. **Enormousness** means 'the quality of being enormous or extremely large', as in 'The little boy was scared by the enormousness of the elephant' and 'the enormousness of their estates'.

enquiry and **inquiry** are frequently used interchangeably, as in 'make enquiries/inquiries about her health'. However some people see a distinction between them and use **enquiry** for ordinary requests for information, as in 'make enquiries about the times of trains'. They use **inquiry** only for 'investigation', as in 'The police have begun a murder inquiry' and 'launch an inquiry into the hygiene standards of the food firm'.

enrol is frequently misspelt. Note the single *l*, but note also that the *l* doubles in the past tense and past participle and the present participle, as in **enrolled, enrolling**. However, the noun **enrolment**, as in 'The enrolment of students takes place tomorrow', has a single *l*. In American English the word is spelt **enroll**. **Enrol** means 'to become a member of a class, society, etc, as in 'She plans to enrol in an aerobics class' and 'to make a member of a class, society, etc, as in 'The tutor will enrol more students next week'.

enthral is frequently misspelt. Note the single *l*, but note that the *l* doubles in the past tense and past participle and the present participle, as in **enthralled** and **enthralling**. However, note the single *l* in **enthralment**. In American English the word is spelt **enthrall**. **Enthral** means 'to bewitch, to capture the attention of', as in 'Her performance will enthral the critics'.

envelop and **envelope** are not interchangeable. **Envelop** means 'to wrap up, to enclose, to surround completely', as in 'He enveloped his daughter in his arms' and 'Mist enveloped the mountain tops'. **Envelope** means 'a paper wrapper for a letter, etc', as in 'put the sheets of paper in a large envelope'. **Envelop** is pronounced en-*vel*-op. The preferred pronunciation of envelope is *en*-vel-op although some people pronounce it *on*-vel-op.

enviable and **envious** are both formed from the noun 'envy' but they mean different things. **Enviable** means 'arousing envy, desirable', as in 'an enviable lifestyle' and 'an enviable optimistic attitude to life'. **Envious** means 'showing or expressing envy', as in 'envious eyes following the expensively dressed woman' and 'They were envious of her lifestyle'.

equable and **equitable** are liable to be confused. **Equable** means 'moderate, not given to extremes', as in 'live in an equable climate' and 'have an equable temperament'. **Equitable** means 'fair, just', as in 'We felt that the judge had come to an equitable decision'.

equal can be followed either by the preposition 'with' or the preposition 'to', but the two constructions are not interchangeable. **Equal to** is used in such sentences as 'He wished to climb the hill but his strength was not equal to the task'. **Equal with** is used in such sentences as 'After many hours of playing the two players remained equal with each other' and 'The women in the factory are seeking a pay scale equal with that of men'.

equally should not be followed by 'as'. Examples of it used correctly include 'Her brother is an expert player but she is equally talented' and 'He is trying hard but his competitors are trying equally hard'. These should not read 'but she is equally as talented' nor 'but his competitors are trying equally as hard'.

Esq. is the abbreviation for 'Esquire'. It is sometimes used rather formally when addressing a letter to a man, as in 'Peter Jones, Esq.' It should not be used with Mr. 'Mr Peter Jones, Esq.' is wrong.

-ess is a suffix that used routinely to be added to a noun to form the femine form, as in 'authoress, editress, poetess, sculptress'. This practice is now often seen as patronizing to women and sexist, and **-ess** is being used less and less. What were once considered masculine forms, as 'author, editor, poet, sculptor', are now considered to be neutral forms applying to either sex. The suffix is still found in such words as 'princess', 'countess', 'hostess' and 'waitress', and sometimes in 'actress'.

et al is the abbreviation of the Latin phrase *et alii*, meaning 'and others'. It is used in lists to indicate that there are more of the same, as in 'She loves Bach, Beethoven, Mozart et al'. The phrase is usually used in a formal context, but it is sometimes used humorously in informal contexts as in 'Uncle Fred, Uncle Jim et al'.

etc is the abbreviation of the Latin phrase *et cetera*, meaning 'and other things, and the rest', as in 'potatoes, carrots, turnips, etc', 'curtains, carpets, rugs, etc'. It can also be spelt **etc.** (with a full stop).

ethnic is a word that causes some confusion. It means 'of a group of people classified according to race, nationality, culture, etc', as in 'a cosmopolitan country with a wide variety of ethnic groups'. It is frequently used loosely to mean 'relating to race', as in 'violent clashes thought to be ethnic in origin', or 'foreign' as in 'prefer ethnic foods to British foods'.

euphemism is 'a more indirect, pleasanter, milder, etc, way of saying something'. 'To join one's forefathers' is a **euphemism** for 'to die'. 'To be tired and emotional' is a euphemism for 'to be drunk'.

evade and **avoid** are similar in meaning but not identical. **Evade** means 'to keep away from by cunning or deceit', as in 'The criminal evaded the police by getting his friend to impersonate him'. **Avoid** means simply 'to keep away from', as in 'Women avoid that area of town at night'.

evasion and **avoidance** are frequently applied to the non-payment of income tax but they are not interchangeable. Tax **avoidance** refers to 'the legal nonpayment of tax by clever means'. Tax **evasion** refers to 'the illegal means of avoiding tax by cunning and dishonest means'.

even should be placed carefully in a sentence since its position can influence the meaning. Compare 'He didn't even acknowledge her' and 'He didn't acknowledge even her'. and 'He doesn't even like Jane , let alone love her' and 'He hates the whole family—he doesn't like even Jane'. This shows that **even** should be placed immediately before the word it refers to in order to avoid ambiguity. In spoken English people often place it where it feels most natural, before the verb as in 'He even finds it difficult to relax on holiday'. To be absolutely correct this should be 'He finds it difficult to relax even on holiday' or 'Even on holiday he finds it difficult to relax'.

ever is sometimes added to 'who', 'what', where, etc', as a separate word for emphasis, as in 'Who ever did that terrible thing?' and 'Where ever did you find that?'. Where there is no question of emphasis, **ever** is joined on to the relevant pronoun. Examples include 'Whoever she is, she must be a bad mother' and 'Wherever he goes she goes'.

every is used with singular nouns. Related words, such as verbs and pronouns, are in the singular too, as in 'Every man must provide his own work clothing'. Some people use a plural pronoun in certain situations in order to avoid sexism in language, as in 'Every worker must supply their own work clothing'. This is to avoid the sexism of 'Every worker must supply his own clothing'. It is possible to avoid both sexism and ungrammatical constructions by using 'Every worker must supply his/her clothing', which can be rather clumsy. Alternatively, the whole sentence can be put in the plural, as in 'All the workers must supply their own work clothing'.

everybody and **everyone** can be used interchangeably. They both take singular verbs, as in 'Everyone has expressed the wish to stay' and 'Everybody wishes the war to end'. **Every one** as two words is used when emphasis is required, as in 'Every one of the workers wanted to stay' and 'Every one of the machines was damaged'.

ex- as a prefix means 'former', as in 'the ex-manager' and 'his ex-wife'. It is usually attached to the noun it describes with a hyphen. As a noun, used informally, **ex** means 'former wife, husband or partner'. as in 'He still visits his ex'. **Ex-directory** means 'not listed in the telephone directory', as in 'choose to have an ex-directory number after having received a series of nuisance calls'.

exaggerate is liable to be misspelt. Note the double *g* and single *r*. Note also the *e* before the *r*. The word means 'to describe as being larger, greater, etc, than is the case', as in 'exaggerate the difficulty of the job' and 'exaggerate how poor he is'.

exceedingly and **excessively** are not the same. **Exceedingly** means 'extremely, to a very great extent', as in 'She was exceedingly beautiful' and 'It was exceedingly kind of them to help'. **Excessively** means 'immoderately, to too great an extent, beyond measure', as in 'It was excessively annoying of him to interfere' and 'He was excessively fond of alcohol'.

except is commoner than **except for**. **Except** is used in such sentences as 'They are all dead except his father', 'He goes every day except Sunday'. **Except for** is used at the beginning of sentences, as in 'Except for Fred, all the workers were present', and where **except** applies to a longish phrase, as in 'There was no one present except for the maid cleaning the stairs' and 'The house was silent except for the occasional purring of the cat'. When followed by a pronoun, this should be in the accusative or objective, as in 'There was no one there except *him*' and 'Everyone stayed late except *me*'.

exceptionable and **exceptional** are both related to the noun 'exception' but they mean different things. **Exceptionable** describes something that someone might take exception to or object to, as in 'They found his behaviour exceptionable' and 'behaviour that was not at all exceptionable'. **Exceptional** means 'out of the ordinary, unusual', as in 'an exceptional talent'. It often means 'unusually good, superior', as in 'have an exceptional singing voice' and 'serve exceptional food and drink'.

excessively *see* **exceedingly**.

exercise and **exorcise** are liable to be confused because they sound alike. However, they are completely different in meaning. **Exercise** as a noun means 'physical exertion', as in 'sitting in front of the television taking little exercise' or 'a set of energetic movements' as in 'doing exercises in the morning'. It can also mean 'a piece of school work', as in 'pupils completing maths exercises'.

It is as a verb that **exercise** is most likely to be confused with **exorcise**. **Exercise** as a verb means 'to take part in physical exertion', 'to perform a series of energetic movements', as in 'The girls liked to exercise to music'. It also means 'to make use of, to employ', as in 'He was charged with the offence but exercised his right to remain silent'. **Exorcise** means 'to rid of evil spirits', as in 'ask a priest to exorcise the haunted house'. **Exercise** and **exorcise** are both frequently misspelt. It is a common error to put a *c* after the *x* in both words. Note that **exercise** is not one of the verbs that can end in *-ize*.

exhausting and **exhaustive** are both formed from the verb 'exhaust' but they mean different things. **Exhausting** means 'extremely tiring', as in 'an exhausting climb up the hill' and 'have an exhausting day at the office'. **Exhaustive** means 'thorough, comprehensive', as in 'police making an exhaustive search of the grounds for the murder weapon'.

exhilarate is often misspelt. Note the *lar* combination. It is a common error to put *ler*. The word means 'to make excited, to rouse, to thrill', as in 'exhilarated by a drive in a fast car', 'exhilarated by their walk in the hills'.

expeditious and **expedient** are liable to be confused but have quite different meanings. Expeditious means 'rapid', as in 'send the parcel by the most expeditious method possible'. **Expedient** means 'most convenient, most advantageous', as in 'The government was only interested in what was politically expedient' and 'choose the most expedient method, no matter how immoral'.

explicable is now usually pronounced with the emphasis on the second syllable (ex-*plik*-ibl). Formerly it was commonly pronounced with the emphasis on the first syllable (*ex*-plikibl).

explicit and **implicit** are liable to be confused although they are virtually opposites. **Explicit** means 'direct, clear', as in 'The instructions were not explicit enough' and 'Give explicit reasons for your decision'. **Explicit** is often used in modern usage to mean 'with nothing hidden or implied', as in 'explicit sex scenes'. **Implicit** means 'implied, not directly expressed', as in 'There was an implicit threat in their warning' and 'an implicit criticism in his comments on their actions'. **Implicit** also means 'absolute and unquestioning', as in 'an implicit faith in his ability to succeed' and 'an implicit confidence in her talents'.

exquisite has two possible pronunciations. It is most usually pronounced with the emphasis on the first syllable (*ex*-kwis-it) but some prefer to put the emphasis on the second syllable (iks-*kwis*-it). The word means 'beautiful, delicate', as in 'exquisite jewellery' and 'exquisite workmanship'. It can also mean 'acute', as in 'the exquisite pain of rejected love'.

extant and **extinct** are liable to be confused although they are opposites. **Extant** means 'still in existence', as in 'customs of ancient origin that are still extant in the village', 'a species of animal that is no longer extant'. **Extinct** means 'no longer in existence', as in 'Dinosaurs have been extinct for millions of years', and 'no longer active', as in 'extinct volcanoes' and 'extinct passion'. Note the spelling of **extinct**, which is frequently misspelt.

extinct *see* **extant**.

extinguish is frequently misspelt. Note the *gui* combination. The word means 'to put out, to cause to stop burning', as in 'firemen extinguishing the flames' and 'extinguish the passion'.

extraordinary can cause problems with pronunciation and spelling. The *a* is silent in the pronunciation. Note the *a* before *o* in the spelling. Remember it is made up of 'extra' and 'ordinary'.

extravagant is frequently misspelt. Note the single *g*.

extrovert and **introvert** are liable to be confused although they are opposites. **Extrovert** refers to 'a person who is more interested in what is going on around him/her than in his/her own thoughts and feelings, such a person usually being outgoing and sociable', as in 'She is a real extrovert who loves to entertain the guests at parties'. **Introvert** refers to 'a person who is more concerned with his/her own thoughts and feelings than with what is going around him/her, such a person usually being shy and reserved', as in 'an introvert who hates having to speak in public' and 'introverts who prefer to stay at home than go to parties'. Both **extrovert** and **introvert** can be adjectives as well as nouns, as in 'extrovert behaviour' and 'introvert personality'. Note the spelling of **extrovert**. It was formerly spelt with an *a* instead of an *o*.

F

façade can cause problems both with regard to spelling and pronunciation. It is French in origin and, although it has been part of the English language for some time, it still usually retains the cedilla under the *c* (*ç*). In modern usage there is a growing tendency to punctuate less and less, and as this tendency also applies to the use of accents **facade** is also found. The word is pronounced fa-*sahd* and means 'front', as in 'a building with an imposing façade', and 'outward appearance', as in 'hide her grief behind a façade of happiness'.

facetious is commonly misspelt. Note that the vowels appear in alphabetical order (*aeiou*). It means 'humorous, flippant', as in 'You shouldn't make facetious remarks about so grave a subject' and 'a facetious young woman who does not take anything seriously'.

facility and faculty are liable to be confused in the sense of 'ability'. **Facility** means 'ease or skill in doing something', as in 'admire his facility with words'. **Faculty** means 'a particular natural talent or power', as in 'her faculty for learning foreign languages'. **Facility** also means 'something that makes it possible or easier to do something'. In this sense it is usually plural (**facilities**), when it often refers to equipment or buildings, as in 'sports facilities'. **Facilities** is sometimes used to mean 'toilet', as in 'Ask the garage owner if we can use his facilities'.

fahrenheit *see* **Celsius**.

family name is used in politically correct language instead of **maiden name** since this is thought to imply that all women are virgins before they are married. Thus 'Her family name was Jones' would be used instead of 'Her maiden name was Jones'. Another politically correct term is **birth name**, as in 'Her birth name was Jones'.

faint and feint are sometimes confused. **Faint** as an adjective means either 'not clear, not strong', as in 'hear a faint noise' and 'bear a faint resemblance', or 'giddy, feeling as though one were about to lose consciousness', as in 'She asked if she could sit down as she felt faint'. As a verb it means 'to lose consciousness', as in 'She turned pale and fainted'. As an adjective **feint** is used on stationery to mean 'with faintly printed fine lines', as in 'a pad with feint pages'. In this sense **feint** is sometimes spelt **faint**. **Feint** as a noun means 'a pretended movement intended to distract someone', as in 'His opponent was misled when the boxer made a feint with his left fist'.

fait accompli is a French phrase that has been adopted into English. It refers to 'something that has been done and cannot be undone or changed', as in 'Her parents disapproved of him but by the time they found about the wedding it was a fait accompli and there was nothing they could do about it'. It is pronounced fayt a-kom-*plee*.

fantastic literally means 'relating to fantasy, fanciful, strange', as in 'fantastic dreams' and 'tales of fantastic events'. In modern usage it is often used informally to mean 'exceptionally good, excellent', as in 'have a fantastic holiday' and 'be a fantastic piano player'. It can also mean in informal usage 'very large', as in 'pay a fantastic sum of money'.

farther and further are not used interchangeably in all situations in modern usage. **Farther** is mainly restricted to sentences where physical distance is involved, as in 'It is farther to Glasgow from here than it is to Edinburgh'. **Further** can also be used in this sense, as in 'It is further to the sea than I thought'. When referring to time or extent, **further** is used, as in 'Further time is required to complete the task' and 'The police have ordered further investigations'. It can also mean 'additional', as in 'We shall require further supplies'. **Further**, unlike **farther**, can be used as a verb to mean 'to help the progress or development about', as in 'further the cause of freedom'.

fascinate is often misspelt. Note the *c* after the *s*. The word means 'to attract greatly, to capture the attention of', as in 'They were fascinated by the explorer's tales of adventure'.

fatal and fateful are liable to be confused although they mean different things. **Fatal** means 'causing death', as in 'involved in a fatal accident' and 'contract a fatal illness', or 'causing ruin or disaster', as in 'His plans for expansion proved fatal to the company' and 'The thief made a fatal mistake and was caught by the police'. **Fateful** means 'important and decisive, having important consequences', as in 'He never arrived home on that fateful night' and 'They eventually got married after that first fateful meeting'.

faux pas is a French phrase that has been adopted into the English language. It means 'a social blunder, an indiscreet or embarrassing remark or deed', as in 'The hostess made a faux pas when she asked after her guest's wife, not knowing that they had divorced last year'. **Faux** is pronounced to rhyme with *foe*, and **pas** is pronounced *pa*.

fax is an abbreviation of 'facsimile' and refers to 'an electronic system for transmitting documents using telephone lines'. As a noun **fax** can refer to the machine transmitting the documents, as in 'the fax has broken down again'; to the system used in the transmission, as in 'send the report by fax'; and the document or documents so transmitted, as in 'He replied to my fax at once'.

faze and phase are liable to be confused because they sound alike. However, they have totally different meanings. **Faze** is a verb meaning 'to fluster or disconcert', as in 'He was completely fazed by the interviewer's question—he could think of nothing to say'. **Phase** is primarily a noun meaning 'stage', as in 'the next phase of the development plans' and 'teachers going through a defiant phase'. **Phase** can also be a verb, found principally in the phrases **phase in** and **phase out**, which mean respectively 'to introduce gradually' and 'to withdraw gradually', as in 'The changes in the educational system are to be phased in over three years' and 'The old system of staffing will be phased out over the next few months'.

fearful and **fearsome** are both adjectives derived from the noun 'fear' but they mean different things. **Fearful** means 'scared, nervous', as in 'fearful children stumbling through the dark woods' and 'The burglars were fearful of being sent to prison'. It also means informally 'very bad, terrible', as in 'what a fearful mess he's in!' **Fearsome** means 'causing fear, frightening', as in 'fearsome wild animals' and 'It was a fearsome sight to behold'.

feasible is liable to be misspelt. Note the '-ible' ending. It means 'capable of being done or achieved, practicable', as in 'trials being carried out to find out if the suggested project is feasible'. In modern usage it is frequently used rather loosely to mean 'possible, probable or likely', as in 'It is just feasible that it might rain'.

February causes problems both with spelling and pronunciation. With reference to spelling note the first *r* between the *b* and *u*. It is a common error to omit this. The correct pronunciation is *feb*-roo-ari, but this is often simplified in informal speech to *feb*-ra-ri.

feint see **faint**.

ferment and **foment** can both mean 'to excite, to stir up', as in 'Troublemakers out to ferment discontent' and 'People out to foment trouble in the crowd'. Both words have other meanings that do not relate to each other. **Ferment** means 'to undergo the chemical process known as fermentation', as in 'home-made wine fermenting in the basement'. **Foment** means 'to apply warmth and moisture to in order to lessen pain or discomfort', as in 'foment the old man's injured hip'.

fetid has two possible pronunciations and two possible spellings. The first syllable can rhyme either with 'met' or 'meet'. With reference to spelling, **foetid** is a rarer alternative spelling.

fête is French in origin and is usually spelt, even in English, with a circumflex over the first *e*. It means 'an outdoor entertainment with the sale of goods, amusement stalls, etc, often held to make money for charity or a good cause', as in 'The proceeds of the village fête went towards the repair of the church roof'. It can be pronounced either to rhyme with 'mate' or 'met'. **Fête** can also be a verb meaning 'to honour or entertain lavishly', as in 'the winning football team were fêted by the whole town when they returned home'.

fetus see **foetus**.

female, feminine and **feminist** all relate to women but they are by no means interchangeable. **Female** refers to the sex of a person, animal or plant, as in 'the female members of the group', 'the female wolf and her cubs' and 'the female reproductive cells'. It refers to the childbearing sex and contrasts with 'male'. **Feminine** means 'having qualities that are considered typical of women or are traditionally associated with women', as in 'wear feminine clothes', 'take part in supposedly feminine pursuits, such as cooking and sewing' and 'feminine hairstyles'. It is the opposite of 'masculine'. It can be used of men as well as women, when it is usually derogatory, as in 'He has a very feminine voice' and 'He walks in a very feminine way'. When applied in a derogatory way to a man, **feminine** means much

the same as **effeminate**. **Feminine** also applies to the gender of words, as in 'Lioness is the feminine form of lion'. **Feminist** means 'referring to feminism', 'feminism' being 'a movement based on the belief that women should have the same rights, opportunities, etc', as in 'management trying to avoid appointing anyone with feminist ideas' and 'Equal opportunities is one of the aims of the feminist movement'.

few and **a few** do not convey exactly the same meaning. **Few** is used to mean the opposite of 'many', as in 'We expected a good many people to come but few did' and 'Many people entered the competition but few won a prize'. The phrase **a few** is used to mean the opposite of 'none', as in 'We didn't expect anyone to turn up but a few did' and 'We thought that none of the students would get a job but a few did'.

fewer see **less**.

fiancé and **fiancée** are respectively the masculine and feminine forms of 'the person to whom one is engaged', as in 'She introduced her fiancé to her parents' and 'He gave his fiancée a magnificent engagement ring'. **Fiancé** and **fiancée** are derived from French and follow the French spelling. Note the acute accent on the *é* of **fiancé** and **fiancée** and the additional *e* on **fiancée**. Both words are pronounced in the same way—fi-*on*-say.

fictional and **fictitious** are both derived from the noun 'fiction' and are interchangeable in the sense of 'imagined, invented', as in 'a fictional character based on an old man whom he used to know' and 'The events in the novel are entirely fictitious'. However, **fictitious** only is used in the sense of 'invented, false', as in 'an entirely fictitious account of the accident' and 'think up fictitious reasons for being late'.

fill in and **fill out** are both used to mean 'to complete a form, etc, by adding the required details', as in 'fill in/fill out an application form for a passport'. In British English **fill in** is the more common term, although **fill out** is the accepted term in American English.

finance can be pronounced in two ways. The commoner pronunciation has the emphasis on the second syllable and the first syllable pronounced like the fin of a fish (fin-*ans*). The alternative pronunciation has emphasis on the first syllable, which then is pronounced as fine (*fin*-ans). As a noun the word means 'money, capital, funding', as in 'provide the finance for the project'. As a verb it means 'to provide the money for, to pay for', as in 'expect her parents to finance her trip round the world'.

first and **firstly** are now both considered acceptable in lists, although formerly **firstly** was considered unacceptable. Originally the acceptable form of such a list was as in 'There are several reasons for staying here. First, we like the house, secondly we have pleasant neighbours, thirdly we hate moving house'. Some users now prefer to use the adjectival forms of 'second' and 'third' when using **first**, as in 'He has stated his reasons for going to another job. First, he has been offered a higher salary, second, he has more opportunities for promotion, third, he will have a company car'. As indicated, **firstly** is now quite acceptable and is the form preferred by many people, as in 'They have several reasons for not having a car. Firstly they have very little money, secondly, they live right next to the bus-stop, thirdly, they feel cars are not environmentally friendly'.

fish and **fishes** are both found as plural forms of 'fish', but **fish** is by far the more widely used form, as in 'He keeps tropical fish', 'Some fish live in fresh water and some in the sea' and 'there are now only three fish in the tank'. **Fishes** is rarely used but when it is, it is usually used to refer to different species of fish, as in 'He is comparing the fishes of the Pacific Ocean with those of the Indian Ocean'. **Fish** can also be used in this case.

first name see **Christian name**.

flaccid, meaning 'soft and limp', as in 'repelled by the sight of his flaccid flesh' causes problems both with reference to spelling and pronunciation. In spelling note the double *c*. As for pronunciation, **flaccid** is usually pronounced *flak*-sid but *flas*-id is a rarer alternative.

flair and **flare** are liable to be confused because they sound alike. However, they mean entirely different things. **Flair** refers to 'a natural aptitude or talent', as in 'She has a real flair for dress designing', or to 'stylishness or attractiveness', as in 'She always dresses with flair, although she does not spend much money on clothes'. As a noun, **flare** refers to a 'a bright, sudden unsteady flame', as in 'From the sea they caught sight of the flare of the bonfire on the hilltop', or 'a signal in the form of light used at sea', as in 'The captain of the sinking ship used flares to try to attract the attention of passing vessels'. As a verb **flare** means either 'to burn brightly and unsteadily', as in 'The match flared in the darkness', or 'to burst into activity', as in 'Tempers flare when the two families get together'. It also means 'to become wider at the bottom', as in 'skirts flaring at the knee'.

flak originally referred to 'gunfire aimed at enemy aircraft', as in 'Pilots returning across the English Channel encountered heavy flak'. In modern usage it is also applied to 'severe criticism', as in 'the government receiving flak for raising taxes'.

flammable and **inflammable** both mean 'easily set on fire, burning easily', as in 'Children's nightclothes should not be made of flammable/inflammable material' and 'The chemical is highly flammable/inflammable'. **Inflammable** is frequently misused because some people wrongly regard it as meaning 'not burning easily', thinking that it is like such words as 'incredible', 'inconceivable' and 'intolerant' where the prefix 'in' means 'not'.

flare see **flair**.

flaunt and **flout** are liable to be confused although they mean different things. **Flaunt** means 'to show off, to display in an ostentatious way', as in 'flaunting her new clothes in front of the other children who were envious of her' and 'flaunting her generous bust'. **Flout** means 'to disobey or disregard openly or scornfully', as in 'expelled for flouting school rules' and 'flout convention by not wearing evening dress'.

fleshly and **fleshy** are not interchangeable although they are both derived from the noun 'flesh'. **Fleshly** means 'referring to the body as opposed to the spirit', as in 'more interested in fleshly pleasure than in prayer'. **Fleshy** means either 'soft and pulpy, as in 'ripe, fleshy peaches', or 'plump', as in 'Women with fleshy upper arms should avoid sleeveless dresses'.

flounder and **flounce** are liable to be confused although they have different meanings. **Flounder** means 'to move with difficulty or clumsily, to struggle helplessly', as in 'walkers floundering in the swampy ground' and 'to hesitate or make mistakes', as in 'The politician answered the first few questions easily but

floundered when the interviewer asked him about his policies'. **Founder** means 'to sink', as in 'The ship hit some rocks and foundered' and 'to fail, to collapse', as in 'His business foundered for lack of enough capital' and 'The campaign foundered when the mayor withdrew his support'.

flout see **flaunt**.

flotsam and **jetsam** are often used together to refer to 'miscellaneous objects, odds and ends', as in 'We have moved most of the furniture to the new house—there's just the flotsam and jetsam left', and 'vagrants, tramps', as in 'people with no pity in their hearts for the flotsam and jetsam of society'. In the phrase **flotsam and jetsam** they are used as though they meant the same thing but this is not the case. Both words relate to the remains of a wrecked ship, but **flotsam** refers to 'the wreckage of the ship found floating in the water', as in 'The coastguards knew the ship must have broken up when they saw bits of flotsam near the rocks', while **jetsam** refers to 'goods and equipment thrown overboard from a ship in distress in order to lighten it', as in 'The coastguards were unable to find the ship although they found the jetsam'.

flounder see **founder**.

flu and **flue** are liable to be confused although they have entirely different meanings. **Flu** is a shortened form of 'influenza', as in 'He is off work with flu', 'She caught flu and had to cancel her skiing trip'. It is much more commonly used than 'influenza', which is restricted to very formal or technical contexts, as in 'an article on the dangers of influenza in a medical journal'. Note that **flu** is no longer spelt with an initial apostrophe although the spelling '**flu** was formerly common. **Flue** means 'a channel or pipe through which smoke, hot air or fumes pass from a boiler, etc, usually to a chimney', as in 'The boiler is not working properly as the flue needs to be cleaned'.

fluorescent, as in 'fluorescent lighting' or 'fluorescent paint', is frequently misspelt. Note the *uo* combination, the *sc* and *ent*.

focus as a verb has two possible spellings in its past participle and past tense. Formerly only **focused** was considered acceptable but in modern usage **focussed** is also considered acceptable. The same applies to the present participle and so **focusing** and **focussing** are both acceptable. **Focus** as a verb means 'to adjust the focus of', as in 'focus a camera'; 'to become able to see clearly', as in 'His eyes gradually began to focus in the darkened room'; 'to cause to be concentrated at a point', as in 'focus the sun's rays through a magnifying glass'; 'to concentrate (one's attention or mind) on', as in 'unable to focus his mind on the problem' and 'the committee should focus on improving the financial situation'.

As a noun **focus** has two possible plural forms. Of these **focuses** (not **focusses**) is the more common in modern usage except in very technical contexts when **foci** is used. **Focus** as a noun means 'the point at which rays of light or sound meet', as in 'the focus of the sun's rays'; 'the point at which the outline of something is most clearly seen', as in 'The trees on the horizon are not yet in focus'; 'a device or adjustment on a lens to produce a clearer image', as in 'a camera with a faulty focus'; 'centre of interest, attention, etc', as in 'The focus of the meeting was on getting the plans for the new road rejected' and 'In that dress she was the focus of attention'.

foetid *see* fetid.

foetus and fetus are both possible spellings of a word meaning 'a young human or animal that has developed within the womb but has not yet reached the stage of being born', as in 'doctors worrying about giving the pregnant woman a drug that might harm the foetus'. Originally fetus was restricted to American English but it is becoming increasingly used in British English also, as in 'a fetus liable to abort'. The adjective formed from foetus/fetus is foetal/fetal.

foment *see* ferment.

forbear and forebear are interchangeable in one meaning of forbear only. Forbear is a verb meaning 'to refrain from', as in 'I hope she can forbear from pointing out that she was right' and this cannot be spelt forebear. However, forebear meaning 'ancestor' can also be spelt forbear, as in 'One of his *forebears/forbears* received a gift of land from Henry VIII'.

The verb forbear is pronounced with the emphasis on the second syllable as for-*bair*. The nouns forbear and forebear are pronounced alike with the emphasis on the first syllable as *for*-bair. the past tense of the verb forbear is forbore, as in 'He forbore to mention that he was responsible for the mistake'.

forever can be spelt as two words when it means 'eternally, for all time', as in 'doomed to separate forever/for ever' and 'have faith in the fact that they would dwell forever/for ever with Christ'. In the sense of 'constantly or persistently', only forever is used, as in 'His wife was forever nagging' and 'the child was forever asking for sweets'.

formally and formerly are liable to be confused because they sound alike. Formally means 'in a formal way', as in 'dress very formally for the dinner' and 'address the meeting formally'. Formerly means 'previously, before, at an earlier time', as in 'Formerly the committee used to meet twice per month' and 'He was formerly chairman of the board'.

former and latter are opposites. Former refers to 'the first of two people or things mentioned' while latter refers to 'the second of two people or things mentioned', as in 'He was given two options, either to stay in his present post but accept less money or to be transferred to another branch of the company. He decided to accept the former/latter option'. Former also means

'previous, at an earlier time', as in 'He is a former chairman of the company' and 'She is a former holder of the championship title'.

formerly *see* formally.

formidable may be pronounced with the emphasis on the first syllable as *for*-mid-ibl or with the emphasis on the second syllable as for-*mid*-ibl. The first of these is the more widely used. The word means 'causing fear or apprehension', as in 'The sight of the raging torrent was a formidable prospect'; 'difficult to deal with', as in 'a formidable task'; 'arousing respect', as in 'a formidable opponent' and 'a formidable list of qualifications'.

forte causes problems with pronunciation. The usual pronunciation in is *for*-tay but it can also be pronounced as single syllable fort. The word means 'someone's strong point', as in 'Putting people at their ease is not her forte' and 'The chef's forte is desserts'. There is also a musical word forte meaning 'loud' or loudly'. It is of Italian origin and is pronounced either *for*-ti or *for*-tay.

forward and forwards are not interchangeable in all contexts. They are interchangeable in the adverbial sense of forward meaning 'towards the front', as in 'He took a step forward/forwards' and 'facing forward/forwards'. Forwards is never used as an alternative for forward as an adjective, as in 'forward planning'. Nor is forwards ever used in idiomatic phrasal verbs such as 'look forward', 'put forward', 'come forward', as in 'look forward to a happy retirement', 'put forward new proposals' and 'appeal to witnesses to come forward'.

founder *see* flounder.

foyer causes pronunciation problems. The most widely used pronunciation is foi-ay but it can also be pronounced fwah-yay following the original French pronunciation. It means 'an entrance hall in a hotel, theatre, etc'.

fulfil is frequently misspelt. Note that neither *l* is doubled. However the second *l* is doubled in the past tense and past participle as fulfilled and in the present participle as fulfilling. In American English the usual spelling is fulfill.

further *see* farther.

G

gaff and gaffe are liable to be confused because they sound alike. Gaff means 'a rod with an iron hook for pulling a large fish out of the water', as in 'The anglers in the boat reached for the gaff when they saw the size of the fish'. It is more commonly found in the slang phrase **blow the gaff**, meaning 'to reveal a secret', as in 'The thieves refused to tell the police where they had hidden the stolen money but the wife of one of them blew the gaff'. Gaffe means 'a social blunder, an indiscreet remark or deed', as in 'He wore a sports jacket to the dinner party and realized that he had made a gaffe when he saw everyone else in evening dress'.

gallop, meaning to go or ride fast, as in 'try to get the horse to gallop', is frequently misspelt. Note the double *l* and single *p*. The past tense, past participle and present participle are even more likely to be misspelt. The *p* does not double, as **galloped** and **galloping**. Thus we have 'horses which galloped across the plains' and 'watch the ponies galloping'.

gamble and gambol are liable to be confused because they sound alike although they mean different thing. Gamble is much more common than gambol and means 'to play games of chance for money', as in 'He gambles all night at the casino', or 'to bet, wager or risk money on something uncertain', as in 'He gambled all his money on the horse in the last race' and 'He gambled all his savings on a risky business venture'. Gambol means 'to skip about', as in 'Lambs used to gambol in the fields here'. The single *l* doubles in the past tense, past participle and present participle as **gambolled** and **gambolling**. Thus 'The lion cubs gambolled around their mother' and 'Watch the children gambolling on the beach'.

gaol see jail.

-gate is a modern suffix which is added to a noun to indicate something scandalous. Most of the words so formed are short-lived and forgotten about almost as soon as they are invented. In modern usage they are frequently used to apply to sexual scandals, but originally **-gate** was restricted to some form of political scandal. The suffix is derived from **Watergate**, and refers to a political scandal in the United States during President Richard Nixon's re-election campaign in 1972 when Republican agents were caught breaking into the headquarters of the Democratic Party in Washington, called the Watergate Building. The uncovering of the attempts to cover up the break-in led to Richard Nixon's resignation.

gauge, meaning 'measure, standard', as in 'petrol gauge' and 'a gauge of his intelligence', is frequently misspelt. Note that the *a* comes before the *u*. It is a common error to put them the wrong way round.

gay originally meant 'merry, light-hearted', as in 'the gay laughter of children playing' and 'everyone feeling gay at the sight of the sunshine'. Although this mean-

ing still exists in modern usage, it is rarely used since **gay** has come to be an accepted word for 'homosexual', as in 'gay rights' and 'gay bars'. Although the term can be applied to men or women it is most commonly applied to men, the corresponding word for women being **lesbian**. There is a growing tendency among homosexuals to describe themselves as **queer**, a term that was formerly regarded as being offensive.

geriatric is frequently found in medical contexts to mean 'elderly' or 'old', as in 'an ever-increasing number of geriatric patients' and 'a shortage of geriatric wards'. In such contexts **geriatric** is not used in a belittling or derogatory way, **geriatrics** being the name given to the branch of medicine concerned with the health and diseases of elderly people. However, **geriatric** is often used in the general language to refer to old people in a derogatory or scornful way, as in 'geriatric shoppers getting in the way' or 'geriatric drivers holding up the traffic'.

gibe and jibe both mean 'to jeer at, mock, make fun of', as in 'rich children gibing/jibing at the poor children for wearing out-of-date clothes'. Gibe and jibe are nouns as well as verbs as in 'politicians tired of the gibes/jibes of the press'.

gipsy and gypsy are both acceptable spellings, as in 'gipsies/gypsies travelling through the country in their caravans'. Some people object to the word **gipsy** or **gypsy**, preferring the word traveller, as in 'councils being asked to build sites for travellers'. The term **traveller** is used to apply to a wider range of people who travel the country, as in 'New Age travellers', and not just to gipsies, who are Romany in origin.

girl means 'a female child or adolescent', as in 'separate schools for girls and boys' and 'Girls tend to mature more quickly than boys'. However it is often applied to a young woman, or indeed to a woman of any age, as in 'He asked his wife if she was going to have a night out with the girls from the office'. Many women object to this use, regarding it as patronizing, although the user of the term does not always intend to convey this impression.

glamorous is frequently misspelt. Note that there is no *u* before the *r*, although there is one in **glamour**. Glamorous means 'beautiful, stylish, elegant', as in 'glamorous filmstars'.

glutton see gourmand.

gobbledygook and gobbledegook are both acceptable spellings of a word meaning 'pretentious language that is difficult to understand, often found in official documents', as in 'The leaflets were meant to explain how to apply for a grant but they were written in gobbledygook'.

gorilla and guerilla are liable to be confused because they sound alike. They are completely different in meaning. Gorilla is a type of large African ape, as in

'The zoo has several gorillas'. It is also used informally to describe a large, powerful, often ugly and brutal man, as in 'The gangster has a gang of gorillas to protect him'. **Guerilla**, which can also be spelt **guerrilla**, means 'a member of an irregular army who fights in small, secret groups', as in 'The army were shot at by guerillas hiding in the hills'. Both words are pronounced alike as gir-*il*-a.

gourmand and **gourmet** and **glutton** all have reference to food but they do not mean quite the same thing. **Gourmand** refers to 'a person who likes food and eats a lot of it', as in 'Gourmands tucking into huge helpings of the local food'. It means much the same as **glutton**, but **glutton** is a more condemnatory term, as in 'gluttons stuffing food into their mouths'. **Gourmet** is a more refined term, being used to refer to 'a person who enjoys food and who is discriminating and knowledgeable about it', as in 'gourmets who spend their holidays seeking out good local restaurants and produce'. In modern usage **gourmet** is often used as an adjective to mean 'high-class, elaborate, expensive', as in 'gourmet restaurants' and 'gourmet foods'.

graffiti is frequently misspelt. Note the double *f* and single *t*. The word is used of 'unofficial writing and drawings, often of an obscene nature, on the walls of public places', as in 'trying to clean the graffiti from the walls of the public toilets'. Graffiti is Italian in origin and is actually the plural form of **graffito**, meaning a single piece of writing or drawing, but this is now hardly ever used in English.

gratuitous is liable to be misspelt and misunderstood. Note the *ui* combination. The word means 'uncalled-for, without good reason, unwarranted, unnecessary', as in 'resent her gratuitous advice' and 'upset by her gratuitous insults'.

gray *see* **grey**.

green is used to mean 'conserved with the conservation of the environment', as in 'a political party concerned with green issues' and 'buy as many green products as possible'. The word is derived from German *grün*, the political environmental lobby having started in West Germany, as it was then called.

grievous causes problems with reference to both spelling and pronunciation. Note the *ie* combination and the absence of *i* before *ou*. It is pronounced *gree*-vus. **Grievous** means 'causing grief or suffering', as in 'grievous bodily harm', or 'serious, grave', as in 'a grievous crime'.

grey and **gray** are both acceptable spellings. In British English, however, **grey** is the more common, as in 'different shades of grey' and 'grey hair', but **gray** is the standard form in American English.

guarantee is frequently misspelt. Note the *u* before the *a* and the *a* after the *r*. It means 'a promise or assurance that certain conditions will be fulfilled', as in 'under the terms of the manufacturer's guarantee'.

guerilla, guerrilla *see* **gorilla**.

gynaecology is frequently misspelt. Note the *y* after the *g* and the *ae* combination after the *n*. **Gynaecology** refers to 'the study and treatment of disorders of women, specially of the female reproductive system', as in 'have an appointment at the gynaecology department'. The American English spelling is **gynecology**.

gypsy *see* **gipsy**.

H

haemorrhage is frequently misspelt. Note the *ae* and the *rrh* combinations. It can be either a noun meaning 'excessive loss of blood', as in 'a haemorrhage from the womb after the birth of the baby', or a verb meaning 'to bleed heavily', as in 'haemorrhaging badly after the birth of the baby'. In American English the word is spelt **hemorrhage**.

hail and **hale** are liable to be confused. They are pronounced alike but have different meanings. **Hail** refers to frozen rain, as in 'get caught in a storm of hail', or to 'something coming in great numbers and with force', as in 'a hail of bullets'. As a verb it means 'to fall as hail', as in 'It began to hail', or 'to come down fast and with force', as in 'Bullets hailed down on them'. There is another word **hail**, which is a verb that means 'to call to in order to attract attention', as in 'He hailed a friend on the other side of the street'; 'to acknowledge enthusiastically as in 'hail him as their new leader' and 'hail his new painting as a masterpiece'; 'to come from', as in 'She hails from a small town up north'. **Hale** means 'healthy and strong' and is frequently found in the phrase 'hale and hearty', as in 'he was very ill but he is hale and hearty again'.

hallo, hello and **hullo** are all acceptable spellings of a word used in greeting, as in 'Hallo/hello/hullo, I didn't expect to see you here' and 'He was in a hurry and didn't stop to say "hallo/hello/hullo"'.

handicap is frequently misspelt in the past tense, past participle and present participle, as in 'physically handicapped people' and 'handicapping circumstances'. The word **handicap** is disliked by some people because they feel it is too negative a term. There is as yet no widespread alternative apart from **disabled**, although various suggestions have been made as part of the politically correct language movement, such as **physically challenged** and **differently abled**.

hangar and **hanger** are liable to be confused since they sound alike. However, they have totally different meanings. **Hangar** refers to 'a building for housing aircraft', as in 'a hangar holding four small aircraft'. **Hanger** refers to 'an apparatus on which clothes are hung', as in 'The hotel didn't provide enough hangars for their clothes'.

hanged and **hung** are both past participles and past tenses of the verb 'to hang' but they are used in different contexts. **Hanged** is restricted to the sense of 'hang' that means 'to suspend by the neck until dead', as in 'He was hanged for murder' and 'She hanged herself while depressed'. **Hung** is used in the other sense of 'hang', as in 'They hung the picture on the wall by the door' and 'A towel hung from the rail'.

hanger *see* **hangar**.

harass causes problems with reference both to spelling and pronunciation. Note the single *r* and the double *s*. It is a common error to put double *r* and single *s*. There

are two possible pronunciations. Traditionally it is pronounced with the stress on the first syllable, as *har*-as. However, in modern usage there is an increasing tendency to put the emphasis on the second syllable, as har-*as*, which is how the word is pronounced in America.

hard and **soft** are both terms applied to drugs. **Hard drugs** refer to 'strong drugs that are likely to be addictive', as in 'Heroin and cocaine are hard drugs'. **Soft drugs** refer to 'drugs that are considered unlikely to cause addiction', as in 'cannabis and other soft drugs'.

hardly is used to indicate a negative idea. Therefore a sentence or clause containing it does not require another negative. Sentences, such as 'I couldn't hardly see him' and 'He left without hardly a word' are *wrong*. They should read 'I could hardly see him' and 'He left with hardly a word'. **Hardly** is followed by 'when', not 'than', as in 'Hardly had he entered the house when he collapsed', although the 'than' construction is very common.

hare-brained is frequently misspelt as 'hair-brained'. It means 'foolish', as in 'a hare-brained scheme to make money'.

height is a simple word that is frequently misspelt. Note the *ei* and the *gh* combination. As well as meaning 'the distance from the bottom to the top of a person or object', as in 'measure the child's height', it can mean 'the highest point of something', as in 'at the height of his career', or 'the most intense or extreme point of something', as in 'at the height of their passion'.

heinous, meaning 'very wicked', as in 'a heinous crime', causes problems both with reference to spelling and pronunciation. Note the *ei*. It is most commonly pronounced *hay*-nis, although *hee*-nis also exists.

hello *see* **hallo**.

he/she is a convention used to avoid sexism. Before the rise of feminism anyone referred to, whose sex was not specified, was assumed to be male, as in 'Each pupil must take his book home' and 'Every driver there parked his car illegally'. The only exception to this occurred in situations that were thought to be particularly appropriate to women, as in 'The cook should make her own stock' and 'The nurse has left her book behind'. In modern usage where attempts are made to avoid sexism either **he/she** or 'he or she' is frequently used, as in 'Each manager is responsible for his/her department' or 'It is a doctor's duty to explain the nature of the treatment to his or her patient'. People who regard this convention as being clumsy should consider restructuring the sentence or putting it in the plural, as in 'All managers are responsible for their departments'. Some users prefer to be ungrammatical and use a plural pronoun with a singular noun, as in 'Every pupil should take their books home'.

hereditary and **heredity** are liable to be confused. **Hereditary** is an adjective meaning 'passed on from parent to child, genetically transmitted', as in 'suffer from a hereditary disease', or 'passed on from parent to child, inherited', as in 'a hereditary title'. **Heredity** is the noun from which **hereditary** is derived, as in 'part of his genetic heredity' and 'The disease can be put down to heredity'.

heterosexism refers to 'discrimination and prejudice by a heterosexual person against a homosexual one', as in 'He was convinced that he had not got the job because he was gay—that the employer had been guilty of heterosexism'.

historic and **historical** are both adjectives formed from the noun history' but they are not interchangeable. **Historic** refers to events that are important enough to earn, or have earned, a place in history, as in 'Nelson's historic victory at Trafalgar' and 'the astronaut's historic landing on the moon'. It can be used loosely to mean 'extremely memorable', as in 'attend a historic party'. **Historical** means 'concerning past events', as in 'historical studies', or 'based on the study of history, as in 'take into consideration only historical facts' and 'produce historical evidence'.

hoard and **horde** are liable to be confused. They sound alike but they have completely different meanings. **Hoard** refers to 'a collected and reserved store', as in 'the miser's hoard of money' and 'a hoard of old comics'. It can also be a verb meaning 'to collect and store', as in 'hoarding food because they thought it was going to be rationed' and 'squirrels hoarding nuts for the winter'. **Horde** refers to 'a large crowd of people, a multitude', as in 'Hordes of people arrived to see the pop star arriving at the theatre'.

honorary and **honourable** are liable to be confused. They are both derived from the noun **honour**, but they mean different things. **Honorary** means 'given as an honour rather than acquired through the usual channels', as in 'an honorary degree', or 'unpaid', as in 'the honorary secretary' and 'an honorary post'. **Honourable** means 'showing honour', as in 'an honourable man' and 'the honourable thing to do', and 'worthy of honour', as in 'perform honourable deeds in battle'.

hopefully has two meanings. The older meaning is 'with hope', as in 'The child looked hopefully at the sweet-shop window' and 'It is better to travel hopefully than to arrive'. A more recent meaning, which is disliked by some people, means 'it is to be hoped that', as in 'Hopefully we shall soon be there'.

horde *see* **hoard**.

hospitable can be pronounced in two ways. The more traditional pronunciation has the emphasis on the first syllable, as *hos*-pit-ibl. In modern usage it is sometimes pronounced with the emphasis on the second syllable, as hos-*pit*-ibl. The word means 'showing or giving hospitality, generous to guests', as in 'He is very hospitable and is always having people to stay' and 'a most hospitable hostess who fed her guests very well'.

hullo *see* **hallo**.

human and **humane** are liable to be confused. **Human** means either 'referring to human beings', as in 'not fit for human habitation', or 'kindly', as in 'He holds a very important position but he is a very human person'. **Humane** means 'showing kindness, sympathy or understanding', as in 'their humane attitude to prisoners of war' and 'Be humane and put the dying animal to sleep'.

humanism and **humanitarianism** are liable to be confused. **Humanism** is a philosophy that values greatly human beings and their rôle, and rejects the need for religion, as in 'She was brought up as a Christian but she decided to embrace humanism in later life'. **Humanitarianism** refers to the philosophy and actions of people who wish to improve the lot of their fellow human beings and help them, as in 'humanitarians trying to help the refugees by taking them food and clothes'.

humorous is frequently misspelt. Note the *o* before the *r*. It is liable to be confused with 'humour' and an extra *u* added before the *r*.

hung *see* **hanged**.

hygiene is liable to be misspelt. Note the *y* after the *h*, not *i*. It means 'the study and practice of cleanliness and good health', as in 'poor standards of hygiene in the hotel kitchens'.

hyper- and **hypo-** are liable to be confused. They sound rather similar but they are opposites. **Hyper-** means 'above, excessively', as in 'hyperactive', 'hyperexcitable'. **Hypo-** means 'under, beneath', as in 'hypothermia'.

I

-**ible** *see* -**able**.

identical in modern usage can be followed by either 'with' or 'to'. Formerly only 'with' was considered correct, as in 'His new suit is identical with the one he bought last year'. Now 'to' is also considered acceptable, as in 'a brooch identical to one which he bought for his wife'.

idioms are expressions the meanings of which are different from the literal meanings of the individual words that they contain. Thus 'straight from the shoulder', 'have a finger in every pie' and 'have one's back to the wall' are all idioms.

idiosyncrasy is frequently misspelt. Note the *y* after the *s*, and the *asy* combination, not *acy*. It means 'a particular and individual way of behaving, thinking, etc', as in 'It was one of his idiosyncrasies always to buy yellow cars'.

idle and **idol** are liable to be confused since they sound alike. They mean entirely different things. **Idle** is an adjective meaning 'inactive, not functioning', as in 'machines lying idle', and 'lazy', as in 'too idle to get up and do any work'. **Idol** refers to 'something or someone that one worships or admires', as in 'worship idols carved from wood', 'Her elder brother was her idol' and 'pop stars who are the idols of teenagers'.

idyllic causes problems both with reference to spelling and pronunciation. Note the *y* and double *l*. It is pronounced with the emphasis on the second syllable and the first syllable is usually pronounced to rhyme with 'lid', as in id-*il*-ik. The first syllable is sometimes pronounced with 'wide', as in *id*-il-ik. The word means 'peaceful and pleasant, perfect', as in 'a cottage in an idyllic setting'.

i.e. is the abbreviation of a Latin phrase *id est*, meaning 'that is', as in 'He is a lexicographer, i.e. a person who edits dictionaries'. It is mostly used in written, rather than formal contexts.

illegible and **eligible** are liable to be confused although they have completely different meanings. **Illegible** means 'impossible to decipher, make out or read', as in 'unable to understand the message because of her totally illegible handwriting'. **Eligible** means 'qualified, suitable', as in 'several candidates who were eligible for the post' and 'eligible bachelors'. **Illegible** is pronounced with the emphasis on the the second syllable (il-*lej*-ibl) but **eligible** is pronounced with the emphasis on the first syllable (*el*-ij-ibl).

illegible and **unreadable** are not totally interchangeable. **Illegible** refers to something that is impossible to make out or decipher, as in 'her handwriting is practically illegible'. **Unreadable** can also mean this, as in 'unreadable handwriting', but it can also mean 'unable to be read with understanding or enjoyment', as in 'His writing is so full of jargon that it is unreadable'.

illicit and **elicit** are liable to be confused. They sound alike although they have totally different meanings. **Illicit** means 'unlawful', as in 'the sale of illicit drugs', or 'against the rules of society', as in 'His wife did not know about his illicit affair with his secretary'. **Elicit** means 'to draw out, often with difficulty', as in 'We finally succeeded in eliciting a response from them' and 'All attempts at eliciting the truth from the boy failed'. Both words sound alike, with the emphasis on the second syllable as il-*lis*-it.

illusion *see* **allusion**.

illusion *see* **delusion**.

imaginary and **imaginative** are liable to be confused. They are related but do not mean the same thing. **Imaginary** means 'existing only in the imagination, unreal', as in 'The child has an imaginary friend'. **Imaginative** means 'having a vivid or creative imagination', as in 'An imaginative child who was always inventing her own games', and 'indicating or using a vivid or creative imagination', as in 'an imaginative adventure story'.

imbroglio means 'a confused, complicated or embarrassing situation', as in 'politicians getting involved in an international imbroglio during the summit conference'. It is liable to be misspelt and mispronounced. Note the *g* which is liable to be omitted erroneously as it is not pronounced. It is pronounced im-*bro*-lio with emphasis on the second syllable which rhymes with 'foe'. **Imbroglio** is used only in formal or literary contexts.

immigrant *see* **emigrant**.

immoral *see* **amoral**.

impasse causes problems with reference to meaning, spelling and pronunciation. It means 'a difficult position or situation from which there is no way out, deadlock', as in 'The negotiations between management and workers have reached an impasse with neither side being willing to compromise'. Note the final *e* in the spelling. The first syllable can be pronounced 'am', or 'om' in an attempt at following the original French pronunciation, although in modern usage it is frequently totally anglicized as 'im'.

impeccable is frequently misspelt. Note the -*able*, not -*ible*, and the double *c*. The word means 'faultless, free from error or defect', as in 'The pianist gave an impeccable performance' and 'It was a difficult situation but his behaviour was impeccable'.

impious is frequently misspelt. The emphasis should be on the first syllable as *im*-pi-us. This is unlike 'impiety' where the stress is on the second syllable. **Impious** means 'showing a lack of respect for God or religion'.

implicit *see* **explicit**.

imply and **infer** are often used interchangeably but they in fact are different in meaning. **Imply** means 'to suggest, to hint at', as in 'We felt that she was implying that he was lying' and 'She did not actually say that

973

there was going to be a delay but she implied it'. **Infer** means 'to deduce, to conclude', as in 'From what the employer said we inferred that there would be some redundancies' and 'From the annual financial reports observers inferred the company was about to go bankrupt'. Note that **infer** doubles the *r* when adding '-ed' or '-ing' to form the past tense, past participle or present participle as **inferred** and **inferring**.

impracticable and **impractical** are liable to be confused. **Impracticable** means 'impossible to put into practice, not workable', as in 'In theory the plan is fine but it is impracticable in terms of costs'. **Impractical** means 'not sensible or realistic', as in 'It is impractical to think that you will get there and back in a day'; 'not skilled at doing or making things', as in 'He is a brilliant academic but he is hopelessly impractical'.

inapt and **inept** are similar in meaning in one sense of **inept**. **Inapt** means 'inappropriate, unsuitable', as in 'The speaker's remarks were totally inapt', 'make a few inapt comments on the situation' and 'inapt behaviour'. **Inept** can mean much the same as this except that it suggests also clumsiness', as in 'embarrassed by his inept remarks'. **Inept** also means 'unskilful, clumsy', as in 'his inept handling of the situation' and 'make an inept attempt at mending the roof'.

incomparable is liable to be mispronounced. The emphasis should be on the second syllable and not the third. It should be pronounced in-*kom*-pir-ibl. **Incomparable** means 'without compare', as in 'her incomparable kindness' and in 'his incomparable rendition of the song'.

incredible and **incredulous** are liable to be confused although they mean different things. **Incredible** means 'unbelievable' or 'difficult to believe', as in 'I find his account of the accident totally incredible' and 'It is incredible that everyone accepts his story'. It also means 'amazing', as in 'earn an incredible amount of money'. **Incredulous** means 'not believing, disbelieving', as in 'His incredulous listeners stared at him'.

indefinite article *see* **a**.

indefinitely is frequently misspelt. Note the *i* before the *t*. Many people wrongly put an *a*. It means 'for an unspecified time', as in 'You could wait indefinitely for a car exactly like that'.

independent is frequently misspelt. Note the final *e*. It is never spelt with an *a*. See **dependant**.

indexes and **indices** are both plural forms of 'index'. In modern usage **indexes** is the more common form in general language, as in 'Indexes are essential in large reference books'. An **index** in this sense is 'an alphabetical list given at the back of a book as a guide to its contents'. The form **indices** is mostly restricted to technical contexts, such as mathematical information. **Indices** is pronounced in-dis-is and is the Latin form of the plural.

indict and **indite** are liable to be confused since they are pronounced alike but they have different meanings. **Indict** means 'to charge, to accuse', as in 'He has been indicted on a charge of murder'. **Indite** is a rarer word meaning 'to write down', as in 'The headmaster indited the names of the culprits on an official report'. The words are both pronounced with the emphasis on the second syllable which rhymes with 'light' as in-*dit*.

indispensable is frequently misspelt. Note the -*able* ending, not -*ible*. It means 'absolutely essential', as in 'He now finds his computer indispensable' and 'Since both parents work full time a good nanny is indispensable'.

indite *see* **indict**.

individual refers to 'a single person as opposed to a group', as in 'The rights of the community matter but so do the rights of the individual'. **Individual** is also sometimes used instead of 'person', but in such cases it is often used in a disapproving or belittling way, as in 'What an unpleasant individual she is!' and 'The individual who designed that building should be shot'.

indoor and **indoors** are not interchangeable. **Indoor** is an adjective, as in 'have an indoor match' and 'indoor games'. **Indoors** is an adverb, as in 'children playing outdoors instead of watching television indoors' and 'sleep outdoors on warm evenings instead of indoors'.

inequality and **inequity** are liable to be confused although they mean different things. **Inequality** means 'lack of equality, the state of being unequal or different', as in 'an inequality in the pay structures of the male and female workers' and 'fight against racial inequalities in the job market'. **Inequity** means 'unfairness, unjustness', as in 'feel that there was a certain inequity in the judge's decision'.

infectious *see* **contagious**.

infer *see* **imply**.

infinite and **infinitesimal** are similar in meaning but are not interchangeable. **Infinite** means 'without limit', as in 'infinite space', or 'very great', as in 'have infinite patience' and 'He seems to have an infinite capacity for hard work'. **Infinitesimal** means 'very small, negligible', as in 'an infinitesimal difference in size' and 'an infinitesimal increase'. **Infinitesimal** is pronounced with the emphasis on the fourth syllable in-fin-it-*es*-im-il.

inflammable *see* **flammable**.

influenza *see* **flu**.

informer and **informant** both refer to 'a person who provides information' but they are used in different contexts. **Informer** is used to refer to 'a person who gives information to the police or authorities about a criminal, fugitive, etc', as in 'The local police have a group of informers who tell them what is going on in the criminal underworld' and 'The resistance worker was caught by the enemy soldier when an informer told them about his activities'. An **informant** provides more general information, as in 'My informant keeps me up-to-date with changes in personnel'.

ingenious and **ingenuous** are liable to be confused. They look rather alike but they mean completely different things. **Ingenious** means 'clever, inventive', as in 'an ingenious device for opening wine bottles' and 'It was ingenious of her to find a quick way to get to the new house'. **Ingenuous** means 'innocent' or 'naive', as in 'so ingenuous as to believe his lies'.

in-law is usually found in compounds such as 'mother-in-law' and 'father-in-law'. When these compounds are in the plural the *s* should be added to the first word of the compound, not to **in-law**, as in 'mothers-in-law' and 'fathers-in-law'.

in lieu, which means 'instead of', as in 'receive extra pay in lieu of holidays', causes problems with pronunciation. It may be pronounced in lew or in loo.

innocuous is frequently misspelt. Note the double *n* and the *ouo* combination. It means 'harmless', as in 'He has a reputation for fierceness but he seems fairly innocuous' and 'It seemed an innocuous remark but she was upset by it'.

input used to be a technical term with particular application to computers. This meaning still exists and **input** can refer to the data, power, etc, put into a computer. As a verb it means 'to enter data into a computer', as in 'input the details of all the travel resorts in the area'. In modern usage it is frequently used in general language to mean 'contribution', as in 'Everyone is expected to provide some input for tomorrow's conference'. It is even found in this sense as a verb, as in 'input a great deal to the meeting'.

inquiry *see* **enquiry**.

install and **instal** are now both considered acceptable spellings. **Install** was formerly considered to be the only correct spelling and it is still the more common. The *l* is doubled in **instal** in the past participle, past tense and present participle as **installed, installing**. It means 'to put in', as in 'he installed a new television set'. The noun is spelt **instalment**.

instantaneously and **instantly** are interchangeable. Both mean 'immediately, at once', as in 'They obeyed instantaneously/instantly' and 'The accident victims were killed instantly/instantaneously'.

instil is often misspelt 'instill'. Note the single *l*. It means 'to introduce gradually', as in 'instil a sense of responsibility into children'. The *l* doubles in the past participle, past tense and present participle as **instilled** and **instilling**.

intense and **intensive** are not interchangeable. Intense means 'very strong, extreme', as in 'an intense desire to scream' and 'unable to tolerate the intense cold on the icy slopes'. **Intensive** means 'thorough', as in 'conduct an intensive search', and 'concentrated', as in 'an intensive course in first aid' and 'intensive bombing'.

interment and **internment** mean different things. **Interment** means 'burial', as in 'delay the interment of the bodies until a post mortem takes place'. **Internment** means 'imprisonment, especially of prisoners-of-war, etc', as in 'released at the end of the war after several years of internment'. In both **interment** and **internment** the emphasis is on the second syllable.

interpretative and **interpretive** are both forms of the same word. They mean 'interpreting', as in 'an interpretative/interpretive study of his poetry'.

introvert *see* **extrovert**.

invalid refers to two different words. If it is pronounced with the emphasis on the second syllable, as in-*val*-id it means 'not valid, no longer valid', as in 'This visa becomes invalid after six months'. If it is pronounced with the emphasis on the first syllable, as *in*-val-id, it means 'a person who is ill', as in 'The doctor has arrived to see the invalid'.

invent *see* **discover**.

inventory is liable to be pronounced wrongly. Unlike the word 'invention', the emphasis is on the first syllable as *in*-ven-tri or *in*-ven-tor-i. **Inventory** means 'a detailed list of goods in a house, etc,' as in 'Take an inventory of the furniture before you rent the house'.

inward and **inwards** are not used interchangeably. **Inward** is an adjective, as in 'an inward curve' and 'No one could guess her inward feelings'. **Inwards** is an adverb, as in 'toes turning inwards' and 'thoughts turning inwards'. **Inward** can be used as an adverb in the same way as **inwards**.

IQ is the abbreviation of 'intelligence quotient', as in 'He has a high IQ. It is always written in capital letters and is sometimes written with full stops and sometimes not, according to preference.

irascible is frequently misspelt. Unlike 'irritable' it has a single *r*. Note the *c* and the *-ible* ending. It means 'easily roused to anger', as in 'The children were told not to disturb the irascible old man'.

irony is 'the expression of one's meaning by saying the direct opposite of one's thoughts', as in 'This is a fine state of affairs' when in fact things have gone wrong. The adjective is **ironic**, as in 'make ironic remarks'.

irrelevant is frequently misspelt. Note the double r and the *-ant* ending.

irreparable is frequently both mispronounced and misspelt. Note the double *r*, the *a* before the *r* and the *-able* ending. It should be pronounced with the emphasis on the second syllable, as ir-*rep*-ar-abl. The word means 'unable to be put right', as in 'Being abused as a child inflicted irreparable mental damage on him'. It is usually applied to abstract nouns, **unrepairable** being used for objects, as in 'shoes that are unrepairable'. **Unrepairable** is pronounced with the emphasis on the third syllable (*pair*) which rhymes with 'care'.

irrespective is followed by the preposition 'of'. The phrase means 'not taking account of, not taking into consideration', as in 'All can go on the trip, irrespective of age'.

irrevocable is frequently misspelt and mispronounced. Note the double *r* and the *-able* ending. It is pronounced with the emphasis on the second syllable, as ir-*rev*-ok-ibl. When applied to legal judgements, etc, it is sometimes pronounced with the emphasis on the third syllable, as ir-rev-*ok*-ibl. The word means 'unable to be changed or revoked', as in 'Their decision to get divorced is irrevocable' and 'The jury's decision is irrevocable'.

-ise and **-ize** are both verb endings. In British English there are many verbs that can be spelt ending in either **-ise** or **-ize**, as 'computerise/ize', 'economise/ize', 'finalise/ize', 'hospitalise/ize', 'modernise/ize', 'organise/ize', 'realise/ize', 'theorise/ize'. There are a few verbs that cannot be spelt **-ize**. These include 'advertise', 'advise', 'comprise', 'despise', 'exercise', 'revise', 'supervise' and 'televise'.

-ism is a suffix originally used to form nouns indicating doctrine or system, as in 'Thatcherism' and 'Marxism'. This use is still current but **-ism** is now commonly used to indicate discrimination, as in 'ageism', 'racism', 'sexism'. The agent nouns from nouns ending in **-ism** in the latter sense end in **-ist**, as 'ageist', 'racist', 'sexist'.

itinerary is frequently misspelt. Note the *e* before the first *r*, and the *a* before the second *r*.

its and **it's** are liable to be confused. **Its** is an adjective meaning 'belonging to it', as in 'The house has lost its charm' and 'The dog does not like its kennel'. **It's** means 'it is', as in 'Do you know if it's raining?' and 'It's not fair to expect her to do all the chores'.

-ize *see* **-ise**.

J

jail and **gaol** are both acceptable spellings although jail is the more common. They mean 'prison' and can be both nouns and verbs, as in 'sent to jail/gaol for killing his wife' and 'jail/gaol him for his part in the bank robbery'.

jargon refers to the technical or specialized language used by a particular group, e.g. doctors, computer engineers, sociologists, etc, to communicate with each other within their specialty. It should be avoided in the general language as it will not be clear to the ordinary person exactly what is meant.

jersey *see* **cardigan**.

jeopardize is liable to be misspelt. Note the *o*. It is pronounced *jep*-er-dise and means 'to put at risk', as in 'He jeopardizes his career by his unpunctuality.'

jetsam *see* **flotsam**.

jettison is frequently misspelt. Note the double *t* and single *s*. In the past tense, past participle and present participle the *n* is not doubled, as **jettisoned** and **jettisoning**. It means 'to throw out, especially in order to make a ship, aircraft, etc, lighter', as in 'The ship's captain decided to jettison most of the cargo'. It also means 'to abandon, reject', as in 'They have had to jettison their plans for expansion because of lack of money'.

jewellery and **jewelry** are both acceptable spellings, as in 'A great deal of jewellery/jewelry was stolen in the robbery', but **jewellery** is the more common spelling in British English.

jibe *see* **gibe**.

jodhpurs, meaning 'trousers worn when horse-riding', is frequently misspelt. Note the *h*, which is liable to be omitted since it is silent, or put in the wrong place. The word is pronounced *jod*-purs.

judgement and **judgment** are both acceptable spellings, as in 'accept the judgement/judgment of the referee', although in British English **judgement** is slightly more common. **Judgment** is used in legal contexts.

judicial and **judicious** are liable to be confused but they are completely different in meaning. **Judicial** means 'referring to a court of law', as in 'judicial proceedings' and 'a judicial inquiry'. **Judicious** means 'having or showing good sense or judgement, wise', as in ' a judicious choice of words' and 'a judicious course of action'.

just is liable to be put in the wrong place in a sentence. It should be placed before the word it refers to, as in 'He has just one book left to sell', not 'He just has one book left to sell'. **Just** in the sense of 'in the very recent past' is used with the perfect tense, as in 'They have just finished the job', not 'They just finished the job'.

K

kaleidoscope is frequently misspelt. Note the *ei* and the first *o*. It is pronounced with the emphasis on the second syllable, which rhymes with 'my', as kal-*i*-do-skop. **Kaleidoscope** refers to 'a kind of toy consisting of a tube containing small loose pieces of coloured glass and mirrors which reflect the glass pieces to form changing patterns when the tube is turned', as in 'The child was fascinated by the changing colours of the kaleidoscope'. It also means 'a constantly and rapidly changing pattern', as in 'The Eastern market was a kaleidoscope of colour', or 'a succession of changing phases', as in 'the kaleidoscope of international politics'.

kerb *see* **curb**.

khaki is frequently misspelt. Note the *h* after the first *k*. It is liable either to be omitted in error or put in the wrong place. **Khaki** is pronounced kah-ki and refers to 'a yellowish brown colour', as in 'Military uniforms are often khaki in colour'.

kidnap is liable to be misspelt in the past tense, past participle and present participle when it doubles the *p* as **kidnapped, kidnapping.** The agent noun, 'one who kidnaps', is spelt **kidnapper. Kidnap** means 'to take away by force and illegally, often with a view to obtaining money or having specified demands met', as in 'The president's daughter was kidnapped by a gang who asked her father for a huge ransom' and 'The terrorists kidnapped the foreign diplomat and would not let him go unless some of their number were released from prison in his country'.

kilometre has two possible pronunciations in modern usage. It can be pronounced with the emphasis on the first syllable, as *kil*-o-meet-er, or with the emphasis on the second syllable, as kil-*om*-it-er. The first of these is the more traditional pronunciation but the second is becoming common. The word means 'the metric unit of length', as in 'It is 200 kilometres from there to Paris'.

kind should be used with a singular noun, as 'This kind of accident can be avoided'. This should not read 'These kind of accidents can be avoided'. Similarly 'The children do not like that kind of film' is correct, not 'The children do not like those kind of films'. A plural noun can be used if the sentence is rephrased as 'Films of that kind are not liked by children'.

   Kind of, meaning 'rather', as in 'That restaurant's kind of dear' and 'She's kind of tired of him', is informal and should be avoided in formal contexts.

kindly can be either an adjective or adverb. The adjective means 'kind, friendly, sympathetic', as in 'A kindly lady took pity on the children and lent them some money to get home' and 'She gave them a kindly smile'. The adverb means 'in a kind manner', as in 'We were treated kindly by the local people' and 'They will not look kindly on his actions'.

kneeled and **knelt**, the past tense and past participle of the verb 'to kneel', are both acceptable spellings although **knelt** is more common, as in 'He knelt and asked for forgiveness' and 'She knelt down to look under the car'.

knit in modern usage is becoming increasingly used as a noun to mean 'a knitted garment', as in 'a shop selling beautifully coloured knits'.

knowledgeable is frequently misspelt. Note the *d*, which is often omitted in error, the *e* after the *g*, which is also liable to be omitted in error, and the -*able* ending. **Knowledgeable** means 'knowing a lot, well-informed', as in 'take advice from people more knowledgeable than himself' and 'He is extremely knowledgeable on the subject of ancient Greece'.

L

laboratory is frequently mispronounced. It should be pronounced with the emphasis on the second syllable, as lab-*or*-a-tor-i or lab-*or*-a-tri. In American English the emphasis is on the first syllable. The word refers to a 'room or building where scientific work, such as research and experiments, is carried out', as in 'collect the results of the blood tests from the laboratory'.

laborious is frequently misspelt. Note that there is no *u* before *r*. It is not spelt like 'labour'. It means 'needing much effort', as in 'It was a laborious task to move all the books from the attic', or 'showing signs of effort, not fluent or flowing', as in 'His laborious style of prose is difficult to read'.

labyrinth is liable to be misspelt. Note the *y* before the *r* and the *i* after *r*. It means 'a network of winding paths, passages, etc, through which it is difficult to find one's way', as in 'a labyrinth of underground passages underneath the castle' and 'unable to find one's way around the labyrinth of regulations'.

lady and woman cause controversy. Lady is objected to by many people when it is used instead of woman. Formerly, and still in some circles, it was regarded as a polite form of woman, as in '"Please get up and give that lady a seat", said the mother to her son'. Indeed, woman was thought to be rather insulting. For many people woman is now the preferred term and lady is seen as classist, because it is associated with nobility, privilege, etc, or condescending. However, lady is still quite commonly used, particularly when women are being addressed in a group, as in '"Ladies, I hope we can reach our sales target", said the manager' and 'Come along, ladies the bus is about to leave'. Phrases, such as dinner lady and cleaning lady are thought by some to be condescending but others still find woman rather insulting.

laid and lain are liable to be confused. Laid is the past participle and past tense of lay, 'to put, place', as in 'They have laid a new carpet in the dining room' and 'We laid the blanket on the ground'. Lain is the past participle of lie, 'to rest in a horizontal position', as in 'He had lain there for hours before they found him'. See also lay.

lama and llama are liable to be confused although they have completely different meanings. Llama means 'a kind of South American animal', as in 'go to see the llama enclosure in the zoo'. Lama refers to a monk who is member of the order of Lamaism, a form of Buddhism in Tibet and Mongolia, as in 'lamas gathering for prayer'.

lamentable is frequently mispronounced. It should be pronounced with the emphasis on the first syllable, as *lam*-en-tabl. However it is becoming common to place the emphasis on the second syllable in the same way that 'lament' does. It means 'deplorable, regrettable', as in 'showing a lamentable lack of consideration for other people's feelings'.

languor is frequently misspelt. Note the *uo* combination and note that there is not a *u* before the *r*. It means 'weariness, listlessness, laziness', as in 'people full of languor on that hot, still afternoon'. The adjective from languor is languorous, as in 'feeling languorous after drinking so much wine at lunch'.

last is liable to cause confusion because it is not always clear which meaning is meant. Last as an adjective has several meanings. It can mean 'final', as in 'That was the musician's last public appearance—he died shortly after'; 'coming after all others in time or order', as in 'December is the last month in the year', 'The last of the runners reached the finishing tape'; 'latest, most recent', as in 'Her last novel is not as good as her earlier ones'; 'previous, preceding', as in 'This chapter is interesting but the last one was boring'. In order to avoid confusion it is best to use a word other than last where ambiguity is likely to arise. An example of a sentence which could cause confusion is 'I cannot remember the title of his last book', which could mean either 'his latest book' or 'his final book'.

latter see former.

lavatory see toilet.

lay and lie are liable to be confused. They are related but are used in different contexts. Lay means 'to put or place' and is a transitive verb, i.e. it takes an object. It is found in such sentences as 'Ask them to lay the books carefully on the table' and 'They are going to lay a new carpet in the bedroom'. Lie, meaning 'to rest in a horizontal position', is an intransitive verb, i.e. it does not take an object. It is found in such sentences as 'They were told to lie on the ground' and 'Snow is apt to lie on the mountain tops for a long time'. The confusion between the two words arises from the fact that lay is also the past tense of lie, as in 'He lay still on the ground' and 'Snow lay on the mountain tops'. The past tense of lay is laid, as in 'They laid the books on the table'. There is another verb lie, meaning 'to tell falsehoods, not to tell the truth', as in 'He was told to lie to the police'. The past tense of lie in this sense is lied, as in 'We suspect that he lied but we cannot prove it'. See also laid.

lead and led are liable to be confused. Lead, pronounced to rhyme with 'feed', is a verb meaning 'to guide, to show the way to, especially by going in front of', as in 'He lead the police to the spot where he had found the murdered man'. Lead, pronounced to rhyme with 'fed, means 'a kind of metal', as in 'replace water pipes made of lead'. Led, which also rhymes with fed, is thus pronounced in the same way as lead in the sense of metal. It is the past participle and past tense of the verb lead, as in 'He had led the search party to the wrong place' and 'The guide led the climbers to the top of the mountain'.

leading question is often used wrongly. It should be used to mean 'a question that is so worded as to invite (or lead to) a particular answer desired by the questioner', as in 'The judge refused to allow the barrister to ask the witness the question on the grounds that it was a leading question'. However, it is often used wrongly to mean 'a question that is difficult, unfair or embarrassing'.

leaned and **leant** are both acceptable forms of the past participle and past tense of the verb 'to lean', as in 'He had *leaned/leant* the ladder against the garage wall' and he *leaned/leant* on the gate and watched the cows'. **Leaned** is pronounced leend or lent, and **leant** is pronounced lent.

leaped and **leapt** are both acceptable forms of the past participle and past tense of the verb 'to leap', as in 'He *leaped/leapt* to his feet and shouted out' and 'The dog had *leaped/leapt* over the fence'. **Leaped** is pronounced either leept or leapt, and **leapt** is pronounced lept.

learn and **teach** are liable to be confused. **Learn** means 'to gain information or knowledge about', as in 'She learnt Spanish as a child', or 'to gain the skill of', as in 'She is learning to drive'. **Teach** means 'to give instruction in, to cause to know something or be able to do something', as in 'She taught her son French' and 'She taught her son to swim'. **Learn** is frequently used wrongly instead of **teach**, as in 'She learnt us to drive'.

learned and **learnt** are both acceptable forms of the past participle and past tense of the verb 'to learn', as in 'She has now *learned/learnt* to drive' and 'They *learned/learnt* French at school'. **Learned** in this sense can be pronounced either lernd or leant. However, **learned** can also be an adjective, meaning 'having much knowledge, erudite', as in 'an learned professor', or 'academic', as in 'learned journals'. It is pronounced *ler*-ned.

leave and **let** are not interchangeable. **Leave go** should not be substituted for **let go** in such sentences as 'Do not let go of the rope'. 'Do not leave go of the rope' is considered to be incorrect. However both **leave alone** and **let alone** can be used in the sense of 'to stop disturbing or interfering with', as in '*Leave/let* the dog alone or it will bite you' and '*leave/let* your mother alone—she is not feeling well'. **Leave alone** can also mean 'leave on one's own, cause to be alone', as in 'Her husband went away and left her alone', but **let alone** cannot be used in this sense. **Let alone** can also mean 'not to mention, without considering', as in 'They cannot afford proper food, let alone a holiday', but **leave alone** should not be used in this sense.

led *see* **lead**.

legible and **readable** are not interchangeable. **Legible** means 'able to be deciphered or made out', as in 'His writing is scarcely legible'. **Readable** can also be used in this sense, as in 'His handwriting is just not readable'. However **readable** is also used to mean 'able to be read with interest or enjoyment', as in 'He is an expert on the subject but I think his books are simply not readable' and 'I find her novels very readable but my friend does not like her style'.

legion has three meanings. It refers to 'a unit of the ancient Roman army', as in 'Caesar's legions', and to 'a very large number', as in 'the pop star has legions of admirers'. As an adjective **legion** means 'very many, numerous', as in 'His faults are legion'.

legionnaire is frequently misspelt. Note the double *n*. The word refers to 'a member, or former member, of a military legion, for example, the French Foreign Legion'. In modern usage it is most likely to be found in the phrase **legionnaires' disease**, a kind of pneumonia first discovered in 1976 at a meeting of the American Legion.

leisure is frequently misspelt. Note the *ei* combination. It is pronounced *lezh*-er. In American English it is pronounced *leezh*-er. **Leisure** means 'time spent away from work or duties', as in 'He works a lot of overtime and has very little leisure'. It is frequently used as an adjective, as in 'leisure time' and 'leisure pursuits'.

lend and **loan** can cause confusion. **Lend** is used as a verb in British English to mean 'to allow someone the use of temporarily', as in 'Can you lend me a pen?' and 'His father refused to lend him any money'. **Loan** is a noun meaning 'something lent, the temporary use of', as in 'They thanked her for the loan of her car'. In American English **loan** is used as a verb to mean **lend**, and this use is becoming common in Britain although it is still regarded as not quite acceptable.

length, as in 'measure the length of the room', is frequently misspelt. Note the *g*, which is sometimes wrongly omitted.

lengthways and **lengthwise** are used interchangeably, as in 'fold the tablecloth lengthways/lengthwise' and 'measure the room lengthwise/lengthways'.

lengthy and **long** are not interchangeable. **Lengthy** means 'excessively long', as in 'We had a lengthy wait before we saw the doctor' and 'It was such a lengthy speech that most of the audience got bored'. **Lengthy** is frequently misspelt. Note the *g*.

leopard is frequently misspelt. Note the *o*. It is the name of a wild animal of the cat family, as in 'leopards stalking deer'.

less and **fewer** are often confused. Less means 'a smaller amount or quantity of' and is the comparative form of 'little'. It is found in sentences such as 'less milk', 'less responsibility' and 'less noise'. **Fewer** means 'a smaller number of' and is the comparative of 'few'. It is found in sentences such as 'buy fewer bottles of milk', 'have fewer responsibilities', 'have fewer opportunities' and 'hear fewer noises'. **Less** is commonly wrongly used where **fewer** is correct. It is common but ungrammatical to say or write 'less bottles of milk' and 'less queues in the shops during the week'.

leukaemia is frequently misspelt. Note the *eu*, *ae* and *ia* combinations. It is pronounced with the emphasis on the second syllable, as loo-*kee*-mia. The word refers to 'a type of cancer in which there is an abnormal increase in the number of white corpuscles', as in 'children suffering from leukaemia'.

liable to and **likely to** both express probability. They mean much the same except that **liable to** suggests that the probability is based on past experience or habit. 'He is liable to lose his temper' suggests that he has been in the habit of doing so in the past. 'He is likely to lose his temper' suggests that he will probably lose his temper, given the situation, but that the probability is not based on how he has reacted in the past. This distinction is not always adhered to, and some people use the terms interchangeably.

liaison, meaning 'communication and cooperation', as in 'Liaison between departments is essential', is frequently misspelt. Note the *i* before the *s*. This is often omitted in error. Note also the *i* before the *s* in **liaise**, which means 'to act as a link or go-between', as in 'You must liaise with your colleague in the other department'.

libel and **slander** both refer to defamatory statements against someone but they are not interchangeable. **Libel** refers to defamation that is written down, printed or drawn, as in 'The politician sued the newspaper for libel when it falsely accused him of fraud'. **Slander** refers to defamation in spoken form, as in 'She heard that one of her neighbours was spreading slander about her'. Both **libel** and **slander** can act as verbs, as in 'bring a suit against the newspaper for libelling him' and 'think that one of her neighbours was slandering her'. Note that the verb **libel** doubles the *l* in the past participle, past tense and present participle, as **libelled** and **libelling**.

library, meaning a collection of books or the place where it is kept, should be pronounced *lib*-ra-ri although it is quite often pronounced *lib*-ri.

licence and **license** are liable to cause confusion in British English. **Licence** is a noun meaning 'an official document showing that permission has been given to do, use or own something', as in 'require a licence to have a stall in the market', 'have a licence to drive a car', and 'apply for a pilot's licence'. **License** is a verb meaning 'to provide someone with a licence', as in 'The council have licensed him as a street trader', 'The restaurant has been licensed to sell alcohol'. Note **licensed grocer** and **licensing laws** but **off-licence**. In American English both the noun and verb are spelt **license**.

lie *see* **lay**.

lieu *see* **in lieu**.

lieutenant is often misspelt. Note the *ieu* combination. In British English the word is pronounced lef-*ten*-ant. The word originally referred to an army or naval rank but is also used to mean 'a deputy, a chief assistant', as in 'The owner of the factory was unavailable but we talked to some of his lieutenants'.

lifelong and **livelong** are liable to be confused. **Lifelong** means 'lasting a lifetime', as in 'He never realized his lifelong ambition of going to Australia' and 'her lifelong membership of the society'. **Livelong** is found in rather literary contexts and means 'whole, entire', as in 'The children played on the beach the livelong day'. In **livelong** the first syllable is pronounced like 'live', as in 'live a long time'.

lighted and **lit** can both be used as the past participle and past tense of the verb 'to light'. **Lit** is the more common form, as in 'We lit the fire early' and 'They lit the birthday candles'. **Lighted** is used when the past participle is used as an adjective, as in 'children playing with lighted matches' and 'The fire was started by a lighted match being thrown away'.

lightning and **lightening** are liable to be confused because they sound alike. **Lightning** refers to 'flashes of light produced by atmospheric electricity', as in 'The child was afraid of thunder and lightning' and 'He was hit by lightning and was killed'. **Lightning** is also used as an adjective meaning 'happening very quickly, suddenly or briefly', as in 'The police made a lightning strike on the nightclub', 'She made a lightning decision to go on holiday', and 'The visitors made a lightning tour of the factory'. **Lightening** is the present participle of the verb 'to lighten', as in 'lightening her hair with peroxide' and 'Lightening his work load is a priority'.

light years are a measure of distance, not time. A **light year** is the distance travelled by light in one year (about six million, million miles) and is a term used in astronomy. **Light years** are often referred to in an informal context when time, not distance, is involved, as in 'Owning their own house seemed light years away' and 'It seems light years since we had a holiday'.

likable *see* **likeable**.

like tends to cause confusion. It is a preposition meaning 'resembling, similar to', as in 'houses like castles', 'gardens like jungles', 'actors like Olivier', 'She looks like her mother', 'She plays like an expert', 'The child swims like a fish' and 'Like you, he cannot stand cruelty to animals'. To be grammatically correct **like** should not be used as a conjunction. Thus 'The house looks like it has been deserted' is incorrect. It should read 'The house looks as though/if it has been deserted'. Similarly, 'Like his mother said, he has had to go to hospital' should read 'As his mother said, he has had to go to hospital'.

likeable and **likable** are both acceptable spellings. The word means 'pleasant, agreeable, friendly', as in 'He is a likeable/likable young man'.

likely to *see* **liable to**.

lineage and **linage** do not mean the same thing. **Lineage** refers to 'line of descent, ancestry', as in 'a family of noble lineage'. **Linage** is rather a specialist term meaning 'number of written or printed lines', as in 'The freelance journalist was paid on a linage basis'. **Linage** can also be spelt **lineage**.

liqueur and **liquor** are liable to be confused. **Liqueur** refers to 'a sweet alcoholic drink taken after dinner', as in 'have a liqueur with one's coffee'. **Liquor** refers to 'any strong alcoholic drink', as in 'prefer soft drinks to liquor'.

liquidate and **liquidize** are liable to be confused. **Liquidate** is frequently used in a financial context. It means 'to settle or pay', as in 'to liquidate a debt'; 'to terminate the operations of a firm by assessment of debts and use the assets towards paying off the debts', as in 'forced to liquidate the firm'; 'to convert into cash', as in 'liquidate one's assets'. In an informal context **liquidate** means 'to kill', as in 'paid to liquidate a member of the enemy gang'. **Liquidize** means 'to make liquid, especially to pulverize into a pulp', as in 'liquidize the vegetables to make a soup'.

liquor *see* **liqueur**.

lit *see* **lighted**.

literal, literary and **literate** are liable to be confused. **Literal** means 'word for word, exact', as in 'a literal translation', 'a literal interpretation of the words'. **Literary** means 'referring to literature', as in 'come from a literary background', 'have literary interests' and 'literary criticism'. **Literate** means 'able to read and write', as in 'children who are leaving school scarcely literate', and 'well-educated', as in 'a very literate family'.

literally is frequently used simply to add emphasis to an idea rather than to indicate that the word, phrase, etc, used is to be interpreted word for word. Thus, 'She was literally tearing her hair out' does not mean that she was pulling her hair out by the handful but that she was very angry, anxious, frustrated, etc.

literary *see* **literal**.

livelong *see* **lifelong**.

livid and **lurid** are liable to be confused although they mean different things. **Livid** means 'discoloured, of a greyish tinge', as in 'a livid bruise on her face', and 'furious', as in 'When he saw his damaged car he was livid'. **Lurid** means 'sensational, shocking', as in 'give the lurid details about finding the body', and 'garish, glaringly bright', as in 'wear a lurid shade of green'.

living room *see* **sitting room**.

loan *see* **lend**.

loath, loathe and **loth** are not all interchangeable. **Loath** and **loth** mean 'reluctant, unwilling', as in 'We were loath/loth to punish the children' and 'They are loath/loth to move house again'. **Loathe** means 'to hate very much, to detest', as in 'She loathes dishonesty' and 'The rivals loathe each other'. The *th* in **loath** and **loth** is pronounced as the *th* in 'bath', but the *th* in **loathe** is pronounced like the *th* in 'bathe'.

longevity, meaning 'long life', is liable to be mispronounced. It should be pronounced lon-*jev*-iti. Some people pronounce it lon-*gev*-iti, but this is rarer.

loo *see* **toilet**.

loose, loosen and **lose** are liable to be confused. **Loose** and **loosen** are related but not **lose**. **Loose** is an adjective meaning 'not tight', as in 'His clothes are loose now that he has lost weight', and 'free, not confined', as in 'The cows are loose'. It is also a verb meaning 'to undo', as in 'loose the knot', or 'set free', as in 'loose the pack of hounds'. **Loosen** means 'to make less tight', as in 'He has put on weight and so he has had to loosen his belt'. **Lose** is a verb meaning 'not to be able to find, to mislay', as in 'I always lose one glove' and 'They may lose their way'. **Loose** is pronounced loos, but **lose** is pronounced looz.

lose *see* **loose**.

lots of and **a lot of**, meaning 'many' and 'much', should be used only in informal contexts', as in '"I've got lots of toys," said the child' and 'You're talking a lot of rubbish'. They should be avoided in formal prose.

loth *see* **loath**.

lounge *see* **sitting room**.

low and **lowly** are not interchangeable. **Low** means 'not high', as in 'a low fence', 'a low level of income', 'speak in a low voice' and 'her low status in the firm'. It can also mean 'despicable, contemptible', as in 'That was a low trick' or 'He's a low creature'. **Lowly** means 'humble', as in 'of lowly birth' and 'the peasant's lowly abode'.

lowly *see* **low**.

lunch and **luncheon** both refer to a meal eaten in the middle of the day. **Lunch**, as in 'a business lunch' and 'have just a snack for lunch', is by far the more usual term. **Luncheon**, as in 'give a luncheon party for the visiting celebrity', is a very formal word and is becoming increasingly uncommon. *See also* **dinner**.

lurid *see* **livid**.

luxuriant, luxurious and **luxury** are liable to be confused. They have completely different meanings. **Luxuriant** means 'profuse, growing thickly and strongly', as in 'the luxuriant vegetation of the area' and 'her luxuriant hair'. **Luxurious** means 'referring to or characterized by luxury', as in 'a luxurious lifestyle' and 'live in luxurious surroundings'. **Luxury** is a noun meaning 'great ease or comfort based on wealth', as in 'live in luxury' and 'a hotel providing luxury'. It also means 'something that is enjoyable but is not essential and is usually expensive', as in 'no money for luxuries' and 'spend money on luxuries such as champagne'. **Luxury** can be used as an adjective, as in 'a luxury hotel' and 'a shop selling luxury goods'.

M

macabre, meaning 'connected with death' or 'gruesome', as in 'a macabre tale about attacks on people in the graveyard' and 'policemen sickened by a particularly macabre murder', is liable to be misspelt. Note the *re* ending.

machinations, meaning 'devious plots or schemes', as in 'They were plotting to kill the king but their machinations were discovered', should be pronounced mak-in-*ay*-shunz but mash-in *ay*-shunz is becoming increasingly common in modern usage.

madam and madame are liable to be confused. Madam is the English-language form of the French madame. It is a form of formal of address for a woman, as in 'Please come this way, madam'. It is used in formal letters when the name of the woman being written to is not known, as in 'Dear Madam'. Madam can be written either with a capital letter or a lower-case letter. Madam is pronounced *mad*-am, with the emphasis on the first syllable. Madame, which is the French equivalent of 'Mrs', is occasionally found in English, as in Madame Tussaud's, and is pronounced in the same way as madam. In French madame is pronounced ma-*dam*.

majority and minority are opposites. Majority means 'more than half the total number of', as in 'The majority of the pupils live locally' and 'the younger candidate received the majority of the votes'. Minority means less than half the total number of', as in 'A small minority of the football fans caused trouble' and 'Only a minority of the committee voted against the motion'. Majority and minority should not be used to describe the greater or lesser part of a single thing. Thus it is wrong to say 'The majority of the book is uninteresting'.

male, masculine and mannish all refer to the sex that is not female but the words are used in different ways. Male is the opposite of 'female' and refers to the sex of a person or animal, as in 'no male person may enter', 'a male nurse', 'a male elephant' and 'the male reproductive system'. Masculine is the opposite of 'feminine' and refers to people or their characteristics. It refers to characteristics, etc, that are traditionally considered to be typically male. Examples of its use include 'a very masculine young man', 'a deep, masculine voice'. It can be used of women, as in 'She has a masculine walk' and 'She wears masculine clothes'. When used of women it is often derogatory and is sometimes replaced with mannish, which is derogatory, as in 'women with mannish haircuts'. Male can also be used as a noun, as in 'the male of the species' 'of the robins, the male is more colourful' and 'the title can be held only by males'.

man causes a great deal of controversy. To avoid being sexist it should be avoided when it really means 'person'. 'We must find the right man for the job' should read 'We must find the right person for the job'. Similarly, 'All men have a right to a reasonable standard of living' should read 'All people have a right to a reasonable standard of living' or 'Everyone has a right to a reasonable standard of living'. Problems also arise with compounds, such as 'chairman'. In such situations 'person' is often used, as in 'chairperson'. Man is also used to mean 'mankind, humankind', as in 'Man is mortal' and 'Man has the power of thought'. Some people also object to this usage and consider it sexist. They advocate using 'humankind' or 'the human race'.

manageable is liable to be misspelt. Note the *e* before the ending -*able*. It means 'able to be controlled, easily controlled', as in 'a task of scarcely manageable proportions' and 'The nanny will not take the job unless the children are manageable'.

mandatory is liable to be mispronounced. The emphasis should be on the first syllable, as *man*-da-tor-i. It means 'required by law, compulsory', as in 'A visa is mandatory for some countries' and 'He was fined for not making the mandatory payment'.

manoeuvre is frequently misspelt. Note the *oeu* combination and the -*re* ending. In American English the *o* is omitted and the ending is *er*. It means 'a movement or action, especially one requiring skill and dexterity', as in 'We were admiring the manoeuvres of the skaters', and 'a skilful, and often complicated and deceptive plan', as in 'his manoeuvres to discredit his boss and obtain his job'. Manoeuvre is also a verb meaning 'to move or position, especially with skill or dexterity', as in 'racing drivers manoeuvring their cars on a muddy circuit', and 'to guide or manipulate skilfully and usually cunningly', as in 'She manoeuvred herself into a position of trust'.

mantel and mantle are liable to be confused. Mantel is more usually called mantelpiece and refers to 'a shelf above a fireplace', as in 'a vase of flowers on the mantelpiece'. Mantelpiece is frequently misspelt as 'mantlepiece'. Mantle is an old word for a cloak and is now found mostly in the sense of 'covering', as in 'a mantle of autumn leaves on the grass'.

many is used in more formal contexts rather than 'a lot of' or 'lots of', as in 'The judge said the accused had had many previous convictions'. Many is often used in the negative in both formal and informal contexts, as in 'They don't have many friends' and 'She won't find many apples on the trees now'.

margarine causes confusion with reference to pronunciation. Formerly the usual pronunciation was mar-ga-reen but now the most common pronunciation is mar-ja-reen. It refers to 'a substitute for butter'.

masculine *see* male.

masterful and masterly are liable to be confused although they mean different things. Masterful means 'able to control others, dominating', as in 'She likes masterful men' and 'The country needs a masterful ruler'. **Masterly** means 'very skilful', as in 'admire his masterly handling of the situation' and 'their masterly defeat of the opposing team'.

mattress is often misspelt. Note the double *t* and double *s*. The word means 'a fabric case filled with soft or springy material used for sleeping on', as in 'He likes to sleep on a firm mattress'.

may *see* **can**.

maybe and **may be** are liable to be confused although they have different meanings. **Maybe** means 'perhaps', as in 'Maybe they lost their way' and 'He said, "Maybe" when I asked him if he was going'. It is used in more informal contexts than 'perhaps'. **May be** is used in such sentences as 'He may be poor but he is very generous' and 'They may be a little late'.

mayoress means 'the wife or partner of a male mayor', as in 'an official dinner for the mayor and mayoress'. A mayor who is a woman is called either 'mayor' or 'lady mayor'.

meaningful originally meant 'full of meaning', as in 'make very few meaningful statements' and 'There was a meaningful silence'. In modern usage it has come to mean 'important, significant, serious', as in 'not interested in a meaningful relationship' and 'seeking a meaningful career'. The word now tends to be very much over-used.

means in the sense of 'way, method' can be either a singular or plural noun, as in 'The means of defeating them is in our hands' and 'Many different means of financing the project have been investigated'. **Means** in the sense of 'wealth' and 'resources' is plural, as in 'His means are not sufficient to support two families'.

media gives rise to confusion. In the form of **the media** it is commonly applied to the press, to newspapers, television and radio, as in 'The politician claimed that he was being harassed by the media'. **Media** is a plural form of 'medium', meaning 'means of communication', as in 'television is a powerful medium'. In modern usage **media** is beginning to be used as a singular noun, as in 'The politician blamed a hostile media for his misfortunes', but this is still regarded as being an incorrect use.

mediaeval and **medieval** are both acceptable spellings. **Mediaeval** was formerly the only acceptable spelling in British English and **medieval** was considered the American spelling. However, in modern usage **medieval** is the more common term in British English. The word means 'relating to the Middle Ages', as in 'medieval knights' and 'medieval castles'.

mediocre is liable to be misspelt. Note the *-re* ending It is a common error to make this *-er*. It means 'not very good, of indifferent quality', as in 'a mediocre pupil unlikely to do well in the exam' and 'His work is at best mediocre'. It is pronounced meed-i-*ok*-er, with the emphasis on the third syllable.

melted and **molten** are not interchangeable although they are both formed the verb 'to melt'. **Melted** is the past participle and the past tense of 'melt', as in 'The ice cream had melted all over the child's clothes' and 'The chocolate melted in the heat'. **Molten** means 'melted or made liquid by heating to very high temperature', as in 'molten rock' and 'molten lava'.

memento is liable to be misspelt. Note the *e* following the first *m*. It is a common error to put *o* instead. The plural form is either **mementos** or **mementoes**. **Memento** refers to 'something kept as a reminder', as in

'He bought her a scarf as a memento of their trip to Paris'.

metal and **mettle** are liable to be confused because they sound alike. **Metal** refers to 'a member of a group of mineral substances that are opaque and good conductors of heat and electricity', as in 'appliances made of metal' and 'cutlery made of plastic, not metal'. **Mettle** means 'endurance, courage, strength of character', as in 'show his mettle by learning to walk again' and 'give the candidates a chance to prove their mettle'.

metaphor is a figure of speech in which a word or phrase is used to suggest a similarity to something else. The similarity is not introduced by 'like' or 'as' as it is in the case of a 'simile'. Examples include 'She was a rose among thorns' and 'Their new product is the jewel in the firm's crown', 'He is a pillar of the community' and 'His mother is a clinging vine'.

meter *see* **metre**.

mettle *see* **metal**.

middle *see* **centre**.

migraine causes problems with regard to pronunciation. It is pronounced *mee*-grayn in British English but the American pronunciation of *mi*-grayn, in which the first syllable rhymes with 'eye', is sometimes used in Britain. **Migraine** refers to 'a severe and recurrent type of headache, often accompanied by vomiting', as in 'She had to lie down in a darkened room because of her migraine'.

mileage and **milage** are both acceptable spellings for 'the distance travelled or measured in miles', as in 'The car is a bargain, given the low mileage'. However, **mileage** is much more common than **milage**. The word also means informally 'benefit, advantage', as in 'The politician got a lot of mileage from the scandal surrounding his opponent' and 'There's not much mileage in pursuing that particular line of inquiry'.

militate and **mitigate** are liable to be confused. **Militate** means 'to have or serve as a strong influence against', as in 'Their lack of facts militated against the success of their application' and 'His previous record will militate against his chances of going free'. **Mitigate** means 'to alleviate', as in 'try to mitigate the suffering of the refugees', or 'moderate', as in 'mitigate the severity of the punishment'.

millenium is liable to be misspelt. Note the double *n* which is frequently omitted in error. The plural form is **millennia**. **Millennium** refers to 'a period of 1000 years', as in 'rock changes taking place over several millennia'. In religious terms it refers to 'the thousand-year reign of Christ prophesied in the Bible'.

millionaire is liable to be misspelt. Note the single *n*. It means 'a person who has a million pounds or dollars' or 'a very wealthy person', as in 'millionaires who spend all their time travelling around the world'.

mimic is liable to be misspelt in its past participle, past tense and present tense. These are respectively **mimicked** and **mimicking**. Note the *k* in these forms. The word means 'to imitate', as in 'The pupil was mimicking the teacher when she walked into the room'. Note that the noun **mimicry** does not have a *k*.

miniature is frequently misspelt. Note the *i* after the *n*. This is often omitted in error. It means 'very small in size', as in 'beautiful miniature coffee cups' and 'a miniature bottle of whisky'. It can also be a noun meaning 'a very small copy or model', as in 'a miniature of the Tower of London', or 'a very small detailed painting', as in 'admire the miniatures in the art gallery'.

minority *see* **majority**.

minuscule is liable to be misspelt. Note the *u* before the *s*. It is a common error to put an *i*. The word is pronounced *min*-iskyool. It means 'extremely small, tiny', as in 'only a minuscule amount of coffee left'.

miscellaneous is very frequently misspelt. Note the *c* after the *s*, the double *l* and the *-eous* ending. The word means 'of various kinds', as in 'a miscellaneous collection of articles for the jumble sale' and 'Some money will have to be allocated for miscellaneous expense'.

mischievous is frequently misspelt and mispronounced. Note the *ie* combination and the absence of *i* before *ous*. It is pronounced *mis*-chiv-is, not mis-*cheev*-is.

Miss *see* **Ms**.

misspelled and **misspelt** are often wrongly spelt. Note the double *s*. Both **misspelled** and **misspelt** are acceptable spellings of the past tense and past participle of the verb 'to misspell'. **Misspell** means 'to spell wrongly'.

misuse *see* **abuse**.

mitigate *see* **militate**.

mnemonic refers to 'something that aids the memory'. For example, some people use a **mnemonic** in the form of a verse to remind them how to spell a word or to recall a date. The word is liable to be misspelt and mispronounced. Note the initial *m*, which is silent. **Mnemonic** is pronounced nim-*on*-ik, with the emphasis on the second syllable.

moccasin is frequently misspelt. Note the double *c* and single *s*. The word refers to 'a flat-soled shoe made of soft leather', as in 'She was wearing moccasins and so he did not hear her approach'.

modern and **modernistic** are not quite the same. **Modern** means 'referring to the present time or recent times', as in 'the politics of modern times' and 'a production of Shakespeare's *Twelfth Night* in modern dress'. It also means 'using the newest techniques, equipment, buildings, etc, as in 'a modern shopping centre' and 'a modern office complex'. **Modernistic** means 'characteristic of modern ideas, fashions, etc, and is often used in a derogatory way, as in 'She says she hates that modernistic furniture'.

modus vivendi refers to 'a practical, sometimes temporary, arrangement or compromise by which people who are in conflict can live or work together', as in 'The two opposing parties on the committee will have to reach a modus vivendi if any progress is to be made'. It is a Latin phrase that literally means 'a way of living' and is pronounced *mo*-dus viv-*en*-di.

molten *see* **melted**.

momentary and **momentous** are liable to be confused. They look rather similar but they are completely different in meaning. **Momentary** means 'lasting for a very short time', as in 'There was a momentary pause' and 'enjoy a momentary success'. It is derived from the noun 'moment' in the sense of 'a very brief period of time'. **Momentous** means 'very important, of great significance', as in 'a momentous incident that led to war'. It is derived from the noun 'moment' in the sense of 'importance, significance', as in 'a meeting of moment'. In **momentary** the emphasis is on the first syllable, as *mom*-en-tar-i or *mom*-en-tri. In **momentous** the stress is on the second syllable, as mom-*en*-tus.

moral and **morale** are liable to be confused although they are different in meaning. **Moral** means 'concerning the principles of right and wrong', as in 'the decline of moral standards' and 'criticize his actions on moral grounds'. **Morale** means 'state of confidence, enthusiasm, etc', as in 'It was a blow to his morale when he failed to get the job' and 'The morale of the country was very low during the recession'. **Moral** is pronounced with the emphasis on the first syllable, as in *mor*-al. **Morale** is pronounced with the emphasis on the second syllable'.

more is used to form the comparative of adjectives and adverbs that do not form the comparative by adding *-er*. This usually applies to longer adjectives, as in 'more beautiful', 'more gracious', 'more useful', and 'more flattering'. **More** should not be used with adjectives that have a comparative ending already. Thus it is wrong to write 'more happier'. **Most** is used in the same way to form the superlative of adjectives and adverbs, as in 'most beautiful', 'most gracious' etc.

Moslem *see* **Muslim**.

most *see* **more**.

motif and **motive** are liable to be confused although they have entirely different meanings. **Motif** refers to 'a theme or idea that is repeated and developed in a work of music or literature', as in 'a motif of suicide runs through the whole novel'. It also means 'a decorative design or pattern', as in 'curtains with a flower motif'. **Motive** refers to 'the reason for a course of action', as in 'There appears to have been no motive for the murder' and 'What was her motive in telling lies about him?' **Motif** is pronounced with the emphasis on the second syllable, as mo-*teef*. **Motive** is pronounced with the emphasis on the first syllable, as *mo*-tiv.

motive *see* **motif**.

movable and **moveable** are both possible spellings but **movable** is the more common, as in 'movable possessions' and 'machines with movable parts'.

Ms, Mrs and **Miss** are all used before the names of women in addressing them and in letter-writing. Formerly **Mrs** was used before the name of a married woman and **Miss** before the name of an unmarried woman or girl. In modern usage **Ms** is often used instead of **Miss** or **Mrs**. This is sometimes because the marital status of the woman is not known and sometimes from a personal preference. Many people feel that since no distinction is made between married and unmarried men when they are being addressed, no distinction should be made between married and unmarried women. On the other hand some people, particularly older women, object to the use of **Ms**.

much, except in negative sentences, is used mainly in rather formal contexts, as in 'They own much property'. 'A great deal of' is often used instead, as in 'They own a great deal of property'. In informal contexts 'a lot of' is often used instead of **much**, as in 'a lot of rubbish' not 'much rubbish'. **Much** is used in negative sentences, as in 'They do not have much money'.

Muslim and **Moslem** refer to to 'a follower of the Islamic faith'. In modern usage **Muslim** is the preferred term rather than the older spelling **Moslem**.

N

naïve causes problems with reference to both spelling and pronunciation. It can be spelt either **naïve** or **naive** and is pronounced ni-*eev*, with the emphasis on the second syllable, and the first syllable rhyming with 'my'. The accent on the *i* (called a diaeresis) indicates that the two vowels *a* and *i* are to be pronounced separately. **Naive** means either 'innocent' or 'too ready to believe what one is told', as in 'You would have to be incredibly naive to believe his excuses'.

naturalist and **naturist** are liable to be confused. They look rather similar but have completely different meanings. **Naturalist** refers to 'a person who studies animals, birds and plants', as in 'naturalists collecting some of the local wild flowers'. **Naturist** refers to 'a person who practises naturism or nudism', as in 'naturists with their own secluded beaches'. **Naturist** can also be an adjective, as in 'naturist beaches'.

naught and **nought** are not totally interchangeable. **Naught** means 'nothing', as in 'All his projects came to naught', and is rather a formal or literary word in this sense. **Naught** is also a less usual spelling of **nought**, which means 'zero' when it is regarded as a number, as in 'nought point one (0.1)'.

naval and **navel** are liable to be confused. They sound alike but they have entirely different meanings. **Naval** means 'referring to the navy', as in 'a naval base' and 'naval personnel'. **Navel** refers to 'a small hollow in the middle of the abdomen where the umbilical cord was attached at birth', as in 'The baby has an infection in the navel'.

nearby and **near by** can cause problems. **Nearby** can be either an adjective, as in 'the nearby village', or an adverb, as in 'Her mother lives nearby'. **Near by** is an adverb, as in 'He doesn't have far to go—he lives near by'. In other words, the adverbial sense can be spelt either **nearby** or **near by**.

necessarily is traditionally pronounced with the emphasis on the first syllable, but this is often very difficult to say except when one is speaking exceptionally carefully. Because of this difficulty it is often pronounced with the emphasis on the third syllable although it is considered by many people to be incorrect.

necessary is frequently misspelt. Note the single *c* and double *s*. It means 'that cannot be done without', as in 'make only necessary purchases' and 'It may be necessary to take him to hospital'.

née is used to indicate the maiden or family name of a married woman, as in 'Jane Jones, née Smith'. It is derived from French, being the feminine form of the French word for 'born'. It can be spelt either with an acute accent or not—**née** or **nee**.

negligent and **negligible** are liable to be confused. **Negligent** means 'not giving proper attention, careless', as in 'mothers accused of being negligent by not making sure their children attend school' and 'He said that his wife had died because of a negligent doctor'. **Negligible** means 'extremely small', as in 'a negligible difference between the prices' and 'lose a negligible amount of weight'. Note the -*ible* ending in **negligible**.

neither as an adjective or a pronoun takes a singular verb, as in 'Neither parent will come' and 'Neither of them wishes to come'. In the **neither ... nor** construction, a singular verb is used if both parts of the construction are singular, as in 'Neither Jane nor Mary was present'. If both parts are plural the verb is plural, as in 'Neither their parents nor their grandparents are willing to look after them'. If the construction involves a mixture of singular and plural, the verb traditionally agrees with the subject that is nearest it, as in 'Neither her mother nor her grandparents are going to come' and 'Neither her grandparents nor her mother is going to come'. If pronouns are used, the nearer one governs the verb as in 'Neither they nor he is at fault' and 'Neither he nor they are at fault'.

never in the sense of 'did not', as in 'He never saw the other car before he hit it', should be used in only very informal contexts. **Never** means 'at no time, on no occasion', as in 'He will never agree to their demands' and 'She has never been poor'. It is also used as a negative for the sake of emphasis, as in 'He never so much as smiled'.

nevertheless and **none the less** mean the same thing, as in 'He has very little money. Nevertheless/none the less he gives generously to charity'. **None the less** is usually written as three words but **nevertheless** is spelt as one word. In modern usage **none the less** is sometimes written as one word, as **nonetheless**.

next and **this** can cause confusion. **Next** in one of its senses is used to mean the day of the week, month of the year, season of the year, etc, that will follow next, as in 'They are coming next Tuesday', 'We are going on holiday next June' and 'They to be married next summer'. **This** can also be used in this sense and so ambiguity can occur. Some people use **this** to refer to the very next Tuesday, June, summer, etc, and use **next** for the one after that. Thus someone might say on Sunday, 'I'll see you next Friday', meaning the first Friday to come, but someone else might take that to mean a week on from that because they would refer to the first Friday to come as 'this Friday'. The only solution is to make sure exactly which day, week, season, etc, the other person is referring to.

nice originally meant 'fine, subtle, requiring precision', as in 'There is rather a nice distinction between the two words', but it is widely used in the sense of 'pleasant, agreeable, etc', as in 'She is a nice person' and 'We had a nice time at the picnic'. It is overused and alternative adjectives should be found to avoid this, as in 'She is an amiable person' and 'We had an enjoyable time at the picnic'.

niceness and **nicety** are both nouns formed from 'nice' but they do not mean the same thing. **Niceness** is the noun from 'nice' in the sense of 'pleasant, agreeable', as in 'They appreciated the niceness of the old lady' and 'The niceness of the climate is the best part of the holiday resort'. **Nicety** is the noun from 'nice' in the sense of 'fine, subtle', as in 'the nicety of the distinction between the two words'.

niche causes problems with reference to both pronunciation and spelling'. The most common pronunciation is *nitch*, but *neech*, following the French pronunciation, is also a possibility. Note the absence of *t* in the spelling.

nimby *see* **acronym**.

nobody *see* **no one**.

none can be used with either a singular verb or plural verb. Examples of sentences using a singular verb include 'There is none of the food left' and 'None of the work is good enough' and 'None of the coal is to be used today'. In sentences where none is used with a plural noun the verb was traditionally still singular, as in 'None of the books is suitable' and 'None of the parcels is undamaged'. This is still the case in formal contexts but, in the case of informal contexts, a plural verb is often used in modern usage, as in 'None of these things are any good'.

none the less *see* **nevertheless**.

no one and **no-one** are interchangeable but the word is never written 'noone', unlike 'everyone'. **No one** and **no-one** are used with a singular verb, as in 'No one is allowed to leave' and 'No one is anxious to leave'. They are used by some people with a plural personal pronoun or possessive case when attempts are being made to avoid sexism, as in 'No one is expected to take their child away', although the singular form is grammatically correct, as in 'No one is expected to take his/her child away'. 'No one is expected to take his child away' is sexist. Nobody is interchangeable with no one, as in 'You must tell no one/nobody about this'.

nor is used as part of the **neither ... nor** construction, and this is dealt with under **neither**. It is also used in such constructions as 'He plays neither golf nor tennis' and 'We were given neither food nor drink' and 'He does not watch television. Nor does he go to the cinema'. In some contexts **nor** is interchangeable with **or**, as in 'The shop is not open on Saturday nor/or Sunday' and 'They have no food nor/or drink'. **Nor** can be used at the start of a sentence, as in 'He does not believe her. Nor does he trust her'.

notable *see* **noticeable**.

noticeable and **notable** are liable to be confused. They are both related to 'note' but they mean different

things. **Noticeable** means 'obvious', as in 'She had a noticeable bruise on her cheek' and 'The hostile atmosphere between them was noticeable to everyone'. **Notable** means 'of note, remarkable', as in 'his notable achievements in the world of business' and 'one of the most notable poets of the century'.

not only is frequently used in a construction with 'but also', as in 'We have not only the best candidate but also the most efficient organization' and 'The organizers of the fete not only made a great deal of money for charity but also gave a great many people a great deal of pleasure'.

nought *see* **naught**.

noxious and **obnoxious** are liable to be confused. They both refer to unpleasantness or harmfulness but they are used in different contexts. **Noxious** is used of a substance, fumes, etc, and means 'harmful, poisonous', as in 'firemen overcome by noxious fumes' and 'delinquent children having a noxious influence on the rest of the class'. **Obnoxious** means 'unpleasant, nasty, offensive', as in 'He has the most obnoxious neighbours' and 'The child's parents let him off with the most obnoxious behaviour'. **Noxious** is used in formal and technical contexts rather than **obnoxious**.

nubile originally meant 'old enough to marry, marriageable' as in 'he has five nubile daughters'. In modern usage **nubile** is frequently used in the sense of 'sexually attractive', as in 'admiring the nubile girls sunbathing on the beach' and 'nubile models posing for magazine illustrations'.

numbers can be written in either figures or words. It is largely a matter of taste which method is adopted. As long as the method is consistent it does not really matter. Some establishments, such as a publishing house or a newspaper office, will have a house style. For example, some of them prefer to have numbers up to 10 written in words, as in 'They have two boys and three girls'. If this system is adopted, guidance should be sought as to whether a mixture of figures and words in the same sentence is acceptable, as in 'We have 12 cups but only six saucers', or whether the rule should be broken in such situations as 'We have twelve cups but only six saucers'.

nutritional and **nutricious** are liable to be confused. They both refer to 'nutrition, the process of giving and receiving nourishment' but mean different things. **Nutritional** means 'referring to nutrition', as in 'doubts about the nutritional value of some fast foods' and 'people who do not receive the minimum nutritional requirements'. **Nutritious** means 'nourishing, of high value as a food', as in 'nourishing homemade soups' and 'something slightly more nourishing than a plate of chips'.

O

O and **Oh** are both forms of an exclamation made at the beginning of a sentence. **Oh** is the usual spelling, as in 'Oh well. It's Friday tomorrow' and 'Oh dear, the baby's crying again'. **O** is considerably rarer and is used in literary contexts in poetry, hymns etc, as in 'O come all ye faithful'. Both **Oh** and **O** are always spelt with an initial capital letter.

object refers to the noun, pronoun or phrase that is affected by the action of the verb. In the sentence 'He eventually married the girl', 'girl' is the object. In the sentence 'They beat him up badly', 'him' is the object. In the sentence 'She received a bunch of flowers', 'bunch of flowers' is the object. An object may be *direct* or *indirect*. The examples shown above are all *direct objects*. In the sentence 'She gave the child a book', 'book' is the *direct object* and 'the child' is the *indirect object*. In the sentence 'I bought him an apple', 'him' is the *indirect object*. In the case of *indirect objects*, it is usually possible to rephrase the sentences in which they appear, putting 'to' or 'for' before the *indirect object*, as in 'She gave a book to the child' and 'I bought an apple for him'. *See* **subject**.

Object can also mean 'aim, goal'—*see* **objective** and **subjective**.

Object is also a verb meaning 'to say that one is not in favour of something, to protest', as in 'They objected to the fact that the decision was taken in their absence'. In the verb sense, **object** is pronounced with the emphasis on the second syllable, as ob-*ject*.

objective and **subjective** are opposites. **Objective** means 'not influenced by personal feelings, attitudes, or prejudices', as in 'She is related to the person accused and so she cannot give an objective view of the situation' and 'It is important that all members of a jury are completely objective'. **Subjective** means 'influenced by personal feelings, attitudes and prejudices', as in 'It is only natural to be subjective in situations regarding one's children' and 'She wrote a very subjective report on the conference and did not stick to the facts'. **Objective** can also be a noun in the sense of 'aim, goal', as in 'Our objective was to make as much money as possible'. **Object** can also be used in this sense, as in 'Their main object is to have a good time'.

oblivious means 'unaware of, unconscious of, not noticing'. Traditionally it is followed by the preposition 'of', as in 'The lovers were oblivious of the rain' and 'When he is reading he is completely oblivious of his surroundings'. In modern usage its use with the preposition 'to' is also considered acceptable, as in 'They were oblivious to the fact that he was cheating them' and 'sleep soundly, oblivious to the noise'.

obnoxious *see* **noxious**.

obscene and **pornographic** are not interchangeable. **Obscene** means 'indecent, especially in a sexual way, offending against the accepted standards of decency', as

in 'obscene drawings on the walls of the public toilet' and 'When his car was damaged he let out a stream of obscene language'. **Pornographic** means 'intended to arouse sexual excitement', as in 'pornographic videos' and 'magazines with women shown in pornographic poses'. **Obscene** is frequently misspelt. Note the *c* after the *s*.

observance and **observation** are liable to be confused. They are both derived from the verb 'to observe' but from different senses of it. **Observance** is derived from 'observe' in the sense of 'obey, comply with', as in 'the observance of school rules' and 'the observance of local customs'. It also refers to 'a ritual act or practice', as in 'religious observances'. **Observation** is derived from the verb 'to observe' meaning 'to see, to notice', as in 'keep the patient under observation' and 'From his observation of them they appeared to be acting strangely'. **Observation** also means 'a remark', as in 'The inspector made a few critical observations about the state of the restaurant's kitchens'.

occasion is frequently misspelt. Note the double *c* and single *s*. It is a common error to put a single *c* and double *s*. **Occasion** is a noun meaning 'a particular time', as in 'happen on more than one occasion', and 'a special event or celebration', as in 'the dinner was a formal occasion'. More rarely **occasion** can be used as a verb but it should be restricted to rather formal situations. It means 'to cause, to bring about', as in 'His remarks occasioned a family feud'.

occurrence is very frequently misspelt. Note the double *c*, double *r* and *-ence* ending. It comes from the verb **occur**, 'to happen'. Note also **occurred** and **occurring**. **Occurrence** means 'an event, incident, happening', as in 'Robbery is an everyday occurrence there' and 'The occurrence of tuberculosis is on the increase'.

oculist *see* **optician**.

of is sometimes wrongly used instead of the verb 'to have', as in 'He must of known she was lying' instead of 'He must have known she was lying'. The error arises because the two constructions sound alike when not emphasized.

off is liable to be misspelt as 'of'. Note 'run off', 'keep off the grass', 'take one's coat off', 'a house off the main street'. The spelling 'of' is totally wrong in phrases such as these. **Off** is used by some people instead of 'from', as in 'He bought the radio off a street trader'. This use should be avoided except in informal contexts.

offence is liable to be misspelt. Note the *c*. It is a common error to put *s* in the British English spelling. **Offense** is the standard American spelling.

officious and **official** are liable to be confused. They sound and look rather alike but they have different meanings. **Official** means 'authorized', as in 'receive an official pass to the conference' and 'The police have released an official statement', and 'formal', as in 'an official reception for the visiting diplomat'. **Officious** means 'too ready to give orders, offer advice, bossy, interfering, self-important', as in 'told by the officious woman behind the desk that I would have to provide other documentation' and 'The child who had lost the money for her fare was put off the bus by an officious inspector'.

Oh *see* **O**.

OK and **okay** are both acceptable spellings of an informal word indicating agreement or approval, as in 'OK/okay, I'll come with you', 'We've at last been given the OK/okay to begin building'. When the word is used as a verb it is more usually spelt **okay** because of the problem in adding endings, as in 'They've okayed our plans at last'. **OK** is sometimes written with full stops as **O.K.**

older *see* **elder**.

omelette is frequently misspelt. Note the double *t* and first *e*. This *e* is not sounded in the pronunciation. It is pronounced with the emphasis on the first syllable, as *om*-lit. **Omelet** is the American English spelling.

omission is frequently misspelt. Note the single *m*. The word means 'the act of leaving out', as in 'the accidental omission of his name from the list of invitations'.

one is used in formal situations to indicate an indefinite person where 'you' would be used in informal situations, as in 'One should not believe all one hears' and 'One should be kind to animals'. This construction can sound rather affected. Examples of the informal 'you' include 'You would've thought he would've had more sense' and 'You wouldn't think anyone could be so stupid'. **One** when followed by 'of the' and a plural noun takes a singular verb, as in 'One of the soldiers was killed' and 'One of the three witnesses has died'. However, the constructions 'one of those … who' and one of the … that' take a plural verb, as in 'He is one of those people who will not take advice' and 'It is one of those houses that are impossible to heat'.

only must be carefully positioned in written sentences to avoid confusion. It should be placed before, or as close as possible before, the word to which it refers. Compare 'She drinks only wine at the weekend', 'She drinks wine only at the weekend' and 'Only she drinks wine at the weekend'. In spoken English, where the intonation of the voice will indicate which word **only** applies to it may be placed in whichever position sounds most natural, usually between the subject and the verb, as in 'She only drinks wine at the weekend'.

onomatopoeia refers to 'the combination of sounds in a word that imitates or suggests the sound of what the word refers to'. 'Crackle', as in 'The fire crackled', 'hiss', as in 'The snake began to hiss', 'rumble', as in 'The thunder rumbled' are all examples of **onomatopoeia**. The word is frequently misspelt. Note the *oeia* combination.

onto and **on to** are both acceptable forms in sentences such as 'The cat leapt onto/on to the table' and 'He jumped from the plane onto/on to the ground'. However, in sentences such as 'It is time to move on to another city' **onto** is not a possible alternative'.

onward and **onwards** are not interchangeable. **Onward** is an adjective, as in 'onward motion' and 'onward progress'. **Onwards** is an adverb, as in 'march onwards' and 'proceed onwards'.

optician, ophthalmologist, optometrist and **oculist** all refer to 'a person who is concerned with disorders of the eyes' but they are not interchangeable. **Dispensing**

optician refers to 'a person who makes and sells spectacles or contact lenses'. **Ophthalmic optician** refers to 'a person who tests eyesight and prescribes lenses'. **Optometrist** is another term for this. **Ophthalmologist** refers to 'a doctor who specializes in disorders of the eyes' and **oculist** is another name for this. **Ophthalmologist** is frequently misspelt. Note the *h* after the *p*. It is pronounced of-thal-mol-*ol*-oj-ist.

optimum means 'the most favourable or advantageous condition, situation, amount, degree, etc', as in 'A temperature of 20° is optimum for these plants'. It is mostly used as an adjective meaning 'most favourable or advantageous', as in 'the optimum speed to run the car at', 'the optimum time at which to pick the fruit' and 'the optimum amount of water to give the plants'. It should not be used simply as a synonym for 'best'.

optometrist *see* **optician**.

or is accompanied by a singular verb when it connects singular subjects, as in 'Dessert will be ice cream or fruit salad' and 'Tuesday or Wednesday would be a suitable day'. A plural verb is used if the subjects are plural, as in 'Oranges or peaches are suitable' and 'Roses or carnations are possibilities'. If there is a combination of singular and plural subjects the verb agrees with the subject that is nearest to it, as in 'One very large cake or several small ones have been ordered' and 'Several small cakes or one very large one has been ordered'.

oral *see* **aural**.

orientate and **orient** are both acceptable forms of the same word. **Orientate** is the more common in British English but the shorter form, **orient**, is preferred by some people and is the standard form in American English. They are verbs meaning 'to get one's bearings', as in 'difficult to orientate/orient themselves in the mist on the mountain'; 'to adjust to new surroundings', as in 'It takes some time to orientate/orient oneself in a new job'; 'to direct at', as in 'The course is orientated/oriented at older students'; 'to direct the interest of to', as in 'try to orientate/orient students towards the sciences'.

orthopaedic and **paediatric** are liable to be confused. They both apply to medical specialties but they are different. **Orthopaedic** means 'referring to the treatment of disorders of the bones', as in 'attend the orthopaedic clinic with an injured back'. **Paediatric** means 'referring to the treatment of disorders associated with children', as in 'Her little boy is receiving treatment from a paediatric consultant'. In American English these are respectively spelt **orthopedic and pediatric**.

other than can be used when **other** is an adjective or pronoun, as in 'There was no means of entry other than through a trap door' and 'He disapproves of the actions of anyone other than himself'. Traditionally it should not be used as an adverbial phrase, as in 'It was impossible to get there other than by private car'. In such constructions **otherwise than** should be used, as in 'It is impossible to get there otherwise than by private car.' However, **other than** used adverbially is common in modern usage.

otherwise traditionally should not be used as an adjective or pronoun, as in 'Pack your clothes, clean or otherwise' and 'We are not discussing the advantages, or otherwise, of the scheme at this meeting'. It is an adverb, as in 'We are in favour of the project but he obviously thinks otherwise' and 'The hours are rather long but otherwise the job is fine'. *See* **other than**.

outdoor and **outdoors** are not interchangeable. **Outdoor** is an adjective, as in 'encourage the children to take part in outdoor activities' and 'have an outdoor party'. **Outdoors** is an adverb, as in 'children going outdoors to play' and 'hold the party outdoors'.

outrageous is liable to be misspelt. Note the *e*. The word means 'shocking, offensive', as in 'their outrageous behaviour at the church service', and 'unconventional', as in 'wearing outrageous hats'.

outward and **outwards** are not completely interchangeable. **Outward** is an adjective, as in 'the outward journey', but it is also a possible alternative to **outwards**, the adverb, as in 'toes turned outwards/outward'.

owing to *see* **due to**.

P

p *see* **pence**.

pace is a Latin word adopted into English where it means 'with due respect to', usually preceding a statement of disagreement, as in 'Pace Robert Louis Stevenson, but I do not think it is better to travel hopefully than to arrive' and 'Pace your parents, but you might well find that school days are not the happiest days of your life'. It is used in formal, literary or facetious contexts and is pronounced *pah*-chay.

paediatric *see* **orthopaedic**.

palate, palette and **pallet** are liable to be confused. They sound alike but they have completely different meanings. **Palate** means either 'the top part of the inside of one's mouth', as in 'have a sore throat and palate' and 'a cleft palate', or 'sense of taste, the ability to distinguish one taste from another', as in 'Sweet things do not appeal to my palate' and 'His wine merchant complimented him on his palate'. **Palette** refers to 'the board on which an artist's colours are mixed', as in 'mix a beautiful shade of purple on his palette'. **Pallet** refers to a large platform for carrying or storing goods', as in 'put a pallet of books on the fork-lift truck', or 'a hard bed or straw mattress', as in 'wounded soldiers lying on pallets'.

panacea and **placebo** are liable to be confused. **Panacea** means 'a universal remedy for all ills and troubles', as in 'The new government does not have a panacea for the country's problems'. It is often used loosely to mean any remedy for any problem, as in 'She thinks that a holiday will be a panacea for his unhappiness'. **Panacea** is pronounced pan-a-*see*-a. **Placebo** refers to 'a supposed medication that is just a harmless substance given to a patient as part of a drugs trial etc', as in 'She was convinced the pills were curing her headaches but the doctor has prescribed her a placebo'. It is pronounced pla-*see*-bo.

panic causes spelling problems with reference to the past participle, past tense and present participle as **panicked** and **panicking**, as in 'They panicked when they smelt the smoke' and 'The panicking audience rushed for the exit'. Note also **panicky**, as in 'She got a bit panicky when she heard the footsteps behind her'.

paraffin is frequently misspelt. Note the single *r* and double *f*. The word refers to 'a type of oil used in heaters and lights', as in 'paraffin lamps'.

parallel is frequently misspelt. Note the single *r* and double *l* and single *l*. Note also that the *l* does not double in the past participle and present participle, as **paralleled** and **paralleling**. The word means 'of lines having the same distance between them at every point' and 'exactly corresponding', as in 'a parallel case'. As a verb it means 'to be equal to', as in 'His comparison has never been paralleled', and 'to be comparable to or similar to', as in 'His experience of the firm paralleled hers'.

paralyse is frequently misspelt. Note the *yse* ending. In American English it is spelt **paralyze**. The word means 'to prevent from moving', as in 'The accident paralysed him from the waist down' and 'to prevent from functioning', as in 'The strike paralysed the factory for weeks'.

parameter is a mathematical term that is very loosely used in modern usage to mean 'limit, boundary, framework' or 'limiting feature or characteristic', as in 'work within the parameters of our budget and resources'. The word is over-used and should be avoided where possible. The emphasis is on the second syllable as par-*am*-it-er.

paranoid is an adjective meaning 'referring to a mental disorder, called **paranoia**, characterized by delusions of persecution and grandeur', as in 'a paranoid personality'. In modern usage it is used loosely to mean 'distrustful, suspicious of others, anxious etc', as in 'It is difficult to get to know him—he's so paranoid' and 'paranoid about people trying to get his job', when there is no question of actual mental disorder. **Paranoia** is pronounced par-a-*noy*-a.

paraphernalia means 'all the bits and pieces of equipment required for something', as in 'all the paraphernalia needed to take a baby on holiday', 'put his angling paraphernalia in the car'. Strictly speaking it is a plural noun but it is now frequently used with a singular verb, as in 'The artist's paraphernalia was lying all over the studio'. **Paraphernalia** is liable to be misspelt. Note the *er* before the *n*.

parentheses *see* **brackets**.

parliament is liable to be misspelt. Note the *i* before the *a*. It is pronounced *par*-la-ment. It refers to 'a legislative assembly or authority'. When it refers to a particular assembly, such as the British one, it is usually spelt with a capital letter.

parlour *see* **sitting room**.

particular means 'special, exceptional', as in 'a matter of particular importance', or 'individual', as in 'Have you a particular person in mind?', and 'concerned over details, fastidious', as in 'very particular about personal hygiene'. **Particular** is often used almost meaninglessly, as in 'this particular dress' and 'this particular car', when **particular** does not add much to the meaning.

partner can be used to indicate one half of an established couple, whether the couple are married or living together, as in 'Her partner was present at the birth of the child'.

passed and **past** are liable to be confused. **Passed** is the past participle and past tense of the verb 'to pass', as in 'She has already passed the exam' and 'They passed an old man on the way'. **Past** is used as a noun, as in 'He was a difficult teenager but that is all in the past now' and 'He has a murky past'. It is also used as an adjective, as in 'I haven't seen him in the past few weeks' and 'Her past experiences affected her opinion of men'. **Past** can also be a preposition, as in 'We drove past their new house', 'It's past three o'clock' and 'He's past caring'. It can also be an adverb, as in 'He watched the athletes running past' and 'The boat drifted past'.

patent, in British English, is usually pronounced *pay*-tent, as in 'patent leather dancing shoes'. **Patent** in the sense of 'obvious', as in 'his patent dislike of the situation' and 'It was quite patent that she loved him' is also pronounced in that way. **Patent** in the sense of 'a legal document giving the holder the sole right to make or sell something and preventing others from imitating it', as in 'take out a patent for his new invention', can be pronounced either *pay*-tent or *pat*-ent. **Patent** in this last sense can also be a verb, as in 'He should patent his invention as soon as possible'.

peaceable and **peaceful** are interchangeable in some meanings. Both **peaceable** and **peaceful** can mean 'not quarrelsome or aggressive, peace-loving', as in 'He is a peaceable person but his neighbours are always trying to pick a quarrel' and 'peaceful nations unwilling to go to war'. They can also both mean 'without fighting or disturbance, non-violent', as in 'try to reach a peaceable settlement' and 'take part in a peaceful demonstration'. **Peaceful** means 'characterized by peace, calm, quiet', as in 'a peaceful spot for a quiet holiday' and 'peaceful country scene'. **Peaceable** is frequently misspelt. Note the *e* before the second *a* and note the *-able*, not *-ible*, ending.

pedal and **peddle** are liable to be confused. They sound alike but have different meanings. **Pedal** refers to a 'foot-operated lever', as in 'The pedal on his bicycle broke' and 'the soft pedal on a piano'. It is also a verb meaning 'to operate a pedal', as in 'pedal the bicycle slowly uphill'. **Peddle** is a verb meaning 'to sell small articles from house to house or from place to place, to hawk', as in 'tinkers peddling clothes pegs and paper flowers around the village'. It also means 'to put forward or spread', as in 'peddle his agnostic theories'. In modern usage **peddle** is often used of selling drugs, as in 'evil men peddling hard drugs to young people'.

peddle *see* **pedal**.

peddler and **pedlar** are not interchangeable in British English. **Peddler** refers particularly to 'a person who peddles drugs', as in 'drug-peddlers convicted and sent to prison'. **Pedlar** refers to 'a person who sells small articles from house to house or from place to place', as in 'pedlars selling ribbons at the fair'.

pedlar *see* **peddler**.

pejorative is liable to be mispronounced. In modern usage it is pronounced with the emphasis on the second syllable, as in pi-*jor*-at-iv. It means 'expressing criticism or scorn, derogatory, disparaging', as in 'It was unsportsmanlike to make pejorative remarks about his rival'.

pence, p and **pennies** are liable to be confused. **Pence** is the plural form of 'penny', as in 'There are a hundred pence in the pound'. It is commonly found in prices, as in 'apples costing 10 pence each'. **Pence** has become much more common than 'pennies', which tends to be associated with pre-decimalization money (the British currency was decimalized in 1972), as in 'There were twelve pennies in one shilling'. **Pence** is sometimes used as though it were singular, as in 'have no one-pence pieces'. In informal contexts **p** is often used, as in 'Have you got a 10p (pronounced ten pee) piece' and

'Those chocolate bars are fifteen p'. **Pence** in compounds is not pronounced in the same way as pence was pronounced in compounds before decimalization. Such words as 'ten pence' are now pronounced *ten pens*, with equal emphasis on each word. In pre-decimalization days it was pronounced *ten*-pens, with the emphasis on the first word.

pennies *see* **pence**.

people is usually a plural noun and so takes a plural verb, as in 'The local people were annoyed at the stranger's behaviour' and 'People were being asked to leave'. In the sense of 'nation', 'race' or 'tribe' it is sometimes treated as a singular noun, as in 'the nomadic peoples of the world'. **People** acts as the plural of 'person', as in 'There's room for only one more person in that car but there's room for three people in this one'. In formal or legal contexts **persons** is sometimes used as the plural of 'person', as in 'The lift had a notice saying "Room for six persons only"'.

per means 'for each' and is used to express rates, prices, etc, as in 'driving at 60 miles per hour', 'cloth costing £5 per square metre', 'The cost of the trip is £20 per person' and 'The fees are £1000 a term per child'. It can also mean 'in each', as in 'The factory is inspected three times per year'.

per capita is a formal expression meaning 'for each person', as in 'The cost of the trip will be £300 per capita'. It is a Latin phrase which has been adopted into English and literally means 'by heads'. It is pronounced per *ka*-pi-ta.

per cent is usually written as two words. It is used adverbially in combination with a number in the sense of 'in or for each hundred', as in '30 per cent of the people are living below the poverty line'. The number is sometimes written in figures, as in 'Fifty per cent of the staff are married'. The symbol % is often used instead of the words 'per cent', especially in technical contexts, as in 'make savings of up to 30%'. **Per cent** in modern usage is sometimes used as a noun, as in 'They have agreed to lower the price by half a per cent'.

percentage refers to 'the rate, number or amount in each hundred', as in 'the number of unemployed people expressed as a percentage of the adult population' and 'What percentage of his salary is free?'. It is also used to mean proportion, as in 'Only a small percentage of last year's students have found jobs' and 'A large percentage of the workers are in favour of a strike' 'In modern usage it is sometimes used to mean 'a small amount' or 'a small part', as in 'Only a percentage of the students will find work'.

perceptible and **perceptive** are liable to be confused. They look and sound rather similar but they mean different things. **Perceptible** means 'noticeable, recognizable', as in 'There was no perceptible difference in her appearance even after all those years' and 'There has been a perceptible improvement in her work'. **Perceptive** means 'quick to notice and understand', as in 'She was perceptive enough to realize that she was not welcome, although her hosts tried to hide the fact', and 'having or showing understanding or insight, discerning', as in 'She wrote a perceptive analysis of his poetry'.

perpetrate and **perpetuate** are liable to be confused. **Perpetrate** means 'to commit, to perform', as in 'perpetrate a crime' and 'perpetrate an act of violence'. **Perpetuate** means 'to cause to continue', as in 'perpetuate the myth that women are helpless' and 'His behaviour will simply perpetuate his reputation as a villain'.

perquisite *see* **prerequisite**.

per se is a Latin phrase that has been adapted into English and means 'in itself', as in 'The substance is not per se harmful but it might be so if it interacts with other substances' and 'Television is not per se bad for children'. It should be used only in formal contexts.

persecute and **prosecute** are liable to be confused. They look and sound rather similar but they mean different things. **Persecute** means 'to treat cruelly, to oppress, to harass', as in 'The Christians in ancient Rome were persecuted for their beliefs' and 'Some of the pupils persecuted the new boy because he was so different from them'. **Prosecute** means 'to take legal action against', as in 'He was prosecuted for embezzling money from the company' and 'Shoplifters will be prosecuted'. It also means 'to follow, to continue to be occupied with', as in 'prosecute a new line of inquiry' and 'prosecute his musical career'. This meaning should be restricted to formal contexts.

person is now used in situations where 'man' was formerly used to avoid sexism in language'. It is used when the sex of the person being referred to is either unknown or not specified, as in 'They are advertising for another person for the warehouse'. It often sounds more natural to use 'someone', as in 'They are looking for someone to help out in the warehouse'. **Person** is often used in compounds, as in **chairperson, spokesperson** and **salesperson**, although some people dislike this convention and some compounds, such as **craftsperson**, have not really caught on. **Person** has two possible plurals. *See* **people**. **Person with** and **people with** are phrases advocated in 'politically correct' language to avoid negative terms such as 'victim', 'sufferer', as in 'person with Aids'.

personal and **personnel** are liable to be confused. **Personal** is an adjective meaning 'of or affecting a person', as in 'carry out the scheme for personal gain' and 'her personal belongings'; 'of or belonging to a particular person rather than a group', as in 'state her personal opinion rather than the official company policy'; 'done in person', as in 'thanks to her personal intervention'; 'of the body', as in 'personal hygiene'; 'critical of a person's character, etc', as in 'upset by her personal remarks'. **Personnel** refers to 'the people employed in a workplace, such as an an office, shop, factory, etc, considered collectively', as in 'personnel officer, 'personnel department', 'Some of the local firms are beginning to recruit more personnel' and 'cut back on personnel during the recession'. It is rather a formal word and is best restricted to a business situation, such as recruitment advertisements. Words such as 'staff', 'workers' and 'employees' can be used instead. **Personnel** is liable to be misspelt. Note the double *n* and single *l*.

phase *see* **faze**.

phenomenal means 'referring to a phenomenon'. It is often used to mean 'remarkable, extraordinary', as in 'a phenomenal atmospheric occurrence', and in modern usage it is also used loosely to mean 'very great', as in 'a phenomenal increase in the crime rate' and 'a phenomenal achievement'. This use is usually restricted to informal contexts.

phenomenon is a singular noun meaning 'a fact, object, occurrence, experience, etc, that can be perceived by the senses rather than by thought or intuition', as in 'She saw something coming out of the lake but it remained an unexplained phenomenon', and 'a strange, unusual or remarkable fact, event or person of some particular significance', as in 'Single parenthood is one of the phenomena of the 1990s'. The plural is **phenomena**, as in 'natural phenomena'. It is a common error to treat **phenomena** as a singular noun. Note the spelling of **phenomenon** as it is liable to be misspelt.

phlegm causes problems with reference to both spelling and pronunciation. Note the *g*, which is often omitted in error. The word is pronounced *flem* and refers to 'a thick mucus secreted by respiratory passages, especially when one has a cold etc', as in 'cough up phlegm'. It also refers to 'slowness to act, react or feel, indifference', as in 'She seemed to face the crisis with an amazing amount of phlegm'. The adjective from this is phlegmatic, meaning 'slow to act, react or feel, indifferent, calm', as in 'require a phlegmatic temperament to cope with all the crises in the office'.

phobia refers to 'an abnormal or irrational fear or aversion', as in 'She is consulting a psychiatrist about her phobia about birds' and 'try to cure his phobia about flying'. It is often used loosely in modern usage to mean 'dislike', as in 'a phobia about people with red hair', or 'obsession', as in 'She has a phobia about her weight.' **Phobia** is liable to be misspelt. Note the *ph*.

phone, which is a short form of 'telephone', is not regarded as being as informal as it once was. It is quite acceptable in sentences such as 'He is going to buy a mobile phone', 'There is an extension phone in the kitchen'. It can also be used as a verb, as in 'Could you phone back tomorrow?' and 'Phone the doctor—it's an emergency'. Telephone is used only in very formal or official contexts', as in 'Please telephone for an application form'. 'If you wish to make an appointment with Mr Jones you will have to telephone his secretary'. Note that **phone** is now spelt without an apostrophe.

phoney and **phony** are both acceptable spellings but **phoney** is the more common in British English. The word means 'pretending or claiming to be what one is not, fake', as in 'He has a phoney American accent' and 'There's something phoney about him'.

photo is an abbreviation of 'photograph' which is usually used in an informal context, as in 'His mother is showing his girlfriend his baby photos', 'He's boring everybody with his holiday photos'. In more formal and official contexts 'photograph' is used, as in 'Assemble the children for the school photograph' and 'Enclose the photographs with the passport application form'. The plural of **photo** is **photos**. It is not generally used as a verb.

picnic causes problems with regard to the past participle, past tense and present participle. They add a *k* after the final *c* before the endings are added, as in **picnicked** and **picnicking**, as in 'They picnicked by the river' and 'We were picnicking on wine'. Note also **picnicker**, as in 'Picnickers should not leave litter'.

pidgin and **pigeon** are liable to be confused. **Pidgin** refers to 'a language that is a mixture of two other languages', as in 'unable to understand the local people who were speaking pidgin English'. **Pigeon** is 'a type of bird of the dove family', as in 'pigeons eating crumbs as we were eating our sandwiches'.

pièce de résistance is a French phrase that has been adopted into English meaning 'the most important or impressive item', as in 'His portrait of his wife was the pièce de résistance of the exhibition'. The phrase is liable to be misspelt. Note the accent on the *e* of **pièce** which should not be omitted or it becomes 'piece'.

Note also the accent on the first *e* of **résistance**. The phrase is pronounced pyes-de-re-*zist*-ahns.

pigeon *see* **pidgin**.

placebo *see* **panacea**.

plain and **plane** are liable to be confused since they sound alike. However, they have completely different meanings. **Plain** can be an adjective with several meanings. It means 'easy to see, hear or understand, clear', as in 'It was plain that she was unhappy' and 'speak in plain English so that you will be understood'; 'frank, not trying to deceive', as in 'the plain truth'; 'simple, not decorated or fancy', as in 'a plain style of dressing' and 'plain food'; 'without a pattern', as in 'prefer a plain material'; 'not beautiful', as in 'People said that she was the plain one of the family'. **Plain** as a noun refers to 'a large area of flat, treeless land', as in 'grow wheat on the plains'. **Plane** as a noun means 'the shortened form of aeroplane', as in 'Travelling by plane will be quicker'; 'a flat or level surface', as in 'create a plane by levelling the surface'; 'a level or standard', as in 'His mind is on a different plane from ours' and 'reach a higher plane of development'; 'a tool for smoothing surfaces', as in 'use a plane to smooth out the imperfections in the wood'. Note the **plain** in the phrase **plain sailing**, as in 'She thought it would be plain sailing once she got a place of her own but there were problems'. It is a common error to put **plane**. *See* **plane**.

plaintiff and **plaintive** are liable to be confused because they sound similar. However, they have completely different meanings. **Plaintiff** refers to 'a person who brings a legal action against someone', as in 'It was the accused's mother who was the plaintiff'. **Plaintive** means 'sounding sad, mournful', as in 'the plaintive cries of hungry children' and 'the plaintive sound of the bagpipes'.

plane and **aeroplane** mean the same thing, both referring to a 'a machine that can fly and is used to carry people and goods'. In modern usage **plane** is the usual term, as in 'The plane took off on time' and 'nearly miss the plane'. **Aeroplane** is slightly old-fashioned or unduly formal, as in 'Her elderly parents say that they refuse to travel by aeroplane'. The American English spelling is **airplane**. Note that **plane** is not spelt with an apostrophe although it is a shortened form. *See also* **plain**.

pleaded and **pled** mean the same thing, both being the past tense and past participle of the verb 'to plead'. **Pleaded** is the usual form in British English, as in 'They pleaded with the tyrant to spare the child's life' and 'The accused was advised to plead guilty'. **Pled** is the usual American spelling.

plenty is used only informally in some contexts. It is acceptable in formal and informal contexts when it is followed by the preposition 'of', as in 'We have plenty of food', or when it is used as a pronoun without the 'of' construction, as in 'You can borrow some food from us—we have plenty'. Some people think its use as an adjective, as in 'Don't hurry—we have plenty time' and 'There's plenty food for all in the fridge', should be restricted to informal contexts. As an adverb it is a acceptable in both formal and informal contexts in such sentences as 'Help yourself—we have plenty more'. However, such sentences as 'The house is plenty big enough for them' is suitable only for very informal or slang contexts'.

plurals cause many problems. Most words in English add *s* to form the plural, as in 'cats', 'machines' and 'boots'. However, words ending in -*s*, -*x*, -*z*, -*ch* and -*sh* add *es*, as in 'buses', 'masses', 'foxes', 'fezzes or fezes', 'churches' and 'sashes'. Nouns ending in a consonant followed by *y* have -*ies* in the plural, as 'fairies' and 'ladies', but note 'monkey', where the *y* is preceded by a vowel and becomes 'monkeys'. Proper nouns ending in *y* add *s*, as in 'the two Germanys'. Some words ending in *f* have *ves* in the plural, as 'wives' and 'halves', but some simply add *s* to the singular form, as 'beliefs'. Some words ending in *f* can either add *s* or change to *ves*, as 'hoofs or hooves'. Words ending in *o* cause problems as some end in *oes* in the plural, as 'potatoes' and 'tomatoes', and some end in *s*, as in 'pianos', while some can be spelt either way and have to be learned or looked up in a dictionary etc. Shortened forms, such as 'photo' and 'video', add simply *s*, as 'photos', 'videos'. Some words have the same form in the plural as they do in the singular, such as 'sheep' and 'deer'. Some are plural in form already and so do not change,. These include 'trousers' and 'scissors'. Several words in English have irregular plural forms which just have to be learned or looked up in a dictionary, etc. These include 'men', 'mice' and 'feet'. Some foreign words adopted into English used to retain the foreign plural form in English but this is becoming less common and, at the very least there is now often an English-formed alternative, as 'gateaux/gateaus', 'index/indices', 'formulae/formulas', 'appendixes/appendices'. However, several nouns of foreign extraction retain the foreign-style plural in English, such as 'criteria' and 'crises'.

p.m. *see* **a.m.**

poignant is liable to be misspelt. Note the *g*, which is silent. It is pronounced *poy*-nyant. The word means 'affecting one's feelings deeply, distressing', as in 'a poignant tale of an orphan child'.

politic and **political** are liable to be confused although they are completely different in meaning. **Politic** means 'prudent, wise', as in 'He thought it politic not to mention that he knew that his boss had been fined for speeding'. **Political** means 'referring to politics', as in 'political parties' and 'the end of his political career'. **Politic** is pronounced with the emphasis on the first syllable, as *pol*-it-ik, but **political** is pronounced with the emphasis on the second syllable as pol-*it*-ic-al.

political correctness is a modern movement aiming to remove all forms of prejudice in language, such as sexism, racism and discrimination against disabled people. Its aims are admirable but in practice many of the words and phrases suggested by advocates of political correctness are rather contrived or, indeed, ludicrous. The adjective is **politically correct**.

pore and **pour** are liable to be confused because they sound alike. **Pore** as a verb means 'to look at or study intently', as in 'They pored over the old document looking for the site of the treasure'. **Pour** means 'to cause to flow', as in 'she poured milk from the jug', or 'to flow in large amounts', as in 'Water poured from the burst pipe'. **Pore** can also be a noun when it means 'one of the tiny openings on the surface of the skin', as in 'clogged pores'.

portrait is liable to be misspelt. Note the first *r*. The word means 'a painting, drawing or photograpgh of a person or animal, particularly one which concentrates on the face', as in 'portraits of his ancestors hanging on the walls of the dining room'.

portray is liable to be misspelt. Note the first *r*. It means 'to paint or draw', as in 'The queen was portrayed in her coronation robes'; 'to describe', as in 'In his autobiography his father is portrayed as a bully'; 'and to act the part of', as in 'The actress portrayed Desdemona in *Othello*'.

Portuguese is liable to be misspelt. Note the *u* after the *g*. It is the adjective from 'Portugal'.

possessives are indicated in English by either apostrophes or the preposition 'of', as in 'the boy's books', Jim's car', the dogs' kennels', 'the key of the back door' and 'The soldiers of the king'. When the 'of' construction is used of people, an apostrophe is often used as well, as in 'a colleague of her husband's'. The 'of' construction is usually used of things rather than people, as in 'The catch of the garden gate is broken', and it is usually used when geographical regions are being referred to, as in 'the forests of Scandinavia'. If the possession in question refers to more than one person the apostrophe goes on the last owner mentioned, as in 'John and Mary's beautiful house'. In the case of compound nouns, the apostrophe goes on the last word, as in 'the lady-in-waiting's role'. For the position of the apostrophe in **possessives** *see* **apostrophe**.

posthumous causes problems with both spelling and pronunciation. Note the *h*, which is often omitted in error since it is silent in pronunciation. The word is pronounced *post*-ewmus with the emphasis on the first syllable, which rhymes with 'lost'. The word means 'happening or given after death', as in 'a posthumous novel' and 'a posthumous medal'. The adverb **posthumously** means 'after one's death', as in 'The soldier's son was born posthumously'.

pour *see* **pore**.

practicable and **practical** should not be used interchangeably. **Practicable** means 'able to be done or carried out, able to be put into practice', as in 'His schemes seem fine in theory but they are never practicable'. **Practical** has several meanings, such as 'concerned with action and practice rather than with theory', as in 'He has studied the theory but has no practical experience of the job'; 'suitable for the purpose for which it was made', as in 'practical shoes for walking'; 'useful', as in 'a practical device with a wide range of uses'; 'clever at doing and making things', as in 'She's very practical when it comes to dealing with an emergency'; 'virtual', as in 'He's not the owner but he's in practical control of the firm'.

practically can mean 'in a practical way', as in 'Practically, the scheme is not really possible', but in modern usage it is usually used to mean 'virtually', as in 'He practically runs the firm although he is not the manager', and 'almost', as in 'The driver of that car practically ran me over'.

practice and **practise** are not interchangeable. **Practice** is a noun, as in 'She has gone to netball practice', 'It is time to put the plan into practice', 'It is accepted practice to tip the waiters', 'object to some of the practices of the religious sect' and 'Our doctor has retired from the practice'. **Practise** is the verb form, as in 'He practises the piano every evening', 'We must practise economy if we are to remain solvent', 'He is a medical doctor but he has not practised for years' and 'He is a Catholic but he no longer practises his religion'. Note that **practise** is not one of the verbs that can end in *-ize*. In American English both the noun and the verb are spelt **practice**.

pray and **prey** are liable to be confused. They sound alike but they have completely different meanings. **Pray** means 'to speak to God, to make requests of God', as in 'pray and sing hymns in church on Sundays' and 'pray to God that the pardon will arrive in time', or 'to ask a favour from, to beg', as in 'They prayed to the tyrant to release their brother'. **Prey** is a noun meaning 'an animal or bird hunted and killed by another animal or bird', as in 'The lion had its prey, a deer, in its mouth'. It also means 'a person who is exploited or harmed by another, a victim', as in 'The old lady was easy prey for the con man'. **Prey** is also a verb meaning 'to hunt and kill as prey', as in 'Eagles prey on small animals', and 'to trouble greatly, to obsess', as in 'His part in the crime preyed on his mind'.

precede and **proceed** are liable to be confused because they sound alike but they mean different things. **Precede** means 'to go in front of', as in 'The guide preceded us into the room', 'to come in front of', as in 'The text is preceded by a long introduction' and 'He preceded her as chairman'. **Proceed** means 'to go on, to continue', as in 'Work is proceeding at an even pace' and 'We were told to proceed with our work', or 'to make one's way, to go', as in 'They were proceeding up the street in a drunken manner'.

precipitate and **precipitous** are liable to be confused. **Precipitate** as an adjective means 'violently hurried', as in 'When the thief saw the policeman he made a precipitate dash from the room', 'sudden', as in 'Her precipitate disappearance from the firm', and 'rash, impulsive', as in 'We thought his action in leaving the firm was rather precipitate'. **Precipitous** means 'very steep, like a precipice', as in 'It was almost impossible to climb the precipitous slope'. **Precipitate** is also a verb meaning to cause something to happen suddenly or sooner than expected, to hasten', as in 'His setting fire to the bicycle shed precipitated his expulsion from the school', or 'to throw', as in 'His sudden departure precipitated the whole office into a state of confusion'. In the pronunciation of both the verb and the adjective, the emphasis is on the second syllable, but in the case of the verb the last syllable rhymes with 'gate' whereas in the case of the adjective the last syllable is pronounced to rhyme with 'hat'. Thus the pronunciation of the adjective is pri-*sip*-i-tat, and that of the verb pri-sip-it-ayt.

prefer is followed by the preposition 'to' not 'than', as in 'She prefers dogs to cats', 'They prefer Paris to London' and 'They prefer driving to walking'. **Prefer** causes spelling problems with regard to the past participle, past tense and present participle. Note that the final *r* of **prefer** doubles before the '-ed' and '-ing' are added, as **preferred** and **preferring**. The word means 'to like better', as in 'She preferred the country to the town'.

premier and **première** are liable to be confused. **Premier** means 'leading, principle', as in 'He is the premier authority on genetic engineering in the country'. **Première** refers to 'the first performance of a film, play, etc', as in 'attend the world première of his latest film'. It is now also a verb, as in 'His latest film was premiered in London'. **Premier** is pronounced *prem*-ier. Première is pronounced *prem*-i-ay or *prem*-i-ayr. **Première** is liable to be misspelt. Note the final *e*. The word is usually spelt with a grave accent over the second *e*.

premise *see* **premises**.

premises and **premise**. are liable to be confused. **Premises** refers to 'a building including any outbuildings and grounds', as in 'the car sales showroom has moved to new premises'. **Premises** is a plural noun and so takes a plural verb, as in 'Their present premises are too small for the volume of business'. **Premise** is a singular noun meaning 'assumption, hypothesis', as in 'His advice was based on the premise that they had enough capital for the project'. It is also spelt **premiss**.

premiss *see* **premises**.

prerequisite and **perquisite** are liable to be confused although they are completely different in meaning. **Perquisite** means 'money or goods given as a right in addition to one's pay', as in 'various perquisites such as a company car'. It is frequently abbreviated to 'perks', as in 'The pay's not very much but the perks are good'. **Prerequisite** refers to 'something required as a condition for something to happen or exist', as in 'Passing the exam is a prerequisite for his getting the job' and 'A certain amount of studying is a prerequisite of passing the exam'.

prescribe and **proscribe** are liable to be confused. They sound similar but are completely different in meaning. **Prescribe** means 'to advise or order the use of, especially a medicine or remedy', as in 'The doctor prescribed antibiotics' and 'The doctor prescribed complete bed rest'. It also means 'to lay down as a rule or law', as in 'School regulations prescribe that all pupils wear school uniform'. **Proscribe** means 'to prohibit', as in 'proscribe the carrying of guns', and 'to outlaw or exile', as in 'proscribe the members of the clan who betrayed the chief'. In some cases the words are virtually opposite in meaning. Compare 'The lecturer has prescribed several books which must be read by the end of term' and 'The government has proscribed several books that are critical of them'.

prestige is liable to be mispronounced. It is pronounced prez-*teezh* and means 'the respect, status or renown derived from achievement, distinction, wealth, glamour etc', as in 'He suffered a loss of prestige when he lost all his money' and 'He enjoys the prestige of being chairman of the company'.

prevaricate and **procrastinate** are liable to be confused although they have completely different meanings. **Prevaricate** means 'to try to avoid telling the truth by speaking in an evasive or misleading way', as in 'She prevaricated when the police asked her where she had been the previous evening'. **Procrastinate** means 'to delay or postpone action', as in 'The student has been procrastinating all term but now he has to get to grips with his essay'.

preventative and **preventive** both mean 'preventing or intended to prevent, precautionary', as in 'If you think the staff are stealing from the factory you should take preventative/preventive measures' and 'Preventative/preventive medicine seeks to prevent disease and disorders rather than cure them'. **Preventive** is the more frequently used of the two terms.

prey *see* **pray**.

prima facie is a Latin phrase that has been adopted into English. It means 'at first sight, based on what seems to be so' and is mainly used in legal or very formal contexts, as in 'The police say they have prima facie evidence for arresting him but more investigation is required'. The phrase is pronounced *pri*-ma *fay*-shee.

primarily is traditionally pronounced with the emphasis on the first syllable, as *prim*-ar-el-i. Since this is difficult to say unless one is speaking very slowly and carefully, it is becoming increasingly common to pronounce it with the emphasis on the second syllable, as prim-*err*-el-i. It means 'mainly', as in 'He was primarily interested in the creative side of the business' and 'The course is primarily a practical one'.

primeval and **primaeval** are both acceptable forms of the word meaning 'of the earliest period in the history of the world, very ancient', as in 'primeval rocks'. In modern usage **primeval** is the more common term although **primaeval** was formerly the more usual term.

principal and **principle** are liable to be confused. They sound alike but they have different meanings. **Principal** means 'chief, main', as in 'his principal reason for leaving' and 'her principal source of income'. **Principal** is also a noun meaning 'head', as in 'the principal of the college'. **Principle** means 'a basic general truth', as in 'according to scientific principles', and 'a guiding rule for personal behaviour', as in 'It is against his principles to lie'.

principle *see* **principal**.

prise and **prize** are liable to cause confusion. The verb 'to force open' can be spelt either **prise** or **prize**, as in 'prise/prize open the chest with an iron bar'. **Prise** is the more common spelling. **Prize** has another meaning for which prise cannot be substituted. It means 'an award or reward', as in 'He won first prize in the tennis competition', and 'something won in a lottery etc', as in 'He won first prize on the football pools'. **Prize** can also be a verb meaning 'to value highly', as in 'She prizes her privacy'.

privilege is liable to be misspelt. Note the *i* before the *l*, and the *e* before the *g*. It refers to 'a special right or advantage', as in 'the privileges conferred on ambassadors' and 'enjoy the privileges of being a senior executive'.

procrastinate *see* **prevaricate**.

professor is liable to be misspelt. Note the single *f* and the double *s*. The word means 'a senior university lecturer', as in 'The professor is retiring from the chair of English this year'.

prognosis *see* **diagnosis**.

programme and **program** are liable to cause confusion. In British English **programme** is the acceptable spelling in such senses as in 'a television programme', 'put on a varied programme of entertainment' 'buy a theatre programme' and 'launch an ambitious programme of expansion'. However, in the computing sense **program** is used. **Programme** can also be a verb meaning 'to plan, to schedule', as in 'programme the trip for tomorrow'; 'to cause something to conform to a particular set of instructions', as in 'programme the central heating system'; or 'to cause someone to behave in a particular way, especially to conform to particular instructions', as in 'Her parents have programmed her to obey them implicitly'. In the computing sense of 'to provide with a series of coded instructions', the verb is spelt **program** and the *m* is doubled to form the past participle, past tense and present participle, as **programmed** and **programming**. In American English **program** is the accepted spelling for all senses of both noun and verb.

prophecy and **prophesy** are liable to confused. **Prophecy** is a noun meaning 'prediction', as in 'Some of the old woman's prophecies came true'. **Prophesy** is a verb meaning 'to predict', as in 'The old woman had prophesied the disaster that befell the village' and 'They prophesied that the recession would be over in a year'. **Prophecy** is pronounced with the emphasis on the first syllable, as *pro*-fi-si. **Prophesy** is also pronounced with the emphasis on the first syllable, but the last syllable rhymes with 'eye' as *pro*-fi-si.

proscribe *see* **prescribe**.

prosecute *see* **persecute**.

prostate and **prostrate** are liable to be confused although they are completely different in meaning. **Prostate** refers to 'a gland around the neck of the bladder in men', as in 'have a prostate complaint' and 'contract cancer of the prostate'. **Prostrate** means 'lying face downwards', as in 'The injured rider was lying prostrate on the ground', 'overcome by', as in 'prostrate with grief', and 'exhausted, helpless', as in 'a country competely prostrate after the war'. **Prostrate** is also a verb meaning 'to throw oneself face down on the ground, for example, as a sign of submission', as in 'The soldiers prostrated themselves before the emperor', 'to overcome', as in 'Grief prostrated her', and 'to make helpless or exhausted', as in 'prostrated following a bout of flu'.

protagonist was originally a term for 'the chief character in a drama', as in 'Hamlet is the protagonist in the play that bears his name'. It then came to mean also 'the leading person or paticipant in an event, dispute, etc', as in 'The protagonists on each side of the dispute had a meeting'. In modern usage it can now also mean 'a leading or notable supporter of a cause, movement, etc,'as in 'She was one of the protagonists of the feminist movement'.

protein is liable to be misspelt. Note the *ei* combination. It is an exception to the 'i before e' rule. **Protein** refers to 'a substance that is an important body-building part of the diet of humans and animals', as in 'Meat, eggs and fish are sources of protein'.

provided and **providing** are used interchangeably, as in 'You may go, provided/providing that you have finished your work' and 'He can borrow the car provided/providing he pays for the petrol'. 'That' is optional. The phrases mean 'on the condition that'.

psychiatry is liable to be misspelt. Note the initial *p* and the *y* after the *s*. It is pronounced si-*ki*-i-tri and refers to 'the branch of medicine that deals with disorders of the mind'.

publicly is liable to be misspelt. There is no *k* before the *l*. It is a common error to spell it 'publically'. The word means 'not in private, in front of other people', as in 'He publicly admitted that he was at fault'.

pudding *see* **dessert**.

pupil and **student** are not interchangeable. **Pupil** refers to 'a child or young person who is at school', as in 'primary school pupils and secondary school pupils', **Student** refers to 'a person who is studying at a place of further education, at a university or college', as in 'students trying to find work during the vacations'. In modern usage senior **pupils** at secondary school are sometimes known as **students**. In American English student refers to people at school as well as to people in further education. **Pupil** can also refer to 'a person who is receiving instruction in something from an expert' as in 'The piano teacher has several adult pupils'. **Student** can also refer to 'a person who is studying a particular thing', as in 'In his leisure time he is a student of local history'.

purposefully and **purposely** are not interchangeable. **Purposefully** means 'determinedly', as in 'He strode purposefully up to the front of the hall and addressed the meeting'. **Purposely** means 'on purpose, deliberately', as in 'He didn't leave his book behind by accident—he did it purposely'.

Q

quasi- is Latin in origin and means 'as if, as it were'. In English it is combined with adjectives in the sense of 'seemingly, apparently, but not really', as in 'He gave a quasi-scientific explanation of the occurrence which convinced many people but did not fool his colleagues', or 'partly, to a certain extent but not completely', as in 'It is a quasi-official body which does not have full powers'. **Quasi-** can also be combined with nouns to mean 'seeming, but not really', as in 'a quasi-socialist who is really a capitalist' and 'a quasi-Christian who will not give donations to charity'. **Quasi-** has several possible pronunciations. It can be pronounced *kway*-zi, *kway*-si or *kwah*-si

quay is liable to be mispronounced. The spelling of the word does not suggest the pronunciation, which is *key*. It means 'a landing place', as in 'ships unloading at the quay'.

queer in the sense of 'homosexual' was formerly used only in a slang and derogatory or offensive way. However, it is now used in a non-offensive way by homosexual people to describe themselves, as an alternative to 'gay'.

question *see* **beg the question; leading question.**

questionnaire is liable to be misspelt. Note the double *n*. Formerly the acceptable pronunciation was kes-tyon-*air*, but in modern usage kwes-chon-*air* is more common. The word refers to 'a list of questions to be answered by a number of people as part of a survey or collection of statistics', as in 'People entering the supermarket were asked to fill in a questionnaire on their shopping habits' and 'Householders were asked to complete a questionnaire on their electrical equipment'.

quick is an adjective meaning 'fast, rapid', as in 'a quick method', 'a quick route' and 'a quick walker'. It should not be used as an adverb, as in 'Come quick', in formal contexts since this is grammatically wrong.

quite has two possible meanings when used with adjectives. It can mean 'fairly, rather, somewhat', as in 'She's quite good at tennis but not good enough to play in the team' and 'The house is quite nice but it's not what we're looking for'. Where the indefinite article is used, **quite** precedes it, as in 'quite a good player' and 'quite a nice house'. 'Quite can also mean 'completely, totally', as in 'We were quite overwhelmed by their generosity' and 'It is quite impossible for him to attend the meeting'.

R

rack and wrack are liable to be confused. Rack refers to 'a framework for storing and displaying things', as in 'a luggage rack' and 'a vegetable rack'. It is also the name given historically to an instrument of torture, consisting of a frame on which a person lay with wrists and ankles tied and had their arms stretched in one direction and their legs in the other, as in 'prisoners on the rack'. The verb rack means 'to cause to suffer pain or great distress to', as in 'cancer patients racked with agony', 'racked with uncertainty' and 'nerve-racking'. The phrase 'rack one's brains' means 'to try hard to think of or remember', as in 'racking his brains to remember their address'. Wrack is a rarer word that refers to 'a kind of seaweed' or 'a remnant of something that has been destroyed'. Rack and wrack are interchangeable in the phrase rack/wrack and ruin—'neglect, decay, destruction', as in 'Since the owner has been ill the business has gone to rack/wrack and ruin'.

racket and racquet are liable to be confused. Either racket or racquet may be used to indicate 'a kind of implement with a stringed frame used in sport for striking the ball', as in 'tennis racket/racquet' and 'badminton racket/racquet'. Racket also means 'a loud noise', as in 'neighbours complaining about the racket made by the party guests' and 'children making a racket running up and down stairs'. Racket also refers to 'a dishonest or illegal way of making money', as in 'a drug racket' and 'a racket involving forged currency'.

raise and raze are liable to be confused. They sound alike but have completely different meanings. Raise means 'to move to a higher position', as in 'raise the flag', 'raise prices' and 'raise morale'. Raze means 'to destroy completely', as in 'The invading army razed the village to the ground'.

raison d'être is French in origin and is used in English to mean 'a reason, a justification for the existence of', as in 'Her children are her raison d'être' and 'His only raison d'être is his work'. The phrase is liable to be misspelt. Note the accent (^) on the first e. It is pronounced ray-zon detr.

rang and rung are liable to be confused. Rang is the past tense of the verb 'to ring', as in 'She rang the bell', and rung is the past participle, as in 'They had rung the bell'.

rara avis is French in origin and means literally 'rare bird'. In English it is used to refer to 'a rare or unusual person or thing', as in 'a person with such dedication to a company is a rara avis'. It is pronounced ray-ra ayv-is or ra-ra ay-vis.

ravage and ravish are liable to be confused. They sound rather similar although they have different meanings. Ravage means 'to cause great damage to, to devastate', as in 'low-lying areas ravaged by floods' and 'a population ravaged by disease', or 'to plunder, to rob', as in 'neighbouring tribes ravaging their territory'. Ravish means either 'to delight greatly, to enchant', as in 'The audience were ravished by the singer's performance'. It also means 'to rape', as in 'The girl was ravished by her kidnappers', but this meaning is rather old-fashioned and is found only in formal or literary contexts.

raze see raise.

re, meaning 'concerning, with reference to', as in 'Re your correspondence of 26 November', should be restricted to business or formal contexts.

re- is a common prefix, meaning 'again', in verbs. In most cases it is not followed by a hyphen, as in 'retrace one's footsteps', 'a retrial ordered by the judge' and 'reconsider his decision'. However, it should be followed by a hyphen if its absence is likely to lead to confusion with another word, as in 're-cover a chair'/'recover from an illness', 're-count the votes'/'recount a tale of woe', 'the re-creation of a 17th-century village for a film set'/'play tennis for recreation' and 're-form the group'/'reform the prison system'. In cases where the second element of a word begins with e, re- is traditionally followed by a hyphen, as in 're-educate', re-entry' and 're-echo', but in modern usage the hyphen is frequently omitted.

readable see legible.

receipt is frequently misspelt. Note the ei combination in line with the 'i before e except after c' rule. Note also p, which is not pronounced. Receipt is pronounced ri-seet and means either 'the act of receiving', as in 'on receipt of your letter', or 'a written statement that money, goods, etc, have been received', as in 'Keep the receipt in case you want to return the goods'.

recommend is frequently misspelt. Note the single c and double m. The word means 'to suggest as suitable, to praise as suitable', as in 'I can thoroughly recommend this brand of face cream', and 'to suggest as advisable, to advise', as in 'He recommends that we reduce expenditure'.

reconnaissance is frequently misspelt. Note the single c, double n, and double s. It is pronounced ri-kon-i-sins and means 'an exploration or survey of an area', as in 'troops engaged in reconnaissance' and 'undertake an aerial reconnaissance of the area where the child was lost'.

re-cover, recover see re-.

re-creation, recreation see re-.

refer causes problems with regard to its past participle, past tense and present participle. The r doubles before the addition of '-ed' or '-ing', as in referred and referring, as in 'He referred to her good work in his speech' and 'He was not referring to the present holder of the post'. Note, however, reference with a single r.

referendum causes problems with regard to its plural form. It has two possible plural forms, referendums or referenda. In modern usage referendums is the more

998

usual plural. **Referendum** means 'the referring of an issue of public importance to a general vote by all the people of a country', as in 'hold a referendum on whether to join the EC'.

re-form, reform *see* **re-**.

refrigerator is frequently misspelt. Note the *-or* ending, the *er* in the middle and the absence of *d*. It is a common error to include a *d* because of confusion with 'fridge'.

registry office and **register office** are interchangeable, although **registry office** is the more common term in general usage. The words refer to 'an office where civil marriage ceremonies are performed and where births, marriages and deaths are recorded', as in 'She wanted to be married in church but he preferred a registry office ceremony' and 'register the child's birth at the local registry office'.

reign and **rein** are liable to be confused. **Reign** is the time during which a king or queen reigns', as in 'during the reign of George V'. **Rein** refers to 'one of the leather straps that control a horse', as in 'The coachman let go of the reins and the horse bolted'. **Reins**, the plural of **rein**, refers to 'a means of control or restraint', as in 'The deputy president held the reins of power'. Both **reign** and **rein** can also be verbs. **Reign** means 'to rule as king or queen', as in 'a monarch who reigned for more than fifty years'. **Rein** as a verb is found in the phrase **rein in**, meaning 'to restrain or stop', as in 'rein in the horse'.

relevant is liable to be misspelt. Note the *-ant* ending. It means 'connected with what is being discussed, happening, done, etc', as in 'collect all the relevant information' and 'police noting details relevant to the case'.

reminiscences is frequently misspelt. Note the *sc* combination. The word refers to 'remembered experiences', as in 'listening to the old woman's reminiscences of her childhood days'. **Reminiscent** is an adjective meaning either 'thinking or talking about past events', as in 'in reminiscent mood', or 'reminding one of, suggesting someone or something', as in 'The style of the artist is reminiscent of Monet'.

requisite *see* **perquisite**.

rhyme and **rime** are liable to be confused. They sound alike but have completely different meanings. **Rhyme** refers to 'a word which is like another in its final sound', as in 'tailor and sailor are rhymes', 'rough and puff are rhymes' and 'dilatory and military are rhymes'. **Rhyme** can also be a verb, as in 'tailor rhymes with sailor'. **Rime** refers to 'a thick white frost', as in 'fields covered with rime'.

rhythm is frequently misspelt. Note the first *h* and the *y*. It means 'a regular repeated pattern of sounds or beats', as in 'the fast rhythm of the dance music'.

rigorous is frequently misspelt. Note the absence of *u* before the second *r*. It is unlike **rigour** in this respect. **Rigorous** means 'severe, strict', as in 'the rigorous discipline of the army', 'harsh, unpleasant', as in 'rigorous weather conditions', and 'strict, detailed', as in 'with rigorous attention to the small print of the agreement'.

rigour and **rigor** are liable to be confused. They look similar but they have completely different meanings. **Rigour** means 'severity, strictness', as in 'the rigour of the punishment', and 'harshness, unpleasantness', as in 'the rigour of the climate' (in this sense it is often in the plural, **rigours**), and 'strictness, detailedness', as in 'the rigour of the editing'. **Rigor** is a medical term meaning 'rigidity', as in 'muscles affected by rigor', or 'a feeling of chilliness often accompanied by feverishness', as in 'infectious diseases of which rigor is one of the symptoms'. **Rigor** is also short for **rigor mortis**, meaning 'the stiffening of the body that occurs after death'. The first syllable of **rigour** is pronounced to rhyme with 'big', but **rigor** can be pronounced either in this way or with the *i* pronounced as in 'ride'

role can be spelt either with a circumflex, as **rôle**, or not, as **role**. **Role** is the more common spelling in modern usage. The word means 'part', as in 'play the role of Hamlet' and 'She had to play the role of mother and of father.' It can also be used to mean 'function, position', as in 'the role of play in a child's development'.

roof causes problems with regard to its plural form. The usual plural is **roofs**, which can be pronounced either as it is spelt, to rhyme with 'hoofs', or to rhyme with 'hooves'.

rout and **route** are liable to be confused. They look similar but are pronounced differently and have completely different meanings'. **Rout** as a noun means 'overwhelming defeat', as in 'the rout of the opposing army', and as a verb 'to defeat utterly', as in 'Their team routed ours last time'. **Route** refers to 'a way of getting somewhere', as in 'the quickest route' and 'the scenic route'. **Route** can also be a verb meaning 'to arrange a route for, to send by a certain route', as in 'route the visitors along the banks of the river'. **Rout** is pronounced to rhyme with 'shout'. **Route** is pronounced to rhyme with 'brute'.

rug *see* **carpet**.

rung *see* **rang**.

S

's and s' *see* **apostrophe**.

sacrilegious is frequently misspelt. Note the *i* before the *l* and the *e* before the g. It is a common error to confuse it with the pattern of 'religious'. **Sacrilegious** is the adjective from 'sacrilege' and means 'showing disrespect for something holy', as in 'the sacrilegious act of destroying the altar'.

salon and **saloon** are liable to be confused. **Salon** in modern usage is most frequently found as a name given to certain businesses, as 'own a hairdressing salon' and 'visit a beauty salon'. Formerly it was used to refer to a room in a large house where guests were received and also to 'a regular gathering of notable guests at the house of a noble lady or wealthy lady', as in 'hold a literary salon'.

sank, sunk and **sunken** are liable to be confused. **Sank** is the past tense of the verb 'to sink', as in 'The ship sank without trace'. **Sunk** is also used in this sense, as in 'The dog sunk its teeth into the postman's leg', but **sank** is the more common form. The past participle of 'sink' is **sunk**, as in 'We have sunk all our money in the business'. **Sunken** is a form of the past participle usually used as an adjective, as in 'sunken treasure' and 'sunken cheeks'.

scarfs and **scarves** are both acceptable spellings of the plural of 'scarf', meaning a piece of cloth worn around the neck or the head', as in 'a silk scarf at her neck' and 'wearing a head scarf'.

sceptic and **septic** are liable to be confused, particularly with regard to their pronunciation. **Sceptic** is pronounced *skep*-tik and refers to 'a person who has doubts about accepted beliefs, principles, etc', as in 'The rest of the family are deeply religious but he is a sceptic'. **Septic** is pronounced *sep*-tik and means 'infected with harmful bacteria', as in 'a wound that turned septic' and 'have a septic finger'.

schedule, meaning 'plan or timetable', as in 'work that is behind schedule' and 'try to work out a revision schedule well before the exams', is usually pronounced *shed*-yool in British English. However, the American English pronunciation *sked*-yool is now sometimes found in British usage.

Scotch, Scots and **Scottish** are liable to be confused. **Scotch** is restricted to a few set phrases, such as 'Scotch whisky', 'Scotch broth' and 'Scotch mist'. As a noun **Scotch** refers to 'Scotch whisky', as in 'have a large Scotch with ice'. **Scots** as an adjective is used in such contexts as 'Scots accents', 'Scots people' and 'Scots attitudes'. As a noun **Scots** refers to the Scots language, as in 'He speaks standard English but he uses a few words of Scots.' The noun **Scot** is used to refer to 'a Scottish person', as in 'Scots living in London'. **Scottish** is found in such contexts as 'Scottish literature', 'Scottish history' and 'Scottish culture'.

sculpt and **sculpture** are interchangeable as verbs meaning 'to make sculptures, to practise sculpting', as in 'commissioned to sculpt/sculpture a bust of the chairman of the firm' and 'She both paints and sculpts/sculptures.

seasonal and **seasonable** are liable to be confused. They are both adjectives formed from the noun 'season' but they have different meanings. **Seasonal** means 'happening during a particular season, varying with the seasons', as in 'Hotel work is often seasonal' and 'a recipe that uses seasonal vegetables'. **Seasonable** means 'suitable for or appropriate to', as in 'seasonable weather'.

start *see* **commence**.

secretary is liable to be misspelt. Note the *-ary* ending. It is pronounced *sek*-re-tri and refers to 'a person employed to deal with correspondence, typing, filing, making appointments, etc', as in 'Her secretary is dealing with all her phone calls today'. It also refers to 'a person appointed in a society, club, etc, to deal with correspondence, take minutes, keep records, etc, as in 'elected secretary of tennis club'.

seize, meaning 'to take hold of suddenly and by force, to grab', as in 'The kidnappers seized the child' and 'seize the opportunity to escape', is frequently misspelt. Note the *ei* combination, which is an exception to the '*i* before *e* except after *c*' rule.

sensual and **sensuous** are liable to be confused. **Sensual** means 'relating to physical (often sexual) pleasure, enjoying or giving physical pleasure', as in 'the sensual pleasures of eating and drinking'. **Sensuous** means 'relating to the senses, giving pleasure to the senses', as in 'the sensuous feel of silk' and 'the sensuous appeal of the music'.

sentiment and **sentimentality** are liable to be confused. They are related but have different shades of meaning. **Sentiment** means 'feeling, emotion', as in 'His actions were the result of sentiment not rationality'. It also means 'attitude, opinion', as in 'a speech full of anti-Christian sentiments'. **Sentimentality** is the noun from the adjective **sentimental** and means 'over-indulgence in tender feelings', as in 'dislike the sentimentality of the love songs' and 'She disliked her home town but now speaks about it with great sentimentality'.

separate, is frequently misspelt. Note the *a* following the *p*. It is a common error to put *e* in that position. As an adjective **separate** means 'forming a unit by itself, existing apart', as in 'occupy separate rooms' and 'lead separate lives'. It also means 'distinct, different', as in 'happening on five separate occasions' and 'separate problems'. As a verb **separate** means 'to divide', as in 'The roads separate further up'; 'to cause to divide', as in 'separate the group'; 'to keep apart', as in 'A river separates the two parts of the estate'; 'to stop living together', as in 'The child's parents have recently separated'.

sewed and **sewn** are interchangeable as the past participle of the verb 'to sew', as in 'She has sewed/sewn patches on the torn parts of the trousers'. When the participle is used as an adjective, **sewn** is the more common form, as in 'badly sewn seams'. **Sewed** is also the past tense of 'to sew', as in 'She sewed the garment by hand'.

sexism in language has been an issue for some time, and various attempts have been made to avoid it. For example, 'person' is often used where 'man' was traditionally used and 'he/she' substituted for 'he' in situations where the sex of the relevant person is unknown or unspecified.

ship see **boat**.

siege is frequently misspelt. Note the *ie* combination. It follows the '*i* before *e* except after *c*' rule, but it is a common error to put *ei* instead. **Siege** means 'the surrounding of a town, fortress, etc, in order to capture it'.

sine qua non is a Latin phrase that has been adopted into English and means 'essential condition, something that is absolutely necessary', as in 'It is a sine qua non of the agreement that the rent is paid on time'. It is used only in formal or legal contexts.

sitting room, **living room**, **lounge** and **drawing room** all refer to 'a room in a house used for relaxation and the receiving of guests'. Which word is used is largely a matter of choice. Some people object to the use of **lounge** as being pretentious but it is becoming increasingly common. **Drawing room** is a more formal word and applies to a room in rather a grand residence.

skilful, as in 'admire his skilful handling of the situation' is frequently misspelt. Note the single *l* before the *f*. In American English the word is spelt **skillful**.

slander see **libel**.

sometime and **some time** are liable to be confused. **Sometime** means 'at an unknown or unspecified time', as in 'We must get together sometime' and 'I saw her sometime last year'. There is a growing tendency in modern usage to spell this as **some time**. Originally **some time** was restricted to meaning 'a period of time', as in 'We need some time to think'.

spelled and **spelt** are both acceptable forms of the past tense and past participle of the verb 'to spell', as in 'They spelled/spelt the word wrongly' and 'He realized that he had spelled/spelt the word wrongly'.

spoiled and **spoilt** are both acceptable forms of the past tense and past participle of the verb 'to spoil', as in 'They spoiled/spoilt that child' and 'They have spoiled/spoilt that house with their renovations'. When the past participle is used adjectivally, **spoilt** is the usual form, as in 'a spoilt child'.

stadium causes problems with regard to its plural form. **Stadiums** and **stadia** are both acceptable. **Stadium** is derived from Latin and the original plural form followed the Latin and was **stadia**. However, anglicized plural forms are becoming more and more common in foreign words adopted into English, and **stadiums** is now becoming the more usual form.

stanch and **staunch** are both acceptable spellings of the word meaning 'to stop the flow of', as in 'stanch/staunch the blood from the wound in his head' and 'try to stanch/staunch the tide of violence'. **Staunch** also means 'loyal, firm', as in 'the team's staunch supporters'.

stank and **stunk** are liable to be confused. **Stank** and **stunk** can both act as the past tense of the verb 'to stink', as in ' The rotten cheese stank' and 'He stunk of

stale beer'. **Stunk** can also act as the past participle, as in 'This room has stunk of cigarette smoke for days'.

stationary and **stationery** are liable to be confused. They sound alike but have completely different meanings. **Stationary** means 'not moving, standing still', as in 'stationary vehicles'. **Stationery** refers to 'writing materials', as in 'office stationery'. An easy way to differentiate between them is to remember that **stationery** is bought from a 'stationer', which, like 'baker' and 'butcher', ends in -*er*.

staunch see **stanch**.

stimulant and **stimulus** are liable to be confused. Formerly the distinction between them was quite clear but now the distinction is becoming blurred. Traditionally **stimulant** refers to 'a substance, such as a drug, that makes a person more alert or more active', as in 'Caffeine is a stimulant'. **Stimulus** traditionally refers to 'something that rouses or encourages a person to action or greater effort', as in 'The promise of more money acted as a stimulus to the work force and they finished the job in record time'. In modern usage the words are beginning to be used interchangeably. In particular, **stimulus** is used in the sense of **stimulant** as well as being used in its own original sense.

storey and **story** are liable to be confused. They sound alike but have completely different meanings. **Storey** means 'level of a building, floor', as in 'a multi-storey car park' and 'They live on the second storey of the house'. **Story** means 'a tale', as in 'tell the children a bedtime story'. The plural of **storey** is **stories** and the plural of **story** is **stories**. In American English, **story** is used for both meanings.

straight away and **straightaway** are both acceptable ways of spelling the expression for 'without delay, at once', as in 'attend to the matter straight away/straightaway'.

straitened and **straightened** are liable to be confused. They sound alike but have completely different meanings. **Straitened** means 'severely restricted' and is most commonly found in the phrase 'in straitened circumstances', which means 'in extremely difficult financial circumstances'. **Straightened** is the past tense and participle of the verb 'to straighten', as in 'They have straightened the road out' and 'with her straightened hair'.

strata see **stratum**.

stratagem and **strategy** are liable to be confused. They look and sound similar but they have different meanings. **Stratagem** means 'a scheme or trick', as in 'think of a stratagem to mislead the enemy' and 'devise a stratagem to gain entry to the building'. **Strategy** refers to 'the art of planning a campaign', as in 'generals meeting to put together a battle strategy', and 'a plan or policy, particularly a clever one, designed for a particular purpose', as in 'admire the strategy which he used to win the game'.

stratum and **strata** are liable to be confused. **Stratum** is the singular form and **strata** is the plural form of a word meaning 'a layer or level', as in 'a stratum of rock' and 'different strata of society'. It is a common error to use **strata** as a singular noun.

student see **pupil**.

subconscious and **unconscious** are used in different contexts. **Subconscious** means 'concerning those areas or activities of the mind of which one is not fully aware', as in 'a subconscious hatred of her parents' and 'a subconscious desire to hurt her sister'. **Unconscious**

means 'unaware', as in 'She was unconscious of his presence' and 'unconscious of the damage which he had caused', and 'unintentional', as in 'unconscious humour' and 'an unconscious slight'. **Unconscious** also means 'having lost consciousness, insensible', as in 'knocked unconscious by the blow to his head'.

subjective see **objective**.

subsequent see **consequent**.

subsidence has two acceptable pronunciations. It can be pronounced either sub-*sid*-ens, with the emphasis on the middle syllable which rhymes with 'hide', or *sub*-sid-ens, with the emphasis on the first syllable and with the middle syllable rhyming with 'hid'. **Subsidence** means 'falling or sinking', as in 'the subsidence of houses in that street'.

such and **like** are liable to be confused. **Such** is used to introduce examples, as in 'herbs, such as chervil and parsley' and 'citrus fruits, such as oranges and lemons'. **Like** introduces comparisons. 'She hates horror films like *Silence of the Lambs*', and 'Very young children, like very old people, have to be kept warm.'

suit and **suite** are liable to be confused. They look similar but they have completely different meanings. **Suit** has several meanings. These include 'a set of clothes', as in 'He was wearing a tweed three-piece suit' (a jacket, trousers and waistcoat in the same material) and 'She was married in a white suit, rather than a dress'; 'one of the four sets of playing cards', as in 'Which suit is trump?'; and 'an action in a court of law', as in 'bring a suit against her ex-husband for non-payment of maintenance'. **Suite** refers to 'a set of furniture', as in 'prefer non-matching chairs to the traditional three-piece suite' (a sofa and two armchairs in the same material); 'a set of rooms', as in 'book a suite at an expensive hotel' and 'the hotel's honeymoon suite'; and 'a musical composition consisting of three or more related parts', as in 'a ballet suite'. Note the *e* at the end of **suite**. **Suit** is pronounced *soot* or *syoot*. **Suite** is pronounced *sweet*.

supercilious is liable to be misspelt. Note the *c* and single *l*. It means 'condescending, disdainful', as in 'She treats unemployed people in a very supercilious way'.

supersede is frequently misspelt. Note the *-sede* ending. It is a common error to put *-cede* here, along the lines of 'precede'. **Supersede** means 'to take the place of, to replace', as in 'Word processors have superseded typewriters in many offices'.

supervise is frequently misspelt. Note the *-ise* ending. This is not one of the verbs that can be spelt ending in *-ize*. **Supervise** means 'to oversee', as in 'the teacher who was supervising the children in the playground' and 'a senior worker supervising the work of the trainees'.

supper see **dinner**.

susceptible is frequently misspelt. Note the *sc* combination and the *-ible*, not *-able*, ending. **Susceptible** means 'easily affected or influenced' and is frequently followed by the preposition 'to', as in 'children who are susceptible to colds' and 'people who are susceptible to political propaganda'.

swam and **swum** are not interchangeable. **Swam** is the past tense of the verb 'to swim', as in 'They swam ashore'. **Swum** is the past participle of the same verb, as in 'The children have swum for long enough'.

swingeing and **swinging** are liable to be confused. They look similar but they have completely different meanings. **Swinging** is simply the present participle of the verb 'to swing', as in 'children swinging on the gate'. It is also rather a dated term for 'lively and modern', as in 'the swinging sixties'. **Swingeing** means 'severe', as in 'swingeing cuts in public spending'. Note the *e* in **swingeing**. Note also the pronunciation of **swingeing**. It is pronounced *swin*-jing, not like swinging.

syndrome in its original meaning refers to 'a set of symptoms and signs that together indicate the presence of a physical or mental disorder', as in 'Down's syndrome'. In modern usage it is used loosely to indicate 'any set of events, actions, characteristics, attitudes that together make up, or are typical of, a situation', as in 'He suffers from the "I'm all right Jack" syndrome and doesn't care what happens to anyone else' and 'They seem to be caring people but they are opposing the building of an Aids hospice in their street—a definite case of "the not in my back yard" syndrome'.

T

target in its verb form, meaning 'to aim at', causes spelling problems with regard to its past participle, past tense and present participle. They are respectively **targeted** and **targeting**, as in 'resources targeted at the poorest section of the community' and 'the need for targeting their advertising campaign at young people.'

tariff is liable to be misspelt. Note the single *r* and double *f*. It means either 'duty to be paid on imported goods', as in 'the tariff payable on imported cars', or 'a list of fixed charges in a hotel, restaurant, etc', as in 'The hotel tariff is hanging behind the bedroom door' and 'the lunch tariff hanging outside the restaurant'.

tea *see* **dinner**.

teach *see* **learn**.

telephone *see* **phone**.

televise is frequently misspelt. Note the *-ise* ending. It is a common error to spell it with an *-ize* ending. It is helpful to remember the *s* of 'television'.

terminal and **terminus** in some contexts are interchangeable. They both refer to 'the end of a bus route, the last stop on a bus route, the building at the end of a bus route', as in 'The bus doesn't go any further—this is the terminus/terminal', but **terminus** is the more common term in this sense. They can also both mean 'the end of a railway line, the station at the end of a railway line', but **terminal** is the more common term in this sense. **Terminal** can refer to 'a building containing the arrival and departure areas for passengers at an airport' and 'a building in the centre of a town for the arrival and departure of air passengers'. **Terminal** also refers to 'a point of connection in an electric circuit', as in 'the positive and negative terminals', and 'apparatus, usually consisting of a keyboard and screen, for communicating with the central processor in a computing system', as in 'He has a dumb terminal so he can read information but not input it'. As an adjective **terminal** means 'of, or relating to, the last stage in a fatal illness', as in 'a terminal disease' and 'terminal patients'.

terminus *see* **terminal**.

tête-à-tête, meaning 'an intimate conversation between two people', as in 'have a tête-à-tête with her best friends about her marital problems', is liable to be misspelt. Note the circumflex accent on the first *e* of each **tête** and the accent on the *a*. The phrase has been adopted into English from French.

than is used to link two halves of comparisons or contrasts, as in 'Peter is considerably taller than John is', 'He is older than I am' and 'I am more informed about the situation than I was yesterday'. Problems arise when the relevant verb is omitted. In order to be grammatically correct, the word after 'than' should take the subject form if there is an implied verb, as in 'He is older than I (am)'. However this can sound stilted, as in 'She works harder than he (does)', and in informal contexts this usually becomes 'She works harder than him'. If there is no implied verb, the word after **than** is in the object form, as in 'rather you than me!'

their and **there** are liable to be confused because they sound similar. **There** means 'in, to or at that place', as in 'place it there' and 'send it there'. **Their** is the possessive of 'they', meaning 'of them, belonging to them', as in 'their books' and 'their mistakes'.

their and **they're** are liable to be confused because they sound similar. **Their** is the possessive of 'they', meaning 'of them, belonging to them', as in 'their cars' and 'their attitudes'. **They're** is a shortened form of 'they are', as in 'They're not very happy' and 'They're bound to lose'.

they, used in conjunction with 'anyone', everyone', 'no one' and 'someone', is increasingly replacing 'he' or 'she', although to do so is ungrammatical. The reason for this is to avoid the sexism of using 'he' when the sex of the person being referred to is either unknown or unspecified, and to avoid the clumsiness of 'he/she' or 'he or she'. Examples of **they** being so used include 'Everyone must do their best' and 'No one is to take their work home'.

they're *see* **their**.

this *see* **next**.

threshold is liable to be misspelt. Note the single *h*. It is a common error to put double *h*. **Threshold** means either 'doorway', as in 'meet the other visitor on the threshold', or 'the beginning', as in 'on the threshold of a new career'.

till and **until** are more or less interchangeable except that **until** is slightly more formal, as in 'They'll work till they drop' and 'Until we assess the damage we will not know how much the repairs will cost'.

tobacconist is frequently misspelt. Note the single *b*, the double *c* and the single *n*. A **tobacconist** refers to 'a person or shop that sells tobacco, cigarettes and cigars'.

toilet, **lavatory**, **loo** and **bathroom** all have the same meaning but the context in which they are used sometimes varies. **Toilet** is the most widely used of the words and is used on signs in public places. The informal **loo** is also very widely used. **Lavatory** is less common nowadays although it was formerly regarded by all but the working class and lower-middle class as the most acceptable term. **Bathroom** in British English usually refers to 'a room containing a bath', but in American English it is the usual word for **toilet**. **Ladies** and **gents** are terms for **toilet**, particularly in public places. **Powder room** also means this, as does the American English **rest room**.

town *see* **city**.

trade names should be written with a capital letter, as in 'Filofax' and 'Jacuzzi'. When trade names are used as verbs they are written with a lower case letter, as in 'hoover the carpet'.

trafficker is frequently misspelt. Note the *k*. The word means 'a person who deals in or trades in something, particularly something illegal or dishonest', as in 'drugs traffickers'. Note also **trafficked** and **trafficking** but **traffic**.

trait is traditionally pronounced *tray* but *trayt* is also an acceptable pronunciation in modern usage. It means an element or quality in someone's personality', as in 'One of his least attractive traits is his habit of blaming other people for his mistakes'.

tranquillity, meaning 'peace, peaceful state', as in 'disturb the tranquillity of the countryside', is liable to be misspelt. Note the double *l*.

travel causes problems with regard to the past participle, past tense and present participle. The *l* doubles before '-ed' and '-ing' are added, as **travelled** and **travelling**, as in 'They travelled to many parts of the world' and 'nervous when travelling by car'. Note also **traveller**, as in 'travellers in foreign lands'. In American English the *l* is not doubled, as **traveled**, **traveling** and **traveler**.

troop and **troupe** are liable to be confused. **Troop** refers to 'a military unit', as in 'the officer in charge of the troop', or to 'a group or collection of people or animals', as in 'Troops of people arrived at the demonstration from all over the country'. **Troupe** refers to 'a company of actors or performers', as in 'a troupe of acrobats'.

try to and **try and** are interchangeable in modern usage. Formerly **try and** was considered suitable only in spoken and very informal contexts, but it is now considered acceptable in all but the most formal contexts, as in 'Try to/and do better' and 'They must try to/and put the past behind them'.

twelfth, as in 'December is the twelfth month of the year', is liable to be both mispronounced and misspelt. The *f* is frequently omitted in error in pronunciation and spelling.

U

ultra is used as a prefix meaning 'going beyond', as in 'ultraviolet' and 'ultrasound', or 'extreme, very', as in 'ultra-sophisticated', ultra-modern, and 'ultra-conservative'. Compounds using it may be spelt with or without a hyphen. Words such as 'ultrasound' and 'ultraviolet' are usually spelt as one word, but words with the second sense of **ultra**, such as 'ultra-sophisticated', are often hyphenated.

unaware and **unawares** are not interchangeable. **Unaware** is an adjective meaning 'not aware, not conscious of', as in 'He was unaware that he was being watched' and 'She was unaware of his presence', and 'ignorant, having no knowledge of', as in 'politically unaware'. **Unawares** is an adverb meaning 'without being aware, without noticing, unintentionally', as in 'I must have dropped my keys unawares' and 'The child dropped her gloves unawares', or 'by surprise, unexpected, without warning', as in 'The enemy attack took them unawares' and 'The snowstorm caught the climbers unawares'.

unconscious see **subconscious**.

underhand and **underhanded** are interchangeable in the sense of 'sly, deceitful', as in 'He used underhand/underhanded methods to get the job' and 'It was underhand/underhanded of him to not to tell her that he was leaving'. **Underhand** is the more common of the two terms.

under way, meaning 'in progress', is traditionally spelt as two words, as in 'Preparations for the conference are under way'. In modern usage it is frequently spelt as one word, as in 'The expansion project is now underway'. It is a common error to write 'under weigh'.

undoubtedly, as in 'He is undoubtedly the best player in the team' and 'Undoubtedly we shall be a little late', is liable to be misspelt. A common error is to spell it 'Undoubtably', probably in confusion with 'indubitably'. **Undoubtedly** means the same as 'without a doubt'.

unexceptionable and **unexceptional** are liable to be confused. They look and sound rather similar but they have different meanings. **Unexceptionable** means 'not liable to be criticized or objected to, inoffensive, satisfactory', as in 'His behaviour was quite unexceptionable' and 'I found her remarks quite unexceptionable'. **Unexceptional** means 'ordinary, not outstanding or unusual', as in 'She was supposed to be a brilliant player but her performance was unexceptional' and 'an unexceptional student'.

uninterested see **disinterested**.

unique traditionally means being the only one of its kind', as in 'a unique work of art' and 'everyone's fingerprints are unique' and so cannot be modified by such words as 'very', 'rather', 'more', etc, although it can be modified by 'almost' and 'nearly'. In modern usage **unique** is often used to mean 'unrivalled, unparalleled, outstanding', as in 'a unique opportunity' and 'a unique performance'.

unreadable see **illegible**.

unrepairable see **irreparable**.

until see **till**.

unwanted and **unwonted** are liable to be confused. They sound alike but they have completely different meanings. **Unwanted** means 'not wanted', as in 'give unwanted furniture to a charity shop', 'an unwanted pregnancy' and 'feel unwanted'. **Unwonted** means 'not customary, not usual', as in 'behave with unwonted courtesy' and 'a feeling of unwonted optimism'. **Unwonted** is not pronounced in the same way as **unwanted**. It is pronounced un-*wont*-ed with the second syllable pronounced as 'won't'.

up and **upon** mean the same and are virtually interchangeable, except that **upon** is slightly more formal. Examples include 'sitting on a bench', 'the carpet on the floor', 'the stamp on the letter', caught with the stolen goods on him' and 'something on his mind'; and 'She threw herself upon her dying mother's bed', 'a carpet of snow upon the ground' and 'Upon his arrival he went straight upstairs'.

upward and **upwards** are not interchangeable. **Upward** is used as an adjective, as in 'on an upward slope' and 'an upward trend in prices'. **Upwards** is an adverb, as in 'look upwards to see the plane'.

urban and **urbane** are liable to be confused. They look similar but they have completely different meanings. **Urban** means 'of a town or city', as in 'urban dwellers' and 'in an urban setting'. **Urbane** means 'smoothly elegant and sophisticated', as in 'an urbane wit' and 'an urbane man of the world'.

usable and **useable** are both acceptable spellings, as in 'furniture which is no longer usable/useable' and 'crockery which is scarcely usable/useable'. **Usable** is more common.

V

vacation, meaning 'holiday', in British English is mostly restricted to a university or college situation, as in 'students seeking paid employment during their vacation'. In American English it is the usual word for 'holiday'.

vaccinate is liable to be misspelt. Note the double c and single n. The word means 'to inject a vaccine into to prevent a particular disease', as in 'vaccinate the children against tuberculosis'. Vaccine refers to 'a substance that is injected into the bloodstream and protects the body against a disease by making it have a mild form of the disease', as in 'a vaccine against smallpox'.

vacuum is liable to be misspelt. Note the single c and double u. It refers to 'a space that is completely empty of all matter and gases', as in 'create a total vacuum'.

variegated is liable to be misspelt. Note the e between the i and the g. It means 'varied in colour, speckled or mottled with different colours', as in 'variegated leaves'. It is pronounced vayr-i-gayt-ed.

verbal and oral are liable to be confused. Oral means 'expressed in speech', as in 'an oral, rather than a written examination'. Verbal means 'expressed in words', as in 'He asked for an instruction diagram but he was given verbal instructions' and 'They were going to stage a protest match but they settled for a verbal protest'. It is also used to mean 'referring to the spoken word, expressed in speech', as in 'a verbal agreement'. Because of these two possible meanings, the use of verbal can lead to ambiguity. In order to clarify the situation, oral should be used when 'expressed in speech' is meant. Verbal can also mean referring to verbs, as in 'verbal endings'. For more information on oral see aural.

vice versa means 'the other way round, with the order reversed', as in 'He will do his friend's shift and vice versa' and 'Mary dislikes John and vice versa'. It is pronounced vis-e ver-sa, vi-si ver-sa or vis ver-sa and is derived from Latin.

vigorous is liable to be misspelt. Note the absence of u before r, unlike the noun vigour. It means 'strong and energetic', as in 'vigorous young men playing football', or 'forceful', as in 'vigorous debate' and 'vigorous criticism'.

vis-à-vis means 'in relation to', as in 'their performance vis-à-vis their ability' and 'the company's policy vis-à-vis early retirement'. It is pronounced vee-za-vee and is derived from French. Note the accent on the a.

vitamin is pronounced vit-a-min, with the first syllable rhyming with 'lit' in British English. In American English the first syllable rhymes with 'light'. The word refers to 'one of a group of substances which are essential for healthy life, different ones occurring in different foods', as in a 'sufferer from a deficiency of vitamin B6' and 'Citrus fruits are a source of vitamin C'.

victuals, meaning 'food', as in 'children requiring nourishing victuals', is liable to be mispronounced. It is pronounced vitlz.

W

-ways see -wise.

weaved, **wove** and **woven** can cause problems. **Wove** is the usual past tense of the verb 'to weave', as in 'She wove the cloth on a hand loom', 'The spider wove a web' and 'The children wove a garland of flowers'. However, in the sense of 'to move along by twisting and turning' **weaved** is the past tense, as in 'The cyclist weaved in and out of the traffic' and 'The drunks weaved their way home'. **Woven** is the past participle of all but 'the twisting and turning' sense, as in 'She had woven the cloth herself' and 'The children had woven garlands'. **Weaved** is the past participle, as in 'She has weaved her way through the traffic'.

weird is liable to be misspelt. Note the *ei* combination. The word means 'strange, uncanny, unnatural', as in 'see weird figures in the mist' and 'hear weird cries in the night'. It also means 'unusual, bizarre, unconventional', as in 'wear weird clothes' and 'have a weird sense of humour'.

wet and **whet** are liable to be confused. **Wet** means 'to cover with moisture', as in 'Wet the clay before using it' and 'wet one's lips'. **Whet** means 'to sharpen', as in 'whet the blade of the sword', and 'to stimulate, excite', as in 'whet his appetite for adventure'.

what ever and **whatever** are not interchangeable. **What ever** is used when 'ever' is used for emphasis, as in 'What ever does he think he's doing?' and 'What ever is she wearing'. **Whatever** means 'anything, regardless of what, no matter what', as in 'Help yourself to whatever you want' and 'Whatever he says I don't believe him'.

whet see **wet**.

which and **what** can cause problems. In questions **which** is used when a limited range of alternatives is suggested, as in 'Which book did you buy in the end?' and **what** is used in general situations, as in 'What book did you buy?'

whisky and **whiskey** both refer to a strong alcoholic drink distilled from grain. **Whisky** is made in Scotland and **whiskey** in Ireland and America. **Whisky** is the usual British English spelling.

who and **whom** cause problems. **Who** is the subject of a verb, as in 'Who told you?', 'It was you who told her' and 'the girls who took part in the play'. **Whom** is the object of a verb or preposition, as in 'Whom did he tell?', 'To whom did you speak?' and 'the people from whom he stole'. In modern usage **whom** is falling into disuse, especially in questions, except in formal contexts. **Who** is used instead even although it is ungrammatical, as in 'Who did you speak to?' **Whom** should be retained when it is a relative pronoun, as in 'the man whom you saw', 'the person to whom he spoke' and 'the girl to whom she gave the book'.

whose and **who's** are liable to be confused. They sound alike but have different meanings. **Whose** means 'of whom' or 'of which', as in 'the woman whose child won', 'the boy whose leg was broken', 'Whose bicycle is that?' and 'the firm whose staff went on strike'. **Who's** is a shortened form of 'who is', as in 'Who's that?', 'Who's first in the queue?' and 'Who's coming to the cinema?'

wilful is liable to be misspelt. Note the single *l* before *f*, and the final single *l*. It means 'done deliberately, unintentional', as in 'wilful damage done to the phone box', or 'headstrong, obstinate', as in 'a wilful child'. In American English the word is spelt with a double *l*, as 'willful'.

-**wise** and -**ways** cause problems. Added to nouns, -**wise** can form adverbs of manner indicating either 'in such a position or direction', as in 'lengthwise' and 'clockwise', and 'in the manner of', as in 'crabwise'. In modern usage -**wise** is frequently used to mean 'with reference to', as in 'Weatherwise it was fine', 'Workwise all is well' and 'Moneywise they're not doing too well'. The suffix -**ways** has a more limited use. It means 'in such a way, direction or manner of', as in 'lengthways' and 'sideways'.

withhold is sometimes misspelt. Note the double *h*. It means 'to keep back', as in 'withhold evidence'.

woman see **lady**.

worship causes problems with regard to the past tense, past participle and present participle as **worshipped, worshipping**. Note also **worshipper** but **worshipful**.

wove see **weaved**.

wrack see **rack**.

XYZ

Xerox causes problems with regard to both spelling and pronunciation. It is a registered trademark for 'a type of photographic process used for copying documents, etc', as in 'a Xerox photocopier', or 'a copy made using this process', as in 'a Xerox of the contract'. Since it is a registered trademark the noun must be spelt with a capital letter. **Xerox** can also be a verb meaning 'to copy a document using the Xerox process' and can be spelt with either a capital letter or a lower-case letter, as in 'Please Xerox/xerox these letters before posting them'.

Xmas is sometimes used as an alternative and shorter form of 'Christmas'. It is common only in a written informal context and is used mainly in commercial situations, as in 'Xmas cards on sale here' and 'Get your Xmas tree here'. When pronounced it is the same as 'Christmas'. The X derives from the Greek *chi*, the first letter of *Christos*, the Greek word for Christ.

X-ray is usually written with an initial capital letter when it is a noun meaning 'a photograph made by means of X-rays showing the bones or organs of the body', as in 'take an X-ray of the patient's chest'. Another term for the noun **X-ray** is 'radiograph'. As a verb it is also usually spelt with an initial capital, as 'After the accident he had his leg X-rayed', but it is sometimes spelt with an initial lower-case letter, as in 'have his chest x-rayed'.

yoghurt is the most usual spelling of the word for 'a type of semi-liquid consisting of milk fermented by added bacteria', as in 'have yoghurt and fruit for breakfast', but **yogurt** and **yoghourt** are also acceptable spellings. It is usually pronounced yog-ert, but yoh-gert is also a possible pronunciation and is the standard one in American English.

yoke and **yolk** are liable to be confused. They sound alike but have completely different meanings. **Yolk**, referring to 'the yellow part of an egg', as in 'The yolk of this egg is too soft', is the commoner of the two words. **Yoke** has several meanings. It means 'a connecting bar', as in 'the yoke across the necks of the oxen' and 'a peasant carrying two pails of water on a yoke'; 'a pair of oxen', as in 'owning three yoke of oxen'; 'an oppres-

sive control', as in 'under the yoke of the cruel tyrant'; 'the part of a garment fitting round the shoulders or hips from which the rest of the garment hangs', as in 'a sweater with a contrasting-coloured yolk'. Both words are pronounced yok to rhyme with 'poke'.

you is used in informal or less formal situations to indicate an indefinite person referred to as 'one' in formal situations. Examples include 'You learn a foreign language more quickly if you spend some time in the country where it is spoken', 'You would think that they would make sure that their staff are polite', 'You can get used to anything in time' and 'You have to experience the situation to believe it'. **You** in this sense must be distinguished from **you** meaning the second person singular', as in 'You have missed your bus', 'You must know where you left your bag' and 'You have to leave now'. *See* **one**.

your and **you're** are liable to be confused. **Your** is a possessive adjective meaning 'belonging to you, of you', as in 'That is your book and this is mine', 'Your attitude is surprising' and 'It is your own fault'. **You're** is a shortened form of 'you are', as in 'You're foolish to believe him', 'You're going to be sorry' and 'You're sure to do well. Note the spelling of the pronoun **yours**, as in 'This book is yours' and 'Which car is yours?' It should not be spelt with an apostrophe as it is not a shortened form of anything.

yours *see* **your**.

yuppie *see* **acronyms**.

zigzag when used in its verb form, meaning 'to move or form a zigzag', has the final *g* doubled to give **zigzagging** and **zigzagged**.

zinc causes spelling problems with reference to the past participle, past tense and present participle when the word is used in its verb form, meaning 'to cover with zinc'. Other words ending in *c* (such as panic, etc) usually have a vowel before the *c* so a *k* is added before the suffixes -ing and -ed. This would give **zincking** and **zincked**, but because of the presence of the consonant *n*, the substitution of *c* by *k*, to give **zinking** and **zinked**, is considered preferable.